THE AUTHORITY SINCE 1868

THE WORLD ALMANAC®

AND BOOK OF FACTS

1994

PAN BOOKS

London, Sydney and Auckland

THE WORLD ALMANAC®
AND BOOK OF FACTS
1994

Editor: Patricia Burgess
Research Assistance: Teresa Chris
Sports Research: Paul Stevens
Design: Judith Robertson
Index: Kathie Gill

Acknowledgements

The editor would like to thank all those who contributed to this edition of *The World Almanac*. They include Alison Classe, Bruce Drake, Mike Gautrey, Ian Gordon, Catherine Hurley, Debra Johnson, Arthur Kilgore, Peter Meyer, Daniel O'Leary and Paul Stevens.

The editor also acknowledges with thanks the many letters of helpful comment and criticism from readers of *The World Almanac*, and invites further suggestions and observations. The volume of letters received makes it impossible to reply to each individually, but every communication is read, and all comments and suggestions receive careful attention. Correspondence should be sent to: The Editor, World Almanac, Pan Books, Cavaye Place, London SW10 9PG.

THE WORLD ALMANAC AND BOOK OF FACTS 1994
UK edition published by Pan Books Ltd,
Cavaye Place, London SW10 9PG
9 8 7 6 5 4 3 2 1

ISBN 0 330 32748 8

Typeset by Parker Typesetting Service, Leicester, England
Printed and bound by BPCC Hazell Books, Aylesbury, Bucks

CONTENTS

STOP PRESS

Haiti

Robert Malval was sworn in as Haiti's new pro-democracy prime minister, Sep. 2. However, violence continued to escalate, and the U.N. reimposed economic sanctions, Oct. 13.

Cambodia

Leaders of the coalition government in Cambodia announced, Sep. 3, that their country would in future be a constitutional monarchy with Prince Norodom Sihanouk as king.

Philippines

The body of former president Ferdinand Marcos, who died in exile in Honolulu in 1989, was flown into the Philippines for reburial, Sep. 7. On Sep. 24 Imelda Marcos was sentenced to 18–24 years in prison for criminal graft. She was released on bail pending an appeal.

South Africa

At least 23 people were shot dead and 25 injured, Sep. 8, when gunmen opened fire on a queue of black people at a taxi rank in Wadeville, near Johannesburg.

Middle East Peace Agreement

Yitzhak Rabin of Israel and Yasser Arafat of the Palestine Liberation Organization shook hands, Sep. 13, after signing a peace deal which would return the occupied territories to the Palestinians and give them self-rule.

Demjanjuk Freed

Ukrainian-born John Demjanjuk, cleared by an Israel court of being the sadistic mass killer "Ivan the Terrible", was freed, Sep. 19.

Australian Republic "Agreed"

In an audience with the Queen, Sep. 19, Australia's prime minister, Paul Keating, claimed that Australia wanted to become a republic and appoint its own head of state. The Queen reportedly said that she would "act on the advice of her ministers . . . and on any decision made by the Australian people".

Booker Prizes

Midnight's Children by Salman Rushdie was named the best Booker Prize winner of the past 25 years, Sep. 20. Roddy Doyle won this year's prize with *Paddy Clarke Ha Ha Ha*, Oct. 26.

Alabama Train Crash

Forty-four people were killed and a further 10 were missing, Sep. 20, when a bridge collapsed near Mobile, Alabama, plunging a train and its 206 passengers into alligator-infested waters.

Russia

Following Boris Yeltsin's dissolution of Parliament, Sep. 21, hardline opponents took over the Moscow White House. They remained there in a state of siege until Oct. 4, when Yeltsin sent in troops and tanks. The ensuing gun battle left a number of dead and many injured.

South Africa

Nelson Mandela, speaking in the U.N. General Assembly on Sep. 24, called for an end to the economic sanctions imposed on the country, but asked for a retention of the arms embargo until a government of national unity had been elected.

Crisis in Georgia

An attempt to suppress the self-declared sovereignty of Abkhazia degenerated into war. Many were killed, and Sukhumi, the last Georgian stronghold of the region, finally fell to separatist rebels, Sep. 27.

Indian Earthquake

As many as 25,000 people were feared dead in an earthquake (6.5) that hit a highly populated area of Maharashtra, Sep. 30.

Somalia

The United States was forced to re-evaluate its presence in Somalia, Oct. 4, when a videotape was released showing a dead U.S. soldier being dragged through the streets of Mogadishu and an injured U.S. helicopter pilot being interrogated.

Birmingham Six

An Old Bailey judge recommended, Oct. 7, that charges against 3 former West Midlands detectives accused of fabricating evidence should be dropped because media comment made it impossible for them to have a fair trial.

Pakistan

After an inconclusive result in the general election, Oct. 6, the Pakistan People's Party eventually gained a majority through the support of other parties, and Benazir Bhutto was voted in as prime minister.

Greece

Andreas Papandreou and his socialist party won the general election, Oct. 10.

London Riot

An anti-racist march by 25,000 people, Oct. 16, ended in violence, with more than 70 people, including 12 police officers, being injured.

Poland

President Lech Walesa appointed Waldemar Pawlak as prime minister, Oct. 18.

Burundi

Military leaders staged a coup, Oct. 21, overthrowing the president, Melchior Ndadaye.

Northern Ireland

Ten people were killed and 50 injured when an IRA bomb exploded in the Shankill Road, Oct. 23.

Canada

The Liberal Party won a landslide victory in the general election, Oct. 26.

Nobel Prizes

(Each 1993 prize included a cash award of about £550,000.)

Chemistry: Kerry Mullis of San Diego, who invented the "polymerase chain reaction", a method of analysing DNA, shared the prize with British-born Michael Smith, whose work on genetic engineering opened the way to curing hereditary diseases.

Economics: U.S. professors Robert W. Fogel and Douglass C. North were awarded the prize for "research in economic history by applying economic theory and quantitative methods in order to explain economic and institutional change".

Literature: U.S. novelist Toni Morrison became the first black woman to win the award. Her writings, which explore the position of black people in society, were praised by the Swedish Academy for a "visionary force and poetic import".

Medicine: British-born Dr Richard Roberts and American Dr Phillip Sharp were awarded the prize for their discovery of "split genes" in 1977. They discovered that genes could be present as separate segments in DNA, thus radically altering the view of genetic development during evolution. The discovery is also important to research into the development of cancer and other diseases.

Peace: Nelson Mandela and President F. W. de Klerk won the prize for their efforts to end apartheid in South Africa and bring about majority rule.

Physics: U.S. astronomers Russell Hulse and Joseph Taylor, both of Princeton University, won the prize for discovering the first indirect proof of the existence of gravity waves.

Obituaries

Hervé Villechaize, 50; U.S. actor, famous as Tattoo in *Fantasy Island* TV series; Sep. 4.
Claude Renoir, 78; French cinematographer; Sep. 5.
Raymond Burr, 76; U.S. actor (*Perry Mason, Ironside*); Sep. 12.
Torkel Opsahl, 62; Norwegian diplomat & peace negotiator; Sep. 16.
Leonard Parkin, 64; British journalist & newscaster; Sep. 20.
Sir John Moores, 97; British pools magnate; Sep. 25.
Peter de Vries, 83; U.S. comic novelist; Sep. 28.
Alex Lyon, 61; British Labour politician; Sep. 30.
Agnes de Mille, 84; U.S. choreographer; Oct. 5.
Cyril Cusack, 82; Irish stage & film actor; Oct. 7.
Andy Stewart, 59; Scottish singer; Oct. 11.
Lord Jo Grimond, 80; former Liberal leader; Oct. 24.
Vincent Price, 82; U.S. film actor; Oct. 25.
Federico Fellini, 73; Italian film director; Oct. 31.
River Phoenix, 22; U.S. film actor; Oct. 31.

INDEX

— M —

—T—

—V—

—W—

2nd UK EDITION

The World Almanac

and Book of Facts for 1994

TOP TEN NEWS STORIES

• "Black Wednesday" (September 16) marked the day when the pound fell below its floor against the deutschmark and made an ignominious withdrawal from the ERM. Some £4.4 billion was spent in propping up the pound during the crisis, and nerves in the money markets caused £20 billion to be wiped off share values. The long period of economic chaos came to a head in May when Norman Lamont was finally forced to resign. On the bright side, the recession was declared to be over, a claim supported by increases in manufacturing industries and exports.

• Uproar greeted the Government's announcement of 31 pit closures in October. The threat of 30,000 job losses immediately and a further 70,000 in support industries aroused almost universal condemnation and the Government was forced to backtrack. A reprieve was granted to 21 pits, and the other 10 were saved when the High Court ruled the closures illegal. Less than 6 months later, however, the Commons approved plans to give a permanent reprieve to only 12 pits and to privatize the coal industry as soon as possible.

• Maastricht captured the headlines for many months, largely thanks to backbench Tory rebels, who threatened to vote against ratification of the treaty if it failed to include the Social Chapter (a guarantee of certain minimal employment rights to European workers). The Government lost a vote on this issue in July, but won the following day by staking everything on a vote of confidence. The treaty was ratified in August.

• Severe embarrassment was brought to the Government in November when the Matrix-Churchill trial collapsed. Three executives of the company had been charged with flouting export controls by supplying arms to Iraq during the Iran–Iraq war. It emerged, however, that they had done so with the knowledge of Government ministers.

• Following accounts of Serbian attacks on aid convoys and the rape of thousands of Muslim women, Yugoslavia was expelled from the UN and subjected to an economic blockade. Over the ensuing months various peace proposals foundered and a U.S. plan to bomb Serb positions and rearm the Muslims was rejected by European leaders. NATO, however, approved possible Serb targets to facilitate humanitarian assistance, and Serb troops began to withdraw from the mountains overlooking Sarajevo.

• As international gifts of food and other supplies to the starving of Somalia continued to be stolen by warring factions, the 3,500-strong peacekeeping force despatched in November was supplemented with 30,000 U.S. troops in December. Although order was restored, fighting continued to break out, and foreigners became targets for random attacks. A transitional government, consisting of 74 representatives, was agreed in March. UN troops then became the focus of terrorist attacks, Pakistani and U.S. peacekeepers being among the first victims.

• Russia was plunged into crisis in September when Pres. Boris Yeltsin ordered the dissolution of parliament and announced that he would rule by decree until December. Vice Pres. Alexander Rutskoi condemned the move as a coup d'état, and was sworn in as acting president at an emergency session of parliament. Yeltsin justified his move by saying that the parliament had become obstructive and that it was time to change to a bicameral legislature. Britain, France and the U.S. all expressed their support of Yeltsin after he promised to hold free and fully democratic elections. In an effort to squeeze out Rutskoi and his followers, the parliament building was surrounded by troops, and water, electricity and telephones were cut off. By the end of the month it appeared that the hard-liners had lost the battle.

• In what some saw as a cynical move to offset the bad publicity of various Royal Family crises, it was announced that the Queen would begin to pay income tax. Although the deal is to include very generous tax exemptions, it also excludes younger members of the family from the Civil List, meaning that the Queen will assume responsibility for their income.

• Bill Clinton was elected 42nd president of the United States in November, the first Democrat to be elected since Jimmy Carter in 1976. Clinton become the first minority president – with clearly less than half of the total popular vote – since 1968. The Democrats continued to control both houses of Congress by large margins.

• Only a few days before the second marriage of the Princess Royal, it was announced that the Prince and Princess of Wales were to separate. Given the years of speculation about their relationship, the announcement came as something of an anti-climax.

That "Nice" Mr Major

Just 4 months after Prime Minister John Major led his Conservative party to election victory, **Apr. 9**, the euphoria was replaced with the trench-like mentality of a government under siege, lurching from scandal to crisis. It was a year of -Gates, U-turns and record low poll ratings. How did John Major's popularity go from the highest since Winston Churchill's during World War II to the lowest in the history of polling?

The party limped into the summer recess already bruised by the protracted scandal that ended in David Mellor's resignation, **Sep. 25**. Since the Danish referendum, there had been worrying signals that the ratification of the Maastricht Treaty, the policy with which Major had become personally identified, would not proceed smoothly. These two themes were to dog the Prime Minister's year: misbehaviour by Government ministers and the European Community.

The Exchange Rate Mechanism (ERM) came under pressure as speculation about a realignment of currencies intensified. Major and his chancellor, Norman Lamont, resisted calls for an interest rate increase, with Lamont's statement intended to remove any "scintilla of doubt" that there would be any devaluation or leaving of the ERM. The London Conference on Bosnia, **Aug. 25**, which achieved little (other than declarations that later proved hollow) was superseded by preoccupation with the sterling crisis and the imminent French referendum on Maastricht. Crucial though a "Yes" vote seemed to John Major, then President of the Community, he declined an invitation, **Aug. 29**, to appear on French television to promote acceptance of the treaty. Major publicly stood by his Chancellor and, **Sep. 11**, underlined his support for Lamont's ERM stance in a speech to industry. None the less, on "Black Wednesday", **Sep. 16**, sterling was withdrawn from the ERM after the Bank of England spent an estimated £10–12 billion fruitlessly propping up the pound in the currency markets. After this, speculation over challenges to the leadership began. Tales of the Prime Minister's "lonely" life started appearing in the press, with hints that his health was not good. Major bounced back, winning an emergency Commons debate backing his economic policies, **Sep. 23**, two days after a narrow "Eurovictory" in the French referendum.

But the rift within the party over Europe, together with continuing economic gloom, fuelled the growing dissatisfaction with Major's performance. In a MORI poll, **Oct. 4**, he achieved the lowest popularity rating since the election. Major was further wounded by accusations in the published memoirs of former chancellor Nigel Lawson, that he was not capable of dealing with Treasury issues. The Prime Minister remained defiantly optimistic, despite the pound's slumping to a new low and shares suffering the biggest fall since the Stock Exchange crash in 1987. Margaret Thatcher, looming more malevolently than ever, chose the eve of the party conference, **Oct. 8**, to denigrate Major's economic policy in the *European* newspaper. Major replied with a resoundingly patriotic speech to the party conference in which he pledged always to put Britain's interests first. In the hour-long speech, which used the words "Britain" or "British" 52 times, he also called on his friend, Michael "Tarzan" Heseltine to "don his loin cloth and get out his club" and take on the local bureaucracy impeding small businesses. He also railed against the scourge of new age travellers and the lack of motorway facilities.

Any momentum gained by the strident optimism of the conference was abruptly halted by "Tarzan"'s announcement, **Oct. 15**, of the decision to close 31 coal mines with the projected loss of 30,000 jobs. Although Michael Heseltine was largely the focus of public wrath, John Major was also held responsible, and his popularity now plummeted to the lowest ever recorded in the history of polling. Inside the party trouble was brewing again over Maastricht as the "Eurosceptics" threatened the paving motion to put the bill back on the agenda in the Commons. Major retaliated in what was now becoming a familiar obdurate style by adopting a high-risk strategy: threatening a general election if he lost the vote to continue with the ratification process. Despite anger and bemusement at these macho tactics, Major won a 3-vote majority on the second reading of the bill in the House of Commons. He announced that he would postpone the final stages of ratification until after the second Danish referendum.

Questions now started to be asked about whether or not John Major knew the guidelines for trade with Iraq were being broken: had he seen the correspondence of his under-ministers that acknowledged the breach while he was at the Foreign Office? Major denied it, and instituted an official inquiry into the allegations, **Nov. 16**. At the same time, Chancellor Lamont was coming under fire for more than his handling of the economy. Reports appeared in the newspapers of his failure to pay his Access bill despite numerous reminders. Speculation over the purchase of wine and cigarettes at a branch of Threshers was compounded by the revelation that taxpayers were footing the bill for his legal costs, incurred in the eviction of a sex therapist from his private property. Major, once again, stood by his Chancellor, despite calls for his resignation.

While the economy finally started to show signs of recovery as the year drew to a close, John Major's fortunes continued on the downturn, though the European Summit in Edinburgh, the last under his tenure as President, provided no major disasters. The country's attention was somewhat diverted by the Prime Minister's announcement, **Dec. 10**, that the Prince and Princess of Wales were to separate. But Major's own personal life came under scrutiny as rumours once again circulated about the state of his and his wife's health after a punishing round of foreign trips. A chill was felt in Anglo-American relations after it was revealed that Conservative Central Office had helped provide the Republican party with records of the newly elected President Clinton's time in England during the 1960s. The High Court delivered its own snub, **Dec. 21**, by ruling the pit closures programme unlawful.

The New Year brought little respite. Major's son, James, was banned by the Football Association, **Jan. 23**, for 35 days for punching an opponent during a match. The attacks against the Prime Minister were further personalized as a story appeared in the *New Statesman*, while he was away in India, alluding to rumours of an affair with a caterer. Major announced, **Jan. 28**, from Muscat airport, that his solicitors had issued writs against the journal and another magazine in which the allegations appeared. Other rumours of a rift between President Clinton and Major over troop deployment in Bosnia further threatened the other "special relationship".

With the ERM again in turmoil, Major staged another public display of support for Norman Lamont, **Feb. 31**. In a speech at the Carlton Club the following day he attempted to confront growing uneasiness about crime, especially juvenile crime, urging the country to "condemn more, understand less". The jobless took this literally, organizing a demonstration at Westminster as the unemployment total topped 3 million, **Feb. 19**. On a visit to the United States, Major was forced to defend the current social and economic state of Britain on US television, **Feb. 26**.

Major's popularity continued to flag and marketing consultants urged him to dig out his election soapbox and to revive his image. The announcement of the addition of VAT to fuel bills in the Budget, **Mar. 16**, had been greeted with as much public acclaim as the poll tax. As his 50th birthday approached, the Eurosceptics presented John Major with the first defeat on Maastricht, ignoring his vigorous pleas for support. The announcement of a reprieve for 12 of the pits, **Mar. 25**, in the closure programme was scorned as too little too late and did little to change the tide of public discontent with the Prime Minister's leadership.

With the subdued celebrations of his first anniversary as Prime Minister came the achievement (of sorts) of his desire for a classless society: Major was now equally unpopular with all classes. He ignored Baroness Thatcher's intervention in foreign policy, with her call to arm the Bosnian Muslims. A biography of his wife, Norma Major, was deemed to be more interesting than the one on the PM. But, despite everything, continuing signs of an economic upturn and the increasingly likely prospect of a victory on Maastricht seemed to herald a shift in Major's fortunes. On **Apr. 27** Major and Lamont hailed the official end to the recession.

Spring, however, brought a return to calamity. The Government suffered the biggest swing to the left in history to lose the Newbury by-election to the Liberal Democrats, **May 6**. They also endured severe losses in the local authority elections on the same date. Major was forced to admit that his government had been given a "bloody nose" and to examine the compromise proposals on the controversial school tests, which were held to be partly responsible for the poor showing in the local elections. Lamont was forced to regret his untimely bout of over-optimism in Newbury when he was finally forced to resign, **May 27**, in the Cabinet reshuffle.

As mutterings about a leadership challenge grew louder, Major replied to his critics, assuring the Conservative Women's Conference that "I'm fit, I'm well, I'm here and staying." Michael Mates, Minister for Northern Ireland, was, on the other hand, forced to leave, **June 25**, after links between him and the fugitive financier Asil Nadir were exposed. Another of Major's ministers, Michael Heseltine, suffered a heart attack in the same week.

The final vote on Maastricht, sans Social Chapter, was viewed as the ultimate test of Major's leadership. In 2 nights of intense Parliamentary intrigue, the bill was passed by 40 votes, after it had been harnessed to a vote of confidence in a desperate attempt to make rebels toe the party line. Another humiliating reverse, **July 29**, at the Christchurch by-election notwithstanding, Major felt able to ask, in a supposedly off-the-record comment to a TV interviewer, "How come a wimp like me keeps on winning?" And for once, the Prime Minister's popularity came out of its tailspin when, in the same interview, he referred to three anti-Maastricht cabinet colleagues as "bastards". That nice Mr Major appears to be not, in spite of everything, letting them get him down.

Bill Clinton's Year

by Bruce Drake, managing editor, U.S. National Public Radio

Bill Clinton arrived at the White House with an ambitious domestic agenda. The sheer volume of proposals and policy initiatives he set in motion stood in sharp contrast to the previous 8 years of relative inactivity on the domestic front under the Bush administration and the second term of Ronald Reagan.

The 2 most important issues Clinton had promised to tackle – the economy and health care reform – by themselves would have required of any new administration an enormous investment of political will and energy. But Clinton also chose to press ahead quickly on a wide range of issues: lifting the ban on gays-in-the-military, seeking passage of a highly controversial U.S.–Mexico–Canada free trade agreement, pressing campaign finance reform and welfare reform, enacting a national service programme to let young people repay federal education loans, proposing an anti-crime programme, launching a programme to streamline government and devising a timber policy for the northwest that balanced economic and environmental interests.

It was not surprising, therefore, that Clinton had a difficult first year in office. He was elected with a less than overwhelming mandate for so sweeping an agenda, having won only 43% of the vote. And, to carry out his programme, he first had to take control of the government – no small challenge after 12 years in which the Republicans were in charge of the executive branch.

Ultimately, Clinton won a hard-fought victory on his top priority, a deficit reduction package. But the narrowness of that victory, and the fact that it inspired little enthusiasm among many Americans, raised questions about the strength of his presidency.

On foreign affairs, Clinton was confronted with a more complicated geopolitical map than his predecessors. The competition with the Soviet Union and communist world, which had been the central focus of American policy-making for more than 4 decades, had given way to less clearcut questions about what role the U.S. should play in restoring order or keeping the peace in countries like Bosnia and Somalia.

William Jefferson Clinton took the oath of office as the nation's 42nd President on January 20. At 46 the former Arkansas governor represented a generational shift in the White House, having been born after World War II and having come of age during the turbulent era of the civil rights battles and Vietnam.

Clinton used his brief inaugural address and his first days in office to set a new tone now that the Democrats had control of both the White House and Congress. He promised "an end to the era of deadlock and drift, and a new season of American renewal". He underlined the break with recent Republican administrations by signing a series of executive orders. One imposed higher ethical standards on top officials of the executive branch. Another overturned 5 restrictions on abortions that had been imposed under the previous Republican administrations.

The first legislation he signed as President was a bill providing workers with up to 12 weeks of unpaid leave in order to tend to family needs and crises. The signing of the family leave bill was a symbolic moment for Clinton and fellow Democrats because it was a key part of their agenda which had been stymied under the previous Republican administration.

Clinton had promised to be ready with an economic package and health care reform within his first 100 days. But it was immediately clear that the magnitude of the econonic and political challenges facing his new administration would force Clinton to alter some of his economic goals and to put health care off until September.

A series of reports before he took office pointed to a steadily worsening deficit. The deficit threat increasingly drove Clinton's decision-making because, as he later told the nation's governors in

August, "unless we did something about it we would not have the capacity to deal with a whole range of other issues" during his term in office.

One casualty of his rising concern about the deficit was his campaign promise to enact a middle-class tax cut – a promise that had helped his cause during the Democratic presidential primaries. Instead, he outlined a package of tax hikes and spending reductions totalling $493 billion and called for new government spending through a $16 billion economic stimulus bill to create jobs, fund public works projects, aid education and increase social welfare services.

Clinton said his programme represented "a new direction" and an end to Republican economic policies. He did in fact turn the nation away from the low-tax policies of the Reagan–Bush years. But in putting the emphasis on deficit reduction, he set in motion the political forces that removed much of the "new Democrat" imprint he sought to put on the economic package, such as his domestic "investment" initiatives.

The first casualty was his economic stimulus bill. Republicans, despite their minority status, found new strength in their use of the filibuster and succeeded in killing Clinton's economic stimulus package. The Republican critics skewered the bill as one that would worsen the deficit and do little to spur the economy. Senate Democrats tried and failed 4 times to muster the 60 votes necessary to break the filibuster and gave up on April 21.

Emboldened by their victory over the economic stimulus bill, Republicans turned to Clinton's deficit reduction package and assailed Democrats for once again pursuing policies that resulted in more taxes on Americans. Ultimately, Republicans voted as a block against the plan in both the House and Senate and Clinton had to struggle to hold the support of enough Democrats to win passage. He faced revolts from liberal and conservative wings of the party. In the House, conservative Democrats wanted more spending cuts, tighter caps on entitlement programmes like Medicare, and fewer taxes; in the Senate, Democrats wanted to steer the plan away from tax increases to spending cuts, but opposed the broad-based energy tax. Liberals exerted counter-pressure on Clinton as members of the increasingly influential Congressional Black Caucus and others decried the move towards more domestic cutbacks.

The final package was put together after painstaking negotiations and compromises. It kept to Clinton's original target of almost $500 billion in deficit reduction, relying on $255 billion in spending cuts and $241 billion in tax increases. But Clinton's broad-based energy tax, which he had proposed as the fairest approach, gave way to a much more modest 4.3 cents a gallon gasoline tax; his "investment" proposals were cut roughly by half; a tax break aimed at encouraging business investment in new equipment was greatly whittled down and increases he had sought in social spending were cut back.

The House approved the plan by the bare margin of 218–216 while, in the Senate, Vice President Gore had to cast a tie-breaking vote to get a 51–50 victory.

Critics believed Clinton made several mistakes that indicated he had lessons to learn as a new president. They said he failed to mount an effective public campaign for the package, letting the Republicans instead define it as a Democratic tax hike; that important elements of the original plan, like the broad-based energy tax, were lost because Clinton was seen as too willing to bargain away parts of the package for votes; and that Clinton had erred by believing he could prevail with Democratic votes alone; rather than bolstering his support by courting moderate Republicans earlier in the process.

Health care, with all the competing interests involved, promised to be another tough political battle for an administration that had already gone through the political wringer on the Budget. However, supporters hoped that different dynamics would be at work, in part because the immediate benefit of reform would be more apparent to Americans than the results of the deficit reduction plan, and in part because the Clinton administration had learned the hard way about the importance of laying the political groundwork early with Congress.

The plan, to be fully in place by 1997, was aimed at providing a standard package of health benefits for all Americans, including the estimated 37 million who had no insurance. The benefits were designed to be comparable to the kind of coverage that employees of big corporations generally received. The major share of the cost would be borne largely by requiring all employers to pick up 80% of their workers' health care premiums (which some Republicans said was tantamount to a tax) and from cost savings in Medicare and Medicaid. In addition, the plan depended on measures to sharply curb the increase in health care costs.

Clinton unveiled the programme before a joint session of Congress on September 22, but because it was presented so late in the year, significant congressional action on the plan was not expected until 1994.

Clinton faced another major fight in the autumn – securing passage of the North American Free Trade Agreement originally negotiated with Mexico and Canada during the Bush Administration. The pact would erase tariffs and other barriers to trade among the 3 nations.

Clinton's support for the agreement was one of the ways he separated himself during the campaign from traditional Democrats, many of whom sided with organized labour, which feared the loss of jobs to Mexico. Clinton sought to make the pact more palatable to fellow Democrats by negotiating side agreements bringing labour and environmental standards more in line with those in the U.S., but a number of important Democrats still refused to back him.

The President's political judgement was questioned by many in Washington when he turned almost immediately after his inauguration to the issue of gays in the military. Clinton announced his intention of lifting the ban, despite intense opposition from the Joint Chiefs of Staff and many on Capitol Hill.

In July, after difficult negotiations with Pentagon chiefs and Capitol Hill, Clinton announced what he called "an honourable compromise" that allowed homosexuals to serve as long as they were discreet about their orientation. The compromise, dubbed "don't ask, don't tell, don't pursue", permitted gays to serve in the military as long as they kept their orientation to themselves. It prohibited commanders from investigating military personnel on suspicion or hearsay of homosexual activity, but did allow them to discharge gay soldiers if such behaviour were proved.

At about the same time that the gay issue erupted, Clinton was faced with an uproar over his first choice for Attorney General, an insurance company executive named Zoe Baird, because Baird had employed an illegal alien couple at her family home in violation of a 1986 immigration law. Baird withdrew as a nominee, only to give way to another embarrassing controversy when Clinton's next choice, U.S. District Judge Kimba Wood, was reported to have employed an illegal alien as a babysitter (although, unlike Baird, she had done so at a time when it was not illegal). The White House decided not to formally nominate her. (In the end, Clinton selected Janet Reno, a Florida state attorney in Miami, who proved to be a popular choice.)

Clinton ran into even more serious trouble over his nomination of University of Pennsylvania Law Professor Lani Guinier to be Assistant Attorney General in charge of civil rights enforcement. Guinier was attacked for published views on strengthening minority influence in government. Though supporters claimed her writings were being distorted, critics dubbed her a "quota queen", and called her antidemocratic. Clinton abandoned the nomination on June 3, saying he had not previously read her writings but now that he had, he found them "difficult to defend".

There were a number of other miscues that undermined Clinton's image and distracted from important issues at hand. In May press reports that Clinton got a $200 haircut from Christophe of Beverly Hills while Air Force One sat on the runway at Los Angeles dominated media coverage of his administration for days and gave the President a huge public relations black eye.

White House staffers also triggered an unnecessary controversy in May when they moved to dismiss the staff of the White House travel office, whose most visible job was in arranging charters for the press who accompanied Clinton on trips. The firings prompted charges that the dismissals came at the behest of friends and relatives of Clinton who either wanted a share of the travel business, or jobs in the office. There were also accusations that the FBI had been misused by Clinton aides to support its case against the fired staffers. The White House backed down and ultimately issued a report saying that its own staff had acted inappropriately.

While Clinton often expressed irritation with press focus on his administration's difficulties, by late spring he and other aides conceded that the White House needed "tighter coordination". Clinton bolstered his staff by bringing in as counsellor David Gergen, who had been an adviser to Republican presidents but was reputed to have great skills in helping his bosses get their message across. The addition of Gergen and other changes in key staff positions added up to a far more extensive shake-up of the White House staff than usually took place so early in an administration.

Clinton was also criticized for failing to develop a coherent foreign policy framework. Whether or not the criticism was valid, Clinton did come to the presidency less versed in foreign policy than many of his predecessors. He was also determined to keep his focus on domestic affairs and make U.S. economic security a priority in foreign policy considerations.

Clinton's most consistent foreign policy effort was his determination to help Russia through its transition to political and economic democracy. He firmly supported Russian president Boris Yeltsin whom he met in Vancouver on April 4, and helped engineer increased economic aid to Russia on the part of the U.S. and its allies. The U.S. did not play a pivotal role in the breakthrough that resulted in a peace agreement between Israel and the Palestine Liberation Organization that was signed at the White House on September 13. But Clinton did promise that the U.S. would do everything possible to make the pact politically viable in the Middle East.

But his most visible problems during the first year were the bloody war in Bosnia and the effort to restore order in Somalia. Both of these were areas where there was little public enthusiasm for major U.S. commitments and where administration officials were confronted by an array of unappetizing choices.

During the presidential campaign, Clinton had freely criticized former President Bush for not taking a more aggressive American role in stopping the bloodshed in Bosnia, where the republic's Serbs had made huge territorial gains at the expense of the outgunned Muslim population. But on taking office, the administration's policy wavered several times between threats of possible U.S. military action and following the European Community's lead in seeking to bring about a negotiated solution to the conflict.

In September, after yielding to European resistance to military measures, Clinton made clear to Bosnian President Alija Izetbegovic that the U.S. was unlikely to use force and indicated that the Bosnian Muslims should try to get the best deal they could through negotiations, even though their bargaining position had greatly worsened since the beginning of the year.

Clinton took more assertive action on Somalia as the humanitarian mission there to safeguard the supply line of food increasingly took on the form of a police action to put down powerful warlords as a step towards enabling the country to reconstitute itself. When the United Nations peacekeeping contingent found itself unable to cope with Mohamed Farrah Aidid, the most powerful warlord, Clinton approved the use of U.S. forces to break Aidid's power. Administration officials found themselves caught between the belief that the UN mission might collapse if the U.S. withdrew and the fact that there was not the same kind of public support for an American commitment to restore order as there was earlier for the largely humanitarian mission that ensured the supply of food. Defence Secretary Les Aspin said that the U.S. would remain until there was order in Somalia, but many on Capitol Hill openly questioned the extent of U.S. involvement. In September the Senate voted 90 to 7 to insist that Clinton get congressional authorization if he wanted to keep U.S. forces in Somalia after November.

The public verdict on the first act of the Clinton Presidency indicated that Clinton had not yet accomplished one of the most important political tasks before him – broadening his base of support from the 43% of Americans who elected him. A *Washington Post*/ABC news poll in August found his overall approval rating after roughly 200 days in office to be 51% negative and 45% positive, generally in line with other major polls. His biggest triumph of the year – the budget victory – did not improve these standings because Americans were so evenly divided about whether they supported or opposed the economic plan. A *USA Today*/CNN/Gallup poll concluded, based on his approval ratings, that Americans had given Clinton "Cs" for his first six months in office – the lowest grade for any president at the same point in his term since Eisenhower.

Future in the Balance? The UN in 1993

by Arthur Kilgore

A past candidate for the post of Secretary General of the United Nations observed that, given the feats expected of the person, the limited resources available to achieve tasks, the restrictive conditions under which one worked and the range of personal qualities essential for someone to accomplish what is required, it had to be the world's most impossible job. It would not be surprising to find such sentiments echoed in the thoughts of the current Secretary General, Boutros Boutros-Ghali. Since his appointment in 1991 Boutros Ghali has had to undertake substantial reform to streamline the organization while assignments have been piled high by member states and funds have dwindled. Indeed, by the beginning of October 1993 the Secretary General calculated that the coffers had run dry and that the numerous UN peacekeeping operations would be in jeopardy unless financial relief was received quickly.

Yet rarely has the UN attained the prominence in world affairs that it has enjoyed in the past three years. After decades of what appeared to be terminal marginalization in world politics, the end of the Cold War heralded a new era for the UN, placing it at the centre of a "New World Order". Its role now included opposing aggressors, calming lethal conflicts, ushering new states into the world, overseeing elections, resolving long-standing political disputes and helping the innocent victims of disasters, both natural and manmade. The UN has seldom been out of the headlines since the late-1980s. But in 1993 those headlines, and the stories that lie beneath them, have become increasingly negative as the UN is criticized for failing in its duties in Somalia, Bosnia, Angola and elsewhere, while being simultaneously castigated for bad management practices back at headquarters. This situation, wherein the UN system is saddled with commitments beyond its capacity to carry them, led Boutros Ghali to remark wryly that the UN now suffers from "too much credibility".

It may be seen as scant consolation, perhaps even ominous portent, but the UN's predecessor, the League of Nations, founded in 1919, suffered similar censure. The League, like the UN, was a global organization primarily concerned with problems of international peace and security. Unlike the UN, there were numerous detractors from the beginning. The high ideals that marked US President Woodrow Wilson's proposals for a "peace without victors" and a postwar organization were transformed in the negotiations at Versailles into a punitive peace to be enforced by the League, prompting John Maynard Keynes to remark acidly, "If I were the Germans, I wouldn't sign for a moment." Charles Treveleyan, Liberal MP, and an ardent supporter of the concept of the League during World War I, despaired "of seeing good fruit come from so rotten a tree" when he observed the machinations to exclude the Soviet Union from the new organization.

By the outbreak of World War II the League's reputation for managing security problems was irreparably damaged. During the 1930s the evidence against the League mounted as it responded inadequately to the Japanese and Italian invasions of China and Ethiopia respectively, failed to effect the disarmament promised in its Covenant, found no significant role in mitigating the world economic depression, and failed utterly to halt the slide towards World War II. Moreover, the League never achieved universality, with key powers always missing from its councils. The US never joined the organization, Japan left it in the early-1930s, and Germany and the Soviet Union were to be eventually admitted only to depart shortly after their arrival. It had some triumphs, particularly on the economic and social side, but the prevailing consensus by 1940 was that the league had failed.

Despite the verdict on the League's record, plans were laid during World War II for a "second generation" of global organization to maintain international peace and security. In June 1945 51 states signed the UN Charter in San Francisco. Much in the Charter was either directly derivative of the League Covenant or the codification of practice that had emerged under the League – old wine in new bottles – but the cosmetic name change helped dissociate the UN from the aura of failure surrounding its predecessor. This strategy was significant in enticing the US, with its historic aversion to "entangling alliances" and the USSR, which had finally joined the League in 1936 only to find itself ignominiously expelled three years later for its invasion of Finland (by an organization that had remained remarkably tolerant of Japanese, German and Italian expansionism throughout the 1930s), to enlist in the new organization. These two superpowers of the post-war era were unlikely to buy a discredited organization, but their participation was deemed essential for any global organization to work. A new name served to make the UN more palatable to states that had previously rejected the League.

The drafters of the UN Charter also attempted to correct some of the design faults in the Covenant. The organization was not linked to any post-war peace agreements, thereby pre-empting any potential loss of legitimacy for the UN should the peace be judged unjust in the fashion of the Versailles Treaty. Decision-making was streamlined. Unanimous voting, used in both chambers of the League, was replaced by majority voting in both the UN General Assembly and Security Council, with the right to veto resolutions restricted to five permanent powers in the Security Council – the US, USSR, UK, France and China. Only one body, the Security Council, was to deal with peace and security issues. Chapter 7 of the Charter empowered the UN, like the League before it, to take strong collective enforcement action against an aggressor, up to and including the use of military force. But Article 43 of this Chapter was intended to give teeth to the system of collective security, by providing for the creation of a UN force that would be available at all times for UN action.

Perhaps the greatest attribute of the new organization was that it was a far more political animal, moving away from the rigid and idealistic legalism that had characterized the League. This more political nature, it was assumed, would give the UN greater flexibility to cope with the vicissitudes of the international political system.

High hopes for the UN were shattered by the onset of Cold War between the superpowers shortly after the end of World War II. Frequent resort to the veto in the Security Council by one or other of the superpowers blocked action on international peace and security.

Cold War antagonisms also soured the work of the more rhetorical forum of the General Assembly. The main change here was a shift in the balance of voting power. With the decolonization of the British and French empires in the late-1950s and 1960s, the superpowers' role was reversed in the General Assembly, with the US appearing isolated and defiant of international opinion as a Socialist/Third World coalition passed numerous, apparently hostile, resolutions. Substantive action on matters of peace and security occurred largely outside the UN, employing instead either existing security arrangements such as NATO and the Warsaw Pact, or, as in the case of the Strategic Arms Limitation Talks (SALT) and the Intermediate Nuclear Force reduction talks (INF), the medium of superpower summits.

One outgrowth of the deadlock in the Security Council and the marginalization of the UN in matters of peace and security was the practice of UN peacekeeping. Under Chapter 6 of the UN Charter, the UN was to seek peaceful methods for the settlement of international disputes. Under Chapter 7, it was authorized to use coercive measures against an aggressor. Peacekeeping (often cited as 'chapter six and a half') has no basis in the Charter but involves the deployment of forces under UN auspices to pacify a conflict, oversee a ceasefire or undertake other neutral activities to help the parties to a dispute maintain a disposition towards peace.

The UN Secretary General most closely associated with the developments of peacekeeping, Dag Hammarskjöld, recognized that by the mid-1950s the Cold War had rendered the UN impotent in certain areas of the world, such as Europe, where the superpowers claimed vital interests; and on certain issues, such as nuclear disarmament, which were judged to be the prerogative of the superpowers. He was also aware that newly emerging states fell into neither superpower's sphere of influence but were destined to become a potentially dangerous focus of Cold War rivalry, unless some alternative to superpower intervention was on offer.

One of the first peacekeeping operations was the United Nations Emergency Force (UNEF I) dispatched to the Sinai in 1956 to separate Israeli and Egyptian forces and encourage the withdrawal of British and French troops in the aftermath of the Suez Crisis. A subsequent peacekeeping force, the UN Operation in the Congo (ONUC) in 1960 was to plunge the practice of UN peacekeeping into bitter controversy. Originally conceived to allay the threat to superpower intervention, ONUC soon became embroiled in a civil war and abandoned its neutral role when it took enforcement action against rebel secessionists in Katanga province. ONUC's actions in the Congo and Hammarskjöld's independent attitude excited the hostility of the Soviet Union and France and nearly caused the financial collapse of the UN. ONUC had been the largest and most expensive operation ever undertaken by the UN, but the Soviet Union and France refused to pay their contributions because they disapproved of the operation. The compromise reached among the permanent powers to resolve the crisis ensured that Hammarskjöld's successors were more diplomatically circumspect about their role in matters relating to Security Council actions, while subsequent peacekeeping operations were smaller scale affairs with more limited mandates, making them less apt to be politically controversial. Although further peacekeeping operations were put into the field in the 1960s and early 1970s, there was a detectable and growing disillusion with the practice, given the mixed record and dubious achievements of the early wave of operations. There was to be a 10-year hiatus between the formation of the United Nations Interim Force in the Lebanon (UNIFIL) in 1978 and the creation of the next UN peacekeeping force.

The experience of UN peacekeeping during the Cold War was mirrored in the economic and social activities of the organization – initial and highly touted accomplishments were soon displaced by bitter controversy. Among the triumphs of the UN system in this area was the eradication of smallpox through a vaccination campaign of the World Health Organization (WHO) and UNESCO's efforts in the preservation of great cultural artefacts such as the restoration of Angkor Wat in Cambodia or the rescue of the temples of Abu Simbel in Egypt. By the 1960s however, the large number of new and poor states which had joined the UN during the previous decade, began to use the organization as a forum to voice their discontent with the international economic and social system. Most of the complaints were aimed at the United States and former colonial powers such as Britain and France. The height of this so-called North-South debate was reached in 1974 with the Declaration and Programme of Action on a New International Economic Order, a resolution passed at a special session of the General Assembly calling for a large transfer of "real resources" from North to South.

The North's response to these developments was strong and by the mid-1980s brought the UN to a period of crisis. Third World and Socialist states were accused of exercising "a tyranny of the majority" and charged with using the UN organizations for subsidized agitation. The UN was characterized as inefficient and overly bureaucratic. In some instances Western states withdrew from UN organizations they perceived as having particularly bad records; the US departed from the ILO in 1977 over the granting of observer status to the Palestine Liberation Organization, while the US and Britain left UNESCO in 1984 and 1985 respectively, disgruntled with the management of the organization by its Senegalese Director General, Amadou-Mahtar M'bow, and with the political slant of programmes adopted during his era.

The most debilitating blow in this struggle for the UN was delivered by the US Senate in the form of the Kassebaum Amendment to the Foreign Relations Act of 1985. The amendment specified that the United States was to withhold 20 per cent of its contribution to the UN until such time as reforms were instituted that would give major contributors greater say in "decisions of budgetary consequence". The impact of the withholdings, later compounded by additional cuts, meant that the US paid only about a quarter of its obligatory contribution to the UN. As the US provides 25 per cent of the core UN budget, these moves plunged the organization into immediate financial crisis.

The events of the mid-1980s marked the nadir of the UN's fortunes. Internal changes and international events coincided to perform a miracle resuscitation of the organization in the late 1980s. UN Secretary General Javier Pérez de Cuéllar responded to financial pressures by appointing a group of 18 experts to review the fiscal and management policies of the UN and propose reforms. The reforms instituted proved satisfactory and in 1988 the US administration promised to restore full funding to the UN.

Other factors also prompted a rethink among major contributor countries about the usefulness of the UN. In particular, new problems with international dimensions, such as AIDS, environmental degradation, drug trafficking and mass flows of refugees across state boundaries began to appear, giving rise to a "New Agenda" in international politics. At just the moment when member states seemed content to consign the UN to the diplomatic rubbish bin, its serviceability became all too evident, re-emphasizing to those states which had been most dismissive of the UN the collaborative purposes for which they had created the organization.

Most significant of all were the momentous changes in the Soviet Union which would eventually lead to the collapse of Communist rule in the country, the break-up of the union, and the end of the Cold War. The reformist regime of Mikhail Gorbachev struck a new, positive attitude towards the UN, reversing a traditional Soviet aversion to multilateral diplomacy. The Soviets announced in 1988 that they would pay their long-standing arrears on the peacekeeping account. They also advocated a more active role for the UN in maintaining international peace and security.

The more positive attitudes of the US and the USSR were reinforced by a British initiative in 1986 to establish regular meetings of the permanent members of the Security Council to enable them to coordinate their approach to problems prior to discussion in the Security Council. The fruits of the new-found consensus in the Security Council soon appeared. In 1987, after years of impasse in the Security Council, a strongly worded resolution on a ceasefire in the Iran–Iraq war was passed, which laid the groundwork for a cessation of hostilities and the establishment of the United Nations Iran–Iraq Military Observer Group (UNIIMOG) to supervise the disengagement of forces. This was rapidly followed by the creation of UN peacekeeping forces for other problem areas of the world, including Namibia, Afghanistan, Angola and Central America. Indeed, between 1988 and 1992 the UN had proposed the initiation of 16 peacekeeping missions, 3 more than had been created in the entire 43 years of UN operation before 1988. As if to augur a new dawn for peacekeeping, UN forces were awarded the Nobel Prize for Peace in 1988. By the beginning of 1993 the UN had mounted some of the most ambitious peacekeeping operations in its history, including the United Nations Protection Force (UNPROFOR) in territories of the former Yugoslavia, the United Nations Transitional Authority in Cambodia (UNTAC), and the United Nations Operation in Somalia (UNOSOM).

The high-water mark of post-Cold War cooperation on security in the UN occurred in 1990–91, as member states moved to meet the challenge posed by the August 1990 Iraqi invasion of Kuwait. The Security Council took a number of strong measures against Iraq under Chapter 7 of the UN Charter, including the imposition of an air and sea blockade, before passing Resolution 678 authorizing the use of force to remove Iraq from Kuwaiti territory. The consequent Operation Desert Storm marked the first time since the Korean War that forces were dispatched with the sanction of the UN to repel an aggressor. The exact role of the UN was problematic since allied armies in the Gulf War were not under the control of the Security Council and did not march under a UN flag. Instead, the forces were predominantly US troops and the chain of command was primarily a US one with some of the participating countries retaining individual control over the units they contributed. This was not how the founders of the UN had envisioned the application of Charter provisions on peace and security, but the peculiarities of the Gulf operation did not deter advocates of the UN from reading into the Iraq case the revival of collective security under the UN.

Not only did the end of the Cold War appear to have been the key that unlocked the door which had been closed on UN collective security operations throughout most of its existence, it also seemed to strengthen the resolve of the major powers to imbue the organization with new, previously uncontemplated powers. The passage of Resolution 688, dubbed by some as the mother of all resolutions, in the summer of 1991, raised the possibility of the UN acquiring unprecedented powers to intervene into a state to protect the rights of its own citizens, in contradistinction to the guarantees of sovereignty and non-interference found in the Charter. In particular, this resolution was used as the basis for the protection of the Kurdish population of northern Iraq from the vengeful reprisal of the Saddam Hussein government in the aftermath of the Gulf War.

The year 1993 has proved to be a severely testing one for the revived post-Cold War UN. As far as peacekeeping is concerned, a proliferation of operations is clearly not synonymous with increased effectiveness. UNPROFOR has often found its primary task of delivering humanitarian aid blocked by determined parties to the conflict in Bosnia and Croatia and has stood by helplessly as people have been starved, tortured and killed in ethnic conflict of heinous brutality.

In Somalia, UN peacekeepers resumed control of the operation there, under the designation UNOSOM II, in May, following operation Restore Hope, which saw US Marines landed at Mogadishu in December 1992 to ensure delivery of food aid and disarm warring clans. Despite US claims to have pacified the situation, UNOSOM troops failed to provide a security framework in the country and instead became the object of vilification by one of the factions led by the warlord, Mohamad Farah Aidid. On 6 June, 24 Pakistani UN troops were killed in an attack by Aidid supporters. American helicopter gunships launched an assault on a supposed Aidid stronghold in reprisal, killing innocent bystanders in the process and further embroiling the UN operation in the civil war. By the end of the summer, the cracks in the Somali operation were clearly visible. As Italy and the United States quarrelled openly about positioning and command of Italian troops attached to UNOSOM, Secretary General Boutros Boutros-Ghali called for larger numbers of troops to be sent to Somalia and for member states to provide additional financial and military support to the operation, and Congressional leaders in the United States began to wonder aloud whether the US had become bogged down in a quagmire. As in the 1960s, so in the 1990s – the more complicated a conflict grew, the more the capacity of the UN to maintain a sustained and clearly defined role began to be questioned.

In Cambodia the UN managed to oversee elections in May, despite numerous difficulties along the way. The fragility of the consequent political settlement in that country notwithstanding, what had been the largest and most expensive UN operation ever (until troop levels in Somalia were increased) stuck to its timetable for withdrawal in autumn 1993. The dangers of such a situation, however, were emphasized in Angola, where the work of the United

Nations Angola Verification Mission (UNAVEM) was unstitched when the Union for the Total Liberation of Angola (UNITA) under Jonas Savimbi refused to accept the election results and renewed the civil conflict there, while charging the UN with bias. What had been judged to have been a successful peacekeeping operation began to look more like a waste of time.

The UN has enjoyed a measure of success in some of its actions on peace and security. One of the most notable of these was the capitulation of the Haitian regime that had overthrown the elected government of Father Jean-Bertrand Aristide, under strain from the comprehensive economic sanctions imposed by the Security Council. However, other sanctions imposed on Iraq, Libya and Serbia have had little noticeable effect on the political behaviour of the target governments and have been subjected to criticism for the suffering they cause among the innocent.

Recognition of the shortcomings of UN machinery for peace and security is widespread and recommendations for reform have been heard from all quarters, not the least of which was the Secretary General's own report to the Security Council in June 1992, entitled *Agenda for Peace*. Among the proposals of Boutros-Ghali was that forces be made available on call to the UN by member states, both for purposes of peacekeeping and enforcement actions. He also recommended that Article 43 be resurrected and that negotiations on a UN force be initiated. Sir Brian Urquhart, a former UN Under-Secretary General, proposed in an article in the *New York Review of Books*, that a standing UN volunteer force be established which would be separate from any national force.

Another issue under consideration is the structure of the Security Council. In a time when Germany and Japan are being pressed to assume greater responsibilities in the management of the international system, it has been argued that they must be made permanent members of the Security Council to reflect their financial and political status. At the same time the legitimacy of Britain and France continuing to hold veto power has been questioned, especially since Japan and Germany now contribute twice as much financially to the UN as do these former great powers. In the summer of 1993 the US threw its weight behind the idea of Security Council reform, including expansion in the number of permanent seats as well as overall membership. The sum of all these suggestions is that the UN machinery for peace and security is creaking loudly and in desperate need of oil to enable it to cope with the sudden and accelerated demands placed on it in the post-Cold War world.

On the economic and social side too, weaknesses of the system continue to make themselves felt, even though the earlier antagonism between North and South has largely dissipated. In an effort to reform UN management, Boutros-Ghali reorganized the Secretariat in 1992, eliminating a number of middle management positions and consolidating a number of offices in newly created departments headed by Under-Secretary Generals. One such example is the Department for Humanitarian Affairs (DHA), set up to coordinate UN humanitarian assistance activities. Although intended as a more authoritative replacement for the Office of the United Nations Disaster Relief Coordinator, the DHA has not been able to assert a clear-cut role in coordinating relief operations as old structures, prerogatives and habits persist, and disarray often continues to prevail in the field.

The experience of the UN in the last year has served to eliminate the misimpression that the end of the Cold War was all that was needed to enable the UN to assume the full and effective role in international affairs its founders intended. The happy set of circumstances that produced the euphoria about the UN flower finally blossoming in the late 1980s and early 1990s has now yielded to the realization that the likelihood of UN success is no greater than in the past. This in turn has raised a pertinent question – just how ill-prepared is the existing UN to meet the challenges of the post-Cold War future?

Favourite People of British Youth, 1993–94

Sport
Linford Christie, athlete
Sally Gunnell, athlete

Television
Jack Dee, comedian
Roseanne Arnold, comedienne

Politics
John Smith, leader of the Labour Party
Betty Boothroyd, Speaker of the House of Commons

Cinema
Steve Martin, actor & comedian
Whoopi Goldberg, actress

Music
Phil Collins, pop singer & actor
Whitney Houston, pop singer

Writing
Roald Dahl, British author
Judy Blume, U.S. author

CHRONOLOGY OF THE YEAR'S EVENTS

Reported Month by Month in 3 Categories: National, International and General 1 Sep. 1992 – 31 Aug. 1993

SEPTEMBER

National

Education – Her Majesty's Inspectorate reported "limited confidence" in the GCSE examination, designed to cater for 90% of academic ability in secondary school pupils. With successes increasing every year since its introduction in 1988, HMI suspected the exam was too easy. On **Sep. 4** Education Sec. John Patten said that the examiners must put their own house in order, but did not rule out the abolition of the GCSE. Meanwhile, the British Institute of Managers described the "A" level system as "fundamentally flawed". On **Sep. 10** the National Curriculum Council recommended greater emphasis on spelling, grammar and standard English, plus a cannon of great works, and tests for 14-year-olds on Shakespeare. On **Sep. 15** junior education minister Nigel Forman told vice-chancellors of the new universities created from polytechnics to tighten up the monitoring of degree standards and that the growing number of first-class degrees would have to be justified. In stark contrast to their English counterparts, the Welsh schools inspectors declared themselves satisfied, **Sep. 26**, that the GCSE worked well.

Money Crisis and Black Wednesday – With the money markets in turmoil on **Sep. 10**, the pound brushed the ERM (Exchange Rate Mechanism) floor – the point at which the Government would have to raise exchange rates. Prime Minister John Major insisted that the conquest of inflation was the centre of economic policy and that rather than devalue sterling, interest rates would rise if necessary. Chancellor of the Exchequer Norman Lamont likewise held firm as over the following days the European money system showed signs of cracking. Currency speculators attacked the lira, which devalued 7%. On **Sep. 16**, "Black Wednesday', the pound came into line for frenzied attack in the markets. Billions were spent in propping it up, and interest rates shot from 10 to 12 to 15% – to no avail. On **Sep. 17** sterling plunged out of the ERM, and British membership was suspended. Politically, this was seen as a double blow to John Major, who as chancellor had taken Britain into the ERM. On **Sep. 22** Norman Lamont completed the U-turn, with interest rates dropped to 9%, and on **Sep. 24** the prime minister announced in Parliament that there would be no quick return to the ERM. According to the business information group Dun & Bradford, **Sep. 30**, more than 1,220 companies were going to the wall every week in Britain. Company failure in the first 9 months of the year was up by 40%.

Law and Order – The Home Office announced, **Sep. 18**, that Britain's 130,000 police officers were to receive a 6.5% pay increase, putting them at the top of the public servants' pay range for the fourth consecutive year. On **Sep. 22** Home Sec. Kenneth Clarke ruled out the idea of a national police force, and added that inept or lazy officers should be improved or removed "fairly and sensitively".

Ethics and the Law – On **Sep. 21** Dr Nigel Cox, who gave a lethal dose of potassium chloride to a terminally ill patient, was convicted of attempted murder at Winchester Crown Court. He was sentenced to 12 months' imprisonment, suspended for 1 year. On **Sep. 25** Kiranjit Ahluwalia, jailed for life for killing her violent husband by setting fire to him, was freed at the Old Bailey after pleading guilty to manslaughter on the grounds of diminished responsibility.

Minister Resigns – Heritage Sec. David Mellor, who had been ragged in the tabloid press since mid-July for his liaison with actress Antonia de Sancha, resigned **Sep. 25**. Ironically, his long-awaited resignation finally occurred because of a quite different "unsuitable friendship". It was reported that Mellor and his family had been entertained by Mona Bauwens, the daughter of a PLO (Palestine Liberation Organization) fund-raiser, at her villa in Marbella.

Lies, Damned Lies and Opinion Polls – A state-of-the-nation poll published in the *Guardian*, **Sep. 14**, found that more British voters favoured a close relationship with the European Community (even if it meant some loss of sovereignty) than reject it. Support had waned, however, for privatization, the retention of Britain's nuclear deterrent and making the conquest of inflation a higher priority than that of employment. On **Sep. 20** a poll carried out for the *Independent on Sunday* found that if a referendum on ratification of the Maastricht Treaty were to be held, as in France, then 24% of those polled would vote yes, 47% no, and 29% would not commit themselves either way.

International

France Votes Yes to Maastricht – France approved the European Community's Treaty on European Union that had been negotiated in Maastricht, the Netherlands, in 1991. On **Sep. 2** the office of Prime Minister John Major said that, in the event that French voters rejected the treaty, the British government would withdraw from Parliament the bill to ratify it. On **Sep. 3** former Prime Minister Margaret Thatcher, an opponent of the treaty, charged that tying the value of the British pound to that of the German mark had prolonged Britain's recession. Major, **Sep. 7**, rejected calls for a referendum on the treaty in Britain. He discounted fears that a Europe united by the treaty would smother national identities. In France the campaign for the treaty was led by Pres. François Mitterrand, who denied that Germany would dominate a unified European Community and that French culture would be submerged. In the **Sep. 20** referendum, the French approved the treaty, but with only 51% voting in favour. France thus joined Greece, Ireland and Luxembourg in completing ratification. Danish Premier Poul Schlutter said, **Sep. 22**, that Denmark, where the treaty had been rejected, would vote again on it in 1993.

Taiwan, Saudi Arabia to Get U.S. Jets – Pres. George Bush announced, **Sep. 2**, that he had approved the sale of 150 F-16 fighter jets to the Republic of China (Taiwan). The People's Republic of China, **Sep. 3**, denounced the sale as a violation of an agreement in 1982 that curbed arms sales to Taiwan. On **Sep. 11** Bush said his administration had approved the sale of 72 F-15 fighter jets to Saudi Arabia. Israel, **Sep. 13**, objected to the sale but indicated no attempt would be made to get Congress to disapprove it. The manufacturers benefiting from the sales were General Dynamics Corp. and McDonnell Douglas Corp., respectively. Some Democrats charged that the sales represented attempts by Bush to buy votes in an election year.

United Nations Expels Yugoslavia – The U.N. General Assembly voted to oust Yugoslavia because of its involvement in the war in Bosnia-Herzegovina. The risk involved in bringing relief supplies to the Bosnians was apparent, **Sep. 3**, when an Italian plane bringing U.N. aid crashed without explanation near Sarajevo. Four crew members were killed. On **Sep. 8** 2 French U.N. peacekeeping officers were killed outside Sarajevo when their convoy was struck by mortar and machine-gun fire. Before the General Assembly vote, **Sep. 22**, Premier Milan Panic of Yugoslavia argued that expulsion would just strengthen the hand of "militant nationalists" in Belgrade. He condemned the "ethnic cleansing" policy practised by the Serbs in Croatia and Bosnia. The Assembly vote was 127–6, with 26 abstentions, although the word "expel" was not included in the resolution. Rather, Yugoslavia's seat was declared vacant. This was the first time that a U.N. member had been removed from the organization.

Middle East Talks Remain Stalled – Arab and Israeli negotiators met again in Washington for a new round of talks, **Sep. 3**, and Israeli Prime Minister Yitzhak Rabin subsequently said that a land-for-peace agreement was likely. Pres. Hafez al-Assad, **Sep. 9**, said publicly for the first time that Syria was willing to seek a peace treaty with Israel. On **Sep. 14**, however, Syria's delegation said that Israel must withdraw from the occupied territories before a treaty could be negotiated.

Maoist Guerrilla Leader Seized in Peru – Abimael Guzmán Reynoso, leader of Sendero Luminoso (Shining Path), a Maoist guerrilla organization, was seized by police in Peru, **Sep. 12**. Three other guerrilla leaders were also captured in raids on 2 houses in Lima, the capital. Shining Path's 12-year rebellion had resulted in 25,000 deaths.

General

Biggest Bankrupt – Kevin, youngest son of deceased newspaper proprietor Robert Maxwell, became Britain's biggest bankrupt, **Sep. 4**. Liquidators trying to trace millions stolen from the Maxwell empire's pension funds filed a bankruptcy order of £406.5 million against him.

U.N. Acts in Famine Crisis –The United Nations stepped up its efforts to reduce the death toll from famine in Africa. The U.S. expanded its own airlift, announcing, **Sep. 4**, that it would deliver food to 2 towns in Somalia and to another in Kenya. The first 40 soldiers, all Pakistani, of a U.N. peacekeeping force arrived in Somalia, **Sep. 14**, to make sure that food reached the needy. The country was plagued by war as well as famine, and one military commander had opposed the U.N. role, arguing that his forces could distribute donated food. The population of Sudan was also suffering as the result of civil war. A U.N. official found, **Sep. 16**, that the city of Juba, which was swollen with refugees to a population of 300,000, was in desperate need of food. Altogether, some 3 million people in the country had left their homes in search of food or to escape the fighting.

50th Shuttle Trip Focuses on Science – The 50th U.S. shuttle mission began, **Sep. 12**, when the orbiter *Endeavour* was launched in Florida. The crew included the first black woman in space, the first married couple to travel in space together, and the first Japanese citizen to ride in a shuttle. Japan was the source of 34 of the 43 experiments planned for the flight. The *Endeavour* landed in Florida on **Sep. 20**.

London Zoo Struggles On – Threatened with closure by the end of the month, London Zoo announced, **Sep. 24**, the development of a kit to indicate when she-elephants are capable of conception. The zoo's candidate was found to be in the mood and trucked off to meet a male elephant from Chester. To finance the tryst a "jumbo weekend" was organized "to maintain the zoo's existence in people's minds. Many think it is still closed," said chief executive Dr Jo Gibbs.

Boy Wins Suit to Get new Parents – A 12-year-old boy won a suit in a Florida circuit court in Orlando, **Sep. 25**, that ended the parental rights of his natural mother and allowed his foster parents to adopt him. The case may have been the first in which family rights were ended as a result of a legal action brought by a child. During the trial the boy, Gregory Kingsley, testified that his mother, Rachel, had not visited him for almost 2 years while he was in foster care.

OCTOBER

National

The Economy – On **Oct. 1** John Major described Chancellor Lamont as "brilliant". Official figures showed, **Oct. 3**, that gold and currency reserves had shrunk by £4.4 billion after propping up the pound during recent crises. With the pound 15% down against the German mark since Black Wednesday, £20 billion was wiped off share values, **Oct. 15**. The Confederation of British Industry accused the Government of "dancing in the dark". On **Oct. 22** the British Chamber of Commerce reported falls in sales, orders, investment, employment and confidence. The diagnosis was "the second leg of a double dip depression". In his Mansion House speech, **Oct. 30**, one of the traditional occasions for the review of economic policy, the Chancellor spoke of "rebalancing" after the departure from the ERM, and in an address notably short on specifics, indicated that the defeat of inflation was no longer a burning priority. Growth and economic confidence were to be encouraged, though Mr Lamont noted in passing that the latter was an "elusive quality" and "could not be drawn like a rabbit out of a hat".

Unemployment – Job losses for the first week of October stood at 9,701, including 91 field officers from the Construction Industry Training Board. Their task had been to seek jobs for young people in the building trades. The unemployment total was 9.9%, or 2.8 million.

Tory Trials and Tribulations – At the Conservative party conference in Brighton on **Oct. 6** ex-party chairman Norman Tebbit rose to denounce John Major to the party faithful, urging him to "pursue policies to restore our economy . . . and manage affairs for ourselves in our own interests". This was during an uncharacteristically robust and bitter debate on the Maastricht Treaty. Mr Major was clearly embarrassed, and his difficulties over Europe and the economy further damaged his credibility with the party throughout the month. On **Oct. 21** an article in *The Times* described the prime minister as lonely, withdrawn, mistrustful and underfed. Despite vigorous denials from Downing Street officials, the newspaper stuck by the story. A Mori poll in the

Guardian, **Oct. 22**, showed the prime minister to be the least popular ever, with only 16% satisfied with his performance.

Terrorism Strikes Again – Between **Oct. 7** and **25** the IRA caused 14 explosions in and around London. The bombs, placed in litter bins, cars and on railway tracks, injured a total of 11 people. The one fatality came at lunchtime, **Oct. 11**, from a bomb in The Sussex pub, Covent Garden.

House Prices – Figures released **Oct. 9** showed that house prices had fallen by 2.8% in September, the equivalent of a one-third price cut over a year. There had also been a sharp drop in sales.

Motor Troubles – Decreasing sales in the car market caused Ford to announce, **Oct. 9**, their third price cut of the year. Some dealers were instructed to make reductions of as much as £2,000. Industry minister Tim Sainsbury would not respond to pleas from the motor industry for the Government to "spell out its programme for development of our manufacturing base".

Crisis in the Coal Industry – The government announced, **Oct. 13**, the closure of 31 pits at the end of the week, with the loss of 30,000 jobs. While trade unions claimed, **Oct. 14**, that redundancies could number 100,000, the High Court put a temporary halt on the closure the following day. Anger and horror at the government's attitude came from all walks of life and all political persuasions, including the Tory backbenches. Demonstrations abounded. Bowing to public pressure, the government announced, **Oct. 19**, a temporary reprieve for 21 pits, to be followed by a complete energy policy inquiry. After 3 days of concessions, the pit closure bill scraped through the House of Commons, **Oct. 21**, by 13 votes.

BCCI Report Points Finger – Lord Justice Bingham's report on the collapse of the Bank of Credit and Commerce International was released **Oct. 22**. It was heavily critical of the Bank of England, which had ignored repeated warnings of fraud within BCCI. Chancellor Norman Lamont told the Commons that legislation was being prepared which would give the Bank of England power to close banks that were not properly regulated.

Police Heckle Home Secretary – At a meeting of the Police Federation (the rank and filer's trade union) Home Sec. Kenneth Clarke was treated to a gruff attack on the criminal justice system, particularly its failure to deal with young offenders. With characteristic pugnacity Mr Clarke responded that the force should stop complaining and get on with the job if it wanted the public's respect. He was heckled and booed from the floor.

International

U.S. Senate Approves Treaty on Nuclear Weapons – The Senate, **Oct. 1**, approved a treaty, signed in 1991, that would reduce the number of strategic (long-range) weapons held by the U.S. and 4 independent states that were formerly part of the Soviet Union. Under its terms, the number of U.S. warheads would drop from 12,646 (in 1990) to 8,556, and the number of Russian warheads would decline from 11,012 held by the Soviet Union (in 1990) to 6,163. Three former Soviet republics, Belarus, Kazakhstan and Ukraine, would have no nuclear weapons. Of the 4 former Soviet republics, only Kazakhstan had approved the treaty so far.

Brazil's President Resigns, Faces Trial – The president of Brazil, Fernando Collor de Mello, surrendered his powers, **Oct. 2**. He faced trial in the Senate on accusations of complicity in a multimillion-dollar bribery scheme. Collor's wife was also under investigation, for allegedly embezzling money from a federal charity that she operated. Vice Pres. Itamar Augusto Franco became acting president, **Oct. 2**.

Peru Rebel Leader Gets Life Term – Abimael Guzmán Reynoso, leader of Shining Path, the Maoist guerrilla movement in Peru, who had been captured in September, was sentenced, **Oct. 7**, to life in prison after being convicted of treason. The judge, who wore a hood to protect his identity, said that Guzmán had been responsible for 20,000 deaths and $20 billion in damages that had occurred during the 12-year war. Meanwhile, the rebellion continued. On **Oct. 10** Shining Path guerrillas killed 44 people in the village of Ayacucho.

Vietnam Offers Help on Missing Combatants – Pres. George Bush said, **Oct. 23**, that Vietnam had agreed to provide to the U.S. all documents, photographs and personal effects relating to American servicemen still missing after the Vietnam War. The U.S. listed 2,265 Americans as unaccounted for in Indo-China. These included men known to be dead whose bodies had not been recovered.

General

Genetic Mapping – A landmark in genetic research was reached, **Oct. 1**, when an international team of scientists published a map of the DNA sequence in human chromosome 21. The project aims eventually to map the entire human genetic make-up at an estimated cost of $200 million (£113 million).

Guilty as Charged – Home Secretary Kenneth Clarke failed, **Oct. 2**, to recommend a free pardon for Derek Bentley, who was hanged in January 1953 for the murder of a policeman. Bentley's accomplice Christopher Craig had fired the fatal shot, but was too young to be executed. A previous application for a pardon was turned down 20 years ago.

It Was 30 Years Ago Today – It took 17 takes to get a satisfactory recording, but the Beatles' first chart success, "Love Me Do", was eventually released on **Oct. 5**, 1962. On the other side of the Atlantic 30 years ago, Bob Dylan released his debut album on **Oct. 16**. Stars gathered to celebrate the thirtieth anniversaries of both releases.

Heavenly Disaster – Comet Swift-Tuttle, which regularly crosses the Earth's orbit, could collide with the planet on Aug. 14, 2126, Dr Duncan Steel of the Anglo-Australian Observatory announced **Oct. 26**. It was such a collision about 65 million years ago which may have wiped out the dinosaurs, but the odds against impact in 2126 were quoted as 400 to 1.

NOVEMBER

National

Racism in Legal Profession – Statistics released by the Council of Legal Education, **Nov. 1**, revealed that black students at the Bar's law school had 3 times the failure rate of their white peers. The Society of Black Lawyers said that this was the greatest disparity between black and white anywhere in the educational system. An independent survey commissioned by the Lord Chancellor's department and the Bar Council revealed, **Nov. 25**, that the legal profession is male-dominated, institutionally discriminatory against women, and with those in positions of power refusing to acknowledge it.

Law and Order – **Nov. 2** saw the opening of a 6-month inquiry chaired by Sir Patrick Sheehy, charged with producing recommendations which would allow more effective use of police resources. Initial considerations included enhanced salaries for more competent officers and powers to dismiss the inept. Targets for equal opportunities were also on the agenda, as were a police university and an ombudsman to replace the present Police Complaints Authority.

Great Britain and Europe – Prime Minister Major's bill towards ratification of the Maastricht Treaty lurched through the House of Commons, **Nov. 4**. Despite furious activity by the whips, 26 Tories voted against their government, but the Liberal Democrats came to Major's rescue and a carefully worded motion was carried by 3 votes. The next day Brussels was "appalled" to learn the price of victory, which was that final ratification might still take over a year, despite previous guarantees to the contrary. On **Nov. 9** European Community foreign ministers told Foreign Sec. Douglas Hurd that he must produce a firm timetable soon, but there was respite for the British, **Nov. 11**, when Chancellor Helmut Kohl said he was content that ratification could wait as late as the end of 1993.

Important Court Cases – Invoking rights granted under the 1992 Children's Act, an 11-year-old girl from Leeds won a court order, **Nov. 5**, allowing her to leave her mother's home and return to the couple who had previously fostered her. The girl is thought to be the youngest person to make a successful application since the introduction of the Act. The General Medical Council decided, **Nov. 17**, not to strike off Dr Nigel Cox, who gave a terminally ill patient a lethal injection. Welcoming the result, Dr Cox called for a public debate on euthanasia. A High Court judge ruled, **Nov. 19**, that Tony Bland, who had been in a persistent vegetative state since the Hillsborough football disaster 3½ years ago, could "die with dignity". The ruling allowed for the withdrawal of liquid food and antibiotics which had maintained his existence.

Economic Indicators – At the Institute of Directors' annual conference, **Nov. 8**, business confidence was reported to be at its lowest since the Gulf War, with declining profits and dwindling order books, particularly in the south. A report by the Joseph Rowntree Foundation, published **Nov. 12**, showed that one in five home-owners who had bought during the last 5 years now found their property worth less than their mortgage – almost double the number of a year ago. Negative equity was estimated at £2.68 billion, compared with £1.2 billion in 1991. The same day Chancellor Lamont's autumn statement imposed the first pay policy since the 1970s, with pay rises for 5 million public sector workers limited to 1½% over the following year. Lamont also announced a £1.3 billion cut in the defence budget over the next 3 years, tax relief on new investment for industrialists, and a 1% cut in interest rates. The Chancellor was generally congratulated for neat manoeuvring in a tight corner, but some gloss came off the next day when it was announced that factory output for September was the lowest since January. MPs voted, **Nov. 25**, to freeze their annual salary of £30,854 for 1 year, but were promised a "catch-up" settlement later.

Matrix-Churchill Trial Collapses – The trial of 3 former executives of the Matrix-Churchill machine tools firm, charged with avoiding export controls, collapsed **Nov. 9**. What did emerge was that the British Government had connived at contravening its own policy. From 1988 to 1990 it had promoted the sale to Iraq of equipment used in its war with Iran, despite all claims to the contrary. By **Nov. 13** it was clear that the Foreign Office knew of this when John Major was foreign secretary. On **Nov. 16** an inquiry under Lord Justice Scott was set up to look at the affair. John Major admitted that as chancellor in 1990 he had been aware of the sales.

Unemployment – The Ministry of Defence announced, **Nov. 12**, the loss of 2,000 naval support jobs and closure of the Portland naval base in Dorset. Figures released by the Department of Employment, **Nov. 17**, showed that the number of people out of work and claiming benefits had virtually doubled since the spring of 1990. On **Nov. 19** a total of 10,000 job losses was announced, half of them by British Rail.

Education – A report published **Nov. 12** by her Majesty's Inspectorate found that girls get better preparation for adulthood in an all-girls school. They are more self-confident, have higher expectations than girls in mixed schools and the overall quality of their lessons is higher, too. Education Sec. John Patten claimed, **Nov. 19**, an "information revolution" as the first national school-by-school tables of "A"-level and GCSE results in England were published. In fact, the figures were incomplete, as some schools had boycotted the exercise, results from sixth-form and further education colleges had not been included, and there was further confusion about the way other schools had been listed. Critics called the tables "a sham" and a waste of money, and head teachers across the country responded with volleys of complaint. In Parliament, **Nov. 24**, John Patten promised more results in years to come, but conceded that the tables would have to be improved.

International

Rushdie Reward Increased – In Iran, **Nov. 2**, Ayatollah Hassan Sanei announced that his Khordid 15 Foundation was increasing the $1 million reward for killing author Salman Rushdie. The announcement came after Rushdie had been cordially received in Germany, Iran's largest trading partner.

U.S. Presidential Election – Gov. Bill Clinton of Arkansas was elected 42nd president of the U.S. on **Nov. 3**. His running mate on the Democratic ticket, Sen. Albert Gore Jr., of Tennessee, was elected vice president. Clinton and Gore carried 32 states and the District of Columbia and thereby won 370 electoral votes. Pres. George Bush, the Republican candidate, and his running mate, Vice Pres. Dan Quayle, carried 18 states for a total of 168 electoral votes. In the nationwide popular vote, the official tally gave Clinton 44,908,254 (43%), Bush 39,102,343 (38%), independent candidate H. Ross Perot 19,741,065 (19%), and all other candidates 666,744 (1%). The Democrats held control of both houses of Congress. They emerged from the voting with a 57–42 margin in the Senate, with one seat to be determined in a runoff. In the House the Republicans gained 10 seats, but the Democrats still held a 258–176 majority, with 1 independent. Altogether, there would be 110 new faces in the House, representing the biggest turnover since 1948. The new House would contain record numbers of women (47), blacks (38) and Hispanics (17).

U.N. Authorizes Blockade of Yugoslavia – The U.N. Security Council authorized a naval blockade as a means of enforcing its economic sanctions against Yugoslavia. On **Nov. 9** the ethnic Serb leader in Bosnia proposed a partition of Bosnia along ethnic lines. Much of Bosnia's territory had already been divided up by Serbs and Croats, and the Serb leader, Radovan Karadzic, recommended that the permanent partition be based on how the territory was then controlled. The U.N. Council adopted its blockade resolution, **Nov. 16**, by a 13–0 vote with 2 abstentions. Ships of all nations were empowered to halt and inspect vessels entering or leaving Yugoslav waters. The Council, however, did not act on an appeal from Muslim states that Bosnia be exempted from an arms embargo imposed in 1991 on Yugoslavia and all former Yugoslav republics.

Germany Confronts Fascism – Neo-Nazi violence, which had been on the rise in Germany, claimed more victims in November. Extreme right-wing organizations had focused their anger on a provision in Germany's constitution that guaranteed that any refugee could seek political asylum in Germany. Although most applicants were ultimately rejected, they were allowed to remain in Germany and receive benefits while their status was being considered. Some 1,800 acts of violence against those seeking asylum had been reported in 1992. In Berlin, **Nov. 8**, 350,000 people demonstrated against right-wing violence, and a similar protest drew 100,000 in Bonn, **Nov. 14**. Police in Halbe, south of Berlin, blocked an attempted march by neo-Nazis, **Nov. 15**. A Turkish woman and 2 Turkish girls, members of a family of "guest workers" who had lived in Germany for 2 decades, were killed in Moelln, **Nov. 23**, by a firebomb. Their deaths brought to 16 the number of people killed in right-wing attacks in 1992. Under a provision of the constitution, the government announced, **Nov. 27**, that it was banning the Nationalist Front, a neo-Nazi group.

Ex-Communists Win Lithuanian Election – On **Nov. 15**, in the second round of Lithuania's parliamentary elections, former communists of the Democratic Labour Party (DLP) secured a majority in the Supreme Council. The DLP won at least 79 of the 141 seats to 35 for the Sajudis nationalist movement, which had run the government.

Czechs, Slovaks Move Towards Separation – The Czech and Slovak regional parliaments adopted a joint resolution, **Nov. 17**, authorizing the separation of Czechoslovakia into 2 separate, independent republics. The Czechoslovak Federal Assembly (parliament) approved a constitutional amendment, **Nov. 25**, permitting the federation to dissolve without a national referendum.

Senators in Vietnam for MIA Inquiry – Three U.S. senators and a general travelled to Southeast Asia to seek information on 2,265 American servicemen who were missing in action during the Vietnam War. The delegation, headed by Sen. John Kerry (D, Mass), met with Vietnamese Pres. Le Duc Anh in Hanoi, **Nov. 18**, and visited Laos, **Nov. 19**. Members of the delegation also travelled to the Mekong River Delta and Danang province, **Nov. 20**, to investigate reports of American MIAs living there. The Vietnamese gave their visitors personal effects of dead or captured Americans, including photographs, letters, diaries, wallets and uniforms.

U.S., Europe Reach Compromise on Trade – Negotiators from the U.S. and the European Community achieved a breakthrough in trade talks, **Nov. 20**. For years the U.S. had pressed European countries to reduce their subsidies on farm products. Subsidies for oilseed products had been a particular sticking point. Oilseed trade was relatively insignificant, but farm lobbies from France and the U.S. had prevented agreement. In the compromise the U.S. accepted more modest limits on subsidies than it had sought, and the Europeans agreed to across-the-board limits. French negotiators, however, objected strongly to the agreement.

Nations Act Again on Ozone Threat – Delegates from 87 nations met in Copenhagen and agreed to accelerate their schedule for phasing out chemicals that damaged the Earth's ozone layer. Under the agreement of **Nov. 25**, some chemicals would be regulated for the first time. Chlorofluorocarbons (CFCs), chemicals thought to be most harmful to the ozone, would be phased out by 1996 rather than 2000.

U.S. Offers to Intervene in Somalia – The U.S. moved towards a humanitarian intervention in Somalia, where thieves had seized most of the food and other supplies being shipped from other countries to starving people. Lawrence Eagleburger, the acting U.S. secretary of state, meeting with U.N. Secretary General Boutros Boutros-Ghali in New York, **Nov. 26**, offered the use of as many as 30,000 American troops. The U.N. force in Somalia consisted of 500 Pakistani peace-keepers, and 3,000 from other countries were due to arrive soon. On **Nov. 30** Boutros-Ghali endorsed immediate military action in Somalia.

Another Coup Thwarted in Venezuela – For the second time in less than a year, military rebels sought to overthrow the government of Venezuela. On **Nov. 27** the rebels, aided by some civilians, seized a television station and 2 air bases. Planes bombed the presidential palace and other sites in Caracas, the capital. The insurgents denounced Pres. Carlos Andres Perez for his alleged disregard for poor people, and they pledged to install a "real democracy". Forces supporting the government overcame the rebellion by the afternoon of **Nov. 27**. The death toll from the brief conflict was reported to be at least 169.

General

Fischer Defeats Spassky in Chess – Former world chess champion Bobby Fischer, playing in public for the first time in 2 decades, defeated Boris Spassky, from whom he won the title in 1972, in a match in Belgrade. Their contest ended, **Nov. 5**, when Fischer won for the tenth time in the 30 games that they played. Spassky won 5 games, and the rest were draws. A Yugoslav businessman had put up the money for the competitors. Fischer, as the winner, received $3.35 million, and Spassky received $1.65 million. On **Dec. 15** Fischer was indicted by a federal grand jury in Washington, D.C., on a charge that he had violated sanctions against Yugoslavia by playing in Belgrade.

Royal Rumbles – The Princess of Wales issued a statement, **Nov. 6**, saying that she found reports of her disagreements with the Queen and the Duke of Edinburgh "untrue and particularly hurtful". This unprecedented move served to increase speculation over the state of the Wales's marriage. The couple had been widely regarded as ill at ease with each other on a recent tour of Korea.

Historic Church Decision – In an all-day debate, **Nov. 11**, the Church of England Synod decided to accept the ordination of women priests. The issue was settled by 2 votes from the House of Laity. Threats of schism receded as appeals for calm and reflection came from both sides.

Catholic Church Issues new Catechism – A new universal catechism of the Roman Catholic Church was issued, **Nov. 16**, by a commission that had devoted 6 years to the task of revising the 400-year-old text. The compilation of teachings embraced many issues that were of modern-day origin. For example, the catechism warned drivers against alcohol and "an immoderate taste for speed" that put themselves and others in danger. Economic sins cited for the first time included embezzlement, tax fraud and forgery. The catechism remained conservative on social issues, declaring, for example, "Human life must be totally respected and protected from the moment of conception." It asserted that homosexuals "do not choose their homosexual condition" and urged that they be "treated with respect, compassion and sensitivity", but it also called on gays to remain chaste. The document declared that "Jews were not collectively responsible for the death of Jesus . . . All sinners were responsible for Christ's Passion."

Windsor Castle Damaged by Fire – On the morning of **Nov. 20** fire broke out at Windsor Castle and raged throughout the night. State apartments were damaged and valuable artefacts destroyed. St George's Hall, built in 1362 for the Knights of the Garter, collapsed in a spectacular blaze. It later emerged that British Heritage, responsible for historic buildings, had been refused permission to survey areas of the castle when electrical, gas and other services had been installed over the past 3 years. During the following week Heritage Sec. Peter Brooke announced that the taxpayer would be footing the £50 million repair bill. This refuelled debate about the cost of keeping the Royal Family, and for the first time ever the House of Commons public accounts committee ordered an investigation into state spending on 5 royal palaces, including Windsor Castle and Buckingham Palace. During one of her speeches, **Nov. 24**, the Queen mentioned that she was having an "annus horribilis".

DECEMBER

National

Terrorism Campaign Continues – An IRA incendiary bomb exploded in central Belfast, **Dec. 1**, injuring 27 people. The same day a van containing half a ton of explosive was made safe in London's Tottenham Court Road. On **Dec. 3** 64 people were injured when 2 bombs exploded "without effective warning" in Manchester. A car bomb went off, **Dec. 9**, outside a north London station, but nobody was hurt. However, 11 people, including 4 police officers, were injured, **Dec. 10**, when 2 explosions occurred at Wood Green shopping centre in London. The London Irish community expressed "frustration, resignation and despair". Two more bombs went off in Oxford Street, **Dec. 16**, and 4 people were slightly hurt. Trade and Industry Sec. Michael Heseltine announced, **Dec. 21**, that the government would in future act as an insurer of last resort to commercial property damaged by terrorist activity. This was after the insurance industry had announced exclusions from commercial policies.

Industry Struggles On – It was announced, **Dec. 3**, that the recession and cuts in military spending would bring closure next year of the famous Cammell Laird shipyard, ending 130 years of shipbuilding on Merseyside. 900 jobs would go and an estimated 1,500 more in related supply industries. The Confederation of British Industry reported, **Dec. 21**, that wage settlements had dropped to their lowest level for 12 years, with 1 in 3 manufacturers imposing a pay freeze.

Job Losses Escalate – On **Dec. 4** 16,000 job losses were announced by the Post Office, 3,000 by the Ford motor company, and 13,000 by the arms makers Royal Ordnance. Five days later Granada Television announced that up to 250 jobs would be lost in "streamlining". Figures released **Dec. 18** showed those out of work and claiming benefit to total 2,908,900 – the highest figure for 5½ years. In the southeast unemployment rose above 10% for the first time since the 1930s.

Child Abuse Report – A committee on the systematic abuse of children in care in Leicestershire, chaired by Norman Warner, was released on **Dec. 7**. It made 4 final recommendations: more rigorous procedures for the selection of staff; a new strategy for staff development and training; an urgent review of the health and education needs of children in residential care; and better planning of children's services. It was estimated that there were 11,250 children in residential care in England at the end of March 1992.

Police Ethics Code Introduced – An ethics code aimed at "changing the culture" of the police was launched **Dec. 8**. The 11-point draft statement was drawn up by police staff associations and the Home Office. Integrity, fairness, tolerance and courtesy were emphasized; colleagues should be supported in the course of duty, and malpractice should be reported. The Police Federation, which represents rank and file officers, thought the code unnecessary. A Home Office survey released the same day showed 3 out of 4 people were satisfied with the police. However, almost half of Afro-Caribbeans interviewed were not: they were 50% more likely to be stopped than whites if driving a vehicle, and 4 times more likely if on foot. Overall, 76% of whites thought the police did a good job, 62% of Asians shared their opinion, and so did 52% of Afro-Caribbeans.

Cardiff 3 Released – Steve Miller, Tony Paris and Yusuf Abdullahi, jailed for life in 1988 for the murder of Lynette White, were freed by the Court of Appeal, **Dec. 10**. This was the first significant successful appeal involving a prosecution after the introduction of the Police and Criminal Evidence Act, which was devised to deal with abuse in police investigations. South Wales police announced, **Dec. 21**, that no action would be taken against officers criticized by the Court of Appeal, and that the case would not be reopened.

Edinburgh Summit a Success for Britain – The European Community Summit opened in Edinburgh, **Dec. 11**. The way was cleared for a second Danish referendum on the Maastricht Treaty next year, and though John Major won plaudits for his skill as a negotiator, he was firmly told that Britain must itself ratify the treaty by June 1993. Tardiness, it was alleged, would result in Denmark and Britain being left behind in a two-speed Europe. European finance ministers meeting separately in Edinburgh agreed plans to combat recession and boost employment – including £4 billions of borrowing for investment in infrastructure and industry. Outside the summit 25,000 Scots took the opportunity to demonstrate for home rule. John Major said he would "take stock", but he flatly rejected the idea of an Edinburgh parliament.

Health Cuts Continue – The British Medical Association's consultants' committee warned, **Dec. 11**, that consultants from all over the country were being told to restrict or stop the treatment of certain patients in the last quarter of the year. This was because contracts with health districts were being completed ahead of schedule, and no extra money was available until April. Health Sec. Virginia Bottomley said that consultants should cooperate with managers in responding to the challenge of planning NHS resources through the entire year.

Prisons Criticized – The National Association for the Care and Resettlement of Offenders together with the Association of Chief Officers of Probation reported, **Dec. 14**, that children as young as 13 may be spending time in "suicide-inducing conditions of prisons and remand centres". The report followed a 6-month survey of juveniles remanded while awaiting trial in England and Wales.

New School Grants; National Curriculum – Education minister Baroness Blatch announced, **Dec. 15**, £23 million in grants to 118 schools which planned to improve technical facilities. In future, she said, such schools would be able to select up to 10% of pupils on their academic aptitude in technology. This was seen by critics as a move away from the principle of comprehensive intake, and the National Union of Teachers claimed to detect the reintroduction of selection. The National Union of Head Teachers, which comprises 90% of primary school heads, urged its members, **Dec. 21**, to boycott the Government's request for 2% of schools to pilot national curriculum tests for 11-year-olds. The tests were flawed and the Government had scorned teachers' opinions, said the union. Ministers replied that the teachers were scared of accountability. Despite the reservations of examination advisers and the NUT over their validity, the Government published league tables or results for last summer's national curriculum tests for 7-year-olds. The top authority was Harrow and the bottom, Cleveland. Her Majesty's Inspectorate released a report, **Dec. 29**, on 2 years' operation of the national curriculum. It said that there were few signs of teachers' more regular record-keeping doing anything to improve pupils' work. Primary science and some aspects of English were the only exceptions "to any discernible general rise in standards".

Pit Closures Stopped – On **Dec. 21** the High Court outlawed the Government's October attempts to close the coal mines. British Coal was ordered to drop plans for the immediate shutdown of 10 pits, and to agree a review procedure with the unions which would include independent scrutiny.

International

Yeltsin Accepts a New Premier – Russian Pres. Boris Yeltsin, **Dec. 1**, appealed for an extension of his emergency powers, which would allow him to choose the government and control economic policy. A motion by conservative deputies to impeach Yeltsin, **Dec. 1**, received fewer than 400 votes in the 1,041-member body. Yeltsin's opponents failed, **Dec. 5**, to pass constitutional amendments that would have put the cabinet under parliamentary control. The conservatives were more successful, **Dec. 9**, narrowly rejecting the confirmation as premier of Yegor Gaidar, Yeltsin's choice, who had served as acting premier since June. Gaidar had designed Yeltsin's economic-reform programme, which had not yet produced many positive results. After vowing, **Dec. 10**, that he would keep Gaidar as acting premier, Yeltsin, **Dec. 14**, joined with the Congress in supporting the confirmation of Deputy Premier Viktor Chernomyrdin as the new premier. He had been a deputy premier in charge of energy. Yeltsin, **Dec. 19**, cut short a visit to China when he heard that the new premier was being pressured to choose a conservative cabinet. However, the cabinet list, approved by Yeltsin, **Dec. 23**, contained most economic reformers who had served under Gaidar.

German Parties Agree to Curb Refugees – A German prosecutor said, **Dec. 1**, that 2 young men had admitted a fire-bombing in Moelln in November that had killed a Turkish woman and 2 Turkish girls. They had been among the victims of violent neo-Nazi protests against the law allowing any foreigner to seek refuge or asylum in Germany. On **Dec. 6** Germany's 2 major parties, the Christian Democratic Union and the Social Democrats, reached an agreement to modify the law, under which 400,000 had entered Germany in 1992. Would-be refugees would now be turned back if they were citizens of countries deemed by parliament to be free of political persecution. The government, **Dec. 10**, banned a second right-wing party for inciting racial hatred.

U.S.-Led Force Enters Somalia – A U.N.-sanctioned military force, led by American troops, arrived in Somalia to ensure the delivery of food to starving people. The U.N. Security Council, voting unanimously, **Dec. 3**, authorized the intervening forces to use "all necessary means" to deliver the food, and the Council also called on warring factions to cease fighting. Pres. George Bush said, **Dec. 4**, that the mission was humanitarian, but that the U.S. would not allow "armed gangs" to condemn "their own people . . . to death by starvation". Some 1,800 Marines entered the capital, Mogadishu, **Dec. 9**, and began to restore the airport runway so that it could receive planes carrying food and supplies. Armed Somalis had fled elsewhere. U.S. Navy ships were deployed in the Indian Ocean. Units of the French Foreign Legion helped patrol the capital. On **Dec. 10** Marines and Legionnaires killed 2 Somalis in a van that was speeding towards a roadblock. The nation's 2 principal warlords signed a peace agreement, **Dec. 11**, in Mogadishu. U.S. and French troops entered Baidoa, a city hard-hit by famine, **Dec. 16**. Marines, **Dec. 20**, occupied the southern coastal city of Kismayu, following a massacre of more than 100 of its citizens by the forces of the local warlord. A civilian employee of the U.S.Army was killed, **Dec. 23**, when his truck struck a mine. Within the next few days, U.S., French and Italian troops occupied other towns that needed food. Pres. Bush arrived in Somalia, **Dec. 31**, visited the U.S. Embassy in Mogadishu, and toured a schoolhouse where he greeted children recovering from hunger and illness.

Razing of Mosque Ignites Violence in India – Hindus in India destroyed a Muslim mosque and provoked new sectarian conflict. The mosque, built in 1528 in the northern Indian city of Ayodhya, stood on a site that Hindus said was the birthplace of the Hindu deity Ram. They wanted to build a temple there in his honour. On **Dec. 6** militant Hindus tore down the mosque, using sledgehammers and bare hands. Violent clashes between Hindus and Muslims followed, and within 3 days the death toll stood at more than 700. On **Dec. 13** the government said 1,210 people had been killed and 4,600 wounded.

Israel Deports 415 Palestinians – An Israeli border policeman was kidnapped, **Dec. 13**, by Hamas, a fundamentalist Muslim organization, and his body was found **Dec. 15**. The Israeli cabinet voted unanimously, **Dec. 16**, to expel 415 Palestinians who were Hamas sympathizers. They were rounded up and taken to the Lebanese border, **Dec. 17**, and, after the Israeli Supreme Court declined to block the expulsion, they were sent into Lebanese territory controlled by Israel. The expulsions, which were illegal under international law, were internationally condemned. On previous occasions, the Israelis had ousted a total of 66 Palestinians. Lebanon barred the Palestinians from proceeding beyond the border area, forcing them to camp in a no man's land without food and supplies. The U.N. Security Council, **Dec. 18**, unanimously condemned the expulsion.

Ex-Dissident Wins Korean Presidency – Kim Young Sam, a longtime opponent of Korean governments, won the presidency of South Korea, **Dec. 18**, as the candidate of the ruling Democratic Liberal Party. He won with 42% in a large field. His principal challenger, Kim Dae Jung, was also a prominent dissident. Kim Young Sam would succeed Pres. Roh Tae Woo in February.

President of Serbia Re-Elected – Pres. Slobodan Milosevic of Serbia was re-elected, **Dec. 20**. Official results, reported **Dec. 23**, gave him 56% of the vote to 35% for his principal challenger, Premier Milan Panic. Panic had blamed Milosevic for the civil war with Bosnia. U.S. Sec. of State Lawrence Eagleburger had charged that Milosevic bore some of the responsibility for Serbian atrocities committed in Bosnia. One of Milosevic's political allies charged in parliament, **Dec. 29**, that Panic was a foreign agent. Panic had come from California in 1992 to assume the premiership. In a no-confidence vote, **Dec. 29**, parliament ousted Panic as premier.

U.S. Downs Iraqi Plane in "No-Fly Zone" – An Iraqi warplane, a Soviet-made MiG jet, was shot down, **Dec. 27**, by a U.S. fighter plane after it entered the so-called no-fly zone in southern Iraq. The U.S., Britain and France had created the zone in August to help protect Shiite Muslims in the area from Iraqi attack.

U.S., Russia Agree on Nuclear Arms Treaty – The U.S. and Russia announced an agreement, **Dec. 29**, on the terms of a treaty that would reduce their strategic nuclear arms by two-thirds. The details of the agreement, the second Strategic Arms Reduction Treaty (START), were worked out by Sec. of State Lawrence Eagleburger and Foreign Minister Andrei Kozyrev. The broad outlines of the treaty had been determined at a summit meeting of presidents George Bush and Boris Yeltsin in June. The final terms were agreed to only a few days before Bush and Yeltsin were scheduled to meet again.

President of Brazil Resigns – Pres. Fernando Collor de Mello of Brazil resigned in December. Vice Pres. Itamar Franco had been serving as acting president since October, pending outcome of a Senate trial of Collor on corruption charges. Collor resigned, **Dec. 29**, hours after the Senate convened an impeachment trial. Franco was sworn in as president. At the trial, witnesses testified that they had had to pay large bribes to win government contracts. The Senate voted, **Dec. 30**, 76–3 to convict Collor. Collor and some of his relatives also faced criminal charges that they had received millions of dollars illegally.

General

Worst Floods in 10 Years – Gales battered Britain, **Dec. 2**. The worst hit areas were southwest England and South Wales, where flooded homes and schools were unusable and routes impassable.

Baby Mix-up – Two babies were reunited with their real parents, **Dec. 5**, after a mix-up at the Princess Anne Maternity Hospital. Both babies were born Nov. 24 and sent home after 3 days, then one set of parents noticed that the name tag on their child was wrong. DNA tests subsequently proved that a mistake had been made.

Royal Separation; Royal Marriage – The prime minister announced, **Dec. 9**, that the Prince and Princess of Wales would in future be living apart. It was said that the couple had no plans to divorce and that both would participate fully in the unbringing of their 2 sons. The Church of England quickly asserted that the constitutional position with regard to succession was unaffected. Three days later, **Dec. 12**, the Princess Royal married Commander Tim Lawrence at Crathie Church in Scotland.

Fifth TV Channel – The prospects for what would have been Britain's fifth national terrestrial television channel were effectively crushed, **Dec. 18**. The Independent Television Commission decided not to award a licence to Channel 5 Holdings, the sole bidder, finding its business plan unsatisfactory.

JANUARY

National

Mental Health Provisions Scrutinized – A diagnosed schizophrenic underwent 5 hours' surgery, **Jan. 1**, after climbing into the lions' enclosure at London Zoo and being mauled. On **Jan. 3** Health Sec. Virginia Bottomley called for a shake-up of the 1983 Mental Health Act and talks on whether the law should allow for compulsory treatment of the mentally ill living in the community. The implications for civil liberties caused concern, but it was widely agreed that care in the community needed much further consideration.

National Curriculum – After teachers complained at the delay, Education Sec. John Patten announced, **Jan. 6**, publication of the anthology on which 14-year-olds would be tested next June. Shakespeare, Chaucer, Wordsworth, Dickens and Wilde were represented, while Derek Walcott, R. S. Thomas and Patricia Pogson carried the 20th-century flame. Critical reports from the schools' inspectorate and the National Curriculum Council encouraged John Patten, **Jan. 18**, to call for more whole-class teaching and "plain, old-fashioned common sense". It was seen as a move away from mixed ability classes and generalized projects. Labour attacked the calls as fanatical and the unions called them "an unwarranted and irrelevant interference".

Unemployment and the Economy – Another tranche of job losses came, **Jan. 7**. The Burton clothing chain announced 1,000 cuts, and 1,000 jobs to be made part time. The St Ivel dairy company reported 80 cuts, and the credit card processor First Data Resources, 500. On **Jan. 21** John Major admitted that a jobless total of 2,973,500 was "deeply disappointing". The Confederation of British Industry's quarterly survey reported, **Jan. 26**, that though output and orders were still falling, business confidence had jumped. And on the same day the Government unexpectedly cut interest rates by 1%, to their lowest level for 5 years.

House Prices Fall Further – The Halifax, Britain's largest building society, published its house price survey, **Jan. 7**. This showed a 0.6% fall in December, as opposed to a 0.1% rise in November. The average price had fallen by 7.8% in the year up to December after dropping 3.5% in 1991.

Press Reforms – Sir David Calcutt presented his proposals for press reform, **Jan. 8**. The present Press Complaints Commission (PCC) would be abolished and replaced by a statutory body chaired by a judge. Legislation would be framed to make electronic bugging and telephone interception illegal, and newspapers that breached press guidelines would be fined and ordered to print corrections. The Cabinet gave a qualified welcome to Calcutt's proposals, **Jan. 14**. The need for new criminal offences was supported, but the PCC was merely recommended to reform itself. Newspapers united in condemning the outcome, described by the *Sunday Times* as "the most draconian attempt to gag the press this country has ever seen".

High-flying Dirty Tricks – Finding British Airways guilty of mounting a campaign of subterfuge against its rival Virgin Atlantic, **Jan. 11**, the High Court ordered it to pay £610,000 damages, about £3 million costs and to apologize unreservedly. BA's dirty tricks had included feeding disinformation to the press, trawling through Virgin's rubbish bins and hacking into its computer system.

Council Found Responsible for Teen Burglar – Leeds Council was fined £600, **Jan. 13**, after a 15-year-old in its care was convicted of burglary. This was believed to be the first such verdict under the Criminal Justice Act 1991, whereby parents or councils may be prosecuted for crimes committed by children in their care.

Rail Future Revealed – The Government unveiled its Railway Bill, **Jan. 22**, a blueprint for privatization. It proposed to separate the track from passenger and freight services, and that private companies be invited to tender for various individual franchises. The Central Transport Consultative Committee, the passengers' watchdog, greeted the bill as "a journey to nowhere".

Prime Minister Sues for Libel – Writs were issued, **Jan. 28**, by John Major and caterer Clare Latimer against the magazines *New Statesmen* and *Scallywag*. The publications had printed unsubstantiated allegations of an affair between the litigants.

International

Czech, Slovak States Established – On **Jan. 1** the 2 independent states of the Czech Republic and Slovakia were founded as a result of the division of Czechoslovakia. Slovaks generally celebrated, but Czechs were reported to have mixed feelings about the amicable divorce. Vaclav Havel, a former president of Czechoslovakia, was elected president of the Czech Republic, **Jan. 26**. Michal Kovac, an economist, was elected president of Slovakia, **Feb. 15**.

Division of Bosnia Proposed – Talks aimed at ending the devastating civil war in Bosnia and Herzegovina opened in Geneva, **Jan. 2**. The conference co-chairmen, Cyrus Vance and Lord Owen, representing the U.N. and the European Community, respectively, proposed to split Bosnia into 10 semi-autonomous provinces. Pres. Alija Izetbegovic of Bosnia visited the U.S., **Jan. 7** and **8**, seeking Western military aid. A European Community investigation found, **Jan. 8**, that Bosnian Serbs had raped up to 20,000 Muslim women and girls. Deputy Premier Hakija Turajlic of Bosnia was assassinated, **Jan. 8**, by Serbian militiamen, even though he was travelling under the protection of U.N. troops. The U.S. State Dept. said, **Jan. 19**, that Serbian atrocities against Bosnian Muslims and Croats "dwarfs anything seen in Europe since Nazi times". The Croatian army, **Jan. 22**, attacked a Serbian-held enclave on the Adriatic Sea; the Serbians launched a counter-attack, **Jan. 27**.

Bush, Yeltsin Sign Arms Treaty – Pres. George Bush and Russian Pres. Boris Yeltsin signed the 2nd Strategic Arms Reduction Treaty (START II) in Moscow, **Jan. 3**. It required the signatories to cut their long-range nuclear arsenals by about two-thirds from existing levels. START II would not be implemented until the other signatories to START I – Ukraine, Belarus and Kazakhstan – honoured the terms of that treaty. Ukraine and Belarus had yet to ratify START I.

U.N. Forces in Somalia – After snipers fired on U.S. Marines in Mogadishu, the Marines, **Jan. 7**, raided the compound of one of the Somali warlords. No Americans were injured in the exchange of fire, but many Somalis fled or were killed or captured. Representatives of 14 Somali factions, meeting in Addis Ababa, the capital of Ethiopia, **Jan. 15**, signed a nationwide ceasefire. They agreed to relinquish their heavy artillery to the U.S.-led forces until a government was established. Militias were to be disarmed. U.S. and Belgian troops, **Jan. 25**, enforced the ceasefire by routing Somali guerrillas advancing on the city of Kismayu. A U.S. Marine, shot on patrol in Mogadishu, **Jan. 25**, became the 3rd American to be killed in the U.S.-led relief operation.

Former East German Leader Freed – Erich Honecker, former leader of the Communist regime in East Germany, was freed from jail in January. He had been on trial for manslaughter in connection with the deaths of East Germans who had attempted to escape to West Germany before the reunification of Germany in 1989. Berlin's Constitutional Court held, **Jan. 12**, that further detention of Honecker, who had terminal liver cancer, would violate his human rights. The manslaughter charges were dropped, **Jan. 12**, and another court dismissed corruption charges against Honecker, **Jan. 13**. On **Jan. 13–14** he flew to Chile to join his wife.

Allies Launch Air Attack in Iraq – U.S., French and British warplanes attacked missile batteries and radar stations in Iraq, **Jan. 13**. The White House said, **Jan. 13**, that Iraq had attempted to position anti-aircraft surface-to-air missiles in the southern no-fly zone created to protect Shiite Muslims from Iraqi attack. Before the attack, Pres. George Bush had consulted with Allied governments, Congressional leaders and the staff of Pres.-elect Bill Clinton. On **Jan. 13** Bush sent 1,250 Army troops to Kuwait to guard against Iraqi incursions. In the northern no-fly zone, established to protect the Kurdish population, a U.S. fighter plane, **Jan. 17**, downed an Iraqi fighter. The Iraqi government said, **Jan. 19**, after more Allied attacks, that it would no longer harass Allied planes patrolling the no-fly zones and that it would guarantee the safety of U.N. arms experts conducting inspections in Iraq. The ruling council said its action was a gesture of goodwill towards the incoming Clinton administration. U.S. planes again attacked air-defence installations, **Jan. 22** and **23**.

Israel Drops Ban on Contacts with PLO – The Israeli parliament, **Jan. 19**, overturned the law barring Israelis from contact with members of the Palestine Liberation Organization. Although the government of Prime Minister Yitzhak Rabin remained opposed to direct contacts with the PLO, the law's repeal represented an attempt to revive the Middle East peace negotiations. Israel's deportation in December of more than 400 Palestinians remained a source of controversy. U.N. Secretary-Gen. Boutros Boutros-Ghali urged the Security Council, **Jan. 26**, to do whatever was necessary to force Israel to take back the deportees. The Israeli Supreme Court ruled, **Jan. 28**, that the expulsions were legal.

U.S. Presidential Inauguration – Bill Clinton (officially William Jefferson Clinton) was inaugurated **Jan. 20** as the 42nd president of the U.S. Before a large throng of dignitaries and citizens, he and Vice-President-elect Al Gore took the oath for their respective offices. In his inaugural address Clinton said, "There is nothing wrong with America that cannot be cured by what is right with America."

General

Asteroids in the News – Photographs were released by NASA, **Jan. 3**, of a 4-mile-long asteroid named Toutatis which passed within 2.2 million miles of the Earth in December. Scientists said, **Jan. 7**, that a much smaller asteroid, which exploded 5 miles above the ground in 1908, had a force of 1,000 Hiroshima-sized nuclear weapons and had levelled trees over an area of hundreds of square miles in Siberian forest.

Drink Driving Campaign Disappoints – Figures released by the Association of Chief Police Officers, **Jan. 4**, revealed that between Dec. 19 and Jan. 1 in England and Wales 300 drivers per day had been breathalysed as over the limit. The number of fatal road accidents was up by 6% over last year, despite what the police described as a "shocking" TV campaign showing the dying victim of a drunken driver.

Major Oil Spill in Shetland – The Liberian-registered tanker *Braer* ran on to rocks off south Shetland, **Jan. 5**, spilling 84,000 tonnes of oil into the sea. Hurricane-force winds pounded the ship for several days, making it impossible for salvage contractors to board her. Although wildlife suffered, crops were condemned and some fishing grounds were closed, the scale of the disaster was found to be far less than anticipated, **Jan. 22**. However, ecologists warned that some effects might be inconspicuous but none the less serious.

BBC Policy Revealed – John Birt, the new director-general of the BBC, presented the policy document *Extending Choice*, **Jan. 11**. While proferring a service of high quality and originality, it foresaw more efficiency, openness and accountability, and the clearing away of red tape, territorialism and confusion.

Nations Sign Chemical Weapons Ban – After 24 years of negotiations, more than 120 countries began to sign a treaty in Paris, **Jan. 13**, that would forbid the manufacture, stockpiling and use of chemical weapons. Twenty-nine toxic chemicals and 14 "families" of compounds would be banned outright or tightly controlled if they had both military and civilian uses. Countries were given 10 years to destroy any existing stockpiles of chemical weapons. The U.S., Russia and Iraq openly possessed chemical weapons, but 20 other nations were suspected to have them as well. Although the U.S. and Russia agreed to sign the treaty, Iraq did not.

FEBRUARY

National

Privatization Plans – At the beginning of the month the Government sketched further stages in its privatization programme. Seven sections of the British Rail network were being groomed for sell-off: the east coast line, 2 sections in the southwest, the London to Southend "Misery Line", Scotrail in its entirety, the Gatwick Express and the Isle of Wight line. Ministers were also considering plans for a £5 billion flotation of the Post Office. Sorting offices would be put out to franchise by competitive tender, and the figure below which the Royal Mail has a monopoly on post would be reduced from £1 to 75p.

Interest Rates and the Pound – The Government's cut in interest rates, **Feb. 1**, sent the pound to a new low, and its lowest against the dollar since 1986. EC countries blamed the cuts for turmoil in the Exchange Rate Mechanism, and this was echoed in the City, where critics failed to descry any coherent economic policy at all. By **Feb. 3** the pound was at its lowest ever against the mark, franc and yen. An analysis published in the *Guardian*, **Feb. 27**, calculated that defending the pound on Black Wednesday had cost the country £5 billion.

Warrington Hit by Bomb – At midnight on **Feb. 26** two men were captured and a third got away after a car chase along the M62. A policeman was shot and taken to hospital. At 4 a.m. came an explosion at Warrington gasworks. One gasholder was destroyed and another left to burn. The IRA struck again next day in Camden High Street, London. Eighteen people were injured, 2 seriously, when a bomb exploded in a waste bin.

Education Wrangles Continue – The National Union of Teachers voted by a large majority, **Feb. 4**, to refuse to invigilate, mark or administer the proposed tests for 14-year-olds, unless they were modified. They described them as ill-prepared, bureaucratic and unworkable. Education Sec. John Patten accused the NUT, **Feb. 7**, of trying to undermine the national curriculum. He incidentally revealed that publicity to promote the tests had trebled his department's yearly estimate for publications expenses. On **Feb. 12** Jersey refused to be a trial ground for the test. The island's director of studies felt that they had "no relevance to our young people".

Housing Market Still Depressed – A negative equity survey by Newcastle University reported, **Feb. 7**, that 27% of homes bought between 1987 and 1991 were now worth less than the mortgage. The survey noted that the phenomenon of negative equity had only recently spread to the north of the country.

Unemployment – The National Westminster Bank announced, **Feb. 8**, that it was to lose 4,000 jobs this year. On **Feb. 11** it emerged that spending on social security was running £3.7 billion ahead of last year's estimate. In the 10 days leading up to **Feb. 15** 17 local authorities sustained a total of 3,529 job losses. Unemployment topped 3 million, **Feb. 18**, having risen for 33 successive months. According to Department of the Environment figures, the southern half of Britain was for once bearing the brunt, with Greater London and the southeast hit hardest of all. Following further job losses at the Rosyth Naval Dockyard,

Feb. 23, and at ICI and British Gas, **Feb. 25**, captains of industry and trade union leaders called for radical government measures to staunch the loss of employment.

Health of the Nation – Department of Health figures released **Feb. 8** showed hospital waiting lists at a record high and rising at a rate equivalent to 16% per annum. A Government paper, *Making London Better*, released **Feb. 16**, sketched plans for the capital's future health care: 870-year-old St Bartholomew's hospital would survive only if merged with the Royal London Hospital; Guy's and St Thomas's would also merge, as would University College Hospital and the Middlesex. On **Feb. 21** Health Sec. Virginia Bottomley confirmed that the 14 regional health authorities would be retained to keep an overview of the revised NHS.

Scathing Reports on Child Abuse Case – Two reports were released **Feb. 8** concerning the affair of Frank Beck, jailed in November 1991 for the systematic abuse of youngsters in his care in Leicestershire children's homes. A Government inquiry found that senior managers had failed abysmally in basic scrutiny, while a police inquiry found that police handling of complaints against Beck had been incompetent, negligent and compounded by lack of understanding of child abuse. The report recommended that police be given powers to tell employers about suspected child abusers.

Maastricht Treaty – On **Feb. 10** Lord Tebbitt rose to thunder against that "foul abomination", the Maastricht Treaty, and the Tory Euro-sceptics laid plans to support a Labour amendment to include the Social Chapter in the Maastricht bill. Foreign Sec. Douglas Hurd and Prime Minister John Major appeared willing to throw Europe into chaos, with the bold retort that if they were forced to back the Social Chapter, they wouldn't sign the treaty. Having claimed for the previous 3 weeks that success for Labour and the Social Chapter would derail the whole treaty, Douglas Hurd, **Feb. 15**, produced the hitherto unseen legal opinion that a Commons vote for the Social Chapter could, in effect, be ignored. At an emergency debate, **Feb. 22**, the Attorney General was forced to give an extremely legal account of Hurd's contention, and the bill continued to halt and stumble its way through Parliament. Meanwhile, Chancellor Kohl was publicly insisting that all 12 EC countries must approve Maastricht for it to be implemented.

Inflation Down Again – Thanks to January's recession-driven price-cutting, inflation reached 1.7%, **Feb. 12** – its lowest since 1967. Chancellor Lamont hastened to say that this would not be used to support further interest rate cuts.

Child Killers Spark National Revulsion – Two-year-old Jamie Bulger was found dead in Liverpool, **Feb. 12**, and two 10-year-old boys were subsequently charged with his abduction and murder. The case provoked horror and a national examining of consciences. John Major called for a crusade against criminality, and Home Sec. Kenneth Clarke said he would bring forward proposals on custodial sentences for young offenders.

Prime Minister Wins Damages – The High Court awarded £60,000 damages against the *New Statesman* magazine, **Feb. 15**, in response to writs for libel issued by John Major and Clare Latimer in January.

Racist Attacks on Increase – According to anti-racist monitoring groups, **Feb. 20**, racial attacks have reached unprecedented levels in Britain. Eight people were killed in 1992, and Home Office figures show a 75% increase in attacks over the period 1988–91.

International

Israel Offers Compromise on Deportees – Israeli Prime Minister Yitzhak Rabin made a proposal, **Feb. 1**, to defuse the controversy over some 400 Palestinians it had deported. Israel would allow 100 of the deportees to return right away, though most of them would be imprisoned, and the remaining exiles could return home in a year. But the deportees declared, **Feb. 2**, that they would all remain in no man's land between Israel and Lebanon until all could return to Israel.

Fighting Resumes in Somalia – Sec. of State Warren Christopher reported, **Feb. 1**, that he and U.N. Secretary Gen. Boutros Boutros-Ghali had agreed that U.S. soldiers in Somalia should soon be replaced by a U.N. peace-keeping force. The American withdrawal from the southern port city of Kismayu was delayed, **Feb. 22**, by fighting between Somali factions. Rioting and demonstrations against foreigners erupted in Mogadishu, the capital, **Feb. 24**. Protesters fired on U.N. offices, the U.S. diplomatic mission and hotels where foreigners stayed. Four Americans were wounded. An attacking clan leader was warned to pull out of Kismayu and on **Feb. 26**, 71 of his soldiers surrendered to international forces.

President, Premier Clash in Zaire: 1,000 Killed – Fighting erupted in Zaire in late January and early February after soldiers and shopkeepers protested against the introduction of new high-denomination banknotes. Soldiers loyal to Pres. Mobutu Sese Seko fought with rebel soldiers, and about 1,000 people were killed. Premier Etienne Tshisekedi declared the new paper money to be worthless, and on **Feb. 4** he called for foreign military intervention to restore order. Mobutu, **Feb. 5**, rejected appeals from foreign diplomats that he step down as president, and he dismissed Tshisekedi, who refused to leave office. On **Feb. 24** soldiers and tanks surrounded the legislature in the capital, Kinshasa, and Mobutu insisted that the lawmakers accept the banknotes. The legislators agreed, **Feb. 26**, to cooperate with Mobutu.

Food and Medicine Dropped Over Bosnia – The United States began parachuting food and medical supplies into Muslim-held areas of Bosnia and Herzegovina in February. On **Feb. 10** Sec. of State Warren Christopher said that the Clinton administration would actively engage in the Vance–Owen negotiations and would "tighten the enforcement of economic sanctions, increase political pressure on Serbia and deter Serbia from widening the war". By a unanimous vote, the U.N. Security Council, **Feb. 22**, approved the creation of an international court to prosecute war crimes in the former Yugoslavia. Operating under the 1949 Geneva Convention, the court would be the first of its kind since those who judged accused war criminals after World War II. In a statement issued **Feb. 25**, Pres. Bill Clinton said he had ordered air drops over Bosnia to proceed "strictly for humanitarian purposes". The action represented the first unilateral U.S. military involvement in the Yugoslav conflict. The supplies were to be dropped by unarmed transport flying at high altitude without fighter escorts. The first mission, to aid the beseiged Muslims of Cerska, took place on **Feb. 28**.

South African Transition Approved – The government of South Africa and the African National Congress reached agreement, **Feb. 12**, on a plan that would lead to black-majority rule in 1999. In the first step, South Africans of all races would elect a 400-seat assembly in 1994. The assembly would serve as a parliament until 1999 and would write a new constitution. A new president, chosen from the most successful party, would need cabinet approval for all major decisions. Not all blacks welcomed the plan. Mangosuthu Buthelezi, president of the Inkatha Freedom Party, objected vigorously, **Feb. 13**, and he appeard to support greater regional autonomy. The left-wing Pan African Congress also protested, **Feb. 15**. The ANC, **Feb. 18**, approved the transition plan, although some ANC leaders said the transition period was too long.

Mulroney Steps Down in Canada – Prime Minister Brian Mulroney of Canada announced, **Feb. 24**, he would resign as leader of the Progressive Conservative Party and as prime minister as soon as a successor was chosen at a party convention. Given Mulroney's popularity rating of only 17%, his resignation was seen as likely to enhance the chances of his party in the national election that would take place in late 1993. Canada's economy was in a deep recession, and the 7% value-added tax adopted by the government in 1991 was unpopular. Mulroney's tenure of 8½ years had been noteworthy for the establishment of free trade with the U.S. and for his failure to resolve conflicts between Canadians of English and French descent.

Terrorist Explosion in New York – A powerful bomb exploded in an underground parking garage beneath the World Trade Center in New York City, **Feb. 26**, killing 6 people and forcing the temporary closing of the complex. The explosion left a crater 200 feet wide and several storeys deep within the garage. The Port Authority of New York and New Jersey operates the complex, including an underground train station where many people were trapped for a while under rubble. Four Port Authority workers were killed as they ate lunch in their underground office. A 5th victim died of a heart attack after the explosion. The 6th victim's body was not recovered from the rubble until **Mar. 15**. About 50,000 people had to be evacuated from the buildings. Most of the occupants of the 110-storey towers had to walk down stairwells through dense smoke. More than 1,000 suffered injuries, mostly smoke inhalation.

Religious Cult Shootout – Four federal agents were killed, **Feb. 28**, during an unsuccessful raid on the compound of a religious cult near Waco, Tex. At least 2 cultists were killed and 16 agents were wounded. The Branch Davidians, a Christian group, had broken away from the Davidians, who in turn had left the Seventh-Day Adventist Church. The leader of the Branch Davidians, David Koresh, had said that he was the messiah and that he believed the apocalypse would occur soon. Koresh claimed more than 100 people lived in the compound, named Mount Carmel, including Koresh's many wives and children. After an investigation, 100 agents of the U.S. Bureau of Alcohol, Tobacco and Firearms attempted to approach the compound by surprise, **Feb. 28**, carrying warrants to search the premises for illegal guns and explosives and to arrest Koresh. But Koresh had apparently been warned of the ATF's plans, and the exchange of fire occurred. ATF agents were allowed to retrieve their comrades who had been hit. Then, ATF personnel, joined by hundreds of officers from federal, state and local agencies, surrounded and laid siege to the compound.

General

New Polar Record Set by Britons – Explorers Sir Ranulph Fiennes and Michael Stroud set a new record, **Feb. 5**, for the longest unsupported polar journey on foot. Each dragged a 420-lb sledge 1,257 miles across Antarctica, raising money for research into multiple sclerosis. Exhausted and frostbitten, they abandoned their project, **Feb. 11**, after 1,355 miles.

Queen to Pay Tax – Although figures were not made public, it was announced, **Feb. 11**, that the Queen would begin paying income tax. The deal took a year to negotiate and includes the country's biggest tax allowance. All gifts and bequests from the Queen to the Prince of Wales are to be exempt from income tax, there will be no tax on the use of the royal yacht, train or flight, and official duties of the Prince of Wales and his wife are tax deductible – as is the £1.5 million spent on various members of the Royal Family from revenue generated by the Duchy of Lancaster.

Newspaper Apologizes to Queen – On **Feb. 15** the *Sun* published a front-page apology for "unintentionally" causing offence by publishing a transcript of her Christmas message to the nation before it had been broadcast. The paper also offered to donate £20,000 to Save the Children Fund.

Renewed Call to Kill Rushdie – On the fourth anniversary of the fatwa on Salman Rushdie, **Feb. 14**, Ayatollah Khamanei urged Muslims with access to the author to kill him. In a television interview, **Feb. 20**, Rushdie declared himself exasperated by the deafening silence from politicians over his cause, and said that he had asked for a formal meeting with the prime minister. John Major responded positively.

Manchester Bids for Olympics – Manchester's bid to host the 2000 Olympiad was launched **Feb. 17**. The government pledged £2 billion to finance the games.

BBC Director General in Tax Scandal – John Birt, new director general of the BBC and a full-time employee of the Corporation, was reported, **Feb. 28**, to be avoiding tax by being paid as a freelance consultant. This meant he was taxed on whatever he chose to pay himself from his private company, John Birt Productions Ltd. His "administration expenses" included £3,666 for "wardrobe".

MARCH

National

Unemployment – A report by the National Association of Citizens Advice Bureaux, **Mar. 2**, said that employers were using the current economic slump to cut pay, increase hours and sack staff unfairly. On the same day, Sheffield council workers voted to take a 3.25% pay cut in order to save 140 jobs. Rolls-Royce announced, **Mar. 11**, that 5,000 jobs would disappear over the next 2 years, mostly in its aerospace division.

National Schools Tests Hit More Trouble – It was announced, **Mar. 2**, that teachers responsible for conducting and marking the tests for 14-year-olds would be supported by at least 2,000 extra auditors, at a cost of £5 million. The National Association of Schoolmasters/Union of Women Teachers voted overwhelmingly, **Mar. 9**, to boycott all national tests in every primary and secondary school in England

and Wales. Government education advisers warned, **Mar. 17**, that the national curriculum and its testing methods were becoming so bureaucratic and complicated that schools might sink under the weight.

Health Scares – The Government announced, **Mar. 2**, that prescription charges would rise on April 1 from £3.75 to £4.25 – an increase of 13%. In the week of **Mar. 14** there emerged 3 cases of HIV-positive doctors having treated patients in England and Wales. One case involved 17,000 patients over 10 years. Health Sec. Virginia Bottomley ruled out compulsory testing of health workers, but did order a review of existing guidelines to protect patients from infection by health workers.

Police Reorganization – Paul Condon, the new Commissioner of the Metropolitan Police, revealed plans, **Mar. 3**, to reduce London's 8 police areas to 5, and to put more officers back on the beat. He also said that racism was the most important item on the justice agenda, and that a Metropolitan Charter would appear later in the year. Speaking at a conference, **Mar. 5**, Home Sec. Kenneth Clarke announced the future publication of league tables comparing the performances of police forces. The idea was condemned as invidious by Home Office officials and senior police officers.

Enormous Bank Losses – On **Mar. 4** there were demands for the chairman's resignation when Barclay's Bank revealed to a "stunned" stock market a pre-tax loss of £242 million for 1992, compared with £533 million profit in 1991.

Maastricht Treaty – After 14 solid days of Commons debate on the treaty, plans for its progress through the next parliamentary session were in disarray. At the Conservative Central Council meeting in Harrogate the Prime Minister appealed for party unity, but the Cabinet lined up to lambast the rebels who were obstructing the bill. On **Mar. 8** 26 Conservatives voted against the Government, and 22 abstained or did not vote. This meant that Labour's Amendment 28 was sustained and thus triggered a report stage – yet further delay to ratification of the treaty.

Prevention of Terrorism Act Renewed – MPs voted 329–202 on **Mar. 10** to renew the Prevention of Terrorism Act. Stiffer sentences were introduced for the handling of terrorist funds, failure to report suspicion or knowledge of such funds, and for warning terrorists of police investigation.

Protests at Mine Closures – After a unanimous vote for the action, the National Union of Mineworkers' executive decided, **Mar. 11**, that April 2 would be the first date for a series of 24-hour strikes in protest at the Government's pit closure plans. After 5 months' reworking, Trade and Industry Sec. Michael Heseltine's much-delayed White paper on the future of coal appeared, **Mar. 25**. Of the 31 pits previously condemned, 12 were temporarily reprieved. Up to £5 million in subsidies was to be available for British Coal to win sales to the electricity supply industry, and the coal industry would be privatized at the earliest practical opportunity. There was emotional reaction by a substantial minority of Tory dissenters, but it died away and the bill was passed easily, **Mar. 29**.

Budget Gives Nasty Surprise – Chancellor Norman Lamont's spring Budget, **Mar. 16**, signalled a £10 billion tax increase, but was designed, commentators said, to nurture a hoped-for economic recovery. (*See* Economics section for full details.) The measure that aroused most ire was the proposed imposition of 8% VAT on domestic fuel and power in 1994, rising to 17.5% in 1995. On **Mar. 19**, in response to widespread anger that the elderly and poor would be hardest hit, the Government pledged extra payment to 10 million benefit recipients, but there was no commitment to compensate people in full. An all-party parliamentary committee was appointed, **Mar. 24**, to investigate the implications of VAT on domestic fuel.

Terrorist Bombs Kill Children – Two bombs exploded within seconds of one another, **Mar. 20**, in a crowded Warrington shopping centre. Three-year-old Jonathan Ball was killed and 56 people were injured, 21 seriously. Police said that a deliberately misleading warning had been given by the IRA. Five days later, 12-year-old Tim Parry, who had taken the full force of the second bomb, died in hospital. The deaths provoked widespread revulsion. Some 15,000 people attended a peace rally in Dublin, **Mar. 28**, and Gerry Adams, president of Sinn Fein, said that the IRA must know their violent action was unacceptable.

Privatization Blunder – The Public Accounts Committee severely criticized the Government, **Mar. 29**, for its first attempt at privatizing the Post Office. It revealed that Girobank had been sold to the Alliance & Leicester Building Society at a loss of £70 million.

International

Bosnian Serbs Reject Peace Plan – Efforts to bring peace to Bosnia and Herzegovina enjoyed only limited success in March. Peace talks resumed, **Mar. 1**, at U.N. headquarters in New York. U.S. officials said, **Mar. 1**, that Pres. Bill Clinton had warned Pres. Slobodan Milosevic of Serbia that the U.S. would take military action if Serbia permitted civil war to spread to its Kosovo region, which was populated mostly by Muslim ethnic Albanians. In the first days of March the U.S. continued to airdrop food and supplies into Bosnia. In a letter released **Mar. 2**, the Bosnian Serb leader, Radovan Karadzic, warned that the ill-advised American humanitarian effort could cause the local conflict to expand even to a world war. Reports from Bosnia indicated that the Serbs were continuing to advance and to commit atrocities, and were still blocking U.N. truck convoys seeking to provide humanitarian aid to besieged towns. Gen. Philippe Morillon, the U.N. commander in Bosnia, went to the besieged Muslim town of Srebrenica, **Mar. 12**, and residents persuaded him to stay to protect them from massacre at the hands of the Serbs. A U.N. effort to airlift sick and wounded Muslims from Srebrenica was suspended, **Mar. 24**, when Serbs shelled the landing zone. In New York, **Mar. 25**, Bosnian Muslims joined Croat leaders in endorsing the Vance-Owen plan to divide Bosnia into 10 semi-autonomous provinces, but Karadzic rejected the plan, and it was reported that Bosnian Serbs opposed it because most natural and industrial resources would remain in Muslim and Croat control. A U.N. truck convoy reached Srebrenica, **Mar. 28**, and the trucks took out several thousand refugees, **Mar. 29–31**.

U.N. Peace Force Approved for Somalia – U.N. Secretary-Gen. Boutros Boutros-Ghali proposed, **Mar. 3**, that a U.N. peacekeeping force replace the U.S.-led coalition forces in Somalia. The U.N. Security Council, **Mar. 26**, approved unanimously a resolution to send 28,000 soldiers and 2,800 civilians to Somalia. The troops would come from about 24 countries, and the civilians would run Somalia, which currently lacked a government. U.N.-sponsored talks in Ethiopia resulted in agreement, **Mar. 27**, by Somali leaders to the creation of a transitional government. Under the plan, a council of 74 representatives would lead the country until a national government could be formed.

Standoff with Texas Cult Continues – The armed confrontation between federal authorities and the Branch Davidian religious cult continued throughout March. Most of the Davidians remained inside their compound near Waco, Texas. During the month more than 30 people, mostly children, left or were freed from the compound by the cult leader, David Koresh. Fewer than 100, including at least 17 children, remained. Koresh said, **Mar. 2**, that he and his followers would surrender if his 58-minute taped monologue were broadcast on the radio. Although several stations played the tape, Koresh then said that God had told him to wait. Agents cut off the compound's electricity, **Mar. 12**, and concentrated floodlights on the compound at night, beginning **Mar. 14**. Two cultists came out, **Mar. 15**, to meet with federal officials, but negotiations made no headway. Three cult members who had left the compound earlier were indicted, **Mar. 30**, for conspiracy to murder federal officers. Four agents had been killed in an unsuccessful assault on the compound in February.

N.Y. Bombing Suspects Arrested – Five men were arrested in March in connection with the February bombing at the World Trade Center in New York City. In Jersey City, N.J., **Mar. 4**, FBI agents arrested Mohammed Salameh, a Jordanian-born Palestinian who lived in Jersey City. According to authorities, Salameh was a follower of Sheikh Omar Abdel Rahman, described as a spiritual leader of radical Islamic groups. Investigators had found fragments of a yellow Ford van at the site of the explosion and believed it had carried the bomb. They traced its vehicle identification number to a van rented by Salameh in Jersey City 3 days before the explosion. Salameh had notified the truck-rental agency that the van had been stolen, and when he returned to the agency to get a refund on a $400 deposit, he was arrested. The FBI said that his apartment contained evidence that he had been involved in making a bomb. A second man, Ibrahim Elgabrowny, was arrested, **Mar. 4**, in Brooklyn, N.Y. after resisting authorities as they searched his apartment in connection with the investigation. A chemical engineer, Nidal Ayyad, was arrested, **Mar. 10**, at his Maplewood, N.J. apartment. The FBI said he had had contacts with Salameh and had the expertise to make explosives. The 3 suspects were indicted in New York City, **Mar. 17**. Sheikh Rahman denied, **Mar. 18**, that he had been involved in the bombing. Mahmud Abouhalima was turned over to U.S. authorities by the Egyptian government and arrested on the plane, **Mar. 24**, upon arrival in the U.S. Abouhalima was reported to have been seen with Salameh the morning of the bombing. A fifth suspect, Bilal Alkaisi, was arrested on **Mar. 25**, the day after he turned himself in at FBI offices in Newark, N.J. Allegedly, Alkaisi was sighted at a N.J. storage shed containing materials to make explosives. Later, a timing mechanism was found in Alkaisi's apartment. A sixth man, Ramzi Ahmed Yousef, was indicted, **Mar. 31**, in connection with the bombing. Yousef, who shared an apartment with Salameh, was at large, and it was not known whether he was still in the U.S.

Doctor Killed by Opponent of Abortion – A doctor was shot dead, **Mar. 10**, outside an abortion clinic in Pensacola, Florida. The gunman, Michael Griffin, surrendered to police and accepted responsibility for the shooting. The victim, David Gunn, had performed many abortions in Pensacola and elsewhere. Demonstrations, sometimes becoming violent, had become commonplace at abortion clinics across the United States. Griffin was a member of Rescue America, an anti-abortion organization. Don Teshman, national director of Rescue America, said, **Mar. 10**, that Dr Gunn's death was unfortunate but that "it's also true that quite a number of babies' lives will be saved".

Yeltsin Struggles to Keep His Powers – For several weeks during March, Russian Pres. Boris Yeltsin resisted attempts by his adversaries in the Congress of People's Deputies to curtail his powers. The congress, elected in 1989, was dominated by former Communists. On **Mar. 12** the congress repudiated an agreement of December 1992 extending the president's powers to rule by decree. It also cancelled an April referendum in which the people were to vote on the relative powers of congress and the president. While most of Russia was undergoing a painful adjustment to a market economy, the congress, **Mar. 13**, called for a slower transition to a market system. At a press conference in Moscow, **Mar. 16**, with French Pres. François Mitterrand, Yeltsin said a serious threat hung over democracy and reforms in Russia. Mitterrand said the West would continue to support the reform process in Russia. Yeltsin announced, **Mar. 20**, that he had signed a decree asserting "special powers" and that there would be a referendum **Apr. 25** on his presidency as well as a vote on a new constitution. Yeltsin's major cabinet ministers rallied behind him, **Mar. 21**, but the vice-president, Gen. Aleksandr Rutskoi, said Yeltsin's decree was unconstitutional. On **Mar. 21** the Supreme Soviet, Russia's smaller standing parliament, asked the Constitutional Court to rule on Yeltsin's assumption of special powers. On **Mar. 23** the court found, by a 10–3 vote, that Yeltsin had violated 9 provisions of the constitution. The court said Yeltsin could not ask the public to choose between presidential and parliamentary control. Ruslan Khasbulatov, chairman of the Congress of People's Deputies, called, **Mar. 23**, for Yeltsin's impeachment. Pres. Bill Clinton, **Mar. 23**, publicly backed Yeltsin and "the historic movement toward democratic political reform in Russia". Yeltsin's decree was published, **Mar. 24**, with softer language containing no reference to special powers. Yeltsin and other leaders then sought to avoid further confrontation. On **Mar. 26** the chairman of the Constitutional Court, Valery Zorkin, offered a compromise plan for government, and Yeltsin acknowledged that mistakes had been made in his economic reform programme. But congress deputies responded negatively to a compromise plan between Yeltsin and Khasbulatov, and on **Mar. 28** a vote to impeach Yeltsin fell just 72 votes short – 689 were needed. On **Mar. 29** the Congress of People's Deputies approved an **Apr. 25** referendum, but also terminated Yeltsin's powers to rule by decree.

North Korea Exits from Nuclear Treaty – North Korea announced its withdrawal, **Mar. 12**, from the Nuclear Nonproliferation Treaty. More than 150 countries had signed the treaty, which sought to restrict the spread of nuclear-weapons technology and sales. North Korea gave as reasons for its withdrawal: joint military exercises by U.S. and South Korean forces in South Korea, as well as "unjust acts" by the International Atomic Energy Agency. The agency had asked to inspect suspicious sites in North Korea. South Korea's Foreign Ministry stated, **Mar. 12**, that North Korea's withdrawal "heightens the suspicion that it is developing nuclear arms".

Bombs Kill 300 in India – Bombs that exploded in Bombay and Calcutta in March killed more than 300 people and left 1,100 injured. An explosion at the Bombay Stock Exchange, **Mar. 12**, killed about 50 people, and within 90 minutes 10 more bombs had claimed additional lives at banks, government offices, hotels, an airline office and a shopping complex. Bombay police charged 2 men with the bombings, **Mar. 15**. At least 80 people were killed in Calcutta, **Mar. 17**, when an explosion destroyed 2 apartment buildings. Another bomb exploded in a Calcutta train station, **Mar. 19**. Bombay police said, **Mar. 19**, that a Muslim family in Bombay with links to organized crime had played a role in that city's bombings.

China's Parliament Elects new President – The National People's Congress, the parliament of China, convened **Mar. 15**. Major actions taken by the 2,977 delegates reflected decisions already made by Deng Xiaoping, China's paramount ruler, and other leaders. Premier Li Peng, **Mar. 15**, called for continued economic reform under the leadership of the Communist party. Jiang Zemin, the general secretary of the party, was elected president, **Mar. 27**. He succeeded Yang Shangkun, who did not seek another term. Li was re-elected as premier, **Mar. 28**, but in something of a surprise more than 10% of the delegates voted against him or abstained. On **Mar. 29** the delegates approved a new constitution that used the phrase "socialist market economy" to characterize the regime's capitalist-style reforms.

Salvadorean Army Blamed in Atrocities – A U.N. commission reported, **Mar. 15**, that it had concluded that most of the human-rights abuses during El Salvador's civil war had been committed by the U.S.-supported Salvadorean army. The commission had interviewed almost 20,000 Salvadoreans. The commission linked some leaders of the Nationalist Republican Alliance (ARENA) party, which now ruled El Salvador, to death squads that operated during the 12-year-long war, which ended in 1992. The commission declared that no current members of the country's Supreme Court were capable of fairness in dealing with those accused of human-rights abuses. Defence Minister Gen. Ren-Emilio Ponce, linked by the commission to the killing in 1989 of 6 Jesuit priests and 2 women, had already offered to resign. The report by the commission also said that the late Roberto d'Aubuisson, founder of ARENA, had probably ordered the slaying of Archbishop Oscar Arnulfo Romero in 1980. The report blamed the left-wing Farabundo Mart-National Liberation Front for the assassination of many public officials. On **Mar. 20** ARENA and other right-wing factions successfully supported approval by the National Assembly of an amnesty for those who had committed atrocities during the war. The amnesty ended any prospects for prosecutions for human-rights abuses.

Clinton Meets Exiled President of Haiti – The Rev. Jean-Bertrand Aristide, who had been elected president of Haiti and then ousted in a military coup, met with Pres. Bill Clinton in Washington, **Mar. 16**. Clinton said he would seek to restore Aristide to power and that the U.S. would not support "continuation of an illegal government in Haiti".

Conservatives Win French Election – Conservative parties won an overwhelming majority of the seats in the French National Assembly in elections held in March. A trend towards the right was apparent in the first round of voting, **Mar. 21**, and after the run-off elections, **Mar. 28**, the Conservatives had won 484 of the 577 seats. Scandals and an unemployment rate of 10.5% had turned many voters against the governing Socialist party. The results meant that Premier Pierre Bérégovoy would have to step down. On **Mar. 29** Pres. François Mitterrand, a Socialist, named as premier Edouard Balladur, a member of the neo-Gaullist Rally for the Republic party.

Israel's Likud Bloc Names New Leader – The Likud bloc, the principal opposition party in Israel, elected a new leader in March. After Likud was defeated by the Labour party in the 1992 election, the outgoing prime minister, Yitzhak Shamir, announced that he would step down as party leader. On **Mar. 25** Likud members chose Benjamin Netanyahu, a former deputy foreign minister, as their new leader in a nationwide primary. At age 43, he was a generation younger than most prominent Israeli political leaders.

General

Resignation That Never Was – John Birt gave up his freelance status, **Mar. 1**, and joined the BBC payroll. Staff unions called for his resignation and that of the chairman, Marmaduke Hussey, who had approved Birt's original financial arrangement. A meeting of the BBC's board of governors, **Mar. 18**, decided that neither Birt's nor Hussey's resignation would be in the interests of the corporation.

It's an Ill Wind – Retailing at £22 a time, a royal divorce mug hit the shops, **Mar. 10**, and was reported to be selling well. It depicted the Princess Royal and ex-husband Captain Mark Phillips.

Resignation That Was – The London Stock Exchange accepted the resignation of chief executive Peter Rawlins, **Mar. 11**. This followed the abandonment of Taurus, the automated share settlement system which was to have facilitated "paperless trading". About £450 million was written off.

Milestone in Organ Transplants – Cambridge University announced, **Mar. 12**, that it had bred a pig with a human heart. A fertilized egg was taken from a "large white sow", injected with human genes, then placed in the womb of another sow. The result was described as an important milestone in the programme to breed animals as organ donors for humans.

Disease Genes Identified – The journal *Nature* reported, **Mar. 4**, that the gene whose mutation caused amyotrophic lateral sclerosis (also known as Lou Gehrig's disease) had been identified. The disorder causes muscles to waste away and leads to death for most patients within 5 years. The discovery was hailed as "a major breakthrough", but it was stressed that "at this point we do not have a therapy". On **Mar. 26** the journal *Cell* reported that scientists from England, Wales and the U.S. had identified the gene responsible for Huntingdon's disease, which involves degeneration of the basal ganglia, 2 nerve clusters in the brain. Again, researchers said the discovery of the gene was a major breakthrough, but no treatment for the disease was imminent.

APRIL

National

Law and Order – At the beginning of the month security firm Group 4 took over the first private prison escort contract, covering the East Midlands and Humberside. Its published business plan stated the primary task as "keeping prisoners in custody". By **Apr. 16** seven had escaped. It was reported, **Apr. 22**, that Avon and Somerset police had carried out the first trials of a U.S.-made baton, which extends from 7 inches to 21 inches, to give protection from knife attacks. The police's stated preference was for a side-handled baton, but the Home Sec. considered that it would give the force an over-aggressive appearance. The Police Complaints Authority annual report, issued **Apr. 2**, revealed that it considered 9,200 complaints against the police during 1992, of which 904 (9.8%) resulted in disciplinary proceedings, and 97 in criminal charges. The report also noted that too many officers escape disciplinary action by taking early retirement on medical grounds. (Proceedings are abandoned when an officer leaves the service.)

Child Support Agency Launched – The Government's Child Support Agency, employing 5,000 staff, began work, **Apr. 5**, tracking down absent fathers to impose child maintenance obligation on them. The exercise was predicted to save £530 million in social security payments to lone parents. However, mainstream childen's charities condemned it as crude for deducting maintenance pound-for-pound from income support, and claimed that lone mothers might face reprisals from the fathers they might be forced to name.

National School Tests Wrangle Continues – Following a High Court ruling that a boycott of the summer tests would not be unlawful, the moderate Association of Teachers and Lecturers joined forces, **Apr. 10**, with other teaching unions to back a boycott. Further National Curriculum Council proposals appeared, **Apr. 15**, which would extend Government power over how English is spoken in schools, and a compulsory list of great authors for study. In an interview, **Apr. 25**, John Patten said that there was pressure from within his party to introduce legislation that would outlaw industrial action against the national curriculum.

End of Recession Signalled – Figures released **Apr. 12** showed an overall rise of 1.2% in house prices in February, but an overall fall of 1.2% in the last quarter of 1992. Central Statistical Office figures showed, **Apr. 14**, that manufacturing production was up by 1.2% in February – the largest rise since March 1989. The Public Sector Borrowing Requirement for March was £9.5 billion – the highest monthly figure ever. Gross domestic productivity figures, released **Apr. 27**, showed a growth of 0.2% per quarter.

Lesbian Foster Parents Win Case – A lesbian couple won the right to become short-term foster parents, **Apr. 20**, after a 5-year struggle with Hampshire County Council. The decision was hailed as a milestone in the eradication of prejudice, but the deputy director of Hampshire social services, who had long been an advocate of the couple, said: "This is not a charter for any particular group. It's simply the approval of a couple who have something to offer who happen to be lesbian."

Massive IRA Bomb Hits City – One person was killed and 45 injured when the biggest ever peacetime bomb exploded in the City of London, **Apr. 24**. In this act of "economic terrorism", designed to disrupt financial trading and cause chaos in the capital, many buildings, including the NatWest Tower, were severely damaged. Early estimates reckoned that the damage would cost taxpayers £1 billion. Financial markets reopened only 2 days later, **Apr. 26**, and later that day the police announced that more than 10 people had been arrested in connection with the bombing.

International

Foreign Aid, Russian Voters Give Yeltsin a Lift – Russia's beleaguered president, Boris Yeltsin, strengthened his hand in April by obtaining promises of international financial assistance and by getting a vote of confidence in a national referendum. Pres. Bill Clinton said, **Apr. 1**, that support for the Yeltsin government was related to continued U.S. economic growth. Yeltsin was embroiled in a power struggle with conservatives sympathetic with the former communist regime. Great Britain, **Apr. 1**, and Canada, **Apr. 2**, announced packages of financial aid to Russia. Representatives of Russia and its creditor nations agreed in Paris, **Apr. 2**, to reschedule about 75% of the $20 billion Russia owed in principal and interest in 1993. Clinton and Yeltsin met at a summit in Vancouver, Canada, **Apr. 3** and **4**. Clinton pledged $1.6 billion in aid. Of this, $894 million consisted of credits and grants for food. Other large sums would help Russia launch investment initiatives and dismantle and store elements of its nuclear arsenal. The Group of 7 nations – the world's leading industrial democracies – announced a $28.4 billion package of aid at a meeting in Tokyo, **Apr. 15**. In their communiqué, the G-7 nations stated that continued democratic reform in Russia was "essential to world peace". The United States and Japan also announced separate commitments of $1.8 billion, the U.S. pledge being in addition to Clinton's previous promise of support. In the **Apr. 25** referendum, 58% of those who voted declared that they had confidence in Yeltsin, and 53% said they approved of his social and economic policies. A court had held that a simple majority of those voters actually participating in the referendum would be sufficient to decide those 2 questions. Proposals for early parliamentary and presidential elections failed because they were not supported by a majority of all registered voters. Yeltsin, **Apr. 29**, proposed a new constitution that would abolish the Congress of People's Deputies and create a 2-chamber parliament. Under Yeltsin's draft, the president would have the power to disband parliament and call new elections in certain circumstances.

Macedonia Joins United Nations –On **Apr. 8** Macedonia became a member of the United Nations under the formal, but temporary, designation as the Former Yugoslav Republic of Macedonia. A permanent name would be the subject of negotiations with Greece, which had expressed concerns that the use of the name "Macedonia" indicated that the new country was eyeing the territory of the Greek province of Macedonia.

U.S. Planes Bomb Iraqi Positions – Four U.S. planes patrolling the no-fly zone in northern Iraq, **Apr. 9**, were fired on by Iraqi anti-aircraft guns, U.S. officials reported. The U.S. planes then bombed the Iraqi positions. Iraq denied initiating the exchange. No U.S. planes were damaged.

Black South African Leader Assassinated – Chris Hani, a secretary general of the South African Communist Party and a leader of the African National Congress, was shot fatally in the driveway of his home in a Johannesburg suburb, **Apr. 10**. Januzu Walus, a Pole who had become a South African citizen, was seized by police, and a pistol in his possession was identified as the weapon used in the assassination. On **Apr. 14**, designated as a day of mourning for Hani, as many as 8 people were killed and hundreds injured as demonstrations turned violent. Clive Derby-Lewis, a leader of the Conservative Party, was arrested, **Apr. 17**, in connection with Hani's death. More than 80,000 attended Hani's funeral, **Apr. 19**, and 4 million black workers went on strike for the day. On **Apr. 21** 5 more people were held in connection with the assassination. Two were questioned and released.

Bosnian Serbs Reject Peace Plan – The self-proclaimed Bosnian Serb parliament in Bijeljina rejected in late April the U.N.-supported peace plan that would divide Bosnia and Herzegovina into regions based on ethnic make-up. The military situation in Bosnia had grown more complex, **Apr. 16**, when an alliance between Muslims and Croats broke down and they began to fight each other. The U.N. Security Council, **Apr. 17**, reaffirmed sanctions against the Yugoslav Federation – Serbia and Montenegro – for its support of the Bosnian Serb forces. A ceasefire agreement signed, **Apr. 18**, by Serbs and the Muslim defenders of Srebrenica provided that the town became a "safe area" for civilians under U.N. auspices. Yugoslav leaders, **Apr. 26**, urged the Bosnian Serbs to endorse the U.N. peace plan, but the Bosnian Serb parliament voted unanimously that day not to approve it. Pres. Bill Clinton, **Apr. 26**, committed the United States to the support of the U.N. sanctions, which went into effect **Apr. 27**. The sanctions froze Yugoslav assets abroad and banned shipment in or out of Yugoslavia, by land or water, of most products. The Serbian parliament in Belgrade, **Apr. 28**, endorsed the U.N. peace plan.

Clinton, Miyazawa Disagree on Trade – Pres. Bill Clinton and Japanese Prime Minister Kiichi Miyazawa failed to see eye to eye on trade issues when they met at the White House, **Apr. 16**. Clinton supported a policy of managed trade, in which market-share goals would be established in the Japanese market for products from the United States and other countries. Miyazawa rejected this concept and said later at a news conference that free trade "cannot be realized with managed trade". Clinton had also asserted during their meeting that Japan did not have an open market and that hidden barriers turned away exports to Japan.

Second Verdict in Rodney King Case – Los Angeles remained quiet in April after a federal jury found 2 police officers guilty and 2 others not guilty of violating the civil rights of Rodney King, a black motorist whom they had arrested and beaten in 1991. In April 1992 the 4 Los Angeles policemen, all white, had been acquitted by an all-white jury of all but one of the state charges brought as a result of King's beating. That verdict had been followed by widespread urban rioting that left 52 dead and caused $1 billion in property damages. The jury at the second trial, which included 2 blacks and 1 hispanic, returned its verdict **Apr. 17**. They found officer Laurence Powell, who had delivered most of the blows, guilty of violating King's right to be free from an arrest made with unreasonable force. Koon, the ranking officer present, was convicted of allowing the violation to occur. The other defendants, Theodore Briseno and Timothy Wind, were acquitted.

Italians Vote for Government Reforms – Allegations of corruption involving many leading Italian politicians produced a backlash in April. In a referendum held **Apr. 18** and **19**, 82% of voters endorsed an end to strict proportional representation in the Senate, the upper parliamentary chamber. Proportionality meant that even very small parties could gain representation. Weak and unstable coalition governments were the result. Legislation would be required to end proportional representation in the Chamber of Deputies, the lower parliamentary body. In other referendum results, voters also supported, overwhelmingly, an end to state financing for political parties. Premier Giuliano Amato, a Socialist, submitted his resignation, **Apr. 22**. Seven of his ministers had been touched by scandal. Pres. Oscar Luigi Scalfaro, **Apr. 26**, chose Carlo Azeglio Ciampi, the central bank governor and a political independent, as Amato's successor. Ciampi's broad-based government took office **Apr. 29**. Ciampi's government was immediately threatened when the Chamber of Deputies resisted lifting the immunity of former Socialist Premier Bettino Craxi, so he could be charged in 6 separate corruption cases. The Chamber eventually relented and lifted immunity for the least serious of the allegations.

Seventy-two Die as Texas Cult's Compound Burns – The confrontation between the Branch Davidians and law-enforcement officials ended tragically, **Apr. 19**, when the religious cult's compound near Waco, Tex., burned to the ground. At least 72 died in the inferno, 17 of them children. Hopes, sometimes based on assurances by Koresh, that he would lead his followers out of the compound peacefully were repeatedly dashed. On the morning of the fire, the 51st day of the siege, Koresh said that there were 95 people in the compound. A total of 37 others had left since the confrontation began. On that day, the FBI decided to make a move. Shortly after 6 a.m. armoured vehicles moved forward, knocked holes in the walls of the compound, and released teargas inside. The FBI said that those inside responded with gunfire. Shortly after 12 p.m. flames appeared at a window. The fire spread rapidly, and the compound was levelled within 30 minutes. Nine people fled from the compound during the fire. No fire trucks arrived in time to control the blaze. Two cultists who had escaped claimed that there had been no plans for a mass suicide and that the fire had been started when one of the armoured vehicles had knocked over a container of fuel. Arson investigators concluded, **Apr. 26**, that the fire had been deliberately set by those inside the compound.

General

Doubt Cast on Value of AIDS Drug – A report published **Apr. 3** called into question the value of the drug AZT in combating the onset of AIDS symptoms. The study, sponsored by the British Medical Research Council and the French National Aids Research Agency, showed that the drug did not slow the rate of progression to AIDS or death, when groups who did and did not take AZT were compared.

Richest Person in Britain Opens Home to Public – Figures in the *Sunday Times*, **Apr. 4**, showed that the Queen is still the richest person in Britain, with more than £5 billion in her private and public fortunes. To add to the coffers, it was announced, **Apr. 29**, that

Buckingham Palace would be opened to the public for 8 weeks beginning Aug. 7. The £8 admission fee would help pay the cost of repairing Windsor Castle, which had been damaged by fire in 1992.

Another Great Disillusionment – Professor Ardito Desio of Milan University announced, **Apr. 20**, that Mount Everest is 6 feet shorter than previously claimed. The new calculations, which involved bouncing laser beams off prisms on the summit, showed that Everest is 29,022 feet 7.2 inches (8,846.1 metres) above sea level.

TB on Increase – In an unprecedented move, **Apr. 24**, the World Health Organization declared TB a global health emergency. About one-third of the world population is believed to be infected by the "greatest single killer".

MAY

National

Government Shaken; Chancellor Resigns – It was a month of climbdown and setback for the Government, beginning **May 4**, when Labour's amendment on the social chapter of the Maastricht Treaty was reluctantly accepted. This development ensured that the bill's progress drifted further into chaos. On **May 6** came a double blow when the Newbury by-election was lost with a 28% swing to the Liberal Democrats, and the Conservatives lost most of their heartland in the county council elections. John Major's leadership was questioned and a Cabinet reshuffle seemed imminent. According to an ICM poll, **May 12**, Government support was at its lowest level in 7 years. the Prime Minister gained some vindication in one direction when Denmark voted yes to Maastricht in a second referendum, **May 18**. Following weeks of speculation, Chancellor Norman Lamont resigned, **May 27**, to be replaced by Kenneth Clarke. Michael Howard filled Clarke's shoes as Home Sec.

More National Curriculum Setbacks – Education Sec. John Patten suffered further embarrassment, **May 5**, when the Conservative peer Lord Skidelsky resigned from the Schools Examination and Assessment Council over the national curriculum tests. "I refuse to be implicated in a procedure so inept and so ill calculated to produce a reputable outcome," said the peer. This was followed the next day by the resignation of senior adviser Dr John Marenbon. The National Association of Head Teachers (NAHT) advised its members not to cooperate with any supply teachers used to administer the tests. The NAHT also suggested that results should not be passed on to feature in "meaningless league tables". Faced with further evidence that parents were in sympathy with the teachers, John Patten made a surprise announcement, **May 11**, that next year's tests would be scaled down. He insisted, however, that this summer's programme would go ahead as planned.

Nadir Jumps Bail – Asil Nadir, chairman of the crashed conglomerate Polly Peck, jumped his £3.5 million bail, **May 5**, and turned up in Northern Cyprus. He stood accused of theft and false accounting involving £150 million, and announced that he had absconded to avoid an unfair hearing. It emerged over the following days that the Serious Fraud Office had received several anonymous warnings of Nadir's imminent departure. At the end of the month questions were being asked in Parliament as to why the Northern Ireland Sec. Michael Mates had given Nadir a watch inscribed "Don't let the buggers grind you down". The minister had also complained several times to the Attorney General about Nadir's treatment by the law.

Stealing up on Health – Hospital waiting lists stood at just below 1 million, according to Department of Health figures issued **May 10** – a record total and up 8.3% on the previous 12 months. Ministers, however, pointed to the 29% drop in those waiting more than a year for treatment. A DoH report released the next day estimated that thefts and other crimes cost the NHS around £600 million per annum. The Royal College of Nursing released a survey, **May 17**, which showed that almost 2 in 3 nurses believed that there were too few staff on their ward to provide proper patient care.

Law and Order Reforms – After continual protests from magistrates and judges about the absurd anomalies arising from sections of the Criminal Justice Act (whereby fines are assessed on a scale linked to the offender's income), Home Sec. Kenneth Clarke announced, **May 13**, that the income-related unit fines would be abolished within 6 weeks. In another U-turn he announced the lifting of restrictions on taking previous convictions into account when sentencing. The maximum sentence for death by drunken or dangerous driving was to be doubled from 5 to 10 years, and the new offence of committing crime on bail was to be introduced. On **May 19** the Home Sec. received a frosty reception at the Police Federation conference, particularly on the issue of putative reform in disciplinary procedure. In surprising contrast, his Labour Shadow, Tony Blair, was rapturously applauded for defending disciplinary safeguards. The conference also voted for the wider use of firearms in the face of increasing violence.

Industrial and Economic Struggles – Receivers were called in to the Tyneside shipyard Swan Hunter, **May 13**, amid fears of the industry's terminal decline. Swan Hunter maintained that its plight was not helped by an outstanding debt of £20 million for work done for the Ministry of Defence. The MoD disputed the figure. On **May 19** Treasury Chief Sec. Michael Portillo said that he would "court unpopularity" with a spending review designed to halve the national deficit of £50 billion. The announcement caused much speculation on both sides of the House. Mr Portillo later conceded that universal child benefit was not negotiable.

Compact Disc Pricing Battle – The Office of Fair Trading announced, **May 14**, that record companies and retailers alleged to be running a price cartel on compact discs would be investigated by the Monopolies and Mergers Commission. This process could take up to a year to complete, but if it found against the retailers, the Sec. of Trade and Industry could cut prices to a level he considered satisfactory.

Nurse Found Guilty of Child Murders – Nurse Beverley Allitt was found guilty, **May 17**, on 13 counts – 4 of murder, 3 of attempted murder and 6 of harming children. All the crimes had been committed while she worked in the children's ward of Grantham Hospital. Experts said that Allitt suffered from Munchausen's Syndrome by Proxy, which caused her to inflict harm on others in order to subject them to medical treatment. Evidence emerged that she had persistently harmed herself as a student nurse. The hospital management had been warned of this but had chosen to discount it. Allitt was sentenced to life imprisonment.

Good and Bad Rail News – British Rail's £130 million international terminal at Waterloo opened on time and within budget, **May 17**. However, delays to the Channel Tunnel and the rail link to the capital meant that there would be no trains for at least a year. Transport Sec. John MacGregor announced, **May 24**, that 18 more sections of railway were to join the Government's privatization plan, then had immediately to mollify determined protest from his own party. Pressed on the future of railcards and other concessionary fares, he said that they would not be mandatory under a new regime, but tried to suggest a flexible position.

"Guildford 4" Officers Cleared – Three former police officers accused of fabricating evidence against the men subsequently convicted of the Guildford pub bombings in 1975, were cleared by the High Court, **May 19**. Lawyers for the Guildford 4 said that more than a dozen issues surrounding the case remained unsolved.

International

President of Sri Lanka Assassinated – Pres. Ranasinghe Premadasa of Sri Lanka was assassinated in May. Earlier, on **Apr. 23**, opposition leader Lalith Athulathmudali had also been assassinated, during a campaign rally. The gunman fled, but police, **Apr. 24**, produced the body of a man they said was the killer. On **May 1**, during a parade in Colombo, the capital, a suicide bomber riding a bicycle set off explosives strapped to his body that killed a total of 24 people, including the president and the bomber. Within hours, Prime Min. Dingiri Banda Wijetunge was sworn in as president. Although the Liberation Tigers of Tamil Eelam denied responsibility, the government blamed the Tamil separatist organization for the attack.

Bosnian Serb Voters Defiant in Referendum – The Bosnian Serb parliament, for the third time, and Bosnian Serb voters, in a referendum, rejected a U.N. peace plan for Bosnia and Herzegovina in May. Radovan Karadzic, leader of the Bosnian Serbs, signed the Vance–Owen peace plan, **May 2**, but said his assent was subject to the approval of the self-proclaimed Bosnian Serb parliament. The parliament turned down the plan, **May 6**, but voted to submit it to a referendum of all Bosnian Serbs. Pres. Slobodan Milosevic of Serbia, **May 6**, ordered a halt to the delivery of arms and fuel to the Bosnian Serbs. The U.N. Security Council, **May 6**, declared Sarajevo, the Bosnian capital, and 5 other cities that were Muslim strongholds to be "safe areas" where non-combatants could seek safety from Serb forces. The Council voted to send 50 military monitors to each city. European foreign ministers, meeting in Brussels, **May 10**, turned down Pres. Bill Clinton's proposal to increase pressure on the Bosnian Serbs, including air strikes on Serb positions and the rearming of the Muslims. Milosevic, **May 11**, urged cancellation of the forthcoming referendum and attempted to call a meeting of legislators from all the Serbian population areas of the Balkans. In the **May 15–16** referendum, 96% of the 1.1 million Bosnian Serbs polled voted against the peace plan and, according to the announced results, the same percentage favoured the creation of an independent Serb state within Bosnia. Karadzic, **May 16**, declared the peace plan to be dead and declared that he now represented Republic Srpska, the new Serb state. On **May 18**, however, Muslims and Croats in Bosnia agreed to a ceasefire and to some of the terms of the peace plan. On **May 22** France, Great Britain, Russia, Spain and the U.S. approved a joint policy calling for a negotiated settlement of the war. Alija Izetbegovic, the Muslim president of Bosnia, rejected negotiations, **May 23**. The U.N. Security Council, **May 25**, voted unanimously to establish a war-crimes tribunal, capable of imposing prison terms, to deal with atrocities in the war.

Body of Cult Leader Identified – Investigators said, **May 2**, that they had identified the body of David Koresh, leader of the Branch Davidian cult who had died with scores of his followers when a fire destroyed their compound near Waco, Tex., in April. Aside from being badly burned, the body had a bullet wound in the middle of the forehead. It appeared that Koresh was fatally shot prior to the fire's destruction of the compound. A team of therapists reported, **May 3**, on their interviews with 19 of the 21 children who had left the compound during the 7 weeks it was under siege. They said that the children had been beaten and deprived of food as a means of discipline. The children said Koresh had "wives" as young as 11. Investigators of the fire reported, **May 4**, at least 2 dozen of the victims' bodies had bullet wounds.

U.N. Assumes Control in Somalia – **May 4** saw the conclusion of the first phase of the relief mission in Somalia. Lieut.-Gen. Robert Johnson of the U.S. Marine Corps handed authority to Lieut.-Gen Cevik Bir of Turkey, the U.N. military commander. This was the first time U.S. troops served under U.N. leadership. The U.S.-led mission, begun in December, had essentially cleared the streets of the cities of weapons, and the distribution of food had brought an end to mass starvation. Clan warfare, starvation and disease had claimed 350,000 lives in Somalia in 1992. The U.N.-controlled force was projected to reach 28,000 troops, including 5,000 Americans.

7th Man Charged in Trade Center Bombing – A 7th man was charged, **May 6**, in connection with the bombing in February at the World Trade Center in New York City. Authorities said that the latest suspect, Mohammad Ahmad Ajaj, had arrived in the U.S. in September 1992 carrying instructions on how to construct a bomb like the one used in New York. Five other suspects linked to the bombing were also in custody, and one remained at large.

State-Owned Enterprises Privatized in Poland – The Polish parliament completed action, **May 7**, on legislation to transfer control of 600 state-owned enterprises to investment funds. Shares in the funds would be distributed to adult Poles at a nominal charge. At the insistence of former Communist deputies and some members of the right-wing National Christian Union, distribution would be free to pensioners and to civil servants who had not received pay increases in 1991. Financiers from Western countries would manage the funds. With the legislation's approval, the World Bank authorized $750 million in new loans to Poland.

"Star Wars" Defence Plan Abandoned – U.S. Defence Sec. Les Aspin announced, **May 13**, that research on the Strategic Defence Initiative (SDI) better known by its nickname, "Star Wars", would be discontinued. Pres. Ronald Reagan had proposed SDI in Mar. 1983. The programme envisioned creation of a defensive shield against incoming missile attacks, and $30 billion had been spent on research over 10 years. Aspin said that the study of ground-based defences against missiles would continue under a scaled-down Ballistic Missile Defence Organization.

Denmark Approves Maastricht Treaty – Danish citizens, voting in a referendum, **May 18**, reversed a position they had taken a year earlier and ratified, by a 57% majority, the Maastricht Treaty on greater European unity. The Danish government had won concessions from its partners in the European Community, allowing Denmark to opt out of close cooperation on defence and monetary matters. The treaty, previously given final ratification by 9 other of the EC's 12 members, still awaited final approval in Great Britain and faced potential legal challenges in Germany.

Venezuelan President Faces Corruption Trial – The Supreme Court of Venezuela ruled, **May 20** that grounds existed to try Pres. Carlos Andres Perez for misappropriating $17 million in government funds. the Senate, **May 21**, authorized the Court to try Perez, who was suspended from office. The president of the Senate, Octavio Legape, became acting president. The Venezuelan Congress had 30 days to elect a president to serve until Feb. 2, 1994, the end of Perez's term.

Cardinal Shot to Death in Mexico – Cardinal Juan Jesus Posadas Ocampo, the archbishop of Guadalajara, Mex., was shot to death at Guadalajara's international airport, **May 24**. He had been driven to the airport in a limousine, and was to welcome a representative from the Vatican. His car was caught in a shoot-out between members of 2 drug cartels, and he may have been mistaken for a leader of a cartel. Six other people were killed. Police detained 2 suspects, but most of the gunmen got away.

Bomb Kills 5 at Museum in Florence – A car bomb exploded, **May 27**, near the renowned Uffizi Gallery in Florence, Italy, one of Europe's greatest art museums. Five people were killed and about two dozen injured. Three paintings by relatively minor artists were destroyed and about 30 were damaged. Masterpieces by Botticelli and Michaelangelo survived behind shatterproof glass. Authorities believed that the Florence explosion and other recent terrorist acts were the work of the Mafia, which might be signalling that it had not been crippled by the recent round-up of hundreds of alleged mobsters.

Germany Tightens Asylum Policy – Germany's parliament completed action, **May 28**, on constitutional changes that would restrict access to persons seeking asylum in Germany. More than 1 million people seeking asylum had entered Germany in the past 4 years, and about 1.8 million Turks had been admitted as "guest workers". Under the changed policy, Germany would rebuff would-be immigrants from nations that Germany deemed free of persecution, and asylum-seekers crossing Germany's land borders would be turned back. On **May 29** 5 members of a Turkish family in Solingen were killed when their home was firebombed. Attacks on foreigners in Germany were reportedly up sharply in 1993.

Clinton Compromises on China Trade – Pres. Bill Clinton, **May 28**, extended most-favoured-nation (MFN) trading status for China for one year. Most U.S trading partners are granted MFN, which provides relatively low tarriffs for imports into the U.S. In a compromise that sought to mollify both U.S. business interests and human-rights advocates, Clinton conditioned MFN on improvement in China's human rights record, including the release of political prisoners and better treatment for prisoners. China's trading status would be reviewed again in 1994.

General

Relief at Last – The days of poking around plaster casts with knitting needles to get at elusive itches drew to an end, **May 3**, when Andy Thomas of Staffordshire launched his "Vent-a-Cast". The device, consisting of 2 flexible tubes and an air compressor, will ventilate the plaster around any broken limb, keeping it cool and itch-free.

British Woman Scales Everest – At 7.41 a.m. BST on **May 17** journalist Rebecca Stephens became the first British woman to climb Mount Everest. She was accompanied by 2 sherpas, after former Royal Marine John Barry had dropped out of the final assault owing to cold and altitude fatigue.

Ireland Legalizes Homosexuality – Ireland's Fianna Fail–Labour coalition government delivered the first of a series of promised social reforms, **May 18**. Homosexual acts were legalized, with the age of consent being set at 17.

Only in America? – Legal and sexual history was made by a California court, **May 20** when a worker at a whirlpool bath factory was awarded $375,000 for emotional distress, $82,000 in economic losses and $550,000 in putative damages. He had been sexually harassed by his female boss.

JUNE

National

Burglaries Escalate – A London-wide operation was launched by the Metropolitan Police, **June 1**, encouraging people to come forward as informers. Regular information would be rewarded with cash. This was in response to the capital's ever-increasing burglary statistics (500 per day or 1 every 3 minutes). The launch was immediately followed by a swoop involving 2,000 police in 617 raids, and a resultant 385 arrests. In an interview, **June 20**, Paul Condon, Commissioner of the Metropolitan Police, feared that pressure of crime would create an armed police force by degrees over the next 10–20 years.

PM at Low Ebb – A Gallup Poll published **June 3** found John Major at the lowest level of popularity since opinion was first sought about prime ministerial performance. Against a background of rumour that Major was exhausted, isolated and depressed. Party Chairman Sir Norman Fowler rallied to him, saying, "John Major is at his best precisely when the pressure is greatest."

Prisons Criticized – A report by the Prison Reform Trust described life in The Wolds, Britain's first privatized prison, as boring, aimless, violent and drug-ridden. Group 4, in charge of The Wolds, responded, **June 4**, that the report was factually inaccurate.

National Tests Begin – Despite a boycott by all the major teaching unions, the national tests for 14-year-olds finally began **June 7**. Next day the National Union of Teachers published alternative proposals for testing. These were weighted in favour of teacher assessment rather than exam papers. On **June 22** it was announced that sex education would become compulsory in all schools in England and Wales.

AIDS and HIV on Increase – Dept. of Health figures released **June 14** revealed that in a quarter of all current HIV-positive cases the virus had been transmitted by heterosexual contact. The rate of infection among gay men and drug users was falling, but was projected to increase among heterosexuals. On **June 25** the Dept. launched a "travel safe" campaign, with a leaflet warning of the dangers of contracting HIV in certain foreign countries.

Change in Economic Strategy – In his Guildhall speech, **June 15**, Chancellor Kenneth Clarke said, "Low inflation cannot be the sole end of economic policy," and was thus seen to be differing from his predecessor. Clarke also asserted that competitiveness was increasing, but that with Government borrowing running at £1 billion per week, all services provided by the state would be under sharp scrutiny. Figures appearing **June 18** showed that during May inflation had held at 1.3% and that the jobless total had fallen to 2,913,800. Labour insisted that these figures had been massaged downwards.

Asil Nadir and the Tories – To the embarrassment of his party, Northern Ireland Security Minister Michael Mates accused MI6, **June 19**, of being behind the prosecution of runaway businessman Asil Nadir. It subsequently came to light that Nadir had contributed £440,000 to Tory Party funds, albeit unofficially. As more rumours flew about covert funding, Nadir claimed that he could implicate other ministers who had tried to woo his loyalty. On **June 23** it emerged that Mates had written to the Attorney General criticizing the Nadir investigation. The following day, bowing to ever-increasing pressure, Mates resigned. In his resignation speech, **June 30**, he left the Cabinet reeling and the Commons in uproar after implying that the Serious Fraud Office, the Inland Revenue, the police and City interests had conspired to deny Nadir justice.

International

Military Ousts Guatemala President – Pres. Jorge Serrano Elias was forced from office in June. On **May 25** he had instituted executive rule and imprisoned opponents to "purge the state of corruption". International criticism followed, and Guatemala's business, labour and academic communities united in opposition to the president's move. On **June 1** the constitutional court urged implementation of its earlier ruling that the action by the president was unconstitutional. Later on **June 1**, Defence Minister Jose Domingo Garcia Samayoa announced that the armed forces, acting in response to appeals from the judiciary and the public, had forced Serrano out. On **June 2** Serrano flew to El Salvador. On the night of **June 5–6** Congress elected as president the nation's human rights ombudsman, Ramiro de Leon Carpio. On **June 7** he dismissed the defence minister and reassigned several military commanders in an apparent effort to confirm civilian authority over the armed forces. Meanwhile, Serrano sought, and received, asylum in Panama.

Moderate Yugoslav President Ousted – Pres. Dobrica Cosic of Yugoslavia was voted out of office by Parliament, **June 1**. Pres. Slobodan Milosevic of Serbia, the principal component of what was left of Yugoslavia, was a leader in the move to remove Cosic, who had angered Serbian hardliners by urging Bosnian Serbs to accept an international peace plan. Eight U.S. military officers arrived, **June 18**, in the former Yugoslav Republic of Macedonia to help plan the development of a U.N. force that would seek to prevent the Bosnian conflict from spreading into Macedonia. Representatives of the 3 factions in Bosnia and Herzegovina met in Geneva, **June 23**, to consider a Serb-Croat plan to divide the country into 3 autonomous areas based on ethnicity.

Cambodian Parties to Share Power – Two Cambodian parties that had received the most support in a U.N.-sponsored election agreed in June to share power. The election was the key element in the 1991 peace accord, under which the nation's 4 leading factions agreed to end their 14-year civil war. The voting for a constituent assembly was completed on **May 28**, and by early June tabulations showed that Funcinpec, the French acronym for the royalist party, had received more than 45% of the vote. The incumbent Cambodian People's Party (CPP) had 39%. On **June 3** Prince Norodom Sihanouk, the nation's dominant political figure and former monarch, installed himself as prime minister and sought to form a coalition government between Funcinpec and the Vietnamese-installed CPP. Sihanouk named his son, Prince Norodom Ranariddh, the Funcinpec leader, and Hun Sen, the CPP leader, as co-equal deputy premiers. His son, however, balked at the arrangement in a message made public **June 4**, in which he said he could not work with those who, he charged, had assassinated members of the royalist party. Prince Sihanouk withdrew, **June 6**, from the brokering process on the advice of his astrologers, he said. The new constituent assembly, **June 14**, granted Prince Sihanouk the powers he deemed necessary to "save our nation". Ranariddh said, **June 14**, that the Khmer Rouge, a Communist faction that had imposed brutal rule on Cambodia in the past, was willing to give up the territory it controlled and drop its demand for a place in the government. On **June 18** Ranariddh and Hun Sen agreed to serve as co-presidents and to divide up cabinet posts.

U.S. Attacks Iraq Because of Plot to Kill Bush – The U.S. fired missiles at Iraq's intelligence headquarters in Baghdad in June in retaliation for an Iraqi plot to kill former Pres. George Bush. Fourteen men charged in the plot went on trial in Kuwait, **June 5**. One testified, **June 5**, that Iraqi intelligence had trained them and ordered them to kill Bush during his visit to Kuwait in April. On **June 26**, in a televised speech, Pres. Bill Clinton said, "The Iraqi attack against President Bush was an attack against our country," and he announced that the U.S. had launched an attack on Iraq's intelligence complex. Early on **June 27**, Iraq time, 23 Tomahawk missiles had been fired from 2 U.S. ships in the Persian Gulf. The main headquarters building was badly damaged. Iraq said, **June 27**, that 8 people had been killed in the attack and a dozen wounded, and it denied the existence of a plot. On **June 29** a U.S. plane fired on an Iraqi anti-aircraft battery in the southern no-fly zone after it reportedly locked its radar on a U.S. squadron.

U.S., Allies Attack Somali Warlord – The level of conflict between U.N. peacekeeping forces and a Somali warlord escalated rapidly in June. On **June 5**, 23 Pakistani members of the peacekeeping force were killed in a series of attacks in Mogadishu, the capital, after the U.N. troops had inspected munitions depots controlled by Gen. Mohammed Farah Aidid. Aidid was the strongest of the warlords in the city and principal figure in the bloody Somali civil war. Americans came to the rescue of the Pakistanis, and 3 were wounded. Although Aidid denied responsibility for the deaths of the peacekeepers, U.S. helicopters bombed 3 of his arms caches. The U.N. Security Council, **June 6**, condemned the attacks on the peacekeepers and demanded that those responsible be punished. On **June 12** U.S helicopters and gunships destroyed 4 of Aidid's arms depots. Ground troops from several countries then moved in to seize heavy weapons, ammunition and 200 of Aidid's men. U.S planes, **June 13**, attacked a compound owned by a financial supporter of Aidid. These actions were overshadowed, **June 13**, when Pakistanis fired into a crowd of demonstrators protesting against the attacks on Aidid, killing 20 and wounding 50. On **June 14** and **16** U.S. planes attacked other targets linked to Aidid, and on **June 17**, U.N. troops stormed his headquarters, but Aidid was not present.

North Korea Reverses Itself on Nuclear Treaty – North Korea announced in June that it would suspend its withdrawal from the Nuclear Nonproliferation Treaty. Although North Korea and the U.S. did not have diplomatic relations, delegations from the 2 nations met at the UN in early June. In a joint statement, issued **June 11**, they said that North Korea had decided to suspend its withdrawal. North Korea, however, did not agree to allow inspection of its nuclear-energy facilities, as mandated by the treaty. The statement said the 2 nations had pledged not to threaten or use force against each other and had promised not to interfere in each other's internal affairs.

Woman Becomes Canada's Prime Minister – Kim Campbell became Canada's 19th prime minister in June, and she also became the first woman to hold the office. Prime Minister Brian Mulroney had announced his retirement, and on **June 13** his Progress Conservative Party, which held a majority in Parliament, voted on a successor as party leader at a convention in Ottawa. The leading contenders were Campbell, 46, the defence minister, who had degrees in political studies and law, and Jean Charest, 34, the environment minister. Campbell defeated Charest, 53% to 47%, on the second ballot. Campbell, who was from British Columbia, was sworn in as prime minister **June 25**. She reduced the number of ministers in her cabinet from 39 to 25 and the number of government departments from 32 to 23. Charest was named deputy prime minister.

U.N. Imposes Oil Ban on Haiti – The U.N. Security Council, **June 16**, voted to impose a worldwide ban on oil shipments to Haiti and also voted to ban arms shipments and freeze Haitian assets abroad. The object was to force Haitian military leaders to accept the return of the Rev. Jean-Bertrand Aristide, Haiti's elected president. The sanctions became effective **June 23**. Talks sponsored by the U.N. opened in New York, **June 27**, between Aristide and Lt.-Gen. Raoul Cedras, representing Haiti's military government.

Senate Approves Clinton Budget Bill – The Senate in June narrowly approved the budget bill that incorporated Pres. Bill Clinton's deficit-reduction programme. The Democratic members of the Senate Finance Committee, **June 16**, abandoned the broad-based energy (BTU) tax, which Clinton had supported and which had been included in the bill approved by the House. The committee Democrats substituted a 4.3-cents-per-gallon tax increase on transportation fuels, which would yield far less revenue than the BTU tax. On **June 25** the Senate divided, 49–49, on the bill, with 2 senators absent. All voting Republicans opposed it, and they were joined by 6 Democrats. The bill passed on the tie-breaking vote cast by Vice Pres. Al Gore. A conference committee would reconcile differences between the Senate and House versions of the bill.

Japan's Government Falls – Premier Kiichi Miyazawa lost a no-confidence vote in the Japanese parliament, **June 18**. The vote was 255–220, with 39 members of his own Liberal Democratic Party (LDP) voting against the government. Miyazawa had served as premier since 1991, a period of serious economic recession. He had been criticized for failing to move forcefully against widespread corruption in Japanese politics. As a result of the vote in parliament, new elections would be held on July 18. On **June 2** more than 40 LDP dissidents resigned from the party and on **June 23** they announced they had formed a new party, the Renaissance party.

Kurdish Militants Attack Turks in Europe – Kurdish militants, seeking to call attention to their 9-year struggle to establish an independent Kurdish state, attacked Turkish diplomatic missions and businesses in more than two dozen European cities, **June 24**. Twenty people were taken hostage, then released, at the Turkish consulate in Munich. Hostages were also taken in Marseille. One Kurdish demonstrator was shot to death in Bern. Other incidents of vandalism, or some form of demonstration, occurred in Stockholm, Copenhagen, London, Geneva, Zurich and 20 German cities.

FBI Arrests 9 in 2nd New York Bomb Plot – On **June 24** the FBI arrested 8 men who, it was alleged, were plotting to bomb several sites in New York City and to assassinate the secretary-general of the U.N. and the president of Egypt, among others. The men were charged, **June 24**, with conspiracy in federal court in Manhattan, and 5 of them were charged with attempted bombing. Five of the men had come to the U.S. carrying Sudanese passports, and 6 worshipped at the mosque of Sheikh Omar Abdel Rahman. The sheikh had ties with several of the suspects charged in the bombing of the World Trade Center in February. Emad Salem, who had been a translator and bodyguard for the sheikh, was identified, **June 25**, as an informer who had secretly taped conversations among the alleged plotters. A 9th suspect was arrested and charged with conspiracy to transport explosives on **June 30**.

General

Tankers Collide in Channel – Despite sophisticated radar equipment and lookouts, 2 ships collided in the English Channel, **June 3**. BP tanker *British Trent*, carrying 24,000 tonnes of unleaded petrol, sustained a gaping hole in the bow and burst into flames after hitting the bulk carrier *Western Winner*. At least 7 people died as the surrounding water caught fire.

England on Slippery Slope – Two striking metaphors for the nation's malaise appeared in June. Crowds gathered at Scarborough to watch a former hotel, Holbeck Hall, slide slowly but inexorably down the cliffs and into the North Sea. A further intimation of moral enfeeblement was that, after a 12-year battle, McDonald's fast-food chain breached the final defence and established a branch in Hampstead, north London. The right to bring burgers to the burghers was won in the teeth of opposition from Melvyn Bragg and Margaret Drabble, to name but two of the bijou enclave's population.

Pessimism Voiced at AIDS Conference – More than 14,000 people attended the 9th International Conference on AIDS, which opened in Berlin, **June 7**. Reports indicated that the number of people infected with the AIDS virus continued to rise worldwide, with especially sharp increases in Africa and South-east Asia. In Thailand 450,000 were infected, up from 50,000 in 3 years. Confirming a report first published in April, scientists said, **June 8**, that the anti-viral drug AZT provided no long-term benefit in delaying the onset of symptoms and the death of

AIDS patients. A research team headed by Dr Jonas Salk said, **June 9**, that use of an experimental AIDS vaccine, on which much hope had been focused, had not slowed the course of the disease or lessened its severity in those who had received it.

Woody Allen Denied Custody – A custody battle between film director Woody Allen and actress Mia Farrow ended, **June 7**, when New York state Supreme Court Justice Elliott Wilk awarded custody of the 3 children to Farrow. In 1992 Farrow, who had never married Allen, accused him of molesting their daughter. Allen had then filed a custody suit. It was subsequently learned that Allen was having an affair with one of Farrow's adopted children. Wilk, in his decision, described Allen as untrustworthy and insensitive.

Japan's Crown Prince Marries – Crown Prince Naruhito of Japan and Masako Owada were married, **June 9**, in a traditional Shinto ceremony at the Imperial Palace in Tokyo. The bride had been educated at Harvard and Oxford universities and had been a trade negotiator in the Japanese foreign service. She was the first woman with a career to join the royal family.

JULY

National

Plot Thickens in Nadir Case – It became clear, **July 1**, that the Inland Revenue had indeed supplied information regarding Asil Nadir to the Serious Fraud Office. This was in breach of legal requirements, though the Attorney General rejected Michael Mates's demand for an independent inquiry. The following day the existence of a forged letter was reported, which had attempted to smear former Cabinet ministers over Nadir and Party donations. Nadir remained in Northern Cyprus, secure in the diminishing likelihood of a fair trial.

Sheehy Police Report Released – The Sheehy inquiry into police pay and conditions finally reported at the beginning of July. It contained 272 proposals. Chiefly, it suggested that automatic pay rises be replaced by performance-related merit awards, that fixed-term contracts be introduced, and that the ranks of chief inspector, chief superintendent and deputy chief constable be abolished. The Police Federation immediately predicted conflict if the Government adopted the proposals, and this was echoed, **July 19**, by the Association of Chief Police Officers. The following day 20,000 police officers met at Wembley to demonstrate their displeasure.

Health Ups and Downs – A Labour Party survey published at the beginning of the month showed that for the first time since records began more than 1 million people were awaiting hospital treatment. Health Sec. Virginia Bottomley countered that for every 100 people treated before the NHS changes in 1991, 113 were now receiving attention. A review undertaken by the Dept. of Health revealed, **July 13**, that some leading hospitals that attracted special funding for research were, in fact, producing only mundane work in this area. Great Ormond Street Hospital for Children and the Royal Marsden Hospital were named. Official figures, appearing **July 30**, showed that NHS income raised by charging private patients had increased by one third in the first year of the market-style changes, being £140.8 million for 1991–2.

Important Legal Developments – Controversy erupted, **July 6**, when the Royal Commission on Criminal Justice proposed abolishing the automatic right of all defendants to trial by jury. The legal establishment was united in its opposition to the change. More dissatisfaction with the law occurred **July 15**. A young man under the influence of drink and drugs was slashing tyres when he was confronted by a man with a hammer who told him to stop. The young man stabbed him to death and was subsequently found not guilty of murder by a jury. After strident protests from the deceased's relatives, it emerged that in 1980, 1985 and 1989 the Law Commissioners had urged that the law be amended to cover just such a case where, if self-defence were taken too far, a murder suspect might be found guilty of manslaughter. "The most important constitutional ruling this century" occurred, **July 27**, when Law Lords said that former Home Sec. Kenneth Baker had been in contempt when he had defied an order banning the deportation of a Zairean asylum-seeker 2 years ago. The ruling established that the courts can stop a minister taking action pending a court hearing on its legality.

Big Defence Cuts – Defence Sec. Malcolm Rifkind announced, **July 5**, "ground-breaking" changes to the defence system. The budget would be £23.5 million, down £240 million on the previous year, but still about £500 per head of population. The Navy suffered the most severe reduction in equipment and manpower, while the RAF lost staff but gained a missile system, and the army gained tanks and personnel.

Slight Recovery from Recession – Central Statistical Office figures released **July 13** showed a 1.8% jump in manufacturing output during May – a trend which had continued since sterling left the ERM the previous September. Unemployment showed a similar improvement, **July 15**, when official figures showed the unemployed total as 2,865,000, the fifth successive monthly drop. On **July 22** it was reported that high street sales had risen 1.3% in June, and the trade gap with non-EC countries was at its narrowest for 2 years.

"Unqualified" Teachers Mooted – A Dept. of Education circular, **July 15**, unveiled plans to allow non-graduates to teach infants after 1 year's in-school training. The news was greeted without enthusiasm by the National Association of Headteachers, which advised schools to boycott the idea.

More Maastricht Manoeuvres – Despite the impassioned oratory of Baroness Thatcher, **July 14**, the Lords rejected a motion calling for a referendum on Maastricht 445–176. However, an unforeseen obstacle was provided by Lord Rees-Mogg, **July 19**, when he won a judicial review in the High Court. His contention was that to incorporate the demands of the Maastricht Treaty into domestic law was legally and constitutionally flawed. After fraught dealing and counter-dealing, the Government was defeated in the Commons, **July 22**, when a desperate attempt to ratify the treaty without its Social Chapter was defeated 324–316. Some 23 Conservatives voted with the Opposition. A "haggard" John Major made his last stand with a catch-all motion which amounted to a vote of confidence, the loss of which would have meant a general election. This shook the Party back into order and was easily won, **July 23**. The Prime Minister's authority was in tatters, though he regained some respect when he called 3 Cabinet colleagues "bastards" in off-the-record remarks which were inadvertently recorded. At the end of the month, the pro-Europeans had the satisfaction of seeing the Rees-Mogg attack comprehensively dismissed by the High Court.

By-Election Blow to Government – At the Christchurch by-election, **July 29**, the Conservatives saw a 23,015 majority blown away with a 35% swing to the Liberal Democrats. The turnout was almost 75%.

International

Date Set for Open South Africa Election – Negotiators announced in Johannesberg, **July 2**, that South Africa's first election open to all races would be held on Apr. 27, 1994. The announcement was also made in Washington, D.C., by Pres. F. W. de Klerk and Nelson Mandela, president of the African National Congress. Pres. Bill Clinton met separately at the White House, **July 2**, with de Klerk and Mandela. While in the U.S., de Klerk amd Mandela criticized each other's policies, but both promoted South Africa as a stable country worthy of foreign investment.

Haitian Leader to Return to Power – The Rev. Jean-Bertrand Aristide, the deposed president of Haiti, and Lt. Gen. Raoul Cedras, who led the coup in 1991 that ousted him, reached an agreement, **July 3**, that would put Aristide back in power by October. The agreement, brokered by the U.N. and signed in New York City, provided for an end to embargoes that the U.N. and the Organization of American States had imposed on Haiti. Pres. Bill Clinton, **July 4**, backed the agreement and pledged financial support to Haiti.

Flood Devastates Parts of Midwest – A flood that was worse than anyone in the Midwest could remember surged down the Mississippi River and its tributaries in the summer of 1993. Fifty people died in drownings or other flood-related accidents, and the lives of tens of thousands of others were disrupted. Heavy rains in the winter, spring and summer left the ground saturated, and the excess water formed lakes. Ultimately, all of the overflow found its way downstream. Many record flood crests were set, and hundreds of levees collapsed or were overrun. All of Iowa and large portions of 8 other states were declared Federal disaster areas. Press. Bill Clinton, **July 4**, visited Davenport, Iowa, in the first of 4 trips to the region. The Mississippi River, a major commercial artery for the Midwest, was closed to barge traffic, **July 6**, from Sioux City, Iowa, to St Louis. The collapse of a levee, **July 11**, flooded Des Moines' water treatment plant and left 250,000 people without drinking water. In St Louis, **July 14**, Clinton said he would ask Congress to provide funds for flood relief. On **July 16** the rising Missouri and Mississippi rivers converged near St Charles, Mo., 20 miles upstream from their normal confluence. The flood, **July 17**, knocked out the Bayview Bridge, connecting Quincy, Ill., and West Quincy, Mo., the only crossing on the Mississippi for about 200 miles. Clinton, Vice Pres. Al Gore, 8 governors and other officials met in Arnold, Mo., **July 17**, to map strategy to overcome the disaster. Tap water became available in Des Moines, **July 22**, but was not yet safe to drink. By **July 26**, disaster areas had been declared in Illinois, Iowa, Kansas, Minnesota, Missouri, Nebraska, North Dakota, South Dakota and Wisconsin. In Kansas City, Mo., **July 28**, the Missouri River crested at 48.9 feet, 17 feet above flood stage. In Des Moines, **July 30**, tap water was declared safe to drink. But also on **July 30** the flooding of a highway virtually cut off access from the north to Jefferson City, the capital of Missouri.

Leaders of "G–7" Nations Attend Summit – The heads of government of the world's 7 leading industrial nations, the so-called Group of 7, met in Tokyo in July. The seven nations are the U.S., Canada, France, Germany, Great Britain, Italy and Japan. On **July 7**, the opening date of the summit, trade ministers from the U.S., Canada, Japan and the European Community announced an agreement that, if implemented, would eliminate tarriffs on a wide range of manufactured products, including construction equipment, furniture, farm equipment and pharmaceuticals. The leaders, **July 8**, declared their commitment to "the territorial integrity of Bosnia and Herzegovina" and said they could not accept a settlement dictated by Serbs and Croats at the expense of Bosnian Muslims. Pres. Boris Yeltsin of Russia joined the meeting, **July 8**, and on **July 9** the G–7 nations announced a $3 billion loan package for Russia. The leaders declared, **July 9**, that their highest priority was the conclusion of trade talks being conducted under auspices of the General Agreement on Tarriffs and Trade. Pres. Bill Clinton and Premier Kiichi Miyazawa announced a bilateral trade agreement, **July 10**. Japan said it would take steps to reduce its large trade surplus with the U.S.; however, the U.S. agreed not to insist on Japan's acceptance of numerical market-share goals for foreign products.

Clinton Visits South Korea – Pres. Bill Clinton visited South Korea in July. He addressed the parliament, **July 10**, and on **July 11** visited U.S. military personnel guarding the demilitarized zone between North and South Korea. Clinton warned North Korea that any use of nuclear weapons would mean the end of their country, and he said he would support tougher sanctions against North Korea if it did not open its nuclear-energy sites to international inspection. He said the U.S. would not remove any of its 36,000 troops from South Korea.

Bosnian Factions Support Federation – Ethnic leaders in Bosnia and Herzegovina agreed in July to support creation of a loose federation in the embattled state. Seven of the 10 members of Bosnia's collective presidency, meeting in Zagreb, Croatia, **July 11**, said that they had agreed that Bosnia's government "should be along the lines of a federal state" in which Muslims, Croats and Serbs would have equal rights as citizens. Serb, Croat and Muslim leaders met in Geneva in late July under the cloud of increased fighting around the capital city of Sarajevo. On **July 30** they agreed to the establishment of ethnically based republics in a loose federation. The central government would be responsible only for trade and external relations. Each republic would have its own currency and armed forces. The Serbs would get 60% of Bosnia's territory, even though they constituted only about 31% of the prewar population. The Muslims, who made up 44% of the prewar population, would receive 25 to 30% of Bosnia's land area. The remaining 10 to 15% would become Croat-controlled. The Croats composed 17% of the prewar population.

U.N. Removes Italian General in Somalia – Four journalists were killed in Mogadishu by Somalis, **July 12**, when they went to the scene of an attack by an American helicopter on a stronghold of Somali warlord Mohammed Farah Aidid. On **July 14** the U.N. announced the removal of Gen. Bruno Loi, commander of the Italian force participating in the Somali operation, because he had refused to engage his troops in the conflict with Aidid.

Voters Desert Japan's Ruling Party – Japan's voters went to the polls, **July 18**, to elect members of the lower house of the Diet (parliament), and no political party emerged with a majority of the seats. The Liberal Democratic Party (LDP) had held a majority in the Diet since the party's founding in 1955, but many of its leaders had been implicated in corrupt activities in recent years, and the party had seemed unable or unwilling to institute political reform. The LDP had won 275 of the 511 seats in the 1990 election, but in July it took only 223 seats. The strength of the Social Democratic Party also declined, from 136 to 70 seats. Three centrist parties recently organized by LDP defectors captured 103 seats with their reform platforms. Prime Minister Kiichi Miyazawa resigned as LDP leader, **July 22**. On **July 28**, 7 parties formed a coalition that excluded the LDP, and on **July 29** they chose as their candidate for prime minister Morihiro Hosokawa, who had bolted the LDP in 1992 and formed the Japan New Party.

U.S. Policy on Gays in the Military – Pres. Bill Clinton, **July 19**, announced the circumstances under which homosexual men and women could serve in the U.S. military. The directive issued by Defence Secretary Les Aspin endorsed the "don't ask, don't tell, don't pursue" approach. Clinton had once promised to repeal outright the 50-year-old ban on homosexuals in the military, and the members of the joint chiefs of staff had initially opposed any modification in it. The administration's policy provided that enlistees would not be asked about their sexual orientation. Once in the service, they could visit bars or read publications that catered for homosexuals, and they could attend rallies on behalf of homosexual rights if they wore civilian clothes. Commission of homosexual acts, however, would be the basis for dismissal from the service. Commanding officers could not initiate investigations on the basis of rumours or hearsay, but only if there was credible information. The order would take effect in October. The joint chiefs supported the policy, but some gay rights leaders said Clinton had reneged on his earlier commitment.

Israeli Attacks Kill 130 in Lebanon – Two guerrilla groups, Hezbollah and the Popular Front for the Liberation of Palestine, launched attacks on Israeli soldiers in the Israeli "security zone" in southern Lebanon in July. By late July, 7 Israelis had been killed. Beginning **July 25**, Israeli forces struck back at guerrilla bases and towns in southern Lebanon with air raids and artillery. Hezbollah guerrillas, **July 25**, then shelled towns in northern Israel, causing 2 fatalities. A ceasefire went into effect, **July 31**, after Lebanon and Syria reportedly said they would take steps to stop the guerrilla attacks. The Israeli bombardment of 70 villages had killed about 130, mostly civilians, wounded approximately 500, destroyed up to 10,000 homes and driven as many as 300,000 people from their homes.

Court Overturns War Crimes Conviction – The Supreme Court of Israel, **July 29**, overturned the conviction and death sentence on John Demjanjuk. Born in Ukraine, he had served in the Soviet army and claimed that he had been captured by the Germans in World War II. After the war, he moved to the U.S. He was stripped of his U.S. citizenship in 1986 when the government concluded he had lied about his Nazi past. In 1986 he was extradited to Israel and in 1988 found guilty of brutal mistreatment of Jews at the Nazi death camp at Treblinka. Evidence showed that he had been trained by his Nazi captors as a death-camp guard, and survivors of the camp identified him as a guard known as Ivan the Terrible. Subsequently, evidence from Soviet KGB files indicated that the notorious Ivan was another Ukrainian, Ivan Marchenko. The KGB files also indicated that Demjanjuk had been a guard at 2 other camps, but the Israeli Supreme Court threw out the conviction because he had been tried as Ivan the Terrible, not for crimes committed elsewhere. The court also said it would be unreasonable to initiate new charges against Demjanjuk.

General

Mystery Illness in Cuba – An illness of unknown origin had afflicted 46,000 Cubans by early July. The illness became apparent during the winter, and by spring as many as 4,000 new cases were being reported each week. Two patterns of symptoms had emerged. One involved impairment of vision, though not blindness. The second affected the nerves and was characterized by a tingling sensation in the hands and feet, muscle cramps and weakness in the legs. Some of those with nerve damage suffered hearing loss and difficulty with swallowing, speaking and urinating. Delegations of scientists from other countries visited Cuba to study the problem. Possible causes included nutritional deficiency, viral infection, chronic cyanide poisoning and an unidentified toxin. Dr Jorge Antelo, Cuba's health minister, said, **July 1**, that the number of reported cases had declined soon after the government began to distribute multivitamin pills to the country. He said 25,000 people had been hospitalized, usually for up to 20 days, and that "much evidence points to a new disease".

Definitely Blue Blood – Following comparison of DNA from 9 skeletons found 2 years ago in eastern Russia with blood samples donated by the Duke of Edinburgh and 2 other relatives of the ill-fated Romanovs, it was announced, **July 7**, that 5 of the skeletons were "virtually beyond doubt" those of the Tsar and his family. They were killed by Bolsheviks after the Russian Revolution.

BBC Brouhaha Continues – The struggle for the soul of the BBC continued, **July 13**, when the distinguished correspondent Mark Tully claimed in a Radio Academy lecture that Director General John Birt ruled by fear, that accountancy was all and that programme quality was degenerating. Birt responded that if costs were not controlled, the Corporation would go broke. He was then attacked by ex-Director General Alasdair Milne, who said that allegations about lack of prudence were "a blanket of lies".

Homosexuality Linked to Genes – In an article in the journal *Science*, published **July 16**, researchers reported that they had linked male homosexuality to a small region of the X chromosome. In a study of 40 pairs of gay brothers, the researchers found that 33 pairs had identical pieces at the tip of the chromosome. Investigating the subjects' relatives, they also found a higher than expected number of homosexual men among the maternal uncles and among male cousins who were the sons of their mother's sisters. This suggested that one or more genes that disposed an individual towards homosexuality were being passed through the maternal line. Researchers emphasized that the mystery of sexual orientation was complex and had not yet been resolved.

British Drug Smugglers Released – After 3 years' incarceration in Thailand, Patricia Cahill and Karyn

Smith were pardoned by King Bhumibol and released, **July 21**. Their case inspired national interest, not least because they were aged only 17 and 18 when arrested. Although heroin worth £4 million had been found in their luggage, it was alleged that it had been planted. It emerged that John Major had intervened in February, asking for a pardon on humanitarian grounds without questioning the convictions.

Upsetting the Balance of Nature – Despite attempts by the authorities to suppress the alarming truth, China is facing a large population imbalance, it was reported at the end of July. In some provinces there are already 120 boys to 100 girls, which means that many of today's young boys will not be able to find wives in 20 years' time. The imbalance is attributed to women aborting female foetuses after scans reveal their sex.

AUGUST

National

School League Tables Abandoned – Education Sec. John Patten announced, **Aug. 2**, that he was abandoning the idea of league tables for schools based on the testing of 7- and 14-year-olds. Tables of truancy rates would also be abandoned. Figures appearing **Aug. 19** showed that 40% of A-level passes were within the top 3 grades. However, with 40,000 hopefuls chasing 26,000 university places it was expected that the universities would be especially astringent in selecting undergraduates – particularly in the arts, humanities and social sciences, which were the most over-subscribed subjects. GCSE results for England and Wales, released **Aug. 24**, showed the sixth successive rise in pass rates, with about 1% more in the top 3 grades.

Deportation Death – Scotland Yard's specialist deportation unit had its activities suspended, **Aug. 3**, while the death of Joy Gardner was investigated. The Jamaican woman, who had exceeded her leave to stay in Britain, went into a coma during the course of her arrest and died in hospital. By **Aug. 9** it was known that the arresting officers had sat on her, gagged her with adhesive tape and that she was "effectively dead on arrival at hospital". The following day the post-mortem recorded the cause of death as suffocation. The following day the post-mortem recorded the cause of death as suffocation. The Home Office admitted, **Aug. 13**, that Joy Gardner's solicitor had been informed of her deportation only on the day of her arrest, and that this was usual policy.

Cost of Hospital Opt-outs – It was stated, **Aug. 4**, that the bill for preparing hospitals and health units to opt out of health authority control and set up as trusts over the period 1990–93 had come to £73 million. Dept. of Health figures showed, **Aug. 7**, that the average cost of a patient during the first year of the market-style NHS has risen by 8% and stood at £1,000 per week.

Economic Revival in the Air – Hopes for a cut in interest rates and increased confidence in economic recovery saw the stock market buoyant, **Aug. 9**, when more than £3 billion was added to share values. A further £10 billion was added, **Aug. 18**, and another £7 billion, **Aug. 25**. However, inflation had edged up to 1.4% in July.

U-turn on Criminal Justice Act – Following widespread criticism of the Criminal Justice Act, it was ruled, **Aug. 16**, that judges and magistrates could again take account of any previous offences when passing sentence.

Compensation for Wrongful Arrest – The Metropolitan Police made a first-ever compensation payment, **Aug. 17**, when 3 people who had been wrongfully arrested under the Prevention of Terrorism Act received £6,000 each.

Future of British Gas – A long-awaited report by the Monopolies and Mergers Commission on the future of British Gas appeared, **Aug. 17**. It suggested splitting it into 2 separate companies and depriving it of the sole right to supply domestic consumers. A possible 20,000 jobs could disappear. Consultation and a decision from the Government was expected later in the year.

Report on First Privatized Prison – Judge Stephen Tumin's report on The Wolds, Britain's first privatized prison, appeared **Aug. 25**. It said that the facilities were excellent but underused, and that there was a pervasive air of lethargy with too much sleeping. In terms of management there were areas of uncertainty between the contracting parties: who, for example, should pay for electricity and gas?

Cancer Treatment Errors – It was announced, **Aug. 26**, that 18,000 cases of cancer diagnosed at the Royal Orthopaedic Hospital, Birmingham, over the past 8 years were to be reviewed. The announcement followed the discovery of 42 errors in the allocation of cancer treatment. Health Sec. Virginia Bottomley promptly announced new guidelines for medical staff in reporting incompetent colleagues.

Richest and Poorest – After number-crunching the 1991 census and taking into account conditions of employment, housing, health and car ownership, a league table of deprivation was published, **Aug. 10**. The 5 most deprived areas were given as Knowsley, Manchester, Liverpool, Hackney and Tower Hamlets. The 5 least deprived areas were Wokingham, Hart, Surrey Heath, Newbury and the Isles of Scilly.

International

Demjanjuk Remains in Israeli Custody – Although John Demjanjuk's conviction in the "Ivan the Terrible" case was overturned in July, he remained in detention in Israel in August. On **Aug. 1**, an Israeli Supreme Court panel issued a restraining order keeping him in custody until prosecutors decided whether to try him on other alleged concentration-camp activites during World War II. The 6th U.S. Circuit Court of Appeals held, **Aug. 3**, that he should be allowed to return to the United States while other charges were under review. The court asserted that any retrial of Demjanjuk in Israel would violate international law. Israel's justice ministry said, **Aug. 4**, that the court's ruling was not binding in Israel. Israel's Supreme Court, Aug. 18, ordered that Demjanjuk be set free, but then heard arguments that their decision be delayed.

NATO Weighs Military Action in Bosnia – A role for NATO in the Bosnian crisis became a centre of attention in August. A U.S. State Dept. spokesman said, **Aug. 1**, that the United States might strike Serb targets in Bosnia with or without the concurrence of NATO. Pres. Bill Clinton said, **Aug. 2**, however, that "we are working with the allies. We're going to try to work through to a common position." NATO ambassadors, **Aug. 3**, agreed to begin planning possible military action against the Serbs if that were necessary to prevent interference with humanitarian assistance in the war zone. NATO, **Aug. 9**, approved a list of possible Serb targets. Serb troops, **Aug. 10**, began withdrawing from mountains overlooking Sarajevo, the capital, and U.N. military observers prepared to take their place. In Geneva, **Aug. 16**, Croatian, Muslim and Serbian representatives tentatively agreed to the eventual demilitarization of Sarajevo in favour of U.N. administration.

U.S. Floods Leave Heavy Damage – "The Great Flood of 1993", as it was inevitably dubbed, receded in August, leaving considerable damage in 9 states. In St Louis the Mississippi River finally peaked at a record 49.4 feet (14.96 metres), **Aug. 1**, about 2.5 feet (72cm) below the top of the flood wall. It was reported, **Aug. 9**, that an estimated 8 million acres had been flooded and that 12 million more acres were too wet to grow crops. State and federal officials put total damage estimates at $12 billion, with nearly $8 billion of this suffered by farmers. The final death toll appeared to be 50, and nearly 70,000 people were made homeless.

Israel, Palestinians Near Agreement – A tense month in Middle East negotiations took a dramatically encouraging turn at the end of August, and it appeared that a plan for limited Palestinian self-rule might soon be approved. Yasser Arafat, chairman of the Palestine Liberation Organization, caused a rift in the ranks, **Aug. 3**, when he asked his negotiation delegation to offer more concessions to Israel than they were prepared to accept. For one thing, Arafat was willing to postpone discussion on the status of Jerusalem. The Palestinian delegates rejected Arafat's terms and presented their own proposal to U.S Secretary of State Warren Christopher. The PLO announced, **Aug. 5**, that Arafat had ordered a restructuring of the PLO bureaucracy in order to overcome serious financial problems. Israeli and Palestinian officials reported, **Aug. 5**, that an Israeli cabinet minister and a senior adviser to Arafat had met, an historic initial contact between the old enemies. In January 1993 the Israeli Knesset (parliament) had repealed a law prohibiting contacts between Israeli citizens and PLO members. Two Palestinian delegates to the peace talks had reportedly decided, **Aug. 7**, to resign in protest over Arafat's direct intervention in the negotiations. But then a compromise was announced, **Aug. 12**. Seven delegates were made a formal part of the PLO decision-making process, and were appointed to the PLO committee that directed peace-talk strategy. Foreign Minister Shimon Perez of Israel announced, **Aug. 13**, that even though the delegates representing the Palestinians were now officially part of the PLO, Israel would continue to negotiate with them. Never before had Israel been willing to negotiate with the PLO. Deploring this shift, former Israeli Prime Minister Yitzhak Shamir called the PLO a "murderous organization". On **Aug. 15** about 400 Palestinian men who had been deported from Israel to southern Lebanon in 1992 agreeed to Israel's terms for their return. Some would be returned to prison. Norway's Foreign Minister Johan Joergan Holst confirmed, **Aug. 30**, reports that he had mediated in talks between the PLO and the Israeli government, beginning in April, that were separate from the publicly known peace talks. Most of the meetings had taken place in Norway. While much of the world rejoiced at the news, hard-liners on both sides were outraged as details of a tentative agreement came out, and one radical Palestinian leader appeared to call for Arafat's assassination. Perez told the Knesset, **Aug. 30**, "This is the beginning of the end" of Israel's dispute with the Palestinians. The Israeli government, **Aug. 31**, approved in principle a plan for interim Palestinian self-rule. Self-rule would be established in the Gaza Strip and in the historic biblical town of Jericho on the West Bank within a few months. Later, self-rule would be extended to the rest of the West Bank, excepting the Israeli settlements. Internationally supervised elections would be held in the occupied territories. Negotiations on the status of Jerusalem would begin within 2 years. In the affected areas Israel would control overall security, but the Palestinians would control taxation, education, health, welfare and the police.

Italy Reforms Electoral System – Italy's parliament gave final approval, **Aug. 4**, to a new means for electing its members. Parliament's response came as one reaction to public outrage over widespread political scandals. Previously, seats had been allocated according to proportional representation. With many parties winning seats, it had proved difficult to form stable coalition governments. From now on, 75% of the seats would be awarded to the candidate in each district who received the most votes. The remaining 25% of the seats would be distributed according to proportional representation.

2 in Rodney King Case Sentenced – On **Aug. 4** a federal judge sentenced Stacey Koon and Laurence Powell to 2½ years in prison for violating Rodney King's civil rights. The 1992 acquittal of the 2 officers and 2 other policemen in the beating of King had resulted in widespread protests and violence in Los Angeles and elsewhere, with the loss of 50 lives. In announcing sentences that were lighter than the federal guidelines, the judge expressed the view that most of the blows delivered to King and recorded on an amateur videotape had been lawful. He said that King's behaviour had "contributed significantly" to the beating. Although many in the black community in Los Angeles objected to the sentences, the city remained calm.

Nail-biting Vote on U.S. Budget – After a long debate of great intensity and acrimony, Congress in August narrowly approved Pres. Clinton's bill to reduce Federal budget deficits by $496 billion over 5 years. The bill, centrepiece of Clinton's economic recovery programme, included raising taxes on high earners, imposing a 2.9% Medicare tax on all salary incomes and increasing the tax on gasoline. Public opinion surveys showed Americans about equally divided on the bill. The House approved it, **Aug. 5**, by a bare 218–216 margin. The following day the Senate divided 50–50, and the bill finally passed with the tie-breaking vote of Vice-Pres. Al Gore.

Reformer Becomes Premier of Japan – Morihiro Hosokawa, who had left the ruling Liberal Democratic Party in 1992, was elected premier of Japan in August as head of a coalition of reform-minded parties. The July election for seats in the Diet (parliament) had proved inconclusive, and Hosokawa became the candidate for premier of 7 parties. In the 511-member Diet, **Aug. 6**, Hosokawa received a majority, 262 votes, to 224 for the new LDP leader, Yohei Kono. Hosokawa, at 55, was much younger than most recent Japanese premiers. He was from Kumamoto prefecture, on the island of Kyushu, and was a descendant of a family that had ruled Kumamoto from the 17th to the 19th centuries. He was governor of Kumamoto in 1992 when he quit the LDP in protest at political and bureaucratic corruption. Also on **Aug. 6**, Takako Doi, former head of the

Socialist Party, became the first woman elected Speaker of parliament. Hosokawa's cabinet, announced **Aug. 9**, included 3 women, the most ever in a Japanese cabinet. He said he would seek quick enactment of political-reform laws. He also pledged, **Aug. 10**, to take steps to reduce Japan's large trade surplus with the United States and other nations. He also stated that World War II was, for Japan, "a war of aggression and it was wrong". His acknowledgement of Japanese guilt went beyond that made by any other previous government official.

4 U.S. Soldiers Killed in Somalia – Four U.S. soldiers were killed, **Aug. 8**, in Mogadishu, the capital of Somalia, when a remote-controlled land mine exploded under their jeep. The soldiers were part of the U.N. peacekeeping force. In all, 12 U.S. troops and a civilian Army employee had been killed in combat in Somalia since December.

Sudan on List of Supporters of Terrorism – The U.S. State Dept. informed the government of Sudan, **Aug. 18**, that the country would be added to the list of nations that the United States regarded as supporters of international terrorism. The department had concluded that the Sudan had trained Islamic militants who had committed terrorist acts. Other countries on the department's list included Cuba, Iran, Iraq, Libya, North Korea and Syria.

Political Hostages Freed in Nicaragua – Two rival political groups seized hostages in Nicaragua in August, but all of them were freed without harm. On **Aug. 19** a band of re-armed former Contra rebels, now called Re-contras, seized a 38-member government delegation visiting their mountain camp. They demanded that Gen. Humberto Ortega Saavedra, a Marxist Sandinista, be ousted as defence minister. In retaliation, former Sandinista soldiers, **Aug. 20**, seized 34 conservative political leaders in Managua, the capital. The vice-president and the president of the Assembly were among the captives. Some of the original hostages were released by both sides, **Aug. 21** and **22**, but then, on **Aug. 22**, leftists seized 9 journalists who had been covering the story. On **Aug. 25** all the remaining hostages were released.

General

Monster Hit at Box Office – Steven Spielberg's *Jurassic Park*, which opened in the UK in mid-July, grossed £24 million in only 20 days, it was announced **Aug. 7**. The film thus broke the country's previous box-office record, held by *Ghost*, of £23 million. On its opening day in the U.S., the long-awaited Spielberg film grossed $18.2 million (£12 million).

Wimbledon Common Murder Charge – Colin Stagg, aged 30, was charged, **Aug. 17**, with the murder of Rachel Nickell. The brutal attack, which took place in broad daylight in July 1992, appalled the country, as the young mother's 2-year-old child witnessed her being stabbed 49 times.

Flash in the Pan – When the Mutant Ninja Turtles held sway as children's heroes, miniature turtles were bought in their thousands as pets. Now they really are mutating, in the south of France, where the hot climate and lack of predators are producing 10-ft-long carnivores with an aggressive disposition. The innocent originals were flushed down toilets or tipped into lakes when their appeal wore off. Now they return to bite swimmers. It was reported, **Aug. 17**, that experts predict "pandemonium".

Satellite Falls Silent Near Mars – The Mars Observer spacecraft ceased communicating from space in August as it approached Mars, its destination. The Observer, which cost $980 million, had been launched in September 1992. Contact with ground controllers was lost **Aug. 21**, 3 days before the spacecraft was to orbit the red planet. The spacecraft was to map the surface of Mars and obtain information on its geology in anticipation of a possible manned visit.

Historical Anniversaries

1894 – 100 Years Ago

The 35-mile Manchester Ship Canal, connecting the River Irwell to Liverpool and the Irish Sea, opened to traffic, **Jan. 1**. It was officially opened by Queen Victoria **May 21**.

The Local Government Act, implemented **Mar. 1**, established parish councils and gave women equality with men as voters and candidates for council elections.

Prime Minister William Gladstone resigned, **Mar. 3**, having split the Liberal Party over Home Rule. He was succeeded by Lord Rosebery.

Chancellor W. V. Harcourt introduced death duties in his Budget, **Apr. 11**.

Lord Rosebery attempted to draw Britain closer to the Triple Alliance (between Germany, Austria-Hungary and Italy), which shaped European diplomacy in the years leading up to World War I. His attempts were thwarted by Germany, **June 24**.

Marks' and Spencer's first "Penny Bazaar" was opened in Cheetham Hill, Manchester, **Sep. 24**.

Alfred Dreyfus, a French army officer, was arrested for betraying state secrets to the Germans, **Oct. 15**. Sentenced to life imprisonment on Devil's Island, he was subsequently found to be completely innocent of all charges.

Attracting 9 exhibitors, the first Motor Show opened in the Champs Elysées, Paris, **Dec. 11**.

Science and technology: Lord (John) Rayleigh and William Ramsay discovered the inert gas they named argon. James Dewar liquefied oxygen. Thomas Edison's "Kinetoscope", invented in 1887, was given its first public showing in New York City.

Literature: *The Memoirs of Sherlock Holmes* by Arthur Conan Doyle; *Prisoner of Zenda* by Anthony Hope; *The Jungle Book* by Rudyard Kipling; *Trilby* by George du Maurier; *Pudd'nhead Wilson* by Mark Twain; *History of Trade Unionism* by Sidney and Beatrice Webb.

Journalism: *The Yellow Book*, a London periodical, which gained fame through art director Aubrey Beardsley's provocative drawings.

Art: *Femme à sa toilette* by Edgar Degas, and *La Toilette* by American artist Mary Cassatt were exhibited in Paris. Louis Comfort Tiffany invented and trademarked a process for staining glass to achieve radiantly iridescent colours, which he used to create "art nouveau"-style lamps, vases, jewellery and windows.

Theatre: *Arms and the Man* by George Bernard Shaw staged in London.

Ballet: *L'Après-midi d'un faun*, with music by Claude Debussy, in Paris.

Opera: *Thaïs* by Jules Massenet.

Popular songs: "Humoresque" by Anton Dvořák.

Sport: Everton beat Liverpool 3-0 at Goodison Park in the first match between the two Merseyside teams. The first U.S. Open golf tournament was held at St Andrew Golf Club in Yonkers, N.Y.

Miscellaneous: Pêche Melba – a scoop of vanilla ice-cream on a cooked peach half with a purée of raspberries topped by almond slivers – was created by August Escoffier at London's Savoy Hotel. The dessert was made in honour of Dame Nellie Melba, the Australian diva.

1944 – 50 Years Ago

The penultimate year of World War II saw the RAF drop 2,300 tons of bombs on Berlin, **Jan. 20**. The scale of the bombing provoked protests in the House of Lords.

On D-Day, **June 6**, some 176,000 Allied troops, under the command of Gen. Dwight D. Eisenhower, landed at 5 beaches along a 50-mile stretch of Normandy coastline. The date marked the start of the reconquest of France, and the beginning of the end for the Axis forces. The Battle of the Bulge in the Ardennes Forest of Belgium, **Dec. 16–27**, was the last major counter-offensive.

In the Pacific, Japanese forces were retreating. U.S. forces headed by Gen. Douglas MacArthur returned to the Philippines, **Oct. 20**, and 4 separate operations of a 6-day naval battle in Leyte Gulf marked the effective end of the Japanese fleet. The kamikaze, or suicide plane, was first used during the Leyte campaign.

Pay-as-you-earn income tax, devised by Sir Cornelius Gregg, was introduced **Feb. 10**.

R. A. Butler's Education Bill, implemented in **May**, created a 3-tier system of free secondary state schools – grammar, technical and modern. Selection for each was to be on the basis of the 11+ exam.

Forty-four nations were represented at a conference at Bretton Woods, **July 1**, to formulate International Monetary Policy.

Representatives of Britain, China, the U.S. and the USSR met at Dumbarton Oaks, Washington DC, to discuss postwar world organization, **Aug. 21–Oct. 7**. Proposals would become the basis for the United Nations charter.

Pres. Franklin D. Roosevelt was re-elected to a fourth term, **Nov. 7**, and would be the only U.S. president to do so.

The U.S. Congress created the rank of General of the Army ("5-star general"), **Dec. 15**, for Dwight D. Eisenhower, Douglas MacArthur, George C. Marshall and Henry Arnold.

The first large-scale automatic digital computer was built by the IBM Corporation at Harvard University to the specifications of Prof. Howard H. Aiken. The Harvard-IBM Automatic Sequence Controlled Calculator, or Mark I, had more than 750,000 parts, was 51 feet long and weighed 5 tons. It performed a multiplication in about 6 seconds.

Science: Quinine was synthesized for the first time.

Literature: *Fair Stood the Wind for France* by H. E. Bates; *Dangling Man* by Saul Bellow; *Winter Tales* by Isak Dinesen; *Four Quartets* by T. S. Eliot; *The Razor's Edge* by W. Somerset Maugham; *Agustino* by Alberto Moravia; *English Social History* by G. M. Trevelyan.

Art: *Three Studies for Figures at the Base of a Crucifix* by Francis Bacon; *Plantation Road* by Thomas Hart Benton; *Pelvis III* by Georgia O'Keeffe; *Christ on the Cross*, Graham Sutherland.

Theatre: *Antigone* by Jean Anouilh, and *No Exit* by Jean-Paul Sartre, both in Paris; *I Remember Mama* by John Druten, with the young Marlon Brando.

Music: Béla Bartók's violin concerto; Paul Hindemith, *Herodias* (opera).

Musicals: *On the Town*, in New York – music by Leonard Bernstein, lyrics by Betty Comden and Adolph Green, dances derived from the ballet *Fancy Free* by Jerome Robbins.

Films: *Henry V*, with Laurence Olivier; Sergei Eisenstein's *Ivan the Terrible*, Part I; Alfred Hitchcock's *Lifeboat*, with Tallulah Bankhead, William Bendix, John Hodiak, Canada Lee; Preston Sturges's *Hail the Conquering Hero*, with Eddie Bracken, Ella Raines; Otto Preminger's *Laura*, with Clifton Webb, Gene Tierney, Dana Andrews; Billy Wilder's *Double Indemnity*, with Barbara Stanwyck, Fred MacMurray, Edward G. Robinson; George Cukor's *Gaslight*, with Ingrid Bergman, Charles Boyer; Howard Hawks's *To Have and Have Not*, with Humphrey Bogart, Lauren Bacall; *National Velvet*, with Mickey Rooney and 12-year-old Elizabeth Taylor; Vincente Minnelli's *Meet Me in St Louis*, with Judy Garland; Leo McCarey's *Going My Way*, with Bing Crosby, Barry Fitzgerald.

Pop songs: "I'll Walk Alone"; "Don't Fence Me In"; "Nancy (with the Laughing Face)"; "Rum and Coca-Cola"; "You're Nobody Till Somebody Loves You"; "You Always Hurt the One You Love".

1969 – 25 Years Ago

A human being walked on the moon for the first time, **July 20**, when U.S. astronaut Neil Armstrong left the lunar module of Apollo 11. He announced, "That's one small step for man, one giant leap for mankind." Armstrong was joined by Edwin "Buzz" Aldrin; the two astronauts deposited a lunar capsule and an American flag on the moon.

Richard M. Nixon was inaugurated as the 37th U.S. president, Spiro T. Agnew as vice-president, **Jan. 20**.

The London School of Economics was closed for the month of **Feb.** because of student protests and sit-ins.

The Victoria line opened on the London Underground system, **Mar. 7**.

The world's first entirely artificial heart, made of Dacron and plastic, was implanted into a human, **Apr. 4**, by Dr Denton A. Cooley of Houston, Texas. The patient lived until **Apr. 8**.

Bernadette Devlin won a by-election in Mid-Ulster, **Apr. 17**, becoming the youngest MP (21) since William Pitt in 1781.

Riots broke out in Belfast and Londonderry, and Catholics erected barricades in Bogside, **Apr. 19**. British troops arrived, **Apr. 21**, to guard key positions. After 3 days of street fighting, **Aug. 12–15**, the army assumed responsibility for security and police in the province.

U.S. B-52s dropped almost 3,000 tons of bombs on enemy positions near the Cambodian border, **Apr. 24**, the heaviest bombing raid in the Vietnam War.

The *QE2* departed on her maiden voyage, **May 2**.

Britain lowered the voting age from 21 to 18, **May 12** – the first change since 1928.

Pres. Nixon met with South Vietnam pres. Nguyen Van Thieu, **June 8**, and announced the start of U.S. troop withdrawal and a "Vietnamization" policy.

Prince Charles was invested as Prince of Wales at Caernarvon Castle, **July 1**.

The body of 28-year-old Mary Jo Kopechne was retrieved, **July 19**, from a car that had plunged off Chappaquiddick Island, Mass. Senator Edward Kennedy, who had been driving the car, failed to report the accident to the police for 10 hours.

Actress Sharon Tate and 4 others were found murdered, **Aug. 9**, in Los Angeles; Charles Manson and several members of his cult were arrested.

The Woodstock Music and Art Fair at Bethel, N.Y., attracted up to 400,000 young people for 4 days in **mid-Aug.** Performers included Jimi Hendrix, Richie Havens, Joan Baez, Jefferson Airplane, the Who and the Grateful Dead. Despite traffic jams, inadequate food and water, heavy rain and widespread drug use, the general atmosphere was one of peaceful celebration. The Isle of Wight music festival, **Aug. 29–31**, attracted 150,000 pop fans; the headline performer was Bob Dylan.

North Vietnamese leader Ho Chi Minh died, **Sep. 3**, aged 79 after 15 years as president.

Concorde made its first supersonic flight, **Oct. 1**.

The 7-sided 50-pence piece was introduced to replace the 10-shilling note, **Oct. 14**.

The Divorce Reform Act, making the breakdown of a marriage adequate grounds for divorce, came into force **Oct. 22**.

Building work began in **Nov.** on the National Theatre complex on London's South Bank.

News reports, **Nov. 16**, charged a U.S. infantry unit with massacring My Lai, a village in South Vietnam, on Mar. 16, 1968; more than 450 villagers, including women and children, were said to have been murdered.

The House of Commons and the House of Lords voted, **Dec. 16–18**, for the permanent abolition of the death penalty.

Literature: *The French Lieutenant's Woman* by John Fowles; *Bruno's Dream* by Iris Murdoch; *Ada* by Vladimir Nabokov; *The Godfather* by Mario Puzo; *Portnoy's Complaint* by Philip Roth; *Slaughterhouse Five* by Kurt Vonnegut. The first Booker Prize was awarded to P. H. Newby for *Something to Answer For.*

Art: *Orange Yellow Orange* by Mark Rothko; *The Finn* by Andrew Wyeth.

Theatre: *Forty Years On* by Alan Bennett; *Early Morning* by Edward Bond; *To Be Young, Gifted and Black* by Lorraine Hansberry; *Last of the Red Hot Lovers* by Neil Simon.

Musicals: Britain's longest-running music show, *The Black and White Minstrel Show*, at London's Victoria Palace, closed after 4,354 performances in 7 years.

Films: Dennis Hopper's *Easy Rider*, with Hopper, Peter Fonda, Jack Nicholson; John Schlesinger's *Midnight Cowboy*, with Dustin Hoffman, John Voight; Sam Peckinpah's *The Wild Bunch*, with William Holden, Robert Ryan, Ernest Borgnine; George Roy Hill's *Butch Cassidy and the Sundance Kid*, with Paul Newman, Robert Redford, Katharine Ross; Sidney Pollack's, *They Shoot Horses, Don't They?*, with Jane Fonda; Henry Hathaway's *True Grit*, with John Wayne.

Sport: Boris Spassky became world chess champion, beating Tigran Petrosian. Pancho Gonzalez and Charlie Pasarell played a record 112-game singles match on Wimbledon's Centre Court. It lasted 5 hours and 12 minutes.

Miscellaneous: Colour television was introduced on BBC1 and ITV in **Sep.**

POPULATION

Improved health care and contraception have had marked effects on the population of the United Kingdom. By 2021 nearly one in five people will be over 65, as opposed to only one in ten in 1951. Meanwhile, young people under 16 are decreasing in numbers – from 14.3 million in 1971 to 11.7 million in 1991. The counties with the fastest growing populations (over 1% per year) are Buckinghamshire, Cambridgeshire, Cornwall and Dorset. The greatest falls in population have occurred in Belfast and the islands of Scotland.

Since deregulation in 1992, which gave greater freedom of movement within the EC, increased numbers of UK nationals are living abroad. Of the 392,000 British ex-patriates living in other EC countries in 1990, two-fifths were resident in Germany and Spain. At the same time 876,000 nationals of other EC countries were resident in the UK, and more than two-thirds were Irish. Over the period 1987–1991 more migrants entered the United Kingdom than left.

As far as international migration is concerned, the major source has been people seeking asylum (six in ten applicants are from Africa and three in ten are from Asia). Between 1986 and mid-1991 applications for asylum in the United Kingdom increased tenfold, but figures have halved since new measures were introduced to deter multiple and fraudulent applications.

Population Summary

Source: CSO

Thousands

	United Kingdom			England and Wales			Wales	Scotland			Northern Ireland		
	Persons	Males	Females	Persons	Males	Females	Persons	Persons	Males	Females	Persons	Males	Females
Enumerated population: census figures													
1801	–	–	–	8,893	4,255	4,638	587	1,608	739	869	–	–	–
1851	22,259	10,855	11,404	17,928	8,781	9,146	1,163	2,889	1,376	1,513	1,442	698	745
1901	38,237	18,492	19,745	32,528	15,729	16,799	2,013	4,472	2,174	2,298	1,237	590	647
1911	42,082	20,357	21,725	36,070	17,446	18,625	2,421	4,761	2,309	2,452	1,251	603	648
1921[1]	44,027	21,033	22,994	37,887	18,075	19,811	2,656	4,882	2,348	2,535	1,258	610	648
1931[1]	46,038	22,060	23,978	39,952	19,133	20,819	2,593	4,843	2,326	2,517	1,243	601	642
1951	50,225	24,118	26,107	43,758	21,016	22,742	2,599	5,096	2,434	2,662	1,371	668	703
1961	52,709	25,481	27,228	46,105	22,304	23,801	2,644	5,179	2,483	2,697	1,425	694	731
1966[2]	53,788	26,044	27,745	47,136	22,841	24,295	2,663	5,168	2,479	2,689	1,485	724	761
1971	55,515	26,952	28,562	48,750	23,683	25,067	2,731	5,229	2,515	2,714	1,536	755	781
1981	55,848	27,104	28,742	49,155	23,873	25,281	2,792	5,131	2,466	2,664	1,533[3]	750	783
1991	56,467	27,344	29,123	49,890	24,182	25,707	–	4,999	2,392	2,606	1,578	769	809
Usually resident													
1981	55,089	26,803	28,286	48,522	23,625	24,897	2,750	5,035	2,428	2,607	1,532	749	783
Resident population: mid-year estimates													
1958	51,652	24,887	26,765	45,109	21,744	23,365	2,615	5,141	2,460	2,682	1,402	684	719
1959	51,956	25,043	26,913	45,386	21,885	23,501	2,623	5,163	2,472	2,690	1,408	686	722
1960	52,372	25,271	27,102	45,775	22,097	23,678	2,629	5,178	2,482	2,696	1,420	692	728
1961	52,807	25,528	27,279	46,196	22,347	23,849	2,635	5,184	2,485	2,698	1,427	696	732
1962	53,292	25,826	27,465	46,657	22,631	24,026	2,652	5,198	2,495	2,703	1,437	700	737
1963	53,625	25,992	27,633	46,973	22,787	24,186	2,664	5,205	2,500	2,705	1,447	705	741
1964	53,991	26,191	27,800	47,324	22,978	24,346	2,677	5,208	2,501	2,707	1,458	711	747
1965	54,350	26,368	27,982	47,671	23,151	24,521	2,693	5,210	2,501	2,709	1,468	716	752
1966	54,643	26,511	28,132	47,966	23,296	24,671	2,702	5,201	2,496	2,704	1,476	719	757
1967	54,959	26,673	28,286	48,272	23,451	24,821	2,710	5,198	2,496	2,702	1,489	726	763
1968	55,214	26,784	28,429	48,511	23,554	24,957	2,715	5,200	2,498	2,702	1,503	733	770
1969	55,461	26,908	28,553	48,738	23,666	25,072	2,722	5,208	2,503	2,706	1,514	739	776
1970	55,632	26,992	28,641	48,891	23,738	25,153	2,729	5,214	2,507	2,707	1,527	747	781
1971	55,928	27,167	28,761	49,152	23,897	25,255	2,740	5,236	2,516	2,720	1,540	755	786
1972	56,097	27,259	28,837	49,327	23,989	25,339	2,755	5,231	2,513	2,717	1,539	758	782
1973	56,223	27,332	28,891	49,459	24,061	25,399	2,773	5,234	2,515	2,719	1,530	756	774
1974	56,236	27,349	28,887	49,468	24,075	25,393	2,785	5,241	2,519	2,722	1,527	755	772
1975	56,226	27,361	28,865	49,470	24,091	25,378	2,795	5,232	2,516	2,716	1,524	753	770
1976	56,216	27,360	28,856	49,459	24,089	25,370	2,799	5,233	2,517	2,716	1,524	754	770
1977	56,190	27,345	28,845	49,440	24,076	25,364	2,801	5,226	2,515	2,711	1,523	754	769
1978	56,178	27,330	28,849	49,443	24,067	25,375	2,804	5,212	2,509	2,704	1,523	754	770
1979	56,240	27,373	28,867	49,508	24,113	25,395	2,810	5,204	2,505	2,699	1,530	755	773
1980	56,330	27,411	28,919	49,603	24,156	25,448	2,816	5,194	2,501	2,693	1,533	755	778
1981	56,352	27,409	28,943	49,634	24,160	25,474	2,814	5,180	2,495	2,685	1,538	754	784
1982	56,306	27,386	28,920	49,601	24,143	25,459	2,807	5,167	2,490	2,677	1,538	754	784
1983	56,347	27,417	28,931	49,654	24,176	25,478	2,808	5,150	2,485	2,665	1,543	756	788
1984	56,460	27,487	28,973	49,764	24,244	25,519	2,807	5,146	2,484	2,662	1,551	760	791
1985	56,618	27,574	29,044	49,924	24,330	25,594	2,812	5,137	2,481	2,656	1,558	763	795
1986	56,763	27,647	29,116	50,075	24,403	25,672	2,821	5,121	2,475	2,646	1,567	768	798
1987	56,930	27,737	29,193	50,243	24,493	25,750	2,836	5,112	2,471	2,641	1,575	773	802
1988	57,065	27,813	29,253	50,393	24,576	25,817	2,857	5,094	2,462	2,632	1,578	774	804
1989	57,236	27,907	29,330	50,562	24,669	25,893	2,873	5,091	2,460	2,630	1,583	777	806
1990	57,411	28,013	29,398	50,719	24,766	25,953	2,881	5,102	2,467	2,636	1,589	780	809
1991[4]	57,649	28,132	29,517	50,955	24,892	26,063	2,886	5,100	2,462	2,638	1,594	778	817

(1) Figures for Northern Ireland are estimated. The population at the census of 1926 was 1,257 thousand (608 thousand males and 649 thousand females). (2) Except for Northern Ireland, where a full census was taken, figures are based on the 10 per cent sample census. (3) The figures include 44,500 non-enumerated persons. (4) The population estimates for mid-1991 are provisional. They are based on early 1991 Census results, and are therefore not comparable with estimates for 1982 to 1990, which were based on the 1981 Census, and will be revised in due course.

Population Changes

Source: CSO

Thousands

	Population at beginning of period[1]	Average annual change: Total increase or decrease(–)	Births	Deaths[2]	Excess of births over deaths	Net civilian migration	Other adjustments[3]
United Kingdom							
1901–1911	38,237	385	1,091	624	467	–82	
1911–1921	42,082	195	975	689	286	–92	
1921–1931	44,027	201	824	555	268	–67	
1931–1951	46,038	213	793	603	190	+22	
1951–1961	50,290	252	839	593	246	–7	+13
1961–1971	52,807	310	962	638	324	–32	+18
1971–1981	55,928	42	736	666	69	–44	+17
1981–1991	56,352	130	757	655	103	21	6
1991–2001[4]	57,649	161	800	639	161	0	
2001–2011	59,174	86	736	650	86	0	
2011–2021	60,033	71	750	679	71	0	
England and Wales							
1901–1911	32,528	354	929	525	404	–50	
1911–1921	36,070	182	828	584	244	–62	
1921–1931	37,887	207	693	469	224	–17	
1931–1951	39,952	193	673	518	155	+38	
1951–1961	43,815	238	714	516	197	+30	+10
1961–1971	46,196	296	832	560	272	+7	+16
1971–1981	49,152	48	638	585	53	–18	+13
1981–1991	49,634	132	664	576	89	36	8
1991–2001[4]	50,955	162	709	564	145	17	
2001–2011	52,526	98	656	574	81	17	
2011–2021	53,510	90	674	600	73	17	
Scotland							
1901–1911	4,472	29	131	76	54	–25	
1911–1921	4,761	12	118	82	36	–24	
1921–1931	4,882	–4	100	65	35	–39	
1931–1951	4,843	13	92	67	25	–11	–1
1951–1961	5,102	8	95	62	34	–28	+2
1961–1971	5,184	3	97	63	34	–32	+2
1971–1981	5,236	–6	70	64	6	–15	+4
1981–1991	5,180	–9	66	63	3	–10	0
1991–2001[4]	5,100	–4	65	60	5	–10	
2001–2011	5,026	–13	58	60	–2	–10	
2011–2021	4,900	–17	55	62	–7	–10	
Northern Ireland							
1901–1911	1,237	1	31	23	8	–6	
1911–1921	1,251	1	29	22	7	–6	
1921–1931	1,258	–2	30	21	9	–11	
1931–1951	1,243	6	28	18	10	–4	
1951–1961	1,373	5	30	15	15	–9	–
1961–1971	1,427	11	33	16	17	–7	+1
1971–1981	1,540	0	28	17	11	–11	0
1981–1991	1,538	6	27	16	12	–5	1
1991–2001[4]	1,594	3	26	15	11	–7	
2001–2011	1,622	0	23	16	7	–7	
2011–2021	1,623	–2	22	17	5	–7	

(1) Census enumerated population up to 1951; mid-year estimates of resident population from 1951 to 1991 and mid-1989 based projections of resident population thereafter. (2) Including deaths of non-civilians and merchant seamen who died outside the country. These numbered 577,000 in 1911–1921 and 240,000 in 1931–1951 for England and Wales; 74,000 in 1911–1921 and 34,000 in 1931–1951 for Scotland; and 10,000 in 1911–1926 for Northern Ireland. (3) For England and Wales, changes in Armed Forces, in visitor balance and other adjustments. (4) Population at the beginning of the period is the provisional rebased mid-year Estimate for 1991 and is therefore not fully consistent with the total increase/decrease figures, which are calculated from the 1989 based projections of the population at mid-1991.

Age Distribution of the Enumerated Population

Source: CSO

Thousands

	England and Wales				Scotland				Northern Ireland			
	1961	1971	1981	1991	1961	1971	1981	1991	1961	1971	1981	1991
Persons: all ages	46,105	48,750	48,522	49,890	5,179.3	5,229.0	5,035.3	4,998.6	1,425.0	1,536.1	1,532.2	1,577.8
Under 5	3,597	3,905	2,910	3,316	469.2	444.3	308.4	317.2	146.5	156.2	130.8	128.3
Under 16	11,233	12,246	10,773	10,013	1,413.9	1,438.1	1,167.0	1,010.3	437.0	483.9	443.3	409.9
Under 18	12,576	13,574	12,418	11,263	1,567.5	1,596.7	1,350.8	1,139.8	487.5	534.9	502.9	460.6
5–14	6,987	7,671	7,053	6,110	869.9	910.5	769.6	629.5	265.6	300.8	283.1	257.0
15–29	8,925	10,236	10,859	10,908	1,034.1	1,099.2	1,183.1	1,099.2	299.2	343.2	366.9	375.9
30–44	9,263	8,593	9,541	10,593	1,000.3	912.7	947.2	1,069.9	262.5	253.4	272.4	310.7

(Continued)

Thousands

	England and Wales				Scotland				Northern Ireland			
	1961	1971	1981	1991	1961	1971	1981	1991	1961	1971	1981	1991
Persons: 45–64	11,836	11,849	10,884	10,919	1,256.9	1,217.9	1,116.3	1,115.4	307.3	316.5	295.2	306.9
65–74	3,520	4,178	4,488	4,505	358.4	426.5	444.3	440.3	92.3	108.2	116.2	117.1
75 and over	1,976	2,318	2,786	3,539	190.5	217.9	266.5	326.7	51.6	57.8	67.8	82.0
Pensionable age aggregate	6,858	8,007	8,611	9,367	695.3	803.7	847.6	908.5	180.1	204.9	220.6	236.4
Under 1	764	774	619	677	97.8	86.0	66.1	63.9	30.8	31.1	27.1	24.7
1 and under 2	725	761	622	671	94.3	86.4	65.0	62.4	29.8	30.9	27.4	25.2
2–4	2,107	2,370	1,669	1,968	277.1	271.9	177.3	190.8	86.0	94.2	76.2	78.3
5–9	3,262	4,044	3,207	3,123	420.7	468.4	344.4	317.6	132.4	157.1	134.3	129.1
10–14	3,725	3,627	3,846	2,988	449.1	442.1	425.2	311.9	133.2	143.7	148.8	127.8
15–19	3,201	3,314	4,020	3,205	374.1	392.3	446.6	332.1	120.2	126.4	144.5	127.5
20–24	2,878	3,731	3,564	3,731	333.0	390.4	394.3	374.5	93.8	114.9	122.3	126.1
25–29	2,846	3,191	3,275	3,971	327.0	316.4	342.2	392.6	85.2	101.9	99.9	122.2
30–34	2,984	2,871	3,656	3,623	332.5	300.6	358.7	375.2	86.5	86.7	98.7	113.4
35–39	3,242	2,786	3,092	3,308	347.3	300.8	300.3	337.9	90.9	82.4	92.5	99.3
40–44	3,037	2,935	2,792	3,662	320.5	311.3	288.1	356.7	85.1	84.3	81.2	97.9
45–49	3,229	3,135	2,689	3,074	342.6	322.8	285.7	297.4	87.0	86.0	76.1	89.9
50–54	3,221	2,897	2,785	3,720	342.0	295.8	289.6	280.8	82.0	80.0	76.0	76.5
55–59	2,928	2,976	2,877	2,567	312.5	306.3	289.8	272.0	72.5	78.5	75.1	71.0
60–64	2,458	2,841	2,533	2,559	259.0	293.0	251.3	265.0	65.7	72.0	68.0	69.3
65–69	1,979	2,400	2,426	2,491	204.6	247.2	240.8	246.8	52.2	60.3	63.4	64.9
70–74	1,542	1,778	2,062	2,014	153.9	179.3	203.5	193.4	40.1	47.9	52.8	52.1
75–79	1,069	1,185	1,458	1,663	105.4	115.2	142.5	156.0	27.0	29.9	34.6	40.2
80–84	605	707	821	1,113	57.9	65.6	78.3	102.7	16.2	17.5	20.5	25.0
85 and over	302	425	507	763	27.2	37.2	45.6	67.9	8.4	10.4	12.7	16.6
Males: all ages	22,304	23,683	23,625	24,183	2,482.7	2,514.6	2,428.5	2,392.0	694.2	754.7	749.5	769.1
Under 5	1,846	2,003	1,492	1,696	240.1	228.5	158.3	162.4	75.4	80.3	66.8	65.9
Under 16	5,756	6,288	5,526	5,129	723.5	737.9	598.3	517.6	224.4	249.0	277.6	209.9
Under 18	6,440	6,971	6,368	5,770	800.7	818.7	691.9	583.8	249.8	275.2	258.3	236.0
5–14	3,578	3,940	3,619	3,132	445.2	466.7	394.5	322.5	136.2	154.9	145.6	131.3
15–29	4,502	5,184	5,506	5,438	507.8	554.4	599.7	543.4	148.8	176.0	187.9	190.1
30–44	4,612	4,337	4,794	5,270	486.5	446.9	471.2	527.8	127.1	124.9	135.8	154.2
45–64	5,663	5,728	5,331	5,409	588.6	573.5	531.9	537.4	145.5	151.2	140.3	148.2
65–74	1,419	1,755	1,971	2,023	143.7	174.5	188.9	191.4	40.0	45.9	50.0	51.5
75 and over	684	737	912	1,215	71.0	70.3	83.9	106.6	21.3	21.4	23.0	27.8
Pensionable age aggregate	2,102	2,492	2,882	3,238	214.6	244.8	272.8	298.1	61.3	67.4	73.0	79.3
Under 1	393	397	317	346	49.9	44.2	33.8	32.7	15.9	15.9	13.8	12.7
1 and under 2	372	390	319	343	48.4	44.5	33.4	31.8	15.4	15.9	14.1	13.0
2–4	1,080	1,215	857	1,006	141.8	139.8	91.0	98.0	44.1	48.5	38.9	40.2
5–9	1,616	1,671	2,074	1,600	215.1	240.1	176.3	162.5	68.1	81.1	69.3	66.2
10–14	1,907	1,865	1,972	1,532	230.1	226.5	218.2	160.0	68.1	73.7	76.4	65.1
15–19	1,622	1,696	2,054	1,636	187.4	199.4	227.8	168.7	60.3	65.1	74.4	65.7
20–24	1,434	1,876	1,805	1,845	159.4	196.6	199.8	184.4	46.9	59.3	62.5	63.8
25–29	1,446	1,612	1,648	1,958	161.0	158.3	172.2	190.3	41.6	51.6	51.0	60.4
30–34	1,502	1,460	1,835	1,801	162.8	148.1	180.5	183.3	41.6	43.5	49.7	55.7
35–39	1,616	1,410	1,554	1,646	170.5	147.4	149.5	167.0	43.9	40.7	46.1	49.7
40–44	1,494	1,467	1,405	1,824	153.2	151.4	141.3	177.3	41.6	40.7	40.0	48.6
45–49	1,584	1,552	1,351	1,537	163.9	157.0	139.5	146.9	42.1	41.7	37.1	44.5
50–54	1,575	1,412	1,381	1,361	164.3	139.6	139.6	136.3	39.6	39.1	36.3	37.5
55–59	1,408	1,434	1,403	1,275	147.3	143.2	138.4	130.4	34.4	37.4	35.5	34.1
60–64	1,096	1,330	1,196	1,236	113.2	133.7	114.4	123.7	29.4	33.1	31.4	31.9
65–69	819	1,063	1,100	1,153	83.4	106.6	105.7	111.3	23.0	26.4	28.2	29.2
70–74	600	692	871	870	60.2	67.9	83.2	80.0	17.0	19.5	21.8	22.2
75–79	389	410	544	651	40.2	39.4	50.9	58.4	11.3	11.6	12.8	15.4
80–84	205	217	248	375	21.7	20.5	22.5	32.6	6.7	6.4	6.7	8.2
85 and over	90	110	119	189	9.0	10.4	10.5	15.5	3.2	3.5	3.5	4.0
Females: all ages	23,801	25,067	24,897	25,707	2,696.6	2,714.3	2,606.8	2,607.0	730.8	781.4	782.7	808.8
Under 5	1,751	1,902	1,418	1,620	229.1	215.8	150.1	154.7	71.2	75.9	64.0	62.3
Under 16	5,477	5,958	5,248	4,884	690.5	700.2	568.6	492.6	212.6	234.8	215.7	200.0
Under 18	6,136	6,603	6,050	5,493	766.9	778.0	658.9	556.0	237.8	259.7	244.6	224.6
5–14	3,410	3,732	3,434	2,979	424.8	443.8	375.1	307.0	129.4	145.9	137.5	125.7
15–29	4,423	5,052	5,353	5,469	526.4	544.8	583.4	555.7	150.4	167.2	178.8	185.8
30–44	4,651	4,256	4,747	5,323	513.8	465.7	475.9	542.1	135.4	128.5	136.6	156.5
45–64	6,172	6,122	5,554	5,510	668.3	644.4	584.4	577.9	161.9	165.3	154.9	158.7
65–74	2,102	2,423	2,517	2,482	214.8	252.0	255.4	248.9	52.3	62.2	66.2	65.6
75 and over	1,292	1,581	1,875	2,325	119.5	147.7	182.5	220.0	30.3	36.4	44.8	54.2
Pensionable age aggregate	4,756	5,515	5,729	6,130	480.7	559.0	574.8	610.4	118.9	137.5	147.5	157.1
Under 1	371	377	303	331	47.9	41.8	32.3	31.2	14.9	15.1	13.4	12.0
1 and under 2	353	371	303	328	45.9	41.9	31.6	30.5	14.4	15.0	13.3	12.2
2–4	1,027	1,154	812	962	135.3	132.1	86.2	93.0	41.9	45.8	37.3	38.1
5–9	1,592	1,970	1,560	1,523	205.7	228.3	168.1	155.1	64.3	76.0	65.0	62.9
10–14	1,818	1,762	1,875	1,456	219.1	215.5	207.0	151.8	65.0	69.9	72.4	62.7
15–19	1,579	1,618	1,966	1,569	186.7	192.9	218.8	163.4	60.0	61.2	70.1	61.8
20–24	1,444	1,855	1,760	1,887	173.7	193.8	194.6	190.1	46.9	55.6	59.8	62.2
25–29	1,400	1,579	1,627	2,013	166.0	158.1	170.0	202.2	43.6	50.3	48.9	61.7
30–34	1,483	1,411	1,822	1,822	169.7	152.4	178.3	191.8	44.9	43.2	49.0	57.6
35–39	1,626	1,376	1,538	1,663	176.9	153.4	150.8	170.8	47.0	41.7	46.4	49.5

(Continued)

Thousands

	England and Wales				Scotland				Northern Ireland			
	1961	1971	1981	1991	1961	1971	1981	1991	1961	1971	1981	1991
40–44	1,543	1,468	1,387	1,838	167.2	159.9	146.9	179.3	43.4	43.6	41.2	49.3
45–49	1,645	1,584	1,338	1,536	178.8	165.8	146.2	150.4	44.9	44.4	39.0	45.4
50–54	1,646	1,485	1,404	1,359	177.9	156.2	150.1	144.5	42.5	41.0	39.7	39.0
55–59	1,520	1,542	1,474	1,292	165.2	163.1	151.3	141.5	38.2	41.1	39.6	36.8
60–64	1,362	1,511	1,337	1,323	146.4	159.3	136.8	141.3	36.3	39.0	36.6	37.3
65–69	1,160	1,336	1,326	1,338	121.1	140.6	135.1	135.4	29.2	33.8	35.2	35.7
70–74	942	1,086	1,191	1,144	93.7	111.4	120.3	113.4	23.1	28.4	31.0	29.8
75–79	680	776	914	1,012	65.2	75.8	91.6	97.5	15.7	18.3	21.8	24.8
80–84	401	490	573	739	36.2	45.1	55.8	70.0	9.4	11.1	13.8	16.7
85 and over	212	315	388	574	18.2	26.8	35.1	52.4	5.2	6.9	9.2	12.5

(1) 1981 data cover the "usually resident" population and are not strictly comparable with earlier data. (2) The figures for Northern Ireland have been revised using a new estimate of 44,500 non-enumerated persons in the 1981 Census.

Population: by Age and Ethnic Group, 1989–1991

Great Britain

Source: CSO

Percentages and thousands

Ethnic group	Age group (percentages) 0–15	16–29	30–44	45–59	60 and over	All ages (=100%) (thousands)
West Indian or Guyanese	*24*	*30*	*19*	*19*	*9*	456
Indian	*29*	*25*	*25*	*14*	*6*	793
Pakistani	*44*	*23*	*20*	*11*	*3*	486
Bangladeshi	*46*	*26*	*15*	*11*	*3*	127
Chinese	*25*	*28*	*29*	*13*	*5*	137
African	*31*	*28*	*28*	*10*	*2*	150
Arab	*23*	*30*	*33*	*9*	*5*	67
Mixed	*54*	*24*	*13*	*6*	*3*	310
Other	*27*	*27*	*31*	*10*	*4*	155
All ethnic minority groups	*34*	*26*	*22*	*13*	*5*	2,682
White	*19*	*21*	*21*	*17*	*21*	51,805
Not stated	*36*	*22*	*16*	*11*	*15*	496
All ethnic groups[1]	*20*	*22*	*21*	*17*	*20*	54,983

(1) Including White and Not Stated.

Household Composition: Census 1991

Source: CSO

Figures are a 10 per cent sample

Number of families in household and family type	All households	Tenure of households in permanent buildings: Owner occupied	Rented: From council or new town	Rented: Privately	With no car
Great Britain					
All households	2,144,128	513,821	453,053	148,875	709,536
Households with no family	634,444	189,351	175,891	81,448	393,647
One person	564,309	172,989	163,433	64,979	365,660
Two or more persons	70,135	16,362	12,458	16,469	27,987
Households with one family	1,489,817	320,551	272,204	66,762	311,333
Married couple family	1,184,737	283,752	169,241	39,574	188,937
With no children	520,806	203,743	78,541	21,521	114,507
With dependent child(ren)	480,192	30,334	64,013	14,266	52,623
With non-dependent child(ren) only	183,739	49,675	26,687	3,787	21,807
Cohabiting couple family	113,882	5,314	21,704	15,400	22,421
With no child(ren)	71,783	3,838	6,692	12,399	11,719
With dependent child(ren)	37,447	984	13,833	2,807	10,003
With non-dependent child(ren) only	4,652	492	1,179	194	699
Lone-parent family	191,198	31,485	81,259	11,788	99,975
With dependent child(ren)	112,246	7,081	56,068	8,272	68,866
With non-dependent child(ren) only	78,952	24,404	25,191	3,516	31,109
Household with two or more families	19,867	3,919	4,958	665	4,556
England and Wales					
All households	1,945,836	481,331	383,759	139,401	625,281
Households with no family	572,512	176,468	149,763	76,209	350,019
One person	508,343	161.279	139,259	60,834	325,350
Two or more persons	64,169	15,189	10,504	15,375	24,669
Households with one family	1,355,052	301,119	229,753	62,558	271,283
Married couple family	1,077,931	266,725	141,124	36,877	164,533
With no children	476,219	191,992	66,135	20,232	101,476
With dependent child(ren)	435,815	28,102	53,441	13,140	44,829
With non-dependent child(ren) only	165,897	46,631	21,548	3,505	18,228
Cohabiting couple family	106,365	5,074	19,230	14,673	19,945
With no child(ren)	67,238	3,663	5,762	11,825	10,410
With dependent child(ren)	34,803	935	12,433	2,662	8,924
With non-dependent child(ren) only	4,324	476	1,035	186	611
Lone-parent family	170,756	29,320	69,399	11,008	86,805
With at dependent child(ren)	100,420	6,595	48,397	7,726	60,106

(Continued)

Figures are a 10 per cent sample

Number of families in household and family type	All households	Tenure of households in permanent buildings: Owner occupied	Rented: From council or new town	Rented: Privately	With no car
England and Wales *(Continued)*					
With non-dependent child(ren) only	70,336	22,725	21,002	3,282	26,699
Households with two or more families	18,272	3,744	4,243	634	3,979
Scotland					
All households	198,292	32,490	68,626	9,474	84,255
Households with no family	101,932	12,003	27,128	5,230	43,620
One person	55,966	11,710	24,174	4,145	40,310
Two or more persons	5,066	1,173	1,954	1,094	3,318
Households with one family	134,706	19,432	42,451	4,204	40,060
Married couple family	100,806	17,027	28,117	2,697	24,404
With no children	44,687	11,751	12,406	1,289	13,031
With dependent child(ren)	44,377	2,232	10,572	1,126	7,794
With non-dependent child(ren) only	17,842	3,044	5,139	282	3,579
Cohabiting couple family	7,517	240	2,444	727	2,476
With no child(ren)	4,545	176	930	674	1,309
With dependent child(ren)	2,644	49	1,400	146	1,079
With non-dependent child(ren)	328	18	144	8	88
Lone-parent family	20,442	2,165	11,780	780	13,170
With dependent child(ren)	11,826	486	7,671	546	8,760
With non-dependent child(ren) only	8,016	1,679	4,189	234	4,410
Households with two or more families	1,696	175	717	31	577

Births

Annual averages or calendar years

Source: CSO

United Kingdom	Live births: Total	Male	Female	Sex ratio	Rates[1]: Crude birth rate[2]	General fertility rate[3]	TPFR[4]	Still-births	Still-birth rate
1900–02	1,095	558	537	1,037	28.6	115.1	–	–	–
1910–12	1,037	528	508	1,039	24.6	99.4	–	–	–
1920–22	1,018	522	496	1,052	23.1	93,0	–	–	–
1930–32	750	383	367	1,046	16.3	66.5	–	–	–
1940–42	723	372	351	1,062	15.0	–	1.89	26	–
1950–52	803	413	390	1,061	16.0	73.7	2.21	18	–
1960–62	946	487	459	1,063	17.9	90.3	2.80	18	–
1970–72	880	453	427	1,064	15.8	82.5	2.36	12	13
1980–82	735	377	358	1,053	13.0	62.5	1.83	5	7
1978	687	353	334	1,059	12.2	60.8	1.76	6	8
1979	735	378	356	1,061	13.1	64.1	1.86	6	8
1980	754	386	368	1,050	13.4	64.9	1.89	6	7
1981	731	375	356	1,053	13.0	62.1	1.81	5	7
1982	719	369	350	1,054	12.8	60.6	1.78	5	6
1983	721	371	351	1,058	12.8	60.2	1.77	4	6
1984	730	373	356	1,049	12.9	60.3	1.77	4	6
1985	751	385	366	1,053	13.3	61.4	1.80	4	6
1986	755	387	368	1,053	13.3	61.1	1.78	4	5
1987	776	398	378	1,053	13.6	62.3	1.82	4	5
1988	788	403	384	1,049	13.8	63.2	1.84	4	5
1989	777	398	379	1,051	13.6	62.4	1.81	4	5
1990	799	409	390	1,049	13.9	64.2	1.84	4	5
1991	793	406	386	1,052	13.8	63.8	1.82	4	5

(1) Rates are based on a new series of population estimates which use a new definition and population base taking into account the 1981 Census results. (2) Rate per 1,000 population. (3) Rate per 1,000 women aged 15–44. (4) Total period fertility rate is the average number of children which would be born per woman if women experienced the age-specific fertility rates of the period in question throughout their child-bearing life span. UK figures for years 1970–72 and earlier are estimates.

Birth Occurrence Inside and Outside Marriage

Source: CSO

Thousands

Year	Inside marriage: All ages	Under 20	20–24	25–29	Over 30	Mean age (years)	Outside marriage: All ages	Under 20	20–24	25–29	Over 30	Mean age (years)
United Kingdom												
1961	890	55	273	280	282	27.7	54	13	17	10	13	25.5
1971	828	70	301	271	185	26.4	74	24	25	13	12	23.8
1981	640	36	193	231	180	27.3	91	30	33	16	13	23.4
1985	609	24	169	233	183	27.7	142	42	54	27	19	23.6
1986	597	21	159	231	185	27.9	158	45	60	31	22	23.7
1987	598	18	153	235	192	28.1	178	48	68	37	26	23.9
1988	590	16	144	235	195	28.2	198	51	76	42	29	24.1
1989	571	14	130	229	198	28.4	207	49	79	46	32	24.3
1990	576	13	121	223	209	28.6	223	51	83	53	37	24.5
1991	556	10	109	224	213	28.9	236	50	87	58	41	24.8
Great Britain												
1961	859	53	264	270	272	27.7	53	13	17	10	13	25.5
1971	797	68	293	261	176	26.4	73	24	25	13	12	23.8
1981	614	34	186	223	171	27.2	89	29	32	16	13	23.3
1985	584	23	162	224	175	27.7	139	41	52	27	19	22.7
1986	572	20	153	222	177	27.9	155	44	59	30	22	22.9

(Continued)

Thousands

Year	Inside marriage: All ages	Under 20	20–24	25–29	Over 30	Mean age (years)	Outside marriage: All ages	Under 20	20–24	25–29	Over 30	Mean age (years)
Great Britain *(Continued)*												
1987	574	17	147	227	184	28.0	174	46	66	36	25	23.4
1988	566	16	138	226	186	28.2	194	49	74	42	29	23.6
1989	549	13	125	220	190	28.4	202	48	77	45	32	24.2
1990	554	12	116	225	201	28.6	218	49	81	52	36	24.6
1991	535	10	105	216	205	28.9	231	48	85	57	41	24.8

Marital Condition: Census Figures

Source: CSO

Thousands

	United Kingdom: Males 1971	Males 1981[1]	Males 1991	Females 1971	Females 1981[1]	Females 1991	England and Wales: Males 1971	Males 1981[1]	Males 1991	Females 1971	Females 1981[1]	Females 1991
All ages:												
Single	12,014	11,860	12,306	11,055	10,585	11,047	10,399	10,363	10,827	9,513	9,199	9,677
Married	13,976	13,563	13,071	14,050	13,630	13,209	12,433	12,042	11,585	12,488	12,093	11,691
Widowed	762	749	818	3,139	3,182	3,306	666	657	720	2,773	2,808	2,918
Divorced	200	606	1,149	318	863	1,560	185	563	1,051	293	797	1,421
Age groups												
0–14: Single	6,873	5,861	5,510	6,515	5,564	5,248	5,942	5,111	4,828	5,633	4,852	4,599
15–19: Single	1,921	2,328	1,861	1,713	2,152	1,763	1,661	2,031	1,628	1,477	1,878	1,542
Married	40	26	9	159	101	29	35	22	8	140	88	21
Widowed	–	–	–	–	–	1	–	–	–	–	–	1
Divorced	–	–	1	–	1	1	–	–	–	–	1	1
20–24: Single	1,350	1,536	1,844	848	1,080	1,613	1,186	1,350	1,629	737	945	1,425
Married	779	517	238	1,244	896	493	687	443	205	1,107	782	431
Widowed	–	1	–	2	2	2	–	1	–	2	2	2
Divorced	3	12	11	10	34	32	3	11	49	9	31	29
25–34: Single	703	973	1,748	374	534	1,246	617	866	1,567	320	471	1,111
Married	2,727	2,802	2,286	2,940	3,113	2,751	2,414	2,469	1,998	2,597	2,753	2,408
Widowed	4	5	4	14	15	14	3	4	5	12	13	12
Divorced	41	154	210	67	230	337	38	143	190	61	212	304
35–44: Single	363	346	753	247	195	326	315	304	485	206	167	286
Married	2,828	2,806	3,001	2,868	2,836	3,109	2,502	2,487	2,651	2,525	2,505	2,749
Widowed	15	13	15	57	48	48	13	11	13	48	41	41
Divorced	51	169	352	72	230	468	47	157	322	66	212	425
45–54: Single	325	288	289	298	200	170	278	251	253	248	167	145
Married	2,913	2,617	2,647	2,885	2,577	2,616	2,593	2,319	2,348	2,565	2,276	2,312
Widowed	53	44	38	218	176	135	46	38	32	187	149	118
Divorced	30	134	290	75	164	351	46	124	265	69	151	321
55–59: Single	140	148	118	177	127	82	118	128	102	148	105	69
Married	1,397	1,326	1,180	1,290	1,259	1,115	1,248	1,184	1,045	1,151	1,124	983
Widowed	56	53	40	246	214	156	48	46	34	213	186	134
Divorced	21	50	102	33	65	117	20	47	94	30	60	107
60–64: Single	125	115	121	207	125	99	105	98	105	173	104	82
Married	1,268	1,120	1,122	1,095	1,018	1,027	1,135	1,003	998	982	911	912
Widowed	87	72	72	380	316	284	75	62	62	330	274	245
Divorced	16	35	76	27	51	92	15	33	70	25	47	84
65–74: Single	158	183	178	392	305	213	130	154	152	328	254	176
Married	1,550	1,732	1,751	1,242	1,403	1,477	1,391	1,558	1,572	1,122	1,266	1,329
Widowed	253	252	255	1,075	1,062	993	220	220	223	948	934	871
Divorced	15	41	82	27	67	114	14	38	76	26	62	105
75 and over: Single	58	82	93	285	304	288	47	69	78	243	257	243
Married	474	616	837	326	426	591	428	558	760	298	389	540
Widowed	294	310	394	1,148	1,348	1,671	259	276	352	1,034	1,208	1,496
Divorced	3	10	25	7	22	49	2	9	24	6	20	46

(1) 1981 data cover the "resident" population and are not strictly comparable with earlier data. The 1991 figures include the population resident in absent households not included in 1981. The 1971 data covers the enumerated population.

Marriages

United Kingdom

Source: CSO

Thousands and percentages

	1971	1976	1981	1986	1988	1989	1990
Marriage (thousands)							
First marriage for both partners	369	282	263	254	253	252	241
First marriage for one partner only							
Bachelor/divorced woman	21	30	32	34	34	35	34
Bachelor/widow	4	4	3	2	2	2	2
Spinster/divorced man	24	32	36	38	39	38	37
Spinster/widower	5	4	3	2	2	2	2
Second (or subsequent) marriage for both partners							
Both divorced	17	34	44	48	50	50	47
Both widowed	10	10	7	6	5	5	5
Divorced man/widow	4	5	5	4	4	4	4
Divorced woman/widower	5	5	5	5	5	5	4
Total marriages	459	406	398	394	394	392	375
Remarriages[1] as a percentage of all marriages	*20*	*31*	*34*	*35*	*36*	*36*	*36*
Remarriages[1] of the divorced as a percentage of all marriages	*15*	*26*	*31*	*33*	*33*	*34*	*34*

(1) Remarriage for one or both partners.

Marriage and Divorce: EC Comparison, 1981 and 1990

Source: CSO

Rates

	Marriages per 1,000 eligible population		Divorces per 1,000 existing marriages	
	1981	1990	1981	1990
United Kingdom[1]	7.1	6.8	11.9	12.6
Belgium	6.5	6.5	6.1	8.7
Denmark	5.0	6.1	12.1	12.8
France[2]	5.8	5.1	6.8	8.4
Germany (Fed. Rep.)	5.8	6.6	7.2	8.1
Greece	7.3	5.8	2.5	–
Irish Republic	6.0	5.0	0.0	0.0
Italy	5.6	5.4	0.9	2.9
Luxembourg[2]	5.5	6.1	5.9	10.0
Netherlands	6.0	6.4	8.3	8.1
Portugal	7.7	7.3	2.8	–
Spain	5.4	5.5	1.1	–

(1) 1990 column for marriages contains 1989 data and divorce column contains 1987 data. (2) 1990 column for divorces contains 1989 data.

Divorce: by Duration of Marriage

Great Britain

Source: CSO

Percentages and thousands

	Year of divorce			
	1961	1971	1981	1990
Duration of marriage *(percentages)*				
0–2 years	1.2	1.2	1.5	9.5
3–4 years	10.1	12.2	19.0	13.7
5–9 years	30.6	30.5	29.1	27.5
10–14 years	22.9	19.4	19.6	17.9
15–19 years	13.9	12.6	12.8	12.9
20–24 years	21.2	9.5	8.6	9.3
25–29 years		5.8	4.9	4.9
30 years and over		8.9	4.5	4.1
All durations (=100%) (thousands)	27.0	79.2	155.6	165.7

Divorce: by Sex and Age

England and Wales

Source: CSO

Rates[1]

	1961	1971	1981	1990
Males				
Aged 16 and over	2.1	5.9	11.9	12.2
16–24	1.4	5.0	17.7	21.6
25–29	3.9	12.5	27.6	29.0
30–34	4.1	11.8	22.8	25.1
35–44	3.1	7.9	17.0	17.9
45 and over	1.1	3.1	4.8	5.0
Females				
Aged 16 and over	2.1	5.9	11.9	12.1
16–24	2.4	7.5	22.3	23.4
25–29	4.5	13.0	26.7	27.3
30–34	3.8	10.5	20.2	22.7
35–44	2.7	6.7	14.9	15.6
45 and over	0.9	2.8	3.9	3.9

(1) Per 1,000 married population.

Deaths

United Kingdom: annual averages or calendar years

Source: CSO

Number

	All ages[1]	Under 1 year	1–4	5–9	10–14	15–19	20–24	25–34	35–44	45–54	55–64	65–74	75–84	85 and over
Males														
1900–02	340,664	87,242	37,834	8,429	4,696	7,047	8,766	19,154	24,739	30,488	37,610	39,765	28,320	6,563
1910–12	303,703	63,885	29,452	7,091	4,095	5,873	6,817	16,141	21,813	28,981	37,721	45,140	29,140	7,283
1920–22	284,876	48,044	19,008	6,052	3,953	5,906	6,572	13,663	19,702	29,256	40,583	49,398	34,937	7,801
1930–32	284,249	28,840	11,276	4,580	2,890	5,076	6,495	12,327	16,326	29,376	47,989	63,804	45,247	10,022
1940–42	314,643	24,624	6,949	3,400	2,474	4,653	4,246	11,506	17,296	30,082	57,076	79,652	59,733	12,900
1950–52	307,312	14,105	2,585	1,317	919	1,498	2,289	5,862	11,074	27,637	53,691	86,435	79,768	20,131
1960–62	318,850	12,234	1,733	971	871	1,718	1,857	3,842	8,753	26,422	63,009	87,542	83,291	26,605
1970–72	335,166	9,158	1,485	1,019	802	1,778	2,104	3,590	7,733	24,608	64,898	105,058	82,905	30,027
1980–82[2]	330,495	4,829	774	527	652	1,999	1,943	3,736	6,568	19,728	54,159	105,155	98,488	31,936
1969	337,800	9,894	1,713	998	800	1,808	1,999	3,595	8,116	25,167	68,265	104,219	82,325	28,901
1970	334,355	9,713	1,556	978	773	1,752	2,131	3,585	7,836	24,399	66,657	103,589	81,996	29,390
1971	328,537	9,366	1,439	1,055	834	1,802	2,091	3,524	7,735	24,242	63,657	102,139	81,183	29,470
1972	342,605	8,393	1,460	1,024	801	1,779	2,092	3,661	7,629	25,184	64,379	109,448	85,535	31,220
1973	338,788	7,783	1,438	978	790	1,819	2,213	3,953	7,530	25,434	61,970	108,871	85,172	30,837
1974	337,263	7,180	1,307	858	775	1,895	1,968	3,820	7,448	25,864	59,703	110,718	84,491	31,236
1975	335,006	6,392	1,139	829	842	1,871	2,018	3,845	7,006	24,630	58,581	110,126	86,653	31,074
1976	341,910	5,706	1,036	798	769	1,978	1,994	3,867	6,976	23,663	59,703	112,234	90,710	32,476
1977	329,924	5,350	918	744	702	1.892	1,947	3,864	6,752	22,787	57,214	108,677	88,569	30,508
1978	336,395	5,220	866	726	729	2,067	2,055	3,944	6,912	22,439	57,381	110,384	92,574	31,098
1979	339,568	5,447	748	708	707	2,042	1,969	4,012	6,868	21,828	56,944	110,172	96,026	32,097
1980	332,370	5,174	792	609	659	2,022	1,940	3,786	6,698	20,577	55,176	107,089	96,301	31,547
1981	329,145	4,759	771	517	666	2,008	1,919	3,761	6,544	19,740	53,770	104,950	97,881	31,859
1982	329,971	4,555	760	456	632	1,966	1,971	3,661	6,462	18,867	53,531	103,426	101,281	32,403
1983	328,824	4,230	695	469	609	1,834	1,899	3,601	6,537	18,238	54,493	100,469	103,038	32,712
1984	321,095	3,995	725	423	580	1,708	1,999	3,595	6,425	17,647	53,715	95,420	102,513	32,350
1985	331,562	4,003	728	393	583	1,612	2,031	3,452	6,728	17,316	52,502	97,458	109,241	35,515
1986	327,160	4,219	653	384	444	1,676	2,067	3,668	6,712	16,814	50,352	95,987	108,123	36,061
1987	318,282	4,105	657	377	470	1,612	2,125	3,776	6,793	15,950	47,675	93,348	105,773	35,621
1988	319,119	4,110	680	433	460	1,525	2,160	3,983	6,860	16,016	46,001	91,893	107,082	37,916
1989	320,193	3,799	699	414	398	1,537	2,118	3,968	6,832	15,560	43,693	90,304	109,450	41,421
1990	314,601	3,614	674	376	406	1,487	2,197	4,354	6,991	15,507	41,983	88,458	107,451	41.103
1991[2]	314,427	3,377	636	395	404	1,417	2,049	4,270	7,102	15,493	40,256	88,014	107,416	43,598
Females														
1900–02	322,058	68,770	36,164	8,757	5,034	6,818	8,264	18,702	21,887	25,679	34,521	42,456	34,907	10,099
1910–12	289,608	49,865	27,817	7,113	4,355	5,683	6,531	15,676	19,647	24,481	32,813	46,453	37,353	11,828
1920–22	274,772	35,356	17,323	5,808	4,133	5,729	6,753	14,878	18,121	24,347	34,026	48,573	45,521	14,203

(Continued)

Number

Females	All ages[1]	Under 1 year	1–4	5–9	10–14	15–19	20–24	25–34	35–44	45–54	55–64	65–74	75–84	85 and over
1930–32	275,336	21,072	9,995	3,990	2,734	4,721	5,931	12,699	15,373	24,695	39,471	59,520	56,250	18,886
1940–42	296,646	17,936	5,952	2,743	2,068	4,180	5,028	11,261	14,255	23,629	42,651	70,907	71,377	24,658
1950–52	291,597	10,293	2,098	880	625	1,115	1,717	5,018	8,989	18,875	37,075	75,220	92,848	36,844
1960–62	304,871	8,887	1,334	627	522	684	811	2,504	6,513	16,720	36,078	73,118	105,956	51,117
1970–72	322,968	6,666	1,183	654	459	718	900	2,110	5,345	15,594	36,177	75,599	109,539	68,024
1980–82	330,269	3,561	585	355	425	733	772	2,099	4,360	12,206	32,052	72,618	117,760	82,743
1969	321,737	7,189	1,280	579	423	714	918	2,125	5,874	15,824	37,725	77,206	108,385	63,495
1970	321,030	7,002	1,181	648	467	662	957	2,118	5,501	15,527	36,652	76,033	108,485	65,798
1971	316,541	6,798	1,129	649	493	721	866	2,105	5,267	15,358	35,621	73,502	107,056	66,976
1972	331,333	6,198	1,238	665	416	770	878	2,107	5,267	15,897	36,260	77,261	113,076	71,300
1973	330,904	5,646	1,060	610	455	803	847	1,166	5,145	15,822	34,733	77,067	113,393	73,157
1974	330,096	5,172	981	581	503	736	805	2,070	5,038	15,972	34,342	76,929	112,492	74,475
1975	327,471	4,798	860	540	405	751	813	2,211	4,897	15,054	33,904	75,459	112,838	74,941
1976	338,889	4,070	735	516	484	724	786	2,264	4,737	14,912	34,468	76,950	118,246	79,997
1977	325,219	3,933	720	431	450	750	839	2,148	4,583	13,905	33,395	74,573	113,872	75,620
1978	330,782	3,908	715	480	497	818	823	2,343	4,719	13,914	33,353	75,433	115,730	78,049
1979	336,009	4,026	617	428	462	701	738	2,244	4,544	13,667	33,274	75,610	118,859	80,839
1980	329,149	3,938	596	409	442	771	811	2,157	4,460	12,583	32,349	73,672	116,461	80,500
1981	328,829	3,402	599	352	424	738	737	2,083	4,309	12,275	31,625	72,476	117,458	82,351
1982	332,830	3,342	561	304	410	689	767	2,057	4,312	11,759	32,183	71,705	119,362	85,379
1983	330,277	3,126	568	318	374	719	698	1,914	4,318	11,384	32,197	69,266	118,940	86,455
1984	323,823	3,005	537	304	344	665	722	1,932	4,269	10,947	32,262	66,432	116,649	85,756
1985	339,094	3,027	574	314	355	626	729	1,852	4,397	10,581	32,010	68,505	122,445	93,679
1986	333,575	2,961	561	275	307	635	769	1,882	4,387	10,211	29,954	67,313	120,663	93,657
1987	326,060	2,972	550	265	288	614	733	1,974	4,454	10,177	29,037	65,570	117,266	92,160
1988	330,059	2,951	552	264	251	612	745	1,915	4,615	9,887	28,154	65,020	117,731	97,362
1989	337,540	2,743	551	271	268	598	773	1,955	4,506	9,834	27,324	64,575	120,975	103,167
1990	327,198	2,658	489	249	273	534	700	1,967	4,463	9,718	26,350	62,019	116,357	101,421
1991[2]	314,427	3,377	636	395	404	1,417	2,049	4,270	7,102	15,493	40,256	88,014	107,416	43,598

(1) In some years the totals include a small number of persons whose age was not stated. (2) Provisional.

Migration Into and Out of the United Kingdom

Source: CSO

A migrant into the United Kingdom is defined as a person who has resided abroad for a year or more and on entering has declared the intention to reside here for a year or more; and *vice versa* for a migrant from the United Kingdom. Estimates are derived from the International Passenger Survey (IPS), a sample survey covering the principal air and sea routes between the United Kingdom and overseas but excluding routes to and from the Irish Republic. Migration between the Channel Islands and the Isle of Man and the rest of the world has been excluded from these tables. The figures include British citizens as well as people subject to immigration control.

Thousands

	Total			Professional and managerial			Manual and clerical			Not gainfully employed[1]		
	Persons	Males	Females	Persons	Males	Females	Persons	Males	Females	Persons	Males	Females
Inflow												
1981	153	82	70	45	32	13	23	14	9	84	37	48
1982	201	100	101	43	34	9	38	18	20	120	48	72
1983	202	107	95	55	40	15	36	21	15	110	46	64
1984	201	102	99	59	41	18	32	15	17	110	46	64
1985	232	99	133	65	38	26	32	16	16	134	44	90
1986	250	120	130	76	52	24	46	21	25	128	47	81
1987	211	104	107	62	43	18	48	21	27	101	39	62
1988	216	109	107	67	44	23	44	26	18	105	40	66
1989	250	110	140	75	47	28	49	22	26	126	40	86
1990	267	135	132	93	61	32	53	26	27	121	48	72
1991	267	122	144	80	51	29	56	23	33	131	48	83
Outflow												
1981	232	133	100	67	50	17	60	38	22	105	44	60
1982	257	133	124	66	47	19	65	36	29	126	50	76
1983	184	90	94	51	32	18	35	19	16	98	38	60
1984	164	80	83	51	32	19	34	16	19	78	32	46
1985	174	91	83	51	36	15	36	18	17	87	36	50
1986	213	107	106	77	55	21	38	17	22	98	35	63
1987	209	107	102	63	38	26	56	28	28	90	41	48
1988	237	125	113	68	44	23	52	25	27	118	55	63
1989	205	108	97	70	44	27	49	23	26	86	41	45
1990	231	113	118	75	47	27	56	25	31	100	41	59
1991	239	120	119	82	48	34	50	28	21	108	44	63
Balance												
1981	−79	−50	−29	−22	−19	−4	−37	−24	−13	−20	−8	−13
1982	−56	−33	−23	−23	−13	−10	−27	−18	−9	−6	−2	−4
1983	+17	+17	–	+5	+8	−3	+1	+1	−1	+12	+8	+4
1984	+37	+22	+16	+8	+8	–	−3	−1	−2	+32	+14	+18
1985	+58	+8	+51	+13	+2	+11	−3	−2	−1	+48	+8	+40
1986	+37	+13	+24	−1	−4	+3	+8	+5	+3	+30	+12	+18
1987	+2	−3	+5	−1	+6	−7	−8	−7	−1	+12	−2	+13
1988	−21	−15	−6	−1	−1	–	−8	+1	−9	−13	−16	+3
1989	+44	+1	+43	+5	+4	+1	−1	−1	+1	+40	−1	+41
1990	+36	+22	+14	+19	+14	+5	−3	+1	−4	+21	+7	+13
1991	28	2	26	−2	3	−5	6	−5	11	24	4	19

(1) Includes housewives, students, children and retired persons.

ECONOMICS

Compiled by Debra Johnson, lecturer in economics, University of Humberside

Recent Economic Performance

Despite numerous sightings of the "green shoots" of recovery over the previous eighteen months, it was only in the first quarter of 1993 that Gross Domestic Product (GDP) growth was above (1.1%) its level of a year earlier – the first time there has been year-on-year growth since the third quarter of 1990. In the summer of 1993 it is still too early to talk about a sustained and strong recovery: while the steep falls in economic activity are undoubtedly over, the signals from a whole range of economic indicators remain mixed, and the worsening economic situation in Europe does not bode well for the UK's main export markets.

The Household Sector

After the consumer boom and the accompanying increase in personal indebtedness of the late 1980s, consumer spending, which accounts for about two-thirds of GDP, was severely depressed during the recent recession: in 1992 consumers' expenditure was more than 2% below 1990 levels in real terms. Spending in most sectors has been stagnant, but it has plummeted in some: spending on furniture and related durable goods fell 10% in real terms between 1989 and 1992 as a result of the collapse in the housing sector, and spending on cars and other vehicles fell a massive 27% in the same period, as individuals, beset by concerns over job security and debt, extended the period between the purchase of new vehicles.

Some life has returned to consumer spending in 1993. Monthly retail sales figures are volatile but, on balance, they point to increased activity. After two to three desperate years, 1993 has been much better for the motor industry with new car registrations on an upward trend and rising by 11% in May. Building societies and estate agents, anxious to restore confidence to a badly battered housing market, have reported increased numbers of enquiries, sales and even prices. However, the evidence of a sustained housing market recovery is, as yet, far from conclusive. Although the housing market clearly benefits from the lower level of interest rates which have emerged since the UK's departure from the ERM and from the higher stamp duty threshold announced in the March 1993 budget, recovery will remain halting while unemployment remains high and hundreds of thousands of house-owners, who bought their property at the height of the late 1980s property boom, are trapped in their homes by the 1990s' phenomenon of negative equity.

The evidence of recovery in the consumer sector suggests not so much a sustained recovery as yet but rather that the economy is turning the corner. Economists have been taken by surprise, however, by the reported falls in unemployment which have taken place during the first half of 1993. Employment usually does not expand until recovery is well underway. If this trend continues, recovery in consumer spending could accelerate as the fear of unemployment, which has reined back spending, recedes.

Manufacturing and Investment

After a year of stagnant manufacturing output in 1992, 1993 manufacturing growth appears to be consistently positive with figures for the early part of the year suggesting increased output in the 2–3% range over the same period of 1992. Apart from food, drink and tobacco, manufacturing output growth has been spread relatively evenly across sectors. Confederation of British Industry (CBI) surveys point to a continuation of this trend in the coming months.

British manufacturing received a competitive filip from the devaluation of sterling, which took place after the pound's departure from the Exchange Rate Mechanism in September 1992, particularly as the expected inflationary boost from increased import prices has not materialized: companies have, so far, absorbed the increased input prices in their margins. Some strengthening of the pound against European currencies is underway in mid-summer. Competitiveness has also been reinforced by wage settlements, which are at their lowest level for some decades.

Two factors may intervene to limit any surges in UK manufacturing growth. First, destocking may not yet have run its full course. Consequently, any further increase in demand could be partially met by further stock rundowns. Secondly, Western European economies, which currently account for about two-thirds of UK exports, have embarked upon potentially severe recessions.

The External Sector

Deterioration in the current account usually marks recovery from recession as industry starts to rebuild its stocks of imported raw materials and capital equipment. However, the UK's current account, following its recession-induced improvement in 1991, deteriorated markedly in 1992 (to a deficit of £12 billion) and there are concerns that balance of payments constraints may inhibit the economy as it moves out of recession. Early estimates for 1993 indicate that the situation continues to worsen.

UK exports of goods and services continued to perform well relative to the rest of the economy in 1992, but imports accelerated at an even faster rate, and the visible trade balance continues to deteriorate. Invisible transactions are more erratic, but there are some encouraging signs of improvements in the performance of financial and other services.

Government Policy

The context of government economic decision-making has changed drastically since September 1992 when sterling abandoned the Exchange Rate Mechanism. The currency has been left to find its own level and the government has greater scope to run a more relaxed monetary policy, especially in relation to interest rates. Subsequent statements by senior ministers indicate that an early return to the ERM is not on the cards.

Current government preoccupations are focused on the need to restore order to public finances, which ran out of control during the recession, to foster recovery and to carry through the privatization of British Rail. The mastery of inflation has been the main economic policy objective since 1979. Inflation is currently at its lowest level for many years. Although more in the background than hitherto, the retail price index remains a key indicator for the government.

The 1993 Budget

The March 1993 Budget was the last spring budget. Henceforth, government expenditure and revenue plans will be announced together towards the end of the year rather than expenditure in the autumn and revenue in the spring. The first combined Budget is scheduled for the end of 1993 and will be presented by the new Chancellor, Kenneth Clarke.

The prime aim of the latest budget was to repair the damage done to public finances by the recession, which has simultaneously reduced government revenue and, given rising unemployment, increased demands on the public purse. Consequently, the Public Sector Borrowing Requirement (PSBR) is forecast to reach £50 billion (equivalent to 8% of GDP) during the 1993–94 financial year. This contrasts sharply with the late 1980s when the government managed to repay some of the national debt.

Correction of the deficit requires tax increases, public spending cuts or both – unpalatable options for politicians. Rather than increase taxes in the current tax year, which could choke off the nascent recovery, the Chancellor chose to defer his revenue-raising measures (namely the restriction of tax reliefs, the introduction of VAT on domestic fuel and power, and the 1% increase on employees' national insurance contributions) until 1994 and beyond.

VAT on domestic fuel, in particular, has given rise to serious dissension among government backbenchers and the Opposition in view of the disproportionate impact of this tax on less well-off groups. Further controversy is expected when the government finishes its review of long-term spending plans. This review has given rise to speculation that long-established spending commitments on social security and state pensions are under threat.

Despite the spending review, the medium-term outlook for public expenditure depends most on general economic performance. If recovery strengthens, public sector finances could be quickly transformed and the PSBR could be within the Maastricht criteria of no more than 3% of GDP within 3–4 years. However, an unsustained or weak recovery will require much stronger action than the additional £6.7 billion in revenue which the March 1993 budget measures will yield in 1994–95 (£10.3 billion in 1995–96).

Summary of the 1993 Budget

Economic Forecast
- Growth of 1.25% in 1993 with recovery gathering pace in the second half of the year and reaching 3% in the first half of 1994.
- Current account deficit of £17.5 billion for 1993.
- Underlying inflation of 3.75% by the end of 1993.

Monetary Policy
- Money supply (M0 — cash in circulation) target of 0–4% and 3–9% for M4.

Public Sector Finances
- Public sector borrowing requirement of £50 billion in 1993–94 – equivalent to 8% of GDP.

Income Tax
- No change in basic and top rate tax.
- 20% band widened by £500 to first £2,500 of taxable income from 1/4/93 and to first £3,000 in 1994.
- Personal allowances, married couples' allowance and inheritance tax threshold of £150,000 frozen.
- Self-assessment for income tax to be introduced in 1996–97.

National Insurance
- No change in employer's contributions, but main rate for employees and self-employed to increase by 1% in 1994.

Housing
- Stamp duty threshold doubled to £60,000.
- Tax relief on mortgage interest limited to 20% from April 1994.

Motoring
- 2.7p on a litre of unleaded petrol and 3.3p on leaded petrol to pay for the abolition of car tax in autumn 1992.
- Vehicle excise duty on cars, taxis and vans to rise by £15 to £125.
- Scale charges on company cars to rise 8% and car fuel scale charges by 20%.
- Discount on high business mileage abolished from 1994.
- Company cars to be taxed according to list price rather than engine size.

Business Taxation
- Advance corporation tax rate reduced to 22.5% for 1993–94 financial year and to 20% from April 1994.

Small Businesses
- Business rates constant in real terms.
- Reduced penalties on late VAT returns and misdeclarations.
- Capital gains tax relief when entrepreneurs reinvest proceeds from the sale of shares in their own businesses in new unquoted trading companies.
- Traders able to claim VAT relief on bad debts after 6 months.

Unemployment
- Vocational education programme to finance 30,000 unemployed to take full-time courses.
- 10,000 additional places on business start-up schemes for those wishing to start their own businesses.

Excise
- Duties on spirits unchanged; 5% increase in wine and beer duties.
- Duty on tobacco products increased by 6.5%.

Value Added Tax (VAT)
- Extension of VAT to domestic fuel and power at a rate of 8% from April 1994 and 17.5% from 1995.
- Small business threshold raised to £37,600.

Consumers' Expenditure at Current Market Prices: Classified by Commodity

Source: CSO

£ million

	1982	1983	1984	1985	1986	1987	1988	1989	1990	1991	1992
Durable goods:											
Cars, motorcycles and other vehicles	7,407	9,112	8,978	9,853	11,485	13,429	17,384	19,926	18,877	16,426	15,935

(Continued)

£ million

	1982	1983	1984	1985	1986	1987	1988	1989	1990	1991	1992
Durable goods *(Continued)*											
Furniture and floor coverings	3,615	3,883	3,971	4,193	4,514	5,059	6,180	6,434	6,205	6,360	6,695
Other durable goods	4,417	5,255	5,689	6,120	6,837	7,750	8,612	8,983	9,164	9,482	9,504
Total	**15,439**	**18,250**	**18,638**	**20,166**	**22,836**	**26,238**	**32,176**	**35,343**	**34,246**	**32,268**	**32,134**
Other goods:											
Food (household expenditure)	26,490	28,061	29,274	30,657	32,561	34,429	36,587	39,264	41,869	44,053	45,402
Beer	6,450	7,138	7,734	8,416	8,902	9,398	10,039	10,677	11,745	12,775	13,539
Other alcoholic drink	5,553	6,132	6,582	7,235	7,502	8,053	8,715	9,132	9,993	10,780	11,621
Tobacco	5,881	6,209	6,622	7,006	7,471	7,653	7,945	8,175	8,683	9,746	10,247
Clothing other than footwear	8,857	9,824	10,656	12,132	13,663	14,599	15,824	16,543	17,196	17,309	17,140
Footwear	2,068	2,296	2,512	2,780	2,998	3,085	3,210	3,400	3,679	3,725	3,815
Energy products	15,027	16,220	16,973	18,578	18,243	18,678	19,343	20,518	22,493	25,065	25,603
Other goods	17,212	18,764	20,637	23,054	26,110	28,893	32,718	36,388	38,641	40,339	42,314
Services:											
Rents, rates and water charges[1]	22,558	24,057	25,214	27,382	29,987	32,747	36,422	40,239	38,895	42,558	48,694
Other services[2]	45,115	50,077	55,419	61,541	72,757	83,750	99,078	110,853	122,971	129,235	136,097
Total consumers' expenditure	**170,650**	**187,028**	**200,261**	**218,947**	**243,030**	**267,523**	**302,057**	**330,532**	**350,411**	**367,853**	**386,606**

(1) Before providing for depreciation and stock appreciation. (2) Including the adjustments for international travel, etc. and final expenditure by private non-profit-making bodies serving persons.

Gross Domestic Fixed Capital Formation

Source: CSO

£ million

Analysis by sector and type of asset

	Private sector[1]	General government[1]	Public corporations[1]	Vehicles, ships and aircraft	Plant and machinery	Other new buildings and works[1]	Dwellings Private	Dwellings Public	Total
Revalued at 1985 prices									
1987	55,807	7,470	4,476	6,648	25,943	21,687	10,734	2,741	67,753
1988	66,361	6,649	4,385	7,113	29,855	24,879	12,999	2,549	77,395
1989	70,046	8,292	4,659	7,777	33,591	26,333	12,290	3,006	82,997
1990	66,647	9,834	3,983	7,022	32,739	27,109	10,506	3,088	80,464
1991	59,733	9,547	3,249	5,839	29,357	26,501	8,754	2,078	72,529
1992	58.076	10,376	3,611	5,452	29,955	26,037	8,586	2,033	72,063
Seasonally adjusted									
1989 Q1	17,732	1,784	1,054	1,821	8,364	6,440	3,334	611	20,570
Q2	17,362	1,928	1,217	1,913	8,722	6,386	2,762	724	20,507
Q3	16,914	2,172	1,194	2,000	8,248	6,551	2,715	766	20,280
Q4	17,124	2,400	1,154	1,966	8,177	6,623	3,024	888	20,678
1990 Q1	17,590	2,712	954	2,012	8,609	6,662	2,938	1,034	21,255
Q2	17,347	2,220	944	1,766	8,413	6,781	2,862	689	20,511
Q3	16,282	2,394	1,057	1,680	8,047	6,768	2,535	704	19,734
Q4	15,428	2,508	1,028	1,564	7,670	6,898	2,171	661	18,964
1991 Q1	15,620	2,140	918	1,484	7,542	6,825	2,298	529	18,678
Q2	14,788	2,327	835	1,524	7,337	6,500	2,059	530	17,950
Q3	14,653	2,563	763	1,233	7,300	6,750	2,190	506	17,979
Q4	14,672	2,517	733	1,598	7,178	6,426	2,207	513	17,922
1992 Q1	14,401	2,712	828	1,389	7,429	6,436	2,130	557	17,941
1990 Q2	14,576	2,495	816	1,354	7,369	6,645	2,053	466	17,887
Q3	14,714	2,495	984	1,346	7,543	6,564	2,236	504	18,193
Q4	14,385	2,674	983	1,363	7,614	6,392	2,167	506	18,042

(1) Including transfer costs of land and buildings.

£ million

Analysis by industry group

	Extraction of mineral oil and natural gas	All other energy and water supply	Manu-facturing	Distribution, hotels and catering repairs[1]	Transport and communi-cation[1,2]	Financial and business services etc[1]	Other industries and services[1,3]	Dwellings	Transfer cost of land and buildings	Total
Revalued at 1985 prices										
1987	1,928	3,975	10,048	6,995	6,281	10,819	9,879	13,475	3,287	67,753
1988	1,941	4,096	11,198	8,360	7,228	13,822	11,606	15,548	3,596	77,395
1989	2,165	4,348	12,395	7,812	8,128	17,275	12,990	15,296	2,588	82,997
1990	2,713	4,700	11,759	6,998	7,430	17,214	13,719	13,594	2,337	80,464
1991	4,027	5,211	10,655	6,938	7,321	12,260	13,057	10,832	2,246	72,529
1992	4,666	5,696	10,313	–	–	–	–	10,619	1,994	72,063
Seasonally adjusted										
1989 Q1	493	1,104	2,864	1,954	2,122	4,198	–	3,945	717	20,570
Q2	502	1,019	3,168	1,960	2,306	4,078	–	3,486	688	20,507
Q3	563	1,121	3,173	1,943	1,756	4,358	–	3,481	590	20,280
Q4	603	1,116	3,077	1,897	2,016	4,174	3,287	3,912	596	20,678

(Continued)

£ million

	Extraction of mineral oil and natural gas	All other energy and water supply	Manufacturing	Distribution, hotels and catering repairs[1]	Transport and communication[1,2]	Financial and business services etc[1]	Other industries and services[1,3]	Dwellings	Transfer cost of land and buildings	Total
	Analysis by industry group									
Revalued at 1985 prices										
1990 Q1	640	1,196	3,174	1,893	1,967	4,188	3,611	3,972	615	21,255
Q2	675	1,150	3,019	1,802	1,726	4,641	3,338	3,551	609	20,511
Q3	688	1,188	2,814	1,686	1,875	4,356	3,342	3,239	545	19,734
Q4	710	1,166	2,752	1,617	1,862	4,029	3,428	2,832	568	18,964
1991 Q1	889	1,174	2,710	1,755	2,006	3,497	3,046	2,827	585	18,678
Q2	936	1,357	2,661	1,676	1,882	3,247	3,283	2,589	564	17,950
Q3	1,096	1,293	2,612	1,729	1,685	2,825	3,502	2,696	572	17,979
Q4	1,106	1,387	2,672	1,778	1,748	2,691	3,226	2,720	525	17,922
1992 Q1	1,141	1,223	2,477	1,772	1,728	2,642	3,351	2,687	483	17,941
Q2	1,283	1,418	2,569	1,533	1,411	2,394	3,157	2,519	465	17,887
Q3	1,081	1,546	2,602	–	–	–	–	2,740	605	18,193
Q4	1,161	1,509	2,665	–	–	–	–	2,673	441	18,042

(1) No estimates of an acceptable quality for 1989 and 1990 are available. (2) In this series capital formation in imported ships is included at the time of delivery instead of when the expenditure takes place. (3) Covers agriculture, forestry and fishing construction and other service industries.

Summary of UK Government Income and Expenditure

Source: CSO

£ million

	1981	1982	1983	1984	1985	1986	1987	1988	1989	1990	1991
Current Receipts											
Taxes on income	36,134	40,282	43,344	46,655	51,643	52,239	55,702	61,852	70,275	77,262	75,105
Taxes on expenditure	42,465	46,467	49,500	52,675	56,592	62,947	69,074	76,511	80,925	79,067	83,023
Social security contributions	15,916	18,095	20,780	22,322	24,210	26,165	28,642	32,108	33,025	34,775	36,643
Community charge	–	–	–	–	–	–	–	–	619	8,811	8,162
Gross trading surplus[1]	236	216	50	−117	265	155	−75	−32	199	17	119
Rent, etc[2]	4,715	4,857	4,836	5,373	5,510	4,101	4,347	4,117	3,902	4,202	4,302
Interest and dividends, etc	4,456	5,292	5,097	5,129	6,242	5,890	6,020	6,243	7,073	6,489	5,975
Miscellaneous current transfers	177	187	222	217	229	266	363	394	431	504	370
Computed charge for consumption of non-trading capital	1,948	2,017	2,081	2,187	2,372	2,583	2,804	3,110	3,448	3,693	3,890
Total	**106,047**	**117,413**	**125,910**	**134,342**	**147,063**	**154,346**	**166,877**	**184,303**	**199,897**	**214,820**	**217,589**
Current Expenditure											
Current expenditure on goods and services	53,426	58,346	63,706	67,573	71,433	76,798	82,545	88,619	95,581	105,802	118,009
Non-trading capital consumption	1,948	2,017	2,081	2,187	2,372	2,583	2,804	3,110	3,448	3,693	3,890
Subsidies	6,369	5,811	6,269	7,537	7,225	6,187	6,173	5,940	5,692	6,217	5,878
Current grants to personal sector	31,242	36,584	39,856	43,020	46,813	50,984	52,494	54,087	56,793	61,983	71,767
Current grants paid abroad (net)	1,607	1,789	1,930	2,099	3,427	2,233	3,277	3,248	4,278	4,635	1,049
Debt interest	12,719	13,952	14,208	15,777	17,483	17,164	17,999	18,169	18,706	18,544	17,097
Total current expenditure	**107,311**	**118,499**	**128,050**	**138,193**	**148,753**	**155,949**	**165,292**	**173,173**	**184,498**	**200,874**	**217,690**
Balance current surplus[1]	−1,264	−1,086	−2,140	−3,851	−1,690	−1,603	1,585	11,130	15,399	13,946	−101
Total	**106,047**	**117,413**	**125,910**	**134,342**	**147,063**	**154,346**	**166,877**	**184,303**	**199,897**	**214,826**	**217,589**

(1) Before providing for depreciation. (2) Includes royalties and licence fees on oil and gas production.

General UK Government Expenditure

Source: CSO

£ billion

Function	1981	1986	1990	1991
Defence	12.6	19.1	22.9	27.3
Public order and safety	4.3	6.8	10.9	12.8
Education	14.3	19.3	26.7	29.5
Health	13.4	19.2	27.7	30.9
Social security	31.1	49.9	62.9	73.9
Housing and community amenities	7.1	8.1	7.8	9.1
Recreational and cultural affairs	1.6	2.4	3.7	3.9
Fuel and energy	0.3	−1.2	−3.9	−5.0
Agriculture, forestry and fishing	1.7	2.1	2.6	2.4
Mining, mineral resources, manufacturing and construction	3.6	1.9	1.2	1.7
Transport and communication	4.2	3.7	9.5	6.7
General public services	4.6	6.3	10.7	9.2
Other economic affairs and services	2.9	4.1	6.9	5.5
Other expenditure	15.4	20.5	25.2	19.7
Total expenditure	**117.1**	**162.2**	**214.8**	**227.5**

(1) Includes privatization proceeds.

Gross Domestic Product: by Category of Expenditure[1]

Source: CSO

£ million, 1985 prices

	At market prices													
	Final expenditure on goods and services at market prices													
		General government final consumption												
	Consumers' expenditure[1]	Central government	Local authorities	Total	Gross domestic fixed capital formation	Value of physical increase in stocks and work in progress[2]	Total domestic expenditure[1]	Exports of goods and services	Total final expenditure[1]	*less* Imports of goods and services	Statistical discrepancy (expenditure adjustment)[4]	Gross domestic product at market prices[1]	*less* Factor cost adjustment[3]	Gross domestic product at factor cost[4]
1985	217,618	45,879	27,926	73,805	60,353	821	352,597	102,208	454,805	98,866	144	356,083	49,367	306,716
1986	231,172	46,684	28,422	75,106	61,813	737	368,828	107,052	475,880	105,662	−188	370,030	52,312	317,718
1987	243,279	46,753	29,281	76,034	67,753	1,158	388,224	113,094	501,318	113,916	316	387,718	55,539	332,179
1988	264,096	46,942	29,544	76,486	77,395	4,010	421,987	112,989	534,976	127,458	–	407,131	57,727	349,404
1989	272,917	47,365	29,819	77,184	82,997	2,657	435,755	117,256	553,011	137,281	–	415,730	59,032	356,698
1990	274,744	48,627	31,062	79,689	80,464	−1,110	433,787	123,049	556,836	138,720	−207	417,909	58,929	358,980
1991	269,083	50,229	32,053	82,282	72,529	−3,418	420,476	123,265	543,741	134,436	−748	408,557	58,375	350,182
1992	269,575	49,563	32,529	82,092	72,063	−1,323	422,407	125,643	548,050	141,349	−685	406,016	57,467	348,549
Seasonally adjusted														
1988 Q1	64,882	11,764	7,418	19,182	18,439	143	102,646	27,919	130,565	30,017	–	100,548	14,164	86,384
Q2	65,246	11,798	7,373	19,171	19,513	−15	103,915	28,823	132,738	31,459	–	101,279	14,322	86,957
Q3	66,575	11,532	7,394	18,926	19,515	1,288	106,304	28,541	134,845	32,729	–	102,116	14,457	87,659
Q4	67,393	11,848	7,359	19,207	19,928	2,594	109,122	27,706	136,828	33,640	–	103,188	14,784	88,404
1989 Q1	67,546	11,704	7,410	19,114	20,974	1,281	108,915	28,803	137,718	34,481	–	103,237	14,422	88,815
Q2	68,370	11,636	7,394	19,030	20,773	1,030	109,203	28,703	137,906	34,231	–	103,675	14,785	88,890
Q3	68,274	12,105	7,492	19,597	20,572	1,112	109,555	29,463	139,018	34,791	–	104,227	14,890	89,337
Q4	68,727	11,920	7,523	19,443	20,678	−766	108,082	30,287	138,369	33,778	–	104,591	14,935	89,656
1990 Q1	68,673	12,058	7,550	19,608	21,255	−295	109,241	30,915	140,156	35,049	−36	105,071	14,848	90,223
Q2	69,121	12,268	7,718	19,986	20,511	43	109,661	31,271	140,932	35,321	−48	105,563	15,039	90,524
Q3	68,547	12,114	7,860	19,974	19,734	40	108,295	30,301	138,596	34,403	−58	104,135	14,672	89,463
Q4	68,403	12,187	7,934	20,121	18,964	−898	106,590	30,562	137,152	33,947	−65	103,140	14,370	88,770
1991 Q1	67,904	12,177	7,951	20,128	18,678	−739	105,971	29,896	135,867	33,130	−161	102,576	14,497	88,079
Q2	67,203	12,783	8,010	20,793	17,950	−1,472	104,474	30,962	135,436	33,394	−184	101,858	14,529	87,329
Q3	67,070	12,667	8,038	20,705	17,979	−876	104,878	31,365	136,243	33,922	−199	102,122	14,638	87,484
Q4	66,906	12,602	8,054	20,656	17,922	−331	105,153	31,042	136,195	33,990	−204	102,001	14,711	87,290
1992 Q1	66,712	12,469	8,093	20,562	17,941	182	105,397	30,999	136,396	34,794	−174	101,428	14,406	87,022
Q2	67,418	12,638	8,118	20,756	17,887	−495	105,566	31,614	137,180	35,722	−171	101,287	14,303	86,984
Q3	67,637	12,219	8,149	20,368	18,193	−299	105,899	31,398	137,297	35,619	−170	101,508	14,333	87,175
Q4	67,808	12,237	8,169	20,406	18,042	−711	105,545	31,632	137,177	35,214	−170	101,793	14,425	87,368

(1) These series are affected by the abolition of domestic rates and the introduction of the Community Charge. For details, see notes in the UK National Accounts article in the latest edition of *UK Economic Accounts*. (2) Includes quarterly alignment adjustment. For explanation see notes in the UK National Accounts article in the latest edition of *UK Economic Accounts*. (3) Represents taxes on expenditure less subsidies, both valued at 1985 prices. (4) GDP is estimated in seasonally adjusted form only. Therefore whilst seasonally and unadjusted versions exist of the residual error, the attribution of statistical discrepancies in the expenditure-based and income-based estimates can be made only in seasonally adjusted form.

Personal Income, Expenditure and Saving

Source: CSO

£ million

	Personal income before tax: Wages, salaries and forces' pay	Employers' contributions	Current grants from general government	Other personal income	Total[1]	*Less* United Kingdom taxes on income (payments)	*Less* Social security contributions	*Less* Miscellaneous current deductions	Community Charge	Total personal disposable income[2,3,4]	Consumers' expenditure[4]	Balance: personal saving[3]	Saving ratio[5]	Real personal disposable income at 1985 prices[6]	Index of real personal disposable income (1985=100)
1987	200,143	29,389	52,494	76,738	358,764	43,386	28,642	2,128	–	284,608	264,880	19,728	*6.9*	261,398	108.3
1988	223,250	32,107	54,087	89,284	398,728	48,290	32,108	2,347	–	315,983	298,796	17,187	*5.4*	276,362	114.5
1989	248,537	35,048	56,793	101,255	441,633	53,517	33,025	2,441	619	352,031	327,386	24,645	*7.0*	290,943	120.5
1990	275,441†	38,698†	62,002†	113,991†	490,132†	61,778†	34,651†	2,569	8,666	382,468†	348,576†	33,892†	*8.9†*	299,355†	124.0†
1991	289,918	41,010	71,570	118,868	521,366	63,860	36,670	2,544†	8,212	410,080	367,991	42,089	*10.3*	298,639	123.7
1992	299,370	43,555	82,667	124,698	550,290	64,864	37,497	2,722	7,877	437,330	386,606	50,724	*11.6*	304,944	124.6
Seasonally adjusted															
1987 Q1	47,897	7,116	12,851	18,459	86,323	10,464	6,849	516		68,494	63,605	4,889	*7.1*	63,690	105.5
Q2	49,297	7,233	13,170	18,948	88,648	10,779	7,011	521		70,337	64,990	5,347	*7.6*	65,109	107.9
Q3	50,682	7,420	13,179	19,437	90,718	11,046	7,259	536		71,877	67,207	4,670	*6.5*	65,800	109.0
Q4	52,267	7,620	13,294	19,894	93,075	11,097	7,523	555		73,900	69,078	4,822	*6.5*	66,799	110.7
1988 Q1	53,577	7,762	13,420	20,487	95,246	12,135	7,709	577		74,825	71,787	3,038	*4.1*	66,944	110.9
Q2	54,937	7,902	13,349	22,331	98,519	11,598	7,896	581		78,444	73,419	5,025	*6.4*	68,968	114.3
Q3	56,546	8,120	13,668	22,556	100,890	11,967	8,188	589		80,146	75,909	4,237	*5.3*	69,619	115.4
Q4	58,190	8,323	13,650	23,910	104,073	12,590	8,315	600		82,568	77,681	4,887	*5.9*	70,831	117.4
1989 Q1	59,853	8,413	13,643	23,871	105,780	12,717	8,393	603		84,067	79,283	4,784	*5.7*	70,979	117.6
Q2	61,273	8,525	14,315	25,858	109,971	12,996	8,320	607		87,842	81,140	6,702	*7.6*	73,274	121.4
Q3	62,785	8,835	14,354	25,657	111,631	13,647	8,155	633		88,990	82,399	6,591	*7.4*	73,127	121.2
Q4	64,626	9,275	14,481	25,869	114,251	14,157	8,157	598		91,132	84,564	6,568	*7.2*	73,563	121.9
1990 Q1	66,582†	9,314†	14,831	27,332†	118,059†	14,779†	8,613†	658		93,802†	85,772†	8,030†	*8.6†*	74,495†	123.5
Q2	68,595	9,566	15,469	27,805	121,435	15,272	8,728	661		93,955	86,630	7,325	*7.8*	74,510	123.5†
Q3	69,766	9,827	15,615	29,019	124,227	16,064	8,544	633		96,166	87,610	8,556	*8.9*	74,933	124.2
Q4	70,498	9,991	16,087†	29,835	126,411	15,663	8,766	617		98,545	88,564	9,981	*10.1*	75,417	125.0
1991 Q1	71,496	10,025	16,614	29,539	127,674	15,951	9,409	653		98,841	89,425	9,416	*9.6*	74,620	123.7
Q2	72,153	10,136	17,670	30,408	130,367	16,136	9,127	637†		102,670	91,385	11,285	*11.1*	75,112	124.6
Q3	72,926	10,349	18,423	29,151	130,849	15,896	8,944	606		103,605	92,941	10,664	*10.4*	74,503	123.6
Q4	73,343	10,500	18,863	29,770	132,476	15,877	9,190	648		104,964	94,240	10,724	*10.0*	74,404	123.0
1992 Q1	74,749	10,532	19,721	31,788	136,790	17,884	9,871	653		106,583	94,657	11,926	*11.5*	74,681	124.2
Q2	74,840	10,713	20,272	31,045	136,870	16,878	9,151	666		108,140	96,215	11,925	*11.0*	75,775	123.8
Q3	74,548	11,257	21,017	31,561	138,383	15,691	8,924	692		111,040	97,342	13,698	*12.3*	77,156	126.1
Q4	74,731	10,848	21,828	31,683	139,090	15,297	9,708	706		111,342	98,610	12,732	*11.4*	76,563	125.1
1993 Q1	–	–	–	–	–	–	–	–		–	100,124	–	–	–	–

(1) Before providing for depreciation and stock appreciation. (2) Equals total personal income before tax *less* payments of taxes on income, social security contributions and other current transfers. (3) Before providing for depreciation, stock appreciation and additions to tax reserves. (4) This series is affected by the abolition of domestic rates and the introduction of the community charge. (5) Personal saving as a percentage of total personal disposable income. (6) Personal disposable income revalued by the implied consumers' expenditure deflator (1985=100). † = figures revised since previous update.

National Insurance Fund
(Years ended 31 March)

Source: CSO

£ thousand

	1981/82	1982/83	1983/84	1984/85	1985/86	1986/87	1987/88	1988/89	1989/90	1990/91
Receipts										
Opening balance	5,177,647	4,194,593	4,164,605	4,742,324	5,165,213	5,400,988	5,858,038	7,481,287	10,634,672	10,852,343
Contributions	14,354,078	16,663,862	18,167,156	19,421,971	21,222,636	22,778,266	26,050,756	27,928,397	29,970,363	32,098,174
Compensation for SSP & SMP payments	–	–	–	–	–	–	–	–	–	40,600[5]
Consolidated Fund supplement	2,490,200	2,642,891	2,866,800	2,654,055	2,210,245	2,463,600	2,184,725	1,686,175	–	1,308,600
Reimbursements for industrial injury benefit payments	–	–	–	–	–	–	–	–	–	17,342[5]
Income from investments	608,233	514,038	506,882	533,732	557,951	619,805	607,863	794,860	1,060,702	1,048,515
Other receipts	96,210	87,859	92,792	96,196	61,778	176,987	194,933	1,081	1,018	965,763
Total	**22,726,368**	**24,103,243**	**25,798,235**	**27,448,278**	**29,217,823**	**31,439,646**	**28,207,349**	**38,076,800**	**41,666,755**	**47,236,816**
Expenditure										
Total benefits[1]	**17,676,334**	**19,073,084**	**20,220,929**	**21,333,736**	**22,929,064**	**24,611,284**	**25,442,704**	**28,352,408**	**30,126,298**	**33,339,702**
Unemployment	1,758,436	1,550,329	1,544,676	1,623,021	1,637,596	1,787,975	1,516,649	1,147,832	764,593	928,086
Sickness	643,782	514,251	267,108	287,455	280,026	190,643	203,623	202,078	214,228	237,644
Invalidity	1,441,266	1,672,580	1,959,334	2,239,461	2,451,527	2,791,026	3,098,571	3,500,571	3,993,974	4,794,989
Maternity	180,600	157,100	145,400	166,727	169,820	174,117	53,216	27,873	31,140	35,515
Widows' pensions	715,700	751,204	798,752	812,834	829,160	854,709	869,360	880,456	883,822	951,918
Guardians' allowances[2] } Child's special allowance	2,340	2,240	2,130	1,824	1,542	1,680	1,534	1,449	1,452	1,735
Retirement pensions	12,387,182	13,844,825	14,932,644	15,622,324	16,949,265	18,162,400	19,057,883	19,951,518	23,634,711	25,800,660
Death grants	17,245	17,335	17,132	17,422	18,661	18,842	2,694	–	–	–
Injury	49,173	47,564	7,573	342	–	–	–	–	–	–
Disablement[3]	323,517	353,326	379,730	392,235	419,054	453,052	466,658	464,466	483,320	419,756
Death[2]	48,280	52,430	55,550	56,640	60,279	63,163	58,602	60,760	–	47,920
Pensioners' lump sum payments	103,413	104,500	105,500	107,600	107,618	109,660	109,690	111,710	114,780	118,259
Other benefits	5,400	5,400	5,400	5,000	4,516	4,017	4,224	3,695	4,278	3,222
Payments in lieu of benefits foregone[3]	26,223	31,176	11,569	10,825	9,775	–	–	–	–	–
Other payments	391	287	316	10,736	1,709	7,782	4,785	8,262	–	9,623
Administration	732,927	749,321	746,097	833,569	838,124	765,699	830,539	896,458	891,925	1,056,787
Transfers to Northern Ireland	95,900	84,770	77,000	95,000	60,000	175,000	155,000	185,000	210,000	225,000
Personal pensions	–	–	–	–	–	–	–	–	–	42,224[5]
Total	**18,531,775**	**19,938,638**	**21,055,911**	**22,283,065**	**23,838,672**	**25,559,765**	**26,438,028**	**27,442,128**	**31,289,692**	**34,706,980**
Accumulated funds	**4,194,593**	**4,164,605**	**4,742,324**	**5,165,213**	**5,379,151**	**5,879,881**	**7,481,287**	**10,624,672**	**10,579,741**	**12,530,598**

(1) The total benefits figure for Northern Ireland in 1984/85 and 1985/86 includes payments in lieu of benefit foregone. (2) Including figures of Child's special allowance for Northern Ireland. (3) From 1.4.90, industrial injury benefits are no longer paid out of the National Insurance Fund; this amount is reimbursement for expenditure incurred by the fund for the period 1.4.90 to 31 12.90. (4) Payments to the Post Office, British Telecommunications, Consolidated and Trading Funds (from 1986/7 Estains payments not shown separately and are included with Sickness Benefit together with Injury Benefit. Estains arrangements were abolished on 25.8 86). (5) Figures provided for Northern Ireland only.

Summary of Government Expenditure on Social Services and Housing

(Years Ended 31 March)

Source: CSO

£ million

	1981/82	1982/83	1983/84	1984/85	1985/86	1986/87	1987/88	1988/89	1989/90	1990/91	1991/92
Education[1]	14,088	15,158	16,084	16,681	17,439	19,013	20,764	22,317	–	–	–
National Health Service	13,267	14,385	15,383	16,312	17,344	18,629	20,482	22,938	25,168	28,194	31,286
Personal social services	2,420	2,552	2,789	2,940	3,467	3,414	3,856	4,355	4,872	5,591	6,103
Welfare foods	52	70	86	98	113	120	124	102	105	115	145
Social security benefits	29,968	33,946	37,190	40,211	43,246	47,008	47,955	48,523	51,969	55,802	60,649
Housing	4,764	4,353	4,744	4,643	4,348	3,967	4,151	3,453	4,941	4,560	5,333
Total government expenditure	**64,559**	**70,464**	**76,276**	**80,885**	**85,957**	**92,151**	**97,332**	**101,688**	–	–	–
Current expenditure	60,629	66,500	71,567	76,163	81,439	87,882	92,673	97,732	–	–	–
Capital expenditure	3,930	3,964	4,709	4,722	4,518	4,269	4,659	3,956	–	–	–
Total government expenditure	**64,559**	**70,464**	**76,276**	**80,885**	**85,957**	**92,151**	**97,332**	**101,688**	–	–	–
Central government	47,932	52,884	57,222	61,282	65,440	70,548	73,555	76,767	–	–	–
Local authorities	16,627	17,580	19,054	19,603	20,517	21,603	23,777	24,921	–	–	–
Total government expenditure	**64,559**	**70,464**	**76,276**	**80,885**	**85,957**	**92,151**	**97,332**	**101,688**	–	–	–

(1) Includes school meals and milk.

Value of United Kingdom Imports[1]

Source: CSO

£ million

	1991	1992	1992 Q4	1993 Q1	1993[2] Jan	1993 Feb	1993 Mar
0. Food and live animals chiefly for food	10,389.3	11,401.9	3,105.1	1,068.8	347.2	316.4	405.2
00. Live animals other than animals of division 03	203.3	211.3	83.5	7.0	1.1	4.9	1.0
01. Meat and meat preparations	1,845.0	2,033.0	514.6	94.6	31.5	20.2	42.8
02. Dairy products and birds' eggs	871.0	1,111.4	350.1	53.7	19.2	19.4	15.1
03. Fish (not marine animals), crustaceans, and aquatic invertebrates and preparations thereof	978.5	996.0	258.0	166.4	56.7	50.3	59.5
04. Cereals and cereal preparations	818.5	1,004.2	340.8	30.5	11.4	7.6	11.5
05. Vegetables and fruit	3,002.6	3,118.3	743.3	325.7	103.5	100.9	121.4
06. Sugar, sugar preparations and honey	681.2	761.8	217.4	123.0	37.3	31.4	54.2
07. Coffee, tea, cocoa, spices and manufactures thereof	869.7	890.5	241.4	152.0	53.3	48.4	50.4
08. Feeding stuff for animals (not including unmilled cereals)	619.1	716.9	209.9	100.3	27.8	28.6	43.9
09. Miscellaneous edible products and preparations	500.4	558.7	146.2	15.6	5.3	4.7	5.5
1. Beverages and tobacco	1,936.1	2,025.5	651.7	107.5	39.6	24.9	43.1
11. Beverages	1,464.8	1,565.0	510.6	42.0	16.8	10.6	14.6
12. Tobacco and tobacco manufactures	471.3	460.5	141.1	65.6	22.8	14.4	28.5
2. Crude materials, inedible, except fuels	4,678.3	4,668.7	1,155.3	929.0	260.6	341.6	326.8
21. Hides, skins and fur skins, raw	68.8	76.8	20.9	11.2	2.7	3.7	4.8
22. Oil seeds and oleaginous fruit	224.0	228.5	56.3	42.9	17.7	12.1	13.1
23. Crude rubber (including synthetic and reclaimed)	223.6	228.9	61.4	31.9	10.6	9.3	12.0
24. Cork and wood	1,043.7	1,025.1	246.6	201.0	68.2	63.0	69.8
25. Pulp and waste paper	608.0	629.6	149.7	121.8	40.0	34.9	46.9
26. Textile fibres (other than wool tops and other combed wool) and their wastes (not manufactured into yarn or fabric)	452.6	480.7	117.4	70.5	25.0	20.4	25.0
27. Crude fertilizers other than those of division 56, and crude minerals (excluding coal, petroleum and precious stones)	284.8	264.0	67.3	180.1	8.8	113.6	57.8
28. Metalliferous ores and metal scrap	1,232.7	1,163.5	279.3	216.1	71.4	66.0	78.8
29. Crude animal and vegetable materials	540.1	571.7	156.7	53.4	16.2	18.6	18.6
3. Mineral fuels, lubricants and related materials	7,510.7	6,988.0	1,864.2	1,592.3	508.6	469.3	614.4
33. Petroleum, petroleum products and related materials	5,773.6	5,302.7	1,462.4	1,319.1	411.0	382.5	525.6
32, 34 and 35. Coal, coke, gas and electric current	1,737.1	1,685.3	401.7	273.2	97.7	86.8	88.8
4. Animal and vegetable oils, fats and waxes	387.5	422.8	116.1	52.6	16.1	19.0	17.5
5. Chemicals and related products	10,978.6	11,618.5	3,048.1	986.7	307.5	283.1	378.0
51. Organic chemicals	2,618.4	2,792.6	720.3	241.3	75.3	69.2	96.8
52. Inorganic chemicals	1,033.5	950.2	277.1	100.0	33.1	21.3	45.3
53. Dyeing, tanning and colouring materials	620.9	687.0	178.1	68.0	21.9	20.6	25.6
54. Medicinal and pharmaceutical products	1,371.2	1,663.4	478.2	194.3	62.6	59.9	71.8
55. Essential oils and perfume materials; toilet, polishing and cleansing materials	798.1	941.1	259.2	60.7	17.1	18.7	24.8
56. Fertilizers (other than those of group 272)	283.0	257.4	55.2	37.6	10.8	12.2	14.7
57. Plastic in primary forms	2,053.1	2,008.5	494.5	109.1	36.1	33.0	40.0
58. Plastics in non-primary forms	976.6	1,028.2	260.9	70.0	21.4	21.6	27.0
59. Chemical materials and products, n.e.s.	1,223.7	1,290.1	324.5	88.0	29.3	26.7	32.0
6. Manufactured goods classified chiefly by material	20,519.9	20,666.6	5,176.8	2,823.6	881.9	931.2	101.4
61. Leather, leather manufactures n.e.s., and dressed fur skins	185.9	187.3	52.4	22.5	7.6	6.0	8.9
62. Rubber manufactures n.e.s.	872.2	995.9	205.9	91.8	29.2	28.4	34.3
63. Cork and wood manufactures (excluding furniture)	821.2	847.3	216.1	144.3	53.4	42.5	48.4

(Continued)

£ million

	1991	1992	1992 Q4	1993 Q1	1993[2] Jan	1993 Feb	1993 Mar
64. Paper, paperboard and articles of paper pulp, of paper or of paperboard	3,868.4	3,801.3	939.3	520.4	160.3	157.8	202.3
65. Textile yarn, fabrics, made-up articles n.e.s. and related products	3,738.0	3,940.5	1,045.9	431.0	149.3	132.2	149.4
66. Non-metallic mineral manufactures n.e.s.	3,332.9	3,217.8	764.2	766.7	235.9	286.7	244.1
67. Iron and steel	2,620.2	2,513.9	584.3	161.5	45.3	54.6	61.6
68. Non-ferrous metals	2,557.9	2,589.7	652.1	426.3	120.7	143.1	162.4
69. Manufactures of metal n.e.s.	2,523.1	2,572.9	656.5	259.0	80.1	79.9	99.1
7. Machinery and transport equipment	43,101.6	47,320.5	12,576.9	6,621.1	1,993.5	2,043.9	2,583.7
71. Power generating machinery and equipment	3,345.5	3,611.8	962.0	569.0	156.8	186.6	225.5
72. Machinery specialized for particular industries	3,005.6	3,207.3	834.8	304.6	97.2	90.4	117.0
73. Metalworking machinery	860.7	800.8	177.8	83.0	25.0	21.9	36.1
74. General industrial machinery and equipment n.e.s. and machine parts n.e.s.	4,202.8	4,517.9	1,185.7	447.3	135.3	139.1	173.0
75. Office machines and automatic data processing equipment	7,586.5	8,362.1	2,431.3	1,454.3	497.3	419.9	537.1
76. Telecommunications and sound recording and reproducing apparatus and equipment	3,351.2	3,554.7	1,154.9	630.1	209.7	188.2	232.2
77. Electrical machinery, apparatus and appliances n.e.s. and electrical parts thereof (including non-electrical counterpart) n.e.s. of electrical household type equipment)	7,078.4	7,738.1	2,237.5	1,305.0	414.1	405.1	485.9
78. Road vehicles (including air-cushion vehicles)	10,227.2	12,118.6	2,932.1	722.8	228.6	236.8	257.4
79. Other transport equipment	3,443.7	3,409.3	660.9	1,105.0	229.6	356.0	519.4
8. Miscellaneous manufactured articles	17,559.3	19,109.0	5,283.4	2,968.2	934.0	963.6	1,070.6
81. Prefabricated buildings, sanitary plumbing, heating and lighting fixtures and fittings n.e.s.	368.3	390.4	110.5	27.3	9.3	8.8	9.2
82. Furniture and parts thereof, bedding, mattresses, mattress supports, cushions and similar stuffed furnishings	1,004.7	1,053.8	273.5	95.5	28.6	28.7	38.2
83. Travel goods, handbags and similar containers	285.1	311.7	81.0	59.5	21.5	20.2	17.7
84. Articles of apparel and clothing accessories	4,128.5	4,478.0	1,186.8	814.7	296.3	261.0	257.4
85. Footwear	1,169.0	1,152.4	291.6	168.7	56.3	54.2	58.2
87. Professional, scientific and controlling instruments and apparatus n.e.s.	2,525.1	2,620.9	685.9	449.7	132.9	137.6	179.1
88. Photographic apparatus, equipment and supplies and optical goods n.e.s., watches and clocks	1,565.5	1,635.0	447.2	235.9	69.6	78.9	87.4
89. Miscellaneous manufactured articles n.e.s.	6,513.3	7,466.9	2,207.0	1,116.9	319.4	374.1	423.4
5–8. Manufactured goods	92,159.4	98,714.5	26,085.1	13,381.6	4,117.0	4,221.9	5,042.8
9. Commodities and transactions not classified elsewhere	1,724.7	1,622.5	409.2	294.6	85.6	114.4	94.6
Total United Kingdom imports	118,786.0	125,843.9	33,386.7	17,426.5	5,374.7	5,507.5	6,544.3

(1) The numbers on the left hand side of the table refer to the Section and Division code numbers of the *Standard International Trade Classification*, Revision 3, which was introduced in January 1988. (2) As from January 1993 figures represent trade with non-EC areas and countries only. n.e.s. = not elsewhere specified.

Value of United Kingdom Exports[1]

Source: CSO

£ million

	1991	1992	1992 Q4	1993 Q1	1993[2] Jan	1993 Feb	1993 Mar
0. Food and live animals chiefly for food	4,715.8	5,291.1	1,606.7	412.7	118.0	128.2	166.5
00. Live animals other than animals of division 03	288.4	339.2	132.3	18.2	12.7	2.8	2.6
01. Meat and meat preparations	672.6	826.7	260.5	15.6	4.6	4.7	6.3
02. Dairy products and birds' eggs	451.9	534.5	146.7	35.1	8.3	9.1	17.8
03. Fish (not marine animals), crustaceans, and aquatic invertebrates and preparations thereof	574.4	567.8	186.3	18.9	4.0	5.1	9.8
04. Cereals and cereal preparations	1,102.8	1,203.5	333.7	145.1	33.3	48.0	63.8
05. Vegetables and fruit	298.5	330.6	114.4	19.5	5.4	6.3	7.8
06. Sugar, sugar preparations and honey	247.5	301.0	79.8	36.3	11.6	12.5	12.2
07. Coffee, tea, cocoa, spices and manufactures thereof	465.2	509.4	156.2	75.0	23.1	24.6	27.3
08. Feeding stuff for animals (not including unmilled cereals)	302.6	337.4	101.8	18.0	5.2	5.2	7.6
09. Miscellaneous edible products and preparations	311.7	341.1	94.9	31.0	9.7	9.9	11.3
1. Beverages and tobacco	3,031.8	3,417.3	1,028.5	457.9	131.0	149.3	177.6
11. Beverages	2,251.7	2,447.6	735.9	318.7	79.8	108.6	130.3
12. Tobacco and tobacco manufactures	780.3	969.7	292.6	139.2	51.2	40.8	47.2
2. Crude materials, inedible, except fuels	1,919.7	1,879.4	504.8	244.9	86.6	75.9	82.4
21. Hides, skins and fur skins, raw	135.1	130.9	37.0	20.0	6.9	5.4	7.7
22. Oil seeds and oleaginous fruit	52.6	36.6	19.6	0.2	–	0.1	0.1
23. Crude rubber (including synthetic and reclaimed)	198.1	209.0	57.4	18.5	6.0	5.4	7.1
24. Cork and wood	27.9	29.7	8.9	1.2	0.2	0.4	0.5
25. Pulp and waste paper	38.8	38.9	8.6	1.4	0.4	0.5	0.5
26. Textile fibres (other than wool tops and other combed wool) and their wastes (not manufactured into yarn or fabric)	466.2	487.7	128.4	63.2	20.9	20.1	22.1
27. Crude fertilizers other than those of division 56, and crude minerals (excluding coal, petroleum and precious stones)	365.5	366.5	97.0	48.0	18.8	13.9	15.4
28. Metalliferous ores and metal scrap	526.9	457.8	118.1	82.9	30.6	26.5	25.8
29. Crude animal and vegetable materials	108.5	122.3	29.9	9.5	2.7	3.6	3.2

(Continued)

£ million

	1991	1992	1992 Q4	1993 Q1	1993[2] Feb	1993 Mar	1993 Apr
3. Mineral fuels, lubricants and related materials	7,169.0	6,929.1	2,051.0	696.9	201.3	237.5	258.0
33. Petroleum, petroleum products and related materials	6,814.1	6,625.7	1,966.8	685.9	196.8	235.6	253.0
32, 34 and 35. Coal, coke, gas and electric current	355.0	303.3	84.0	11.0	4.5	1.9	4.6
4. Animal and vegetable oils, fats and waxes	95.9	86.0	21.1	7.8	3.4	2.0	2.4
5. Chemicals and related products	13,788.6	14,974.1	3,959.4	1,857.4	521.6	593.5	742.3
51. Organic chemicals	3,468.4	3,699.0	928.6	416.1	126.6	127.5	162.0
52. Inorganic chemicals	1,000.6	1,184.6	320.2	110.0	25.5	42.5	42.0
53. Dyeing, tanning and colouring materials	1,216.4	1,281.5	324.8	172.7	49.8	54.3	68.6
54. Medicinal and pharmaceutical products	2,556.1	2.992.8	851.8	449.3	112.0	152.6	184.7
55. Essential oils and perfume materials; toilet, polishing and cleansing materials	1,298.4	1,469.3	393.4	174.4	46.7	57.3	70.4
56. Fertilizers (other than those of group 272)	103.2	110.6	27.5	5.0	2.6	1.5	0.9
57. Plastic in primary forms	1,332.9	1,325.8	338.9	128.8	40.8	38.1	49.9
58. Plastics in non-primary forms	786.9	812.4	223.0	85.5	25.2	27.7	32.6
59. Chemical materials and products, n.e.s.	2,025.7	2,098,1	551.4	315.7	92.5	92.0	131.2
6. Manufactured goods classified chiefly by material	15,581.1	15,481.9	4,179.7	1,765.7	479.9	536.7	749.2
61. Leather, leather manufactures n.e.s., and dressed fur skins	258.0	265.4	72.1	45.1	12.4	14.9	17.8
62. Rubber manufactures n.e.s.	887.9	975.6	273.1	96.3	23.6	31.6	41.1
63. Cork and wood manufactures (excluding furniture)	116.4	129.3	34.6	10.0	2.5	2.7	4.7
64. Paper, paperboard and articles of paper pulp, of paper or of paperboard	1,623.8	1,730.3	466.0	158.1	47.0	51.6	59.5
65. Textile yarn, fabrics, made-up articles n.e.s. and related products	2,349.0	2,457.5	664.5	245.1	71.5	76.1	97.5
66. Non-metallic mineral manufactures n.e.s.	3,177.1	2,955.4	779.2	418.5	3.3†	97.7	217.5
67. Iron and steel	3,011.3	3,004.8	786.0	327.4	88.4	120.0	119.0
68. Non-ferrous metals	1,975.2	1,752.5	525.4	195.3	56.6	57.5	81.2
69. Manufactures of metal n.e.s.	2,182.4	2,211.1	578.7	269.9	74.4	84.6	110.8
7. Machinery and transport equipment	43,627.1	44,243.0	12,598.0	5,347.0	1,608.4	1,627.6	2,111.2
71. Power generating machinery and equipment	5,073.1	5,535.4	1,547.0	916.3	285.0	262.2	369.2
72. Machinery specialized for particular industries	3,922.1	4,031.7	1,088.4	604.2	180.9	200.6	222.7
73. Metalworking machinery	812.5	700.0	167.5	102.0	31.8	28.2	42.0
74. General industrial machinery and equipment n.e.s. and machine parts n.e.s.	4,520.6	4,576.1	1,195.6	676.4	210.5	218.8	247.1
75. Office machines and automatic data processing equipment	6,590.9	6,616.7	1,976.9	679.2	202.6	203.5	273.2
76. Telecommunications and sound recording and reproducing apparatus and equipment	2,942.8	2,857.3	883.5	327.6	86.4	106.3	135.0
77. Electrical machinery, apparatus and appliances n.e.s. and electrical parts thereof (including non-electrical counterpart) n.e.s. of electrical household type equipment)	5,709.7	6,353.5	1,833.9	806.0	226.8	245.2	334.0
78. Road vehicles (including air-cushion vehicles)	8,555.4	8,890.2	2,592.3	636.5	182.5	197.8	256.2
79. Other transport equipment	5,500.2	4,682.2	1,313.1	598.8	201.9	165.0	231.8
8. Miscellaneous manufactured articles	13,140.4	13,963.1	3,788.6	1,780.8	481.6	557.4	741.8
81. Prefabricated buildings, sanitary plumbing, heating and lighting fixtures and fittings n.e.s.	267.3	273.6	76.1	31.3	8.5	10.5	12.3
82. Furniture and parts thereof, bedding, mattresses, mattress supports, cushions and similar stuffed furnishings	564.2	620.4	173.0	55.1	13.6	17.0	24.5
83. Travel goods, handbags and similar containers	72.4	75.7	21.8	11.2	3.0	2.9	5.3
84. Articles of apparel and clothing accessories	1,920.1	2,083.8	642.5	164.9	41.5	54.5	68.9
85. Footwear	314.8	340.7	96.8	45.1	12.4	14.3	18.5
87. Professional, scientific and controlling instruments and apparatus n.e.s.	2,992.7	3,076.3	803.3	460.4	127.5	159.9	172.9
88. Photographic apparatus, equipment and supplies and optical goods n.e.s., watches and clocks	1,266.1	1,379.4	376.3	179.0	44.1	55.9	79.0
89. Miscellaneous manufactured articles n.e.s.	5,742.9	6,113.1	1,598.7	833.9	231.0	242.6	360.3
5–8. Manufactured goods	86,137.2	88,662.1	24,525.7	10,751.0	3,091.4	3,315.2	4,344.4
9. Commodities and transactions not classified elsewhere	1.807.6	2,024.9	573.6	314.7	94.1	121.8	98.9
Total United Kingdom exports	**104.877.0**	**108,290.0**	**30,311.4**	**12,886.0**	**3,725.9**	**4,030.0**	**5,130.1**

(1) The numbers on the left hand side of the table refer to the Section and Division code numbers of the *Standard International Trade Classification*, Revision 3, which was introduced in January 1988. (2) As from January 1993 figures represent trade with non-EC areas and countries only. n.e.s. = not elsewhere specified.

Worldwide Value of Exports and Imports

Source: CSO

£ million, seasonally adjusted

	European Community	Rest of Western Europe	E Europe & former USSR	North America	Other OECD	Oil exporting countries	Other countries	Total
Exports								
1986	35,025	6,730	1,275	12,063	2,829	5,494	8,923	72,782
1987	39,497	7,415	1,241	12,992	3,195	5,220	9,786	79,760
1988	41,052	7,210	1,285	12,794	3,520	5,019	10,009	82,072
1989	47,540	7,987	1,473	14,437	4,519	5,831	11,084	93,798
1990	55,072	9,039	1,480	14,972	4,828	5,572	12,173	103,691
1991	59,412	8,608	1,253	13,134	3,986	5,717	12,063	104,816
1992	60,512	8,543	1,702	13,983	3,991	5,999	12,587	108,298

(Continued)

	European Community	Rest of Western Europe	E Europe & former USSR	North America	Other OECD	Oil exporting countries	Other countries	Total
Imports								
1986	44,727	11,718	1,477	9,995	6,100	2,061	8,842	85,658
1987	49,736	12,710	1,696	10,781	6,722	1,699	10,243	94,043
1988	55,958	13,831	1,629	12,903	7,817	2,085	11,663	106,556
1989	63,807	15,155	1,781	15,929	8,514	2,313	13,659	122,000
1990	65,956	15,717	1,798	16,753	8,413	2,974	13,748	126,086
1991	61,308	14,306	1,691	15,740	8,104	2,786	14,165	118,867
1992	65,620	14,459	1,644	15,718	9,036	3,082	15,552	125,896

Internal Purchasing Power of the Pound (based on RPI)[1,2]

Source: CSO

pence

	Year in which purchasing power was 100p															
	1977	1978	1979	1980	1981	1982	1983	1984	1985	1986	1987	1988	1989	1990	1991	1992
1977	100	108	123	145	162	176	184	193	205	212	221	232	250	273	289	300
1978	92	100	113	134	150	163	170	178	189	196	204	214	231	252	267	277
1979	81	88	100	118	132	143	150	157	167	173	180	189	203	223	236	244
1980	69	75	85	100	112	122	127	133	142	146	152	160	172	189	200	207
1981	62	67	76	89	100	109	114	119	127	131	136	143	154	169	179	185
1982	57	62	70	82	92	100	105	110	116	120	125	132	142	155	164	171
1983	54	59	67	79	88	96	100	105	111	115	120	126	136	148	157	163
1984	52	56	64	75	84	91	95	100	106	110	114	120	129	141	150	155
1985	49	53	60	71	79	86	90	94	100	103	108	113	122	133	141	146
1986	47	51	58	68	76	83	87	91	97	100	104	109	118	129	136	142
1987	45	49	56	66	74	80	84	88	93	96	100	105	113	124	131	136
1988	43	47	53	63	70	76	79	83	88	92	95	100	108	118	125	130
1989	40	43	49	58	65	71	74	77	82	85	88	93	100	109	116	120
1990	37	40	45	53	59	64	67	71	75	78	81	85	91	100	106	110
1991	35	37	42	50	56	61	64	67	71	73	76	80	86	94	100	104
1992	33	36	41	48	54	59	61	64	68	71	74	77	83	91	96	100

(1) To find the purchasing power of the pound in 1992, given that it was 100 pence in 1980, select the column headed 1980 and look at the 1992 row. The result is 48 pence. (2) These figures are calculated by taking the inverse ratio of the respective annual averages of the General Index of Retail Prices. See p. 62.

UK Index of Retail Prices: Rates of Change

Source: CSO

The rate of growth in retail prices in the United Kingdom, often referred to as the rate of inflation, is measured by changes in the Retail Prices Index (RPI). This index monitors the change from month to month in the cost of a representative "basket" of goods and services of the sort bought by a typical household. It is an important macroeconomic indicator which is used widely in pay negotiations, contractual arrangements, and the up-rating of benefits, savings and securities. An error in the index of just one tenth of 1 per cent would directly affect government expenditure and receipts by around £80 million in total in a year.

	Average annual percentage change						Weights	
	1961–71	1971–76	1976–81	1981–86	1986–91	1990–91	1961	1992
General Index								
All items	4.6	14.5	13.4	5.5	6.4	5.9	1,000	1,000
All items, except housing	–	–	12.8	5.0	5.5	7.6	913	808
Food	4.7	17.4	11.7	4.6	5.1	5.2	350	151
Catering[1]	4.5[3]	17.0	15.1	6.7	7.6	10.0	–	47
Alcoholic drink	4.9	11.6	14.0	7.1	7.3	12.4	71	77
Tobacco	3.8	12.0	15.9	10.3	6.0	14.3	80	32
Housing	5.8	13.3	17.3	8.5	11.1	−1.8	87	192
Fuel and light	5.4	16.4	15.8	5.9	4.6	7.9	55	46
Clothing and footwear	2.9	11.9	8.4	1.9	3.6	3.0	106	63
Pensioner Indices[2]								
All items, except housing								
One-person housholds	4.8[4]	15.5	12.8	5.2	5.2	7.1	–	–
Two-person housholds	4.8[4]	15.5	12.8	5.3	5.3	7.3	–	–

(1) Described as 'Meals bought and consumed outside the home' prior to 1987. (2) Pensioner Indices relate to households in which at least 75 per cent of total income is derived from state pensions and benefits. (3) Not separately identified until 1968; the figure relates to 1968–1971. (4) Figure relates to 1962–1971.

Length of Time Necessary to Work to Pay for Selected Commodities and Services

(Great Britain)

Source: CSO

	Married couple with husband only working[1]							
	1971[2]		1981[2]		1986[2]		1992[2]	
	Hrs	mins	Hrs	mins	Hrs	mins	Hrs	mins
1 large loaf (white sliced)		9		8		6		5
1lb of rump steak		56		59		46		33
500g of butter (home produced)		19		19		16		12
1 pint of fresh milk		5		4		4		3
1 dozen eggs (55–60g)		22		17		15		9
100g of coffee (instant)		22		20		21		11
1 pint of beer (draught bitter)		14		13		13		12
20 cigarettes (king size filter)		22		20		21		19
Motor car licence	40	31	27	3	25	39	16	43
Colour television licence	19	27	13	8	14	37	12	9
1 litre of petrol (4 star)		8		8		6		5

(1) Length of time necessary for married man on average hourly male adult earnings for all industries and services, with non-earning wife and two children under 11, to work so that his net income pays for the various goods. (2) At April.

Consumer Price Indices: International Comparisons

	Percentage changes over 12 months[1]					
	1992 Dec	1993 Jan	1993 Feb	1993 Mar	1993 Apr	1993 May
European Community countries						
United Kingdom	2.6	1.7	1.8	1.9	1.3	1.3
Belgium	2.4	2.8	2.8	2.9	2.9	2.7
Denmark	1.5	1.5	1.3	1.1	1.1	–
France	1.9	2.1	2.2	2.2	2.1	–
Germany (West)	3.7	4.4	4.2	4.2	4.3	4.2
Greece	14.3	14.5	14.5	16.4	16.2	–
Irish Republic[2]	–	–	1.9	–	–	–
Italy	4.7	4.4*	4.4*	4.2*	4.1*	4.0*
Luxembourg	2.9	3.5	3.8	3.7	3.8	–
Netherlands	2.9	2.6	2.6	2.4	2.4	–
Portugal	8.5	8.5	8.0	7.3	6.2	–
Spain	5.3	4.7	4.0	4.0	4.6	–
EC 12 average	**3.6**	**3.6***	**3.5***	**3.5***	**3.3***	–
Other G7 countries[3]						
Canada	2.1	2.0	2.3	1.9	1.8	
Japan	1.2	1.2	1.4	1.2	0.9	–
U.S.A.	2.9	3.3	3.2	3.1	3.2	–
G7 average	**2.7**	**2.9***	**2.9***	**2.8***	**2.7***	–
Various other countries						
Australia[2]	–	–	1.2	–	–	–
Austria	4.2	4.1	3.7	3.9	3.9	–
Finland	2.1	2.9	2.9	2.7	2.6	–
New Zealand[2]	–	–	1.0	–	–	–
Norway	2.2	2.5	2.6	2.5	2.6	–
Sweden	1.8	4.7	4.9	4.9	5.1	
Switzerland	3.4	3.5	3.4	3.7	3.8	–

(1) For countries other than the United Kingdom, percentages are calculated from rounded series rebased to 1985 = 100. They must thus differ from official national sources. (2) Only quarterly figures are available. (3) The four European members of the "Group of Seven" countries are the United Kingdom, France, Germany and Italy.
*Provisional figure

Economic Evaluations

How well is Great Britain doing?

Source: SCPR's *British Social Attitudes* survey, 9th Report, ed. R. Jowell *et al* (Dartmouth Publishing, 1992)

	Percentage agreeing					
	Scotland	North	Wales	Midlands	London	South
Do you think:						
prices will go up a lot in next year?	45	49	53	43	41	41
unemployment will go up a lot in next year?	24	20	24	18	18	17
unemployment is of greater concern than inflation to you and your family?	33	34	31	27	28	26
income has fallen behind prices in the last year?	47	53	58	51	50	50
expect income to fall behind prices in the next year	45	50	54	48	42	46
living on household income is difficult?	24	26	30	24	27	21
Britain's industrial performance will decline over the next year?	29	24	22	21	26	23

Government Intervention

Source: SCPR's *British Social Attitudes* survey, 9th Report, ed. R. Jowell *et al* (Dartmouth Publishing, 1992)

Do you support:	Percentage supporting
Wage controls	33
Price controls	60
Reducing health and education spending	7
Increasing subsidies for private industry	58
Reducing defence spending	55
Government incentives for job-sharing	70
Government setting up job-creating projects	84
Cutting interest rates	90
Controls on HP and credit	81
Cutting down on foreign goods	67

Stock of Dwellings

(Great Britain)

Source: CSO

	1985	1986	1987	1988[2]	1989[3]	1990	1991[2]
Estimated annual gains and losses (thousands)							
Gains: New construction	196.9	205.8	216.3	231.8	211.0	189.8	177.8
Other	16.6	18.3	18.2	15.5	15.5	13.3	13.1
Losses: Slum clearance	10.6	8.7	8.3	6.8	6.8	7.1	6.9
Other	11.4	9.6	9.8	11.9	9.2	9.5	10.2
Net gain	191.4	205.8	216.3	228.7	210.5	186.5	173.8
Stock at end of year[1]	21,825	22,030	22,247	22,476	22,686	22,872	23,046
Estimated tenure distribution at end of year (percentage)							
Owner occupied	*61.7*	*62.7*	*63.8*	*65.1*	*66.3*	*67.2*	*67.7*
Rented: From local authorities and new towns	*26.9*	*26.2*	*25.4*	*24.4*	*23.2*	*22.3*	*21.8*
From housing associations	*2.5*	*2.5*	*2.6*	*2.6*	*2.8*	*3.0*	*3.1*
From private owners including other tenures	*9.0*	*8.6*	*8.2*	*7.9*	*7.6*	*7.5*	*7.4*

Note: For statistical purposes the stock estimates are expressed to the nearest thousand, but should not be regarded as accurate to the last digit. (1) Estimates are based on data from the 1971 and 1981 Censuses. (2) Provisional.

Building Societies' Mortgage Interest Rates

(United Kingdom)

Source: CSO

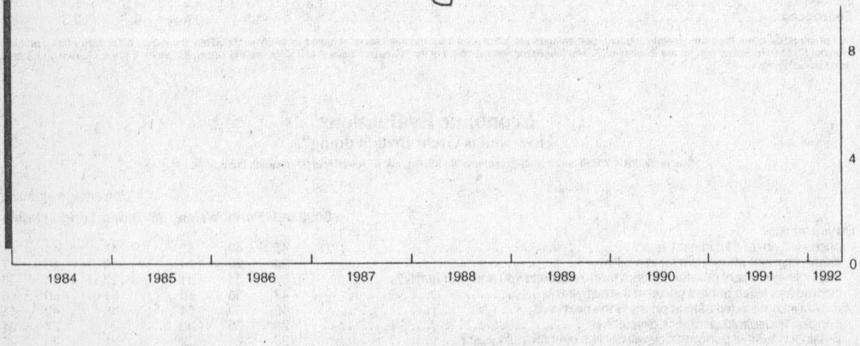

Balance of Payments of the United Kingdom

Source: CSO

£ million

	1980	1981	1982	1983	1984	1985	1986	1987	1988	1989	1990	1991
Current account												
Visible trade												
Exports (fob)	47,149	50,668	55,331	60,700	70,265	77,991	72,627	79,153	80,346	92,389	102,036	103,413
Imports (fob)	45,792	47,416	53,421	62,237	75,601	81,336	82,186	90,735	101,970	116,987	120,653	113,703
Visible balance	**1,357**	**3,251**	**1,911**	**−1,537**	**−5,336**	**−3,345**	**−9,559**	**−11,582**	**−21,624**	**−24,598**	**−18,617**	**−10,290**
Invisibles												
Credits	41,041	57,085	65,162	65,569	77,249	80,022	77,253	79,896	88,041	108,465	115,728	116,164
Debits	39,555	53,589	62,423	60,267	70,102	73,799	67,507	72,473	81,937	104,271	113,192	112,195
Invisibles balance	**1,487**	**3,496**	**2,741**	**5,302**	**7,146**	**6,222**	**9,747**	**7,423**	**6,103**	**4,195**	**2,535**	**3,969**
of which:												
Services balance	*3,653*	*3,792*	*3,022*	*4,064*	*4,519*	*6,687*	*6,808*	*6,745*	*4,574*	*4,685*	*4,966*	*4,990*
Interest, profits and dividends balance	*−182*	*1,251*	*1,460*	*2,831*	*4,357*	*2,646*	*5,096*	*4,078*	*5,047*	*4,088*	*2,466*	*328*
Transfers balance	*−1,984*	*−1,547*	*−1,741*	*−1,593*	*−1,730*	*−3,111*	*−2,157*	*−3,400*	*−3,518*	*−4,578*	*−4,897*	*−1,349*
Current balance	**2,843**	**6,748**	**4,649**	**3,765**	**1,811**	**2,878**	**−187**	**−4,159**	**−15,520**	**−20,404**	**−14,380**	**−6,321**
Transactions in external assets and liabilities[1]												
Investment overseas by UK residents												
Direct	−4,867	−6,005	−4,091	−5,417	−6,033	−8,456	−12,038	−19,215	−20,880	−21,521	−9,592	−10,261
Portfolio	−3,310	−4,467	−7,565	−7,350	−9,759	−16,755	−22,095	−7,201	−8,600	−31,283	−12,031	−30,908
Total UK investment overseas	**−8,175**	**−10,474**	**−11,656**	**−12,768**	**−15,792**	**−25,211**	**−34,133**	**−12,014**	**−29,480**	**−52,804**	**−21,623**	**−41,169**
Investment in the United Kingdom by overseas residents												
Direct	4,355	2,932	3,027	3,386	−181	3,865	4,987	8,478	10,236	17,145	18,593	12,045
Portfolio	1,431	257	−11	1,701	1,288	9,671	11,785	19,210	14,387	13,239	6,234	16,627
Total overseas investment in the United Kingdom	**5,786**	**3,189**	**3,016**	**5,087**	**1,107**	**13,536**	**16,772**	**27,688**	**24,623**	**30,384**	**24,827**	**28,672**
Foreign currency lending abroad by UK banks[2]	−29,836	−36,900	−16,520	−16,165	−9,427	−20,209	−47,861	−45,787	−14,890	−24,113	−33,327	27,394
Foreign currency borrowing abroad by UK banks[2]	30,505	36,763	19,942	17,199	18,635	25,295	58,568	43,143	20,403	33,012	34,000	−14,802
Net foreign currency transactions of UK banks	**669**	**−137**	**3,422**	**1,034**	**9,208**	**5,086**	**10,707**	**−2,644**	**5,513**	**8,899**	**673**	**12,592**
Sterling lending abroad by UK banks	−2,778	−3,019	−4,046	−2,278	−4,932	−1,815	−5,817	−4,640	−4,625	−2,919	−3,919	4,837
Sterling borrowing and deposit liabilities abroad of UK banks	3,044	2,497	4,479	4,094	6,155	4,148	5,559	9,457	13,815	10,875	12,179	−9,222
Net sterling transactions of UK banks	**266**	**−522**	**433**	**1,816**	**1,223**	**2,333**	**−258**	**4,817**	**9,190**	**7,956**	**8,260**	**−4,385**
Deposits with and lending to banks abroad by UK non-bank private sector	−2,502	−1,864	−598	863	−3,213	−1,305	−3,109	−4,632	−3,980	−9,473	−5,722	−3,580
Borrowing from banks abroad by:												
UK non-bank private sector	471	1,042	985	73	−2,215	2,618	3,817	2,035	3,971	7,081	7,916	13,032
Public corporations	−15	−178	−36	−35	−47	64	−31	−166	−253	−1,132	−127	−49
General government	−40	−192	58	78	49	87	100	104	−10	−65	−461	−65

(Continued)

	1980	1981	1982	1983	1984	1985	1986	1987	1988	1989	1990	1991
												£ million
Official reserves (additions to –, drawings on +)	–291	2,419	1,421	607	908	–1,758	–2,891	–12,012	–2,761	5,440	–77	–2,662
Other external assets of:												
UK non-bank private sector and public corporations	–209	–1,026	126	–161	1,281	528	1,656	254	1,201	1,611	–3,740	–4,707
General government	351	93	–161	–478	–743	–730	–509	–796	–891	–942	–1,227	–894
Other external liabilities of:												
UK non-bank private sector and public corporations	301	224	119	–15	558	732	567	1,448	1,682	13,710	5,649	10,710
General government	–553	–14	351	–661	–89	–64	78	1,725	841	2,251	1,158	–2,246
Net transactions in assets and liabilities	**–3,940**	**–7,436**	**–2,519**	**–4,562**	**–7,766**	**–4,082**	**–7,234**	**5,810**	**9,645**	**12,916**	**13,682**	**5,249**
Allocation of special drawing rights	**180**	**158**	–	–	–	–	–	–	–	–	–	–
Balancing item	**917**	**530**	**–2,130**	**797**	**5,955**	**1,204**	**7,047**	**–1,651**	**5,875**	**7,488**	**2,399**	**–1,072**

(1) Assets: increase – /decrease +. Liabilities: increase + /decrease –. (2) This item consists of UK residents' deposits with banks in the International Monetary Fund (IMF) reporting area supplemented by fiduciary accounts with Swiss banks and deposits with branches of US banks in Panama. (3) Covers predominately borrowing from commercial banks in the IMF reporting area, the European Investment Bank and the United States Export–Import Bank. fob = free on board.

General Index of Retail Prices[1]

Source: CSO

The Retail Prices Index measures the change from month to month in the average level of prices and services purchased by most households in the United Kingdom. The expenditure pattern on which the index is based is revised each year using information from the Family Expenditure Survey. The expenditure of certain higher income households and households of retired people dependent mainly on social security benefits is excluded. The index covers a large and representative selection of more than 600 separate goods and services, for which price movements are regularly measured in 180 towns throughout the country. More than 120,000 separate price quotations are used in compiling the index.

	All items	All items except seasonal food[2]	Food	Alcoholic drink	Tobacco	Housing	Fuel and light	Durable household goods	Clothing and footwear	Transport and vehicles	Miscel-laneous goods	Services	Meals bought and consumed outside the home
15 January 1974 = 100													
Annual averages													
1982	320.4	322.0	299.3	341.0	413.3	358.3	433.3	243.8	210.5	343.5	325.8	331.6	341.7
1983	335.1	337.1	308.8	366.4	440.9	367.1	465.4	250.4	214.8	366.3	345.6	342.9	364.0
1984	351.8	353.1	326.1	387.7	489.0	400.7	478.8	256.7	214.6	374.7	364.7	357.3	390.8
1985	373.2	375.4	336.3	412.1	532.4	452.3	499.3	263.9	222.9	392.5	392.2	381.3	413.3
1986	385.9	387.9	347.3	430.6	584.9	478.1	506.0	266.7	229.2	390.1	409.2	400.5	439.5
1987 Jan 1	394.5	396.4	354.0	100.0	602.9	502.4	506.1	265.6	230.8	399.7	413.0	408.8	454.8

(Continued)

		All items	Food and catering	Alcohol and tobacco	Housing and household expenditure	Personal expenditure	Travel and leisure	All items except seasonal food[2]	All items except food	Seasonal food[2]	Non-seasonal food	All items except housing	Consumer durables
13 January 1987 = 100													
Weights 1991		*1000*	*198*	*109*	*353*	*101*	*239*	*976*	*849*	*24*	*127*	*808*	*128*
Weights 1992		*1000*	*199*	*116*	*344*	*99*	*242*	*978*	*848*	*22*	*130*	*828*	*127*
Annual averages													
1987		101.9	101.4	101.2	102.1	101.4	102.6	101.9	102.0	101.6	101.0	101.6	101.2
1988		106.9	105.7	105.7	108.4	105.2	107.2	107.0	107.3	102.4	105.0	105.8	103.7
1989		115.2	111.9	110.8	121.9	111.2	112.8	115.5	116.1	105.0	111.6	111.5	107.2
1990		126.1	120.8	120.5	139.0	117.6	119.8	126.4	127.4	116.4	119.9	119.2	111.3
1991		133.5	128.6	136.2	142.2	123.6	128.9	133.8	135.1	121.6	126.3	128.3	114.8
1992		138.5	132.6	146.8	144.2	126.9	136.8	139.1	140.5	114.7	130.6	134.3	115.5
1990 Aug	14	128.1	121.7	123.0	142.5	117.2	121.4	128.5	129.6	112.2	121.4	120.3	110.7
Sep	11	129.3	120.3	123.5	143.6	119.3	123.5	129.8	131.1	111.5	121.8	121.6	112.5
Oct	16	130.3	122.5	124.4	144.8	120.3	124.6	130.7	132.2	111.8	121.9	122.6	113.2
Nov	13	130.0	123.4	124.6	143.8	121.1	123.7	130.4	131.7	114.5	122.4	122.7	113.8
Dec	11	129.9	124.1	125.1	143.8	121.1	122.4	130.2	131.4	119.2	122.6	122.6	114.1
1991 Jan	15	130.2	124.9	126.0	144.2	118.6	122.8	130.4	131.6	121.2	123.1	122.7	110.7
Feb	12	130.9	126.2	126.8	145.0	119.7	123.1	131.1	132.2	125.9	124.0	123.5	111.8
Mar	12	131.4	126.4	127.3	145.5	120.9	123.6	131.6	132.8	124.4	124.4	123.9	113.0
Apr	16	133.1	128.5	136.9	141.7	123.6	127.5	133.3	134.5	125.6	125.8	127.6	115.2
May	14	133.5	128.6	137.9	141.5	124.2	128.9	133.8	135.1	122.5	126.2	128.5	116.0
Jun	11	134.1	129.8	138.4	141.7	124.6	129.4	134.3	135.5	126.0	127.1	129.3	116.1
Jul	16	133.8	128.8	139.1	141.0	122.3	130.6	134.2	135.4	117.3	126.8	129.2	113.2
Aug	13	134.1	129.7	139.6	140.9	122.7	130.9	134.4	135.6	121.6	127.3	129.8	113.9
Sep	10	134.6	129.1	140.0	141.3	125.6	131.6	135.2	136.4	114.9	127.4	130.4	116.2
Oct	15	135.1	129.4	140.3	141.0	126.7	132.8	135.6	136.9	116.1	127.4	131.1	116.9
Nov	12	135.6	130.4	140.8	141.3	127.0	133.1	135.9	137.3	121.3	127.8	131.7	117.3
Dec	10	135.7	130.9	141.0	141.6	127.0	132.9	136.0	137.4	122.7	128.0	131.8	117.6
1992 Jan	14	135.6	131.9	141.8	141.7	123.5	132.9	135.9	137.1	125.2	129.0	131.6	113.2
Feb	11	136.3	132.6	142.3	142.2	124.7	133.7	136.6	137.8	126.0	129.7	132.3	114.4
Mar	10	136.7	133.0	142.7	141.9	126.1	134.6	137.0	138.2	124.8	130.2	133.0	115.7
Apr	14	138.8	132.8	146.6	144.8	127.3	136.9	139.2	140.7	122.4	130.1	134.4	116.2
May	12	139.3	133.4	147.3	145.1	127.5	137.5	139.7	141.2	120.9	131.0	134.9	116.4
Jun	11	139.3	133.1	147.6	145.0	127.7	137.8	139.9	141.3	117.4	131.0	135.0	116.4
Jul	16	138.8	131.9	148.1	145.0	125.0	137.8	139.6	141.1	105.8	130.9	134.3	113.1
Aug	13	138.9	132.2	148.4	145.2	125.0	137.7	139.7	141.2	107.0	131.1	134.4	113.5
Sep	10	139.4	132.0	148.7	145.6	128.2	137.7	140.3	141.8	104.0	131.1	134.9	116.0
Oct	15	139.9	132.4	149.2	145.8	129.3	138.3	140.7	142.3	106.5	131.1	134.9	116.0
Nov	12	139.7	132.4	149.5	145.1	129.2	138.4	140.5	142.1	106.3	130.9	135.6	116.8
Dec	10	139.2	133.4	149.8	143.4	128.7	138.0	139.9	141.3	110.6	131.5	135.7	117.1
1993 Jan	14	137.9	133.8	150.6	140.7	125.2	137.2	138.6	139.7	112.2	131.7	135.0	112.8
Feb	11	138.8	135.0	151.1	141.2	126.9	138.2	139.4	140.5	114.6	132.9	136.0	114.5
Mar	10	139.3	136.1	151.6	140.5	128.6	139.0	139.8	140.8	116.3	133.9	137.0	115.9

(1) Following the recommendation of the Retail Price Index Advisory Committee, the index has been re-referenced to make 13 January 1987 = 100. (2) Seasonal food is defined as: items of food the prices of which show significant seasonal variations. These are fresh fruit and vegetables, fresh fish, eggs and home-killed lamb.

UK Mortgages, Arrears and Possessions[1]: 1989

Source: CSO

Thousands

	Number of mortgages	Loans in arrears at end-period: By 6–12 months	Loans in arrears at end-period: By over 12 months	Properties taken into possession in period
1981	6,336	21.5	–	4.9
1982	6,518	27.4	5.5	6.9
1983	6,846	29.4	7.5	8.4
1984	7,313	48.3	9.5	12.4
1985	7,717	57.1	13.1	19.3
1986	8,138	52.1	13.0	24.1
1987	8,283	55.5	15.0	26.4
1988	8,564	42.8	10.3	18.5
1989	9,125	66.8	13.8	15.8
1990	9,415	123.1	36.1	43.9
1991	9,815	183.6	91.7	75.5
1992[1]	9,840	191.3	113.9	35.8

(1) As estimated by the Council of Mortgage Lenders at 31 December in each year, except 1992, 30 June. Estimates cover only members of the Council; these account for 90 per cent of all mortgages outstanding.

Financial Institutions

The City of London is one of the world's main financial centres. Major deregulation in recent years has had profound effects on the way financial institutions operate and has blurred the distinctions among different types of institution.

The Bank of England

The Bank of England is the central bank of the United Kingdom. It was founded in 1694 as a commercial bank with private shareholders and only brought into public ownership in 1946. However, long before that date, the Bank had acquired all the attributes of a central bank.

Nowadays, the Bank has many tasks, but all are related in some way towards maintaining:

1. the value of the nation's money;
2. the soundness of the financial system;
3. the efficiency and competitiveness of the financial system.

In order to achieve these objectives, the Bank of England acts as:

Banker to the government: The Bank arranges government borrowing, invests surplus government funds in the money markets, manages the gold and foreign exchange reserves and manages the national debt. The purchase and sale of Treasury Bills (stock with a 3–6 month life) by the Bank through the discount houses enable the Bank to manage liquidity in the money markets. The government's borrowing requirement (PSBR) is funded by the sale of gilt-edged stock.

Banker to other banks: The settlement of financial imbalances among banks and between the banks and government takes place daily via accounts of commercial banks with the Bank of England. This clearing role fosters efficient operation of the banking system and enables the Bank to monitor the flow of funds between the government and the private sector.

Banker to other central banks: Other central banks keep accounts and gold at the Bank of England and carry out foreign exchange and bullion transactions in London through the Bank.

Issuer of banknotes: Since 1844 the Bank of England has been the monopoly issuer of banknotes in England and Wales. The Royal Mint issues coin. Banks in Scotland and Northern Ireland issue their own notes, but the majority of these must usually be backed by Bank of England notes.

Implementation of monetary policy: The ultimate responsibility for UK monetary policy lies with the Treasury. If the UK government were to commit the UK to European Monetary Union, this responsibility would be transferred to European institutions and the Bank of England would become an independent Central Bank along the lines of the Bundesbank in Germany.

In recent years, short-term interest rates, which the Bank influences through its daily operations in the money markets, have been the key instrument of monetary policy. Since the UK departure from the ERM in September 1992, the constraints of using interest rates to maintain sterling within its permitted fluctuations bands have gone and monetary policy has been relaxed.

Supervisor of commercial banks: The Banking Act of 1979, reinforced in 1987, formalized the Bank of England's powers to authorize and supervise deposit-taking institutions in the UK (except for building societies). In order to operate in the UK, a bank must obtain and retain authorization from the Bank of England. Authorization requires banks to maintain adequate capital and appropriate provision against bad debt. Failure of an authorized bank entitles depositors to limited compensation from a Deposit Protection Fund which is administered by the Bank but financed by levies on the commercial banks.

Commercial Banks

Over 500 commercial banks are authorized to operate in the UK. Roughly half of these were incorporated in the UK, and half are the branches of banks incorporated overseas. Banks from over 72 countries maintain a presence in the UK.

Banks in the UK are not homogeneous, although increasingly their functions overlap. The main categories are:

The large clearing or high street banks: the retail banks which operate millions of small accounts for individuals. In recent years, they have transformed themselves into financial supermarkets by expanding their range of services into mortgages, pensions, insurance, share dealing and unit trusts, among others. High street banks have also acquired their own merchant banking arms.

Merchant banks: these operate as wholesale banks for industry, large private clients and government. Deregulation has also extended the range of merchant bank activities, which now include:

- Corporate finance – advice on takeovers, mergers and new issues
- Wholesale banking services, including export credits and foreign exchange dealing
- Eurocurrency and Eurobond business
- Fund management – pension funds, investment and unit trusts
- Specialized services, such as commodities, shipping, property, etc.

Foreign banks: dominated by the large Japanese and American banks, these banks originally set up in London to finance trade between their domestic market and the UK. Latterly, they have been attracted by London's more liberal financial regulations, by its well-developed foreign exchange markets and its central role in the Eurobond and Eurocurrency markets.

Nationwide savings banks: such as National Girobank and the National Savings Bank.

Capital Markets

Companies raise funds for investment from their own resources (i.e. retained profits), commercial borrowing or through the issue of shares, debentures, bonds, etc. The Stock Exchange is the traditional market for securities. Following "Big Bang" in 1986 various restrictive stock exchange practices were abolished, resulting in the takeover of long-established stockbroking and jobbing firms by merchant banks, retail banks and foreign banks, and tremendous changes in the process of buying and selling stocks and shares.

Despite the government's attempts to encourage a greater proportion of the population to own shares through privatization issues, the vast majority of share dealing is carried out on behalf of institutional investors, namely:

Insurance companies: insurance companies regularly invest over £100 million in UK and overseas securities.

Pension funds: which invest the regular contributions of a fund's members with a view to providing a retirement pension. Almost 100,000 occupational pension funds exist in the UK, and the largest funds, such as those of British Coal and British Telecom, each have over £10 billion of assets under management. Total occupational pension fund assets have been valued at over £300 billion.

Investment and unit trusts: Both unit and investment trusts aim to spread investment risk. However, they operate in different ways: an investment trust is a company which invests the funds of its shareholders in the shares of other companies. Unit trusts issue units that represent the holdings of a range of shares. In 1991 unit trusts invested around £5.5 billion in UK securities and almost £10 billion in overseas securities. This compares with a unit trust investment of £24.5 billion in domestic securities and almost £30 billion in overseas securities.

Building Societies

In addition to its traditional role of borrowing and lending for house purchase, today's building society, spurred on by competition from banks in the mortgage market, offers a full range of financial services, including cheque accounts, credit cards, insurance, pensions and foreign exchange.

Building societies developed from nineteenth-century self-help mutual societies; members deposited regular savings in order to finance the construction of houses. The great building society expansion began in the post-war years with the rapid spread of home ownership. Since the early 1970s, deposits in building societies have exceeded those in retail banks.

As a result of their historical origins, building societies have no shareholders but are owned by their members – that is, the depositors. Until the 1986 Building Societies Act, building societies were subject to stricter reserve asset requirements than banks and were restricted in the range of services they could offer and the investments they could undertake. The 1986 Act changed all this. Building societies gained the freedom to compete with banks on all levels, and may even become banks themselves. To date the Abbey National is the only building society that has gone down this route.

Insurance

Although beset with major problems in recent years, London remains the world's most important insurance centre, and over half its insurance business originates overseas. Three main groups participate in the London market:

1. Insurance and re-insurance companies: Over 800 insurance companies are authorized to operate in the UK. In addition to life and non-life business, an important part of their activity is concerned with re-insurance, a process whereby an insurer seeks to spread his or her risk by re-insuring with one or more other companies.

2. Lloyd's: In 1688 Lloyd's of London began life as a coffee house where merchants met to conduct business, particularly marine insurance – a sector in which Lloyd's remains the world leader. However, nowadays, non-marine business and re-insurance dominate its activities.

Lloyd's uniqueness stems from the unlimited personal liability of its "names" – private individuals with personal wealth of at least £250,000. A name belongs to and provides capital to a Lloyd's syndicate. Each syndicate is managed by an underwriting agent who appoints professional underwriters to operate on the syndicate's behalf. Business is conducted through brokers who negotiate with the underwriters on the floor of Lloyd's.

Lloyd's existence, at least in its present form, is in serious doubt. 1990 losses (reported in June 1993) were £2.91 billion and followed losses of £2.06 billion in 1989 and £510 million in 1988. Losses of this magnitude combined with litigation over allegations of malpractice in some syndicates threaten to ruin thousands of names. Lloyd's is attempting to attract new limited liability capital from the corporate sector but the institution's future is still finely balanced.

3. Insurance brokers and intermediaries: Brokers advise and arrange insurance, ranging from individual life cover to the safeguarding of major investments for multinational companies.

Bank of England Balance Sheet

Source: CSO

£ million

	1979 Dec	1980 Dec	1981 Dec	1982 Dec	1983 Dec	1984 Dec	1985 Dec	1986 Dec	1987 Dec	1988 Dec	1989 Dec	1990 Dec	1991 Dec
Issue Department													
Liabilities:													
Notes in circulation	10,089	10,611	11,001	11,271	12,152	12,610	12,612	14,119	14,654	16,071	16,849	17,283	17,466
Notes in Banking Department	11	14	24	4	8	10	8	11	6	9	11	7	4
Assets:													
Government securites[1]	8,635	8,430	6,329	3,217	4,699	1,888	938	2,718	9,783	10,339	13,946	14,672	11,791
Other securities	1,465	2,195	4,696	8,058	7,461	10,732	11,682	11,412	4,877	5,741	2,914	2,618	5,679
Banking Department													
Liabilities:													
Total[2]	1,999	1,162	2,039	2,754	2,356	2,595	2,328	2,606	3,059	3,203	5,398	8,613	5,825
Public deposits[3]	20	33	40	41	44	99	83	86	100	94	69	44	104
Special deposits[4]	805	–	–	–	–	–	–	–	–	–	–	–	–
Bankers' deposits[5]	462	487	482	647	650	787	848	932	1,064	1,310	1,750	1,842	1,813
Reserves and other accounts	697	627	1,503	2,051	1,647	1,694	1,382	1,574	1,880	1,784	3,565	6,713	3,894
Assets:													
Total	2,000	1,162	2,039	2,754	2,356	2,595	2,328	2,618	3,053	3,385	5,870	7,080	6,196
Government securities	1,462	447	433	456	383	460	579	474	559	882	1,354	1,432	1,346
Advances and other accounts	161	175	1,026	1,283	947	894	719	701	1,064	661	726	2,146	2,443
Premises, equipment and other securities	365	526	556	1,011	1,018	1,231	1,022	1,420	1,430	1,651	3,307	5,030	2,031
Notes and coin	12	15	24	4	8	10	8	11	6	9	11	7	5

(1) Including the historic liability of the Treasury of £11 million. (2) The only liability not shown separately is the Bank's capital (held by the Treasury) which has been constant at £14.6 million. (3) Excluding local authorities' and public corporations' deposits, which are included under Reserves and other accounts. (4) Deposits called from institutions are not at their free disposal. Until 19 August 1981, all banks and finance houses which observed the common reserve ratio were liable for calls to lodge special deposits. With effect from 20 August 1981 only reporting institutions with eligible liabilities of £10 million or more are liable for special deposit calls. This item also includes deposits under the supplementary special deposits scheme which was in force on three occasions before 1980. (5) Up to 19 August 1981 these constituted the current accounts held at the Bank by the banks and discount houses. From the introduction of new arrangements for monetary control on 20 August, they consist of operational deposits held mainly by the clearing banks and non-operational cash ratio deposits for which institutions authorized under the Banking Act are liable.

Value of Notes in Circulation
(Years to end-February)

Source: Bank of England

£ millions

	1993	1990	1991	1992
£1[1]	58	62	61	59
£5	1,163	1,539	1,373	1,166
£10[1]	5,348	5,866	5,810	5,743
£20	6,101	4,380	4,847	5,288
£50	2,732	2,292	2,375	2,515
Other notes[2]	1,563	882	909	1,350
Total	**16,965**	**15,021**	**15,375**	**16,121**

(1) No £1 notes have been issued since 1984. (2) Includes higher value notes used internally in the Bank, e.g. as cover for the note issues of banks of issue in Scotland and Northern Ireland in excess of their permitted issues.

Number of New Notes Issued Each Year
(Years to end-February)

Source: Bank of England

millions

	1993	1990	1991	1992
£5	318	424	507	355
£10*	752	627	619	638
£20	329	194	252	489
£50	23	22	24	21
Total	**1,422**	**1,267**	**1,402**	**1,503**

*The £10 note remains the most commonly used denomination. Of the other denominations, usage of £20 notes (particularly by banks and building societies for issue through cash dispensers and automated teller machines) continues to grow rapidly, while demand for £5 notes continues to decline.

London Clearing Banks' Base Rates[1]
Percentage Rates Operative Between Dates Shown

Source: CSO

Date	Per cent	Date	Per cent	Date	Per cent	Date	Per cent	Date	Per cent	Date	Per cent
1981		1983		1985		1986		1988		1989	
Mar. 11	*12*	Jan. 12	*11*	Jan. 11	*10½*	Jan. 9	*12½*	Feb. 2	*9*	May 24	*14*
Sept. 16	*14*	Mar. 15	*10½*	Jan. 14	*12*	Mar. 19	*11½*	Mar. 17	*8½*	Oct. 5	*15*
Oct. 1	*16*	Apr. 15	*10*	Jan. 28	*14*	Apr. 8	*11–11½*	Apr. 11	*8*		
Oct. 14	*15½*	June 15	*9½*	Mar. 20	*13½–14*	Apr. 9	*11*	May 18	*7½*	1990	
Nov. 9	*15*	Oct. 4	*9*	Mar. 21	*13½*	Apr. 21	*10½*	June 3	*8*	Oct. 8	*14*
Dec. 3	*14½*			Mar. 29	*13–13½*	May 27	*10*	June 6	*8–8½*		
		1984		Apr. 2	*13–13¼*	Oct. 10	*11*	June. 7	*8½*	1991	
1982		Mar. 7	*8¾–9*	Apr. 12	*12¾–13*			June 22	*9*	Feb. 13	*13½*
Jan. 22	*14*	Mar. 15	*8½–8¾*	Apr. 19	*12½–12¾*	1987		June 29	*9½*	Feb. 27	*13*
Feb. 25	*13½*	May 10	*9–9¼*	June 12	*12½*	Mar. 10	*10½*	July 5	*10*	Mar. 22	*12½*
Mar. 12	*13*	June 27	*9¼*	July 15	*12–12½*	Mar. 19	*10*	July 19	*10½*	Apr. 12	*12*
June 8	*12½*	July 9	*10*	July 16	*12*	Apr. 29	*9½*	Aug. 8	*10½–11*	May 24	*11½*
July 13	*12*	July 12	*12*	July 29	*11½–12*	May 11	*9*	Aug. 9	*11*	July 12	*11*
Aug. 2	*11½*	Aug. 9	*11½*	July 30	*11½*	Aug. 7	*10*	Aug. 25	*11–12*	Sep. 4	10½
Aug. 18	*11*	Aug. 10	*11*			Oct. 26	*9½*	Aug. 26	*12*		
Aug. 31	*10½*	Aug. 20	*10½*			Nov. 5	*9*	Nov. 25	*13*	1992	
Oct. 7	*10*	Nov. 7	*10*			Dec. 4	*8½*			May 5	10
Oct. 14	*9½*	Nov. 20	*9¾–10*								
Nov. 4	*9*	Nov. 23	*9½–9¾*								
Nov. 26	*10–10¼*										

(1) Each bank has a single base rate, which may sometimes differ from those of other banks. The rates of interest charged by the London clearing banks for their advances to customers and their discounting of trade bills are, in general, linked to their own individually declared base rates. The rates charged for advances depend on the nature and status of the customer; most lending is between 1 per cent and 5 per cent higher than base rate. Some lending is related to market rates instead of base rates.

Bank Lending to UK Residents[1]: Amounts Outstanding

Source: CSO

£ million

	3rd Weds. in Nov.		End Nov.				
	1985	1986	1987	1988	1989[2]	1990	1991
Total to UK residents	**168,280**	**203,069**	**242,899**	**304,996**	**413,663**	**451,611**	**476,664**
Loans and advances	154,919	189,671	230,752	289,518	395,971	433,619	459,585
of which in sterling	*119,819*	*141,492*	*181,771*	*236,679*	*317,233*	*363,395*	*376,038*
Acceptances	13,361	13,398	12,146	15,478	17,692	17,992	17,075
of which in sterling	*12,407*	*12,768*	*11,706*	*15,016*	*17,062*	*17,545*	*16,735*
Agriculture, forestry and fishing							
Total	5,878	6,088	6,080	6,530	6,836	7,118	7,124
of which in sterling	*5,859*	*6,048*	*6,041*	*6,461*	*6,697*	*6,990*	*7,018*
Energy and water supply							
Total	4,888	4,421	4,197	3,983	4,682	4,997	6,715
of which in sterling	*2,107*	*1,416*	*1,804*	*1,960*	*2,174*	*2,913*	*3,711*
Oil and extraction of natural gas	3,072	2,723	2,731	3,161	3,797	3,792	5,224
Other energy industries	1,310	1,090	988	723	701	1,027	1,285
Water supply	506	608	478	99	185	178	235
Manufacturing industry							
Total	27,433	29,648	29,900	40,688	51,175	54,291	51,588
of which in sterling	*22,353*	*23,289*	*23,396*	*31,204*	*35,280*	*39,136*	*37,391*
Extraction of minerals and ores	805	644	650	719	1,252	1,019	1,410
Metal manufacturing	1,268	1,106	1,118	1,456	1,803	2,123	1,816
Mineral products	960	1,072	930	1,100	1,471	1,922	1,932
Chemical industry	2,016	2,124	2,074	2,107	3,003	3,334	2,978
Mechanical engineering	2,162	2,158	2,136	2,603	3,404	3,751	3,463
Electrical engineering	3,628	3,548	3,460	4,604	5,916	5,586	5,733
Motor vehicles	1,352	1,742	952	1,274	1,480	1,797	1,775
Other transport equipment	1,474	1,515	1,444	1,585	1,390	1,604	1,678

(Continued)

£ million

	3rd Weds. in Nov.		End Nov.				
	1985	1986	1987	1988	1989[2]	1990	1991
Manufacturing industry *(Continued)*							
Other engineering and metal goods	1,989	1,982	1,811	2,527	3,263	3,299	2,966
Food, drink and tobacco	4,595	6,029	6,039	9,328	9,542	10,796	10,350
Textiles, leather, clothing and footwear	1,796	1,720	2,041	2,500	3,347	3,220	3,056
Other manufacturing	5,388	6,009	7,246	10,885	15,304	15,841	14,431
Construction							
Total	5,074	5,675	7,203	10,751	15,135	17,335	16,414
of which in sterling	*4,614*	*5,253*	*6,677*	*9,841*	*13,682*	*15,729*	*14,452*
Garages, distribution, hotels and catering							
Total	22,388	24,362	27,525	32,832	42,010	44,648	45,106
of which in sterling	*17,057*	*18,572*	*20,794*	*25,388*	*32,320*	*36,710*	*36,689*
Retail motor trades	2,246	2,486	2,794	3,172	4,302	4,869	5,168
Other retail distribution	6,621	7,215	8,365	10,118	13,832	14,602	13,510
Wholesale distribution	9,973	10,600	10,654	12,358	14,016	13,258	13,687
Hotels and catering	3,548	4,060	5,712	7,184	9,859	11,919	12,709
Transport							
Total	3,509	3,559	3,402	4,221	5,298	6,758	7,110
of which in sterling	*2,356*	*2,396*	*3,144*	*2,953*	*3,884*	*5,035*	*5,247*
Air transport	502	456	418	548	1,010	1,535	1,854
Other transport	3,007	3,103	2,984	3,673	4,289	5,223	5,257
Postal services and telecommunications							
Total	339	304	441	997	1,455	809	914
of which in sterling	*177*	*162*	252	*681*	*1,135*	*589*	*774*
Financial							
Total	32,574	55,504	69,532	80,754	103,654	111,396	130,287
of which in sterling	*18,072*	*30,032*	*41,175*	*53,698*	*63,970*	*76,554*	*82,618*
Building societies	2,064	3,362	4,015	6,759	6,317	7,704	9,725
Investment and unit trusts	3,462	3,725	6,483	6,777	7,928	5,387	6,759
Insurance companies and pension funds	2,370	2,906	3,928	3,336	4,356	4,257	3,723
Leasing companies	6,660	7,799	10,181	11,283	16,003	22,125	24,644
Other financial	18,018	25,050	30,137	37,361	48,830	49,768	49,884
Securities dealers, stockbrokers, jobbers, etc.[3]	–	13,706	62,536	57,670	73,627	84,336	120,345
Business and other services							
Total	25,094	25,185	31,764	46,119	66,489	77,028	77,755
of which in sterling	*18,644*	*21,905*	*28,667*	*41,646*	*58,849*	*70,726*	*71,862*
Central and local government	2,144	1,380	1,300	1,554	1,952	1,768	2,038
Property companies	7,109	9,349	13,360	21,348	31,963	38,996	39,674
Hiring of movables	771	918	1,064	1,070	1,740	1,706	1,427
Other services	15,070	13,538	16,040	22,146	30,834	34,557	34,620
Persons							
Total (loans and advances only)	41,102	48,323	62,854	78,120	116,929	127,232	133,656
of which in sterling	*40,991*	*48,145*	*62,629*	*77,879*	*116,306*	*126,560*	*133,008*
Bridging finance for house purchase	832[4]	25,296	34,861	44,596	78,289	85,539	90,193
Other house purchase	20,167						
Other advances to persons	20,103	20,127	27,994	33,525	38,639	41,692	43,463

(1) This is a series of statistics based on the Standard Industrial Classification 1980 and comprises loans, advances and acceptances by all monthly reporting institutions other than members of the London Discount Market Association (LDMA). The table includes lending under the Department of Trade and Industry special scheme for domestic shipbuilding, secured money placed with money brokers and gilt-edged jobbers, time deposits placed with and certificates of deposit issued by building societies. (2) From 1989 Abbey National's data have been included. (3) From end November 1986 lending to securities dealers, stockbrokers and stock jobbers (including money placed with the stock exchange money brokers and gilt-edged market makers) is shown separately within the Financial sector. Such lending was previously included in the "Other services" line of "Business and other services". (4) Now published as House Purchase.

Composition of Consumer Credit

(United Kingdom)

Source: CSO

Percentages and £ billion

	1981	1986	1987	1988	1989	1990	1991
Bank credit card lending	11.7	17.4	16.7	15.8	15.0	17.1	18.3
Bank loans[1]	65.0	61.7	62.6	64.8	65.9	64.0	63.0
Finance houses[2]	8.8	11.8	11.9	10.9	10.8	10.4	10.3
Insurance companies	2.2	2.7	2.5	2.3	2.2	2.3	2.5
Retailers	12.2	6.4	6.0	5.6	4.9	4.7	4.7
Building Society loans[3]	–	–	0.2	0.7	1.2	1.5	1.4
Credit outstanding at end of year (=100%) (£ billion)	15.5	30.1	36.2	42.5	48.4	52.6	53.6

(1) Banks and all other institutions authorized to take deposits under the Banking Act 1987. (2) Finance houses and other credit companies. (3) Building Society loans are Class 3, unsecured loans to individuals or companies.

Individual Insolvencies

Source: CSO

Number

	1980	1981	1982	1983	1984	1985	1986	1987	1988	1989	1990	1991
England and Wales												
Bankruptcies[1,2]	3,986	5,075	5,654	6,981	8,178	6,730	7,093	6,994	7,717	8,138	12,058	22,632
Individual voluntary arrangements[3]	–	–	–	–	–	–	–	404	779	1,224	1,927	3,002
Deeds of arrangement	52	76	46	51	51	48	62	29	11	3	2	6
Total	**4,038**	**5,151**	**5,700**	**7,032**	**8,229**	**6,778**	**7,155**	**7,427**	**8,507**	**9,365**	**13,987**	**25,640**
Scotland												
Sequestrations[4]	150	181	213	282	292	298	437	818	1,401	2,301	4,350	7,665
Northern Ireland												
Bankruptcies[5,6]	41	70	78	103	114	150	193	134	164	238	286	344
Deeds of arrangement	–	–	–	–	–	–	–	–	–	–	–	24
Total	**41**	**70**	**78**	**103**	**114**	**150**	**193**	**134**	**164**	**238**	**286**	**368**

(1) Comprises receiving and administration orders under the Bankruptcy Act 1914 and bankruptcy orders under the Insolvency Act 1986. (2) Orders later consolidated or rescinded are included in these figures. (3) Introduced under the Insolvency Act 1986. (4) Sequestrations awarded but not brought into operation are included in these figures. (5) Comprises bankruptcy adjudication orders, arrangement protection orders and orders for the administration of estates of deceased insolvents. (6) Orders later set aside or dismissed are included in these figures.

Company Insolvencies

Source: CSO

Number

2602,0110	1980	1981	1982	1983	1984	1985	1986	1987	1988	1989	1990	1991
England and Wales												
Compulsory liquidations	2,935	2,771	3,745	4,807	5,260	5,761	5,204	4,116	3,667	4,020	5,977	8,368
Creditors' voluntary liquidations	3,955	5,825	8,322	8,599	8,461	9,137	9,201	7,323	5,760	6,436	9,074	13,459
Total	**6,890**	**8,596**	**12,067**	**13,406**	**13,721**	**14,898**	**14,405**	**11,439**	**9,427**	**10,456**	**15,051**	**21,827**
Scotland												
Compulsory liquidations	135	158	177	263	272	306	299	253	228	229	251	304
Creditors' voluntary liquidations	244	280	326	258	251	231	212	203	168	199	219	312
Total	**379**	**438**	**503**	**521**	**523**	**537**	**511**	**456**	**396**	**438**	**470**	**616**
Northern Ireland												
Compulsory liquidations	8	16	10	15	19	36	56	59	58	69	70	106
Creditors' voluntary liquidations	66	83	111	96	64	75	108	91	68	56	62	73
Total	**74**	**99**	**121**	**111**	**83**	**111**	**164**	**150**	**126**	**125**	**132**	**179**

Self-Administered Pension Funds: Market Value of Assets

(United Kingdom)

Source: CSO

£ million, end-year

	1981	1982	1983	1984	1985	1986	1987	1988	1989	1990
Total pension funds[1]										
Total net assets	65,682	86,907	111,375	139,290	168,059	211,220	227,551	267,446	338,950	302,670
Short-term assets	2,694	3,190	4,809	7,012	7,728	10,359	14,963	18,156	22,438	24,759
British government securities	13,022	18,984	22,631	25,608	29,648	32,511	34,022	34,814	31,894	27,940
UK local authority long-term debt	156	160	181	163	149	153	181	184	102	32
Overseas government securities	120	422	518	772	1,203	1,313	1,367	1,968	4,187	5,442
UK company securities	30,129	39,257	50,990	68,263	86,005	111,169	124,334	134,556	168,993	152,496
Overseas company securities	6,321	9,742	15,566	18,483	22,998	33,076	27,937	42,028	63,570	48,995
Loans and mortgages	450	480	493	524	459	383	244	300	288	258
UK land, property and ground rents	9,782	10,654	11,293	12,796	13,853	15,311	18,068	23,666	26,959	26,363
Overseas land, property and ground rents[2]	–	996	1,300	2,022	1,666	1,728	1,728	1,835	1,880	1,006
Property unit trusts	1,678	2,076	2,308	2,582	2,661	2,351	1,772	2,500	2,089	1,656
Other assets	2,141	1,849	2,574	3,401	4,494	6,086	6,420	10,283	19,215	17,574
Long-term borrowing	−447	−451	−525	−1,114	−1,250	−1,126	−1,122	346	303	220
Short-term liabilities	−364	−452	−763	−1,222	−1,555	−2,094	−2,363	2,498	2,362	3,631

(1) These figures cover funded schemes only and therefore exclude the main superannuation arrangements in the central government sector. (2) Prior to 1982 figures are included with "Other assets".

Building Societies[1]

Great Britain (until 1985), United Kingdom (from 1986)

Source: CSO

Number and balance sheets

	1979	1980	1981	1982	1983	1984	1985	1986[2]	1987	1988	1989	1990	1991
Societies on register (Number)	287	273	253	227	206	190	167	151	138	130	126	117	110
Share investors (Thousands)	27,878	30,636	33,388	36,607	37,711	39,380	39,996	40,559	41,967	43,816	36,805	36,948	37,925
Depositors (Thousands)	797	915	995	1,094	1,200	1,550	2,149	2,850	3,648	4,306	4,490	4,229	4,698
Borrowers (Thousands)	5,251	5,383	5,490	5,645	5,928	6,314	6,657	7,023	7,182	7,369	6,699	6,724	6,998
Liabilities (£ million):													
Shares	42,023.1	48,914.6	55,463.4	64,968.0	75,197.3	88,087.0	102,331.8	115,550.8	129,954.3	149,791.1	143,359.3	160,538.2	177,519.4
Deposits and loans	1,289.8	1,762.0	2,576.9	3,531.6	5,601.4	8,425.6	10,751.5	16,862.2	20,571.8	26,528.5	30,532.5	40,695.5	49,516.6
Taxation and other	835.2	1,228.5	1,495.3	1,729.6	1,583.1	2,067.1	2,767.5	2,250.4	2,569.1	2,953.4	3,071.6	3,847.1	3,093.9
General reserves	1,640.9	1,887.9	2,279.0	2,803.3	3,487.0	4,109.1	4,912.6	5,939.0	7,001.7	8,466.0	8,680.7	10,200.1	11,430.4
Subordinates Debt	–	–	–	–	–	–	–	–	–	1,105.1	1,368.0	1,561.4	2,419.4
Assets (£ million): total	45,789.1	53,792.9	61,814.6	73,032.5	85,868.8	102,688.8	120,763.4	140,602.5	160,096.9	188,844.2	187,012.1	216,148.3	243,979.7
Mortgages	36,800.5	42,437.0	48,874.8	56,695.7	67,473.5	81,881.9	96,764.5	115,669.4	130,870.4	153,015.4	151,491.7	175,745.4	196,945.6
Investments	7,436.9	8,878.0	10,106.4	12,430.4	13,641.1	15,746.8	16,177.4	16,353.9	17,689.6	20,964.9	30,932.2	250,050.9	39,513.6
Cash	928.0	1,728.1	1,949.9	2,925.2	3,676.3	3,861.2	6,507.4	7,105.0	9,590.4	11,748.1			
Other	623.8	749.8	883.6	981.2	1,077.9	1,198.9	1,314.1	1,474.2	1,946.4	3,115.7	4,588.2	6,032.0	7,520.5

Current transactions (£ million)

	1979	1980	1981	1982	1983	1984	1985	1986[2]	1987	1988	1989	1990[5]	1991
Shares:													
Received	18,849.4	21,916.5	26,126.9	32,434.8	40,204.5	54,251.7	76,151.5	83,866.9	97,503.5	111,716.9	97,386.2	–	–
Interest thereon	3,297.7	4,699.4	4,795.7	5,298.6	5,095.6	6,318.8	8,269.5	8,498.5	9,141.7	9,852.6	11,775.6	–	–
Withdrawn (including interest)	16,313.6	19,726.1	24,373.0	28,218.0	34,813.3	47,759.0	70,444.9	79,262.9	92,024.6	100,991.8	87,744.1	–	–
Deposits:													
Received	678.4	1,091.2	1,571.5	2,029.3	4,801.4	11,244.2	17,924.9	28,100.8	38,325.7	58,637.2	62,271.1	–	–
Interest thereon	97.2	148.2	186.6	273.2	327.4	581.5	853.7	1,263.7	1,683.7	2,170.0	2,887.8	–	–
Withdrawn (including interest)	749.0	785.2	964.1	1,389.2	3,001.2	8,966.1	16,244.5	23,239.2	35,957.5	54,924.7	54,149.8	–	–
Mortgages:													
Advances	9,002.3	9,503.4	12,005.3	15,036.4	19,346.5	23,770.9	26,530.8	35,913.2	36,034.0	47,374.9	42,032.2	43,081	42,948.0
Repayments of principal	3,805.4	3,867.9	5,566.9	7,214.0	8,316.8	9,345.2	11,650.8	16,976.3	19,864.6	25,002.8	37,862.3	–	–
Interest[3]	4,082.5	5,912.9	6,398.1	7,030.7	6,845.9	8,843.5	12,027.6	12,820.0	14,306.7	15,965.1	18,395.5	–	–
Management expenses	449.3	589.6	731.6	874.6	1,002.2	1,109.9	1,264.9	1,437.4	1,668	2,074.7	2,093.2	2,363	2,581.0
Percentage rate of interest[4]													
Paid on shares	*8.43*	*10.34*	*9.19*	*8.80*	*7.27*	*7.74*	*8.69*	*7.80*	*7.45*	*7.04*	*8.03*	–	–
Paid on deposits	*7.67*	*9.77*	*8.71*	*9.12*	*7.24*	*8.30*	*8.92*	*9.15*	*9.00*	*9.21*	*10.12*	–	–
Received on mortgage advances	*11.94*	*14.92*	*14.01*	*13.32*	*11.03*	*11.84*	*13.47*	*12.07*	*11.61*	*11.25*	*12.21*	–	–

(1) The figures for each year relate to accounting years ending on dates between 1 February of that year and 31 January of the following year. (2) 1988 and subsequent years include Northern Ireland societies, responsibility for which was acquired under the Building Societies Act 1986. (3) Includes amounts recoverable from HM Government under Option Mortgage Scheme and MIRAS (Mortgage interest relief at source). (4) Based on the mean of the amounts outstanding at the end of the previous and the current year. (5) Apart from Mortgage Advances and Management expenses, no new data are available for 1990 and 1991. This is due to procedure changes.

End-Year Assets and Liabilities of Investment Trust Companies, Unit Trusts and Property Unit Trusts[1]

Source: CSO

£ million

	1979	1980	1981	1982	1983	1984	1985	1986	1987	1988	1989	1990	1991
Investment trust companies													
Short-term assets and liabilities (net):	202	230	283	249	154	487	346	438	1,461	619	1,217	1,227	908
Cash and UK bank deposits	163	187	210	186	273	396	401	455	1,296	574	883	1,010	790
Other short-term assets	213	216	221	269	244	475	684	575	618	403	751	501	544
Short-term liabilities	–174	–173	–148	–206	–363	–384	–739	–592	–453	–358	–417	–284	–426
Medium and long-term liabilities and capital:	–7,194	–8,546	–9,188	–10,241	–13,419	–15,722	–17,325	–21,055	–20,445	–19,834	–24,386	–20,250	–23,313
Issued share and loan capital	–1,951	–2,013	–2,211	–2,087	–2,258	–2,325	–2,558	–3,237	–4,042	–4,335	–4,692	–5,193	–5,100
Foreign currency borrowing	–342	–280	–228	–361	–538	–449	–557	–406	–610	–427	–342	–318	–344
Other borrowing	–12	–24	–69	–88	–100	–102	–85	–178	–344	–306	–316	–265	–316
Reserves and provisions, etc.	–4,889	–6,229	–6,680	–7,705	–10,523	–12,846	–14,125	–17,234	–15,449	–14,766	–19,036	–14,474	–17,553
Investments:	6,996	8,352	8,904	10,051	13,371	15,312	17,040	20,692	19,066	19,298	23,251	19,108	22,497
British government securities	320	266	183	199	310	300	438	311	595	360	177	326	417
UK company securities													
Loan capital and preference shares	134	132	136	129	172	128	262	378	494	878	903	687	722
Ordinary and deferred shares	4,160	4,620	4,673	4,604	5,306	6,074	7,603	8,957	9,144	8,817	11,121	9,878	10,687
Overseas company securities:													
Loan capital and preference shares	75	98	203	344	396	416	478	725	476	581	454	257	358
Ordinary and deferred shares	2,139	3,042	3,514	4,256	6,570	7,563	7,368	9,356	7,482	8,116	10,259	7,392	9,146
Other investments	168	194	195	519	617	831	891	965	875	546	337	568	1,167
Unit trusts													
Short-term assets and liabilities:	209	179	254	348	569	901	1,179	1,392	2,996	1,682	2,286	2,457	1,982
Cash and UK bank deposits	178	126	210	189	475	651	1,141	1,115	3,325	1,630	2,174	2,158	1,785
Other short-term assets	89	90	90	204	205	420	462	792	662	469	513	759	643
Short-term liabilities	–58	–37	–46	–45	–111	–170	–424	–515	–991	–417	–401	–460	–446
Foreign currency borrowing	–35	–12	–3	–58	–123	–128	–475	–190	–685	–9	–70	–34	–38
Investments	3,600	4,629	5,369	7,309	10,843	13,997	18,433	30,309	33,024	39,592	55,783	41,609	50,525
British government securities	52	72	175	322	415	566	512	538	663	480	393	411	480
UK company securities													
Loan capital and preference shares	76	64	106	154	225	283	505	961	1,518	1,610	1,779	1,337	1,530
Ordinary and deferred shares	2,758	3,357	3,566	4,457	5,954	8,201	10,884	16,424	20,510	23,123	30,324	25,530	29,526
Overseas company securities:													
Loan capital and preference shares	6	14	31	49	58	109	249	424	398	535	476	347	515
Ordinary and deferred shares	688	1,081	1,454	2,229	4,091	4,689	6,179	11,747	9,720	13,640	22,528	13,791	18,072
Other assets	20	41	37	98	100	149	104	215	215	204	283	193	402
Property unit trusts													
Short-term assets and liabilities (net)	135	152	158	146	180	147	67	85	49	71	78	136	37
Property	757	951	1,271	1,321	1,426	1,364	928	987	672	857	1,020	948	540
Other assets	49	166	259	216	333	439	341	200	186	196	26	21	–
Long-term borrowing	–60	–50	–69	–67	–77	–81	–40	–29	–16	–	–6	–6	–4

Note: Assets are shown as being positive: liabilities as being negative. (1) Investments are at market value.

Gold Reserves of Central Banks and Governments

Source: IMF, *International Financial Statistics*

(Million fine troy ounces)

Year end	All countries[1]	Belgium	Canada	France	Germany	Italy	Japan	Netherlands	Switzerland	United Kingdom	United States
1974	1,020.24	42.17	21.95	100.93	117.61	82.48	21.11	54.33	83.20	21.03	275.97
1975	1,018.71	42.17	21.95	100.93	117.61	82.48	21.11	54.33	83.20	21.03	274.71
1976	1,014.23	42.17	21.62	101.02	117.61	82.48	21.11	54.33	83.28	21.03	274.68
1977	1,029.19	42.45	22.01	101.67	118.30	82.91	21.62	54.63	83.28	22.23	277.55
1978	1,036.82	42.59	22.13	101.99	118.64	83.12	23.97	54.78	83.28	22.83	276.41
1979	944.44	34.21	22.18	81.92	95.25	66.71	24.23	43.97	83.28	18.25	264.60
1980	952.99	34.18	20.98	81.85	95.18	66.67	24.23	43.94	83.28	18.84	264.32
1981	953.72	34.18	20.46	81.85	95.18	66.67	24.23	43.94	83.28	19.03	264.11
1982	949.16	34.18	20.26	81.85	95.18	66.67	24.23	43.94	83.28	19.01	264.03
1983	947.84	34.18	20.17	81.85	95.18	66.67	24.23	43.94	83.28	19.01	263.39
1984	946.79	34.18	20.14	81.85	95.18	66.67	24.23	43.94	83.28	19.03	262.79
1985	949.39	34.18	20.11	81.85	95.18	66.67	24.23	43.94	83.28	19.03	262.65
1986	949.11	34.18	19.72	81.85	95.18	66.67	24.23	43.94	83.28	19.01	262.04
1987	944.49	33.63	18.52	81.85	95.18	66.67	24.23	43.94	83.28	19.01	262.38
1988	944.92	33.67	17.14	81.85	95.18	66.67	24.23	43.94	83.28	19.00	261.87
1989	938.95	30.23	16.10	81.85	95.18	66.67	24.23	43.94	83.28	18.99	261.93
1990	940.29	30.23	14.76	81.85	95.18	66.67	24.23	43.94	83.28	18.94	261.91
1991	939.58	30.23	12.96	81.85	95.18	66.67	24.23	43.94	83.28	18.89	261.91
1992	930.30	25.04	9.94	81.85	95.18	66.67	24.23	43.94	83.28	18.61	261.91

(1) Covers IMF members with reported gold holdings. For countries not listed above, see *International Financial Statistics*, a monthly publication of the International Monetary Fund.

Royal Mint

Llantrisant, Pontyclun, Mid-Glamorgan CF7 8YT
Tel: 0443 222111

The Royal Mint has produced coinage for over 1100 years, making it one of the oldest manufacturing institutions in the UK. In 1968 it moved from its original site near the Tower of London to larger premises at Llantrisant in South Wales in order to accommodate the introduction of decimalization and an increasing export business.

The Mint is responsible for the production and issue of United Kingdom coinage. The Chancellor of the Exchequer is the official "Master of the Mint" but, in practice, day-to-day operations are the responsibility of the Deputy Master, Anthony Garrett, acting as Chief Executive.

In addition to the 1000 or so Royal Mint staff, a regular staff of Ministry of Defence police are also based at the Llantrisant site, charged with the security of the Mint. The Royal Mint operates as a cashless society and visitors are not permitted to take coins on to the site. Plastic tokens are used for internal transactions.

The Royal Mint produces ordinary circulating coins and coinage blanks for approximately 100 countries as well as special Proof and Uncirculated quality collectors' coins, military and civil decorations and medals, gold bullion coins, tokens, commemorative medals, executive gifts, and royal and official seals.

All new designs are submitted to the Royal Mint Advisory Committee which advises on the designs of coins and medals. The Committee was approved by King George V in 1922. The President of the Committee is HRH the Duke of Edinburgh and the appointment of members is approved by The Queen.

Royal Mint Production

Set in 35 acres in South Wales, the Royal Mint combines the latest technology with traditional skills such as engraving and silversmithing to produce coins and medals.

The production of coins involves three separate processes: the engraving of dies, the manufacture of coin-sized discs or blanks and the striking of the blanks on the coining presses to transform them into coins.

Four large furnaces with a combined capacity of over 20,000 tonnes a year ensure continuous casting of metal, and X-ray fluorescence spectrometry is used to check its composition. The Royal Mint recently introduced a number of high-speed coining presses, each of which can produce over 700 coins a minute.

All circulating coins are subjected to rigorous control checks through a statistical sampling technique that tests for the correct weight, size and surface quality.

Proof coins are struck to a much higher quality than ordinary circulating coins. Each coin blank is highly polished and struck with polished dies to ensure that the design detail is perfectly captured.

Royal Mint Output

	£ million
Total sales value for 1992/93	104.00
Profits for 1992/93	11.80
Export sales for 1992/93	54.53
Cumulative sales since 1975	1,339.00
Cumulative profits since 1975	134.80
Cumulative export sales since 1975	819.75

Coins in Circulation

	millions
£1	1,035
50p	600
20p	1,410
10p	980*
5p	2,620
2p	3,700
1p	6,000
Approx. total in UK	16,345

*At 31 March 1993 there were 980 million new 10p coins in circulation, plus 300 million old 10p coins. The latter ceased to be legal tender on 30 June 1993.

Economic and Monetary Union (EMU)

Economic and monetary union in Europe was envisaged by the founding fathers of the European Community as the final stage of European integration. However, it was not until the late 1980s, when the single market looked like becoming reality, that EMU moved firmly to the top of the agenda. EMU involves:

- an independent European central bank
- a common monetary policy within Europe
- a single European currency

EMU supporters claim it will:

1. Eliminate transaction costs in intra-Community trade.
2. Remove uncertainty about exchange rates, interest rates and inflation.
3. Complete the economic integration process begun by the Treaty of Rome in 1957 and continued by the Single Market initiative.

The Maastricht Treaty, signed by all EC member states in December 1991, sets out the stages which will be followed for the attainment of EMU. Stage 2, which involves the establishment of monetary institutions which will govern EMU, will begin on 1 January 1994. Stage 3, which will irrevocably fix exchange rates and create a single currency, could begin as early as January 1997 – but only if a majority of member states meet the following convergence criteria:

- budget deficits no greater than 3% of GDP
- national debt no more than 60% of GDP
- currencies within the narrow band of the ERM for two years without realignment
- inflation rates no more than 1.5 percentage points above the average of the three best performing member states
- long-range interest rates within 2 percentage points of the average of the lowest three

Gathering recession in Europe is seriously lessening the likelihood of sufficient member states meeting the criteria by 1997. However, the Treaty provides for those states which do meet the criteria to go ahead with EMU before the end of the century.

According to EC law, all member states must ratify

a treaty before it comes into effect. This has proved problematic. In Denmark ratification requires a referendum: in 1992, the Danes voted against Maastricht, and it was only in May 1993, after concessions to Danish concerns at the December 1992 Edinburgh Summit, that the Danes voted for the treaty. Controversy has raged over Maastricht in the British parliament, but Britain will ratify, albeit some time after all other member states.

Shareholders as a Percentage of the Adult Population

Great Britain

Source: CSO

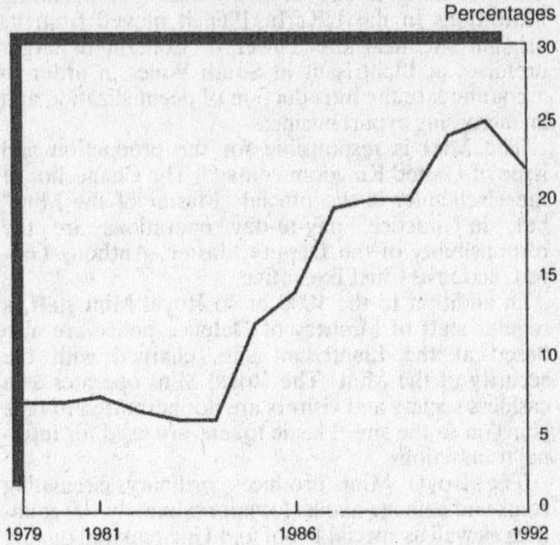

Global Stock Markets

Source: Morgan Stanley

(in local currencies)

Index[1]	Aug. 26, 1993	52-week range	
The World	456.7	456.9–	367.3
E.A.F.E.[2]	566.3	570.2–	427.6
Australia	400.3	400.3–	289.8
Austria	427.1	427.1–	315.6
Belgium	458.0	469.5–	358.1
Canada	421.5	422.7–	355.5
Denmark	768.8	795.7–	556.5
Finland	109.0	114.0–	37.5
France	638.2	638.2–	471.0
Germany	281.1	285.1–	213.1
Hong Kong	5172.1	5294.1–	3589.8
Ireland	178.8	181.0–	104.4
Italy	533.0	533.0–	266.0
Japan	962.5	982.3–	719.1
Malaysia	289.9	289.9–	181.8
Netherlands	418.6	422.2–	318.4
New Zealand	99.2	100.8–	62.3
Norway	748.5	782.3–	461.4
Singapore	974.7	974.7–	718.3
Spain	264.8	264.8–	144.9
Sweden	1640.6	1763.0–	787.2
Switzerland	311.5	314.1–	216.1
United Kingdom	934.2	934.8–	677.1
United States	431.7	431.7–	376.7

(1) Base: Jan. 1, 1970 = 100. (2) Europe, Australia, Far East Index.

Economic and Financial Glossary

Annual Percentage Rate (APR): The amount of compound interest when all costs associated with the loan are collected as interest. UK law requires lenders to quote APR in addition to the basic interest rate.

Appreciation: An increase in the value of a currency relative to other currencies. This term is used during times of freely floating exchange rates. (A decrease in the value of a currency in a fixed or semi-fixed system is termed "devaluation".)

Balance of payments: The accounts of a country's debits and credits with the rest of the world. The balance of payments is made up of the current account (the balance of trade and invisibles) and the capital account (the flow of money for international investment, grants and loans).

Bear Market: A market in which prices are falling.

Bull Market: A market in which prices are rising.

Business Expansion Scheme (BES): A scheme introduced in 1981 intended to foster small businesses by offering investors substantial income tax relief. The demise of the scheme was announced in the 1992 Budget.

Current account: The combined balance on the visible and invisibles trade account.

Depreciation: A decrease in the value of a currency relative to other currencies. This term is used during times of freely floating exchange rates (a decrease in the value of a currency in a fixed or semi-fixed system is termed "devaluation").

Devaluation: A decision to reduce the value of a currency within a fixed or semi-fixed exchange rate system. A devaluation makes exports more competitive but makes imports more expensive and can increase inflationary pressure if a country has a high propensity to import.

Discount house: An institution peculiar to the London money market, which buys and sells Treasury bills, acting as the middle-man between the Bank of England and the commercial money markets.

Disposable income: Total household income minus income tax and national insurance contributions.

Dividend: The proportion of a company's profits which is distributed to shareholders.

Dow Jones Industrial Average: A measure of stock market prices based on 30 leading companies on the New York Stock Exchange (compare **FTSE 100**).

Equities: Shares representing an ownership stake in a company.

Eurobonds: Bonds sold in countries other than the country of the currency in which the issue is denominated.

Eurocurrency: Currency held by institutions outside the country of issue. Eurodollars, for example, are US dollars acquired by banks outside the US.

European Currency Unit (ECU): Notional currency used by the EC. The ECU is the average of the currencies of EC member states, weighted according to the size of national income and intra-Community trade. The weights are re-assessed every 5 years. The ECU is used as a means to settle inter-government debt and, increasingly, by private-sector firms in cross-border transactions.

Exchange Rate Mechanism (ERM): A semi-fixed system of exchange rates in which each currency which is a member of the mechanism is allowed to fluctuate by plus or minus 2.5%. The system was introduced by the European Community in 1979, since when there have been a number of realignments. The UK and Italy withdrew from ERM in September 1992.

Fiscal policy: Taxation policy. An increase in taxes and/or a reduction in government spending reflect a tighter fiscal policy, while lower taxes and/or increased spending signal a looser fiscal stance and a boost to aggregate demand.

Friendly society: A mutual insurance company which is owned by its members, i.e. those who pay the premiums. Friendly societies have traditionally been used as retail institutions.

FTSE 100 (Footsie): A measure of stock market prices based on the 100 leading companies quoted on the London Stock Exchange.

Gilts: Fixed interest government securities traded on the stock exchange with a term generally ranging between 5 and 40 years.

Gross domestic product (GDP): The market value of all goods and services bought for final use during a specific period, usually a quarter or year.

Gross national product (GNP): GDP plus the income of domestic residents arising from investment abroad minus income earned in the domestic market by those resident abroad.

Inflation: Ongoing increases in prices.

Invisible trade: Trade in services such as banking, insurance, tourism, civil aviation and shipping.

Joint venture: Investment by two companies in a specific business venture over which they both have partial control. The collaboration is for a particular project only and cooperation stops far short of mergers and takeovers.

Management buyout: The purchase of a company by its management. Assistance from financial institutions is often required.

Merger: The combining of two companies into one.

Monetary policy: Government policy relating to the money supply, interest rates and the exchange rate.

National debt: The debt of the national government.

National Insurance: Deductions from wages and salaries that fund the UK social security scheme which covers unemployment benefit, sickness benefits, old age pensions, maternity benefits, child allowances and other state benefits.

National Savings: Government savings schemes, including national savings certificates, premium bonds and some gilt-edged securities. The government promotes new savings instruments when its borrowing is high.

Negative equity: The situation in which house-owners find themselves when the value of their mortgage is greater than the value of their property.

Per capita income: GDP or GNP divided by the number of people in the population.

Producer price indices: Measurements of changes in wholesale prices. Indices are produced for changes in input prices (i.e. the prices of materials and fuels purchased) and of the wholesale prices of the output of individual sectors.

Public Sector Borrowing Requirement (PSBR): The amount of government borrowing required to fund shortfalls between government revenue and expenditure.

Real terms: Money values corrected for inflation.

Recession: A modest decline in economic activity. Increasingly, a recession is being defined more specifically as two or more successive declines in real GDP.

Retail Prices Index (RPI): The most commonly used measure of inflation in the UK. An index number, published monthly, which represents the weighted average of the prices of goods in a representative basket of goods purchased by the final consumer.

Savings ratio: The amount of household income saved as a percentage of disposable income.

Seasonal adjustment: Statistical changes made to compensate for regular fluctuations in data that are so great that they distort data and make comparisons meaningless.

Supply-side economics: The school of economic thought which emphasizes the importance of increasing production efficiency as a means of revitalizing the economy. The use of incentives to capital and labour are advocated to raise output.

Takeover: The passing of control of one publicly quoted company to another by sale or merger. A friendly takeover occurs when the acquired company's management agrees to the merger; an unfriendly takeover occurs when management is opposed to the merger.

Trade balance: The difference between the value of imports and exports. The trade account is in deficit when imports exceed exports and in surplus when exports exceed imports.

Treasury bills: Instruments for short-term government borrowing.

Visible trade: The import and export of goods.

TAXATION

Compiled by Peter Meyer, finance director

This section aims to provide an understanding of the nature and operation of the current UK taxation environment. It should be regarded only as a general guide. Your tax office or local Customs and Excise office can provide further free advice and it may be advisable, if considering taking action, to consult a professional adviser.

Central taxation within the UK has been levied and collected by Parliament since 1689, with this right being limited to the House of Commons since 1911. However, all taxes are still collected in the name of the ruling monarch and are regarded as belonging to the Crown. There are 2 main ways in which taxes are levied.

1. Direct Taxes

Income Tax and *Capital Gains Tax* are levied annually on individuals, partnerships and trusts. *Corporation Tax* is levied annually on incorporated entities. These three taxes, together with *Inheritance Tax* (principally paid by individuals at death), are referred to as direct taxes. Taxpayers are assessed by, and pay taxes directly over to, the Inland Revenue, whose staff are employed by the Treasury and constitute the main administrative arm within Government responsible for the collection of taxes.

2. Indirect Taxes

The three other groups of taxes or duties which are collected by the Customs and Excise, also responsible to the Treasury, are referred to as indirect taxes. They are *Value Added Tax* (VAT), *Customs and Excise Duties* and *Car Tax*. Although incurred by the consumer, these taxes are paid over to the Customs and Excise by collecting agents. Lastly, among formal taxes, there is *Stamp Duty*, payable on transfers of property and certain securities. This tax is indirect in nature, but is in fact collected by the Inland Revenue.

National Insurance Contributions

Although not a formal tax, National Insurance (NHI) Contributions constitute a levy upon earnings and go towards funding the social welfare and health care commitments of the Government. As such, they have many of the properties of a tax and are also collected by the Inland Revenue.

Income Tax

Income Tax is payable on income earned in the UK and also income earned overseas which has been remitted to the UK.

Rates of Tax

Since the introduction of unified tax in 1973, income tax has been assessed at *basic* rate (currently 25%). The 1992 Finance Act introduced a *lower* rate (currently 20%) for the first £2,000 of taxable income (£2,500 for 1993/94) and a *higher* marginal rate or rates have existed at various figures above the basic rate (currently fixed at 40%).

The rates applicable since 1984/85 are given in the table below. 1993/94 rates are based upon the provisions of the March 1993 Budget and subsequent Finance Act.

Rates of Income Tax

Source: CSO

	1984/85		1985/86		1986/87		1987/88		1988/89	
	Slice of taxable income	Rate per cent	Slice of taxable income	Rate per cent	Slice of taxable income	Rate per cent	Slice of taxable income	Rate per cent	Slice of taxable income	Rate per cent
	£		£		£		£		£	
Lower rate	–	–	–	–	–	–	–	–	–	–
Basic rate	1–15,400	*30*	1–16,200	*30*	1–17,200	*29*	1–17,900	*27*	1–19,300	*25*
Higher rates	15,401–18,200	*40*	16,201–19,200	*40*	17,201–20,200	*40*	17,901–20,400	*40*	over 19,300	*40*
	18,201–23,100	*45*	19,201–24,400	*45*	20,201–25,400	*45*	20,401–25,400	*45*	–	–
	23,101–30,600	*50*	24,401–32,300	*50*	25,401–33,300	*50*	25,401–33,300	*50*	–	–
	30,601–38,100	*55*	32,301–40,200	*55*	33,301–41,200	*55*	33,301–41,200	*55*	–	–
	over 38,100	*60*	over 40,200	*60*	over 41,200	*60*	over 41,200	*60*	–	–

	1989/90		1990/91		1991/92		1992/93		1993/94	
	Slice of taxable income	Rate per cent	Slice of taxable income	Rate per cent	Slice of taxable income	Rate per cent	Slice of taxable income	Rate per cent	Slice of taxable income	Rate per cent
	£		£		£		£		£	
Lower rate	–	–	–	–	–	–	1–2,000	*20*	1–2,500	*20*
Basic rate	1–20,700	*25*	1–20,700	*25*	1–23,700	*25*	2,001–23,700	*25*	2,501–23,700	*25*
Higher rates	over 20,700	*40*	over 20,700	*40*	over 23,700	*40*	over 23,700	*40*	over 23,700	*40*

Assessment and Collection

For taxpayers in trade, Income Tax is collected by direct assessment, based upon a return supported by suitably prepared accounts or records. However, for taxpayers in earned employment it is collected at source under the Pay As You Earn (PAYE) scheme and many taxpayers make no return. Income Tax due on interest from savings is generally deducted at source, as is tax on dividends and other distributions.

Income Tax is assessed in tax years which run from 6 April to the following 5 April.

Who Pays Income Tax?

Income Tax is payable by all individuals, male or female, while they are alive and by all partnerships and corporate bodies while they are in existence. By dint of legislation or practice, however, the following are *not* normally required to pay tax:

- Diplomats enjoying immunity
- Charities (except on their *trading* income)
- Non-residents
- Housing associations
- Mutual companies
- Agricultural societies
- Local authorities
- Trade unions
- Pension funds
- Scientific research associations
- Visiting armed funds

Others exempted from paying tax include statutory bodies such as the BBC and Docks Authorities on their statutory income, the British Museum and the Historic Buildings and Monuments Commission.

Taxable Income

Taxable income is the money amount (or deemed equivalent money amount in the case of any benefits-in-kind) received as part of the following:

- Income from trade, business or professional activity
- Income from employment, including pensions
- Interest income, dividends and other income returns on capital such as annuities
- Rent or other income from property
- Royalties

Income from trade or employment is often referred to as earned income, while the last three categories above are known as unearned or investment income. Since abolition of the investment income surcharge in 1984, the distinction between the two forms of income has been of only minor technical importance.

Non-Taxable Income

Income or cash received in the following forms is not taxed:

- Gifts and inheritances
- Profits from sale of assets
- Gambling profits
- Lottery prizes
- Scholarships, grants and prizes for achievement
- Golden handshakes (up to certain limits)
- Capital part of a life annuity
- Interest on National Savings Certificates
- Interest on a Post Office Savings Bank account (up to £70)
- Income received under a Deed of Covenant
- Income from letting furnished accommodation in one's main residence (up to £3,250)
- Wedding presents from an employer
- Wound, disability, gallantry, Nazi victims' and war widows' pensions
- Income from additional services within the Armed Forces
- Final bonuses on Save As You Earn (SAYE) and certain bonds
- Lump sum payments from a pension fund
- Interest on post-war credits
- Repayment supplements for any tax
- Most social security payments
- Awards made by a court
- Receipts under Statute or Royal Charter
- Statutory Adoption Allowances
- Personal Equity Plan (PEP) dividend income
- Payments under Profit-related pay (PRP) arrangements
- Beneficial ownership of-woodlands income

How Tax Is Organized

For administrative reasons, taxable income is divided into Schedules, sometimes subdivided into Cases (sections). These are of more importance to legislators and practitioners than to the average taxpayer, but may well be mentioned in correspondence or discussion.

Schedule A taxes all rent in respect of land in the UK. This includes ground rent, licence fees for hoardings, parking fees, service charges and short-lease premiums.

Schedule B was abolished in the 1988/89 tax year. It originally covered income from farming but was very shortly limited to profits from UK woodlands managed on a commercial basis. Tax was payable by the occupier on 1 January in the year of assessment.

Schedule C taxes any dividend payable in the UK from public revenue. The tax is levied only on the paying agent – usually a bank. Most income from UK Government Securities is assessed under Schedule D, Case III, below.

Schedule D, *Case I* taxes trades, while ***Case II*** taxes vocations and professions. Definition of trading has been left to case law, since this has not been fully defined by statute. It may nevertheless be rather loosely defined as "operations of a commercial nature capable of producing a profit". There is a slender line between trading income taxable under this Schedule and, say, capital gains from investment activities, so discretion is required. For example, investing in a commodity or a related traded option does not necessarily constitute trading, but dealing in commodities or related options does. Marginal cases will generally be decided according to the motive behind the initial acquisition.

The fact that a trade is illegal does not render it free from tax; thus, for example, prostitution and drug dealing have been the subject of tax assessments. However, generally speaking, if a person cannot profit from an activity (e.g. because it is charitable work done without remuneration or benefit), he or she will not be taxed.

The profits assessable to tax are often those of a period (known as a *basis period*) which relates to an earlier *accounting period*, as follows:

Year of Assessment	Basis Period
1. Start of business to next 5 April	Actual (i.e. the exact period of months)
2. First complete tax year	First 12 months' trading
3. Second complete tax year	Previous year (or First 12 months, if no previous year)
4. Thereafter	Previous year
5. Final year up to close of business	Actual

If a trade lasts no more than 4 years in total, all years are converted to an actual basis. The taxpayer has an option to be assessed on an actual basis in years 2 and 3, and the Inland Revenue has the option to raise assessments on an actual basis in the pre-penultimate and penultimate years. Special rules operate for partnerships and changes of accounting date.

Expenses may be deducted if wholly and exclusively incurred for the purpose of the trade. *Capital Allowances* in respect of eligible capital expenditure may be deducted as if they were a trade expense. Allowances – now only in the form of *writing down allowance* (i.e. spread over a number of years) and a balancing allowance or charge – are principally available on industrial buildings, hotels, plant and machinery and motor vehicles, although other minor categories of asset also apply.

Schedule D, *Case III* taxes interest income, annuities and other annual payments which include:

- Discounts (including deep discounts) and interest on Government Securities on securities sold
- Savings bank interest
- Mining rents and royalties
- Small maintenance orders

Case III income is normally assessed on a preceding (tax) year basis with rules as follows:

Year of Assessment	Basis of Assessment
1. From initiation to next 5 April	Income earned in actual period
2. Second year of operation	Income earned in actual period
3. Third year	Previous tax year's income
4. Thereafter	Income earned in actual period

The taxpayer may elect to have the third year of operation taxed on an actual basis. The Inland Revenue will assess the higher of actual and previous year's income in the penultimate year of operation. Rules on the start and end of operations are not completely fixed, e.g. a large increase to a building society account *may* constitute a new source of funds and a new operation.

Almost all receipts of income will have had basic rate tax deducted at source, with the taxpayer regarded as having paid tax on a gross income amount. The taxpayer will thus only be liable for further tax if his taxable income reaches the higher rates of tax (see the worked example, p. 82).

Schedule D, *Case IV* taxes income from secured debts or claims held overseas, and ***Case V*** taxes income from assets held overseas by a UK resident. Tax is assessed as it arises for UK residents and domiciles, and as it is remitted to the UK for persons not ordinarily resident or domiciled in the UK. Income is taxed on the full amount arising (or received on a remittance basis), with relief for allowable expenses, annuities, etc., and for overseas taxation incurred.

Schedule D, *Case VI* taxes annual income arising under a number of guises, of which the following are perhaps the most significant:

- Income from furnished lettings
- Income from bondwashing, i.e. holding a bond for the period of income accrual between payment dates (since 27 February 1986)
- Underwriting commission
- Insurance company commission

Tax is assessed on an actual year basis unless the Inland Revenue directs otherwise.

Schedule E taxes all income from employment, including pensions. Income coming into this category would include all cash or benefits received from an employer and also any tips or gifts, etc., received from customers.

As a general rule, all sums of money paid over to an employee are likely to be taxable, but the following main items are specifically excluded from tax:

- Reimbursement of expenses incurred
- Wedding presents
- Prizes for achievement
- Christmas presents and/or Christmas parties up to the value of £50 a head
- Testimonial payments

Since 6 April 1989 income has been assessed in the year in which it is received. Prior to that date it was taxed in the year in which it was earned.

Schedule E is applied according to residence:

Case I taxes those individuals *ordinarily resident* in the UK for all income.
Case II taxes those *resident* in the UK for UK income.
Case III taxes those *not resident* in the UK for UK income.

A taxpayer has only one domicile for tax purposes, although he may have more than one residence. The *domicile* is the taxpayer's natural home by dint of birth, choice or dependency. *Residence* is the place where a taxpayer lives; a UK *resident* is one who spends six months a year in the UK, with accommodation available all year, and who makes habitual and substantial visits to the UK. An *ordinarily resident* taxpayer is one who normally lives in the UK and his absences are only temporary or infrequent.

Income from employment abroad is subject to a 100% deduction if earned in a 365-day period, during which the taxpayer spent no more than 62 consecutive days in the UK and/or no more than one-sixth of the time spent overseas in total.

All fringe benefits or "perks" are taxable as income. They could encompass anything from free coffee to a company car, free parking, beneficial or interest-free loans, board and lodging, subsidized canteen, medical insurance and luncheon or gift vouchers. Should the employer be prepared to pay the tax in respect of any benefit received, this payment of tax is itself assessable as a benefit in kind and gives rise to a further tax assessment.

Certain expenses may be offset against income if wholly, necessarily or exclusively incurred in the performance of duties. These are:

- Professional fees and subscriptions to bodies relevant to employment

- Overalls and clothing of a specialized nature
- Tools provided by the taxpayer
- Travel and other expenses such as home telephone
- Pension contributions by the taxpayer

Tax-free charitable donations by employees under a Give As You Earn (GAYE) scheme are offsetable against Schedule E income up to certain limits (£900 p.a. for 1993/94). Gift Aid, introduced in 1990, permits charities to reclaim the income of Corporation Tax paid by a donor on large gifts (those over £250 for 1993/94).

Company Cars

Employees earning in excess of £8,500 p.a. (including benefits) and all company directors are assessable on the taxable value of a car and any fuel provided by the employer. For 1994/95 provision has been made for a revised basis of assessing taxable value, based upon a percentage (30%) of the value of the car at purchase. The following tables indicate the method of establishing the taxable value of a car and fuel provided in the current and prior tax years.

Car Scale Benefit Rates

Taxable value[1] of the benefit applied to a car with an original market value and engine capacity[2] (where applicable) of:	1984/85 Under 4 years old	1984/85 Over 4 years old	1985/86 Under 4 years old	1985/86 Over 4 years old	1986/87 Under 4 years old	1986/87 Over 4 years old	1987/88 Under 4 years old	1987/88 Over 4 years old	1988/89 Under 4 years old	1988/89 Over 4 years old
£16,000 or lower										
– up to 1300cc	375	250	–	–	–	–	–	–	–	–
– 1301–1800cc	480	320	–	–	–	–	–	–	–	–
– 1801cc and above	750	500	–	–	–	–	–	–	–	–
£16,001 to £24,000	1,100	740	–	–	–	–	–	–	–	–
£24,001 and above	1,725	1,150	–	–	–	–	–	–	–	–
£17,500 or lower										
– up to 1300cc	–	–	410	275	–	–	–	–	–	–
– 1301–1800cc	–	–	525	350	–	–	–	–	–	–
– 1801cc and above	–	–	825	550	–	–	–	–	–	–
£17,501 to £26,500	–	–	1,200	800	–	–	–	–	–	–
£26,501 and above	–	–	1,900	1,270	–	–	–	–	–	–
£19,250 or lower										
– up to 1300cc	–	–	–	–	450	300	–	–	–	–
– 1301–1800cc	–	–	–	–	575	380	–	–	–	–
– 1801cc and above	–	–	–	–	900	600	–	–	–	–
£19,251 to £29,000	–	–	–	–	1,320	875	–	–	–	–
£29,001 and above	–	–	–	–	2,100	1,400	–	–	–	–
£19,250 or lower										
– up to 1400cc	–	–	–	–	–	–	525	350	1,050	700
– 1401–2000cc	–	–	–	–	–	–	700	470	1,400	940
– 2001cc and above	–	–	–	–	–	–	1,100	725	2,200	1,450
£19,251 to £29,000	–	–	–	–	–	–	1,450	970	2,900	1,940
£29,001 and above	–	–	–	–	–	–	2,300	1,530	4,600	3,060

	1989/90 Under 4 years old	1989/90 Over 4 years old	1990/91 Under 4 years old	1990/91 Over 4 years old	1991/92 Under 4 years old	1991/92 Over 4 years old	1992/93 Under 4 years old	1992/93 Over 4 years old	1993/94 Under 4 years old	1993/94 Over 4 years old
£19,250 or lower										
– up to 1400cc	1,400	950	1,700	1,150	2,050	1,400	2,140	1,460	2,310	1,580
– 1401–2000cc	1,850	1,250	2,200	1,500	2,650	1,800	2,770	1,880	2,990	2,030
– 2001cc and above	2,950	1,950	3,550	2,350	4,250	2,850	4,440	2,980	4,800	3,220
£19,251 to £29,000	3,850	2,600	4,600	3,100	5,500	3,700	5,750	3,870	6,210	4,180
£29,001 and above	6,150	4,100	7,400	4,900	8,900	5,900	9,300	6,170	10,040	6,660

(1) The taxable value of the car assessed is *increased* by 50% if business mileage is less than 2,501 miles a year; it is *reduced* by 50% if business mileage is more than 18,000 miles a year. (2) Provision has been made in tax legislation for vehicles with no recognized engine capacity, with differing values applicable in each year.

Car Fuel Scale Benefit Rates[1]

Taxable value of fuel provided free[3] for a car with an engine size[4] of:	1984/85	1985/86	1986/87	1987/88	1988/89	1989/90	1990/91	1991/92	1992/93 Petrol	1992/93 Diesel[2]	1993/94 Petrol	1993/94 Diesel
Up to 1300cc	375	410	450	–	–	–	–	–	–	–	–	–
1301–1800cc	480	525	575	–	–	–	–	–	–	–	–	–
1801cc and above	750	825	900	–	–	–	–	–	–	–	–	–
Up to 1400cc	–	–	–	480	480	480	480	480	500	460	600	550
1401–2000cc	–	–	–	600	600	600	600	600	630	460	760	550
2001cc and above	–	–	–	900	900	900	900	900	940	590	1,130	710

(1) For the years 1984/85 to 1992/93, but not 1993/94, the scale benefit is reduced by 50% if the taxpayer's use exceeds 18,000 miles in any tax year. (2) Different rates have applied to petrol and diesel-driven cars since 6 April 1992. Previously, no distinction was made. (3) The scale benefit is reduced to nil if the taxpayer is required to pay for all fuel provided for private use and does so. (4) Provision has been made in tax legislation for vehicles with no recognized engine capacity, with differing values applicable in each year.

Redundancy (Termination) Payments

Terminations are deemed to arise when an employee is constructively dismissed (rather than resigning or retiring), and tax relief in general applies only to such situations. The question of whether a termination or retirement is involved depends on a number of factors, including the employee's age and whether he was seeking alternative employment. The final judgement rests with the Inland Revenue.

Payments made on termination to compensate for loss of a contractual right are regarded as earned income and (since 5 April 1988) are fully taxed above £30,000. *Ex gratia* payments made are also taxable unless made on death or permanent disability, or to members of the armed forces, or to employees whose work was substantially overseas. From 6 April 1982 to 5 April 1988 voluntary payments were tax-free up to £25,000, with tapered relief for amounts up to £75,000.

Pensions

Pensions may be paid by the Government (via the State Earnings Related Pension Scheme (SERPS) since 1978) or via company or private schemes. Each operates differently, with different contribution and benefit arrangements permissible under Inland Revenue guidelines. The area is complex and cannot be covered here in detail; see the Inland Revenue leaflet IR 121. Successive governments have encouraged the establishment of personal pensions by the following favourable tax treatments:

- Contributions are tax-deductible
- Pension funds pay no tax on income
- Lump sums on retirement are tax-free

These concenssions are, however, subject to many restrictions, as indeed are the pensions payable. Again, this topic cannot be covered here in detail. Suffice it to say that all pensions received are treated as earned income and are assessable under Schedule E.

Social Security Payments

Most social security payments are tax-free. These include:

- Child Benefit
- Child's special allowance
- Christmas bonuses paid
- Death grant
- Guardian's allowance
- Housing benefit
- Industrial disablement benefit
- Invalidity pensions (but not allowances)
- Maternity grants and allowances (but not maternity pay)
- Mobility allowance
- Severe disablement and sickness benefit (but not statutory sick pay)
- Social Fund payments such as Family Credit and Income Support (the latter being dependent on availability for employment)
- War pensions (but not widows' pensions)
- Workmen's compensation scheme payments

PAYE

Employers are required by law to operate the Pay As You Earn (PAYE) scheme for all employees earning above the minimum wage, and to deduct National Insurance (NHI) Contributions. Every employer is given a PAYE number by his allocated tax office and every employee has a PAYE tax code. It is up to the employer to obtain the correct code and ensure that the correct amount of tax is deducted. If the employer does not have a certificate or other direct notification, he must apply an "emergency" tax code, which always causes the employee to pay too much tax. The employee gets a proper tax code by sending a completed tax return to the employer's PAYE office.

The tax code is arrived at after taking into account as much information as may be known about allowances, charges, reliefs and other income sources, with the aim of obtaining a proportion of the final tax payment every pay day.

Profit-Related Pay

Profit-Related Pay was introduced in 1987 to encourage employers to pay employees according to the fortunes of their employers. Half of any amounts received under such a scheme were received free of income tax, until 1 April 1991, with all payments tax-free since that date.

Allowances

Every individual may have at least one *personal allowance* set against his or her income for tax purposes each year. Some individuals may be entitled to more. The available allowances, together with their cash values, are set out in the table below.

Income Tax: Allowances and Reliefs

Source: CSO

	1984/85	1985/86	1986/87	1987/88	1988/89	1989/90	1990/91	1991/92	1992/93	1993/94
Personal allowances										
Personal allowance	£2,055	£2,205	£2,335	£2,425	£2,605	£2,785	£3,005	£3,295	£3,445	£3,445
Married man's allowance[1]	£3,155	£3,455	£3,655	£3,795	£4,095	£4,375	–	–	–	–
Married couple's allowance[2]	–	–	–	–	–	–	£1,720	£1,720	£1,720	£1,720
Wife's earned income allowance[3]	£2,055	£2,205	£2,335	£2,425	£2,605	£2,785	–	–	–	–
Age allowance[4]:										
Married (either partner over 65 but neither partner over 75)	£3,955	£4,255	£4,505	£4,675[4]	£5,035[4]	£5,385	–	–	–	–
Married couple's allowance[2] (either partner over 65 but neither partner over 75)	–	–	–	–	–	–	£2,145	£2,355	£2,465	£2,465
Married (either partner over 75)	£3,955	£4,255	£4,505	£4,845[4]	£5,205[4]	£5,565	–	–	–	–
Married couple's allowance[2] (either partner over 75)	–	–	–	–	–	–	£2,185	£2,395	£2,505	£2,505
Personal (over 65 but under 75)	£2,490	£2,690	£2,850	£2,960	£3,180	£3,400	£3,670	£4,020	£4,200	£4,200
Personal (over 75)	£2,490	£2,690	£2,850	£3,070	£3,310	£3,540	£3,820	£4,180	£4,370	£4,370
Income limit	£8,100	£8,800	£9,400	£9,800	£10,600	£11,400	£12,300	£13,500	£14,200	£14,200
Marginal fraction	2/3	2/3	2/3	2/3	2/3	1/2	1/2	1/2	1/2	1/2
Additional personal allowance[5]	£1,150	£1,250	£1,320	£1,370	£1,490	£1,590	£1,720	£1,720	£1,720	£1,720
Widow's bereavement allowance[6]	£1,150	£1,250	£1,320	£1,370	£1,490	£1,590	£1,720	£1,720	£1,720	£1,720
Dependent relative allowance[7]:										
Maintained by single woman	£145	£145	£145	£145	–	–	–	–	–	–
Other cases	£100	£100	£100	£100	–	–	–	–	–	–
Limit of relative's income	£1,804	£1,901	£1,901	£1,901	–	–	–	–	–	–
Daughter's or son's services allowance[8]	£55	£55	£55	£55	–	–	–	–	–	–
Housekeeper allowance[9]	£100	£100	£100	£100	–	–	–	–	–	–
Blind person's allowance[10]	£360	£360	£360	£540	£540	£540	£1,080	£1,080	£1,080	£1,080
Life assurance relief[11]										
(Percentage of gross premium)	*15.0* or Nil	*15.0* or Nil	*15.0* or Nil	*15.0* or Nil	*15.0* or Nil	*15.0* or Nil	*15.0* or Nil	*15.0* or Nil	*15.0* or Nil	*15.0* or Nil

(1) The married man's allowance was that for a full year, payable instead of the personal allowance. In the year of marriage the allowance is reduced by one twelfth of the difference between the married and single personal allowances for each complete month (beginning on the sixth day of each calendar month) prior to the date of marriage. (2) Following the introduction of Independent Taxation from 1990–91 the married couple's allowance is introduced. It is payable in addition to the personal allowance. The married couple's allowance will initially be set against the husband's income. If there is any surplus this will be transferred to the wife. There will continue to be higher allowances for elderly taxpayers aged 65 to 74 or 75 and over. (3) The wife's earned income allowance has as its maximum value the amount shown: Where the earned income was less, the allowance is reduced to the actual amount of earned income. From 1990–91, under Independent Taxation, the allowance is abolished and wives obtain a personal allowance. (4) The age allowance replaces the single or married allowances, provided the taxpayer's income is below the limit shown. For incomes in excess of the limit, the allowance is reduced by £2 for each additional £3 of income until the ordinary single or married allowance is reached. For 1989–90 the allowance was reduced by £1 for each additional £2 of income. The relief was due where the taxpayer (or, prior to 1990–91, wife living with him) was aged 65 or over in the year of assessment. For 1987–88 et seq there is additional relief at a higher age. For 1987–88 and 1988–89 the increased relief was available to those aged 80 or over in the year of assessment. For 1989–90 and 1990–91 the increased level of relief is available to those aged 75 and over. The married age allowances were abolished in 1990–91, under Independent Taxation and replaced by age-related married couple's allowances. (5) The additional personal allowance may be claimed by a single parent (or by a married man if his wife is totally incapacitated) who maintains a resident child at his or her own expense. (6) Widow's bereavement allowance is due to a widow in the year of her husband's death and in the following year provided the widow has not remarried before the beginning of that year. (7) The dependent relative allowance was due to a taxpayer who maintained, wholly or partially, either (a) an aged or infirm relative, or (b) his or his wife's separated, divorced or widowed mother. The relative's income had to be below the limits shown in order for the full allowances to be given (the limit was equal to the basic National Insurance Retirement Pension). The allowance was reduced by the excess of the relative's income over the income limit. (8) The daughter's or son's services allowance could be claimed by an aged or infirm taxpayer who maintained a daughter or son on whose services the taxpayer or his wife were dependent. (9) The housekeeper allowance could be claimed by a widow or widower who had a resident housekeeper. (10) The blind person's allowance is due to a registered blind taxpayer and up to 1980–81 was reduced by the amount of any tax-free blindness disability pension which was receivable. Prior to 1990–91 where both spouses were blind the married man received two blind person's allowances. (11) Relief on life assurance premiums was given by deduction from the premium payable. From 1984–85, it is confined to policies made before 14 March 1984. (12) Allowances and reliefs for 1993/94 are based upon the provisions of the March 1993 Budget and ensuing Finance Act. (13) From 1994/95 the following reliefs and allowances are restricted to the 20% lower rate tax band: married couple's allowance, additional personal allowance, widow's bereavement allowance, maintenance payments, mortgage interest payments.

Reliefs, Charges and Other Deductions

Various reliefs are given from taxation by tax law or concessions. These are as follows:

Loss Relief provided by trading losses, which may be set against other income in the same tax year or against future profits from the same trade.

Top-slicing Reliefs, which are available in respect of lease premiums, copyright income, patent rights and certain life assurance profits. These seek to remove the unfairness from being taxed at a higher rate in one tax year when the income was earned over several.

Double Taxation Relief, where the same income is taxed in two countries, so that the total cost is no more than the higher of the two rates.

Stock Relief, which was available from 1974/5 to 1983/4 and sought to relieve the inflationary elements in stock profits.

In addition, certain annual payments or charges are available for set-off against taxable income. These include a number of legally enforceable payments and other obligations. Particular items are:

Annual payments under Deeds of Covenant. Since 14 March 1988, these are deductible only if made to a charity. Prior to that, they were deductible in all cases.

Interest relief on a qualifying loan or mortgage, up to a set limit (currently £30,000 for a house mortgage). Since 1983/4, this relief is usually given by deduction at source under the Mortgage Interest Relief at Source (MIRAS) scheme. From 6 April 1991 the amount of tax relief has been restricted to basic rate only and from 6 April 1994 this will be further restricted to lower rate (20%) only.

Medical insurance premiums paid for those aged 60 or more.

Independent Taxation

Since 6 April 1990, under the provisions for independent taxation, married women have become taxpayers in their own right. This brought to an end the legal situation which had existed since 1806 whereby a wife was regarded as her husband's chattel and all her income was his. All married women are now assessable and responsible for the payment of tax on their income, and are required where necessary to complete annual tax returns.

Since 1990 there has been only one personal allowance granted to all taxpayers, with an additional married couple's allowance. This latter allowance, given only to legally married couples who are living together, is given first to the husband. Only then, if he cannot use it, is it passed to his wife. Married couples are treated as husband and wife until separated or divorced.

All other allowances for Income Tax or Capital Gains Tax are now aimed at individuals rather than married couples, and each spouse has the full benefit of the basic rate tax band. This has both benefits and drawbacks. For example, Age Allowance is now restricted by only one income rather than two, but reliefs for annual charges, such as Life Assurance Relief or Covenants, are restricted to the relevant spouse's income only.

Tax Computations

The procedure for calculating an individual's tax liability is basically as set out below:

	£
Income from trade or employment	x
Less: Allowable expenses (of trade or employment)	(x)
Capital Allowances (for trade, if applicable)	(x)
Other income (including income grossed up at basic rate for any tax already deducted at source)	x
Less: Annual charges on income	(x)
Personal allowances	(x)
Amount chargeable to tax (also known as Total taxable income)	(x)

Tax assessed (at the rates applicable by band for the above total, also known as Tax borne)	(x)
Less: Tax deducted at source	(x)
Net tax underpaid or overpaid	(x)

Note: Before 1984 it was usual to deduct *Annual charges* from investment income before earned income to reduce the higher rates which then applied to investment income.

A worked example will make the procedure clearer. Assume the case of Sidney Clarke, who is employed as an accountant on a salary of £50,000 p.a. His employers allow him to use a 2-litre car costing £15,000 for business and private use in which he does average business mileage. He is a member of a professional body whose tax-allowable membership subscription amounts to £100. He receives annual dividend income of £100 from privatized shares and £500 in interest income. He has been married for several years. His tax computation (using 1993/4 data) appears below.

As may be seen from the calculations, Sidney Clarke has underpaid Income Tax. This is because his investment income has been taxed only at basic rate (25%) in the case of his interest income, and at the lower rate (20%) in the case of his dividends, but the rest of his income causes him to be assessed overall at 40%. The amount of his underpayment of tax on which he has been assessed is therefore £125. (Note: It is assumed that his PAYE code takes account of all other benefits and reliefs.)

Worked example: Sidney Clarke, Accountant

				£
Salaried income from employment				55,000
Benefits from employment (car) assessed as				2,990
Allowable expense				(100)
				57,890
Other income	*Received*	*Related tax credit*	*Grossed up*	
Dividends	£100	£25	£125	125
Interest	£500	£167	£667	667
				58,682
Personal allowance				(3,445)
Married couple's allowance				(1,720)
Amount chargeable to tax				£53,517
Tax assessed:				
Lower rate:	20% on	£2,500		500
Basic rate:	25% on	£21,700		5,425
Higher rate:	40% on	£30,317		11,727
		£53,517		17,652
Tax deducted at source:				
Dividends		£25		
Interest		£167		
PAYE		£17,335		
		£17,527		
				(17,527)
Net tax underpaid				£125

Capital Gains Tax

Capital Gains Tax (CGT) applies to gains on the disposal of capital assets and is payable by any taxpayer who sells, destroys, loses, exchanges or gives away an asset in the UK (or overseas if a UK resident). All reportable transactions must be notified to the Inland Revenue on purchase or sale through the Annual Return process and since 6 April 1989, tax has been payable at the highest marginal Income Tax rate. Despite the advent of Independent Taxation (see p. 76), transfers between spouses are *not* considered to be disposals, although tax on a wife's gains since 6 April 1990 is the liability of the wife.

CGT was introduced in the 1965 Finance Act, although it has been subject to considerable modification since, last consolidated in the Capital Gains Tax Act 1979.

Assessment and Collection

Taxpayers are assessed in the Income Tax year (6 April to 5 April), based upon a return supported (if needed) by documentary records of purchase and sale. As a taxpayer, you are expected to notify the Inland Revenue of all *Chargeable assets acquired* and all individual disposals where a settlement value in excess of £10,000 and a chargeable gain in excess of £1,000 is involved. Processes for assessments and penalties are the same as for Income Tax. CGT is always payable on 1 December after the end of the tax year.

Who Pays Capital Gains Tax

CGT is payable by individuals, trusts and partnerships. Companies pay Corporation Tax on their Capital Gains at the CGT rate. Tax is charged on any person or body resident or ordinarily resident in the UK. The Crown, certain quasi-governmental and international organizations, charities, housing associations, friendly societies and trade unions are among those exempt from the tax.

Taxable Gains

All gains over the annual limit (£5,800 per person for 1993/94) are chargeable, however no chargeable gains can arise on *exempted assets*. The principal items coming under this heading are:

- Your home (or your *main residence* if more than one is owned)
- Your chattels, i.e. personal possessions, worth less than £6,000 (£3,000 before 1989) at the time of disposal
- Motor vehicles, boats and other wasting assets, i.e. assets which normally lose value the longer held
- Life assurance policies
- Government Securities and qualifying Corporate Bonds, National Savings Certificates, British Savings Bonds and SAYE contracts
- Building society permanent interest-bearing shares
- Business Expansion Scheme (BES) investments (since 1986/7)
- Decorations for valour or gallantry
- British money and any foreign currency obtained for personal expenditure

In addition, no chargeable gain arises on the following disposals:

- Transactions between husband and wife
- Gifts to charities, housing associations or for the public benefit (e.g. to the British Museum)
- Disposals within a Personal Equity Plan (PEP)
- Legacies

Unit Trusts and Investment Trusts pay no Capital Gains Tax on investments, although holders of units or shares pay tax on any gains from sales of these. *Hold-over relief* is available on the transfer of certain assets by a joint claim by transferrer and transferee. This has the effect of reducing the value of the asset by the gain accruing to the transferrer.

Indexation and Losses

An indexation allowance, based on the increase in the Retail Price Index since 31 March 1982 (or from date of acquisition if later), can be used to reduce a gain. Since 6 April 1985, this may also be used to create or increase any loss arising on disposal. Losses may be offset against gains in a tax year or carried forward as an offset against future years. *Bed and breakfasting* is the means by which taxpayers may legitimately crystallize a loss (or gain) by selling shares or units and buying them back on the following day.

Private Residence

Gains from the disposal of a single or main private residence are exempt from tax. A taxpayer (and a married couple) are permitted to have only one private residence for this purpose and special rules exist where, for example, a second home is purchased or acquired or a part of the home is used for business purposes, or if the home is wholly or partly let. In these cases, any issues are generally determined on the basis of fact, i.e. by dint of usage in the case of the main residence and by floor space in apportioning the exempt and chargeable parts of the home. Further guidance is available in an Inland Revenue leaflet (CGT 4) entitled "Capital Gains Tax – Owner-Occupied Houses".

Shares and Securities

Particular rules have always operated for gains from share investments. Government Securities have ceased to be exempt since 1 July 1986. Special provisions exist for valuing quoted and unquoted shares and for rights, bonus and scrip issues. There are options regarding valuations of holdings at particular dates, and indexation and pooling arrangements which follow on from this. The area is quite complex and merits either further detailed investigation or professional advice. Some additional guidance is available in an Inland Revenue leaflet (CGT 13) "Capital Gains Tax – The Indexation Allowance for Quoted Shares".

Businesses

Businesses are taxed on the gain in the value of business assets since established, incorporated or acquired. Special reliefs exist to mitigate the effect of taxation in certain circumstances when assets are transferred to a new owner. *Roll-over relief* is given when an existing business is incorporated (i.e. the assets are transferred to a company) or when a business replaces an asset sold with another eligible asset for use in the business. *Retirement relief* is given when an individual reaches 55 or retires earlier due to ill-health. Further details are provided in an Inland Revenue leaflet (CGT 6) "Capital Gains Tax – Retirement Relief on Disposal of a Business".

Calculation of Capital Gains

The capital gain for tax purposes in a tax year is obtained through the following seven steps:

1. Determine the value attaching to the disposal – by reference to consideration (cash received) or, in the case of gifts or as a general reference point, market value.
2. Establish the gain, after allowing for the costs of acquiring, enhancing or disposing of the asset.
3. Apply indexation.
4. Identify whether any business reliefs apply.
5. Determine whether the relief (£6,000) on chattels reduces or eliminates any gains.
6. Claim the annual exemption.
7. Determine whether to apply losses brought forward or occurring in the year.

There is much scope for the tax planning of financial arrangements, for example, by deferring a disposal. It may be of benefit to taxpayers to consider such action under suitable advice during the course of the tax year.

Inheritance Tax

Tax has been levied on transfers at death since the end of the 19th century. The original tax, Estate Duty (also known as "death duties"), gave way in 1974 to Capital Transfer Tax, which sought to tax almost all transfers of capital at any time. This tax applied with varying rates and provisions until 18 March 1986, when it went through substantial change and was renamed Inheritance Tax. It is a tax on individuals, with husband and wife treated separately, and is principally payable on transfers made at death or in the 7 years preceding. It also operates (at half the rate at death) for lifetime transfers which are above and beyond those exempted from tax and cumulatively add to more than a ceiling amount (£150,000 for 1993/4).

Administration and Collection

Inheritance Tax is collected by the Inland Revenue and is assessed on returns by executors or personal representatives on behalf of the deceased. There are penalties for failure to render an account or return or to answer summons, and for fraudulent or negligent information. Generally, a return has to be made within 12 months of any transfer. Tax, however, is already payable 6 months after the same date, with interest accruing on a daily basis if unpaid.

Lifetime Transfers

All gifts, including Potentially Exempt Transfers (PETs) made within 7 years of death, are taxable once the total amount of such gifts or transfers exceeds the lifetime transfer ceiling (£150,000 for 1993/4).

Certain conditions apply under the *reservation rules*, which also existed under Estate Duty. These take effect where a transfer has been made with a reservation, such as where the transferrer continues to enjoy some benefit after passing on title. An example of this might be where a parent gives away his home to a child but continues to live in it. In such a situation, the gift will normally be treated as if it had been transferred on the date such a benefit finally ceases.

For the purposes of establishing the value of a transfer, the (open) market value at the time of the transfer is applied. The total value of the transfers on death or in the 7 years before will be taxed on a cumulative or "top-sliced" basis, adding the cumulative value of transfers in the 7 years before death to the estate passed at death.

Tapering relief is available to reduce the Inheritance Tax payable at death on lifetime transfers – at the rates of 20, 40, 60 and 80% in the fourth, fifth, sixth and seventh years after transfer respectively. Other reliefs are available for business property, agricultural land and buildings, woodlands, shares representing a controlling interest in a company and minority shareholdings in an unquoted company.

Exempt Transfers

Certain transfers are exempt from Inheritance Tax. These are:

- Transfers made as normal expenditure and paid out of income.
- Transfers up to £3,000 in any one tax year, with unused relief carried forward one year only.
- Small gifts (currently defined as £250 per individual donee).
- Marriage gifts by parents (up to £5,000 per parent), grandparents (up to £2,500 per grandparent), bride and groom (up to £2,500 to each other), other people (up to £1,000 per person).
- Transfers between spouses (but only up to £55,000 if to a non-UK-domiciled spouse).
- Gifts to charities, political parties, for the public benefit or for the national purpose.
- Gifts to housing associations and employee trusts.

Transfers on Death

A single rate of Inheritance Tax is applicable on death and has been fixed at 40% since 15 March 1988. (For the 2 years prior to that differential rates applied, and before 1986 the Capital Transfer Tax was effective, also with differential rates.) Transfers between spouses are exempt from this tax.

For the purposes of calculating liability, funeral expenses and overseas property disposal expenses may be deducted, and legacies which would form exempt lifetime transfers are also exempt at death.

Certain reliefs, known as *loss relief* and *quick succession relief*, are available to mitigate hardship caused by loss of value on sale or by the early death of a legatee.

Corporation Tax

Corporation Tax was introduced in 1965 and replaced Income Tax on companies. It is payable by all companies, clubs and associations operating in or from the United Kingdom. UK-resident companies are assessed on any income (profits) arising anywhere in the world, and non-resident companies are assessed on their UK income. The tax is assessed in the same way as Income Tax and uses the same schedules, with the same basic rules governing taxability of income and allowability of expense. Another tax, Petroleum Revenue Tax (PRT), is an additional tax payable by oil companies under the same broad aegis.

As for Income Tax, amendments to legislation are contained in Finance Acts, consolidated from time to time, the last occasion being in the Income and Corporation Taxes Act 1988.

Assessment and Collection

Tax is collected by direct assessment based upon accounting years which run from 1 April to 31 March and is generally payable 9 months after the company's year-end. Companies must pay Advanced Corporation Tax (ACT) on dividends and certain distributions. The tax is deductible from the final Corporation Tax liability for the year and thus should normally be only a pre-payment rather than an expense. If the amount of ACT exceeds the company's UK Corporation Tax liability for any reason, the ACT may be carried forward, or back for up to 6 accounting years, or else surrendered to a subsidiary. Companies with substantial overseas earnings may, however, find that there is a difficulty in utilizing this relief and it may need to be carried forward as an unrelieved expense. From 6 April 1993 the rate of ACT is 22.5/77.5 of the amount of dividend, paid after deducting any franked investment income paid. From 5 April 1994 the rate of ACT will be 20/80.

Rates of Corporation Tax

Income (profits) for an accounting period (which may be shorter, but no longer, than 12 months) are determined on normal taxation principles. The rate of tax is fixed for an accounting period ending on 31 March, with apportionment to periods before and after if the accounting period overlaps this date.

The Corporation Tax rate has been progressively reduced as follows for the years ending 31 March:

Year	Rate
1985	45%
1986	40%

1987–90	35%
1991	34%
1993–94	33%

A small companies rate is applied where profits do not exceed certain limits (independently of the actual size of the company). The limits and rates have been as follows for the years ending 31 March:

Year	Limit	Rate
1985–86	£100,000	30%
1987	£100,000	29%
1988	£100,000	27%
1989	£100,000	25%
1990	£150,000	25%
1991	£200,000	25%
1992–94	£250,000	25%

A marginal small companies rate relief applies for profits up to £1,250,000, such that the first £250,000 of profits are taxed at the small companies rate with a marginal rate (35% for 1993/94) applying for the remaining amount. The small companies rate has not been available for close investment companies (essentially companies in which shares are closely held) since 31 March 1989.

Capital gains have been taxed at the Corporation Tax rate since 17 March 1987. Prior to that date, an effective 30% rate was applied, as for individuals, but with no annual exemptions. The change means the rate for capital gains is currently 33% for 1993/4, but could be at the small companies rate of 25% if insufficient profits arise.

Groups of Companies

Each company within a group is separately assessed on its profits and capital gains. Where one company makes a loss, however, a claim may be made to offset this loss against the profits of another company in the same group. Claims may also be made to avoid payment of ACT or the deduction of Income Tax on payment of interest between group companies. Capital transfers between companies of the group similarly incur no tax liability on any capital gain arising.

Value Added Tax

Value Added Tax (VAT) was introduced in the UK in 1973 and replaced the old Purchase Tax and Selective Employment Tax. It has been progressively introduced within the European Community (it was a condition of UK membership) and the world's major economies. The tax is simple to operate and understand and inexpensive for governments to collect. However, there are many complicated elements and this guide can only touch the surface of the issues involved.

Administration and Collection

In the United Kingdom VAT is charged on all types of goods or services forming a taxable supply in the UK, unless these are specified as exempt or zero-rated. As a direct tax, it is charged and collected only by those taxable companies or individuals who are registered for VAT purposes. (For 1993/4 this means those with taxable turnover of £37,600 or more.) Qualification for registration is fairly complex, and late notification can have unfortunate and penal consequences. If you think you may be eligible, you should contact your local Customs and Excise (VAT) office for more details.

Taxable persons effectively bear and charge on (where possible) tax on the value added by their business. The tax borne is the difference between the *Input Tax* paid over to suppliers and the *Output Tax* charged to customers. Input and Output Tax are accounted for in quarterly returns (monthly for certain taxpayers), and a net payment is generally made over to Customs and Excise at that time.

In general, VAT inspectors have extremely wide powers, with both criminal and civil penalties available since July 1985. Inter alia, VAT inspectors have (and exercise) the right to inspect a trader's records to ensure compliance with regulations and (with good cause) to enter and search premises and persons at any time.

Types of Supply

Goods or services supplied may be any of the following:

Standard-rated (and chargeable for 1993/4 at 17½%)
Zero-rated (i.e. chargeable, but currently the rate is set at zero)
Exempt (i.e. outside the scope of the system)

To the non-registered, the zero-rated and exempt categories mean that no VAT is payable. However, VAT-registered suppliers may relieve Input Tax paid on zero-rated goods, but not that on exempt goods (see right). Partial exemption of a business occurs where some sales of goods or services fall within the tax and the rest do not. In such circumstances, only part of the Input Tax is relieved and the rest must be borne as a business expense.

Input Tax Disallowances

Relief for Input Tax can be obtained by offset against Output Tax due or by repayment. Certain items are not relievable and the tax must be borne by the registered person. These include cars, business entertainment expenses and goods acquired for personal use.

Exempt Supplies

Exempt supplies include the following groups of goods or services:

- Land
- Insurance
- Postal services
- Betting, gaming and lottery activities
- Finance, including banking and broking activities
- Education and incidental services
- Health and welfare
- Burial and cremation
- Trade unions and professional bodies
- Sports competitions
- Works of art, etc.
- Fund-raising events by charities and other qualifying bodies

Zero-rated Supplies

Items are zero-rated if they fall within one of the following groups:

- Food
- Water and sewerage services
- Books, including the Talking Books for the Blind service

- News services
- Power and fuel
- Construction of buildings
- Protected buildings
- International goods and services
- Transport
- Caravans
- Houseboats
- Gold
- Banknotes
- Drugs and medicines
- Children's clothing and footwear
- Aids for the handicapped

Tax Point and Tax Invoice

The point at which liability to tax occurs is known as the tax point. Special rules exist to prevent manipulation of dates, either for deferment of VAT, to take advantage of tax rate changes or for any other reason. The tax point is essentially the date at which a tax invoice is raised and (with two main exceptions) is the date when the supply of goods or services is made – or made available – to the customer. The two exceptions relate to when an invoice is issued subsequently – in which case it must be within 14 days of supply – or when payment is made in advance, in which case the date of receipt becomes the tax point. Under certain circumstances the Customs and Excise office may accept different tax points, for which they will provide written permission.

Stamp Duty

Stamp Duty is a tax on documents rather than transactions, but becomes payable on transfers of certain assets. It was introduced in 1891. As a tax, it has affected fewer and fewer activities.

Duty is payable at the rate of 0.5% on all sales of shares and marketable securities and at 1% on sales of land and other property (including new leasehold premiums) with a value in excess of £60,000 (as from 16 March 1993, with a limit of £30,000 operating prior to that date). It is payable at rates from 1% to 24% on the rent of new leases.

Several reliefs are available and include exemptions for:

- Gifts
- Transfers between *associated companies*

National Insurance Contributions

National Insurance is an insurance premium rather than a tax, but it long ago lost most of its links with insurance and is now more in the nature of a second Income Tax. It is collected from most taxpayers by their employers under the PAYE scheme, and there are 4 classes involved.

Class 1	Paid by employees at a variable rate
Class 1A	Paid by the employer on employees' car and fuel benefits
Class 2	Paid by the self-employed at a fixed rate
Class 3	A voluntary contribution payable by an individual (e.g. a widow) who would otherwise not be eligible for social security benefits
Class 4	Paid by the self-employed at a variable rate

EMPLOYMENT & SOCIAL SECURITY

News of bankruptcies, job losses and redundancies dominated the employment scene in 1992/3. The young were hardest hit, with one in five males and one in seven females under 19 being unemployed. Among the ethnic minorities, the Pakistani/Bangladeshi community suffered the worst unemployment – almost 25%.

The number of men in the labour force has remained fairly static in recent years, but the number of working women has continued to grow. Indeed, it is estimated that women will make up 45% of the civilian labour force by 2001. This is partly attributed to low birth rates in the 1970s and partly to a rise in the average age at which women have children.

The ageing population of the United Kingdom means that it also has an ageing workforce. Those over 45 currently outnumber those under 24 by 3.2 million, but the gap is predicted to widen to 5.2 million by 2001.

Between 1971 and 1992 there was a 40% fall in the number of employees in manufacturing. This meant that only one-fifth of all employees were in manufacturing, while nearly three-quarters were in services. In tandem with this change, six out of ten self-employed people were in the services sector. In recent times the areas of biggest growth have been banking and finance.

Despite suspicions to the contrary, men in the UK work longer hours than in the rest of Europe – an average of 44 hours per week. British women, on the other hand, are second only to the Dutch in working the shortest hours in Europe – an average of 30.5 hours per week. However, 45% of British women are part-time workers.

Continuing the trend for good industrial relations, only 800,000 working days were lost through strikes in 1991, the lowest figure since records began 100 years ago.

Distribution of the Workforce

At mid-June each year

Source: CSO

Thousands, seasonally adjusted

United Kingdom	1979	1980	1981	1982	1983	1984	1985	1986	1987	1988	1989	1990	1991[11]
Workforce[1]	26,580	26,759	26,697	26,610	26,633	27,309	27,743	27,877	28,007	28,347	28,480	28,530	28,340
Males	16,174	16,247	16,288	16,175	16,113	16,350	16,509	16,442	16,414	16,427	16,346	16,323	16,240
Females	10,406	10,511	10,409	10,435	10,519	10,959	11,234	11,435	11,663	11,920	12,134	12,208	12,100
Unemployed[2,3,4,5]	1,068	1,274	2,176	2,521	2,905	2,897	3,019	3,121	2,836	2,295	1,785	1,611	2,293
Males	770	910	1,605	1,848	2,028	2,040	2,100	2,154	1,979	1,600	1,276	1,189	1,739
Females	297	363	571	673	778	857	919	967	858	695	510	422	554
Workforce in employment[6]	25,365	25,301	24,323	23,889	23,611	24,226	24,530	24,559	25,084	25,922	26,693	26,918	26,043
Males	15,328	15,242	14,569	14,213	13,961	14,201	14,294	14,173	14,341	14,746	15,069	15,133	14,498
Females	10,037	10,059	9,754	9,676	9,650	10,025	10,236	10,386	10,744	11,176	11,624	11,785	11,544
HM Forces[7]	314	323	334	324	322	326	326	322	319	316	308	303	297
Males	299	307	317	309	306	310	309	305	302	300	291	286	278
Females	15	16	17	15	16	16	16	16	16	16	16	18	19
Self-employed persons (with or without employees)[8]	1,906	2,013	2,119	2,169	2,219	2,496	2,614	2,633	2,869	2,998	3,253	3,298	3,143
Males	1,550	1,622	1,694	1,699	1,703	1,901	1,976	1,993	2,157	2,264	2,487	2,511	2,396
Females	357	391	425	471	517	595	637	640	712	734	766	786	747
Employees in employment[9]	23,145	22,965	21,870	21,395	21,054	21,229	21,414	21,379	21,586	22,266	22,670	22,894	22,259
Males	13,480	13,313	12,558	12,205	11,944	11,895	11,908	11,748	11,705	11,978	11,999	12,076	11,613
Females	9,665	9,652	9,312	9,190	9,109	9,334	9,506	9,631	9,881	10,288	10,671	10,818	10,646
of whom													
Total, production and construction industries	9,215	8,911	8,068	7,621	7,232	7,080	6,992	6,777	6,688	6,746	6,753	6,686	6,247
Total, all manufacturing industries	7,258	6,944	6,230	5,873	5,538	5,424	5,377	5,242	5,171	5,215	5,208	5,167	4,846
Work-related Government Training Programmes[10]	–	–	–	–	16	175	176	226	311	343	462	423	343
Males	–	–	–	–	8	95	100	127	177	205	291	260	211
Females	–	–	–	–	8	80	76	99	134	138	171	163	132

Note: Because the figures have been rounded independently totals may differ from the sum of the components. Also the totals may include some employees whose industrial classification could not be ascertained.

(1) The workforce is the workforce in employment plus the claimant unemployed. (2) From October 1982 new basis (claimants); see article in *Employment Gazette*, December 1982, page S20. (3) From October 1980 the figures are affected by the introduction in Great Britain of fortnightly payment of unemployment benefit. This is estimated to have resulted in an artificial increase of 20,000 (13,000 males and 7,000 females) in the count of the unemployed and therefore a corresponding reduction should be made when comparing the 1980 figures with those of earlier years. (4) From April 1983, the figures of unemployment reflect the effects of the provisions in the Budget for some men aged 60 and over who no longer have to sign on at an unemployment office. It is estimated that 132,500 men were affected over the period April to June 1983, and a further 29,300 were affected in July and August 1983, the total effect was a reduction in the coverage of the unemployment count of 161,800. (5) Due to a change in the compilation of the unemployment stastistics to remove over-recording (see *Employment Gazette*, March/April 1986, pp. 107–108), unadjusted figures from February 1986 are not directly comparable with earlier figures. It is estimated that the change reduced the total UK count by 50,000 on average. (6) The workforce in employment comprises employees in employment, the self-employed, HM Forces and work-related government training programmes. (7) HM Forces figures, provided by the Ministry of Defence, represent the total number of UK service personnel, male and female, in HM Regular Forces, wherever serving and including those on release leave. (8) Estimates of the self-employed up to mid-1989 are based on the 1981 Census of population and the results of the Labour Force Surveys. A detailed description of the current estimates is given in the article on p. 182 of the April 1990 edition of *Employment Gazette*. (9) Estimates of employees in employment from December 1987 to August 1989 include an allowance based on the Labour Force Survey to compensate for persistent undercounting in the regular sample enquiries (*Employment Gazette*, October 1989, p. 56). For all dates, individuals with two jobs as employees of different employers are counted twice. (10) Includes all participants on government training and employment programmes who are receiving some work experience on their placement but who do not have a contract of employment (those with a contract are included in the employees in employment series). The numbers are not subject to seasonal adjustment. (11) Estimates from September 1989 are based on data provided by the New Panel of employers (see article on p. 191 of the April 1992 edition of *Employment Gazette*).

Employees in Employment[1]

United Kingdom

Source: CSO

Thousands

	1971	1979	1981	1983	1986	1990	1991	1992
All industries	22,139	23,173	21,892	21,067	21,387	22,899	22,229	21,758
of which								
Males	13,726	13,487	12,562	11,940	11,744	12,069	11,592	11,253
Females	8,413	9,686	9,331	9,127	9,644	10,830	10,637	10,504
Manufacturing	8,065	7,253	6,222	5,525	5,227	5,138	4,793	4,589
Services	11,627	13,580	13,468	13,501	14,297	15,945	15,744	15,644
Other	2,447	2,340	2,203	2,042	1,863	1,817	1,692	1,524
Employees in employment by SIC[2] division								
Agriculture, forestry and fishing	450	380	363	350	329	298	291	283
Energy and water supply	798	722	710	648	545	449	439	403
Other minerals and ore extraction, etc.	1,282	1,147	939	817	729	721	657	635
Metal goods, engineering and vehicles	3,709	3,374	2,923	2,548	2,372	2,310	2,139	2,030
Other manufacturing industries	3,074	2,732	2,360	2,159	2,126	2,106	1,997	1,924
Construction	1,198	1,239	1,130	1,044	989	1,070	962	839
Distribution, catering and repairs	3,686	4,257	4,172	4,118	4,298	4,822	4,686	4,605
Transport and communication	1,556	1,479	1,425	1,345	1,298	1,382	1,349	1,324
Banking, finance, insurance, etc	1,336	1,647	1,739	1,875	2,166	2,744	2,687	2,639
Other services	5,049	6,197	6,132	6,163	6,536	6,996	7,022	7,076

(1) As at June each year (2) Standard Industrial Classification.

Self-employed[1]

Great Britain

Source: CSO

Thousands

	Standard Industrial Classification (1980)	1971	1979	1981	1983	1986	1989	1990	1992
All industries[2]	0–9	1,953	1,842	2,058	2,160	2,799	3,182	3,222	3,212
of which									
Males		1,556	1,494	1,641	1,652	2,109	2,428	2,449	2,422
Females		397	348	417	508	690	754	773	791
Manufacturing	2–4	129	140	146	150	257	280	272	348
Services	6–9	1,199	1,102	1,274	1,355	1,694	1,934	1,981	1,871
Other	0, 1, 5	625	601	638	656	844	967	969	981
Employees in employment by SIC division									
Agriculture, forestry and fishing	0	282	257	250	246	265	243	247	294
Energy and water supply	1	0	1	1	1	3	2	3	11
Other minerals and ore extraction, etc	2	4	6	7	9	20	13	18	27
Metal goods, engineering and vehicles	3	35	42	46	46	83	83	85	107
Other manufacturing industries	4	90	92	93	95	154	185	168	214
Construction	5	342	343	388	409	575	722	718	676
Distribution, catering and repairs	6	726	636	698	701	823	824	809	746
Transport and communication	7	65	87	99	92	120	162	172	173
Banking, finance, insurance, etc	8	148	145	188	214	299	372	409	447
Other services	9	261	234	288	348	452	576	591	506

(1) At spring each year. (2) Includes workplace outside the UK and industry group not stated.

Economic activity: 1981[1]

Great Britain: all residents

Source: CSO

Thousands

	Total	Age last birthday							
		Under 20	20–24	25–34	35–44	45–54	55–59	60–64	65 and over
Males: total population (aged 16 and over)	19,929	1,821	2,004	3,835	3,250	3,011	1,542	1,310	3,155
Total economically inactive (aged 16 and over)	4,430	645	218	110	71	109	130	333	2,815
Students	896	627	193	60	13	4	–	–	–
Retired	2,923	–	–	–	3	10	28	181	2,702
Permanently sick	512	8	13	31	43	86	98	147	85
Other	99	10	11	18	12	9	5	5	28

(Continued)

Thousands

		Age last birthday							
	Total	Under 20	20–24	25–34	35–44	45–54	55–59	60–64	65 and over
Total economically active	15,499	1,177	1,787	3,725	3,180	2,902	1,412	977	340
Self-employed (included above)	1,840	23	103	435	496	407	160	120	95
In employment	13,736	949	1,492	3,326	2,902	2,648	1,263	822	333
Working full-time	13,374	933	1,476	3,299	2,881	2,625	1,243	788	130
Working part-time	362	17	17	27	21	24	20	33	203
Out of employment	1,763	227	294	399	278	253	149	156	7
Seeking work	1,595	222	286	374	246	214	122	129	5
Temporarily sick	168	5	9	25	32	39	27	27	3
Females: total population (aged 16 and over)	21,687	1,746	1,954	3,797	3,223	3,039	1,625	1,474	4,830
Total economically inactive (aged 16 and over)	11,809	760	602	1,733	1,112	1,032	776	1,144	4,651
Students	862	672	139	34	13	4	–	–	–
Retired	1,785	–	–	–	3	10	38	298	1,437
Permanently sick	357	6	11	26	33	62	58	31	130
Other	8,806	82	451	1,673	1,064	958	680	815	3,083
Total economically active	9,878	986	1,352	2,064	2,110	2,007	849	330	179
Self-employed (included above)	457	5	23	100	128	107	43	26	26
In employment	9,146	814	1,196	1,909	2,014	1,912	802	324	174
Working full-time	5,602	776	1,092	1,163	975	1,013	417	117	50
Working part-time	3,543	38	104	746	1,039	899	385	207	125
Out of employment	732	172	157	155	96	95	47	6	5
Seeking work	645	165	147	139	79	72	36	4	3
Temporarily sick	88	7	10	16	17	22	11	2	2

(1) During the week before the census (5 April 1981).

The Best 50 Companies for Women

Source: Scarlett MacGwire, *Best Companies for Women*, Pandora Books, 1992

The companies were selected from a total of 500 on the basis of their answers to questionnaires about policy concerning women. The answers were assessed on a sector-by-sector basis: it seemed unfair to judge an engineering company employing very few women, for instance, against a finance company with a large female workforce. At least three women were interviewed from each company, of whom at least one was a mother.

Companies were rated on eight areas: **Equal opportunities policy** – showing how discrimination was avoided; **Equal opportunities recruitment** – to ensure enough women were hired at all levels; **Monitoring** – making sure policies worked; **Positive action** – from announcing targets on recruitment and promotion to women-only training courses; **Crèches**; **Careers breaks** – up to five years off after giving birth; **Jobshares**; **Flexible hours** – any type of part-time arrangements.

Yes ✓ No ✗

	Equal opps policy	Equal opps recruitment	Monitoring	Positive action	Crèche	Career breaks	Job-shares	Flexible hours
Councils								
Cambridge City Council	✓	✓	✓	✗	✗	✓	✓	✓
Edinburgh District Council	✓	✓	✓	✓	✓	✗	✓	✓
Gloucestershire County Council	✓	✓	✓	✓	✓	✓	✓	✓
Leicester City Council	✓	✓	✓	✓	✓	✓	✓	✓
London Borough of Islington	✓	✓	✓	✓	✓	✓	✓	✓
Oxfordshire County Council	✓	✓	✓	✓	✓	✓	✓	✓
Sheffield City Council	✓	✓	✓	✓	✗	✓	✓	✓
Engineering								
British Aerospace	✓	✓	✓	✓	✓	✗	✗	✓
Brown & Root (UK)	✓	✗	✗	✗	✗	✗	✓	✓
General Electric Company	✓	✓	✓	✗	✓	✓	✓	✓
Lucas Industries	✓	✓	✓	✓	✗	✗	✗	✓
Ove Arup	✓	✓	✗	✗	✗	✓	✗	✓
The Rover Group	✓	✓	✓	✓	✓	✗	✓	✗
Finance								
Alliance & Leicester Building Society	✓	✓	✗	✗	✗	✓	✓	✓
Barclays Bank	✓	✓	✓	✗	✗	✓	✓	✓
Halifax Building Society	✓	✓	✓	✗	✗	✓	✓	✓
Legal & General	✓	✓	✓	✗	✗	✓	✓	✓
Midland Bank	✓	✓	✓	✓	✓	✓	✓	✓
National Westminster Bank	✓	✓	✓	✓	✗	✓	✓	✓
Prudential Corporation	✓	✓	✓	✓	✓	✓	✓	✓
Royal Bank of Scotland	✓	✓	✓	✗	✗	✓	✓	✓
Sun Life of Canada	✓	✓	✗	✗	✗	✗	✓	✓
TSB	✓	✓	✓	✓	✓	✓	✓	✓
Hi-Tech								
Bull HN Information Systems	✓	✓	✗	✗	✗	✓	✓	✓
International Computers	✓	✓	✓	✗	✗	✓	✓	✓
Rank Xerox	✓	✓	✓	✓	✗	✓	✓	✓
Manufacturing								
Imperial Chemical Industries	✓	✓	✓	✓	✓	✓	✓	✓
Mars Confectionery	✓	✓	✓	✓	✓	✓	✗	✓
Smith's	✓	✓	✗	✗	✗	✗	✓	✓
Media								
BBC	✓	✓	✓	✓	✓	✓	✓	✓
Channel 4	✓	✓	✓	✗	✗	✗	✓	✓

(Continued)

Yes ✓ No ×

	Equal opps policy	Equal opps recruitment	Monitoring	Positive action	Crèche	Career breaks	Job-shares	Flexible hours
Media *(Continued)*								
London Weekend Television	✓	✓	✓	✓	✓	×	×	✓
Research & Development Services	×	×	✓	×	✓	×	×	✓
Thames Television	✓	✓	✓	✓	✓	×	✓	✓
Yorkshire Television	✓	✓	✓	×	×	×	✓	✓
Oil companies								
British Petroleum	✓	✓	✓	✓	✓	✓	✓	✓
Esso	✓	✓	✓	×	×	✓	×	✓
Shell	✓	✓	✓	✓	×	✓	✓	✓
Public and private services								
The British Council	✓	✓	✓	✓	✓	✓	✓	✓
British Rail	✓	✓	✓	✓	×	✓	✓	✓
British Telecom	✓	✓	✓	×	×	✓	✓	✓
The Civil Service	✓	✓	✓	✓	✓	✓	✓	✓
National & Local Government Officers Association	✓	✓	×	×	✓	✓	✓	✓
*National Health Service	✓	✓	✓	✓	✓	✓	✓	✓
Croydon District Health Authority	✓	✓	✓	×	×	✓	✓	✓
Retail								
Boots the Chemist	✓	✓	✓	×	×	✓	✓	✓
Littlewoods	✓	✓	✓	✓	×	✓	✓	✓
Marks & Spencer	✓	✓	✓	×	×	✓	✓	✓
Sainsbury's	✓	✓	✓	×	✓	✓	✓	✓
Voluntary organizations								
Oxfam	✓	✓	✓	×	✓	×	✓	✓

*Arrangements vary according to the health authority.

Economic Activity of Women with Children: 1989–1991

Great Britain

Source: CSO

Percentages

	Professional or employer/ manager	Intermediate and junior non-manual	Skilled manual	Semi-skilled manual	Unskilled manual	All women aged 16–59
Youngest child aged 0–4						
Working full-time	34	14	15	8	2	13
Working part-time	27	31	31	23	49	30
Unemployed	2	4	5	5	3	4
Economically inactive	35	50	48	63	45	52
Youngest child aged 5–9						
Working full-time	48	21	30	14	3	21
Working part-time	30	49	43	49	64	48
Unemployed	2	4	4	4	7	4
Economically inactive	20	26	23	33	26	26
Youngest child aged 10 and over						
Working full-time	63	36	37	22	5	33
Working part-time	28	43	42	44	70	44
Unemployed	1	2	4	3	4	3
Economically inactive	8	18	18	29	21	20
No dependent children						
Working full-time	78	60	52	41	12	55
Working part-time	9	20	21	24	51	21
Unemployed	2	4	4	7	5	4
Economically inactive	10	15	22	26	31	18
All women aged 16–59						
Working full-time	67	44	39	28	8	40
Working part-time	16	28	29	30	56	29
Unemployed	2	4	4	6	5	4
Economically inactive	14	23	27	35	31	26

Average Weekly and Hourly Earnings and Hours of Full-time Employees on Adult Rates

Great Britain

New Earnings Survey: April of each year

Source: CSO

	All industries				Manufacturing industries[1]			
	Average weekly earnings[2]	Average hours[3]	Average hourly earnings[2,3] including overtime	Average hourly earnings[2,3] excluding overtime	Average weekly earnings[2]	Average hours[3]	Average hourly earnings[2,3] including overtime	Average hourly earnings[2,3] excluding overtime
	£		p	p	£		p	p
All adults								
1985	171.0	40.4	416.8	412.7	174.7	41.9	411.8	404.8
1986	184.7	40.4	450.8	446.8	188.6	41.9	444.4	437.7
1987	198.9	40.4	484.7	481.1	202.0	42.0	474.1	467.6
1988	218.4	40.6	529.2	525.9	219.4	42.3	509.4	501.7
1989	239.7	40.7	580.7	578.5	239.5	42.5	555.3	547.9
1990	263.1	40.5	636.8	634.4	262.8	42.4	609.1	601.1
1991	284.7	40.0	700.2	698.3	280.7	41.3	669.0	661.9

(Continued)

	All industries				Manufacturing industries[1]			
	Average weekly earnings[2] £	Average hours[3]	Average hourly earnings[2,3] including overtime p	Average hourly earnings[2,3] excluding overtime p	Average weekly earnings[2] £	Average hours[3]	Average hourly earnings[2,3] including overtime p	Average hourly earnings[2,3] excluding overtime p
All men								
1985	192.4	41.9	452.5	449.9	192.6	42.9	444.3	438.6
1986	207.5	41.8	488.9	486.6	207.8	42.9	479.1	474.0
1987	224.0	41.9	527.3	526.2	222.3	43.0	511.0	506.5
1988	245.8	42.1	573.6	573.1	242.3	43.3	549.8	544.1
1989	269.5	42.3	627.6	629.0	264.6	43.6	598.4	593.7
1990	295.6	42.2	687.8	689.2	289.2	43.4	655.0	649.7
1991	318.9	41.5	755.3	756.9	308.1	42.1	720.4	715.4
Manual men								
1985	163.6	44.5	368.0	356.8	172.6	44.6	386.8	373.8
1986	174.4	44.5	392.6	380.8	183.4	44.5	411.6	398.5
1987	185.5	44.6	416.5	404.3	195.9	44.7	437.6	423.8
1988	200.6	45.0	445.7	431.5	212.3	45.2	468.5	451.7
1989	217.8	45.3	480.9	466.2	230.6	45.5	506.2	488.7
1990	237.2	45.2	524.6	508.5	250.0	45.2	551.3	532.4
1991	253.1	44.4	569.9	554.1	261.8	43.7	598.4	580.2
Non-manual men								
1985	225.0	38.6	574.7	573.2	232.0	39.3	582.0	580.7
1986	244.9	38.6	627.3	625.8	255.7	39.3	641.0	640.0
1987	265.9	38.7	679.9	679.3	273.7	39.4	684.1	684.0
1988	294.1	38.7	748.8	748.3	300.5	39.4	744.9	744.1
1989	323.6	38.8	823.3	824.0	331.5	39.6	821.9	822.8
1990	354.9	38.7	901.6	902.1	364.1	39.6	903.4	903.8
1991	375.7	38.7	954.9	956.3	379.2	39.5	942.9	944.5
All women								
1985	126.4	37.3	334.0	332.4	114.7	38.8	294.4	291.5
1986	137.2	37.3	362.5	360.7	123.2	38.8	316.1	313.3
1987	148.1	37.5	388.4	386.2	133.4	39.0	339.2	335.9
1988	164.2	37.6	431.3	429.0	144.3	39.2	365.8	362.3
1989	182.3	37.6	480.2	478.2	159.1	39.1	403.9	400.2
1990	201.5	37.5	530.1	527.9	177.1	39.1	447.5	443.5
1991	222.4	37.4	591.1	589.1	192.9	38.8	494.4	490.6
Manual women								
1985	101.3	39.5	256.9	252.9	104.5	40.0	261.7	257.3
1986	107.5	39.5	273.0	269.2	111.6	40.0	278.9	274.6
1987	115.3	39.7	292.0	287.4	119.6	40.3	297.2	291.9
1988	123.6	39.8	310.5	305.6	127.9	40.5	315.5	309.6
1989	134.9	39.9	338.7	333.3	138.2	40.4	341.8	335.0
1990	148.0	39.8	372.4	366.1	152.8	40.5	377.1	369.3
1991	159.2	39.7	401.4	395.2	162.1	40.0	405.6	398.3
Non-manual women								
1985	133.8	36.6	359.1	357.6	126.8	37.4	336.5	334.7
1986	145.7	36.7	390.6	388.8	136.7	37.4	363.2	361.2
1987	157.2	36.8	418.0	415.9	149.1	37.5	391.6	389.4
1988	175.5	36.9	467.7	465.3	163.3	37.6	430.0	427.5
1989	195.0	36.9	521.9	519.7	182.8	37.6	481.6	479.5
1990	215.5	36.9	575.5	573.1	202.8	37.6	530.8	528.5
1991	236.8	36.8	638.1	636.0	221.8	37.6	585.6	583.1

(1) Results for manufacturing industries relate to Divisions 2, 3 and 4 of the 1980 SIC (Standard Industrial Classification). (2) The figures are gross before deductions. Generally they exclude the value of earnings in kind, but include payment such as overtime (except where otherwise stated), bonus, commission and shift premiums for the pay period. (3) The estimates given relate only to employees for whom normal basic hours were reported. (4) Manual and non-manual results for 1986–1989 inclusive and the first row of figures for 1990 are based on the list of Key Occupations for Statistical Purposes (KOS). Results for 1991 and the second row of figures for 1990 are based on the Standard Occupational Classification (SOC).

Average Earnings Index: All Employees

Great Britain

Source: CSO

1988 = 100

	Agriculture and forestry[1]	Coal and coke[2]	Mineral oil and natural gas	Electricity, gas, other energy and water supply	Metal processing and manufacturing	Mineral extraction and manufacturing	Chemicals and man-made fibres	Mechanical engineering	Electrical and electronic engineering	Motor vehicles and parts	Other transport equipment	Metal goods and instruments	Food, drink and tobacco	Textiles
1989	108.0	113.3	110.3	109.8	107.2	109.4	109.0	109.8	109.5	109.9	112.7	107.9	109.3	107.4
1990	120.0	125.0	126.7	121.6	115.5	119.1	122.6	119.3	119.3	119.5	125.6	117.5	121.7	117.6
1991	132.1	141.9	140.4	134.2	122.8	125.9	134.0	130.2	129.5	129.1	136.2	124.7	134.6	128.1
1991														
January	118.7	137.8	139.6	125.7	123.2	122.3	126.3	124.2	123.6	124.5	135.0	119.9	127.0	120.8
February	122.0	141.0	131.5	127.8	114.9	121.9	129.7	126.6	125.3	124.8	132.4	121.8	128.4	121.9
March	120.9	142.7	136.0	126.4	116.9	122.2	135.4	127.8	127.3	124.9	135.7	122.0	131.3	123.1
April	129.9	139.3	140.0	127.8	127.2	123.7	129.9	129.1	127.1	139.4	139.2	122.6	135.5	124.5
May	126.4	140.6	140.8	140.9	119.5	125.8	130.7	129.2	129.4	126.7	133.2	123.9	135.9	126.7
June	127.1	142.2	141.7	129.0	119.8	128.0	131.6	131.6	132.1	131.2	135.5	124.4	135.5	129.7
July	134.4	139.7	145.1	133.4	128.6	127.5	132.4	131.0	131.0	131.3	136.0	127.4	134.5	132.9
August	160.4	141.5	140.8	140.8	125.9	126.5	134.6	130.5	129.3	124.9	136.2	124.3	134.3	130.6
September	147.6	140.7	140.4	146.1	120.8	127.2	135.5	130.6	129.6	127.0	135.3	126.7	134.7	129.7
October	137.6	141.8	141.1	136.2	130.1	127.3	136.8	132.6	131.7	129.1	139.8	125.9	135.0	131.6
November	130.4	152.7	141.1	139.1	121.8	128.5	140.6	134.5	133.0	131.5	139.0	128.0	141.3	132.0
December	129.7	142.8	146.5	137.6	125.2	130.2	144.4	135.1	134.6	134.3	137.6	129.4	141.5	133.9

(Continued)

	Leather, footwear and clothing	Paper products, printing and publishing	Rubber, plastics, timber and other manufacturing	Construction	Distribution and repairs	Hotels and catering	Transport and communication[3]	Banking, finance and insurance	Public administration	Education and health	Other services[4]	Whole economy
1988	100.0	100.0	100.0	100.0	100.0	100.0	100.0	100.0	100.0	100.0	100.0	100.0
1989	107.1	106.1	107.7	111.8	108.6	107.6	107.6	109.9	108.8	108.6	111.3	109.1
1990	115.8	113.5	117.5	124.6	117.3	118.4	118.8	121.2	120.7	118.0	122.9	119.7
1991	123.7	121.6	126.0	134.6	124.7	128.8	128.6	129.4	130.0	129.1	132.7	129.3
1991												
January	119.1	117.0	120.3	129.7	120.1	123.6	125.1	126.5	125.7	122.3	125.8	124.3
February	120.1	116.1	122.8	130.8	120.8	124.3	124.8	123.7	126.5	122.6	128.5	124.7
March	121.9	118.0	122.9	131.9	125.5	124.3	125.9	134.9	126.9	123.5	130.7	127.5
April	122.6	119.1	123.7	133.4	124.3	125.0	126.5	126.8	125.7	126.4	129.7	127.4
May	123.6	120.1	125.6	132.1	124.8	127.6	126.8	127.6	127.5	127.9	130.6	128.1
June	125.8	122.5	127.9	137.4	125.7	129.8	125.7	129.4	126.9	129.1	132.3	129.2
July	124.8	123.4	127.2	137.0	125.5	128.7	127.8	129.0	131.7	133.9	130.8	130.5
August	123.3	122.9	125.4	132.5	124.8	132.1	130.6	128.3	131.1	136.3	134.9	130.8
September	123.9	124.0	126.8	134.8	125.1	129.6	133.7	127.5	133.7	131.5	133.4	130.8
October	125.5	123.5	128.1	135.5	123.6	129.6	131.7	128.3	136.0	130.0	135.6	130.9
November	126.7	125.5	129.3	137.8	128.4	131.8	133.2	135.2	134.5	131.4	138.2	133.3
December	126.6	127.2	132.1	142.4	128.1	138.6	131.9	135.7	134.2	134.1	142.1	134.5

(1) England and Wales only. (2) The index series for this group has been based on average 1985 excluding January and February figures which were seriously affected by a dispute in the coal mining industry. (3) Excluding sea transport. (4) Excluding private domestic and personal services.

Redundancy Rates: By Region, Spring 1992

United Kingdom

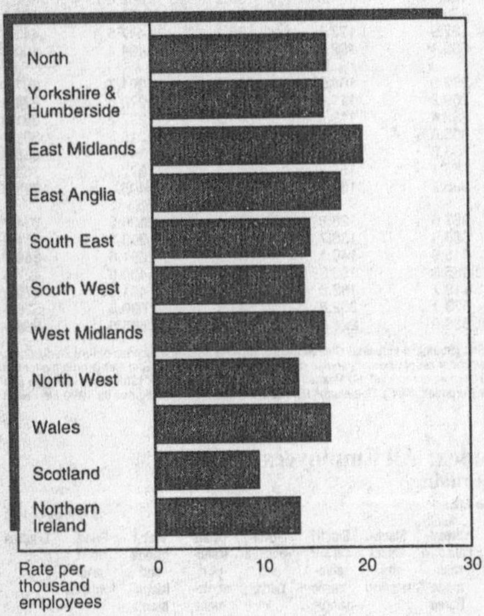

Average Hours Usually Worked[1] Per Week[2]: EC Comparison, 1990

Source: CSO

Hours

	Males	Females	All persons
United Kingdom	44.0	30.5	37.8
Belgium	38.1	32.1	35.8
Denmark	37.0	31.7	34.5
France	39.8	34.7	37.5
Germany (Fed. Rep.)	39.6	32.8	36.8
Greece	40.5	37.8	39.5
Irish Republic	41.0	35.1	38.6
Italy	39.5	35.3	38.0
Luxembourg	40.3	35.6	38.7
Netherlands	35.8	25.9	32.1
Portugal	42.9	38.7	41.1
Spain	40.9	37.2	39.7
EUR 12	40.4	33.1	37.4

(1) Employees only. (2) Excludes meal breaks but includes paid and unpaid overtime.

Rates of Unemployment

Analysis by standard regions: seasonally adjusted

Source: CSO

Percentages

Annual averages	1981	1982	1983	1984	1985	1986	1987	1988	1989	1990	1991
United Kingdom	8.1	9.5	10.5	10.7	10.9	11.1	10.0	8.1	6.3	5.8	8.1
Great Britain	8.0	9.4	10.3	10.6	10.8	11.0	9.8	7.9	6.1	5.6	7.9
North	11.7	13.3	14.6	15.2	15.4	15.3	14.1	11.9	9.9	8.7	10.4
Yorkshire and Humberside	8.8	10.3	11.4	11.7	12.0	12.5	11.3	9.3	7.4	6.7	8.7
East Midlands	7.4	8.4	9.5	9.8	9.8	10.0	9.0	7.1	5.4	5.1	7.2
East Anglia	6.3	7.4	8.0	7.9	8.1	8.5	7.3	5.2	3.6	3.7	5.8
South East	5.5	6.7	7.5	7.8	8.1	8.3	7.2	5.4	3.9	4.0	7.0
South West	6.8	7.8	8.7	9.0	9.3	9.5	8.1	6.2	4.5	4.4	7.1
West Midlands	10.0	11.9	12.9	12.7	12.8	12.9	11.4	8.9	6.6	6.0	8.6
North West	10.2	12.1	13.3	13.6	13.7	13.7	12.5	10.4	8.5	7.7	9.4
Wales	10.4	12.1	12.9	13.2	13.6	13.5	12.0	9.8	7.3	6.6	8.7
Scotland	9.9	11.3	12.3	12.6	12.9	13.3	13.0	11.3	9.3	8.1	8.7
Northern Ireland	12.7	14.4	15.5	15.9	15.9	17.2	17.0	15.6	14.6	13.4	13.7

Unemployment Rates: International Comparison

Source: CSO

Percentages

	Annual averages												
	1979	1980	1981	1982	1983	1984	1985	1986	1987	1988	1989	1990	1991
United Kingdom	5.0	6.4	9.8	11.3	12.4	11.7	11.2	11.2	10.2	8.5	7.1	6.8	8.7
Belgium	8.2	8.8	10.8	12.6	12.1	12.1	11.3	11.2	11.0	9.7	8.1	7.2	7.1
France	5.9	6.3	7.4	8.1	8.3	9.7	10.2	10.4	10.5	10.0	9.4	9.0	9.5
Germany (Fed. Rep.)	3.2	3.0	4.4	6.1	8.0	7.1	7.2	6.4	6.2	6.2	5.6	4.9	4.3
Italy	7.6	7.5	7.8	8.4	8.8	9.4	9.6	10.5	10.9	11.0	10.9	10.3	9.9
Netherlands	5.4	6.0	8.5	11.4	12.0	11.8	10.6	9.9	9.6	9.2	8.3	7.5	7.0
Portugal	–	–	–	–	7.9	8.4	8.5	8.4	7.0	5.7	5.0	4.6	4.1
Spain	8.5	11.2	13.9	15.8	17.2	20.0	21.4	21.0	20.1	19.1	16.9	15.9	16.0
Australia	6.2	6.0	5.7	7.1	9.9	8.9	8.2	8.0	8.1	7.2	6.1	6.9	9.5
Canada	7.4	7.4	7.5	10.9	11.8	11.2	10.4	9.5	8.8	7.7	7.5	8.1	10.2
Finland	5.9	4.6	4.8	5.3	5.4	5.2	5.0	5.3	5.0	4.5	3.4	3.4	7.5
Japan	2.1	2.0	2.2	2.4	2.6	2.7	2.6	2.8	2.8	2.5	2.3	2.1	2.1
Sweden	2.1	2.0	2.5	3.2	3.5	3.1	2.8	2.7	1.9	1.6	1.4	1.5	2.7
United States	5.8	7.0	7.5	9.5	9.5	7.4	7.1	6.9	6.1	5.4	5.2	5.4	6.6

Contributory Benefits[1] Expenditure and Recipients[2]

Great Britain

Source: CSO

£ million and thousands

	Expenditure (£ million)				Recipients[2] (thousands)			
	1976–77	1981–82	1986–87	1991–92	1976–77	1981–82	1986–87	1991–92
Retirement pensions	5,662	12,126	17,779	25,538	8,250	9,015	9,575	9,920
Widow's benefit	466	738	886	983	490	460	430	350
Invalidity benefit	585	1,370	2,673	5,255	510	660	935	1,325
Lump sum payments to contributory pensioners	–	101	107	114	–	10,100	10,700	11,400
Unemployment benefit	559	1,702	1,734	1,506	625	1,220	1,005	650
Sickness benefit	552	680	179	268	520	445	100	120
Statutory sick pay	–	–	757	724	–	–	320	345
Maternity allowance	60	158	168	39	80	125	110	20
Statutory maternity pay	–	–	–	344	–	–	–	85
Death grant	15	17	18	–	–	–	–	–
Industrial disablement benefit	167	315	440	–	200	260	285	–
Industrial death benefit	26	47	61	–	30	30	30	–
Administration and miscellaneous services[3]	571	733	733	1,154	–	–	–	–

(1) Benefit structures have changed over the time period. Consult the DSS Department Reports or Social Security Statistics for more details. (2) Estimated average number receiving benefit at any one time, except for lump sum payments and death grants, which because they are single payments are the total number paid in each year. (3) Figure for 1976–77 represents administration cost of both contributory and non-contributory benefits.

Weekly Rates of Principal Social Security Benefits

Source: CSO

£

	1980 Nov	1985 Nov	1990 Apr	1991 Apr	1992 Apr
Unemployment benefit:[1]					
Men and women	20.65	30.45	37.35	41.40	43.10
Sickness benefit:[1]					
Men and women	20.65	29.15	35.70	39.60	41.20
Invalidity benefit:					
Invalidity pension	26.00	38.30	46.90	52.00	54.15
Invalidity allowance:					
High rate	5.45	8.05	10.00	11.10	11.55
Middle rate	3.45	5.10	6.20	6.90	7.20
Low rate	1.75	2.55	3.10	3.45	3.60
Increase for dependants:					
Adult	15.60	23.00	28.20	31.25	32.55
Each child	7.50	8.05	9.65	10.70	10.85
Attendance allowance:					
Higher rate	21.65	30.60	37.55	41.65	43.35
Lower rate	14.45	20.45	25.05	27.10	28.95
Mobility allowance[2]	14.50	21.40	26.25	29.80	–
Maternity benefit:					
Maternity allowance for insured women	20.65	29.15	35.70	40.60	46.30
Death grant[3]	30.00	30.00	–	–	–
Guardians' allowance	7.50	8.05	9.65	10.70	10.85
Widow's benefit:					
Widow's pension	27.15	38.30	46.90	52.00	54.15
Widowed mother's allowance	27.15	38.30	46.90	52.00	54.15
Addition for each child	7.50	8.05	9.65	10.70	10.85

£

	1980 Nov	1985 Nov	1990 Apr	1991 Apr	1992 Apr
Retirement pension:[4]					
Single person	27.15	38.30	46.90	52.00	54.15
Married couple	43.45	61.30	75.10	83.25	86.70
Non-contributory retirement pension:					
Man or woman	16.30	23.00	28.20	31.25	32.55
Married woman	9.80	13.75	16.85	18.70	19.45
Industrial injuries benefit:					
Injury benefit	23.40	–	–	–	–
Disablement pension at 100 per cent rate	44.30	62.50	76.60	84.90	88.40
Widow's or widower's pension	27.70	38.85	46.90	52.00	54.15
Increase for dependants:[5]					
Adult	12.75	18.80	23.05	25.55	26.60
Each child	1.25	–	–	–	–
Child benefit:					
First child	4.75	7.00	7.25	8.25	9.65
Subsequent children	–	–	–	–	7.80
Family Credit[6] (maximum awards payable):					
Families with 1 child					
Child under 11	17.00	25.00	44.60	48.00	51.40
Child 11–15	17.00	25.50	50.50	54.40	58.25
Child 16 and over	17.00	26.00	54.15	58.35	62.45
Child age 18	–	–	61.45	66.25	70.90
Increase for each additional child					
Child under 11	1.50	2.50	8.25	9.70	10.40

(Continued)

£

	1980 Nov	1985 Nov	1990 Apr	1991 Apr	1992 Apr
Child 11–15	1.50	3.00	14.15	16.10	17.25
Child 16 and over	1.50	3.50	17.80	20.05	21.45
Child age 18	–	–	25.10	27.95	29.90
War pension:					
Ex-private (100 per cent assessment)	44.30	62.50	76.60	84.90	89.00
War widow	35.30	49.80	60.95	67.60	70.35
Supplementary benefits:[9,14]					
Weekly scale rate of requirements[10]					
Married couple[11]					
Ordinary rate	34.60	47.85	–	–	–
Long-term rate	43.45	60.00	–	–	–
Single householder:[12]					
Ordinary rate	21.30	29.50	–	–	–
Long-term rate	27.15	37.50	–	–	–
Non-householder aged:					
18 or over					
Ordinary rate	17.05	23.60	–	–	–
Long-term rate	21.70	30.00	–	–	–
16–17					
Ordinary rate	13.10	18.20	–	–	–
Long-term rate	–	23.00	–	–	–
Increase for children aged:					
11–15	10.90	15.10	–	–	–

£

	1980 Nov	1985 Nov	1990 Apr	1991 Apr	1992 Apr
Under 10	7.30	10.10	–	–	–
Income Support:					
Personal allowances[13]					
Single					
aged 16–17 either	–	–	21.90	23.65[15]	25.55
or depending on their circumstances	–	–	28.80	31.15[16]	33.60
aged 18–24	–	–	28.80	31.15	33.60
aged 25 or over	–	–	36.70	39.65	42.45
Couple					
both aged under 18	–	–	43.80	47.30	50.60
one or both 18 or over	–	–	57.60	62.25	66.60
Lone parent					
aged 16–17 either	–	–	21.90	23.65	25.55
or depending on their circumstances	–	–	28.80	31.15[16]	33.60
aged 18 or over	–	–	36.70	39.65	42.45
Dependant children and young people					
aged under 11		–	12.35	13.35[17]	14.55
aged 11–15	–	–	18.25	19.75	21.40
aged 16–17	–	–	21.90	23.65	25.65
aged 18	–	–	28.80	31.15	33.60

(1) Persons under the age of 18 are entitled to the appropriate adult rate. (2) Mobility allowance was introduced from 1 January 1976 at the £5.00 rate. Disability living allowance has replaced Mobility allowance from April 1992. (3) Death grant is not payable in respect of the death of a person who on 4 July 1948 was aged 65 or over (men) and 60 or over (women). This benefit was abolished from April 1987 and replaced by payments from Social Fund. (4) Retirement pensioners over 80 receive 25p addition. (5) An allowance for one adult dependant is payable, where appropriate, with unemployment benefit, sickness benefit, retirement pension, injury benefit and maternity allowance. Allowances for dependent children are payable with any of these benefits. Changes in these increases take effect from the same date as the main benefits. (6) Injury benefit ceased on 6 April 1983. (7) Child dependency addition was abolished from 24 November 1984. (8) Family credit superseded Family Income Supplement from April 1988. (9) Supplementary pension is paid to people over age 65 (men) or 60 (women). Supplementary allowance is paid to people below those ages. Persons aged 80 years and over are entitled to a further 25p. (10) Scale rates for normal requirements other than rent. (11) Including couples as man and wife. (12) Including any single person who is directly responsible for rent. (13) In addition to personal allowances, a claimant may also be entitled to a premium(s). The types of premium are family, lone parent, pensioner, higher pensioner, disability, severe disability and disabled child. (14) Supplementary Benefit was replaced by Income Support from April 1988. (15) From October 1991 the rate was £23.90. (16) From October 1991 the rate was £31.40. (17) From October 1991 each rate increased by 25p.

Trade Unions: Numbers and Membership

United Kingdom

Source: CSO

	Number of unions	Total membership: Millions	Total membership: As a percentage of civilian workforce in employment[1]	Percentage change in membership since previous year
1976	473	12.4	*50.5*	*+3.0*
1977	481	12.8	*52.4*	*+3.7*
1978	462	13.1	*52.6*	*+2.1*
1979	453	13.3	*52.8*	*+1.3*
1980	438	12.9	*52.9*	*−2.6*
1981	414	12.1	*51.0*	*−6.5*
1982	408	11.6	*49.8*	*−4.2*
1983	394	11.2	*47.4*	*−3.1*
1984	375	11.0	*45.6*	*−2.2*
1985	370	10.8	*44.6*	*−1.6*
1986	335	10.5	*43.2*	*−2.6*
1987	330	10.5	*41.5*	*−0.6*
1988	315	10.4	*39.8*	*−0.9*
1989	309	10.2	*37.9*	*−2.1*
1990	287	9.9	*37.7*	*−2.1*

(1) As at December for years 1984 onwards, previously based on mid-year estimates.

Trade Unions (TUC Affiliated)

(as at Jan. 1993)

Source: TUC

Membership figures appear in brackets after the union name.

Amalgamated Engineering and Electrical Union (622,622)
110 Peckham Road, London SE15 5EL
Tel: 071-703 4231
Fax: 071-701 7862
Secretary: Gavin Laird

Associated Society of Locomotive Engineers and Firemen (18,866)
9 Arkwright Road, London NW3 6AB
Tel: 071-431 0275
Fax: 071-794 6406
Secretary: Derrick Fullick

Association of First Division Civil Servants (10,683)
2 Caxton Street, London SW1H 0QH
Tel: 071-222 6242
Fax: 071-222 5926
Secretary: Elizabeth Symons

Association of University Teachers (32,960)
United House, 1 Pembridge Road, London W11 3HJ
Tel: 071-221 4370
Fax: 071-727 6547
Secretary: David Triesman

Bakers, Food and Allied Workers' Union (34,328)
Stanborough House, Great North Road, Stanborough, Welwyn Garden City, Hertfordshire AL8 7TA
Tel: 07072 60150
Secretary: Joe Marino

Banking, Insurance and Finance Union (162,429)
Sheffield House, 1b Amity Grove,
London SW20 0LG
Tel: 081-946 9151
Fax: 081-879 3728
Secretary: Leif Mills

British Actors' Equity Association (44,379)
Guild House, Upper St Martin's Lane,
London WC2H 9EG
Tel: 071-379 6000
Fax: 071-379 7001
Secretary: Ian McGarry

British Air Line Pilots' Association (5,391)
81 New Road, Harlington, Hayes,
Middlesex UB3 5BG
Tel: 081-759 9331
Fax: 081-564 7957
Secretary: Chris Darke

British Association of Colliery Management (6,694)
BACM House, 317 Nottingham Road,
Old Basford, Nottingham NG7 7DP
Tel: 0602 785819
Secretary: John Meads

Broadcasting, Entertainment, Cinematograph and Theatre Union (45,206)
111 Wardour Street, London W1V 4AY
Tel: 071-437 8506
Fax: 071-437 8268
Secretary: Tony Hearn

Card Setting Machine Tenters' Society (88)
48 Scar End Lane, Staincliffe, Dewsbury,
West Yorkshire WF12 4NY
Tel: 0924 400206
Secretary: Anthony John Moorhouse

Ceramic and Allied Trades Union (25,929)
Hillcrest House, Garth Street, Hanley,
Stoke-on-Trent ST1 2AB
Tel: 0782 272755
Secretary: Alf Clowes

Chartered Society of Physiotherapy (24,416)
14 Bedford Row, London WC1R 4ED
Tel: 071-242 1941
Fax: 071-831 4509
Secretary: Toby Simon

Civil and Public Services Association (124,023)
160 Falcon Road, London SW11 2LN
Tel: 071-924 2727
Fax: 071-924 1847
Secretary: Barry Reamsbottom

Communication Managers' Association (17,292)
Hughes House, Ruscombe Road, Twyford,
Reading, Berks RG10 9JD
Tel: 0734 342300
Fax: 0734 342087
Secretary: Terry Deegan

Confederation of Health Service Employees[1] (201,993)
Glen House, High Street, Banstead,
Surrey SM7 2LH
Tel: 0737 353322
Fax: 0737 370079
Secretary: Hector Mackenzie

Educational Institute of Scotland (47,169)
46 Moray Place, Edinburgh EH3 6BH
Tel: 031-225 6244
Fax: 031-220 3151
Secretary: Jim Martin

Electrical and Plumbing Industries Union (4,100)
Park House, 64/66 Wandsworth Common
North Side, London SW18 2SH
Tel: 081-874 0458
Fax: 081-877 1160
Secretary: John Aitkin

Engineering and Fastener Trade Union (240)
42 Galton Road, Warley, West Midlands B67 5JU
Tel: 021-429 2594
Secretary: James Burdis

Engineers' and Managers' Association (39,716)
Flaxman House, Gogmore Lane, Chertsey,
Surrey KT16 9JW
Tel: 0932 564131
Fax: 0932 567707
Secretary: Tony Cooper

Film Artistes' Association (1,937)
61 Marloes Road, London W8 6LE
Tel: 071-937 4567
Secretary: Michael Reynel

Fire Brigades Union (51,881)
Bradley House, 68 Coombe Road,
Kingston-upon-Thames, Surrey KT2 7AE
Tel: 081-541 1765
Fax: 081-546 5187
Secretary: Ken Cameron

Furniture, Timber and Allied Trades Union (34,785)
'Fairfields', Roe Green, Kingsbury,
London NW9 0PT
Tel: 081-204 0273
Fax: 081-204 2073
Secretary: Colin Christopher

General Union of Associations of Loom Overlookers (530)
9 Wellington Street, St Johns,
Blackburn BB1 8AF
Tel: 0254 51760
President: D. Rishton

GMB (862,785)
22/24 Worple Road, London SW19 4DD
Tel: 081-947 3131
Fax: 081-944 6552
Secretary: John Edmonds

Graphical, Paper and Media Union (270,983)
Keys House, 63–67 Bromham Road,
Bedford MK40 2AG
Tel: 0234 351521
Fax: 0234 270580
Secretary: Tony Dubbins

Hospital Consultants and Specialists Association (2,351)
Number One, Kingsclere Road, Overton,
Basingstoke, Hampshire RG25 3JP
Tel: 0256 771777
Fax: 0256 770999
Secretary: Stephen J. Charkham

Inland Revenue Staff Federation (57,011)
Douglas Houghton House, 231 Vauxhall Bridge Road, London SW1V 1EH
Tel: 071-834 8254
Fax: 071-630 6258
Secretary: Clive Brooke

Institution of Professionals, Managers and Specialists (90,434)
75–79 York Road, London SE1 7AQ
Tel: 071-928 9951
Fax: 071-928 5996
Secretary: Bill Brett

Iron and Steel Trades Confederation (63,000)
Swinton House, 324 Gray's Inn Road, London WC1X 8DD
Tel: 071-837 6691
Fax: 071-278 8378
Secretary: Keith Brookman

Manufacturing Science Finance (604,000)
Park House, 64/66 Wandsworth Common North Side, London SW18 2SH
Tel: 081-871 2100
Fax: 081-877 1160
Secretary: Roger Lyons

Military and Ochestral Musical Instrument Makers Trade Society (44)
2 Whitehouse Avenue, Borehamwood, Hertfordshire WD6 1HD
Secretary: Mr F. McKenzie

Musicians' Union (36,979)
60–62 Clapham Road, London SW9 0JJ
Tel: 071-582 5566
Fax: 071-582 9805
Secretary: Dennis Scard

National and Local Government Officers' Association[1] (759,735)
1 Mabledon Place, London WC1H 9AJ
Tel: 071-388 2366
Fax: 071-387 6692
Secretary: Alan Jinkinson

National Association of Colliery Overmen, Deputies and Shotfirers (5,750)
Simpson House, 48 Nether Hall Road, Doncaster, South Yorshire DN1 2PZ
Tel: 0302 368015
Fax: 0302 341945
Secretary: Peter McNestry

National Association of Co-operative Officials (4,364)
Coronation House, Arndale Centre, Manchester M4 2HW
Tel: 061-834 6029
Secretary: Lindsay Ewing

National Association of Licensed House Managers (10,603)
9 Coombe Lane, London SW20 8NE
Tel: 081-947 3080
Secretary: John Madden

National Association of Probation Officers (6,765)
3–4 Chivalry Road, London SW11 1HT
Tel: 071-223 4887
Secretary: Bill Beaumont

National Association of Schoolmasters/Union of Women Teachers (121,142)
5 King Street, London WC2E 8HN
Tel: 071-379 9499
Fax: 071-497 8262
Secretary: Nigel De Gruchy

NATFHE – University and College Lecturers' Union (73,517)
27 Britannia Street, London WC1X 9JP
Tel: 071-837 3636
Fax: 071-837 4403
Secretary: Geoff Woolf

National Communications Union (150,703)
Greystoke House, 150 Brunswick Road, London W5 1AW
Tel: 081-998 2981
Fax: 081-991 1410
Secretary: Tony Young

National League of the Blind and Disabled (2,510)
2 Tenterden Road, London N17 8BE
Tel: 081-808 6030
Secretary: Michael Barrett

National Union of Civil and Public Servants (112,761)
124–130 Southwark Street, London SE1 0TU
Tel: 071-928 9671
Fax: 071-620 2707
Secretary: John Sheldon (acting)

National Union of Domestic Appliance and General Operatives (2,400)
Imperial Buildings, Corporation Street, Rotherham, South Yorkshire S60 1PB
Tel: 0709 382820
Secretary: Tony McCarthy

National Union of Insurance Workers (17,582)
27 Old Gloucester Street, London WC1N 3AF
Tel: 071-405 6798
Secretary: Ken Perry

National Union of Journalists (29,074)
Acorn House, 314–320 Gray's Inn Road, London WC1X 8DP
Tel: 071-278 7916
Fax: 071-837 8143
Secretary: John Foster

National Union of Knitwear, Footwear and Apparel Trades (54,588)
The Grange, Earls Barton, Northampton NN6 0JH
Tel: 0604 810326
Fax: 0604 812496
Secretary: Helen McGrath

National Union of Lock and Metal Workers (4,666)
Bellamy House, Wilkes Street, Willenhall, West Midlands WV13 2BS
Tel: 0902 366651/2
Fax: 0902 368035
Secretary: Michael Bradley

National Union of Marine, Aviation and Shipping Transport Officers (18,520)
Oceanair House, 750–760 High Road, London E11 3BB
Tel: 081-989 6677
Fax: 081-530 1015
Secretary: John Newman

National Union of Mineworkers (44,352)
Holly Street, Sheffield, South Yorkshire S1 2GT
Tel: 0742 766900
Fax: 0742 766400
President: Arthur Scargill

National Union of Public Employees[1] (551,165)
Civic House, 20 Grand Depot Road,
London SE18 6SF
Tel: 081-854 2244
Fax: 081-316 7770
Secretary: Rodney Bickerstaffe

National Union of Rail, Maritime and Transport Workers (114,101)
Unity House, Euston Road, London NW1 2BL
Tel: 071-387 4771
Fax: 071-387 4123
Secretary: Jimmy Knapp

National Union of Scalemakers (750)
1st Floor, Queensway House, 57 Livery Street,
Birmingham B3 1HA
Tel: 021-236 8998
Secretary: Arthur Smith

National Union of Teachers (164,718)
Hamilton House, Mabledon Place,
London WC1H 9BD
Tel: 071-388 6191
Fax: 071-387 8458
Secretary: Doug McAvoy

Northern Carpet Trades' Union (721)
22 Clare Road, Halifax HX1 2HX
Tel: 0422 360492
Fax: 0422 321146
Secretary: Keith Edmondson

Power Loom Carpet Weavers' and Textile Workers' Union (2,167)
Carpet Weavers Hall, Callows Lane,
Kidderminster DY10 2JG
Tel: 0562 823192
Secretary: Ron White

Prison Officers' Association (27,225)
Cronin House, 245 Church Street,
London N9 9HW
Tel: 081-803 0255
Fax: 081-803 1761
Secretary: David Evans

Rossendale Union of Boot, Shoe and Slipper Operatives (2,273)
7 Tenterfield Street, Waterfoot, Rossendale,
Lancashire BB4 7BA
Tel: 0706 215657
Secretary: Michael Murray

Scottish Prison Officers' Association (4,099)
21 Calder Road, Saughton, Edinburgh EH11 3PF
Tel: 031-443 8105
Fax: 031-444 0657
Secretary: William Goodall

Scottish Union of Power-Loom Overlookers (60)
3 Napier Terrace, Dundee, Tayside DD2 2SL
Tel: 0382 612196
Secretary: Jim Reilly

Sheffield Wool Shear Workers' Union (16)
50 Bankfield Road, Malin Bridge, Sheffield,
South Yorkshire S6 4RD
Secretary: Mr R. Cutler

Society of Radiographers (12,815)
14 Upper Wimpole Street, London W1M 8BN
Tel: 071-935 5726
Fax: 071-487 3483
Secretary: Bryan Macey

Society of Shuttlemakers (19)
211 Burnley Road, Colne, Lancashire BB8 2JD
Tel: 0282 866716
Fax: 0282 866716
Secretary: Leslie Illingworth

Society of Telecom Executives (25,027)
1 Park Road, Teddington, Middlesex TW11 0AR
Tel: 081-943 5181
Fax: 081-943 2532
Secretary: Simon Petch

Transport and General Workers' Union (TGWU) (1,126,631)
Transport House, Smith Square,
London SW1P 3JB
Tel: 071-828 7788
Fax: 071-630 5861
Secretary: Bill Morris

Transport Salaried Staffs' Association (37,705)
Walkden House, 10 Melton Street,
London NW1 2EJ
Tel: 071-387 2101
Secretary: Richard Rosser

Union of Communication Workers (186,849)
UCW House, Crescent Lane, London SW4 9RN
Tel: 071-622 9977
Fax: 071-720 6853
Secretary: Alan Tuffin

Union of Construction, Allied Trades and Technicians (202,334)
UCATT House, 177 Abbeville Road,
London SW4 9RL
Tel: 071-622 2442
Fax: 071-720 4081
Secretary: George Brumwell

Union of Shop, Distributive and Allied Workers (341,349)
Oakley, 188 Wilmslow Road, Fallowfield,
Manchester M14 6LJ
Tel: 061-224 2804
Fax: 061-257 2566
Secretary: Garfield Davies

Union of Textile Workers (1,951)
Foxlowe, Market Place, Leek,
Staffordshire ST13 6AD
Tel: 0538 382068
Secretary: Alf Hitchmough

United Road Transport Union (18,500)
76 High Lane, Chorlton-cum-Hardy,
Manchester M21 1FD
Tel: 061-881 6245
Fax: 061-862 9127
Secretary: David Higginbottom

Writers' Guild of Great Britain (1,685)
430 Edgware Road, London W2 1EH
Tel: 071-723 8074
Secretary: Walter Jeffrey

Yorkshire Association of Power-Loom Overlookers (450)
Inveresk House, 31 Houghton Place,
Bradford BD1 3RG
Tel: 0274 727966
Secretary: Tony Barrow

Total membership **7,786,885**
(Total women members – as notified to the TUC) 2,323,312

(1) The Confederation of Health Service Employees, the National and Local Government Officers' Association and the National Union of Public Employees merged, 1 July 1993, to form UNISON.

Political Funds of Trade Unions, 1991

Source: Certification Office for Trade Unions & Employers' Associations

	Number of Members contribution to the Political Fund	Number of Members exempt from contributing to the Political Fund	POLITICAL FUND (a)			
			Income	Expenditure	Fund at beginning of year	Fund at end of year
	(b) (1)	(b) (2)	£ (3)	£ (4)	£ (5)	£ (6)
Amalgamated Engineering Union	397,071	225,551	941,066	974,581	114,161	80,646
Associated Society of Locomotive Engineers and Firemen	18,055	811	59,932	48,524	59,761	71,169
Association of Her Majesty's Inspectors of Taxes	2,406	113	7,167	–	8,622	15,789
Bakers Food and Allied Workers Union	33,419	909	50,106	51,801	6,560	4,865
Broadcasting and Entertainment Trades Alliance	5,879	9(c)	12,379	43,454	65,509	34,434
Ceramic and Allied Trades Union	25,214	69	85,236	57,836	57,685	85,085
Civil and Public Services Association	1	–	1	–	(4,369)	(4,368)
Communication Managers Association	16,782	510	26,554	29,841	69,276	65,989
Confederation of Health Service Employees	186,267	15,726	434,760	428,501	147,024	153,283
Educational Institute of Scotland	44,610	1,605	65,172	9,974	96,684	151,882
Electrical Electronic Telecommunication and Plumbing Union	267,921	42,396	367,562	328,515	296,265	335,312
Fire Brigades Union	36,693	11,530	108,617	76,056	103,316	135,877
Furniture Timber and Allied Trades Union	30,346	4,439	37,515	36,350	9,063	10,228
General Union of Associates of Loom Overlookers	334	341	–	575	881	306
GMB	735,033	63,915	2,607,000	3,000,000	2,686,000	2,293,000
Inland Revenue Staff Federation	52,995	2,298	124,765	59,338	318,592	384,019
Institution of Professionals, Managers and Specialists	78,995	2,402	47,397	21,030	63,495	89,862
Iron and Steel Trades Confederation	30,758	7,930	84,116	96,256	45,894	33,754
Manufacturing Science and Finance Union	274,307	329,693	493,000	601,000	342,000	234,000
Musicians Union	33,442	1,903	16,476	18,915	24,375	21,936
National and Local Government Officers Association	630,109	46,806	1,915,596	984,359	2,943,668	3,874,905
National Association of Colliery Overmen Deputies and Shotfirers	5,696	54	23,259	18,064	44,485(d)	49,680
National Association of Colliery Overmen Deputies and Shotfirers Durham Area	478	–	2,990	2,475	(1,351)	(836)
National Association of Schoolmasters and Union of Women Teachers	100,285	58,795	53,401	10,246	170	43,325
National Association of Teachers in Further and Higher Education	63,711	2,796	79,048	8,984	157,551	227,615
National Communications Union (Engineering and Clerical Groups) – Engineering Group	86,151	22,801	326,353	308,211	110,267	128,409
National Communications Union (Engineering and Clerical Groups) – Clerical Group	31,754	3,131	73,945	35,871	130,043	168,117
National Graphical Association (1982) (e)	57,790	43,102	236,877	154,826	575,427	657,478
National League of the Blind and Disabled	1,601	73	2,782	2,952	4,921	4,751
National Union of Civil and Public Servants	111,644	1,117	140,470	15,004	354,719	480,185
National Union of Domestic Appliances and General Operatives	650	12	1,091	1,087	82	86
National Union of Insurance Workers	15,631	3,025	26,384	7,504	47,577	66,457
National Union of Knitwear, Footwear and Apparel Trades	52,500	849	98,020	76,593	84,438	105,865
National Union of Lock and Metal Workers	4,646	46	2,763	555	5,783	7,991
National Union of Mineworkers	40,703	65,316	378,801	860,560	995,482	513,723
National Union of Public Employees	535,406	15,759	2,111,746	1,693,695	943,005	1,361,056
National Union of Rail, Maritime and Transport Workers	112,104	2,034	346,363	403,984	305,666	248,045
National Union of Scalemakers	2	1,039	17	1	289	305
National Union of Tailors and Garment Workers (f)	56,395	10,235	–	10,433	128,509	118,076
Power Loom Carpet Weavers and Textile Workers Union	2,149	18	2,051	546	6,210	7,715
Rossendale Union of Boot, Shoe and Slipper Operatives	2,252	21	107	51	2,090	2,146
Scottish Carpet Workers Union	760	–	664	213	479	930
Society of Graphical and Allied Trades 1982 (SOGAT) (e)	82,731	74,610	180,577	198,525	250,248	232,300

(Continued)

	Number of Members contribution to the Political Fund (b) (1)	Number of Members exempt from contributing to the Political Fund (b) (2)	POLITICAL FUND (a) Income £ (3)	Expenditure £ (4)	Fund at beginning of year £ (5)	Fund at end of year £ (6)
Society of Telecom Executives	13,712	11,315	55,993	13,100	126,901	169,794
Society of Union Employees (NUPE)	164	–	78	–	2,604(d)	2,682
Transport and General Workers Union	997,182	21,786	3,286,916	3,260,499	4,739,078	4,765,495
Transport Salaried Staffs Association	34,150	5,880	81,380	74,479	105,801	112,702
Union of Communication Workers	179,634	11,988	407,060	534,408	223,397	96,049
Union of Construction Allied Trades and Technicians	171,947	23,013	240,000	198,087	(31,126)	10,787
Union of Democratic Mineworkers	14,690	82	10,050	9,770	18,320	18,600
Union of Shop Distributive and Allied Workers	311,905	29,444	738,837	719,268	452,237	471,806
Union of Textile Workers	1,887	64	3,977	2,967	1,334	2,344
Total for the 52 unions with political funds for 1991	**5,990,947**	**1,167,361**	**16,396,417**	**15,489,864**	**17,239,098**	**18,145,651**
Total for the 54 unions with political funds for 1990	6,113,457	1,207,470	15,639,595	12,709,976	14,331,580	17,261,199

(a) The information in the table relates to the position at the end of 1991 and therefore to unions which were in existence at that time. (b) It should be noted that columns (1) and (2) do not necessarily add up to a union's total membership. This is because, in the case of some trade unions, total membership includes various classes of special category members (e.g. honorary, retired, unemployed) who are members under the union's rules but who are neither required to pay the political levy nor to seek formal exemption. The number of members exempt from contributing to the Political Fund relates to those members who have completed a political exemption notice. (c) This figure is a transitional once. (d) This figure has been changed from last year's report due to later information. (e) These unions amalgamated on 30/9/91 to form the Graphical Paper and Media Union. (f) This union transferred its engagements to GMB on 1/3/91.

Power of Trade Unions, Business and Government

Do you think trade unions, business and government have too much power?

Source: SCPR's *British Social Attitudes* survey, 9th Report, ed. R. Jowell *et al.* (Dartmouth Publishing, 1992)

	1985	1986	1987	1989	1990
Percentage saying that each has 'too much' or 'far too much' power:					
Trade unions	54	53	48	40	35
Business and industry	21	27	26	36	28
Government	48	50	44	54	47

Ideological Differences by Region, 1989–91 Combined

Source: SCPR's *British Social Attitudes* survey, 9th Report, ed. R. Jowell *et al.* (Dartmouth Publishing, 1992)

	Scotland	North	Wales	Midlands	London	South
Percentage agreeing that:						
Unemployment benefit is too low and causes hardship	67	57	62	50	51	41
Government should redistribute income from the better off to the less well-off	58	54	55	47	51	43
Ordinary people do not get their fair share of the nation's wealth	69	71	65	67	66	59
Big business benefits owners at the expense of the workers	56	56	61	53	53	47
There is one law for the rich and one for the poor	65	71	71	67	63	63
Unemployment should be a higher priority than inflation	58	56	58	53	55	46

AGRICULTURE & FISHING

Hedgerows, for centuries a distinctive feature of British farmland, have suffered from modern agricultural developments. Estimates by the Institute of Terrestrial Ecology indicate that 53,000 miles of hedgerow were lost between 1984 and 1990. Most of this loss was due to neglect, but at least a third was grubbed up by farmers to aid mechanized farming. Now, instead of being subsidized to rip out hedgerows, farmers are being paid to replant and repair them, slowing the decline for the first time this century. One of the national schemes currently operating allows farmers to reclaim from the Ministry of Agriculture 50% of the cost of providing hedges, gates and stiles. A second scheme, run by the Countryside Commission, pays farmers £2 a metre for hedge laying and £1.50 for coppicing.

While conservationists welcome the incentives, they point out that Britain had 495,000 miles of hedgerow in 1947 compared with 203,000 in 1993, so much work remains to be done.

Number of Workers Employed in Agriculture[1,2,3]

United Kingdom: at June in each year

Source: CSO

Thousands

	Regular workers					Seasonal or casual workers			All workers			Salaried managers[4]
		Whole-time		Part-time								
	Total	Male	Female	Male	Female	Total	Male	Female	Total	Male	Female	
1983	228.3	152.2	15.5	31.3	29.4	97.9	56.9	41.0	326.2	240.3	85.9	7.8
1984	220.8	145.6	15.2	30.7	29.4	95.6	56.7	38.8	316.3	233.0	83.4	7.8
1985	218.0	141.6	15.1	31.5	29.8	97.2	58.1	39.1	315.2	231.1	84.1	8.3
1986	210.3	134.1	14.8	32.2	29.1	95.3	57.2	38.1	305.5	223.5	82.1	8.3
1987	202.1	126.9	14.6	31.5	29.0	93.4	55.8	37.6	295.5	214.2	81.3	7.9
1988	195.5	120.4	14.6	31.5	29.2	92.7	56.1	37.6	288.2	207.8	80.3	7.9
1989	187.7	114.0	15.1	30.8	27.8	88.3	54.0	34.3	276.0	198.8	77.2	7.8
1990	184.6	109.5	15.5	31.5	28.1	90.5	55.5	34.9	275.1	196.5	78.5	8.1
1991	178.3	104.6	14.9	31.1	27.6	86.6	53.8	32.8	264.9	189.6	75.3	7.9

(1) Figures exclude school children, farmers, partners and directors and their wives. (2) Figures include estimated figures for Scotland. (3) Includes estimates for minor holdings in England and Wales. (4) Great Britain only.

Average Weekly Earnings[1] and Hours of Agricultural Workers

Great Britain

Source: CSO

	1980	1981	1982	1983	1984	1985	1986	1987	1988	1989	1990	1991
Men[2]												
Earnings	86.26	96.52	106.87	117.02	123.11	134.67	141.32	148.61	154.62	167.33	187.28	207.03
Hours	46.4	46.9	46.7	46.7	46.2	46.9	46.8	46.6	47.10	46.6	46.8	47.3
Youths[3]												
Earnings	56.66	62.15	69.40	76.02	80.20	85.81	89.83	95.34	98.20	109.56	122.58	129.99
Hours	44.8	44.9	45.0	45.5	44.7	44.8	45.5	45.9	44.80	45.1	46.4	45.1
Females												
Earnings	65.53	70.35	80.36	87.70	93.47	102.06	107.77	121.78	124.82	137.45	153.70	157.15
Hours	42.1	41.7	42.9	42.6	41.7	42.7	42.6	42.6	42.80	43.5	43.3	42.6

(1) Total earnings of hired regular whole-time workers, including payments-in-kind valued, where applicable, in accordance with Agricultural Wages Orders. (2) Aged 20 and over. (3) Aged under 20 years.

Agriculture – Land Use

United Kingdom: Area at the June census[1]

Source: CSO

Thousand hectares

	1981	1982	1983	1984	1985	1986	1987	1988	1989	1990	1991
Cereals											
Wheat	1,491	1,663	1,695	1,939	1,902	1,997	1,994	1,886	2,083	2,013	1,980
Barley	2,327	2,222	2,143	1,978	1,965	1,916	1,830	1,878	1,652	1,515	1,393
Oats	144	129	108	106	133	97	99	120	119	107	1,393
Mixed corn	11	10	8	8	7	7	6	5	5	4	4
Rye	6	6	7	6	8	7	7	7	7	8	9
Potatoes											
Early crop	24	25	24	198	191	178	177	180	175	177	177
Main crop	167	167	171								
Fodder crops											
Field beans[2]	45	40	34	32	45	60	91	154	129	139	131
Turnips and swedes[3]	79	71	66	64	62	59	56	54	51	46	42
Fodder beet and mangolds[3]	5	5	5	8	12	13	13	12	11	12	13
Maize for threshing or stockfeeding	18	16	15	16	20	23	24	24	25	34	44
Kale, cabbage, savoys, kohlrabi, rape for stockfeeding	49	43	40	39	37	33	30	28	25	24	25
Peas harvested dry[4]	–	–	29	56	92	91	117	107	86	77	72
Other crops for stockfeeding	26	31	25	22	20	20	15	14	10	9	10
Horticultural crops[5]											
Orchards and small fruit	62	60	58	56	55	53	53	52	51	50	48
Vegetables grown in the open:											
Brussels sprouts	13	13	11	11	11	11	10	10	8	7	8

(Continued)

Thousand hectares

	1981	1982	1983	1984	1985	1986	1987	1988	1989	1990	1991
Horticultural crops[5] *(Continued)*											
Cabbage (all kinds), kale, cauliflower and broccoli[6]	26	27	25	25	24	26	25	26	27	26	26
Carrots	14	14	13	14	14	14	13	15	15	15	16
Parsnips		3	2	3	3	3	3	3	3	4	3
Turnips and swedes[7]	3	3	–	–	–	–	–	–	–	–	–
Beetroot	2	2	2	2	2	2	2	2	2	2	2
Onions, salad and dry bulb	8	9	8	8	9	9	9	9	8	9	9
Beans (broad, runner and French)	11	12	11	10	11	10	10	10	10	8	9
Green peas	55	56	47	46	53	52	42	46	48	51	46
Peas, for harvesting dry[8]	28	27	18	–	–	–	–	–	–	–	–
Celery	1	1	1	1	1	1	1	1	1	1	1
Sweet corn	–	–	1	1	1	1	1	1	1	1	2
Hardy nursery stock bulbs and other flowers grown in the open:											
Hardy nursery stock	7	7	7	7	7	7	7	8	8	8	8
Bulbs	5	5	4	4	4	4	4	5	5	5	5
Other flowers	1	1	1	1	1	1	1	1	1	2	1
Area under glass	2	2	2	2	2	2	2	2	2	2	2
Other crops											
Sugar beet	210	204	199	199	205	205	202	201	197	194	196
Rape grown for oilseed	125	174	222	269	296	299	388	347	321	390	440
Hops[9]	6	6	6	5	5	4	4	4	4	4	3,405
Other crops not for stockfeeding	7	6	7	6	11	18	19	24	25	41	27,500
Bare fallow	76	55	97	42	41	48	42	58	65	63	530
Total tillage	**5,071**	**5,127**	**5,124**	**5,196**	**5,265**	**5,287**	**5,313**	**5,311**	**5,202**	**5,075**	**915**
All grasses under five years old	1,911	1,859	1,846	1,794	1,796	1,723	1,691	1,613	1,534	1,578	1,581
All arable	6,982	6,986	6,970	6,990	7,061	7,011	7,004	6,924	6,736	6,653	6,601
All grasses five years old and over	5,103	5,097	5,107	5,105	5,019	5,077	5,112	5,161	5,251	5,264	5,267
Total crops and grass	**12,085**	**12,083**	**12,078**	**12,095**	**12,080**	**12,088**	**12,116**	**12,085**	**11,987**	**11,917**	**11,868**
Rough grazings											
Sole rights	5,021	4,984	4,927	4,895	4,872	4,829	4,743	4,712	4,710	4,680	5,937
Common (estimated)	1,214	1,214	1,212	1,212	1,216	1,216	1,216	1,216	1,236	1,236	6,506
Woodland on agricultural holdings	277	285	292	299	312	316	322	333	347	354	–
All other land on agricultural holdings	211	217	227	218	223	227	225	229	273	323	344
Total area of agricultural land	**18,808**	**18,783**	**18,735**	**18,720**	**18,703**	**18,676**	**18,622**	**18,575**	**18,553**	**18,510**	**24,086**
Total area of the United Kingdom	**24,089**	**24,088**	**24,088**	**24,088**	**24,085**	**24,086**	**24, 086**	**24, 086**	**24,086**	**24,086**	**18,487**

(1) Figures include estimates for minor holdings not surveyed at the June census in England and Wales. (2) Prior to 1986 collected as "Beans for stockfeeding" in England and Wales. (3) See footnote 5 to table below. (4) Includes "Peas for harvesting dry for both human consumption and stockfeeding" from 1984 onwards. (5) Figures relate to land usage at 1 June and are not necessarily good indicators of production as for some crops more than one crop may be obtained in each season or a crop may overlap two seasons. (6) Excludes kale from 1983 which is included with "Other vegetables". (7) From 1983 included with "Other vegetables". (8) Following a change in definition in 1986 "Peas for harvesting dry for human consumption" is not included with "Peas harvested dry for stockfeeding". Data from 1984 reflect this change. (9) Collected as England only.

Estimated Quantity of Crops and Grass Harvested[1,2]

United Kingdom

Source: CSO

Thousand tonnes

	1981	1982	1983	1984	1985	1986	1987	1988	1989	1990	1991	1992
Cereals												
Wheat	8,707	10,317	10,802	14,969	12,046	13,911	11,940	11,751	14,033	14,033	14,363	–
Barley	10,227	10,956	9,980	11,072	9,740	10,014	9,229	8,778	8,073	7,911	7,627	–
Oats	619	575	466	517	614	503	454	548	529	530	523	–
Mixed corn for threshing	44	39	35	35	31	29	26	22	18	17	15	–
Rye for threshing	24	27	24	28	35	32	32	34	36	40	49	–
Maize for threshing[3]	–[4]	–[4]	–[4]	–[4]	–[4]	–[4]	–	–	–	–	–	–
Potatoes												
Early crop[4,8]	383	432	322	396	401	361	391	420	366	437	359	–
Main crop[4,8]	5,732	6,498	5,527	6,982	6,462	6,051	6,306	6,470	5,884	6,037	5,906	–
Fodder crops												
Beans for stockfeeding	125	120	105	125	155	230	294	–	–	–	–	–
Turnips, swedes[5]	4,795	4,575	3,655	3,960	3,300	3,855	3,451	3,325	2,720	–	–	–
Fodder beet and mangolds[5]	320	370	295	570	815	845	782	735	600	–	–	–
Maize for threshing or stockfeeding[3]	635	635	550	580	770	915	782	875	940	–	–	–
Rape for stockfeeding										–		
Kale, cabbage, savoys and kohlrabi	2,195	1,985	1,660	1,805	1,555	1,380	1,320	735	600	–	–	–
Peas harvested dry for stockfeeding	–	–	85	170	215	330	310	–	–	–	–	–
Other crops												
Sugar beet[6]	7,395	10,005	7,495	9,015	7,715	8,120	7,992	8,150	8,115	–	–	–
Rape grown for oilseed	325	580	565	925	895	965	1,326	–	–	–	–	–
Hops	9	10	9	8	6	5	5	5	5	5	–	–
Hay[7]												
From all grasses under five years old	6,775	6,550	6,000	5,700	4,650	4,675	–	–	–	–	–	–
From all grasses five years old and over	–	–	–	–	–	–	–	–	–	–	–	–
Horticultural crops												
Vegetables grown in the open												
Brussels sprouts	197	223	154	169	152	168	173	165	134	102	105	–
Cabbage (including savoys and spring greens)	546	610	518	670	683	688	698	743	704	659	655	–
Cauliflowers	325	353	299	344	356	360	370	376	364	332	342	–
Carrots	711	725	555	572	600	635	549	675	587	573	641	–

(Continued)

Thousand tonnes

	1981	1982	1983	1984	1985	1986	1987	1988	1989	1990	1991	1992
Horticultural crops *(Continued)*												
Parsnips	53	55	51	57	62	68	64	70	55	54	59	–
Turnips and swedes	109	145	135	143	140	163	161	171	137	158	162	–
Beetroot	97	105	94	115	114	95	104	105	97	93	99	–
Onions, dry bulb	232	231	175	238	268	247	298	299	223	235	231	–
Onions, salad	25	27	25	22	25	30	31	30	27	24	28	–
Leeks	40	43	44	53	60	71	72	71	74	70	72	–
Broad beans	17	19	17	21	19	14	13	15	15	16	24	–
Runner beans including French	69	92	65	77	65	67	52	56	48	30	41	41
Peas, green for market	25	28	23	27	26	20	14	14	10	9	9	9
Peas, green for processing	277	238	198	241	206	239	229	226	229	252	254	234
Celery	50	51	46	57	53	65	53	58	56	49	54	54
Lettuce	134	161	155	153	166	158	174	194	175	167	167	–
Rhubarb	41	39	29	26	26	28	31	27	25	26	24	–
Protected crops												
Tomatoes	125	121	121	129	125	131	123	130	152	139	141	–
Cucumbers	54	56	61	68	71	76	81	99	101	105	133	–
Lettuce	37	45	49	48	49	50	47	52	49	51	50	–
Fruit crops												
Total Dessert Apples	152	216	186	184	161	163	165	134	253	158	173	–
Total Culinary Apples	80	147	126	163	145	139	123	134	185	152	157	–
Pears	49	40	54	48	51	47	66	32	43	37	39	–
Plums	16	34	36	34	24	33	36	23	11	8	25	–
Cherries	3	7	3	5	5	4	4	2	3	2	2	–
Soft Fruit	105	109	124	114	111	109	107	104	96	94	101	–

(1) UK gross production in calendar years; for horticultural crops and potatoes it is in crop years. (2) Except for sugar beet and hops, the production area for England and Wales is the area returned at the June census together with estimates for very small holdings (known as minor holdings). In Scotland and Northern Ireland the area returned at June is also the production area except that estimates for minor holdings are included in Scotland for potatoes and in Northern Ireland for barley, oats and potatoes. (3) From 1979 maize for threshing is included with maize for stockfeeding. (4) Revised basis of calculation adopted which prevents direct comparison with post-1980 figures and earlier years. (5) Before 1977 fodder beet was included with turnips and swedes for stockfeeding. In 1977, as a result of changes in the census categories, fodder beet was included with mangolds in England and Wales but continued to be included with turnips and swedes for stockfeeding in Scotland and Northern Ireland. Scotland collected fodder beet separately for the first time in 1986. (6) The production area for sugar beet is provided by British Sugar plc. (7) The production of hay in England and Wales is calculated from the area cut for hay and actually harvested and does not include the area mown for silage, drying or seed; the production of hay in Scotland and Northern Ireland is calculated from the area cut for hay only and does not include grass mown for silage or drying. (8) Potatoes for 1990 – provisional figures only.

Landed Weight and Value of Fish

United Kingdom

Source: CSO

	Landed weight (Thousand tonnes)							Value (£ thousand)						
	1985	1986	1987	1988	1989	1990	1991	1985	1986	1987	1988	1989	1990	1991
Total all fish	**762.1**	**716.9**	**790.4**	**742.0**	**671.8**	**621.5**	**562.3**	**323,825**	**361,680**	**435,162**	**402,893**	**394,346**	**430,503**	**396,469**
Total wet fish	**687.2**	**629.3**	**679.3**	**645.5**	**580.4**	**528.4**	**477.7**	**258,904**	**284,161**	**339,223**	**310,412**	**299,354**	**329,491**	**310,042**
Demersal:														
Catfish	1.4	1.5	1.6	1.6	1.8	1.7	1.7	755	1,035	1,318	1,223	1,557	1,816	1,785
Cod	90.0	76.5	93.4	77.7	68.2	60.4	51.8	69,945	69,140	86,312	74,849	69,568	76,759	69,243
Dogfish	13.8	11.6	13.6	13.0	11.3	110.8	9.9	4,550	6,376	7,201	7,066	7,762	8,944	8,485
Haddock	132.2	131.0	102.4	97.6	71.9	490.8	46.2	67,757	79,019	78,079	68,708	61,918	59,369	52,915
Hake	2.7	3.0	3.3	3.6	4.0	4.59	4.5	3,851	4,549	5,540	6,389	7,699	11,610	11,931
Halibut	0.1	0.1	0.1	0.1	0.1	0.1	0.2	365	372	446	482	442	1,171	639
Lemon sole	5.7	5.0	5.3	5.4	5.0	5.7	5.7	7,137	8,265	9,018	8,788	8,945	10,887	11,021
Plaice	20.4	21.3	25.7	27.3	26.2	25.3	21.0	13,821	16,048	22,541	22,348	20,400	23,815	27,932
Redfish	0.2	0.1	0.2	0.2	0.2	0.3	0.6	75	56	62	71	101	189	425
Saithe (Coalfish)	14.4	17.7	15.2	14.4	11.7	12.2	13.5	3,874	6,361	7,077	5,657	4,868	5,834	7,869
Skate and ray	7.0	6.9	8.6	8.4	7.4	7.3	6.7	2,992	3,908	4,742	4,796	4,596	5,326	5,206
Sole	2.7	3.2	3.1	3.0	2.9	3.1	2.4	9,093	14,500	16,991	14,067	14,370	14,274	10,651
Turbot	0.5	0.6	0.7	0.7	0.5	0.6	0.6	1,976	2,607	3,612	3,690	3,014	3,481	3,275
Whiting	50.2	41.1	51.9	45.6	38.4	38.3	38.4	18,997	18,460	25,198	21,143	20,834	26,085	21,477
Livers[1]	–	–	–	–	–	0	1	1	1	–	–	–	0	–
Roes	0.5	0.5	0.5	0.5	0.4	0.4	0.3	390	348	499	473	457	446	213
Other demersal	60.5	63.1	55.0	66.9	63.0	54.2	41.7	21,596	25,660	35,690	37,198	41,861	48,193	49,139
Total	**402.3**	**383.2**	**381.3**	**366.0**	**313.1**	**274.3**	**345.8**	**227,175**	**256,705**	**304,326**	**276,948**	**268,392**	**298,649**	**282,287**
Pelagic:														
Herring	95.4	106.1	100.3	93.2	99.4	98.8	92.4	11,493	11,881	12,213	11,244	11,257	11,705	9,778
Mackerel[2]	174.2	132.1	189.4	176.1	157.9	146.6	124.9	18,694	14,766	21,484	20,791	18,702	18,043	16,424
Other pelagic	15.4	7.9	8.3	10.2	10.0	8.7	14.6	1,543	809	1,200	1,429	1,003	1,094	1,558
Total	**285.0**	**246.1**	**298.0**	**279.5**	**267.4**	**254**	**231.9**	**31,730**	**27,456**	**34,897**	**33,464**	**30,962**	**30,842**	**27,755**
Total shell fish	**74.8**	**87.6**	**111.1**	**96.5**	**91.3**	**93.1**	**84.6**	**64,920**	**77,519**	**95,939**	**92,481**	**94,992**	**101,012**	**86,427**
Cockles	7.8	19.4	39.0	24.6	14.8	19.6	20.4	476	1,165	4,285	3,276	1,274	1,663	2,049
Crab	13.5	12.6	13.5	15.2	14.1	16	9.2	8,557	9,599	11,400	13,908	14,143	15,064	8,181
Lobster	1.1	1.0	1.1	1.3	1.3	1.3	1.1	8,030	7,680	9,346	10,163	10,650	11,115	8,618
Mussels	5.8	6.3	4.9	6.9	9.0	6.6	6.3	467	541	543	906	1,190	923	942
Nephrop (Norway lobster)	24.8	25.4	24.2	27.4	27.0	25.4	25.1	31,548	39,119	43,007	44,585	42,122	49,659	44,289
Oysters[3]	0.5	0.6	0.1	0.1	0.5	0.2	0.3	734	845	241	225	179	4,367	294
Shrimps[4]	0.8	1.4	3.3	1.7	1.8	1.2	0.2	711	1,254	2,346	1,785	2,627	1,959	217
Whelks	1.6	2.0	2.7	2.0	1.2	0.8	1.6	355	418	665	473	251	175	336
Other shell fish	18.9	18.9	22.3	17.3	22.0	22.0	20.6	14,042	16,898	24,106	17,165	22,556	16,087	21,501

(1) Including the raw equivalent of any liver oils landed. (2) Includes transhipments of mackerel or herring, i.e. caught by British vessels but not actually landed at British ports. These quantities are transhipped to foreign vessels and are later recorded as exports. (3) The weight of oysters is calculated on the basis of one tonne being equal to 15,748 oysters in England and Wales. (4) From 1986, data for prawn is also included.

Processed Food and Animal Feedingstuffs: Production

United Kingdom

Source: CSO

Thousand tonnes

	1981	1982	1983	1984	1985	1986	1987	1988	1989	1990	1991
Flour milling:											
Wheat milling: total	4,753	4,616	4,478	5,044	4,749	4,830	4,919	5,112	5,032	4,875	4,790
Home produced	3,178	3,172	3,256	3,948	3,614	3,082	3,825	3,356	4,161	4,273	4,180
Imported	1,575	1,444	1,222	1,096	1,135	1,748	1,094	1,756	871	605	610
Flour produced	3,596	3,504	3,426	3,608	3,647	3,702	3,874	3,973	3,928	3,879	3,846
Offals produced	1,174	1,121	1,050	1,076	1,092	1,107	1,067	1,157	1,076	999	969
Oat milling:											
Oat milled by oatmeal millers	144	138	144	144	148	157	161	183	221	230	211
Products of oat milling	85	82	81	87	89	96	100	109	129	133	123
Seed crushing:											
Oilseeds and nuts processed	1,724	1,706	1,342	1,188	1,213	1,272	1,526	1,870	1,725	1,877	1,720
Crude oil produced, including production of maize oil	449	431	398	383	407	431	561	659	589	630	597
Oilcake and meal produced, excluding castor meal, cocoa cake and meal	1,241	1,240	945	790	841	823	923	1,162	1,077	1,193	1,077
Production of home-killed meat: total including meat subsequently canned	2,188	2,107	2,264	2,318	2,353	2,260	2,366	2,220	2,215	2,277	2,352
Beef	1,053	961	1,046	1,146	1,150	1,058	1,115	944	976	1,000	1,017
Veal	5	5	6	6	5	4	3	2	1	2	2
Mutton and lamb	263	264	287	288	303	289	296	322	366	370	386
Pork	710	728	763	708	723	747	784	796	709	740	777
Offal	157	149	161	170	171	162	168	156	162	165	170
Production of poultry meat[5]	747	813	805	847	869	919	969	1,050	993	1,025	1,063
Production of bacon and ham, including meat subsequently canned	200	197	212	208	203	206	199	196	206	175	172
Production of milk products:											
Butter	172	216	241	206	202	222	176	140	130	138	112
Cheese (including farmhouse)	242	244	245	246	256	259	266	300	279	312	298
Condensed milk: includes skim concentrate and condensed milk used in manufacture of chocolate crumb	219	225	194	184	181	174	180	183	207	204	198
Milk powder: excluding buttermilk and whey powder											
Full cream	29	34	35	53	61	57	94	104	95	70	73
Skimmed	251	296	302	223	241	268	194	137	133	166	133
Cream, fresh and sterilized: including farm cream[1]	77	75	74	59	45	39	51	53	60	64	74
Sugar: production from home-grown sugar-beet (as refined sugar)	1,092	1,418	1,062	1,314	1,210	1,318	1,226	1,304	1,267	1,241	1,220
Production of compound fats:											
Margarine and other table spreads[3]	398	399	387	382	378	460	464	469	489	475	465
Solid cooking fats	153	157	153	115	108	104	107	104	121	121	115
Production of other processed foods:											
Jam and marmalade	173	177	168	174	182	174	175	174	181	–	–
Syrup and treacle	60	52	52	56	56	52	53	53	52	51	51
Canned vegetables[2]	753	810	811	789	786	782	723	701	732[3]	–	–
Canned and bottled fruit[2]	29	39	42	42	39	35	41	36	37	–	–
Soups, canned and powdered	261	286	301	302	333	314	329	314	–	–	–
Canned meat	95	86	93	98	98	86	93	86	118	91	147
Canned fish	6	5	4	7	8	7	6	8	9	–	–
Biscuits, total disposals of home produced	632	622	698	643	704	709	699	724	–	–	–
Breakfast cereals, other than oatmeal and oatmeal flakes	219	229	233	248	249	264	259	273	–	–	–
Glucose	434	446	449	472	460	472	452	499	542	546	557
Production of soft drinks (million litres):											
Concentrated	503	523	570	602	511	544	558	566	555	–	–
Unconcentrated	2,231	2,458	2,642	2,690	2,899	3,417	3,713	3,628	4,112	4,316	–
Compound feedingstuffs: total	10,943	11,855	12,234	10,743	10,420	11,187	10,625	10,729	11,115	11,363	11,361
Cattle food	4,538	5,012	5,456	4,382	4,116	4,486	3,826	3,780	3,947	3,909	3,781
Calf food	436	478	504	422	401	402	352	345	347	324	278
Pig food	2,169	2,317	2,292	2,099	2,142	2,186	2,189	2,180	2,158	2,276	2,360
Poultry food	3,445	3,640	3,532	3,331	3,229	3,473	3,589	3,672	3,616	3,812	3,857
Other compounds	355	408	450	509	532	640	670	753	1,045	1,042	1,088

TIME SERIES. The figures relate to periods of 52 weeks (53 weeks in 1981 and 1987), with the following exceptions which are on calendar year basis: butter, cheese, cream, canned meat, soft drinks, condensed milk and milk powder, canned vegetables, canned and bottled fruit, jam and marmalade and soups.

(1) Excludes cream made from the residual fat of low-fat milk production. (2) From 1981 the method of collecting these figures has changed. They are therefore not comparable with previous years. (3) Provisional figures. (4) Table spreads are only included from 1986 onwards. (5) Total of fowl, ducks, geese and turkeys.

Cattle, Sheep, Pigs and Poultry on Agricultural Holdings[1]

United Kingdom: at June in each year

Source: CSO

Thousands

	1981	1982	1983	1984	1985	1986	1987	1988	1989	1990	1991
Cattle and Calves:											
Dairy herd	3,191	3,250	3,333	3,281	3,150	3,138	3,042	2,911	2,865	2,847	2,770
Beef herd	1,420	1,389	1,358	1,351	1,333	1,308	1,343	1,373	1,495	1,599	1,666
Heifers in calf (first calf)	863	851	847	811	874	879	774	834	793	757	733
Bulls for service	84	84	83	80	78	76	74	75	78	82	81
Other cattle:											
Two years old and over	963	937	904	905	852	769	732	726	733	722	678
One year old and under two	3,041	3,057	3,059	3,069	3,012	2,819	2,749	2,669	2,600	2,654	2,581
Six months old and under one year	1,876	1,890	1,924	1,949	1,905	1,876	1,844	1,702	1,775	1,746	1,695
Under six months old	1,699	1,786	1,783	1,768	1,707	1,668	1,599	1,581	1,637	1,652	1,662
Total	**13,138**	**13,244**	**13,290**	**13,213**	**12,911**	**12,533**	**12,158**	**11,872**	**11,977**	**12,059**	**11,866**
Sheep and lambs:											
Breeding ewes	12,528	12,909	13,310	13,648	13,893	14,252	14,780	15,461	16,154	16,760	16,944
Rams for service	358	366	383	393	406	419	437	461	491	500	503
Other sheep	3,584	3,748	3,764	3,680	3,763	3,961	4,107	4,433	4,740	4,515	4,232
Lambs under one year old	15,628	16,044	16,612	17,080	17,566	18,384	19,377	20,587	21,582	22,023	21,942
Total	**32,097**	**33,067**	**34,069**	**34,802**	**35,628**	**37,016**	**38,701**	**40,942**	**42,967**	**43,799**	**43,621**
Pigs:											
Breeding herd	836	864	856	800	828	824	820	804	757	769	786
Boars for service	43	45	45	42	44	44	44	43	42	43	45
Gilts not yet in pig	87	89	82	77	80	79	81	73	74	85	89
Barren sows for fattening[2]	11	12	15	12	12	12	11	12	10	10	10
Other pigs:											
110 kg and over[2]	90	117	100	91	89	80	67	62	45	51	40
80 kg and under 110 kg	638	630	605	599	589	603	615	621	613	620	652
50 kg and under 80 kg	1,776	1,824	1,868	1,787	1,813	1,863	1,890	1,898	1,779	1,741	1,767
20 kg and under 50 kg	2,227	2,281	2,362	2,198	2,260	2,270	2,253	2,263	2,131	2,109	2,143
Under 20 kg	2,119	2,163	2,241	2,082	2,151	2,163	2,160	2,204	2,058	2,022	2,065
Total	**7,828**	**8,023**	**8,174**	**7,689**	**7,865**	**7,937**	**7,942**	**7,980**	**7,509**	**7,449**	**7,596**
Poultry:											
Fowls:											
Growing pullets	14,219	14,766	11,828	12,536	12,503	12,502	12,230	11,236	9,411	10,452	11,016
Laying flock	44,473	44,792	41,127	40,573	39,538	38,096	38,498	37,389	33,957	33,468	33,273
Breeding flock	6,117	6,457	6,012	6,396	6,104	6,334	7,146	6,879	6,788	7,107	7,238
Table birds	57,830	60,075	58,887	59,341	61,311	63,807	70,754	75,305	70,042	73,588	75,701
Total	**122,639**	**126,091**	**117,854**	**118,846**	**119,456**	**120,740**	**128,628**	**130,809**	**120,198**	**124,615**	**127,228**
Ducks[3]	1,333	1,443	1,566 (Ducks and Geese)	1,530 (Ducks and Geese)	1,654 (Ducks and Geese)	1,747 (Ducks and Geese)	1,757 (Ducks and Geese)	1,836 (Ducks and Geese)	2,101 (Ducks and Geese)	2,216 (Ducks and Geese)	2,191 (Ducks and Geese)
Geese[3]	148	157									
Turkeys	8,167	7,672	8,198	7,134	7,864	–	–	–	–	–	–
Total	**132,286**	**135,363**	**127,618**	**127,507**	**128,968**	–	–	–	–	–	–

(1) Figures from 1979 onwards include estimates for minor holdings not surveyed at the June census in England and Wales. Excludes Scotland except for years 1979, 1983 and 1984. (2) Barren sows for fattening in Northern Ireland are included with "Other pigs weighing 110 kg and over". (3) Excludes data for Scotland 1978, 1980, 1981, 1982.

Forestry

End of period

Source: CSO

Area – thousand hectares
Volume – million cubic metres

	1980/81	1981/82	1982/83	1983/84	1984/85	1985/86	1986/87	1987/88	1988/89	1989/90	1990/91	1991/92
	Years ending 31 March											
Forest area[1]												
United Kingdom	2,121	2,142	2,233	2,258	2,277	2,301	2,328	2,368	2,364	2,400	2,410	2,425
Great Britain	2,054	2,075	2,165[5]	2,189	2,207	2,230	2,256	2,285	2,291	2,327	2,336	2,350
Northern Ireland	67	67	68	69	70	71	72	73	73	73	74	75
Forestry Commission (Great Britain)												
Productive woodland	896	905	909	902	892	889	890	888	888	865[6]	859	855
Plantations and plantable land acquired during year[2]	1.1	2.1	−3.0	−13.7	−15.3	−7.3	−3.7	−4.7	−2.5	−4.5	−0.8	−4.2
New planting[3]	11.6	11.0	9.0	8.4	5.2	4.3	5.3	5.0	4.1	4.1	3.5	3.1
Replanting[3]	5.0	5.5	5.8	6.7	6.0	7.3	8.0	8.1	8.5	7.9	7.7	8.3
Volume of timber removed[4]	2.5	2.7	2.8	3.0	2.9	3.1	3.2	3.4	3.6	3.6	3.6	3.9
Total estates	1,264	1,259	1,251	1,209	1,181	1,166	1,157	1,148	1,143	1,140	1,133	1,128
Private forestry (Great Britain)												
Productive woodland	873	886	1,084[5]	1,116	1,145	1,171	1,195	1,227	1,231	1,266	1,281	1,298
New planting[2]	8.7	12.6	12.5	16.9	16.6	19.4	19.4	24.0	25.4	15.6	15.5	14.3
Replanting[3]	3.3	3.5	3.2	3.2	3.2	4.6	4.6	5.0	4.9	6.3	7.1	7.9
Volume of timber removed[4]	2.3	2.0	2.2	1.8	2.0	2.2	2.4	2.6	3.0	3.0	3.0	2.8

	1980	1981/82	1982/83	1983/84	1984/85	1985/86	1986/87	1987/88	1988/89	1989/90	1990/91	1991/92
State afforestation in Northern Ireland												
Land under plantation	53.9	54.4	55.2	56.3	56.6	57.3	57.9	58.4	58.3	58.5	58.8	60.6
Plantable land acquired during year	0.8	0.3	0.6	0.4	0.1	0.2	0.5	0.4	0.4	0.6	0.4	0.3
Total area planted during year[3]	1.1	1.1	1.2	1.1	1.0	1.2	1.0	1.0	1.0	1.0	1.0	0.9
Total estates	71.5	71.9	72.5	73.2	73.3	73.5	73.9	74.1	74.3	74.6	74.8	75.1

(1) Includes unproductive woodland. (2) Net area acquired. (3) Total area now shows areas of New planting (planting on ground not previously carrying forest) and areas of Replanting (replacing trees after felling). (4) Calendar year ending previous December. (5) The apparent increase in 1982/83 is a result of data from the Census of Woodlands and Trees becoming available. The change is entirely in the private sector of the industry. (6) The apparent decrease in 1989/90 is mainly the result of re-classification of certain woodland types within the Forestry Commission.

TRADE & TRANSPORTATION

Estimated Traffic on All Roads in Great Britain

Source: CSO

Billion vehicle kilometres

	1981	1982	1983	1984	1985	1986	1987	1988	1989	1990	1991[1]
All motor vehicles	276.33	283.88	288.02	303.07	309.59	325.23	350.47	375.71	406.9	410.88	411.6
Cars and taxis[2]	219.62	227.50	231.45	244.30	250.46	264.44	284.63	305.41	331.3	335.9	335.2
Two-wheeled motor vehicles	8.90	9.25	8.31	8.16	7.37	7.07	6.71	6.03	5.9	5.6	5.4
Buses and coaches	3.47	3.49	3.65	3.81	3.66	3.69	4.08	4.33	4.5	4.6	4.8
Light vans[3]	23.39	23.18	23.15	24.48	25.17	26.49	28.98	32.06	35.4	35.7	37.2
Other goods vehicles	20.95	20.46	21.45	22.33	22.94	23.53	26.06	27.90	29.8	29.1	29.0
Total goods vehicles	**44.34**	**43.64**	**44.60**	**46.81**	**48.11**	**50.02**	**55.04**	**59.96**	**65.2**	**64.8**	**66.2**
Pedal cycles	5.46	6.41	6.40	6.41	6.08	5.48	5.74	5.24	5.2	5.3	5.2

(1) Provisional. (2) This category includes three-wheeled cars; excludes all vans whether licensed for private or for commercial use. (3) Not exceeding 30 cwt unladen weight.

Length of Public Roads in Great Britain

At 1 April in each year

Source: CSO

Kilometres

	1980	1981	1982	1983	1984	1985	1986	1987	1988	1989	1990	1991
Motorway[1]	2,556	2,646	2,692	2,741	2,786	2,813	2,920	2,975	2,992	2,995	3,070	3,099
Trunk	12,282	12,269	12,209	12,231	12,271	12,201	12,439	12,419	12,480	12,623	12,597	12,356
Principal	34,298	34,656	34,700	34,819	34,753	34,800	34,868	34,987	34,939	35,039	35,149	35,629
Others[2]	290,497	292,749	294,341	295,985	297,779	298,885	299,849	302,314	303,904	305,946	307,142	308,962
Total	**339,633**	**342,320**	**343,942**	**345,776**	**347,589**	**348,699**	**350,076**	**352,695**	**354,315**	**356,602**	**357,958**	**360,046**

(1) Including local authority motorways, the percentage of which is small, less than 5% (2) Excluding unsurfaced roads and green lanes.

Motor Vehicles Currently Licensed[1,2]

Source: CSO

Great Britain

Thousands

	1981	1982	1983	1984	1985	1986	1987	1988	1989	1990	1991
Total	**19,347**	**19,762**	**20,209**	**20,765**	**21,157**	**21,699**	**22,152**	**23,302**	**24,196**	**24,673**	**24,511**
Private cars[3]	14,943	15,303	15,543	16,055	16,454	16,981	17,421	18,432	19,248	19,742	19,737
Other vehicles[3]	1,548	1,585	1,709	1,770	1,804	1,879	1,952	2,095	2,199	2,247	2,215
Private and light goods[3]	16,491	16,888	17,252	17,825	18,258	18,860	19,373	20,527	21,447	21,989	21,952
Up to 50 c.c.	472	489	474	449	423	389	352	312	280	248	207
Other	899	881	816	776	725	676	626	600	595	585	543
Motor cycles, etc: total	1,371	1,370	1,290	1,225	1,148	1,065	978	912	875	833	750
Public road passenger vehicles: total	110	111	113	116	120	125	129	132	122	115	109
Buses, coaches, taxis, etc											
Not over 8 passengers	40	43	46	49	53	57	58	59	49	42	38
Over 8 passengers	70	68	68	67	67	68	71	73	73	73	71
Goods[4,5]	488	477	496	497	486	484	484	503	505	482	449
Agricultural tractors, etc[6]	365	371	376	375	374	371	374	383	384	375	346
Other licensed vehicles[7]	95	91	86	82	78	73	68	83	77	71	65
Crown vehicles	37	37	39	39	39	39	39	38	38	37	36
All other exempt vehicles	390	417	582	631	656	681	706	722	747	770	804
Exempt from licence duty: total[8]	427	454	621	670	695	720	744	761	785	807	840

(1) Since 1978, censuses have been taken annually on 31 December and are obtained from a full count of licensing records held at DVLA Swansea. Prior to this, figures were compiled from a combination of DVLA data and records held at Local Taxation offices. (2) Excludes vehicles officially registered by the Armed Forces. (3) Includes all vehicles used privately. Mostly consists of private cars and vans. However, from October 1990, goods vehicles less than 3,500 kg gross vehicle weight are now included in this category. (4) Mostly goods vehicles over 3,500 kg gross vehicle weight but includes farmers' and showmen's vehicles that are less than 3,500 kg. (5) Includes agricultural vans and lorries, showmen's goods vehicles licensed to draw trailers. (6) Includes combine harvesters, mowing machines, digging machines, mobile cranes and works trucks. (7) Includes three-wheelers, pedestrian-controlled vehicles and showmen's haulage and recovery vehicles. New tax class introduced January 1988. (8) From 1980 includes electric vehicles which are now exempt from licence duty.

Northern Ireland[1]

Number

	1980	1981	1982	1983	1984	1985	1986	1987[3]	1988[4]	1989	1990	1991
Private cars, etc.	364,590	365,000	388,030	411,780	430,660	405,090	415,050	434,237	443,081	456,611	481,090	498,471
Cycles and tricycles	14,720	14,550	15,500	14,790	15,700	12,360	10,820	8,946	8,957	9,460	10,167	9,684
Public road passenger vehicles:												
total	2,270	2,510	2,210	2,200	2,780	2,460	2,450	3,258	3,333	2,962	2,786	2,887
Taxis up to 4 seats	710	840	720	940	1,240	860	940	1,087	1,128	741	603	656
Buses, coaches, over 4 seats	1,560	1,670	1,490	1,260	1,540	1,600	1,510	2,171	2,205	2,221	2,183	2,231
General (HGV) goods vehicles:												
total	38,900	33,760	34,060	29,450	34,510	26,650	23,610	22,789	22,547	23,514	16,191	13,907
Unladen weight:												
Not over 1,525 kg	16,720	13,190	15,490	10,530	15,440	8,850	7,830	29,009	–	–	–	–
Over 1,525 and not over 12,000 kg	6,710	6,140	5,730	9,690	9,310	8,070	7,690	17,521	17,524	18,424	–	–
Over 12,000 kg	10,740	10,510	11,660	7,740	8,230	7,960	6,880	7,318	–	–	–	–
Farmers' goods vehicles[2]	4,620	3,770	1,090	1,440	1,430	1,630	1,090	5,101	4,858	4,948	4,962	4,994

(Continued)

Number

	1980	1981	1982	1983	1984	1985	1986	1987[3]	1988[4]	1989	1990	1991
Tractors for general haulage	80	130	70	50	90	120	100	148	144	120	–	–
Tower wagons	20	20	–	10	20	20	19	21	22	–	–	–
Agricultural tractors and engines, etc[4]	9,580	7,660	9,150	9,870	9,840	8,370	7,310	6,806	7,640	7,965	8,021	7,199
Other	–	–	–	–	–	–	–	–	–	–	513	403
Vehicles exempt from duty: total	12,288	13,215	13,610	13,764	13,208	13,681	13,615	13,308	15,427	17,144	–	–
Government owned	7,978	9,395	9,390	9,604	10,258	11,071	11,115	4,458	5,021	5,142	5,211	5,120
Other: Ambulances	70	10	290	342	358	203	324	41	49	56	74	98
Fire engines	60	110	140	40	50	80	50	14	210	234	162	250
Other exempt	4,180	3,700	3,790	3,778	2,542	2,327	2,126	8,795	10,147	11,712	13,937	15,305
Total	**442,348**	**436,695**	**462,560**	**481,854**	**506,698**	**468,611**	**472,855**	**489,344**	**500,985**	**517,656**	**543,114**	**558,318**

(1) Licences current at any time during the quarter ended December. (2) Owned by a farmer and available for hauling produce and requisites for his farm. (3) Licences current at 31 March 1988. (4) Licences current at 31 December 1988.

World Motor Vehicle Production, 1950–1992

Source: American Automobile Manufacturers Association

Thousands

Year	Canada	Europe	Japan	United States	Other	World Total
1992	1,968	17,244	12,499	9,702	5,964	47,377
1991	1,873	17,527	13,245	8,811	5,040	46,496
1990	1,928	18,761	13,487	9,783	4,496	48,345
1989	2,002	18,979	13,026	10,874	4,220	49,101
1988	1,949	18,234	12,700	11,214	4,113	48,210
1987	1,635	17,548	12,249	10,925	3,546	45,903
1986	1,854	16,727	12,260	11,335	3,121	45,297
1985	1.933	16,015	12,271	11,653	2,939	44,811
1984	1,829	15,290	11,465	10,925	2,549	42,058
1983	1,525	15,706	11,112	9,225	2,187	39,755
1982	1,276	14,808	10,732	6,986	2,311	36,113
1981	1,289	14,439	11,180	7,943	2,379	37,230
1980	1,324	15,445	11,043	8,010	2,692	38,514
1970	1,160	13,033	5,289	8,284	1,637	29,403
1960	398	6,837	482	7,905	866	16,488
1950	388	1,991	32	8,006	160	10,577

Note: As far as can be determined, production refers to vehicles locally manufactured.

World Motor Vehicle Production, 1992

Source: American Automobile Manufacturers Association

Country	Passenger Cars	Commercial Vehicles	Total
Argentina	220,498	41,445	261,943
Australia	279,550	4,858	284,408
Austria	23,479	4,491	27,970
Belgium	222,680	75,392	298,072
Brazil	814,423	257,141	1,071,564
Canada	1,024,739	943,758	1,988,497
China	180,000	900,000	1,080,000
CIS	930,000	600,000	1,530,000
Czechoslovakia	202,450	26,608	229,058
France	3,329,490	438,310	3,767,800
Germany	4,863,721	330,221	5,193,942
Hungary	12,000	6,000	18,000
India	153,867	170,518	324,385
Italy	1,476,627	209,860	1,686,487
Japan	9,378,694	3,120,590	12,499,284
Korea, South	1,306,752	422,944	1,729,696
Malaysia	117,773	11,414	129,187
Mexico	778,413	304,678	1,083,091
Netherlands	94,019	23,973	117,992
Poland	200,000	30,000	230,000
Spain	1,790,615	331,272	2,121,887
Sweden	293,499	63,096	358,595
United Kingdom	1,291,880	248,453	1,540,333
United States	5,663,284	4,038,218	9,701,502
Yugoslavia	116,391	9,250	125,641
Total	**34,764,844**	**12,612,490**	**47,377,334**

Rates of Vehicle Excise Duty

(as from 18 March 1993)

Source: Department of Transport

1. Private/light goods vehicles (i.e. goods vehicles not over 3500 kg gross vehicle weight)

	12 month rate £	6 months rate £
Private Vehicles, Light Vans, Estate Cars, etc.	125.00	68.75
Vehicles constructed before 1.1.47	70.00	38.50
Light Goods Farmer's	85.00	46.75
Light Goods Showman's	85.00	46.75

2. Bicycles, tricycles (not over 450 kg)

		12 month rate £	6 months rate £
Motor cycles (with or without sidecar)	Not Over 150cc	15.00	–
	Over 150cc up to 250cc	35.00	–
	All other motorcycles	55.00*	30.25
Tricycles	Not Over 150cc	15.00	–
	All other tricycles	55.00*	30.25

*If constructed before 1.1.33, weighs not more than 101.6 kg and of more than 250cc, the rate is £30.00.

Cars[1] and Car Ownership: 1981 and 1990

Source: CSO

	1981				1990			
	Percentage of households without the regular use of a car	Percentage of households with regular use of[1] One car only	Two or more cars	Cars per 1,000 pop.	Percentage of households without the regular use of a car	Percentage of households with regular use of[1] One car only	Two or more cars	Cars per 1,000 pop.
Great Britain	39	45	15	281	33	44	23	363
North	48	41	10	227	42	43	16	295
Yorkshire & Humberside	46	43	12	245	38	46	16	323
East Midlands	37	47	15	273	31	44	24	351
East Anglia	31	51	18	321	26	47	26	420
South East	36	46	19	316	28	44	28	396
Greater London	45	42	14	287	38	42	19	355
Rest of South East	30	48	22	336	23	45	32	420
South West	31	51	18	329	25	48	27	410
West Midlands	38	46	16	290	35	42	24	386
North West	45	42	13	250	37	44	20	338
England	39	45	16	288	32	44	23	372
Wales	38	47	15	271	30	49	21	346
Scotland	49	40	11	217	42	41	17	294
Northern Ireland	40	46	14	237	34	47	19	302

(1) Includes cars and vans normally available to the household.

Driving Licence Costs

Source: DVLA

Provisional Driving Licences	On or after 01.02.93
First licence	£21
(if Highway Code required	£21.99)
Renewal of licence issued before 1.10.82	£21
Renewal after disqualification	
• If imposed before 1.11.88	FREE
• If imposed on or after 1.11.88	£12
• For certain drink/drive offences	*
Duplicate licence	£6
Exchange licence (removal of endorsements)	£6
Replacement licence (change of name/address)	FREE
Exchange licence for first full licence	FREE
Medical Renewal	FREE
Medical Renewal – over 70	£6 (if 3 yearly issue)
(You will be advised when a fee (£6) is required for renewal of licences of less than 3 years duration)	

Full Driving Licences	On or after 01.02.93
First GB licence	£21
(but if you have already paid £10, £15, £17 for your provisional licence)	FREE
Renewal licence if last full licence was issued after 1.1.76	£6
Renewal after age 70	£6
Renewal after disqualification	
• If imposed before 1.11.88	FREE
• If imposed on or after 1.11.88	£12
• For certain drink/drive offences	*
Duplicate licence	£6
Exchange licence (removal of endorsement, claiming an additional category if your licence has full entitlement)	£6
Exchanging a Northern Ireland full licence for a first GB full licence	£6
Medical Renewal	FREE
Medical Renewal – over 70	£6 (if 3 yearly issue)
(You will be advised when a fee (£6) is required for renewal of licences of less than 3 years duration)	
Replacement licence (change of name or address)	FREE

You can obtain further driving licence information from the *Driver Enquiry Unit*, DVLC, Swansea SA6 7JL. Tel: 0792 772151
If you have queries about vehicle licensing or registration, you should contact the *Vehicle Enquiry Unit*. Tel. 0792 772134

*You will be advised about the fee when you renew your licence.

Driving Test Costs

	Weekday	Saturday
Car	£23.50	£35.00
Motorcycle (accompanied)	£34.00	£44.00
LGV/PCV	£55.50	£75.00

Driving Test Pass Rates

United Kingdom[1]

Source: CSO

Millions and percentages

	Tests conducted (millions)	Pass rate (percentages) Men	Women	All
1980	1.96	53.0	41.5	47.3
1981	2.03	52.9	42.5	47.6
1982	2.01	53.1	42.9	48.1
1983	1.89	53.8	43.7	48.7
1984	1.78	54.3	44.2	49.1
1985	1.84	54.2	43.7	48.6
1986	1.95	54.1	43.8	49.7
1987	1.98	55.6	46.1	50.7
1987	2.03	56.2	46.3	51.7
1988	2.05	57.2	47.2	52.0
1989	1.99	57.3	47.7	52.2
1990	2.04	57.3	48.5	51.3
1991	1.85	57.3	46.6	51.3

(1) Prior to 1986 coverage is for Great Britain only.

Road Deaths[1]: International Comparison, 1990

Source: CSO

	Road vehicles per 1,000 population	Rate of road deaths per 100,000 population	Rate of road deaths per 100,000 motor vehicles	Rate of car user deaths per billion car kilometres[2]
United Kingdom	439	9.4	21	7.1
Belgium[4]	462	19.9	43	23.3
Denmark	420	12.3	29	9.8
France	512	19.9	39	–
Germany (Fed. Rep.)	586	12.6	22	11.3
Greece[4]	277	19.9	72	–
Irish Republic	301	13.6	45	10.7
Italy[3]	604	12.4	21	–
Luxembourg[3,4]	584	17.9	31	–
Netherlands	453	9.2	20	8.8
Portugal[3,4]	365	31.5	86	–
Spain	432	23.2	54	55.4
Austria	546	20.3	37	–
Finland	472	13.0	28	10.3
German (Dem. Rep.)[4]	420	19.1	45	33.0
Hungary[4]	223	23.1	104	–
Norway	554	7.8	14	–
Sweden	523	9.1	17	–
Switzerland	605	13.9	23	9.8
Yugoslavia[3]	157	19.5	124	–
Japan	615	11.8	19	16.0
USA[4]	773	17.9	23	9.9

(1) Road deaths are normally counted as those which occur within 30 days of the accident. (2) United Kingdom figure relates only to Great Britain. (3) 1989 data. (4) The number of road vehicles and deaths per 100,000 motor vehicles excludes mopeds.

MOT Tests

The Department of Transport specifies that cars, motorcycles, motor caravans, light goods and dual-purpose vehicles more than three years old must be tested for roadworthiness every year. Private passenger vehicles and private service vehicles must be tested every year regardless of age.

It is an offence to use on a public road a vehicle of testable age that does not have a current test certificate.

Test Fees
(as from 1 January 1993)

Class	Vehicle	Fee
I	Solo motorcycles	£10.35
II	Motorcycles with or without sidecar	£17.30
III	3-wheeled vehicles under 450 kg unladen	£20.30
IV	Private cars & goods vehicles under 3000 kg, including minibuses with 8 passenger seats, motor caravans and dual-purpose vehicles	£24.00
V	Private passenger vehicles, including ambulances, with 12 or more seats	£30.35
		(weekday/Saturday)
VI	Public Service Vehicles (PSV) 9–12 passenger seats:	£29.80/£49.80
	Retest after failure	£14.90/£24.90
	13 or more passenger seats:	£42.70/£70.20
	Retest after failure	£21.00/£34.75
VII	Light goods vehicles (LGV) between 3000 & 3500 kg unladen	£34.70/£54.20
	Retest after failure	£17.60/£27.10
	Trailer	£17.90/£30.20
	Retest after failure	£9.70/£15.80

MOT Checks

Lighting equipment: front lamps, rear lamps, headlamps, headlamp aim, stop lamps, rear reflectors, direction indicators.

Steering & suspension: steering controls, steering mechanism, power steering, transmission shafts, stub axle assemblies, wheel bearings, suspension, shock absorbers.

Brakes: service brake condition, parking brake condition, service brake performance, parking brake performance, service brake balance.

Tyres & wheels: tyre type, tyre condition, roadwheels.

Seat belts: security of mountings, condition, operation.

General items: windscreen washers, windscreen wipers, horn, exhaust system, silencer, vehicle structure.

If your vehicle fails the test and you want to continue using it on the road it must be repaired immediately.

Retesting
(Classes I–V)

If the vehicle is left at a station that undertakes repairs for repair and retest, the retest is free.

A full fee is payable if the vehicle is *not* repaired at the testing station which carries out the test, or if the vehicle is submitted for retesting more than 14 days after being failed.

Half the full test fee is payable if the vehicle is taken away from the testing station which did the test and returned for repair and retest to that or any other testing station within 14 days of being failed.

Only one free retest is permissable per MOT.

Road Accident Casualty Rates

Great Britain

Source: CSO

Rate per 100 million vehicle kilometres

	1981	1982	1983	1984	1985	1986	1987	1988	1989	1990	1991[2]
Pedal cyclists:											
Killed	5.7	4.6	5.1	5.4	4.7	5.0	4.9	4.7	5.7	4.9	4.1
Killed or seriously injured	101	93	100	103	93	96	90	93	99	87	72
All severities	465	440	480	485	446	479	457	494	552	501	424
Two-wheel motor vehicle riders:											
Killed	11	10	10	11	10	10	10	10	9	11	9
Killed or seriously injured	223	217	220	222	224	213	189	193	182	184	139
All severities	694	690	699	711	701	680	628	657	548	646	502
Car drivers:											
Killed	0.6	0.6	0.5	0.5	0.5	0.5	0.5	0.4	0.5	0.4	0.4
Killed or seriously injured	9	9	7	7	7	6	6	6	5	5	5
All severities	37	37	32	33	34	34	32	33	33	34	33
Bus and coach drivers:											
Killed	0.1	0.1	0.1	0.1	0.0	0.0	0.0	0.1	0.0	0.1	–
Killed or seriously injured	2	2	2	2	1	2	1	1	1	2	1
All serverities	15	14	13	12	15	14	13	13	15	14	13
Light Goods Vehicle drivers:											
Killed	0.4	0.3	0.3	0.3	0.3	0.3	0.3	0.3	0.3	0.2	0.2
Killed or seriously injured	6	5	4	4	4	4	4	4	3	3	3
All severities	24	23	19	19	21	22	20	20	19	18	16
Heavy Goods Vehicle drivers:											
Killed	0.2	0.3	0.2	0.3	0.2	0.3	0.2	0.2	0.2	0.2	0.2
Killed or seriously injured	3	3	3	3	3	3	3	2	2	2	2
All severities	11	12	11	12	12	12	11	11	11	11	11
All road users:[1]											
Killed	2.1	2.0	1.8	1.8	1.6	1.6	1.4	1.4	1.3	1.3	1.1
Killed or seriously injured	30	30	26	25	24	22	19	19	17	16	14
All severities	115	115	105	105	101	97	87	89	84	82	76

(1) Includes other road users and road user not reported. (2) Rate based on provisional traffic estimates.

Buses and Coaches[1]

Great Britain

Source: CSO

	1980	1981	1982	1983	1984	1985/6	1986/7	1987/8	1988/9	1989/90	1990/91
Number of vehicles	69.1	69.9	70.7	70.2	68.8	67.9	69.5	71.7	72.0	72.6	72.1
Single deck	43.6	44.7	44.8	44.9	43.2	42.9	45.1	47.6	48.5	49.8	49.9
Double deck	25.6	25.2	25.9	25.3	25.6	25.0	24.5	24.1	23.5	22.8	22.2
London Buses Ltd[2]	6.2	5.9	6.2	5.6	5.7	5.2	5.1	5.0	5.1	5.0	5.20
Metropolitan PTCs[3]	10.3	10.1	9.9	9.6	9.5	9.1	8.6	8.4	8.4	8.2	8.1
Municipal PTCs[3]	5.7	5.5	5.3	5.3	5.3	5.2	5.1	5.4	5.6	5.5	5.5
National Bus Company[4,5]	16.0	15.3	15.0	14.6	14.5	14.7	16.4	16.4	–	–	–
Scottish Bus Group[4]	3.6	3.4	3.3	3.1	3.1	3.4	3.4	3.1	3.1	2.8	2.7
Independent operators[5]	27.4	29.7	31.0	31.9	30.8	30.3	30.9	33.5	–	–	–
NBC and Independents	–	–	–	–	–	–	–	–	49.8	51.0	50.6
Vehicle kilometres (millions)	3,280	3,227	3,206	3,280	3,314	3,323	3,414	3,664	3,735	3,847	3,838
London Buses Ltd[2]	279	282	265	264	268	262	251	245	249	253	261
Metropolitan PTCs[3]	510	487	485	482	486	488	458	485	485	486	476
Municipal PTCs[3]	241	233	232	231	235	233	237	257	278	284	275
National Bus Company[4,5]	1,026	973	972	969	981	979	1,042	1,047	–	–	–
Scottish Bus Group[4]	203	206	200	202	201	210	210	204	207	209	195
Independent operators[5]	1,020	1,048	1,051	1,131	1,142	1,152	1,216	1,425	–	–	–
NBC and Independents	–	–	–	–	–	–	–	–	2,516	2,605	2,632
Passenger journeys (millions)	6,783	6,278	6,097	6,210	6,237	6,176	5,897	5,907	5,805	5,682	5,470
London Buses Ltd[2]	1,183	1,081	1,043	1,089	1,163	1,147	1,122	1,167	1,140	1,090	1,068
Metropolitan PTCs[3]	1,973	1,814	1,765	1,796	1,826	1,847	1,605	1,504	1,444	1,385	1,287
Municipal PTCs[3]	952	886	854	854	837	799	761	718	721	681	634
National Bus Company[4,5]	1,669	1,529	1,479	1,460	1,440	1,453	1,415	1,400	–	–	–
Scottish Bus Group[4]	339	322	314	319	311	320	307	287	284	255	236
Independent operators[5]	666	647	642	691	659	609	688	831	–	–	–
NBC and independents	–	–	–	–	–	–	–	–	2,216	2,272	2,244
Passenger receipts (£ million)	1,637	1,745	1,908	2,024	2,085	2,219	2,268	2,389	2,514	2,724	2,853
London Buses Ltd[2]	207	209	254	266	264	292	288	292	307	336	360
Metropolitan PTCs[3]	328	334	364	379	389	406	417	431	450	470	475
Municipal PTCs[3]	160	173	181	196	210	220	220	228	239	255	268
National Bus Company[4,5]	491	520	543	573	593	629	636	640	–	–	–
Scottish Bus Group[4]	109	117	127	134	136	140	138	130	131	128	127
Independent operators[5]	342	393	437	476	494	532	570	668	–	–	–
NBC and Independents	–	–	–	–	–	–	–	–	1,387	1,534	1,622

(1) Includes trams. (2) 1979–83 London Transport Executive; 1984 London Regional Transport; 1985 onwards London Regional Buses Ltd. (3) Including ex-PTCs. (4) Including former NBC or SBG operators. (5) Following structural changes to the industry, data for 1988/89 onwards are not shown separately for ex-NBC and independent operators.

Driving Abroad

As a Visitor

If you wish to drive abroad, check with your local AA, RAC, RSAC or NBRC office whether you need, and are entitled to, an International Driving Permit (IDP). Where appropriate, these organizations will issue an IDP. You do not have to be a member, but you will need to show your full licence or prove that you hold one. IDPs are not available from any other source.

As a New Resident

If you go to live permanently in another country, you may be able to apply to exchange a valid full GB licence for that country's licence. EC countries permit an exchange (on surrender of your GB licence) within one year of becoming resident. For other countries check with the driver licensing authorities on arrival.

British Rail: Passenger Business, and Investment

Great Britain

Source: CSO

	1976	1981	1986–87	1991–92
Passenger business				
Passenger carriages (thousands)	17.1	16.2	13.7	11.8
Passenger kilometres per passenger carriage (millions)	1.7	1.8	2.3	2.7
Passenger receipts per passenger kilometre (pence)[1]	6.2	6.2	6.3	6.6
PSO and PTE grant per passenger kilometre (pence)[1]	4.0	4.6	3.3	3.1
Investment (£ million)	609	496	546	1,005

(1) Adjusted for general inflation by the GDP market price deflator (1991–92 prices).

British Rail: Performance Indicators

Great Britain

Source: CSO

Percentages

	1986–87	1990–91[1]	1991–92
Percentage of trains arriving within punctuality target[2]			
InterCity	85	85	84
Network SouthEast	91	90	91
Regional			
Express and long rural	91	90	92
Urban and short rural	–	–	90
Percentage of trains cancelled			
InterCity	0.8	2.2	2.2
Network SouthEast	1.6	2.1	1.3
Regional	0.5	2.7	1.5

(1) Severe winter weather affected some services. (2) InterCity and Regional (express and long rural), 10 minutes; Network SouthEast and Regional (urban and short rural), 5 minutes.

Accidents on Railways

Great Britain

Source: CSO

Number

	1981	1982	1983	1984	1985	1986	1987	1988	1989	1990	1991/92
Train accidents											
Number of accidents: total[1]	1,014	998	1,255	1,359	1,240	1,171	1,165	1,330	1,434	1,283	960
Collisions	280	250	315	300	282	266	290	296	329	290	187
Derailments	148	173	220	230	229	192	193	231	192	183	144
Running into level-crossing gates and other obstructions	353	284	363	471	440	451	391	486	510	473	340
Fires	165	163	165	168	191	174	191	229	283	257	225
Miscellaneous	68	128	192	190	98	88	101	88	120	80	64
Persons killed	7	11	10	30	6	27	11	40	18	4	11
Passengers	4	–	2	18	–	8	3	34	6	–	2
Railway staff	1	8	1	6	–	5	1	2	6	1	2
Others	2	3	7	6	6	14	7	4	6	3	7
Persons injured	195	264	218	475	380	510	396	705	405	243	391
Passengers	127	150	88	386	261	342	310	615	312	157	307
Railway staff	34	92	93	68	88	137	65	68	71	73	65
Others	34	22	37	21	31	31	21	22	22	13	19
Other accidents through movement of railway vehicles											
Persons killed	58	40	53	41	55	41	57	53	41	75	73
Passengers	31	18	25	21	31	24	36	34	25	37	53
Railway staff	21	17	24	14	16	8	11	11	8	19	9
Others	6	5	4	6	8	9	10	8	8	19	11
Persons injured	2,450	1,946	2,459	2,486	2,489	2,443	2,776	2,810	2,769	2,777	2,360
Passengers	2,218	1,822	2,341	2,400	2,383	2,346	2,689	2,721	2,698	2,658	2,254
Railway staff	219	121	97	73	96	80	84	85	63	116	104
Others	13	3	21	13	10	17	3	4	8	3	2
Other accidents on railway premises											
Persons killed	11	6	6	5	13	4	37	4	10	5	10
Passenger	4	2	2	–	2	1	29	1	2	2	3
Railway staff	5	2	3	5	9	3	4	3	4	2	6
Others	2	2	1	–	2	–	4	–	4	1	1
Persons injured	7,379	6,490	6,590	6,267	6,295	6,528	6,614	7,351	7,628	6,978	6,900
Passengers	2,657	2,571	3,381	3,473	3,518	3,577	3,650	4,035	4,429	3,647	–
Railway staff	4,530	3,740	2,981	2,530	2,533	2,691	2,761	3,142	3,001	3,118	3,335
Others	192	179	228	264	244	260	203	174	198	213	146
Trespassers and suicides											
Persons killed	369	296	358	339	318	325	317	374	298	285	334
Persons injured	127	141	153	128	128	120	101	129	92	123	92

(1) The figures from 1982 onwards include accidents to non-passenger trains on non-passenger lines not previously reported.

Number of Journeys and Distance Travelled per Person per Week: 1988–1990

Great Britain

Source: CSO

Number of journeys and miles travelled

	Journey purpose									
	To or from work	In course of work	Education	Escorting: Work	Escorting: Education	Shopping	Other personal business	Social or entertainment	Holidays/ day trips/ other	All purposes
Number of journeys per person per week										
0–15 years	0.1	–	2.2	0.3	0.4	1.4	1.0	3.2	2.5	11.0
16–59 years										
Males	6.8	1.7	0.3	0.6	0.2	2.6	2.0	3.9	1.7	19.9
Females	3.9	0.5	0.3	0.3	0.7	3.5	1.7	3.7	1.8	16.5
60 years and over	0.7	0.2	–	0.1	–	3.3	1.6	2.7	1.4	10.0
All ages	3.2	0.6	0.6	0.4	0.3	2.8	1.6	3.4	1.8	14.9
Distance travelled per person per week (miles)										
0–15 year	0.3	0.2	7.8	1.6	0.9	7.0	4.9	25.9	21.1	69.8
16–59 years										
Males	63.8	34.6	2.1	2.7	0.9	13.6	12.9	38.3	21.9	190.9
Females	24.0	5.0	2.2	1.7	1.9	17.6	10.1	35.3	22.6	120.7
60 years and over	4.9	2.5	–	0.6	0.2	13.9	7.7	23.1	18.7	71.6
All ages	26.0	11.7	2.9	1.7	1.1	13.4	9.3	31.5	21.4	119.0

Consumers' Expenditure per Head[1] on Transport

United Kingdom

Source: CSO

£ per week at 1985 prices and percentages

	1971	1976	1981	1984	1986	1989	1990	1991
Net purchase of motor vehicles, spares and accessories	2.54	2.43	2.85	3.34	3.81	4.83	4.33	3.53
Maintenance and running of motor vehicles	0.94	1.36	1.51	1.64	1.66	2.05	2.68	2.04
Railway fares[2]	0.47	0.43	0.46	0.49	0.52	0.55	0.55	0.52
Bus and coach fares[2]	0.99	0.91	0.69	0.65	0.62	0.62	0.62	0.57
Other travel and transport[3]	0.73	0.89	1.41	1.52	1.85	2.56	2.55	2.63
All transport and vehicles	5.67	6.01	6.93	7.65	8.47	10.60	10.73	9.30
Expenditure on transport and vehicles as a percentage of total consumers' expenditure	*10.2*	*9.9*	*10.4*	*10.7*	*10.7*	*11.6*	*11.7*	*10.3*

(1) Average weekly expenditure per head of population. (2) Includes purchase of season tickets. (3) Includes purchase and maintenance of other vehicles and boats.

United Kingdom International Passenger Movement by Sea and Air

Arrivals plus departures by country of embarkation or landing

Source: CSO

Thousands

	1981	1982	1983	1984	1985	1986	1987	1988	1989	1990	1991
All passenger movements											
By sea	25,222	26,359	26,776	26,205	26,287	26,797	26,103	24,994	28,967	29,650	31,128
Air	42,962	43,477	45,244	49,984	51,772	56,555	65,742	70,524	74,424	76,417	71,889
Irish Republic:											
By sea	2,422	2,621	2,761	2,875	2,866	2,628	2,581	2,434	2,737	2,773	2,037
By air	1,806	1,726	1,645	1,714	1,807	2,107	2,721	3,521	4,091	4,436	3,948
Total	**4,228**	**4,347**	**4,406**	**4,589**	**4,673**	**4,735**	**5,302**	**5,955**	**6,828**	**7,209**	**5,985**
European continent and Mediterranean Sea area[5]											
By sea: total	22,603	23,628	23,856	23,172	23,241	24,026	22,357	22,399	26,071	26,876	27,849
Belgium	4,714	4,678	4,415	4,608	4,411	3,792	3,626	3,232	3,444	3,588	3,510
France[6]	14,734	15,747	16,140	15,353	15,645	16,867	16,530	15,975	19,246	20,104	21,248
Netherlands	1,958	1,968	2,210	2,191	2,207	2,258	2,090	2,218	2,365	2,508	2,459
Other European Community[7]	772	808	705	656	589	649	671	590	591	383	416
Other countries	425	427	386	364	389	459	440	384	425	293	252
By air: total	28,598	30,087	31,652	35,469	36,199	41,186	47,599	49,955	51,560	51,834	46,373
Belgium and Luxembourg	816	807	881	1,014	1,080	1,092	1,236	1,365	1,443	1,553	1,351
Denmark	510	490	548	592	613	622	670	696	780	883	909
Federal Republic of Germany	3,948	2,998	3,006	3,384	3,644	3,820	4,347	4,492	4,800	5,591	5,115
France	3,105	3,193	3,275	3,537	3,736	3,667	4,236	4,883	5,702	6,231	5,918
Italy	2,335	2,378	2,494	2,582	2,583	2,714	3,065	3,095	3,311	3,453	3,079
Netherlands	1,813	1,843	1,808	2,014	2,227	2,311	2,659	2,896	3,070	3,291	3,162
Norway	543	585	616	647	721	706	725	850	792	864	769
Portugal[1]	954	1,050	1,152	1,329	1,649	2,043	2,263	2,156	2,137	2,249	2,193
Sweden	450	433	454	502	511	566	644	753	842	943	835
Switzerland	1,469	1,576	1,711	1,875	2,016	2,112	2,325	2,490	2,656	2,737	2,541
Greece	2,095	2,123	2,006	2,301	2,875	3,349	3,980	3,796	3,526	3,577	3,459
Spain[2]	7,159	8,635	9,571	11,217	9,513	12,678	14,800	14,865	14,234	11,853	8,406
Yugoslavia	492	476	480	605	813	899	1,070	1,046	1,053	1,145	257
Eastern Europe	454	360	408	476	590	543	629	751	852	994	1,081
Middle East countries[4]	1,490	1,513	1,556	1,563	1,596	1,609	1,638	1,622	1,716	1,716	1,619
Austria	228	240	258	300	364	381	528	707	851	907	844
Rest of other Western Europe[3]	1,736	1,385	1,429	1,531	1,669	2,072	2,784	3,492	3,795	3,847	3,622

(Continued)

Thousands

	1981	1982	1983	1984	1985	1986	1987	1988	1989	1990	1991
Rest of world											
By sea: total	35.4	22.6	35.5	36.1	42.4	36.2	40.8	33.6	31.1	21.7	34.0
United States of America	27.5	16.9	28.7	28.9	35.1	31.4	36.0	30.7	29.3	18.0	29.5
Canada	1.9	1.4	1.7	1.1	1.1	1.5	2.4	–	–	–	–
Australia	2.0	1.7	1.3	1.6	2.1	1.0	1.0	1.1	0.4	1.7	1.7
New Zealand	0.5	0.4	0.2	0.2	–	0.4	0.4	0.2	0.1	0.3	0.3
South Africa	0.6	0.2	1.4	2.3	2.3	0.9	0.2	0.6	0.1	0.7	0.8
West Africa	0.4	0.2	0.2	0.2	0.1	0.2	0.2	0.3	0.1	0.3	0.5
British West Indies and Bermuda	0.1	–	0.2	–	–	–	–	–	–	–	0.1
Other countries	2.4	1.6	1.7	1.6	1.4	0.9	0.9	0.5	1.0	0.5	0.8
By air: total	14,289	13,767	14,412	15,733	16,740	16,781	19,224	21,156	22,991	24,398	24,073
United States of America	6,132	5,334	5,783	6,517	6,970	6,345	7,745	8,587	9,447	10,244	9,697
Canada	1,451	1,370	1,367	1,387	2,228	1,501	1,684	1,879	1,996	2,088	1,853
Australasia	509	539	500	509	509	494	531	573	486	615	753
North Africa	765	687	684	648	717	737	872	932	930	859	604
Rest of Africa	1,257	1,277	1,268	1,231	1,303	1,254	1,184	1,249	1,321	1,445	1,542
South America	123	100	83	82	95	106	122	150	192	249	285
Latin America and Caribbean	454	433	361	–	–	–	–	–	–	–	–
Indian sub-continent	671	683	634	628	676	719	786	897	1,037	1,109	908
Japan	253	264	264	303	337	356	459	549	699	822	820
Rest of Asia	933	978	1,038	1,115	1,233	1,340	1,517	1,610	1,820	1,951	1,988
Pleasure cruises beginning and/or ending at United Kingdom seaports	162	86	124	121	137	107	125	127	129	153	172

(1) Includes Azores and Madeira. (2) Includes Canary Islands. (3) Includes Cyprus, Faroes, Finland, Gibraltar, Iceland, Malta, Turkey, Indian Ocean Islands. (4) Includes Israel, Iran, Iraq, Jordan, Kuwait, Lebanon, Gulf States, Saudi Arabia, United Arab Emirates, Yemeni Arab Republic, Yemeni People's Republic. (5) Includes North Africa and Middle East Mediterranean countries. (6) Includes hovercraft passengers. (7) Greece, Portugal and Spain have been included in this grouping from 1977 onwards, even though they joined the EC in 1981 and 1986 respectively.

Air Traffic Between the United Kingdom and Abroad[1]

Aircraft flights and passengers carried

Source: CSO

Thousands

	1981	1982	1983	1984	1985	1986	1987	1988	1989	1990	1991
Flights											
United Kingdom airlines											
Scheduled services	149.7	143.5	141.9	151.3	170.8	177.5	188.5	216.9	245.0	271.0	250.5
Non-scheduled services	162.2	176.3	184.9	214.0	196.2	198.8	219.2	225.5	221.3	207.9	202.6
Overseas airlines[2]											
Scheduled services	152.0	154.3	155.2	160.9	172.8	195.8	222.8	249.8	269.9	294.8	300.4
Non-scheduled services	31.9	37.3	36.5	40.2	39.5	43.6	45.2	43.0	46.1	45.5	34.6
Total	**495.8**	**511.4**	**518.5**	**566.3**	**579.3**	**615.8**	**675.7**	**735.2**	**782.3**	**819.2**	**788.1**
Passengers carried											
United Kingdom airlines											
Scheduled services	13,559.0	12,214.7	12,140.0	13,174.2	14,854.3	15,082.9	17,473.8	19,237.6	21,863.2	25,316.8	23,721.6
Non-scheduled services	12,128.9	13,216.9	14,661.9	16,643.7	15,529.0	12,929.7	22,250.5	23,062.1	22,558.8	19,679.1	19,715.2
Overseas airlines[2]											
Scheduled services	15,398.8	15,520.5	16,065.6	17,623.0	18,815.6	19,409.5	22,441.5	25,029.3	26,517.8	28,224.4	26,719.4
Non-scheduled services	2,645.4	3,180.1	3,417.4	3,713.9	3,663.8	4,186.0	4,412.8	4,086.5	4,325.6	4,187.9	3,078.8
Total	**43,732.0**	**44,131.9**	**46,284.9**	**51,154.8**	**52,862.7**	**51,608.1**	**66,578.6**	**71,415.5**	**75,265.3**	**77,408.2**	**72,785.0**

(1) Excludes travel to and from the Channel Islands. (2) Includes airlines of overseas UK Territories.

Passenger Airline[1] Accidents

United Kingdom

Source: CSO

	Passenger casualties			Crew casualties		Thousand aircraft stage flights per fatal accident	Million aircraft km flown per fatal accident	Thousand passengers carried per passenger killed	Millon passenger km flown per passenger killed	Fatal accidents		Passengers killed per hundred million passenger km
	Number of fatal accidents	Killed	Seriously injured	Killed	Seriously injured					per 100,000 aircraft stage fights	per hundred millon aircraft km	
1950–54	7	194	9	28	4	107.4	61.8	46.1	50.0	0.93	1.62	1.99
1955–59	7	123	28	29	8	158.3	92.1	155.2	158.5	0.63	1.09	0.63
1960–64	5	104	35	21	6	303.7	182.3	373.4	390.6	0.33	0.55	0.25
1965–69	6	273	2	32	2	282.7	194.9	222.2	255.2	0.35	0.52	0.39
1970–74	2	167	5	14	2	897.4	737.6	466.3	657.7	0.11	0.14	0.15
1975–79	1	54	6	9	–	1,797.2	1,481.6	1,697.0	3,240.0	0.06	0.07	0.03
1980–84	–	–	4	–	–	–	–	–	–	–	–	–
1985–89	2	47	–	1	–	1,220.0	1,014.5	303.1	6,262.9	0.08	0.10	0.02
1986	–	–	–	–	–	–	–	–	–	–	–	–
1987	–	–	–	–	–	–	–	–	–	–	–	–
1988	–	–	–	–	–	–	–	–	–	–	–	–
1989	1	47	67	–	7	2,682.4	2,295.6	3,515.0	7,353.6	0.04	0.04	0.01
1990	–	–	–	–	–	–	–	–	–	–	–	–

(1) Including services of UK Airways Corporations (reconstituted as the British Airways Board in 1973) and private companies. Excluding accidents involving the deaths of third parties only.

Passenger Traffic: International Comparison[1], 1980 and 1990

Source: CSO

Billion passenger kilometres

	Cars and taxis		Buses and coaches		Rail excluding metro systems		All modes	
	1980	1990	1980	1990	1980	1990	1980	1990
Great Britain[2]	389.4	590.9	52.0	46.0	30.3	33.2	471.2	669.7
Belgium[3]	61.8	75.0	9.1	10.0	7.0	6.5	77.8	91.5
Denmark[4]	38.3	53.7	7.3	8.9	4.3	4.9	49.9	67.4
France	452.5	587.7	38.1	41.3	54.7	63.8	545.3	692.8
Germany (Fed. Rep.)[5]	466.5	588.4	65.5	55.5	40.5	44.4	572.6	688.3
Greece	–	–	5.8	5.0	1.5	2.0	–	–
Irish Republic	–	–	–	–	1.0	1.2	–	–
Italy[2]	324.0	494.0	78.7	85.0	39.6	45.5	442.3	624.5
Luxembourg	–	–	–	–	0.3	0.3	–	–
Netherlands	101.8	133.9	9.8	13.1	8.9	11.1	120.5	158.1
Portugal	40.1	65.0	7.8	10.3	6.1	5.7	54.0	81.0
Spain	130.9	163.0	28.1	40.6	14.8	16.8	173.8	220.3
Austria[2]	48.4	63.7	13.4	14.0	7.6	8.6	69.3	86.3
Czechoslovakia	–	–	33.8	43.4	15,4	19.3	–	–
Finland	33.9	46.8	8.4	8.5	3.2	3.3	45.5	58.6
German (Dem. Rep.)[2]	–	–	24.3	23.0	22.0	24.0	–	–
Hungary	–	–	–	–	14.7	11.4	–	–
Norway[2]	31.4	41.0	4.3	4.0	2.4	2.1	38.1	47.1
Sweden[2]	66.7	86.2	7.3	9.0	7.0	6.1	81.0	101.3
Switzerland	55.1	66.0	4.8	5.8	9.2	12.7	69.1	84.5
Yugoslavia	–	–	29.6	26.2	10.4	11.3	–	–
Japan	341.5	570.0	90.2	110.0	314.5	370.0	746.2	1,050.0
USA[6]	3,220.0	4,250.0	44.1	39.0	17.7	21.1	3,281.8	4,310.1
USSR	–	–	389.9	546.6	332.1	417.2	–	–

(1) National vehicles on national territory except where otherwise stated. (2) Includes foreign cars and taxis in Great Britain, foreign buses and coaches in the German Dem. Rep. and all foreign vehicles Italy, Austria, Norway and Swedish. (3) Excludes taxis. (4) Includes buses and coaches abroad in 1980. (5) Includes buses and coaches abroad in 1990 but excludes firms with fewer than 6 vehicles. (6) Includes only buses and coaches.

Air Distances Between Selected World Cities in Statute Miles

Point-to-point measurements are usually from City Hall.

	Bangkok	Beijing	Berlin	Cairo	Cape Town	Caracas	Chicago	Hong Kong	Hono-lulu	Lima
Bangkok	...	2,046	5,352	4,523	6,300	10,555	8,570	1,077	6,609	12,244
Beijing	2,046	...	4,584	4,698	8,044	8,950	6,604	1,217	5,077	10,349
Berlin	5,352	4,584	...	1,797	5,961	5,238	4,414	5,443	7,320	6,896
Cairo	4,523	4,698	1,797	...	4,480	6,342	6,141	5,066	8,848	7,726
Cape Town	6,300	8,044	5,961	4,480	...	6,366	8,491	7,376	11,535	6,072
Caracas	10,555	8,950	5,238	6,342	6,366	...	2,495	10,165	6,021	1,707
Chicago	8,570	6,604	4,414	6,141	8,491	2,495	...	7,797	4,256	3,776
Hong Kong	1,077	1,217	5,443	5,066	7,376	10,165	7,797	...	5,556	11,418
Honolulu	6,609	5,077	7,320	8,848	11,535	6,021	4,256	5,556	...	5,947
London	5,944	5,074	583	2,185	5,989	4,655	3,958	5,990	7,240	6,316
Los Angeles	7,637	6,250	5,782	7,520	9,969	3,632	1,745	7,240	2,557	4,171
Madrid	6,337	5,745	1,165	2,087	5,308	4,346	4,189	6,558	7,872	5,907
Melbourne	4,568	5,643	9,918	8,675	6,425	9,717	9,673	4,595	5,505	8,059
Mexico City	9,793	7,753	6,056	7,700	8,519	2,234	1,690	8,788	3,789	2,639
Montreal	8,338	6,519	3,740	5,427	7,922	2,438	745	7,736	4,918	3,970
Moscow	4,389	3,607	1,006	1,803	6,279	6,177	4,987	4,437	7,047	7,862
New York	8,669	6,844	3,979	5,619	7,803	2,120	714	8,060	4,969	3,639
Paris	5,877	5,120	548	1,998	5,786	4,732	4,143	5,990	7,449	6,370
Rio de Janeiro	9,994	10,768	6,209	6,143	3,781	2,804	5,282	11,009	8,288	2,342
Rome	5,494	5,063	737	1,326	5,231	5,195	4,824	5,774	8,040	6,750
San Francisco	7,931	5,918	5,672	7,466	10,248	3,902	1,859	6,905	2,398	4,518
Singapore	883	2,771	6,164	5,137	6,008	11,402	9,372	1,605	6,726	11,689
Stockholm	5,089	4,133	528	2,096	6,423	5,471	4,331	5,063	6,875	7,166
Tokyo	2,865	1,307	5,557	5,958	9,154	8,808	6,314	1,791	3,859	9,631
Warsaw	5,033	4,325	322	1,619	5,935	5,559	4,679	5,147	7,366	7,215
Washington, D.C.	8,807	6,942	4,181	5,822	7,895	2,047	596	8,155	4,838	3,509

	London	Los Angeles	Madrid	Mel-bourne	Mexico City	Mon-treal	Mos-cow	New Delhi	New York	Paris
Bangkok	5,944	7,637	6,337	4,568	9,793	8,338	4,389	1,813	8,669	5,877
Beijing	5,074	6,250	5,745	5,643	7,753	6,519	3,607	2,353	6,844	5,120
Berlin	583	5,782	1,165	9,918	6,056	3,740	1,006	3,598	3,979	548
Cairo	2,185	7,520	2,087	8,675	7,700	5,427	1,803	2,758	5,619	1,998
Cape Town	5,989	9,969	5,308	6,425	8,519	7,922	6,279	5,769	7,803	5,786
Caracas	4,655	3,632	4,346	9,717	2,234	2,438	6,177	8,833	2,120	4,732
Chicago	3,958	1,745	4,189	9,673	1,690	745	4,987	7,486	714	4,143
Hong Kong	5,990	7,240	6,558	4,595	8,788	7,736	4,437	2,339	8,060	5,990
Honolulu	7,240	2,557	7,872	5,505	3,789	4,918	7,047	7,412	4,969	7,449
London	...	5,439	785	10,500	5,558	3,254	1,564	4,181	3,469	214
Los Angeles	5,439	...	5,848	7,931	1,542	2,427	6,068	7,011	2,451	5,601
Madrid	785	5,848	...	10,758	5,643	3,448	2,147	4,530	3,593	655
Melbourne	10,500	7,931	10,758	...	8,426	10,395	8,950	6,329	10,359	10,430
Mexico City	5,558	1,542	5,643	8,426	...	2,317	6,676	9,120	2,090	5,725
Montreal	3,254	2,427	3,448	10,395	2,317	...	4,401	7,012	331	3,432
Moscow	1,564	6,068	2,147	8,950	6,676	4,401	...	2,698	4,683	1,554
New York	3,469	2,451	3,593	10,359	2,090	331	4,683	7,318	...	3,636
Paris	214	5,601	655	10,430	5,725	3,432	1,554	4,102	3,636	...

(Continued)

	London	Los Angeles	Madrid	Melbourne	Mexico City	Montreal	Moscow	New Delhi	New York	Paris
Rio de Janeiro	5,750	6,330	5,045	8,226	4,764	5,078	7,170	8,753	4,801	5,684
Rome	895	6,326	851	9,929	6,377	4,104	1,483	3,684	4,293	690
San Francisco	5,367	347	5,803	7,856	1,887	2,543	5,885	7,691	2,572	5,577
Singapore	6,747	8,767	7,080	3,759	10,327	9,203	5,228	2,571	9,534	6,673
Stockholm	942	5,454	1,653	9,630	6,012	3,714	716	3,414	3,986	1,003
Tokyo	5,959	5,470	6,706	5,062	7,035	6,471	4,660	3,638	6,757	6,053
Warsaw	905	5,922	1,427	9,598	6,337	4,022	721	3,277	4,270	852
Washington, D.C.	3,674	2,300	3,792	10,180	1,885	489	4,876	7,500	205	3,840

	Rio de Janeiro	Rome	San Francisco	Singapore	Stockholm	Tehran	Tokyo	Vienna	Warsaw	Wash., D.C.
Bangkok	9,994	5,494	7,931	883	5,089	3,391	2,865	5,252	5,033	8,807
Beijing	10,768	5,063	5,918	2,771	4,133	3,490	1,307	4,648	4,325	6,942
Berlin	6,209	737	5,672	6,164	528	2,185	5,557	326	322	4,181
Cairo	6,143	1,326	7,466	5,137	2,096	1,234	5,958	1,481	1,619	5,822
Cape Town	3,781	5,231	10,248	6,008	6,423	5,241	9,154	5,656	5,935	7,895
Caracas	2,804	5,195	3,902	11,402	5,471	7,320	8,808	5,372	5,559	2,047
Chicago	5,282	4,824	1,859	9,372	4,331	6,502	6,314	4,698	4,679	596
Hong Kong	11,009	5,774	6,905	1,605	5,063	3,843	1,791	5,431	5,147	8,155
Honolulu	8,288	8,040	2,398	6,726	6,875	8,070	3,859	7,632	7,366	4,838
London	5,750	895	5,367	6,747	942	2,743	5,959	771	905	3,674
Los Angeles	6,330	6,326	347	8,767	5,454	7,682	5,470	6,108	5,922	2,300
Madrid	5,045	851	5,803	7,080	1,653	2,978	6,706	1,128	1,427	3,792
Melbourne	8,226	9,929	7,856	3,759	9,630	7,826	5,062	9,790	9,598	10,180
Mexico City	4,764	6,377	1,887	10,327	6,012	8,184	7,035	6,320	6,337	1,885
Montreal	5,078	4,104	2,543	9,203	3,714	5,880	6,471	4,009	4,022	489
Moscow	7,170	1,483	5,885	5,228	716	1,532	4,660	1,043	721	4,876
New York	4,801	4,293	2,572	9,534	3,986	6,141	6,757	4,234	4,270	205
Paris	5,684	690	5,577	6,673	1,003	2,625	6,053	645	852	3,840
Rio de Janeiro	...	5,707	6,613	9,785	6,683	7,374	11,532	6,127	6,455	4,779
Rome	5,707	...	6,259	6,229	1,245	2,127	6,142	477	820	4,497
San Francisco	6,613	6,259	...	8,448	5,399	7,362	5,150	5,994	5,854	2,441
Singapore	9,785	6,229	8,448	...	5,936	4,103	3,300	6,035	5,843	9,662
Stockholm	6,683	1,245	5,399	5,936	...	2,173	5,053	780	494	4,183
Tokyo	11,532	6,142	5,150	3,300	5,053	4,775	...	5,689	5,347	6,791
Warsaw	6,455	820	5,854	5,843	494	1,879	5,689	347	...	4,472
Washington, D.C.	4,779	4,497	2,441	9,662	4,183	6,341	6,791	4,438	4,472	...

Busiest UK Airports, 1992

Source: BAA

Airport	No. passengers (thousands)	Airport	No. passengers (thousands)
London, Heathrow	44,964.4	Belfast	2,241.3
London, Gatwick	19,842.4	Aberdeen	2,146.5
Manchester	11,677.9	Luton	1,943.1
Glasgow	4,670.3	Newcastle	1,941.6
Birmingham	3,651.6	Jersey	1,595.8
Edinburgh	2,539.2	East Midlands	1,250.5
London, Stansted	2,332.4	Bristol	1,025.9

Important Waterways and Canals

The St. Lawrence & Great Lakes Waterway, the largest inland navigation system on the continent, extends from the Atlantic ocean to Duluth at the western end of Lake Superior, a distance of 2,342 miles. With the deepening of channels and locks to 27 ft., ocean carriers are able to penetrate to ports in the Candian interior and the American midwest.

The major canals are those of the St. Lawrence Great Lakes waterway – the 3 canals of the St. Lawrence Seaway, with their 7 locks, providing navigation for vessels of 26-foot draught from Montreal to Lake Ontario; the Welland Ship Canal, with its 8 locks, by-passing the Niagara River between Lake Ontario and Lake Erie, and the Sault Ste. Marie Canal and lock between Lake Huron and Lake Superior. These 16 locks overcome a drop of 580 ft. from the head of the lakes to Montreal. From Montreal to Lake Ontario the former bottleneck of narrow, shallow canals and of slow passage through 22 locks has been overcome, giving faster and safer movement for larger vessels. The current locks and linking channels now accommodate all but the largest ocean-going vessels and the upper St. Lawrence and Great Lakes are open to 80% of the world's saltwater fleet.

Subsidiary Canadian canals or branches include the St. Peters Canal between Bras d'Or Lakes and the Atlantic Ocean in Nova Scotia; the St. Ours and Chambly Canals on the Richelieu River, Quebec; the Ste. Anne and Carillon Canals on the Ottawa River; the Rideau Canal between the Ottawa River and Lake Ontario, the Trent and Murrary Canals between Lake Ontario and Georgian Bay in Ontario, and the St. Andrew's Canal on the Red River. The commercial value of these canals is not great but they are maintained to control water levels and permit the passage of small vessels and pleasure craft. The Canso Canal, completed 1957, permits shipping to pass through the causeway connecting Cape Breton Island with the Nova Scotia mainland.

The Welland Canal overcomes the 326-ft. drop of Niagara Falls and the rapids of the Niagara River. It has 8 locks, each 859 ft. long, 80 ft. wide and 30 ft. deep. Regulations permit ships of 730-ft. length and 75-ft. beam to transit.

Major Merchant Fleets of the World

Source: Maritime Administration, U.S. Department of Commerce

Fleets of ocean-going steam and motor ships totalling 1 million gross tons or over as of Jan. 1, 1993. Excludes ships operating exclusively on the Great Lakes and inland waterways and special types such as channel ships, icebreakers, cable ships and merchant ships owned by any military force. Gross tonnage is a volume measurement; each cargo gross ton represents 100 cubic ft. of enclosed space. Deadweight tonnage is the carrying capacity of a ship in tons (2,240 lb). Tonnage figures may not add, due to rounding.

(tonnage in thousands)

	Total			Type of Vessel: Freighters			Type of Vessel: Bulk Carriers			Type of Vessel: Tankers		
	No. of Ships	Gross Tons	Dwt. Tons	No. of Ships	Gross Tons	Dwt. Tons	No. of Ships	Gross Tons	Dwt. Tons	No. of Ships	Gross Tons	Dwt. Tons
All Countries[1]	23,753	402,217	656,591	12,339	101,635	123,179	5,420	138,712	246,983	5,642	156,683	285,009
Australia	74	2,313	3,495	21	241	271	30	1,007	1,685	23	1,065	1,539
Bahamas	818	19,412	32,173	380	4,003	5,213	147	4,343	7,690	242	10,062	19,034
Bermuda	62	3,150	5,369	18	177	200	9	204	347	35	2,769	4,822
Brazil	220	5,131	8,783	59	543	698	77	2,434	4,250	83	2,163	3,834
Bulgaria*	117	1,266	1,880	59	371	463	37	603	949	19	290	468
China*	1,231	12,631	19,388	752	5,364	7,438	285	5,433	9,181	170	1,661	2,685
Cyprus	1,251	20,050	35,630	616	4,085	5,996	488	10,858	19,840	140	5,046	9,765
Denmark	281	4,335	6,309	189	2,294	2,563	14	555	1,029	78	1,486	2,717
France	106	3,020	4,742	45	1,003	1,084	6	103	153	48	1,853	3,485
Germany	419	4,462	5,672	351	3,475	4,263	22	522	853	39	327	513
Greece	904	24,431	46,101	193	1,540	2,258	458	11,834	22,134	231	10,898	21,639
Hong Kong	200	7,085	11,981	64	1,135	1,286	104	4,821	8,839	31	1,039	1,853
India	296	6,029	10,036	97	914	1,339	119	2,928	4,994	77	2,162	3,693
Indonesia	365	1,588	2,514	247	842	1,310	19	181	268	92	549	922
Iran	124	4,421	8,228	38	385	533	50	1,058	1,757	36	2,978	5,938
Isle of Man	68	1,498	2,583	28	275	314	12	311	543	28	912	1,726
Italy	468	6,411	9,737	172	1,346	1,355	60	2,317	4,208	217	2,473	4,110
Japan	913	21,109	32,562	351	3,849	3,077	251	8,653	15,992	296	8,407	13,437
Korea, South	422	6,383	10,238	225	1,996	2,307	130	3,869	7,013	67	518	918
Kuwait	43	2,208	3,792	13	281	370	0	0	0	30	1,927	3,422
Latvia	118	1,023	1,316	75	431	425	0	0	0	43	592	891
Liberia	1,568	55,139	97,173	367	5,911	6,363	540	17,333	32,001	639	31,143	58,679
Luxembourg	51	1,609	2,605	16	199	225	17	881	1,630	17	496	745
Malaysia	185	1,865	2,779	107	666	926	24	468	842	54	731	1,001
Malta	752	10,569	17,971	343	2,286	3,313	255	5,209	9,163	147	3,002	5,468
Marshall Islands	31	2,031	4,002	4	86	102	18	625	1,163	9	1,320	2,097
Netherlands	367	3,240	4,265	285	1,950	2,403	19	393	638	68	766	1,206
Norway	737	20,230	35,371	193	1,860	2,049	219	6,114	11,079	311	11,866	22,173
Panama	3,171	49,589	79,414	1,719	13,966	16,325	717	17,115	29,587	704	18,169	33,375
Philippines	534	7,979	13,420	239	1,382	1,833	251	6,202	10,871	39	360	699
Poland	212	2,780	4,046	119	980	1,111	85	1,671	2,740	5	109	185
Romania	255	2,701	4,135	193	1,147	1,535	50	1,110	1,820	12	444	780
Russia	1,363	10,036	13,370	1,006	5,509	6,369	135	2,092	3,209	211	2,378	3,781
Saint Vincent	431	4,344	7,114	285	1,625	2,313	97	1,881	3,286	47	823	1,503
Singapore	493	9,525	15,377	227	2,706	3,168	82	2,514	4,480	184	4,305	7,729
Spain	222	2,116	3,904	130	350	558	30	530	959	61	1,234	2,384
Sweden	172	2,467	3,157	90	1,079	1,035	10	220	374	67	1,011	1,723
Taiwan	215	5,955	9,146	134	2,444	2,852	60	2,537	4,622	21	974	1,672
Turkey	339	3,817	6,583	189	715	1,039	93	2,239	3,987	54	849	1,551
United Kingdom	154	2,749	3,081	58	1,062	1,032	19	139	209	59	1,159	1,731
United States[2]	603	15,406	22,500	349	6,824	7,232	23	574	991	220	7,825	14,180
Vanuatu	119	2,018	3,021	55	644	599	52	1,115	1,948	11	253	472

(1) Includes Combination Passenger & Cargo Ships. (2) Excludes non-merchant type and/or Navy-owned vessels that are currently in the Nat. Reserve Fleet. * = source material limited.

Notable Ocean Passages by Ships

Compiled by N. R. P. Bonsor

Sailing Vessels

Date	Ship	From	To	Nautical miles	Time D. H. M	Speed (knots)
1846	*Yorkshire*	Liverpool	New York	3,150	16. 0. 0	8.46†
1853	*Northern Light*	San Francisco	Boston	—	76. 6. 0	—
1854	*James Baines*	Boston Light	Light Rock	—	12. 6. 0	—
1854	*Flying Cloud*	New York	San Francisco	15,091	89. 0. 0	7.07†
1868-9	*Thermopylae*	Liverpool	Melbourne	—	63.18.15	—
—	*Red Jacket*	New York	Liverpool	3,150	13. 1.25	10.05†
—	*Starr King*	50 S. Lat	Golden Gate	—	36. 0. 0	—
—	*Golden Fleece*	Equator	San Francisco	—	12.12. 0	—
1905	*Atlantic*	Sandy Hook	England	3,013	12. 4. 0	10.32

Atlantic Crossing by Passenger Steamships

Date	Ship		From	To	Nautical miles	Time D. H. M	Speed (knots)
1819 (22/5 - 20/6)	*Savannah* (a)	US	Savannah	Liverpool	—	29. 4. 0	—
1838 (7/5 - 22/5)	*Great Western*	Br	New York	Avonmouth	3,218	14.15.59	9.14
1840 (4/8 - 14/8)	*Britannia* (b)	Br	Halifax	Liverpool	2,610	9.21.44	10.98†
1854 (28/6 - 7/7)	*Baltic*	US	Liverpool	New York	3,037	9.16.52	13.04
1856 (6/8 - 15/8)	*Persia*	Br	Sandy Hook	Liverpool	3,046	8.23.19	14.15†

(Continued)

Atlantic Crossing by passenger Steamships *(Continued)*

Date	Ship		From	To	Nautical miles	Time D. H. M	Speed (knots)
1876 (16/12-24/12)	*Britannic*	Br	Sandy Hook	Queenstown	2,882	7.12.41	15.94
1895 (18/5 - 24/5)	*Lucania*	Br	Sandy Hook	Queenstown	2,897	5.11.40	22.00
1898 (30/3 - 5/4)	*Kaiser Wilhelm der Grosse*	Ger	Needles	Sandy Hook	3,120	5.20. 0	22.29
1901 (10/7 - 17/7)	*Deutschland*	Ger	Sandy Hook	Eddystone	3,082	5.11. 5	23.51
1907 (6/10 - 10/10)	*Lusitania*	Br	Queenstown	Sandy Hook	2,780	4.19.52	23.99
1924 (20/8 - 25/8)	*Mauretania*	Br	Ambrose	Cherbourg	3,198	5. 1.49	26.25
1929 (17/7 - 22/7)	*Bremen**	Ger	Cherbourg	Ambrose	3,164	4.17.42	27.83
1933 (27/6 - 2/7)	*Europa*	Ger	Cherbourg	Ambrose	3,149	4.16.48	27.92
1933 (11/8 - 16/8)	*Rex*	It	Gibraltar	Ambrose	3,181	4.13.58	28.92
1935 (30/5 - 3/6)	*Normandie**	Fr	Bishop Rock	Ambrose	2,971	4. 3. 2	29.98
1938 (10/8 - 14/8)	*Queen Mary*	Br	Ambrose	Bishop Rock	2,938	3.20.42	31.69
1952 (11/7 - 15/7)	*United States*	US	Bishop Rock	Ambrose	2,906	3.12.12	34.51
1952 (3/7 - 7/7)	*United States** (e)	US	Ambrose	Bishop Rock	2,942	3.10.40	35.59
			Other Ocean Passages				
1928 (June)	USS *Lexington*		San Pedro	Honolulu	2,226	3. 0.36	30.66
1944 (July-Sep)	*St. Roch* (c) (Can)		Halifax	Vancouver	7,295	86. 0. 0	—
1945 (16/7 - 19/7)	USS *Indianapolis* (d)		San Francisco	Oahu, Hawaii	2,091	3. 2.20	28.07
1945 (26/11)	USS *Lake Champlain*		Gibraltar	Newport News	3,360	4. 8.51	32.04
1950 (July-Aug)	USS *Boxer*		Japan	San Francisco	5,000	7.18.36	26.80†
1951 (1/6 - 9/6)	USS *Philippine Sea*		Yokohama	Alameda	5,000	7.13. 0	27.62†
1958 (25/2 - 4/3)	USS *Skate* (f)		Nantucket	Portland, England	3,161	8.11. 0	15.57
1958 (23/3 - 29/3)	USS *Skate* (f)		Lizard, England	Nantucket	—	7. 5. 0	—
1958 (23/7 - 7/8)	USS *Nautilus* (g)		Pearl Harbor	Iceland (via N. Pole)	—	15. 0. 0	—
1960 (16/2 - 10/5)	USS *Triton* (h)		New London	Rehoboth, Del	41,500	84. 0. 0	20.59†
1960 (15/8 - 20/8)	USS *Seadragon* (i)		Baffin Bay	NW Passage, Pac	850	6. 0. 0	—
1962 (30/10 - 11/11)	*African Comet** (U.S.)		New York	Cape Town	6,786	12.16.22	22.03
1973 (20/8)	*Sea-Land Exchange* (k) (U.S.)		Bishop Rock	Ambrose	2,912	3.11.24	34.92
1973 (24/8)	*Sea-Land Trade* (U.S.)		Kobe	Race Rock, BC	4,126	5. 6. 0	32.75

† The time taken and/or distance covered is approximate and so, therefore, is the average speed.
* Maiden voyage. (a) The *Savannah*, a fully rigged sailing vessel with steam auxiliary (over 300 tons, 98.5 ft. long, beam 25.8 ft., depth 12.9 ft.) was launched in the East River in 1818. It was the first ship to use steam in crossing any ocean. It was supplied with engines and detachable iron paddle wheels. On its famous voyage it used steam 105 hours. (b) First Cunard liner. (c) First ship to complete NW Passage in one season. (d) Carried Hiroshima atomic bomb in World War II. (e) Set world speed record; average speed eastbound on maiden voyage 35.59 knots (about 41 m.p.h.). (f) First atomic submarine to cross Atlantic both ways submerged. (g) World's first atomic submarine also first to make undersea voyage under polar ice cap, 1,830 miles from Point Barrow, Alaska, to Atlantic Ocean, Aug. 1-4, 1958, reaching North Pole Aug. 3. Second undersea transit of the North Pole made by submarine USS *Skate* Aug. 11, 1958, during trip from New London, Conn., and return. (h) World's largest submarine. Nuclear-powered *Triton* was submerged during nearly all its voyage around the globe. It duplicated the route of Ferdinand Magellan's circuit (1519-1522) 30,708 miles, starting from St. Paul Rocks off the NE coast of Brazil, Feb. 24-Apr. 25, 1960, then sailed to Cadiz, Spain, before returning home. (i) First underwater transit of NW Passage. (k) Fastest freighter crossing of Atlantic.

Shortest Navigable Distances Between Ports

Source: *Distances Between Ports* (Pub. 151, 7th Edition 1993) Defense Mapping Agency Hydrographic/Topographic Center

Distances shown are in nautical miles (1,852 metres or about 6,076.115 feet). For statute miles, multiply by 1.15.

FROM	TO	Distance
New York, New York	Barcelona, Spain	3,714
	Cape Town, South Africa	6,786
	Cherbourg, France	3,134
	Copenhagen, Denmark	3,826
	Galveston, Texas	1,935
	Glasgow, Scotland	3,210
	Hamburg, Germany	3,654
	Havana, Cuba	1,186
	Helsinki, Finland	4,289
	Oslo, Norway	3,704
	Piraeus, Greece	4,688
	Southampton, England	3,169
Montreal, Canada	Algiers, Algeria	3,842
	Barcelona, Spain	3,959
	Cape Town, South Africa	7,118
	Gibraltar[3]	3,429
	Halifax, Nova Scotia	895
	Havana, Cuba	2,528
	Istanbul, Turkey	5,226
	Kingston, Jamaica	3,269
	Lagos, Nigeria	5,170
	Marseille, France	4,116
	Naples, Italy	4,406
	Oslo, Norway	3,165
	Piraeus, Greece	4,856
	Port Said, Egypt	5,348
	Southampton, England	2,913

FROM	TO	Distance
Colón[1], Panama	Buenos Aires, Argentina	5,385
	Copenhagen, Denmark	5,233
	Galveston, Texas	1,508
	Gibraltar[3]	4,332
	Hamburg, Germany	5,061
	Helsinki, Finland	5,696
	Lagos, Nigeria	5,049
	Lisbon, Portugal	4,152
	Oslo, Norway	5,053
	Piraeus, Greece	5,759
	Port Said, Egypt	6,251
	St. John's, Newfoundland	2,695
	Southampton, England	4,576
San Francisco, Calif.	Bombay, India	9,794
	Calcutta, India	9,384
	Colón, Panama	3,264
Vancouver, Canada	Calcutta, India	8,727
	Melbourne, Australia	7,365
Panamá, Panama	Jakarta, Indonesia	10,603
Port Said, Egypt	Ho Chi Minh City, Vietnam	5,684
	Hong Kong	6,489
	Manila, Philippines	6,365
	Melbourne, Australia	7,886
	Singapore	5,035
	Yokohama, Japan	7,024
Cape Town[2], South Africa	Jakarta, Indonesia	5,276
	Melbourne, Australia	5,719
	Singapore	5,614
Singapore	Jakarta, Indonesia	525

(1) Colón on the Atlantic is 44 nautical miles from Panamá (port) on the Pacific. (2) Cape Town is 35 nautical miles northwest of the Cape of Good Hope. (3) Gibraltar (port) is 24 nautical miles east of the Strait of Gibraltar.

INDUSTRY

Information about the structure of industry in the United Kingdom is gleaned from the Census of Production. Census forms are sent to approximately one quarter of businesses employing 20–49 people, to half of businesses employing 50–99 people, and to all businesses employing more than 100 people.

The Standard Industrial Classification (SIC) is a system of classification according to industry. Designed to correspond as far as possible with EC activity classification, it has been in use since 1983.

Gross Domestic Product by Industry[1]

Source: CSO

£ million

	1981	1982	1983	1984	1985	1986	1987	1988	1989	1990	1991
Agriculture, forestry and fishing	4,839	5,508	5,346	6,445	5,725	6,193	6,299	6,149	6,965	7,102	8,772
Energy and water supply[2]	23,521	26,127	30,100	29,781	32,696	24,098	24,901	22,542	22,474	24,334	28,273
Manufacturing	54,826	59,472	62,151	67,236	73,432	79,010	84,589	93,504	101,015	106,995	104,283
Construction	13,027	14,100	15,733	16,995	17,904	20,277	23,760	28,512	32,365	36,085	33,686
Distribution; hotels and catering; repairs	27,463	30,350	33,403	36,500	40,839	45,492	49,618	57,378	63,429	70,151	73,024
Transport and communication	16,182	17,481	18,530	20,161	21,725	23,511	25,792	28,684	31,262	34,031	34,755
Banking, finance, insurance, business services and leasing	26,019	28,728	34,614	37,683	44,758	52,058	59,386	67,021	80,561	87,260	88,179
Ownership of dwellings	13,895	15,044	15,945	16,769	18,175	19,501	21,013	23,255	25,154	30,719	34,839
Public administration, national defence and compulsory social security	16,287	17,418	18,875	20,212	21,466	23,069	24,984	27,058	28,622	31,524	34,786
Education and health services	20,618	21,297	23,337	24,649	26,567	30,035	33,136	37,170	41,094	45,143	49,643
Other services[2]	12,039	13,344	15,189	16,767	18,602	20,774	23,379	26,573	29,274	30,983	33,915
Total	227,716	248,869	273,223	293,198	321,889	344,018	376,866	417,846	462,215	504,327	524,155
less Adjustment for financial services	9,705	11,147	11,893	13,681	15,029	17,153	17,555	19,668	25,401	26,740	27,171
Statistical discrepancy (income adjustment)	744	509	−247	535	−144	−683	−1,014	−886	−634	160	17
Gross domestic product (average estimate)	218,755	238,231	261,038	280,052	306,716	326,182	358,297	397,292	436,180	477,747	497,001

(1) The contribution of each industry to the gross domestic product before providing for depreciation but after providing for stock appreciation. (2) Comprising classes 92, 94, 96 and 00 of the Standard Industrial Classification, Revised 1980.

International Manufacturing Productivity and Labour Costs

Source: Bureau of Labor Statistics, U.S. Dept. of Labor (1982 = 100)

Output per hour

Country	1960	1965	1970	1975	1980	1985	1988	1989	1990	1991
Canada	51.6	66.1	76.9	90.1	99.9	119.8	117.1	118.0	121.2	121.7
France	30.7	41.4	58.5	72.7	90.6	108.8	120.6	126.4	127.7	129.1
West Germany	38.5	51.2	67.0	84.5	98.4	112.9	115.6	120.6	124.8	125.4
Italy	28.9	40.0	54.3	67.1	95.5	122.3	130.5	134.5	138.8	145.2
Japan	18.6	28.1	52.0	69.6	92.1	112.0	126.6	133.1	138.1	146.5
Norway	47.8	58.0	74.5	88.6	96.3	116.0	119.7	124.2	127.1	133.5
Sweden	36.5	50.4	69.6	86.4	96.4	112.6	117.3	117.6	118.2	122.4
United Kingdom	49.4	58.4	70.8	83.7	89.9	117.8	137.3	143.9	145.1	149.8
United States	58.4	72.1	77.2	89.4	96.6	114.8	132.1	133.1	136.6	128.1

Unit Labour Costs in U.S. dollars

Country	1960	1965	1970	1975	1980	1985	1988	1989	1990	1991
Canada	40.6	34.4	44.1	63.6	83.1	88.2	110.8	121.5	128.4	138.1
France	32.2	37.4	36.2	78.8	125.2	87.8	132.4	122.1	148.0	150.0
Germany	21.7	27.2	35.8	74.1	121.2	85.0	157.8	147.7	175.8	184.6
Italy	29.6	37.6	46.2	90.2	116.3	87.5	137.9	138.9	171.0	174.6
Japan	26.2	32.5	35.9	79.6	106.7	88.2	185.3	173.4	167.4	185.8
Norway	18.7	23.2	29.8	69.2	110.2	85.7	145.2	137.7	157.6	150.7
Sweden	31.0	36.6	42.5	86.9	130.2	85.7	140.9	145.7	172.5	175.5
United Kingdom	23.4	27.0	28.7	54.9	118.1	77.4	111.8	106.4	126.2	133.0
United States	38.3	36.3	46.3	59.8	86.7	96.8	93.0	95.8	96.5	109.8

NOTE: The data relate to all employed persons (wage & salary, the self-employed and unpaid family workers) in the U.S. and Canada, and all employees (wage & salary earners) in the other countries.

International Index of Hourly Compensation Costs for Production Workers in Manufacturing, 1991

Source: Bureau of Labor Statistics, U.S. Dept. of Labor (Index: U.S. = 100)

Country or area	1975	1980	1985	1986	1987	1988	1989	1990	1991
United States	100	100	100	100	100	100	100	100	100
Australia	87	86	63	64	70	81	86	87	86
Austria	68	87	56	78	97	100	95	114	113
Belgium	101	133	69	93	111	112	106	127	126
Brazil	14	14	9	11	10	10	12	18	17
Canada	91	85	83	83	88	97	103	108	112
Denmark	99	110	62	84	108	109	101	120	117
Finland	72	83	63	81	99	112	116	139	133

(Continued)

Country or area	1975	1980	1985	1986	1987	1988	1989	1990	1991
France	71	91	58	78	91	93	88	102	99
Germany	100	125	74	101	126	131	124	145	143
Greece	27	38	28	31	34	38	38	45	NA
Hong Kong	12	15	13	14	15	17	19	22	23
Ireland	48	60	46	60	69	72	68	79	77
Israel	35	39	31	39	47	55	54	57	–
Italy	73	81	57	76	91	94	95	110	111
Japan	48	57	49	70	80	92	88	85	93
Korea	5	10	10	10	12	17	23	26	28
Luxembourg	100	121	59	80	96	99	95	112	NA
Mexico	NA	NA	12	8	8	9	11	12	14
Netherlands	103	122	67	92	112	114	105	122	120
New Zealand	50	54	34	42	50	59	55	56	54
Norway	107	118	81	102	128	136	131	147	144
Portugal	25	21	12	16	19	20	20	25	27
Singapore	13	15	19	17	17	19	22	25	28
Spain	41	60	37	49	58	63	64	78	82
Sri Lanka	4	2	2	2	2	2	2	NA	NA
Sweden	113	127	74	94	112	121	122	141	143
Switzerland	96	112	74	104	126	129	117	140	141
Taiwan	6	10	12	13	17	20	25	27	29
United Kingdom	52	75	48	57	66	75	73	84	87

NA = not available

Industrial Stoppages

United Kingdom

Source: CSO

Thousands

	1986	1987	1988	1989	1990	1991
Working days lost through all stoppages in progress: total	**1,920**	**3,546**	**3,702**	**4,128**	**1,903**	**761**
Analysis by industry						
Coal extraction	143	217	222	50	59	29
Other energy and water	6	9	16	20	39	4
Metals, minerals and chemicals	192	60	70	42	42	27
Engineering and vehicles	744	422	1,409	617	922	160
Other manufacturing industries	135	115	151	91	106	35
Construction	33	22	17	128	14	14
Transport and communication	190	1,705	1,491	624	177	60
Public admin., sanitary services and education	449	939	254	2,237	175	362
Medical and health services	11	6	36	151	345	1
All other industries and services	20	53	30	167	20	69
Analysis by number of working days lost in each stoppage						
Under 250 days	48	48	33	30	28	15
250 and under 500 days	50	54	34	28	24	16
500 and under 1,000 days	89	88	78	51	45	34
1,000 and under 5,000 days	369	360	310	221	216	123
5,000 and under 25,000 days	381	388	325	365	286	205
25,000 and under 50,000 days	258	118	127	234	216	190
50,000 days and over	726	2,490	2,795	3,198	1,087	178
Working days lost per 1,000 employees all industries and services	90	164	166	182	83	34
Workers directly and indirectly involved: total	**720**	**887**	**790**	**727**	**298**	**176**
Analysis by industry						
Coal extraction	87	98	92	25	15	6
Other energy and water	2	2	2	10	18	2
Metals, minerals and chemicals	17	9	10	7	5	2
Engineering and vehicles	147	174	137	99	92	34
Other manufacturing industries	30	19	29	12	11	15
Construction	8	4	4	20	5	6
Transport and communication	72	207	321	112	68	12
Public admin., sanitary services and education	348	361	161	414	70	87
Medical and health services	4	4	31	9	10	–
All other industries and services	6	10	4	19	3	11
Analysis by duration of stoppage						
Not more than 5 days	369	308	381	194	185	133
Over 5 but not more than 10 days	47	66	280	97	24	2
Over 10 but not more than 20 days	24	153	19	388	27	11
Over 20 but not more than 30 days	58	25	22	8	21	3
Over 30 but not more than 50 days	17	23	57	12	22	1
Over 50 days	206	313	32	29	19	26
Numbers of stoppages in progress: total	**1,074**	**1,016**	**781**	**701**	**630**	**369**
Analysis by industry						
Coal extraction	351	296	154	146	87	32
Other energy and water	10	6	6	7	7	3
Metals, minerals and chemicals	62	36	50	40	36	17
Engineering and vehicles	202	209	162	126	132	67
Other manufacturing industries	85	98	75	63	45	30
Construction	26	24	16	40	12	18
Transport and communication	145	191	176	79	124	37
Public admin., sanitary services and education	132	99	104	154	164	124
Medical and health services	35	24	21	18	13	6

(Continued)

	1986	1987	1988	1989	1990	1991
All other industries and services	34	41	31	31	16	35
Analysis of number of stoppages by duration						
Not more than 5 days	836	784	587	553	476	270
Over 5 but not more than 10 days	108	103	89	52	44	20
Over 10 but not more than 20 days	65	78	60	45	45	24
Over 20 but not more than 30 days	23	23	17	18	20	15
Over 30 but not more than 50 days	18	12	12	18	22	10
Over 50 days	24	16	16	15	23	30

Notes: These figures exclude details of stoppages involving fewer than ten workers or lasting less than one day except any in which the aggregate number of working days lost exceeded 100.
There may be some under-recording of small or short stoppages; this would have much more effect on the total of stoppages than of working days lost.
Some stoppages which affected more than one industry group have been counted under each of the industries but only once in the totals.
Stoppages have been classified using Standard Industrial Classification 1980.
The figures have been rounded to the nearest 100 workers and 1,000 working days; the sums of the constituent items may not, therefore, agree precisely with the totals shown.
Classifications by size are based on the full duration of stoppages where these continue into the following year.
Working days lost per thousand employees are based on the latest available mid-year (June) estimates of employees in employment.

Coal: Average Number of Wage-earners on Colliery Books[1]

United Kingdom: years ended March

Source: CSO

Thousands

	1981/82	1982/83	1983/84	1984/85	1985/86	1986/87	1987/88	1988/89	1989/90	1990/91	1991/92
Scottish	18.3	16.9	14.5	12.3	8.8	6.0	4.3	3.3	1.8	1.5	1.4
North East	30.4	27.6	24.5	22.2	19.7	15.9	12.9	11.5	9.9	9.1	7.8
Selby[3]	–	–	–	–	–	–	–	–	–	3.6	7.5
North Yorkshire[2]	14.8	14.4	13.6	12.7 }	22.8	19.0	16.5	12.9	11.1	8.5	–
Barnsley[2]	15.1	15.0	14.3	13.6 }							
Doncaster[2]	15.9	15.0	13.9	12.8 }	22.0	16.9	15.5	13.7	11.3	8.2	10.7[6]
South Yorkshire[2]	16.3	15.5	14.7	13.7 }							
North Derbyshire	12.0	11.8	11.1	10.1	9.7	8.2	12.7[4]	10.8[4]	10.7[4]	8.6[4]	–
North Nottingham[2]	18.1	17.8	17.1	16.5 }	27.2	24.5	20.3	16.4	13.9	13.4	13.0
South Nottingham[2]	15.3	14.8	13.7	11.7 }							
South Midlands and Kent	16.1	15.2	13.6	12.6	11.4	9.3	0.8[5]	0.7[5]	0.3[5]	–	–
Western	21.5	20.3	19.1	17.5	16.3	13.5	11.5	10.3	6.3	5.5	–
South Wales	24.8	23.4	21.5	19.7	16.7	12.1	9.9	7.4	4.5	2.5	–
Midland and Wales	–	–	–	–	–	–	–	–	–	–	12.0[6]
Total	218.5	207.7	191.5	175.4	154.6	125.4	104.4	86.9	69.8	60.9	52.3

(1) Collieries operated by the British Coal Corporation (BCC). (2) With effect from 1985/86 BCC altered its regional structure and incorporated Barnsley into North Yorkshire Area, Doncaster into South Yorkshire Area and merged North and South Nottingham into Nottinghamshire Area. See also note 3. (3) Selby (previously part of North Yorkshire) became a separate BCC Area with effect from 1990/91. (4) From 1987/88 figures relate to BCC's Central Area (previously North Derbyshire and South Midlands). (5) From 1987/88 figures relate to BCC's Kent Area only. Mining operations ceased on 29 July 1989. See also footnote 4. (6) With effect from October 1991 the three Areas of Central, North Western and South Wales have been replaced by a single amalgamated Midland and Wales Area. North Yorkshire has ceased to operate as a separate area; its operation has been transferred to the Selby and South Yorkshire Areas.

Iron and Steel Supplies, Deliveries and Stocks

Source: CSO

	1980[3]	1981	1982	1983	1984	1985	1986	1987	1988	1989	1990	1991
								Finished product weight – thousand tonnes				
Supply, disposal and consumption												
UK producers' home deliveries	8,224	9,175	8,790	8,757	9,036	8,917	8,337	9,197	10,780	10,907	9,711	7,951
Imports excl. steelworks receipts	3,977	2,738	2,988	2,760	2,691	2,924	3,409	3,595	4,228	4,424	4,446	4,509
Total deliveries to home market (a)	12,201	11,913	11,978	11,517	11,727	11,841	11,745	12,792	15,007	15,331	14,157	12,009
Total exports (producers', consumers', merchants')	2,553	3,718	3,281	3,812	3,843	4,562	4,922	6,057	6,168	6,180	6,550	7,444
Exports by UK producers	2,165	3,514	3,045	3,502	3,527	4,156	4,804	5,815	5,902	5,973	6,370	7,082
Derived consumers' and merchants' exports (b)	388	204	236	310	316	406	118	242	266	207	180	362
Net home disposals (a)–(b)	11,813	11,541	11,542	11,207	11,411	11,435	11,628	12,549	14,742	15,124	13,977	12,098
Consumers' and merchants' stock change[1]	–674	–713	–370	–300	+170	–180	–310	+100	+30	+220	–290	–400
Estimated home consumption	12,487	12,164	11,912	11,507	11,241	11,615	11,938	12,449	14,712	14,904	14,267	12,498
Stocks												
Producers – ingots and semi-finished steel	1,196	1,243	1,056	1,072	1,130	1,629	1,121	1,198	1,311	1,182	1,245	1,035
– finished steel	1,655	1,560	1,488	1,548	1,633	1,604	1,657	1,701	1,633	1,692	1,563	1,719
Consumers	2,870	2,330	2,110	1,800	1,830	1,640	1,380	1,430	1,480	1,700	1,590	1,400
Merchants	1,413	1,240	1,090	1,100	1,240	1,250	1,200	1,250	1,230	1,230	1,050	840
								Crude steel equivalent – million tonnes				
Estimated home consumption												
Crude steel production[2]	11.28	15.57	13.70	14.99	15.12	15.72	14.72	17.41	18.95	18.74	17.84	16.47
Producers' stock change[1]	–1.12	–0.06	–0.33	+0.10	+0.18	+0.60	–0.69	+0.20	+0.06	–0.09	–0.08	–0.07
Re-usable material	0.09	0.06	0.08	0.10	0.07	0.08	0.08	0.10	0.08	0.10	0.10	0.07
Total supply from home sources	12.49	15.69	14.11	14.99	15.01	15.20	15.49	17.31	18.97	18.93	18.02	16.61
Total imports[4]	5.99	4.30	4.74	4.07	4.34	4.54	4.95	5.06	5.95	6.25	8.96	6.21
Total exports[4]	3.31	4.83	4.45	4.73	4.80	5.62	6.01	7.26	7.39	7.49	7.60	8.72
Net home disposals	15.17	15.16	14.70	14.33	14.55	14.12	14.43	15.11	17.53	17.69	16.32	14.10
Consumers' and merchants' stock change[1]	–0.88	–0.93	–0.48	–0.38	+0.22	–0.23	–0.39	+0.13	+0.04	+0.29	–0.37	–0.50
Estimated home consumption	16.05	16.09	15.18	14.71	14.33	14.35	14.82	14.98	17.49	17.40	16.69	14.60

TIME SERIES. The figures relate to periods of 52 weeks (53 weeks in 1981).
Note: Figures in the above table have been amended to reflect the Iron and Steel Statistics Bureau's revised definition of the iron and steel industry.

(1) Increases in stock are shown as + and decreases in stock (i.e. deliveries from stock) as –. (2) Includes liquid steel for castings. (3) Statistics for 1980 were affected by the steel strike. (4) Based on HM Customs Statistics, reflecting total trade rather than producers' trade.

Non-ferrous Metals

United Kingdom

Source: CSO

Thousand tonnes

	1980	1981	1982	1983	1984	1985	1986	1987	1988	1989	1990	1991
Copper												
Production of refined copper:												
Primary	68.3	59.8	63.2	67.5	69.5	63.9	62.4	54.0	49.3	48.6	47.0	16.6
Secondary	93.0	76.3	71.0	76.8	67.4	61.6	63.2	68.3	74.7	70.4	74.6	53.5
Home consumption:												
Refined	409.2	333.1	355.4	358.0	352.9	346.5	339.6	327.7	327.7	324.7	317.2	269.4
Scrap (metal content)	121.2	128.0	128.4	109.6	132.5	131.5	135.3	137.7	132.1	129.7	126.3	118.5
Stocks (end of period)[1,2]	82.0	62.0	69.3	75.8	43.4	37.6	31.6	11.7	13.8	15.9	20.1	9.3
Analysis of home consumption (Refined and scrap):[3] total	530.4	461.1	483.8	467.6	485.4	477.9	474.9	465.4	459.8	454.4	443.5	387.9
Wire[4]	255.7	215.2	226.0	227.0	226.9	225.4	229.6	220.3	217.8	221.7	220.2	191.9
Rods, bars and sections	65.7	56.3	58.8	58.9	67.9	64.6	61.4	62.5	57.3	55.5	54.4	52.7
Sheet, strip and plate	80.1	63.4	69.2	59.9	67.7	66.9	62.4	62.5	66.3	59.2	54.4	37.1
Tubes	78.1	77.2	80.8	80.1	81.3	79.6	80.4	79.1	77.5	77.7	73.0	65.5
Castings and miscellaneous	50.8	48.9	49.0	41.7	41.5	41.4	41.2	41.0	40.9	40.4	41.5	40.7
Zinc												
Slab zinc:												
Production	86.7	81.7	79.3	87.7	85.6	74.3	85.9	81.4	76.0	79.8	93.3	100.7
Home consumption	181.3	185.4	181.6	177.2	182.2	189.3	181.9	188.1	192.8	194.5	189.0	173.3
Stocks (end of period)	19.7	16.1	16.0	19.3	15.9	15.5	15.3	14.0	13.2	13.9	12.0	11.1
Other zinc (metal content):												
Consumption	62.3	56.1	57.8	54.4	54.0	53.3	53.4	52.6	51.7	49.6	52.4	50.1
Analysis of home consumption (slab and scrap): total	243.6	241.5	239.3	231.6	236.2	242.6	235.3	240.7	244.4	244.1	241.3	223.7
Brass	66.7	56.8	59.3	56.6	61.8	58.3	55.1	55.8	54.1	51.1	51.5	47.2
Galvanized products	69.1	80.1	83.5	86.6	90.5	90.5	87.2	95.8	101.4	104.3	100.5	86.8
Zinc sheet and strip	19.1	15.9	14.1	8.6	5.7	5.8	4.6	4.0	4.1	4.0	3.6	3.6
Zinc alloy die castings	37.7	40.1	37.5	39.7	34.9	43.2	44.8	44.0	43.5	43.1	44.4	45.4
Zinc oxide	26.6	21.5	18.7	20.6	19.6	23.4	23.7	22.8	23.2	21.7	21.2	20.5
Other products	24.4	27.2	26.1	19.6	23.8	21.4	20.1	18.3	18.2	19.8	20.2	20.2
Refined lead												
Production[5,6]	324.8	333.4	306.2	322.2	338.4	327.2	328.6	347.0	373.8	350.0	329.4	300.6
Home consumption[6,7]												
Refined lead	295.5	265.8	271.9	292.9	295.3	274.3	282.1	287.5	302.5	301.3	301.6	266.4
Scrap and remelted lead[6]	10.0	8.2	9.9	14.3	19.8	29.0	27.0	36.6	37.0	35.0	32.5	33.9
Stocks (end of period)[8]												
Lead bullion	115.7	94.6	13.6	14.8	18.0	13.4	16.1	26.1	18.6	17.0	18.0	22.4
Refined soft lead at consumers	19.7	21.3	25.7	28.1	28.2	29.5	28.3	24.4	26.7	25.7	22.3	21.6
In LME warehouses (UK)	19.0	39.5	53.7	60.3	34.8	27.5	18.5	2.8	–	11.0	12.1	–
Analysis of home consumption (refined and scrap): total	305.5	274.0	281.8	307.1	315.4	303.6	309.1	324.1	339.4	336.4	334.0	300.2
Cables	21.7	19.4	20.9	19.2	15.1	13.1	13.0	10.0	11.0	12.6	10.4	8.6
Batteries (excluding oxides)	49.3	41.5	43.7	43.3	46.9	47.4	47.6	48.0	49.2	50.5	51.0	52.2
Oxides and compounds												
Batteries	49.3	37.7	45.0	44.4	43.9	49.6	46.7	49.0	51.4	51.7	52.8	54.4
Other uses	81.9	75.9	73.5	74.7	75.1	72.1	72.4	82.7	76.8	72.0	73.7	55.8
Sheets and pipes	50.9	51.7	53.6	77.2	84.3	77.6	84.5	86.1	102.4	98.1	96.8	81.3
White lead	0.9	0.7	0.7	0.5	0.4	0.4	–	–	–	–	–	–
Solder	9.7	9.6	9.0	8.4	7.7	7.9	7.6	7.4	9.0	9.1	8.0	7.7
Alloys	11.9	7.1	7.9	11.2	10.9	11.2	11.5	13.6	13.5	13.4	14.0	12.2
Other uses	29.9	30.4	27.6	28.3	31.1	27.0	26.0	27.3	26.1	28.3	27.5	28.1
Tin												
Tin ore (metal content):												
Production	3.0	3.9	4.2	4.1	5.0	5.2	4.3	3.6	3.4	4.0	4.2	1.1
Tin metal[10]:												
Production[11]	11.4	12.9	13.6	13.3	13.8	14.8	14.9	17.0	16.8	10.8	12.0	5.2
Home consumption[11]	9.9	10.9	10.4	10.2	10.0	9.4	9.7	9.8	10.2	10.2	10.4	10.2
Exports and re-exports[12]	7.0	6.3	5.4	1.0	11.1	7.3	13.6	14.8	14.0	5.4	5.7	2.9
Stocks (end of period):												
Consumers	1.1	1.1	0.9	0.9	1.0	1.0	1.0	1.0	1.0	1.0	1.0	1.0
Merchants and others	–	–	–	–	–	–	–	–	–	–	–	–
Analysis of home consumption (excluding scrap): total	9.9	10.9	10.4	10.2	10.0	9.4	9.7	9.8	10.2	10.2	10.4	10.2
Tinplate	3.1	4.3	4.0	3.8	3.7	3.4	3.3	3.6	3.4	3.6	3.6	3.6
Alloys	3.6	3.4	3.4	3.2	3.1	3.1	3.1	3.2	3.4	3.4	3.4	3.3
Solder	0.9	1.0	0.8	0.9	0.8	0.8	0.9	0.9	1.0	1.0	1.0	1.0
Other uses	2.3	2.2	2.2	2.2	2.4	2.1	2.5	2.1	2.3	2.2	2.4	2.3
Primary aluminium[13]												
Production	374.4	339.2	240.8	252.5	287.9	275.4	275.9	295.4	300.2	297.3	289.8	293.5[12]
Despatches to consumers	520.9	446.2	399.2	418.3	448.3	436.0	451.2	461.6	541.3	494.2	520.2	485.4
Secondary aluminium												
Production	162.1	148.0	114.6	128.3	143.9	127.6	116.4	116.7	105.8	109.5	120.9	136.5
Despatches to consumers	161.0	148.8	114.9	127.5	142.1	126.6	117.2	120.9	107.3	117.2	127.2	146.8
Exports	–	59.2	40.0	37.7	42.1	40.7	42.2	36.7	45.0	66.7	65.1	70.7
Fabricated aluminium												
Total despatches[14]	521.1	444.3	455.4	460.5	473.8	466.0	–	–	–	–	–	–
Rolled products[15]	199.4	165.8	173.7	174.9	191.2	194.6	215.5	224.4	225.7	236.2	261.0	269.4
Extrusions and tubes[16]	183.6	161.2	169.6	177.7	174.5	168.9	–	–	–	–	–	–
Wire products	33.3	31.6	31.9	29.2	28.9	29.9	27.3	27.0	20.9	24.5	15.5	–
Castings	101.9	83.3	78.3	77.0	77.5	72.6	73.3	74.8	–	–	–	–
Forgings	2.9	2.3	1.9	1.7	1.7	–	–	–	–	–	–	–
Foil products (Aluminium content)	40.4	37.8	[19]	[19]	[19]	[19]	[19]	–	–	–	–	–

(Continued)

Thousand tonnes

	1980	1981	1982	1983	1984	1985	1986	1987	1988	1989	1990	1991
Magnesium and magnesium alloys												
Production[17]	2.8	1.9	1.8	[19]	[19]	[19]	[19]	[19]	[19]	[19]	–	–
Consumption: total[18]	5.4	4.1	4.1	[19]	[19]	[19]	[19]	[19]	[19]	[19]	–	–
Refined nickel												
Production (including ferro-nickel)	19.3	25.4	6.9	23.2	22.3	17.8	30.9	29.5	28.0	26.1	26.5	29.0

(1) Unwrought copper (electrolytic, fire refined and blister). (2) Reported stocks of refined copper held by consumers and those held in London Metal Exchange (LME) warehouses in the United Kingdom. (3) Copper content. (4) Consumption for high-conductivity copper and cadmium copper wire represented by consumption of wire rods, production of which for export is also included. (5) Lead reclaimed from secondary and scrap material and lead refined from bullion and domestic ores. (6) From 1975, figures for production and consumption of refined lead include antimonial lead, and for scrap and remelted lead, exclude secondary antimonial lead. (7) Including toll transactions involving fabrication. (8) Excluding government stocks. (9) Includes values for White Lead wef 1986. (10) Including production from imported scrap and residues refined on toll. (11) Primary and secondary metal. (12) Including re-exports on toll transactions. (13) Including primary alloys. (14) Includes wrought, cast and forged products, and excludes foil products. (15) Includes foil stock and excludes foil products. (16) Excluding forging bars, wirebars, and almost two-thirds of despatches of hot-rolled rod. (17) Primary and remelt alloys. (18) Despatches to consumers of primary metal, primary and remelt alloys. (19) Data no longer obtainable.

Cotton, Man-made Fibres and Wool

United Kingdom

Source: CSO

	Unit	1980	1981	1982	1983	1984	1985	1986	1987	1988	1989	1990	1991
Raw cotton[1]													
Imports	Thousand	69	48	54	50	48	54	52	55	48	43	32	23
Home consumption: total	tonnes	69	46	45	45	44	44	47	51	43	39	28	19
Stocks (end of period)	"	9	6	5	5	4	4	3	4	4	3	1	1
Cotton waste													
Imports	"	26.5	22.6	30.2	28.9	27.0	28.7	24.3	28.1	28.4	29.2	36.1	31.3
Cotton linters													
Imports	"	29.9	25.7	37.8	24.8	31.7	38.4	23.1	23.6	13.6	18.0	13.7	16.1
Man-made fibres[2]													
Production: total	"	449.7	394.7	333.6	389.3	383.3	330.2	288.0	276.7	280.1	272.5	273.2	267.3
Continuous filament yarn	"	162.6	126.3	89.3	102.6	102.5	99.1	100.8	99.0	105.3	108.5	101.7	92.6
Staple fibre	"	287.2	268.4	244.3	286.6	280.9	231.1	187.2	177.7	174.9	164.0	171.5	174.7
Cotton and man-made fibre yarn	Thousand tonnes												
Production of single yarn:													
Cotton[3]	"	61.3	42.5	42.3	40.9	38.0	38.6	39.8	41.8	35.4	28.4	22.5	12.5
Cotton mixture yarn	"	18.4	15.5	15.6	17.1	17.2	16.5	15.9	16.4	16.5	15.4	13.8	12.7
Spun man-made fibre yarn	"	31.2	25.5	26.5	28.2	28.9	30.1	31.3	33.1	30.0	24.2	21.7	16.7
Cotton waste yarn[4]	"	10.8	8.5	8.7	9.0	9.3	9.5	8.6	9.0	8.3	7.7	7.5	7.9
Other waste yarn	"	2.3	1.9	1.7	2.1	2.6	3.8	3.9	4.1	3.9	3.2	2.0	1.7
Production of doubled yarn	"	49.1	39.8	34.1	30.6	29.8	32.6	31.8	31.4	31.1	30.0	25.9	23.2
Spindle activity[5]:													
Single yarn spindles: total (ring equivalent)	Millions	1.53	1.17	1.04	0.96	0.95	0.93	0.90	0.86	0.82	0.69	NA	–
Doubling spindles	"	0.22	0.17	0.12	0.11	0.10	0.09	0.09	0.08	0.08	0.08	NA	–
Yarn consumed in cotton and man-made fibre weaving:													
Cotton and waste yarns	Thousand	45.5	35.9	35.8	36.2	39.0	39.5	37.0	37.0	31.4	30.3	27.8	23.9
Mixtures yarn[6]	tonnes	–	–	15.4	16.7	15.1	15.9	17.2	15.9	17.2	15.6	15.3	13.6
Man-made fibres: total	"	62.5	50.3	45.0	41.7	45.7	50.4	51.6	52.4	49.8	49.9	50.4	47.1
Continuous filament yarn	"	50.7	39.4	35.0	31.9	35.0	37.5	38.2	37.2	34.5	35.3	34.4	31.8
Spun yarn	"	11.8	10.9	10.0	9.8	10.7	12.9	13.4	15.2	15.3	14.6	16.0	15.3
Cotton and man-made fibre weaving													
Production of woven cloth:	Million linear metres												
Cotton		314	278	261	255	265	274	275	245	219	206	168	154
Man-made fibres	"	298.9	229.9	204.8	176	182.7	206.6	217.7	214.7	212.5	217.4	216.3	193.3
Cotton/man-made fibre mixtures	"	51.2	42.9	45.7	52.3	55.9	48.1	44.7	44.6	44.6	41.5	43.6	39.1
Loom activity													
Average number of looms running on cotton and man-made fibres	Thousands	32.9	26.2	19.8	16.9	14.7	14.0	13.3	12.6	11.6	11.6	10.6	–
Wool													
Virgin wool (clean weight):	Million kg												
Production		34	33	33	33	37	40	40	42	44	47	45	–
Imports	"	67	76[7]	71	77	82	90	83	98	89	77	62	65
Exports[8]	"	25	27[7]	24[7]	26	28	28	31	34	34	33	27	26
Stocks at 31 August	"	42	39	21	19	20	23	22	22	21	21	20	28
Consumption:													
Wool	"	92.3	88.2	88.1	90.0	94.9	96.6	100.2	104.0	104.5	97.2	93.6	87.9
Hair	"	6.4	6.6	5.9	6.6	7.2	7.9	7.5	8.3	7.0	6.5	5.9	5.6
Man-made fibres	"	53.1	51.6	48.8	51.5	50.4	53.9	57.6	56.2	53.9	45.9	40.6	37.7
Other fibres[9]	"	15.0	11.5	10.1	10.1	9.0	9.3	8.8	9.8	10.0	8.9	6.4	5.6
Tops													
Production: total	"	65.8	70.1	66.5	70.3	76.0	81.8	83.6	83.1	80.0	69.1	60.5	61.9
Wool and hair	"	39.1	38.7	37.3	38.5	42.9	44.5	43.8	43.8	42.8	38.7	34.2	36.0
Man-made fibres	"	26.7	31.4	29.2	31.8	33.2	37.3	39.8	39.3	37.2	30.4	26.3	25.9
Worsted yarns[10]:													
Production	"	52.8	51.6	53.4	55.6	59.6	61.8	64.8	66.3	60.2	52.4	47.2	44.8
Semi-worsted yarns[10]:													
Production	"	7.1	7.2	8.1	9.4	6.5	7.5	10.2	12.5	13.5	12.7	11.4	7.6
Woollen yarn[7]:													
Production	"	81.2	72.0	53.4	56.2	60.5	64.3	72.9	76.7	78.3	74.9	72.7	66.1

(Continued)

Wool *(Continued)*

	Unit	1980	1981	1982	1983	1984	1985	1986	1987	1988	1989	1990	1991
Woven woollen and worsted fabrics[11]:	Million square												
Deliveries	metres	118.2	96.7	100.3	94.0	90.7	90.9	93.1	90.3	89.0	85.4	79.0	72.0
Blankets:													
Deliveries	„	15.0	9.9	9.4	8.3	9.3	8.9	6.9	6.7	7.2	7.0	7.3	6.2

TIME SERIES. Figures for consumption of raw cotton, and production and consumption of cotton and man-made fibre yarn are for periods of 52 weeks (53 weeks in 1980 and 1986).

(1) From 1978 figures for consumption of raw cotton are for calendar months. (2) Figures are based on returns from producers (excluding waste) and include all man-made fibres in commercial production. (3) Excluding waste yarns. (4) Yarns wholly of cotton waste, cotton yarn spun on condenser system and mixture yarns of cotton and cotton waste. (5) Average of numbers running in last week of each month. Waste spinning spindles are excluded. (6) Figures prior to 1982 are not provided. (7) Estimated. (8) Including imported wool and wool from imported skins, scoured, etc. in the United Kingdom. (9) Including noils, broken tops, wastes, mungo and shoddy. (10) Including all yarn spun on the worsted system. (11) Includes mixture and man-made fibre fabrics classified as wool or worsted, but excludes blankets.

Inorganic Chemicals

Source: CSO

Thousand tonnes

	1980	1981	1982	1983	1984	1985	1986	1987	1988	1989	1990	1991
Materials used for the manufacture of sulphuric acid												
Zinc concentrates:												
Consumption	242.6	188.7	210.2	238.1	243.6	237.3	242.8	220.7	195.6	216.8	255.6	241.3
Spent oxide:												
Consumption	10.6	7.6	6.1	6.6	1.3	–	–	–	–	–	–	–
Stocks (end of period)	0.9	0.8	8.1	4.7	4.7	–	–	–	–	–	–	–
Sulphur:												
Consumption (for acid production)[1]	1,064.1	911.9	805.7	824.2	828.1	784.9	719.1	657.9	700.0	660.0	594.6	547.8
Stocks (end of period)[1]	48.7	50.5	36.7	32.1	45.8	31.0	18.8	21.1	22.3	18.4	13.7	14.5
Sulphuric acid[2]												
Production	3,380.7	2,888.9	2,587.3	2,628.7	2,654.2	2,525.1	2,329.8	2,157.7[2]	2,257.5	2,148.1	1,996.1	1,852.4
Consumption[3]: total	3,241.2	2,899.2	2,586.6	2,809.7	2,786.0	2,667.0	2,479.6	2,335.3	2,439.2	2,318.4	2,155.3	2,002.3
Fertilizers	1,042.8	901.2	749.3	857.1	739.4	661.3	508.4	335.8	246.5	149.3	61.1	30.4
All other chemical uses[4]	1,571.1	1,998.0	1.837.3	1,952.6	2,047.0	2,005.7	1,971.1	1,999.5	2,192.8	2,169.1	2,094.3	1,971.9
Metallurgy	50.4	–	–	–	–	–	–	–	–	–	–	–
Other (incl. Textiles)	576.3	–	–	–	–	–	–	–	–	–	–	–
Stocks (emd of period)	145.0	151.2	122.3	113.0	118.8	106.9	91.5	72.7	76.9	86.7	94.0	72.1

(1) Filter cake and boiler bottom are excluded. (2) As 100 per cent acid. (3) Including recovered and imported acid. (4) Figures from 1981 include Metallurgy and other (incl. Textiles).

Organic Chemicals Production[1]

Source: CSO

Thousand tonnes[2]

	1980	1981	1982	1983	1984	1985	1986	1987	1988	1989	1990	1991
Ethylene[3]	1,094.9	1,235.5	1,115.4	1,154.6	1,324.3	1,446.5	1,740.1	1,797.9	2,005.2	1,975.4	1,498.1	1,794.9
Propylene[3]	572.7	736.6	824.2	831.9	975.8	973.2	864.2	874.9	850.4	796.8	751.3	834.3
Butadiene[3]	191.9	207.9	228.8	237.7	259.2	297.6	192.9	231.4	239.7	225.9	198.1	197.5
Benzene[4]	825.5	751.9	569.5	725.9	754.7	834.9	852.8	911.6	872.8	1,024.9	702.0	869.7
Toluene[5]	170.1	179.0	–[8]	–[8]	–[8]	164.8	–	–	–	–	–	–
Formaldehyde[6]	123.9	113.0	107.2	97.8	103.6	123.7	103.2	113.5	111.6	79.7	42.8	59.6
Propyl alcohols	61.4	–[9]	–	–	–	–	–	–	–	–	–	–
Acetone	122.6	111.2	135.3	121.8	161.5	146.8	123.2	117.9	127.5	130.3	128.5	125.3
Phenol (synthetic)	–	109.7	140.0	143.2	184.4	117.5	52.9	–	–	–	–	–
Phthalic anhydride	46.3	61.1	73.0	–[9]	–	–	–	–	–	–	–	–
Ethyl alcohol[7] (Thousand hectolitres of alcohol)	1,810.6	1,839.4	2,071.5	2,398.1	3,043.3	2,509.5	2,538.0	2,980.1	2,968.1	2,886.9	3,061.8	2,959.3

(1) Figures relate to total production, i.e. "captive use" is included. (2) Except for ethyl alcohol, which is measured in thousand hectolitres of alcohol. (3) Produced from oil base, other than for use as fuel. (4) Includes production obtained by dealkylation of toluene (excludes production from coal). (5) Includes that used for the production of benzene, but excludes production from coal. (6) Including paraformaldehyde (expressed as 100 per cent formaldehyde). (7) Industrial alcohol made from molasses and derived from other processes. The figures include a small quantity of beverage spirits produced by rectification of spirits distilled from molasses. In the financial year ended 31 March 1985 this amounted to about 13.21 thousand hectolitres of alcohol a month. (8) Figures suppressed for disclosure reasons. (9) No longer published in the *Business Monitor* series.

Timber

United Kingdom

Source: CSO

Thousand cubic metres

	1978	1979	1980	1981	1982	1983	1984	1985	1986	1987	1988	1989	1990	1991
Softwood														
Deliveries:														
Imported	6,709	7,053	6,131	5,649	6,237	6,895	6,650	6,441	7,010	–	–	–	–	–
Home grown[1,2]	299	302	388	428	595	618	594	641	781	819	909	832	–	–
Stocks (end of period):														
Imported	1,798	1,959	1,846	1,646	1,494	1,729	1,765	1,435	1,429	–	–	–	–	–

(Continued)

	1978	1979	1980	1981	1982	1983	1984	1985	1986	1987	1988	1989	1990	1991
Total	**7,008**	**7,355**	**6,519**	**6,077**	**6,832**	**7,513**	**7,244**	**7,082**	**7,788**	–	–	–	–	–
Hardwood														
Deliveries:														
Imported	842	964	766	717	740	951	841	830	855	–	–	–	–	–
Home grown[1,2]	170	149	108	85	74	78	47	63	89	63	59	59	–	–
Stocks (end of period):														
Imported	270	300	228	223	232	272	271	249	241	–	–	–	–	–
Total	**1,012**	**1,113**	**874**	**802**	**814**	**1,029**	**888**	**893**	**944**	–	–	–	–	–
Imported plywood														
Deliveries	1,059	1,159	830	972	920	1,068	1,019	1,090	1,119	–	–	–	–	–
Stocks (end of period)	196	216	142	209	130	191	212	163	247	–	–	–	–	–
Mining timber														
Production:														
Sawn	373.5	372.3	407.6	407.2	428.3	415.2	135.6	306.8	335.9	300.2	281.7	253.4	243.4	215.7
Round	140.4	137.1	152.6	149.7	136.3	124.2	45.8	94.9	87.9	65.3	48.8	38.7	31.8	24.2
Total	**513.8**	**509.5**	**560.2**	**556.9**	**564.6**	**539.4**	**181.4**[3]	**401.7**	**423.8**	**365.5**	**330.5**	**292.1**	**275.2**	**239.9**
Consumption:														
Sawn	384.0	382.2	424.4	415.8	429.4	415.5	135.6	306.8	335.9	300.2	281.7	253.4	243.4	215.7
Round[4]	215.1	202.0	214.6	198.1	175.9	149.6	48.2	101.0	94.2	68.9	48.8	38.7	31.8	24.2
Stocks (end of period):														
Sawn	55.2	57.2	70.3	54.2	64.7	61.2	62.0	43.4	43.2	30.2	37.7	23.0	26.4	19.1
Round	134.7	103.5	45.2	96.1	62.6	39.9	27.7	21.0	18.0	10.5	10.4	7.0	4.9	3.2
Wood chipboard														
Production[3]	366.5	597.9	606.7	524.7	514.6	518.5	541.4	728.0	–	–	–	–	–	–
Stocks (end of period)	37.2	32.6	55.4	24.1	45.5	39.4	38.5	47.8	–	–	–	–	–	–

TIME SERIES. Figures for wood chipboard relate to periods of 52 weeks (53 weeks in 1982).

(1) Up to and including 1979 sales of home-grown timber and of plywood are by firms employing 25 or more people and from 1980 by firms employing 35 or more people.
(2) Home-grown excludes mining timber and relates to sawn and planed only. Home-grown hardwood also excludes planed timber. (3) Reduction due to the miners' strike.
(4) As from February 1988 imported materials no longer used for mining purposes.

Fertilizers

Years ending 31 May[1]

Source: CSO

Thousand tonnes

	1979	1980	1981	1982	1983	1984	1985	1986	1987	1988	1989	1990	1991
Deliveries to UK agriculture													
N (nitrogen): – nutrient content													
Straight	638	701	695	785	896	857	903	850	883	802	673.1	706.0	627.9
Compounds	522	544	468	476	529	476	471	445	472	498	491.3	513.5	462.1
P_2O_5 (phosphate)	394	394	372	379	407	395	404	367	355	354	334.0	332.9	278.4
K_2O (potash)	395	425	386	407	467	465	477	454	446	444	429.0	443.2	365.3
Compounds – total weight	3,024	3,120	2,819	2,922	3,260	3,082	3,167	3,022	2,997	3,129	3,034.0	2,964.3	2,744.0

(1) From 1990 the year ended is 30 June.

Minerals

Source: Bureau of Mines, U.S. Dept. of the Interior, as of mid-1992

Aluminium: the second most abundant metal element in the Earth's crust. Bauxite is the main source of aluminium; convert to aluminium equivalent by multiplying by 0.211. Guinea and Australia have 49% of the world's reserves.

Chromium: some two-thirds of the world's chromite production is in Kazakhstan and South Africa. The chemical and metallurgical industries use about 80% of the chromite produced.

Cobalt: used in superalloys for jet engines; chemicals (paint driers, catalysts, magnetic coatings); permanent magnets; and cemented carbides for cutting tools. Principal cobalt-producing countries include Zaire, Zambia and the former USSR.

Columbium: used mostly as an additive in steelmaking and in superalloys. Brazil and Canada are the world's leading producers. There is no UK columbium mining industry.

Copper: main uses of copper are in building construction, electrical and electronic products, industrial machinery and equipment, transportation and consumer and general products. The leading producer is Chile, followed by the U.S., Poland, Russia, Peru, Kazakhstan, Australia and China. The UK produced over 70,000 tonnes of copper in 1991.

Gold: used mainly in jewellery and crafts, the electronics and other industries, and dentistry. South Africa has about half of the world's resources; significant quantities are also present in the U.S., Canada, the former USSR and Brazil.

Iron ore: the source of primary iron for the world's iron and steel industries. Major iron ore producers include the former USSR, Brazil, Australia and China.

Lead: the U.S., Australia, China and the former USSR are the world's largest producers of lead. It is used mainly in petrol, batteries, construction sheeting, sporting ammunition and TV tubes. The UK produced 300,000 tonnes in 1991.

Manganese: essential to iron and steel production. The U.S., Japan and Western Europe are all nearly deficient in economically minable manganese. South Africa and the former USSR have over 80% of the world's reserves.

Nickel: vital to the stainless steel industry and played a key role in the development of the chemical and aerospace industries. Leading producers include the former USSR, Canada, Australia and New Caledonia.

Platinum-group Metals: the platinum group comprises 6 closely related metals: platinum, palladium, rhodium, ruthenium, iridium and osmium. They commonly occur together in nature and are among the scarcest of the metallic elements. They are mainly consumed in the following industries: automotive, electrical and electronic, and dental. The former USSR and South Africa have nearly all the world's reserves.

Silver: used in the following industries: photography, electrical and electronic products, sterling ware, electroplated ware and jewellery. Silver is mined in more than 60 countries.

Tantalum: a refractory metal with unique electrical, chemical and physical properties used mostly to produce electronic components, mainly tantalum capacitors. Australia, Brazil, Canada and Thailand are the leading producers.

Titanium: a metal which is mostly used in jet engines, airframes, and space and missile applications. It is produced in Ukraine, Russia, Kazakhstan, Japan, the western and central U.S., the United Kingdom and China.

Vanadium: used as an alloying element in steel, as an alloying agent in aerospace titanium alloys, and as a catalyst in the production of sulphuric acid and maleic anhydride. The former USSR and South Africa are the world's largest producers.

Zinc: used as a protective coating on steel, as die-castings, as an alloying metal with copper to make brass, and as a component of chemical compounds in rubber and paints. It is mined in over 50 countries, with Canada the leading producer, followed by Australia, the former USSR, Peru, China and the U.S. The UK produced 100,000 tonnes in 1991.

Minerals Production

Great Britain

Source: CSO

Thousand tonnes

	1981	1982	1983	1984	1985	1986	1987	1988	1989	1990	1991
Limestone	62,850	69,114	75,753	75,533	77,567	81,207	93,617	103,410	107,908	99,775	91,999
Sandstone	9,611	10,803	12,199	12,529	10,870	11,337	13,804	16,031	16,748	14,952	12,928
Igneous rock	25,323	29,987	30,733	29,969	31,720	34,038	39,529	44,636	46,809	49,542	46,008
Clay/shale	18,799	20,323	22,403	17,817	18,909	17,169	17,862	18,534	19,011	15,864	13,038
Industrial sand	4,451	4,123	4,026	4,328	4,178	4,108	4,029	4,340	4,380	4,132	4,201
Chalk	11,756	11,616	12,430	12,022	12,023	12,511	13,444	14,516	13,877	13,129	10,317
Fireclay	992	850	689	757	831	940	900	1,057	1,052	892	867
Barium sulphate	63.3	81.1	36.0	62.7	107.3	86.8	76.8	76.2	70.0	67.6	85.5
Calcium fluoride	255.5	200.8	131.3	136.7	167.4	133.4	120.4	103.7	122.1	118.5	77.9
Copper	0.6	0.6	0.7	0.7	0.6	0.6	0.8	0.7	0.5	1.0	0.2
Lead	7.0	4.0	3.8	2.4	4.0	0.6	0.7	1.2	2.2	1.4	0.2
Tin	3.7	4.2	4.0	5.2	4.3	3.8	3.7	3.4	3.8	3.4	2.3
Zinc	10.9	10.2	8.9	7.5	5.3	5.7	6.6	5.5	5.8	6.7	1.0
Iron ore: crude	703	392	262	246	147	291	246	227	4	4	–
Iron ore: iron content	162	85	57	53	31	77	56	50	2	2	–
Calcspar	20	18	10	7	6	10	–	23	22	34	8
China clay (including ball clay)	3,508	3,358	3,346	3,607	3,762	3,780	4,054	4,352	4,190	4,042	3,744
Chert and flint	10	–	174	17	22	14	16	11	–	14	5
Fuller's earth	205	243	267	286	292	248	–	277	265	228	202
Lignite	–	–	1	2	5	7	6	18	4	5	3
Rock salt	1,350	2,209	1,316	1,569	2,030	2,040	1,855	877	594	815	2,088
Salt from brine	1,454	1,554	1,394	1,423	1,552	1,510	1,554	1,426	–	–	1,319
Salt in brine	3,916	3,874	3,601	4,134	3,563	3,305	3,672	3,827	–	–	–
Anhydrite	47	67	51	56	59	53	–	–	–	–	–
Dolomite	13,936	13,727	14,983	14,228	14,953	15,851	17,037	19,861	21,271	20,674	19,454
Gypsum	2,897	2,674	2,916	3,082	3,130	3,363	–	–	–	–	–
Slate[1]	350	785	494	157	158	242	322	708	590	359	360
Soapstone and talc	18	19	16	19	20	12	12	14	15	15	11
Sand and gravel (land-won)	77,951	79,287	88,002	87,092	87,813	90,215	95,409	110,516	110,504	98,993	85,479
Sand and gravel (marine-dredged)	11,501	11,919	12,797	12,582	13,792	15,284	16,220	19,638	20,728	17,179	12,439

Northern Ireland

Thousand tonnes

	1981	1982	1983	1984	1985	1986	1987	1988	1989	1990
Chalk	–	–	–	–	–	–	–	–	–	–
Clay and shale	–	–	–	–	–	397	409	–	–	–
Sand and gravel	3,738	3,665	3,207	3,506	3,627	4,226	3,634	3,871	4,554	4,030
Basalt and igneous rock (other than granite)	5,449	6,151	6,140	6,856	6,717	6,731	6,380	7,324	7,463	7,691
Limestone	2,281	2,609	3,249	3,707	3,057	3,436	3,041	2,409	3,485	2,866
Grit and conglomerate	2,622	2,524	2,532	2,578	2,307	2,693	2,573	2,870	2,845	3,090
Diatomite	–	–	–	–	–	–	–	–	–	–
Granite	–	–	–	–	–	189	107	–	–	–
Sandstone	–	–	–	–	–	–	–	–	–	–
Rock salt	–	–	–	–	–	–	–	–	–	–

(1) Includes waste used for constructional fill, and powder and granules used in manufacturing.

World Mineral Reserve Base

Source: Bureau of Mines, U.S. Dept. of the Interior, as of 1993

Mineral	Reserve Base[1]
Aluminium	28,000 mln. metric tons[2]
Chromium	6,800 mln. metric tons
Cobalt	8,800 thou. metric tons
Columbium	4,200 kilograms
Copper	590 mln. metric tons
Gold	51,000 metric tons
Iron	230,000 mln. metric tons[3]
Lead	125 mln. metric tons
Manganese	4,860,000 thousand metric tons
Nickel	110,000 thousand metric tons
Platinum-group Metals	66 mln. kilograms
Silver	420,000 metric tons
Tantalum	35 mln. kilograms.
Titanium	595 mln. metric tons
Vanadium	27,000 thousand metric tons
Zinc	325 mln. metric tons

(1) Includes demonstrated resources that are currently economic (reserves), marginally economic (marginal reserves), and some of those that are currently sub-economic. (2) Bauxite. (3) Crude ore.

World Silver Production

Source: Bureau of Mines, U.S. Dept. of the Interior

Year	Tonnes
1930	7,736
1935	6,865
1940	8,565
1945	5,039
1950	6,323
1955	6,967
1960	7,505
1965	8,007
1970	9,670
1975	9,428
1980	10,556
1985	13,051
1986	12,970
1987	14,019
1988	15,484
1989	16,041
1990	16,216
1991	15,692
1992	15,345

World Gold Production

Source: Bureau of Mines, U.S. Dept. of the Interior

(Troy Ounces)

		Africa			North and South America				Other			
Year	World prod.	South Africa	Ghana	Zaire[r]	United States	Canada	Mexico	Colombia	Australia	China	Philip-pines	USSR
1972	44,843,374	29,245,273	724,051	80,377	1,449,943	2,078,567	146,061	188,137	754,866	NA	606,730	NA
1975	38,476,371	22,937,820	523,889	115,743	1,052,252	1,653,611	144,710	308,864	526,821	NA	502,577	NA
1977	38,906,145	22,501,886	480,884	96,542	1,100,347	1,733,609	212,709	257,070	624,270	NA	558,554	NA
1978	38,983,019	22,648,558	402,034	32,151	998,832	1,735,077	202,003	246,446	647,579	NA	586,531	NA
1979	38,768,978	22,617,179	362,000	73,947	964,390	1,644,265	190,364	269,369	596,910	NA	535,166	NA
1980	39,197,315	21,669,468	353,000	96,452	969,782	1,627,477	195,991	510,439	547,591	NA	753,452	8,425,000
1982	43,082,814	21,355,111	331,000	135,033	1,465,686	2,081,230	214,349	472,674	866,815	1,800,000	834,439	8,550,000
1984	46,929,444	21,860,933	287,000	321,507	2,084,615	2,682,786	270,998	730,670	1,295,963	1,900,000	827,149	8,650,000
1985	49,283,691	21,565,230	299,363	257,206	2,427,232	2,815,118	265,693	1,142,385	1,881,491	1,950,000	1,062,997	8,700,000
1986	51,534,056	20,513,665	287,127	257,206	3,739,015	3,364,700	250,615	1,285,878	2,413,842	2,100,000	1,296,400	8,850,000
1987	53,033,614	19,176,500	327,598	385,809	4,947,040	3,724,000	256,822	853,600	3,558,954	2,300,000	1,048,081	8,850,000
1988	60,308,973	19,965,611	355,620	401,884	6,459,534	4,334,338	292,508	932,822	5,046,059	2,507,758	980,019	8,925,046
1989	65,335,998	19,530,290	429,470	340,798	8,543,449	5,127,850	276,914	948,640	6,544,702	2,893,567	964,265	9,773,826
1990	68,632,896	19,454,414	541,419	299,002	9,458,395	5,381,166	268,073	943,689	7,849,186	3,215,074	790,619	9,709,524
1991	69,083,682	19,323,014	845,886	282,927	9,542,501	5,676,278	287,331	1,120,260	7,530,283	3,858,089	801,775	8,359,193
1992	72,269,724	19,737,341	997,670	257,206	10,581,581	5,081,393	321,507	1,189,578	7,716,178	4,501,104	771,618	8,101,987*

r = revised to reflect improved data. NA = not available. * = USSR as constituted prior to December 1991.

Building Materials and Components: Production[1]

Great Britain

Source: CSO

	Unit	1979	1980	1981	1982	1983	1984	1985	1986	1987	1988	1989	1990	1991
Building bricks (excluding refractory and glazed)	Millions	4,887	4,562	3,725	3,517	3,806	4,012	4,100	3,971	4,222	4,682	4,654	3,802	3,212
Cement[2]	Thousand	16,140	14,805	12,729	12,962	13,396	13,481	13,339	13,413	14,311	16,506	16,849	14,740	–
Building sand[3,4]	tonnes	18,983	18,005	15,675	17,044	19,151	18,187	18,346	20,423	20,620	23,415	23,290	20,948	18,573[11]
Concreting sand[4]	"	29,455	26,699	25,427	25,242	26,720	28,172	28,694	30,347	32,823	39,174	41,223	37,213	29,456[11]
Gravel[4,5]	"	54,056	51,454	48,351	48,920	54,929	53,316	54,564	54,729	58,185	67,566	66,718	58,010	46,907[11]
Crushed rock aggregates:[6]	Thousand													
used as roadstone (coated)	tonnes	14,413	14,366	13,179	17,739	18,562	17,424	18,188	19,239	22,599	28,860	23,733	26,430	–
roadstone (uncoated)	"	41,785	42,896	35,949	35,259	38,522	36,660	41,168	44,185	50,784	54,187	66,015	61,742	–
fill and ballast	"	31,722	31,619	31,049	37,129	40,416	42,234	42,426	45,227	53,411	59,989	59,689	54,640	–
concrete aggregate	"	15,588	13,653	11,205	12,721	14,582	14,360	13,214	13,715	15,443	17,978	19,366	18,804	–
Ready-mixed concrete[2]	Million m^3	24.4	22.4	19.9	20.7	21.5	20.8	21.6	21.5	24.4	28.8	29.6	26.8	22.0
Fibre cement products	Thousand tonnes	405.5	352.2	265.6	261.7	239.5	255.5	252.6	217.4	205.4	251.0	220.7	234.7	133.7
Clay roofing tiles[2,7]	Thousand	2,265	1,698	1,635	1,632	2,206	2,051	2,143	2,587	3,019	3,459	3,756	2,912	2,191
Concrete roofing tiles	m^2	28,263	28,813	23,345	25,551	33,243	34,685	27,870	30,843	34,707	38,818	35,787	31,510	26,359
Concrete building blocks:[2]														
dense aggregate	"	22,298	21,014	18,911	23,918	29,186	31,907	30,431	33,483	36,548	44,404	45,564	39,297	32,456
lightweight aggregate	"	28,407	23,779	20,896	23,395	25,544	24,378	21,867	27,515	31,121	33,530	31,041	23,768	18,581
aerated concrete	"	22,385	22,027	15,758	16,372	20,912	25,358	22,147	26,156	29,328	32,095	31,394	28,089	23,594
Concrete pipes[2,7]	Thousand	1,063	692	648	694	744	701	571	630	533	700	717	737	722
Roofing slates[8]	tonnes	14.5	17.7	16.3	22.7	18.4	22.0	34.0	34.7	45.6	40.9	46.6	44.1	41.0
Slates (damp-proof course)[8]	"													
Gypsum (excluding anhydrite)	"	3,396	3,264	2,667	2,566	2,978	3,155	3,074	3,253	–[10]	–	–	–	–
Plaster	"	949	960	775	764	855	912	876	912	–[10]	–	–	–	–
Plasterboard	Thousand m^2	113,961	111,132	101,987	107,867	120,819	127,668	122,599	134,501	–[10]	–	–	–	–

(Continued)

	Unit	1979	1980	1981	1982	1983	1984	1985	1986	1987	1988	1989	1990	1991
Unglazed floorquarries[2,7]	Thousand	1,220	1,123	1,007	949	1,013	1,000	1,061	1,075	1,078	2,681[12]	1,180	1,070	1,037
Unglazed tiles[2,7]	m^2	2,099	2,332	2,085	1,357	1,146	1,277	1,102	1,207	1,175	–[12]	1,521	1,349	1,371
Copper tubing[2,9]	Thousand tonnes	79	69	68	72	74	–[10]	–	–	–	–	–	–	–

(1) The figures are summaries of returns made by manufacturers and producers. They represent total production and not merely the quantities available for building purposes. (2) United Kingdom. (3) Including sand used in the production of sand lime bricks. (4) From 1979 figures represent volume sold, not production. (5) Figures include hoggin, concrete aggregate, other purposes (excluding fill) and fill. (6) From 1979 figures represent volume sold, not production. (7) Figures represent volume sold, not production. (8) From 1985 figures refer to slates used for architectural and cladding uses, roofing and damp-proof courses. (9) Figures relate to the production of copper tubes for all purposes including those used in the construction industry. (10) Series discontinued. (11) Provisional. (12) Unglazed floorquarries and unglazed tiles figures merged for 1988.

Merchant Shipbuilding[1]

United Kingdom

Source: CSO

	1981	1982	1983	1984	1985	1986	1987	1988	1989	1990	1991
Total Gross new orders[2]											
Number	72	57	45	90	58	61	37	41	42	35	21
Thousand gross tonnes[3,4]	482	355	172	127	291	146	163	26	534	92	614
£ million	383	313	279	224	330	280	277	84	430	216	–
For Overseas Registration											
Number	26	21	12	3	8	28	10	1	13	14	6
Thousand gross tonnes[3,4]	386	123	80	1	77	97	112	1	500	67	114
£ million	251	151	82	6	59	102	78	–	301	–	242
Total Orders on hand[5]											
Number	99	88	63	97	65	74	65	56	55	57	47
Thousand gross tonnes[3,4]	1,117	990	562	301	387	426	305	265	698	657	1,163
£ million	783	720	563	444	515	609	622	562	840	819	1,128
For Overseas Registration											
Number	26	35	24	10	8	31	31	18	19	25	22
Thousand gross tonnes[3,4]	386	384	195	95	73	140	160	123	548	565	600
£ million	271	339	194	85	64	135	144	102	340	445	576
Total Completions											
Number	51	67	68	56	86	48	43	41	43	33	31
Thousand gross tonnes[3,4]	217	453	540	411	225	106	247	31	106	134	110
£ million	194	408	390	311	259	175	278	106	157	238	209
For Overseas Registration											
Number	10	12	22	18	10	5	10	5	12	8	10
Thousand gross tonnes[3,4]	101	104	276	141	101	29	53	4	78	52	82
£ million	57	57	200	128	81	30	47	10	63	–	–

(1) Merchant registered ships of 100 gross tonnes and over built in the United Kingdom (including drilling ships but excluding floating platform drilling rigs). (2) Includes vessels which may have been cancelled at a late stage. (3) From 1984, tonnages conform to the 1969 IMO Convention on the tonnage measurement of ships. Earlier years relate to gross registered tonnes. (4) Tonnages are only accurately measured on completion: earlier figures are estimates. (5) Includes both vessels under construction and those not yet commenced.

Motor Vehicle Production

United Kingdom

Source: CSO

Number

	1981	1982	1983	1984	1985	1986	1987	1988	1989	1990	1991
Motor vehicles											
Passenger cars: total	**954,650**	**887,679**	**1,044,597**	**908,906**	**1,047,973**	**1,018,962**	**1,142,683**	**1,226,835**	**1,299,082**	**1,295,610**	**1,236,900**
1,000 c.c. and under	229,189	197,153	194,064	161,884	183,383	162,090	153,214	129,446	133,135	93,039	26,621
Over 1,000 c.c. but not over 1,600 c.c.	526,498	547,676	723,289	637,868	694,876	665,093	718,046	764,289	716,784	809,219	830,530
Over 1,600 c.c. but not over 2,800 c.c.	153,957	97,536	77,504	56,587	109,437	134,802	205,067	260,231	375,309	325,116	338,877
Over 2,800 c.c.	45,006	45,314	49,740	52,567	60,277	56,977	66,356	72,869	73,854	68,236	40,872
Commercial vehicles: total	229,555	268,798	244,514	224,825	265,973	228,685	246,728	317,343	326,590	270,346	217,141
Of which:											
Light commercial vehicles	157,744	189,094	175,338	157,963	195,475	175,825	188,858	250,053	267,135	230,510	184,005
Trucks:											
Under 7.5 tonnes	14,294	16,367	12,792	13,057	14,601	12,451	15,697	19,732	17,687	10,515	8,833
Over 7.5 tonnes	41,152	43,469	34,850	31,945	33,716	22,718	22,834	24,887	21,083	13,674	11,766
Motive units for articulated vehicles	3,921	6,761	5,918	5,361	6,154	5,351	5,343	6,171	5,827	3,327	2,700
Buses, coaches and mini buses:											
Single deck buses	9,903	11,518	13,870	14,811	14,842	11,180	13,397	15,836	14,140	11,782	9,426
Double deck buses	2,541	1,589	1,746	1,688	1,185	1,160	599	664	718	538	411

TIME SERIES. Figures for motor vehicles relate to periods of 52 weeks (53 weeks in 1983 and 1988).

Alcoholic Drink
United Kingdom

Source: CSO

	Unit	1980	1981	1982	1983	1984	1985	1986	1987	1988	1989	1990	1991
Spirits[1]													
Production	Thousand hectolitres of alcohol	4,907	3,251	3,021	2,898	2,986	3,124	2,966	3,136	3,568	4,211	4,676	4,476
Released for home consumption													
Imported:													
Rum	"	86	80	73	73	75	77	78	81	90	88	–	–
Brandy	"	71	64	66	69	70	77	79	82	90	85	–	–
Other	"	57	58	59	65	71	72	74	86	89	85	–	–
Home produced:													
Whisky (mature)[3]	"	502	477	448	445	434	461	456	446	452	430	413	383
Gin	"	144	130	124	137	133	139	131	128	135	124	–	–
Other	"	136	136	122	127	129	148	151	161	179	187	–	–
Total[2]	"	**996**	**945**	**891**	**916**	**912**	**974**	**971**	**983**	**1,035**	**1,000**	**980**	**912**
Beer[4]													
Production	Thousand hectolitres	64,830	61,721	59,786	60,324	60,105	59,655	59,446	59,906	60,145	60,015	59,653	57,359
Released for home consumption													
Home produced	"	63,188	60,024	58,668	59,586	59,241	58,431	57,911	58,519	58,913	58,679	58,026	55,515
Imported	"	2,302	2,293	2,252	2,646	2,841	3,076	3,302	3,454	4,350	4,533	5,067	5,329
Total	"	**65,490**	**62,317**	**60,920**	**62,232**	**62,082**	**61,507**	**61,213**	**61,973**	**63,263**	**63,212**	**63,093**	**60,844**
Imported wine/wine of fresh grapes													
Released for home consumption													
Heavy	"	1,257	1,191	1,074	1,079	1,022	861	559	489	451	406	378	357
Light	"	2,581	2,941	3,132	3,512	4,152	4,525	5,061	5,474	5,680	5,871	5,892	5,980
Sparkling	"	183	196	193	218	224	257	281	315	352	392	365	317
Total	"	**4,022**	**4,328**	**4,399**	**4,810**	**5,398**	**5,644**	**5,902**	**6,278**	**6,483**	**6,669**	**6,635**	**6,654**
British wine/made-wine													
Released for home consumption	"	515	539	509	549	492	538	528	561	593	591	706	702
Cider and perry													
Released for home consumption	"	2,255	2,409	2,899	3,258	3,259	3,174	3,233	3,226	3,103	3,272	3,621	3,738

(1) Potable spirits distilled. (2) Breakdown of minor spirits not available for 1990. (3) Before April 1983, the figures represent quantities of all mature home-produced spirits. (4) From 1976 the figures take account of brewing at high gravity with the addition of some brewing liquor after fermentation.

Tobacco Products
United Kingdom

Source: CSO

	Unit	1981	1982	1983	1984	1985	1986	1987	1988	1989	1990	1991
Released for home consumption												
Cigarettes:												
Home produced	Thousand million	108.3	100.6	100.6	93.4	88.6	83.3	90.1	87.9	87.5	87.4	85.3
Imported	"	1.5	1.8	2.0	6.4	11.1	11.7	12.2	9.4	10.3	10.3	10.3
Total	"	**109.8**	**102.3**	**102.6**	**99.9**	**99.7**	**95.0**	**102.3**	**97.3**	**95.9**	**97.8**	**95.6**
Cigars:	Million kg											
Home produced	"	2.2	2.3	2.4	2.4	2.3	2.3	2.4	2.4	2.3	2.1	1.9
Imported	"	0.7	0.4	0.2	0.2	0.2	0.2	0.2	0.2	0.2	0.2	0.1
Total	"	**2.9**	**2.7**	**2.7**	**2.5**	**2.5**	**2.5**	**2.6**	**2.6**	**2.4**	**2.3**	**2.0**
Hand-rolling tobacco:												
Home produced	"	6.2	6.2	5.9	5.4	5.1	4.8	4.8	4.5	4.3	4.1	4.1
Imported	"	–	–	–	–	–	–	–	–	–	–	0.1
Total	"	**6.2**	**6.3**	**5.9**	**5.4**	**5.1**	**4.8**	**4.8**	**4.5**	**4.8**	**4.1**	**4.2**
Other smoking and chewing tobacco:												
Home produced	"	3.5	3.3	3.1	3.0	2.9	2.7	2.6	2.5	2.2	2.1	2.0
Imported	"	–	–	–	–	–	–	–	–	0.1	0.1	0.1
Total	"	**3.5**	**3.3**	**3.1**	**3.0**	**2.9**	**2.7**	**2.6**	**2.5**	**2.6**	**2.2**	**2.1**

Net Central Government Expenditure on Research and Development[3]

Source: CSO

£ million

	1984–85	1985–86	1986–87	1987–88	1988–89	1989–90[1]	1990–91	1991–92[2]
Exploration and exploitation of the Earth	73.9	77.1	79.4	85.2	95.5	119.9	141.5	125.3
Infrastructure and general planning of land-use	60.3	54.1	65.5	66.8	66.8	71.6	75.7	86.2
Control of environmental pollution	51.6	53.3	48.7	56.1	58.2	53.4	73.9	85.1
Protection and promotion of human health	158.1	163.0	190.0	203.9	217.7	257.9	285.4	301.0
Production, distribution and rational utilization of energy	207.8	204.9	187.6	170.4	177.3	157.7	150.0	120.4
Agricultural production and technology	205.5	203.5	198.1	196.1	206.3	194.9	202.1	204.0
Industrial production and technology	288.0	435.3	443.6	411.8	394.8	451.6	472.7	404.8
Social structures and relationships	43.9	55.8	62.3	70.5	95.5	100.4	109.3	116.9
Exploration and exploitation of space	80.8	127.9	123.9	129.8	146.4	145.1	155.8	165.1
Research financed from General University Funds	630.0	669.0	720.0	795.6	830.4	890.8	918.8	960.4
Non-oriented research	281.0	183.8	192.8	209.3	215.9	222.9	247.7	245.5
Other civil research	11.4	12.4	14.2	13.6	13.8	11.9	11.7	13.0
Defence[2]	1,961.6	2,110.8	2,040.9	2,009.1	1,984.9	2,153.5	2,308.2	2,246.2
Total	4,054.2	4,351.0	4,367.1	4,418.0	4,503.6	4,831.2	5,152.6	5,073.9

(1) Data for 1989–90 have been revised. (2) Provisional. (3) Using European Community objectives for R&D expenditure.

Expectations of Industrial Performance

How do you think British industry will perform over the coming year?

Source: SCPR's *British Social Attitudes* survey, 9th Report, ed. R. Jowell *et al.* (Dartmouth Publishing, 1992)

Percentage

	1989	1990	1991
Improve a lot	5	3	4
Improve a little	25	16	17
Stay much the same	47	50	39
Decline a little	12	19	23
Decline a lot	4	7	12

British Industrial Profits

Who do you think benefits most from the profits made by British firms, and who do you think **should** profit?

Source: SCPR's *British Social Attitudes* survey, 9th Report, ed. R. Jowell *et al.* (Dartmouth Publishing, 1992)

Percentages

	Do benefit	Should benefit
Mainly their owners or shareholders	65	18
Mainly their directors and managers	25	3
Mainly their employees	4	44
The public generally	4	32

British Industrial Priorities

What do you think firms are *most likely* to do with their profits, and what do you think *should* be their first priority?

Source: SCPR's *British Social Attitudes* survey, 9th Report, ed. R. Jowell *et al.* (Dartmouth Publishing, 1992)

Percentages

	Where profits *would* go	Where profits *should* go
Investment		
New machinery or technology	20	26
Training the workforce	2	11
Researching new products	6	5
Workforce benefits		
Pay rise	6	27
Improved conditions	2	12
Customer benefit		
Lower prices	4	14
Shareholders/managers		
Increased dividends	34	3
Bonus to top management	20	*

* = less than 0.5 per cent.

ENERGY

The oil and gas reserves in the United Kingdom and around its coastline are very important national resources. In 1975 the UK produced less than 2 million tonnes of oil, but over the next decade this rose to nearly 130 million tonnes. Production has since declined and in 1991 stood at 90 million tonnes. At the end of that year there were 46 offshore and 19 onshore fields in production. As in other years, production was significantly restricted by continuing maintenance work, including the installation of emergency shutdown valves, and for general refurbishment.

Major Energy Developments

Source: Energy Information Administration, U.S. Dept. of Energy, *International Energy Annual 1991*

World Primary Energy Production Trends

Since 1981, the world's total output of primary energy – petroleum, natural gas, coal, hydro-electricity and nuclear electricity – has increased steadily at an average annual rate of 2.4%. World production increased from 279 quadrillion Btu in 1982 to 346 quadrillion Btu in 1991. In 1991 world production of petroleum was more than 66 million barrels per day, the equivalent of 136 quadrillion Btu.

Over the past 10 years petroleum has been the world's most heavily used type of energy. Between 1982 and 1991 production increased by more than 8 million barrels per day. Africa had the largest production gain, followed by the Far East and Oceania, and Western Europe. Their combined gains over the past 10 years were 5.6 million barrels per day, nearly 68% of the worldwide increase. In North America, Eastern Europe and the former USSR average daily production fell by 0.6 and 2.0 million barrels per day. Production by OPEC (Organization of Petroleum Exporting Countries) increased by 5.4 million barrels per day. In North America declines in oil production in the U.S. were largely offset by production increases in Canada and Mexico.

Major Energy Producers and Consumers

In 1991 three countries – the U.S., the former USSR and China – were the leading producers and consumers of world energy. These three countries produced 47% and consumed 48% of the world's total energy. The former USSR and the U.S. were the world's largest producers of energy in 1991, supplying 39% of the world's total energy. The United States consumed 23% of the world's total energy – more than any other country. The former USSR produced over 36% of the world's natural gas, followed by the U.S. with approximately 25%. The world's leading coal producers were China and the U.S., who produced 22.2 and 21.6 quadrillion Btu respectively – 48% of the world's total coal. While the former USSR and China produced more energy than they consumed, the U.S. consumed 20% more than it produced – an imbalance of 13.6 quadrillion Btu of energy.

World's Major Producers of Primary Energy, 1991

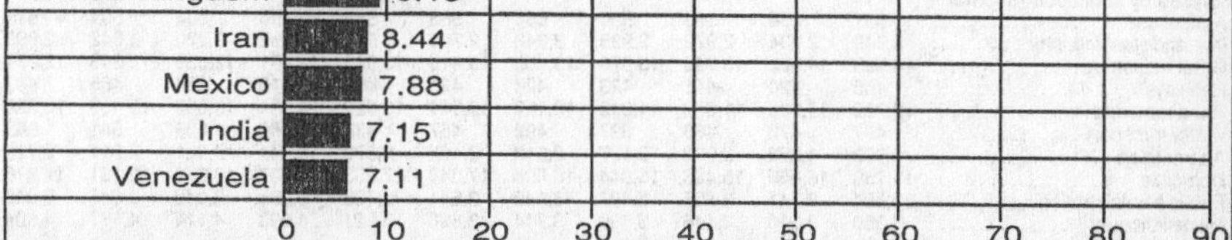

SOURCE: Energy Information Administration: International Energy Annual 1991: Quadrillion Btu

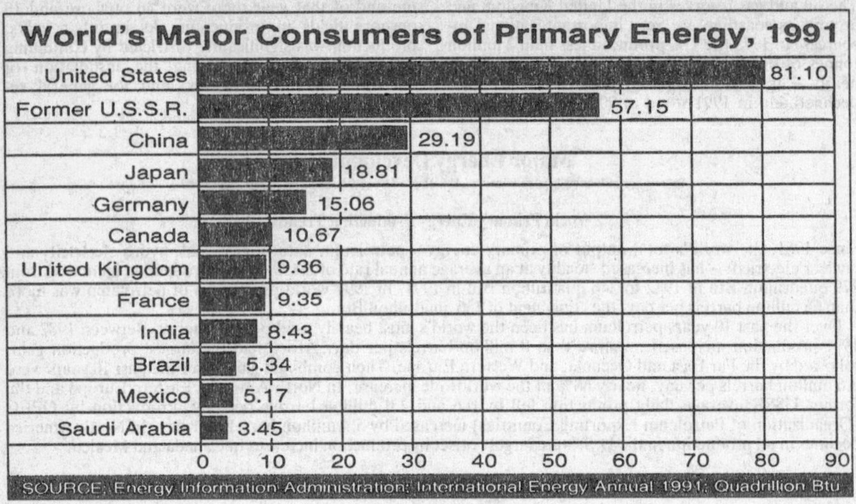

Total Inland Energy Consumption

United Kingdom

Source: CSO

Million therms[1]

	1981	1982	1983	1984	1985	1986	1987	1988	1989	1990	1991
Inland energy consumption of primary fuels and equivalents	78,740	77,315	77,673	77,352	81,050	83,269	84,037	84,702	84,902	85,710	88,049
Coal[2]	28,926	26,978	27,229	19,348	25,734	27,790	28,472	27,625	26,749	26,666	26,455
Petroleum[3]	28,117	28,189	27,046	33,924	29,167	28,711	27,953	29,661	30,232	30,955	31,009
Primary electricity[4]	3,677	4,218	4,708	4,958	5,583	5,859	6,138	7,038	7,746	7,278	8,142
Natural gas[5]	18,020	17,930	18,690	19,122	20,565	20,907	21,473	20,378	20,175	20,811	22,441
less Energy used by fuel producers and losses in conversion and distribution	23,819	23,036	23,630	23,462	24,731	25,449	25,805	25,906	26,572	27,098	27,598
Total consumption by final users	54,921	54,279	54,043	53,890	56,319	57,820	58,232	58,796	58,330	58,612	60,451
Analysed by type of fuel											
Coal (direct use)	4,748	4,831	4,640	3,840	4,814	4,902	4,257	3,866	3,381	3,071	3,258
Coke and breeze	2,039	1,850	1,945	1,983	2,118	1,933	2,121	2,225	2,107	1,958	1,841
Other solid fuel[6]	523	512	502	316	439	422	436	381	331	320	317
Coke oven gas	264	240	252	213	305	309	326	306	295	289	272
Natural gas (direct use)[7]	16,631	16,691	16,797	17,186	18,253	18,517	19,103	18,366	18,066	18,504	19,936
Electricity	7,521	7,371	7,486	7,654	7,987	8,217	8,834	9,054	9,226	9,366	9,590
Petroleum (direct use)	23,191	22,772	22,412	22,691	22,397	23,519	23,155	24,954	24,924	25,104	25,235
Other fuels (direct use)[8]	4	12	9	7	6	1	–	–	–	–	–
Analysed by class of consumer											
Agriculture	557	558	566	550	564	565	544	536	502	504	514
Iron and steel industry	3,249	2,934	2,972	2,935	3,048	2,790	3,081	3,262	3,220	3,042	2,895
Other industries	14,893	14,502	13,748	13,376	13,469	13,418	13,085	12,881	12,539	12,348	12,371
Railways[9]	466	420	441	423	428	425	408	416	388	465	483
Road transport	10,722	11,035	11,372	11,912	12,142	12,944	13,522	14,384	15,007	15,409	15,298
Water transport	437	472	480	527	498	457	438	460	538	541	565
Air transport	1,993	1,982	2,022	2,137	2,216	2,432	2,572	2,741	2,901	2,911	2,728
Domestic	15,750	15,569	15,488	15,044	16,698	17,348	17,253	16,737	16,073	16,191	17,876
Public administration	3,504	3,441	3,497	3,497	3,540	3,544	3,405	3,285	3,049	3,045	3,246
Miscellaneous[10]	3,350	3,366	3,446	3,490	3,714	3,898	3,921	4,093	4,114	4,177	4,504

(1) Estimates of the gross calorific values used for converting the statistics for the various fuels to therms are given in the *Digest of United Kingdom Energy Statistics 1991*. (2) Including net trade and stock change in other solid fuels. (3) Refinery throughput of crude oil, *plus* net foreign trade and stock change in petroleum products. Liquid fuels derived from coal (which are included in coal consumption) and petroleum products not used as fuels (chemical feedstock, industrial and white spirits, lubricants, bitumen and wax) are excluded. (4) Primary electricity comprises produced electricity in the UK at nuclear, natural flow, hydro and wind stations, *plus* net imports of electricity. The figures represent the notional thermal input of fossil fuel that would have been needed to produce the same quantities of electricity at the efficiency of contemporary UK conventional steam power stations. (5) Natural gas includes both indigenous and imported natural gas and colliery methane piped to the surface and consumed at collieries or sold. (6) Including briquettes, ovoids, Phurnacite, Coalite, Rexco, etc. (7) Figures for Natural gas up to 1988 include Town gas. Data for consumption of Town gas in 1988 and previous years may be found in earlier editions of *The Annual Abstract of Statistics*. (8) Liquid fuels derived from coal. (9) Including fuel used at transport premises from 1990. (10) Including fuel used at transport premises prior to 1990.

Coal Production[1]

Great Britain: Years ended March

Source: CSO

Million tonnes

	1981/82	1982/83	1983/84	1984/85[2]	1985/86[3]	1986/87	1987/88	1988/89	1989/90	1990/91	1991/92
Scottish	7.22	6.62	5.27	0.30	4.26	3.43	2.59	1.90	1.90	2.14	2.22
North East	13.41	12.42	10.91	0.38	9.50	10.17	10.22	10.30	10.04	8.96	7.55
Selby[4]	–	–	–	–	–	–	–	–	–	5.94	14.28
North Yorkshire[3]	8.26	8.39	7.55	0.32 }	13.90	14.24	14.30	15.85	13.26	10.06	–
Barnsley[3]	8.40	8.13	6.19	0.12 }							
Doncaster[3]	7.12	6.78	5.82	0.01 }	12.48	12.49	11.55	13.23	10.87	8.58	13.38[7]
South Yorkshire[3]	7.23	7.33	6.57	0.17 }							
North Derbyshire	8.48	8.15	6.29	1.44	6.21	6.04	10.57[5]	10.87[5]	10.66[5]	9.60[6]	–
North Nottingham[3]	12.26	12.36	11.60	9.16 }	18.67	18.06	17.61	17.15	16.50	16.89	17.22
South Nottingham[3]	8.54	8.25	6.97	5.59 }							
South Midlands and Kent	8.64	8.17	6.65	4.98	6.74	6.14	0.35[6]	0.44[6]	0.14[6]	–	–
Western	11.08	10.78	9.08	4.82	9.38	10.09	9.55	9.73	6.92	6.39	–
South Wales	7.56	6.88	6.58	0.29	6.63	6.48	5.01	4.98	3.37	3.15	–
Midlands and Wales	–	–	–	–	–	–	–	–	–	–	15.92[7]
Total – Saleable mined coal	108.20	104.26	89.48	27.58	87.76	87.14	81.75	84.44	73.55	71.71	70.57

TIME SERIES. Figures relate to periods of 52 weeks. For 1989/90, figures relate to 52 weeks estimate for period ended 31 March 1990.

(1) Collieries operated by the British Coal Corporation (BCC). Excludes coal extracted in work on capital account (0.59 million tonnes in 1990/91). (2) Production was affected by a national overtime ban from 1 November 1983 and by wider industrial action from 12 March 1984. (3) With effect from 1985/86 the BCC altered their regional structure and incorporated Barnsley into North Yorkshire Area, Doncaster into South Yorkshire Area and merged North and South Nottingham into Nottinghamshire Area. See also note 4. (4) Selby (previously part of North Yorkshire) became a separate BCC Area with effect from 1990/91. (5) From 1987/88 figures relate to BCC's Central Area (previously North Derbyshire and South Midlands). (6) From 1987/88 figures relate to BCC's Kent Area only. Mining operations ceased on 29 July 1989. See also footnote 5.

Electricity Generation, Supply and Consumption

United Kingdom

Source: CSO

Gigawatt-hours[6]

	1981	1982	1983	1984	1985	1986	1987	1988	1989	1990	1991
Electricity generated:											
Major generating companies[1]: total	259,731	255,439	260,436	265,990	279,972	282,258	282,745	288,511	292,896	298,495	301,176
Conventional steam stations	220,259	209,957	208,514	209,121	216,255	221,426	226,426	222,887	219,712	230,376	229,190
Nuclear stations	34,043	40,001	45,776	49,498	56,354	54,005	50,282	58,867	66,740	61,306	66,329
Gas turbines and oil engines	509	517	356	1,947	1,084	508	487	464	529	432	355
Hydro-electric stations:											
Natural flow	3,917	3,884	3,892	3,368	3,447	4,098	3,474	4,171	4,002	4,393	3,777
Pumped storage	1,003	1,080	1,897	2,055	2,831	2,221	2,075	2,121	1,910	1,982	1,523
Other (mainly wind)	–	–	–	1	1	1	–	1	2	–	3
Other generators[2]: total	17,971	17,344	17,037	16,553	17,659	18,813	19,367	19,593	20,929	20,483	20,956
Conventional steam stations[3]	13,580	12,700	12,216	11,435	12,271	13,057	13,688	14,332	15,279	15,355	16,037
Nuclear stations	3,926	3,971	4,152	4,481	4,740	5,074	4,956	4,589	4,994	4,441	4,214
Hydro-electric stations (natural flow)	465	673	669	637	648	682	723	672	657	687	706
All generating companies: total	277,702	272,783	277,473	282,543	297,631	301,071	302,112	308,104	313,825	318,979	322,132
Conventional steam stations[3]	233,839	222,657	220,730	220,556	228,526	234,483	240,114	237,219	234,991	245,732	245,227
Nuclear stations	37,969	43,972	49,928	53,979	61,094	59,079	55,238	63,238	71,734	65,747	70,543
Gas turbines and oil engines	509	517	356	1,947	1,084	508	487	464	529	432	355
Hydro-electric stations:											
Natural flow	4,382	4,557	4,561	4,005	4,095	4,780	4,198	4,843	4,659	5,080	4,482
Pumped storage	1,003	1,080	1,897	2,055	2,831	2,221	2,075	2,121	1,910	1,982	1,523
Other (mainly wind)	–	–	–	1	1	1	–	1	2	4	3
Electricity used on works: total	17,799	17,704	18,115	18,332	19,643	19,602	19,600	20,198	20,234	19,553	20,083
Major generating companies[1]	16,429	16,380	16,794	17,011	18,235	18,105	18,041	18,694	18,610	17,891	18,420
Other generators[2]	1,370	1,324	1,321	1,321	1,408	1,497	1,559	1,504	1,624	1,691	1,663
Electricity supplied (gross)											
Major generating companies[1]: total	243,302	239,059	243,642	248,979	261,737	264,154	264,704	269,817	274,286	280,604	282,757
Conventional steam stations[4]	208,589	198,822	197,600	200,240	205,906	209,977	214,836	211,502	208,675	218,957	217,947
Nuclear stations	29,818	35,310	40,344	43,407	49,694	47,484	43,947	51,699	59,312	54,964	59,265
Gas turbines and oil engines[4]	–	–	–	–	–	475	454	430	494	403	310
Hydro-electric stations:											
Natural flow	3,906	3,873	3,882	3,358	3,435	4,087	3,460	4,160	3,992	4,384	3,767
Pumped storage	989	1,054	1,816	1,974	2,701	2,129	2,006	2,025	1,812	1,892	1,465
Other (mainly wind)	–	–	–	–	–	1	–	1	2	3	3
Other generators[2]: total	16,637	16,024	15,719	15,168	16,184	17,316	17,809	18,089	19,305	18,792	19,293
Conventional steam stations[3]	12,801	11,943	11,486	10,685	11,467	12,278	12,831	13,478	14,362	14,409	15,095
Nuclear stations	3,373	3,411	3,567	3,849	4,073	4,359	4,257	3,942	4,290	3,700	3,496
Hydro-electric stations (natural flow)	463	670	666	634	645	679	720	669	654	684	702
All generating companies: total	259,939	255,083	259,361	264,148	277,922	281,469	282,512	287,906	293,592	299,396	302,050
Conventional steam stations[3,4]	221,390	210,765	209,086	210,925	217,373	222,255	227,667	224,980	223,037	233,366	233,042
Nuclear stations	33,191	38,721	43,911	47,256	53,767	51,843	48,205	55,642	63,602	58,664	62,761
Gas turbines and oil engines[4]	–	–	–	–	–	475	454	430	494	403	310
Hydro-electric stations:											
Natural flow	4,369	4,543	4,548	3,992	4,080	4,766	4,180	4,829	4,645	5,067	4,469
Pumped storage	989	1,054	1,816	1,974	2,701	2,129	2,006	2,025	1,812	1,892	1,465
Other (mainly wind)	–	–	–	–	–	1	–	1	2	3	3
Electricity used in pumping											
Major generating companies[1]	1,196	1,272	2,337	2,613	3,494	2,993	2,804	2,888	2,572	2,626	2,109
Electricity supplied (net): total	258,743	253,811	257,024	261,535	274,427	278,476	279,708	285,018	291,019	296,770	299,942
Major generating companies[1]	242,106	237,787	241,305	246,367	258,242	261,160	261,899	266,929	271,714	277,978	280,649
Other generators[2]	16,637	16,024	15,719	15,168	16,184	17,316	17,809	18,089	19,305	18,792	19,293

(Continued)

Gigawatt-hours[6]

	1981	1982	1983	1984	1985	1986	1987	1988	1989	1990	1991
Net imports	–	–	–	–	–	4,256	11,636	12,830	12,631	11,943	16,407
Electricity available	258,743	253,811	257,024	261,535	274,427	282,732	291,344	297,848	303,650	308,713	316,349
Losses in transmission etc.[5]	20,410	20,662	21,371	21,070	22,637	22,914	22,958	23,343	24,251	24,293	25,508
Electricity consumption: total[5]	238,333	233,149	235,653	240,465	251,790	259,818	268,386	274,505	279,399	284,420	290,841
Fuel industries[5]	–	–	–	8,297	9,236	9,505	9,492	9,163	9,001	9,986	9,794
Final users: total[5]	–	–	–	232,168	242,554	250,313	258,894	265,342	270,398	274,434	281,048
Industrial sector[5]	94,213	90,289	89,683	86,503	88,009	88,800	93,137	97,143	99,417	100,643	99,570
Domestic sector	84,440	82,790	82,950	83,898	88,228	91,826	93,254	92,362	92,270	93,793	98,098
Other sectors[5]	59,680	60,070	63,020	61,767	66,317	69,687	72,503	75,837	78,711	79,997	83,380

(1) Generating companies corresponding to the old public sector supply system, i.e. National Power, PowerGen, Nuclear Electric, National Grid Company, Scottish Power, Hydro-Electric, Scottish Nuclear, North Ireland Electricity, Midlands Electricity and South Western Electricity. (2) Larger establishments in the industrial and transport sectors generating 1 Gigawatt-hour or more a year. The prototype reactors operated by the United Kingdom Atomic Energy Authority and by British Nuclear Fuels plc are included. (3) For other generators, conventional steam stations cover all types of stations, including combined heat and power plants, other than nuclear and hydro-electric stations. (4) Prior to 1986 gas turbines and oil engines are included with conventional steam stations. (5) Until 1983 consumption by fuel industries is included with industrial sector consumption. The figures for consumption, and hence losses, in these years are subject to some estimation. (6) 1 Gigawatt-hour equals 1 million Kilowatt hours.

Indigenous Production, Refinery Receipts, Arrivals and Shipments of Oil[1]

Source: CSO

Thousand tonnes

	1981	1982	1983	1984	1985	1986	1987	1988	1989	1990	1991
Total indigenous petroleum production[2]	89,480	103,219	115,045	126,065	127,642	127,053	123,351	114,459	91,827	91,602	91,256
Crude petroleum[3]:											
Refinery receipts total	76,616	76,705	76,344	78,450	78,653	79,666	80,363	83,925	88,840	59,735	92,523
Indigenous[4]	37,769	40,294	44,815	45,304	43,231	38,780	38,794	40,582	39,585	37,754	35,932
Others[5]	2,486	3,162	2,366	2,196	1,095	1,006	939	730	904	916	772
Net foreign arrivals[6]	36,361	33,249	29,163	30,950	34,327	39,880	40,630	42,613	48,351	51,065	55,819
Foreign trade											
Arrivals[6]	36,855	33,754	30,324	32,272	35,576	41,209	41,541	44,272	49,500	52,710	57,084
Shipments											
Indigenous	51,149	60,195	67,397	77,271	79,335	83,341	80,043	69,965	49,130	54,022	52,378
Other[7]	494	505	1,161	1,363	1,416	1,635	1,113	1,967	1,332	1,878	1,424
Petroleum products											
Foreign trade											
Arrivals[6]	9,402	12,524	9,907	23,082	13,101	11,767	8,570	9,219	9,479	11,005	10,140
Shipments[6]	12,793	13,585	14,674	14,234	17,038	17,726	17,056	17,176	17,873	18,002	20,677
Net arrivals[6]	−3,391	−1,061	−4,767	+8,848	−3,937	−5,959	−8,486	−7,957	−8,394	−6,997	−10,537
Bunkers[8]	2,073	2,583	2,019	2,248	2,118	2,091	1,668	1,831	2,396	2,538	2,486

(1) The term indigenous is used in this table for convenience to include oil from the UK Continental Shelf as well as the small amounts produced on the mainland. (2) Crude oil *plus* condensates and petroleum gases derived at onshore treatment plants. (3) Includes process (partly refined) oils. (4) Includes condensate for distillation. (5) Mainly recycled products. (6) Foreign trade as recorded by the petroleum industry and may differ from figures published in *Overseas Trade Statistics*. (7) Re-exports of imported crude which may include some indigenous oil in blend. (8) International marine bunkers.

Oil and Gas Reserves, 1991

United Kingdom Continental Shelf

Source: CSO

	Oil (million tonnes)	Gas (billion cubic metres)
Fields already discovered		
Proven reserves	2,020	1,345
Probable reserves	675	695
Possible reserves	730	570
Total initial reserves in present discoveries	2,020–3,425	1,345–2,610
of which:		
Already recovered	1,465	804
Estimates in potential future discoveries	540–3,395	260–1,252
Total recoverable reserves	2,560–6,820	1,605–3,862

Production of Primary Fuels

United Kingdom

Source: CSO

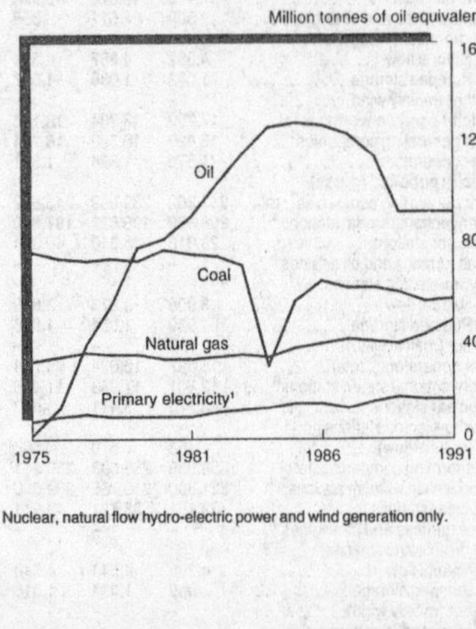

(1) Nuclear, natural flow hydro-electric power and wind generation only.

World Crude Oil and Natural Gas Reserves, Jan. 1, 1992

Source: Energy Information Administration; *Annual Energy Review 1992*

Region and Country	Crude Oil (billion barrels) *Oil and Gas Journal*	Crude Oil (billion barrels) *World Oil*	Natural Gas (trillion cubic feet) *Oil and Gas Journal*	Natural Gas (trillion cubic feet) *World Oil*
North America	**81.6**	**81.7**	**335.3**	**334.0**
Canada	5.6	6.1	96.7	96.0
Mexico	51.3	50.9	71.5	71.0
United States	24.7	24.7	167.1	167.1
Central and South America	**68.5**	**73.1**	**167.0**	**186.9**
Argentina	1.6	1.5	20.4	22.7
Bolivia	0.1	0.1	4.5	4.1
Brazil	2.8	3.0	4.0	4.4
Colombia	1.9	1.7	3.9	3.6
Ecuador	1.6	1.7	3.9	3.9
Trinidad and Tobago	0.5	0.6	8.9	8.7
Venezuela	59.1	62.7	110.0	128.5
Other	0.9	1.8	11.4	11.0
Western Europe	**14.7**	**22.2**	**181.4**	**215.5**
Denmark	0.8	0.7	4.1	4.0
Germany	0.4	0.3	8.8	8.2
Italy	0.7	0.7	11.4	11.4
Netherlands	0.1	0.1	69.6	68.9
Norway	7.6	15.3	60.7	96.7
United Kingdom	4.0	4.1	19.2	19.2
Other	1.1	1.0	7.6	7.1
Eastern Europe and former USSR	**58.5**	**61.8**	**1,763.5**	**1,871.3**
Former USSR	57.0	59.9	1,750.0	1,853.4
Other[1]	1.5	1.9	13.5	17.9
Middle East	**661.6**	**596.6**	**1,319.1**	**1,344.9**
Bahrain	0.1	0.1	6.0	5.9
Iran	92.9	62.5	600.4	600.0
Iraq	100.0	100.0	95.0	109.4
Kuwait	96.5	95.2	48.5	51.8
Oman	4.3	4.4	9.9	13.0
Qatar	3.7	2.9	162.0	162.0
Saudi Arabia	260.3	261.9	184.5	184.5
United Arab Emirates	98.1	65.8	199.3	195.7
Other	5.7	3.8	13.5	22.6
Africa	**60.5**	**75.5**	**310.2**	**334.0**
Algeria	9.2	9.9	116.5	128.1
Cameroon	0.4	0.4	3.9	3.9
Egypt	4.5	3.5	12.4	12.0
Libya	22.8	38.4	43.0	43.5
Nigeria	17.9	17.9	104.7	120.1
Tunisia	1.7	1.8	3.0	3.2
Other	4.0	3.6	26.7	23.2
Far East and Oceania	**44.1**	**56.4**	**299.3**	**389.3**
Australia	1.5	2.1	15.1	75.4
Brunei	1.3	1.1	11.2	11.9
China	24.0	30.0	35.4	35.0
India	6.1	6.1	25.8	25.8
Indonesia	6.6	11.8	64.8	104.3
Malaysia	3.0	3.6	59.1	59.1
New Zealand	0.2	0.2	3.4	3.4
Pakistan	0.2	0.4	22.6	26.7
Thailand	0.3	0.3	13.6	14.7
Other	0.9	0.8	48.3	33.0
World Total	**989.4**	**967.1**	**4,375.8**	**4,675.9**

(1) Albania, Bulgaria, Czechoslovakia, Hungary, Poland and Romania.

Notes: Data for Kuwait and Saudi Arabia include half of the reserves in the Neutral Zone between the 2 countries. All reserve figures except those for the USSR and natural gas reserves in Canada are proved reserves recoverable with present technology and prices. USSR figures are "explored reserves", which include proved, probable and some possible. The Canadian natural gas figure includes proved and some probable. The latest Energy Information Administration data for the United States are for Dec. 31, 1991. Sum of components may not equal total due to independent rounding.

World Nuclear Power

Source: International Atomic Energy Agency, Dec. 31, 1992

Country	Reactors in Operation: No. of Units	Reactors in Operation: Total MW(e)[1]	Reactors under Construction: No. of Units	Reactors under Construction: Total MW(e)[1]	Nuclear Electricity Supplied, 1992: TW(e).h[1]	Nuclear Electricity Supplied, 1992: % of Total	Total Operating Experience to December 31, 1992: Years	Total Operating Experience to December 31, 1992: Months
Argentina	2	935	1	692	6.6	14.4	28	7
Belgium	7	5,484	—	—	40.9	59.9	114	7
Brazil	1	626	1	1,245	1.8	0.7	10	9
Bulgaria	6	3,538	—	—	11.6	32.5	65	6
Canada	21	14,874	1	881	76.0	15.2	283	2
China	1	288	2	1,812	0.5	0.1	1	1
Cuba	—	—	2	816	—	—	—	—
Czech Republic	4	1,632	2	1,784	12.3	20.7	26	8
Finland	4	2,310	—	—	18.2	33.2	55	9
France	55	57,688	5	7,125	321.7	72.9	709	10
Germany	21	22,559	—	—	150.0	30.1	448	0
Hungary	4	1,729	—	—	13.1	48.4	30	2
India	9	1,593	5	1,010	5.6	3.3	101	3
Iran	—	—	2	2,392	—	—	—	—
Italy	—	—	—	—	—	—	81	0
Japan	44	34,238	9	8,129	217.0	27.7	556	11
Kazakhstan, Rep. of.	1	135	—	—	0.5	0.6	19	6
Korea, South	9	7,220	3	2,550	58.5	53.2	72	1
Lithuania, Rep. of	2	2,760	1	1,380	15.6*	80.0*	14	6
Mexico	1	654	1	654	3.0	3.2	3	4
Netherlands	2	504	—	—	3.8	4.9	43	9
Pakistan	1	125	—	—	0.5	1.2	21	3
Romania	—	—	5	3,155	—	—	—	—
Russia	28	18,893	18	14,175	119.6	11.8	439	9
South Africa	2	1,842	—	—	9.3	6.0	16	2
Spain	9	7,101	—	—	53.4	36.4	119	8
Sweden	12	10,002	—	—	60.8	43.2	183	2
Switzerland	5	2,952	—	—	22.1	39.6	88	10
Ukraine	15	13,020	6	5,700	71.0*	25.0*	128	11
United Kingdom	37	12,066	1	1,188	69.1	23.2	962	10
United States	109	98,729	3	3,480	618.8	22.3	1,702	4
Total	**412**	**323,497**	**68**	**58,168**	**1981.3**	—	**6,329**	**4**

(1) 1 terawatt-hour (TW(e).h) = 10^6 megawatt-hour (MW(e).h). For an average power plant, 1 TW(e).h = 0.39 megatonnes of coal equivalent (input) and 0.23 megatonnes of oil equivalent (input). * = IAEA estimate.

World's Largest Capacity Hydro Plants

Source: U.S. Committee on Large Dams, of the Intl. Commission on Large Dams, Sep. 1993

Rank order	Name	Country	Rated capacity now (MW)	Rated capacity planned (MW)
1	Turukhansk (Lower Tunguska)*	USSR		20,000
2	Itaipu	Brazil/Paraguay	7,400	13,320
3	Grand Coulee	USA	6,495	10,830
4	Guri (Raúl Leoni)	Venezuela	10,300	10,300
5	Tucuruí	Brazil	2,640	7,260
6	Sayano Shushensk*	USSR	6,400	6,400
7=	Corpus Posadas	Argentina/Paraguay	4,700	6,000
7=	Krasnoyarsk	USSR	6,000	6,000
9	La Grande 2	Canada	5,328	5,328
10	Churchill Falls	Canada	5,225	5,225
11	Xingo	Brazil	3,012	5,020

* Planned or under construction.

Rank order	Name	Country	Rated capacity now (MW)	Rated capacity planned (MW)
12	Tarbela	Pakistan	1,750	4,678
13=	Bratsk	USSR	4,500	4,500
13=	Ust-Ilim	USSR	3,675	4,500
15	Cabora Bassa	Mozambique	2,425	4,150
16	Boguchany	USSR		4,000
17=	Rogun*	USSR		3,600
17=	Oak Creek	USA	3,600	3,600
19	Paulo Afonso I	Brazil	1,524	3,409
20	Pati*	Argentina		3,300
21=	Ilha Solteira	Brazil	3,200	3,200
21=	Brumley Gap*	USA	3,200	3,200
23	Chapetón*	Argentina		3,000
24	Gezhouba	China	2,715	2,715
25=	John Day	USA	2,160	2,700
25=	Nurek	USSR	900	2,700
25=	Yacyreta*	Argentina/Paraguay		2,700

Major Dams of the World

Source: U.S. Committee on Large Dams, of the Intl. Commission of Large Dams, Sep. 1993

World's Highest Dams

Rank order	Name	Country	Height above lowest formation (metres)
1	Rogun*	USSR	335
2	Nurek	USSR	300
3	Grand Dixence	Switzerland	285
4	Inguri	USSR	272
5=	Chicoasén	Mexico	261
5=	Tehri*	India	261
7	Kishau*	India	253
8=	Ertan	China	245
8=	Sayano-Shushensk*	USSR	245
10	Guavio*	Colombia	243
11	Mica	Canada	242
12	Mauvoisin	Switzerland	237
13	Chivor	Colombia	237
14	El Cajón	Honduras	234
15	Chirkei	USSR	233
16	Oroville	USA	230
17	Bhakra	India	226
18	Hoover	USA	221
19	Contra	Switzerland	220
20	Mratinje	Yugoslavia	220

* Under construction.

World's Largest Volume Embankment Dams

Rank order	Name	Country	Volume cubic metres × 1000
1	Tarbela	Pakistan	148,500
2	Fort Peck	USA	96,050
3	Tucurui	Brazil	85,200
4	Ataturk*	Turkey	85,000
5	Yacireta*	Argentina	81,000
6	Rogun*	USSR	75,500
7	Oahe	USA	70,339
8	Guri	Venezuela	70,000
9	Parambikulam	India	69,165
10	High Island West	Hong Kong	67,000
11	Gardiner	Canada	65,000
12	Afsluitdijk	Netherlands	63,400
13	Mangla	Pakistan	63,379
14	Oroville	USA	59,635
15	San Luis	USA	59,559
16	Nurek	USSR	58,000
17	Tanda	Pakistan	57,250
18	Garrison	USA	50,843
19	Chochiti	USA	50,228
20	Oosterschelde	Netherlands	50,000

* Under construction.

World's Largest Capacity Man-made Reservoirs

Rank order	Name	Country	Capacity cubic metres × 1000
1	Owen Falls	Uganda	204,800
2	Bratsk	USSR	169,000
3	Aswan (High)	Egypt	162,000
4	Kariba	Zimbabwe/Zambia	160,368
5	Akosombo	Ghana	147,960
6	Daniel Johnson	Canada	141,851
7	Guri	Venezuela	135,000
8	Krasnoyarsk	USSR	73,300
9	W A C Bennett (Portage Mt.)	Canada	70,309
10	Zeya	USSR	68,400

* Under construction

Rank order	Name	Country	Capacity cubic metres × 1000
11	Cabora Bassa	Mozambique	63,000
12	La Grande 2	Canada	61,715
13	La Grande 3	Canada	60,020
14	Ust-Ilim	USSR	59,300
15	Boguchany*	USSR	58,200
16	Kuibyshev	USSR	58,000
17	Serra de Mesa	Brazil	54,400
18	Caniapiscau Barrage KA 3	Canada	53,790
19	Bukhtarma	USSR	49,800
20	Ataturk	Turkey	48,700

EDUCATION

Alongside the increase in working mothers has been a sevenfold increase in the number of places for 3–5-year-olds in nurseries and playgroups and with registered childminders. Although the average size of nursery schools continues to increase, that of comprehensives has fallen. Over the past decade the proportion of comprehensive schools with over 1000 pupils fell from 40% to 23%.

While there has been a major shift from selective to comprehensive education over the last 20 years, independent schools continue to attract 7% of all pupils in Great Britain.

The National Curriculum for 5–16-year-olds, incorporating formal assessments at the ages of 7, 11, 14 and 16, was introduced to state schools in autumn 1989. It has attracted much criticism from the teaching profession, who claim loss of autonomy in the classroom, massively increased administration and results which tell nothing they don't already know about their pupils. The government has responded by making changes to the curriculum and testing procedures, but remains firm in its commitment to both.

The General Certificate of Secondary Education (GCSE) was introduced in England, Wales and Northern Ireland in 1988, replacing the GCE and CSE examinations. "A" levels remain unchanged, but the Advanced Supplementary ("AS") exam, introduced in 1989, runs alongside "A" levels, taking about half the teaching and study time of an "A" level course. Pupils in Scotland and Wales often take alternative national exams – SCOTVEC in Scotland and the Certificate of Education in Wales.

Despite recent allegations about falling standards, many more pupils are leaving school with qualifications than they did 20 years ago. Whereas only 4 in 10 left school in 1970/71 with one GCSE pass at grades A–C, the figure for 1989/90 was up to 6 in 10 boys and 7 in 10 girls.

In public exams girls outperformed boys in English, biology, French and history, while boys outperformed girls in maths, physics, geography and chemistry.

One of the largest areas of growth has been in part-time education. Between 1970 and 1990 the overall number of part-time students rose 2½ times to 427,000. Within this figure, however, the number of female students increased eightfold. The Open University accounts for 22% of part-time students.

UK Government Expenditure on Education

Years ended 31 March

Source: CSO

£ million

2601,111	1980/81	1981/82	1982/83	1983/84	1984/85	1985/86	1986/87	1987/88	1988/89	1989[7]/90	1990/91
Current expenditure											
Nursery schools	52	57	63	67	70	74	81	4,771	5,259	5,654	–
Primary schools	2,840	3,093	3,255	3,337	3,483	3,705	4,157				
Secondary schools	3,695	4,143	4,435	4,675	4,850	5,066	5,583	6,027	6,437	6,483	–
Special schools	443	500	543	583	620	667	727	812	888	989	–
Further and adult education[1]	1,591	1,812	1,987	2,157	2,260	2,377	2,625	2,895	3,277	2,705[5]	–
Training of teachers: tuition	78	83	93	86	93	110	142	156			
PCFC sector[2]	–	–	–	–	–	–	–	–	–	1,024	–
Universities[1]	1,264	1,277	1,388	1,497	1,562	1,608	1,654	1,824	1,958	2,104	–
Other education expenditure	516	553	599	656	697	736	871	900	1,009	1,195	–
Related current expenditure:											
Training of teachers: residence[3]	15	15	18	20	18	19	19	–	–	–	–
School welfare[4]	20	23	27	30	33	37	40	56	70	91	–
Meals and milk	479	480	499	519	527	532	559	546	469	485	–
Youth service and physical training	148	169	192	209	227	239	211	246	277	328	–
Maintenance grants and allowances to pupils and students	630	702	759	825	850	838	806	764	900	934	–
Transport of pupils	215	234	253	262	268	275	290	300	311	304	–
Miscellaneous expenditure	3	3	4	4	5	5	5	6	10	17	–
Total current expenditure[5]	11,989	13,144	14,116	14,967	15,563	16,288	17,770	19,240	20,865	22,353	–
Capital expenditure											
Nursery schools	6	4	4	6	7	8	7	192	246	314	–
Primary schools	174	136	128	141	154	164	180				
Secondary schools	274	233	239	232	217	223	187	213	195	397	–
Special schools	26	22	21	20	12	17	23	11	33	38	–
Further and adult education	129	108	139	141	144	149	149	174	180	164	–
Training of teachers	2	2	3	2	3	3	3	3			
PCFC sector[2]	–	–	–	–	–	–	–	–	–	90	–
Universities	117	117	116	139	121	140	156	158	172	196	–
Other education expenditure	10	10	13	14	12	11	10	32	22	41	–
Related capital expenditure*	23	19	20	22	23	23	24	21	25	33	–
Total capital expenditure[5]	761	651	683	717	693	738	739	804	873	1,273	–
VAT refunds to local authorities	189	189	240	259	266	284	345	357	399	477	–
Total expenditure											
Central government	1,779	1,797	2,022	2,222	2,288	2,398	2,618	2,746	3,025	4,337	–
Local authorities	11,160	12,187	13,017	13,721	14,233	14,911	16,235	17,655	19,112	19,765	–
Total government expenditure[6]	12,939	13,984	15,039	15,943	16,521	17,309	18,853	20,401	22,137	24,102	–
Gross domestic product (average estimate) at market prices	237,798	260,950	285,691	309,788	331,873	362,876	390,732	432,357	481,081	522,297	582,859
Expenditure as a percentage of GDP	*5.4*	*5.4*	*5.4*	*5.3*	*5.0*	*4.8*	*4.8*	*4.7*	*4.6*	*4.6*	–

(1) Including tuition fees. (2) The Polytechnics and Colleges Funding Council sector (PCFC), applicable from 1989/90. (3) With effect from 1987/88 included with maintenance grants and allowances. (4) Expenditure on the school health service is included in the National Health Service. (5) Due to rounding, constituent figures may not sum to totals. (6) Excludes additional adjustment to allow for capital consumption made for National Accounts purposes amounting to £1,040m in 1989/90. (7) Provisional.

Education and Day Care of Children Under Five

United Kingdom

Source: CSO

Thousands and percentages

	1966	1971	1976	1981	1986[1]	1989	1990	1991
Children under 5 in schools[2] (thousands)								
Public sector schools								
Nursery schools – full-time	26	20	20	22	19	17	17	16
– part-time	9	29	54	67	77	65	67	68
Primary schools – full-time	220	263	350	281	306	317	346	357
– part-time	–	38	117	167	228	273	286	303
Non-maintained schools – full-time	21	19	19	19	20	26	27	28
– part-time	2	14	12	12	15	18	19	20
Special schools – full-time	2	2	4	4	4	4	4	4
– part-time	–	–	1	1	2	2	2	2
Total	280	384	576	573	671	722	769	799
As a percentage of all children aged 3 or 4	*15.0*	*20.5*	*34.5*	*44.3*	*46.7*	*49.1*	*51.2*	*52.8*
Day care places[3] (thousands)								
Local authority day nurseries[4]	21	23[2]	35	32	33	34	33	32
Local authority playgroups				5	5	4	3	3
Registered day nurseries[5]	75	296	401	23	29	64[6]		88
Registered playgroups				433	473	480	491	502
Registered child minders[6,7]	32	90	86	110[5]	157	216	238	273
Total[5]	128	409	522	603[5]	698	783	830	899

(1) Data for 1985 have been used for Scotland for children under 5 in schools. (2) Pupils aged under 5 at December/January of academic year. (3) Figures for 1966 and 1971 cover England and Wales at end-December 1966 and end-March 1972 respectively. From 1976 data are at end-March except for the Northern Ireland component, which is at end-December of the preceding year up to 1988. (4) The Scottish component included in the 1991 column relates to 1990. (5) No figures are available for registered nurseries in Scotland for 1988 and later. Estimates have been made for the purpose of obtaining a United Kingdom total. (6) Because of a different method of collection of data relating to registered child minders between 1978 and 1981, these figures are less reliable. (7) Includes child minders provided by local authorities.

Number of Schools[1] or Departments and Establishments of Higher and Further Education

Academic years[2]

Source: CSO

	1981/82	1982/83	1983/84	1984/85	1985/86	1986/87	1987/88	1988/89	1989/90	1990/91[12]
United Kingdom: Public sector schools										
Nursery	1,254	1,259	1,260	1,257	1,262	1,271	1,298	1,312	1,337	1,364
Primary	26,072	25,755	25,326	24,993	24,756	24,609	24,482	24,344[3]	24,268	24,135
Secondary	5,506	5,437	5,328	5,262	5,161	5,091	5,020	4,894	4,876	4,790
Non-maintained[3]	2,635	2,637	2,619	2,599	2,538	2,544	2,546	2,542[3]	2,492	2,508
Special	1,994	1,989	1,972	1,949	1,923	1,915	1,900	1,873	1,851	1,824
Universities (including Open University)	46	46	46	46	46	46	46	46	46	48
PCFC sector: Polytechnics[4]	31	31	31	30	30	30	30	30	30	32
Other[5]	–	–	–	–	–	–	–	–	56	53
Other HE/FE: Vocational colleges and C of Ed										
Public sector[6]	729	729	728	693	697	677	673	675	624	587
Assisted[7]	58	57	57	56	56	52	51	51	25	26
Adult education centres (England and Wales)	4,318	4,542	4,513	4,227	2,878[8]	2,523	2,632	2,782	2,669	2,656
England: Public sector schools										
Nursery	582	575	565	561	560	558	558	559	564	566
Primary	20,650	20,384	20,020	19,734	19,549	19,432	19,319	19,232	19,162	19,047
Secondary	4,622	4,553	4,444	4,382	4,286	4,221	4,153	4,035	3,976	3,897
Non-maintained	2,340	2,344	2,333	2,313	2,274	2,276	2,273	2,271	2,283	2,289
Special	1,571	1,562	1,548	1,529	1,493	1,470	1,443	1,414	1,398	1,380
Universities (including Open University)	35	35	35	35	35	35	35	35	35	37
PCFC sector: Polytechnics	29	29	29	29	29	29	29	29	29	31
Other[5]	–	–	–	–	–	–	–	–	56	53
Other HE/FE establishments										
Maintained and assisted	459	450	439	437	436	422	417	415	375	370
Grant-aided	34	33	33	32	31	29	29	30	6	6
Adult education centres	3,747	3,958	3,938	3,684	2,616[8]	2,718	2,412	2,494	2,399	2,315
Wales: Public sector schools										
Nursery	64	64	65	61	59	59	58	56	55	54
Primary	1,873	1,844	1,821	1,796	1,774	1,762	1,753	1,743	1,729	1,717
Secondary	241	238	236	237	237	234	233	232	231	230
Non-maintained	71	73	70	67	69	69	67	66	67	71
Special	73	71	69	68	67	65	65	64	62	61
Universities	1	1	1	1	1	1	1	1	1	1
Polytechnics	1	1	1	1	1	1	1	1	1	1
Other major establishments										
Maintained and assisted	43	43	43	43	39	39	39	40	36	36
Grant-aided	1	1	1	1	1	1	1	1	1	1
Adult education centres	571	584	575	543	258[8]	205	220	288	270	341
Scotland: Public sector schools										
Nursery	527	537	546	551	559	568	596	612	633	659
Primary	2,499	2,489	2,461	2,443	2,425	2,417	2,418	2,384	2,378	2,372
Secondary	439	442	444	440	440	440	438	434	429	424
Non-maintained[3]	136	132	127	131	106	111	118	118	123	131
Special[3]	324	330	330	328	339	356	346	349	345	337
Universities	8	8	8	8	8	8	8	8	8	8

(Continued)

	1981/82	1982/83	1983/84	1984/85	1985/86	1986/87	1987/88	1988/89	1989/90	1990/91[12]
Vocational further education colleges										
Education authority										
Day	64	67	64	52	50	49	49	49	46	46
Evening	105	111	124	104	115	109	111	114	110	110
Central institutions	14	14	14	14	16	16	15	15	13	13
Voluntary bodies	–	–	–	–	–	–	–	–	–	–
Colleges of education	7	7	7	7	7	5	5	5	5	5
Northern Ireland: Public sector schools										
Nursery	81	83	84	84	84	86	86	85	85	85
Primary	1,050	1,038	1,024	1,020	1,008	998	992	985[3]	999	999
Secondary[9]	204	204	204	203	198	196	196	193	240	239
Non-maintained[10]	88	88	89	88	89	87	88	87[3]	19	17
Special[11]	26	26	25	24	24	24	46[11]	46[11]	46[11]	46
Universities	2	2	2	2	2	2	2	2	2	2
Colleges of education	3	3	3	3	2	2	2	2	2	2
Polytechnics	1	1	1	–	–	–	–	–	–	–
Further education colleges	26	26	26	26	26	26	26	26	26	24

(1) Schools (excluding independent) in Scotland and Northern Ireland with more than one department have been counted once for each department. (2) Schools are counted at January except for Scotland and Wales when the count is at September. Further education establishments are counted at 1 November – England and Wales, October – Scotland and Northern Ireland. University establishments at 31 December. (3) Including for Scotland grant-aided nursery schools. (4) Includes the Polytechnic of Wales. (5) 56 institutions transferred from LEA maintained and grant-aided sector wef 89/90. (6) Maintained and assisted colleges in England and Wales, education authority colleges in Scotland, Stranmillis College of Education and education authority/education and library board colleges in Northern Ireland. (7) Direct grant colleges in England and Wales, central institutions, voluntary bodies and colleges of education in Scotland, voluntary colleges of education in Northern Ireland. (8) Excludes youth clubs and centres; these were included in years prior to 1985–86. (9) Wef 89/90 includes Voluntary Grammar Schools formerly within independent sector. (10) Excludes Voluntary Grammar Schools transferred to maintained sector wef 89/90. (11) Wef 1987/88 includes 22 schools which were the responsibility of Northern Ireland Department of Health and Social Security up to 31 March 1987. (12) Provisional.

Number of Pupils and Teachers: Pupil/Teacher Ratios

United Kingdom: at January[1]

Source: CSO

Thousands

	1980	1981	1982	1983	1984	1985	1986	1987	1988	1989	1990	1991[7]
All schools or departments[2]												
Total												
Pupils												
Full-time and full-time equivalent of part-time	10,770.9	10,525.3	10,234.7	9,949.7	9,724.7	9,544.3	9,384.5[5]	9,245.6[6]	9,100.7	9,022.7	9,009.9	9,062.3
Teachers[3]	590.2	579.1	568.1	559.6	554.1	546.0	540.3[5]	537.4[6]	531.1	528.0	528.1	526.8
Pupils per teacher:												
United Kingdom[3]	18.2	18.2	18.0	17.8	17.6	17.5	17.4[5]	17.2[6]	17.1	17.1	17.1	17.2
England	18.4	18.2	18.1	17.9	17.6	17.6	17.4	17.2	17.2	17.1	17.2	17.3
Wales	18.6	18.5	18.5	18.3	18.1	18.2	18.2	18.2	18.0	18.1	18.1	18.2
Scotland	16.8	16.7	16.7	16.6	16.4	16.2	–	–	15.8	15.7	15.3	15.2
Northern Ireland	19.0	18.9	18.9	18.7	18.7	18.6	18.5	18.4	18.4	18.3	18.3	18.1
Public sector schools or departments												
Nursery												
Pupils												
Full-time and full-time equivalent of part-time	54.9	55.5	55.8	56.3	57.2	57.3	56.9[5]	57.5[6]	57.6	58.4	59.4	60.4
Teachers[3]	2.5	2.6	2.6	2.6	2.6	2.6	2.6[5]	2.7[6]	2.7	2.7	2.7	2.8
Pupils per teacher	21.6	21.5	21.6	21.8	21.7	21.8	21.7[5]	21.2[6]	21.4	21.6	21.8	21.6
Primary												
Pupils												
Full-time and full-time equivalent of part-time	5,317.1	5,087.3	4,870.0	4,659.0	4,549.7	4,513.6	4,520.8	4,550.3	4,598.9	4,662.8	4,747.7	4,812.3
Teachers[3]	237.0	227.8	218.7	211.1	207.1	205.0	205.8	208.7	210.1	213.3	217.7	219.2
Pupils per teacher	22.4	22.3	22.3	22.1	22.0	22.0	22.0	21.8	21.9	21.9	21.8	22.0
Secondary												
Pupils												
Full-time and full-time equivalent of part-time	4,636.2	4,606.3	4,558.5	4,493.6	4,384.2	4,243.6	4,080.0	3,902.4	3,701.5	3,551.7	3,491.6	3,473.3
Teachers[3]	283.4	281.6	278.5	277.0	274.5	267.7	260.5	253.8	244.9	237.0	233.7	229.1
Pupils per teacher	16.4	16.4	16.4	16.2	16.0	15.9	15.7	15.4	15.1	15.0	14.9	15.2
Special schools[4]												
Pupils												
Full-time and full-time equivalent of part-time	149.3	147.2	145.0	142.7	137.7	133.1	130.0	124.9	120.9	117.6	114.6	112.5
Teachers[3]	19.8	19.8	19.7	19.7	19.7	19.7	19.6	19.5	19.3	19.2	19.4	19.4
Pupils per teacher	7.5	7.4	7.4	7.3	7.0	6.8	6.6	6.4	6.3	6.1	5.9	5.8

(1) In Scotland and in Wales the school census date is September whereas that for the rest of the United Kingdom remains at January. (2) From 1980 onwards includes non-maintained schools or departments, including independent schools in Scotland. (3) Figures of teachers and of pupil/teacher ratios take account of the full-time equivalent of part-time teachers. (4) Public sector only up to and including 1979. (5) Includes 1984–85 data for Scotland. (6) Includes 1987–88 data for Scotland. (7) Provisional.

School Pupils[1]

United Kingdom

Source: CSO

Thousands

	1961	1971	1981[2]	1991[2]
Public sector schools				
(full- and part-time)				
Nursery schools	31	50	89	105
Primary schools				
Under fives	} 4,906	{ 301	459	842
Other primary[3]		5,601	4,712	4,113
Secondary schools				
Under school leaving age	–	–	4,202	3,044
Over school leaving age	–	–	404	429
All secondary schools[4]	3,165	3,555	4,606	3,473
Total public sector	8,102	9,507	9,866	8,533
Independent schools	680	621	619	613
Special schools[5]				
(full-time equivalent)	77	103	147	114
All schools	8,859	10,230	10,632	9,260

(1) Part-time pupils are counted as one (except for special schools). (2) Figures for Scottish components are at previous September. (3) In Scotland 11-year-olds are customarily in primary schools. (4) Excluding public sector special schools. (5) Includes public and non-maintained sector.

Class Sizes as Taught[1]

England

Source: CSO

	1977	1981	1986	1991
Primary schools				
Percentage of classes taught by:				
One teacher in classes with				
1–20 pupils	*16*	*20*	*17*	*12*
21–30 pupils	*46*	*55*	*58*	*62*
31 or more pupils	*34*	*22*	*19*	*19*
Two or more teachers	*4*	*3*	*6*	*7*
Average size of class (numbers)	28	26	26	27
Number of classes (thousands)	171	161	142	147
Secondary schools				
Percentage of classes taught by:				
One teacher in classes with				
1–20 pupils	*42*	*44*	*46*	*44*
21–30 pupils	*42*	*45*	*45*	*47*
31 or more pupils	*12*	*8*	*6*	*4*
Two or more teachers	*4*	*2*	*3*	*5*
Average size of class (numbers)	22	22	21	21
Number of classes (thousands)	165	174	155	130

(1) Class size related to one selected period in each public sector school on the day of the count in January. Middle schools are either primary or secondary for this table.

Pupils with Special Needs in Public Sector and Assisted Schools

United Kingdom: at January[1]

Source: CSO

(i) Numbers of public sector and assisted special schools, full-time pupils and teachers

[12]	1980	1981	1982	1983	1984	1985	1986	1987	1988	1989	1990	1991[12]
Hospital schools[2]												
Schools:												
Public sector	145	141	132	125	117	111	98	88	79	68	60	48
Assisted	4	4	3	3	3	2	2	1	1	1	–	–
Total	149	145	135	128	120	113	100	89	80	69	60	48
Full-time pupils (thousands)	7.8	7.3	6.7	6.2	5.3	4.8	4.6	3.2	3.0	2.8	1.6	0.9
Teachers (thousands)[3]												
Full-time teachers	1.2	1.2	1.1	1.0	0.9	0.8	0.7	0.6	0.6	0.5	0.4	0.4
Other special schools or departments[4]												
Schools:												
Public sector	1,760	1,763	1,759	1,763	1,757	1,742	1,726	1,739	1,736	1,723	1,712	1,695
Assisted	115	112	109	107	104	103	95	96	92	89	89	87
Day	1,412	1,412	1,412	1,393	1,488	1,469	1,464	1,174[5]	1,500	1,499	1,540	1,522
Boarding	463	463	456	477	373	376	357	281[5]	328	313	261	260
Total	1,875	1,875	1,868	1,870	1,861	1,845	1,821	1,835	1,828	1,812	1,801	1,782
Full-time pupils (thousands):												
Blind and partially sighted	3.7	3.5	3.3	3.2	[6]	[6]	[6]	[6]	[6]	[6]	[6]	–
Deaf and partially hearing	5.6	5.3	5.0	4.7	[6]	[6]	[6]	[6]	[6]	[6]	[6]	–
Delicate and physically handicapped	18.0	17.3	16.8	16.2	[6]	[6]	[6]	[6]	[6]	[6]	[6]	–
Maladjusted	15.0	14.7	14.5	14.8	[6]	[6]	[6]	[6]	[6]	[6]	[6]	–
Educationally sub-normal and mentally handicapped[5]	92.1	92.8	92.9	92.2	[6]	[6]	[6]	[6]	[6]	[6]	[6]	–
Epileptic	1.9	1.8	1.6	1.6	[6]	[6]	[6]	[6]	[6]	[6]	[6]	–
Speech defect	3.5	3.1	2.5	2.3	[6]	[6]	[6]	[6]	[6]	[6]	[6]	–
Autistic[6]	0.6	0.7	0.6	0.6	[6]	[6]	[6]	[6]	[6]	[6]	[6]	–
Total	140.7	139.2	137.3	135.5	132.1	128.8	126.0	120.4	117.7	114.1	112.1	110.8
Teachers (thousands)												
Full-time teachers	17.6	17.7	17.7	17.8	17.9	17.8	17.7	17.7[7]	[8]	[8]	[8]	–
Full-time equivalent of part-time teachers	0.7	0.7	0.7	0.7	0.7	0.8	0.8	0.8[7]	18.7	18.7	19.0	19.1

(1) In Wales the school census date is September whereas that for the rest of the United Kingdom remains at January. (2) England, Wales and Northern Ireland only. (3) Excluding part-time teachers in hospital schools, full-time equivalent in 1988 was 36. (4) In the 1986 column, data for Scotland relate to 1984/85. (5) Information on individual handicaps ceased to be collected in 1984. (6) England and Wales only. (7) Including 1984–85 data for Scotland. (8) Data on full-time teachers no longer collected separately.

(ii) Pupils with statements of special needs in other public sector schools

	1986	1987	1988	1989	1990	1991[12]
Public sector primary schools[9]	22.8[11]	24.0	28.5	31.8	35.0	40.3
Public sector secondary schools[10]	15.4[11]	17.4	21.8	25.7	29.4	34.8
Total	38.2	41.3	50.2	57.4	64.4	75.2

(9) Including middle schools deemed primary. (10) Including middle schools deemed secondary. (11) Including estimated primary/secondary split for Wales. (12) Provisional.

Secondary Schools' Performance: England 1992

LEA AREA (sorted by A-level results)	GCSE results: % of pupils in age group obtaining the following grades: 5 or more A–C	5 or more A–F	1 or more A–C	1 or more A–G	A/AS results: % entered for at least 1A/AS level	Average A/AS level points per pupil
Trafford	36.6	81.3	65.2	92.5	95.8	18.4
Dudley	35.1	85.9	64.6	96.0	95.1	17.7
Sutton	45.6	86.3	72.4	94.3	93.2	17.2
North Yorkshire	42.6	87.2	67.9	95.0	89.3	16.7
Buckinghamshire	42.1	81.7	66.5	88.2	85.2	16.6
Bury	40.5	87.1	68.4	93.7	89.3	16.2
Lancashire	36.5	80.1	62.8	91.3	87.4	16.2
Sefton	36.7	80.8	65.8	92.1	85.7	15.9
Sheffield	29.2	78.3	56.4	88.1	95.3	15.9
Cheshire	40.1	83.5	66.8	91.3	88.5	15.8
Barnsley	24.1	74.1	49.7	90.1	90.3	15.7
Lincolnshire	36.6	83.3	66.1	94.0	94.7	15.7
Barnet	42.6	82.9	72.6	90.0	84.4	15.5
Derbyshire	36.1	86.4	63.9	94.3	92.1	15.5
Shropshire	40.2	89.9	66.9	96.5	88.5	15.5
Cumbria	37.5	83.7	64.0	93.0	91.9	15.4
Bolton	35.3	79.1	61.8	90.4	84.8	15.3
Warwickshire	37.0	86.9	67.1	95.1	92.2	15.2
Kirklees	31.5	79.0	59.0	91.0	85.6	15.1
Dorset	40.9	89.1	69.6	96.2	90.2	15.0
Stockport	40.2	84.6	67.6	93.0	77.7	14.7
Berkshire	40.1	85.2	68.2	91.5	89.0	14.7
Cleveland	29.8	77.6	56.6	89.0	81.9	14.7
Staffordshire	33.2	82.6	61.8	92.6	88.3	14.7
Tameside	29.9	82.5	59.9	91.7	80.9	14.6
Leeds	30.0	73.0	55.0	85.9	86.5	14.6
Wiltshire	40.0	86.6	68.6	95.8	92.1	14.6
Birmingham	25.1	73.0	55.8	86.6	73.5	14.5
Harrow	49.7	92.3	79.0	97.6	100.0	14.4
Wigan	39.3	84.3	66.5	94.0	89.1	14.4
Calderdale	32.6	76.5	59.9	90.0	90.0	14.4
Hereford and Worcester	37.8	84.7	65.2	93.4	88.9	14.4
Sunderland	28.2	77.2	57.5	92.1	75.5	14.2
St Helens	30.5	76.3	59.3	89.7	85.9	14.1
Wirral	36.4	80.9	60.3	92.0	85.9	14.1
Kent	36.9	82.8	64.7	92.1	88.4	14.1
Essex	36.7	85.7	67.1	93.5	87.1	14.0
Kingston upon Thames	46.3	88.1	75.2	93.5	83.9	13.9
Manchester	18.6	59.9	45.7	77.0	70.4	13.9
Newcastle upon Tyne	26.8	72.7	51.7	86.0	97.4	13.9
Cambridgeshire	39.5	86.6	68.0	93.6	91.4	13.9
Gloucestershire	40.0	81.3	67.6	88.7	84.3	13.9
Solihull	41.7	86.8	71.1	96.6	82.6	13.8
Rotherham	29.7	79.1	56.3	93.0	84.1	13.8
Bedfordshire	34.9	87.5	67.2	94.6	91.2	13.8
West Sussex	46.1	90.1	75.4	94.9	88.1	13.8
Somerset	40.7	83.7	69.9	95.3	92.0	13.6
Wakefield	27.8	76.5	56.4	91.1	84.3	13.5
Hertfordshire	43.6	87.8	72.7	93.5	93.3	13.5
Walsall	31.4	78.1	59.3	90.1	89.9	13.4
Hampshire	39.3	85.6	69.3	93.5	78.6	13.4
Humberside	30.8	81.6	56.9	91.5	84.3	13.4
Leicestershire	33.2	83.1	63.2	92.5	80.6	13.4
Oxfordshire	41.2	85.8	69.4	93.4	91.0	13.4
Oldham	27.1	74.1	56.3	86.9	89.7	13.3
Nottinghamshire	29.8	81.2	58.2	91.9	91.1	13.3
Surrey	43.9	88.3	72.7	93.9	83.1	13.3
Rochdale	26.0	71.3	54.4	84.2	88.8	13.1
Devon	37.8	86.5	68.4	94.5	90.0	13.1
Durham	31.8	79.9	60.8	92.6	88.9	13.1
Doncaster	27.6	75.1	53.1	88.9	82.6	12.9
Bradford	22.7	72.1	51.3	87.8	69.8	12.9
Camden	34.6	72.5	68.0	86.5	81.4	12.6
Salford	25.2	74.6	54.3	88.8	72.2	12.6
Croydon	38.0	83.3	69.5	93.2	72.8	12.5
Isle of Wight	34.9	87.7	65.2	97.0	84.5	12.5
Bromley	44.2	86.5	73.4	91.8	89.1	12.4
Wolverhampton	24.7	76.4	55.7	89.8	88.3	12.3
East Sussex	39.7	85.0	70.4	93.2	82.9	12.3
Enfield	32.4	82.4	66.4	91.8	85.7	12.2
Havering	38.4	87.0	70.1	94.3	93.2	12.2
Avon	36.1	84.7	66.3	93.0	89.3	12.2
Northants	36.2	85.5	65.8	94.7	90.6	12.2
Liverpool	21.4	66.3	48.3	83.3	79.5	12.1
Cornwall	38.1	87.0	70.5	95.3	87.5	12.1
Redbridge	37.3	83.7	71.5	92.3	83.7	12.0
Suffolk	39.0	90.0	67.5	96.1	92.1	12.0
Norfolk	34.9	82.5	66.1	92.3	88.2	11.9
Northumberland	37.9	86.3	65.7	93.9	88.3	11.9
South Tyneside	29.9	82.2	59.6	92.7	79.2	11.8
Hammersmith and Fulham	26.6	67.6	56.1	82.2	88.1	11.7
Bexley	34.3	84.1	64.4	93.7	91.3	11.6
North Tyneside	34.6	84.4	60.9	90.9	85.5	11.4
Hillingdon	32.5	77.7	61.4	84.9	80.7	11.3
Merton	33.2	81.6	63.1	90.0	70.2	11.3
Ealing	26.8	75.3	61.0	87.5	69.5	10.9
Gateshead	28.5	77.2	56.9	90.6	90.4	10.9
Sandwell	21.9	75.5	50.5	90.1	65.5	10.4
Kensington and Chelsea	28.1	69.2	62.0	86.5	60.0	10.3
Islington	19.5	55.9	52.4	76.3	68.8	10.2
Coventry	32.8	81.3	63.2	91.8	88.2	10.2
Hounslow	34.9	81.0	66.9	90.3	74.7	9.9
Hackney	19.3	63.4	53.0	81.5	53.2	9.6
Wandsworth	26.2	72.3	58.0	87.9	73.9	9.6
Waltham Forest	25.8	79.2	61.6	91.4	54.7	9.6
Westminster/Corp of London	23.9	68.6	60.2	87.0	73.3	9.0
Brent	28.8	77.2	60.8	89.7	51.9	9.0
Haringey	24.0	67.1	58.4	81.3	75.1	9.0
Greenwich	23.4	71.1	55.5	84.3	87.7	8.4
Lewisham	25.2	70.7	56.3	86.5	81.1	8.4
Newham	20.7	67.8	53.9	82.9	69.4	8.1
Knowsley	16.3	59.6	44.8	80.5	62.7	7.9
Barking and Dagenham	15.5	76.0	45.8	86.8	88.5	7.3
Southwark	15.1	62.4	45.4	80.3	56.9	7.2
Tower Hamlets	16.0	59.9	53.8	79.5	56.9	5.6
Lambeth	18.2	59.5	48.0	75.9	26.2	4.2
Richmond upon Thames	42.5	85.9	71.1	91.9	0.0	0.0
Isles of Scilly	57.1	100.0	92.9	100.0	0.0	0.0
England	**38.1**	**82.0**	**65.5**	**91.3**	**86.1**	**15.0**

Qualifications of School-leavers

United Kingdom

Source: CSO

Thousands

	1978/79	1979/80	1980/81[1]	1981/82	1982/83[1]	1983/84	1984/85[1]	1985/86	1986/87	1987/88	1988/89	1989/90
Boys and girls												
Leavers with GCSE/GCE 'A' level/ SCE 'H' grade passes												
2 or more 'A', 3 or more 'H'	117	121	122	133	131	136	127	127	129	131	137	146
1 'A', 1 or 2 'H'	31	33	32	36	37	37	34	34	34	33	31	33
Leavers with GCSE/GCE 'O' level/ CSE/SCE 'O' grades alone												
5 or more A–C awards/CSE grade 1[2]	83	85	81	90	91	95	93	95	92	97	100	93
1–4 A–C awards/CSE grade 1[2]	241	242	228	240	244	243	232	231	233	210	206	190

(Continued)

Thousands

	1978/79	1979/80	1980/81[1]	1981/82	1982/83[1]	1983/84	1984/85[1]	1985/86	1986/87	1987/88	1988/89	1989/90
No higher grades												
1 or more other grades			284	293	293	295	283	283	284	241	212	184
No GCSE/GCE/SCE or CSE qualifications	427	434	119	121	105	108	98	101	95	86	67	60
Total school leavers	900	915	865	913	902	914	866	871	867	797	753	706
Boys												
Leavers with GCSE/GCE 'A' level/ SCE 'H' grade passes												
2 or more 'A', 3 or more 'H'	64	64	65	69	68	70	67	66	66	67	69	72
1 'A', 1 or 2 'H'	15	16	15	17	17	17	15	16	16	16	14	16
Leavers with GCSE/GCE 'O' level/ CSE/SCE 'O' grades alone												
5 or more A–C awards/CSE grade 1[2]	38	39	37	41	42	44	43	44	42	42	45	41
1–4 A–C awards/CSE grade 1[2]	116	115	109	115	116	114	108	108	109	100	100	93
No higher grades												
1 or more other grades			149	154	155	155	151	151	152	132	118	105
No GCSE/GCE/SCE or CSE qualifications	228	234	68	69	62	64	57	59	56	51	40	36
Total school leavers	461	469	442	466	460	464	441	444	442	409	387	362
Girls												
Leavers with GCSE/GCE 'A' level/ SCE 'H' grade passes												
2 or more 'A', 3 or more 'H'	54	58	57	64	63	65	60	61	62	64	68	74
1 'A', 1 or 2 'H'	17	17	17	19	20	20	19	18	18	17	17	17
Leavers with GCSE/GCE 'O' level/ CSE/SCE 'O' grades alone												
5 ore more A–C awards/CSE grade 1[2]	45	45	44	49	49	50	50	51	50	55	55	52
1–4 A–C awards/SCE grade 1[2]	125	127	120	125	128	129	124	123	124	110	106	97
No higher grades												
1 or more other grades			135	139	138	140	131	132	132	108	94	79
No GCSE/GCE/SCE or CSE qualifications	199	200	51	51	44	45	42	43	39	35	27	24
Total school leavers	439	446	423	447	442	450	425	427	425	388	366	344
The number of pupils who left school in Great Britain with no GCSE/GCE/ SCE or CSE qualifications were as follows:	135	132	119	113	105	102	98	95	90	81	62	57

(1) Great Britain only. (2) 'O' grades in Scotland and 'O' levels in England, Wales and Northern Ireland have been awarded in bands A to E; awards in bands A to C can be regarded as equivalent to what were previously rated as passes.

Numbers and Percentages Continuing Education Aged 16 and Over

United Kingdom: 1990–91[3]

Source: CSO

Home students

	All students	Age at 31 August 1990: 16	17	18	16–18	19–20	21–24	25 and over
Number in thousands								
Total population	–	726	771	822	2,319	1,752	3,670	–
Full-time and sandwich students								
Schools	523	295	197	28	519	4	–	–
Further education	472	154	129	71	354	38	24	56
Higher education	666	1	9	102	112	265	182	107
Universities	312	–	5	53	57	134	83	37
Undergraduates	273	–	5	53	57	134	62	20
Postgraduates	39	–	–	–	–	–	22	16
Polytechnics and other HE establishments	355	–	4	50	54	131	99	70
Undergraduates	338	–	4	50	54	131	91	62
Postgraduates	16	–	–	–	–	1	7	8
Total full-time and sandwich students	1,660	449	334	202	985	307	206	163
Part-time students								
Further education	2,988	140	139	119	397	123	265	1,934
Day students	1,294	98	104	77	278	71	168	746
Adult education centres[1]	506	7	2	3	13	29	102	362
Other	788	90	102	74	265	71	65	384
Evening only students	1,694	42	35	42	119	52	97	1,188
Adult education centres[1]	928	24	12	14	51	52	182	644
Other	766	18	23	28	68	52	97	545
Higher education[2]	365	–	1	9	11	36	69	248
Universities	51	–	–	–	–	1	6	45
Undergraduates	11	–	–	–	–	1	2	8
Postgraduates	41	–	–	–	–	–	4	37
Polytechnics and other HE establishments	264	–	1	9	11	35	61	156
Undergraduates	233	–	1	9	11	35	58	128
Postgraduates	31	–	–	–	–	–	3	28
Open University	49	–	–	–	–	–	2	47
Total part-time students	3,353	140	140	128	408	159	333	2,182
All full-time and part-time students	5,013	589	474	330	1,393	466	539	2,345

(Continued)

Home students

	All students	Age at 31 August 1990: 16	17	18	16–18	19–20	21–24	25 and over
As percentage of population								
Full-time and sandwich students								
Schools	–	40.6	25.5	3.4	22.4	0.2	–	–
Further education	–	21.2	16.7	8.7	15.3	2.1	0.7	–
Higher education	–	0.1	1.1	12.5	4.8	15.1	5.0	
Universities	–	–	0.6	6.4	2.5	7.7	2.3	–
Undergraduates	–	–	0.6	6.4	2.5	7.6	1.7	–
Postgraduates	–	–	–	–	–	–	0.6	–
Polytechnics and other HE establishments	–	0.1	0.5	6.1	2.3	7.5	2.7	–
Undergraduates	–	0.1	0.5	6.0	2.3	7.5	2.5	–
Postgraduates	–	–	–	–	–	–	0.2	–
Total full-time and sandwich students	–	61.9	43.3	24.5	42.5	17.5	5.6	–
Part-time students								
Further education	–	19.3	18.0	14.4	17.1	7.0	7.2	–
Day students	–	13.5	13.5	9.3	12.0	4.0	4.6	–
Adult education centres[1]	–	1.0	0.3	0.4	0.6	1.7	2.8	–
Other	–	12.4	13.2	9.0	11.4	4.0	1.8	–
Evening only students	–	5.8	4.6	5.1	5.1	3.0	2.6	–
Adult education centres	–	3.3	1.6	1.7	2.2	2.9	5.0	–
Other	–	2.5	3.0	3.3	2.9	3.0	2.6	–
Higher education[2]	–	–	0.2	1.2	0.5	2.1	1.9	–
Universities	–	–	–	–	–	–	0.2	–
Undergraduates	–	–	–	–	–	–	–	–
Postgraduates	–	–	–	–	–	–	0.1	–
Polytechnics and other HE establishments	–	–	0.2	1.1	0.5	2.0	1.7	–
Undergraduates	–	–	0.2	1.1	0.5	2.0	1.6	–
Postgraduates	–	–	–	–	–	–	0.1	–
Open University	–	–	–	–	–	–	0.1	–
Total part-time students	–	19.3	18.2	15.6	17.6	9.1	9.1	–
All full-time and part-time students	–	81.2	61.5	40.1	60.1	26.6	14.7	–

(1) Including estimated age detail for 1,434,500 students aged 16 years in adult education centres; excluding youth clubs and centres, 77,000 in 1984–85 (England). Excluding 618,900 students in 1989/90 on courses run by responsible bodies for whom age detail was not available. (2) Excluding 81,700 students (1990–91) enrolled on nursing and paramedical courses at Department of Health establishments. (3) Provisional.

Universities[1]: Full-time Students and Areas of Study

United Kingdom: Academic years

Source: CSO

Thousands

	1984/85[2]	1985/86[3]	1986/87	1987/88	1988/89	1989/90	1990/91
Medicine and dentistry:							
Men		15.2	14.9	14.8	14.7	14.5	14.2
Women	26.8	11.5	11.5	11.5	11.8	12.0	12.2
Subjects allied to medicine:							
Men		3.0	3.1	3.1	3.3	3.5	3.8
Women	8.1	5.7	5.8	5.9	6.1	6.7	7.6
Biological sciences:							
Men		10.1	10.4	10.5	10.8	11.2	11.8
Women	20.3	10.5	10.9	11.3	11.9	13.2	14.4
Agriculture and related subjects:							
Men		3.6	3.7	3.7	3.7	3.6	3.6
Women	6.2	2.6	2.7	2.6	2.7	2.7	2.8
Physical sciences:							
Men		20.9	20.9	20.5	20.6	21.5	22.2
Women	27.1	6.3	6.4	6.7	6.9	7.6	8.4
Mathematical sciences:							
Men		13.8	14.0	14.7	15.7	16.8	17.9
Women	18.1	4.7	4.6	4.6	5.0	5.5	6.1
Engineering and technology:							
Men		36.7	37.3	37.4	37.1	37.9	39.2
Women	39.4	3.6	4.0	4.3	4.7	5.1	5.8
Architecture, building and planning:							
Men		4.0	3.9	4.0	4.0	4.1	4.5
Women	5.0	1.3	1.4	1.5	1.6	1.8	1.8
Social studies:							
Men		24.1	24.6	24.7	25.7	26.4	28.0
Women	42.9	19.6	20.6	21.3	22.7	23.4	25.2
Business and administrative studies:							
Men		9.2	9.5	10.1	10.7	11.6	12.1
Women	13.3	5.3	5.9	6.5	7.0	7.7	7.9
Mass communications and documentation:							
Men		0.4	0.4	0.4	0.5	0.6	0.7
Women	0.9	0.7	0.7	0.6	0.8	0.9	1.0
Languages and related disciplines:							
Men		10.0	9.9	9.8	10.2	10.6	11.4
Women	30.9	21.2	21.2	21.5	22.4	23.7	25.2
Humanities:							
Men		9.4	9.8	9.9	10.1	10.7	11.5
Women	17.8	7.9	8.0	8.2	8.5	9.2	10.1
Creative arts:							
Men		1.9	1.9	2.0	2.3	2.3	2.3
Women	4.1	2.5	2.8	2.9	3.4	3.6	3.5

(Continued)

Thousands

	1984/85[2]	1985/86[3]	1986/87	1987/88	1988/89	1989/90	1990/91
Education:							
Men	11.0	4.7	5.0	4.4	4.4	4.4	4.4
Women		6.4	6.6	6.6	7.3	8.2	8.9
Multidisciplinary:							
Men	33.3	17.8	18.2	18.4	19.2	20.0	20.8
Women		15.5	15.7	16.6	17.9	19.9	21.1

(1) Excludes the Open University. (2) Includes Ulster Polytechnic which merged with the University of Ulster in October 1984. (3) A new subject classification was introduced in 1985 when certain subjects were reclassified and combinations of subjects were classified separately for the first time.

Degrees and Diplomas Obtained by Full-time Students[1]

Calendar years

Source: CSO

Number

	1980	1981	1982	1983	1984	1985	1986	1987	1988	1989	1990
Degrees											
First degrees – honours: Men	35,127	36,018	36,696	37,103	36,940	36,119	35,823	35,845	36,735	37,473	38,324
Women	21,344	22,563	24,723	25,636	25,577	26,122	25,988	26,601	27,799	28,578	30,121
First degrees – ordinary[3]: Men	7,704	7,743	7,387	7,520	7,031	6,057	5,405	5,518	5,520	5,301	4,973
Women	3,975	4,218	4,272	4,659	4,293	3,911	3,696	3,853	3,702	3,601	3,745
Higher degrees: Men	14,414	14,746	14,864	15,565	15,593	16,802	17,354	18,559	19,176	20,424	20,905
Women	4,511	4,803	5,209	5,671	5,936	6,754	7,219	8,008	8,676	9,794	10,419
Total: Men	57,245	58,507	58,947	60,188	59,564	58,978	58,582	60,059	61,431	63,198	64,202
Women	29,830	31,584	33,754	35,966	35,806	36,787	36,903	38,475	40,177	41,973	44,285
Diplomas and certificates: Men	7,044	7,260	7,572	6,853	6,613	6,447	5,867	6,800	6,659	6,621	6,712
Women	5,754	6,015	6,208	5,547	5,587	5,751	5,706	6,303	6,611	6,599	7,000

(1) Excluding the Open University. (2) Includes Ulster Polytechnic, which merged with the University of Ulster in October 1984. (3) Includes some degrees where the class is not recorded.

Student Grants and Loans – Real Value and Parental Contributions

England & Wales

Source: CSO

	Standard maintenance grant[1] (£)	Index of the real value of the grant deflated by: Retail prices index	Index of the real value of the grant deflated by: Average earnings index	Average assessed contribution by parents[2] (percentages)	Student loans[3] (£) (maximum)
1980/81	1,430	2,811	3,481	*13*	–
1981/82	1,535	2,708	3,362	*14*	–
1982/83	1,595	2,623	3,211	*19*	–
1983/84	1,660	2,597	3,146	*20*	–
1984/85	1,775	2,652	3,130	*25*	–
1985/86	1,830	2,581	2,979	*30*	–
1986/87	1,901	2,603	2,886	*30*	–
1987/88	1,972	2,592	2,751	*31*	–
1988/89	2,050	2,545	2,614	*31*	–
1989/90	2,155	2,488	2,520	*31*	–
1990/91	2,265	2,358	2,438	–	420
1991/92	2,265	2,265	2,265	–	580

(1) Excludes those studying in London and those studying elsewhere living in the parental home. Prior to 1982/83 Oxford and Cambridge were also excluded. Since 1984/85 the grant has included an additional travel allowance of £50. (2) Assuming full payment of parental and other contributions, including a notional assessment in respect of students for whom fees only were paid by LEAs. (3) At current prices. The amounts quoted are for students studying outside London and living away from home. Different amounts are payable in the final year.

The Largest Universities[1] in the World

Source: Russell Ash, *The Top Ten of Everything*

	University	Students
1	State University of New York, USA	369,318
2	University of Mexico, Mexico	327,000
3	University of Buenos Aires, Argentina	248,453
4	University of Paris, France	244,096
5	University of Calcutta, India	235,162
6	University of Guadalajara, Mexico	217,022
7	University of Rajasthan, India	192,039
8	University of Rome, Italy	180,000
9	University of Bombay, India	162,000
10	University of California, USA	145,727

(1) Certain universities listed, such as the State University of New York and the University of Paris, are divided into numerous separate centres and figures are for the totals of all centres.

The Oldest Universities in Great Britain

Source: Russell Ash, *The Top Ten of Everything*

	University	Founded
1	Oxford	1249
2	Cambridge	1284
3	St Andrews	1411
4	Glasgow	1451
5	Aberdeen	1495
6	Edinburgh	1583
7	Durham	1832
8	London	1836
9	Manchester	1851
10	Newcastle	1852

The Largest Universities in the UK*

Source: Russell Ash, *The Top Ten of Everything*

	University	Full-time students†
1	London	51,392
2	Manchester	20,098
3	Leeds	14,453
4	Oxford	14,288
5	Cambridge	13,290
6	Glasgow	13,638
7	Edinburgh	12,607
8	Birmingham	12,304
9	Ulster	10,972
10	Liverpool	9,565

*Excluding Open University. †Undergraduates and postgraduates.

The Largest Libraries in the World

Source: Russell Ash, *The Top Ten of Everything*

Library	Location	Founded	Books
Library of Congress	Washington, DC, USA	1800	26,000,000
British Library	London, UK	1753[1]	18,000,000
Harvard University Library	Cambridge, MA, USA	1638	11,874,148
State V.I. Lenin Library of the USSR	Moscow, Russia	1862	11,750,000
New York Public Library	New York, NY, USA	1848	9,834,933[1]
Biblioteca Academiei Republicii Socialiste Romania	Bucharest, Romania	1867	9,255,556
Bibliothèque Nationale	Paris, France	1480	9,000,000
Yale University Library	New Haven, CT, USA	1701	8,862,768
State M.E. Saltykov-Shchedrin State Public Library	St Petersburg, Russia	1795	8,000,000
University of Illinois	Urbana, IL, USA	1867	7,748,736

(1) Founded as part of the British Museum, 1753; became an independent body, 1973. (2) Reference holdings only; a further 15,000,000 books are held in the various NYPL lending library branches.

The 10 Largest Libraries in the UK

Source: Russell Ash, *The Top Ten of Everything*

	Library	Location	Founded	Books
1	British Library	London	1753	18,000,000
2=	Bodleian Library	Oxford	1602	6,000,000
2=	National Library of Scotland	Edinburgh	1682	6,000,000
4	National Library of Wales	Aberystwyth	1907	5,000,000
5	University of Cambridge	Cambridge	c1400	4,850,000
6	Lancashire County Library	Preston	1924	3,697,640
7=	Hampshire County Library	Winchester	1925	3,500,000
7=	John Rylands University Library of Manchester*	Manchester	1851	3,500,000
9	Kent County Library	Maidstone	1921	3,300,000
10	Birmingham Public Library	Birmingham	1861	2,600,000

*In 1972 the John Rylands Library (founded 1900) was amalgamated with Manchester University Library (1851).

In addition to the books held by these libraries, many have substantial holdings of manuscripts, periodicals and other printed material: the Bodleian Library, for example, has almost 1,000,000 maps.

British and Irish Universities

The following list includes all the British polytechnics that won university status in 1992, The undergraduate colleges that constitute the universities of Oxford, Cambridge and London appear alphabetically in italics under the main university entry. Colleges within the University of Wales are listed as main (bold) entries.

Aberdeen University
Regent Walk, Aberdeen AB9 1FX
Tel: 0224 272000

Aberystwyth University
PO Box 2, Aberystwyth, Dyfed SY23 2AX
Tel: 0970 622021

Anglia Poly University
(previously Anglia Poly)
Victoria Road South, Chelmsford, Essex CM1 1LL
Tel: 0245 493131

Aston University
Aston Triangle, Birmingham B4 7ET
Tel: 021-359 3611

Bangor University
Bangor, Gwynedd LL57 2DG
Tel: 0248 351151

Bath University
Claverton Down, Bath BA2 7AY
Tel: 0225 826826

Belfast University
University Road, Belfast BT7 1NN
Tel: 0232 245133

Birmingham University
Edgbaston, Birmingham B15 2TT
Tel: 021-414 3344

Bournemouth University
(formerly Bournemouth Poly)
Talbot Campus, Fern Barrow, Poole, Dorset BH12 5BB
Tel: 0202 524111

Bradford University
Bradford, West Yorkshire BD7 1DP
Tel: 0274 733466

Brighton University
(formerly Brighton Poly)
Lewes Road, Brighton, East Sussex BN2 4AT
Tel: 0273 600900

Bristol University
Senate House, Tyndall Ave, Bristol BS8 1TH
Tel: 0272 303030

Brunel University
Uxbridge, Middx UB8 3PH
Tel: 0895 274000

Buckingham University
Hunter Street, Buckingham MK18 1EG
Tel: 0280 814080

Buckland University College
Ewert Place, Oxford OX2 7YT
Tel: 0865 53570

Cambridge University
(consisting of 28 undergraduate colleges)
Cambridge CB2 1TN
Tel: 0223 332200 (registry)

Christ's College (m/f)
Cambridge CB2 3BU
Tel: 0223 334953

Churchill College (m/f)
Cambridge CB3 0DS
Tel: 0223 336202

Clare College (m/f)
Cambridge CB2 1TL
Tel: 0223 333246

Corpus Christi College (m/f)
Cambridge CB2 1RH
Tel: 0223 338056

Downing College (m/f)
Cambridge CB2 1DQ
Tel: 0223 334800

Emmanuel College (m/f)
Cambridge CB2 3AP
Tel: 0223 334200

Fitzwilliam College (m/f)
Cambridge CB3 0DG
Tel: 0223 332000

Girton College (m/f)
Cambridge CB3 0JG
Tel: 0223 338999

Gonville & Caius College (m/f)
Cambridge CB2 1TA
Tel: 0223 332447

Jesus College (m/f)
Cambridge CB5 8BL
Tel: 0223 357626

King's College (m/f)
Cambridge CB2 1ST
Tel: 0223 350411

Lucy Cavendish College (f/mature)
Lady Margaret Road, Cambridge CB3 0BU
Tel: 0223 332190

Magdalene College (m/f)
Cambridge CB3 0AG
Tel: 0223 332100

New Hall (f)
Huntingdon Road, Cambridge CB3 0DF
Tel: 0223 351721

Newnham College (f)
Cambridge CB3 9DF
Tel: 0223 335700

Pembroke College (m/f)
Cambridge CB2 1RF
Tel: 0223 338100

Peterhouse (m/f)
Cambridge CB2 1RD
Tel: 0223 338200

Queens' College (m/f)
Cambridge CB3 9ET
Tel: 0223 335522

Robinson College (m/f)
Cambridge CB3 9AN
Tel: 0223 311431

St Catharine's College (m/f)
Cambridge CB2 1RL
Tel: 0223 338300

St Edmund's College (m/f)
Cambridge CB3 0BN
Tel: 0223 350398

St John's College (m/f)
Cambridge CB2 1TP
Tel: 0223 338600

Selwyn College (m/f)
Cambridge CB3 9QD
Tel: 0223 335846

Sidney Sussex College (m/f)
Cambridge CB2 3HU
Tel: 0223 338800

Trinity College (m/f)
Cambridge CB2 1TQ
Tel: 0223 338400

Trinity Hall (m/f)
Cambridge CB2 1TJ
Tel: 0223 332537

Wolfson College (m/f)
Cambridge CB3 9BB
Tel: 0223 335900

Cardiff University
PO Box 68, Cardiff CF1 3XA
Tel: 0222 874000

Central England University
(formerly Birmingham Poly)
Perry Barr, Birmingham B42 2SU
Tel: 021-331 5000

(Continued)

Central Lancashire University
(formerly Lancashire Poly & Preston Poly)
Preston PR1 2TQ
Tel: 0772 201201

City University
Northampton Square, London EC1V 0HB
Tel: 071-477 8022

Coventry University
(formerly Coventry Poly)
Priory Street, Coventry CV1 5FB
Tel: 0203 631313

De Montfort University
(formerly Leicester Poly)
The Gateway, Leicester LE1 9BH
Tel: 0533 551551

Derby University
(formerly Derbyshire College)
Kedleston Road, Derby DE3 1GB
Tel: 0332 47181

Dublin City University
Dublin 9
Tel: 7045000

Dundee University
Dundee DD1 4HN
Tel: 0382 23181

Durham University
Old Shire Hall, Durham DH1 3HP
Tel: 091-374 2000

East Anglia University
Norwich, Norfolk NR4 7TJ
Tel: 0603 56161

East London University
(formerly East London Poly)
Longbridge Road, Dagenham, Essex RM8 2AS
Tel: 081-590 7722

Edinburgh University
Old College, South Bridge, Edinburgh EH8 9YL
Tel: 031-650 4360

Essex University
Wivenhoe Park, Colchester CO4 3SQ
Tel: 0206 873333

Exeter University
Northcote House, The Queen's Drive, Exeter EX4 4QJ
Tel: 0392 263263

Glamorgan University
(formerly Wales Poly)
Pontypridd, Mid Glamorgan CF37 1DL
Tel: 0443 480480

Glasgow Caledonian University
(formerly Glasgow Poly)
Cowcaddens Road, Glasgow G4 0BA
Tel: 041-331 3000

Glasgow University
Glasgow G12 8QQ
Tel: 041-339 8855

Greenwich University
(formerly Thames Poly)
Wellington Street, London SE18 6PF
Tel: 081-316 8590

Heriot-Watt University
Riccarton, Edinburgh EH14 4AS
Tel: 031-449 5111

Hertfordshire University
(formerly Hatfield Poly)
College Lane, Hatfield, Herts AL10 9AB
Tel: 0707 284000

Huddersfield University
(formerly Huddersfield Poly)
Queensgate, Huddersfield HD1 3DH
Tel: 0484 422288

Hull University
Hull HU6 7RX
Tel: 0482 46311

Humberside University
(formerly Humberside Poly)
Cottingham Road, Hull HU6 7RT
Tel: 0482 440550

Keele University
Staffs ST5 5BG
Tel: 0782 621111

Kent University
Canterbury, Kent CT2 7NZ
Tel: 0227 764000

Kingston University
(formerly Kingston Poly)
Penrhyn Road, Kingston upon Thames KT1 2EE
Tel: 081-547 2000

Lampeter University
Dyfed SA48 7ED
Tel: 0570 422351

Lancaster University
University House, Lancaster LA1 4YW
Tel: 0524 65201

Leeds Metropolitan University
(formerly Leeds Poly)
Calverley Street, Leeds LS1 3HE
Tel: 0532 832600

Leeds University
Leeds LS2 9JT
Tel: 0532 431751

Leicester University
University Road, Leicester LE1 7RH
Tel: 0533 522522

Limerick University
Plassey Technological Park, Limerick
Tel: 333644

Liverpool John Moores University
(formerly Liverpool Poly)
Rodney House, 70 Mount Pleasant, Liverpool L3 5UX
Tel: 051-231 2121

Liverpool University
PO Box 147, Liverpool L69 3BX
Tel: 051-794 2000

London Guildhall University
(formerly City of London Poly)
117 Houndsditch, London EC3A 7BU
Tel: 071-320 1000

London University
(consisting of 22 undergraduate colleges)
Senate House, Malet Street, London WC1E 7HU
Tel: 071-636 8000

Birkbeck College
Malet Street, London WC1E 7HX
Tel: 071-580 6622

Charing Cross & Westminster Medical School
The Reynolds Building, St Dunstan's Road, London W6 8RP
Tel: 081-846 1234

Courtauld Institute of Art
Somerset House, Strand, London WC2R 0RN
Tel: 071-872 0220

Goldsmiths' College
New Cross, London SE14 6NW
Tel: 081-692 7171

Heythrop College
Kensington Square, London W8 5HQ
Tel: 071-580 6941

Imperial College
South Kensington, London SW7 2AZ
Tel: 071-589 5111

Institute of Archaeology
(part of University College)
31–34 Gordon Square, London WC1H 0PY
Tel: 071-387 7050

Jews' College
Albert Road, Hendon, London NW4 2SG
Tel: 081-203 6427

King's College
Strand, London WC2R 2LS
Tel: 071-836 5454

King's College School of Medicine & Dentistry
Bessemer Road, London SE5 9PJ
Tel: 071-274 6222

London Hospital Medical School
Turner Street, London E1 2AD
Tel: 071-377 7000

London School of Economics (LSE)
Houghton Street, London WC2A 1AE
Tel: 071-405 7686

Queen Mary & Westfield College
Mile End Road, London E1 4NS
Tel: 071-975 5555

Royal Free Hospital School of Medicine
Rowland Hill Street, London NW3 2PF
Tel: 071-794 0500

Royal Holloway & Bedford New College
Egham Hill, Egham, Surrey TW20 0EX
Tel: 0784 434455

Royal Veterinary College
Royal College Street, London NW1 0TU
Tel: 071-387 2898

School of Oriental & African Studies (SOAS)
Thornhaugh Street, Russell Square, London WC1H 0XG
Tel: 071-637 2388

School of Pharmacy
29/39 Brunswick Square, London WC1N 1AX
Tel: 071-837 7651

School of Slavonic & East European Studies (SSEES)
Senate House, Malet Street, London WC1E 7HU
Tel: 071-637 4934

Slade School of Fine Art
(part of University College)
Gower Street, London WC1E 6BT
Tel: 071-387 7050

St Bartholomew's Hospital Medical School
West Smithfield, London EC1A 7BE
Tel: 071-982 6000

St George's Hospital Medical School
Cranmer Terrace, Tooting, London SW17 0RE
Tel: 081-672 9944

St Mary's Hospital Medical School
(part of Imperial College)
Paddington, London W2 1PG
Tel: 071-723 1252

United Medical & Dental Schools (UMDS)
Lambeth Palace Road, London SE1 7EH
Tel: 071-922 8013

University College
Gower Street, London WC1E 6BT
Tel: 071-387 7050

Wye College
Ashford, Kent TN25 5AH
Tel: 0233 812401

Loughborough University
Loughborough, Leics LE11 3TU
Tel: 0509 263171

Manchester Metropolitan University
(formerly Manchester Poly)
All Saints, Manchester M15 6BH
Tel: 061-247 2000

Manchester University
Manchester M13 9PL
Tel: 061-275 2000
(see also UMIST)

Mater Dei Institute of Education
Clonliffe Road, Dublin 3
Tel: 376027

Middlesex University
(formerly Middlesex Poly)
White Hart Lane, London N17 8HR
Tel: 081-362 5000

Milltown Institute of Theology & Philosophy
Milltown Park, Dublin 6
Tel: 2698486

Napier University
(formerly Napier Poly)
219 Colinton Road, Edinburgh EH14 1DJ
Tel: 031-444 2266

Newcastle University
6 Kensington Terrace, Newcastle upon Tyne NE1 7RU
Tel: 091-222 6000

Northumbria University
(formerly Newcastle Poly)
Ellison Place, Newcastle upon Tyne NE1 8ST
Tel: 091-232 6002

Nottingham Trent University
(formerly Nottingham Poly)
Burton Street, Nottingham NG1 4BU
Tel: 0602 418418

Nottingham University
Nottingham NG7 2RD
Tel: 0602 484848

Open University
Walton Hall, Milton Keynes MK7 6AA
Tel: 0908 274066

Oxford Brookes University
(formerly Oxford Poly)
Headington, Oxford OX3 0BP
Tel: 0865 741111

(Continued)

Oxford University
(consisting of 28 undergraduate colleges)
Oxford OX1 2JD
Tel: 0865 270000 (registry)

Balliol College (m/f)
Oxford OX1 3BJ
Tel: 0865 277777

Brasenose College (m/f)
Oxford OX1 4AJ
Tel: 0965 277823

Christ Church (m/f)
Oxford OX1 1DP
Tel: 0865 276151

Corpus Christi College (m/f)
Oxford OX1 4JF
Tel: 0865 276700

Exeter College (m/f)
Oxford OX1 3DP
Tel: 0865 279600

Hertford College (m/f)
Oxford OX1 3BW
Tel: 0865 279400

Jesus College (m/f)
Oxford OX1 3DW
Tel: 0865 279700

Keble College (m/f)
Oxford OX1 3PG
Tel: 0865 272727

Lady Margaret Hall (m/f)
Oxford OX2 6QA
Tel: 0865 274300

Lincoln College (m/f)
Oxford OX1 3DR
Tel: 0865 279800

Magdalen College (m/f)
Oxford OX1 4AU
Tel: 0865 276000

Manchester College (m/f – mature)
Mansfield Road, Oxford OX1 3TD
Tel: 0865 271006

Mansfield College (m/f)
Oxford OX1 3TF
Tel: 0865 270999

Merton College (m/f)
Oxford OX1 4JD
Tel: 0865 276310

New College (m/f)
Oxford OX1 3BN
Tel: 0865 248541

Oriel College (m/f)
Oxford OX1 4EW
Tel: 0865 276555

Pembroke College (m/f)
Oxford OX1 1DW
Tel: 0865 276444

Queen's College (m/f)
Oxford OX1 4AW
Tel: 0865 279120

Regent's Park College (m/f)
Pusey Street, Oxford OX1 2LB
Tel: 0865 59887

Somerville College (f)
Oxford OX2 6HD
Tel: 0865 270600

St Catherine's College (m/f)
Oxford OX1 3UJ
Tel: 0865 271700

St Edmund Hall (m/f)
Oxford OX1 4AR
Tel: 0865 279000

St Hilda's College (f)
Oxford OX4 1DY
Tel: 0865 276884

St Hugh's College (m/f)
Oxford OX2 6LE
Tel: 0865 274900

St John's College (m/f)
Oxford OX1 3JP
Tel: 0865 277300

St Peter's College (m/f)
Oxford OX1 2DL
Tel: 0865 278900

Trinity College (m/f)
Oxford OX1 3BH
Tel: 0865 279900

University College (m/f)
Oxford OX1 4BH
Tel: 0865 276602

Wadham College (m/f)
Oxford OX1 3PN
Tel: 0865 277946

Worcester College (m/f)
Oxford OX1 2HB
Tel: 0865 278300

Paisley University
(formerly Paisley College)
High Street, Paisley PA1 2BE
Tel: 041-848 3000

Plymouth University
(formerly SouthWest Poly)
Drake Circus, Plymouth PL4 8AA
Tel: 0752 600600

Pontifical University of Maynooth
Maynooth, Co. Kildare
Tel: 6285222

Portsmouth University
(formerly Portsmouth Poly)
University House, Winston Churchill Avenue, Portsmouth PO1 2UP
Tel: 0705 876543

Queen's University of Belfast
(see Belfast University)

Reading University
Whiteknights, Reading RG6 2AH
Tel: 0734 875123

Robert Gordon University
(formerly Robert Gordon Institute)
Schoolhill, Aberdeen AB9 1FR
Tel: 0224 633611

Salford University
Salford, Greater Manchester M5 4WT
Tel: 061-745 5000

Sheffield Hallam University
(formerly Sheffield Poly)
Pond Street, Sheffield S1 1WB
Tel: 0742 720911

Sheffield University
Western Bank, Sheffield S10 2TN
Tel: 0742 768555

South Bank University
(formerly South Bank Poly)
Borough Road, London SE1 0AA
Tel: 071-928 8989

Southampton University
Southampton SO9 5NH
Tel: 0703 595000

Staffordshire University
(formerly Staffordshire Poly)
College Road, Stoke-on-Trent ST4 2DE
Tel: 0782 744531

St Andrews University
College Gate, St Andrews, Fife KY16 9AJ
Tel: 0334 76161

Stirling University
Stirling FK9 4LA
Tel: 0786 67043

St Patrick's College
Maynooth, Co. Kildare
Tel: (01) 6285222

Strathclyde University
Glasgow G1 1XQ
Tel: 041-552 4400

Sunderland University
(formerly Sunderland Poly)
Langham Tower, Ryhope Road, Sunderland SR2 7EE
Tel: 091-515 2000

Surrey University
Guildford, Surrey GU2 5XH
Tel: 0483 300800

Sussex University
Falmer, Brighton, Sussex BN1 9RH
Tel: 0273 678416

Swansea University
Singleton Park, Swansea SA2 8PP
Tel: 0792 205678

Teesside University
(formerly Teesside Poly)
Middlesbrough, Cleveland TS1 3BA
Tel: 0642 218121

Thames Valley University
(formerly West London Poly)
St Mary's Road, London W5 5RF
Tel: 081-579 5000
or
Wellington Street, Slough, Berks SL1 1YG
Tel: 0753 534585

Trinity College
Dublin 2
Tel: 6772941

Ulster University
Cromore Road, Coleraine, Co. Londonderry BT52 1SA
Tel: 0265 44141

UMIST (University of Manchester Institute of Science & Technology)
PO Box 88, Sackville Street, Manchester M60 1QD
Tel: 061-236 3311

University College Cork
Cork
Tel: 276871

University College Dublin
Belfield, Dublin 4
Tel: 2693244

University College Galway
Galway
Tel: 24411

Wales College of Medicine
Heath Park, Cardiff CF4 4XN
Tel: 0222 747747

Wales University
(Consists of 6 colleges: Aberystwyth, Bangor, Cardiff, Lampeter, Swansea and Wales College of Medicine. See individual entries.)

Warwick University
Coventry CV4 7AL
Tel: 0203 523523

Westminster University
(formerly Central London Poly)
309 Regent Street, London W1R 8AL
Tel: 071-911 5000

West of England University
(formerly Bristol Poly)
Coldharbour Lane, Frenchay, Bristol BS16 1QY
Tel: 0272 656261

Wolverhampton University
(formerly Wolverhampton Poly)
Wulfruna Street, Wolverhampton WV1 1SB
Tel: 0902 321000

York University
Heslington, York YO1 5DD
Tel: 0904 433535

HEALTH

Increasing awareness of the link between diet and health has had the greatest effect on British people in recent years. Sales of red meat, milk, potatoes and alcohol are down, but those of poultry, cheese and fruit are up.

Improved public health has rid the UK of many life-threatening diseases, but the World Health Organization recently declared tuberculosis to be a global emergency requiring concerted government action to minimize deaths. In 1992 there were 5,802 cases of TB in Britain, 1,794 of them in London.

Expectation of Life

United Kingdom

Source: CSO

Expectation of life	1901	1931	1961	1981	1991	2001
	Years					
Males						
At birth	45.5	58.4	67.9	70.8	73.2	74.5
At age:						
1 year	53.6	62.1	68.6	70.7	72.8	74.0
10 years ...	50.4	55.6	60.0	62.0	64.0	65.2
20 years ...	41.7	46.7	50.4	52.3	54.2	55.4
40 years ...	26.1	29.5	31.5	33.2	35.1	36.2
60 years ...	13.3	14.4	15.0	16.3	17.6	18.7
80 years ...	4.9	4.9	5.2	5.7	6.3	7.0

Expectation of life	1901	1931	1961	1981	1991	2001
	Years					
Females						
At birth	49.0	62.4	73.8	76.8	78.8	79.9
At age:						
1 year	55.8	65.1	74.2	76.6	78.3	79.3
10 years ...	52.7	58.6	65.6	67.8	69.5	70.5
20 years ...	44.1	49.6	55.7	57.9	59.6	60.6
40 years ...	28.3	32.4	36.5	38.5	40.0	41.0
60 years ...	14.6	16.4	19.0	20.8	21.9	22.7
80 years ...	5.3	5.4	6.3	7.5	8.3	8.8

Stress: How Much Can Affect Your Health?

Source: Reprinted with permission from the *Journal of Psychosomatic Research*, Vol. 11, pp. 213-218, T.H. Holmes, M.D., R.H. Rahe, M.D.; The Social Readjustment Rating Scale 1967, Pergamon Press, Ltd.

Change, both good and bad, can create stress and stress, if sufficiently severe, can lead to illness. Drs. Thomas Holmes and Richard Rahe, psychiatrists at the University of Washington in Seattle, developed the Social Readjustment Rating Scale. In their study, they gave a point value to stressful events. The psychiatrists discovered that in 79 percent of the persons studied, major illness followed the accumulation of stress-related changes totaling over 300 points in one year.

The Social Readjustment Rating Scale

Life Event	Value
Death of Spouse	100
Divorce	73
Marital separation from mate	65
Detention in jail or other institution	63
Death of a close family member	63
Major personal injury or illness	53
Marriage	50
Being fired at work	47
Marital reconciliation with mate	45
Retirement from work	45
Major change in the health or behavior of a family member	44
Pregnancy	40
Sexual difficulties	39
Gaining a new family member (e.g., through birth, adoption, moving in, etc.)	39
Major business readjustment (e.g., merger, reorganization, bankruptcy, etc.)	39
Major change in financial state (e.g., a lot worse off or a lot better off than usual)	38
Death of a close friend	37
Changing to a different line of work	36
Major change in the number of arguments with spouse (e.g., either a lot more or a lot less than usual regarding child-rearing, personal habits, etc.)	35
Taking out a mortgage or loan for a major purchase (e.g. for a home, business, etc.)	31
Foreclosure on a mortgage or loan	30
Major change in responsibilities at work (e.g., promotion, demotion, lateral transfer)	29
Son or daughter leaving home (e.g., marriage, attending college, etc.)	29
In-law troubles	29
Outstanding personal achievement	28
Wife beginning or ceasing work outside the home	26
Beginning or ceasing formal schooling	26
Major change in living conditions (e.g., building a new home, remodeling, deterioration of home or neighborhood)	25
Revision of personal habits (dress, manners, association, etc.)	24
Troubles with the boss	23
Major change in working hours or conditions	20
Change in residence	20
Changing to a new school	20
Major change in usual type and/or amount of recreation	19
Major change in church activities (e.g., a lot more or a lot less than usual)	19
Major change in social activities (e.g., clubs, dancing, movies, visiting, etc.)	18
Taking out a mortgage or loan for a lesser purchase (e.g., for a car, TV, freezer, etc.)	17
Major change in sleeping habits (a lot more or a lot less sleep, or change in part of day when asleep)	16
Major change in number of family get-togethers (e.g., a lot more or a lot less than usual)	15
Major change in eating habits (a lot more or a lot less food intake, or very different meal hours or surroundings)	15
Vacation	13
Christmas	12
Minor violations of the law (e.g., traffic tickets, jay-walking, disturbing the peace, etc.)	11

Exercise and Health

Do you think the amount of exercise a person takes generally affects their health?

Source: SCPR's *British Social Attitudes* survey, 9th Report, ed. R. Jowell *et al.* (Dartmouth Publishing, 1992)

	Percentage
A great deal	41.2
Quite a bit	46.5
Not very much	6.9
Hardly at all	3.8
Don't know	1.1

Immunization Schedule for Children

Source: *Immunization Against Infectious Diseases*, HMSO, 1992

Childhood immunization means protection against eight major diseases: polio, measles, mumps, rubella (German measles), whooping cough (pertussis), diphtheria, tetanus, and Haemophilus influenzae b (Hib) infections. Check the table and ask your doctor if your child is up to date on vaccines. It could save a life or prevent disability. Measles, mumps, rubella, polio, pertussis, diphtheria, Haemophilus infections and tetanus are not just harmless childhood illnesses. All of them can cripple or kill. All are preventable. In order to be completely protected against diphtheria, tetanus and pertussis, your child needs a shot of the combination diphtheria-tetanus-pertussis (DTP) vaccine at 2, 3 and 4 months, and a diphtheria-tetanus booster prior to school entry. The same applies to protection against polio. At 12 to 15 months your child should have a shot for measles, mumps and rubella (MMR). Children in high-risk populations should be tested for tuberculosis soon after birth. Immunization against TB is given between the ages of 10 and 13 years with the BCG (Bacillus Calmet Guerin) vaccine. Hib vaccine is due at 2, 3 and 4 months. At 15 to 19 years a tetanus booster shot may be given.

Individual circumstances may warrant decisions differing from the immunization guidelines given here.

Adolescents and adults should consult with their physicians about further vaccinations. Those without natural immunity or proper immunization against childhood diseases like measles, mumps, rubella and polio may be at increased risk from such diseases and their complications; in addition, tetanus should be boosted periodically. Various ages, occupations, lifestyles, environmental risks and outbreaks of disease may also call for adult immunization.

	DTP	DT booster	Polio	TB test	BCG	MMR	Hib[3]	Tetanus
Newborn				X[1]				
2 months	X		X				X	
3 months	X		X				X	
4 months	X		X				X	
12-15 months						X		
4-5 years		X[2]	X[2]					
10-13 years					X			
15-19 years								X

(1) In high-prevalence populations. (2) Pre-school booster. (3) Introduced in Oct. 1992, this vaccination is on offer to all children under 4 years until Oct. 1993.

Immunization of Children

United Kingdom

Source: CSO

	1971[1]	1976	1981	1986	1990–91[2]
	Percentages				
Percentage immunized[3]					
Diphtheria	80	73	82	85	93
Whooping cough	78	39	46	66	84
Poliomyelitis	80	73	82	85	92
Tetanus	80	73	82	85	92
Measles	46	45	54	71	89

(1) England and Wales only. (2) Scotland figures are for 1991. (3) Children born two years earlier and immunized by the end of the specified year.

Children and Young Persons on the Child Protection Registers: 1991[1]

England & Wales

Source: CSO

Thousands and rates

	Boys	Girls
Children aged (thousands)		
Under 1	1.6	1.5
1–4	8.1	7.3
5–9	7.8	7.5
10–15	5.5	6.8
16 and over	0.6	1.2
All children	23.5	24.3
Children aged (rates[2])		
Under 1	4.5	4.5
1–4	5.9	5.6
5–9	4.7	4.8
10–15	3.0	3.9
16 and over	0.8	1.9
All children	4.0	4.3

(1) At 31 March. (2) Rates per 1,000 population in each age group.

Notifications of Selected Infectious Diseases

United Kingdom

Source: CSO

Thousands and numbers

	1951	1961	1971	1976	1981	1986	1987	1988	1989	1990	1991
Notifications (thousands)											
Infective jaundice[1]	–	–	17.9	7.6	11.0	4.3	4.4	6.4	8.3	9.8	9.9
Whooping cough	194.9	27.3	19.4	4.4	21.5	39.9	17.4	5.9	13.6	16.9	6.3
Measles	636.2	788.8	155.2	68.4	61.7	90.2	46.1	90.6	31.0	15.6	11.7
Tuberculosis											
Respiratory[2]	–	22.9	10.8	9.1	6.8	5.4	4.5	4.5	4.6	4.5	4.5
Other[2]	–	3.4	3.0	2.6	2.5	1.5	1.2	1.3	1.4	1.5	1.7
Meningococcal meningitis[3]	–	–	0.6	0.7	0.5	0.9	1.1	1.3	1.3	1.1	1.1
Notifications (numbers)											
Malaria[4]	217	107	268	1,243	1,328	1,744	1,264	1,333	1,538	1,566	1,651
Typhoid fever[5]	214	105	136	216	195	167	148	181	173	190	186
Paratyphoid fever[5]	1,218	347	109	78	82	93	67	188	100	103	102

(1) Viral hepatitis for Scotland, and for England and Wales from 1989. (2) From 1984, categories overlap, therefore some cases will be included in respiratory. (3) England and Wales only. (4) Great Britain only until 1989. United Kingdom from 1990. (5) Great Britain only for 1951 and 1961.

Selected Causes of Death: 1951 and 1991

United Kingdom

Source: CSO

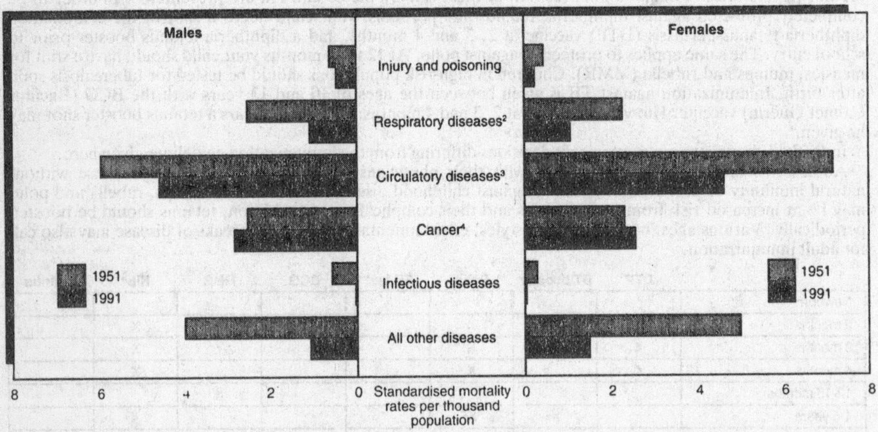

(2) In 1984 the coding procedure was changed, reducing the number of deaths assigned to respiratory causes. (3) Includes heart attacks and strokes. (4) The figures for neoplasms include both malignant and benign cancers.

Infant Mortality

United Kingdom[1]

Source: CSO

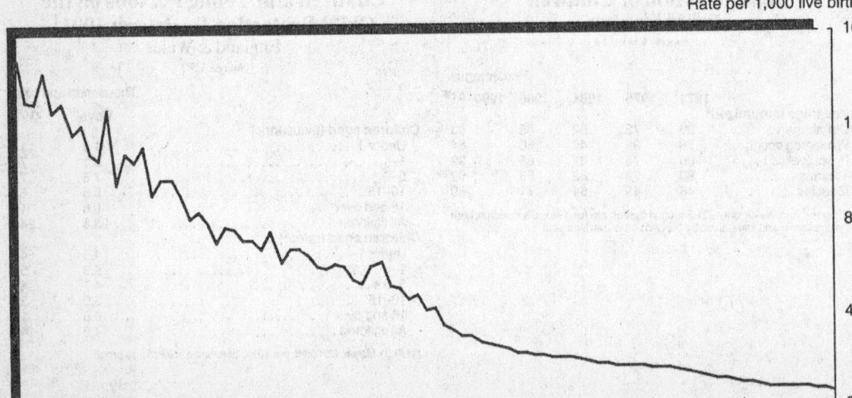

(1) From 1901 to 1921 rates are for Great Britain

Accidental Deaths

Great Britain

Source: CSO

Cause of death	1971	1981	1986[1]	1991[1]
			Numbers	
Railway accident	212	95	99	90
Road accident[2]	7,970	4,880	5,565	5,042
Other transport accident	219	143	235	109
Accident at home or in residential accommodation[3]	7,045	–	5,522	4,717
Accident elsewhere[3]	3,807	–	2,620	2,427
Total accidental deaths	**19,246**	**15,097**	**14,024**	**12,377**

(1) On 1 January 1986 a new certificate for deaths within the first 28 days of life was introduced in England and Wales. It is not possible to assign one underlying cause of death from this certificate. The 1986 and 1990 figures for England and Wales exclude deaths under 28 days. (2) These figures are not comparable with those issued by the Department of Transport. Road deaths are normally counted as those which occur within 30 days of the accident. (3) Late effects of accidental injury are included in the individual cause figures for Scotland, but are excluded from the total.

Injuries at Work[1]

Source: CSO

	Fatal			Major[2]			Over 3 days[3]		
	1988/89	1989/90	1990/91	1988/89	1989/90	1990/91	1988/89	1989/90	1990/91
Agriculture, forestry and fishing	46	53	52	583	505	558	1,615	1,626	1,422
Agriculture and horticulture	40	48	42	527	455	491	1,298	1,354	1,215
Forestry	5	4	10	53	45	60	291	232	182
Fishing[4]	1	1	–	3	5	7	26	40	25
Energy and water supply industries[5,6]	205	31	27	1,267	1,146	1,074	13,738	11,705	10,276
Coal extraction and manufacture of solid fuels	21	20	12	769	665	549	6,427	5,084	4,253
Coke ovens	–	1	–	8	9	6	104	106	53
Extraction of mineral oil and natural gas[5,6]	172	2	12	64	75	95	692	693	701
Mineral oil processing	2	3	–	33	42	36	154	164	147
Nuclear fuels industry	–	–	–	12	13	9	313	288	211
Production and distribution of electricity, gas and other forms of energy	8	3	3	324	273	299	4,721	4,224	3,899
Water supply industry	2	2	–	57	69	80	1,327	1,146	1,012
Extraction of minerals and ores other than fuels; manufacture of metals, mineral products and chemicals	35	36	30	1,681	1,554	1,414	11,150	11,480	10,501
Extraction and preparation of metalliferous ores/extraction of minerals nes*	8	3	9	180	163	128	788	784	687
Metal manufacture	8	6	5	517	415	354	3,430	3,188	2,991
Manufacture of non-metallic mineral products	11	19	11	474	403	408	3,251	3,676	3,297
Chemical industry	8	8	5	498	559	508	3,557	3,725	3,439
Man-made fibres industry	–	–	–	12	14	16	124	107	87
Metal goods, engineering and vehicles industries	33	48	29	2,645	2,762	2,609	20,076	21,774	20,467
Manufacture of metal goods	11	9	3	682	746	668	4,459	5,082	4,573
Mechanical engineering	11	20	14	828	836	772	5,043	5,459	5,137
Manufacture of office machinery and data processing equipment	–	–	–	29	40	27	205	207	217
Electrical and electronic engineering	2	9	3	366	369	437	3,192	3,267	3,087
Manufacture of motor vehicles parts thereof	5	2	5	400	384	333	4,019	4,355	4,141
Manufacture of other transport equipment	4	6	4	303	337	324	2,911	3,097	3,062
Instrument engineering	–	2	–	37	50	48	247	307	250
Other manufacturing industries	33	31	39	3,188	3,181	2,900	25,043	26,900	25,581
Food, drink and tobacco industries	7	10	13	1,255	1,333	1,192	12,932	14,301	13,687
Textile industry	5	2	6	269	248	214	1,891	1,989	1,745
Leather and leather goods industry	–	–	1	19	16	20	119	144	124
Footwear and clothing industry	–	–	1	106	92	108	885	822	723
Timber and wooden furniture industries	5	11	8	631	586	515	2,579	2,602	2,471
Manufacture of paper and paper products; printing and publishing	10	4	4	446	434	395	3,289	3,359	3,349
Processing of rubber and plastics	5	3	6	387	415	400	2,970	3,257	3,106
Other manufacturing industries	1	1	–	75	57	56	378	426	376
Total manufacturing industries	101	115	98	7,514	7,497	6,923	56,269	60,154	56,549
Construction	137	154	124	3,660	4,107	3,838	17,566	18,487	18,243
Distributive trades, hotels and catering; repairs	39	35	32	2,091	2,244	2,337	12,516	14,652	15,991
Transport and communication	45	46	53	1,271	1,324	1,526	13,240	14,883	15,817
Banking and finance, insurance, business services and leasing	10	10	9	213	277	316	1,183	1,466	1,593
Other services	25	31	38	4,359	4,482	4,454	44,574	43,655	42,169
Unclassified	1	–	–	138	124	196	3,921	481	828
Total reported to enforcement authorities[6]	609	475	433	21,096	21,706	21,222	164,622	167,109	162,888

(1) Included work-related injuries to employees and self-employed persons reported to enforcing authorities under the Reporting of Injuries, Diseases and Dangerous Occurrences Regulations (RIDDOR) 1985. (2) As defined in RIDDOR. (3) Injuries causing incapacity for normal work for more than 3 days. (4) Excludes sea fishing. (5) Includes figures for the oil and gas industry collected under offshore safety legislation. (6) Includes the 167 fatalities, 11 major injuries and 50 over 3-day injuries of the Piper Alpha disaster, 6 July 1988. *nes = not elsewhere specified.

Basic First Aid

First aid experts stress that knowing what to do for an injured person until a doctor or trained person gets to an accident scene can save a life, especially in cases of stoppage of breath, severe bleeding, and shock.

People with special medical problems, such as diabetes, cardiovascular disease, epilepsy, or allergy, are also urged to wear some sort of emblem identifying it, as a safeguard against use of medication that might be injurious or fatal in an emergency. Emblems may be obtained from Medic Alert, 17 Bridge Wharf, 156 Caledonian Road, London N1 9UU; tel. 071-833 3034.

Most accidents occur in homes. National Safety Council figures show that home accidents exceed those in other locations, such as in cars, at work, or in public places.

In all cases, get medical assistance as soon as possible.

Animal bite — Wound should be washed with soap under running water and animal should be caught alive for rabies test.

Asphyxiation — Start mouth-to-mouth resuscitation immediately after getting patient to fresh air.

Bleeding — Elevate the wound above the heart if possible. Press hard on wound with sterile compress until bleeding stops. Send for doctor if it is severe.

Burn — If mild, with skin unbroken and no blisters, plunge into ice water until pain subsides. Apply a dry dressing if necessary. Send for physician if burn is severe. Apply sterile compresses and keep patient quiet and comfortably warm until doctor's arrival. Do not try to clean burn, or to break blisters.

Chemical in eye — With patient lying down, pour cupsful of water immediately into corner of eye, letting it run to other side to remove chemicals thoroughly. Cover with sterile compress. Get medical attention immediately.

Choking — Use back slaps to dislodge obstruction, keeping the patient's head low and asking him to cough at the same time. (See **Abdominal Thrust**)

Convulsions — Place person on back on bed or rug. Loosen clothing. Turn head to side. Do not place a blunt object between the victim's teeth. If convulsions do not stop, get medical attention immediately.

Cut (minor) — Apply mild antiseptic and sterile compress after washing with soap under warm running water.

Drowning — (See Mouth-to-Mouth Resuscitation) Artificial breathing must be started at once, before victim is out of the water, if possible. If the victim's stomach is bloated with water, put victim on stomach, place hands under stomach, and lift. If no pulse is felt, begin cardio-pulmonary resuscitation. This should only be done by those professionally trained. If necessary, treat for shock. (See **Shock**)

Electric shock — If possible, turn off power. Don't touch victim until contact is broken; pull him from contact with electrical source using rope, wooden pole, or loop of dry cloth. Start mouth-to-mouth resuscitation if breathing has stopped.

Foreign body in eye — Touch object with moistened corner of handkerchief if it can be seen. If it cannot be seen or does not come out after a few attempts, take patient to doctor. Do not rub eye.

Fainting — If victim feels faint, lower head to knees. Lay him down with head turned to side if he becomes unconscious. Loosen clothing and open windows. Keep patient lying quietly for at least 15 minutes after he regains consciousness. Call doctor if faint lasts for more than a few minutes.

Fall — Send for physician if patient has continued pain. Cover wound with sterile dressing and stop any severe bleeding. Do not move patient unless absolutely necessary — as in case of fire — if broken bone is suspected. Keep patient warm and comfortable.

Loss of Limb — If a limb is severed, it is important to protect the limb properly so that it can possibly be reattached to the victim. After the victim is cared for, the limb should be placed in a clean plastic bag, garbage can or other suitable container. Pack ice around the limb on the OUTSIDE of the bag to keep the limb cold. Call ahead to the hospital to alert them of the situation.

Poisoning — Call doctor. Use antidote listed on label if container is found. Except for lye, other caustics, and petroleum products, induce vomiting unless victim is unconscious. Give milk if poison or antidote is unknown.

Shock (injury-related) — Keep the victim lying down; if uncertain as to his injuries, keep him flat on his back. Maintain the victim's normal body temperature; if the weather is cold or damp, place blankets or extra clothing over and under the victim; if weather is hot, provide shade.

Snakebite — Immediately get victim to a hospital. If there is mild swelling or pain, apply a constricting band 2 to 4 inches above the bite.

Sting from insect — If possible, remove stinger and apply solution of ammonia and water, or paste of baking soda. Call physician immediately if body swells or patient collapses.

Unconsciousness — Send for doctor and place person on his back. Start resuscitation if he stops breathing. Never give food or liquids to an unconscious person.

Abdominal Thrust

For victims of choking the British Red Cross recommends slaps on the back, provided the patient is bent over with the head held low and coughs at the same time. If this fails, the recommended treatment is the Heimlich manoeuvre, named after its creator, Dr. Henry Heimlich.

- Get behind the victim and wrap your arms around him above his waist.
- Make a fist with one hand and place it, with the thumb knuckle pressing inward, just below the point of the "v" of the rib cage.
- Grasp the wrist with the other hand and give one or more upward thrusts or hugs.
- Start mouth-to-mouth resuscitation if breathing stops.

Mouth-to-Mouth Resuscitation

Stressing that your breath can save a life, the Red Cross gives the following directions for mouth-to-mouth resuscitation if the victim is not breathing:

- Determine consciousness by tapping the victim on the shoulder and asking loudly, "Are you okay?"
- Tilt the victim's head back so that his chin is pointing upward. Do not press on the soft tissue under the chin, as this might obstruct the airway. If you

suspect that an accident victim might have neck or back injuries, open the airway by placing the tips of your index and middle fingers on the corners of the victim's jaw to lift it forward without tilting the head.

- Place your cheek and ear close to the victim's mouth and nose. Look at the victim's chest to see if it rises and falls. Listen and feel for air to be exhaled for about 5 seconds.
- If there is no breathing, pinch the victim's nostrils shut with the thumb and index finger of your hand that is pressing on the victim's forehead. Another way to prevent leakage of air when the lungs are inflated is to press your cheek against the victim's nose.
- Blow air into victim's mouth by taking a deep breath and then sealing your mouth tightly around the victim's mouth. Initially, give two, quick (approx. 1.5 seconds each), full breaths without allowing the lungs to deflate completely between each breath.
- Watch the victim's chest to see if it rises.
- Stop blowing when the victim's chest is expanded. Raise your mouth; turn your head to the side and listen for exhalation.
- Watch the chest to see if it falls.
- Repeat the blowing cycle until the victim starts breathing.
- **Note:** Infants (up to one year) and children (1 to 8 years) should be administered mouth-to-mouth resuscitation as described above, except for the following:
- Do not tilt the head as far back as an adult's head.
- Both the mouth and nose of the infant should be sealed by the mouth.
- Give breaths to a child once every four seconds.
- Blow into the infant's mouth and nose once every three seconds with less pressure and volume than for a child.

Nutritive Value of Food (Calories, Proteins, etc.)

Source: Home and Garden Bulletin No. 72; available from Supt. of Documents, U. S. Government Printing Office, Washington, DC 20402

Food	Measure	Grams	Food Energy (calories)	Protein (grams)	Fat (grams)	Saturated fats (grams)	Carbohydrate (grams)	Calcium (milligrams)	Iron (milligrams)	Vitamin A (I.U.)	Thiamin (milligrams)	Riboflavin (milligrams)
Dairy products												
Cheese, cheddar	1 oz.	28	115	7	9	6.1	T	204	.2	300	.01	.11
Cheese, cottage	7.3 oz	210	220	26	9	6.0	6	126	.3	340	.04	.34
Cheese, cream	1 oz.	28	100	2	10	6.2	1	23	.3	400	T	.06
Cheese, Swiss	1 oz.	28	105	8	8	5.0	1	272	T	240	.01	.10
Half-and-Half (milk & cream)	1 tbsp.	15	20	T	2	1.1	1	16	T	20	.01	.02
Cream, sour	1 tbsp.	15	25	T	3	1.6	1	14	T	90	T	.02
Milk, whole	8 fl oz.	244	150	8	8	5.1	11	291	.1	310	.09	.40
Milk, nonfat (skimmed)	8 fl oz.	244	85	8	T	.3	12	302	.1	500	.09	.37
Milkshake, chocolate	10.6 oz.	300	355	9	8	5.0	63	396	.9	260	.14	.67
Ice Cream, hardened	4.6 oz.	133	270	5	14	8.9	32	176	.1	540	.05	.33
Sorbet	6.7 oz.	193	270	2	4	2.4	59	103	.3	190	.03	.09
Yogurt, fruit-flavoured	8 oz.	227	230	10	3	1.8	42	343	.2	120	.08	.40
Eggs												
Fried in butter	1	46	85	5	6	2.4	1	26	.9	290	.03	.13
Hard-boiled	1	50	80	6	6	1.7	1	28	1.0	260	.04	.14
Scrambled in butter (milk added)	1	64	95	6	7	2.8	1	47	.9	310	.04	.16
Fats & oils												
Butter	1 tbsp.	14	100	T	12	7.2	T	3	T	430	T	T
Margarine	1 tbsp.	14	100	T	12	2.1	T	3	T	470	T	T
Salad dressing, blue cheese	1 tbsp.	15	75	1	8	1.6	1	12	T	30	T	.02
Salad dressing, French	1 tbsp.	16	65	T	6	1.1	3	2	1	—	—	—
Salad dressing, Italian	1 tbsp.	15	85	T	9	1.6	1	2	T	T	T	T
Mayonnaise	1 tbsp.	14	100	T	11	2.0	T	3	.1	40	T	.01
Meat, poultry, fish												
Bluefish, baked with butter or margarine	3 oz.	85	135	22	4	—	0	25	0.6	40	.09	.08
Clams, raw, meat only	3 oz.	85	65	11	1	—	2	59	5.2	90	.08	.15
Crabmeat, white or king, canned	4.7 oz.	135	135	24	3	.6	1	61	1.1	—	.11	.11
Fish fingers, breaded, cooked, frozen	1 oz.	28	50	5	3	—	2	3	.1	0	.01	.02
Salmon, pink, canned	3 oz.	85	120	17	5	.9	0	167	.7	60	.03	.16
Sardines, Atlantic, canned in oil	3 oz.	85	175	20	9	3.0	0	372	2.5	190	.02	.17
Prawns, deep fried	3 oz.	85	190	17	9	2.3	9	61	1.7	—	.03	.07
Tuna, canned in oil	3 oz.	85	170	24	7	1.7	0	7	1.6	70	.04	.10
Bacon, grilled or fried crisp	2 slices	15	85	4	8	2.5	T	2	.5	0	.08	.05
Minced beef, dry-fried, 10% fat	3 oz.	85	185	23	10	4.0	0	10	3.0	20	.08	.20
Roast beef, relatively lean	3 oz.	85	165	25	7	2.8	0	11	3.2	10	.06	.19
Beef steak, lean and fat	3 oz.	85	330	20	27	11.3	0	9	2.5	50	.05	.15
Beef & vegetable stew	8.5 oz.	245	220	16	11	4.9	15	29	2.9	2,400	.15	.17
Lamb, chop, lean and fat	3.1 oz.	89	360	18	32	14.8	0	8	1.0	—	.11	.19
Liver, beef	3 oz.	85	195	22	9	2.5	5	9	7.5	45,390	.22	3.56
Ham, lean and fat	3 oz.	85	245	18	19	6.8	0	8	2.2	0	.40	.15
Pork, chop, lean and fat	2.7 oz.	78	305	19	25	8.9	0	9	2.7	0	.75	.22
Bologna	1 slice	28	85	3	8	3.0	T	2	.5	—	.05	.06
Frankfurter, cooked	1	56	170	7	15	5.6	1	3	.8	—	.08	.11
Sausage, pork chipolata, cooked	1	13	60	2	6	2.1	T	1	.3	0	.10	.04
Veal, cutlet, braised or grilled	3 oz.	85	185	23	9	4.0	0	9	2.7	—	.06	.21
Chicken, drumstick, fried, bones removed	1.3 oz.	38	90	12	4	1.1	T	6	.9	50	.03	.15
Chicken, half, grilled, bones removed	6.2 oz.	176	240	42	7	2.2	0	16	3.0	160	.09	.34

(Continued)

	Measure	Grams	Food Energy (calories)	Protein (grams)	Fat (grams)	Saturated fats (grams)	Carbohydrate (grams)	Calcium (milligrams)	Iron (milligrams)	Vitamin A (I.U.)	Thiamin (milligrams)	Riboflavin (milligrams)
Fruits & products												
Apple, raw, 2¾ in. diam.	1	138	80	T	1	—	20	10	.4	120	.04	.03
Apple juice	8 fl oz.	248	120	T	T	—	30	15	1.5	—	.02	.05
Apricots, raw	3	107	55	1	T	—	14	18	.5	2,890	.03	.04
Banana, raw	1	119	100	1	T	—	26	10	.8	230	.06	.07
Cantaloupe melon, 5 in. diam.	½	477	80	2	T	—	20	38	1.1	9,240	.11	.08
Cherries, sweet, raw	10	68	45	1	T	—	12	15	.3	70	.03	.04
Fruit cocktail, canned, in heavy syrup	8.9 oz.	255	195	1	T	—	50	23	1.0	360	.05	.03
Grapefruit, raw, medium, white	½	241	45	1	T	—	12	19	.5	10	.05	.02
Grapes, Thompson seedless	10	50	35	T	T	—	9	6	.2	50	.03	.02
Lemonade (citron pressé), frozen, diluted	8 fl oz.	248	105	T	T	—	28	2	.1	10	.01	.02
Orange, 2⅝ in. diam.	1	131	65	1	T	—	16	54	.5	260	.13	.05
Orange juice, frozen, diluted	8 fl oz.	249	120	2	T	—	29	25	.2	540	.23	.03
Peach, raw, 2½ in. diam.	1	100	40	1	T	—	10	9	.5	1,330	.02	.05
Raisins, seedless	5 oz.	145	420	4	T	—	112	90	5.1	30	.16	.12
Strawberries, whole	5.2 oz.	149	55	1	1	—	13	31	1.5	90	.04	.10
Watermelon, 4 by 8 in. wedge	1 wedge	926	110	2	1	—	27	30	2.1	2,510	.13	.13
Grain products												
Bagel, egg	1	55	165	6	2	.5	28	9	1.2	30	.14	.10
Boston cream pie with custard filling, 1/12 of cake		69	210	3	6	1.9	34	46	.7	140	.09	.11
Bran flakes (40% bran), added sugar, salt, iron, vitamins	1.2 oz.	35	105	4	1	—	28	19	12.4	1,650	.41	.49
Bread, white, enriched	1 slice	25	70	2	1	.2	13	21	.6	T	.10	.06
Bread, whole wheat	1 slice	28	65	3	1	.1	14	24	.8	T	.09	.03
Brownies, with nuts, from commercial recipe	1	20	85	1	4	.9	13	9	.4	20	.03	.02
Cake, angel food, 1/12 of cake	1	53	135	3	T	—	32	50	.2	0	.03	.08
Cake, pound, 1/17 of loaf	1	33	160	2	10	2.5	16	6	.5	80	.05	.06
Cookies, chocolate chip, from home recipe	4	40	205	2	12	3.5	24	14	.8	40	.06	.06
Corn flakes, added sugar, salt, iron, vitamins	1 oz.	25	95	2	T	—	21	*	0.6	1,180	.29	.35
Crackers, graham	2	14	55	1	1	.3	10	6	.5	0	.02	.08
Crackers, saltines	4	11	50	1	1	.3	8	2	.5	0	.05	.05
Cupcake, 2½ in. diam., with chocolate icing	1	36	130	2	5	2.0	21	47	.4	60	.05	.06
Danish pastry, round piece	1	65	275	5	15	4.7	30	33	1.2	200	.18	.19
Doughnut, cake type	1	25	100	1	5	1.2	13	10	.4	20	.05	.05
Macaroni cheese, from home recipe	7 oz.	200	430	17	22	8.9	40	362	1.8	860	.20	.40
Muffin, corn	1	40	125	3	4	1.2	19	42	.7	120	.10	.10
Noodles, enriched, cooked	5.5 oz.	160	200	7	2	—	37	16	1.4	110	.22	.13
Oatmeal or rolled oats	8.4 oz.	240	130	5	2	.4	23	22	1.4	0	.19	.05
Fruitcake, dark, 1/30 of loaf	1	15	55	1	2	.5	9	11	.4	20	.02	.02
Pie, apple, 1/7 of pie	1	135	345	3	15	3.9	51	11	.9	40	.15	.11
Pie, cherry, 1/7 of pie	1	135	350	4	15	4.0	52	19	.9	590	.16	.12
Pie, lemon meringue, 1/7 of pie	1	120	305	4	12	3.7	45	17	1.0	200	.09	.12
Pie, pecan, 1/7 of pie	1	118	495	6	27	4.0	61	55	3.7	190	.26	.14
Pizza, cheese, 1/8 of 12 in. diam. pie	1	60	145	6	4	1.7	22	86	1.1	230	.16	.18
Popcorn, popped, plain	0.2 oz.	6	25	1	T	T	5	1	.2	—	—	.01
Pretzels, stick	10	3	10	T	T	—	2	1	T	0	.01	.01
Rice, puffed, added iron, thiamin, niacin	½ oz.	15	60	1	T	—	13	3	.3	0	.07	.01
Rolls, enriched, brown & serve	1	26	85	2	2	.4	14	20	.5	T	.10	.06
Rolls, frankfurter & hamburger	1	40	120	3	2	.5	21	30	.8	T	.16	.10
Scone, 2 in. diam., from home recipe	1	28	105	2	5	1.2	13	34	.4	T	.08	.08
Spaghetti with meat balls & tomato sauce	8.5 oz.	248	330	19	12	3.3	39	124	3.7	1,590	.25	.30
Wheat, shredded, plain	1	25	90	2	1	—	20	11	.9	0	.06	.03
Legumes, nuts, seeds												
Beans, cooked	6 oz.	180	210	14	1	—	38	90	4.9	0	.25	.13
Peanuts, roasted in oil, salted	5 oz.	144	840	37	72	13.7	27	107	3.0	—	.46	.19
Peanut butter	1 tbsp.	16	95	4	8	1.5	3	9	.3	—	.02	.02
Sunflower seeds	5 oz.	145	810	35	69	8.2	29	174	10.3	70	2.84	.33
Sugars & sweets												
Boiled sweets	1 oz.	28	110	0	T	—	28	6	.5	0	0	0
Caramels	1 oz.	28	115	1	3	1.6	22	42	.4	T	.01	.05
Chocolate, milk	1 oz.	28	145	2	9	5.5	16	65	.3	80	.02	.10
Fudge, chocolate	1 oz.	28	115	1	3	1.3	21	22	.3	T	.01	.03
Honey	1 tbsp.	21	65	T	0	0	17	1	.1	0	T	.01
Jams & Preserves	1 tbsp.	20	55	T	T	—	14	4	.2	T	T	.01
Jelly	8.5 oz.	240	140	4	0	0	34	—	—	—	—	—
Sugar, white, granulated	1 tbsp.	12	45	0	0	0	12	0	T	0	0	0
Vegetables												
Asparagus, canned, spears	4 spears	80	15	2	T	—	3	15	1.5	640	.05	.08
Beans, green, from frozen, cut	5 oz.	135	35	2	T	—	8	54	.9	780	.09	.12
Broccoli, cooked	1 stalk	180	45	6	1	—	8	158	1.4	4,500	.16	.36
Cabbage, raw, coarsely shredded or sliced	2.5 oz.	70	15	1	T	—	4	34	.3	90	.04	.04
Carrots, raw, 7½ by 1⅛ in.	1	72	30	1	T	—	7	27	.5	7,930	.04	.04
Celery, raw	1 stalk	40	5	T	T	—	2	16	.1	110	.01	.01
Corn, sweet, cooked	1 ear	140	70	2	1	—	16	2	.5	310	.09	.08
Gherkins, dill, whole	1	65	5	T	T	—	1	17	.7	70	T	.01
Kale, cooked	6.5 oz.	190	65	7	1	—	10	357	1.5	14,820	.21	.38
Lettuce, Iceberg, chopped	2 oz.	55	5	T	T	—	2	11	.3	180	.03	.03
Mushrooms, raw	2.5 oz.	70	20	2	T	—	3	4	.6	T	.07	.32
Olives, pickled, green	4 medium	16	15	T	2	.2	T	8	.2	40	—	—

(Continued)

	Measure	Grams	Food Energy (calories)	Protein (grams)	Fat (grams)	Saturated fats (grams)	Carbohydrate (grams)	Calcium (milligrams)	Iron (milligrams)	Vitamin A (I.U.)	Thiamin (milligrams)	Riboflavin (milligrams)
Onions, raw, chopped	6 oz.	170	65	3	T	—	15	46	.9	T	.05	.07
Peas, frozen, cooked	5.5 oz.	160	110	8	T	—	19	30	3,0	960	.43	.14
Potatoes, baked, peeled	1	156	145	4	T	—	33	14	1.1	T	.15	.07
Potatoes, frozen, French fried	10	50	110	2	4	1.1	17	5	.9	T	.07	.01
Potatoes, mashed, milk added	7 oz.	210	135	4	2	.7	27	50	.8	40	.17	.11
Potato crisps	10	20	115	1	8	2.1	10	8	.4	T	.04	.01
Potato salad	8.5 oz.	250	250	7	7	2.0	41	80	1.5	350	.20	.18
Spinach, chopped, from frozen	7 oz.	205	45	6	1	—	8	232	4.3	16,200	.14	.31
Sweet potatoes, baked in skin, peeled	1	114	160	2	1	—	37	46	1.0	9,230	.10	.08
Tomatoes, raw	1	135	25	1	T	—	6	16	.6	1,110	.07	.05
Tomato soup, prepared with water	8 fl oz.	245	90	2	3	.5	16	15	.7	1,000	.05	.05
Miscellaneous												
Beer	12 fl. oz.	360	150	1	0	0	14	18	T	—	.01	.11
Gin, rum, vodka, whisky, 86 proof	1½ fl. oz.	42	105	—	—	0	T	—	—	—	—	—
Wine, table	3½ fl. oz.	102	85	T	0	0	4	9	.4	—	T	.01
Cola-type beverage	12 fl. oz.	369	145	0	0	0	37	—	—	0	0	0
Ginger ale	12 fl. oz.	366	115	0	0	0	29	—	—	0	0	0
Ice lolly, 3 fl. oz.	1	95	70	0	0	0	18	0	T	0	0	0

T — Indicates trace * — Varies by brand

Ideal Weight Ranges
(stones and pounds)

Source: Weight Watchers

WOMEN

Height without shoes	Age: 25 & over	23–24	21–22	19–20	18
4′6″	7.8–6.4	7.6–6.2	7.5–6.1	7.3–6.0	7.1–5.13
4′7″	7.9–6.6	7.7–6.4	7.6–6.2	7.4–6.1	7.2–6.0
4′8″	7.10–6.8	7.8–6.6	7.7–6.4	7.5–6.3	7.3–6.2
4′9″	7.12–6.10	7.10–6.8	7.8–6.7	7.6–6.6	7.4–6.5
4′10″	8.1–6.12	7.13–6.10	7.11–6.9	7.8–6.8	7.7–6.7
4′11″	8.4–7.1	8.2–6.12	8.1–6.11	7.13–6.10	7.11–6.9
5′0″	8.7–7.4	8.5–7.2	8.3–7.0	8.1–6.13	8.0–6.12
5′1″	8.10–7.7	8.9–7.5	8.7–7.4	8.5–7.3	8.4–7.2
5′2″	9.0–7.10	8.13–7.9	8.11–7.8	8.9–7.7	8.7–7.6
5′3″	9.4–7.13	9.3–7.11	9.1–7.10	9.0–7.9	8.13–7.8
5′4″	9.9–8.2	9.8–8.0	9.6–7.13	9.5–7.12	9.4–7.11
5′5″	9.13–8.6	9.12–8.4	9.10–8.2	9.8–8.1	9.7–8.0
5′6″	10.3–8.10	10.2–8.8	10.0–8.6	9.12–8.5	9.11–8.4
5′7″	10.7–9.0	10.6–8.12	10.4–8.11	10.2–8.10	10.0–8.9
5′8″	10.11–9.4	10.10–9.2	10.8–9.0	10.6–8.12	10.4–8.11
5′9″	11.1–9.8	11.0–9.7	10.12–9.6	10.10–9.5	10.8–9.4
5′10″	11.5–9.12	11.4–9.11	11.2–9.10	11.0–9.9	10.11–9.7
5′11″	11.9–10.2	11.8–10.1	11.6–10.0	11.4–9.13	11.1–9.12
6′0″	11.13–10.6	11.12–10.5	11.10–10.4	11.8–10.3	11.6–10.2
6′1″	12.3–10.10	12.2–10.9	12.0–10.8	11.12–10.7	11.10–10.6
6′2″	12.7–11.0	12.6–10.13	12.4–10.12	12.2–10.11	12.0–10.10

MEN

Height without shoes	Age: 25 & over	23–24	21–22	19–20	18
5′0″	9.12–8.3	9.11–8.2	9.9–8.0	9.7–7.12	8.10–7.11
5′1″	10.1–8.6	10.0–8.5	9.12–8.3	9.10–8.1	9.0–8.0
5′2″	10.4–8.9	10.2–8.8	10.0–8.6	9.13–8.4	9.4–8.3
5′3″	10.8–8.12	10.7–8.11	10.5–8.9	10.3–8.7	9.9–8.6
5′4″	10.12–9.1	10.11–9.0	10.9–8.12	10.7–8.10	10.5–8.8
5′5″	11.2–9.4	11.1–9.3	10.13–9.1	10.11–8.13	10.9–8.12
5′6″	11.7–9.8	11.6–9.7	11.4–9.5	11.2–9.3	11.0–9.2
5′7″	11.12–9.12	11.11–9.10	11.9–9.8	11.7–9.7	11.5–9.6
5′8″	12.2–10.2	12.1–10.0	11.13–9.12	11.11–9.10	11.9–9.9
5′9″	12.6–10.6	12.5–10.4	12.3–10.2	12.1–10.1	11.11–10.0
5′10″	12.11–10.10	12.10–10.8	12.7–10.6	12.5–10.4	12.2–10.3
5′11″	13.2–11.0	13.1–10.12	12.13–10.10	12.11–10.8	12.9–10.7
6′0″	13.7–11.4	13.6–11.2	13.4–11.0	13.2–10.12	12.12–10.11
6′1″	13.12–11.8	13.11–11.6	13.8–11.4	13.7–11.2	13.5–11.1
6′2″	14.3–11.13	14.2–11.11	14.0–11.9	13.12–11.7	13.10–11.6
6′3″	14.8–12.4	14.7–12.2	14.5–12.0	14.3–11.12	14.2–11.11
6′4″	14.13–12.9	14.12–12.7	14.10–12.5	14.8–12.3	14.6–12.2

GIRLS

Height	Age: 10	11	12	13	14	15	16	17
3′11″	3.13–3.6	–	–	–	–	–	–	–
4′0″	4.2–3.7	4.5–3.9	–	–	–	–	–	–
4′1″	4.5–3.8	4.9–3.10	4.13–3.11	–	–	–	–	–
4′2″	4.8–3.9	4.11–3.11	5.1–3.13	5.3–4.4	–	–	–	–

(Continued)

GIRLS

Height	Age 10	11	12	13	14	15	16	17
4'3"	4.11–3.12	5.0–3.13	5.3–4.1	5.6–4.6	6.0–4.7	–	–	–
4'4"	5.0–4.2	5.3–4.3	5.6–4.4	5.9–4.8	6.4–4.11	6.7–5.7	–	–
4'5"	5.3–4.3	5.6–4.6	5.9–4.7	5.12–4.10	6.6–5.1	6.9–5.8	6.10–5.9	6.12–5.10
4'6"	5.5–4.6	5.7–4.9	5.11–4.10	6.1–4.12	6.7–5.4	6.10–5.9	6.11–5.10	7.1–5.12
4'7"	5.7–4.8	5.8–4.12	6.0–4.13	6.4–5.0	6.8–5.6	6.11–5.10	6.12–5.11	7.1–5.13
4'8"	5.9–4.10	5.10–5.1	6.3–5.2	6.7–5.3	6.10–5.8	6.12–5.11	6.13–5.12	7.2–6.1
4'9"	5.13–4.12	6.0–5.4	6.6–5.5	6.10–5.6	6.13–5.11	7.1–6.0	7.2–6.1	7.3–6.4
4'10"	6.2–5.0	6.3–5.6	6.9–5.7	6.13–5.9	7.2–6.0	7.4–6.3	7.5–6.4	7.6–6.6
4'11"	6.5–5.5	6.6–5.8	6.12–5.10	7.2–5.12	7.5–6.3	7.7–6.6	7.8–6.7	7.10–6.8
5'0"	6.8–5.10	6.9–5.11	7.0–5.12	7.5–6.2	7.8–6.6	7.10–6.9	7.12–6.10	7.13–6.11
5'1"	6.11–5.12	6.13–6.0	7.3–6.2	7.8–6.4	7.11–6.10	7.13–6.13	8.0–7.0	8.1–7.1
5'2"	7.0–6.0	7.4–6.2	7.6–6.5	7.11–6.8	8.0–7.0	8.3–7.3	8.5–7.4	8.6–7.5
5'3"	7.3–6.3	7.6–6.5	7.8–6.8	8.0–6.12	8.3–7.3	8.10–7.5	8.11–7.6	8.12–7.7
5'4"	7.5–6.6	7.8–6.9	7.11–6.13	8.3–7.2	8.6–7.6	8.12–7.8	9.0–7.9	9.2–7.10
5'5"	7.7–6.10	7.10–7.0	7.13–7.4	8.6–7.6	8.9–7.9	9.0–7.11	9.3–7.12	9.5–7.13
5'6"	–	7.13–7.5	8.4–7.8	8.9–7.10	8.12–7.13	9.5–8.1	9.6–8.2	9.8–8.3
5'7"	–	8.2–7.9	8.8–7.12	8.12–8.0	9.1–8.4	9.8–8.6	9.9–8.7	9.11–8.8
5'8"	–	–	8.12–8.2	9.1–8.5	9.4–8.7	9.9–8.8	9.12–8.9	10.0–8.10
5'9"	–	–	9.1–8.6	9.4–8.10	9.7–8.12	10.1–9.0	10.2–9.2	10.4–9.3
5'10"	–	–	–	9.8–9.1	9.11–9.2	10.3–9.4	10.6–9.6	10.8–9.7
5'11"	–	–	–	9.12–9.6	10.1–9.7	10.6–9.9	10.10–9.10	10.12–9.11
6'0"	–	–	–	–	10.5–9.10	10.8–9.12	10.11–10.0	11.2–10.1
6'1"	–	–	–	–	10.10–10.0	11.1–10.2	11.4–10.4	11.6–10.5

BOYS

Height	Age 10	11	12	13	14	15	16	17
3'11"	3.10–3.6	–	–	–	–	–	–	–
4'0"	3.13–3.8	4.1–3.9	–	–	–	–	–	–
4'1"	4.1–3.10	4.2–3.11	–	–	–	–	–	–
4'2"	4.3–3.12	4.4–3.13	4.6–4.0	–	–	–	–	–
4'3"	4.6–4.2	4.7–4.3	4.8–4.4	–	–	–	–	–
4'4"	4.9–4.4	4.10–4.5	4.11–4.6	–	–	–	–	–
4'5"	4.12–4.7	4.13–4.8	5.0–4.9	5.1–4.10	–	–	–	–
4'6"	5.1–4.9	5.2–4.10	5.3–4.11	5.5–4.12	–	–	–	–
4'7"	5.5–5.0	5.6–5.1	5.7–5.2	5.9–5.3	5.10–5.4	–	–	–
4'8"	5.10–5.5	5.11–5.6	5.13–5.7	6.1–5.8	6.3–5.9	–	–	–
4'9"	5.12–5.9	6.0–5.10	6.2–5.11	6.5–5.13	6.6–6.0	6.11–6.2	–	–
4'10"	6.2–5.12	6.3–5.13	6.4–6.0	6.9–6.4	6.10–6.5	7.2–6.8	7.10–6.11	–
4'11"	6.6–6.2	6.7–6.3	6.8–6.4	6.13–6.9	7.0–6.10	7.6–6.12	7.12–7.0	8.2–7.3
5'0"	6.10–6.6	6.11–6.7	6.12–6.8	7.3–6.12	7.5–7.0	7.10–7.2	8.1–7.4	8.5–7.7
5'1"	6.13–6.9	7.1–6.11	7.2–6.12	7.7–7.2	7.10–7.3	8.0–7.5	8.4–7.8	8.8–7.10
5'2"	7.3–6.13	7.5–7.1	7.6–7.2	7.11–7.6	8.1–7.8	8.4–7.10	8.8–7.12	8.11–8.0
5'3"	7.6–7.2	7.8–7.4	7.10–7.6	8.1–7.9	8.13–8.6	8.8–8.1	8.11–8.2	9.0–8.5
5'4"	7.9–7.4	7.11–7.6	8.0–7.10	8.5–7.13	8.9–8.2	8.11–8.4	9.1–8.6	9.4–8.7
5'5"	7.12–7.7	8.0–7.9	8.4–8.0	8.9–8.3	8.13–8.5	9.1–8.7	9.4–8.10	9.7–8.11
5'6"	–	8.4–7.13	8.8–8.4	8.13–8.6	9.3–8.9	9.5–8.11	9.7–9.0	9.11–9.1
5'7"	–	8.8–8.3	8.12–8.7	9.4–8.9	9.7–8.13	9.8–9.2	9.10–9.4	10.1–9.5
5'8"	–	–	9.2–8.10	9.7–8.12	9.11–9.3	9.12–9.6	10.0–9.7	10.5–9.8
5'9"	–	–	9.6–8.13	9.10–9.1	10.0–9.7	10.2–9.10	10.4–9.12	10.9–9.13
5'10"	–	–	–	10.0–9.4	10.5–9.11	10.5–10.0	11.1–10.1	11.6–10.2
5'11"	–	–	–	10.4–9.9	10.9–10.1	11.1–10.4	11.6–10.5	12.0–10.6
6'0"	–	–	–	–	10.13–10.6	11.2–10.8	11.9–10.9	12.2–10.10
6'1"	–	–	–	–	11.3–10.10	11.9–10.10	11.12–10.13	12.7–11.0
6'2"	–	–	–	–	–	11.11–11.3	12.2–11.4	13.0–11.5
6'3"	–	–	–	–	–	12.7–11.8	12.12–11.9	13.8–11.10
6'4"	–	–	–	–	–	13.3–11.13	13.9–12.0	13.13–12.1

Food and Nutrition

Food contains proteins, carbohydrates, fats, water, vitamins and minerals. Nutrition is the way your body takes in and uses these ingredients to maintain proper functioning.

Recently issued dietary guidelines recommended substantial cuts in the amount of fat, sugar and salt we eat. They also stress the importance of increasing the amount of fibre consumed. (Adults should try to eat at least 30g a day.)

A healthy diet is a balanced one that provides all the nutrients a body requires. These can be divided into the following 6 groups.

Protein

Proteins, composed of amino acids, are indispensable in the diet. They build, maintain, and repair the body. Best sources: eggs, milk, fish, meat, poultry, soybeans, nuts. High quality proteins such as eggs, meat, or fish supply all 8 amino acids needed in the diet.

Fats

Fats provide energy by furnishing calories to the body, and by carrying vitamins A, D, E, and K. They are the most concentrated source of energy in the diet. Best sources: butter, margarine, salad oils, nuts, cream, egg yolks, most cheeses, lard, meat.

Carbohydrates

Carbohydrates provide energy for body function and activity by supplying immediate calories. The carbohydrate group includes sugars, starches, fiber, and starchy vegetables. Best sources: grains, legumes, nuts, potatoes, fruits.

Water

Water dissolves and transports other nutrients throughout the body, aiding the processes of digestion, absorption, circulation, and excretion. It helps regulate body temperature.

Vitamins

Vitamin A – promotes good eyesight and helps keep the skin and mucous membranes resistant to infection. Best sources: liver, carrots, sweet potatoes, kale, turnips, fortified milk.

Vitamin B1 (thiamine) – prevents beriberi. Essential to carbohydrate metabolism and health of nervous system.

Vitamin B2 (riboflavin) – protects skin, mouth, eye, eyelids, and mucous membranes. Essential to protein and energy metabolism. Best sources: liver, milk, meat, poultry, broccoli, mushrooms.

Vitamin B6 (pyridoxine) – important in the regulation of the central nervous system and in protein metabolism. Best sources: whole grains, meats, nuts, brewers' yeast.

Vitamin B12(cobalamin) – needed to form red blood cells. Best sources: liver, meat, fish, eggs, soybeans.

Niacin – maintains the health of skin, tongue, and digestive system. Best sources: poultry, peanuts, fish, offal, enriched flour and bread.

Other B vitamins – biotin, choline, folic acid (folacin), inositol, PABA (para-aminobenzoic acid), pantothenic acid.

Vitamin C (ascorbic acid) – maintains collagen, a protein necessary for the formation of skin, ligaments, and bones. It helps heal wounds and mend fractures, and aids in resisting some types of virus and bacterial infections. Best sources: citrus fruits and juices, turnips, broccoli, Brussels sprouts, potatoes and sweet potatoes, tomatoes, cabbage.

Vitamin D – important for bone development. Best sources: sunlight, fortified milk and milk products, fish-liver oils, egg yolks, offal.

Vitamin E (tocopherol) – helps protect red blood cells. Best sources: vegetable oils, wheat germ, whole grains, eggs, peanuts, offal, margarine, green leafy vegetables.

Vitamin K – necessary for formation of prothrombin, which helps blood to clot. Also made by intestinal bacteria. Best dietary sources: green leafy vegetables, tomatoes.

Minerals

Calcium – the most abundant mineral in the body, works with phosphorus in building and maintaining bones and teeth. Best sources: milk and milk products, cheese, and blackstrap molasses.

Phosphorus – the 2d most abundant mineral, performs more functions than any other mineral, and plays a part in nearly every chemical reaction in the body. Best source: whole grains, cheese, milk.

Iron – Necessary for the formation of myoglobin, which transports oxygen to muscle tissue, and hemoglobin, which transports oxygen in the blood. Best sources: offal, beans, green leafy vegetables, and shellfish.

Other minerals – chromium, cobalt, copper, fluorine, iodine, magnesium, manganese, molybdenum, potassium, selenium, sodium, sulfur, and zinc.

Recommended Daily Dietary Allowances

Source: Food and Nutrition Board, Natl. Academy of Sciences – Natl. Research Council; 1989

				Fat soluble vitamins					Water soluble vitamins							Minerals						
	Age (years) and sex group	Weight (lbs.)	Protein (grams)	Vitamin A[1]	Vitamin D[2]	Vitamin E[3]	Vitamin K	Vitamin C	Thiamin (mg.)	Riboflavin (mg.)	Niacin (mg.)[4]	Vitamin B_6 (mg.)	Folate (micrograms)	Vitamin B_{12} (micrograms)	Calcium (mg.)	Phosphorus (mg.)	Magnesium (mg.)	Iron (mg.)	Zinc (mg.)	Iodine (micrograms)	Selenium (micrograms)
Infants . .	to 5 mos.	13	13	375	7.5	3	5	30	0.3	0.4	5	0.3	25	0.3	400	300	40	6	5	40	10
	to 1 yr.	20	14	375	10	4	10	35	0.4	0.5	6	0.6	35	0.5	600	500	60	10	5	50	15
Children .	1-3	29	16	400	10	6	15	40	0.7	0.8	9	1.0	50	0.7	800	800	80	10	10	70	20
	4-6	44	24	500	10	7	20	45	0.9	1.1	12	1.1	75	1.0	800	800	120	10	10	90	20
	7-10	62	28	700	10	7	30	45	1.0	1.2	13	1.4	100	1.4	800	800	170	10	10	120	30
Males . . .	11-14	99	45	1000	10	10	45	50	1.3	1.5	17	1.7	150	2.0	1200	1200	270	12	15	150	40
	15-18	145	59	1000	10	10	65	60	1.5	1.8	20	2.0	200	2.0	1200	1200	400	12	15	150	50
	19-24	160	58	1000	10	10	70	60	1.5	1.7	19	2.0	200	2.0	1200	1200	350	10	15	150	70
	25-50	174	63	1000	5	10	80	60	1.5	1.7	19	2.0	200	2.0	800	800	350	10	15	150	70
	51+	170	63	1000	5	10	80	60	1.2	1.4	15	2.0	200	2.0	800	800	350	10	15	150	70
Females .	11-14	101	46	800	10	8	45	50	1.1	1.3	15	1.4	150	2.0	1200	1200	280	15	12	150	45
	15-18	120	44	800	10	8	55	60	1.1	1.3	15	1.5	180	2.0	1200	1200	300	15	12	150	50
	19-24	128	46	800	10	8	60	60	1.1	1.3	15	1.6	180	2.0	1200	1200	280	15	12	150	55
	25-50	138	50	800	5	8	65	60	1.1	1.3	15	1.6	180	2.0	800	800	280	15	12	150	55
	51+	143	50	800	5	8	65	60	1.0	1.2	13	1.6	180	2.0	800	800	280	10	12	150	55

(1) Retinol equivalents. (2) Micrograms of cholecalciferol. (3) Milligrams alpha-tocopherol equivalents. (4) Niacin equivalents.

Food Poisoning[1]

United Kingdom

Source: CSO

	Rates per million population				
	1971	1976	1981	1986	1991
United Kingdom	149	200	231	338	674
North	104	79	260	283	787
Yorkshire & Humberside	107	386	209	292	962
East Midlands	81	162	177	274	648
East Anglia	111	109	114	272	457
South East	131	159	203	362	686
South West	199	220	164	356	597
West Midlands	122	144	190	264	614
North West	175	186	234	331	585
England	133	184	201	323	678
Wales	211	192	188	437	941
Scotland	289	384	571	476	576
Northern Ireland	70	133	88	174	399

(1) Formal notifications in England and Wales; formal notifications and cases ascertained by other means in Scotland and Northern Ireland.

Alcohol Units

In recent years the medical profession has devised a method of quantifying alcohol intake, which allows drinkers to keep a more accurate record of their consumption. The following drinks are each worth 1 unit:

- ½ pint ordinary beer
- 30 ml/1 fl oz of spirits
- small glass (2 fl oz) of sherry or fortified wine
- glass of wine (4 fl oz)

To keep within a safe limit men should drink no more than 21 units a week, and women no more than 14 units. If you are consuming more than these recommended limits on a regular basis, try cutting down by, say, 5 units a week, and allowing yourself no more than 4 "drinking days".

Alcohol Consumption[1]

England & Wales

Source: CSO

	Units[2] of alcohol			
	Males		Females	
	1987	1989	1987	1989
Professional	11.4	10.2	4.3	5.3
Managerial and junior professional	15.4	15.0	6.1	5.3
Other non-manual	14.0	11.8	5.3	3.5
Skilled manual	15.4	13.1	4.6	4.1
Semi-skilled manual	12.5	16.3	3.4	3.2
Unskilled manual	17.3	14.8	3.7	4.1
All persons aged 16 and over	14.5	13.9	4.8	4.2

(1) Average number of units consumed in the seven days before interview. (2) See above. One unit is roughly equivalent to 8½ grammes of absolute alcohol.

Cancer's 7 Warning Signals*

Source: American Cancer Society

1. A change in bowel or bladder habits.
2. A sore that does not heal.
3. Unusual bleeding or discharge.
4. Thickening or lump in breast or elsewhere.
5. Indigestion or difficulty in swallowing.
6. Obvious change in wart or mole.
7. Nagging cough or hoarseness.

*If you have a warning signal, see your doctor.

Cancer Prevention

Source: American Cancer Society

PRIMARY PREVENTION: steps that can be taken to avoid those factors that might lead to the development of cancer.

Smoking The Royal College of Physicians estimates that around 100,000 deaths in the UK each year are caused by smoking. In fact, smoking accounts for about 30% of all cancer deaths. Those who smoke two or more packets of cigarettes a day have lung cancer mortality rates 15-25 times greater than non-smokers.

Nutrition Risk for colon, breast and uterine cancers increases in obese people. High-fat diets may contribute to the development of cancers of the breast, colon and prostate. High-fibre foods may help reduce the risk of colon cancer. A varied diet containing plenty of vegetables and fruits rich in vitamins A and C may reduce the risk for a wide range of cancers. Salt-cured, smoked and nitrite-cured foods have been linked to oesophageal and stomach cancer.

Sunlight Most of the non-melanoma skin cancer diagnosed each year in is considered to be sun-related. Such exposure is a major factor in the development of melanoma, and the incidence increases for those living near the Equator. There are about 3,120 new cases of malignant melanoma in the UK each year.

Alcohol Oral cancer and cancers of the larynx, throat, oesophagus, and liver occur more frequently among heavy drinkers of alcohol, especially when accompanied by cigarette smoking or chewing tobacco.

Smokeless tobacco Use of chewing tobacco or snuff increases the risk of cancers of the mouth, larynx, throat and oesophagus.

Oestrogen Oestrogen treatment to control menopausal symptoms can increase the risk of endometrial cancer. However, including progesterone in oestrogen replacement therapy helps to minimize this risk. Use of oestrogen by menopausal women needs careful discussion between the women and their doctors, while research continues.

Radiation Excessive exposure to ionizing radiation can increase cancer risk. Most medical and dental X rays are adjusted to deliver the lowest dose possible without sacrificing image quality. Excessive radon exposure in the home may increase the risk of lung cancer, especially in cigarette smokers. If levels are found to be too high, remedial actions should be taken.

Occupational hazards Exposure to several different industrial agents (including nickel, chromate, asbestos and vinyl chloride) increases the risk of various cancers. Risk of lung cancer from asbestos is greatly increased when combined with smoking.

SECONDARY PREVENTION: steps to be taken to diagnose a cancer or precursor as early as possible after it has developed.

Breast examination British health authorities recommend regular breast self-examination, preferably at the same time each month. Any unusual changes should be notified to a GP. A special X-ray called a mammogram is available free to all women between the ages of 50 and 64, the age range which appears most susceptible to breast cancer. The test may be offered earlier if a woman's medical background warrants it.

Smear test For cervical cancer, women aged 20-64 who are or have been sexually active should have a cervical cancer smear test and pelvic examination at least every 5 years. Women in whom abnormalities have been found may be offered smears at more frequent intervals – usually every year.

Cervical Cancer: Deaths and Screening

Great Britain

Source: CSO

Thousands and percentages

	1976	1981	1983	1984	1985	1986	1987–88	1988–89
Deaths	2.4	2.2	2.2	2.1	2.2	2.2	2.1	2.1
Smears taken	2,923	3,442	3,669	3,911	4,455	4,468	4,754	5,032
Smears as a percentage of women aged 15 and over	13.3	15.2	16.0	17.0	19.3	19.2	20.4	21.5

Heart and Blood Vessel Disease

Source: American Heart Association, Dallas, and the Chest, Heart & Stroke Assn., London

Warning Signs of Heart Attack

- Uncomfortable pressure, fullness, squeezing or pain in the centre of the chest lasting two minutes or longer
- Pain may radiate to the shoulder, arm, neck or jaw
- Sweating may accompany pain or discomfort
- Nausea and vomiting may also occur
- Shortness of breath, dizziness, or fainting may accompany other signs

It is advisable to take immediate action at the onset of these symptoms. Delay may prove fatal.

Warning Signs of Stroke

- Sudden temporary weakness or numbness of face or limbs on one side of the body
- Temporary loss of speech, or trouble speaking or understanding speech
- Temporary dimness or loss of vision, particularly in one eye
- Unexplained dizziness, unsteadiness, or sudden falls

Some Major Risk Factors

Cholesterol – There is clear-cut evidence that high blood cholesterol levels can lead to coronary artery disease, and there is also some evidence that cholesterol may contribute to cerebral artery disease, particularly in young people. To avoid the danger it is advisable to reduce intake of foods rich in animal fats.

Cigarettes – Smokers of 20 cigarettes a day have more than twice the risk of heart attack and 3 times the risk of a stroke than non-smokers.

Contraceptive pill – Studies have shown that there is an increased risk of stroke among younger women taking the pill where there is a family history of arterial disease. There is also evidence that severe migraine sufferers taking the pill have an increased risk of stroke.

High blood pressure – This is known to increase the risk of stroke, heart attack, kidney failure and congestive heart failure. It is wise to have blood pressure checked every 4 years until the age of 40, then every 2 years thereafter.

High blood sugar – Strokes are more common, especially among women, where there is a personal or family history of diabetes.

Obesity – Excess weight often creates a tendency to high blood pressure (see above). Cholesterol levels may also be high, so it is worth restricting intake of fats and carbohydrates.

Smoking Behaviour of Children[1]

England & Wales

Source: CSO

Percentages and numbers

	1982	1986	1988[2]	1990[2]
Smoking behaviour (percentages)				
Boys				
Regular smokers	11	7	7	9
Occasional smokers	7	5	5	6
Used to smoke	11	10	8	7
Tried smoking once	26	23	23	22
Never smoked	45	55	58	56
Sample size (= 100%) (numbers)	1,460	1,676	1,489	1,643
Girls				
Regular smokers	11	12	9	11
Occasional smokers	9	5	5	6
Used to smoke	10	10	9	7
Tried smoking once	22	19	19	18
Never smoked	49	53	59	58
Sample size (= 100%) (numbers)	1,514	1,508	1,529	1,478

(1) Aged 11–15 years. (2) England only.

Effects of Commonly Abused Drugs

Source: National Institute on Drug Abuse

Alcohol

Effects: Like sedatives, it is a central nervous system depressant. In small doses, it has a tranquilizing effect on most people, although it appears to stimulate others. Alcohol first acts on those parts of the brain which affect self-control and other learned behaviors, which often leads to the aggressive behavior associated with some people who drink.

Dangers: In large doses, alcohol can dull sensation and impair muscular coordination, memory, and judgment. Taken in larger quantities over a long period of time, alcohol can damage the liver and heart and can cause permanent brain damage. A large dose of alcohol can interfere with the part of the brain that controls breathing. The respiratory failure which results can bring death. Delirium tremens, the most extreme manifestation of alcohol withdrawal, can also cause death.

Risks during pregnancy: Women who drink heavily during pregnancy (more than 3 ounces of alcohol per day or about 2 mixed drinks) run a higher risk of delivering babies with physical, mental and behavioral abnormalities.

Dependence: Repeated drinking produces tolerance to the drug's effects and dependence. The drinker's body then needs alcohol to function. Once dependent, drinkers experience withdrawal symptoms when they stop drinking.

Hallucinogens ("psychodelics")

What are they? Drugs which affect perception, sensation, thinking, self-awareness, and emotion.

(1) **LSD (lysergic acid diethylamide),** a synthetic, is converted from lysergic acid which comes from fungus (ergot).

Effects: Vary greatly according to dosage, personality of the user, and conditions under which the drug is used. Basically, it causes changes in sensation. Vision alters; users describe changes in depth perception and in the meaning of the perceived object. Illusions and hallucinations often occur. Physical reactions range from minor changes such as dilated pupils, a rise in temperature and heartbeat, or a slight increase in blood pressure, to tremors. High doses can greatly alter the state of consciousness. Heavy use of the drug may produce flashbacks, recurrences of some features of a previous LSD experience days or months after the last dose.

Dangers: After taking LSD, a person loses control over normal thought processes. Although many perceptions are pleasant, others may cause panic or may make a person believe that he or she cannot be harmed. Longer-term harmful reactions include anxiety and depression, or "breaks from reality" which may last from a few days to months. Heavy users sometimes develop signs of organic brain damage, such as impaired memory and attention span, mental confusion, and difficulty with abstract thinking. It is not known yet whether such mental changes are permanent.

(2) **Mescaline:** Comes from peyote cactus and its effects are similar to those of LSD.

Marijuana ("grass", "pot", "weed")

What is it? A common plant (*Cannabis sativa*), its chief psychoactive ingredient is delta-9-tetrahydrocannabinol, or THC. The amount of THC in the marijuana cigarette (joint) primarily determines its psychoactive potential.

Effects: Most users experience an increase in heart rate, reddening of the eyes, and dryness in the mouth and throat. Studies indicate the drug temporarily impairs short-term memory, alters sense of time, and reduces the ability to perform tasks requiring concentration, swift reactions, and coordination. Many feel that their hearing, vision, and skin sensitivity are enhanced by the drug, but these reports have not been objectively confirmed by research. Feelings of euphoria, relaxation, altered sense of body image, and bouts of exaggerated laughter are also commonly reported.

Dangers: Scientists believe marijuana can be particularly harmful to lungs because users typically inhale the unfiltered smoke deeply and hold it in their lungs for prolonged periods of time. Marijuana smoke has been found to have more cancer-causing agents than are found in cigarette smoke (see above). Because marijuana use increases heart rate as much as 50% and brings on chest pain in people who have a poor blood supply to the heart (and more rapidly than tobacco smoke does), doctors believe people with heart conditions or who are at high risk for heart ailments, should not use marijuana. Findings also suggest that regular use may reduce fertility in women and that men with marginal fertility or endocrine functioning should avoid marijuana use.

Risks during pregnancy: Research is limited, but scientists believe marijuana which crosses the placental barrier, may have a toxic effect on embryos and fetuses.

Bad reactions: Most commonly reported immediate adverse reaction to marijuana use is the "acute panic anxiety reaction," usually described as an exaggeration of normal marijuana effects in which intense fears of losing control accompany severe anxiety. The symptoms often disappear in a few hours when the acute drug effects have worn off.

Dependence: Tolerance to marijuana, the need to take more and more of the drug over time to get the original effect, has been proven in humans and animals. Physical dependence has been demonstrated in research subjects who ingested an amount equal to smoking 10 to 20 joints a day. When the drug was discontinued, subjects experienced withdrawal symptoms— irritability, sleep disturbances, loss of appetite and weight, sweating, and stomach upset.

Narcotics

What are they? Drugs that relieve pain and often induce sleep. The opiates, which are narcotics, include opium and drugs derived from opium, such as morphine, codeine, and heroin. Narcotics also include certain synthetic chemicals that have a morphine-like action, such as methadone.

Which are abused? Heroin ("junk," "smack") accounts for 85% of narcotic abuse in the UK. Sometimes medicinal narcotics are also abused, including paregoric containing codeine, and methadone, meperidine, and morphine.

Dangers: Physical dangers depend on the specific drug, its source, and the way it is used. Most medical problems are caused by the uncertain dosage level, use of unsterile needles and other paraphernalia, contamination of the drug, or combination of a narcotic with other drugs, rather than by the effects of the heroin (or another narcotic) itself. The life expectancy of a heroin addict who injects the drug intravenously is significantly lower than that of one who does not. An overdose can result in death. If, for example, an addict obtains pure heroin and is not tolerant of the dose, he or she may die minutes after injecting it. Infections from unsterile needles, solutions, syringes, cause many diseases. Serum hepatitis is common. Skin abscesses, inflammation of the veins and congestion of the lungs also occur.

Dependence: Anyone can become heroin dependent if he or she takes the drug regularly. Although environmental stress and problems of coping have often been considered as factors that lead to heroin addiction, physicians do not agree that some people just have an "addictive personality" and are prone to dependence. All we know for certain is that continued use of heroin causes dependence.

Withdrawal: When a heroin-dependent person stops taking the drug, withdrawal begins within 4-6 hours after the last injection. Full-blown withdrawal symptoms—which include shaking, sweating, vomiting, a running nose and eyes, muscle aches, chills, abdominal pains, and diarrhea—begin some 12-16 hours after the last injection. The intensity of symptoms depends on the degree of dependence.

Phencyclidine (PCP or "angel dust")

What is it? A drug that was developed as a surgical anesthetic for humans in the late 1950s. PCP was soon restricted to its only current legal use as a veterinary anesthetic and tranquilizer.

Effects: Vary according to dosage. Low doses may provide the usual releasing effects of many psychoactive drugs. A floaty euphoria is described, sometimes associated with a feeling of numbness (part of the drug's anesthetic effects). Increased doses produce an excited, confused intoxification, which may include muscle rigidity, loss of concentration and memory, visual disturbances, delirium, feelings of isolation, convulsions, speech impairment, violent behavior, fear of death, and changes in the user's perceptions of their bodies.

Dangers: PCP intoxication can produce violent and bizarre behavior even in people not otherwise prone to such behavior. Violent actions may be directed at themselves or others and often account for serious injuries and death. More people die from accidents caused by the erratic behavior produced by the drug than from the drug's direct effect on the body. A temporary, schizophrenic-like psychosis, which can last for days or weeks, has also occurred in users of moderate or higher doses.

Sedatives (Tranquillizers, sleeping pills)

What are they? Drugs which depress the central nervous system, more appropriately called sedative-hypnotics because they include drugs which calm the nerves (the sedation effect) and produce sleep (the hypnotic effect). Of drugs in this class, barbiturates ("barbs", "downers", "reds") have the highest rate of abuse and misuse. The most commonly abused barbiturates include pentobarbital (Nembutal), secobarbital (Seconal), and amobarbital (Amytal). These all have legitimate use as sedatives or sleeping aids. Among the most commonly abused nonbarbiturate drugs are glutethimide (Doriden), meprobamate (Miltown), methyprylon (Noludar), ethchlorvynol (Placidyl), and methaqualone (Sopor, Quaalude). These are prescribed to help people sleep. Benzodiazepines, especially diazepam (Valium), prescribed to relieve anxiety, are commonly abused, and their rate of abuse and misuse is increasing.

Dangers: These can kill. Barbiturate overdose is implicated in nearly one-third of all reported drug-induced deaths. Accidental deaths may occur when a user takes an unintended larger or repeated dose of sedatives because of confusion or impairment in judgment caused by initial intake of the drug. With lesser, but still large doses, users can go into coma. Moderately large doses often produce an intoxicated stupor. Users' speech is often slurred, memory vague, and judgment impaired. Taken along with alcohol, the combination can be fatal. Tranquilizers act somewhat differently from other sedatives and are considered less hazardous. But even by themselves, or in combination with other drugs (especially alcohol and other sedatives) they can be quite dangerous.

Dependence: Potential for dependence is greatest with barbiturates, but all sedatives, tranquilizers, can be addictive. Barbiturate withdrawal is often more severe than heroin withdrawal.

Stimulants ("Uppers")

What are they? A class of drugs which stimulate the central nervous system and produce an increase in alertness and activity.

(1) **Amphetamines** promote a feeling of alertness and increase in speech and general physical activity. Under medical supervision, the drugs are taken to control appetite.

Effects and dangers: Even small, infrequent doses can produce toxic effects in some people. Restlessness, anxiety, mood swings, panic, circulatory and cardiac disturbances, paranoid thoughts, hallucinations, convulsions, and coma have all been reported. Heavy, frequent doses can produce brain damage which results in speed disturbances and difficulty in turning thoughts into words. Death can result from injected amphetamine overdose. Long-term users often have acne resembling a measles rash; trouble with teeth, gums and nails, and dry lifeless hair. As heavy users who inject amphetamines accumulate larger amounts of the drug in their bodies, the resulting toxicity can produce amphetamine psychosis. People in this extremely suspicious, paranoid state, frequently exhibit bizarre, sometimes violent behavior.

Dependence: People with a history of sustained low-dose use quite often become dependent and feel they need the drug to get by.

(2) **Cocaine** is a stimulant extracted from the leaves of the coca plant. It is available in many forms, the most

available of which is cocaine hydrochloride. Cocaine hydrochloride is often used medically as a local anesthetic, but is also sold illegally on the street in large pieces called rocks. Street cocaine is a white, crystal-like powder that is most commonly inhaled or snorted, though some users ingest, inject, or smoke a form of the drug called freebase or crack.

Freebase and **crack** are formed by chemically converting street cocaine to a purified substance that is more suitable for smoking. Smoking freebase or crack produces a shorter, but more intense high than other ways of using the drug. It is the most direct and rapid means of getting the drug to the brain, and because larger amounts are reaching the brain more quickly, the effects of the drug are more intense and the dangers associated with its use are greater.

Ice, or crystal methamphetamine, is another stimulant that can be smoked and which has many of the same euphoric and adverse effects as crack.

Effects: The drug's usual effects are dilated pupils and increased blood pressure, heart rate, breathing rate, and body temperature. Even small doses may elicit feelings of euphoria; illusions of increased mental and physical strength and sensory awareness; and a decrease in hunger, pain, and the perceived need for sleep. Large doses significantly magnify these effects, sometimes causing irrational behavior and confusion.

Dangers: Paranoia is not an uncommon response to heavy doses. Psychosis may be triggered in users prone to mental instability. Repeated inhalation often results in nostril and nasal membrane irritation. Some regular users have reported feelings of restlessness, irritability, and anxiety. Others have experienced hallucinations of touch, sight, taste, or smell. When people stop using cocaine after taking it for a long time, they frequently become depressed. They tend to fight off this depression by taking more cocaine, just as in the up/down amphetamine cycle. Cocaine is toxic. Although few people realize it, overdose deaths, though rare, have occurred as a result of injecting, ingesting and even snorting cocaine. The deaths are a result of seizures followed by respiratory arrest and coma, or sometimes by cardiac arrest. Other dangers associated with cocaine include the risk of infection, such as hepatitis, resulting from the use of unsterile needles and the risk of fire or explosion resulting from the use of volatile substances necessary for freebase preparation.

Dependence: Cocaine is not a narcotic; no evidence suggests that it produces a physical dependence. However, cocaine is psychologically a very dangerous, dependence-producing drug. Smoking freebase or crack increases this risk of dependence.

(3) **Caffeine** may be the world's most popular drug. It is primarily consumed in coffee and tea, but is also found in cocoa, cola and other soft drinks, as well as in many over-the-counter medicines.

Effects: Two to four cups of coffee increase heart rate, body temperature, urine production, and gastric juice secretion. Caffeine can also raise sugar levels and cause tremors, loss of coordination, decreased appetite, and postponement of fatigue. It can interfere with the depth of sleep and the amount of dream sleep by causing more rapid eye movement (REM) sleep at first, but less than average over an entire night. Extremely high doses may cause diarrhea, sleeplessness, trembling, severe headache, and nervousness.

Dependence: A form of physical dependence may result with regular consumption. In such cases, withdrawal symptoms may occur if caffeine use is stopped or interrupted. These symptoms include headache, irritability, and fatigue. Tolerance may develop with the use of six to eight cups or more a day. A regular user of caffeine who has developed a tolerance may also develop a craving for the drug's effects.

Dangers: Poisonous doses of caffeine have occurred occasionally and have resulted in convulsions, breathing failure, and even death. However, it is almost impossible to die from drinking too much coffee or tea. The deaths that have been reported have resulted from the misuse of tablets containing caffeine.

Tobacco

Effects and dangers: Nicotine, the active ingredient in tobacco, acts as a stimulant on the heart and nervous system. When tobacco smoke is inhaled the immediate effects on the body are a faster heart beat and elevated blood pressure. These effects, however, are quickly dissipated. Tar (in the smoke) contains many carcinogens. These compounds, many of which are in polluted air but are found in vastly greater quantities in cigarette smoke, have been identified as major causes of cancer and respiratory difficulties. Even relatively young smokers can have shortness of breath, nagging cough, or develop cardiovascular and respiratory difficulties. A third principal component of cigarette smoke, carbon monoxide, is also a cause of some of the more serious health effects of smoking. Carbon monoxide can reduce the blood's ability to carry oxygen to body tissues and can promote the development of arteriosclerosis (hardening of the arteries). Long-term effects of smoking cigarettes are emphysema, chronic bronchitis, heart disease, lung cancer, and cancer in other parts of the body.

Risks during pregnancy: Women who smoke during pregnancy are more likely to have babies that weigh less.

New Drug Addicts Notified

United Kingdom

Source: CSO

Numbers

	1973	1981	1986	1989	1990	1991
Type of drug						
Heroin	508	1,660	4,855	4,883	5,819	6,328
Methadone	328	431	659	682	1,469	2,180
Dipipanone	28	473	116	109	154	155
Cocaine	132	174	520	527	633	882
Morphine	226	355	343	259	296	185
Pethidine	27	45	33	36	39	37
Dextromoradine	28	59	97	75	78	89
Opium	0	0	23	15	14	12
Others	2	4	4	1	4	1
Total addicts notified[1]	**806**	**2,248**	**5,325**	**5,639**	**6,923**	**8,007**

(1) As an addict can be reported as addicted to more than one notifiable drug, the figures for individual drugs cannot be added together to produce totals.

Contraception Methods[1]

Great Britain

Source: CSO

Percentages

	1976[2]	1983[3,4]	1986[3]	1991[3]
Non-surgical				
Pill	29	28	26	23
IUD	6	6	8	5
Condom	14	13	13	16
Cap/Diaphragm	2	1	2	1

(Continued)

	1976[2]	1983[3,4]	1986[3]	1991[3]
				Percentages
Non-surgical *(Continued)*				
Withdrawal	5	4	4	3
Safe period	1	1	2	1
Other	1	1	1	1
Surgical				
Female sterilization	7	11	11	12
Male sterilization	6	10	12	13
Total using at least one method	68	75	75	70

(1) Women aged 16–49. (2) Family Formation Survey, 1976. (3) General Household Survey, 1983, 1986 and 1991. (4) Women aged 18–44.

Abortions

England & Wales

Source: CSO

Percentages and thousands

	1971	1976	1981	1986	1991
Single women					
Under 16	5.2	6.7	5.0	4.2	2.7
16–19	39.2	44.7	42.7	35.2	26.9
20–34	52.3	45.5	50.2	58.6	67.6
35–44	1.5	1.5	1.7	1.9	2.8
45 and over	0.0	0.0	0.0	0.0	0.0
Age not known	1.7	1.5	0.4	0.0	–
Total (=100%) (thousands)	**44.3**	**50.9**	**70.0**	**93.0**	**118.9**
Married women					
Under 16	–	–	–	–	–
16–19	1.4	2.3	2.0	1.5	1.2
20–34	63.5	65.7	66.5	67.8	69.6
35–44	32.1	29.1	30.0	29.8	28.4
45 and over	0.9	1.0	1.0	0.8	0.9
Age not known	2.0	1.9	0.5	0.0	–
Total (=100%) (thousands)	**41.5**	**40.3**	**42.4**	**38.2**	**39.2**

Selected Sexually Transmitted Diseases

United Kingdom

Source: CSO

Thousands

	1971	1981	1986	1991[3]
New cases seen				
Male				
Syphilis	2	3	2	1
Gonorrhoea	43	37	28	13
Herpes simplex	3[1]	7	11	11
Non-specific genital infection	65	99	119	80
Female				
Syphilis	1	1	1	1
Gonorrhoea	20	21	18	8
Herpes simplex	1[1]	5	9	11
Non-specific genital infection	14[2]	33	56	44

(1) England and Wales only. (2) Excludes Scotland. (3) 1990 for England, but 1991–92 for Wales and Northern Ireland and 1991 for Scotland.

Organ Transplants

United Kingdom

Source: CSO

Numbers

	Organ transplanted			
	Heart & lung	Heart	Kidney	Liver
1981	0	24	905	11
1982	0	36	1,033	21
1983	1	53	1,144	20
1984	10	116	1,443	51
1985	37	137	1,336	88
1986	51	176	1,493	127
1987	72	243	1,485	172
1988	101	274	1,575	241
1989	94	295	1,732	295
1990	95	329	1,730	359

AIDS Cases and Related Deaths and HIV Antibody Positive Reports

United Kingdom: to end June 1992

Source: CSO

Numbers

	AIDS						
	Cases		Related deaths		HIV antibody positive reports		
	Males	Females	Males	Females	Males	Females	Not known
Exposure category							
Sexual intercourse							
between men	4,681	–	2,981	–	10,761	–	–
between men and women	340	219	172	96	1,011	1,117	12
Injecting drug use (IDU)	291	80	174	51	1,746	694	9
Blood							
blood factor (e.g. haemophilia)	307	4	232	3	1,236	10	–
blood/tissue transfer (e.g. transfusion)	31	47	23	30	99	88	1
Mother to child	25	35	10	17	60	61	1
Other/undetermined	67	13	45	5	762	158	42
Total	**5,742**	**398**	**3,637**	**202**	**15,675**	**2,128**	**65**

National Health Service

The NHS was founded in 1948 to provide health care to all citizens of the United Kingdom, regardless of their ability to pay. The principles of the NHS were outlined in 1944 in the economist William Beveridge's report to the war-time coalition government – *Social Insurance and Allied Services*. After the war Beveridge's ideas met with considerable opposition from the medical profession, but this opposition was overcome by the persuasive Labour health minister, Aneurin Bevan.

The NHS is funded partly out of employers' and employees' National Insurance contributions and partly from general taxation. Some diagnostic services and treatments are free to patients requiring them; for other needs, such as spectacles, dentistry and drugs prescribed by GPs, most patients bear at least part of the cost. Often there are exemptions for such groups as children, pregnant women and those on income support.

Recent governments have introduced charges for certain previously free items such as eye tests. NHS consultations with GPs and specialists, as well as NHS hospital treatment as an in- or out-patient, remain free.

Around 10% of the British have private medical insurance, but there is interaction between the public and private sectors, with many consultants working for both. Virtually everyone, privately insured or not, is registered with a general practitioner (GP) under the NHS.

Administration of the Health Service

	Govt. dept. responsible	Administered locally by
England	Department of Health	Regional Health Authorities District Health Authorities
Wales	Welsh Office	District Health Authorities
Scotland	Scottish Office Home & Health Department	Health Boards
N. Ireland	Department of Health & Social Services in Northern Ireland	Area Health & Social Services Councils

Though widely admired overseas, the NHS comes in for perennial criticism at home because it is unable to keep up with demand. This problem is at least partly related to the increasing range of treatments available as medical science progresses, coupled with the needs of an ageing population.

While critics argue that the service is seriously underfunded, Conservative governments have sought to increase efficiency through administrative changes, some of which have brought allegations – vehemently denied – of "creeping privatization".

One year into its current term of office the government was coming in for criticism on two fronts. On the one hand there was widespread concern over rumours of plans to close specialist units and hospitals, notably Harefield, famous as the heart transplant centre. On the other hand it was claimed that the government was missing the opportunity for radical reform. Market incentives were being grafted on, piecemeal, to a centrally managed system, where some had hoped for the creation of a fully market-driven service.

Health Service Reforms

The National Health Service and Community Care Act of 1990 introduced a number of alterations to the way the health service is managed and funded, creating an "internal market" where money is supposed to follow patients. The provisions of the Act are as follows:

- Hospitals can opt to become "self-governing trusts" instead of being run by the local health authority.
- Large GP practices can become budget-holders, funded by health authorities to buy services for patients from hospitals.
- Health authorities can purchase health care on behalf of local residents. Private and public hospitals are supposed to compete for the work, and contracts between health authorities and hospitals lay down quality, quantity and cost of services to be supplied.

The Patient's Charter (an offshoot of the Citizen's Charter) committed the NHS to keeping no one waiting for treatment for more than 2 years, but press reports in July 1992 claimed that only 4 out of 13 English health regions (the fourteenth region did not supply data) were succeeding in meeting this target.

Preventive Medicine

The current government places emphasis on the notion that prevention is better than cure. This conviction entails not only offering incentives to GPs to screen their patients for diseases such as cervical cancer, but also encouraging the public to take responsibility for their own health.

A White Paper, "The Health of the Nation", published in July 1992, outlined 5 major areas for action, in each of which it set targets for percentage reductions in the number of victims:

- heart disease and strokes
- cancers
- mental illness
- sexual health
- accidents

"Risk factor target" areas for action included:

- reduction of smoking
- improvements to diet
- reduction of the incidence of high blood-pressure
- containment of the HIV virus

The Paper outlined a promotional campaign, applying only to England. Critics of the proposals said they failed to tackle the connection between poor health and poverty, and that any campaign to reduce smoking would be undermined by the government's refusal to ban cigarette advertising.

UK Government Expenditure on the National Health Service

Years ended 31 March

Source: CSO

£ million

	1984/85	1985/86	1986/87	1987/88	1988/89	1989/90	1990/91	1991/92
Current expenditure								
Central government:								
Hospitals and Community Health Services[1] and Family Health Services[2]	14,976	15,932	17,086	18,870	21,110	22,197	25,540	28,278
Administration	473	475	553	627	682	855	979	1,113
less Payments by patients:								
Hospital services	−84	−92	−99	−106	−347	−407	−95	−369
Pharmaceutical services	−149	−158	−204	−256	−202	−242	−228	−240
Dental services	−197	−225	−261	−290	−282	−340	−395	−502
Ophthalmic services	−52	−14	−1	−1	–	–	–	–
Total	−482	−489	−565	−653	−831	−989	−743	−1,111
Departmental administration	137	142	171	193	206	223	264	320
Other central services	218	283	324	336	326	471	535	658
Total current expenditure	15,322	16,343	17,569	19,373	21,493	23,757	26,575	29,258
Capital expenditure								
Central government	990	1,091	1,160	1,212	1,309	2,071	2,040	2,028
Total expenditure								
Central government	16,312	17,434	18,729	20,585	22,802	24,828	28,615	31,286

(1) Including the school health service. (2) General Medical Services have been included in the expenditure of the Health Authorities. Therefore, Hospitals and Community Health Services and Family Practitioner Services (now Family Health Services) are not identifiable separately.

Distribution of NHS Waiting Time

England

Source: CSO

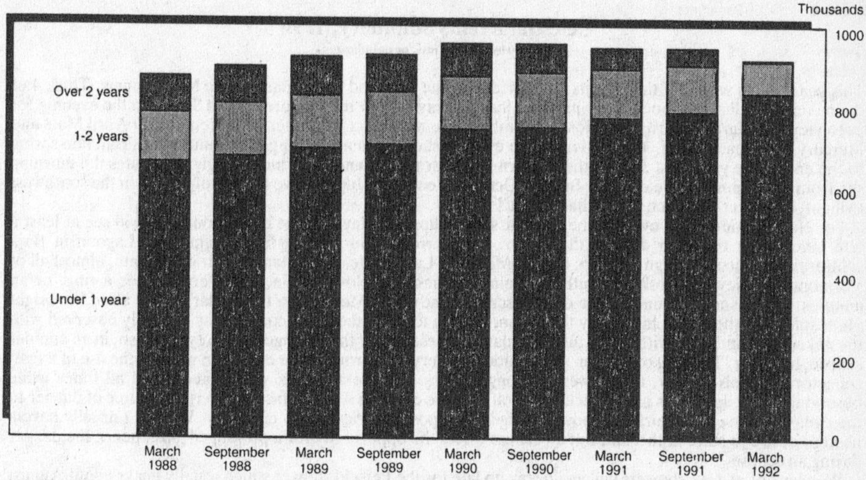

Family Practitioner and Dental Services

United Kingdom

Source: CSO

	General medical and pharmaceutical services						General dental services	
	Number of doctors[1] in practice (thousands)	Average number of patients per doctor (thousands)	Prescriptions dispensed[2] (millions)	Average total cost per prescription (£)	Average number of prescriptions per person	Average prescription cost[3] per person (£)	Number of dentists[4] in practice (thousands)	Average number of persons per dentist (thousands)
1961	23.6	2.25	233.2	0.41	4.7	1.9	11.9	4.4
1971	24.0	2.39	304.5	0.77	5.6	4.3	12.5	4.5
1981	27.5	2.15	370.0	3.46	6.6	23.0	15.2	3.7
1985	29.7	2.01	393.1	4.77	7.0	33.4	17.0	3.3
1986	30.2	1.99	397.5	5.11	7.0	36.0	17.3	3.3
1987	30.7	1.97	413.6	5.47	7.3	40.0	17.6	3.2
1988	31.2	1.94	427.7	5.91	7.5	44.1	18.0	3.2
1989	31.5	1.91	435.8	6.26	7.5	47.2	18.4	3.1
1990	31.6	1.89	446.6	6.68	7.8	52.1	18.6	3.2
1991	31.7	1.90	467.8	7.14	8.2	58.5	18.6	3.1

(1) Unrestricted principals only, i.e. medical practitioners who provide the full range of general medical services and whose lists are not limited to any particular group of persons. In a few cases (about 20), they may be relieved of the liability to have patients assigned to them or be exempted from liability to emergency calls out-of-hours from patients other than their own. Doctors may also practise in the general medical services as restricted principals, assistants or trainees. (2) Prescriptions dispensed by general practitioners are excluded. (3) Total cost including dispensing fees and cost. (4) Principals plus assistants.

Aspects of Primary Care Seen as in Need of Improvement

Source: SCPR's *British Social Attitudes* survey, 9th Report, ed. R. Jowell *et al.* (Dartmouth Publishing, 1992)

	1987	1989	1990	1991
Percentage saying that each is in need of improvement ('a lot' or 'some')*				
GPs' appointment systems	47	45	41	44
Amount of time GP gives to each patient	33	34	31	29
Waiting areas at GPs' surgeries	n/a	n/a	28	27
Being able to choose which GP to see	29	30	27	26
Quality of medical treatment by GPs	26	27	24	26

*The order of the items is according to the amount of criticism they attracted in 1991. The question about waiting areas was not asked in 1987 or 1989.

Access to the NHS

It has been suggested that the National Health Service should be available only to those with lower incomes. This would mean that contributions and taxes could be lower and most people would then take out medical insurance and pay for health care. Do you support or oppose this idea?

Source: SCPR's *British Social Attitudes* survey, 9th Report, ed. R. Jowell *et al.* (Dartmouth Publishing, 1992)

Percentages

	1983	1986	1989	1990
Support...................	29	27	22	22
Oppose....................	64	67	74	74

Satisfaction with the NHS

Source: SCPR's *British Social Attitudes* survey, 9th Report, ed. R. Jowell *et al.* (Dartmouth Publishing, 1992)

Percentages

	1983	1986	1989	1990	1991
Very satisfied	11	6	6	7	7
Quite satisfied........	44	34	30	30	33
Neither satisfied nor dissatisfied	20	19	18	15	19
Quite dissatisfied	18	23	25	27	23
Very dissatisfied......	7	16	21	20	18

ASTRONOMY AND CALENDAR

Edited by Dr Kenneth L. Franklin, Astronomer Emeritus, American Museum of Natural History-Hayden Planetarium

Celestial Events Summary, 1994

(Greenwich Mean Time, or as indicated)

This year begins with 3 of the planets conjoined with the Sun, and on January 11 the Moon is new. Thus, 4 of the naked-eye planetary bodies are invisible, leaving only Jupiter in the morning and Saturn in the evening for us to view. In March Saturn has 2 close encounters, one with Mars, the other with Mercury. In April Mars and Mercury brush each other. Venus gives a fine evening show from mid-spring to mid-autumn. From late spring to the end of the year, first Jupiter then Saturn liven our nights, and Mars increasingly dominates the morning sky from late summer to year's end. In early October Venus and Jupiter give us a bit of a show in the southwest twilight, but never get much closer than about 7°.

For North America *the* event is the annular solar eclipse of May 10. The entire continent will see at least a bite taken from the solar disc by the Moon. In a narrow band starting from Scammon's Lagoon in Baja California, Mexico, through El Paso, central Missouri, Lakes Erie and Ontario, central NY state, almost all of Vermont and New Hampshire, southern Maine and most of Nova Scotia, observers will see a ring, or an annulus, of the Sun surrounding the dark obscuring disc of the Moon. In a total solar eclipse all of the bright photosphere of the Sun is hidden by the Moon. During totality, the Sun's corona may be safely observed with the naked eye, and even with powerful binoculars or telescopes with no danger to the eye. Not so, in an annular eclipse, however. The ring of the Sun still unhidden is very dangerous to the eye, even without the use of a light collector. For this reason, the viewer is strongly advised to use adequate eye protection at all times while observing this eclipse. It is not the eclipse, itself, but the exposed solar surface which is the source of danger to the eye. Of course, that surface, and the danger, is exposed to view every clear day. We don't usually have a need or desire to stare at the sun, but an eclipse offers the opportunity for a prolonged gaze, hence the danger during an eclipse.

Watchers of meteor showers will again stay up late for the Perseid shower which usually peaks about August 11–12. The swift streaks of light crossing the sky are caused by chunks – meteoroids – of comet Swift-Tuttle as they crash into our upper atmosphere. That comet passed our way in 1992 after an absence from our neighbourhood of 130 years, so the region behind it should be much more cluttered with debris than the region in front of it. Avid observers will watch the skies all week surrounding this date because the cloud of meteoroids is somewhat stretched out along the comet's path and beside it, thus giving us a protracted viewing period, perhaps even greater than this shower's usual 4–5-day duration.

Whenever notice is given in the following listing of some celestial object passing close to another, we may not see the actual event, but regard the notice that the evenings before and after that time will be good times to see the relative movements in our ever-changing, dramatic sky.

January

Mercury begins this year lost in the Sun's glare, passing superior conjunction, beyond the Sun, on the 3rd.

Venus follows Mercury to superior conjunction on the 17th, also lost in the Sun's light, coming to easy view in mid-spring in evening twilight.

Mars, in conjunction last December 27, is mingling with the inferior planets at this time, but will be visible in the morning sky in early March.

Jupiter, the brightest planet until mid-spring, can be seen these mornings in Libra, becoming an evening object after passing opposition April 30.

Saturn looks like a first magnitude star low in the evening twilight all this month.

Moon passes Jupiter on the 6th, Saturn on the 15th, the other planets too close to the Sun to observe the Moon's passage.

Jan. 2 – Earth at perihelion, 91.4 million miles from the Sun.

Jan. 3 – Mercury at superior conjunction entering the evening sky, nearly 134 million miles from us, beyond the Sun.

Jan. 4 – Quadrantid meteor shower.

Jan. 6 – Moon passes 3° south of Jupiter.

Jan. 11 – Neptune in conjunction with the Sun, about 2,900 million miles away.

Jan. 12 – Uranus in conjunction with the Sun, over 1,900 million miles away.

Jan. 15 – Moon passes 7° north of Saturn.

Jan. 17 – Venus in superior conjunction beyond the Sun, 159 million miles from us, entering the evening sky.

Jan. 19 – Sun enters Capricornus.

February

Mercury may be briefly visible in the southwest evening twilight early this month, passing very close to Saturn on the evening of the 1st.

Venus, while technically in the evening sky, is too deep in the evening twilight to be seen.

Mars is similarly invisible, until late in the month, but in the morning sky.

Jupiter is stationary on the 28th, thus beginning its retrograde motion, westward among the stars, prior to opposition April 30.

Saturn may be visible for the first few days of the month, perhaps pointing out Mercury on the evening of the 1st, but soon thereafter enters the evening twilight to be lost to view until mid-March.

Moon passes Jupiter on the 3rd, Neptune and Uraqnus on the 8th.

Feb. 2 – Mercury passes 1.3° north of Saturn, seen close the evening of the 1st.

Feb. 3 – Moon passes 3° south of Jupiter.

Feb. 4 – Mercury at greatest elongation, 18° east of the Sun.

Feb. 8 – Moon passes 3° north of Neptune and 5° north of Uranus.

Feb. 10 – Mercury stationary, beginning its retrograde motion, westward against the background stars, prior to inferior conjunction.

Feb. 16 – Sun enters Aquarius.

Feb. 20 – Mercury in inferior conjunction, between

the Earth and the Sun, less than 60 million miles away, entering the morning sky,

Feb. 21 – Saturn in conjunction with the Sun, beyond it, to enter our morning sky, 999 million miles away.

Feb. 27 – Mercury passes 4° north of Mars.

Feb. 28 – Jupiter stationary, beginning its retrograde, westward, motion.

March

Mercury rises southeast of the Sun all month, passing just 0.3° south of Saturn about 20:00 on the 23rd.

Venus may become visible very low in the evening twilight after mid-month.

Mars, looking like a star a bit fainter than 1st magnitude in Aquarius for most of the year, passes only 0.4° north of slightly brighter Saturn on the 13th, about 22:00.

Jupiter, in Libra, is 2° north of the Moon on the 2nd and the 29th.

Saturn has close encounters this month with Mars on the 14th, and Mercury on the 24th, its passing of the Moon on the 11th being a distant 7°.

Moon passes Jupiter on the 2nd, Neptune and Uranus on the 7th, Mercury and Mars on the 10th, Saturn on the 11th, Venus on the 13th and Jupiter on the 29th.

Mar. 2 – Moon passes 2° south of Jupiter.

Mar. 4 – Pluto stationary, beginning retrograde, westward, motion; Mercury stationary, resuming direct, eastward, motion.

Mar. 7 – Moon passes 4° south of Uranus and 5° south of Neptune.

Mar. 10 – Moon passes 5° south of Mercury and 7° south of Mars.

Mar. 11 – Moon passes 7° south of Saturn; Sun enters Pisces.

Mar. 13 – Moon passes 5° south of Venus.

Mar. 14 – Mars passes 0.4° north of Saturn.

Mar. 19 – Mercury at greatest elongation, 28° west of the Sun.

Mar. 20 – Vernal equinox; spring begins in the northern hemisphere at 20:28.

Mar. 24 – Mercury 0.3° south of Saturn.

Mar. 29 – Moon passes 2° south of Jupiter.

April

Mercury, nearly 1.5 magnitudes brighter, passes close to Mars on the 4th, but soon moves into the morning twilight, thus lost to view.

Venus is becoming more prominent in the western evening sky, so close to the thin crescent Moon on the evening of the 12th as to be occulted, its shadow passing across our Arctic regions, a good photo opportunity.

Mars in Pisces after the 1st week, passes close to Mercury on the 4th.

Jupiter, at magnitude minus 2.5, coming to opposition on the 30th, still dominates the night sky, but evenings belong to Venus at magnitude minus 3.9.

Saturn continues to take over the morning sky in Aquarius, about as bright as Mars.

Moon passes Neptune on the 3rd, Uranus on the 4th, Saturn on the 7th, Mars and Mercury on the 9th, occults Venus on the 12th, and passes Jupiter on the 26th.

Apr. 3 – Moon passes 4° north of Neptune.

Apr. 4 – Mercury passes 1.5° south of Mars; Moon passes 5° north of Uranus.

Apr. 9 – Moon passes 6° north of Mars and 7° north of Mercury.

Apr. 12 – Moon passes 1.0° north of Venus, occulting it for viewers in the Arctic regions.

Apr. 18 – Sun enters Aries.

Apr. 25 – Neptune stationary, beginning its retrograde motion.

Apr. 26 – Moon passes 3° south of Jupiter.

Apr. 30 – Jupiter at opposition, 411 million miles away; Mercury in superior conjunction, 123 million miles away.

May

Mercury, by the 20th, may become easily visible in the northwest twilight after sunset, lower and fainter than brilliant Venus which sets over an hour later.

Venus, in Taurus, may be seen north of Aldebaran on the 4th, and is north of the thin crescent Moon on the evening of the 12th.

Mars continues to linger in the low morning sky, as it slides across constellations, in Aries before the end of the month

Jupiter, now in the sky all night, is the brightest object continuously visible, surpassed only by the fleeting Moon, and by Venus, who leaves the sky early for her beauty sleep.

Saturn is slowly brightening, heading for its late summer opposition when its turn to patrol the sky all night comes around September 1.

Moon passes Neptune and Uranus on the 1st, Saturn on the 5th, Mars on the 8th, eclipses the Sun on the 10th, passes Venus on the 13th, Jupiter on the 23rd, partially enters the Earth's shadow on the 25th, and on the 28th, again passes Uranus and Neptune.

May 1 – Uranus stationary; Moon passes 4° north of Neptune; Moon passes 5° north of Uranus.

May 5 – Venus passes 6° north of Aldebaran; Moon passes 6° south of Saturn.

May 8 – Moon passes 4° north of Mars.

May 10 – Annular eclipse of the Sun.

May 13 – Moon passes 4° south of Venus; Sun enters Taurus.

May 15 – Mercury passes 8° north of Aldebaran.

May 17 – Pluto at opposition, 2,723 million miles from us.

May 23 – Moon passes 3° south of Jupiter.

May 25 – Partial eclipse of the Moon.

May 27 – Moon passes 4° north of Neptune and 5° north of Uranus.

May 30 – Mercury at greatest elongation, 23° east of the Sun.

June

Mercury, although fairly well placed for viewing, is turning its dark side towards us as it heads for inferior conjunction on the 25th, thus becoming fainter in our sky.

Venus, passing Pollux and the Moon this month at unspectacular distances, is becoming more spectacular by just being in our western evening sky well after sunset.

Mars' most exciting adventure this month, other than entering Taurus about the 22nd, is being about 2° from the thin crescent Moon in the dawn sky of the 6th.

Jupiter, in Virgo, is brighter and yellower than Spica to its west.

Saturn is a bright, 1st magnitude object in Aquarius, not known for bright objects.

Moon passes Saturn on the 1st, Mars on the 6th, Mercury on the 11th, Venus on the 12th, Jupiter on the 19th, Neptune on the 24th, Uranus on the 25th and Saturn, again, on the 28th.

June 1 – Moon passes 7° north of Saturn.
June 6 – Moon passes 2° north of Mars.
June 10 – Venus passes 5° south of Pollux.
June 11 – Moon passes 3° south of Mercury.
June 12 – Mercury stationary, beginning its retrograde motion; Moon passes 7° south of Venus.
June 19 – Moon passes 3° south of Jupiter.
June 20 – Sun enters Gemini.
June 21 – Summer solstice at 14:48; summer begins in the northern hemisphere.
June 24 – Saturn stationary, beginning its retrograde motion; Moon passes 4° north of Neptune.
June 25 – Moon passes 5° north of Uranus; Mercury at inferior conjunction, 51.7 million miles away.
June 28 – Moon passes 7° north of Saturn.

July

Mercury is in the morning sky virtually the entire month, but not easy to see.

Venus passes Regulus, the bright star of Leo, by a little over 2 Moon diameters on the 10th.

Mars, in Taurus all month, is occulted by the moon on the 5th.

Jupiter is stationary on the 2nd, resuming its direct motion, again heading for Libra.

Saturn continues to lurk in Aquarius, passed only by the Moon on the 26th.

Moon occults Mars on the 5th, passes Mercury on the 7th, Venus on the 12th, Jupiter on the 16th, Neptune and Uranus on the 22nd, and Saturn on the 26th.

July 2 – Jupiter stationary, resuming its direct motion.
July 5 – Moon occults Mars; Earth at aphelion, 94.4 million miles from the Sun.
July 6 – Mercury stationary, resuming its direct motion.
July 7 – Moon passes 1.3° south of Mars, occulting it.
July 10 – Venus passes 1.1° north of Regulus.
July 12 – Moon passes 7° south of Venus.
July 14 – Neptune at opposition, 2,710 million miles away.
July 16 – Moon passes 3° south of Jupiter.
July 17 – Uranus at opposition, almost 1,734 million miles away; Mercury at greatest elongation, 21° west of the Sun.
July 18 – Mars passes 5° north of Aldebaran.
July 20 – Sun enters Cancer.
July 22 – Moon passes 4° north of Neptune, and 5° north of Uranus.
July 26 – Moon passes 7° north of Saturn.
July 30 – Mercury 3° north of Pollux.

August

Mercury is lost in the Sun all month.

Venus is at greatest elongation, 46° east of the Sun on the 24th, appearing like a half moon in telescopes.

Mars continues its dogged round of the sky all month, moving into Gemini about the 15th

Jupiter decreases its distance from Venus, fading slightly as Venus grows still brighter.

Saturn attains its greatest brilliancy this year, but never getting brighter than 0.5 magnitude.

Moon passes Mars on the 3rd, Venus on the 10th, Jupiter on the 13th, Neptune and Uranus on the 18th, and Saturn on the 22nd.

Aug. 3 – Moon passes 3° south of Mars.
Aug. 9 – Pluto stationary.
Aug. 10 – Moon passes 3° south of Venus; Sun enters Leo.
Aug. 11 – Watch for Perseid meteor shower tonight and tomorrow night.
Aug. 13 – Mercury in superior conjunction, over 125 million miles away; Moon passes 2° south of Jupiter.
Aug. 18 – Moon passes 4° north of Neptune and 5° north of Uranus.
Aug. 22 – Moon passes 7° north of Saturn.
Aug. 24 – Venus at greatest elongation, 46° east of the Sun.
Aug. 31 – Venus 0.7° south of Spica.

September

Mercury is in the evening sky all month and half of October, appearing as a zero magnitude star to the left of the set Sun in the evening twilight, passing 0.1° south of Spica on the 21st, a binocular and telescope photo opportunity.

Venus achieves greatest brilliancy on the 28th, minus 4.6 magnitude, putting nearby Jupiter in his place, after a pleasant encounter with the crescent Moon on the evening of the 8th.

Mars begins to brighten almost imperceptibly in preparation for its show at the end of the year, sneaking into Cancer just as the month ends.

Jupiter closes in on Venus, just to lose the spectacle to the traditional evening star, but providing a pleasant supporting role to the passing Moon on the evenings of the 9th and 10th.

Saturn, at opposition on the 1st, has the whole night to itself, after the evening show in the west, and before the challenging Mars to the east.

Moon passes Mars on the 1st, Mercury on the 7th, Venus and Jupiter on the 9th, Neptune and Uranus on the 14th, Saturn on the 18th, and Mars, again, on the 29th.

Sep. 1 – Moon passes 4° south of Mars; Saturn at opposition, about 808 million miles from us.
Sep. 7 – Moon passes 3° south of Mercury.
Sep. 16 – Moon passes 2° north of Venus and 1.4° south of Jupiter.
Sep. 14 – Moon passes 4° north of Neptune and 5° north of Uranus.
Sep. 16 – Sun enters Virgo.
Sep. 18 – Moon passes 7° north of Saturn.
Sep. 21 – Mercury passes 0.1° south of Spica.
Sep. 23 – Autumnal equinox; autumn begins in the northern hemisphere at 06:19.
Sep. 24 – Mars passes 6° south of Pollux.
Sep. 26 – Mercury at greatest elongation, 26° east of the Sun.
Sep. 28 – Venus at greatest brilliancy.
Sep. 29 – Moon passes 6° south of Mars.

October

Mercury, except for the 1st week, and then only for very dedicated observers, is lost to view in the solar glare.

Venus and Jupiter are about 7° apart in the N–S direction, Venus considerably more to the left in the evening twilight, and it will plunge into the brighter parts of the twilight before Jupiter.

Mars, in Cancer all month, continues to brighten during the rest of the year.

Jupiter plays with a stand-offish Venus for the rest of the month, but remains visible with some difficulty into November.

Saturn takes over the night sky as Venus and Jupiter leave, but Mars is becoming a serious contender.

Moon passes Mercury on the 6th, Venus and Jupiter on the 7th, occulting Jupiter, passes Neptune and Uranus on the 12th, Saturn on the 15th, and Mars on the 28th.

Oct. 2 – Uranus and Neptune stationary, resuming their direct motions.

Oct. 6 – Moon passes 3° north of Mercury.

Oct. 7 – Moon passes 7° north of Venus, 0.7° south of Jupiter, occulting it; Venus is 34 million miles away, Jupiter, over 578 million miles.

Oct. 9 – Mercury stationary, beginning its retrograde motion.

Oct. 12 – Moon passes 4° north of Neptune, 5° north of Uranus; Venus stationary, beginning its retrograde motion.

Oct. 15 – Moon passes 7° north of Saturn.

Oct. 21 – Mercury at inferior conjunction, 62 million miles from us; Orionid meteor shower.

Oct. 28 – Moon passes 7° south of Mars.

Oct. 29 – Mercury stationary, resuming its direct motion.

Oct. 30 – Sun enters Libra.

November

Mercury is a morning object early in the month, passing Venus on the 12th.

Venus emerges into the morning sky, taking charge by mid-November, passing Mercury on the 12th.

Mars leaves Cancer for Leo on the 6th, brightening by half a magnitude this month.

Jupiter is lost to view all month, passing through conjunction on the 17th.

Saturn is alone in the evening sky, still faithful to Aquarius.

Moon passes Mercury on the 2nd, totally eclipses the Sun on the 3rd, passes Neptune and Uranus on the 8th, Saturn on the 11th, has a penumbral eclipse on the 18th, passes Mars on the 25th, and Venus on the 30th.

Nov. 2 – Moon passes 4° south of Mercury; Venus in inferior conjunction.

Nov. 3 – Mercury passes 4° north of Spica; Total solar eclipse.

Nov. 6 – Mercury at greatest elongation, 10° west of the Sun.

Nov. 8 – Moon passes 4° north of Neptune and 6° north of Uranus.

Nov. 9 – Saturn stationary, resuming its direct motion.

Nov. 14 – Moon passes 7° north of Saturn.

Nov. 12 – Mercury 5° north of Venus.

Nov. 17 – Jupiter in conjunction with the Sun, 593 million miles away; Leonid meteor shower.

Nov. 18 – Moon in penumbral eclipse.

Nov. 20 – Pluto in conjunction with the Sun, nearly 2,851 million miles from Earth..

Nov. 22 – Sun enters Scorpius.

Nov. 25 – Moon passes 8° south of Mars.

Nov. 29 – Sun enters Ophiuchus.

Nov. 30 – Moon passes 2° south of Venus.

December

Mercury is lost to view all month, passing superior conjunction on the 14th.

Venus is at greatest brilliancy in the dawn sky on the 9th.

Mars stays in Leo, slowing its direct motion, passing 2° north of Regulus on the 8th, and brightening over a half magnitude during the month.

Jupiter emerges from the dawn solar glare early in the month, quickly moving into Scorpius from Libra, where it has spent the year.

Saturn, prominent in our western sky after sunset, remains in Aquarius.

Moon passes Neptune on the 5th, Uranus on the 6th, Saturn on the 9th, Mars on the 23rd, Venus on the 29th, and occults Jupiter on the 30th.

Dec. 5 – Moon passes 4° north of Neptune.

Dec. 6 – Moon passes 6° north of Uranus.

Dec. 8 – Mars passes 2° north of Regulus.

Dec. 9 – Moon passes 7° north of Saturn; Venus at greatest brilliancy.

Dec. 13 – Geminid meteor shower.

Dec. 14 – Mercury in superior conjunction, nearly 135 million miles away.

Dec. 16 – Sun enters Sagittarius.

Dec. 22 – Winter solstice; winter begins in the northern hemisphere at 02:23.

Dec. 23 – Moon passes 9° south of Mars.

Dec. 29 – Moon passes 3° south of Venus.

Dec. 30 – Moon occults Jupiter.

Planets and the Sun

The planets of the solar system, in order of their mean distance from the sun, are Mercury, Venus, Earth, Mars, Jupiter, Saturn, Uranus, Neptune and Pluto. Both Uranus and Neptune are visible through good field glasses, but Pluto is so distant and so small that only large telescopes or long-exposure photographs can make it visible.

Since Mercury and Venus are nearer to the sun than is the Earth, their motions about the sun are seen from the Earth as wide swings first to one side of the sun and then to the other, although they are both passing continuously around the sun in orbits that are almost circular. When their passage takes them either between the Earth and the sun, or beyond the sun as seen from the Earth, they are invisible to us. Because of the laws which govern the motions of planets about the sun, both Mercury and Venus require much less time to pass between the Earth and the sun than around the far side of the sun, so their periods of visibility and invisibility are unequal.

The planets that lie further from the sun than does the Earth may be seen for longer periods of time and are invisible only when they are so located in our sky that they rise and set about the same time as the sun when, of course, they are overwhelmed by the sun's great brilliance. None of the planets has any light of its own; each shines only by reflecting sunlight from its surface. Mercury and Venus, because they are between the Earth and the sun, show phases very much as the moon does. The planets further from the sun are always seen as full, although Mars does occasionally present a slightly gibbous phase – like the moon when not quite full.

The planets move rapidly among the stars because they are very much nearer to us. The stars are also in motion, some of them at tremendous speeds, but they are so far away that their motion does not change their apparent positions in the heavens sufficiently for anyone to perceive that change in a single lifetime. The very nearest star is about 7,000 times as far away as the most distant planet.

Planets of the Solar System

Mercury

Mercury, nearest planet to the sun, is the second smallest of the nine planets known to be orbiting the sun. Its diameter is 3,100 miles and its mean distance from the sun is 36,000,000 miles.

Mercury moves with great speed in its journey about the sun, averaging about 30 miles a second to complete its circuit in 88 of our days. Mercury rotates upon its axis over a period of nearly 59 days, thus exposing all of its surface periodically to the sun. It is believed that the surface passing before the sun may have a temperature of about 800° F., while the temperature on the side turned temporarily away from the sun does not fall as low as might be expected. This night temperature has been described by Russian astronomers as "room temperature" — possibly about 70°. This would contradict the former belief that Mercury did not possess an atmosphere, for some sort of atmosphere would be needed to retain the fierce solar radiation that strikes Mercury. A shallow but dense layer of carbon dioxide would produce the "greenhouse" effect, in which heat accumulated during exposure to the sun would not completely escape at night. The actual presence of a carbon dioxide atmosphere is in dispute. Other research, however, has indicated a nighttime temperature approaching −300°.

This uncertainty about conditions upon Mercury and its motion arise from its shorter angular distance from the sun as seen from the Earth, for Mercury is always too much in line with the sun to be observed against a dark sky, but is always seen during either morning or evening twilight.

Mariner 10 made 3 passes by Mercury in 1974 and 1975. A large fraction of the surface was photographed from varying distances, revealing a degree of cratering similar to that of the moon. An atmosphere of hydrogen and helium may be made up of gases of the solar wind temporarily concentrated by the presence of Mercury. The discovery of a weak but permanent magnetic field was a surprise. It has been held that both a fluid core and rapid rotation were necessary for the generation of a planetary magnetic field. Mercury may demonstrate these conditions to be unnecessary, or the field may reveal something about the history of Mercury.

Venus

Venus, slightly smaller than the Earth, moves about the sun at a mean distance of 67,000,000 miles in 225 of our days. Its synodical revolution — its return to the same relationship with the Earth and the sun, which is a result of the combination of its own motion and that of the Earth — is 584 days. Every 19 months, then, Venus will be nearer to the Earth than any other planet of the solar system. The planet is covered with a dense, white, cloudy atmosphere that conceals whatever is below it. This same cloud reflects sunlight efficiently so that when Venus is favorably situated, it is the third brightest object in the sky, exceeded only by the sun and the moon.

Spectral analysis of sunlight reflected from Venus' cloud tops has shown features that can best be explained by identifying the material of the clouds as sulphuric acid (oil of vitriol). Infrared spectroscopy from a balloon-borne telescope nearly 20 miles above the Earth's surface gave indications of a small amount of water vapor present in the same region of the atmosphere of Venus. In 1956, radio astronomers at the Naval Research Laboratories in Washington, D. C., found a temperature for Venus of about 600° F., in marked contrast to minus 125° F., previously found at the cloud tops. Subsequent radio work confirmed a high temperature and produced evidence for this temperature to be associated with the solid body of Venus. With this peculiarity in mind, space scientists devised experiments for the U.S. space probe Mariner 2 to perform when it flew by in 1962. Mariner 2 confirmed the high temperature and the fact that it pertained to the ground rather than to some special activity of the atmosphere. In addition, Mariner 2 was unable to detect any radiation belts similar to the Earth's so-called Van Allen belts. Nor was it able to detect the existence of a magnetic field even as weak as 1/100,000 of that of the Earth.

In 1967, a Russian space probe, Venera 4, and the American Mariner 5 arrived at Venus within a few hours of each other. Venera 4 was designed to allow an instrument package to land gently on the planet's surface via parachute. It ceased transmission of information in about 75 minutes when the temperature it read went above 500° F. After considerable controversy, it was agreed that it still had 20 miles to go to reach the surface. The U.S. probe, Mariner 5, went around the dark side of Venus at a distance of about 6,000 miles. Again, it detected no significant magnetic field but its radio signals passed to Earth through Venus' atmosphere twice — once on the night side and once on the day side. The results are startling. Venus' atmosphere is nearly all carbon dioxide and must exert a pressure at the planet's surface of up to 100 times the Earth's normal sea-level pressure of one atmosphere. Since the Earth and Venus are about the same size, and were presumably formed at the same time by the same general process from the same mixture of chemical elements, one is faced with the question: which is the planet with the unusual history — Earth or Venus?

Radar astronomers using powerful transmitters as well as sensitive receivers and computers have succeeded in determining the rotation period of Venus. It turns out to be 243 days clockwise — in other words, contrary to the spin of most of the other planets and to its own motion around the sun. If it were exactly 243.16 days, Venus would always present the same face toward the Earth at every inferior conjunction. This rate and sense of rotation allows a "day" on Venus of 117.4 Earth days. Any part of Venus will receive sunlight on its clouds for over 58 days and will be in darkness for 58 days. Recent radar observations have shown surface features below the clouds. Large craters, continent-sized highlands, and extensive, dry "ocean" basins have been identified.

Mariner 10 passed Venus before traveling on to Mercury in 1974. The carbon dioxide molecule found in such abundance in the atmosphere is rather opaque to certain ultraviolet wavelengths, enabling sensitive television cameras to take pictures of the Venusian cloud cover. Photos radioed to Earth show a spiral pattern in the clouds from equator to the poles.

In December, 1978, two U. S. Pioneer probes arrived at Venus. One went into orbit about Venus, the other split into 5 separate probes targeted for widely-spaced entry points to sample different conditions. The instrumentation ensemble was selected on the basis of previous missions that had shown the range of conditions to be studied. The probes confirmed expected high surface temperatures and high winds aloft. Winds of about 200 miles per hour, there, may account for the transfer of heat into the night side in spite of the low rotation speed of the planet. Surface winds were light at the time, however. Atmosphere and cloud chemistries were examined in detail, providing much data for continued analysis. The probes detected 4 layers of clouds and more light on the surface than expected solely from sunlight. This light allowed Russian scientists to obtain at least two photos showing rocks on the surface. Sulphur seems to play a large role in the chemistry of Venus, and reactions involving sulphur may be responsible for the glow. To learn more about the weather and atmospheric circulation on Venus, the orbiter takes daily photos of the daylight side cloud cover. It confirms the cloud pattern and its circulation shown by Mariner 10. The ionosphere shows large variability. The orbiter's radar operates in 2 modes: one, for ground elevation variability, and the second for ground reflectivity in 2 dimensions, thus "imaging" the surface. Radar maps of the entire planet that show the features mentioned above have been produced.

The Venus orbiter Magellan was launched May 5, 1989. It was equipped to observe Venus by a side-scanning radar system, together with one to gather data on variations in elevations directly beneath the craft. Magellan has mapped all but a small fraction of the planet. The side-looking radar illuminates the surface and its features with radio waves and records the strength and distance of returning echoes. Computer processing produces what seems to be a view of the landscape as if seen through a clear atmosphere from above, near sunset, with a resolution better than about a mile on Venus.

Craters over 20 miles wide are believed to have been caused by impacting bodies. One 150 mile-wide crater, the largest found to date, has been named for Margaret Mead. Smaller craters are probably due to volcanic action. The largest such caldera has been named Sakajawea. Many lava flows have been seen, and some old craters and plains seem to be filled with lava.

Most of the surface is believed to be younger than 1000 to 500 million years old. Modifications of previously existing surface features have been due to tectonic actions such as faulting, and to weathering. Tectonic actions in general are distinctly different from such actions on Earth. The intense heat at the surface of Venus can prevent the surface materials from cooling to the same brittle condition as on Earth. The same actions on Earth, thus, may produce somewhat different results on Venus. Although there are deep regions, somewhat similar to our ocean basins, there is no water to fill them. There seems to be no activity on Venus similar to our moving tectonic plates, but there may be local stretching and compressing that produce rift valleys and higher plains and mountains. Although there is no weathering due to water on Venus, the action of winds is in evidence. Extensive sand dunes have been seen, and wind-blown deposits indicate stable wind patterns for very long periods of time.

Despite deterioration in the physical condition of the orbiter, Magellan continues to function in adapted capacities.

Mars

Mars is the first planet beyond the Earth, away from the sun. Mars' diameter is about 4,200 miles, although a determination of the radius and mass of Mars by the space-probe Mariner 4, which flew by Mars on July 14, 1965 at a distance of less than 6,000 miles, indicated that these dimensions were slightly larger than had been previously estimated. While Mars' orbit is also nearly circular, it is somewhat more eccentric than the orbits of many of the other planets, and Mars is more than 30 million miles farther from the sun in some parts of its year than it is at others. Mars takes 687 of our days to make one circuit of the sun, traveling at about 15 miles a second. Mars rotates upon its axis in almost the same period of time that the Earth does — 24 hours and 37 minutes. Mars' mean distance from the sun is 141 million miles, so that the temperature on Mars would be lower than that on the Earth even if Mars' atmosphere were about the same as ours. The atmosphere is not, however, for Mariner 4 reported that atmospheric pressure on Mars is between 1% and 2% of the Earth's atmospheric pressure. This thin atmosphere appears to be largely carbon dioxide. No evidence of free water was found.

There appears to be no magnetic field about Mars. This would eliminate the previous conception of a dangerous radiation belt around Mars. The same lack of a magnetic field would expose the surface of Mars to an influx of cosmic radiation about 100 times as intense as that on Earth.

Deductions from years of telescopic observation indicate that 5/8ths of the surface of Mars is a desert of reddish rock, sand, and soil. The rest of Mars is covered by irregular patches that appear generally green in hues that change through the Martian year. These were formerly held to be some sort of primitive vegetation, but with the findings of Mariner 4 of a complete lack of water and oxygen, such growth does not appear possible. The nature of the green areas is now unknown. They may be regions covered with volcanic salts whose color changes with changing temperatures and atmospheric conditions, or they may be gray, rather than green. When large gray areas are placed beside large red areas, the gray areas will appear green to the eye.

Mars' axis of rotation is inclined from a vertical to the plane of its orbit about the sun by about 25° and therefore Mars has seasons as does the Earth, except that the Martian seasons are longer because Mars' year is longer. White caps form about the winter pole of Mars, growing through the winter and shrinking in summer. These polar caps are now believed to be both water ice and carbon dioxide ice. It is the carbon dioxide that is seen to come and go with the seasons. The water ice is apparently in many layers with dust between them, indicating climatic cycles.

The canals of Mars have become more of a mystery than they were before the voyage of Mariner 4. Markings forming a network of fine lines crossing much of the surface of Mars have been seen there by men who have devoted much time to the study of the planet, but no canals have shown clearly enough in previous photographs to be universally accepted. A few of the 21 photographs sent back to Earth by Mariner 4 covered areas crossed by canals. The pictures show faint, ill-defined, broad, dark markings, but no positive identification of the nature of the markings.

Mariners 6 & 7 in 1969 sent back many more

photographs of higher quality than those of the pioneering Mariner 4. These pictures showed cratering similar to the earlier views, but in addition showed 2 other types of terrain. Some regions seemed featureless for many square miles, but others were chaotic, showing high relief without apparent organization into mountain chains or craters.

Mariner 9, the first artificial body to be placed in an orbit about Mars, has transmitted over 10,000 photographs covering 100% of the planet's surface. Preliminary study of these photos and other data shows that Mars resembles no other planet we know. Using terrestrial terms, however, scientists describe features that seem to be clearly of volcanic origin. One of these features is Nix Olympica, (now called Olympus Mons), apparently a shield volcano whose caldera is over 50 miles wide, and whose outer slopes are over 300 miles in diameter, and which stands about 90,000 feet above the surrounding plain. Some features may have been produced by cracking (faulting) of the surface and the sliding of one region over or past another. Many craters seem to have been produced by impacting bodies such as may have come from the nearby asteroid belt. Features near the south pole may have been produced by glaciers that are no longer present. Flowing water, non-existent on Mars at the present time, probably carved canyons, one 10 times longer and 3 times deeper than the Grand Canyon.

Although the Russians landed a probe on the Martian surface, it transmitted for only 20 seconds. In 1976, the U.S. landed 2 Viking spacecraft on the Martian surface. The landers had devices aboard to perform chemical analyses of the soil in search of evidence of life. The results have been inconclusive. The 2 Viking orbiters have returned the best pictures yet of Martian topographic features. Many features can be explained only if Mars once had large quantities of flowing water.

Mars' position in its orbit and its speed around that orbit in relation to the Earth's position and speed bring Mars fairly close to the Earth on occasions about two years apart and then move Mars and the Earth too far apart for accurate observation and photography. Every 15-17 years, the close approaches are especially favorable to close observation.

Mars has 2 satellites, discovered in 1877 by Asaph Hall. The outer satellite, Deimos, revolves around Mars in about 31 hours. The inner satellite, Phobos, whips around Mars in a little more than 7 hours, making 3 trips around the planet each Martian day. Mariner and Viking photos show these bodies to be irregularly shaped and pitted with numerous craters. Phobos also shows a system of linear grooves, each about 1/3-mile across and roughly parallel. Phobos measures about 8 by 12 miles and Deimos about 5 by 7.5 miles in size.

Jupiter

Jupiter is the largest of the planets. Its equatorial diameter is 88,000 miles, 11 times the diameter of the Earth. Its polar diameter is about 6,000 miles shorter. This is an equilibrium condition resulting from the liquidity of the planet and its extremely rapid rate of rotation: a Jupiter day is only 10 Earth hours long. For a planet this size, this rotational speed is amazing, and it moves a point on Jupiter's equator at a speed of 22,000 miles an hour, as compared with 1,000 miles an hour for a point on the Earth's equator. Jupiter is at an average distance of 480 million miles from the sun and takes almost 12 of our years to make one complete circuit of the sun.

The only directly observable chemical constituents of Jupiter's atmosphere are methane (CH_4) and ammonia (NH_3), but it is reasonable to assume the same mixture of elements available to make Jupiter as to make the sun. This would mean a large fraction of hydrogen and helium must be present also, as well as water (H_2O). The temperature at the tops of the clouds may be about minus 260° F. The clouds are probably ammonia ice crystals, becoming ammonia droplets lower down. There may be a space before water ice crystals show up as clouds: in turn, these become water droplets near the bottom of the entire cloud layer. The total atmosphere may be only a few hundred miles in depth, pulled down by the surface gravity (= 2.64 times Earth's) to a relatively thin layer. Of course, the gases become denser with depth until they may turn into a slush or a slurry. Perhaps there is no surface — no real interface between the gaseous atmosphere and the body of Jupiter. Pioneers 10 and 11 provided evidence for considering Jupiter to be almost entirely liquid hydrogen. Long before a rocky core about the size of the Earth is reached, hydrogen mixed with helium becomes a liquid metal at very high temperature and pressure. Jupiter's cloudy atmosphere is a fairly good reflector of sunlight and makes it appear far brighter than any of the stars.

Fourteen of Jupiter's 17 or more satellites have been found through Earth-based observations. Four of the moons are large and bright, rivaling our own moon and the planet Mercury in diameter, and may be seen through a field glass. They move rapidly around Jupiter and their change of position from night to night is extremely interesting to watch. The other satellites are much smaller and in all but one instance much farther from Jupiter and cannot be seen except through powerful telescopes. The 4 outermost satellites are revolving around Jupiter clockwise as seen from the north, contrary to the motions of the great majority of the satellites in the solar system and to the direction of revolution of the planets around the sun. The reason for this retrograde motion is not known, but one theory is that Jupiter's tremendous gravitational power may have captured 4 of the minor planets or asteroids that move about the sun between Mars and Jupiter, and that these would necessarily revolve backward. At the great distance of these bodies from Jupiter — some 14 million miles — direct motion would result in decay of the orbits, while retrograde orbits would be stable. Jupiter's mass is more than twice the mass of all the other planets put together, and accounts for Jupiter's tremendous gravitational field and so, probably, for its numerous satellites and its dense atmosphere.

In December, 1973, Pioneer 10 passed about 80,000 miles from the equator of Jupiter and was whipped into a path taking it out of our solar system in about 50 years, and beyond the system of planets, on June 13, 1983. In December, 1974, Pioneer 11 passed within 30,000 miles of Jupiter, moving roughly from south to north, over the poles.

Photographs from both encounters were useful at the time but were far surpassed by those of Voyagers I and II. Thousands of high resolution multi-color pictures show rapid variations of features both large and small. The Great Red Spot exhibits internal counterclockwise rotation. Much turbulence is seen in adjacent material passing north or south of it. The satellites Amalthea, Io, Europa, Ganymede, and Callisto were photographed, some in great detail. Each is individual and unique, with no similarities to other known planets or satellites. Io has active volcanoes that probably have ejected material into a doughnut-shaped ring enveloping its orbit about Jupiter. This is not to be confused with the thin flat disk-like ring closer to Jupiter's surface. Now that such a ring has been seen by the Voyagers, older uncertain observations from Earth can be reinterpreted as early sightings of this structure.

Neptune

Neptune, currently the most distant planet from the sun (until 1999), lies at an average distance of 2.8 billion miles. It was the last planet visited in Voyager II's epic 12 year trek from Earth. While much new information was immediately perceived, much more must await further analysis of the tremendous amount of data returned from the spacecraft.

As with the other giant planets, there may be no solid surface to give real meaning to a measure of a diameter. However, a mean value of 30,600 miles may be assigned to a diameter between atmosphere levels where the pressure is about the same as sea level on Earth, as determined by radio experimenters. A different radio observational technique gave evidence of a rotation period for the bulk of Neptune of 16.1 hours, a shorter value than the 18.2 hours given by the clouds seen in the blue atmosphere. Neptune orbits the sun in 164 years in nearly a circular orbit.

Voyager II, which passed 3000 miles from Neptune's north pole, found a magnetic field which is considerably asymmetric to the planet's structure, similar, but not so extreme, to that found at Uranus.

Neptune's atmosphere was seen to be quite blue, with quickly changing white clouds often suspended high above an apparent surface. In that apparent surface were found features, one of which was reminiscent of the Great Red Spot of Jupiter, even to the counterclockwise rotation expected in a high-pressure system in the southern hemisphere. Atmospheric constituents are mostly hydrocarbon compounds. Although lightning and auroras have been found on other giant planets, only the aurora phenomenon has been seen on Neptune.

Six new satellites were discerned around Neptune, one confirming a 1981 sighting that was then difficult to recover for proper identification. Five of these satellites orbit Neptune in a half day or less. Of the eight satellites of Neptune, the largest, Triton, is in a retrograde orbit suggesting that it was captured rather than being co-eval with Neptune. Triton is sufficiently large to raise significant tides on Neptune which will one day, say 100 million years from now, cause Triton to come close enough to Neptune for it to be torn apart. Nereid was found in 1949, and is in a long looping orbit suggesting it, too, was captured. Each of the satellites that has been photographed by the two Voyagers in the planetary encounters has been different from any of the other satellites, and certainly from any of the planets. Only about half of Triton has been observed, but its terrain shows cratering and a strange regional feature described as resembling the skin of a cantaloupe. Triton has a tenuous atmosphere of nitrogen with a trace of hydrocarbons, and evidence of active geysers injecting material into it. At minus 238 degrees Celsius, Triton is one of the coldest objects in the solar system observed by Voyager II.

In addition to the satellite system, Voyager II confirmed the existence of at least three rings composed of very fine particles. There may some clumpiness in their structure, but the known satellites may not contribute to the formation or maintenance of the rings, as they have in other systems.

As with the other giant planets, Neptune is emitting more energy than it receives from the sun, Voyager finding the excess to be 2.7 times the solar contribution. These excesses are thought to be cool ing from internal heat sources and from the heat of formation of the planets.

Saturn

Saturn, last of the planets visible to the unaided eye, is almost twice as far from the sun as Jupiter, almost 900 million miles. It is second in size to Jupiter but its mass is much smaller. Saturn's specific gravity is less than that of water. Its diameter is about 71,000 miles at the equator; its rotational speed spins it completely around in a little more than 10 hours, and its atmosphere is much like that of Jupiter, except that its temperature at the top of its cloud layer is at least 100° lower. At about 300° F. below zero, the ammonia would be frozen out of Saturn's clouds. The theoretical construction of Saturn resembles that of Jupiter; it is either all gas, or it has a small dense center surrounded by a layer of liquid and a deep atmosphere.

Until Pioneer 11 passed Saturn in September 1979 only 10 satellites of Saturn were known. Since that time, the situation is quite confused. Added to data interpretations from the fly-by are Earth-based observations using new techniques while the rings were edge-on and virtually invisible. It was hoped that the Voyager I and II fly-bys would help sort out the system. It is now believed that Saturn has at least 22 satellites, some sharing orbits. The Saturn satellite system is still confused.

Saturn's ring system begins about 7,000 miles above the visible disk of Saturn, lying above its equator and extending about 35,000 miles into space. The diameter of the ring system visible from Earth is about 170,000 miles; the rings are estimated to be no thicker than 10 miles. In 1973, radar observation showed the ring particles to be large chunks of material averaging a metre on a side.

Voyager I and II observations showed the rings to be considerably more complex than had been believed, so much so that interpretation will take much time. To the untrained eye, the Voyager photographs could be mistaken for pictures of a colorful phonograph record.

Uranus

Voyager II, after passing Saturn in August 1981, headed for a rendezvous with Uranus culminating in a fly-by January 24, 1986. This encounter answered many questions, and raised others.

Uranus, discovered by Sir William Herschel on Mar. 13, 1781, lies at a distance of 1.8 billion miles from the sun, taking 84 years to make its circuit around our star. Uranus has a diameter of about 32,000 miles and spins once in some 16.8 hours, according to fly-by data. One of the most fascinating features of Uranus is how far it is tipped over. Its north pole lies 98° from being directly up and down to its orbit plane. Thus, its seasons are extreme. When the sun rises at the north pole, it stays up for 42 years; then it sets and the north pole will be in darkness (and winter) for 42 years.

The satellite system of Uranus, consisting of at least 15 moons, (the 5 largest having been known before the fly-by) have orbits lying in the plane of the planet's equator. In that plane there is also a complex of rings, 9 of which were discovered in 1978. Invisible from Earth, the 9 original rings were found by observers watching Uranus pass before a star. As they waited, they saw their photoelectric equipment register several short eclipses of the star. Then the planet occulted the star as expected. After the star came out from behind Uranus, the star winked out several more times. Subsequent observations and analyses indicated the 9 narrow, nearly opaque rings circling Uranus. Evidence from the Voyager II fly-by has shown the ring particles to be predominantly a yard or so in diameter.

In addition to the 10 new, very small satellites, Voyager II returned detailed photos of the 5 large satellites. As in the case of other satellites newly observed in the Voyager program, these bodies proved to be entirely different from each other and any others. Miranda has grooved markings, reminiscent of Jupiter's Ganymede, but often arranged in a chevron pattern. Ariel shows rifts and channels. Umbriel is extremely dark, prompting some observers to regard its surface as among the oldest in the system. Titania has rifts and fractures, but not the evidence of flow found on Ariel. Oberon's main feature is its surface saturated with craters, unrelieved by other formations.

The structure of Uranus is subject to some debate. Basically, however, it may have a rocky core surrounded by a thick icy mantle on top of which is a crust of hydrogen and helium that gradually becomes an atmosphere. Perhaps continued analysis of the wealth of data returned by Voyager II will shed some light on this problem.

Pluto

Although Pluto on the average stays about 3.6 billion miles from the sun, its orbit is so eccentric that its minimum distance of 2.7 billion miles is less than the current distance of Neptune. Thus Pluto, until 1999, is temporarily planet number 8 from the sun. At its mean distance, Pluto takes 247.7 years to cir cumnavigate the sun, a 3/2 resonance with Neptune. Until recently that was about all that was known of Pluto.

About a century ago, a hypothetical planet was believed to lie beyond Neptune and Uranus because neither planet followed the paths predicted by astronomers even when all known gravitational influences were considered. Little more than a guess, a mass of one Earth was assigned to the mysterious body and mathematical searches were begun. Amid some controversy about the validity of the predictive process, Pluto was found nearly where it was predicted to be. It was found by Clyde Tombaugh at the Lowell Observatory in Flagstaff, Ariz., in 1930.

At the U.S. Naval Observatory, also in Flagstaff, on July 2, 1978, James Christy obtained a photograph of Pluto that was distinctly elongated. Repeated observations of this shape and its variation were convincing evidence of the discovery of a satellite of Pluto, now named Charon. Subsequent observations show it to be 750 miles across, at a distance of over 12,000 miles from Pluto, and taking 6.4 days to move around Pluto. In this same length of time Pluto and Charon each rotate once around their individual axes. The Pluto-Charon system thus appears to rotate as virtually a ridged body. Gravitational laws allow these interactions to give us the mass of Pluto as 0.0020 of the Earth. This mass, together with a new diameter for Pluto of 1,430 miles makes the density about twice that of water. Theorists predict a rocky core for Pluto surrounded by a thick mantle of ice.

It is now clear that Pluto, the body found by Tombaugh, could not have influenced Neptune and Uranus to go astray. As a result, theorists are again at work looking for a new planet X.

Because the rotational axis of the system is tipped from the reference plane of the solar system by about 98°.3, similar to that of Uranus, there is only a short interval every half solar period when Pluto and Charon alternately eclipse each other. Analysis of the variations in light in and out of the recent eclipses has led to the diameters quoted above, and to interesting knowledge of other aspects of the system. Each component is approximately spherical, but they are otherwise different. Pluto is red, Charon grey. Charon has a surface identified as water ice; Pluto's surface is frozen methane. There are large regions on Pluto that are dark, others, light; Pluto has spots, and, perhaps, polar caps. Although extremely cold, Pluto's methane surface produces a tenuous atmosphere that may be slowly escaping into space, per haps going to Charon. When Pluto occulted a star, the star's light faded in such a way as to have passed through a haze layer lying above the planet's surface, indicating an inversion of temperatures, 110°K above, and 50°K below, suggesting Pluto has primitive weather.

There are tentative plans for a space-craft reconnaissance of the Pluto system, thus completing direct, close-up observation of each of the planets of the solar system.

Greenwich Sidereal Time for 0^h GMT, 1994

(Add 12 hours to obtain Right Ascension of Mean Sun)

Date		h	m	Date		h	m	Date		h	m	Date		h	m
Jan.	1	06	41.7	Apr.	1	12	36.5	July	10	19	10.8	Oct.	8	01	05.6
	11	07	21.1		11	13	15.9		20	19	50.2		18	01	45.0
	21	08	0.5		21	13	55.4		30	20	29.6		28	02	24.4
	31	08	40.0	May	1	14	34.8	Aug.	9	21	09.0	Nov.	7	03	03.9
Feb.	10	09	19.4		11	15	14.2		19	21	48.5		17	03	43.3
	20	09	58.8		21	15	53.6		29	22	27.9		27	04	22.7
Mar.	2	10	38.2		31	16	33.1	Sept.	8	23	07.3	Dec.	7	05	02.1
	12	11	17.7	June	10	17	12.5		18	23	46.7		17	05	41.6
	22	11	57.1		20	17	51.9		28	00	26.2		27	06	21.0
					30	18	31.3								

Astronomical Signs and Symbols

☉	The Sun	⊕	The Earth	♅	Uranus	□	Quadrature
☾	The Moon	♂	Mars	♆	Neptune	☍	Opposition
☿	Mercury	♃	Jupiter	♇	Pluto	☊	Ascending Node
♀	Venus	♄	Saturn	☌	Conjunction	☋	Descending Node

Two heavenly bodies are in "conjunction" (☌) when they are due north and south of each other, either in Right Ascension (with respect to the north celestial pole) or in Celestial Longitude (with respect to the north ecliptic pole). If the bodies are seen near each other, they will rise and set at nearly the same time. They are in "opposition" (☍) when their Right Ascensions differ by exactly 12 hours, or their Celestial Longitudes differ by 180°. One of the two objects in opposition will rise while the other is setting. "Quadrature" (□) refers to the arrangement when the coordinates of two bodies differ by exactly 90°. These terms may refer to the relative positions of any two bodies as seen from the Earth, but one of the bodies is so frequently the sun that mention of the sun is omitted; otherwise both bodies are named. The geocentric angular separation between sun and object is termed "elongation". Elongation is limited only for Mercury and Venus; the "greatest elongation" for each of these bodies is noted in the appropriate tables and is approximately the time for longest observation. When a planet is in its "ascending" (☋) or "descending" (☊) node, it is passing northward or southward, respectively, through the plane of the Earth's orbit, across the celestial circle called the ecliptic. The term "perihelion" means nearest to the sun, and "aphelion," farthest from the sun. An "occultation" of a planet or star is an eclipse of it by some other body, usually the moon.

Planetary Configurations, 1994

Greenwich Mean Time (0 designates midnight; 12 designates noon; * = star; ■ = moon)

Mo.	d.	h.	m.		
Jan.	2	06	-		⊕ closest to ☉; perihelion
	3	20	-	☌ ☿ ☉	Superior conj
	6	22	-	☌ ♃ ☽	♃ 3° N
	11	08	-	☌ ♆ ☉	
	12	17	-	☌ ♅ ☉	
	15	00	-	☌ ♄ ☽	♄ 7° S
	17	02	-	☌ ♀ ☉	
Feb.	2	04	-	☌ ☿ ♄	☿ 1°.3 N
	3	08	-	☌ ♃ ☽	♃ 3° N
	4	21	-		☿ Gr. elong; 18° E of ☉
	8	08	-	☌ ♆ ☽	♆ 3° S
	8	12	-	☌ ♅ ☽	♅ 5° S
	10	18	-		☿ stationary
	20	08	-	☌ ☿ ☉	Inferior conj.
	21	17	-	☌ ♄ ☉	
	27	01	-	☌ ☿ ♂	☿ 4° N
	28	21	-		♃ stationary
Mar.	2	16	-	☌ ♃ ☽	♃ 2°N
	4	01	-		♇ stationary
	4	12	-		☿ stationary
	7	16	-	☌ ♆ ☽	♆ 4° S
	7	21	-	☌ ♅ ☽	♅ 5° S
	10	04	-	☌ ☿ ☽	☿ 5° S
	10	23	-	☌ ♂ ☽	♂ 7° S
	11	04	-	☌ ♄ ☽	♄ 7° S
	13	17	–	☌ ♀ ☽	♀ 5° S
	14	10	-	☌ ♂ ♃	♂ 0.4° N
	19	02	-		☿ Gr. elong; 28° W of ☉
	20	28	-		Vernal equinox; spring begins in Northern Hemisphere
	24	08	-	☌ ☿ ♄	☿ 0°.3 S
	29	23	-	☌ ♃ ☽	♃ 2° N
Apr.	3	22	-	☌ ♆ ☽	♆ 4° S
	4	02	-	☌ ☿ ♂	☿ 1°.5 S
	4	04	-	☌ ♅ ☽	♅ 5° S
	7	16	-	☌ ♄ ☽	♄ 7° S
	9	02	-	☌ ♂ ☽	♂ 6° S
	9	11	-	☌ ☿ ☽	☿ 7° S
	12	23	-	☌ ♀ ☽	♀ 1°.0 S; occultation
	25	09	-		♆ stationary
	26	05	-	☌ ♃ ☽	♃ 3° N
	30	09	-	☍ ♄ ☉	
	30	10	-	☌ ☿ ☉	Superior conj.
May	1	01	-		♅ stationary
	1	06	-	☌ ♆ ☽	♆ 4° S
	1	12	-	☌ ♅ ☽	♅ 5° S
	5	00	-	☌ ♀ *	♀ 6° N at Aldebaran
	5	03	-	☌ ♄ ☽	♄ 7° S
	8	04	-	☌ ♂ ☽	♂ 4°S
	10	17	-	☌ ☽ ☉	Annular solar eclipse
	13	06	-	☌ ♀ ☽	♀ 4° N
	15	11	-	☌ ☿ *	☿ 8° N at Aldebaran
	17	20	-	☍ ♇ ☉	
	23	11	-	☌ ♃ ☽	♃ 3° N
	25	04	-	☍ ☽ ☉	Partial lunar eclipse
	28	14	-	☌ ♆ ☽	♆ 4° S
	28	20	-	☌ ♅ ☽	♅ 5° S
	30	07	-		☿ Gr. elong; 23° E of ☉
June	1	12	-	☌ ♄ ☽	♄ 7° S
	6	05	-	☌ ♂ ☽	♂ 2° S
	10	05	-	☌ ♀ *	♀ 5° S of Pollux
	11	00	-	☌ ☿ ☽	☿ 3° N
	12	12	-		☿ stationary
	12	13	-	☌ ♀ ☽	♀ 7° N
	19	16	-	☌ ♃ ☽	♃ 3° N
	21	14	48		Summer solstice; summer begins in Northern Hemisphere
	24	04	-		♄ stationary
	24	23	-	☌ ♆ ☽	♆ 4° S
	25	05	-	☌ ♅ ☽	♅ 5° S
	25	10	-	☌ ☿ ☉	Inferior conj.
	28	21	-	☌ ♄ ☽	♄ 7° S°
July	2	16	-		♃ stationary
	5	05	-	☌ ♂ ☽	♂ 0°.3 N; occultation
	5	19	-		⊕ farthest from ☉; aphelion
	6	20	-		☿ stationary
	7	13	-	☌ ☿ ☽	☿ 1°.3 S
	10	17	-	☌ ♀ *	♀ 1°.1 N of Regulus
	12	12	-	☌ ♀ ☽	♀ 7° N
	14	16	-	☍ ♆ ☉	
	16	23	-	☌ ♃ ☽	♃ 3° N
	17	04	-	☍ ♅ ☉	
	17	14	-		☿ Gr. elong; 21° W of ☉
	18	21	-	☌ ♂ *	♂ 5° N of Aldebaran
	22	07	-	☌ ♆ ☽	♆ 4° S
	22	12	-	☌ ♅ ☽	♅ 5° S
	26	04	-	☌ ♃ ☽	♃ 7° S
	31	07	-	☌ ☿ *	☿ 6° S of Pollux
Aug.	3	04	-	☌ ♂ ☽	♂ 3° N
	9	14	-		♇ stationary
	10	23	-	☌ ♀ ☽	♀ 3° N
	13	01	-	☌ ☿ ☉	Superior conj.
	13	07	-	☌ ♄ ☽	♄ 2° N
	18	14	-	☌ ♆ ☽	♆ 4° S
	18	18	-	☌ ♅ ☽	♅ 5° S
	22	10	-	☌ ♄ ☽	♄ 7° S
	24	23	-		♀ Gr. elong; 46° E of ☉
	31	21	-	☌ ♀ *	♀ 0°.7 S of Spica
Sept.	1	03	-	☌ ♂ ☽	♂ 4° N
	1	17	-	☍ ♄ ☉	
	7	09	-	☌ ☿ ☽	☿ 3° N
	9	01	-	☌ ♀ ☽	♀ 2° S
	9	20	-	☌ ♄ ☽	♄ 1°.4 N
	14	19	-	☌ ♆ ☽	♆ 4° S
	14	23	-	☌ ♅ ☽	♅ 5° S
	18	13	-	☌ ♄ ☽	♄ 7° S
	21	13	-	☌ ☿ *	☿ 0° 1 S of Spica
	23	06	19		Autumnal equinox; autumn begins in Northern Hemisphere
	24	15	-	☌ ♂ *	♂ 6° S of Pollux
	26	16	-		☿ Gr. elong; 26° E of ☉
	28	22	-		♀ Gr. brilliancy

Mo.	d.	h.	m.		
	29	22	-	☌ ♂ ☽	♂ 6° N
Oct.	2	03	-		♅ stationary
	2	14	-		♆ stationary
	6	18	-	☌ ☿ ☽	☿ 3° S
	7	10	-	☌ ♀ ☽	♀ 7° S
	7	12	-	☌ ♃ ☽	♃ 0°.7 N; occultation
	9	09	-		☿ stationary
	12	01	-	☌ ♆ ☽	♆ 4° S
	12	04	-	☌ ♅ ☽	♅ 5° S
	12	23	-		♇ stationary
	15	16	-	☌ ♄ ☽	♄ 7° S
	21	05	-	☌ ☿ ☉	Inferior conj.
	28	13	-	☌ ♂ ☽	♂ 7° N
	29	17	-		☿ stationary
Nov.	2	10	-	☌ ☿ ☽	☿ 4° N
	2	23	-	☌ ♀ ☉	Inferior conj.
	3	01	-	☌ ☿ *	☿ 4° N of Spica
	3	14	-	☌ ☽ ☉	otal solar eclipse
	6	01	-		☿ Gr. elong; 19° W of ☉
	8	08	-	☌ ♆ ☽	♆ 4° S
	8	12	-	☌ ♅ ☽	♅ 6° S
	9	21	-		♄ stationary
	11	21	-	☌ ♄ ☽	♄ 7° S
	12	18	-	☌ ☿ ♀	☿ 5° N
	17	20	-	☌ ♄ ☉	
	18	07	-	☍ ☽ ☉	Penumbral lunar eclipse
	20	13	-	☌ ♇ ☉	
	25	20	-	☌ ♂ ☽	♂ 8° N
	30	14	-	☌ ♀ ☽	♀ 2° N
Dec.	5	19	-	☌ ♆ ☽	♆ 4° S
	6	00	-	☌ ♅ ☽	♅ 6° S
	8	08	-	☌ ♂ *	♂ 2° N of Regulus
	9	05	-	☌ ♄ ☽	♄ 7° S
	9	11	-		♀ Gr. brilliancy
	14	03	-	☌ ☿ ☉	Superior conj.
	22	02	23		Winter solstice; winter begins in Northern Hemisphere
	23	15	-	☌ ♂ ☽	♂ 9° N
	29	05	-	☌ ♀ ☽	♀ 3° N
	30	00	-	☌ ♃ ☽	♃ 1°.1 S; occultation

Rising and Setting of Planets, 1994

Greenwich Mean Time (0 designates midnight)

Venus, 1994

Date		20° N. Latitude Rise	Set	30° N. Latitude Rise	Set	40° N. Latitude Rise	Set	50° N. Latitude Rise	Set	60° N. Latitude Rise	Set
Jan.	1	6:21	17:14	6:43	16:52	7:10	16:25	7:48	15:47	8:57	14:38
	11	6:35	17:31	6:56	17:10	7:21	16:44	7:58	16:08	9:02	15:04
	21	6:46	17:48	7:04	17:30	7:27	17:07	8:00	16:35	8:54	15:40
	31	6:53	18:05	7:08	17:50	7:28	17:31	7:54	17:05	8:37	16:22
Feb.	10	6:57	18:22	7:09	18:10	7:23	17:55	7:43	17:36	8:14	17:05
	20	6:58	18:37	7:06	18:29	7:16	18:20	7:28	18:07	7:48	17:48
Mar.	2	6:58	18:51	7:01	18:47	7:06	18:43	7:11	18:38	7:20	18:30
	12	6:56	19:04	6:56	19:05	6:55	19:07	6:53	19:08	6:50	19:12
	22	6:55	19:18	6:50	19:23	6:43	19:30	6:34	19:39	6:21	19:53
Apr.	1	6:54	19:31	6:45	19:41	6:33	19:53	6:17	20:10	5:51	20:36
	11	6:55	19:46	6:41	20:00	6:24	20:17	6:01	20:41	5:23	21:20
	21	6:58	20:02	6:41	20:19	6:19	20:41	5:48	21:12	4:57	22:05
May	1	7:04	20:18	6:43	20:39	6:18	21:05	5:41	21:42	4:35	22:48
	11	7:13	20:34	6:50	20:57	6:21	21:26	5:40	22:08	4:22	23:26
	21	7:25	20:49	7:01	21:13	6:31	21:43	5:47	22:27	4:23	23:51
	31	7:39	21:01	7:15	21:25	6:46	21:54	6:02	22:37	4:40	23:59
June	10	7:53	21:11	7:32	21:32	7:04	22:00	6:24	22:39	5:12	23:50
	20	8:08	21:16	7:49	21:35	7:35	21:59	6:50	22:33	5:51	23:30
	30	8:21	21:18	8:05	21:34	7:45	21:53	7:18	22:20	6:53	23:04
July	10	8:32	21:16	8:20	21:28	8:06	21:42	7:45	22:02	7:13	22:34
	20	8:42	21:12	8:34	21:19	8:24	21:29	8:11	21:41	7:50	22:01
	30	8:49	21:05	8:46	21:08	8:41	21:12	8:35	21:18	8:26	21:27
Aug.	9	8:55	20:56	8:56	20:55	8:56	20:54	8:57	20:53	8:59	20:51
	19	8:59	20:45	9:04	20:40	9:10	20:34	9:18	20:26	9:30	20:13
	29	9:01	20:33	9:10	20:24	9:21	20:13	9:36	19:57	9:59	19:34
Sept.	8	9:00	20:19	9:13	20:06	9:29	19:50	9:51	19:28	10:25	18:53
	18	8:55	20:02	9:11	19:45	9:32	19:25	10:00	18:56	10:47	18:09
	28	8:42	19:40	9:02	19:20	9:26	18:56	10:00	18:22	10:59	17:23
Oct.	8	8:19	19:10	8:40	18:48	9:07	18:21	9:45	17:43	10:53	16:35
	18	7:40	18:29	8:01	18:07	8:28	17:40	9:07	17:01	10:16	15:52
	28	6:42	17:37	7:02	17:18	7:27	16:53	8:01	16:19	9:01	15:19
Nov.	7	5:36	16:43	5:52	16:27	6:12	16:08	6:39	15:40	7:24	14:56
	17	4:37	15:57	4:49	15:44	5:04	15:29	5:25	15:09	5:58	14:36
	27	3:55	15:22	4:05	15:12	4:18	15:00	4:35	14:42	5:01	14:16
Dec.	7	3:29	14:58	3:39	14:48	3:51	14:36	4:07	14:20	4:32	13:55
	17	3:15	14:42	3:26	14:31	3:39	14:18	3:56	14:00	4:24	13:32
	27	3:09	14:32	3:22	14:19	3:37	14:04	3:57	13:43	4:30	13:11

Mars, 1994

Date		20° N. Latitude Rise	Set	30° N. Latitude Rise	Set	40° N. Latitude Rise	Set	50° N. Latitude Rise	Set	60° N. Latitude Rise	Set
Jan.	1	6:32	17:23	6:54	17:01	7:22	16:34	8:01	15:55	9:11	14:44
	11	6:25	17:18	6:46	16:57	7:13	16:31	7:50	15:53	8:57	14:47
	21	6:17	17:14	6:37	16:54	7:02	16:29	7:37	15:54	8:38	14:53
	31	6:08	17:10	6:26	16:51	6:49	16:28	7:21	15:57	8:15	15:03
Feb.	10	5:57	17:06	6:14	16:49	6:34	16:29	7:02	16:01	7:49	15:14
	20	5:46	17:01	6:00	16:47	6:18	16:29	6:42	16:05	7:21	15:26
Mar.	2	5:33	16:57	5:45	16:45	6:00	16:30	6:20	16:10	6:51	15:39
	12	5:20	16:51	5:29	16:42	5:41	16:31	5:56	16:15	6:21	15:51
	22	5:06	16:46	5:12	16:39	5:21	16:31	5:32	16:20	5:49	16:03
Apr.	1	4:51	16:40	4:55	16:36	5:00	16:31	5:07	16:24	5:17	16:14
	11	4:35	16:34	4:37	16:32	4:39	16:31	4:41	16:29	4:45	16:25
	21	4:20	16:27	4:10	16:20	4:17	16:30	4:15	16:33	4:12	16:36
May	1	4:04	16:21	4:01	16:25	3:56	16:30	3:50	16:36	3:40	16:47
	11	3:49	16:14	3:43	16:21	3:35	16:29	3:24	16:40	3:07	16:57
	21	3:34	16:07	3:25	16:16	3:14	16:27	2:59	16:43	2:35	17:07

Mars, 1994

Date		20° N. Latitude Rise	Set	30° N. Latitude Rise	Set	40° N. Latitude Rise	Set	50° N. Latitude Rise	Set	60° N. Latitude Rise	Set
	31	3:19	16:01	3:07	16:12	2:53	16:26	2:34	16:46	2:04	17:17
June	10	3:04	15:54	2:51	16:07	2:34	16:24	2:11	16:48	1:33	17:26
	20	2:50	15:47	2:35	16:03	2:15	16:22	1:48	16:50	1:03	17:35
	30	2:37	15:40	2:20	15:57	1:58	16:19	1:27	16:50	0:35	17:43
July	10	2:24	15:32	2:05	15:52	1:41	16:16	1:07	16:50	0:09	17:49
	20	2:12	15:25	1:52	15:45	1:26	16:11	0:50	16:48	23:43	17:53
	30	2:01	15:16	1:39	15:37	1:12	16:05	0:34	16:43	23:22	17:53
Aug.	9	1:49	15:07	1:28	15:29	1:00	15:57	0:20	16:37	23:05	17:50
	19	1:38	14:56	1:16	15:19	0:48	15:47	0:07	16:27	22:52	17:42
	29	1:27	14:45	1:05	15:07	0:37	15:35	23:56	16:15	22:42	17:30
Sept.	8	1:16	14:32	0:54	14:54	0:27	15:21	23:46	16:01	22:34	17:13
	18	1:04	14:18	0:43	14:39	0:16	15:06	23:37	15:44	22:29	16:52
	28	0:51	14:02	0:31	14:22	0:06	14:48	23:28	15:24	22:25	16:28
Oct.	8	0:38	13:45	0:18	14:04	23:53	14:28	23:19	15:02	22:21	16:01
	18	0:23	13:27	0:05	13:45	23:41	14:07	23:09	14:39	22:15	15:33
	28	0:06	13:06	23:48	13:23	23:27	13:44	22:58	14:13	22:09	15:03
Nov.	7	23:47	12:44	23:31	13:00	23:12	13:19	22:44	13:47	22:00	14:31
	17	23:26	12:21	23:12	12:35	22:54	12:53	22:29	13:18	21:48	13:59
	27	23:04	11:55	22:50	12:09	22:33	12:25	22:10	12:49	21:32	13:27
Dec.	7	22:38	11:27	22:25	11:40	22:09	11:56	21:47	12:18	21:12	12:53
	17	22:09	10:56	21:56	11:09	21:41	11:24	21:20	11:45	20:46	12:19
	27	21:35	10:22	21:23	10:35	21:08	10:50	20:47	11:11	20:13	11:44

Jupiter, 1994

Date		20° N. Latitude Rise	Set	30° N. Latitude Rise	Set	40° N. Latitude Rise	Set	50° N. Latitude Rise	Set	60° N. Latitude Rise	Set
Jan.	1	2:07	13:30	2:18	13:18	2:33	13:03	2:52	12:44	3:23	12:13
	11	1:34	12:55	1:46	12:43	2:01	12:28	2:21	12:08	2:53	11:36
	21	1:00	12:20	1:12	12:08	1:27	11:52	1:48	11:32	2:21	10:59
	31	0:25	11:44	0:37	11:32	0:53	11:16	1:14	10:55	1:48	10:21
Feb.	10	23:45	11:07	*0:01	10:55	0:17	10:39	0:39	10:17	1:13	9:43
	20	23:07	10:30	23:20	10:17	23:36	10:01	*0:02	9:39	0:36	9:04
Mar.	2	22:28	9:51	22:41	9:38	22:57	9:22	23:19	9:00	23:53	8:26
	12	21:48	9:11	22:01	8:58	22:17	8:42	22:38	8:20	23:12	7:46
	22	21:06	8:30	21:19	8:17	21:34	8:01	21:56	7:40	22:29	7:06
Apr.	1	20:23	7:48	20:36	7:35	20:51	7:20	21:12	6:59	21:45	6:26
	11	19:40	7:05	19:52	6:53	20:07	6:38	20:27	6:17	20:59	5:45
	21	18:55	6:21	19:07	6:10	19:21	5:55	19:41	5:35	20:12	5:04
May	1	18:10	5:38	18:22	5:26	18:36	5:12	18:55	4:53	19:25	4:23
	11	17:25	4:54	17:37	4:43	17:50	4:29	18:09	4:11	18:38	3:42
	21	16:41	4:11	16:52	4:00	17:05	3:47	17:23	3:29	17:51	3:01
	31	15:57	3:28	16:08	3:18	16:21	3:05	16:38	2:47	17:06	2:20
June	10	15:15	2:46	15:25	2:36	15:38	2:23	15:55	2:06	16:22	1:39
	20	14:33	2:05	14:44	1:55	14:56	1:42	15:13	1:25	15:39	0:59
	30	13:53	1:25	14:03	1:15	14:16	1:02	14:33	0:45	14:59	0:19
July	10	13:14	0:46	13:25	0:35	13:37	0:23	13:54	0:06	14:21	23:35
	20	12:37	0:08	12:47	23:53	13:00	23:41	13:17	23:23	13:44	22:56
	30	12:00	23:27	12:11	23:16	12:24	23:03	12:42	22:45	13:09	22:17
Aug.	9	11:25	22:50	11:36	22:39	11:50	22:26	12:08	22:08	12:36	21:39
	19	10:51	22:15	11:02	22:04	11:16	21:50	11:35	21:31	12:05	21:01
	29	10:18	21:40	10:29	21:28	10:44	21:14	11:04	20:54	11:35	20:23
Sept.	8	9:45	21:06	9:57	20:54	10:12	20:39	10:33	20:18	11:05	19:46
	18	9:13	20:33	9:26	20:20	9:42	20:04	10:03	19:43	10:37	19:09
	28	8:42	20:00	8:56	19:47	9:12	19:30	9:34	19:08	10:10	18:32
Oct.	8	8:12	19:27	8:26	19:14	8:43	18:56	9:06	18:33	9:44	17:55
	18	7:42	18:55	7:56	18:41	8:14	18:23	8:38	17:59	9:18	17:19
	28	7:12	18:24	7:27	18:09	7:45	17:50	8:11	17:25	8:52	16:43
Nov.	7	6:42	17:52	6:58	17:37	7:17	17:17	7:43	16:51	8:26	16:08
	17	6:13	17:21	6:29	17:05	6:49	16:45	7:16	16:17	8:01	15:32
	27	5:43	16:50	6:00	16:33	6:20	16:13	6:49	15:44	7:36	14:57
Dec.	7	5:14	16:19	5:31	16:02	5:52	15:40	6:21	15:11	7:10	14:22
	17	4:44	15:48	5:01	15:30	5:23	15:08	5:54	14:38	6:44	13:48
	27	4:14	15:16	4:32	14:58	4:54	14:36	5:25	14:05	6:17	13:13

*2nd Rise 23:58 (30° N. Latitude)

*2nd Set 23:58 (50° N. Latitude)

Saturn, 1994

Date		20° N. Latitude Rise	Set	30° N. Latitude Rise	Set	40° N. Latitude Rise	Set	50° N. Latitude Rise	Set	60° N. Latitude Rise	Set
Jan.	1	9:34	20:56	9:46	20:44	10:00	20:30	10:20	20:10	10:51	19:39
	11	8:58	20:21	9:09	20:10	9:24	19:55	9:43	19:36	10:13	19:06
	21	8:22	19:47	8:33	19:35	8:47	19:22	9:06	19:03	9:35	18:34
	31	7:47	19:12	7:57	19:01	8:11	18:48	8:29	18:30	8:57	18:02
Feb.	10	7:11	18:38	7:22	18:28	7:34	18:15	7:52	17:58	8:19	17:30
	20	6:36	18:04	6:46	17:54	6:58	17:42	7:15	17:25	7:41	16:59
Mar.	2	6:00	17:30	6:10	17:20	6:22	17:08	6:38	16:53	7:03	16:28
	12	5:25	16:56	5:34	16:47	5:46	16:35	6:01	16:20	6:25	15:56
	22	4:49	16:22	4:58	16:13	5:09	16:02	5:24	15:47	5:47	15:24
Apr.	1	4:14	15:47	4:22	15:38	4:33	15:28	4:47	15:14	5:09	14:52
	11	3:38	15:12	3:46	15:04	3:56	14:54	4:10	14:40	4:31	14:19
	21	3:02	14:37	3:10	14:29	3:19	14:19	3:32	14:06	3:53	13:46

Saturn, 1994

Date		20° N. Latitude Rise	Set	30° N. Latitude Rise	Set	40° N. Latitude Rise	Set	50° N. Latitude Rise	Set	60° N. Latitude Rise	Set
May	1	2:25	14:01	2:33	13:54	2:42	13:44	2:55	13:32	3:14	13:12
	11	1:48	13:25	1:56	13:18	2:05	13:08	2:17	12:56	2:36	12:37
	21	1:11	12:48	1:18	12:41	1:27	12:32	1:39	12:20	1:58	12:02
	31	0:33	12:11	0:40	12:04	0:49	11:55	1:01	11:43	1:19	11:25
June	10	23:51	11:33	*0:02	11:26	0:11	11:17	0:22	11:05	0:40	10:47
	20	23:12	10:54	23:19	10:47	23:28	10:38	23:40	10:27	*0:01	10:09
	30	22:33	10:15	22:40	10:07	22:49	9:59	23:00	9:47	23:18	9:29
July	10	21:53	9:34	22:00	9:27	22:09	9:18	22:21	9:06	22:39	8:48
	20	21:13	8:54	21:20	8:46	21:29	8:37	21:41	8:25	22:00	8:06
	30	20:32	8:12	20:39	8:05	20:49	7:55	21:01	7:43	21:20	7:24
Aug.	9	19:51	7:30	19:58	7:22	20:08	7:13	20:21	7:00	20:41	6:40
	19	19:09	6:48	19:17	6:40	19:27	6:30	19:40	6:17	20:01	5:56
	29	18:28	6:05	18:36	5:57	18:46	5:47	19:00	5:33	19:21	5:12
Sept.	8	17:46	5:23	17:54	5:14	18:05	5:04	18:19	4:50	18:41	4:28
	18	17:04	4:40	17:13	4:31	17:24	4:21	17:38	4:06	18:01	3:44
	28	16:23	3:58	16:32	3:49	16:43	3:38	16:58	3:23	17:21	3:00
Oct.	8	15:42	3:16	15:51	3:07	16:02	2:56	16:17	2:41	16:41	2:17
	18	15:01	2:35	15:10	2:26	15:22	2:14	15:37	1:59	16:01	1:35
	28	14:20	1:55	14:30	1:45	14:42	1:33	14:57	1:18	15:21	0:54
Nov.	7	13:41	1:15	13:50	1:05	14:02	0:54	14:17	0:38	14:42	0:14
	17	13:02	0:36	13:11	0:26	13:23	0:15	13:38	23:55	14:02	23:31
	27	12:23	23:53	12:32	23:44	12:44	23:33	12:59	23:17	13:23	22:53
Dec.	7	11:45	23:16	11:54	23:07	12:05	22:55	12:20	22:40	12:44	22:17
	17	11:07	22:39	11:16	22:30	11:27	22:19	11:42	22:04	12:05	21:41
	27	10:30	22:03	10:39	21:54	10:50	21:43	11:04	21:29	11:26	21:07
				*2nd Rise 23:58						*2nd Rise 23:27	

Calculation of Risetimes

The *Daily Calendar* pages contain rise and set times for the Sun and Moon for the Greenwich Meridian at north latitudes 20°, 30°, 40°, 50° and 60°. You probably live somewhere west of the Greenwich meridian, 0° longitude, and within the range of latitudes in the table. Notice that from day to day, the values for the sun at any particular latitude do not change very much. This slow variation for the sun means that no important correction needs to be made from one day to the next, once a proper correction for your latitude has been made. Thus, whenever it rises or sets at the 0° meridian, that will also be the time of that phenomenon at your Standard Time meridian. Any correction necessary for you to be able to observe that phenomenon from your location will be to account for your distance from the Standard Time meridian, and for your latitude.

The moon, however, moves its own diameter, about a half degree, in an hour, or about 12°.5 in one complete turn of the Earth – one day. Most of this is eastward against the background stars of the sky, but some is also north or south of the equator. If there is little change on the same day of the times over the range of latitudes, the moon is near the celestial equator. All of this motion considerably affects the times of rise or set, as you can see from the adjacent entries in the table. Thus, it is necessary also to take your longitude into account in addition to your latitude. If you have no need for total accuracy, simply note that the time will be between the four values you find surrounding your location and the dates of interest.

The process of finding more accurate corrections is called interpolation. In the example, linear interpolation involving simple differences is used. In extreme cases, higher order interpolation should be used. If such cases are important to you, it is suggested that you make a plot of the times, draw smooth curves through the plots, and interpolate by eye between the relevant curves. Some people find this exercise fun.

Let's find the time of the June Full Moon in Brandon, Manitoba. First, find Brandon's latitude and longitude.

I. Brandon, Manitoba
 49° 51′ 00″ N
 99° 57′ 00″ W

IA. Convert these values to decimals:
 51 ÷ 60 = 0°.85
 49 + .85 = 49°.85

 57 ÷ 60 = 0°.95
 99 + .95 = 99°.95

IB. Fraction Brandon lies between latitudes 50° and 60°:
 49°.85 − 40° = 9.85; 9.85 ÷ 10 = .985

IC. Fraction world must turn between Greenwich and Brandon:
 99.95 ÷ 360 = .278

ID. The CST meridian is 90°, thus 99°.95 is 99.95 − 90 = 9.95 degrees west of the CST. In 24 hours there are 24 × 60 = 1440 minutes; 1440 ÷ 360 = 4 minutes for every degree around the Earth. So events happen
 4 × 9.95 = 40
minutes later for Brandon than on the CST meridian of 90°.

IE. The values in IB and IC are the interpolates for Brandon; ID is the time correction from local to standard time for Brandon. These values need never be calculated for Brandon again.

IIA. We need the Greenwich times for moonrise at latitudes 50° and 60°, and for June 23 and 24, the day of Full Moon and the next day.

	Lat. 50°	Diff.	Lat. 60°
June 23	20:04	55	20:59
June 24	20:48	45	21:33

IIB. We want IB and the June 23 time difference:
 .985 × 55 = 54
 Add this to the June 23 time:
 20:04 + 54 = 20:58
 And for June 24:
 .985 × 45 = 44
 20:48 + 44 = 21:92
 These two times are for the latitude of

Brandon, but for the Greenwich meridian.

IIC. To get the time for Brandon, take the difference in the times just determined,

21:92 − 20:58 = 34

and find what fraction of this one-day difference occurred while the Earth turned from Greenwich to Brandon, 0.278:

.278 × 34 = 9.4 minutes after 20:58

Thus, 20:58 + 9 = 21:07, the time the moon will rise at the 90° CST meridian, at the latitude of Brandon.

IID. Events happen at Brandon 40 minutes later than at the 90° meridian, therefore

21:07 + 40 = 21:47 CST at Brandon on June 23.

However, the date is in the Daylight Time period, so we must add a 1 hour correction. Finally, Brandon's moonrise is 22:47 CAT on June 23, 1994.

Star Tables

These tables include stars of visual magnitude 2.5 and brighter. Co-ordinates are for mid-1994. Where no parallax figures are given, the trigonometric parallax figure is smaller than the margin for error and the distance given is obtained by indirect methods. Stars of variable magnitude designated by v.

To find the time when the star is on meridian, subtract R.A.M.S. of the sun table on page 172 from the star's right ascension, first adding 24h to the latter, if necessary. Mark this result P.M., if less than 12h; but if greater than 12, subtract 12h and mark the remainder A.M.

	Star	Magnitude	Parallax ″	Light yrs.	Right ascen. h. m.	Declination ° ′
α	Andromedae (Alpheratz)	2.06	0.02	90	0 08.1	29 04
β	Cassiopeiae	2.27v	0.07	45	0 08.9	59 07
α	Phoenicis	2.39	0.04	93	0 26.0	−42 20
α	Cassiopeiae (Schedir)	2.23	0.01	150	0 40.2	56 30
β	Ceti	2.04	0.06	57	0 43.3	−18 01
γ	Cassiopeiae	2.47v	0.03	96	0 56.4	60 41
β	Andromedae	2.06	0.04	76	1 09.4	35 35
α	Eridani (Achernar)	0.46	0.02	118	1 37.5	−57 16
γ	Andromedae	2.26		260	2 03.5	42 18
α	Arietis	2.00	0.04	76	2 06.9	23 26
o	Ceti	2.00v	0.01	103	2 19.1	−3 00
α	Ursae Min. (Pole Star)	2.02v		680	2 25.8	89 14
β	Persei (Algol)	2.12v	0.03	105	3 07.8	40 56
α	Persei	1.80	0.03	570	3 23.9	49 51
α	Tauri (Aldebaran)	0.85v	0.05	68	4 35.6	16 30
β	Orionis (Rigel)	0.12v		900	5 14.3	−8 12
α	Aurigae (Capella)	0.08	0.07	45	5 16.3	46 00
γ	Orionis (Bellatrix)	1.64	0.03	470	5 24.8	6 21
β	Tauri (El Nath)	1.65	0.02	300	5 25.9	28 36
δ	Orionis	2.23v		1500	5 31.7	−0 18
ϵ	Orionis	1.70		1600	5 35.9	−1 12
ζ	Orionis	2.05	0.02	1600	5 40.5	−1 57
κ	Orionis	2.06	0.01	2100	5 47.5	−9 40
α	Orionis (Betelgeuse)	0.50v		520	5 54.9	7 24
β	Aurigae	1.90	0.04	88	5 59.1	44 57
β	Canis Majoris	1.98	0.01	750	6 22.5	−17 57
α	Carinae (Canopus)	−0.72	0.02	98	6 23.8	−52 42
γ	Geminorum	1.93	0.03	105	6 37.4	16 24
α	Canis Majoris (Sirius)	−1.46	0.38	8.7	6 44.9	−16 42
ϵ	Canis Majoris	1.50		680	6 58.4	−28 58
δ	Canis Majoris	1.86		2100	7 08.2	−26 23
η	Canis Majoris	2.44		2700	7 23.9	−29 18
α	Geminorum (Castor)	1.99	0.07	45	7 34.2	31 54
α	Canis Minoris (Procyon)	0.38	0.29	11.3	7 39.0	5 14
β	Geminorum (Pollux)	1.14	0.09	35	7 45.0	28 02
ζ	Puppis	2.25		2400	8 03.4	−39 59
γ	Velorum	1.82		520	8 09.4	−47 19
ϵ	Carinae	1.86		340	8 22.4	−59 30
δ	Velorum	1.96	0.04	76	8 44.6	−54 41
δ	Velorum	2.21	0.02	750	9 07.8	−43 25
β	Carinae	1.68	0.04	86	9 13.1	−69 42
ι	Carinae	2.25		750	9 16.9	−59 15
κ	Velorum	2.50	0.01	470	9 21.9	−54 59
α	Hydrae	1.98	0.02	94	9 27.3	−8 38
α	Leonis (Regulus)	1.35	0.04	84	10 08.1	12 00
γ	Leonis	1.90	0.02	90	10 19.7	19 55
β	Ursae Majoris (Merak)	2.37	0.04	78	11 01.5	56 25
α	Ursae Majoris (Dubhe)	1.79	0.03	105	11 03.4	61 47
β	Leonis (Denebola)	2.14	0.08	43	11 48.8	14 36
γ	Ursae Majoris (Phecda)	2.44	0.02	90	11 53.5	53 44
α	Crucis	1.58		370	12 26.3	−63 04
γ	Crucis	1.63		220	12 30.9	−57 05
γ	Centauri	2.17		160	12 41.2	−48 56
β	Crucis	1.25v		490	12 47.4	−59 40
ϵ	Ursae Majoris (Alioth)	1.77v	0.01	68	12 53.8	55 59
ζ	Ursae Majoris (Mizar)	2.05	0.04	88	13 23.7	54 57
α	Virginis (Spica)	0.97v	0.02	220	13 24.9	−11 08
ϵ	Centauri	2.30v		570	13 39.5	−53 26
γ	Ursae Majoris (Alkaid)	1.86		210	13 47.3	49 20
β	Centauri	0.61v	0.02	490	14 03.4	−60 21
θ	Centauri	2.06	0.06	55	14 06.4	−36 21
α	Bootis (Arcturus)	−0.04	0.09	36	14 15.4	19 13
η	Centauri	2.31v		390	14 35.2	−42 08
α	Centauri	−0.01	0.75	4.3	14 39.2	−60 49
α	Lupi	2.30v		430	14 41.6	−47 22
ϵ	Bootis	2.40	0.01	103	14 44.7	27 06
β	Ursae Minoris	2.08	0.03	105	14 50.7	74 11
α	Coronae Borealis	2.23v	0.04	76	15 34.5	26 44
δ	Scorpii	2.32		590	16 00.0	−22 36
α	Scorpii (Antares)	0.96v	0.02	520	16 29.1	−26 25
α	Trianguli Australis	1.92	0.02	82	16 48.1	−69 01
ϵ	Scorpii	2.29	0.05	66	16 49.8	−34 17
η	Ophiuchi	2.43	0.05	69	17 10.1	−15 43
λ	Scorpii	1.63v		310	17 33.2	−37 06
α	Ophiuchi	2.08	0.06	58	17 34.7	12 34
θ	Scorpii	1.87	0.02	650	17 36.9	−43 00
κ	Scorpii	2.41v		470	17 42.1	−39 02
γ	Draconis	2.23	0.02	108	17 56.5	51 29
ϵ	Sagittarii	1.85	0.02	124	18 23.8	−34 23
α	Lyrae (Vega)	0.03	0.12	26.5	18 36.8	38 47
ϵ	Sagittarii	2.02		300	18 54.9	−26 18
α	Aquilae (Altair)	0.77	0.20	16.5	19 50.5	8 51
γ	Cygni	2.20		750	20 22.0	40 14
α	Pavonis	1.94		310	20 25.2	−56 45
α	Cygni (Deneb)	1.25		1600	20 41.2	45 16
ϵ	Cygni	2.46	0.04	74	20 46.0	33 57
α	Cephei	2.44	0.06	52	21 18.4	62 34
ϵ	Pegasi	2.39		780	21 43.9	9 51
α	Gruis	1.74	0.05	64	22 07.9	−46 59
β	Gruis	2.11v		280	22 42.3	−46 55
α	Piscis Austrinis (Fomalhaut)	1.16	0.14	22.6	22 57.3	−29 39
β	Pegasi	2.42v	0.02	210	23 03.5	28 03
α	Pegasi	2.49	0.03	109	23 04.5	15 11

Constellations

Culturally, constellations are imagined patterns among the stars that, in some cases, have been recognized through millenia of tradition. In the early days of astronomy, knowledge of the constellations was necessary in order to function as an astronomer. For today's astronomers, constellations are simply areas on the entire sky in which interesting objects await observation and interpretation.

Because western culture has prevailed in establishing modern science, equally viable and interesting constellations and celestial traditions of other cultures (of Asia or Africa, for example) are not well known outside of their regions of origin. Even the patterns with which we are most familiar today have undergone considerable change over the centuries, because the western heritage embraces teachings of cultures disparate in time as well as place.

Today, students of the sky the world over recognize 88 constellations that cover the entire celestial sphere. Many of these have their origins in ancient days; many are "modern," contrived out of unformed stars by astronomers a few centuries ago. Unformed stars were those usually too faint or inconveniently placed to be included in depicting the more prominent constellations. When astronomers began to travel to South Africa in the 16th and 17th centuries, they found a sky that itself was unformed, and showing numerous brilliant stars. Thus, we find constellations in the southern hemisphere like the "air pump," the "microscope," the "furnace," and other technological marvels of the time, as well as some arguably traditional forms, such as the "fly."

Many of the commonly recognized constellations had their origins in Asia Minor. These were adopted by the Greeks and Romans who translated their names and stories into their own languages, some details being modified in the process. After the declines of these cultures, most such knowledge entered oral tradition, or remained hidden in monastic libraries. Beginning in the 8th century, the Moslem explosion spread through the Mediterranean world. Wherever possible, everything was translated into Arabic to be taught in the universities the Moslems established all over their new-found world.

In the 13th century, Alphonsus XX of Spain, an avid student of astronomy, succeeded in having Claudius Ptolemy's *Almagest,* as its Arabian title was known, translated into Latin. It thus became widely available to European scholars. In the process, the constellation names were translated, but the star names were retained in their Arabic forms. Transliterating Arabic into the Roman alphabet has never been an exact art, so many of the star names we use today only "seem" Arabic to all but scholars.

Names of stars often indicated what parts of the traditional figures they represented: Deneb, the tail of the swan; Betelgeuse, the armpit of the giant. Thus, the names were an indication of the position in the sky of a particular star, provided one recognized the traditional form of the mythic figure.

In English, usage of the Latin names for the constellations couples often inconceivable creatures, represented in unimaginable configurations, with names that often seem unintelligible. Avoiding traditional names, astronomers may designate the brighter stars in a constellation with Greek letters, usually in order of brightness. Thus, the "alpha star" is often the brightest star of that constellation. The "of" implies possession, so the genitive (possessive) form of the constellation name is used, as in Alpha Orionis, the first star of Orion (Betelgeuse). Astronomers usually use a 3-letter form for the constellation name, understanding it to be read as either the nominative or genitive case of the name.

Until the 1920's, astronomers used curved boundaries for the constellation areas. As these were rather arbitrary at best, the International Astronomical Union adopted boundaries that ran due north-south and east-west, much like the contiguous states of the United States.

Within these boundaries, and occasionally crossing them, popular "asterisms" are recognized: the Big Dipper is a small part of Ursa Major, the big bear; the Sickle is the traditional head and mane of Leo, the lion; one of the horntips of Taurus, the bull, properly belongs to Auriga, the charioteer; the northeast star of the Great Square of Pegasus is Alpha Andromedae.

It is unlikely that further change will occur in the realm of the celestial constellations.

Name	Genitive	Abbreviation	Meaning
Andromeda	Andromedae	And	Chained Maiden
Antlia	Antliae	Ant	Air Pump
Apus	Apodis	Aps	Bird of Paradise
Aquarius	Aquarii	Aqr	Water Bearer
Aquila	Aquilae	Aql	Eagle
Ara	Arae	Ara	Altar
Aries	Arietis	Ari	Ram
Auriga	Aurigae	Aur	Charioteer
Bootes	Bootis	Boo	Herdsmen
Caelum	Caeli	Cae	Chisel
Camelopardalis	Camelopardalis	Cam	Giraffe
Cancer	Cancri	Cnc	Crab
Canes Venatici	Canum Venaticorum	CVn	Hunting Dogs
Canis Major	Canis Majoris	CMa	Great Dog
Canis Minor	Canis Minoris	CMi	Little Dog
Capricornus	Capricorni	Cap	Sea-goat
Carina	Carinae	Car	Keel
Cassiopeia	Cassiopeiae	Cas	Queen
Centaurus	Centauri	Cen	Centaur
Cepheus	Cephei	Cep	King
Cetus	Ceti	Cet	Whale
Chamaeleon	Chamaeleontis	Cha	Chameleon
Circinus	Circini	Cir	Compasses (art)
Columba	Columbae	Col	Dove
Coma Berenices	Comae Berenices	Com	Berenice's Hair
Corona Australis	Coronae Australis	CrA	Southern Crown

Name	Genitive	Abbreviation	Meaning
Corona Borealis	Coronae Borealis	CrB	Northern Crown
Corvus	Corvi	Crv	Crow
Crater	Crateris	Crt	Cup
Crux	Crucis	Cru	Cross (southern)
Cygnus	Cygni	Cyg	Swan
Delphinus	Delphini	Del	Dolphin
Dorado	Doradus	Dor	Goldfish
Draco	Draconis	Dra	Dragon
Equuleus	Equulei	Equ	Little Horse
Eridanus	Eridani	Eri	River
Fornax	Fornacis	For	Furnace
Gemini	Geminorum	Gem	Twins
Grus	Gruis	Gru	Crane (bird)
Hercules	Herculis	Her	Hercules
Horologium	Horologii	Hor	Clock
Hydra	Hydrae	Hya	Water Snake (female)
Hydrus	Hydri	Hyi	Water Snake (male)
Indus	Indi	Ind	Indian
Lacerta	Lacertae	Lac	Lizard
Leo	Leonis	Leo	Lion
Leo Minor	Leonis Minoris	LMi	Little Lion
Lepus	Leporis	Lep	Hare
Libra	Librae	Lib	Balance
Lupus	Lupi	Lup	Wolf
Lynx	Lyncis	Lyn	Lynx

Name	Genitive	Abbreviation	Meaning
Lyra	Lyrae	Lyr	Lyre
Mensa	Mensae	Men	Table Mountain
Microscopium	Microscopii	Mic	Microscope
Monoceros	Monocerotis	Mon	Unicorn
Musca	Muscae	Mus	Fly
Norma	Normae	Nor	Square (rule)
Octans	Octantis	Oct	Octant
Ophiuchus	Ophiuchi	Oph	Serpent Bearer
Orion	Orionis	Ori	Hunter
Pavo	Pavonis	Pav	Peacock
Pegasus	Pegasi	Peg	Flying Horse
Perseus	Persei	Per	Hero
Phoenix	Phoenicis	Phe	Phoenix
Pictor	Pictoris	Pic	Painter
Pisces	Piscium	Psc	Fishes
Piscis Austrinius	Piscis Austrini	PsA	Southern Fish
Puppis	Puppis	Pup	Stern (deck)
Pyxis	Pyxidis	Pyx	Compass (sea)
Reticulum	Reticuli	Ret	Reticle
Sagitta	Sagittae	Sge	Arrow
Sagittarius	Sagittarii	Sgr	Archer
Scorpius	Scorpii	Sco	Scorpion
Sculptor	Sculptoris	Scl	Sculptor
Scutum	Scuti	Sct	Shield
Serpens	Serpentis	Ser	Serpent
Sextans	Sextantis	Sex	Sextant
Taurus	Tauri	Tau	Bull
Telescopium	Telescopii	Tel	Telescope
Triangulum	Trianguli	Tri	Triangle
Triangulum Australe	Trianguli Australis	TrA	Southern Triangle
Tucana	Tucanae	Tuc	Toucan
Ursa Major	Ursae Majoris	UMa	Great Bear
Ursa Minor	Ursae Minoris	UMi	Little Bear
Vela	Velorum	Vel	Sail
Virgo	Virginis	Vir	Maiden
Volans	Volantis	Vol	Flying Fish
Vulpecula	Vulpeculae	Vul	Fox

Aurora Borealis and Aurora Australis

The Aurora Borealis, also called the Northern Lights, is a broad display of rather faint light in the northern skies at night. The Aurora Australis, a similar phenomenon, appears at the same time in southern skies. The aurora appears in a wide variety of forms. Sometimes it is seen as a quiet glow, almost foglike in character; sometimes as vertical streamers in which there may be considerable motion; sometimes as a series of luminous expanding arcs. There are many colors, with white, yellow, and red predominating.

The auroras are most vivid and most frequently seen at about 20 degrees from the magnetic poles, along the northern coast of the North American continent and the eastern part of the northern coast of Europe. They have been seen as far south as Key West and as far north as Australia and New Zealand, but rarely.

While the cause of the auroras is not known beyond question, there does seem to be a definite correlation between auroral displays and sun-spot activity. It is thought that atomic particles expelled from the sun by the forces that cause solar flares speed through space at velocities of 400 to 600 miles per second. These particles are entrapped by the Earth's magnetic field, forming what are termed the Van Allen belts. The encounter of these clouds of the solar wind with the Earth's magnetic field weakens the field so that previously trapped particles are allowed to impact the upper atmosphere. The collisions between solar and terrestrial atoms result in the glow in the upper atmosphere called the aurora. The glow may be vivid where the lines of magnetic force converge near the magnetic poles.

The auroral displays appear at heights ranging from 50 to about 600 miles and have given us a means of estimating the extent of the Earth's atmosphere.

The auroras are often accompanied by magnetic storms whose forces, also guided by the lines of force of the Earth's magnetic field, disrupt electrical communication.

Eclipses, 1994

(Greenwich Mean Time)

There are four eclipses during 1994, two of the sun and two of the moon.

I. Annular eclipse of the Sun, May 10

The partial phases of this eclipse are visible throughout North America, from south of Panama to beyond the North Pole, including far eastern Siberia, Bering Strait, Greenland, Iceland, the Scandinavian peninsula, and as a sunset phenomenon in parts of western Europe and western Africa; the Hawaiian Islands experience a partial phase at sunrise.

The path of annularity begins in the eastern Pacific Ocean, southeast of Hawaii, passes over the middle of the Baja Peninsula, enters the United States at El Paso, passes through central Missouri, over Lakes Erie and Ontario, central New York State, portions of New England, and portions of the Canadian Maritime Provinces.

Circumstances of the Eclipse

Event	Date	h	m
Eclipse begins	May 10	14	12.2
Central eclipse begins	10	15	23.3
Central eclipse at local noon	10	17	19.8
Central eclipse ends	10	18	59.5
Eclipse ends	10	20	10.6

Maximum duration: 6 min 08.5 sec

II. Partial eclipse of the Moon, May 25

The beginning of the umbral phase visible in the United States (except for the far west, Alaska and Hawaii), southeastern and central Canada, Mexico, Central America, South America, the southern tip of Greenland, Iceland, most of Antarctica, most of Africa, most of Europe, the southeastern North Pacific Ocean, the eastern South Pacific Ocean, the Atlantic Ocean and the southwestern Indian Ocean. The end of the umbral phase is generally visible in the United States (except Alaska and Hawaii), Canada (except for the northwest), Mexico, Central America, South America, the southern tip of Greenland, most of Antarctica, southern and western Africa, the southern United Kingdom, southern and western France, the Iberian Peninsula, the southeastern North Pacific Ocean, the eastern South Pacific Ocean and the Atlantic Ocean.

Circumstances of the Eclipse

Event	Date	h	m
Moon enters penumbra	May 25	1	17.9
Moon enters umbra	25	2	37.3
Middle of eclipse	25	3	30.3
Moon leaves umbra	25	4	23.3
Moon leaves penumbra	25	5	42.7

Magnitude of the eclipse: 0.249

III. Total eclipse of the Sun, November 3

The partial phases are visible in South America, parts of Antarctica, including the Palmer Peninsula, and parts of southern Africa.

The path of totality begins in the eastern Pacific Ocean, enters South America in southern Peru, crosses northern Chile, parts of Argentina, Paraguay and southern Brazil, and the South Atlantic Ocean. The path of totality ends south of Madagascar.

Circumstances of the Eclipse

Event	Date	h	m
Eclipse begins	Nov. 3	11	05.0
Central eclipse begins	3	12	02.7
Central eclipse at local noon	3	13	47.1
Central eclipse ends	3	15	15.4
Eclipse ends	3	16	13.1

Maximum duration: 4 min 27.6 sec

IV. Penumbral eclipse of the Moon, November 18

The beginning of the penumbral phases generally visible in North America, Greenland, Iceland, the Arctic regions, Central America, South America, Hawaii, western Africa, Europe, extreme western Asia, the Palmer Peninsula of Antarctica, the eastern Pacific Ocean, and most of the Atlantic Ocean. The end is generally visible in North America, Greenland, Iceland, the Arctic regions, Central America, western South America, Hawaii, northeastern Asia, eastern Australia, New Zealand, the Pacific Ocean, and western North Atlantic Ocean.

Circumstances of the Eclipse

Event	Date	h	m
Moon enters penumbra	Nov. 18	4	25.7
Middle of eclipse	18	6	43.9
Moon leaves penumbra	18	9	02.1

Penumbral magnitude of the eclipse: 0.908

Total Eclipses, 1900–2000

Date	Duration m s	Width miles	Path of Totality
1900 May 28	2 10	57	Mexico, US, Spain, N. Africa
1901 May 18	6 28	147	Indian Ocean, Sumatra, Borneo, New Guinea
1903 Sept. 21	2 11	150	Indian Ocean, Antarctica
1904 Sept. 9	6 19	145	Pacific Ocean
1905 Aug. 30	3 46	119	Canada, Spain, N. Africa, Arabia
1907 Jan. 14	2 24	117	Russia, China, Mongolia
1908 Jan. 3	4 13	92	Pacific Ocean
1908 Dec. 23h	0 11	6	S. America, Atlantic Ocean, Indian Ocean
1909 June 17h	0 23	32	Greenland, Russia
1910 May 9	4 15	370	Antarctica
1911 Apr. 28	4 57	118	Pacific Ocean
1912 Apr. 17h	0 01	1	Atlantic Ocean, Europe, Russia
1912 Oct. 10	1 55	52	Colombia, Brazil, Atlantic Ocean
1914 Aug. 21	2 14	105	Greenland, Europe, Middle East
1916 Feb. 3	2 36	67	Colombia, Venezuela, Atlantic Ocean
1918 June 8	2 22	70	Pacific Ocean, US
1919 May 29	6 50	152	S. America, Atlantic Ocean, Africa
1921 Oct. 1	1 52	180	Antarctica
1922 Sept. 21	5 58	140	Indian Ocean, Australia
1923 Sept. 10	3 36	103	Pacific Ocean, S. California, Mexico
1925 Jan. 24	2 32	128	Great Lakes, NE US, Atlantic Ocean
1926 Jan. 14	4 10	91	Africa, Indian Ocean, Borneo
1927 June 29	0 50	48	England, Scandinavia, Arctic Ocean, Siberia
1929 May 9	5 06	120	Indian Ocean, Malaya, Philippines
1930 Apr. 28h	0 01	1	Pacific Ocean, US, Canada
1930 Oct. 21	1 55	52	S. Pacific Ocean
1932 Aug. 31	1 44	96	Arctic Ocean, Canada, New England
1934 Feb. 14	2 52	76	Borneo, Pacific Ocean
1936 June 19	2 31	82	Greece, Turkey, Soviet Union, Japan
1937 June 8	7 04	155	Pacific Ocean, Peru
1938 May 29	4 04	420	S. Atlantic Ocean
1939 Oct. 12	1 32	260	Antarctica
1940 Oct. 1	5 35	135	Colombia, Brazil, Atlantic Ocean, S. Africa
1941 Sept. 21	3 21	88	Soviet Union, China, Pacific Ocean
1943 Feb. 4	2 39	142	Japan, Pacific Ocean, Alaska
1944 Jan. 25	4 08	90	Peru, Brazil, W. Africa
1945 July 9	1 15	57	US, Canada, Greenland, Scandinavia, USSR
1947 May 20	5 13	121	S. America, Atlantic Ocean, Africa
1948 Nov. 1	1 55	52	Africa, Indian Ocean
1950 Sept. 12	1 13	83	Arctic Ocean, Siberia, Pacific Ocean
1952 Feb. 25	3 09	85	Africa, Middle East, Soviet Union
1954 June 30	2 35	95	US, Canada, Iceland, Europe, Middle East
1955 June 20	7 07	157	SE Asia, Philippines, Pacific Ocean
1956 June 8	4 44	266	S. Pacific Ocean
1958 Oct. 12	5 10	129	Pacific Ocean, Chile, Argentina
1959 Oct. 2	3 01	75	New England, Atlantic Ocean, Africa
1961 Feb. 15	2 45	160	Europe, Soviet Union
1962 Feb. 5	4 08	91	Borneo, New Guinea, Pacific Ocean
1963 July 20	1 39	63	Pacific Ocean, Alaska, Canada, Maine
1965 May 30	5 15	123	New Zealand, Pacific Ocean
1966 Nov. 12	1 57	52	Pacific Ocean, S. America, Atlantic Ocean
1968 Sept. 22	0 39	64	Soviet Union, China
1970 Mar. 7	3 27	95	Pacific Ocean, Mexico, eastern US, Canada
1972 July 10	2 35	109	Siberia, Alaska, Canada
1973 June 30	7 03	159	Atlantic Ocean, Central Africa, Indian Ocean
1974 June 20	5 08	214	Indian Ocean, Australia
1976 Oct. 23	4 46	123	Africa, Indian Ocean, Australia
1977 Oct. 12	2 37	61	Pacific Ocean, Colombia, Venezuela
1979 Feb. 26	2 49	185	NW US, Canada, Greenland
1980 Feb. 16	4 08	92	Africa, Indian Ocean, India, Burma, China
1981 July 31	2 02	67	Soviet Union, Pacific Ocean
1983 June 11	5 10	123	Indian Ocean, Indonesia, New Guinea
1984 Nov. 22	1 59	53	New Guinea, Pacific Ocean
1985 Nov. 12	1 58	430	Antarctica
1986 Oct. 3h	0 01	1	N. Atlantic Ocean
1987 Mar. 29h	0 07	3	S. Atlantic Ocean, Africa
1988 Mar. 18	3 46	104	Sumatra, Borneo, Philippines, Pacific Ocean
1990 July 22	2 32	125	Finland, Soviet Union, Aleutian Islands
1991 July 11	6 53	160	Hawaii, Mexico, C. America, Colombia, Brazil
1992 June 30	5 20	182	S. Atlantic Ocean
1994 Nov. 3	4 23	117	Peru, Bolivia, Paraguay, Brazil
1995 Oct. 24	2 09	48	Iran, India, SE Asia
1997 Mar. 9	2 50	221	Mongolia, Siberia
1998 Feb. 26	4 08	94	Galapagos Islands, Panama, Colombia, Venezuela
1999 Aug. 11	2 22	69	Europe, Middle East, India

Note: "h" indicates annular-total hybrid eclipse.

The Planets and the Solar System

Planet	Mean daily motion "	Orbital velocity miles per sec.	Sidereal revolution days	Synodical revolution days	Dist. from sun in millions of mi. Max.	Min.	Dist. from Earth in millions of mi. Max.	Min.	Light at[1] perihelion	aphelion
Mercury ...	14732	29.75	88.0	115.9	43.4	28.6	136	50	10.58	4.59
Venus	5768	21.76	224.7	583.9	67.7	66.8	161	25	1.94	1.89
Earth	3548	18.51	365.3	—	94.6	91.4	—	—	1.03	0.97
Mars	1886	14.99	687.0	779.9	155.0	128.5	248	35	0.524	0.360
Jupiter	299	8.12	4331.8	398.9	507.0	460.6	600	368	0.0408	0.0336
Saturn	120	5.99	10760.0	378.1	937.5	838.4	1031	745	0.01230	0.00984
Uranus	42	4.23	30684.0	369.7	1859.7	1669.3	1953	1606	0.00300	0.00250
Neptune ...	21	3.38	60188.3	367.5	2821.7	2760.4	2915	2667	0.00114	0.00109
Pluto	14	2.95	90466.8	366.7	4551.4	2756.4	4644	2663	0.00114	0.00042

(1) Light at perihelion and aphelion is solar illumination in units of mean illumination at Earth.

Planet	Mean longitude of:* ascending node °	'	"	perihelion °	'	"	Inclination* of orbit to ecliptic °	'	"	Mean* distance**	Eccentricity* of orbit	Mean longitude at the epoch* °	'	"
Mercury	48	16	4	77	22	24	7	00	18	0.387098	0.205307	214	37	25
Venus	76	37	55	131	29	21	3	23	41	0.702333	0.006774	306	33	46
Earth	0	0	0	102	50	45	0	0	0	1.000001	0.016711	343	52	31
Mars	49	31	1	335	57	44	1	50	59	1.523679	0.093396	56	22	37
Jupiter	100	24	36	14	14	44	1	18	13	5.202603	0.048486	232	42	23
Saturn	113	37	8	92	57	8	2	29	21	9.554910	0.055527	344	56	27
Uranus	73	58	42	172	55	34	0	46	23	19.218450	0.046297	291	10	12
Neptune	131	43	31	48	2	52	1	46	14	30.110390	0.008988	292	38	33
Pluto***	110	13	37	224	0	32	17	08	9	39.810100	0.254949	229	37	8

* Consistent for the standard Epoch: 1994 September 5 Ephemeris Time. ** Astronomical units. *** Consistent for the standard epoch: 1993 August 1 Ephemeris Time.

Sun and planets	Semi-diameter at unit distance ' "	at mean least dist.	in miles mean s.d.	Volume ⊕=1.	Mass. ⊕=1.	Density ⊕=1.	Sidereal period of rotation d.	h.	m.	s.	Gravity at surface ⊕=1.	Reflecting power Pct.	Probable temperature °F.
Sun	959.62	——	432449	1297370	332946	0.26	24	16	48		27.9	——	+ 10,000
Mercury	3.37	5.5	1515	0.0559	0.0553	1.00	58	15	30		0.37	0.11	+ 620
Venus	8.34	30.1	3760	0.8541	0.8150	0.97	243	R			0.88	0.65	+ 900
Earth	——	——	3963	1.000	1.000	1.00		23	56	6.7	1.00	0.37	+ 72
Moon	2.40	932.4	1080	0.020	0.0123	0.62	27	7	43		0.17	0.12	– 10
Mars	4.69	8.95	2108.5	0.1506	0.1074	0.73	24	37	26		0.38	0.15	– 10
Jupiter	98.35	23.4	44419	1403	317.89	0.25		9	3	30	2.64	0.52	– 240
Saturn	82.83	9.7	37448	832	95.18	0.13		10	39	22	1.15	0.47	– 300
Uranus	35.4	1.9	15881	63	14.54	0.23		17	14	R	1.15	0.40	– 340
Neptune	33.4	1.2	15387	55	17.15	0.30		16	6		1.12	0.35	– 370
Pluto	1.9	0.05	714	0.006	0.0020	0.37	6	9	17		0.04	0.5	? ?

R = retrograde of Venus and Uranus.

The Sun

The sun, the controlling body of our solar system, is a star whose dimensions cause it to be classified among stars as average in size, temperature, and brightness. Its proximity to the Earth makes it appear to us as tremendously large and bright. A series of thermonuclear reactions involving the atoms of the elements of which it is composed produces the heat and light that make life possible on Earth.

The sun has a diameter of 864,000 miles and is distant, on the average, 92,900,000 miles from the Earth. It is 1.41 times as dense as water. The light of the sun reaches the Earth in 499.012 seconds or slightly more than 8 minutes. The average solar surface temperature has been measured by several indirect methods which agree closely on a value of 6,000° Kelvin or about 10,000° F. The interior temperature of the sun is about 35,000,000 F.°.

When sunlight is analyzed with a spectroscope, it is found to consist of a continuous spectrum composed of all the colors of the rainbow in order, crossed by many dark lines. The "absorption lines" are produced by gaseous materials in the atmosphere of the sun. More than 60 of the natural terrestrial elements have been identified in the sun, all in gaseous form because of the intense heat of the sun.

Spheres and Corona

The radiating surface of the sun is called the **photosphere**, and just above it is the **chromosphere.** The chromosphere is visible to the naked eye only at times of total solar eclipses, appearing then to be a pinkish-violet layer with occasional great prominences projecting above its general level. With proper instruments the chromosphere can be seen or photographed whenever the sun is visible without waiting for a total eclipse. Above the chromosphere is the **corona,** also visible to the naked eye only at times of total eclipse. Instruments also permit the brighter portions of the corona to be studied whenever conditions are favorable. The pearly light of the corona surges millions of miles from the sun. Iron, nickel, and calcium are believed to be principal contributors to the composition of the corona, all in a state of extreme attenuation and high ionization that indicates temperatures on the order of a million degrees Fahrenheit.

Sunspots

There is an intimate connection between sunspots and the corona. At times of low sunspot activity, the fine streamers of the corona will be much longer above the sun's equator than over the polar regions of the sun, while during high sunspot activity, the corona extends fairly evenly outward from all regions of the sun, but to a much greater distance in space. Sunspots are dark, irregularly-shaped regions whose diameters may reach tens of thousands of miles. The average life of a sunspot group is from two to three weeks, but there have been groups that have lasted for more than a year, being carried repeatedly around as the sun rotated upon its axis. The record for the duration of a sunspot is 18 months. Sunspots reach a low point every 11.3 years, with a peak of activity occurring irregularly between two successive minima.

The sun is 400,000 times as bright as the full moon and gives the Earth 6 million times as much light as do all the other stars put together. Actually, most of the stars that can be easily seen on any clear night are brighter than the sun.

The Zodiac

The sun's apparent yearly path among the stars is known as the **ecliptic.** The zone 16° wide, 8° on each side of the ecliptic, is known as the **zodiac.** Inside of this zone are the apparent paths of the sun, moon, earth, and major planets. Beginning at the point on the ecliptic which marks the position of the sun at the vernal equinox, and thence proceeding eastward, the zodiac is divided into twelve signs of 30° each, as shown herewith.

These signs are named from the twelve constellations of the zodiac with which the signs coincided in the time of the astronomer Hipparchus, about 2,000 years ago. Owing to the precession of the equinoxes, that is to say, to the retrograde motion of the equinoxes along the ecliptic, each sign in the zodiac has, in the course of 2,000 years, moved backward 30° into the constellation west of it; so that the sign Aries is now in the constellation Pisces, and so on. The vernal equinox will move from Pisces into Aquarius about the middle of the 26th century. The signs of the zodiac with their Latin and English names are as follows:

Spring	1. ♈ Aries.	The Ram.
	2. ♉ Taurus.	The Bull.
	3. ♊ Gemini.	The Twins.
Summer	4. ♋ Cancer.	The Crab.
	5. ♌ Leo.	The Lion.
	6. ♍ Virgo.	The Virgin.
Autumn	7. ♎ Libra.	The Balance.
	8. ♏ Scorpius.	The Scorpion.
	9. ♐ Sagittarius.	The Archer.
Winter	10. ♑ Capricorn.	The Goat.
	11. ≈ Aquarius.	The Water Bearer.
	12. ♓ Pisces.	The Fishes.

Moon's Phases, 1994

(Greenwich Mean Time)

New Moon				First Q				Full Moon				Last Q				Perigee			Apogee		
Month	**Day**	**h**	**m**	**Month**	**Day**	**h**	**m**	**Month**	**Day**	**h**	**m**	**Month**	**Day**	**h**	**m**	**Month**	**Day**	**h**	**Month**	**Day**	**h**
												Jan.	5	00	00	Jan.	6	1	Jan.	19	5
Jan.	11	23	10	Jan.	19	20	27	Jan.	27	13	23	Feb.	3	08	06	Jan.	31	4	Feb.	16	2
Feb.	10	14	30	Feb.	18	17	47	Feb.	28	01	15	Mar.	4	16	53	Feb.	27	22	Mar.	15	17
Mar.	12	07	05	Mar.	20	12	14	Mar.	27	11	09	Apr.	3	02	55	Mar.	28	6	Apr.	12	0
Apr.	11	00	17	Apr.	19	02	34	Apr.	25	19	45	May	2	14	32	Apr.	25	17	May	9	2
May	10	17	07	May	18	12	50	May	25	03	39	June	1	04	02	May	24	3	June	5	13
June	9	08	26	June	16	19	56	June	23	11	33	June	30	19	31	June	21	7	July	3	5
July	8	21	37	July	16	01	12	July	22	22	16	July	30	12	40	July	18	18	July	30	23
Aug.	7	08	45	Aug.	14	05	57	Aug.	21	06	47	Aug.	29	06	41	Aug.	12	23	Aug.	27	18
Sept.	5	18	33	Sept.	12	11	34	Sept.	19	20	00	Sept.	28	00	23	Sept.	8	14	Sept.	24	12
Oct.	5	03	55	Oct.	11	19	17	Oct.	19	12	18	Oct.	27	16	44	Oct.	6	14	Oct.	22	2
Nov.	3	13	35	Nov.	10	06	14	Nov.	18	06	57	Nov.	26	07	04	Nov.	4	0	Nov.	18	5
Dec.	2	23	54	Dec.	9	21	06	Dec.	18	02	17	Dec.	25	19	06	Dec.	2	12	Dec.	15	8
																Dec	30	23			

Astronomical Constants: Speed of Light

The following were adopted in 1968, in accordance with the resolutions and recommendations of the International Astronomical Union (Hamburg 1964): Speed of light, 299,792.5 kilometers per second, or about 186,282.3976 statute miles per second; solar parallax, 8″.794; constant of nutation, 9″.210; and constant of aberration, 20″.496.

The Moon

The moon completes a circuit around the Earth in a period whose mean or average duration is 27 days 7 hours 43.2 minutes. This is the moon's sidereal period. Because of the motion of the moon in common with the Earth around the sun, the mean duration of the lunar month — the period from one new moon to the next new moon — is 29 days 12 hours 44.05 minutes. This is the moon's synodical period.

The mean distance of the moon from the Earth according to the American Ephemeris is 238,857 miles. Because the orbit of the moon about the Earth is not circular but elliptical, however, the maximum distance from the Earth that the moon may reach is 252,710 miles and the least distance is 221,463 miles. All distances are from the center of one object to the center of the other.

The moon's diameter is 2,160 miles. If we deduct the radius of the moon, 1,080 miles, and the radius of the Earth, 3,963 miles from the minimum distance or perigee, given above, we shall have for the nearest approach of the bodies' surfaces 216,420 miles.

The moon rotates on its axis in a period of time exactly equal to its sidereal revolution about the Earth — 27.321666 days. The moon's revolution about the Earth is irregular because of its elliptical orbit. The moon's rotation, however, is regular and this, together with the irregular revolution, produces what is called "libration in longitude" which permits us to see first farther around the east side and then farther around the west side of the moon. The moon's variation north or south of the ecliptic permits us to see farther over first one pole and then the other of the moon and this is "libration in latitude." These two libration effects permit us to see a total of about 60% of the moon's surface over a period of time. The hidden side of the moon was photographed in 1959 by the Soviet space vehicle Lunik III. Since then many excellent pictures of nearly all of the moon's surface have been transmitted to Earth by Lunar Orbiters launched by the U.S.

The tides are caused mainly by the moon, because of its proximity to the Earth. The ratio of the tide-raising power of the moon to that of the sun is 11 to 5.

Harvest Moon and Hunter's Moon

The Harvest Moon, the full moon nearest the Autumnal Equinox, ushers in a period of several successive days when the moon rises soon after sunset. This phenomenon gives farmers in temperate latitudes extra hours of light in which to harvest their crops before frost and winter come. The 1994 Harvest Moon falls on Sept. 19 GMT. Harvest moon in the south temperate latitudes falls on March 27.

The next full moon after Harvest Moon is called the Hunter's Moon, accompanied by a similar phenomenon but less marked; — Oct. 19, northern hemisphere; May 25, southern hemisphere.

The Earth: Size, Definitions of Time, Seasons

Size and Dimensions

The Earth is the fifth largest planet and the third from the sun. Its mass is 6 sextillion, 588 quintillion short tons. Using the parameters of an ellipsoid adopted by the International Astronomical Union in 1964 and recognized by the International Union of Geodesy and Geophysics in 1967, the length of the equator is 24,901.55 miles, the length of a meridian is 24,859.82 miles, the equatorial diameter is 7,926.41 miles, and the area of this reference ellipsoid is approximately 196,938,800 square miles.

The Earth is considered a solid, rigid mass with a dense core of magnetic, probably metallic material. The outer part of the core is probably liquid. Around the core is a thick shell or mantle of heavy crystalline rock which in turn is covered by a thin crust forming the solid granite and basalt base of the continents and ocean basins. Over broad areas of the Earth's surface the crust has a thin cover of sedimentary rock such as sandstone, shale, and limestone formed by weathering of the Earth's surface and deposition of sands, clays, and plant and animal remains.

The temperature in the Earth increases about 1°F. with every 100 to 200 feet in depth, in the upper 100 kilometers of the Earth, and the temperature near the core is believed to be near the melting point of the core materials under the conditions at that depth. The heat of the Earth is believed to be derived from radioactivity in the rocks, pressures developed within the Earth, and original heat (if the Earth in fact was formed at high temperatures).

Atmosphere of the Earth

The Earth's atmosphere is a blanket composed of nitrogen, oxygen, and argon, in amounts of about 78, 21, and 1% by volume. Also present in minute quantities are carbon dioxide, hydrogen, neon, helium, krypton, and xenon.

Water vapor displaces other gases and varies from nearly zero to about 4% by volume. The height of the **ozone** layer varies from approximately 12 to 21 miles above the Earth. Traces exist as low as 6 miles and as high as 35 miles. Traces of methane have been found.

The atmosphere rests on the Earth's surface with the weight equivalent to a layer of water 34 ft. deep. For about 300,000 ft. upward the gases remain in the proportions stated. Gravity holds the gases to the Earth. The weight of the air compresses it at the bottom, so that the greatest density is at the Earth's surface. Pressure, as well as density, decreases as height increases because the weight pressing upon any layer is always less than that pressing upon the layers below.

The temperature of the air drops with increased height until the **tropopause** is reached. This may vary from 25,000 to 60,000 ft. The atmosphere below the tropopause is the **troposphere;** the atmosphere for about twenty miles above the tropopause is the **stratosphere,** where the temperature generally increases with height except at high latitudes in winter. A temperature maximum near the 30-mile level is called the **stratopause.** Above this boundary is the **mesosphere** where the temperature decreases with height to a minimum, the **mesopause,** at a height of 50 miles. Extending above the mesosphere to the outer fringes of the atmosphere is the **thermosphere,** a region where temperature increases with height to a value measured in thousands of degrees Fahrenheit. The lower portion of this region, extending from 50 to about 400 miles in altitude, is characterized by a high ion density, and is thus called the **ionosphere.** The outer region is called **exosphere;** this is the region where gas molecules traveling at high speed may escape into outer space, above 600 miles.

Latitude, Longitude

Position on the globe is measured by means of meridians and parallels. Meridians, which are imaginary lines drawn around the Earth through the poles, determine **longitude.** The meridian running through Greenwich, England, is the **prime meridian of longitude,** and all others are either east or west. Parallels, which are imaginary circles parallel with the equator, determine **latitude.** The length of a degree of longitude varies as the cosine of the latitude. At the equator a degree is 69.171 statute miles; this is gradually reduced toward the poles. Value of a longitude degree at the poles is zero.

Latitude is reckoned by the number of degrees north or south of the equator, an imaginary circle on the Earth's surface everywhere equidistant between the two poles. According to the IAU Ellipsoid of 1964, the length of a degree of latitude is 68.708 statute miles at the equator and varies slightly north and south because of the oblate form of the globe; at the poles it is 69.403 statute miles.

Definitions of Time

The Earth rotates on its axis and follows an elliptical orbit around the sun. The rotation makes the sun appear to move across the sky from East to West. It determines day and night and the complete rotation, in relation to the sun, is called the **apparent** or **true solar day.** This varies but an average determines the **mean solar day** of 24 hours.

The mean solar day is in universal use for civil purposes. It may be obtained from apparent solar time by correcting observations of the sun for the equation of time, but when high precision is required, the mean solar time is calculated from its relation to sidereal time. These relations are extremely complicated, but for most practical uses, they may be considered as follows:

Sidereal time is the measure of time defined by the diurnal motion of the vernal equinox, and is determined from observation of the meridian transits of stars. One complete rotation of the Earth relative to the equinox is called the **sidereal day.** The **mean sidereal day** is 23 hours, 56 minutes, 4.091 seconds of mean solar time.

The **Calendar Year** begins at 12 o'clock midnight precisely local clock time, on the night of Dec. 31-Jan. 1. The day and the calendar month also begin at midnight by the clock. The interval required for the Earth to make one absolute revolution around the sun is a **sidereal year;** it consisted of 365 days, 6 hours, 9 minutes, and 9.5 seconds of mean solar time (approximately 24 hours per day) in 1900, and is increasing at the rate of 0.0001-second annually.

The **Tropical Year,** on which the return of the seasons depends, is the interval between two consecutive returns of the sun to the vernal equinox. The tropical year consists of 365 days, 5 hours, 48 minutes, and 46 seconds in 1900. It is decreasing at the rate of 0.530 seconds per century.

In 1956 the unit of time interval was defined to be identical with the second of **Ephemeris Time,** 1/31,556,925.9747 of the tropical year for 1900 January 0d 12th hour E.T. A physical definition of the second based on a quantum transition of cesium (atomic second) was adopted in 1964. The atomic second is equal to 9,192,631,770 cycles of the emitted radiation. In 1967 this atomic second was adopted as the unit of time interval for the Int. System of Units.

The Zones and Seasons

The five zones of the Earth's surface are Torrid, lying between the Tropics of Cancer and Capricorn; North Temperate, between Cancer and the Arctic Circle; South Temperate, between Capricorn and the Antarctic Circle; The Frigid Zones, between the polar Circles and the Poles.

The inclination or tilt of the Earth's axis with respect to the sun determines the seasons. These are commonly marked in the North Temperate Zone, where spring begins at the vernal equinox, summer at the summer solstice, autumn at the autumnal equinox and winter at the winter solstice.

In the South Temperate Zone, the seasons are reversed. Spring begins at the autumnal equinox, summer at the winter solstice, etc.

If the Earth's axis were perpendicular to the plane of the Earth's orbit around the sun there would be no change of seasons. Day and night would be of nearly constant length and there would be equable conditions of temperature. But the axis is tilted 23° 27′ away from a perpendicular to the orbit and only in March and Sept. is the axis at right angles to the sun.

The points at which the sun crosses the equator are the equinoxes, when day and night are most nearly equal. The points at which the sun is at a maximum distance from the equator are the solstices. Days and nights are then most unequal.

In June the North Pole is tilted 23° 27′ toward the sun and the days in the northern hemisphere are longer than the nights, while the days in the southern hemisphere are shorter than the nights. In December the North Pole is tilted 23° 27′ away from the sun and the situation is reversed.

The Seasons in 1994

In 1994 the 4 seasons will begin as follows (Greenwich Mean Time).

		Date	GMT
Vernal Equinox	**Spring**	Mar. 20	20:28
Summer Solstice	**Summer**	June 21	14:48
Autumnal Equinox	**Autumn**	Sept. 23	06:19
Winter Solstice	**Winter**	Dec. 22	02:23

Poles of the Earth

The geographic (rotation) poles, or points where the Earth's axis of rotation cuts the surface, are not absolutely fixed in the body of the Earth. The pole of rotation describes an irregular curve about its mean position.

Two periods have been detected in this motion: (1) an annual period due to seasonal changes in barometric pressure, load of ice and snow on the surface and to other phenomena of seasonal character; (2) a period of about 14 months due to the shape and constitution of the Earth.

In addition there are small but as yet unpredictable irregularities. The whole motion is so small that the actual pole always remains within a circle of 30 or 40 feet in radius centered at the mean position of the pole.

The pole of rotation for the time being is of course the pole having a latitude of 90° and an indeterminate longitude.

Magnetic Poles

The **north magnetic pole** of the Earth is that region where the magnetic force is vertically downward and the **south magnetic pole** that region where the magnetic force is vertically upward. A compass placed at the magnetic poles experiences no directive force in azimuth.

There are slow changes in the distribution of the Earth's magnetic field. These changes were once attributed in part to a periodic movement of the magnetic poles around the geographical poles, but later evidence refutes this theory and points, rather, to a slow migration of "disturbance" foci over the Earth.

There appear shifts in position of the magnetic poles due to the changes in the Earth's magnetic field. The center of the area designated as the north magnetic pole was estimated to be in about latitude 70.5° N and longitude 96° W in 1905; from recent nearby measurements and studies of the secular changes, the position in 1970 is estimated as latitude 76.2° N and longitude 101° W. Improved data rather than actual motion partly account for the change.

The position of the south magnetic pole in 1912 was near 71° S and longitude 150° E; the position in 1970 is estimated at latitude 66° S and longitude 139.1° E.

The direction of the horizontal components of the magnetic field at any point is known as magnetic north at that point, and the angle by which it deviates east or west of true north is known as the magnetic declination, or in the mariner's terminology, the **variation of the compass.**

A compass without error points in the direction of

magnetic north. (In general this is *not* the direction of the magnetic north pole.) If one follows the direction indicated by the north end of the compass, he will travel along a rather irregular curve which eventually reaches the north magnetic pole (though not usually by a great-circle route). However, the action of the compass should not be thought of as due to any influence of the distant pole, but simply as an indication of the distribution of the Earth's magnetism at the place of observation.

Rotation of the Earth

The speed of rotation of the Earth about its axis has been found to be slightly variable. The variations may be classified as:

(A) **Secular.** Tidal friction acts as a brake on the rotation and causes a slow secular increase in the length of the day, about 1 millisecond per century.

(B) **Irregular.** The speed of rotation may increase for a number of years, about 5 to 10, and then start decreasing. The maximum difference from the mean in the length of the day during a century is about 5 milliseconds. The accumulated difference in time has amounted to approximately 44 seconds since 1900. The cause is probably motion in the interior of the Earth.

(C) **Periodic.** Seasonal variations exist with periods of one year and six months. The cumulative effect is such that each year the Earth is late about 30 milliseconds near June 1 and is ahead about 30 milliseconds near Oct. 1. The maximum seasonal variation in the length of the day is about 0.5 millisecond. It is believed that the principal cause of the annual variation is the seasonal change in the wind patterns of the Northern and Southern Hemispheres. The semiannual variation is due chiefly to tidal action of the sun, which distorts the shape of the Earth slightly.

The secular and irregular variations were discovered by comparing time based on the rotation of the Earth with time based on the orbital motion of the moon about the Earth and of the planets about the sun. The periodic variation was determined largely with the aid of quartz-crystal clocks. The introduction of the cesium-beam atomic clock in 1955 made it possible to determine in greater detail the nature of the irregular and periodic variations.

Morning and Evening Stars, 1994

(GMT)

	Morning	Evening
Jan.	Mercury, Jan. 1 to 3 Venus, Jan. 1 to 17 Mars, Jan. 1 Jupiter, Jan. 1 Uranus, from Jan. 12 Neptune, from Jan. 11 Pluto, Jan. 1	Mercury, from Jan. 3 Venus, from Jan. 17 Saturn, Jan. 1 Uranus, Jan. 1 to 12 Neptune, Jan. 1 to 11
Feb.	Mercury, from Feb. 20 Mars Jupiter Saturn, from Feb. 21 Uranus Neptune Pluto	Mercury, to Feb. 20 Venus Saturn, to Feb. 21
Mar.	Mercury Jupiter Saturn Uranus Neptune Pluto	Venus
Apr.	Mercury, to Apr. 30 Mars Jupiter, to Apr. 30 Saturn Uranus Neptune Pluto	Mercury, from Apr. 30 Venus Jupiter, from Apr. 30
May	Mars Saturn Uranus Neptune Pluto, to May 17	Mercury Venus Jupiter Pluto, from May 17
June	Mercury, from Jun. 25 Mars Saturn Uranus Neptune	Mercury, to Jun. 25 Venus Jupiter Pluto
July	Mercury Mars Saturn Uranus, to July 17 Neptune, to July 14	Venus Jupiter Uranus, from July 17 Neptune, from July 14 Pluto
Aug.	Mercury, to Aug. 13 Mars Saturn	Mercury, from Aug. 13 Jupiter Uranus Neptune Pluto
Sept.	Mars Saturn, to Sept. 1	Mercury Venus Jupiter Saturn, from Sept. 1 Uranus Neptune Pluto
Oct.	Mercury, from Oct. 21 Mars	Mercury, to Oct. 21 Venus Jupiter Saturn Uranus Neptune Pluto
Nov.	Mercury Venus, from Nov. 2 Mars Jupiter, from Nov. 17 Pluto, from Nov. 20	Venus, to Nov. 2 Jupiter, to Nov. 17 Saturn Uranus Neptune Pluto, to Nov. 20
Dec.	Mercury, to Dec. 17 Venus Jupiter Pluto	Mercury, from Dec. 14 Saturn Uranus Neptune

Chronological Eras, 1994

The year 1994 of the Christian Era marks the 430th anniversary of Shakespeare's birth.

Era	Year	Begins in 1994	
Byzantine	7503	Sept.	14
Jewish	5755	Sept.	5 (sunset)
Roman (Ab Urbe Condita)	2747	Jan.	14
Nabonassar (Babylonian)	2743	Apr.	25
Japanese	2654	Jan.	1
Grecian (Seleucidae)	2306	Sept. or Oct.	14 / 14
Diocletian	1711	Sept.	11
Indian (Saka)	1916	Mar.	22
Mohammedan (Hegira)	1415	June	9

Chronological Cycles, 1994

Dominical Letter	B	Golden Number (Lunar Cycle).....	XIX	Roman Indiction	2
Epact	17	Solar Cycle........................	15	Julian Period (year of)..........	6707

Twilight

Twilight is that evening period of waning light from the time of sunset to dark, often termed dusk. Morning twilight, a time of increasing light, is called dawn. The source of this light is the sun shining on the atmosphere above the observer. Twilight is a time of very slowly changing sky illumination with no abrupt variations. Nevertheless, there are three commonly accepted divisions in this smooth continuum defined by the distance the sun lies below the astronomical horizon: civil twilight, nautical twilight and astronomical twilight. The astonomical horizon is that great circle lying 90° from the zenith, the point directly over the observer's head. Twilight ends in the evening or begins in the morning at a particular time. Nominally, evening events are repeated in reverse order in the morning.

Civil twilight is that time between the moment of sunset, when the sun's apparent upper edge is just at the horizon until the centre of the sun is 6° directly below the horizon. After this time, a newspaper becomes increasingly difficult to read.

Nautical twilight ends when the sun's centre is 12° below the horizon. By this time the bright stars used by navigators have appeared and the horizon may still be seen. After this time, the horizon is more obscure, preventing navigators from making star sights.

Astronomical twilight ends in the evening when the sun is 18° below the horizon, and the sky is dark enough, at least away from the sun's location, to allow astronomical work to proceed. Sunlight, however, is still shining on the higher levels of the atmosphere from the observer's zenith to the horizon toward the sun. Although not named as a period of twilight, when the sun is 24° below the horizon, no part of the observer's atmosphere, even toward the sun, receives any sunlight.

In the tropics the sun moves nearly vertically, accomplishing its 6°, 12° or 18° depression very quickly. In the polar regions the sun's diurnal motion may actually be nearly along the horizon, prolonging the twilight period, or even not permitting darkness to fall at all. In mid-latitudes civil twilight may last about half an hour, nautical an hour, and astronomers can go to work in about 90 minutes.

The twilight tables given in *The World Almanac* are for astronomical twilight, and presented for reference only. Although the instant of the sun's horizontal depression may be calculated precisely, the phenomena associated with the event are sufficiently imprecise that the table is not recalculated each year.

Astronomical Twilight – Meridian of Greenwich[1]

Date 1993[1]	20° Begin	20° End	30° Begin	30° End	40° Begin	40° End	50° Begin	50° End	60° Begin	60° End
	h m	h m	h m	h m	h m	h m	h m	h m	h m	h m
Jan. 1	5 16	6 50	5 30	6 35	5 45	6 21	6 00	6 07	6 18	5 49
11	5 19	6 56	5 33	6 43	5 46	6 30	6 00	6 17	6 15	6 01
21	5 21	7 01	5 32	6 51	5 43	6 40	5 55	6 30	6 06	6 18
Feb. 1	5 21	7 07	5 29	6 58	5 38	6 51	5 45	6 44	5 51	6 38
11	5 18	7 11	5 24	7 05	5 29	7 01	5 32	6 59	5 32	7 01
21	5 13	7 15	5 17	7 12	5 17	7 12	5 16	7 14	5 09	7 23
Mar. 1	5 08	7 18	5 08	7 19	5 06	7 21	4 59	7 29	4 44	7 45
11	5 00	7 21	4 58	7 24	4 50	7 32	4 38	7 46	4 12	8 12
21	4 52	7 24	4 45	7 32	4 33	7 44	4 14	8 04	3 37	8 43
Apr. 1	4 42	7 28	4 31	7 39	4 14	7 57	3 47	8 25	2 53	9 21
11	4 32	7 32	4 18	7 47	3 56	8 09	3 20	8 47	2 03	10 10
21	4 23	7 36	4 04	7 54	3 37	8 23	2 52	9 11	0 37	11 47
May 1	4 14	7 41	3 52	8 04	3 19	8 37	2 22	9 39		
11	4 08	7 46	3 41	8 13	3 03	8 53	1 49	10 09		
21	4 02	7 52	3 32	8 22	2 48	9 07	1 13	10 46		
June 1	3 58	7 58	3 26	8 30	2 36	9 20	0 21	11 52		
11	3 56	8 03	3 22	8 36	2 29	9 30				
21	3 57	8 06	3 22	8 40	2 28	9 35				
July 1	3 59	8 07	3 25	8 41	2 30	9 35				
11	4 03	8 06	3 30	8 39	2 40	9 30				
21	4 08	8 03	3 39	8 33	2 52	9 18	1 12	11 23		
Aug. 1	4 15	7 56	3 48	8 23	3 09	9 01	1 49	10 20		
11	4 20	7 50	3 56	8 13	3 22	8 46	2 21	9 46		
21	4 24	7 41	4 05	8 01	3 34	8 27	2 47	9 15		
Sept. 1	4 29	7 31	4 14	7 46	3 51	8 08	3 13	8 43	1 40	10 02
11	4 32	7 20	4 20	7 33	4 02	7 50	3 33	8 16	2 36	9 12
21	4 35	7 11	4 26	7 19	4 14	7 31	3 52	7 52	3 11	8 31
Oct. 1	4 38	7 02	4 33	7 05	4 25	7 13	4 10	7 28	3 41	7 54
11	4 40	6 53	4 40	6 53	4 35	6 58	4 26	7 05	4 07	7 23
21	4 43	6 47	4 45	6 44	4 45	6 43	4 41	6 46	4 32	6 55
Nov. 1	4 46	6 41	4 52	6 34	4 56	6 30	4 58	6 27	4 56	6 27
11	4 50	6 38	4 59	6 28	5 06	6 21	5 13	6 14	5 17	6 08
21	4 55	6 36	5 06	6 25	5 16	6 15	5 26	6 04	5 37	5 52
Dec. 1	5 00	6 37	5 13	6 24	5 25	6 11	5 38	5 58	5 53	5 42
11	5 06	6 40	5 20	6 26	5 34	6 12	5 48	5 57	6 06	5 38
21	5 11	6 45	5 25	6 30	5 39	6 16	5 55	6 00	6 15	5 40
31	5 15	6 50	5 30	6 35	5 44	6 21	6 00	6 06	6 18	5 48

(1) Although the instant of the sun's horizontal depression may be calculated precisely, the phenomena associated with astronomical twilight are sufficiently imprecise that the table is not re-calculated each year.

1st Month — January 1994 — 31 days

Greenwich Mean Time

NOTE: Light numbers indicate Sun. **Dark** numbers indicate **Moon**. *Degrees are North Latitude.*

FM = full moon; LQ = last quarter; NM = new moon; FQ = first quarter.

CAUTION: Must be converted to local time. For instructions see page 176.

Day of month	week year	Sun on Meridian / **Moon phase** h	m	s	Sun's Declination °	′	20° Rise Sun / **Moon** h m	20° Set Sun / **Moon** h m	30° Rise Sun / **Moon** h m	30° Set Sun / **Moon** h m	40° Rise Sun / **Moon** h m	40° Set Sun / **Moon** h m	50° Rise Sun / **Moon** h m	50° Set Sun / **Moon** h m	60° Rise Sun / **Moon** h m	60° Set Sun / **Moon** h m
1	Sa	12	3	32	–23	2	6 35	17 32	6 56	17 11	7 22	16 45	7 59	16 09	9 02	15 05
	1						**21 09**	**9 06**	**21 03**	**9 14**	**20 56**	**9 23**	**20 47**	**9 36**	**20 32**	**9 55**
2	Su	12	4	0	–22	57	6 35	17 33	6 56	17 12	7 22	16 46	7 59	16 10	9 02	15 06
	2						**22 07**	**9 48**	**22 06**	**9 52**	**22 05**	**9 56**	**22 03**	**10 01**	**22 01**	**10 09**
3	Mo	12	4	28	–22	52	6 36	17 33	6 56	17 13	7 22	16 47	7 58	16 11	9 01	15 08
	3						**23 05**	**10 30**	**23 09**	**10 29**	**23 13**	**10 27**	**23 20**	**10 25**	**23 30**	**10 22**
4	Tu	12	4	56	–22	46	6 36	17 34	6 57	17 13	7 22	16 48	7 58	16 12	9 01	15 10
	4						**– –**	**11 13**	**– –**	**11 07**	**– –**	**11 00**	**– –**	**10 50**	**– –**	**10 35**
5	We	12	5	23	–22	40	6 36	17 35	6 57	17 14	7 22	16 49	7 58	16 13	9 00	15 11
	5	**0**	**0**	**LQ**			**0 04**	**11 57**	**0 12**	**11 47**	**0 23**	**11 34**	**0 37**	**11 17**	**1 00**	**10 50**
6	Th	12	5	49	–22	33	6 37	17 35	6 57	17 15	7 22	16 50	7 58	16 14	8 59	15 13
	6						**1 04**	**12 44**	**1 17**	**12 30**	**1 33**	**12 12**	**1 55**	**11 48**	**2 30**	**11 09**
7	Fr	12	6	15	–22	26	6 37	17 36	6 57	17 16	7 22	16 51	7 57	16 15	8 58	15 15
	7						**2 05**	**13 35**	**2 22**	**13 17**	**2 42**	**12 55**	**3 11**	**12 25**	**3 59**	**11 34**
8	Sa	12	6	41	–22	18	6 37	17 36	6 57	17 17	7 22	16 52	7 57	16 17	8 57	15 17
	8						**3 07**	**14 29**	**3 26**	**14 09**	**3 50**	**13 44**	**4 24**	**13 10**	**5 22**	**12 10**
9	Su	12	7	6	22	10	6 37	17 37	6 57	17 17	7 22	16 53	7 57	16 18	8 56	15 19
	9						**4 07**	**15 26**	**4 27**	**15 06**	**4 53**	**14 40**	**5 29**	**14 04**	**6 32**	**13 01**
10	Mo	12	7	31	–22	01	6 37	17 38	6 57	17 18	7 22	16 54	7 56	16 19	8 55	15 21
	10						**5 05**	**16 25**	**5 25**	**16 06**	**5 50**	**15 41**	**6 26**	**15 06**	**7 27**	**14 06**
11	Tu	12	7	55	–21	52	6 37	17 38	6 57	17 19	7 21	16 55	7 56	16 21	8 54	15 23
	11	**23**	**10**	**NM**			**5 59**	**17 24**	**6 17**	**17 07**	**6 40**	**16 45**	**7 12**	**16 15**	**8 05**	**15 23**
12	We	12	8	18	–21	43	6 33	17 39	6 57	17 20	7 21	16 56	7 55	16 22	8 52	15 25
	12						**6 48**	**18 22**	**7 03**	**18 08**	**7 22**	**17 50**	**7 49**	**17 26**	**8 32**	**16 45**
13	Th	12	8	41	–21	33	6 38	17 40	6 57	17 21	7 21	16 57	7 54	16 23	8 51	15 27
	13						**7 32**	**19 17**	**7 44**	**19 07**	**7 59**	**18 54**	**8 19**	**18 36**	**8 51**	**18 08**
14	Fr	12	9	3	–21	23	6 38	17 40	6 57	17 21	7 21	16 58	7 54	16 25	8 50	15 29
	14						**8 13**	**20 10**	**8 21**	**20 04**	**8 31**	**19 56**	**8 45**	**19 45**	**9 06**	**19 28**
15	Sa	12	9	25	–21	12	6 38	17 41	6 57	17 22	7 20	16 59	7 53	16 26	8 48	15 31
	15						**8 51**	**21 01**	**8 55**	**20 59**	**9 01**	**20 56**	**9 07**	**20 53**	**9 18**	**20 47**
16	Su	12	9	46	–21	01	6 38	17 42	6 57	17 23	7 20	17 00	7 52	16 28	8 46	15 34
	16						**9 28**	**21 51**	**9 28**	**21 53**	**9 28**	**21 55**	**9 28**	**21 58**	**9 29**	**22 03**
17	Mo	12	10	6	–20	50	6 38	17 42	6 56	17 24	7 19	17 01	7 51	16 29	8 45	15 36
	17						**10 03**	**22 40**	**9 59**	**22 45**	**9 55**	**22 53**	**9 49**	**23 02**	**9 39**	**23 17**
18	Tu	12	10	25	–20	38	6 38	17 43	6 56	17 25	7 19	17 02	7 50	16 31	8 43	15 38
	18						**10 39**	**23 28**	**10 31**	**23 38**	**10 22**	**23 50**	**10 10**	**– –**	**9 51**	**– –**
19	We	12	10	44	–20	25	6 38	17 44	6 56	17 26	7 18	17 03	7 50	16 32	8 41	15 41
	19	**20**	**27**	**FQ**			**11 16**	**– –**	**11 04**	**– –**	**10 51**	**– –**	**10 32**	**0 06**	**10 04**	**0 32**
20	Th	12	11	2	–20	13	6 38	17 44	6 56	17 27	7 18	17 05	7 49	16 34	8 40	15 43
	20						**11 55**	**0 18**	**11 40**	**0 31**	**11 23**	**0 47**	**10 58**	**1 09**	**10 20**	**1 45**
21	Fr	12	11	19	–19	60	6 38	17 45	6 55	17 27	7 17	17 06	7 48	16 36	8 38	15 45
	21						**12 36**	**1 08**	**12 19**	**1 24**	**11 58**	**1 44**	**11 29**	**2 12**	**10 41**	**2 58**
22	Sa	12	11	35	–19	46	6 38	17 46	6 55	17 28	7 17	17 07	7 47	16 37	8 36	15 48
	22						**13 22**	**2 00**	**13 03**	**2 18**	**12 39**	**2 41**	**12 06**	**3 14**	**11 10**	**4 08**
23	Su	12	11	51	–19	33	6 38	17 46	6 55	17 29	7 16	17 08	7 45	16 39	8 34	15 50
	23						**14 11**	**2 52**	**13 51**	**3 12**	**13 26**	**3 37**	**12 50**	**4 12**	**11 50**	**5 12**
24	Mo	12	12	6	–19	19	6 37	17 47	6 54	17 30	7 15	17 09	7 44	16 40	8 32	15 53
	24						**15 04**	**3 44**	**14 45**	**4 04**	**14 20**	**4 30**	**13 44**	**5 05**	**12 44**	**6 06**
25	Tu	12	12	20	–19	4	6 37	17 48	6 54	17 31	7 15	17 10	7 43	16 42	8 30	15 55
	25						**16 01**	**4 36**	**15 42**	**4 55**	**15 19**	**5 19**	**14 47**	**5 52**	**13 52**	**6 49**
26	We	12	12	33	–18	49	6 37	17 48	6 54	17 32	7 14	17 12	7 42	16 44	8 28	15 58
	26						**16 59**	**5 26**	**16 44**	**5 43**	**16 24**	**6 04**	**15 57**	**6 33**	**15 12**	**7 20**
27	Th	12	12	45	–18	34	6 37	17 49	6 53	17 33	7 13	17 13	7 41	16 45	8 26	16 01
	27	**13**	**23**	**FM**			**17 59**	**6 14**	**17 47**	**6 28**	**17 32**	**6 45**	**17 12**	**7 08**	**16 39**	**7 44**
28	Fr	12	12	57	–18	19	6 37	17 49	6 53	17 34	7 12	17 14	7 39	16 47	8 23	16 03
	28						**18 59**	**7 01**	**18 51**	**7 10**	**18 42**	**7 22**	**18 29**	**7 38**	**18 09**	**8 02**
29	Sa	12	13	8	–18	3	6 36	17 50	6 52	17 34	7 12	17 15	7 38	16 49	8 21	16 06
	29						**19 58**	**7 45**	**19 55**	**7 50**	**19 52**	**7 56**	**19 47**	**8 05**	**19 40**	**8 17**
30	Su	12	13	18	–17	47	6 36	17 51	6 52	17 35	7 11	17 16	7 37	16 50	8 19	16 08
	30						**20 58**	**8 29**	**21 00**	**8 29**	**21 03**	**8 29**	**21 06**	**8 30**	**21 11**	**8 31**
31	Mo	12	13	27	–17	30	6 36	17 51	6 51	17 36	7 10	17 18	7 35	16 52	8 17	16 11
	31						**21 58**	**9 12**	**22 05**	**9 08**	**22 13**	**9 02**	**22 25**	**8 55**	**22 43**	**8 45**

2nd Month — February 1994 — 28 days

Greenwich Mean Time

NOTE: Light numbers indicate Sun. **Dark** numbers indicate **Moon**. *Degrees are North Latitude.*

FM = full moon; LQ = last quarter; NM = new moon; FQ = first quarter.

CAUTION: Must be converted to local time. For instructions see page 176.

Day of month	week year	Sun on Meridian **Moon phase** h m s	Sun's Declination ° '	20° Rise Sun **Moon** h m	20° Set Sun **Moon** h m	30° Rise Sun **Moon** h m	30° Set Sun **Moon** h m	40° Rise Sun **Moon** h m	40° Set Sun **Moon** h m	50° Rise Sun **Moon** h m	50° Set Sun **Moon** h m	60° Rise Sun **Moon** h m	60° Set Sun **Moon** h m
1	Tu	12 13 35	−17 13	6 36	17 52	6 51	17 37	7 09	17 19	7 34	16 54	8 14	16 14
	32			**22 59**	**9 57**	**23 10**	**9 48**	**23 24**	**9 37**	**23 43**	**9 22**	**– –**	**9 00**
2	We	12 13 43	−16 56	6 35	17 52	6 50	17 38	7 08	17 20	7 33	16 56	8 12	16 16
	33			**23 59**	**10 43**	**– –**	**10 30**	**– –**	**10 14**	**– –**	**9 52**	**0 14**	**9 17**
3	Th	12 13 50	−16 39	6 35	17 53	6 49	17 39	7 07	17 21	7 31	16 57	8 10	16 19
	34	**8 6 LQ**		**– –**	**11 32**	**0 15**	**11 16**	**0 34**	**10 55**	**1 00**	**10 27**	**1 44**	**9 41**
4	Fr	12 13 56	−16 21	6 35	17 53	6 49	17 40	7 06	17 22	7 30	16 59	8 07	16 21
	35			**1 00**	**12 35**	**1 19**	**12 06**	**1 41**	**11 42**	**2 14**	**11 09**	**3 08**	**10 13**
5	Sa	12 14 1	−16 03	6 34	17 54	6 48	17 40	7 05	17 24	7 28	17 01	8 05	16 24
	36			**2 00**	**13 20**	**2 20**	**13 00**	**2 45**	**12 34**	**3 21**	**11 59**	**4 22**	**10 57**
6	Su	12 14 5	−15 45	6 34	17 55	6 47	17 41	7 04	17 25	7 26	17 02	8 02	16 27
	37			**2 58**	**14 17**	**3 18**	**13 57**	**3 43**	**13 32**	**4 19**	**12 57**	**5 21**	**11 56**
7	Mo	12 14 09	−15 27	6 33	17 55	6 47	17 42	7 03	17 26	7 25	17 04	8 00	16 29
	38			**3 51**	**15 15**	**4 10**	**14 57**	**4 34**	**14 34**	**5 08**	**14 01**	**6 04**	**13 07**
8	Tu	12 14 12	−15 8	6 33	17 56	6 46	17 43	7 02	17 27	7 23	17 06	7 57	16 32
	39			**4 41**	**16 12**	**4 58**	**15 56**	**5 19**	**15 37**	**5 47**	**15 10**	**6 34**	**14 25**
9	We	12 14 14	−14 49	6 32	17 56	6 45	17 44	7 01	17 28	7 22	17 08	7 55	16 35
	40			**5 27**	**17 07**	**5 40**	**15 55**	**5 57**	**16 40**	**6 20**	**16 19**	**6 56**	**15 46**
10	Th	12 14 15	−14 29	6 32	17 57	6 44	17 45	6 59	17 30	7 20	17 09	7 52	16 37
	41	**14 30 NM**		**6 09**	**18 01**	**6 19**	**17 52**	**6 31**	**17 42**	**6 47**	**17 29**	**7 13**	**17 07**
11	Fr	12 14 15	−14 10	6 32	17 57	6 44	17 45	6 58	17 31	7 18	17 11	7 50	16 40
	42			**6 48**	**18 52**	**6 54**	**18 48**	**7 01**	**18 43**	**7 11**	**18 36**	**7 26**	**18 25**
12	Sa	12 14 15	−13 50	6 31	17 58	6 43	17 46	6 57	17 32	7 16	17 13	7 47	16 43
	43			**7 25**	**19 42**	**7 27**	**19 43**	**7 29**	**19 43**	**7 33**	**19 42**	**7 28**	**19 42**
13	Su	12 14 14	−13 30	6 30	17 58	6 42	17 47	6 56	17 33	7 15	17 15	7 44	16 45
	44			**8 01**	**20 32**	**7 59**	**20 36**	**7 57**	**20 41**	**7 53**	**20 47**	**7 49**	**20 58**
14	Mo	12 14 12	−13 10	6 30	17 59	6 41	17 48	6 55	17 34	7 13	17 16	7 42	16 48
	45			**8 37**	**21 21**	**8 31**	**21 29**	**8 24**	**21 38**	**8 14**	**21 52**	**8 00**	**22 12**
15	Tu	12 14 10	−12 50	6 29	17 59	6 40	17 49	6 53	17 36	7 11	17 18	7 39	16 51
	46			**9 13**	**22 10**	**9 04**	**22 21**	**8 52**	**22 36**	**8 37**	**22 55**	**8 13**	**23 26**
16	We	12 14 6	−12 29	6 29	18 00	6 39	17 49	6 52	17 37	7 09	17 20	7 36	16 53
	47			**9 51**	**23 00**	**9 39**	**23 14**	**9 23**	**23 32**	**9 01**	**23 56**	**8 27**	**– –**
17	Th	12 14 2	−12 8	6 28	18 00	6 38	17 50	6 51	17 38	7 07	17 21	7 33	16 56
	48			**10 32**	**23 30**	**10 16**	**– –**	**9 56**	**– –**	**9 30**	**– –**	**8 46**	**0 39**
18	Fr	12 13 58	−11 47	6 28	18 01	6 37	17 51	6 49	17 39	7 06	17 23	7 31	16 58
	49	**17 47 FQ**		**11 15**	**– –**	**10 57**	**0 07**	**10 34**	**0 29**	**10 03**	**0 59**	**9 11**	**1 49**
19	Sa	12 13 52	−11 26	6 27	18 01	6 37	17 52	6 48	17 40	7 04	17 25	7 28	17 01
	50			**12 02**	**0 41**	**11 42**	**1 00**	**11 18**	**1 24**	**10 43**	**1 58**	**9 45**	**2 55**
20	Su	12 13 46	−11 05	6 26	18 01	6 36	17 52	6 47	17 41	7 02	17 27	7 25	17 04
	51			**12 52**	**1 32**	**12 32**	**1 52**	**12 07**	**2 17**	**11 32**	**2 52**	**10 32**	**3 53**
21	Mo	12 13 39	−10 43	6 26	18 02	6 35	17 53	6 45	17 42	7 00	17 28	7 22	17 06
	52			**13 46**	**2 24**	**13 27**	**2 43**	**13 03**	**3 07**	**12 29**	**3 42**	**11 32**	**4 40**
22	Tu	12 13 32	−10 21	6 25	18 02	6 34	17 54	6 44	17 44	6 58	17 30	7 19	17 09
	53			**14 42**	**3 14**	**14 25**	**3 32**	**14 04**	**3 54**	**13 34**	**4 25**	**12 45**	**5 16**
23	We	12 13 24	−9 59	6 24	18 03	6 33	17 55	6 43	17 45	6 56	17 32	7 17	17 11
	54			**15 41**	**4 02**	**15 27**	**4 18**	**15 10**	**4 36**	**14 46**	**5 02**	**14 08**	**5 44**
24	Th	12 13 15	−9 37	6 24	18 03	6 32	17 55	6 41	17 46	6 54	17 33	7 14	17 14
	55			**16 41**	**4 50**	**16 31**	**5 01**	**16 19**	**5 15**	**16 02**	**5 35**	**15 36**	**6 05**
25	Fr	12 13 6	−9 15	6 23	18 03	6 31	17 56	6 40	17 47	6 52	17 35	7 11	17 16
	56			**17 42**	**5 35**	**17 36**	**5 43**	**17 30**	**5 52**	**17 21**	**6 04**	**17 08**	**6 22**
26	Sa	12 12 56	−8 53	6 22	18 04	6 30	17 57	6 38	17 48	6 50	17 37	7 08	17 19
	57	**1 15 FM**		**18 43**	**6 20**	**18 43**	**6 23**	**18 42**	**6 26**	**18 42**	**6 31**	**18 41**	**6 37**
27	Su	12 12 46	−8 31	6 22	18 04	6 28	17 57	6 37	17 49	6 48	17 38	7 05	17 22
	58			**19 45**	**7 05**	**19 50**	**7 03**	**19 55**	**7 01**	**20 03**	**6 57**	**20 16**	**6 52**
28	Mo	12 12 35	−8 8	6 21	18 05	6 27	17 58	6 35	17 50	6 46	17 40	7 02	17 24
	59			**20 47**	**7 51**	**20 57**	**7 44**	**21 09**	**7 36**	**21 25**	**7 24**	**21 51**	**7 07**

3rd Month March 1994 31 days

Greenwich Mean Time

NOTE: Light numbers indicate Sun. **Dark** numbers indicate **Moon**. *Degrees are North Latitude.*

FM = full moon; LQ = last quarter; NM = new moon; FQ = first quarter.

CAUTION: Must be converted to local time. For instructions see page 176.

Day of month week year	Sun on Meridian **Moon phase** h m s	Sun's Declination °	20° Rise Sun **Moon** h m	20° Set Sun **Moon** h m	30° Rise Sun **Moon** h m	30° Set Sun **Moon** h m	40° Rise Sun **Moon** h m	40° Set Sun **Moon** h m	50° Rise Sun **Moon** h m	50° Set Sun **Moon** h m	60° Rise Sun **Moon** h m	60° Set Sun **Moon** h m
1 Tu	12 12 23	–7 45	6 20	18 05	6 26	17 59	6 34	17 51	6 44	17 52	6 59	17 27
60			**21 50**	**8 39**	**22 04**	**8 27**	**22 21**	**8 13**	**22 45**	**7 54**	**23 24**	**7 25**
2 We	12 12 11	–7 23	6 19	18 05	6 25	10 00	6 32	17 53	6 42	17 34	6 56	17 29
61			**22 53**	**9 29**	**23 10**	**9 13**	**23 32**	**8 55**	**– –**	**8 29**	**– –**	**7 47**
3 Th	12 11 59	–6 60	6 19	18 06	6 24	18 00	6 31	17 54	6 40	17 45	6 53	17 32
62			**23 54**	**10 21**	**– –**	**10 03**	**– –**	**9 41**	**0 02**	**9 09**	**0 52**	**8 17**
4 Fr	12 11 46	–6 37	6 18	18 06	6 23	18 01	6 29	17 55	6 38	17 47	6 51	17 34
63	**16 53 LQ**		**– –**	**11 16**	**0 14**	**10 57**	**0 38**	**10 32**	**1 12**	**9 57**	**2 11**	**8 58**
5 Sa	12 11 32	–6 14	6 17	18 06	6 22	18 02	6 28	17 56	6 36	17 48	6 48	17 37
64			**0 53**	**12 13**	**1 13**	**11 53**	**1 38**	**11 28**	**2 14**	**10 53**	**3 15**	**9 52**
6 Su	12 11 19	–5 50	6 16	18 07	6 21	18 02	6 26	17 57	6 34	17 50	6 45	17 39
65			**1 48**	**13 10**	**2 07**	**12 52**	**2 31**	**12 28**	**3 05**	**11 55**	**4 02**	**10 59**
7 Mo	12 11 5	–5 27	6 15	18 07	6 20	18 03	6 25	17 58	6 32	17 52	6 42	17 42
66			**2 38**	**14 07**	**2 56**	**13 50**	**3 17**	**13 30**	**3 47**	**13 02**	**4 36**	**12 14**
8 Tu	12 10 50	–5 04	6 15	18 07	6 19	18 04	6 23	17 58	6 29	17 63	6 39	17 44
67			**3 25**	**15 02**	**3 39**	**14 39**	**3 57**	**14 32**	**4 22**	**14 10**	**5 01**	**13 33**
9 We	12 10 35	–4 40	6 14	18 08	6 17	18 04	6 22	18 00	6 27	17 55	6 36	17 47
68			**4 07**	**15 55**	**4 18**	**15 45**	**4 32**	**15 34**	**4 50**	**15 18**	**5 19**	**14 52**
10 Th	12 10 20	–4 17	6 13	18 08	6 16	18 05	6 20	18 01	6 25	17 56	6 33	17 49
69			**4 47**	**16 46**	**4 54**	**16 41**	**5 03**	**16 34**	**5 15**	**16 25**	**5 34**	**16 10**
11 Fr	12 10 4	–3 53	6 12	18 08	6 15	18 06	6 19	18 02	6 23	17 58	6 30	17 52
70			**5 24**	**17 37**	**5 28**	**17 35**	**5 32**	**17 33**	**5 37**	**17 31**	**5 46**	**17 27**
12 Sa	12 9 49	–3 30	6 11	18 09	6 14	18 06	6 17	18 03	6 21	18 00	6 27	17 54
71	**7 5 NM**		**6 00**	**18 26**	**6 00**	**18 28**	**5 59**	**18 31**	**5 59**	**18 36**	**5 57**	**18 42**
13 Su	12 9 32	–3 06	6 10	18 09	6 13	18 07	6 15	18 04	6 19	18 01	6 24	17 57
72			**6 36**	**19 15**	**6 32**	**19 21**	**6 27**	**19 29**	**6 20**	**19 40**	**6 09**	**19 56**
14 Mo	12 9 16	–2 42	6 10	18 09	6 12	18 07	6 14	18 05	6 17	18 03	6 21	17 59
73			**7 12**	**20 04**	**7 04**	**20 14**	**6 55**	**20 26**	**6 41**	**20 43**	**6 21**	**21 10**
15 Tu	12 8 59	–2 19	6 09	18 10	6 10	18 08	6 12	18 06	6 14	18 04	6 18	18 02
74			**7 50**	**20 53**	**7 39**	**21 07**	**7 24**	**21 23**	**7 05**	**21 46**	**6 36**	**22 23**
16 We	12 8 42	–1 55	6 08	18 10	6 09	18 09	6 11	18 08	6 12	18 06	6 15	18 04
75			**8 29**	**21 43**	**8 15**	**22 00**	**7 57**	**22 20**	**7 32**	**22 48**	**6 53**	**23 34**
17 Th	12 8 25	–1 31	6 07	18 10	6 08	18 09	6 09	18 09	6 10	18 08	6 12	18 07
76			**9 11**	**22 34**	**8 54**	**22 52**	**8 33**	**23 15**	**8 04**	**23 47**	**7 16**	**– –**
18 Fr	12 8 8	–1 08	6 06	18 10	6 07	18 10	6 07	18 10	6 08	18 09	6 09	18 09
77			**9 56**	**23 24**	**9 37**	**23 44**	**9 14**	**– –**	**8 41**	**– –**	**7 46**	**0 41**
19 Sa	12 7 50	–0 44	6 05	18 11	6 06	18 11	6 06	18 11	6 06	18 11	6 06	18 11
78			**10 44**	**– –**	**10 24**	**– –**	**10 00**	**0 08**	**9 25**	**0 42**	**8 27**	**1 41**
20 Su	12 7 33	–0 20	6 04	18 11	6 04	18 11	6 04	18 12	6 04	18 12	6 03	18 14
79	**12 14 FQ**		**11 35**	**0 14**	**11 16**	**0 34**	**10 52**	**0 58**	**10 18**	**1 33**	**9 20**	**2 31**
21 Mo	12 7 15	0 3	6 04	18 11	6 03	18 12	6 02	18 13	6 01	18 14	6 00	18 16
80			**12 29**	**1 03**	**12 11**	**1 22**	**11 49**	**1 45**	**11 18**	**2 17**	**10 25**	**3 11**
22 Tu	12 6 57	0 27	6 03	18 12	6 02	18 12	6 01	18 14	5 59	18 16	5 57	18 19
81			**13 25**	**1 51**	**13 10**	**2 08**	**12 51**	**2 28**	**12 24**	**2 56**	**11 41**	**3 42**
23 We	12 6 39	0 51	6 02	18 12	6 01	18 13	5 59	18 15	5 57	18 17	5 54	18 21
82			**14 23**	**2 38**	**14 11**	**2 51**	**13 56**	**3 08**	**13 36**	**3 30**	**13 04**	**4 05**
24 Th	12 6 21	1 14	6 01	18 12	5 59	18 14	5 58	18 16	5 55	18 19	5 50	18 24
83			**15 22**	**3 24**	**15 14**	**3 33**	**15 05**	**3 45**	**14 52**	**4 00**	**14 32**	**4 24**
25 Fr	12 6 2	1 38	6 00	18 12	5 58	18 14	5 56	18 17	5 53	18 20	5 47	18 26
84			**16 22**	**4 08**	**16 19**	**4 13**	**16 16**	**4 20**	**16 11**	**4 28**	**16 04**	**4 40**
26 Sa	12 5 44	2 2	5 59	18 13	5 57	18 15	5 54	18 18	5 50	18 22	5 44	18 28
85			**17 24**	**4 53**	**17 26**	**4 54**	**17 29**	**4 54**	**17 32**	**4 55**	**17 38**	**4 55**
27 Su	12 5 26	2 25	5 58	18 13	5 56	18 15	5 53	18 19	5 48	18 24	5 41	18 31
86	**11 9 FM**		**18 28**	**5 39**	**18 35**	**5 35**	**18 43**	**5 29**	**18 55**	**5 22**	**19 14**	**5 11**
28 Mo	12 5 8	2 49	5 57	18 13	5 55	18 16	5 51	18 20	5 46	18 25	5 38	18 33
87			**19 32**	**6 27**	**19 44**	**6 18**	**19 59**	**6 07**	**20 19**	**5 52**	**20 51**	**5 28**
29 Tu	12 4 49	3 12	5 57	18 13	5 53	18 17	5 49	18 21	5 44	18 27	5 35	18 36
88			**20 38**	**7 18**	**20 53**	**7 04**	**21 13**	**6 48**	**21 40**	**6 25**	**22 25**	**5 49**
30 We	12 4 31	3 35	5 56	18 14	5 42	18 17	5 48	18 22	5 42	18 28	5 32	18 38
89			**21 42**	**8 11**	**22 00**	**7 54**	**22 24**	**7 33**	**22 56**	**7 04**	**23 51**	**6 17**
31 Th	12 4 13	3 59	5 55	18 14	5 51	18 18	5 46	18 23	5 40	18 30	5 29	18 41
90			**22 44**	**9 08**	**23 04**	**8 49**	**23 29**	**8 25**	**– –**	**7 51**	**– –**	**6 55**

4th Month April 1994 30 days

Greenwich Mean Time

NOTE: Light numbers indicate Sun. **Dark** numbers indicate **Moon**. *Degrees are North Latitude.*

FM = full moon; LQ = last quarter; NM = new moon; FQ = first quarter.

CAUTION: Must be converted to local time. For instructions see page 176.

Day of month / week / year	Sun on Meridian / Moon phase (h m s)	Sun's Declination (° ′)	20° Rise Sun / Moon (h m)	20° Set Sun / Moon (h m)	30° Rise Sun / Moon (h m)	30° Set Sun / Moon (h m)	40° Rise Sun / Moon (h m)	40° Set Sun / Moon (h m)	50° Rise Sun / Moon (h m)	50° Set Sun / Moon (h m)	60° Rise Sun / Moon (h m)	60° Set Sun / Moon (h m)
1 Fr	12 3 55	4 22	5 54	18 14	5 50	18 18	5 45	18 24	5 37	18 31	5 26	18 43
91			23 42	10 06	– –	9 46	– –	9 21	0 03	8 46	1 03	7 46
2 Sa	12 3 37	4 45	5 53	18 14	5 49	18 19	5 43	18 25	5 35	18 33	5 23	18 46
92			– –	11 05	0 01	10 46	0 26	10 22	1 00	9 48	1 58	8 51
3 Su	12 3 20	5 8	5 52	18° 15	5 47	18 20	5 41	18 26	5 33	18 35	5 20	18 48
93	2 55 LQ		0 35	12 02	0 53	11 45	1 15	11 24	1 46	10 54	2 37	10 05
4 Mo	12 3 2	5 31	5 51	18 15	5 46	18 20	5 40	18 27	5 31	18 36	5 17	18 50
94			1 23	12 58	1 38	12 44	1 57	12 27	2 23	12 02	3 05	11 23
5 Tu	12 2 45	5 54	5 50	18 15	5 45	18 21	5 38	18 28	5 29	18 38	5 14	18 53
95			2 07	13 52	2 19	13 41	2 34	13 28	2 54	14 10	3 25	12 42
6 We	12 2 27	6 17	5 50	18 16	5 44	18 22	5 37	18 29	5 27	18 39	5 11	18 55
96			2 47	14 43	2 55	14 37	3 06	14 28	3 19	14 17	3 41	13 59
7 Th	12 2 11	6 39	5 49	18 16	5 43	18 22	5 35	18 30	5 25	18 41	5 08	18 58
97			3 25	15 33	3 29	15 31	3 35	15 27	3 42	15 23	3 54	15 15
8 Fr	12 1 54	7 2	5 48	18 16	5 42	18 23	5 34	18 31	5 22	18 42	5 05	19 00
98			4 01	16 22	4 02	16 24	4 03	16 25	4 04	16 27	4 06	16 30
9 Sa	12 1 37	7 24	5 47	18 16	5 40	18 23	5 32	18 32	5 20	18 44	5 02	19 03
99			4 37	17 11	4 34	17 16	4 30	17 22	4 25	17 31	4 17	17 44
10 Su	12 1 21	7 47	5 46	18 17	5 39	18 24	5 30	18 33	5 18	18 45	4 49	19 05
100			5 13	18 00	5 06	18 09	4 58	18 20	4 47	18 34	4 30	18 58
11 Mo	12 1 5	8 9	5 45	18 17	5 38	18 25	5 29	18 34	5 16	18 47	4 56	19 08
101	0 17 NM		5 50	18 49	5 39	19 01	5 27	19 16	5 10	19 37	4 43	20 10
12 Tu	12 0 50	8 31	5 45	18 17	5 37	18 25	5 27	18 35	5 14	18 49	4 53	19 10
102			6 29	19 39	6 15	19 54	5 58	20 13	5 36	20 39	5 00	21 22
13 We	12 0 34	8 53	5 44	18 18	5 36	18 26	5 26	18 36	5 12	18 50	4 50	19 12
103			7 10	20 29	6 54	20 47	6 33	21 08	6 06	21 39	5 21	22 30
14 Th	12 0 19	9 15	5 43	18 18	5 35	18 26	5 24	18 37	5 10	18 52	4 47	19 15
104			7 53	21 19	7 35	21 38	7 13	22 02	6 41	22 36	5 49	23 32
15 Fr	12 0 5	9 36	5 42	18 18	5 34	18 27	5 23	18 38	5 08	18 53	4 44	19 17
105			8 40	22 09	8 21	22 29	7 57	22 53	7 23	23 27	6 26	– –
16 Sa	11 59 50	9 58	5 42	18 18	5 33	18 28	5 21	18 39	5 06	18 55	4 41	19 20
106			9 30	22 58	9 10	23 17	8 46	23 40	8 12	– –	7 14	0 26
17 Su	11 59 36	10 19	5 41	18 19	5 31	18 28	5 20	18 40	5 04	18 56	4 38	19 22
107			10 21	23 45	10 03	– –	9 40	– –	9 08	0 13	8 14	1 08
18 Mo	11 59 23	10 40	5 40	18 19	5 30	18 29	5 18	18 41	5 02	18 58	4 36	19 25
108			11 15	– –	10 59	0 03	10 39	0 24	10 11	0 53	9 24	1 42
19 Tu	11 59 9	11 1	5 39	18 19	5 29	18 29	5 17	18 42	5 00	19 00	4 33	19 27
109	2 34 FQ		12 10	0 31	11 57	0 46	11 41	1 04	11 18	1 28	10 42	2 07
20 We	11 58 56	11 22	5 38	18 20	5 28	18 30	5 15	18 43	4 58	19 01	4 30	19 30
110			13 07	1 15	12 57	1 27	12 46	1 40	12 30	1 59	12 05	2 27
21 Th	11 58 44	11 42	5 38	18 20	5 27	18 31	5 14	18 44	4 56	19 03	4 27	19 32
111			14 05	1 59	14 00	2 06	13 53	2 15	13 45	2 26	13 32	2 44
22 Fr	11 58 32	12 3	5 37	18 20	5 26	18 31	5 13	18 45	4 54	19 04	4 24	19 35
112			15 04	2 42	15 04	2 45	15 03	2 48	15 03	2 53	15 02	2 59
23 Sa	11 58 20	12 23	5 36	18 21	5 25	18 32	5 11	18 46	4 52	19 06	4 21	19 37
113			16 05	3 27	16 10	3 25	16 15	3 22	16 23	3 19	16 35	3 14
24 Su	11 58 9	12 43	5 36	18 21	5 23	18 33	5 10	18 47	4 50	19 07	4 18	19 40
114			17 09	4 13	17 18	4 06	17 30	3 58	17 46	3 47	18 11	3 30
25 Mo	11 57 58	13 3	5 35	18 21	5 23	18 33	5 08	18 48	4 48	19 09	4 15	19 42
115	19 45 FM		18 15	5 02	18 28	4 51	18 45	4 37	19 09	4 18	19 47	3 49
26 Tu	11 57 48	13 22	5 34	18 22	5 22	18 34	5 07	18 49	4 46	19 10	4 13	19 45
116			19 21	5 55	19 38	5 39	19 59	5 21	20 30	4 55	21 20	4 13
27 We	11 57 39	13 41	5 34	18 22	5 21	18 35	5 06	18 50	4 44	19 12	4 10	19 47
117			20 26	6 51	20 46	6 33	21 10	6 10	21 44	5 39	22 42	4 47
28 Th	11 57 29	14 0	5 33	18 22	5 20	18 35	5 04	18 51	4 42	19 14	4 07	19 50
118			21 29	7 51	21 48	7 31	22 13	7 07	22 48	6 32	23 47	5 33
29 Fr	11 57 21	14 19	5 32	18 23	5 19	18 36	5 03	18 52	4 41	19 15	4 04	19 52
119			22 26	8 52	22 44	8 32	23 08	8 08	23 40	7 33	– –	6 35
30 Sa	11 57 13	14 38	5 32	18 23	5 18	18 36	5 02	18 53	4 39	19 17	4 02	19 55
120			23 18	9 52	23 34	9 34	23 54	9 12	– –	8 41	0 34	7 48

5th Month May 1994 31 days

Greenwich Mean Time

NOTE: Light numbers indicate Sun. **Dark** numbers indicate **Moon**. *Degrees are North Latitude*.

FM = full moon; LQ = last quarter; NM = new moon; FQ = first quarter.

CAUTION: Must be converted to local time. For instructions see page 176.

Day of month	week year	Sun on Meridian **Moon phase** h m s	Sun's Declina-tion ° ′	20° Rise Sun **Moon** h m	20° Set Sun **Moon** h m	30° Rise Sun **Moon** h m	30° Set Sun **Moon** h m	40° Rise Sun **Moon** h m	40° Set Sun **Moon** h m	50° Rise Sun **Moon** h m	50° Set Sun **Moon** h m	60° Rise Sun **Moon** h m	60° Set Sun **Moon** h m
1	Su	11 57 5	14 56	5 31	18 23	5 17	18 37	5 01	18 54	4 37	19 18	3 59	19 57
	121			**– –**	**10 50**	**– –**	**10 35**	**– –**	**10 17**	**0 22**	**9 50**	**1 07**	**9 08**
2	Mo	11 56 58	15 14	5 30	18 24	5 17	18 38	4 59	18 55	4 35	19 20	3 56	20 00
	122	**14 32 LQ**		**0 04**	**11 46**	**0 17**	**11 34**	**0 33**	**11 20**	**0 55**	**11 00**	**1 30**	**10 28**
3	Tu	11 56 51	15 32	5 30	18 24	5 16	18 38	4 58	18 56	4 33	19 21	3 53	20 02
	123			**0 46**	**12 39**	**0 56**	**12 31**	**1 07**	**12 22**	**1 23**	**12 08**	**1 48**	**11 47**
4	We	11 56 46	15 50	5 29	18 24	5 15	18 39	4 57	18 57	4 32	19 23	3 51	20 05
	124			**1 25**	**12 30**	**1 31**	**13 26**	**1 38**	**13 21**	**1 47**	**13 15**	**2 02**	**13 04**
5	Th	11 56 40	16 7	5 29	18 25	5 14	18 40	4 56	18 58	4 30	19 24	3 48	20 07
	125			**2 02**	**14 19**	**2 04**	**14 19**	**2 06**	**14 19**	**2 09**	**14 19**	**2 14**	**14 19**
6	Fr	11 56 35	16 24	5 28	18 25	5 13	18 40	4 55	18 59	4 28	19 26	3 45	20 09
	126			**2 38**	**15 08**	**2 36**	**15 12**	**2 33**	**15 17**	**2 30**	**15 23**	**2 26**	**15 33**
7	Sa	11 56 31	16 41	5 28	18 26	5 12	18 41	4 53	19 00	4 27	19 27	3 43	20 12
	127			**3 14**	**15 57**	**3 08**	**16 04**	**3 01**	**16 14**	**2 52**	**16 27**	**2 38**	**16 47**
8	Su	11 56 28	16 58	5 27	18 26	5 12	18 42	4 52	19 01	4 25	19 29	3 40	20 14
	128			**3 50**	**16 46**	**3 41**	**16 57**	**3 30**	**17 11**	**3 14**	**17 29**	**2 51**	**17 59**
9	Mo	11 56 25	17 14	5 27	18 26	5 11	18 42	4 51	19 02	4 24	19 30	3 38	20 17
	129			**4 28**	**17 35**	**4 16**	**17 49**	**4 00**	**19 07**	**3 39**	**18 32**	**3 07**	**19 11**
10	Tu	11 56 22	17 30	5 26	18 27	5 10	18 43	4 50	19 03	4 22	19 32	3 35	20 19
	130	**17 7 NM**		**5 09**	**18 25**	**4 53**	**18 42**	**4 34**	**19 03**	**4 08**	**19 32**	**3 26**	**20 21**
11	We	11 56 20	17 46	5 26	18 27	5 09	18 44	4 49	19 04	4 20	19 33	3 33	20 22
	131			**5 52**	**19 16**	**5 34**	**19 34**	**5 12**	**19 58**	**4 42**	**20 30**	**3 52**	**21 26**
12	Th	11 56 19	18 1	5 25	18 28	5 09	18 44	4 48	19 05	4 19	19 35	3 30	20 24
	132			**6 38**	**20 06**	**6 19**	**20 26**	**5 55**	**20 50**	**5 22**	**21 24**	**4 26**	**22 22**
13	Fr	11 56 18	18 16	5 25	18 28	5 08	18 45	4 47	19 06	4 17	19 36	3 28	20 26
	133			**7 26**	**20 55**	**7 07**	**21 14**	**6 43**	**21 38**	**6 09**	**22 12**	**5 10**	**23 08**
14	Sa	11 56 18	18 31	5 24	18 28	5 07	18 46	4 46	19 07	4 16	19 38	3 25	20 29
	134			**8 17**	**21 43**	**7 59**	**22 01**	**7 35**	**22 23**	**7 02**	**22 53**	**6 07**	**23 44**
15	Su	11 56 18	18 45	5 24	18 29	5 07	18 46	4 45	9 08	4 15	19 39	3 23	20 31
	135			**9 10**	**22 29**	**8 53**	**22 44**	**8 32**	**23 03**	**8 03**	**23 29**	**7 14**	**– –**
16	Mo	11 56 19	18 60	5 24	18 29	5 06	18 47	4 44	19 09	4 13	19 40	3 21	20 34
	136			**10 04**	**23 13**	**9 50**	**23 25**	**9 32**	**23 40**	**9 08**	**– –**	**8 28**	**0 11**
17	Tu	11 56 21	19 13	5 23	18 30	5 06	18 47	4 43	19 10	4 12	19 42	3 18	20 36
	137			**10 59**	**23 55**	**10 48**	**– –**	**10 35**	**– –**	**10 17**	**0 01**	**9 48**	**0 33**
18	We	11 56 23	19 27	5 23	18 30	5 05	18 48	4 42	19 11	4 11	19 43	3 16	20 38
	138	**12 50 FQ**		**11 55**	**– –**	**11 48**	**0 04**	**11 40**	**0 14**	**11 28**	**0 29**	**11 11**	**0 50**
19	Th	11 56 25	19 40	5 23	18 30	5 04	18 49	4 42	19 12	4 09	19 44	3 14	20 40
	139			**12 51**	**0 37**	**12 49**	**0 42**	**12 46**	**0 47**	**12 42**	**0 54**	**12 36**	**1 05**
20	Fr	11 56 29	19 53	5 22	18 31	5 04	18 49	4 41	19 13	4 08	19 46	3 12	20 43
	140			**13 50**	**1 19**	**13 52**	**1 19**	**13 55**	**1 19**	**13 58**	**1 20**	**14 05**	**1 19**
21	Sa	11 56 32	20 5	5 22	18 31	5 03	18 50	4 40	19 14	4 07	19 47	3 10	20 45
	141			**14 50**	**2 03**	**14 57**	**1 58**	**15 06**	**1 53**	**15 17**	**1 45**	**15 36**	**1 34**
22	Su	11 56 36	20 18	5 22	18 32	5 03	18 51	4 39	19 14	4 06	19 48	3 08	20 47
	142			**15 53**	**2 49**	**16 04**	**2 40**	**16 18**	**2 29**	**16 38**	**2 14**	**17 10**	**1 51**
23	Mo	11 56 41	20 29	5 22	18 32	5 03	18 51	4 39	19 15	4 04	19 50	3 06	20 49
	143			**16 58**	**3 39**	**17 13**	**3 25**	**17 32**	**3 09**	**17 59**	**2 47**	**18 44**	**2 12**
24	Tu	11 56 46	20 41	5 21	18 32	5 02	18 52	4 38	19 16	4 03	19 51	3 04	20 51
	144			**18 04**	**4 33**	**18 22**	**4 16**	**18 45**	**3 55**	**19 17**	**3 26**	**20 12**	**2 40**
25	We	11 56 52	20 52	5 21	18 33	5 02	18 52	4 37	19 17	4 02	19 52	3 02	20 54
	145	**3 39 FM**		**19 08**	**5 31**	**19 28**	**5 12**	**19 53**	**4 48**	**20 28**	**4 15**	**21 27**	**3 19**
26	Th	11 56 58	21 3	5 21	18 33	5 01	18 53	4 37	19 18	4 01	19 53	3 00	20 56
	146			**20 10**	**6 32**	**20 29**	**6 12**	**20 53**	**5 48**	**21 27**	**5 13**	**22 24**	**4 13**
27	Fr	11 57 4	21 13	5 21	18 34	5 01	18 53	4 36	19 19	4 00	19 55	2 58	20 58
	147			**21 06**	**7 34**	**21 23**	**7 16**	**21 45**	**6 52**	**22 15**	**6 19**	**23 05**	**5 23**
28	Sa	11 57 11	21 23	5 20	18 34	5 01	18 54	4 35	19 19	3 59	19 56	2 56	21 00
	148			**21 56**	**8 36**	**22 11**	**8 19**	**22 29**	**7 59**	**22 53**	**7 30**	**23 33**	**6 42**
29	Su	11 57 19	21 33	5 20	18 34	5 00	18 55	4 35	19 20	3 58	19 57	2 55	21 01
	149			**22 42**	**9 35**	**22 53**	**9 21**	**23 06**	**9 05**	**23 25**	**8 42**	**23 53**	**8 06**
30	Mo	11 57 27	21 42	5 20	18 35	5 00	18 55	4 34	19 21	3 58	19 58	2 53	21 03
	150			**23 23**	**10 30**	**23 30**	**10 21**	**23 39**	**10 09**	**23 51**	**9 53**	**– –**	**9 28**
31	Tu	11 57 36	21 51	5 20	18 35	5 00	18 56	4 34	19 22	3 57	19 59	2 51	21 05
	151			**– –**	**11 23**	**– –**	**11 18**	**– –**	**11 11**	**– –**	**11 02**	**0 09**	**10 48**

6th Month — June 1994 — 30 days

Greenwich Mean Time

NOTE: Light numbers indicate Sun. **Dark** numbers indicate **Moon**. *Degrees are North Latitude.*

FM = full moon; LQ = last quarter; NM = new moon; FQ = first quarter.

CAUTION: Must be converted to local time. For instructions see page 176.

Day of month	week / year	Sun on Meridian / **Moon phase** (h m s)	Sun's Declination (° ′)	20° Rise Sun / **Moon** (h m)	20° Set Sun / **Moon** (h m)	30° Rise	30° Set	40° Rise	40° Set	50° Rise	50° Set	60° Rise	60° Set
1	We	11 57 44	21 59	5 20	18 36	4 59	18 56	4 33	19 22	3 56	20 00	2 50	21 07
	152	**4 2 LQ**		**0 01**	**12 14**	**0 04**	**12 13**	**0 08**	**12 11**	**0 14**	**12 09**	**0 22**	**12 05**
2	Th	11 57 54	22 8	5 20	18 36	4 59	18 57	4 33	19 23	3 55	20 01	2 48	21 09
	153			**0 38**	**13 04**	**0 37**	**13 06**	**0 36**	**13 09**	**0 36**	**13 14**	**0 34**	**13 20**
3	Fr	11 58 4	22 15	5 20	18 36	4 59	18 57	4 33	19 24	3 55	20 02	2 47	21 10
	154			**1 14**	**13 53**	**1 09**	**13 59**	**1 04**	**14 07**	**0 57**	**14 17**	**0 46**	**14 34**
4	Sa	11 58 14	22 23	5 20	18 37	4 59	18 58	4 32	19 25	3 54	20 03	2 46	21 12
	155			**1 50**	**14 41**	**1 42**	**14 51**	**1 32**	**15 04**	**1 19**	**15 20**	**0 59**	**15 47**
5	Su	11 58 24	22 30	5 20	18 37	4 59	18 58	4 32	19 25	3 53	20 04	2 44	21 13
	156			**2 27**	**15 31**	**2 16**	**15 44**	**2 02**	**16 00**	**1 43**	**16 23**	**1 13**	**16 59**
6	Mo	11 58 35	22 36	5 20	18 37	4 59	18 59	4 32	19 26	3 53	20 05	2 43	21 15
	157			**3 07**	**16 21**	**2 53**	**16 37**	**2 35**	**16 57**	**2 10**	**17 24**	**1 31**	**18 10**
7	Tu	11 58 46	22 42	5 20	18 38	4 58	18 59	4 31	19 26	3 52	20 05	2 42	21 16
	158			**3 49**	**17 11**	**3 32**	**17 29**	**3 11**	**17 52**	**2 42**	**18 24**	**1 55**	**19 17**
8	We	11 58 57	22 48	5 20	18 38	4 58	19 00	4 31	19 27	3 52	20 06	2 41	21 18
	159			**4 34**	**18 02**	**4 16**	**18 21**	**3 52**	**18 45**	**3 20**	**19 19**	**2 26**	**20 17**
9	Th	11 59 9	22 54	5 20	18 39	4 58	19 00	4 31	19 28	3 52	20 07	2 40	21 19
	160	**8 26 NM**		**5 23**	**18 52**	**5 03**	**19 11**	**4 39**	**19 36**	**4 05**	**20 10**	**3 07**	**21 07**
10	Fr	11 59 21	22 58	5 20	18 39	4 58	19 01	4 31	19 28	3 51	20 08	2 39	21 20
	161			**6 13**	**19 41**	**5 54**	**19 59**	**5 30**	**20 22**	**4 57**	**20 54**	**4 00**	**21 47**
11	Sa	11 59 33	23 3	5 20	18 39	4 58	19 01	4 31	19 29	3 51	20 08	2 39	21 21
	162			**7 06**	**20 28**	**6 49**	**20 44**	**6 27**	**21 04**	**5 56**	**21 32**	**5 04**	**22 17**
12	Su	11 59 46	23 7	5 20	18 40	4 58	19 01	4 31	19 29	3 51	20 09	2 38	21 22
	163			**8 00**	**21 12**	**7 45**	**21 26**	**7 26**	**21 42**	**7 00**	**22 05**	**6 17**	**22 40**
13	Mo	11 59 58	23 11	5 20	18 40	4 58	19 02	4 31	19 30	3 51	20 10	2 37	21 23
	164			**8 55**	**21 55**	**8 43**	**22 05**	**8 28**	**22 17**	**8 08**	**22 33**	**7 35**	**22 58**
14	Tu	12 0 11	23 14	5 20	18 40	4 58	19 02	4 31	19 30	3 50	20 10	2 37	21 24
	165			**9 50**	**22 37**	**9 42**	**22 43**	**9 32**	**22 50**	**9 18**	**22 59**	**8 57**	**23 14**
15	We	12 0 24	23 17	5 20	18 40	4 58	19 02	4 31	19 30	3 50	20 11	2 36	21 25
	166			**10 45**	**23 18**	**10 42**	**23 20**	**10 37**	**23 22**	**10 30**	**23 24**	**10 20**	**23 28**
16	Th	12 0 36	23 20	5 21	18 41	4 59	19 03	4 31	19 31	3 50	20 11	2 36	21 26
	167	**19 56 FQ**		**11 42**	**24 00**	**11 42**	**23 57**	**11 43**	**23 54**	**11 44**	**23 49**	**11 46**	**23 42**
17	Fr	12 0 49	23 22	5 21	18 41	4 59	19 03	4 31	19 31	3 50	20 12	2 36	21 26
	168			**12 40**	**– –**	**12 45**	**– –**	**12 51**	**– –**	**13 00**	**– –**	**13 13**	**23 57**
18	Sa	12 1 2	23 24	5 21	18 41	4 59	19 03	4 31	19 31	3 50	20 12	2 36	21 27
	169			**13 39**	**0 43**	**13 49**	**0 36**	**14 01**	**0 27**	**14 17**	**0 15**	**14 43**	**– –**
19	Su	12 1 15	23 25	5 21	18 41	4 59	19 04	4 31	19 32	3 50	20 12	2 36	21 27
	170			**14 41**	**1 30**	**14 55**	**1 18**	**15 12**	**1 04**	**15 36**	**0 45**	**16 14**	**0 15**
20	Mo	12 1 28	23 26	5 21	18 42	4 59	19 04	4 31	19 32	3 50	20 13	2 36	21 27
	171			**15 45**	**2 20**	**16 02**	**2 50**	**16 23**	**1 46**	**16 53**	**1 20**	**17 43**	**0 39**
21	Tu	12 1 41	23 26	5 21	18 42	4 59	19 04	4 31	19 32	3 51	20 13	2 36	21 28
	172			**16 49**	**3 14**	**17 08**	**2 56**	**17 32**	**2 34**	**18 06**	**2 03**	**19 04**	**1 11**
22	We	12 1 54	23 26	5 22	18 42	5 00	19 04	4 31	19 32	3 51	20 13	2 36	21 28
	173			**17 51**	**4 13**	**18 11**	**3 54**	**18 36**	**3 29**	**19 10**	**2 55**	**20 10**	**1 56**
23	Th	12 2 7	23 26	5 22	18 42	5 00	19 04	4 32	19 33	3 51	20 13	2 36	21 28
	174	**11 33 FM**		**18 50**	**5 15**	**19 09**	**4 55**	**19 32**	**4 31**	**20 04**	**3 56**	**20 59**	**2 57**
24	Fr	12 2 20	23 25	5 22	18 43	5 00	19 05	4 32	19 33	3 51	20 13	2 37	21 28
	175			**19 44**	**6 17**	**20 00**	**5 59**	**20 20**	**5 37**	**20 48**	**5 06**	**21 33**	**4 13**
25	Sa	12 2 33	23 24	5 22	18 43	5 00	19 05	4 32	19 33	3 52	20 13	2 37	21 28
	176			**20 33**	**7 18**	**20 46**	**7 03**	**21 01**	**6 45**	**21 23**	**6 19**	**21 57**	**5 36**
26	Su	12 2 45	23 22	5 23	18 43	5 01	19 05	4 33	19 33	3 52	20 13	2 38	21 27
	177			**21 17**	**8 17**	**21 26**	**8 05**	**21 37**	**7 51**	**21 52**	**7 32**	**22 15**	**7 01**
27	Mo	12 2 58	23 20	5 23	18 43	5 01	19 05	4 33	19 33	3 53	20 13	2 38	21 27
	178			**21 57**	**9 12**	**22 02**	**9 05**	**22 09**	**8 56**	**22 17**	**8 44**	**22 30**	**8 24**
28	Tu	12 3 10	23 18	5 23	18 43	5 01	19 05	4 33	19 33	3 53	20 13	2 39	21 27
	179			**22 36**	**10 05**	**22 37**	**10 02**	**22 38**	**9 58**	**22 40**	**9 53**	**22 43**	**9 44**
29	We	12 3 22	23 15	5 23	18 43	5 02	19 05	4 34	19 33	3 54	20 13	2 40	21 26
	180			**23 12**	**10 56**	**23 10**	**10 57**	**23 06**	**10 58**	**23 02**	**11 00**	**22 55**	**11 02**
30	Th	12 3 34	23 12	5 24	18 43	5 02	19 05	4 34	19 33	3 54	20 13	2 41	21 26
	181	**19 31 LQ**		**23 49**	**11 46**	**23 42**	**11 51**	**23 34**	**11 57**	**23 24**	**12 05**	**23 07**	**12 17**

7th Month — July 1994 — 31 days

Greenwich Mean Time

NOTE: Light numbers indicate Sun. **Dark** numbers indicate **Moon**. *Degrees are North Latitude*.

FM = full moon; LQ = last quarter; NM = new moon; FQ = first quarter.

CAUTION: Must be converted to local time. For instructions see page 176.

Day of month	week / year	Sun on Meridian / **Moon phase** h	m	s	Sun's Declination °	′	20° Rise Sun / **Moon** h m	20° Set Sun / **Moon** h m	30° Rise Sun / **Moon** h m	30° Set Sun / **Moon** h m	40° Rise Sun / **Moon** h m	40° Set Sun / **Moon** h m	50° Rise Sun / **Moon** h m	50° Set Sun / **Moon** h m	60° Rise Sun / **Moon** h m	60° Set Sun / **Moon** h m
1	Fr	12	3	46	23	8	5 24	18 43	5 02	19 05	4 35	19 33	3 55	20 12	2 42	21 25
	182						**– –**	**12 35**	**– –**	**12 44**	**– –**	**12 54**	**23 47**	**13 09**	**23 21**	**13 31**
2	Sa	12	3	57	23	4	5 24	18 43	5 03	19 05	4 35	19 33	3 55	20 12	2 43	21 24
	183						**0 26**	**13 25**	**0 16**	**13 37**	**0 04**	**13 51**	**– –**	**14 12**	**23 38**	**14 44**
3	Su	12	4	9	23	0	5 25	18 43	5 03	19 05	4 36	19 32	3 56	20 12	2 44	21 23
	184						**1 05**	**14 14**	**0 51**	**14 29**	**0 35**	**14 48**	**0 13**	**15 14**	**23 59**	**15 56**
4	Mo	12	4	20	22	55	5 25	18 44	5 04	19 05	4 36	19 32	3 57	20 11	2 45	21 22
	185						**1 46**	**15 05**	**1 30**	**15 22**	**1 10**	**15 44**	**0 43**	**16 14**	**– –**	**17 04**
5	Tu	12	4	30	22	50	5 25	18 44	5 04	19 05	4 37	19 32	3 58	20 11	2 47	21 21
	186						**2 30**	**15 55**	**2 12**	**16 14**	**1 49**	**16 38**	**1 18**	**17 11**	**0 26**	**18 07**
6	We	12	4	40	22	44	5 26	18 44	5 04	19 05	4 37	19 32	3 58	20 10	2 48	21 20
	187						**3 17**	**16 46**	**2 58**	**17 05**	**2 34**	**17 30**	**2 00**	**18 04**	**1 03**	**19 02**
7	Th	12	4	50	22	38	5 26	18 44	5 05	19 05	4 38	19 31	3 59	20 10	2 49	21 19
	189						**4 07**	**17 36**	**3 48**	**17 55**	**3 23**	**18 18**	**2 49**	**18 51**	**1 51**	**19 46**
8	Fr	12	5	0	22	31	5 26	18 43	5 05	19 04	4 39	19 31	4 00	20 09	2 51	21 18
	198	**21**	**37**	**NM**			**5 00**	**18 24**	**4 41**	**18 41**	**4 18**	**19 02**	**3 46**	**19 32**	**2 52**	**20 20**
9	Sa	12	5	9	22	25	5 27	18 43	5 06	19 04	4 39	19 31	4 01	20 09	2 52	21 17
	190						**5 54**	**19 10**	**5 38**	**19 25**	**5 18**	**19 43**	**4 49**	**20 07**	**4 03**	**20 46**
10	Su	12	5	18	22	17	5 27	18 43	5 06	19 04	4 40	19 30	4 02	20 08	2 54	21 15
	191						**6 49**	**19 55**	**6 36**	**20 06**	**6 20**	**20 19**	**5 57**	**20 38**	**5 21**	**21 06**
11	Mo	12	5	26	22	10	5 28	18 43	5 07	19 04	4 41	19 30	4 03	20 07	2 56	21 14
	192						**7 45**	**20 37**	**7 36**	**20 44**	**7 24**	**20 53**	**7 08**	**21 05**	**6 43**	**21 23**
12	Tu	12	5	34	22	02	5 28	18 43	5 07	19 04	4 41	19 29	4 04	20 07	2 58	21 12
	193						**8 41**	**21 19**	**8 36**	**21 22**	**8 29**	**21 26**	**8 21**	**21 30**	**8 07**	**21 38**
13	We	12	5	42	21	53	5 28	18 43	5 08	19 03	4 42	19 29	4 05	20 06	2 59	21 11
	194						**9 38**	**22 00**	**9 37**	**21 59**	**9 36**	**21 57**	**9 34**	**21 55**	**9 32**	**21 52**
14	Th	12	5	49	21	45	5 29	18 43	5 08	19 03	4 43	19 28	4 06	20 05	3 01	21 09
	195						**10 35**	**22 43**	**10 38**	**22 37**	**10 43**	**22 30**	**10 49**	**22 21**	**10 58**	**22 07**
15	Fr	12	5	55	21	26	5 29	18 43	5 09	19 03	4 43	19 28	4 07	20 04	3 03	21 07
	196						**11 33**	**23 27**	**11 41**	**23 17**	**11 51**	**23 05**	**12 05**	**22 49**	**12 26**	**22 23**
16	Sa	12	6	1	21	26	5 29	18 43	5 09	19 02	4 44	19 27	4 08	20 03	3 05	21 06
	191	**1**	**12**	**FQ**			**12 33**	**– –**	**12 45**	**– –**	**13 00**	**23 44**	**13 21**	**23 21**	**13 55**	**22 44**
17	Su	12	6	6	21	16	5 30	18 42	5 10	19 02	4 45	19 27	4 09	20 02	3 07	21 04
	198						**13 34**	**0 15**	**13 50**	**0 01**	**14 09**	**– –**	**14 37**	**23 59**	**15 22**	**23 11**
18	Mo	12	6	11	21	6	5 30	18 42	5 11	19 02	4 46	19 26	4 11	20 01	3 09	21 02
	199						**14 36**	**1 06**	**14 54**	**0 49**	**15 17**	**0 28**	**15 50**	**– –**	**16 44**	**23 50**
19	Tu	12	6	15	20	56	5 30	18 42	5 11	19 01	4 47	19 25	4 12	20 00	3 11	21 00
	200						**15 37**	**2 01**	**15 57**	**1 42**	**16 21**	**1 19**	**16 56**	**0 46**	**17 55**	**– –**
20	We	12	6	19	20	45	5 31	18 42	5 12	19 01	4 47	19 25	4 13	19 59	3 13	20 58
	201						**16 36**	**3 00**	**16 56**	**2 41**	**17 20**	**2 16**	**17 53**	**1 41**	**18 50**	**0 42**
21	Th	12	6	22	20	33	5 31	18 41	5 12	19 00	4 48	19 24	4 14	19 58	3 15	20 56
	202						**17 32**	**4 01**	**17 49**	**3 42**	**18 11**	**3 19**	**18 41**	**2 46**	**19 31**	**1 50**
22	Fr	12	6	24	20	22	5 32	18 41	5 13	19 00	4 49	19 23	4 15	19 57	3 17	20 54
	203	**20**	**16**	**FM**			**18 23**	**5 02**	**18 37**	**4 45**	**18 55**	**4 25**	**19 20**	**3 56**	**19 59**	**3 09**
23	Sa	12	6	26	20	10	5 32	18 41	5 13	18 59	4 50	19 22	4 17	19 55	3 19	20 52
	204						**19 09**	**6 01**	**19 20**	**5 48**	**19 33**	**5 32**	**19 52**	**5 09**	**20 20**	**4 33**
24	Su	12	6	28	19	58	5 32	18 40	5 14	18 59	4 51	19 22	4 18	19 54	3 22	20 50
	205						**19 52**	**6 59**	**19 59**	**6 49**	**20 07**	**6 38**	**20 19**	**6 22**	**20 37**	**5 57**
25	Mo	12	6	29	19	45	5 33	18 40	5 15	18 58	4 52	19 21	4 19	19 53	3 24	20 47
	206						**20 31**	**7 53**	**20 34**	**7 48**	**20 38**	**7 42**	**20 43**	**7 33**	**20 51**	**7 19**
26	Tu	12	6	29	19	32	5 33	18 40	5 15	18 57	4 53	19 20	4 21	19 51	3 26	20 45
	207						**21 09**	**8 46**	**21 08**	**8 45**	**21 07**	**8 44**	**21 06**	**8 42**	**21 03**	**8 39**
27	We	12	6	28	19	19	5 33	18 39	5 16	18 57	4 53	19 19	4 22	19 50	3 28	20 43
	208						**21 46**	**9 37**	**21 42**	**9 40**	**21 36**	**9 44**	**21 28**	**9 49**	**21 16**	**9 56**
28	Th	12	6	27	19	5	5 34	18 39	5 16	18 56	4 54	19 18	4 23	19 49	3 31	20 41
	209						**22 24**	**10 27**	**22 15**	**10 34**	**22 05**	**10 43**	**21 51**	**10 54**	**21 29**	**11 12**
29	Fr	12	6	26	18	51	5 34	18 38	5 17	18 56	4 55	19 17	4 25	19 47	3 33	20 38
	210						**23 02**	**11 17**	**22 50**	**11 27**	**22 36**	**11 40**	**22 16**	**11 58**	**21 45**	**12 26**
30	Sa	12	6	24	18	37	5 35	18 38	5 18	18 55	4 56	19 16	4 26	19 46	3 35	20 36
	211	**12**	**40**	**LQ**			**23 42**	**12 07**	**23 27**	**12 20**	**23 09**	**12 37**	**22 44**	**13 00**	**22 04**	**13 38**
31	Su	12	6	21	18	23	5 35	18 38	5 18	18 54	4 57	19 15	4 27	19 44	3 38	20 33
	212						**– –**	**12 57**	**– –**	**13 13**	**23 46**	**13 33**	**23 17**	**14 01**	**22 29**	**14 48**

8th Month — August 1994 — 31 days

Greenwich Mean Time

NOTE: Light numbers indicate Sun. **Dark** numbers indicate **Moon**. *Degrees are North Latitude*.

FM = full moon; LQ = last quarter; NM = new moon; FQ = first quarter.

CAUTION: Must be converted to local time. For instructions see page 176.

Day of month	week year	Sun on Meridian / **Moon phase** h m s	Sun's Declination ° ′	20° Rise Sun / **Moon** h m	20° Set Sun / **Moon** h m	30° Rise Sun / **Moon** h m	30° Set Sun / **Moon** h m	40° Rise Sun / **Moon** h m	40° Set Sun / **Moon** h m	50° Rise Sun / **Moon** h m	50° Set Sun / **Moon** h m	60° Rise Sun / **Moon** h m	60° Set Sun / **Moon** h m
1	Mo	12 6 18	18 8	5 35	18 37	5 19	18 53	4 58	19 14	4 29	19 43	3 40	20 31
	213			**0 25**	**13 47**	**0 07**	**14 05**	**– –**	**14 28**	**23 55**	**15 00**	**23 01**	**15 53**
2	Tu	12 6 14	17 53	5 36	18 37	5 19	18 53	4 59	19 13	4 30	19 41	3 42	20 28
	214			**1 10**	**14 38**	**0 51**	**14 57**	**0 28**	**15 21**	**– –**	**15 54**	**23 44**	**16 52**
3	We	12 6 9	17 37	5 36	18 36	5 20	18 52	5 00	19 12	4 32	19 40	3 45	20 26
	215			**1 59**	**15 27**	**1 39**	**15 47**	**1 15**	**16 10**	**0 41**	**16 44**	**– –**	**17 40**
4	Th	12 6 4	17 22	5 36	18 36	5 21	18 51	5 01	19 11	4 33	19 38	3 47	20 23
	216			**2 50**	**16 16**	**2 31**	**16 34**	**2 08**	**16 57**	**1 35**	**17 28**	**0 39**	**18 19**
5	Fr	12 5 59	17 6	5 37	18 35	5 21	18 50	5 02	19 10	4 34	19 36	3 49	20 21
	217			**3 44**	**17 04**	**3 27**	**17 20**	**3 05**	**17 39**	**2 36**	**18 06**	**1 46**	**18 48**
6	Sa	12 5 52	16 49	5 37	18 34	5 22	18 50	5 03	19 08	4 36	19 35	3 52	20 18
	218			**4 39**	**17 50**	**4 25**	**18 02**	**4 07**	**18 18**	**3 42**	**18 39**	**3 01**	**19 11**
7	Su	12 5 45	16 33	5 37	18 34	5 22	18 49	5 04	19 07	4 37	19 33	3 54	20 16
	219	**8 45 NM**		**5 36**	**18 34**	**5 25**	**18 43**	**5 11**	**18 53**	**4 53**	**19 08**	**4 23**	**19 30**
8	Mo	12 5 38	16 16	5 38	18 33	5 23	18 48	5 05	19 06	4 39	19 31	3 57	20 13
	220			**6 33**	**19 17**	**6 26**	**19 22**	**6 18**	**19 27**	**6 06**	**19 35**	**5 48**	**19 46**
9	Tu	12 5 30	15 59	5 38	18 33	5 24	18 47	5 06	19 05	4 40	19 30	3 59	20 10
	221			**7 31**	**19 59**	**7 28**	**20 00**	**7 25**	**20 00**	**7 21**	**20 00**	**7 14**	**20 01**
10	We	12 5 21	15 42	5 38	18 32	5 24	18 46	5 06	19 04	4 42	19 28	4 01	20 08
	222			**8 29**	**20 43**	**8 31**	**20 28**	**8 33**	**20 33**	**8 37**	**20 26**	**8 42**	**20 16**
11	Th	12 5 12	15 24	5 39	18 31	5 25	18 45	5 07	19 02	4 43	19 26	4 04	20 05
	223			**9 27**	**21 27**	**9 34**	**21 18**	**9 42**	**21 08**	**9 53**	**20 54**	**10 11**	**20 32**
12	Fr	12 5 2	15 6	5 39	18 31	5 25	18 44	5 08	19 01	4 45	19 24	4 06	20 02
	224			**10 27**	**22 14**	**10 38**	**22 01**	**10 51**	**21 46**	**11 10**	**21 25**	**11 40**	**20 52**
13	Sa	12 4 52	14 48	5 39	18 30	5 26	18 43	5 09	19 00	4 46	19 23	4 09	19 59
	225			**11 28**	**23 04**	**11 43**	**22 48**	**12 01**	**22 28**	**12 26**	**22 01**	**13 07**	**21 17**
14	Su	12 4 41	14 30	5 40	18 30	5 27	18 42	5 10	18 58	4 48	19 21	4 11	19 57
	226	**5 57 FQ**		**12 29**	**23 57**	**12 47**	**23 39**	**13 09**	**23 16**	**13 39**	**22 44**	**14 30**	**21 51**
15	Mo	12 4 30	14 11	5 40	18 29	5 27	18 41	5 11	18 57	4 49	19 19	4 13	19 54
	227			**13 30**	**– –**	**13 49**	**– –**	**14 13**	**– –**	**14 47**	**23 36**	**15 44**	**22 38**
16	Tu	12 4 17	13 53	5 40	18 28	5 28	18 40	5 12	18 56	4 51	19 17	4 16	19 51
	228			**14 28**	**0 53**	**14 48**	**0 34**	**15 12**	**0 10**	**15 46**	**– –**	**16 44**	**23 38**
17	We	12 4 5	13 34	5 40	18 27	5 28	18 39	5 13	18 54	4 52	19 15	4 18	19 48
	229			**15 24**	**1 52**	**15 42**	**1 33**	**16 04**	**1 09**	**16 36**	**0 35**	**17 28**	**– –**
18	Th	12 3 52	13 15	5 41	18 27	5 29	18 38	5 14	18 53	4 54	19 13	4 21	19 45
	230			**16 15**	**2 51**	**16 31**	**2 34**	**16 50**	**2 12**	**17 17**	**1 42**	**18 00**	**0 51**
19	Fr	12 3 38	12 55	5 41	18 26	5 29	18 37	5 15	18 52	4 55	19 11	4 23	19 42
	231			**17 02**	**3 50**	**17 15**	**3 35**	**17 30**	**3 17**	**17 51**	**2 52**	**18 24**	**2 11**
20	Sa	12 3 24	12 36	5 41	18 25	5 30	18 36	5 16	18 50	4 57	19 09	4 25	19 40
	232			**17 46**	**4 47**	**17 55**	**4 36**	**18 06**	**4 23**	**18 20**	**4 04**	**18 43**	**3 34**
21	Su	12 3 9	12 16	5 42	18 24	5 31	18 35	5 17	18 49	4 58	19 07	4 28	19 37
	233	**6 47 FM**		**18 27**	**5 42**	**18 32**	**5 35**	**18 38**	**5 27**	**18 46**	**5 15**	**18 58**	**4 56**
22	Mo	12 2 54	11 56	5 42	18 24	5 31	18 34	5 18	18 47	5 00	19 05	4 30	19 34
	234			**19 06**	**6 36**	**19 06**	**6 33**	**19 08**	**6 29**	**19 09**	**6 24**	**19 11**	**6 17**
23	Tu	12 2 39	11 36	5 42	18 23	5 32	18 33	5 19	18 46	5 01	19 03	4 33	19 31
	235			**19 43**	**7 28**	**19 40**	**7 29**	**19 37**	**7 30**	**19 32**	**7 32**	**19 24**	**7 35**
24	We	12 2 23	11 15	5 42	18 22	5 32	18 32	5 20	18 44	5 03	19 01	4 35	19 28
	236			**20 21**	**8 18**	**20 14**	**8 24**	**20 06**	**8 30**	**19 55**	**8 38**	**19 38**	**8 51**
25	Th	12 2 7	10 55	5 43	18 21	5 33	18 31	5 21	18 43	5 04	18 59	4 37	19 25
	237			**20 59**	**9 09**	**20 49**	**9 17**	**20 36**	**9 28**	**20 19**	**9 43**	**19 53**	**10 06**
26	Fr	12 1 50	10 34	5 43	18 21	5 33	18 30	5 22	18 41	5 06	18 57	4 40	19 22
	238			**21 38**	**9 59**	**21 25**	**10 11**	**21 09**	**10 26**	**20 46**	**10 46**	**20 10**	**11 20**
27	Sa	12 1 33	10 13	5 43	18 20	5 34	18 29	5 23	18 40	5 07	18 55	4 42	19 19
	239			**22 20**	**10 49**	**22 04**	**11 04**	**21 44**	**11 22**	**21 17**	**11 48**	**20 33**	**12 30**
28	Su	12 1 15	9 52	5 43	18 19	5 35	18 27	5 24	18 38	5 08	18 53	4 45	19 16
	240			**23 04**	**11 39**	**22 46**	**11 56**	**22 24**	**12 17**	**21 53**	**12 47**	**21 01**	**13 37**
29	Mo	12 0 57	9 31	5 44	18 18	5 35	18 26	5 25	18 37	5 10	18 51	4 47	19 13
	241	**6 41 LQ**		**23 50**	**12 29**	**23 32**	**12 27**	**23 08**	**13 10**	**22 35**	**13 43**	**21 39**	**14 38**
30	Tu	12 0 39	9 10	5 44	18 17	5 36	18 25	5 25	18 35	5 11	18 49	4 49	19 10
	242			**– –**	**13 18**	**– –**	**13 37**	**23 58**	**14 01**	**23 24**	**14 34**	**22 28**	**15 31**
31	We	12 0 21	8 48	5 44	18 16	5 36	18 24	5 26	18 34	5 13	18 47	4 52	19 07
	243			**0 40**	**14 07**	**0 21**	**14 25**	**– –**	**14 48**	**– –**	**15 20**	**23 29**	**16 13**

9th Month **September 1994** 30 days

Greenwich Mean Time

NOTE: Light numbers indicate Sun. **Dark** numbers indicate **Moon**. *Degrees are North Latitude*.

FM = full moon; LQ = last quarter; NM = new moon; FQ = first quarter.

CAUTION: Must be converted to local time. For instructions see page 176.

Day of month	week / year	Sun on Meridian / **Moon phase** h m	s	Sun's Declination ° ′	20° Rise Sun / **Moon** h m	20° Set Sun / **Moon** h m	30° Rise Sun / **Moon** h m	30° Set Sun / **Moon** h m	40° Rise Sun / **Moon** h m	40° Set Sun / **Moon** h m	50° Rise Sun / **Moon** h m	50° Set Sun / **Moon** h m	60° Rise Sun / **Moon** h m	60° Set Sun / **Moon** h m
1	Th	12 0	2	8 27	5 44	18 15	5 37	18 23	5 27	18 32	5 14	18 45	4 54	19 4
	244				**1 32**	**14 55**	**1 14**	**15 11**	**0 52**	**15 32**	**0 21**	**16 00**	**– –**	**16 47**
2	Fr	11 59	43	8 5	5 45	18 15	5 37	18 22	5 28	18 30	5 16	18 42	4 56	19 01
	245				**2 26**	**15 41**	**2 11**	**15 55**	**1 51**	**16 12**	**1 24**	**16 35**	**0 40**	**17 13**
3	Sa	11 59	24	7 43	5 45	18 14	5 38	18 20	5 29	18 29	5 17	18 40	4 59	18 58
	246				**3 22**	**16 26**	**3 10**	**16 36**	**2 54**	**16 49**	**2 33**	**17 07**	**1 58**	**17 34**
4	Su	11 59	4	7 21	5 45	18 13	5 38	18 19	5 30	18 27	5 19	18 38	5 01	18 55
	247				**4 19**	**17 10**	**4 11**	**17 16**	**4 00**	**17 24**	**3 45**	**17 35**	**3 22**	**17 51**
5	Mo	11 58	44	6 59	5 45	18 12	5 39	18 18	5 31	18 26	5 20	18 36	5 04	18 52
	248	**18 33**	**NM**		**5 17**	**17 53**	**5 13**	**17 56**	**5 07**	**17 58**	**5 00**	**18 02**	**4 48**	**18 07**
6	Tu	11 58	24	6 36	5 45	18 11	5 39	18 17	5 32	18 24	5 22	18 34	5 06	18 49
	249				**6 17**	**18 37**	**6 17**	**18 35**	**6 17**	**18 32**	**6 17**	**18 29**	**6 17**	**18 23**
7	We	11 58	4	6 14	5 46	18 10	5 40	18 16	5 33	18 22	5 23	18 32	5 08	18 46
	250				**7 17**	**19 23**	**7 21**	**19 16**	**7 27**	**19 08**	**7 35**	**18 57**	**7 47**	**18 39**
8	Th	11 57	43	5 52	5 46	18 09	5 41	18 14	5 34	18 21	5 25	18 30	5 11	18 43
	251				**8 18**	**20 10**	**8 27**	**19 59**	**8 36**	**19 46**	**8 54**	**19 27**	**9 19**	**18 59**
9	Fr	11 57	23	5 29	5 46	18 8	5 41	18 13	5 35	18 19	5 26	18 27	5 13	18 40
	252				**9 20**	**21 00**	**9 33**	**20 46**	**9 50**	**20 27**	**10 12**	**20 03**	**10 49**	**19 23**
10	Sa	11 57	2	5 6	5 46	18 08	5 42	18 12	5 36	18 18	5 28	18 25	5 15	18 37
	253				**10 23**	**21 53**	**10 39**	**21 36**	**10 59**	**21 14**	**11 28**	**20 44**	**12 16**	**19 55**
11	Su	11 56	41	4 44	5 46	18 07	5 42	18 11	5 37	18 16	5 29	18 23	5 18	18 34
	254				**11 24**	**22 49**	**11 43**	**22 30**	**12 06**	**22 07**	**12 38**	**21 34**	**13 34**	**20 38**
12	Mo	11 56	20	4 21	5 47	18 06	5 43	18 09	5 38	18 14	5 31	18 21	5 20	18 31
	255	**11 34**	**FQ**		**12 24**	**23 47**	**12 43**	**23 28**	**13 07**	**23 04**	**13 40**	**22 31**	**14 38**	**21 34**
13	Tu	11 55	59	3 58	5 47	18 05	5 43	18 08	5 39	18 13	5 32	18 19	5 22	18 28
	256				**13 20**	**– –**	**13 38**	**– –**	**14 01**	**– –**	**14 33**	**23 35**	**15 26**	**22 42**
14	We	11 55	38	3 35	5 47	18 04	5 44	18 07	5 40	18 11	5 34	18 16	5 25	18 25
	257				**14 11**	**0 46**	**14 28**	**0 28**	**14 48**	**0 06**	**15 16**	**– –**	**16 02**	**23 29**
15	Th	11 55	16	3 12	5 47	18 03	5 44	18 06	5 41	18 09	5 35	18 14	5 27	18 22
	258				**14 59**	**1 44**	**15 13**	**1 28**	**15 29**	**1 09**	**15 52**	**0 43**	**16 28**	**– –**
16	Fr	11 54	55	2 49	5 48	18 02	5 45	18 04	5 42	18 08	5 37	18 12	5 29	18 19
	259				**15 43**	**2 40**	**15 53**	**2 28**	**16 06**	**2 13**	**16 22**	**1 53**	**16 48**	**1 19**
17	Sa	11 54	33	2 26	5 48	18 01	5 45	18 03	5 42	18 06	5 38	18 10	5 32	18 16
	260				**16 24**	**3 35**	**16 31**	**3 27**	**16 38**	**3 16**	**16 49**	**3 02**	**17 04**	**2 40**
18	Su	11 54	12	2 3	5 48	18 00	5 46	18 02	5 43	18 04	5 40	18 08	5 34	18 13
	261				**17 03**	**4 28**	**17 06**	**4 24**	**17 09**	**4 18**	**17 12**	**4 11**	**17 18**	**3 59**
19	Mo	11 53	50	1 39	5 48	17 59	5 46	18 01	5 44	18 03	5 41	18 05	5 36	18 10
	262	**20 0**	**FM**		**17 41**	**5 20**	**17 40**	**5 20**	**17 38**	**5 19**	**17 35**	**5 18**	**17 32**	**5 17**
20	Tu	11 53	29	1 16	5 48	17 58	5 47	17 59	5 45	18 01	5 43	18 03	5 39	18 07
	263				**18 19**	**6 11**	**18 13**	**6 15**	**18 07**	**6 19**	**17 58**	**6 25**	**17 45**	**6 34**
21	We	11 53	8	0 53	5 49	17 57	5 48	17 58	5 46	17 59	5 44	18 01	5 41	18 04
	264				**18 57**	**7 01**	**18 48**	**7 09**	**18 37**	**7 18**	**18 22**	**7 30**	**18 00**	**7 49**
22	Th	11 52	46	0 30	5 49	17 57	5 48	17 57	5 47	17 58	5 46	17 59	5 43	18 01
	265				**19 36**	**7 51**	**19 24**	**8 02**	**19 09**	**8 15**	**18 48**	**8 34**	**18 17**	**9 03**
23	Fr	11 52	25	0 6	5 49	17 56	5 49	17 56	5 48	17 56	5 47	17 57	5 46	17 58
	266				**20 16**	**8 41**	**20 01**	**8 55**	**19 43**	**9 12**	**18 18**	**9 36**	**18 37**	**10 14**
24	Sa	11 52	4	–0 17	5 49	17 55	5 49	17 54	5 49	17 54	5 49	17 54	5 48	17 55
	267				**20 59**	**9 31**	**29 42**	**9 48**	**20 21**	**10 08**	**19 52**	**10 36**	**19 04**	**11 23**
25	Su	11 54	44	–0 41	5 49	17 54	5 50	17 53	5 50	17 53	5 50	17 52	5 51	17 52
	268				**21 44**	**10 21**	**21 26**	**10 39**	**21 03**	**11 02**	**20 31**	**11 33**	**19 38**	**12 26**
26	Mo	11 51	23	–1 4	5 50	17 53	5 50	17 52	5 51	17 51	5 52	17 50	5 53	17 49
	269				**22 32**	**11 10**	**22 13**	**11 29**	**21 50**	**11 53**	**21 17**	**12 25**	**20 22**	**13 21**
27	Tu	11 51	2	–1 27	5 50	17 52	5 51	17 51	5 52	17 49	5 53	17 48	5 55	17 46
	270				**23 22**	**11 59**	**23 04**	**12 17**	**22 42**	**12 40**	**22 10**	**13 13**	**21 16**	**14 07**
28	We	11 50	42	–1 51	5 50	17 51	5 51	17 50	5 53	17 48	5 55	17 46	5 58	17 42
	271	**0 23**	**LQ**		**– –**	**12 46**	**23 58**	**13 03**	**23 37**	**13 25**	**23 09**	**13 54**	**22 21**	**14 43**
29	Th	11 50	22	–2 14	5 50	17 50	5 52	17 48	5 54	17 36	5 56	17 43	6 00	17 39
	272				**0 14**	**13 32**	**– –**	**13 47**	**– –**	**14 05**	**– –**	**14 31**	**23 35**	**15 12**
30	Fr	11 50	2	–2 37	5 51	17 49	5 53	17 47	5 55	17 45	5 58	17 41	6 02	17 36
	273				**1 08**	**14 16**	**0 54**	**14 28**	**0 37**	**14 43**	**0 13**	**15 03**	**– –**	**15 35**

10th Month — October 1994 — 31 days

Greenwich Mean Time

NOTE: Light numbers indicate Sun. **Dark** numbers indicate **Moon**. *Degrees are North Latitude.*

FM = full moon; LQ = last quarter; NM = new moon; FQ = first quarter.

CAUTION: Must be converted to local time. For instructions see page 176.

Day of month	week / year	Sun on Meridian / **Moon phase** h	m	s	Sun's Declination °	'	20° Rise Sun / **Moon** h m	20° Set Sun / **Moon** h m	30° Rise Sun / **Moon** h m	30° Set Sun / **Moon** h m	40° Rise Sun / **Moon** h m	40° Set Sun / **Moon** h m	50° Rise Sun / **Moon** h m	50° Set Sun / **Moon** h m	60° Rise Sun / **Moon** h m	60° Set Sun / **Moon** h m
1	Sa	11	49	43	–3	1	5 51	17 48	5 53	17 46	5 56	17 43	5 59	17 39	6 05	17 33
	274						**2 04**	**15 00**	**1 53**	**15 08**	**1 40**	**15 19**	**1 22**	**15 33**	**0 54**	**15 54**
2	Su	11	49	24	–3	24	5 51	17 47	5 54	17 45	5 57	17 41	6 01	17 37	6 07	17 30
	275						**3 00**	**15 43**	**2 54**	**15 48**	**2 46**	**15 53**	**2 35**	**16 00**	**2 17**	**16 11**
3	Mo	11	49	5	–3	47	5 51	17 47	5 54	17 43	5 58	17 40	6 03	17 35	6 09	17 27
	276						**3 59**	**16 27**	**3 57**	**16 27**	**3 54**	**16 27**	**3 50**	**16 27**	**3 45**	**16 27**
4	Tu	11	48	47	–4	10	5 52	17 46	5 55	17 42	5 59	17 38	6 04	17 33	6 12	17 24
	277						**4 59**	**17 12**	**5 01**	**17 08**	**5 04**	**17 02**	**5 08**	**16 55**	**5 15**	**16 43**
5	We	11	48	29	–4	34	5 52	17 45	5 55	17 41	6 00	17 36	6 06	17 30	6 14	17 21
	278	**3**	**55**	**NM**			**6 01**	**18 00**	**6 98**	**17 51**	**6 16**	**17 40**	**6 28**	**17 25**	**6 47**	**17 02**
6	Th	11	48	11	–4	57	5 52	17 44	5 56	17 40	6 01	17 35	6 07	17 28	6 17	17 18
	279						**7 04**	**18 50**	**7 16**	**18 37**	**7 30**	**18 21**	**7 49**	**17 59**	**8 21**	**17 25**
7	Fr	11	47	53	–5	20	5 52	17 43	5 57	17 39	6 02	17 33	6 09	17 26	6 19	17 15
	280						**8 09**	**19 44**	**8 24**	**19 28**	**8 43**	**19 08**	**9 09**	**18 40**	**9 52**	**17 54**
8	Sa	11	47	36	–5	43	5 53	17 42	5 57	17 38	6 03	17 32	6 10	17 24	6 22	17 12
	281						**9 13**	**20 41**	**9 31**	**20 23**	**9 53**	**10 00**	**10 24**	**19 28**	**11 16**	**18 34**
9	Su	11	47	20	–6	5	5 53	17 42	5 58	17 36	6 04	17 30	6 12	17 22	6 24	17 10
	282						**10 15**	**21 40**	**10 34**	**21 21**	**10 58**	**20 58**	**11 31**	**20 24**	**12 28**	**19 28**
10	Mo	11	47	4	–6	28	5 53	17 41	5 58	17 35	6 05	17 29	6 13	17 20	6 26	17 07
	283						**11 14**	**22 40**	**11 33**	**22 22**	**11 56**	**21 59**	**12 28**	**21 27**	**13 23**	**20 34**
11	Tu	11	46	48	–6	51	5 53	17 40	5 59	17 34	6 06	17 27	6 15	17 18	6 29	17 04
	284	**19**	**17**	**FQ**			**12 08**	**23 39**	**12 25**	**23 23**	**12 46**	**23 03**	**13 15**	**22 35**	**14 03**	**21 49**
12	We	11	46	33	–7	14	5 54	17 39	6 00	17 33	6 06	17 26	6 17	17 16	6 31	17 01
	285						**12 57**	**– –**	**13 12**	**– –**	**13 29**	**– –**	**13 54**	**23 45**	**14 32**	**23 09**
13	Th	11	46	18	–7	36	5 54	17 38	6 00	17 32	6 08	17 24	6 18	17 14	6 34	16 58
	286						**13 42**	**9 36**	**13 53**	**0 23**	**14 07**	**0 07**	**14 25**	**– –**	**14 54**	**– –**
14	Fr	11	46	4	–7	59	5 54	17 37	6 01	17 31	6 09	17 22	6 20	17 12	6 36	16 55
	287						**14 24**	**1 31**	**14 31**	**1 22**	**14 40**	**1 10**	**14 52**	**0 54**	**15 11**	**0 29**
15	Sa	11	45	50	–8	21	15 55	17 37	6 02	17 30	6 10	17 21	6 21	17 10	6 39	16 52
	288						**15 03**	**2 24**	**15 07**	**2 19**	**15 11**	**2 12**	**15 17**	**2 02**	**15 26**	**1 48**
16	Su	11	45	37	–8	43	5 55	17 36	6 02	17 29	6 11	17 20	6 23	17 07	6 41	16 49
	289						**15 41**	**3 16**	**15 41**	**3 14**	**15 40**	**3 12**	**15 40**	**3 09**	**15 39**	**3 05**
17	Mo	11	45	25	–9	5	5 55	17 35	6 03	17 27	6 12	17 18	6 25	17 05	6 44	16 46
	290						**16 18**	**4 06**	**16 14**	**4 09**	**16 09**	**4 11**	**16 03**	**4 15**	**15 53**	**4 21**
18	Tu	11	45	13	–9	27	5 56	17 34	6 04	17 26	6 13	17 17	6 26	17 03	6 46	16 43
	291						**16 56**	**4 56**	**16 48**	**5 02**	**16 39**	**5 10**	**16 26**	**5 20**	**16 07**	**5 35**
19	We	11	45	1	–9	49	5 56	17 34	6 04	17 25	6 14	17 15	6 28	17 01	6 49	16 40
	292	**12**	**18**	**FM**			**17 34**	**5 46**	**17 23**	**5 56**	**17 10**	**6 07**	**16 51**	**6 23**	**16 23**	**6 49**
20	Th	11	44	50	–10	11	5 56	17 33	6 05	17 24	6 15	17 14	6 29	16 59	6 51	16 38
	293						**18 14**	**6 36**	**18 99**	**6 49**	**17 43**	**7 03**	**17 20**	**7 26**	**16 42**	**8 01**
21	Fr	11	44	40	–10	32	5 57	17 32	6 06	17 23	6 16	17 12	6 31	16 58	6 54	16 35
	294						**18 56**	**7 26**	**18 40**	**7 41**	**18 20**	**8 00**	**17 52**	**8 27**	**17 07**	**9 11**
22	Sa	11	44	31	–10	53	5 57	17 32	6 06	17 22	6 18	17 11	6 33	16 56	6 56	16 32
	295						**19 41**	**8 16**	**19 23**	**8 33**	**19 01**	**8 55**	**18 30**	**9 25**	**17 38**	**10 16**
23	Su	11	44	22	–11	15	5 58	17 31	6 07	17 21	6 19	17 10	6 34	16 54	6 59	16 29
	296						**20 27**	**9 05**	**20 09**	**9 24**	**19 46**	**9 47**	**19 13**	**10 19**	**18 18**	**11 13**
24	Mo	11	44	14	–11	36	5 58	17 30	6 08	17 20	6 20	17 08	6 36	16 52	7 01	16 26
	297						**21 16**	**9 54**	**10 58**	**10 12**	**20 35**	**10 35**	**20 03**	**11 08**	**19 09**	**12 02**
25	Tu	11	44	7	–11	56	5 58	17 30	6 08	17 19	6 21	17 07	6 38	16 50	7 04	16 24
	298						**22 07**	**10 40**	**21 50**	**10 58**	**21 28**	**11 20**	**20 58**	**11 51**	**20 09**	**12 42**
26	We	11	44	0	–12	17	5 59	17 29	6 09	17 18	6 22	17 06	6 39	16 48	7 06	16 21
	299						**22 59**	**11 26**	**22 44**	**11 42**	**22 25**	**12 02**	**21 59**	**21 29**	**21 17**	**13 13**
27	Th	11	43	54	–12	38	5 59	17 28	6 10	17 18	6 23	17 04	6 41	16 46	7 09	16 18
	300	**16**	**44**	**LQ**			**23 52**	**12 10**	**23 40**	**12 23**	**23 25**	**12 39**	**23 05**	**13 02**	**22 32**	**13 37**
28	Fr	11	43	49	–12	58	6 00	17 28	6 11	17 17	6 24	17 03	6 43	16 44	7 11	16 15
	301						**– –**	**12 52**	**– –**	**13 02**	**– –**	**13 15**	**– –**	**13 31**	**23 51**	**13 57**
29	Sa	11	43	45	–13	18	6 00	17 27	6 11	17 16	6 25	17 02	6 44	16 43	7 14	16 13
	302						**0 46**	**13 34**	**0 38**	**13 41**	**0 27**	**13 48**	**0 13**	**13 59**	**– –**	**14 14**
30	Su	11	43	41	–13	38	6 00	17 27	6 12	17 15	6 26	17 00	6 46	16 41	7 16	16 10
	303						**1 42**	**14 17**	**1 38**	**14 19**	**1 32**	**14 21**	**1 25**	**14 25**	**1 14**	**14 30**
31	Mo	11	43	38	–13	58	6 01	17 26	6 13	17 14	6 28	16 59	6 47	16 39	7 19	16 07
	304						**2 39**	**15 00**	**2 40**	**14 58**	**2 40**	**14 55**	**2 40**	**14 52**	**2 40**	**14 46**

11th Month **November 1994** **30 days**

Greenwich Mean Time

NOTE: Light numbers indicate Sun. **Dark** numbers indicate **Moon.** *Degrees are North Latitude.*

FM = full moon; LQ = last quarter; NM = new moon; FQ = first quarter.

CAUTION: Must be converted to local time. For instructions see page 176.

Day of month week year		Sun on Meridian **Moon phase** h m	s	Sun's Declina-tion °		20° Rise Sun **Moon** h m	20° Set Sun **Moon** h m	30° Rise Sun **Moon** h m	30° Set Sun **Moon** h m	40° Rise Sun **Moon** h m	40° Set Sun **Moon** h m	50° Rise Sun **Moon** h m	50° Set Sun **Moon** h m	60° Rise Sun **Moon** h m	60° Set Sun **Moon** h m
1	Tu	11 43	37	–14	17	6 01	17 26	6 14	17 13	6 29	16 58	6 49	16 37	7 21	16 05
	305					**3 39**	**15 46**	**3 44**	**15 39**	**3 50**	**15 31**	**3 57**	**15 20**	**4 10**	**15 03**
2	We	11 43	35	–14	36	6 02	17 25	6 14	17 12	6 30	16 57	6 51	16 36	7 24	16 02
	306					**4 42**	**16 35**	**4 51**	**16 24**	**5 02**	**16 10**	**5 18**	**15 52**	**5 42**	**15 23**
3	Th	11 43	35	–14	55	6 02	17 25	6 15	17 12	6 31	16 56	6 52	16 34	7 27	16 00
	307	**13 35**	**NM**			**5 46**	**17 28**	**6 00**	**17 13**	**6 16**	**16 55**	**6 39**	**16 30**	**7 16**	**15 50**
4	Fr	11 43	36	–15	14	6 03	17 24	6 16	17 11	6 32	16 55	6 54	16 32	7 29	15 57
	308					**6 53**	**18 25**	**7 09**	**18 07**	**7 30**	**17 45**	**7 59**	**17 15**	**8 47**	**16 25**
5	Sa	11 43	37	–15	32	6 03	17 24	6 17	17 10	6 33	16 53	6 56	16 31	7 32	15 55
	309					**7 58**	**19 25**	**8 17**	**19 06**	**8 40**	**18 43**	**9 13**	**18 10**	**10 08**	**17 14**
6	Su	11 43	39	–15	51	6 04	17 23	6 18	17 09	6 34	16 52	6 57	16 29	7 34	15 52
	310					**9 01**	**20 27**	**9 20**	**20 09**	**9 44**	**19 45**	**10 17**	**19 13**	**11 13**	**18 17**
7	Mo	11 43	42	–16	09	6 04	17 23	6 18	17 09	6 36	16 51	6 59	16 28	7 37	15 50
	311					**9 59**	**21 29**	**10 17**	**21 12**	**10 39**	**20 51**	**11 10**	**20 21**	**12 01**	**19 32**
8	Tu	11 43	46	–16	26	6 05	17 23	6 19	17 08	6 37	16 50	7 01	16 26	7 39	15 47
	312					**10 52**	**22 29**	**11 08**	**22 15**	**11 27**	**21 57**	**11 53**	**21 33**	**12 35**	**20 53**
9	We	11 43	50	–16	44	6 05	17 22	6 20	17 07	6 38	16 49	7 02	16 25	7 42	15 45
	313					**11 40**	**23 26**	**11 52**	**23 15**	**12 07**	**23 02**	**12 27**	**22 44**	**12 59**	**22 15**
10	Th	11 43	56	–17	1	6 06	17 22	6 21	17 07	6 39	16 48	7 04	16 23	7 45	15 42
	314	**6 14**	**FQ**			**12 23**	**– –**	**12 32**	**– –**	**12 42**	**– –**	**12 56**	**23 54**	**13 18**	**23 36**
11	Fr	11 44	2	–17	18	6 06	17 21	6 22	17 06	6 40	16 47	7 06	16 22	7 47	15 40
	315					**13 04**	**0 20**	**13 08**	**0 13**	**13 14**	**0 05**	**13 22**	**– –**	**13 34**	**– –**
12	Sa	11 44	9	–17	34	6 07	17 21	6 22	17 06	6 41	16 47	7 07	16 20	7 50	15 38
	316					**13 42**	**1 12**	**13 43**	**1 10**	**13 44**	**1 06**	**13 45**	**1 01**	**13 47**	**0 54**
13	Su	11 44	17	–17	50	6 08	17 21	6 23	17 03	6 42	16 46	7 09	16 19	7 52	15 36
	317					**14 19**	**2 03**	**14 16**	**2 04**	**14 12**	**2 05**	**14 08**	**2 07**	**14 01**	**2 10**
14	Mo	11 44	26	–18	6	6 08	17 21	6 24	17 05	6 44	16 45	7 11	16 18	7 55	15 33
	318					**14 56**	**2 53**	**14 49**	**2 58**	**14 41**	**3 04**	**14 31**	**3 12**	**14 15**	**3 24**
15	Tu	11 44	35	–18	22	6 09	17 20	6 25	17 04	6 45	16 44	7 12	16 16	7 57	15 31
	319					**15 34**	**3 42**	**15 24**	**3 51**	**15 12**	**4 01**	**14 55**	**4 15**	**14 30**	**4 38**
16	We	11 44	46	–18	37	6 09	17 20	6 26	17 04	6 46	16 43	7 14	16 15	8 00	15 29
	320					**16 13**	**4 32**	**16 99**	**4 44**	**15 44**	**4 58**	**15 22**	**5 18**	**14 48**	**5 50**
17	Th	11 44	57	–18	52	6 10	17 20	6 26	17 03	6 47	16 42	7 16	16 14	8 02	15 27
	321					**16 54**	**5 22**	**16 39**	**5 36**	**16 20**	**5 54**	**15 53**	**6 20**	**15 10**	**7 00**
18	Fr	11 45	9	–19	7	6 10	17 20	6 27	17 03	6 48	16 42	7 17	16 13	8 05	15 25
	322	**6 57**	**FM**			**17 38**	**6 12**	**17 21**	**6 28**	**16 59**	**6 49**	**16 29**	**7 19**	**15 39**	**8 07**
19	Sa	11 45	22	–19	21	6 11	17 20	6 28	17 02	6 49	16 41	7 19	16 12	8 07	15 23
	323					**18·24**	**7 01**	**18 06**	**7 20**	**17 43**	**7 42**	**17 10**	**8 14**	**16 16**	**9 08**
20	Su	11 45	36	–19	35	6 12	17 19	6 29	17 02	6 50	16 40	7 20	16 10	8 10	15 21
	324					**19 12**	**7 50**	**18 54**	**8 09**	**18 31**	**8 32**	**17 58**	**9 05**	**17 03**	**10 00**
21	Mo	11 45	50	–19	49	6 12	17 19	6 30	17 02	6 52	16 40	7 22	16 09	8 12	15 19
	325					**20 02**	**8 38**	**19 45**	**8 56**	**19 23**	**9 18**	**18 52**	**9 50**	**18 00**	**10 42**
22	Tu	11 46	6	–20	2	6 13	17 19	6 31	17 01	6 53	16 39	7 23	16 08	8 14	15 17
	326					**20 54**	**9 24**	**20 38**	**9 40**	**20 18**	**10 01**	**19 51**	**10 29**	**19 06**	**11 16**
23	We	11 46	22	–20	15	6 13	17 19	6 31	17 01	6 54	16 39	7 25	16 07	8 17	15 15
	327					**21 46**	**10 07**	**21 32**	**10 22**	**21 16**	**10 39**	**20 54**	**11 04**	**20 18**	**11 42**
24	Th	11 46	39	–20	27	6 14	17 19	6 32	17 01	6 55	16 38	7 26	16 06	8 19	15 14
	328					**22 38**	**10 50**	**22 28**	**11 01**	**22 16**	**11 15**	**22 00**	**11 34**	**21 34**	**12 03**
25	Fr	11 46	57	–20	39	6 15	17 19	6 33	17 01	6 56	16 38	7 28	16 06	8 21	15 12
	329					**23 32**	**11 31**	**23 26**	**11 39**	**23 18**	**11 48**	**23 08**	**12 01**	**22 53**	**12 20**
26	Sa	11 47	15	–20	51	6 15	17 19	6 34	17 00	6 57	16 37	7 29	16 05	8 24	15 10
	330	**7 4**	**LQ**			**– –**	**12 11**	**– –**	**12 15**	**– –**	**12 20**	**– –**	**12 26**	**– –**	**12 36**
27	Su	11 47	35	–21	2	6 16	17 19	6 35	17 00	6 58	16 37	7 31	16 04	8 26	15 09
	331					**0 26**	**12 53**	**0 24**	**12 52**	**0 22**	**12 52**	**0 19**	**12 52**	**0 14**	**12 51**
28	Mo	11 47	55	–21	13	6 17	17 19	6 36	17 00	6 59	16 36	7 32	16 03	8 28	15 07
	332					**1 23**	**13 35**	**1 25**	**13 31**	**1 28**	**13 25**	**1 32**	**13 18**	**1 39**	**13 07**
29	Tu	11 48	15	–21	24	6 17	17 19	6 36	17 00	7 00	16 36	7 34	16 03	8 30	15 06
	333					**2 22**	**14 21**	**2 29**	**14 12**	**2 37**	**14 01**	**2 49**	**13 47**	**3 07**	**13 24**
30	We	11 48	37	–21	34	6 18	17 19	6 37	17 00	7 01	16 36	7 35	16 02	8 32	15 04
	334					**3 23**	**15 10**	**3 35**	**14 58**	**3 48**	**14 42**	**4 07**	**14 20**	**4 38**	**13 47**

12th Month — December 1994 — 31 days

Greenwich Mean Time

NOTE: Light numbers indicate Sun. **Dark** numbers indicate **Moon**. *Degrees are North Latitude*.

FM = full moon; LQ = last quarter; NM = new moon; FQ = first quarter.

CAUTION: Must be converted to local time. For instructions see page 176.

Day of month	week year	Sun on Meridian / Moon phase h m s	Sun's Declination ° ′	20° Rise Sun/Moon h m	20° Set Sun/Moon h m	30° Rise Sun/Moon h m	30° Set Sun/Moon h m	40° Rise Sun/Moon h m	40° Set Sun/Moon h m	50° Rise Sun/Moon h m	50° Set Sun/Moon h m	60° Rise Sun/Moon h m	60° Set Sun/Moon h m
1	Th	11 48 59	−21 44	6 18	17 19	6 38	17 00	7 02	16 35	7 36	16 01	8 34	15 03
	335			**4 28**	**16 04**	**4 43**	**15 48**	**5 01**	**15 28**	**5 27**	**15 01**	**6 09**	**14 16**
2	Fr	11 49 22	−21 53	6 19	17 20	6 39	17 00	7 03	16 35	7 38	16 01	8 36	15 02
	336	**23 54 NM**		**5 34**	**17 03**	**5 51**	**16 45**	**6 13**	**16 22**	**6 44**	**15 50**	**7 36**	**14 57**
3	Sa	11 49 45	−22 2	6 20	17 20	6 40	17 00	7 04	16 35	7 39	16 00	8 38	15 01
	337			**6 39**	**18 06**	**6 58**	**17 47**	**7 22**	**17 23**	**7 55**	**16 49**	**8 52**	**15 53**
4	Su	11 50 9	−22 10	6 20	17 20	6 40	17 00	7 05	16 35	7 40	16 00	8 40	15 00
	338			**7 42**	**19 10**	**8 00**	**18 52**	**8 23**	**18 29**	**8 56**	**17 57**	**9 50**	**17 04**
5	Mo	11 50 34	−22 18	6 21	17 20	6 41	17 00	7 06	16 35	7 41	15 59	8 42	14 59
	339			**8 39**	**20 13**	**8 56**	**19 57**	**9 17**	**19 38**	**9 45**	**19 11**	**10 32**	**18 26**
6	Tu	11 50 59	−22 26	6 22	17 20	6 42	17 00	7 07	16 35	7 43	15 59	8 44	14 58
	340			**9 31**	**21 13**	**9 45**	**21 01**	**10 02**	**20 46**	**10 25**	**20 25**	**11 02**	**19 51**
7	We	11 51 25	−22 33	6 22	17 20	6 43	17 00	7 08	16 35	7 44	15 59	8 46	14 57
	341			**10 18**	**22 11**	**10 28**	**22 03**	**10 41**	**21 52**	**10 58**	**21 38**	**11 24**	**21 16**
8	Th	11 51 51	−22 40	6 23	17 21	6 43	17 00	7 09	16 35	7 45	15 59	8 47	14 56
	342			**11 01**	**23 06**	**11 07**	**23 01**	**11 15**	**22 56**	**11 25**	**22 49**	**11 41**	**22 37**
9	Fr	11 52 17	−22 46	6 23	17 21	6 44	17 00	7 10	16 35	7 46	15 58	8 49	14 55
	343	**21 6 FQ**		**11 41**	**23 58**	**11 43**	**23 58**	**11 46**	**23 57**	**11 50**	**23 56**	**11 56**	**23 55**
10	Sa	11 52 44	−22 52	6 24	17 21	6 45	17 01	7 11	16 35	7 47	15 58	8 50	14 55
	344			**12 19**	**– –**	**12 17**	**– –**	**2 16**	**– –**	**12 13**	**– –**	**12 09**	**– –**
11	Su	11 53 12	−22 57	6 25	17 22	6 45	17 01	7 11	16 35	7 48	15 58	8 52	14 54
	345			**12 56**	**0 49**	**12 51**	**0 52**	**12 45**	**0 57**	**12 36**	**1 02**	**12 23**	**1 11**
12	Mo	11 53 40	−23 2	6 25	17 22	6 46	17 01	7 12	16 35	7 49	15 58	8 53	14 54
	346			**13 34**	**1 38**	**13 25**	**1 46**	**13 14**	**1 55**	**13 00**	**2 07**	**12 38**	**2 25**
13	Tu	11 54 8	−23 7	6 26	17 22	6 47	17 01	7 13	16 35	7 50	15 58	8 55	14 54
	347			**14 12**	**2 28**	**14 01**	**2 39**	**13 46**	**2 52**	**13 26**	**3 10**	**12 55**	**3 38**
14	We	11 54 36	−23 11	6 26	17 23	6 47	17 02	7 14	16 35	7 51	15 58	8 56	14 53
	348			**14 53**	**3 18**	**14 38**	**3 31**	**14 20**	**3 48**	**13 55**	**4 11**	**13 15**	**4 49**
15	Th	11 55 5	−23 14	6 27	17 23	6 48	17 02	7 14	16 36	7 52	15 58	8 57	14 53
	349			**15 36**	**4 07**	**15 19**	**4 23**	**14 58**	**4 43**	**14 29**	**5 11**	**13 41**	**5 57**
16	Fr	11 55 34	−23 18	6 28	17 23	6 49	17 02	7 15	16 36	7 53	15 59	8 58	14 53
	350			**16 21**	**4 57**	**16 03**	**5 15**	**15 40**	**5 37**	**15 08**	**6 08**	**14 15**	**7 01**
17	Sa	11 56 3	−23 20	6 28	17 24	6 49	17 03	7 16	16 36	7 53	15 59	8 59	14 53
	351			**17 09**	**5 47**	**16 50**	**6 05**	**16 27**	**6 29**	**15 54**	**7 01**	**14 59**	**7 56**
18	Su	11 56 32	−23 22	6 29	17 24	6 50	17 03	7 16	16 37	7 54	15 59	9 00	14 53
	352	**2 17 FM**		**17 59**	**6 35**	**17 40**	**6 53**	**17 18**	**7 16**	**16 46**	**7 49**	**15 53**	**8 43**
19	Mo	11 57 2	−23 24	6 29	17 25	6 50	17 04	7 17	16 37	7 55	15 59	9 01	14 53
	353			**18 50**	**7 22**	**18 33**	**7 39**	**18 13**	**8 01**	**17 44**	**8 30**	**16 56**	**9 19**
20	Tu	11 57 31	−23 25	6 30	17 25	6 51	17 04	7 18	16 37	7 55	16 00	9 01	14 54
	354			**19 42**	**8 07**	**19 28**	**8 22**	**19 10**	**8 41**	**18 46**	**9 07**	**18 07**	**9 48**
21	We	11 58 1	−23 26	6 30	17 26	6 52	17 04	7 18	16 38	7 56	16 00	9 02	14 54
	355			**20 34**	**8 50**	**20 23**	**9 02**	**20 10**	**9 17**	**19 51**	**9 38**	**19 21**	**10 11**
22	Th	11 58 31	−23 26	6 31	17 26	6 52	17 05	7 19	16 38	7 56	16 01	9 02	14 55
	356			**21 27**	**9 31**	**21 20**	**9 40**	**21 11**	**9 51**	**20 58**	**10 06**	**20 39**	**10 29**
23	Fr	11 59 1	−23 26	6 31	17 27	6 53	17 06	7 19	16 39	7 57	16 01	9 03	14 55
	357			**22 21**	**10 11**	**22 17**	**10 17**	**22 13**	**10 23**	**22 07**	**10 32**	**21 59**	**10 45**
24	Sa	11 59 31	−23 25	6 32	17 27	6 53	17 06	7 20	16 39	7 57	16 02	9 03	14 56
	358			**23 15**	**10 52**	**23 16**	**10 53**	**23 17**	**10 54**	**23 18**	**10 57**	**23 20**	**11 00**
25	Su	12 0 0	−23 24	6 32	17 28	6 53	17 07	7 20	16 40	7 58	16 03	9 03	14 57
	359	**19 6 LQ**		**– –**	**11 32**	**– –**	**11 30**	**– –**	**11 26**	**– –**	**11 22**	**– –**	**11 15**
26	Mo	12 0 30	−23 23	6 33	17 28	6 54	17 07	7 20	16 41	7 58	16 03	9 04	14 58
	360			**0 11**	**12 15**	**0 16**	**12 08**	**0 22**	**12 00**	**0 31**	**11 48**	**0 44**	**11 31**
27	Tu	12 1 00	−23 21	6 33	17 29	6 54	17 07	7 21	16 41	7 58	16 04	9 04	14 59
	361			**1 09**	**13 01**	**1 18**	**12 50**	**1 30**	**12 36**	**1 45**	**12 18**	**2 10**	**11 50**
28	We	12 1 29	−23 18	6 34	17 30	6 55	17 08	7 21	16 42	7 58	16 05	9 04	15 00
	362			**2 10**	**13 50**	**2 23**	**13 36**	**2 39**	**13 18**	**3 02**	**12 53**	**3 38**	**12 14**
29	Th	12 1 59	−23 15	6 34	17 30	6 55	17 09	7 21	16 43	7 58	16 06	9 03	15 01
	363			**3 13**	**14 45**	**3 29**	**14 27**	**3 49**	**14 06**	**4 18**	**13 36**	**5 05**	**12 47**
30	Fr	12 2 28	−23 12	6 34	17 31	6 55	17 10	7 22	16 44	7 59	16 07	9 03	15 02
	364			**4 17**	**15 44**	**4 35**	**15 25**	**4 58**	**15 02**	**5 31**	**14 29**	**6 25**	**13 33**
31	Sa	12 2 57	−23 8	6 35	17 31	6 56	17 10	7 22	16 44	7 59	16 07	9 03	15 03
	365			**5 20**	**16 46**	**5 39**	**16 28**	**6 03**	**16 04**	**6 36**	**15 31**	**7 32**	**14 35**

Julian and Gregorian Calendars; Leap Year; Century

Calendars based on the movements of sun and moon have been used since ancient times, but none has been perfect. The Julian calendar, under which western nations measured time until A.D.1582, was authorized by Julius Caesar in 46 B.C., the year 709 of Rome. His expert was a Greek, Sosigenes. The Julian calendar, on the assumption that the true year was 365 1/4 days long, gave every fourth year 366 days. The Venerable Bede, an Anglo-Saxon monk, announced in A.D.730 that the 365 1/4-day Julian year was 11 min., 14 sec. too long, making a cumulative error of about a day every 128 years, but nothing was done about it for over 800 years.

By 1582 the accumulated error was estimated to have amounted to 10 days. In that year Pope Gregory XIII decreed that the day following Oct. 4, 1582, should be called Oct. 15, thus dropping 10 days.

However, with common years 365 days and a 366-day leap year every fourth year, the error in the length of the year would have recurred at the rate of a little more than 3 days every 400 years. So 3 of every 4 centesimal years (ending in 00) were made common years, not leap years. Thus 1600 was a leap year, 1700, 1800 and 1900 were not, but 2000 will be. **Leap years** are those divisible by 4 except centesimal years, which are common unless divisible by 400.

The Gregorian calendar was adopted at once by France, Italy, Spain, Portugal and Luxembourg. Within 2 years most German Catholic states, Belgium and parts of Switzerland and the Netherlands were brought under the new calendar, and Hungary followed in 1587. The rest of the Netherlands, along with Denmark and the German Protestant states made the change in 1699-1700 (German Protestants retained the old reckoning of Easter until 1776).

The British government imposed the Gregorian calendar on all its possessions, including the American colonies, in 1752. The British decreed that the day following Sept. 2, 1752, should be called Sept. 14, a loss of 11 days. All dates preceding were marked O.S., for Old Style. In addition, New Year's Day was moved to Jan. 1 from Mar. 25 (e.g. under the old reckoning, Mar. 24, 1700 had been followed by Mar. 25, 1701). George Washington's birth date, which was Feb. 11, 1731, O.S., became Feb. 22, 1732, N.S. In 1753 Sweden too went Gregorian, retaining the old Easter rules until 1844.

In 1793 the French revolutionary government adopted a calendar of 12 months of 30 days each with 5 extra days in September of each common year and a 6th extra day every 4th year. Napoleon reinstated the Gregorian calendar in 1806.

The Gregorian system later spread to non-European regions, first in the European colonies, then in the independent countries, replacing traditional calendars at least for official purposes. Japan in 1873, Egypt in 1875, China in 1912 and Turkey in 1917 made the change, usually in conjunction with political upheavals. In China, the republican government began reckoning years from its 1911 founding — e.g. 1948 was designated the year 37. After 1949, the Communists adopted the Common, or Christian Era, year count, even for the traditional lunar calendar.

In 1918 the revolutionary government in Russia decreed that the day after Jan. 31, 1918, Old Style, would become Feb. 14, 1918, New Style. Greece followed in 1923. (In Russia the Orthodox Church has retained the Julian calendar, as have various Middle Eastern Christian sects.) For the first time in history, all major cultures have one calendar.

To change from the Julian to the Gregorian calendar, add 10 days to dates Oct. 5, 1582, through Feb. 28, 1700; after that date add 11 days through Feb. 28, 1800; 12 days through Feb. 28, 1900; and 13 days through Feb. 28, 2100.

A **century** consists of 100 consecutive calendar years. The 1st century A.D. consisted of the years 1 through 100. The 20th century consists of the years 1901 through 2000 and will end Dec. 31, 2000. The 21st century will begin Jan. 1, 2001.

Julian Calendar

To find which of the 14 calendars printed on pages 202-203 applies to any year, starting Jan. 1, under the Julian system, find the century for the desired year in the three left-hand columns below; read across. Then find the year in the four top rows; read down. The number in the intersection is the calendar designation for that year.

Year (last two figures of desired year)

Century			00	01 29 57 85	02 30 58 86	03 31 59 87	04 32 60 88	05 33 61 89	06 34 62 90	07 35 63 91	08 36 64 92	09 37 65 93	10 38 66 94	11 39 67 95	12 40 68 96	13 41 69 97	14 42 70 98	15 43 71 99	16 44 72	17 45 73	18 46 74	19 47 75	20 48 76	21 49 77	22 50 78	23 51 79	24 52 80	25 53 81	26 54 82	27 55 83	28 56 84
0	700	1400	12	7	1	2	10	5	6	7	8	3	4	5	13	1	2	3	11	6	7	1	9	4	5	6	14	2	3	4	12
100	800	1500	11	6	7	1	9	4	5	6	14	2	3	4	12	7	1	2	10	5	6	7	8	3	4	5	13	1	2	3	11
200	900	1600	10	5	6	7	8	3	4	5	13	1	2	3	11	6	7	1	9	4	5	6	14	2	3	4	12	7	1	2	10
300	1000	1700	9	4	5	6	14	2	3	4	12	7	1	2	10	5	6	7	8	3	4	5	13	1	2	3	11	6	7	1	9
400	1100	1800	8	3	4	5	13	1	2	3	11	6	7	1	9	4	5	6	14	2	3	4	12	7	1	2	10	5	6	7	8
500	1200	1900	14	2	3	4	12	7	1	2	10	5	6	7	8	3	4	5	13	1	2	3	11	6	7	1	9	4	5	6	14
600	1300	2000	13	1	2	3	11	6	7	1	9	4	5	6	14	2	3	4	12	7	1	2	10	5	6	7	8	3	4	5	13

The Julian Period

How many days have you lived? To determine this, you must multiply your age by 365, add the number of days since your last birthday until today, and account for all leap years. Chances are your answer would be wrong. Astronomers, however, find it convenient to express dates and long time intervals in days rather than in years, months and days. This is done by placing events within the Julian period.

The Julian period was devised in 1582 by Joseph Scaliger and named after his father Julius (not after the Julian calendar). Scaliger had Julian Day (JD) 1 begin at noon, Jan. 1, 4713 B.C., the most recent time that three major chronological cycles began on the same day – 1) the 28-year solar cycle, after which dates in the Julian calendar (e.g. Feb. 11) return to the same days of the week (e.g. Monday); 2) the 19-year lunar cycle, after which the phases of the moon return to the same dates of the year; and 3) the 15-year indiction cycle, used in ancient Rome to regulate taxes. It will take 7980 years to complete the period, the product of 28, 19, and 15.

Noon of Dec. 31, 1993 marks the beginning of JD 2,449,353; that many days will have passed since the start of the Julian period. The JD at noon of any date in 1994 may be found by adding to this figure the day of the year for that date, which is given in the left hand column in the chart below. Simple JD conversion tables are used by astronomers.

Gregorian Calendar

Pick desired year from table below or on page 202 (for years 1803 to 2080). The number shown with each year shows which calendar to use for that year, as shown on pages 202-203. (The Gregorian calendar was inaugurated Oct. 15, 1582. From that date to Dec. 31, 1582, use calendar 6.)

1583-1802

1583 . 7	1603 . 4	1623 . 1	1643 . 5	1663 . 2	1683 . 6	1703 . 2	1723 . 6	1743 . 3	1763 . 7	1783 . 4
1584 . 8	1604 .12	1624 . 9	1644 .13	1664 .10	1684 .14	1704 .10	1724 .14	1744 .11	1764 . 8	1784 .12
1585 . 3	1605 . 7	1625 . 4	1645 . 1	1665 . 5	1685 . 2	1705 . 5	1725 . 2	1745 . 6	1765 . 3	1785 . 7
1586 . 4	1606 . 1	1626 . 5	1646 . 2	1666 . 6	1686 . 3	1706 . 6	1726 . 3	1746 . 7	1766 . 4	1786 . 1
1587 . 5	1607 . 2	1627 . 6	1647 . 3	1667 . 7	1687 . 4	1707 . 7	1727 . 4	1747 . 1	1767 . 5	1787 . 2
1588 .13	1608 .10	1628 .14	1648 .11	1668 . 8	1688 .12	1708 . 8	1728 .12	1748 . 9	1768 .13	1788 .10
1589 . 1	1609 . 5	1629 . 2	1649 . 6	1669 . 3	1689 . 7	1709 . 3	1729 . 7	1749 . 4	1769 . 1	1789 . 5
1590 . 2	1610 . 6	1630 . 3	1650 . 7	1670 . 4	1690 . 1	1710 . 4	1730 . 1	1750 . 5	1770 . 2	1790 . 6
1591 . 3	1611 . 7	1631 . 4	1651 . 1	1671 . 5	1691 . 2	1711 . 5	1731 . 2	1751 . 6	1771 . 3	1791 . 7
1592 .11	1612 . 8	1632 .12	1652 . 9	1672 .13	1692 .10	1712 .13	1732 .10	1752 .14	1772 .11	1792 . 8
1593 . 6	1613 . 3	1633 . 7	1653 . 4	1673 . 1	1693 . 5	1713 . 1	1733 . 5	1753 . 2	1773 . 6	1793 . 3
1594 . 7	1614 . 4	1634 . 1	1654 . 5	1674 . 2	1694 . 6	1714 . 2	1734 . 6	1754 . 3	1774 . 7	1794 . 4
1595 . 1	1615 . 5	1635 . 2	1655 . 6	1675 . 3	1695 . 7	1715 . 3	1735 . 7	1755 . 4	1775 . 1	1795 . 5
1596 . 9	1616 .13	1636 .10	1656 .14	1676 .11	1696 . 8	1716 .11	1736 . 8	1756 .12	1776 . 9	1796 .13
1597 . 4	1617 . 1	1637 . 5	1657 . 2	1677 . 6	1697 . 3	1717 . 6	1737 . 3	1757 . 7	1777 . 4	1797 . 1
1598 . 5	1618 . 2	1638 . 6	1658 . 3	1678 . 7	1698 . 4	1718 . 7	1738 . 4	1758 . 1	1778 . 5	1798 . 2
1599 . 6	1619 . 3	1639 . 7	1659 . 4	1679 . 1	1699 . 5	1719 . 1	1739 . 5	1759 . 2	1779 . 6	1799 . 3
1600 .14	1620 .11	1640 . 8	1660 .12	1680 . 9	1700 . 6	1720 . 9	1740 .13	1760 .10	1780 .14	1800 . 4
1601 . 2	1621 . 6	1641 . 3	1661 . 7	1681 . 4	1701 . 7	1721 . 4	1741 . 1	1761 . 5	1781 . 2	1801 . 5
1602 . 3	1622 . 7	1642 . 4	1662 . 1	1682 . 5	1702 . 1	1722 . 5	1742 . 2	1762 . 6	1782 . 3	1802 . 6

Lunar Calendar, Chinese New Year, Vietnamese Tet

The ancient Chinese lunar calendar is divided into 12 months of either 29 or 30 days (compensating for the fact that the mean duration of the lunar month is 29 days, 12 hours, 44.05 minutes). The calendar is synchronized with the solar year by the addition of extra months at fixed intervals.

The Chinese calendar runs on a sexagenary cycle, i.e. 60 years. The cycles 1876-1935 and 1936-1995, with the years grouped under their twelve animal designations, are printed below. A new cycle will begin in 1996 and last until 2055. The year 1994 (lunar year 4692) is found in the eleventh column under Dog, and is known as a "Year of the Dog". Readers can find the animal name for the year of their birth, marriage, etc., in the same chart. (Note: the first 3-7 weeks of each of the Western years belong to the previous Chinese year and animal designation.)

Both the Western (Gregorian) and traditional lunar calendars are used publicly in China and North and South Korea, and two New Year's celebrations are held. On Taiwan, in overseas Chinese communities, and in Vietnam, the lunar calendar has been used only to set the dates for traditional festivals, with the Gregorian system in general use.

The four-day Chinese New Year, Hsin Nien, the three-day Vietnamese New Year festival, Tet, and the three- to four-day Korean festival, Suhl, begin at the first new moon after the sun enters Aquarius. The day may fall, therefore, between Jan. 21 and Feb. 19 of the Gregorian calendar. Feb. 10, 1994 marks the start of the new Chinese year. The date is fixed according to the date of the new moon in the Far East. Since this is west of the International Date Line, the date may be one day later than that of the new moon in the United Kingdom.

Rat	Ox	Tiger	Hare (Rabbit)	Dragon	Snake	Horse	Sheep (Goat)	Monkey	Rooster	Dog	Pig
1876	1877	1878	1879	1880	1881	1882	1883	1884	1885	1886	1887
1888	1889	1890	1891	1892	1893	1894	1895	1896	1897	1898	1899
1900	1901	1902	1903	1904	1905	1906	1907	1908	1909	1910	1911
1912	1913	1914	1915	1916	1917	1918	1919	1920	1921	1922	1923
1924	1925	1926	1927	1928	1929	1930	1931	1932	1933	1934	1935
1936	1937	1938	1939	1940	1941	1942	1943	1944	1945	1946	1947
1948	1949	1950	1951	1952	1953	1954	1955	1956	1957	1958	1959
1960	1961	1962	1963	1964	1965	1966	1967	1968	1969	1970	1971
1972	1973	1974	1975	1976	1977	1978	1979	1980	1981	1982	1983
1984	1985	1986	1987	1988	1989	1990	1991	1992	1993	1994	1995
1996	1997	1998	1999	2000	2001	2002	2003	2004	2005	2006	2007

Days Between Two Dates

Table covers period of two ordinary years. Example—Days between Feb. 10, 1989 and Dec. 15, 1990; subtract 41 from 714; answer is 673 days. For leap year, such as 1992, one day must be added: final answer is 674.

Date	Jan.	Feb.	Mar.	April	May	June	July	Aug.	Sept.	Oct.	Nov.	Dec.
1	1	32	60	91	121	152	182	213	244	274	305	335
2	2	33	61	92	122	153	183	214	245	275	306	336
3	3	34	62	93	123	154	184	215	246	276	307	337
4	4	35	63	94	124	155	185	216	247	277	308	338
5	5	36	64	95	125	156	186	217	248	278	309	339
6	6	37	65	96	126	157	187	218	249	279	310	340
7	7	38	66	97	127	158	188	219	250	280	311	341
8	8	39	67	98	128	159	189	220	251	281	312	342
9	9	40	68	99	129	160	190	221	252	282	313	343
10	10	41	69	100	130	161	191	222	253	283	314	344
11	11	42	70	101	131	162	192	223	254	284	315	345
12	12	43	71	102	132	163	193	224	255	285	316	346
13	13	44	72	103	133	164	194	225	256	286	317	347
14	14	45	73	104	134	165	195	226	257	287	318	348
15	15	46	74	105	135	166	196	227	258	288	319	349
16	16	47	75	106	136	167	197	228	259	289	320	350
17	17	48	76	107	137	168	198	229	260	290	321	351
18	18	49	77	108	138	169	199	230	261	291	322	352
19	19	50	78	109	139	170	200	231	262	292	323	353
20	20	51	79	110	140	171	201	232	263	293	324	354
21	21	52	80	111	141	172	202	233	264	294	325	355
22	22	53	81	112	142	173	203	234	265	295	326	356
23	23	54	82	113	143	174	204	235	266	296	327	357
24	24	55	83	114	144	175	205	236	267	297	328	358
25	25	56	84	115	145	176	206	237	268	298	329	359
26	26	57	85	116	146	177	207	238	269	299	330	360
27	27	58	86	117	147	178	208	239	270	300	331	361
28	28	59	87	118	148	179	209	240	271	301	332	362
29	29	—	88	119	149	180	210	241	272	302	333	363
30	30	—	89	120	150	181	211	242	273	303	334	364
31	31	—	90	—	151	—	212	243	—	304	—	365

Date	Jan.	Feb.	Mar.	April	May	June	July	Aug.	Sept.	Oct.	Nov.	Dec.
1	366	397	425	456	486	517	547	578	609	639	670	700
2	367	398	426	457	487	518	548	579	610	640	671	701
3	368	399	427	458	488	519	549	580	611	641	672	702
4	369	400	428	459	489	520	550	581	612	642	673	703
5	370	401	429	460	490	521	551	582	613	643	674	704
6	371	402	430	461	491	522	552	583	614	644	675	705
7	372	403	431	462	492	523	553	584	615	645	676	706
8	373	404	432	463	493	524	554	585	616	646	677	707
9	374	405	433	464	494	525	555	586	617	647	678	708
10	375	406	434	465	495	526	556	587	618	648	679	709
11	376	407	435	466	496	527	557	588	619	649	680	710
12	377	408	436	467	497	528	558	589	620	650	681	711
13	378	409	437	468	498	529	559	590	621	651	682	712
14	379	410	438	469	499	530	560	591	622	652	683	713
15	380	411	439	470	500	531	561	592	623	653	684	714
16	381	412	440	471	501	532	562	593	624	654	685	715
17	382	413	441	472	502	533	563	594	625	655	686	716
18	383	414	442	473	503	534	564	595	626	656	687	717
19	384	415	443	474	504	535	565	596	627	657	688	718
20	385	416	444	475	505	536	566	597	628	658	689	719
21	386	417	445	476	506	537	567	598	629	659	690	720
22	387	418	446	477	507	538	568	599	630	660	691	721
23	388	419	447	478	508	539	569	600	631	661	692	722
24	389	420	448	479	509	540	570	601	632	662	693	723
25	390	421	449	480	510	541	571	602	633	663	694	724
26	391	422	450	481	511	542	572	603	634	664	695	725
27	392	423	451	482	512	543	573	604	635	665	696	726
28	393	424	452	483	513	544	574	605	636	666	697	727
29	394	—	453	484	514	545	575	606	637	667	698	728
30	395	—	454	485	515	546	576	607	638	668	699	729
31	396	—	455	—	516	—	577	608	—	669	—	730

Latitude, Longitude & Altitude of World Cities

City	Lat. N ° ′ ″	Long. W ° ′ ″	Alt* feet
Athens, Greece	37 58 00N	23 44 00E	300
Bangkok	13 45 00N	100 30 00E	0
Beijing, China	39 54 00N	116 28 00E	600
Berlin, Germany	52 32 00N	13 25 00E	110
Jerusalem, Israel	31 47 00N	35 13 00E	2,500
Johannesburg, So. Afr.	26 10 00S	28 02 00E	5,740
Kathmandu	27 40 00N	86 30 00E	4,500
London, UK (Greenwich)	51 30 00N	0 0 0	245
Los Angeles, USA	34 03 15N	118 114 28E	340
Mecca	21 25 00N	39 50 00E	6,562
Mexico City	19 25 34	99 07 00	7,347
Moscow, Russia	55 45 00N	37 42 00E	394
New Delhi, India	28 38 00N	77 12 00E	770
New York, USA	40 45 06N	73 59 39E	55
Paris, France	48 50 14N	2 20 14E	300
Rio de Janeiro, Brazil	22 53 43S	43 13 22W	30
Rome, Italy	41 53 00N	12 30 00E	95
Sydney, Australia	33 52 00S	151 12 00E	25
Tokyo, Japan	35 45 00N	139 45 00E	30
Tripoli	32 54 00N	13 11 00E	0
Warsaw, Poland	52 15 00N	21 00 00E	360
Wellington	41 17 00S	174 47 00E	0

*At downtown business area.

Standard Time Differences – World Cities

The time indicated in the table is fixed by law and is called the legal time, or, more generally, Standard Time. Use of Daylight Saving Time varies widely. At 12:00 noon, Greenwich Mean Time, the standard time (in 24-hour time) in foreign cities is as follows:

City	Time	City	Time	City	Time	City	Time
Addis Ababa	15 00	Caracas	08 00	Le Havre	13 00	Rio de Janeiro	09 00
Alexandria	14 00	Casablanca	12 00	Leningrad	15 00	Rome	13 00
Amsterdam	13 00	Chicago	06 00	Lima	07 00	Santiago	08 00
Anchorage	02 00	Copenhagen	14 00	Lisbon	12 00	Seoul	21 00
Athens	14 00	Dacca	18 00	Los Angeles	04 00	Shanghai	20 00
Auckland	24 00	Darwin	21 30	Madrid	13 00	Singapore	20 00
Baghdad	15 00	Delhi	17 30	Manila	20 00	Stockholm	13 00
Bangkok	19 00	Denver	05 00	Mecca	15 00	Sydney	22 00
Beijing	20 00	Gdańsk	13 00	Melbourne	22 00	Tashkent	18 00
Berlin	13 00	Geneva	13 00	Mexico City	06 00	Tehran	15 30
Bogotá	07 00	Havana	07 00	Montevideo	09 00	Tel Aviv	14 00
Bombay	17 30	Helsinki	14 00	Moscow	15 00	Tokyo	21 00
Brussels	13 00	Ho Chi Minh City	19 00	Nagasaki	21 00	Valparaiso	08 00
Bucharest	14 00	Hong Kong	20 00	New York	07 00	Vladivostok	22 00
Budapest	13 00	Istanbul	14 00	Oslo	13 00	Vienna	13 00
Buenos Aires	09 00	Jakarta	19 00	Paris	13 00	Warsaw	13 00
Cairo	14 00	Jerusalem	14 00	Perth	20 00	Wellington	24 00
Calcutta	17 30	Johannesburg	14 00	Prague	13 00	Yokohama	21 00
Cape Town	14 00	Karachi	17 00	Rangoon	18 30	Zurich	13 00

Perpetual Calendar

The number shown for each year indicates which Gregorian calendar to use. For 1583-1802, or for Julian calendar, see pages 199-200. For years 1803-1820, use numbers for 1983-2000, respectively.

1821 2	1847 6	1873 4	1899 1	1925 5	1951 2	1977 7	2003 4	2029 2	2055 6
1822 3	1848 14	1874 5	1900 2	1926 6	1952 10	1978 1	2004 12	2030 3	2056 14
1823 4	1849 2	1875 6	1901 3	1927 7	1953 5	1979 2	2005 7	2031 4	2057 2
1824 12	1850 3	1876 14	1902 4	1928 8	1954 6	1980 10	2006 1	2032 12	2058 3
1825 7	1851 4	1877 2	1903 5	1929 3	1955 7	1981 5	2007 2	2033 7	2059 4
1826 1	1852 12	1878 3	1904 13	1930 4	1956 8	1982 6	2008 10	2034 1	2060 12
1827 2	1853 7	1879 4	1905 1	1931 5	1957 3	1983 7	2009 5	2035 2	2061 7
1828 10	1854 1	1880 12	1906 2	1932 13	1958 4	1984 8	2010 6	2036 10	2062 1
1829 5	1855 2	1881 7	1907 3	1933 1	1959 5	1985 3	2011 7	2037 5	2063 2
1830 6	1856 10	1882 1	1908 11	1934 2	1960 13	1986 4	2012 8	2038 6	2064 10
1831 7	1857 5	1883 2	1909 6	1935 3	1961 1	1987 5	2013 3	2039 7	2065 5
1832 8	1858 6	1884 10	1910 7	1936 11	1962 2	1988 13	2014 4	2040 8	2066 6
1833 3	1859 7	1885 5	1911 1	1937 6	1963 3	1989 1	2015 5	2041 3	2067 7
1834 4	1860 8	1886 6	1912 9	1938 7	1964 11	1990 2	2016 13	2042 4	2068 8
1835 5	1861 3	1887 7	1913 4	1939 1	1965 6	1991 3	2017 1	2043 5	2069 3
1836 13	1862 4	1888 8	1914 5	1940 9	1966 7	1992 11	2018 2	2044 13	2070 4
1837 1	1863 5	1889 3	1915 6	1941 4	1967 1	1993 6	2019 3	2045 1	2071 5
1838 2	1864 13	1890 4	1916 14	1942 5	1968 9	1994 7	2020 11	2046 2	2072 13
1839 3	1865 1	1891 5	1917 2	1943 6	1969 4	1995 1	2021 6	2047 3	2073 1
1840 11	1866 2	1892 13	1918 3	1944 14	1970 5	1996 9	2022 7	2048 11	2074 2
1841 6	1867 3	1893 1	1919 4	1945 2	1971 6	1997 4	2023 1	2049 6	2075 3
1842 7	1868 11	1894 2	1920 12	1946 3	1972 14	1998 5	2024 9	2050 7	2076 11
1843 1	1869 6	1895 3	1921 7	1947 4	1973 2	1999 6	2025 4	2051 1	2077 6
1844 9	1870 7	1896 11	1922 1	1948 12	1974 3	2000 14	2026 5	2052 9	2078 7
1845 4	1871 1	1897 6	1923 2	1949 7	1975 4	2001 2	2027 6	2053 4	2079 1
1846 5	1872 9	1898 7	1924 10	1950 1	1976 12	2002 3	2028 14	2054 5	2080 9

1 1995

JANUARY

S	M	T	W	T	F	S
1	2	3	4	5	6	7
8	9	10	11	12	13	14
15	16	17	18	19	20	21
22	23	24	25	26	27	28
29	30	31				

FEBRUARY

S	M	T	W	T	F	S
			1	2	3	4
5	6	7	8	9	10	11
12	13	14	15	16	17	18
19	20	21	22	23	24	25
26	27	28				

MARCH

S	M	T	W	T	F	S
			1	2	3	4
5	6	7	8	9	10	11
12	13	14	15	16	17	18
19	20	21	22	23	24	25
26	27	28	29	30	31	

APRIL

S	M	T	W	T	F	S
						1
2	3	4	5	6	7	8
9	10	11	12	13	14	15
16	17	18	19	20	21	22
23	24	25	26	27	28	29
30						

MAY

S	M	T	W	T	F	S
	1	2	3	4	5	6
7	8	9	10	11	12	13
14	15	16	17	18	19	20
21	22	23	24	25	26	27
28	29	30	31			

JUNE

S	M	T	W	T	F	S
				1	2	3
4	5	6	7	8	9	10
11	12	13	14	15	16	17
18	19	20	21	22	23	24
25	26	27	28	29	30	

JULY

S	M	T	W	T	F	S
						1
2	3	4	5	6	7	8
9	10	11	12	13	14	15
16	17	18	19	20	21	22
23	24	25	26	27	28	29
30	31					

AUGUST

S	M	T	W	T	F	S
		1	2	3	4	5
6	7	8	9	10	11	12
13	14	15	16	17	18	19
20	21	22	23	24	25	26
27	28	29	30	31		

SEPTEMBER

S	M	T	W	T	F	S
					1	2
3	4	5	6	7	8	9
10	11	12	13	14	15	16
17	18	19	20	21	22	23
24	25	26	27	28	29	30

OCTOBER

S	M	T	W	T	F	S
1	2	3	4	5	6	7
8	9	10	11	12	13	14
15	16	17	18	19	20	21
22	23	24	25	26	27	28
29	30	31				

NOVEMBER

S	M	T	W	T	F	S
			1	2	3	4
5	6	7	8	9	10	11
12	13	14	15	16	17	18
19	20	21	22	23	24	25
26	27	28	29	30		

DECEMBER

S	M	T	W	T	F	S
					1	2
3	4	5	6	7	8	9
10	11	12	13	14	15	16
17	18	19	20	21	22	23
24	25	26	27	28	29	30
31						

2

JANUARY

S	M	T	W	T	F	S
	1	2	3	4	5	6
7	8	9	10	11	12	13
14	15	16	17	18	19	20
21	22	23	24	25	26	27
28	29	30	31			

FEBRUARY

S	M	T	W	T	F	S
				1	2	3
4	5	6	7	8	9	10
11	12	13	14	15	16	17
18	19	20	21	22	23	24
25	26	27	28			

MARCH

S	M	T	W	T	F	S
				1	2	3
4	5	6	7	8	9	10
11	12	13	14	15	16	17
18	19	20	21	22	23	24
25	26	27	28	29	30	31

APRIL

S	M	T	W	T	F	S
1	2	3	4	5	6	7
8	9	10	11	12	13	14
15	16	17	18	19	20	21
22	23	24	25	26	27	28
29	30					

MAY

S	M	T	W	T	F	S
		1	2	3	4	5
6	7	8	9	10	11	12
13	14	15	16	17	18	19
20	21	22	23	24	25	26
27	28	29	30	31		

JUNE

S	M	T	W	T	F	S
					1	2
3	4	5	6	7	8	9
10	11	12	13	14	15	16
17	18	19	20	21	22	23
24	25	26	27	28	29	30

JULY

S	M	T	W	T	F	S
1	2	3	4	5	6	7
8	9	10	11	12	13	14
15	16	17	18	19	20	21
22	23	24	25	26	27	28
29	30	31				

AUGUST

S	M	T	W	T	F	S
			1	2	3	4
5	6	7	8	9	10	11
12	13	14	15	16	17	18
19	20	21	22	23	24	25
26	27	28	29	30	31	

SEPTEMBER

S	M	T	W	T	F	S
						1
2	3	4	5	6	7	8
9	10	11	12	13	14	15
16	17	18	19	20	21	22
23	24	25	26	27	28	29
30						

OCTOBER

S	M	T	W	T	F	S
	1	2	3	4	5	6
7	8	9	10	11	12	13
14	15	16	17	18	19	20
21	22	23	24	25	26	27
28	29	30	31			

NOVEMBER

S	M	T	W	T	F	S
				1	2	3
4	5	6	7	8	9	10
11	12	13	14	15	16	17
18	19	20	21	22	23	24
25	26	27	28	29	30	

DECEMBER

S	M	T	W	T	F	S
						1
2	3	4	5	6	7	8
9	10	11	12	13	14	15
16	17	18	19	20	21	22
23	24	25	26	27	28	29
30	31					

3

JANUARY

S	M	T	W	T	F	S
		1	2	3	4	5
6	7	8	9	10	11	12
13	14	15	16	17	18	19
20	21	22	23	24	25	26
27	28	29	30	31		

FEBRUARY

S	M	T	W	T	F	S
					1	2
3	4	5	6	7	8	9
10	11	12	13	14	15	16
17	18	19	20	21	22	23
24	25	26	27	28		

MARCH

S	M	T	W	T	F	S
					1	2
3	4	5	6	7	8	9
10	11	12	13	14	15	16
17	18	19	20	21	22	23
24	25	26	27	28	29	30
31						

APRIL

S	M	T	W	T	F	S
	1	2	3	4	5	6
7	8	9	10	11	12	13
14	15	16	17	18	19	20
21	22	23	24	25	26	27
28	29	30				

MAY

S	M	T	W	T	F	S
			1	2	3	4
5	6	7	8	9	10	11
12	13	14	15	16	17	18
19	20	21	22	23	24	25
26	27	28	29	30	31	

JUNE

S	M	T	W	T	F	S
						1
2	3	4	5	6	7	8
9	10	11	12	13	14	15
16	17	18	19	20	21	22
23	24	25	26	27	28	29
30						

JULY

S	M	T	W	T	F	S
	1	2	3	4	5	6
7	8	9	10	11	12	13
14	15	16	17	18	19	20
21	22	23	24	25	26	27
28	29	30	31			

AUGUST

S	M	T	W	T	F	S
				1	2	3
4	5	6	7	8	9	10
11	12	13	14	15	16	17
18	19	20	21	22	23	24
25	26	27	28	29	30	31

SEPTEMBER

S	M	T	W	T	F	S
1	2	3	4	5	6	7
8	9	10	11	12	13	14
15	16	17	18	19	20	21
22	23	24	25	26	27	28
29	30					

OCTOBER

S	M	T	W	T	F	S
		1	2	3	4	5
6	7	8	9	10	11	12
13	14	15	16	17	18	19
20	21	22	23	24	25	26
27	28	29	30	31		

NOVEMBER

S	M	T	W	T	F	S
					1	2
3	4	5	6	7	8	9
10	11	12	13	14	15	16
17	18	19	20	21	22	23
24	25	26	27	28	29	30

DECEMBER

S	M	T	W	T	F	S
1	2	3	4	5	6	7
8	9	10	11	12	13	14
15	16	17	18	19	20	21
22	23	24	25	26	27	28
29	30	31				

4

JANUARY

S	M	T	W	T	F	S
			1	2	3	4
5	6	7	8	9	10	11
12	13	14	15	16	17	18
19	20	21	22	23	24	25
26	27	28	29	30	31	

FEBRUARY

S	M	T	W	T	F	S
						1
2	3	4	5	6	7	8
9	10	11	12	13	14	15
16	17	18	19	20	21	22
23	24	25	26	27	28	

MARCH

S	M	T	W	T	F	S
						1
2	3	4	5	6	7	8
9	10	11	12	13	14	15
16	17	18	19	20	21	22
23	24	25	26	27	28	29
30	31					

APRIL

S	M	T	W	T	F	S
		1	2	3	4	5
6	7	8	9	10	11	12
13	14	15	16	17	18	19
20	21	22	23	24	25	26
27	28	29	30			

MAY

S	M	T	W	T	F	S
				1	2	3
4	5	6	7	8	9	10
11	12	13	14	15	16	17
18	19	20	21	22	23	24
25	26	27	28	29	30	31

JUNE

S	M	T	W	T	F	S
1	2	3	4	5	6	7
8	9	10	11	12	13	14
15	16	17	18	19	20	21
22	23	24	25	26	27	28
29	30					

JULY

S	M	T	W	T	F	S
		1	2	3	4	5
6	7	8	9	10	11	12
13	14	15	16	17	18	19
20	21	22	23	24	25	26
27	28	29	30	31		

AUGUST

S	M	T	W	T	F	S
					1	2
3	4	5	6	7	8	9
10	11	12	13	14	15	16
17	18	19	20	21	22	23
24	25	26	27	28	29	30
31						

SEPTEMBER

S	M	T	W	T	F	S
	1	2	3	4	5	6
7	8	9	10	11	12	13
14	15	16	17	18	19	20
21	22	23	24	25	26	27
28	29	30				

OCTOBER

S	M	T	W	T	F	S
			1	2	3	4
5	6	7	8	9	10	11
12	13	14	15	16	17	18
19	20	21	22	23	24	25
26	27	28	29	30	31	

NOVEMBER

S	M	T	W	T	F	S
						1
2	3	4	5	6	7	8
9	10	11	12	13	14	15
16	17	18	19	20	21	22
23	24	25	26	27	28	29
30						

DECEMBER

S	M	T	W	T	F	S
	1	2	3	4	5	6
7	8	9	10	11	12	13
14	15	16	17	18	19	20
21	22	23	24	25	26	27
28	29	30	31			

5

JANUARY

S	M	T	W	T	F	S
				1	2	3
4	5	6	7	8	9	10
11	12	13	14	15	16	17
18	19	20	21	22	23	24
25	26	27	28	29	30	31

FEBRUARY

S	M	T	W	T	F	S
1	2	3	4	5	6	7
8	9	10	11	12	13	14
15	16	17	18	19	20	21
22	23	24	25	26	27	28

MARCH

S	M	T	W	T	F	S
1	2	3	4	5	6	7
8	9	10	11	12	13	14
15	16	17	18	19	20	21
22	23	24	25	26	27	28
29	30	31				

APRIL

S	M	T	W	T	F	S
			1	2	3	4
5	6	7	8	9	10	11
12	13	14	15	16	17	18
19	20	21	22	23	24	25
26	27	28	29	30		

MAY

S	M	T	W	T	F	S
					1	2
3	4	5	6	7	8	9
10	11	12	13	14	15	16
17	18	19	20	21	22	23
24	25	26	27	28	29	30
31						

JUNE

S	M	T	W	T	F	S
	1	2	3	4	5	6
7	8	9	10	11	12	13
14	15	16	17	18	19	20
21	22	23	24	25	26	27
28	29	30				

JULY

S	M	T	W	T	F	S
			1	2	3	4
5	6	7	8	9	10	11
12	13	14	15	16	17	18
19	20	21	22	23	24	25
26	27	28	29	30	31	

AUGUST

S	M	T	W	T	F	S
						1
2	3	4	5	6	7	8
9	10	11	12	13	14	15
16	17	18	19	20	21	22
23	24	25	26	27	28	29
30	31					

SEPTEMBER

S	M	T	W	T	F	S
		1	2	3	4	5
6	7	8	9	10	11	12
13	14	15	16	17	18	19
20	21	22	23	24	25	26
27	28	29	30			

OCTOBER

S	M	T	W	T	F	S
				1	2	3
4	5	6	7	8	9	10
11	12	13	14	15	16	17
18	19	20	21	22	23	24
25	26	27	28	29	30	31

NOVEMBER

S	M	T	W	T	F	S
1	2	3	4	5	6	7
8	9	10	11	12	13	14
15	16	17	18	19	20	21
22	23	24	25	26	27	28
29	30					

DECEMBER

S	M	T	W	T	F	S
		1	2	3	4	5
6	7	8	9	10	11	12
13	14	15	16	17	18	19
20	21	22	23	24	25	26
27	28	29	30	31		

6 1993

JANUARY

S	M	T	W	T	F	S
					1	2
3	4	5	6	7	8	9
10	11	12	13	14	15	16
17	18	19	20	21	22	23
24	25	26	27	28	29	30
31						

FEBRUARY

S	M	T	W	T	F	S
	1	2	3	4	5	6
7	8	9	10	11	12	13
14	15	16	17	18	19	20
21	22	23	24	25	26	27
28						

MARCH

S	M	T	W	T	F	S
	1	2	3	4	5	6
7	8	9	10	11	12	13
14	15	16	17	18	19	20
21	22	23	24	25	26	27
28	29	30	31			

APRIL

S	M	T	W	T	F	S
				1	2	3
4	5	6	7	8	9	10
11	12	13	14	15	16	17
18	19	20	21	22	23	24
25	26	27	28	29	30	

MAY

S	M	T	W	T	F	S
						1
2	3	4	5	6	7	8
9	10	11	12	13	14	15
16	17	18	19	20	21	22
23	24	25	26	27	28	29
30	31					

JUNE

S	M	T	W	T	F	S
		1	2	3	4	5
6	7	8	9	10	11	12
13	14	15	16	17	18	19
20	21	22	23	24	25	26
27	28	29	30			

JULY

S	M	T	W	T	F	S
				1	2	3
4	5	6	7	8	9	10
11	12	13	14	15	16	17
18	19	20	21	22	23	24
25	26	27	28	29	30	31

AUGUST

S	M	T	W	T	F	S
1	2	3	4	5	6	7
8	9	10	11	12	13	14
15	16	17	18	19	20	21
22	23	24	25	26	27	28
29	30	31				

SEPTEMBER

S	M	T	W	T	F	S
			1	2	3	4
5	6	7	8	9	10	11
12	13	14	15	16	17	18
19	20	21	22	23	24	25
26	27	28	29	30		

OCTOBER

S	M	T	W	T	F	S
					1	2
3	4	5	6	7	8	9
10	11	12	13	14	15	16
17	18	19	20	21	22	23
24	25	26	27	28	29	30
31						

NOVEMBER

S	M	T	W	T	F	S
	1	2	3	4	5	6
7	8	9	10	11	12	13
14	15	16	17	18	19	20
21	22	23	24	25	26	27
28	29	30				

DECEMBER

S	M	T	W	T	F	S
			1	2	3	4
5	6	7	8	9	10	11
12	13	14	15	16	17	18
19	20	21	22	23	24	25
26	27	28	29	30	31	

7 1994

JANUARY

S	M	T	W	T	F	S
						1
2	3	4	5	6	7	8
9	10	11	12	13	14	15
16	17	18	19	20	21	22
23	24	25	26	27	28	29
30	31					

FEBRUARY

S	M	T	W	T	F	S
		1	2	3	4	5
6	7	8	9	10	11	12
13	14	15	16	17	18	19
20	21	22	23	24	25	26
27	28					

MARCH

S	M	T	W	T	F	S
		1	2	3	4	5
6	7	8	9	10	11	12
13	14	15	16	17	18	19
20	21	22	23	24	25	26
27	28	29	30	31		

APRIL

S	M	T	W	T	F	S
					1	2
3	4	5	6	7	8	9
10	11	12	13	14	15	16
17	18	19	20	21	22	23
24	25	26	27	28	29	30

MAY

S	M	T	W	T	F	S
1	2	3	4	5	6	7
8	9	10	11	12	13	14
15	16	17	18	19	20	21
22	23	24	25	26	27	28
29	30	31				

JUNE

S	M	T	W	T	F	S
			1	2	3	4
5	6	7	8	9	10	11
12	13	14	15	16	17	18
19	20	21	22	23	24	25
26	27	28	29	30		

JULY

S	M	T	W	T	F	S
					1	2
3	4	5	6	7	8	9
10	11	12	13	14	15	16
17	18	19	20	21	22	23
24	25	26	27	28	29	30
31						

AUGUST

S	M	T	W	T	F	S
	1	2	3	4	5	6
7	8	9	10	11	12	13
14	15	16	17	18	19	20
21	22	23	24	25	26	27
28	29	30	31			

SEPTEMBER

S	M	T	W	T	F	S
				1	2	3
4	5	6	7	8	9	10
11	12	13	14	15	16	17
18	19	20	21	22	23	24
25	26	27	28	29	30	

OCTOBER

S	M	T	W	T	F	S
						1
2	3	4	5	6	7	8
9	10	11	12	13	14	15
16	17	18	19	20	21	22
23	24	25	26	27	28	29
30	31					

NOVEMBER

S	M	T	W	T	F	S
		1	2	3	4	5
6	7	8	9	10	11	12
13	14	15	16	17	18	19
20	21	22	23	24	25	26
27	28	29	30			

DECEMBER

S	M	T	W	T	F	S
				1	2	3
4	5	6	7	8	9	10
11	12	13	14	15	16	17
18	19	20	21	22	23	24
25	26	27	28	29	30	31

8

JANUARY

S	M	T	W	T	F	S
1	2	3	4	5	6	7
8	9	10	11	12	13	14
15	16	17	18	19	20	21
22	23	24	25	26	27	28
29	30	31				

FEBRUARY

S	M	T	W	T	F	S
			1	2	3	4
5	6	7	8	9	10	11
12	13	14	15	16	17	18
19	20	21	22	23	24	25
26	27	28	29			

MARCH

S	M	T	W	T	F	S
				1	2	3
4	5	6	7	8	9	10
11	12	13	14	15	16	17
18	19	20	21	22	23	24
25	26	27	28	29	30	31

APRIL

S	M	T	W	T	F	S
1	2	3	4	5	6	7
8	9	10	11	12	13	14
15	16	17	18	19	20	21
22	23	24	25	26	27	28
29	30					

MAY

S	M	T	W	T	F	S
		1	2	3	4	5
6	7	8	9	10	11	12
13	14	15	16	17	18	19
20	21	22	23	24	25	26
27	28	29	30	31		

JUNE

S	M	T	W	T	F	S
					1	2
3	4	5	6	7	8	9
10	11	12	13	14	15	16
17	18	19	20	21	22	23
24	25	26	27	28	29	30

JULY

S	M	T	W	T	F	S
1	2	3	4	5	6	7
8	9	10	11	12	13	14
15	16	17	18	19	20	21
22	23	24	25	26	27	28
29	30	31				

AUGUST

S	M	T	W	T	F	S
			1	2	3	4
5	6	7	8	9	10	11
12	13	14	15	16	17	18
19	20	21	22	23	24	25
26	27	28	29	30	31	

SEPTEMBER

S	M	T	W	T	F	S
						1
2	3	4	5	6	7	8
9	10	11	12	13	14	15
16	17	18	19	20	21	22
23	24	25	26	27	28	29
30						

OCTOBER

S	M	T	W	T	F	S
	1	2	3	4	5	6
7	8	9	10	11	12	13
14	15	16	17	18	19	20
21	22	23	24	25	26	27
28	29	30	31			

NOVEMBER

S	M	T	W	T	F	S
				1	2	3
4	5	6	7	8	9	10
11	12	13	14	15	16	17
18	19	20	21	22	23	24
25	26	27	28	29	30	

DECEMBER

S	M	T	W	T	F	S
						1
2	3	4	5	6	7	8
9	10	11	12	13	14	15
16	17	18	19	20	21	22
23	24	25	26	27	28	29
30	31					

9

JANUARY

S	M	T	W	T	F	S
	1	2	3	4	5	6
7	8	9	10	11	12	13
14	15	16	17	18	19	20
21	22	23	24	25	26	27
28	29	30	31			

FEBRUARY

S	M	T	W	T	F	S
				1	2	3
4	5	6	7	8	9	10
11	12	13	14	15	16	17
18	19	20	21	22	23	24
25	26	27	28	29		

MARCH

S	M	T	W	T	F	S
					1	2
3	4	5	6	7	8	9
10	11	12	13	14	15	16
17	18	19	20	21	22	23
24	25	26	27	28	29	30
31						

APRIL

S	M	T	W	T	F	S
	1	2	3	4	5	6
7	8	9	10	11	12	13
14	15	16	17	18	19	20
21	22	23	24	25	26	27
28	29	30				

MAY

S	M	T	W	T	F	S
			1	2	3	4
5	6	7	8	9	10	11
12	13	14	15	16	17	18
19	20	21	22	23	24	25
26	27	28	29	30	31	

JUNE

S	M	T	W	T	F	S
						1
2	3	4	5	6	7	8
9	10	11	12	13	14	15
16	17	18	19	20	21	22
23	24	25	26	27	28	29
30						

JULY

S	M	T	W	T	F	S
	1	2	3	4	5	6
7	8	9	10	11	12	13
14	15	16	17	18	19	20
21	22	23	24	25	26	27
28	29	30	31			

AUGUST

S	M	T	W	T	F	S
				1	2	3
4	5	6	7	8	9	10
11	12	13	14	15	16	17
18	19	20	21	22	23	24
25	26	27	28	29	30	31

SEPTEMBER

S	M	T	W	T	F	S
1	2	3	4	5	6	7
8	9	10	11	12	13	14
15	16	17	18	19	20	21
22	23	24	25	26	27	28
29	30					

OCTOBER

S	M	T	W	T	F	S
		1	2	3	4	5
6	7	8	9	10	11	12
13	14	15	16	17	18	19
20	21	22	23	24	25	26
27	28	29	30	31		

NOVEMBER

S	M	T	W	T	F	S
					1	2
3	4	5	6	7	8	9
10	11	12	13	14	15	16
17	18	19	20	21	22	23
24	25	26	27	28	29	30

DECEMBER

S	M	T	W	T	F	S
1	2	3	4	5	6	7
8	9	10	11	12	13	14
15	16	17	18	19	20	21
22	23	24	25	26	27	28
29	30	31				

10

JANUARY

S	M	T	W	T	F	S
		1	2	3	4	5
6	7	8	9	10	11	12
13	14	15	16	17	18	19
20	21	22	23	24	25	26
27	28	29	30	31		

FEBRUARY

S	M	T	W	T	F	S
					1	2
3	4	5	6	7	8	9
10	11	12	13	14	15	16
17	18	19	20	21	22	23
24	25	26	27	28	29	

MARCH

S	M	T	W	T	F	S
						1
2	3	4	5	6	7	8
9	10	11	12	13	14	15
16	17	18	19	20	21	22
23	24	25	26	27	28	29
30	31					

APRIL

S	M	T	W	T	F	S
		1	2	3	4	5
6	7	8	9	10	11	12
13	14	15	16	17	18	19
20	21	22	23	24	25	26
27	28	29	30			

MAY

S	M	T	W	T	F	S
				1	2	3
4	5	6	7	8	9	10
11	12	13	14	15	16	17
18	19	20	21	22	23	24
25	26	27	28	29	30	31

JUNE

S	M	T	W	T	F	S
1	2	3	4	5	6	7
8	9	10	11	12	13	14
15	16	17	18	19	20	21
22	23	24	25	26	27	28
29	30					

JULY

S	M	T	W	T	F	S
		1	2	3	4	5
6	7	8	9	10	11	12
13	14	15	16	17	18	19
20	21	22	23	24	25	26
27	28	29	30	31		

AUGUST

S	M	T	W	T	F	S
					1	2
3	4	5	6	7	8	9
10	11	12	13	14	15	16
17	18	19	20	21	22	23
24	25	26	27	28	29	30
31						

SEPTEMBER

S	M	T	W	T	F	S
	1	2	3	4	5	6
7	8	9	10	11	12	13
14	15	16	17	18	19	20
21	22	23	24	25	26	27
28	29	30				

OCTOBER

S	M	T	W	T	F	S
			1	2	3	4
5	6	7	8	9	10	11
12	13	14	15	16	17	18
19	20	21	22	23	24	25
26	27	28	29	30	31	

NOVEMBER

S	M	T	W	T	F	S
						1
2	3	4	5	6	7	8
9	10	11	12	13	14	15
16	17	18	19	20	21	22
23	24	25	26	27	28	29
30						

DECEMBER

S	M	T	W	T	F	S
	1	2	3	4	5	6
7	8	9	10	11	12	13
14	15	16	17	18	19	20
21	22	23	24	25	26	27
28	29	30	31			

11 1992

JANUARY

S	M	T	W	T	F	S
			1	2	3	4
5	6	7	8	9	10	11
12	13	14	15	16	17	18
19	20	21	22	23	24	25
26	27	28	29	30	31	

FEBRUARY

S	M	T	W	T	F	S
						1
2	3	4	5	6	7	8
9	10	11	12	13	14	15
16	17	18	19	20	21	22
23	24	25	26	27	28	29

MARCH

S	M	T	W	T	F	S
1	2	3	4	5	6	7
8	9	10	11	12	13	14
15	16	17	18	19	20	21
22	23	24	25	26	27	28
29	30	31				

APRIL

S	M	T	W	T	F	S
			1	2	3	4
5	6	7	8	9	10	11
12	13	14	15	16	17	18
19	20	21	22	23	24	25
26	27	28	29	30		

MAY

S	M	T	W	T	F	S
					1	2
3	4	5	6	7	8	9
10	11	12	13	14	15	16
17	18	19	20	21	22	23
24	25	26	27	28	29	30
31						

JUNE

S	M	T	W	T	F	S
	1	2	3	4	5	6
7	8	9	10	11	12	13
14	15	16	17	18	19	20
21	22	23	24	25	26	27
28	29	30				

JULY

S	M	T	W	T	F	S
			1	2	3	4
5	6	7	8	9	10	11
12	13	14	15	16	17	18
19	20	21	22	23	24	25
26	27	28	29	30	31	

AUGUST

S	M	T	W	T	F	S
						1
2	3	4	5	6	7	8
9	10	11	12	13	14	15
16	17	18	19	20	21	22
23	24	25	26	27	28	29
30	31					

SEPTEMBER

S	M	T	W	T	F	S
		1	2	3	4	5
6	7	8	9	10	11	12
13	14	15	16	17	18	19
20	21	22	23	24	25	26
27	28	29	30			

OCTOBER

S	M	T	W	T	F	S
				1	2	3
4	5	6	7	8	9	10
11	12	13	14	15	16	17
18	19	20	21	22	23	24
25	26	27	28	29	30	31

NOVEMBER

S	M	T	W	T	F	S
1	2	3	4	5	6	7
8	9	10	11	12	13	14
15	16	17	18	19	20	21
22	23	24	25	26	27	28
29	30					

DECEMBER

S	M	T	W	T	F	S
		1	2	3	4	5
6	7	8	9	10	11	12
13	14	15	16	17	18	19
20	21	22	23	24	25	26
27	28	29	30	31		

12

JANUARY

S	M	T	W	T	F	S
				1	2	3
4	5	6	7	8	9	10
11	12	13	14	15	16	17
18	19	20	21	22	23	24
25	26	27	28	29	30	31

FEBRUARY

S	M	T	W	T	F	S
1	2	3	4	5	6	7
8	9	10	11	12	13	14
15	16	17	18	19	20	21
22	23	24	25	26	27	28
29						

MARCH

S	M	T	W	T	F	S
	1	2	3	4	5	6
7	8	9	10	11	12	13
14	15	16	17	18	19	20
21	22	23	24	25	26	27
28	29	30	31			

APRIL

S	M	T	W	T	F	S
				1	2	3
4	5	6	7	8	9	10
11	12	13	14	15	16	17
18	19	20	21	22	23	24
25	26	27	28	29	30	

MAY

S	M	T	W	T	F	S
						1
2	3	4	5	6	7	8
9	10	11	12	13	14	15
16	17	18	19	20	21	22
23	24	25	26	27	28	29
30	31					

JUNE

S	M	T	W	T	F	S
		1	2	3	4	5
6	7	8	9	10	11	12
13	14	15	16	17	18	19
20	21	22	23	24	25	26
27	28	29	30			

JULY

S	M	T	W	T	F	S
				1	2	3
4	5	6	7	8	9	10
11	12	13	14	15	16	17
18	19	20	21	22	23	24
25	26	27	28	29	30	31

AUGUST

S	M	T	W	T	F	S
1	2	3	4	5	6	7
8	9	10	11	12	13	14
15	16	17	18	19	20	21
22	23	24	25	26	27	28
29	30	31				

SEPTEMBER

S	M	T	W	T	F	S
			1	2	3	4
5	6	7	8	9	10	11
12	13	14	15	16	17	18
19	20	21	22	23	24	25
26	27	28	29	30		

OCTOBER

S	M	T	W	T	F	S
					1	2
3	4	5	6	7	8	9
10	11	12	13	14	15	16
17	18	19	20	21	22	23
24	25	26	27	28	29	30
31						

NOVEMBER

S	M	T	W	T	F	S
	1	2	3	4	5	6
7	8	9	10	11	12	13
14	15	16	17	18	19	20
21	22	23	24	25	26	27
28	29	30				

DECEMBER

S	M	T	W	T	F	S
			1	2	3	4
5	6	7	8	9	10	11
12	13	14	15	16	17	18
19	20	21	22	23	24	25
26	27	28	29	30	31	

13

JANUARY

S	M	T	W	T	F	S
					1	2
3	4	5	6	7	8	9
10	11	12	13	14	15	16
17	18	19	20	21	22	23
24	25	26	27	28	29	30
31						

FEBRUARY

S	M	T	W	T	F	S
	1	2	3	4	5	6
7	8	9	10	11	12	13
14	15	16	17	18	19	20
21	22	23	24	25	26	27
28	29					

MARCH

S	M	T	W	T	F	S
		1	2	3	4	5
6	7	8	9	10	11	12
13	14	15	16	17	18	19
20	21	22	23	24	25	26
27	28	29	30	31		

APRIL

S	M	T	W	T	F	S
					1	2
3	4	5	6	7	8	9
10	11	12	13	14	15	16
17	18	19	20	21	22	23
24	25	26	27	28	29	30

MAY

S	M	T	W	T	F	S
1	2	3	4	5	6	7
8	9	10	11	12	13	14
15	16	17	18	19	20	21
22	23	24	25	26	27	28
29	30	31				

JUNE

S	M	T	W	T	F	S
			1	2	3	4
5	6	7	8	9	10	11
12	13	14	15	16	17	18
19	20	21	22	23	24	25
26	27	28	29	30		

JULY

S	M	T	W	T	F	S
					1	2
3	4	5	6	7	8	9
10	11	12	13	14	15	16
17	18	19	20	21	22	23
24	25	26	27	28	29	30
31						

AUGUST

S	M	T	W	T	F	S
	1	2	3	4	5	6
7	8	9	10	11	12	13
14	15	16	17	18	19	20
21	22	23	24	25	26	27
28	29	30	31			

SEPTEMBER

S	M	T	W	T	F	S
				1	2	3
4	5	6	7	8	9	10
11	12	13	14	15	16	17
18	19	20	21	22	23	24
25	26	27	28	29	30	

OCTOBER

S	M	T	W	T	F	S
						1
2	3	4	5	6	7	8
9	10	11	12	13	14	15
16	17	18	19	20	21	22
23	24	25	26	27	28	29
30	31					

NOVEMBER

S	M	T	W	T	F	S
		1	2	3	4	5
6	7	8	9	10	11	12
13	14	15	16	17	18	19
20	21	22	23	24	25	26
27	28	29	30			

DECEMBER

S	M	T	W	T	F	S
				1	2	3
4	5	6	7	8	9	10
11	12	13	14	15	16	17
18	19	20	21	22	23	24
25	26	27	28	29	30	31

14

JANUARY

S	M	T	W	T	F	S
						1
2	3	4	5	6	7	8
9	10	11	12	13	14	15
16	17	18	19	20	21	22
23	24	25	26	27	28	29
30	31					

FEBRUARY

S	M	T	W	T	F	S
		1	2	3	4	5
6	7	8	9	10	11	12
13	14	15	16	17	18	19
20	21	22	23	24	25	26
27	28	29				

MARCH

S	M	T	W	T	F	S
			1	2	3	4
5	6	7	8	9	10	11
12	13	14	15	16	17	18
19	20	21	22	23	24	25
26	27	28	29	30	31	

APRIL

S	M	T	W	T	F	S
						1
2	3	4	5	6	7	8
9	10	11	12	13	14	15
16	17	18	19	20	21	22
23	24	25	26	27	28	29
30						

MAY

S	M	T	W	T	F	S
	1	2	3	4	5	6
7	8	9	10	11	12	13
14	15	16	17	18	19	20
21	22	23	24	25	26	27
28	29	30	31			

JUNE

S	M	T	W	T	F	S
				1	2	3
4	5	6	7	8	9	10
11	12	13	14	15	16	17
18	19	20	21	22	23	24
25	26	27	28	29	30	

JULY

S	M	T	W	T	F	S
						1
2	3	4	5	6	7	8
9	10	11	12	13	14	15
16	17	18	19	20	21	22
23	24	25	26	27	28	29
30	31					

AUGUST

S	M	T	W	T	F	S
		1	2	3	4	5
6	7	8	9	10	11	12
13	14	15	16	17	18	19
20	21	22	23	24	25	26
27	28	29	30	31		

SEPTEMBER

S	M	T	W	T	F	S
					1	2
3	4	5	6	7	8	9
10	11	12	13	14	15	16
17	18	19	20	21	22	23
24	25	26	27	28	29	30

OCTOBER

S	M	T	W	T	F	S
1	2	3	4	5	6	7
8	9	10	11	12	13	14
15	16	17	18	19	20	21
22	23	24	25	26	27	28
29	30	31				

NOVEMBER

S	M	T	W	T	F	S
			1	2	3	4
5	6	7	8	9	10	11
12	13	14	15	16	17	18
19	20	21	22	23	24	25
26	27	28	29	30		

DECEMBER

S	M	T	W	T	F	S
					1	2
3	4	5	6	7	8	9
10	11	12	13	14	15	16
17	18	19	20	21	22	23
24	25	26	27	28	29	30
31						

Standard Time, Daylight Saving Time, and Others

Source: Defense Mapping Agency Hydrographic/Topographic Center; U.S. Dept. of Transportation

Standard Time

Standard time is reckoned from Greenwich, England, recognized as the Prime Meridian of Longitude. The world is divided into 24 zones, each 15° of arc, or one hour in time apart. The Greenwich meridian (0°) extends through the center of the initial zone, and the zones to the east are numbered from 1 to 12 with the prefix "minus" indicating the number of hours to be subtracted to obtain Greenwich Time. Each zone extends 71/2 ° on either side of its central meridian.

Westward zones are similarly numbered, but prefixed "plus" showing the number of hours that must be added to get Greenwich Time. While these zones apply generally to sea areas, it should be noted that the Standard Time maintained in many countries does not coincide with zone time.

The United States and possessions are divided into eight standard Time zones, as set forth by the Uniform Time Act of 1966, which also provides for the use of Daylight Saving Time therein. Each zone is approximately 15° of longitude in width. All places in each zone use, instead of their own local time, the time counted from the transit of the "mean sun" across the Standard Time meridian which passes near the middle of that zone.

These time zones are designated as Atlantic, Eastern, Central, Mountain, Pacific, Yukon, Alaska-Hawaii, and Bering (Samoa), and the time in these zones is basically reckoned from the 60th, 75th, 90th, 105th, 120th, 135th, 150th and 165th meridians west of Greenwich. The line wanders to conform to local geographical regions. The time in the various zones is earlier than Greenwich Time by 4, 5, 6, 7, 8, 9, 10, and 11 hours respectively.

24-Hour Time

24-hour time is widely used in scientific work throughout the world, and in operations of the Armed Forces. In Europe it is frequently used by the transportation networks in preference to the 12-hour a.m. and p.m. system. With the 24-hour system the day begins at midnight and is designated 0000 through 2359.

International Date Line

The Date Line is a zig-zag line that approximately coincides with the 180th meridian, and it is where the calendar dates are separated. The date must be advanced one day when crossing in a westerly direction and set back one day when crossing in an easterly direction.

The line is deflected eastward through the Bering Strait and westward of the Aleutians to prevent separating these areas by date. The line is again deflected eastward of the Tonga and New Zealand Islands in the South Pacific for the same reason.

Daylight Saving Time

Daylight Saving Time is achieved by advancing the clock one hour. Adjusting clock time to be able to use the added daylight on summer evenings is common throughout the world.

Western Europe is on daylight saving time generally from the last Sunday in March to the last Sunday in September; however, the United Kingdom continues until the last Sunday in October.

Russia, which lies over 11 time zones, maintains its standard time 1 hour fast of the zone designation. Additionally, it proclaims daylight saving time, as does Europe.

China lies across 5 time zones, but has decreed that the entire country be placed on Greenwich time plus 8 hours, with daylight saving time from April 12 to September 12.

North America lies over 8 times zones and is on daylight saving time from the last Sunday in April to the last Sunday in October.

Many of the countries in the Southern Hemisphere maintain daylight saving time generally from October to March; however, most countries near the equator do not deviate from standard time.

SCIENCE & TECHNOLOGY

Inventions and Discoveries

Invention	Date	Inventor	Nation.
Adding machine	1642	Pascal	French
Adding machine	1885	Burroughs	U.S.
Aeroplane, automatic pilot	1912	Sperry	U.S.
Aeroplane, experimental	1896	Langley	U.S.
Aeroplane, hydro	1911	Curtiss	U.S.
Aeroplane jet engine	1939	Ohain	German
Aeroplane with motor	1903	Wright bros.	U.S.
Aerosol spray	1926	Rotheim	Norwegian
Air brake	1868	Westinghouse	U.S.
Air conditioning	1911	Carrier	U.S.
Air pump	1654	Guericke	German
Airship	1852	Giffard	French
Airship, rigid dirigible	1900	Zeppelin	German
Arc welder	1919	Thomson	U.S.
Aspartame	1965	Schlatter	U.S.
Autogyro	1920	de la Cierva	Spanish
Automobile, differential gear	1885	Benz	German
Automobile, electric	1892	Morrison	U.S.
Automobile, exp'mtl	1864	Marcus	Austrian
Automobile magneto	1897	Bosch	German
Automobile, petrol	1889	Daimler	German
Automobile, petrol	1892	Duryea	U.S.
Automobile self-starter	1911	Kettering	U.S.
Automobile silencer	...	Maxim, H.P.	U.S.
Babbitt metal	1839	Babbitt	U.S.
Bakelite	1907	Baekeland	Belg., U.S.
Balloon	1783	Montgolfier	French
Barometer	1643	Torricelli	Italian
Bicycle, modern	1885	Starley	English
Bifocal lens	1780	Franklin	U.S.
Block signals, railway	1867	Hall	U.S.
Bomb, depth	1916	Tait	U.S.
Bottle machine	1895	Owens	U.S.
Braille printing	1829	Braille	French
Burner, gas	1855	Bunsen	German
Calculating machine	1833	Babbage	English
Calculator, electronic pocket	1972	Van Tassel	U.S.
Camera, Kodak	1888	Eastman, Walker	U.S.
Camera, Polaroid Land	1948	Land	U.S.
Car coupler	1873	Janney	U.S.
Carburettor, petrol	1893	Maybach	German
Card time-recorder	1894	Cooper	U.S.
Carding machine	1797	Whittemore	U.S.
Carpet sweeper	1876	Bissell	U.S.
Cassette, audio	1963	Philips Co.	Dutch
Cassette, videotape	1969	Sony	Japanese
Cash register	1879	Ritty	U.S.
Cathode ray oscilloscope	1897	Braun	German
Cathode ray tube	1878	Crookes	English
CAT scan (computerized tomography)	1973	Hounsfield	English
Cellophane	1908	Brandenberger	Swiss
Celluloid	1870	Hyatt	U.S.
Cement, Portland	1824	Aspdin	English
Chronometer	1761	Harrison	English
Circuit breaker	1925	Hilliard	U.S.
Circuit, integrated	1959	Kilby, Noyce, Texas Instr	U.S
Clock, pendulum	1657	Huygens	Dutch
Coaxial cable system	1929	Affel, Espenschied	U.S.
Coke oven	1893	Hoffman	Austrian
Compressed air rock drill	1871	Ingersoll	U.S.
Comptometer	1887	Felt	U.S.
Computer, automatic sequence	1944	Aiken et al.	U.S.
Computer, mini	1960	Digital Corp	U.S.
Condenser microphone (telephone)	1916	Wente	U.S.
Contraceptive, oral	1954	Pincus, Rock	U.S.
Corn, hybrid	1917	Jones	U.S.
Cotton gin	1793	Whitney	U.S.
Cream separator	1878	DeLaval	Swedish
Cultivator, disc	1878	Mallon	U.S.
Cystoscope	1878	Nitze	German
Diesel engine	1895	Diesel	German
Disc, compact	1972	RCA	U.S.
Disc, floppy	1970	IBM	U.S.

Invention	Date	Inventor	Nation.
Disc player, compact	1979	Sony, Philips Co	Japanese, Dutch
Disc, video	1972	Philips Co	Dutch
Dynamite	1866	Nobel	Swedish
Dynamo, continuous current	1871	Gramme	Belgian
Dynamo, hydrogen cooled	1915	Schuler	U.S.
Electric battery	1800	Volta	Italian
Electric fan	1882	Wheeler	U.S.
Electrocardiograph	1903	Einthoven	Dutch
Electroencephalograph	1929	Berger	German
Electromagnet	1824	Sturgeon	English
Electron spectrometer	1944	Deutsch, Elliott, Evans	U.S.
Electron tube multigrid	1913	Langmuir	U.S.
Electroplating	1805	Brugnatelli	Italian
Electrostatic generator	1929	Van de Graaff	U.S.
Engine, automatic transmission	1910	Fottinger	German
Engine, coal-gas 4-cycle	1876	Otto	German
Engine, compression ignition	1883	Daimler	German
Engine, electric ignition	1883	Benz	German
Engine, gas, compound	1926	Eickemeyer	U.S.
Engine, jet	1930	Whittle	English
Engine, petrol	1872	Brayton, Geo.	U.S.
Engine, petrol	1889	Daimler	German
Engine, steam, piston	1705	Newcomen	English
Engine, steam, piston	1769	Watt	Scottish
Engraving, half-tone	1852	Talbot	U.S.
Fibreglass	1938	Owens-Corning	U.S.
Fibre optics	1955	Kapany	English
Filament, tungsten	1913	Coolidge	U.S.
Flanged rail	1831	Stevens	U.S.
Flatiron, electric	1882	Seely	U.S.
Food, frozen	1924	Birdseye	U.S.
Freon (low-boiling fluorine compounds	1930	Midgley, et al.	U.S.
Furnace (for steel)	1858	Siemens	German
Galvanometer	1820	Sweigger	German
Gas discharge tube	1922	Hull	U.S.
Gas lighting	1792	Murdoch	Scottish
Gas mantle	1885	Welsbach	Austrian
Geiger counter	1913	Geiger	German
Glass, laminated safety	1909	Benedictus	French
Glider	1853	Cayley	English
Gun, breechloader	1811	Thornton	U.S.
Gun, Browning	1897	Browning	U.S.
Gun, magazine	1875	Hotchkiss	U.S.
Gun, silencer	1908	Maxim, H.P.	U.S.
Guncotton	1847	Schoenbein	German
Gyrocompass	1911	Sperry	U.S.
Gyroscope	1852	Foucault	French
Harvester-thresher	1818	Lane	U.S.
Heart, artificial	1982	Jarvik	U.S.
Helicopter	1939	Sikorsky	U.S.
Hydrogen bomb	1952	Government scientists	U.S.
Hydrometer	1768	Baume	French
Ice-making machine	1851	Gorrie	U.S.
Iron lung	1928	Drinker, Slaw	U.S.
Kaleidoscope	1817	Brewster	Scottish
Kinetoscope	1889	Edison	U.S.
Lacquer, nitrocellulose	1921	Flaherty	U.S.
Lamp, arc	1847	Staite	English
Lamp, fluorescent	1938	General Electric, Westinghouse	U.S.
Lamp, incandescent	1879	Edison	U.S.
Lamp, incand., frosted	1924	Pipkin	U.S.
Lamp, incand., gas	1913	Langmuir	U.S.
Lamp, Klieg	1911	Kliegl, A.&J.	U.S.
Lamp, mercury vapour	1912	Hewitt	U.S.
Lamp, miner's safety	1816	Davy	English
Lamp, neon	1909	Claude	French
Lathe, turret	1845	Fitch	U.S.
Launderette	1934	Cantrell	U.S.

(Continued)

Invention	Date	Inventor	Nation.
Lens, achromatic	1758	Dollond	English
Lens, fused bifocal	1908	Borsch	U.S.
Leyden jar (condenser)	1745	von Kleist	German
Lift brake	1852	Otis	U.S.
Lift, push button	1922	Larson	U.S.
Lightning rod	1752	Franklin	U.S.
Linoleum	1860	Walton	English
Linotype	1884	Mergenthaler	U.S.
Lock, cylinder	1851	Yale	U.S.
Locomotive, electric	1851	Vail	U.S.
Locomotive, exp'mtl	1802	Trevithick	English
Locomotive, exp'mtl	1812	Fenton, et al	English
Locomotive, exp'mtl	1813	Hedley	English
Locomotive, exp'mtl	1814	Stephenson	English
Locomotive practical	1829	Stephenson	English
Locomotive, 1st U.S.	1830	Cooper, P.	U.S.
Loom, power	1785	Cartwright	English
Loudspeaker, dynamic	1924	Rice, Kellogg	U.S.
Machine gun	1861	Gatling	U.S.
Machine gun, improved	1872	Hotchkiss	U.S.
Machine gun (Maxim)	1883	Maxim, H.S.	U.S., Eng.
Magnet, electro	1828	Henry	U.S.
Mantle, gas	1885	Welsbach	Austrian
Mason jar	1858	Mason, J.	U.S.
Match, friction	1827	John Walker	English
Mercerized textiles	1843	Mercer, J.	English
Meter, induction	1888	Shallenberg	U.S.
Metronome	1816	Maelzel	German
Microcomputer	1973	Truong, et al	French
Micrometer	1636	Gascoigne	English
Microphone	1877	Berliner	U.S.
Microprocessor	1971	Intel Corp.	U.S.
Microscope, compound	1590	Janssen	Dutch
Microscope, electronic	1931	Knoll, Ruska	German
Microscope, field ion	1951	Mueller	German
Monitor, warship	1861	Ericsson	U.S.
Monotype	1887	Lanston	U.S.
Motor, AC	1892	Tesla	U.S.
Motor, DC	1837	Davenport	U.S.
Motor, induction	1887	Tesla	U.S.
Motorcycle	1885	Daimler	German
Movie machine	1894	Jenkins	U.S.
Movie, panoramic	1952	Waller	U.S.
Movie, talking	1927	Warner Bros.	U.S.
Mower, lawn	1831	Budding, Ferrabee	English
Mowing machine	1822	Bailey	U.S.
Neoprene	1930	Carothers	U.S.
Nylon	1937	Du Pont lab	U.S.
Nylon, synthetic	1930	Carothers	U.S.
Oil cracking furnace	1891	Gavrilov	Russian
Oil-filled power cable	1921	Emanueli	Italian
Oleomargarine	1869	Mege-Mouries	French
Ophthalmoscope	1851	Helmholtz	German
Paper	105	Lun	Chinese
Paper machine	1809	Dickinson	U.S.
Parachute	1785	Blanchard	French
Pen, ballpoint	1938	Biro	Hungarian
Pen, fountain	1884	Waterman	U.S.
Pen, steel	1780	Harrison	English
Pendulum	1583	Galileo	Italian
Percussion cap	1807	Forsythe	Scottish
Petrol, cracked	1913	Burton	U.S.
Petrol, high octane	1930	Ipatieff	Russian
Petrol, lead ethyl	1922	Midgley	U.S.
Phonograph	1877	Edison	U.S.
Photo, colour	1892	Ives	U.S.
Photo film, celluloid	1893	Reichenbach	U.S.
Photo film, transparent	1884	Eastman, Goodwin	U.S.
Photoelectric cell	1895	Elster	German
Photographic paper	1835	Talbot	U.S.
Photography	1835	Talbot	English
Photography	1835	Daguerre	French
Photography	1816	Niepce	French
Photophone	1880	Bell	U.S.-Scot.
Phototelegraphy	1925	Bell Labs	U.S.
Piano	1709	Cristofori	Italian
Piano, player	1863	Fourneaux	French
Pin, safety	1849	Hunt	U.S.
Pistol (revolver)	1836	Colt	U.S.
Plough, cast iron	1785	Ransome	English
Plough, disc	1896	Hardy	U.S.
Pneumatic hammer	1890	King	U.S.

Invention	Date	Inventor	Nation.
Powder, smokeless	1884	Vieille	French
Printing press, rotary	1845	Hoe	U.S.
Printing press, web	1865	Bullock	U.S.
Propeller, screw	1804	Stevens	U.S.
Propeller, screw	1837	Ericsson	Swedish
Pulsars	1967	Bell	English
Punch card accounting	1889	Hollerith	U.S.
Quasars	1963	Schmidt	U.S.
Radar	1940	Watson-Watt	Scottish
Radio amplifier	1906	De Forest	U.S.
Radio beacon	1928	Donovan	U.S.
Radio crystal oscillator	1918	Nicolson	U.S.
Radio receiver, cascade tuning	1913	Alexanderson	U.S.
Radio receiver, heterodyne	1913	Fessenden	U.S.
Radio transmitter triode modulation	1914	Alexanderson	U.S.
Radio tube diode	1905	Fleming	English
Radio tube oscillator	1915	De Forest	U.S.
Radio tube triode	1906	De Forest	U.S.
Radio, signals	1895	Marconi	Italian
Radio, magnetic detector	1902	Marconi	Italian
Radio FM 2-path	1933	Armstrong	U.S.
Rayon (acetate)	1895	Cross	English
Rayon (cuprammonium)	1890	Despeissis	French
Rayon (nitrocellulose)	1884	Chardonnet	French
Razor, electric	1917	Schick	U.S.
Razor, safety	1895	Gillette	U.S.
Reaper	1834	McCormick	U.S.
Record, cylinder	1887	Bell, Tainter	U.S.
Record, disc	1887	Berliner	U.S.
Record, long-playing	1947	Goldmark	U.S.
Record, wax cylinder	1888	Edison	U.S.
Refrigerator car	1868	David	U.S.
Resin, synthetic	1931	Hill	English
Richter scale	1935	Richter, Gutenberg	U.S.
Rifle, repeating	1860	Spencer	U.S.
Rocket engine	1926	Goddard	U.S.
Rubber, vulcanized	1839	Goodyear	U.S.
Saccharin	1879	Remsen, Fahlberg	U.S.
Saw, band	1808	Newberry	English
Saw, circular	1777	Miller	English
Sewing machine	1846	Howe	U.S.
Shoe-sewing machine	1860	McKay	U.S.
Shrapnel shell	1784	Shrapnel	English
Shuttle, flying	1733	Kay	English
Sleeping-car	1865	Pullman	U.S.
Slide rule	1620	Oughtred	English
Soap, hardwater	1928	Bertsch	German
Spectroscope	1859	Kirchoff, Bunsen	German
Spectroscope (mass)	1918	Dempster	U.S.
Spinning jenny	1767	Hargreaves	English
Spinning mule	1779	Crompton	English
Steamboat, exp'mtl	1778	Jouffroy	French
Steamboat, exp'mtl	1785	Fitch	U.S.
Steamboat, exp'mtl	1787	Rumsey	U.S.
Steamboat, exp'mtl	1788	Miller	Scottish
Steamboat, exp'mtl	1803	Fulton	U.S.
Steamboat, exp'mtl	1804	Stevens	U.S.
Steamboat, practical	1802	Symington	Scottish
Steamboat, practical	1807	Fulton	U.S.
Steam car	1770	Cugnot	French
Steam turbine	1884	Parsons	English
Steel (converter)	1856	Bessemer	English
Steel alloy	1891	Harvey	U.S.
Steel alloy, high-speed	1901	Taylor, White	U.S.
Steel, electric	1900	Heroult	French
Steel, manganese	1884	Hadfield	English
Steel, stainless	1916	Brearley	English
Stereoscope	1838	Wheatstone	English
Stethoscope	1819	Laennec	French
Stethoscope, binaural	1840	Cammann	U.S.
Stock ticker	1870	Edison	U.S.
Storage battery, rechargeable	1859	Plante	French
Stove, electric	1896	Hadaway	U.S.
Submarine	1891	Holland	U.S.
Submarine, even keel	1894	Lake	U.S.
Submarine, torpedo	1776	Bushnell	U.S.
Superconductivity (BCS theory)	1957	Bardeen, Cooper, Schreiffer	U.S.

(Continued)

Invention	Date	Inventor	Nation.
Tank, military	1914	Swinton	English
Tape recorder, magnetic	1899	Poulsen	Danish
Teflon	1938	Du Pont	U.S.
Telegraph, magnetic	1837	Morse	U.S.
Telegraph, quadruplex	1864	Edison	U.S.
Telegraph, railroad	1887	Woods	U.S.
Telegraph, wireless high frequency	1895	Marconi	Italian
Telephone	1876	Bell	U.S.-Scot.
Telephone amplifier	1912	De Forest	U.S.
Telephone, automatic	1891	Stowger	U.S.
Telephone, radio	1900	Poulsen, Fessenden	Danish
Telephone, radio	1906	De Forest	U.S.
Telephone, radio, l. d.	1915	AT&T	U.S.
Telephone, recording	1898	Poulsen	Danish
Telephone, wireless	1899	Collins	U.S.
Telescope	1608	Lippershey	Neth.
Telescope	1609	Galileo	Italian
Telescope, astronomical	1611	Kepler	German
Teletype	1928	Morkrum, Kleinschmidt	U.S.
Television, electronic	1927	Farnsworth	U.S.
Television, iconoscope	1923	Zworykin	U.S.
Television (mech. scanner)	1923	Baird	Scottish
Thermometer	1593	Galileo	Italian
Thermometer	1730	Reaumur	French
Thermometer, mercury	1714	Fahrenheit	German
Time recorder	1890	Bundy	U.S.
Time, self-regulator	1918	Bryce	U.S.
Toaster, automatic	1918	Strite	U.S.
Tool, pneumatic	1865	Law	English
Torpedo, marine	1804	Fulton	U.S.
Tractor, crawler	1904	Holt	U.S.
Transformer AC	1885	Stanley	U.S.
Transistor	1947	Shockley, Brattain, Bardeen	U.S.
Trolley car, electric	1884-87	Van DePoele, Sprague	U.S.
Tungsten, ductile	1912	Coolidge	U.S.
Tupperware	1945	Tupper	U.S.
Turbine, gas	1849	Bourdin	French
Turbine, hydraulic	1849	Francis	U.S.
Turbine, steam	1884	Parsons	English
Type, movable	1447	Gutenberg	German
Typewriter	1867	Sholes, Soule, Glidden	U.S.
Tyre, double-tube	1845	Thomson	Scottish
Tyre, pneumatic	1888	Dunlop	Scottish
Vacuum cleaner, electric	1907	Spangler	U.S.
Velcro	1948	de Mestral	Swiss
Video game ("Pong")	1972	Buschnel	U.S.
Video home system (VHS)	1975	Matsushita, JVC	Japanese
Washer, electric	1901	Fisher	U.S.
Welding, atomic hydrogen	1924	Langmuir, Palmer	U.S.
Welding, electric	1877	Thomson	U.S.
Wind tunnel	1912	Eiffel	French
Wire, barbed	1874	Glidden	U.S.
Wire, barbed	1875	Haisn	U.S.
Wrench, double-acting	1913	Owen	U.S.
X-ray tube	1913	Coolidge	U.S.
Zip fastener	1891	Judson	U.S.

Discoveries and Innovations: Chemistry, Physics, Biology, Medicine

	Date	Discoverer	Nation
Acetylene gas	1862	Berthelot	French
ACTH	1927	Evans, Long	U.S.
Adrenalin	1901	Takamine	Japanese
Aluminium, electrolytic process	1886	Hall	U.S.
Aluminium, isolated	1825	Oersted	Danish
Anaesthesia, ether	1842	Long	U.S.
Anaesthesia, local	1885	Koller	Austrian
Anaesthesia, spinal	1898	Bier	German
Aniline dye	1856	Perkin	English
Anti-rabies	1885	Pasteur	French
Antiseptic surgery	1867	Lister	English
Antitoxin, diphtheria	1891	Von Behring	German
Argyrol	1897	Bayer	German
Arsphenamine	1910	Ehrlich	German
Aspirin	1889	Dresser	German
Atabrine	...	Mietzsch, et al.	German
Atomic numbers	1913	Moseley	English
Atomic theory	1803	Dalton	English
Atomic time clock	1947	Libby	U.S.
Atom-smashing theory	1919	Rutherford	English
Bacitracin	1945	Johnson, et al.	U.S.
Bacteria (described)	1676	Leeuwenhoek	Dutch
Barbital	1903	Fischer	German
Bleaching powder	1798	Tennant	English
Blood, circulation	1628	Harvey	English
Bordeaux mixture	1885	Millardet	French
Bromine from sea	1924	Edgar Kramer	U.S.
Calcium carbide	1888	Wilson	U.S.
Calculus	1670	Newton	English
Camphor synthetic	1896	Haller	French
Canning (food)	1804	Appert	French
Carbomycin	1952	Tanner	U.S.
Carbon oxides	1925	Fisher	German
Chloamphenicol	1947	Burkholder	U.S.
Chlorine	1774	Scheele	Swedish
Chloroform	1831	Guthrie, S.	U.S.
Chlortetracycline	1948	Duggen	U.S.
Classification of plants and animals	1735	Linnaeus	Swedish
Cocaine	1860	Niermann	German
Combustion explained	1777	Lavoisier	French
Conditioned reflex	1914	Pavlov	Russian
Cortisone	1936	Kendall	U.S.
Cortisone, synthesis	1946	Sarett	U.S.
Cosmic rays	1910	Gockel	Swiss
Cyanamide	1905	Frank, Caro	German
Cyclotron	1930	Lawrence	U.S.
DDT (not applied as insecticide until 1939)	1874	Zeidler	German
Deuterium	1932	Urey, Brickwedde, Murphy	U.S.
DNA (structure)	1951	Crick Watson Wilkins	English U.S. English
Electric resistance (law)	1827	Ohm	German
Electric waves	1888	Hertz	German
Electrolysis	1852	Faraday	English
Electromagnetism	1819	Oersted	Danish
Electron	1897	Thomson, J.	English
Electron diffraction	1936	Thomson, G. Davisson	English U.S.
Electroshock treatment	1938	Cerletti, Bini	Italian
Erythromycin	1952	McGuire	U.S.
Evolution, natural selection	1858	Darwin	English
Falling bodies, law	1590	Galileo	Italian
Gases, law of combining volumes	1808	Gay-Lussac	French
Geometry, analytic	1619	Descartes	French
Gold (cyanide process for extraction)	1887	MacArthur, Forest	British
Gravitation, law	1687	Newton	English
Holograph	1948	Gabor	British
Human heart transplant	1967	Barnard	S. African
Human immunodeficiency virus identified	1984	Montagnier, Gallo	French, U.S.
Indigo, synthesis of	1880	Baeyer	German
Induction, electric	1830	Henry	U.S.
Insulin	1922	Banting, Best, Macleod	Canadian, Scottish
Intelligence testing	1905	Binet, Simon	French
In vitro fertilization	1978	Steptoe, Edwards	English
Isoniazid	1952	Hoffman-La-Roche Domagk	U.S. German
Isotopes, theory	1912	Soddy	English
Laser (light amplification by stimulated emission of radiation)	1958	Townes,	

(Continued)

	Date	Discoverer	Nation
		Schawlow	U.S.
Light, velocity	1675	Roemer	Danish
Light, wave theory	1690	Huygens	Dutch
Lithography	1796	Senefelder	Bohemian
Lobotomy	1935	Egas Moniz	Portuguese
LSD-25	1943	Hoffman	Swiss
Mendelian laws	1866	Mendel	Austrian
Mercator projection (map)	1568	Mercator (Kremer)	Flemish
Methanol	1661	Boyle	Irish
Milk condensation	1853	Borden	U.S.
Molecular hypothesis	1811	Avogadro	Italian
Motion, laws of	1687	Newton	English
Neomycin	1949	Waksman, Lechevalier	U.S.
Neutron	1932	Chadwick	English
Nitric acid	1648	Glauber	German
Nitric oxide	1772	Priestley	English
Nitroglycerin	1846	Sobrero	Italian
Oil cracking process	1891	Dewar	U.S.
Oxygen	1774	Priestley	English
Oxytetracycline	1950	Finlay, et al.	U.S.
Ozone	1840	Schonbein	German
Paper, sulphite process	1867	Tilghman	U.S.
Paper, wood pulp, sulphate process	1884	Dahl	German
Penicillin	1929	Fleming	Scottish
practical use	1941	Florey, Chain	English
Periodic law and table of elements	1869	Mendeleyev	Russian
Planetary motion, laws	1609	Kepler	German
Plutonium fission	1940	Kennedy, Wahl, Seaborg, Segre	U.S.
Polymyxin	1947	Ainsworth	English
Positron	1932	Anderson	U.S.
Proton	1919	Rutherford	N. Zealand
Psychoanalysis	1900	Freud	Austrian
Quantum theory	1900	Planck	German
Quasars	1963	Matthews, Sandage	U.S.
Quinine synthetic	1946	Woodward, Doering	U.S.
Radioactivity	1896	Becquerel	French
Radium	1898	Curie, Pierre Curie, Marie	French Pol.-Fr.
Relativity theory	1905	Einstein	German
Reserpine	1949	Jal Vaikl	Indian
Schick test	1913	Schick	U.S.
Silicon	1823	Berzelius	Swedish
Smallpox eradication	1979	World Health Organization	United Nations
Streptomycin	1945	Waksman	U.S.
Sulphadiazine	1940	Roblin	U.S.
Sulphanilamide	1935	Bovet, Trefouel	French
Sulphanilamide theory	1908	Gelmo	German
Sulphapyridine	1938	Ewins, Phelps	English
Sulphathiazole	...	Fosbinder, Walter	U.S.
Sulphuric acid	1831	Phillips	English
Sulphuric acid, lead	1746	Roebuck	English
Thiacetazone	1950	Belmisch, Mietzsch, Domagk	German
Tuberculin	1890	Koch	German
Uranium fission (theory)	1939	Hahn, Meitner, Strassmann Bohr Fermi Einstein, Pegram, Wheeler	German Danish Italian U.S.
Uranium fission, atomic reactor	1942	Fermi, Szilard	U.S.
Vaccine, measles	1954	Enders, Peebles	U.S.
Vaccine, meningococcus A.	1971	Gotschlich	U.S.
Vaccine, meningococcus C.	1968	Gotschlich	U.S.
Vaccine, polio	1953	Salk	U.S.
Vaccine, polio, oral	1955	Sabin	U.S.
Vaccine, rabies	1885	Pasteur	French
Vaccine, smallpox	1796	Jenner	English
Vaccine, typhus	1909	Nicolle	French
Van Allen belts, radiation	1958	Van Allen	U.S.
Vitamin A	1913	McCollum, Davis	U.S.
Vitamin B	1916	McCollum	U.S.
Vitamin C	1928	Szent-Gyorgyi, King	U.S.
Vitamin D	1922	McCollum	U.S.
Wassermann test	1906	Wassermann	German
Xerography	1938	Carlson	U.S.
X-ray	1895	Roentgen	German

Chemical Elements, Atomic Weights, Discoverers

Atomic weights, based on the exact number 12 as the assigned atomic mass of the principal isotope of carbon, carbon 12, are provided through the courtesy of the International Union of Pure and Applied Chemistry and Butterworth Scientific Publications.

For the radioactive elements, with the exception of uranium and thorium, the mass number of either the isotope of longest half-life (*) or the better known isotope (**) is given.

Chemical element	Symbol	Atomic number	Atomic weight	Year discov.	Discoverer
Actinium	Ac	89	227*	1899	Debierne
Aluminium	Al	13	26.9815	1825	Oersted
Americium	Am	95	243*	1944	Seaborg, et al.
Antimony	Sb	51	121.75	1450	Valentine
Argon	Ar	18	39.948	1894	Rayleigh, Ramsay
Arsenic	As	33	74.9216	13th c.	Albertus Magnus
Astatine	At	85	210*	1940	Corson, et al.
Barium	Ba	56	137.34	1808	Davy
Berkelium	Bk	97	249**	1949	Thompson, Ghiorso, Seaborg
Beryllium	Be	4	9.0122	1798	Vauquelin
Bismuth	Bi	83	208.980	15th c.	Valentine
Boron	B	5	10.811a	1808	Gay-Lussac, Thenard
Bromine	Br	35	79.904b	1826	Balard
Cadmium	Cd	48	112.40	1817	Stromeyer
Caesium	Cs	55	132.905	1860	Bunsen, Kirchhoff
Calcium	Ca	20	40.08	1808	Davy
Californium	Cf	98	251*	1950	Thompson, et al.
Carbon	C	6	12.01115a	B.C.	unknown
Cerium	Ce	58	140.12	1803	Klaproth
Chlorine	Cl	17	35.453b	1774	Scheele
Chromium	Cr	24	51.996b	1797	Vauquelin

(Continued)

Chemical element	Symbol	Atomic number	Atomic weight	Year discov.	Discoverer
Cobalt	Co	27	58.9332	1735	Brandt
Copper	Cu	29	63.546b	B.C.	unknown
Curium	Cm	96	247*	1944	Seaborg, James, Ghiorso
Dysprosium	Dy	66	162.50	1886	Boisbaudran
Einsteinium	Es	99	254*	1952	Ghiorso, et al.
Erbium	Er	68	167.26	1843	Mosander
Europium	Eu	63	151.96	1901	Demarcay
Fermium	Fm	100	257*	1953	Ghiorso, et al.
Fluorine	F	9	18.9984	1771	Scheele
Francium	Fr	87	223*	1939	Perey
Gadolinium	Gd	64	157.25	1886	Marignac
Gallium	Ga	31	69.72	1875	Boisbaudran
Germanium	Ge	32	72.59	1886	Winkler
Gold	Au	79	196.967	B.C.	unknown
Hafnium	Hf	72	178.49	1923	Coster, Hevesy
Hahnium	Ha	105	262*	1970	Ghiorso, et al.
Hassium	Hs	108	265*	1984	Münzenberg, et al.
Helium	He	2	4.0026	1868	Janssen, Lockyer
Holmium	Ho	67	164.930	1878	Soret, Delafontaine
Hydrogen	H	1	1.00797a	1766	Cavendish
Indium	In	49	114.82	1863	Reich, Richter
Iodine	I	53	126.9044	1811	Courtois
Iridium	Ir	77	192.2	1804	Tennant
Iron	Fe	26	55.847b	B.C.	unknown
Krypton	Kr	36	83.80	1898	Ramsay, Travers
Lanthanum	La	57	138.91	1839	Mosander
Lawrencium	Lr	103	262*	1961	Ghiorso, T. Sikkeland, A.E. Larsh, and R.M. Latimer
Lead	Pb	82	207.19	B.C.	unknown
Lithium	Li	3	6.939	1817	Arfvedson
Lutetium	Lu	71	174.97	1907	Welsbach, Urbain
Magnesium	Mg	12	24.312	1829	Bussy
Manganese	Mn	25	54.9380	1774	Gahn
Meitnerium	Mt	109	266*	1982	Münzenberg, at el.
Mendelevium	Md	101	258*	1955	Ghiorso, et al.
Mercury	Hg	80	200.59	B.C.	unknown
Molybdenum	Mo	42	95.94	1782	Hjelm
Neodymium	Nd	60	144.24	1885	Welsbach
Neon	Ne	10	20.183	1898	Ramsay, Travers
Neptunium	Np	93	237*	1940	McMillan, Abelson
Nickel	Ni	28	58.71	1751	Cronstedt
Nielsbohrium	Ns	107	262*	1981	Münzenberg, et al.
Niobium[1]	Nb	41	92.906	1801	Hatchett
Nitrogen	N	7	14.0067	1772	Rutherford
Nobelium	No	102	259*	1958	Ghiorso, et al.
Osmium	Os	76	190.2	1804	Tennant
Oxygen	O	8	15.9994a	1774	Priestley, Scheele
Palladium	Pd	46	106.4	1803	Wollaston
Phosphorus	P	15	30.9738	1669	Brand
Platinum	Pt	78	195.09	1735	Ulloa
Plutonium	Pu	94	242**	1940	Seaborg, et al.
Polonium	Po	84	210**	1898	P. and M. Curie
Potassium	K	19	39.102	1807	Davy
Praseodymium	Pr	59	140.907	1885	Welsbach
Promethium	Pm	61	147**	1945	Glendenin, Marinsky, Coryell
Protactinium	Pa	91	231*	1917	Hahn, Meitner
Radium	Ra	88	226*	1898	P. & M. Curie, Bemont
Radon	Rn	86	222*	1900	Dorn
Rhenium	Re	75	186.2	1925	Noddack, Tacke, Berg
Rhodium	Rh	45	102.905	1803	Wollaston
Rubidium	Rb	37	85.47	1861	Bunsen, Kirchhoff
Ruthenium	Ru	44	101.07	1845	Klaus
Rutherfordium	Rf	104	261*	1969	Ghiorso, et al.
Samarium	Sm	62	150.35	1879	Boisbaudran
Scandium	Sc	21	44.956	1879	Nilson
Selenium	Se	34	78.96	1817	Berzelius
Silicon	Si	14	28.086a	1823	Berzelius
Silver	Ag	47	107.868b	B.C.	unknown
Sodium	Na	11	22.9898	1807	Davy
Strontium	Sr	38	87.62	1790	Crawford
Sulphur	S	16	32.064a	B.C.	unknown
Tantalum	Ta	73	180.948	1802	Ekeberg
Technetium	Tc	43	99**	1937	Perrier and Segre
Tellurium	Te	52	127.60	1782	Von Reichenstein
Terbium	Tb	65	158.924	1843	Mosander
Thallium	Tl	81	204.37	1861	Crookes
Thorium	Th	90	232.038	1828	Berzelius
Thulium	Tm	69	168.934	1879	Cleve
Tin	Sn	50	118.69	B.C.	unknown
Titanium	Ti	22	47.90	1791	Gregor
Tungsten (Wolfram)	W	74	183.85	1783	d'Elhujar
Uranium	U	92	238.03	1789	Klaproth
Vanadium	V	23	50.942	1830	Sefstrom
Xenon	Xe	54	131.30	1898	Ramsay, Travers
Ytterbium	Yb	70	173.04	1878	Marignac
Yttrium	Y	39	88.905	1794	Gadolin
Zinc	Zn	30	65.37	B.C.	unknown

(Continued)

Chemical element	Symbol	Atomic number	Atomic weight	Year discov.	Discoverer
Zirconium	Zr	40	91.22	1789	Klaproth

(1) Formerly Columbium. (a) Atomic weights so designated are known to be variable because of natural variations in isotopic composition. The observed ranges are: hydrogen±0.0001; boron±0.003; carbon±0.005; oxygen±0.0001; silicon±0.001; sulphur±0.003. (b) Atomic weights so designated are believed to have the following experimental uncertainties: chlorine±0.001; chromium±0.001; iron±0.003; bromine±0.001; silver±0.001; copper±0.001.

Computer Glossary

Source: *Electronic Computer Glossary* by Alan Freedman, The Computer Language Co. Inc., 1992

acoustic coupler: a device that connects a terminal or computer to the handset of a telephone. It may also include the *modem.*

address: a number of a particular memory or disk location.

analog: of or relating to the representation of an object that resembles the original. For example, the telephone system converts sound waves into electrical impulses.

arithmetic logic unit (ALU): a part of the *central processing unit (CPU)* that performs arithmetic operations and logical comparisons.

artificial intelligence (AI): a broad range of computer applications that resemble human intelligence and behaviour, such as understanding speech, making judgements and learning.

ASCII: an acronym for American Standard Code for Information Interchange; a widely used binary code for storing data, often used to transfer data from one system to an incompatible system.

assembly language: a low-level, machine-orientated language using mnemonics to represent each machine-language instruction. Each CPU has its own assembly language.

authorization code: an identification number or password used to gain access to a computer system.

back up: to make a copy of important data to be used if the current file is destroyed.

BASIC: an acronym for Beginner's All-purpose Symbolic Instruction Code; a computer language used by many small and personal computer systems.

baud rate: the number of changes in an electrical line per second. Often used as the measurement of printer or modem speed. One baud equals one bit per second or more.

binary: composed of 2 components or possible states. Often represented as a 0 or 1; true or false; or on or off.

binary code: a representation of the base-2 number system in which the only allowable digits are 0 and 1.

bit: short for binary digit; a single binary digit (0 or 1) or the smallest unit of information stored in a computer, such as a memory cell.

board: short for printed circuit board; a flat board that holds chips and other electronic components connected by "printed" electronically conductive pathways.

boot: to start the computer.

bubble memory: a memory that circulates tiny bubble-like magnetic bits in a solid-state structure. Not widely used.

buffer: a temporary place to put information for processing when it is being transferred from one device to another.

bug: a mistake that occurs in a program within a computer or in the unit's electrical system.

bus: a common channel, or pathway, between hardware devices, either internally between computer components, or externally between stations in a communications network.

byte: an 8-bit sequence of binary digits. Each byte corresponds to 1 character of data, representing a single letter, number, or symbol.

C: a high-level programming language often used to write commercial products due to its transportability to many different computer systems.

C+30+30: an object-orientated version of the C programming language.

cache: a memory unit between the main memory and the CPU that accelerates retrieval of data and instructions.

CAD/CAM: abbreviation for computer-aided design/computer-aided manufacturing.

cathode ray tube (CRT): a vacuum tube used as a display screen in a terminal or TV. Term usually used to refer to the entire terminal.

CD-ROM: an acronym for Compact Disk – Read Only Memory; general term applied to a variety of storage formats by which audio, text and graphics are retrieved by a laser beam that scans tracks of microscopic holes in a rotating compact disk. The disk can store over 600 million characters, but the user cannot store new information or alter the existing information.

central processing unit (CPU): the part within the computer that interprets and executes the instructions the user gives the system. It is composed of an arithmetic logic unit, a control unit and a small amount of memory.

channel: a high-speed metal or optical fibre pathway between a computer and its peripheral devices, or in telecommunications, any pathway between systems.

chip: a common term for an integrated circuit, a collection of interconnected micro-miniature electronic components.

client/server: *local area network (LAN)* architecture in which the user's PC is the client and the network *file server* contains the database.

COBOL: an acronym for Common Business Orientated Language; one of the most widely used business programming languages.

code: a set of machine symbols that represents data or instructions; also to write a program.

command: an action statement or order to the computer.

compiler: a program that translates a high-level language, such as COBOL or C, into machine code or assembly language.

computer: a programmable machine that accepts, processes and displays data.

connect time: the time a user at a terminal (a workstation away from the main computer) is logged on to a computer system.

cursor: the movable symbol on the computer monitor that marks the place where the operator is working.

cybernetics: the comparative study of human and machine processes in order to understand the similarities and differences. Often used in the development of *artificial intelligence.*

database: a large amount of data stored in a well-

organized format and managed by a database management system, a program that allows access to the information.
Data Encryption Standard (DES): the U.S. National Institute of Standards and Technology system for encryption of commercial data. DES uses a binary number as a key for encryption and offers more than 72 quadrillion combinations.
data glove: a glove used to report the position of a user's hand in *virtual reality* systems.
debug: to eliminate a mistake within a computer program or in the unit's electrical system.
dedicated: designed for single use.
density: the number of bits that can be stored in a linear inch.
desktop publishing: the use of a personal computer to produce high-quality output (camera-ready hard copy or digital files) ready for commercial printing.
diagnostics: software programs that test the operational capability of hardware components.
digital: of or relating to the representation, manipulation, or transmission of data by discrete signals, or on-off signals.
digitize: to convert an analog, or continuous, signal into a digital form.
DIP switch: an abbreviation for dual in-line package switch; a set of toggle switches built into the housing commonly used to mount a chip and used to encode various kinds of information, such as the amount of memory or the type of monitor in a computer system.
directory: an index of files on a disk.
disk: a revolving magnetized plate on which information and programs are stored. See also *floppy disk.*
disk drive: a peripheral machine that rotates a storage disk in order to read or record information.
documentation: user or operator instructions that come with some hardware and software that tell how to use the material.
DOS: stands for disk operating system, a generic term for the operating system; also a single-user operating system commonly used on IBM-compatible PCs.
download: to transmit data from a central to a remote computer; from a file server to a workstation; or from a computer to a floppy disk.
dumb terminal: a terminal without processing capability and dependent upon a main computer.
dump: a printout of the contents of memory or a file.
electronic mail: transmission of memos and messages over a *network.* Also called e-mail.
encryption: the encoding of data for security purposes by converting the standard data code into proprietary code that must be decoded to be used.
fax: facsimile, the communication of a printed page between remote locations using a scanner, printer and fax modem.
field: the physical unit of data in a record.
file: any collection data treated as a single unit.
file server: a computer that stores data and programs that are shared by many users in a network.
floppy disk: a small, inexpensive removable disk used to record and store information. It must be used in conjunction with a disk drive.
flops: an acronym for floating-point operations per second; used as a measurement of processing speed in supercomputers.
font: a set of type characters of a particular design and size.
foreground/background: an operating system prioritizing method in multi-tasking computer systems. Programs running in the foreground have highest priority.
format: arrangement by which data are stored or displayed.
FORTRAN: an acronym for Formula Translator; a high-level computer language and compiler widely used for scientific, engineering, or mathematical purposes.
function: in programming, a routine, or set of instructions, that performs a particular task.
gigabyte: one billion bytes.
global memory: the shared central memory of a multiple-processor system, as opposed to the local memory of individual processors.
groupware: interactive software designed for several users working together on one project.
hacker: a person with great technical skills in the computer field; the term is sometimes used in a derogatory sense to refer to people who gain unauthorized access to computer systems and data banks.
hard copy: printed computer output.
hard disk: a magnetic disk made of metal and covered with a magnetic recording surface. In PCs, hard disks are often installed inside the computer for increased storage capacity.
hardware: the physical apparatus that makes up a computer – chips, transformers, boards and wires. Also used to describe various pieces of equipment, including the CPU, printer, modem and CRT.
hexadecimal: refers to the base-16 number system, which is used to condense binary-based codes, such as bytes, for more efficient computer processing.
integrated circuit (IC): the formal name for a *chip.*
intelligent terminal: a terminal with built-in processing capability. It has memory, but no disk or tape storage.
interface: a connection and interaction between hardware, software and the user.
Internet: a network of computer networks, both domestic and foreign, involving millions of scientists and other users.
joystick: a hand-held lever than can be tilted in different directions to control the movement of the cursor on the terminal screen.
K: abbreviation for kilobyte, used to denote 1,024 units of stored matter.
key: a sequence of symbols used to encrypt and decrypt data.
keyboard: a set of input keys; also used as a verb meaning to type data into a computer for processing.
language: any set of compiled, unified, or related commands or instructions that are understandable to a computer.
laptop computer: a portable computer that usually weighs less than 12 pounds (5.4 kg) and has a self-contained power supply.
light-emitting diode (LED): a display technology that utilizes a semiconductor device that emits light when a current passes through it.
light pen: an input device in which directions are given to the computer by touching the terminal screen with a light-sensitive stylus.
liquid crystal display (LCD): a digital display mechanism made up of character-forming segments of a liquid crystal material sandwiched between polarizing and reflecting pieces of glass; commonly used in watches and laptop computers.
load: the actual operation of putting information and data into the computer or memory.
local area network (LAN): a computer system that links computers, computer workstations, printers and other peripheral devices in a network for transmitting data between users situated near one another. Local

area networks can be connected to a supercomputer centre to provide ready access to powerful machines.
loop: in programming, the repetition of some function within the program.
machine language: a set of binary-code instructions capable of being understood by a computer without translation.
machine readable: any paper form or storage medium that can be automatically read by the computer.
mainframe computer: the largest type of computer, usually capable of processing data quickly and able to serve many users simultaneously.
master file: a collection of records pertaining to one of the main subjects of an information system.
megabyte: one million bytes.
memory: the computer's internal storage capacity.
menu: programs, functions, or other choices displayed on the monitor for user selection.
microcomputer: a computer that uses a microprocessor for its CPU. All personal computers are microcomputers.
microprocessor: a complete CPU on a single chip.
minicomputer: an intermediate computer system sized between the very small microcomputer and the large mainframe computer.
modem: an acronym for modulator-demodulator. A device that enables data to be transmitted between computers, generally over telephone lines, but sometimes via fibre-optic cable or radio frequency.
monitor: a high-resolution screen used to display the output of a computer.
mouse: a rectangular, hand-held object that when slid across a flat surface may be used as a pointing and drawing device.
multi-tasking: the ability to run more than one program on one computer at the same time.
nanosecond: one-billionth of a second.
network: in communications, terminals and computers linked together with the ability to interact with each other. In database management, a database design.
nibble: half a byte, or four bits.
noise: extraneous, random disturbances that degrade or disrupt data communications.
notebook computer: a portable computer that weighs less than 5 pounds (2.25 kg).
object-oriented programming: a programming method with formalized rules for developing self-contained software routines that can be re-used in other program applications, allowing greater programming flexibility.
on-line: immediately accessible by a computer's CPU.
operating system: a master control program that runs the computer and acts as a scheduler and traffic cop. Also known as DOS to most microcomputer users.
optical character reader (OCR): a device capable of recognizing characters in a special typeface.
optical fibre: an ultra-thin strand of glass with the ability to carry billions of bits of encoded data per second when pulses of laser light are beamed through it.
opto-electronics: a technology that joins light and electricity. OCRs, laser printers and CD-ROMs are examples of opto-electronic devices.
Pascal: a high-level programming language originally designed as a teaching tool, but now very common among microcomputer users.
password: a word or code used to identify an authorized user.
PC: an abbreviation for personal computer; a microcomputer that serves one user.
peripheral: any hardware device connected to a computer, such as keyboards, printers, or joy sticks.
pixel: an acronym for picture element; the smallest display element on a video display screen.
ports: connectors for attaching peripherals to a computer's main *board*.
printer: a device that converts computer output into printed images.
program: a sequence of detailed, coded instructions telling a computer how to perform a specific function.
RAM: an abbreviation for Random Access Memory; same as *memory*. Contents of RAM may be retrieved and altered by the user.
random access: the ability to retrieve records in a file directly without reading any previous records.
realtime processing: computer processing fast enough to provide an immediate response to problems as they occur.
record: a group of related fields that are used to store data about a subject.
ROM: an abbreviation for Read Only Memory; a permanent memory.
sector: a defined portion of concentric track on a disk.
semiconductor: a solid-state substance that can be electrically altered, such as a transistor.
software: the programs, or sets of instructions, that tell the computer what to do.
solid-state: an electronic component or circuit composed of a solid material operating by electromagnetic action without the need for mechanical action.
spreadsheet: any software program that simulates a paper spreadsheet, or worksheet, in which columns of numbers are totalled.
supercomputers: a term applied to the fastest, most powerful computers at a given time; supercomputers typically are used to solve scientific problems that involve the manipulation of large amounts of data.
superconductor: a material that has almost no resistance to the flow of electricity.
telecommuting: working at home and communicating via computer with the office.
teleconferencing: to communicate with a number of people simultaneously via telephone lines with audio, video, or computer connections.
terminal: a keyboard and display unit (usually a CRT) that allows a person to communicate with a computer. See also *dumb terminal* and *intelligent terminal*.
timesharing: the simultaneous use of a computer by more than one person, as in a *local area network*.
track: a concentric band on a magnetic disk that contains a specified amount of data.
translate: to change programming codes from high-level language, such as BASIC, Pascal, or C+30 +30, into low-level machine language.
user-friendly: hardware or software that is easy to learn and use.
user interface: hardware and software that provide the interface between the user and the computer.
UNIX: a multi-user operating system that runs on a wide variety of computers.
virtual memory: the use of hard disk storage to expand effective memory capability.
virtual reality: interaction with a computer to create an artificial reality that projects the user into a 3-dimensional space.
virus: a destructive program that is secretly attached to an existing program. Once a virus program is run it

begins to alter or delete data, or cause other computer system malfunctions, whenever the pre-existing program is run.
voice recognition: the understanding of spoken words by a machine.
window: a separate viewing area on a display screen.
wireless modem: a radio the user can connect to a computer in order to receive data over a designated frequency operated by a wireless service provider.
word: the basic storage unit of a computer's operation; a sequence of bits (commonly from 8 to 32) occupying a single storage location and processed as a unit by the computer.
word processor: a text creation and editing program or system that allows electronic writing and correcting of documents.
workstation: a high-performance, single-user microcomputer or minicomputer, any terminal or personal computer, or in a *local area network*, a PC that serves a single user.
worm: a destructive program that reproduces itself and deletes data from a computer's memory.
write-access: authorization to record or alter data stored in a computer.

AEROSPACE

Notable Crewed Space Flights

Sources: National Aeronautics and Space Administration and *The World Almanac*

The following table does not include aerospacecraft, such as the U.S. Space Shuttle.

Crew, date	Mission name	Orbits[1]	Duration	Remarks
Yuri A. Gagarin (12/4/61)	Vostok 1	1	1h 48m	1st manned orbital flight
Alan B. Shepard Jr. (5/5/61)	Mercury-Redstone 3	(2)	15m 22s	1st American in space
Virgil I. Grissom (21/7/61)	Mercury-Redstone 4	(2)	15m 37s	Spacecraft sank. Grissom rescued
Gherman S. Titov (6–7/8/61)	Vostok 2	16	25h 18m	1st space flight of more than 24 hrs
John H. Glenn Jr. (20/2/62)	Mercury-Atlas 6	3	4h 55m 23s	1st American in orbit
M. Scott Carpenter (24/5/62)	Mercury-Atlas 7	3	4h 56m 05s	Manual retrofire error caused 250 mile landing overshoot
Andrian G. Nikolayev (11–15/8/62)	Vostok 3	64	94h 22m	Vostok 3 and 4 made 1st group flight
Pavel R. Popovich (12–15/8/62)	Vostok 4	48	70h 57m	On 1st orbit it came within 3 miles of Vostok 3
Walter M. Schirra Jr. (3/10/62)	Mercury-Atlas 8	6	9h 13m 11s	Then-closest splashdown to target (4.5 miles)
L. Gordon Cooper (15–16/5/63)	Mercury-Atlas 9	22	34h 19m 49s	1st U.S. evaluation of effects on man of one day in space
Valery F. Bykovsky (14–19/6/63)	Vostok 5	81	119h 06m	Vostok 5 and 6 made 2d group flight
Valentina V. Tereshkova (16–19/6/63)	Vostok 6	48	70h 50m	1st woman in space
Vladimir M. Komarov, Konstantin P. Feoktistov, Boris B. Yegorov (12/10/64)	Voskhod 1	16	24h 17m	1st 3-man orbital flight: 1st without space suits
Pavel I. Belyayev, Aleksei A. Leonov (18/3/65)	Voskhod 2	17	26h 02m	Leonov made 1st "space walk" (10 min.)
Virgil I. Grissom, John W. Young (23/3/65)	Gemini-Titan III	3	4h 53m 00s	1st manned spacecraft to change its orbital path
James A. McDivitt, Edward H. White 2d, (3–7/6/65)	Gemini-Titan IV	62	97h 56m 11s	White was 1st American to "walk in space" (20 min.)
L. Gordon Cooper Jr., Charles Conrad Jr. (21–29/8/65)	Gemini-Titan V	120	190h 55m 14s	1st use of fuel cells for electric power; evaluated guidance and navigation system
Frank Borman, James A. Lovell Jr. (4–18/12/65)	Gemini-Titan VII	206	330h 35m 31s	Longest duration Gemini flight
Walter M. Schirra Jr., Thomas P. Stafford (15–16/12/65)	Gemini-Titan VI-A	16	25h 51m 24s	Completed world's 1st space rendezvous with Gemini 7
Neil A. Armstrong, David R. Scott (16–17/3/66)	Gemini-Titan VIII	6.5	10h 41m 26s	1st docking of one space vehicle with another; mission aborted, control malfunction
Thomas P. Stafford, Eugene A. Cernan (3–6/6/66)	Gemini-Titan IX-A	45	72h 21m	Closest splashdown to recovery vessel (769.6 yds)
John W. Young, Michael Collins (18–21/7/66)	Gemini-Titan X	43	70h 46m 39s	1st use of Agena target vehicle's propulsion systems
Charles Conrad Jr., Richard F. Gordon Jr. (12–15/9/66)	Gemini-Titan XI	44	71h 17m 08s	Docked, made 2 revolutions of Earth tethered; set Gemini altitude record (739.2 miles)
James A. Lovell Jr., Edwin E. Aldrin Jr. (11–15/11/66)	Gemini-Titan XII	59	94h 34m 31s	Final Gemini mission; record 51/2 hrs of extravehicular activity
Vladimir M. Komarov (23/4/67)	Soyuz 1	17	26h 40m	Crashed after re-entry killing Komarov
Walter M. Schirra Jr., Donn F. Eisele, R. Walter Cunningham (11–22/10/68)	Apollo-Saturn 7	163	260h 09m 03s	1st manned flight of Apollo spacecraft command-service module only
Georgi T. Beregovoi (26–30/10/68)	Soyuz 3	64	94h 51m	Made rendezvous with unmanned Soyuz 2
Frank Borman, James A. Lovell Jr., William A. Anders (21–27/12/68)	Apollo-Saturn 8	10[3]	147h 00m 42s	1st flight to moon (command-service module only); views of lunar surface televised to Earth
Vladimir A. Shatalov (14–17/1/69)	Soyuz 4	45	71h 14m	Docked with Soyuz 5
Boris V. Volyanov, Aleksei S. Yeliseyev,				Docked with Soyuz 4; Yeliseyev

(Continued)

Crew, date	Mission name	Orbits[1]	Duration	Remarks
Yevgeny V. Khrunov (15–18/1/69)	Soyuz 5	46	72h 46m	and Khrunov transferred to Soyuz 4
James A. McDivitt, David R. Scott, Russell L. Schweickart (3–13/3/69)	Apollo-Saturn 9	151	241h 00m 54s	1st manned flight of lunar module
Thomas P. Stafford, Eugene A. Cernan, John W. Young (18–26/5/69)	Apollo-Saturn 10	31[4]	192h 03m 23s	1st lunar module orbit of moon
Neil A. Armstrong, Edwin E. Aldrin Jr., Michael Collins (16–24/7/69)	Apollo-Saturn 11	30[3]	195h 18m 35s	1st lunar landing made by Armstrong and Aldrin; collected 48.5 lb of soil, rock samples; lunar stay time 21h, 36m, 21 s
Georgi S. Shonin, Valery N. Kubasov (11–16/10/69)	Soyuz 6	79	118h 42m	1st welding of metals in space
Anatoly V. Filipchenko, Vladislav N. Volkov, Viktor V. Gorbatko (12–17/10/69)	Soyuz 7	79	118h 41m	Space lab construction tests made; Soyuz 6, 7 and 8 — 1st time 3 spacecraft 7 crew orbited Earth at once
Charles Conrad Jr., Richard F. Gordon, Alan L. Bean (14–24/11/69)	Apollo-Saturn 12	45[3]	244h 36m 25s	Conrad and Bean made 2d moon landing; collected 74.7 lb of samples, lunar stay time 31 h, 31 m
James A. Lovell Jr., Fred W. Haise Jr., John L. Swigart Jr. (11–17/4/70)	Apollo-Saturn 13	...	142h 54m 41s	Aborted after service module oxygen tank ruptured; crew returned safely using lunar module oxygen and power
Alan B. Shepard Jr., Stuart A. Roosa, Edgar D. Mitchell (31/1–9/2/71)	Apollo-Saturn 14	34[3]	216h 01m 57s	Shepard and Mitchell made 3d moon landing, collected 96 lb of lunar samples; lunar stay 33 h, 31 m
Georgi T. Dobrovolsky, Vladislav N. Volkov, Viktor I. Patsayev (6–30/6/71)	Soyuz 11	360	569h 40m	Docked with Salyut space station; and orbited in Salyut for 23 days; crew died during re-entry from loss of pressurization
David R. Scott, Alfred M. Worden, James B. Irwin (26/7–7/8/71)	Apollo-Saturn 15	74[3]	295h 11m 53s	Scott and Irwin made 4th moon landing; 1st lunar rover use; 1st deep space walk; 170 lb of samples; 66 h, 55 m, stay
Charles M. Duke Jr., Thomas K. Mattingly, John W. Young (16–27/4/72)	Apollo-Saturn 16	64[3]	265h 51m 05s	Young and Duke made 5th moon landing; collected 213 lb of lunar samples; lunar stay line 71 h, 2 m
Eugene A. Cernan, Ronald E. Evans, Harrison H. Schmitt (7–19/12/72)	Apollo-Saturn 17	75[3]	301h 51m 59s	Cernan and Schmitt made 6th manned lunar landing; collected 243 lb of samples; record lunar stay of 75 h
Charles Conrad Jr., Joseph P. Kerwin, Paul J. Weitz (25/5–22/6/73)	Skylab 2	...	672h 49m 49s	1st American manned orbiting space station; made long-flights tests, crew repaired damage caused during boost
Alan L. Bean, Jack R. Lousma, Owen K. Garriott (28/7–25/9/73)	Skylab 3	...	1,427h 09m 04s	Crew systems and operational tests, exceeded pre-mission plans for scientific activities; space walk total 13h, 44 m
Gerald P. Carr, Edward G. Gibson, William Pogue (16/11/73–8/2/74)	Skylab 4	...	2,017h 16m 30s	Final Skylab mission; record space walk of 7 h, 1 m, record space walks total for a mission 22 h, 21 m
Alexi Leonov, Valeri Kubasov (15–21/7/75)	Soyuz 19	96	143h 31m	
Vance Brand, Thomas P. Stafford, Donald K. Slayton (15–24/7/75)	Apollo 18	136	217h 30m	U.S.–USSR joint flight. Crews linked up in space, conducted experiments, shared meals and held a joint news conference
Leonid Kizim, Vladmir Solovyov, Oleg Atkov (8/2–2/10/84)	Salyut 7	...	237 days	Set space endurance record (since broken)

(1) The U.S. measures orbital flights in revolutions, while the Soviets use "orbits". (2) Suborbital. (3) Moon orbits in command module. (4) Moon orbits.

Fire aboard spacecraft Apollo I on the ground at Cape Kennedy, Fla., killed Virgil I. Grissom, Edward H. White and Roger B. Chaffee on Jan. 27, 1967. They were the only U.S. astronauts killed in space tests.

U.S. Space Shuttle Missions

Name, date	Crew
Columbia (12-14/4/81)	Robert L. Crippen, John W. Young.
Columbia (12-14/11/81)	Joe Engle, Richard Truly.
Columbia (22-30/3/82)	Jack Lousma, C. Gordon Fullerton.
Columbia (27/6-4/7/82)	Thomas Mattingly 2d, Henry Hartsfield Jr.
Columbia (11-16/11/82)	Vance Brand, Robert Overmyer, William Lenoir, Joseph Allen.
Challenger (4-9/4/83)	Paul Weitz, Karol Bobko, Story Musgrave, Donald Peterson.
Challenger (18-24/6/83)	Robert L. Crippen, Norman Thagard, John Fabian, Frederick Hauck, Sally K. Ride (1st U.S. woman in space).
Challenger (30/8-5/9/83)	Richard Truly, Daniel Brandenstein, William Thornton,Guion Bluford (1st U.S. black in space), Dale Gardner.
Columbia (28/11-8/12/83)	John Young, Brewster Shaw Jr., Robert Parker, Owen Garriott, Byron Lichtenberg, Ulf Merbold.
Challenger (3-11/2/84)	Vance Brand, Robert Gibson, Ronald McNair, Bruce McCandless, Robert Stewart.
Challenger (6-13/4/84)	Robert L. Crippen, Francis R. Scobee, George D. Nelson, Terry J. Hart, James D. Van Hoften.
Discovery (30/8-5/9/84)	Henry W. Hartsfield Jr., Michael L. Coats, Steven A. Hawley, Judith A. Resnik, Richard M. Mullane, Charles D. Walker.
Challenger (5-13/10/84)	Robert L. Crippen, Jon A. McBride, Kathryn D. Sullivan, Sally K. Ride, Marc Garneau (first Canadian), David C. Leestma, Paul D. Scully-Power.
Discovery (8-16/11/84)	Frederick H. Hauck, David M. Walker, Dr. Anna L. Fisher, Joseph P. Allen, Dale A. Gardner.
Discovery (24-27/1/85)	Thomas K. Mattingly, Loren J. Shriver, James F. Buchli, Ellison S. Onizuka, Gary E. Payton.
Discovery (12-19/4/85)	Karol J. Bobko, Donald E. Williams, Sen. Jake Garn, Charles D. Walker, Jeffrey A. Hoffman, S. David Griggs, M. Rhea Seddon.
Challenger (29/4-6/5/85)	Robert F. Overmyer, Frederick D. Gregory, Don L. Lind, Taylor G. Wang, Lodewijk van den Berg, Norman Thagard, William Thornton.
Discovery (17-24/6/85)	John O. Creighton, Shannon W. Lucid, Steven R. Nagel, Daniel C. Brandenstein, John W. Fabian, Prince Sultan Salman al-Saud (first Arab), Patrick Baudry.
Challenger (29/7-6/8/85)	Roy D. Bridges Jr., Anthony W. England, Karl G. Henize, F. Story Musgrave, C. Gordon Fullerton, Loren W. Acton, John-David F. Bartoe.
Discovery (27/8-3/9/85)	John M. Lounge, James D. van Hoften, William F. Fisher, Joe H. Engle, Richard O. Covey.
Atlantis (4-7/10/85)	Karol J. Bobko, Ronald J. Grabe, David C. Hilmers, William A. Pailes, Robert C. Stewart.
Challenger (30/10-6/11/85)	Henry W. Hartsfield Jr., Steven R. Nagel, Bonnie J. Dunbar, James F. Buchli, Guion S. Bluford Jr., Ernst Messerschmid, Reinhard Furrer, Wubbo J. Ockels.
Atlantis (26/11-3/12/85)	Brewster H. Shaw Jr., Bryan D. O'Connor, Charles Walker, Rodolfo Neri (first Mexican), Jerry L. Ross, Sherwood C. Spring, Mary L. Cleave.
Columbia (12-18/1/86)	Robert L. Gibson, Charles F. Bolden Jr., George D. Nelson, Bill Nelson (first congressman), Franklin R. Chang-Diaz, Steven A. Hawley, Robert J. Cenker.
Challenger (28/1/86 – exploded after takeoff)	Francis R. Scobee, Michael J. Smith, Ronald E. McNair, Ellison S. Onizuka, Judith A. Resnik, Gregory B. Jarvis, Sharon Christa McAuliffe.
Discovery (29/9-3/10/88)	Frederick H. Hauck, Richard O. Covey, David C. Hilmers, George D. Nelson, John M. Lounge.
Atlantis (3-6/12/88)	Robert L. Gibson, Guy S. Gardner, Richard M. Mullane, Jerry L. Ross, William M. Shepherd.
Discovery (13-18/3/89)	Michael L. Coats, John E. Blaha, James F. Buchli, Robert C. Springer, James P. Bagian.
Atlantis (4-8/5/89)	David M. Walker, Ronald J. Grabe, Mary L. Cleave, Norman E. Thagard, Mark C. Lee.
Columbia (8-13/8/89)	Brewster H. Shaw Jr., Richard N. Richards, David C. Leestma, James C. Adamson, Mark N. Brown.
Atlantis (18-23/10/89)	Donald E. Williams, Michael J. McCulley, Shannon W. Lucid, Ellen S. Baker, Franklin R. Chang-Diaz.
Discovery (22-27/11/89)	Frederick D. Gregory, John E. Blaha, Manley L. Carter, F. Story Musgrave, Katherine C. Thornton.
Columbia (9-20/1/90)	Daniel C. Brandenstein, Bonnie J. Dunbar, James D. Wetherbee, Marsha S. Ivins, G. David Low.
Atlantis (28/2-4/3/90)	John O. Creighton, John H. Casper, David C. Hilmers, Richard M. Mullane, Pierre J. Thuot.

(Continued)

Name, date	Crew
Discovery (24-29/4/90)	Bruce McCandless 2d, Kathryn D. Sullivan, Loren J. Shriver, Charles F. Bolden Jr., Steven A. Hawley.
Discovery (6-10/10/90)	Richard N. Richards, Robert D. Cabana, Bruce E. Melnick, William M. Shepherd, Thomas D. Akers.
Atlantis (15-20/11/90)	Richard O. Covey, Frank L. Culbertson, Robert C. Springer, Carl J. Meade, Charles D. Gemar.
Columbia (2-10/12/90)	Vance D. Brand, Guy S. Gardner, Jeffrey A. Hoffman, John M. Lounge, Robert A.R. Parker, Samuel T. Durrance, Ronald A. Parise.
Atlantis (5-11/4/91)	Stephen R. Nagel, Kenneth D. Cameron, Linda M. Godwin, Jerry L. Ross, Jerome Apt.
Discovery (28/4-6/5/91)	Michael L. Coats, L. Blaine Hammond Jr., Guion S. Bluford Jr., Gregory J. Harbaugh, Richard J. Hieb, Donald R. McMonagle, Charles L. Veach.
Columbia (5-14/6/91)	Byron O. O'Connor, Sidney M. Gutierrez, James P. Bagian, Margaret Rhea Seddon, Francis A. Gaffney, Millie Hughes-Fulford, Tamara E. Jernigan.
Atlantis (2-11/8/91)	John E. Blaha, Michael A. Baker, Shannon W. Lucid, G. David Low, James C. Adamson.
Discovery (12-18/9/91)	John O. Creighton, Kenneth S. Reightler Jr., Charles D. Gemar, James F. Buchli, Mark N. Brown.
Atlantis (24/11-1/12/91)	Frederick D. Gregory, Terrence T. Hendricks, F. Story Musgrave, James S. Voss, Mario Runco Jr., Thomas J. Hennen.
Discovery (22-30/1/92)	Ronald J. Grabe, Stephen S. Oswald, Norman E. Thagard, William E. Readdy, David Hilmers, Roberta L. Bondar, Ulf Merbold.
Atlantis (24/3-2/4/92)	Charles F. Bolden Jr., Brian Duffy, Michael Foale, David C. Leestma, Kathryn D. Sullivan, Bryon K. Lichtenberg, Dirk D. Frimout.
Endeavour (7-16/5/92)	Daniel C. Brandenstein, Kevin C. Chilton, Thomas Dakers, Richard J. Hieb, Kathryn C. Thornton, Bruce E. Melnick, Pierre J. Thout.
Columbia (25/6-9/7/92)	Richard N. Richards, Kenneth D. Bowersox, Bonnie J. Dunbar, Ellen S. Baker, Lawrence J. DeLucas, Carl J. Meade, Eugene H. Trinh. *Set duration record for shuttle flight.*

Notable U.S. Uncrewed and Planetary Missions

Source: National Aeronautics and Space Administration

Spacecraft	Launch date (GMT)	Mission	Remarks
Mariner 2	Aug. 27, 1962	Venus	Passed within 22,000 miles from Venus 14/12/62; contact lost 3/1/63 at 54 million miles
Ranger 7	July 28, 1964	Moon	Yielded over 4,000 photos
Mariner 4	Nov. 28, 1964	Mars	Passed behind Mars 14/7/65; took 22 photos from 6,000 miles
Ranger 8	Feb. 17, 1965	Moon	Yielded over 7,000 photos
Surveyor 3	Apr. 17, 1967	Moon	Scooped and tested lunar soil
Mariner 5	June 14, 1967	Venus	In solar orbit; closest Venus fly-by 19/10/67
Mariner 6	Feb. 25, 1969	Mars	Came within 2,000 miles of Mars 31/7/69; sent back data, photos
Mariner 7	Mar. 27, 1969	Mars	Came within 2,000 miles of Mars 5/8/69
Mariner 9	May 30, 1971	Mars	First craft to orbit Mars 13/11/71; sent back over 7,000 photos
Pioneer 10	Mar. 3, 1972	Jupiter	Passed Jupiter 3/12/73; exited the solar system 14/6/83
Mariner 10	Nov. 3, 1973	Venus, Mercury	Passed Venus 5/2/74; arrived Mercury 29/3/74. First time gravity of one planet (Venus) used to whip spacecraft towards another (Mercury)
Viking 1	Aug. 20, 1975	Mars	Landed on Mars 20/7/76; did scientific research, sent photos; functioned 6½ years
Viking 2	Sept. 9, 1975	Mars	Landed on Mars 3/9/76; functioned 3½ years
Voyager 1	Sept. 5, 1977	Jupiter, Saturn	Encountered Jupiter 5/3/79; Saturn 13/11/80
Voyager 2	Aug. 20, 1977	Jupiter, Saturn, Uranus, Neptune	Encountered Jupiter 9/7/79; Saturn 26/8/81; Uranus 8/1 and 27/1/86; Neptune 24/8/89
Pioneer Venus 1	May 20, 1978	Venus	Entered Venus orbit 4/12/78; spent 14 years studying planet; ceased operating 19/10/92
Pioneer Venus 2	Aug. 8, 1978	Venus	Encountered Venus 9/12/78; probes impacted on surface
Magellan	May 4, 1989	Venus	Orbit and map Venus; monitoring geological activity on surface; still operating in outer solar system
Titan IV	June 14, 1989	Orbit Earth	First of 41 such rockets whose primary purpose is defence
Galileo	Oct. 18, 1989	Jupiter	Used Earth's gravity to propel it towards Jupiter; encountered Venus, Feb. 1991

Summary of Worldwide Payloads, 1986–92

(A payload is something carried into space by a rocket)

Source: National Aeronautics and Space Administration

Year	Total[1]	USSR/CIS[2]	United States	Japan	European Space Agency	India	China
1986	132	114	9	3	0	—	3
1987	133	116	9	3	1	—	1
1988	136	107	15	2	2	2	3
1989	129	95	22	4	2	0	0
1990	160	96	31	7	1	1	5
1991	156	101	30	2	4	1	1
1992[3]	128	77	27	3	1	2	2
Total	4,300	2,838	1,158	56	31	15	32

(1) Includes launches in countries not shown. (2) Figures for 1986–91 are for the Soviet Union; 1992 is for the Commonwealth of Independent States. (3) Includes launches in prior years not shown.

Notable Proposed U.S. Space Missions

Source: National Aeronautics and Space Administration

Year	Month	Mission	Purpose
1994	Feb.	Wind (a)	Will determine solar wind input to Earth's magnetosphere.
1994		International Microgravity Laboratory – 2 (b)	Spacelab mission to study materials, fluid and life sciences.
1996		Mars Environmental Survey Pathfinder (a)	Technical demonstration of Mars Environmental Survey.
1996		X-ray Timing Explorer (a)	Study temporal variability in compact X-ray emitting objects.
1997		Cassini (a)	Study of Saturn's atmosphere, rings, magnetosphere and moons.
1998		Earth Observing System (a)	Provide long-term data sets of interactions between Earth's land, atmosphere, water and life.
1998, 1999		Advanced X-ray Astrophysics Facility (2 spacecraft) (a)	Study of dark matter, stellar evolution, galactic clusters.
TBD		Pluto Fast Fly-by (a)	First fly-by of Pluto for photographic survey and other studies.
2001		Space Infrared Telescope Facility (a)	High sensitivity observations of celestial sources.

(a) Launched by expendable rocket. (b) Carried aboard shuttle. TBD = to be determined.

International Aviation and Space Records

The National Aeronautic Association of the USA, 1815 North Fort Myer Dr., Arlington, VA 22209, representative in the United States of the Fédération Aéronautique Internationale, is the certifying agency for world aviation and space records. The International Aeronautical Federation was formed in 1905 by representatives from Belgium, France, Germany, Great Britain, Spain, Italy, Switzerland and the United States, with headquarters in Paris. Regulations for the control of official records were signed Oct. 14, 1905.

World absolute records are defined as maximum performance, regardless of class or type of aircraft used. Absolute records for space flight (Class K, spacecraft, and Class P, aerospacecraft) are kept separately. All other records, also international in scope, are termed "World Class" records and are divided into 17 classes, including: Class A, free balloons; Class B, airships; Class C-1, aeroplanes; Class C-2, sea-planes; Class C-3, amphibians; Class D, gliders; and Class E, rotorcrafts, such as helicopters. Classes are subdivided into four groups based on their power source: Group I – piston engine, Group II – turboprop, Group III – jet engine, Group IV – rocket engine. Sometimes there are also further divisions for weight subclasses, such as Class C-1d, which is a light aeroplane weighing 3,858 to 6,614 pounds. All FAI course records listed here were accomplished in Class C-1 landplanes. A partial listing of world records follows (records to Jan. 1, 1993).

World Absolute Records – Maximum Performance in Any Class

Speed over a straight course – 2,193.16 mph – Capt. Elden W. Joersz, USAF, Lockheed SR-71; Beale AFB, Cal., July 28, 1976.

Speed over a closed circuit – 2,092.294 mph – Maj. Adolphus H. Bledsoe Jr., USAF, Lockheed SR-71; Beale AFB, Cal., July 27, 1976.

Speed around the world, non-stop, non-refuelled – 115.65 mph – Richard Rutan & Jeana Yeager, U.S., Voyager, Edwards AFB, Cal., Dec. 14-23, 1986.

Altitude – (123,523.58 feet) – Alexander Fedotov, USSR, E-266M; Podmoskovnoye, USSR, Aug. 31, 1977.

Altitude in horizontal flight – 85,068.997 ft. – Capt. Robert C. Helt, USAF, Lockheed SR-71; Beale AFB, Cal., July 28, 1976.

Spacecraft (Class K)

Duration – 365 days, 22 hours, 39 minutes, 47 seconds – Vladimir Titov, Musa Manarov, USSR, Soyuz TM4; Dec. 21, 1987 – Dec 21, 1988.

Altitude– 234,672.5 mi. – Frank Borman, James A. Lovell Jr., William Anders, Apollo 8; Dec. 21-27, 1968.

Greatest mass lifted – 282,197 lbs. – Frank Borman, James A. Lovell Jr., William Anders, Apollo 8; Dec. 21-27, 1968.

Distance – 87,436,800 mi. – Anatoly Beresovoy & Valentin Lebedev, USSR, Salyut 7, Soyuz T5, Soyuz T7; May 13-Dec. 10, 1982.

"World Class" Records

Free Balloons (Class A)

Altitude – (113,739.9 ft.) – Cmdr. Malcolm D. Ross, USNR; Lee Lewis Memorial Winzen Research Balloon; Gulf of Mexico, May 4, 1961.

Distance – (5,208.67 mi.) – Ben Abruzzo; Raven Experimental; Nagashima, Japan to Covello, Cal., Nov. 9-12, 1981.

Duration –137 hr., 5 min., 50 sec. – Ben Abruzzo, Larry Newman, and Maxie Anderson; Double Eagle II; Presque Isle, Maine to Miserey, France (3,107.61 mi.); Aug. 12-17, 1978.

Aeroplanes (Class C-I, Group I)

Distance, closed circuit – 24,986.727 mi. – Richard Rutan & Jeana Yeager, U.S., Voyager; Edwards AFB, Cal., Dec. 14-23, 1986.

Speed for 100 kilometres (62.137 miles) without payload – 469.549 mph – Jacqueline Cochran, U.S.; North American P-51; Coachella Valley, Cal., Dec. 10, 1947.

Speed for 1,000 kilometres (621.369 miles) without payload – 431.09 mph – Jacqueline Cochran, U.S.; North American P-51; Santa Rosasummit, Cal. – Flagstaff, Ariz. course, May 24, 1948.

Speed for 5,000 kilometres (3,106.849 miles) without payload – 338.39 mph – Capt. James Bauer, USAF, Boeing B-29; Dayton, Oh., June 28, 1946.

Speed around the world – 203.64 mph – D.N. Dalton, Australia; Beechcraft Duke; Brisbane, Aust., July 20-25, 1975. Time: 5 days, 2 hours, 19 min., 57 sec.

Light Aeroplanes (Class C-1d, Group I)

Great Circle distance without landing – 7,929.71 mi. – Peter Wilkins, Australia, Piper Malibu, Sydney, Aust. to Phoenix, Ariz., Mar. 30-Apr. 1, 1987.

Speed for 100 kilometres – (62,137 miles) in a closed circuit – 322.780 mph – Ms R. M. Sharpe, Great Britain; Vickers Supermarine Spitfire 5-B; Wolverhampton, June 17, 1950.

Aeroplanes (Class C-1, Group II)

Great Circle distance without landing – 8,732.09 mi. – Lt. Col. Edgar L. Allison Jr., USAF, Lockheed HC-130 Hercules aircraft; Taiwan to Scott AFB, Ill.; Feb. 20, 1972.

Altitude – (51,014 ft.) – Donald R. Wilson, U.S.; LTV L450F aircraft; Greenville, Tex., Mar. 27, 1972.

Speed for 1,000 kilometres (621.369 miles) without payload – 541.449 mph – Ivan Soukhomline, USSR; TU-114 aircraft; Sternberg, USSR; Mar. 24, 1960.

Speed for 5,000 kilometres (3,106.849 miles) without payload – 545.072 mph – Ivan Soukhomline, USSR; TU-114 aircraft, Sternberg, USSR; Apr. 9, 1960.

Speed around the world – 304.80 mph – Joe Harnish, U.S., Gulfstream Commander 695A, Elkhart, Ind., Mar. 21-24, 1983.

Aeroplanes (Class C-1, Group III)

Great Circle distance without landing – 12,532.28 mi. – Maj. Clyde P. Evely, USAF, Boeing B-52-H, Kadena, Okinawa to Madrid, Spain, Jan. 10-11, 1962.

Distance in a closed circuit – 12,521.78 mi. – Vladimir Tersky, USSR, AN-124, Podmoskovnoye, USSR, May 6-7, 1987.

Altitude – 123,523.58 ft. – Alexander Fedotov, USSR; E-226M aeroplane; Podmoskovnoye, USSR, Aug. 31, 1977.

Speed for 100 kilometres in a closed circuit – 1,618.7 mph – Alexander Fedotov, USSR; E-266 aeroplane, Apr. 8, 1973.

Speed for 500 kilometres in a closed circuit – 1,852.61 mph – Mikhail Komarov, USSR; E-266 aeroplane, Oct. 5, 1967.

Speed for 1,000 kilometres in a closed circuit – 2,092.294 mph – Maj. Adolphus H. Bledsoe Jr., USAF; Lockheed SR-71; Beale AFB, Cal., July 27, 1976.

Speed for 2,000 kilometres without payload – 1,250.42 mph – S. Agapov, USSR; Podmoscovnde, USSR; July 20, 1983.

Speed around the world – 637.71 mph – Allen E. Paulson, U.S., Gulfstream IV, Houston, Tex., Feb. 26-28, 1988.

Gliders (Class D-1 – single seater)

Distance, straight line – 907.7 mi. – Hans Werner Grosse, West Germany; ASK12 sailplane; Luebeck to Biarritz, Apr. 25, 1972.

Distance to a goal & return – 1,023.25 mi. – Thomas Knauff, U.S. Nimbus III; Williamsport, Pa., Apr. 25, 1983.

Helicopters (Class E-1)

Great Circle distance without landing – 2,213.04 mi. – Robert G. Ferry, U.S.; Hughes YOH-6A helicopter;

Culver City, Cal., to Ormond Beach, Fla., Apr. 6-7, 1966.

Speed around the world – 35.40 mph – H. Ross Perot Jr.; Bell 206 L-11 Long Ranger N39112; Dallas, Tex.-Dallas, Tex.; Sept. 1-30, 1982; 29 days, 3 hrs., – min., 13 sec.

FAI Course Records

Los Angeles to New York – 1,214.65 mph – Capt. Robert G. Sowers, USAF; Convair B-58 Hustler; elapsed time: 2 hrs. 58.71 sec., Mar. 5, 1962.

New York to Los Angeles – 1,081.80 mph – Capt. Robert G. Sowers, USAF; Convair B-58 Hustler; elapsed time: 2 hrs. 15 min. 50.08 sec., Mar. 5, 1962.

London to New York – 1,021.54 mph – Capt. Peter Horton, U.S.; British Airways Concorde G-BOAF; elapsed time: 3 hrs. 22 min.; Mar. 14, 1990.

Baltimore to Moscow, USSR – 563.36 mph – Col. James B. Swindal, USAF; Boeing VC-137 (707); elapsed time: 8 hrs. 33 min. 45.4 sec., May 19, 1963.

New York to London – 1,806.964 mph – Maj. James V. Sullivan, USAF; Lockheed SR-71; elapsed time 1 hr. 54 min. 56.4 sec., Sept. 1, 1974.

London to Los Angeles – 1,435.587 mph – Capt. Harold B. Adams, USAF; Lockheed SR-71; elapsed time: 3 hrs. 47 min. 39 sec., Sept. 13, 1974.

Aircraft Operating Statistics, 1992

Source: Air Transport Assn. of America
(Figures are averages for most commonly used models)

	Number of seats	Speed airborne (mph)	Flight length (miles)	Fuel (gallons per hour)	Aircraft operating cost per hour
B747-400	403	534	4,375	3,361	$7,098
B747-100	399	520	3,094	3,507	5,905
L-1011-100/200	293	495	1,519	2,362	4,072
DC-10-10	282	488	1,387	2,189	4,056
A300-600	266	474	1,206	1,686	3,917
DC-10-30	265	522	2,962	2,607	4,595
B767-300	224	489	2,087	1,485	3,384
B757-200	188	458	1,105	996	2,293
B767-200	187	483	2,064	1,434	2,956
A320-100/200	149	441	944	757	1,868
B727-200	148	430	689	1,242	2,263
B737-400	145	400	564	769	1,743
MD-80	142	419	662	889	1,842
B737-300	131	415	633	739	1,768
DC-9-50	122	387	453	890	1,640
B727-100	117	429	638	1,137	2,220
B737-100/200	112	387	444	793	1,735
DC-9-30	102	381	441	794	1,658
F-100	99	361	388	690	1,445
DC-9-10	77	361	359	727	1,439

Notable Around the World and Intercontinental Trips

	From/To	Miles	Time	Date
Nellie Bly	New York/New York		72d 06h 11m	1889
George Francis Train	New York/New York		67d 12h 03m	1890
Charles Fitzmorris	Chicago/Chicago		60d 13h 29m	1901
J. W. Willis Sayre	Seattle/Seattle		54d 09h 42m	1903
J. Alcock-A.W. Brown (1)	Newfoundland/Ireland	1,960	16h 12m	June 14-15, 1919
Two U.S. Army aeroplanes	Seattle/Seattle	26,103	35d 01h 11m	1924
Richard E. Byrd (2)	Spitsbergen/N. Pole	1,545	15h 30m	May 9, 1926
Amundsen-Ellsworth-Nobile Expedition	Spitsbergen/Teller, Alaska		80h	May 11-14,1926
E.S. Evans and L. Wells (N. Y. World) (3)	New York/New York	18,400	28d 14h 36m 05s	June 16-July 14, 1926
Charles Lindbergh (4)	New York/Paris	3,610	33h 29m 30s	May 20-21, 1927
Amelia Earhart, W. Stultz, L. Gordon	Newfoundland/Wales		20h 40m	June 17-18, 1928
Graf Zeppelin	Friedrichshafen, Ger./Lakehurst, N.J.	6,630	4d 15h 46m	Oct. 11-15, 1928
Graf Zeppelin	Friedrichshafen, Ger./Lakehurst, N.J.	21,700	20d 04h	Aug. 14-Sept. 4, 1929
Wiley Post and Harold Gatty (Monoplane Winnie Mae)	New York/New York	15,474	8d 15h 51m	July 1, 1931
C. Pangborn-H. Herndon Jr. (5)	Misawa, Japan/Wenatchee, Wash.	4,458	41h 34m	Oct. 3-5, 1931
Amelia Earhart (6)	Newfoundland/Ireland	2,026	14h 56m	May 20-21, 1932
Wiley Post (Monoplane Winnie Mae) (7)	New York/New York	15,596	115h 36m 30s	July 15-22, 1933
Hindenburg Zeppelin	Lakehurst, N.J./Frankfurt, Ger.		42h 53m	Aug. 9-11, 1936
H. R. Ekins (Scripps-Howard Newspapers in race) (Zeppelin Hindenburg to Germany, aeroplanes from Frankfurt)	Lakehurst, N.J./Lakehurst, N.J.	25,654	18d 11h 14m 33s	Sept, 30-Oct. 19, 1936
Howard Hughes and 4 assistants	New York/New York	14,824	3d 19h 08m 10s	July 10-13, 1938
Douglas Corrigan	New York/Dublin		28h 13m	July 17-18, 1938
Mrs. Clara Adams				

(Continued)

	From/To	Miles	Time	Date
(Pan American Clipper)	Port Washington, N.Y./Newark, N.J.		16d 19h 04m	June 28-July 15, 1939
Globemaster, U.S. Air Transport Command	Wash., D.C./Wash., D.C.	23,279	149h 44m	Oct. 4, 1945
Capt. William P. Odom (A-26 Reynolds Bombshell)	New York/New York	20,000	78h 55m 12s	Apr. 12-16, 1947
America, Pan American 4-engine Lockheed Constellation (8)	New York/New York	22,219	101h 32m	June 17-30, 1947
Col. Edward Eagan	New York/New York	20,559	147h 15m	Dec. 13, 1948
USAF B-50 Lucky Lady II (Capt. James Gallagher) (9)	Ft. Worth, Tex./Ft. Worth, Tex.	23,452	94h 01m	Feb. 26-Mar. 2, 1949
Col. D. Schilling, USAF (10)	England/Limestone, Maine	3,300	10h 01m	Sept. 22, 1950
C.F. Blair Jr.	Norway/Alaska	3,300	10h 29m	May 29, 1951
Two U.S. S-55	Massachusetts/Scotland	3,410	42h 30m	July 15-31, 1952
Canberra Bomber (11)	N. Ireland/Newfoundland	2,073	04h 34m	Aug. 26, 1952
	Newfoundland/N. Ireland	2,073	03h 25m	Aug. 26, 1952
Three USAF B-52 Stratofortresses (12)	Merced, Cal./Cal.	24,325	45h 19m	Jan. 15-18, 1957
Max Conrad	Chicago/Rome	5,000	34h 03m	Mar. 5-6, 1959
USSR TU-114 (13)	Moscow/New York	5,092	11h 06m	June 28, 1959
Boeing 707-320	New York/Moscow	c.5090	08h 54m	July 23, 1959
Peter Gluckmann (solo)	San Francisco/San Francisco	22,800	29d	Aug. 22-Sept. 20, 1959
Sue Snyder	Chicago/Chicago	21,219	62h 59m	June 22-24, 1960
Max Conrad (solo)	Miami/Miami	25,946	8d 18h 35m 57s	Feb. 28-Mar. 8, 1961
Sam Miller & Louis Fodor	New York/New York		46h 28m	Aug. 3-4, 1963
Robert & Joan Wallick	Manila/Manila	23,129	05d 06h 17m 10s	June 2-7, 1966
Arthur Godfrey, Richard Merrill, Fred Austin, Karl Keller	New York/New York	23,333	86h 09m 01s	June 4-7, 1966
Trevor K. Brougham	Darwin, Australia/Darwin	24,800	5d 05h 57m	Aug. 5-10, 1972
Walter H. Mullikin, Albert Frink, Lyman Watt, Frank Cassaniti, Edward Shields	New York/New York	23,137	1d 22h 50s	May 1-3,1976
David Kunst (15)	Waseca, Minn./Waseca, Minn.	14,500	4yrs 3mos 16d	June 10, 1970-Oct. 5, 1974
Arnold Palmer	Denver/Denver	22,985	57h 25m 42s	May 17-19, 1976
Boeing 747 (14)	San Francisco/San Francisco	26,382	54h 07m 12s	Oct. 28-31, 1977
Concorde	London/Wash., D.C.	1,023 mph	03h 34m 48s	May 29, 1976
Concorde	Paris/New York	1,037.50 mph	03h 30m 11s	Aug. 22, 1978
Richard Rutan & Jeana Yeager (16)	Edwards AFB, Cal.	24,986	09d 03m 44s	Dec. 14-23, 1986

(1) Non-stop transatlantic flight. (2) Polar flight. (3) Mileage by train and auto, 4,110; by plane, 6,300; by steamship, 8,000. (4) Solo transatlantic flight in the Ryan monoplane the "Spirit of St. Louis". (5) Non-stop Pacific flight. (6) Woman's transoceanic solo flight. (7) First to fly solo around northern circumference of the world, also first to fly twice around the world. (8) Inception of regular commercial global air service. (9) First non-stop round-the-world flight, refuelled 4 times in flight. (10) Non-stop jet transatlantic flight. (11) Transatlantic round trip on same day. (12) First non-stop global flight by jet planes; refuelled in flight by KC-97 aerial tankers; average speed approx. 525 mph. (13) Non-stop between Moscow and New York. (14) Speed record around the world over both the Earth's poles. (15) First to circle the Earth on foot. (16) Circled the Earth nonstop without refuelling.

ENGINEERING ACHIEVEMENTS

Some Notable Tall Structures*

Structure	Height (ft)	Storeys
CN Tower, Toronto	1821	—
Sears Tower, Chicago	1454	110
Empire State Building (plus TV tower), New York	1414	102
World Trade Center (2 towers), New York	1368/1362	110/110
Bank of China, Hong Kong	1209	72
Amoco Building, Chicago	1136	80
John Hancock Center, Chicago	1127	100
Chrysler Building, New York	1046	77
First Interstate World Center, Los Angeles	1017	73
Texas Commerce Tower, Houston	1002	75
Eiffel Tower, Paris	984	—

Structure	Height (ft)	Storeys
Messe Turm Building, Frankfurt	841	70
Canary Wharf tower, London	800	59
Palace of Science & Culture, Warsaw	790	42
Moscow State University (including spire)	787	39
Tour Maine, Paris	751	64
MLC Centre, Sydney	748	60
Ikebukuro office tower, Tokyo	742	60
Carlton Centre, Johannesburg	722	50
Overseas-Chinese Banking Corp., Singapore	660	52
Ukraine Hotel, Moscow	650	60
Natwest Tower, London	600	50

*Excluding buildings in the USA under 1000ft tall.

The Tallest Churches in the World

Source: Russell Ash, *The Top Ten of Everything*

	Church	Year completed	Height m	ft
1	Chicago Methodist Temple	1924	173	568
2	Ulm Cathedral	1890	161	528
3	Cologne Cathedral	1880	156.4	513
4	Rouen Cathedral	1523*	148	485
5	St Nicholas, Hamburg	1847	145	475
6	Notre Dame, Strasbourg	1439	142	465
7	St Peter's, Rome	1612	140	458
8	St Stephen's Cathedral, Vienna	1433	136	446
9=	Amiens Cathedral, France	1260	134	440
9=	St Michael, Hamburg	1906	134	440
	Salisbury Cathedral	*1375*	*123*	*404*

* The cast-iron spire was added around 1822.

Longest Bridges in the UK

Source: Russell Ash, *The Top Ten of Everything*

	Bridge	Completed	Length of main span m	ft
1	Humber Estuary	1980	1,410	4,626
2	Forth Road Bridge	1964	1,006	3,300
3	Severn Bridge	1966	988	3,240
4	Firth of Forth	1890	521	1,710
5	Tamar, Saltash	1961	335	1,100
6	Runcorn-Widnes	1961	330	1,082
7	Clifton Suspension	1864	214	702
8	Menai Straits	1834	176	579
9	Tyne Bridge, Newcastle	1930	162	531
10=	Medway (M2 Motorway)	1963	152	500
10=	George Street, Newport	1964	152	500

Notable International Bridges

Angostura, suspension type, span 2,336 feet, 1967 at Ciudad Bolivar, Venezuela. Total length, 5,507.

Bendorf Bridge on the Rhine River, 5 mi. north of Coblenz, completed 1965, is a 3-span cement girder bridge, 3,378 ft. overall length, 101 ft. wide, with the main span 682 ft.

Bosporus Bridge linking Europe and Asia opened at Istanbul in 1973, at 3,524 ft. is the fifth longest suspension bridge in the world.

Gladesville Bridge at Sydney, Australia, has the longest concrete arch in the world (1,000 ft. span).

Humber Bridge, with a suspension span of 4,626 ft., the longest in the world, crosses the Humber estuary 5 miles west of the city of Kingston upon Hull, England. Unique in a large suspension bridge are the towers of reinforced concrete instead of steel.

Second Narrow's Bridge, Canada's longest railway lift span connecting Vancouver and North Vancouver over Burrard Inlet.

Oland Island Bridge in Sweden was completed in 1972. It is 19,882 feet long, Europe's longest.

Oosterscheldebrug, opened Dec. 15, 1965, is a 3.125-mile causeway for automobiles over a sea arm in Zeeland, the Netherlands. It completes a direct connection between Flushing and Rotterdam.

Rio-Niteroi, Guanabara Bay, Brazil, completed in 1972, is world's longest continuous box and plate girder bridge, 8 miles, 3,363 feet long, with a centre span of 984 feet and a span on each side of 656 feet.

Tagus River Bridge near Lisbon, Portugal, has a 3,323-ft. main span. Opened Aug. 6, 1966, it was named Salazar Bridge after the former premier.

Zoo Bridge across the Rhine at Cologne, with steel box girders, has a main span of 850 ft.

World's Longest Railway Tunnels

Source: Railway Directory & Year Book. Tunnels over 5 miles in length.

Tunnel	Date	Miles	Operating railway	Country
Seikan	1985	33.5	Japanese Railway	Japan
Dai-shimizu	1979	14	Japanese Railway	Japan
Simplon No. 1 and 2	1906, 1922	12	Swiss Fed. & Italian St.	Switz.-Italy
Kanmon	1975	12	Japanese Railway	Japan
Apennine	1934	11	Italian State	Italy
Rokko	1972	10	Japanese Railway	Japan
Mt. MacDonald	1989	9.1	Canadian Pacific	Canada
Gotthard	1882	9	Swiss Federal	Switzerland
Lotschberg	1913	9	Bern-Lotschberg-Simplon	Switzerland
Hokuriku	1962	9	Japanese Railway	Japan
Mont Cenis (Frejus)	1871	8	Italian State	France-Italy
Shin-Shimizu	1961	8	Japanese Railway	Japan
Aki	1975	8	Japanese Railway	Japan
Cascade	1929	8	Burlington Northern	U.S.
Flathead	1970	8	Burlington Northern	U.S.

Channel Tunnel

1880 – The first attempt to bore a tunnel under the English Channel was made, using a machine designed by Colonel Beaumont. The tunnel, which was about 2.4m (8 ft) in diameter, started from an access shaft and was approximately 2km (1¼ miles) long when the project was halted in 1882. A similar tunnel was also started in France from a shaft sunk near Sangatte.
1922 – A trial bore was made at Folkestone, using a Whitaker machine which cut a tunnel about 3m (10 ft) in diameter.
1974 – Work began on a much larger tunnel system, similar to that which has now been built. Access tunnels (adits) were bored on both sides of the Channel, and 400m (440 ft) of service tunnel was constructed before work was abandoned at the beginning of 1975.
1986 – A twin-bore rail tunnel design was selected by the French and British governments, 20 Jan.
1987 – UK tunnelling began on 1 Dec. at Shakespeare Cliff, near Folkestone.
1988 – French tunnelling began at Sangatte on 28 Feb.
1990 – Half of the total tunnelling work, 75.7km (45 miles), was completed 21 April. By 13 Aug. two-thirds was complete.

The first contact between the French and British workings was made on 30 Oct. with a probe 100m (330 ft) long.

Breakthrough in the undersea service tunnel on 1 Dec. allowed the first people to cross dryshod between France and England for 12,000 years.
1991 – Rail tunnel breakthroughs achieved on 22 May and 28 June.
1993 – Eurotunnel opening postponed from summer 1993 to spring 1994.

Eurotunnel Facts

- The Eurotunnel system consists of 3 parallel tunnels: 2 single-track rail tunnels and a smaller service tunnel.
- All 3 tunnels are 50km (30 miles), running for 38km (23 miles) under the Channel, and were bored at an average depth of 40m (130 ft) below the sea-bed.
- The finished diameter of the rail tunnels is 7.6m (25 ft), while the service tunnel is 4.8m (16 ft).
- The service tunnel is linked to the rail tunnels by 130 cross-passages which occur every 375m (400 yds).
- The rail tunnels are brought together at 2 undersea crossover caverns, making it possible for trains to cross from one track to the other.
- The crossovers divide the length of the rail tunnels into 3 equal sections, any of which can be closed off in an emergency or for maintenance.
- The 2 rail tunnels are 30m (100 ft) apart, and no closer than 8m (25 ft) to the walls of the service tunnel.
- The specially designed tunnel boring machines (TBMs) often completed over 300m (1000 ft) of tunnel in a week.
- The tunnelling generated 7 million cubic metres of spoil – enough to fill Wembley Stadium 13 times over.
- The service will operate 24 hours a day, with passenger vehicle shuttles at approximately 15-minute intervals during peak hours, 20-minute intervals at other times of day, and once an hour at night.
- The total projected cost of the tunnel (as at mid-1993) was £8.4 billion.

Safety Features

When asked for their views on the Channel tunnel, most people express a fear of being trapped under the sea. However, as the tunnel is about 40m (130 ft) below the sea-bed, the sea itself does not present a significant hazard. It would take an earthquake unprecedented in this region to rupture the tunnel lining; even then, pumps are provided to deal with such emergencies.

The risk of collision has been eliminated by building 2 railway tunnels which have only a single track and carry trains in only one direction. Concrete walkways on both sides are designed to hold the shuttle wagons upright in the event of derailment.

Driver error, the most common cause of rail collisions, will be rendered negligible thanks to Automatic Train Protection (ATP). If a driver ignores warning signals, ATP will take over and stop the train.

The risk of fire has been reduced substantially by eliminating the chances of collision. Other possible causes of fire are, apparently, very few, but extensive precautions have been taken to ensure rapid detection and suppression.

Lorries and trailers will be carried separately from cars and passengers. Hazardous loads, such as fuels and toxic chemicals, will be banned.

All life-sustaining systems (electricity, ventilation, communications, etc.) have been duplicated several times over to ensure that if one system fails, another is available.

Rabies and the Channel Tunnel

Thanks to stringent quarantine measures, the British Isles have been free of rabies for many years. To keep it so the Eurotunnel consortium have taken measures to prevent rabies-susceptible animals, such as cats, dogs, foxes and rodents, from entering or passing through the tunnel. These measures comprise:

- A security/perimeter fence, with animal-proof mesh buried below ground, surrounding the terminals. There will also be surveillance to detect the passage of animals at terminal entrances.
- A high-security fence around the tunnel portals, with animal-proof mesh buried below ground, and an environment at the portals which will be hostile to animals. There will also be round-the-clock surveillance.
- Electrified barriers at each end of the undersea sections of all three tunnels will prevent the passage of animals in the event that they have passed through the first two lines of defence.

Permanent control operations – baiting and trapping, and measures to ensure that there is no food source in the tunnels to attract animals – will keep the terminal areas and tunnels free of rats and other rodents. Structures such as service pipes, drain channels, ducts and cable entries will be meshed off.

METEOROLOGY

Britain's Weather: Sep. 1992–Aug. 1993

(All average figures based on 1951–80 average)

Warmest	Coldest	Sunniest	Cloudiest	Wettest	Driest
September (cool, cloudy & wet)					
Folkestone 18.0°C	Lerwick 12.0°C	Folkestone 164 hrs	Weston-super-Mare 53 hrs sun	Eskdalemuir 206 mm	Lowestoft 35 mm
October (very cold, especially northern England)					
Guernsey 13.7°C	Eskdalemuir 8.3°C	Folkestone 134 hrs	Eskdalemuir 67 hrs sun	Folkestone 155 mm	Leuchars 22 mm
November (wet & dull, especially in the west)					
Guernsey 13.1°C	Eskdalemuir 6.6°C	Leuchars 88 hrs	Lerwick 27 hrs sun	Eskdalemuir 274 mm	Skegness 44 mm
December (cold & rather dry)					
Guernsey 9.4°C	Eskdalemuir 3.5°C	Brighton 67 hrs	Lerwick 11 hrs sun	Morecambe 120 mm	Lowestoft 37 mm
January (dull & mild; very wet in Scotland)					
Guernsey 11.1°C	Eskdalemuir 4.8°C	Aberdeen 60 hrs	Lerwick 11 hrs sun	Eskdalemuir 294 mm	Scarborough 38 mm
February (cloudy, mild & very dry)					
Leuchars 9.0°C	Lerwick 5.5°C	Guernsey 62 hrs	Stornoway 20 hrs sun	Lerwick 63 mm	Leuchars 3 mm
March (mild & dry)					
Guernsey 11.4°C	Lerwick 6.4°C	Folkestone 155 hrs	Lerwick 75 hrs sun	Lerwick 109 mm	Folkestone 7 mm
April (wet, cloudy & mild)					
Ross-on-Wye 13.3°C	Lerwick 8.0°C	Guernsey 185 hrs	Eskdalemuir 75 hrs sun	Eskdalemuir 171 mm	Folkestone 41 mm
May (wet & cloudy)					
Brighton 16.6°C	Wick 10.1°C	Stornoway 215 hrs	Wick 103 hrs sun	Eskdalemuir 161 mm	Guernsey 27 mm
June (cloudy)					
Ross-on-Wye 21.0°C	Lerwick 12.2°C	Folkestone 259 hrs	Wick 88 hrs sun	Stornoway 93 mm	Lowestoft 24 mm
July (cool & cloudy)					
Lowestoft 20.3°C	Lerwick 12.5°C	Ross-on-Wye 222 hrs	Wick 45 hrs sun	Eskdalemuir 132 mm	Scarborough 34 mm
August (chilly & generally dry)					
Ross-on-Wye 20.5°C	Lerwick 12.5°C	Guernsey 271 hrs	Lerwick 83 hrs sun	Scarborough 114 mm	Ross-on-Wye 18 mm

UK Weather Records: 1900–1993

		Place	Date
Highest temperature:	98.8°F (37.1°C)	Cheltenham, Gloucestershire	3/8/90
Lowest temperature:	−17°F (−27.2°C)	Braemar, Grampian	10/1/82
Wettest day:	11 inches (279.4 mm)	Martinstown, Dorset	18/7/55
Wettest hour:	3.6 inches (92.2mm)	Maidenhead, Berkshire	12/7/01
Windiest day:	150 knots (172 mph)	Cairngorm, Grampian/ Highland	20/3/86

1990: Warmest Year on Record

NASA's Goddard Inst. recorded the average global temperature in 1990 at **59.81 degrees**, the warmest since 1880. The British Meteorological Office reported that no year had been as warm since they began keeping records in 1850, and said that 6 of the 7 warmest years of the 20th century had occurred during the 1980s.

Explanation of Normal Temperatures

Normal temperatures are based on records for the 30-year period from 1951–1980 inclusive. To obtain the average maximum or minimum temperature for any month, the daily temperatures are added; this total is then divided by the number of days in that month.

The normal maximum temperature for January, for example, is obtained by adding the average maximums for Jan. 1951, Jan. 1952, etc., through to Jan. 1980. The total is then divided by 30. The normal minimum temperature is obtained in a similar manner by adding the average minimums for each January in the 30-year period and dividing by 30. The normal temperature for January is half of the sum for the normal maximum and minimum temperatures for that month. The mean temperature for any one day is half the total of the maximum and minimum temperatures for that day.

International Temperature and Precipitation

Source: Environmental Data Service, U.S. Commerce Department

A standard period of 30 years has been used to obtain the average daily maximum and minimum temperatures and precipitation. The length of record of extreme maximum and minimum temperatures includes all available years of data for a given location and is usually for a longer period.

Station	Elev. Ft.	Temperature °F Average Daily January Max.	Min.	July Max.	Min.	Extreme Max.	Min.	Average annual precipitation (inches)
Addis Ababa, Ethiopia	8,038	75	43	69	50	94	32	48.7
Algiers, Algeria	194	59	49	83	70	107	32	30.0
Amsterdam, Netherlands	5	40	34	69	59	95	3	25.6
Athens, Greece	351	54	42	90	72	109	20	15.8
Auckland, New Zealand	23	73	60	56	46	90	33	49.1
Bangkok, Thailand	53	89	67	90	76	104	50	57.8
Beirut, Lebanon	111	62	51	87	73	107	30	35.1
Belgrade, Yugoslavia	453	37	27	84	61	107	−14	24.6
Berlin, Germany	187	35	26	74	55	96	−15	23.1
Bogota, Colombia	8,355	67	48	64	50	75	30	41.8
Bombay, India	27	88	62	88	75	110	46	71.2
Bucharest, Romania	269	33	20	86	61	105	−18	22.8
Budapest, Hungary	394	35	26	82	61	103	−10	24.2
Buenos Aires, Argentina	89	85	63	57	42	104	22	37.4
Cairo, Egypt	381	65	47	96	70	117	34	1.1
Capetown, South Africa	56	78	60	63	45	103	28	20.0
Caracas, Venezuela	3,418	75	56	78	61	91	45	32.9
Casablanca, Morocco	164	63	45	79	65	110	31	15.9
Copenhagen, Denmark	43	36	29	72	55	91	−3	23.3
Damascus, Syria	2,362	53	36	96	64	113	21	8.6
Dublin, Ireland	155	47	35	67	51	86	8	29.7
Geneva, Switzerland	1,329	39	29	77	58	101	−1	33.9
Havana, Cuba	80	79	65	89	75	104	43	48.2
Hong Kong	109	64	56	87	78	97	32	85.1
Istanbul, Turkey	59	45	36	81	65	100	17	31.5
Jerusalem, Israel	2,654	55	41	87	63	107	26	19.7
Lagos, Nigeria	10	88	74	83	74	104	60	72.3
La Paz, Bolivia	12,001	63	43	62	33	80	26	22.6
Lima, Peru	394	82	66	67	57	93	49	1.6
London, England	149	44	35	73	55	99	9	22.9
Los Angeles, USA	340	67	48	84	64	107	54	14.8
Madrid, Spain	2,188	47	33	87	62	102	14	16.5
Manila, Philippines	49	86	69	88	75	101	58	82.0
Mexico City, Mexico	7,340	66	42	74	54	92	24	23.0
Moscow, Russia	505	21	9	76	55	96	−27	24.8
Nairobi, Kenya	5,971	77	54	69	51	87	41	37.7
New York, USA	55	37	25	83	67	104	−2	41.7
Oslo, Norway	308	30	20	73	56	93	−21	26.9
Paris, France	164	42	32	76	55	105	1	22.3
Prague, Czechoslovakia	662	34	25	74	58	98	−16	19.3
Reykjavik, Iceland	92	36	28	58	48	74	4	33.9
Rome, Italy	377	54	39	88	64	104	20	29.5
San Salvador, El Salvador	2,238	90	60	89	65	105	45	70.0
Santiago, Chile	1,706	85	53	59	37	99	24	14.2
Sao Paolo, Brazil	2,628	77	63	66	53	100	32	57.3
Shanghai, China	16	47	32	91	75	104	10	45.0
Singapore	33	86	73	88	75	97	66	95.0
Stockholm, Sweden	146	31	23	70	55	97	−26	22.4
Sydney, Australia	62	78	65	60	46	114	35	46.5
Teheran, Iran	3,937	45	27	99	72	109	−5	9.7
Tokyo, Japan	19	47	29	83	70	101	17	61.6
Tripoli, Libya	72	61	47	85	71	114	33	15.1
Vienna, Austria	664	34	26	75	59	98	−14	25.6
Warsaw, Poland	294	30	21	75	56	98	−22	22.0
Washington, D.C., USA	25	41	22	87	64	104	−18	40.3

The Meaning of "One Inch of Rain"

An acre of ground contains 43,560 square feet. Consequently, a rainfall of 1 inch over 1 acre of ground would mean a total of 6,272,640 cubic inches of water. This is the equivalent of 3,630 cubic feet.

As a cubic foot of pure water weighs about 62.4 pounds, the exact amount varying with the density, it follows that the weight of a uniform coating of 1 inch of rain over 1 acre of surface would be 226,512 pounds, or about 101 tons. The weight of 1 imperial gallon of pure water is about 10.431 pounds. Consequently a rainfall of 1 inch over 1 acre of ground would mean 37,864 gallons of water.

Tides and Their Causes

Source: NOAA, National Ocean Service, U.S. Department of Commerce

The tides are a natural phenomenon involving the alternating rise and fall in the large fluid bodies of the Earth caused by the combined gravitational attraction of the sun and moon. The combination of these two variable force influences produces the complex recurrent cycle of the tides. Tides may occur in both oceans and seas, to a limited extent in large lakes, the atmosphere, and, to a very minute degree, in the Earth itself. The period between succeeding tides varies as the result of many factors and force influences.

The tide-generating force represents the difference between (1) the centrifugal force produced by the revolution of the Earth around the common center-of-gravity of the Earth-moon system and (2) the gravitational attraction of the moon acting upon the Earth's overlying waters. Since, on the average, the moon is only 238,852 miles from the Earth compared with the sun's much greater distance of 92,956,000 miles, this closer distance outranks the much smaller mass of the moon compared with that of the sun, and the moon's tide-raising force is, accordingly, 2⅕ times that of the sun.

The effect of the tide-generating forces of the moon and sun acting tangentially to the Earth's surface (the so-called "tractive force") tends to cause a maximum accumulation of the waters of the oceans at two diametrically opposite positions on the surface of the Earth and to withdraw compensating amounts of water from all points 90° removed from the positions of these tidal bulges. As the Earth rotates beneath the maxima and minima of these tide-generating forces, a sequence of two high tides, separated by two low tides, ideally is produced each day (*semidiurnal* tide).

Twice in each lunar month, when the sun, moon, and Earth are directly aligned, with the moon between the Earth and the sun (at new moon) or on the opposite side of the Earth from the sun (at full moon), the sun and the moon exert their gravitational force in a mutual or additive fashion. The highest high tides and lowest low tides are produced. These are called *spring* tides. At two positions 90° in between, the gravitational forces of the moon and sun — imposed at right angles—tend to counteract each other to the greatest extent, and the range between high and low tides is reduced. These are called *neap* tides. This semi-monthly variation between the spring and neap tides is called the *phase inequality*.

The inclination of the moon's monthly orbit to the equator and the inclination of the sun during the Earth's yearly orbit to the equator produce a difference in the height of succeeding high tides and in the extent of depression of succeeding low tides which is known as the *diurnal inequality*. In most cases, this produces a type of tide called a *mixed* tide. In extreme cases, these phenomena can result in only one high tide and one low each tide (*diurnal* tide). There are also other monthly and yearly variations in the tide due to the elliptical shape of the orbits themselves.

The actual range of tide in the waters of the open oceans may amount to only 1–3. However, as the ocean tide approaches shoal waters and its effects are augmented the tidal range may be greatly increased. In Nova Scotia along the narrow channel of the Bay of Fundy, the range of tides or difference between high and low waters, may reach 43½ feet or more (under spring tide conditions) due to resonant amplification.

In every case, actual high or low tide can vary considerably from the average, due to weather conditions such as strong winds, abrupt barometric pressure changes, or prolonged periods of extreme high or low pressure.

Heat Index

The index is a measure of the contribution that high humidity makes with abnormally high temperatures in reducing the body's ability to cool itself. For example, the index shows that for an actual air temperature of 100 degrees Fahrenheit and a relative humidity of 50 percent, the effect on the human body would be same as 120 degrees. Sunstroke and heat exhaustion are likely when the heat index reaches 105. This index is a measure of what hot weather "feels like" to the average person for various temperatures and relative humidities.

Relative Humidity	Air Temperature* 70	75	80	85	90	95	100	105	110	115	120
	Apparent Temperature*										
0%	64	69	73	78	83	87	91	95	99	103	107
10%	65	70	75	80	85	90	95	100	105	111	116
20%	66	72	77	82	87	93	99	105	112	120	130
30%	67	73	78	84	90	96	104	113	123	135	148
40%	68	74	79	86	93	101	110	123	137	151	
50%	69	75	81	88	96	107	120	135	150		
60%	70	76	82	90	100	114	132	149			
70%	70	77	85	93	106	124	144				
80%	71	78	86	97	113	136					
90%	71	79	88	102	122						
100%	72	80	91	108							

*Degrees Fahrenheit.

Sea Areas Around the British Isles

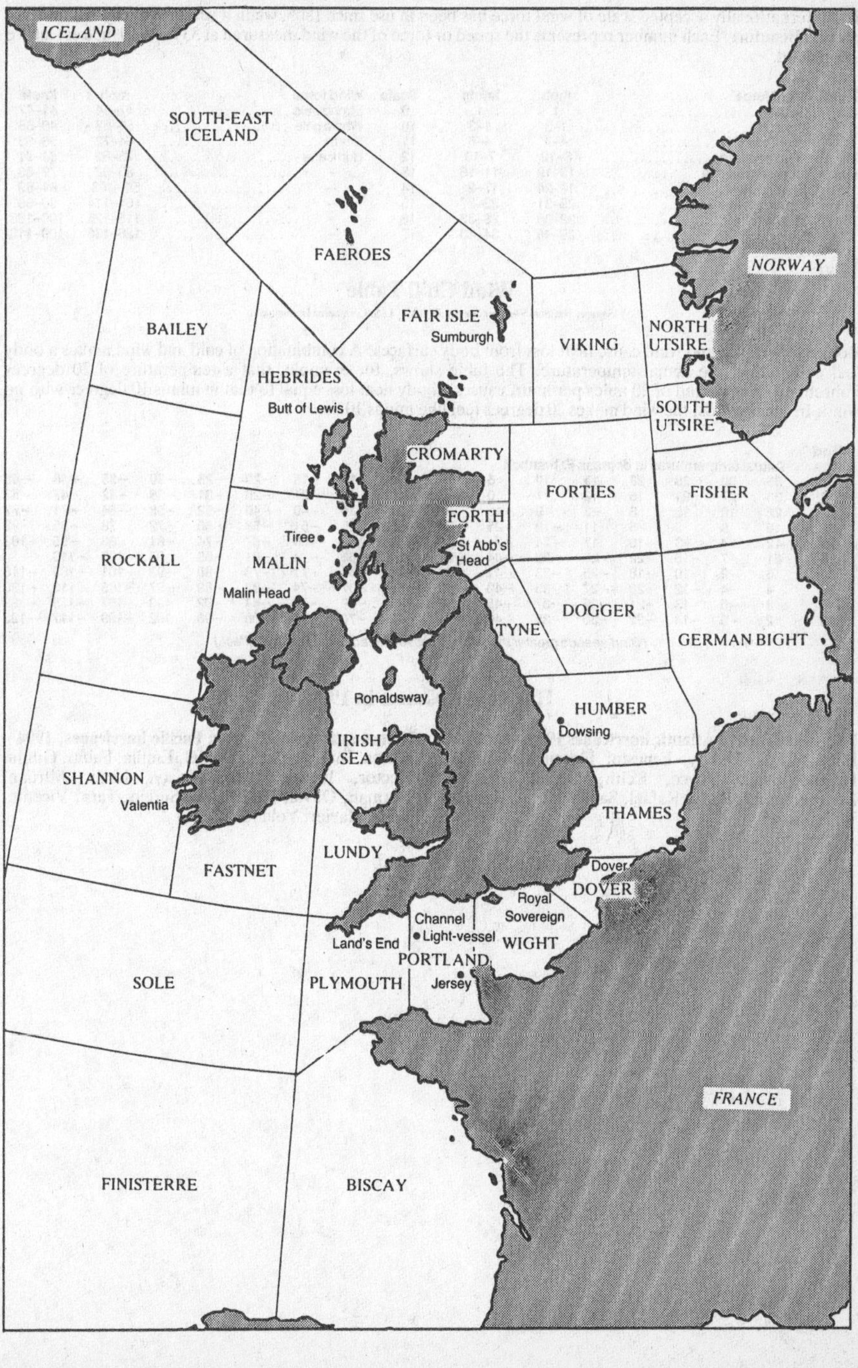

Beaufort Scale

The internationally accepted scale of wind force has been in use since 1805, when it was devised by Admiral Sir Francis Beaufort. Each number represents the speed or force of the wind measured at 33 feet (10 metres) above the ground.

Scale	Wind force	mph	knots
0	Calm	1	1
1	Light air	1–3	1–3
2	Slight breeze	4–7	4–6
3	Gentle breeze	8–12	7–10
4	Moderate breeze	13–18	11–16
5	Fresh breeze	19–24	17–21
6	Strong breeze	25–31	22–27
7	High wind	32–38	28–33
8	Gale	39–46	34–40
9	Strong gale	47–54	41–47
10	Whole gale	55–63	48–55
11	Storm	64–72	56–63
12	Hurricane	73–82	64–71
13	–	83–92	72–80
14	–	93–103	81–89
15	–	104–114	90–99
16	–	115–125	100–108
17	–	126–136	109–118

Wind Chill Table

Source: National Weather Service, NOAA, U.S. Commerce Department

Both temperature and wind cause heat loss from body surfaces. A combination of cold and wind makes a body feel colder than the actual temperature. The table shows, for example, that a temperature of 20 degrees Fahrenheit, plus a wind of 20 miles per hour, causes a body heat loss equal to that in minus 10 degrees with no wind. In other words, the wind makes 20 degrees feel like minus 10.

Wind speed (mph)	Actual temperatures in degrees Fahrenheit																
	35	30	25	20	15	10	5	0	−5	−10	−15	−20	−25	−30	−35	−40	−45
5	33	27	21	16	12	7	0	−5	−10	−15	−21	−26	−31	−36	−42	−47	−52
10	22	16	10	3	−3	−9	−15	−22	−27	−34	−40	−46	−52	−58	−64	−71	−77
15	16	9	2	−5	11	−18	−25	−31	−38	45	−51	−58	−65	−72	78	−85	−92
20	12	4	−3	−10	17	−24	−31	−39	−46	53	−60	−67	−74	−81	88	−95	−103
25	81	−7	−15	22	−29	−36	−44	−51	59	−66	−74	−81	−88	96	−103	−110	
30	6	−2	−10	−18	−25	−33	−41	−49	−56	−64	−71	−79	−86	−93	−101	−109	−116
35	4	−4	−12	−20	−27	−35	−43	−52	−58	−67	−74	−82	−89	−97	−105	−113	−120
40	3	−5	−13	−21	−29	−37	−45	−53	−60	−69	−76	−84	−92	100	−107	−115	−123
45	2	−6	−14	−22	−30	−38	−46	−54	−62	−70	−78	−85	−93	102	−109	−117	−125

(Wind speeds greater than 45 mph have little additional chilling effect.)

Hurricane Names in 1994

Names assigned to Atlantic hurricanes 1994 – Alberto, Beryl, Chris, Debby, Ernesto, Florence, Gordon, Helene, Isaac, Joyce, Keith, Leslie, Michael, Nadine, Oscar, Patty, Rafael, Sandy, Tony, Valerie, William.

Names assigned to Eastern Pacific hurricanes, 1994 – Aletta, Bud, Carlotta, Daniel, Emilia, Fabio, Gilma, Hector, Ileana, John, Kristy, Lane, Miriam, Norman, Olivia, Paul, Rosa, Sergio, Tara, Vicente, Willa, Xavier, Yolanda, Zeke.

ENVIRONMENT

Nine out of ten people claim to be interested in the environment, and recent improvements tend to support this claim. Many people now recognize the useful contribution that can be made by changes in their own behaviour, such as using recycled paper and conserving energy.

Regular bulletins about the shrinking ozone layer continue to keep people alert to the dangers of environmental damage. Indeed, the effectiveness of the message can be seen in the dramatic fall of CFC sales for use in aerosols – a drop of 75% between 1988 and 1990.

Water quality has also improved. Three-quarters of UK bathing waters met EC standards in 1991, and although there were 25,000 reported pollution incidents in Britain in 1991, only a few hundred resulted in prosecutions.

Of particular importance to children's health is the 75% drop in lead emissions from petrol between 1975 and 1990. Sulphur dioxide, a major pollutant and constituent of acid rain, has dropped by 40% over the last 20 years. Other atmospheric pollutants, such as carbon dioxide, have also been reduced, but this is largely because of cutbacks in industry arising from the recession.

British People's Environmental Concerns

How concerned are you about each of these environmental issues?

Source: SCPR's *British Social Attitudes* survey, 9th Report, ed. R. Jowell *et al.* (Dartmouth Publishing, 1992)

Percentages

	Very concerned	A bit concerned	Not very concerned	Not at all concerned	Don't know/ can't say
Insecticides, fertilizers and chemical sprays?	48.7	35.6	11.2	3.1	0.9
Disposal of sewage?	63.8	26.5	5.4	2.5	1.3
Thinning of the ozone layer?	51.8	31.7	9.7	2.7	3.5
Risks from núclear power stations?	49.2	29.9	14.0	5.2	1.1
The growth in the world's population?	38.1	35.2	20.1	4.2	1.8
The "greenhouse effect" – a rise in the world's temperature?	40.9	37.2	13.6	4.5	3.2
Using up the earth's remaining coal, oil and gas?	38.4	39.5	15.2	4.1	1.9
The quality of drinking water?	49.3	31.5	13.9	4.2	0.4
The loss of plant and animal species?	54.2	32.4	9.0	2.4	1.4
The transport and disposal of dangerous chemicals?	65.9	24.5	6.7	1.4	1.0

Personal Actions Taken to Improve the Environment, 1991–92

Great Britain

Source: CSO

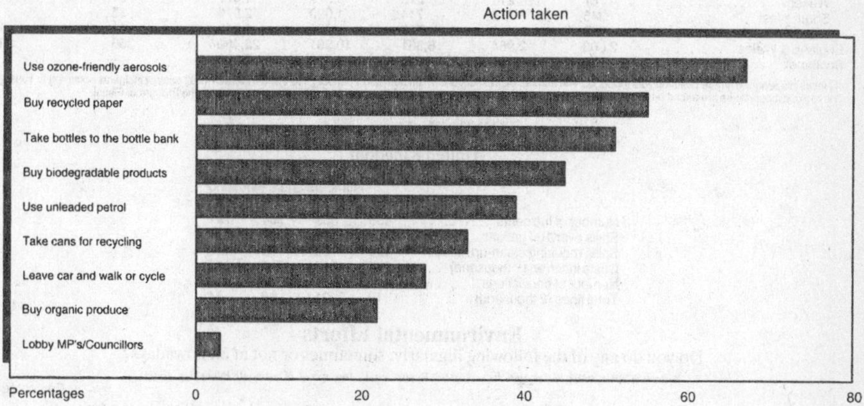

Membership of Selected Voluntary Environmental Organizations

Great Britain

Source: CSO

Thousands

	1971	1981	1991
Civic Trust[1]	214	–	222
Council for the Protection of Rural England	21	29	45
Friends of the Earth[2]	1	18	111
National Trust	278	1,046	2,152
National Trust for Scotland	37	110	234
Ramblers Association	22	37	87
Royal Society for Nature Conservation	64	143	250
Royal Society for the Protection of Birds	98	441	852
Woodland Trust	–	20	150
World Wide Fund for Nature	12	60	227

(1) Members of local amenity societies registered with the Civic Trust. (2) England and Wales only. Friends of the Earth (Scotland) is a separate organization founded in 1978.

Carbon Dioxide Emissions[1]: International Comparison

Source: CSO

Tonnes of carbon dioxide per head

	1960	1970	1980	1989
United Kingdom	11.8	12.1	10.4	10.1
Belgium	9.2	13.2	13.0	10.7
Denmark	6.6	13.0	12.3	10.1
France	5.8	8.4	8.9	6.7
Germany (Fed. Rep.)	9.6	12.2	13.1	11.1
Greece	1.0	2.5	5.0	7.2
Irish Republic	3.6	6.5	7.4	8.6
Italy	2.0	5.3	6.4	6.9
Luxembourg	46.0	46.8	34.1	28.2
Netherlands	6.6	10.1	10.9	10.4
Portugal	0.9	1.4	2.7	4.0
Spain	1.5	3.0	5.5	5.3
USA	15.9	20.6	20.1	19.4
Japan	2.4	6.9	7.6	8.1

(1) All fossil fuels, energy use only.

Average Household Water Use, 1991

Source: CSO

Percentages

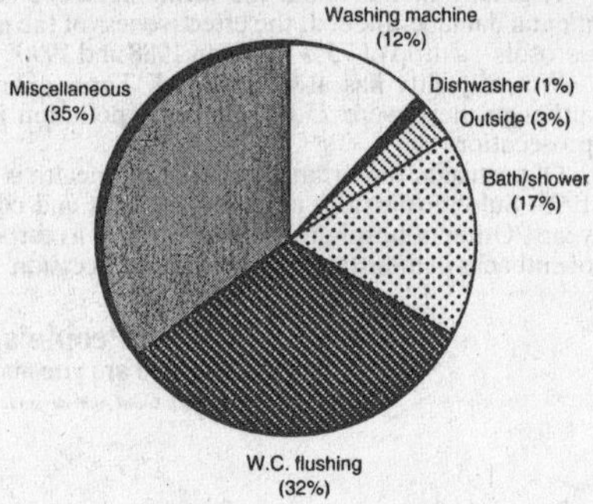

Water Pollution Incidents[1]: 1991

Great Britain

Source: CSO

Numbers

	Cause of pollution incident						
	Industrial	Farm	Sewage/ sewerage	Other	Total	Prosecutions[2]	Outstanding cases
North West	336	469	986	1,229	3,020	73	36
Northumbria	123	79	486	475	1,163	23	4
Severn Trent	608	402	1,329	2,016	4,355	48	0
Yorkshire	323	264	734	894	2,215	27	29
Anglian	194	212	570	1,164	2,140	37	12
Thames	211	78	416	1,234	1,939	46	7
Southern	168	93	376	1,098	1,735	5	13
Wessex	67	218	215	577	1,077	21	0
South West	345	718	714	1,099	2,876	35	3
Welsh[3]	428	421	525	575	1,949	41	15
England & Wales	2,803	2,954	6,351	10,361	22,469	356	119
Scotland[4]	758	567	880	1,003	3,208	–	–

(1) Incidents reported where pollution was found. (2) The number of prosecutions taken between 1 January 1991 and 31 March 1992 against incidents occurring in 1991. (3) The regional boundaries are based on river catchment areas and not county borders. (4) In Scotland 65 incidents were referred to the Procurator Fiscal.

Oil Spills Reported

United Kingdom

Source: CSO

Numbers and £ thousand

	1986	1988	1989	1990
Number of incidents	436	559	764	791
Spills over 100 gallons	103	110	132	174
Spills requiring clean-up	126	120	160	136
Costs incurred (£ thousand)	134	217	234	1,193
Number of convictions	7	15	30	22
Total fines (£ thousand)	19	21	48	54

Environmental Efforts

Do you do any of the following regularly, sometimes or not at all nowadays?

Source: SCPR's *British Social Attitudes* survey, 9th Report, ed. R. Jowell *et al.* (Dartmouth Publishing, 1992)

Percentages

	Does			Intends to		
	Regularly	Sometimes	Not at all	Yes	No	Don't know
Return bottles, tins, newspapers and so on for recycling?	32.4	30.8	36.3	12.0	18.5	5.0
Buy organically grown fruit and vegetables?	7.8	38.3	52.8	7.7	36.8	5.9
Buy toiletries or cosmetics not tested on animals?	33.1	34.0	29.7	5.0	18.4	4.6
Buy environment-friendly washing powders or detergents?	31.0	30.7	35.2	5.9	22.6	5.5
Choose to eat less meat?	25.5	26.7	47.0	3.3	40.8	1.4
Choose products made out of recycled materials?	23.2	47.7	27.7	4.6	18.1	3.7
Make a conscious effort to save electricity?	47.8	31.8	19.9	5.9	11.4	1.6
Cut back on driving your car?	12.1	18.2	35.4	3.9	28.8	1.5
Buy environment-friendly aerosols?	55.4	25.8	17.2	2.0	12.1	2.0
Refuse unnecessary packaging or wrapping?	17.4	32.4	49.3	8.3	32.6	5.4
Buy free-range chicken or eggs?	38.7	33.3	26.7	3.9	18.8	2.8

Nuclear Power

Source: SCPR's *British Social Attitudes* survey, 9th Report, ed. R. Jowell *et al.* (Dartmouth Publishing, 1992)

	1983	1984	1985	1986	1987	1989	1990	1991
Percentage saying that . . .								
Nuclear power stations create very serious risks for the future	35	37	30	49	37	40	43	40
Waste from nuclear electricity stations has a very serious effect	63	69	58	72	60	67	64	58

Public Opinion on Environmental Problems: International Comparison, 1991

Source: CSO

	Percentage of people who think the problem is very serious		
	Greenhouse effect	Acid rain	Ozone layer damage
United Kingdom	65	72	73
Belgium	63	75	74
Denmark	67	68	72
France	64	74	77
Germany (Fed. Rep.)	79	74	83
Germany (Dem. Rep.)	77	76	83
Greece	89	85	91
Irish Republic	65	64	73
Italy	79	77	85
Luxembourg	85	84	88
Netherlands	55	70	66
Portugal	75	74	83
Spain	76	78	82
European Community	72	74	80

New Tree Planting

Source: CSO

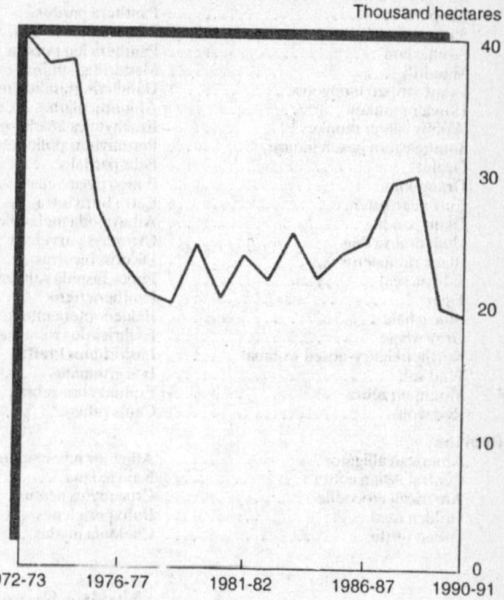

Some Endangered World Species

Sources: Fish and Wildlife Service, U.S. Dept. of Interior, and IUCN *Red List*, as of 30 July 1992

The species are arranged alphabetically by their common name (bat, bear, cheetah, deer, dolphin, etc.)

Common name	Scientific name	Range
Birds		
White cockatoo	Cacatua alba	Mollucas (Indonesia)
California condor	Gymnogyps californianus	U.S. (Ore., Cal.)
Hooded crane	Grus monacha	Japan, USSR
Whooping crane	Grus americana	Canada, U.S.
Whited-necked crow	Corvus leucognaphalus	U.S. (P.R.), Dominican Rep.
Eskimo curlew	Numenius borealis	Alaska and N. Canada
Bald eagle	Haliaeetus leucocephalus	U.S. (most states), Canada
American peregrine falcon	Falco peregrinus anatum	Canada to Mexico
Hawaiian hawk	Buteo solitarius	U.S. (Hi.)
Crested ibis	Nipponia nippon	China, Japan
Indigo macaw	Anodorhynchus leari	Brazil
West African ostrich	Struthio camelus spatzi	Spanish Sahara
Golden parakeet	Aratinga guarouba	Brazil
Australian parrot	Geopsittacus occidentalis	Australia
Attwater's greater prairie-chicken	Tympanuchus cupido attwateri	U.S. (Tex.)
Bachman's warbler (wood)	Vermivora bachmanii	U.S. (Southeast), Cuba
Kirtland's warbler (wood)	Dendroica kirtlandii	U.S., Canada, Bahama Is.
Ivory-billed woodpecker	Campephilus principalis	U.S. (Southcentral and Southeast), Cuba
Fish		
Cave catfish	Clarias cavernicola	Namibia
Bonytail chub	Gila elegans	U.S. (Ariz., Cal., Col., Nev., Ut., Wyo.)
Trout cod	Maccullochella macquariensis	Australia
Adriatic salmon	Salmothymus obtusirostris	Yugoslavia
Common sturgeon	Acipenser sturio	Europe
Gila trout	Salmo gilae	U.S. (Ariz., N.M.)
Mammals		
Asian wild ass	Equus hemionus	Southwestern & Central Asia
Polar bear	Ursus maritimus	Arctic
Broad-tail beaver	Castor canadensis frondator	Mexico
European bison	Bison bonasus	Poland, USSR
Bobcat	Felis rufus escuinapae	Central Mexico
Brown or grizzly bear	Ursus arctos horribilis	U.S. (48 conterminous states)
Chartreuse chamois	Rupicapra rupicapra cartusiana	France
Cheetah	Acinonyx jubatus	Africa to India
Chimpanzee	Pan troglodytes	Eq. Africa
Eastern cougar	Felis concolor cougar	Eastern N.A.
Columbian white-tailed deer	Odocoileus virginianus leucurus	U.S. (Wash., Ore.)
Pyrenean desman	Galemys pyrenaicus	France, Portugal, Spain
Chinese river dolphin	Lipotes vexillifer	China
Indus river dolphin	Platanista minor	Pakistan
Indian elephant	Elephas maximus	Southcentral, Southeast Asia
Gorilla	Gorilla gorilla	Central & W. Africa
South African hedgehog	Atelerix frontalis	South Africa

(Continued)

Common name	Scientific name	Range
Mammals *(Continued)*		
Pygmy hippopotamus	Choeropsis liberiensis	West Africa
Mongoose lemur	Lemur mongoz	Madagascar, Comoros
Leopard	Panthera pardus	Africa, Asia
Snow leopard	Panthera uncia	Asia
Asiatic lion	Panthera leo persica	Turkey to India
Mandrill	Mandrillus sphinx	Cameroon, Congo, Eq. Guinea, Gabon
Giant-striped mongoose	Galidictis grandidiensis	Madagascar
Howler monkey	Alouatta pigra	Mexico to S. America
Woolly spider monkey	Brachyteles arachnoides	Brazil
Southeastern beach mouse	Peromyscus polionotus phasma	U.S. (Fla.)
Ocelot	Felis pardalis	U.S. (Tex., Ariz.)
Orang-utan	Pongo pygmaeus	Borneo, Sumatra
European otter	Lutra lutra lutra	Eurasia
Giant panda	Ailuropoda melanoleuca	China
Utah prairie dog	Cynomys parvidens	U.S. (Ut.)
Black rhinoceros	Diceros bicornis	Sub-Saharan Africa
Saimaa seal	Phoca hispida saimensis	Finland
Tiger	Panthera tigris	Asia
Blue whale	Balaenoptera musculus	All oceans
Grey whale	Eschrichtius robustus	N. Pacific Ocean
Northern hairy-nosed wombat	Lasiorhinus krefftii	Australia
Wild yak	Bos grunniens	China (Tibet), India
Mountain zebra	Equus zebra zebra	South Africa
Red wolf	Canis rufus	U.S. (Southeast to central Tex.)
Reptiles		
American alligator	Alligator mississippiensis	U.S (Southeastern)
Central Asian cobra	Naja oxiana	Central Asia
American crocodile	Crocodylus acutus	U.S. (Fla.)
Golden toad	Bufo periglenes	Costa Rica
Green turtle	Chelonia mydas	Tropical seas & Medit.

Native Species at Risk, 1991

Great Britain

Source: CSO

	Number of native species	Number extinct	Number endangered	Number vulnerable	Number rare
Plants					
Stoneworts	29	2	4	6	6
Lichens	1,500	25	57	63	176
Liverworts/mosses	1,000	16	30	59	117
Ferns and related plants	69	0	3	2	3
Seed plants	1,425	19	48	91	151
Animals					
Leeches	16	0	0	0	1
Non-marine molluscs	200	0	10	7	11
Larger non-marine crustaceans	70	1	2	1	2
Spiders/harvestmen/pseudoscorpions	670	0	22	31	29
Mayflies	47	0	1	2	1
Dragonflies/damselflies	41	3	1	2	3
Stoneflies	33	1	0	1	0
Grasshoppers/crickets/cockroaches	30	0	3	2	1
True bugs	540	7	13	6	53
Caddis flies	196	2	7	7	8
Butterflies/moths	2,400	22	21	22	55
Beetles	3,900	64	132	84	266
Bees/wasps/ants	520	31	27	20	54
Flies	6,000	13	208	223	312
Freshwater fish[1]	41	2	2	3	2
Amphibians	6	0	1	1	0
Non-marine reptiles	6	0	2	0	0

(1) Includes fish which leave the sea to breed in fresh water.

Speeds of Animals

Source: *Natural History* magazine, March 1974. © The American Museum of Natural History, 1974.

Animal	Mph	Animal	Mph	Animal	Mph
Cheetah	70	Mongolian wild ass	40	Human	27.89
Pronghorn antelope	61	Greyhound	39.35	Elephant	25
Wildebeest	50	Whippet	35.50	Black mamba snake	20
Lion	50	Rabbit (domestic)	35	Six-lined race runner	18
Thomson's gazelle	50	Mule deer	35	Wild turkey	15
Quarterhorse	47.5	Jackal	35	Squirrel	12
Elk	45	Reindeer	32	Pig (domestic)	11
Cape hunting dog	45	Giraffe	32	Chicken	9
Coyote	43	White-tailed deer	30	Spider (Tegenaria atrica)	1.17
Grey fox	42	Wart hog	30	Giant tortoise	0.17
Hyena	40	Grizzly bear	30	Three-toed sloth	0.15
Zebra	40	Cat (domestic)	30	Garden snail	0.03

Most of these measurements are for maximum speeds over approximate quarter-mile distances. Exceptions are the lion and elephant, whose speeds were clocked in the act of charging; the whippet, which was timed over a 200-yard course; the cheetah timed over a 100-yard distance; human, timed for a 15-yard segment of a 100-yard run (of 13.6 seconds); and the black mamba, six-lined race runner, spider, giant tortoise, three-toed sloth and garden snail, which were measured over various small distances.

Mammals: Orders and Major Families

Subclass Theria
Infraclass Placentalia

(Columns: Family — Suborder / Infraorder / Superfamily — Order)

Order Carnivora

- Suborder Fissipedia (toe-footed)
  - Superfamily Canoidea — Canoids have long snouts and unretractable claws.
    - **Canidae:** wolf, dog, jackal, fox
    - **Ursidae:** bear, giant panda
    - **Procyonidae:** coati, racoon, lesser panda
    - **Mustelidae:** badger, weasel, skunk, otter
  - Superfamily Feloidea — Feloids have retractable claws.
    - **Felidae:** cat, leopard, lion, tiger, cheetah
    - **Hyaenidae:** hyena, aardwolf
    - **Viverridae:** mongoose, civet
- Suborder Pinnipedia (fin-footed)
  - **Otariidae:** eared seals, sea lion
  - **Odobenidae:** walrus
  - **Phocidae:** earless seals

Most carnivora also eat some plants and insects.

Order Artiodactyla — The artiodactyla have an even number of toes.

- Suborder Suiformes
  - Suina
    - **Suidae:** pig
    - **Tayassuidae:** peccary
  - Ancodonta
    - **Hippopotamidae:** hippopotamus
- Tylopoda
  - **Camelidae:** camel, llama
- Ruminantia
  - **Giraffidae:** giraffe, okapi
  - **Cervidae:** deer, moose, reindeer, wapiti (elk)
  - **Antilocapridae:** pronghorn
  - Bovoidea
    - Family Bovidae — All ruminants have 4-chamber stomachs and chew cuds.
      - Subfamily
        - **Bovinae:** cattle, eland, kudu, bison, yak
        - **Hippotraginae:** sable, oryx, waterbuck
        - **Acelaphinae:** hartebeest, wildebeest (gnu)
        - **Antilopinae:** gazelle, springbok, saiga
        - **Caprinae:** sheep, goat, musk ox

Order Perissodactyla — The perissodactyla have an odd number of toes.

- Family
- Hippomorpha
  - **Equidae:** horse, donkey zebra
- Ceratomorpha
  - **Tapiridae:** tapir
  - **Rhinocerotidae:** rhinoceros

Order Rodentia — Rodents are the most numerous of all mammals. Rodent suborders are distinguished by the placement of a major jaw muscle.

- Sciuromorpha
  - **Aplodontidae:** mountain beaver
  - **Sciuridae:** chipmunk, squirrel, marmot
- Myomorpha
  - **Cricetidae:** field mice, lemming, muskrat, hamster, gerbil
  - **Muridae:** rat, Old World mice
  - **Heteromyidae:** New World mice
  - **Geomyidae:** gopher
  - **Dipodidae:** jerboa
- Caviomorpha
  - **Chinchillidae:** chinchilla
  - **Dasyproctidae:** agouti, paca
  - **Erethizontidae:** New World porcupine
- **Hystricidae:** Old World porcupine
- **Castoridae:** beaver

Order Chiroptera

- Bats - various familes

Order Lagomorpha

- **Leporidae:** rabbit, hare
- **Ochotonidae:** pika

Order Pholidata

- **Manidae:** pangolin

Order Insectivora

- **Erinaceidae:** hedgehog
- **Talpidae:** mole
- **Saricidae:** some shrews

Order Edentate (toothless)

- Loricata
  - **Dasypodidae:** armadillo
- Pilosa
  - **Bradypodidae:** sloth
- Vermilingua
  - **Myrmecophagidae:** hairy anteater

Order Cetacea

- Odontoceti (toothed)
  - **Physeteridae:** sperm whale
  - **Monodontidae:** narwhal, beluga
  - **Phocoenidae:** porpoise
  - **Delphinidae:** dolphin, killer whale
- Mysticeti (baleen)
  - **Eschrichtiidae:** gray whale
  - **Balaenidae:** right whale
  - **Balaenopteridae:** humpback whale

Order Sirenea

- Manatee, dugong

Order Proboscidea

- **Elephantidae:** elephant

Order Primates — Most primates have opposable thumbs; all but man have opposable big toes.

- Prosimii — The prosimians usually have longer snouts than anthropoids.
  - **Tupaiidae:** tree shrew
  - **Lemuridae:** lemur
  - **Daubentoniidae:** aye-aye
  - **Lorisidae:** loris, potto
  - **Tarsiidae:** tarsier
- Anthropoidea
  - **Callitrichidae:** marmoset
  - **Cebidae:** New World monkeys (flat-nosed)
  - **Cercopithecidae:** baboon, Old World monkeys (long-nosed, bare buttocks)
  - **Hylobatidae:** gibbon
  - **Pongidae** (great apes): gorilla, chimpanzee, orangutan
  - **Hominidae:** human

Infraclass Marsupialia

Order Marsupicanivora

- Dasyuroidea
  - **Dasyuridae:** mouse- and ratlike, Tasmanian devil
  - **Notoryctidae:** molelike
  - **Thylacinidae:** wolflike
- Didelphoidea
  - **Didelphidae:** American opossums

Order Paucituberculata

- **Caenolestidae:** ratlike So. America only

Order Peramalina

- **Peramelidae:** bandicoot

Order Diprodonta

- Phalangeroidea
  - **Burramyidae:** mouse- and squirrellike
  - **Macropodidae:** kangaroo, wallaby
  - **Petauridae:** squirrellike, some Australian possums
  - **Phalangeridae:** cuscus, some Australian possums
- Tarsipedoidea
  - **Tarsipedidae:** honey possum
- Vombatoidea
  - **Vombatidae:** wombat
  - **Phascolarctidae:** koala

Subclass Prototheria

Order Monotremata

- **Ornithorhynchidae:** duck-billed platypus
- **Tachyglossidae:** echidna (spiny anteater)

Gestation, Longevity and Incubation of Animals

Average longevity figures were supplied by Ronald T. Reuther. They refer to animals in captivity; the potential life span of animals is rarely attained in nature. Maximum longevity figures are from *The Biology Data Book*, 1972. Figures on gestation and incubation are averages based on estimates by leading authorities.

Animal	Gestation (days)	Average longevity (years)	Maximum longevity (yrs., mos.)
Ass	365	12	35-10
Baboon	187	20	35-7
Bear: Black	219	18	36-10
Grizzly	225	25	–
Polar	240	20	34-8
Beaver	122	5	20-6
Bison	278	15	–
Camel, bactrian	406	12	29-5
Cat (domestic)	63	12	28
Chimpanzee	231	20	44-6
Chipmunk	31	6	8
Cow	284	15	30
Deer (white-tailed)	201	8	17-6
Dog (domestic)	61	12	20
Elephant (African)	–	35	60
Elephant (Asian)	645	40	70
Elk	250	15	26-6
Fox (red)	52	7	14
Giraffe	425	10	33-7
Goat (domestic)	151	8	18
Gorilla	257	20	39-4
Guinea pig	68	4	7-6
Hippopotamus	238	25	–
Horse	330	20	46
Kangaroo	42	7	–
Leopard	98	12	19-4
Lion	100	15	25-1
Monkey (rhesus)	164	15	–
Moose	240	12	–
Mouse (meadow)	21	3	–
Mouse (dom. white)	19	3	3-6
Opossum (American)	14-17	1	–
Pig (domestic)	112	10	27
Puma	90	12	19
Rabbit (domestic)	31	5	13
Rhinoceros (black)	450	15	–
Rhinoceros (white)	–	20	–
Sea lion (California)	350	12	28
Sheep (domestic)	154	12	20
Squirrel (grey)	44	10	–
Tiger	105	16	26-3
Wolf (maned)	63	5	–
Zebra (Grant's)	365	15	–

Animal	Incubation time (days)
Chicken	21
Duck	30
Goose	30
Pigeon	18
Turkey	26

Major Venomous Animals

Snakes

Coral snake – 2 to 4 ft. long, in Americas south of Canada; bite is nearly painless; very slow onset of paralysis, difficulty breathing; mortality high without antivenin.

Rattlesnake – 2 to 8 ft. long, throughout W. Hemisphere. Rapid onset of symptoms of severe pain, swelling; mortality low, but amputation of affected limb is sometimes necessary; antivenin. Probably higher mortality rate for Mojave rattler.

Cottonmouth water moccasin – up to 5 ft. long, wetlands of southern U.S. from Virginia to Texas. Rapid onset of symptoms of severe pain, swelling; mortality low, but tissue destruction can be extensive; antivenin.

Copperhead – less than 4 ft. long, from New England to Texas; pain and swelling; very seldom fatal; antivenin seldom needed.

Bushmaster – up to 12 ft. long, wet tropical forests of C. and S. America; few bites occur, but mortality rate is high.

Barba Amarilla or **Fer-de-lance** – up to 7 ft. long, from tropical Mexico to Brazil; severe tissue damage common; moderate mortality; antivenin.

Asian pit vipers – from 2 to 5 ft. long throughout Asia; reactions and mortality vary but most bites cause tissue damage and mortality is generally low.

Sharp-nosed pit viper or **One Hundred Pace Snake** – up to 5 ft. long, in southern Vietnam and Taiwan, China; the most toxic of Asian pit vipers; very rapid onset of swelling and tissue damage, internal bleeding; moderate mortality; antivenin.

Boomslang – under 6 ft. long, in African savannahs; rapid onset of nausea and dizziness, often followed by slight recovery and then sudden death from internal hemorrhaging; bites rare, mortality high; antivenin.

European vipers – from 1 to 3 ft. long; bleeding and tissue damage; mortality low; antivenins.

Puff adder – up to 5 ft. long, fat; south of the Sahara and throughout the Middle East; rapid large swelling, great pain, dizziness; moderate mortality often from internal bleeding; antivenin.

Gaboon viper – over 6 ft. long, fat; 2-inch fangs; south of the Sahara; massive tissue damage, internal bleeding; few recorded bites.

Saw-scaled or carpet viper – up to 2 ft. long, in dry areas from India to Africa; severe bleeding, fever; high mortality, causes more human fatalities than any other snake; antivenin.

Desert horned viper – in dry areas of Africa and western Asia; swelling and tissue damage; low mortality; antivenin.

Russell's viper or tic-palonga – over 5 ft. long, throughout Asia; internal bleeding; moderate mortality rate; bite reports common; antivenin.

Black mamba – up to 14 ft. long, fast-moving; S. and C. Africa; rapid onset of dizziness, difficulty breathing, erratic heart-beat; mortality high, nears 100% without antivenin.

Kraits – in S. Asia; rapid onset of sleepiness; numbness; up to 50% mortality even with antivenin treatment.

Common or Asian cobra – 4 to 8 ft. long, throughout S. Asia; considerable tissue damage, sometimes paralysis; mortality probably not more than 10%; antivenin.

King cobra – up to 16 ft. long, throughout S. Asia; rapid swelling, dizziness, loss of consciousness, difficulty breathing, erratic heart-beat; mortality varies sharply with amount of venom involved, most bites involve non-fatal amounts; antivenin.

Yellow or Cape cobra – 7 ft. long, in southern Africa; most toxic venom of any cobra; rapid onset of swelling, breathing and cardiac difficulties; mortality high without treatment; antivenin.

Ringhals, or spitting, cobra – 5 ft. and 7 ft. long; southern Africa; squirt venom through holes in front of fangs as a defense; venom is severely irritating and can cause blindness.

Australian brown snakes – very slow onset of symptoms of cardiac or respiratory distress; moderate mortality; antivenin.

Tiger snake – 2 to 6 ft. long, S. Australia; pain, numbness, mental disturbances with rapid onset of paralysis; may be the most deadly of all land snakes though antivenin is quite effective.

Death adder – less than 3 ft. long, Australia; rapid onset of faintness, cardiac and respiratory distress; at least 50% mortality without antivenin.

Taipan – up to 11 ft. long, in Australia and New Guinea; rapid paralysis with severe breathing difficulty; mortality nears 100% without antivenin.

Sea snakes – throughout Pacific, Indian oceans except NE Pacific; almost painless bite, variety of muscle pain, paralysis; mortality rate low, many bites are not envenomed; some antivenins.

Notes: Not all snake bites by venomous snakes are actually envenomed. Any animal bite, however, carries the danger of tetanus and anyone suffering a venomous snake bite should seek medical attention. Antivenins are not certain cures; they are only an aid in the treatment of bites. Mortality rates above are for envenomed bites; low mortality, up to 2% result in death; moderate, 2–5%; high, 5–15%. Even when the victim recovers fully, prolonged hospitalization and extensive medical procedures are usually required.

Lizards

Gila monster – up to 24 inches long with heavy body and tail, in high desert in southwest U.S. and N. Mexico; immediate severe pain followed by vomiting, thirst, difficulty swallowing, weakness approaching paralysis; no recent mortality.

Mexican beaded lizard – similar to Gila monster, Mexican west coast; reaction and mortality rate similar to Gila monster.

Insects

Ants, bees, wasps, hornets, etc. Global distribution. Usual reaction is piercing pain in area of sting. Not directly fatal, except in cases of massive multiple stings. Many people suffer allergic reactions – swelling, rashes, partial paralysis – and a few may die within minutes from severe sensitivity to the venom (anaphylactic shock).

Spiders, scorpions

Black widow – small, round-bodied with hour-glass marking; the widow and its relatives are found around the world in tropical and temperate zones; sharp pain, weakness, clammy skin, muscular rigidity, breathing difficulty and, in small children, convulsions; low mortality; antivenin.
Recluse or fiddleback and brown spiders – small, oblong body; throughout U.S.; pain with later ulceration at place of bite; in severe cases fever, nausea, and stomach cramps; ulceration may last months; very low mortality.
Atrax spiders – several varieties, often large, in Australia; slow onset of breathing, circulation difficulties; low mortality.
Tarantulas – large, hairy spiders found around the world; American tarantulas, and probably all others, are harmless, though their bite may cause some pain and swelling.
Scorpions – crab-like body with stinger in tail, various sizes, many varieties throughout tropical and subtropical areas; various symptoms may include severe pain spreading from the wound, numbness, severe emotional agitation, cramps; severe reactions include vomiting, diarrhea, respiratory failure; low mortality, usually in children; antivenins.

Sea Life

Sea wasps – jellyfish, with tentacles up to 30 ft. long, in the S. Pacific; very rapid onset of circulatory problems; high mortality largely because of speed of toxic reaction; antivenin.
Portuguese man-of-war – jellyfish-like, with tentacles up to 70 ft. long, in most warm water areas; immediate severe pain; not fatal, though shock may cause death in a rare case.
Octopuses – global distribution, usually in warm waters; all varieties produce venom but only a few can cause death; rapid onset of paralysis with breathing difficulty.
Stingrays – several varieties of differing sizes, found in tropical and temperate seas and some fresh water; severe pain, rapid onset of nausea, vomiting, breathing difficulties; wound area may ulcerate, gangrene may appear; seldom fatal.
Stonefish – brownish fish which lies motionless as a rock on bottom in shallow water; throughout S. Pacific and Indian oceans; extraordinary pain, rapid paralysis; low mortality.
Cone-shells – molluscs in small, beautiful shells in the S. Pacific and Indian oceans; shoot barbs into victims; paralysis; low mortality.

Measuring Earthquakes

Earthquakes are measured either on the Mercalli Scale of intensity or the Richter Scale of magnitude. The value given on the Mercalli Scale measures the power of a quake at a given place and varies according to how far the observer is from the epicentre. The Richter Scale, being logarithmic, gives more precise measurements of the energy released during an earthquake. For example, a quake of magnitude 5 is ten times more powerful than one of magnitude 4, magnitude 6 is ten times more powerful than 5, and so on.

Mercalli Scale		Approx. equivalent on Richter Scale at a depth of 6 miles (10 km)
1	Not felt, except under ideal conditions	–
2	Felt by a few at rest. Delicately suspended objects swing	2.5
3	Felt noticeably indoors. Standing cars may rock	–
4	Felt generally indoors. People awakened; windows rattled	3.5
5	Felt generally. Some falling plaster; dishes, windows broken	4.5
6	Felt by all. Chimneys damaged, furniture moved; difficult to walk	–
7	People run outdoors. Felt in moving cars. Moderate damage	5.5
8	General alarm. Damage to weak structures; monuments and walls fall	6.0
9	Total destruction of weak structures; ground fissured	7.0
10	Panic. Strongest buildings survive, ground badly cracked, rails bent	–
11	Few buildings survive. Broad fissures; underground pipes broken	8.0
12	Total destruction. Ground waves seen; uncontrollable panic	8.6

WEIGHTS AND MEASURES

Source: Based on information from the National Institute of Standards and Technology, U.S. Dept. of Commerce

Two systems of weights and measures exist side by side in the United Kingdom today: the Imperial System (yards, pounds and gallons) and the Metric System (metres, kilograms and litres). The Système International d'Unités (SI) is a fuller version of the Metric System and was designed to meet the specific needs of science and technology. Seven units have been adopted to serve as the base for the International System, as follows: **length** – metre; **mass** – kilogram; **time** – second; **electric current** – ampere; **thermodynamic temperature** – kelvin; **amount of substance** – mole; **luminous intensity** – candela.

The U.S. Customary System is based on the British Imperial System, but is now different from it. For example, the U.S. pint contains 16 fl oz, while the Imperial pint contains 20. Some of the other U.S. variations appear in the information that follows.

International System Prefixes

The following prefixes, in combination with the basic unit names, provide the multiples and submultiples in the International System. For example, the unit name "metre" with the prefix "kilo" added produces "kilometre", meaning "1,000 metres".

Prefix	Symbol	Multiples	Equivalent
exa	E	10^{18}	quintillionfold
peta	P	10^{15}	quadrillionfold
tera	T	10^{12}	trillionfold
giga	G	10^{9}	billionfold
mega	M	10^{6}	millionfold
kilo	k	10^{3}	thousandfold
hecto	h	10^{2}	hundredfold
deca	da	10	tenfold

Prefix	Symbol	Submultiples	Equivalent
deci	d	10^{-1}	tenth part
centi	c	10^{-2}	hundredth part
milli	m	10^{-3}	thousandth part
micro	µ	10^{-6}	millionth part
nano	n	10^{-9}	billionth part
pico	p	10^{-12}	trillionth part
femto	f	10^{-15}	quadrillionth part
atto	a	10^{-18}	quintillionth part

Metric Weights and Measures

Linear Measure

10 millimetres (mm)	= 1 centimetre (cm)
10 centimetres	= 1 decimetre (dm) = 100 millimetres
10 decimetres	= 1 metre (m) = 1,000 millimetres
10 metres	= 1 decametre (dam)
10 decametres	= 1 hectometre (hm) = 100 metres
10 hectometres	= 1 kilometre (km) = 1,000 metres

Area Measure

100 square millimetres (mm^2)	= 1 square centimetre (cm^2)
10,000 square centimetres	= 1 square metre (m^2) = 1,000,000 square millimetres
100 square metres	= 1 are (a)
100 ares	= 1 hectare (ha) = 10,000 square metres
100 hectares	= 1 square kilometre (km^2) = 1,000,000 square metres

Fluid Volume Measure

10 millilitres (ml)	= 1 centilitre (cl)
10 centilitres	= 1 decilitre (dl) = 100 millilitres
10 decilitres	= 1 litre (l or L) = 1,000 millilitres
10 litres	= 1 decalitre (dal)
10 decalitres	= 1 hectolitre (hl) = 100 litres
10 hectolitres	= 1 kilolitre (kl) = 1,000 litres

Cubic Measure

1,000 cubic millimetres (mm^3)	= 1 cubic centimetre (cm^3)
1,000 cubic centimetres	= 1 cubic decimetre (dm^3) = 1,000,000 cubic millimetres
1,000 cubic decimetres	= 1 cubic metre (m^3) = 1 stere = 1,000,000 cubic centimetres = 1,000,000,000 cubic millimetres

Weight

10 milligrams (mg)	= 1 centigram (cg)
10 centigrams	= 1 decigram (dg) = 100 milligrams
10 decigrams	= 1 gram (g) = 1,000 milligrams
10 grams	= 1 decagram (dag)
10 decagrams	= 1 hectogram (hg) = 100 grams
10 hectograms	= 1 kilogram (kg) = 1,000 grams
1,000 kilograms	= 1 tonne or metric ton (t)

Imperial Weights and Measures

Linear Measure

12 inches (in)	= 1 foot (ft)
3 feet	= 1 yard (yd)
5½ yards	= 1 rod (rd), pole, or perch (16½ feet)
40 rods	= 1 furlong (fur)= 220 yards= 660 feet
8 furlongs	= 1 statute mile (mi) = 1,760 yards = 5,280 feet
3 miles	= 1 league = 5,280 yards = 15,840 feet
6076.11549 feet	= 1 International Nautical Mile

Liquid Measure

When necessary to distinguish the liquid pint or quart from the dry pint or quart, the word "liquid" or the abbreviation "liq" should be used with the name or abbreviation of the liquid unit.

4 gills	= 1 pint (pt) = 34.65 cubic inches
2 pints	= 1 quart (qt) = 69.3 cubic inches
4 quarts	= 1 gallon (gal) = 277.2 cubic inches = 8 pints = 32 gills

Area Measure

Squares and cubes of units are sometimes abbreviated by using "superior" figures. For example, ft^2 means square foot, and ft^3 means cubic foot.

144 square inches	= 1 square foot (ft^2)
9 square feet	= 1 square yard (yd^2) = 1,296 square inches
30¼ square yards	= 1 square rod (rd^2) = 272¼ square feet
160 square rods	= 1 acre = 4,840 square yards = 43,560 square feet
640 acres	= 1 square mile (mi^2)

Cubic Measure

1 cubic foot (ft^3)	= 1,728 cubic inches (in^3)
27 cubic feet	= 1 cubic yard (yd^3)

Gunter's or Surveyors' Chain Measure

7.92 inches (in)	= 1 link
100 links	= 1 chain (ch) = 4 rods = 22 yards
80 chains	= 1 mile (mi) = 320 rods = 5,280 feet

Troy Weight

24 grains	= 1 pennyweight (dwt)
20 pennyweights	= 1 ounce troy (oz t) = 480 grains
12 ounces troy	= 1 pound troy (lb t) = 240 pennyweights = 5,760 grains

Dry Measure

When necessary to distinguish the dry pint or quart from the liquid pint or quart, the word "dry" should be used in combination with the name or abbreviation of the dry unit.

2 pints (pt)	= 1 quart (qt) = 69.3 cubic inches
8 quarts	= 1 peck (pk) = 554.4 cubic inches = 16 pints
4 pecks	= 1 bushel (bu) = 2,217.6 cubic inches = 32 quarts

Avoirdupois Weight

When necessary to distinguish the avoirdupois ounce or pound from the troy ounce or pound, the word "avoirdupois" or the abbreviation "avdp" should be used in combination with the name or abbreviation of the avoirdupois unit.

(The "grain" is the same in avoirdupois and troy weight.)

$27\frac{11}{32}$ grains	= 1 dram (dr)
16 drams	= 1 ounce (oz) = 437½ grains
16 ounces	= 1 pound (lb) = 256 drams = 7,000 grains
14 pounds	= 1 stone
2 stones	= 1 quarter = 28 pounds
4 quarters	= 1 hundredweight (cwt) = 112 pounds
20 hundredweights	= 1 ton = 2,240 pounds*

The "short" or "net" hundredweight and ton, used commercially in the U.S., are worth 100 pounds and 2000 pounds respectively. Americans refer to the Imperial measures as "gross" or "long".

Tables of Equivalents

Equivalents involving decimals are, in most instances, rounded off to the third decimal place except where they are exact, in which cases these exact equivalents are so designated.

Lengths

1 angstrom (Å)	0.1 nanometre (exactly) 0.0001 micrometre (exactly) 0.0000001 millimetre (exactly) 0.000000004 inch
1 centimetre (cm)	0.3937 inch
1 chain (ch)	66 feet (exactly) 20.1168 metres
1 decimetre (dm)	3.937 inches
1 degree (geographical)	364,566.929 feet 69.047 miles (avg.) 111.123 kilometres (avg.)
-of latitude	68.708 miles at equator 69.403 miles at poles
-of longitude	69.171 miles at equator
1 decametre (dam)	32.808 feet
1 fathom	6 feet 1.8288 metres (exactly)
1 foot (ft)	0.3048 metres (exactly)
1 furlong (fur)	10 chains (exactly) 660 feet (exactly) ⅛ statute mile (exactly) 201.168 metres
1 hand (height measure for horses from ground to top of shoulders)	4 inches
1 inch (in)	2.54 centimetres (exactly)
1 kilometre (km)	0.621 mile 3,281.5 feet
1 league (land)	3 miles 4.828 kilometres
1 link	7.92 inches (exactly) 0.201 metre
1 metre (m)	39.37 inches 1.094 yards
1 micrometre (μm, the Greek letter mu)	0.001 millimetre (exactly) 0.00003937 inch
1 mil	0.001 inch (exactly) 0.0254 millimetre (exactly)
1 mile (mi) (statute or land)	5,280 feet (exactly) 1.609 kilometres
1 international nautical mile (nmi)	1.852 kilometres (exactly) 1.150779 miles 6,076.11549 feet
1 millimetre (mm)	0.03937 inch
1 nanometre (nm)	0.001 micrometre (exactly) 0.00000003937 inch
1 pica (typography)	12 points
1 point (typography)	0.013837 inch (exactly) 0.351 millimetre
1 rod (rd), pole, or perch	16½ feet (exactly) 5.029 metres
1 yard (yd)	0.9144 metre (exactly)

Areas or Surfaces

1 acre	43,560 square feet (exactly) 4,840 square yards 0.405 hectare
1 are (a)	119.599 square yards 0.025 acre
1 bolt (cloth measure):	
length	100 yards (on modern looms)
width	42 inches (usually, for cotton) 60 inches (usually, for wool)
1 hectare (ha)	2.471 acres
1 square centimetre (cm^2)	0.155 square inch
1 square decimetre (dm^2)	15.500 square inches
1 square foot (ft^2)	929.030 square centimetres
1 square inch (in^2)	6.4516 square centimetres (exactly)
1 square kilometre (km^2)	247.104 acres 0.386 square mile
1 square metre (m^2)	1.196 square yards 10.764 square feet
1 square mile (mi^2)	258.999 hectares
1 square millimetre (mm^2)	0.002 square inch
1 square rod (rd^2) sq. pole, or sq. perch	25.293 square metres
1 square yard (yd^2)	0.836 square metre

Capacities or Volumes

1 barrel (bbl) liquid	36 gallons (water) 42 gallons (oil)
1 bushel (bu) (Imperial) (struck measure)	1.032 U.S. bushels struck measure 2,219.36 cubic inches
1 bushel (bu) (U.S.) (struck measure)	2,150.42 cubic inches (exactly) 35.239 litres 2,747.715 cubic inches
1 cord (cd) firewood	128 cubic feet (exactly)
1 cubic centimetre (cm^3)	0.061 cubic inch
1 cubic decimetre (dm^3)	61.024 cubic inches
1 cubic inch (in^3)	0.576 fluid ounce 4.613 fluid drams 16.387 cubic centimetres
1 cubic foot (ft^3)	6.229 gallons 28.317 cubic decimetres
1 cubic metre (m^3)	1.308 cubic yards

1 cubic yard (yd^3)	0.765 cubic metre
1 cup (U.S.)	8 fluid ounces (exactly)
1 dram, fluid (fl dr)	0.961 U.S. fluid dram 0.217 cubic inch 3.552 millilitres
1 decalitre (dal)	2.200 gallons 0.945 pecks
1 gallon (gal)	277.42 cubic inches 1.201 U.S. gallons 4.546 litres 160 fluid ounces (exactly)
1 gallon (gal) (U.S.)	231 cubic inches (exactly) 3.785 litres 0.833 Imperial gallon 128 U.S. fluid ounces (exactly)
1 gill (gi)	8.672 cubic inches 5 fluid ounces (exactly) 0.139 litre
1 hectolitre (hl)	21.997 gallons 2.749 bushels
1 litre (l) (1 cubic decimetre exactly)	1.760 pints 61.025 cubic inches
1 millilitre (ml) (1 cu cm exactly)	0.281 fluid dram 16.890 minims 0.061 cubic inch
1 ounce, fluid (fl oz) (Imperial)	0.961 U.S. fluid ounce 1.734 cubic inches 28.412 millilitres
1 ounce, fluid (U.S.)	1.805 cubic inches 29.573 millilitres 1.041 Imperial fluid ounces
1 peck (pk)	10.581 litres
1 pint (pt), liquid	34.65 cubic inches (exactly) 0.568 litre
1 quart (qt)	69.354 cubic inches 1.032 U.S. dry quarts 1.201 U.S. liquid quarts
1 quart (qt) dry (U.S.)	67.201 cubic inches 1.101 litres 0.969 British quart
1 quart (qt) liquid (U.S.)	57.75 cubic inches (exactly) 0.946 litre 0.833 British quart
1 tun	210 gallons

Weights or Masses

1 assay ton* (AT)	29.167 grams

*Used in assaying. The assay ton bears the same relation to the milligram that a "short" or "net" ton of 2,000 pounds avoirdupois bears to the ounce troy; hence the weight in milligrams of precious metal obtained from one assay ton of ore gives directly the number of troy ounces to the net ton.

1 bale (cotton measure)	500 pounds in U.S. 750 pounds in Egypt
1 carat (c)	200 milligrams (exactly) 3.086 grains
1 dram avoirdupois (dr avdp)	$27^{11}/_{32}$ (=27.344) grains 1.772 grams
gamma, see microgram	
1 grain	64.799 milligrams
1 gram	15.432 grains 0.035 ounce, avoirdupois
1 hundredweight (cwt)	112 pounds (exactly) 50.802 kilograms
1 kilogram (kg)	2.205 pounds
1 microgram (μg, the Greek letter mu in combination with the letter g)	0.000001 gram (exactly)
1 milligram (mg)	0.015 grain
1 ounce, avoirdupois (oz avdp)	437.5 grains (exactly) 0.911 troy ounce 28.350 grams
1 ounce, troy (oz t)	480 grains (exactly) 1.097 avoirdupois ounces 31.103 grams
1 pennyweight (dwt)	1.555 grams
1 pound, avoirdupois (lb avdp)	7,000 grains (exactly) 1.215 troy pounds 453.59237 grams (exactly)
1 pound, troy (lb t)	5,760 grains (exactly) 0.823 avoirdupois pound 373.242 grams
1 ton	2,240 pounds (exactly) 1.12 short or net tons (exactly) 1.016 metric tons
1 tonne (metric ton) (t)	2,204.623 pounds 0.984 ton

Miscellaneous Measures

Calibre – the diameter of a gun bore. In the U.S., calibre is traditionally expressed in hundredths of inches, say, .22 or .30. In Britain, calibre is often expressed in thousandths of inches, say, .270 or .465. Now, it is commonly expressed in millimetres, such as the 5.56 mm M16 rifle. The calibre of heavier weapons has long been expressed in millimetres, e.g. the 81 mm mortar, the 105 mm howitzer (light), the 155 mm howitzer (medium or heavy).

Naval guns' calibre refers to the barrel length as a multiple of the bore diameter. A 5-inch, 50-calibre naval gun has a 5-inch bore and a barrel length of 250 inches.

Carat – a measure of the amount of alloy per 24 parts in gold. Thus 24-carat gold is pure; 18-carat gold is one-quarter alloy.

Decibel (dB) – a measure of the relative loudness or intensity of sound. A 20-decibel sound is 10 times louder than a 10-decibel sound; 30 decibels is 100 times louder; 40 decibels is 1,000 times louder, etc. One decibel is the smallest difference between sounds detectable by the human ear. A 120-decibel sound is painful.

Decibels	Sounds like
10	a light whisper
20	quiet conversation
30	normal conversation
40	light traffic
50	typewriter, loud conversation
60	noisy office
70	normal traffic, quiet train
80	rock music, subway
90	heavy traffic, thunder
100	jet plane at takeoff

Em – a printer's measure designating the square width of any given type size. Thus, an em of 10-point type is 10 points. An en is half an em.

Gauge – a measure of shotgun bore diameter. Gauge numbers originally referred to the number of lead balls of the gun barrel diameter in a pound. Thus, a 16-gauge shotgun's bore was smaller than a 12-gauge shotgun's. Today, an international agreement assigns millimetre measures to each gauge, thus:

Gauge	Bore diameter in mm
6	23.34
10	19.67
12	18.52
14	17.60
16	16.81
20	15.90

Horsepower – the power needed to lift 550-pounds one foot in one second, or to lift 33,000 pounds one foot in one minute. Equivalent to 746 watts or 2,546.0756 Btu/h.

Knot – a measure of the speed of ships. A knot equals 1 nautical mile per hour.

TABLES OF INTERRELATION OF UNITS OF MEASUREMENT

Bold face type indicates exact values

Units of Length

Units	Inches	Links	Feet	Yards	Rods	Chains	Miles	cm	Metres
1 inch =	**1**	0.126	0.083	0.027	0.005	0.001	0.000016	**2.54**	**0.0254**
1 link =	**7.92**	**1**	**0.66**	**0.22**	**0.04**	**0.01**	**0.000125**	20.117	0.2011
1 foot =	**12**	1.515	**1**	0.333	0.060	0.015	0.000	**30.48**	**0.3048**
1 yard =	**36**	4.545	**3**	**1**	0.181	0.045	0.000568	**91.44**	**0.9144**
1 rod =	**198**	**25**	**16.5**	**5.5**	**1**	**0.25**	**0.003125**	502.92	5.0292
1 chain =	**792**	**100**	**66**	**22**	**4**	**1**	**0.0125**	2,011.68	20.1168
1 mile =	**63,360**	**8,000**	**5,280**	**1,760**	**320**	**80**	**1**	**160,934.4**	**1,609.344**
1 cm =	0.393	0.049	0.032	0.010	0.001	0.0004	0.000006	**1**	**0.01**
1 metre =	39.37	4.970	3.280	1.093	0.198	0.049	0.000621	**100**	**1**

Units of Area

Units	Sq. inches	Sq. links	Sq. feet	Sq. yards	Sq. rods	Sq. chains
1 sq. inch =	**1**	0.015	0.006	0.0007	0.000025	0.000001
1 sq. link =	62.726	**1**	**0.4356**	**0.0484**	**0.0016**	**0.0001**
1 sq. foot =	**144**	2.295	**1**	0.1111	0.003673	0.000229
1 sq. yard =	**1,296**	20.661	**9**	**1**	0.033057	0.002066
1 sq. rod =	**39,204**	**625**	**272.25**	**30.25**	**1**	**0.0625**
1 sq. chain =	**627,264**	**10,000**	**4,356**	**484**	**16**	**1**
1 acre =	**6,272,640**	**100,000**	**43,560**	**4,840**	**160**	**10**
1 sq. mile =	**4,014,489,600**	**64,000,000**	**27,878,400**	**3,097,600**	**102,400**	**6,400**
1 sq. cm =	0.155	0.002	0.0010	0.0001	0.000003	0.000000247
1 sq. metre =	1,550.003	24.710	10.763	1.1959	0.039536	0.002471
1 hectare =	15,500,031	247,104	107,639.1	11,959.90	395.3670	24.71044

Units	Acres	Sq. miles	Sq. cm	Sq. metres	Hectares
1 sq. inch =	0.000000159	0.000000000249	**6.4516**	**0.00064516**	0.000000065
1 sq. link =	**0.00001**	**0.000000015625**	404.6856	0.04046856	0.000004047
1 sq. foot =	0.000022956	0.000000035870	929.0341	0.09290341	0.000009290
1 sq. yard =	0.000206611	0.000000322830	**8361.2736**	**0.83612736**	0.000083613
1 sq. rod =	**0.00625**	**0.000009765625**	252,929.5	25.2929	0.002529295
1 sq. chain =	**0.1**	**0.00015625**	4,046,873	404.6873	0.04046873
1 acre =	**1**	**0.0015625**	40,468.73	4046.873	0.4046873
1 sq. mile =	**640**	**1**	25,899,881,103	2,589,988.11	258.998811034
1 sq. cm =	0.000000024	0.000000000038	**1**	**0.0001**	**0.00000001**
1 sq. metre =	0.000247104	0.000000386102	**10,000**	**1**	**0.0001**
1 hectare =	2.471044	0.003861006	**100,000,000**	**10,000**	**1**

Units of Mass Not Greater than Pounds and Kilograms

Units	Grains	Pennyweights	Avdp drams	Avdp ounces
1 grain =	**1**	0.04166667	0.03657143	0.00228571
1 pennyweight =	**24**	**1**	0.8777143	0.05485714
1 dram avdp =	**27.34375**	1.139323	**1**	**0.0625**
1 ounce avdp =	**437.5**	18.22917	**16**	**1**
1 ounce troy =	**480**	**20**	17.55429	1.097143
1 pound troy =	**5760**	**240**	210.6514	13.16571
1 pound avdp =	**7000**	291.6667	**256**	**16**
1 milligram =	0.015432	0.000643015	0.000564383	0.000035274
1 gram =	15.43236	0.6430149	0.5643834	0.03527396
1 kilogram =	15,432.36	643.0149	564.3834	35.27396

Units	Troy ounces	Troy pounds	Avdp pounds	Milligrams	Grams	Kilograms
1 grain =	0.00208333	0.000173611	0.000142857	**64.79891**	**0.06479891**	0.000064799
1 pennyw't. =	**0.05**	0.004166667	0.003428571	**1,555.17384**	**1.55517384**	0.001555174
1 dram avdp =	0.05696615	0.004747179	0.00390625	1,771.845195	1.771845195	0.001771845
1 oz avdp =	0.911458 3	0.07595486	**0.0625**	**28,349.523125**	**28.349523125**	0.02834952
1 oz troy =	**1**	0.083333333	0.06857143	**31,103.4768**	**31.1034768**	0.03110348
1 lb troy =	**12**	**1**	0.8228571	**373,241.7216**	**373.2417216**	0.373241722
1 lb avdp =	14.58333	1.215278	**1**	**453,592.37**	**453.59237**	**0.45359237**
1 milligram =	0.000032151	0.000002679	0.000002205	**1**	**0.001**	**0.000001**
1 gram =	0.03215075	0.002679229	0.002204623	**1000**	**1**	**0.001**
1 kilogram =	32.15075	2.679229	2.204623	**1,000,000**	**1000**	**1**

Units of Mass Not Less than Avoirdupois Ounces

Units	Avdp oz	Avdp lb	Hundredweights	Tons	Kilograms	Tonnes
1 oz avdp =	**1**	**0.0625**	0.000558	0.000027902	0.028349523	0.000028350
1 lb avdp =	**16**	**1**	0.008928	0.000446429	**0.45359237**	0.000453592
1 cwt =	**1,792**	**112**	**1**	**0.05**	50.802337	0.0508368
1 ton =	**35,840**	**2,240**	**20**	**1**	**1016.0469088**	1.016046909
1 kg =	35.27396	2.204623	0.019684	0.000984207	**1**	**0.001**
1 tonne =	35,273.96	2,204.623	19.6841	0.9842065	**1000**	**1**

(Continued)

Units of Volume

Units	Cubic inches	Cubic feet	Cubic yards	Cubic cm	Cubic dm	Cubic metres
1 cubic inch =	1	0.000578704	0.000021433	16.387064	0.016387	0.000016387
1 cubic foot =	1,728	1	0.03703704	28,316.846592	28.316847	0.028316847
1 cubic yard =	46,656	27	1	764,554.857984	764.554858	0.764554858
1 cubic cm =	0.06102374	0.000035315	0.000001308	1	0.001	0.000001
1 cubic dm =	61.02374	0.03531467	0.001307951	1,000	1	0.001
1 cubic metre	61,023.74	35.31467	1.307951	1,000,000	1000	1

Units of Capacity (Liquid Measure)

Units	Minims	Fluid drams	Fluid ounces	Gills	Pints
1 minim =	1	0.0166667	0.00208333	0.0004166	0.000104167
1 fluid dram =	60	1	0.125	0.03125	0.0078125
1 fluid ounce =	480	8	1	0.20	0.05
1 gill =	2,400	40	5	1	0.20
1 pint =	9,600	160	20	4	1
1 quart =	19,200	320	40	8	2
1 gallon =	76,800	1,280	160	32	8
1 cubic inch =	276.78	4.613	0.576	0.1152	0.0288
1 cubic foot =	478275.84	7971.264	995.328	9.066	49.766
1 millilitre =	16.889	0.281	0.0352	0.00704	0.00176
1 litre =	16,889.42	281.490	35.18628	7.03725	1.759314

Units	Quarts	Gallons	Cubic inches	Cubic feet	Litres
1 minim =	0.000052	0.000013	0.0036166	0.000002092	0.000592
1 fl. dram =	0.003312	0.00078	0.217	0.0001255	0.0035525
1 fl. oz =	0.025	0.00625	1.734	0.00110034	0.0284201
1 gill =	0.125	0.025	8.6625	0.005013	0.1421009
1 pint =	0.5	0.125	34.65	0.020052	0.5684033
1 quart =	1	0.25	69.354	0.0401354	1.1368067
1 gallon =	4	1	277.42	0.1605439	3.785411784
1 cubic in. =	0.0144	0.0036	1	0.0005787037	0.016387064
1 cubic foot =	24.883	6.22075	1728	1	28.316846592
1 litre =	0.879657	0.199736	61.02374	0.03531467	1

Units of Capacity (Dry Measure)

Units	Pints	Quarts	Pecks	Bushels	Cubic inches	Litres
1 peck =	16	8	1	0.25	537.605	9.092
1 bushel =	64	32	4	1	2150.42	36.368
1 cubic inch =	0.028835	0.011475	0.0018021	0.0004505	1	0.0163837
1 litre =	1.759314	0.879657	0.1099571	0.0274892	61.02374	1

Paper Sizes

International

Based on a rectangle with an area of 1 sq metre (A0). The length of the long side is simply halved to find the next size down. (It is usual to quote the upright side first.) Larger sizes are called 2A, 3A and so on, indicating twice the size of A0, etc.

A Series

Used mainly for books and magazines. A4 is commonly used as office stationery.

	mm		mm		mm
A0	1149 × 841	A4	297 × 210	A8	74 × 52
A1	841 × 594	A5	210 × 148	A9	52 × 37
A2	594 × 420	A6	148 × 105	A10	37 × 26
A3	420 × 297	A7	105 × 74		

B Series

Used for large items, such as posters.

	mm		mm		mm
B0	1414 × 1000	B4	353 × 250	B8	88 × 62
B1	1000 × 707	B5	250 × 176	B9	62 × 44
B2	707 × 500	B6	176 × 125	B10	44 × 31
B3	500 × 353	B7	125 × 88		

C Series

Used for envelopes

	mm
C4	324 × 229
C5	229 × 162
C6	162 × 114

DL Series

Long sizes usually obtained by folding the long side of the A Series into 3, 4 or 8 equal parts parallel to the short side.

	mm
DL	220 × 110

Imperial

These sizes are still occasionally used in printing.

	Inches		Inches
Foolscap	17 × 13½	Demy	22½ × 17½
Double foolscap	27 × 17	Double demy	35 × 22½
Quad foolscap	34 × 27	Quad demy	45 × 35
Crown	20 × 15	Music demy	20 × 15½
Double crown	30 × 20	Medium	23 × 18
Quad crown	40 × 30	Royal	25 × 20
Double quad crown	60 × 40	Super Royal	27½ × 20½
Post	19¼ × 15½	Elephant	28 × 23
Double post	31½ × 19½	Imperial	30 × 22
Double large post	33 × 21		

Paper Quantities

24 or 25 sheets = 1 quire
20 quires = 1 ream
480 or 500 sheets = 1 ream

Where alternatives are given, the higher figure was originally to allow for waste. It has now become the standard quantity.

Electrical Units

The **watt** is the unit of power (electrical, mechanical, thermal, etc.). Electrical power is given by the product of the voltage and the current.

Energy is sold by the **joule,** but in common practice the billing of electrical energy is expressed in terms of the **kilowatt-hour,** which is 3,600,000 joules or 3.6 megajoules.

The **horsepower** is a non-metric unit sometimes used in mechanics. It is equal to 746 watts.

The **ohm** is the unit of electrical resistance and represents the physical property of a conductor that offers a resistance to the flow of electricity, permitting just 1 ampere to flow at 1 volt of pressure.

Compound Interest

Compounded Annually

Principal	Period	4%	5%	6%	7%	8%	9%	10%	12%	14%	16%
£100	1 day	0.011	0.014	0.016	0.019	0.022	0.025	0.027	0.033	0.038	0.044
	1 week	0.077	0.096	0.115	0.134	0.153	0.173	0.192	0.230	0.268	0.307
	6 months	2.00	2.50	3.00	3.50	4.00	4.50	5.00	6.00	7.00	8.00
	1 year	4.00	5.00	6.00	7.00	8.00	9.00	10.00	12.00	14.00	16.00
	2 years	8.16	10.25	12.36	14.49	16.64	18.81	21.00	25.44	29.96	34.56
	3 years	12.49	15.76	19.10	22.50	25.97	29.50	33.10	40.49	48.15	56.09
	4 years	16.99	21.55	26.25	31.08	36.05	41.16	46.41	57.35	68.90	81.06
	5 years	21.67	27.63	33.82	40.26	46.93	53.86	61.05	76.23	92.54	110.03
	6 years	26.53	34.01	41.85	50.07	58.69	67.71	77.16	97.38	119.50	143.64
	7 years	31.59	40.71	50.36	60.58	71.38	82.80	94.87	121.07	150.23	182.62
	8 years	36.86	47.75	59.38	71.82	85.09	99.26	114.36	147.60	185.26	227.84
	9 years	42.33	55.13	68.95	83.85	99.90	117.19	135.79	177.31	225.19	280.30
	10 years	48.02	62.89	79.08	96.72	115.89	136.74	159.37	210.58	270.72	341.14
	12 years	60.10	79.59	101.22	125.22	151.82	181.27	213.84	289.60	381.79	493.60
	15 years	80.09	107.89	139.66	175.90	217.22	264.25	317.72	447.36	613.79	826.55
	20 years	119.11	165.33	220.71	286.97	366.10	460.44	572.75	864.63	1,274.35	1,846.08

Ancient Measures

Biblical

Cubit	=	21.8 inches
Omer	=	0.45 peck
		3.964 litres
Ephah	=	10 omers
Shekel	=	0.497 ounce
		14.1 grams

Greek

Cubit	=	18.3 inches
Stadion	=	607.2 or 622 feet
Obolos	=	715.38 milligrams
Drachma	=	4.2923 grams
Mina	=	0.9463 pounds
Talent	=	60 mina

Roman

Cubit	=	17.5 inches
Stadium	=	202 yards
As, libra, pondus	=	325.971 grams, .71864 pounds

Weight of Water

1	cubic inch	.0360 pound
12	cubic inches	.433 pound
1	cubic foot	62.4 pounds
1	cubic feet	112.0 pounds
35.96	cubic feet	2240.0 pounds
1	imperial gallon	10.0 pounds
11.2	imperial gallons	112.0 pounds
224	imperial gallons	2240.0 pounds
1	U.S. gallon	8.33 pounds
13.45	U.S. gallons	112.0 pounds
269.0	U.S. gallons	2240.0 pounds

Density of Gases and Vapours

at 0°C and 760 mmHg (kilograms per cubic metre)

Source: National Institute of Standards and Technology

Gas	Wgt.	Gas	Wgt.	Gas	Wgt.
Acetylene	1.171	Ethylene	1.260	Methyl fluoride	1.545
Air	1.293	Fluorine	1.696	Mono methylamine	1.38
Ammonia	.759	Helium	.178	Neon	.900
Argon	1.784	Hydrogen	.090	Nitric oxide	1.341
Arsine	3.48	Hydrogen bromide	3.50	Nitrogen	1.250
Butane-iso	2.60	Hydrogen chloride	1.639	Nitrosyl chloride	2.99
Butane-n	2.519	Hydrogen iodide	5.724	Nitrous oxide	1.997
Carbon dioxide	1.977	Hydrogen selenide	3.66	Oxygen	1.429
Carbon monoxide	1.250	Hydrogen sulphide	1.539	Phosphine	1.48
Carbon oxysulphide	2.72	Krypton	3.745	Propane	2.020
Chlorine	3.214	Methane	.717	Silicon tetrafluoride	4.67
Chlorine monoxide	3.89	Methyl chloride	2.25	Sulphur dioxide	2.927
Ethane	1.356	Methyl ether	2.091	Xenon	5.897

Boiling and Freezing Points of Water

Water boils at 212°F at sea level. For every 550 feet above sea level, the boiling point of water decreases by about 1°F. Methyl alcohol boils at 148°F. Average human oral temperature is 98.6°F. Water freezes at 32°F. Although "Centigrade" is still frequently used, the International Committee on Weights and Measures and the National Institute of Standards have recommended since 1948 that this scale be called "Celsius".

Temperature Conversion Table

The numbers in **bold face type** refer to the temperature either in degrees Celsius or Fahrenheit which are to be converted. If converting from degrees Fahrenheit to Celsius, the equivalent will be found in the column on the left, while if converting from degrees Celsius to Fahrenheit the answer will be found in the column on the right.

For temperatures not shown. To convert Fahrenheit to Celsius subtract 32 degrees and multiply by 5, divide by 9; to convert Celsius to Fahrenheit, multiply by 9, divide by 5 and add 32 degrees.

Celsius		Fahrenheit	Celsius		Fahrenheit	Celsius		Fahrenheit
−273.2	**−459.7**	....	−17.8	**0**	32	35.0	**95**	203
−184	**−300**	....	−12.2	**10**	50	36.7	**98**	208.4
−169	**−273**	−459.4	− 6.67	**20**	68	37.8	**100**	212
−157	**−250**	−418	− 1.11	**30**	86	43	**110**	230
−129	**−200**	−328	4.44	**40**	104	49	**120**	248
−101	**−150**	−238	10.0	**50**	122	54	**130**	266
− 73.3	**−100**	−148	15.6	**60**	140	60	**140**	284
− 45.6	**− 50**	− 58	21.1	**70**	158	66	**150**	302
− 40.0	**− 40**	− 40	23.9	**75**	167	93	**200**	392
− 34.4	**− 30**	− 22	26.7	**80**	176	121	**250**	482
− 28.9	**− 20**	− 4	29.4	**85**	185	149	**300**	572
− 23.3	**− 10**	14	32.2	**90**	194			

Breaking the Sound Barrier; Speed of Sound

The prefix Mach is used to describe supersonic speed. It derives from Ernst Mach, a Czech-born German physicist, who contributed to the study of sound. When a plane moves at the speed of sound it is Mach 1. When twice the speed of sound it is Mach 2. When it is near but below the speed of sound its speed can be designated at less than Mach 1, for example, Mach .90. Mach is defined as "in jet propulsion, the ratio of the velocity of a rocket or a jet to the velocity of sound in the medium being considered."

When a plane passes the sound barrier – flying faster than sound travels – listeners in the area hear thunderclaps, but those aboard the aircraft do not hear them.

Sound is produced by vibrations of an object and is transmitted by alternate increase and decrease in pressures that radiate outward through a material media of molecules – somewhat like waves spreading out on a pond after a rock has been tossed into it.

The frequency of sound is determined by the number of times the vibrating waves undulate per second, and is measured in cycles per second. The slower the cycle of waves, the lower the frequency. As frequencies increase, the sound is higher in pitch.

Sound is audible to human beings only if the frequency falls within a certain range. The human ear is usually not sensitive to frequencies of less than 20 vibrations per second, or more than about 20,000 vibrations per second – although this range varies among individuals. Anything at a pitch higher than the human ear can hear is termed ultrasonic.

Intensity or loudness is the strength of the pressure of these radiating waves, and is measured in decibels. The human ear responds to intensity in a range from zero to 120 decibels. Any sound with pressure over 120 decibels is painful.

The speed of sound is generally placed at 1,088 feet per second at sea level at 32°F. It varies in other temperatures and in different media. Sound travels faster in water than in air, and even faster in iron and steel. If in air it travels a mile in 5 seconds, it does a mile under water in 1 second, and through iron in ⅓ of a second. It travels through ice cold vapour at approximately 4,708 feet per second, ice-cold water, 4,938; granite, 12,960; hardwood, 12,620; brick, 11,960; glass, 16,410 to 19,690; silver, 8,658; gold, 5,717.

Colours of the Spectrum

Colour, an electromagnetic wave phenomenon, is a sensation produced through the excitation of the retina of the eye by rays of light. The colours of the spectrum may be produced by viewing a light beam refracted by passage through a prism, which breaks the light into its wavelengths.

Customarily, the primary colours of the spectrum are thought of as those 6 monochromatic colours that occupy relatively large areas of the spectrum: red, orange, yellow, green, blue, and violet. However, Sir Isaac Newton named a 7th, indigo, situated between blue and violet on the spectrum. Aubert estimated (1865) the solar spectrum to contain approximately 1,000 distinguishable hues of which, according to Rood (1881), 2 million tints and shades can be distinguished; Luckiesh stated (1915) that 55 distinctly different hues have been seen in a single spectrum.

Many physicists recognize only 3 primary colours: red, yellow, and blue (Mayer, 1775); red, green, and violet (Thomas Young, 1801); red, green, and blue (Clerk Maxwell, 1860).

The colour sensation of black is due to complete lack of stimulation of the retina, that of white to complete stimulation. The infra-red and ultra-violet rays, below the red (long) end of the spectrum and above the violet (short) end respectively, are invisible to the naked eye. Heat is the principal effect of the infra-red rays and chemical action that of the ultra-violet rays.

Common Fractions Reduced to Decimals

8ths	16ths	32ds	64ths		8ths	16ths	32ds	64ths		8ths	16ths	32ds	64ths	
			1	.015625				23	.359375				45	.703125
		1	2	.03125	3	6	12	24	.375			23	46	.71875
			3	.046875				25	.390625				47	.734375
	1	2	4	.0625			13	26	.40625	6	12	24	48	.75
			5	.078125				27	.421875				49	.765625
		3	6	.09375		7	14	28	.4375			25	50	.78125
			7	.109375				29	.453125				51	.796875
1	2	4	8	.125			15	30	.46875		13	26	52	.8125
			9	.140625				31	.484375				53	.828125
		5	10	.15625	4	8	16	32	.5			27	54	.84375
			11	.171875				33	.515625				55	.859375
	3	6	12	.1875			17	34	.53125	7	14	28	56	.875

8ths	16ths	32ds	64ths	
			13	.203125
		7	14	.21875
			15	.234375
2	4	8	16	.25
			17	.265625
		9	18	.28125
			19	.296875
	5	10	20	.3125
			21	.328125
		11	22	.34375

8ths	16ths	32ds	64ths	
			35	.546875
	9	18	36	.5625
			37	.578125
		19	38	.59375
			39	.609375
5	10	20	40	.625
			41	.640625
		21	42	.65625
			43	.671875
	11	22	44	.6875

8ths	16ths	32ds	64ths	
			57	.890625
		29	58	.90625
			59	.921875
	15	30	60	.9375
			61	.953125
		31	62	.96875
			63	.984375
8	16	32	64	1.

Wine Measures

Wine bottle (standard): 75 cl = 22.5 fl oz

For champagne only:

Magnum	2 bottles = 150 cl
Jeroboam	2 magnums = 4 bottles
Rehoboam	3 magnums = 6 bottles
Methuselah	4 magnums = 8 bottles
Salmanazar	6 magnums = 12 bottles
Balthazar	8 magnums = 16 bottles
Nebuchadnezzar	10 magnums = 20 bottles

Mathematical Formulas

To find the CIRCUMFERENCE of a:

Circle – Multiply the diameter by 3.14159265 (usually 3.1416).

To find the AREA of a:

Circle – Multiply the square of the diameter by .785398 (usually .7854).

Rectangle – Multiply the length of the base by the height.

Sphere (surface) – Multiply the square of the radius by 3.1416 and multiply by 4.

Square – Multiply the length of one side by 2.

Trapezoid – Add the two parallel sides, multiply by the height and divide by 2.

Triangle – Multiply the base by the height and divide by 2.

To find the VOLUME of a:

Cone – Multiply the square of the radius of the base by 3.1416, multiply by the height, and divide by 3.

Cube – Multiply the length of one edge by 3.

Cylinder – Multiply the square of the radius of the base by 3.1416 and multiply by the height.

Pyramid – Multiply the area of the base by the height and divide by 3.

Rectangular Prism – Multiply the length by the width by the height.

Sphere – Multiply the cube of the radius by 3.1416, multiply by 4 and divide by 3.

Playing Cards and Dice Chances

Poker Hands

Hand	Number possible	Odds against
Royal flush	4	649,739 to 1
Other straight flush	36	72,192 to 1
Four of a kind	624	4,164 to 1
Full house	3,744	693 to 1
Flush	5,108	508 to 1
Straight	10,200	254 to 1
Three of a kind	54,912	46 to 1
Two pairs	123,552	20 to 1
One pair	1,098,240	4 to 3 (1.37 to 1)
Nothing	1,302,540	1 to 1
Total	**2,598,960**	

Dice
(Probabilities on 2 dice)

Total	Odds against (Single toss)	Total	Odds against (Single toss)
2	35 to 1	8	31 to 5
3	17 to 1	9	8 to 1
4	11 to 1	10	11 to 1
5	8 to 1	11	17 to 1
6	31 to 5	12	35 to 1
7	5 to 1		

Dice
(Probabilities of consecutive winning plays)

No. consecutive wins	By 7,11, or point	No. consecutive wins	By 7,11, or point
1	244 in 495	6	1 in 70
2	6 in 25	7	1 in 141
3	3 in 25	8	1 in 287
4	1 in 17	9	1 in 582
5	1 in 34		

Bridge

The odds – against suit distribution in a hand of 4-4-3-2 are about 4 to 1, against 5-4-2-2 about 8 to 1, against 6-4-2-1 about 20 to 1, against 7-4-1-1 about 254 to 1, against 8-4-1-0 about 2,211 to 1, and against 13-0-0-0 about 158,753,389,899 to 1.

Measures of Force and Pressure

Dyne = force necessary to accelerate a 1-gram mass 1 centimetre per second squared = 0.000072 poundal

Poundal = force necessary to accelerate a 1-pound mass 1 foot per second squared = 13,825.5 dynes = 0.138255 newtons

Newton = force needed to accelerate a 1-kilogram mass 1 metre per second squared

Pascal (pressure) = 1 newton per square metre = 0.020885 pound per square foot

Atmosphere (air pressure at sea level) = 2,116.102 pounds per square foot = 14.6952 pounds per square inch = 1.0332 kilograms per square centimetre = 101,323 newtons per square metre.

Large Numbers

U.S.	Number of zeros	French British, German
million	6	million
billion	9	milliard
trillion	12	billion
quadrillion	15	1,000 billion
quintillion	18	trillion
sextillion	21	1,000 trillion
septillion	24	quadrillion
octillion	27	1,000 quadrillion
nonillion	30	quintillion
decillion	33	1,000 quintillion

Note: The U.S. billion is used worldwide in statistical information.

Roman Numerals

I	–	1	VI	–	6	XI	–	11	L	–	50	CD	–	400	$\overline{X}$	–	10,000
II	–	2	VII	–	7	XIX	–	19	LX	–	60	D	–	500	$\overline{L}$	–	50,000
III	–	3	VIII	–	8	XX	–	20	XC	–	90	CM	–	900	$\overline{C}$	–	100,000
IV	–	4	IX	–	9	XXX	–	30	C	–	100	M	–	1,000	$\overline{D}$	–	500,000
V	–	5	X	–	10	XL	–	40	CC	–	200	$\overline{V}$	–	5,000	$\overline{M}$	–	1,000,000

THE POLITICAL SCENE

Compiled by Alison Classe

The first year of the Conservative Party's fourth consecutive term of office was inevitably a turbulent one, beginning as it did in the midst of the UK's worst recession since the 1930s. The April 1992 election had been won partly on the strength of promises that recovery was just around the corner, but in the event that corner proved agonizingly long in the turning.

Unemployment continued to increase for the remaining months of 1992. The government's, and in particular the Prime Minister's, popularity sank to an unprecedented low, according to opinion polls. Local government elections in May 1993 brought the Conservatives defeat in all but one of the county councils contested.

By summer 1993 polls in the run-up to the Christchurch by-election showed the Tories trailing well behind the Liberal Democratic party in what was a previously safe Conservative seat.

This unpopularity revealed an electorate unconvinced by the clear, though not dramatic, indications that recovery was at last beginning. Unemployment had by this time decreased in several consecutive months and the previously somnolent housing market was stirring.

As the *Economist* pointed out, with unemployment still standing at 10.4% during May, it would take more than the remarkably low inflation rate of 1.3% to cause Britons to sing and dance in the streets. Moreover, given the alarming size of the Public Sector Borrowing Requirement, it looked as if stringent spending cuts, probably in the area of social services, were in the offing. Yet for all these woes, Britain was the only major EC economy expected to grow during 1993.

Controversy at Home and Abroad

In October 1992 Michael Heseltine, President of the Board of Trade, heralded what appeared to be the demise of the British coal industry when he announced plans to close 31 mines. These plans were later modified in response to a public outcry, and to the High Court's judgment that there should have been consultation with the miners. However, the resultant reprieves seemed likely to be temporary for the most part. Meanwhile, a controversial bill promoting the privatization of British Rail also made its way through Parliament.

An ongoing row over educational policy came to a head in spring 1993 over the question of English tests for 14-year-olds. Although the concept and substance of the tests were widely attacked, and the tests boycotted, Education Secretary John Patten stuck by the principle of testing. Other domestic areas for debate included reforms to the police and judicial systems, proposed in the wake of various well-publicized miscarriages of justice.

The EC was at the eye of several of the storms that beset the government. Black Wednesday (16 September) saw Britain's embarrassing withdrawal from the Exchange Rate Mechanism [see Economics section] – embarrassing because of the denials that preceded it and the expensive market interventions with which the Treasury had attempted to avert the necessity of withdrawing.

Maastricht [see European Community section] was a constant source of parliamentary antagonism, and of internal division within the government. A crisis came in July 1993 when for a moment the Maastricht Treaty appeared to threaten the government's future. Tory rebels opposed to the bill allied themselves with the Opposition to vote for an amendment in support of the Social Chapter. The government heaved a sigh of relief when rebels returned to the fold to support a confidence motion. However, although the government was saved, many commentators had doubts about the future of the Prime Minister.

As a member of the EC and the UN, Britain played its part in the international effort to end fighting and relieve suffering in Bosnia and Herzegovina, the current focus for the seemingly interminable territorial struggle in the former Yugoslavia. Though it could not be accused of dragging its heels – it contributed 2,400 of the 9,000-strong peacekeeping force in Bosnia in summer 1993 – Britain was reluctant to support the US's calls for air strikes. The calls for peacekeeping troops both in the Balkans and in Somalia brought into question the viability of the defence cuts currently underway in pursuit of the "Peace Dividend."

Party Politics

The "green shoots of recovery" so long promised by Chancellor of the Exchequer Norman Lamont came too late to save his job, and he was sacked by John Major in a cabinet reshuffle in May 1993. His replacement, former Home Secretary Kenneth Clarke, was an unknown quantity as far as economics were concerned. Some argued that having a Chancellor untainted by economic ideology might prove to be beneficial. Meanwhile, Michael Howard moved into the job of Home Secretary.

Other ministerial casualties during the first 18 months of this government included David Mellor, Minister for Heritage, who eventually resigned in September 1992 after a prolonged bout of scandal-mongering by the tabloid papers. Another reluctant departure came in June 1993, when Michael Mates, minister of state for Northern Ireland, resigned following revelations about his (and other ministers') association with Asil Nadir, former head of the Polly Peck empire. Nadir, who stood accused of business malpractices, had jumped bail and fled to Northern Cyprus.

Reports of Nadir's contributions to Tory party funds began a debate about party funding. At the same time, the Labour party discussed constitutional changes relating to its relationship with the trade unions. Labour leader John Smith tried to steer the party towards the abandonment of the system of block votes, whereby union delegates wielded what many felt to be a disproportionate share of power over the party's choice of parliamentary candidates. Predictably, the "one man one vote" proposals encountered union resistance, but many Labour members saw them as crucial to the future electoral success of the party.

The Constitution

The functions of any government comprise the legislature, the executive and the judiciary. Under the (unwritten) constitution of the UK, these functions, though linked, are allocated as follows:

- Legislature (making law)
  - Parliament, consisting of:
    The House of Commons
    The House of Lords
    The Crown
- Executive (administering law)
  - The Cabinet
  - Government departments (ministers plus civil servants, e.g. the Department of Health) and agencies (e.g. the Department of Health's Medicines Control Agency)
  - Public corporations (such as the BBC)
  - Local authorities
- Judiciary (interpreting the law and adjudicating between disputants)
  - The courts

Here we look at the political aspects of central government: the legislature and the Cabinet.

The Electoral System

The Commons, or lower house of Parliament, is elected; general elections must be called at least every five years. By-elections must be held if a Member of Parliament (MP) dies or resigns.

Every citizen of the UK over 18 is entitled to vote, with a few exceptions such as peers, those serving a criminal sentence and people confined in institutions for the mentally ill. As of the 1992 election, UK citizens who have been resident overseas for up to 20 years were for the first time allowed to vote, a controversial change alleged to favour the Conservative Party (formerly the limit had been five years).

The country is divided into geographical constituencies, each of which contains a similar number of voters and is represented by one MP. Despite frequent calls for proportional representation, particularly from the Liberal Democrats, voting continues to be on a first-past-the-post system, meaning that the winner in each constituency is the candidate who polls the largest number of votes. This system helps to explain the fact that for the past century and a half there have been only two parties of significant size in Parliament at any one time. In the 1992 election, for instance, the Liberal Democrats won 17.8% of the votes but only 3% of the seats.

Candidates are put forward by constituency branches of the political parties, or may stand independently. Each candidate or his/her party pays a deposit of £500 which is returned only if the candidate polls more than 5% of the votes.

Parliament

Parliament is the legislative arm of government. It consists of the House of Commons, the House of Lords and the Crown (i.e. the Monarch).

The House of Commons

The House of Commons currently consists of 651 members. Its main business is:

- to debate and pass legislation
- to monitor and debate the activities of the Cabinet and government departments
- to raise money for public expenditure by approving taxation
- to safeguard the rights of the citizen.

Members of the party in government sit on one side of the chamber facing the rest. Government ministers and their opposition shadows are called "front-benchers"; the rest are "back-benchers". Parliamentary activities are presided over by the Speaker (after the 1992 election, Betty Boothroyd) who, though drawn from the ranks of MPs, is for the purposes of the office regarded as politically neutral.

Remuneration for back-benchers is £30,854. They can also claim travel and accommodation expenses, plus an allowance of £40,380 to cover staff and offices both at Westminster and in their constituency (July 1993 figures).

Issues raised for debate in the Commons are called *motions*. Motions can lead to *resolutions*, i.e. expressions of collective opinion or to *orders* in which the House instructs someone to do something. A debate often concludes with a *division* in which members vote by physically walking into the Government or Opposition lobby. They are counted on the way in. Short of a revolt, a Government with an overall majority can almost always secure a victory in a debate on a matter of policy.

The major opportunities for MPs to raise subjects for discussion are during *Question Time*, when ministers are available for questioning (each afternoon at 2.45 for 45 minutes), and the *Adjournment Debate*, which may take place in the evening between 10 and 10.30 p.m., before the House rises.

The House of Lords

The unelected upper house of the UK Parliament is the older of the two houses, tracing its origins back to Anglo-Saxon times. It consists of:

- hereditary peers
- life peers, many of them former MPs
- the "Lords Spiritual": 24 bishops and 2 archbishops
- Law Lords or "Lords of Appeal in Ordinary"

There are about 1,200 peers altogether, of whom around a quarter attend on an average day, though rarely seen "backwoodsmen", usually Tory hereditary peers, will turn out to vote on important issues. They are not paid a salary but receive expenses up to a fixed level per day of attendance.

Besides its legislative function, the House of Lords forms part of the judiciary since it is the highest Court of Appeal for the UK (except for criminal cases in Scotland). Appeals are heard by the Law Lords and Lord Chancellor. The Lord Chancellor, appointed by the Prime Minister, acts as the Speaker within the Lords. He sits on the "Woolsack", a special red seat whose origins go back to the Middle Ages when wool underpinned the British economy.

As they are not subject to re-election, members of the House of Lords have fewer political axes to grind than the Commons. The House therefore provides a forum for airing the issues of the day in an impartial atmosphere. However, many critics of the House consider the concept of an unelected house and in particular of a hereditary peerage to be essentially undemocratic.

The Crown

The governmental power of the monarch is nowadays purely symbolic. The Queen opens and closes parliamentary sessions, appoints the Prime Minister and gives assent to all new legislation, but in this and other matters is effectively obliged to follow the advice of the Cabinet (officially "Ministers of the Crown") and Prime Minister, in whom the real political power is vested.

Whips

The title "Whip" derives from the whippers-in of fox-hunting who keep the hounds in line; parliamentary Whips have a similar function. They are MPs or peers appointed by their party to manage the parliamentary behaviour, and in particular the attendance and voting, of members of the party. They circulate weekly letters, also known as "whips", to let members know which debates they are expected to attend. Defiance of a three-line whip (i.e. failure to attend an occasion which is underlined three times in the letter) usually leads to suspension from the party.

Although they have a low profile, Whips, especially government Whips, exercise substantial power. They not only "persuade" party members to toe the line in debates and divisions, but also influence the parliamentary timetable, the constitution of Committees and the appointment of junior ministers.

Committees

The function of Select and Standing committees has changed over the years, making their names rather confusing in the light of their current character.

Standing Committees are not permanent but are set up on an ad hoc basis to review a specific item, such as a proposed piece of legislation, and in particular to carry out the committee stage of a Public Bill. Select Committees, on the other hand, are usually set up on a more permanent basis with a watching brief for a particular topic.

Other types of committee include Joint Committees made up from both Houses. One such committee is responsible for vetting the legal validity of Statutory Instruments ("delegated legislation" proposed by ministries or local authorities to save parliamentary time) before they are debated by the House or a Standing Committee.

Standing Committees

When a Bill is referred to a Standing Committee after its Second Reading, the Committee of Selection identifies the MPs to be included in it. MPs from each of the main parties are included in approximate proportion to their representation in the House of Commons as a whole. Whips and government departments can ask for particular MPs to be included, and MPs may nominate themselves for inclusion. There are 16–50 members in each Standing Committee, and a usual maximum of 10 Standing Committees at any one time.

As well as reviewing Bills, Standing Committees can also debate Statutory Instruments and EC legislation on behalf of Parliament. Scottish and Welsh Standing Committees, each comprising all MPs for the relevant country, debate Bills relating specifically to those countries.

Select Committees

Select Committees are constituted, normally for the life of a Parliament, to specialize in a particular area, sifting evidence and reporting to the House. They usually have about 12 members. The scope of their activities often corresponds with one or more government departments, and there are also committees on "domestic" subjects such as Members' Interests (i.e. business associations that might influence Parliamentary behaviour and must therefore be declared). Ad hoc committees are sometimes set up.

Most Select Committees are attached to the House of Commons, but some, such as the Committee on the European Communities, are attached to the Lords.

Select Committees impose an element of accountability on the government by subjecting Cabinet decisions to independent scrutiny by MPs of all parties, many of whom accumulate substantial expertise in their chosen area. In the summer of 1992 a controversial new rule was introduced whereby Conservative MPs were allowed to sit on a Select Committee for no more than 12 consecutive years. Some saw this change as a ploy by the party managers to oust Tory backbencher Nicholas Winterton, chairman of the Select Committee on Health for 13 years and an outspoken critic of Government policy.

How Laws Are Enacted

A proposed law is introduced into Parliament in the form of a Bill. There are Private Bills – legislation put forward from outside Parliament, often to grant new legal powers to local authorities and nationalized industries – but the majority are Public Bills, which may be either Government Bills or Private Members' Bills.

Government Bills

A Bill can originate in either House, and passes through that House first. More controversial Bills usually start life in the Commons. Either way, the Bill has to be processed by both Houses before it becomes law.

Bills are drafted by civil servants at the behest of the government department concerned.

Stages of a Government Bill

Prior to the introduction of a new piece of legislation, the Government will sometimes publish a *Green Paper*, a preliminary discussion document outlining a number of alternative approaches to canvass the views of interested parties both inside and outside Parliament. A *White Paper*, usually issued shortly before the introduction of a Bill, will contain a firmer account of the legislation to be introduced.

First Reading. The Bill is formally introduced into Parliament by being mentioned in the daily Order Paper.

Second Reading. Once the Bill has been printed, this initial debate and vote on the general principles of the Bill take place. It is possible, though uncommon, for a Government Bill to be rejected at this stage.

Committee Stage. The Bill is examined in detail either by a special Standing Committee (see p. 240) or by a Committee of the Whole House in the case of a very important or urgent Bill. Occasionally a Bill may be referred to a Select Committee (also explained earlier), or different parts of the Bill may be referred to several committees. (In the case of the House of Lords, a Committee of the Whole House is more usual.) Amendments may be made in committee and in this case the Bill will be reprinted.

Report Stage. The findings of the committee are reviewed by the House. Further amendments can be made. This stage is bypassed if the committee stage took the form of a Committee of the Whole House.

Third Reading. The Bill is debated and voted on for the last time.

These stages are repeated for both Houses. If the Lords amend a Commons bill, a certain amount of toing and froing ensues until an agreement is reached. Until 1911 the Lords had the power to veto a Bill. Nowadays they can only delay it by a year at most, and they have no power to amend a Budget or Finance Bill.

Royal Assent. The Crown must formally approve each piece of legislation, though it has no power to withhold assent and has not attempted to do so since 1707. Once assented to, the Bill is published by Her Majesty's Stationery Office as an Act. The Act may take effect immediately or at a specified future date.

Private Members' Bills

To become law, a Private Member's Bill has to pass through the same stages of debate and approval as a Government Bill. The main difference is that because of the way it is introduced a Private Member's Bill is less likely to have the necessary time allocated to pass through all the stages and become law.

A back-bencher who wants to propose legislation has to join in a ballot at the beginning of each parliamentary session. 400 MPs normally do so; 20 names are drawn and these MPs are given priority in getting their proposals discussed. Those who do not get a place in the ballot can still introduce a Bill, though not until the Ballot Bills have been introduced and approved for their second reading. These Bills stand a poor chance of becoming law, but occasionally an uncontroversial Bill will go through all the stages on a single day.

Private Members' Bills can also be introduced under the Ten-Minute Rule, which allows a short speech to be made after Question Time on Tuesdays and Wednesdays. Introducing a Bill in this way is more a way of airing a topic than an attempt to get legislation introduced on that occasion.

There is insufficient time to debate all the Ballot Bills, so only the top 7 or so stand a good chance. Otherwise, unless a Bill is so uncontroversial that it can go through all its stages without debate, it has little prospect of finding its way on to the Statute Book. An exception to this rule is that certain legislation on controversial topics, such as abortion, is often put forward as a Private Member's Bill but with Government support. These Bills have a better chance of success than normal Private Members' Bills.

The Cabinet

The Cabinet, appointed by the Prime Minister, is composed of about 20 senior members of the party in power. In it is vested the executive power of the government. It makes policy and runs government departments. In addition, it is in overall control of the legislative activities of Parliament in the sense that it oversees the drafting of most Bills and can virtually decide which ones are given parliamentary time. However, Parliament as a whole has the ultimate say in what legislation gets passed.

Most, though not all, Cabinet ministers have responsibility for a government department. They are assisted by an array of 100-plus ministers and junior ministers who are attached to government departments but are not members of the Cabinet.

The majority of ministers are drawn from the House of Commons and the remainder are from the Lords.

In accordance with the "doctrine of collective responsibility", the Cabinet acts as if its decisions are unanimous. Cabinet ministers voicing dissent from Government policy put themselves in a precarious position. Any dissidents must eventually either resign or comply with the majority feeling.

From a constitutional point of view, the Cabinet forms a link between the Executive and Legislative arms of Government.

Privy Council

Though it was formerly the main executive arm of the Government, most of the Privy Council's responsibilities have now been taken over by the Cabinet (which was originally a sub-committee of the Privy Council). The full Council convenes only when a new king or queen accedes to the throne or is to marry. Other responsibilities are discharged by committees of the Privy Council.

One of these is the Judicial Committee. Its 5 judges act as a final court of appeal for the Isle of Man, Channel Islands and some British dependencies and Commonwealth countries. It was said in the 1930s that "the jurisdiction of the Privy Council . . . embraces more than one-fourth part of the world", but since then the bulk of its work has disappeared as it has ceased to hear appeals from Canada, India, Australia and former Dominions in Africa and elsewhere. Domestic appeals that come within the committee's jurisdiction include those from medical and veterinary disciplinary tribunals and those against the proposals of the Church Commissioners.

The Privy Council retains a miscellany of functions, many of which involve advising the Monarch on the approval of "Orders in Council". These can cover issues ranging from changes to the method of government of a colony, through the dissolution of Parliament to the appointment of governors of the BBC. One of the Council's duties during 1992 has been to approve the transformation of the country's polytechnics into universities.

Cabinet ministers automatically become Privy Counsellors. Others can be appointed to the Council on special recommendation of the Prime Minister. The total number of Privy Counsellors is currently around 400. The name of a Privy Counsellor is prefixed by the title "Right Honourable".

Citizen's Charter

The Citizen's Charter, brainchild of John Major, is described as "a bold programme to improve public services in the 1990s". As outlined in a White Paper published in July 1991, it addresses not only services still in the public sector, such as state schools, the police, the Post Office and public transport, but also privatized utilities like electricity. Its intention appears to be to compensate for the fact that many of these services have a captive customer base, and therefore are not motivated to please their customers, by imposing targets and objectives relating to customer care.

The more specific proposals announced under the Charter umbrella include:

- limits on the permissible waiting times for certain NHS treatments
- better liaison between schools and parents, and publication of "league tables" comparing schools' exam results
- improved procedures for tenants on council estates to get repairs done
- compensation for British Rail passengers when services fall below a prescribed standard of punctuality, with plans for progressive privatization of the rail service
- promotion of competition in the delivery of letters
- incentives for contractors to complete motorway repairs within the agreed timescales.

General proposals include:

- publication of league tables and other information allowing the public to compare the performance of education authorities, health authorities and councils
- better information to be given to the public about service level targets compared with actual performance
- employees of public services to wear name badges and give their names when writing or speaking on the phone
- lay experts to be appointed to the inspectorates responsible for ensuring quality of services such as schools
- appointments of regulators for some services which do not yet have them, such as post and railways
- easier complaints procedures with adjudication at local level.

Individual charters for Government departments, agencies and public sector bodies were planned to follow the White Paper.

The Charter had a mixed reception. Most applauded the notion of inculcating a more customer-friendly attitude among public "servants" who all too often have behaved like anything but servants. The main criticism was that the Charter was thin in the area of implementation; in particular, it was doubted that funding would be forthcoming to help hard-pressed services such as the NHS meet their new performance targets. There was scepticism as to whether the organizations concerned would compete for the accolade of the "Chartermark" as hotly as the White Paper seemed to anticipate.

Following the 1992 election William Waldegrave was given the job of implementing the Charter initiative, assisted.by an advisory panel of industrialists. A few months later, as Britain prepared for its presidency of the EC, it became clear that John Major would seek to introduce a European Citizen's Charter. It was expected that this initiative would not only add an element of accountability to the Brussels bureaucracy, but would also seek to privatize some aspects of its work.

Women in Government

The Act of Parliament entitling women to stand for election was passed in 1918, the same year in which women acquired the vote (on similar terms to men, except that they had to be over 30 – the age for males was 21). These changes followed 50 years of vigorous campaigning by women such as the Pankhursts; bills to introduce women's suffrage had been repeatedly introduced since philosopher John Stuart Mill first initiated a parliamentary debate on the subject in 1867.

In a general election that took place at the end of 1918, 17 women stood as candidates (about 1% of the total number) and just one, Countess Constance Markievicz, was elected. A member of the Irish republican party Sinn Fein, she never took her seat as she was in prison on suspicion of pro-German activity during WW1.

The first woman MP actually to appear in the House of Commons was Nancy, Viscountess Astor, a Conservative who won her seat at a by-election in 1919; her husband had just vacated the seat because he had become a peer on the death of his father. In 1923 she became the first woman to introduce a successful Bill; it was against the sale of alcohol to those under 18.

Two more women had by this time been returned in by-elections, and another two were elected in the 1922 general election. The first woman to become a Cabinet minister was Labour's Margaret Bondfield, who was elected in 1923, became a junior minister in 1924 and joined the Cabinet as Minister of Labour in 1929. She also became a member of the Privy Council.

The number of women returned at elections between 1929 and 1979 varied between 9 and 29. In 1979 only 19 women were returned; it was also the election that made Margaret Thatcher, who since 1975 had been leader of the Conservative Party, Britain's first woman Prime Minister. She continued in office for 11½ years – longer than any other 20th-century Prime Minister – until ousted by her party. During her term of office she appointed no female Cabinet ministers.

Women have always been notably under-represented in Parliament, and it is only now that any effort is being made to redress the balance. For instance, since 1988 the Labour Party has ruled that when a prospective parliamentary candidate is selected at least one woman must be shortlisted.

In the 1992 general election 60 women were returned as MPs. Following the election, Betty Boothroyd was chosen by the Commons as its Speaker (presiding officer who chairs proceedings). Perhaps taking note of criticism for including no women in his first Cabinet, John Major appointed two in his post-election reshuffle: Gillian Shephard became Secretary of State for Employment (moved to Agriculture in May 1993) and Virginia Bottomley became Secretary of State for Health. After the Labour Party's leadership election in July Margaret Beckett became the Party's first female deputy leader.

Women in the Commons

Source: CSO

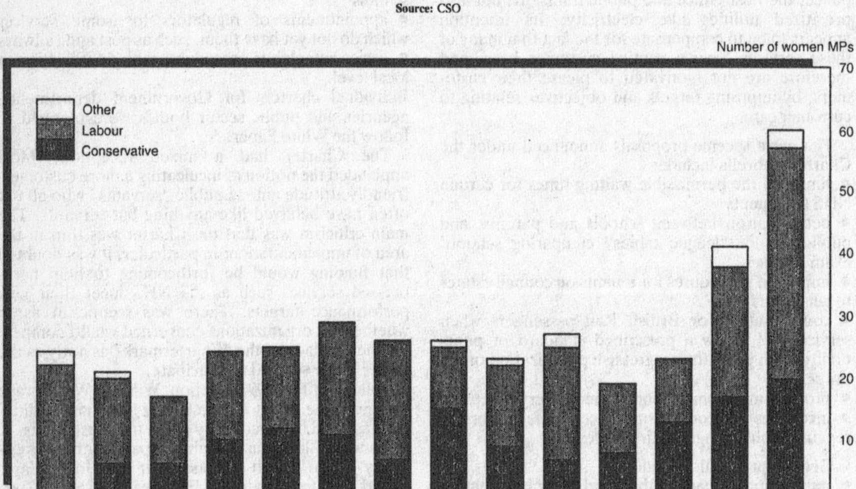

Political Parties

Conservative and Unionist Party

32 Smith Square, London SW1P 3HH
Tel: 071-222 9000
Chairman: Sir Norman Fowler, MP

The Conservative Party has its roots in the old Tory Party, whose origins date back to the 17th century. The name "Conservative" came into use during the 19th century, specifically after the Reform Act of 1832. The party embraces a range of right-of-centre opinion, its overall complexion changing according to the leadership. It moved to the right under Margaret Thatcher.

John Major presents Conservatism as the politics of a "classless society", implying a meritocratic one in which social mobility allows individual effort and ability to be rewarded, regardless of social origins. However, this calls the position of the less able into question. Critics of the government point to the fact that the rich have got richer and the poor poorer under Conservative rule, and some accuse the Conservatives of being bent on dismantling the Welfare State.

Originally representing the interests of the land-owning classes, the Conservative Party has succeeded in attracting working-class supporters as well as middle-class ones. However, it recruits relatively few working-class members to its ranks compared with Labour.

In electoral terms, the Conservative Party, currently enjoying its fourth successive term of office, is the most successful party in post-war Britain. To some extent, however, this success reflects the electoral system, and the fact that political opposition in England is divided between the Labour Party and Liberal Democrats.

Democratic Unionist Party (DUP)

296 Albert Bridge Road, Belfast BT5 4GX
Tel: 0232 458597
Chairman: James McClure

The DUP is almost synonymous with its leader, the outspoken – some would say demagogic – Protestant minister Ian Paisley. Along with the Ulster Unionist Party, it represents those who want Northern Ireland to remain part of the United Kingdom. The DUP's supporters are predominantly working class. The Party, which describes itself as "a hard-line and traditional Unionist party", for "a war against the IRA" and for devolved government. It dates from 1971.

Labour Party

150 Walworth Road, London SE17 1JT
Tel: 071-701 1234
Chairman: John Evans, MP

The Labour Party was formed in 1900 by a group of Socialist societies and trade unions who wanted a working-class voice to be heard in Parliament. Today, although its constitution retains expressions of commitment to Socialism, the Labour Party has moved somewhat to the right in an attempt to gain wider appeal. Arguably it is more aligned politically with the Social Democratic parties of continental Europe than with any Socialist parties.

Although Labour retains strong links with the trade unions, there are moves to "democratize" the party by reducing the unions' influence in certain areas. The rightward shift has brought accusations of "champagne socialism", and some consider that the Labour Party has diluted its policies to the extent that it is not strongly enough differentiated from the Liberal Democrats.

However, Labour remains Britain's main party of opposition. Since the war it has alternated with the Conservative Party as the party of government.

Liberal Democrats

4 Cowley Street, London SW1P 3NB
Tel: 071-222 7999
President: Charles Kennedy, MP

The Liberal Party was formed in the mid-19th century from the earlier Whigs. It was one of the two major parties between the 1860s and World War I. It came to stand for the interests of the middle classes, also enjoying some working-class support.

Subsequently overshadowed by the Labour Party, the Liberals rebuilt their support during the 1960s and early 1970s. In 1981 the liberals forged an alliance with the Social Democratic Party, formed after a split within the Labour Party. The Liberals and SDP merged in 1988 to create a single party of the centre, which adopted the name "Liberal Democrats" the following year.

The Liberal Democrats' most conspicuous successes come at by-elections and in local government elections. They campaign for proportional representation, without which their chances of success in a general election remain remote.

Plaid Cymru

51 Cathedral Road, Cardiff CF1 9HD
Tel: 0222 231944
Chairman: John Dixon

"The Party of Wales" was founded in 1925 as an amalgam of two earlier nationalist groupings. It did not win representation at Westminster until the party's president, Gwynfor Evans, took Camarthen in a 1966 by-election. In the current government there are four Plaid Cymru MPs, more than ever before.

Plaid Cymru aims to establish an elected assembly in Wales as a first step towards independence. It also campaigns for the wider use of the Welsh language, and, like the Scottish National Party, represents a range of local interests at Westminster.

Scottish National Party (SNP)

6 North Charlotte Street, Edinburgh EH2 4JH
Tel: 031-226 3661
National Convenor: Alex Salmond, MP

In 1934 the Scottish National Party was formed from the coming together of various parties started during the 1920s. The first SNP member of parliament was returned in a by-election of 1945. The party embraces a range of political views, the common thread being the desire for an independent Scotland with its own Parliament.

Although the Party enjoys considerable support in Scotland – it received 21.5% of Scottish votes cast in the 1992 general election – it suffers, like other minority parties, from the current electoral system in terms of its ability to translate those votes into seats.

Social Democratic and Labour Party (SDLP)

Cranmore House, 611C Lisburn Road, Belfast BT9 7GT
Tel: 0232 668100
Chairman: Mark Durkan

Northern Ireland's SDLP was founded in 1970 as a nationalist party of moderate aims, in contrast with the extremist Provisional Sinn Fein which has IRA connections. The SDLP campaigns for equal rights for Roman Catholics, and wants eventually to bring about a united Ireland by democratic means. While its electoral fortunes have been mixed, the SDLP claims success in promoting the vision of a peaceful settlement in Northern Ireland.

Ulster Unionist Party

3 Glengall Street, Belfast BT12 5AE
Tel: 0232 324601
President: Josias Cunningham

The Ulster Unionist Party, like the Democratic Unionist Party, exists to ensure that Northern Ireland remains within the UK. Also like the DUP, it has strong affinities with the Protestant Orange Order. Unlike the DUP, however, its appeal is chiefly to the middle-class voter.

The party traces its origins to the Ulster Unionist Council, which first met in 1905. During the period when Ulster had its own Parliament, from 1921 to 1972, all the prime ministers came from the Unionist Party.

HM Government

(As at July 1993)

Members of the Cabinet

Prime Minister, First Lord of the Treasury and Minister for the Civil Service – Rt. Hon. John Major MP
Lord Chancellor – Rt. Hon. Lord Mackay of Clashfern
Secretary of State for Foreign and Commonwealth Affairs – Rt. Hon. Douglas Hurd CBE MP
Chancellor of the Exchequer – Rt. Hon. Kenneth Clarke MP
Secretary of State for the Home Department – Rt. Hon. Michael Howard QC MP
President of the Board of Trade (Secretary of State for Trade and Industry) – Rt. Hon. Michael Heseltine MP
Secretary of State for Transport – Rt. Hon. John MacGregor OBE MP
Secretary of State for Defence – Rt. Hon. Malcolm Rifkind QC MP
Lord Privy Seal and Leader of the House of Lords – Rt. Hon. Lord Wakeham
Lord President of the Council and Leader of the House of Commons – Rt. Hon. Antony Newton OBE MP
Minister of Agriculture, Fisheries and Food – Rt. Hon. Gillian Shephard MP
Secretary of State for the Environment – Rt. Hon. John Gummer QC MP
Secretary of State for Wales – Rt. Hon. John Redwood MBE MP
Secretary of State for Social Security – Rt. Hon. Peter Lilley MP
Chancellor of the Duchy of Lancaster – Rt. Hon. William Waldegrave MP
Secretary of State for Scotland – Rt. Hon. Ian Lang MP
Secretary of State for National Heritage – Rt. Hon. Peter Brooke QC MP
Secretary of State for Northern Ireland – Rt. Hon. Sir Patrick Mayhew QC MP
Secretary of State for Education and Science – Rt. Hon. John Patten MP
Secretary of State for Health – Rt. Hon. Virginia Bottomley JP MP
Secretary of State for Employment – Rt. Hon. David Hunt MP
Chief Secretary to the Treasury – Rt. Hon. Michael Portillo MP

Law Officers

Attorney-General – Rt. Hon. Sir Nicholas Lyell QC MP
Lord Advocate – Rt. Hon. Lord Rodger of Earlsferry QC
Solicitor-General – Sir Derek Spencer QC MP
Solicitor-General for Scotland – Thomas Dawson Esq QC

Ministers Not in the Cabinet

Parliamentary Secretary to the Treasury – Rt. Hon. Richard Ryder OBE MP
Minister for Overseas Development – Rt. Hon. Baroness Chalker of Wallasey
Ministers of State, Foreign and Commonwealth Office –
Rt. Hon. Douglas Hogg QC MP
Rt. Hon. Tristan Garel-Jones MP
Rt. Hon. Alistair Goodlad MP
Financial Secretary to the Treasury – Stephen Dorrell Esq MP
Paymaster General – Rt. Hon. Sir John Cope MP
Ministers of State, Home Office –
Rt. Hon. Earl Ferrers DL
Peter Lloyd Esq MP
Michael Jack Esq MP
Ministers of State, Department of Trade and Industry –
Minister for Industry – Rt. Hon. Tim Sainsbury MP
Minister for Energy – Tim Eggar Esq MP
Minister for Trade – Richard Needham Esq MP
Ministers of State, Department of Transport –
Minister for Public Transport – Roger Freeman Esq MP
Minister for Aviation and Shipping – Earl of Caithness

Minister of State, Ministry of Agriculture, Fisheries and Food – David Maclean Esq MP
Ministers of State, Ministry of Defence –
Minister of State for the Armed Forces – Rt. Hon. Archibald Hamilton MP
Minister of State for Defence Procurement – Jonathan Aitken Esq MP
Ministers of State, Department of the Environment –
Minister for Housing and Planning – Sir George Young Bt MP
Minister for Local Government and Inner Cities – David Curry Esq MP
Minister for the Environment and Countryside – David Maclean Esq MP
Minister of State, Welsh Office – Rt. Hon. Sir Wyn Roberts MP
Minister of State, Department of Social Security–
Minister for Social Security and Disabled People – Rt. Hon. Nicholas Scott MBE MP
Minister of State, Scottish Office – Rt. Hon. Lord Fraser of Carmyllie QC
Ministers of State, Northern Ireland Office –
Robert Atkins Esq MP
Sir Michael Wheeler MP
Minister of State, Department of Education and Science – Baroness Blatch CBE
Minister of State, Department of Health –
Minister for Health – Dr Brian Mawhinney MP
Minister of State, Department of Employment –
Michael Forsyth Esq MP

Opposition Front Bench Spokespersons

(As at July 1993)

Leader of the Opposition	Rt. Hon. John Smith MP
Deputy Leader (also Leader of the House and Campaigns Coordinator)	Rt. Hon. Margaret Beckett MP* Nick Brown MP
Chief Whip	Derek Foster MP*
Deputy Chief Whip	Don Dixon MP
Chairman PLP	Doug Hoyle MP*
Agriculture, Food & Rural Affairs	Elliot Morley MP Dale Campbell-Savours MP
Citizen's Charter & Women	George Robertson MP* Brian Wilson MP Lewis Moonie MP (Science & Technology) Kate Hoey MP
Defence, Disarmament & Arms Control	Dr David Clark MP* Dr John Reid MP George Foulkes MP Eric Martlew MP
Development & Cooperation	Michael Meacher MP* Tony Worthington MP
Disabled People's Rights	Barry Sheerman MP
Education	Ann Taylor MP* Jeff Rooker MP Win Griffiths MP Tony Lloyd MP†
Employment	John Prescott MP* Joyce Quin MP Tony Lloyd MP* Sam Galbraith MP
Environment (Local Govt.)	Jack Straw MP* John Battle MP Doug Henderson MP Keith Vaz MP Peter Pike MP Tony Banks MP (London Affairs)
Foreign & Commonwealth Affairs	Dr John Cunningham MP* George Robertson MP Allan Rogers MP* Bruce Grocott MP*
Health & Community Care	David Blunkett MP* Dawn Primarolo MP David Hinchcliffe MP Ian McCartney MP
Home Affairs	Tony Blair MP* Joan Ruddock MP Alun Michael MP Graham Allen MP
Law Officers	Rt. Hon. John Morris QC MP John Fraser MP
Lord Chancellor's Dept.	Paul Boateng MP
National Heritage	Marjorie Mowlam MP* Robin Corbett MP Tom Pendry MP
Northern Ireland	Kevin McNamara MP Roger Stott MP Bill O'Brien MP
Scotland	Tom Clarke MP* Henry McLeish MP John McFall MP Maria Fyfe MP
Social Security	Donald Dewar MP* Keith Bradley MP Llin Golding MP
Trade & Industry	Robin Cook MP* Martin O'Neill MP (Energy) Derek Fatchett MP Nigel Griffiths MP Stuart Bell MP Jim Cousins
Transport	Frank Dobson MP* Peter Snape MP Joan Walley MP Tony Banks MP (London Affairs)
Treasury & Economic Affairs	Gordon Brown MP* Harriet Harman MP* (Chief Secretary to the Treasury) Nicholas Brown MP Andrew Smith MP Alistair Darling MP
Wales	Ron Davies MP* Paul Murphy MP Rhodri Morgan MP

* Members of the Shadow Cabinet.
† Responsible for coordinating policies on education and training.

Prime Ministers of Great Britain

(W=Whig; T=Tory; Cl=Coalition; P=Peelite; L=Liberal; C=Conservative; La=Labour)

Sir Robert Walpole (W)	1721-1742
Earl of Wilmington (W)	1742-1743
Henry Pelham (W)	1743-1754
Duke of Newcastle (W)	1754-1756
Duke of Devonshire (W)	1756-1757
Duke of Newcastle (W)	1757-1762
Earl of Bute (T)	1762-1763
George Grenville (W)	1763-1765
Marquess of Rockingham(W)	1765-1766
William Pitt the Elder (Earl of Chatham) (W)	1766-1768
Duke of Grafton (W)	1768-1770
Frederick North (Lord North) (W)	1770-1782
Marquess of Rockingham(W)	1782
Earl of Shelburne (W)	1782-1783
Duke of Portland (Cl)	1783
William Pitt the Younger(T)	1783-1801
Henry Addington (T)	1801-1804
William Pitt the Younger(T)	1804-1806
William Wyndham Grenville, Baron Grenville (W)	1806-1807
Duke of Portland (T)	1807-1809
Spencer Perceval (T)	1809-1812
Earl of Liverpool (T)	1812-1827
George Canning (T)	1827
Viscount Goderich (T)	1827-1828
Duke of Wellington (T)	1828-1830
Earl Grey (W)	1830-1834
Viscount Melbourne (W)	1834
Sir Robert Peel (T)	1834-1835
Viscount Melbourne (W)	1835-1841
Sir Robert Peel (T)	1841-1846
Lord John Russell (later Earl) (W)	1846-1852
Earl of Derby (T)	1852
Earl of Aberdeen (P)	1852-1855
Viscount Palmerston (L)	1855-1858
Earl of Derby (C)	1858-1859
Viscount Palmerston (L)	1859-1865
Earl Russell (L)	1865-1866
Earl of Derby (C)	1866-1868
Benjamin Disraeli (C)	1868
William E. Gladstone (L)	1868-1874
Benjamin Disraeli (C)	1874-1880
William E. Gladstone (L)	1880-1885
Marquess of Salisbury (C)	1885-1886
William E. Gladstone (L)	1886
Marquess of Salisbury (C)	1886-1892
William E. Gladstone (L)	1892-1894
Earl of Rosebery (L)	1894-1895
Marquess of Salisbury (C)	1895-1902
Arthur J. Balfour (C)	1902-1905
Sir Henry Campbell-Bannerman (L)	1905-1908
Herbert H. Asquith (L)	1908-1915
Herbert H. Asquith (L)	1915-1916
David Lloyd George (Cl)	1916-1922
Andrew Bonar Law (C)	1922-1923
Stanley Baldwin (C)	1923-1924
James Ramsay MacDonald(La)	1924
Stanley Baldwin (C)	1924-1929
James Ramsay MacDonald(La)	1929-1931
James Ramsay MacDonald(Cl)	1931-1935
Stanley Baldwin (Cl)	1935-1937
Neville Chamberlain (Cl)	1937-1940
Winston Churchill (Cl)	1940-1945
Winston Churchill (C)	1945
Clement Attlee (La)	1945-1951
Sir Winston Churchill(C)	1951-1955
Sir Anthony Eden (C)	1955-1957
Harold Macmillan (C)	1957-1963
Sir Alec Douglas-Home(C)	1963-1964
Harold Wilson (La)	1964-1970
Edward Heath (C)	1970-1974
Harold Wilson (La)	1974-1976
James Callaghan (La)	1976-1979
Margaret Thatcher (C)	1979-1990
John Major (C)	1990-

Members of the House of Commons

(As at July 1993)

Party	Member (Birthdate)	Constituency
Lab	Abbott, Ms Diane Julie (27/9/53)	Hackney North & Stoke Newington
Lab	Adams, Mrs Katherine (Irene) (27/12/47)	Paisley North
Lab	*Ainger, Nicholas Richard (Nick) (24/10/49)	Pembroke
Con	*Ainsworth, Peter Michael (16/11/56)	Surrey, East
Lab	*Ainsworth, Robert William (Bob) (19/6/52)	Coventry, North East
Con	Aitken, Jonathan William Patrick (30/8/42)	Thanet, South
Con	Alexander, Richard Thain (29/6/34)	Newark
Con	Alison, Rt. Hon. Michael James Hugh (27/6/26)	Selby
Con	Allason, Rupert William Simon (8/11/51)	Torbay
Lab	Allen, Graham William (11/1/53)	Nottingham, North
LD	Alton, David Patrick Paul (15/3/51)	Liverpool, Mossley Hill
Con	Amess, David Anthony Andrew (26/3/52)	Basildon
Con	#Ancram, Michael (7/7/45)	Devizes
Lab	Anderson, Donald (17/6/39)	Swansea, East
Lab	*Anderson, Ms Janet (6/12/49)	Rossendale & Darwen
Con	Arbuthnot, James Norwich (4/8/52)	Wanstead & Woodford
Lab	Armstrong, Ms Hilary Jane (30/11/45)	North West Durham
Con	Arnold, Jacques (27/8/47)	Gravesham
Con	Arnold, Sir Thomas Richard (25/1/47)	Hazel Grove
Con	Ashby, David Glynn(14/5/40)	North West Leicestershire
LD	Ashdown, Rt. Hon. Jeremy John Durham (Paddy) (27/2/41)	Yeovil
Lab	Ashton, Joseph William (Joe) (9/10/33)	Bassetlaw
Con	Aspinwall, Jack Heywood (15/2/33)	Wansdyke
Con	Atkins, Robert James (5/2/46)	South Ribble
Con	Atkinson, David Anthony (24/3/40)	Bournemouth, East
Con	*Atkinson, Peter Landreth (19/1/43)	Hexham
Lab	*Austin-Walker, John Eric (21/8/44)	Woolwich
Con	Baker, Rt. Hon. Kenneth Wilfred, CH (3/11/34)	Mole Valley
Con	Baker, Nicholas Brian (23/11/38)	North Dorset
Con	Baldry, Anthony Brian (Tony) (10/7/50)	Banbury
Con	*Banks, Matthew Richard William (21/6/61)	Southport
Con	Banks, Robert George (18/1/37)	Harrogate
Lab	Banks, Tony (8/4/43)	Newham, North West
Lab	Barnes, Harold (Harry) (22/7/36)	North East Derbyshire
Lab	Barron, Kevin John (26/10/46)	Rother Valley
Con	*Bates, Michael Walton (26/5/61)	Langbaurgh
Con	Batiste, Spencer Lee (5/6/45)	Elmet
Lab	Battle, John Dominic (26/4/41)	Leeds, West
Lab	*Bayley, Hugh (9/1/52)	York
Lab	Beckett, Margaret Mary (15/1/43)	Derby, South
UU	Beggs, Roy (20/2/36)	East Antrim
LD	Beith, Alan James (20/4/43)	Berwick-upon-Tweed
Lab	Bell, Stuart (16/5/38)	Middlesbrough
Con	Bellingham, Henry Campbell (29/3/55)	North West Norfolk
Con	Bendall, Vivian Walter Hough (14/12/38)	Ilford, North
Lab	Benn, Rt. Hon. Anthony Neil Wedgwood (Tony) (3/4/25)	Chestefield
Lab	Bennett, Andrew Francis (9/3/39)	Denton & Reddish
Lab	Benton, Joseph Edward (Joe) (28/9/33)	Bootle

(Continued)

Party	Member (Birthdate)	Constituency
Con	*Beresford, Sir Alexander Paul (6/4/46)	Croydon, Central
Lab	Bermingham, Gerald Edward (Gerry) (20/8/40)	St Helens, South
Lab	*Berry, Roger Leslie (4/7/48)	Kingswood
Lab	*Betts, Clive James Charles (13/1/50)	Sheffield, Attercliffe
Con	Biffen, Rt. Hon. William John (3/11/30)	North Shropshire
Con	Blackburn, Dr John Graham (2/9/33)	Dudley, West
Lab	Blair, Anthony Charles Lynton (Tony) (6/5/53)	Sedgefield
Lab	Blunkett, David (6/6/47)	Sheffield, Brightside
Lab	Boateng, Paul Yaw (14/6/51)	Brent, South
Con	Body, Sir Richard Bernard Frank Stewart (18/5/27)	Holland with Boston
Con	Bonsor, Sir Nicholas Cosmo, Bt (9/12/42)	Upminster
Con	*Booth, Vernon Edward Hartley (17/7/46)	Finchley
The Speaker	Boothroyd, Rt. Hon. Betty (8/10/29)	West Bromwich West
Con	Boswell, Timothy Eric (Tim) (2/12/42)	Daventry
Con	Bottomley, Peter James (30/7/44)	Eltham
Con	Bottomley, Rt. Hon. Virginia Hilda Brunette Maxwell (12/3/48)	South West Surrey
Con	Bowden, Andrew, MBE (8/4/30)	Brighton, Kemptown
Con	Bowis, John Crocket, OBE (2/8/45)	Battersea
Lab	*Boyce, James (Jimmy) (6/9/47)	Rotherham
Lab	Boyes, Roland (12/2/37)	Houghton & Washington
Con	Boyson, Rt. Hon. Sir Rhodes (11/5/25)	Brent, North
Lab	Bradley, Keith John Charles (17/5/50)	Manchester, Withington
Con	*Brandreth, Gyles Daubeney (8/3/48)	City of Chester
Lab	Bray, Dr Jeremy William (29/6/30)	Motherwell, South
Con	Brazier, Julian William Hendy (24/7/53)	Canterbury
Con	Bright, Graham Frank James (2/4/42)	Luton, South
Con	Brooke, Rt. Hon. Peter Leonard, CH (3/3/34)	City of London & Westminster, South
Lab	Brown, James Gordon (20/2/51)	Dunfermline, East
Con	Brown, Michael Russell (3/7/51)	Brigg & Cleethorpes
Lab	Brown, Nicholas Hugh (13/6/50)	Newcastle-upon-Tyne, East
Con	*Browning, Mrs Angela Frances (4/12/46)	Tiverton
Con	Bruce, Ian Cameron (14/3/47)	Dorset, South
LD	Bruce, Malcolm Gray (17/11/44)	Gordon
Con	Budgen, Nicholas William (3/11/37)	Wolverhampton, South West
Lab	*Burden, Richard Haines (1/9/54)	Birmingham, Northfield
Con	Burns, Simon High McGuigan (6/9/52)	Chelmsford
Con	Burt, Alistair James Hendrie (25/5/55)	Bury, North
Con	Butcher, John Patrick (13/2/46)	Coventry, South West
Con	*Butler, Peter (10/6/51)	Milton Keynes, North East
Con	Butterfill, John Valentine, FRICS (14/2/41)	Bournemouth, West
Lab	*Byers, Stephen John (13/4/53)	Wallsend
Lab	Caborn, Richard George (6/10/43)	Sheffield, Central
Lab	Callaghan, James (Jim) (28/1/27)	Heywood & Middleton
Lab	*Campbell, Mrs Anne MA (Cantab), FIS, FRSS (6/4/40)	Cambridge
Lab	Campbell, Ronald (Ronnie) (14/8/43)	Blyth Valley
LD	Campbell, Walter Menzies CBE QC (22/5/41)	Fife, North East
Lab	Campbell-Savours, Dale Norman (23/8/43)	Workington
Lab	Canavan, Dennis Andrew (8/8/42)	Falkirk, West
Lab	*Cann, James Charles (Jamie) (28/6/46)	Ipswich
LD	Carlile, Alexander Charles QC (Alex) (12/2/48)	Montgomery
Con	Carlisle, John Russell (28/8/42)	Luton, North
Con	Carlisle, Kenneth Melville (25/3/41)	Lincoln
Con	Carrington, Matthew Hadrian Marshall (17/9/46)	Fulham
Con	Cartiss, Michael Reginald Harry (11/3/38)	Great Yarmouth
Con	Cash, William Nigel Paul (Bill) (10/5/40)	Stafford
Con	Channon, Rt. Hon. Henry Paul Guinness (9/10/38)	Southend, West
Con	Chapman, Sydney Brookes (17/10/35)	Chipping Barnet
Lab	*Chisholm, Malcolm George Richardson (7/3/49)	Edinburgh, Leith
Con	Churchill, Winston Spencer (10/10/40)	Davyhulme
Lab	*Clapham, Michael (15/5/43)	Barnsley, West & Penistone
Con	*Clappison, William James (14/9/56)	Hertsmere
Lab	Clark, Dr David George (19/10/39)	South Shields
Con	Clark, Dr Michael (8/8/35)	Rochford
Lab	*Clarke, Eric Lionel (9/4/33)	Midlothian
Con	Clarke, Rt. Hon. Kenneth Harry, QC (2/7/40)	Rushcliffe
Lab	Clarke, Thomas, CBE (Tom) (10/1/41)	Monklands, West
Lab	Clelland, David Gordon (30/6/43)	Tyne Bridge
Con	*Clifton-Brown, Geoffrey Robert ARICS (23/3/53)	Cirencester & Tewkesbury
Lab	Clwyd, Ann (21/3/37)	Cynon Valley
Con	*Coe, Sebastian Newbold MBE (29/9/56)	Falmouth & Camborne
Lab	*Coffey, Ann (31/8/46)	Stockport
Lab	Cohen, Harry Michael (10/12/49)	Leyton
Con	Colvin, Michael Keith Beale (27/9/32)	Romsey & Waterside
Con	*Congdon, David Leonard (16/10/49)	Croydon, North East
Lab	*Connarty, Michael (3/9/47)	Falkirk, East
Con	Conway, Derek Leslie TD (15/2/53)	Shrewsbury & Atcham
Lab	Cook, Francis (Frank) (3/11/55)	Stockton, North
Lab	Cook, Robert Finlayson (Robin) (28/2/46)	Livingston
Con	Coombs, Anthony Michael Vincent (18/11/52)	Wyre Forest
Con	Coombs, Simon Christopher (21/2/47)	Swindon
Con	Cope, Rt. Hon. Sir John Ambrose (13/5/37)	Northavon
Lab	Corbett, Robin (22/12/33)	Birmingham, Erdington
Lab	Corbyn, Jeremy Bernard (26/5/49)	Islington, North
Con	Cormack, Patrick Thomas, FSA (18/5/39)	South Staffordshire
Lab	*Corston, Ms Jean Ann (5/5/42)	Bristol, East
Con	Couchman, James Randall (11/2/42)	Gillingham
Lab	Cousins, James Mackay (Jim) (24/2/44)	Newcastle-upon-Tyne, Central

(Continued)

Party	Member (Birthdate)	Constituency
Lab	Cox, Thomas Michael (Tom) (30/6/30)	Tooting
Con	Cran, James Douglas (28/1/44)	Beverley
Con	Critchley, Julian Michael Gordon (3/12/30)	Aldershot
Lab	Cryer, George Robert (Bob) (3/12/34)	Bradford, South
Lab	Cummings, John Scott (6/7/43)	Easington
Lab	Cunliffe, Lawrence Francis (25/3/29)	Leigh
Lab	*Cunningham, James Dolan (Jim) (4/2/41)	Coventry, South East
Lab	Cunningham, Dr John Anderson (Jack) (4/8/39)	Copeland
Con	Currie, Mrs Edwina (13/9/46)	South Derbyshire
Con	Curry, David Maurice (13/6/44)	Skipton & Ripon
PC	*Dafis, Cynog Glyndwr (1/4/38)	Ceredigion & Pembroke North
Lab	Dalyell, Thomas (Tam) (9/8/32)	Linlithgow
Lab	Darling, Alistair Maclean (28/11/53)	Edinburgh, Central
Lab	*Davidson, Ian Graham (8/9/50)	Glasgow, Govan
Lab	#Davies, Bryan (9/11/39)	Oldham Central & Royton
Lab	Davies, Rt. Hon. David John (9/10/38)	Llanelli
Con	Davies, Quentin (29/5/44)	Stamford & Spalding
Lab	Davies, Ronald (Ron) (6/8/46)	Caerphilly
Con	Davis, David Michael (23/12/48)	Boothferry
Lab	Davis, Terence Anthony Gordon (Terry) (5/1/38)	Birmingham, Hodge Hill
Con	Day, Stephen Richard (30/10/48)	Cheadle
Lab	*Denham, John Yorke (15/7/53)	Southampton, Itchen
Con	*Deva, Niranjan Joseph DL (Nirj) (11/5/48)	Brentford & Isleworth
Con	Devlin, Timothy Robert (Tim) (13/6/59)	Stockton, South
Lab	Dewar, Donald Campbell (21/8/37)	Glasgow, Garscadden
Con	Dickens, Geoffrey Kenneth JP (26/8/31)	Littleborough & Saddleworth
Con	Dicks, Terence Patrick (Terry) (17/3/37)	Hayes & Harlington
Lab	Dixon, Donald (Don) (6/3/29)	Jarrow
Lab	Dobson, Frank Gordon (15/3/40)	Holborn & St Pancras
Lab	*Donohoe, Brian (10/9/48)	Cunninghame, South
Con	Dorrell, Stephen James (25/3/52)	Loughborough
Con	Douglas-Hamilton, Lord James Alexander, MA, LLB (31/7/42)	Edinburgh, West
Con	Dover, Denshore Ronald (Den) (4/4/48)	Chorley
Lab	*Dowd, James Patrick (Jim) (5/3/51)	Lewisham, West
Con	*Duncan, Alan James Carter (31/3/57)	Rutland & Melton
Con	*Duncan-Smith, George Iain (9/4/54)	Chingford
Con	Dunn, Robert John (14/7/46)	Dartford
Lab	Dunnachie, James Francis (Jimmy) (17/11/30)	Glasgow, Pollok
Lab	Dunwoody, Hon Mrs Gwyneth Patricia (12/12/30)	Crewe & Nantwich
Con	Durant, Sir Robert Anthony Belvis (9/1/28)	Reading, West
Con	Dykes, Hugh John Maxwell (17/5/39)	Harrow, East
Lab	*Eagle, Ms Angela (17/2/61)	Wallasey
Lab	Eastham, Kenneth (11/8/27)	Manchester, Blackley
Con	Eggar, Timothy John Crommelin (Tim) (19/12/51)	Enfield, North
Con	*Elletson, Harold Daniel Hope (8/12/60)	Blackpool, North
Con	Emery, Sir Peter Frank Hannibal (27/2/26)	Honiton
Lab	Enright, Derek Anthony (2/8/35)	Hemsworth
Lab	*Etherington, William (Bill) (17/7/41)	Sunderland, North
Con	Evans, David John (23/4/35)	Welwyn Hatfield
Lab	Evans, John (19/10/30)	St Helens, North
Con	*Evans, Jonathan Peter (2/6/50)	Brecon & Radnor
Con	*Evans, Nigel Martin (10/11/57)	Ribble Valley
Con	*Evans, Roger Kenneth (18/5/47)	Monmouth
Con	Evennett, David Anthony (3/6/49)	Erith & Crayford
SNP	Ewing, Mrs Margaret Anne (1/9/45)	Moray
Con	*Faber, David James Christian (7/7/61)	Westbury
Con	*Fabricant, Michael Louis David (12/6/50)	Mid Staffordshire
Con	Fairbairn, Sir Nicholas Hardwick, QC (24/12/33)	Perth & Kinross
Lab	Fatchett, Derek John (8/8/45)	Leeds, Central
Lab	Faulds, Andrew Matthew William (1/3/23)	Warley, East
Con	Fenner, Dame Peggy Edith, DBE, DL (12/11/22)	Medway
Con	Field, Barry John Anthony (7/7/46)	Isle of Wight
Lab	Field, Frank (16/7/42)	Birkenhead
Con	Fishburn, John Dudley (8/6/46)	Kensington
Lab	Fisher, Mark (29/10/44)	Stoke-on-Trent, Central
Lab	Flynn, Paul Phillip (9/2/35)	Newport, West
2nd DCWM	Fookes, Dame Janet Evelyn, DBE (21/2/36)	Plymouth, Drake
Con	Forman, Francis Nigel (25/3/43)	Carshalton & Wallington
Con	Forsyth, Michael Bruce (16/10/54)	Stirling
UU	Forsythe, Clifford (24/8/29)	Antrim, South
Con	Forth, Eric (9/9/44)	Mid-Worcestershire
Lab	Foster, Derek (25/6/37)	Bishop Auckland
LD	*Foster, Donald Michael Ellison (Don) (31/3/47)	Bath
Lab	Foulkes, George (21/1/42)	Carrick, Cumnock & Doon Valley
Con	Fowler, Rt. Hon. Sir Peter Norman (2/2/38)	Sutton Coldfield
Con	Fox, Sir John Marcus, MBE (11/6/27)	Shipley
Con	*Fox, Dr Liam (22/9/61)	Woodspring
Lab	Fraser, John Denis (30/1/34)	Norwood
Con	Freeman, Roger Norman (27/5/42)	Kettering
Con	French, Douglas Charles ,(20/3/44)	Gloucester
Con	Fry, Peter Derek, MA (26/5/31)	Wellingborough
Lab	Fyfe, Mrs Maria (25/11/38)	Glasgow, Maryhill
Lab	Galbraith, Samuel Laird (Sam) (18/10/45)	Strathkelvin & Bearsden
Con	Gale, Roger James (20/8/43)	Thanet, North

(Continued)

Party	Member (Birthdate)	Constituency
Con	*Gallie, Philip Roy (3/1/39)	Ayr
Lab	Galloway, George (30/6/55)	Glasgow, Hillhead
Lab	*Gapes, Michael John (4/9/52)	Ilford, South
Con	Gardiner, Sir George Arthur, KCMG (3/3/35)	Reigate
Con	Garel-Jones, Rt. Hon. William Armand Thomas Tristan (28/2/41)	Watford
Con	*Garnier, Edward Henry (26/10/52)	Harborough
Lab	Garrett, John Laurence (8/9/31)	Norwich, South
Lab	George, Bruce Thomas (1/7/42)	Walsall, South
Lab	*Gerrard, Neil Francis (3/7/42)	Walthamstow
Lab	Gilbert, Rt. Hon. Dr John William (5/4/27)	Dudley, East
Con	Gill, Christopher John Fred, RD (3/6/36)	Ludlow
Con	*Gillan, Mrs Cheryl Elise Kendall (21/4/52)	Chesham & Amersham
Lab	Godman, Dr Norman Anthony (19/4/38)	Greenock & Port Glasgow
Lab	*Godsiff, Roger Duncan (28/6/46)	Birmingham, Small Heath
Lab	Golding, Mrs Llinos (Llin) (30/6/33)	Newcastle-under-Lyme
Con	Goodlad, Rt. Hon. Alastair Robertson (4/7/43)	Eddisbury
Con	Goodson-Wickes, Dr Charles (7/11/45)	Wimbledon
Lab	Gordon, Ms Mildred (24/8/23)	Bow & Poplar
Con	Gorman, Mrs Teresa Ellen (15/9/31)	Billericay
Con	Gorst, John Michael (28/6/28)	Hendon, North
Lab	Gould, Bryan Charles (11/2/39)	Dagenham
Lab	Graham, Thomas (30/6/44)	Renfrew West & Inverclyde
Lab	Grant, Bernard Alexander Montgomery (Bernie) (17/2/44)	Tottenham
Con	Grant, Sir John Anthony (29/5/25)	South West Cambridgeshire
Con	Greenway, Harry (4/10/34)	Ealing, North
Con	Greenway, John Robert (15/2/46)	Ryedale
Lab	Griffiths, Nigel (20/5/55)	Edinburgh, South
Con	Griffiths, Peter Harry Steve (24/5/28)	Portsmouth, North
Lab	Griffiths, Winston James (Win) (11/2/43)	Bridgend
Lab	Grocott, Bruce Joseph (1/11/40)	The Wrekin
Con	Grylls, Sir William Michael John (21/2/34)	North West Surrey
Con	Gummer, Rt. Hon. John Selwyn (26/11/39)	Suffolk Coastal
Lab	*Gunnell, John (1/10/33)	Leeds, South & Morley
Con	Hague, William Jefferson (26/3/61)	Richmond, Yorks
Lab	Hain, Peter Gerald (16/2/50)	Neath
Lab	*Hall, Mike Thomas (20/9/52)	Warrington, South
Con	Hamilton, Rt. Hon. Peter Archibald Gavin (Archie) (30/12/41)	Epsom & Ewell
Con	Hamilton, Mostyn Neil (9/3/49)	Tatton
Con	Hampson, Dr Keith (14/8/43)	Leeds, North West
Con	Hanley, Jeremy James (17/11/45)	Richmond & Barnes
Con	Hannam, Sir John Gordon (2/8/29)	Exeter
Lab	*Hanson, David George (5/7/57)	Delyn
Lab	Hardy, Peter (17/2/29)	Wentworth
Con	Hargreaves, Andrew Raikes (15/5/55)	Birmingham, Hall Green
Lab	Harman, Ms Harriet Ruth (30/7/50)	Peckham
Con	Harris, David Anthony (1/11/37)	St Ives
LD	*Harvey, Nick (3/8/61)	North Devon
Con	Haselhurst, Alan Gordon Barraclough (23/6/37)	Saffron Walden
Lab	Hattersley, Rt. Hon. Roy Sydney George (28/12/32)	Birmingham, Sparkbrook
Con	*Hawkins, John Nicholas (Nick) (27/3/57)	Blackpool, South
Con	#Hawksley, Philip Warren (10/3/43)	Halesowen & Stourbridge
Con	Hayes, Jeremy Joseph James (Jerry) (20/4/53)	Harlow
Con	*Heald, Oliver (15/12/54)	North Hertfordshire
Con	Heath, Rt. Hon. Sir Edward Richard George, KG, MBE (9/7/16)	Old Bexley & Sidcup
Con	Heathcoat-Amory, David Phillip, FCA (21/3/49)	Wells
Lab	Henderson, Douglas John (Doug) (9/6/49)	Newcastle-upon-Tyne, North
SDLP	*Hendron, Dr Joseph Gerard (Joe) (12/11/32)	Belfast, West
Con	*Hendry, Charles (6/5/59)	High Peak
Lab	*Heppell, John (3/11/48)	Nottingham, East
Con	Heseltine, Rt. Hon. Michael Ray Dibden (21/3/33)	Henley
Con	Hicks, Robert Adrian (18/1/38)	South East Cornwall
Con	Higgins, Rt. Hon. Terence Langley, DL (18/1/28)	Worthing
Lab	*Hill, Trevor Keith (28/7/43)	Streatham
Con	Hill, Stanley James Allen (21/12/26)	Southampton, Test
Lab	Hinchcliffe, David Martin (14/10/48)	Wakefield
Lab	Hoey, Miss Catharine Letitia (Kate) (21/6/48)	Vauxhall
Con	Hogg, Rt. Hon. Douglas Martin, QC (5/2/45)	Grantham
Lab	Hogg, Norman (12/3/38)	Cumbernauld & Kilsyth
Lab	Home Robertson, John David (5/12/48)	East Lothian
Lab	Hood, James (Jimmy) (11/5/49)	Clydesdale
Lab	*Hoon, Geoffrey William (Geoff) (6/12/53)	Ashfield
Con	#Horam, John Rhodes (7/5/39)	Orpington
Con	Hordern, Sir Peter Maudslay DL (18/4/29)	Horsham
Con	Howard, Rt. Hon. Michael, QC (7/7/41)	Folkestone & Hythe
Con	Howarth, Alan Thomas, CBE (11/6/44)	Stratford-on-Avon
Lab	Howarth, George Edward (29/6/49)	Knowsley, North
Con	Howell, Rt. Hon. David Arthur Russell (18/1/36)	Guildford
Con	Howell, Ralph Frederic (25/5/23)	North Norfolk
Lab	Howells, Dr Kim Scott (11/11/46)	Pontypridd
Lab	Hoyle, Eric Douglas Harvey (Doug) (17/2/30)	Warrington, North
Lab	*Hughes, Kevin Michael (15/12/52)	Doncaster, North
Con	Hughes, Robert Gurth (Robert G) (14/7/51)	Harrow, West
Lab	Hughes, Robert (3/1/32)	Aberdeen, North
Lab	Hughes, Royston John, DL (Roy) (9/6/25)	Newport, East
LD	Hughes, Simon Henry Ward (17/5/51)	Southwark & Bermondsey
SDLP	Hume, John (18/1/34)	Foyle
Con	Hunt, Rt. Hon. David James Fletcher, MBE (21/5/42)	Wirral West

(Continued)

Party	Member (Birthdate)	Constituency
Con	Hunt, Sir John Leonard (27/10/39)	Ravensbourne
Con	Hunter, Andrew Robert Frederick (8/1/43)	Basingstoke
Con	Hurd, Rt. Hon. Douglas Richard, CBE (8/3/30)	Witney
Lab	*Hutton, John Matthew Patrick (6/5/55)	Barrow & Furness
Lab	Illsley, Eric Evelyn (9/4/55)	Barnsley, Central
Lab	Ingram, Adam Paterson, JP (1/2/47)	East Kilbride
Con	Jack, John Michael 17/9/46)	Fylde
Lab	*Jackson, Miss Glenda May (9/5/36)	Hampstead & Highgate
Lab	*Jackson, Ms Helen Margaret (19/5/39)	Sheffield, Hillsborough
Con	Jackson, Robert Victor (24/9/46)	Wantage
Lab	*Jamieson, David Charles (18/5/47)	Plymouth, Devonport
Lab	Janner, Hon. Greville Ewan, QC (11/7/28)	Leicester, West
Con	*Jenkin, Hon. Bernard Christison, MA (Cantab) (9/4/59)	Colchester, North
Con	Jessel, Toby Francis Henry (11/7/34)	Twickenham
Con	Johnson Smith, Sir Geoffrey DL (16/4/24)	Wealden
LD	Johnston, Sir David Russell (28/7/32)	Inverness, Nairn & Lochaber
Con	Jones, Gwilym Haydn (30/7/47)	Cardiff, North
PC	Jones, Ieuan Wyn (22/5/49)	Ynys Mon
Lab	*Jones, Jonathan Owen (Jon Owen) (19/4/54)	Cardiff, Central
Lab	*Jones, Dr Lynne Mary (26/4/51)	Birmingham, Selly Oak
Lab	Jones, Martyn David, MI Biol (1/3/47)	Clwyd, South West
LD	*Jones, Nigel David (30/3/48)	Cheltenham
Con	Jones, Robert Brannock (26/9/50)	West Hertfordshire
Lab	Jones, Stephen Barry (26/6/38)	Alyn & Deeside
Con	Jopling, Rt. Hon. Thomas Michael DL (10/12/30)	Westmorland & Lonsdale
Lab	*Jowell, Tessa Jane Douglas (17/9/47)	Dulwich
Lab	Kaufman, Rt. Hon. Gerald Bernard (21/6/30)	Manchester, Gorton
Lab	*Keen, David Alan (25/11/37)	Feltham & Heston
Con	Kellett-Bowman, Dame Mary Elaine, DBE (8/7/24)	Lancaster
LD	Kennedy, Charles Peter (25/11/59)	Ross, Cromarty & Skye
Lab	*Kennedy, Jane Elizabeth (4/5/58)	Liverpool, Broadgreen
Con	Key, Simon Robert (22/4/45)	Salisbury
Lab	*Khabra, Piara Singh (20/11/24)	Ealing, Southall
UPUP	Kilfedder, James Alexander, BA, BL (16/7/28)	North Down
Lab	Kilfoyle, Peter (9/6/46)	Liverpool, Walton
Con	King, Rt. Hon. Thomas Jeremy (Tom), CH (13/6/33)	Bridgwater
Lab	Kinnock, Rt. Hon. Neil Gordon (28/3/42)	Islwyn
Con	Kirkhope, Timothy John Robert (29/4/45)	Leeds, North East
LD	Kirkwood, Archibald Johnstone (Archy) (22/5/46)	Roxburgh & Berwickshire
Con	Knapman, Roger Maurice (20/2/44)	Stroud
Con	*Knight, Mrs Angela Ann (31/10/50)	Erewash
Con	Knight, Gregory (Greg) (4/4/49)	Derby, North
Con	Knight, Dame Joan Cristabel Jill, DBE (9/7/23)	Birmingham, Edgbaston
Con	Knox, David Laidlaw (30/5/33)	Staffordshire, Moorlands
Con	*Kynoch, George Alexander Bryson (7/10/46)	Kincardine & Deeside
Con	*Lait, Mrs Jacqueline Anne Harkness (Jacqui) (10/12/47)	Hastings & Rye
Con	Lamont, Rt. Hon. Norman Stewart Hughson (8/5/42)	Kingston upon Thames
Con	Lang, Rt. Hon. Ian Bruce (27/6/40)	Galloway & Upper Nithsdale
Con	Lawrence, Ivan John, QC (24/12/36)	Burton
Con	*Legg, Barry Charles (30/5/49)	Milton Keynes, South West
Con	Leigh, Edward Julian Egerton (20/7/50)	Gainsborough & Horncastle
Lab	Leighton, Ronald (Ron) (24/1/30)	Newham, North East
Con	Lennox-Boyd, Hon. Mark Alexander (4/5/43)	Morecambe & Lunesdale
Con	Lester, James Theodore (Jim) (23/5/32)	Broxtowe
Lab	Lestor, Miss Joan (13/11/31)	Eccles
Lab	Lewis, Terence (Terry) (29/12/35)	Worsley
Con	*Lidington, David Roy (30/6/56)	Aylesbury
Con	Lightbown, David Lincoln (30/11/32)	South East Staffordshire
Con	Lilley, Rt. Hon. Peter Bruce (23/8/43)	St Albans
Lab	Litherland, Robert Kenneth (Bob) (23/6/30)	Manchester, Central
Lab	Livingstone, Kenneth Robert (Ken) (17/6/45)	Brent, East
Lab	Lloyd, Anthony Joseph (Tony) (25/2/50)	Stretford
Con	Lloyd, Peter Robert Cable (12/11/37)	Fareham
PC	*Llwyd, Elfyn (26/9/51)	Meirionnydd Nant Conwy
1st DCWM	Lofthouse, Geoffrey (18/12/25)	Pontefract & Castleford
Con	Lord, Michael Nicholson (17/10/38)	Suffolk, Central
Lab	Loyden, Edward (Eddie) (3/5/23)	Liverpool, Garston
Con	*Luff, Peter James (18/2/55)	Worcester
Con	Lyell, Rt. Hon. Sir Nicholas Walter, QC (6/12/38)	Mid Bedfordshire
LD	*Lynne, Elizabeth (Liz) (22/1/48)	Rochdale
Lab	MacDonald, Calum Alastair (7/5/56)	Western Isles
Con	MacGregor, Rt. Hon. John Roddick Russell, OBE (14/2/37)	South Norfolk
Con	MacKay, Andrew James (27/8/49)	East Berkshire
Lab	*MacKinlay, Andrew Stuart (24/4/49)	Thurrock
Con	Maclean, David John (16/5/53)	Penrith & the Border
LD	Maclennan, Robert Adam Ross (26/6/36)	Caithness & Sutherland
Lab	Madden, Maxwell Francis (Max) (29/10/41)	Bradford, West
LD	Maddock, Diana (19/5/45)	Christchurch
Con	Madel, William David (6/8/38)	South West Bedfordshire
UU	Maginnis, Kenneth (Ken) (21/1/38)	Fermanagh & South Tyrone
Lab	Mahon, Mrs Alice (28/9/37)	Halifax
Con	*Maitland, Lady Olga Helen (23/5/44)	Sutton & Cheam
Con	Major, Rt. Hon. John (29/3/43)	Huntingdon
SDLP	Mallon, Seamus (17/8/36)	Newry & Armagh

(Continued)

Party	Member (Birthdate)	Constituency
Con	#Malone, Peter Gerald (21/7/50)	Winchester
Lab	*Mandelson, Peter Benjamin (21/10/53)	Hartlepool
Con	Mans, Keith Douglas Rowland (10/2/47)	Wyre
Lab	Marek, Dr John (24/12/40)	Wrexham
Con	Marland, Paul (19/3/40)	West Gloucestershire
Con	Marlow, Antony Rivers (Tony) (17/6/40)	Northampton, North
Lab	Marshall, David (7/5/41)	Glasgow, Shettleston
Lab	Marshall, James (13/3/41)	Leicester, South
Con	Marshall, John Leslie (19/8/40)	Hendon, South
Con	Marshall, Sir Robert Michael (21/6/30)	Arundel
Con	Martin, David John Pattison (5/2/45)	Portsmouth, South
Lab	Martin, Michael John (3/7/45)	Glasgow, Springburn
Lab	Martlew, Eric Anthony (1/3/49)	Carlisle
Con	Mates, Michael John (9/6/34)	East Hampshire
Con	Mawhinney, Dr Brian Stanley (2/7/40)	Peterborough
Lab	Maxton, John Alston (5/5/36)	Glasgow, Cathcart
Con	Mayhew, Rt. Hon. Sir Patrick Barnabas Burke, QC (11/9/29)	Tunbridge Wells
Lab	McAllion, John (13/2/48)	Dundee, East
Lab	McAvoy, Thomas McLaughlin (15/11/27)	Glasgow, Rutherglen
Lab	McCartney, Ian (25/4/51)	Makerfield
UDUP	McCrea, Rev Robert Thomas William, DC (6/8/48)	Mid-Ulster
Lab	McFall, John (14/10/44)	Dumbarton
SDLP	McGrady, Edward Kevin, FCA (Eddie) (3/6/35)	South Down
Lab	McKelvey, William (1/7/34)	Kilmarnock & Loudoun
Lab	McLeish, Henry Baird (15/6/48)	Fife, Central
Con	McLoughlin, Patrick Allen (30/11/57)	West Derbyshire
Lab	McMaster, Gordon (13/2/60)	Paisley, South
Con	McNair-Wilson, Sir Patrick Michael Ernest David (28/5/29)	New Forest
Lab	McNamara, Joseph Kevin (5/9/34)	Kingston upon Hull, North
Lab	McWilliam, John David (16/5/41)	Blaydon
Lab	Meacher, Michael Hugh (4/11/39)	Oldham, West
Lab	Meale, Joseph Alan (31/7/49)	Mansfield
Con	Mellor, David John, QC (12/3/49)	Putney
Con	#Merchant, Piers Ralph Garfield (2/1/51)	Beckenham
Lab	Michael, Alun Edward, JP (22/8/43)	Cardiff, South & Penarth
LD	Michie, Mrs Janet Ray (4/2/34)	Argyll & Bute
Lab	Michie, William (Bill) (24/11/35)	Sheffield, Heeley
Lab	*Milburn, Alan (27/1/58)	Darlington
Lab	*Miller, Andrew Peter (23/3/49)	Ellesmere Port & Neston
Con	*Milligan, Stehen David Wyatt (12/5/48)	Eastleigh
Con	Mills, Iain Campbell (21/4/40)	Meriden
Con	Mitchell, Andrew John Bower (23/3/56)	Gedling
Lab	Mitchell, Austin Vernon (19/9/34)	Great Grimsby
Con	Mitchell, Sir David Bower (20/6/28)	North West Hampshire
Con	Moate, Roger Denis (12/5/38)	Faversham
UU	Molyneaux, Rt. Hon. James Henry (27/8/20)	Lagan Valley
Con	Monro, Sir Hector Seymour Peter (4/10/22)	Dumfries
Con	Montgomery, Sir William Fergus (25/11/27)	Altrincham & Sale
Lab	Moonie, Dr Lewis George (25/2/47)	Kirkcaldy
Lab	Morgan, Hywel Rhodri (29/9/39)	Cardiff, West
Lab	Morley, Elliot Anthony (6/7/52)	Glanford & Scunthorpe
Lab	Morris, Rt. Hon. Alfred (23/3/28)	Manchester, Wythenshawe
Lab	*Morris, Ms Estelle (17/6/52)	Birmingham, Yardley
Lab	Morris, Rt. Hon. John, QC (5/11/31)	Aberavon
CWM	Morris, Michael Wolfgang Laurence (25/11/36)	Northampton, South
Con	Moss, Malcolm Douglas (6/3/43)	North East Cambridgeshire
Lab	Mowlam, Miss Marjorie, PhD (18/9/49)	Redcar
Lab	*Mudie, George Edward (6/2/45)	Leeds, East
Lab	Mullin, Christopher John (Chris) (12/12/47)	Sunderland, South
Lab	Murphy, Paul Peter (25/11/48)	Torfaen
Con	Needham, Richard Francis (9/1/42)	North Wiltshire
Con	Nelson, Richard Anthony (11/6/48)	Chichester
Con	Neubert, Sir Michael Jon (3/9/33)	Romford
Con	Newton, Rt. Hon. Anthony Harold, OBE (Tony) (29/8/37)	Braintree
Con	Nicholls, Patrick Charles Martyn (14/11/48)	Teignbridge
Con	Nicholson, David John (17/8/44)	Taunton
Con	Nicholson, Miss Emma Harriet (16/10/41)	Devon, West & Torridge
Con	Norris, Steven John (24/5/45)	Epping Forest
Lab	Oakes, Rt. Hon. Gordon James (22/6/31)	Halton
Lab	*O'Brien, Michael (Mike) (19/6/54)	North Warwickshire
Lab	O'Brien, William (25/1/29)	Normanton
Lab	O'Hara, Edward (Eddie) (1/10/37)	Knowsley South
Lab	*Olner, William John (Bill) (9/5/42)	Nuneaton
Lab	O'Neill, Martin John (6/1/45)	Clackmannan
Con	Onslow, Rt. Hon. Cranley Gordon Douglas (8/6/26)	Woking
Con	Oppenheim, Phillip Anthony Charles Lawrence (20/3/56)	Amber Valley
Lab	Orme, Rt. Hon. Stanley (Stan) (5/4/23)	Salford, East
Con	#Ottaway, Richard Geoffrey James (24/5/45)	Croydon, South
Con	Page, Richard Lewis (22/2/41)	South West Hertfordshire
Con	Paice, James Edward Thornton (24/4/49)	Cambridgeshire, South East
UDUP	Paisley, Rev Ian Richard Kyle (6/4/26)	North Antrim
Lab	Parry, Robert (Bob) (8/1/33)	Liverpool, Riverside
Lab	Patchett, Terry (11/7/40)	Barnsley, East
Con	Patnick, Cyril Irvine, OBE (15/10/29)	Sheffield, Hallam
Con	Patten, Rt. Hon. John Haggitt Charles (17/7/45)	Oxford, West & Abingdon

(Continued)

Party	Member (Birthdate)	Constituency
Con	Pattie, Rt. Hon. Sir Geoffrey Edwin (17/1/36)	Chertsey & Walton
Con	Pawsey, James Francis (21/8/33)	Rugby & Kenilworth
Con	Peacock, Mrs Elizabeth Joan, JP (4/9/37)	Batley & Spen
Lab	Pendry, Thomas (Tom) (10/6/34)	Stalybridge & Hyde
Con	*Pickles, Eric Jack (20/4/52)	Brentwood & Ongar
Lab	*Pickthall, Colin (13/9/44)	West Lancashire
Lab	Pike, Peter Leslie (26/6/37)	Burnley
Lab	*Pope, Greg James (29/8/60)	Hyndburn
Con	Porter, David John (16/4/48)	Waveney
Con	Porter, George Barrington (Barry) (11/6/39)	Wirral, South
Con	Portillo, Rt. Hon. Michael Denzil Xavier (26/5/53)	Enfield, Southgate
Lab	Powell, Raymond (Ray) (19/6/28)	Ogmore
Con	Powell, William Rhys (3/8/48)	Corby
Lab	*Prentice, Bridget Theresa (28/12/52)	Lewisham, East
Lab	*Prentice, Gordon (28/1/51)	Pendle
Lab	Prescott, John Leslie (31/5/38)	Kingston-upon-Hull, East
Lab	Primarolo, Ms Dawn (2/5/54)	Bristol, South
Lab	*Purchase, Kenneth (8/1/39)	Wolverhampton, North East
Lab	Quin, Ms Joyce Gwendolen (26/11/44)	Gateshead, East
Lab	Radice, Giles Heneage (4/10/36)	North Durham
Lab	Randall, Stuart Jeffrey (22/6/36)	Kingston-upon-Hull, West
Con	Rathbone, John Rankin (Tim), FRSA (17/3/33)	Lewes
Lab	#Raynsford, Wyvill Richard Nicholls (Nick) (28/1/45)	Greenwich
Lab	Redmond, Martin (15/8/37)	Don Valley
Con	Redwood, John Alan (15/6/51)	Wokingham
Lab	Reid, Dr John (8/5/47)	Motherwell, North
LD	Rendel, David (15/4/49)	Newbury
Con	Renton, Rt. Hon. Ronald Timothy (Tim) (28/5/32)	Mid-Sussex
Con	*Richards, Roderick (Rod) (12/3/47)	Clwyd, North West
Lab	Richardson, Josephine (Jo) (28/8/23)	Barking
Con	Riddick, Graham Edward Galloway (30/6/55)	Colne Valley
Con	Rifkind, Rt. Hon. Malcolm Leslie, QC (21/6/46)	Edinburgh, Pentlands
Con	*Robathan, Andrew Robert George (17/7/51)	Blaby
Con	Roberts, Rt. Hon. Sir Ieuan Wyn Pritchard (10/7/30)	Conwy
Lab	Robertson, George Islay Macneill (12/4/46)	Hamilton
Con	*Robertson, Raymond Scott (11/12/59)	Aberdeen, South
Lab	Robinson, Geoffrey (25/5/38)	Coventry, North West
Con	#Robinson, Mark Noel Foster (26/12/46)	Somerton & Frome
UDUP	Robinson, Peter David (29/12/48)	Belfast, East
Lab	*Roche, Mrs Barbara Maureen (13/4/54)	Hornsey & Wood Green
Con	Roe, Mrs Marion Audrey (1/7/36)	Broxbourne
Lab	Rogers, Allan Ralph (24/10/32)	Rhondda
Lab	Rooker, Jeffrey William (Jeff) (5/6/41)	Birmingham, Perry Barr
Lab	Rooney, Terence Henry (Terry) (11/11/50)	Bradford North
Lab	Ross, Ernest (Ernie) (27/7/42)	Dundee, West
UU	Ross, William (4/2/36)	Londonderry, East
Con	Rowe, Andrew John Bernard (11/9/35)	Mid Kent
Lab	Rowlands, Edward (Ted) (23/1/40)	Merthyr Tydfil & Rhymney
Lab	Ruddock, Ms Joan Mary (28/12/43)	Lewisham, Deptford
Con	Rumbold, Rt. Hon. Dame Angela Claire Rosemary, DBE (11/8/32)	Mitcham & Morden
Con	Ryder, Rt. Hon. Richard Andrew, OBE (4/2/49)	Mid Norfolk
Con	Sackville, Thomas Geoffrey (Tom) (26/10/50)	Bolton, West
Con	Sainsbury, Rt. Hon. Timothy Alan Davan (11/6/32)	Hove
SNP	Salmond, Alexander Elliott Anderson (Alex) (31/12/54)	Banff & Buchan
Con	Scott, Rt. Hon. Nicholas Paul, MBE (5/8/33)	Chelsea
Lab	Sedgemore, Brian Charles (17/3/37)	Hackney, South & Shoreditch
Con	Shaw, David Lawrence (14/11/50)	Dover
Con	Shaw, Sir John Giles Dunkerley (16/11/31)	Pudsey
Lab	Sheerman, Barry John (17/8/40)	Huddersfield
Lab	Sheldon, Rt. Hon. Robert Edward (13/9/23)	Ashton-under-Lyne
Con	Shephard, Rt. Hon. Gillian Patricia (22/1/40)	South West Norfolk
Con	Shepherd, Colin Ryley (13/1/38)	Hereford
Con	Shepherd, Richard Charles Scrimgeour (6/12/42)	Aldridge Brownhills
Con	Shersby, Julian Michael (17/2/33)	Uxbridge
Lab	Shore, Rt. Hon. Peter David (20/5/24)	Bethnal Green & Stepney
Lab	Short, Clare (15/2/46)	Birmingham, Ladywood
Lab	*Simpson, Alan (20/9/48)	Nottingham, South
Con	Sims, Roger Edward (27/1/30)	Chislehurst
Con	Skeet, Sir Trevor Herbert Harry, KT, LLB (28/1/18)	North Bedfordshire
Lab	Skinner, Dennis Edward (11/2/32)	Bolsover
Lab	Smith, Andrew (1/2/51)	Oxford, East
Lab	Smith, Christopher Robert (Chris) (24/7/51)	Islington, South & Finsbury
Con	Smith, Sir Dudley Gordon (14/11/26)	Warwick & Leamington
Lab	Smith, Rt. Hon. John, QC (13/9/38)	Monklands, East
Lab	*Smith, Llewellyn (16/4/44)	Blaenau Gwent
Con	Smith, Timothy John (Tim) (5/10/47)	Beaconsfield
UU	Smyth, Rev William Martin, BA, BD (15/6/31)	Belfast, South
Lab	Snape, Peter Charles (12/2/42)	West Bromwich, East
Con	Soames, Hon. Arthur Nicholas Winston (12/2/48)	Crawley
Lab	Soley, Clive Stafford (7/5/39)	Hammersmith
Lab	Spearing, Nigel John (8/10/30)	Newham, South
Con	Speed, Herbert Keith, RD (11/3/34)	Ashford
Lab	#Spellar, John Francis (5/8/47)	Warley, West
Con	#Spencer, Sir Derek Harold, QC (31/3/36)	Brighton, Pavilion
Con	Spicer, Sir James Wilton (4/10/25)	West Dorset

(Continued)

Party	Member (Birthdate)	Constituency
Con	Spicer, William Michael Hardy (22/1/43)	South Worcestershire
Con	*Spink, Dr Robert Michael (1/8/48)	Castle Point
Con	*Spring, Richard John Grenville (24/9/46)	Bury St Edmunds
Con	#Sproat, Iain Macdonald (8/11/38)	Harwich
Lab	*Squire, Mrs Rachel Anne (13/7/54)	Dunfermline, West
Con	Squire, Robin Clifford (12/7/44)	Hornchurch
Con	Stanley, Rt. Hon. Sir John Paul (19/1/42)	Tonbridge & Malling
LD	Steel, Rt. Hon. Sir David Martin Scott, KBE (31/3/38)	Tweeddale, Ettrick & Lauderdale
Con	Steen, Anthony David (22/7/39)	South Hams
Lab	Steinberg, Gerald Neil (Gerry) (20/4/45)	City of Durham
Con	*Stephen, Michael (25/9/42)	Shoreham
Con	Stern, Michael Charles (3/8/42)	Bristol, North West
Lab	*Stevenson, George William (30/8/38)	Stoke on Trent, South
Con	Stewart, John Allan (1/7/42)	Eastwood
Lab	Stott, Roger, CBE (7/8/43)	Wigan
Lab	Strang, Dr Gavin Steel (10/7/43)	Edinburgh, East
Lab	Straw, John Whitaker (Jack) (3/8/46)	Blackburn
Con	*Streeter, Gary Nicholas (2/10/55)	Plymouth, Sutton
Con	Sumberg, David Anthony Gerald (2/1/41)	Bury, South
Con	*Sweeney, Walter Edward (23/4/49)	Vale of Glamorgan
Con	*Sykes, John David (24/8/56)	Scarborough
Con	Tapsell, Sir Peter Hannay Bailey (1/2/30)	East Lindsey
Con	Taylor, Sir Edward Macmillian (Teddy) (18/4/37)	Southend, East
Con	Taylor, Ian Colin, MBE (18/4/45)	Esher
UU	Taylor, Rt. Hon. John David (John D) (24/12/37)	Strangford
Con	Taylor, John Mark (John M) (19/8/41)	Solihull
LD	Taylor, Matthew Owen John (3/1/63)	Truro
Lab	Taylor, Mrs Winifred Ann (2/7/47)	Dewsbury
Con	Temple-Morris, Peter (12/2/38)	Leominster
Con	*Thomason, Kenneth Roy (14/12/44)	Bromsgrove
Con	Thompson, Sir Donald (13/11/31)	Calder Valley
Con	Thompson, Hugh Patrick (21/10/35)	Norwich, North
Lab	Thompson, John (Jack) (27/8/28)	Wansbeck
Con	Thornton, George Malcolm (3/4/39)	Crosby
Con	Thurnham, Peter Giles (21/8/38)	Bolton, North East
Lab	*Tipping, Simon Patrick (Paddy) (24/10/49)	Sherwood
Con	Townend, John Ernest, FCA (12/6/34)	Bridlington
Con	Townsend, Cyril David (21/12/37)	Bexleyheath
Con	Tracey, Richard Patrick (8/2/43)	Surbiton
Con	Tredinnick, David Arthur Stephen (19/1/50)	Bosworth
Con	*Trend, Michael St John (19/4/52)	Windsor & Maidenhead
UU	Trimble, William David (15/10/44)	Upper Bann
Con	Trotter, Neville Guthrie (27/1/32)	Tynemouth
Lab	Turner, Dennis (26/8/42)	Wolverhampton, South East
Con	Twinn, Dr Ian David (26/4/50)	Edmonton
LD	#Tyler, Paul Archer, CBE (29/10/41)	North Cornwall
Con	Vaughan, Sir Gerard Folliott (11/6/23)	Reading, East
Lab	Vaz, Nigel Keith Anthony Standish, BA (Cantab) (26/11/56)	Leicester, East
Con	Viggers, Peter John (13/3/38)	Gosport
Con	Waldegrave, Rt. Hon. William Arthur (15/8/46)	Bristol, West
Con	Walden, George Gordon Harvey, CMG (15/9/39)	Buckingham
UU	Walker, Alfred Cecil, JP (17/12/34)	Belfast, North
Lab	Walker, Rt. Hon. Harold (12/7/27)	Doncaster, Central
Con	Walker, William Connoll (Bill) (20/2/29)	North Tayside
LD	Wallace, James Robert (25/8/54)	Orkney & Shetland
Con	Waller, Gary Peter Anthony (24/6/45)	Keighley
Lab	Walley, Joan Lorraine (23/1/49)	Stoke-on-Trent, North
Con	Ward, John Devereux, CBE (8/3/25)	Poole
Lab	Wardell, Gareth Lodwig (29/11/44)	Gower
Con	Wardle, Charles Frederick (23/8/39)	Bexhill & Battle
Lab	Wareing, Robert Nelson (20/8/30)	Liverpool, West Derby
Con	*Waterson, Nigel (12/10/50)	Eastbourne
Lab	Watson, Michael Goodall (Mike) (1/5/49)	Glasgow, Central
Con	Watts, John Arthur (19/4/47)	Slough
Con	Wells, Petrie Bowen (4/8/35)	Hertford & Stortford
SNP	Welsh, Andrew, MA (Hons) (15/4/44)	Angus, East
Con	Wheeler, Sir John Daniel, JP DL (1/5/40)	Westminster, North
Con	Whitney, Raymond William, OBE (Ray) (28/11/30)	Wycombe
Con	*Whittingdale, John Flasby Lawrance, OBE (16/10/59)	Colchester South & Maldon
Lab	*Wicks, Malcolm Hunt (1/7/47)	Croydon, North West
Con	Widdecombe, Miss Ann Noreen (4/10/47)	Maidstone
Con	Wiggin, Alfred William, TD (Jerry) (24/2/37)	Weston-super-Mare
PC	Wigley, Dafydd (1/4/43)	Caernarfon
Con	Wilkinson, John Arbuthnot Duncane (23/9/40)	Ruislip-Northwood
Con	*Willetts, David Lindsay (9/3/56)	Havant
Lab	Williams, Rt. Hon. Alan John (14/10/30)	Swansea, West
Lab	Williams, Alan Wynne (Alan W) (21/12/45)	Carmarthen
Con	Wilshire, David (16/9/43)	Spelthorne
Lab	Wilson, Brian David Henderson (13/12/48)	Cunninghame, North
Lab	Winnick, David Julian (26/6/33)	Walsall, North
Con	Winterton, Jane Ann (6/3/41)	Congleton
Con	Winterton, Nicholas Raymond (31/3/38)	Macclesfield
Lab	Wise, Mrs Audrey (30/6/35)	Preston
Con	Wolfson, Geoffrey Mark (7/4/34)	Sevenoaks
Con	Wood, Timothy John Rogerson (13/8/40)	Stevenage

(Continued)

Party	Member (Birthdate)	Constituency
Lab	Worthington, Anthony (Tony) (11/10/41)	Clydebank & Milngavie
Lab	Wray, James (28/4/38)	Glasgow, Provan
Lab	*Wright, Anthony Wayland (Tony) (11/3/48)	Cannock & Burntwood
Con	Yeo, Timothy Stephen Kenneth (Tim) (20/3/45)	South Suffolk
Lab	Young, David Wright (12/10/30)	Bolton, South-East
Con	Young, Sir George Samuel Knatchbull, Bt (16/7/41)	Ealing, Acton

* Indicates a Member who has not previously served in the House. # Indicates a Member, who, though not a Member immediately before the April 1992 election, has previously served in the House (not necessarily for the same constituency).

Political Constituencies and MPs: By County

(As at July 1993)

Greater London

BARKING & DAGENHAM
- Barking .... Ms Jo Richardson (La)
- Dagenham .... Bryan Gould (La)

BARNET
- Chipping Barnet .... Sydney Chapman (C)
- Finchley .... Hartley Booth (C)
- Hendon North .... John Gorst (C)
- Hendon South .... John Marshall (C)

BEXLEY
- Bexleyheath .... Cyril Townsend (C)
- Erith & Crayford .... David Evennett (C)
- Old Bexley & Sidcup .... Sir Edward Heath (C)

BRENT
- East .... Ken Livingstone (La)
- North .... Sir Rhodes Boyson (C)
- South .... Paul Boateng (La)

BROMLEY
- Beckenham .... Piers Merchant (C)
- Chislehurst .... Roger Sims (C)
- Orpington .... John Horam (C)
- Ravensbourne .... Sir John Hunt (C)

CAMDEN
- Hampstead & Highgate .... Miss Glenda Jackson (La)
- Holborn & St Pancras .... Frank Dobson (La)

CITY OF LONDON – see WESTMINSTER

CROYDON
- Central .... Sir Paul Beresford (C)
- North East .... David Congdon (C)
- North West .... Malcolm Wicks (La)
- South .... Richard Ottaway (C)

EALING
- Acton .... Sir George Young Bt (C)
- North .... Harry Greenway (C)
- Southall .... Piara Khabra (La)

ENFIELD
- Edmonton .... Dr Ian Twinn (C)
- North .... Tim Eggar (C)
- Southgate .... Michael Portillo (C)

GREENWICH
- Eltham .... Peter Bottomley (C)
- Greenwich .... Nick Raynsford (La)
- Woolwich .... John Austin-Walker (La)

HACKNEY
- North & Stoke Newington .... Ms Diane Abbott (La)
- South & Shoreditch .... Brian Sedgemore (La)

HAMMERSMITH & FULHAM
- Fulham .... Matthew Carrington (C)
- Hammersmith .... Clive Soley (La)

HARINGEY
- Hornsey & Wood Green .... Mrs Barbara Roche (La)
- Tottenham .... Bernie Grant (La)

HARROW
- East .... Hugh Dykes (C)
- West .... Robert G. Hughes (C)

HAVERING
- Hornchurch .... Robin Squire (C)
- Romford .... Sir Michael Neubert (C)
- Upminster .... Sir Nicholas Bonsor (C)

HILLINGDON
- Hayes & Harlington .... Terry Dicks (C)
- Ruislip-Northwood .... John Wilkinson (C)
- Uxbridge .... Michael Shersby (C)

HOUNSLOW
- Brentford & Isleworth .... Nirj Deva (C)
- Feltham & Heston .... Alan Keen (La)

ISLINGTON
- North .... Jeremy Corbyn (La)
- South & Finsbury .... Chris Smith (La)

KENSINGTON & CHELSEA
- Chelsea .... Nicholas Scott (C)
- Kensington .... Dudley Fishburn (C)

KINGSTON UPON THAMES
- Kingston upon Thames .... Norman Lamont (C)
- Surbiton .... Richard Tracey JP (C)

LAMBETH
- Norwood .... John Fraser (La)
- Streatham .... Keith Hill (La)
- Vauxhall .... Miss Kate Hoey (La)

LEWISHAM
- Deptford .... Mrs Joan Ruddock (La)
- East .... Bridget Prentice (La)
- West .... Jim Dowd (La)

MERTON
- Mitcham & Morden .... Dame Angela Rumbold (C)
- Wimbledon .... Dr Charles Goodson-Wickes (C)

NEWHAM
- North East .... Ron Leighton (La)
- North West .... Tony Banks (La)
- South .... Nigel Spearing (La)

REDBRIDGE
- Ilford North .... Vivian Bendall (C)
- Ilford South .... Mike Gapes (La)
- Wanstead & Woodford .... James Arbuthnot (C)

RICHMOND UPON THAMES
- Richmond & Barnes .... Jeremy Hanley (C)
- Twickenham .... Toby Jessel (C)

SOUTHWARK
- Dulwich .... Ms Tessa Jowell (La)
- Peckham .... Ms Harriet Harman (La)
- Southwark & Bermondsey .... Simon Hughes (LD)

SUTTON
- Carshalton & Wallington .... Nigel Forman (C)
- Sutton & Cheam .... Lady Olga Maitland (C)

TOWER HAMLETS
- Bethnal Green & Stepney .... Peter Shore (La)
- Bow & Poplar .... Ms Mildred Gordon (La)

WALTHAM FOREST
- Chingford .... Iain Duncan-Smith (C)
- Leyton .... Harry Cohen (La)
- Walthamstow .... Neil Gerrard (La)

WANDSWORTH
- Battersea .... John Bowis (C)
- Putney .... David Mellor (C)
- Tooting .... Tom Cox (La)

WESTMINSTER (& CITY OF LONDON)
- City of London & Westminster South .... Peter Brooke (C)
- Westminster North .... Sir John Wheeler (C)

Metropolitan Counties

GREATER MANCHESTER

BOLTON
- North East .... Peter Thurnham (C)
- South East .... David Young (La)
- West .... Tom Sackville (C)

BURY
- North .... Alistair Burt (C)
- South .... David Sumberg (C)

(Continued)

MANCHESTER
Blackley....Kenneth Eastham (La)
Central....Bob Litherland (La)
Gorton....Gerald Kaufman (La)
Withington....Keith Bradley (La)
Wythenshawe....Alfred Morris (La)
Stretford (part)....Tony Lloyd (La)
TRAFFORD
Altrincham & Sale....Sir Fergus Montgomery (C)
Davyhulme....Winston Churchill (C)
Stretford (part)....Tony Lloyd (La)
Oldham
Littleborough & Saddleworth (part)....Geoffrey Dickens (C)
Oldham Central & Royton....Bryan Davies (La)
Oldham West....Michael Meacher (La)
ROCHDALE
Heywood & Middleton....Jim Callaghan (La)
Littleborough & Saddleworth (part)....Geoffrey Dickens (C)
Rochdale....Ms Liz Lynne (LD)
SALFORD
Eccles....Miss Joan Lestor (La)
Salford East....Stan Orme (La)
Worsley (part)....Terry Lewis (La)
STOCKPORT
Cheadle....Stephen Day (C)
Denton & Reddish (part)....Andrew Bennett (La)
Hazel Grove....Sir Thomas Arnold (C)
Stockport....Ann Coffey (La)
TAMESIDE
Ashton under Lyne....Robert Sheldon (La)
Denton & Reddish (part)....Andrew Bennett (La)
Stalybridge & Hyde....Tom Pendry (La)
WIGAN
Leigh....Lawrence Cunliffe (La)
Makerfield....Ian McCartney (La)
Wigan....Roger Stott (La)
Worsley (part)....Terry Lewis (La)

MERSEYSIDE

KNOWSLEY
North....George Howarth (La)
South....Eddie O'Hara (Lab)
LIVERPOOL
Broadgreen....Jane Kennedy (La)
Garston....Eddie Loyden (La)
Mossley Hill....David Alton (LD)
Riverside....Robert Parry (La)
Walton....Peter Kilfoyle (La)
West Derby....Robert Wareing (La)
ST HELENS
North....John Evans (La)
South....Gerald Bermingham (La)
SEFTON
Bootle....Joe Benton (La)
Crosby....Sir Malcolm Thornton (C)
Southport....Matthew Banks (C)
WIRRAL
Birkenhead....Frank Field (La)
Wallasey....Ms Angela Eagle (La)
Wirral South....Barry Porter (C)
Wirral West....David Hunt (C)

TYNE & WEAR

GATESHEAD
Blaydon....John McWilliam (La)
Gateshead East....Ms Joyce Quin (La)
Tyne Bridge (part)....David Clelland (La)
NEWCASTLE UPON TYNE
Central....Jim Cousins (La)
East....Nicholas Brown (La)
North....Doug Henderson (La)
Tyne Bridge (part)....David Clelland (La)
NORTH TYNESIDE
Tynemouth....Neville Trotter (C)
Wallsend....Stephen Byers (La)
SOUTH TYNESIDE
Jarrow....Don Dixon (La)
South Shields....Dr David Clark (La)
SUNDERLAND
Houghton & Washington....Roland Boyes (La)
Sunderland North....William Etherington (La)
Sunderland South....Chris Mullin (La)

WEST MIDLANDS

BIRMINGHAM
Edgbaston....Dame Jill Knight (C)
Erdington....Robin Corbett (La)
Hall Green....Andrew Hargreaves (C)
Hodge Hill....Terry Davis (La)
Ladywood....Ms Clare Short (La)
Northfield....Richard Burden (La)
Perry Barr....Jeff Rooker (La)
Selly Oak....Dr Lynne Jones (La)
Small Heath....Roger Godsiff (La)
Sparkbrook....Roy Hattersley (La)
Sutton Coldfield....Sir Norman Fowler (C)
Yardley....Ms Estelle Morris (La)
COVENTRY
North East....Robert Ainsworth (La)
North West....Geoffrey Robinson (La)
South East....Jim Cunningham (La)
South West....John Butcher (C)
DUDLEY
East....Dr John Gilbert (La)
West....Dr John Blackburn (C)
Halesowen & Stourbridge....Warren Hawksley (C)
SANDWELL
Warley East....Andrew Faulds (La)
Warley West....John Spellar (La)
West Bromwich East....Peter Snape (La)
West Bromwich West....Betty Boothroyd (The Speaker)
SOLIHULL
Meriden....Iain Mills (C)
Solihull....John Mark Taylor (C)
WALSALL
Aldridge-Brownhills....Richard Shepherd (C)
Walsall North....David Winnick (La)
Walsall South....Bruce George (La)
WOLVERHAMPTON
North East....Ken Purchase (La)
South East....Dennis Turner (La)
South West....Nicholas Budgen (C)

YORKSHIRE-SOUTH

BARNSLEY
Central....Eric Illsley (La)
East....Terry Patchett (La)
West and Penistone....Michael Clapham (La)
DONCASTER
Central....Sir Harold Walker (La)
North....Kevin Hughes (La)
Don Valley....Martin Redmond (La)
ROTHERHAM
Rotherham....Jimmy Boyce (La)
Rother Valley....Kevin Barron (La)
Wentworth....Peter Hardy (La)
SHEFFIELD
Attercliffe....Clive Betts (La)
Brightside....David Blunkett (La)
Central....Richard Caborn (La)
Hallam....Irvine Patnick (C)
Heeley....Bill Michie (La)
Hillsborough....Helen Jackson (La)

YORKSHIRE-WEST

BRADFORD
Bradford North....Terry Rooney (La)
Bradford South....Bob Cryer (La)
Bradford West....Max Madden (La)
Keighley....Gary Waller (C)
Shipley....Sir Marcus Fox (C)
CALDERDALE
Calder Valley....Sir Donald Thompson (C)
Halifax....Mrs Alice Mahon (La)
KIRKLEES
Batley & Spen....Mrs Elizabeth Peacock (C)
Colne Valley....Graham Riddick (C)
Dewsbury....Mrs Ann Taylor (La)
Huddersfield....Barry Sheerman (La)
LEEDS
Elmet....Spencer Batiste (C)
Leeds Central....Derek Fatchett (La)
Leeds East....George Mudie (La)
Leeds North East....Timothy Kirkhope (C)
Leeds North West....Dr Keith Hampson (C)
Leeds West....John Battle (La)
Leeds South & Morley....John Gunnell (La)
Normanton (part)....William O'Brien (La)
Pudsey....Sir Giles Shaw (C)
WAKEFIELD
Hemsworth....Derek Enright (La)
Normanton (part)....William O'Brien (La)
Pontefract & Castleford....Geoffrey Lofthouse (1st DCWM)
Wakefield....David Hinchliffe (La)

(Continued)

Non-Metropolitan Counties

AVON
Bath .... Don Foster (LD)
Bristol East .... Ms Jean Corston (La)
Bristol North West .... Michael Stern (C)
Bristol South .... Ms Dawn Primarolo (La)
Bristol West .... William Waldegrave (C)
Kingswood .... Roger Berry (La)
Northavon .... Sir John Cope (C)
Wansdyke .... Jack Aspinwall (C)
Weston-super-Mare .... Jerry Wiggin TD (C)
Woodspring .... Dr Liam Fox (C)
BEDFORDSHIRE
Mid-Bedfordshire .... Sir Nicholas Lyell (C)
North Bedfordshire .... Sir Trevor Skeet (C)
South West Bedfordshire .... David Madel (C)
North Luton .... John Carlisle (C)
Luton South .... Graham Bright (C)
BERKSHIRE
East Berkshire .... Andrew MacKay (C)
Newbury .... David Rendel (LD)
Reading East .... Sir Gerard Vaughan (C)
Reading West .... Sir Tony Durant (C)
Slough .... John Watts (C)
Windsor & Maidenhead .... Michael Trend (C)
Wokingham .... John Redwood (C)
BUCKINGHAMSHIRE
Aylesbury .... David Lidington (C)
Beaconsfield .... Tim Smith (C)
Buckingham .... George Walden (C)
Chesham & Amersham .... Mrs Cheryl Gillan (C)
Milton Keynes North East .... Peter Butler (C)
Milton Keynes South West .... Barry Legg (C)
Wycombe .... Ray Whitney (C)
CAMBRIDGESHIRE
Cambridge .... Mrs Anne Campbell (La)
Huntingdon .... John Major (C)
Peterborough .... Dr Brian Mawhinney (C)
North East Cambridgeshire .... Malcolm Moss (C)
South East Cambridgeshire .... James Paice (C)
South West Cambridgeshire .... Sir Anthony Grand (C)
CHESHIRE
City of Chester .... Gyles Brandreth (C)
Congleton .... Mrs Ann Winterton (C)
Crewe & Nantwich .... Mrs Gwyneth Dunwoody (La)
Eddisbury .... Alastair Goodlad (C)
Ellesmere Port & Neston .... Andrew Miller (La)
Halton .... Gordon Oakes (La)
Macclesfield .... Nicholas Winterton (C)
Tatton .... Neil Hamilton (C)
Warrington North .... Doug Hoyle (La)
Warrington South .... Mike Hall (La)
CLEVELAND
Langbaurgh .... Michael Bates (C)
Hartlepool .... Peter Mandelson (La)
Middlesbrough .... Stuart Bell (La)
Redcar .... Marjorie Mowlam (La)
Stockton North .... Frank Cook (La)
Stockton South .... Tim Devlin (C)
CORNWALL & THE ISLES OF SCILLY
Falmouth & Camborne .... Sebastian Coe (C)
North Cornwall .... Paul Tyler (LD)
St Ives .... David Harris (C)
South East Cornwall .... Robert Hicks (C)
Truro .... Matthew Taylor (LD)
CUMBRIA
Barrow & Furness .... John Hutton (La)
Carlisle .... Eric Martlew (La)
Copeland .... Dr John Cunningham (La)
Penrith & The Border .... David Maclean (C)
Westmorland & Lonsale .... Michael Jopling (C)
Workington .... Dale Campbell-Savours (La)
DERBYSHIRE
Amber Valley .... Phillip Oppenheim (C)
Bolsover .... Dennis Skinner (La)
Chesterfield .... Tony Benn (La)
Derby North .... Greg Knight (C)
Derby South .... Mrs Margaret Beckett (La)
Erewash .... Mrs Angela Knight (C)
High Peak .... Charles Hendry (C)
North East Derbyshire .... Harry Barnes (La)
South Derbyshire .... Mrs Edwina Currie (C)
West Derbyshire .... Patrick McLoughlin (C)
DEVON
Exeter .... Sir John Hannam (C)
Honiton .... Sir Peter Emery (C)
North Devon .... Nick Harvey (LD)
Plymouth Devonport .... David Jamieson (La)
Plymouth Drake .... Dame Janet Fookes (2nd DCWM)
Plymouth Sutton .... Gary Streeter (C)
South Hams .... Anthony Steen (C)
Teignbridge .... Patrick Nicholls (C)
Tiverton .... Mrs Angela Browning (C)
Torbay .... Rupert Allason (C)
West Devon & Torridge .... Emma Nicholson (C)
DORSET
Bournemouth East .... David Atkinson (C)
Bournemouth West .... John Butterfill (C)
Christchurch .... Diana Maddock (LD)
North Dorset .... Nicholas Baker (C)
Poole .... John Ward (C)
South Dorset .... Ian Bruce (C)
West Dorset .... Sir James Spicer (C)
DURHAM
Bishop Auckland .... Derek Foster (La)
City of Durham .... Gerry Steinberg (La)
Darlington .... Alan Milburn (La)
Easington .... John Cummings (La)
North Durham .... Giles Radice (La)
North West Durham .... Ms Hilary Armstrong (La)
Sedgefield .... Tony Blair (La)
ESSEX
Basildon .... David Amess (C)
Billericay .... Mrs Teresa Gorman (C)
Braintree .... Tony Newton (C)
Brentwood & Ongar .... Eric Pickles (C)
Castle Point .... Dr Robert Spink (C)
Chelmsford .... Simon Burns (C)
Colchester North .... Bernard Jenkin (C)
Colchester South & Maldon .... John Whittingdale (C)
Epping Forest .... Steven Norris (C)
Harlow .... Jerry Hayes (C)
Harwich .... Iain Sproat (C)
Rochford .... Dr Michael Clark (C)
Saffron Walden .... Alan Haselhurst (C)
Southend East .... Sir Teddy Taylor (C)
Southend West .... Paul Channon (C)
Thurrock .... Andrew MacKinlay (La)
GLOUCESTERSHIRE
Cheltenham .... Nigel Jones (LD)
Cirencester & Tewkesbury .... Geoffrey Clifton-Brown (C)
Gloucester .... Douglas French (C)
Gloucester West .... Paul Marland (C)
Stroud .... Roger Knapman (C)
HAMPSHIRE
Aldershot .... Julian Critchley (C)
Basingstoke .... Andrew Hunter (C)
East Hampshire .... Michael Mates (C)
Eastleigh .... Stephen Milligan (C)
Fareham .... Peter Lloyd (C)
Gosport .... Peter Viggers (C)
Havant .... David Willetts (C)
New Forest .... Sir Patrick McNair-Wilson (C)
North West Hampshire .... Sir David Mitchell (C)
Portsmouth North .... Peter Griffiths (C)
Portsmouth South .... David Martin (C)
Romsey & Waterside .... Michael Colvin (C)
Southampton Itchen .... John Denham (La)
Southampton Test .... James Hill (C)
Winchester .... Gerry Malone (C)
HEREFORD & WORCESTER
Bromsgrove .... Roy Thomason (C)
Hereford .... Colin Shepherd (C)
Leominster .... Peter Temple-Morris (C)
Mid Worcestershire .... Eric Forth (C)
South Worcestershire .... Michael Spicer (C)
Worcester .... Peter Luff (C)
Wyre Forest .... Anthony Coombs (C)
HERTFORDSHIRE
Broxbourne .... Mrs Marion Roe (C)
Hertford & Stortford .... Bowen Wells (C)
Hertsmere .... James Clappison (C)
North Hertfordshire .... Oliver Heald (C)
South West Hertfordshire .... Richard Page (C)
St Albans .... Peter Lilley (C)
Stevenage .... Timothy Wood (C)
Watford .... Tristan Garel-Jones (C)
Welwyn Hatfield .... David Evans (C)
West Hertfordshire .... Robert Jones (C)
HUMBERSIDE
Beverley .... James Cran (C)
Boothferry .... David Davis (C)
Bridlington .... John Townend (C)
Brigg & Cleethorpes .... Michael Brown (C)

(Continued)

Glanford & Scunthorpe .... Elliot Morley (La)
Great Grimsby .... Austin Mitchell (La)
Kingston upon Hull East ..... John Prescott (La)
Kingston upon Hull North .... Kevin McNamara (La)
Kingston upon Hull West ..... Stuart Randall (La)
ISLE OF WIGHT
Isle of Wight .... Barry Field (C)
KENT
Ashford .... Sir Keith Speed (C)
Canterbury .... Julian Brazier (C)
Dartford .... Robert Dunn (C)
Dover .... David Shaw (C)
Faversham .... Roger Moate (C)
Folkestone & Hythe .... Michael Howard (C)
Gillingham .... James Couchman (C)
Gravesham .... Jacques Arnold (C)
Maidstone .... Miss Ann Widdecombe (C)
Medway .... Dame Peggy Fenner (C)
Mid Kent .... Andrew Rowe (C)
Sevenoaks .... Mark Wolfson (C)
Thanet North .... Roger Gale (C)
Thanet South .... Jonathan Aitken (C)
Tonbridge & Malling .... Sir John Stanley (C)
Tunbridge Wells .... Sir Patrick Mayhew (C)
LANCASHIRE
Blackburn .... Jack Straw (La)
Blackpool North .... Harold Elletson (C)
Blackpool South .... Nick Hawkins (C)
Burnley .... Peter Pike (La)
Chorley .... Den Dover (C)
Fylde .... Michael Jack (C)
Hyndburn .... Greg Pope (La)
Lancaster .... Dame Elaine Kellett-Bowman (C)
Morecambe & Lunesdale .... Mark Lennox-Boyd (C)
Pendle .... Gordon Prentice (La)
Preston .... Mrs Audrey Wise (La)
Ribble Valley .... Nigel Evans (C)
Rossendale & Darwen .... Ms Janet Anderson (La)
South Ribble .... Robert Atkins (C)
West Lancashire .... Colin Pickthall (La)
Wyre .... Keith Mans (C)
LEICESTERSHIRE
Blaby .... Andrew Robathan (C)
Bosworth .... David Tredinnick (C)
Harborough .... Edward Garnier (C)
Leicester East .... Keith Vaz (La)
Leicester South .... James Marshall (La)
Leicester West .... Greville Janner (La)
Loughborough .... Stephen Dorrell (C)
North West Leicestershire ... David Ashby (C)
Rutland & Melton .... Alan Duncan (C)
LINCOLNSHIRE
East Lindsey .... Sir Peter Tapsell (C)
Gainsborough & Horncastle ... Edward Leigh (C)
Grantham .... Douglas Hogg (C)
Holland with Boston .... Sir Richard Body (C)
Lincoln .... Kenneth Carlisle (C)
Stamford & Spalding .... Quentin Davies (C)
MIDDLESEX (ceased to exist as an administrative county 31/3/65)
NORFOLK
Great Yarmouth .... Michael Carttiss (C)
Mid-Norfolk .... Richard Ryder (C)
North Norfolk .... Ralph Howell (C)
North West Norfolk .... Henry Bellingham (C)
South Norfolk .... John MacGregor (C)
South West Norfolk .... Gillian Shephard (C)
Norwich North .... Patrick Thompson (C)
Norwich South .... John Garrett (La)
NORTHAMPTONSHIRE
Corby .... William Powell (C)
Daventry .... Tim Boswell (C)
Kettering .... Roger Freeman (C)
Northampton North .... Tony Marlow (C)
Northampton South .... Michael Morris (CWM)
Wellingborough .... Peter Fry (C)
NORTHUMBERLAND
Berwick-upon-Tweed .... Alan Beith (LD)
Blyth Valley .... Ronnie Campbell (La)
Hexham .... Peter Atkinson (C)
Wansbeck .... Jack Thompson (La)
NOTTINGHAMSHIRE
Ashfield .... Geoff Hoon (La)
Bassetlaw .... Joe Ashton (La)
Broxtowe .... Jim Lester (C)
Gedling .... Andrew Mitchell (C)
Mansfield .... Alan Meale (La)
Newark .... Richard Alexander (C)
Nottingham East .... John Heppell (La)
Nottingham North .... Graham Allen (La)
Nottingham South .... Alan Simpson (La)
Rushcliffe .... Kenneth Clarke (C)
Sherwood .... Paddy Tipping (La)
OXFORDSHIRE
Banbury .... Tony Baldry (C)
Henley .... Michael Heseltine (C)
Oxford East .... Andrew Smith (La)
Oxford West & Abingdon ...... John Patten (C)
Wantage .... Robert Jackson (C)
Witney .... Douglas Hurd (C)
SHROPSHIRE
Ludlow .... Christopher Gill (C)
North Shropshire .... John Biffen (C)
Shrewsbury & Atcham .... Derek Conway (C)
Wrekin .... Bruce Grocott (La)
SOMERSET
Bridgwater .... Tom King (C)
Somerton & Frome .... Mark Robinson (C)
Taunton .... David Nicholson (C)
Wells .... David Heathcoat-Amory (C)
Yeovil .... Paddy Ashdown (LD)
STAFFORDSHIRE
Burton .... Sir Ivan Lawrence (C)
Cannock & Burntwood .... Dr Tony Wright (La)
Mid Staffordshire .... Michael Fabricant (C)
Newcastle-under-Lyme .... Mrs Llin Golding (La)
Stoke-on-Trent Central ...... Mark Fisher (La)
Stoke-on-Trent North .... Ms Joan Walley (La)
Stoke-on-Trent South .... George Stevenson (La)
South East Staffordshire .... David Lightbown (C)
South Staffordshire .... Patrick Cormack (C)
Stafford .... Bill Cash (C)
Staffordshire Moorlands ..... David Knox (C)
SUFFOLK
Bury St Edmunds .... Richard Spring (C)
Central Suffolk .... Michael Lord (C)
Ipswich .... Jamie Cann (La)
South Suffolk .... Tim Yeo (C)
Suffolk Coastal .... John Gummer (C)
Waveney .... David Porter (C)
SURREY
Chertsey & Walton .... Sir Geoffrey Pattie (C)
Surrey East .... Peter Ainsworth (C)
Epsom & Ewell .... Archie Hamilton (C)
Esher .... Ian Taylor (C)
Guildford .... David Howell (C)
Mole Valley .... Kenneth Baker (C)
North West Surrey .... Sir Michael Grylls (C)
Reigate .... Sir George Gardiner (C)
South West Surrey .... Virginia Bottomley (C)
Spelthorne .... David Wilshire (C)
Woking .... Cranley Onslow (C)
SUSSEX EAST
Bexhill & Battle .... Charles Wardle (C)
Brighton Kemptown .... Andrew Bowden (C)
Brighton Pavilion .... Sir Derek Spencer (C)
Eastbourne .... Nigel Waterson (C)
Hastings & Rye .... Mrs Jacqui Lait (C)
Hove .... Tim Sainsbury (C)
Lewes .... Tim Rathbone (C)
Wealden .... Sir Geoffrey Johnson Smith (C)
SUSSEX WEST
Arundel .... Sir Michael Marshall (C)
Chichester .... Anthony Nelson (C)
Crawley .... Nicholas Soames (C)
Horsham .... Sir Peter Hordern (C)
Mid Sussex .... Tim Renton (C)
Shoreham .... Michael Stephen (C)
Worthing .... Terence Higgins (C)
WARWICKSHIRE
North Warwickshire .... Mike O'Brien (La)
Nuneaton .... Bill Olner (La)
Rugby & Kenilworth .... James Pawsey (C)
Stratford-on-Avon .... Alan Howarth (C)
Warwick & Leamington .... Sir Dudley Smith (C)
WILTSHIRE
Devizes .... Michael Ancram (C)
North Wiltshire .... Richard Needham (C)
Salisbury .... Robert Key (C)
Swindon .... Simon Coombs (C)
Westbury .... David Faber (C)
YORKSHIRE NORTH
Harrogate .... Robert Banks (C)
Richmond (Yorks) .... William Hague (C)
Ryedale .... John Greenway (C)
Scarborough .... John Sykes (C)
Selby .... Michael Alison (C)
Skipton & Ripon .... David Curry (C)
York .... Hugh Bayley (La)

(Continued)

Northern Ireland

ANTRIM
East .... Roy Beggs (UU)
North .... Dr Ian Paisley (UDUP)
South .... Clifford Forsythe (UU)
BELFAST
East .... Peter Robinson (UDUP)
North .... Cecil Walker (UU)
South .... Rev. Martin Smyth (UU)
West .... Dr Joe Hendron (SDLP)
DOWN
North .... Sir James Kilfedder (UPUP)
South .... Eddie McGrady (SDLP)

Fermanagh & South Tyrone ..... Ken Maginnis (UU)
Foyle .... John Hume (SDLP)
Lagan Valley .... James Molyneaux (UU)
Londonderry East .... William Ross (UU)
Newry & Armagh .... Seamus Mallon (SDLP)
Strangford .... John D. Taylor (UU)
Ulster Mid .... Rev. William McCrea (UDUP)
Upper Bann .... David Trimble (UU)

Scotland

BORDERS REGION
Roxburgh & Berwickshire ..... Archy Kirkwood (LD)
Tweeddale, Ettrick
& Lauderdale .... Sir David Steel (LD)
CENTRAL REGION
Clackmannan .... Martin O'Neill (La)
Falkirk East .... Michael Connarty (La)
Falkirk West .... Dennis Canavan (La)
Stirling .... Michael Forsyth (C)
DUMFRIES & GALLOWAY REGION
Dumfries .... Sir Hector Monro (C)
Galloway & Upper Nithsdale .. Ian Lang (C)
FIFE REGION
Dunfermline East .... Gordon Brown (La)
Dunfermline West .... Ms Rachel Squire (La)
Fife Central .... Henry McLeish (La)
Fife North East .... Menzies Campbell (LD)
Kirkcaldy .... Dr Lewis Moonie (La)
GRAMPIAN REGION
Aberdeen North .... Robert Hughes (La)
Aberdeen South .... Raymond Robertson (C)
Banff & Buchan .... Alex Salmond (SNP)
Gordon .... Malcolm Bruce (LD)
Kincardine & Deeside .... George Kynoch (C)
Moray .... Mrs Margaret Ewing (SNP)
HIGHLAND REGION
Caithness & Sutherland .... Robert Maclennan (LD)
Inverness, Nairn & Lochaber .. Sir Russell Johnston (LD)
Ross, Cromarty & Skye .... Charles Kennedy (LD)
LOTHIAN REGION
East Lothian .... John Horne Robertson (La)
EDINBURGH Central .... Alistair Darling (La)
East .... Dr Gavin Strang (La)
Leith .... Malcolm Chisholm (La)
Pentlands .... Malcolm Rifkind (C)
South .... Nigel Griffiths (La)
West .... Lord James Douglas-Hamilton (C)
Linlithgow .... Tam Dalyell (La)
Livingston .... Robin Cook (La)
Midlothian .... Eric Clarke (La)
STRATHCLYDE REGION
Argyll & Bute .... Mrs Ray Michie (LD)

Ayr .... Phil Gallie (C)
Carrick, Cumnock &
Doon Valley .... George Foulkes (La)
Clydebank & Milngavie .... Tony Worthington (La)
Clydesdale .... Jimmy Hood (La)
Cumbernauld & Kilsyth .... Norman Hogg (La)
Cunninghame North .... Brian Wilson (La)
Cunninghame South .... Brian Donohoe (La)
Dumbarton .... John McFall (La)
Eastwood .... Allan Stewart (C)
East Kilbride .... Adam Ingram (La)
Greenock & Port Glasgow .... Dr Norman Godman (La)
GLASGOW Cathcart .... John Maxton (La)
Central .... Mike Watson (La)
Garscadden .... Donald Dewar (La)
Govan .... Ian Davidson (La)
Hillhead .... George Galloway (La)
Maryhill .... Mrs Maria Fyfe (La)
Pollok .... Jimmy Dunnachie (La)
Provan .... James Wray (La)
Rutherglen .... Thomas McAvoy (La)
Shettleston .... David Marshal (La)
Springburn .... Michael Martin (La)
Hamilton .... George Robertson (La)
Kilmarnock & Loudoun .... William McKelvey (La)
Monklands East .... John Smith (La)
Monklands West .... Tom Clarke (La)
Motherwell North .... Dr John Reid (La)
Motherwell South .... Dr Jeremy Bray (La)
Paisley North .... Mrs Irene Adams (Lab)
Paisley South .... Gordon McMaster (Lab)
Renfrew West & Inverclyde ... Thomas Graham (La)
Strathkelvin & Bearsden ... Sam Galbraith (La)
TAYSIDE REGION
Angus East .... Andrew Welsh (SNP)
Dundee East .... John McAllion (La)
Dundee West .... Ernie Ross (La)
North Tayside .... Bill Walker (C)
Perth & Kinross .... Sir Nicholas Fairbairn (C)
ISLANDS AREAS
Orkney & Shetland .... James Wallace (LD)
Western Isles .... Calum Macdonald (La)

Wales

CLWYD
Alyn & Deeside .... Barry Jones (La)
Clwyd North West .... Rod Richards (C)
Clwyd South West .... Martyn Jones (La)
Delyn .... David Hanson (La)
Wrexham .... Dr John Marek (La)
DYFED
Carmarthen .... Dr Alan W Williams (La)
Ceredigion & Pembroke North . Cynog Dafis (PC)
Llanelli .... Denzil Davies (La)
Pembroke .... Nick Ainger (La)
GWENT
Blaenau Gwent .... Llew Smith (La)
Islwyn .... Neil Kinnock (La)
Monmouth .... Roger Evans (C)
Newport East .... Roy Hughes DL (La)
Newport West .... Paul Flynn (La)
Torfaen .... Paul Murphy (La)
GWYNEDD
Caernarfon .... Dafydd Wigley (PC)
Conwy .... Sir Wyn Roberts (C)
Meirionnydd Nant Conwy ..... Elfyn Llwyd (PC)
Ynys Mon .... Ieuan Wyn Jones (PC)

MID GLAMORGAN
Bridgend .... Win Griffiths (La)
Caerphilly .... Ron Davies (La)
Cynon Valley .... Ann Clwyd (La)
Merthyr Tydfil & Rhymney ..... Ted Rowlands (La)
Ogmore .... Ray Powell (La)
Pontypridd .... Dr Kim Howells (La)
Rhondda .... Allan Rogers (La)
POWYS
Brecon & Radnor .... Jonathan Evans (C)
Montgomery .... Alex Carlile (LD)
SOUTH GLAMORGAN
Cardiff Central .... Jon Owen Jones (La)
Cardiff North .... Gwilym Jones (C)
Cardiff South & Penarth ..... Alun Michael (La)
Cardiff West .... Rhodri Morgan (La)
Vale of Glamorgan .... Walter Sweeney (C)
WEST GLAMORGAN
Aberavon .... John Morris (La)
Gower .... Gareth Wardell (La)
Neath .... Peter Hain (La)
Swansea East .... Donald Anderson (La)
Swansea West .... Alan Williams (La)

Votes Recorded in Parliamentary General Elections and By-Elections

Source: CSO

Percentages and thousands

	General Election 3/5/79	May 1979 to June 1983	General Election 9/6/83	June 1983 to June 1987	General Election 11/6/87	June 1987 to Sept 1991	General Election 9/4/92
Number of by-elections	–	20	–	31	–	21	–
Turnout *(percentages)*[1]	76.1	61.2	72.7	62.4	75.3	57.4	76.3
Votes recorded, by party (percentage of all votes)							
Conservative	43.9	23.8	42.4	16.0	42.3	22.8	41.8
Labour	36.9	25.7	27.6	14.9	30.8	39.5	35.2
Social Liberal Democrats[2]	13.8	9.0	13.7	15.0	12.8	17.6	17.0
Social Democratic Party[2]	0	14.2	11.6	5.6	9.7	3.7	–
Plaid Cymru	0.4	0.5	0.4	0.3	0.4	2.6	0.4
Scottish National Party	1.6	1.7	1.1	–	1.3	5.0	1.9
Northern Ireland Parties[3]	2.2	23.3	2.5	47.4[4]	2.2	4.3	2.1
Green Party[4]	0.1	0.3	0.2	–	0.3	1.9	0.6
Others	1.1	1.6	0.5	0.8	0.2	2.7	1.1
Total (=100%) (thousands)	31,221	715	30,671	1,979	32,530	759	33,275

(1) Estimated by dividing the number of votes cast by the number of people on the electoral registers in force at the time of the elections. (2) The Social Democratic Party (SDP) was launched on 26 March 1981. In the 1983 and 1987 General Elections the Liberals and SDP contested seats as the Liberal-SDP Alliance. In 1988 the Social and Liberal Democrats formed, after which the Democrats and the SDP contested elections separately. In June 1990 the SDP disbanded. (3) On 17 December 1985 all 15 Ulster Unionist MPs resigned their seats and sought re-election as a protest against the Anglo-Irish Agreement. The 15 by-elections were held on 23 January 1986. (4) Known as the Ecology Party before 1987.

Number of MPs Elected Per Party

Source: CSO

	23 Feb 1950	25 Oct 1951	26 May 1955	8 Oct 1959	15 Oct 1964	31 Mar 1966	18 June 1970[1]	28 Feb 1974	10 Oct 1974	3 May 1979	9 June 1983	11 June 1987	9 Apr 1992
Total MPs	625	625	630	630	630	630	630	635	635	635	650	650	651
Conservative	297	320	344	364	303	253	330	296	276	339	396	375	336
Labour	315	295	277	258	317	363	287	301	319	268	209	229	271
Liberal	9	6	6	6	9	12	6	14	13	11	17	17	20
Social Democratic Party	–	–	–	–	–	–	–	–	–	–	6	5	–
Scottish National Party	–	–	–	–	–	–	1	7	11	2	2	3	3
Plaid Cymru	–	–	–	–	–	–	–	2	3	2	2	3	4
Other[1]	4	4	3	2	1	2	6	15	13	13	18	18	17

(1) The Speaker is included in Other.

Proportional Representation

Source: SCPR's *British Social Attitudes* survey, 9th Report, ed. R. Jowell *et al.* (Dartmouth Publishing, 1992)

	Percentage agreeing
We should change the voting system to allow smaller political parties to get a fairer share of MPs	36.6
We should keep the voting system as it is to produce more effective government	57.6
Don't know	5.0

Attitudes Towards Government Intervention

Do you agree that it is the government's responsibility to do the following?

Source: SCPR's *British Social Attitudes* survey, 9th Report, ed. R. Jowell *et al.* (Dartmouth Publishing, 1992)

	Percentage agreeing					
	Scotland	North	Wales	Midlands	London	South
Provide a job for everyone who wants one	35	36	33	30	27	23
Provide a decent standard of living for the unemployed	51	42	44	35	35	30
Reduce income differences between the rich and the poor	44	46	45	36	41	30

Trust in Government

How much do you trust British governments of *any* party to place the needs of the nation above the interests of their own political party?

Source: SCPR's *British Social Attitudes* survey, 9th Report, ed. R. Jowell *et al.* (Dartmouth Publishing, 1992)

	Percentage
Just about always	3.8
Most of the time	29.4
Only some of the time	49.9
Almost never	13.7
Don't know/can't say	2.6

The Future of Northern Ireland

Source: SCPR's *British Social Attitudes* survey, 9th Report, ed. R. Jowell *et al.* (Dartmouth Publishing, 1992)

	Britain			Northern Ireland		
	1989	1990	1991	1989	1990	1991
There should be a united Ireland	55	56	54	24	25	22
British troops should be withdrawn	59	60	58	32	32	25

Members of the House of Lords

(As at 8 July 1993)

Title abbreviations: Abp = Archbishop; B = Baroness; Bp = Bishop; C = Countess; D = Duke; E = Earl; L = Baron/Lord; Ly = Lady; M = Marquess; V = Viscount.

Party allegiance is shown for those in receipt of a party whip.
Party abbreviations: Con = Conservative; Dem = Liberal Democrat; Ind = Independent; Lab = Labour. Peers with nothing against their name have not declared their party affiliation.

Lords Spiritual

Party	Name
–	Bristol, Bp
–	Canterbury, Abp
–	Chelmsford, Bp.
–	Chester, Bp.
–	Chichester, Bp.
–	Coventry, Bp.
–	Durham, Bp.
–	Exeter, Bp.
–	Guildford, Bp.
–	Lichfield, Bp.
–	Lincoln, Bp.
–	Liverpool, Bp.
–	London, Bp.
–	Newcastle, Bp.
–	Norwich, Bp.
–	Peterborough, Bp.
–	Portsmouth, Bp.
–	Ripon, Bp.
–	St Albans, Bp.
–	St Edmundsbury and Ipswich, Bp.
–	Salisbury, Bp.
–	Sheffield, Bp.
–	Southwark, Bp.
–	Winchester, Bp.
–	Worcester, Bp.
–	York, Abp.

Hereditary Peers
(including Peers of 1st Creation)

Party	Name
Con	Aberconway, L
Con	Abercorn, D.
Con	Aberdare, L.
Ind	Aberdeen and Temair, M.
Ind	Abergavenny, M.
Con	Abinger, L.
Ind	Acton, L.
Dem	Addington, L.
Con	Addison, V.
Ind	Adrian, L.
Ind	Ailesbury, M.
Con	Ailsa, M.
Dem	Airedale, L.
Ind	Airlie, E.
Ind	Alanbrooke, V.
Ind	Albemarle, E.
Con	Aldenham, L.
Con	Aldington, L.
Con	Alexander of Tunis, E
Ind	Allenby of Megiddo, V.
Con	Allendale, V.
–	Alvingham, L.
Ind	Amherst of Hackney, L.
Ind	Ampthill, L.
Ind	Amwell, L.
–	Anglesey, M.
Con	Annaly, L.
Con	Annandale and Hartfell, E.
Ind	Arbuthnott, V.
Con	Argyll, D.
Con	Arran, E.
Con	Ashbourne, L.
Ind	Ashburton, L.
–	Ashcombe, L.
Ind	Ashton of Hyde, L.
Con	Astor, V.
Con	Astor of Hever, L.
Con	Atholl, D.
Ind	Attlee, E.
Con	Auckland, L.
–	Audley, L.
Dem	Avebury, L.

Party	Name
Con	Aylesford, E.
–	Baden-Powell, L.
–	Bagot, L.
–	Baillieu, L.
Ind	Baldwin of Bewdley, E.
Con	Balfour, E.
Ind	Balfour of Burleigh, L.
Ind	Balfour of Inchrye, L.
Con	Banbury of Southam, L.
Ind	Barnard, L.
–	Basing, L.
–	Bath, M.
Con	Bathurst, E.
Con	Bearsted, V.
–	Beatty, E.
–	Beaufort, D.
Con	Beaverbrook, L.
–	Bedford, D.
Con	Belhaven and Stenton, L.
–	Belper, L.
Con	Belstead, L.
–	Berkeley, L.
Con	Bessborough, E.
Con	Bethell, L.
–	Bicester, L.
Con	Biddulph, L
Con	Birdwood, L.
Ind	Birkett, L.
Con	Blakenham, V.
Ind	Bledisloe, V.
Con	Blyth, L.
–	Bolingbroke and St John, V.
Con	Bolton, L.
Con	Borthwick, L.
–	Borwick, L.
Con	Boston, L.
–	Boyd of Merton, V.
Ind	Boyne, V.
Con	Brabazon of Tara, L.
Ind	Brabourne, L.
–	Bradbury, L.
Con	Bradford, E.
Ind	Brain, L.
Con	Brassey of Apethorpe, L.
Con	Braybrooke, L.
Con	Braye, B.
–	Breadalbane, L.
Con	Brentford, V.
Con	Bridgeman, V.
Ind	Bridges, L.
–	Bridport, V.
–	Bristol, M.
Ind	Broadbridge, L.
Con	Brocket, L.
–	Brooke and Warwick, E.
Con	Brookeborough, V.
Con	Brougham and Vaux, L.
–	Broughshane, L.
–	Brownlow, L.
Con	Bruntisfield, L.
Con	Buccleuch and Queensberry, D.
Ind	Buchan, E.
Con	Buckinghamshire, E.
Ind	Buckmaster, V.
–	Burden, L.
–	Burgh, L.
–	Burnham, L.
Con	Burton, L.
–	Bute, M.
Con	Byron, L.
Con	Cadman, L.
–	Cadogan
Ind	Cairns, E.
Con	Caithness, E.
Con	Caldecote, V.

Party	Name
–	Calthorpe, L.
–	Calverley, L.
Con	Camden, M.
Ind	Camoys, L.
–	Camrose, V.
–	Carew, L.
Ind	Carlisle, E.
Ind	Carnarvon, E.
Con	Carnock, L.
–	Carrick, E.
Con	Carrington, L.
Con	Cathcart, E.
–	Catto, L.
–	Cawdor, E.
Con	Cawley, L.
Ind	Chandos, V.
–	Chatfield, L.
Con	Chelmsford, V.
Con	Chesham, L.
	Chetwode, L.
Con	Chichester, E.
Con	Chilston, V.
Ind	Cholmondeley, M.
Ind	Chorley, L.
–	Churchill, V.
Con	Churston, L.
–	Citrine, L.
Ind	Clancarty, E.
Con	Clanwilliam, E.
–	Clarendon, E.
Ind	Clifford of Chudleigh, L.
Con	Clinton, L.
Con	Clitheroe, L.
Ind	Clwyd, L.
Con	Clydesmuir, L.
Dem	Cobbold, L.
–	Cobham, V.
Con	Cochrane of Cults, L.
Con	Coleraine, L.
–	Coleridge, L.
Ind	Colgrain, L.
Con	Colville of Culross, V.
Con	Colwyn, L.
–	Colyton, L.
Ind	Combermere, V.
Ind	Congleton, L.
–	Conyngham, M.
Con	Cork and Orrery, E.
Ind	Cornwallis, L.
Con	Cottenham, E.
Con	Cottesloe, L.
Con	Courtown, E.
Con	Coventry
Ind	Cowdray, V.
Con	Cowley, E.
Ind	Craigavon, V.
Con	Craigmyle, L.
Con	Cranbourne, V.
Con	Cranbrook, E.
Con	Cranworth, L.
Con	Crathorne, L.
–	Craven, E.
Con	Crawford and Balcarres, E.
Con	Crawshaw, L.
Con	Croft, L.
–	Cromartie, E.
Con	Cromer, E.
Ind	Cromwell, L.
Ind	Crook, L.
Con	Cross, V.
Con	Cullen of Ashbourne, L.
Ind	Cunliffe, L.
Ind	Dacre, B.
–	Dalhousie, E.
Ind	Darcy (de Knayth), B.

(Continued)

Party	Name
–	Daresbury, L.
–	Darling, L.
Con	Darnley, E.
–	Dartmouth, E.
–	Darwen, L.
–	Daryngton, L.
Con	Daventry, V.
Con	Davidson, V.
Dem	Davies, L.
–	de Clifford, L.
Con	De Freyne, L.
Con	De La Warr, E.
Con	De L'Isle, V.
–	De Mauley, L.
–	De Ramsey, L.
–	De Ros, L.
Con	De Saumarez, L.
–	De Villiers, L.
–	Delamere, L.
Dem	Denbigh, E.
Con	Denham, L.
Con	Denman, L.
–	Deramore, L.
–	Derby, E.
Con	Derwent, L.
–	Devon, E.
Ind	Devonport, V.
Ind	Devonshire, D.
Ind	Dickinson, L.
Con	Digby, L.
Con	Dilhorne, V.
–	Dinevor, L.
Con	Donegall, M.
Con	Donoughmore, E.
Con	Dormer, L.
Ind	Dowding, L.
–	Downe, V.
Con	Downshire, M.
Ind	Drogheda, E.
–	Ducie, E.
Con	Dudley, E.
Con	Dudley, B.
–	Dulverton, L.
Con	Dundee, E.
Con	Dundonald, E.
–	Dunleath, L.
–	Dunmore, E.
Ind	Dunrossil, V.
–	Dysart, C.
–	Ebury, V.
Con	Eccles, V.
–	Edinburgh, D.
Con	Effingham, E.
–	Eglinton, E.
–	Egmont, E.
Ind	Eldon, E.
Con	Elgin and Kincardine, E.
Con	Elibank, L.
Con	Ellenborough, L.
Con	Elphinstone, L.
Con	Elton, L.
–	Ely, M.
Ind	Enniskillen, E.
Con	Erne, E.
Ind	Erroll, E.
Con	Erroll of Hale, L.
–	Erskine of Rerrick, L.
Dem	Esher, V.
Ind	Essex, E.
Ind	Exeter, M.
–	Exmouth, V.
Con	Fairfax, of Cameron, L.
Con	Fairhaven, L.
Dem	Falkland, V.
Con	Falmouth, V.
Ind	Faringdon, L.
Con	Ferrers, E.
Ind	Feversham, L.
–	Fife, D.
Con	Fisher, L.
–	FitzWalter, L.
–	Foley, L.
Con	Forbes, L.
Con	Forester, L.
Ind	Forres, L.
–	Fortescue, E.
–	Forteviot, L.
–	Freyberg, L.

Party	Name
–	Furness, V.
–	Gage, V.
Con	Gainford, L.
Ind	Gainsborough, E.
Con	Galloway, E.
Con	Geddes, L.
–	Gerard, L.
Lab	Gifford, L.
Con	Gisborough, L.
Dem	Gladwyn, L.
Con	Glanusk, L.
Dem	Glasgow, E.
Con	Glenarthur, L.
Dem	Glenconner, L.
–	Glendevon, L.
Con	Glendyne, L.
–	Glentoran, L.
Ind	Gloucester, D.
Ind	Gorell, L
Con	Gormanston, V.
Con	Goschen, V.
–	Gosford, E.
Ind	Gough, V.
Con	Gowrie, E.
Con	Grafton, D.
Con	Granard, E.
Ind	Grantchester, L.
–	Grantley, L
–	Granville, E.
Con	Gray, L.
–	Greenhill, L.
Ind	Greenway, L.
–	Greenwood, V.
Lab	Grenfell, L.
–	Gretton, L.
Dem	Grey, E.
–	Grey of Codnor, L.
Con	Gridley, L.
Con	Grimston of Westbury, L.
Con	Grimthorpe, L.
–	Guilford, E.
Con	Hacking, L.
Con	Haddington, E.
Ind	Haden-Guest, L.
Con	Haig, E.
Con	Halifax, E.
Ind	Halsbury, E.
Con	Hambleden, V.
Ind	Hamilton and Brandon, D.
Con	Hamilton of Dalzell, L.
Ind	Hampden, V.
Dem	Hampton, L.
Ind	Hankey, L.
Dem	Hanworth, V.
Con	Harding of Petherton, L.
Ind	Hardinge, V.
Con	Hardinge of Penshurst, L.
Con	Hardwicke, E.
–	Harewood, E.
Con	Harlech, L
Con	Harmsworth, L.
–	Harrington, E.
–	Harris, L.
Con	Harrowby, E.
Con	Harvey of Tasburgh, L.
Con	Hastings, L.
–	Hatherton, L.
–	Hawke, L.
Ind	Hayter, L.
–	Hazlerigg, L.
Ind	Head, V.
Ind	Headfort, M.
Ind	Hemingford, L.
Con	Hemphill, L.
Con	Henley, L.
Dem	Henniker, L.
–	Hereford, V.
–	Herries, Ly.
–	Herschell, L.
Con	Hertford, M.
Con	Hesketh, L.
–	Heytesbury, L.
–	Hill, V.
Con	Hindlip, L.
Con	Hives, L.
–	Hollenden, L.
Con	HolmPatrick, L.
Con	Hood, V.

Party	Name
–	Horder, L.
Con	Hothfield, L.
–	Howard de Walden, L.
–	Howard of Penrith, L.
Con	Howe, E.
–	Howick of Glendale, L.
Ind	Huntingdon, E.
Con	Huntly, M.
Ind	Hylton, L.
Ind	Iddesleigh, E.
Ind	Ilchester, E.
–	Iliffe, L.
Con	Inchcape, E.
Ind	Inchyra, L.
Ind	Ingleby, V.
Con	Inglewood, L.
–	Inverforth, L.
Con	Ironside, L.
–	Iveagh, E.
Con	Jeffreys, L.
Con	Jellicoe, E.
–	Jersey, E.
–	Joicey, L.
Con	Kemsley, V.
Con	Kenilworth, L.
Lab	Kennet, L.
–	Kensington, L.
–	Kenswood, L.
Ind	Kent, D.
–	Kenyon, L.
–	Kershaw, L.
Con	Keyes, L.
Lab	Kilbracken, L.
Ind	Killanin, L.
Con	Killearn, L.
Ind	Kilmarnock, L.
Con	Kimberley, E.
Con	Kindersley, L.
Ind	Kinloss, Ly
Con	Kinnaird, L.
Con	Kinnoull, E.
–	Kinross, L.
Ind	Kintore, E.
Dem	Kirkwood, L.
Con	Kitchener, E.
Con	Knollys, V.
Con	Knutsford, V.
–	Lambert, V.
–	Lansdowne, M.
–	Latham, L
–	Latymer, L.
Con	Lauderdale, E.
Ind	Lawrence, L.
Con	Layton, L.
Ind	Leathers, V.
Con	Leconfield and Egremont, L.
–	Leicester, E.
Con	Leigh, L.
–	Leighton of Saint Mellons
–	Leinster, D.
–	Leven and Melville, E.
Con	Leverhulme, V.
Con	Lichfield, E.
–	Lilford, L.
Con	Limerick, E.
–	Lincoln, E.
Con	Lindsay, E.
–	Lindsay of Birker, L.
Con	Lindsay and Abingdon, E.
Con	Linlithgow, M
Lab	Listowel, E.
Con	Liverpool, E.
Ind	Lloyd-George of Dwyfor, E.
–	Londesborough, L.
–	Londonderry, M.
Con	Long, V.
Lab	Longford, E.
Con	Lonsdale, E.
Con	Lothian, M.
Ind	Loudoun, C.
Con	Lovat, L.
–	Lovelace, E.
–	Lucan, E.
Con	Lucas, L.
Con	Lucas of Chilworth, L.
Con	Luke, L.
Con	Lyell, L.
Ind	Lytton, E.

(Continued)

Party	Name
–	Lyveden, L.
Con	MacAndrew, L.
Ind	Macclesfield, E.
–	Macdonald of Gwaenysgor, L.
–	McGowan, L.
Con	Mackintosh of Halifax, V.
–	Maclay, L.
Dem	McNair, L.
Con	Macpherson of Drumochter, L.
Con	Malmesbury, E.
–	Malvern, V.
Ind	Manchester, D.
Con	Mancroft, L.
Con	Manners, L.
Con	Mansfield, E.
Con	Manton, L.
Ind	Mar, C.
Con	Mar and Kellie, E.
–	Marchamley, L.
Con	Marchwood, V.
Con	Margadale, L.
–	Margesson, V.
–	Marks of Broughton, L.
Con	Marlborough, D.
Ind	Martonmere, L.
–	Massereene and Ferrard, V.
Con	May, L.
	Meath, E.
Lab	Melchett, L.
Con	Melville, V.
Con	Merrivale, L.
Con	Mersey, V.
Dem	Meston, L.
–	Methuen, L.
Con	Middleton, L.
–	Midleton, V.
Ind	Milford, L.
Con	Mills, V.
Ind	Milne, L.
Lab	Milner of Leeds, L.
Con	Milverton, L.
Ind	Minto, E.
–	Monck, V.
Ind	Monckton of Brenchley, V.
–	Moncrieff, L.
Con	Monk Bretton, L.
Lab	Monkswell, L.
–	Monsell, V.
Ind	Monson, L.
Con	Montagu of Beaulieu, L.
Con	Monteagle of Brandon, L.
Con	Montgomery of Alamein, V.
–	Montrose, D.
Ind	Moran, L.
–	Moray, E.
Con	Morley, E.
Con	Morris, L.
Ind	Morris of Kenwood, L.
–	Morrison, L.
–	Morton, E.
Con	Mostyn, L.
Con	Mottistone, L.
–	Mount Edgcumbe, E.
Ind	Mountbatten of Burma, C.
Con	Mountevans, L.
Con	Mountgarrey, V.
Con	Mowbray and Stourton, L.
Con	Moyne, L.
–	Moynihan, L.
Con	Munster, E.
Con	Nairne, Ly.
Ind	Napier and Ettrick, L.
Ind	Napier of Magdala, L.
Ind	Nathan, L.
Con	Nelson, E.
Con	Nelson of Stafford, L.
Ind	Netherthorpe, L.
Con	Newall, L.
Con	Newton, L.
Con	Noel-Buxton, L.
Con	Norfolk, D.
Ind	Normanby, M.
–	Normanton, E.
Con	Norrie, L.
–	Northampton, M.
Ind	Northbourne, L.
Con	Northbrook, L.
Con	Northesk, E.
–	Northumberland, D.
–	Norton, L.
–	Norwich, V.
–	Nunburnholme, L.
Dem	Ogmore, L.
Con	O'Hagan, L.
–	O'Neill, L.
Con	Onslow, E.
–	Oranmore and Browne, L.
Con	Orkney, E.
–	Ormonde, M.
Ind	Oxford and Asquith, E.
Con	Oxfuird, V.
Ind	Palmer, L.
–	Parmoor, L.
Con	Peel, E.
Con	Pembroke and Montgomery, E.
Con	Pender, L.
Con	Penrhyn, L.
Ind	Perth, E.
Ind	Petre, L.
–	Phillimore, L.
–	Piercy, L.
Con	Plunket, L.
–	Plymouth, E.
Con	Poltimore, L.
Con	Polwarth, L.
Lab	Ponsonby of Shulbrede, L.
Ind	Poole, L.
Ind	Portland, E.
Con	Portman, V.
Con	Portsmouth, E.
–	Powerscourt, V.
–	Powis, E.
Dem	Queensberry, M.
Con	Radnor, E.
Ind	Raglan, L.
Con	Ranfurly, E.
Con	Rankeillour, L.
–	Rathcavan, L.
Ind	Rathcreedan, L.
–	Ravensdale, L.
–	Ravensworth, L.
Con	Rayleigh, L.
Lab	Rea, L.
Con	Reading, M.
Con	Reay, L.
Dem	Redesdale, L.
Con	Remnant, L.
Con	Rennell, L.
Con	Renwick, L.
–	Revelstoke, L.
Ind	Richmond Lennox and Gordon, D.
Ind	Ridley, V.
Dem	Ritchie of Dundee, L.
–	Riverdale, L.
Ind	Robertson of Oakridge, L.
–	Roborough, L.
–	Rochdale, V.
Dem	Rochester, L.
Con	Rockley, L.
Con	Rodney, L.
Con	Rollo, L.
Con	Romney, E.
–	Rootes, L.
–	Rosebery, E.
Ind	Rosslyn, E.
–	Rossmore, L.
–	Rothermere, V.
Con	Rotherwick, L.
–	Rothes, E.
Ind	Rothschild, L.
–	Rowallan, L.
Con	Roxburghe, D.
Ind	Rugby, L.
Ind	Runciman of Doxford, V.
Dem	Russell, E.
Ind	Russell of Liverpool, L.
–	Rutland, D.
Con	Sackville, L.
Con	Saint Albans, D.
Con	St Aldwyn, E.
Con	St Davids, V.
Con	St Germans, E.
–	St Helens, L.
Ind	St John of Bletso, L.
Con	Saint Levan, L.
Con	Saint Oswald, L.
–	St Vincent, V.
Con	Salisbury, M.
Ind	Saltoun of Abernethy, Ly.
–	Samuel, VB.
Con	Sandford, L.
Ind	Sandhurst, L.
Con	Sandys, L.
Con	Savile, L.
–	Saye and Sele, L.
Con	Scarborough, E.
–	Scarsdale, V.
Con	Seafield, E.
Con	Selborne, E.
–	Selby, V.
Con	Selkirk, E.
Con	Selsdon, L.
Con	Sempill, Ly.
Con	Shaftesbury, E.
Ind	Shannon, E.
Ind	Shaughnessy, L.
Lab	Shepherd, L.
Ind	Sherfield, L.
Con	Shrewsbury, E.
Con	Shuttleworth, L.
Ind	Sidmouth, V.
–	Silsoe, L.
Dem	Simon, V.
–	Simon of Wythenshawe, L.
Con	Sinclair, L.
–	Sinclair of Cleeve, L.
–	Sinha, L.
Con	Skelmersdale, L.
–	Sligo, M.
Ind	Slim, V.
Ind	Snowdon, E.
Ind	Somerleyton, L.
Ind	Somers, L.
Ind	Somerset, D.
–	Sondes, E.
Ind	Soulbury, V.
–	Southampton, L.
Ind	Spencer, E.
Ind	Spens, L.
Con	Stafford, L.
–	Stair, E.
Ind	Stamp, L.
Con	Stanley of Alderley, L.
Con	Stockton, E.
Lab	Strabolgi, L.
–	Stradbroke, E.
Ind	Strafford, E.
–	Strang, L.
Con	Strange, B.
Ind	Strathalmond, L.
Con	Strathcarron, L.
Con	Strathclyde, L.
Con	Strathcona and Mount Royal, L.
–	Stratheden and Campbell, L.
Con	Strathmore and Kinghorne, E.
–	Strathspey, L.
–	Stuart of Findhorn, V.
Con	Sudeley, L.
Con	Suffield, L.
Con	Suffolk and Berkshire, E.
–	Sutherland, D.
–	Sutherland, C.
Con	Swansea, L.
Con	Swaythling, L.
Con	Swinfen, L.
Con	Swinton, E.
–	Sysonby, L.
–	Tankerville, E.
–	Tedder, L.
Ind	Temple of Stowe, E.
Ind	Tenby, V.
–	Tennyson, L.
Ind	Terrington, L.
Con	Teviot, L.
Con	Teynham, L.
–	Thomson of Fleet, L.
Ind	Thurlowe, L.
Dem	Thurso, V.
Con	Tollemache, L.
Ind	Tonypandy, V.
Con	Torphichen, L.
Con	Torrington, V.
Con	Townshend, M.
Con	Trefgarne, L.

(Continued)

Party	Name
Con	Trenchard, V.
Con	Trevethin and Oaksey, L.
–	Trevor, L.
Ind	Tryon, L.
Ind	Tweeddale, M.
Con	Tweedsmuir, L.
Con	Ullswater, V.
Con	Vaux of Harrowden, L.
–	Vernon, L.
–	Verulam, E.
Con	Vestey, L.
Con	Vivian, L.
Con	Wakeshurst, L.
Con	Waldegrave, E.
Ind	Wales, P.
Ind	Walpole, L.
–	Walsingham, L.
Con	Wardington, L.
Con	Waterford, M.
Con	Watkinson, V.
Ind	Waverley, V.
Con	Wedgwood, L.
Con	Weir, V.
Con	Wellington, D.
Con	Wemyss and March, E.
Con	Westbury, L.
Con	Westminster, D.
Ind	Westmorland, E.
Ind	Westwood, L.
–	Wharncliffe, E.
Ind	Wharton, B.
Con	Whitelaw, V.
Con	Wigram, L.
Con	Willoughby de Broke, L.
–	Willoughby de Eresby, B.
–	Wilson, L.
–	Wilton, E
–	Wimborne, V.
–	Winchester, M.
Dem	Winchilsea and Nottingham, E.
Conm	Windlesham, L.
Con	Wise, L.
Ind	Wolverton, L.
Con	Woolton, E.
–	Wraxall, L.
Ind	Wrenbury, L.
Ind	Wrottesley, L.
–	Wyfold, L.
Con	Wynford, L.
Con	Yarborough, E.
Ind	York, D.
Ind	Younger of Leckie, V.
Con	Zetland, M.
Con	Zouche of Haryngworth, L.

Life Peers

Party	Name
Ind	Ackner, L.
Ind	Alexander of Potterhill, L.
Con	Alexander of Weedon, L.
Ind	Allen of Abbeydale, L.
–	Alport, L.
Con	Amery of Lustleigh, L.
Ind	Annan, L.
Lab	Archer of Sandwell, L.
Con	Archer of Weston-Super-Mare, L.
Lab	Ardwick, L.
Ind	Armstrong of Ilminster, L.
Lab	Ashley of Stoke, L.
Dem	Aylestone, L.
Ind	Bancroft, L.
Dem	Banks, L.
Con	Barber, L.
Ind	Barbner of Tewkesbury, L.
Lab	Barnett, L.
Con	Bauer, L.
Dem	Beaumont of Whitley, L.
Con	Bellwin, L.
Con	Beloff, L.
Ind	Benson, L.
Lab	Birk, B.
Lab	Blackstone, B.
Con	Blake, L.
Ind	Blanch, L.
Con	Blatch, B.
Lab	Blease, L.
Con	Boardman, L.

Party	Name
Dem	Bonham-Carter, L.
Lab	Boston of Faversham, L.
Lab.	Bottomley, L.
Con	Boyd-Carpenter, L.
Con	Braine of Wheatley, L.
Ind	Bramall, L.
Ind	Brandon of Oakbrook, L.
Ind	Bridge of Harwich, L.
Ind.	Briggs, L.
Ind	Brightman, L.
Con	Brigstocke, B.
Lab	Brimelow, L.
–	Brooke of Ystradfellte, B.
Ind	Brookes, L.
Lab	Brooks of Tremorfa, L.
Ind	Browne-Wilkinson, L.
Lab	Bruce of Donington, L.
Ind	Bullock, L.
Ind	Butterfield, L.
Con	Butterworth, L.
Con	Buxton of Alsa, L.
Lab	Callaghan of Cardiff, L.
Ind	Cameron of Lochbroom, L.
Con	Campbell of Alloway, L.
Con	Campbell of Croy, L.
Lab	Campbell of Eskan, L.
Con	Carlisle of Bucklow, L.
Lab	Carmichael of Kelvingrove, L.
Con	Carnegy of Lour, B.
Con	Carr of Hadley, L.
Lab	Carter, L.
Ind	Carver, L.
Lab	Castle of Blackburn, B.
Con	Cavendish of Furness, L.
Con	Cayzer, L.
Ind	Chalfont, L.
Con	Chalker of Wallasey, B.
Ind	Chapple, L.
Ind	Charteris of Amisfield, L.
Con	Chelmer, L.
Con	Chilver, L.
–	Chitnis, L.
Con	Clark of Kempston, L.
Lab	Cledwyn of Penrhos, L.
Lab	Clinton-Davis, L.
Con	Cockfield, L.
Lab	Cocks of Hartcliffe, L.
Ind	Coggan, L.
Lab	Collison, L.
Con	Colnbrook, L.
Con	Constantine of Stanmore, L.
Ind	Cooke of Islandreagh, L.
Con	Cox, B.
Ind	Craig of Radley, L.
Con	Craigton, L.
Conm	Crickhowell, L.
Ind	Croham, L.
Dem	Cudlipp, L.
Con	Cumberlege, B.
Con	Dacre of Glanton, L.
Ind	Dainton, L.
Lab	David, B.
Lab	Dean of Beswick, L.
Con	Deedes, L.
Lab	Delacourt-Smith of Alteryn, B.
–	Delfont, L.
Lab	Denington, B.
Ind	Denning, L.
Con	Denton of Wakefield, B.
Lab	Desai, L.
–	Diamond, L.
Dem	Donaldson of Kingsbridge, L.
Ind	Donaldson of Lymington, L.
Lab	Donoughue, L.
Lab	Dormand of Easington, L.
Ind	Dunn, B.
Lab	Eatwell, L.
Con	Eccles of Moulton, B.
Con	Eden of Winton, L.
Ind	Elis-Thomas, L.
Con	Elles, B.
Con	Elliot of Harwood, B.
Con	Elliott of Morpeth, L.
–	Elystan-Morgan, L.
Ind	Emslie, L.
Lab	Ennals, L.
Lab	Ewing of Kirkford, L.
Dem	Ezra, L.

Party	Name
Con	Faithfull, B.
Lab	Falkender, B.
Con	Fanshawe of Richmond, L.
Con	Finsberg, L.
Lab	Fisher of Rednal, B.
–	Fitt, L.
Con	Flather, B
Ind	Flowers, L.
Dem	Foot, L.
Con	Forte, L.
Con	Fraser of Carmyllie, L.
Con	Fraser of Kilmorack
Lab	Gallacher, L.
Lab	Galpern, L.
Con	Gardner of Parkes, B.
Dem	Geraint, L.
Ind	Gibson, L.
Con	Gibson-Watt, L.
Con	Gilmour of Craigmillar, L.
Lab	Glenamara, L.
Ind	Goff of Chieveley, L.
Ind	Goodman, L.
Con	Goold, L.
Ind	Grade, L.
Lab	Graham of Edmonton, L.
Ind	Granville of Eye, L.
Con	Gray of Contin, L.
Lab	Greene of Harrow Weald, L.
Ind	Greenhill of Harrow, L.
Lab	Gregson, L.
Ind	Grey of Naunton, L.
Ind	Griffiths, L.
Con	Griffiths of Fforestfach, L.
Dem	Grimond, L.
Con	Hailsham of Saint Marylebone, L.
Dem	Hamwee, B.
Con	Hanson, L.
Con	Harmar-Nicholls, L.
Dem	Harris of Greenwich, L.
Ind	Harris of High Cross, L.
Ind	Hartwell, L.
Con	Harvey of Prestbury, L.
Con	Harvington, L.
Con	Haslam, L.
Con	Hayhoe, L
Lab	Healey, L.
Ind	Henderson of Brompton, L.
Ind	Hill-Norton, L.
Lab	Hilton of Eggardon, B.
Lab	Hirshfield, L.
Con	Holderness, L.
Lab	Hollick, L.
Lab	Hollis of Heigham, B.
Dem	Holme of Cheltenham, L
Con	Home of the Hirsel, L.
Con	Hooper, B.
Dem	Hooson, L.
Lab	Houghton of Sowerby, L.
Con	Howe of Aberavon, L.
Lab	Howell, L.
Lab	Howie of Troon, L.
Lab	Hughes, L.
Dem	Hunt, L.
Ind	Hunt of Tanworth, L.
Ind	Hunter of Newington, L.
Dem	Hutchinson of Lullington, L.
Ind	Hylton-Foster, B.
Con	Ingrow, L.
Lab	Irvine of Lairg, L.
Lab	Jacques, L.
Ind	Jakobovits, L.
Ind	James of Holland Park, B.
Ind	Jauncey of Tullichettle, L.
Lab	Jay, L.
Lab	Jay of Paddington, B.
Lab	Jeger, B.
Con	Jenkin of Roding, L.
Dem	Jenkins of Hillhead, L.
Lab	Jenkins of Putney, L.
Lab	John-Mackie, L.
Con	Johnston of Rockport, L.
Con	Joseph, L.
Lab	Judd, L.
Ind	Kadoorie, L.
Lab	Kagan, L.
Con	Keith of Castleacre, L.
Ind	Keith of Kinkel, L.
Con	Kimball, L.

(Continued)

Party	Name
Con	King of Wartnaby, L.
Ind	Kings Norton, L.
Lab	Kirkhill, L.
Ind	Kissin, L.
Ind	Knights, L.
Con	Laing of Dunphail, L.
Ind	Lane, L.
Con	Lane of Horsell, L.
Con	Lawson of Blaby, L.
Lab	Lever of Manchester, L.
Ind	Lewin, L.
Ind	Lewis of Newnham, L.
Lab	Llewelyn-Davies of Hastcoe, B.
Lab	Lockwood, B.
Lab	Lovell-Davis, L.
Ind	Lowry, L.
Con	McAlpine of West Green, L.
Lab	Macaulay of Bragar, L.
Lab	McCarthy, L.
Ind	McCluskey, L.
Con	McColl of Dulwich, L.
Con	McFadzean, L.
Con	Macfarlane of Bearsden, L.
Ind	McFarlane of Llandaff, B.
Dem	McGregor of Durris, L.
Lab	McIntosh of Haringey, L.
Con	Mackay of Ardbrecknish, L.
Con	Mackay of Clashfern, L.
Ind	Mackenzie-Stuart, L.
Dem	Mackie of Benshie, L.
Ind	MacLehose of Beoch, L.
Con	Macleod of Borve, B.
Dem	Mais, L.
Lab	Mallalieu, B.
Con	Marlesford, L.
Ind	Marsh, L.
Ind	Marshall of Goring, L.
Ind	Masham of Ilton, B.
Lab	Mason of Barnsley, L.
–	Matthews, L.
Con	Maude of Stratford-upon-Avon, L.
Dem	Mayhew, L.
–	Mellish, L.
Lab	Merlyn-Rees, L.
Lab	Mishcon, L.
Lab	Molloy, L.
Con	Moore of Lower Marsh, L.
Ind	Moore of Wolvercote, L.
Lab	Morris of Castle Morris, L.
Ind	Morton of Shuna, L.
Con	Moyola, L.
Lab	Mulley, L.
Lab	Murray of Epping Forest, L.
–	Murray of Newhaven, L.
Con	Murton of Lindisfarne, L.
Ind	Mustill, L.
Lab	Nicol, B.
Lab	Northfield, L.
Con	Nugent of Guildford, L.
Ind	O'Brien of Lothbury, L.
Ind	O'Cathain, B.
Ind	Oliver of Aylmerton, L.
Con	Oppenheim-Barnes, B.
Lab	Oram, L.
Con	Orr-Ewing, L.
Ind	Owen, L.
Ind	Palumbo, L.
Con	Park of Monmouth, B.
Con	Parkinson, L.
Lab	Parry, L.
Con	Pearson of Rannoch, L.
Con	Perry of Southwark, B.
Dem	Perry of Walton, L.
Lab	Peston, L.
Con	Peyton of Yeovil, L.
Con	Pike, B.
Lab	Pitt of Hampstead, L.
Lab	Plant of Highfield, L.
Con	Platt of Writtle, B.
Ind	Plowden, L.
Con	Plumb, L.
Con	Plummer of St Marylebone, L.
Ind	Porritt, L.
Ind	Porter of Luddenham, L.
Con	Prentice, L.
Con	Prior, L.
Con	Pritchard, L.
Lab	Prys-Davies, L.
Con	Pym, L.
Con	Quinton, L.
Con	Rawlinson of Ewell, L.
Ind	Rayne, L.
–	Rayner, L.
Con	Rees, L.
Ind	Rees-Mogg, L.
Con	Reigate, L.
Con	Renfrew of Kaimsthorn, L.
Con	Renton, L.
Lab	Richard, L.
Ind	Richardson, L.
Ind	Richardson of Duntisbourne, L.
Con	Rippon of Hexham, L.
Ind	Rix, L.
–	Robens of Woldingham, L.
Dem	Robson of Kiddington, B.
Con	Rodger of Earlsferry, L.
Dem	Rodgers of Quarry Bank, L.
Ind	Roll of Ipsden, L.
Ind	Roskill, L.
Ind	Runcie, L.
–	Ryder of Eaton Hastings, L.
Ind	Ryder of Warsaw, B.
–	Sainsbury, L.
Con	Sainsbury of Preston Candover, L.
Con	St John of Fawsley, L.
Con	Sanderson of Bowden, L.
Lab	Scanlon, L.
Ind	Scarman, L.
Ind	Schon, L.
Con	Seccombe, B.
Dem	Seear, B.
Lab	Sefton of Garston, L.
Lab	Serota, B.
Lab	Shackleton, L.
Con	Sharp of Grimsdyke, L.
Con	Sharples, B.
Ind	Shawcross, L.
Con	Sieff of Brimpton, L.
Ind	Simon of Glaisdale, L.
Con	Skidelsky, L.
Ind	Slynn of Hadley, L.
Ind	Smith, L.
Lab	Soper, L.
Con	Soulsby of Swaffham Prior, L.
Lab	Stallard, L.
Ind	Stedman, B.
Con	Sterling of Plaistow, L.
Con	Stevens of Ludgate, L.
Con	Stewartby, L.
Con	Stodart of Leaston, L.
Lab	Stoddart of Swindon, L.
Ind	Stokes, L.
Ind	Tanlaw, L.
Lab	Taylor of Blackburn, L.
Ind	Taylor of Gosforth, L.
Lab	Taylor of Gryfe, L.
Con	Taylor of Hadfield, L.
Con	Tebbit, L.
Ind	Templeman, L.
Con	Thatcher, B.
Con	Thomas of Gwydir, L.
Con	Thomas of Swynnerton, L.
Dem	Thomson of Monifieth, L.
Con	Thorneycroft, L.
Ind	Todd, L.
Ind	Tombs, L.
Dem	Tordoff, L.
Con	Tranmire, L.
Con	Trumpington, B.
Lab	Turner of Camden, B.
Lab	Varley, L.
Con	Vickers, B.
Con	Vinson, L.
Con	Waddington, L.
Con	Wade of Chorlton, L.
Con	Wakeham, L.
Con	Walker of Worcester, L.
Lab	Wallace of Campsie, L.
Lab	Wallace of Coslany, L.
Ind	Walton of Detchant, L.
Ind	Warnock, B.
Ind	Weatherill, L.
Lab	Wedderburn of Charlton, L.
Ind	Weidenfeld, L.
Ind	Weinstock, L.
Dem	Whaddon, L.
Lab	White, B.
Con	White of Hull, L.
Dem	Wigoder, L.
Ind	Wilberforce, L.
Dem	Williams of Crosby
Lab	Williams of Elvel, L.
Lab	Williams of Mostyn, L.
–	Wilson of Langside, L.
Lab	Wilson of Rievaul L.
Ind	Wilson of Tillyorn, L.
Dem	Winstanley, L.
Con	Wolfson, L.
Con	Wolfson of Sunningdale, L.
Ind	Woolf, L.
Ind	Wyatt of Weeford, L.
Con	Young, B.
Lab	Young of Dartington, L.
Con	Young of Graffham, L.
Con	Younger of Prestwick, L.

Government Officers – Forms of Address

Source: Debrett's

Cabinet Ministers are invariably Privy Counsellors, *see* below.

Members of Parliament According to rank, but adding the initials "MP" after title or name and honours.

Minister of the Crown If a Privy Counsellor, *see* below, otherwise *see* Member of Parliament or Grade of Peerage (p. 412). The social form of "Dear Secretary of State" or "Dear Minister" may be used if the matter concerns the Department.

Prime Minister, The *See* Privy Counsellors. The social form of "Dear (Mr) Prime Minister" may be used if the matter concerns his office.

Privy Counsellors, also spelt Privy Councillors – LETTERS *Superscription*, "The Right Hon. ——", but if a peer then as such, followed by the letters "PC" *after* all Orders and Decorations. *Commencement, etc*, according to the rank of the individual. Privy Counsellors of Northern Ireland, which are no longer created, are entitled to the prefix of Right Hon. and are included in this section. Members of the Privy Council of Canada are entitled to the style of "Hon." for life. *Commencement*, as for Esquire (*see* p. 413) or appropriate rank.

Privy Counsellors, Wives of They enjoy no special style or precedence as such.

Secretary of State *See* Minister of the Crown *and* Privy Counsellors.

CIVIL SERVICE

The Civil Service consists of 19 principal departments (outlined below) which have a permanent staff to administer central government policies. Each department is headed by a government-appointed minister, but the transitory nature of ministerial appointments means that the smooth running of the department rests heavily on the knowledge and experience of the permanent staff. The Permanent Secretary or Permanent Under Secretary is the most senior civil servant within a ministry.

Ministry of Agriculture, Fisheries & Food

Whitehall Place, London SW1A 2HH
Tel: 071-270 3000
Responsibilities include: agriculture, horticulture, fisheries, food safety and quality, related environmental and rural issues in England, EC common agricultural and fisheries policies, single European market.
Minister: Gillian Shephard, MP
Permanent Secretary: Sir Derek Andrews

Ministry of Defence

Main Building, Whitehall, London SW1A 2HB
Tel: 071-218 9000
Responsibilities include: control, administration and support of the armed forces.
Defence Secretary: Malcolm Rifkind, MP
Permanent Under Secretary: Sir Christopher France

Department of Education & Science

Sanctuary Building, Great Smith Street, London SW1P 3BT
Tel: 071-925 5000
Responsibilities include: education, sport and recreation in England; universities in Great Britain; promotion of civil science in Britain and overseas.
Education Secretary: John Patten, MP
Permanent Secretary: Sir John Caines

Duchy of Lancaster

Lancaster Place, Strand, London WC2E 7ED
Tel: 071-836 8277
Responsibilities include: Citizen's Charter; the Civil Service; science and technology.
Chancellor: William Waldegrave, MP
Second Permanent Secretary: Richard Mottram

Department of Employment

Caxton House, Tothill Street, London SW1H 9NF
Tel: 071-273 3000
Responsibilities include: policy and legislation on employment and training; health and safety at work; industrial relations, wages councils and equal opportunities; small firms and tourism; statistics on labour and industrial matters in Great Britain; the Employment Service; the Careers Service in England; international representation on employment matters.
Employment Secretary: David Hunt, MP
Permanent Secretary: Sir Geoffrey Holland

Department of the Environment

2 Marsham Street, London SW1P 3EB
Tel: 071-276 3000
Responsibilities include: planning and regional development policies; local government; new towns; housing; construction; inner city matters; environmental protection; water; the countryside; conservation; historic buildings and ancient monuments in England; Property Services Agency in Great Britain.
Environment Secretary: John Gummer, MP
Permanent Secretary: Sir Terence Heiser

Foreign & Commonwealth Office

Downing Street, London SW1A 2AL
Tel: 071-270 3000
Responsibilities include: overseas relations; British consular facilities abroad.
Foreign Secretary: Douglas Hurd, MP
Permanent Under Secretary: Sir David Gillmore

Department of Health

Richmond House, 79 Whitehall, London SW1A 2NS
Tel: 071-210 3000
Responsibilities include: National Health Service; local authority personal social services, including those for children, the elderly and the infirm; ambulance service.
Health Secretary: Virginia Bottomley, MP
Permanent Secretary: G. A. Hart

Home Office

50 Queen Anne's Gate, London SW1H 9AT
Tel: 071-273 3000
Responsibilities include: administration of justice; criminal law; treatment of offenders; prison service; the police; crime prevention; fire and civil defence services; licensing laws; scrutiny of local authority by-laws; control of firearms and dangerous drugs; electoral matters in England and Wales; passports, immigration and nationality; race relations and sex discrimination; matters relating to the Channel Islands and the Isle of Man.
Home Secretary: Michael Howard, MP
Permanent Under Secretary: Sir Clive Whitmore

Lord Chancellor's Department

House of Lords, London SW1A 0PW
Tel: 071-219 3000
Responsibilities include: civil, county and Supreme courts, civil law, legal aid schemes, appointing and advising on the appointment of judges and magistrates.
Lord Chancellor: Lord Mackay of Clashfern
Permanent Secretary: T. S. Legg

Department of National Heritage

2–4 Cockspur Street, London SW1Y 5DH
Tel: 071-270 3000
Responsibilities include: arts, sport and broadcasting; national lottery.
Heritage Secretary: Peter Brooke, MP
Permanent Secretary: G. H. Phillips

Northern Ireland Office

Whitehall, London SW1A 2AZ
Tel: 071-210 3000
Responsibilities include: constitutional developments; law and order; security; electoral matters; also oversees the work of the Northern Ireland departments: Agriculture, Economic Development and Education.
Northern Ireland Secretary: Sir Patrick Mayhew
Permanent Under Secretary: J. A. Chilcot

Overseas Development Administration

94 Victoria Street, London SW1E 5JL
Tel: 071-917 7000
Responsibilities include: administering financial and technical assistance to overseas countries.
Minister: Baroness Lynda Chalker
Permanent Secretary: T. P. Lankester

Scottish Office

Dover House, Whitehall, London SW1A 2AU
Tel: 071-270 3000
Responsibilities include: agriculture, fisheries, education, law and order, environmental protection, local government, housing, roads, tourism, energy, sport, legal services and some aspects of social work and health. The responsibilities are divided between five departments (Agriculture & Fisheries, Environment, Education, Home & Health, Industry), supported by Central Services, which include the Solicitor's Office, the Information Directorate, and the Divisions of Personnel, Management and Organization.
Scottish Secretary: Ian Lang, MP
Permanent Under Secretary: Sir Russell Hillhouse

Department of Social Security

Richmond House, 79 Whitehall, London SW1A 2NS
Tel: 071-210 3000
Responsibilities include: social security system in Great Britain. Three executive agencies cover the main aspects of the Department's work: the Information Technology Services Agency; the Benefits Agency; and the Contribution Agency. In addition, the Resettlement Agency runs residential units designed to help single homeless people.
Social Security Secretary: Peter Lilley, MP
Permanent Secretary: Sir Michael Partridge

Department of Trade & Industry

Ashdown House, 123 Victoria Street, London SW1E 6RB
Tel: 071-215 5000
Responsibilities include: industrial and commercial policy; promoting enterprise and competition; information about new methods and opportunities; investor and consumer protection; business/education links; international trade policy; commercial relations and export promotion; company law; insolvency; radio regulation; patents and copyright protection in Great Britain. Since the reshuffle after the 1992 General Election, the Department of Energy has been merged with the DTI. Its responsibilities include policies for all forms of energy, the efficient use and development of new sources and government liaison with energy industries.
President of the Board of Trade: Michael Heseltine, MP
Permanent Secretary: Sir Peter Gregson

Department of Transport

2 Marsham Street, London SW1P 3EB
Tel: 071-276 3000
Responsibilities include: land, sea and air transport; London Transport; British Rail; international transport agreements; shipping and ports; marine pollution; road safety; local authority transport.
Transport Secretary: John MacGregor, MP
Permanent Under Secretary: A. P. Brown

The Treasury

Parliament Street, London SW1P 3AG
Tel: 071-270 5000
Responsibilities include: public finance and expenditure; staffing and pay within the Civil Service.
Chancellor of the Exchequer: Kenneth Clarke, MP
Permanent Secretary: Sir Terence Burns

Welsh Office

Gwydyr House, Whitehall, London SW1A 2ER
Tel: 071-270 3000
Responsibilities include: education; Welsh language and culture; agriculture and fisheries; forestry; local government; housing; water; environmental protection; sport; town and country planning; roads; tourism; implementation of European Regional Development Fund in Wales; civil emergencies.
Welsh Secretary: John Redwood, MP
Permanent Secretary: Sir Richard Lloyd Jones

Civil Service Staff

At 1 April in each year

Source: CSO

Full-time equivalents[1] (thousands)

	1981	1982	1983	1984	1985	1986	1987	1988	1989	1990	1991	1992
Agriculture, Fisheries and Food	13.6	13.1	12.7	12.1	12..1	11.7	11.3	11.1	10.9	10.7	11.0	10.8
Chancellor of the Exchequer's Departments:	114.9	121.0	117.4	112.4	111.9	111.0	110.1	108.6	109.1	109.2	109.6	111.6
Customs and Excise	26.8	26.2	25.4	25.1	25.4	25.1	25.8	26.3	26.4	26.9	27.0	26.4
Inland Revenue	75.6	74.0	73.1	69.8	69.8	69.3	67.8	66.6	67.0	66.0	65.7	68.9
Department for National Savings	10.0	9.1	8.3	8.0	7.8	7.8	7.7	7.4	7.3	7.0	6.7	6.3
Treasury and others	2.5	11.7	10.6	9.5	8.9	8.8	8.8	8.3	8.3	9.3	10.1	10.0
Education and Science	3.6	3.5	3.5	2.4	2.4	2.4	2.4	2.5	2.5	2.6	2.7	2.7
Employment	53.8	58.7	57.9	56.4	54.7	55.7	60.5	58.3	55.0	52.4	49.0	57.1
Energy	1.2	1.1	1.1	1.1	1.1	1.0	1.0	1.0	1.1	1.2	1.2	1.1
Environment	47.0	42.1	39.4	36.6	35.8	34.9	34.2	33.0	30.6	29.2	25.8	23.2
Foreign and Commonwealth	11.4	11.1	11.1	10.0	9.8	9.6	9.5	9.6	9.6	9.5	9.9	10.0
Health	–	–	–	–	–	–	–	–	8.9	5.4	4.7	6.9
Home	35.4	34.6	35.1	36.4	36.6	37.5	37.6	39.2	40.8	42.7	44.1	49.7
Industry	8.8	8.3	7.7	–	–	–	–	–	–	–	–	–
Scotland	13.6	13.4	13.1	12.8	13.0	12.9	13.0	13.0	12.3	12.6	12.9	13.1
Social Security	–	–	–	–	–	–	–	–	85.5	83.0	81.0	78.3
Social Services	100.1	98.0	96.4	92.6	94.9	94.9	97.7	102.3	–	–	–	–
Trade	9.3	8.9	8.9	–	–	–	–	–	–	–	–	–
Trade and Industry	–	–	–	14.7	14.8	14.8	14.8	14.6	14.7	13.6	13.4	12.7
Transport	13.7	13.0	13.0	14.2	14.4	14.7	12.3	14.1	14.1	15.5	15.3	15.0
Wales	2.3	2.3	2.2	2.2	2.3	2.3	2.3	2.2	2.2	2.3	2.3	2.4
Other civil departments	31.3	20.2	20.5	20.9	21.2	21.5	25.1	26.7	30.7	31.0	30.9	31.3
Total Ministry of Defence	229.6	216.9	208.9	199.2	174.0	169.5	164.0	143.4	141.3	141.4	140.2	139.5
Total civil and defence departments	689.6	666.4	648.9	624.0	599.0	594.4	597.8	579.6	569.2	562.4	553.9	565.3
of which Non-industrials	539.9	528.0	518.5	504.3	498.0	498.2	507.5	506.6	499.8	495.2	490.0	504.2
Industrials	149.7	138.4	130.4	119.7	101.0	96.2	90.3	73.0	69.4	67.2	63.9	61.1
Total civil departments	460.0	449.4	440.0	424.8	425.0	424.9	433.8	436.2	427.9	421.0	413.7	425.9

NOTE: figures may not add due to rounding. (1) Part-time employees are counted as half units.

LOCAL GOVERNMENT

In the United Kingdom local government is administered by elected local authorities, whose power and duties are determined by parliament. The authorities' responsibilities include schools, social welfare, housing, environmental planning and public health. In England they operate under the aegis of the relevant government department, although the Department of the Environment is the main link between them and central government. In Scotland, Wales and Northern Ireland local authorities deal with the Scottish Office, the Welsh Office and the Department of the Environment for Northern Ireland respectively.

Structure

Greater London has 32 *borough councils*, plus the Corporation of the City of London. The other main conurbations outside London (Greater Manchester, Merseyside, South Yorkshire, Tyne & Wear, West Midlands and West Yorkshire), which are known as metropolitam counties, are administered by 36 *district councils*. The remaining 47 counties of England and Wales (the shire counties) operate a two-tier system: *county councils* provide large-scale services, such as public health, while *district councils* oversee such things as street cleaning.

Mainland Scotland also operates a two-tier system: the 9 regions each have a regional authority and they are further divided into 53 *district councils*. Three *island councils* oversee Orkney, Shetland and the Western Isles.

Northern Ireland has 26 *district councils* which deal with many local needs, but *statutory bodies*, such as the Northern Ireland Housing Executive, are responsible for specific major services. *Area boards* are responsible for administering education, health, libraries and welfare services.

Consultations, initiated by the government in April 1991, are continuing to discuss the abolition of the two-tier structure in England, Scotland and Wales, and the introduction of single, all-purpose authorities.

Elections

In most of England (including Greater London), Wales and Northern Ireland councillors are elected every four years. However, all other metropolitan districts and some non-metropolitan districts elect one-third of their councillors each year between county council elections. Scottish elections take place every two years, but alternate between regional and district, so councillors still hold office for four years.

Next Local Elections

	County Councils	Met District Councils	Non-Met District Councils	London Borough	Regional & Island
England:	1997	1994	1994* 1995†	1994	
Wales:	1997		1994* 1995†		
Scotland:			1994* 1995†		1994
N. Ireland:			1997†		

* in districts where one third of the council retires each year.
† where the whole council retires every four years.

Political Composition of Local Councils

(as at 7 May 1993)

Abbreviations: A = Liberal/SDP Alliance; C = Conservative; Com = Communist; Dem = Democrat; Dem Lab = Democratic Labour; Grn = Green; Ind = Independent; Ind C = Independent Conservative; Ind Lab = Independent Labour; Lab = Labour; Lib = Liberal; LD = Social and Liberal Democrat; MK = Mebyon Kernow; NP = Non-Political/Non-Party; PC = Plaid Cymru; RA = Ratepayers'/Residents' Association; SDP = Social Democratic Party; SNP = Scottish National Party; Vac = Vacant.

ENGLAND

County Councils

Avon .... Lab 33, C 25, LD 18
Bedfordshire .... Lab 31, C 28, LD 13, Ind 1
Berkshire .... LD 33, Lab 24, C 16, Ind 2, R 1
Buckinghamshire .... C 39, LD 16, Lab 13, Ind 3
Cambridgeshire........ C 33, Lab 21, LD 21, Ind 1, Lib 1
Cheshire .... Lab 35, C 22, LD 14
Cleveland .... Lab 51, C 14, LD 12
Cornwall .... LD 42, Ind 21, Lab 8, C 6, Lib 1, Others 1
Cumbria .... Lab 39, C 27, LD 14, Ind 3
Derbyshire .... Lab 55, C 21, LD 7, Ind 1
Devon .... LD 41, Lab 21, C 18, Ind 4, Lib 1
Dorset .... LD 38, C 29, Lab 6, Ind 4
Durham.................. Lab 56, C 6, LD 6, Ind 4
East Sussex .... LD 30, C 22, Lab 18
Essex .... Lab 33, C 32, LD 32, Ind 1
Gloucestershire........ LD 30, Lab 20, C 10, Ind 2, Others 1
Hampshire .... LD 48, C 29, Lab 24, Ind 1
Hereford & Worcester... C 25, Lab 24, LD 23, Ind 4
Hertfordshire .... Lab 30, C 27, LD 19, Ind 1
Humberside .... Lab 43, C 22, LD 10
Isle of Wight .... LD 28, C 9, Ind 6
Kent...................... C 40, Lab 30, LD 29
Lancashire ... . Lab 53, C 35, LD 10, Vac 1
Leicestershire .... Lab 37, C 31, LD 17
Lincolnshire .... C 32, Lab 25, LD 15, Ind 4
Norfolk .... C 34, Lab 32, LD 16, Ind 2
Northamptonshire...... Lab 36, C 27, LD 5
Northumberland ...... Lab 40, C 13, LD 11, Others 2
North Yorkshire .... LD 35, C 29, Lab 23, Ind 9
Nottinghamshire .... Lab 59, C 23, LD 6
Oxfordshire .... C 25, Lab 24, LD 20, Grn 1
Shropshire .... C 26, Lab 23, LD 13, Ind 4
Somerset .... LD 41, C 13, Lab 2, Ind 1
Staffordshire .... Lab 53, C 22, LD 4, Others 3
Suffolk................. Lab 31, C 26, LD 19, Ind 4
Surrey .... C 34, LD 29, Lab 8, RA 3, Ind 2
Warwickshire .... Lab 30, C 19, LD 10, Ind 1, Others 1, R 1
West Sussex .... LD 34, C 26, Lab 10, R 1
Wiltshire .... LD 33, C 18, Lab 17

Greater London Borough Councils

Barking & Dagenham ... Lab 44, RA 3, Lib 1
Barnet .... C 38, Lab 18, LD 3, Vac 1
Bexley .... C 35, Lab 18, LD 9
Brent .... C 31, Lab 26, LD 6, Dem Lab 2, Ind 1
Bromley .... C 43, Lab 11, LD 6
Camden .... Lab 42, C 15, LD 2
City of Westminster..... C 45, Lab 15
Croydon .... C 41, Lab 29
Ealing .... C 40, Lab 30
Enfield................. C 35, Lab 31
Greenwich .... Lab 44, C 12, SDP 4, Lib 2
Hackney .... Lab 46, C 6, LD 6, Ind Lab 1, Ind Lib 1

(Continued)

Hammersmith and Fulham	Lab 28, C 22
Haringey	Lab 43, C 16
Harrow	C 32, Lab 13, LD 11, Ind C 4, Ind 3
Havering	Lab 25, C 19, RA 13, LD 6
Hillingdon	C 35, Lab 34
Hounslow	Lab 44, C 15, LD 1
Islington	Lab 49, LD 3
Kensington & Chelsea	C 39, Lab 14, Vac 1
Kingston upon Thames	C 25, LD 17, Lab 7, Vac 1
Lambeth	Lab 40, C 20, LD 4
Lewisham	Lab 58, C 6, LD 3
Merton	Lab 29, C 22, Ind 5, Ind Lab 1
Newham	Lab 55, C 3, LD 2
Redbridge	C 42, Lab 18, LD 3
Richmond upon Thames	LD 48, C 4
Southwark	Lab 36, LD 21, C 6, Vac 1
Sutton	LD 32, C 18, Lab 6
Tower Hamlets	LD 29, Lab 21
Waltham Forest	Lab 30, C 16, LD 11
Wandsworth	C 48, Lab 13

Metropolitan District Councils

Greater Manchester

Bolton	Lab 39, C 16, LD 4, Ind Lab 1
Bury	Lab 24, C 22, LD 2
Manchester	Lab 82, LD 12, C 5
Oldham	Lab 33, LD 19, C 7, Ind 1
Rochdale	Lab 23, LD 20, C 16, Ind 1
Salford	Lab 54, C 6
Stockport	LD 26, C 17, Lab 17, Ind 3
Tameside	Lab 48, C 7, Ind 1, Vac 1
Trafford	C 37, Lab 22, LD 4
Wigan	Lab 61, LD 8, C 2, Ind 1

Merseyside

Knowsley	Lab 60, C 3, Ind 3
Liverpool	Lab 38, LD 37, Others 19, C 2, Ind 2, Lib 1
St Helens	Lab 33, LD 15, C 6
Sefton	Lab 27, C 25, LD 17
Wirral	Lab 31, C 29, LD 6

South Yorkshire

Barnsley	Lab 63, C 2, RA 1
Doncaster	Lab 54, C 9
Rotherham	Lab 64, C 2
Sheffield	Lab 67, C 11, LD 9

Tyne and Wear

Gateshead	Lab 56, LD 7, C 1, Ind 1, Lib 1
Newcastle upon Tyne	Lab 61, LD 11, C 6
North Tyneside	Lab 37, C 16, Lib 7
South Tyneside	Lab 55, LD 4, Other 1
Sunderland	Lab 64, C 8, LD 3

West Midlands

Birmingham	Lab 60, C 43, LD 13, Ind 1
Coventry	Lab 42, C 12
Dudley	C 36, Lab 35, Vac 1
Sandwell	Lab 42, C 24, LD 6
Solihull	C 24, Lab 15, LD 6, RA 6
Walsall	Lab 24, C 23, LD 9, Ind 4
Wolverhampton	Lab 29, C 28, LD 3

West Yorkshire

Bradford	Lab 50, C 38, LD 2
Calderdale	Lab 25, C 22, LD 7
Kirklees	Lab 41, C 19, LD 10, Ind 2
Leeds	Lab 67, C 23, LD 8, Ind 1
Wakefield	Lab 55, C 6, Ind 1, Other 1

Non-Metropolitan District Councils

(*one-third of councillors retire each year, except in years of County Council elections)

Adur*	LD 22, C 14, Ind 2, Lab 1
Allerdale	Lab 31, C 11, Ind 7, Ind C 4, LD 2
Alnwick	LD 15, C 7, Ind 5, Lab 2
Amber Valley*	Lab 24, C 17, Ind 2
Arun	C 36, LD 12, Lab 7, Grn 1
Ashfield	Lab 32, C 1
Ashford	C 29, LD 11, Lab 5, Ind 1, Others 3
Aylesbury Vale	C 29, LD 22, Ind 6, Lab 1
Babergh	C 15, Ind 10, Lab 6, LD 5, Others 5, Vac 1
Barrow-in-Furness*	Lab 18, C 18, Ind 2
Basildon*	C 26, Lab 13, LD 3
Basingstoke & Deane*	C 30, Lab 15, LD 11, NP 3
Bassetlaw*	Lab 30, C 17, Ind 1, Ind Lab 1, LD 1
Bath*	C 24, LD 17, Lab 7
Berwick-upon-Tweed	LD 11, Ind 6, C 1, Lab 1, Others 3
Beverley	C 31, Lib 19, Lab 2, Ind 1
Blaby	C 30, LD 4, Ind 3, Ind C 1, Lab 1
Blackburn*	Lab 37, C 19, LD 4
Blackpool	Lab 27, C 12, LD 5
Blyth Valley	Lab 28, LD 19
Bolsover	Lab 34, RA 2, Ind 1
Boothferry	C 18, Lab 12, Ind 5
Boston	C 10, Ind 8, Lib 8, Lab 8
Bournemouth	LD 27, C 20, Lab 6, Ind 3
Bracknell Forest	C 32, Lab 7, LD 1
Braintree	C 23, Lab 21, LD 6, RA 4, Ind 2
Breckland	C 33, Lab 8, Ind 5, LD 1, Others 16
Brentwood*	LD 24, C 14, Lab 1
Bridgnorth	C 11, Ind 8, LD 4, Ind Lab 2, NP 2, Lab 1, Others 5
Brighton*	Lab 25, C 23
Bristol*	Lab 44, C 18, LD 5, Vac 1
Broadland*	C 27, Ind 8, LD 8, Lab 6
Bromsgrove	C 26, Lab 14, LD 1
Broxbourne*	C 36, Lab 4, LD 2
Broxtowe	C 28, Lab 15, LD 5
Burnley*	Lab 35, C 8, LD 5
Cambridge*	Lab 21, LD 12, C 9
Cannock Chase*	Lab 29, C 9, LD 3, Ind 1
Canterbury	LD 23, C 19, Lab 7
Caradon	Ind 23, LD 9, C 5, RA 3, Lab 1
Carlisle*	Lab 30, C 18, LD 2, Ind 1
Carrick	LD 24, C 8, Ind 8, Lab 4, Ind C 1
Castle Morpeth	Ind 9, LD 9, Lab 9, C 7
Castle Point	C 36, Lab 3
Charnwood	C 34, Lab 15, LD 2, Ind 1
Chelmsford	C 29, LD 21, Ind 3, Lab 2
Cheltenham*	LD 22, C 12, Lab 3, Ind 2, Others 2
Cherwell*	C 32, Lab 15, LD 3, Ind 2
Chester*	C 24, Lab 18, LD 16, Ind 2
Chesterfield	Lab 31, LD 11, C 5
Chester-le-Street	Lab 27, Ind 4, C 1, Lib 1
Chichester	C 34, LD 14, Ind 2
Chiltern	C 39, LD 9, RA 2
Chorley*	Lab 22, C 20, Ind 3, LD 3
Christchurch	C 13, Ind 12
Cleethorpes	Lab 16, C 12, LD 11, Ind 1
Colchester*	LD 30, C 21, Lab 7, RA 2
Congleton*	LD 19, C 16, Lab 10
Copeland	Lab 28, C 20, Ind 3
Corby	Lab 23, LD 2, C 1, Ind 1
Cotswold	Ind 16, C 9, LD 3, Others 16
Craven*	C 13, LD 12, Ind 6, Lab 3
Crawley*	Lab 22, C 9, LD 1
Crewe & Nantwich*	Lab 31, C 24, LD 2
Dacorum	C 38, Lab 16, LD 4
Darlington	Lab 30, C 18, Ind 2, LD 2
Dartford	C 25, Lab 20, RA 2
Daventry*	C 20, Lab 10, LD 3, Ind 2
Derby*	C 22, Lab 22
Derbyshire Dales	C 24, LD 9, Lab 3, Ind C 2, Ind 1
Derwentside	Lab 38, Ind 14, C 2
Dover	C 28, Lab 21, LD 4
Durham	Lab 28, LD 15, Ind 6
Easington	Lab 43, Ind 4, Ind Lab 4, LD 4
Eastbourne*	LD 17, C 13
East Cambridgeshire	Ind 10, C 6, LD 4, Ind C 1, Lab 1, Others 15
East Devon	C 41, LD 11, Ind 3, Grn 2, Ind C 1, Lib 1, Other 1
East Dorset	C 19, LD 13, RA 2, Ind 1, Vac 1
East Hampshire	LD 20, C 16, Ind 6
East Hertfordshire	C 32, LD 12, Ind 3, Lab 2, RA 1
Eastleigh*	C 20, LD 18, Lab 6
East Lindsey	Ind 43, C 8, LD 5, Lab 4
East Northamptonshire	C 24, Lab 9, LD 3
East Staffordshire	Lab 23, C 19, LD 4
East Yorkshire	C 16, Ind 13, Lab 5, LD 5, SDP 3, Vac 1
Eden	Ind 24, RA 8, LD 4, Ind C 1
Ellesmere Port & Neston	Lab 30, C 11
Elmbridge*	C 23, RA 19, LD 10, Lab 8
Epping Forest*	C 30, Lab 13, RA 10, SDP 3, LD 2, Ind 1
Epsom & Ewell	RA 30, LD 6, Lab 3
Erewash	Lab 27, C 22, Ind 2, LD 1
Exeter*	Lab 16, C 14, LD 5, Lib 1
Fareham*	C 30, LD 8, Lab 4

(Continued)

Fenland	C 28, Lab 6, Ind 4, LD 3
Forest Heath	C 12, Ind 9, LD 3, Lab 1
Forest of Dean	Lab 25, Ind 9, LD 6, C 3, Ind C 1, Others 5
Fylde	C 23, RA 9, Ind 6, LD 4, Others 13
Gedling	C 38, Lab 15, LD 3, Ind 1
Gillingham*	LD 17, C 15, Lab 10
Glanford	C 17, Ind 11, Grn 3, NP 3
Gloucester*	Lab 16, C 13, LD 5, Ind 1
Gosport*	LD 17, C 8, Lab 3, Ind 2
Gravesham	C 22, Lab 22
Great Grimsby*	Lab 29, C 13, LD 2, Ind 1
Great Yarmouth*	Lab 29, C 18, LD 1
Guildford	C 19, LD 19, Lab 6, Ind 1
Halton*	Lab 44, LD 7, C 2
Hambleton	C 24, Ind 13, LD 5, SDP 3, Lab 2
Harborough	C 18, LD 12, Ind 4, Lab 3
Harlow*	Lab 37, C 7, LD 3, Vac 1
Harrogate*	LD 29, C 22, Lab 4, Ind 2, Grn 1, Lib 1, SDP 1
Hart*	C 16, LD 12, Ind 7
Hartlepool*	Lab 28, C 12, LD 6, Ind 1
Hastings*	C 14, Lab 9, LD 9
Havant*	C 20, Lab 12, Ind 5, LD 5
Hereford*	LD 22, Lab 4, C 1
Hertsmere*	C 23, Lab 12, LD 3, Ind 1
High Peak	Lab 16, C 15, LD 10, Ind 3
Hinckley & Bosworth	C 21, LD 10, Lab 3
Holderness	Ind 20, LD 7, NP 4
Horsham	C 28, LD 16, Ind 2
Hove	C 21, Lab 6, LD 3
Huntingdonshire*	C 42, LD 7, Lab 3, Ind 1
Hyndburn*	Lab 32, C 12, LD 3
Ipswich*	Lab 33, C 15
Kennet	C 16, Ind 11, LD 9
Kerrier	LD 16, Lab 12, Ind 7, C 5, Lib 1
Kettering	Lab 20, C 11, LD 8, Ind 6
King's Lynn & West Norfolk	C 33, Lab 16, LD 5, Ind 4
Kingston upon Hull*	Lab 57, LD 2, C 1
Kingswood	Lab 26, C 18, LD 5, Ind 1
Lancaster	Lab 24, C 15, Ind 14, LD 7
Langbaurgh-on-Tees	Lab 32, C 20, LD 7
Leicester	Lab 37, C 13, LD 6
Leominster*	Ind 17, LD 9, C 6, Lab 2, Grn 1, Vac 1
Lewes	LD 27, C 18, Ind 3
Lichfield	C 37, Lab 15, Ind Lab 3, Ind 1
Lincoln*	Lab 30, C 3
Luton	Lab 28, C 11, LD 9
Macclesfield*	C 34, LD 13, Lab 10, RA 3
Maidstone*	C 27, LD 16, Lab 8, Ind 4
Maldon	C 13, Ind 9, LD 6, Ind C 1, Lab 1
Malvern Hills	Ind 18, LD 16, C 14, Lab 2, Grn 1
Mansfield	Lab 38, C 5, LD 2, Vac 1
Medina	C 18, LD 13, Ind 3, Lab 2
Melton	C 18, LD 8
Mendip	LD 23, C 13, Ind 4, Lab 3
Mid Bedfordshire	C 40, NP 5, Lab 3, LD 3, Ind 2
Mid Devon	Ind 27, LD 9, Lib 2, Lab 1, Other 1
Middlesbrough	Lab 38, C 9, LD 5, Ind 1
Mid Suffolk	C 17, LD 10, Lab 8, Ind 5
Mid Sussex*	C 34, LD 13, Ind 5, Lab 2
Milton Keynes*	Lab 21, C 15, LD 9, Ind 1
Mole Valley*	LD 17, C 14, Ind 9, Lab 1
Newark & Sherwood	Lab 28, C 19, LD 4, Ind 3
Newbury	LD 24, C 20, Ind 1
Newcastle under Lyme*	Lab 36, C 10, LD 10
New Forest	LD 29, C 23, Ind 6
Northampton	Lab 21, C 18, LD 4
Northavon	LD 25, C 20, Lab 11, Ind 1
North Bedfordshire*	C 25, Lab 15, LD 10, Ind 3
North Cornwall	Ind 30, LD 5, Lab 2, C 1
North Devon	LD 26, Ind 16, C 2
North Dorset	Ind 21, LD 12
NE Derbyshire	Lab 35, C 12, Ind 3, LD 3
North Hertfordshire*	C 25, Lab 17, RA 3, LD 3, Ind 1, Vac 1
North Kesteven	C 10, Ind 10, NP 7, Lab 6, LD 5, Ind C 1
North Norfolk	C & Ind All 24, Ind 7, Lab 6, LD 5, Others 4
North Shropshire	NP 28, C 5, Lab 4, Ind 3
N Warwickshire	Lab 20, C 12, Ind 1, LD 1
NW Leicestershire	Lab 24, C 12, Ind 4
North Wiltshire	LD 29, C 24, Ind 4, Lab 3
Norwich*	Lab 35, LD 10, C 3
Nottingham	Lab 37, C 17, Ind 1
Nuneaton & Bedworth*	Lab 36, C 9
Oadby & Wigston*	LD 19, C 7
Oswestry	C 8, Ind 8, Lab 6, Lib 3
Oxford*	Lab 35, C 10, LD 6
Pendle*	Lab 27, LD 17, C 7

Penwith*	C 11, Lab 10, Ind 7, LD 4, Others 2
Peterborough*	Lab 23, C 19, Lib 5, LD 1
Plymouth	Lab 41, C 19
Poole	LD 16, C 13, Vac 1
Portsmouth*	C 17, Lab 14, LD 7, Vac 1
Preston*	Lab 33, C 19, LD 5
Purbeck*	C 11, Ind 6, LD 5
Reading*	Lab 29, C 11, LD 4, Ind 1
Redditch*	Lab 20, C 9
Reigate & Banstead	C 24, Lab 11, LD 10, RA 2, Ind 1
Restormel	LD 23, Ind 13, C 2, Lab 1
Ribble Valley	C 24, LD 13, Ind 1, Lab 1
Richmondshire	Ind 27, LD 3, C 1, Ind C 1, Others 2
Rochester upon Medway	C 21, Lab 21, LD 8
Rochford*	LD 19, C 12, Lab 7, RA 2
Rossendale*	Lab 22, C 14
Rother	C 20, LD 16, Ind 6, Lab 3
Rugby*	C 21, Lab 14, RA 6, Ind 3, LD 3
Runnymede*	C 28, Lab 7, RA 4, Ind 2, Grn 1
Rushcliffe	C 43, LD 6, Lab 5
Rushmoor*	C 30, LD 9, Lab 6
Rutland	Ind 9, C 6, LD 4, Vac 1
Ryedale	LD 20, Ind 14, C 6, Lab 2
St Albans*	C 23, LD 23, Lab 10, Ind 1
St Edmundsbury	C 26, Lab 11, LD 5, Ind 2, Vac 1
Salisbury	C 31, Ind 9, LD 9, Lab 5, RA 4
Scarborough	Lab 16, C 15, Ind 10, LD 8
Scunthorpe*	Lab 33, C 6, SDP 1
Sedgefield	Lab 33, LD 7, Ind 5, C 2, Others 2
Sedgemoor	C 26, Lab 12, LD 7, Ind 4
Selby	C 22, Lab 13, Ind 10, LD 3
Sevenoaks	C 31, Ind 11, LD 11
Shepway	LD 33, C 18, Lab 3, Ind 2
Shrewsbury & Atcham*	C 21, Lab 19, LD 6, Ind 2
Slough*	Lab 29, C 5, Lib 3, LD 2
Southampton*	Lab 30, C 9, LD 6
South Bedfordshire*	C 37, Lab 9, LD 6, Vac 1
South Bucks	C 30, Ind 10, LD 1
South Cambridgeshire*	C 24, Ind 22, Lab 5, LD 4
South Derbyshire	Lab 20, C 12, Ind C 2
Southend-on-Sea*	C 25, LD 8, Lab 6
South Hams	C 23, Ind 8, LD 4, Ind C 1, Lab 1, Others 7
South Herefordshire*	Ind 30, C 4, LD 3, Vac 2
South Holland	Ind 15, Lab 9, C 5, Ind 1, Others 9
South Kesteven	C 25, Lab 13, Ind 10, LD 8, Lib 1
South Lakeland*	C 17, LD 15, Ind 14, Lab 6
South Norfolk	A 22, C 22, Ind 3
South Northants	C 28, Ind 9, Lab 2, LD 1
South Oxfordshire	C 29, LD 8, Ind 5, Lab 5
South Ribble	C 33, Lab 15, LD 6
South Shropshire	NP 13, C 6, Ind 6, LD 3, Ind C 1, Lab 1, Others 13
South Somerset	LD 41, C 14, Ind 5
South Staffordshire	C 37, Lab 8, Ind 3, LD 1
South Wight	LD 12, C 7, Ind 5
Spelthorne	C 33, Lab 4, LD 3
Stafford	C 29, Lab 18, LD 13
Staffordshire Moorlands	RA 23, Ind C 14, Lab 9, Ind 6, LD 4
Stevenage*	Lab 32, C 4, LD 3
Stockton-on-Tees	Lab 26, C 17, LD 11, Ind Lab 1
Stoke-on-Trent*	Lab 48, C 12
Stratford-upon-Avon*	C 28, LD 19, Ind 7, Lab 1
Stroud*	C 22, Lab 16, LD 9, Grn 5, Ind 3
Suffolk Coastal	C 37, Ind 8, Lab 7, LD 3
Surrey Heath	C 31, LD 4, Lab 1
Swale*	C 20, Lab 14, LD 14, Ind 1
Tamworth*	Lab 21, C 8, Ind 1
Tandridge*	C 20, LD 18, Lab 4
Taunton Deane	LD 29, C 13, Lab 7, Ind 4
Teesdale	Ind 21, Lab 7, C 2, LD 1
Teignbridge	Ind 24, C 19, LD 11, Lab 4
Tendring	LD 21, C 18, Lab 11, RA 4, Ind 3, Ind C 2, Other 1
Test Valley	C 28, LD 13, Ind 2, NP 1
Tewkesbury	Ind 19, C 7, LD 6, Lab 2, Vac 2
Thamesdown*	Lab 33, C 14, LD 6, Ind 1
Thanet	C 29, Lab 14, Ind 9, LD 2
Three Rivers*	C 21, LD 18, Lab 9
Thurrock*	Lab 29, C 9, Ind 1
Tonbridge & Malling*	C 32, LD 17, Lab 6
Torbay*	LD 21, C 12, Lab 2, Ind 1
Torridge	NP 18, C 5, Ind 4, Lab 4, LD 4, Grn 1
Tunbridge Wells*	C 30, LD 14, Lab 3, Ind 1
Tynedale	C 17, Lab 14, LD 9, Ind 7
Uttlesford	C 25, LD 10, Ind 6, Lab 1
Vale of White Horse	C 29, LD 18, Ind 2, Lab 2
Vale Royal	Lab 32, C 24, LD 3, Ind 1, RA 1

(Continued)

Wansbeck	Lab 44, Lib 2
Wansdyke	C 23, Lab 20, Ind 3, LD 1
Warrington	Lab 42, LD 9, C 8
Warwick	C 24, Lab 10, LD 8, RA 3
Watford*	Lab 22, C 11, LD 3
Waveney*	Lab 26, C 17, LD 5
Waverley	C 29, LD 28, Lab 2
Wealden	C 44, LD 11, Ind 3
Wear Valley	LD 28, Lab 8, Ind 4
Welling	C 19, Lab 11, Ind 3, Lib 1
Welwyn Hatfield*	C 24, Lab 23
West Devon	Ind 17, LD 6, C 5, Grn 1, Lab 1
West Dorset	C 18, NP 14, LD 11, Lab 5, Ind 4, Ind C 1, SDP 1, Vac 1
West Lancashire*	C 28, Lab 26, LD 1
West Lindsey*	Ind 11, C 10, LD 9, Lab 7
West Oxfordshire*	Ind 20, C 15, LD 8, Lab 6
West Somerset	Ind 22, C 5, Lab 3, LD 1, Vac 1
West Wiltshire	LD 21, C 9, Ind 3, Lib 3, Lab 2, Others 2
Weymouth & Portland*	Lab 10, C 10, LD 10, Ind 3, RA 1, Other 1
Winchester*	C 23, LD 22, Lab 6, Others 3, Ind 1
Windsor & Maidenhead	C 26, LD 25, RA 7
Woking*	C 19, LD 11, Lab 5
Wokingham*	C 34, LD 19, Lab 1
Woodspring	C 35, LD 14, Ind 4, Lab 4, Grn 1, Vac 1
Worcester*	Lab 23, C 11, Ind 1, LD 1
Worthing*	C 22, LD 14
Wrekin	Lab 33, C 10, LD 2, Ind 1
Wychavon	C 32, LD 10, Lab 6, Ind 1
Wycombe	C 38, LD 10, Lab 9, Ind 2, RA 1
Wyre	C 32, Lab 17, LD 5, Ind 1, RA 1
Wyre Forest*	Lab 21, LD 11, C 9, Ind 1
York*	Lab 34, C 7, LD 4

WALES

County Councils

Clwyd	Lab 32, Ind 17, C 8, LD 3, PC 3, Vac 1
Dyfed	Ind 31, Lab 22, LD 8, PC 7, R 1, C 1
Gwent	Lab 55, C 6, LD 1, PC 1
Gwynedd	Ind 27, PC 18, Lab 9, LD 7, C 1
Mid Glamorgan	Lab 60, PC 10, Ind 3, C 1
Powys	Ind 38, Lab 4, LD 4
South Glamorgan	Lab 40, C 12, LD 8, PC 1, Ind 1
West Glamorgan	Lab 46, Ind 7, C 3, LD 3, PC 1, Vac 1

District Councils

Aberconwy	Lab 11, LD 10, C 9, Ind 6, PC 1, Others 4
Alyn & Deeside	Lab 28, C 8, Ind 4, LD 2, PC 1
Arfon	Ind 14, PC 14, Lab 8, LD 2, Other 1
Blaenau Gwent	Lab 31, RA 5, Ind 3, PC 2, C 1, Lib 1, Vac 1
Brecknock	Ind 29, Lab 13, LD 2
Cardiff	Lab 39, C 16, LD 9, Ind 1
Carmarthen	Ind 27, Lab 6, PC 2, LD 1, RA 1
Ceredigion	Ind 31, LD 9, PC 3, Lab 1
Colwyn	Ind 12, LD 12, C 7, Lab 3
Cynon Valley	Lab 26, PC 10, Ind 1, Other 1
Delyn	Ind 24, Lab 12, LD 3, PC 2, C 1
Dinefwr	Lab 16, Ind 11, PC 3, NP 1, Vac 1
Dwyfor	PC 7, Others 22
Glyndŵr	Ind 25, Lab 7, LD 2, PC 1
Islwyn	Lab 30, PC 5
Llanelli	Lab 20, LD 3, Grn 2, Ind 2, Ind Lab 1, PC 1, Others 6
Lliw Valley	Lab 22, Ind 6, PC 4, C 1
Meirionnydd	PC 13, Lab 4, Others 24
Merthyr Tydfil	Lab 21, RA 6, Ind 3, PC 1, Others 3
Monmouth	C 22, Lab 14, Ind 3, LD 1
Montgomeryshire	Ind 36, Lab 4, LD 4, C 1, PC 1
Neath	Lab 25, PC 5, SDP 2, Com 1, Ind 1
Newport	Lab 40, C 7
Ogwr	Lab 39, C 8, Ind Lab 1, LD 1
Port Talbot	Lab 21, RA 6, SDP 2, Ind 1, LD 1
Preseli Pembrokeshire	Ind 34, Lab 2, C 1, LD 1, Vac 2
Radnorshire	Ind 28, Lab 5
Rhondda	Lab 26, PC 4, RA 3
Rhuddlan	Ind 21, Lab 11
Rhymney Valley	Lab 27, PC 13, Ind 3, RA 2, Other 1
South Pembrokeshire	NP 25, Lab 2, PC 2, Vac 1
Swansea	Lab 30, C 11, LD 6, Ind 5
Taff-Ely	Lab 19, PC 14, C 2, LD 2, RA 1, SDP 1
Torfaen	Lab 36, LD 4, Ind 2, C 1, Com 1
Vale of Glamorgan	Lab 23, C 18, Ind C 3, RA 3, Ind 1
Wrexham Maelor	Lab 28, LD 5, C 4, Ind 3, NP 3, Lib 1, PC 1
Ynys Môn	NP 22, PC 8, Lab 5, Ind 3, C 1

SCOTLAND

Regional and Island Councils

Borders	Ind 13, LD 6, C 2, SNP 2
Central	Lab 22, SNP 6, C 5, Ind 1
Dumfries & Galloway	Ind 17, Lab/Ind Lab 11, SNP 3, LD 2, C 1, Other 1
Fife	Lab 30, LD 10, C 2, SNP 2, Com 1, Ind 1
Grampian	Lab 17, SNP 14, C 12, LD 10, Ind 3, Ind Lab 1
Highland	Ind 34, Lab 10, LD 3, Ind LD 2, SNP 2, C 1, Grn 1
Lothian	Lab 34, C 12, LD 2, SNP 1
Orkney	NP 24
Shetland	Ind 15, Lab 2, Others 7, Vac 1
Strathclyde	Lab 90, C 5, LD 4, Ind 3, SNP 1
Tayside	Lab 18, C 14, SNP 10, LD 2, Ind 1, Ind Lab 1
Western Isles	Ind 30

District Councils

Aberdeen	Lab 27, LD 13, C 10, SNP 2
Angus	SNP 13, C 6, Ind 1, Other 1
Annandale & Eskdale	LD 10, Ind 5, Lab 1
Argyll & Bute	Ind 8, LD 4, C 3, SNP 3, Lab 1, Others 7
Badenoch & Strathspey	Ind 11
Banff & Buchan	Ind 10, SNP 7, LD 1
Bearsden & Milngavie	C 5, LD 4, Lab 1
Berwickshire	C 8, Ind 3, LD 1
Caithness	Ind 15, Lib 1
Clackmannan	Lab 8, SNP 3, C 1
Clydebank	Lab 8, SNP 2, C 1, Ind 1
Clydesdale	Lab 9, SNP 4, Ind 2, C 1
Cumbernauld & Kilsyth	Lab 7, SNP 5
Cumnock & Doon Valley	Lab 10
Cunninghame	Lab 20, C 6, SNP 3, Other 1
Dumbarton	Lab 7, C 4, SNP 3, Ind 1, NP 1
Dundee	Lab 26, C 12, SNP 6
Dundermline	Lab 22, LD 5, SNP 4, C 2, Other 1
East Kilbride	Lab 12, C 2, SNP 2
East Lothian	Lab 9, C 7, SNP 1
Eastwood	C 8, Ind 2, Lab 1, Other 1
Edinburgh	Lab 32, C 22, LD 5, SNP 3
Ettrick & Lauderdale	Ind 14, Lab 1, SNP 1
Falkirk	Lab 16, SNP 14, C 3, Ind 3
Glasgow	Lab 54, C 5, SNP 2, Ind 2, Others 2, LD 1
Gordon	Ind 9, LD 5, C 2
Hamilton	Lab 15, LD 2, C 2, Ind 1
Inverclyde	Lab 11, LD 8, C 1
Inverness	Ind 13, Lab 8, LD 5, Lib 1, SNP 1
Kilmarnock & Loudoun	Lab 8, C 7, SNP 3
Kincardine & Deeside	Ind 5, C 5, LD 1, SNP 1
Kirkcaldy	Lab 26, SNP 7, Ind 3, LD 2, C 2
Kyle & Carrick	Lab 16, C 7, Ind C 1, Ind Lab 1
Lochaber	Ind 4, Lab 4, Others 4, SNP 3
Midlothian	Lab 12, C 2, SNP 1
Monklands	Lab 17, SNP 3
Moray	Ind 9, SNP 7, Lab 1, C 1
Motherwell	Lab 22, SNP 4, C 2, Ind 2
Nairn	Ind 8, C 1, SNP 1
Nithsdale	Lab 9, Ind 8, SNP 5, C 5, LD 1
North East Fife	LD 12, C 4, Ind 2
Perth & Kinross	C 11, SNP 9, Lab 5, Ind 2, LD 2
Renfrew	Lab 31, C 6, SNP 5, LD 2, Lib 1
Ross & Cromarty	Ind 16, SNP 4, Lab 1, C 1
Roxburgh	Ind 7, LD 4, NP 2, C 1, SNP 1, Other 1
Skye & Lochalsh	Ind 10, SNP 1
Stewartry	Ind 11, C 1
Stirling	C 10, Lab 10
Strathkelvin	Lab 9, C 6
Sutherland	Ind 14
Tweeddale	Ind 6, LD 2, Lab 1, SNP 1
West Lothian	Lab 12, SNP 9, Ind 3
Wigtown	Ind 10, SNP 2, Lab 1, C 1

Local Government Finance

In England, Scotland and Wales funds are raised by imposing a *council tax* on most adults. The charge is based on average property values divided into 8 bands (A–H). Those in the highest band (H) will pay up to 3 times more than those in the lowest band (A). One-person households, students and apprentices receive a 25% discount. (Student halls of residence and other households where all the adult residents are students are exempt from the council tax.) People on very low incomes or dependent on income support receive rebates of up to 100%. Others exempt from the tax include hospital patients, full-time school pupils, prisoners and members of religious orders.

Northern Ireland has a system of domestic rates rather than the council tax.

The council tax will account for 23% of the £38 billion in local government expenditure in 1993/94. The remainder will be met by Revenue Support Grant (£17 billion), business rates (£11.6 billion) and use of reserves (£0.5 billion). These figures represent about £2,000 per household.

A scheme of transitional relief will apply to the first 2 years of the council tax to ensure that households do not face an unreasonable increase in their bill compared with the community charge. This is calculated automatically and does not need to be applied for. The cost of transitional relief in the first year is estimated at £340 million.

Expenditure and Income of Local Authorities

Years ended 31 March

Source: CSO

£ million

	1980/81	1981/82	1982/83	1983/84	1984/85	1985/86	1986/87	1987/88	1988/89	1989/90	1990/91
United Kingdom											
Total expenditure:											
On capital works	5,861.0	5,635.7	6,899.5	7,876.6	8,093.9	7,253.5	7,603.5	8,213.9	8,895.4	11,761.3	8,863.8
Other	33,971.1	37,477.8	40,509.2	43,272.9	45,481.9	47,339.7	50,289.5	54,881.0	59,328.1	64,281.8	76,495.4
Total income[1]	40,160.9	44,120.0	47,901.8	50,442.7	52,355.7	54,779.4	56,251.2	59,827.3	65,476.2	70,197.3	–
England and Wales											
Total expenditure:											
On capital works	5,176.0	4,903.3	6,111.8	6,918.0	7,228.7	6,443.1	6,666.3	7,103.5	8,384.7	10,726.4	7,576.7
Other	30,337.5	33,441.0	36,142.3	38,573.3	40,544.5	42,138.3	44,783.4	48,270.6	52,275.6	55,539.1	68,872.1
Total income[1]	35,915.8	39,311.2	42,617.6	44,718.7	46,602.7	48,581.4	49,873.3	52,734.6	57,873.7	61,731.8	66,190.8
Scotland											
Total expenditure:											
On capital works	660.9	707.3	763.6	929.4	840.0	891.5	912.2	1,079.4	1,142.1	1,262.1	1,249.7
Other	3,536.8	3,926.2	4,245.0	4,566.5	4,794.1	5,048.2	5,352.0	5,721.8	6,198.0	6,793.2	7,429.8
Total income[1]	4,125.0	4,672.6	5,133.1	5,558.7	5,581.8	6,046.4	6,235.1	6,922.5	7,438.3	8,288.7	–
Northern Ireland											
Total expenditure:											
On capital works	24.1	25.1	24.1	29.2	25.2	33.3	25.0	31.0	34.0	36.0	37.4
Other	96.8	110.6	121.9	133.1	143.3	153.2	154.1	166.9	167.3	179.4	193.5
Total income[1]	120.1	136.2	151.1	165.3	168.8	151.6	142.8	170.2	164.2	176.8	187.5

(1) "Capital" and "Other" figures cannot be added to give a "Total" figure because of double counting of loan charges, which are scored as both "Capital" and "Other" expenditure.

Council Taxes 1993/94, England

Years ended 31 March

Source: Department of the Environment

	Band C Council Tax for notifiable authority[1] £	Council Tax for Area (Band C) 2 Adults[2] £	Band in which average (median) dwelling falls[3]	Average Council Tax per dwelling[4] £	Average Community Charge per dwelling 1992/93[5] £	Average rates per household 1989/90[6] £
Greater London						
City of London	352	368	E	344	260	661
Camden	492	638	D	641	563	714
Greenwich	550	696	C	599	347	536
Hackney	475	621	C	502	567	546
Hammersmith & Fulham	342	488	D	506	360	592
Islington	474	620	D	566	544	679
Kensington & Chelsea	295	441	F	513	317	555
Lambeth	414	560	C	472	519	516
Lewisham	313	459	C	408	292	483
Southwark	409	555	C	423	252	452
Tower Hamlets	328	474	C	395	307	424
Wandsworth	253	399	D	398	0	358
Westminster	117	262	E	305	54	785
Barking & Dagenham	318	448	C	389	344	447
Barnet	359	488	E	551	492	711
Bexley	328	458	D	472	450	459
Brent	402	531	D	516	498	968

(Continued)

	Band C Council Tax for notifiable authority[1] £	Council Tax for Area (Band C) 2 Adults[2] £	Band in which average (median) dwelling falls[3]	Average Council Tax per dwelling[4] £	Average Community Charge per dwelling 1992/93[5] £	Average rates per household 1989/90[6] £
Greater London *(Continued)*						
Bromley	324	453	D	522	388	469
Croydon	328	458	D	477	396	499
Ealing	377	507	D	512	522	634
Enfield	393	522	D	538	498	590
Haringey	516	646	D	631	644	904
Harrow	362	492	D	550	510	614
Havering	346	476	D	480	496	501
Hillingon	337	467	D	499	527	601
Hounslow	415	545	D	565	504	655
Kingston upon Thames	335	465	D	521	444	583
Merton	314	443	D	464	417	501
Newham	403	532	C	438	547	628
Redbridge	337	467	D	477	458	447
Richmond upon Thames	351	481	E	562	428	626
Sutton	333	463	D	490	471	573
Waltham Forest	394	524	C	453	492	583
Metropolitan Police	114					
London Fire & CD Authority	16					
Greater Manchester						
Greater Manchester Police Authority	37					
Greater Manchester Fire & CD Authority	15					
Bolton	478	530	A	418	507	447
Bury	488	540	B	464	549	564
Manchester	604	656	A	434	513	593
Oldham	502	554	A	427	503	438
Rochdale	539	591	A	456	583	474
Salford	576	628	A	465	532	526
Stockport	522	574	C	531	587	577
Tameside	569	621	A	468	575	469
Trafford	404	456	C	431	447	554
Wigan	526	578	A	459	548	508
Merseyside						
Merseyside Police Authority	38					
Merseyside Fire & CD Authority	15					
Knowsley	545	598	A	443	550	597
Liverpool	592	645	A	445	674	561
Sefton	501	554	B	481	569	573
St Helens	494	547	A	427	531	533
Wirral	560	613	B	507	601	708
South Yorkshire						
South Yorkshire Police Authority	37					
South Yorkshire Fire & CD Authority	19					
Barnsley	477	534	A	400	402	409
Doncaster	466	522	A	387	429	483
Rotherham	563	619	A	469	505	462
Sheffield	514	570	A	423	471	527
Tyne and Wear						
Northumbria Police Authority	37					
Tyne and Wear Fire & CD Authority	15					
Gateshead	566	619	A	446	451	420
Newcastle upon Tyne	652	704	A	513	561	515
North Tyneside	576	628	A	482	572	560
South Tyneside	529	582	A	423	497	434
Sunderland	481	534	A	382	484	412
West Midlands						
West Midlands Police Authority	38					
West Midlands Fire & CD Authority	15					
Birmingham	531	584	B	444	521	526
Coventry	557	610	B	466	566	573
Dudley	465	518	B	439	549	567
Sandwell	491	543	A	394	567	522
Solihull	409	462	C	475	494	595
Walsall	473	526	B	418	568	611
Wolverhampton	440	493	A	376	567	587
West Yorkshire						
West Yorkshire Police Authority	38					
West Yorkshire Fire & CD Authority	19					
Bradford	404	460	B	367	472	406
Calderdale	490	546	B	434	375	432
Kirklees	502	559	B	448	428	390
Leeds	478	534	B	418	530	409
Wakefield	520	576	A	438	490	441

(Continued)

	Band C Council Tax for notifiable authority[1] £	Council Tax for Area (Band C) 2 Adults[2] £	Band in which average (median) dwelling falls[3]	Average Council Tax per dwelling[4] £	Average Community Charge per dwelling 1992/93[5] £	Average rates per household 1989/90[6] £
COUNTY COUNCILS						
Avon	454					
Bath	0	454	C	426	425	470
Bristol	168	621	B	505	647	548
Kingswood	66	519	C	480	562	508
Northavon	93	546	C	534	570	568
Wansdyke	94	548	C	559	591	540
Woodspring	79	533	C	508	549	596
Bedfordshire	387					
Luton	68	455	B	371	453	662
Mid Bedfordshire	67	455	C	456	450	634
North Bedfordshire	61	448	C	423	464	584
South Bedfordshire	96	483	C	475	535	705
Berkshire	399					
Bracknell Forest	63	461	C	487	472	543
Newbury	71	470	D	512	477	544
Reading	141	540	C	511	573	516
Slough	20	419	C	383	391	494
Windsor & Maidenhead	1	400	E	477	455	634
Wokingham	90	489	E	585	521	682
Buckinghamshire	383					
Aylesbury Vale	69	452	D	493	416	561
Chiltern	90	473	E	629	496	878
Milton Keynes	132	516	C	469	559	545
South Bucks	64	447	E	605	418	871
Wycombe	145	528	D	567	569	719
Cambridgeshire	390					
Cambridge	121	511	C	475	587	620
East Cambridgeshire	19	408	C	384	449	414
Fenland	65	455	B	382	453	390
Huntingdonshire	−4	386	C	353	373	465
Peterborough	85	475	B	376	492	474
South Cambridgeshire	4	394	D	428	399	575
Cheshire	467					
Chester	76	543	C	519	586	560
Congleton	49	516	C	502	555	549
Crewe and Nantwich	72	539	B	464	560	519
Ellesmere Port & Neston	81	548	B	474	594	558
Halton	107	574	A	439	598	469
Macclesfield	56	523	D	571	529	646
Vale Royal	92	559	C	535	611	508
Warrington	52	520	B	458	542	503
Cleveland	456					
Hartlepool	126	582	A	431	563	467
Langbaurgh-on-Tees	151	607	B	480	652	567
Middlesbrough	111	567	A	442	584	520
Stockton-on-Tees	104	560	B	448	562	572
Cornwall	416					
Caradon	79	495	C	443	453	380
Carrick	94	510	C	475	492	388
Kerrier	93	509	B	437	498	356
North Cornwall	70	486	C	443	450	386
Penrith	75	491	C	417	414	344
Restormel	72	488	B	422	461	380
Cumbria	465					
Allerdale	45	510	A	409	445	372
Barrow-in-Furness	155	620	A	463	508	352
Carlisle	88	553	B	434	573	407
Copeland	75	540	A	408	485	356
Eden	65	530	C	492	481	374
South Lakeland	76	541	C	537	507	450
Derbyshire	466					
Amber Valley	65	531	B	457	519	463
Bolsover	78	544	A	410	417	425
Chesterfield	70	536	A	416	518	463
Derby	52	518	A	397	493	540
Derbyshire Dales	69	535	C	558	544	520
Erewash	63	529	B	421	530	486
High Peak	78	544	B	500	547	471
North East Derbyshire	96	562	B	484	577	523
South Derbyshire	60	526	B	472	543	527

(Continued)

	Band C Council Tax for notifiable authority[1] £	Council Tax for Area (Band C) 2 Adults[2] £	Band in which average (median) dwelling falls[3]	Average Council Tax per dwelling[4] £	Average Community Charge per dwelling 1992/93[5] £	Average rates per household 1989/90[6] £
Devon	400					
East Devon	41	442	D	453	425	434
Exeter	83	483	C	420	435	401
Mid Devon	83	483	C	469	479	368
North Devon	77	477	C	434	463	345
Plymouth	102	502	B	374	520	438
South Hams	38	438	D	447	397	424
Teignbridge	92	492	C	474	466	424
Torbay	77	477	C	395	445	488
Torridge	66	466	C	414	421	306
West Devon	78	478	C	478	472	385
Dorset	384					
Bournemouth	64	448	C	399	453	480
Christchurch	53	437	D	447	407	507
East Dorset	74	458	D	519	505	584
North Dorset	29	412	C	419	391	406
Poole	44	428	C	426	417	517
Purbeck	47	431	D	443	379	442
West Dorset	64	448	C	452	431	379
Weymouth & Portland	92	476	B	413	473	404
Durham	413					
Chester-le-Street	100	513	A	396	533	448
Darlington	110	523	A	411	531	478
Derwentside	213	626	A	460	511	402
Durham	85	499	A	401	532	460
Easington	150	563	A	389	448	364
Sedgefield	86	499	A	371	450	416
Teesdale	96	509	B	468	454	316
Wear Valley	146	559	A	416	426	372
East Sussex	391					
Brighton	86	477	C	387	472	537
Eastbourne	135	526	C	453	527	587
Hastings	86	477	B	380	432	466
Hove	76	467	C	405	423	508
Lewes	89	481	C	477	478	577
Rother	98	489	D	486	457	571
Wealden	97	488	D	534	499	543
Essex	384					
Basildon	200	584	C	546	578	781
Braintree	84	468	C	448	473	544
Brentford	62	446	D	518	413	780
Castle Point	171	555	C	508	506	637
Chelmsford	95	479	D	502	482	667
Colchester	93	477	C	450	451	555
Epping Forest	92	472	D	536	468	745
Harlow	494	878	C	776	547	748
Maldon	75	459	C	466	422	619
Rochford	66	450	D	465	456	688
Southend-on-Sea	75	459	C	392	398	629
Tendring	88	472	C	406	400	545
Thurrock	105	488	C	434	487	660
Uttlesford	86	470	D	524	454	684
Gloucestershire	451					
Cheltenham	73	524	C	473	518	491
Cotswold	85	536	D	581	501	532
Forest of Dean	107	558	C	533	547	378
Gloucester	68	519	B	430	494	406
Stroud	115	565	C	566	601	463
Tewkesbury	−29	422	C	414	461	497
Hampshire	328					
Basingstoke & Deane	63	391	C	405	437	464
East Hampshire	97	426	D	493	499	555
Eastleigh	108	436	C	429	467	494
Fareham	66	395	C	401	407	540
Gosport	109	438	B	371	458	435
Hart	87	415	D	483	460	634
Havant	132	461	C	426	475	504
New Forest	85	413	D	434	409	474
Portsmouth	76	404	B	315	312	407
Rushmoor	76	404	C	383	477	507
Southampton	88	416	B	325	436	402
Test Valley	67	395	D	423	420	510
Winchester	79	407	D	463	404	550
Hereford and Worcester	383					
Bromsgrove	70	453	C	476	497	506

(Continued)

	Band C Council Tax for notifiable authority[1] £	Council Tax for Area (Band C) 2 Adults[2] £	Band in which average (median) dwelling falls[3]	Average Council Tax per dwelling[4] £	Average Community Charge per dwelling 1992/93[5] £	Average rates per household 1989/90[6] £
Hereford and Worcester *(Continued)*						
Hereford	59	442	B	371	464	317
Leominster	70	453	D	465	423	337
Malvern Hills	85	468	C	484	499	478
Redditch	114	497	B	437	530	478
South Herefordshire	48	431	D	465	421	353
Worcester	107	490	B	420	495	464
Wychavon	77	460	C	463	491	517
Wyre Forest	109	492	C	447	507	448
Hertfordshire	396					
Broxbourne	64	469	D	513	458	617
Dacorum	60	457	D	488	446	670
East Hertfordshire	79	475	D	532	456	648
Hertsmere	92	489	D	568	468	761
North Hertfordshire	68	464	C	479	453	672
St Albans	76	472	E	543	482	735
Stevenage	142	539	C	491	575	697
Three Rivers	112	508	D	608	538	816
Watford	111	507	D	514	529	626
Welwyn Hatfield	146	544	D	579	603	748
Humberside	464					
Beverley	71	535	C	506	554	614
Boothferry	69	534	B	454	464	416
Cleethorpes	133	598	B	466	606	496
East Yorkshire	32	496	B	425	489	444
Glanford	85	549	B	464	582	473
Great Grimsby	144	609	A	444	602	451
Holderness	73	537	B	462	575	484
Kingston upon Hull	99	563	A	384	490	397
Scunthorpe	116	581	A	420	543	502
Isle of Wight	409					
Medina	69	478	C	422	424	448
South Wight	86	495	C	478	472	501
Kent	383					
Ashford	55	439	C	448	437	449
Canterbury	101	484	C	455	461	420
Dartford	97	480	C	469	477	402
Dover	96	479	C	434	431	372
Gillingham	65	449	C	403	437	391
Gravesham	41	425	C	417	416	441
Maidstone	103	486	D	509	516	433
Rochester upon Medway	61	445	C	397	169	376
Sevenoaks	85	469	D	567	466	474
Shepway	112	495	C	458	489	475
Swale	54	437	C	395	437	340
Thanet	86	470	B	392	409	425
Tonbridge and Malling	86	470	D	517	478	439
Tunbridge Wells	78	461	D	498	429	435
Lancashire	472					
Blackburn	81	552	A	415	542	333
Blackpool	106	577	B	433	594	463
Burnley	86	558	A	410	429	299
Chorley	73	545	B	474	556	427
Fylde	58	530	C	507	492	520
Hyndburn	92	564	A	425	470	311
Lancaster	76	547	B	457	532	405
Pendle	111	582	A	442	437	299
Preston	108	580	B	450	547	418
Ribble Valley	66	538	C	555	536	446
Rossendale	124	596	A	483	467	352
South Ribble	65	537	C	476	535	425
West Lancashire	72	544	B	489	558	524
Wyre	64	535	C	492	504	456
Leicestershire	379					
Blaby	56	436	C	400	460	515
Charnwood	106	486	C	458	539	503
Harborough	79	459	C	468	496	567
Hinckley and Bosworth	4	383	C	352	427	486
Leicester	199	579	A	404	585	431
Melton	69	449	C	452	485	471
North West Leicestershire	82	461	B	408	495	470
Oadby and Wigston	96	475	C	431	545	540
Rutland	80	460	C	471	461	539
Lincolnshire	400					
Boston	66	466	A	362	467	367

(Continued)

	Band C Council Tax for notifiable authority[1] £	Council Tax for Area (Band C) 2 Adults[2] £	Band in which average (median) dwelling falls[3]	Average Council Tax per dwelling[4] £	Average Community Charge per dwelling 1992/93[5] £	Average rates per household 1989/90[6] £
Lincolnshire *(Continued)*						
East Lindsey	30	430	B	348	446	356
Lincoln	67	467	A	338	449	340
North Kesteven	60	460	B	393	455	396
South Holland	48	448	B	364	474	385
South Kesteven	52	452	B	405	432	393
West Lindsey	71	471	B	409	459	378
Norfolk	399					
Breckland	47	447	B	382	445	401
Broadland	50	450	C	431	480	466
Great Yarmouth	62	462	B	356	471	376
King's Lynn and West Norfolk	52	451	B	377	412	369
North Norfolk	41	440	C	391	376	385
Norwich	130	529	B	388	509	426
South Norfolk	51	451	C	433	443	456
Northamptonshire	391					
Corby	73	465	A	351	493	454
Daventry	65	457	C	447	479	564
East Northamptonshire	52	443	B	394	435	429
Kettering	67	458	B	375	451	442
Northampton	91	482	B	379	490	531
South Northamptonshire	86	478	C	488	457	536
Wellingborough	−174	218	B	182	257	436
Northumberland	437					
Northumbria Police Authourity	37					
Alnwick	69	542	B	479	474	438
Berwick-upon-Tweed	44	518	B	415	454	390
Blyth Valley	127	601	A	449	575	493
Castle Morpeth	96	570	C	574	578	601
Tynedale	83	557	C	534	556	458
Wansbeck	141	615	A	444	480	429
North Yorkshire	387					
Craven	69	456	C	448	386	351
Hambleton	−10	377	C	404	372	452
Harrogate	128	515	C	513	505	488
Richmondshire	58	445	C	415	400	443
Ryedale	53	440	C	438	426	389
Scarborough	56	443	B	365	384	366
Selby	68	455	C	432	439	396
York	72	459	B	374	411	322
Nottinghamshire	459					
Ashfield	70	529	A	404	519	386
Bassetlaw	76	535	A	434	543	436
Broxtowe	53	512	B	434	514	482
Gedling	70	529	B	464	510	503
Mansfield	143	602	A	451	567	422
Newark and Sherwood	101	561	B	477	534	444
Nottingham	101	560	A	392	512	438
Rushcliffe	48	507	C	510	492	561
Oxfordshire	414					
Cherwell	31	445	C	413	406	533
Oxford	109	523	D	527	604	648
South Oxfordshire	92	506	D	566	590	601
Vale of White Horse	39	454	D	496	498	580
West Oxfordshire	23	437	D	450	446	532
Shropshire	403					
Bridgnorth	63	467	C	480	483	464
North Shropshire	94	497	C	480	497	417
Oswestry	79	482	B	401	477	377
Shrewsbury and Atcham	75	478	C	426	486	450
South Shropshire	64	467	C	459	469	363
The Wrekin	170	573	B	469	588	471
Somerset	412					
Mendip	69	481	C	471	518	459
Sedgemoor	71	484	C	436	514	472
South Somerset	85	498	C	474	518	464
Taunton Deane	29	441	C	414	475	453
West Somerset	45	458	C	435	506	459
Staffordshire	386					
Cannock Chase	124	510	B	427	530	475
East Staffordshire	77	463	B	391	469	436
Lichfield	64	450	C	446	463	594
Newcastle-under-Lyme	98	484	B	398	511	448

(Continued)

	Band C Council Tax for notifiable authority[1] £	Council Tax for Area (Band C) 2 Adults[2] £	Band in which average (median) dwelling falls[3]	Average Council Tax per dwelling[4] £	Average Community Charge per dwelling 1992/93[5] £	Average rates per household 1989/90[6] £
Staffordshire *(Continued)*						
South Staffordshire	46	432	C	431	484	583
Stafford	73	459	C	425	466	500
Staffordshire Moorlands	106	492	C	456	537	453
Stoke-on-Trent	114	500	A	349	540	383
Tamworth	65	451	B	375	491	484
Suffolk	381					
Babergh	44	425	C	413	464	466
Forest Heath	28	409	B	294	348	408
Ipswich	182	562	B	442	572	489
Mid Suffolk	49	429	C	414	456	448
St Edmundsbury	63	444	C	411	460	434
Suffolk Coastal	57	438	C	418	428	519
Waveney	58	438	B	362	460	403
Surrey	394					
Elmbridge	140	539	E	675	577	796
Epsom & Ewell	62	467	E	562	537	773
Guildford	99	493	D	574	542	604
Mole Valley	67	461	E	586	464	599
Reigate and Banstead	90	488	D	575	508	657
Runnymede	24	418	D	480	418	551
Spelthorne	65	470	D	532	496	512
Surrey Heath	78	472	E	586	514	688
Tandridge	91	485	E	616	535	581
Waverley	84	478	E	580	499	656
Woking	80	474	D	539	521	642
Warwickshire	445					
North Warwickshire	142	587	C	536	663	587
Nuneaton and Bedworth	140	585	B	487	640	576
Rugby	66	511	C	471	550	576
Stratford-on-Avon	67	513	D	562	532	686
Warwick	68	513	C	519	520	670
West Sussex	356					
Adur	157	514	C	474	486	488
Arun	120	476	C	472	398	465
Chichester	56	413	D	452	339	479
Crawley	127	484	C	472	459	460
Horsham	67	424	D	492	388	465
Mid Sussex	85	441	D	494	390	538
Worthing	109	465	C	428	393	443
Wiltshire	398					
Kennet	38	436	C	446	413	471
North Wiltshire	74	471	C	487	472	446
Salisbury	41	438	C	446	416	495
Thamesdown	94	492	C	429	483	443
West Wiltshire	76	474	C	459	455	440
All Purpose Authority						
Isles of Scilly	334	334	F	402	203	344

(1) The 1993/94 average council tax amount set by each authority expressed in terms of band C, 2-adult dwellings (i.e. the amount set for a band C, 2-adult dwelling in each part of the authority, weighted by the taxbase for each part of the authority). Figures for billing authorities include parish precepts. (2) The 1993/94 average headline council tax (expressed in terms of band C, 2-adult dwellings) for the area of each billing authority. It is calculated as the sum of the council taxes for the relevant notifiable authorities shown in column 1. (3) The valuation band in which the average (median) dwelling falls. (4) The implied council tax per dwelling (after discounts and exemptions for students and visiting forces, but before transitional relief and council tax benefit) for the area of the billing authority, i.e. on the same basis as the headline council taxes shown in column 2. It is calculated as the average (band D) council tax multiplied by the taxbase used for tax-setting, divided by the total number of dwellings on the valuation list (adjusted to exclude uninhabitable dwellings and unoccupied dwellings only recently completed). (5) The average 1992/93 community charge per dwelling (before transitional relief and community charge benefit), calculated as 1992/93 community charge income divided by the number of dwellings used to calculate the average council tax per dwelling shown in column 4. (6) The average rate bill per household in 1989/90 (before rate rebates but after domestic rate relief grant).

Council Taxes[1] 1993/94, Scotland

Source: Scottish Office

Authority	Region/ Island Band C Council Tax £	District Band C Council Tax £	Total Band C Council Tax[2] £	Band in which averages (median) dwelliing falls	Average Council Tax per dwelling 1993/94 £	Average Council Tax per dwelling 1992/93 £	Average rates per household 1988/89[3] £
Borders	324			B			
Berwickshire		58	382	B	354	291	322.03
Ettrick & Lauderdale		90	414	B	378	317	324.98
Roxburgh		88	412	B	355	319	324.04
Tweeddale		84	409	C	424	299	343.93

(Continued)

Authority	Region/ Island Band C Council Tax £	District Band C Council Tax £	Total Band C Council Tax[2] £	Band in which averages (median) dwelling falls	Average Council Tax per dwelling 1993/94 £	Average Council Tax per dwelling 1992/93 £	Average rates per household 1988/89[3] £
Central	370			B			
Clackmannan		147	516	B	434	505	420.07
Falkirk		71	441	B	360	411	397.79
Stirling		165	535	C	528	524	548.21
Dumfries & Galloway	336			C			
Annandale & Eskdale		105	441	C	407	408	357.37
Nithsdale		115	451	B	410	391	372.13
Stewartry		60	396	C	386	360	373.22
Wigtown		109	445	B	389	396	331.61
Fife	396			B			
Dunfermline		104	500	B	425	439	433.00
Kirkcaldy		133	529	B	421	441	428.99
North East Fife		140	536	C	518	450	489.71
Grampian	346			C			
Aberdeen City		138	484	C	433	351	386.13
Banff & Buchan		84	430	B	351	319	308.02
Gordon		76	422	D	447	301	348.42
Kincardine & Deeside		52	398	D	440	277	351.49
Moray		80	426	B	354	290	299.13
Highland	352			C			
Badenoch & Strathspey		88	440	D	387	345	348.97
Caithness		85	437	A	335	326	288.71
Inverness		80	432	C	402	338	392.76
Lochaber		125	477	C	442	347	331.93
Nairn		96	448	C	444	358	387.82
Ross & Cromarty		121	473	C	428	372	336.33
Sky & Lochalsh		97	449	C	394	363	232.58
Sutherland		91	443	B	348	347	227.92
Lothian	392			C			
East Lothian		120	512	C	493	548	556.58
Edinburgh City		195	587	C	554	607	563.99
Midlothian		111	503	C	461	529	521.61
West Lothian		77	469	B	387	489	480.36
Strathclyde	330			B			
Argyll & Bute		151	481	C	405	475	424.05
Bearsden & Milngavie		112	442	E	570	461	838.63
Clydebank		172	501	B	382	475	444.75
Clydesdale		176	506	B	410	501	480.51
Cumbernauld & Kilsyth		129	459	B	364	442	517.39
Cumnock & Doon Valley		135	465	A	332	448	409.07
Cunninghame		137	467	B	370	449	488.35
Dumbarton		177	507	C	457	602	554.85
East Kilbride		152	482	C	431	494	539.33
Eastwood		70	400	E	494	395	746.03
Glasgow East		208	538	B	407	501	483.07
Hamilton		178	508	B	410	492	524.93
Inverclyde		148	478	A	364	470	488.10
Kilmarnock & Loudoun		138	468	B	365	439	460.99
Kyle & Carrick		196	526	C	490	529	549.55
Monklands		178	508	A	372	501	496.65
Motherwell		148	477	A	347	453	476.18
Renfrew		160	490	B	410	510	514.04
Strathkelvin		177	507	D	510	513	575.61
Tayside	369			B			
Angus		88	457	B	387	367	393.19
Dundee City		185	554	B	422	430	452.42
Perth & Kinross		98	467	C	449	395	428.78
Orkney	356		356	B	295	313	155.19
Shetland	354		354	B	298	287	364.72
Western Isles	412		412	B	293	206	193.73

(1) Excluding water charges. (2) In Scotland the levying authority is the Region or Island. The total Council Tax, Community Charge or Rates bill consists of the Regional charge added to the District charge. (The Islands are unitary authorities and therefore have no District element.) (3) Community Charge came into operation in Scotland in 1989/90, so 1988/89 was the last year of the domestic rating system.

Council Taxes 1993/94, Wales

Source: Welsh Office

Authority	Band C Council Tax (excluding county tax) £	Band C Council Tax (including county tax) £	Band in which averages (median) dwellling falls	Average Council Tax per dwelling £	Community Charge payable 1992/93 £	Average rates per household 1988/89* £
Alyn & Deeside	65	340	C	344	317	429
Colwyn	47	322	C	317	308	408
Delyn	64	339	C	344	309	414
Glyndwr	44	320	C	315	255	352
Rhuddlan	60	336	C	315	328	406
Wrexham Maelor	64	340	B	317	289	392
Carmarthen	48	310	C	313	243	254
Ceredigion	56	318	D	324	256	265
Dinefwr	49	310	C	300	220	223
Llanelli	96	354	B	305	295	287
Preseli Pembrokeshire	40	302	C	301	264	254
South Pembrokeshire	28	290	C	292	244	278
Blaenau Gwent	43	269	A	209	202	249
Islwyn	46	272	B	235	236	280
Monmouth	56	282	D	335	273	394
Newport	55	277	C	261	297	392
Torfaen	53	278	B	243	279	333
Aberconwy	61	295	C	295	299	349
Arfon	59	292	B	259	248	279
Dwyfor	46	279	C	276	236	283
Meirionnydd	73	307	B	283	273	280
Ynys Mon	68	301	C	292	282	315
Cynon Valley	46	255	A	200	201	226
Merthyr Tydfil	42	251	A	195	242	252
Ogwr	42	253	C	239	227	334
Rhondda	40	249	A	184	161	180
Rhymney Valley	44	256	B	218	274	302
Taff Ely	65	277	B	258	293	328
Brecknock	63	279	D	297	251	314
Montgomeryshire	51	267	C	273	241	253
Radnorshire	48	264	D	276	246	245
Cardiff	56	258	C	255	287	389
Vale of Glamorgan	63	265	D	296	276	373
Port Talbot	41	313	B	268	237	297
Lliw Valley	41	313	C	286	237	299
Neath	70	342	B	301	243	302
Swansea	49	321	C	305	302	442

*The amount raised by local taxation by the 1993/94 total chargeable dwellings for Council Tax.

Council Tax Bands

Source: Department of the Environment

Band A	up to£40,000
Band B	£40,000–£52,000
Band C	£52,00–£68,000
Band D	£68,000–£88,000
Band E	£88,000–£120,000
Band F	£120,000–£160,000
Band G	£160,000–£320,000
Band H	£320,000+

Local Dignitaries – Forms of Address

Source: Debrett's

Lady Mayoress – *As for* Lord Mayor's wife.

Lord Mayor – LETTERS The Lord Mayors of London, York, Belfast and Cardiff have the privilege of being styled "The Rt. Hon."; and permission to use this style has also been granted to the Lord Mayors of Sydney (NSW), Melbourne (Vic.), Adelaide (S. Aust.), Perth (W. Aust.), Brisbane (Queensland) and Hobart (Tasmania). *Superscription*, "The Rt. Hon. the Lord Mayor of —", or "(Henry —,) The Rt. Hon. Lord Mayor of —". (The prefix of Right Hon. is not retained after retirement from office.) (*See also* "Lord Provost" p. 291.) *Commencement*, "My Lord", or less formally, "Dear Lord Mayor". *Superscription* for other Lord Mayors "The Right Worshipful the Lord Mayor of —".

Lord Mayor's Wife or Lady Mayoress – LETTERS *Superscription*, "The Lady Mayoress". In other respects as Knight's or Esquire's wife (*see* p. 413).

Mayor (whether man or woman) – LETTERS *Superscription* (if Mayor of a City), "The Right Worshipful the Mayor of —"; (if a Mayor of a Borough or Town Mayor), "The Worshipful the Mayor of —". *Commencement*, "Sir (or Madam)". In other respects as an Esquire or an Esquire's wife (*see* p. 413). The form "Dear Mr Mayor" may be used for a man or woman.

LAW AND ORDER

Compiled by Daniel O'Leary

In the United Kingdom separate legal systems have grown up in England and Wales, in Scotland and in Northern Ireland. However, all are based on a combination of statute law (law deriving from Parliamentary legislation) and the common law (law deriving from court decisions), both nowadays increasingly supplemented by EC law.

In England and Wales, at least, the traditional view that Parliament is sovereign has meant the supremacy of statute law over all other law, but as a result of the UK's entry into the European Community it is now arguable that the UK's Parliament and its law is subject to Community law.

Civil Law & Criminal Law

Each of the legal systems makes the same basic distinction between civil and criminal law. Civil law is concerned with the compensation of the individual who has suffered loss or damage at the hands of another, for example by breach of contract or a negligent act. Criminal law is concerned to punish those who have committed crimes, i.e. offences against the state, such as murder or theft.

In a criminal case it is the Crown, that is the State, which prosecutes the accused (defendant) and attempts to prove his guilt, whereas in a civil case the innocent party (plaintiff) himself sues the breaching or negligent party (defendant). Conviction of a criminal offence may result in imprisonment or a fine, whereas the establishment of liability in a civil action generally leads to an order for the compensation of the injured party.

Who Administers the Law?

The legal profession itself is divided into 2 main groups – barristers and solicitors. In England and Wales a lawyer must practise as one or the other.

Solicitors

The solicitor's role has often been compared with that of the GP – he is usually the public's first point of contact with the legal system. Solicitors practise either in partnership or as a sole practitioners. They cannot yet advocate in the High Court, although they can, and increasingly do, advocate in the lower courts.

Barristers

Barristers, much fewer in number, are generally specialists whom a solicitor will employ to provide expert legal opinion and/or appear in court to argue the client's case. They alone are entitled to advocate in the High Court, but they are not entitled to deal directly with the public.

Barristers are self-employed but invariably operate in groups (chambers), thereby pooling experience and reducing administrative costs. In England and Wales they must belong to one of the four Inns of Court, where, in fact, most have their chambers. Each of the Inns is a self-governing body, medieval in original, responsible for the conduct of its members. The comparable body for solicitors is the Law Society, also situated in London.

In the UK both barristers and solicitors owe a double duty – to work in the best interests of their clients, but also to the court not to deceive it in any way. In order to preserve professional standards, both barristers and solicitors are subject to strict disciplinary codes; for example, a lawyer cannot arrange to be paid out of a client's compensation since such an arrangement is deemed prejudicial to his duty to the court.

Judges

A proportion of barristers is invited to become Queen's Counsel ("take silk"). It is largely from this cadre of senior barristers that the judiciary is chosen by the Lord Chancellor. In England and Wales there are various ranks of judge, from Recorder, Circuit and High Court judges, to the judges of the Court of Appeal, presided over by the Master of the Rolls. The most senior judges are the so-called Law Lords of the House of Lords, presided over by the Lord Chancellor, the most senior lawyer in the land and a member of the Cabinet.

In Scotland the most senior judge is the Lord President who presides over the Lords of Session. Below them are 6 Sheriffs Principal and subordinate Sheriffs who sit in judgment in Sheriff's Courts.

Magistrates

In addition to judges, some 30,000 magistrates try the less serious criminal offences in Magistrates' Courts. The majority of magistrates are unpaid and are not legally qualified, but they are advised on points of law by a qualified Clerk.

Courts

Crime is dealt with at a number of levels, depending on the seriousness of the offence. In England and Wales nearly all criminal cases begin in **Magistrates' Courts.** Some categories of serious offence, such as rape or murder, can only be tried before a judge and jury ("on indictment") and these cases will be transferred to the **Crown Court** for trial. If convicted in the Crown Court, the defendant can appeal against both conviction and sentence to the **Court of Appeal** and thence to the **House of Lords**, which is the final appeal court. The House of Lords is also the final appeal court for many Commonwealth jurisdictions. Minor offences, such as careless driving, are dealt with in the Magistrates' Court before a bench of magistrates ("summarily").

A person convicted in the Magistrates' Court can appeal against both conviction and sentence to the Crown Court. A third category of offence, for example theft, can be tried either in the Magistrates' Court or the Crown Court, depending on the views of the magistrates and the wishes of the defendant.

In Scotland the hierarchy of courts in criminal cases ascends from **District Court** to **Sheriffs' Court**, then to the **High Court of Justiciary** in Edinburgh where the most serious criminal cases are heard.

Most civil cases in England and Wales are heard in the local **County Court**, unless the value of the action is less than £1000, in which cases there are special arbitration facilities. Where the value of the action exceeds £50,000 or the issues of law are especially complex, the trial takes place in the High Court.

The **High Court** is divided as follows:

- Chancery, dealing with property and succession matters
- Queen's Bench, dealing with commercial and maritime matters
- Family Division, dealing with family-related cases

Two recent pieces of legislation, the Children Act 1989 and the Child Support Act 1991, have substantially altered the manner in which the Family Division deals with children and absent parents. The first Act re-emphasizes both the importance of the child's welfare in the court's decision-making process and its duty to avoid delay in reaching any decision. The Act also redefines the type of orders the court can make in relation to children but stresses that the court ought to make no order unless it is satisfied that it is clearly better for the child that an order is made.

The second Act is designed to tackle the problem of absent parents refusing to take financial responsibility for the maintenance of their children. It imposes a statutory duty to maintain a qualifying child and establishes a new agency both to make the necessary assessment as to the level of maintenance required and to trace defaulting parents. Consequently, the court's former powers to make financial orders in respect of children have been considerably curtailed by the new Act.

Any party to an action in the County or High Courts can appeal to the Court of Appeal and from there to the House of Lords, as in criminal cases the final court of appeal.

In Scotland the Sheriff's Court tries all actions where the value of the action is less than £1500. Actions of greater value are tried in a **Court of Session** in Edinburgh.

In Northern Ireland the system of courts resembles that of England and Wales, except that in terrorist cases no juries are employed to obviate the risk of intimidation.

Citizens' Rights

As a result of a unique process of evolution, the constitution of the UK is not to be found written down in a single document. One result of this is that there is no written summary of the citizens' rights comparable to the prescriptive rights guaranteed by the US Constitution. Instead, the "rights" of the UK citizen have traditionally been located in his freedom to do or say anything which is not contrary to the law. Thus, for example, a citizen's freedom of speech is actually his freedom to say anything which does not libel or threaten another, or incite the commission of some criminal offence.

The UK is, however, signatory to the European Convention on Human Rights, which specifies certain basic rights such as freedom of thought, conscience and religion, and the courts will in some circumstances take note of these prescriptive rights. The Convention is not, however, part of UK law. Therefore the UK citizen who maintains that his rights under the Convention have been breached must petition the European Court of Human Rights rather than a UK court for a hearing.

The Police

In the UK the maintenance of public order, the prevention of crime and the apprehension of criminals is in the hands of the police, some 150,000 strong. The police force is actually not a single service but a body comprised of 52 separate local forces, each headed by a chief constable appointed by the local police authority to which he is answerable for the efficiency of his force.

London is policed by the Metropolitan and City of London police forces. These two forces jointly operate the Fraud Squad, a unit specializing in the investigation of criminal fraud, and a number of other specialist units such as the Drugs Intelligence Unit. The Metropolitan force is additionally responsible nationwide for anti-terrorist duties.

Powers and Privileges

British police officers have no special privileges or immunities under the law, apart from those strictly necessary for the performance of their duties. The police are subject to codes governing the detention, treatment and questioning of suspects and any breach of these codes may impair the prosecution case against a suspect and leave the police officer concerned open to civil or criminal action.

The police have wide powers of search and arrest, but again these are subject to strict guidelines. Failure to comply with these may mean a search has been illegal or an arrest wrongful. Although the police remain unarmed (apart from a truncheon) in the normal course of their duties, firearms are issued if circumstances warrant. In 1991 police fired on 5 occasions which resulted in death or injury.

Rights After Arrest

Once arrested, a person has the statutory right to consult a solicitor (the one phone call allowed) and to have a third party informed of his arrest. On arrest, before questioning and at certain times thereafter the police are under a duty to caution the suspect as to his right to silence, and no prejudicial conclusion can be drawn from the exercise of this right. A suspect has to be charged within a certain specified time or released.

Charging a Suspect

If charged, a suspect can be kept in custody or released on bail pending trail. There is a statutory right to bail, which will only be refused by magistrates if it can be demonstrated that there are substantial grounds for refusing bail. The court may grant bail subject to conditions – for example, that the accused report at specified times to a local police station.

It is for the police to decide whether there is sufficient evidence to charge a suspect. However, in England and Wales it is the duty of the **Crown Prosecution Service** (CPS) to decide whether to prosecute. If a prosecution is launched, the CPS will provide the prosecution lawyers or, if necessary, brief barristers to conduct the prosecution.

In Scotland the Lord Advocate and Crown Counsel conduct prosecutions in the High Court. In the District and Sheriffs' Courts this task is performed by Procurators Fiscal.

In Northern Ireland the police themselves prosecute minor offences, while the Department of Public Prosecutions for Northern Ireland prosecutes all indictable offences.

Trials

Criminal trials in the UK normally take place in open court – if in the Crown Court before a judge and jury, and if in the Magistrates' Court before a bench of magistrates. The task of the prosecution is to prove the guilt of the accused. However, it is also duty bound to reveal to the defence any evidence which may assist the defence case.

Under British law the accused is presumed innocent until proven guilty. The task of the defence is to demonstrate that the prosecution has failed to prove the guilt of the defendant. The role of the judge is to determine what types of evidence ought to be admitted, to clarify points of law and to instruct the jury in what circumstances to acquit or convict the accused. This is known as the adversarial system and contrasts with the inquisitorial method used in most Continental European countries.

Juries

It is for the jury to decide whether the guilt of the accused has been proven. In England and Wales juries number 12 randomly selected members of the public. In Scotland the number is 15. If the jury decides to convict, it is for the judge alone to decide what sentence is appropriate. If the jury decides not to convict, the accused will be found not guilty and acquitted. In Scotland a jury may also bring in a verdict of "not proven", which also leads to acquittal. Any mentally competent adult can be summoned for jury service unless he or she is a member of an excluded class, e.g. recently convicted criminals.

Penal Institutions

In 1991 the UK's prison population numbered some 50,000. In recent years there has been a concerted effort to reduce that number by means of suspended sentences, probation and fining. UK courts may also order payment of compensation and confiscation of property. However, throughout the UK there is a mandatory sentence of life imprisonment for murder.

Sentences are served in various types of institution, from "open" to high security establishments in which the most dangerous types of criminal are incarcerated. There are separate prisons for women. Young offenders (those between 14 and 21 at the time of conviction) can be held in Young Offenders' Institutions, although here too there has been an attempt to reduce the numbers by meting out alternative forms of punishment.

Tribunals

In addition to the courts, a wide variety of tribunals exists to handle particular matters speedily and efficiently. Among the best known are industrial tribunals, which deal with matters relating to employment; the Lands Tribunal, dealing with land valuation and rating; and the Copyright Tribunal which handles copyright disputes.

Legal Aid

A state-funded legal aid scheme exists to assist those on low incomes to take legal action.

Criminal legal aid helps meet the expenses of an accused's defence.

Civil legal aid assists either the plaintiff in meeting the costs of his suit, or the defendant in meeting the cost of defending the action.

Legal aid exists in 2 forms. **Legal Advice and Assistance** covers up to 2 hours legal work prior to the taking of proceedings. **Legal Aid proper** covers the assisted person's legal costs thereafter. In both types of legal aid the applicant himself may have to contribute towards his legal costs. The actual amount will vary depending on the applicant's income and capital savings. The effect of recent changes to the eligibility threshold for Legal Aid has been to reduce the number of people eligible and to increase the level of personal contribution of those who remain so.

Legal aid additionally is subject to a merit test, the local Legal Aid Board (LAB) having to be satisfied in a civil action that the applicant's case is sufficiently strong to be worth funding; and in a criminal case that there is a real risk of loss of liberty or reputation to the applicant if convicted. Legal aid should be regarded as a loan rather than as a gift since in a civil action the LAB will reimburse itself out of the damages awarded to an assisted person, should this be necessary.

Legal Aid and Legal Advice and Assistance

England & Wales

Source: CSO

Thousands and percentages

	1971 –72	1976 –77	1981 –82	1986 –87	1987 –88	1988 –89	1989 –90	1990 –91	1991 –92
Civil aid: certificates issued[1]									
(thousands)									
Matrimonial proceedings	154	155	112	126	125	119	128	138	146
Other cases	49	56	79	119	122	128	131	158	207
Total	202	211	191	245	247	247	259	296	353
Criminal legal aid: applications granted									
Total, all criminal proceedings and appeals[2] (thousands)	167	362	443	620	628	652	643	658	669
Legal advice and assistance[3]									
Type of case (percentages)									
Matrimonial and family	–	56	48	41	40	40	40	38	35
Criminal	–	15	23	23	22	22	22	22	21
Other	–	29	29	36	38	38	38	40	44
Claims paid (thousands)	–	292	649	981	1,077	995	1,029	1,041	1,230

(1) After 1975–76 data refer to offers of certificates accepted, some of which will have been issued in an earlier year. (2) Calendar years. 1971 is shown under 1971–72, etc. Includes care proceedings. (3) Scheme began on 2 April 1973.

The Bench – Forms of Address

Source: Debrett's

Judge of City of London Court *As for* Circuit Judge.

Judge in Commonwealth and Overseas Territories The title of "The Right Honourable" is borne for life by the Chief Justice of Canada. The title of "Honourable" during tenure of office is borne by Chief Justices and Judges of the High Court of Australia, and the Supreme Courts of New South Wales, Victoria, Queensland, S. Aust, W. Aust, Tasmania, NZ, and the Judges of the Supreme and Exchequer Courts, and the Chief Justices and Judges of certain other Courts in the provinces of Canada; also such Chief Justices and Judges of those Courts as may be specially permitted to bear it after retirement. *Superscription*, "The Hon. the Chief Justice", or "The Hon. Mr Justice —". Judges of the Supreme Courts in Commonwealth Countries are styled "The Honourable".

Judge, Circuit LETTERS *Superscription*, "His Honour Judge —". PERSONAL ADDRESS "Sir", but when on the Bench, "Your Honour". The prefix of "His Honour", but not "Judge", is retained after retirement from office, but personal address as "Judge" or "Judge Brown" may be continued unofficially in retirement.

Judges of High Court (men) LETTERS *Superscription* (official) "The Hon. Mr Justice —"; private, "Sir John —". *Commencement*, "Sir". PERSONAL ADDRESS, "Sir", but when on the Bench, "My Lord", or "Your Lordship". *See also* Lord Chief Justice of England, Master of the Rolls, Lord Justice of Appeal *and* Lord of Appeal in Ordinary.

Judges of High Court (women) LETTERS *Superscription* (official) "The Hon. Mrs Justice —"; private, "Dame Mary Smith". *Commencement*, "Madam". PERSONAL ADDRESS, "Madam", but when on the Bench "My Lady" or "Your Ladyship".

Justice of the Peace PERSONAL ADDRESS When on the Bench, "Your Worship", and in other respects as an Esquire (*see* p. 413). The letters JP are usually put after the name.

Lord Advocate LETTERS *Superscription*, "The Rt. Hon. The Lord Advocate", or "The Rt. Hon. (George) —". In other respects as an Esquire (*see* p. 413). (The prefix of Rt. Hon. is not retained after retirement from office, unless a Member of the Privy Council.)

Lord Chancellor LETTERS *Superscription*, "The Rt. Hon. The Lord High Chancellor". In other respects as a peer according to his rank (*see* p. 412).

Lord Chief Justice LETTERS *Superscription*, "The Lord Chief Justice of England", or "To the Right Hon. Lord —, Lord Chief Justice of England". In other respects as a Judge, except when of noble rank, when he is addressed according to his degree (*see* p. 412).

Lord Justice Clerk and Lord Justice General *See* Lord of Session, but addressed as "The Rt. Hon. the Lord Justice Clerk and the Rt. Hon. the Lord Justice General".

Lord Justice of Appeal LETTERS *Superscription*, "The Right Hon. Lord Justice —", or "To the Right Hon. Sir (Robert) —". In other respects as a Judge of High Court.

Lord of Appeal-in-Ordinary *See* Baron (p. 412).

Lord of Session, Scottish LETTERS *Superscription*, "The Hon. Lord —". In other respects as a Baron, but children have no courtesy styles. *See also* Lord Justice Clerk *and* Lord Justice General.

Lord of Sessions's Wife or Widow LETTERS *Superscription*, "Lady —". In other respects as Baron's wife (*see* p. 413).

Lord Provost LETTERS *Superscription*, The Lord Provosts of Edinburgh and Glasgow are addressed as "The Rt. Hon. the Lord Provost" while in office. The prefix may be placed before the name of the holder in the case of the Lord Provost of Edinburgh. In other respects as a Baron. The Lord Provost of Perth, Dundee and Aberdeen are styled "The Lord Provosts of —".

Lord Provost's Wife *As for* the wife of an Esquire (*see* p. 413). The style "Lady Provost" is incorrect.

Master of the Rolls LETTERS *Superscription*, "The Right Hon. the Master of the Rolls", or "The Right Hon. —", according to his rank. *Commencement*, as Judge. PERSONAL ADDRESS, "Sir", but when on the Bench, "My Lord", or "Your Lordship".

Queen's Counsel LETTERS *Superscription*, "— Esq., QC". In other respects as an Esquire (*see* p. 413). The letters are used after the name by Circuit Judges, but not by High Court Judges.

Police Forces: Authorized Establishment and Strength

End of Year

Source: CSO

Number

	1981	1982	1983	1984	1985	1986	1987	1988	1989	1990	1991
England and Wales											
Regular police											
Authorized establishment[1]	120,008	120,125	120,447	120,679	120,903	121,785	122,648	123,551	124,667	125,646	126,325
Strength:											
Men	107,379	108,517	108,519	108,102	107,960	108,225	109,773	109,900	110,466	110,790	110,396
Women	10,702	10,935	10,995	11,001	11,213	11,600	12,492	13,007	13,695	14,352	14,898
Seconded[2]:											
Men	1,424	1,419	1,407	1,388	1,439	1,617	1,716	1,730	1,815	1,787	1,670
Women	70	80	82	82	90	108	121	122	134	161	163
Additional constables[3]:											
Men	90	89	84	83	79	88	70	69	75	85	73
Women	1	1	2	–	1	1	–	–	1	5	3
Special constables											
Enrolled strength:											
Men	11,813	11,932	11,743	11,749	11,550	11,140	10,927	10,578	10,390	10,483	11,592
Women	2,791	3,228	3,588	4,307	4,611	4,930	5,282	5,210	5,199	5,419	6,480
Scotland											
Regular police[4]											
Authorized establishment	13,195	13,205	13,261	13,283	13,377	13,489	13,569	13,707	13,813	13,981	14,046
Strength[5]:											
Men	12,379	12,433	12,435	12,415	12,455	12,504	12,470	12,498	12,656	12,583	12,566
Women	749	719	713	722	761	838	933	1,020	1,158	1,258	1,357
Central service[5,6]:											
Men	54	55	65	61	69	70	73	65	69	67	64
Women	2	2	2	2	1	2	3	3	4	6	6
Seconded[5,7]:											
Men	78	73	68	67	67	88	85	88	92	98	103
Women	5	4	3	3	3	4	5	7	8	8	6
Additional regular police:											
Authorized establishment[4]	67	62	60	88	88	86	73	64	64	64	91
Strength	66	62	60	88	88	86	73	64	64	64	93
Part-time auxiliaries[8]											
Strength:											
Men	2,612	2,528	2,439	2,250	1,846	1,755	1,561	1,514	1,521	1,475	1,436
Women	202	208	204	203	200	209	216	233	279	312	342
Northern Ireland											
Royal Ulster Constabulary											
Strength:											
Men	6,622	7,017	7,328	7,487	7,610	7,581	7,591	7,568	7,571	7,535	7,510
Women	712	701	675	640	649	653	645	659	688	708	707
Royal Ulster Constabulary Reserve											
Strength:											
Men	4,350	4,385	4,105	4,102	4,199	4,127	4,319	4,268	4,200	4,097	4,069
Women	520	455	388	337	309	287	325	386	425	449	491

(1) Total of establishments of individual forces *plus* the Metropolitan Regional Crime Squad and additional constables in the Metropolitan Police. (2) Regional Crime Squads, other inter-force units and officers in central service. (3) Excluding additional constables in the Metropolitan Police Force. (4) From 1976, officers employed at ports, airports and oil-related industries are no longer included in "Regular police" but included in "Additional regular police". (5) "Strength" includes central service and seconded police. (6) Instructors at Training Establishments, etc. formerly shown as secondments. (7) Scottish Crime Squad, Officers on courses, etc. (8) Including special constables (enrolled strength).

Notifiable Offences Recorded by the Police

England and Wales

Source: CSO

Thousands

	1981	1982	1983	1984	1985	1986	1987	1988	1989	1990	1991
Violence against the person	100.2	108.7	111.3	114.2	121.7	125.5	141.0	158.2	177.0	184.7	190.3
Sexual offences[1]	19.4	19.7	20.4	20.2	21.5	22.7	25.2	26.5	29.7	29.0	29.4
Burglary	718.4	805.4	808.3	892.9	866.7	931.6	900.1	817.8	825.9	1,006.8	1,219.5
Robbery	20.3	22.8	22.1	24.9	27.5	30.0	32.6	31.4	33.2	36.2	45.3
Theft and handling stolen goods	1,603.2	1,755.9	1,705.9	1,808.0	1,884.1	2,003.9	2,052.0	1,931.3	2,012.8	2,374.4	2,761.1
Fraud and forgery	106.7	123.1	121.8	126.1	134.8	133.4	133.0	133.9	134.5	147.9	174.7
Criminal damage	386.7	417.8	443.3	497.8	539.0	583.6	589.0	594.0	630.1	733.4	821.1
Other offences[2]	8.9	9.0	13.8	15.0	16.7	16.7	19.3	22.7	27.6	31.1	34.6
Total	2,963.8	3,262.4	3,247.0	3,499.1	3,611.9	3,847.4	3,892.2	3.715.8	3,870.7	4,543.6	5,276.2

(1) Includes from the beginning of 1983 offences of "Gross indecency with a child". (2) Includes from the beginning of 1983 offences of "Trafficking in controlled drugs".

Clear-up Rates for Notifiable Offences

Source: CSO

Percentages

	England & Wales			Scotland			Northern Ireland		
	1971[2]	1990	1991	1971[2]	1990	1991	1971[2]	1990[3]	1991[3]
Notifiable offences recorded									
Violence against the person	82[2]	77	77	87[2]	82[7]	81	28[2]	62	62
Sexual offences[4], of which	76	76[5]	76	77	79	77	87	92	87
rape and attempted rape	–	74	76	81	79	79	–	88	80
Burglary	37	25	23	26	16	15	30	22	21
Robbery	42	26	23	21	28	27	18	18	17
Drugs trafficking	–	98	97	–	99	100	–	100	82
Theft and handling stolen goods[5]	43	30[4]	28	37	24	23	43	36	34
of which, theft of vehicles	–	26	24	36	24	21	–	31	29
Fraud and forgery	83	61	55	80	69	70	79	74	67
Criminal damage[6]	34[4]	22[3]	19	32	20	19	43	36	32
Other notifiable offences[5,7]	92[5]	95[6]	96	85	97	98	42	79	79
Total notifiable offences	45[4]	32[3]	29	38	32	31	32	38	36

(1) Offences in 1978 and earlier years were "Indictable". Scottish figures of "crime" have been recompiled to approximate to the classification of notifiable offences in England & Wales and Northern Ireland. However, because of differences in the legal system, recording and counting practices and classification problems, Scottish figures are not comparable with those for England & Wales and Northern Ireland. (2) Not precisely comparable with later years. (3) These figures no longer include assault on police and communicating false information regarding a bomb hoax. These offences have been removed from the categories "Violence against the person" and "Other notifiable offences". (4) Includes offences of "gross indecency with a child" in England and Wales in 1990 and 1991. (5) Offences of "abstracting electricity" for England and Wales are included in "Other offences" in 1971 and "Theft and handling stolen goods" in 1990 and 1991. (6) In England and Wales excludes criminal damage valued at £20 or less. In Northern Ireland, the 1971 figure excludes criminal damage valued at £25 or less; the 1990 and 1991 figures exclude criminal damage valued at £200 or less. (7) Includes "trafficking in controlled drugs" in England and Wales since 1983.

Prison Population

United Kingdom

Source: CSO

Numbers and rates

	1986	1987	1988	1989	1990	1991
Males						
Prisoners aged 21 and over serving:						
Up to 18 months	11,480	10,771	9,911	9,265	8,397	8,650
Over 18 months and up to 4 years	9,878	10,617	11,308	11,488	10,059	9,791
Over 4 years less than life	6,835	7,989	9,073	10,011	10,505	10,890
Life sentences	2,680	2,852	3,019	3,178	3,299	3,450
All sentenced male prisoners	30,873	32,229	33,311	33,943	32,260	32,781
Rate per 100,000 male population aged 21 and over	160	165	170	171	162	163
Females						
Prisoners aged 21 and over serving:						
Up to 18 months	618	576	507	465	423	444
Over 18 months and up to 4 years	306	404	406	381	314	266
Over 4 years less than life	125	172	218	284	330	339
Life sentences	72	77	82	92	97	102
All sentenced female prisoners	1,121	1,229	1,213	1,222	1,164	1,151
Rate per 100,000 female population aged 21 and over	5	6	6	6	5	5

Sex and Age of Offenders

Magistrates' Courts and the Crown Court, England and Wales

Source: CSO

Thousands

	1981	1982	1983	1984	1985	1986	1987	1988	1989	1990	1991[1]
Males					Indictable offences						
All ages	397.9	407.7	397.0	387.4	382.5	331.7	336.4	337.5	293.7	295.7	293.5
10 and under 14 years	15.1	13.6	11.6	10.9	9.1	6.1	4.3	3.7	2.8	2.6	2.3
14 and under 17 years	62.3	59.5	54.4	52.8	48.1	37.7	34.3	29.6	21.2	19.5	17.2
17 and under 21 years	113.9	119.6	115.3	114.0	114.0	98.9	99.9	97.2	83.0	84.8	83.1
21 years and over	206.6	215.1	215.8	209.6	211.3	189.0	198.0	207.1	186.8	188.8	190.8
					Summary offences						
All ages	1,437.1	1,358.8	1,411.7	1,298.3	1,247.3	1,252.6	972.5	974.5	993.7	968.9	956.3
10 and under 14 years	2.7	2.2	2.2	1.8	1.5	1.0	0.7	0.6	0.9	0.9	0.8
14 and under 17 years	27.0	24.5	23.5	20.0	16.9	12.8	10.4	9.2	12.3	11.0	9.2
17 and under 21 years	215.8	213.2	212.2	192.3	183.1	171.5	148.9	145.6	154.8	149.0	129.5
21 years and over	1,191.6	1,118.9	1,173.8	1,084.2	1,045.7	1,067.3	812.6	819.1	825.7	807.9	816.8
Females					Indictable offences						
All ages	65.5	66.1	62.7	59.9	59.0	50.0	47.5	46.1	43.0	44.0	41.9
10 and under 14 years	1.8	1.7	1.3	1.0	0.9	0.5	0.3	03	02	0.2	0.2
14 and under 17 years	7.5	7.0	6.1	5.4	5.0	3.7	3.1	2.9	2.3	2.3	2.2
17 and under 21 years	14.6	15.1	14.8	14.4	14.8	12.7	12.2	11.5	10.7	10.9	10.3
21 years and over	41.6	42.3	40.5	39.0	38.4	33.1	31.9	31.4	29.8	30.6	29.2
					Summary offences						
All ages	175.6	169.4	190.4	183.0	189.3	227.4	175.2	176.4	179.1	185.3	194.1
10 and under 14 years	0.1	0.1	0.1	0.1	0.1	0.1	[1]	[1]	[1]	–	–
14 and under 17 years	1.8	1.5	1.4	1.2	1.0	0.7	0.6	0.5	0.5	0.7	0.6
17 and under 21 years	14.7	14.8	16.7	14.9	14.5	14.9	12.4	12.9	14.2	14.3	13.6

	1981	1982	1983	1984	1985	1986	1987	1988	1989	1990	1991[1]
21 years and over	158.9	153.1	172.3	166.7	173.8	211.6	162.2	163.0	164.3	170.4	179.8
Companies, etc.											
Indictable offences	1.2	1.3	1.4	2.2	2.3	2.4	2.5	2.7	2.9	3.1	2.2
Summary offences	27.4	29.1	32.4	32.3	30.4	30.0	20.7	18.2	19.6	17.6	17.2

(1) Provisional.

Offences of Guilty Offenders

Magistrates' Courts and the Crown Court, England and Wales

Source: CSO

Thousands

	1981	1982	1983	1984	1985	1986	1987	1988	1989	1990	1991[3]
Offenders[1] of all ages found guilty					**Indictable offences**						
Violence against the person:											
Murder	0.1	0.1	0.1	0.2	0.2	0.2	0.2	0.2	0.2	0.2	0.2
Manslaughter	0.3	0.2	0.2	0.2	0.3	0.3	0.3	0.3	0.3	0.2	0.2
Wounding	48.7	49.6	49.5	45.8	45.3	40.9	45.6	50.9	53.7	50.9	45.5
Other offences of violence against the person	1.7	1.7	1.6	1.6	1.7	1.5	1.8	2.1	1.5	1.2	1.2
Sexual offences	6.9	6.6	6.4	5.6	6.0	5.5	6.2	7.2	7.3	6.6	5.5
Burglary	76.4	76.5	72.7	72.7	69.4	56.3	54.2	48.4	43.4	43.6	46.1
Robbery	4.1	4.4	4.0	4.3	4.4	4.2	4.4	4.3	4.6	4.8	4.8
Theft and handing stolen goods	232.2	238.7	224.9	219.2	216.3	183.2	175.9	163.4	134.5	134.3	133.5
Fraud and forgery	25.7	24.9	25.6	25.7	25.5	22.8	22.5	22.7	22.3	21.9	21.2
Criminal damage	11.8	11.4	12.1	11.5	11.5	10.1	10.6	11.8	9.4	11.2	10.2
Other offences (excluding motoring)	29.0	31.2	33.4	33.5	34.3	29.1	35.6	43.7	51.1	56.9	34.4
Motoring offences	27.7	29.8	30.5	29.2	29.0	27.5	29.1	31.3	11.3	11.1	11.3
Total	464.6	475.1	461.0	449.4	443.9	381.5	386.4	386.3	339.5	342.8	337.6
					Summary offences						
Assaults	11.2	11.1	10.7	11.4	10.5	9.6	10.8	11.5	14.7	17.3	16.5
Betting and gaming	0.5	0.5	0.6	0.3	0.3	0.1	0.1	–	0.1	–	–
Breach of local or other regulations .	15.8	14.7	14.4	13.3	12.5	13.0	12.6	11.0	10.1	12.6	8.5
Intoxicating Liquor Laws:											
Drunkenness	97.2	96.4	96.2	60.5	49.2	38.0	42.3	45.3	42.9	37.8	29.4
Other offences	6.5	4.9	4.5	3.5	2.8	3.0	2.7	3.8	2.8	2.2	1.5
Education Acts	3.0	2.9	2.5	2.7	2.9	3.1	2.9	2.8	2.8	3.0	2.8
Game Laws	1.9	1.7	1.9	1.8	1.5	1.4	1.4	1.3	1.2	1.1	1.0
Labour Laws	0.4	0.3	0.2	0.3	0.2	0.2	0.1	0.1	0.1	0.1	0.1
Summary offences of criminal damage and malicious damages .	37.8	36.6	38.6	39.0	38.5	34.2	35.4	35.2	36.6	33.9	28.5
Offences by prostitutes	4.1	5.8	10.4	8.6	9.2	9.1	8.2	8.8	11.1	11.5	10.9
Railway offences	17.4	15.4	15.9	13.3	11.9	9.7	8.3	9.2	9.9	8.3	5.4
Revenue Laws	73.6	72.7	107.8	108.7	114.3	121.9	107.4	113.4	108.5	104.9	115.6
Motoring offences (summary)......	1210.5	1,128.0	1,161.7	1,083.2	1,052.0	1,066.2	738.1	713.9	722.3	704.6	713.1
Vagrancy Acts	2.9	2.0	1.6	1.3	0.9	0.8	0.9	1.0	1.8	1.9	2.1
Wireless Telegraphy Acts	49.6	61.9	67.5	77.2	80.6	128.6	120.4	124.3	123.4	126.4	138.7
Others summary offences	107.5	100.7	99.7	88.3	79.7	72.8	76.6	87.6	104.5	106.1	93.4
Total	1,640.1	1,555.9	1,634.5	1,513.5	1,467.0	1,510.0	1,168.3	1,169.1	1,193.0	1,171.8	1.167.5
Persons aged under 17 found guilty[2]					**Indictable offences**						
Violence against the person	7.3	7.3	6.7	6.0	5.6	4.4	4.2	4.3	4.0	3.5	3.2
Sexual offences	0.6	0.6	0.6	0.5	0.5	0.4	0.4	0.4	0.3	0.3	0.3
Burglary	25.8	23.0	21.2	20.7	18.1	12.9	11.0	9.1	7.5	6.8	5.9
Robbery	1.0	1.0	0.8	1.0	0.9	0.8	0.8	0.8	0.4	1.0	1.0
Theft and handling stolen goods ...	44.6	42.9	38.0	36.1	32.7	25.1	21.4	17.6	10.7	9.8	8.6
Fraud and forgery	1.1	0.9	0.8	0.8	0.8	0.6	0.5	0.4	0.3	0.3	0.2
Criminal damage	3.1	2.8	2.9	2.6	2.4	1.8	1.6	1.5	1.2	1.3	1.1
Other offences (excluding motoring)	0.7	0.7	0.6	0.7	0.6	0.5	0.9	1.1	1.2	1.3	0.6
Motoring offences	2.4	2.5	1.9	1.9	1.6	1.4	1.2	1.2	0.2	0.3	0.3
Total	86.6	81.8	73.3	70.2	63.2	48.0	42.0	36.5	26.5	24.6	21.9
					Summary offences						
Highway Acts and motoring summary offences:											
Offences with pedal cycles	2.4	2.1	2.2	1.9	1.3	0.7	0.4	0.2	0.2	0.2	0.1
Other	15.5	11.2	10.9	9.1	7.8	7.4	4.5	3.8	3.8	3.6	2.7
Breach of local or other regulations .	0.9	0.8	0.8	0.6	0.5	0.4	0.3	0.1	0.1	0.1	0.1
Summary offences of criminal damage and malicious damage ..	7.1	6.0	6.2	5.3	5.0	3.9	3.1	2.5	2.2	1.8	1.4
Railway offences	0.7	0.7	0.7	0.6	0.4	0.2	0.2	0.2	0.1	0.1	0.1
Other summary offences	5.1	7.5	6.5	5.6	4.5	2.1	3.2	3.6	7.4	6.9	6.2
Total	31.7	28.3	27.1	23.1	19.5	14.6	11.6	10.4	13.9	12.7	10.6

(1) Includes "Companies", etc. (2) Figures for persons aged under 17 are included in the totals for all offenders above. (3) Provisional.

Dealing with Crime

What do British people think of the following measures?

Source: SCPR's *British Social Attitudes* survey, 9th Report, ed. R. Jowell *et al* (Dartmouth Publishing, 1992)

Percentages

	Strongly agree	Agree	Neither agree nor disagree	Disagree	Strongly disagree	Can't choose
People who break the law should be given stiffer sentences	33.7	37.0	17.0	7.3	1.5	2.4
People convicted of murder should be subject to the death penalty	31.6	21.7	11.3	16.1	13.5	4.7

British Attitudes to Law and Order

Source: SCPR's *British Social Attitudes* survey, 9th Report, ed. R. Jowell *et al* (Dartmouth Publishing, 1992)

In general would you say that people should obey the law without exception, or are there exceptional occasions on which people should follow their consciences even if it means breaking the law?

	Percentage
Obey law without exception	51.7
Follow conscience on occasions	46.6
Don't know	1.2

Are there any circumstances in which you might break a law to which you were very strongly opposed?

	Percentage
Yes	33.9
No	57.2
Don't know	8.2

Public Expenditure on Justice and Law[1]

United Kingdom

Source: CSO

£ million and percentages

	1981	1986	1990	1991
Police	2,433	3,691	5,351	6,324
Prisons	613	1,071	1,722	1,918
Legal Aid	160	345	613	755
Probation	102	148	220	262
Parliament	243	530	664	780
Law Courts	757	1,219	2,640	3,204
Total	4,308	7,004	11,210	13,243
As a percentage of general Government expenditure	*3.7*	*4.3*	*5.2*	*6.0*

(1) Costs are not included for social work staff employed in Scotland on aspects related to the criminal justice system which in England and Wales are undertaken by the probation service.

Prison Population[1]: International Comparison, 1991

Source: CSO

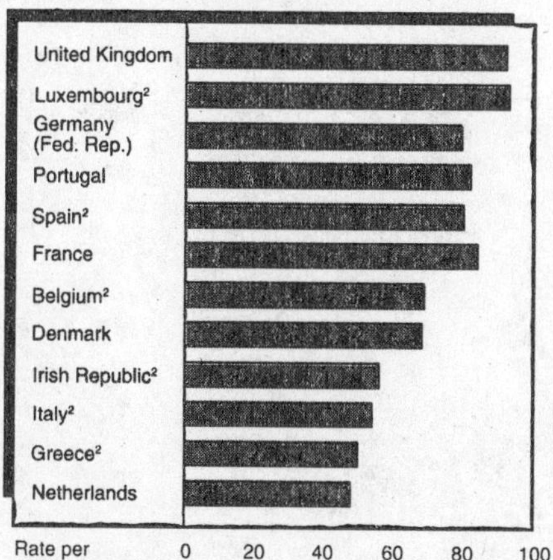

(1) At 1 September. (2) 1989.

Victims of One or More Crimes[1]: By Ethnic Origin and Type of Offence, 1987

England & Wales

Source: CSO

Percentages and numbers

	Ethnic origin of victim		
	White	Afro-Caribbean	Asian
Percentage who were victims of each offence			
Household vandalism	5	4	6
Burglary	6	10	6
Vehicles (owners)			
Vandalism	9	9	14
All thefts[2]	18	26	20
Bicyle theft (owners)	4	8	2
Other household theft	6	6	8
Assault	3	7	4
Threats	2	4	5
Robbery/theft from person	1	3	3
Other personal thefts	4	6	3
Sample size (numbers)	9,874	733	996

(1) Based on incidents occurring over the full recall period. (2) Includes theft of and from vehicles and attempted theft.

Ages of Consent in Europe

(As at end June 1993)

Compiled by Peter Tatchell, author of *Europe in the Pink: Lesbian & Gay Equality in the New Europe* (GMP, 1992)

Country	Heterosexual	Lesbian	Gay
Albania	14	14	14
Austria	14	14	18
Belgium	16	16	16
Bosnia-Herzegovina	14	14	Illegal
Bulgaria[1]	14	18 (14?)	18 (14?)
Belarus[1]	18 (16?)	18 (16?)	Illegal[2]
Croatia	14	14	18
Cyprus	16	16	Illegal[3]
Czech Rep.	15	15	15
Denmark[4]	15/18	15/18	15/18
Estonia[1,5]	14/16	14	16
Finland[4]	16/18	18/21	18/21
France	15	15	15
Germany (ex-East)[6]	14	14	14
Germany (ex-West)[6]	14	14	18
Gibraltar	18	18	18
Greece	15	15	15/17[7]
Hungary	14	18	18
Iceland	14	14	14
Ireland, Republic of	17	17	17
Italy[8]	14/16	14/16	14/16
Latvia[1]	18 (16?)	18 (16?)	18 (16?)
Liechtenstein	14	14	18
Lithuania[1]	18 (16?)	18 (16?)	18 (16?)
Luxembourg	16	16	16
Macedonia	14	14	Illegal
Malta[4,9]	12/18	12/18	12/18
Moldova[1]	18 (16?)	18 (16?)	Illegal[2]
Montenegro	14	14	14
Netherlands[9]	12/16	12/16	12/16
Norway	16	16	16
Poland	15	15	15
Portugal[9]	12/16	12/16	12/16
Romania[1]	16 (14?)	Illegal	Illegal
Russia[1]	18 (16?)	18 (16?)	18 (16?)
San Marino[8]	14/16	14/16	14/16
Serbia	14	14	Illegal
Slovakia	15	15	15
Slovenia	14	14	14
Spain[4,9]	12/18	12/18	12/18
Sweden	15	15	15
Switzerland[4,10]	16/20	16/20	16/20
Turkey[11]	15/18	15/18	15/18
Ukraine[1]	18 (16?)	18 (16?)	18 (16?)
United Kingdom[12]	16	16	21

(1) There is conflicting information from London embassies, ministries of justice, lawyers and human rights groups about the ages of consent in some of the ex-communist countries. Therefore, as well as listing the age cited by the most authoritative sources, the age claimed by other sources is also listed in brackets thus (?). (2) Only sodomy is a specific criminal offence. Other homosexual acts are, in theory, lawful, with the age of consent being the same as for heterosexual behaviour. (3) The European Court of Human Rights in 1993 ordered Cyprus to lift its ban on male homosexuality. Decriminalization is expected in the near future. (4) The higher age applies in cases where an older person, such as parent or teacher, has a position of trust or authority over a younger person. (5) The Estonian age of consent is 14 for women and 16 for men, regardless of sexual orientation, and is based on the assumption that males reach sexual maturity later than women. (6) Since German reunification, there is an interim situation whereby East Germany's laws concerning homosexuality still apply in the eastern half of the country, and West Germany's laws remain in force in the western half. The German government has announced its intention to introduce a common age of consent of 16 for heterosexual, lesbian and gay sex. (7) In Greece the "seduction" of a man under 17 by a man over 18 is an offence. (8) Sex with 14- and 15-year-olds is punishable only if they are "sexually innocent" and make a complaint. (9) Sex with persons between the lower and higher ages is prosecuted only if the younger person or his/her parent or guardian files a formal complaint. (10) Sex with a person under 16 is not prosecuted if there is no more than 3 years' difference in the partners' ages. If there is more than 3 years' difference, but the older person is under 20 and there are mitigating circumstances, the authorities can waive a prosecution. (11) The higher age applies to sexual intercourse (vaginal and anal), and the lower age to all other sexual acts. (12) In Northern Ireland the age of consent for heterosexual and lesbian relations is 17.

THE EUROPEAN COMMUNITY

Compiled by Mike Gautrey

The European Community (EC) is the collective designation of three organizations with common membership:

- the European Coal and Steel Community (ECSC), established in 1952
- the European Atomic Energy Community (Euratom), established in 1958
- the European Economic Community (EEC), established in 1958

Members are European countries with certain shared political, social and above all economic aims. At present there are 12 full members, those marked with an asterisk (*) being founder members:

Belgium*
Denmark (since 1973)
France*
Germany*
Greece (since 1981)
Ireland (since 1973)
Italy*
Luxembourg*
Netherlands*
Portugal (since 1986)
Spain (since 1986)
United Kingdom (since 1973)

Some 60 nations in Africa, the Caribbean and the Pacific are affiliated under the Lomé Convention with a view to facilitating trade and development.

Origins and Aims

The basis for the foundation of the European Community lay in a proposal made by former French prime minister Robert Schuman in 1950 to pool the coal and steel resources of western Europe. The Paris Treaty, signed on 18 April 1951 by representatives of the 6 original member states and ratified by their parliaments over the months that followed, led to the setting up of the ECSC in Luxembourg on 25 August 1952. The aim was the creation of a "common market" for coal and steel.

An inter-governmental conference of ESCS members in 1956 produced the 2 Treaties of Rome establishing the EEC and Euratom. They came into force on 1 January 1958 with the establishment of the 2 headquarters in Brussels. Euratom's essential function was as a focus for nuclear research cooperation, but once again a central aim in both cases was to create a common market.

Establishing the common market involved the removal of all tariffs and quotas between member states so as to permit the free movement of people, goods, services and capital – the so-called 4 freedoms – under conditions of fair competition within the EEC. This was to be one means of attaining the goals of enhanced economic activity, increased stability and ever-greater standards of living; the other was the gradual rapprochement of member states' economic policies. In addition, there were to be common agricultural, fisheries and external trade policies and a harmonization of social policy.

A merger of the 3 communities' executives was effected on 1 July 1967, creating a single Council to make policy decisions and a single Commission to make policy proposals. The other 2 Community institutions, the European Parliament (established in 1958) and the European Court of Justice (established in 1957), had both been common to the 3 since 1958.

On 14 February 1984 the European Parliament adopted the treaty establishing the European Union, while the Single European Act, signed in February 1986 and coming into force on 1 July 1987, represented a further significant step along the same road. By 1992, the European internal market was to be complete and the Community would effectively have no internal frontiers. The aim was now economic and monetary union, while foreign policy cooperation was to be institutionalized and measures were to be taken to make the Community itself more effective and democratic.

This process was set to be further consolidated with the signing on 7 February 1992 of the Treaty of Maastricht, due to be ratified by 1 January 1993. It sets a timetable towards achieving the 3 specific objectives of a single European currency (the ecu), a single monetary policy, and the establishment of a European Central Bank, after 1 January 1999. However, its future was placed in some doubt after market pressures on the more vulnerable Community currencies brought one of its central pillars, the Exchange Rate Mechanism (ERM) of the European Monetary System (EMS), to the point of collapse: with Britain and Italy already, in September 1992, having suspended participation in the mechanism and France desperate to avoid doing so, the hitherto strict range within which Community currencies were permitted to float was drastically relaxed in August 1993. This virtually ensured derailment of the second stage of economic and monetary union, due to begin on 1 January 1994 and entailing the coordination of monetary policy among members.

The EC has had its own budget since 1975, funded through customs duties and agricultural levies on imports from outside the Community, a proportion of member states' VAT receipts and, since 1989, a "fourth resource" based on GNP. The current spending ceiling represents 1.2% of the Community's GDP (66,500 million ecus, a little over £50,000 million).

The Council of the European Communities

More often referred to as the Council of Ministers, the Council is the Community's policy decision-making body. As the only institution whose members directly represent national governments, it comprises 12 government ministers, one from each member state, meeting in Brussels and Luxembourg. While constitutionally there has been a single Council since 1967, in practice composition varies with the matter under consideration. Thus, although the Council will normally comprise the Council of Foreign Ministers, it may at other times be constituted by the Council of Finance Ministers, the Council of Agriculture Ministers, and so on, each holding power of decision.

In a further refinement, since December 1974 the heads of state or government of Community countries, accompanied by their foreign ministers, have met twice a year, together with the President of the Commission, in a regular summit known as the European Council. These meetings coincide with the 6-monthly rotation of the Council's presidency and are hosted by the presiding country.

Council meetings normally have their agenda shaped by formal proposals from the Commission, taking decisions unanimously (required where the

Council departs from such proposals), or by a simple majority or a qualified majority, according to the treaty article forming the legal basis of the proposal. Votes of member states are weighted for majority voting: France, Germany, Italy and the UK have 10 votes each, Spain 8, Belgium, Greece, the Netherlands and Portugal 5, Denmark and Ireland 3 and Luxembourg 2. A qualified majority requires 54 of these 76 votes and, for a decision not based on a Commission proposal to pass, at least 8 of the 12 members must vote in favour.

The European Commission

Constituting the executive arm of the Community and guardian of its treaties, the European Commission exists to propose and plan policy and steer it through the Council of Ministers. It also acts as a mediator between member governments and as a monitor of breaches of Community law, if necessary taking cases before the European Court.

The Commission comprises 17 members (2 each from France, Germany, Italy, Spain and the UK, and 1 each from Belgium, Denmark, Greece, Ireland, the Netherlands and Portugal). Appointed jointly by member governments for a 4-year renewable term, they are answerable to the Community as a whole, independently of any national interest. The President and 6 vice-presidents hold office for a 2-year renewable term. France's Jacques Delors was in 1992 reappointed President for a fifth term.

Decisions are reached by simple majority vote at the weekly Brussels meetings of the Commission. Under the Treaties of Rome, the Commission can issue regulations, which are binding on all member states as regards ends but not means; decisions, binding on particular governments, enterprises and individuals; and recommendations and opinions, which are not binding.

The Commission's work is structured into 23 directorates-general, responsibility for which is shared among the members. For the 4-year term beginning January 1993, British Commission members were Sir Leon Brittan (Vice-President with responsibility for international trade matters) and Bruce Millan (responsible for regional policy).

The Commission has a staff of over 11,000 and 9 working languages.

The European Parliament

While the European Parliament does not have the full legislative powers of a national parliament, which in the Community have rested largely with the Council of Ministers, it nevertheless carries much greater importance now than at its establishment in Strasbourg in March 1958 as the European Parliamentary Assembly (adopting its present name in 1962).

As well as exercising advisory and supervisory powers in relation to both the Commission and the Council (it can dismiss the former on a two-thirds majority for a motion of censure), the Parliament has possessed considerable budgetary powers since the Community acquired its own financial resources in the 1970s. It now has the final say on all expenditure which does not stem directly from Community legislation. Thus, it determines, for example, the operating expenditure of the European Regional Development Fund and the European Social Fund, and that on industrial policy, and on research and energy. It is the Parliament which adopts the budget of the Community and which has the power to amend and increase it within specified limits.

Despite the primacy of the Council, the Parliament is an integral part of the Community's legislative process. Its opinion on Commission proposals must be taken into account, and if by an absolute majority it rejects a common position of the Council, the latter may then act only by unanimity. The Single European Act of 1987 increased the Parliament's influence on Community legislation on the single market, and the Council also needs the Parliament's assent to seek any enlargement of the Community.

Since June 1979, the 518 members have been directly elected by the citizens of the 12 member countries for 5-year terms. Belgium has 24 seats, Denmark 16, France 81, Germany 81, Greece 24, Ireland 15, Italy 81, Luxembourg 6, the Netherlands 25, Portugal 24, Spain 60 and the UK 81. However, members sit not in national but in political groups, of which there are 11 as of 1992. The largest are the left-of-centre Socialist Group (180 members) and the right-of-centre Group of the European People's Party–Christian Democrat Group (128 members). Normally sitting in Strasbourg, with its committees meeting in Brussels, the Parliament employs 3,000 staff.

UK Constituencies and Their MEPs

(as at August 1993)

Source: *Vacher's European Companion*, Vachers Publications

Con = Conservative; DUP = Democratic Unionist Party; Lab = Labour; OUP = Official Unionist Party; SDLP = Social Democrat & Labour Party; SNP = Scottish National Party.

ENGLAND
(66 members)

Bedfordshire South **Peter Beazley** (Con)
(Bedfordshire South West, Hertfordshire North, Hertfordshire West, Luton North, Luton South, Milton Keynes, Stevenage)

Birmingham East **Christine Crawley** (Lab)
(Edgbaston, Erdington, Hall Green, Hodge Hill, Northfield, Selly Oak, Small Heath, Sparkbrook and Yardley)

Birmingham West **John Tomlinson** (Lab)
(Aldridge Brownhills, Birmingham Ladywood, Birmingham Perry Barr, Sutton Coldfield, Walsall North, Walsall South, West Bromwich East, West Bromwich West)

Bristol **Ian White** (Lab)
(Bath, the Bristol seats of East, North West, South and West, Kingswood, Northavon, Wansdyke)

(Continued)

Cambridge & Bedfordshire North **Sir Fred Catherwood** (Con)
(Bedfordshire Mid, Bedfordshire North, Cambridge, Cambridgeshire North East, Cambridgeshire South West, Huntingdon, Peterborough)

Cheshire East **Brian Simpson** (Lab)
(Congleton, Crewe and Nantwich, Macclesfield, Staffordshire Moorlands, Tatton, Warrington North, Warrington South)

Cheshire West **Lyndon Harrison** (Lab)
(Birkenhead, City of Chester, Eddisbury, Ellesmere Port and Neston, Halton, Wallasey, Wirral South, Wirral West)

Cleveland & Yorkshire North **David Bowe** (Lab)
(Hartlepool, Langbaurgh, Middlesborough, Redcar, Richmond (Yorks), Skipton and Ripon, Stockton North, Stockton South)

Cornwall & Playmouth **Christopher Beazley** (Con)
(Cornwall North, Cornwall South East, Falmouth and Camborne, Plymouth Devonport, Plymouth Drake, Plymouth Sutton, St Ives, Truro)

Cotswolds **Lord Plumb** (Con)
(Banbury, Cheltenham, Cirencester and Tewkesbury, Gloucester, Stratford-on-Avon, Stroud, Witney)

Cumbria & Lancashire North **Lord Inglewood** (Con)
(Barrow and Furness, Carlisle, Copeland, Lancaster, Morecambe and Lunesdale, Penrith and the Border, Westmorland and Lunesdale, Workington, Wyre)

Derbyshire **Geoffrey Hoon** (Lab)
(Amber Valley, Ashfield, Bolsover, Derby North, Derby South, Derbyshire West, Erewash, High Peak)

Devon **Lord O'Hagan** (Con)
(Devon North, Devon West and Torridge, Exeter, Honiton, South Hams, Teignbridge, Tiverton, Torbay)

Dorset East & Hampshire West **Bryan Cassidy** (Con)
(Bournemouth East, Bournemouth West, Christchurch, Dorset North, Dorset South, New Forest, Poole, Romsey and Waterside)

Durham **Stephen Hughes** (Lab)
(Bishop Auckland, Blaydon, Darlington, Durham, City of Durham North, Durham North West, Easington, Sedgefield)

Essex North East **Anne McIntosh** (Con)
(Braintree, Colchester North, Colchester South and Maldon, Harwich, Rochford, Saffron Walden, Southend East, Southend West)

Essex South West **Patricia Rawlings** (Con)
(Basildon, Billericay, Brentwood and Ongar, Castle Point, Chelmsford, Epping Forest, Harlow Thurrock)

Greater Manchester Central **Edward Newman** (Lab)
(Altrincham and Sale, Davyhulme, the Manchester seats of Blackley, Central, Gorton, Withington and Wythenshawe, Stretford)

Greater Manchester East **James Ford** (Lab)
(Ashton under Lyne, Cheadle, Denton and Reddish, Hazel Grove, Oldham Central and Royton, Oldham West, Stalybridge and Hyde, Stockport)

Greater Manchester West **Gary Titley** (Lab)
(Bolton North East, Bolton South East, Bolton West, Bury North, Bury South, Eccles, Salford East, Worsley)

Hampshire Central **Edward Kellett-Bowman** (Con)
(Aldershot, Basingstoke, Eastleigh, Hampshire North West, Southampton Itchen, Southampton Test, Winchester)

Hereford & Worcester **Sir James Scott-Hopkins** (Con)
(Bromsgrove, Gloucestershire West, Hereford, Leominster, Worcester, Worcestershire Mid, Worcestershire South, Wyre Forest)

Hertfordshire **Derek Prag** (Con)
(Broxbourne, Hertford and Stortford, Hertfordshire South West, Hertsmere, St Albans, Watford, Welwyn Hatfield)

Humberside **Peter Crampton** (Lab)
(Beverley, Bridlington, Brigg and Cleethorpes, Great Grimsby, Hull East, Hull North, Hull West)

Kent East **Christopher Jackson** (Con)
(Ashford, Canterbury, Dover, Faversham, Folkestone and Hythe, Maidstone, Thanet North, Thanet South)

Kent West **Ben Patterson** (Con)
(Dartford, Gillingham, Gravesham, Kent Mid, Medway, Sevenoaks, Tonbridge and Malling, Tunbridge Wells)

Lancashire Central **Michael Welsh** (Con)
(Blackpool North, Blackpool South, Chorley, Fylde, Lancashire West, Preston, Ribble Valley, South Ribble)

Lancashire East **Michael Hindley** (Lab)
(Blackburn, Burnley, Heywood and Middleton, Hyndburn, Littleborough and Saddleworth, Pendle, Rochdale, Rossendale and Darwin)

Leeds **Michael McGowan** (Lab)
(Elmet, the Leeds seats of Central, East, North East, North West, South and Morley, and West, Pudsey)

Leicester **Mel Read** (Lab)
(Bosworth, Leicester East, Leicester South, Leicester West, Loughborough, Nuneaton, Rutland and Melton, Warwickshire North)

Lincolnshire **William Newton Dunn** (Con)
(Bassetlaw, Gainsborough and Horncastle, Grantham, Holland with Boston, Lincoln, Lindsey East, Newark, Stamford and Spalding)

London Central **Stan Newens** (Lab)
(Chelsea, City of London and Westminster South, Fulham, Hampstead and Highgate, Holborn and St Pancras, Islington North, Islington South and Finsbury, Kensington, Westminster North)

London East **Carole Tongue** (Lab)
(Barking, Dagenham, Hornchurch, Ilford North, Ilford South, Newham North East, Romford, Upminster, Wanstead and Woodford)

London North **Pauline Green** (Lab)
(Chipping Barnet, Edmonton, Enfield North, Enfield Southgate, Finchley, Hendon North, Hendon South, Hornsey and Wood Green, Tottenham)

London North East **Alf Lomas** (Lab)
(Bethnal Green and Stepney, Bow and Poplar, Chingford, Hackney North and Stoke Newington, Hackney South and Shoreditch, Leyton Newham North West, Newham South, Walthamstow)

London North West **Lord Bethell** (Con)
(Brent East, Brent North, Brent South, Harrow East, Harrow West, Hayes and Harlington, Ruislip-Northwood, Uxbridge)

London South & Surrey East **James Moorhouse** (Con)
(Carshalton and Wallington, Croydon Central, Croydon North East, Croydon North West, Croydon South, Reigate, Surrey East, Sutton and Cheam)

London South East **Peter Price** (Con)
(Beckenham, Bexleyhealth, Chislehurst, Eltham, Erith and Crayford, Greenwich, Old Bexley and Sidcup, Orpington, Ravensbourne, Woolwich)

London South Inner **Richard Balfe** (Lab)
(Dulwich, Lewisham Deptford, Lewishman East, Lewisham West, Norwood, Peckham, Southwark and Bermondsey, Streatham, Vauxhall)

London South West **Anita Pollack** (Lab)
(Battersea, Epsom and Ewell, Kingston upon Thames, Mitcham and Morden, Putney, Surbiton, Tooting, Wimbledon)

London West **Michael Elliott** (Lab)
(Brentford and Isleworth, Ealing Acton, Ealing North, Ealing Southall, Feltham and Heston, Hammersmith, Richmond and Barnes, Twickenham)

Merseyside East **Terry Wynn** (Lab)
(Knowsley North, Knowsley South, Leigh, Liverpool Garston, Makerfield, St Helens North, St Helens South, Wigan)

Merseyside West **Ken Stewart** (Lab)
(Bootle, Crosby, the Liverpool seats of Broadgreen, Mossley Hill, Riverside, Walton, and West Derby, Southport)

Midlands Central **Christine Oddy** (Lab)
(The Coventry seats of North East, North West, South East, and South West, Meriden, Rugby and Kenilworth, Solihull, Warwick and Leamington)

Midlands West **John Bird** (Lab)
(Dudley East, Dudley West, Halesowen and Stourbridge, Warley East, Warley West, Wolverhampton North East, Wolverhampton South East, Wolverhampton South West)

Norfolk **Paul Howell** (Con)
(Great Yarmouth, the Norfolk seats of Mid, North, North West, South and South West, Norwich North, Norwich South)

Northamptonshire **Anthony Simpson** (Con)
(Blaby, Corby, Daventry, Harborough, Kettering, Northampton North, Northampton South, Wellingborough)

Northumbria **Gordon Adam** (Lab)
(Berwick-upon-Tweed, Blyth Valley, Hexham, Newcastle upon Tyne Central, North Tynemouth, Wallsend, Wansbeck)

Nottingham **Ken Coates** (Lab)
(Broxtowe, Gedling, Mansfield, Nottingham East, Nottingham North, Nottingham South, Rushcliffe, Sherwood)

Oxford & Buckinghamshire **James Elles** (Con)
(Aylesbury, Beaconsfield, Buckingham, Chesham and Amersham, Henley, Oxford East, Oxford West and Abingdon, Wycombe)

Sheffield **Roger Barton** (Lab)
(Chesterfield, Derbyshire North East, the Sheffield seats of Attercliffe, Brightside, Central, Hallam, Heeley, and Hillsborough)

Shropshire & Stafford **Sir Christopher Prout** (Con)
(Cannock and Burntwood, Ludlow, Newcastle-under-Lyme, Shrewsbury and Atcham, Shropshire North, Stafford, Staffordshire South, The Wrekin)

Somerset & Dorset West **Margaret Daly** (Con)
(Bridgwater, Dorset West, Somerton and Frome, Taunton, Wells, Weston-super-Mare, Woodspring, Yeovil)

Staffordshire East **George Stevenson** (Lab)
(Burton, Derbyshire South, Staffordshire South East, Leicestershire North West, Staffordshire Mid, Stoke-on-Trent Central, Stoke-on-Trent North, Stoke-on Trent South)

Suffolk **Amédée Turner** (Con)
(Bury St Edmunds, Cambridgeshire South East, Ipswich, Suffolk Central, Suffolk Coastal, Suffolk South, Waveney)

Surrey West **Tom Spencer** (Con)
(Chertsey and Walton, Esher, Guildford, Mole Valley, Surrey North West, Surrey South West, Woking)

Sussex East **Sir Jack Stewart-Clark** (Con)
(Bexhill and Battle, Brighton Kemptown, Brighton Pavilion, Eastbourne, Hastings and Rye, Hove, Lewes, Wealden)

Sussex West **Madron Seligman** (Con)
(Arundel, Chichester, Crawley, Horsham, Shoreham, Sussex Mid, Worthing)

Thames Valley **John Stevens** (Con)
(Berkshire East, Reading East, Reading West, Slough, Spelthorne, Windsor and Maidenhead, Wokingham)

Tyne & Wear **Alan Donnelly** (Lab)
(Gateshead East, Houghton and Washington, Jarrow, Newcastle upon Tyne East, South Shields, Sunderland North, Sunderland South, Tyne Bridge)

Wight & Hampshire East **Richard Simmonds** (Con)
(Fareham, Gosport, Hampshire East, Havant, Isle of Wight, Portsmouth North, Portsmouth South)

Wiltshire **Dr Caroline Jackson** (Con)
(Devizes, Newbury, Salisbury, Swindon, Wantage, Westbury, Wiltshire North)

York **Edward McMillan Scott** (Con)
(Boothferry, Glanford and Scunthorpe, Harrogate, Ryedale, Scarborough, Selby, York)

Yorkshire South **Norman West** (Lab)
(Barnsley Central, Barnsley East, Doncaster Central, Doncaster North, Don Valley, Rotherham, Rother Valley, Wentworth)

Yorkshire South West **Thomas Megahy** (Lab)
(Barnsley West and Penistone, Colne Valley, Dewsbury, Hemsworth, Huddersfield, Normanton, Pontefract and Castleford, Wakefield)

Yorkshire West **Barry Seal** (Lab)
(Batley and Spen, Bradford North, Bradford South , Bradford West, Calder Valley, Halifax, Keighley, Shipley)

SCOTLAND
(8 members)

Glasgow **Janey Buchan** (Lab)
(The Glasgow seats of Cathcart Central, Carscadden, Govan, Hillhead, Maryhill, Pollok, Provan, Shettleston, and Springburn)

Highlands & Islands **Winifred Ewing** (SNP)
(Argyll and Bute, Caithness and Sutherland, Inverness, Nairn and Lochaber, Moray, Ross, Cromarty and Skye, Orkney and Shetland, Western Isles)

Lothians **David Martin** (Lab)
(The Edinburgh seats of Central, East, Leith, Pentlands, South and West, Linlithgow, Livingston, Midlothian)

Mid Scotland & Fife **Alex Falconer** (Lab)
(Clackmannan, Dunfermline East, Dunfermline West, Falkirk East, Falkirk West, Fife Central, Fife North East, Kirkcaldy, Perth and Kinross, Stirling)

Scotland North East **Henry McGubbin** (Lab)
(Aberdeen North, Aberdeen South, Angus East Banff and Buchan, Dundee East, Dundee West, Gordon, Kincardine and Deeside, Tayside North)

South of Scotland **Alex Smith** (Lab)
(Ayr, Carrick, Cumnock and Doon Valley, Clydesdale, Cunninghame South, Dumfries, Galloway and Upper Nithsdale, East Lothian, Roxburgh and Berwickshire, Tweeddale, Ettrick and Lauderdale)

Strathclyde East **Kenneth Collins** (Lab)
(Cumbernauld and Kilsyth, East Kilbride, Glasgow

Rutherglen, Hamilton, Kilmarnock and Loudoun, Monklands East, Monklands West, Motherwell North, Motherwell South)
Strathclyde West **Hugh McMahon** (Lab)
(Clydebank and Milngavie, Cunninghame North, Dumbarton, Eastwood, Greenock and Port Glasgow, Paisley North, Paisley South, Renfrew West and Inverclyde, Strathkelvin and Bearsden)

WALES
(4 members)

Mid & West Wales **David Morris** (Lab)
(Brecon and Radnor, Carmarthen, Ceredigion and Pembroke North, Gower, Llanelli, Neath, Pembroke, Swansea East, Swansea West)
North Wales **Joe Wilson** (Lab)
(Alyn and Deeside, Caernarfon, Clwyd North West, Clwyd South West, Conwy, Delyn Meirionnydd)
South East Wales **Llewellyn Smith** (Lab)
(Blaenau Gwent, Caerphilly, Cynon Valley, Islwyn, Merthyr Tydfil and Rhymney, Monmouth, Newport East, Newport West, Rhondda, Torfaen)
South Wales **Wayne David** (Lab)
(Bridgend, the Cardiff seats of Central, North, South and Penarth, and West, Ogmore, Pontypridd, Vale of Glamorgan)

NORTHERN IRELAND
(3 members)

Rev Ian Paisley DUP
John Hume SDLP
James Nicholson OUP
Northern Ireland MEPs are elected by proportional representation and therefore do not have constituencies.

Rates of Participation in EC Elections

Source: CSO

Percentages

	1979	1984	1989
United Kingdom	32.8	32.5	36.0
Belgium	91.4	92.1	93.0
Denmark	47.8	54.0	46.0
France	61.2	57.4	50.4
Germany (Fed. Rep.)	65.7	56.8	61.5
Greece	–	78.4	77.7
Irish Republic	63.6	47.6	68.5
Italy	86.0	83.4	81.5
Luxembourg	88.9	88.8	87.0
Netherlands	58.2	50.9	47.2
Portugal	–	–	51.2
Spain	–	–	54.8
EUR 12	62.5(1)	59.4(2)	58.5

(1) EUR 9. (2) EUR 10.

The European Court of Justice

Ultimately, the Community's most powerful institution in the sense that it has the final say in what can and cannot be done under Community treaties and conventions, the European Court of Justice is also, ironically, its least well known. (It is often confused, for example, with the European Court of Human Rights in Strasbourg.)

Based in Luxembourg, the court adjudicates, at the request of national courts, on disputes arising from the interpretation and application of Community law. It arbitrates between member states and can judge complaints from individuals or corporate bodies about the effects of Community legislation. At the request of a Community institution, government or individual, it can also quash any measure adopted by the Commission, the Council or a national government which is incompatible with the treaties.

The 13 judges constituting the court – 1 from each member state plus another to ensure an uneven number, chosen by the larger states in rotation – are appointed for a renewable term of 6 years, electing a president from among themselves for a 3-year term. There is an 800-strong staff and an annual budget of about £58 million.

The court may sit in public hearings, administrative meetings or judges' deliberations, and there is both written and oral procedure. Judgments are always collective, representing either consensus or the majority opinion; minority opinions are not revealed. Judgments are mandatory in all member states.

The court's workload has greatly increased in recent years, and to ease it a lower-tier Court of First Instance was created in 1989, with responsibility for competition cases and EC staff disputes.

Britain and Europe

Over the years Britain has garnered a not entirely unjustified reputation as the EC's most reluctant member. When the idea of a European common market first gained currency in the 1950s, Britain, led by the ageing prime minister Winston Churchill, preferred to put its faith in the links with its imperial past offered by trade with the Commonwealth.

By the time the Conservative government had come round to the European idea, lodging a first membership application on 10 August 1961, the Franco-German axis of the 6 founder members was well established. French president Charles de Gaulle, mistrustful of Britain's affinity with the United States, doubted the sincerity of its commitment. France vetoed the application and negotiations were broken off in January 1962.

A second attempt to join the Community was made on 10 May 1967 by the Labour government of Harold Wilson, itself deeply divided over the issue. De Gaulle this time refused to allow negotiations to begin. It was not until he quit the political scene that they finally began, on 30 June 1970, under the newly elected Conservative government of noted European enthusiast Edward Heath. The treaty of accession, ratified by the Commons on 28 October 1971, was signed on 22 January 1972, and the UK, together with Denmark and Ireland, became an official member of the new Community of 9 on 1 January 1973.

A second Wilson administration, elected the following year, sought to renegotiate the terms of accession. Labour anti-Europeans led by left-wing minister Tony Benn urged the holding of a referendum on British membership. After an often bitter campaign, the result on 5 June 1975 was a two-thirds majority for remaining within the Community. Continued British membership was at last assured, although few seemed to see cause for celebration. One who did was former Labour Chancellor Roy Jenkins, appointed first British President of the Commission in 1977.

Although over the 1960s and 1970s Conservatives had usually been more eager to embrace the European ideal than Labour politicians, it was with the arrival of Margaret Thatcher in 10 Downing Street that Britain actually began to be perceived as anti-European. De Gaulle's old transatlantic bugbear enjoyed something of a revival as the Thatcher–Reagan tandem set its own new international agenda.

For Mrs Thatcher, the Community, which she perceived as having moved away from its original free-market concept to become a socialistic bureaucracy, was above all a source of subsidy to the inefficient, particularly with its Common Agricultural Policy. She demanded a reduction in the UK's budgetary contribution, which in a compromise agreement in the Council of Ministers was secured in May 1980.

Throughout the Thatcher years Britain seemed at odds with the rest of Europe, particularly after the appointment of French socialist Jacques Delors as President of the Commission in 1985. Then came a sudden u-turn in monetary policy with the decision in October 1990 to allow sterling to become a full member of the Exchange-Rate Mechanism (ERM) of the European Monetary System (EMS). It heralded a change in Conservative leadership, and the signs were that new prime minister John Major had a more flexible stance towards the Community, although economic problems forced his government to suspend ERM membership in late 1992.

From Maastricht to Sarajevo

Conceived as a schedule of implementation for European Economic and Monetary Union, the Treaty of Maastricht became a millstone around the neck of more than one head of government. Although over the course of 1992 eight Community members ratified it with little or no discussion following an overwhelming parliamentary or – in Ireland's case – popular majority, three were convulsed by debates indissolubly linked to the political fortunes of their respective leaders, and a fourth – Germany – was obliged to wait adjudication on a legal challenge to the treaty's constitutionality. As a result, doubt began to be cast on the future of the European project as a whole, at least in its elaborately ambitious Maastricht version.

France's referendum became a plebiscite on the increasingly unpopular personality politics which had characterized a decade under President François Mitterand, a process exacerbated by an excess of xenophobia fuelled from the extreme right. French public and political opinion, traditionally Europhile, was surprisingly divided as voters belatedly woke up to the treaty's deeper implications for national sovereignty and joined a debate long since rehearsed by the British. The outcome was a tiny margin in favour.

Three months earlier, Denmark's own referendum had already dramatically altered the shape of events as the Danes voted against, albeit by a similarly narrow margin. Under the terms of the treaty, non-ratification by one member meant that implementation could not go ahead, and there was speculation – which the French result did not entirely dispel – that the European juggernaut would be abruptly halted.

In Britain the verdicts of the Danish and French peoples were grist to the mill of those on the right of the Conservative Party, known as the "Eurosceptics", who were rallied by Margaret Thatcher in increasingly open revolt against the faltering leadership of her successor. John Major had ruled out any possibility of a British Maastricht referendum, the result of which was likely to be even less favourable.

He had seen to it that the treaty included specific provision for the UK to opt out, if it wished, of the third stage of European monetary union foreseen by the treaty (implementing a central banking system and single currency from 1999). And alone of the 12, the country was to be unaffected by the Social Chapter, guaranteeing European workers certain minimal employment rights. In order to obtain the necessary parliamentary approval, he thus found himself obliged to walk a fine political line between those of his own party for whom European union had gone quite far enough, and opposition parties concerned that Britain was being left behind the rest. Seeking a breathing space by declaring that British ratification depended on what happened next in Denmark, he only incurred greater wrath from the Community partners, who began to talk of a two-speed Europe.

Matters went from bad to worse as, with the economy deep in recession, irresistible pressure on an overvalued pound forced the government to suspend membership of the Exchange Rate Mechanism (ERM), which had been a symbol of increased British commitment to the goal of monetary union.

To some extent a second Danish referendum brought relief. Having negotiated British-style opt-outs on economic and monetary union, among other things, new Danish prime minister Poul Nyrup Rasmussen secured a 57% approval rating for the treaty. Clearly reservation about the path from Maastricht to European Union were not restricted to Britain. The concept for which it claimed credit, "subsidiarity", or the devolution of decision-making to the most practicable local level, seemed central to a Europe of scaled-down expectations. Even Chancellor Helmut Kohl's German government affirmed its right to opt out if parliament saw fit.

After a humiliating Commons defeat for the Government's motion on Maastricht in July 1993, British ratification was finally made possible only by the risky expedient of tying approval of the treaty to a vote of confidence in the Major administration, passed the following day. The treaty was ratified on 2 August 1993. But it was clear that the governing Conservative party remained deeply divided over the issue.

The Copenhagen summit in June 1993 opened the door to 1995 membership for Austria, Finland, Norway and Sweden, and foresaw the eventual entry of six east European states. It also recognized the need for economic renewal to combat recession and halt the decline in EC competitiveness. But perhaps more significant was a Community failure which illustrated the stark reality that genuine European unity remained a far distant dream. While the summit leaders wrung their hands in impotence, the bloody Yugoslavian war raged on unabated at its doorstep.

THE COMMONWEALTH

The Commonwealth of Nations is an association of 50 independent states loosely joined by a common interest based on having been parts of the British Empire. The combined population of the Commonwealth is 1300 million and its symbolic head is Queen Elizabeth II.

Members
(and date of joining)

United Kingdom (1931)

The following members recognize the Queen, represented by a governor-general, as their head of state:
Antigua and Barbuda (1981)
Australia (1931)
Bahamas (1973)
Barbados (1966)
Belize (1981)
Canada (1931)
Grenada (1974)
Jamaica (1962)
Mauritius (1968)
New Zealand (1931)
Papua New Guinea (1975)
St Kitts and Nevis (1983)
St Lucia (1979)
St Vincent and the Grenadines (1979)
Solomon Islands (1978)
Tuvalu (special member) (1978)

The following members have their own heads of state:
Bangladesh (1972)
Botswana (1966)
Brunei (1984)
Cyprus (1961)
Dominica (1978)
The Gambia (1965)
Ghana (1957)
Guyana (1966)
India (1947)
Kenya (1963)
Kiribati (1979)
Lesotho (1966)
Malawi (1964)
Malaysia (1957)
The Maldives (1982)
Malta (1964)
Namibia (1990)
Nauru (special member) (1968)
Nigeria (1960)
Pakistan (1947, resigned 1972, rejoined 1989)
Seychelles (1976)
Sierra Leone (1961)
Singapore (1965)
Sri Lanka (1948)
Swaziland (1968)
Tanzania (1961)
Tonga (1970)
Trinidad and Tobago (1962)
Uganda (1962)
Vanuatu (1980)
Western Samoa (1970)
Zambia (1964)
Zimbabwe (1980)

Fiji, the Republic of Ireland and South Africa left the Commonwealth in 1987, 1949 and 1961 respectively.

Special members may take part in all Commonwealth activities, apart from Commonwealth Heads of Government meetings.

The formula for the Commonwealth was outlined in 1926 by the Inter-Imperial Relations Committee under the chairmanship of Lord Balfour. This formula was given legal substance by the Statute of Westminster in 1931. The founder members of the Commonwealth were the UK and the then Dominions of Australia, Canada, the Irish Free State, Newfoundland, New Zealand and South Africa.

The Commonwealth facilitates consultation among member states through meetings of prime ministers and finance ministers. Heads of government meet every two years and decisions are reached in private, by consensus rather than voting, and the results made public in a communiqué. Members consult on economic, scientific, education, financial, legal and military matters, and try to coordinate policies.

The *Commonwealth Secretariat*, established in 1965 by the Commonwealth heads of government, is a permanent neutral body funded by all member states. It organizes meetings and conferences, disseminates information and mediates in disputes.

The *Commonwealth Fund for Technical Cooperation* provides assistance for developing countries within the Commonwealth. It aims to improve technical, industrial and managerial skills, and promotes the exchange of these skills between the developing countries.

Commonwealth Country Dependencies

Britain
Anguilla
Bermuda
British Antarctic Territory
British Indian Ocean Territory
British Virgin Islands
Cayman Islands
Falkland Islands
Gibraltar
Hong Kong
Montserrat
Pitcairn, Ducie, Henderson and Oeno
South Georgia and the South Sandwich Islands
St Helena and Dependencies (Ascension and Tristan da Cunha)
Turks and Caicos Islands

Britain oversees the internal security, defence and foreign affairs of these territories, but is committed to giving independence where it is wanted and practicable.

The Falkland Islands and Gibraltar are both subjects of territorial claims – the former by Argentina and the latter by Spain. In both cases the British Government is committed to honouring the wishes of the people in retaining links with Britain.

Hong Kong will cease to be a British Dependency after 30 June 1997. It will then become a Special Administrative Region (SAR) of China, but retain its own government and legislature for all matters apart from defence and foreign affairs.

Australia
Norfolk Island
Heard Island
McDonald Island
Cocos (Keeling) Islands
Christmas Island
Asmore and Cartier Islands
Coral Sea Islands

New Zealand
Cook Islands
Niue
Tokelau Islands

While members may cooperate on matters of defence and be signatories to such treaties as NATO, the Commonwealth is not a military alliance. In recent years its function as a trading bloc has been somewhat overshadowed by the European Community.

ARTS & MEDIA

Notable Films of the Year

Sept. 1992–Aug. 1993

Film/Stars/Director

Aladdin/Robin Williams, Jonathan Freeman, Gilbert Gottfried/John Musker, Ron Clemens
Benny and Joon/Johnny Depp, Mary Stuart Masterson, Aiden Quinn/Jeremiah Chechik
Bob Roberts/Tim Robbins, Giancarlo Esposito, Gore Vidal/Tim Robbins
The Bodyguard/Kevin Costner, Whitney Houston/ Mike Jackson
Chaplin/Robert Downey Jr, Dan Aykroyd, Anthony Hopkins/Richard Attenborough
Cliffhanger/Sylvester Stallone, John Lithgow, Janine Turner/Renny Harlin
The Crying Game/Stephen Rea, Miranda Richardson, Jaye Davidson/Neil Jordan
Dave/Kevin Kline, Sigourney Weaver/Ivan Reitman
Damage/Jeremy Irons, Juliette Binoche/Louis Malle
Dennis the Menace/Walter Matthau, Mason Gamble, Christopher Lloyd/Nick Castle
Dracula/Gary Oldman, Winona Ryder, Anthony Hopkins/Francis Ford Coppola
Falling Down/Michael Douglas, Robert Duvall, Barbara Hershey/Joel Schumacher
A Few Good Men/Tom Cruise, Jack Nicholson, Demi Moore, Kevin Bacon/Rob Reiner
The Firm/Tom Cruise, Ed Harris, Holly Hunter, Hal Holbrook/Sidney Pollack
The Fugitive/Harrison Ford, Tommy Lee Jones/ Andrew Davies
Glengarry Glen Ross/Al Pacino, Jack Lemmon, Ed Harris, Alec Baldwin/James Foley
Groundhog Day/Bill Murray, Andie McDowell/ Harold Ramis
Hero/Dustin Hoffman, Geena Davis, Andy Garcia/ Stephen Frears
Hoffa/Jack Nicholson, Danny DeVito, Armand Assante/Danny DeVito
Home Alone 2/Macaulay Culkin, Joe Pesci, Daniel Stern/John Hughes
Honeymoon in Vegas/James Caan, Nicolas Cage, Sarah Jessica Parker/Andrew Berg
Husbands and Wives/Woody Allen, Mia Farrow, Judy Davis, Blythe Danner/Woody Allen
Indecent Proposal/Robert Redford, Demi Moore, Woody Harrelson/Adrian Lyne
In the Line of Fire/Clint Eastwood, John Malkovich, Rene Russo/Wolfgang Peterson
Jurassic Park/Sam Neill, Laura Dern, Jeff Goldblum/ Steven Spielberg
Last Action Hero/Arnold Schwarzenegger, Austin O'Brien/John McTiernan
The Last of the Mohicans/Daniel Day-Lewis, Madeleine Stowe/Michael Mann
Lorenzo's Oil/Susan Sarandon, Nick Nolte/George Miller
Lost in Yonkers/Richard Dreyfuss, Mercedes Ruehl, Irene Worth/Martha Coolidge
Mad Dog and Glory/Robert De Niro, Uma Thurman, Bill Murray/John McNaughton
Made in America/Whoopi Goldberg, Ted Danson/ Richard Benjamin
Malcolm X/Denzel Washington, Angela Bassett, Al Freeman, Jr./Spike Lee
Map of the Human Heart/Patrick Bergin, Anne Parillaud/Vincent Ward
Matinee/John Goodman, Cathy Moriarty/Joe Dante
Mr Saturday Night/Billy Crystal, David Paymer/Billy Crystal
Much Ado About Nothing/Kenneth Branagh, Emma Thompson, Michael Keaton/Kenneth Branagh
Night and the City/Robert De Niro, Jessica Lange/ Irwin Winkler
Of Mice and Men/Gary Sinise, John Malkovich, Sherilyn Fenn/Gary Sinise
Passion Fish/Mary McDonnell, Alfre Woodard/John Sayles
Point of No Return/Bridget Fonda, Gabriel Byrne, Harvey Keitel/John Badham
Posse/Mario Van Peebles, Charles Lane, Big Daddy Kane/Mario Van Peebles
Rising Sun/Sean Connery, Wesley Snipes/Philip Kaufman
Scent of a Woman/Al Pacino, Chris O'Donnel/Martin Brest
Sliver/Sharon Stone, William Baldwin, Tom Berenger/Phillip Noyce
Sniper/Tom Berenger, Billy Zane/Luis Llosa
Sleepless in Seattle/Tom Hanks, Meg Ryan/Nora Ephron
Under Siege/Steven Seagal, Tommy Lee Jones, Gary Busey/Andrew Davis
Unforgiven/Clint Eastwood, Gene Hackman, Morgan Freeman/Clint Eastwood
What's Love Got to Do With It?/Angela Bassett, Laurence Fishburne/Brian Gibson

Top UK Film Grosses: 1992

Source: *BFI Film & Television Handbook 1994*

Film	Revenue £
Patriot Games	6,542,299
Alien 3	6,522,103
The Lawnmower Man	3,622,720
Peter's Friends	3,017,357
Howards End	2,735,992
Blame It on the Bellboy	2,606,840
The Muppet Christmas Carol	2,531,873
Chaplin	1,764,462
Carry on Columbus	1,672,337
The Lover	1,375,697
The Crying Game	1,257,510
City of Joy	856,859
Hear My Song	739,989
The Playboys	545,000
The Naked Lunch	542,019

UK Attendance at Cinemas[1]

Source: CSO

Percentages

	1984	1986	1988	1990	1991
Ages					
7–14	73	87	84	85	80
15–24	59	82	81	87	88
25–34	49	65	64	79	70
35–44	45	60	61	70	70
45 and over	13	25	34	41	39
All persons aged 7 and over	38	53	56	64	61

(1) Percentage attending at least once in any given year.

National Film & Television Archive, 1914–79

Source: BFI

The British Film Institute has compiled the following working list of 360 key films from the early days of cinema to the end of the 1970s.

1914
Cabiria, Giovanni Pastrone

1915
The Birth of a Nation, D. W. Griffith

1916
Les Vampires, Louis Feuillade
Intolerance, D. W. Griffith
Joan the Woman, Cecil B. DeMille
Judex, Louis Feuillade

1918
J'accuse, Abel Gance
Tih Minh, Louis Feuillade

1919
Karin Ingmarsdot, Victor Sjöström
True Heart Susie, D. W. Griffith
Die Austernprinzessin (The Oyster Princess), Ernst Lubitsch
Das Cabinet des Dr Caligari (The Cabinet of Dr Caligari), Robert Wiene

1921
La Roue, Abel Gance

1922
Foolish Wives, Erich von Stroheim

1923
Gunnar Hedes Saga, Mauritz Stiller
Die Nibelungen – ein Deutsches Heldenlied I: Siegfrieds Tod, Fritz Lang

1924
Neobychainiye Priklucheniya Mistera, Lev Kuleshov
Vesta v Stranye Bolshevikov (The Extraordinary Adventures of Mr West in the Land of the Bolsheviks), Lev Kuleshov
Die Nibelungen – ein Deutsches Heldenlied II: Kriemhilds Rache, Fritz Lang
Der Letzte Mann (The Last Man), Friedrich W. Murnau
The Navigator, Buster Keaton, Donald Crisp
Inhumaine, Marcel l'Herbier

1925
Stachka (Strike), Sergei Eisenstein
Greed, Erich von Stroheim
The Gold Rush, Charles Chaplin
The Freshman, F. Newmeyer, S. Taylor
Visages d'Enfants (Faces of Children), Jacques Feyder
The Unholy Three, Tod Browning
Variété (Vaudeville), E.A. Dupont
Tumbleweeds, King Baggot
Bronenosets Potyomkin (Battleship Potemkin), Sergei Eisenstein
Metropolis, Fritz Lang

1926
Mat' (Mother), V. Pudovkin
Po Zakonu (Dura Lex), Lev Kuleshov
Hands Up!, Clarence Badger
Flesh and the Devil, Clarence Brown
The Lodger: A Story of the London Fog, Alfred Hitchcock
The Strong Man, Frank Capra
Geheimnisse einer Seele (Secrets of a Soul), G. W. Pabst
Faust – eine Deutsch Volkssage, Friedrich W. Murnau
Kurutta Ippeiji (A Page of Madness), Teinosuke Kinugasa
Napoleon, Abel Gance

1929
Sunrise – A Song of Two Humans, Friedrich W. Murnau
Un Chapeau de Paille d'Italie (An Italian Straw Hat), René Clair
Berlin, die Sinfonie eine Großstadt (Berlin, Symphony of a City), Walter Ruttmann
The Crowd, King Vidor
Love, Edmund Goulding
La Passion de Jeanne d'Arc (The Passion of Joan of Arc), Carl Dreyer
The Man Who Laughs, Paul Leni

1928
The Docks of New York, Josef von Sternberg
Steamboat Bill, Jr, Charles F. Reisner
Dom na Trubnoi (The House on Trubnaya Square), Boris Barnet
Oktyabr (October), Sergei Eisenstein
The Wind, Victor Sjöström
Queen Kelly, Erich von Stroheim
Heimkehr, Joe May
Die Buchse der Pandora (Pandora's Box), G. W. Pabst
L'Argent, Marcel l'Herbier
Chelovek s Kinoapparatom (The Man with a Movie Camera), Dziga Vertov
Asphalt, Joe May
Spione (The Spy), Fritz Lang

1929
Blackmail (silent version), Alfred Hitchcock
Die Wunderbare Luge der Nina Petrowna, Hans Schwarz
Piccadilly (silent version), E. A. Dupont
Menschen am Sonntag (People on Sunday), Robert Siodmak, Edgar G. Ulmer
Applause, Rouben Mamoulian

1930
The Big Trail, Raoul Walsh
Zemlja (Earth), Alexander P. Dovzhenko
Der Blaue Engel (The Blue Angel), Josef von Sternberg
L'Age d'Or, Luis Buñuel
Little Caesar, Mervyn LeRoy
All Quiet on the Western Front, Lewis Milestone
Ariane, Paul Czinner

1931
Frankenstein, James Whale
Die 3 Groschenoper (The Threepenny Opera), G. W. Pabst
The Public Enemy, William A. Wellman
M, Fritz Lang
Le Million, René Clair
La Chienne, Jean Renoir
City Lights, Charles Chaplin

(Continued)

Marius, Alexander Korda

1932
Love Me Tonight, Rouben Mamoulian
Vampyr (The Strange Adventure of David Gray), Carl Dreyer
Boudu Sauvé des Eaux (Boudu Saved from Drowning), Jean Renoir
Tavaszi Zapor (Marie – A Hungarian Legend), Paul Fejös
Scarface, Shame of a Nation, Howard Hawks
The Most Dangerous Game, Ernest B. Schoedsack, Irving Pichel
Liebelei, Max Ophüls

1933
42nd Street, Lloyd Bacon
King Kong, Ernest B. Schoedsack, Merian C. Cooper
Chuncan (Spring Silkworms), Cheng Bugao
Tianming (Daybreak), Sun Yu
Queen Christina, Rouben Mamoulian
Hallelujah, I'm a Bum, Lewis Milestone
Zoo in Budapest, Rowland V. Lee
Duck Soup, Leo McCarey

1934
L'Atalante, Jean Vigo
La Signora di Tutti, Max Ophüls
It Happened One Night, Frank Capra
It's a Gift, Norman Z. McLeod
The Scarlet Empress, Josef von Sternberg
Shennu (The Goddess), Wu Yonggang

1935
Toni, Jean Renoir
Novyi Gulliver (The New Gulliver), Aleksander Ptushko
La Kermesse Héroique (Carnival in Flanders), Jacques Feyder
First a Girl, Victor Saville
A Night at the Opera, Sam Wood
Tsuma Yo Bara No Yoni (Wife, Be Like a Rose), Mikio Naruse
Bride of Frankenstein, James Whale

1936
La Belle Équipe, Julien Duvivier
Triumph des Willens (Triumph of the Will), Leni Riefenstahl
Modern Times, Charles Chaplin
Le Roman d'un Tricheur (Diary of a Cheat), Sacha Guitry
Rembrandt, Alexander Korda
Things to Come, William Cameron Menzies
Swing Time, George Stevens
Show Boat, James Whale
Cesar, Marcel Pagnol
Way Out West, James W. Horne

1937
Pepe le Moko, Julien Duvivier
Nothing Sacred, William A. Wellman
La Grande Illusion, Jean Renoir
Malu Tianshi (Street Angel), Yuan Muzhi
Les Perles de la Couronne (The Peals of the Crown), Sacha Guitry, Christian-Jacque
Snow White and the Seven Dwarfs, David Hand
Un Carnet de Bal (Life Dances On), Julien Duvivier
Oh! Mr Porter, Marcel Varnel

1938
Bringing up Baby, Howard Hawks
Jezebel, William Wyler
Olympia, Leni Riefenstahl
La Bête Humaine, Jean Renoir
Quai des Brumes, Marcel Carné
Aleksandr Nevskii (Alexander Nevsky), Sergei Eisenstein
Varastettu Kuolema (Stolen Death), Nyrki Tapiovaara

1939
The Wizard of Oz, Victor Fleming
Only Angels Have Wings, Howard Hawks
La Règle du Jeu (The Rules of the Game), Jean Renoir
Stagecoach, John Ford
Le Jour se Lève, Marcel Carné
Zangiku Monogatari (The Story of Late Chrysanthemums), Kenji Mizoguchi

1940
The Grapes of Wrath, John Ford
The Thief of Bagdad, Ludwig Berger, Michael Powell, Tim Whelan, Zoltan Korda
Fantasia, Walt Disney Productions

1941
Remorques (Stormy Waters), Jean Grémillon
Citizen Kane, Orson Welles
Sullivan's Travels, Preston Sturges

1942
La Nuit Fantastique (The Fantastic Night), Marcel l'Herbier
The Magnificent Ambersons, Orson Welles
Ossessione, Luchino Visconti
Went The Day Well?, Alberto Cavalcanti
The Palm Beach Story, Preston Sturges
To Be or Not to Be, Ernst Lubitsch
Casablanca, Michael Curtiz

1943
Le Corbeau (The Raven), Henri-Georges Clouzot
Douce, Claude Autant-Lara
Cat People, Jacques Tourneur
The Life and Death of Colonel Blimp, Michael Powell, Emeric Pressburger
Fires Were Started, Humphrey Jennings
I Walked with a Zombie, Jacques Tourneur
Les Anges du Pêche, Robert Bresson
Millions Like Us, Frank Launder, Sidney Gilliat

1944
Ivan Groznyi (Ivan the Terrible, Parts 1 & 2), Sergei Eisenstein
Henry V, Laurence Olivier
Meet Me in St Louis, Vincente Minnelli
Laura, Otto Preminger
Double Indemnity, Billy Wilder
To Have and Have Not, Howard Hawks

1945
Les Enfants du Paradis, Marcel Carné
Brief Encounter, David Lean
Roma Citta Aperta (Rome, Open City), Roberto Rossellini
A Walk in the Sun, Lewis Milestone
I Know Where I'm Going!, Michael Powell, Emeric Pressburger

(Continued)

Les Dames du Bois de Boulogne, Robert Bresson
GI Joe, William A. Wellman

1946
La Belle et la Bête (Beauty and the Beast), Jean Cocteau
The Big Sleep, Howard Hawks
My Darling Clementine, John Ford
The Best Years of Our Lives, William Wyler
A Matter of Life and Death, Michael Powell, Emeric Pressburger
Leave Her to Heaven, John M. Stahl
Great Expectations, David Lean

1947
Odd Man Out, Carol Reed
The Ghost and Mrs Muir, Joseph Mankiewicz
Quai des Orfèvres, Henri-Georges Clouzot
Black Narcissus, Michael Powell, Emeric Pressburger
Red River, Howard Hawks
Yijiang Chunshui Xiang Dong Liu (The Spring River Flows East), Chi Chusen, Zheng Junli
Jour de Fète, Jacques Tati

1948
Ladri di Biciclette (Bicycle Thieves), Vittorio de Sica
Letter from an Unknown Woman, Max Ophüls
Fort Apache, John Ford
The Red Shoes, Michael Powell, Emeric Pressburger
Moonrise, Frank Borzage
Une Si Jolie Petite Plage, Yves Allégret

1949
White Heat, Raoul Walsh
Gun Crazy, Joseph H. Lewis
Wuya Yu Maque (Crows and Sparrows), Zheng Junli
Kind Hearts and Coronets, Robert Hamer
She Wore a Yellow Ribbon, John Ford
Les Enfants Terribles, Jean-Pierre Melville
The Third Man, Carol Reed
La Beauté du Diable, René Clair

1950
Cyrano de Bergerac, Michael Gordon
In a Lonely Place, Nicholas Ray
The Asphalt Jungle, John Huston
Los Olvidados, Luis Buñuel
Orphée, Jean Cocteau
Rio Grande, John Ford
Wagon Master, John Ford
Sunset Boulevard, Billy Wilder
Rashomon, Akira Kurosawa
La Ronde, Max Ophüls
Froken Julie (Miss Julie), Alf Sjöberg

1951
The Medium, Gian-Carlo Menotti
Strangers on a Train, Alfred Hitchcock
The Thing from Another World, Christian Nyby
Singin' in the Rain, Stanley Donen, Gene Kelly

1952
High Noon, Fred Zinnemann
Ikiru (Living), Akira Kurosawa
The Quiet Man, John Ford
Jeux Interdits (Forbidden Games), René Clement
Casque d'Or, Jacques Becker
El, Luis Buñuel

1953
Les Vacances de Monsieur Hulot, Jacques Tati
Shane, George Stevens
The Band Wagon, Vincente Minnelli
From Here to Eternity, Fred Zinnemann
Tokyo Monogatari (Tokyo Story), Yasujiro Ozu
The Big Heat, Fritz Lang
The Sun Shines Bright, John Ford
I Vitelloni Federico Fellini

1954
Sansho Dayu, Kenji Mizoguchi
Shichinin No Samurai (The Seven Samurai), Akira Kurosawa
Pokolenie (A Generation), Andrzej Wajda
On the Waterfront, Elia Kazan
A Star Is Born, George Cukor

1955
Richard III, Laurence Olivier
Lola Montes, Max Ophüls
French Cancan, Jean Renoir
Bob le Flambeur, Jean-Pierre Melville
Kiss Me Deadly, Robert Aldrich
The Man from Laramie, Anthony Mann
Shin Heike Monogatari (New Tales of Taira Clan), Kenji Mizoguchi
Pather Panchali, Satyajit Ray

1956
The Searchers, John Ford
Aparajito (The Unvanquished), Satyajit Ray
Un Condamne à Mort s'Est Echappé (A Man Escaped), Robert Bresson
Invasion of the Body Snatchers, Don Siegel
The Tall T, Budd Boetticher
Det Sjunde Inseglet (The Seventh Seal), Ingmar Bergman
Written on the Wind, Douglas Sirk

1957
Smultronstallet (Wild Strawberries), Ingmar Bergman
Kanal, Andrzej Wajda
Buye Cheng (City Without Night), Tang Ziaodan
Paths of Glory, Stanley Kubrick
Kumonosu-Jo (Throne of Blood), Akira Kurosawa
La Casa del Angel (The House of the Angel), Leopoldo Torre Nilsson
Forty Guns, Sam Fuller

1958
Apur Sansar (The World of Apu), Satyajit Ray
Popiol i Diament (Ashes and Diamonds), Andrzej Wajda
Eroica, Andrzej Munk
Vertigo, Alfred Hitchcock
Enjo (Conflagration), Kon Ichikawa
Touch of Evil, Orson Welles
Rio Bravo, Howard Hawks
Jalsaghar (The Music Room), Satyajit Ray
Ningen No Joken I (The Human Condition: No Greater Love), Masaki Kobayashi
Paris Nous Appartient, Jacques Rivette

1959
Les Quatre Cent Coups (The Four Hundred Blows), François Truffaut
Shadows, John Cassavetes
Ningen No Joken II (The Human Condition: Road to Eternity), Masaki Kobayashi
Hiroshima Mon Amour, Alain Resnais
Les Cousins, Claude Chabrol

(Continued)

Some Like It Hot, Billy Wilder
Pickpocket, Robert Bresson
L'Avventura, Michelangelo Antonioni
A Bout de Souffle (Breathless), Jean-Luc Godard
Peeping Tom, Michael Powell

1960
Ningen No Joken III (The Human Condition: A Soldier's Prayer), Masaki Kobayashi
Rocco e i suoi Fratelli/Rocco et ses Frères, Luchino Visconti
Psycho, Alfred Hitchcock
Lola/Donna di Vita, Jacques Demy
One-Eyed Jacks, Marlon Brando
Dama s Sobachkoi (The Lady With the Little Dog), Josef Heifitz

1961
Accattone, Pier Paolo Pasolini
Viridiana, Luis Buñuel
The Deadly Companions, Sam Peckinpah
Jules et Jim, François Truffaut
L'Année Dernière à Marienbad (Last Year in Marienbad), Alain Resnais
Il Posto, Ermanno Olmi
Lolita, Stanley Kubrick

1962
Cléo de 5 à 7, Agnès Varda
Noz w Wodzie (Knife in the Water), Roman Polanski
The Manchurian Candidate, John Frankenheimer
Thérèse Desqueyroux, Georges Franju
Ride the High Country, Sam Peckinpah
The Man Who Shot Liberty Valance, John Ford

1963
The Nutty Professor, Jerry Lewis
This Sporting Life, Lindsay Anderson
The Servant, Joseph Losey
Le Feu Follet, Louis Malle
Yukinojo Henge (An Actor's Revenge), Kon Ichikawa
Le Mépris, Jean-Luc Godard
The Birds, Alfred Hitchcock
Judex, Georges Franju
8½, Federico Fellini

1964
Vidas Secas, Nelson Pereira dos Santos
Marnie, Alfred Hitchcock
Charulata, Satyajit Ray
Les Parapluies de Cherbourg, Jacques Demy
Wutai Jiemei (Two Stage Sisters), Xie Jin

1965
Szegenylegenyek (The Round-up), Mikós Jancsó
Repulsion, Roman Polanski
Pierrot le Fou, Jean-Luc Godard
Pugni in Tasca (Fists in the Pocket), Marco Bellocchio

1966
Le Deuxième Souffle, Jean-Pierre Melville
Mouchette, Robert Bresson
Andrei Roublev, Andrei Tarkovsky

1967
Le Samouraï/Frank Costello Faccia d'Angelo, Jean-Pierre Melville
Hori, Ma Panenko (The Fireman's Ball), Milos Forman
The St Valentine's Day Massacre, Roger Corman
Bonnie and Clyde, Arthur Penn
Belle de Jour, Luis Buñuel

1968
If..., Lindsay Anderson
Night of the Living Dead, George A. Romero
2001: A Space Odyssey (70mm), Stanley Kubrick
La Hora de los Hornos (Hour of the Furnaces), O. Getino, F. Solanos
C'Era una Volta il West (Once Upon a Time in the West), Sergio Leone
Memorias del Subdessarrollo (Memoirs of Underdevelopment), Tomás Gutiérrez Alea
The Wild Bunch, Sam Peckinpah

1969
Hsia Nu (A Touch of Zen), Hu Jinquan (King Hu)
Mash, Robert Altman

1970
XI, Nu, Ai, Le (Four Moods), Bei Jingrui, Hu Jinguan
Strategia del Ragno, Bernardo Bertolucci
Le Boucher, Claude Chabrol
Il Conformista, Bernardo Bertolucci
Performance, Nicolas Roeg, Donald Cammell

1971
Blanche, Walerian Borowczyk
Play Misty for Me, Clint Eastwood

1972
Ai Nu (Intimate Confessions of a Chinese Courtesan), Chu Yuan
Viskningar Och Rop (Cries and Whispers), Ingmar Bergman
Tout Va Bien, Jean-Luc Godard, Jean-Pierre Gorin
The Godfather, Francis Ford Coppola

1973
Mean Streets, Martin Scorsese
Angst essen Seele auf (Fear Eats the Soul), Rainer Werner Fassbinder
El Espiritu de la Colmena (Spirit of the Beehive), Victor Erice
La Nuit Americaine, François Truffaut

1974
Chinatown, Roman Polanski
Alice in den Städten (Alice in the Cities), Wim Wenders
The Godfather, Part II, Francis Ford Coppola

1975
Maynila Sa Mga Kuko Ng Liwanag (Manila: in the Claws of Neon), Lino Brocka
O Thiassos (The Travelling Players), Theo Angelopoulos

1976
Ai No Corrida (In the Realm of the Senses), Nagisa Oshima
The Shootist, Don Siegel
Assault on Precinct 13, John Carpenter
Taxi Driver, Martin Scorsese
Cadaveri Eccellenti (Illustrious Corpses), Francesco Rosi
Voskhozhdenie (The Ascent), Larissa Shepitko

1977
Close Encounters of the Third Kind – Special Edition,

(Continued)

Steven Spielberg
Annie Hall, Woody Allen

1978
Prae Kow (The Scar), Cherd Songsri
L'Albero degli Zoccoli (The Tree of the Wooden Clogs), Ermanno Olmi

1979
Apocalypse Now, Francis Ford Coppola
Sürü (The Herd), Zeki Okten

U.S. National Film Registry

In accordance with the National Film Preservation Act passed by Congress in 1988, 25 films deemed "culturally, historically, or aesthetically significant" are selected each year.

Films Chosen in 1989

The Best Years of Our Lives (1946)
Casablanca (1942)
Citizen Kane (1941)
The Crowd (1928)
Dr Strangelove (or, How I Learned to Stop Worrying and Love the bomb) (1964)
The General (1927)
Gone With the Wind (1939)
The Grapes of Wrath (1940)
High Noon (1952)
Intolerance (1916)
The Learning Tree (1969)
The Maltese Falcon (1941)
Mr Smith Goes to Washington (1939)
Modern Times (1936)
Nanook of the North (1921)
On the Waterfront (1954)
The Searchers (1956)
Singin' in the Rain (1952)
Snow White and the Seven Dwarfs (1937)
Some Like It Hot (1959)
Star Wars (1977)
Sunrise (1927)
Sunset Boulevard (1950)
Vertigo (1958)
The Wizard of Oz (1939)

Films Chosen in 1990

All About Eve (1950)
All Quiet on the Western Front (1930)
Bringing Up Baby (1938)
Dodsworth (1936)
Duck Soup (1933)
Fantasia (1940)
The Freshman (1925)
The Godfather (1972)
The Great Train Robbery (1903)
Harlan County, U.S.A. (1976)
How Green Was My Valley (1941)
It's a Wonderful Life (1946)
Killer of Sheep (1977)
Love Me Tonight (1932)
Meshes of the Afternoon (1943)
Ninotchka (1939)
Primary (1960)
Raging Bull (1980)
Rebel Without a Cause (1955)
Red River (1948)
The River (1937)
Sullivan's Travels (1941)
Top Hat (1935)
The Treasure of the Sierra Madre (1948)
A Woman Under the Influence (1974)

Films Chosen in 1991

The Battle of San Pietro (1945)
The Blood of Jesus (1941)
Chinatown (1974)
City Lights (1931)
David Holzman's Diary (1968)
Frankenstein (1931)
Gertie the Dinosaur (1914)
Gigi (1958)
Greed (1924)
High School (1968)
I Am a Fugitive From a Chain Gang (1932)
The Italian (1915)
King Kong (1933)
Lawrence of Arabia (1962)
The Magnificent Ambersons (1942)
My Darling Clementine (1946)
Out of the Past (1947)
A Place in the Sun (1951)
The Poor Little Rich Girl (1917)
The Prisoner of Zenda (1937)
Shadow of a Doubt (1943)
Sherlock, Jr. (1924)
Tevya (1939)
Trouble in Paradise (1932)
2001: A Space Odyssey (1968)

Films Chosen in 1992

Adam's Rib (1949)
Annie Hall (1977)
The Bank Dick (1940)
Big Business (1929)
The Big Parade (1925)
The Birth of a Nation (1915)
Bonnie and Clyde (1967)
Carmen Jones (1954)
Castro Street (1966)
Detour (1946)
Dog Star Man (1964)
Double Indemnity (1944)
Footlight Parade (1933)
The Gold Rush (1925)
Letter from an Unknown Woman (1948)
Morocco (1930)
Nashville (1975)
The Night of the Hunter (1955)
Paths of Glory (1957)
Psycho (1960)
Ride the High Country (1962)
Salesman (1969)
Salt of the Earth (1954)
What's Opera, Doc? (1957)
Within Our Gates (1920)

West End Openings: Jan.–July 1993

Source: Society of West End Theatre

Plays

Title	Theatre	Opened
The Game of Love and Chance	Cottesloe	12/1/93
King Baby	The Pit	19/1/93
King Lear	Royal Court	21/1/93
The Day After Tomorrow	Cottesloe	4/2/93
No Man's Land	Comedy	8/2/93
Trelawny of the Wells	Olivier	18/2/93
Playland	Donmar	2/3/93

(Continued)

The Deep Blue Sea	Apollo	18/3/93
The Gift of the Gorgon	Wyndham's	23/3/93
Fires in the Mirror	Royal Court	24/3/93
Macbeth	Olivier	1/4/93
The School of Night	The Pit	16/4/93
The Beggar's Opera	Barbican	7/4/93
Arcadia	Lyttleton	13/4/93
The Treatment	Royal Court	20/4/93
A Jovial Crew	Barbican	22/4/93
Don't Fool with Love/The Blind Men	Donmar	22/4/93
Somewhere	Cottesloe	24/4/93
The Neighbour	Cottesloe	24/4/93
On the Ledge	Lyttleton	27/4/93
Hove	Cottesloe	28/4/93
The Last Yankee	Duke of York's	5/5/93
He Who Saw Everything	Cottesloe	12/5/93
Juno and the Paycock	Albery	19/5/93
The Changeling	The Pit	25/5/93
Antony and Cleopatra	Barbican	26/5/93
The Taming of the Shrew	Open Air	1/6/93
Translations	Donmar	9/6/93
Lysistrata	Old Vic	14/6/93
The Desire Paths	Royal Court	15/6/93
Romeo and Juliet	Open Air	16/6/93
Inadmissible Evidence	Lyttleton	17/6/93
The Odyssey	The Pit	22/6/93
The Winter's Tale	Barbican	23/6/93
Separate Tables	Albery	28/6/93
Oleanna	Royal Court	30/6/93
The Mountain Giants	Cottesloe	14/7/93
The Taming of the Shrew	Barbican	20/7/93
Misha's Party	The Pit	21/7/93

Thrillers

Title	Theatre	Opened
The Invisible Man	Vaudeville	16/2/93
Murder Is Easy	Duke of York's	23/2/93

Musicals

Title	Theatre	Opened
Robin, Prince of Sherwood	Piccadilly	3/2/93
Crazy for You	Prince Edward	3/2/93
City of Angels	Prince of Wales	30/3/93
Sweeney Todd	Cottesloe	2/6/93
Leonardo, a Portrait of Love	Strand	3/6/93
Sunset Boulevard	Adelphi	29/6/93
Grease	Dominion	15/7/93
Lust	Haymarket	19/7/93
A Connecticut Yankee	Open Air	28/7/93

Comedies

Title	Theatre	Opened
On the Piste	Garrick	24/2/93
The Importance of Being Earnest	Aldwych	9/3/93
As You Like It	Barbican	21/4/93
The California Dream Men	Piccadilly	11/5/93
Present Laughter	Globe	23/6/93
Much Ado About Nothing	Queen's	6/7/73

Opera

Title	Venue	Opened
Carmen	Coliseum	13/1/93
Stiffelio	ROH	25/1/93
Rigoletto	Coliseum	4/2/93
Il Barbiere di Siviglia	ROH	8/2/93
Don Pasquale	Coliseum	19/2/93
Turandot	ROH	20/2/93
Cosi Fan Tutte	Sadler's Wells	22/2/93
Falstaff	Sadler's Wells	23/2/93
Le Damnation de Faust	ROH	8/3/93
The Duel of Tancredi and Clorinda/ Bluebeard's Castle	Coliseum	17/3/93
Pelleas and Melisande	ROH	24/3/93
Fidelio	ROH	30/3/93
The Queen of Spades	Coliseum	3/4/93
Jenufa	ROH	20/4/93
Ariodante	Coliseum	28/4/93
Baby Doll	Cottesloe	6/5/93
The Barber of Seville	Coliseum	8/5/93
Otello	ROH	10/5/93
Macbeth	Coliseum	20/5/93
La Bohème	ROH	24/5/93
Inquest of Love	Coliseum	5/6/93
The Magic Flute	Coliseum	14/6/93
Attila	ROH	14/6/93
Tosca	ROH	16/6/93
The Cunning Little Vixen	ROH	24/6/93
Don Giovanni	ROH	6/7/93
Eugene Onegin	ROH	13/7/93

Operetta

Title	Venue	Opened
The Mikado	Coliseum	4/3/93
Orpheus in the Underworld	Sadler's Wells	19/4/93
The Pirates of Penzance	Sadler's Wells	22/4/93

Ballet/Dance

Title	Venue	Opened
The Dream/Tales of Beatrix Potter	ROH	2/1/93
Cinderella	ROH	4/1/93
Apollo/The Judas Tree/Symphony in C	ROH	12/1/93
Alice	Sadler's Wells	12/1/93
The Sleeping Beauty	ROH	30/1/93
Paramour/Twilight/Don Quixote Pas de Deux/Facade/The Green Table	Sadler's Wells	2/2/93
Hobson's Choice	Sadler's Wells	5/2/93
The Snow Queen	Sadler's Wells	9/2/93
The Firebird/Tombeaux/In the Middle/Somewhat Elevated	ROH	11/2/93
Forget Me Not	Sadler's Wells	2/3/93
Antic	Sadler's Wells	15/3/93
Mr C/Sissi	Sadler's Wells	25/3/93
Opera/The Miraculous Mandarin	Sadler's Wells	29/3/93
Don Quixote	ROH	7/4/93
Ballet Imperial/Gloria/Still Life at the Penguin Café	ROH	30/4/93
Swan Lake	ROH	13/5/93
In Ballo/Passomezzo/Stamping Ground/Jardi Tancat	Sadler's Wells	18/5/93
Shorthand/Passomezzo/Stoolgame/ Step Lightly	Sadler's Wells	19/5/93
Prodigal Son/La Ronde/Checkmate	ROH	4/6/93
Emanuelle Enchanted	Royal Court	7/6/93
Echoes of Harlem	Royal Court	10/6/93
Tango para Dos	Sadler's Wells	22/6/93
Romeo and Juliet	Coliseum	29/6/93
Swan Lake	Coliseum	2/7/93
La Bayadère	Coliseum	15/7/93
Le Corsaire	Coliseum	19/7/93
Raymonda (Act III)/Seven Silences of Salome/The Savoy Suite	Savoy	20/7/93
Les Sylphides/Sphinx/The Savoy Suite	Savoy	22/7/93
The Sleeping Beauty	Coliseum	22/7/93
The Sleeping Beauty	ROH	26/7/93
Swan Lake	RFH	27/7/93
Concerto/Job/Choreartium	ROH	28/7/93

Children's Shows

Title	Theatre	Opened
Mr A's Amazing Maze Plays	Cottesloe	4/3/93

Longest-Running West End Productions

(as at May 1993)

Source: Society of West End Theatre

Production	Years	Months
1. *The Mousetrap* (Thriller)	40	6
2. *Cats* (Musical)	12	0
3. *Starlight Express* (Musical)	9	2
4. *Les Miserables* (Musical)	7	7
5. *The Phantom of the Opera* (Musical)	6	7
6. *Blood Brothers* (Musical)	4	10
7. *The Woman in Black* (Thriller)	4	3
8. *Miss Saigon* (Musical)	3	8
9. *Buddy* (Musical)	3	7
10. *Five Guys Named Moe* (Musical)	2	5
11. *Don't Dress for Dinner* (Comedy)	2	2
12. *Joseph and the Amazing Technicolor Dreamcoat* (Musical)	1	11
13. *It Runs in the Family* (Comedy)	–	9
14. *Kiss of the Spider Woman* (Musical)	–	7
15. *An Ideal Husband* (Play)	–	6

West End Productions: 1992

Plays	60
Musicals	21
Comedies	6
Revue/Cabaret	1
Plays with Music	2
Thrillers	2
Children's Shows	3
Pantomime	0
Opera	46
Operetta	2
Ballet	36
Dance	14
Total	**193**

Arts Councils Grants 1993/4

Source: Arts Council

Grants and awards are made to hundreds of companies throughout the UK. Below are listed the top 15 recipients in the fields of dance, drama and music.

Dance

		£
1.	Royal Ballet	11,655,487
2.	English National Ballet	3,603,000
3.	Scottish Ballet	1,904,000
4.	London Contemporary Dance Theatre	942,600
5.	Rambert Dance Company	906,500
6.	Northern Ballet Theatre	879,800
7.	Adzido Dance Company	508,400
8.	Diversions Welsh Repertory Dance Company	242,000
9.	Kinetics of Social Harmony (KOSH)	169,200
10.	Dance Umbrella	145,800
11.	Kokuma	127,800
12.	Shobana Jeyasingh	126,600
13.	Siobhan Davies Dance Company	120,500
14.	Adventures in Motion Pictures	117,300
15.	Dundee Rep. Dance Company	105,000

Drama

		£
1.	Royal National Theatre	11,167,000
2.	Royal Shakespeare Theatre	8,470,000
3.	Royal Exchange Theatre, Manchester	1,322,000
4.	English Stage Company	861,000
5.	Leicester Theatre Trust	817,700
6.	Leeds Theatre Trust	787,000
7.	Birmingham Repertory Theatre	716,000
8.	Nottingham Theatre Trust	673,800
9.	Crucible Theatre Trust	672,600
10.	Liverpool Repertory Theatre	540,500
11.	Glasgow Citizens' Theatre	535,377
12.	Edinburgh Royal Lyceum Theatre Co.	534,296
13.	Theatre Royal, Plymouth	505,200
14.	Bristol Old Vic Trust	500,000
15.	Northern Stage Company	369,500

Music

		£
1.	English National Opera	11,655,000
2.	Royal Opera House	7,865,513
3.	Welsh National Opera	6,262,000
4.	Scottish Opera	4,460,000
5.	Opera North	3,815,000
6.	Royal Scottish National Orchestra	1,821,750
7.	Bournemouth Orchestras	1,484,400
8.	Royal Liverpool Philharmonic Society	1,482,800
9.	Hallé Concerts Society	1,251,000
10.	London Symphony Orchestra	1,128,500
11.	London Philharmonic Orchestra	1,128,500
12.	Birmingham Symphony Orchestra	1,149,000
13.	Scottish Chamber Orchestra	880,000
14.	Philharmonia Orchestra	711,500
15.	Northern Sinfonia Concert Society	625,800

Regional Arts Boards Grants 1993/4

Source: Arts Council

	£
Eastern Arts	4,035,100
East Midlands Arts	2,684,200
London Arts Board	10,510,100
Northern Arts	5,143,900
North West Arts	4,965,000
Southern Arts	2,838,100
South East Arts	2,635,700
South West Arts	2,863,500
West Midlands Arts	3,703,600
Yorkshire & Humberside Arts	4,4538,500
Scottish Arts Council	23,246,000
Welsh Arts Council	13,020,000

Arts Council Expenditure

United Kingdom

Source: CSO

Percentage and £ thousand

	1971 –72	1981 –82	1986 –87	1991 –92
National companies[1]	29	27	24	27
Regional Arts Associations	5	11	19	18
Art	5	6	5	4
Drama	20	18	15	13
Music	20	19	17	15
Dance	4	4	5	5
Literature	2	2	1	1
Other[2]	15	12	15	17
Total (= 100%) (£ thousand)	12,096	83,028	136,870	214,963

(1) Includes the English National Opera in London and on tour, the National Theatre (in three auditoria), the Royal Opera and the Royal Ballet Companies in London and on tour, and the Royal Shakespeare Company in Stratford-on-Avon and in London. (2) Includes arts centres and community projects (including the South Bank Board), training in the arts, incentive funding and general operating costs.

Some Notable British Opera Companies

Source: *British Music Year Book 1992*, Rhinegold Publishing, 241 Shaftesbury Ave, London WC2H 8EH

Company	Music director
Buxton International Festival Opera	Anthony Hose
City of Birmingham Touring Opera	Paul Herbert & Simon Halsey
D'Oyly Carte Opera Company	John Pryce-Jones
Early English Opera Society	David Roblou
English National Opera	Mark Elder
Glyndebourne Festival Opera	Andrew Davis
Glyndebourne Touring Opera	Ivon Bolton
Mecklenburgh Opera	Anne Manson
New Opera Company Ltd	Leon Lovett
Opera Factory	Mark Wigglesworth
Opera North	Paul Daniel
Opera Northern Ireland	Kenneth Montgomery
Royal Opera	Bernard Haitink
Scottish Opera	John Mauceri
Welsh National Opera	Carlo Rizzi

Some Notable British Dance Companies

Source: *British Music Year Book 1992*, Rhinegold Publishing, 241 Shaftesbury Ave, London WC2H 8EH

Company	Director
Birmingham Royal Ballet (formerly Sadler's Wells Royal Ballet)	Peter Wright
English National Ballet	Ivan Nagy
London City Ballet	Harold King
London Contemporary Dance Theatre	Nancy Duncan
Northern Ballet Theatre	Christopher Gable
Rambert Dance Company	Richard Alston
Royal Ballet	Anthony Dowell
Scottish Ballet	Jane Somerville

Some Notable British Orchestras

Source: *British Music Year Book 1992*, Rhinegold Publishing, 241 Shaftesbury Ave, London WC2H 8EH

Orchestra	Principal conductor/ Musical director
Academy of Ancient Music	Christopher Hogwood
Academy of St Martin in the Fields	Sir Neville Marriner
BBC Philharmonic	Jan Pascal Tortelier
BBC Scottish Symphony	Jerzy Maksymiuk
BBC Symphony	Andrew Davis
BBC Welsh Symphony	Tadaaki Otaka
Bournemouth Symphony	Andrew Litton
City of Birmingham Symphony	Simon Rattle
City of Glasgow Philharmonic	Iain Sutherland
English Chamber	Jeffrey Tate
English Philharmonia	Paul Daniel
English Philharmonic	Octav Calleya
Hallé	Kent Nugano
Henry Wood Chamber	John Landor
Liverpool Sinfonietta	Anthony Ridley
London Baroque Players	Roger Norrington
London Chamber	Christopher Warren-Green
London Festival	Ross Pople
London Orpheus	James Gaddarn
London Philharmonic	Franz Welser-Müst
London Sinfonia	Gordon Heard
London Symphony	Michael Tilson Thomas
Northern Sinfonia	Richard Hickox
Royal Liverpool Philharmonic	Libor Pesek
Royal Philharmonic	Vladimir Ashkenazy
Scottish Chamber	Jukka-Pekka Saraste
Wren Orchestra of London	Hilary Davan Wetton

UK Television Viewing

Source: CSO

	1986	1987	1988	1989	1990	1991
	Hours and minutes per week					
Social class[1]						
AB	20:47	20:54	20:14	19:48	19:31	18:51
C1	23:05	24:05	23:41	23:11	23:12	23:56
C2	25:18	24:40	25:25	25:00	24:13	26:57
DE	33:11	31:47	31:44	30:57	30:13	31:56
All persons	25:54	25:25	25:21	24:44	23:51	26:04
Reach[2]	Percentages					
Daily	78	76	77	78	77	79
Weekly	94	93	94	94	94	94

(1) See Social class categories, p. 581. (2) Percentage of UK population aged 4 and over who viewed TV for at least three consecutive minutes.

Top 20 Networked Programmes*

June 1992–May 1993

Source: Broadcasters' Audience Research Board

Programme	Transmitted	Channel	Audience (millions)
1. *Coronation Street*	Mon. 22 Mar.	ITV	20.73
2. *Only Fools and Horses*	Fri. 25 Dec.	BBC1	20.13
3. *EastEnders*	Mon. 25 Jan.	BBC1	19.96
4. *Inspector Morse*	Wed. 13 Jan.	ITV	18.77
5. *Merry Xmas Mr Bean*	Tue. 29 Dec.	ITV	18.48
6. *More Aunties Bloomers*	Sun. 27 Dec.	BBC1	18.45
7. *Neighbours*	Wed. 13 Jan.	BBC1	18.29
8. *One Foot in the Grave*	Sun. 7 Mar.	BBC1	17.99
9. *The Bill*	Fri. 26 mar.	ITV	17.73
10. *You've Been Framed*	Sun. 31 Jan.	ITV	17.67
11. *Birds of a Feather*	Fri. 25 Nov.	BBC1	16.88
12. *Touch of Frost*	Sun. 6 Nov.	ITV	16.82
13. *Casualty*	Sat. 5 Dec.	BBC1	16.64
14. *Home and Away*	Mon. 23 Nov.	ITV	16.62
15. *Heartbeat*	Sun. 16 May	BBC1	16.47
16. *This Is Your Life*	Wed. 4 Nov.	ITV	15.82
17. *Darling Buds of May*	Sun. 21 Mar.	BBC1	15.46
18. *Grand National*	Sat. 3 Apr.	BBC1	15.17
19. *Barrymore*	Sat. 20 Feb.	ITV	14.34
20. *Mr Bean in Room 426*	Wed. 17 Feb.	ITV	14.31

(Continued)

* Excluding multiple screenings.

Hiring of Pre-recorded VCR Tapes

Source: CSO

	1986	1989	1990	1991
Domestic video population[1] (millions)	9.66	13.80	14.80	15.55
Hiring of video tapes[2]				
Percentage hiring tapes during previous 7 days	30	30	26	22
Number of tapes hired per week (millions)	6.5	8.0	7.3	6.4

(1) Estimated number of households in possession of at least one video cassette recorder based on a survey of 13,000 households per quarter. (2) Figures refer to households in possession of a video cassette recorder.

UK Radio Listening

Source: CSO

	1987	1988	1989	1990	1991
	Hours and minutes per week				
Age group					
4–15 years	2:07	2:13	2:21	2:26	2:40
16–34	11:18	11:40	12:07	12:28	12:43
35–64	10:16	10:33	11:10	11:42	11:53
65 years and over	8:44	8:49	9:00	9:18	9:40
All aged 4 years and over	8:52	9:12	9:46	10:12	10:27
Reach[1]	Percentages				
Daily	43	43	44	45	47
Weekly	74	73	74	74	76

(1) Percentage of UK population aged 4 and over who listened to radio for at least half a programme a day.

National Newspapers – Daily Circulation

Source: *Willings Press Guide*, 1993

Daily Express	1,529,273
Daily Mail	1,735,737
Daily Mirror	2,803,193
Daily Sport	250,000
Daily Star	805,571
Daily Telegraph	1,038,792
Financial Times	288,495
The Guardian	411,509
The Independent	372,243
The Racing Post	45,184
The Sporting Life	69,670
The Sun	3,554,833
The Times	381,854
Today	539,284

Reading of National Newspapers: 1971 and 1991

Great Britain

Source: CSO

	Percentage of adults reading each paper in 1991			Percentage of each age group reading each paper in 1991				Readership[1] (millions)		Readers per copy (numbers)
	Males	Females	All adults	15–24	25–44	45–64	65 and over	1971	1991	1991
Daily newspapers										
The Sun	25	19	22	28	23	20	17	8.5	9.9	2.7
Daily Mirror	25	19	22	23	21	24	21	13.8	10.0	2.7
Daily Mail	10	9	10	9	9	11	10	4.8	4.3	2.5
Daily Express	8	8	8	7	6	10	10	9.7	3.6	2.4
Daily Star	8	4	6	7	7	5	3	–	2.6	3.1
Daily Telegraph	6	5	6	3	4	7	7	3.6	2.4	2.3
The Guardian	4	3	3	4	4	3	1	1.1	1.2	2.9
Today	3	2	3	3	4	2	1	–	1.4	3.0
The Times	3	1	2	3	2	3	1	1.1	1.0	2.6
The Independent	3	2	2	3	3	2	1	–	1.0	2.8
Financial Times	2	1	2	1	2	2	–	0.7	0.6	3.7
Any daily newspaper[2]	66	57	62	61	59	65	62	–	–	–
Sunday newspapers										
News of the World	31	26	28	37	30	26	21	15.8	12.8	2.7
Sunday Mirror	22	19	20	23	20	21	17	13.5	9.1	3.2
The People	16	14	15	13	13	17	15	14.4	6.5	2.9
Sunday Express	13	12	13	14	13	13	9	10.4	5.6	2.9
Mail on Sunday	10	10	10	8	8	12	13	–	4.5	2.8
The Sunday Times	9	7	8	9	9	9	4	3.7	3.5	3.1
Sunday Telegraph	4	3	4	3	3	5	4	2.1	1.7	3.0
The Observer	4	4	4	4	5	4	3	2.4	1.8	3.3
Independent on Sunday	4	2	3	4	4	2	1	–	0.2	3.5
Any Sunday newspaper[3]	73	69	71	72	70	74	68	–	–	–

(1) Defined as the average issue readership and represents the number of people who claim to have read or looked at one or more copies of a given publication during a period equal to the interval at which the publication appears. (2) Includes the above newspapers plus the *Daily Record*. (3) Includes the above newspapers plus the *Sunday Post*, *Sunday Mail*, *Scotland on Sunday* and *Sunday Sport*.

Most Popular Magazines: 1971 and 1991

Great Britain

Source: CSO

	Percentage of adults reading each magazine in 1991			Percentage of each age group reading each magazine in 1991				Readership[1] (millions)		Readers per copy (numbers)
	Males	Females	All adults	15–24	25–44	45–64	65 and over	1971	1991	1991
General magazines										
Radio Times	14	14	14	17	14	17	12	9.5	6.3	–
TV Times	14	14	14	19	14	16	12	9.9	6.3	–
Reader's Digest	14	12	13	8	12	18	14	9.2	5.8	3.9
What Car	7	2	4	8	6	5	1	–	2.0	14.3
National Geographic	5	3	4	4	4	4	2	–	1.7	–
Exchange and Mart	6	2	4	5	5	5	1	–	1.6	10.8
Women's magazines[2]										
Woman's Own	3	16	10	11	11	11	8	7.2	4.4	4.8
Bella	4	15	10	12	11	12	7	–	4.4	–
Women's Weekly	2	11	6	3	4	7	11	4.7	2.8	2.7
Woman	2	12	7	7	9	8	5	8.0	3.1	3.5
Best	2	10	6	9	8	7	3	–	2.8	3.6
Prima	2	10	6	7	8	8	2	–	2.5	3.2

(1) Defined as the average issue readership and represents the number of people who claim to have read, or looked at, one or more copies of a given publication during a period equal to the interval at which the publication appears. (2) The age analysis for women's magazines includes male readers.

British Bestsellers: Jan.–Dec. 1992

Source: Bookwatch, based on appearances in the *Sunday Times* bestseller lists and sales statistics from a panel of UK bookshops

Hardback General

1. *Diana: Her True Story*, Andrew Morton (O'Mara)
2. *Sex*, Madonna (Secker & Warburg)
3. *Pole to Pole*, Michael Palin (BBC)
4. *The Guinness Book of Records*, ed. Peter Matthews (Guinness)
5. *Mr Bean's Diary*, Rowan Atkinson & Robin Driscoll (Boxtree)
6. *A Brief History of Time*, Stephen Hawking (Bantam Press)
7. *One Hundred Days*, Sandy Woodward (HarperCollins)
8. *Michelin Red Guide: France 1992* (Michelin)
9. *Storm Command*, Peter de la Billière (HarperCollins)
10. *Wild Swans*, Jung Chang (HarperCollins)

Hardback Fiction

1. *The Queen and I*, Sue Townsend (Methuen)
2. *Mostly Harmless*, Douglas Adams (Heinemann)
3. *Driving Force*, Dick Francis (Michael Joseph)
4. *Fatherland*, Robert Harris (Hutchinson)
5. *The Silence of the Lambs & Red Dragon*, Thomas Harris (Peerage/Bounty Books)
6. *Gerald's Game*, Stephen King (Hodder)
7. *A Dubious Legacy*, Mary Wesley (Bantam Press)
8. *Small Gods*, Terry Pratchett (Gollancz)
9. *The Way Through the Woods*, Colin Dexter (Macmillan)
10. *The House of Women*, Catherine Cookson (Bantam Press)

Paperback General

1. *A Year in Provence*, Peter Mayle (Pan)
2. *Diana: Her True Story*, Andrew Morton (O'Mara)
3. *Toujours Provence*, Peter Mayle (Pan)
4. *Seasons of My Life*, Hannah Hauxwell (Arrow)
5. *The Tree and Shrub Expert*, Dr David Hessayon (pbi)
6. *Proms 1992* (BBC)
7. *The Flower Expert*, Dr David Hessayon (pbi)
8. *Gardens of England and Wales Open to the Public 1992* (National Gardens Scheme)
9. *Complete Hip and Thigh Diet*, Rosemary Conley (Arrow)
10. *Complete Cookery Course*, Delia Smith (BBC)

Paperback Fiction

1. *Polo*, Jilly Cooper (Corgi)
2. *As the Crow Flies*, Jeffrey Archer (Coronet)
3. *The Liar*, Stephen Fry (Mandarin)
4. *My Beloved Son*, Catherine Cookson (Corgi)
5. *The Rag Nymph*, Catherine Cookson (Corgi)
6. *Remember*, Barbara Taylor Bradford (Grafton)
7. *The Rector's Wife*, Joanna Trollope (Black Swan)
8. *Elephant Song*, Wilbur Smith (Pan)
9. *Needful Things*, Stephen King (NEL)
10. *Heartbeat*, Danielle Steel (Corgi)

Children's Bestsellers of 1992

1. *Matilda*, Roald Dahl (Puffin)
2. *Fudge-a-Mania*, Judy Blume (Piper)
3. *Very Hungry Caterpillar*, Eric Carle (Picture Puffin)
4. *Esio Trot*, Roald Dahl (Puffin)
5. *Animals of Farthing Wood*, Colin Dann (Mammoth)
6. *Incredible Cross-Sections*, Stephen Biesty (Dorling Kindersley)
7. *The Minpins*, Roald Dahl (Cape)
8. *Where's Spot?*, Eric Hill (Picture Puffin)
9. *The Baby's Catalogue*, Janet & Allan Ahlberg (Picture Puffin)
10. *The Carpet People*, Terry Pratchett (Doubleday)

Public Lending Right

Instituted in 1982, PLR is a government-funded scheme which pays authors a fee for every occasion their books are borrowed. The figures are based on a sample of 30 public libraries, then multiplied by the total number of libraries to arrive at a total *estimated* figure. For the year July 1991 to June 1992 the money available for distribution was £3,945,000; the Rate per Loan was 1.86 pence, and 97 authors received the £6,000 maximum.

Most Borrowed Modern Authors

The following authors, listed alphabetically, each achieved over 1 million loans during the period July 1991 to June 1992. Also listed are some of their most popular titles for that year.

Allan & Janet Ahlberg (C) – *Funny Bones; Starting School*
Virginia Andrews – *Dawn; Gates of Paradise; Fallen Hearts; Web of Dreams*
Enid Blyton (C) – Numerous titles
Agatha Christie – Numerous titles
Catherine Cookson – *Bill Bailey; The Black Candle; The Cultured Handmaiden; A Dinner of Herbs; The Gillyvors; Goodbye Hamilton; Harrogate Secret; The Moth; My Beloved Son*
Roald Dahl (C) – *The BFG; Charlie and the Chocolate Factory; Danny, the Champion of the World; The Enormous Crocodile; George's Marvellous Medicine; The Magic Finger; Matilda; Revolting Rhymes; The Twits; The Witches*
Len Deighton – *Hook; Mamista; Spy Line; Spy Sinker*
Elizabeth Ferrars – Numerous titles
Dick Francis – *Bolt; Break In; Comeback; The Danger; The Edge; Hot Money; Longshot; Straight*
René Goscinny (C) – Numerous *Asterix* titles

(Continued)

Jack Higgins – *Cold Harbour; The Eagle Has Flown; Memoirs of a Dance Hall Romeo; Night of the Fox; A Season in Hell*
Victoria Holt – *The Captive; The Road to Paradise Island; The Silk Vendetta; Snare of Serpents*
Lena Kennedy – *The Dandelion Seed; Down Our Street; Eve's Apples; The Inn on the Marsh; Owen Oliver*
Stephen King – *The Dark Half*
Ed McBain – Numerous titles
Ellis Peters – Numerous titles
Ruth Rendell – *The Copper Peacock and Other Stories; The Bridesmaid*
Wilbur Smith – *Elephant Song; Golden Fox; A Time to Die*
Danielle Steel – *Daddy; Fine Things; Full Circle; Heartbeat; Kaleidoscope; Message from Nam; Star*; Wanderlust; *Zoya*

(C) = Children's author

Most Borrowed Classic Authors

200,000 to 500,000 loans	100,000+ loans
Jane Austen	Charlotte Brontë
Charles Dickens	Sir Arthur Conan Doyle
Thomas Hardy	George Eliot
D. H. Lawrence	C. S. Forrester
A. A. Milne	E. M. Forster
J. R. R. Tolkien	Rudyard Kipling
Anthony Trollope	Somerset Maugham
	E. Nesbit
	George Orwell
	Virginia Woolf

Best-selling Records: July 1992–June 1993

Source: CIN Ltd.

Top 10 Singles

1. "I Will Always Love You", Whitney Houston
2. "Rhythm Is a Dancer", Snap
3. "Would I Lie to You", Charles & Eddie
4. "All That She Wants", Ace of Base
5. "No Limit", 2 Unlimited
6. "(I Can't Help) Falling in Love with You", UB40
7. "Oh Carolina", Shaggy
8. "End of the Road", Boyz II Men
9. "Heal the World", Michael Jackson
10. "Ain't No Doubt", Jimmy Nail

Top 10 Pop Albums

1. *The Bodyguard*, Original soundtrack
2. *Automatic for the People*, R.E.M.
3. *Now That's What I Call Music 23*, Various
4. *Cher's Greatest Hits: 1965–92*, Cher
5. *Glittering Prize 81/92*, Simple Minds
6. *Timeless (The Classics)*, Michael Bolton
7. *Back to Front*, Lionel Richie
8. *Gold – Greatest Hits*, Abba
9. *Pop! The First 20 Hits*, Erasure
10. *Stars*, Simply Red

Top 10 Classical Albums

1. *Gorecki Symphony No. 3*, David Zinman/LSO/Upshaw
2. *Beethoven's Violin Concerto*, Nigel Kennedy/Klaus Tennstedt
3. *Essential Opera*, Various
4. *The Best of the Classical Bits*, Various
5. *Vivaldi's Four Seasons*, Nigel Kennedy/ECO
6. *Essential Ballet*, Various
7. *The Ultimate Opera Collection*, Various
8. *Classic Commercials*, Various
9. *The Essential Mozart*, Various
10. *Pavarotti in Hyde Park*, Luciano Pavarotti

AWARDS – MEDALS – PRIZES

Nobel Prize Winners

Alfred B. Nobel (1833–1896), inventor of dynamite, bequeathed $9,000,000, the interest to be distributed yearly to those who had most benefited mankind in physics, chemistry, medicine-physiology, literature and peace. Prizes in these five areas were first awarded in 1901. The first Nobel Memorial Prize in Economic Science was awarded in 1969, funded by the central bank of Sweden. No awards given for years omitted. In 1992 each prize was worth approximately £550,000. (For 1993 awards, see Stop Press.)

Physics

1992 Georges Charpak, French
1991 Pierre-Giles de Gennes, French
1990 Richard E. Taylor, Can.; Jerome I. Friedman, Henry W. Kendall, both U.S.
1989 Norman F. Ramsey, U.S.; Hans G. Dehmelt, German-U.S. & Wolfgang Paul, German
1988 Leon M. Lederman, Melvin Schwartz, Jack Steinberger, all U.S.
1987 K. Alex Muller, Swiss; J. Georg Bednorz, W. German
1986 Ernest Ruska, German; Gerd Binnig, W. German; Heinrich Rohrer, Swiss
1985 Klaus von Klitzing, W. German
1984 Carlo Rubbia, Italian; Simon van der Meere, Dutch
1983 Subrahmanyan Chandrasekhar, William A. Fowler, both U.S.
1982 Kenneth G. Wilson, U.S.
1981 Nicolass Bloembergen, Arthur Schaalow, both U.S.; Kai M. Siegbahn, Swedish
1980 James W. Cronin, Val L. Fitch, U.S.
1979 Steven Weinberg, Sheldon L. Glashow, both U.S.; Abdus Salam, Pakistani
1978 Pyotr Kapitsa, USSR; Arno Penzias, Robert Wilson, both U.S.
1977 John H. Van Vleck, Philip W. Anderson, both U.S.; Nevill F. Mott, British
1976 Burton Richter, U.S.
Samuel C.C. Ting, U.S.
1975 James Rainwater, U.S.;
Ben Mottelson, U.S.-Danish; Aage Bohr, Danish
1974 Martin Ryle, British
Antony Hewish, British
1973 Ivar Giaever, U.S.
Leo Esaki, Japan
Brian D. Josephson, British
1972 John Bardeen, U.S.
Leon N. Cooper, U.S.
John R. Schrieffer, U.S.
1971 Dennis Gabor, British
1970 Louis Neel, French
Hannes Alfven, Swedish
1969 Murray Gell-Mann, U.S.
1968 Luis W. Alvarez, U.S.
1967 Hans A. Bethe, U.S.
1966 Alfred Kastler, French
1965 Richard P. Feynman, U.S.
Julian S. Schwinger, U.S.
Shinichiro Tomonaga, Japanese
1964 Nikolai G. Basov, USSR
Aleksander M. Prochorov, USSR
Charles H. Townes, U.S.
1963 Maria Goeppert-Mayer, U.S.
J. Hans D. Jensen, German
Eugene P. Wigner, U.S.
1962 Lev. D. Landau, USSR
1961 Robert Hofstadter, U.S.
Rudolf L. Mossbauer, German
1960 Donald A. Glaser, U.S.
1959 Owen Chamberlain, U.S.
Emilio G. Segre, U.S.
1958 Pavel Cherenkov, Ilya Frank, Igor Y. Tamm, all USSR
1957 Tsung-dao Lee, Chen Ning Yang, both U.S.
1956 John Bardeen, U.S.
Walter H. Brattain, U.S.
William Shockley, U.S.
1955 Polykarp Kusch, U.S.
Willis E. Lamb, U.S.
1954 Max Born, British
Walter Bothe, German
1953 Frits Zernike, Dutch
1952 Felix Bloch, U.S.
Edward M. Purcell, U.S.
1951 Sir John D. Cockroft, British
Ernest T. S. Walton, Irish
1950 Cecil F. Powell, British
1949 Hideki Yukawa, Japanese
1948 Patrick M. S. Blackett, British
1947 Sir Edward V. Appleton, British
1946 Percy Williams Bridgman, U.S.
1945 Wolfgang Pauli, U.S.
1944 Isidor Isaac Rabi, U.S.
1943 Otto Stern, U.S.
1939 Ernest O. Lawrence, U.S.
1938 Enrico Fermi, U.S.
1937 Clinton J. Davisson, U.S.
Sir George P. Thomson, British
1936 Carl D. Anderson, U.S.
Victor F. Hess, Austrian
1935 Sir James Chadwick, British
1933 Paul A. M. Dirac, British
Erwin Schrödinger, Austrian
1932 Werner Heisenberg, German
1930 Sir Chandrasekhara V. Raman, Indian
1929 Prince Louis-Victor de Broglie, French
1928 Owen W. Richardson, British
1927 Arthur H. Compton, U.S.
Charles T. R. Wilson, British
1926 Jean B. Perrin, French
1925 James Franck, Gustav Hertz, both German
1924 Karl M. G. Siegbahn, Swedish
1923 Robert A. Millikan, U.S.
1922 Niels Bohr, Danish
1921 Albert Einstein, Ger.-U.S.
1920 Charles E. Guillaume, French
1919 Johannes Stark, German
1918 Max K. E. L. Planck, German
1917 Charles G. Barkla, British
1915 Sir William H. Bragg, British
Sir William L. Bragg, British
1914 Max von Laue, German
1913 Heike Kamerlingh-Onnes, Dutch
1912 Nils G. Dalen, Swedish
1911 Wilhelm Wien, German
1910 Johannes D. van der Waals, Dutch
1909 Carl F. Braun, German
Guglielmo Marconi, Italian
1908 Gabriel Lippmann, French
1907 Albert A. Michelson, U.S.
1906 Sir Joseph J. Thomson, British
1905 Philipp E. A. von Lenard, German
1904 John W. Strutt, Lord Rayleigh, British
1903 Antoine Henri Becquerel, French
Marie Curie, Polish-French
Pierre Curie, French
1902 Hendrik A. Lorentz, Pieter Zeeman, both Dutch
1901 Wilhelm C. Roentgen, German

Chemistry

1992 Rudolph Marcus, Can.-U.S.
1991 Richard R. Ernst, Swiss
1990 Elias James Corey, U.S.
1989 Thomas R. Cech, Sidney Altman, both U.S.
1988 Johann Deisenhofer, Robert Huber, Hartmut Michel, all W. German
1987 Donald J. Cram, Charles J. Pederson, both U.S.; Jean-Marie Lehn, French
1986 Dudley Herschbach, Yuan T. Lee, both U.S.; John C. Polanyi, Canadian
1985 Herbert A. Hauptman, Jerome Karle, both U.S.
1984 Bruce Merrifield, U.S.
1983 Henry Taube, Canadian
1982 Aaron Klug, S. African
1981 Kenichi Fukui, Japan; Roald Hoffmann, U.S.
1980 Paul Berg., U.S.; Walter Gilbert, U.S.; Frederick Sanger, U.K.
1979 Herbert C. Brown, U.S.
George Wittig, German
1978 Peter Mitchell, British
1977 Ilya Prigogine, Belgian
1976 William N. Lipscomb, U.S.
1975 John Cornforth, Austral.-Brit., Vladimir Prelog, Yugo.-Swiss.
1974 Paul J. Flory, U.S.
1973 Ernst Otto Fischer, W. German
Geoffrey Wilkinson, British
1972 Christian B. Anfinsen, U.S.
Stanford Moore, U.S.
William H. Stein, U.S.
1971 Gerhard Herzberg, Canadian
1970 Luis F. Leloir, Arg.
1969 Derek H. R. Barton, British
Odd Hassel, Norwegian
1968 Lars Onsager, U.S.
1967 Manfred Eigen, German
Ronald G. W. Norrish, British
George Porter, British
1966 Robert S. Mulliken, U.S.
1965 Robert B. Woodward, U.S.
1964 Dorothy C. Hodgkin, British
1963 Giulio Natta, Italian
Karl Ziegler, German
1962 John C. Kendrew, British
Max F. Perutz, British
1961 Melvin Calvin, U.S.
1960 Willard F. Libby, U.S.
1959 Jaroslav Heyrovsky, Czech
1958 Frederick Sanger, British
1957 Sir Alexander R. Todd, British
1956 Sir Cyril N. Hinshelwood, British
Nikolai N. Semenov, USSR
1955 Vincent du Vigneaud, U.S.
1954 Linus C. Pauling, U.S.
1953 Hermann Staudinger, German
1952 Archer J. P. Martin, British
Richard L. M. Synge, British
1951 Edwin M. McMillan, U.S.
Glenn T. Seaborg, U.S.
1950 Kurt Alder, German
Otto P. H. Diels, German
1949 William F. Giauque, U.S.
1948 Arne W. K. Tiselius, Swedish
1947 Sir Robert Robinson, British
1946 James B. Sumner, John H. Northrop, Wendell M. Stanley, U.S.
1945 Artturi I. Virtanen, Finnish
1944 Otto Hahn, German
1943 Georg de Hevesy, Hungarian
1939 Adolf F. J. Butenandt, German
Leopold Ruzicka, Swiss
1938 Richard Kuhn, German
1937 Walter N. Haworth, British
Paul Karrer, Swiss
1936 Peter J. W. Debye, Dutch
1935 Frederic Joliot-Curie, French
Irene Joliot-Curie, French
1934 Harold C. Urey, U.S.
1932 Irving Langmuir, U.S.
1931 Friedrich Bergius, German
Karl Bosch, German
1930 Hans Fischer, German
1929 Sir Arthur Harden, British
Hans von Euler-Chelpin, Swedish
1928 Adolf O. R. Windaus, German
1927 Heinrich O. Wieland, German
1926 Theodor Svedberg, Swedish

1925 Richard A. Zsigmondy, German
1923 Fritz Pregl, Austrian
1922 Francis W. Aston, British
1921 Frederick Soddy, British
1920 Walther H. Nernst, German
1918 Fritz Haber, German
1915 Richard M. Willstatter, German
1914 Theodore W. Richards, U.S.
1913 Alfred Werner, Swiss
1912 Victor Grignard, French
Paul Sabatier, French
1911 Marie Curie, Polish-French
1910 Otto Wallach, German
1909 Wilhelm Ostwald, German
1908 Ernest Rutherford, British
1907 Eduard Buchner, German
1906 Henri Moissan, French
1905 Adolf von Baeyer, German
1904 Sir William Ramsay, British
1903 Svante A. Arrhenius, Swedish
1902 Emil Fischer, German
1901 Jacobus H. van't Hoff, Dutch

Physiology or Medicine

1992 Edwin Krebs, Edmond Fischer, both U.S.
1991 Edwin Neher, Bert Sakmann, both German
1990 Joseph E. Murray, E. Donnall Thomas, both U.S.
1989 J. Michael Bishop, Harold E. Varmus, both U.S.
1988 Gertrude B. Elion, George H. Hitchings, both U.S; Sir James Black, British
1987 Susumu Tonegawa, Japanese
1986 Rita Levi-Montalcini, It.-U.S., Stanley Cohen, U.S.
1985 Michael S. Brown, Joseph L. Goldstein, both U.S.
1984 Cesar Milstein, Brit.-Argentinian; Georges J. F. Koehler, German; Niels K. Jerne, Brit.-Danish
1983 Barbara McClintock, U.S.
1982 Sune Bergstrom, Bengt Samuelsson, both Swedish; John R. Vane, British
1981 Roger W. Sperry, David H. Hubel, Tosten N. Wiesel, all U.S.
1980 Baruj Benacerraf, George Snell, both U.S.; Jean Dausset, France
1979 Alian M. Cormack, U.S.
Geoffrey N. Hounsfield, British
1978 Daniel Nathans, Hamilton O. Smith, both U.S.; Werner Arber, Swiss
1977 Rosalyn S. Yalow, Roger C.L. Guillemin, Andrew V. Schally, U.S.
1976 Baruch S. Blumberg, U.S.
Daniel Carleton Gajdusek, U.S.
1975 David Baltimore, Howard Temin, both U.S.; Renato Dulbecco, Ital.-U.S.
1974 Albert Claude, Lux.-U.S.; George Emil Palade, Rom.-U.S.; Christian René de Duve, Belg.
1973 Karl von Frisch, Ger.; Konrad Lorenz, Ger.-Austrian; Nikolaas Tinbergen, Brit.
1972 Gerald M. Edelman, U.S.
Rodney R. Porter, British
1971 Earl W. Sutherland Jr., U.S.
1970 Julius Axelrod, U.S.
Sir Bernard Katz, British
Ulf von Euler, Swedish
1969 Max Delbruck, Alfred D. Hershey, Salvador Luria, all U.S.
1968 Robert W. Holley, H. Gobind Khorana, Marshall W. Nirenberg, all U.S.
1967 Ragnar Granit, Swedish; Haldan Keffer Hartline, U.S.; George Wald, U.S.
1966 Charles B. Huggins, Francis Peyton Rous, both U.S.
1965 Francois Jacob, Andre Lwoff, Jacques Monod, all French
1964 Konrad E. Bloch, U.S.
Feodor Lynen, German
1963 Sir John C. Eccles, Australian
Alan L. Hodgkin, British
Andrew F. Huxley, British
1962 Francis H. C. Crick, British
James D. Watson, U.S.
Maurice H. F. Wilkins, British
1961 Georg von Bekesy, U.S.
1960 Sir F. MacFarlane Bumet, Australian
Peter B. Medawar, British
1959 Arthur Kornberg, U.S.
Severo Ochoa, U.S.
1958 George W. Beadle, U.S.
Edward L. Tatum, U.S.
Joshua Lederberg, U.S.
1957 Daniel Bovet, Italian
1956 Andre F. Cournand, U.S.
Werner Forssmann, German
Dickinson W. Richards Jr., U.S.
1955 Alex H. T. Theorell, Swedish
1954 John F. Enders, Frederick C. Robbins, Thomas H. Weller, all U.S.
1953 Hans A. Krebs, British
Fritz A. Lipmann, U.S.
1952 Selman A. Waksman, U.S.
1951 Max Theiler, U.S.
1950 Philip S. Hench, Edward C. Kendall, both U.S.
Tadeus Reichstein, Swiss
1949 Walter R. Hess, Swiss
Antonio Moniz, Portuguese
1948 Paul H. Müller, Swiss
1947 Carl F. Cori, Gerty T. Cori, both U.S.
Bernardo A. Houssay, Arg.
1946 Hermann J. Muller, U.S.
1945 Ernst B. Chain, British
Sir Alexander Fleming, British
Sir Howard W. Florey, British
1944 Joseph Erlanger, U.S.
Herbert S. Gasser, U.S.
1943 Henrik C. P. Dam, Danish
Edward A. Doisy, U.S.
1939 Gerhard Domagk, German
1938 Corneille J. F. Heymans, Belgian
1937 Albert Szent-Gyorgyi, Hung.-U.S.
1936 Sir Henry H. Dale, British
Otto Loewi, U.S.
1935 Hans Spemann, German
1934 George R. Minot, Wm. P. Murphy, G. H. Whipple, all U.S.
1933 Thomas H. Morgan, U.S.
1932 Edgar D. Adrian, British
Sir Charles S. Sherrington, Brit.
1931 Otto H. Warburg, German
1930 Karl Landsteiner, U.S.
1929 Christiaan Eijkman, Dutch
Sir Frederick G. Hopkins, British
1928 Charles J. H. Nicolle, French
1927 Julius Wagner-Jauregg, Austrian
1926 Johannes A. G. Fibiger, Danish
1924 Willem Einthoven, Dutch
1923 Frederick G. Banting, Canadian
John J. R. Macleod, Scottish
1922 Archibald V. Hill, British
Otto F. Meyerhof, German
1920 Schack A. S. Krogh, Danish
1919 Jules Bordet, Belgian
1914 Robert Barany, Austrian
1913 Charles R. Richet, French
1912 Alexis Carrel, French
1911 Allvar Gullstrand, Swedish
1910 Albrecht Kossel, German
1909 Emil T. Kocher, Swiss
1908 Paul Ehrlich, German
Elie Metchnikoff, French
1907 Charles L. A. Laveran, French
1906 Camillo Golgi, Italian
Santiago Ramón y Cajal, Sp.
1905 Robert Koch, German
1904 Ivan P. Pavlov, Russian
1903 Niels R. Finsen, Danish
1902 Sir Ronald Ross, British
1901 Emil A. von Behring, German

Literature

1992 Derek Walcott, St. Lucian
1991 Nadine Gordimer, South African
1990 Octavio Paz, Mexican
1989 Camilo José Cela, Spanish
1988 Naguib Mahfouz, Egyptian
1987 Joseph Brodsky, USSR-U.S.
1986 Wole Soyinka, Nigerian
1985 Claude Simon, French
1984 Jaroslav Siefert, Czech.
1983 William Golding, British
1982 Gabriel Garcia Marquez, Colombian-Mex.
1981 Elias Canetti, Bulgarian-British
1980 Czeslaw Milosz, Polish-U.S.
1979 Odysseus Elytis, Greek
1978 Isaac Bashevis Singer, U.S. (Yiddish)
1977 Vicente Aleixandre, Spanish
1976 Saul Bellow, U.S.
1975 Eugenio Montale, Italian
1974 Eyvind Johnson, Harry Edmund Martinson, both Swedish
1973 Patrick White, Australian
1972 Heinrich Böll, W. German
1971 Pablo Neruda, Chilean
1970 Aleksandr I. Solzhenitsyn, Russ.
1969 Samuel Beckett, Irish
1968 Yasunari Kawabata, Japanese
1967 Miguel Angel Asturias, Guate.
1966 Samuel Joseph Agnon, Israeli
Nelly Sachs, Swedish
1965 Mikhail Sholokhov, Russian
1964 Jean-Paul Sartre, French (Prize declined)
1963 Giorgos Seferis, Greek
1962 John Steinbeck, U.S.
1961 Ivo Andric, Yugoslavian
1960 Saint-John Perse, French
1959 Salvatore Quasimodo, Italian
1958 Boris L. Pasternak, Russian (Prize declined)
1957 Albert Camus, French
1956 Juan Ramon Jimenez, Span.
1955 Halldor K. Laxness, Icelandic
1954 Ernest Hemingway, U.S.
1953 Sir Winston Churchill, British
1952 Francois Mauriac, French
1951 Pär F. Lagerkvist, Swedish
1950 Bertrand Russell, British
1949 William Faulkner, U.S.
1948 T.S. Eliot, British
1947 André Gide, French
1946 Hermann Hesse, Swiss
1945 Gabriela Mistral, Chilean
1944 Johannes V. Jensen, Danish
1939 Frans E. Sillanpaa, Finnish
1938 Pearl S. Buck, U.S.
1937 Roger Martin du Gard, French
1936 Eugene O'Neill, U.S.
1934 Luigi Pirandello, Italian
1933 Ivan A. Bunin, French
1932 John Galsworthy, British
1931 Erik A. Karlfeldt, Swedish
1930 Sinclair Lewis, U.S.
1929 Thomas Mann, German
1928 Sigrid Undset, Norwegian
1927 Henri Bergson, French
1926 Grazia Deledda, Italian
1925 George Bernard Shaw, British
1924 Władysław S. Reymont, Polish
1923 William Butler Yeats, Irish
1922 Jacinto Benavente, Spanish
1921 Anatole France, French
1920 Knut Hamsun, Norwegian
1919 Carl F. G. Spitteler, Swiss
1917 Karl A. Gjellerup, Danish
Henrik Pontoppidan, Danish
1916 Verner von Heidenstam, Swed.
1915 Romain Rolland, French
1913 Rabindranath Tagore, Indian
1912 Gerhart Hauptmann, German
1911 Maurice Maeterlinck, Belgian
1910 Paul J. L. Heyse, German
1909 Selma Lagerlöf, Swedish
1908 Rudolf C. Eucken, German
1907 Rudyard Kipling, British
1906 Giosue Carducci, Italian
1905 Henryk Sienkiewicz, Polish
1904 Frederic Mistral, French
José Echegaray, Spanish
1903 Björnsterne Björnson, Norwegian
1902 Theodor Mommsen, German
1901 René F. A Sully-Prudhomme, French

Nobel Memorial Prize in Economic Science

1992 Gary Becker, U.S.

1991 Ronald H. Coase, Br.–U.S.
1990 Harry M. Markowitz, William F. Sharpe, Merton H. Miller, all U.S.
1989 Trygve Haavelmo, Norwegian
1988 Maurice Allais, French
1987 Robert M. Solow, U.S.
1986 James M. Buchanan, U.S.
1985 Franco Modigliani, It.-U.S.
1984 Richard Stone, British
1983 Gerard Debreu, Fr.-U.S.
1982 George J. Stigler, U.S.
1981 James Tobin, U.S.
1980 Lawrence R. Klein, U.S.
1979 Theodore W. Schultz, U.S.
Sir Arthur Lewis, British
1978 Herbert A. Simon, U.S.
1977 Bertil Ohlin, Swedish
James E. Meade, British
1976 Milton Friedman, U.S.
1975 Tjalling Koopmans, Dutch-U.S.
Leonid Kantorovich, USSR
1974 Gunnar Myrdal, Swed.
Friedrich A. von Hayek, Austrian
1973 Wassily Leontief, U.S.
1972 Kenneth J. Arrow, U.S.
John R. Hicks, British
1971 Simon Kuznets, U.S.
1970 Paul A. Samuelson, U.S.
1969 Ragnar Frisch, Norwegian
Jan Tinbergen, Dutch

Peace

1992 Rigoberta Menchú, Guatemalan
1991 Daw Aung San Suu Kyi, Myanmarese
1990 Mikhail S. Gorbachev, USSR
1989 Dalai Lama, Tibetan
1988 United Nations Peacekeeping Forces
1987 Oscar Arias Sanchez, Costa Rican
1986 Elie Wiesel, Romanian-U.S.
1985 Intl. Physicians for the Prevention of Nuclear War, U.S.
1984 Bishop Desmond Tutu, So. African
1983 Lech Walesa, Polish
1982 Alva Myrdal, Swedish; Alfonso Garcia Robles, Mexican
1981 Office of U.N. High Commissioner for Refugees
1980 Adolfo Perez Esquivel, Argentine
1979 Mother Teresa of Calcutta, Albanian-Indian
1978 Anwar Sadat, Egyptian
Menachem Begin, Israeli
1977 Amnesty International
1976 Mairead Corrigan, Betty Williams, N. Irish
1975 Andrei Sakharov, USSR
1974 Eisaku Sato, Japanese, Sean MacBride, Irish
1973 Henry Kissinger, U.S.
Le Duc Tho, N. Vietnamese (Tho declined)
1971 Willy Brandt, W. German
1970 Norman E. Borlaug, U.S.
1969 Intl. Labor Organization
1968 Rene Cassin, French
1965 U.N. Children's Fund (UNICEF)
1964 Martin Luther King Jr., U.S.
1963 International Red Cross, League of Red Cross Societies
1962 Linus C. Pauling, U.S.
1961 Dag Hammarskjöld, Swedish
1960 Albert J. Luthuli, South African
1959 Philip J. Noel-Baker, British
1958 Georges Pire, Belgian
1957 Lester B. Pearson, Canadian
1954 Office of the UN High Commissioner for Refugees
1953 George C. Marshall, U.S.
1952 Albert Schweitzer, French
1951 Leon Jouhaux, French
1950 Ralph J. Bunche, U.S.
1949 Lord John Boyd Orr of Brechin Mearns, British
1947 Friends Service Council, Brit. Amer. Friends Service Com.
1946 Emily G. Balch, John R. Mott, both U.S.
1945 Cordell Hull, U.S.
1944 International Red Cross
1938 Nansen International Office for Refugees
1937 Viscount Cecil of Chelwood, Brit.
1936 Carlos de Saavedra Lamas, Arg.
1935 Carl von Ossietzky, German
1934 Arthur Henderson, British
1933 Sir Norman Angell, British
1931 Jane Addams, U.S.
Nicholas Murray Butler, U.S.
1930 Nathan Söderblom, Swedish
1929 Frank B. Kellogg, U.S.
1927 Ferdinand E. Buisson, French
Ludwig Quidde, German
1926 Aristide Briand, French
Gustav Stresemann, German
1925 Sir J. Austen Chamberlain, Brit.
Charles G. Dawes, U.S.
1922 Fridtjof Nansen, Norwegian
1921 Karl H. Branting, Swedish
Christian L. Lange, Norwegian
1920 Leon V.A. Bourgeois, French
1919 Woodrow Wilson, U.S.
1917 International Red Cross
1913 Henri La Fontaine, Belgian
1912 Elihu Root, U.S.
1911 Tobias M.C. Asser, Dutch
Alfred H. Fried, Austrian
1910 Permanent Intl. Peace Bureau
1909 Auguste M. F. Beernaert, Belg.
Paul H. B. B. d'Estournelles de Constant, French
1908 Klas P. Arnoldson, Swedish
Fredrik Bajer, Danish
1907 Ernesto T. Moneta, Italian
Louis Renault, French
1906 Theodore Roosevelt, U.S.
1905 Baroness Bertha von Suttner, Austrian
1904 Institute of International Law
1903 Sir William R. Cremer, British
1902 Elie Ducommun, Charles A. Gobat, both Swiss
1901 Jean H. Dunant, Swiss
Frédéric Passy, French

Film, Theatre, Television & Radio Awards

ALFs

(presented by the London Film Critics' Circle, Jan. 1993)
Source: London Film Critics' Circle

Film of the year: *Unforgiven* (USA), dir. Clint Eastwood
Director of the year: Robert Altman, *The Player*
Screenwriter of the year: Michael Tolkin, *The Player*
Actor of the year: Robert Downey Jr., *Chaplin*
Actress of the year: Judy Davis, *Husbands and Wives*, *Barton Fink*, *Naked Lunch*
Non-British newcomer of the year: Baz Luhrman, dir. and co-screenwriter, *Strictly Ballroom*
British film of the year: *Howards End* (UK), dir. James Ivory
British producer of the year: Stephen Woolley, *The Crying Game*
British director of the year: Neil Jordan, *The Crying Game*
British screenwriter of the year: Neil Jordan, *The Crying Game*
British actor of the year: Daniel Day Lewis, *Last of the Mohicans*
British actress of the year: Emma Thompson, *Howards End*
British technical achievement of the year: Roger Deakins, cinematographer, *Barton Fink*
Foreign language film of the year: *Raise the Red Lantern* (China), dir. Zhang Yimou
Special award: Freddie Francis, cinematographer, director and producer
Dilys Powell award: Freddie Young, "for lifetime achievement as a cinematographer/director"

BAFTA Awards

(presented by the British Academy of Film & Television Arts, March 1993, for 1992 productions)
Source: *Screen International* magazine

BAFTA special award 1993: Dame Maggie Smith
Academy fellowship: Sydney Samuelson, CBE
Michael Balcon award for outstanding British contribution to cinema: Kenneth Branagh
Alan Clarke award for outstanding creative contribution to television: Keith Todd
Alexander Korda award for best British film: *The Crying Game*, dir. Neil Jordan

FILM
Best film: *Howards End*, dir. James Ivory
Best director: Robert Altman, *The Player*
Best original screenplay: *Husbands and Wives*, Woody Allen
Best adapted screenplay: *The Player*, Michael Tolkin
Best actress: Emma Thompson, *Howards End*
Best actor: Robert Downey Jr, *Chaplin*
Best supporting actress: Miranda Richardson, *Damage*
Best supporting actor: Gene Hackman, *Unforgiven*
Best original film music: David Hirschfielder, *Strictly Ballroom*
Best foreign film: *Raise the Red Lantern*, dir. Zhang Yimou
Best short film: *Omnibus*, dir. Sam Karmann
Best short animated film: *Daumier's Law*, dir. Geoff Dunbar

TELEVISION
Best single drama: *An Ungentlemanly Act*, Bradley Adams/Stuart Urban
Best drama serial: *Anglo-Saxon Attitudes*, Andrew Brown/Diarmuid Lawrence/Andrew Davies
Best drama series: *Inspector Morse*, Dierdre Keir
Best factual series: *Pandora's Box*, Adam Curtis
Best light entertainment programme/series: *Noel's House Party*, Michael Leggo
Best comedy programme/series: *Absolutely Fabulous*, Jon Plowman/Bob Spiers/Jennifer Saunders
Best actuality coverage: Serbian Prison Camps discovery, Penny Marshall/Ian Williams
Best actress: Helen Mirren, *Prime Suspect 2*
Best actor: John Thaw, *Inspector Morse*
Best light entertainment performance: Joanna Lumley, *Absolutely Fabulous*
Best original television music: Jeff Beck & Jed Leiber, *Frankie's House*
Best children's programme (entertainment/drama): *The Borrowers*, Grainne Marmion/John Henderson/Richard Carpenter
Best children's programme (documentary/educational): *Art Attack*, Tim Edmunds
Flaherty documentary award: *The Man Who Loves Gary Lineker* (Video Diaries), Bob Long/Dr Yili Hasani
Huw Wheldon award (best arts programme): *Angela Carter's Curious Room* Omnibus), Kim Evans

42nd Berlin Film Festival Awards

(presented Feb. 1993)
Source: *Screen International* magazine

GOLDEN BEAR
Grand prix (shared): *The Women from the Lake of Scented Souls* (China), dir. Xie Fei; *The Wedding Banquet* (China-Taiwan), dir. Ang Lee
SILVER BEARS
Special jury prize: *Arizona Dream* (France), dir. Emir Kusturica
Best director: Andrew Birkin, *The Cement Garden* (UK)
Best actor: Denzel Washington, *Malcolm X* (USA), dir. Spike Lee
Best actress: Michelle Pfeiffer, *Love Field* (USA)
Blue Angel (Grand Prize): *Le Jeune Werther* (France), dir. Jacques Doillon

BFI Awards

(presented by the British Film Institute, September 1993)
Source: *British Film Institute*

BFI Fellowships: Clint Eastwood, Sir Denis Forman and Maureen O'Hara
BFI Award for Innovation: *Sweet Thames*, dir. Mark Harrison
Archival Achievement Award: Adam Curtis, prod. *Pandora's Box*
Mari Kuttna Award Animation: An Vrombaut, *Little Wolf*
Michael Powell Book Award: David Thomson, *Showman: The Life of David O. Selznick*
Grierson Award (for best documentary): Nick Broomfield, *Aileen Wuornos: The Selling of a Serial Killer*
Sutherland Trophy (for best first feature shown at the National Film Theatre during the year): *Vacas* (Cows), dir. Julio Medem
Career in the Industry: Eleanor Fazan, choreographer

British Comedy Awards

Source: Michael Hurll Television

Top TV Comedy Actress: Stephanie Cole
Best TV Comedy Drama: *Murder Most Horrid*
Top TV Comedy Actor: David Jason
Top Variety Performer: Les Dawson
Top Channel 4 Entertainment Presenter: Clive Anderson
Best BBC Sitcom: *One Foot in the Grave*
Best Comedy Film Award: *Hear My Song*
Top BBC Entertainment Presenter: Bruce Forsyth
Best Radio Comedy: *On the Hour*
Top TV Comedy Newcomer: Alan Cumming
Top Comedy Club Performer: Jo Brand
Top ITV Entertainment Presenter: Des O'Connor
Top Female Comedy Performer: Ruby Wax
Best Channel 4 Sitcom: *Desmond's*
Top Male Comedy Performer: Rory Bremner
Best Entertainment Series: *Have I Got News for You*
Lifetime Achievement Award: Eric Sykes
WGGB Award for Top Comedy Writer: David Renwick
Best ITV Sitcom: *Men Behaving Badly*
Best New TV Comedy: *Bottom*
Top TV Comedy Personality: Paul Merton

45th Cannes Film Festival Awards

(presented May 1993)

Golden Palm (joint): *The Piano* (Australia), dir. Jane Campion, and *Farewell to My Concubine* (China), dir. Chen Kaige
Special jury prize: *Faraway, So Close!* (Germany), dir. Wim Wenders
Jury prize (joint): *Raining Stones* (UK), dir. Ken Loach, and *The Puppetmaster* (Taiwan), dir. Hou Hsaio Hsien
Best director: Mike Leigh, *Naked*
Best actor: David Thewlis, *Naked*
Best actress: Holly Hunter, *The Piano*
Golden Camera (Best First Film): *The Smell of the Green Papaya* (Vietnam), dir. Tran Anh Hung
Short Film (Golden Palm): *Coffee and Cigarettes* (US), dir. Jim Jarmusch
Best Film in Competition (Int. Critics' Award): *The Puppetmaster*

50th Golden Globe Awards

(presented Jan. 1993)
Source: *Screen International* magazine

FILM
Best drama: *Scent of a Woman*, dir. Martin Brest
Best comedy/musical: *The Player*, dir. Robert Altman
Best foreign language film: *Indochine*, dir. Regis Wargnier
Best actor (drama): Al Pacino, *Scent of a Woman*
Best actor (comedy/musical): Tim Robbins, *The Player*
Best supporting actor: Gene Hackman, *Unforgiven*
Best actress (drama): Emma Thompson, *Howards End*
Best actress (comedy/musical): Miranda Richardson, *Enchanted April*
Best supporting actress: Joan Plowright, *Enchanted April*
Best director: Clint Eastwood, *Unforgiven*
Best screenplay: Bo Goldman, *Scent of a Woman*
Best original score: Alan Menken, *Aladdin*
Best original song: Alan Menken (song) and Tim Rice (lyrics), *Aladdin*
Special achievement: Robin Williams, voice of the Genie, *Aladdin*
Lifetime achievement: Lauren Bacall

Laurence Olivier Awards

(presented April 1993)

Source: *Society of West End Theatre*

Best actor: Robert Stephens, *Henry IV, Parts 1 & 2*
Best actress: Alison Steadman, *The Rise and Fall of Little Voice*
Best director of a musical: Nicholas Hytner, *Carousel*
Best director of a play: Stephen Daldry, *An Inspector Calls*
Best revival: *An Inspector Calls*
Best comedy performance: Simon Cadell, *Travels with My Aunt*
Best new dance production: *The Judas Tree*, Royal Ballet
Best new opera production: *Stiffelio*, Royal Opera
Best musical revival: *Carousel*
Best entertainment: *Travels with My Aunt*
Best actress in a musical: Joanna Riding, *Carousel*
Best actor in a musical: Henry Goodman, *Assassins*
***Observer* award for outstanding achievement:** Almeida Theatre, Islington, "for giving glamour and a good name to the fringe"
Special award for lifetime achievement: the late Sir Kenneth MacMillan
BBC award for best play: *Six Degrees of Separation* by John Guare
American Express award for best musical: *Crazy for You*
Best comedy: *The Rise and Fall of Little Voice* by Jim Cartwright
Best costume designer: William Dudley, *Heartbreak House*, *Pygmalion* and *The Rise and Fall of Little Voice*
Best lighting designer: Howell Binkley, *Kiss of the Spider Woman*
Best set designer: Ian MacNeil, *An Inspector Calls*
Outstanding achievement in opera: Sir Edward Downes, conductor of *The Fiery Angel* and *Stiffelio*
Outstanding achievement in dance: Siobhan Davies, choreographer of *Winnsboro Cotton Mill Blues*
Best choreographer: Susan Stroman, *Crazy for You*
Best actress in a supporting role: Barbara Leigh-Hunt, *An Inspector Calls*
Best actor in a supporting role: Julian Glover, *Henry IV, Parts 1 & 2*
Best supporting performance in a musical: Janie Dee, *Carousel*

Oscars (Academy Awards)

1927–28

Actor: Emil Jannings, *The Way of All Flesh.*
Actress: Janet Gaynor, *Seventh Heaven.*
Director: Frank Borzage, *Seventh Heaven;* Lewis Milestone, *Two Arabian Knights.*
Picture: *Wings*, Paramount.

1928–29

Actor: Warner Baxter, *In Old Arizona.*
Actress: Mary Pickford, *Coquette.*
Director: Frank Lloyd, *The Divine Lady.*
Picture: *Broadway Melody*, MGM.

1929–30

Actor: George Arliss, *Disraeli.*
Actress: Norma Shearer, *The Divorcee.*
Director: Lewis Milestone, *All Quiet on the Western Front.*
Picture: *All Quiet on the Western Front*, Univ.

1930–31

Actor: Lionel Barrymore, *Free Soul.*
Actress: Marie Dressler, *Min and Bill.*
Director: Norman Taurog, *Skippy.*
Picture: *Cimarron*, RKO.

1931–32

Actor: Fredric March, *Dr. Jekyll and Mr. Hyde;* Wallace Beery, *The Champ* (tie).
Actress: Helen Hayes, *Sin of Madelon Claudet.*
Director: Frank Borzage, *Bad Girl.*
Picture: *Grand Hotel*, MGM.
Special: Walt Disney, *Mickey Mouse.*

1932–33

Actor: Charles Laughton, *Private Life of Henry VIII.*
Actress: Katharine Hepburn, *Morning Glory.*
Director: Frank Lloyd, *Cavalcade.*
Picture: *Cavalcade*, Fox.

1934

Actor: Clark Gable, *It Happened One Night.*
Actress: Claudette Colbert, *It Happened One Night.*
Director: Frank Capra, *It Happened One Night.*
Picture: *It Happened One Night*, Columbia.

1935

Actor: Victor McLaglen, *The Informer.*
Actress: Bette Davis, *Dangerous.*
Director: John Ford, *The Informer.*
Picture: *Mutiny on the Bounty*, MGM.

1936

Actor: Paul Muni, *Story of Louis Pasteur.*
Actress: Luise Rainer, *The Great Ziegfeld.*
Sup. Actor: Walter Brennan, *Come and Get It.*
Sup. Actress: Gale Sondergaard, *Anthony Adverse.*
Director: Frank Capra, *Mr. Deeds Goes to Town.*
Picture: *The Great Ziegfeld*, MGM.

1937

Actor: Spencer Tracy, *Captains Courageous.*
Actress: Luise Rainer, *The Good Earth.*
Sup. Actor: Joseph Schildkraut, *Life of Emile Zola.*
Sup. Actress: Alice Brady, *In Old Chicago.*
Director: Leo McCarey, *The Awful Truth.*
Picture: *Life of Emile Zola*, Warner.

1938

Actor: Spencer Tracy, *Boys Town.*
Actress: Bette Davis, *Jezebel.*
Sup. Actor: Walter Brennan, *Kentucky.*
Sup. Actress: Fay Bainter, *Jezebel.*
Director: Frank Capra, *You Can't Take It With You.*
Picture: *You Can't Take It With You*, Columbia.

1939

Actor: Robert Donat, *Goodbye Mr. Chips.*
Actress: Vivien Leigh, *Gone With the Wind.*
Sup. Actor: Thomas Mitchell, *Stage Coach.*
Sup. Actress: Hattie McDaniel, *Gone With the Wind.*
Director: Victor Fleming, *Gone With the Wind.*
Picture: *Gone With the Wind*, Selznick International.

1940

Actor: James Stewart, *The Philadelphia Story.*
Actress: Ginger Rogers, *Kitty Foyle.*
Sup. Actor: Walter Brennan, *The Westerner.*
Sup. Actress: Jane Darwell, *The Grapes of Wrath.*
Director: John Ford, *The Grapes of Wrath.*
Picture: *Rebecca*, Selznick International.

1941

Actor: Gary Cooper, *Sergeant York.*
Actress: Joan Fontaine, *Suspicion.*
Sup. Actor: Donald Crisp, *How Green Was My Valley.*
Sup. Actress: Mary Astor, *The Great Lie.*
Director: John Ford, *How Green Was My Valley.*
Picture: *How Green Was My Valley*, 20th Century-Fox.

1942

Actor: James Cagney, *Yankee Doodle Dandy.*
Actress: Greer Garson, *Mrs. Miniver.*
Sup. Actor: Van Heflin, *Johnny Eager.*
Sup. Actress: Teresa Wright, *Mrs. Miniver.*
Director: William Wyler, *Mrs. Miniver.*
Picture: *Mrs. Miniver*, MGM.

1943

Actor: Paul Lukas, *Watch on the Rhine.*
Actress: Jennifer Jones, *The Song of Bernadette.*
Sup. Actor: Charles Coburn, *The More the Merrier.*
Sup. Actress: Katina Paxinou, *For Whom the Bell Tolls.*
Director: Michael Curtiz, *Casablanca.*
Picture: *Casablanca*, Warner.

1944

Actor: Bing Crosby, *Going My Way.*
Actress: Ingrid Bergman, *Gaslight.*
Sup. Actor: Barry Fitzgerald, *Going My Way.*
Sup. Actress: Ethel Barrymore, *None But the Lonely Heart.*
Director: Leo McCarey, *Going My Way.*
Picture: *Going My Way*, Paramount.

1945

Actor: Ray Milland, *The Lost Weekend*.
Actress: Joan Crawford, *Mildred Pierce*.
Sup. Actor: James Dunn, *A Tree Grows in Brooklyn*.
Sup. Actress: Anne Revere, *National Velvet*.
Director: Billy Wilder, *The Lost Weekend*.
Picture: *The Lost Weekend*, Paramount.

1946

Actor: Fredric March, *Best Years of Our Lives*.
Actress: Olivia de Havilland, *To Each His Own*.
Sup. Actor: Harold Russell, *The Best Years of Our Lives*.
Sup. Actress: Anne Baxter, *The Razor's Edge*.
Director: William Wyler, *The Best Years of Our Lives*.
Picture: *The Best Years of Our Lives*, Goldwyn, RKO.

1947

Actor: Ronald Colman, *A Double Life*.
Actress: Loretta Young, *The Farmer's Daughter*.
Sup. Actor: Edmund Gwenn, *Miracle on 34th Street*.
Sup. Actress: Celeste Holm, *Gentleman's Agreement*.
Director: Elia Kazan, *Gentleman's Agreement*.
Picture: *Gentleman's Agreement*, 20th Century-Fox.

1948

Actor: Laurence Olivier, *Hamlet*.
Actress: Jane Wyman, *Johnny Belinda*.
Sup. Actor: Walter Huston, *Treasure of Sierra Madre*.
Sup. Actress: Claire Trevor, *Key Largo*.
Director: John Huston, *Treasure of Sierra Madre*.
Picture: *Hamlet*, Two Cities Film, Universal International.

1949

Actor: Broderick Crawford, *All the King's Men*.
Actress: Olivia de Havilland, *The Heiress*.
Sup. Actor: Dean Jagger, *Twelve O'Clock High*.
Sup. Actress: Mercedes McCambridge, *All the King's Men*.
Director: Joseph L. Mankiewicz, *Letter to Three Wives*.
Picture: *All the King's Men*, Columbia.

1950

Actor: Jose Ferrer, *Cyrano de Bergerac*.
Actress: Judy Holliday, *Born Yesterday*.
Sup. Actor: George Sanders, *All About Eve*.
Sup. Actress: Josephine Hull, *Harvey*.
Director: Joseph L. Mankiewicz, *All About Eve*.
Picture: *All About Eve*, 20th Century-Fox.

1951

Actor: Humphrey Bogart, *The African Queen*.
Actress: Vivien Leigh, *A Streetcar Named Desire*.
Sup. Actor: Karl Malden, *A Streetcar Named Desire*.
Sup. Actress: Kim Hunter, *A Streetcar Named Desire*.
Director: George Stevens, *A Place in the Sun*.
Picture: *An American in Paris*, MGM.

1952

Actor: Gary Cooper, *High Noon*.
Actress: Shirley Booth, *Come Back, Little Sheba*.
Sup. Actor: Anthony Quinn, *Viva Zapata*
Sup. Actress: Gloria Grahame, *The Bad and the Beautiful*.
Director: John Ford, *The Quiet Man*.
Picture: *Greatest Show on Earth*, C.B. DeMille, Paramount.

1953

Actor: William Holden, *Stalag 17*.
Actress: Audrey Hepburn, *Roman Holiday*.
Sup. Actor: Frank Sinatra, *From Here to Eternity*.
Sup. Actress: Donna Reed, *From Here to Eternity*.
Director: Fred Zinnemann, *From Here to Eternity*.
Picture: *From Here to Eternity*, Columbia.

1954

Actor: Marlon Brando, *On the Waterfront*.
Actress: Grace Kelly, *The Country Girl*.
Sup. Actor: Edmond O'Brien, *The Barefoot Contessa*.
Sup. Actress: Eva Marie Saint, *On the Waterfront*.
Director: Elia Kazan, *On the Waterfront*.
Picture: *On the Waterfront*, Horizon-American, Colum.

1955

Actor: Ernest Borgnine, *Marty*.
Actress: Anna Magnani, *The Rose Tattoo*.
Sup. Actor: Jack Lemmon, *Mister Roberts*.
Sup. Actress: Jo Van Fleet, *East of Eden*.
Director: Delbert Mann, *Marty*.
Picture: *Marty*, Hecht and Lancaster's Steven Prods., U.A.

1956

Actor: Yul Brynner, *The King and I*.
Actress: Ingrid Bergman, *Anastasia*.
Sup. Actor: Anthony Quinn, *Lust for Life*.
Sup. Actress: Dorothy Malone, *Written on the Wind*.
Director: George Stevens, *Giant*.
Picture: *Around the World in 80 Days*, Michael Todd, U.A.

1957

Actor: Alec Guinness, *The Bridge on the River Kwai*.
Actress: Joanne Woodward, *The Three Faces of Eve*.
Sup. Actor: Red Buttons, *Sayonara*.
Sup. Actress: Miyoshi Umeki, *Sayonara*.
Director: David Lean, *The Bridge on the River Kwai*.
Picture: *The Bridge on the River Kwai*, Columbia.

1958

Actor: David Niven, *Separate Tables*.
Actress: Susan Hayward, *I Want to Live*.
Sup. Actor: Burl Ives, *The Big Country*.
Sup. Actress: Wendy Hiller, *Separate Tables*.
Director: Vincente Minnelli, *Gigi*.
Picture: *Gigi*, Arthur Freed Production, MGM.

1959

Actor: Charlton Heston, *Ben-Hur*.
Actress: Simone Signoret, *Room at the Top*.
Sup. Actor: Hugh Griffith, *Ben-Hur*.
Sup. Actress: Shelley Winters, *Diary of Anne Frank*.
Director: William Wyler, *Ben-Hur*.
Picture: *Ben-Hur*, MGM.

1960

Actor: Burt Lancaster, *Elmer Gantry*.
Actress: Elizabeth Taylor, *Butterfield 8*.
Sup. Actor: Peter Ustinov, *Spartacus*.
Sup. Actress: Shirley Jones, *Elmer Gantry*.
Director: Billy Wilder, *The Apartment*.
Picture: *The Apartment*, Mirisch Co., U.A.

1961

Actor: Maximilian Schell, *Judgment at Nuremberg*.
Actress: Sophia Loren, *Two Women*.
Sup. Actor: George Chakiris, *West Side Story*.
Sup. Actress: Rita Moreno, *West Side Story*.
Director: Jerome Robbins, Robert Wise, *West Side Story*.
Picture: *West Side Story*, United Artists.

1962

Actor: Gregory Peck, *To Kill a Mockingbird*.
Actress: Anne Bancroft, *The Miracle Worker*.
Sup. Actor: Ed Begley, *Sweet Bird of Youth*.
Sup. Actress: Patty Duke, *The Miracle Worker*.
Director: David Lean, *Lawrence of Arabia*.
Picture: *Lawrence of Arabia*, Columbia.

1963

Actor: Sidney Poitier, *Lilies of the Field*.
Actress: Patricia Neal, *Hud*.
Sup. Actor: Melvyn Douglas, *Hud*.
Sup. Actress: Margaret Rutherford, *The V.I.P.s*.
Director: Tony Richardson, *Tom Jones*.
Picture: *Tom Jones*, Woodfall Prod., UA-Lopert Pictures.

1964

Actor: Rex Harrison, *My Fair Lady*.
Actress: Julie Andrews, *Mary Poppins*.
Sup. Actor: Peter Ustinov, *Topkapi*.
Sup. Actress: Lila Kedrova, *Zorba the Greek*.
Director: George Cukor, *My Fair Lady*.
Picture: *My Fair Lady*, Warner Bros.

1965

Actor: Lee Marvin, *Cat Ballou*.
Actress: Julie Christie, *Darling*.
Sup. Actor: Martin Balsam, *A Thousand Clowns*.
Sup. Actress: Shelley Winters, *A Patch of Blue*.
Director: Robert Wise, *The Sound of Music*.
Picture: *The Sound of Music*, 20th Century-Fox.

1966

Actor: Paul Scofield, *A Man for All Seasons*.
Actress: Elizabeth Taylor, *Who's Afraid of Virginia Woolf ?*
Sup. Actor: Walter Matthau, *The Fortune Cookie*.
Sup. Actress: Sandy Dennis, *Who's Afraid of Virginia Woolf ?*
Director: Fred Zinnemann, *A Man for All Seasons*.
Picture: *A Man for All Seasons*, Columbia.

1967

Actor: Rod Steiger, *In the Heat of the Night*.
Actress: Katharine Hepburn, *Guess Who's Coming to Dinner*.
Sup. Actor: George Kennedy, *Cool Hand Luke*.
Sup. Actress: Estelle Parsons, *Bonnie and Clyde*.
Director: Mike Nichols, *The Graduate*.
Picture: *In the Heat of the Night*.

1968

Actor: Cliff Robertson, *Charly*.
Actress: Katharine Hepburn, *The Lion in Winter*; Barbra Streisand, *Funny Girl* (tie).
Sup. Actor: Jack Albertson, *The Subject Was Roses*.
Sup. Actress: Ruth Gordon, *Rosemary's Baby*.
Director: Sir Carol Reed, *Oliver*
Picture: *Oliver*

1969

Actor: John Wayne, *True Grit*.
Actress: Maggie Smith, *The Prime of Miss Jean Brodie*.
Sup. Actor: Gig Young, *They Shoot Horses, Don't They?*
Sup. Actress: Goldie Hawn, *Cactus Flower*.
Director: John Schlesinger, *Midnight Cowboy*.
Picture: *Midnight Cowboy*.

1970
Actor: George C. Scott, *Patton* (refused).
Actress: Glenda Jackson, *Women in Love*.
Sup. Actor: John Mills, *Ryan's Daughter*.
Sup. Actress: Helen Hayes, *Airport*.
Director: Franklin Schaffner, *Patton*.
Picture: *Patton*.

1971
Actor: Gene Hackman, *The French Connection*.
Actress: Jane Fonda, *Klute*.
Sup. Actor: Ben Johnson, *The Last Picture Show*.
Sup. Actress: Cloris Leachman, *The Last Picture Show*.
Director: William Friedkin, *The French Connection*.
Picture: *The French Connection*.

1972
Actor: Marlon Brando, *The Godfather* (refused).
Actress: Liza Minnelli, *Cabaret*.
Sup. Actor: Joel Grey, *Cabaret*.
Sup. Actress: Eileen Heckart, *Butterflies Are Free*.
Director: Bob Fosse, *Cabaret*.
Picture: *The Godfather*.

1973
Actor: Jack Lemmon, *Save the Tiger*.
Actress: Glenda Jackson, *A Touch of Class*.
Sup. Actor: John Houseman, *The Paper Chase*.
Sup. Actress: Tatum O'Neal, *Paper Moon*.
Director: George Roy Hill, *The Sting*.
Picture: *The Sting*.

1974
Actor: Art Carney, *Harry and Tonto*.
Actress: Ellen Burstyn, *Alice Doesn't Live Here Anymore*.
Sup. Actor: Robert DeNiro, *The Godfather, Part II*.
Sup. Actress: Ingrid Bergman, *Murder on the Orient Express*.
Director: Francis Ford Coppola, *The Godfather, Part II*.
Picture: *The Godfather, Part II*.

1975
Actor: Jack Nicholson, *One Flew Over the Cuckoo's Nest*.
Actress: Louise Fletcher, *One Flew Over the Cuckoo's Nest*.
Sup. Actor: George Burns, *The Sunshine Boys*.
Sup. Actress: Lee Grant, *Shampoo*.
Director: Milos Forman, *One Flew Over the Cuckoo's Nest*.
Picture: *One Flew Over the Cuckoo's Nest*.

1976
Actor: Peter Finch, *Network*.
Actress: Faye Dunaway, *Network*.
Sup. Actor: Jason Robards, *All the President's Men*.
Sup. Actress: Beatrice Straight, *Network*.
Director: John G. Avildsen, *Rocky*.
Picture: *Rocky*.

1977
Actor: Richard Dreyfuss, *The Goodbye Girl*.
Actress: Diane Keaton, *Annie Hall*.
Sup. Actor: Jason Robards, *Julia*.
Sup. Actress: Vanessa Redgrave, *Julia*.
Director: Woody Allen, *Annie Hall*.
Picture: *Annie Hall*.

1978
Actor: Jon Voight, *Coming Home*.
Actress: Jane Fonda, *Coming Home*.
Sup. Actor: Christopher Walken, *The Deer Hunter*.
Sup. Actress: Maggie Smith, *California Suite*.
Director: Michael Cimino, *The Deer Hunter*.
Picture: *The Deer Hunter*.

1979
Actor: Dustin Hoffman, *Kramer vs. Kramer*.
Actress: Sally Field, *Norma Rae*.
Sup. Actor: Melvyn Douglas, *Being There*.
Sup. Actress: Meryl Streep, *Kramer vs. Kramer*.
Director: Robert Benton, *Kramer vs. Kramer*.
Picture: *Kramer vs. Kramer*.

1980
Actor: Robert DeNiro, *Raging Bull*.
Actress: Sissy Spacek, *Coal Miner's Daughter*.
Sup. Actor: Timothy Hutton, *Ordinary People*.
Sup. Actress: Mary Steenburgen, *Melvin & Howard*.
Director: Robert Redford, *Ordinary People*.
Picture: *Ordinary People*.

1981
Actor: Henry Fonda, *On Golden Pond*.
Actress: Katharine Hepburn, *On Golden Pond*.
Sup. Actor: John Gielgud, *Arthur*.
Sup. Actress: Maureen Stapleton, *Reds*.
Director: Warren Beatty, *Reds*.
Picture: *Chariots of Fire*.

1982
Actor: Ben Kingsley, *Gandhi*.
Actress: Meryl Streep, *Sophie's Choice*.
Sup. Actor: Louis Gossett, Jr., *An Officer and a Gentleman*.
Sup. Actress: Jessica Lange, *Tootsie*.
Director: Richard Attenborough, *Gandhi*.
Picture: *Gandhi*.

1983
Actor: Robert Duvall, *Tender Mercies*.
Actress: Shirley MacLaine, *Terms of Endearment*.
Sup. Actor: Jack Nicholson, *Terms of Endearment*.
Sup. Actress: Linda Hunt, *The Year of Living Dangerously*.
Director: James L. Brooks, *Terms of Endearment*.
Picture: *Terms of Endearment*.

1984
Actor: F. Murray Abraham, *Amadeus*.
Actress: Sally Field, *Places in the Heart*.
Sup. Actor: Haing S. Ngor, *The Killing Fields*.
Sup. Actress: Peggy Ashcroft, *A Passage to India*.
Director: Milos Forman, *Amadeus*.
Picture: *Amadeus*.

1985
Actor: William Hurt, *Kiss of the Spider Woman*.
Actress: Geraldine Page, *The Trip to Bountiful*.
Sup. Actor: Don Ameche, *Cocoon*.
Sup. Actress: Anjelica Huston, *Prizzi's Honor*.
Director: Sydney Pollack, *Out of Africa*.
Picture: *Out of Africa*.

1986
Actor: Paul Newman, *The Color of Money*.
Actress: Marlee Matlin, *Children of a Lesser God*.
Sup. Actor: Michael Caine, *Hannah and Her Sisters*.
Sup. Actress: Dianne Wiest, *Hannah and Her Sisters*.
Director: Oliver Stone, *Platoon*.
Picture: *Platoon*.

1987
Actor: Michael Douglas, *Wall Street*.
Actress: Cher, *Moonstruck*.
Sup. Actor: Sean Connery, *The Untouchables*.
Sup. Actress: Olympia Dukakis, *Moonstruck*.
Director: Bernardo Bertolucci, *The Last Emperor*.
Picture: *The Last Emperor*.

1988
Actor: Dustin Hoffman, *Rain Man*.
Actress: Jodie Foster, *The Accused*.
Sup. Actor: Kevin Kline, *A Fish Called Wanda*.
Sup. Actress: Geena Davis, *The Accidental Tourist*.
Director: Barry Levinson, *Rain Man*.
Picture: *Rain Man*.

1989
Actor: Daniel Day-Lewis, *My Left Foot*.
Actress: Jessica Tandy, *Driving Miss Daisy*.
Sup. Actor: Denzel Washington, *Glory*.
Sup. Actress: Brenda Fricker, *My Left Foot*.
Director: Oliver Stone, *Born on the Fourth of July*.
Picture: *Driving Miss Daisy*.

1990
Actor: Jeremy Irons, *Reversal of Fortune*.
Actress: Kathy Bates, *Misery*.
Sup. Actor: Joe Pesci, *Goodfellas*.
Sup. Actress: Whoopi Goldberg, *Ghost*.
Director: Kevin Costner, *Dances With Wolves*.
Picture: *Dances With Wolves*.

1991
Actor: Anthony Hopkins, *The Silence of the Lambs*.
Actress: Jodie Foster, *The Silence of the Lambs*.
Sup. Actor: Jack Palance, *City Slickers*.
Sup. Actress: Mercedes Ruehl, *The Fisher King*.
Director: Jonathan Demme, *The Silence of the Lambs*.
Picture: *The Silence of the Lambs*.

1992
Picture: *Unforgiven*.
Actor: Al Pacino, *Scent of a Woman*.
Actress: Emma Thompson, *Howards End*.
Sup. Actor: Gene Hackman, *Unforgiven*.
Sup. Actress: Marisa Tomei, *My Cousin Vinny*.
Director: Clint Eastwood, *Unforgiven*.
Foreign-language Film: *Indochine*, France.
Original Screenplay: Neil Jordan, *The Crying Game*.
Adapted Screenplay: Ruth Prawer Jhabvala, *Howards End*.
Cinematography: Philippe Rousselot, *A River Runs Through It*.
Editing: Joel Cox, *Unforgiven*.
Original Score: Alan Menken, *Aladdin*.
Original Song: "Whole New World", from *Aladdin*, Alan Menken, Tim Rice.
Art Direction: Luciana Arrighi, Ian Whittaker, *Howards End*.
Costume Design: Eiko Ishioka, *Bram Stoker's Dracula*.
Make-up: Greg Cannom, Michele Burke, Matthew W. Mungle, *Bram Stoker's Dracula*.
Visual Effects: Ken Ralston, Doug Chiang, Doug Smythe, Tom Woodruff Jr., *Death Becomes Her*.
Sound: Chris Jenkins, Doug Hemphill, Mark Smith, Simon Kaye, *The Last of the Mohicans*.
Documentary Feature: *The Panama Deception*.

Documentary Short Subject: *Educating Peter.*
Short Film, Live: *Omnibus.*
Short Film, Animated: *Mona Lisa Descending a Staircase.*
Honorary Award: Federico Fellini.
Jean Hersholt Humanitarian Awards: Audrey Hepburn, Elizabeth Taylor.
Academy Award of Merit: Chadwell O'Connor.
Gordon E. Sawyer Award, for technical achievement: Erich Kaestner.

Royal Television Society Awards

(presented May 1993)

Entertainment: *Victoria Wood's All Day Breakfast Show* (BBC)
Situation comedy: *One Foot in the Grave* (BBC)
Single documentary: *Katie & Eilish – Siamese Twins* (Yorkshire Television)
Documentary series: *Pandora's Box – The League of Gentlemen* (BBC)
Team award: *The Big Breakfast* (Planet 24 for Channel 4)
Arts: *Bookmark – Miss Pym's Day Out* (BBC)
Outside broadcasts: *Last Night of the Proms* (BBC)
Technique: Lee Eynon for the videotape editing of the *Barcelona Olympics*, British medals sequence (BBC)
Regional programme: *The Snow Show* (Gallus Besom Productions for BBC Scotland)
Regional documentary: *Tuesday Special: Caution – Our Hands Are Tied* (Central Independent Television)
Children's factual: *Newsround Special – SOS: The Suffering of Somalia* (BBC)
Children's entertainment: *What's that Noise!* (BBC)
Children's drama: *The Borrowers* (Working Title Production for BBC)
Performance awards: David Jason "for the range, depth . . . and sheer volume of his work"; Julia Sawalha, *Absolutely Fabulous*
Writer's award: Andy Hamilton and Guy Jenkin, *Drop the Dead Donkey*
Drama serial: *Goodbye Cruel World* (BBC)
Drama series: *Between the Lines – Out of the Game* (BBC in association with Island World Productions)
Single drama: *Hedd Wyn* (Pendefig production for Channel 4 Wales)
Judges' award: Anna Home, head of children's programmes, BBC Television, and Lewis Rudd, controller, young people's programmes, Central Productions
Cyril Bennett award (for outstanding contribution to television programming): Charles Wheeler
Gold medal: Sir Michael Checkland, "for his achievements in ensuring the survival and success of . . . the BBC"

Sony Radio Awards 1993

(Gold; Silver; Bronze)

Outstanding Sports Broadcast: *Barcelona Olympics*, BBC Radio 5; *The London Marathon*, Capital 95.8 FM; *Five Aside – Paralympics*, BBC Radio 5.
Outstanding Special Event: *Coca Cola National Music Day*, MCM Networking (UK) Ltd for Independent Radio; *The 40th Birthday Concert of the BBC Concert Orchestra*, BBC Radio 2; *MacDiarmid*, BBC Radio Scotland.
Magazine/Special Interest Programme: *Punters*, BBC Radio 4; *The Shocking History of Phosphorus*, BBC Radio Scotland for BBC Radio 4; *Word of Mouth*, BBC Radio 4.
Sports Reporter of the Year: Jonathan Agnew, BBC Radio 3 and 5; John Rawling, BBC Radio 5; Martin Fisher, BBC Radio Nottingham.
Breakfast Show – Contemporary Music: *Tony Blackburn Breakfast Show*, Capital Gold; *Simon Mayo Breakfast Show*, BBC Radio One FM; *Signal Radio Breakfast Show*, Signal Radio.
Breakfast Show – Non-Contemporary Music: Nick Bailey, Classic FM; Sarah Lucas, Classic FM; *Kevin King at Breakfast*, South Coast Radio.
Response to a News Event: *Ayodhya*, BBC Radio Leicester; *Manchester Bombs*, Piccadilly Gold; *Castlemorton Common – May 1992*, BBC Hereford & Worcester.
News and Current Affairs Sequence: *Good Morning Ulster*, BBC Radio Ulster; *News 92*, BBC Radio One FM; *The World Tonight*, BBC Radio 4.
Breakfast Show – Speech Based: *Mike Carlton's Morning Report*, LBC Newstalk 97.3 FM; *The Breakfast Show*, BBC Radio Nottingham; *Stephen Rhodes Breakfast Show*, BBC Radio Shropshire.
News and Current Affairs Programme: *File on 4 – Feltham Remand Centre*, BBC Radio 4; *Europhile*, BBC 4; *The Clash of Absolutes: The Politics of Abortion*, BBC Radio 4.
Local Broadcaster of the Year: David Dunseith, BBC Radio Ulster; Peter Adamson, BBC Radio Humberside; Steve Penk, Piccadilly Key 103.
Phone-in: *Hayes Over Britain*, BBC Radio 2; *The Open Line*, Clyde 1FM & Clyde 2; *Talk Back*, BBC Radio Newcastle.
Documentary/Feature: *Soundtrack: Jason and the Thunderbirds*, BBC Radio 4; *The Hospital*, BBC Radio 4; *Michael Jackson – King of Pop*, Capital 95.8 FM.
Specialist Music Programme: *Scotland's Music*, BBC Radio Scotland; *Mixing It*, BBC Radio 3; *Classic Opera Guide*, Classic FM.
Art Programme or Feature: *Larks Ascending*, BBC Radio 4; *Barcelobra*, BBC Radio 3; *GLR Picture Show*, BBC GLR.
Popular Music Programme: *Unsung Heroes*, Unique Broadcasting for BBC Radio One FM; *In Search of the Last Riff*, BBC Radio One FM; *Michael Jackson – King of Pop*, Capital 95.8 FM.
Use of Comedy/Comedy Show: *Knowing Me, Knowing You*, BBC Radio 4; *The Nick Revell Show*, BBC Radio 4; *The Light Entertainment Show*, BBC Radio 2.
Music Programming: *Friel's Fancy*, BBC Radio Ulster; *The Neil Fox Show*, Capital 95.8 FM; *Hit the North*, BBC Radio 5.
Outstanding Service to the Community: *Year of Action*, BBC Radio Nottingham; *The BRMB Walkathon*, BRMB; *Tell It Like It Is*, BBC Radio One FM.
Newcomer: Tom Bright, Radio Wave 96.5; Clare Ashford, Capital 95.8 FM; Phil Sellars, BBC Radio Stoke.
News Reporter of the Year: Malcolm Brabant, BBC Radio 4; Feargal Keane, BBC Radio 4; Mark Coles, BBC Radio 4.
Best Actor: Keith Clifford, *Randle's Scandals*, BBC Radio 4; Kerry Shale, *The Set Up*, BBC Radio 5; Anthony Sher, *Singer*, BBC Radio 4.
Best Actress: Miriam Margolyes, *The Queen and I*, BBC Radio 4; Rachel Joyce, *Darling Peidi*, BBC Radio 4.
Society of Authors Award for Best Dramatization/Adaptation: *Weir of Hermiston*, BBC Radio Scotland/Radio 4; *Humphrey Clinker*, BBC Radio 4; *Canterbury at War*, BBC Radio Kent.

Drama Production: *The Master and Margarita*, BBC World Service/BBC Radio 4; *A Fake's Progress*, BBC Radio 4; *The Adventures of Tintin by Hergé*, BBC Radio 5, and *The Way We Live Now*, BBC Radio 3.
Best Original Script: *A Matter of Sex*, BBC Radio 4; *Kitty Wilkinson*, BBC Radio 4; *Down the Wanderers*, LBC, and *Lost for Words*, BBC World Service.
Local Station of the Year: Fox FM.
Metropolitan Station of the Year: Clyde 2.
National Station of the Year: Classic FM.
Sony Special Award: Misha Glenny.
Radio Academy Creative Award: David Hatch.
National Broadcaster of the Year: John Peel.
Gold Award: Humphrey Lyttleton.

Tony Awards 1993
(US stage awards named after Antoinette Perry)

Play: Tony Kushner, *Angels in America*
Leading actor: Ron Leibman, *Angels in America*
Leading actress: Madeline Kahn, *The Sisters Rosensweig*
Featured actor: Stephen Spinella, *Angels in America*
Featured actress: Debra Monk, *Redwood Curtain*
Direction: George C. Wolfe, *Angels in America*

Musical: *Kiss of the Spider Woman*
Revival: *Anna Christie*
Leading actor: Brent Carver, *Kiss of the Spider Woman*
Leading actress: Chita Rivera, *Kiss of the Spider Woman*
Featured actor: Anthony Crivello, *Kiss of the Spider Woman*
Featured actress: Andrea Martin, *My Favourite Year*
Direction: Des McAnuff, *Tommy*
Book: Terence McNally, *Kiss of the Spider Woman*
Original score: John Kander & Fred Ebb, *Kiss of the Spider Woman*, and Pete Townsend, *Tommy*
Scenic design: John Arnone, *Tommy*
Costume design: Florence Klotz, *Kiss of the Spider Woman*
Lighting design: Chris Parry, *Tommy*
Choreography: Wayne Cilento, *Tommy*

British Literary Awards 1992/3

James Tait Black Memorial Prize (£1500 each)
Fiction: Ian Sinclair, *Downriver*
Biography: Adrian Desmond & James R. Moore, *Darwin*

Booker Prize for Fiction (£22,000)
Michael Ondaatje, *The English Patient*, and Barry Unsworth, *Sacred Hunger*

Guardian Fiction Prize (£1000)
Alasdair Gray, *Poor Things*

Hawthornden Prize (£750)
Ferdinand Mount, *Of Love and Asthma*

Mail on Sunday John Llewellyn Rhys Prize (£5000)
Matthew Kneale, *The Sweet Thames*

NCR Book Award for Non-fiction (£25,000; £1500 each to 3 runners-up)
Peter Hennessy, *Never Again: Britain 1945–51*

W. H. Smith Literary Award (£10,000)
March 1993: Michèle Roberts, *Daughters of the House*

Sunday Express Book of the Year Award (£20,000)
Hilary Mantel, *A Place of Greater Safety*

Betty Trask Award (£10,000; £7000 to first runner-up; £5000 for next runner-up; £2000 each for last 2 runners-up)
June 1993: Mark Blackaby, *You'll Never Be Here Again*

Whitbread Book of the Year Award (£20,250, plus £1750 for each of 5 category winners)
Fiction : Alasdair Gray, *Poor Things*
Biography: Victoria Glendinning, *Trollope*

Yorkshire Post Book of the Year (£1200)
John Gross, *Shylock*

Pulitzer Prize in Letters, 1993

Fiction: Robert Olen Butler, *A Good Scent from a Strange Mountain*

Drama: Tony Kushner, *Angels in America: Millennium Approaches*

History: Gordon S. Wood, *The Radicalism of the American Revolution*

Biography or Autobiography: David McCullough, *Truman*

American Poetry: Louise Glück, *The Wild Iris*

General Non-Fiction: Gary Wills, *Lincoln at Gettysburg*

British Press Awards 1993
(presented by the *UK Press Gazette*)

Journalist of the Year: Maggie O'Kane, *The Guardian*

Reporter of the Year: David Hencke, *The Guardian*

Reporting Team of the Year: *Financial Times* Robert Maxwell Investigation team

Cecil King Young Journalist of the Year: Andrew Malone, *Scotland on Sunday*

David Blundy Award: Allister Sparkes, *The Observer*

Provincial Journalist of the Year: Steve Davies, *Southampton Advertiser*

Arthur Sandles Travel and Leisure Writer of the Year: Alexander Frater, *The Observer*

David Holden International Reporters of the Year: Ed Vulliamy and Maggie O'Kane, *The Guardian*

Critic of the Year: Allison Pearson, *Independent on Sunday*

Columnist of the Year: Simon Jenkins, *The Times*

Feature Writer of the Year: Lynda Lee-Potter, *Daily Mail*

Sports Journalist of the Year: Hugh McIlvanney, *The Observer*

Specialist Writer of the Year: Anatole Kaletsky, *The Times*

Magazine Writer of the Year: Russell Miller, *Sunday Times* magazine

Chairman's Awards: Ray Snoddy, *Financial Times*; Andrew Morton

Music Awards

The Brit Awards 1993

Best Male Singer: Mick Hucknall
Best Female Singer: Annie Lennox
Best Album: *Diva*, Annie Lennox
Best British Group: Simply Red
Best Producer: Peter Gabriel
Best Newcomer: Tasmin Archer
Best Soundtrack: *Wayne's World*
Best Single: "Could It Be Magic", Take That
Best International Artist: Prince
Best International Group: REM
Best International Newcomer: Nirvana
Best Music Video: *Stay*, Shakespear's Sister
Best Classical Recording: Nigel Kennedy, Beethoven's *Violin Concerto*, con. Klaus Tennstedt
Best Live Band: U2
Outstanding Contribution: Rod Stewart

The Gramophone Awards

(presented Oct. 1992)
Source: *Gramophone* magazine

Record of the Year: Beethoven, *Symphonies*, Chamber Orchestra of Europe/Nikolaus Harnoncourt (Teldec)
Best Baroque Recording (vocal): Handel, *Giullio Cesare*, Larmore; Schlick; Fink; Ragin; Zanasi; Lallouette; Visse; Concerto Cologne/Jacobs (Harmonia Mundi)
Best Baroque Recording (non-vocal): Rameau, *Harpsichord Works*, Rousset (L'Oiseau-Lyre)
Best Chamber Recording: Szymanowski, *String Quartets: No. 1 in C major, Opus 37, No. 2 Opus 56*; Webern, *Slow Movement*, Carmina Quartet (Denon)
Best Choral Recording: Britten, *War Requiem, Opus 66*; *Sinfonia da Requiem, Opus 20*; *Ballad of Heroes, Opus 14*; Harper/Langridge/Hill/Shirley-Quirk/St Paul's Cathedral Choir/London Symphony Chorus and Orchestra/Hickox (Chandos)
Best Concerto Recording: Medtner, *Piano Concertos: No. 2 in C minor, Opus 50*; *No. 3 in E minor, Opus 60*, Demidenko/BBC Scottish Symphony Orchestra/Maksymiuk (Hyperion)
Best Contemporary Recording: Tavener, *The Protecting Veil*; *Thrinos*; Britten, *Solo Cello Suite No. 3, Opus 87*, Isserlis/London Symphony Orchestra/Rozhdestvensky (Virgin Classics)
Best Early Music Recording: *The Rose and the Ostrich Feather*, music from the Eton Choirbook, Volume 1, The Sixteen Christophers (Collins Classics)
Best Engineered Recording: Britten, *War Requiem, Opus 66*; *Sinfonia da Requiem, Opus 20*; *Ballad of Heroes, Opus 14*, Harper/Langridge/Hill/Shirley-Quirk/St Paul's Cathedral Choir/London Symphony Chorus and Orchestra/Hickox (Chandos)
Best Historical Recording (vocal): *Covent Garden on Record, Volumes 1–4*, 143 singers with various accompaniments (Pearl)
Best Historical Recording (non-vocal): *The Elgar Edition, Volume 1*, London Symphony Orchestra/Royal Albert Hall Orchestra/Elgar (EMI)
Best Instrumental Recording: Alkan, *25 Preludes dans les tons majeurs et mineurs, Opus 31*; Shostakovich, *24 Preludes, Opus 34*, Mustonen (Decca)
Best Music Theatre Recording: Bernstein, *Candide*, Hadley/Anderson/Green/Ludwig/Gedda/Jones/Ollmann/Jenkins/Stuart/Treleaven/Benson/Bayley/London Symphony Chorus and Orchestra/Bernstein (Deutsche Gramophon)
Best Opera Recording: Richard Strauss, *Die Frau ohne schatten*, Varady/Domingo/Behrens/van Dam/Runkel/Dohmen/Jo/Gambill/Vienna Boys' Choir/Vienna State Opera Chorus/Vienna Philharmonic Orchestra/Solti (Decca)
Best Orchestral Recording: Beethoven, *Symphonies*, Chamber Orchestra of Europe/Harnoncourt (Teldec)
Best Solo Vocal Recording: Schubert, *Lieder*, Fassbaender/Reimann (Deutsche Gramophon)
Special Achievement Award: The Abbey Road Studios, 1931–92
Artist of the Year: Dame Kiri Te Kanawa
Lifetime Achievement: Sir Georg Solti
Young Artist of the Year: Bryn Terfel

Grammy Awards

Source: National Academy of Recording Arts & Sciences

1958
Record: Domenico Modugno, *Nel Blu Dipinto Di Blu (Volare)*.
Album: Henry Mancini, *The Music from Peter Gunn*.

1959
Record: Bobby Darin, *Mack the Knife*.
Album: Frank Sinatra, *Come Dance With Me*.

1960
Record: Percy Faith, *Theme from a Summer Place*.
Album: Bob Newhart, *Button Down Mind*.

1961
Record: Henry Mancini, *Moon River*.
Album: Judy Garland, *Judy at Carnegie Hall*.

1962
Record: Tony Bennett, *I Left My Heart in San Francisco*.
Album: Vaughn Meader, *The First Family*.

1963
Record: Henry Mancini, *The Days of Wine and Roses*.
Album: *The Barbra Streisand Album*.

1964
Record: Stan Getz and Astrud Gilberto, *The Girl from Ipanema*.
Album: Stan Getz and Astrud Gilberto, *Getz/Gilberto*.

1965
Record: Herb Alpert, *A Taste of Honey*.
Album: Frank Sinatra, *September of My Years*.

1966
Record: Frank Sinatra, *Strangers in the Night*.
Album: Frank Sinatra, *A Man and His Music*.

1967
Record: 5th Dimension, *Up, Up and Away*.
Album: The Beatles, *Sgt. Pepper's Lonely Hearts Club Band*.

1968
Record: Simon & Garfunkel, *Mrs. Robinson*.
Album: Glen Campbell, *By the Time I Get to Phoenix*.

1969
Record: 5th Dimension, *Aquarius/Let the Sunshine In*.
Album: Blood, Sweat and Tears, *Blood, Sweat and Tears*.

1970
Record: Simon & Garfunkel, *Bridge Over Troubled Water*.
Album: Simon & Garfunkel, *Bridge Over Troubled Water*.

1971
Record: Carole King, *It's Too Late*.
Album: Carole King, *Tapestry*.

1972
Record: Roberta Flack, *The First Time Ever I Saw Your Face*.
Album: *The Concert For Bangla Desh*.

1973
Record: Roberta Flack, *Killing Me Softly with His Song*.
Album: Stevie Wonder, *Innervisions*.

1974
Record: Olivia Newton-John, *I Honestly Love You.*
Album: Stevie Wonder, *Fulfullingness' First Finale.*

1975
Record: Captain & Tennille, *Love Will Keep Us Together.*
Album: Paul Simon, *Still Crazy After All These Years.*

1976
Record: George Benson, *This Masquerade.*
Album: Stevie Wonder, *Songs in the Key of Life.*

1977
Record: Eagles, *Hotel California.*
Album: Fleetwood Mac, *Rumours.*

1978
Record: Billy Joel, *Just the Way You Are.*
Album: Bee Gees, *Saturday Night Fever.*

1979
Record: The Doobie Brothers, *What a Fool Believes.*
Album: Billy Joel, *52nd Street.*

1980
Record: Christopher Cross, *Sailing.*
Album: Christopher Cross, *Christopher Cross.*

1981
Record: Kim Carnes, *Bette Davis Eyes.*
Album: John Lennon, Yoko Ono, *Double Fantasy.*

1982
Record: Toto, *Rosanna.*
Album: Toto, *Toto IV.*

1983
Record: Michael Jackson, *Beat It.*
Album: Michael Jackson, *Thriller.*

1984
Record: Tina Turner, *What's Love Got to Do With It.*
Album: Lionel Richie, *Can't Slow Down.*

1985
Record: USA for Africa, *We Are the World.*
Album: Phil Collins, *No Jacket Required.*

1986
Record: Steve Winwood, *Higher Love.*
Album: Paul Simon, *Graceland.*

1987
Record: Paul Simon, *Graceland.*
Album: U2, *The Joshua Tree.*

1988
Record: Bobby McFerrin, *Don't Worry, Be Happy.*
Album: George Michael, *Faith.*

1989
Record: Bette Midler, *Wind Beneath My Wings.*
Album: Bonnie Raitt, *Nick of Time.*

1990
Record: Phil Collins, *Another Day in Paradise.*
Album: Quincy Jones, *Back on the Block.*

1991
Record: Natalie Cole, with Nat 'King' Cole, *Unforgettable.*
Album: Natalie Cole, with Nat 'King' Cole, *Unforgettable.*

1992
Record: Eric Clapton, *Tears in Heaven.*
Album: Eric Clapton, *Unplugged.*
Song: Eric Clapton, *Tears in Heaven.*
New Artist: Arrested Development.
Female Pop Vocalist: k. d. lang, *Constant Craving.*
Male Pop Vocalist: Eric Clapton, *Tears in Heaven.*
Duo or Group Pop Vocal: Celine Dion and Peabo Bryson, *Beauty and the Beast.*
Traditional Pop Vocalist: Tony Bennett, *Perfectly Frank.*
Pop-musical Performance: *Beauty and the Beast*, Nurenberg Symphony Orchestra.
Female Rock Vocalist: Melissa Etheridge, *Ain't It Heavy.*
Male Rock Vocalist: Eric Clapton, *Unplugged.*
Rock Duo or Group: U2, *Achtung Baby.*
Hard Rock: Red Hot Chili Peppers, *Give It Away.*
Metal: Nine-Inch Nails, *Wish.*
Rock Instrumental Performance: Stevie Ray Vaughan and Double Trouble, *Little Wing.*
Rock Song: Eric Clapton and Jim Gordon, *Layla.*

Eurovision Song Contest

Source: BBC

	Winner						
	Country	**Song**	**Singer**	**British entry**	**Singer**	**Placed**	**Location**
1956	Switzerland	*Refrain*	Lys Assia	No entry	No entry	–	Lugano
1957	Netherlands	*Net Als Toen*	Corry Brokken	*All*	Patricia Bredin	7th	Frankfurt-am-Main
1958	France	*Dors, mon amour*	André Claveau	No entry	No entry	–	Hilversum
1959	Netherlands	*Een Beetje*	Teddy Scholten	*Single Little Birdie*	Pearl Carr & Teddy Johnson	2nd	Cannes
1960	France	*Tom Pillibi*	Jacqueline Boyer	*Looking High, High, High*	Bryan Johnson	2nd	London
1961	Luxembourg	*Nous, les amoureux*	Jean-Claude Pascal	*Are You Sure?*	The Allisons	2nd	Cannes
1962	France	*Un premier amour*	Isabelle Aubret	*Ring-a-ding Girl*	Ronnie Carroll	Tied 4th	Luxembourg
1963	Denmark	*Dansevise*	Grethe & Jorgen Ingmann	*Say Wonderful Things*	Ronnie Carroll	4th	London
1964	Italy	*Non ho l'ete*	Gigliola Cinquetti	*I Love the Little Things*	Matt Monro	2nd	Copenhagen
1965	Luxembourg	*Poupée de cire, poupée de son*	France Gall	*I Belong*	Kathy Kirby	2nd	Naples
1966	Austria	*Merci chérie*	Udo Jurgens	*A Man without Love*	Kenneth McKellar	9th	Luxembourg
1967	UK	*Puppet on a String*	Sandie Shaw	–	–	–	Vienna
1968	Spain	*La, La, La*	Massiel	*Congratulations*	Cliff Richard	2nd	London
1969	Tie: France	*Un jour, un enfant*	Frida Boccara	–	–	–	Madrid
	Netherlands	*De Troubadour*	Lennie Kuhr				
	Spain	*Vivo Cantando*	Salome				
	UK	*Boom-bang-a-bang*	Lulu				
1970	Ireland	*All Kinds of Everything*	Dana	*Knock, Knock, Who's There?*	Mary Hopkin	2nd	Amsterdam
1971	Monaco	*Un banc, un arbre, une rue*	Sévérine	*Jack in the Box*	Clodagh Rodgers	4th	Dublin
1972	Luxembourg	*Après toi*	Vicky Leandros	*Beg, Steal or Borrow*	The New Seekers	2nd	Edinburgh

(Continued)

	Winner						
	Country	Song	Singer	British entry	Singer	Placed	Location
1973	Luxembourg	*Tu te reconnaitras*	Anne-Marie David	*Power to all Our Friends*	Cliff Richard	3rd	Luxembourg
1974	Sweden	*Waterloo*	Abba	*Long Live Love*	Olivia Newton-John	Tie 4th	Brighton
1975	Netherlands	*Ding-dinge-dong*	Teach-In	*Let Me Be the One*	The Shadows	2nd	Stockholm
1976	UK	*Save Your Kisses for Me*	Brotherhood of Man	–	–	–	The Hague
1977	France	*L'oiseau et l'enfant*	Marie Myriam	*Rock Bottom*	Lynsey de Paul & Mike Moran	2nd	London
1978	Israel	*A-ba-ni-bi*	Izhar Cohen & The Alpha Beta	*Bad Old Days*	Co-Co	11th	Paris
1979	Israel	*Hallelujah*	Milk and Honey	*Mary Ann*	Black Lace	7th	Jerusalem
1980	Ireland	*What's Another Year?*	Johnny Logan	*Love Enough for Two*	Prima Donna	3rd	The Hague
1981	UK	*Making Your Mind Up*	Buck's Fizz	–	–	–	Dublin
1982	Germany	*Ein Bisschen frieden*	Nicole	*One Step Further*	Bardo	7th	Harrogate
1983	Luxembourg	*Si la vie est un cadeau*	Corinne Hermès	*I'm Never Giving Up*	Sweet Dreams	6th	Munich
1984	Sweden	*Diggi Loo, Diggi Ley*	Herrey's	*Love Games*	Bell & the Devotions	7th	Luxembourg
1985	Norway	*La det Swinge*	Bobbysocks!	*Love Is*	Vikki	4th	Gothenburg
1986	Belgium	*J'aime la vie*	Sandra Kim	*Runner in the Night*	Ryder	7th	Bergen
1987	Ireland	*Hold Me Now*	Johnny Logan	*Only the Night*	Rikki	13th	Brussels
1988	Switzerland	*Ne partez-pas sans moi*	Céline Dion	*Go*	Scott Fitzgerald	2nd	Dublin
1989	Yugoslavia	*Rock Me*	Riva	*Why Do I Always Get It Wrong?*	Live Report	2nd	Lausanne
1990	Italy	*Insieme: 1992*	Toto Cutugno	*Give a Little Love Back to the World*	Emma	6th	Zagreb
1991	Sweden	*Captured by a Love Storm*	Carola	*A Message to Your Heart*	Samantha Janus	10th	Rome
1992	Ireland	*Why Me?*	Linda Martin	*One Step Out of Time*	Michael Ball	2nd	Malmo
1993	Ireland	*In Your Eyes*	Niamh Kavanagh	*Better the Devil You Know*	Sonia	2nd	Millstreet

New Year Honours 1993: Highlights

Life Peer

Shirley Williams, founder member and former president of the Social Democratic Party

Privy Counsellor

Baroness Emily Blatch, minister of state for education

Knights Bachelor

Malcolm Arnold, composer
David Frost, broadcaster and journalist
Anthony Hopkins, actor

Commander, Royal Victorian Order

John Julius Norwich, writer and broadcaster
Jocelyn Stevens, newspaper proprietor
Sir Antony Jay, politician

Companion of Honour

Sir V. S. Pritchett, writer

Dame Commander, Order of the British Empire

Catherine Cookson, novelist
Annette Penhaligon, political activist
Margaret Price, opera singer

Commander, Order of the British Empire

Leslie Crowther, television personality
Jimmy Young, broadcaster

Order of the British Empire

Kate Adie, television news correspondent
Roy Castle, entertainer
David Coleman, television sports presenter
Evelyn Glennie, musician
Gordon Strachan, footballer

Member, Order of the British Empire

Chris Boardman, cyclist and Olympic gold medallist
Sharron Davies, swimmer
Sally Gunnell, athlete and Olympic gold medallist
Sean Kerly, hockey player

Queen's Birthday Honours 1993: Highlights

Life Peer

Sir Richard Attenborough, film director
Sir Ralf Dahrendorf, warden, St Anthony's College, Oxford
Robin Leigh Pemberton, former governor, Bank of England
Sir Yehudi Menuhin, violinist

Dame Commander, order of the British Empire

Thora Hird, actress
Muriel Spark, novelist

Knight Commander, Order of the British Empire

Sir Peter Parker, former head of British Rail

(Continued)

Commander, Order of the British Empire

Louise Botting, financial consultant and broadcaster
Paul Hamlyn, publisher
Felicity Palmer, opera singer
Alan Tuffin, union leader

Order of the British Empire

Michael Aspel, television presenter
Phil Drabble, naturalist and broadcaster
Rumer Godden, novelist
Anna Home, head of BBC children's programmes
David Jason, actor
Mike Leigh, film director
Bob Monkhouse, television presenter
Patricia Routledge, actress
Sir Ranulph Fiennes, explorer

Member, Order of the British Empire

Percy Edwards, ornithologist
Harold Larwood, cricketer

Queen's Awards for Export, Technology & Environmental Achievement

Awarded 21 April 1993

These awards are given to a team or company as a whole, rather than to an individual, and were instituted to recognize and encourage outstanding achievement.

Further information and application forms may be obtained from: The Queen's Award Office, Dean Bradley House, 52 Horseferry Road, London SW1P 2AG; tel. 071-222 2277.

Exports

AES Engineering, Rotherham and Bradford: Four-fold increase in exports of mechanical seals since 1989.
ASM (Orchestra) Ltd, t/a The Acxademy of St Martin in the Fields, London: Non-subsidized orchestra founded by Sir Neville Marriner gains over two-thirds of its earnings from overseas concert performances and sale of recordings.
Advent Communications, Chesham: Portable earth terminals for the transmission of television or data.
Airwair, Wellingborough: Makes "Dr Martens" branded footwear for export.
Appletise, Woking: Sparkling apple juice.
A. E. Arthur, King's Lynn: Developed new models of dressmakers' dummy to break into Japanese market.
Autovalet Systems International, London: Microprocessor controlled automatic dispensers for issue of workwear in hospitals, industry, hotels and leisure centres.
BCB International, Cardiff: Leisure and safety equipment for outdoor pursuits.
BT & D Technologies, Ipswich: Optoelectronic components for advanced telecommunications, data communication and cable television systems.
Edward Baker, Sudbury: Pet food products.
Banque Paribas Export Finance Unit, London: Export credit finance.
Bioscot, Edinburgh: Monoclonal and polyclonal antibodies for use as blood reagents.
Booster Electric Vehicles, Huddersfield: Electric scooters for the disabled and elderly.
Borden decorative Products (Transprints Division), Morecambe: Transfer paper for printing of fabrics.
CADCentre, Cambridge: Software.
Canadian Pizza Crust Co (UK), Salford: Pizza bases and fillings.
Carron Bathrooms, Falkirk: Luxury acrylic baths styled to customer requirements.
Caterham Cars, Caterham: Super Seven sports car.
Chadwicks of Bury, Bury: Aluminium foil lids for dairy, food and soft drinks industries.
Churchill Tableware, Stoke-on-Trent: Earthenware tableware and mugs.
ConvaTec, Deeside: Stoma care products and modern wound dressings.
Cookson Entek, Newcastle upon Tyne: Polyethylene-based separator materials for lead acid batteries.
The Copyrights Company, Milton, near Banbury: Licensing agency for merchandise featuring copyright designs owned by the writers and artists it represents.
Croda Kerr, Liverpool: Fire extinguishing chemicals.
Derwent MacDee, Doncaster: Plastic plumbing and sanitary ware.
Desurvey, Birkenhead: Hi-tech engineering design services for offshore oil and gas industries.
Dunphy Combustion, Rochdale: Industrial burners.
Dynacast International, Alcester: Small, high-volume, high-precision components in metals and plastics.
Epitaxial Products International, Cardiff: Epitaxially coated semiconductor wafers grown to customer specifications for advanced electronics.
Europalite, Mansfield: Road traffic separators, barrier systems and signs.
Europressings, Cardiff: Decorative steel pressings for outer wraps on video recorders, compact disc players and computers.
FMC Corporation (UK), Wellhead Equipment Division, Dunfermline: Surface and subsea oil wellhead equipment.
Financial Times Group, London: Newspaper.
Ford Motor Company, Brentwood: Motor manufacturers.
Foster Refrigerator (UK), King's Lynn: Refrigeration units.
Foster Wheeler Energy, Reading: Engineering, management and construction services to energy industry.
GEC ALSTHOM Transmission & Distribution Projects, Stafford: High voltage DC converters, static VAR compensators, heavy duty rectifiers and DC circuit breakers.
Gaffney, Cline & Associates, Alton: Consultants to petroleum and other energy-related organizations.
The Good Book Guide, London: Independent book review magazine with international ordering service.
Griffith Laboratories, Somercotes: Breadcrumb manufacturers.
Hanover Displays, Lewes: Electronic signs.
Harrison & Sons, High Wycombe: Security printing.
Hilditch & Key (Wholesale Division), Glenrothes: Shirt manufacturers.
A. E. Holt, Leicester: Sock manufacturers.
John Horsfall & Sons, Halifax: Manufactures blankets, specializing in airline industry.
Howmet Ltd, Exeter Casting, Exeter: Precision casting for aerospace and industrial gas turbine industries.
ICL MID Range Systems, Bracknell: DRS 6000 series computers and associated UNIX products.
It's At (UK), London: High fashion ladies' garments.

IXI, Cambridge: Develops and supplies UNIX open system.
Johnson Matthey, Catalytic Systems Division, European Catalyst Group, Royston: Autocatalysts for control of motor vehicle exhaust emissions.
Jotun-Henry Clark, London: Paints for marine, offshore and industrial use.
Junior Hagen, London: Trimmings for fashion industry.
Justerini & Brooks, London: Wine merchant and Scotch whisky producer.
KCC Process Equipment, Sunbury-on-Thames: Process plant equipment for oil and natural gas production.
Kacy, London: Ladies' garments.
John Laing International, Hemel Hempstead: Construction and project management.
Lightfoot Surfaces, Doddington: Seamless rubber flooring for use in stables, etc.
Linnhoff March, Knutsford: Consultancy to large energy users on Pinch Technology (Process Information on the Control of Heating).
Lion Cabinets, Leeds: Mild steel enclosures and mountings for computer peripherals.
Lofthouse of Fleetwood, Fleetwood: Manufacturer of Fisherman's Friend lozenges.
Lothian Coated Fabrics, Prestonpans: Textile finishing.
Lowndes Lambert Group Holdings, London: Insurance broker.
Macallan-Glenlivet, Craigellachie: Malt whisky.
Madge Networks, Chalfont St Giles: Token ring networking products for use in computing.
Marks and Spencer, London: Chain store which exports clothing, home furnishings and foods under St Michael trademark.
Mayflower Glass, East Boldon: Glass sculptures of ships in bottles.
R. Mears & Co, London: Insurance and reinsurance brokers.
Morane, Banbury: Manufacturers of machinery and plastic film for lamination.
National Pig Development Company, Driffield: Genetically advanced purebred and hybrid pig breeding stock.
Newley Goodman, Tipton: Lingerie fastenings.
Newsround International Airfreight, High Wycombe: Freight forwarders.
Nissan Motor Manufacturing (UK), Sunderland: Subsidiary of Nissan Motor Co Ltd.
Nylon Hosiery Company Limited, Hinckley: Ladies' hosiery.
Omega Diagnostics Ltd, Alloa: Medical diagnostics test kits.
Otodynamics, Hatfield: Electronic hearing test equipment.
PED (Staden), Northampton: Thermal processing plant.
PPE, Harlow: Point-of-sale display equipment and leaflet dispensers.
Pauls Malt, Newmarket: Producer of malt for beer and whisky.
Pearsalls Sutures, Somerset: Materials for surgical sutures.
Peboc, Anglesey: Vitamin D3 products and organic fine chemicals.
Pfizer, Sandwich: Pharmaceutical and animal health products.
Pig Improvement Company, Abingdon: Genetically improved breeding pigs.
Pilkington Micronics, Deeside: Flat glass, precision-worked for use in liquid crystal displays, optical disc substrates and magnetic disc substrates.
Pointing, Prudhoe: Colours and flavours for food processing and pharmaceutical industries.
Porton Speywood, Wrexham: Hyate C, pharmaceutical product for treatment of haemophilia.
Powell Duffryn International Fuels, Harpenden: Coal trading.
Psygnosis, Liverpool: Develops and manufactures computer games.
Racal Radar Defence Systems, Chessington: Manufacturers naval electronic warfare equipment and other products.
Randox Laboratories, Crumlin, Co Antrim: Manufacturers diagnostic kits and enzymes for medical and veterinary applications.
Really Useful Group, London: Theatrical producers, theatre licensers, music publishers, record producers and theatre owners.
Redwood International, Hemel Hempstead: Develops and markets Uniplex business software.
Reyrolle, Hebburn: Manufactures high-voltage switchgear and protection components for electricity supply industry.
Riggarna UK, Christchurch: Rod-rigging systems for yachts, and advanced tensile structures for buildings.
Felix Rosenstiel's Widow and Son, London: Fine art publisher.
STC Submarine Systems, Greenwich: Installs submarine telecommunications, on a turnkey basis, worldwide.
St Brendans Irish Cream, Londonderry: Manufacturer of cream liqueurs.
Schroder Capital Management, London: Manages international equity portfolios for overseas clients, mainly trustees of pension funds.
Shelbourne Reynolds Engineering, Bury St Edmunds: Manufacturer of agricultural harvesting machinery.
Fokker Division of Short Brothers, Belfast: Wings for Fokker 100 aircraft.
Sigmaform UK, Wellingborough: Heat-shrinkable cable jointing and accessories.
Silent Channel Products, Huntingdon: Manufactures rubber seals and bodyside mouldings for automotive industry.
Slinger Group, Blackburn: Meat producers.
Steward Hughes, Eastleigh: Produces condition-monitoring equipment for engineering applications, and provides consultancy services.
TSS, Oxfordshire: Design and manufactures marine instruments.
Tacolin, Winsford: Cast embossed polythene film for hygiene and sanitary products.
Charles W. Taylor & Son, South Shields: Castings for gas turbine engines, pumps, and other high-integrity engineering applications.
Edward Thompson (Printers), Sunderland: Games for interactive TV shows, newspapers, and general promotions.
Thor Ceramics, Glasgow: Graphitic industrial ceramics for the control of the flow of steel in continuous casting processes.
Titus International, Iver: Fittings and fasteners for furniture assembly.
Torquemeters, Northampton: Torquemeters and associated equipment to measure shaft horsepower produced or required to drive rotating machines.
Transatlantic Clothing Company Inc Aero Leathers, Galashiels: Leather outer clothing.
University of Strathclyde Graduate Business School, Glasgow: Part-time Master of Business Administra-

tion degree.
Vascutek, Inchinnan: Sterile implantable vascular grafts for treatment of diseased or damaged arteries.
Vauxhall Motors, Luton: Motor manufacturers.
Voltech Instruments, Abingdon: Instrumentation for power electronics market.

Technology

BT Laboratories, Optical Research Division, Ipswich: Development of metal organic vapour phase epitaxy technique for making semiconductor devices for optoelectronics industry.
Bridon Ropes, Brifen Department, Doncaster: Development of wire rope safety fence for use in central reserve and verge of roads.
Marine Technology, Castrol, Reading: Cyltech 80, a marine diesel lubricant.
Crown Berger, Darwen: For loop reactor system to replace the traditional batch reactor process for production of emulsion polymers.
Glacier Vandervell, Kilmarnock: For Glacier AS124, a bimetallic bearing material.
Holroyd, Rochdale: For fully automatic cutter grinders which overcome disadvantages in existing machines through software control of six axes simultaneously.
Huntleigh Healthcare, Cardiff: Development of intelligent obstetric and vascular pocket dopplers.
ICL Corporate Systems, Manchester: Development of Series 39 SX mainframe computer system.
Insignia Solutions, High Wycombe: Development of system which emulates an IBM personal computer on a wide range of otherwise incompatible computers.
Intavent, Reading: Development of laryngeal mask, which is more secure than a face mask but less invasive than an endotrachael tube, both traditional ways of anaesthetizing patients.
Joint Replacement Instrumentation, London: For furlong (R) H-A-C Coated Hip Prosthesis.
Kelvin Hughes, Ilford: High resolution navigational radar for commercial vessels on inland waterways.
Land Rover Power Train, Solihull: For 200 Tdi diesel engine which overcomes poor high-speed performance and high emission and noise levels normally found with direct injection diesel engines.
Martin-Baker Aircraft Company, Uxbridge: Development of ejection seat selected as United States Navy aircrew common ejection seat.
NextBase, Ashford: For computerized route planning system.
Oxford Applied Research, Witney: For developing reactive atom/radical source for use in developing thin film devices, particularly high temperature superconductors.
P. P. Payne, Nottingham: Development of pressure sensitive adhesive tear tape as easy opening device for flexible packaging.
Pitman-Moore, Uxbridge: For automatic cattle wormer.
pneuPAC, Luton: Development of portable gas-powered lung ventilators.
Raychem, Swindon: For heat shrinkable, fabric, composite technology for use in sealing and protecting splice joints in telecommunication networks.
S & S International, Berkhamsted: Development of anti-virus toolkit by use of an interpreted language data base.
Smiths Industries Aerospace & Defence Systems – Integrated Display Systems, Cheltenham: Development of multi-purpose colour display for high performance aircraft.
Solid State Logic, Oxford: For digital audio post production system, widely used for video and film.
Tronic Electronic Services, Ulverston: Development of connector for interconnection of electrical cables in heavily contaminated sea water.
ZENECA, Grangemouth Works: Development of improved process for production of hexaconazole and flutriafol which reduces costs and volume of waste.

Environment

Agricultural Genetics Co, MicroBio Division, Royston: MicroBio Division gains award jointly with Horticultural Research International for development of insect pathogenic products as alternatives to synthetic pesticides.
BEWT (Water Engineers), Alcester: Development of systems capable of reducing metal content of effluent solutions and of recovering the metal as a high quality electrolytic product for re-use.
Edwards High Vacuum International, Crawley: Development of rotary mechanical pumps, which are unlubricated.
FKI Babcock Roby, Oldbury: Development of gas and oil-fired boilers with low emissions of nitrogen oxides.
Non-Ferrous Metal Treatment Team, Foundry Division, Tamworth: Development of pollution-free portable foundry degassing unit.
Horticulture Research International, Wellesbourne: Gains award jointly with the Agricultural Genetics Co for development of insect parasitic nematode products as alternatives to synthetic pesticides.
Johnson Matthey Catalytic Systems Division, Royston: Development of autocatalysts to reduce carbon monoxide, hydrocarbon and nitrogen oxide content of motor vehicle exhausts.
Kerry Ultrasonics, Hitchen: Development of ultrasonic cleaning systems which replace CFC solvents.
Pilkington Glass Limited, St Helens: Development of Pilkington K Glass which offers a 30 per cent reduction in heat loss, compared to conventional double glazing.
Ricardo Consulting Engineers, Shoreham-by-Sea: Application of tumbling air motion for car engines, achieving combustion optimization.
Ricoh UK Products Ltd, Telford: Elimination of CFC in production of photocopiers.
Sericol Limited, Broadstairs: Development of water-based screen printing inks.

PEOPLE

Selected International Figures of the Present

Name (Birthplace)	Birthdate
Agnelli, Giovanni (Turin, Italy)	12/3/21
Alfonsin, Raul (Chascomus, Argentina)	12/3/27
Amado, Jorge (Bahia, Brazil)	1/8/12
Andreotti, Giulio (Rome, Italy)	14/1/19
Angelou, Maya (St Louis, Mo.)	4/4/28
Aquino, Cory (Tarlac Province, Philippines)	25/1/33
Arafat, Yasser (Jerusalem, Palestine)	1929
Arens, Moshe (Kaumas, Lithuania)	27/12/25
Arias-Sanchez, Oscar (Heredia, Costa Rica)	13/9/41
Aristide, Jean-Bertrand (Port Salut, Haiti)	15/7/53
Ashrawi, Hanan (Ramallat, Palestine)	1946
Aung San Suu Kyi (Rangoon, Burma)	19/6/45
Baker, James A. (Houston, Tex.)	28/4/30
Banda, Dr Hastings (Malawi)	14/5/05
Bandaranaike, Sirimavo (Ratnapura, Sri Lanka)	17/4/16
Barnard, Dr Christiaan (Beaufortwest, S. Africa)	9/11/22
Barre, Raymond (Saint-Denis, Réunion)	12/4/24
Bhutto, Benazir (Karachi, Pakistan)	21/6/53
Black, Shirley Temple (Santa Monica, Cal.)	23/4/28
Bond, Alan (Fremantle, Australia)	22/4/38
Boutros-Ghali, Boutros (Cairo, Egypt)	14/11/22
Brown, Helen Gurley (Green Forest, Ark.)	18/2/22
Brown, Jerry (San Francisco, Cal.)	7/4/38
Bruntland, Gro Harlem (Oslo, Norway)	2/4/39
Buchwald, Art (Mt. Vernon, N.Y.)	20/10/25
Buckley, William F. (New York, N.Y.)	24/11/25
Bush, Barbara (Rye, N.Y.)	8/6/25
Bush, George (Milton, Mass)	12/6/24
Campell, Kim (Port Alberni, British Columbia)	10/3/47
Cardin, Pierre (San Biagio di Callatla, Italy)	7/7/22
Carter, Jimmy (Plains, Ga.)	1/10/24
Carter, Rosalynn (Plains, Ga.)	18/8/27
Cela, Camilo Jose (Ira Flavia, Spain)	11/5/16
Charles, Dr Eugenia (Pointe Michel, Dominica)	15/5/19
Chirac, Jacques (Paris, France)	29/11/32
Chomsky, Noam (Pennsylvania, USA)	7/12/28
Clinton, Bill (Hope, Arkansas)	11/8/46
Clinton, Hillary Rodham (Chicago, Ill.)	26/10/47
Courrèges, André (Pau, France)	9/3/23
Cousteau, Jacques (St André de Cubzac, France)	11/6/10
Cronkite, Walter (St. Joseph, Mo.)	4/11/16
Cuomo, Mario (Queens, N.Y.)	15/6/32
Dalai Lama (Taktser, Tibet)	6/7/35
Delors, Jacques (Paris, France)	20/7/25
Derrida, Jacques (El Bia, Algeria)	15/7/30
Dinkins, David (Trenton, N.J.)	10/7/27
Dukakis, Michael S. (Boston, Mass.)	3/11/33
Fabius, Laurent (Paris, France)	20/8/46
Ferraro, Geraldine (Newburgh, N.Y.)	26/8/35
Ferre, Gianfranco (Legnano, Italy)	15/8/44
Fischer, Bobby (Chicago, Illinois)	9/3/43
Fitzgerald, Dr Garrett (Dublin, Ireland)	9/2/26
Fitzwater, Marlin (Salina, Kan.)	24/11/42
Ford, Betty (Chicago, Ill.)	8/4/18
Ford, Gerald, R. (Omaha, Neb.)	14/7/13
Friedman, Milton (Brooklyn, N.Y.)	31/7/12
Gaddafy, Muammar al- (nr. Sirte, Libya)	1942
Galbraith, John Kenneth (Ontario, Can.)	15/10/08
Genscher, Hans-Dietrich (Reideburg, Germany)	21/3/27
Giscard d'Estaing, Valéry (Koblenz, Germany)	2/2/26
Givenchy, Hubert de (Beauvais, France)	21/2/27
Glemp, Cardinal Jozef (Inowroclaw, Poland)	18/12/29
Gorbachev, Mikhail (Privalnaye, USSR)	2/3/31
Gorbachev, Raisa (Rubtsovsk, USSR)	1934
Gore, Al (Washington DC)	31/3/48
Gore, Tipper (Washington DC)	19/8/48
Graham, Billy (Charlotte, N.C.)	7/11/18
Greer, Germaine (Melbourne, Australia)	29/1/39
Haughey, Charles (Castlebar, Co. Mayo)	16/9/25
Havel, Vaclav (Prague, Czechoslovakia)	5/10/36
Hawke, Bob (Bordertown, S. Australia)	9/12/29
Hefner, Hugh (Chicago, Ill.)	9/4/26
Helms, Jesse (Monroe, N.C.)	18/10/21
Heyerdahl, Dr Thor (Larvik, Norway)	6/10/14
Iacocca, Lee A. (Allentown, Pa.)	15/10/24
Jackson, Jesse (Greenville, S.C.)	8/10/41
Kael, Pauline (Petaluma, Calif.)	19/6/19
Karan, Donna (Forest Hill, N.Y.)	2/10/48
Karpov, Anatoly (Zlatoust, USSR)	23/5/51
Keating, Paul (Sydney, Australia)	18/1/44

Name (Birthplace)	Birthdate
Kennedy, Edward M. (Brookline, Mass.)	22/2/32
King, Coretta Scott (Marion, Ala.)	27/4/27
King Hassan II of Morocco	9/7/29
King Hussein of Jordan	14/11/35
Kirkpatrick, Jeane (Duncan, Okla.)	19/11/26
Kissinger, Henry (Fuerth, Germany)	27/5/23
Klein, Calvin (New York, N.Y.)	19/11/42
Koch, Edward I. (New York, N.Y.)	12/12/24
Kohl, Helmut (Ludwigshafen, Germany)	3/4/30
Lauren, Ralph (Bronx, N.Y.)	14/10/39
Levi-Strauss, Prof. Claude (Brussels, Belgium)	28/11/08
Mahfouz, Naguib (Cairo, Egypt)	11/12/11
Mandela, Nelson (Transkei, S. Africa)	1918
Mandela, Winnie (Transkei, S. Africa)	1934
Milosz, Czeslaw (Sateinial, Lithuania)	3/6/11
Mitterrand, François (Jarnac, France)	26/10/16
Miyazawa, Kiichi (Tokyo, Japan)	8/10/19
Monaco Royal Family	
Prince Rainier III (Monaco)	31/5/23
Prince Albert (Monte Carlo, Monaco)	14/3/58
Princess Caroline (Monte Carlo, Monaco)	23/1/57
Princess Stephanie (Monaco-Ville, Monaco)	1/2/65
Mondale, Walter (Ceylon, Minn.)	5/1/28
Mosimann, Anton (Switzerland)	23/2/47
Moynihan, Daniel P. (Tulsa, Okla.)	16/3/27
Mubarak, Hosni (Kafr El-Moseilha, Minuffya Gov'nate)	4/5/28
Mugabe, Robert (Kutama, Rhodesia)	21/2/24
Mulroney, Brian (Baie Comeau, Canada)	20/3/39
Murdoch, Rupert (Melbourne, Australia)	11/3/31
Nader, Ralph (Winsted, Conn.)	27/2/34
Nakasone, Yasuhiro (Takasaki, Japan)	27/5/18
Newton, Helmut (Berlin, Germany)	31/10/20
Nixon, Richard (Yorba Linda, Cal.)	9/1/13
Noor al Hussein, Queen of Jordan (Washington, D.C.)	23/8/51
O'Brien, Conor Cruise (Dublin, Ireland)	3/11/17
O'Connor, Cardinal John (Philadelphia, Pa.)	15/1/20
Onassis, Jacqueline (Southampton, N.Y.)	28/7/29
O'Reilly, Tony (Dublin, Ireland)	7/5/36
Packer, Kerry (Sydney, Australia)	17/12/37
Paglia, Camille (Endicott, N.Y.)	1942
Papandreou, Andreas (Chios, Greece)	5/2/19
Pauling, Linus (Portland, Ore.)	28/2/01
Paz, Octavio (Mexico City, Mexico)	31/3/14
Perez, Shimon (Wolozyn, Poland)	16/8/23
Perot, H. Ross (Texarcana, Tex.)	27/6/30
Pope John Paul II (Krakow, Poland)	18/5/20
Powell, Gen. Colin (New York, N.Y.)	5/4/37
Rabin, Yitzak (Jerusalem, Palestine)	1/3/22
Reagan, Nancy (New York, N.Y.)	6/7/23
Reagan, Ronald (Tampico, Ill.)	6/2/11
Ride, Sally K. (Encino, Calif.)	1952
Robinson, Mary (Ballina, Ireland)	21/5/44
Rubik, Erno (Budapest, Hungary)	13/7/44
Sagan, Carl (New York, N.Y.)	9/11/34
Saint Laurent, Yves (Oran, Algeria)	1/8/36
Salinger, Pierre (San Francisco, Cal.)	14/6/25
Salk, Jonas (New York, N.Y.)	28/10/14
Samaranch, Juan (Barcelona, Spain)	17/7/20
Sassoon, Vidal (London)	17/1/28
Scharansky, Natan (Donetsk, USSR)	20/1/48
Stephen, Sir Ninian (Oxford)	15/6/23
Schwarzkopf, H. Norman (Trenton, N.J.)	22/8/34
Shamir, Yitzak (Kuzinoy, Poland)	3/11/14
Shevardnadze, Eduard (Mamati, USSR)	25/1/28
Spock, Benjamin (New Haven, Conn.)	2/5/03
Sununu, John H. (Havana, Cuba)	2/7/39
Suzman, Helen (Germiston, S. Africa)	8/11/17
Teresa, Mother (Skopje, Macedonia)	27/8/10
Terkel, Studs (New York, N.Y.)	16/5/12
Trudeau, Pierre (Montreal, Canada)	18/10/19
Trump, Donald (New York, N.Y.)	1946
Turner, Ted (Cincinnati, Oh.)	1938
Vance, Cyrus (Clarksburg, W. Virginia)	27/2/17
Waldheim, Kurt (Vienna, Austria)	21/12/18
Walesa, Lech (Popowo, Poland)	29/9/43
Westheimer, Ruth (Germany)	1928
Whitlam, Gough (Melbourne, Australia)	11/7/16
Wickramasinghe, Prof. Nalin (Colombo, Sri Lanka)	20/1/39
Wiesenthal, Simon (Buczacz, Poland)	31/12/08
Yeltsin, Boris (Sverdlovsk, USSR)	1/2/31
Young, Andrew (New Orleans, La.)	12/3/32

Widely Known British People of the Present

(Media personalities and popular figures not listed in other categories – as at mid-1993. See Political Scene section for politicians.)

Name (Birthplace)	Birthdate
Adie, Kate (Sunderland)	19/9/45
Armstrong, Fiona (Preston, Lancs)	28/11/56
Armstrong, Pamela (Borneo)	25/8/51
Aspel, Michael (London)	12/1/33
Attenborough, Sir David (Leicester)	8/5/26
Baker, Cheryl (Bethnal Green, London)	8/3/55
Baker, Danny (Deptford, London)	22/6/57
Bannister, Sir Roger (Harrow, Middx)	23/3/29
Barnes, Carol (Norwich, Norfolk)	13/9/54
Beaumont, Bill (Preston, Lancs)	9/3/52
Bellamy, David (London)	18/1/33
Birt, John (Liverpool)	10/12/44
Black, Conrad (Montreal, Canada)	25/8/44
Bragg, Melvyn (Carlisle, Cumbria)	6/10/39
Campbell, Gavin (Letchworth, Herts)	17/3/46
Carpenter, Harry (London)	17/10/25
Carpenter, Sue (London)	17/5/56
Chalmers, Judith (Manchester)	10/10/36
Coleman, David (Alderley Edge, Cheshire)	26/4/26
Cook, Sue (Ruislip, Middx)	30/3/49
Cox, Doc (Sheffield, Yorks)	1/7/46
Craven, John (Leeds)	16/8/41
Davey, Bernard (Belfast, N. Ireland)	29/3/43
Davies, Dickie (Wallasey, Cheshire)	30/4/33
Diamond, Anne (Birmingham, W. Midlands)	8/9/54
Dimbleby, David (London)	28/10/38
Dimbleby, Jonathan (Aylesbury, Bucks)	31/7/40
Edmonds, Noel (London)	22/12/48
Everett, Kenny (Seaforth, Liverpool)	25/12/44
Fish, Michael (Eastbourne, E. Sussex)	27/4/44
Ford, Anna (Tewkesbury, Glos)	2/10/43
Freud, Emma (London)	25/1/62
Gascoigne, Bamber (London)	24/1/35
Grant, Russell (Hillingdon, Middx)	5/2/52
Gray, Muriel (Glasgow, Scotland)	30/8/61
Greene, Sarah (London)	24/10/59
Gregg, Anne (Belfast, N. Ireland)	11/2/40
Gubba, Tony (Manchester)	23/9/43
Hann, Judith (Littleover, Derbyshire)	8/9/42
Hayton, Philip (Keighley, Yorkshire)	2/11/47
Heiney, Paul (Sheffield, Yorks)	20/4/49
Hill, Alex (Glasgow, Scotland)	9/8/54
Hill, Jimmy (Balham, London)	27/7/28
Holness, Bob (Vryheid, S. Africa)	12/11/32
James, Clive (Sydney, Australia)	7/10/40
Judd, Lesley (London)	20/12/46
Kelly, Chris (Cuddington, Cheshire)	24/4/40
Kelly, Henry (Dublin, Ireland)	18/4/46
Kennedy, Sarah (Wallington, Surrey)	8/7/50
Kilroy-Silk, Robert (Birmingham, W. Midlands)	18/5/42
Lawley, Sue (Dudley, Worcs)	14/7/46
Lewis, Martyn (Swansea, W. Glam)	7/4/45
Lloyd, Sian (Maesteg, Mid Glam)	3/7/58
Lynam, Desmond (Ennis, Co. Clare)	17/9/42
Magnusson, Magnus (Reykjavik, Iceland)	12/10/19
McGaskill, Ian (Glasgow, Scotland)	28/7/38
McDonald, Trevor (Trinidad)	16/8/39
Michelmore, Cliff (Cowes, Isle of Wight)	11/12/19
Moore, Brian (Benenden, Kent)	28/2/32
Muir, Frank (Broadstairs, Kent)	5/2/20
Nicholson, Mavis (Briton Ferry, W. Glam)	19/10/30
Norden, Denis (Hackney, London)	6/2/22
Norman, Barry (London)	21/8/33
Owen, Nick (Berkhamsted, Herts)	10/2/47
Parsons, Nicholas (Grantham, Lincs)	10/11/28
Paxman, Jeremy (Leeds, Yorks)	11/5/50
Pettifer, Julian (Malmesbury, Wilts)	21/7/35
Philbin, Maggie (Manchester)	23/6/55
Pilger, John (Sydney, Australia)	1/10/39
Rantzen, Esther (Berkhamsted, Herts)	22/6/40
Rayner, Claire (London)	22/1/31
Rice, Anneka (Cowbridge, S. Glam)	4/10/58
Rippon, Angela (Plymouth, Devon)	12/10/44
Robinson, Anne (Crosby, Liverpool)	26/9/44
Robinson, Jancis (Cumbria)	22/4/50
Robinson, Robert (Liverpool)	17/12/27
Ross, Jonathan (London)	17/11/60
Ross, Nick (London)	7/8/47
Schofield, Philip (Oldham, Lancs)	1/4/62
Serle, Chris (Bristol, Avon)	13/7/43
Singleton, Valerie (Hitchin, Herts)	9/4/37
Sissons, Peter (Liverpool)	17/7/42
Smith, Mike (Hornchurch, Essex)	23/4/55
Snow, Jon (Ardingley, Sussex)	28/9/47
Stewart, Alistair (Emsworth, Hants)	22/6/52
Stoppard, Dr Miriam (Newcastle, Tyne & Wear)	12/5/37
Strachan, Michaela (Ewell, Surrey)	7/4/66
Suchet, John (London)	29/3/44
Tarrant, Chris (Reading, Berks)	10/10/46
Thrower, Debbie (Nairobi, Kenya)	17/11/57
Vine, David (Barnstaple, Devon)	3/1/28
Whicker, Alan (Cairo, Egypt)	2/8/25
Witchell, Nicholas (Cosford, Shropshire)	23/9/53
Wogan, Terry (Co. Limerick, Eire)	3/8/38

Noted Political Figures of the Past

(Full lists of British prime ministers and U.S. presidents appear on pages 254 and 407)

Abu Bakr, 573-634, Mohammedan leader, first caliph, chosen successor to Mohammed.

Dean Acheson, 1893-1971, (U.S.) secretary of state, chief architect of cold war foreign policy.

Konrad Adenauer, 1876-1967, (G.) West German chancellor.

Emilio Aguinaldo, 1869-1964, (Philip.) revolutionary, fought against Spain and the U.S.

Akbar, 1542-1605, (Ind.) greatest Mogul emperor of India.

Salvador Allende Gossens, 1908-1973, (Chil.) president, advocate of democratic socialism.

Herbert H. Asquith, 1852-1928, (Br.) Liberal prime minister, instituted an advanced programme of social reform.

Nancy Astor, 1879–1964, (U.S./Br.) first woman MP in British parliament.

Atahualpa, ?-1533, Inca (ruling chief) of Peru.

Kemal Atatürk, 1881-1938, (Turk.) founded modern Turkey.

Clement Attlee, 1883-1967, (Br.) Labour party leader, prime minister, enacted national health, nationalized many industries.

Manuel Azana, 1880–1940, (Sp.) president, supported republic, ousted by Gen. Franco, died in exile.

Mikhail Bakunin, 1814-1876, (R.) revolutionary, leading exponent of anarchism.

Arthur J. Balfour, 1848-1930, (Br.) as foreign secretary under Lloyd George, issued Balfour Declaration expressing official British approval of Zionism.

Bernard M. Baruch, 1870-1965, (U.S.) financier, gvt. adviser.

Fulgencio Batistá y Zaldívar, 1901-1973, (Cub.) ruler overthrown by Castro.

Lord Beaverbrook, 1879-1964, (Br.) financier, statesman, newspaper owner.

Menachem Begin, 1914–1992, (Isr.) Israeli prime minister, won 1978 Nobel Peace Prize.

Eduard Benes, 1884-1948, (Cze.) president during interwar and post-WW II eras.

David Ben-Gurion, 1886-1973, (Isr.) first premier of Israel.

Lavrenti Beria, 1899-1953, (USSR) Communist leader prominent in political purges under Stalin.

Aneurin Bevan, 1897-1960, (Br.) Labour party leader, key figure in establishing NHS.

Ernest Bevin, 1881-1951, (Br.) Labour party leader, foreign minister, helped lay foundation for NATO.

Zulfiqar Ali Bhutto, 1928–1979, (Pak.) president, instituted basic reforms, overthrown by military, executed.

Otto von Bismarck, 1815-1898, (G.) statesman known as the Iron Chancellor, uniter of Germany, 1870.

Léon Blum, 1872-1950, (F.) socialist leader, writer, headed first Popular Front government.

Simón Bolívar, 1783-1830, (Vnz.) South American revolutionary who liberated much of the continent from Spanish rule.

Robert Boothby, 1900–1986, (Br.) outspoken Conservative party politician, championed European unity long before EC was founded.

Cesare Borgia, 1476-1507, (It.) soldier, politician, an outstanding figure of the Italian Renaissance.

Leonid Brezhnev, 1906-1982, (USSR) leader of the Soviet Union, 1964-82.

Aristide Briand, 1862-1932, (F.) foreign minister, chief architect of Locarno Pact and anti-war Kellogg-Briand Pact.

Nikolai Bukharin, 1888-1938, (USSR) communist leader.

Robert Castlereagh, 1769-1822, (Br.) foreign secretary, guided Grand Alliance against Napoleon.

Camillo Benso Cavour, 1810-1861, (It.) statesman, largely responsible for uniting Italy under the House of Savoy.

Nicolae Ceausescu, 1918-1989, Romanian Communist leader, head of state, 1967-1989.

Austen Chamberlain, 1863-1937, (Br.) Conservative party leader, largely responsible for Locarno Pact of 1925.

Neville Chamberlain, 1869-1940, (Br.) Conservative prime minister whose appeasement of Hitler led to Munich Pact.

Chiang Kai-shek, 1887-1975, (Ch.) Nationalist Chinese president whose govt. was driven from mainland to Taiwan.

Chou En-lai, 1898-1976, (Ch.) diplomat, prime minister, a leading figure of the Chinese Communist party.

Winston Churchill, 1874-1965, (Br.) prime minister, soldier, author, guided Britain through WW 2.

Galeazzo Ciano, 1903-1944, (It.) fascist foreign minister, helped create Rome-Berlin Axis, executed by Mussolini.

Henry Clay, 1777-1852, (U.S.) "The Great Compromiser", one of most influential pre-Civil War political leaders.

Georges Clemenceau, 1841-1929, (F.) twice premier, Wilson's chief antagonist at Paris Peace Conference after WW 1.

DeWitt Clinton, 1769-1828, (U.S.) political leader, responsible for promoting idea of the Erie Canal.

Robert Clive, 1725-1774, (Br.) first administrator of Bengal, laid foundation for British Empire in India.

Jean Baptiste Colbert, 1619-1683, (F.) statesman, influential under Louis XIV, created the French navy.

Stafford Cripps, 1889-1952, (Br.) politician, highly respected chancellor of the exchequer, 1947–50.

Oliver Cromwell, 1599-1658, (Br.) Lord Protector of England, led parliamentary forces during Civil War.

Curzon of Kedleston, 1859-1925, (Br.) viceroy of India, foreign secretary, major force in dealing with post-WW 1 problems in Europe and Far East.

Édouard Daladier, 1884-1970, (F.) radical socialist politician, arrested by Vichy government, interned by Germans until liberation in 1945.

Georges Danton, 1759-1794, (F.) a leading figure in the French Revolution.

Jefferson Davis, 1808-1889, (U.S.) president of the Confederate States of America.

Charles G. Dawes, 1865-1951, (U.S.) statesman, banker, advanced Dawes Plan to stabilize post-WW 1 German finances.

Benjamin Disraeli, 1804-1881, (Br.) prime minister, considered founder of modern Conservative party.

Engelbert Dollfuss, 1892-1934, (Aus.) chancellor, assassinated by Austrian Nazis.

Andrea Doria, 1466-1560, (It.) Genoese admiral, statesman, called "Father of Peace" and "Liberator of Genoa".

Alexander Dubcek, 1921–1992, (Cze.) statesman whose attempted liberalization was crushed, 1968.

John Foster Dulles, 1888-1959, (U.S.) secretary of state under Eisenhower, cold war policy maker.

François "Papa Doc" Duvalier, 1907-1971, (Haiti) president, dictator who enforced rule with brutal secret police (Tonton Macoute) and voodoo.

Friedrich Ebert, 1871-1925, (G.) Social Democratic movement leader, instrumental in bringing about Weimar constitution.

Sir Anthony Eden, 1897-1977, (Br.) foreign secretary, prime minister during Suez invasion of 1956.

Dwight D. Eisenhower, 1890-1969, (U.S.) 34th president, received surrender of Germans in WW2.

Ludwig Erhard, 1897-1977, (G.) economist, West German chancellor, led nation's economic rise after WW 2.

Francisco Franco, 1892-1975, (Sp.) leader of rebel forces during Spanish Civil War and dictator of Spain.

Benjamin Franklin, 1706-1790, (U.S.) printer, publisher, author, inventor, scientist, diplomat.

Louis de Frontenac, 1620-1698, (F.) governor of New France (Canada); encouraged explorations, fought Iroquois.

Hugh Gaitskell, 1906-1963, (Br.) Labour party leader, major force in reversing its stand for unilateral disarmament.

Léon Gambetta, 1838-1882, (F.) statesman, politician, one of the founders of the Third Republic.

Indira Gandhi, 1917-1984, (Ind.) succeeded father, Jawaharlal Nehru, as prime minister, assassinated.

Mohandas K. Gandhi, 1869-1948, (Ind.) political leader, ascetic, led nationalist movement against British rule.

Giuseppe Garibaldi, 1807-1882, (It.) patriot, soldier, a leading figure in the Risorgimento, the Italian unification movement.

Alcide de Gasperi, 1881-1954, (It.) premier, founder of the Christian Democratic party.

Charles de Gaulle, 1890-1970, (F.) general, statesman, and first president of the Fifth Republic.

Genghis Khan, c. 1167-1227, Mongol conqueror, ruler of vast Asian empire.

William E. Gladstone, 1809-1898, (Br.) prime minister 4 times, dominant force of Liberal party from 1868 to 1894.

Paul Joseph Goebbels, 1897-1945, (G.) Nazi propagandist, master of mass psychology.

Klement Gottwald, 1896-1953, (Cze.) communist leader ushered communism into his country.

Antonio Gramsci, 1891-1937, (It.) founder of Italian Communist Party.

Ché (Ernesto) Guevara, 1928-1967, (Arg.) guerrilla leader, prominent in Cuban revolution, killed in Bolivia.

Haile Selassie, 1891-1975, (Eth.) emperor, maintained monarchy through invasion, occupation, internal resistance.

Dag Hammarskjöld, 1905-1961, (Swe.) statesman, UN secretary general.

John Hancock, 1737-1793, (U.S.) revolutionary leader, first signer of Declaration of Independence.

Patrick Henry, 1736-1799, (U.S.) major revolutionary figure, remarkable orator.

Édouard Herriot, 1872-1957, (F.) Radical Socialist leader, twice premier, president of National Assembly.

Theodor Herzl, 1860-1904, (Aus.) founder of modern Zionism.

Rudolf Hess, 1894-1987, (G.) deputy leader, Nazi Party; secretly flew to Scotland, May 1941, to negotiate peace, interned, then imprisoned for life at Spandau.

Heinrich Himmler, 1900-1945, (G.) chief of Nazi SS and Gestapo, primarily responsible for the Holocaust.

Paul von Hindenburg, 1847-1934, (G.) field marshal, president.

Hirohito, 1902-1989; emperor of Japan from 1926.

Adolf Hitler, 1889-1945, (G.) dictator, founder of National Socialism; wrote *Mein Kampf*, strategy for world domination.

Ho Chi Minh, 1890-1969, (Viet.) North Vietnamese president, Vietnamese Communist leader, national hero.

Harry L. Hopkins, 1890-1946, (U.S.) New Deal administrator, closest adviser to FDR during WW 2.

Samuel Houston, 1793-1863, (U.S.) leader of struggle to win control of Texas from Mexico.

Enver Hoxha, 1908-1985, (Alb.) Stalinist dictator.

Hubert H. Humphrey, 1911-1978, (U.S.) Minnesota Democrat, senator, vice president, spent 32 years in public service.

Abdul Aziz Ibn Saud, c. 1888-1953, (S. Arab.) founder of Saudi Arabia and its first king.

Dolores Ibarruri, "La Pasionaria", 1895-1989, (Sp.) communist politician and revolutionary heroine.

Jean Jaurès, 1859-1914, (Fr.) socialist leader, founded *L'Humanité* newspaper, 1904.

Muhammed Ali Jinnah, 1876-1948, (Pak.) founder, first governor-general of Pakistan.

Benito Juarez, 1806-1872, (Mex.) rallied countrymen against foreign threats, sought to create democratic, federal republic.

Thomas Jefferson, 1743-1826, (U.S.) 3rd president, wrote basic draft of Declaration of Independence.

Kamehameha I, c. 1758-1819, (Haw.) founder, first monarch of unified Hawaii.

John F. Kennedy, 1917-1963, (U.S.) 35th president, the youngest and first Roman Catholic president in U.S. history; assassinated.

Robert F. Kennedy, 1925-1968, (U.S.) attorney general, senator, assassinated while seeking presidential nomination.

Jomo Kenyatta, 1881-1970, (Ken.) first prime minister of independent Kenya, 1963, becoming president, 1964.

Aleksandr Kerensky, 1881-1970, (R.) revolutionary, served as premier after Feb. 1917 revolution until Bolshevik overthrow.

Ruhollah Khomeini, 1900-1989, (Iran), religious leader with Islamic title "ayatollah", directed overthrow of shah, 1979, became source of political authority in succeeding governments.

Nikita Khrushchev, 1894-1971, (USSR) premier, first secretary of Communist party, initiated de-Stalinization.

Martin Luther King, 1929-1968, (U.S.) Baptist minister and civil

rights leader; assassinated.
Lajos Kossuth, 1802-1894, (Hun.) principal figure in 1848 Hungarian revolution.
Pyotr Kropotkin, 1842-1921, (R.) anarchist, championed the peasants but opposed Bolshevism.
Kublai Khan, c. 1215-1294, Mongol emperor, founder of Yan dynasty in China.
Béla Kun, 1886-c.1939, (Hun.) communist, member of 3d International, tried to foment worldwide revolution.
Pierre Laval, 1883-1945, (F.) politician, Vichy foreign minister, executed for treason.
Andrew Bonar Law, 1858-1923, (Br.) Conservative party politician, led opposition to Irish home rule.
Jennie Lee, 1904-1988, (Br.) socialist politician, campaigned tirelessly against poverty.
Vladimir Ilyich Lenin (Ulyanov), 1870-1924, (USSR) revolutionary, founder of Bolshevism, Soviet leader 1917-1924.
Ferdinand de Lesseps, 1805-1894, (F.) diplomat, engineer, conceived idea of Suez Canal.
René Levesque, 1922-1987 (Can.) premier of Quebec, 1976-85; led unsuccessful fight to separate from Canada.
Abraham Lincoln, 1809–1865, (U.S.) 16th president, held office throughout Civil War; assassinated.
Liu Shao-ch'i, c.1898-1974, (Chi.) communist leader, fell from grace during "cultural revolution".
Maximilian Litvinov, 1876-1951, (USSR) revolutionary, commissar of foreign affairs, favoured cooperation with Western powers.
David Lloyd George, 1863-1945, (Br.) Liberal party prime minister, laid foundations for modern welfare state.
Henry Cabot Lodge, 1850-1924, (U.S.) Republican senator, led opposition to participation in League of Nations.
Huey P. Long, 1893-1935, (U.S.) Louisiana political demagogue, governor, assassinated.
Rosa Luxemburg, 1871-1919, (G.) revolutionary, leader of the German Social Democratic party and Spartacus party.
J. Ramsay MacDonald, 1866-1937, (Br.) first Labour party prime minister of Great Britain.
Harold Macmillan, 1895-1987 (Br.) prime minister of Great Britain, 1957-63.
Makarios III, 1913-1977, (Cyp.) Greek Orthodox archbishop, first president of Cyprus.
Malcolm X (Malcolm Little), 1925-1965, (U.S.) black separatist leader, assassinated.
Mao Tse-tung, 1893-1976, (Chi.) chief Chinese Marxist theorist, soldier, led Chinese revolution establishing his nation as an important communist state.
Jean Paul Marat, 1743-1793, (F.) revolutionary, politician, identified with radical Jacobins, assassinated.
José Martí, 1853-1895, (Cub.) patriot, poet, leader of Cuban struggle for independence.
Jan Masaryk, 1886-1948, (Cze.) foreign minister, died by mysterious suicide following communist coup.
Thomas G. Masaryk, 1850-1937, (Cze.) statesman, philosopher, first president of Czechoslovak Republic.
Jules Mazarin, 1602-1661, (F.) cardinal, statesman, prime minister under Louis XIII and queen regent Anne of Austria.
Giuseppe Mazzini, 1805-1872, (It.), reformer dedicated to the Risorgimento, 19th-century movement for the political and social renewal of Italy.
Tom Mboya, 1930-1969, (Ken.) political leader, instrumental in securing independence for his country.
Joseph R. McCarthy, 1908-1957, (U.S.) senator notorious for his witch hunt for communists in the government.
Cosimo I de' Medici, 1519-1574, (It.) Duke of Florence, grand duke of Tuscany.
Lorenzo de' Medici, the Magnificent, 1449-1492, (It.) merchant prince, a towering figure in Italian Renaissance.
Catherine de Medicis, 1519-1589, (F.) queen consort of Henry II, regent of France, influential in Catholic-Huguenot wars.
Golda Meir, 1898-1979, (Isr.) prime minister, 1969-74.
Klemens W.N.L. Metternich, 1773-1859, (Aus.) statesman, arbiter of post-Napoleonic Europe.
Anastas Mikoyan, 1895-1978, (USSR) prominent Soviet leader from 1917; president 1964-65.
Guy Mollet, 1905-1975, (F.) social politician, resistance leader.
Vyacheslav Molotov, 1809–1986, (R.) Stalinist politician; Finns named crude petrol bomb after him.
Gouverneur Morris, 1752-1816, (U.S.) statesman, diplomat, financial expert who helped plan decimal coinage system.
Wayne Morse, 1900-1974, (U.S.) senator, long-time critic of Vietnam War.
Oswald Mosley, 1896-1980, (Br.) right-wing politician, founder of the British Union of Fascists, 1932.
Muhammad Ali, 1769?-1849, (Egy.), pasha, founder of dynasty that encouraged emergence of modern Egyptian state.
Benito Mussolini, 1883-1945, (It.) dictator and leader of the Italian fascist state.
Imre Nagy, c. 1895-1958, (Hun.) communist premier, assassinated after Soviets crushed 1956 uprising.
Gamal Abdel Nasser, 1918-1970, (Egy.) leader of Arab unification, second Egyptian president.
Jawaharlal Nehru, 1889-1964, (Ind.) prime minister, guided India through its early years of independence.
Ngo Dinh Diem, 1901-1963, (Viet.) South Vietnamese president, assassinated in government take-over.
Kwame Nkrumah, 1909-1972, (Gha.) dictatorial prime minister, deposed in 1966.
Frederick North, 1732-1792, (Br.) prime minister, his inept policies led to loss of American colonies.
Daniel O'Connell, 1775-1847, (Ir.) political leader, known as The Liberator.
Omar, c.581-644, Mohammedan leader, 2d caliph, led Islam to become an imperial power.
Ignace Paderewski, 1860-1941, (Pol.) statesman, pianist, composer, briefly prime minister, an ardent patriot.
Viscount Palmerston, 1784-1865, (Br.) Liberal prime minister, foreign minister, embodied British nationalism.
George Papandreou, 1888-1968, (Gk.) Republican politician, served three times as prime minister.
Franz von Papen, 1879-1969, (G.) politician, played major role in overthrow of Weimar Republic and rise of Hitler.
Charles Stewart Parnell, 1846-1891, (Ir.) nationalist leader, "uncrowned king of Ireland".
Lester Pearson, 1897-1972, (Can.) diplomat, Liberal party leader, prime minister.
Robert Peel, 1788-1850, (Br.) reformist prime minister, founder of Conservative party.
Juan Perón, 1895-1974, (Arg.) president, dictator.
Henri Philippe Pétain, 1856–1951, (Fr.) head of state, puppet of German occupying forces, WW2; sentenced to death for treason, 1945, but reprieved and imprisoned for life.
Józef Pilsudski, 1867-1935, (Pol.) statesman, instrumental in re-establishing Polish state in the 20th century.
Charles Pinckney, 1757-1824, (U.S.) founding father, his Pinckney plan was largely incorporated into constitution.
William Pitt, the Elder, 1708-1778, (Br.) statesman, called the "Great Commoner", transformed Britain into imperial power.
William Pitt, the Younger, 1759-1806, (Br.) prime minister during French Revolutionary wars.
Georgi Plekhanov, 1857-1918, (R.) revolutionary, social philosopher, called "father of Russian Marxism".
Raymond Poincaré, 1860-1934, (F.) 9th president of the Republic, advocated harsh punishment of Germany after WW 1.
Georges Pompidou, 1911-1974, (F.) Gaullist political leader, president from 1969 to 1974.
Grigori Potemkin, 1739-1791, (R.) field marshal, favourite of Catherine II.
Jeannette Rankin, 1880-1973, (U.S.) pacifist, first woman member of U.S. Congress.
Walter Rathenau, 1867-1922, (G.) industrialist, social theorist, statesman.
Paul Reynaud, 1878-1966, (F.) statesman, premier in 1940 at the time of France's defeat by Germany.
Syngman Rhee, 1875-1965, (Kor.) first president of the Republic of Korea.
Cecil Rhodes, 1853-1902, (Br.) imperialist, industrial magnate, established Rhodes scholarships in his will.
Cardinal de Richelieu, 1585-1642, (F.) statesman, known as "red eminence", chief minister to Louis XIII.
Maximilien Robespierre, 1758-1794, (F.) leading figure of French Revolution, responsible for much of Reign of Terror.
Nelson Rockefeller, 1908-1979, (U.S.) Republican gov. of N.Y., 1959-73; U.S. vice president, 1974-77.
Eleanor Roosevelt, 1884-1962, (U.S.) humanitarian, United Nations diplomat.
Franklin D. Roosevelt, 1882–1945, (U.S.) 32nd president, 5th cousin of Theodore Roosevelt, first to use radio for "fireside chats".
Theodore Roosevelt, 1858-1919, (U.S.) 26th president, fought corruption of politics by big business.
Elihu Root, 1845-1937, (U.S.) lawyer, statesman, diplomat, leading Republican supporter of the League of Nations.
John Russell, 1792-1878, (Br.) Liberal prime minister during the Irish potato famine.
Anwar el-Sadat, 1918-1981, (Egy.) president, 1970-1981, promoted peace with Israel; assassinated.
António de O. Salazar, 1899-1970, (Por.) statesman, long-time dictator.
José de San Martin, 1778-1850, South American revolutionary, protector of Peru.
Eisaku Sato, 1901-1975, (Jap.) prime minister, presided over Japan's post-WW II emergence as major world power.
Philipp Scheidemann, 1865-1939, (G.) Social Democratic leader, first chancellor of the German republic.
Robert Schuman, 1886-1963, (F.) statesman, founded European Coal and Steel Community.
Kurt Schuschnigg, 1897-1977, (Aus.) chancellor, unsuccessful in stopping his country's annexation by Germany.

Carlo Sforza, 1872-1952, (It.) foreign minister, anti-fascist.
Emmanuel Shinwell, 1884-1986, (Br.) socialist politician; began nationalization of coal industry and introduced 5-day week for miners.
Wladyslaw Sikorski, 1881-1943, (Pol.) soldier and prime minister, ran govt.-in-exile in London, WW2.
Sitting Bull, c. 1831-1890, (Native Amer.) Sioux leader in Battle of Little Bighorn over George A. Custer, 1876; fostered Ghost Dance religion.
Jan C. Smuts, 1870-1950, (S.Af.) statesman, philosopher, soldier, prime minister.
Christopher Soames, 1920-1987, (Br.) politician and statesman; negotiated independence for Zimbabwe.
Paul Henri Spaak, 1899-1972, (Bel.) statesman, socialist leader.
Josef Stalin, 1879-1953, (USSR) Soviet dictator, 1924-53.
Edwin M. Stanton, 1814-1869, (U.S.) Lincoln's secretary of war during the Civil War.
Adlai E. Stevenson, 1900-1965, (U.S.) Democratic leader, diplomat, Illinois governor, presidential candidate.
Gustav Stresemann, 1878-1929, (G.) chancellor, foreign minister, dedicated to regaining friendship for post-WW 1 Germany.
Achmed Sukarno, 1901-1970, (Indo.) dictatorial first president of the Indonesian republic.
Sun Yat-sen, 1866-1925, (Chi.) revolutionary, leader of Kuomintang, regarded as the father of modern China.
Robert A. Taft, 1889-1953, (U.S.) conservative Senate leader, called "Mr Republican".
Charles de Talleyrand, 1754-1838, (F.) statesman, diplomat, the major force of the Congress of Vienna of 1814-15.
U Thant, 1909-1974 (Bur.) statesman, UN secretary-general.
Norman M. Thomas, 1884-1968, (U.S.) social reformer, 6 times unsuccessful Socialist party presidential candidate.
Josip Broz Tito, 1892-1980, (Yug.) president of Yugoslavia from 1953, World War 2 guerrilla chief, postwar rival of Stalin, leader of 3d world movement.
Palmiro Togliatti, 1893-1964, (It.) major leader of Italian Communist party.
Hideki Tojo, 1885-1948, (Jap.) statesman, soldier, prime minister during most of WW 2.
François Toussaint l'Ouverture, c. 1744-1803, (Hai.) patriot, martyr, thwarted French colonial aims.
Leon Trotsky, 1879-1940, (USSR) revolutionary, founded Red Army, expelled from party in conflict with Stalin.
Rafael L. Trujillo Molina, 1891-1961, (Dom.) absolute dictator, assassinated.
Harry S. Truman, 1884–1972, (U.S.) 33rd president, authorized use of atomic bomb on Hiroshima and Nagasaki.
Moise K. Tshombe, 1919-1969, (Con.) politician, president of secessionist Katanga, premier of Republic of Congo (Zaire).
William M. Tweed, 1823-1878, (U.S.) politician, absolute leader of Tammany Hall, NYC's Democratic political machine.
Walter Ulbricht, 1893-1973, (G.) communist leader of German Democratic Republic.
Eamon de Valéra, 1882-1975, (Ir.) statesman, led fight for Irish independence.
Eleutherios Venizelos, 1864-1936, (Gk.) most prominent Greek statesman in early 20th century; expanded territory.
Hendrik F. Verwoerd, 1901-1966, (S.Af.) prime minister, rigorously applied apartheid policy despite protest.
Balthazar Johannes Vorster, 1915-1983, (S.Af.) prime minister, then president; enforced strict maintenance of apartheid.
Robert Walpole, 1676-1745, (Br.) statesman, generally considered Britain's first prime minister.
George Washington, 1732-1799, (U.S.) first president of U.S.
Chaim Weizmann, 1874-1952, (Br.) Zionist leader, scientist, first Israeli president.
Woodrow Wilson, 1856-1924, (U.S.) 28th president, helped negotiate peace with Germans, 1918.
Emiliano Zapata, c. 1879-1919, (Mex.) revolutionary, major influence on modern Mexico.
Muhammad Zia ul-Haq, 1924–1988, (Pak.) president tried to impose Islamic fundamentalism on Pakistan after ordering execution of his predecessor, Ali Bhutto; assassinated.

Notable Military and Naval Leaders of the Past

Creighton Abrams, 1914-1974, (U.S.) commanded forces in Vietnam, 1968-72.
Harold Alexander, 1891-1969, (Br.) led Allied invasion of Italy, WW2, 1943.
Edmund Allenby, 1861-1936, (Br.) in Boer War, WW1; led Egyptian expeditionary force, 1917-18.
Benedict Arnold, 1741-1801, (U.S.) victorious at Saratoga; tried to betray West Point to British, Amer. Revolutionary War.
Henry "Hap" Arnold, 1886-1950, (U.S.) commanded Army Air Force in WW2.
Claude Auchinleck, 1884–1981, (Br.) commanded force at Narvik, 1940; won first battle of Alamein; commander in India, 1943–7.
Pierre Beauregard, 1818-1893, (U.S.) Confederate general ordered bombardment of Ft. Sumter that began the Civil War.
Gebhard von Blücher, 1742-1819, (G.) helped defeat Napoleon at Waterloo.
Napoleon Bonaparte, 1769-1821, (F.) defeated Russia and Austria at Austerlitz, 1805; invaded Russia, 1812; defeated at Waterloo, 1815.
Edward Braddock, 1695-1755, (Br.) commanded forces in French and Indian War.
Omar N. Bradley, 1893-1981, (U.S.) headed U.S. ground troops in Normandy invasion, WW2, 1944.
Mark Clark, 1896-1984, (U.S.) led forces in WW2 and Korean War.
Karl von Clausewitz, 1780-1831, (G.) wrote books on military theory.
Lucius D. Clay, 1897-1978, (U.S.) led Berlin airlift, 1948-49.
Henry Clinton, 1738-1795, (Br.) commander of forces in American Revolutionary War, 1778-81.
Cochise, c. 1815-1874, (Native Amer.) Chief of Chiricahua band of Apache Indians in Arizona.
Charles Cornwallis, 1738-1805, (Br.) victorious at Brandywine, 1777; surrendered at Yorktown, Amer. Revolutionary War.
Crazy Horse, 1849-1877, (U.S.) Sioux war chief victorious at Little Big Horn.
George A. Custer, 1839-1876, (U.S.) cavalry general defeated and killed at Little Big Horn.
Moshe Dayan, 1915-1981, (Isr.) army general and foreign minister, directed campaigns in the 1967, 1973 Arab-Israeli wars.
Stephen Decatur, 1779-1820, (U.S.) naval hero of Barbary wars, War of 1812.
Anton Denikin, 1872-1947, (R.) led White forces in Russian civil war.
George Dewey, 1837-1917, (U.S.) destroyed Spanish fleet at Manila, 1898, Spanish-American War.
Hugh C. Dowding, 1883-1970, (Br.) headed RAF during WW2, 1936-40.
Jubal Early, 1816-1894, (U.S.) Confederate general led raid on Washington, Civil War, 1864.
Dwight D. Eisenhower, 1890-1969, (U.S.) commanded Allied forces in Europe, WW2.
David Farragut, 1801-1870, (U.S.) Union admiral captured New Orleans, Mobile Bay, Civil War.
Ferdinand Foch, 1851-1929, (F.) headed victorious Allied armies, WW1, 1918.
Nathan Bedford Forrest, 1821-1877, (U.S.) Confederate general led cavalry raids against Union supply lines, Civil War.
Frederick the Great, 1712-1786, (G.) led Prussia in the Seven Years War.
Geronimo, 1829-1909 (Native Amer.) leader of Chiricahua band of Apache Indians.
Charles G. Gordon, 1833-1885, (Br.) led forces in China, Crimean War; killed at Khartoum.
Ulysses S. Grant, 1822-1885, (U.S.) headed Union army, Civil War, 1864-65; forced Lee's surrender, 1865.
Heinz Guderian, 1888-1953, (G.) tank theorist, led panzer forces in Poland, France, Russia, WW2.
Douglas Haig, 1861-1928, (Br.) led British armies in France, WW1, 1915-18.
Sir Arthur Travers Harris, 1895-1984, (Br.) led Britain's WW2 bomber command.
Richard Howe, 1726-1799, (Br.) commanded navy in Amer. Revolutionary War, 1776-78; June 1 victory against French, 1794.
William Howe, 1729-1814, (Br.) commanded forces in American Revolutionary War, 1776-78.
Hastings "Pugs" Ismay, 1887–1965, (Br.) chief staff officer in Churchill's War Cabinet.
Thomas (Stonewall) Jackson, 1824-1863, (U.S.) Confederate general led Shenandoah Valley campaign, Civil War.
Joseph Joffre, 1852-1931, (F.) headed Allied armies, won Battle of the Marne, WW1, 1914.
John Paul Jones, 1747-1792, (U.S.) commanded *Bonhomme Richard* in victory over Serapis, Amer. Revolutionary War, 1779.
Horatio H. Kitchener, 1850-1916, (Br.) led forces in Boer War; victorious at Khartoum; organized army in WW1.
Lavrenti Kornilov, 1870-1918, (R.) Commander-in-Chief, 1917; led counter-revolutionary march on Petrograd.
Mikhail Kutuzov, 1745-1813, (R.) fought French at Borodino, Napoleonic Wars, 1812; abandoned Moscow; forced French retreat.
Marquis de Lafayette, 1757-1834, (F.) aided American cause in Amer. Revolutionary War.
T(homas) E. Lawrence (of Arabia), 1888-1935, (Br.) organized revolt of Arabs against Turks in WW1.
Robert E. Lee, 1807-1870, (U.S.) Confederate general defeated

at Gettysburg, Civil War; surrendered to Grant, 1865.

Lyman Lemnitzer, 1899-1988, (U.S.) WW2 hero, later general, chairman of Joint Chiefs of Staff.

Douglas MacArthur, 1880-1964, (U.S.) commanded forces in SW Pacific in WW2; headed occupation forces in Japan, 1945-51; UN commander in Korean War.

Duke of Marlborough, 1650-1722, (Br.) led forces against Louis XIV in War of the Spanish Succession.

George C. Marshall, 1880-1959, (U.S.) chief of staff in WW2; devised Marshall Plan.

George B. McClellan, 1826-1885, (U.S.) Union general, commanded Army of the Potomac, Civil War, 1861-62.

George Meade, 1815-1872; (U.S.) commanded Union forces at Gettysburg, Civil War.

Helmuth von Moltke, 1800-1891; (G.) victorious in Austro-Prussian, Franco-Prussian wars.

Louis de Montcalm, 1712-1759, (F.) headed troops in Canada, French and Indian War; defeated at Quebec, 1759.

Bernard Law Montgomery, 1887-1976, (Br.) stopped German offensive at Alamein, WW2, 1942; helped plan Normandy invasion.

Louis Mountbatten, 1900-1979, (Br.) Supreme Allied Commander of SE Asia, WW2, 1943-46.

Joachim Murat, 1767-1815, (F.) leader of cavalry at Marengo, 1800; Austerlitz, 1805; and Jena, 1806, Napoleonic Wars.

Horatio Nelson, 1758-1805, (Br.) naval commander destroyed French fleet at Trafalgar.

Michel Ney, 1769-1815, (F.) commanded forces in Switzerland, Austria, Russia, Napoleonic Wars; defeated at Waterloo.

Chester Nimitz, 1885-1966, (U.S.) commander of naval forces in Pacific in WW2.

George S. Patton, 1885-1945, (U.S.) led assault on Sicily, 1943, 3d Army invasion of German-occupied Europe, WW2.

Oliver Perry, 1785-1819, (U.S.) won Battle of Lake Erie in War of 1812.

John Pershing, 1860-1948, (U.S.) commanded Mexican border campaign, 1916; American expeditionary forces in WW1.

Henri Philippe Pétain, 1856-1951, (F.) defended Verdun, 1916; headed Vichy government in WW2.

Charles Portal, 1893-1971, (Br.) marshal of RAF for most of WW2.

Erwin Rommel, 1891-1944, (G.) headed Afrika Korps, WW2.

Karl von Rundstedt, 1875-1953, (G.) supreme commander in West, WW2, 1943-45.

Aleksandr Samsonov, 1859-1914, (R.) led invasion of E. Prussia, WW1, defeated at Tannenberg, 1914.

William T. Sherman, 1820-1891, (U.S.) Union general, sacked Atlanta during "march to the sea", Civil War, 1864.

Joseph W. Stilwell, 1883-1946, (U.S.) headed forces in the China, Burma, India theatre in WW2.

J. E. B. Stuart, 1833–1864, (U.S.) Confederate cavalry commander, Civil War.

George H. Thomas, 1816-1870, (U.S.) saved Union army at Chattanooga, 1863; victorious at Nashville, 1864, Civil War.

Semyon Timoshenko, 1895-1970, (USSR) defended Moscow, Stalingrad, WW2; led winter offensive, 1942-43.

Alfred von Tirpitz, 1849-1930, (G.) responsible for submarine blockade in WW1.

George Washington, 1732-1799, (U.S.) led Continental army, Amer. Revolutionary War, 1775-83.

Archibald Wavell, 1883-1950, (Br.) commanded forces in N. and E. Africa, and SE Asia in WW2.

Duke of Wellington, 1769-1852, (Br.) defeated Napoleon at Waterloo.

James Wolfe, 1727-1759, (Br.) captured Quebec from French, French and Indian War, 1759.

Georgi Zhukov, 1895-1974, (USSR) defended Moscow, 1941, led assault on Berlin, WW2.

Noted Writers of the Past

Louisa May Alcott, 1832-1888, (U.S.) novelist. *Little Women.*

Sholom Aleichem, 1859-1916. (R.) Yiddish writer. *Tevye's Daughter, Adventures of Mottel, The Old Country.*

Vicente Aleixandre, 1898-1984, (Sp.) poet. *La destrucción o el amor, Dialogolos del conocimiento.*

Horatio Alger, 1832-1899, (U.S.) "rags-to-riches" books.

Hans Christian Andersen, 1805-1875, (Den.) author of fairy tales. *The Princess and the Pea, The Ugly Duckling.*

Matthew Arnold, 1822-1888, (Br.) poet, critic. "Thrysis," "Dover Beach," "The Gypsy Scholar"; "Culture and Anarchy".

Jane Austen, 1775-1817, (Br.) novelist. *Pride and Prejudice, Sense and Sensibility, Emma, Mansfield Park, Persuasion.*

Isaac Babel, 1894-1941, (R.) short-story writer, playwright. *Odessa Tales, Red Cavalry.*

Honoré de Balzac, 1799-1850, (Fr.) novelist. *Le Père Goriot, Cousine Bette, Eugénie Grandet, The Human Comedy.*

James M. Barrie, 1860-1937, (Br.) playwright, novelist. *Peter Pan, Dear Brutus, What Every Woman Knows.*

H.E. Bates, 1905-1974, (Br.) novelist and short-story writer. *The Woman Who Had Imagination, The Two Sisters, The Darling Buds of May.*

Charles Baudelaire, 1821-1867, (Fr.) symbolist poet. *Les Fleurs du Mal.*

L. Frank Baum, 1856-1919, (U.S.) writer. Wizard of Oz series of children's books.

Simone de Beauvoir, 1908-1986, (Fr.) novelist, essayist. *The Second Sex, Memoirs of a Dutiful Daughter.*

Samuel Beckett, 1906-1989, (Ir.) novelist, playwright, in French and English. *Waiting for Godot, Endgame* (plays); *Murphy, Watt, Molloy* (novels).

Brendan Behan, 1923-1964, (Ir.) playwright. *The Quare Fellow, The Hostage, Borstal Boy.*

Robert Benchley, 1889-1945, (U.S.) humorist. *From Bed to Worse, My Ten Years in a Quandary.*

Arnold Bennett, 1867-1931, (Br.) novelist and short-story writer. *The Old Wives' Tale, Clayhanger, Riceyman Steps.*

E.F. Benson, 1867-1940, (Br.) novelist. *Dodo, Queen Lucia.*

Ambrose Bierce, 1842-1914, (U.S.) short-story writer, journalist. *In the Midst of Life, The Devil's Dictionary.*

William Blake, 1757-1827, (Br.) poet, artist. *Songs of Innocence, Songs of Experience, The Marriage of Heaven and Hell.*

Giovanni Boccaccio, 1313-1375, (It.) poet, storyteller. *Decameron, Filostrato.*

Jorge Luis Borges, 1900-1986 (Arg.) short-story writer, poet, essayist. *Labyrinths.*

James Boswell, 1740-1795, (Br.) biographer. *The Life of Samuel Johnson, A Journal of a Tour of the Hebrides.*

Bertolt Brecht, 1898-1956, (G.) dramatist, poet. *The Threepenny Opera, Mother Courage and Her Children.*

Vera Brittain, 1893-1970, (Br.) writer and feminist. *Testament of Youth.*

Anne Brontë, 1820-1849, (Br.) novelist. *The Tenant of Wildfell Hall.*

Charlotte Brontë, 1816-1855, (Br.) novelist. *Jane Eyre.*

Emily Brontë, 1818-1848, (Br.) novelist. *Wuthering Heights.*

Elizabeth Barrett Browning, 1806-1861, (Br.) poet. *Sonnets from the Portuguese, Aurora Leigh.*

Robert Browning, 1812-1889, (Br.) poet. "My Last Duchess", "Fra Lippo Lippi", *The Ring and the Book.*

Pearl Buck, 1892-1973, (U.S.) novelist. *The Good Earth.*

Mikhail Bulgakov, 1891-1940, (R.) novelist, playwright. *The Heart of a Dog, The Master and Margarita.*

John Bunyan, 1628-1688, (Br.) writer. *Pilgrim's Progress.*

Ivy Compton-Burnett, 1884-1969, (Br.) novelist. *A House and Its Head, A Family and a Fortune.*

Robert Burns, 1759-1796, (Br.) poet. "Flow Gently, Sweet Afton", "My Heart's in the Highlands", "Auld Lang Syne".

Edgar Rice Burroughs, 1875-1950, (U.S.) novelist. *Tarzan of the Apes.*

George Gordon Lord Byron, 1788-1824, (Br.) poet. *Don Juan, Childe Harold, Manfred, Cain.*

Italo Calvino, 1923-1985 (It.) novelist, short-story writer. *If on a Winter's Night a Traveller . . .*

Albert Camus, 1913-1960, (F.) novelist. *The Plague, The Stranger, Caligula, The Fall.*

Lewis Carroll, 1832-1898, (Br.) writer, mathematician. *Alice's Adventures in Wonderland, Through the Looking Glass.*

Karel Čapek, 1890-1938, (Czech.) playwright, novelist, essayist. *R.U.R. (Rossum's Universal Robots).*

Giacomo Casanova, 1725-1798, (It.) adventurer, memoirist.

Willa Cather, 1876-1947, (U.S.) novelist, essayist. *O Pioneers, My Antonia, Death Comes for the Archbishop.*

Miguel de Cervantes Saavedra, 1547-1616, (Sp.) novelist, dramatist, poet. *Don Quixote de la Mancha.*

Raymond Chandler, 1888-1959, (U.S.) writer of detective fiction. Philip Marlowe series.

Geoffrey Chaucer, c. 1340-1400, (Br.) poet. *The Canterbury Tales, Troilus and Criseyde.*

John Cheever, 1912-1982, (U.S.) short-story writer, novelist. *The Wapshot Scandal,* "The Country Husband".

Anton Chekhov, 1860-1904, (R.) short-story writer, dramatist. *Uncle Vanya, The Cherry Orchard, The Three Sisters.*

G.K. Chesterton, 1874-1936, (Br.) critic, novelist. Father Brown series of mysteries.

Agatha Christie, 1891-1976, (Br.) mystery writer. *And Then There Were None, Murder on the Orient Express.*

Jean Cocteau, 1889-1963, (F.) writer, visual artist, film-maker. *The Beauty and the Beast, Enfants Terribles.*

Samuel Taylor Coleridge, 1772-1834, (Br.) poet, critic. "Kubla Khan", "The Rime of the Ancient Mariner", "Christabel".

(Sidonie) Colette, 1873-1954, (F.) novelist. *Claudine, Gigi.*

Joseph Conrad, 1857-1924, (Br.) novelist. *Lord Jim, Heart of Darkness, The Nigger of the "Narcissus", Nostromo.*

James Fenimore Cooper, 1789-1851, (U.S.) novelist. *Leather-Stocking Tales.*

Pierre Corneille, 1606-1684, (F.) dramatist. *Medée, Le Cid, Horace, Cinna, Polyeucte.*

Hart Crane, 1899-1932, (U.S.) poet. "The Bridge".

Stephen Crane, 1871-1900, (U.S.) novelist, short-story writer. *The Red Badge of Courage,* "The Open Boat".

e.e. cummings, 1894-1962, (U.S.) poet. *Tulips and Chimneys.*

Roald Dahl, 1916-1990, (Br.-U.S.) writer. *Charlie and the Chocolate Factory.*

Gabriele d'Annunzio, 1863-1938, (It.) poet, novelist, dramatist. *The Child of Pleasure, The Intruder, The Victim.*

Dante Alighieri, 1265-1321, (It.) poet. *The Divine Comedy.*

Daniel Defoe, 1660-1731, (Br.) writer. *Robinson Crusoe, Moll Flanders, Journal of the Plague Year.*

Walter de la Mare, 1873-1956, (Br.) poet. *The Listeners, Come Hither,* "The Traveller".

Charles Dickens, 1812-1870, (Br.) novelist. *David Copperfield, Oliver Twist, Great Expectations, The Pickwick Papers.*

Emily Dickinson, 1830-1886, (U.S.) poet.

Isak Dinesen (Karen Blixen), 1885-1962, (Dan.) author. *Out of Africa, Seven Gothic Tales, Winter's Tales.*

John Donne, 1573-1631, (Br.) poet. *Songs and Sonnets.*

John Dos Passos, 1896-1970, (U.S.) novelist. *U.S.A.*

Fyodor Dostoyevsky, 1821-1881, (R.) novelist. *Crime and Punishment, The Brothers Karamazov, The Possessed.*

Arthur Conan Doyle, 1859-1930, (Br.) novelist, created Sherlock Holmes mystery series.

Theodore Dreiser, 1871-1945, (U.S.) novelist. *An American Tragedy, Sister Carrie.*

John Dryden, 1631-1700, (Br.) poet, dramatist, critic. *All for Love, Mac Flecknoe, Absalom and Achitopel.*

Alexandre Dumas, 1802-1870, (F.) novelist, dramatist. *The Three Musketeers, The Count of Monte Cristo.*

Alexandre Dumas (fils), 1824-1895, (F.) dramatist, novelist. *La Dame aux camélias, Le Demi-monde.*

George Eliot (Mary Ann, later Marian, Evans), 1819-1880, (Br.) novelist. *Adam Bede, Silas Marner, Middlemarch, The Mill on the Floss, Daniel Deronda.*

T.S. Eliot, 1888-1965, (Br.) poet, critic. *The Waste Land,* "The Love Song of J. Alfred Prufrock", *Four Quartets.*

Ralph Waldo Emerson, 1803-1882, (U.S.) poet, essayist. "Brahma", "Nature", "The Over-Soul", "Self-Reliance".

William Faulkner, 1897-1962, (U.S.) novelist. *Sanctuary, Light in August, The Sound and the Fury, Absalom, Absalom!*

Henry Fielding, 1707-1754, (Br.) novelist. *Tom Jones.*

F. Scott Fitzgerald, 1896-1940, (U.S.) short-story writer, novelist. *The Great Gatsby, Tender Is the Night.*

Gustave Flaubert, 1821-1880, (F.) novelist. *Madame Bovary.*

C.S. Forester, 1899-1966, (Br.) novelist. Horatio Hornblower series, *The African Queen.*

E.M. Forster, 1879-1970, (Br.) novelist. *A Passage to India, Howard's End.*

Anatole France, 1844-1924. (F.) writer. *Penguin Island, My Friend's Book, Le Crime de Sylvestre Bonnard.*

Robert Frost, 1874-1963, (U.S.) poet. "Birches", "Fire and Ice", "Stopping by Woods on a Snowy Evening".

John Galsworthy, 1867-1933, (Br.) novelist, dramatist. *The Forsyte Saga, A Modern Comedy.*

Erle Stanley Gardner, 1889-1970, (U.S.) novelist. Perry Mason series of mysteries.

Elizabeth Gaskell, 1810-1865, (Br.) novelist. *Cranford, North and South, Wives and Daughters.*

Jean Genet, 1911-1986, (Fr.) playwright, novelist. *The Blacks, The Maids, The Balcony.*

André Gide, 1869-1951, (F.) writer. *The Immoralist, The Pastoral Symphony, Strait Is the Gate.*

Jean Giraudoux, 1882-1944, (F.) novelist, dramatist. *Electra, The Madwoman of Chaillot, Ondine, Tiger at the Gate.*

Johann W. von Goethe, 1749-1832, (G.) poet, dramatist, novelist. *Faust, The Sorrows of Young Werther.*

Nikolai Gogol, 1809-1852, (R.) short-story writer, dramatist, novelist. *Dead Souls, The Inspector General.*

Oliver Goldsmith, 1730?-1774, (Br.-Ir.) writer. *The Vicar of Wakefield, She Stoops to Conquer.*

Maxim Gorky, 1868-1936, (R.) writer. *The Lower Depths.*

Edmund Gosse, 1849-1928, (Br.) critic, translator and biographer. *Father and Son.*

Kenneth Grahame, 1859-1932, (Br.) novelist. *The Wind in the Willows.*

Robert Graves, 1895-1985, (Br.) poet, classical scholar, novelist. *I, Claudius, The White Goddess.*

Thomas Gray, 1716-1771, (Br.) poet. "Elegy Written in a Country Churchyard", "The Progress of Poesy".

Kate Greenaway, 1846-1901, (br.) children's writer and illustrator. *Under the Window, Marigold Garden.*

Graham Greene, 1904-1991, (Br.) novelist. *The Power and the Glory, The Heart of the Matter, The Ministry of Fear.*

Zane Grey, 1875-1939, (U.S.) writer of western stories.

Jakob Grimm, 1785-1863, (G.) philologist, folklorist. *German Methodology, Grimm's Fairy Tales.*

Wilhelm Grimm, 1786-1859, (G.) philologist, folklorist. *Grimm's Fairy Tales.*

Rider Haggard, 1856-1925, (Br.) novelist. *King Solomon's Mines, She.*

Dashiell Hammett, 1894-1961, (U.S.) writer of detective fiction, created Sam Spade.

Knut Hamsun, 1859-1952 (Nor.) novelist. *Hunger.*

Thomas Hardy, 1840-1928, (Br.) novelist, poet. *The Return of the Native, Tess of the D'Urbervilles, Jude the Obscure.*

Joel Chandler Harris, 1848-1908, (U.S.) short-story writer. Uncle Remus series.

Moss Hart, 1904-1961, (U.S.) playwright. *Once in a Lifetime, You Can't Take It With You, The Man Who Came to Dinner.*

Nathaniel Hawthorne, 1804-1864, (U.S.) novelist, short-story writer. *The Scarlet Letter,* "The Artist of the Beautiful".

William Hazlitt, 1778-1830, (Br.) essayist and critic. *The Spirit of the Age.*

Heinrich Heine, 1797-1856, (G.) poet. *Book of Songs.*

Lillian Hellman, 1905-1984, (U.S.) playwright, memoirist, "The Little Foxes", *An Unfinished Woman, Pentimento.*

Ernest Hemingway, 1899-1961, (U.S.) novelist, short-story writer. *A Farewell to Arms, For Whom the Bell Tolls.*

O. Henry (W.S. Porter), 1862-1910, (U.S.) short-story writer. "The Gift of the Magi".

G.A. Henty, 1832-1902, (Br.) adventure stories. *Colonel Thorndyke's Secret.*

Hermann Hesse, 1877-1962, (G.) novelist, poet. *Death and the Lover, Steppenwolf, Siddhartha.*

Oliver Wendell Holmes, 1809-1894, (U.S.) poet, novelist. *The Autocrat of the Breakfast-Table.*

Gerald Manley Hopkins, 1844-1889, (Br.) poet. "The Wreck of the *Deutschland*", "The Windhover", "Pied Beauty".

Alfred E. Housman, 1859-1936, (Br.) poet. *A Shropshire Lad.*

Victor Hugo, 1802-1885, (F.) poet, dramatist, novelist. *Notre Dame de Paris, Les Misérables.*

Aldous Huxley 1894-1963, (Br.) writer. *Brave New World.*

Henrik Ibsen, 1828-1906, (Nor.) dramatist, poet. *A Doll's House, Ghosts, The Wild Duck, Hedda Gabler.*

Washington Irving, 1783-1859, (U.S.) writer. "Rip Van Winkle", "The Legend of Sleepy Hollow".

Christopher Isherwood, 1904-1986, (Br.) novelist. *Mr Norris Changes Trains, Goodbye to Berlin.*

Henry James, 1843-1916, (U.S.) novelist, short-story writer, critic. *The Portrait of a Lady, The American, Daisy Miller.*

M.R. James, 1862-1936, (Br.) short-story writer. "Oh, Whistle and I'll Come to You, My Lad", *Ghost Stories of an Antiquary.*

Jerome K. Jerome, 1859-1927, (Br.) historian and novelist. *Three Men in a Boat.*

Samuel Johnson, 1709-1784, (Br.) author, scholar, critic. *Dictionary of the English Language.*

Ben Jonson, 1572-1637, (Br.) dramatist, poet. *Volpone.*

James Joyce, 1882-1941, (Ir.) writer. *Ulysses, Dubliners, A Portrait of the Artist as a Young Man, Finnegans Wake.*

Franz Kafka, 1883-1924, (G.) novelist, short-story writer. *The Trial, Amerika, The Castle, The Metamorphosis.*

George S. Kaufman, 1889-1961, (U.S.) playwright. *The Man Who Came to Dinner, You Can't Take It With You, Stage Door.*

Nikos Kazantzakis, 1883?-1957, (Gk.) novelist. *Zorba the Greek, A Greek Passion.*

John Keats, 1795-1821, (Br.) poet. "Ode on a Grecian Urn", "Ode to a Nightingale", "La Belle Dame Sans Merci".

Charles Kingsley, 1819-1875, (Br.) historian and novelist. *Westward Ho!, The Water-Babies.*

Rudyard Kipling, 1865-1936, (Br.) author, poet. "The White Man's Burden", "Gunga Din", *The Jungle Book.*

Jean de la Fontaine, 1621-1695, (F.) poet. *Fables choisies.*

Pär Lagerkvist, 1891-1974, (Swed.) poet, dramatist, novelist. *Barabbas, The Sybil.*

Selma Lagerlöf, 1858-1940, (Swed.) novelist. *Jerusalem, The Ring of the Lowenskolds.*

Alphonse de Lamartine, 1790-1869, (F.) poet, novelist, statesman. *Méditations poétiques.*

Charles Lamb, 1775-1834, (Br.) essayist. *Specimens of English Dramatic Poets, Essays of Elia, Tales from Shakespeare.*

Giuseppe di Lampedusa, 1896-1957, (It.) novelist. *The Leopard.*

Ring Lardner, 1885-1933, (U.S.) short-story writer, humorist. *You Know Me, Al.*

Philip Larkin, 1922–1985, (Br.) poet. *The Whitsun Weddings.*

D. H. Lawrence, 1885-1930, (Br.) novelist. *Sons and Lovers, Women in Love, Lady Chatterley's Lover.*

Edward Lear, 1812-1888, (Br.) writer and artist. *A Book of Nonsense,* "The Owl and the Pussycat".

Mikhail Lermontov, 1814-1841, (R.) novelist, poet. "Demon",

Hero of Our Time.

Alain-René Lesage, 1668-1747, (F.) novelist. *Gil Blas de Santillane.*

Sinclair Lewis, 1885-1951, (U.S.) novelist. *Babbitt, Arrowsmith, Dodsworth, Main Street.*

Hugh Lofting, 1886-1947, (Br.) writer. Dr Doolittle series of children's books.

Jack London, 1876-1916, (U.S.) novelist, journalist. *Call of the Wild, The Sea-Wolf.*

Henry Wadsworth Longfellow, 1807-1882, (U.S.) poet. *Evangeline, The Song of Hiawatha.*

Robert Lowell, 1917-1977, (U.S.) poet. "Lord Weary's Castle", "For the Union Dead".

Rose Macaulay, 1812-1958, (Br.) novelist. *Potterism, The Towers of Trebizond.*

Niccolò Machiavelli, 1469-1527, (It.) writer, statesman. *The Prince, Discourses on Livy.*

Louis MacNeice, 1907-1963, (Br.) poet and playwright. *Autumn Journal, The Burning Perch, The Dark Tower.*

Bernard Malamud, 1914-1986, (U.S.) short story writer, novelist. "The Magic Barrel", *The Assistant, The Fixer.*

Stéphane Mallarmé, 1842-1898, (F.) poet. *The Afternoon of a Faun.*

Thomas Malory, ?-1471, (Br.) writer. *Morte d'Arthur.*

André Malraux, 1901-1976, (F.) novelist. *Man's Fate.*

Osip Mandelstam, 1891-1938, (R.) poet. *Stone, Tristia.*

Thomas Mann, 1875-1955, (G.) novelist, essayist. *Buddenbrooks, Death in Venice, The Magic Mountain.*

Olivia Manning, 1908-1980, (Br.) novelist. *The Balkan Trilogy.*

Ngaio Marsh, 1899-1982, (N.Z.) detective novelist. Creator of Roderick Alleyn.

Katherine Mansfield, 1888-1923, (N.Z.-Br.) short-story writer. "Bliss", "The Garden Party".

Christopher Marlowe, 1564-1593, (Br.) dramatist, poet. *Tamburlaine the Great, Dr Faustus, The Jew of Malta.*

Andrew Marvell, 1621-1678, (Br.) poet and satirist. "To His Coy Mistress", "Last Instructions to a Painter".

John Masefield, 1878-1967, (Br.) poet. "Sea Fever", "Cargoes", *Salt Water Ballads.*

W. Somerset Maugham, 1874-1965, (Br.) author. *Of Human Bondage, The Razor's Edge, The Moon and Sixpence.*

Guy de Maupassant, 1850-1893, (F.) novelist, short-story writer. "A Life", "Bel-Ami", "The Necklace".

François Mauriac, 1885-1970, (F.) novelist, dramatist. *Viper's Tangle, The Kiss to the Leper.*

Vladimir Mayakovsky, 1893-1930, (R.) poet, dramatist. *The Cloud in Trousers.*

Mary McCarthy, 1912-1989, (U.S.) critic, novelist. *Memories of a Catholic Girlhood.*

Carson McCullers, 1917-1967, (U.S.) novelist. *The Heart Is a Lonely Hunter, Member of the Wedding.*

Herman Melville, 1819-1891, (U.S.) novelist, poet. *Moby Dick, Typee, Billy Budd, Omoo.*

H.L. Mencken, 1880-1956, (U.S.) author, critic, editor. *Prejudices, The American Language.*

George Meredith, 1828-1909, (Br.) novelist, poet. *The Ordeal of Richard Feverel, The Egoist.*

Prosper Mérimée, 1803-1870, (F.) author. *Carmen.*

Edna St. Vincent Millay, 1892-1950, (U.S.) poet. *The Harp Weaver and Other Poems, A Few Figs from Thistles.*

A.A. Milne, 1882-1956, (Br.) author. *Winnie-the-Pooh.*

John Milton, 1608-1674, (Br.) poet. *Paradise Lost.*

Mishima Yukio (Hiraoka Kimitake), 1925-1970, (Jap.) writer. *Confessions of a Mask.*

Gabriela Mistral, 1889-1957, (Chil.) poet. *Sonnets of Death, Desolación, Tala, Lagar.*

Margaret Mitchell, 1900-1949, (U.S.) novelist. *Gone With the Wind.*

Nancy Mitford, 1904-1973, (Br.) novelist. *The Pursuit of Love, Love in a Cold Climate, Noblesse Oblige.*

Jean-Baptiste Molière, 1622-1673, (F.) dramatist. *Le Tartuffe, Le Misanthrope, Le Bourgeois Gentilhomme.*

Ferenc Molnár, 1878-1952, (Hung.) dramatist, novelist. *Liliom, The Guardsman, The Swan.*

Michel de Montaigne, 1533-1592, (F.) essayist. *Essais.*

Thomas More, 1478-1535, (Br.) writer. *Utopia.*

H.H. Munro (Saki), 1870-1916, (Br.) writer. *Reginald, The Chronicles of Clovis, Beasts and Super-Beasts.*

Murasaki (Shikibu), Lady, c. 978-1031?, (Jap.) novelist. *The Tale of Genji.*

John Middleton Murry, 1889-1957, (Br.) critic and writer. *The Problem of Style.*

Alfred de Musset, 1810-1857, (F.) poet, dramatist. *Confession d'un enfant du siècle.*

Vladimir Nabokov, 1899-1977, (Rus.-U.S.) novelist. *Lolita.*

Ogden Nash, 1902-1971, (U.S.) poet. *Hard Lines, I'm a Stranger Here Myself, The Private Dining Room.*

Pablo Neruda, 1904-1973, (Chil.) poet. *Twenty Love Poems and One Song of Despair, Toward the Splendid City.*

Edith Nesbit, 1858-1924, (Br.) children's writer. *The Wouldbegoods, The Railway Children.*

Harold Nicolson, 1886-1968, (Br.) writer and critic. *Swinburne, Some People.*

Nostradamus, 1503-1566, (Fr.) astrologer and physician. *Centuries.*

Flann O'Brien (Brian Ó Nualláin; aka Myles na Gopaleen), 1911-1966, (Ir.) novelist. *At Swim-Two-Birds, The Third Policeman.*

Sean O'Casey, 1884-1964, (Ir.) dramatist. *Juno and the Paycock, The Plough and the Stars.*

Flannery O'Connor, 1925-1964, (U.S.) novelist, short-story writer. *Wise Blood,* "A Good Man Is Hard to Find".

Clifford Odets, 1906-1963, (U.S.) playwright. *Waiting for Lefty, Awake and Sing, Golden Boy, The Country Girl.*

John O'Hara, 1905-1970, (U.S.) novelist, short-story writer. *From the Terrace, Appointment in Samarra, Pal Joey.*

Omar Khayyam, c. 1028-1122, (Per.) poet. *Rubaiyat.*

Eugene O'Neill, 1888-1953, (U.S.) playwright. *Emperor Jones, Anna Christie, Long Day's Journey into Night.*

Baroness Orczy, 1865-1947, (Hung.-Br.) novelist. *The Scarlet Pimpernel.*

Joe Orton, 1933-1967, (Br.) playwright. *Entertaining Mr Sloane, What the Butler Saw.*

George Orwell, 1903-1950, (Br.) novelist, essayist. *Animal Farm, Nineteen Eighty-Four.*

Wilfred Owen, 1893-1918, (Br.) poet. "Strange Meeting", "Anthem for Doomed Youth", "Dulce et Decorum Est".

Thomas (Tom) Paine, 1737-1809, (U.S.) writer, political theorist. *Common Sense.*

Dorothy Parker, 1893-1967, (U.S.) poet, short-story writer. *Enough Rope, Laments for the Living.*

Boris Pasternak, 1890-1960, (R.) poet, novelist. *Doctor Zhivago, My Sister, Life.*

Alan Paton, 1903-1988, (S.Af.) novelist. *Cry, the Beloved Country.*

Mervyn Peake, 1911-1968, (Br.) novelist. *Titus Groan, Gormenghast, Titus Alone.*

Samuel Pepys, 1633-1703, (Br.) public official, diarist.

S. J. Perelman, 1904-1979, (U.S.) humorist. *The Road to Miltown, Under the Spreading Atrophy.*

Francesco Petrarca, 1304-1374, (It.) poet. *Africa, Trionfi, Canzoniere, On Solitude.*

Arthur Wing Pinero, 1855–1936, (Br.) playwright. *The Second Mrs Tanqueray, Trelawny of the "Wells".*

Luigi Pirandello, 1867-1936, (It.) novelist, dramatist. *Six Characters in Search of an Author.*

Sylvia Plath, 1932-1963, (U.S.) poet. *The Colossus, Ariel.*

Edgar Allan Poe, 1809-1849, (U.S.) poet, short-story writer, critic. "Annabel Lee", "The Raven", "The Purloined Letter".

Alexander Pope, 1688-1744, (Br.) poet. *The Rape of the Lock, An Essay on Man.*

Beatrix Potter, 1866-1943, (Br.) children's writer and illustrator. *The Tale of Peter Rabbit, Squirrel Nutkin, Jemima Puddleduck.*

Ezra Pound, 1885-1972, (U.S.) poet. *Cantos.*

J.B. Priestley, 1894-1984, (Br.) novelist, playwright and critic. *The Good Companions, Time and the Conways, An Inspector Calls.*

Marcel Proust, 1871-1922, (F.) novelist. *A la recherche du temps perdu (Remembrance of Things Past).*

Alexander Pushkin, 1799-1837, (R.) poet, prose writer. *Boris Godunov, Eugene Onegin, The Bronze Horseman.*

Barbara Pym, 1913-1980, (Br.) novelist. *Excellent Women, A Glass of Blessings, Quartet in Autumn.*

François Rabelais, 1495-1553, (F.) writer. *Tiers livre, Gargantua, Pantagruel.*

Jean Racine, 1639-1699, (F.) dramatist. *Andromaque, Phèdre, Bérénice, Britannicus.*

Ayn Rand, 1905-1982 (Rus.-U.S.) novelist, philosopher. *The Fountainhead, Atlas Shrugged.*

Terence Rattigan, 1911-1977, (Br.) playwright. *French Without Tears, The Winslow Boy, Separate Tables.*

Erich Maria Remarque, 1898-1970, (Ger.-U.S.) novelist. *All Quiet on the Western Front.*

Mary Renault, 1905-1983, (Br.) historical novelist. *The King Must Die, The Bull from the Sea.*

Jean Rhys, 1890-1979, (W.Ind) novelist. *Good Morning, Midnight, Wide Sargasso Sea.*

Samuel Richardson, 1689-1761, (Br.) novelist. *Clarissa Harlowe, Pamela; or, Virtue Rewarded.*

Rainer Maria Rilke, 1875-1926, (G.) poet. *Life and Songs, Duino Elegies, Poems from the Book of Hours.*

Arthur Rimbaud, 1854-1891, (F.) poet. *A Season in Hell.*

Theodore Roethke, 1908-1963, (U.S.) poet. *Open House, The Waking, The Far Field.*

Romain Rolland, 1866-1944, (F.) novelist, biographer. *Jean-Christophe.*

Pierre de Ronsard, 1524-1585, (F.) poet. *Sonnets pour Hélène, La Françiade.*

Christina Rossetti, 1830-1894, (Br.) poet. "Up-hill", "A Birthday", *Goblin Market and Other Poems.*

Edmond Rostand, 1868-1918, (F.) poet, dramatist. *Cyrano de Bergerac.*

Damon Runyon, 1880-1946, (U.S.) short-story writer, journalist. *Guys and Dolls, Blue Plate Special.*

John Ruskin, 1819-1900, (Br.) critic, social theorist. *Modern Painters, The Seven Lamps of Architecture.*

Vita Sackville-West, 1892-1962, (Br.) poet and novelist. *The Land, All Passion Spent.*

Antoine de Saint-Exupéry, 1900-1944, (F.) writer. *Wind, Sand and Stars, Le Petit Prince.*

George Sand (Amandine Aurore Dupine), 1804-1876, (F.) novelist. *Consuelo, The Haunted Pool, The Master Bell-Ringer.*

Carl Sandburg, 1878-1967, (U.S.) poet. *The People, Yes; Chicago Poems, Smoke and Steel, Harvest Poems.*

George Santayana, 1863-1952, (U.S.) poet, essayist, philosopher. *The Sense of Beauty, The Realms of Being.*

William Saroyan, 1908-1981, (U.S.) playwright, novelist. *The Time of Your Life, The Human Comedy.*

Jean-Paul Sartre, 1905-1980, (Fr.) philosopher, novelist, playwright, *Nausea, No Exit, Being and Nothingness.*

Siegfried Sassoon, 1886-1967, (Br.) poet. *Vigils, Sequences.*

Dorothy L. Sayers, 1893-1957, (Br.) detective novelist, translator. Creator of Lord Peter Wimsey.

Friedrich von Schiller, 1759-1805, (G.) dramatist, poet, historian. *Don Carlos, Maria Stuart, Wilhelm Tell.*

Sir Walter Scott, 1771-1832, (Br.) novelist, poet. *Ivanhoe.*

Jaroslav Seifert, 1902-1986, (Cz.) poet.

Dr Seuss (Theodor Seuss Geisel), 1904-1991, (U.S.) children's writer and illustrator. *The Cat in the Hat.*

William Shakespeare, 1564-1616, (Br.) dramatist, poet. *Romeo and Juliet, Hamlet, King Lear, Julius Caesar, The Merchant of Venice, Othello, Macbeth, The Tempest;* sonnets.

George Bernard Shaw, 1856-1950, (Ir.-Br.) playwright, critic. *St Joan, Pygmalion, Major Barbara, Man and Superman.*

Mary Wollstonecraft Shelley, 1797-1851, (Br.) novelist. *Frankenstein.*

Percy Bysshe Shelley, 1792-1822, (Br.) poet. *Prometheus Unbound, Adonais,* "Ode to the West Wind", "To a Skylark".

Richard B. Sheridan, 1751-1816, (Br.) dramatist. *The Rivals, School for Scandal.*

Mikhail Sholokhov, 1906-1984 (R.) writer. *And Quiet Flows the Don.*

Upton Sinclair, 1878-1968, (U.S.) novelist. *The Jungle.*

Isaac Bashevis Singer, 1904-1991, (Pol.-U.S.) novelist, short-story writer, in Yiddish. *The Magician of Lubin.*

Stevie Smith, 1902-1971, (Br.) poet and novelist. "Not Waving But Drowning", *Novel on Yellow Paper.*

Tobias Smollett, 1721-1771, (Br.) novelist and satirist. *The Adventures of Roderick Random, The Expedition of Humphry Clinker.*

Noel Streatfeild, 1895-1986, (Br.) children's writer. *Ballet Shoes, Curtain Up.*

Edmund Spenser, 1552-1599, (Br.) poet. *The Faerie Queen.*

Christina Stead, 1903-1983 (Austral.) novelist, short-story writer. *The Man Who Loved Children.*

Richard Steele, 1672-1729, (Br.) essayist, playwright, began the *Tatler* and *Spectator* magazines. *The Conscious Lovers.*

Gertrude Stein, 1874-1946, (U.S.) writer. *Three Lives.*

John Steinbeck, 1902-1968, (U.S.) novelist. *Grapes of Wrath, Of Mice and Men, Winter of Our Discontent.*

Stendhal (Marie Henri Beyle), 1783-1842, (F.) novelist. *The Red and the Black, The Charterhouse of Parma.*

Laurence Sterne, 1713-1768, (Br.) novelist. *Tristram Shandy.*

Wallace Stevens, 1879-1955, (U.S.) poet. *Harmonium, The Man With the Blue Guitar, Notes Toward a Supreme Fiction.*

Robert Louis Stevenson, 1850-1894, (Br.) novelist, poet, essayist. *Treasure Island, A Child's Garden of Verses.*

Harriet Beecher Stowe, 1811-1896, (U.S.) novelist. *Uncle Tom's Cabin.*

Lytton Strachey, 1880-1932, (Br.) biographer, critic. *Eminent Victorians, Queen Victoria, Elizabeth and Essex.*

August Strindberg, 1849-1912, (Swed.) dramatist, novelist. *The Father, Miss Julie, The Creditors.*

Jonathan Swift, 1667-1745, (Br.) writer. *Gulliver's Travels.*

Algernon C. Swinburne, 1837-1909, (Br.) poet, critic. *Atalanta in Calydon.*

John M. Synge, 1871-1909, (Ir.) poet, dramatist. *Riders to the Sea, The Playboy of the Western World.*

Rabindranath Tagore, 1861-1941, (Ind.) author, poet. *Sadhana, The Realization of Life, Gitanjali.*

Booth Tarkington, 1869-1946, (U.S.) novelist. *Seventeen, Alice Adams, Penrod.*

Sara Teasdale, 1884-1933, (U.S.) poet. *Helen of Troy and Other Poems, Rivers to the Sea, Flame and Shadow.*

Alfred Lord Tennyson, 1809-1892, (Br.) poet. *Idylls of the King, In Memoriam,* "The Charge of the Light Brigade".

William Makepeace Thackeray, 1811-1863, (Br.) novelist. *Vanity Fair, Henry Esmond, Pendennis.*

Dylan Thomas, 1914-1953, (Br.) poet. *Under Milk Wood, A Child's Christmas in Wales.*

Henry David Thoreau, 1817-1862, (U.S.) transcendentalist thinker, writer. *Walden.*

James Thurber, 1894-1961, (U.S.) humorist, cartoonist. "The Secret Life of Walter Mitty", *My Life and Hard Times.*

J.R.R. Tolkien, 1892-1973, (Br.) writer. *Lord of the Rings.*

Leo Tolstoy, 1828-1910, (R.) novelist, short-story writer. *War and Peace, Anna Karenina,* "The Death of Ivan Ilyich".

Ben Travers, 1886-1980, (Br.) novelist and playwright. *Rookery Nook, A Cuckoo in the Nest.*

Anthony Trollope, 1815-1882, (Br.) novelist. *The Warden, Barchester Towers,* The Palliser novels.

Ivan Turgenev, 1818-1883, (R.) novelist, short-story writer. *Fathers and Sons, First Love, A Month in the Country.*

Mark Twain (Samuel Clemens), 1835-1910, (U.S.) novelist, humorist. *The Adventures of Huckleberry Finn, Tom Sawyer.*

Sigrid Undset, 1881-1949, (Nor.) novelist, poet. *Kristin Lavransdatter.*

Alison Uttley, 1884-1976, (Br.) children's writer. "Little Grey Rabbit", "Sam Pig".

Paul Valéry, 1871-1945, (F.) poet, critic. *La Jeune Parque, The Graveyard by the Sea.*

Jules Verne, 1828-1905, (F.) novelist. *Twenty Thousand Leagues Under the Sea.*

François Villon, 1431-1463?, (F.) poet. *Le Petit et le Grand Testament.*

Voltaire (François-Marie Arouet), 1694-1778, (Fr.) novelist, dramatist and critic. *Candide.*

Evelyn Waugh, 1903-1966, (Br.) novelist. *Decline and Fall, Vile Bodies, The Loved One.*

H.G. Wells, 1866-1946, (Br.) novelist. *The Time Machine, The Invisible Man, The War of the Worlds.*

Rebecca West, 1893-1983 (Br.) critic. *Black Lamb and Grey Falcon.*

Edith Wharton, 1862-1937, (U.S.) novelist. *The Age of Innocence, The House of Mirth, Ethan Frome.*

Antonia White, 1899-1979, (Br.) novelist. *Frost in May.*

E.B. White, 1899-1985 (U.S.), essayist, novelist. *Here Is New York, Charlotte's Web, Stuart Little.*

T.H. White, 1906-1964, (Br.) author. *The Once and Future King, A Book of Beasts.*

Walt Whitman, 1819-1892, (U.S.) poet. *Leaves of Grass.*

Oscar Wilde, 1854-1900, (Ir.) playwright, story-writer. *The Picture of Dorian Gray, The Importance of Being Earnest.*

Laura Ingalls Wilder, 1867-1957, (U.S.) novelist. *Little House on the Prairie* series of children's books.

Thornton Wilder, 1897-1975, (U.S.) playwright. *Our Town, The Skin of Our Teeth, The Matchmaker.*

Tennessee Williams, 1912-1983 (U.S.) playwright. *A Streetcar Named Desire, Cat on a Hot Tin Roof, The Glass Menagerie.*

William Carlos Williams, 1883-1963, (U.S.) poet. *Tempers, Al Que Quiere!, Paterson.*

P.G. Wodehouse, 1881-1975, (Br.-U.S.) humorist. Creator of Jeeves and Bertie Wooster, *Anything Goes.*

Thomas Wolfe, 1900-1938, (U.S.) novelist. *Look Homeward, Angel, You Can't Go Home Again, Of Time and the River.*

Virginia Woolf, 1882-1941, (Br.) novelist, essayist. *Mrs Dalloway, To the Lighthouse, The Waves, A Room of One's Own.*

William Wordsworth, 1770-1850, (Br.) poet. "Tintern Abbey", "Ode: Intimations of Immortality", *The Prelude.*

John Wyndham, 1903-1969, (Br.) novelist. *The Day of the Triffids, The Midwich Cuckoos.*

William Butler Yeats, 1865-1939, (Ir.) poet, playwright. *The Wild Swans at Coole, The Tower, Last Poems.*

Émile Zola, 1840-1902, (F.) novelist. *Nana, La Bête humaine.*

Poets Laureate of England

There is no authentic record of the origin of the office of Poet Laureate of England. According to the historian and poet laureate Thomas Warton, there was a Versificator Regis, or King's Poet, in the reign of Henry III (1216-1272), and he was paid 100 shillings a year. Geoffrey Chaucer (1340-1400) assumed the title of Poet Laureate, and in 1389 got a royal grant of a yearly allowance of wine. In the reign of Edward IV (1461-1483), John Kay held the post. Under Henry VII (1485-1509), Andrew Bernard was the Poet Laureate, and was succeeded under Henry VIII (1509-1547) by John Skelton.

Next came Edmund Spenser, who died in 1599; then Samuel Daniel, appointed 1599, and then Ben Jonson, 1619. Sir William D'Avenant was appointed in 1637. He was a godson of William Shakespeare.

Others were John Dryden, 1670; Thomas Shadwell, 1688; Nahum Tate, 1692; Nicholas Rowe, 1715; the Rev. Laurence Eusden, 1718; Colley Cibber, 1730; William Whitehead, 1757, on the refusal of Gray; Rev. Thomas Warton, 1785, on the refusal of Mason; Henry J. Pye, 1790; Robert Southey, 1813, on the refusal of Sir Walter Scott; William Wordsworth, 1843; Alfred, Lord Tennyson, 1850; Alfred Austin, 1896; Robert Bridges, 1913; John Masefield, 1930; Cecil Day Lewis, 1967; Sir John Betjeman, 1972; Ted Hughes, 1984.

U.S. Poets Laureate

Robert Penn Warren, the poet, novelist, and essayist, was named the country's first official Poet Laureate on Feb. 26, 1986. The only writer to have won the Pulitzer Prize for fiction and poetry (twice), Warren was chosen by Daniel J. Boorstin, the Librarian of Congress. The appointment began in September, 1986. Other appointments, all beginning in September, are: Richard Wilbur, 1987; Howard Nemerov, 1988; Mark Strand, 1990; Joseph Brokdsky, 1991; Mona Van Duyn (the first female poet laureate), 1992; Rita Dove (the first black poet laureate), 1993.

Notable Living Fiction Writers and Playwrights

Name (Birthplace)	Birthdate
Ackroyd, Peter (London)	5/10/49
Albee, Edward (Washington, D.C.)	12/3/28
Amis, Kingsley (London)	16/4/22
Amis, Martin (Oxford)	25/8/49
Arden, John (Barnsley, Yorks)	26/10/30
Atwood, Margaret (Ottawa, Ontario)	18/11/39
Ayckbourn, Alan (London)	12/4/39
Bailey, Paul (Battersea, London)	16/2/37
Bainbridge, Beryl (Liverpool)	21/11/34
Ballard, J.G. (Shanghai, China)	15/11/30
Banks, Lynn Reid (London)	31/7/29
Banville, John (Wexford, Ireland)	8/12/45
Barker, Howard (Dulwich, London)	28/6/46
Barnes, Julian (Leicester)	19/1/46
Barth, John (Cambridge, Md.)	27/5/30
Bawden, Nina (London)	19/1/25
Beattie, Ann (Washington, D.C.)	7/9/47
Bellow, Saul (Quebec, Canada)	10/7/15
Benchley, Peter (New York, N.Y.)	8/5/40
Bennett, Alan (Leeds, Yorks)	9 /5/34
Billington, Rachel (Oxford)	11/5/42
Blume, Judy (Elizabeth, N.J.)	12/2/38
Bolt, Robert (Sale, Manchester)	15/8/24
Bond, Edward (London)	18/7/34
Boyd, William (Accra, Ghana)	7/3/52
Bradbury, Malcolm (Sheffield, Yorks)	7/9/32
Bradbury, Ray (Waukegan, Ill.)	22/8/20
Bragg, Melvyn (Carlisle, Cumbria)	6/10/39
Brenton, Howard (Portsmouth, Hants)	13/12/42
Brokaw, Tom (Webster, S. Dak.)	6/2/40
Brook, Peter (London)	21/3/25
Brookner, Anita (London)	16/7/28
Burgess, Anthony (Manchester)	25/2/17
Byatt, A.S. (Sheffield, Yorks)	24/8/36
Canetti, Elias (Ruschuk, Bulgaria)	25/7/05
Carey, Peter (Victoria, Australia)	7/5/43
Clarke, Arthur C. (Minehead, Somerset)	16/12/17
Clancy, Tom (Baltimore, Md.)	1947
Clavell, James (England)	10/10/24
Cleary, Beverly (McMinnville, Ore.)	1916
Coetzee, J.M. (Cape Town, S. Africa)	9/2/40
Crichton, Michael (Chicago, Ill.)	23/10/42
Davies, Robertson (Thamesville, Ontario)	28/8/13
Deighton, Len (London)	18/2/29
Delaney, Shelagh (Salford, Lancs)	25/11/39
Desai, Anita (Mussoorie, India)	24/6/37
De Vries, Peter (Chicago, Ill.)	27/2/10
Didion, Joan (Sacramento, Cal.)	12/5/34
Doctorow, E.L. (New York, N.Y.)	6/1/31
Drabble, Margaret (Sheffield, Yorks)	5/6/39
Ellison, Ralph (Oklahoma City, Okla.)	1/3/14
Fitzgerald, Penelope (Lincoln)	17/12/16
Fo, Dario (San Giano, Italy)	24/3/36
Forster, Margaret (Carlisle, Cumbria)	25/5/38
Forsyth, Frederick (Ashford, Kent)	1938
Fowles, John (Leigh-on-Sea, Essex)	31/3/26
Fox, Paula (New York, N.Y.)	22/4/23
Frame, Janet (Dunedin, New Zealand)	28/8/24
Frayn, Michael (Mill Hill, London)	8/9/33
French, Marilyn (New York, N.Y.)	21/11/29
Friedan, Betty (Peoria, Ill.)	4/2/21
Friel, Brian (Omagh, Co. Tyrone)	9/1/29
Fry, Christopher (Bristol, Avon)	18/12/07
Gardam, Jane (Coatham, Yorks)	11/7/28
Geisel, Theodore ("Dr Seuss", Springfield, Mass.)	2/3/04
Gems, Pam (Bransgore, Hants)	1/8/25
Godden, Rumer (Sussex)	10/12/07
Goldman, William (Chicago, Ill.)	12/8/31
Gordimer, Nadine (Springs, S. Africa)	2/11/23
Gordon, Mary (Long Island, N.Y.)	8/12/49
Gray, Simon (Hayling Island, Hants)	21/10/36
Griffiths, Trevor (Manchester)	4/4/35
Guare, John (New York, N.Y.)	5/2/38
Hailey, Arthur (Luton, England)	5/4/20
Hall, Willis (Leeds, Yorks)	6/4/29
Hampton, Christopher (Fayal, Azores)	26/1/46
Hare, David (Sussex)	5/6/47
Heller, Joseph (Brooklyn, N.Y.)	1/5/23
Hersey, John (Tientsin, China)	17/6/14
Highsmith, Patricia (Fort Worth, Tex.)	19/1/21
Hill, Susan (Scarborough, Yorks)	5/2/42
Hinton, S.E. (Tulsa, Okla.)	1948
Howard, Elizabeth Jane (London)	26/3/23
Hulme, Keri (Christchurch, New Zealand)	9/3/47
Irving, John (Exeter, N.H.)	2/3/42
James, P.D. (Oxford)	3/8/20
Jhabvala, Ruth Prawer (Cologne, Germany)	7/5/27
Johnston, Jennifer (Ireland)	12/1/30
Jong, Erica (New York, N.Y.)	26/3/42
Keillor, Garrison (Anoka, Minn.)	7/8/42
Keneally, Thomas (Sydney, Australia)	7/10/35
Kerr, Jean (Scranton, Pa.)	10/7/23
Kesey, Ken (La Junta, Cal.)	17/9/35
King, Stephen (Portland, Me.)	21/9/47
Kingston, Maxine Hong (Stockton, Cal.)	27/10/40
Krantz, Judith (New York, N.Y.)	9/1/28
Kundera, Milan (Brno, Czechoslovakia)	1/4/29
Le Carré, John (Poole, Dorset)	19/10/31
Lee, Laurie (Stroud, Glos)	26/6/14
LeGuin, Ursula (Berkeley, Cal.)	21/10/29
Leigh, Mike (Salford, Lancs)	20/2/43
Leonard, Elmore (New Orleans, La.)	11/10/25
Lessing, Doris (Kermanshah, Persia)	22/10/19
Levin, Ira (New York, N.Y.)	27/8/29
Lively, Penelope (Cairo, Egypt)	17/3/33
Lodge, David (London)	28/1/35
Ludlum, Robert (New York, N.Y.)	25/5/27
Lurie, Alison (Chicago, Ill.)	3/9/26
Mailer, Norman (Long Branch, N.J.)	31/1/23
Mamet, David (Chicago, Ill.)	30/11/47
Mantel, Hilary (Derbyshire)	1952
Marquez, Gabriel Garcia (Aracata, Colombia)	6/3/28
McEwan, Ian (Aldershot, Hants)	21/6/48
McGahern, John (Dublin, Ireland)	12/11/34
Mercer, David (Wakefield, Yorks)	27/6/28
Michener, James A. (New York, N.Y.)	3/2/07
Miller, Arthur (New York, N.Y.)	17/10/15
Moore, Brian (Belfast, N. Ireland)	25/8/21
Morley, Sheridan (Ascot, Berks)	5/12/41
Morrison, Toni (Lorain, Oh.)	18/2/31
Mortimer, John (Hampstead, London)	21/4/23
Mortimer, Penelope (Rhyl, Flint)	19/9/18
Murdoch, Iris (Dublin, Ireland)	15/7/19
Naipaul, V.S. (Trinidad)	17/8/32
Narayan, R.K. (Madras, India)	10/10/06

Name (Birthplace)	Birthdate
Nichols, Peter (Bristol, Avon)	31/7/27
Oates, Joyce Carol (Lockport, N.Y.)	16/6/38
O'Brien, Edna (Tuamgraney, Ireland)	15/12/31
O'Faolain, Julia (London)	6/6/32
O'Faolain, Sean (Cork, Ireland)	22/2/1900
Osborne, John (London)	12/12/29
Owen, Alun (Liverpool)	24/11/25
Oz, Amos (Jerusalem, Palestine)	4/5/39
Ozick, Cynthia (New York, N.Y.)	17/4/28
Piercy, Marge (Detroit, Mich.)	31/3/36
Pinter, Harold (Hackney, London)	10/10/30
Plater, Alan (Jarrow, Tyne & Wear)	15/4/35
Poliakoff, Stephen (London)	1951
Potok, Chaim (New York, N.Y.)	17/2/29
Potter, Dennis (Coleford, Glos)	17/5/35
Powell, Anthony (London)	21/12/05
Pritchett, V.S. (Ipswich, Suffolk)	16/12/1900
Puzo, Mario (New York, N.Y.)	15/10/20
Pynchon, Thomas (Glen Cove, N.Y.)	8/5/37
Raphael, Frederic (Chicago, Ill.)	14/8/31
Rendell, Ruth (London)	17/2/30
Richler, Mordecai (Montreal, Quebec)	27/1/31
Rosenthal, Jack (London)	8/9/31
Roth, Philip (Newark, N.J.)	19/3/33
Rubens, Bernice (Cardiff, Glam.)	26/7/28
Rushdie, Salman (Bombay, India)	19/6/47
St Aubin de Teran, Lisa (London)	2/10/53
Salinger, J.D. (New York, N.Y.)	1/1/19
Sendak, Maurice (New York. N.Y.)	10/6/28
Shaffer, Anthony (Liverpool)	15/5/26
Shaffer, Peter (Liverpool)	15/5/26
Sharpe, Tom (London)	30/3/38

Name (Birthplace)	Birthdate
Shepard, Sam (Ft. Sheridan, Ill.)	5/11/43
Silver, Joan Micklin (Omaha, Neb.)	25/5/35
Simon, Neil (New York, N.Y.)	4/7/27
Spark, Muriel (Edinburgh, Scotland)	1/2/18
Spillane, Mickey (Brooklyn, N.Y.)	9/3/18
Stoppard, Tom (Zlin, Czechoslovakia)	3/7/37
Storey, David (Wakefield, Yorks)	13/7/33
Styron, William (Newport News, Va.)	11/6/25
Swift, Graham (London)	4/5/49
Tennant, Emma (London)	20/10/37
Terson, Peter (Newcastle, Tyne & Wear)	24/2/32
Theroux, Paul (Medford, Mass.)	10/4/41
Thomas, D.M. (Redruth, Cornwall)	27/1/35
Tremain, Rose (London)	2/8/43
Trevor, William (Mitchelstown, Co. Cork)	24/5/28
Tyler, Anne (Minneapolis, Minn.)	25/10/41
Updike, John (Shillington, Pa.)	18/3/32
Uris, Leon (Baltimore, Md.)	3/8/24
Van der Post, Laurens (Philippolis, S. Africa)	13/12/06
Vidal, Gore (West Point, N.Y.)	3/10/25
Vonnegut, Kurt Jr. (Indianapolis, Ind.)	11/11/22
Walker, Alice (Eatonton, Ga.)	9/2/44
Wambaugh, Joseph (East Pittsburgh, Pa.)	22/1/37
Waterhouse, Keith (Leeds, Yorks)	6/2/29
Weldon, Fay (Alvechurch, Worcs)	22/2/31
Welty, Eudora (Jackson, Miss.)	13/4/09
Wesker, Arnold (Stepney, London)	24/5/32
Wilson, A.N. (Stone, Staffs)	27/10/50
Wilson, Snoo (Reading, Berks)	2/8/48
Winterson, Jeanette (Lancs)	1959
Wolfe, Tom (Richmond, Va.)	2/3/31
Wouk, Herman (New York, N.Y.)	27/5/15

Noted Philosophers and Religionists of the Past

Pierre Abelard, 1079-1142, (F.) philosopher, theologian, and teacher, used dialectic method to support Christian dogma.

Felix Adler, 1851-1933, (U.S.) German-born founder of the Ethical Culture Society.

Thomas Aquinas, 1225-1274, (It.) Roman Catholic saint, founder of system declared official Catholic philosophy; *Summa Theologica*.

Aristotle, 384–322 BC, (Gr.) philosopher, emphasized direct observation of nature.

St. Augustine, 354-430, Latin bishop considered the founder of formalized Christian theology.

Averroes, 1126-1198, (Sp.) Islamic philosopher.

Roger Bacon, c.1214-1294, (Br.) philosopher and scientist.

Bahaullah (Mirza Husayn Ali), 1817-1892, (Pers.) founder of Bahai faith.

Karl Barth, 1886-1968, (Swi.) theologian, a leading force in 20th-century Protestantism.

Thomas à Becket, 1118-1170, (Br.) archbishop of Canterbury, opposed Henry II.

St. Benedict, c.480-547, (It.) founded the Benedictines.

Jeremy Bentham, 1748-1832, (Br.) philosopher, reformer, founder of Utilitarianism.

Henri Bergson, 1859-1941, (F.) philosopher of evolution.

George Berkeley, 1685-1753, (Ir.) philosopher, churchman.

St. Bernard of Clairvaux, 1090–1153, (Fr.) theologian and influential Cistercian.

John Biddle, 1615-1662, (Br.) founder of English Unitarianism.

Jakob Boehme, 1575-1624, (G.) theosophist and mystic.

William Brewster, 1567-1644, (Br.) headed Pilgrims, signed Mayflower Compact.

Emil Brunner, 1889-1966, (Swi.) Protestant theologian.

Giordano Bruno, 1548-1600, (It.) philosopher, first to state the cosmic theory.

Martin Buber, 1878-1965, (G.) Jewish philosopher, theologian, wrote *I and Thou*.

Buddha (Siddhartha Gautama), c.563-c.483 BC, (Ind.) philosopher, founded Buddhism.

John Calvin, 1509-1564, (F.) theologian, a key figure in the Protestant Reformation.

Rudolph Carnap, 1891-1970, (U.S.) German-born philosopher, a founder of logical positivism.

William Ellery Channing, 1780-1842, (U.S.) clergyman, early spokesman for Unitarianism.

Auguste Comte, 1798-1857, (F.) philosopher, the founder of positivism.

Confucius, 551-479 BC, (Chi.) founder of Confucianism.

John Cotton, 1584-1652, (Br.) Puritan theologian.

Thomas Cranmer, 1489-1556, (Br.) churchman, wrote much of *Book of Common Prayer;* promoter of English Reformation.

René Descartes, 1596-1650, (F.) philosopher, mathematician, "father of modern philosophy".

John Dewey, 1859-1952, (U.S.) philosopher, educator; helped inaugurate the progressive education movement.

Denis Diderot, 1713-1784, (F.) philosopher, creator of first modern encyclopedia.

Mary Baker Eddy, 1821-1910, (U.S.) founder of Christian Science, wrote *Science and Health*.

(Desiderius) Erasmus, c.1466-1536, (Du.) Renaissance humanist, wrote *On the Freedom of the Will*.

Johann Fichte, 1762-1814, (G.) philosopher, the first of the Transcendental Idealists.

George Fox, 1624-1691, (Br.) founder of Society of Friends.

St. Francis of Assisi, 1182-1226, (It.) founded Franciscans.

al Ghazali, 1058-1111, Islamic philosopher.

Georg W. Hegel, 1770-1831, (G.) Idealist philosopher.

Martin Heidegger, 1889-1976, (G.) existentialist philosopher, affected fields ranging from physics to literary criticism.

Johann G. Herder, 1744-1803, (G.) philosopher, cultural historian; a founder of German Romanticism.

David Hume, 1711-1776, (Br.) philosopher, historian.

Jan Hus, 1369-1415, (Cz.) religious reformer.

Edmund Husserl, 1859-1938, (G.) philosopher, founded the Phenomenological movement.

Thomas Huxley, 1825-1895, (Br.) philosopher, educator.

Ignatius of Loyola, 1491-1556, (Sp.) founder of the Jesuits.

William Inge, 1860-1954, (Br.) theologian, explored the mystic aspects of Christianity.

William James, 1842-1910, (U.S.) philosopher, psychologist; advanced theory of the pragmatic nature of truth.

Karl Jaspers, 1883-1969, (G.) existentialist philosopher.

Immanuel Kant, 1724-1804, (G.) metaphysician, pre-eminent founder of modern critical philosophy; *Critique of Pure Reason*.

Thomas à Kempis, c.1380-1471, (G.) theologian, probably wrote *Imitation of Christ*.

Søren Kierkegaard, 1813-1855, (Dan.) philosopher, considered the father of Existentialism.

John Knox, 1505-1572, (Br.) leader of the Protestant Reformation in Scotland.

Lao-Tzu, 604-531 BC, (Ch.) philosopher, considered the founder of the Taoist religion.

Gottfried von Leibniz, 1646-1716, (G.) philosopher, mathematician, influenced German Enlightenment.

Martin Luther, 1483-1546, (G.) leader of the Protestant Reformation, founded Lutheran church.

Maimonides, 1135-1204, (Sp.) Jewish philosopher.

Jacques Maritain, 1882-1973, (F.) Neo-Thomist philosopher.

Cotton Mather, 1663-1728, (U.S.) defender of orthodox Puritanism; founded Yale, 1701.

Philip Melanchthon, 1497-1560, (G.) theologian, humanist; an important voice in the Reformation.

Thomas Merton, 1915-1968, (U.S.) Trappist monk, spiritual writer; *The Seven-Storey Mountain*.

Mohammed, c.570-632, Arab prophet of the religion of Islam.

George E. Moore, 1873-1958, (Br.) ethical theorist.

Elijah Muhammad, 1897-1975, (U.S.) leader of the Black Muslim sect.

Heinrich Muhlenberg, 1711-1787, (G.) organized the Lutheran Church in America.

John H. Newman, 1801-1890, (Br.) Roman Catholic cardinal, led Oxford Movement; *Apologia pro Vita Sua*.

Reinhold Niebuhr, 1892-1971, (U.S.) Protestant theologian, social and political critic.

Friedrich Nietzsche, 1844-1900, (G.) moral philosopher; *The Birth of Tragedy, Thus Spake Zarathustra*.

Blaise Pascal, 1623-1662, (F.) philosopher, mathematician.

St. Patrick, c.389-c.461, took Christianity to Ireland.

St. Paul, ?-c.67, a founder of Christianity; his epistles are first Christian theological writing.

Charles S. Peirce, 1839-1914, (U.S.) philosopher, logician; originated concept of Pragmatism, 1878.

Plato, 427?–347? BC, (Gr.) philosopher, argued for independent reality of ideas; *Republic*.

Josiah Royce 1855-1916, (U.S.) idealist philosopher.

Bertrand Russell, 1872-1970, (Br.) philosopher and writer; *An Inquiry into Meaning and Truth*.

Charles T. Russell, 1852-1916, (U.S.) founder of Jehovah's Witnesses.

Girolamo Savonarola, 1452–1498, (It.) prior, attacked corruption in politics and papacy.

Fredrich von Schelling, 1775-1854, (G.) philosopher of romantic movement.

Friedrich Schleiermacher, 1768-1834, (G.) theologian, a founder of modern Protestant theology.

Arthur Schopenhauer, 1788-1860, (G.) philosopher, emphasized human will as a means to understanding.

Joseph Smith, 1805-1844, (U.S.) founded Latter Day Saints (Mormon) movement, 1830.

Socrates, 469–399 BC, (Gr.) philosopher, refined dialectic method.

Herbert Spencer, 1820-1903, (Br.) philosopher of evolution.

Baruch Spinoza, 1632-1677, (Du.) rationalist philosopher.

John Stuart Mill, 1806–1873, (Br.) philosopher, economist; *Essay on Liberty*.

Daisetz Teitaro Suzuki, 1870-1966, (Jap.) Buddhist scholar.

Emanuel Swedenborg, 1688-1772, (Swe.) philosopher and mystic.

Pierre Teilhard de Chardin, 1881-1955, (F.) Jesuit theologian, palaeontologist; explored synthesis of natural science & religion.

Paul Tillich, 1886-1965, (U.S.) German-born philosopher and theologian; brought depth psychology to Protestantism.

John Wesley, 1703-1791, (Br.) theologian, evangelist; founded Methodism.

Alfred North Whitehead, 1861-1947, (Br.) philosopher, mathematician; *Principia Mathematica* (with Bertrand Russell).

William of Occam, c.1285-c.1349, (Br.) medieval scholastic philosopher.

Roger Williams, c.1603-1683, (U.S.) clergyman, championed religious freedom and separation of church and state.

Ludwig Wittgenstein, 1889-1951, (Aus.) philosopher, influenced language philosophy.

John Wycliffe, 1320-1384, (Br.) theologian, reformer.

Brigham Young, 1801-1877, (U.S.) Mormon leader after Smith's assassination, colonized Utah.

Huldrych Zwingli, 1484-1531, (Swi.) theologian, led Swiss Protestant Reformation.

Noted Social Reformers and Educators of the Past

Jane Addams, 1860-1935, (U.S.) co-founder of Hull House; won Nobel Peace Prize, 1931.

Elizabeth Garrett Anderson, 1836-1917, (Br.) doctor who pioneered entry of women to medical profession.

Susan B. Anthony, 1820-1906, (U.S.) a leader in temperance, anti-slavery, and women's suffrage movements.

Thomas Arnold, 1795-1842, (Br.) educator, headmaster of Rugby School, whose reforms spread throughout English public schools.

Robert Baden-Powell, 1857-1941, (Br.) founder of the Boy Scouts and Girl Guides.

Thomas Barnardo, 1845-1905, (Br.) social reformer, pioneer in the care of destitute children.

Clara Barton, 1821-1912, (U.S.) organizer of the American Red Cross.

Henry Ward Beecher, 1813-1887, (U.S.) clergyman, abolitionist.

Annie Besant, 1847-1933, (Br.) campaigner for birth control, trade unions and atheism.

Aneurin (Nye) Bevan, 1897-1960, (Br.) politician who pioneered the National Health System.

William Beveridge, 1879-1963, (Br.) social reformer and economist; 2 of his books formed the basis of the Welfare State.

Sarah G. Blanding, 1899-1985, (U.S.), head of Vassar College, 1946-64.

Amelia Bloomer, 1818-1894, (U.S.) social reformer, women's rights advocate.

William Booth, 1829-1912, (Br.) founded the Salvation Army.

John Brown, 1800-1859, (U.S.) abolitionist who led murder of 5 pro-slavery men, was hanged.

Nicholas Murray Butler, 1862-1947, (U.S.) educator headed Columbia Univ., 1902-45; won Nobel Peace Prize, 1931.

Frances X. (Mother) **Cabrini**, 1850-1917, (U.S.) Italian-born nun founded charitable institutions; first American canonized.

Edith Cavell, 1865-1915, (Br.) nurse and trainer of nurses in Belgium, WW1; executed by Germans for helping allied soldiers to escape.

Clarence Darrow, 1857-1938, (U.S.) lawyer, defender of "underdog", opponent of capital punishment.

Eugene V. Debs, 1855-1926, (U.S.) labour leader, led Pullman strike, 1894; 4-time Socialist presidential candidate.

Melvil Dewey, 1851-1931, (U.S.) devised decimal system of library-book classification.

Dorothea Dix, 1802-1887, (U.S.) crusader for humane care of mentally ill.

W.E.B. DuBois, 1868-1963, (U.S.) Negro-rights leader, educator, and writer.

Havelock Ellis, 1859-1939, (Br.) sexologist who wrote serious but controversial books: *Man and Woman, The Erotic Rights of Women*.

Mrs Henry Fawcett (Millicent Garrett), 1847-1929, (Br.) suffragist who opposed militancy of the Pankhursts.

Friedrich Froebel, 1782-1852 (G.) founder of first kindergarten; introduced idea of creative play.

Giovanni Gentile, 1875-1944, (It.) philosopher, educator; reformed Italian educational system.

Emma Goldman, 1869-1940, (Rus.-U.S.) published anarchist *Mother Earth*, birth control advocate.

Michael Harrington, 1928-1989, (U.S.) revealed poverty in affluent U.S. in *The Other America*, 1963.

John Holt, 1924-1985, (U.S.) educator and author, *How Children Fail*.

Helen Keller, 1880-1968, (U.S.) crusader for better treatment for the handicapped.

Martin Luther King Jr., 1929-1968, (U.S.) civil rights leader; won Nobel Peace Prize, 1964.

Alexander Meiklejohn, 1872-1964, (U.S.) British-born educator, championed academic freedom and experimental curricula.

Karl Menninger, 1893-1991, (U.S.) with brother William made Menninger Clinic, and Menninger Foundation in Topeka, Kans., the center of U.S. psychiatry.

Maria Montessori, 1870-1952 (It.) doctor and educator who stressed the development of the senses.

Lucretia Mott, 1793-1880, (U.S.) reformer, pioneer feminist.

Philip Murray, 1886-1952, (U.S.) Scottish-born labour leader.

Florence Nightingale, 1820-1910, (Br.) founder of modern nursing.

Emmeline Pankhurst, 1858-1928, (Br.) woman suffragist.

Johann Pestalozzi, 1746-1827, (Swi.) pioneer of education for all; the Pestalozzi Villages, which educate war orphans and the children of developing countries, were founded to commemorate his work.

Dora Russell, 1894-1986, (Br.) political activist who promoted birth control, the rights of women and educational reform.

Earl of Shaftesbury (A.A. Cooper), 1801-1885, (Br.) social reformer.

Elizabeth Cady Stanton, 1815-1902, (U.S.) women's suffrage pioneer.

Lucy Stone, 1818-1893, (U.S.) feminist, abolitionist.

Marie Stopes, 1880-1958, (Br.) founded first birth-control clinic in England, 1921.

Harriet Tubman, c.1820-1913, (U.S.) abolitionist, ran Underground Railroad.

Booker T. Washington, 1856-1915, (U.S.) educator, reformer; championed vocational training for blacks.

Walter F. White, 1893-1955, (U.S.) headed NAACP, 1931-55.

William Wilberforce, 1759-1833, (Br.) social reformer, prominent in struggle to abolish the slave trade.

Emma Hart Willard, 1787-1870, (U.S.) pioneered higher education for women.

Mary Wollstonecraft, 1759-1797 (Br.) feminist writer; *Vindication of the Rights of Women*; *Thoughts on the Education of Daughters*.

Noted Historians, Economists and Social Scientists of the Past

Brooks Adams, 1848-1927, (U.S.) historian, political theoretician; *The Law of Civilization and Decay.*

Henry Adams, 1838-1911, (U.S.) historian; *History of the United States of America, The Education of Henry Adams.*

Francis Bacon, 1561-1626, (Br.) philosopher, essayist, and statesman; applied scientific induction to philosophy.

George Bancroft, 1800-1891, (U.S.) historian, wrote 10-volume *History of the United States.*

Bede (the Venerable), c.673-735, (Br.) scholar historian whose writings virtually comprise the learning of his time.

Bruno Bettelheim, 1903-1990, (Aust.-U.S.) psychoanalyst specializing in autistic children; *The Uses of Enchantment.*

Louis Blanc, 1811-1882, (F.) Socialist leader and historian whose ideas were a link between utopian and Marxist socialism.

Edmund Burke, 1729-1797, (Br.) parliamentarian and political philosopher; influenced many Federalists.

Joseph Campbell, 1904-1987, (U.S.) wrote books on mythology, folklore.

Thomas Carlyle, 1795-1881, (Br.) historian, critic; *Sartor Resartus, Past and Present, The French Revolution.*

Edward Channing, 1856-1931, (U.S.) historian, wrote 6-volume *A History of the United States.*

Benedetto Croce, 1866-1952, (It.) philosopher, statesman, and historian; *Philosophy of the Spirit.*

Ariel Durant, 1898-1981, (U.S.) historian, collaborated with husband on 11-volume *The Story of Civilization.*

Will Durant, 1885-1981, (U.S.) historian. *The Story of Civilization, The Story of Philosophy.*

Emile Durkheim, 1858-1917, (F.) a founder of modern sociology; *The Rules of Sociological Method.*

Friedrich Engels, 1820-1895, (G.) political writer, with Marx wrote the *Communist Manifesto.*

Irving Fisher, 1867-1947, (U.S.) economist, contributed to the development of modern monetary theory.

Edward Gibbon, 1737-1794, (Br.) historian; *The History of the Decline and Fall of the Roman Empire.*

Francesco Guicciardini, 1483-1540, (It.) historian, wrote *Storia d'Italia*, principal historical work of the 16th century.

Thomas Hobbes, 1588-1679, (Br.) political philosopher; *Leviathan.*

John Maynard Keynes, 1883-1946, (Br.) economist, principal advocate of deficit spending.

Lucien Lévy-Bruhl, 1857-1939, (F.) philosopher, studied the psychology of primitive societies; *Primitive Mentality.*

John Locke, 1632-1704, (Br.) philosopher; *Essay Concerning Human Understanding.*

Konrad Lorenz, 1904-1989, (Aus.) ethologist, pioneer in study of animal behaviour.

Thomas B. Macauley, 1800-1859, (Br.) historian, statesman.

Bronislaw Malinowski, 1884-1942, (Pol.) considered the father of social anthropology.

Thomas R. Malthus, 1766-1834, (Br.) economist, famed for *Essay on the Principle of Population.*

Karl Mannheim, 1893-1947, (Hung.) sociologist, historian; *Ideology and Utopia.*

Karl Marx, 1818-1883, (G.) political philosopher, proponent of modern communism; *Communist Manifesto, Das Kapital.*

Giuseppe Mazzini, 1805-1872, (It.) political philosopher.

Margaret Mead, 1901-1978, (U.S.) cultural anthropologist, popularized field; *Coming of Age in Samoa.*

John Stuart Mill, 1806-1873, (Br.) philosopher, political economist; *Essay on Liberty.*

Theodor Mommsen, 1817-1903, (G.) historian; *The History of Rome.*

Charles-Louis Montesquieu, 1689-1755, (F.) social philosopher; *The Spirit of Laws.*

Lewis Mumford, 1895-1990, (U.S.) sociologist, critic, *The Culture of Cities.*

Gunnar Myrdal, 1898-1987 (Swe.) economist, social scientist.

José Ortega y Gasset, 1883-1955, (Sp.) philosopher, advocated control by elite; *The Revolt of the Masses.*

Robert Owen, 1771-1858, (Br.) political philosopher, reformer; pioneer in cooperative movement.

Vilfredo Pareto, 1848-1923, (It.) economist, sociologist.

Nikolaus Pevsner, 1902-1983, (G.-Br.) art historian; *The Buildings of England.*

Marco Polo, c.1254-1324, (It.) narrated an account of his travels to China.

William Prescott, 1796-1859, (U.S.) early American historian; *The Conquest of Peru.*

Pierre Joseph Proudhon, 1809-1865, (F.) social theorist, the father of anarchism; *The Philosophy of Property.*

François Quesnay, 1694-1774, (F.) economic theorist, demonstrated circular flow of economic activity through society.

David Ricardo, 1772-1823, (Br.) economic theorist, advocated free international trade.

Jean-Jacques Rousseau, 1712-1778, (F.) social philosopher, the father of romantic sensibility; *Discours sur l'origine de l'inégalité.*

Ferdinand de Saussure, 1857-1913, (Swi.) a founder of modern linguistics.

Hjalmar Schacht, 1877-1970, (G.) economist; Reichsbank president.

Joseph Schumpeter, 1883-1950, (U.S.) Czech.-born economist, championed big business, capitalism.

Albert Schweitzer, 1875-1965, (G.) Alsatian-born social philosopher, theologian, medical missionary.

George Simmel, 1858-1918, (G.) sociologist, philosopher; helped establish German sociology.

B.F. Skinner, 1904-1989, (U.S.) psychologist, championed behaviourism.

Adam Smith, 1723-1790, (Br.) economist, advocated laissez-faire economy and free trade.

Oswald Spengler, 1880-1936, (G.) philosopher and historian; *The Decline of the West.*

Hippolyte Taine, 1828-1893, (F.) historian, basis of naturalistic school; *The Origins of Contemporary France.*

A(lan) **J**(ohn) **P**(ercivale) **Taylor**, 1906-1989, (Br.) historian, *The Origins of the Second World War.*

Nikolaas Tinbergen, 1907-1988, (Dutch-Br.) ethologist, pioneer in study of animal behaviour.

Alexis de Tocqueville, 1805-1859, (F.) political scientist, historian; *Democracy in America.*

Arnold Toynbee, 1889-1975, (Br.) historian; *A Study of History.*

Heinrich von Treitschke, 1834-1896, (G.) historian, political writer; *A History of Germany in the 19th Century.*

George Trevelyan, 1838-1928, (Br.) historian, statesman; favoured "literary" over "scientific" history; *History of England.*

Barbara Tuchman, 1912-1989, (U.S.) author of popular history books, *The Guns of August, The March of Folly.*

Thorstein B. Veblen, 1857-1929, (U.S.) economist, social philosopher; *The Theory of the Leisure Class.*

Giovanni Vico, 1668-1744, (It.) historian, philosopher; regarded by many as first modern historian. *New Science.*

Voltaire (F.M. Arouet), 1694-1778, (F.) philosopher, historian, writer of "philosophical romances"; *Candide.*

Izaak Walton, 1593-1683, (Br.) wrote biographies, political-philosophical study of fishing, *The Compleat Angler.*

Sidney J., 1859-1947, and wife **Beatrice**, 1858-1943, **Webb** (Br.) leading figures in Fabian Society and British Labour Party.

Max Weber, 1864-1920, (G.) sociologist. *The Protestant Ethic and the Spirit of Capitalism.*

Noted Scientists of the Past

Howard H. Aiken, 1900-1973, (U.S.) mathematician, credited with designing forerunner of digital computer.

Albertus Magnus, 1193-1280, (G.) theologian, philosopher, established medieval Christian study of natural science.

André-Marie Ampère, 1775-1836, (F.) scientist known for contributions to electrodynamics.

Amedeo Avogadro, 1776-1856, (It.) chemist, physicist, advanced important theories on properties of gases.

John Bardeen, 1908-1991, (U.S.) co-inventor of the transistor that led to modern electronics.

A.C. Becquerel, 1788-1878, (F.) physicist, pioneer in electrochemical science.

A.H. Becquerel, 1852-1908, (F.) physicist, discovered radioactivity in uranium.

Alexander Graham Bell, 1847-1922, (U.S.) inventor, first to patent and commercially exploit the telephone, 1876.

Daniel Bernoulli, 1700-1782, (Swi.) mathematician, advanced kinetic theory of gases and fluids.

Jöns Jakob Berzelius, 1779-1848, (Swe.) chemist, developed modern chemical symbols and formulas.

Henry Bessemer, 1813-1898, (Br.) engineer, invented Bessemer steel-making process.

Louis Blériot, 1872-1936, (F.) engineer, pioneer aviator, invented and constructed monoplanes.

Niels Bohr, 1885-1962, (Dan.) physicist, leading figure in the development of quantum theory.

Max Born, 1882-1970, (G.) physicist known for research in quantum mechanics.

Satyendranath Bose, 1894-1974, (In.) physicist, chemist, mathematician known for Bose statistics, forerunner of modern quantum theory.

Walter Brattain, 1902-1987, (U.S.) inventor, worked on invention of transistor.

Werner von Braun, 1912-1977, (G.-U.S.) pioneered development of rockets for warfare and space exploration.

Louis de Broglie, 1893-1987, (F.) physicist, best known for wave theory.

Robert Bunsen, 1811-1899, (G.) chemist, invented Bunsen burner.

Luther Burbank, 1849-1926, (U.S.) plant breeder whose work developed plant breeding into a modern science.

Vannevar Bush, 1890-1974, (U.S.) electrical engineer, developed differential analyser, first electronic analogue computer.

Alexis Carrel, 1873-1944, (F.) surgeon, biologist, developed methods of suturing blood vessels and transplanting organs.

George Washington Carver, 1860?-1943, (U.S.) agricultural chemist at Tuskegee Institute, discovered hundreds of uses for peanut, sweet potato, soybean.

Henry Cavendish, 1731-1810, (Br.) chemist, physicist, discovered hydrogen.

James Chadwick, 1891-1974, (Br.) physicist, discovered the neutron.

Jean M. Charcot, 1825-1893, (F.) neurologist known for work on hysteria, hypnotism, sclerosis.

Albert Claude, 1899-1983, (Belg.) a founder of modern cell biology.

John D. Cockcroft, 1897-1967, (Br.) nuclear physicist, constructed first atomic particle accelerator with E.T.S. Walton.

Nicholas Copernicus, 1473-1543, (Pol.) astronomer who first described solar system, with Earth as one of planets revolving around sun.

William Crookes, 1832-1919, (Br.) physicist, chemist, discovered thallium, invented a cathode-ray tube, radiometer.

Marie Curie, 1867-1934, (Pol.-F.) physical chemist known for work on radium and its compounds.

Pierre Curie, 1859-1906, (F.) physical chemist known for work with his wife on radioactivity.

Gottlieb Daimler, 1834-1900, (G.) engineer, inventor, pioneer automobile manufacturer.

John Dalton, 1766-1844, (Br.) chemist, physicist, formulated atomic theory, made first table of atomic weights.

Charles Darwin, 1809-1882, (Br.) naturalist, established theory of organic evolution; *Origin of Species.*

Humphry Davy, 1778-1829, (Br.) chemist, research in electrochemistry led to isolation of potassium, sodium, calcium, barium, boron, magnesium and strontium.

Lee De Forest, 1873-1961, (U.S.) inventor, pioneer in development of wireless telegraphy, sound pictures, television.

Max Delbruck, 1907-1981, (U.S.) pioneer in modern molecular genetics.

Rudolf Diesel, 1858-1913, (G.) mechanical engineer, patented Diesel engine.

Thomas Dooley, 1927-1961, (U.S.) "jungle doctor", noted for efforts to supply medical aid to underdeveloped countries.

Christian Doppler, 1803-1853, (Aus.) physicist, demonstrated Doppler effect (change in energy wavelengths caused by motion).

Thomas A. Edison, 1847-1931, (U.S.) inventor, held over 1,000 patents, including incandescent electric lamp, phonograph.

Paul Ehrlich, 1854-1915, (G.) bacteriologist, pioneer in modern immunology and bacteriology.

Albert Einstein, 1879-1955, (Ger.-U.S.) theoretical physicist, known for formulation of relativity theory.

John F. Enders, 1897-1985, (U.S.) virologist who helped discover vaccines against polio, measles and mumps.

Leonhard Euler, 1707-1783, (Swiss), mathematician, physicist, author of first calculus book.

Gabriel Fahrenheit, 1686-1736, (G.) physicist, introduced Fahrenheit scale for thermometers.

Michael Faraday, 1791-1867, (Br.) chemist, physicist, known for work in field of electricity.

Pierre de Fermat, 1601-1665, (F.) mathematician, discovered analytic geometry, founded modern theory of numbers and calculus of probabilities.

Enrico Fermi, 1901-1954, (It.) physicist, one of chief architects of the nuclear age.

Galileo Ferraris, 1847-1897, (It.) physicist, electrical engineer, discovered principle of rotary magnetic field.

Richard Feynman, 1918-1988, (U.S.) a leading theoretical physicist of the postwar generation.

Camille Flammarion, 1842-1925, (F.) astronomer, popularized study of astronomy.

Alexander Fleming, 1881-1955, (Br.) bacteriologist, discovered penicillin.

Jean B.J. Fourier, 1768-1830, (F.) mathematician, discovered theorem governing periodic oscillation.

James Franck, 1882-1964, (G.) physicist, proved value of quantum theory.

Sigmund Freud, 1856-1939, (Aus.) psychiatrist, founder of psychoanalysis.

Galileo Galilei, 1564-1642, (It.) astronomer, physicist, a founder of the experimental method.

Luigi Galvani, 1737-1798, (It.) physician, physicist, known as founder of galvanism.

Carl Friedrich Gauss, 1777-1855, (G.) mathematician, astronomer, physicist, made important contributions to almost every field of physical science, founded a number of new fields.

Joseph Gay-Lussac, 1778-1850, (F.) chemist, physicist, investigated behaviour of gases, discovered law of combining volumes.

Josiah W. Gibbs, 1839-1903, (U.S.) theoretical physicist, chemist, founded chemical thermodynamics.

Robert H. Goddard, 1882-1945 (U.S.) physicist, father of modern rocketry.

George W. Goethals, 1858-1928, (U.S.) army engineer, built the Panama Canal.

William C. Gorgas, 1854-1920, (U.S.) sanitarian, U.S. army surgeon-general, his work to prevent yellow fever, malaria helped ensure construction of Panama Canal.

Ernest Haeckel, 1834-1919, (G.) zoologist, evolutionist, a strong proponent of Darwin.

Otto Hahn, 1879-1968, (G.) chemist, worked on atomic fission.

J.B.S. Haldane, 1892-1964, (Br.) scientist, known for work as geneticist and application of mathematics to science.

James Hall, 1761-1832, (Br.) geologist, chemist, founded experimental geology, geochemistry.

Edmund Halley, 1656-1742, (Br.) astronomer, calculated the orbits of many planets.

William Harvey, 1578-1657, (Br.) physician, anatomist, discovered circulation of the blood.

Hermann von Helmholtz, 1821-1894, (G.) physicist, anatomist, physiologist, made fundamental contributions to physiology, optics, electrodynamics, mathematics, meteorology.

William Herschel, 1738-1822, (Br.) astronomer, discovered Uranus.

Heinrich Hertz, 1857-1894, (G.) physicist, his discoveries led to wireless telegraphy.

David Hilbert, 1862-1943, (G.) mathematician, formulated first satisfactory set of axioms for modern Euclidean geometry.

Frederick Gowland Hopkins, 1887-1975, (Br.) biochemist, specializing in amino acids and vitamins.

Edwin P. Hubble, 1889-1953, (U.S.) astronomer, produced first observational evidence of expanding universe.

Alexander von Humboldt, 1769-1859, (G.) explorer, naturalist, propagator of earth sciences, originated ecology, geophysics.

Julian Huxley, 1887-1975, (Br.) biologist, a gifted exponent and philosopher of science.

Edward Jenner, 1749-1823, (Br.) physician, discovered vaccination.

William Jenner, 1815-1898, (Br.) physician, pathological anatomist.

Frédéric Joliot-Curie, 1900-1958, (F.) physicist, with his wife continued work of Curies on radioactivity.

Irène Joliot-Curie, 1897-1956, (F.) physicist, continued work of Curies in radioactivity.

James P. Joule, 1818-1889, (Br.) physicist, determined relationship between heat and mechanical energy (conservation of energy).

Carl Jung, 1875-1961, (Swi.) psychiatrist, founder of analytical psychology.

Wm. Thomson Kelvin, 1824-1907, (Br.) mathematician, physicist, known for work on heat and electricity.

Sister Elizabeth Kenny, 1886-1952, (Austral.) nurse, developed method of treatment for polio.

Johannes Kepler, 1571-1630, (G.) astronomer, discovered important laws of planetary motion.

Joseph Lagrange, 1736-1813, (F.) geometer, astronomer, worked in all fields of analysis, and number theory, and analytical and celestial mechanics.

Jean B. Lamarck, 1744-1829, (F.) naturalist, forerunner of Darwin in evolutionary theory.

Edwin Land, 1910-1991, (U.S.) invented Polaroid camera.

Irving Langmuir, 1881-1957, (U.S.) physical chemist, his studies of molecular films on solid and liquid surfaces opened new fields in colloid research and biochemistry.

Pierre S. Laplace, 1749-1827, (F.) astronomer, physicist, put forth nebular hypothesis of origin of solar system.

Antoine Lavoisier, 1743-1794, (F.) chemist, founder of modern chemistry.

Ernest O. Lawrence, 1901-1958, (U.S.) physicist, invented the cyclotron.

Louis Leakey, 1903-1972, (Br.) anthropologist, discovered important fossils, remains of early hominids.

Anton van Leeuwenhoek, 1632-1723, (Du.) microscopist, father of microbiology.

Gottfried Wilhelm Leibniz, 1646-1716, (G.) mathematician, developed theories of differential and integral calculus.

Justus von Liebig, 1803-1873, (G.) chemist, established quantitative organic chemical analysis.

Joseph Lister, 1827-1912, (Br.) pioneer of antiseptic surgery.

Percival Lowell, 1855-1916, (U.S.) astronomer, predicted the existence of Pluto.

Louis (1864-1984) and **Auguste Lumière,** 1862-1954, (Fr.) invented cinematograph, first mechanism to project moving pictures on screen.

Guglielmo Marconi, 1874-1937, (It.) physicist, known for his development of wireless telegraphy.

James Clerk Maxwell, 1831-1879, (Br.) physicist, known especially for his work in electricity and magnetism.

Maria Goeppert Mayer, 1906-1972, (G.-U.S.) physicist, independently developed theory of structure of atomic nuclei.

Lise Meitner, 1878-1968, (Aus.) physicist whose work contributed to the development of the atomic bomb.

Gregor J. Mendel, 1822-1884, (Aus.) botanist, known for his experimental work on heredity.

Franz Mesmer, 1734-1815, (G.) physician, developed theory of animal magnetism.

Albert A. Michelson, 1852-1931, (U.S.) physicist, established speed of light as a fundamental constant.

Robert A. Millikan, 1868-1953, (U.S.) physicist, noted for study of elementary electronic charge and photoelectric effect.

Thomas Hunt Morgan, 1866-1945, (U.S.) geneticist, embryologist, established chromosome theory of heredity.

Isaac Newton, 1642-1727, (Br.) natural philosopher, mathematician, discovered law of gravitation, laws of motion.

Robert N. Noyce, 1927-1989, (U.S.) inventor of the microchip, which revolutionized the electronics industry.

J. Robert Oppenheimer, 1904-1967, (U.S.) physicist, director of Los Alamos during development of the atomic bomb.

Wilhelm Ostwald, 1853-1932, (G.) physical chemist, philosopher, chief founder of physical chemistry.

Robert Morris Page, 1903-1992, (U.S.) research director of U.S. Naval Research Laboratory, a leading figure in development of radar technology.

Louis Pasteur, 1822-1895, (F.) chemist, originated process of pasteurization.

Max Planck, 1858-1947, (G.) physicist, originated and developed quantum theory.

Henri Poincaré, 1854-1912, (F.) mathematician, physicist, influenced cosmology, relativity and topology.

Joseph Priestley, 1733-1804, (Br.) chemist, one of the discoverers of oxygen.

Isidor Rabi, 1899-1988 (U.S.) physicist, pioneered atom exploration.

Walter S. Reed, 1851-1902, (U.S.) army pathologist, bacteriologist, proved mosquitos transmit yellow fever.

Bernhard Riemann, 1826-1866, (G.) mathematician, contributed to development of calculus, complex variable theory and mathematical physics.

Wilhelm Roentgen, 1845-1923, (G.) physicist, discovered X-rays.

Ronald Ross, 1857-1932, (Br.) biologist, discovered cause of malaria.

Bertrand Russell, 1872-1970, (Br.) logician, philosopher, one of the founders of modern logic, wrote *Principia Mathematica*.

Ernest Rutherford, 1871-1937, (Br.) physicist, discovered the atomic nucleus.

Albert B. Sabin, 1906–1993, (Rus.–U.S.) virologist, developed oral polio vaccine, 1954.

Giovanni Schiaparelli, 1835-1910, (It.) astronomer, hypothesized canals on the surface of Mars.

Angelo Secchi, 1818-1878, (It.) astronomer, pioneer in classifying stars by their spectra.

Harlow Shapley, 1885-1972, (U.S.) astronomer, noted for his studies of the galaxy.

Charles P. Steinmetz, 1865-1923, (G.-U.S.) electrical engineer, developed basic ideas on alternating current systems.

Leo Szilard, 1898-1964, (Hung.-U.S.) physicist, helped create first sustained nuclear reaction.

Nikola Tesla, 1856-1943, (Croat-U.S.) electrical engineer, contributed to most developments in electronics.

Rudolf Virchow, 1821-1902, (G.) pathologist, a founder of cellular pathology.

Alessandro Volta, 1745-1827, (It.) physicist, pioneer in electricity.

Alfred Russell Wallace, 1823-1913, (Br.) naturalist, proposed concept of evolution similar to Darwin.

Barnes Wallis, 1887-1979, (Br.) aircraft designer, inventor of the "bouncing bomb".

August von Wasserman, 1866-1925, (G.) bacteriologist, discovered reaction used as test for syphilis.

James E. Watt, 1736-1819, (Br.) mechanical engineer, inventor, invented modern steam condensing engine.

Alfred L. Wegener, 1880-1930, (G.) meteorologist, geophysicist, postulated theory of continental drift.

Norbert Wiener, 1894-1964, (U.S.) mathematician, founder of the science of cybernetics.

Sewall Wright, 1889-1988 (U.S.) a leading evolutionary theorist.

Ferdinand von Zeppelin, 1838-1917 (G.) soldier, aeronaut, airship designer.

Noted Business Leaders, Industrialists and Philanthropists of the Past

Max Aitken, 1879-1964, (Can.-Br.) newspaper magnate (*Daily Express, Sunday Express, Evening Standard*).

Elizabeth Arden (F.N. Graham), 1884-1966, (U.S.) Canadian-born founder of cosmetics empire.

Philip D. Armour, 1832-1901, (U.S.) industrialist, streamlined meat packing.

John Jakob Astor, 1763-1848, (U.S.) German-born fur trader, banker, real estate magnate; at death, richest in U.S.

Herbert Austin, 1866-1941, (Br.) motor manufacturer and philanthropist, especially to hospitals.

Jesse Boot, 1850-1931, (Br.) pharmacist and philanthropist, founded one of largest retail chemist organizations in world.

James B. (Diamond Jim) Brady, 1856-1917, (U.S.) financier, philanthropist, legendary bon vivant.

Montague Burton, 1885-1952, (Br.) multiple tailor and philanthropist; endowed numerous chairs in industrial and international relations.

Adolphus Busch, 1839-1913, (U.S.) German-born businessman, established brewery empire.

Billy Butlin, 1899-1980, (Br.) pioneer of holiday camps; philanthropist, especially to children's charities.

George Cadbury, 1839-1922, (Br.) chocolate manufacturer and social reformer; actively supported Adult School Movement to increase literacy.

Asa Candler, 1851-1929, (U.S.) founded Coca-Cola Co.

Andrew Carnegie, 1835-1919, (U.S.) Scots-born industrialist, founded U.S. Steel; financed over 2,800 libraries.

William Colgate, 1783-1857, (U.S.) British-born businessman, philanthropist; founded soap-making empire.

Jay Cooke, 1821-1905, (U.S.) financier, sold $1 billion in Union bonds during Civil War.

Ezra Cornell, 1807-1874, (U.S.) businessman, philanthropist; headed Western Union, established univ.

Erastus Corning, 1794-1872, (U.S.) financier, headed N.Y. Central.

Samuel Courtauld, 1876-1947, (Br.) textile manufacturer, financed gallery and college for the study of art history.

Samuel Cunard, 1787-1865, (Can.) pioneered trans-Atlantic steam navigation.

George T. Delacorte, 1893-1991, (U.S.) publisher; Central Park donations included Alice in Wonderland statue.

Walt Disney, 1901-1966, (U.S.) pioneer in cinema animation, built entertainment empire.

Herbert H. Dow, 1866-1930, (U.S.) Canadian-born founder of chemical co.

James Duke, 1856-1925, (U.S.) founded American Tobacco, Duke Univ.

Eleuthère I. du Pont, 1771-1834, (U.S.) French-born gunpowder manufacturer; founded one of world's largest business empires.

William C. Durant, 1861-1947, (U.S.) industrialist, formed General Motors.

George Eastman, 1854-1932, (U.S.) inventor, manufacturer of photographic equipment.

Marshall Field, 1834-1906, (U.S.) merchant, founded Chicago's largest department store.

Harvey Firestone, 1868-1938, (U.S.) industrialist, founded tyre company.

Henry M. Flagler, 1830-1913, (U.S.) financier, helped form Standard Oil; developed Florida as resort state.

Malcolm Forbes, 1919-1990, (U.S.) publisher, *Forbes* magazine.

Henry Ford, 1863-1947, (U.S.) auto maker, developed first popular low-priced car.

Henry Ford II, 1917-1987, (U.S.) headed auto company founded by grandfather.

William Foyle, 1885-1957 (Br.) bookseller, founded what was once the largest bookshop in the world.

Hugh Fraser, 1903-1966, (Br.) founder House of Fraser department stores; philanthropist.

Henry C. Frick, 1849-1919, (U.S.) industrialist, helped organize U.S. Steel.

Jakob Fugger (Jakob the Rich), 1459-1525, (G.) headed leading banking house, trading concern, in 16th-century Europe.

Alfred C. Fuller, 1885-1973, (U.S.) Canadian-born businessman, founded brush co.

Jean Paul Getty, 1892-1976, (U.S.) founded oil empire.

Amadeo P. Giannini, 1870-1949, (U.S.) founded Bank of America.

Stephen Girard, 1750-1831, (U.S.) French-born financier, philanthropist; richest man in U.S. at his death.

Jay Gould, 1836-1892, (U.S.) railroad magnate, financier, speculator.

Hetty Green, 1834-1916, (U.S.) financier, the "witch of Wall St."; richest woman in U.S. in her day.

Meyer Guggenheim, 1828-1905, (U.S.) Swiss-born merchant, philanthropist; built merchandising, mining empires.
Edward Guinness, 1847-1927, (Ir.) Brewing heir and philanthropist.
Armand Hammer, 1898-1990, (U.S.) headed Occidental Petroleum; promoted U.S.-Soviet ties.
Edward H. Harriman, 1848-1909, (U.S.) railroad financier, administrator; headed Union Pacific.
William Randolph Hearst, 1863-1951, (U.S.) a dominant figure in American journalism; built vast publishing empire.
Henry J. Heinz, 1844-1919, (U.S.) founded food empire.
James J. Hill, 1838-1916, (U.S.) Canadian-born railroad magnate, financier; founded Great Northern Railway.
Conrad N. Hilton, 1888-1979, (U.S.) intl. hotel chain founder.
Howard Hughes, 1905-1976, (U.S.) industrialist, financier, movie maker.
Walter L. Jacobs, 1898-1985, (U.S.) founder of the first rental car agency, which later became Hertz.
Howard Johnson, 1896-1972, (U.S.) founded restaurant chain.
Will K. Kellogg, 1860-1951, (U.S.) businessman, philanthropist, founded breakfast food co.
Samuel H. Kress, 1863-1955, (U.S.) businessman, art collector, philanthropist; founded "dime store" chain.
Ray A. Kroc, 1902-1984, (U.S.) builder of McDonald's fast food empire; owner, San Diego Padres baseball team.
Alfred Krupp, 1812-1887, (G.) armaments magnate.
Allen Lane, 1902-1970, (Br.) publisher, founder of Penguin Books.
William Lever, 1851-1925, (Br.) soap manufacturer, introduced profit-sharing and medical benefits for employees; founded Port Sunlight, model industrial town.
John Lewis, 1885-1963, (Br.) retail chain founder and industrial reformer; made all employees partners and introduced profit-sharing.
Thomas Lipton, 1850-1931, (Br.) merchant, built tea empire.
Daniel Macmillan, 1813-1857, and **Alexander Macmillan**, 1818-1896, (both Br.) booksellers, founded one of the world's largest publishing companies.
Michael Marks, 1863-1907, and **Thomas Spencer**, 1852-1905, (both Br.) founders of penny bazaar, which grew into UK's largest retailing chain.
James McGill, 1744-1813, (Can.) Scots-born fur trader, founded univ.
Andrew W. Mellon, 1855-1937, (U.S.) financier, industrialist; benefactor of National Gallery of Art.
Charles E. Merrill, 1885-1956, (U.S.) financier, developed firm of Merrill Lynch.
John Pierpont Morgan, 1837-1913, (U.S.) most powerful figure in finance and industry at the turn of the century.
William Morris, 1877-1963, (Br.) car manufacturer and philanthropist who donated millions to causes for the alleviation of human suffering.
Samuel Newhouse, 1895-1979, (U.S.) publishing and broadcasting magnate, built communications empire.
Aristotle Onassis, 1900-1975, (Gr.) shipping magnate.
Ernest Oppenheimer, 1880-1972, (Br.) industrialist in gold, diamonds and minerals; philanthropist.
William S. Paley, 1901-1989, (U.S.) built CBS communications empire.
James C. Penney, 1875-1971, (U.S.) businessman, developed department store chain.
William C. Procter, 1862-1934, (U.S.) headed soap co.
Arthur Rank, 1888-1972, (Br.) flour mill heir, creator of British film industry.
Austin Reed, 1873-1954, (Br.) founder of retail chain, with branches on the *Queen Mary* and *Queen Elizabeth*.
John D. Rockefeller, 1839-1937, (U.S.) industrialist, established Standard Oil; became world's wealthiest person.
John D. Rockefeller Jr., 1874-1960, (U.S.) philanthropist, established foundation; provided land for United Nations.
Charles Rolls, 1877-1910, (Br.) car dealer, co-founder of Rolls-Royce company.
Meyer A. Rothschild, 1743-1812, (G.) founded international banking house.
Joseph Rowntree, 1836-1925, (Br.) chocolate manufacturer and philanthropist.
Henry Royce, 1863-1933, (Br.) engineer, co-founder of Rolls-Royce company.
Richard W. Sears, 1863-1914, (U.S.) founded mail-order co.
Gordon Selfridge, 1858-1947, (U.S.-Br.) founder of London's first department store.
(Ernst) Werner von Siemens, 1816-1892, (G.) industrialist, inventor.
Alfred P. Sloan, 1875-1966, (U.S.) industrialist, philanthropist; headed General Motors.
A. Leland Stanford, 1824-1893, (U.S.) railroad official, philanthropist; founded univ.
Thomas Sopwith, 1888-1989, (Br.) founder Sopwith Aviation Company, 1912; designed successful WW1 biplane, Sopwith "Camel".
Nathan Strauss, 1848-1931, (U.S.) German-born merchant, philanthropist; headed Macy's.
Levi Strauss, c.1829-1902, (U.S.) jeans manufacturer.
Clement Studebaker, 1831-1901, (U.S.) wagon, carriage manufacturer.
Henry Tate, 1819-1899, (Br.) sugar merchant and philanthropist, financed Tate Gallery, London.
James Walter Thompson, 1847-1928, (U.S.) ad executive.
Theodore N. Vail, 1845-1920, (U.S.) organized Bell Telephone system, headed ATT.
Cornelius Vanderbilt, 1794-1877, (U.S.) financier, established steamship, railroad empires.
DeWitt Wallace, 1890-1981, (U.S.) and **Lila Wallace**, 1890-1984, (U.S.) co-founders of *Reader's Digest* magazine, philanthropists.
Aaron Montgomery Ward, 1843-1913, (U.S.) established first mail-order firm.
Thomas J. Watson, 1874-1956, (U.S.) headed IBM, 1924-49.
John Hay Whitney, 1905-1982, (U.S.) publisher, sportsman, philanthropist.
Frank W. Woolworth, 1852-1919, (U.S.) created chain of stores around world selling low-priced goods.
William Wrigley Jr., 1861-1932, (U.S.) founded chewing gum company.

Noted Artists and Sculptors of the Past

Artists are painters unless otherwise indicated.

Albrecht Altdorfer, 1480-1538, (Ger.) landscapist. *Battle of Alexander*.
Andrea del Sarto, 1486-1530, (It.) frescoes. *Madonna of the Harpies*.
Fra Angelico, c. 1400-1455, (It.) Renaissance muralist. *Madonna of the Linen Drapers' Guild*.
John James Audubon, 1785-1851, (U.S.) *Birds of America*.
Francis Bacon, 1909-1992, (Br.) *Three Studies for Figures at the Base of a Crucifixion*; *Study for a Red Pope*.
Hans Baldung Grien, 1484-1545, (Ger.) *Todentanz*.
Ernst Barlach, 1870-1938, (Ger.) Expressionist sculptor. *Man Drawing a Sword*.
Frédéric-Auguste Bartholdi, 1834-1904, (Fr.) *Liberty Enlightening the World*; *Lion of Belfort*.
Fra Bartolommeo, 1472-1517, (It.) *Vision of St. Bernard*.
Aubrey Beardsley, 1872-1898, (Br.) illustrator. *Salome*; *Lysistrata*.
Max Beckmann, 1884-1950, (Ger.) Expressionist. *The Descent from the Cross*.
Gentile Bellini, 1426-1507, (It.) Renaissance. *Procession in St. Mark's Square*.
Giovanni Bellini, 1428-1516, (It.) *St. Francis in Ecstasy*.
Jacopo Bellini, 1400-1470, (It.) *Crucifixion*.
Thomas Hart Benton, 1889-1975, (U.S.) American regionalist. *Threshing Wheat*; *Arts of the West*.
Gianlorenzo Bernini, 1598-1680, (It.) Baroque sculpture. *The Assumption*.
William Blake, 1752-1827, (Br.) engraver. *Book of Job*; *Songs of Innocence*; *Songs of Experience*.
Rosa Bonheur, 1822-1899, (Fr.) *The Horse Fair*.
Pierre Bonnard, 1867-1947, (Fr.) Intimist. *The Breakfast Room*.
Gutzon Borglum, 1871-1941, (U.S.) sculptor. *Mt. Rushmore Memorial*.
Hieronymus Bosch, 1450-1516, (Flem.) religious allegories. *The Crowning with Thorns*.
Sandro Botticelli, 1444-1510, (It.) Renaissance. *Birth of Venus*.
Constantin Brancusi, 1876-1957, (Rom.) Non-objective sculptor. *Flying Turtle*; *The Kiss*.
Frank Brangwyn, 1867-1956, (Belg.-Br.) painter, etcher and designer, particularly noted for murals.
Georges Braque, 1882-1963, (Fr.) Cubist. *Violin and Palette*.
Pieter Bruegel the Elder, c. 1525-1569, (Flem.) *The Peasant Dance*.
Pieter Bruegel the Younger, 1564-1638, (Flem.) *Village Fair*; *The Crucifixion*.
Edward Burne-Jones, 1833-1898, (Br.) medieval and mythical subjects. *The Sleeping Beauty*; *The Beguiling of Merlin*.
Alexander Calder, 1898-1976, (U.S.) sculptor. *Lobster Trap and Fish Tail*.
Michelangelo Merisi da Caravaggio, 1573-1610, (It.) Baroque. *The Supper at Emmaus*.
Carlo Carra, 1881-1966, (It.) Metaphysical school. *Lot's Daughters*.
Mary Cassatt, 1845-1926, (U.S.) Impressionist. *Woman*

Bathing.
Benvenuto Cellini, 1500-1571, (It.) Mannerist sculptor, goldsmith. *Perseus*.
Paul Cézanne, 1839-1906, (Fr.) *Card Players*; *Mont-Sainte-Victoire with Large Pine Trees*.
Marc Chagall, 1887-1985, (Rus.) Jewish life and folklore. *I and the Village*.
Jean Siméon Chardin, 1699-1779, (Fr.) still lifes. *The Kiss*; *The Grace*.
Giovanni Cimabue, 1240-1302, (It.) Byzantine mosaicist. *Madonna Enthroned with St. Francis*.
Claude Lorrain, 1600-1682, (Fr.) ideal-landscapist. *The Enchanted Castle*.
John Constable, 1776-1837, (Br.) landscapist. *The Haywain*; *Salisbury Cathedral from the Bishop's Grounds*.
Jean-Baptiste-Camille Corot, 1796-1875, (Fr.) landscapist. *Souvenir de Mortefontaine*; *Pastorale*.
Correggio, 1494-1534, (It.) Renaissance muralist. *Mystic Marriages of St. Catherine*.
John Sell Cotman, 1782-1842, (Br.) landscapist, Norwich School; *Greta Bridge*.
Gustave Courbet, 1819-1877, (Fr.) Realist. *The Artist's Studio*.
Lucas Cranach the Elder, 1472-1553, (Ger.) Protestant Reformation portraitist. *Luther*.
Richard Dadd, 1818-1887, (Br.) biblical scenes, mythological subjects and fairy life.
Salvador Dalí, 1904-1989, (Sp.) Surrealist. *Persistence of Memory*.
Honoré Daumier, 1808-1879, (Fr.) caricaturist. *The Third-Class Carriage*.
Jacques-Louis David, 1748-1825, (Fr.) Neoclassicist. *The Oath of the Horatii*.
Edgar Degas, 1834-1917, (Fr.) *The Ballet Class*.
Eugène Delacroix, 1789-1863, (Fr.) Romantic. *Massacre at Chios*.
Paul Delaroche, 1797-1856, (Fr.) historical themes. *Children of Edward IV*.
Luca della Robbia, 1400-1482, (It.) Renaissance terracotta artist. *Cantoria* (singing gallery), Florence cathedral.
Donatello, 1386-1466, (It.) Renaissance sculptor. *David*; *Gattamelata*.
Jean Dubuffet, 1902-1985, (Fr.) painter, sculptor, printmaker. *Group of Four Trees*.
Marcel Duchamp, 1887-1968, (Fr.) *Nude Descending a Staircase*.
Raoul Dufy, 1877-1953, (Fr.) Fauvist. *Chateau and Horses*.
Albrecht Dürer, 1471-1528, (Ger.) Renaissance engraver, woodcuts. *St. Jerome in His Study*; *Melencolia I*; *Apocalypse*.
Anthony van Dyck, 1599-1641, (Flem.) Baroque portraitist. *Portrait of Charles I Hunting*.
Thomas Eakins, 1844-1916, (U.S.) Realist. *The Gross Clinic*.
Jacob Epstein, 1880-1959, (Br.) religious and allegorical sculptor. *Genesis*; *Ecce Homo*.
Jan van Eyck, 1380-1441, (Flem.) naturalistic panels. *Adoration of the Lamb*.
Anselm Feuerbach, 1829-1880, (Ger.) Romantic classicism. *Judgement of Paris*; *Iphigenia*.
Jean-Honoré Fragonard, 1732-1806, (Fr.) Rococo. *The Swing*.
Daniel Chester French, 1850-1931, (U.S.) *The Minute Man of Concord*; seated Lincoln, Lincoln Memorial, Washington, D.C.
Caspar David Friedrich, 1774-1840, (Ger.) Romantic landscapes. *Man and Woman Gazing at the Moon*.
Thomas Gainsborough, 1727-1788, (Br.) portraitist. *The Blue Boy*.
Paul Gauguin, 1848-1903, (Fr.) Post-impressionist. *The Tahitians*.
Lorenzo Ghiberti, 1378-1455, (It.) Renaissance sculptor. *Gates of Paradise* baptistry doors, Florence.
Alberto Giacometti, 1901-1966, (It.) attenuated sculptures of solitary figures. *Man Pointing*.
Eric Gill, 1882-1940, (Br.) stonecarver, engraver and typographer. *Mankind, Creation of Adam*; Perpetua and Gill Sans Serif typefaces.
Giorgione, c. 1477-1510, (It.) Renaissance. *The Tempest*.
Giotto di Bondone, 1267-1337, (It.) Renaissance. *Presentation of Christ in the Temple*.
François Girardon, 1628-1715, (Fr.) Baroque sculptor of classical themes. *Apollo Tended by the Nymphs*.
Vincent van Gogh, 1853-1890, (Du.) *The Starry Night*; *Sunflowers*; *L'Arlesienne*.
Francisco de Goya y Lucientes, 1746-1828, (Sp.) *The Naked Maja*; *The Disasters of War* (etchings).
El Greco, 1541-1614, (Gr.-Sp.) *View of Toledo*.
Matthias Grünewald, 1480-1528, (Ger.) mystical religious themes. *The Resurrection*.
Frans Hals, c. 1580-1666, (Du.) portraitist. *Laughing Cavalier*; *Gypsy Girl*.
Dame Barbara Hepworth, 1903-1975, (Br.) sculptor. *Single Form*, UN building, New York.
William Hogarth, 1697-1764, (Br.) caricaturist. *The Rake's Progress*.
Katsushika Hokusai, 1760-1849, (Jap.) printmaker. *Crabs*.
Hans Holbein the Elder, 1460-1524, (Ger.) late Gothic. *Presentation of Christ in the Temple*.
Hans Holbein the Younger, 1497-1543, (Ger.) portraitist. *Henry VIII*; *Anne of Cleves*.
Winslow Homer, 1836-1910, (U.S.) marine themes. *Marine Coast*; *High Cliff*.
Edward Hopper, 1882-1967, (U.S.) realistic urban scenes. *Sunlight in a Cafeteria*.
William Holman Hunt, 1827-1910, (Br.) Pre-Raphaelite. *The Light of the World*; *The Scapegoat*.
Jean-Auguste-Dominique Ingres, 1780-1867, (Fr.) Classicist. *Valpinçon Bather*.
Vasily Kandinsky, 1866-1944, (Rus.) Abstractionist. *Capricious Forms*.
Paul Klee, 1879-1940, (Swi.) Abstractionist. *Twittering Machine*.
Gustav Klimt, 1862-1918, (Aus.) avant-garde images. *The Kiss*.
Laura Knight, 1877-1970, (Br.) first woman elected to the Royal Academy. *Charivari*; war paintings from Nuremberg trials.
Oskar Kokoschka, 1886-1980, (Aus.) Expressionist. *View of Prague*.
Kathe Kollwitz, 1867-1945, (Ger.) printmaker, social justice themes. *The Peasant War*.
Gaston Lachaise, 1882-1935, (U.S.) figurative sculptor. *Standing Woman*.
John La Farge, 1835-1910, (U.S.) muralist. *Red and White Peonies*.
Edwin Landseer, 1802-1873, (Br.) sentimental animal subjects. *Monarch of the Glen*; sculpted the lions in Trafalgar Square.
Bernard Leach, 1887-1979, (Br.) potter, much influenced by Japanese style.
Fernand Léger, 1881-1955, (Fr.) machine art. *The Cyclists*.
Peter Lely, 1618-1680, (Br.) court painter to Charles II. *Windsor Beauties*; *Admirals*.
Leonardo da Vinci, 1452-1519, (It.) *Mona Lisa*; *Last Supper*; *The Annunciation*.
Jacques Lipchitz, 1891-1973, (Fr.) Cubist sculptor. *Harpist*.
Filippini Lippi, 1457-1504, (It.) Renaisasance. *The Vision of St Bernard*.
Fra Filippo Lippi, 1406-1469, (It.) Renaissance. *Coronation of the Virgin*.
Aristide Maillol, 1861-1944, (Fr.) sculptor. *The Mediterranean*.
Eduard Manet, 1832-1883, (Fr.) forerunner of Impressionism. *Luncheon on the Grass*; *Olympia*.
Andrea Mantegna, 1431-1506, (It.) Renaissance frescoes. *Triumph of Caesar*.
Masaccio, 1401-1428, (It.) Renaissance. *The Tribute Money*.
Henri Matisse, 1869-1954, (Fr.) Fauvist. *Woman with the Hat*.
Michaelangelo Buonarroti, 1475-1564, (It.) *Pietà*; *David*; *Moses*; *The Last Judgement*; Sistine Ceiling.
John Everett Millais, 1829–1896, (Br.) Pre-Raphaelite. *The Boyhood of Raleigh*; *Christ in the House of His Parents*; *Ophelia*.
Jean-François Millet, 1814-1875, (Fr.) painter of peasant subjects. *The Gleaners*; *The Man with a Hoe*.
Joan Miró, 1893-1983, (Sp.) Exuberant colours, playful images. *Catalan Landscape*; *Dutch Interior*.
Amedeo Modigliani, 1884-1920, (It.) *Reclining Nude*.
Piet Mondrian, 1872-1944, (Du.) Abstractionist. *Composition in Red and Yellow and Blue*.
Claude Monet, 18040-1926, (Fr.) Impressionist. *The Bridge at Argenteuil*; *Haystacks*.
Henry Moore, 1898-1986, (Br.) sculptor of large-scale, abstract works. *Reclining Figure* (several).
Gustave Moreau, 1826-1898, (Fr.) Symbolist. *The Apparition*; *Dance of Salome*.
Grandma Moses, 1860-1961, (U.S.) folk painter. *Out for the Christmas Trees*.
Berthe Morisot, 1841-1895, (F.) impressionist. *The Cradle*; *In the Dining Room*.
Edvard Munch, 1863-1944, (Nor.) Expressionist. *The Cry*.
Alfred Munnings, 1878-1959, (Br.) animal artist, particularly noted for gipsies and their horses.
Bartolomé Murillo, 1618-1682, (Sp.) Baroque religious artist. *Vision of St. Anthony*; *The Two Trinities*.
Paul Nash, 1889-1946 (Br.) war artist. *The Menin Road*; *Totes Meer*.
Barnett Newman, 1905-1970, (U.S.) Abstract Expressionist. *Stations of the Cross*.
Isamu Noguchi, 1904-1988, (U.S.) trad. Japanese art, modern techniques.
Georgia O'Keeffe, 1887-1986, (U.S.) Southwest motifs. *Cow's Skull*.
Pietro Perugino, 1446-1523, (It.) Renaissance. *Delivery of the Keys to St. Peter*.
Pablo Picasso, 1881-1973, (Sp.) *Guernica*; *Dove*; *Head of a Woman*.
Piero della Francesca, c. 1415-1492, (It.) Renaissance. *Duke of*

Urbino; Flagellation of Christ.

Camille Pissarro, 1830-1903, (Fr.) Impressionist. *Morning Sunlight.*

Jackson Pollock, 1912-1956, (U.S.) Abstract Expressionist. *Autumn Rhythm.*

Nicolas Poussin, 1594-1665, (Fr.) Baroque pictorial classicism. *St John on Patmos.*

Maurice B. Prendergast, c. 1860-1924, (U.S.) Post-impressionist water-colourist. *Umbrellas in the Rain.*

Pierre-Paul Prud'hon, 1758-1823, (Fr.) Romanticist. *Crime Pursued by Vengeance and Justice.*

Pierre Cècile Puvis de Chavannes, 1824-1898, (Fr.) muralist, *The Poor Fisherman.*

Raphael Sanzio, 1483-1520, (It.) Renaissance. *Disputa; School of Athens; Sistine Madonna.*

Man Ray, 1890-1976, (U.S.) Dadaist. *Observing Time; The Lovers.*

Odilon Redon, 1840-1916, (Fr.) Symbolist lithographer. *In the Dream.*

Rembrandt van Rijn, 1606-1669, (Du.) *The Bridal Couple; The Night Watch.*

Frederic Remington, 1861-1909, (U.S.) painter, scultptor, portrayer of the American West. *Bronco Buster.*

Pierre-Auguste Renoir, 1841-1919, (Fr.) Impressionist. *The Luncheon of the Boating Party.*

Joshua Reynolds, 1723-1792, (Br.) portraitist. *Mrs Siddons as the Tragic Muse.*

Diego Rivera, 1886-1957, (Mex.) frescoes. *The Fecund Earth.*

Norman Rockwell, 1894-1978, (U.S.) illustrator. *Saturday Evening Post* covers.

Auguste Rodin, 1840-1917, (Fr.) sculptor. *The Thinker; The Burghers of Calais.*

Dante Gabriel Rossetti, 1828-1882, (Br.) Pre-Raphaelite. *Girlhood of Mary Virgin; Beata Beatrix.*

Mark Rothko, 1903-1970, (U.S.) Abstract Expressionist. *Light, Earth and Blue.*

Georges Rouault, 1871-1958, (Fr.) Expressionist. *The Old King.*

Henri Rousseau, 1844-1910, (Fr.) primitive exotic themes. *The Snake Charmer.*

Theodore Rousseau, 1812-1867, (Sw.-Fr.) landscapist. *Under the Birches; Evening.*

Peter Paul Rubens, 1577-1640, (Flem.) Baroque. *Mystic Marriage of St. Catherine.*

Jacob van Ruisdael, c. 1628-1682, (Du.) landscapist. *Jewish Cemetery.*

Salomon van Ruysdael, c. 1600-1670, (Du.) landscapist. *River with Ferry-Boat.*

Andrea Sansovino, 1460-1529, (It.) Renaissance sculptor. *Baptism of Christ.*

Jacopo Sansovino, 1486-1570, (It.) Renaissance sculptor. *St. John the Baptist.*

John Singer Sargent, 1856-1925, (U.S.) Edwardian society portraitist. *The Wyndham Sisters, Madam X.*

Georges Seurat, 1859-1891, (Fr.) Pointillist. *Sunday Afternoon on the Island of Grande Jette.*

Gino Severini, 1883-1966, (It.) Futurist and Cubist. *Dynamic Hieroglyph of the Bal Tabarin.*

Ben Shahn, 1898-1969, (U.S.) social and political thermes. Sacco and Vanzetti series; *Seurat's Lunch; Handball.*

Walter Sickert, 1860-1942, (Br.) Post-impressionist. *Ennui; Conversation.*

Alfred Sisley, 1839-1899, (F.) Impressionist. *Hampton Court Bridge; Rue de la Machine.*

John F. Sloan, 1871-1951, (U.S.) depictions of New York City. *Wake of the Ferry.*

David Smith, 1906-1965, (U.S.) welded metal sculpture. *Hudson River Landscape; Zig; Cubi* series.

Stanley Spencer, 1891-1959, (Br.) religious subjects. *The Resurrection: Cookham.*

George Stubbs, 1724-1806, (Br.) animal paintings, particularly horses. *Mares and Foals in a River Landscape; Hambletonian Rubbing Down.*

Graham Sutherland, 1903-1980, (Br.) landscapes, religious subjects and portraits. *Crucifixion; Somerset Maugham.*

Yves Tanguy, 1900-1955, (Fr.) Surrealist. *Rose of the Four Winds.*

Giovanni Battista Tiepolo, 1696-1770, (It.) Rococo frescoes. *The Crucifixion.*

Jacopo Tintoretto, 1518-1594, (It.) Mannerist. *St. George and the Dragon; The Last Supper.*

Titian, c. 1485-1576, (It.) Renaissance. *Venus and the Lute Player; The Bacchanal.*

J(oseph) M(allord) W(illiam) Turner, 1775-1851, (Br.) Romantic landscapist. *Snow Storm.*

Paolo Uccello, 1397-1475, (It.) Gothic-Renaissance. *The Rout of San Romano.*

Maurice Utrillo, 1883-1955, (Fr.) Impressionist. *Sacré-Coeur de Montmartre.*

John Vanderlyn, 1775-1852, (U.S.) Neo-classicist. *Ariadne Asleep on the Island of Naxos.*

Diego Velázquez, 1599-1660, (Sp.) Baroque. *Las Meninas; Portrait of Juan de Pareja.*

Jan Vermeer, 1632-1675, (Du.) interior genre subjects. *Young Woman with a Water Jug.*

Paolo Veronese, 1528-1588, (It.) devotional themes, vastly peopled canvases. *The Temptation of St. Anthony.*

Andrea del Verrocchio, 1435-1488, (It.) Florentine sculptor. *Celleoni.*

Maurice de Vlaminck, 1876-1958, (Fr.) Fauvist landscapist. *The Storm.*

Andy Warhol, 1928-1987, (U.S.) Pop Art. *Campbell's Soup Cans.*

Antoine Watteau, 1684-1721, (Fr.) Rococo painter of "scenes of gallantry". *The Embarkation of Cythera.*

George Frederic Watts, 1817-1904. (Br.) painter and sculptor of grandiose allegorical themes. *Hope; Physical Energy.*

James McNeill Whistler, 1834-1903, (U.S.) *Arrangement in Grey and Black, No. 1; The Artist's Mother.*

Grant Wood, 1891-1942, (U.S.) Midwestern regionalist. *American Gothic; Daughters of Revolution.*

Ossip Zadkine, 1890-1967, (Rus.) School of Paris sculptor. *The Destroyed City; Musicians; Christ.*

Notable Architects and Some of Their Achievements

Alvar Aalto, 1898–1976, (Fin.) Finlandia Hall, Helsinki; Vasksenniska church, Imatra.

Robert Adam, 1728–1792, (Br.) Home House, Portman Square; Culzean Castle, Ayrshire.

Charles Barry, 1795–1860, (Br.) Halifax Town Hall; Houses of Parliament, London.

Edward M. Barry, 1830–1880, (Br.) Royal Opera House, Covent Garden.

Isambard Kingdom Brunel, 1806–1859, (Br.) Clifton Suspension Bridge; Temple Meads station, Bristol.

Marcel Breuer, 1902–1981, (Hun.–U.S.) Whitney Museum of American Art, N.Y.C. (with Hamilton Smith).

William Burges, 1827–1881, (Br.) Cork Cathedral, Ireland; Trinity College, Hartford, Conn.

Daniel H. Burnham, 1846–1912, (U.S.) Union Station, Wash. D.C.; Flatiron, N.Y.C.

Lewis Cubitt, 1799–1883, (Br.) King's Cross Station, London.

Norman Foster, b. 1935, (Br.) Hong Kong & Shanghai Bank, Hong Kong; Sainsbury Centre, University of East Anglia.

Maxwell Fry, 1899–1987, (Br.) Village College, Impington; College of Engineering, Liverpool University.

R. Buckminster Fuller, 1895–1983, (U.S.) U.S. Pavilion, Expo 67, Montreal (geodesic domes).

Antoní Gaudí, 1852–1926, (Sp.) Sagrada Familia church, Barcelona; Casa Milá flats, Barcelona.

Walter Gropius, 1883–1969, (G.–U.S.) Pan Am Building, N.Y.C., (with Pietro Belluschi).

Nicholas Hawksmoor, 1661–1736, (Br.) Church of St George-in-the-East, Stepney; mausoleum, Castle Howard, Yorkshire.

Inigo Jones, 1573–1652, (Br.) Queen's House, Greenwich; Banqueting House, London; Covent Garden square and church.

Denys Lasdun, b.1914, (Br.) National Theatre, London; University of East Anglia, Norwich.

Le Corbusier (Charles-Edouard Jeanneret), 1887–1966, (F.) Salvation Army hostel, Paris; Swiss House, Paris Cité Universitaire; Unité d'Habitation, Marseille.

Edwin Lutyens, 1869–1944, (Br.) Castle Drogo, Devon; Viceroy's House, Delhi; Cenotaph, London.

Charles Rennie Mackintosh, 1868–1928, (Br.) Miss Cranston's Tea-rooms, Glasgow; School of Art, Glasgow.

Ludwig Mies van der Rohe, 1886–1969, (G.–U.S.) Seagram Building, N.Y.C., (with Philip C. Johnson); National Gallery, Berlin.

John Nash, 1752–1835, (Br.) Blaise Hamlet, Glos.; Cumberland Terrace, Regents Park; Regent Street, London; Brighton Pavilion.

I(eoh) M(ing) Pei, b. 1917, (U.S.) National Center for Atmospheric Research, Boulder, Col.; East Wing, Natl. Gallery of Art, Wash. D.C.; Pyramid, The Louvre, Paris.

Gio Ponti, 1891–1979, (It.) Pirelli building, Milan; Faculty of Mathematics, Rome University.

Richard Rogers, b. 1933, (Br.) Pompidou Centre, Paris (with Renzo Piano); Lloyd's building, London.

Eero Saarinen, 1910–1961, (Fin.–U.S.) Gateway to the West Arch, St. Louis; Trans World Flight Center, N.Y.C.

Basil Spence, 1907–1976, (Br.) Coventry Cathedral; Knightsbridge Barracks, London; Sussex University.

James Stirling, 1926–1992, (Br.) Clore Gallery, London; Staatsgalerie, Stuttgart.

John Vanbrugh, 1664–1726, (Br.) Castle Howard, Yorkshire;

Blenheim Palace, Oxfordshire.

Charles Voysey, 1857–1941, (Br.) Annesley Lodge, Hampstead; Hog's Back, Guildford; The Orchard, Chorley Wood.

Clough Williams-Ellis, 1883–1978, (Br.) Portmeirion, N. Wales.

Christopher Wren, 1632–1723, (Br.) St. Paul's Cathedral, London (and 51 City churches); Greenwich Hospital, London; Trinity College Library, Cambridge.

Some Noted Cartoonists

Charles Addams, 1912–1988, (U.S.) macabre cartoons.

Brad Anderson, b. 1924, (U.S.) "Marmaduke".

Tex Avery, 1908–1980, **Friz Freleng**, b. 1905?, **Chuck Jones**, b. 1912, (all U.S.) animators of Bugs Bunny, Porky Pig, Daffy Duck.

Henry Bateman, 1887–1970, (Br.) cartoons for *Tatler*; "The Man Who . . ." series illustrating social gaffes.

C. C. Beck, 1910–1989, (U.S.) "Captain Marvel".

Steve Bell, b. 1951, (Br.) "If . . ."; *Guardian* political cartoons.

Mark Boxer, 1931–1988, (Br.) newspaper cartoonist.

Dik Browne, 1917–1989, (U.S.) "Hi & Lois", "Hagar the Horrible".

Mel Calman, b. 1931, (Br.) newspapers, magazines.

Al Capp, 1909–1979, (U.S.) "Li'l Abner".

Jim Davis, b. 1945, (U.S.) "Garfield".

Rudolph Dirks, 1877–1968, (U.S.) "The Katzenjammer Kids".

Walt Disney, 1901–1966, (U.S.) producer of animated cartoons; created Mickey Mouse & Donald Duck.

Steve Ditko, b. 1927, (U.S.) Spider-Man.

Stephen Dowling, 1904–1986, (Br.) "The Ruggles", "Garth".

Ron Embleton, 1930–1988, (Br.) "Biggles", "Black Dagger".

Mort Drucker, b. 1929, (U.S.) *Mad* magazine.

Barry Fantoni, b. 1940, (Br.) magazine cartoons.

Jules Feiffer, b. 1929, (U.S.) satirical *Village Voice* cartoonist.

Michael ffolkes, 1925–1988, (Br.) cartoons for *Punch*, *Daily Telegraph*.

Bud Fisher, 1884–1954, (U.S.) "Mutt & Jeff".

Max Fleischer, 1883–1972, (U.S.) creator of Betty Boop, Popeye cartoons.

Carl Giles, b.1916, (Br.) "Granny" cartoons, *Daily Express*, *Sunday Express*.

Chester Gould, 1900–1985, (U.S.) "Dick Tracy".

Harold Gray, 1894–1968, (U.S.) "Little Orphan Annie".

Matt Groening, b. 1954, (U.S.) "Life Is Hell", "The Simpsons".

Frank Hampson, 1918–1985, (Br.) "Dan Dare".

Bill Hanna, b. 1910, & **Joe Barbera**, b. 1911, (both U.S.) animators of Tom & Jerry, Huckleberry Hound, Yogi Bear, The Flintstones.

Johnny Hart, b. 1931, (U.S.) "BC", "The Wizard of Id".

Michael Heath, b.1935, (Br.) newspapers/magazines; *Punch*, *Private Eye*.

B(ernard) Kliban, 1935–1991, (U.S.) cat books.

Osbert Lancaster, 1908–1986, (Br.) Maudie Littlehampton, (*Daily Express*).

Walter Lantz, b. 1900, (U.S.) Woody Woodpecker.

Gary Larson, b. 1950, (U.S.) "The Far Side".

Stan Lee, b. 1922, (U.S.) Marvel Comics.

Don Martin, b. 1931, (U.S.) *Mad* magazine.

Alex Raymond, 1909–1956, (U.S.) "Flash Gordon"; "Jungle Jim".

Georges Remi (Hergé) 1907–1983, (Fr.) "Tintin".

William Heath Robinson, 1872–1944, (Br.) cartoons for *Penny Illustrated Paper*, the *Sketch*, *Illustrated London News*; humorous drawings of complicated machines for ridiculous purposes.

Gerald Scarfe, b. 1936, (Br.) political cartoons.

Charles Schultz, b. 1922, (U.S.) "Peanuts".

Ronald Searle, b.1920, (Br.) St Trinian's schoolgirls, Nigel Molesworth.

Elzie C. Segar, 1894–1938, (U.S.) "Popeye".

Jerry Siegel, b. 1914, & **Joe Shuster**, b. 1914, (both U.S.) "Superman".

Art Spiegelman, b. 1948, (U.S.) "Raw"; "Maus".

Ralph Steadman, b. 1937, (Br.) newspaper/magazine cartoons.

William Steig, b. 1907, (U.S.) *New Yorker* cartoonist.

James Thurber, 1894–1961, (U.S.) *New Yorker* cartoonist.

Bill Tidy, b. 1934, (Br.) "The Fosdyke Saga", magazine cartoons (*Private Eye*, *Punch*).

Garry Trudeau, b. 1948, (U.S.) "Doonesbury".

Chic Young, 1901–1973, (U.S.) "Blondie".

Classical Composers

Carl Philipp Emanuel Bach, 1714-1788, (G.) Prussian and Wurtembergian Sonatas.

Johann Christian Bach, 1735-1782, (G.) Concertos; sonatas.

Johann Sebastian Bach, 1685-1750, (G.) St. Matthew Passion, The Well-Tempered Clavichord.

Samuel Barber, 1910-1981, (U.S.) Adagio for Strings, Vanessa.

Béla Bartók, 1881-1945, (Hung.) Concerto for Orchestra, The Miraculous Mandarin.

Ludwig van Beethoven, 1770-1827, (G.) Concertos (Emperor); sonatas (Moonlight, Pastorale, Pathétique); symphonies (Eroica).

Vincenzo Bellini, 1801-1835, (It.) La Sonnambula, Norma, I Puritani.

Alban Berg, 1885-1935, (Aus.) Wozzeck, Lulu.

Hector Berlioz, 1803-1869, (F.) Damnation of Faust, Symphonie Fantastique, Requiem.

Leonard Bernstein, 1918-1990, (U.S.) Jeremiah Symphony, West Side Story, Chichester Psalms.

Georges Bizet, 1838-1875, (F.) Carmen, Pearl Fishers.

Arthur Bliss, 1891-1975, (Br.) Ballet (Checkmate), opera (The Olympians), symphony (Morning Heroes).

Ernest Bloch, 1880-1959, (Swiss-U.S.) Schelomo, Voice in the Wilderness, Sacred Service.

Luigi Boccherini, 1743-1805, (It.) Cello Concerto in B Flat, Symphony in C.

Alexander Borodin, 1833-1887, (R.) Prince Igor, In the Steppes of Central Asia.

Johannes Brahms, 1833-1897, (G.) Liebeslieder Waltzes, Rhapsody in E Flat Major, Opus 119 for Piano, Academic Festival Overture; symphonies; quartets.

Benjamin Britten, 1913-1976, (Br.) Peter Grimes, Turn of the Screw, Ceremony of Carols, War Requiem.

Anton Bruckner, 1824-1896, (Aus.) Symphonies (Romantic), Intermezzo for String Quintet.

Ferruccio Busoni, 1866-1924, (It.) Doctor Faust, Comedy Overture.

Diderik Buxtehude, 1637-1707, (Dan.) Cantatas, trio sonatas.

William Byrd, 1543-1623, (Br.) Masses, sacred songs.

Pietro Cavalli, 1602-1676, (It.) Over 40 operas; Ormindo, Calisto.

(Alexis-) Emmanuel Chabrier, 1841-1894, (Fr.) Le Roi Malgré Lui, España.

Gustave Charpentier, 1860-1956, (F.) Opera, Louise.

Frédéric Chopin, 1810-1849, (P.) Polonaises, mazurkas, waltzes, études, nocturnes. Polonaise No. 6 in A Flat Major (Heroic); sonatas.

Eric Coates, 1886-1957, (Br.) Songs, orchestral works; Bird Songs at Eventide, The Three Bears.

Aaron Copland, 1900-1990, (U.S.) Appalachian Spring.

Arcangelo Corelli, 1653-1713, (It.) Concerti grossi.

(Achille-) Claude Debussy, 1862-1918, (F.) Pelléas et Mélisande, La Mer, Prelude à l'après-midi d'un faun.

C.P. Léo Delibes, 1836-1891, (F.) Lakmé, Coppélia, Sylvia.

Frederick Delius, 1862-1934, (Br.) Operas, sonatas, concertos; Koanga, Requiem, Brigg Fair.

Norman Dello Joio, b. 1913, (U.S.), Triumph of St. Joan, Psalm of David.

Gaetano Donizetti, 1797-1848, (It.) Elixir of Love, Lucia di Lammermoor, Daughter of the Regiment.

Paul Dukas, 1865-1935, (Fr.) Sorcerer's Apprentice.

Antonín Dvořák, 1841-1904, (C.) Symphony in E Minor (From the New World).

Edward Elgar, 1857-1934, (Br.) Dream of Gerontius, Pomp and Circumstance.

Manuel de Falla, 1876-1946, (Sp.) La Vida Breve, El Amor Brujo.

Gabriel Fauré, 1845-1924, (Fr.) Requiem, Ballade.

Friedrich von Flotow, 1812-1883, (G.) Martha.

César Franck, 1822-1890, (Belg.) D Minor Symphony.

George Gershwin, 1898-1937, (U.S.) Rhapsody in Blue, American in Paris, Porgy and Bess.

Umberto Giordano, 1867-1948, (It.) André Chénier.

Alexander K. Glazunov, 1865-1936, (R.) Symphonies, Stenka Razin.

Mikhail Glinka, 1804-1857, (R.) Ruslan and Ludmilla.

Christoph W. Gluck, 1714-1787, (G.) Alceste, Iphigénie en Tauride.

Charles Gounod, 1818-1893, (F.) Faust, Romeo and Juliet.

Percy Grainger, 1882-1961 (Austral.-U.S.) Choral works, short orchestral pieces (Country Gardens).

Edvard Grieg, 1843-1907, (Nor.) Peer Gynt Suite, Concerto in A Minor.

George Frideric Handel, 1685-1759, (G.-Br.) Messiah, Xerxes,

Berenice.
Howard Hanson, 1896-1981, (U.S.) Symphonies No. 1 (Nordic) and 2 (Romantic).
Roy Harris, 1898-1979, (U.S.) Symphonies, Amer. Portraits.
Joseph Haydn, 1732-1809, (Aus.) Symphonies (Clock); oratorios; chamber music.
Paul Hindemith, 1895-1963, (G.-U.S.) Mathis der Maler.
Gustav Holst, 1874-1934, (Br.) The Planets.
Arthur Honegger, 1892-1955, (Swiss) Judith, Le Roi David, Pacific 231.
Engelbert Humperdinck, 1854-1921, (G.) Hansel and Gretel.
Charles Ives, 1874-1954, (U.S.) Third Symphony.
Leoš Janáček, 1854-1928, (Cz.) Operas; The Cunning Little Vixen, From the House of the Dead.
Aram Khachaturian, 1903-1978, (Armen.) Gayaneh (ballet), symphonies.
Zoltán Kodály, 1882-1967, (Hung.) Háry János, Psalmus Hungaricus.
Fritz Kreisler, 1875-1962, (Aus.) Caprice Viennois, Tambourin Chinois.
Rodolphe Kreutzer, 1766-1831, (F.) 40 études for violin.
Edouard V.A. Lalo, 1823-1892, (F.) Symphonie Espagnole.
Ruggiero Leoncavallo, 1857-1919, (It.) Pagliacci.
Franz Liszt, 1811-1886, (Hung.) 20 Hungarian rhapsodies; symphonic poems.
Jean-Baptiste Lully, 1632-1687, (It.-Fr.) Ballet and operas; Le Bourgeois Gentilhomme, Alkestis.
Elisabeth Lutyens, 1906-1983, (Br.) Operas, ballet and concertos; Infidelio, Isis and Osiris, The Birthday of the Infanta.
Edward MacDowell, 1861-1908, (U.S.) To a Wild Rose.
Gustav Mahler, 1860-1911, (Aus.) 10 symphonies, Kindertotenlieder.
Pietro Mascagni, 1863-1945, (It.) Cavalleria Rusticana.
Jules Massenet, 1842-1912, (F.) Manon, Le Cid, Thaïs.
Felix Mendelssohn, 1809-1847, (G.) Midsummer Night's Dream, Songs Without Words.
Gian-Carlo Menotti, b. 1911, (It.-U.S.) The Medium, The Consul, Amahl and the Night Visitors.
Olivier Messiaen, 1908-1992, (Fr.) Works for orchestra, piano, organ; Turangalila, The Awakening of the Birds.
Giacomo Meyerbeer, 1791-1864, (G.) Robert le Diable, Les Huguenots.
Darius Milhaud, 1892-1974, (Fr.) Concertos, 18 string quartets; Christopher Columbus (opera), The Creation of the World (ballet).
Claudio Monteverdi, 1567-1643, (It.) Opera; masses; madrigals.
Modest Moussorgsky, 1835-1881, (R.) Boris Godunov, Pictures at an Exhibition.
Wolfgang Amadeus Mozart, 1756-1791, (Aus.) Magic Flute, Marriage of Figaro; concertos; symphonies, etc.
Jacques Offenbach, 1819-1880, (F.) Operas and operettas; Tales of Hoffmann, La Belle Hélène.
Carl Orff, 1895-1982, (G.) Carmina Burana.
Ignace Paderewski, 1860-1941, (Pol.) Minuet in G.
Niccolò Paganini, 1782-1840, (It.) Violinist, many bravura variations for violin.
Giovanni Pierluigi da Palestrina, c. 1525-1594, (It.) Masses; madrigals.
Amilcare Ponchielli, 1834-1886, (It.) La Gioconda.
Francis Poulenc, 1899-1963, (F.) Concertos, Dialogues des Carmelites (opera).
Sergei Prokofiev, 1891-1953, (R.) Concertos, symphonies, operas, ballets; Love for Three Oranges, Romeo and Juliet, Peter and the Wolf.
Giacomo Puccini, 1858-1924, (It.) La Bohème, Manon Lescaut, Tosca, Madame Butterfly.
Henry Purcell, 1659-1695, (Br.) Operas (Dido and Aeneas, The Fairy Queen), songs, sonatas.
Sergei Rachmaninov, 1873-1943, (R.) 24 preludes, 4 concertos, 4 symphonies. Prelude in C Sharp Minor.
Maurice Ravel, 1875-1937, (Fr.) Bolero, Daphnis et Chloe, Rapsodie Espagnole.
Nikolai Rimsky-Korsakov, 1844-1908, (R.) Golden Cockerel, Capriccio Espagnol, Scheherazade, Russian Easter Overture.
Gioacchino Rossini, 1792-1868, (It.) Barber of Seville, Semiramide, William Tell.
Charles Camille Saint-Saëns, 1835-1921, (F.) Samson and Delilah, Danse Macabre.
Antonio Salieri, 1750-1825, (It.) Operas (Falstaff), masses, concertos.
Erik Satie, 1866-1925, (Fr.) Piano solos and duets, ballets (Relâche), operettas, Messe des pauvres.
Alessandro Scarlatti, 1660-1725, (It.) Cantatas; concertos.
Domenico Scarlatti, 1685-1757, (It.) Harpsichord sonatas.
Arnold Schoenberg, 1874-1951, (Aus.) Pelleas and Melisande, Transfigured Night, De Profundis.
Franz Schubert, 1797-1828, (A.) Lieder; symphonies (Unfinished); overtures (Rosamunde).
William Schuman, b. 1910, (U.S.) Credendum, New England Triptych.
Robert Schumann, 1810-1856, (G.) Symphonies, songs.
Dimitri Shostakovich, 1906-1975, (R.) Symphonies, Lady Macbeth of Mzensk, The Nose.
Jean Sibelius, 1865-1957, (Finn.) Finlandia, Karelia.
Alexander Skriabin, 1872-1915, (R.) Prometheus.
Bedřich Smetana, 1824-1884, (Cz.). The Bartered Bride.
Karlheinz Stockhausen, b. 1928, (G.) Kontrapunkte, Kontakte.
Richard Strauss, 1864-1949, (G.) Salome, Elektra, Der Rosenkavalier, Thus Spake Zarathustra.
Igor F. Stravinsky, 1882-1971, (R.-U.S.) Oedipus Rex, Le Sacre du Printemps, Petrushka.
Thomas Tallis, c. 1505-1585, (Br.) Church music; Spem in alium.
Pyotr I. Tchaikovsky, 1840-1893, (R.) Nutcracker Suite, Swan Lake, Eugene Onegin.
Georg Telemann, 1681-1767, (G.) 40 operas, plus chamber music, oratorios, cantatas and concertos.
Ambroise Thomas, 1811-1896, (F.) Mignon.
Virgil Thomson, 1896-1989, (U.S.) Opera, ballet; Four Saints in Three Acts.
Ralph Vaughan Williams, 1872-1958, (Br.) Job (ballet), London Symphony, Sinfonia Antarctica.
Giuseppe Verdi, 1813-1901, (It.) Aida, Rigoletto, Don Carlo, Il Trovatore, La Traviata, Falstaff, Macbeth.
Heitor Villa-Lobos, 1887-1959, (Brz.) Chôros.
Antonio Vivaldi, 1678-1741, (It.) Concertos, The Four Seasons.
Richard Wagner, 1813-1883, (G.) Rienzi, Tannhäuser, Lohengrin, Tristan und Isolde.
William Walton, 1902-1983, (Br.) Façade, Belshazzar's Feast, Troilus and Cressida.
Carl Maria von Weber, 1786-1826, (G.) Operas; Der Freischütz.

Composers of Operettas, Musicals and Popular Music

Richard Adler, b. 1921, (U.S.) *Pajama Game; Damn Yankees.*
Milton Ager, 1893-1979, (U.S.) I Wonder What's Become of Sally; Hard Hearted Hannah; Ain't She Sweet?
Leroy Anderson, 1908-1975, (U.S.) Syncopated Clock.
Paul Anka, b. 1941, (Can.) My Way; She's a Lady; Tonight Show theme.
Harold Arlen, 1905-1986, (U.S.) Stormy Weather; Over the Rainbow; Blues in the Night; That Old Black Magic.
Burt Bacharach, b. 1928, (U.S.) Raindrops Keep Fallin' on My Head; Walk on By; What the World Needs Now is Love.
Ernest Ball, 1878-1927, (U.S.) Mother Machree; When Irish Eyes Are Smiling.
Irving Berlin, 1888-1989 (U.S.) *This is the Army; Annie Get Your Gun; Call Me Madam;* God Bless America; White Christmas.
Leonard Bernstein, 1918-1990, (U.S.) *On the Town; Wonderful Town; Candide; West Side Story.*
Eubie Blake, 1883-1983, (U.S.) *Shuffle Along;* I'm Just Wild about Harry.
Jerry Bock, b. 1928, (U.S.) *Mr. Wonderful; Fiorello; Fiddler on the Roof; The Rothschilds.*
Carrie Jacobs Bond, 1862-1946, (U.S.) I Love You Truly.
Nacio Herb Brown, 1896-1964, (U.S.) Singing in the Rain; You Were Meant for Me; All I Do Is Dream of You.
Hoagy Carmichael, 1899-1981, (U.S.) Stardust; Georgia on My Mind; Old Buttermilk Sky.
George M. Cohan, 1878-1942, (U.S.) Give My Regards to Broadway; You're a Grand Old Flag; Over There.
Cy Coleman, b. 1929, (U.S.) *Sweet Charity;* Witchcraft.
Noel Coward, 1899-1973 (Br.) *Bitter Sweet;* Mad Dogs and Englishmen; Mad About the Boy.
Neil Diamond, b. 1941, (U.S.) I'm a Believer; Sweet Caroline.
Walter Donaldson, 1893-1947, (U.S.) My Buddy; Carolina in the Morning; You're Driving Me Crazy; Makin' Whoopee.
Vernon Duke, 1903-1969, (U.S.) April in Paris.
Bob Dylan, b. 1941, (U.S.) Blowin' in the Wind.
Gus Edwards, 1879-1945, (U.S.) School Days; By the Light of the Silvery Moon; In My Merry Oldsmobile.
Duke Ellington, 1899-1974, (U.S.) Sophisticated Lady; Satin Doll; It Don't Mean a Thing; Solitude.
Sammy Fain, 1902-1989, (U.S.) I'll Be Seeing You; Love Is a Many-Splendored Thing.
Stephen Collins Foster, 1826-1864, (U.S.) My Old Kentucky Home; Old Folks At Home.
Rudolf Friml, 1879-1972, (naturalized U.S.) *The Firefly; Rose Marie; Vagabond King; Bird of Paradise.*
John Gay, 1685-1732, (Br.) *The Beggar's Opera.*
George Gershwin, 1898-1937, (U.S.) Someone to Watch Over Me; I've Got a Crush on You; Embraceable You.

Ferde Grofe, 1892-1972, (U.S.) Grand Canyon Suite.
Marvin Hamlisch, b. 1944, (U.S.) The Way We Were, Nobody Does It Better, *A Chorus Line.*
W. C. Handy, 1873-1958, (U.S.) St. Louis Blues.
Ray Henderson, 1896-1970, (U.S.) *George White's Scandals;* That Old Gang of Mine; Five Foot Two, Eyes of Blue.
Victor Herbert, 1859-1924, (Ir.-U.S.) *Mlle. Modiste; Babes in Toyland; The Red Mill; Naughty Marietta; Sweethearts.*
Jerry Herman, b. 1932, (U.S.) *Hello Dolly; Mame.*
Brian Holland, b. 1941, **Lamont Dozier,** b. 1941, **Eddie Holland,** b. 1939, (all U.S.) Heat Wave; Stop! In the Name of Love; Baby, I Need Your Loving.
Scott Joplin, 1868-1917, (U.S.) Piano compositions and opera, *Treemonisha.*
John Kander, b. 1927, (U.S.) *Cabaret; Chicago; Funny Lady.*
Jerome Kern, 1885-1945, (U.S.) *Sally; Sunny; Show Boat.*
Carole King, b. 1942, (U.S.) Will You Love Me Tomorrow?; Natural Woman; One Fine Day; Up on the Roof.
Burton Lane, b. 1912, (U.S.) *Finian's Rainbow.*
Franz Lehar, 1870-1948, (Hung.) *Merry Widow.*
Jerry Leiber & **Mike Stoller,** both b. 1933, (both U.S.) Hound Dog; Searchin'; Yakety Yak; Love Me Tender.
Mitch Leigh, b. 1928, (U.S.) *Man of La Mancha.*
John Lennon, 1940-1980, & **Paul McCartney,** b. 1942, (both Br.) I Want to Hold Your Hand; She Loves You; Hard Day's Night; Can't Buy Me Love; And I Love Her.
Frank Loesser, 1910-1969, (U.S.) *Guys and Dolls; Where's Charley?; The Most Happy Fella; How to Succeed . . .*
Frederick Loewe, 1901-1988, (Aust.-U.S.) *The Day Before Spring; Brigadoon; Paint Your Wagon; My Fair Lady; Camelot.*
Henry Mancini, b. 1924, (U.S.) Moon River; Days of Wine and Roses; Pink Panther Theme.
Barry Mann, b. 1939, & **Cynthia Weil,** b. 1937, (both U.S.) You've Lost That Loving Feeling, Saturday Night at the Movies.
Jimmy McHugh, 1894-1969 (U.S.) Don't Blame Me; I'm in the Mood for Love; I Feel a Song Coming On.
Alan Menken, b. 1950, (U.S.) *Little Shop of Horrors.*
Joseph Meyer, 1894-1987, (U.S.) If You Knew Susie; California, Here I Come; Crazy Rhythm.
Ivor Novello, 1893-1951, (Br.) *Careless Rapture; The Dancing Years;* Keep the Home Fires Burning.
Jerome "Doc" Pomus, 1925-1991, (U.S.) Save the Last Dance for Me; A Teenager in Love.
Cole Porter, 1893-1964, (U.S.) *Anything Goes; Kiss Me Kate; Can Can; Silk Stockings.*
Smokey Robinson, b. 1940, (U.S.) Shop Around; My Guy; My Girl; Get Ready.
Richard Rodgers, 1902-1979, (U.S.) *Connecticut Yankee; Oklahoma; Carousel; South Pacific; The King and I; The Sound of Music.*
Sigmund Romberg, 1887-1951, (Hung.) *Maytime; The Student Prince; Desert Song; Blossom Time.*
Harold Rome, b. 1908, (U.S.) *Pins and Needles; Call Me Mister; Wish You Were Here; Fanny; Destry Rides Again.*
Vincent Rose, b. 1880-1944, (U.S.) Avalon; Whispering; Blueberry Hill.
Harry Ruby, 1895-1974, (U.S.) Three Little Words; Who's Sorry Now?
Arthur Schwartz, 1900-1984, (U.S.) *The Band Wagon;* Dancing in the Dark; By Myself; That's Entertainment.
Neil Sedaka, b. 1939, (U.S.) Breaking Up Is Hard to Do.
Paul Simon, b. 1942, (U.S.) Sounds of Silence; I Am a Rock; Mrs. Robinson; Bridge Over Troubled Waters.
Stephen Sondheim, b. 1930, (U.S.) *A Little Night Music; Company; Sweeney Todd; Sunday in the Park with George.*
John Philip Sousa, 1854-1932, (U.S.) *El Capitan;* Stars and Stripes Forever.
Oskar Straus, 1870-1954, (Aus.) *Chocolate Soldier.*
Johann Strauss, 1825-1899, (Aus.) *Gypsy Baron; Die Fledermaus;* waltzes: Blue Danube, Artist's Life.
Charles Strouse, b. 1928, (U.S.) *Bye Bye, Birdie; Annie.*
Jule Styne, b. 1905, (Br.-U.S.) *Gentlemen Prefer Blondes; Bells Are Ringing; Gypsy; Funny Girl.*
Arthur S. Sullivan, 1842-1900, (Br.) *H.M.S. Pinafore, Pirates of Penzance; The Mikado.*
Egbert van Alstyne, 1882-1951, (U.S.) In the Shade of the Old Apple Tree; Memories; Pretty Baby.
Jimmy Van Heusen, 1913-1990, (U.S.) Moonlight Becomes You; Swinging on a Star; All the Way; Love and Marriage.
Albert von Tilzer, 1878-1956, (U.S.) I'll Be With You in Apple Blossom Time; Take Me Out to the Ball Game.
Harry von Tilzer, 1872-1946, (U.S.) Only a Bird in a Gilded Cage; On a Sunday Afternoon.
Fats Waller, 1904-1943, (U.S.) Honeysuckle Rose; Ain't Misbehavin'.
Harry Warren, 1893-1981, (U.S.) You're My Everything; We're in the Money; I Only Have Eyes for You.
Jimmy Webb, b. 1946, (U.S.) Up, Up and Away; By the Time I Get to Phoenix; Didn't We?; Wichita Lineman.
Andrew Lloyd Webber, b. 1948, (Br.) *Jesus Christ Superstar, Evita, Cats, The Phantom of the Opera.*
Kurt Weill, 1900-1950, (G.-U.S.) *Threepenny Opera; Lady in the Dark; Knickerbocker Holiday; One Touch of Venus.*
Percy Wenrich, 1887-1952, (U.S.) When You Wore a Tulip; Moonlight Bay; Put On Your Old Gray Bonnet.
Richard A. Whiting, 1891-1938, (U.S.) Till We Meet Again; Sleepytime Gal; Beyond the Blue Horizon; My Ideal.
John Williams, b. 1932, (U.S.) *Jaws, E.T., Star Wars* series, *Raiders of the Lost Ark* series.
Meredith Willson, 1902-1984, (U.S.) *The Music Man.*
Stevie Wonder, b. 1950, (U.S.) You Are the Sunshine of My Life; Signed, Sealed, Delivered, I'm Yours.
Vincent Youmans, 1898-1946, (U.S.) *Two Little Girls in Blue; Wildflower; No, No, Nanette; Hit the Deck; Rainbow; Smiles.*

Lyricists

Howard Ashman, 1950-1991, (U.S.) *Little Shop of Horrors, The Little Mermaid.*
Johnny Burke, 1908-1984, (U.S.) What's New?; Misty; Imagination; Polka Dots and Moonbeams.
Sammy Cahn, 1913–1993, (U.S.) High Hopes; Love and Marriage; The Second Time Around; It's Magic.
Betty Comden, b. 1919 (U.S.) and **Adolph Green,** b. 1915 (U.S.) The Party's Over; Just in Time; New York, New York.
Hal David, b. 1921 (U.S.) What the World Needs Now Is Love; Close to You.
Buddy De Sylva, 1895-1950, (U.S.) When Day Is Done; Look for the Silver Lining; April Showers.
Howard Dietz, 1896-1983, (U.S.) Dancing in the Dark; You and the Night and the Music; That's Entertainment.
Al Dubin, 1891-1945, (U.S.) Tiptoe Through the Tulips; Anniversary Waltz; Lullaby of Broadway.
Fred Ebb, b. 1936 (U.S.) *Cabaret, Zorba, Woman of the Year.*
Dorothy Fields, 1905-1974, (U.S.) On the Sunny Side of the Street; Don't Blame Me; The Way You Look Tonight.
Ira Gershwin, 1896-1983, (U.S.) The Man I Love; Fascinating Rhythm; S'Wonderful; Embraceable You.
William S. Gilbert, 1836-1911, (Br.) *The Mikado; H.M.S. Pinafore, Pirates of Penzance.*
Gerry Goffin, b. 1939, (U.S.) Will You Love Me Tomorrow; Take Good Care of My Baby; Up on the Roof; One Fine Day.
Mack Gordon, 1905-1959, (Pol.-U.S.) You'll Never Know; The More I See You; Chattanooga Choo-Choo.
Oscar Hammerstein II, 1895-1960, (U.S.) Ol' Man River; *Oklahoma; Carousel.*
E. Y. (Yip) Harburg, 1898-1981, (U.S.) Brother, Can You Spare a Dime; April in Paris; Over the Rainbow.
Lorenz Hart, 1895-1943, (U.S.) Isn't It Romantic; Blue Moon; Lover; Manhattan; My Funny Valentine; Mountain Greenery.
DuBose Heyward, 1885-1940, (U.S.) Summertime; A Woman Is a Sometime Thing.
Gus Kahn, 1886-1941, (U.S.) Memories; Ain't We Got Fun.
Alan J. Lerner, 1918-1986, (U.S.) *Brigadoon; My Fair Lady; Camelot; Gigi; On a Clear Day You Can See Forever.*
Johnny Mercer, 1909-1976, (U.S.) Blues in the Night; Come Rain or Come Shine; Laura; That Old Black Magic.
Bob Merrill, b. 1921, (U.S.) People; Don't Rain on My Parade.
Jack Norworth, 1879-1959, (U.S.) Take Me Out to the Ball Game; Shine On Harvest Moon.
Andy Razaf, 1895-1973, (U.S.) Honeysuckle Rose, Ain't Misbehavin', S'posin'.
Tim Rice, b. 1944, (Br.) *Jesus Christ Superstar; Evita; Chess.*
Leo Robin, 1900-1984, (U.S.) Thanks for the Memory; Hooray for Love; Diamonds Are a Girl's Best Friend.
Paul Francis Webster, 1907-1984, (U.S.) I Got It Bad and That Ain't Good; Secret Love; The Shadow of Your Smile; Love Is a Many-Splendored Thing.
Jack Yellen, 1892-1991, (U.S.) Down by the O-Hi-O; Ain't She Sweet; Happy Days Are Here Again.

Noted Jazz Artists

Jazz has been called America's only completely unique contribution to Western culture. The following individuals have made major contributions in this field:

Julian "Cannonball" Adderley, 1928-1975: alto sax.
Louis "Satchmo" Armstrong, 1900-1971: trumpet, singer; originated the "scat" vocal.
Mildred Bailey, 1907-1951: blues singer.
Chet Baker, 1929-1988: trumpet.
Count Basie, 1904-1984: orchestra leader, piano.
Sidney Bechet, 1897-1959: early innovator, soprano sax.
Bix Beiderbecke, 1903-1931: cornet, piano, composer.
Bunny Berigan, 1909-1942: trumpet, singer.
Barney Bigard, 1906-1980: clarinet.
Art Blakey, 1919-1990: drums, leader.
Jimmy Blanton, 1921-1942: bass.
Charles "Buddy" Bolden, 1868-1931: cornet; formed the first jazz band in the 1890s.
Big Bill Broonzy, 1893-1958: blues singer, guitar.
Clifford Brown, 1930-1956: trumpet.
Ray Brown, b. 1926: bass.
Dave Brubeck, b. 1920: piano, combo leader.
Don Byas, 1912-1972: tenor sax.
Harry Carney, 1910-1974: baritone sax.
Benny Carter, b. 1907: alto sax, trumpet, clarinet.
Ron Carter, b. 1937: bass, cello.
Sidney Catlett, 1910-1951: drums.
Charlie Christian, 1919-1942: guitar.
Kenny Clarke, 1914-1985: pioneer of modern drums.
Buck Clayton, b. 1911: trumpet, arranger.
Al Cohn, 1925-1988: tenor sax, composer.
Cozy Cole, 1909-1981: drums.
Ornette Coleman, b. 1930: saxophone; unorthodox style.
John Coltrane, 1926-1967: tenor sax innovator.
Eddie Condon, 1904-1973: guitar, band leader; promoter of Dixieland.
Chick Corea, b. 1941: pianist, composer.
Tadd Dameron, 1917-1965: piano, composer.
Eddie "Lockjaw" Davis, 1921-1986: tenor sax.
Miles Davis, 1926-1992: trumpet; pioneer of cool jazz.
Wild Bill Davison, 1906-1989: cornet, leader; prominent in early Chicago jazz.
Buddy De Franco, b. 1933: clarinet.
Paul Desmond, 1924-1977: alto sax.
Vic Dickenson, 1906-1984: trombone, composer.
Warren "Baby" Dodds, 1898-1959: Dixieland drummer.
Johnny Dodds, 1892-1940: clarinet.
Eric Dolphy, 1928-1964: alto sax, composer.
Jimmy Dorsey, 1904-1957: clarinet, alto sax; band leader.
Tommy Dorsey, 1905-1956: trombone; band leader.
Roy Eldridge, 1911-1989: trumpet, drums, singer.
Duke Ellington, 1899-1974: piano, band leader, composer.
Bill Evans, 1929-1980: piano.
Gil Evans, 1912-1988: composer, arranger, piano.
Ella Fitzgerald, b. 1918: singer.
"Red" Garland, 1923-1984; piano.
Erroll Garner, 1921-1977: piano, composer, "Misty".
Stan Getz, 1927-1991: tenor sax.
Dizzy Gillespie, 1917–1993: trumpet, composer; bop developer.
Benny Goodman, 1909-1986: clarinet, band and combo leader.
Dexter Gordon, 1923-1990: tenor sax; bop-derived style.
Stephane Grappelli, b. 1908: violin.
Bobby Hackett, 1915-1976: trumpet, cornet.
Lionel Hampton, b. 1913: vibes, drums, piano, combo leader.
Herbie Hancock, b. 1940: piano, composer.
W. C. Handy, 1873-1958: composer, "St. Louis Blues".
Coleman Hawkins, 1904-1969: tenor sax; 1939 recording of "Body and Soul" a classic.
Roy Haynes, b. 1926: drums.
Fletcher Henderson, 1898-1952: orchestra leader, arranger; pioneered jazz and dance bands of the 30s.
Woody Herman, 1913-87: clarinet, alto sax, band leader.
Jay C. Higginbotham, 1906-1973: trombone.
Earl "Fatha" Hines, 1905-1983: piano, songwriter.
Johnny Hodges, 1906-1970: alto sax.
Billie Holiday, 1915-1959: singer, "Strange Fruit".
Sam "Lightnin' " Hopkins, 1912-1982: blues singer, guitar.
Mahalia Jackson, 1911-1972: gospel singer.
Milt Jackson, b. 1923: vibes, piano, guitar.
Illinois Jacquet, b. 1922: tenor sax.
Keith Jarrett, b. 1945: technically phenomenal pianist.
Blind Lemon Jefferson, 1897-1930: blues singer, guitar.
Bunk Johnson, 1879-1949: cornet, trumpet.
James P. Johnson, 1891-1955: piano, composer.
J. J. Johnson, b. 1924: trombone, composer.
Elvin Jones, b. 1927: drums.
Jo Jones, 1911-1985: drums.
Philly Joe Jones, 1923-1985: drums.
Quincy Jones, b. 1933: arranger.
Thad Jones, 1923-1986: trumpet, cornet.
Scott Joplin, 1868-1917: composer; "Maple Leaf Rag".
Stan Kenton, 1912-1979: orchestra leader, composer, piano.
Barney Kessel, b. 1923: guitar.
Lee Konitz, b. 1927: alto sax.
Gene Krupa, 1909-1973: drums, band and combo leader.
Scott LaFaro, 1936-1961: bass.
Huddie Ledbetter (Leadbelly), 1888-1949: blues singer, guitarist.
John Lewis, b. 1920: composer, piano, combo leader.
Mel Lewis, 1929-1990: drummer, orchestra leader.
Jimmie Lunceford, 1902-1947: band leader, sax.
Herbie Mann, b. 1930: flute.
Wynton Marsalis, b. 1961: trumpet.
Jimmy McPartland, b. 1907: trumpet.
Marian McPartland, b. 1920: piano.
Glenn Miller, 1904-1944: trombone, dance band leader.
Charles Mingus, 1922-1979: bass, composer, combo leader.
Thelonious Monk, 1920-1982: piano, composer, combo leader; a developer of bop.
Wes Montgomery, 1925-1968: guitar.
"Jelly Roll" Morton, 1885-1941: composer, piano, singer.
Bennie Moten, 1894-1935: piano; an early organizer of large jazz orchestras.
Gerry Mulligan, b. 1927: baritone sax, arranger, leader.
Turk Murphy, 1915-1987: trombone, band leader.
Theodore "Fats" Navarro, 1923-1950: trumpet.
Red Nichols, 1905-1965: cornet, combo leader.
Red Norvo, b. 1908: vibes, band leader.
Anita O'Day, b. 1919: singer.
King Oliver, 1885-1938: cornet, band leader; teacher of Louis Armstrong.
Sy Oliver, 1910-1988: Swing Era arranger, composer, conductor.
Kid Ory, 1886-1973: trombone, "Muskrat Ramble".
Charlie "Bird" Parker, 1920-1955: alto sax, composer; rated by many as the greatest jazz improviser.
Art Pepper, 1925-1982: alto sax.
Oscar Peterson, b. 1925: piano, composer, combo leader.
Oscar Pettiford, 1922-1960: a leading bassist in the bop era.
Bud Powell, 1924-1966: piano; modern jazz pioneer.
Tito Puente, b. 1923: band leader.
Sun Ra, 1915?–1993: big band leader, pianist, composer.
Gertrude "Ma" Rainey, 1886-1939: blues singer.
Don Redman, 1900-1964: composer, arranger; pioneer in the evolution of the large orchestra.
Django Reinhardt, 1910-1953: guitar; Belgian gypsy, first European to influence American jazz.
Buddy Rich, 1917-1987: drums, band leader.
Max Roach, b. 1925: drums.
Sonny Rollins, b. 1929: tenor sax.
Frank Rosolino, 1926-1978: trombone.
Jimmy Rushing, 1903-1972: blues singer.
George Russell, b. 1923: composer, piano.
Pee Wee Russell, 1906-1969: clarinet.
Artie Shaw, b. 1910: clarinet, combo leader.
George Shearing, b. 1919: piano, composer.
Horace Silver, b. 1928: piano, combo leader.
Zoot Sims, 1925-1985: tenor, alto sax; clarinet.
Zutty Singleton, 1898-1975: Dixieland drummer.
Bessie Smith, 1894-1937: blues singer.
Clarence "Pinetop" Smith, 1904-1929: piano, singer; pioneer of boogie woogie.
Willie "The Lion" Smith, 1897-1973: stride style pianist.
Muggsy Spanier, 1906-1967: cornet, band leader.
Billy Strayhorn, 1915-67: composer, piano.
Sonny Stitt, 1924-1982: alto, tenor sax.
Art Tatum, 1910-1956: piano; technical virtuoso.
Billy Taylor, b. 1921: piano, composer.
Cecil Taylor, b. 1933: piano, composer.
Jack Teagarden, 1905-1964: trombone, singer.
Dave Tough, 1908-1948: drums.
Lennie Tristano, 1919-1978: piano, composer.
Joe Turner, 1911-1985: blues singer.
McCoy Tyner, b. 1938: piano, composer.
Sarah Vaughan, 1924-1990: singer.
Joe Venuti, 1904-1978: first great jazz violinist.
Thomas "Fats" Waller, 1904-1943: piano, singer, composer. "Ain't Misbehavin' ".
Dinah Washington, 1924-1963: singer.
Chick Webb, 1902-1939: band leader, drums.
Ben Webster, 1909-1973: tenor sax.
Paul Whiteman, 1890-1967: orchestra leader, a major figure in

the introduction of jazz to a large audience.
Charles "Cootie" Williams, 1908-1985: trumpet, band leader.
Mary Lou Williams, 1914-1981: piano, composer.
Teddy Wilson, 1912-1986: piano, composer.
Kai Winding, 1922-1983: trombone, composer.
Jimmy Yancey, 1894-1951: piano.
Lester "Pres" Young, 1909-1959: tenor sax, composer: a bop pioneer.

Rock & Roll Notables

For more than a quarter of a century, rock & roll has been an important force in popular culture. The following individuals or groups have made a significant impact. Next to each is an associated single record or record album.

Paula Abdul: "Forever Your Girl"
Aerosmith: "Sweet Emotion"
The Allman Brothers Band: "Ramblin' Man"
The Animals: "House of the Rising Sun"
Paul Anka: "Lonely Boy"
The Association: "Cherish"
Frankie Avalon: "Venus"

The Band: "The Weight"
The Beach Boys: "Good Vibrations"
The Beatles: *Sergeant Pepper's Lonely-Hearts Club Band*
The Bee Gees: "Stayin' Alive"
Pat Benatar: "Hit Me With Your Best Shot"
Chuck Berry: "Johnny B. Goode"
The Big Bopper: "Chantilly Lace"
Black Sabbath: "Paranoid"
Blind Faith: "Can't Find My Way Home"
Blondie: "Heart of Glass"
Blood, Sweat and Tears: "Spinning Wheel"
Bon Jovi: *Slippery When Wet*
Gary "U.S". Bonds: "Quarter to Three"
Booker T. and the MGs: "Green Onions"
Earl Bostic: "Flamingo"
David Bowie: "Let's Dance"
James Brown: "Papa's Got a Brand New Bag"
Jackson Browne: "Doctor My Eyes"
Buffalo Springfield: "For What It's Worth"
The Byrds: "Turn! Turn! Turn!"

Canned Heat: "Going Up the Country"
The Cars: "Shake It Up"
Tracy Chapman: "Fast Car"
Ray Charles: "Georgia on My Mind"
Chubby Checker: "The Twist"
Chicago: "Saturday in the Park"
Eric Clapton: "Layla"
The Coasters: "Yakety Yak"
Eddie Cochran: "Summertime Blues"
Phil Collins: "Another Day in Paradise"
Sam Cooke: "You Send Me"
Alice Cooper: "School's Out"
Elvis Costello: "Alison"
Cream: "Sunshine of Your Love"
Credence Clearwater Revival: "Proud Mary"
Crosby, Stills, Nash and Young: "Suite: Judy Blue Eyes"
The Crystals: "Da Doo Ron Ron"

Danny and the Juniors: "At the Hop"
Bobby Darin: "Splish Splash"
Spencer Davis Group: "Gimme Some Lovin' "
Bo Diddley: "Who Do You Love?"
Dion and the Belmonts: "A Teenager in Love"
Dire Straits: *Brothers in Arms*
DJ Jazzy Jeff & the Fresh Prince: "Summertime"
Fats Domino: "Blueberry Hill"
The Doobie Brothers: "What a Fool Believes"
The Doors: "Light My Fire"
The Drifters: "Save the Last Dance for Me"
Bob Dylan: "Like a Rolling Stone"

The Eagles: "Hotel California"
Earth, Wind and Fire: "Shining Star"
Emerson, Lake and Palmer: "From the Beginning"
The Eurythmics: "Sweet Dreams (Are Made of This)"
Everly Brothers: "Wake Up Little Susie"

The Five Satins: "In the Still of the Night"
Fleetwood Mac: *Rumours*
The Four Seasons: "Sherry"
The Four Tops: "I Can't Help Myself"
Aretha Franklin: "Respect"

Marvin Gaye: "I Heard It through the Grapevine"
Grand Funk Railroad: "We're an American Band"
The Grateful Dead: "Truckin' "
Guns 'n' Roses: *Appetite for Destruction*

Bill Haley and the Comets: "Rock Around the Clock"
M.C. Hammer: "U Can't Touch This"
Jimi Hendrix: *Are You Experienced?*
Buddy Holly and the Crickets: "That'll Be the Day"
Whitney Houston: "The Greatest Love"

The Isley Brothers: "This Old Heart of Mine"

The Jackson 5/The Jacksons: "ABC"
Janet Jackson: *Rhythm Nation*
Michael Jackson: *Thriller*
Tommy James & The Shondells: "Crimson and Clover"
Jay and the Americans: "This Magic Moment"
The Jefferson Airplane: "White Rabbit"
Jethro Tull: *Aqualung*
Joan Jett: "I Love Rock 'n' Roll"
Billy Joel: "Piano Man"
Elton John: "Sad Songs"
Janis Joplin: "Me and Bobby McGee"

Chaka Khan: "I Feel for You"
B.B. King: "The Thrill Is Gone"
Carole King: *Tapestry*
The Kinks: "You Really Got Me"
Kiss: "Rock 'n' Roll All Night"
Gladys Knight and the Pips: "Midnight Train to Georgia"

Led Zeppelin: "Stairway to Heaven"
Brenda Lee: "I'm Sorry"
Jerry Lee Lewis: "Whole Lotta Shakin' Going On"
Little Anthony and the Imperials: "Tears on My Pillow"
Little Richard: "Tutti Frutti"
L.L. Cool J: "Mama's Gonna Knock You Out"
Lovin' Spoonful: "Do You Believe in Magic?"
Frankie Lymon: "Why Do Fools Fall in Love?"
Lynyrd Skynyrd: "Freebird"

Madonna: "Material Girl"
The Mamas and the Papas: "Monday, Monday"
Bob Marley: "Jamming"
Martha and the Vandellas: "Dancin' in the Streets"
The Marvelettes: "Please Mr. Postman"
Clyde McPhatter: "Money Honey"
John Mellencamp: "Hurt So Good"
George Michael: *Faith*
Joni Mitchell: "Big Yellow Taxi"
The Monkees: "I'm a Believer"
Moody Blues: "Nights in White Satin"

Rick Nelson: "Hello Mary Lou"

Roy Orbison: "Oh Pretty Woman"

Carl Perkins: "Blue Suede Shoes"
Tom Petty and the Heartbreakers: "Refugee"
Pink Floyd: *The Wall*
Poco: *Deliverin'*
The Police: "Every Breath You Take"
Iggy Pop: "Lust for Life"
Elvis Presley: "Love Me Tender"
The Pretenders: *Learning to Crawl*
Lloyd Price: "Stagger Lee"
Prince: "Purple Rain"
Procul Harum: "A Whiter Shade of Pale"
Public Enemy: "Fight The Power"

Queen: "Bohemian Rhapsody"

The Rascals: "Good Lovin' "
Otis Redding: "The Dock of the Bay"
Lou Reed: "Walk on the Wild Side"
R.E.M: "Losing My Religion"
Righteous Brothers: "You've Lost that Lovin' Feeling"
Johnny Rivers: "Poor Side of Town"
Smokey Robinson and the Miracles: "Tears of a Clown"
The Rolling Stones: "Satisfaction"
The Ronettes: "Be My Baby"
Linda Ronstadt: "You're No Good"
Run D.M.C.: "Raisin' Hell"

Sam and Dave: "Soul Man"
Santana: "Black Magic Woman"
Neil Sedaka: "Breaking Up Is Hard to Do"
Del Shannon: "Runaway"
The Shirelles: "Soldier Boy"
Simon and Garfunkel: "Bridge Over Troubled Water"
Carly Simon: "You're So Vain"
Sly and the Family Stone: "Everyday People"
Patti Smith: "Because the Night"
Southside Johnny and the Asbury Jukes: *This Time*
Dusty Springfield: "You Don't Have to Say You Love Me"
Bruce Springsteen: "Born in the U.S.A".
Steely Dan: "Rikki Don't Lose That Number"
Steppenwolf: "Born to Be Wild"
Rod Stewart: "Maggie Mae"
Sting: "If You Love Somebody, Set Them Free"
Donna Summer: "Work Hard for My Money"
The Supremes: "Stop! In the Name of Love"

Talking Heads: "Once in a Lifetime"
James Taylor: "You've Got a Friend"
The Temptations: "My Girl"
Three Dog Night: "Joy to the World"
Traffic: "Feelin' Alright"
Big Joe Turner: "Shake, Rattle & Roll"
Tina Turner: "What's Love Got to Do with It?"

U2: *Joshua Tree*

Van Halen: "Jump"

Dionne Warwick: "I'll Never Fall in Love Again"
Muddy Waters: "Rollin' Stone"'
Mary Wells: "My Guy"
The Who: "My Generation"
Jackie Wilson: "That's Why"
Stevie Wonder: "You Are the Sunshine of My Life"

The Yardbirds: "For Your Love"
Yes: "Yours Is No Disgrace"

Frank Zappa/Mothers of Invention: *Sheik Yerbouti*

Entertainment Personalities – Where and When Born

Actors, Actresses, Dancers, Directors, Musicians, Producers, Radio-TV Performers, Singers
(As of Aug., 1993)

Name	Birthplace	Born
Abbado, Claudio	Milan, Italy	26/6/33
Abbott, Russ	Chester, Cheshire	16/9/47
Abdul, Paula	San Fernando, Cal.	19/6/62
Abraham, F. Murray	Pittsburgh, Pa.	24/10/39
Ackland, Joss	London	29/2/28
Adams, Edie	Kingston, Pa.	16/4/29
Adams, Maud	Lulea, Sweden	12/2/45
Adjani, Isabelle	W. Germany	27/6/55
Adler, Larry	Baltimore, Md.	10/2/14
Agutter, Jenny	London	20/12/52
Aimée, Anouk	Paris, France	27/4/32
Aitken, Maria	Dublin, Ireland	12/9/45
Albert, Eddie	Rock Island, Ill.	22/4/08
Alda, Alan	New York, N.Y.	28/1/36
Alderton, John	Gainsborough, Lincs	27/11/40
Alexander, Jane	Boston, Mass	28/10/39
Allen, Dave	Tallaght, Co. Dublin	6/7/36
Allen, Steve	New York, N.Y.	26/12/21
Allen, Woody	Brooklyn, N.Y.	1/12/35
Alley, Kirstie	Wichita, Kan.	12/1/55
Allman, Gregg	Nashville, Tenn.	7/12/47
Allyson, June	New York, N.Y.	7/10/17
Alpert, Herb	Los Angeles, Cal.	31/3/35
Altman, Robert	Kansas City, Mo.	20/2/25
Ameche, Don	Kenosha, Wis.	31/5/08
Amsterdam, Morey	Chicago, Ill.	14/12/14
Anderson, Ian	Dunfermline, Scotland	10/8/47
Anderson, Lindsay	Bangalore, India	17/4/23
Anderson, Loni	St. Paul, Minn.	5/8/46
Andersson, Bibi	Stockholm, Sweden	11/11/35
Andress, Ursula	Bern, Switzerland	19/3/38
Andrews, Anthony	London	12/1/48
Andrews, Julie	Walton, Middx.	1/10/35
Anka, Paul	Ottawa, Ont.	30/7/41
Ann-Margret	Stockholm, Sweden	28/4/41
Annis, Francesca	London	14/5/44
Ant, Adam	London	3/11/54
Anton, Susan	Oak Glen, Cal.	12/10/50
Antonioni, Michelangelo	Ferrara, Italy	29/9/12
Apted, Michael	London	10/2/41
Arkin, Alan	New York, N.Y.	26/3/34
Arnaz, Desi Jr.	Los Angeles, Cal.	19/1/53
Arnaz, Lucie	Hollywood, Cal.	17/7/51
Arness, James	Minneapolis, Minn.	26/5/23
Arnold, Roseanne	Salt Lake City, Ut.	3/11/52
Arquette, Rosanna	New York, N.Y.	10/8/59
Arthur, Beatrice	New York, N.Y.	13/5/26
Asher, Jane	London	5/5/46
Ashkenazy, Vladimir	Moscow, USSR	6/7/37
Asner, Ed	Kansas City, Mo.	15/11/29
Assante, Armand	New York, N.Y.	4/10/49
Atkins, Chet	Luttrell, Tenn.	20/6/24
Atkins, Eileen	London	16/6/34
Atkinson, Rowan	Newcastle, Tyne & Wear	6/1/55
Attenborough, David	Leicester	8/5/26
Attenborough, Richard	Cambridge	29/8/23
Audran, Stephane	Versailles, France	8/11/32
Austin, Patti	New York, N.Y.	10/8/48
Autry, Gene	Tioga, Tex.	29/9/07
Avalon, Frankie	Philadelphia, Pa.	18/9/39
Aykroyd, Dan	Ottawa, Ont.	1/7/52
Ayres, Lew	Minneapolis, Minn.	28/12/08
Aznavour, Charles	Paris, France	22/5/24
Bacall, Lauren	New York, N.Y.	16/9/24
Bacon, Kevin	Philadelphia, Pa.	8/7/58
Badel, Sarah	London	30/3/43
Baez, Joan	Staten Island, N.Y.	9/1/41
Baio, Scott	Brooklyn, N.Y.	22/9/61
Baker, Carroll	Johnstown, Pa.	28/5/31
Baker, Colin	London	8/6/43
Baker, George	Varna, Bulgaria	1/4/31
Baker, Joe Don	Groesbeck, Tex.	12/2/36
Bakula, Scott	St. Louis, Mo.	9/10/–
Ball, Bobby	Oldham, Lancs	28/1/44
Ball, Johnny	Bristol, Avon	23/5/38
Balsam, Martin	New York, N.Y.	4/11/19
Bancroft, Anne	New York, N.Y.	17/9/31
Bannerji, Victor	Calcutta, India	15/10/46
Bannen, Ian	Airdrie, Strathclyde	29/6/28
Barber, Frances	Wolverhampton, W. Midlands	1957
Bardot, Brigitte	Paris, France	28/9/34
Barenboim, Daniel	Buenos Aires, Argentina	15/11/42
Barker, Ronnie	Bedford, Beds	25/9/29
Barkin, Ellen	New York, N.Y.	16/4/55
Barkworth, Peter	Margate, Kent	14/1/29
Barrault, Jean-Louis	Vesinet, France	8/9/10
Barrie, Amanda	Ashton-under-Lyne, Lancs	14/9/39
Barron, Keith	Mexborough, S. Yorks	8/8/34
Barry, Gene	New York, N.Y.	14/6/19
Barrymore, Michael	Bermondsey, London	4/5/52
Baryshnikov, Mikhail	Riga, Latvia	28/1/48
Basinger, Kim	Athens, Ga.	8/12/53
Bassey, Shirley	Cardiff, Wales	8/1/37
Bates, Alan	Allestree, Derbyshire	17/2/34
Baxter, Stanley	Glasgow, Scotland	24/5/26
Baye, Nathalie	Mainneville, France	6/7/48
Beacham, Stephanie	London	28/2/47
Beadle, Jeremy	Hackney, London	12/4/48
Beatty, Ned	Louisville, Ky.	6/7/37
Beatty, Warren	Richmond, Va.	30/3/37
Bedelia, Bonnie	New York, N.Y.	25/3/48
Bee Gees		
Gibb, Barry	Isle of Man	1/9/46
Gibb, Robin	" "	22/12/49
Gibb, Maurice	" "	22/12/49
Beery, Noah Jr.	New York, N.Y.	10/8/13
Begley, Ed Jr.	Los Angeles, Cal.	16/9/49
Belafonte, Harry	New York, N.Y.	1/3/27
Bel Geddes, Barbara	New York, N.Y.	31/10/22
Bell, Tom	Liverpool	1932
Bellamy, Ralph	Chicago, Ill.	17/6/04
Bellingham, Linda	Montreal, Canada	31/5/48
Belmondo, Jean-Paul	Neuilly-sur-Seine, France	9/4/33
Belushi, Jim	Chicago, Ill.	15/6/54
Benatar, Pat	Brooklyn, N.Y.	10/1/53
Bening, Annette	Topeka, Kan.	1958
Benjamin, Richard	New York, N.Y.	22/5/38
Bennett, Alan	Leeds, Yorks	9/5/34
Bennett, Hywel	Garnant, Dyfed	8/4/44
Bennett, Lennie	Blackpool, Lancs	26/9/38
Bennett, Tony	New York, N.Y.	3/8/26
Benson, George	Pittsburgh, Pa.	22/3/43

Name	Birthplace	Born
Benson, Robby	Dallas, Tex.	21/1/55
Berenger, Tom	Chicago, Ill.	31/5/50
Beresford, Bruce	Sydney, Australia	1940
Bergen, Candice	Beverly Hills, Cal.	9/5/46
Bergman, Ingmar	Uppsala, Sweden	14/7/18
Berkoff, Steven	London	3/8/37
Berle, Milton	New York, N.Y.	12/7/08
Berman, Shelley	Chicago, Ill	3/2/26
Bernhard, Sandra	Flint, Michigan	6/6/55
Bernsen, Corbin	N. Hollywood, Cal.	7/9/54
Berri, Claude	Paris, France	1/7/34
Berry, Chuck	St. Louis, Mo.	18/10/26
Bewes, Rodney	Bingley, Yorks	27/11/37
Biggins, Christopher	Oldham, Lancs	16/12/48
Bird, John	Nottingham, Notts	22/11/36
Bisset, Jacqueline	Weybridge, Surrey	13/9/44
Bixby, Bill	San Francisco, Cal.	22/1/34
Black, Cilla	Liverpool	27/5/43
Black, Karen	Park Ridge, Ill.	1/7/42
Blackman, Honor	London	22/8/26
Blair, Isla	Bangalore, India	29/9/44
Blair, Linda	St. Louis, Mo.	22/1/59
Blair, Lionel	Montreal, Canada	12/12/31
Blessed, Brian	Yorkshire	9/10/37
Blethyn, Brenda	Ramsgate, Kent	20/2/46
Blier, Bertrand	Paris, France	11/3/39
Bloom, Claire	London	15/2/31
Bochco, Steven	New York, N.Y.	16/12/43
Bogarde, Dirk	London	28/3/20
Bogdanovich, Peter	Kingston, N.Y.	30/7/39
Boht, Jean	Bebington, Cheshire	6/3/36
Bolam, James	Sunderland, Tyne & Wear	16/6/38
Bond, Derek	Glasgow, Scotland	26/1/20
Bond, Gary	Alton, Hants	7/2/40
Bonham-Carter, Helena	London	26/5/66
Bon Jovi, Jon	Sayreville, N.J.	2/3/61
Bono, Sonny	Detroit, Mich.	16/2/35
Boone, Pat	Jacksonville, Fla.	1/6/34
Boorman, John	Shepperton, Middx	18/1/33
Borge, Victor	Copenhagen, Denmark	3/1/09
Borgnine, Ernest	Hamden, Conn.	24/1/17
Bosley, Tom	Chicago, Ill.	1/10/27
Bottoms, Timothy	Santa Barbara, Cal.	30/8/51
Boulting, Roy	Bray, Berks	21/11/13
Bowen, Jim	Heswall, Cheshire	20/8/37
Bowie, David	Brixton, London	8/1/47
Bowles, Peter	London	16/10/36
Boy George	London	14/6/61
Boyle, Katie	Florence, Italy	29/5/26
Branagh, Kenneth	Belfast, N. Ireland	10/12/60
Brando, Marlon	Omaha, Neb.	3/4/24
Brazzi, Rossano	Bologna, Italy	18/9/16
Bremner, Rory	Edinburgh, Scotland	6/4/61
Brendel, Alfred	Wiesenberg, Austria	5/1/31
Brett, Jeremy	Berkswell, W. Midlands	3/11/33
Bridges, Beau	Hollywood, Cal.	9/12/41
Bridges, Jeff	Los Angeles, Cal.	4/12/49
Bridges, Lloyd	San Leandro, Cal.	15/1/13
Briers, Richard	Croydon, Surrey	14/1/34
Briggs, Johnny	Battersea, London	5/9/37
Britton, Tony	Birmingham	9/6/24
Broderick, Matthew	New York, N.Y.	21/3/62
Brolin, James	Los Angeles, Cal.	18/7/40
Bron, Eleanor	Stanmore, Middx	1937
Bronson, Charles	Ehrenfeld, Pa.	3/11/22
Brook, Peter	London	21/3/25
Brooke-Taylor, Tim	Buxton, Derbyshire	17/7/40
Brooks, Mel	New York, N.Y.	28/6/26
Brosnan, Pierce	Co. Meath, Ireland	15/5/53
Brown, Bryan	Sydney, Australia	1947
Brown, James	Pulaski, Tenn.	17/6/28
Bruce, Brenda	Manchester	1922
Bryan, Dora	Southport, Lancs	7/2/24
Bryant, Anita	Barnsdall, Okla.	25/3/40
Bryden, Bill	Greenock, Scotland	12/4/42
Bujold, Genevieve	Montreal, Que.	1/7/42
Bumbry, Grace	St. Louis, Mo.	4/1/37
Burke, Alfred	New Cross, London	28/2/18
Burke, Kathy	London	13/6/64
Burnett, Carol	San Antonio, Tex.	26/4/33
Burns, George	New York, N.Y.	20/1/1896
Burstyn, Ellen	Detroit, Mich.	7/12/32
Buttons, Red	New York, N.Y.	5/2/19
Bygraves, Max	Rotherhithe, London	16/10/20
Byrne, David	Dumbarton, Scotland	14/4/52
Byrne, Gabriel	Dublin, Ireland	1956
Caan, James	New York, N.Y.	26/3/39
Caballe, Montserrat	Spain	12/4/33
Cadell, Simon	London	19/7/50
Caesar, Sid	Yonkers, N.Y.	8/9/22
Cage, Nicholas	Long Beach, Cal.	7/1/64
Caine, Marti	Sheffield, S. Yorks	26/1/45
Caine, Michael	London	14/3/33
Calder-Marshall, Anna	Kensington, London	11/1/47
Calhoun, Rory	Los Angeles, Cal.	8/8/23
Callow, Simon	London	15/6/49
Calloway, Cab	Rochester, N.Y.	25/12/07
Calvert, Phyllis	London	18/2/15
Campbell, Cheryl	Welwyn Garden City, Herts	1949
Campbell, Glen	Billstown, Ark.	22/4/36
Candy, John	Toronto, Ont.	31/10/50
Cannon, Dyan	Tacoma, Wash.	4/1/37
Cara, Irene	New York, N.Y.	18/3/59
Cardinale, Claudia	Tunis, Tunisia	15/4/38
Cargill, Patrick	London	3/6/18
Carmichael, Ian	Hull, Humberside	18/6/20
Carnes, Kim	California	20/7/45
Carney, Art	Mt. Vernon, N.Y.	4/11/18
Carolgees, Bob	Birmingham, W. Midlands	12/5/48
Caron, Leslie	Boulogne, France	1/7/31
Carr, Vikki	El Paso, Tex.	19/7/41
Carradine, David	Hollywood, Cal.	8/10/36
Carradine, Keith	San Mateo, Cal.	8/8/49
Carreras, José	Barcelona, Spain	5/12/47
Carroll, Diahann	Bronx, N.Y.	17/7/35
Carrott, Jasper	Birmingham, W. Midlands	14/3/45
Carson, Frank	Belfast, N. Ireland	6/11/26
Carson, Johnny	Corning, Ia.	23/10/25
Carter, Lynda	Phoenix, Ariz.	24/7/51
Carteret, Anna	Bangalore, India	11/12/42
Cash, Johnny	Kingsland, Ark.	26/2/32
Cashman, Michael	Croydon, Surrey	17/12/50
Cassidy, David	New York, N.Y.	12/4/50
Cassidy, Shaun	Los Angeles, Cal.	27/9/58
Castle, Roy	Scholes, W. Yorks	31/8/32
Cavett, Dick	Gibbon, Neb.	19/11/36
Cazenove, Christopher	Winchester, Hants	17/12/45
Chabrol, Claude	Paris, France	24/6/30
Chamberlain, Richard	Beverly Hills, Cal.	31/3/35
Channing, Carol	Seattle, Wash.	31/1/23
Channing, Stockard	New York, N.Y.	13/2/44
Chaplin, Geraldine	Santa Monica, Cal.	31/7/44
Chapman, Tracy	Cleveland, Oh.	1965
Charisse, Cyd	Amarillo, Tex.	8/3/21
Charles, Ray	Albany, Ga.	23/9/30
Chase, Chevy	New York, N.Y.	8/10/43
Checker, Chubby	Philadelphia, Pa.	3/10/41
Cher	El Centro, Cal.	20/5/46
Christie, Julie	Assam, India	14/4/40
Cilento, Diane	Brisbane, Australia	5/10/33
Cimino, Michael	New York, N.Y.	1940
Clapton, Eric	Surrey	30/3/45
Clarke, Margi	Liverpool	1954
Clark, Petula	Ewell, Surrey	23/5/33
Clayburgh, Jill	New York, N.Y.	30/4/44
Cleese, John	Weston-super-Mare, Avon	27/10/39
Clooney, Rosemary	Maysville, Ky.	23/5/28
Close, Glenn	Greenwich, Conn.	19/4/47
Coburn, James	Laurel, Neb.	31/8/28
Coen, Ethan	St. Louis Park, Minn.	1958
Coen, Joel	St. Louis Park, Minn.	1955
Coffey, Denise	Aldershot, Hants	12/12/36
Colbert, Claudette	Paris, France	18/9/05
Cole, George	London	22/4/25
Cole, Natalie	Los Angeles, Cal.	6/2/50
Coleman, Dabney	Austin, Tex.	3/1/32
Collins, Joan	London	23/5/33
Collins, Judy	Seattle, Wash.	1/5/39
Collins, Lewis	Birkenhead, Cheshire	27/5/46
Collins, Pauline	Exmouth, Devon	3/9/40
Collins, Phil	London	30/1/51
Coltrane, Robbie	Rutherglen, Glasgow	1950
Como, Perry	Canonsburg, Pa.	18/5/12
Connery, Jason	London	11/1/63
Connery, Sean	Edinburgh, Scotland	25/8/30
Connick, Harry Jr.	New Orleans, La.	9/11/67
Conniff, Ray	Attleboro, Mass.	6/11/16
Connolly, Billy	Glasgow, Scotland	24/11/42
Conrad, William	Louisville, Ky.	27/9/20
Conti, Tom	Glasgow, Scotland	22/11/41
Cooder, Ry	Los Angeles, Cal.	15/3/47

Name	Birthplace	Born
Cook, Peter	Torquay, Devon	17/11/37
Cooke, Alistair	Manchester	20/11/08
Coolidge, Rita	Nashville, Tenn.	1/5/45
Coombs, Pat	London	27/8/30
Cooper, Alice	Detroit, Mich.	4/2/48
Cooper, Jackie	Los Angeles, Cal.	15/9/21
Copeland, Stewart	Maclean, Va.	16/7/52
Copperfield, David	Metuchen, N.J.	16/9/56
Coppola, Francis	Detroit, Mich.	7/4/39
Corea, Chick	Chelsea, Mass.	12/6/41
Corbett, Ronnie	Edinburgh, Scotland	4/12/30
Corman, Roger	Detroit, Mich.	5/4/26
Cornwell, Judy	London	22/2/42
Cosby, Bill	Philadelphia, Pa.	12/7/37
Costa-Gavras	Athens, Greece	1933
Costello, Elvis	London	25/8/54
Costner, Kevin	Los Angeles, Cal.	18/1/55
Cotten, Joseph	Petersburg, Va.	15/5/05
Cougar, John	Seymour, Ind.	7/10/51
Courtenay, Tom	Hull, Humberside	25/2/37
Cox, Brian	Dundee, Scotland	1/6/46
Craig, Wendy	Sacriston, Co. Durham	20/6/34
Crain, Jeanne	Barstow, Cal.	25/5/25
Cranham, Kenneth	Dunfermline, Scotland	12/12/44
Craven, Gemma	Dublin, Ireland	1/6/50
Crawford, Michael	Salisbury, Wilts	19/1/42
Cribbins, Bernard	Oldham, Lancs	29/12/28
Crichton, Charles	Wallasey, Cheshire	6/8/10
Crisp, Quentin	Sutton, Surrey	25/12/08
Cronenberg, David	Toronto, Canada	15/5/43
Cronyn, Hume	London, Ont.	18/7/11
Cropper, Anna	Manchester	13/5/38
Crosbie, Annette	Edinburgh, Scotland	12/2/38
Cross, Ben	London	16/12/47
Crowther, Leslie	W. Bridgeford, Notts	6/2/33
Cruise, Tom	Syracuse, N.Y.	3/7/62
Crutchley, Rosalie	London	4/1/21
Cryer, Barry	Leeds, Yorks	23/3/35
Crystal, Billy	Long Beach, N.Y.	14/3/47
Culp, Robert	Oakland, Cal.	16/8/30
Cummings, Constance	Seattle, Wash.	15/5/10
Curry, Tim	Cheshire	19/4/46
Curtis, Jamie Lee	Los Angeles, Cal.	22/11/58
Curtis, Tony	New York, N.Y.	3/6/25
Cusack, Sinead	Ireland	18/2/48
Cushing, Peter	Kenley, Surrey	26/5/13
Dafoe, Willem	Appleton, Wis.	22/7/55
Dahl, Arlene	Minneapolis, Minn.	11/8/28
Dale, Jim	Rothwell, Northants	15/8/35
Dalton, Timothy	Colwyn Bay, Wales	21/3/44
Daltrey, Roger	London	1/3/44
Daly, Tyne	Madison, Wis.	21/2/46
Damone, Vic	Brooklyn, N.Y.	12/6/28
Dance, Charles	Rednal, Shropshire	10/10/46
Daneman, Paul	London	26/10/25
D'Angelo, Beverly	Columbus, Oh.	15/11/54
Daniels, Paul	South Bank, Cleveland	6/4/38
Danner, Blythe	Philadelphia, Pa.	3/2/44
Danson, Ted	San Diego, Cal.	29/12/47
D'Arby, Terence Trent	New York, N.Y.	15/3/62
Davenport, Nigel	Shelford, Cambs	23/5/28
Davidson, Jim	Blackheath, London	13/12/53
Davies, Windsor	Canning Town, London	28/8/30
Davis, Geena	Ware, Mass.	21/1/57
Davis, Judy	Perth, Australia	1956
Davison, Peter	London	1950
Davro, Bobby	Ashford, Middx	13/9/59
Day, Doris	Cincinnati, Oh.	3/4/24
Day, Laraine	Roosevelt, Ut.	13/10/20
Day-Lewis, Daniel	London	29/4/58
DeCarlo, Yvonne	Vancouver, B.C.	1/9/22
Dee, Sandra	Bayonne, N.J.	23/4/42
De Havilland, Olivia	Tokyo, Japan	1/7/16
De la Tour, Frances	Bovingdon, Herts	30/7/44
De Laurentiis, Dino	Torve Annunziata, Italy	8/8/19
Delon, Alain	Sceaux, France	8/11/35
De los Angeles, Victoria	Barcelona, Spain	1923
DeLuise, Dom	Brooklyn, N.Y.	1/8/33
De Mille, Agnes	New York, N.Y.	18/9/05
Demme, Jonathan	Rockville Centre, N.Y.	22/2/44
DeMornay, Rebecca	Santa Rosa, Cal.	29/11/61
Dench, Judi	York	9/12/34
Deneuve, Catherine	Paris, France	22/10/43
Denham, Maurice	Beckenham, Kent	23/12/09
De Niro, Robert	New York, N.Y.	17/8/43

Name	Birthplace	Born
Denison, Michael	Doncaster, S. Yorks	1/11/15
Dennis, Les	Liverpool	12/10/54
Denver, John	Roswell, N.M.	31/12/43
DePalma, Brian	Newark, N.J.	11/9/40
Depardieu, Gerard	Chateauroux, France	27/12/48
Depp, Johnny	Owensboro, Ky.	9/6/63
Derbyshire, Eileen	Urmston, Manchester	6/10/30
Derek, Bo	Long Beach, Cal.	20/11/56
Derek, John	Hollywood, Cal.	12/8/26
Dern, Bruce	Chicago, Ill.	4/6/36
Dern, Laura	Los Angeles, Cal.	1966
DeVito, Danny	Neptune, N.J.	17/11/44
Dey, Susan	Pekin, Ill.	10/12/52
Diamond, Neil	Brooklyn, N.J.	24/1/41
Dickinson, Angie	Kulm, N.D.	30/9/31
Diddley, Bo.	McComb, Miss.	20/12/28
Diller, Phyllis	Lima, Oh.	17/7/17
Dillon, Matt	New Rochelle, N.Y.	18/2/64
Dinsdale, Reece	Normanton, W. Yorks	6/8/59
Distel, Sacha	Paris, France	29/1/33
Dobie, Alan	Wombwell, Yorks	2/6/32
Dobson, Anita	London	29/4/49
Dodd, Ken	Knotty Ash, Liverpool	8/11/29
Domingo, Placido	Madrid, Spain	21/1/41
Domino, Fats	New Orleans, La.	26/2/28
Donahue, Phil	Cleveland, Oh.	21/12/35
Donahue, Troy	New York, N.Y.	27/1/36
Donegan, Lonnie	London	29/4/31
Donner, Clive	London	21/1/26
Donovan	Glasgow, Scotland	10/5/43
Doonican, Val	S. Ireland	3/2/29
Dotrice, Roy	Guernsey	26/5/23
Douglas, Kirk	Amsterdam, N.Y.	9/12/18
Douglas, Michael	New Brunswick, N.J.	25/9/44
Down, Leslie-Anne	London	17/3/54
Dreyfuss, Richard	Brooklyn, N.Y.	29/10/47
Drinkwater, Carole	London	22/4/48
Driver, Betty	Leicester	20/5/20
Duffy, Patrick	Townsend, Mont.	17/3/49
Dukakis, Olympia	Lowell, Mass.	20/6/31
Duke, Patty	New York, N.Y.	14/12/46
Dullea, Keir	Cleveland, Oh.	30/5/36
Dunaway, Faye	Bascom, Fla.	14/1/41
Duncan, Lindsay	Edinburgh, Scotland	7/11/50
Dunham, Joanna	Luton, Beds	6/5/36
Dunlop, Lesley	Newcastle, Tyne & Wear	10/3/56
Durbin, Deanna	Winnipeg, Man.	4/12/21
Durning, Charles	Highland Falls, N.Y.	28/2/23
Dury, Ian	Billericay, Essex	12/5/42
Du Sautoy, Carmen	London	26/2/50
Duttine, John	Barnsley, Yorks	15/5/49
Duvall, Robert	San Diego, Cal.	5/1/31
Duvall, Shelly	Houston, Texas	7/7/49
Dylan, Bob	Duluth, Minn.	24/5/41
Dysart, Richard	Augusta, Me.	30/3/–
Easton, Sheena	Bellshill, Glasgow	27/4/59
Eastwood, Clint	San Francisco, Cal.	31/5/30
Ebsen, Buddy	Belleville, Ill.	2/4/08
Eddington, Paul	London	18/6/27
Eden, Barbara	Tucson, Ariz.	23/8/24
Edwards, Blake	Tulsa, Okla.	26/7/22
Egan, Peter	London	28/9/46
Eggar, Samantha	London	5/3/39
Eichhorn, Lisa	Reading, Pa.	4/2/52
Eikenberry, Jill	New Haven, Conn.	21/1/47
Ekberg, Anita	Malmo, Sweden	29/9/31
Ekland, Britt	Stockholm, Sweden	6/10/42
Elphick, Michael	Chichester, W. Sussex	19/9/46
Enfield, Harry	Sussex	31/5/61
Essex, David	London	23/7/47
Estefan, Gloria	Cuba	1/9/57
Estevez, Emilio	New York, N.Y.	12/5/62
Evans, Linda	Hartford, Conn.	18/11/42
Evans, Robert	New York N.Y.	29/6/30
Everett, Chad	South Bend, Ind.	11/6/36
Everett, Rupert	Norfolk	1959
Everly, Don	Brownie, Ky.	1/2/37
Everly, Phil	Chicago, Ill.	19/1/38
Ewing, Maria	London	27/3/50
Eyre, Ronald	Mapplewell, Yorks	13/3/29
Fabian (Forte)	Philadelphia, Pa.	6/2/43
Fairbanks, Douglas Jr.	New York, N.Y.	9/12/09
Fairchild, Morgan	Dallas, Tex.	2/3/50
Faith, Adam	Acton, London	23/6/40
Faithfull, Marianne	Hampstead, London	29/12/46

Name	Birthplace	Born
Falk, Peter	New York, N.Y.	16/9/27
Farentino, James	Brooklyn, N.Y.	24/2/38
Farr, Jamie	Toledo, Oh.	1/7/34
Farrow, Mia	Los Angeles, Cal.	9/2/45
Fawcett, Farrah	Corpus Christi, Tex.	2/2/47
Faye, Alice	New York, N.Y.	5/5/12
Feliciano, José	Lares, Puerto Rico	10/9/45
Fellini, Federico	Rimini, Italy	20/1/20
Fenn, Sherilyn	Detroit, Mich.	1965
Ferrell, Conchata	Charleston, W. Va.	28/3/43
Ferrer, Jose	Santurce, P.R.	8/1/12
Ferrer, Mel	Elberon, N.J.	25/8/17
Ferry, Bryan	Tyneside	26/9/45
Field, Sally	Pasadena, Cal.	6/11/46
Fielding, Fenella	London	17/11/34
Finlay, Frank	Farnworth, Cheshire	6/8/26
Finney, Albert	Salford, Lancs	9/5/36
Firth, Colin	Grayshott, Hants	10/9/60
Firth, Peter	Bradford, Yorks	27/10/53
Fischer-Dieskau, Dietrich	Berlin, Germany	28/5/25
Fisher, Carrie	Beverly Hills, Cal.	21/10/56
Fisher, Eddie	Philadelphia, Pa.	10/8/28
Fitzgerald, Ella	Newport News, Va.	25/4/18
Fitzgerald, Geraldine	Dublin, Ireland	24/11/13
Flack, Roberta	Black Mountain, N.C.	10/2/39
Fleetwood, Susan	St Andrews, Scotland	21/9/44
Fleming, Rhonda	Hollywood, Cal.	10/8/23
Fletcher, Cyril	Watford, Herts	25/6/13
Flynn, Barbara	Hastings, E. Sussex	5/8/48
Fogelberg, Dan	Peoria, Ill.	13/8/51
Fonda, Bridget	Los Angeles, Cal.	1964
Fonda, Jane	New York, N.Y.	21/12/37
Fonda, Peter	New York, N.Y.	23/2/39
Fontaine, Joan	Tokyo, Japan	22/10/17
Ford, Glenn	Quebec, Canada	1/5/16
Ford, Harrison	Chicago, Ill.	13/7/42
Forman, Milos	Kaslov, Czechoslovakia	18/2/32
Forrest, Frederic	Waxahachie, Tex.	23/12/36
Forsyth, Bill	Glasgow, Scotland	1948
Forsyth, Bruce	Edmonton, London	22/2/28
Forsythe, John	Penns Grove, N.J.	29/1/18
Foster, Barry	Beeston, Notts	1938
Foster, Jodie	New York, N.Y.	19/11/62
Foster, Julia	Lewes, Sussex	1942
Fowlds, Derek	London	2/9/37
Fowler, Harry	Lambeth, London	10/12/26
Fox, Edward	London	13/4/37
Fox, James	London	19/5/39
Fox, Michael J.	Edmonton, Alta.	9/6/61
Franciosa, Anthony	New York, N.Y.	25/10/28
Francis, Connie	Newark, N.J.	12/12/38
Frankenheimer, John	Malba, N.Y.	19/2/30
Franklin, Aretha	Memphis, Tenn.	25/3/42
Franklyn, William	London	22/9/26
Fraser, Liz	London	14/8/35
Frears, Stephen	Leicester	20/6/41
French, Dawn	London	11/10/57
Friedkin, William	Chicago, Ill.	29/8/39
Frost, David	Tenterden, Kent	7/4/39
Fry, Stephen	Hampstead, London	24/8/57
Fugard, Athol	Middleburg, S. Africa	11/6/32
Fullerton, Fiona	Kaduna, Nigeria	10/10/56
Funicello, Annette	Utica, N.Y.	22/10/42
Gabor, Eva	Hungary	1921
Gabor, Zsa Zsa	Hungary	6/2/17
Gabriel, Peter	London	13/5/50
Galway, James	Belfast, N. Ireland	8/12/39
Gambon, Michael	Dublin, Ireland	19/10/40
Garcia, Andy	Havana, Cuba	12/4/56
Garden, Graeme	Aberdeen, Scotland	18/2/43
Garfunkel, Art	New York, N.Y.	13/10/41
Garner, James	Norman, Okla.	7/4/28
Garr, Teri	Lakewood, Oh.	11/12/49
Garson, Greer	Co. Down, N. Ireland	29/9/08
Gascoine, Jill	Lambeth, London	11/4/37
Gaunt, William	Leeds, Yorks	3/4/37
Gayle, Crystal	Paintsville, Ky	9/1/51
Gaynor, Mitzi	Chicago, Ill	4/9/30
Gazzara, Ben	New York, N.Y.	28/8/30
Geeson, Judy	Arundel, Sussex	10/9/48
Geldof, Bob	Dublin, Ireland	5/10/51
Geller, Uri	Israel	20/12/48
George, Susan	Wraysbury, Berks	26/7/50
Gere, Richard	Philadelphia, Pa.	31/8/49
Getty, Estelle	New York, N.Y.	25/7/24
Gibson, Mel	Peekskill, N.Y.	3/1/56
Gielgud, John	London	14/4/04

Name	Birthplace	Born
Gilberto, Astrud	Salvador, Brazil	30/3/40
Gillespie, Robert	Lille, France	9/11/33
Gilliam, Terry	Minneapolis, Minn.	22/11/40
Givens, Robin	New York, N.Y.	27/11/64
Glaser, Paul Michael	Cambridge, Mass	25/3/43
Glass, Phillip	Baltimore, Md.	31/1/37
Glennie, Evelyn	Scotland	18/7/65
Gless, Sharon	Los Angeles, Cal.	31/5/43
Glover, Julian	St John's Wood, London	27/3/35
Godard, Jean-Luc	Paris, France	3/12/30
Goddard, Liza	Smethwick, W. Midlands	20/1/50
Godunov, Alexander	Sakhalin, Is., USSR	28/11/49
Goldberg, Whoopi	New York, N.Y.	13/11/49
Goldblum, Jeff	Pittsburgh, Pa.	22/10/52
Goldsboro, Bobby	Marianna, Fla.	18/1/42
Goodman, John	St. Louis, Mo.	20/6/53
Goodyear, Julie	Bury, Lancs	29/3/45
Gordon, Hannah	Edinburgh, Scotland	9/4/41
Gorme, Eydie	Bronx, N.Y.	16/8/32
Gough, Michael	Malaya	23/11/16
Gould, Elliott	Brooklyn, N.Y.	29/8/38
Grace, Nickolas	West Kirby, Cheshire	21/11/49
Grade, Lew	Odessa, Russia	25/12/06
Granger, Farley	San Jose, Cal.	1/7/25
Grantham, Leslie	Camberwell, London	30/4/46
Graves, Peter	Minneapolis, Minn.	18/3/26
Graves, Rupert	Weston-super-Mare, Somerset	30/6/63
Gray, Charles	Bournemouth, Dorset	29/8/28
Gray, Dulcie	Kuala Lumpur, Malaysia	20/11/19
Gray, Elspet	Inverness, Scotland	12/4/29
Gray, Linda	Santa Monica, Cal.	12/9/40
Grayson, Kathryn	Winston-Salem, N.C.	9/2/22
Greco, Buddy	Philadelphia, Pa.	14/8/26
Green, Al	Forest City, Ark.	13/4/46
Grey, Joel	Cleveland, Oh.	11/4/32
Griffin, Merv	San Mateo, Cal.	6/7/25
Griffith, Melanie	New York, N.Y.	9/8/57
Griffiths, Richard	Cleveland	31/7/47
Grimes, Tammy	Lynn, Mass.	30/1/34
Grodin, Charles	Pittsburgh, Pa.	21/4/35
Grout, James	London	22/10/27
Guillaume, Robert	St. Louis, Mo.	30/11/37
Guillem, Sylvie	Paris, France	23/2/65
Guinness, Alec	London	2/4/14
Guthrie, Arlo	New York, N.Y.	10/7/47
Guttenberg, Steve	New York, N.Y.	24/8/58
Gwilym, Mike	Neath, W. Glam	5/3/49
Hackett, Buddy	Brooklyn, N.Y.	31/8/24
Hackman, Gene	San Bernadino, Cal.	30/1/30
Hagen, Uta	Gottingen, Germany	12/6/19
Haggard, Merle	Bakersfield, Cal.	6/4/37
Hagman, Larry	Weatherford, Tex.	21/9/31
Hale, Gareth	London	15/1/53
Hale, Georgina	Essex	4/8/43
Hall, Arsenio	Cleveland, Oh.	12/2/58
Hall, Daryl	Pottstown, Pa.	11/10/49
Hall, Sir Peter	Bury St Edmunds, Suffolk	22/11/30
Hamel, Veronica	Philadelphia, Pa.	20/11/43
Hamill, Mark	Oakland, Cal.	25/9/51
Hamilton, George	Memphis, Tenn.	12/8/39
Hamlin, Harry	Pasadena, Cal.	30/10/51
Hammer, M.C.	Oakland, Cal.	30/3/62
Hampshire, Susan	London	12/5/42
Hampton, Lionel	Birmingham, Ala.	12/4/13
Hancock, Herbie	Chicago, Ill.	12/4/40
Hancock, Sheila	Blackgang, Isle of Wight	22/2/33
Hanks, Tom	Oakland, Cal.	9/7/56
Hannah, Daryl	Chicago, Ill.	1961
Hardwicke, Edward	London	7/8/32
Hardy, Robert	England	29/10/25
Harper, Gerald	London	15/2/29
Harper, Valerie	Suffern, N.Y.	22/8/40
Harrelson, Woody	Midland, Tex.	23/7/61
Harris, Emmylou	Birmingham, Ala.	2/4/47
Harris, Richard	Co. Limerick, Ireland	1/10/33
Harris, Rolf	Perth, Australia	30/3/30
Harris, Rosemary	Ashby, Suffolk	19/9/30
Harrison, George	Liverpool	25/2/43
Harrison, Kathleen	Blackburn, Lancs	23/2/1898
Harrow, Lisa	New Zealand	25/8/43
Harry, Deborah	Miami, Fla.	1/7/45
Harwood, Ronald	Cape Town, S. Africa	9/11/34
Hauer, Rutger	Netherlands	23/1/44
Haver, June	Rock Island, Ill.	10/6/26
Havers, Nigel	London	6/11/49

Name	Birthplace	Born
Hawn, Goldie	Washington, D.C.	21/11/45
Hawthorne, Nigel	Coventry, W. Midlands	5/4/29
Hayes, Isaac	Covington, Tenn.	20/8/42
Hayes, Patricia	London	22/12/09
Helmond, Katherine	Galveston, Tex.	5/7/34
Hemingway, Margaux	Portland, Ore.	19/2/55
Hemingway, Mariel	Mill Valley, Cal.	21/11/61
Hemmings, David	Guildford, Surrey	18/11/41
Henner, Marilu	Chicago, Ill.	6/4/52
Henry, Lenny	Sedgeley, W. Midlands	29/8/58
Henson, Nicky	London	12/5/45
Hepburn, Katharine	Hartford, Conn.	8/11/09
Hepton, Bernard	Bradford, Yorks	19/10/25
Herman, Pee-Wee	Peekskill, N.Y.	27/8/52
Hershey, Barbara	Los Angeles, Cal.	5/2/48
Herzog, Werner	Munich, Germany	5/9/42
Heston, Charlton	Evanston, Ill.	4/10/24
Hickson, Joan	Kingsthorpe, Northants	5/8/06
Hill, Bernard	Liverpool	17/12/44
Hiller, Wendy	Stockport, Cheshire	15/8/12
Hines, Gregory	New York, N.Y.	14/2/46
Hird, Thora	Morecambe, Lancs	28/5/13
Hirsch, Judd	New York, N.Y.	15/3/35
Hodge, Patricia	Lincolnshire	29/9/46
Hoffman, Dustin	Los Angeles, Cal.	8/8/37
Hogan, Paul	New South Wales, Australia	10/8/39
Holbrook, Hal	Cleveland, Oh.	17/2/25
Holm, Celeste	New York, N.Y.	29/4/19
Holm, Ian	Ilford, Essex	12/9/31
Hood, Morag	Glasgow, Scotland	12/12/42
Hope, Bob	Eltham, London	29/5/03
Hopkins, Anthony	Port Talbot, Wales	31/12/37
Hopper, Dennis	Dodge City, Kansas	17/5/36
Hordern, Michael	Berkhamsted, Herts	3/10/11
Horne, Lena	Brooklyn, N.Y.	30/6/17
Horovitch, David	London	11/8/45
Hoskins, Bob	Bury St Edmunds, Suffolk	26/10/42
Houston, Whitney	E. Orange, N.J.	9/8/63
Howard, Alan	London	5/8/37
Howes, Sally Ann	London, England	20/7/30
Hudd, Roy	Croydon, Surrey	16/5/36
Hughes, Nerys	Rhyl, Clwyd	8/11/41
Hulce, Tom	Whitewater, Wis.	6/12/53
Hull, Rod	Isle of Sheppey, Kent	13/8/35
Humperdinck, Engelbert	Madras, India	3/5/36
Humphries, Barry	Melbourne, Australia	17/2/34
Hunnicutt, Gayle	Texas	6/2/43
Hunter, Holly	Conyers, Ga.	20/3/58
Hunter, Tab	New York, N.Y.	11/7/31
Huppert, Isabelle	Paris, France	16/3/55
Hurt, John	Chesterfield, Derbyshire	22/1/40
Hurt, Mary Beth	Marshalltown, Ia.	26/9/46
Hurt, William	Washington, D.C.	20/3/50
Hussey, Olivia	Buenos Aires, Argentina	17/4/51
Huston, Anjelica	Ireland	8/7/51
Hutton, Betty	Battle Creek, Mich.	26/2/21
Hutton, Lauren	Charleston, S.C.	17/11/43
Hutton, Timothy	Malibu, Cal.	16/8/61
Ian, Janis	New York, N.Y.	7/4/51
Idle, Eric	South Shields, Tyne & Wear	29/3/43
Idol, Billy	London	30/11/55
Ifield, Frank	Australia	30/11/36
Iglesias, Julio	Madrid, Spain	23/9/43
Imrie, Celia	Guildford, Surrey	15/7/52
Irons, Jeremy	Cowes, Isle of Wight	19/9/48
Irving, Amy	Palo Alto, Cal.	10/9/53
Ives, Burl	Hunt Township, Ill.	14/6/09
Ivory, James	Berkeley, Cal.	7/6/28
Jackson, Glenda	Birkenhead, Cheshire	9/5/36
Jackson, Janet	Gary, Ind.	16/5/66
Jackson, Jermaine	Gary, Ind.	11/12/54
Jackson, La Toya	Gary, Ind.	29/5/56
Jackson, Kate	Birmingham, Ala.	29/10/48
Jackson, Michael	Gary, Ind.	29/8/58
Jacobi, Derek	London	22/10/38
Jaffrey, Saeed	Maler Kotla, India	1929
Jagger, Mick	Dartford, Kent	26/7/43
James, Geraldine	Maidenhead, Berks	6/7/50
James, John	Minneapolis, Minn.	18/4/56
James, Polly	Blackburn, Lancs	9/7/41
Jarman, Derek	England	31/1/42
Jarreau, Al	Milwaukee, Wis.	12/3/40
Jarvis, Martin	Cheltenham, Glos	4/8/41

Name	Birthplace	Born
Jason, David	London	2/2/40
Jason-Leigh, Jennifer	Los Angeles, Cal.	1958
Jayston, Michael	Nottingham, Notts	29/10/36
Jefford, Barbara	Plymstock, Devon	26/7/30
Jeffrey, Peter	Bristol, Avon	18/4/29
Jenkins, Megs	Cheshire	21/4/17
Jennings, Waylon	Littlefield, Tex.	15/6/37
Jett, Joan	Philadelphia, Pa.	22/9/60
Jewel, Jimmy	Sheffield, Yorks	4/12/12
Jewison, Norman	Toronto, Ont.	21/7/26
Jhabvala, Ruth Prawer	Cologne, Germany	17/5/27
Joel, Billy	Bronx, N.Y.	9/5/49
John, Elton	Middlesex	25/3/47
Johns, Glynis	Durban, S. Africa	5/10/23
Johns, Stratford	Pietermaritzburg, S. Africa	22/2/25
Johnson, Don	Flatt, Creek, Mo.	15/12/49
Johnson, Richard	Upminster, Essex	30/7/27
Johnson, Van	Newport, R.I.	25/8/16
Jones, Davy	Manchester	30/12/46
Jones, Gemma	London	4/12/42
Jones, Grace	Spanishtown, Jamaica	19/5/52
Jones, Jack	Hollywood, Cal.	14/1/38
Jones, James Earl	Tate Co., Miss.	17/1/31
Jones, Jennifer	Tulsa, Okla.	2/3/19
Jones, Paul	Portsmouth, Hants	24/2/42
Jones, Peter	Wem, Shropshire	12/6/20
Jones, Terry	Colwyn Bay, Clwyd	1/2/42
Jones, Tom	Pontypridd, Mid Glam.	7/6/40
Jones, Tommy Lee	San Saba, Tex.	15/9/46
Jourdan, Louis	Marseilles, France	19/6/19
Julia, Raul	San Juan, P.R.	9/3/40
Kahn, Madeline	Boston, Mass.	29/9/42
Kanaly, Steve	Burbank, Cal.	14/3/46
Kapoor, Shashi	Calcutta, India	18/3/38
Karlin, Miriam	Hampstead, London	23/6/25
Kavner, Julie	Los Angeles, Cal.	7/9/51
Kaye, Stubby	New York, N.Y.	11/11/18
Kazan, Elia	Istanbul, Turkey	7/9/09
Keach, Stacy	Savannah, Ga.	2/6/41
Keaton, Diane	Santa Ana, Cal.	5/1/46
Keaton, Michael	Pittsburgh, Pa.	9/9/51
Keel, Howard	Gillespie, Ill.	13/4/17
Keen, Diane	London	29/7/46
Keith, Penelope	Sutton, Surrey	2/4/40
Keitel, Harvey	Brooklyn, N.Y.	1947
Kellerman, Sally	Long Beach, Cal.	2/6/37
Kelley, DeForesw	Atlanta, Ga.	20/1/20
Kelly, Gene	Pittsburgh, Pa.	23/8/12
Kelly, Matthew	Urmston, Manchester	9/5/50
Kempson, Rachel	Dartmouth, Devon	28/5/10
Kendal, Felicity	Olton, Warks	25/9/46
Kennedy, Cheryl	Enfield, Middx	29/4/47
Kensit, Patsy	London	4/3/68
Kent, Jean	London	29/6/21
Kenwright, Bill	Liverpool	4/9/45
Kercheval, Ken	Wolcottville, Ind.	15/7/35
Kerr, Deborah	Helensburgh, Scotland	30/9/21
Kestelman, Sara	London	12/5/44
Khan, Chaka	Great Lakes, Ill.	23/3/53
Kidder, Margot	Yellowknife, N.W.T.	17/10/48
Kidman, Nicole	Hawaii	1977
Kilmer, Val	Los Angeles, Cal.	31/12/59
King, B. B.	Itta Bena, Miss.	16/9/25
King, Carole	Brooklyn, N.Y.	9/2/42
Kingsley, Ben	Snaiton, Yorkshire	31/12/43
Kinski, Nastassia	Berlin, W. Germany	24/1/60
Kirkbride, Anne	Oldham, Lancs	21/6/54
Kirkland, Gelsey	Bethlehem, Pa.	29/12/53
Kirkwood, Patricia	Pendleton, Lancs	24/2/21
Kitchen, Michael	Leicester	31/10/48
Kitt, Eartha	North, S.C.	26/1/28
Kline, Kevin	St. Louis, Mo.	24/10/47
Klugman, Jack	Philadelphia, Pa.	27/4/22
Knight, Gladys	Atlanta, Ga.	28/5/44
Knopfler, Mark	Glasgow, Scotland	12/8/49
Kossoff, David	London	24/11/19
Kotto, Yaphet	New York, N.Y.	15/11/37
Kramer, Billy J.	Liverpool	19/8/43
Kristofferson, Kris	Brownsville, Tex.	22/6/36
Kubrick, Stanley	Bronx, N.Y.	26/7/28
Kurtz, Swoosie	Omaha, Neb.	6/9/44
Kurosawa, Akira	Tokyo, Japan	23/3/10
LaBelle, Patti	Philadelphia, Pa.	4/10/44
Ladd, Cheryl	Huron, S.D.	12/7/51
Ladd, Diane	Meridian, Miss.	29/11/32

Name	Birthplace	Born
Laine, Cleo	Middlesex	28/10/27
Laine, Frankie	Chicago, Ill.	30/3/13
Lamarr, Hedy	Vienna, Austria	9/11/13
Lamour, Dorothy	New Orleans, La.	10/12/14
Lancaster, Burt	New York, N.Y.	2/11/13
Landen, Dinsdale	Margate, Kent	4/9/32
Landau, Martin	New York, N.Y.	20/6/34
Landis, John	Chicago, Ill.	3/8/50
Lang, Belinda	London	23/12/55
Lange, Hope	Redding Ridge, Conn.	28/11/31
Lange, Jessica	Cloquet, Minn.	20/4/49
Langella, Frank	Bayonne, N.J.	1/1/40
Langford, Bonnie	Hampton Court, Surrey	22/7/64
Lansbury, Angela	London	16/10/25
Lapotaire, Jane	Ipswich, Suffolk	26/12/44
Large, Eddie	Glasgow, Scotland	25/6/42
La Rue, Danny	Cork, Ireland	26/7/27
Lauper, Cyndi	New York, N.Y.	20/6/53
Laurie, Hugh	England	11/6/59
Laurie, Piper	Detroit, Mich.	22/1/32
Lawrence, Steve	Brooklyn, N.Y.	8/7/35
Lawson, Denis	Scotland	27/9/47
Lawson, Leigh	Atherstone, Warks	21/7/43
Laye, Evelyn	London	10/7/1900
Leach, Rosemary	Much Wenlock, Shropshire	18/12/35
Leachman, Cloris	Des Moines, Ia.	4/4/26
LeBon, Simon	Bushey, Herts.	27/10/58
Lee, Brenda	Atlanta, Ga.	11/12/44
Lee, Christopher	London	27/5/22
Lee, Peggy	Jamestown, N.D.	26/5/20
Lee, Spike	Atlanta, Ga.	20/3/57
Legrand, Michel	Paris, France	24/2/32
Leigh, Janet	Merced, Cal.	6/7/27
Leigh, Jennifer Jason	Los Angeles, Cal.	5/2/62
Leigh, Mike	Salford, Lancs	20/2/43
Leigh-Hunt, Barbara	Bath, Avon	14/12/35
Lemmon, Jack	Boston, Mass.	8/2/25
Lennon, Julian	London	8/4/63
Lenska, Rula	St Neots, Hunts	30/9/47
Lewis, Huey	New York, N.Y.	5/7/51
Lewis, Jerry	Newark, N.J.	16/3/26
Lewis, Jerry Lee	Ferriday, La.	29/9/35
Lewis, Shari	New York, N.Y.	17/1/34
Lightfoot, Gordon	Orillia, Ont.	17/11/38
Linden, Jennie	Worthing, W. Sussex	8/12/39
Lindfors, Viveca	Uppsala, Sweden	29/12/20
Lindsay, Robert	Ilkeston, Derbyshire	13/12/49
Lipman, Maureen	Hull, Humberside	10/5/46
Lister, Moira	Cape Town, S. Africa	6/8/23
Little, Rich	Ottawa, Ont.	26/11/38
Little Richard	Macon, Ga.	5/12/32
Little, Syd	Blackpool, Lancs	19/12/42
Lloyd, Emily	London	29/9/70
Lloyd Pack, Roger	London	2/8/44
Locke, Sondra	Shelbyville, Tenn.	28/5/47
Lockhart, June	New York, N.Y.	25/6/25
Locklear, Heather	Los Angeles, Cal.	25/9/61
Loe, Judy	Urmston, Manchester	6/3/47
Logan, Phyllis	Paisley, Scotland	11/1/56
Loggins, Kenny	Everett, Wash.	17/1/47
Lollobrigida, Gina	Subiaco, Italy	4/7/27
Lom, Herbert	Prague, Czechoslovakia	9/1/17
Long, Shelley	Ft. Wayne, Ind.	23/8/49
Longthorne, Joe	Hull, Humberside	31/5/57
Lord, Jack	New York, N.Y.	30/12/22
Loren, Sophia	Rome, Italy	20/9/34
Lott, Felicity	Cheltenham, Glos	1947
Lowe, Rob	Charlottesville, Va.	17/3/64
Loy, Myrna	Helena, Mon.	2/8/05
Lucas, George	Modesto, Cal.	14/5/44
Lulu	Glasgow, Scotland	3/11/48
Lumet, Sidney	Philadelphia, Pa.	25/6/24
Lumley, Joanna	Srinagar, India	1/5/46
Lundgren, Dolph	Stockholm, Sweden	1959
Lunghi, Cherie	London	1953
Lupino, Ida	London	4/2/14
Lynch, David	Missoula, Mont.	20/1/46
Lyndhurst, Nicholas	Emsworth, Hants	21/4/61
Lyne, Adrian	England	1941
Lynn, Gillian	Bromley, Kent	20/2/26
Lynn, Loretta	Butcher Hollow, Ky.	14/4/–
Lynn, Dame Vera	London	20/3/17
Lyttleton, Humphrey	Eton, Berks	23/5/21
Maazel, Lorin	Paris, France	6/3/30
MacCorkindale, Simon	Ely, Cambs.	12/2/52
MacDowell, Andie	Gaffney, S.C.	21/4/58
MacGraw, Ali	Pound Ridge, N.Y.	1/4/38
Mackintosh, Cameron	Enfield, Middlesex	17/10/46
MacLachlan, Kyle	Yakima, Wash.	22/2/59
MacLaine, Shirley	Richmond, Va.	24/4/34
MacNee, Patrick	London	6/2/22
Madoc, Ruth	Norwich, Norfolk	16/4/43
Madonna (Ciccone)	Bay City, Mich.	16/8/58
Majors, Lee	Wyandotte, Mich.	23/4/40
Malahide, Patrick	Berkshire	24/3/45
Malden, Karl	Chicago, Ill.	22/3/13
Malik, Art	Bahawalpur, Pakistan	13/11/52
Malkovich, John	Christopher, Ill.	9/12/53
Malle, Louis	Thumeries, France	30/10/32
Malone, Dorothy	Chicago, Ill.	30/1/25
Mamet, David	Chicago, Ill.	30/11/47
Mancini, Henry	Cleveland, Oh.	16/4/24
Manilow, Barry	New York, N.Y.	17/6/46
Mankowitz, Wolf	London	7/11/24
Mantegna, Joe	Chicago, Ill.	13/11/47
Marceau, Marcel	Strasbourg, France	22/3/23
Margolyes, Miriam	Oxford	18/5/41
Marin, Cheech	Los Angeles, Cal.	13/7/46
Markova, Alicia	London	1/12/10
Marks, Alfred	Holborn, London	28/1/21
Marriner, Neville	Lincoln	15/4/24
Marsh, Jean	London	1/7/34
Marsalis, Wynton	New Orleans, La.	18/10/61
Marsden, Roy	London	25/6/41
Marshall, E.G.	Owatonna, Minn.	18/6/10
Marshall, Penny	Bronx, N.Y.	15/10/43
Martin, Dean	Steubenville, Oh.	17/6/17
Martin, George	London	3/1/26
Martin, Millicent	Romford, Essex	8/6/34
Martin, Steve	Waco, Tex.	14/4/45
Mason, Jackie	Sheboygan, Wis.	9/6/31
Mason, Marsha	St Louis, Mo.	3/4/42
Massey, Anna	Thakeham, Sussex	11/8/37
Massey, Daniel	London	10/10/33
Mastrantonio, Mary Eliz.	Lombard, Ill.	17/11/58
Mastroianni, Marcello	Rome, Italy	28/9/23
Mathis, Johnny	San Francisco, Cal.	30/9/35
Matthau, Walter	New York, N.Y.	1/10/20
Matthews, Francis	York, Yorks	2/9/27
Mature, Victor	Louisville, Ky.	29/1/16
Maughan, Sharon	Liverpool	22/6/51
May, Elaine	Philadelphia, Pa.	21/4/32
Mayall, Rick	Harlow, Essex	7/3/58
Mayfield, Curtis	Chicago, Ill.	3/6/42
Mayo, Virginia	St Louis, Mo.	30/11/20
McCallum, David	Glasgow, Scotland	19/9/33
McCambridge, Mercedes	Joliet, Ill.	17/3/18
McCartney, Paul	Liverpool	18/6/42
McClanahan, Rue	Healdton, Okla.	21/2/36
McClure, Doug	Glendale, Cal.	11/5/35
McCowan, Alec	Tunbridge Wells, Kent	26/5/25
McDowall, Roddy	London	28/9/28
McDowell, Malcolm	Leeds, Yorks	13/6/43
McEnery, Peter	Walsall, W. Midlands	21/2/40
McEwan, Geraldine	Old Windsor, Berks	9/5/32
McGee, Henry	London	14/5/29
McGillis, Kelly	Newport, Cal.	1957
McGoohan, Patrick	New York, N.Y.	19/3/28
McGuire, Dorothy	Omaha, Neb.	14/6/19
McKellen, Ian	Burnley, Lancs	25/5/39
McKellar, Kenneth	Scotland	23/6/27
McKenna, T.P.	Mullagh, Co. Cavan	7/9/29
McKenna, Virginia	London	7/6/31
McKenzie, Julia	Enfield, Middx	17/2/41
McKern, Leo	Sydney, Australia	16/3/20
McLean, Don	New Rochelle, N.Y.	2/10/45
McManus, Mark	Hamilton, Lanarks	1940
McQueen, Butterfly	Tampa, Fla.	7/1/11
McShane, Ian	Blackburn, Lancs	29/9/42
McTeer, Janet	Newcastle, Tyne & Wear	8/8/61
Mehta, Zubin	Bombay, India	29/4/36
Melanie	New York, N.Y.	3/2/47
Mendes, Sergio	Niteroi, Brazil	11/2/41
Menges, Chris	Herefordshire	1941
Menuhin, Yehudi	New York, N.Y.	22/4/16
Merchant, Ismail	Bombay, India	25/12/36
Mercouri, Melina	Athens, Greece	18/10/25
Meredith, Burgess	Cleveland, Oh.	16/11/08
Metcalf, Laurie	Carbondale, Ill.	16/6/55
Michael, George	Watford, Herts	26/6/63
Michell, Keith	Adelaide, Australia	1/12/28
Middlemass, Frank	England	28/5/19

Name	Birthplace	Born
Midler, Bette	Paterson, N.J.	1/12/45
Miles, Sarah	Ingatestone, Essex	31/12/41
Miles, Vera	near Boise City, Okla.	23/8/29
Miller, Ann	Houston, Tex.	12/4/19
Miller, Jonathan	London	21/7/34
Miller, Mitch	Rochester, N.Y.	4/7/11
Milligan, Spike	India	16/4/18
Mills, Donna	Chicago, Ill.	11/12/42
Mills, Hayley	London	18/4/46
Mills, John	Nr. Elmham, Norfolk	22/2/08
Mills, Juliet	London	21/11/41
Milsap, Ronnie	Robinsville, N.C.	16/1/44
Minnelli, Liza	Los Angeles, Cal.	12/3/46
Miou-Miou	Paris, France	22/1/50
Mirren, Helen	Southend, Essex	1946
Mitchell, Joni	McLeod, Alta.	7/11/43
Mitchell, Warren	London	1926
Mitchum, Robert	Bridgeport, Conn.	6/8/17
Molina, Alfred	London	24/5/53
Monkhouse, Bob	Beckenham, Kent	1/6/28
Montalban, Ricardo	Mexico City, Mexico	25/11/20
Montgomery, Elizabeth	Hollywood, Cal.	15/4/33
Moody, Ron	London	8/1/24
Moore, Demi	Roswell, N.M.	11/11/62
Moore, Dudley	London	19/4/35
Moore, Mary Tyler	Brooklyn, N.Y.	29/12/37
Moore, Melba	New York, N.Y.	29/10/45
Moore, Roger	London	14/10/27
Moore, Stephen	London	11/12/37
Moreau, Jeanne	Paris, France	23/1/28
Moreno, Rita	Humacao, P.R.	11/12/31
Moricone, Ennio	Rome, Italy	10/11/28
Morrison, Van	Belfast, N. Ireland	31/8/45
Mount, Peggy	Southend-on-Sea, Essex	2/5/16
Mulligan, Richard	New York, N.Y.	13/11/32
Murphy, Brian	Ventnor, Isle of Wight	25/9/39
Murphy, Eddie	Brooklyn, N.Y.	3/4/61
Murphy, Michael	Los Angeles, Cal.	5/5/38
Murray, Barbara	London	27/9/29
Murray, Bill	Evanston, Ill.	21/9/50
Muti, Riccardo	Naples, Italy	28/7/41
Nash, Graham	Blackpool, Lancs	2/2/42
Neal, Patricia	Packard, Ky.	20/1/26
Neeson, Liam	Ballymeena, N. Ireland	1952
Neill, Sam	New Zealand	1948
Nelligan, Kate	London, Ontario	16/3/51
Nelson, Judd	Portland, Me.	28/11/59
Nelson, Willie	Abbott, Tex.	30/4/33
Nero, Franco	Italy	1941
Nettles, John	St Austell, Cornwall	1948
Newman, Nanette	Northampton, Northants	29/5/39
Neuwirth, Bebe	Newark, N.J.	31/12/56
New Kids on the Block		
Knight, Jonathan	Worcester, Mass.	29/11/68
Knight, Jordan	Worcester, Mass.	17/5/70
McIntyre, Joe	Needham, Mass.	31/12/72
Wahlberg, Donnie	Boston, Mass.	17/8/69
Wood, Danny	Boston, Mass.	14/5/69
Newhart, Bob	Oak Park, Ill.	29/9/29
Newley, Anthony	Hackney, London	24/9/31
Newman, Paul	Cleveland, Oh.	26/1/25
Newton, Wayne	Norfolk, Va.	3/4/42
Newton-John, Olivia	Cambridge	26/9/47
Nicholas, Paul	Peterborough, Cambs	3/12/45
Nichols, Mike	Berlin, Germany	6/11/31
Nicholson, Jack	Neptune, N.J.	28/4/37
Nicks, Stevie	Phoenix, Ariz.	26/5/48
Nielsen, Leslie	Regina, Sask.	11/2/26
Nilsson, Birgit	Karup, Sweden	17/5/18
Nimmo, Derek	Liverpool	19/9/32
Nimoy, Leonard	Boston, Mass.	26/3/31
Nolte, Nick	Omaha, Neb.	8/2/40
Norman, Jessye	Augusta, Ga.	15/9/45
Novak, Kim	Chicago, Ill.	13/2/33
Nunn, Trevor	Ipswich, Suffolk	14/1/40
Oates, John	New York, N.Y.	7/4/48
O'Brien, Margaret	San Diego, Cal.	15/1/37
Ocean, Billy	Trinidad	21/1/50
O'Connor, Des	Stepney, London	12/1/32
O'Connor, Donald	Chicago, Ill.	28/8/25
O'Connor, Sinéad	Dublin, Ireland	8/12/67
O'Connor, Tom	Bootle, Lancs	31/10/39
Oddie, Bill	Rochdale, Lancs	7/7/41
O'Hara, Maureen	Dublin, Ireland	17/8/20
O'Herlihy, Dan	Wexford, Ireland	1/5/19
Oldman, Gary	London	21/3/58

Name	Birthplace	Born
Olin, Ken	Chicago, Ill.	30/7/54
O'Mara, Kate	Leicester	10/8/39
O'Neal, Ryan	Los Angeles, Cal.	20/4/41
O'Neal, Tatum	Los Angeles, Cal.	5/11/63
Ophuls, Marcel	Frankfurt, Germany	1/11/27
Orlando, Tony	New York, N.Y.	3/4/44
Osbourne, Ozzy	Birmingham, W. Midlands	3/12/46
O'Shea, Milo	Dublin, Ireland	2/6/26
Osmond, Donny	Ogden, Ut.	9/12/57
Osmond, Marie	Ogden, Ut.	13/10/59
O'Sullivan, Maureen	Boyle, Ireland	17/5/11
O'Sullivan, Richard	Chiswick, London	7/5/44
O'Toole, Peter	Connemara, Ireland	2/8/32
Owen, Alun	Liverpool	24/11/25
Owen, Bill	Acton Green, London	14/3/14
Pace, Norman	Dudley, Worcs	17/2/53
Pacino, Al	New York, N.Y.	25/4/40
Page, Patti	Claremore, Okla	8/11/27
Pagett, Nicola	Cairo, Egypt	15/5/45
Paige, Janis	Tacoma, Wash.	16/9/22
Pakula, Alan J.	New York, N.Y.	7/4/28
Palance, Jack	Lattimer, Pa.	18/2/20
Palin, Michael	Suffolk	5/5/43
Palmer, Geoffrey	London	6/4/27
Papas, Irene	Greece	9/3/26
Parfitt, Judy	Sheffield, Yorks	7/11/—
Parker, Alan	London	14/2/44
Parker, Eleanor	Cedarville, Oh.	26/6/22
Parsons, Estelle	Lynn, Mass.	20/11/27
Parton, Dolly	Sevierville, Tenn.	19/1/46
Pasco, Richard	London	18/7/26
Patinkin, Mandy	Chicago, Ill.	30/11/52
Pavarotti, Luciano	Modena, Italy	12/10/35
Peck, Gregory	La Jolla, Cal.	5/4/16
Peck, Bob	Leeds, Yorks	23/8/45
Pendergrass, Teddy	Philadelphia, Pa.	26/3/50
Penhaligon, Susan	Manila, Philippines	3/7/49
Penn, Sean	Burbank, Cal.	17/8/60
Peppard, George	Detroit, Mich.	1/10/28
Perlman, Itzhak	Tel Aviv, Israel	31/8/45
Perlman, Rhea	Brooklyn, N.Y.	31/3/48
Perrine, Valerie	Galveston, Tex.	3/9/43
Pertwee, Bill	Amersham, Bucks	21/7/26
Pertwee, Jon	London	7/7/19
Pesci, Joe	Newark, N.J.	9/2/43
Peters, Bernadette	New York, N.Y.	28/2/48
Petherbridge, Edward	Bradford, Yorks	3/8/36
Petty, Tom	Gainesville, Fla.	20/10/53
Pfeiffer, Michelle	Santa Ana, Cal.	29/4/57
Phillips, Arlene	London	22/5/43
Phillips, Leslie	London	20/4/24
Phillips, Michelle	Long Beach, Cal.	4/6/44
Phillips, Sian	Bettws, Gwent	14/5/34
Pickup, Ronald	Chester, Cheshire	7/6/40
Pigott-Smith, Tim	Rugby, Warks	13/5/46
Pitt, Brad	Missouri	18/12/65
Phoenix, River	Madras, Ore.	23/8/70
Planer, Nigel	London	22/2/55
Pleasence, Donald	Worksop, Notts	5/10/19
Pleshette, Suzanne	New York, N.Y.	31/1/37
Plowright, Joan	Scunthorpe, Lincs	28/10/29
Plummer, Christopher	Toronto, Ont.	13/12/27
Poitier, Sidney	Miami, Fla.	20/2/27
Polanski, Roman	Paris, France	18/8/33
Pollard, Su	Nottingham, Notts	8/11/49
Ponti, Carlo	Milan, Italy	11/12/13
Porter, Eric	London	8/4/28
Powell, Robert	Salford, Lancs	1/6/44
Powers, Stefanie	Hollywood, Cal.	2/11/42
Praed, Michael	Gloucester, Glos	1/4/60
Prentiss, Paula	San Antonio, Tex	4/3/39
Presley, Priscilla	New York, N.Y.	24/5/45
Preston, Billy	Houston, Tex.	9/9/46
Previn, André	Berlin, Germany	6/4/29
Price, Leontyne	Laurel, Miss.	10/2/27
Pride, Charlie	Sledge, Miss.	18/3/39
Prince	Minneapolis, Minn.	7/6/58
Principal, Victoria	Japan	3/1/50
Pringle, Bryan	Glascote, Staffs	19/1/35
Protheroe, Brian	Salisbury, Wilts	16/5/44
Prowse, Juliet	Bombay, India	25/9/37
Pryce, Jonathan	Holywell, Clwyd	1/6/47
Pryor, Richard	Peoria, Ill.	1/12/40
Quaid, Dennis	Houston, Tex.	9/4/54
Quaid, Randy	Houston, Tex.	1/10/50

Name	Birthplace	Born
Quayle, Anna	Birmingham, W. Midlands	6/10/37
Quick, Diana	Kent	23/11/46
Quilley, Denis	London	26/12/27
Quinn, Anthony	Chihuahua, Mexico	21/4/15
Quirke, Pauline	London	8/7/59
Rachins, Alan	Cambridge, Mass.	10/10/47
Rafelson, Bob	New York, N.Y.	1933
Raffin, Deborah	Los Angeles	13/3/53
Raitt, Bonnie	Burbank, Cal.	8/11/49
Rambo, Dack	Delano, Cal.	13/11/41
Rampling, Charlotte	Sturmer, Essex	5/2/46
Rawls, Lou	Chicago, Ill.	1/12/36
Reddy, Helen	Melbourne, Australia	25/10/41
Redford, Robert	Santa Monica, Cal.	18/8/37
Redgrave, Lynn	London	8/3/43
Redgrave, Vanessa	London	30/1/37
Reed, Oliver	London	13/2/38
Rees, Angharad	Wales	1949
Rees, Roger	Aberystwyth, Dyfed	5/5/44
Reeve, Christopher	New York, N.Y.	25/9/52
Reeves, Keanu	Beirut, Lebanon	2/9/64
Reid, Beryl	Hereford	17/6/20
Reiner, Rob	Bronx, N.Y.	6/3/45
Reynolds, Burt	Waycross, Ga.	11/2/36
Reynolds, Debbie	El Paso, Tex.	1/4/32
Rhys-Jones, Griff	Cardiff, S. Glam.	16/11/53
Rich, Charlie	Forest City, Ark.	14/12/32
Richard, Cliff	Lucknow, India	14/10/40
Richard, Wendy	Middlesborough, Cleveland	20/7/46
Richards, Keith	Kent	18/12/43
Richardson, Joely	London	9/1/65
Richardson, Miranda	Lancs	3/3/58
Richardson, Natasha	London	11/5/63
Richie, Lionel	Tuskegee, Ala.	20/6/50
Rickman, Alan	London	1946
Riegert, Peter	New York, N.Y.	11/4/47
Rigg, Diana	Doncaster, S. Yorks	20/7/38
Ringwald, Molly	Rosewood, Cal.	14/2/68
Ritt, Martin	New York, N.Y.	2/3/20
Rivera, Chita	Washington, D.C.	23/1/33
Rivers, Joan	Brooklyn, N.Y.	8/6/37
Rix, Brian	Cottingham, Yorks	27/1/24
Roache, William	Ilkeston, Derbyshire	25/4/32
Robards, Jason Jr.	Chicago, Ill.	26/7/22
Roberts, Julia	Smyrna, Ga.	1/4/67
Robinson, Smokey	Detroit, Mich.	19/2/40
Robinson, Tony	London	15/8/46
Rodgers, Anton	Wisbech, Cambs	10/1/33
Roeg, Nicolas	London	15/8/28
Rogers, Ginger	Independence, Mo.	16/7/11
Rogers, Kenny	Houston, Tex.	21/8/38
Rogers, Mimi	Coral Gables, Fla.	27/1/57
Rogers, Roy	Cincinnati, Oh.	5/11/12
Rogers, Ted	Kennington, London	20/7/35
Romero, Cesar	New York, N.Y.	15/2/07
Ronstadt, Linda	Tucson, Ariz.	15/7/46
Rooney, Mickey	Brooklyn, N.Y.	23/9/20
Ross, Annie	Mitcham, Surrey	25/7/30
Ross, Diana	Detroit, Mich.	26/3/44
Ross, Katharine	Hollywood, Cal.	29/1/42
Rossellini, Isabella	Rome, Italy	18/6/52
Rostropovich, Mstislav	Baku, USSR	12/3/27
Rourke, Mickey	Miami, Fla.	1956
Routledge, Patricia	Birkenhead, Cheshire	17/2/29
Rowlands, Gena	Cambria, Wis.	19/6/34
Rushton, Willie	London	18/8/37
Russell, Jane	Bemidji, Minn.	21/6/21
Russell, Ken	Southampton, Hants	3/7/27
Russell, Kurt	Springfield, Mass.	17/3/51
Russell, Theresa	San Diego, Cal.	20/3/57
Ruttan, Susan	Oregon City, Ore.	16/9/50
Ryan, Meg	Fairfield, Conn.	19/11/63
Rydell, Bobby	Philadelphia, Pa.	26/4/42
Ryder, Winona	Winona, Minn.	1971
Sachs, Andrew	Berlin, Germany	7/4/30
Saint, Eve Marie	Newark, N.J.	4/7/24
Sainte-Marie, Buffy	Maine	20/2/41
Sallis, Peter	Twickenham, Middx	1/2/21
Samms, Emma	London	28/8/60
Sarandon, Susan	New York, N.Y.	4/10/46
Sarrazin, Michael	Quebec City, Que.	22/5/40
Saunders, Jennifer	Sleaford, Lincs	12/7/58
Savalas, Telly	Garden City, N.Y.	21/1/24
Sayle, Alexei	Liverpool	7/8/52
Sayles, John	Schenectady, N.Y.	28/9/50
Scaggs, Boz	Dallas, Tex.	8/6/44
Scales, Prunella	Sutton, Surrey	22/6/32
Scheider, Roy	Orange, N.J.	10/11/32
Schell, Maria	Vienna, Austria	5/1/26
Schell, Maximilian	Vienna, Austria	8/12/30
Schlesinger, John	London	16/2/26
Schloendorff, Volker	Wiesbaden, Germany	31/3/39
Schwarzenegger, Arnold	Graz, Austria	30/7/47
Schwarzkopf, Elisabeth	Jarotschin, Poland	9/12/15
Scofield, Paul	Hurstpierpoint, Surrey	21/1/22
Scorsese, Martin	New York, N.Y.	17/11/42
Scott, George C.	Wise, VA.	18/10/27
Scott, Lizabeth	Scranton, Pa.	29/9/22
Scott, Ridley	South Shields, Tyne & Wear	1939
Scott, Terry	Watford, Herts	4/5/27
Seagal, Steven	Lansing, Mich.	10/4/51
Seagrove, Jenny	Kuala Lumpur, Malaysia	4/7/57
Seal, Elizabeth	Genoa, Italy	28/8/33
Sebastian, John	New York, N.Y.	17/3/44
Secombe, Harry	Swansea, Glam.	8/9/21
Sedaka, Neil	New York, N.Y.	13/3/39
Seeger, Pete	New York, N.Y.	3/5/19
Segal, George	Great Neck, N.Y.	13/2/34
Selleck, Tom	Detroit, Mich.	29/1/45
Sessions, John	Scotland	11/1/53
Seymour, Jane	Middlesex	15/2/51
Shandling, Garry	Tuscon, Ariz.	29/11/49
Shane, Paul	Rotherham, S. Yorks	19/6/40
Shankar, Ravi	India	7/4/20
Sharif, Omar	Alexandria, Egypt	10/4/32
Shatner, William	Montreal, Que.	22/3/31
Shaw, Fiona	Cork, Ireland	1955
Shaw, Martin	Birmingham, W. Midlands	21/1/45
Shaw, Sandie	London	26/2/47
Shearer, Moira	Scotland	17/1/26
Sheedy, Ally	New York, N.Y.	12/6/62
Sheen, Charlie	Santa Monica, Cal.	3/9/65
Sheen, Martin	Dayton, Oh.	3/8/40
Shepard, Sam	Ft. Sheridan, Ill.	5/11/43
Shepherd, Cybill	Memphis, Tenn.	18/2/49
Shepherd, Jack	Leeds, Yorks	29/10/40
Sheridan, Dinah	Hampstead Garden Suburb	17/9/20
Sherrin, Ned	Low Ham, Somerset	18/2/31
Shields, Brooke	New York, N.Y.	31/5/65
Shire, Talia	New York, N.Y.	25/4/46
Shore, Dinah	Winchester, Tenn.	1/3/17
Siegel, Don	Chicago, Ill.	26/10/12
Sills, Beverly	Brooklyn, N.Y.	25/5/29
Silvera, Carmen	Toronto, Canada	2/6/38
Simmons, Jean	London	31/1/29
Simon, Carly	New York, N.Y.	25/6/45
Simon, Paul	Newark, N.J.	5/11/42
Simone, Nina	Tyron, N.C.	21/2/33
Sims, Joan	Laindon, Essex	9/5/30
Sinatra, Frank	Hoboken, N.J.	12/12/15
Sinden, Donald	Plymouth, Devon	9/10/23
Sinden, Jeremy	London	14/6/50
Skelton, Red (Richard)	Vincennes, Ind.	18/7/13
Slater, Christian	New York, N.Y.	19/8/69
Smith, Jaclyn	Houston, Tex.	26/10/47
Smith, Liz	Scunthorpe, Lincs	11/12/25
Smith, Maggie	Ilford, Essex	28/12/34
Smith, Mel	London	3/12/52
Smits, Jimmy	New York, N.Y.	9/7/55
Smothers, Dick	New York, N.Y.	20/11/39
Smothers, Tom	New York, N.Y.	2/2/37
Solti, Georg	Budapest, Hungary	21/10/12
Somers, Suzanne	San Bruno, Cal.	16/10/46
Sommer, Elke	Berlin, Germany	5/11/41
Sothern, Anne	Valley City, N.D.	22/1/09
Soul, David	Chicago, Ill.	28/8/43
Spacek, Sissy	Quitman, Tex.	25/12/49
Spelling, Aaron	Dallas, Tex.	22/4/28
Spielberg, Steven	Cincinnati, Oh.	18/12/47
Spinetti, Victor	Cwm, Monmouth	2/9/33
Spriggs, Elizabeth	Buxton, Derbyshire	18/9/29
Springfield, Dusty	London	16/4/39
Springsteen, Bruce	Freehold, N.J.	23/9/49
Stack, Robert	Los Angeles, Cal.	13/1/19
Staff, Kathy	Dakinfield, Cheshire	12/7/28
Stafford-Clark, Max	Cambridge	17/3/41
Stallone, Sylvester	New York, N.Y.	6/7/46
Stamp, Terence	Stepney, London	22/7/39

Name	Birthplace	Born
Standing, John	London	16/8/34
Stanton, Harry Dean	Kentucky	14/7/46
Stapleton, Jean	New York, N.Y.	19/1/23
Stapleton, Maureen	Troy, N.Y.	21/6/25
Starr, Ringo	Liverpool	7/7/40
Steadman, Alison	Liverpool	26/8/46
Steafel, Sheila	S. Africa	26/5/35
Steele, Tommy	Bermondsey, London	17/12/36
Steenburgen, Mary	Newport, Ariz.	8/2/53
Steiger, Rod	W. Hampton, N.Y.	14/4/25
Stephens, Robert	Bristol, Avon	14/7/31
Stephenson, Pamela	Australia	4/12/50
Stern, Isaac	Kreminiecz, Russia	21/7/20
Stevens, Cat	London	21/7/48
Stevens, Connie	Brooklyn, N.Y.	8/8/38
Stewart, James	Indiana, Pa.	20/5/08
Stewart, Patrick	Mirfield, Yorks	13/7/40
Stewart, Rod	London	10/1/45
Stilgoe, Richard	Camberley, Surrey	28/3/43
Stills, Stephen	Dallas, Tex.	3/1/45
Sting (G. Sumner)	Newcastle, Tyne & Wear	2/10/51
St. James, Susan	Los Angeles, Cal.	14/8/46
St. John, Jill	Los Angeles, Cal.	19/8/40
Stockwell, Dean	Hollywood, Cal.	5/3/36
Stoltz, Eric	American Samoa	1961
Stone, Oliver	New York, N.Y.	15/9/46
Stone, Sharon	Meadville, Pa.	1958
Streep, Meryl	Summit, N.Y.	22/6/49
Streisand, Barbra	Brooklyn, N.Y.	24/4/42
Stride, John	London	11/7/36
Stritch, Elaine	Detroit, Mich.	2/2/26
Stubbs, Imogen	Rothbury, Northumberland	20/2/61
Stubbs, Una	London	1/5/37
Styne, Jule	London	31/12/05
Summer, Donna	Boston, Mass.	31/12/48
Sutherland, Donald	St. John, New Brunswick	17/7/34
Sutherland, Joan	Sydney, Australia	7/11/26
Sutherland, Keifer	London	20/12/66
Suchet, David	London	2/5/46
Sugden, Mollie	Keighley, Yorks	21/7/22
Suzman, Janet	Johannesburg, S. Africa	9/2/39
Swayze, Patrick	Houston, Tex.	18/8/54
Swift, Clive	Liverpool	9/2/36
Swit, Loretta	Passaic, N.J.	4/11/37
Sykes, Eric	Oldham, Lancs	1924
Syms, Sylvia	London	1934
Szabo, Istvan	Budapest, Hungary	18/2/38
Mr. T (Lawrence Tero)	Chicago, Ill.	21/5/52
Tandy, Jessica	London, England	7/6/09
Tarbuck, Jimmy	Liverpool	6/2/40
Tavernier, Bertrand	Lyons, France	25/4/41
Taylor, Elizabeth	London	27/2/32
Taylor, James	Boston, Mass.	12/3/48
Taylor, Rod	Sydney, Australia	11/1/29
Te Kanawa, Kiri	Gisborne, New Zealand	6/3/44
Temple, Shirley	Santa Monica, Cal.	23/4/28
Tennant, Victoria	London	30/9/50
Tewson, Josephine	Hampstead, London	26/2/41
Tharp, Twyla	Portland, Ind.	1/7/41
Thaw, John	Manchester	3/1/42
Theodorakis, Mikis	Athens, Greece	1925
Thompson, Emma	London	15/4/59
Thorne, Angela	Karachi, India	25/1/39
Threlfall, David	Manchester	3/1/53
Tiegs, Cheryl	Minnesota	27/9/47
Timothy, Christopher	Bala, Gwynedd	14/10/40
Tiny Tim	New York, N.Y.	12/4/23
Tomlin, Lily	Detroit, Mich.	1/9/39
Tomlinson, David	Henley-on-Thames, Oxon	7/5/17
Toomey, Regis	Pittsburgh, Pa.	13/8/02
Topol	Tel Aviv, Israel	9/9/35
Torme, Mel	Chicago, Ill.	13/9/25
Torn, Rip	Temple, Tex.	6/2/31
Townshend, Pete	London	19/5/45
Toye, Wendy	London	1/5/17
Travanti, Daniel J.	Kenosha, Wis.	7/3/40
Travis, Randy	Marshville, N.C.	4/5/59
Travolta, John	Englewood, N.J.	18/2/54
Trintignant, Jean Louis	France	11/12/30
Tucker, Michael	Baltimore, Md.	6/2/44
Tune, Tommy	Wichita Falls, Tex.	28/2/39
Turner, Kathleen	Springfield, Mo.	19/6/54
Turner, Lana	Wallace, Ida.	8/2/20
Turner, Tina	Nutbush, Tenn.	26/11/39
Turturro, John	New York, N.Y.	28/2/57
Tushingham, Rita	Liverpool	14/3/40

Name	Birthplace	Born
Tutin, Dorothy	London	8/4/30
Twiggy (Lesley Hornby)	Neasden, London	19/9/46
Tyson, Cicely	New York, N.Y.	19/12/33
Uggams, Leslie	New York, N.Y.	25/5/43
Ullman, Tracey	Slough, Bucks	30/12/59
Ullman, Liv	Tokyo, Japan	16/12/38
Ustinov, Peter	London	16/4/21
Vaccaro, Brenda	Brooklyn, N.Y.	18/11/39
Vadim, Roger	Paris, France	26/1/28
Valli, Frankie	Newark, N.J.	3/5/37
Vandross, Luther	New York, N.Y.	20/4/51
Van Dyke, Dick	West Plains, Mo.	13/12/25
Van Pallandt, Nina	Copenhagen, Denmark	15/7/32
Varda, Agnes	Brussels, Belgium	30/5/28
Vaughn, Robert	New York, N.Y.	22/11/32
Vernon, Richard	Reading, Berks	7/3/25
Voight, Jon	Yonkers, N.Y.	29/12/38
Von Stade, Frederica	Somerville, N.J.	1/6/45
Von Sydow, Max	Lund, Sweden	10/4/29
Wagner, Lindsay	Los Angeles, Cal.	22/6/49
Wagner, Robert	Detroit, Mich.	10/2/30
Waits, Tom	Pomona, Cal.	7/12/49
Wajda, Andrzej	Suwalki, Poland	6/3/26
Walken, Christopher	New York, N.Y.	31/3/43
Walker, Zena	Birmingham, W. Midlands	7/3/34
Wallach, Eli	Brooklyn, N.Y.	7/12/15
Walters, Julie	Birmingham, W. Midlands	22/2/50
Wanamaker, Sam	Chicago, Ill.	14/6/19
Wanamaker, Zoe	New York, N.Y.	13/5/49
Ward, Rachel	London	1957
Ward, Simon	London	19/10/41
Warden, Jack	Newark, N.J.	18/9/20
Warner, David	Manchester	29/7/41
Warren, Lesley Ann	New York, N.Y.	16/8/46
Warwick, Dionne	E. Orange, N.J.	12/12/41
Washington, Denzel	Mt. Vernon, N.Y.	28/12/54
Waterman, Dennis	Clapham, London	24/2/48
Waterston, Sam	Cambridge, Mass.	15/11/40
Watford, Gwen	London	10/9/27
Watling, Dilys	Fulmer Chase, Bucks	5/5/46
Watling, Jack	Chingford, Essex	13/1/23
Watson, Moray	Sunningdale, Berks	25/6/28
Watts, Charlie	London	2/6/41
Wax, Ruby	Chicago, Ill.	19/4/53
Weaver, Dennis	Joplin, Mo.	4/6/24
Weaver, Sigourney	New York, N.Y.	8/10/49
Weir, Peter	Sydney, Australia	8/8/44
Weitz, Bruce	Norwalk, Conn.	27/5/43
Welch, Elizabeth	New York, N.Y.	27/2/09
Welch, Raquel	Chicago, Ill.	5/9/40
Weld, Tuesday	New York, N.Y.	27/8/43
Welland, Colin	Liverpool	4/7/34
Wendt, George	Chicago, Ill.	17/10/48
Wenham, Jane	Southampton, Hants	26/11/—
Wertmuller, Lina	Rome, Italy	14/8/28
West, Timothy	Bradford, Yorks	20/10/34
Whalley-Kilmer, Joanne	Salford, Lancs	1964
Whately, Kevin	Tyneside	6/2/51
White, Barry	Galveston, Tex.	12/9/44
White, Betty	Oak Park, Ill.	17/1/22
Whitelaw, Billie	Coventry, W. Midlands	6/6/38
Whitfield, June	London	11/11/25
Widmark, Richard	Sunrise, Minn.	26/12/14
Wiest, Dianne	Kansas City, Mo.	28/3/48
Wilby, James	Rangoon, Burma	20/2/58
Wilcox, Paula	Manchester	13/12/49
Wilder, Billy	Vienna, Austria	22/6/06
Wilder, Gene	Milwaukee, Wis.	11/6/35
Williams, Andy	Wall Lake, Ia.	3/12/30
Williams, Billy Dee	New York, N.Y.	6/4/37
Williams, Esther	Los Angeles, Cal.	8/8/23
Williams, JoBeth	Houston, Tex.	1953
Williams, Michael	Manchester	9/7/35
Williams, Robin	Chicago, Ill.	21/7/52
Williams, Treat	Rowayton, Conn.	1/12/51
Williamson, Nicol	Hamilton, Strathclyde	14/9/38
Willis, Bruce	W. Germany	19/3/55
Wilson, Flip	Jersey City, N.J.	8/12/33
Wilson, Mary	Greenville, Miss.	6/3/44
Wilson, Nancy	Chillicothe, Oh.	20/2/37
Wilson, Richard	Greenock, Renfrewshire	9/7/36
Wilton, Penelope	Scarborough, Yorks	3/6/46
Windsor, Barbara	Whitechapel, London	6/8/37
Windsor, Frank	Walsall, Staffs	12/7/27
Winfrey, Oprah	Kosciusko, Miss.	29/1/54
Winger, Debra	Cleveland, Oh.	16/5/55

Name	Birthplace	Born
Winkler, Henry	New York, N.Y.	30/10/45
Winner, Michael	London	30/10/35
Winters, Shelley	St. Louis, Mo.	18/8/22
Winwood, Steve	Birmingham, W. Midlands	12/5/48
Wisdom, Norman	London	4/2/25
Withers, Googie	Karachi, Pakistan	12/3/17
Wonder, Stevie	Saginaw, Mich.	13/5/50
Wood, Victoria	Prestwich, Lancs	19/5/53
Woodward, Edward	Croydon, Surrey	1/6/30
Woodward, Joanne	Thomasville, Ga.	27/2/30
Woodward, Tim	London	24/4/53
Wooldridge, Susan	London	1956
Worth, Irene	Nebraska	23/6/16
Wray, Fay	Alberta, Canada	10/9/07
Wright, Teresa	New York, N.Y.	27/10/18
Wyman, Jane	St. Joseph, Mo.	4/1/14
Wynette, Tammy	Red Bay, Ala.	5/5/42
Yates, Peter	Aldershot, Hants	24/7/29
York, Michael	Fulmer, Bucks	27/3/42
York, Susannah	London	9/1/42
Young, Loretta	Salt Lake City, Ut.	6/1/13
Young, Neil	Toronto, Ont	12/11/45
Young, Robert	Chicago, Ill.	22/2/07
Young, Sean	Louisville, Ky.	20/11/59
Zappa, Frank	Baltimore, Md.	21/12/40
Zeffirelli, Franco	Florence, Italy	12/2/23
Zimbalist, Efrem Jr.	New York, N.Y.	30/11/23
Zuckerman, Pinchas	Tel Aviv, Israel	16/7/48

Entertainment Personalities of the Past

(as of mid-1993)

Born	Died	Name
1895	1974	Abbott, Bud
1930	1985	Addams, Dawn
1902	1986	Aherne, Brian
1931	1989	Ailey, Alvin
1906	1964	Allen, Gracie
1922	1987	Andrews, Eamonn
1909	1992	Andrews, Dana
1911	1989	Andrews, Harry
1887	1933	Arbuckle, Fatty (Roscoe)
1908	1990	Arden, Eve
1900	1976	Arlen, Richard
1868	1946	Arliss, George
1900	1971	Armstrong, Louis
1917	1986	Arnaz, Desi
1890	1956	Arnold, Edward
1900	1991	Arthur, Jean
1907	1991	Ashcroft, Peggy
1904	1988	Ashton, Sir Frederick
1899	1987	Astaire, Fred
1906	1987	Astor, Mary
1905	1967	Auer, Mischa
1906	1986	Baddeley, Hermione
1918	1990	Bailey, Pearl
1906	1975	Baker, Josephine
1904	1983	Balanchine, George
1911	1989	Ball, Lucille
1902	1968	Bankhead, Tallulah
1890	1955	Bara, Theda
1810	1891	Barnum, Phineas T.
1879	1959	Barrymore, Ethel
1882	1942	Barrymore, John
1878	1954	Barrymore, Lionel
1897	1963	Barthelmess, Richard
1924	1992	Bartholomew, Freddie
1914	1984	Basehart, Richard
1904	1984	Basie, Count
1921	1987	Bass, Alfie
1923	1985	Baxter, Anne
1874	1937	Baylis, Lilian
1889	1949	Beery, Wallace
1901	1970	Begley, Ed
1949	1982	Belushi, John
1906	1964	Bendix, William
1904	1965	Bennett, Constance
1931	1990	Bennett, Jill
1910	1990	Bennett, Joan
1894	1974	Benny, Jack
1903	1978	Bergen, Edgar
1915	1982	Bergman, Ingrid
1895	1976	Berkeley, Busby
1844	1923	Bernhardt, Sarah
1911	1960	Bjoerling, Jussi
1930	1987	Blakely, Colin
1908	1989	Blanc, Mel
1928	1972	Blocker, Dan
1909	1979	Blondell, Joan
1899	1957	Bogart, Humphrey
1904	1987	Bolger, Ray
1903	1960	Bond, Ward
1892	1981	Bondi, Beulah
1905	1965	Bow, Clara
1899	1978	Boyer, Charles
1912	1985	Brambell, Wilfrid
1904	1979	Brent, George
1891	1951	Brice, Fanny
1933	1992	Brown, Georgia
1926	1966	Bruce, Lenny
1895	1953	Bruce, Nigel
1910	1982	Bruce, Virginia
1915	1985	Brynner, Yul
1891	1957	Buchanan, Jack
1912	1984	Bull, Peter
1923	1990	Bunnage, Avis
1885	1970	Burke, Billie
1925	1984	Burton, Richard
1893	1971	Byington, Spring
1918	1977	Cabot, Sebastian
1899	1986	Cagney, James
1895	1956	Calhern, Louis
1923	1977	Callas, Maria
1865	1940	Campbell, Mrs Patrick
1892	1964	Cantor, Eddie
1923	1990	Capucine
1898	1992	Carey, Joyce
1950	1983	Carpenter, Karen
1906	1988	Carradine, John
1892	1972	Carroll, Leo G.
1905	1965	Carroll, Nancy
1910	1963	Carson, Jack
1873	1921	Caruso, Enrico
1876	1973	Casals, Pablo
1929	1989	Cassavetes, John
1893	1969	Castle, Irene
1887	1918	Castle, Vernon
1873	1938	Chaliapin, Feodor
1918	1961	Chandler, Jeff
1883	1930	Chaney, Lon
1905	1973	Chaney Jr., Lon
1942	1981	Chapin, Harry
1889	1977	Chaplin, Charles
1949	1990	Charleson, Ian
1888	1972	Chevalier, Maurice
1923	1990	Clancy, Tom
1920	1966	Clift, Montgomery
1932	1963	Cline, Patsy
1911	1976	Cobb, Lee J.
1877	1961	Coburn, Charles
1919	1965	Cole, Nat (King)
1891	1958	Colman, Ronald
1914	1984	Coogan, Jackie
1892	1986	Cooper, Lady Diana
1901	1961	Cooper, Gary
1888	1971	Cooper, Gladys
1918	1989	Corbett, Harry
1914	1968	Corey, Wendell
1893	1974	Cornell, Katherine
1906	1959	Costello, Lou
1893	1980	Courtneidge, Cicely
1899	1973	Coward, Noël
1908	1983	Crabbe, Buster
1911	1986	Crawford, Broderick
1908	1977	Crawford, Joan
1942	1973	Croce, Jim
1903	1977	Crosby, Bing
1910	1986	Crothers, Scatman
1907	1988	Cruickshank, Andrew
1908	1990	Cummings, Robert
1900	1990	Cugat, Xavier
1878	1968	Currie, Finlay
1927	1986	Dainty, Billy
1923	1965	Dandridge, Dorothy
1901	1971	Daniels, Bebe
1906	1990	Danvers-Walker, Bob
1936	1973	Darin, Bobby
1921	1965	Darnell, Linda
1908	1989	Davis, Bette
1927	1991	Davis, Miles
1925	1990	Davis, Sammy Jr.
1931	1955	Dean, James
1908	1983	Del Rio, Dolores
1892	1983	Demarest, William
1881	1959	DeMille, Cecil B.
1901	1974	DeSica, Vittorio
1902	1992	Dietrich, Marlene
1901	1966	Disney, Walt
1945	1988	Divine
1905	1958	Donat, Robert
1906	1988	Dorati, Antal
1931	1984	Dors, Diana
1901	1981	Douglas, Melvyn
1904	1990	Drake, Fabia
1909	1951	Duchin, Eddy
1889	1965	Dumont, Margaret
1878	1927	Duncan, Isadora
1898	1990	Dunne, Irene
1893	1980	Durante, Jimmy
1907	1968	Duryea, Dan
1914	1993	Eckstine, Billy
1901	1967	Eddy, Nelson
1920	1988	Edwards, Jimmy
1899	1974	Ellington, Duke
1941	1974	Elliot, Cass
1888	1976	Evans, Edith
1883	1939	Fairbanks, Douglas
1914	1970	Farmer, Frances
1912	1986	Farr, Derek
1933	1982	Feldman, Marty
1912	1953	Ferrier, Kathleen
1898	1985	Fetchit, Stepin
1896	1992	Ffrangcon-Davies, Gwen
1898	1979	Fields, Gracie
1879	1946	Fields, W.C.
1916	1977	Finch, Peter
1909	1959	Flynn, Errol
1880	1942	Fokine, Michel
1905	1982	Fonda, Henry
1920	1978	Fontaine, Frank
1919	1991	Fonteyn, Margot
1895	1973	Ford, John
1904	1961	Formby, George
1927	1987	Fosse, Bob
1857	1928	Foy, Eddie
1908	1987	Fraser, Bill
1887	1966	Frawley, William
1901	1960	Gable, Clark
1905	1990	Garbo, Greta
1922	1990	Gardner, Ava
1913	1952	Garfield, John
1922	1969	Garland, Judy
1939	1984	Gaye, Marvin
1906	1984	Gaynor, Janet
1890	1957	Gigli, Beniamino

Born	Died	Name
1895	1936	Gilbert, John
1897	1987	Gingold, Hermione
1898	1968	Gish, Dorothy
1896	1993	Gish, Lillian
1916	1987	Gleason, Jackie
1915	1984	Gobbi, Tito
1905	1990	Goddard, Paulette
1882	1974	Goldwyn, Samuel
1909	1986	Goodman, Benny
1897	1988	Goossens, Leon
1923	1985	Gordon, Noele
1896	1985	Gordon, Ruth
1916	1973	Grable, Betty
1894	1991	Graham, Martha
1925	1981	Grahame, Gloria
1904	1986	Grant, Cary
1915	1987	Greene, Lorne
1918	1985	Greene, Richard
1879	1954	Greenstreet, Sydney
1921	1987	Greenwood, Joan
1910	1970	Grenfell, Joyce
1912	1967	Guthrie, Woody
1925	1981	Haley, Bill
1898	1989	Hall, Henry
1847	1919	Hammerstein, Oscar
1924	1968	Hancock, Tony
1901	1987	Handl, Irene
1892	1949	Handley, Tommy
1893	1964	Hardwicke, Cedric
1892	1957	Hardy, Oliver
1911	1937	Harlow, Jean
1908	1990	Harrison, Rex
1934	1988	Harty, Russell
1928	1973	Harvey, Laurence
1910	1973	Hawkins, Jack
1914	1988	Hawtrey, Charles
1888	1949	Hay, Will
1917	1975	Hayward, Susan
1918	1987	Hayworth, Rita
1910	1971	Heflin, Van
1901	1987	Heifetz, Jascha
1909	1986	Helpmann, Robert
1922	1985	Henderson, Dickie
1942	1970	Hendrix, Jimi
1936	1990	Henson, Jim
1910	1969	Henie, Sonja
1908	1992	Henreid, Paul
1929	1993	Hepburn, Audrey
1913	1987	Herman, Woody
1925	1992	Hill, Benny
1899	1980	Hitchcock, Alfred
1917	1987	Hobley, McDonald
1918	1981	Holden, William
1922	1965	Holiday, Judy
1915	1959	Holliday, Billie
1890	1982	Holloway, Stanley
1936	1959	Holly, Buddy
1898	1978	Homolka, Oscar
1902	1972	Hopkins, Miriam
1904	1989	Horowitz, Vladimir
1886	1970	Horton, Edward Everett
1874	1926	Houdini, Harry
1902	1988	Houseman, John
1902	1980	Houston, Renée
1893	1943	Howard, Leslie
1916	1988	Howard, Trevor
1921	1992	Howerd, Frankie
1925	1985	Hudson, Rock
1906	1987	Huston, John
1884	1950	Huston, Walter
1936	1990	Ireland, Jill
1838	1905	Irving, Henry
1895	1980	Iturbi, Jose
1923	1990	Jackson, Gordon
1911	1972	Jackson, Mahalia
1924	1980	Jacques, Hattie
1891	1984	Jaffe, Sam
1903	1991	Jagger, Dean
1930	1980	Janssen, David
1902	1987	Jochum, Eugen
1930	1988	Joffrey, Robert
1899	1992	Johns, Mervyn
1908	1982	Johnson, Celia
1886	1950	Jolson, Al
1943	1970	Joplin, Janis

Born	Died	Name
1908	1989	Karajan, Herbert von
1887	1969	Karloff, Boris
1913	1987	Kaye, Danny
1787	1833	Kean, Edmund
1895	1966	Keaton, Buster
1909	1993	Keeler, Ruby
1928	1982	Kelly, Grace
1926	1959	Kendall, Kay
1934	1988	Kinnear, Roy
1928	1984	Korner, Alexis
1919	1962	Kovacs, Ernie
1913	1964	Ladd, Alan
1895	1967	Lahr, Bert
1919	1973	Lake, Veronica
1902	1986	Lanchester, Elsa
1936	1991	Landon, Michael
1853	1929	Langtry, Lillie
1921	1959	Lanza, Mario
1870	1950	Lauder, Harry
1899	1962	Laughton, Charles
1890	1965	Laurel, Stan
1923	1984	Lawford, Peter
1898	1952	Lawrence, Gertrude
1908	1991	Lean, David
1940	1973	Lee, Bruce
1914	1970	Lee, Gypsy Rose
1888	1976	Lehmann, Lotte
1913	1967	Leigh, Vivien
1922	1976	Leighton, Margaret
1940	1980	Lennon, John
1898	1981	Lenya, Lotte
1900	1987	LeRoy, Mervyn
1906	1972	Levant, Oscar
1905	1980	Levene, Sam
1902	1971	Lewis, Joe E.
1919	1987	Liberace
1820	1887	Lind, Jenny
1894	1989	Lillie, Beatrice
1893	1971	Lloyd, Harold
1870	1922	Lloyd, Marie
1916	1990	Lockwood, Margaret
1901	1988	Loewe, Frederick
1909	1942	Lombard, Carole
1902	1977	Lombardo, Guy
1904	1964	Lorre, Peter
1909	1990	Loss, Joe
1898	1986	Love, Bessie
1915	1984	Lowe, Arthur
1892	1947	Lubitsch, Ernst
1907	1989	Luckham, Cyril
1882	1956	Lugosi, Bela
1892	1977	Lunt, Alfred
1915	1989	MacColl, Ewan
1903	1965	MacDonald, Jeanette
1922	1987	Mackay, Fulton
1908	1991	MacMurray, Fred
1921	1986	MacRae, Gordon
1908	1973	Magnani, Anna
1930	1989	Mangano, Silvana
1914	1988	Manio, Jack de
1932	1967	Mansfield, Jayne
1905	1980	Mantovani, Annunzio
1897	1975	March, Frederic
1945	1981	Marley, Bob
1910	1989	Marshall, Arthur
1890	1966	Marshall, Herbert
1913	1990	Martin, Mary
1924	1987	Marvin, Lee
1888	1964	Marx, Arthur (Harpo)
1901	1979	Marx, Herbert (Zeppo)
1890	1977	Marx, Julius (Groucho)
1886	1961	Marx, Leonard (Chico)
1893	1977	Marx, Milton (Gummo)
1909	1984	Mason, James
1896	1983	Massey, Raymond
1907	1981	Matthews, Jessie
1885	1957	Mayer, Louis B.
1926	1989	McAnally, Ray
1905	1990	McCrea, Joel
1895	1952	McDaniel, Hattie
1923	1986	McKenna, Siobhan
1883	1959	McLaglen, Victor
1930	1980	McQueen, Steve
1861	1931	Melba, Nellie
1890	1963	Menjou, Adolphe
1908	1984	Merman, Ethel

Born	Died	Name
1905	1986	Milland, Ray
1904	1944	Miller, Glenn
1913	1955	Miranda, Carmen
1880	1940	Mix, Tom
1930	1985	Monro, Matt
1926	1962	Monroe, Marilyn
1921	1992	Montand, Yves
1904	1981	Montgomery, Robert
1906	1974	Moorehead, Agnes
1926	1984	Morecambe, Eric
1908	1992	Morley, Robert
1943	1971	Morrison, Jim
1932	1982	Morrow, Vic
1915	1977	Mostel, Zero
1926	1986	Moult, Ted
1903	1990	Muggeridge, Malcolm
1895	1967	Muni, Paul
1907	1990	Murdoch, Richard
1924	1971	Murphy, Audie
1904	1986	Neagle, Anna
1940	1985	Nelson, Rick
1888	1982	Nesbitt, Cathleen
1907	1986	Nichols, Dandy
1944	1988	Nico
1890	1950	Nijinsky, Vaslav
1909	1983	Niven, David
1899	1968	Novarro, Ramon
1893	1951	Novello, Ivor
1938	1993	Nureyev, Rudolf
1860	1926	Oakley, Annie
1928	1982	Oates, Warren
1911	1979	Oberon, Merle
1915	1985	O'Brien, Edmond
1899	1983	O'Brien, Pat
1937	1989	Ogdon, John
1908	1968	O'Keefe, Dennis
1883	1942	Oliver, Edna May
1907	1989	Olivier, Laurence
1936	1988	Orbison, Roy
1899	1985	Ormandy, Eugene
1876	1949	Ouspenskaya, Maria
1860	1941	Paderewski, Ignace
1924	1987	Page, Geraldine
1889	1954	Pallette, Eugene
1914	1986	Palmer, Lilli
1881	1940	Pasternack, Josef A.
1885	1931	Pavlova, Anna
1910	1986	Pears, Peter
1932	1992	Perkins, Anthony
1923	1986	Phoenix, Patricia
1915	1963	Piaf, Edith
1893	1979	Pickford, Mary
1897	1984	Pidgeon, Walter
1898	1963	Pitts, Zasu
1904	1963	Powell, Dick
1912	1982	Powell, Eleanor
1892	1984	Powell, William
1913	1958	Power, Tyrone
1945	1987	Pré, Jacqueline du
1905	1986	Preminger, Otto
1935	1977	Presley, Elvis
1918	1987	Preston, Robert
1913	1989	Quayle, Anthony
1946	1989	Radner, Gilda
1895	1980	Raft, George
1890	1967	Rains, Claude
1952	1990	Rappaport, David
1892	1967	Rathbone, Basil
1891	1943	Ray, Charles
1927	1990	Ray, Johnnie
1941	1967	Redding, Otis
1908	1985	Redgrave, Michael
1921	1986	Reed, Donna
1923	1964	Reeves, Jim
1910	1953	Reinhardt, Django
1935	1991	Remick, Lee
1909	1971	Rennie, Michael
1902	1983	Richardson, Ralph
1921	1985	Riddle, Nelson
1907	1974	Ritter, Tex
1905	1969	Ritter, Thelma
1902	1987	Robertson, Fyfe
1898	1976	Robeson, Paul

Born	Died	Name
1869	1954	Robey, George
1893	1973	Robinson, Edward G.
1902	1984	Robson, Flora
1926	1984	Rossiter, Leonard
1922	1987	Rowan, Dan
1887	1982	Rubinstein, Artur
1886	1970	Ruggles, Charles
1911	1976	Russell, Rosalind
Born	Died	Name
1892	1972	Rutherford, Margaret
1909	1973	Ryan, Robert
1909	1990	Sachs, Leonard
1906	1972	Sanders, George
1922	1987	Schidlof, Peter
1882	1951	Schnabel, Artur
1898	1987	Scott, Randolph
1914	1965	Scott, Zachary
1938	1979	Seberg, Jean
1893	1987	Segovia, Andres
1925	1980	Sellers, Peter
1902	1965	Selznick, David O.
1908	1990	Semprini
1884	1960	Sennett, Mack
1889	1990	Seyler, Athene
1932	1990	Seyrig, Delphine
1939	1990	Shannon, Del
1927	1978	Shaw, Robert
1915	1967	Sheridan, Ann
1755	1831	Siddons, Mrs Sarah
1921	1985	Signoret, Simone
1912	1985	Silvers, Phil
1900	1976	Sim, Alastair
1863	1948	Smith, C. Aubrey
1907	1986	Smith, Kate
1854	1932	Sousa, John Philip

Born	Died	Name
1907	1990	Stanwyck, Barbara
1919	1986	Stock, Nigel
1882	1977	Stokowski, Leopold
1885	1957	Stroheim, Erich von
1898	1959	Sturges, Preston
1911	1960	Sullavan, Margaret
1902	1974	Sullivan, Ed
1899	1983	Swanson, Gloria
1893	1957	Talmadge, Norma
1892	1948	Tauber, Richard
1911	1969	Taylor, Robert
1847	1928	Terry, Ellen
1911	1990	Terry-Thomas
1899	1936	Thalberg, Irving
1882	1976	Thorndike, Sybil
1921	1991	Tierney, Gene
1909	1958	Todd, Michael
1903	1968	Tone, Franchot
1867	1957	Toscanini, Arturo
1905	1987	Trapp, Baroness Maria von
1900	1967	Tracy, Spencer
1853	1917	Tree, Herbert Beerbohm
1909	1989	Trinder, Tommy
1920	1987	Troughton, Patrick
1932	1984	Truffaut, François
1919	1986	Tucker, Forrest
1884	1966	Tucker, Sophie
1933	1993	Twitty, Conway
1933	1975	Ure, Mary
1895	1926	Valentino, Rudolph
1901	1986	Vallee, Rudy
1911	1979	Vance, Vivian

Born	Died	Name
1924	1990	Vaughan, Sarah
1908	1987	Vaughan-Thomas, Wynford
1893	1943	Veidt, Conrad
1926	1981	Vera-Ellen
1908	1990	Wall, Max
1887	1980	Walsh, Raoul
1903	1988	Washbourne, Mona
1924	1963	Washington, Dinah
1884	1990	Waters, Elsie
1900	1977	Waters, Ethel
1907	1979	Wayne, John
1891	1966	Webb, Clifton
1915	1985	Welles, Orson
1892	1980	West, Mae
1865	1948	Whitty, May
1912	1979	Wilding, Michael
1905	1987	Williams, Emlyn
1923	1953	Williams, Hank
1926	1988	Williams, Kenneth
1907	1961	Wong, Anna May
1938	1981	Wood, Natalie
1910	1988	Woodhouse, Barbara
1888	1963	Woolley, Monty
1920	1989	Worth, Harry
1902	1981	Wyler, William
1916	1986	Wynn, Keenan
1932	1989	Yana
1913	1978	Young, Gig
1887	1953	Young, Roland
1902	1979	Zanuck, Darryl F.
1869	1932	Ziegfeld, Florenz
1873	1976	Zukor, Adolph

Original Names of Selected Entertainers

Anouk Aimée: Françoise Sorya Dreyfus
Eddie Albert: Edward Albert Heimberger
Alan Alda: Alphonso D'Abruzzo
Jane Alexander: Jane Quigley
Woody Allen: Allen Konigsberg
Julie Andrews: Julia Wells
Eve Arden: Eunice Quedens
Beatrice Arthur: Bernice Frankel
Mary Astor: Lucile Vasconcellos Langhanke
Jean Arthur: Gladys Greene
Fred Astaire: Frederick Austerlitz
Stephane Audran: Colette Ducheville

Lauren Bacall: Betty Joan Perske
Anne Bancroft: Anna Maria Italiano
Brigitte Bardot: Camille Javal
Gene Barry: Eugene Klass
Bonnie Bedelia: Bonnie Culkin
Pat Benatar: Patricia Andrejewski
Robbie Benson: Robert Segal
Tony Bennett: Anthony Benedetto
Busby Berkeley: William Berkeley Enos
Jack Benny: Benjamin Kubelsky
Cilla Black: Priscilla White
Lionel Blair: Lionel Ogus
Dirk Bogarde: Derek van den Bogaerde
Victor Borge: Borge Rosenbaum
David Bowie: David Robert Jones
Boy George: George Alan O'Dowd
Katie Boyle: Caterina Imperiale di Francavilla
Jeremy Brett: Jeremy Huggins
Fanny Brice: Fanny Borach
Morgan Brittany: Suzanne Cupito
Charles Bronson: Charles Buchinski
Mel Brooks: Melvin Kaminsky
Georgia Brown: Lillian Klott
Dora Bryan: Dora Broadbent
Yul Brynner: Taidje Khan
George Burns: Nathan Birnbaum
Ellen Burstyn: Edna Gilhooley
Richard Burton: Richard Jenkins
Red Buttons: Aaron Chwatt

Nicolas Cage: Nicholas Coppola
Michael Caine: Maurice Micklewhite
Maria Callas: Maria Kalogeropoulos
Vikki Carr: Florencia Casillas
Diahann Carroll: Carol Diahann Johnson
Jasper Carrott: Robert Davies
Cyd Charisse: Tula Finklea
Ray Charles: Ray Charles Robinson
Cher: Cherilyn Sarkasian Lapiere
Patsy Cline: Virginia Patterson Hensley
Lee J. Cobb: Leo Jacoby
Claudette Colbert: Lily Chauchoin
Alice Cooper: Vincent Furnier
David Copperfield: David Kotkin
Elvis Costello: Declan Patrick McManus
Lou Costello: Louis Cristillo
Joan Crawford: Lucille Le Sueur
Michael Crawford: Michael Dumbell-Smith
Tom Cruise: Thomas Mapother
Tony Curtis: Bernard Schwartz

Vic Damone: Vito Farinola
Bobby Darin: Walden Waldo Cassotto
Bette Davis: Ruth Elizabeth Davis
Bobby Davro: Robert Nankeville
Doris Day: Doris von Kappelhoff
Yvonne de Carlo: Peggy Middleton
Sandra Dee: Alexandra Zuck
John Denver: Henry John Deutschendorf Jr.
Bo Derek: Cathleen Collins
John Derek: Derek Harris
Susan Dey: Susan Smith
Angie Dickinson: Angeline Brown
Bo Diddley: Elias Bates
Phyllis Diller: Phyllis Driver
Divine: Harris Glen Milstead
Diana Dors: Diana Fluck
Melvyn Douglas: Melvyn Hesselberg
Bob Dylan: Robert Zimmerman

Barbara Eden: Barbara Huffman
Chad Everett: Raymond Cramton
Kenny Everett: Maurice Cole

Douglas Fairbanks: Douglas Ullman
Morgan Fairchild: Patsy McClenny
Adam Faith: Terence Nelhams
Alice Faye: Ann Leppert
Stepin Fetchit: Lincoln Perry
Sally Field: Sally Mahoney
W.C. Fields: William Claude Dukenfield
Peter Finch: William Mitchell
Joan Fontaine: Joan de Havilland
John Ford: Sean O'Fearna
John Forsythe: John Freund
Anthony Franciosa: Anthony Papaleo
Connie Francis: Concetta Franconero

Greta Garbo: Greta Gustafsson
Vincent Gardenia: Vincent Scognamiglio
John Garfield: Julius Garfinkle
Judy Garland: Frances Gumm
James Garner: James Baumgarner
Crystal Gayle: Brenda Gayle Webb
Paulette Goddard: Marion Levy
Whoopi Goldberg: Caryn Johnson
Eydie Gorme: Edith Gormezano
Stewart Granger: James Stewart
Cary Grant: Archibald Leach
Dulcie Gray: Dulcie Bailey
Joel Grey: Joe Katz
Robert Guillaume: Robert Williams

Jean Harlow: Harlean Carpentier
Rex Harrison: Reginald Carey
Laurence Harvey: Larushka Skikne
Helen Hayes: Helen Brown
Susan Hayward: Edythe Marriner
Rita Hayworth: Margarita Cansino
Audrey Hepburn: Edda van Heemstra Hepburn-Ruston
Pee-Wee Herman: Paul Rubenfeld
Barbara Hershey: Barbara Herzstine
Benny Hill: Alfred Hawthorn Hill
William Holden: William Beedle
Judy Holliday: Judith Tuvim
Ian Holm: Ian Cuthbert
Harry Houdini: Ehrich Weiss
John Houseman: Jacques Haussman
Leslie Howard: Leslie Stainer
Rock Hudson: Roy Scherer Jr. (later Fitzgerald)
Engelbert Humperdinck: Arnold Dorsey
Mary Beth Hurt: Mary Supinger
Betty Hutton: Betty Thornberg

Polly James: Polly Devaney
David Janssen: David Meyer
David Jason: David White
Michael Jayston: Michael James
Elton John: Reginald Dwight

Don Johnson: Donald Wayne
Jennifer Jones: Phyllis Isley
Paul Jones: Paul Pond
Tom Jones: Thomas Woodward
Louis Jourdan: Louis Gendre

Boris Karloff: William Henry Pratt
Danny Kaye: David Kaminsky
Diane Keaton: Diane Hall
Michael Keaton: Michael Douglas
Howard Keel: Howard Leek
Penelope Keith: Penelope Hatfield
Chaka Khan: Yvette Stevens
Carole King: Carole Klein
Ben Kingsley: Krishna Banji
Nastassia Kinski: Nastassja Nakszynski

Cheryl Ladd: Cheryl Stoppelmoor
Veronica Lake: Constance Ockleman
Dorothy Lamour: Mary Kaumeyer
Michael Landon: Eugene Orowitz
Mario Lanza: Alfredo Cocozza
Danny La Rue: Daniel Patrick Carroll
Stan Laurel: Arthur Jefferson
Brenda Lee: Brenda Mae Tarpley
Bruce Lee: Lee Yuen Kam
Gypsy Rose Lee: Rose Louise Hovick
Peggy Lee: Norma Egstrom
Janet Leigh: Jeanette Morrison
Vivien Leigh: Vivian Hartley
Lotte Lenya: Karoline Blamauer
Huey Lewis: Hugh Cregg
Jerry Lewis: Joseph Levitch
Liberace: Wladziu Valentino Liberace
Carole Lombard: Jane Peters
Jack Lord: John Joseph Ryan
Sophia Loren: Sophia Scicoloni
Peter Lorre: Laszio Lowenstein
Myrna Loy: Myrna Williams
Bela Lugosi: Bela Ferenc Blasko
Lulu: Marie Lawrie

Shirley MacLaine: Shirley Beaty
Madonna: Madonna Louise Ciccone
Lee Majors: Harvey Lee Yeary II
Karl Malden: Malden Sekulovich
Jayne Mansfield: Vera Jane Palmer
Fredric March: Frederick Bickel
Dean Martin: Dino Crocetti
Leo McKern: Reginald McKern
Ethel Merman: Ethel Zimmerman
George Michael: Georgios Panayiotou
Ray Milland: Reginald Truscott-Jones
Ann Miller: Lucille Collier
Spike Milligan: Terence Alan Milligan
John Mills: Lewis Ernest Watts
Joni Mitchell: Roberta Joan Anderson
Marilyn Monroe: Norma Jean Mortenson, (later) Baker
Yves Montand: Ivo Levi
Ron Moody: Ronald Moodnick
Demi Moore: Demi Guynes
Eric Morecambe: John Eric Bartholomew
Rita Moreno: Rosita Alverio
Paul Muni: Muni Weisenfreund

Anna Neagle: Florence Robertson
Mike Nichols: Michael Igor Peschowsky

Maureen O'Hara: Maureen Fitzsimmons

Patti Page: Carla Ann Fowler
Nicola Pagett: Nicola Scott
Jack Palance: Walter Palanuik
Lilli Palmer: Lilli Peiser
Bernadette Peters: Bernadette Lazzaro
Edith Piaf: Edith Gassion
Slim Pickens: Louis Lindley
Mary Pickford: Gladys Smith
Stephanie Powers: Stefania Federkiewicz
Paula Prentiss: Paula Ragusa
Robert Preston: Robert Preston Meservey
Prince: Prince Rogers Nelson

Tony Randall: Leonard Rosenberg
Donna Reed: Donna Belle Mullenger
Joan Rivers: Joan Sandra Molinsky
Edward G. Robinson: Emmanuel Goldenberg
Ginger Rogers: Virginia McMath
Roy Rogers: Leonard Slye
Mickey Rooney: Joe Yule Jr.
Lillian Russell: Helen Leonard
Theresa Russell: Theresa Paup
Winona Ryder: Winona Horowitz

Susan St. James: Susan Miller
Susan Sarandon: Susan Tomaling
Randolph Scott: George Randolph Crane
Jane Seymour: Joyce Frankenberg
Omar Sharif: Michael Shalhoub
Martin Sheen: Ramon Estevez
Simone Signoret: Simone Kaminker
Beverly Sills: Belle Silverman
Talia Shire: Talia Coppola
Phil Silvers: Philip Silverman
Suzanne Somers: Suzanne Mahoney
Ann Sothern: Harriette Lake
Robert Stack: Robert Modini
Barbara Stanwyck: Ruby Stevens
Jean Stapleton: Jeanne Murray
Ringo Starr: Richard Starkey
Tommy Steele: Thomas Hicks
Connie Stevens: Concetta Ingolia
Sting: Gordon Sumner
Donna Summer: LaDonna Gaines

Robert Taylor: Spangler Arlington Brugh
Sophie Tucker: Sophia Kalish
Tina Turner: Annie Mae Bullock
Conway Twitty: Harold Lloyd Jenkins

Roger Vadim: Roger Plemiannikov
Rudolph Valentino: Rudolpho D'Antonguolla
Frankie Valli: Frank Castelluccio

John Wayne: Marion Morrison
Raquel Welch: Raquel Tejada
Gene Wilder: Jerome Silberman
Barbara Windsor: Barbara Deeks
Shelly Winters: Shirley Schrift
Googie Withers: Georgette Withers
Stevie Wonder: Stevland Morris
Natalie Wood: Natasha Gurdin
Jane Wyman: Sarah Jane Fulks

Susannah York: Susannah Johnson
Gig Young: Byron Barr

UK HISTORY

BC

15,000

Ice Age ends in Britain.

5000

Sea divides Britain from Europe.

3000

Windmill Hill culture flourishes.

1860

Stonehenge, construction begins.

55

Julius Caesar unsuccessfully invades England.

AD

61

Boudicca, Queen of the Iceni, leads a rebellion against the Romans but is defeated and killed by the Roman governor, Suetonius Paulinus.

77

Roman conquest of Britain; Julius Agricola is imperial governor.

122–38

Hadrian's Wall built by Romans to keep out Scottish tribes.

383

Roman legions begin to leave Britain.

407

Last Roman troops withdraw from Britain.

449

The Jutes, a Germanic people, under Hengest and Horsa conquer Kent.

584

Foundation of the **Anglo-Saxon kingdom of Mercia.**

597

St Augustine, sent by Pope Gregory I to evangelize the country, lands in England.

Venerable Bede completes his history of the Church in England.

787

First Danish invasion.

832–60

Scots and Picts merge under Kenneth Macalpin to form what is to become the kingdom of Scotia.

860s

Danes overrun East Anglia, Northumbria and East Mercia.

871–99

Reign of Alfred the Great, King of Wessex.

878

Alfred decisively defeats the Danes; under the Treaty of Wedmore he rules Wessex in the south, while the Danes rule the north (the Danelaw).

924

Athelstan becomes king of Wessex and effective ruler of most of England.

1016

The Dane Cnut defeats Edmund Ironside to become King of England; becomes king of Denmark (1019) and of Norway (1028). Tired of his sycophantic courtiers, he proved his vulnerability by showing that he could not stop the waves.

1052

Edward the Confessor founds Westminster Abbey.

1066

Battle of Hastings; William of Normandy successfully invades England, kills Harold II, and becomes William the Conqueror.

1070

Hereward the Wake begins a Saxon revolt in the fens of eastern England.

1086

The Domesday Book, a survey of England commissioned by William I, is completed.

1155

Henry II appoints the Archdeacon of Canterbury, Thomas à Becket, as chancellor.

1162

Becket is appointed Archbishop of Canterbury and at once quarrels with Henry II over the Church's rights.

1170

Thomas à Becket murdered in Canterbury Cathedral at behest of king.

1209

Cambridge University founded.

1215

King John signs Magna Carta, to protect feudal rights against royal abuse.

1264

Simon de Montfort and other barons defeat Henry III at the battle of Lewes.

1265

Simon de Montfort becomes king for a year; summons the burgesses from the major towns to Parliament for the first time, thus becoming known as the Father of the House of Commons.

1277

Roger Bacon, Franciscan philosopher, exiled for heresy.

1290

Edward I expels all Jews from England.

1295

Model Parliament of Edward I; knights and burgesses from the shires and towns summoned. First representative parliament.

1296

Anglo-Scottish wars begin and continue for 10 years.

1337

Hundred Years' War between England and France begins. Edward III, provoked by French attacks on English territories in France, declares himself King of France.

1346

Edward III invades France and defeats the French under Philip VI at Crécy, thanks to the superiority of English longbowmen.

1347
Calais captured by the English.

1348
Black Death (bubonic plague) wipes out a third of the population.

1360
Treaty of Bretigny ends the first stage of the Hundred Years' War. Edward III gives up claim to French throne.

1369
Second stage of the war between France and England begins.

1381
Peasant's Revolt in England. Led by Wat Tyler and John Ball, the peasants march on London to protest against taxes and other government policies. Initial success is followed by collapse and ruthless suppresion.

1387
Geoffrey Chaucer begins work on *The Canterbury Tales*.

1431
Joan of Arc, French visionary and military leader, burned to death by the English at Rouen.

1453
Hundred Years' War ends. England's only French possession left is Calais.

1455–87
Wars of the Roses, between the Houses of Lancaster and York, for the English throne.

1476
William Caxton sets up printing press at Westminster.

1483
Murder of the princes – Edward V and his brother Richard – in the Tower, probably by their uncle the Duke of Gloucester, later King Richard III.

1484
Morte d'Arthur, stories about the legendary court of King Arthur, by Sir Thomas Malory, is published by Caxton.

1485
Battle of Bosworth – Henry Tudor defeats and kills Richard III, and becomes Henry VII, first of the Tudor monarchs.

1486
Henry VII marries Elizabeth of York and unites the Houses of Lancaster and York.

1521
Henry VIII named "Defender of the Faith" by Pope Leo X for his opposition to Martin Luther, a German reformer who publicized the corruption of the papacy.

1529–40
English Reformation: Henry VIII breaks with the papacy when it refuses to grant him a divorce from Catherine of Aragon.

1533
Henry marries Anne Boleyn and is excommunicated by Pope Clement VII.

1534
Act of Supremacy: Henry VIII declared supreme head of the Church in England.

1535
Sir Thomas More, Henry's chancellor, executed for failing to take the oath of supremacy.

1536
Dissolution of the monasteries ordered by Henry VIII.

1536–43
Acts of Union unite England and Wales, imposing English law and making English the official language.

1547–53
Protestantism becomes official religion in England under Edward VI.

1553
Nine-day reign of Lady Jane Grey; she is subsequently executed for treason.

1553–58
Mary I ascends throne, intent on restoring Catholicism to England; Protestant laws repealed and heresy laws reintroduced, resulting in many deaths at the stake; queen acquires nickname "Bloody Mary".

1558
England loses Calais, last English possession in France.

1558–1603
Reign of Elizabeth I; moderate Protestantism established.

1587
Mary Queen of Scots, great-niece of Henry VIII and claimant to the English throne, executed by Elizabeth.

1588
The Spanish Armada, a fleet of 130 ships sent by Philip II of Spain to invade England, resoundingly defeated.

c1590–c1613
Plays of Shakespeare written.

1605
Gunpowder Plot to blow up Protestant James I and the Houses of Parliament discovered. Guy Fawkes and the other conspirators arrested and executed.

1611
James I authorized version of the *Bible* completed.

1628
William Harvey demonstrates circulation of the blood.

1642–51
Civil War between the Cavaliers (Royalists) and the Roundheads (Parliamentarians).

1649
Charles I tried for treason and executed.

1653–59
Republic of Oliver Cromwell; Puritanism established, but Jews allowed to return to England.

1665–66
Great Plague of London claims 70,000 lives.

1666
Great Fire of London destroys four-fifths of the City.

1679
Act of Habeas Corpus passed, forbidding imprisonment without trial.

1688

Glorious Revolution: accession of William III and Mary II.

1707

Act of Union unites England and Scotland to form Great Britain.

1720

South Sea Bubble – the boom in South Sea stocks collapses and causes financial panic.

1721

Britain's first prime minister – Sir Robert Walpole – appointed.

1739

John Wesley founds Methodist movement.

1745

Jacobite Rebellion unsuccessfully tries to return the Young Pretender – Charles Edward Stuart – to the throne.

1756–63

Seven Years' War settles rivalry between Britain and France in America and India in Britain's favour.

c. 1750

Industrial Revolution begins.

1767

Spinning jenny invented by James Hargeaves.

1769

James Watt's steam engine patented.

1783

First successful **hot-air balloon.**

1785

Edmund Cartwright's power-loom patented.

1788

First convicts transported from Britain to Australia.

1801

Act of Union formally unites Great Britain and Ireland as the United Kingdom.

1804

Richard Trevithick builds first successful steam locomotive.

1805

Horatio Nelson leads the navy to victory over the Franco-Spanish fleet at Trafalgar.

1807

Slave trade abolished in the British Empire.

1811

Luddite riots in England against mechanized industry.

George III declared insane; Prince of Wales rules as regent.

1820

Cato Street Conspiracy, led by Arthur Thistlewood, plans to assassinate Cabinet ministers, but fails.

1825

Stockton to Darlington railway built.

1829

Catholic Emancipation Act allows Catholics to hold public office.

1831

Michael Faraday discovers magno-electricity.

1833

Factory Act forbids employment of children under 9 in factories.

1834

"Tolpuddle Martyrs"; six Dorset labourers transported to Australia for attempting to form a trade union.

1836

Chartist movement begins to gain votes for all adult males.

1837

Queen Victoria succeeds to the throne.

1840

Penny post introduced.

1846

Corn Laws, which kept the price of bread artificially high, repealed.

1851

Great Exhibition (of technical and industrial prowess) held in London.

1853–56

Crimean War – Britain unites with France, the Ottoman (Turkish) Empire and Sardinia-Piedmont against Russia.

1855

Florence Nightingale reforms nursing during the Crimean War.

1861

Prince Albert dies.

1864

First International, an association of labour and socialist groups, founded in London by Karl Marx.

1868

William Gladstone elected prime minister.

1870

Education Act introduces elementary education for all children and establishes school boards to set up schools where none exist.

1871

Trade unions legalized.

1874

Benjamin Disraeli becomes prime minister.

1875

Government buys **shares in the Suez Canal** from Egypt.

1877

Queen Victoria proclaimed Empress of India.

1880–81

First Boer War – British force suffers massive defeat at Majuba, and Transvaal regains independence.

1885

General Gordon killed at Khartoum 2 days before British relief force arrives to break 10-month siege.

1886

First Home Rule Bill defeated.

1893

Second Home Rule Bill passed in Commons but defeated in Lords.

1899–1902

Second Boer War – British troops quell rebels, killing 20,000 in concentration camps in the process.

1901

Edward VII succeeds to throne.

1903

Mrs Emmeline Pankhurst forms Women's Social and Political Union.

1906

First Labour MPs returned in general election.

1908

Herbert Asquith becomes prime minister.

1909

Old age pensions introduced.

1910

George V succeeds to throne.
Suffragette movement becomes increasingly militant.

1911

Parliament Act reduces the power of the House of Lords.
MPs receive salary for first time.

1912

***Titanic* sinks** with the loss of 1,513 lives.

1914

World War I begins.
Irish Home Rule Act creates separate parliament in Ireland with some MPs in Westminster.

1916

Irish Republican uprising.

1918

World War I ends.
Women over 30 win the right to vote.

1919

Lady Astor becomes the first woman MP to take her seat in the House of Commons.

1920

Communist Party of Great Britain formed.

1921

Irish Free State established.

1922

British Broadcasting Company (BBC) makes first regular broadcast by wireless.

1924

First Labour government elected, with Ramsay MacDonald as prime minister.

1926

General Strike severely disrupts major industries and transport for 9 days, but government manages to maintain essential services.

1928

Alexander Fleming discovers penicillin.
Women entitled to vote on same basis as men (i.e. at age 21).

1930

Unemployment reaches 2 million.

1931

R101 airship explodes on maiden flight to India, ending Britain's enthusiasm for this form of transport.

1936

Edward VIII abdicates after 325 days; George VI succeeds to the throne.

1938

Neville Chamberlain visits Hitler and makes the Munich Agreement, calling it a formula for "peace for our time".

1939

World World II begins when Hitler invades Poland.

1940

Winston Churchill becomes leader of coalition government for duration of the war.
Battle of Britain air victory prevents German invasion.

1941

Rationing of food and clothes begins.

1945

World War II in Europe officially declared over on 8 May.
Labour Party win landslide election victory.

1947

Coal industry nationalized.
School-leaving age raised from 14 to 15.

1948

National Health Service established.
Nationalization of the railways and electricity industry.

1949

Clothes rationing ends.
Nationalization of the gas industry.

1950

Labour government returned with a narrow majority.
Korean War begins; British troops join with those of 15 other UN nations to repel Communist force from N. Korea.

1951

Guy Burgess and Donald Maclean, Soviet agents, defect, causing grave embarrassment to British secret service.
Conservatives win general election; Winston Churchill again prime minister.

1952

Elizabeth II succeeds to throne.
Britain's **first atomic bomb** tested off Australia.

1953

Coronation of Elizabeth II – the first time such a ceremony has been televised.

1954

Food rationing ends.

1955

Churchill resigns; succeeded as prime minister by Anthony Eden.
London declared a "smokeless zone".

1956

British troops withdrawn from Suez Canal Zone.

1957

Premium Bond prize draws begin.
Harold Macmillan becomes prime minister.

1958

Campaign for Nuclear Disarmament (CND) organizes first march from London to Aldermaston.

1959

Conservative government returned with an increased majority.

First stretch of M1 opened to traffic.

1960

"Lady Chatterley" trial; Penguin Books found not guilty of publishing obscene material.

1961

Britain makes **unsuccessful application to join European Economic Community** (EEC).

1962

***Telstar* satellite** brings live television link between US and Europe.

Dr Beeching becomes chairman of British Railways Board and begins a major programme of station closures.

1963

Britain **refused entry** to EEC.

Profumo Affair rocks government.

"Great Train Robbery" – £2.5 million stolen.

Sir Alec Douglas-Home becomes prime minister.

1964

Labour government returned in general election with majority of 5; Harold Wilson prime minister.

1965

Death penalty for murder abolished.

Winston Churchill dies.

1966

Aberfan disaster: slag heap engulfs school and part of village, claiming 144 lives.

Labour government increases majority to 97 in general election.

England wins **World Cup.**

1967

Britain reapplies to join EEC.

1968

British-built **Concorde** makes maiden flight.

1969

Troops sent to quell conflict in Northern Ireland.

1970

Conservatives win general election with a majority of 30; Edward Heath prime minister.

Britain makes **third application** to join EEC.

1971

Terms of **Independence for Rhodesia** announced.

1972

90-day freeze on pay, prices and rent.

Britain assumes **direct rule of Northern Ireland**; Bloody Sunday sees 13 people killed.

1973

Britain enters European Community; Common Agricultural Policy implemented.

Northern Ireland referendum shows a majority of over 500,000 to be in favour of retaining links with Britain.

3-day week introduced to save fuel.

1974

Minority Labour government takes office.

5-day week reintroduced.

General election returns Labour government with a majority of 3.

IRA bombs kill 21 and injure 120 in 2 Birmingham pubs; legislation introduced proscribing IRA.

1975

Margaret Thatcher becomes leader of the Conservative Party.

First live radio broadcast of a Commons debate.

Unemployment reaches over 1 million.

Internment (detention without trial) ends in Northern Ireland.

1976

Harold Wilson resigns; James Callaghan becomes prime minister.

Jeremy Thorpe resigns; David Steel becomes leader of the Liberal Party.

Ian Smith accepts British proposals for majority rule in Rhodesia.

1977

Ian Smith rejects proposals for majority rule.

Labour and Liberal parties form pact.

Diplomatic links severed with Uganda.

1978

World's first test-tube baby born in Britain.

Lib-Lab Pact terminated.

1979

Margaret Thatcher becomes first woman prime minister.

Jeremy Thorpe acquitted in conspiracy trial.

Earl Mountbatten killed by terrorist bomb.

1980

Iranian Embassy siege; 2 hostages shot by gunmen; SAS storms embassy to bring siege to an end.

James Callaghan retires; Michael Foot elected leader of Labour Party.

1981

"Gang of Four" (Roy Jenkins, David Owen, Bill Rodgers and Shirley Williams) announce the formation of a new political party – the Social Democrats.

Rioting breaks out in London, Liverpool and Manchester, apparently caused by conflict with the police.

Hunger strikes at Maze Prison end; 10 have died.

1982

Barbican Centre, London, opened by Queen.

Falklands War begins Apr. 2, ends June 14.

Thames Barrier raised for first time.

Massive anti-nuclear protest at Greenham Common; 30,000 women encircle the site.

1983

Conservatives returned with increased majority.

Neil Kinnock elected leader of the Labour Party.

Greenham Common protests begin against cruise missiles.

1984

Diplomatic links broken with Libya after unlawful killing of WPC Yvonne Fletcher outside Libyan embassy.

Government ban on unions at GCHQ ruled illegal by High Court.

IRA bomb at Conservative Party Conference kills 5.

1985

House of Lords proceedings televised for first time.

British football teams banned indefinitely from European competition after spectator violence at Heysel stadium results in 38 deaths.

1986

Channel Tunnel construction work begins.

Michael Heseltine resigns over **Westland affair**,

followed shortly afterwards by Leon Brittan.

Commons vote to ban corporal punishment in schools.

Jeffrey Archer retires as deputy chairman of Conservative Party after allegations of payments to a prostitute.

1987

Guinness affair begins with sacking of Ernest Saunders and 2 colleagues.

Terry Waite kidnapped in Beirut.

Conservatives elected for third term.

Poll tax plans announced.

David Owen resigns as leader of the SDP, refusing to discuss merger with the Liberals.

Black Monday in the City: stock values drop over £100 billion.

1988

Social and Liberal Democratic (SLD) Party formed by merger of the Liberals and SDP; Paddy Ashdown elected leader.

Conservative MPs revolt against poll tax; government majority cut from 101 to 25.

Pan Am jet blown up by terrorist bomb over Lockerbie.

1989

Salman Rushdie, sentenced to death for blasphemy by Ayatollah Khomeini, goes into hiding.

John Major appointed foreign secretary.

Guildford Four, jailed for pub bombings, released after their convictions are found to be "unsafe".

Nigel Lawson resigns as chancellor of the exchequer when Mrs Thatcher refuses to dismiss Sir Alan Walters, her personal economic adviser; John Major becomes chancellor, and Walters ultimately resigns too.

House of Commons proceedings begin to be televised.

1990

Mortgage rates reach a record high of 15.4%.

Riots at Strangeways Prison; inmates complain of inhumane conditions.

David Owen disbands Social Democrat Party for lack of support.

English football clubs, except Liverpool, readmitted to European competition after 5-year ban following Heysel tragedy.

Queen awarded 50% pay rise; Civil List income reaches £7.9 million.

Ian Gow, Conservative MP, killed by IRA bomb at his home in Sussex.

British forces sent to Gulf after Saddam Hussein's invasion of Kuwait.

British sheep burned alive in lorries by French farmers protesting against meat imports; French government later apologizes and agrees to pay compensation.

Britain rejects single currency by year 2000 at EC summit in Rome.

Sir Geoffrey Howe resigns from Cabinet, publicly disagreeing with Mrs Thatcher's stand on Europe.

Margaret Thatcher withdraws from Conservative leadership contest; John Major becomes prime minister.

Poll tax review announced by Major.

Channel Tunnel boring teams meet in the middle – the first time Britain has been linked to the European continent since the Ice Age 7,000 years ago.

IRA announce Christmas truce.

1991

Gulf War begins, Jan. 17, with massive air and missile attack on Iraq by British, American and Saudi forces; ground war begins 1 week later – 13 British soldiers die, 10,000 Iraqi troops surrender; allied ceasefire announced Jan. 27.

Downing Street Cabinet meeting is target of IRA bomb attack; none present are injured.

Birmingham Six released.

Court of Appeal makes historic ruling that a man can be accused of raping his wife.

Unemployment reaches 2.4 million.

Unpopularity of poll tax with public and MPs alike causes increasing embarrassment to government; a replacement "council tax" is announced – this one to be based on the value of property and to take effect in 1993.

Britain promises £33 million to Kurds who are suffering oppression and severe hardship at the hands of Saddam Hussein.

Dr George Carey enthroned as Archbishop of Canterbury.

Hospitals are allowed to become self-governing trusts.

Prison reform plan pledges to end slopping out by 1994.

Parents' Charter, announced by Education Secretary, aims to privatize school inspectors and to make schools" academic results readily available to parents.

The Children Act, claiming to put the child first and promote the family, comes into force.

John Major announces that every government department will have a minister responsible for promoting women's interests.

Crime in London is found to have risen by almost 20%.

Extra troops move into Belfast after a spate of tit-for-tat killings.

Many shops open in defiance of **Sunday trading laws**, thanks to the confusion between EEC and British rulings.

Britain agrees to a **single European currency** by 1999.

Prison mutiny legislation introduced following violent unrest at Strangeways.

Dangerous Dogs Act introduced.

Robert Maxwell dies in mysterious circumstances, leaving massive debts.

Tottenham 3 are cleared of murdering PC Keith Blakelock in Broadwater Farm riots when police evidence is found to be unreliable.

John Major negotiates an opt-out clause from EMU and promises the other EC members sweeping concessions in return for dropping all references to a federal Europe in the Maastricht Treaty.

1992

Recession continues its strangflehold on the British economy, with the car industry suffering its worst ever slump.

IRA terrorists breach Whitehall security, planting a bomb which explodes 400 yards from Downing Street.

Crime is up 32% under the present government.

Major employers Ford, British Aerospace, British Telecom and BP announce massive job cuts due to trading losses.

Stephen Kisczko, imprisoned for the murder of Lesley Molseed, is freed when it is learned that the police withheld vital information from his original trial.

National lottery of £1 billion "for good causes" is announced by government.

Duke and Duchess of York separate after 5 years of marriage.

Tories win general election, but with a decreased majority.

Neil Kinnock resigns as leader of the Labour Party. He is subsequently replaced by John Smith.

Princess Royal is granted a divorce from Captain Mark Phillips.

Bank base rates drop to a 4-year low of 10%.

Canary Wharf development declared bankrupt.

Judith Ward cleared of M62 coach bombing, for which she had served 18 years in jail.

Urban rioting breaks out in Coventry, and later spreads to Bristol, Burnley and Blackburn.

British soldiers go on the rampage in Northern Ireland when one of their colleagues is seriously injured in a bomb blast.

West Midlands Police escape prosecution for fabricating evidence, despite the clearing of 11 prisoners convicted by the force.

Common Agricultural Policy changes include substantial cuts in the prices paid to farmers, measures to take land out of production and a switch of subsidies from output to incomes.

Maastricht Treaty bill passed in Commons with a 336–92 majority.

Stamp Duty reintroduced in August, having been waived for a year in an effort to revive the depressed housing market.

Unemployment figures reach 2,753,400 in mid-July, the highest for 5 years.

Ulster Defence Association, a Protestant paramilitary organization, is outlawed by Government.

"Union Jack"

The state flag, commonly known as the Union Jack, is properly known as the Union Flag. Its takes its common name from the jack-staff from which it is flown on naval vessels.

The Union Flag is a combination of the flags of England (cross of St George – red cross on a white ground), Scotland (cross of St Andrew – white diagonal cross on a blue ground) and Ireland (cross of St Patrick – red diagonal cross on a white ground). However, the latter has never actually been used as the Irish emblem; it is in fact the heraldic device of the Fitzgerald family, whom Henry II (1154–89) dispatched to subjugate Ireland.

The process of combining the flags began in 1603, when King James became monarch of both Scotland and England. The cross of St Patrick was incorporated in 1801, when Ireland was united with Great Britain. The flag of Wales, a red dragon on a horizontally divided ground of white over green, is not represented in the Union Flag.

Flying the Flag

The broader diagonal band of white should be uppermost (nearest) the flagpole, and the narrower diagonal band of white furthest away from the pole.

The flag is flown on appointed days by command of the Queen between 8 a.m. and sunset. The days are notified to the Department of the Environment.

The National Anthem

The composer and author of *God Save the Queen* are unknown. The anthem was adopted in the mid-18th century, the earliest-known copy of the words dating from a 1745 issue of *Gentleman's Magazine*. The melody dates from much earlier and is the same as that of the national anthem of Liechtenstein, and of *America (My Country 'Tis of Thee)*.

1. God save our gracious Queen,
Long live our noble Queen,
God save the Queen
Send her victorious,
Happy and glorious,
Long to reign over us;
God save the Queen.

2. O Lord our God arise,
Scatter her enemies,
And make them fall.
Confound their politics,
Frustrate their knavish tricks,
On Thee our hopes we fix:
God save us all.

3. Thy choicest gifts in store
On her be pleased to pour;
Long may she reign.
May she defend our laws,
And ever give us cause
To sing with heart and voice
God save the Queen.

WORLD HISTORY

Prehistory: Our Ancestors Take Over

Homo sapiens. The precise origins of *Homo sapiens,* the species to which all humans belong, are subject to broad speculation based on a small number of fossils, genetic and anatomical studies, and the geological record. But most scientists agree that we evolved from ape-like primate ancestors in a process that began millions of years ago.

Current theories trace the first hominid (human-like primate) to Africa where 2 lines of hominids appeared some 5 or 6 million years ago. One was *Australopithecus,* a tool-maker and social animal, who lived from perhaps 4 to 3 million years ago, and then apparently became extinct.

The 2nd was a human line, *Homo habilis*, a large-brained specimen that walked upright and had a dextrous hand. *Homo habilus* lived in semi-permanent camps and had a food-gathering and sharing economy.

Homo erectus, our nearest ancestor, appeared in Africa perhaps 1.75 million years ago, and began spreading into Asia and Europe soon after. It had a fairly large brain and a skeletal structure similar to ours. *Homo erectus* learned to control fire, and probably had primitive language skills. The final brain development to *Homo sapiens* and then to our sub-species *Homo sapiens sapiens* occurred between 500,000 and 50,000 years ago, either in one place — probably Africa — or virtually simultaneously and independently in different places in Africa, Europe, and Asia. There is no question that all modern races are members of the same sub species, *Homo sapiens sapiens.*

The spread of mankind into the remaining habitable continents probably took place during the last ice age up to 100,000 years ago: to the Americas across a land bridge from Asia, and to Australia across the Timor Straits.

Earliest cultures. A variety of cultural modes — in toolmaking, diet, shelter, and possibly social arrangements and spiritual expression, arose as early mankind adapted to different geographic and climatic zones.

Three basic tool-making traditions are recognized by archeologists as arising and often coexisting from one million years ago to the near past: the *chopper tradition,* found largely in E. Asia, with crude chopping tools and simple flake tools; the *flake tradition,* found in Africa and W. Europe, with a variety of small cutting and flaking tools, and the *biface tradition,* found in all of Africa, W. and S. Europe, and S. Asia, producing pointed hand axes chipped on both faces. Later biface sites yield more refined axes and a variety of other tools, weapons, and ornaments using bone, antler, and wood as well as stone.

Only sketchy evidence remains for the different stages in man's increasing control over the environment. Traces of 400,000-year-old covered wood shelters have been found at Nice, France. Scraping tools at Neanderthal sites (200,000-30,000 BC in Europe, N. Africa, the Middle East and Central Asia) suggest the treatment of skins for clothing. Sites from all parts of the world show seasonal migration patterns and exploitation of a wide range of plant and animal food sources.

Painting and decoration, for which there is evidence at the Nice site, flourished along with stone and ivory sculpture after 30,000 years ago; 60 caves in France and 30 in Spain show remarkable examples of wall painting. Other examples have been found in Africa. Proto-religious rites are suggested by these works, and by evidence of ritual cannibalism by Peking Man, 500,000 BC, and of ritual burial with medicinal plants and flowers by Neanderthals at Shanidar in Iraq.

The Neolithic Revolution. Sometime after 10,000 BC, among widely separated human communities, a series of dramatic technological and social changes occurred that are summed up as the Neolithic Revolution. The cultivation of previously wild plants encouraged the growth of permanent settlements. Animals were domesticated as a work force and food source. The manufacture of pottery and cloth began. These techniques permitted a huge increase in world population and in human control over the earth.

No region can safely claim priority as the "inventor" of these techniques. Dispersed sites in Cen. and S. America, S.E. Europe, and the Middle East show roughly contemporaneous (10-8,000 BC) evidence of one or another "neolithic" trait. Dates near 6-3,000 BC have been given for E. and S. Asian, W. European, and sub-Saharan African neolithic remains. The variety of crops — field grains, rice, maize, and roots, and the varying mix of other traits suggest that the revolution occurred independently in all these regions.

History Begins: 4000–1000 BC

Near Eastern cradle. If history began with writing, the first chapter opened in Mesopotamia, the Tigris-Euphrates river valley. Clay tablets with pictographs were used by the Sumerians to keep records after 4000 BC. A **cuneiform** (wedge shaped) script evolved by 3000 BC as a full syllabic alphabet. Neighboring peoples adapted the script to their own language.

Sumerian life centered, from 4000 BC, on large cities (Eridu, Ur, Uruk, Nippur, Kish, Lagash) organized around temples and priestly bureaucracies, with the surrounding plains watered by vast irrigation works and worked with traction plows. Sailboats, wheeled vehicles, potters wheels, and kilns were used. Copper was smelted and tempered in Sumeria from c4000 BC and bronze was produced not long after. Ores, as well as precious stones and metals were obtained through long-distance ship and caravan trade. Iron was used from c2000 BC. Improved ironworking, developed partly by the **Hittites,** became widespread by 1200 BC.

Sumerian political primacy passed among cities and their kingly dynasties. Semitic-speaking peoples, with cultures derived from the Sumerian, founded a succession of dynasties that ruled in Mesopotamia and neighboring areas for most of 1800 years; among them the **Akkadians** (first under Sargon c2350 BC), the Amorites (whose laws, codified by **Hammurabi,** c1792-1750 BC, have Biblical parallels), and the Assyrians, with interludes of rule by the Hittites, Kassites, and Mitanni, all possibly Indo-Europeans. The political and cultural center of gravity shifted northwest with each successive empire.

Mesopotamian learning, maintained by scribes and preserved by successive rulers in vast libraries, was not abstract or theoretical. Algebraic and geometric problems could be solved on a practical basis in construction, commerce, or administration. Systematic lists of astronomical phenomena, plants, animals and stones were kept; medical texts listed ailments and their herbal cures.

The Sumerians worshipped anthropomorphic gods representing natural forces — Anu, god of heaven; Enlil (Ea), god of water. Epic poetry related these and other gods in a hierarchy. Sacrifices were made at **ziggurats** — huge stepped temples. Gods were thought to control all events, which could be foretold using oracular materials. This religious pattern persisted into the first millenium BC.

The Syria-Palestine area, site of some of the earliest urban remains (Jericho, 7000 BC), and of the recently uncovered **Ebla** civilization (fl. 2500 BC), experienced Egyptian cultural and political influence along with Mesopotamian. The **Phoenician** coast was an active commercial center. A phonetic alphabet was invented here before 1600 BC. It became the ancestor of all European, Middle Eastern, Indian, S.E. Asian,

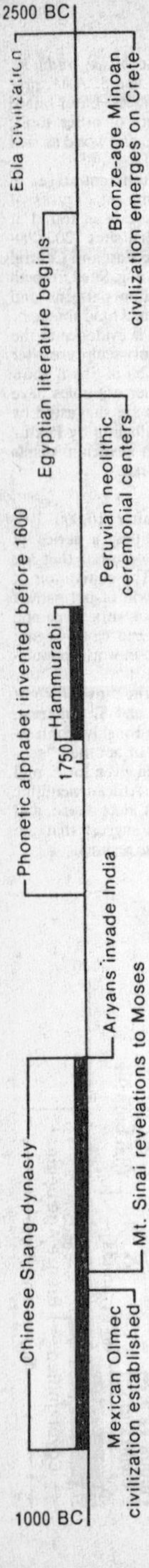

Ethiopian, and Korean alphabets.

Regional commerce and diplomacy were aided by the use of Akkadian as a *lingua franca,* later replaced by Aramaic.

Egypt. Agricultural villages along the Nile were united by 3300 BC into two kingdoms, Upper and Lower Egypt, unified under the Pharaoh Menes c3100 BC; Nubia to the south was added 2600 BC. A national bureaucracy supervised construction of canals and monuments (**pyramids** starting 2700 BC). Brilliant First Dynasty achievements in architecture, sculpture and painting, set the standards and forms for all subsequent Egyptian civilization and are still admired. **Hieroglyphic writing** appeared by 3400 BC, recording a sophisticated literature including romantic and philosophical modes after 2300 BC.

An ordered hierarchy of gods, including totemistic animal elements, was served by a powerful priesthood in Memphis. The pharaoh was identified with the falcon god Horus. Later trends were the belief in an afterlife, and the quasi-monotheistic reforms of **Akhenaton** (c1379-1362 BC).

After a period of conquest by Semitic Hyksos from Asia (c1700-1500 BC), the New Kingdom established an empire in Syria. Egypt became increasingly embroiled in Asiatic wars and diplomacy. Eventually it was conquered by Persia in 525 BC, and it faded away as an independent culture.

India. An urban civilization with a so-far-undeciphered writing system stretched across the Indus Valley and along the Arabian Sea c3000-1500 BC. Major sites are Harappa and **Mohenjo-Daro** in Pakistan, well-planned geometric cities with underground sewers and vast granaries. The entire region (600,000 sq. mi.) may have been ruled as a single state. Bronze was used, and arts and crafts were highly developed. Religious life apparently took the form of fertility cults.

Indus civilization was probably in decline when it was destroyed by **Aryan invaders** from the northwest, speaking an Indo-European language from which all the languages of Pakistan, north India and Bangladesh descend. Led by a warrior aristocracy whose legendary deeds are recorded in the **Rig Veda,** the Aryans spread east and south, bringing their pantheon of sky gods, elaborate priestly (Brahmin) ritual, and the beginnings of the caste system; local customs and beliefs were assimilated by the conquerors.

Europe. On Crete, the bronze-age **Minoan civilization** emerged c2500 BC. A prosperous economy and richly decorative art (e.g. at Knossos palace) was supported by seaborne commerce. Mycenae and other cities in Greece and Asia Minor (e.g. **Troy**) preserved elements of the culture to c1100 BC. Cretan Linear A script, c2000-1700 BC, is undeciphered; Linear B, c1300-1200 BC, records a Greek dialect.

Possible connection between Minoan-Mycenaean monumental stonework, and the great megalithic monuments and tombs of W. Europe, Iberia, and Malta (c4000-1500 BC) is unclear.

China. Proto-Chinese neolithic cultures had long covered northern and southeastern China when the first large political state was organized in the north by the **Shang dynasty** c1500 BC. Shang kings called themselves Sons of Heaven, and presided over a cult of human and animal sacrifice to ancestors and nature gods. The Chou dynasty, starting c1100 BC, expanded the area of the Son of Heaven's dominion, but feudal states exercised most temporal power.

A writing system with 2,000 different characters was already in use under the Shang, with **pictographs** later supplemented by phonetic characters. The system, with modifications, is still in use, despite changes in spoken Chinese.

Technical advances allowed urban specialists to create fine ceramic and jade products, and bronze casting after 1500 BC was the most advanced in the world.

Bronze artifacts have recently been discovered in northern Thailand dating to 3600 BC, hundreds of years before similar Middle Eastern finds.

Americas. Olmecs settled on the Gulf coast of Mexico, 1500 BC, and soon developed the first civilization in the Western Hemisphere. Temple cities and huge stone sculpture date to 1200 BC. A rudimentary calendar and writing system existed. Olmec religion, centering on a jaguar god, and art forms influenced all later Meso-American cultures.

Neolithic ceremonial centers were built on the Peruvian desert coast, c2000 BC.

Classical Era of Old World Civilizations

Greece. After a period of decline during the Dorian Greek invasions (1200-1000 BC), Greece and the Aegean area developed a unique civilization. Drawing upon Mycenaean traditions, Mesopotamian learning (weights and measures, lunisolar calendar, astronomy, musical scales), the Phoenician alphabet (modified for Greek), and Egyptian art, the revived **Greek city-states** saw a rich elaboration of intellectual life. Long-range commerce was aided by metal coinage (introduced by the Lydians in Asia Minor before 700 BC); colonies were founded around the Mediterranean and Black Sea shores (Cumae in Italy 760 BC, Massalia in France c600 BC).

Philosophy, starting with Ionian speculation on the nature of matter and the universe (Thales c634-546 BC), and including mathematical speculation (Pythagoras c580-c500), culminated in Athens in the rationalist idealism of **Plato** (c428-347) and **Socrates** (c470-399); the latter was executed for alleged impiety. **Aristotle** (384-322) united all fields of study in his system. The arts were highly valued. Architecture culminated in the **Parthenon** in Athens (438, sculpture by Phidias); poetry and drama (Aeschylus 525-456) thrived. Male beauty and strength, a chief artistic theme, were enhanced at the gymnasium and the national games at Olympia.

Ruled by local tyrants or oligarchies, the Greeks were never politically united, but managed to resist inclusion in the Persian Empire (Darius defeated at Marathon 490 BC, Xerxes at Salamis, Plataea 479 BC). Local warfare was common; the **Peloponnesian Wars,** 431-404 BC, ended in Sparta's victory over Athens. Greek political power waned, but classical Greek cultural forms spread thoughout the ancient world from the Atlantic to India.

Hebrews. Nomadic Hebrew tribes entered Canaan before 1200 BC, settling among other Semitic peoples speaking the same language. They brought from the desert a **monotheistic faith** said to have been revealed to Abraham in Canaan c1800 BC and to Moses at Mt. Sinai c1250 BC, after the Hebrews' escape from bondage in Egypt. David (ruled 1000-961 BC) and Solomon (ruled 961-922 BC) united the Hebrews in a kingdom that briefly dominated the area. Phoenicians to the north established colonies around the E. and W. Mediterranean (**Carthage** c814 BC) and sailed into the Atlantic.

Palaeontology: The History of Life

All dates are approximate, and are subject to change based on new fossil finds or new dating techniques; but the sequence of events is generally accepted. Dates are in years before the present.

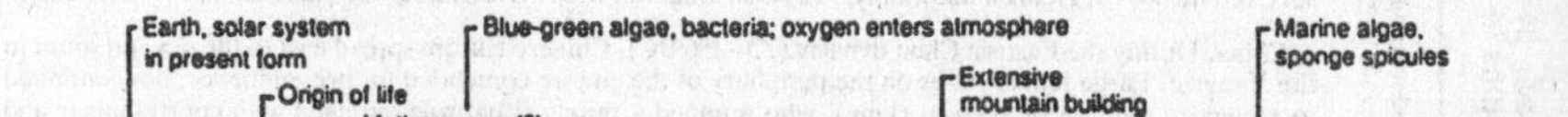

Ancient Near Eastern Civilizations 4000 BC–500 BC

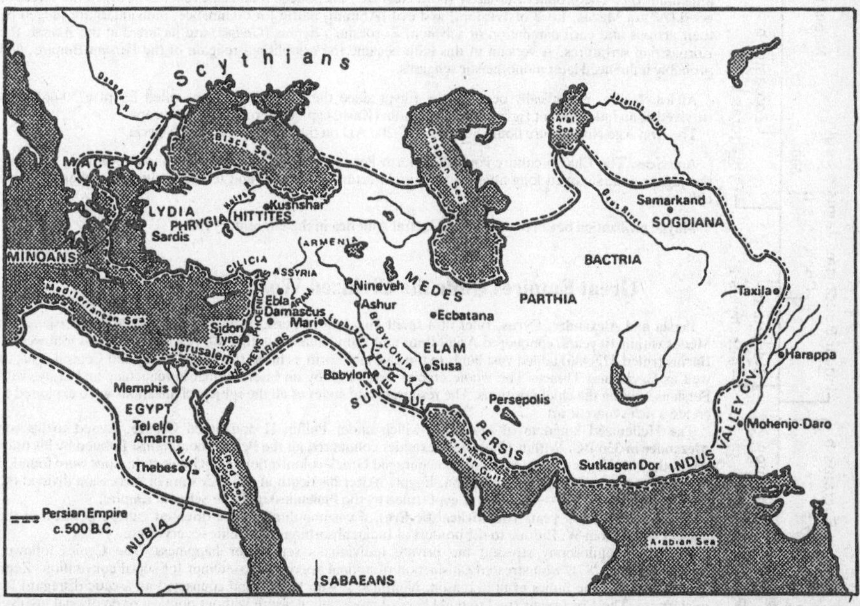

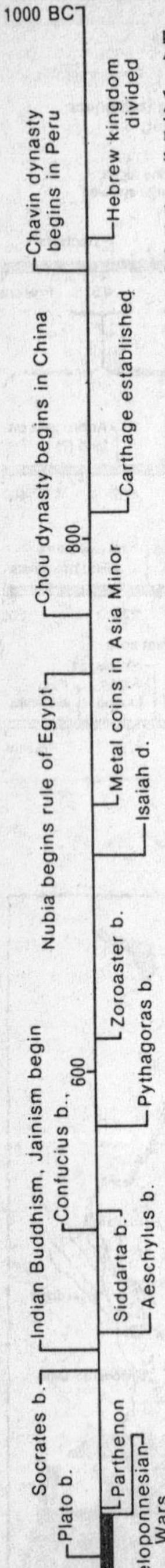

A temple in Jerusalem became the national religious center, with sacrifices performed by a hereditary priesthood. Polytheistic influences, especially of the fertility cult of Baal, were opposed by **prophets** (Elijah, Amos, Isaiah).

Divided into **two kingdoms** after Solomon, the Hebrews were unable to resist the revived Assyrian empire, which conquered Israel, the northern kingdom in 722 BC. Judah, the southern kingdom, was conquered in 586 BC by the Babylonians under Nebuchadnezzar II. But with the fixing of most of the Biblical canon by the mid-fourth century BC, and the emergence of rabbis, arbiters of law and custom, Judaism successfully survived the loss of Hebrew autonomy. A Jewish kingdom was revived under the Hasmoneans (168-42 BC).

China. During the **Eastern Chou** dynasty (770-256 BC), Chinese culture spread east to the sea and south to the Yangtze. Large feudal states on the periphery of the empire contended for pre-eminence, but continued to recognize the Son of Heaven (king), who retained a purely ritual role enriched with courtly music and dance. In the Age of Warring States (403-221 BC), when the first sections of the **Great Wall** were built, the Ch'in state in the West gained supremacy, and finally united all of China.

Iron tools entered China c500 BC, and casting techniques were advanced, aiding agriculture. Peasants owned their land, and owed civil and military service to nobles. Cities grew in number and size, though barter remained the chief trade medium.

Intellectual ferment among noble scribes and officials produced the Classical Age of Chinese literature and philosophy. **Confucius** (551-479 BC) urged a restoration of a supposedly harmonious social order of the past through proper conduct in accordance with one's station and through filial and ceremonial piety. The *Analects,* attributed to him, are revered throughout East Asia. **Mencius** (d. 289 BC) added the view that the Mandate of Heaven can be removed from an unjust dynasty. The Legalists sought to curb the supposed natural wickedness of people through new institutions and harsh laws; they aided the Ch'in rise to power. The Naturalists emphasized the balance of opposites — yin, yang — in the world. **Taoists** sought mystical knowledge through meditation and disengagement.

India. The political and cultural center of India shifted from the Indus to the Ganges River Valley. Buddhism, Jainism, and mystical revisions of orthodox Vedism all developed around 500-300 BC. The *Upanishads,* last part of the *Veda,* urged escape from the illusory physical world. Vedism remained the preserve of the priestly Brahmin caste. In contrast, **Buddhism,** founded by Siddarta Gautama (c563-c483 BC), appealed to merchants in the growing urban centers, and took hold at first (and most lastingly.) on the geographic fringes of Indian civilization. The classic Indian epics were composed in this era: The *Ramayana* perhaps around 300 BC, the *Mahabharata* over a period starting 400 BC.

Northern India was divided into a large number of monarchies and aristocratic republics, probably derived from tribal groupings, when the Magadha kingdom was formed in Bihar c542 BC. It soon became the dominant power. The **Maurya dynasty,** founded by Chandragupta c321 BC, expanded the kingdom, uniting most of N. India in a centralized bureaucratic empire. The third Mauryan king, **Asoka** (ruled c274-236) conquered most of the subcontinent: he converted to Buddhism, and inscribed its tenets on pillars throughout India. He downplayed the caste system and tried to end expensive sacrificial rites.

Before its final decline in India, Buddhism developed the popular worship of heavenly Bodhisatvas (enlightened beings), and produced a refined architecture (stupa—shrine—3 at Sanchi 100 AD) and sculpture (Gandhara reliefs 1-400 AD).

Persia. Aryan peoples (Persians, Medes) dominated the area of present Iran by the beginning of the first millenium BC. The prophet **Zoroaster** (born c628 BC) introduced a dualistic religion in which the forces of good (Ahura Mazda, Lord of Wisdom) and evil (Ahiram) battle for dominance; individuals are judged by their actions and earn damnation or salvaion, Zoroaster's hymns (*Gathas*) are included in the *Avesta,* the Zoroastrian scriptures. A version of this faith became the established religion of the Persian Empire, and probably influenced later monotheistic religions.

Africa. Nubia, periodically occupied by Egypt since the third millennium, ruled Egypt c750-661, and survived as an independent Egyptianized kingdom (**Kush;** capital Meroe) for 1,000 years.

The Iron Age Nok culture flourished c500 BC-200 AD on the Benue Plateau of **Nigeria.**

Americas. The Chavin culture controlled north Peru from 900-200 BC. Its ceremonial centers, featuring the jaguar god, survived long after. Chavin architecture, ceramics, and textiles influenced other Peruvian cultures.

Mayan civilization began to develop in Central America in the 5th century BC.

Great Empires Unite the Civilized World: 400 BC–400 AD

Persia and Alexander. Cyrus, ruler of a small kingdom in Persia from 559 BC, united the Persians and Medes within 10 years, conquered Asia Minor and Babylonia in another 10. His son Cambyses followed by **Darius** (ruled 522-486) added vast lands to the east and north as far as the Indus Valley and Central Asia, as well as Egypt and Thrace. The whole empire was ruled by an international bureaucracy and army, with Persians holding the chief positions. The resources and styles of all the subject civilizations were exploited to create a rich syncretic art.

The Hellenized kingdom of Macedon, which under Phillip II dominated Greece, passed to his son **Alexander** in 336 BC. Within 13 years, Alexander conquered all the Persian dominions. Imbued by his tutor Aristotle with Greek ideals, Alexander encouraged Greek colonization, and Greek-style cities were founded throughout the empire (e.g. Alexandria, Egypt). After his death in 323 BC, wars of succession divided the empire into three parts — **Macedon,** Egypt (ruled by the **Ptolemies**), and the **Seleucid** Empire.

In the ensuing 300 years (the **Hellenistic Era**), a cosmopolitan Greek-oriented culture permeated the ancient world from W. Europe to the borders of India, absorbing native elites everywhere.

Hellenistic philosophy stressed the private individual's search for happiness. The Cynics followed Diogenes (c372-287), who stressed satisfaction of animal needs and contempt for social convention. Zeno (c335-c263) and the Stoics exalted reason, identified it with virtue, and counseled an ascetic disregard for misfortune. The Epicureans tried to build lives of moderate pleasure without political or emotional involve-

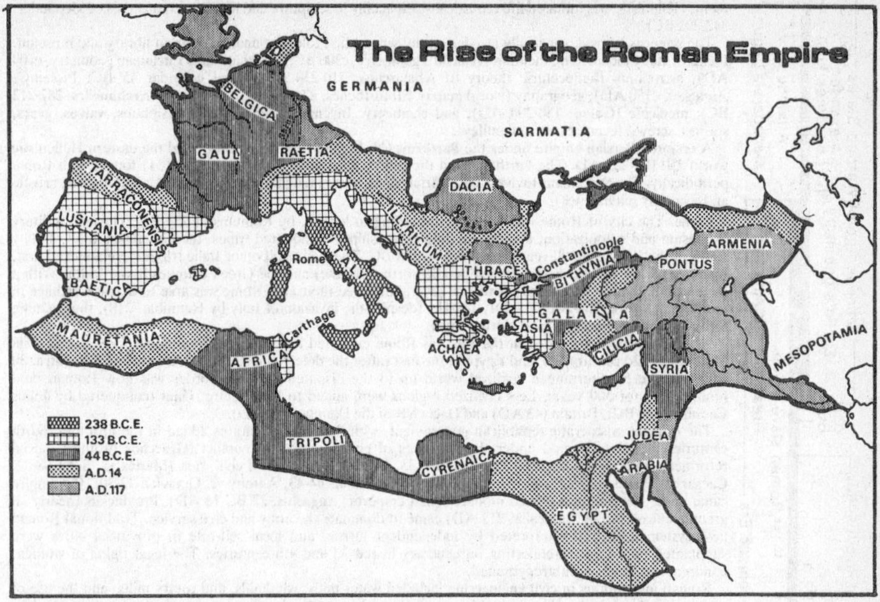
The Rise of the Roman Empire
GERMANIA
SARMATIA
BELGICA
GAUL
RAETIA
TARRACONENSIS
LUSITANIA
BAETICA
DACIA
ILLYRICUM
ITALY
Rome
ARMENIA
PONTUS
Constantinople
THRACE
BITHYNIA
GALATIA
ASIA
ACHAEA
CILICIA
MESOPOTAMIA
MAURETANIA
Carthage
AFRICA
SYRIA
TRIPOLI
JUDEA
CYRENAICA
ARABIA
EGYPT
238 B.C.E.
133 B.C.E.
44 B.C.E.
A.D.14
A.D.117

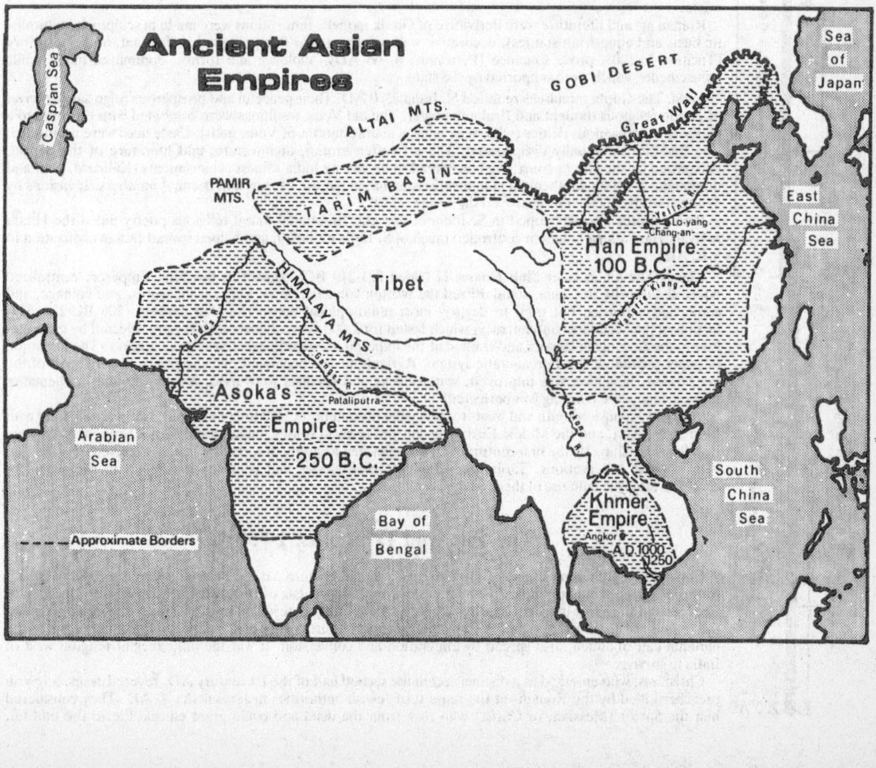
Ancient Asian Empires
Caspian Sea
GOBI DESERT
Sea of Japan
Great Wall
ALTAI MTS.
PAMIR MTS.
TARIM BASIN
Lo-yang
Chang-an
Han Empire 100 B.C.
East China Sea
Tibet
HIMALAYA MTS.
Asoka's Empire 250 B.C.
Pataliputra
Arabian Sea
South China Sea
Khmer Empire
Angkor
A.D.1000 - 1250
Bay of Bengal
Approximate Borders

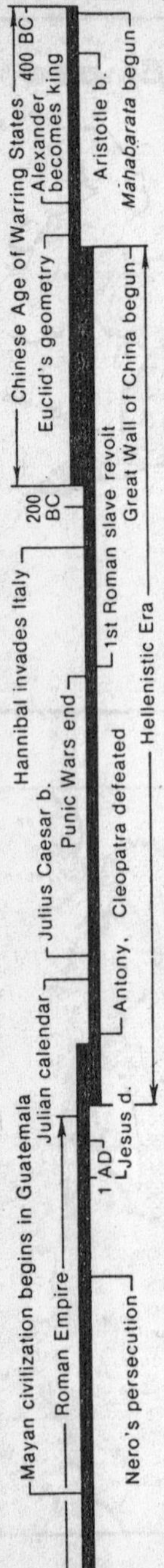

ment. Hellenistic arts imitated life realistically, especially in sculpture and literature (comedies of Menander, 342-292 BC).

The sciences thrived, especially at Alexandria, where the Ptolemies financed a great library and museum. Fields of study included mathematics (**Euclid's** geometry, c300 BC; Menelaus' non-Euclidean geometry, c100 AD); astronomy (heliocentric theory of Aristarchus, 310-230 BC; Julian calendar 45 BC; Ptolemy's *Almagest,* c150 AD); geography (world map of Eratosthenes, 276-194 BC); hydraulics (**Archimedes,** 287-212 BC); medicine (Galen, 130-200 AD), and chemistry. Inventors refined uses for siphons, valves, gears, springs, screws, levers, cams, and pulleys.

A restored Persian empire under the **Parthians** (N. Iranian tribesmen) controlled the eastern Hellenistic world 250 BC-229 AD. The Parthians and the succeeding Sassanian dynasty (229-651) fought with Rome periodically. The **Sassanians** revived Zoroastrianism as a state religion, and patronized a nationalistic artistic and scholarly renaissance.

Rome. The city of Rome was founded, according to legend, by Romulus in 753 BC. Through military expansion and colonization, and by granting citizenship to conquered tribes, the city annexed all of Italy south of the Po in the 100-year period before 268 BC. The Latin and other Italic tribes were annexed first, followed by the Etruscans (a civilized people north of Rome) and the Greek colonies in the south. With a large standing army and reserve forces of several hundred thousand, Rome was able to defeat Carthage in the 3 **Punic Wars,** 264-241, 218-201, 149-146 (despite the invasion of Italy by Hannibal, 218), thus gaining Sicily and territory in Spain and North Africa.

New provinces were added in the East, as Rome exploited local disputes to conquer Greece and Asia Minor in the 2d century BC, and Egypt in the first (after the defeat and suicide of **Antony and Cleopatra,** 30 BC). All the Mediterranean civilized world up to the disputed Parthian border was now Roman, and remained so for 500 years. Less civilized regions were added to the Empire: Gaul (conquered by Julius Caesar, 56-49 BC), Britain (43 AD) and Dacia NE of the Danube (117 AD).

The original aristocratic republican government, with democratic features added in the fifth and fourth centuries BC, deteriorated under the pressures of empire and class conflict (**Gracchus** brothers, social reformers, murdered 133, 121; slave revolts 135, 73). After a series of civil wars (Marius vs. Sulla 88-82, Caesar vs. Pompey 49-45, triumvirate vs. Caesar's assassins 44-43, Antony vs. Octavian 32-30), the empire came under the rule of a deified monarch (first emperor, **Augustus,** 27 BC-14 AD). Provincials (nearly all granted citizenship by Caracalla, 212 AD) came to dominate the army and civil service. Traditional Roman law, systematized and interpreted by independent jurists, and local self-rule in provincial cities were supplanted by a vast tax-collecting bureaucracy in the 3d and 4th centuries. The legal rights of women, children, and slaves were strengthened.

Roman innovations in **civil engineering** included water mills, windmills, and rotary mills, and the use of cement that hardened under water. Monumental architecture (baths, theaters, apartment houses) relied on the arch and the dome. The network of roads (some still standing) stretched 53,000 miles, passing through mountain tunnels as long as 3.5 miles. Aqueducts brought water to cities, underground sewers removed waste.

Roman art and literature were derivative of Greek models. Innovations were made in sculpture (naturalistic busts and equestrian statues), decorative wall painting (as at Pompeii), satire (Juvenal, 60-127), history (Tacitus, 56-120), prose romance (Petronius, d. 66 AD). Violence and torture dominated mass public amusements, which were supported by the state.

India. The **Gupta** monarchs reunited N. India c320 AD. Their peaceful and prosperous reign saw a revival of Hindu religious thought and Brahmin power. The old Vedic traditions were combined with devotion to a plethora of indigenous deities (who were seen as manifestations of Vedic gods). **Caste lines** were reinforced, and Buddhism gradually disappeared. The art (often erotic), architecture, and literature of the period, patronized by the Gupta court, are considered to be among India's finest achievements (Kalidasa, poet and dramatist, fl. c400). Mathematical innovations included the use of zero and decimal numbers. Invasions by White Huns from the NW destroyed the empire c550.

Rich cultures also developed in S. India in this era. Emotional Tamil religious poetry aided the Hindu revival. The Pallava kingdom controlled much of S. India c350-880, and helped spread Indian civilization to S.E. Asia.

China. The Ch'in ruler Shih Huang Ti (ruled 221-210 BC), known as the First Emperor, centralized political authority in China, standardized the written language, laws, weights, measures, and coinage, and conducted a census, but tried to destroy most philosophical texts. The **Han dynasty** (206 BC-220 AD) instituted the Mandarin bureaucracy, which lasted for 2,000 years. Local officials were selected by examination in the Confucian classics and trained at the imperial university and at provincial schools. The invention of **paper** facilitated this bureaucratic system. Agriculture was promoted, but the peasants bore most of the tax burden. Irrigation was improved; water clocks and sundials were used; astronomy and mathematics thrived; landscape painting was perfected.

With the expansion south and west (to nearly the present borders of today's China), trade was opened with India, S.E. Asia, and the Middle East, over sea and caravan routes. Indian missionaries brought Mahayana Buddhism to China by the first century AD, and spawned a variety of sects. Taoism was revived, and merged with popular superstitions. Taoist and Buddhist monasteries and convents multiplied in the turbulent centuries after the collapse of the Han dynasty.

The One God Triumphs: 1-750 AD

Christianity. Religions indigenous to particular Middle Eastern nations became international in the first 3 centuries of the Roman Empire. Roman citizens worshipped **Isis** of Egypt, **Mithras** of Persia, **Demeter** of Greece, and the great mother **Cybele** of Phrygia. Their cults centered on mysteries (secret ceremonies) and the promise of an afterlife, symbolized by the death and rebirth of the god. Judaism, which had begun as the national cult of Judea, also spread by emigration and conversion. It was the only ancient religion west of India to survive.

Christians, who emerged as a distinct sect in the second half of the 1st century AD, revered **Jesus,** a Jewish preacher killed by the Romans at the request of Jewish authorities in Jerusalem c30 AD. They considered him the Savior (Messiah, or Christ) who rose from the dead and could grant eternal life to the faithful, despite their sinfulness. They believed he was an incarnation of the one god worshipped by the Jews, and that he would return soon to pass final judgment on the world. The missionary activities of such early leaders as **Paul of Tarsus** spread the faith, at first mostly among Jews or among quasi-Jews attracted by the Pauline rejection of such difficult Jewish laws as circumcision. Intermittent persecution, as in Rome under Nero in 64 AD, on grounds of suspected disloyalty, failed to disrupt the Christian communities. Each congregation, generally urban and of plebeian character, was tightly organized under a leader (bishop), elders (presbyters or priests), and assistants (deacons). Stories about Jesus (the Gospels) and the early church (Acts) were written down in the late first and early 2nd centuries, and circulated along with letters of Paul. An authoritative canon of these writings was not fixed until the 4th century.

A school for priests was established at Alexandria in the second century. Its teachers (**Origen** c182-251) helped define Christian doctrine and promote the faith in Greek-style philosophical works. Pagan Neoplatonism was given Christian coloration in the works of Church Fathers such as Augustine (354-430). Christian hermits, often drawn from the lower classes, began to associate in monasteries, first in Egypt (St. Pachomius c290-345), then in other eastern lands, then in the West (**St. Benedict's rule,** 529). Popular devotion to saints, especially Mary, mother of Jesus, spread.

Under **Constantine** (ruled 306-337), Christianity became in effect the established religion of the Empire. Pagan temples were expropriated, state funds were used to build huge churches and support the hierarchy, and laws were adjusted in accordance with Christian notions. Pagan worship was banned by the end of the fourth century, and severe restrictions were placed on Judaism.

The newly established church was rocked by doctrinal disputes, often exacerbated by regional rivalries both within and outside the Empire. Chief heresies (as defined by church councils backed by imperial authority) were **Arianism,** which denied the divinity of Jesus; **Donatism,** which rejected the convergence of church and state and denied the validity of sacraments performed by sinful clergy; and the **Monophysite** position denying the dual nature of Christ.

Judaism. First century Judaism embraced several sects, including: the **Sadducees,** mostly drawn from the Temple priesthood, who were culturally Hellenized; the **Pharisees,** who upheld the full range of traditional customs and practices as of equal weight to literal scriptural law, and elaborated synagogue worship; and the **Essenes,** an ascetic, millenarian sect. Messianic fervor led to repeated, unsuccessful rebellions against Rome (66-70, 135). As a result, the Temple was destroyed, and the population decimated.

To avoid the dissolution of the faith, a program of codification of law was begun at the academy of Yavneh. The work continued for some 500 years in Palestine and Babylonia, ending in the final redaction of the **Talmud** (c600), a huge collection of legal and moral debates, rulings, liturgy, Biblical exegesis, and legendary materials.

Islam. The earliest Arab civilization emerged by the end of the 2d millenium BC in the watered highlands of Yemen. Seaborne and caravan trade in frankincense and myrrh connected the area with the Nile and Fertile Crescent. The Minaean, Sabean (Sheba), and Himyarite states successively held sway. By Mohammed's time (7th century AD), the region was a province of Sassanian Persia. In the North, the **Nabataean kingdom** at Petra and the kingdom of Palmyra were first Aramaicized and then Romanized, and finally absorbed like neighboring Judea into the Roman Empire. Nomads shared the central region with a few trading towns and oases. Wars between tribes and raids on settled communities were common, and were celebrated in a poetic tradition that by the 6th century helped establish a classic literary Arabic.

In 611 **Mohammed,** a 40-year-old Arab of Mecca, announced a revelation from the one true God, calling on him to repudiate pagan idolatry. Drawing on elements of Judaism and Christianity, and eventually incorporating some Arab pagan traditions (such as reverence for the black stone at the kaaba shrine in Mecca), Mohammed's teachings, recorded in the **Koran,** forged a new religion, Islam (submission to Allah). Opposed by the leaders of Mecca, Mohammed made a *hejira* (migration) to Medina to the north in 622, the beginning of the Moslem lunar calendar. He and his followers defeated the Meccans in 624 in the first *jihad* (holy war), and by his death (632), nearly all the Arabian peninsula accepted his religious and secular leadership.

Under the first two **caliphs** (successors), Abu Bakr (632-34) and Omar (634-44), Moslem rule was confirmed over Arabia. Raiding parties into Byzantine and Persian border areas developed into campaigns of conquest against the two empires, which had been weakened by wars and by disaffection among subject peoples (including Coptic and Syriac Christians opposed to the Byzantine orthodox church). Syria, Palestine, Egypt, Iraq, and Persia all fell to the inspired Arab armies. The Arabs at first remained a distinct minority, using non-Moslems in the new administrative system, and tolerating Christians, Jews, and Zoroastrians as self-governing "Peoples of the Book," whose taxes supported the empire.

Disputes over the succession, and puritan reaction to the wealth and refinement that empire brought to the ruling strata, led to the growth of schismatic movements. The followers of Mohammed's son-in-law Ali (assassinated 661) and his descendants became the founders of the more mystical **Shi'ite** sect, still the largest non-orthodox Moslem sect. The Karijites, puritanical, militant, and egalitarian, persist as a minor sect to the present.

Under the **Omayyad** caliphs (661-750), the boundaries of Islam were extended across N. Africa and into Spain. Arab armies in the West were stopped at Tours in 732 by the Frank **Charles Martel.** Asia Minor, the Indus Valley, and Transoxiana were conquered in the East. The vast majority of the subject population gradually converted to Islam, encouraged by tax and career privileges. The Arab language supplanted the local tongues in the central and western areas, but Arab soldiers and rulers in the East eventually became assimilated to the indigenous languages.

New Peoples Enter History: 400-900

Barbarian invasions. Germanic tribes infiltrated S and E from their Baltic homeland during the 1st millennium BC, reaching S. Germany by 100 BC and the Black Sea by 214 AD. Organized into large federated tribes under elected kings, most resisted Roman domination and raided the empire in time of civil war (Goths took Dacia 214, raided Thrace 251-269). German troops and commanders came to dominate the Roman armies by the end of the 4th century. **Huns,** invaders from Asia, entered Europe 372, driving more Germans into the western empire. Emperor Valens allowed Visigoths to cross the Danube 376. Huns under

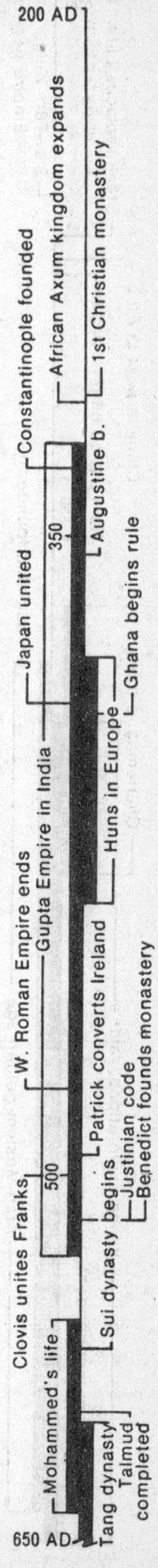

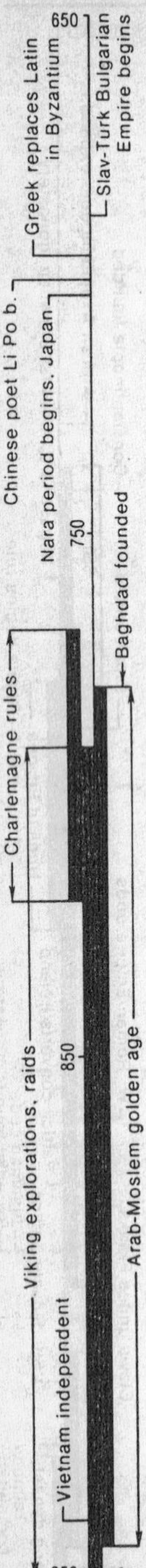

Attila (d. 453) raided Gaul, Italy, Balkans. The western empire, weakened by overtaxation and social stagnation, was overrun in the 5th century. Gaul was effectively lost 406-7, Spain 409, Britain 410, Africa 429-39. Rome was sacked 410 by Visigoths under Alaric, 455 by Vandals. The last western emperor, Romulus Augustulus, was deposed 476 by the Germanic chief Odoacer.

Celts. Celtic cultures, which in pre-Roman times covered most of W. Europe, were confined almost entirely to the British Isles after the Germanic invasions. **St. Patrick** completed the conversion of Ireland (c457-92). A strong monastic tradition took hold. Irish monastic missionaries in Scotland, England, and the continent (Columba c521-597; Columban c543-615) helped restore Christianity after the Germanic invasions. The monasteries became renowned centers of classic and Christian learning, and presided over the recording of a Christianized Celtic mythology, elaborated by secular writers and bards. An intricate decorative art style developed, especially in book illumination (Lindisfarne Gospels, c700, Book of Kells, 8th century).

Successor states. The Visigoth kingdom in Spain (from 419) and much of France (to 507) saw a continuation of much Roman administration, language, and law (Breviary of Alaric 506), until its destruction by the Moslems, 711. The Vandal kingdom in Africa, from 429, was conquered by the Byzantines, 533. Italy was ruled in succession by an Ostrogothic kingdom under Byzantine suzerainty 489-554, direct Byzantine government, and the German Lombards (568-774). The latter divided the peninsula with the Byzantines and the papacy under the dynamic reformer Pope Gregory the Great (590-604) and his successors.

King Clovis (ruled 481-511) united the Franks on both sides of the Rhine, and after his conversion to orthodox Christianity, defeated the Arian Burgundians (after 500) and Visigoths (507) with the support of the native clergy and the papacy. Under the **Merovingian** kings a feudal system emerged: power was fragmented among hierarchies of military landowners. Social stratification, which in late Roman times had acquired legal, hereditary sanction, was reinforced. The Carolingians (747-987) expanded the kingdom and restored central power. **Charlemagne** (ruled 768-814) conquered nearly all the Germanic lands, including LOMBARD Italy, and was crowned Emperor by Pope Leo III in Rome in 800. A centuries-long decline in commerce and the arts was reversed under Charlemagne's patronage. He welcomed Jews to his kingdom, which became a center of Jewish learning (Rashi 1040-1105). He sponsored the "Carolingian Renaissance" of learning under the Anglo-Latin scholar Alcuin (c732-804), who reformed church liturgy.

Byzantine Empire. Under Diocletian (ruled 284-305) the empire had been divided into 2 parts to facilitate administration and defense. Constantine founded **Constantinople,** 330, (at old Byzantium) as a fully Christian city. Commerce and taxation financed a sumptuous, orientalized court, a class of hereditary bureaucratic families, and magnificent urban construction (Hagia Sophia, 532-37). The city's fortifications and naval innovations (Greek fire) repelled assaults by Goths, Huns, Slavs, Bulgars, Avars, Arabs, and Scandinavians. Greek replaced Latin as the official language by c700. Byzantine art, a solemn, sacral, and stylized variation of late classical styles (mosaics at S. Vitale, Ravenna, 526-48) was a starting point for medieval art in E. and W. Europe.

Justinian (ruled 527-65) reconquered parts of Spain, N. Africa, and Italy, codified Roman law (*codex Justinianus,* 529, was medieval Europe's chief legal text), closed the Platonic Academy at Athens and ordered all pagans to convert. Lombards in Italy, Arabs in Africa retook most of his conquests. The Isaurian dynasty from Anatolia (from 717) and the Macedonian dynasty (867-1054) restored military and commercial power. The Iconoclast controversy (726-843) over the permissibility of images, helped alienate the Eastern Church from the papacy.

Arab Empire. Baghdad, founded 762, became the seat of the **Abbasid** Caliphate (founded 750), while Ummayads continued to rule in Spain. A brilliant cosmopolitan civilization emerged, inaugurating an Arab-Moslem golden age. Arab lyric poetry revived; Greek, Syriac, Persian, and Sanskrit books were translated into Arabic, often by Syriac Christians and Jews, whose theology and Talmudic law, respectively, influenced Islam. The arts and music flourished at the court of **Harun al-Rashid** (786-809), celebrated in *The Arabian Nights.* The sciences, medicine, and mathematics were pursued at Baghdad, Cordova, and Cairo (founded 969). Science and Aristotelian philosophy culminated in the systems of Avicenna (980-1037), Averroes (1126-98), and Maimonides (1135-1204), a Jew; all influenced later Christian scholarship and theology. The Islamic ban on images encouraged a sinuous, geometric decorative tradition, applied to architecture and illumination. A gradual loss of Arab control in Persia (from 874) led to the capture of Baghdad by Persians, 945. By the next century, Spain and N. Africa were ruled by Berbers, while Turks prevailed in Asia Minor and the Levant. The loss of political power by the caliphs allowed for the growth of non-orthodox trends, especially the mystical **Sufi** tradition (theologian Ghazali, 1058-1111).

Africa. Immigrants from Saba in S. Arabia helped set up the **Axum** kingdom in Ethiopia in the 2d century (their language, Ge'ez, is preserved by the Ethiopian Church). In the 4th century, when the kingdom became Christianized, it defeated Kushite Meroe and expanded into Yemen. Axum was the center of a vast ivory trade; it controlled the Red Sea coast until c1100. Arab conquest in Egypt cut Axum's political and economic ties with Byzantium.

The Iron Age entered W. Africa by the end of the 1st millennium BC. **Ghana,** the first known sub-Saharan state, ruled in the upper Senegal-Niger region c400-1240, controlling the trade of gold from mines in the S to trans-Sahara caravan routes to the N. The **Bantu** peoples, probably of W. African origin, began to spread E and S perhaps 2000 years ago, displacing the Pygmies and Bushmen of central and southern Africa over a 1,500-year period.

Japan. The advanced Neolithic Yayoi period, when irrigation, rice farming, and iron and bronze casting techniques were introduced from China or Korea, persisted to c400 AD. The myriad Japanese states were then united by the **Yamato** clan, under an emperor who acted as the chief priest of the animistic **Shinto** cult. Japanese political and military intervention in Korea by the 6th century quickened a Chinese cultural invasion, bringing Buddhism, the Chinese language (which long remained a literary and governmental medium), Chinese ideographs and Buddhist styles in painting, sculpture, literature, and architecture (7th c. Horyu-ji temple at Nara). The Taika Reforms, 646, tried to centralize Japan according to Chinese bureaucratic and Buddhist philosophical values, but failed to curb traditional Japanese decentralization. A nativist reaction against the Buddhist **Nara period** (710-94) ushered in the Heian period (794-1185) centered at the new capital, Kyoto. Japanese elegance and simplicity modified Chinese styles in architecture, scroll painting, and literature; the writing system was also simplified. The courtly novel *Tale of Genji* (1010-20) testifies to the enhanced role of women.

Southeast Asia. The historic peoples of southeast Asia began arriving some 2500 years ago from China and Tibet, displacing scattered aborigines. Their agriculture relied on rice and tubers (yams), which they may have introduced to Africa. Indian cultural influences were strongest; literacy and Hindu and Buddhist ideas followed the southern India-China trade route. From the southern tip of Indochina, the kingdom of **Funan** (1st-7th centuries) traded as far west as Persia. It was absorbed by Chenla, itself conquered by the **Khmer Empire** (600-1300). The Khmers, under Hindu god-kings (Suryavarman II, 1113-c1150), built the monumental Angkor Wat temple center for the royal phallic cult. The **Nam-Viet** kingdom in Annam, dominated by China and Chinese culture for 1,000 years, emerged in the 10th century, growing at the expense of the Khmers, who also lost ground in the NW to the new, highly-organized **Thai** kingdom. On Sumatra, the **Srivijaya** Empire at Palembang controlled vital sea lanes (7th to 10th centuries). A Buddhist dynasty, the Sailendras, ruled central **Java** (8th-9th centuries), building at Borobudur one of the largest stupas in the world.

China. The short-lived Sui dynasty (581-618) ushered in a period of commercial, artistic, and scientific achievement in China, continuing under the **T'ang** dynasty (618-906). Such inventions as the magnetic compass, gunpowder, the abacus, and printing were introduced or perfected. Medical innovations included cataract surgery. The state, from the cosmopolitan capital, Ch'ang-an, supervised foreign trade which exchanged Chinese silks, porcelains, and art works for spices, ivory, etc., over Central Asian caravan routes and sea routes reaching Africa. A golden age of poetry bequeathed tens of thousands of works to later generations (Tu Fu 712-70, Li Po 701-62). Landscape painting flourished. Commercial and industrial expansion continued under the **Northern Sung** dynasty (960-1126), facilitated by paper money and credit notes. But commerce never achieved respectability; government monopolies expropriated successful merchants. The population, long stable at 50 million, doubled in 200 years with the introduction of early-ripening rice and the double harvest. In art, native Chinese styles were revived.

Americas. An Indian empire stretched from the Valley of Mexico to Guatemala, 300-600, centering on the huge city **Teotihuacan** (founded 100 BC). To the S, in Guatemala, a high **Mayan** civilization developed, 150-900, around hundreds of rural ceremonial centers. The Mayans improved on Olmec writing and the calendar, and pursued astronomy and mathematics (using the idea of zero). In S. America, a widespread pre-Inca culture grew from **Tiahuanaco** near Lake Titicaca (Gateway of the Sun, c700).

Christian Europe Regroups and Expands: 900-1300

Scandinavians. Pagan Danish and Norse (**Viking**) adventurers, traders, and pirates raided the coasts of the British Isles (Dublin founded c831), France, and even the Mediterranean for over 200 years beginning in the late 8th century. Inland settlement in the W was limited to Great Britain (King Canute, 994-1035) and Normandy, settled under Rollo, 911, as a fief of France. Other Vikings reached Iceland (874), Greenland (c986), and probably N. America (Leif Eriksson c1000). Norse traders (**Varangians**) developed Russian river commerce from the 8th-11th centuries, and helped set up a state at Kiev in the late 9th century. Conversion to Christianity occurred during the 10th century, reaching Sweden 100 years later. Eleventh century Norman bands conquered S. Italy and Sicily. Duke **William of Normandy** conquered England, 1066, bringing continental feudalism and the French language, essential elements in later English civilization.

East Europe. Slavs inhabited areas of E. Central Europe in prehistoric times, and reached most of their present limits by c850. The first Slavic states were in the Balkans (Slav-Turk **Bulgarian Empire,** 680-1018) and Moravia (628). Missions of St. Cyril (whose Greek-based Cyrillic alphabet is still used by S. and E. Slavs) converted Moravia, 863. The Eastern Slavs, part-civilized under the overlordship of the Turkish-Jewish **Khazar** trading empire (7th-10th centuries), gravitated toward Constantinople by the 9th century. The **Kievan state** adopted Eastern Christianity under Prince Vladimir, 989. King Boleslav I (992-1025) began **Poland's** long history of eastern conquest. The Magyars (**Hungarians**), in present-day Hungary since 896, accepted Latin Christianity, 1001.

Germany. The German kingdom that emerged after the breakup of Charlemagne's Empire remained a confederation of largely autonomous states. The Saxon Otto I, king from 936, established the **Holy Roman Empire** of Germany and Italy in alliance with Pope John XII, who crowned him emperor, 962; he defeated the Magyars, 955. Imperial power was greatest under the **Hohenstaufens** (1138-1254), despite the growing opposition of the papacy, which ruled central Italy, and the Lombard League cities. Frederick II (1194-1250) improved administration, patronized the arts; after his death German influence was removed from Italy.

Christian Spain. From its northern mountain redoubts, Christian rule slowly migrated south through the 11th century, when Moslem unity collapsed. After the capture of **Toledo** (1085), the kingdoms of Portugal, Castile, and Aragon undertook repeated crusades of reconquest, finally completed in 1492. Elements of Islamic civilization persisted in recaptured areas, influencing all W. Europe.

Crusades. Pope Urban II called, 1095, for a crusade to restore Asia Minor to Byzantium and conquer the Holy Land from the Turks. Some 10 crusades (to 1291) succeeded only in founding 4 temporary Frankish states in the Levant. The 4th crusade sacked Constantinople, 1204. In Rhineland (1096), England (1290) and France (1306) Jews were massacred or expelled, and wars were launched against Christian heretics (**Albigensian** crusade in France, 1229). Trade in eastern luxuries expanded, led by the Venetian naval empire.

Economy. The agricultural base of European life benefitted from improvements in **plow design** c1000, and by draining of lowlands and clearing of forests, leading to a rural population increase. Towns grew in N. Italy, Flanders, and N. Germany (Hanseatic League). Improvements in **loom design** permitted factory textile production. **Guilds** dominated urban trades from the 12th century. Banking (centered in Italy, 12th-15th century) facilitated long-distance trade.

The Church. The split between the Eastern and Western churches was formalized in 1054. W. and Central

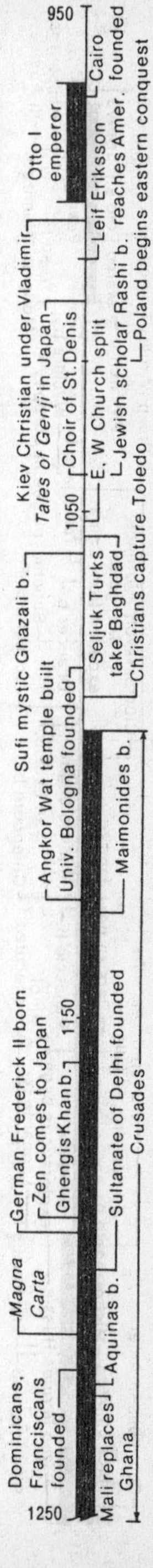

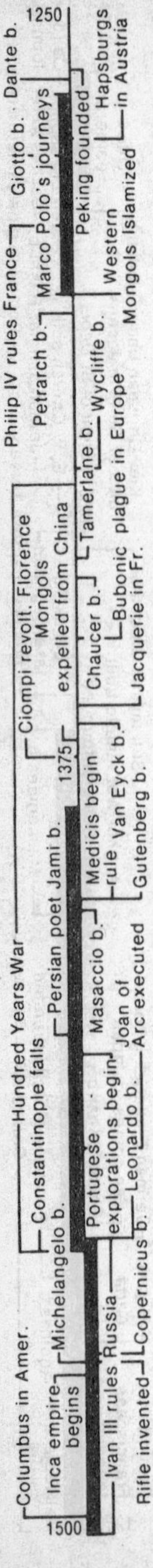

Europe was divided into 500 bishoprics under one united hierarchy, but conflicts between secular and church authorities were frequent (German **Investiture Controversy,** 1075-1122). Clerical power was first strengthened through the international monastic reform begun at Cluny, 910. Popular religious enthusiasm often expressed itself in heretical movements (Waldensians from 1173), but was channelled by the **Dominican** (1215) and **Franciscan** (1223) friars into the religious mainstream.

Arts. Romanesque architecture (11th-12th centuries) expanded on late Roman models, using the rounded arch and massed stone to support enlarged basilicas. Painting and sculpture followed Byzantine models. The literature of **chivalry** was exemplified by the epic (Chanson de Roland, c1100) and by courtly love poems of the troubadours of Provence and minnesingers of Germany. **Gothic architecture** emerged in France (choir of St. Denis, c1040) and spread as French cultural influence predominated in Europe. Rib vaulting and pointed arches were used to combine soaring heights with delicacy, and freed walls for display of stained glass. Exteriors were covered with painted relief sculpture and elaborate architectural detail.

Learning. Law, medicine, and philosophy were advanced at independent **universities** (Bologna, late 11th century), originally corporations of students and masters. Twelfth century translations of Greek classics, especially Aristotle, encouraged an analytic approach. Scholastic philosophy, from Anselm (1033-1109) to Aquinas (1225-74) attempted to reconcile reason and revelation.

Apogee of Central Asian Power; Islam Grows: 1250-1500

Turks. Turkic peoples, of Central Asian ancestry, were a military threat to the Byzantine and Persian Empires from the 6th century. After several waves of invasions, during which most of the Turks adopted Islam, the **Seljuk Turks** took Baghdad, 1055. They ruled Persia, Iraq, and, after 1071, Asia Minor, where massive numbers of Turks settled. The empire was divided in the 12th century into smaller states ruled by Seljuks, Kurds (**Saladin** c1137-93), and Mamelukes (a military caste of former Turk, Kurd, and Circassian slaves), which governed Egypt and the Middle East until the Ottoman era (c1290-1922).

Osman I (ruled c1290-1326) and succeeding sultans united Anatolian Turkish warriors in a militaristic state that waged holy war against Byzantium and Balkan Christians. Most of the Balkans had been subdued, and Anatolia united, when **Constantinople fell,** 1453. By the mid-16th century, Hungary, the Middle East, and North Africa had been conquered. The Turkish advance was stopped at Vienna, 1529, and at the naval battle of Lepanto, 1571, by Spain, Venice, and the papacy.

The Ottoman state was governed in accordance with orthodox Moslem law. Greek, Armenian, and Jewish communities were segregated, and ruled by religious leaders responsible for taxation; they dominated trade. State offices and most army ranks were filled by slaves through a system of child conscription among Christians.

India. Mahmud of Ghazni (971-1030) led repeated Turkish raids into N. India. Turkish power was consolidated in 1206 with the start of the **Sultanate at Delhi.** Centralization of state power under the early Delhi sultans went far beyond traditional Indian practice. Moslem rule of most of the subcontinent lasted until the British conquest some 600 years later.

Mongols. Genghis Khan (c1162-1227) first united the feuding Mongol tribes, and built their armies into an effective offensive force around a core of highly mobile cavalry. He and his immediate successors created the largest land empire in history; by 1279 it stretched from the east coast of Asia to the Danube, from the Siberian steppes to the Arabian Sea. East-West trade and contacts were facilitated (Marco Polo c1254-1324). The western Mongols were Islamized by 1295; successor states soon lost their Mongol character by assimilation. They were briefly reunited under the Turk Tamerlane (1336-1405).

Kublai Khan ruled China from his new capital Peking (founded 1264). Naval campaigns against Japan (1274, 1281) and Java (1293) were defeated, the latter by the Hindu-Buddhist maritime kingdom of Majapahit. The **Yuan** dynasty made use of Mongols and other foreigners (including Europeans) in official posts, and tolerated the return of Nestorian Christianity (suppressed 841-45) and the spread of Islam in the South and West. A native reaction expelled the Mongols, 1367-68.

Russia. The Kievan state in Russia, weakened by the decline of Byzantium and the rise of the Catholic Polish-Lithuanian state, was overrun by the Mongols, 1238-40. Only the northern trading republic of Novgorod remained independent. The grand dukes of Moscow emerged as leaders of a coalition of princes that eventually defeated the Mongols, by 1481. With the fall of Constantinople, the **Tsars** (Caesars) at Moscow (from Ivan III, ruled 1462-1505) set up an independent Russian Orthodox Church. Commerce failed to revive. The isolated Russian state remained agrarian, with the peasant class falling into serfdom.

Persia. A revival of Persian literature, using the Arab alphabet and literary forms, began in the 10th century (epic of Firdausi, 935-1020). An art revival, influenced by Chinese styles, began in the 12th. Persian cultural and political forms, and often the Persian language, were used for centuries by Turkish and Mongol elites from the Balkans to India. Persian mystics from Rumi (1207-73) to Jami (1414-92) promoted **Sufism** in their poetry.

Africa. Two Berber dynasties, imbued with Islamic militance, emerged from the Sahara to carve out empires from the Sahel to central Spain — the **Almoravids,** c1050-1140, and the fanatical **Almohads,** c1125-1269. The Ghanaian empire was replaced in the upper Niger by Mali, c1230-c1340, whose Moslem rulers imported Egyptians to help make **Timbuktu** a center of commerce (in gold, leather, slaves) and learning. The Songhay empire (to 1590) replaced Mali. To the S, forest kingdoms produced refined art works (Ife terra cotta, **Benin** bronzes). Other Moslem states in Nigeria (Hausas) and Chad originated in the 11th century, and continued in some form until the 19th century European conquest. Less developed Bantu kingdoms existed across central Africa.

Some 40 Moslem Arab-Persian trading colonies and city-states were established all along the E. African coast from the 10th century (Kilwa, Mogadishu). The interchange with Bantu peoples produced the **Swahili** language and culture. Gold, palm oil, and slaves were brought from the interior, stimulating the growth of the Monamatapa kingdom of the Zambezi (15th century). The Christian Ethiopian empire (from 13th century) continued the traditions of Axum.

Southeast Asia. Islam was introduced into Malaya and the Indonesian islands by Arab, Persian, and Indian traders. Coastal Moslem cities and states (starting before 1300), enriched by trade, soon dominated the interior. Chief among these was the **Malacca** state, on the Malay peninsula, c1400-1511.

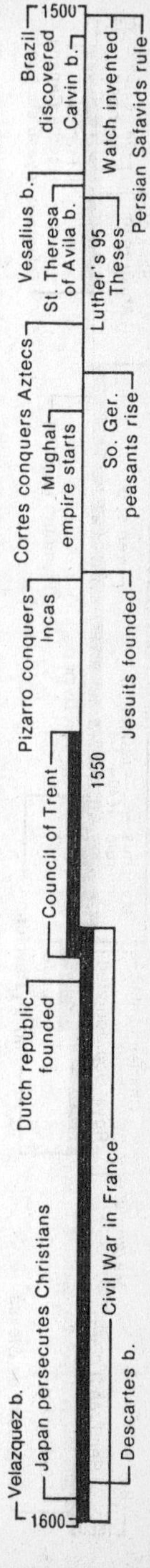

Arts and Statecraft Thrive in Europe: 1350-1600

Italian Renaissance & humanism. Distinctive Italian achievements in the arts in the late Middle Ages (Dante, 1265-1321, Giotto, 1276-1337) led to the vigorous new styles of the Renaissance (14th-16th centuries). Patronized by the rulers of the quarreling petty states of Italy (Medicis in Florence and the papacy, c1400-1737), the plastic arts perfected realistic techniques, including **perspective** (Masaccio, 1401-28, Leonardo 1452-1519). Classical motifs were used in architecture and increased talent and expense were put into secular buildings. The Florentine dialect was refined as a national literary language (Petrarch, 1304-74). Greek refugees from the E strengthened the respect of humanist scholars for the classic sources (Bruni 1370-1444). Soon an international movement aided by the spread of **printing** (Gutenberg c1400-1468), **humanism** was optimistic about the power of human reason (Erasmus of Rotterdam, 1466-1536, Thomas More's *Utopia,* 1516) and valued individual effort in the arts and in politics (Machiavelli, 1469-1527).

France. The French monarchy, strengthened in its repeated struggles with powerful nobles (Burgundy, Flanders, Aquitaine) by alliances with the growing commercial towns, consolidated bureaucratic control under Philip IV (ruled 1285-1314) and extended French influence into Germany and Italy (popes at Avignon, France, 1309-1417). The **Hundred Years War,** 1337-1453, ended English dynastic claims in France (battles of Cr8 cy, 1346, Poitiers, 1356; Joan of Arc executed, 1431). A French Renaissance, dating from royal invasions of Italy, 1494, 1499, was encouraged at the court of Francis I (ruled 1515-47), who centralized taxation and law. French vernacular literature consciously asserted its independence (La Pleiade, 1549).

England. The evolution of England's unique political institutions began with the Magna Carta, 1215, by which King John guaranteed the privileges of nobles and church against the monarchy and assured jury trial. After the Wars of the Roses (1455-85), the **Tudor dynasty** reasserted royal prerogatives (Henry VIII, ruled 1509-47), but the trend toward independent departments and ministerial government also continued. English trade (wool exports from c1340) was protected by the nation's growing maritime power (**Spanish Armada** destroyed, 1588).

English replaced French and Latin in the late 14th century in law and literature (Chaucer, 1340-1400) and English translation of the Bible began (Wycliffe, 1380s). Elizabeth I (ruled 1558-1603) presided over a confident flowering of poetry (Spenser, 1552-99), drama (**Shakespeare,** 1564-1616), and music.

German Empire. From among a welter of minor feudal states, church lands, and independent cities, the **Hapsburgs** assembled a far-flung territorial domain, based in Austria from 1276. The family held the title Holy Roman Emperor from 1452 to the Empire's dissolution in 1806, but failed to centralize its domains, leaving Germany disunited for centuries. Resistance to Turkish expansion brought Hungary under Austrian control from the 16th century. The Netherlands, Luxembourg, and Burgundy were added in 1477, curbing French expansion.

The Flemish painting tradition of naturalism, technical proficiency, and bourgeois subject matter began in the 15th century (Jan Van Eyck, 1366-1440), the earliest northern manifestation of the Renaissance. **Dürer** (1471-1528) typified the merging of late Gothic and Italian trends in 16th century German art. Imposing civic architecture flourished in the prosperous commercial cities.

Spain. Despite the unification of Castile and Aragon in 1479, the 2 countries retained separate governments, and the nobility, especially in Aragon and Catalonia, retained many privileges. Spanish lands in Italy (Naples, Sicily) and the Netherlands entangled the country in European wars through the mid-17th century, while explorers, traders, and conquerors built up a Spanish empire in the Americas and the Philippines.

From the late 15th century, a **golden age** of literature and art produced works of social satire (plays of Lope de Vega, 1562-1635; Cervantes, 1547-1616), as well as spiritual intensity (El Greco, 1541-1614; Velazquez, 1599-1660).

Black Death. The bubonic plague reached Europe from the E in 1348, killing as much as half the population by 1350. Labor scarcity forced a rise in wages and brought greater freedom to the peasantry, making possible **peasant uprisings** (Jacquerie in France, 1358, Wat Tyler's rebellion in England, 1381). In the *ciompi* revolt, 1378, Florentine wage earners demanded a say in economic and political power.

Explorations. Organized European maritime exploration began, seeking to evade the Venice-Ottoman monopoly of eastern trade and to promote Christianity. Expeditions from Portugal beginning 1418 explored the west coast of Africa, until **Vasco da Gama** rounded the Cape of Good Hope in 1497 and reached India. A Portuguese trading empire was consolidated by the seizure of Goa, 1510, and Malacca, 1551. Japan was reached in 1542. Spanish voyages (**Columbus,** 1492-1504) uncovered a new world, which Spain hastened to subdue. Navigation schools in Spain and Portugal, the development of large sailing ships (carracks), and the invention of the rifle, c1475, aided European penetration.

Mughals and Safavids. East of the Ottoman empire, two Moslem dynasties ruled unchallenged in the 16th and 17th centuries. The Mughal empire in India, founded by Persianized Turkish invaders from the NW under Babur, dates from their 1526 conquest of Delhi. The dynasty ruled most of India for over 200 years, surviving nominally until 1857. **Akbar** (ruled 1556-1605) consolidated administration at his glorious court, where Urdu (Persian-influenced Hindi) developed. Trade relations with Europe increased. Under Shah Jahan (1629-58), a secularized art fusing Hindu and Moslem elements flourished in miniature painting and architecture (**Taj Mahal**). Sikhism, founded c1519, combined elements of both faiths. Suppression of Hindus and Shi'ite Moslems in S India in the late 17th century weakened the empire.

Fanatical devotion to the Shi'ite sect characterized the Safavids of Persia, 1502-1736, and led to hostilities with the Sunni Ottomans for over a century. The prosperity and strength of the empire are evidenced by the mosques at its capital, **Isfahan.** The dynasty enhanced Iranian national consciousness.

China. The Ming emperors, 1368-1644, the last native dynasty in China, wielded unprecedented personal power, while the Confucian bureaucracy began to suffer from inertia. European trade (Portugese monopoly

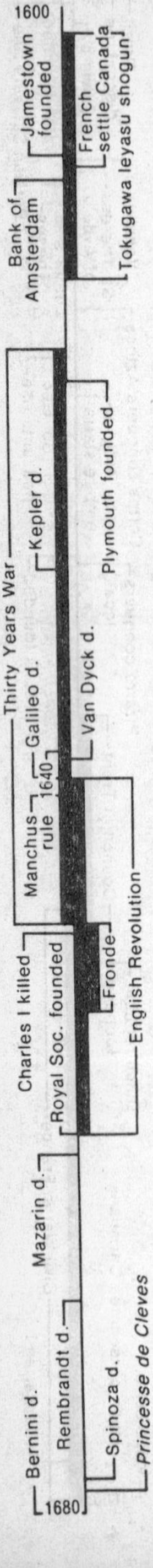

through **Macao** from 1557) was strictly controlled. Jesuit scholars and scientists (Matteo Ricci 1552-1610) introduced some Western science; their writings familiarized the West with China. Chinese technological inventiveness declined from this era, but the arts thrived, especially painting and ceramics.

Japan. After the decline of the first hereditary shogunate (chief generalship) at **Kamakura** (1185-1333), fragmentation of power accelerated, as did the consequent social mobility. Under Kamakura and the Ashikaga shogunate, 1338-1573, the daimyos (lords) and samurai (warriors) grew more powerful and promoted a martial ideology. Japanese pirates and traders plied the China coast. Popular Buddhist movements included the nationalist Nichiren sect (from c1250) and **Zen** (brought from China, 1191), which stressed meditation and a disciplined esthetic (tea ceremony, landscape gardening, judo, Noh drama).

Reformed Europe Expands Overseas: 1500-1700

Reformation begun. Theological debate and protests against real and perceived clerical corruption existed in the medieval Christian world, expressed by such dissenters as Wycliffe (c1320-84) and his followers, the Lollards, in England, and **Huss** (burned as a heretic, 1415) in Bohemia.

Luther (1483-1546) preached that only faith could lead to salvation, without the mediation of clergy or good works. He attacked the authority of the Pope, rejected priestly celibacy, and recommended individual study of the Bible (which he translated, c1525). His 95 Theses (1517) led to his excommunication (1521). **Calvin** (1509-64) said God's elect were predestined for salvation; good conduct and success were signs of election. Calvin in Geneva and Knox (1505-72) in Scotland erected theocratic states.

Henry VIII asserted English national authority and secular power by breaking away from the Catholic church, 1534. Monastic property was confiscated, and some Protestant doctrines given official sanction.

Religious wars. A century and a half of religious wars began with a South German peasant uprising, 1524, repressed with Luther's support. Radical sects—democratic, pacifist, millenarian—arose (Anabaptists ruled Muenster, 1534-35), and were suppressed violently. Civil war in France from 1562 between **Huguenots** (Protestant nobles and merchants) and Catholics ended with the 1598 Edict of Nantes tolerating Protestants (revoked 1685). Hapsburg attempts to restore Catholicism in Germany were resisted in 25 years of fighting; the 1555 Peace of Augsburg guarantee of religious independence to local princes and cities was confirmed only after the **Thirty Years War,** 1618-48, when much of Germany was devastated by local and foreign armies (Sweden, France).

A Catholic Reformation, or **counter-reformation,** met the Protestant challenge, clearly defining an official theology at the Council of Trent, 1545-63. The **Jesuit** order, founded 1534 by Loyola (1491-1556), helped reconvert large areas of Poland, Hungary, and S. Germany and sent missionaries to the New World, India, and China, while the Inquisition helped suppress heresy in Catholic countries. A revival of piety appeared in the devotional literature (Theresa of Avila, 1515-82) and the grandiose Baroque art (Bernini, 1598-1680) of Roman Catholic countries.

Scientific Revolution. The late nominalist thinkers (Ockham, c1300-49) of Paris and Oxford challenged Aristotelian orthodoxy, allowing for a freer scientific approach. But metaphysical values, such as the Neoplatonic faith in an orderly, mathematical cosmos, still motivated and directed subsequent inquiry. **Copernicus** (1473-1543) promoted the heliocentric theory, which was confirmed when Kepler (1571-1630) discovered the mathematical laws describing the orbits of the planets. The Christian-Aristotelian belief that heavens and earth were fundamentally different collapsed when **Galileo** (1564-1642) discovered moving sunspots, irregular moon topography, and moons around Jupiter. He and **Newton** (1642-1727) developed a mechanics that unified cosmic and earthly phenomena. To meet the needs of the new physics, Newton and Leibnitz (1646-1716) invented calculus, Descartes (1596-1650) invented analytic geometry.

An explosion of observational science included the discovery of blood circulation (Harvey, 1578-1657) and microscopic life (Leeuwenhoek, 1632-1723), and advances in anatomy (Vesalius, 1514-64, dissected corpses) and chemistry (Boyle, 1627-91). Scientific research institutes were founded: Florence, 1657, London **(Royal Society),** 1660, Paris, 1666. Inventions proliferated (Savery's steam engine, 1696).

Arts. Mannerist trends of the high Renaissance **(Michelangelo,** 1475-1564) exploited virtuosity, grace, novelty, and exotic subjects and poses. The notion of artistic genius was promoted, in contrast to the anonymous medieval artisan. Private connoisseurs entered the art market. These trends were elaborated in the 17th century **Baroque** era, on a grander scale. Dynamic movement in painting and sculpture was emphasized by sharp lighting effects, use of rich materials (colored marble, gilt), realistic details. Curved facades, broken lines, rich, deep-cut detail, and ceiling decoration characterized Baroque architecture, especially in Germany. Monarchs, princes, and prelates, usually Catholic, used Baroque art to enhance and embellish their authority, as in royal portraits by Velazquez (1599-1660) and Van Dyck (1599-1641).

National styles emerged. In France, a taste for rectilinear order and serenity (Poussin, 1594-1665), linked to the new rational philosophy, was expressed in classical forms. The influence of **classical values** in French literature (tragedies of Racine, 1639-99) gave rise to the "battle of the Ancients and Moderns." New forms included the essay (Montaigne, 1533-92) and novel (*Princesse de Cleves,* La Fayette, 1678).

Dutch painting of the 17th century was unique in its wide social distribution. The Flemish tradition of undemonstrative realism reached its peak in **Rembrandt** (1606-69) and Vermeer (1632-75).

Economy. European economic expansion was stimulated by the new trade with the East, New World gold and silver, and a doubling of population (50 mln. in 1450, 100 mln. in 1600). New business and financial techniques were developed and refined, such as joint-stock companies, insurance, and letters of credit and exchange. The Bank of Amsterdam, 1609, and the Bank of England, 1694, broke the old monopoly of private banking families. The rise of a business mentality was typified by the spread of clock towers in cities in the 14th century. By the mid-15th century, portable clocks were available; the first watch was invented in 1502.

By 1650, most governments had adopted the **mercantile system,** in which they sought to amass metallic wealth by protecting their merchants' foreign and colonial trade monopolies. The rise in prices and the new coin-based economy undermined the craft guild and feudal manorial systems. Expanding industries, such as clothweaving and mining, benefitted from technical advances. Coal replaced disappearing wood as the chief fuel; it was used to fuel new 16th century blast furnaces making cast iron.

New World. The **Aztecs** united much of the Meso-American culture area in a militarist empire by 1519, from their capital, Tenochtitlan (pop. 300,000), which was the center of a cult requiring enormous levels of ritual human sacrifice. Most of the civilized areas of S. America were ruled by the centralized **Inca Empire** (1476-1534), stretching 2,000 miles from Ecuador to N.W. Argentina. Lavish and sophisticated traditions in pottery, weaving, sculpture, and architecture were maintained in both regions.

These empires, beset by revolts, fell in 2 short campaigns to gold-seeking Spanish forces based in the Antilles and Panama. **Cortes** took Mexico, 1519-21; **Pizarro** Peru, 1531-35. From these centers, land and sea expeditions claimed most of N. and S. America for Spain. The Indian high cultures did not survive the impact of Christian missionaries and the new upper class of whites and mestizos. In turn, New World silver, and such Indian products as potatoes, tobacco, corn, peanuts, chocolate, and rubber exercised a major economic influence on Europe. While the Spanish administration intermittently concerned itself with the welfare of Indians, the population remained impoverished at most levels, despite the growth of a distinct South American civilization. European diseases reduced the native population.

Brazil, which the Portuguese reached in 1500 and settled after 1530, and the Caribbean colonies of several European nations developed a plantation economy where sugar cane, tobacco, cotton, coffee, rice, indigo, and lumber were grown commercially by slaves. From the early 16th to the late 19th centuries, some 10 million Africans were transported to **slavery** in the New World.

Netherlands. The urban, Calvinist northern provinces of the Netherlands rebelled against Hapsburg Spain, 1568, and founded an oligarchic mercantile republic. Their strategic control of the Baltic grain market enabled them to exploit Mediterranean food shortages. Religious refugees — French and Belgian Protestants, Iberian Jews — added to the cosmopolitan commercial talent pool. After Spain absorbed Portugal in 1580, the Dutch seized Portuguese possessions and created a vast, though generally short-lived commercial empire in Brazil, the Antilles, Africa, India, Ceylon, Malacca, Indonesia, and Taiwan, and challenged or supplanted Portuguese traders in China and Japan.

England. Anglicanism became firmly established under Elizabeth I after a brief Catholic interlude under "Bloody Mary," 1553-58. But religious and political conflicts led to a rebellion by Parliament, 1642. Roundheads (Puritans) defeated Cavaliers (Royalists); Charles I was beheaded, 1649. The new **Commonwealth** was ruled as a military dictatorship by Cromwell, who also brutally crushed an Irish rebellion, 1649-51. Conflicts within the Puritan camp (democratic Levelers defeated 1649) aided the Stuart restoration, 1660, but Parliament was permanently strengthened and the peaceful **"Glorious Revolution"**, 1688, advanced political and religious liberties (writings of Locke, 1632-1704). British privateers (Drake, 1540-96) challenged Spanish control of the New World, and penetrated Asian trade routes (Madras taken, 1639). N. American colonies (Jamestown, 1607, Plymouth, 1620) provided an outlet for religious dissenters.

France. Emerging from the religious civil wars in 1628, France regained military and commercial great power status under the ministries of **Richelieu** (1624-42), Mazarin (1643-61), and Colbert (1662-83). Under Louis XIV (ruled 1643-1715) royal absolutism triumphed over nobles and local *parlements* (defeat of Fronde, 1648-53). Permanent colonies were founded in Canada (1608), the Caribbean (1626), and India (1674).

Sweden. Sweden seceded from the Scandinavian Union in 1523. The thinly-populated agrarian state (with copper, iron, and timber exports) was united by the Vasa kings, whose conquests by the mid-17th century made Sweden the dominant Baltic power. The empire collapsed in the Great Northern War (1700-21).

Poland. After the union with Lithuania in 1447, Poland ruled vast territories from the Baltic to the Black Sea, resisting German and Turkish incursions. Catholic nobles failed to gain the loyalty of the Orthodox Christian peasantry in the East; commerce and trades were practiced by German and Jewish immigrants. The bloody 1648-49 cossack uprising began the kingdom's dismemberment.

China. A new dynasty, the **Manchus,** invaded from the NE and seized power in 1644, and expanded Chinese control to its greatest extent in Central and Southeast Asia. Trade and diplomatic contact with Europe grew, carefully controlled by China. New crops (sweet potato, maize, peanut) allowed an economic and population growth (300 million pop. in 1800). Traditional arts and literature were pursued with increased sophistication (*Dream of the Red Chamber,* novel, mid-18th century).

Japan. Tokugawa Ieyasu, shogun from 1603, finally unified and pacified feudal Japan. Hereditary daimyos and samurai monopolized government office and the professions. An urban merchant class grew, literacy spread, and a cultural renaissance occurred (haiku of Basho, 1644-94). Fear of European domination led to persecution of Christian converts from 1597, and stringent isolation from outside contact from 1640.

Philosophy, Industry and Revolution: 1700-1800

Science and Reason. Faith in human reason and science as the source of truth and a means to improve the physical and social environment, espoused since the Renaissance (Francis Bacon, 1561-1626), was bolstered by scientific discoveries in spite of theological opposition (**Galileo's forced retraction,** 1633). Descartes applied the logical method of mathematics to discover "self-evident" scientific and philosophical truths, while Newton emphasized induction from experimental observation.

The challenge of reason to traditional religious and political values and institutions began with **Spinoza** (1632-77), who interpreted the Bible historically and called for political and intellectual freedom.

French philosophes assumed leadership of the **"Enlightenment"** in the 18th century. Montesquieu (1689-1755) used British history to support his notions of limited government. Voltaire's (1694-1778) diaries and novels of exotic travel illustrated the intellectual trends toward secular ethics and relativism. Rousseau's (1712-1778) radical concepts of the **social contract** and of the inherent goodness of the common man gave impetus to anti-monarchical republicanism. The *Encyclopedia,* 1751-72, edited by Diderot and d'Alembert, designed as a monument to reason, was largely devoted to practical technology.

In England, ideals of political and religious liberty were connected with empiricist philosophy and science in the followers of Locke. But the extreme **empiricism of Hume** (1711-76) and Berkeley (1685-1753) posed

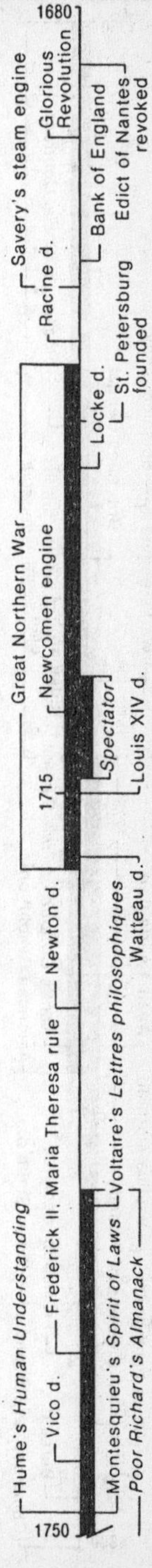

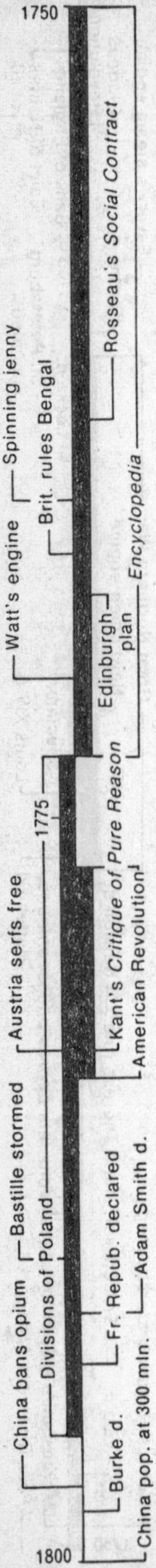

limits to the identification of reason with absolute truth, as did the evolutionary approach to law and politics of Burke (1729-97) and the utilitarianism of Bentham (1748-1832). Adam Smith (1723-90) and other **physiocrats** called for a rationalization of economic activity by removing artificial barriers to a supposedly natural free exchange of goods.

Despite the political disunity and backwardness of most of Germany, German writers participated in the new philosophical trends popularized by Wolff (1679-1754). **Kant's** (1724-1804) **idealism,** unifying an empirical epistemology with *a priori* moral and logical concepts, directed German thought away from skepticism. Italian contributions included work on electricity by Galvani (1737-98) and Volta (1745-1827), the pioneer **historiography of Vico** (1668-1744), and writings on penal reform by Beccaria (1738-94). The American Franklin (1706-90) was celebrated in Europe for his varied achievements.

The growth of the **press** (*Spectator,* 1711-14) and the wide distribution of realistic but sentimental **novels** attested to the increase of a large bourgeois public.

Arts. Rococo art, characterized by extravagant decorative effects, asymmetries copied from organic models, and artificial pastoral subjects, was favored by the continental aristocracy for most of the century (Watteau, 1684-1721), and had musical analogies in the ornamentalized polyphony of late Baroque. The **Neoclassical** art after 1750, associated with the new scientific archeology, was more streamlined, and infused with the supposed moral and geometric rectitude of the Roman Republic (David, 1748-1825). In England, **town planning** on a grand scale began (Edinburgh, 1767).

Industrial Revolution in England. Agricultural improvements, such as the sowing drill (1701) and livestock breeding, were implemented on the large fields provided by enclosure of common lands by private owners. Profits from agriculture and from colonial and foreign trade (1800 volume, £ 54 million) were channelled through hundreds of banks and the **Stock Exchange** (founded 1773) into new industrial processes.

The Newcomen steam pump (1712) aided coal mining. Coal fueled the new efficient steam engines patented by Watt in 1769, and coke-smelting produced cheap, sturdy iron for machinery by the 1730s. The **flying shuttle** (1733) and **spinning jenny** (1764) were used in the large new cotton textile factories, where women and children were much of the work force. Goods were transported cheaply over **canals** (2,000 miles built 1760-1800).

American Revolution. The British colonies in N. America attracted a mass immigration of religious dissenters and poor people throughout the 17th and 18th centuries, coming from all parts of the British Isles, Germany, the Netherlands, and other countries. The population reached 3 million whites and blacks by the 1770s. The small native population was decimated by European diseases and wars with and between the various colonies. British attempts to control colonial trade, and to tax the colonists to pay for the costs of colonial administration and defense clashed with traditions of local self government, and eventually provoked the colonies to rebellion. (*See American Revolution in Index.*)

Central and East Europe. The monarchs of the three states that dominated eastern Europe — Austria, Prussia, and Russia — accepted the advice and legitimation of philosophes in creating more modern, centralized institutions in their kingdoms, enlarged by the division of Poland (1772-95).

Under **Frederick II** (ruled 1740-86) Prussia, with its efficient modern army, doubled in size. State monopolies and tariff protection fostered industry, and some legal reforms were introduced. Austria's heterogeneous realms were legally unified under **Maria Theresa** (ruled 1740-80) and **Joseph II** (1780-90). Reforms in education, law, and religion were enacted, and the Austrian serfs were freed (1781). With its defeat in the Seven Years' War in 1763, Austria lost Silesia and ceased its active role in Germany, but was compensated by expansion to the E and S (Hungary, Slavonia, 1699, Galicia, 1772).

Russia, whose borders continued to expand in all directions, adopted some Western bureaucratic and economic policies under **Peter I** (ruled 1682-1725) and Catherine II (ruled 1762-96). Trade and cultural contacts with the West multiplied from the new Baltic Sea capital, **St. Petersburg** (founded 1703).

French Revolution. The growing French middle class lacked political power, and resented aristocratic tax privileges, especially in light of liberal political ideals popularized by the American Revolution. Peasants lacked adequate land and were burdened with feudal obligations to nobles. Wars with Britain drained the treasury, finally forcing the king to call the **Estates-General** in 1789 (first time since 1614), in an atmosphere of food riots (poor crop in 1788).

Aristocratic resistance to absolutism was soon overshadowed by the reformist Third Estate (middle class), which proclaimed itself the **National Constituent Assembly** June 17 and took the "Tennis Court oath" on June 20 to secure a constitution. The storming of the **Bastille** July 14 by Parisian artisans was followed by looting and seizure of aristocratic property throughout France. Assembly reforms included abolition of class and regional privileges, a Declaration of Rights, suffrage by taxpayers (75% of males), and the **Civil Constitution of the Clergy** providing for election and loyalty oaths for priests. A republic was declared Sept. 22, 1792, in spite of royalist pressure from Austria and Prussia, which had declared war in April (joined by Britain the next year). Louis XVI was beheaded Jan. 21, 1793, Queen Marie Antoinette was beheaded Oct. 16, 1793.

Royalist uprisings in La Vendée and military reverses led to a **reign of terror** in which tens of thousands of opponents of the Revolution and criminals were executed. Radical reforms in the **Convention** period (Sept. 1793-Oct. 1795) included the abolition of colonial slavery, economic measures to aid the poor, support of public education, and a short-lived de-Christianization.

Division among radicals (execution of Hebert, March 1794, Danton, April, and Robespierre, July) aided the ascendance of a moderate **Directory,** which consolidated military victories. **Napoleon Bonaparte** (1769-1821), a popular young general, exploited political divisions and participated in a coup Nov. 9, 1799, making himself first consul (dictator).

India. Sikh and Hindu rebels (Rajputs, Marathas) and Afghans destroyed the power of the Mughals during the 18th century. After France's defeat in the Seven Years War, 1763, Britain was the chief European trade power in India. Its control of inland **Bengal and Bihar** was recognized by the Mughal shah in 1765, who granted the **British East India Co.** (under Clive, 1727-74) the right to collect land revenue there. Despite objections from Parliament (1784 India Act) the company's involvement in local wars and politics led to repeated acquisitions of new territory. The company exported Indian textiles, sugar, and indigo.

Change Gathers Steam: 1800-1840

French ideals and empire spread. Inspired by the ideals of the French Revolution, and supported by the expanding French armies, new republican regimes arose near France: the **Batavian** Republic in the Netherlands (1795-1806), the **Helvetic** Republic in Switzerland (1798-1803), the **Cisalpine** Republic in N. Italy (1797-1805), the **Ligurian** Republic in Genoa (1797-1805), and the **Parthenopean** Republic in S. Italy (1799). A Roman Republic existed briefly in 1798 after Pope Pius VI was arrested by French troops. In Italy and Germany, new nationalist sentiments were stimulated both in imitation of and reaction to France (anti-French and anti-Jacobin peasant uprisings in Italy, 1796-9).

From 1804, when Napoleon declared himself emperor, to 1812, a succession of military victories (Austerlitz, 1805, Jena, 1806) extended his control over most of Europe, through puppet states (**Confederation of the Rhine** united W. German states for the first time and **Grand Duchy of Warsaw** revived Polish national hopes), expansion of the empire, and alliances.

Among the lasting reforms initiated under Napoleon's absolutist reign were: establishment of the Bank of France, centralization of tax collection, codification of law along Roman models (*Code Napoleon*), and reform and extension of secondary and university education. In an 1801 concordat, the papacy recognized the effective autonomy of the French Catholic Church. Some 400,000 French soldiers were killed in the Napoleonic Wars, along with 600,000 foreign troops.

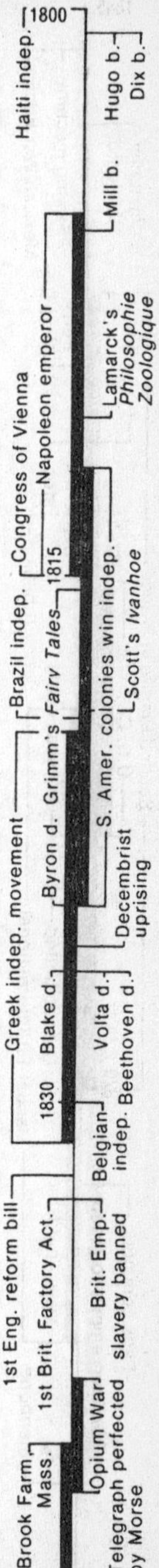

Last gasp of old regime. France's coastal blockade of Europe (**Continental System**) failed to neutralize Britain. The disastrous 1812 invasion of Russia exposed Napoleon's overextension. After an 1814 exile at Elba, Napoleon's armies were defeated at **Waterloo,** 1815, by British and Prussian troops.

At the **Congress of Vienna,** the monarchs and princes of Europe redrew their boundaries, to the advantage of Prussia (in Saxony and the Ruhr), Austria (in Illyria and Venetia), and Russia (in Poland and Finland). British conquest of Dutch and French colonies (S. Africa, Ceylon, Mauritius) was recognized, and France, under the restored Bourbons, retained its expanded 1792 borders. The settlement brought 50 years of international peace to Europe.

But the Congress was unable to check the advance of liberal ideals and of nationalism among the smaller European nations. The 1825 **Decembrist uprising** by liberal officers in Russia was easily suppressed. But an independence movement in **Greece,** stirred by commercial prosperity and a cultural revival, succeeded in expelling Ottoman rule by 1831, with the aid of Britain, France, and Russia.

A constitutional monarchy was secured in France by an **1830 revolution;** Louis Philippe became king. The revolutionary contagion spread to **Belgium,** which gained its independence from the Dutch monarchy, 1830; to **Poland,** whose rebellion was defeated by Russia, 1830-31; and to Germany.

Romanticism. A new style in intellectual and artistic life began to replace Neo-classicism and Rococo after the mid-18th century. By the early 19th, this style, Romanticism, had prevailed in the European world.

Rousseau had begun the reaction against excessive rationalism and skepticism; in education (*Emile,* 1762) he stressed subjective spontaneity over regularized instruction. In Germany, Lessing (1729-81) and Herder (1744-1803) favorably compared the German folk song to classical forms, and began a cult of Shakespeare, whose passion and "natural" wisdom was a model for the Romantic *Sturm und Drang* (storm and stress) movement. **Goethe's** *Sorrows of Young Werther* (1774) set the model for the tragic, passionate genius.

A new interest in **Gothic architecture** in England after 1760 (Walpole, 1717-97) spread through Europe, associated with an aesthetic Christian and mystic revival (Blake, 1757-1827). Celtic, Norse, and German mythology and folk tales were revived or imitated (Macpherson's Ossian translation, 1762, Grimm's *Fairy Tales,* 1812-22). The medieval revival (Scott's *Ivanhoe,* 1819) led to a new interest in history, stressing national differences and organic growth (Carlyle, 1795-1881; Michelet, 1798-1874), corresponding to theories of natural evolution (Lamarck's *Philosophie zoologique,* 1809, Lyell's *Geology,* 1830-33).

Revolution and war fed an obsession with freedom and conflict, expressed by poets (**Byron,** 1788-1824, **Hugo,** 1802-85) and philosophers (**Hegel,** 1770-1831).

Wild gardens replaced the formal French variety, and painters favored rural, stormy, and mountainous landscapes (**Turner,** 1775-1851; **Constable,** 1776-1837). Clothing became freer, with wigs, hoops, and ruffles discarded. Originality and genius were expected in the life as well as the work of inspired artists (Murger's *Scenes from Bohemian Life,* 1847-49). Exotic locales and themes (as in "Gothic" horror stories) were used in art and literature (Delacroix, 1798-1863, **Poe,** 1809-49).

Music exhibited the new dramatic style and a breakdown of classical forms (Beethoven, 1770-1827). The use of folk melodies and modes aided the growth of distinct national traditions (Glinka in Russia, 1804-57).

Latin America. Haiti, under the former slave **Toussaint L'Ouverture,** was the first Latin American independent state, 1800. All the mainland Spanish colonies won their independence 1810-24, under such leaders as **Bolivar** (1783-1830). Brazil became an independent empire under the Portuguese prince regent, 1822. A new class of military officers divided power with large landholders and the church.

United States. Heavy immigration and exploitation of ample natural resources fueled rapid economic growth. The spread of the franchise, public education, and antislavery sentiment were signs of a widespread democratic ethic.

China. Failure to keep pace with Western arms technology exposed China to greater European influence, and hampered efforts to bar imports of opium, which had damaged Chinese society and drained wealth overseas. In the **Opium War,** 1839-42, Britain forced China to expand trade opportunities and to cede Hong Kong.

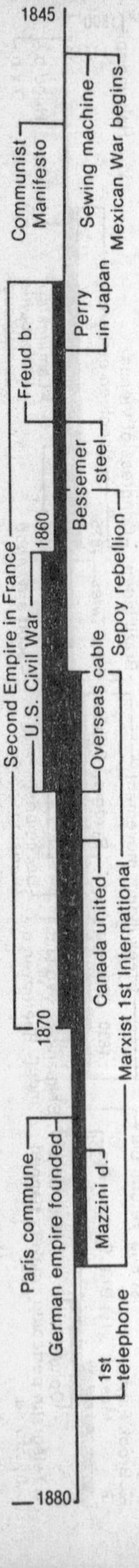

Triumph of Progress: 1840-80

Idea of Progress. As a result of the cumulative scientific, economic, and political changes of the preceding eras, the idea took hold among literate people in the West that continuing growth and improvement was the usual state of human and natural life.

Darwin's statement of the **theory of evolution** and survival of the fittest (*Origin of Species*, 1859), defended by intellectuals and scientists against theological objections, was taken as confirmation that progress was the natural direction of life. The controversy helped define popular ideas of the dedicated scientist and ever-expanding human knowledge of and control over the world (Foucault's demonstration of earth's rotation, 1851, Pasteur's germ theory, 1861).

Liberals following Ricardo (1772-1823) in their faith that unrestrained competition would bring continuous economic expansion sought to adjust political life to the new social realities, and believed that unregulated competition of ideas would yield truth (Mill, 1806-73). In England, successive reform bills (1832, 1867, 1884) gave representation to the new industrial towns, and extended the franchise to the middle and lower classes and to Catholics, Dissenters, and Jews. On both sides of the Atlantic, reformists tried to improve conditions for the mentally ill (Dix, 1802-87), women (Anthony, 1820-1906), and prisoners. Slavery was barred in the British Empire, 1833; the United States, 1865; and Brazil, 1888.

Socialist theories based on ideas of human perfectibility or historical progress were widely disseminated. Utopian socialists like Saint-Simon (1760-1825) envisaged an orderly, just society directed by a technocratic elite. A model factory town, New Lanark, Scotland, was set up by utopian Robert Owen (1771-1858), and utopian communal experiments were tried in the U.S. (Brook Farm, Mass., 1841-7). Bakunin's (1814-76) anarchism represented the opposite utopian extreme of total freedom. Marx (1818-83) posited the inevitable triumph of socialism in the industrial countries through a historical process of class conflict.

Spread of industry. The technical processes and managerial innovations of the English industrial revolution spread to Europe (especially Germany) and the U.S., causing an explosion of industrial production, demand for raw materials, and competition for markets. Inventors, both trained and self-educated, provided the means for larger-scale production (Bessemer steel, 1856, sewing machine, 1846). Many inventions were shown at the 1851 London Great Exhibition at the Crystal Palace, whose theme was universal prosperity.

Local specialization and long-distance trade were aided by a revolution in transportation and communication. Railroads were first introduced in the 1820s in England and the U.S. Over 150,000 miles of track had been laid worldwide by 1880, with another 100,000 miles laid in the next decade. Steamships were improved (*Savannah* crossed Atlantic, 1819). The telegraph, perfected by 1844 (Morse), connected the Old and New Worlds by cable in 1866, and quickened the pace of international commerce and politics. The first commercial telephone exchange went into operation in the U.S. in 1878.

The new class of industrial workers, uprooted from their rural homes, lacked job security, and suffered from dangerous overcrowded conditions at work and at home. Many responded by organizing trade unions (legalized in England, 1824; France, 1884). The U.S. Knights of Labor had 700,000 members by 1886. The First International, 1864-76, tried to unite workers internationally around a Marxist program. The quasi-Socialist Paris Commune uprising, 1871, was violently suppressed. Factory Acts to reduce child labor and regulate conditions were passed (1833-50 in England). Social security measures were introduced by the Bismarck regime in Germany, 1883-89.

Revolutions of 1848. Among the causes of the continent-wide revolutions were an international collapse of credit and resulting unemployment, bad harvests in 1845-7, and a cholera epidemic. The new urban proletariat and expanding bourgeoisie demanded a greater political role. Republics were proclaimed in France, Rome, and Venice. Nationalist feelings reached fever pitch in the Hapsburg empire, as Hungary declared independence under Kossuth, a Slav Congress demanded equality, and Piedmont tried to drive Austria from Lombardy. A national liberal assembly at Frankfurt called for German unification.

But riots fueled bourgeois fears of socialism (Marx and Engels' 1848 *Communist Manifesto*) and peasants remained conservative. The old establishment — The Papacy, the Hapsburgs (using Croats and Romanians against Hungary), the Russian army — was able to rout the revolutionaries by 1849. The French Republic succumbed to a renewed monarchy by 1852 (Emperor Napoleon III).

Great nations unified. Using the "blood and iron" tactics of Bismarck from 1862, Prussia controlled N. Germany by 1867 (war with Denmark, 1864, Austria, 1866). After defeating France in 1870 (annexation of Alsace-Lorraine), it won the allegiance of S. German states. A new **German Empire** was proclaimed, 1871. **Italy,** inspired by Mazzini (1805-72) and Garibaldi (1807-82), was unified by the reformed Piedmont kingdom through uprisings, plebiscites, and war.

The **U.S.,** its area expanded after the 1846-47 Mexican War, defeated a secession attempt by slave states, 1861-65. The Canadian provinces were united in an autonomous **Dominion of Canada,** 1867. Control in **India** was removed from the East India Co. and centralized under British administration after the 1857-58 Sepoy rebellion, laying the groundwork for the modern Indian State. Queen Victoria was named Empress of India, 1876.

Europe dominates Asia. The Ottoman Empire began to collapse in the face of Balkan nationalisms and European imperial incursions in N. Africa (Suez Canal, 1869). The Turks had lost control of most of both regions by 1882. Russia completed its expansion south by 1884 (despite the temporary setback of the Crimean War with Turkey, Britain, and France, 1853-56) taking Turkestan, all the Caucasus, and Chinese areas in the East and sponsoring Balkan Slavs against the Turks. A succession of reformist and reactionary regimes presided over a slow modernization (serfs freed, 1861). Persian independence suffered as Russia and British India competed for influence.

China was forced to sign a series of unequal treaties with European powers and Japan. Overpopulation and an inefficient dynasty brought misery and caused rebellions (Taiping, Moslems) leaving tens of millions dead. Japan was forced by the U.S. (Commodore Perry's visits, 1853-54) and Europe to end its isolation. The Meiji restoration, 1868, gave power to a Westernizing oligarchy. Intensified empire-building gave Burma to Britain, 1824-86, and Indo-China to France, 1862-95. Christian missionary activity followed imperial and trade expansion in Asia.

Respectability. The fine arts were expected to reflect and encourage the progress of morals and manners among the different classes. "Victorian" prudery, exaggerated delicacy, and familial piety were heralded by **Bowdler's** expurgated edition of Shakespeare (1818). Government-supported mass education inculcated a work ethic as a means to escape poverty (Horatio Alger, 1832-99).

The official **Beaux Arts** school in Paris set an international style of imposing public buildings (Paris Opera, 1861-74, Vienna Opera, 1861-69) and uplifting statues (Bartholdi's *Statue of Liberty*, 1885). Realist painting, influenced by photography (Daguerre, 1837), appealed to a new mass audience with social or historical narrative (Wilkie, 1785-1841, Poynter, 1836-1919) or with serious religious, moral, or social messages (pre-Raphaelites, Millet's Angelus, 1858) often drawn from ordinary life. The **Impressionists** (Pissarro, 1830-1903, Renoir, 1841-1919) rejected the central role of serious subject matter in favor of a colorful and sensual depiction of a moment, but their sunny, placid depictions of bourgeois scenes kept them within the respectable consensus.

Realistic **novelists** presented the full panorama of social classes and personalities, but retained sentimentality and moral judgment (Dickens, 1812-70, Eliot, 1819-80, Tolstoy, 1828-1910, Balzac, 1799-1850).

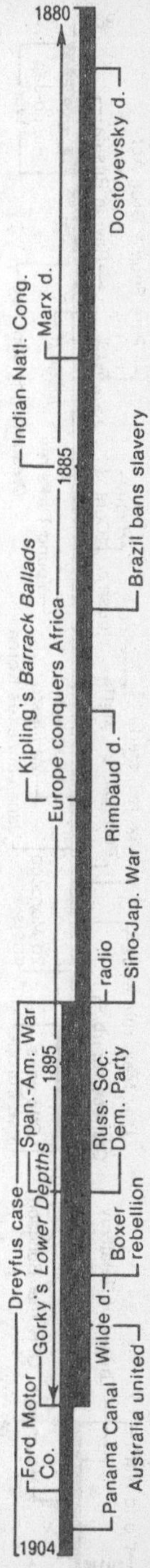

Veneer of Stability: 1880-1900

Imperialism triumphant. The vast **African** interior, visited by European explorers (Barth, 1821-65, Livingstone, 1813-73), was conquered by the European powers in rapid, competitive thrusts from their coastal bases after 1880, mostly for domestic political and international strategic reasons. W. African Moslem kingdoms (Fulani), Arab slave traders (Zanzibar), and Bantu military confederations (Zulu) were alike subdued. Only Christian Ethiopia (defeat of Italy, 1896) and Liberia resisted successfully. France (W. Africa) and Britain ("Cape to Cairo," Boer War, 1899-1902) were the major beneficiaries. The ideology of "the white man's burden" (Kipling, *Barrack Room Ballads*, 1892) or of a "civilizing mission" (France) justified the conquests.

West European foreign capital investment soared to nearly $40 billion by 1914, but most in E. Europe (France, Germany), the Americas (Britain) and the Europeans' colonies. The foundation of the modern interdependent world economy was laid, with cartels dominating raw material trade.

An industrious world. Industrial and technological proficiency characterized the 2 new great powers — **Germany** and the **U.S.** Coal and iron deposits enabled Germany to reach second or third place status in iron, steel, and shipbuilding by the 1900s. German electrical and chemical industries were world leaders. The U.S. post-civil war boom (interrupted by "panics," 1884, 1893, 1896) was shaped by massive immigration from S. and E. Europe from 1880, government subsidy of railroads, and huge private monopolies (Standard Oil, 1870, U.S. Steel, 1901). The **Spanish-American War,** 1898 (Philippine rebellion, 1899-1901) and the Open Door policy in China (1899) made the U.S. a world power.

England led in **urbanization** (72% by 1890), with **London** the world capital of finance, insurance, and shipping. Electric subways (London, 1890), sewer systems (Paris, 1850s), parks, and bargain department stores helped improve living standards for most of the urban population of the industrial world.

Asians assimilate. Asian reaction to European economic, military, and religious incursions took the form of imitation of Western techniques and adoption of Western ideas of progress and freedom. The Chinese "self-strengthening" movement of the 1860s and 70s included rail, port, and arsenal improvements and metal and textile mills. Reformers like **K'ang Yu-wei** (1858-1927) won liberalizing reforms in 1898, right after the European and Japanese "scramble for concessions."

A universal education system in Japan and importation of foreign industrial, scientific, and military experts aided Japan's unprecedented rapid modernization after 1868, under the authoritarian Meiji regime. Japan's victory in the **Sino-Japanese War,** 1894-95, put Formosa and Korea in its power.

In India, the British alliance with the remaining princely states masked reform sentiment among the Westernized urban elite; higher education had been conducted largely in English for 50 years. The **Indian National Congress,** founded in 1885, demanded a larger government role for Indians.

"Fin-de-siècle" sophistication. Naturalist writers pushed realism to its extreme limits, adopting a quasi-scientific attitude and writing about formerly taboo subjects like sex, crime, extreme poverty, and corruption (Flaubert, 1821-80, Zola, 1840-1902, Hardy, 1840-1928). Unseen or repressed psychological motivations were explored in the clinical and theoretical works of **Freud** (1856-1939) and in the fiction of Dostoevsky (1821-81), James (1843-1916), Schnitzler (1862-1931) and others.

A contempt for bourgeois life or a desire to shock a complacent audience was shared by the French **symbolist** poets (Verlaine, 1844-96, Rimbaud, 1854-91), neo-pagan English writers (Swinburne, 1837-1909), continental dramatists (Ibsen, 1828-1906) and satirists (Wilde, 1854-1900). **Nietzsche** (1844-1900) was influential in his elitism and pessimism.

Post-impressionist art neglected long-cherished conventions of representation (Cezanne, 1839-1906) and showed a willingness to learn from primitive and non-European art (Gauguin, 1848-1903, Japanese prints).

Racism. Gobineau (1816-82) gave a pseudo-biological foundation to modern racist theories, which spread in the latter 19th century along with **Social Darwinism,** the belief that societies are and should be organized as a struggle for survival of the fittest. The Medieval period was interpreted as an era of natural Germanic rule (Chamberlain, 1855-1927) and notions of superiority were associated with German national aspirations (Treitschke, 1834-96). **Anti-Semitism,** with a new racist rationale, became a significant political force in Germany (Anti-Semitic Petition, 1880), Austria (Lueger, 1844-1910), and France (Dreyfus case, 1894-1906).

Last Respite: 1900-1909

Alliances. While the peace of Europe (and its dependencies) continued to hold (1907 **Hague Conference** extended the rules of war and international arbitration procedures), imperial rivalries, protectionist trade practices (in Germany and France), and the escalating arms race (British *Dreadnought* battleship launched, Germany widens Kiel canal, 1906) exacerbated minor disputes (German-French Moroccan "crises", 1905, 1911).

Security was sought through alliances: **Triple Alliance** (Germany, Austria-Hungary, Italy) renewed 1902,

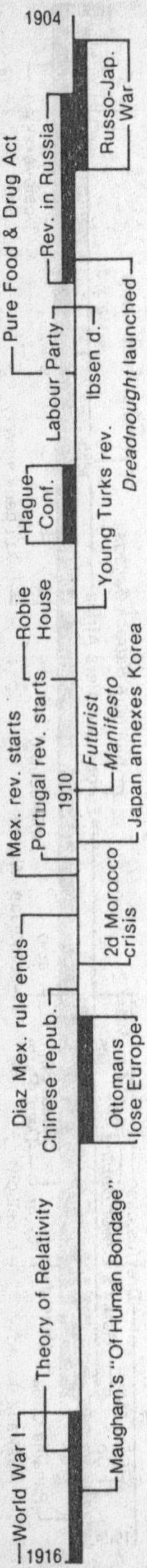

1907; Anglo-Japanese Alliance, 1902; Franco-Russian Alliance, 1899; **Entente Cordiale** (Britain, France), 1904; Anglo-Russian Treaty, 1907; German-Ottoman friendship.

Ottomans decline. The inefficient, corrupt Ottoman government was unable to resist further loss of territory. Nearly all European lands were lost in 1912 to Serbia, Greece, Montenegro, and Bulgaria. Italy took Libya and the Dodecanese islands the same year, and Britain took Kuwait, 1899, and the Sinai, 1906. The **Young Turk** revolution in 1908 forced the sultan to restore a constitution, and introduced some social reform, industrialization, and secularization.

British Empire. British trade and cultural influence remained dominant in the empire, but constitutional reforms presaged its eventual dissolution: the colonies of **Australia** were united in 1901 under a self-governing commonwealth. **New Zealand** acquired dominion status in 1907. The old Boer republics joined Cape Colony and Natal in the self-governing **Union of South Africa** in 1910.

The 1909 Indian Councils Act enhanced the role of elected province legislatures in **India.** The Moslem League, founded 1906, sought separate communal representation.

East Asia. Japan exploited its growing industrial power to expand its empire. Victory in the 1904-05 war against Russia (naval battle of Tsushima, 1905) assured Japan's domination of **Korea** (annexed 1910) and Manchuria (took Port Arthur 1905).

In China, central authority began to crumble (empress died, 1908). Reforms (Confucian exam system ended 1905, modernization of the army, building of railroads) were inadequate and secret societies of reformers and nationalists, inspired by the Westernized **Sun Yat-sen** (1866-1925) fomented periodic uprisings in the south.

Siam, whose independence had been guaranteed by Britain and France in 1896, was split into spheres of influence by those countries in 1907.

Russia. The population of the Russian Empire approached 150 million in 1900. Reforms in education, law, and local institutions (*zemstvos*), and an industrial boom starting in the 1880s (oil, railroads) created the beginnings of a modern state, despite the autocratic tsarist regime. Liberals (1903 Union of Liberation), Socialists (Social Democrats founded 1898, Bolsheviks split off 1903), and populists (Social Revolutionaries founded 1901) were periodically repressed, and national minorities persecuted (anti-Jewish pogroms, 1903, 1905-6).

An industrial crisis after 1900 and harvest failures aggravated poverty in the urban proletariat, and the 1904-05 defeat by Japan (which checked Russia's Asian expansion) sparked the revolution of 1905-06. A **Duma** (parliament) was created, and an agricultural reform (under Stolypin, prime minister 1906-11) created a large class of landowning peasants (kulaks).

The world shrinks. Developments in transportation and communication and mass population movements helped create an awareness of an interdependent world. Early **automobiles** (Daimler, Benz, 1885) were experimental, or designed as luxuries. Assembly-line mass production (Ford Motor Co., 1903) made the invention practicable, and by 1910 nearly 500,000 motor vehicles were registered in the U.S. alone. **Heavier-than-air flights** began in 1903 in the U.S. (Wright brothers), preceded by glider, balloon, and model plane advances in several countries. Trade was advanced by improvements in **ship design** (gyrocompass, 1907), speed (Lusitania crossed Atlantic in 5 days, 1907), and reach (Panama Canal begun, 1904).

The first transatlantic **radio** telegraphic transmission occurred in 1901, 6 years after Marconi discovered radio. Radio transmission of human speech had been made in 1900. Telegraphic transmission of photos was achieved in 1904, lending immediacy to news reports. **Phonographs,** popularized by Caruso's recordings (starting 1902), made for quick international spread of musical styles (ragtime). **Motion pictures,** perfected in the 1890s (Dickson, Lumière brothers), became a popular and artistic medium after 1900; newsreels appeared in 1909.

Emigration from crowded European centers soared in the decade: 9 million migrated to the U.S., and millions more went to Siberia, Canada, Argentina, Australia, South Africa, and Algeria. Some 70 million Europeans emigrated in the century before 1914. Several million Chinese, Indians, and Japanese migrated to Southeast Asia, where their urban skills often enabled them to take a predominant economic role.

Social reform. The social and economic problems of the poor were kept in the public eye by realist fiction writers (Dreiser's *Sister Carrie,* 1900; Gorky's *Lower Depths,* 1902; Sinclair's *Jungle,* 1906), journalists (U.S. **muckrakers** — Steffens, Tarbell), and artists (Ashcan school). Frequent labor strikes and occasional assassinations by anarchists or radicals (Austrian Empress, 1898; King Umberto I of Italy, 1900; U.S. Pres. McKinley, 1901; Russian Interior Minister Plehve, 1904; Portugal's King Carlos, 1908) added to social tension and fear of revolution.

But democratic reformism prevailed. In Germany, Bernstein's (1850-1932) **revisionist Marxism,** downgrading revolution, was accepted by the powerful Social Democrats and trade unions. The British Fabian Society (the Webbs, Shaw) and the Labour Party (founded 1906) worked for reforms such as social security and union rights (1906), while women's suffragists grew more militant. U.S. **progressives** fought big business (Pure Food and Drug Act, 1906). In France, the 10-hour work day (1904) and separation of church and state (1905) were reform victories, as was universal suffrage in Austria (1907).

Arts. An unprecedented period of experimentation, centered in France, produced several new **painting** styles: fauvism exploited bold color areas (Matisse, *Woman with Hat,* 1905); expressionism reflected powerful inner emotions (the Br cke group, 1905); cubism combined several views of an object on one flat surface (Picasso's *Demoiselles,* 1906-07); futurism tried to depict speed and motion (Italian Futurist Manifesto, 1910). **Architects** explored new uses of steel structures, with facades either neo-classical (Adler and Sullivan in U.S.); curvilinear Art Nouveau (Gaudi's Casa Mila, 1905-10); or functionally streamlined (Wright's Robie House, 1909).

Music and **Dance** shared the experimental spirit. Ruth St. Denis (1877-1968) and Isadora Duncan (1878-1927) pioneered modern dance, while Diaghilev in Paris revitalized classic ballet from 1909. Composers explored atonal music (Debussy, 1862-1918) and dissonance (Sch nberg, 1874-1951), or revolutionized classical forms (Stravinsky, 1882-1971), often showing jazz or folk music influences.

War and Revolution: 1910-1919

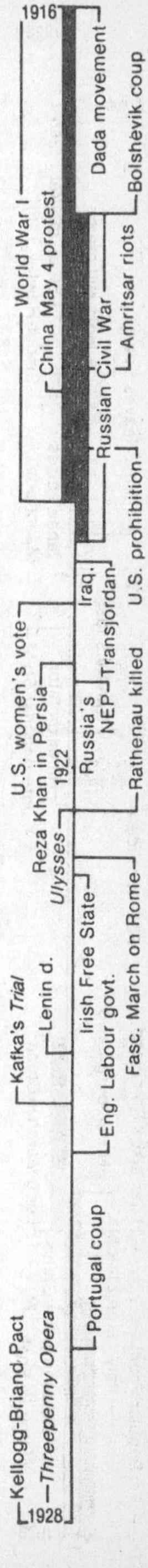

War threatens. Germany under Wilhelm II sought a political and imperial role consonant with its industrial strength, challenging Britain's world supremacy and threatening France, still resenting the loss of Alsace-Lorraine. Austria wanted to curb an expanded Serbia (after 1912) and the threat it posed to its own Slav lands. Russia feared Austrian and German political and economic aims in the Balkans and Turkey. An accelerated arms race resulted: the German standing army rose to over 2 million men by 1914. Russia and France had over a million each, Austria and the British Empire nearly a million each. Dozens of enormous battleships were built by the powers after 1906.

The **assassination of Austrian Archduke Franz Ferdinand** by a Serbian, June 28, 1914, was the pretext for war. The system of alliances made the conflict Europe-wide; Germany's invasion of Belgium to outflank France forced Britain to enter the war. Patriotic fervor was nearly unanimous among all classes in most countries.

World War I. German forces were stopped in France in one month. The rival armies dug **trench networks.** Artillery and improved machine guns prevented either side from any lasting advance despite repeated assaults (600,000 dead at **Verdun,** Feb.-July 1916). Poison gas, used by Germany in 1915, proved ineffective. Over one million U.S. troops tipped the balance after mid-1917, forcing Germany to sue for peace.

In the East, the Russian armies were thrown back (battle of **Tannenberg,** Aug. 20, 1914) and the war grew unpopular. An allied attempt to relieve Russia through Turkey failed (**Gallipoli** 1915). The new Bolshevik regime signed the capitulatory Brest-Litovsk peace in March, 1918. Italy entered the war on the allied side, May 1915, but was pushed back by Oct. 1917. A renewed offensive with Allied aid in Oct.-Nov. 1918 forced Austria to surrender.

The British Navy successfully blockaded Germany, which responded with submarine U-boat attacks; **unrestricted submarine warfare** against neutrals after Jan. 1917 helped bring the U.S. into the war. Other battlefields included Palestine and Mesopotamia, both of which Britain wrested from the Turks in 1917, and the African and Pacific colonies of Germany, most of which fell to Britain, France, Australia, Japan, and South Africa.

From 1916, the civilian populations and economies of both sides were mobilized to an unprecedented degree. Hardships intensified among fighting nations in 1917 (French mutiny crushed in May). Over 10 million soldiers died in the war.

Settlement. At the **Versailles conference** (Jan.-June 1919) and in subsequent negotiations and local wars (Russian-Polish War 1920), the map of Europe was redrawn with a nod to U.S. Pres. Wilson's principle of self-determination. Austria and Hungary were separated and much of their land was given to Yugoslavia (formerly Serbia), Romania, Italy, and the newly independent Poland and Czechoslovakia. Germany lost territory in the West, North, and East, while Finland and the Baltic states were detached from Russia. Turkey lost nearly all its Arab lands to British-sponsored Arab states or to direct French and British rule.

A huge **reparations** burden and partial demilitarization were imposed on Germany. Wilson obtained approval for a League of Nations, but the U.S. Senate refused to allow the U.S. to join.

Russian revolution. Military defeats and high casualties caused a contagious lack of confidence in Tsar Nicholas, who was forced to abdicate, Mar. 1917. A liberal provisional government failed to end the war, and massive desertions, riots, and fighting between factions followed. A moderate socialist government under Kerensky was overthrown in a violent **coup by the Bolsheviks** in Petrograd under Lenin, who disbanded the elected Constituent Assembly, Nov. 1917.

The Bolsheviks brutally suppressed all opposition and ended the war with Germany, Mar. 1918. **Civil war** broke out in the summer between the Red Army, including the Bolsheviks and their supporters, and monarchists, anarchists, nationalities (Ukrainians, Georgians, Poles) and others. Small U.S., British, French and Japanese units also opposed the Bolsheviks, 1918-19 (Japan in Vladivostok to 1922). The civil war, anarchy, and pogroms devastated the country until the 1920 Red Army victory. The wartime total monopoly of political, economic, and police power by the Communist Party leadership was retained.

Other European revolutions. An unpopular monarchy in **Portugal** was overthrown in 1910. The new republic took severe anti-clerical measures, 1911.

After a century of Home Rule agitation, during which **Ireland** was devastated by famine (one million dead, 1846-47) and emigration, republican militants staged an unsuccessful uprising in Dublin, Easter 1916. The execution of the leaders and mass arrests by the British won popular support for the rebels. The Irish Free State, comprising all but the 6 northern counties, achieved dominion status in 1922.

In the aftermath of the world war, radical revolutions were attempted in Germany (**Spartacist** uprising Jan. 1919), **Hungary** (Kun regime 1919), and elsewhere. All were suppressed or failed for lack of support.

Chinese revolution. The Manchu Dynasty was overthrown and a republic proclaimed, Oct. 1911. First president Sun Yat-sen resigned in favor of strongman Yuan Shih-k'ai. Sun organized the parliamentarian **Kuomintang** party.

Students launched protests May 4, 1919 against League of Nations concessions in China to Japan. Nationalist, liberal, and socialist ideas and political groups spread. The **Communist Party** was founded 1921. A communist regime took power in Mongolia with Soviet support in 1921.

India restive. Indian objections to British rule erupted in nationalist riots as well as in the non-violent tactics of Gandhi (1869-1948). Nearly 400 unarmed demonstrators were shot at **Amritsar,** Apr. 1919. Britain approved limited self-rule that year.

Mexican revolution. Under the long Diaz dictatorship (1876-1911) the economy advanced, but Indian and mestizo lands were confiscated, and concessions to foreigners (mostly U.S.) damaged the middle class. A **revolution in 1910** led to civil wars and U.S. intervention (1914, 1916-17). Land reform and a more democratic constitution (1917) were achieved.

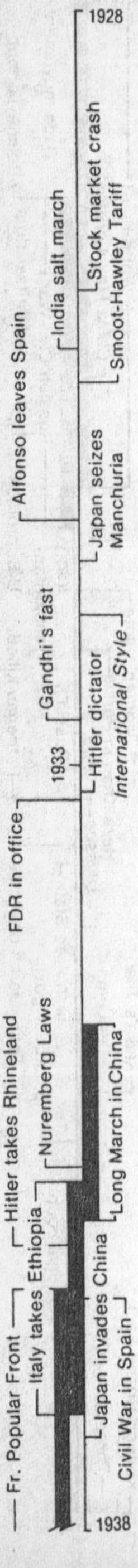

The Aftermath of War: 1920-29

U.S. Easy credit, technological ingenuity, and war-related industrial decline in Europe caused a long economic boom, in which ownership of the new products — autos, phones, radios — became democratized. Prosperity, an increase in women workers, women's suffrage (1920) and drastic change in fashion (flappers, mannish bob for women, clean-shaven men), created a wide perception of social change, despite prohibition of alcoholic beverages (1919-33). Union membership and strikes increased. Fear of radicals led to Palmer raids (1919-20) and Sacco/Vanzetti case (1921-27).

Europe sorts itself out. Germany's liberal **Weimar constitution** (1919) could not guarantee a stable government in the face of rightist violence (Rathenau assassinated 1922) and Communist refusal to cooperate with Socialists. Reparations and allied occupation of the Rhineland caused staggering inflation which destroyed middle class savings, but economic expansion resumed after mid-decade, aided by U.S. loans. A sophisticated, innovative culture developed in architecture and design (Bauhaus, 1919-28), film (Lang, *M*, 1931), painting (Grosz), music (Weill, *Threepenny Opera*, 1928), theater (Brecht, *A Man's a Man*, 1926), criticism (Benjamin), philosophy (Jung), and fashion. This culture was considered decadent and socially disruptive by rightists.

England elected its first labor governments (Jan. 1924, June 1929). A 10-day general strike in support of coal miners failed, May 1926. In **Italy**, strikes, political chaos and violence by small Fascist bands culminated in the Oct. 1922 Fascist March on Rome, which established Mussolini's dictatorship. Strikes were outlawed (1926), and Italian influence was pressed in the Balkans (Albania a protectorate 1926). A conservative dictatorship was also established in **Portugal** in a 1926 military coup.

Czechoslovakia, the only stable democracy to emerge from the war in Central or East Europe, faced opposition from Germans (in the Sudetenland), Ruthenians, and some Slovaks. As the industrial heartland of the old Hapsburg empire, it remained fairly prosperous. With French backing, it formed the Little Entente with Yugoslavia (1920) and **Romania** (1921) to block Austrian or Hungarian irredentism. **Hungary** remained dominated by the landholding classes and expansionist feeling. Croats and Slovenes in **Yugoslavia** demanded a federal state until King Alexander proclaimed a dictatorship (1929). Poland faced nationality problems as well (Germans, Ukrainians, Jews); Pilsudski ruled as dictator from 1926. The Baltic states were threatened by traditionally dominant ethnic Germans and by Soviet-supported communists.

An economic collapse and famine in **Russia,** 1921-22, claimed 5 million lives. The New Economic Policy (1921) allowed land ownership by peasants and some private commerce and industry. Stalin was absolute ruler within 4 years of Lenin's 1924 death. He inaugurated a brutal collectivization program 1929-32, and used foreign communist parties for Soviet state advantage.

Internationalism. Revulsion against World War I led to pacifist agitation, the Kellogg-Briand Pact renouncing aggressive war (1928), and **naval disarmament** pacts (Washington, 1922, London, 1930). But the League of Nations was able to arbitrate only minor disputes (Greece-Bulgaria, 1925).

Middle East. Mustafa Kemal (Ataturk) led **Turkish** nationalists in resisting Italian, French, and Greek military advances, 1919-23. The sultanate was abolished 1922, and elaborate reforms passed, including secularization of law and adoption of the Latin alphabet. Ethnic conflict led to persecution of **Armenians** (over 1 million dead in 1915, 1 million expelled), Greeks (forced Greek-Turk population exchange, 1923), and Kurds (1925 uprising).

With evacuation of the Turks from **Arab** lands, the puritanical Wahabi dynasty of eastern Arabia conquered present Saudi Arabia, 1919-25. British, French, and Arab dynastic and nationalist maneuvering resulted in the creation of two more Arab monarchies in 1921: Iraq and Transjordan (both under British control), and two French mandates: Syria and Lebanon. Jewish immigration into British-mandated **Palestine,** inspired by the Zionist movement, was resisted by Arabs, at times violently (1921, 1929 massacres).

Reza Khan ruled **Persia** after his 1921 coup (shah from 1925), centralized control, and created the trappings of a modern state.

China. The Kuomintang under **Chiang Kai-shek** (1887-1975) subdued the warlords by 1928. The Communists were brutally suppressed after their alliance with the Kuomintang was broken in 1927. Relative peace thereafter allowed for industrial and financial improvements, with some Russian, British, and U.S. cooperation.

Arts. Nearly all bounds of subject matter, style, and attitude were broken in the arts of the period. **Abstract** art first took inspiration from natural forms or narrative themes (Kandinsky from 1911), then worked free of any representational aims (Malevich's suprematism, 1915-19, Mondrian's geometric style from 1917). The **Dada** movement from 1916 mocked artistic pretension with absurd collages and constructions (Arp, Tzara, from 1916). Paradox, illusion, and psychological taboos were exploited by **surrealists** by the latter 1920s (Dali, Magritte). Architectural schools celebrated industrial values, whether vigorous abstract constructivism (Tatlin, *Monument to 3rd International,* 1919) or the machined, streamlined **Bauhaus** style, which was extended to many design fields (Helvetica type face).

Prose writers explored revolutionary narrative modes related to dreams (Kafka's *Trial,* 1925), internal monologue (Joyce's *Ulysses,* 1922), and word play (Stein's *Making of Americans,* 1925). Poets and novelists wrote of modern alienation (Eliot's *Waste Land,* 1922) and aimlessness (Lost Generation).

Sciences. Scientific specialization prevailed by the 20th century. Advances in knowledge and technological aptitude increased with the geometric increase in the number of practitioners. Physicists challenged common-sense views of causality, observation, and a mechanistic universe, putting science further beyond popular grasp (Einstein's general theory of relativity, 1915; Bohr's quantum mechanics, 1913; Heisenberg's uncertainty principle, 1927).

Rise of the Totalitarians: 1930-39

Depression. A worldwide financial panic and economic depression began with the Oct. 1929 U.S. stock market crash and the May 1931 failure of the Austrian Credit-Anstalt. A credit crunch caused international bankruptcies and **unemployment:** 12 million jobless by 1932 in the U.S., 5.6 million in Germany, 2.7 million in England. Governments responded with **tariff restrictions** (Smoot-Hawley Act, 1930; Ottawa Imperial Conference, 1932), which dried up world trade. Government public works programs were vitiated by deflationary budget balancing.

Germany. Years of agitation by violent extremists was brought to a head by the Depression. Nazi leader **Hitler** was named chancellor by Pres. Hindenburg Jan. 1933, and given dictatorial power by the Reichstag in Mar. Opposition parties were disbanded, strikes banned, and all aspects of economic, cultural, and religious life brought under central government and Nazi party control and manipulated by sophisticated propaganda. Severe persecution of Jews began (**Nuremberg Laws** Sept. 1935). Many Jews, political opponents and others were sent to concentration camps (Dachau, 1933) where thousands died or were killed. Public works, renewed conscription (1935), arms production, and a 4-year plan (1936) ended unemployment.

Hitler's expansionism started with reincorporation of the Saar (1935), occupation of the **Rhineland** (Mar. 1936), and annexation of Austria (Mar. 1938). At **Munich,** Sept. 1938, an indecisive Britain and France sanctioned German dismemberment of Czechoslovakia.

Russia. Urbanization and education advanced. Rapid industrialization was achieved through successive **5-year-plans** starting 1928, using severe labor discipline and mass forced labor. Industry was financed by a decline in living standards and exploitation of agriculture, which was almost totally collectivized by the early 1930s (*kolkhoz,* collective farm; *sovkhoz,* state farm, often in newly-worked lands). Successive **purges** increased the role of professionals and management at the expense of workers. Millions perished in a series of man-made disasters: elimination of kulaks (peasant land-owners), 1929-34; severe famine, 1932-33; party purges (Great Purge, 1936-38); suppression of nationalities; and poor conditions in labor camps.

Spain. An industrial revolution during World War I created an urban proletariat, which was attracted to socialism and anarchism; Catalan nationalists challenged central authority. The 5 years after King Alfonso left Spain, Apr. 1931, were dominated by tension between intermittent leftist and anti-clerical governments and clericals, monarchists and other rightists. Anarchist and communist rebellions were crushed, but a July 1936 extreme right rebellion led by Gen. Francisco Franco and aided by Nazi Germany and Fascist Italy succeeded, after a 3-year **civil war** (over 1 million dead in battles and atrocities). The war polarized international public opinion.

Italy. Despite propaganda for the ideal of the Corporate State, few domestic reforms were attempted. An entente with Hungary and Austria, Mar. 1934, a pact with Germany and Japan, Nov. 1937, and intervention by 50-75,000 troops in Spain, 1936-39, sealed Italy's identification with the fascist bloc (anti-Semitic laws after Mar. 1938). Ethiopia was conquered, 1935-37, and **Albania** annexed, Jan. 1939, in conscious imitation of ancient Rome.

East Europe. Repressive regimes fought for power against an active opposition (liberals, socialists, communists, peasants, Nazis). Minority groups and Jews were restricted within national boundaries that did not coincide with ethnic population patterns. In the destruction of **Czechoslovakia, Hungary** occupied southern Slovakia (Nov. 1938) and Ruthenia (Mar. 1939), and a pro-Nazi regime took power in the rest of Slovakia. Other boundary disputes (e.g. Poland-Lithuania, Yugoslavia-Bulgaria, Romania-Hungary) doomed attempts to build joint fronts against Germany or Russia. Economic depression was severe.

East Asia. After a period of liberalism in **Japan,** nativist militarists dominated the government with peasant support. Manchuria was seized, Sept. 1931-Feb. 1932, and a puppet state set up (Manchukuo). Adjacent Jehol (Inner Mongolia) was occupied in 1933. China proper was invaded July 1937; large areas were conquered by Oct. 1938.

In **China** Communist forces left Kuomintang-besieged strongholds in the South in a Long March (1934-35) to the North. The Kuomintang-Communist civil war was suspended Jan. 1937 in the face of threatening Japan.

The democracies. The Roosevelt Administration, in office Mar. 1933, embarked on an extensive program of social reform and economic stimulation, including protection for labor unions (heavy industries organized), social security, public works, wages and hours laws, and assistance to farmers. Isolationist sentiment (1937 Neutrality Act) prevented U.S. intervention in Europe, but military expenditures were increased in 1939.

French political instability and polarization prevented resolution of economic and international security questions. The **Popular Front** government under Blum (June 1936-Apr. 1938) passed social reforms (40-hour week) and raised arms spending. National coalition governments ruled Britain from Aug. 1931, brought some economic recovery, but failed to define a consistent foreign policy until Chamberlain's government (from May 1937), which practiced deliberate **appeasement** of Germany and Italy.

India. Twenty years of agitation for autonomy and then for independence (Gandhi's **salt march,** 1930) achieved some constitutional reform (extended provincial powers, 1935) despite Moslem-Hindu strife. Social issues assumed prominence with peasant uprisings (1921), strikes (1928), Gandhi's efforts for untouchables (1932 "fast unto death"), and social and agrarian reform by the provinces after 1937.

Arts. The streamlined, geometric design motifs of Art Deco (from 1925) prevailed through the 1930s. Abstract art flourished (Moore sculptures from 1931) alongside a new realism related to social and political concerns (**Socialist Realism** the official Soviet style from 1934; Mexican muralists Rivera, 1886-1957, and Orozco, 1883-1949), which was also expressed in fiction and poetry (Steinbeck's *Grapes of Wrath,* 1939; Sandburg's *The People, Yes,* 1936). Modern architecture (*International Style,* 1932) was unchallenged in its use of man-made materials (concrete, glass), lack of decoration, and monumentality (Rockefeller Center, 1929-40). U.S.-made films captured a world-wide audience with their larger-than-life fantasies (*Gone with the Wind,* 1939).

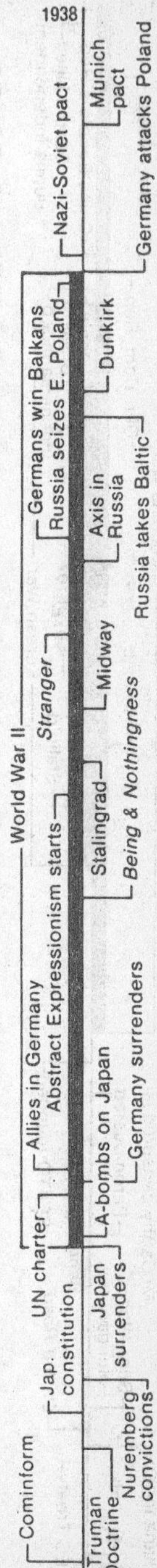

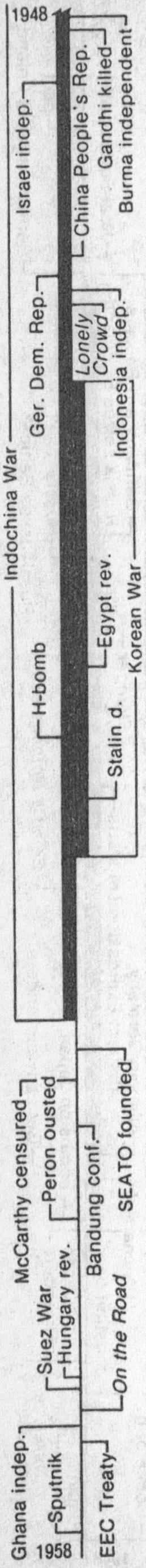

War, Hot and Cold: 1940-49

War in Europe. The Nazi-Soviet non-aggression pact (Aug. '39) freed Germany to attack Poland (Sept.). Britain and France, who had guaranteed Polish independence, declared war on Germany. Russia seized East Poland (Sept.), attacked Finland (Nov.) and took the Baltic states (July '40). Mobile German forces staged **"blitzkrieg"** attacks Apr.-June, '40, conquering neutral Denmark, Norway, and the Low Countries and defeating France; 350,000 British and French troops were evacuated at **Dunkirk** (May). The Battle of Britain, June-Dec. '40, denied Germany air superiority. German-Italian campaigns won the Balkans by Apr. '41. Three million Axis troops **invaded Russia** June '41, marching through Ukraine to the Caucasus, and through White Russia and the Baltic republics to Moscow and Leningrad.

Russian winter counterthrusts, '41-'42 and '42-'43 stopped the German advance (Stalingrad Sept. '42-Feb. '43). With British and U.S. Lend-Lease aid and sustaining great casualties, the Russians drove the Axis from all E. Europe and the Balkans in the next 2 years. Invasions of N. Africa (Nov. '42), Italy (Sept. '43), and Normandy (June '44) brought U.S., British, Free French and allied troops to Germany by spring '45. Germany surrendered May 7, 1945.

War in Asia-Pacific. Japan occupied Indochina Sept. '40, dominated Thailand Dec. '41, attacked Hawaii, the Philippines, Hong Kong, Malaya Dec. 7, 1941. Indonesia was attacked Jan. '42, Burma conquered Mar. 42. Battle of **Midway** (June '42) turned back the Japanese advance. "Island-hopping" battles (Guadalcanal Aug. '42-Jan. '43, **Leyte Gulf** Oct. '44, Iwo Jima Feb.-Mar. '45, Okinawa Apr. '45) and massive bombing raids on Japan from June '44 wore out Japanese defenses. Two U.S. atom bombs, dropped Aug. 6 and 9, forced Japan to surrender Aug. 14, 1945.

Atrocities. The war brought 20th-century cruelty to its peak. Nazi murder camps (Auschwitz) systematically killed 6 million Jews. Gypsies, political opponents, sick and retarded people, and others deemed undesirable were murdered by the Nazis, as were vast numbers of Slavs, especially leaders.

Civilian deaths. German bombs killed 70,000 English civilians. Some 100,000 Chinese civilians were killed by Japanese forces in the capture of Nanking. Severe retaliation by the Soviet army, E. European partisans, Free French and others took a heavy toll. U.S. and British bombing of Germany killed hundreds of thousands, as did U.S. bombing of Japan (80-200,000 at Hiroshima alone). Some 45 million people lost their lives in the war.

Settlement. The United Nations charter was signed in San Francisco June 26, 1945 by 50 nations. The International Tribunal at Nuremberg convicted 22 German leaders for war crimes Sept. '46, 23 Japanese leaders were convicted Nov. '48. Postwar border changes included large gains in territory for the USSR, losses for Germany, a shift westward in Polish borders, and minor losses for Italy. Communist regimes, supported by Soviet troops, took power in most of E. Europe, including Soviet-occupied Germany (GDR proclaimed Oct. '49). Japan lost all overseas lands.

Recovery. Basic political and social changes were imposed on Japan and W. Germany by the western allies (Japan constitution Nov. '46, W. German basic law May '49). U.S. Marshall Plan aid ($12 billion '47-'51) spurred W. European economic recovery after a period of severe inflation and strikes in Europe and the U.S. The British Labour Party introduced a national health service and nationalized basic industries in 1946.

Cold War. Western fears of further Soviet advances (Cominform formed Oct. '47, Czechoslovakia coup, Feb. '48, Berlin blockade Apr.'48-Sept. '49) led to formation of NATO. Civil War in Greece and Soviet pressure on Turkey led to U.S. aid under the Truman Doctrine (Mar. '47). Other anti-communist security pacts were the Org. of American States (Apr. '48) and Southeast Asia Treaty Org. (Sept. '54). A new wave of Soviet purges and repression intensified in the last years of Stalin's rule, extending to E. Europe (Slansky trial in Czechoslovakia, 1951). Only Yugoslavia resisted Soviet control (expelled by Cominform, June '48; U.S. aid, June '49).

China, Korea. Communist forces emerged from World War II strengthened by the Soviet takeover of industrial Manchuria. In 4 years of fighting, the Kuomintang was driven from the mainland; the People's Republic was proclaimed Oct. 1, 1949. Korea was divided by Russian and U.S. occupation forces. Separate republics were proclaimed in the 2 zones Aug.-Sept. '48.

India. India and Pakistan became independent dominions Aug. 15, 1947. Millions of Hindu and Moslem refugees were created by the partition; riots, 1946-47, took hundreds of thousands of lives; Gandhi himself was assassinated Jan. '48. Burma became completely independent Jan. '48; Ceylon took dominion status in Feb.

Middle East. The UN approved partition of Palestine into Jewish and Arab states. Israel was proclaimed May 14, 1948. Arabs rejected partition, but failed to defeat Israel in war, May '48-July '49. Immigration from Europe and the Middle East swelled Israel's Jewish population. British and French forces left Lebanon and Syria, 1946. Transjordan occupied most of Arab Palestine.

Southeast Asia. Communists and others fought against restoration of French rule in Indochina from 1946; a non-communist government was recognized by France Mar. '49, but fighting continued. Both Indonesia and the Philippines became independent, the former in 1949 after 4 years of war with Netherlands, the latter in 1946. Philippine economic and military ties with the U.S. remained strong; a communist-led peasant rising was checked in '48.

Arts. New York became the center of the world art market; abstract expressionism was the chief mode (Pollock from '43, de Kooning from '47). Literature and philosophy explored existentialism (Camus' *Stranger*, 1942, Sartre's *Being and Nothingness*, 1943). Non-Western attempts to revive or create regional styles (Senghor's Negritude, Mishima's novels) only confirmed the emergence of a universal culture. Radio and gramophone records spread American popular music (swing, bebop) around the world.

The American Decade: 1950-59

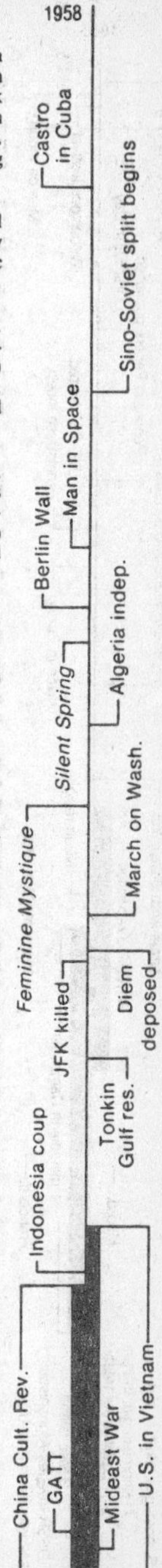

Polite decolonization. The peaceful decline of European political and military power in Asia and Africa accelerated in the 1950s. Nearly all of **N. Africa** was freed by 1956, but France fought a bitter war to retain Algeria, with its large European minority, until 1962. **Ghana,** independent 1957, led a parade of new black African nations (over 2 dozen by 1962), which altered the political character of the UN. Ethnic disputes often exploded in the new nations after decolonization (UN troops in Cyprus 1964; **Nigeria** civil war 1967-70). Leaders of the new states, mostly sharing socialist ideologies, tried to create an Afro-Asian bloc (Bandung Conf. 1955), but Western economic influence and U.S. political ties remained strong (Baghdad Pact, 1955).

Trade. World trade volume soared, in an atmosphere of monetary stability assured by international accords (**Bretton Woods** 1944). In Europe, economic integration advanced (**European Economic Community** 1957, European Free Trade Association 1960). Comecon (1949) coordinated the economies of Soviet-bloc countries.

U.S. Economic growth produced an abundance of consumer goods (9.3 million motor vehicles sold, 1955). Suburban housing tracts changed life patterns for middle and working classes (Levittown 1946-51). **Eisenhower's** landslide election victories (1952, 1956) reflected consensus politics. Censure of McCarthy (Dec. '54) curbed the political abuse of anti-communism. A system of alliances and military bases bolstered U.S. influence on all continents. Trade and payments surpluses were balanced by overseas investments and foreign aid ($50 billion, 1950-59).

USSR. In the "thaw" after Stalin's death in 1953, relations with the West improved (evacuation of Vienna, Geneva summit conference, both 1955). Repression of scientific and cultural life eased, and many prisoners were freed or rehabilitated culminating in **de-Stalinization** (1956). Khrushchev's leadership aimed at consumer sector growth, but farm production lagged, despite the virgin lands program (from 1954). The 1956 Hungarian revolution, the 1960 U-2 spy plane episode, and other incidents renewed East-West tension and domestic curbs.

East Europe. Resentment of Russian domination and Stalinist repression combined with nationalist, economic and religious factors to produce periodic violence. East Berlin workers rioted in 1953, Polish workers rioted in Poznan, June 1956, and a broad-based revolution broke out in Hungary, Oct. 1956. All were suppressed by Soviet force or threats (at least 7,000 dead in Hungary). But Poland was allowed to restore private ownership of farms, and a degree of personal and economic freedom returned to Hungary. Yugoslavia experimented with worker self-management and a market economy.

Korea. The 1945 division of Korea left industry in the North, which was organized into a militant regime and armed by Russia. The South was politically disunited. Over 60,000 North Korean troops invaded the South June 25, 1950. The U.S., backed by the UN Security Council, sent troops. UN troops reached the Chinese border in Nov. Some 200,000 Chinese troops crossed the Yalu River and drove back UN forces. Cease-fire in July 1951 found the opposing forces near the original 38th parallel border. After 2 years of sporadic fighting, an armistice was signed July 27, 1953. U.S. troops remained in the South, and U.S. economic and military aid continued. The war stimulated rapid economic recovery in Japan.

China. Starting in 1952, industry, agriculture, and social institutions were forcibly collectivized. As many as several million people were executed as Kuomintang supporters or as class and political enemies. The Great Leap Forward, 1958-60, unsuccessfully tried to force the pace of development by substituting labor for investment.

Indochina. Ho's forces, aided by Russia and the new Chinese Communist government, fought French and pro-French Vietnamese forces to a standstill, and captured the strategic Dienbienphu camp in May, 1954. The Geneva Agreements divided Vietnam in half pending elections (never held), and recognized Laos and Cambodia as independent. The U.S. aided the anti-Communist Republic of Vietnam in the South.

Middle East. Arab revolutions placed leftist, militantly nationalist regimes in power in Egypt (1952) and Iraq (1958). But Arab unity attempts failed (United Arab Republic joined Egypt, Syria, Yemen 1958-61). Arab refusal to recognize Israel (Arab League economic blockade began Sept. 1951) led to a permanent state of war, with repeated incidents (Gaza, 1955). Israel occupied Sinai, Britain and France took the Suez Canal, Oct. 1956, but were replaced by the UN Emergency Force. The Mossadegh government in Iran nationalized the British-owned oil industry May 1951, but was overthrown in a U.S.-aided coup Aug. 1953.

Latin America. Dictator Juan Peron, in office 1946, enforced land reform, some nationalization, welfare state measures, and curbs on the Roman Catholic Church, but crushed opposition. A Sept. 1955 coup deposed Peron. The 1952 revolution in Bolivia brought land reform, nationalization of tin mines, and improvement in the status of Indians, who nevertheless remained poor. The Batista regime in Cuba was overthrown, Jan. 1959, by Fidel Castro, who imposed a communist dictatorship, aligned Cuba with Russia, and improved education and health care. A U.S.-backed anti-Castro invasion (Bay of Pigs, Apr. 1961) was crushed. Self-government advanced in the British Caribbean.

Technology. Large outlays on research and development in the U.S. and USSR focused on military applications (H-bomb in U.S. 1952, USSR 1953, Britain 1957, intercontinental missiles late 1950s). Soviet launching of the Sputnik satellite, Oct. 1957, spurred increases in U.S. science education funds (National Defense Education Act).

Literature and letters. Alienation from social and literary conventions reached an extreme in the theater of the absurd (Beckett's *Waiting for Godot* 1952), the "new novel" (Robbe-Grillet's *Voyeur* 1955), and avant-garde film (Antonioni's *L'Avventura* 1960). U.S. Beatniks (Kerouac's *On the Road* 1957) and others rejected the supposed conformism of Americans (Riesman's *Lonely Crowd* 1950).

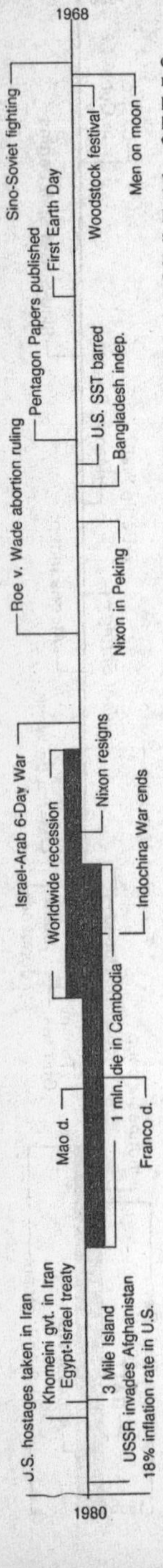

Rising Expectations: 1960-69

Economic boom. The longest sustained economic boom on record spanned almost the entire decade in the capitalist world; the closely-watched GNP figure doubled in the U.S. 1960-70, fueled by Vietnam War-related budget deficits. The **General Agreement on Tariffs and Trade,** 1967, stimulated West European prosperity, which spread to peripheral areas (Spain, Italy, E. Germany). Japan became a top economic power ($20 billion exports 1970). Foreign investment aided the industrialization of Brazil. Soviet 1965 economic reform attempts (decentralization, material incentives) were limited, but growth continued.

Reform and radicalization. Pres. John F. Kennedy, inaugurated 1961, emphasized youthful idealism, vigor; he was assassinated Nov. 22, 1963. A series of political and social reform movements took root in the U.S., later spreading to other countries with the help of ubiquitous U.S. film and television programs and heavy overseas travel (2.2 million U.S. passports issued 1970). Blacks agitated peaceably and with partial success against segregation and poverty (1963 March on Washington, 1964 **Civil Rights Act**); but some urban ghettos erupted in extensive riots (Watts, 1965; Detroit, 1967; King assassination, Apr. 4, 1968). New concern for the poor (Harrington's *Other America,* 1963) led to Pres. Johnson's **"Great Society"** programs (Medicare, Water Quality Act, Higher Education Act, all 1965). Concern with the **environment** surged (Carson's *Silent Spring,* 1962). **Feminism** revived as a cultural and political movement (Friedan's *Feminine Mystique,* 1963, National Organization for Women founded 1966) and a movement for homosexual rights emerged (Stonewall riot, in NYC, 1969). Pope John XXIII called Vatican II, 1962-65, which liberalized Roman Catholic liturgy.

Opposition to U.S. involvement in Vietnam, especially among university students (**Moratorium** protest Nov. '69), turned violent (Weathermen Chicago riots Oct. '69). New Left and Marxist theories became popular, and membership in radical groups swelled (Students for a Democratic Society, Black Panthers). Maoist groups, especially in Europe, called for total transformation of society. In France, students sparked a nationwide strike affecting 10 million workers May-June '68, but an electoral reaction barred revolutionary change.

Arts and styles. The boundary between fine and popular arts were blurred by Pop Art (Warhol) and rock musicals (*Hair*, 1968). Informality and exaggeration prevailed in fashion (beards, miniskirts). A non-political "counterculture" developed, rejecting traditional bourgeois life goals and personal habits, and use of marijuana and hallucinogens spread (Woodstock festival Aug. '69). Indian influence was felt in music (Beatles), religion (Ram Dass), and fashion.

Science. Achievements in space (men on moon July '69) and electronics (lasers, integrated circuits) encouraged a faith in scientific solutions to problems in agriculture ("green revolution"), medicine (heart transplants 1967) and other areas. The harmful effects of science, it was believed, could be controlled (1963 nuclear weapon test ban treaty, 1968 non-proliferation treaty).

China. Mao's revolutionary militance caused disputes with Russia under "revisionist" Khrushchev, starting 1960. The two powers exchanged fire in 1969 border disputes. China used force to capture areas disputed with India 1962. The "Great Proletarian Cultural Revolution" tried to impose a utopian egalitarian program in China and spread revolution abroad; political struggle, often violent, convulsed China 1965-68.

Indochina. Communist-led guerrillas aided by N. Vietnam fought from 1960 against the S. Vietnam government of Ngo Dinh Diem (killed 1963). The U.S. military role increased after the 1964 Tonkin Gulf incident. U.S. forces peaked at 543,400, Apr. '69. Massive numbers of N. Viet troops also fought. Laotian and Cambodian neutrality were threatened by communist insurgencies, with N. Vietnamese aid, and U.S. intrigues.

Third World. A bloc of authoritarian leftist regimes among the newly independent nations emerged in political opposition to the U.S.-led Western alliance, and came to dominate the conference of nonaligned nations (Belgrade 1961, Cairo 1964, Lusaka 1970). Soviet political ties and military bases were established in Cuba, Egypt, Algeria, Guinea, and other countries, whose leaders were regarded as revolutionary heros by opposition groups in pro-Western or colonial countries. Some leaders were ousted in coups by pro-Western groups—Zaire's Lumumba (killed 1961), Ghana's Nkrumah (exiled 1966), and Indonesia's Sukarno (effectively ousted 1965 after a Communist coup failed).

Middle East. Arab-Israeli tension erupted into a brief war June 1967. Israel emerged as a major regional power. Military shipments before and after the war brought much of the Arab world into the Soviet political sphere. Most Arab states broke U.S. diplomatic ties, while Communist countries cut their ties to Israel. Intra-Arab disputes continued: Egypt and Saudi Arabia supported rival factions in a bloody Yemen civil war 1962-70; Lebanese troops fought Palestinian commandos 1969.

East Europe. To stop the large-scale exodus of citizens, E. German authorities built a fortified wall across Berlin Aug. '61. Soviet sway in the Balkans was weakened by Albania's support of China (USSR broke ties Dec. '61) and Romania's assertion of industrial and foreign policy autonomy 1964. Liberalization in Czechoslovakia, spring 1968, was crushed by troops of 5 Warsaw Pact countries. West German treaties with Russia and Poland, 1970, facilitated the transfer of German technology and confirmed post-war boundaries.

Disillusionment: 1970-79

U.S.: Caution and neoconservatism. A relatively sluggish economy, energy and resource shortages (natural gas crunch 1975, gasoline shortage 1979) and environmental problems contributed to a **"limits of growth"** philosophy. Suspicion of science and technology killed or delayed major projects (supersonic transport dropped 1971, DNA recombination curbed 1976, Seabrook A-plant protests 1977-78) and was fed by the Three Mile Island nuclear reactor accident Mar. '79.

Mistrust of big government weakened support for government reform plans among liberals. School busing and racial quotas were opposed (**Bakke decision** June '78); the Equal Rights Amendment for women languished; civil rights for homosexuals were opposed (Dade County referendum June '77).

Completion of communist forces' takeover of **S. Vietnam** (evacuation of U.S. civilians Apr. '75), revelations of Central Intelligence Agency misdeeds (Rockefeller Commission report June '75), and **Watergate** scandals (Nixon quit Aug. '74) reduced faith in U.S. moral and material capacity to influence world affairs. Revelations of Soviet crimes (Solzhenitsyn's *Gulag Archipelago* from 1974) and Russian intervention in Africa aided a revival of anti-Communist sentiment.

Economy sluggish. The 1960s boom faltered in the 1970s; a severe recession in the U.S. and Europe 1974-75 followed a huge oil price hike Dec. '73. Monetary instability (U.S. cut ties to gold Aug. '71), the decline of the dollar, and **protectionist** moves by industrial countries (1977-78) threatened trade. Business investment and spending for research declined. Severe inflation plagued many countries (25% in Britain 1975; 18% in U.S. 1979).

China picks up pieces. After the 1976 deaths of Mao and Chou, a power struggle for the leadership succession was won by pragmatists. A nationwide purge of orthodox Maoists was carried out and the **"Gang of Four"** led by Mao's widow Chiang Ching was arrested.

The new leaders freed over 100,000 political prisoners, and reduced public adulation of Mao. Political and trade ties were expanded with Japan, Europe, and U.S. in the late 1970's, as relations worsened with Russia, Cuba, and Vietnam (4-week invasion by China 1979). Ideological guidelines in industry, science, education, and the armed forces, which the ruling faction said had caused chaos and decline, were reversed (bonuses to workers Dec. '77; exams for college entrance Oct. '77). Severe restrictions on cultural expression were eased (Beethoven ban lifted Mar. '77).

Europe. European unity moves (EEC-EFTA trade accord 1972) faltered as economic problems appeared (Britain floated pound 1972; France floated franc 1974). Germany and Switzerland curbed guest workers from S. Europe. Greece and Turkey quarreled over Cyprus (Turks intervened 1974), Aegean oil rights.

All non-Communist Europe was under democratic rule after free elections were held in **Spain** June '76, 7 months after the death of Franco. The conservative, colonialist regime in **Portugal** was overthrown Apr. '74. In **Greece**, the 7-year-old military dictatorship yielded power in 1974. Northern Europe, though ruled mostly by Socialists (**Swedish** Socialists unseated 1976, after 44 years in power), turned conservative. The **British** Labour government imposed wage curbs 1975, and suspended nationalization schemes. Terrorism in **Germany** (1972 Munich Olympics killings) led to laws curbing some civil liberties. **French** "new philosophers" rejected leftist ideologies and the shaky Socialist-Communist coalition lost a 1978 election bid.

Religion back in politics. The improvement in Moslem countries' political fortunes by the 1950s (with the exception of Central Asia under Soviet and Chinese rule) and the growth of Arab oil wealth, was followed by a resurgence of traditional piety. **Libyan** dictator Qaddafy mixed strict Islamic laws with socialism in his militant ideology, called for an eventual Moslem return to Spain and Sicily. The illegal Moslem Brotherhood in **Egypt** was accused of violence, while extreme Moslem groups bombed theaters, 1977, to protest secular values.

In **Turkey**, the National Salvation Party was the first Islamic group to share power (1974) since secularization in the 1920s. Religious authorities, such as Ayatollah Ruhollah Khomeini, led the **Iranian** revolution and religiously motivated Moslems took part in the insurrection in Saudi Arabia that briefly seized the Grand Mosque in Mecca 1979. Moslem puritan opposition to **Pakistan** Pres. Bhutto helped lead to his overthrow July '77. However, Moslem solidarity could not prevent Pakistan's eastern province **(Bangladesh)** from declaring independence, Dec. '71, after a bloody civil war.

Moslem and Hindu resentment against coerced sterilization in **India** helped defeat the Gandhi government, which was replaced Mar. '77 by a coalition including religious Hindu parties and led by devout Hindu Desai. Moslems in the southern **Philippines,** aided by Libya, conducted a long rebellion against central rule from 1973.

Evangelical Protestant groups grew in numbers and prosperity in the U.S. A revival of interest in Orthodox Christianity occurred among **Russian** intellectuals (Solzhenitsyn). The secularist **Israeli** Labor party, after decades of rule, was ousted in 1977 by conservatives led by Begin, an observant Jew; religious militants founded settlements on the disputed West Bank, part of Biblically-promised Israel. U.S. Reform Judaism revived many previously discarded traditional practices.

The Buddhist Soka Gakkai movement launched the Komeito party in Japan 1964, which became a major opposition party in 1972 and 1976 elections.

Old-fashioned religious wars raged intermittently in **N. Ireland** (Catholic vs. Protestant 1969-   ) and **Lebanon** (Christian vs. Moslem 1975-   ) while religious militancy complicated the Israel-Arab dispute (1973 Israel-Arab war). In spite of a **1979 peace treaty between Egypt and Israel** which looked forward to a resolution of the Palestinian issue, increased religious militancy on the West Bank made a resolution unlikely.

Latin America. Repressive conservative regimes strengthened their hold on most of the continent, with the violent coup against the elected Allende government in **Chile,** Sept. '73, the 1976 military coup in **Argentina,** and coups against reformist regimes in **Bolivia,** 1971 and 1979, and **Peru,** 1976. In Central America, increasing liberal and leftist militancy led to the ouster of the Somoza regime of Nicaragua in 1979 and civil conflict in El Salvador.

Indochina. Communist victory in Vietnam, Cambodia, and Laos by May '75 did not bring peace. Attempts at radical social reorganization left over one million dead in Cambodia 1975-78 and caused hundreds of thousands of ethnic Chinese and others to flee Vietnam ("boat people" 1979). The Vietnamese invasion of Cambodia swelled the refugee population and contributed to widespread starvation in that devastated country.

Russian expansion. Soviet influence, checked in some countries (troops ousted by Egypt 1972) was projected further afield, often with the use of Cuban troops (Angola 1975-89, Ethiopia 1977-88) and aided by a growing navy, merchant fleet, and international banking ability. Détente with the West — 1972 Berlin pact, 1972 strategic arms pact **(SALT)** — gave way to a more antagonistic relationship in the late 1970s, exacerbated by the Soviet invasion of Afghanistan 1979.

Africa. The last remaining European colonies were granted independence **(Spanish Sahara** 1976, **Djibouti** 1977) and, after 10 years of civil war and many negotiation sessions, a black government took over Zimbabwe (Rhodesia) 1979; white domination remained in **S. Africa.** Great power involvement in local wars (Russia in **Angola, Ethiopia;** France in **Chad, Zaire, Mauritania**) and the use of tens of thousands of Cuban troops was denounced by some African leaders as neocolonialism. Ethnic or tribal clashes made Africa the chief world locus of sustained warfare in the late 1970s.

Arts. Traditional modes in painting, architecture, and music, pursued in relative obscurity for much of the 20th century, returned to popular and critical attention in the 1970s. The pictorial emphasis in neorealist and photorealist painting, the return of many architects to detail, decoration, and traditional natural materials, and the concern with ordered structure in musical composition were, ironically, novel experiences for artistic consumers after the exhaustion of experimental possibilities. However, these more conservative styles coexisted with modernist works in an atmosphere of variety and tolerance.

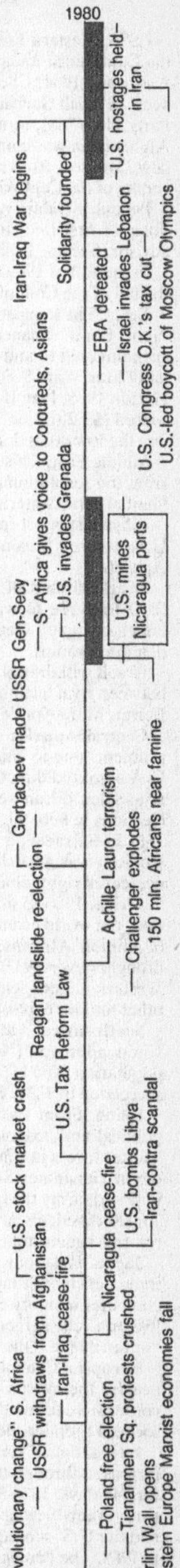

Revitalization of Capitalism, Demand for Democracy: 1980-89

USSR, Eastern Europe. A troublesome 1980-85 for the USSR was followed by 5 years of astonishing change: the **surrender of the Communist monopoly, remaking of the Soviet state, and disintegration of the Soviet empire.** After deaths of Brezhnev 1982, Andropov 1984, Chernenko 1985; harsh treatment of dissent; restriction of emigration; invasion of Afghanistan Dec.'79; Gen. Secy. **Mikhail Gorbachev** (1985-) promoted **glasnost, perestroika,** economic and social reform (Jan.'87), supported by Communist Party (July '88); signed **INF treaty** (Dec.'87). Gorbachev pledged to cut the military budget (1988); military withdrawal from Afghanistan was completed Feb.'89; democratization was not hindered in Poland, Hungary; the Soviet people chose part of the new Congress from competing candidates Mar.'89. At decade's end, Gorbachev was widely considered responsible for the **1989 ending of the Cold War.**

Poland. Solidarity, the labor union founded 1980 by **Lech Walesa,** outlawed 1982, was legalized 1988, after years of unrest. Poland's first free election since the Communist takeover brought Solidarity victory (June '89); Tadeusz Mazowiecki, a Walesa advisor, became Prime Minister in a government with the Communists (Aug.'89).

In the fall of 1989 the failure of Marxist economies in **Hungary, E. Germany, Czechoslovakia, Bulgaria, and Romania** brought the fall of the Communist monopoly, the demand for democracy. The **Berlin Wall** was opened Nov.'89.

U.S. "The Reagan Years" (1981-88) brought the **longest economic boom** in U.S. history via budget and tax cuts, deregulation, "junk bond" financing, leveraged buyouts, mergers and takeovers; a **strong anti-Communist stance,** via increased defense spending, aid to anti-communists in Central America, invasion of Cuba-threatened Grenada, championing of MX missile system and "Star Wars." Four Reagan-Gorbachev summits, 1985-88, climaxed in INF treaty 1987. Financial scandals mounted (E.F. Hutton 1985, Ivan Boesky 1986), the stock market crashed Oct.'87, the trade imbalance grew (esp. with Japan), the budget deficit soared ($3.2 trillion 1988); homelessness, drug abuse (esp. "crack") grew. The Iran-contra affair (North TV testimony July '87) was the low point, but V.P. Bush was elected pres. 1988.

Middle East. This area remained militarily unstable, with sharp divisions on economic, political, racial, and religious lines. In **Iran,** the revolution (1979-80) and violent political upheavals after, brought strong anti-U.S. stance. A dispute with **Iraq** over the Shatt al-Arab waterway became warfare Sept.'80-July'88, with millions killed.

Libya's support for international terrorism caused the U.S. to close the diplomatic mission (May'81), embargo oil (Mar.'82); U.S. accused Muammar al-Qadaffy of aiding terrorists in Dec.'85 Rome, Vienna airport attacks, retaliated by bombing Libya Apr.'86.

Israel affirmed all Jerusalem as its capital (July'80); destroyed an Iraqi atomic reactor 1981; invaded Lebanon 1982, bringing the PLO to agree to withdraw. A **Palestinian uprising,** inc. women, children hurling rocks, bottles at troops, began Dec.'87 in Israeli-occupied Gaza, spread to the West Bank; troops responded with force, killing 300 by 1988's end, with 6,000 more in detention camps.

Israeli withdrawal from **Lebanon** began Feb.'85, ended June'85, as Lebanon continued torn with military and political conflict between rival factions. Premier Karami was assassinated June'87. Artillery duels between Christian East Beirut and Moslem West Beirut, Mar.-Apr. '89, left 200 dead, 700 wounded. At the end of the decade, violence still dominated.

Central America. In **Nicaragua,** the leftist Sandinista National Liberation Front, in power after the 1979 civil war, faced problems due to Nicaragua's military aid to leftist guerrillas in El Salvador, U.S. backing of anti-government contras. The U.S. CIA admitted directing the mining of Nicaraguan ports 1984; U.S. sent aid, humanitarian 1985, military 1986. Profits from secret arms sales to Iran were found diverted to contras 1987. Cease-fire talks between Sandinista government and contras came in 1988, elections in Feb.'90.

In **El Salvador,** a military coup (Oct.'79) failed to halt extreme right-wing violence and left-wing activity. Archbishop Oscar Romero was assassinated Mar.'80; Jan.-June some 4,000 civilians reportedly were killed. In 1984, newly-elected Pres. Duarte decreased rights abuses. Leftist guerrillas continued their offensive 1989.

Africa. 1980-85 marked the rapid decline of the economies of virtually all Africa's 61 countries, due to accelerating desertification, the world economic recession, heavy indebtedness to overseas creditors, rapid population growth, political instability. Some 60 million Africans, almost one-fifth of the population, faced prolonged hunger 1981; much of Africa had one of the worst droughts ever 1983, and by year's end **150 million faced near-famine.** "Live Aid" marathon rock concert (July'85), U.S. and Western nations sent aid Sept.'85. Economic hardship fueled political unrest, coups. Wars in Ethiopia, Sudan, military strife in 6 other nations continued through 1989. AIDS took a heavy toll.

South Africa. Anti-apartheid sentiment gathered force, demonstrations and violent police response grew. South African white voters approved (Nov.'83) the first constitution to give "Coloureds" Asians a voice, while still excluding blacks—70% of the population. The U.S. imposed economic sanctions Aug.'85, 11 Western nations followed in Sept. **P.W. Botha,** '80s president, was succeeded by **F.W. de Klerk,** Sept.'89, on a platform of "evolutionary" change via negotiation with the black population.

China. From 1980 through mid-1989 the Communist Party, under **Chairman Deng Xiaoping,** pursued **far-reaching changes** in political and economic institutions, expanding commercial and technical ties to the industrialized world, increasing the role of market forces in stimulating urban economic development. But Apr. '89 brought the demand for more changes: students camped out in Tiananmen Sq., Beijing; some 100,000 students and workers marched, at least 20 other cities saw protests. Martial law was imposed; army troops crushed protests in Tiananmen Sq., June 3-4 with death toll estimates 500-7,000, up to 10,000 injured, up to 10,000 dissidents arrested, 31 tried and executed. The conciliatory Communist Party chief was ousted; the Politburo adopted reforms against official corruption (July).

Japan. Relations with other nations, esp. U.S., 1980-89, were dominated by **trade imbalances favoring Japan.** In 1985 the U.S. trade deficit with Japan was $49.7 billion, one-third of the total U.S. trade deficit. After Japan was found to sell semiconductors, computer memory chips below cost (Apr.'86), the U.S. was assured a "fair share" of the market, but charged Japan with failing to live up to the agreement Mar.'87. The **Omnibus Trade Bill,** Aug.'88, provided for retaliation; Pres. Bush called Japan's practices "unjustifiable," the law gave Japan 18 months to stop or face trade restrictions.

European Community. With the addition of Greece, Portugal, and Spain, the EC became a **common market of over 300 million people,** the West's largest trading entity. **Margaret Thatcher** became the first British prime minister in this century to win 3 consecutive terms 1987. France elected its first socialist president, **François Mitterrand** 1981, re-elected 1988. Italy elected its first socialist premier, **Bettino Craxi** 1983.

International Terrorism. With the 1979 overthrow of the Shah of Iran, terrorism became a prominent political tactic that increased through the '80s, but with fewer "spectacular" attacks after 1985. Iranian militants held 52 Americans hostage in Iran for 444 days, 1979-81; a TNT-laden suicide terrorist blew up U.S. Marine headquarters in Beirut, killing 241 Americans, while a truck bomb blew up a French paratroop barracks, killing 58, 1984; the *Achille Lauro* was hijacked, an American passenger killed, and the U.S. subsequently intercepted the Egyptian plane flying the terrorists to safety 1985. Incidents rose to 700 in 1985, 1,000+ in 1988. The Pentagon reported 52 terrorist groups Jan.'89.

Assassinations included Egypt's Pres. **Anwar Sadat** 1981; India's Prime Minister **Indira Gandhi** 1984; Lebanese Premier **Rashid Karami** 1987; Pakistan's Pres. **Mohammed Zia ul-Haq** 1988.

The Seven Wonders of the World

These ancient works of art and architecture were considered awe-inspiring in splendor and/or size by the Greek and Roman world of the Alexandrian epoch and later. Classical writers disagreed as to which works made up the list of Wonders, but the following were usually included:

The Pyramids of Egypt: The only surviving Wonder, these monumental structures of masonry located on the west bank of the Nile River above Cairo were built from 3000 to 1800 B.C. as royal tombs. Three—Khufu, Khafra, and Menkaura—were often grouped as the first Wonder of the World. The largest, **The Great Pyramid of Khufu,** or Cheops, is a solid mass of limestone blocks covering 13 acres. It is estimated to contain 2.3 million blocks of stone, the stones themselves averaging 2½ tons and some weighing 30 tons. Its construction reputedly took 100,000 laborers 20 years.

The Hanging Gardens of Babylon: These gardens were laid out on a brick terrace about 400 feet square and 75 feet above the ground. To irrigate the trees, shrubs, and flowers, screws were turned to lift water from the Euphrates River. The gardens were probably built by King Nebuchandnezzar II around 600 B.C. **The Walls of Babylon,** long, thick, and made of colorfully glazed brick, were considered by some to be among the Seven Wonders.

The Statue of Zeus (Jupiter) at Olympia: This statue of the king of the gods showed him seated on a throne. His flesh was made of ivory, his robe and ornaments of gold. Reputedly 40 feet high, the statue was made by Phidias and was placed in the great temple of Zeus in the sacred grove of Olympia around 457 B.C.

The Colossus of Rhodes: A bronze statue of the sun god Helios, the Colossus was worked on for 12 years in the early 200's B.C. by the sculptor Chares. It was probably 120 feet high. A symbol of the city of Rhodes at its height, the statue stood on a promontory overlooking the harbor.

The Temple of Artemis (Diana) at Ephesus: This largest and most complex temple of ancient times was built around 550 B.C. and was made of marble except for its tile-covered wooden roof. It was begun in honor of a non-Hellenic goddess who later became identified with the Greek goddess of the same name. Ephesus was one of the greatest of the Ionian cities.

The Mausoleum at Halicarnassus: The source of our word "mausoleum," this marble tomb was built in what is now southeastern Turkey by Artemisia for her husband Mausolus, an official of the Persian Empire who died in 353 B.C. About 135 feet high, it was adorned with the works of 4 sculptors.

The Pharos (Lighthouse) of Alexandria: This sculpture was designed around 270 B.C., during the reign of King Ptolemy II, by the Greek architect Sostratos. Estimates of its height range from 200 to 600 feet.

Magna Carta

Source: The British Library (copyright)

The original purpose of the Great Charter of 1215 was to define the limitations of royal power. The English barons believed that King John had abused his power by having an arbitrary approach to government and justice, and by implementing a disastrous foreign policy. Under threat of insurrection, the King sealed the charter at Runnymede, but war broke out nonetheless. The charter was subsequently annulled by the pope, but revised and reissued in 1216, 1217 and 1225. Of the 4 original copies in existence, 2 are kept in the British Library, 1 in Salisbury Cathedral and 1 in Lincoln Cathedral. Below is the text of the charter, divided into the traditional 63 chapters (paragraphs).

* = Chapters omitted from 1216 reissue and all subsequent reissues.

Preamble

John, by the grace of God, King of England, Lord of Ireland, Duke of Normandy and Aquitaine, and Count of Anjou: To the Archbishops, Bishops, Abbots, Earls, Barons, Justiciaries, Foresters, Sheriffs, Reeves, Ministers, and all Bailiffs and others, his faithful subjects, Greeting. Know ye that in the presence of God, and for the health of Our soul, and the souls of Our ancestors and heirs, to the honour of God, and the exaltation of Holy Church, and amendment of Our kingdom, by the advice of Our reverend Fathers, Stephen, Archbishop of Canterbury, Primate of all England, and Cardinal of the Holy Roman Church; Henry, Archbishop of Dublin; William of London, Peter of Winchester, Jocelin of Bath and Glastonbury, Hugh of Lincoln, Walter of Worcester, William of Coventry and Benedict of Rochester, Bishops, Master Pandulph, the Pope's subdeacon and familiar; Brother Aymeric, Master of the Knights of the Temple in England; and the noble persons, William Marshal, Earl of Pembroke; William, Earl of Salisbury; William, Earl of Warren; William, Earl of Arundel; Alan de Galloway, Constable of Scotland; Warin Fitz-Gerald, Peter Fitz-Herbert, Hubert de Burgh, Seneschal of Poitou, Hugh de Neville, Matthew Fitz-Herbert, Thomas Basset, Alan Basset, Philip Daubeny, Robert de Roppelay, John Marshal, John Fitz-Hugh, and others, Our liegemen:

The English Church shall be free; grant of liberties to freemen of the kingdom

1. We have, in the first place, granted to God, and by this Our present Charter confirmed for Us and Our heirs forever – That the English Church shall be free and enjoy her rights in their integrity and her liberties untouched. And that We will this so to be observed appears from the fact that We of Our own free will, before the outbreak of the dissensions between Us and Our barons, granted, confirmed and procured to be confirmed by Pope Innocent III the freedom of elections, which is considered most important and necessary to the English Church, which Charter We will both keep Ourself and will it to be kept with good faith by Our heirs forever. We have also granted to all the free men of Our kingdom, for Us and Our heirs forever, all the liberties underwritten, to have and to hold to them and their heirs of Us and Our heirs.

Reliefs for inheritance

2. If any of Our earls, barons, or others who hold of Us in chief by knight's service shall die, and at the time of his death his heir shall be of full age and owe a relief, he shall have his inheritance by ancient relief; to wit, the heir or heirs of an earl of an entire earl's barony, £100; the heir or heirs of a baron of an entire barony, £100; the heir or heirs of a knight of an entire knight's fee, 100*s*. at the most; and he that owes less shall give less, according to the ancient custom of fees.

Under-age heirs

3. If, however, any such heir shall be under age and in ward, he shall, when he comes of age, have his inheritance without relief or fine.

Rights of wards

4. The guardian of the land of any heir thus under age shall take therefrom only reasonable issues, customs and services, without destruction or waste of men or property; and if We shall have committed the wardship of any such land to the sheriff or any other person answerable to Us for the issues thereof, and he commit destruction or waste, We will take an amends from him, and the land shall be committed to 2 lawful and discreet men of that fee, who shall be answerable for the issues to Us or to whomsoever We shall have assigned them. And if We shall give or sell the wardship of any such land to anyone, and he commit destruction or waste upon it, he shall lose the wardship, which shall be committed to 2 lawful and discreet men of that fee, who shall, in like manner, be answerable unto Us as has been aforesaid.

Duties of guardians

5. The guardian, so long as he shall have the custody of the land, shall keep up and maintain the houses, parks, fishponds, pools, mills and other things pertaining thereto, out of the issues of the same, and shall restore the whole to the heir when he comes of age, stocked with ploughs and tillage, according as the season may require and the issues of the land can reasonably bear.

Marriage of heirs

6. Heirs shall be married without loss of station, and the marriage shall be made known to the heir's nearest of kin before it be contracted.

Rights of widows

7. A widow, after the death of her husband, shall immediately and without difficulty have her marriage portion and inheritance. She shall not give anything for her marriage portion, dower, or inheritance which she and her husband held on the day of his death, and she may remain in her husband's house for 40 days after his death, within which time her dower shall be assigned to her.

Remarriage of widows

8. No widow shall be compelled to marry so long as she has a mind to live without a husband, provided, however, that she give security that she will not marry without Our assent, if she holds of Us, or that of the lord of whom she holds, if she holds of another.

Debtors and sureties

9. Neither We nor Our bailiffs shall seize any land or rent for any debt so long as the debtor's chattels are sufficient to discharge the same; nor shall the debtor's sureties be distrained so long as the debtor is able to pay the debt. If the debtor fails to pay, not having the means to pay, then the sureties shall answer the debt, and, if they desire, they shall hold the debtor's lands and rents until they have received satisfaction of the debt which they have paid for him, unless the debtor can show that he has discharged his obligation to them.

Interest on debts

***10.** If anyone who has borrowed from the Jews any sum of money, great or small, dies before the debt has been paid, the heir shall pay no interest on the debt so long as he remains under age, of whomsoever he may hold. If the debt shall fall into Our hands, We will take only the principal sum named in the bond.

Rights of widows and heirs against creditors

***11.** And if any man dies indebted to the Jews, his wife shall have her dower and pay nothing of that debt; if the deceased leaves children under age, they shall have necessaries provided for them in keeping with the estate of the deceased, and the debt shall be paid out of the residue, saving the service due to the deceased's feudal lords. So shall it be done with regard to debts owed persons other than Jews.

Aids only by common counsel

***12.** No scutage or aid [tax or loan] shall be imposed in Our kingdom unless by common counsel thereof, except to ransom Our person, make Our eldest son a knight, and once to marry Our eldest daughter, and for these only a reasonable aid shall be levied. So shall it be with regard to aids from the City of London.

Liberties of London and other towns

13. The City of London shall have all her ancient liberties and free customs, both by land and water. Moreover, We will and grant that all other cities, boroughs, towns and ports shall have all their liberties and free customs.

Calling of council to consent to aids

***14.** For obtaining the common counsel of the kingdom concerning the assessment of aids (other than in the 3 cases aforesaid) or of scutage, We will cause to be summoned, severally by Our letters, the archbishops, bishops, abbots, earls, and great barons; We will also cause to be summoned, generally, by Our sheriffs and bailiffs, all those who hold lands directly of Us, to meet on a fixed day, but with at least 40 days' notice, and at a fixed place. In all letters of such summons We will explain the cause thereof. The summons being thus made, the business shall proceed on the day appointed, according to the advice of those who shall be present, even though not all the persons summoned have come.

Limit on other lords' aids

***15.** We will not in the future grant permission to any man to levy an aid upon his free men, except to ransom his person, make his eldest son a knight, and once to marry his eldest daughter, and on each of these occasions only a reasonable aid shall be levied.

Knight's fee

16. No man shall be compelled to perform more service for a knight's fee or other free tenement than is due therefrom.

Justice to be had at a fixed place

17. Common Pleas shall not follow Our Court, but shall be held in some certain place.

Land disputes to be tried in their counties

18. Recognizances of novel disseisin, mort d'ancestor and darrein presentment shall be taken only in their proper counties, and in this manner: We or, if We be absent from the realm, Our Chief Justiciary shall send 2 justiciaries through each county 4 times a year, and they, together with 4 knights elected out of each county by the people thereof, shall hold the said assizes in the county court, on the day and in the place where that court meets.

Conclusion of assizes

19. If the said assizes cannot be held on the day appointed, so many of the knights and free-holders as shall have been present on that day shall remain as will be sufficient for the administration of justice, according as the business to be done be greater or less.

Fines to be measured by the offence; livelihoods not to be destroyed

20. A free man shall be amerced [fined] for a small fault only according to the measure thereof, and for a greater crime according to its magnitude, saving his position; and in like manner a merchant saving his trade, and a villein saving his tillage, if they should fall under Our mercy. None of these amercements shall be imposed except by the oath of honest men of the neighbourhood.

Same for barons

21. Earls and barons shall be amerced only by their peers, and only in proportion to the measure of the offence.

Same for clergymen

22. No amercement shall be imposed upon a clerk's lay property, except after the manner of the other persons aforesaid, and without regard to the value of his ecclesiastical benefice.

Obligations to build bridges

23. No village or person shall be compelled to build bridges over rivers except those bound by ancient custom and law to do so.

Unauthorized persons not to hold trials

24. No sheriff, constable, coroners, or other of Our bailiffs shall hold pleas of Our Crown.

Ceiling on rents

***25.** All counties, hundreds, wapentakes and tithings (except Our demesne manors) shall remain at the ancient rents without any increase.

Debts owed the Crown

26. If anyone holding a lay fee of Us shall die, and the sheriff or Our bailiff show Our letters patent of summons touching the debt due to Us from the deceased, it shall be lawful for such sheriff or bailiff to attach and catalogue the chattels of the deceased found in the lay fee to the value of that debt, as assessed by lawful men. Nothing shall be removed therefrom until Our whole debt be paid; then the residue shall be given up to the executors to carry out the will of the decreased. If there be no debt due from him to Us, all his chattels shall remain the property of the deceased, saving to his wife and children their reasonable shares.

Intestacy

***27.** If any free man shall die intestate, his chattels shall be distributed by his nearest kinfolk and friends, under supervision of the Church, saving to each creditor the debts owed him by the deceased.

Compensation for taking of private property

28. No constable or other of Our bailiffs shall take corn or other chattels of any man without immediate payment, unless the seller voluntarily consents to postponement of payment.

Castle-guard

29. No constable shall compel any knight to give money in lieu of castle-guard when the knight is willing to perform it in person or (if reasonable cause prevents him from performing it himself) by some other fit man. Further, if We lead or send him into military service, he shall be quit of castle-guard for the time he shall remain in service by Our command.

No taking of horses without consent

30. No sheriff or other of Our bailiffs, or any other man, shall take the horses or carts of any free man for carriage without the owner's consent.

No taking of wood without consent

31. Neither We nor Our bailiffs will take another man's wood for Our castles or for any other purpose without the owner's consent.

Lands of felons

32. We will retain the lands of persons convicted of felony for only a year and a day, after which they shall be restored to the lords of the fees.

Removal of fishweirs

33. All fishweirs shall be entirely removed from the Thames and Medway, and throughout England, except upon the seacoast.

Writ of praecipe

34. The writ called "praecipe" shall not in the future issue to anyone respecting any tenement if thereby a free man may not be tried in his lord's court.

Uniform weights and measures

35. There shall be one measure of wine throughout Our kingdom, and one of ale, and one measure of corn, to wit, the London quarter, and one breadth of dyed cloth, russets, and haberjets, to wit 2 ells within the selvages. As with measures so shall it also be with weights.

Writs upon life or limbs

36. Henceforth nothing shall be given or taken for a writ of inquisition upon life or limbs, but it shall be granted gratis and not be denied.

Crown wardship

37. If anyone holds of Us by fee farm, socage, or burgage, and also holds land of another by knight's service, We will not by reason of that fee farm, socage, or burgage have the wardship of his heir, or the land which belongs to another man's fee; nor will We have the wardship of such fee farm, socage, or burgage unless such fee farm owe knight's service. We will not have the wardship of any man's heir, or the land which he holds of another by knight's service, by reason of any petty serjeanty which he holds of Us by service of rendering Us daggers, arrows, or the like.

No man to be put to his trial upon unsupported accusation

38. In the future no bailiff shall upon his own unsupported accusation put any man to trial without producing credible witnesses to the truth of the accusation.

Free men guaranteed "law of the land"

39. No free man shall be taken, imprisoned, disseised, outlawed, banished, or in any way destroyed, nor will We proceed against or prosecute him except by the lawful judgment of his peers and by the law of the land.

Guarantee of equal justice

40. To no one will We sell, to none will We deny or delay, right or justice.

Free movement for merchants

41. All merchants shall have safe conduct to go and come out of and into England, and to stay in and travel through England by land and water for purposes of buying and selling, free of illegal tolls, in accordance with ancient and just customs, except, in time of war, such merchants as are of a country at war with Us. If any such be found in Our dominion at the outbreak of war, they shall be attached, without injury to their persons or goods, until it be known to Us or Our Chief Justiciary how Our merchants are being treated in the country at war with Us, and if Our merchants be safe there, then theirs shall be safe with Us.

Freedom to leave and re-enter the kingdom

***42.** In the future it shall be lawful (except for a short period in time of war, for the common benefit of the realm) for anyone to leave and return to Our Kingdom safely and securely by land and water, saving his fealty to Us. Excepted are those who have been imprisoned or outlawed according to the law of the land, people of the country at war with Us, and merchants, who shall be dealt with as aforesaid.

Escheats [land reverting to Crown through intestacy]

43. If anyone die holding of any escheat, such as the honour of Wallingford, Nottingham, Boulogne, Lancaster, or other escheats which are in Our hands and are baronies, his heir shall not give any relief or do any service to Us other than he would owe to the baron, if such barony had been in the hands of a baron, and We will hold the escheat in the same manner in which the baron held it.

Forest laws

44. Persons dwelling outside the forest need not in the future come before Our justiciaries of the forest in answer to a general summons unless they be impleaded or are sureties for any person or persons attached for breach of forest laws.

Law appointments

***45.** We will appoint as justiciaries, constables, sheriffs, or bailiffs only such men as know the law of the land and will keep it well.

Wardship of abbeys

46. All barons who have founded abbeys, evidenced by charters of English kings or ancient tenure, shall, as is their due, have the wardship of the same when vacant.

Forest boundaries

47. All forests which have been created in Our time shall forthwith be disafforested. So shall it be done with regard to rivers which have been placed in fence in Our time.

Evil forest customs

***48.** All evil customs concerning forests and warrens, foresters and warreners, sheriffs and their officers, or riverbanks and their conservators shall be immediately enquired into in each county by 12 sworn knights of such county, chosen by honest men of that county, and shall within 40 days after the inquest be completely and irrevocably abolished, provided always that the matter shall have been previously brought to Our knowledge, or that of Our Chief Justiciary if We Ourself shall not be in England.

Return of hostages

***49.** We will immediately return all hostages and charters delivered to Us by Englishmen as security for the peace or for the performance of loyal service.

Ousting of Poitevin favourites

***50.** We will entirely remove from their bailiwicks the kinsmen of Gerard de Athyes, so that henceforth they shall hold no bailiwick in England: Engelard de Cigogné, Peter, Guy and Andrew de Chanceaux, Guy de Cigogné, Geoffrey de Martigny and his brothers, Philip Mark and his brothers, and Geoffrey his nephew, and all their followers.

Banishment of mercenaries

***51.** As soon as peace is restored, We will banish from Our kingdom all foreign knights, bowmen, attendants and mercenaries who have come with horses and arms to the kingdom's hurt.

Restoration of lands and rights

*52. If anyone has been disseised or deprived by Us, without the legal judgment of his peers, of lands, castles, liberties or rights, We will immediately restore the same, and if any dispute shall arise thereupon, the matter shall be decided by judgment of the 25 barons mentioned below in the clause for securing the peace. With regard to all those things, however, of which any man was disseised or deprived, without the legal judgment of his peers, by King Henry Our Father or Our Brother King Richard, and which remain in Our hands or are held by others under Our warranty, We shall have respite during the term commonly allowed to the Crusaders, except as to those matters on which a plea had arisen, or an inquisition had been taken by Our command, prior to Our taking the Cross. Immediately after Our return from Our pilgrimage, or if by chance We should remain behind from it, We will at once do full justice.

Respite during Crusade

*53. Likewise, We shall have the same respite in rendering justice with respect to the disafforestation or retention of those forests which Henry Our Father or Richard Our Brother afforested, and to wardships of lands belonging to another's fee, which We hitherto have held by reason of the fee which some person has held of Us by knight's service, and to abbeys founded in another's fee than Our own, whereto the lord of that fee asserts his right. When We return from Our pilgrimage, or if We remain behind from it, We will forthwith do full justice to the complainants in these matters.

Women's appeals

54. No one shall be arrested or imprisoned upon a woman's appeal for the death of any person other than her husband.

Remission of unlawful fines

*55. All fines unjustly and unlawfully given to Us, and all amercements levied unjustly and against the law of the land, shall be entirely remitted or the matter settled by judgment of the 25 barons of whom mention is made below in the clause for securing the peace, or the majority of them, together with the aforesaid Stephen, Archbishop of Canterbury, if he himself can be present, and any others whom he may wish to bring with him for the purpose; if he cannot be present, the business shall nevertheless proceed without him. If any one or more of the said 25 barons he interested in a suit of this kind, he or they shall be set aside, as to this particular judgment, and another or others, elected and sworn by the rest of the said barons for this occasion only, be substituted in his or their stead.

Restoration of Welsh rights

56. If we have disseised or deprived the Welsh of lands, liberties, or other things, without legal judgment of their peers, in England or Wales, they shall immediately be restored to them, and if a dispute shall arise thereon, the question shall be determined in the Marches by judgment of their peers according to the law of England as to English tenements, the law of Wales as to Welsh tenements, and the law of the Marches as to tenements in the Marches. The same shall the Welsh do to Us and Ours.

Respite during Crusade

*57. But with regard to all those things of which any Welshman was disseised or deprived, without legal judgment of his peers, by King Henry Our Father or Our Brother King Richard, and which We hold in Our hands or others hold under Our warranty, We shall have respite during the term commonly allowed to the Crusaders, except as to those matters whereon a suit had arisen or an inquisition had been taken by Our command prior to Our taking the Cross. Immediately after Our return from Our pilgrimage, or if by chance We should remain behind from it, We will do full justice according to the laws of the Welsh and the aforesaid regions.

Return of Welsh hostages

*58. We will immediately return the son of Llywelyn, all the Welsh hostages, and the charters which were delivered to Us as security for the peace.

Rights of Alexander, King of Scots

*59. With regard to the return of the sisters and hostages of Alexander, King of the Scots, and of his liberties and rights, We will do the same as We would with regard to Our other barons of England, unless it should appear by the charters which We hold of William his father, late King of the Scots, that it ought to be otherwise; this shall be determined by judgment of his peers in Our court.

Liberties to be granted to lesser tenants

60. All the customs and liberties aforesaid, which We have granted to be enjoyed, as far as in Us lies, by Our people throughout Our kingdom, let all Our subjects, whether clerks or laymen, observe, as far as in them lies, toward their dependents.

Committee of barons to enforce Charter

*61. Whereas We, for the honour of God and the amendment of Our realm, and in order the better to allay the discord arisen between Us and Our barons, have granted all these things aforesaid, We, willing that they be forever enjoyed wholly and in lasting strength, do give and grant to Our subjects the following security, to wit, that the barons shall elect any 25 barons of the kingdom at will, who shall, with their utmost power, keep, hold and cause to be kept the peace and liberties which We have granted unto them and by this Our present Charter have confirmed, so that if We, Our Justiciary, bailiffs, or any of Our ministers offend in any respect against any man, or shall transgress any of these articles of peace or security, and the offence he brought before 4 of the said 25 barons, those 4 barons shall come before Us, or Our Chief Justiciary if We are out of the kingdom, declaring the offence, and shall demand speedy amends for the same. If We or, in case of Our being out of the kingdom, Our Chief

Justiciary fail to afford redress within the space of 40 days from the time the case was brought before Us or, in the event of Our having been out of the kingdom, Our Chief Justiciary, the aforesaid 4 barons shall refer the matter to the rest of the 25 barons, who, together with the commonalty of the whole country, shall distrain and distress Us to the utmost of their power, to wit, by capture of Our castles, lands and possessions and by all other possible means, until compensation be made according to their decision, saving Our person and that of Our Queen and children; as soon as redress has been had, they shall return to their former allegiance. Anyone in the kingdom may take oath that, for the accomplishment of all the aforesaid matters, he will obey the orders of the said 25 barons and distress Us to the utmost of his power; and We give public and free leave to everyone wishing to take such oath to do so, and to none will We deny the same. Moreover, all such of Our subjects who shall not of their own free will and accord agree to swear to the said 25 barons, to distrain and distress Us together with them, We will compel to do so by Our command in the manner aforesaid. If any one of the 25 barons shall die or leave the country or be in any way hindered from executing the said office, the rest of the said 25 barons shall choose another in his stead, at their discretion, who shall be sworn in like manner as the others. In all cases which are referred to the said 25 barons to execute, and in which a difference shall arise among them, supposing them all to be present, or in which not all who have been summoned are willing or able to appear, the verdict of the majority shall be considered as firm and binding as if the whole number should have been of one mind. The aforesaid 25 shall swear to keep faithfully all the aforesaid articles and, to the best of their power, to cause them to be kept by others. We will not procure, either by Ourself or any other, anything from any man whereby any of these concessions or liberties may be revoked or abated. If any such procurement be made, let it be null and void; it shall never be made use of either by Us or by any other.

Pardon of ill-will and trespasses

*62. We have also wholly remitted and pardoned all ill-will, wrath and malice which has arisen betwen Us and Our subjects, both clergy and laymen, during the disputes, to and with all men. Moreover, We have fully remitted and, as far as in Us lies, wholly pardoned to and with all, clergy and laymen, all trespasses made in consequence of the said disputes from Easter in the sixteenth year of Our reign till the restoration of peace. Over and above this, We have caused to be made in their behalf letters patent by testimony of Stephen, Archbishop of Canterbury, Henry, Archbishop of Dublin, the Bishops above-mentioned, and Master Pandulph, for the security and concessions aforesaid.

Oath to observe rights of Church and people

*63. Wherefore We will, and firmly charge, that the English Church shall be free, and that all men in Our kingdom shall have and hold all the aforesaid liberties, rights and concessions, well and peaceably, freely, quietly, fully and wholly, to them and their heirs, of Us and Our heirs, in all things and places forever, as is aforesaid. It is moreover sworn, as well on Our part as on the part of the barons, that all these matters aforesaid shall be kept in good faith and without deceit. Witness the above-named and many others. Given by Our hand in the meadow which is called Runnymede, between Windsor and Staines, on the fifteenth day of June in the seventeenth year of Our reign.

Declaration of Independence

The Declaration of Independence was adopted by the Continental Congress in Philadelphia, on July 4, 1776. John Hancock was president of the Congress and Charles Thomson was secretary. A copy of the Declaration, engrossed on parchment, was signed by members of Congress on and after Aug. 2, 1776. On Jan. 18, 1777, Congress ordered that "an authenticated copy, with the names of the members of Congress subscribing the same, be sent to each of the United States, and that they be desired to have the same put upon record." Authenticated copies were printed in broadside form in Baltimore, where the Continental Congress was then in session. The following text is that of the original printed by John Dunlap at Philadelphia for the Continental Congress.

IN CONGRESS, July 4, 1776.

A DECLARATION

By the REPRESENTATIVES of the

UNITED STATES OF AMERICA,

In GENERAL CONGRESS assembled

When in the Course of human Events, it becomes necessary for one People to dissolve the Political Bands which have connected them with another, and to assume among the Powers of the Earth, the separate and equal Station to which the Laws of Nature and of Nature's God entitle them, a decent Respect to the Opinions of Mankind requires that they should declare the causes which impel them to the Separation.

We hold these Truths to be self-evident, that all Men are created equal, that they are endowed by their Creator with certain unalienable Rights, that among these are Life, Liberty, and the Pursuit of Happiness—That to secure these Rights, Governments are instituted among Men, deriving their just Powers from the Consent of the Governed, that whenever any Form of Government becomes destructive of these Ends, it is the Right of the People to alter or to abolish it, and to institute new Government, laying its Foundation on such Principles, and organizing its Powers in such Form, as to them shall seem most likely to effect their Safety and Happiness. Prudence, indeed, will dictate that Governments long established should not be changed for light and transient Causes; and accordingly all Experience hath shewn, that Mankind are more disposed to suffer, while Evils are sufferable, than to right themselves by abolishing the Forms to which they are accustomed. But when a long Train of Abuses and Usurpations, pursuing invariably the same Object, evinces a Design to reduce them under absolute Despotism, it is their Right, it is their Duty, to throw off such Government, and to provide new Guards for their future Security. Such has been the patient Sufferance of these Colonies; and such is now the Necessity which constrains them to alter their former Systems of Government. The History of the present King of Great-Britain is a History of repeated Injuries and Usurpations, all having in direct Object the Establishment of an absolute Tyranny over these States. To prove this, let Facts be submitted to a candid World.

He has refused his Assent to Laws, the most wholesome and necessary for the public Good.

He has forbidden his Governors to pass Laws of immediate and pressing Importance, unless suspended in their Operation till his Assent should be obtained; and when so suspended, he has utterly neglected to attend to them.

He has refused to pass other Laws for the Accommodation of large Districts of People, unless those People would relinquish the Right of Representation in the Legislature, a Right inestimable to them, and formidable to Tyrants only.

He has called together Legislative Bodies at Places unusual, uncomfortable, and distant from the Depository of their Public Records, for the sole Purpose of fatiguing them into Compliance with his Measures.

He has dissolved Representative Houses repeatedly, for opposing with manly Firmness his Invasions on the Rights of the People.

He has refused for a long Time, after such Dissolutions, to cause others to be elected; whereby the Legislative Powers, incapable of Annihilation, have returned to the People at large for their exercise; the State remaining in the mean time exposed to all the Dangers of Invasion from without, and Convulsions within.

He has endeavoured to prevent the Population of these States; for that Purpose obstructing the Laws for Naturalization of Foreigners; refusing to pass others to encourage their Migrations hither, and raising the Conditions of new Appropriations of Lands.

He has obstructed the Administration of Justice, by refusing his Assent to Laws for establishing Judiciary Powers.

He has made Judges dependent on his Will alone, for the Tenure of their Offices, and the Amount and payment of their Salaries.

He has erected a Multitude of new Offices, and sent hither Swarms of Officers to harrass our People, and eat out their Substance.

He has kept among us, in Times of Peace, Standing Armies, without the consent of our Legislatures.

He has affected to render the Military independent of, and superior to the Civil Power.

He has combined with others to subject us to a Jurisdiction foreign to our Constitution, and unacknowledged by our Laws; giving his Assent to their Acts of pretended Legislation:

For quartering large Bodies of Armed Troops among us:

For protecting them, by a mock Trial, from Punishment for any Murders which they should commit on the Inhabitants of these States:

For cutting off our Trade with all Parts of the World:

For imposing Taxes on us without our Consent:

For depriving us, in many Cases, of the Benefits of Trial by Jury:

For transporting us beyond Seas to be tried for pretended Offences:

For abolishing the free System of English Laws in a neighbouring Province, establishing therein an arbitrary Government, and enlarging its Boundaries, so as to render it at once an Example and fit Instrument for introducing the same absolute Rule into these Colonies:

For taking away our Charters, abolishing our most valuable Laws, and altering fundamentally the Forms of our Governments:

For suspending our own Legislatures, and declaring themselves invested with Power to legislate for us in all Cases whatsoever.

He has abdicated Government here, by declaring us out of his Protection and waging War against us.

He has plundered our Seas, ravaged our Coasts, burnt our towns, and destroyed the Lives of our People.

He is, at this Time, transporting large Armies of foreign Mercenaries to complete the works of Death, Desolation, and Tyranny, already begun with circumstances of Cruelty and Perfidy, scarcely paralleled in the most barbarous Ages, and totally unworthy the Head of a civilized Nation.

He has constrained our fellow Citizens taken Captive on the high Seas to bear Arms against their Country, to become the Executioners of their Friends and Brethren, or to fall themselves by their Hands.

He has excited domestic Insurrections amongst us, and has endeavoured to bring on the Inhabitants of our Frontiers, the merciless Indian Savages, whose known Rule of Warfare, is an undistinguished Destruction, of all Ages, Sexes and Conditions.

In every stage of these Oppressions we have Petitioned for Redress in the most humble Terms: Our repeated Petitions have been answered only by repeated Injury. A Prince, whose Character is thus marked by every act which may define a Tyrant, is unfit to be the Ruler of a free People.

Nor have we been wanting in Attentions to our British Brethren. We have warned them from Time to Time of Attempts by their Legislature to extend an unwarrantable Jurisdiction over us. We have reminded them of the Circumstances of our Emigration and Settlement here. We have appealed to their native Justice and Magnanimity, and we have conjured them by the Ties of our common Kindred to disavow these Usurpations, which, would inevitably interrupt our Connections and Correspondence. They too have been deaf to the Voice of Justice and of Consanguinity. We must, therefore, acquiesce in the Necessity, which denounces our Separation, and hold them, as we hold the rest of Mankind, Enemies in War, in Peace, Friends.

We, therefore, the Representatives of the UNITED STATES OF AMERICA, in General Congress, Assembled, appealing to the Supreme Judge of the World for the Rectitude of our Intentions, do, in the Name, and by Authority of the good People of these Colonies, solemnly Publish and Declare, That these United Colonies are, and of Right ought to be, Free and Independent States; that they are absolved from all Allegiance to the British Crown, and that all political Connection between them and the State of Great-Britain, is and ought to be totally dissolved; and that as Free and Independent States, they have full Power to levy War, conclude Peace, contract Alliances, establish Commerce, and to do all other Acts and Things which Independent States may of right do. And for the support of this declaration, with a firm Reliance on the Protection of divine Providence, we mutually pledge to each other our lives, our Fortunes, and our sacred Honor.

JOHN HANCOCK, President

Attest.
CHARLES THOMSON, Secretary.

Signers of the Declaration of Independence

Delegate and state	Vocation	Birthplace	Born	Died
Adams, John (Mass.)	Lawyer	Braintree (Quincy), Mass.	Oct. 30, 1735	July 4, 1826
Adams, Samuel (Mass.)	Political leader	Boston, Mass.	Sept. 27, 1722	Oct. 2, 1803
Bartlett, Josiah (N.H.)	Physician, judge	Amesbury, Mass.	Nov. 21, 1729	May 19, 1795
Braxton, Carter (Va.)	Farmer	Newington Plantation, Va.	Sept. 10, 1736	Oct. 10, 1797
Carroll, Chas. of Carrollton (Md.)	Lawyer	Annapolis, Md.	Sept. 19, 1737	Nov. 14, 1832
Chase, Samuel (Md.)	Judge	Princess Anne, Md.	Apr. 17, 1741	June 19, 1811
Clark, Abraham (N.J.)	Surveyor	Roselle, N.J.	Feb. 15, 1726	Sept. 15, 1794
Clymer, George (Pa.)	Merchant	Philadelphia, Pa.	Mar. 16, 1739	Jan. 23, 1813

Delegate and state	Vocation	Birthplace	Born	Died
Ellery, William (R.I.)	Lawyer	Newport, R.I.	Dec. 22, 1727	Feb. 15, 1820
Floyd, William (N.Y.)	Soldier	Brookhaven, N.Y.	Dec. 17, 1734	Aug. 4, 1821
Franklin, Benjamin (Pa.)	Printer, publisher	Boston, Mass.	Jan. 17, 1706	Apr. 17, 1790
Gerry, Elbridge (Mass.)	Merchant	Marblehead, Mass.	July 17, 1744	Nov. 23, 1814
Gwinnett, Button (Ga.)	Merchant	Down Hatherly, England	c. 1735	May 19, 1777
Hall, Lyman (Ga.)	Physician	Wallingford, Conn.	Apr. 12, 1724	Oct. 19, 1790
Hancock, John (Mass.)	Merchant	Braintree (Quincy), Mass.	Jan. 12, 1737	Oct. 8, 1793
Harrison, Benjamin (Va.)	Farmer	Berkeley, Va.	Apr. 5, 1726	Apr. 24, 1791
Hart, John (N.J.)	Farmer	Stonington, Conn.	c. 1711	May 11, 1779
Hewes, Joseph (N.C.)	Merchant	Princeton, N.J.	Jan. 23, 1730	Nov. 10, 1779
Heyward, Thos. Jr. (S.C.)	Lawyer, farmer	St. Luke's Parish, S.C.	July 28, 1746	Mar. 6, 1809
Hooper, William (N.C.)	Lawyer	Boston, Mass.	June 28, 1742	Oct. 14, 1790
Hopkins, Stephen (R.I.)	Judge, educator	Providence, R.I.	Mar. 7, 1707	July 13, 1785
Hopkinson, Francis (N.J.)	Judge, author	Philadelphia, Pa.	Sept. 21, 1737	May 9, 1791
Huntington, Samuel (Conn.)	Judge	Windham County, Conn.	July 3, 1731	Jan. 5, 1796
Jefferson, Thomas (Va.)	Lawyer	Shadwell, Va.	Apr. 13, 1743	July 4, 1826
Lee, Francis Lightfoot (Va.)	Farmer	Westmoreland County, Va.	Oct. 14, 1734	Jan. 11, 1797
Lee, Richard Henry (Va.)	Farmer	Westmoreland County, Va.	Jan. 20, 1732	June 19, 1794
Lewis, Francis (N.Y.)	Merchant	Llandaff, Wales	Mar., 1713	Dec. 31, 1802
Livingston, Philip (N.Y.)	Merchant	Albany, N.Y.	Jan. 15, 1716	June 12, 1778
Lynch, Thomas Jr. (S.C.)	Farmer	Winyah, S.C.	Aug. 5, 1749	(at sea) 1779
McKean, Thomas (Del.)	Lawyer	New London, Pa.	Mar. 19, 1734	June 24, 1817
Middleton, Arthur (S.C.)	Farmer	Charleston, S.C.	June 26, 1742	Jan. 1, 1787
Morris, Lewis (N.Y.)	Farmer	Morrisania (Bronx County), N.Y.	Apr. 8, 1726	Jan. 22, 1798
Morris, Robert (Pa.)	Merchant	Liverpool, England	Jan. 20, 1734	May 9, 1806
Morton, John (Pa.)	Judge	Ridley, Pa.	1724	Apr., 1777
Nelson, Thos. Jr. (Va.)	Farmer	Yorktown, Va.	Dec. 26, 1738	Jan. 4, 1789
Paca, William (Md.)	Judge	Abingdon, Md.	Oct. 31, 1740	Oct. 23, 1799
Paine, Robert Treat (Mass.)	Judge	Boston, Mass.	Mar. 11, 1731	May 12, 1814
Penn, John (N.C.)	Lawyer	Near Port Royal, Va.	May 17, 1741	Sept. 14, 1788
Read, George (Del.)	Judge	Near North East, Md.	Sept. 18, 1733	Sept. 21, 1798
Rodney, Caesar (Del.)	Judge	Dover, Del.	Oct. 7, 1728	June 29, 1784
Ross, George (Pa.)	Judge	New Castle, Del.	May 10, 1730	July 14, 1779
Rush, Benjamin (Pa.)	Physician	Byberry, Pa. (Philadelphia)	Dec. 24, 1745	Apr. 19, 1813
Rutledge, Edward (S.C.)	Lawyer	Charleston, S.C.	Nov. 23, 1749	Jan. 23, 1800
Sherman, Roger (Conn.)	Lawyer	Newton, Mass.	Apr. 19, 1721	July 23, 1793
Smith, James (Pa.)	Lawyer	Dublin, Ireland	c. 1719	July 11, 1806
Stockton, Richard (N.J.)	Lawyer	Near Princeton, N.J.	Oct. 1, 1730	Feb. 28, 1781
Stone, Thomas (Md.)	Lawyer	Charles County, Md.	1743	Oct. 5, 1787
Taylor, George (Pa.)	Ironmaster	Ireland	1716	Feb. 23, 1781
Thornton, Matthew (N.H.)	Physician	Ireland	1714	June 24, 1803
Walton, George (Ga.)	Judge	Prince Edward County, Va.	1741	Feb. 2, 1804
Whipple, William (N.H.)	Merchant, judge	Kittery, Me.	Jan. 14, 1730	Nov. 28, 1785
Williams, William (Conn.)	Merchant	Lebanon, Conn.	Apr. 23, 1731	Aug. 2, 1811
Wilson, James (Pa.)	Judge	Carskerdo, Scotland	Sept. 14, 1742	Aug. 28, 1798
Witherspoon, John (N.J.)	Clergyman, educator	Gifford, Scotland	Feb. 5, 1723	Nov. 15, 1794
Wolcott, Oliver (Conn.)	Judge	Windsor, Conn.	Dec. 1, 1726	Dec. 1, 1797
Wythe, George (Va.)	Lawyer	Elizabeth City Co. (Hampton), Va.	1726	June 8, 1806

How the Declaration of Independence Was Adopted

On June 7, 1776, Richard Henry Lee, who had issued the first call for a congress of the colonies, introduced in the Continental Congress at Philadelphia a resolution declaring "that these United Colonies are, and of right ought to be, free and independent states, that they are absolved from all allegiance to the British Crown, and that all political connection between them and the state of Great Britain is, and ought to be, totally dissolved."

The resolution, seconded by John Adams on behalf of the Massachusetts delegation, came up again June 10 when a committee of 5, headed by Thomas Jefferson, was appointed to express the purpose of the resolution in a declaration of independence. The others on the committee were John Adams, Benjamin Franklin, Robert R. Livingston, and Roger Sherman.

Drafting the Declaration was assigned to Jefferson, who worked on a portable desk of his own construction in a room at Market and 7th Sts. The committee reported the result June 28, 1776. The members of the Congress suggested a number of changes, which Jefferson called "deplorable." They didn't approve Jefferson's arraignment of the British people and King George III for encouraging and fostering the slave trade, which Jefferson called "an execrable commerce." They made 86 changes, eliminating 480 words and leaving 1,337. In the final form capitalization was erratic. Jefferson had written that men were endowed with "inalienable" rights; in the final copy it came out as "unalienable" and has been thus ever since.

The Lee-Adams resolution of independence was adopted by 12 yeas July 2 — the actual date of the act of independence. The Declaration, which explains the act, was adopted July 4, in the evening.

After the Declaration was adopted, July 4, 1776, it was turned over to John Dunlap, printer, to be printed on broadsides. The original copy was lost and one of his broadsides was attached to a page in the journal of the Congress. It was read aloud July 8 in Philadelphia, Easton, Pa., and Trenton, N.J. On July 9 at 6 p.m. it was read by order of Gen. George Washington to the troops assembled on the Common in New York City (City Hall Park).

The Continental Congress of July 19, 1776, adopted the following resolution:

"Resolved, That the Declaration passed on the 4th, be fairly engrossed on parchment with the title and stile of 'The Unanimous Declaration of the thirteen United States of America' and that the same, when engrossed, be signed by every member of Congress."

Not all delegates who signed the engrossed Declaration were present on July 4. Robert Morris (Pa.), William Williams (Conn.) and Samuel Chase (Md.) signed on Aug. 2, Oliver Wolcott (Conn.), George Wythe (Va.), Richard Henry Lee (Va.) and Elbridge Gerry (Mass.) signed in August and September, Matthew Thornton (N. H.) joined the Congress Nov. 4 and signed later. Thomas McKean (Del.) rejoined Washington's Army before signing and said later that he signed in 1781.

Charles Carroll of Carrollton was appointed a delegate by Maryland on July 4, 1776, presented his credentials July 18, and signed the engrossed Declaration Aug. 2. Born Sept. 19, 1737, he was 95 years old and the last surviving signer when he died Nov. 14, 1832.

Two Pennsylvania delegates who did not support the Declaration on July 4 were replaced.

The 4 New York delegates did not have authority from their state to vote on July 4. On July 9 the New York state convention authorized its delegates to approve the Declaration and the Congress was so notified on July 15, 1776. The 4 signed the Declaration on Aug. 2.

The original engrossed Declaration is preserved in the National Archives Building in Washington.

Lincoln's Address at Gettysburg, 1863

Fourscore and seven years ago our fathers brought forth on this continent a new nation, conceived in liberty and dedicated to the proposition that all men are created equal.

Now we are engaged in a great civil war, testing whether that nation or any nation so conceived and so dedicated can long endure. We are met on a great battle field of that war. We have come to dedicate a portion of that field, as a final resting-place for those who here gave their lives that that nation might live. It is altogether fitting and proper that we should do this.

But, in a larger sense, we can not dedicate — we can not consecrate — we can not hallow — this ground. The brave men, living and dead, who struggled here, have consecrated it, far above our poor power to add or detract. The world will little note, nor long remember, what we say here, but it can never forget what they did here. It is for us the living, rather, to be dedicated here to the unfinished work which they who fought here have thus far so nobly advanced. It is rather for us to be here dedicated to the great task remaining before us — that from these honored dead we take increased devotion to that cause for which they gave the last full measure of devotion — that we here highly resolve that these dead shall not have died in vain — that this nation, under God, shall have a new birth of freedom — and that government of the people, by the people, for the people, shall not perish from the earth.

Presidents of the U.S.

No.	Name	Politics	Born	In	Inaug.	at age	Died	at age
1	George Washington	Fed.	1732, Feb. 22	Va.	1789	57	1799, Dec. 14	67
2	John Adams	Fed.	1735, Oct. 30	Mass.	1797	61	1826, July 4	90
3	Thomas Jefferson	Dem.-Rep.	1743, Apr. 13	Va.	1801	57	1826, July 4	83
4	James Madison	Dem.-Rep.	1751, Mar. 16	Va.	1809	57	1836, June 28	85
5	James Monroe	Dem.-Rep.	1758, Apr. 28	Va.	1817	58	1831, July 4	73
6	John Quincy Adams	Dem.-Rep.	1767, July 11	Mass.	1825	57	1848, Feb. 23	80
7	Andrew Jackson	Dem.	1767, Mar. 15	S.C.	1829	61	1845, June 8	78
8	Martin Van Buren	Dem.	1782, Dec. 5	N.Y.	1837	54	1862, July 24	79
9	William Henry Harrison	Whig	1773, Feb. 9	Va.	1841	68	1841, Apr. 4	68
10	John Tyler	Whig	1790, Mar. 29	Va.	1841	51	1862, Jan. 18	71
11	James Knox Polk	Dem.	1795, Nov. 2	N.C.	1845	49	1849, June 15	53
12	Zachary Taylor	Whig	1784, Nov. 24	Va.	1849	64	1850, July 9	65
13	Millard Fillmore	Whig	1800, Jan. 7	N.Y.	1850	50	1874, Mar. 8	74
14	Franklin Pierce	Dem.	1804, Nov. 23	N.H.	1853	48	1869, Oct. 8	64
15	James Buchanan	Dem.	1791, Apr. 23	Pa.	1857	65	1868, June 1	77
16	Abraham Lincoln	Rep.	1809, Feb. 12	Ky.	1861	52	1865, Apr. 15	56
17	Andrew Johnson	(1)	1808, Dec. 29	N.C.	1865	56	1875, July 31	66
18	Ulysses Simpson Grant	Rep.	1822, Apr. 27	Oh.	1869	46	1885, July 23	63
19	Rutherford Birchard Hayes	Rep.	1822, Oct. 4	Oh.	1877	54	1893, Jan. 17	70
20	James Abram Garfield	Rep.	1831, Nov. 19	Oh.	1881	49	1881, Sept. 19	49
21	Chester Alan Arthur	Rep.	1829, Oct. 5	Vt.	1881	51	1886, Nov. 18	57
22	Grover Cleveland	Dem.	1837, Mar. 18	N.J.	1885	47	1908, June 24	71
23	Benjamin Harrison	Rep.	1833, Aug. 20	Oh.	1889	55	1901, Mar. 13	67
24	Grover Cleveland	Dem.	1837, Mar. 18	N.J.	1893	55	1908, June 24	71
25	William McKinley	Rep.	1843, Jan. 29	Oh.	1897	54	1901, Sept. 14	58
26	Theodore Roosevelt	Rep.	1858, Oct. 27	N.Y.	1901	42	1919, Jan. 6	60
27	William Howard Taft	Rep.	1857, Sept. 15	Oh.	1909	51	1930, Mar. 8	72
28	Woodrow Wilson	Dem.	1856, Dec. 28	Va.	1913	56	1924, Feb. 3	67
29	Warren Gamaliel Harding	Rep.	1865, Nov. 2	Oh.	1921	55	1923, Aug. 2	57
30	Calvin Coolidge	Rep.	1872, July 4	Vt.	1923	51	1933, Jan. 5	60
31	Herbert Clark Hoover	Rep.	1874, Aug. 10	Ia.	1929	54	1964, Oct. 20	90
32	Franklin Delano Roosevelt	Dem.	1882, Jan. 30	N.Y.	1933	51	1945, Apr. 12	63
33	Harry S. Truman	Dem.	1884, May 8	Mo.	1945	60	1972, Dec. 26	88
34	Dwight David Eisenhower	Rep.	1890, Oct. 14	Tex.	1953	62	1969, Mar. 28	78
35	John Fitzgerald Kennedy	Dem.	1917, May 29	Mass.	1961	43	1963, Nov. 22	46
36	Lyndon Baines Johnson	Dem.	1908, Aug. 27	Tex.	1963	55	1973, Jan. 22	64
37	Richard Milhous Nixon (2)	Rep.	1913, Jan. 9	Cal.	1969	56		
38	Gerald Rudolph Ford	Rep.	1913, July 14	Neb.	1974	61		
39	Jimmy (James Earl) Carter	Dem.	1924, Oct. 1	Ga.	1977	52		
40	Ronald Reagan	Rep.	1911, Feb. 6	Ill.	1981	69		
41	George Bush	Rep.	1924, June 12	Mass.	1989	64		
42	Bill (William Jefferson) Clinton	Dem.	1946, Aug. 19	Ark.	1993	46		

(1) Andrew Johnson — a Democrat, nominated vice president by Republicans and elected with Lincoln on National Union ticket. (2) Resigned Aug. 9, 1974.

Vice Presidents of the U.S.

The numerals given vice presidents do not coincide with those given presidents, because some presidents had no vice president and some had more than one.

	Name	Birthplace	Year	Home	Inaug.	Politics	Place of death	Year	Age
1	John Adams	Quincy, Mass.	1735	Mass.	1789	Fed.	Quincy, Mass.	1826	90
2	Thomas Jefferson	Shadwell, Va.	1743	Va.	1797	Dem.-Rep.	Monticello, Va	1826	83
3	Aaron Burr	Newark, N.J.	1756	N.Y.	1801	Dem.-Rep.	Staten Island, N.Y.	1836	80
4	George Clinton	Ulster Co., N.Y.	1739	N.Y.	1805	Dem.-Rep.	Washington, D.C.	1812	73
5	Elbridge Gerry	Marblehead, Mass.	1744	Mass.	1813	Dem.-Rep.	Washington, D.C.	1814	70
6	Daniel D. Tompkins	Scarsdale, N.Y.	1774	N.Y.	1817	Dem.-Rep.	Staten Island, N.Y.	1825	51
7	John C. Calhoun (1)	Abbeville, S.C.	1782	S.C.	1825	Dem.-Rep.	Washington, D.C.	1850	68
8	Martin Van Buren	Kinderhook, N.Y.	1782	N.Y.	1833	Dem.	Kinderhook, N.Y.	1862	79
9	Richard M. Johnson	Louisville, Ky.	1780	Ky.	1837	Dem.	Frankfort, Ky.	1850	70
10	John Tyler	Greenway, Va.	1790	Va.	1841	Whig	Richmond, Va.	1862	71
11	George M. Dallas	Philadelphia, Pa.	1792	Pa.	1845	Dem.	Philadelphia, Pa.	1864	72
12	Millard Fillmore	Summerhill, N.Y.	1800	N.Y.	1849	Whig	Buffalo, N.Y.	1874	74
13	William R. King	Sampson Co., N.C.	1786	Ala.	1853	Dem.	Dallas Co., Ala.	1853	67
14	John C. Breckinridge	Lexington, Ky.	1821	Ky.	1857	Dem.	Lexington, Ky.	1875	54
15	Hannibal Hamlin	Paris, Me.	1809	Me.	1861	Rep.	Bangor, Me	1891	81
16	Andrew Johnson	Raleigh, N.C.	1808	Tenn.	1865	(2)	Carter Co., Tenn	1875	66
17	Schuyler Colfax	New York, N.Y.	1823	Ind.	1869	Rep.	Mankato, Minn.	1885	62
18	Henry Wilson	Farmington, N.H.	1812	Mass.	1873	Rep.	Washington, D.C.	1875	63
19	William A. Wheeler	Malone, N.Y.	1819	N.Y.	1877	Rep.	Malone, N.Y.	1887	68
20	Chester A. Arthur	Fairfield, Vt.	1829	N.Y.	1881	Rep.	New York, N.Y.	1896	57
21	Thomas A. Hendricks	Muskingum Co., Oh.	1819	Ind.	1885	Dem.	Indianapolis, Ind.	1885	66
22	Levi P. Morton	Shoreham, Vt.	1824	N.Y.	1889	Rep.	Rhinebeck, N.Y.	1920	96
23	Adlai E. Stevenson (3)	Christian Co., Ky	1835	Ill.	1893	Dem.	Chicago, Ill.	1914	78
24	Garret A. Hobart	Long Branch, N.J.	1844	N.J.	1897	Rep.	Paterson, N.J.	1899	55
25	Theodore Roosevelt	New York, N.Y.	1858	N.Y.	1901	Rep.	Oyster Bay, N.Y.	1919	60
26	Charles W. Fairbanks	Unionville Centre, Oh.	1852	Ind.	1905	Rep.	Indianapolis, Ind.	1918	66
27	James S. Sherman	Utica, N.Y.	1855	N.Y.	1909	Rep.	Utica, N.Y.	1912	57
28	Thomas R. Marshall	N. Manchester Ind.	1854	Ind.	1913	Dem.	Washington, D.C.	1925	71
29	Calvin Coolidge	Plymnouth, Vt.	1872	Mass.	1921	Rep.	Northampton, Mass.	1933	60
30	Charles G. Dawes	Marietta, Oh.	1865	Ill	1925	Rep.	Evanston Ill.	1951	85
31	Charles Curtis	Topeka, Kan.	1860	Kan.	1929	Rep.	Washington, D.C.	1936	76
32	John Nance Garner	Red River Co., Tex.	1868	Tex.	1933	Dem.	Uvalde, Tex.	1967	98
33	Henry Agard Wallace	Adair County, Ia	1888	Iowa	1941	Dem.	Danbury, Conn.	1965	77
34	Harry S. Truman	Lumar, Mo.	1884	Mo.	1945	Dem.	Kansas City, Mo.	1972	88
35	Alben W. Barkley	Graves County, Ky.	1877	Ky.	1949	Dem.	Lexington, Va.	1956	78
36	Richard M. Nixon	Yorba Linda, Cal.	1913	Cal.	1953	Rep.			
37	Lyndon B. Johnson	Johnson City, Tex.	1908	Tex.	1961	Dem.	San Antonio, Tex.	1973	64
38	Hubert H. Humphrey	Wallace, S.D.	1911	Minn.	1965	Dem.	Waverly, Minn.	1978	66
39	Spiro T. Agnew(4)	Baltimore, Md.	1918	Md.	1969	Rep.			
40	Gerald R. Ford	Omaha, Neb.	1913	Mich.	1973	Rep.			
41	Nelson A. Rockefeller	Bar Harbor, Me.	1908	N.Y.	1974	Rep.	New York, N.Y.	1979	70
42	Walter F. Mondale	Ceylon, Minn.	1928	Minn.	1977	Dem.			
43	George Bush	Milton, Mass.	1924	Tex.	1981	Rep.			
44	Dan Quayle	Indianapolis, Ind.	1947	Ind.	1989	Rep.			
45	Al Gore	Washington, D.C.	1948	Tenn.	1993	Dem.			

(1) John C. Calhoun resigned Dec. 28, 1832 having been elected to the Senate to fill a vacancy. (2) Andrew Johnson – a Democrat nominated by Republicans and elected with Lincoln on the national Union Ticket. (3) Adlai E. Stevenson, 23rd vice president, was grandfather of Democratic candidate for present, 1952 and 1956. (4) Resigned Oct. 10, 1973.

HISTORICAL FIGURES & ROYALTY

Ancient Greeks

Aeschines, orator, 389-314BC.
Aeschylus, dramatist, 525-456BC.
Aesop, fableist, c620-c560BC.
Alcibiades, politician, 450-404BC.
Anacreon, poet, c582-c485BC.
Anaxagoras, philosopher, c500-428BC.
Anaximander, philosopher, 611-546BC.
Antiphon, speechwriter, c480-411BC.
Apollonius, mathematician, c265-170BC.
Archimedes, math. c287-212BC.
Aristophanes, dramatist, c448-380BC.
Aristotle, philosopher, 384-322BC.
Athenaeus, scholar, fl.c200.
Callicrates, architect, fl.5th cent.BC.
Callimachus, poet, c305-240BC.
Cratinus, comic dramatist, 520-421BC.
Democritus, philosopher, c460-370BC.
Demosthenes, orator, 384-322BC.
Diodorus, historian, fl.20BC.
Diogenes, philosopher, c372-c287BC.
Dionysius, historian, d.c7BC.
Empedocles, philosopher, c490-430BC.
Epicharmus, dramatist, c530-440BC.
Epictetus, philosopher, c55-c135.
Epicurus, philosopher, 341-270BC.
Eratosthenes, scientist, c276-194BC.
Euclid, mathematician, fl.c300BC.
Euripides, dramatist, c484-406BC.
Galen, physician, c129-199.
Heraclitus, philosopher, c535-c475BC.
Herodotus, historian, c484-420BC.
Hesiod, poet, 8th cent. BC.
Hippocrates, physician, c460-377BC.
Homer, poet, believed lived c850BC.
Isocrates, orator, 436-338BC.
Menander, dramatist, 342-292BC.
Phidias, sculptor, c500-435BC.
Pindar, poet, c518-c438BC.
Plato, philosopher, c428-c347BC.
Plutarch, biographer, c46-120.
Polybius, historian, c200-c118BC.
Praxiteles, sculptor, 400-330BC.
Pythagoras, phil., math., c580-c500BC.
Sappho, poet, c610-c580BC.
Simonides, poet, 556-c468BC.
Socrates, philosopher, c470-399BC.
Solon, statesman, 640-560BC.
Sophocles, dramatist, c496-406BC.
Strabo, geographer, c63BC-AD24.
Thales, philosopher, c634-c546BC.
Themistocles, politician, c524-c460BC.
Theocritus, poet, c310-250BC.
Theophrastus, phil. c372-c287BC.
Thucydides, historian, fl.5th cent.BC.
Timon, philosopher, c320-c230BC.
Xenophon, historian, c434-c355BC.
Zeno, philosopher, c495-c430BC.

Ancient Latins

Ammianus, historian, c330-395.
Apuleius, satirist, c124-c170.
Boethius, scholar, c480-524
Caesar, Julius, general, 100-44BC.
Catilina, politician, c108-62BC.
Cato (Elder), statesman, 234-149BC.
Catullus, poet, c84-54BC.
Cicero, orator, 106-43BC.
Claudian, poet, c370-c404.
Ennius, poet, 239-170BC.
Gellius, author, c130-c165.
Horace, poet, 65-8BC.
Juvenal, satirist, c60-c127.
Livy, historian, 59BC-AD17.
Lucan, poet, 39-65.
Lucilius, poet, c180-c102BC.
Lucretius, poet, c99-c55BC.
Martial, epigrammatist, c38-c103.
Nepos, historian, c100-c25BC.
Ovid, poet, 43BC-AD17.
Persius, satirist, 34-62.
Plautus, dramatist, c254-c184BC.
Pliny, scholar, 23-79.
Pliny (Younger), author, 62-113.
Quintilian, rhetorician, c35-c97.
Sallust, historian, 86-34BC.
Seneca, philosopher, 4BC-AD65.
Silius, poet, c25-101.
Statius, poet, c45-c96.
Suetonius, biographer, c69-c122.
Tacitus, historian, c56-c120.
Terence, dramatist, 185-c159BC.
Tibullus, poet, c55-c19BC.
Virgil, poet, 70-19BC.
Vitruvius, architect, fl.1st cent.BC.

Ancient Gods

Greek		Roman
Zeus	King of the gods	Jupiter
Hera	Consort of the king/goddess of childbirth	Juno
Aphrodite	Goddess of love	Venus
Apollo	God of the sun/prophecy	Helios
Ares	God of war	Mars
Artemis	Goddess of the hunt/women	Diana
Athena	Goddess of wisdom/patron of the arts	Minerva
Aurora	Goddess of the dawn	Eos
Demeter	Goddess of fertility	Ceres
Dionysus	God of wine	Bacchus
Eros	God of love	Cupid
Gaia	Goddess of the earth	Tellus
Hebe	Cup-bearer to the gods	Juventus
Hephaestus	God of fire & metalwork	Vulcan
Heracles	Deified hero	Hercules
Hermes	Messenger of the gods	Mercury
Hestia	Goddess of the hearth	Vesta
Hypnos	God of sleep	Morpheus
Irene	Goddess of peace	Pax
Nike	Goddess of victory	Victoria
Pan	God of shepherds	Faunus
Persephone	Goddess of vegetation/queen of the underworld	Proserpina
Poseidon	God of earthquakes/the sea	Neptune
Rhea	Mother goddess of Phrygia	Cybele
Tyche	Goddess of luck	Fortuna
Zephyrus	God of the west wind	Favonius

Norse Gods

Relatively little is known about the Norse gods, as documentation is scarce. However, archaeological evidence points to the following roles or associations.

Baldr	Fairest & best of the gods
Bragi	God of poetry
Eir	Goddess of medicine
Forseti	God of lawsuits
Frey	God of rain, sun & fertility
Freyja	Goddess of love & fertility
Frigga	Goddess of married love & the home
Heimdallr	Warden of the gods
Hel	Goddess of death
Hǫðr	Slayer of Baldr
Iðunn	Goddess of eternal youth
Njǫrðr	God of wind, sea & fishing
Norns	Goddesses of the past, present & future
Odin	Principal god & god of war, learning & poetry
Thor	God of thunder & war
Týr	God of victory
Ullr	God of the hunt/vanquisher of winter
Váli	Avenger of Baldr
Valkyries	Goddesses of battle
Víðarr	Son of Odin
Vǫr	Goddess of truth

RULERS OF ENGLAND AND GREAT BRITAIN

Name	England	Began	Died	Age	Rgd
	Saxons and Danes				
Egbert	King of Wessex, won allegiance of all English	829	839	—	10
Ethelwulf	Son, King of Wessex, Sussex, Kent, Essex	839	858	—	19
Ethelbald	Son of Ethelwulf, displaced father in Wessex	858	860	—	2
Ethelbert	2d son of Ethelwulf, united Kent and Wessex	860	866	—	6
Ethelred I	3d son, King of Wessex, fought Danes	866	871	—	5
Alfred	The Great, 4th son, defeated Danes, fortified London	871	899	52	28
Edward	The Elder, Alfred's son, united English, claimed Scotland	899	924	55	25
Athelstan	The Glorious, Edward's son, King of Mercia, Wessex	924	940	45	16
Edmund I	3d son of Edward, King of Wessex, Mercia	940	946	25	6

(Continued)

England

Name		Began	Died	Age	Rgd
Edred	4th son of Edward	946	955	32	9
Edwy	The Fair, eldest son of Edmund, King of Wessex	955	959	18	3
Edgar	The Peaceful, 2d son of Edmund, ruled all English	959	975	32	17
Edward	The Martyr, eldest son of Edgar, murdered by stepmother	975	978	17	4
Ethelred II	The Unready, 2d son of Edgar, married Emma of Normandy	978	1016	48	37
Edmund II	Ironside, son of Ethelred II, King of London	1016	1016	27	0
Canute	The Dane, gave Wessex to Edmund, married Emma	1016	1035	40	19
Harold I	Harefoot, natural son of Canute	1035	1040	—	5
Hardecanute	Son of Canute by Emma, Danish King	1040	1042	24	2
Edward	The Confessor, son of Ethelred II (Canonized 1161)	1042	1066	62	24
Harold II	Edward's brother-in-law, last Saxon King	1066	1066	44	0
	House of Normandy				
William I	The Conqueror, defeated Harold at Hastings	1066	1087	60	21
William II	Rufus, 3d son of William I, killed by arrow	1087	1100	43	13
Henry I	Beauclerc, youngest son of William I	1100	1135	67	35
	House of Blois				
Stephen	Son of Adela, daughter of William I, and Count of Blois	1135	1154	50	19
	House of Plantagenet				
Henry II	Son of Geoffrey Plantagenet (Angevin) by Matilda, dau. of Henry I	1154	1189	56	35
Richard I	Coeur de Lion, son of Henry II, crusader	1189	1199	42	10
John	Lackland, son of Henry II, signed Magna Carta, 1215	1199	1216	50	17
Henry III	Son of John, acceded at 9, under regency until 1227	1216	1272	65	56
Edward I	Longshanks, son of Henry III	1272	1307	68	35
Edward II	Son of Edward I, deposed by Parliament, 1327	1307	1327	43	20
Edward III	Of Windsor, son of Edward II	1327	1377	65	50
Richard II	Grandson of Edw. III, minor until 1389, deposed 1399	1377	1400	33	22
	House of Lancaster				
Henry IV	Son of John of Gaunt, Duke of Lancaster, son of Edw. III	1399	1413	47	13
Henry V	Son of Henry IV, victor of Agincourt	1413	1422	34	9
Henry VI	Son of Henry V, deposed 1461, died in Tower	1422	1471	49	39
	House of York				
Edward IV	Great-great-grandson of Edward III, son of Duke of York	1461	1483	41	22
Edward V	Son of Edward IV, murdered in Tower of London	1483	1483	13	0
Richard III	Crookback, bro. of Edward IV, fell at Bosworth Field	1483	1485	35	2
	House of Tudor				
Henry VII	Son of Edmund Tudor, Earl of Richmond, whose father had married the widow of Henry V; descended from Edward III through his mother, Margaret Beaufort via John of Gaunt. By marriage with dau.of Edward IV he united Lancaster and York	1485	1509	53	24
Henry VIII	Son of Henry VII by Elizabeth, dau. of Edward IV	1509	1547	56	38
Edward VI	Son of Henry VIII, by Jane Seymour, his 3d queen. Ruled under regents. Was forced to name Lady Jane Grey his successor. Council of State proclaimed her queen July 10, 1553. Mary Tudor won Council, was proclaimed queen July 19, 1553. Mary had Lady Jane Grey beheaded for treason, Feb., 1554	1547	1553	16	6
Mary I	Daughter of Henry VIII, by Catherine of Aragon	1553	1558	43	5
Elizabeth I	Daughter of Henry VIII, by Anne Boleyn	1558	1603	69	44

Great Britain

Name		Began	Died	Age	Rgd
	House of Stuart				
James I	James VI of Scotland, son of Mary, Queen of Scots. First to call himself King of Great Britain. This became official with the Act of Union, 1707	1603	1625	59	22
Charles I	Only surviving son of James I; beheaded Jan. 30, 1649	1625	1649	48	24
	Commonwealth, 1649-1660 Council of State, 1649; Protectorate, 1653				
The Cromwells	Oliver Cromwell, Lord Protector	1653	1658	59	—
	Richard Cromwell, son, Lord Protector, resigned May 25, 1659	1658	1712	86	—
	House of Stuart (Restored)				
Charles II	Eldest son of Charles I, died without issue	1660	1685	55	25
James II	2d son of Charles I. Deposed 1688. Interregnum Dec. 11, 1688, to Feb. 13, 1689	1685	1701	68	3
William III	Son of William, Prince of Orange, by Mary, dau. of Charles I	1689	1702	51	13
and Mary II	Eldest daughter of James II and wife of William III		1694	33	6
Anne	2d daughter of James II	1702	1714	49	12
	House of Hanover				
George I	Son of Elector of Hanover, by Sophia, grand-dau. of James I	1714	1727	67	13
George II	Only son of George I, married Caroline of Brandenburg	1727	1760	77	33
George III	Grandson of George II, married Charlotte of Mecklenburg	1760	1820	81	59
George IV	Eldest son of George III, Prince Regent, from Feb., 1811	1820	1830	67	10
William IV	3d son of George III, married Adelaide of Saxe-Meiningen	1830	1837	71	7
Victoria	Dau. of Edward, 4th son of George III; married (1840) Prince Albert of Saxe-Coburg and Gotha, who became Prince Consort	1837	1901	81	63
	House of Saxe-Coburg and Gotha				
Edward VII	Eldest son of Victoria, married Alexandra, Princess of Denmark	1901	1910	68	9
	House of Windsor *Name Adopted July 17, 1917*				
George V	2d son of Edward VII, married Princess Mary of Teck	1910	1936	70	25
Edward VIII	Eldest son of George V; acceded Jan. 20, 1936, abdicated Dec. 11	1936	1972	77	1
George VI	2d son of George V; married Lady Elizabeth Bowes-Lyon	1936	1952	56	15
Elizabeth II	Elder daughter of George VI, acceded Feb. 6, 1952	1952	—	—	—

RULERS OF SCOTLAND

Kenneth I MacAlpin was the first Scot to rule both Scots and Picts, 846 AD.

Duncan I was the first general ruler, 1034. Macbeth seized the kingdom 1040, was slain by Duncan's son, Malcolm III MacDuncan (Canmore), 1057.

Malcolm married Margaret, Saxon princess who had fled from the Normans. Queen Margaret introduced English language and English monastic customs. She was canonized, 1250. Her son Edgar, 1097, moved the court to Edinburgh. His brothers Alexander I and David I succeeded. Malcolm IV, the Maiden, 1153, grandson of David I, was followed by his brother, William the Lion, 1165, whose son was Alexander II, 1214. The latter's son, Alexander III, 1249, defeated the Norse and regained the Hebrides. When he died, 1286, his granddaughter, Margaret, child of Eric of Norway and grandniece of Edward I of England, known as the Maid of Norway, was chosen ruler, but died 1290, aged 8.

John Baliol, 1292-1296. (Interregnum, 10 years).

Robert Bruce (The Bruce), 1306-1329, victor at Bannockburn, 1314.

David II, only son of Robert Bruce, ruled 1329-1371.

Robert II, 1371-1390, grandson of Robert Bruce, son of Walter, the Steward of Scotland, was called The Steward, first of the so-called Stuart line.

Robert III, son of Robert II, 1390-1406.

James I, son of Robert III, 1406-1437.

James II, son of James I, 1437-1460.

James III, eldest son of James II, 1460-1488.

James IV, eldest son of James III, 1488-1513.

James V, eldest son of James IV, 1513-1542.

Mary, daughter of James V, born 1542, became queen when one week old; was crowned 1543. Married, 1558, Francis, son of Henry II of France, who became king 1559, died 1560. Mary ruled Scots 1561 until abdication, 1567. She also married (2) Henry Stewart, Lord Darnley, and (3) James, Earl of Bothwell. Imprisoned by Elizabeth I, Mary was beheaded 1587.

James VI, 1566-1625, son of Mary and Lord Darnley, became King of England on death of Elizabeth in 1603. Although the thrones were thus united, the legislative union of Scotland and England was not effected until the Act of Union, May 1, 1707.

The Longest-reigning British Monarchs[1]

Monarch	Reign	Age at accession	Age at death	Reign years
Victoria	1837–1901	18	81	63
George III	1760–1820	22	81	59
Henry III	1216–72	9	64	56
Edward III	1327–77	14	64	50
Elizabeth I	1558–1603	25	69	44
Elizabeth II	1952–	25	–	41
Henry VI	1422–61 (deposed; d.1471)	8 months	49	38
Henry VIII	1509–47	17	55	37
Charles II	1649–85	19	54	36
Henry I	1100–35	31/32[2]	66/67[2]	35

(1) Excluding the reigns of monarchs before 1066. (2) Henry I's birthdate is unknown, so his age at accession and death are uncertain.

The Queen's Full Title

Elizabeth the Second, by the grace of God of the United Kingdom of Great Britain and Northern Ireland and of Her other Realms and Territories Queen, Head of the Commonwealth, Defender of the Faith.

Order of Succession to the Throne

1 HRH The Prince of Wales
2 HRH Prince William of Wales
3 HRH Prince Henry of Wales
4 HRH The Duke of York
5 HRH Princess Beatrice of York
6 HRH Princess Eugenie of York
7 HRH The Prince Edward
8 HRH The Princess Royal
9 Peter Phillips
10 Zara Phillips
11 HRH The Princess Margaret, Countess of Snowdon
12 Viscount Linley
13 Lady Sarah Armstrong-Jones
14 HRH The Duke of Gloucester
15 Earl of Ulster
16 Lady Davina Windsor
17 Lady Rose Windsor
18 HRH The Duke of Kent
19 Baron Downpatrick
20 Lord Nicholas Windsor
21 Lady Helen Windsor
22 Lord Frederick Windsor
23 Lady Gabriella Windsor
24 HRH Princess Alexandra, The Hon Lady Ogilvy
25 James Ogilvy
26 Marina Mowatt
27 The Earl of Harewood
28 Viscount Lascelles
29 The Hon Alexander Lascelles
30 The Hon Edward Lascelles

The Royal Family – Birthplaces & Birthdates

Queen Elizabeth II (London)	21/4/26
Queen Elizabeth the Queen Mother (Glamis, Scotland)	4/8/1900
Prince Philip, Duke of Edinburgh (Corfu, Greece)	1/6/21
Charles, Prince of Wales (London)	14/11/48
Diana, Princess of Wales (Sandringham, Norfolk)	1/7/61
Prince William of Wales (London)	2/6/81
Prince Henry of Wales (London)	15/9/84
Princess Royal (London)	15/8/50
Prince Andrew, Duke of York (London)	19/2/60
Sarah, Duchess of York (London)	15/10/59
Princess Beatrice (London)	8/8/88
Princess Eugenie (London)	23/3/90
Prince Edward (London)	1/3/64
Princess Margaret (Glamis, Scotland)	21/8/30

Persons of Title – Forms of Address

Source: Debrett's

- **Eldest Sons** of Dukes, Marquesses, and Earls bearing courtesy titles should not be styled "The Rt. Hon." or "The" unless they themselves are Peers or Members of the Privy Council.
- **Formal conclusions to letters to Peers**. The style "I am, my Lord, Your obedient servant" may be used (as applicable), but "Yours faithfully" and "Yours truly" are now more customarily adopted, except for letters to Members of the Royal Family.
- **Succession to hereditary titles**. By custom those who have succeeded to peerages and baronetcies are not so addressed until after their predecessor's funeral.
- **New honours.** Knights and Dames of Orders of Chivalry may use their style of "Sir" and "Dame" and the appropriate letters after their names, and Knights Bachelor their style of "Sir" immediately their honours have been announced. Other recipients of honours may also use the appropriate letters. Peers may use their titles after the patent of creation has passed the Great Seal, when their respective Peerage titles will be announced.

Baron – LETTERS *Superscription*, "The Right Hon. the Lord ——" or socially "The Lord ——". *Commencement*, "My Lord" or socially "Dear Lord ——". PERSONAL ADDRESS, "My Lord".

Baroness – LETTERS *Superscription* if a Baroness in her own right "The Right Hon. the Baroness ——", or socially "The Baroness ——", or "The Right Hon. the Lady ——", or "The Lady ——". If the wife of a Baron "The Right Hon. the Lady ——", or socially "The Lady ——". *Commencement*, "Madam" or socially "Dear Lady ——", PERSONAL ADDRESS, "Madam" (*see also* Baron's Widow).

• If a Baroness in her own right marries a commoner and has issue, the children have the same rank and are addressed as if their father were a Baron.

Baronet – LETTERS *Superscription*, "Sir (Charles) ——Bt." (The abbreviation "Bart." is also sometimes used.) *Commencement*, "Sir". PERSONAL ADDRESS, "Sir" or socially "Dear Sir (Charles) Smith" or "Dear Sir (Charles)".

Baronet's Widow – *As for* Baronet's Wife if present baronet is unmarried. For widows where present incumbent of the title is married "Dowager". As to re-marriage, *see* Widows.

Baronet's Wife – LETTERS *Superscription*, if the daughter (i) of a commoner. "Lady ——"; (ii) of a Baron or a Viscount, "The Hon. Lady ——"; (iii) of an Earl, a Marquess, or a Duke, "Lady (Emily) ——". *Commencement*, "Madam", or socially, "Dear Lady ——". PERSONAL ADDRESS, "Madam".

Baron's Daughter – LETTERS *Superscription*, if married (i) to an esquire, "The Hon. Mrs ——"; (ii) to a knight, or a baronet, "The Hon. Lady ——"; (iii) to the son of a Baron, or Viscount, or to the younger son of an Earl, "The Hon. Mrs ——", or if her husband has a married brother, "The Hon. Mrs (William) ——"; (iv) to the younger son of a Marquess or a Duke, "Lady (Henry) ——". If unmarried, "The Hon. (Mary) ——"; (v) to the eldest son of a Duke, Marquess, or Earl by his courtesy title. (*See also* Duke's Daughter.) *Commencement*, "Madam". PERSONAL ADDRESS, "Madam", or socially if married to an esquire, "Dear Mrs ——", or according to her husband's rank if a Peer.

Baron's Son – LETTERS *Superscription*. "The Hon. (John) ——". *Commencement*, "Sir". PERSONAL ADDRESS, "Sir", or socially, "Dear Mr ——". *See also* Master of ——.

Baron's Son's Widow – *As for* Baron's Son's Wife, so long as she remains a widow. As to re-marriage, *see* Widows.

Baron's Son's Wife – LETTERS *Superscription*, "The Hon. Mrs (Edward) ——", but if the daughter (i) of a Viscount or Baron, "The Hon. Mrs ——"; (ii) of an Earl, a Marquess, or a Duke, "Lady (Ellen)". (*See also* Duke's Daughter.) *Commencement*, "Madam", or socially, if her father is an esquire, "Dear Mrs ——", or according to her father's rank, if a Peer. PERSONAL ADDRESS, "Madam".

Baron's Widow – *As for* Baroness, if present Baron is unmarried. For widows where present incumbent of title is married *see* Dowager. As to re-marriage, *see* Widows.

Countess – LETTERS *Superscription*, "The Rt. Hon. the Countess of ——", or socially "The Countess of ——". In other respects, as Baroness. (*See also* Earl's Widow.) *Commencement*, formally "Madam", socially "Dear Lady ——".

• If a Countess in her own right marries a gentleman of lesser degree than herself, and has issue, the children would have the same rank and are addressed as if their father were an Earl.

Dames of Orders of Chivalry prefix "Dame" to their christian names, adding the initials GCB, GCMG, GCVO, GBE, DCB, DCMG, DCVO or DBE, as the case may be, after the surname. *Commencement*, formally "Madam" or socially "Dear Dame (Edith) ——" or "Dear Dame (Edith)". PERSONAL ADDRESS, "Dame (Edith)".

Divorced Ladies – When a lady is divorced, she loses any precedence which she gained by marriage. With regard to divorced Peeresses, the College of Arms, acting on an opinion of the Lord Chancellor, has long held that such persons cannot claim the privileges or status of Peeresses which they derived from their husbands. Divorced Peeresses are not summoned to a Coronation as Peeresses. The above remarks apply to ladies who have divorced their husbands, as well as to those who have been divorced.

The correct style and description of divorced ladies who have not remarried, nor have taken steps to resume their maiden name with the prefix of Mrs, is as follows.

The former wife of a Peer or courtesy Peer: "Mary, Viscountess ——".

The former wife of a Baronet or Knight: "Mary, Lady ——".

The divorced wife of an "Honourable": "The Hon. Mrs John ——", or alternatively she may prefer to be known as "Mrs Mary ——".

The divorced wife of a younger son of a Duke or Marquess: "Lady John ——", or "Mrs Mary ——".

The divorced wife of an untitled gentleman: "Mrs Mary ——" or initials.

Dowager Lady is addressed according to her rank. Immediately a peer or a baronet marries, the widow of the previous incumbent of the titles becomes "The Dowager"; but if there is more than one widow living of previous incumbents of a title, use must be made of the christian name as a distinction, since the style of Dowager belongs to the senior of the widows for her lifetime. This prefix, however, is very much less used than formerly, use of the christian name generally being preferred. In such cases ladies are addressed as "Right Hon. (Mary) Countess of ——"; or socially as "(Mary), Countess of ——", etc, etc, if a peeress; or, as "Ellen, Lady ——", if a Baronet's widow.

Duchess – LETTERS *Superscription*, "Her Grace the Duchess of ——", or socially "The Duchess of ——". *Commencement*, formally "Madam", or socially "Dear Duchess of ——" or "Dear Duchess". PERSONAL ADDRESS, "Your Grace". (*See also* Duke's Widow, and for "Duchess of the Blood Royal" *see* Princess.)

Duke – LETTERS *Superscription*, "His Grace the Duke of ——" or socially "The Duke of ——". The very formal style of "The Most Noble" is now rarely used. *Commencement*, "My Lord Duke", "Dear Duke of ——", or (more usual) "Dear Duke". PERSONAL ADDRESS, "Your Grace". (For "Duke of the Blood Royal" *see* Prince.)

Duke's Daughter – LETTERS *Superscription*, "Lady (Henrietta) ——". *Commencement*, "Madam", or socially "Dear Lady (Henrietta) ——" or "Dear Lady (Henrietta)". PERSONAL ADDRESS, "Madam".

• If the daughter of a Duke, a Marquess, or an Earl marries a Peer, she is addressed according to the rank of her husband. If she marries the eldest son of a Duke, Marquess or Earl, she is known by her husband's courtesy title, but if the daughter of a *Duke or Marquess* marries the eldest son of an Earl, she is sometimes addressed by the courtesy title of her husband, but she may revert to the style of Lady (Mary) Stavordale, i.e. her own title, followed by her husband's courtesy title. His surname must never be used. This form is invariably used by such ladies after divorce.

Duke's Eldest Son, assumes by courtesy a secondary title of his father, and is addressed personally as if he were a Peer without "The Most Hon." or "The Rt. Hon." *Superscription*, "Marquess of ——" (or as title adopted may be).

Duke's Eldest Son's Daughter is by courtesy addressed as if her father were a Peer.

Duke's Eldest Son's Eldest Son assumed by courtesy the third title of his grandfather, and is addressed personally as if he were a peer, provided such courtesy title is the title of a Peerage vested in his grandfather. *Superscription*, "The Earl of ——" or "Lord ——" (or as title adopted may be).

Duke's Eldest Son's Younger Son is by courtesy addressed as if his father were a Peer.

Duke's Eldest Son's Widow – *As for* Duke's Eldest Son's Wife, so long as she remains a widow. As to re-marriage, *see* Widows.

Duke's Eldest Son's Wife is known by his courtesy title, and is addressed personally as peeress without "The Most Hon." or "The Rt. Hon.".

Duke's Widow – *As for* Duchess, if present Duke is unmarried. For widows where present incumbent of title is married *see* Dowager. As to re-marriage, *see* Widows.

Duke's Younger Son – LETTERS *Superscription*, "Lord (Robert) ——". *Commencement*, formally "My Lord", or socially "Dear Lord Robert". PERSONAL ADDRESS, "My Lord".

Duke's Younger Son's Widow – *As for* Duke's Younger Son's Wife. As to re-marriage, *see* Widows.

Duke's Younger Son's Wife – LETTERS *Superscription*, "Lady (Thomas) ——". *Commencement*, "Madam", socially "Dear Lady Thomas ——", or "Dear Lady Thomas".

Earl – LETTERS *Superscription*, "The Right Hon. the Earl of ——", or socially "The Earl of ——". In other respects as Baron.

Earl's Daughter – *As for* Duke's Daughter.

Earl's Eldest Son bears by courtesy a lesser (usually the second) title of his father, and is addressed as if he were a Peer but without "The Rt. Hon.". *Superscription*, "Viscount ——".

Earl's Eldest Son's Daughter is by courtesy addressed as if her father were a Peer.

Earl's Eldest Son's Son is by courtesy addressed as if his father were a Peer. (If a Scottish earldom, the eldest may be addressed as "The Master of ——". *See* Master.)

Earl's Eldest Son's Widow – *As for* Eldest Son's Wife, so long as she remains a widow. As to re-marriage, *see* Widows.

Earl's Eldest Son's Wife is usually known by his courtesy title (for exception *see* Duke's Daughter), and is addressed personally as if a Peeress but without "The Rt. Hon.".

Earl's Widow – *As for* Countess if present Earl is unmarried. For widows where present incumbent of the title is married *see* Dowager.

Earl's Wife – *As for* Countess.

Earl's Younger Son – *As for* Baron's Son.

Earl's Younger Son's Widow – *As for* Baron's Son's Widow.

Earl's Younger Son's Wife – *As for* Baron's Son's Wife.

Emperor – LETTERS *Superscription*, "His Imperial Majesty". *Commencement*, "Sir" or "Your Imperial Majesty". PERSONAL ADDRESS, "Your Majesty".

Esquire – LETTERS *Superscription*, "(Edward) ——, Esq.". *Commencement*, "Sir". PERSONAL ADDRESS, "Sir".

Esquire's Widow *As for* Esquire's Wife. She continues to use her late husband's christian name unless she re-marries. e.g. Mrs John Smith *not* Mrs Mary Smith.

Esquire's Wife – *Superscription*, "Mrs (Egerton)", or "Mrs (John Egerton)". The former style is applicable if she is the wife of the head of the family, provided that there is no senior widow living, who retains the style for life or until re-marriage. LETTERS *Commencement*, "Madam". PERSONAL ADDRESS, "Madam".

Grandchildren of Peers – If the eldest son of a peer predeceases his father and the grandson succeeds to the peerage held by his grandfather, a Royal Warrant is necessary (when such succession has eventuated) to grant to his younger brothers and his sisters the "rank, title, place, pre-eminence and precedence" which would have been due to them if their fathers had survived to inherit the Peerage.

Knight Bachelor – LETTERS *Superscription*, "Sir (George) ——". In other respects same as Baronet. The letters KB should not be used.

Knight's Wife – *As for* Baronet's Wife. The wife of a clergyman of the Church of England who receives a Knighthood of an Order of Chivalry but consequently not the accolade, retains the style of "Mrs ——".

Knight of an Order of Chivalry *As for* Knight Bachelor, but adding to the superscription the recognized letters of the Order, such as GCB or KCB. Clergymen of the Church of England and Honorary Knights do not receive the accolade, and consequently are addressed by the letters of the Orders but not the prefix "Sir".

Knight's Widow – *As for* Knight's Wife so long as she remains a widow. As to remarriage, *see* Widows.

Life Peer – He is addressed as for an hereditary peer. *As for* Baron.

Life Peer's Son – *As for* Baron's Son.

Life Peer's Daughter – *As for* Baron's Daughter.

Life Peeress *As for* Baroness.

Life Peeress in her own right. She is addressed as for an hereditary peeress. *As for* Baroness.

Lord, in Peerage of Scotland – *As for* Baron.

Marchioness – LETTERS *Superscription*, "The Most Hon. the Marchioness of ——", or socially, "The Marchioness of ——". In other respects as Baroness. *See also* Marquess's Widow.

Marquess – LETTERS *Superscription*, "The Most Hon. the Marquess of ——", or less formally, "The Marquess of ——". In other respects as Baron.

Marquess's Daughter – *As for* Duke's Daughter.

Marquess's Eldest Son *As for* Duke's Eldest Son. *Superscription*, "Earl of ——" (or as title adopted may be).

Marquess's Eldest Son's Daughter is by courtesy addressed as if her father were a peer.

Marquess's Eldest Son's Eldest Son – *As for* Duke's Eldest Son. *Superscription*, "Viscount ——" (or as title adopted may be).

Marquess's Eldest Son's Younger Son is by courtesy addressed as if his father were a Peer, namely "The Hon. ——".

Marquess's Eldest Son's Widow – *As for* Duke's Eldest Son's Widow.

Marquess's Eldest Son's Wife is known by his courtesy title, and is addressed personally as a peeress without "The Rt. Hon.".

Marquess's Widow *As for* Marchioness, if present Marquess is unmarried. For widows where present incumbent of title is married *see* Dowager. As to re-marriage, *see* Widows.

Marquess's Younger Son *As for* Duke's Younger Son.

Marquess's Younger Son's Widow *As for* Duke's Younger Son's Wife. As to re-marriage, *see* Widows.

Marquess's Younger Son's Wife *As for* Duke's Younger Son's Wife.

Master – This title is borne in the *Peerage of Scotland* by the heir apparent or presumptive of a Peer. It is also used by *courtesy* by the eldest son of a Peer by courtesy. In the case of the heir apparent, "Master" is normally used by the eldest son of a Viscount and Lord, as the heirs of the senior grades of the Peerage normally use a courtesy title. He is styled "The Master of ——" (the appropriate title will be found under the Peerage article). If the heir be a woman, she is officially designated "The Mistress of ——" but this title is seldom used. A Master's wife is styled "The Hon. Mrs (Donald Campbell)" or according to her husband's rank.

Peers and Peeresses by courtesy – As commoners they are not addressed as "Rt. Hon." or "The" but "Viscount (Brown)" or appropriate title.

Prince – LETTERS *Superscription*, (i) the son of a Sovereign "His Royal Highness The Prince (Edward)"; (ii) other Princes "His Royal Highness Prince (Michael of Kent)"; (iii) Duke "His Royal Highness The Duke of (Gloucester)". *Commencement*, "Sir". *Conclusion*, "I have the honour to be, Your Royal Highness's most humble and obedient servant". PERSONAL ADDRESS, "Your Royal Highness", and henceforward as "Sir". (*See also* Royal Family.)

Princess – LETTERS *Superscription*, (i) the daughter of a Sovereign "Her Royal Highness The Princess (Anne)"; (ii) other Princesses "Her Royal Highness Princess (Alexandra), the Hon. Mrs (Angus Ogilvy)"; (iii) Duchess "Her Royal Highness The Duchess of (Kent)". A Princess Royal is addressed "Her Royal Highness The Princess Royal". *Commencement*, "Madam". *Conclusion*, "I have the honour to be, Madam, Your Royal Highness's most humble and obedient servant". PERSONAL ADDRESS, "Your Royal Highness", and henceforward as "Ma'am". (*See also* Royal Family.)

Queen Mother – LETTERS *Superscription*, for formal and state documents, "Her Gracious Majesty Queen Elizabeth The Queen Mother", otherwise "Her Majesty Queen Elizabeth The Queen Mother". *Commencement*, as for the Queen Regnant. *Conclusion*, "I have the honour to remain, Madam, Your Majesty's most humble and obedient servant". PERSONAL ADDRESS, as for the Queen Regnant.

Queen Regnant – LETTERS *Superscription*, for formal and state documents, "The Queen's Most Excellent Majesty", otherwise "Her Majesty The Queen", *Commencement* "Madam", or "May it please your Majesty". *Conclusion*, "I have the honour to remain Madam, Your Majesty's most humble and obedient servant". PERSONAL ADDRESS, "Your Majesty", and henceforth as "Ma'am".

Rt. Honourable – This prefix is borne by Privy Counsellors of Great Britain and Northern Ireland, the Governor General of Canada, and Prime Minister and Chief Justice of Canada *for life*; by Earls, Viscounts and Barons (except peers by courtesy) their wives and widows; and certain Lord Mayors (*see* Lord Mayors, p. 287), and Provosts of Edinburgh and Glasgow (*see* Lord Provosts, p. 291) *while in office*.

Royal Dukes – *See* Prince.

Royal Family – On 11 December 1917 it was ordained that "The children of any Sovereign of the United Kingdom and the children of the sons of any such Sovereign and the eldest living son of the eldest son of the Prince of Wales, shall have and at all times hold and enjoy the style, title, or attribute of Royal Highness with their titular dignity of Prince or Princess prefixed to their respective christian names, or with their other titles of honour; and that the grandchildren of the sons of any such Sovereign in the direct male line (save only the eldest living son of the eldest son of the Prince of Wales), shall have the style and the title enjoyed by the children of Dukes." (*See also* Queen Regnant, Queen Mother, Prince *and* Princess.)

Sovereign, The – *See* Queen Regnant.

Titles just announced – *See* introduction to this section.

Viscount – LETTERS *Superscription*, "The Right

Hon. The Viscount ——", or socially "The Viscount ——". In other respects as Baron.

Viscountess – LETTERS *Superscription*, "The Right Hon. The Viscountess ——", or socially, "The Viscountess ——". In other respects as Baroness and Baron's widow. (*See also* Viscount's Widow.)

Viscount's Son, and his Wife or Widow – *As for* Baron's.

Viscount's Widow – *As for* Viscountess if present Viscount is unmarried. For widows where present incumbent of title is married *see* Dowager. As to re-marriage, *see* Widows.

Wales, Prince of – *See* Prince *and* Royal Family.

Widows – A Widow who re-marries loses any title or precedence she gained by her previous marriage, and is not recognized as having any claim to bear the title of her deceased husband. For example, at a coronation or other State ceremonial, the widow of a Peer would not be summoned as a Peeress if she had subsequently married a commoner; and, if having espoused a peer of lesser degree than her former husband, she would only be recognized by the rank acquired by her last marriage. (*See also* Esquire's Widow.)

HISTORICAL PERIODS OF JAPAN

Yamato	c.300-592	Conquest of Yamato plain c. 300 A.D.
Asuka	592-710	Accession of Empress Suiko, 592.
Nara	710-794	Completion of Heijo (Nara), 710; capital moves to Nagaoka, 784.
Heian	794-1192	Completion of Heian (Kyoto), 794
Fujiwara	858-1160	Fujiwara-no-Yoshifusa becomes regent, 858.
Taira	1160-1185	Taira-no-Kiyomori assumes control, 1160; Minamoto-no-Yoritomo victor over Taira, 1185.
Kamakura	1192-1333	Yoritomo becomes shogun, 1192.
Namboku	1334-1392	Restoration of Emperor Godaigo, 1334; Southern Court established by Godaigo at Yoshino, 1336.
Ashikaga	1338-1573	Ashikaga Takauji becomes shogun, 1338.
Muromachi	1392-1573	Unification of Southern and Northern Courts, 1392.
Sengoku	1467-1600	Beginning of the Onin war, 1467
Momoyama	1573-1603	Oda Nobunaga enters Kyoto,1568; Nobunaga deposes last Ashikaga shogun, 1573; Tokugawa Leyasu victor at Sekigahara, 1600.
Edo	1603-1867	Leyasu becomes shogun, 1603.
Meiji	1868-1912	Enthronement of Emperor Mutsuhito (Meiji), 1867; Meiji Restoration and Charter Oath, 1868.
Taisho	1912-1926	Accession of Emperor Yoshihito, 1912.
Showa	1926-1989	Accession of Emperor Hirohito, 1926.
Heisei	1989-	Accession of Emperor Akihito, 1989

RULERS OF FRANCE: KINGS, QUEENS, PRESIDENTS

Caesar to Charlemagne

Julius Caesar subdued the Gauls, native tribes of Gaul (France) 57 to 52 BC. The Romans ruled 500 years. The Franks, a Teutonic tribe, reached the Somme from the East ca. 250 AD. By the 5th century the Merovingian Franks ousted the Romans. In 451 AD, with the help of Visigoths, Burgundians and others, they defeated Attila and the Huns at Châlons-sur-Marne.

Childeric I became leader of the Merovingians 458 AD. His son Clovis I (Chlodwig, Ludwig, Louis), crowned 481, founded the dynasty. After defeating the Alemanni (Germans) 496, he was baptized a Christian and made Paris his capital. His line ruled until Childeric III was deposed, 751.

The West Merovingians were called Neustrians, the eastern Austrasians. Pepin of Herstal (687-714) major domus, or head of the palace, of Austrasia, took over Neustria as dux (leader) of the Franks. Pepin's son, Charles, called Martel (the Hammer) defeated the Saracens at Tours-Poitiers, 732; was succeeded by his son, Pepin the Short, 741, who deposed Childeric III and ruled as king until 768.

His son, Charlemagne, or Charles the Great (742-814) became king of the Franks, 768, with his brother Carloman, who died 771. He ruled France, Germany, parts of Italy, Spain, Austria, and enforced Christianity. Crowned Emperor of the Romans by Pope Leo III in St. Peter's, Rome, Dec. 25, 800 AD. Succeeded by son, Louis I the Pious, 814. At death, 840, Louis left empire to sons, Lothair (Roman emperor); Pepin I (king of Aquitaine); Louis II (of Germany); Charles the Bald (France). They quarreled and by the peace of Verdun, 843, divided the empire.

AD	Name, year of accession
	The Carolingians
843	Charles I (the Bald), Roman Emperor, 875
877	Louis II (the Stammerer), son
879	Louis III (died 882) and Carloman, brothers
885	Charles II (the Fat), Roman Emperor, 881
888	Eudes (Odo) elected by nobles
898	Charles III (the Simple), son of Louis II, defeated by
922	Robert, brother of Eudes, killed in war
923	Rudolph (Raoul) Duke of Burgundy
936	Louis IV, son of Charles III
954	Lothair, son, aged 13, defeated by Capet
986	Louis V (the Sluggard), left no heirs
	The Capets
987	Hugh Capet, son of Hugh the Great
996	Robert II (the Wise), his son
1031	Henry I, his son
1060	Philip I (the Fair), son
1108	Louis VI (the Fat), son
1137	Louis VII (the Younger), son
1180	Philip II (Augustus), son, crowned at Reims
1223	Louis VIII (the Lion), son
1226	Louis IX, son, crusader; Louis IX (1214-1270) reigned 44 years, arbitrated disputes with English King Henry III; led crusades, 1248 (captured in Egypt 1250) and 1270, when he died of plague in Tunis. Canonized 1297 as St. Louis.
1270	Philip III (the Hardy), son
1285	Philip IV (the Fair), son, king at 17
1314	Louis X (the Headstrong), son. His posthumous son, John I, lived only 7 days
1316	Philip V (the Tall), brother of Louis X
1322	Charles IV (the Fair), brother of Louis X
	House of Valois
1328	Philip VI (of Valois), grandson of Philip III
1350	John II (the Good), his son, retired to England
1364	Charles V (the Wise), son
1380	Charles VI (the Beloved), son

(Continued)

AD **Name, year of accession**

1422 Charles VII (the Victorious), son. In 1429 Joan of Arc (Jeanne d'Arc) promised Charles to oust the English, who occupied northern France. Joan won at Orleans and Patay and had Charles crowned at Reims July 17, 1429. Joan was captured May 24, 1430, and executed May 30, 1431, at Rouen for heresy. Charles ordered her rehabilitation, effected 1455.
1461 Louis XI (the Cruel), son, civil reformer
1483 Charles VIII (the Affable), son
1498 Louis XII, great-grandson of Charles V
1515 Francis I, of Angouleme, nephew, son-in-law. Francis I (1494-1547) reigned 32 years, fought 4 big wars, was patron of the arts, aided Cellini, del Sarto, Leonardo da Vinci, Rabelais, embellished Fontainebleau.
1547 Henry II, son, killed at a joust in a tournament. He was the husband of Catherine de Medicis (1519-1589) and the lover of Diane de Poitiers (1499-1566). Catherine was born in Florence, daughter of Lorenzo de Medicis. By her marriage to Henry II she became the mother of Francis II, Charles IX, Henry III and Queen Margaret (Reine Margot) wife of Henry IV. She persuaded Charles IX to order the massacre of Huguenots on the Feast of St. Bartholomew, Aug. 24, 1572, the day her daughter was married to Henry of Navarre.
1559 Francis II, son. In 1548, Mary, Queen of Scots since infancy, was betrothed when 6 to Francis, aged 4. They were married 1558. Francis died 1560, aged 16; Mary ruled Scotland, abdicated 1567.
1560 Charles IX, brother
1574 Henry III, brother, assassinated

House of Bourbon

1589 Henry IV, of Navarre, assassinated. Henry IV made enemies when he gave tolerance to Protestants by Edict of Nantes, 1598. He was grandson of Queen Margaret of Navarre, literary patron. He married Margaret of Valois, daughter of Henry II and Catherine de Medicis; was divorced; in 1600 married Marie de Medicis, who became Regent of France, 1610-17 for her son, Louis XIII, but was exiled by Richelieu, 1631.
1610 Louis XIII (the Just), son. Louis XIII (1601-1643) married Anne of Austria. His ministers were Cardinals Richelieu and Mazarin.
1643 Louis XIV (The Grand Monarch), son. Louis XIV was king 72 years. He exhausted a prosperous country in wars for thrones and territory. By revoking the Edict of Nantes (1685) he caused the emigration of the Huguenots. He said: "I am the state."
1715 Louis XV, great-grandson. Louis XV married a Polish princess; lost Canada to the English. His favorites, Mme. Pompadour and Mme. du Barry, influenced policies. Noted for saying "After me, the deluge".
1774 Louis XVI, grandson; married Marie Antoinette, daughter of Empress Maria Therese of Austria. King and queen beheaded by Revolution, 1793. Their son, called Louis XVII, died in prison, never ruled.

AD **Name, year of accession**

First Republic

1792 National Convention of the French Revolution
1795 Directory, under Barras and others
1799 Consulate, Napoleon Bonaparte, first consul. Elected consul for life, 1802.

First Empire

1804 Napoleon I, emperor. Josephine (de Beauharnais) empress, 1804-09; Marie Louise, empress, 1810-1814. Herson, François (1811-1832), titular King of Rome, later Duke de Reichstadt and "Napoleon II," never ruled. Napoleon abdicated 1814, died 1821.

Bourbons Restored

1814 Louis XVIII king; brother of Louis XVI.
1824 Charles X, brother; reactionary; deposed by the July Revolution, 1830.

House of Orleans

1830 Louis-Philippe, the "citizen king."

Second Republic

1848 Louis Napoleon Bonaparte, president, nephew of Napoleon I. He became:

Second Empire

1852 Napoleon III, emperor; Eugénie (de Montijo) empress. Lost Franco-Prussian war, deposed 1870. Son, Prince Imperial (1856-79), died in Zulu War. Eugénie died 1920.

Third Republic – Presidents

1871 Thiers, Louis Adolphe (1797-1877)
1873 MacMahon, Marshal Patrice M. de (1808-1893)
1879 Grevy, Paul J. (1807-1891)
1887 Sadi-Carnot, M. (1837-1894), assassinated
1894 Casimir-Perier, Jean P. P. (1847-1907)
1895 Fauré, François Félix (1841-1899)
1899 Loubet, Emile (1838-1929)
1906 Fallières, C. Armand (1841-1931)
1913 Poincaré, Raymond (1860-1934)
1920 Deschanel, Paul (1856-1922)
1920 Millerand, Alexandre (1859-1943)
1924 Doumergue, Gaston (1863-1937)
1931 Doumer, Paul (1857-1932), assassinated
1932 Lebrun, Albert (1871-1950), resigned 1940
1940 **Vichy govt.** under German armistice: Henri Philippe Pétain (1856-1951) Chief of State, 1940-1944.
Provisional govt. after liberation: Charles de Gaulle (1890-1970) Oct. 1944-Jan. 21, 1946; Félix Gouin (1884-1977) Jan. 23, 1946; Georges Bidault (1899-1983) June 24, 1946.

Fourth Republic – Presidents

1947 Auriol, Vincent (1884-1966)
1954 Coty, René (1882-1962)

Fifth Republic – Presidents

1959 de Gaulle, Charles André J. M. (1890-1970)
1969 Pompidou, Georges (1911-1974)
1974 Giscard d'Estaing, Valéry (1926-)
1981 Mitterrand, François (1916-)

RULERS OF MIDDLE EUROPE: RISE AND FALL OF DYNASTIES

Carolingian Dynasty

Charles the Great, or Charlemagne, ruled France, Italy, and Middle Europe; established Ostmark (later Austria); crowned Roman emperor by pope in Rome, 800 AD; died 814.

Louis I (Ludwig) the Pious, son; crowned by Charlemagne 814, d. 840.

Louis II, the German, son; succeeded to East Francia (Germany) 843-876.

Charles the Fat, son; inherited East Francia and West Francia (France) 876, reunited empire, crowned emperor by pope, 881, deposed 887.

Arnulf, nephew, 887-899. Partition of empire.

Louis the Child, 899-911, last direct descendant of Charlemagne.

Conrad I, duke of Franconia, first elected German king, 911-918, founded House of Franconia.

Saxon Dynasty; First Reich

Henry I, the Fowler, duke of Saxony, 919-936.

Otto I, the Great, 936-973, son; crowned Holy Roman Emperor by pope, 962.

Otto II, 973-983, son; failed to oust Greeks and Arabs from Sicily.

Otto III, 983-1002, son; crowned emperor at 16.

Henry II, the Saint, duke of Bavaria, 1002-1024, great-grandson of Otto the Great.

House of Franconia

Conrad II, 1024-1039, elected king of Germany.

Henry III, the Black, 1039-1056, son; deposed 3 popes; annexed Burgundy.

Henry IV, 1056-1106, son; regency by his mother, Agnes of Poitou. Banned by Pope Gregory VII, he did penance at Canossa.

Henry V, 1106-1125, son; last of Salic House.

Lothair, duke of Saxony, 1125-1137. Crowned emperor in Rome, 1134.

House of Hohenstaufen

Conrad III, duke of Swabia, 1138-1152. In 2d Crusade.

Frederick I, Barbarossa, 1152-1190; Conrad's nephew.

Henry VI, 1190-1196, took lower Italy from Normans. Son became king of Sicily.

Philip of Swabia, 1197-1208, brother.

Otto IV, of House of Welf, 1198-1215; deposed.

Frederick II, 1215-1250, son of Henry VI; king of Sicily; crowned king of Jerusalem; in 5th Crusade.

Conrad IV, 1250-1254, son; lost lower Italy to Charles of Anjou.

Conradin, 1252-1268, son, king of Jerusalem and Sicily, beheaded. Last Hohenstaufen.

Interregnum, 1254-1273, Rise of the Electors.

Transition

Rudolph I of Hapsburg, 1273-1291, defeated King Ottocar II of Bohemia. Bequeathed duchy of Austria to eldest son, Albert.

Adolph of Nassau, 1292-1298, killed in war with Albert of Austria.

Albert I, king of Germany, 1298-1308, son of Rudolph.

Henry VII, of Luxemburg, 1308-1313, crowned emperor in Rome. Seized Bohemia, 1310.

Louis IV of Bavaria (Wittelsbach), 1314-1347. Also elected was Frederick of Austria, 1314-1330 (Hapsburg). Abolition of papal sanction for election of Holy Roman Emperor.

Charles IV, of Luxemburg, 1347-1378, grandson of Henry VII, German emperor and king of Bohemia, Lombardy, Burgundy; took Mark of Brandenburg.

Wenceslaus, 1378-1400, deposed.

Rupert, Duke of Palatine, 1400-1410.

Hungary

Stephen I, house of Arpad, 997-1038. Crowned king 1000; converted Magyars; canonized 1083. After several centuries of feuds Charles Robert of Anjou became Charles I, 1308-1342.

Louis I, the Great, son, 1342-1382; joint ruler of Poland with Casimir III, 1370. Defeated Turks.

Mary, daughter, 1382-1395, ruled with husband. Sigismund of Luxemburg, 1387-1437, also king of Bohemia. As bro. of Wenceslaus he succeeded Rupert as Holy Roman Emperor, 1410.

Albert, 1438-1439, son-in-law of Sigismund; also Roman emperor as Albert II. *(See under Hapsburg.)*

Ulaszlo I of Poland, 1440-1444.

Ladislaus V, posthumous son of Albert II, 1444-1457. John Hunyadi (Hunyadi Janos), governor (1446-1452), fought Turks, Czechs; died 1456.

Matthias I (Corvinus), son of Hunyadi, 1458-1490. Shared rule of Bohemia, captured Vienna, 1485, annexed Austria, Styria, Carinthia.

Ulaszlo II (king of Bohemia), 1490-1516.

Louis II, son, aged 10, 1516-1526. Wars with Suleiman, Turk. In 1527 Hungary was split between Ferdinand I, Archduke of Austria, bro.-in-law of Louis II, and John Zapolya of Transylvania. After Turkish invasion, 1547, Hungary was split between Ferdinand, Prince John Sigismund (Transylvania) and the Turks.

House of Hapsburg

Albert V of Austria, Hapsburg, crowned king of Hungary, Jan. 1438, Roman emperor, March, 1438, as Albert II; died 1439.

Frederick III, cousin, 1440-1493. Fought Turks.

Maximilian I, son, 1493-1519. Assumed title of Holy Roman Emperor (German), 1493.

Charles V, grandson, 1519-1556. King of Spain with mother co-regent; crowned Roman emperor at Aix, 1520. Confronted Luther at Worms; attempted church reform and religious conciliation; abdicated 1556.

Ferdinand I, king of Bohemia, 1526, of Hungary, 1527; disputed. German king, 1531. Crowned Roman emperor on abdication of brother Charles V, 1556.

Maximilian II, son, 1564-1576.

Rudolph II, son, 1576-1612.

Matthias, brother, 1612-1619, king of Bohemia and Hungary.

Ferdinand II of Styria, king of Bohemia, 1617, of Hungary, 1618, Roman emperor, 1619. Bohemian Protestants deposed him, elected Frederick V of Palatine, starting Thirty Years War.

Ferdinand III, son, king of Hungary, 1625, Bohemia, 1627, Roman emperor, 1637. Peace of Westphalia, 1648, ended war. Leopold I, 1658-1705; Joseph I, 1705-1711; Charles VI, 1711-1740.

Maria Theresa, daughter, 1740-1780, Archduchess of Austria, queen of Hungary; ousted pretender, Charles VII, crowned 1742; in 1745 obtained election of her husband Francis I as Roman emperor and co-regent (d. 1765). Fought Seven Years' War with Frederick II (the Great) of Prussia. Mother of Marie Antoinette, Queen of France.

Joseph II, son, 1765-1790, Roman emperor, reformer; powers restricted by Empress Maria Theresa until her death, 1780. First partition of Poland. Leopold II, 1790-1792.

Francis II, son, 1792-1835. Fought Napoleon. Proclaimed first hereditary emperor of Austria, 1804. Forced to abdicate as Roman emperor, 1806; last use of title. Ferdinand I, son, 1835-1848, abdicated during revolution.

Austro-Hungarian Monarchy

Francis Joseph I, nephew, 1848-1916, emperor of Austria, king of Hungary. Dual monarchy of Austria-Hungary formed, 1867. After assassination of heir, Archduke Francis Ferdinand, June 28, 1914, Austrian diplomacy precipitated World War I.

Charles I, grand-nephew, 1916-1918, last emperor of Austria and king of Hungary. Abdicated Nov. 11-13, 1918, died 1922.

Rulers of Prussia

Nucleus of Prussia was the Mark of Brandenburg. First margrave was Albert the Bear (Albrecht), 1134-1170. First Hohenzollern margrave was Frederick, burgrave of Nuremberg, 1417-1440.

Frederick William, 1640-1688, the Great Elector. Son, Frederick III, 1688-1713, was crowned King Frederick of Prussia, 1701.

Frederick William I, son, 1713-1740.

Frederick II, the Great, son, 1740-1786, annexed Silesia, part of Austria.

Frederick William II, nephew, 1786-1797.

Frederick William III, son, 1797-1840. Napoleonic wars.

Frederick William IV, son, 1840-1861. Uprising of 1848 and first parliament and constitution.

Second and Third Reich

William I, 1861-1888, brother. Annexation of Schleswig and Hanover; Franco-Prussian war, 1870-71, proclamation of German Reich, Jan. 18, 1871, at Versailles; William, German emperor (Deutscher Kaiser), Bismarck, chancellor.

Frederick III, son, 1888.

William II, son, 1888-1918. Led Germany in World War I, abdicated as German emperor and king of Prussia, Nov. 9, 1918. Died in exile in Netherlands June 4, 1941. Minor rulers of Bavaria, Saxony, Wurttemberg also abdicated.

Germany proclaimed a republic at Weimar, July 1, 1919. Presidents: Frederick Ebert, 1919-1925, Paul von Hindenburg-Beneckendorff, 1925, reelected 1932, d. Aug. 2, 1934. Adolf Hitler, chancellor, chosen successor as Leader-Chancellor (Fuehrer & Reichskanzler) of Third Reich. Annexed Austria, March, 1938. Precipitated World War II, 1939-1945. Committed suicide April 30, 1945.

RULERS OF POLAND

House of Piasts

Miesko I, 962?-992; Poland Christianized 966. Expansion under 3 Boleslavs: I, 992-1025, son, crowned king 1024; II, 1058-1079, great-grandson, exiled after killing bishop Stanislav who became chief patron saint of Poland: III, 1106-1138, nephew, divided Poland among 4 sons, eldest suzerain.

1138-1306, feudal division. 1226 founding in Prussia of military order Teutonic Knights. 1226 invasion by Tartars/Mongols.

Vladislav I, 1306-1333, reunited most Polish territories, crowned king 1320. Casimir III the Great, 1333-1370, son, developed economic, cultural life, foreign policy.

House of Anjou

Louis I, 1370-1382, nephew/identical with Louis I of Hungary.

Jadwiga, 1384-1399, daughter, married 1386 Jagiello, Grand Duke of Lituania.

House of Jagelloneans

Vladislav II, 1386-1434, Christianized Lituania, founded personal union between Poland & Lituania. Defeated 1410 Teutonic Knights at Grunwald.

Vladislav III, 1434-1444, son, simultaneously king of Hungary. Fought Turks, killed 1444 in battle of Varna.

Casimir IV, 1446-1492, brother, competed with Hapsburgs, put son Vladislav on throne of Bohemia, later also of Hungary.

Sigismund I, 1506-1548, brother, patronized science & arts, his & son's reign "Golden Age."

Sigismund II, 1548-1572, son, established 1569 real union of Poland and Lituania (lasted until 1795).

Elective kings

Polish nobles proclaimed 1572 Poland a Republic headed by king to be elected by whole nobility.

Stephen Batory, 1576-1586, duke of Transylvania, married Ann, sister of Sigismund II August. Fought Russians.

Sigismund III Vasa, 1587-1632, nephew of Sigismund II. 1592-1598 also king of Sweden. His generals fought Russians, Turks.

Vladislav II Vasa, 1632-1648, son. Fought Russians.

John II Casimir Vasa, 1648-1668, brother. Fought Cossacks, Swedes, Russians, Turks, Tartars (the "Deluge"). Abdicated 1668.

John III Sobieski, 1674-1696. Won Vienna from besieging Turks, 1683.

Stanislav II, 1764-1795, last king. Encouraged reforms; 1791 1st modern Constitution in Europe. 1772, 1793, 1795 Poland partitioned among Russia, Prussia, Austria. Unsuccessful insurrection against foreign invasion 1794 under Kosciuszko, Amer-Polish gen.

1795-1918 Poland under foreign rule

1807-1815 Grand Duchy of Warsaw created by Napoleon I, Frederick August of Saxony grand duke.

1815 Congress of Vienna proclaimed part of Poland +37 Kingdom" in personal union with Russia.

Polish uprisings: 1830 against Russia, 1846, 1848 against Austria, 1863 against Russia—all repressed.

1918-1939 Second Republic

1918-1922 Head of State Jozef Pilsudski. Presidents: Gabriel Narutowicz 1922, assassinated. Stanislav Wojciechowski 1922-1926, had to abdicate after Pilsudski's coup d'état. Ignacy Moscicki, 1926-1939, ruled with Pilsudski as (until 1935) virtual dictator.

1939-1945 Poland under foreign occupation

Nazi aggression Sept. 1939. Polish govt.-in-exile, first in France, then in England. Vladislav Raczkiewicz pres., Gen. Vladislav Sikorski, then Stanislav Mikolajczyk, prime ministers. Polish Committee of Natl. Liberation proclaimed at Lublin July 1944, transformed into govt. Jan. 1, 1945.

RULERS OF DENMARK, SWEDEN, NORWAY

Denmark

Earliest rulers invaded Britain; King Canute, who ruled in London 1016-1035, was most famous. The Valdemars furnished kings until the 15th century. In 1282 the Danes won the first national assembly, Danehof, from King Erik V.

Most redoubtable medieval character was Margaret, daughter of Valdemar IV, born 1353, married at 10 to King Haakon VI of Norway. In 1376 she had her first infant son Olaf made king of Denmark. After his death, 1387, she was regent of Denmark and Norway. In 1388 Sweden accepted her as sovereign. In 1389 she made her grand-nephew, Duke Erik of Pomerania, titular king of Denmark, Sweden, and Norway, with herself as regent. In 1397 she effected the Union of Kalmar of the three kingdoms and had Erik VII crowned. In 1439 the three kingdoms deposed him and elected, 1440, Christopher of Bavaria king (Christopher III). On his death, 1448, the union broke up.

Succeeding rulers were unable to enforce their claims as rulers of Sweden until 1520, when Christian II conquered Sweden. He was thrown out 1522, and in 1523 Gustavus Vasa united Sweden. Denmark continued to dominate Norway until the Napoleonic wars, when Frederick VI, 1808-1839, joined the Napoleonic cause after Britain had destroyed the Danish fleet, 1807. In 1814 he was forced to cede Norway to Sweden and Helgoland to Britain, receiving Lauenburg. Successors Christian VIII, 1839; Frederick VII, 1848; Christian IX, 1863; Frederick VIII, 1906; Christian X, 1912; Frederick IX, 1947; Margrethe II, 1972.

Sweden

Early kings ruled at Uppsala, but did not dominate the country. Sverker, c1130-c1156, united the Swedes and Goths. In 1435 Sweden obtained the Riksdag, or parliament. After the Union of Kalmar, 1397, the Danes either ruled or harried the country until Christian II of Denmark conquered it anew, 1520. This led to a rising under Gustavus Vasa, who ruled Sweden 1523-1560, and established an independent kingdom. Charles IX, 1599-1611, crowned 1604, conquered Moscow. Gustavus II Adolphus, 1611-1632, was called the Lion of the North. Later rulers: Christina, 1632; Charles X, Gustavus 1654; Charles XI, 1660; Charles XII (invader of Russia and Poland, defeated at Poltava, June 28, 1709), 1697; Ulrika Eleanora, sister, elected queen 1718; Frederick I (of Hesse), her husband, 1720; Adolphus Frederick, 1751; Gustavus III, 1771; Gustavus IV Adolphus, 1792; Charles XIII, 1809. (Union with Norway began 1814.) Charles XIV John, 1818. He was Jean Bernadotte, Napoleon's Prince of Ponte Corvo, elected 1810 to succeed Charles XIII. He founded the present dynasty: Oscar I, 1844, Charles XV, 1859; Oscar II, 1872; Gustavus V, 1907; Gustav VI Adolf, 1950; Carl XVI Gustaf, 1973.

Norway

Overcoming many rivals, Harald Haarfager, 872-930, conquered Norway, Orkneys, and Shetlands; Olaf I, great-grandson, 995-1000, brought Christianity into Norway, Iceland, and Greenland. In 1035 Magnus the Good also became king of Denmark. Haakon V, 1299-1319, had married his daughter to Erik of Sweden. Their son, Magnus, became ruler of Norway and Sweden at 6. His son, Haakon VI, married Margaret of Denmark; their son Olaf IV became king of Norway and Denmark, followed by Margaret's regency and the Union of Kalmar, 1397.

In 1450 Norway became subservient to Denmark. Christian IV, 1588-1648, founded Christiania, now Oslo. After Napoleonic wars, when Denmark ceded Norway to Sweden, a strong nationalist movement forced recognition of Norway as an independent kingdom united with Sweden under the Swedish kings, 1814-1905. In 1905 the union was dissolved and Prince Carl of Denmark became Haakon VII. He died Sept. 21, 1957, aged 85; succeeded by son, Olav V, 1957.

RULERS OF THE NETHERLANDS AND BELGIUM

The Netherlands (Holland)

William Frederick, Prince of Orange, led a revolt against French rule, 1813, and was crowned King of the Netherlands, 1815. Belgium seceded Oct. 4, 1830, after a revolt, and formed a separate government. The change was ratified by the two kingdoms by treaty Apr. 19, 1839.

Succession: William II, son, 1840; William III, son, 1849; Wilhelmina, daughter of William III and his 2d wife Princess Emma of Waldeck, 1890; Wilhelmina abdicated, Sept. 4, 1948, in favor of daughter, Juliana. Juliana abdicated Apr. 30, 1980, in favor of daughter, Beatrix.

Belgium

A national congress elected Prince Leopold of Saxe-Coburg King; he took the throne July 21, 1831, as Leopold I. Succession: Leopold II, son 1865; Albert I, nephew of Leopold II, 1909; Leopold III, son of Albert, 1934; Prince Charles, Regent 1944; Leopold returned 1950, yielded powers to son Baudouin, Prince Royal, Aug. 6, 1950, abdicated July 16, 1951. Baudouin I took throne July 17, 1951.

For political history prior to 1830 see articles on the Netherlands and Belgium in Nations section.

ROMAN RULERS

From Romulus to the end of the Empire in the West. Rulers of the Roman Empire in the East sat in Constantinople and for a brief period in Nicaea, until the capture of Constantinople by the Turks in 1453, when Byzantium was succeeded by the Ottoman Empire.

BC	Name
	The Kingdom
753	Romulus (Quirinus)
716	Numa Pompilius
673	Tullus Hostilius
640	Ancus Marcius
616	L. Tarquinius Priscus
578	Servius Tullius
534	L. Tarquinius Superbus
	The Republic
509	Consulate established
509	Quaestorship instituted
498	Dictatorship introduced
494	Plebeian Tribunate created
494	Plebeian Aedileship created
444	Consular Tribunate organized
435	Censorship instituted
366	Praetorship established
366	Curule Aedileship created
362	Military Tribunate elected
326	Proconsulate introduced
311	Naval Duumvirate elected
217	Dictatorship of Fabius Maximus
133	Tribunate of Tiberius Gracchus
123	Tribunate of Gaius Gracchus
82	Dictatorship of Sulla
60	First Triumvirate formed (Caesar, Pompeius, Crassus)
46	Dictatorship of Caesar
43	Second Triumvirate formed (Octavianus, Antonius, Lepidus)
	The Empire
27	Augustus (Gaius Julius Caesar Octavianus)
AD	
14	Tiberius I
37	Gaius Caesar (Caligula)
41	Claudius I
54	Nero
68	Galba
69	Galba; Otho, Vitellius
69	Vespasianus
79	Titus
81	Domitianus

AD	Name
96	Nerva
98	Trajanus
117	Hadrianus
138	Antoninus Pius
161	Marcus Aurelius and Lucius Verus
169	Marcus Aurelius (alone)
180	Commodus
193	Pertinax; Julianus I
193	Septimius Severus
211	Caracalla and Geta
212	Caracalla (alone)
217	Macrinus
218	Elagabalus (Heliogabalus)
222	Alexander Severus
235	Maximinus I (the Thracian)
238	Gordianus I and Gordianus II; Pupienus and Balbinus
238	Gordianus III
244	Philippus (the Arabian)
249	Decius
251	Gallus and Volusianus
253	Aemilianus
253	Valerianus and Gallienus
258	Gallienus (alone)
268	Claudius Gothicus
270	Quintillus
270	Aurelianus
275	Tacitus
276	Florianus
276	Probus
282	Carus
283	Carinus and Numerianus
284	Diocletianus
286	Diocletianus and Maximianus
305	Galerius and Constantius I
306	Galerius, Maximinus II, Severus I
307	Galerius, Maximinus II, Constantinus I, Licinius, Maxentius
311	Maximinus II, Constantinus I, Licinius, Maxentius
314	Maximinus II, Constantinus I, Licinius

AD	Name
314	Constantinus I and Licinius
324	Constantinus I (the Great)
337	Constantinus II, Constans I, Constantius II
340	Constantius II and Constans I
350	Constantius II
361	Julianus II (the Apostate)
363	Jovianus
	West (Rome) and East (Constantinople)
364	Valentinianus I (West) and Valens (East)
367	Valentinianus I with Gratianus (West) and Valens (East)
375	Gratianus with Valentinianus II (West) and Valens (East)
378	Gratianus with Valentinianus II (West) Theodosius I (East)
383	Valentinianus II (West) and Theodosius I (East)
394	Theodosius I (the Great)
395	Honorius (West) and Arcadius (East)
408	Honorius (West) and Theodosius II (East)
423	Valentinianus III (West) and Theodosius II (East)
450	Valentinianus III (West) and Marcianus (East)
455	Maximus (West), Avitus (West); Marcianus (East)
456	Avitus (West), Marcianus (East)
457	Majorianus (West), Leo I (East)
461	Severus II (West), Leo I (East)
467	Anthemius (West), Leo I (East)
472	Olybrius (West), Leo I (East)
473	Glycerius (West), Leo I (East)
474	Julius Nepos (West), Leo II (East)
475	Romulus Augustulus (West) and Zeno (East)
476	End of Empire in West; Odovacar, King, drops title of Emperor; murdered by King Theodoric of Ostrogoths 493 AD

RULERS OF MODERN ITALY

After the fall of Napoleon in 1814, the Congress of Vienna, 1815, restored Italy as a political patchwork, comprising the Kingdom of Naples and Sicily, the Papal States, and smaller units. Piedmont and Genoa were awarded to Sardinia, ruled by King Victor Emmanuel I of Savoy.

United Italy emerged under the leadership of Camillo, Count di Cavour (1810-1861), Sardinian prime minister. Agitation was led by Giuseppe Mazzini (1805-1872) and Giuseppe Garibaldi (1807-1882), soldier, Victor Emmanuel I abdicated 1821. After a brief regency for a brother, Charles Albert was King 1831-1849, abdicating when defeated by the Austrians at Novara. Succeeded by Victor Emmanuel II, 1849-1861.

In 1859 France forced Austria to cede Lombardy to Sardinia, which gave rights to Savoy and Nice to France. In 1860 Garibaldi led 1,000 volunteers in a spectacular campaign, took Sicily and expelled the King of Naples. In 1860 the House of Savoy annexed Tuscany, Parma, Modena, Romagna, the Two Sicilies, the Marches, and Umbria. Victor Emmanuel assumed the title of King of Italy at Turin Mar. 17, 1861. In 1866 he allied with Prussia in the Austro-Prussian War, with Prussia's victory received Venetia. On Sept. 20, 1870, his troops under Gen. Raffaele Cadorna entered Rome and took over the Papal States, ending the temporal power of the Roman Catholic Church.

Succession: Umberto I; 1878, assassinated 1900; Victor Emmanuel III, 1900, abdicated 1946, died 1947; Umberto II, 1946, ruled a month. In 1921 Benito Mussolini (1883-1945) formed the Fascist party and became prime minister Oct. 31, 1922. He made the King Emperor of Ethiopia, 1937; entered World War II as an ally of Hitler. He was deposed July 25, 1943.

At a plebiscite June 2, 1946, Italy voted for a republic; Premier Alcide de Gasperi became chief of state June 13, 1946. On June 28, 1946, the Constituent Assembly elected Enrico de Nicola, Liberal, provisional president. Successive presidents: Luigi Einaudi, elected May 11, 1948, Giovanni Gronchi, Apr. 29, 1955; Antonio Segni, May 6, 1962; Giuseppe Saragat, Dec. 28, 1964; Giovanni Leone, Dec. 29, 1971; Alessandro Pertini, July 9, 1978; Francesco Cossiga, July 9, 1985; Oscar Luigi Scalfaro, May 25, 1992.

RULERS OF SPAIN

From 8th to 11th centuries Spain was dominated by the Moors (Arabs and Berbers). The Christian reconquest established small kingdoms (Asturias, Aragon, Castile, Catalonia, Leon, Navarre, and Valencia). In 1474 Isabella, b. 1451, became Queen of Castile & Leon. Her husband, Ferdinand, b. 1452, inherited Aragon 1479, with Catalonia, Valencia, and the Balearic Islands, became Ferdinand V of Castile. By Isabella's request Pope Sixtus IV established the Inquisition, 1478. Last Moorish kingdom, Granada, fell 1492. Columbus opened New World of colonies, 1492. Isabella died 1504, succeeded by her daughter, Juana "the Mad," but Ferdinand ruled until his death 1516.

Charles I, b. 1500, son of Juana and grandson of Ferdinand and Isabella, and of Maximilian I of Hapsburg; succeeded later as Holy Roman Emperor, Charles V, 1520; abdicated 1556. Philip II, son, 1556-1598, inherited only Spanish throne; conquered Portugal, fought Turks, persecuted non-Catholics, sent Armada against England. Was married to Mary I of England, 1554-1558. Succession: Philip III, 1598-1621; Philip IV, 1621-1665; Charles II, 1665-1700, left Spain to Philip of Anjou, grandson of Louis XIV, who as Philip V, 1700-1746, founded Bourbon dynasty. Ferdinand VI, 1746-1759; Charles III, 1759-1788; Charles IV, 1788-1808, abdicated.

Napoleon now dominated politics and made his brother Joseph King of Spain 1808, but the Spanish ousted him in 1813. Ferdinand VII, 1808, 1814-1833, lost American colonies; succeeded by daughter Isabella II, aged 3, with wife Maria Christina of Naples regent until 1843. Isabella deposed by revolution 1868. Elected king by the Cortes, Amadeo of Savoy, 1870; abdicated 1873. First republic, 1873-74. Alphonso XII, son of Isabella, 1875-85. His posthumous son was Alphonso XIII, with his mother, Queen Maria Christina regent; Spanish-American war, Spain lost Cuba, gave up Puerto Rico, Philippines, Sulu Is., Marianas. Alphonso took throne 1902, aged 16, married British Princess Victoria Eugenia of Battenberg. The dictatorship of Primo de Rivera, 1923-30, precipitated the revolution of 1931. Alphonso agreed to leave without formal abdication. The monarchy was abolished and the second republic established, with socialist backing. Presidents were Niceto Alcala Zamora, to 1936, when Manuel Aza a was chosen.

In July, 1936, the army in Morocco revolted against the government and General Francisco Franco led the troops into Spain. The revolution succeeded by Feb., 1939, when Aza a resigned. Franco became chief of state, with provisions that if he was incapacitated the Regency Council by two-thirds vote may propose a king to the Cortes, which must have a two-thirds majority to elect him.

Alphonso XIII died in Rome Feb. 28, 1941, aged 54. His property and citizenship had been restored.

A succession law restoring the monarchy was approved in a 1947 referendum. Prince Juan Carlos, son of the pretender to the throne, was designated by Franco and the Cortes in 1969 as the future king and chief of state. Upon Franco's death, Nov. 20, 1975, Juan Carlos was proclaimed king, Nov. 22, 1975.

LEADERS IN THE SOUTH AMERICAN WARS OF LIBERATION

Simon Bolivar (1783-1830), Jose Francisco de San Martin (1778-1850), and Francisco Antonio Gabriel Miranda (1750-1816), are among the heroes of the early 19th century struggles of South American nations to free themselves from Spain. All three, and their contemporaries, operated in periods of factional strife, during which soldiers and civilians suffered.

Miranda, a Venezuelan, who had served with the French in the American Revolution and commanded parts of the French Revolutionary armies in the Netherlands, attempted to start a revolt in Venezuela in 1806 and failed. In 1810, with British and American backing, he returned and was briefly a dictator, until the British withdrew their support. In 1812 he was overcome by the royalists in Venezuela and taken prisoner, dying in a Spanish prison in 1816.

San Martin was born in Argentina and during 1789-1811 served in campaigns of the Spanish armies in Europe and Africa. He first joined the independence movement in Argentina in 1812 and in 1817 invaded Chile with 4,000 men over the mountain passes. Here he and Gen. Bernardo O'Higgins (1778-1842) defeated the Spaniards at Chacabuco, 1817, and O'Higgins was named Liberator and became first director of Chile, 1817-23. In 1821 San Martin occupied Lima and Callao, Peru, and became protector of Peru.

Bolivar, the greatest leader of South American liberation from Spain, was born in Venezuela, the son of an aristocratic family. He first served under Miranda in 1812 and in 1813 captured Caracas, where he was named Liberator. Forced out next year by civil strife, he led a campaign that captured Bogota in 1814. In 1817 he was again in control of Venezuela and was named dictator. He organized Nueva Granada with the help of General Francisco de Paula Santander (1792-1840). By joining Nueva Granada, Venezuela, and the present terrain of Panama and Ecuador, the republic of Colombia was formed with Bolivar president. After numerous setbacks he decisively defeated the Spaniards in the second battle of Carabobo, Venezuela, June 24, 1821.

In May, 1822, Gen. Antonio Jose de Sucre, Bolivar's lieutenant, took Quito. Bolivar went to Guayaquil to confer with San Martin, who resigned as protector of Peru and withdrew from politics. With a new army of Colombians and Peruvians Bolivar defeated the Spaniards in a battle at Jun n in 1824 and cleared Peru.

De Sucre organized Charcas (Upper Peru) as Republica Bolivar (now Bolivia) and acted as president in place of Bolivar, who wrote its constitution. De Sucre defeated the Spanish faction of Peru at Ayacucho, Dec. 19, 1824.

Continued civil strife finally caused the Colombian federation to break apart. Santander turned against Bolivar, but the latter defeated him and banished him. In 1828 Bolivar gave up the presidency he had held precariously for 14 years. He became ill from tuberculosis and died Dec. 17, 1830. He is buried in the national pantheon in Caracas.

RULERS OF PRE-REVOLUTIONARY RUSSIA; LEADERS OF THE USSR

First ruler to consolidate Slavic tribes was Rurik, leader of the Russians who established himself at Novgorod, 862 A.D. He and his immediate successors had Scandinavian affiliations. They moved to Kiev after 972 AD and ruled as Dukes of Kiev. In 988 Vladimir was converted and adopted the Byzantine Greek Orthodox service, later modified by Slav influences. Important as organizer and lawgiver was Yaroslav, 1019-1054, whose daughters married kings of Norway, Hungary, and France. His grandson, Vladimir II (Monomakh), 1113-1125, was progenitor of several rulers, but in 1169 Andrew Bogolubski overthrew Kiev and began the line known as Grand Dukes of Vladimir.

Of the Grand Dukes of Vladimir, Alexander Nevsky, 1246-1263, had a son, Daniel, first to be called Duke of Muscovy (Moscow) who ruled 1294-1303. His successors became Grand Dukes of Muscovy. After Dmitri III Donskoi defeated the Tartars in 1380, they also became Grand Dukes of all Russia. Independence of the Tartars and considerable territorial expansion were achieved under Ivan III, 1462-1505.

Tsars of Muscovy—Ivan III was referred to in church ritual as Tsar. He married Sofia, niece of the last Byzantine emperor. His successor, Basil III, died in 1533 when Basil's son Ivan was only 3. He became Ivan IV, "the Terrible"; crowned 1547 as Tsar of all the Russias, ruled till 1584. Under the weak rule of his son, Feodor I, 1584-1598, Boris Godunov had control. The dynasty died, and after years of tribal strife and intervention by Polish and Swedish armies, the Russians united under 17-year-old Michael Romanov, distantly related to the first wife of Ivan IV. He ruled 1613-1645 and established the Romanov line. Fourth ruler after Michael was Peter I. .

Tsars, or Emperors of Russia (Romanovs)—Peter I, 1682-1725, known as Peter the Great, took title of Emperor in 1721. His successors and dates of accession were: Catherine, his widow, 1725; Peter II, his grandson, 1727; Anne, Duchess of Courland, 1730, daughter of Peter the Great's brother, Tsar Ivan V; Ivan VI, 1740, great-grandson of Ivan V, child, kept in prison and murdered 1764; Elizabeth, daughter of Peter I, 1741; Peter III, grandson of Peter I, 1761, deposed 1762 for his consort, Catherine II, former princess of Anhalt Zerbst (Germany) who is known as Catherine the Great; Paul I, her son, 1796, killed 1801; Alexander I, son of Paul, 1801, defeated Napoleon; Nicholas I, his brother, 1825; Alexander II, son of Nicholas, 1855, assassinated 1881 by terrorists; Alexander III, son, 1881.

Nicholas II, son, 1894-1917, last Tsar of Russia, was forced to abdicate by the Revolution that followed losses to Germany in WWI. The Tsar, the Empress, the Tsesarevich (Crown Prince) and the Tsar's 4 daughters were murdered by the Bolsheviks in Ekaterinburg, July 16, 1918.

Provisional Government—Prince Georgi Lvov and Alexander Kerensky, premiers, 1917.

Union of Soviet Socialist Republics

Bolshevik Revolution, Nov. 7, 1917, displaced Kerensky; council of People's Commissars formed, Lenin (Vladimir Ilyich Ulyanov), premier. Lenin died Jan. 21, 1924. Aleksei Rykov (executed 1938) and V. M. Molotov held the office, but actual ruler was Joseph Stalin (Joseph Vissarionovich Djugashvili), general secretary of the Central Committee of the Communist Party. Stalin became president of the Council of Ministers (premier) May 7, 1941, died Mar. 5, 1953. Succeeded by Georgi M. Malenkov, as head of the Council and premier and Nikita S. Khrushchev, first secretary of the Central Committee. Malenkov resigned Feb. 8, 1955, became deputy premier, was dropped July 3, 1957. Marshal Nikolai A. Bulganin became premier Feb. 8, 1955; was demoted and Khrushchev became premier Mar. 27 1958. Khrushchev was ousted Oct. 14-15, 1964, replaced by Leonid I. Brezhnev as first secretary of the party and by Aleksei N. Kosygin as premier. On June 16, 1977, Brezhnev took office as president. Brezhnev died Nov. 10, 1982; 2 days later the Central Committee unanimously elected former KGB head Yuri V. Andropov president. Andropov died Feb. 9, 1984; on Feb. 13, Konstantin U. Chernenko was chosen by Central Committee as its general secretary. Chernenko died Mar. 10, 1985. On Mar. 11, he was succeeded as general secretary by Mikhail Gorbachev, who replaced Andrei Gromyko as president on Oct. 1, 1988. Gorbachev resigned Dec. 25, 1991, and the Soviet Union officially disbanded the next day. A loose Commonwealth of Independent States, made up of 11 of the 15 former Soviet constituent republics, was created.

GOVERNMENTS OF CHINA

(Until 221 BC and frequently thereafter, China was not a unified state. Where dynastic dates overlap, the rulers or events referred to appeared in different areas of China.)

Hsia	c1994BC	c1523BC
Shang	c1523	c1028
Western Chou	c1027	770
Eastern Chou	770	256
Warring States	403	222
Ch'in (first unified empire)	221	206
Han	202BC	220AD
Western Han (expanded Chinese state beyond the Yellow and Yangtze River valleys)	202BC	9AD
Hsin (Wang Mang, usurper)	9AD	23AD
Eastern Han (expanded Chinese state into Indo-China and Turkestan)	25	220
Three Kingdoms (Wei, Shu, Wu)	220	265
Chin (western)	265	317
(eastern)	317	420
Northern Dynasties (followed several short-lived governments by Turks, Mongols, etc.)	386	581
Southern Dynasties (capital: Nanking)	420	589
Sui (reunified China)	581	618
Tang (a golden age of Chinese culture; capital: Sian)	618	906
Five Dynasties (Yellow River basin)	902	960
Ten Kingdoms (southern China)	907	979
Liao (Khitan Mongols; capital: Peking)	947	1125
Sung	960	1279
Northern Sung (reunified central and southern China)	960	1126
Western Hsai (non-Chinese rulers in northwest)	990	1227

Chin (Tartars; drove Sung out of central China)	1115 - 1234	Ch'ing (Manchus, descendents of Tartars)	1644 - 1911
Yuan (Mongols; Kublai Khan made Peking his capital in 1267)	1271 - 1368	Republic (disunity; provincial rulers, warlords)	1912 - 1949
Ming (China reunified under Chinese rule; capital: Nanking, then Peking in 1420)	1368 - 1644	People's Republic of China	1949 - —

Leaders Since 1949

Mao Zedong	Chairman, Central People's Administrative Council, Communist Party (CPC), 1949-1976	Zhao Ziyang	Premier, 1980-88; CPC Chairman, 1987-89
Zhou Enlai	Premier, foreign minister, 1949-1976	Hu Yaobang	CPC Chairman, 1981-1987
Deng Xiaoping	Vice Premier, 1949-1976; 1977-1987	Li Xiannian	President, 1983-1988
Liu Shaoqi	President, 1959-1969	Yong Shang-Kun	President, 1988-1993
Hua Guofeng	Premier, 1976-1980; CPC Chairman, 1976-1981	Li Peng	Premier, 1988-
		Jiang Zemin	President, 1993-

BRITISH ISLES GEOGRAPHY

British Isles Facts & Figures

The British Isles is a geographical term covering England, Scotland, Wales, Northern Ireland and the Republic of Ireland.
Area: 121,544 sq miles (314,798 sq km)

The United Kingdom is the name given to England, Scotland, Wales and Northern Ireland, including most islands.
Area: 94,249 sq miles (244,103 sq km)
Max. length: 787 miles (1,264 km) (Out Stack, off Unst, Shetland Islands to St Agnes, Isles of Scilly)
Max. width: 417 miles (670 km) (western end of County Fermanagh, Northern Ireland, to Lowestoft, Suffolk)

Great Britain includes mainland England, Scotland and Wales. The name came into being with the 1707 Act of Union.
Area: 88,797 sq miles (229,984 sq km)
Max. length: 605 miles (974 km) (Dunnet Head, Caithness, to the Lizard peninsula, Cornwall)
Max. width: 330 miles (531 km) (Ardnamurchan Point, Argyll, to Lowestoft, Suffolk)

England, including all the islands (except the Isle of Man & the Channel Islands) off the English coast, consists of 46 counties.
Area: 52,194 sq miles (135,704 sq km)
Capital: London

English Counties

Name	Area (sq miles/sq km)		Population (at mid-1991)
Avon	538	1,347	919,800
Bedfordshire	494	1,235	514,200
Berkshire	504	1,259	716,500
Buckinghamshire	753	1,883	619,500
Cambridgeshire	1,361	3,402	640,700
Cheshire	933	2,333	937,300
Cleveland	239	598	541,100
Cornwall & Isles of Scilly	1,426	3,564	469,300
Cumbria	2,730	6,825	486,900
Derbyshire	1,052	2,631	915,000
Devon	2,684	6,711	1,008,300
Dorset	1,062	2,654	645,200
Durham	974	2,434	589,800
East Sussex	718	1,795	670,600
Essex	1,469	3,672	1,495,600
Gloucestershire	1,057	2,643	520,600
Greater London	632	1,579	6,378,600
Greater Manchester	515	1,287	2,445,200
Hampshire	1,512	3,780	1,511,900
Hereford & Worcester	1,570	3,926	667,800
Hertfordshire	654	1,636	951,500
Humberside	1,405	3,513	845,200
Isle of Wight	152	381	126,600
Kent	1,492	3,731	1,485,600
Lancashire	1,228	3,070	1,365,100
Leicestershire	1,021	2,553	860,500
Lincolnshire	2,367	5,918	573,900
Merseyside	262	654	1,376,800
Norfolk	2,150	5,375	736,700
Northamptonshire	947	2,368	568,900
Northumberland	2,013	5,032	300,600
North Yorkshire	3,325	8,312	698,800
Nottinghamshire	864	2,161	980,600
Oxfordshire	1,043	2,608	553,800
Shropshire	1,396	3,490	401,600
Somerset	1,381	3,452	459,100
South Yorkshire	624	1,560	1,249,300
Staffordshire	1,086	2,716	1,020,300
Suffolk	1,519	3,707	629,900
Surrey	672	2,679	997,000
Tyne & Wear	216	540	1,087,000
Warwickshire	792	1,980	477,000
West Midlands	360	899	2,500,400
West Sussex	796	1,989	692,800
West Yorkshire	814	2,036	1,984,700
Wiltshire	1,392	3,479	553,300

Wales, including all the islands off the Welsh coast, is a principality, its head being the Prince of Wales. It has 8 counties.
Area: 8,305 sq miles (21,593 sq km)
Capital: Cardiff

Welsh Counties

Name	Area (sq miles/sq km)		Population (at mid-1991)
Clwyd	972	2,430	401,500
Dyfed	2,306	5,766	341,600
Gwent	550	1,376	432,300
Gwynedd	1,545	3,863	238,600
Mid Glamorgan	407	1,017	526,500
Powys	2,031	5,077	116,500
South Glamorgan	166	416	383,300
West Glamorgan	328	820	357,800

Scotland, including all the islands off the Scottish coast, consists of 9 regions and 3 island authority areas.
Area: 30,987 sq miles (80,566 sq km)
Capital: Edinburgh

Scottish Regions

Name	Area (sq miles/sq km)		Population (at mid-1990)
Borders	1,886	4,714	103,500
Central	1,054	2,636	272,100
Dumfries & Galloway	2,558	6,395	148,400
Fife	529	1,307	345,900
Grampian	3,482	8,704	506,100
Highland	10,122	25,303	204,300
Lothian	702	1,755	749,600
Strathclyde	5,541	13,852	2,306,000
Tayside	3,001	7,503	394,000
Island Authority Areas			
Orkney Islands	390	975	19,570
Shetland Islands	563	1,408	22,270
Western Isles	1,156	2,890	30,660

Northern Ireland, under direct rule from Westminster since 1974, consists of 6 counties (Antrim, Armagh, Down, Fermanagh, Londonderry and Tyrone).
Area: 5,452 sq miles (14,120 sq km)
Capital: Belfast

Northern Irish Councils

(Statistics are prepared under District Councils rather than geographical counties.)

Name	Area (sq miles/sq km)		Population (at mid-1991)
Antrim	229	572	65,400
Ards	148	369	295,100
Armagh	269	672	58,100
Ballymena	255	638	57,700
Ballymoney	167	419	98,700
Banbridge	178	445	72,600
Belfast City	48	121	47,600
Carrickfergus	35	87	57,300
Castlereagh	34	85	24,100
Coleraine	194	485	31,000
Cookstown	249	623	48,600
Craigavon	152	381	27,700
Derry City	153	382	29,000
Down	258	646	33,200
Dungannon	312	779	15,000
Fermanagh	750	1,875	72,900
Larne	135	338	49,100
Limavady	235	587	32,100
Lisburn	177	444	78,200
Magherafelt	229	573	43,800
Moyle	198	495	89,700
Newry	358	895	50,600
Newtownabbey	64	160	29,900
North Down	29	74	100,500
Omagh	451	1,129	45,800
Strabane	348	870	35,700

Counties of the United Kingdom

The Republic of Ireland

The Republic of Ireland is divided into 4 provinces, which are further divided into 26 counties.
Area: 27,558 sq miles (68,895 sq km)
Capital: Dublin

Irish Republic Provinces & Counties

Name	Area (sq miles/sq km)		Population (preliminary 1991 figures)
CONNACHT	6,848	17,122	422,909
Galway	2,376	5,940	180,304
Leitrim	610	1,525	25,297
Mayo	2,159	5,398	110,696
Roscommon	985	2,463	51,876
Sligo	718	1,796	54,736
LEINSTER	7,853	19,633	1,860,037
Carlow	359	896	40,946
Dublin	368	921	1,024,429
Kildare	677	1,694	122,516
Kilkenny	824	2,062	73,613
Laoighis	687	1,719	52,325
Longford	417	1,044	30,293
Louth	329	823	90,707
Meath	934	2,336	105,540
Offaly	799	1,998	58,448
Westmeath	705	1,763	61,882
Wexford	940	2,351	102,045
Wicklow	810	2,025	97,293
MUNSTER	9,651	24,127	1,008,443
Clare	1,275	3,188	90,826
Cork	2,984	7,460	409,814
Kerry	1,880	4,701	121,719
Limerick	1,076	2,686	162,856
Tipperary N.R.	798	1,996	57,829
Tipperary S.R.	903	2,258	74,791
Waterford	735	1,838	91,608
ULSTER (part of)	3,205	8,012	232,012
Cavan	756	1,890	52,756
Donegal	1,932	4,831	127,994
Monaghan	516	1,291	51,262

Crown Dependencies

Certain islands off the British coast are dependencies of the Crown rather than part of the United Kingdom. They have their own systems of government, so they have no MPs in the British Parliament. Similarly, they are not members of the EC, but they have a special relationship with it.

Isle of Man is a Crown dependency and has the oldest continuously existing parliament in the world (Tynwald, est. 979 AD).
Area: 221 sq miles (572 sq km)
Capital: Douglas

Jersey is a bailiwick and the largest of the Channel Islands.
Area: 44.8 sq miles (116.2 sq km)
Capital: St Helier

Guernsey is a bailiwick and the second largest of the Channel Islands. The islands of Alderney, Sark, Herm, Brechou, Jethou and Lihou are dependencies of Guernsey.
Area (excluding dependencies): 24.5 sq miles (63.3 sq km)
Capital: St Peter Port

Largest Cities in the UK

(1991 Census)

City	Area (sq miles/sq km)		Population
1. London	632	1,579	6,378,600
2. Birmingham	106	266	938,000
3. Leeds	225	562	677,000
4. Glasgow	79	198	654,000
5. Sheffield	147	367	503,000
6. Bradford	146	366	451,000
7. Liverpool	45	113	450,000
8. Edinburgh	104	261	422,000
9. Manchester	46	116	400,000
10. Bristol	47	109	372,000

Areas of Outstanding Natural Beauty

(United Kingdom)

Area	Size sq. km	sq. miles
Cotswolds	2,038	787
North Pennines	1,983	766
North Wessex Downs	1,730	668
High Weald	1,460	564
Dorset	1,129	436
Sussex Downs	983	380
West Wiltshire Downs	983	380
Cornwall	958	370
Kent Downs	878	339
Chilterns	833	322

Longest National Trails

(United Kingdom)

Trail	Length km	miles
South West Coast path	956	594
Pennine Way	412	256
Thames Path	383	238
Pembrokeshire Coast Path	292	181
Offa's Dyke Path	285	177
North Downs Way	227	141
Cleveland Way	175	109
South Downs Way	171	106
Peddars Way and Norfolk Coast Path	150	93
Ridgeway	137	85

Road Mileage Chart: Republic of Ireland

Source: Irish Tourist Board

Distances are shown in miles

	Athlone	Cork	Donegal	Dublin	Dundalk	Galway	Kilkenny	Killarney	Limerick	Roscommon	Rosslare Harbour	Shannon Airport	Sligo	Waterford
Cork	136
Donegal	114	250
Dublin	78	160	138
Dundalk	90	202	98	53
Galway	58	130	127	136	148
Kilkenny	78	92	192	73	123	107
Killarney	144	54	253	192	219	120	123
Limerick	75	65	184	123	150	65	70	69
Roscommon	20	156	94	91	94	51	98	164	94
Rosslare Harbour	130	129	243	101	153	170	62	171	131	150
Shannon Airport	83	80	176	138	165	57	85	84	15	96	146
Sligo	73	209	41	135	104	86	152	213	144	53	203	136
Waterford	108	78	222	98	151	137	30	120	80	129	51	95	182
Wexford	117	116	231	88	141	157	50	158	118	138	12	133	191	39

Road Mileage Chart: Great Britain

Source: Ordnance Survey (Crown copyright)

Distances are shown in miles

	London	Aberdeen	Aberystwyth	Ayr	Berwick-upon-Tweed	Birmingham	Blackpool	Bournemouth	Braemar	Brighton	Bristol	Cambridge	Cardiff	Carlisle	Doncaster	Dover	Dundee	Edinburgh	Exeter	Fishguard	Fort William	Glasgow	Gloucester	Gt. Yarmouth
Aberdeen	503
Aberystwyth	211	445
Ayr	394	177	317
Berwick-upon-Tweed	338	182	311	134
Birmingham	105	420	114	289	264
Blackpool	226	308	153	180	193	123
Bournemouth	100	564	207	436	412	147	270
Braemar	482	59	405	143	148	377	268	524
Brighton	52	556	235	446	390	163	286	92	534
Bristol	122	493	125	370	352	81	204	82	458	137
Cambridge	54	458	214	357	294	100	208	154	426	106	144
Cardiff	157	490	105	382	368	103	209	117	470	182	45	179
Carlisle	301	221	224	93	87	106	87	343	181	353	277	264	289
Doncaster	159	344	176	235	198	94	94	235	310	211	175	116	197	142
Dover	71	576	282	465	409	176	297	174	553	82	186	125	238	372	231
Dundee	434	67	376	117	113	349	239	495	52	486	430	391	441	152	275	505
Edinburgh	378	125	320	73	57	292	183	439	91	430	373	335	385	96	219	449	56
Exeter	172	569	201	456	428	157	282	82	534	166	76	220	121	353	251	248	506	450
Fishguard	260	491	56	373	393	170	209	234	461	291	154	270	112	280	233	331	432	376	230
Fort William	497	165	430	133	190	392	283	539	125	549	473	460	485	196	338	568	127	144	549	486
Glasgow	397	145	320	33	101	292	183	439	110	449	373	360	385	96	238	468	83	44	449	376	101
Gloucester	109	468	102	330	318	56	174	99	419	133	35	123	56	237	150	180	390	334	111	153	433	333
Gt. Yarmouth	128	495	294	402	345	180	252	228	477	180	241	82	261	309	167	185	442	386	297	350	505	405	205
	76	505	281	439	372	167	275	176	504	128	191	67	246	336	194	125	469	413	248	337	532	432	178	82
	253	439	111	305	311	148	141	288	393	311	206	248	216	212	167	339	364	308	282	167	408	308	180	313
	536	105	486	199	215	458	348	597	75	588	539	493	549	262	351	607	132	158	618	542	66	166	504	518
	663	232	615	328	342	587	478	724	202	715	668	620	680	391	478	734	259	285	744	671	195	295	628	645
	206	364	223	251	185	152	127	282	307	258	233	163	244	158	47	277	272	216	309	280	354	254	198	169
	576	189	499	212	243	471	362	618	159	628	552	539	564	275	417	647	186	216	628	555	79	179	512	584
	297	692	325	570	552	281	405	205	665	289	200	334	245	477	374	366	630	574	123	353	672	573	235	420
	189	327	181	212	156	113	72	255	293	241	194	145	220	119	29	260	258	202	270	237	315	215	159	196
	97	414	153	299	252	39	140	158	378	149	120	68	142	206	74	168	349	283	196	209	402	302	85	140
	131	383	199	274	224	90	128	209	343	183	171	85	193	181	39	202	314	258	247	255	377	277	136	128
	202	341	104	213	219	93	49	234	307	256	161	201	165	120	86	273	272	216	237	160	316	216	126	240
	185	340	141	212	196	80	48	227	306	237	161	151	172	119	51	256	271	215	236	197	315	215	126	205
	274	235	273	149	64	207	129	347	201	326	288	230	304	57	114	345	166	110	364	329	253	148	253	281
	114	475	276	382	328	166	232	214	457	163	221	62	241	289	147	174	422	366	282	330	485	385	186	20
	122	379	164	274	221	50	111	183	353	174	145	83	153	181	43	193	318	262	221	220	377	277	110	142
	489	178	412	125	180	384	275	530	141	541	465	452	477	188	330	560	117	123	533	468	49	92	424	497
	57	483	154	353	324	64	187	90	448	99	74	83	108	260	145	128	413	357	142	205	456	356	52	156
	218	615	247	492	474	203	328	128	587	212	122	263	167	399	297	289	552	496	46	276	595	495	157	343
	70	560	222	430	401	141	264	52	526	48	97	124	142	337	222	130	491	435	118	251	533	433	108	198
	159	360	159	245	190	76	86	216	320	211	161	120	179	152	18	230	291	235	237	215	348	248	126	166
	150	399	77	269	265	45	98	185	357	208	103	145	111	176	99	221	330	274	179	133	372	272	77	225
	77	547	201	417	388	128	251	31	512	61	76	131	121	324	209	143	477	421	105	215	520	420	93	205
	402	228	325	51	158	297	188	444	194	454	378	365	390	101	243	473	167	124	454	381	184	84	343	410
	194	494	73	366	383	119	216	167	483	222	85	217	41	273	217	274	448	392	161	67	469	369	89	294
	193	319	205	214	148	130	96	269	285	245	211	150	244	121	34	264	250	194	287	261	317	217	176	201

	Harwich	Holyhead	Inverness	John o'Groats	Kingston upon Hull	Kyle of Lochalsh	Land's End	Leeds	Leicester	Lincoln	Liverpool	Manchester	Newcastle upon Tyne	Norwich	Nottingham	Oban	Oxford	Plymouth	Portsmouth	Sheffield	Shrewsbury	Southampton	Stranraer	Swansea
Harwich																								
Holyhead	315																							
Inverness	545	474																						
John o'Groats	672	603	129																					
Kingston upon Hull	232	214	374	501																				
Kyle of Lochalsh	611	487	84	189	433																			
Land's End	371	405	741	868	421	752																		
Leeds	223	164	360	487	55	394	394																	
Leicester	135	163	461	588	121	481	320	95																
Lincoln	155	200	427	554	44	456	371	68	51															
Liverpool	235	92	382	511	130	395	361	75	100	118														
Manchester	239	124	373	500	95	394	361	40	92	84	35													
Newcastle upon Tyne	308	247	268	395	121	318	488	92	187	159	155	132												
Norwich	73	293	498	625	149	564	421	176	119	105	220	185	264											
Nottingham	150	171	430	557	90	456	345	70	25	35	98	63	157	122										
Oban	524	400	134	244	346	128	665	307	393	368	308	307	233	477	369									
Oxford	126	209	515	642	192	535	274	168	73	124	157	144	260	145	98	448								
Plymouth	294	328	664	790	355	674	89	316	242	293	283	283	410	343	267	587	185							
Portsmouth	146	288	592	719	269	612	241	244	150	201	234	221	337	186	175	525	77	164						
Sheffield	187	149	393	520	65	427	361	33	62	46	72	38	125	146	37	339	135	283	212					
Shrewsbury	220	103	438	567	146	451	303	109	84	117	58	69	201	205	82	364	106	225	185	82				
Southampton	153	273	579	706	256	599	228	232	137	188	221	208	324	193	162	512	64	151	21	199	170			
Stranraer	435	313	250	379	259	263	578	220	307	282	221	220	158	390	290	176	362	500	438	263	277	425		
Swansea	267	184	535	664	264	548	285	227	158	209	153	187	319	274	169	461	141	206	182	200	118	161	374	
York	228	188	352	479	37	396	411	24	108	75	99	64	84	181	77	309	181	333	258	52	133	245	222	251

National Parks

England & Wales

Brecon Beacons, South Wales
Area: 519 sq miles (1,344 sq km)
Dartmoor, Devon
Area: 365 sq miles (945 sq km)
Exmoor, Devon and Somerset
Area: 265 sq miles (686 sq km)
Lake District, Cumbria
Area: 880 sq miles (2,280 sq km)
Northumberland
Area: 398 sq miles (1,031 sq km)
North Yorks Moors, Yorkshire
Area: 553 sq miles (1,433 sq km)
Peak District, Derbyshire, Staffordshire, S. Yorkshire, Cheshire, W. Yorkshire and Greater Manchester
Area: 542 sq miles (1,404 sq km)
Pembrokeshire Coast, Dyfed
Area: 225 sq miles (583 sq km)
Snowdonia, Gwynedd
Area: 838 sq miles (2,171 sq km)
Yorkshire Dales, N. Yorkshire and Cumbria
Area: 680 sq miles (1,762 sq km)

Northern Ireland

In Northern Ireland the nearest equivalent to National Parks are Countryside Parks, which are administered by the Countryside and Wildlife Branch of the Department of the Environment.

Castle Archdale Country park, Co. Fermanagh
Area: 200 acres (80 hectares)
Crawfordsburn Country Park, Co. Down
Area: 200 acres (80 hectares)
Ness Wood Country Park, Co. Londonderry
Area: 80 acres (32 hectares)
Peatlands Park, Co. Tyrone
Area: 625 acres (250 hectares)
Redburn Country Park, Co. Down
Area: 140 acres (56 hectares)
Roe Valley Country Park, Co. Londonderry
Area: 200 acres (80 hectares)
Scrabo Country Park, Co. Down
Area: 130 acres (52 hectares)

Republic of Ireland

Connemara, Co. Galway
Area: 8 sq miles (20 sq km)
Glenveagh, Co. Donegal
Area: approx. 40 sq miles (100 sq km)
Killarney, Co. Kerry
Area: over 40 sq miles (100 sq km)
Wicklow Mountains, Co. Wicklow
Area: 15 sq miles (37 sq km)

Scotland

Many parts of Scotland have been designated National Scenic Areas. The nearest equivalent to National Parks are Regional Parks, listed below.

Clyde-Muirshiel Regional Park, Strathclyde
Area: 66,063 acres (26,425 hectares)
Fife Regional Park, Fife
Area: 16,250 acres (6,500 hectares)
Loch Lomond Regional Park, Strathclyde & Central
Area: 110,500 acres (44,200 hectares)
Pentland Hills Regional Park, Borders & Lothian
Area: 22,500 acres (9,000 hectares)

Longest Rivers in the UK

Name		Length (miles/km)	
1.	Severn	220	354
2.	Thames	215	344
3.	Trent	185	296
4.	Aire	161	258
5.	Ouse	143	229
6.	Wye	135	216
7.	Tay	117	187
8.	Nene	100	160
9.	Clyde	98½	158
10.	Spey	98	157

Britain's Largest Lakes

Name	Area (sq miles/sq km)		Depth (feet/metres)	
Loch Lomond	28.5	71.2	623.7	189
Loch Ness	22.5	56.2	185.5	56.2
Loch Awe	15.5	38.7	306.9	93
Loch Maree	11.3	28.4	366.3	111
Loch Morar	10.6	26.3	1,019.7	309
Lake Windermere	5.9	14.7	217.8	66
Ullswater	3.5	8.9	204.6	62
Bassenthwaite/ Derwent Water	2.1	5.3		
Coniston	1.9	4.8	184.8	56
Lake Vyrnwy	1.8	4.5	125.4	62

Highest Waterfalls in the British Isles

Name		Height (feet/metres)	
1.	Eas-Coul-Aulin, Highland	658	197
2.	Falls of Glomach, Highland	370	111
3.	Powerscourt Falls, Co. Wicklow	350	105
4.	Pistyll-y-Llyn, Powys/Dyfed	300	90
5.	Pistyll Rhaiadr, Clwyd	240	72
6.	Foyers, Highland	205	62
7.	Falls of Clyde, Strathclyde	204	61
8.=	Falls of Bruar, Tayside	200	60
8.=	Cauldron Snout, Cumbria	200	60
8.=	Grey Mare's Tail, Dumfries & Galloway	200	60

Highest Peaks in the British Isles

Scotland wins hands down in having the most high peaks in the British Isles, so the following list gives the 5 highest peaks in each constituent country.

Scotland

Mountain	Height (feet)	Height (metres)
Ben Nevis, Highland	4,435	1,344
Ben Macdui, Grampian	4,320	1,309
Braeriach, Grampian/Highland	4,273	1,295
Cairn Toul, Grampian	4,267	1,293
Cairn Gorm, Grampian/Highland	4,108	1,245

Wales

Mountain	Height (feet)	Height (metres)
Snowdon, Gwynedd	3,580	1,085
Carnedd Llewelyn, Gwynedd	3,445	1,062
Carnedd Dafydd Gwynedd	3,426	1,044
Glyder Fawr, Gwynedd	3,297	999
Glyder Fach, Gwynedd	3,280	994

Republic of Ireland

Mountain	Height (feet)	Height (metres)
Carrauntoohill, Kerry	3,435	1,041
Beenkeragh, Kerry	3,333	1,010
Caher, Kerry	3,217	975
Ridge of the Reeks, Kerry	c. 3,217	c. 975
Brandon, Kerry	3,145	953

England

Mountain	Height (feet)	Height (metres)
Scafell Pike, Cumbria	3,224	977
Sca Fell, Cumbria	3,181	964
Helvellyn, Cumbria	3,135	950
Skiddaw, Cumbria	3,072	931
Bow Fell, Cumbria	2,977	902

Northern Ireland

Mountain	Height (feet)	Height (metres)
Slieve Donard, Co. Down	2,811	852
Sawel, Co. Tyrone	2,254	683
Sperrin Mtns, Co. Tyrone	2,099	636
(2 unnamed peaks)	1,907	578
Trostan, Co. Antrim	1,828	554

WORLD EXPLORATION & GEOGRAPHY

Early Explorers of the Western Hemisphere

The first people to discover the New World or Western Hemisphere are believed to have walked across a "land bridge" from Siberia to Alaska, an isthmus since broken by the Bering Strait. From Alaska, these ancestors of the Indians spread through North, Central and South America. Anthropologists have placed these crossings at between 18,000 and 14,000 B.C.; but evidence found in 1967 near Puebla, Mex., indicates that people may have reached there as early as 35,000–40,000 years ago.

At first, these people were hunters using flint weapons and tools. In Mexico, about 7000–6000 B.C., they founded farming cultures, developing corn, squash, etc. Eventually, they created complex civilizations – Olmec, Toltec, Aztec and Maya and, in South America, Inca. Carbon-14 tests show humans lived about 8000 B.C. near what are now Front Royal, Va., Kanawha, W. Va. and Dutchess Quarry, N.Y. The Hopewell Culture, based on farming, flourished about 1000 B.C.; remains of it are seen today in large mounds in Ohio and other states.

Norsemen (Norwegian Vikings sailing out of Iceland and Greenland) are credited by most scholars with being the first Europeans to discover America, with at least 5 voyages around 1000 A.D. to areas they called Helluland, Markland, Vinland—possibly Labrador, Nova Scotia or Newfoundland, and New England.

Christopher Columbus, the most famous explorer, was born Cristoforo Colombo in or near Genoa, Italy, probably in 1451, but made his voyages of exploration for the Spanish rulers Ferdinand and Isabella. Dates of his voyages, places he reached, and other information follow:

1492 – First voyage. Left Palos, Spain, Aug. 3 with 88 men (est.). His fleet consisted of 3 vessels – the *Nina*, the *Pinta* and the *Santa Maria*. Landed at San Salvador (Guanahani or Watling Is., Bahamas) Oct. 12. Also Cuba, Hispaniola (Haiti-Dominican Republic); built Fort La Navidad on latter.

1493 – Second voyage, first part, Sept. 25, with 17 ships, 1,500 men. Dominica (Lesser Antilles) Nov. 3; Guadeloupe, Montserrat, Antigua, San Martin, Santa Cruz, Puerto Rico, Virgin Islands. Settled Isabela on Hispaniola. **Second part** (Columbus having remained in Western Hemisphere), Jamaica, Isle of Pines, La Mona Is.

1498 – Third voyage. Left Spain, May 30, 1498, 6 ships. Landed at Trinidad. Saw South American continent, Aug. 1, 1498, but called it Isla Sancta (Holy Island). Entered Gulf of Paria and landed, first time on continental soil. At mouth of Orinoco, Aug. 14, he decided this was the mainland.

1502 – Fourth voyage, 4 caravels, 150 men. St. Lucia, Guanaja off Honduras; Cape Gracias a Dios, Honduras; San Juan River, Costa Rica; Almirante, Portobelo and Laguna de Chiriqui, Panama.

Year	Explorer	Nationality and employer	Area reached or explored
1497	John Cabot	Italian–English	Newfoundland or Nova Scotia
1498	John and Sebastian Cabot	Italian–English	Labrador to Hatteras
1499	Alonso de Ojeda	Spanish	South American coast, Venezuela
1500, Feb.	Vicente y Pinzon	Spanish	South American coast, Amazon River
1500, Apr.	Pedro Alvarez Cabral	Portuguese	Brazil (for Portugal)
1500–02	Gaspar Corte-Real	Portuguese	Labrador
1501	Rodrigo de Bastidas	Spanish	Central America
1513	Vasco Nunez de Balboa	Spanish	Pacific Ocean
1513	Juan Ponce de Leon	Spanish	Florida
1515	Juan de Solis	Spanish	Rio de la Plata
1519	Alonso de Pineda	Spanish	Mouth of Mississippi River
1519	Hernando Cortes	Spanish	Mexico
1520	Ferdinand Magellan	Portuguese–Spanish	Straits of Magellan, Tierra del Fuego
1524	Giovanni da Verrazano	Italian–French	Atlantic coast–New York harbor
1532	Francisco Pizarro	Spanish	Peru
1534	Jacques Cartier	French	Canada, Gulf of St. Lawrence
1536	Pedro de Mendoza	Spanish	Buenos Aires
1536	A.N. Cabeza de Vaca	Spanish	Texas coast and interior
1539	Francisco de Ulloa	Spanish	California coast
1539–41	Hernando de Soto	Spanish	Mississippi River near Memphis
1539	Marcos de Niza	Italian–Spanish	Southwest (now U.S.)
1540	Francisco V. de Coronado	Spanish	Southwest (now U.S.)
1540	Hernando Alarcon	Spanish	Colorado River
1540	Garcia de L. Cardenas	Spanish	Grand Canyon of the Colorado
1541	Francisco de Orellana	Spanish	Amazon River
1542	Juan Rodriguez Cabrillo	Portuguese–Spanish	San Diego harbor
1565	Pedro Menendez de Aviles	Spanish	St. Augustine
1576	Martin Frobisher	English	Frobisher's Bay, Canada
1577–80	Francis Drake	English	California coast
1582	Antonio de Espejo	Spanish	Southwest (named New Mexico)
1584	Amadas & Barlow (for Raleigh)	English	Virginia
1585–87	Sir Walter Raleigh's men	English	Roanoke Is., N.C.
1595	Sir Walter Raleigh	English	Orinoco River
1603–09	Samuel de Champlain	French	Canadian interior, Lake Champlain
1607	Capt. John Smith	English	Atlantic coast
1609–10	Henry Hudson	English–Dutch	Hudson River, Hudson Bay
1634	Jean Nicolet	French	Lake Michigan; Wisconsin
1673	Jacques Marquette, Louis Jolliet	French	Mississippi S to Arkansas
1682	Sieur de La Salle	French	Mississippi S to Gulf of Mexico
1789	Alexander Mackenzie	Canadian	Canadian Northwest

Arctic Exploration

Early Explorers

1587 — John Davis (England). Davis Strait to Sanderson's Hope, 72° 12′ N.

1596 — Willem Barents and Jacob van Heemskerck (Holland). Discovered Bear Island, touched northwest tip of Spitsbergen, 79° 49′ N, rounded Novaya Zemlya, wintered at Ice Haven.

1607 — Henry Hudson (England). North along Greenland's east coast to Cape Hold-with-Hope, 73° 30′, then north of Spitsbergen to 80° 23′. Returning he discovered Hudson's Touches (Jan Mayen).

1616 — William Baffin and Robert Bylot (England). Baffin Bay to Smith Sound.

1728 — Vitus Bering (Russia). Proved Asia and America were separated by sailing through strait.

1733–40 — Great Northern Expedition (Russia). Surveyed Siberian Arctic coast.

1741 — Vitus Bering (Russia). Sighted Alaska from sea, named Mount St. Elias. His lieutenant, Chirikof, discovered coast.

1771 — Samuel Hearne (Hudson's Bay Co.). Overland from Prince of Wales Fort (Churchill) on Hudson Bay to mouth of Coppermine River.

1778 — James Cook (Britain). Through Bering Strait to Icy Cape, Alaska, and North Cape, Siberia.

1789 — Alexander Mackenzie (North West Co., Britain). Montreal to mouth of Mackenzie River.

1806 — William Scoresby (Britain). N. of Spitsbergen to 81° 30′.

1820–3 — Ferdinand von Wrangel (Russia). Completed a survey of Siberian Arctic coast. His exploration joined that of James Cook at North Cape, confirming separation of the continents.

1845 — Sir John Franklin (Britain) was one of many to seek the Northwest Passage—an ocean route connecting the Atlantic and Pacific via the Arctic. His 2 ships (the *Erebus* and *Terror*) were last seen entering Lancaster Sound July, 26.

1881 — The steamer *Jeanette* on an expedition led by Lt. Cmdr. George W. DeLong was trapped in ice and crushed, June 1881. DeLong and 11 crewmen died; 12 others survived.

1888 — Fridtjof Nansen (Norway) crossed Greenland's icecap, 1893–96 – Nansen in Fram drifted from New Siberian Is. to Spitsbergen; tried polar dash in 1895, reached Franz Josef Land.

1897 — Salomon A. Andree (Sweden) and 2 others started in balloon from Danes, Is., Spitsbergen, July 11, to drift across pole to America, and disappeared. Over 33 years later, Aug. 6, 1930, their frozen bodies were found on White Is., 82° 57′ N 29° 52′ E.

1903–06 — Roald Amundsen (Norway) first sailed Northwest Passage.

Discovery of North Pole

Robert E. Peary explored Greenland's coast, 1891–92, tried for North Pole, 1893. In 1900 he reached northern limit of Greenland and 83° 50′ N; in 1902 he reached 84° 06′ N; in 1906 he went from Ellesmere Is. to 87° 06′ N. He sailed in the *Roosevelt,* July, 1908, to winter off Cape Sheridan, Grant Land. The dash for the North Pole began Mar. 1 from Cape Columbia, Ellesmere Land. Peary reached the pole, 90° N, Apr. 6, 1909.

Peary had several supporting groups carrying supplies until the last group turned back at 87° 47′ N. Peary, Matthew Henson, and 4 Eskimos proceeded with dog teams and sleds. They crossed the pole several times, finally built an igloo at 90°, remained 36 hours. Started south, Apr. 7 at 4 p.m., for Cape Columbia. The Eskimos were Coqueeh, Ootah, Eginwah, and Seegloo.

1914 — Donald MacMillan (U.S.). Northwest, 200 miles, from Axel Heiberg Island to seek Peary's Crocker Land.

1915–17 — Vihjalmur Stefansson (Canada) discovered Borden, Brock, Meighen, and Lougheed Islands.

1918–20 — Roald Amundsen sailed Northeast Passage.

1925 — Amundsen and Lincoln Ellsworth (U.S.) reached 87° 44′ N in attempt to fly to North Pole from Spitsbergen.

1926 — Richard E. Byrd and Floyd Bennett (U.S.) first over North Pole by air, May 9.

1926 — Amundsen, Ellsworth, and Umberto Nobile (Italy) flew from Spitsbergen over North Pole May 12, to Teller, Alaska, in dirigible *Norge.*

1928 — Nobile crossed North Pole in airship, May 24, crashed, May 25. Amundsen lost while trying to effect rescue by plane.

North Pole Exploration Records

On Aug. 3, 1958, the *Nautilus,* under Comdr. William R. Anderson, became the first ship to cross the North Pole beneath the Arctic ice.

The nuclear-powered U.S. submarine *Seadragon,* Comdr. George P. Steele 2d, made the first east–west underwater transit through the Northwest Passage during August, 1960. It sailed from Portsmouth N.H., headed between Greenland and Labrador through Baffin Bay, then west through Lancaster Sound and McClure Strait to the Beaufort Sea. Traveling submerged for the most part, the submarine made 850 miles from Baffin Bay to the Beaufort Sea in 6 days.

On Aug. 16, 1977, the Soviet nuclear icebreaker *Arktika* reached the North Pole and became the first surface ship to break through the Arctic ice pack to the top of the world.

On April 30, 1978, Naomi Uemura, a Japanese explorer, became the first man to reach the North Pole alone by dog sled. During the 54-day, 600-mile trek over the frozen Arctic, Uemura survived attacks by a marauding polar bear.

In April, 1982, Sir Ranulph Fiennes and Charles Burton, British explorers, reached the North Pole and became the first to circle the earth from pole to pole. They had reached the South Pole 16 months earlier. The 52,000-mile trek took 3 years, involved 23 people, and cost an estimated $18 million. The expedition was also the first to travel down the Scott Glacier and the first to journey up the Yukon and through the Northwest Passage in a single season.

On May 2, 1986, 6 American and Canadian explorers reached the North Pole assisted only by dogs. They became the first to reach the Pole without mechanical assistance since Robert E. Peary planted a flag there in 1909. The explorers, Americans Will Steger, Paul Schurke, Anne Bancroft, and Geoff Carroll, and Canadians Brent Boddy and Richard Weber completed the 500-mile journey in 56 days.

Antarctic Exploration

Early History

Antarctica has been approached since 1773–75, when Capt. James Cook (Britain) reached 71° 10′ S. Many sea and landmarks bear names of early explorers. Bellingshausen (Russia) discovered Peter I and Alexander I Islands, 1819–21. Nathaniel Palmer (U.S.) discovered Palmer Peninsula, 60° W, 1820, without realizing that this was a continent. James Weddell (Britain) found Weddell Sea, 74° 15′ S, 1823.

First to announce existence of the continent of Antarctica was Charles Wilkes (U.S.), who followed the coast for 1,500 mi., 1840. Adelie Coast, 140° E, was found by Dumont d'Urville (France), 1840. Ross Ice Shelf was found by James Clark Ross (Britain), 1841–42.

1895 — Leonard Kristensen (Norway) landed a party on the coast of Victoria Land. They were the first ashore on the main continental mass. C.E. Borchgrevink, a member of that party, returned in 1899 with a British expedition, first to winter on Antarctica.

1902–04 — Robert F. Scott (Britain) discovered Edward VII Peninsula. He reached 82° 17′ S, 146° 33′ E from McMurdo Sound.

1908–09 — Ernest Shackleton (Britain) introduced the use of Manchurian ponies in Antarctic sledging. He reached 88° 23′ S, discovering a route on to the plateau by way of the Beardmore Glacier and pioneering the way to the pole.

Discovery of South Pole

1911 — Roald Amundsen (Norway) with 4 men and dog teams reached the pole, Dec. 14.

1912 — Capt. Scott reached the pole from Ross Island, Jan. 18, with 4 companions. They found Amundsen's tent. None of Scott's party survived. They were found, Nov. 12.

1928 — First man to use an airplane over Antarctica was Hubert Wilkins (Britain).

1929 — Richard E. Byrd (U.S.) established Little America on Bay of Whales. On 1,600-mi. airplane flight begun, Nov. 28, he crossed South Pole, Nov. 29 with 3 others.

1934–35 — Byrd led 2d expedition to Little America, explored 450,000 sq. mi., wintered alone at weather station, 80° 08′ S.

1934–37 — John Rymill led British Graham Land expedition; discovered that Palmer Peninsula is part of Antarctic mainland.

1935 — Lincoln Ellsworth (U.S.) flew south along Palmer Peninsula's east coast, then crossed continent to Little America, making 4 landings on unprepared terrain in bad weather.

1939–41 — U.S. Antarctic Service built West Base on Ross Ice Shelf under Paul Siple, and East Base on Palmer Peninsula under Richard Black. U.S. Navy plane flights discovered about 150,000 sq. miles of new land.

1940 — Byrd charted most of coast between Ross Sea and Palmer Peninsula.

1946–47 — U.S. Navy undertook Operation Highjump under Byrd. Expedition included 13 ships and 4,000 men. Airplanes photomapped coastline and penetrated beyond pole.

1946–48 — Ronne Antarctic Research Expedition, Comdr. Finn Ronne, USNR, determined the Antarctic to be only one continent with no strait between Weddell Sea and Ross Sea; discovered 250,000 sq. miles of land by flights to 79° S Lat., and made 14,000 aerial photographs over 450,000 sq. miles of land. Mrs. Ronne and Mrs. H. Darlington were the first women to winter on Antarctica.

1955–57 — U.S. Navy's Operation Deep Freeze led by Adm. Byrd. Supporting U.S. scientific efforts for the International Geophysical Year, the operation was commanded by Rear Adm. George Dufek. It established 5 coastal stations fronting the Indian, Pacific, and Atlantic oceans and also 3 interior stations; explored more than 1,000,000 sq. miles in Wilkes Land.

1957–58 — During the International Geophysical year, July 1957, through Dec. 1958, scientists from 12 countries conducted ambitious programs of Antarctic research. A network of some 60 stations on the continent and sub-Arctic islands studied oceanography, glaciology, meteorology, seismology, geomagnetism, the ionosphere, cosmic rays, aurora, and airglow.

Dr. V.E. Fuchs led a 12-man Trans-Antarctic Expedition on the first land crossing of Antarctica. Starting from the Weddell Sea, they reached Scott Station, Mar. 2, 1958, after traveling 2,158 miles in 98 days.

1958 — A group of 5 U.S. scientists led by Edward C. Thiel, seismologist, moving by tractor from Ellsworth Station on Weddell Sea, identified a huge mountain range, 5,000 ft. above the ice sheet and 9,000 ft. above sea level. The range, originally seen by a Navy plane, was named the Dufek Massif, for Rear Adm. George Dufek.

1959 — Twelve nations – Argentina, Australia, Belgium, Chile, France, Japan, New Zealand, Norway, South Africa, the Soviet Union, the United Kingdom, and the U.S. – signed a treaty suspending any territorial claims for 30 years and reserving the continent for research.

1961–62 — Scientists discovered a trough, the Bentley Trench, running from Ross Ice Shelf, Pacific, into Marie Byrd Land, around the end of the Ellsworth Mtns., toward the Weddell Sea.

1962 — First nuclear power plant began operation at McMurdo Sound.

1963 — On Feb. 22 a U.S. plane made the longest nonstop flight ever made in the S. Pole area, covering 3,600 miles in 10 hours. The flight was from McMurdo Station south past the geographical S. Pole to Shackleton Mtns., southeast to the "Area of Inaccessibility" and back to McMurdo Station.

1964 — A British survey team was landed by helicopter on Cook Island, the first recorded visit since its discovery in 1775.

1964 — New Zealanders completed one of the last and most important surveys when they mapped the mountain area from Cape Adare west some 400 miles to Pennell Glacier.

1989 — Two Americans, Victoria Murden and Shirley Metz, became the first women to reach the South Pole overland when they arrived with 9 others on Jan. 17, 1989. The 51-day trek on skis covered 740 miles.

Volcanoes

Source: Global Volcanism Network, Smithsonian Institution

More than 75 per cent of the world's 850 active volcanoes lie within the "Ring of Fire," a zone running along the west coast of the Americas from Chile to Alaska and down the east coast of Asia from Siberia to New Zealand. Twenty per cent of these volcanoes are located in Indonesia. Other prominent groupings are located in Japan, the Aleutian Islands, and Central America. Almost all active regions are found at the boundaries of the large moving plates which comprise the earth's surface. The "Ring of Fire" marks the boundary between the plates underlying the Pacific Ocean and those underlying the surrounding continents. Other active regions, such as the Mediterranean Sea and Iceland, are located on plate boundaries.

Major Historical Eruptions

Approximately 7,000 years ago, Mazama, a 9,900-feet-high volcano in southern Oregon, erupted violently, ejecting ash and lava. The ash spread over the entire northwestern United States and as far away as Saskatchewan, Canada. During the eruption, the top of the mountain collapsed, leaving a caldera 6 miles across and about a half mile deep, which filled with rain water to form what is now called Crater Lake.

In A.D. 79 Vesuvio, or Vesuvius, a 4,190 feet volcano overlooking Naples Bay became active after several centuries of quiescence. On Aug. 24 of that year, a heated mud and ash flow swept down the mountain engulfing the cities of Pompeii, Herculaneum, and Stabiae with debris over 60 feet deep. About 10 percent of the population of the 3 towns was killed.

The largest eruptions in recent centuries have been in Indonesia. In 1883, an eruption similar to the Mazama eruption occurred on the island of Krakatau. On August 27, the 2,640-feet-high peak of the volcano collapsed to 1,000 feet below sea level, leaving only a small portion of the island standing above the sea. Ash from the eruption coloured sunsets around the world for 2 years. A tsunami ("tidal wave") generated by the collapse killed 36,000 people in nearby Java and Sumatra and eventually reached England. A similar, but even more powerful, eruption had taken place 68 years earlier at Tambora volcano on the Indonesian island of Sumbawa.

Notable Active Volcanoes

Name, latest activity	Location	Height (feet)
Africa		
Cameroon (1982)	Cameroon	13,354
Nyirangongo (1977)	Zaire	11,400
Nyamuragira (1991)	Zaire	10,028
Karthala (1977)	Comoro Is.	8,000
Piton de la Fournaise (1991)	Reunion Is.	5,981
Erta-Ale (1992)	Ethiopia	1,650
Antarctica		
Erebus (1991)	Ross Island	12,450
Deception Island (1970)	South Shetland Islands	1,890
Asia-Oceania		
Kliuchevskoi (1991)	Russia	15,584
Kerinci (1987)	Sumatra	12,467
Semeru (1991)	Java	12,060
Slamet (1988)	Java	11,247
Raung (1991)	Java	10,932
On-Take (1991)	Japan	10,049
Mayon (1993)	Philippines	9,991
Merapi (1993)	Java	9,551
Marapi (1988)	Sumatra	9,485
Ruapehu (1992)	New Zealand	9,175
Asama (1991)	Japan	8,300
Niigata Yakeyama (1989)	Japan	8,111
Canlaon (1991)	Philippines	8,070
Alaid (1972)	Kuril Is.	7,662
Ulawun (1992)	New Britain	7,532
Ngauruhoe (1975)	New Zealand	7,515
Chokai (1974)	Japan	7,300
Galunggung (1982)	Java	7,113
Azuma (1978)	Japan	6,700
Pinatubo (1992)	Philippines	5,770
Sangeang Api (1988)	Indonesia	6,351
Nasu (1977)	Japan	6,210
Tiatia (1973)	Kuril Islands	6,013
Manam (1992)	Papua New Guinea	6,000
Soputan (1989)	Indonesia	5,994
Siau (1976)	Indonesia	5,853
Kelud (1990)	Java	5,679
Kirisima (1982)	Japan	5,577
Bagana (1992)	Papua New Guinea	6,558
Akita Komaga take (1970)	Japan	5,449
Gamkonora (1981)	Indonesia	5,364
Aso (1993)	Japan	5,223
Lokon-Empung (1991)	Indonesia	5,187
Bulusan (1988)	Philippines	5,115
Sarycheva (1976)	Kuril Islands	4,960
Karkar (1981)	Papua New Guinea	4,920
Lopevi (1982)	Vanuatu	4,755
Unzen (1993)	Japan	4,462
Ambrym (1991)	Vanuatu	4,376
Awu (1992)	Indonesia	4,350
Sakurajima (1993)	Japan	3,668
Langila (1992)	New Britain	3,586
Suwanosezima (1991)	Japan	2,640
Oshima (1990)	Japan	2,550
Usu (1978)	Japan	2,400
Pagan (1990)	Mariana Is.	1,870
White Island (1993)	New Zealand	1,075
Taal (1988)	Philippines	984
Central America—Caribbean		
Acatenango (1972)	Guatemala	12,992
Fuego (1991)	Guatemala	12,582
Tacana (1988)	Guatemala	12,400
Santiaguito (Santa Maria) (1991)	Guatemala	12,362
Irazu (1992)	Costa Rica	11,260
Turrialba (1992)	Costa Rica	10,650
Poas (1992)	Costa Rica	8,930
Pacaya (1991)	Guatemala	8,346
San Miguel (1992)	El Salvador	6,994
Rincon de la Vieja (1993)	Costa Rica	6,234
El Viejo (San Cristobal)(1991)	Nicaragua	5,840
Ometepe (Concepcion)(1986)	Nicaragua	5,106
Arenal (1993)	Costa Rica	5,092
Momotombo (1982)	Nicaragua	4,199
Soufriere (1979)	St. Vincent	4,048
Telica (1987)	Nicaragua	3,409
South America		
Guallatiri (1987)	Chile	19,882
Lascar (1991)	Chile	19,652
Cotopaxi (1975)	Ecuador	19,347
Tupungatito (1986)	Chile	18,504
Ruiz (1992)	Colombia	17,716
Sangay (1988)	Ecuador	17,159
Guagua Pichincha (1988)	Ecuador	15,696
Purace (1977)	Colombia	15,601
Galeras (1993)	Colombia	13,996
Llaima (1990)	Chile	10,239
Villarrica (1992)	Chile	9,318
Hudson (1991)	Chile	8,580
Alcedo (1970)	Galapagos Is.	3,599
Mid-Pacific		
Mauna Loa (1987)	Hawaii	13,680
Kilauea (1993)	Hawaii	4,077
Mid-Atlantic Ridge		
Beerenberg (1985)	Jan Mayen Is.	7,470
Hekla (1991)	Iceland	4,892
Leirhnukur (1975)	Iceland	2,145
Krafla (1984)	Iceland	2,145
Europe		
Etna (1993)	Italy	11,053
Stromboli (1993)	Italy	3,038
North America		
Colima (1991)	Mexico	14,003
Redoubt (1991)	Alaska	10,197
Iliamna (1978)	Alaska	10,016
Shishaldin (1987)	Aleutian Is.	9,387
Mt. St. Helens (1991)	Washington	8,300+
Pavlof (1988)	Aleutian Is.	8,261
Veniaminof (1987)	Alaska	8,225
El Chichon (1983)	Mexico	7,300
Katmai (1974)	Alaska	6,715
Makushin (1987)	Aleutian Is.	6,680
Great Sitkin (1974)	Aleutian Is.	5,710
Cleveland (1987)	Aleutian Is.	5,675
Gareloi (1982)	Aleutian Is.	5,334
Korovin (1987)	Aleutian Is.	4,852
Akutan (1992)	Aleutian Is.	4,275
Kiska (1990)	Aleutian Is.	4,275
Augustine (1988)	Alaska	3,999
Okmok (1988)	Aleutian Is.	3,519
Seguam (1977)	Alaska	3,458

Notable Volcanic Eruptions

Date	Volcano	Deaths
A.D. 79	Mt. Vesuvius, Italy	16,000
1169	Mt. Etna, Sicily	15,000
1631	Mt. Vesuvius, Italy	4,000
1669	Mt. Etna, Sicily	20,000
1772	Mt. Papandayan, Java	3,000
1792	Mt. Unzen-Dake, Japan	10,400
1815	Tamboro, Java	12,000
Aug. 26-28, 1883	Krakatau, Indonesia	35,000
Apr. 8, 1902	Santa Maria, Guatemala	1,000
May 8, 1902	Mt. Pelée, Martinique	30,000
1911	Mt. Taal, Philippines	1,400
1919	Mt. Kelud, Java	5,000
Jan. 18-21, 1951	Mt. Lamington, New Guinea	3,000
Apr. 26, 1966	Mt. Kelud, Java	1,000
May 18, 1980	Mt. St. Helens, U.S.	60
Nov. 13, 1985	Nevado del Ruiz, Colombia	22,940
Aug. 24, 1986	NW Cameroon	1,700+

Mountains

Height of Mount Everest

Mt. Everest was considered to be 29,002 ft. tall when Edmund Hillary and Tenzing Norgay scaled it in 1953. This triangulation figure had been accepted since 1850. In 1954 the Surveyor General of the Republic of India set the height at 29,028 ft., plus or minus 10 ft. because of snow. The National Geographic Society accepts the new figure, but many mountaineering groups still use 29,002 ft.

In 1987, new calculations based on satellite measurements indicate that the Himalayan peak K-2 rose 29,064 feet above sea level and that Mt. Everest is 800 feet higher. The National Geographic Society has not accepted the revised figure.

United States, Canada, Mexico

Name	Place	Height (feet)
McKinley	Alaska	20,320
Logan	Yukon	19,850
Citlaltepec (Orizaba)	Mexico	18,700
St. Elias	Alas-Yukon	18,008
Popocatepetl	Mexico	17,887
Foraker	Alaska	17,400
Iztaccihuatl	Mexico	17,343
Lucania	Yukon	17,147
King	Yukon	16,971
Steele	Yukon	16,644
Bona	Alaska	16,550
Blackburn	Alaska	16,390
Kennedy	Alaska	16,286
Sanford	Alaska	16,237
South Buttress	Alaska	15,885
Wood	Yukon	15,885
Vancouver	Alas-Yukon	15,700
Churchill	Alaska	15,638
Fairweather	Alas-Yukon	15,300
Zinantecatl (Toluca)	Mexico	15,016
Hubbard	Alas-Yukon	15,015
Bear	Alaska	14,831
Walsh	Yukon	14,780
East Buttress	Alaska	14,730
Matlalcueyetl	Mexico	14,636
Hunter	Alaska	14,573
Alverstone	Alas-Yukon	14,565
Browne Tower	Alaska	14,530
Whitney	Cal	14,494
Elbert	Col	14,433
Massive	Col	14,421
Harvard	Col	14,420
Rainier	Wash	14,410
Williamson	Cal	14,375
Blanca Peak	Col	14,345
La Plata	Col	14,336
Uncompahgre	Col	14,309
Crestone	Col	14,294
Lincoln	Col	14,286
Grays Peak	Col	14,270
Antero	Col	14,269
Torreys	Col	14,267
Castle	Col	14,265
Quandary	Col	14,265
Evans	Col	14,264
Longs Peak	Col	14,256
McArthur	Yukon	14,253
Wilson	Col	14,246
White	Cal	14,246
North Palisade	Cal	14,242
Shavano	Col	14,229
Belford	Col	14,197
Princeton	Col	14,197
Crestone Needle	Col	14,197
Yale	Col	14,196
Bross	Col	14,172
Kit Carson	Col	14,165
Wrangell	Alaska	14,163
Shasta	Cal	14,162
Sill	Cal	14,162
El Diente	Col	14,159
Maroon	Col	14,156
Tabeguache	Col	14,155
Oxford	Col	14,153
Sneffels	Col	14,150
Point Success	Wash	14,150
Democrat	Col	14,148
Capitol	Col	14,130
Liberty Cap	Wash	14,112
Pikes Peak	Col	14,110
Snowmass	Col	14,092
Windom	Col	14,087
Russell	Cal	14,086
Eolus	Col	14,084
Columbia	Col	14,073
Augusta	Alas-Yukon	14,070
Missouri	Col	14,067
Humboldt	Col	14,064

South America

Peak, country	Height (feet)
Aconcagua, Argentina	22,834
Ojos del Salado, Arg.-Chile	22,572
Bonete, Argentina	22,546
Tupungato, Argentina-Chile	22,310
Pissis, Argentina	22,241
Mercedario, Argentina	22,211
Huascaran, Peru	22,205
Llullaillaco, Argentina-Chile	22,057
El Libertador, Argentina	22,047
Cachi, Argentina	22,047
Yerupaja, Peru	21,709
Galan, Argentina	21,654
El Muerto, Argentina-Chile	21,457
Sajama, Bolivia	21,391
Nacimiento, Argentina	21,302
Illimani, Bolivia	21,201
Coropuna, Peru	21,083
Laudo, Argentina	20,997
Ancohuma, Bolivia	20,958
Ausangate, Peru	20,945
Toro, Argentina-Chile	20,932
Illampu, Bolivia	20,873
Tres Cruces, Argentina-Chile	20,853
Huandoy, Peru	20,852
Parinacota, Bolivia-Chile	20,768
Tortolas, Argentina-Chile	20,745
Ampato, Peru	20,702
Condor, Argentina	20,669
Salcantay, Peru	20,574
Chimborazo, Ecuador	20,561
Huancarhuas, Peru	20,531
Famatina, Argentina	20,505
Pumasillo, Peru	20,492
Solo, Argentina	20,492
Polleras, Argentina	20,456
Pular, Chile	20,423
Chani, Argentina	20,341
Aucanquilcha, Chile	20,295
Juncal, Argentina-Chile	20,276
Negro, Argentina	20,184
Quela, Argentina	20,128
Condoriri, Bolivia	20,095
Palermo, Argentina	20,079
Solimana, Peru	20,068
San Juan, Argentina-Chile	20,049
Sierra Nevada, Arg.-Chile	20,023
Antofalla, Argentina	20,013
Marmolejo, Argentina-Chile	20,013
Chachani, Peru	19,931
Licancabur, Argentina-Chile	19,425

The highest point in the West Indies is in the Dominican Republic, Pico Duarte (10,417 ft.)

Africa, Southeast Asia, Australia and New Zealand

Peak, country	Height (feet)
Kilimanjaro, Tanzania	19,340
Kenya, Kenya	17,058
Margherita Pk., Uganda-Zaire	16,763
Jaja, New Guinea	16,500
Trikora, New Guinea	15,585
Mandala, New Guinea	15,420
Ras Dashan, Ethiopia	15,158
Meru, Tanzania	14,979

Peak, country	Height (feet)
Wilhelm, New Guinea	14,793
Karisimbi, Zaire-Rwanda	14,787
Elgon, Kenya-Uganda	14,178
Batu, Ethiopia	14,131
Guna, Ethiopia	13,881
Gughe, Ethiopia	13,780
Toubkal, Morocco	13,661

Peak, country	Height (feet)
Kinabalu, Malaysia	13,455
Cameroon, Cameroon	13,353
Kerinci, Sumatra	12,467
Cook, New Zealand	12,349
Teide, Canary Islands	12,198
Semeru, Java	12,060
Kosciusko, Australia	7,310

Europe

Peak, country, island	Height (feet)
Alps	
Mont Blanc, Fr.-It.	15,771
Monte Rosa (highest peak of group), Switz.	15,203
Dom, Switz.	14,911
Liskamm, It., Switz.	14,852
Weisshom, Switz.	14,780
Taschhorn, Switz.	14,733
Matterhorn, It., Switz.	14,690
Dent Blanche, Switz.	14,293
Nadelhorn, Switz.	14,196
Grand Combin, Switz.	14,154
Lenzpitze, Switz.	14,088
Finsteraarhorn, Switz.	14,022
Castor, Switz.	13,865
Zinalrothorn, Switz.	13,849
Hohberghom, Switz.	13,842
Alphubel, Switz.	13,799
Rimpfischhom, Switz.	13,776
Aletschorn, Switz.	13,763
Strahlhorn, Switz.	13,747
Dent d'Herens, Switz.	13,686

Peak, country, island	Height (feet)
Breithorn, It., Switz.	13,665
Bishorn, Switz.	13,645
Jungfrau, Switz.	13,642
Ecrins, Fr.	13,461
Monch, Switz.	13,448
Pollux, Switz.	13,422
Schreckhorn, Switz.	13,379
Ober Gabelhorn, Switz.	13,330
Gran Paradiso, It.	13,323
Bernina, It., Switz.	13,284
Fiescherhorn, Switz.	13,283
Grunhorn, Switz.	13,266
Lauteraarhorn, Switz.	13,261
Durrenhorn, Switz.	13,238
Allalinhorn, Switz.	13,213
Weissmies, Switz.	13,199
Lagginhorn, Switz.	13,156
Zupo, Switz.	13,120
Fletschhorn, Switz.	13,110
Adlerhorn, Switz.	13,081
Gletscherhorn, Switz.	13,068
Schalihorn, Switz.	13,040

Peak, country, island	Height (feet)
Scerscen, Switz.	13,028
Eiger, Switz.	13,025
Jagerhorn, Switz.	13,024
Rottalhorn, Switz.	13,022
Pyrenees	
Aneto, Sp.	11,168
Posets, Sp.	11,073
Perdido, Sp.	11,007
Vignemale, Fr.-Sp.	10,820
Long, Sp.	10,479
Estats, Sp.	10,304
Montcalm, Sp.	10,105
Caucasus (Europe-Asia)	
El'brus, Russia	18,510
Shkara, Russia	17,064
Dykh Tau, Russia	17,054
Kashtan Tau, Russia	16,877
Dzhangi Tau, Russia	16,565
Kazbek, Russia	16,558

Asia

Peak	Country	Height (feet)
Everest	Nepal-Tibet	29,028
K2 (Godwin Austen)	Kashmir	28,250
Kanchenjunga	India-Nepal	28,208
Lhotse I (Everest)	Nepal-Tibet	27,923
Makalu I	Nepal-Tibet	27,824
Lhotse II (Everest)	Nepal-Tibet	27,560
Dhaulagiri	Nepal	26,810
Manaslu I	Nepal	26,760
Cho Oyu	Nepal-Tibet	26,750
Nanga Parbat	Kashmir	26,660
Annapurna I	Nepal	26,504
Gasherbrum	Kashmir	26,470
Broad	Kashmir	26,400
Gosainthan	Tibet	26,287
Annapurna II	Nepal	26,041
Gyachung Kang	Nepal-Tibet	25,910
Disteghil Sar	Kashmir	25,868
Himalchuli	Nepal	25,801
Nuptse (Everest)	Nepal-Tibet	25,726
Masherbrum	Kashmir	25,660
Nanda Devi	India	25,645
Rakaposhi	Kashmir	25,550
Kamet	India-Tibet	25,447
Namcha Barwa	Tibet	25,445
Gurla Mandhata	Tibet	25,355
Ulugh Muz Tagh	Sinkiang-Tibet	25,340

Peak	Country	Height (feet)
Kungur	Sinkiang	25,325
Tirich Mir	Pakistan	25,230
Makalu II	Nepal-Tibet	25,120
Minya Konka	China	24,900
Kula Gangri	Bhutan-Tibet	24,784
Changtzu (Everest)	Nepal-Tibet	24,780
Muz Tagh Ata	Sinkiang	24,757
Skyang Kangri	Kashmir	24,750
Communism Peak	Tajikistan	24,590
Jongsang Peak	India-Nepal	24,472
Pobedy Peak	Sinkiang-Kyrgyzstan	24,406
Sia Kangri	Kashmir	24,350
Haramosh Peak	Pakistan	24,270
Istoro Nal	Pakistan	24,240
Tent Peak	India-Nepal	24,165
Chomo Lhari	Bhutan-Tibet	24,040
Chamlang	Nepal	24,012
Kabru	India-Nepal	24,002
Alung Gangri	Tibet	24,000
Baltoro Kangri	Kashmir	23,990
Mussu Shan	Sinkiang	23,890
Mana	India	23,860
Baruntse	Nepal	23,688
Nepal Peak	India-Nepal	23,500
Amne Machin	China	23,490
Gauri Sankar	Nepal-Tibet	23,440

Peak	Country	Height (feet)
Badrinath	India	23,420
Nunkun	Kashmir	23,410
Lenin Peak	Tajikistan	23,405
Pyramid	India-Nepal	23,400
Api	Nepal	23,399
Pauhunri	India-Tibet	23,385
Trisul	India	23,360
Kangto	India-Tibet	23,260
Nyenchhen Thanglha	Tibet	23,255
Trisuli	India	23,210
Pumori	Nepal-Tibet	23,190
Dunagiri	India	23,184
Lombo Kangra	Tibet	23,165
Saipal	Nepal	23,100
Macha Pucchare	Nepal	22,958
Numbar	Nepal	22,817
Kanjiroba	Nepal	22,580
Ama Dablam	Nepal	22,350
Cho Polu	Nepal	22,093
Lingtren	Nepal-Tibet	21,972
Khumbutse	Nepal-Tibet	21,785
Hlako Gangri	Tibet	21,266
Mt. Grosvenor	China	21,190
Thagchhab Gangri	Tibet	20,970
Damavand	Iran	18,606
Ararat	Turkey	16,804

Antarctica

Peak	Height (feet)
Vinson Massif	16,864
Tyree	16,290
Shinn	15,750
Gardner	15,375
Epperly	15,100
Kirkpatrick	14,855
Elizabeth	14,698
Markham	14,290
Bell	14,117
Mackellar	14,098
Anderson	13,957

Peak	Height (feet)
Bentley	13,934
Kaplan	13,878
Andrew Jackson	13,750
Sidley	13,720
Ostenso	13,710
Minto	13,668
Miller	13,650
Long Gables	13,620
Dickerson	13,517
Giovinetto	13,412
Wade	13,400

Peak	Height (feet)
Fisher	13,386
Fridtjof Nansen	13,350
Wexler	13,202
Lister	13,200
Shear	13,100
Odishaw	13,008
Donaldson	12,894
Ray	12,808
Sellery	12,779
Waterman	12,730
Anne	12,703

Peak	Height (feet)	Peak	Height (feet)	Peak	Height (feet)
Press	12,566	Campbell	12,434	Astor	12,175
Falla	12,549	Don Pedro Christophersen	12,355	Mohl	12,172
Rucker	12,520	Lysaght	12,326	Frankes	12,064
Goldthwait	12,510	Huggins	12,247	Jones	12,040
Morris	12,500	Sabine	12,200	Gjelsvik	12,008
Erebus	12,450			Coman	12,000

Ocean Areas and Average Depths

Four major bodies of water are recognized by geographers and mapmakers: the Pacific, Atlantic, Indian, and Arctic oceans. The Atlantic and Pacific oceans are considered divided at the equator into the N. and S. Atlantic; the N. and S. Pacific. The Arctic Ocean is the name for waters north of the continental land masses in the region of the Arctic Circle.

	Sq. miles	Avg. depth (feet)		Sq. miles	Avg. depth (feet)
Pacific Ocean	64,186,300	12,925	Hudson Bay	281,900	305
Atlantic Ocean	33,420,000	11,730	East China Sea	256,600	620
Indian Ocean	28,350,500	12,598	Andaman Sea	218,100	3,667
Arctic Ocean	5,105,700	3,407	Black Sea	196,100	3,906
South China Sea	1,148,500	4,802	Red Sea	174,900	1,764
Caribbean Sea	971,400	8,448	North Sea	164,900	308
Mediterranean Sea	969,100	4,926	Baltic Sea	147,500	180
Bering Sea	873,000	4,893	Yellow Sea	113,500	121
Gulf of Mexico	582,100	5,297	Persian Gulf	88,800	328
Sea of Okhotsk	537,500	3,192	Gulf of California	59,100	2,375
Sea of Japan	391,100	5,468			

Principal Ocean Depths

Source: Defense Mapping Agency Hydrographic/Topographic Center, U.S. Dept. of Defense

Name of area	Location		Depth Metres	Depth Fathoms	Depth Feet
Pacific Ocean					
Mariana Trench	11°22′N	142°36′E	10,924	5,973	35,840
Tonga Trench	23°16′S	174°44′W	10,800	5,906	35,433
Philippine Trench	10°38′N	126°36′E	10,057	5,499	32,995
Kermadec Trench	31°53′S	177°21′W	10,047	5,494	32,963
Bonin Trench	24°30′N	143°24′E	9,994	5,464	32,788
Kuril Trench	44°15′N	150°34′E	9,750	5,331	31,988
Izu Trench	31°05′N	142°10′E	9,695	5,301	31,808
New Britain Trench	06°19′S	153°45′E	8,940	4,888	29,331
Yap Trench	08°33′N	138°02′E	8,527	4,663	27,976
Japan Trench	36°08′N	142°43′E	8,412	4,600	27,599
Peru-Chile Trench	23°18′S	71°14′W	8,064	4,409	26,457
Palau Trench	07°52′N	134°56′E	8,054	4,404	26,424
Aleutian Trench	50°51′N	177°11′E	7,679	4,199	25,194
New Hebrides Trench	20°36′S	168°37′E	7,570	4,139	24,836
North Ryukyu Trench	24°00′N	126°48′E	7,181	3,927	23,560
Mid. America Trench	14°02′N	93°39′W	6,662	3,643	21,857
Atlantic Ocean					
Puerto Rico Trench	19°55′N	65°27′W	8,605	4,705	28,232
So. Sandwich Trench	55°42′S	25°56′E	8,325	4,552	27,313
Romanche Gap	0°13′S	18°26′W	7,728	4,226	25,354
Cayman Trench	19°12′N	80°00′W	7,535	4,120	24,721
Brazil Basin	09°10′S	23°02′W	6,119	3,346	20,076
Indian Ocean					
Java Trench	10°19′S	109°58′E	7,125	3,896	23,376
Ob' Trench	09°45′S	67°18′E	6,874	3,759	22,553
Diamantina Trench	35°50′S	105°14′E	6,602	3,610	21,660
Vema Trench	09°08′S	67°15′E	6,402	3,501	21,004
Agulhas Basin	45°20′S	26°50′E	6,195	3,387	20,325
Arctic Ocean					
Eurasia Basin	82°23′N	19°31′E	5,450	2,980	17,881
Mediterranean Sea					
Ionian Basin	36°32′N	21°06′E	5,150	2,816	16,896

Note: Deeper depths have been reported in some of the above areas. However, they are not official unless confirmed by research vessels.

Principal World Rivers

Source: Geological Survey, U.S. Dept. of the Interior

River	Outflow	Length (Miles)	River	Outflow	Length (Miles)	River	Outflow	Length (Miles)
Albany	James Bay	610	Irrawaddy	Bay of Bengal	1,337	Rhine	North Sea	820
Amazon	Atlantic Ocean	4,000	Japura	Amazon River	1,750	Rhone	Gulf of Lions	505
Amu	Aral Sea	1,578	Jordan	Dead Sea	200	Rio de la Plata	Atlantic Ocean	150
Amur	Tatar Strait	2,744	Kootenay	Columbia River	485	Rio Grande	Gulf of Mexico	1,900
Angara	Yenisey River	1,151	Lena	Laptev Sea	2,734	Rio Roosevelt	Aripuana	400
Arkansas	Mississippi	1,459	Loire	Bay of Biscay	634	Saguenay	St. Lawrence R.	434
Back	Arctic Ocean	605	Mackenzie	Arctic Ocean	2,635	St. John	Bay of Fundy	418
Brahmaputra	Bay of Bengal	1,800	Madeira	Amazon River	2,013	St. Lawrence	Gulf of St. Law.	800
Bug, Southern	Dnieper River	532	Magdalena	Caribbean Sea	956	Salween	Andaman Sea	1,500
Bug, Western	Wisla River	481	Marne	Seine River	326	Sao Francisco	Atlantic Ocean	1,988
Canadian	Arkansas River	906	Mekong	S. China Sea	2,600	Saskatchewan	Lake Winnipeg	1,205
Chang Jiang	E. China Sea	3,964	Meuse	North Sea	580	Seine	English Chan.	496
Churchill, Man.	Hudson Bay	1,000	Mississippi	Gulf of Mexico	2,340	Shannon	Atlantic Ocean	230
Churchill, Que.	Atlantic Ocean	532	Missouri	Mississippi	2,315	Snake	Columbia River	1,038
Colorado	Gulf of Calif.	1,450	Murray-Darling	Indian Ocean	2,310	Songhua	Amur River	1,150
Columbia	Pacific Ocean	1,243	Negro	Amazon	1,400	Syr	Aral Sea	1,370
Congo	Atlantic Ocean	2,718	Nelson	Hudson Bay	410	Tajo, Tagus	Atlantic Ocean	626
Danube	Black Sea	1,776	Niger	Gulf of Guinea	2,590	Tennessee	Ohio River	652
Dnieper	Black Sea	1,420	Nile	Mediterranean	4,160	Thames	North Sea	236
Dniester	Black Sea	877	Ob-Irtysh	Gulf of Ob	3,362	Tiber	Tyrrhenian Sea	252
Don	Sea of Azov	1,224	Oder	Baltic Sea	567	Tigris	Shatt al-Arab	1,180
Drava	Danube River	447	Ohio	Mississippi	981	Tisza	Danube River	600
Dvina, North	White Sea	824	Orange	Atlantic Ocean	1,300	Tocantins	Para River	1,677
Dvina, West	Gulf of Riga	634	Orinoco	Atantic Ocean	1,600	Ural	Caspian Sea	1,575
Ebro	Mediterranean	565	Ottawa	St. Lawrence R.	790	Uruguay	Rio de la Plata	1,000
Elbe	North Sea	724	Paraguay	Parana River	1,584	Volga	Caspian Sea	2,290
Euphrates	Shatt al-Arab	1,700	Parana	Rio de la Plata	2,485	Weser	North Sea	454
Fraser	Str. of Georgia	850	Peace	Slave River	1,210	Wisla	Bay of Danzig	675
Gambia	Atlantic Ocean	700	Pilcomayo	Paraguay River	1,000	Xi	S. China Sea	1,200
Ganges	Bay of Bengal	1,560	Po	Adriatic Sea	405	Yellow (See Huang)		
Garonne	Bay of Biscay	357	Purus	Amazon River	2,100	Yenisey	Kara Sea	2,543
Huang	Yellow Sea	3,395	Red	Mississippi	1,290	Yukon	Bering Sea	1,979
Indus	Arabian Sea	1,800	Red River of N.	Lake Winnipeg	545	Zambezi	Indian Ocean	1,700

Lakes of the World

Source: Geological Survey, U.S. Dept. of the Interior

A lake is a body of water surrounded by land. Although some lakes are called seas (such as the Caspian Sea and the Aral Sea), they are lakes by definition.

Name	Continent	Area (sq. mi.)	Length (miles)	Depth (feet)	Elevation (feet)
Caspian Sea	Asia-Europe	143,244	760	3,363	−92
Superior	North America	31,700	350	1,330	600
Victoria	Africa	26,828	250	270	3,720
Aral Sea	Asia	24,904(A)	280	220	174
Huron	North America	23,000	206	750	579
Michigan	North America	22,300	307	923	579
Tanganyika	Africa	12,700	420	4,823	2,534
Baykal	Asia	12,162	395	5,315	1,493
Great Bear	North America	12,096	192	1,463	512
Nyasa	Africa	11,150	360	2,280	1,550
Great Slave	North America	11,031	298	2,015	513
Erie	North America	9,910	241	210	570
Winnipeg	North America	9,417	266	60	713
Ontario	North America	7,550	193	802	245
Balkhash	Asia	7,115	376	85	1,115
Ladoga	Europe	6,835	124	738	13
Chad	Africa	6,300	175	24	787
Maracaibo	South America	5,217	133	115	Sea level
Onega	Europe	3,710	145	328	108
Eyre	Australia	3,600	90	4	−52
Volta	Africa	3,276	250	....	....
Titicaca	South America	3,200	122	922	12,500
Nicaragua	North America	3,100	102	230	102
Athabasca	North America	3,064	208	407	700
Reindeer	North America	2,568	143	720	1,106
Rudolf	Africa	2,473	154	240	1,230
Issyk Kul	Asia	2,355	115	2,303	5,279
Torrens	Australia	2,230	130	....	92
Vanern	Europe	2,156	91	328	144
Nettilling	North America	2,140	67	....	95
Winnipegosis	North America	2,075	141	38	830
Albert	Africa	2,075	100	168	2,030
Kariba	Africa	2,050	175	390	1,590
Nipigon	North America	1,872	72	540	1,050
Gairdner	Australia	1,840	90	....	112
Urmia	Asia	1,815	90	49	4,180
Manitoba	North America	1,799	140	12	813

(A) Probably less because of the diversion of feeder rivers.

The Great Lakes

Source: National Ocean Service, U.S. Dept. of Commerce

The Great Lakes form the largest body of fresh water in the world and with their connecting waterways are the largest inland water transportation unit. Draining the great North Central basin of the U.S., they enable shipping to reach the Atlantic via their outlet, the St. Lawrence R., and also the Gulf of Mexico via the Illinois Waterway, from Lake Michigan to the Mississippi R. A third outlet connects with the Hudson R. and thence the Atlantic via the N. Y. State Barge Canal System. Traffic on the Illinois Waterway and the N.Y. State Barge Canal System is limited to recreational boating and small shipping vessels.

Only one of the lakes, Lake Michigan, is wholly in the United States; the others are shared with Canada. Ships move from the shores of Lake Superior to Whitefish Bay at the east end of the lake, thence through the Soo (Sault Ste. Marie) locks, through the St. Mary's River and into Lake Huron. To reach Gary, and Port of Indiana and South Chicago, Ill., ships move west from Lake Huron to Lake Michigan through the Straits of Mackinac.

Lake Superior is 600 feet above mean water level at Point-au-Père, Quebec, on the International Great Lakes Datum (1955). From Duluth, Minn., to the eastern end of Lake Ontario is 1,156 mi.

	Superior	Michigan	Huron	Erie	Ontario
Length in miles	350	307	206	241	193
Breadth in miles	160	118	183	57	53
Deepest soundings in feet	1,330	923	750	210	802
Volume of water in cubic miles	2,900	1,180	850	116	393
Area (sq. miles) water surface—U.S.	20,600	22,300	9,100	4,980	3,560
Canada	11,100	.....	13,900	4,930	3,990
Area (sq. miles) entire drainage basin—U.S.	16,900	45,600	16,200	18,000	15,200
Canada	32,400	.....	35,500	4,720	12,100
Total Area (sq. miles) U.S. and Canada	**81,000**	**67,900**	**74,700**	**32,630**	**34,850**
Mean surface above mean water level at Point-au-Père, Quebec, aver. level in feet (1900-1988)	600.61	578.34	578.34	570.53	244.74
Latitude, North	46°25'	41°37'	43°00'	41°23'	43°11'
	49°00'	46°06'	46°17'	42°52'	44°15'
Longitude, West	84°22'	84°45'	79°43'	78°51'	76°03'
	92°06'	88°02'	84°45'	83°29'	79°53'
National boundary line in miles	282.8	None	260.8	251.5	174.6
United States shore line (mainland only) miles	863	1,400	580	431	300

Famous Waterfalls

Source: National Geographic Society

The Earth has thousands of waterfalls, some of considerable magnitude. Their importance is determined not only by height but volume of flow, steadiness of flow, crest width, whether the water drops sheerly or over a sloping surface, and in one leap or a succession of leaps. A series of low falls flowing over a considerable distance is known as a cascade.

Estimated mean annual flow, in cubic feet per second, of major waterfalls are: Niagara, 212,200; Paulo Afonso, 100,000; Urubupunga, 97,000; Iguazu, 61,000; Patos-Maribondo, 53,000; Victoria, 35,400; and Kaieteur, 23,400.

Height = total drop in feet in one or more leaps. † = falls of more than one leap; * = falls that diminish greatly seasonally; ** = falls that reduce to a trickle or are dry for part of each year. If river names not shown, they are same as the falls. R. = river; L. = lake; (C) = cascade type.

Name and location	Elevation (Feet)
Africa	
Angola	
Ruacana, Cuene R.	406
Ethiopia	
Fincha	508
Lesotho	
*Maletsunyane	630
Zimbabwe-Zambia	
*Victoria, Zambezi R.	343
South Africa	
*Augrabies, Orange R.	480
† Tugela	2,014
Tanzania-Zambia	
*Kalambo	726
Asia	
India—*Cauvery	330
*Jog (Gersoppa), Sharavathi R.	830
Japan	
*Kegon, Daiya R.	330
Australasia	
Australia	
New South Wales	
Wentworth	614
Wollomombi	1,100
Queensland	
Tully	885
† Wallaman, Stony Cr.	1,137
New Zealand	
Helena	890
† Sutherland, Arthur R.	1,904
Europe	
Austria—† Gastein	492
† Krimml	1,312
France—*Gavarnie	1,385
Great Britain—Scotland	
Glomach	370
Wales	
Rhaiadr	240
Italy—Frua, Toce R. (C)	470
Norway	
Mardalsfossen (Northern)	1,535
† Mardalsfossen (Southern)	2,149
† **Skjeggedal, Nybuai R.	1,378
**Skykje	984
Vetti, Morka-Koldedola R.	900
Sweden	
† Handol	427
Switzerland	
Giessbach (C)	984
† Reichenbach	656
† Simmen	459
Staubbach	984
† Trummelbach	1,312
North America	
Canada	
Alberta	
Panther, Nigel Cr.	600
British Columbia	
† Della	1,443
† Takakkaw, Daly Glacier	1,200
Quebec	
Montmorency	274
Canada—United States	
Niagara: American	182
Horseshoe	173
United States	
California	
*Feather, Fall R.	640
Yosemite National Park	
*Bridalveil	620
*Illilouette	370
*Nevada, Merced R.	594
**Ribbon	1,612
**Silver Strand, Meadow Br.	1,170
*Vernal, Merced R.	317
† **Yosemite	2,425

Name and location	Elevation (Feet)
Colorado	
† Seven, South Cheyenne Cr.	300
Hawaii	
Akaka, Kolekole Str.	442
Idaho	
**Shoshone, Snake R.	212
Kentucky	
Cumberland	68
Maryland	
*Great, Potomac R. (C)	71
Minnesota	
**Minnehaha	53
New Jersey	
Passaic	70
New York	
*Taughannock	215
Oregon	
† Multnomah	620
Tennessee	
Fall Creek	256
Washington	
Mt. Rainier Natl. Park	
Sluiskin, Paradise R.	300
**Snoqualmie	268
Wisconsin	
*Big Manitou, Black R. (C)	165
Wyoming	
Yellowstone Natl. Pk. Tower	132
*Yellowstone (upper)	109
*Yellowstone (lower)	308
Mexico	
El Salto	218
South America	
Argentina-Brazil	
Iguazu	230
Brazil	
Glass	1,325
Patos-Maribondo, Grande R.	115
Paulo Afonso, Sao Francisco R.	275
Colombia	
Catarata de Candelas, Cusiana R.	984
*Tequendama, Bogota R.	427
Ecuador	
*Agoyan, Pastaza R.	200
Guyana	
Kaieteur, Potaro R.	741
Great, Kamarang R.	1,600
† Marina, Ipobe R.	500
Venezuela—	
† *Angel	3,212
Cuquenan	2,000

Highest and Lowest Continental Altitudes

Source: National Geographic Society

Continent	Highest point	Feet	Lowest point (below sea level)	Feet
Asia	Mount Everest, Nepal-Tibet	29,028	Dead Sea, Israel-Jordan	1,312
South America	Mount Aconcagua, Argentina	22,834	Valdes Peninsula, Argentina	131
North America	Mount McKinley, Alaska	20,320	Death Valley, California	282
Africa	Kilimanjaro, Tanzania	19,340	Lake Assal, Djibouti	512
Europe	Mount El'brus, Russia	18,510	Caspian Sea, Russia, Azerbaijan	92
Antarctica	Vinson Massif	16,864	Unknown	
Australia	Mount Kosciusko, New South Wales	7,310	Lake Eyre, South Australia	52

Notable Deserts of the World

Arabian (Eastern), 70,000 sq. mi. in Egypt between the Nile river and Red Sea, extending southward into Sudan.

Atacama, 600 mi. long area rich in nitrate and copper deposits in N. Chile.

Chihuahuan, 140,000 sq. mi. in Tex., N.M., Ariz., and Mexico.

Death Valley, 3,300 sq. mi. in E. Cal. and SW Nev. Contains lowest point below sea level (282 ft.) in Western Hemisphere.

Gibson, 120,000 sq. mi. in the interior of W. Australia.

Gobi, 500,000 sq. mi. in Mongolia and China.

Great Sandy, 150,000 sq. mi. in W. Australia.

Great Victoria, 150,000 sq. mi. in W. and S. Australia.

Kalahari, 225,000 sq. mi. in southern Africa.

Kara-Kum, 120,000 sq. mi. in Turkmenistan.

Kyzyl Kum, 100,000 sq. mi. in Kazakhstan & Uzbekistan.

Libyan, 450,000 sq. mi. in the Sahara extending from Libya through SW Egypt into Sudan.

Lut (Dasht-e Lut), 20,000 sq. mi. in E. Iran.

Mojave, 15,000 sq. mi. in S. Cal.

Namib, long narrow area extending 800 miles along SW coast of Africa.

Nubian, 100,000 sq. mi. in the Sahara in NE Sudan.

Painted Desert, section of high plateau in N. Ariz. extending 150 mi.

Rub al Khali (Empty Quarter), 250,000 sq. mi. in the south Arabian Peninsula.

Sahara, 3,500,000 sq. mi. in N. Africa extending westward to the Atlantic. Largest desert in the world.

Sonoran, 70,000 sq. mi. in SW Ariz. and SE Cal. extending into Mexico.

Syrian, 100,000 sq. mi. arid wasteland extending over much of N. Saudi Arabia, E. Jordan, S. Syria, and W. Iraq.

Taklimakan, 140,000 sq. mi. in Sinkiang Province, China.

Thar (Great Indian), 100,000 sq. mi. arid area extending 400 mi. along India-Pakistan border.

Important Islands and Their Areas

Figure in parentheses shows rank among the world's 10 largest islands; some islands have not been surveyed accurately; in such cases estimated areas are shown.

Location-Ownership

Area in square miles

Arctic Ocean	
Canadian	
Axel Heiberg	15,779
Baffin (5)	183,810
Banks	27,038
Bathurst	7,609
Devon	20,861
Ellesmere (9)	82,119
Melville	16,369
Prince of Wales	12,830
Somerset	9,370
Southampton	15,700
Victoria (10)	81,930
Norwegian	
Svalbard	23,940
Nordaustlandet	5,410
Spitsbergen	15,060
Russian	
Franz Josef Land	8,000
Novaya Zemlya (two is.)	31,730
Wrangel	2,800
Atlantic Ocean	
Anticosti, Canada	3,043
Ascension, UK	34
Azores, Portugal	888
Faial	67

(Continued)

Sao Miguel	291
Bahamas	5,386
Bermuda Is., UK	20
Bioko Is. Equatorial Guinea	785
Block, Rhode Island	10
Canary Is., Spain	2,808
Fuerteventura	668
Gran Canaria	592
Tenerife	795
Cape Breton, Canada	3,970
Cape Verde Is.	1,557
Faeroe Is., Denmark	540
Falkland Is., UK	4,700
Fernando de Noronha Archipelago, Brazil	7
Greenland, Denmark (1)	840,000
Iceland	39,769
Long Island, N. Y.	1,396
Madeira Is., Portugal	307
Marajo, Brazil	15,444
Martha's Vineyard, Mass.	108
Mount Desert, Me.	108
Nantucket, Mass.	57
Newfoundland, Canada	42,030
Prince Edward, Canada	2,184
St. Helena, UK	47
South Georgia, UK	1,450
Tierra del Fuego, Chile and Argentina	18,800
Tristan da Cunha, UK	40

British Isles

Great Britain, mainland (8)	88,797
Channel Islands	75
Guernsey	24
Jersey	45
Sark	2
Hebrides	2,744
Ireland	32,599
Irish Republic	27,136
Northern Ireland	5,463
Man	227
Orkney Is.	390
Scilly Is.	6
Shetland Is.	567
Skye	670
Wight	147

Baltic Sea

Aland Is., Finland	581
Bornholm, Denmark	227
Gotland, Sweden	1,159

Caribbean Sea

Antigua	108
Aruba, Netherlands	75
Barbados	166
Cuba	44,218
Isle of Youth	1,182
Curacao, Netherlands	171
Dominica	290
Guadeloupe, France	687
Hispaniola, Haiti and Dominican Republic	29,371
Jamaica	4,244
Martinique, France	425
Puerto Rico, U.S.	3,435
Tobago	116
Trinidad	1,864
Virgin Is., UK	59
Virgin Is., U.S.	132

Indian Ocean

Andaman Is., India	2,500
Madagascar (4)	226,658
Mauritius	720
Pemba, Tanzania	380
Reunion, France	969
Seychelles	171
Sri Lanka	25,332
Zanzibar, Tanzania	640

Persian Gulf

Bahrain	255

Mediterranean Sea

Balearic Is., Spain	1,936
Corfu, Greece	229
Corsica, France	3,369
Crete, Greece	3,189
Cyprus	3,572
Elba, Italy	86
Euboea, Greece	1,411
Malta	95
Rhodes, Greece	540
Sardinia, Italy	9,262
Sicily, Italy	9,822

Pacific Ocean

Aleutian Is., U.S.	6,821
Adak	289
Amchitka	121
Attu	388
Kanaga	135
Kiska	110
Tanaga	209
Umnak	675
Unalaska	1,064
Unimak	1,600
Canton, Kiribati*	4
Caroline Is.	472
Christmas, Kiribati*	94
Clipperton, France	2
Diomede, Big, Russia	11
Diomede, Little, U.S.	2
Easter, Chile	69
Fiji	7,056
Vanua Levu	2,242
Viti Levu	4,109
Funafuti, Tuvalu*	2
Galapagos Is., Ecuador	3,043
Guadalcanal	2,180
Guam	209
Hainan, China	13,000
Hawaiian Is., U.S.	6,450
Hawaii	4,037
Oahu	593
Hong Kong, UK	29
Japan	145,809
Hokkaido	30,144
Honshu (7)	87,805
Iwo Jima	8
Kyushu	14,114
Okinawa	459
Shikoku	7,049
Kodiak, U.S.	3,670
Marquesas Is., France	492
Marshall Is.	70
Bikini*	2
Nauru	8
New Caledonia, France	6,530
New Guinea (2)	306,000
New Zealand	103,883
Chatham	372
North	44,035
South	58,305
Stewart	674
Northern Mariana Is.	184
Philippines	115,831
Leyte	2,787
Luzon	40,880
Mindanao	36,775
Mindoro	3,790
Negros	4,907
Palawan	4,554
Panay	4,446
Samar	5,050
Quemoy	56
Sakhalin, Russia	29,500
Samoa Is.	1,177
American Samoa	77
Tutuila	52
Samoa (Western)	1,133
Savaii	670
Upolu	429
Santa Catalina, U.S.	72
Tahiti, France	402
Taiwan	13,823
Tasmania, Australia	26,178
Tonga Is.	270
Vancouver, Canada	12,079
Vanuatu	5,700

East Indies

Bali, Indonesia	2,171
Borneo, Indonesia-Malaysia, Brunei (3)	280,100
Celebes, Indonesia	69,000
Java, Indonesia	48,900
Madura, Indonesia	2,113
Moluccas, Indonesia	32,307
New Britain, Papua New Guinea	14,093
New Ireland, Papua New Guinea	3,707
Sumatra, Indonesia (6)	165,000
Timor	13,094

* **Atolls:** Bikini (lagoon area, 230 sq. mi., and area 2 sq. mi.); Canton (lagoon 20 sq. mi., land 4 sq. mi.), Kiribati; Christmas (lagoon 140 sq. mi., land 94 sq. mi.), Kiribati; Funafuti (lagoon 84 sq. mi., land 2 sq. mi.), Tuvalu. **Australia,** often called an island, is a continent.

Islands in minor waters: Manhattan (22 sq mi.), Staten (59 sq. mi.) and Governors (173 acres), all in New York Harbor, U.S.; Isle Royale (209 sq. mi.), Lake Superior, U.S.; Manitoulin (1,068 sq. mi.), Lake Huron, Canada; Pinang (110 sq. mi.), Strait of Malacca, Malaysia; Singapore (239 sq. mi.), Singapore Strait, Singapore.

United States Facts

Source: U.S. Geological Survey; U.S. Bureau of the Census; World Almanac Research

Area for 50 states and D. of C.	Total Land 3,539,289 sq. mi. – Water 79,481 sq. mi.	3,618,770 sq. mi.
Largest state	Alaska	591,004 sq. mi.
Smallest state	Rhode Island	1,212 sq. mi.
Largest county (excludes Alaska)	San Bernardino County, California	20,064 sq. mi.
Smallest county	Kalawo, Hawaii	14 sq. mi.
Northernmost city	Barrow, Alaska	71°17′N.
Northernmost point	Point Barrow, Alaska	71°23′N.
Southernmost city	Hilo, Hawaii	19°43′N.
Southernmost settlement	Naalehu, Hawaii	19°03′N.
Southernmost point	Ka Lae (South Cape), Island of Hawaii	18°55′N. (155°41′W.)
Easternmost city	Eastport, Maine	66°59′02″W.
Easternmost settlement*	Amchitka, Alaska	179°15′E.
Easternmost point*	Semisapochnoi, Alaska	179°52′E.

Westernmost city	West Unalaska, Alaska ... 166°32′W.
Westernmost settlement	Adak Station, Alaska ... 176°39′W.
Westernmost point	Cape Wrangell, Alaska ... 172°27′W.
Highest settlement	Climax, Colorado ... 11,560 ft.
Lowest settlement	Calipatria, California ... –185 ft.
Highest point on Atlantic coast	Cadillac Mountain, Mount Desert Is., Maine ... 1,530 ft.
Oldest national park	Yellowstone National Park (1872), Wyoming, Montana, Idaho ... 3,468 sq. mi.
Largest national park	Wrangell-St. Elias, Alaska ... 13,018 sq. mi.
Largest national monument	Death Valley, California, Nevada ... 3,231 sq. mi.
Highest waterfall	Yosemite Falls – Total in three sections ... 2,425 ft.
	Upper Yosemite Fall ... 1,430 ft.
	Cascades in middle section ... 675 ft.
	Lower Yosemite Fall ... 320 ft.
Longest river	Mississippi-Missouri ... 3,710 mi.
Highest mountain	Mount McKinley, Alaska ... 20,320 ft.
Lowest point	Death Valley, California ... –282 ft.
Deepest lake	Crater Lake, Oregon ... 1,932 ft.
Rainiest spot	Mt. Waialeale, Hawaii ... Annual aver. rainfall 460 inches
Largest gorge	Grand Canyon, Colorado River, Arizona ... 277 miles long, 600 ft. to 18 miles wide, 1 mile deep
Deepest gorge	Hell's Canyon, Snake River, Idaho–Oregon ... 7,900 ft.
Strongest surface wind	Mount Washington, New Hampshire recorded 1934 ... 231 mph
Biggest dam	New Cornelia Tailings, Ten Mile Wash, Arizona ... 274,026,000 cu. yds. material used
Tallest building	Sears Tower, Chicago, Illinois ... 1,454 ft.
Largest building	Boeing 747 Manufacturing Plant, Everett, Washington ... 205,600,000 cu. ft.; covers 47 acres.
Tallest structure	TV tower, Blanchard, North Dakota ... 2,063 ft.
Longest bridge span	Verrazano-Narrows, New York ... 4,260 ft.
Highest bridge	Royal Gorge, Colorado ... 1,053 ft. above water
Deepest well	Gas well, Washita County, Oklahoma ... 31,441 ft.

The 48 Contiguous States

Area for 48 states	Total ... 3,021,295 sq. mi. Land 2,962,031 sq. mi. – Water 59,264 sq. mi.
Largest state	Texas ... 266,807 sq. mi.
Northernmost city	Bellingham, Washington ... 48°46′N.
Northernmost settlement	Angle Inlet, Minnesota ... 49°21′N.
Northernmost point	Northwest Angle, Minnesota ... 49°23′N.
Southernmost city	Key West, Florida ... 24°33′N.
Southernmost mainland city	Florida City, Florida ... 25°27′N.
Southernmost point	Key West, Florida ... 24°33′N.
Easternmost settlement	Lubec, Maine ... 66°58′49″W.
Easternmost point	West Quoddy Head, Maine ... 66°57′W.
Westernmost town	La Push, Washington ... 124°38′W.
Westernmost point	Cape Alava, Washington ... 124°44′W.
Highest mountain	Mount Whitney, California ... 14,494 ft.

* Alaska's Aleutian Islands extend into the eastern hemisphere and therefore technically contain the easternmost point and settlement in the United States.

States: Settled, Capitals, Entry into Union, Area, Rank

The original 13 states – The 13 colonies that seceded from Great Britain and fought the War of Independence (American Revolution) became the 13 states. They were: Delaware, Pennsylvania, New Jersey, Georgia, Connecticut, Massachusetts, Maryland, South Carolina, New Hampshire, Virginia, New York, North Carolina and Rhode Island. The order for the original 13 states is that in which they ratified the Constitution.

State	Settled*	Capital	Entered Union Date	Entered Union Order	Extent in miles (approx. mean) Long	Extent in miles Wide	Area in square miles Land	Area Inland water	Area Total	Rank in area
Ala.	1702	Montgomery	Dec. 14, 1819	22	330	190	50,767	938	51,705	29
Alas.	1784	Juneau	Jan. 3, 1959	49	(a) 1,480	810	570,833	20,171	591,004	1
Ariz.	1776	Phoenix	Feb. 14, 1912	48	400	310	113,508	492	114,000	6
Ark.	1686	Little Rock	June 15, 1836	25	260	240	52,078	1,109	53,187	27
Cal.	1769	Sacramento	Sept. 9, 1850	31	770	250	156,299	2,407	158,706	3
Col.	1858	Denver	Aug. 1, 1876	38	380	280	103,595	496	104,091	8
Conn.	1634	Hartford	Jan. 9, 1788	5	110	70	4,872	147	5,018	48
Del.	1638	Dover	Dec. 7, 1787	1	100	30	1,932	112	2,045	49
D.C.		Washington			...	...	63	6	69	51
Fla.	1565	Tallahassee	Mar. 3, 1845	27	500	160	54,153	4,511	58,664	22
Ga.	1733	Atlanta	Jan. 2, 1788	4	300	230	58,056	854	58,910	21
Ha.	1820	Honolulu	Aug. 21, 1959	50	...	...	6,425	46	6,471	47
Ida.	1842	Boise	July 3, 1890	43	570	300	82,412	1,153	83,564	13
Ill.	1720	Springfield	Dec. 3, 1818	21	390	210	55,645	700	56,345	24
Ind.	1733	Indianapolis	Dec. 11, 1816	19	270	140	35,932	253	36,185	38
Ia.	1788	Des Moines	Dec. 28, 1846	29	310	200	55,965	310	56,275	25
Kan.	1727	Topeka	Jan. 29, 1861	34	400	210	81,778	499	82,277	14
Ky.	1774	Frankfort	June 1, 1792	15	380	140	39,669	740	40,410	37
La.	1699	Baton Rouge	Apr. 30, 1812	18	380	130	44,521	3,230	47,752	31
Me.	1624	Augusta	Mar. 15, 1820	23	320	190	30,995	2,270	33,265	39
Md.	1634	Annapolis	Apr. 28, 1788	7	250	90	9,837	623	10,460	42
Mass.	1620	Boston	Feb. 6, 1788	6	190	50	7,824	460	8,284	45
Mich.	1668	Lansing	Jan. 26, 1837	26	490	240	56,954	1,573	58,527	23
Minn.	1805	St. Paul	May 11, 1858	32	400	250	79,548	4,854	84,402	12
Miss.	1699	Jackson	Dec. 10, 1817	20	340	170	47,233	457	47,689	32

(Continued)

State	Settled*	Capital	Entered Union Date			Entered Union Order	Extent in miles Long (approx. mean)	Extent in miles Wide (approx. mean)	Area in square miles Land	Area in square miles Inland water	Area in square miles Total	Rank in area
Mo.	1735	Jefferson City	Aug.	10,	1821	24	300	240	68,945	752	69,697	19
Mon.	1809	Helena	Nov.	8,	1889	41	630	280	145,388	1,658	147,046	4
Neb.	1823	Lincoln	Mar.	1,	1867	37	430	210	76,644	711	77,355	15
Nev.	1849	Carson City	Oct.	31,	1864	36	490	320	109,894	667	110,561	7
N.H.	1623	Concord	June	21,	1788	9	190	70	8,993	286	9,279	44
N.J.	1660	Trenton	Dec.	18,	1787	3	150	70	7,468	319	7,787	46
N.M.	1610	Santa Fe	Jan.	6,	1912	47	370	343	121,335	258	121,593	5
N.Y.	1614	Albany	July	26,	1788	11	330	283	47,377	1,731	49,108	30
N.C.	1660	Raleigh	Nov.	21,	1789	12	500	150	48,843	3,826	52,669	28
N.D.	1812	Bismarck	Nov.	2,	1889	39	340	211	69,300	1,403	70,702	17
Oh.	1788	Columbus	Mar.	1,	1803	17	220	220	41,004	325	41,330	35
Okla.	1889	Oklahoma City	Nov.	16,	1907	46	400	220	68,655	1,301	69,956	18
Ore.	1811	Salem	Feb.	14,	1859	33	360	261	96,184	889	97,073	10
Pa.	1682	Harrisburg	Dec.	12,	1787	2	283	160	44,888	420	45,308	33
R.I.	1636	Providence	May	29,	1790	13	40	30	1,055	158	1,212	50
S.C.	1670	Columbia	May	23,	1788	8	260	200	30,203	909	31,113	40
S.D.	1859	Pierre	Nov.	2,	1889	40	380	210	75,952	1,164	77,116	16
Tenn.	1769	Nashville	June	1,	1796	16	440	120	41,155	989	42,144	34
Tex.	1682	Austin	Dec.	29,	1845	28	790	660	262,017	4,790	266,807	2
Ut.	1847	Salt Lake City	Jan.	4,	1896	45	350	270	82,073	2,826	84,899	11
Vt.	1724	Montpelier	Mar.	4,	1791	14	160	80	9,273	341	9,614	43
Va.	1607	Richmond	June	25,	1788	10	430	200	39,704	1,063	40,767	36
Wash.	1811	Olympia	Nov.	11,	1889	42	360	240	66,511	1,627	68,139	20
W. Va.	1727	Charleston	June	20,	1863	35	240	130	24,119	112	24,232	41
Wis.	1766	Madison	May	29,	1848	30	310	260	54,426	1,727	56,153	26
Wy.	1834	Cheyenne	July	10,	1908	44	360	280	96,989	820	97,809	9

* First European permanent settlement. (a) Aleutian Islands and Alexander Archipelago are not considered in these lengths.

Federal Indian Reservations and Trust Lands[1]

Source: Bureau of Indian Affairs, U.S. Dept. of the Interior (data as of 1990)

The total American Indian population according to the 1990 Census is 1,878,285.

State	No. of reser.	Tribally owned acreage[2]	Individually owned acreage[2]	No. of persons[3]	Major tribes and/or nations
Alabama	1	230	0	16,504	Poarch Creek
Alaska	1[4]	86,773	1,265,432	85,698	Aleut, Eskimo, Athapascan,[5] Haida, Tlingit, Tsimpshian
Arizona	23	19,775,959	256,879	203,527	Navajo, Apache, Papago, Hopi, Yavapai, Pima
California	96	520,049	66,769	242,164	Hoopa, Paiute, Yurok, Karok, Cherokee
Colorado	2	764,120	2,805	27,776	Ute
Connecticut	1	1,638	0	6,654	Mashantucket Pequot
Florida	4	153,874	0	36,335	Seminole, Miccosukee, Cherokee
Idaho	4	464,077	327,301	13,780	Shoshone, Bannock, Nez Perce
Iowa	1	3,550	0	7,349	Sac and Fox
Kansas	4	7,219	23,763	21,965	Potawatomi, Kickapoo, Iowa
Louisiana	3	415	0	18,541	Chitimacha, Coushatta, Tunica-Biloxi
Maine	3	191,511	0	5,998	Passamaquoddy, Penobscot, Maliseet
Michigan	8	14,411	9,276	55,638	Chippewa, Potawatomi, Ottawa, Cherokee
Minnesota	14	779,138	50,338	49,909	Chippewa, Sioux
Mississippi	1	20,486	0	8,825	Choctaw
Missouri	1	0	374.37		Cherokee
Montana	7	2,663,385	2,911,450	47,679	Blackfeet, Crow, Sioux, Assiniboine, Cheyenne
Nebraska	3	21,742	43,208	12,410	Omaha, Winnebago, Santee Sioux
Nevada	19	1,147,088	78,529	19,637	Paiute, Shoshone, Washoe
New Mexico	25	7,119,982	621,715	134,355	Zuni, Apache, Navajo
New York	8	118,199	0	62,651	Seneca, Mohawk, Onondaga, Oneida
North Carolina	1	56,509	0	80,155	Cherokee, Lumbee
North Dakota	3	214,006	627,289	25,917	Sioux, Chippewa, Mandan, Arikara, Hidatsa
Oklahoma	1[6]	96,839	1,000,165	252,420	Cherokee, Creek, Choctaw, Chickasaw, Osage, Cheyenne, Arapahoe, Kiowa, Comanche
Oregon	7	660,367	135,053	38,496	Warm Springs, Wasco, Paiute, Umatilla, Siletz
Rhode Island	1	1,800	0	4,071	Narragansett
South Dakota	9	2,399,531	2,121,188	50,573	Sioux
Texas	3	4,726	0	65,877	Alabama-Coushatta, Tiwa, Kickapoo
Utah	4	2,284,766	32,838	24,283	Ute, Goshute, Southern Paiute, Navajo
Washington	27	2,250,731	467,785	81,483	Yakima, Lummi, Quinault, Sioux
Wisconsin	11	338,097	80,345	39,387	Chippewa, Oneida, Winnebago
Wyoming	1	1,958,095	101,537	9,479	Shoshone, Arapahoe

(1) As of 1988 the federal government recognized and acknowledged that it had a special relationship with, and a trust responsibility for, 307 federally recognized Indian entities in the continental U.S., plus some 200 tribal entities in Alaska. The term "Indian entities" encompasses Indian tribes, bands, villages, groups, pueblos, Eskimos, and Aleuts, eligible for federal services and classified in the following 3 categories: (a) Officially approved Indian organizations pursuant to federal statutory authority (Indian Reorganization Act; Oklahoma Indian Welfare Act and Alaska Native Act). (b) Officially approved Indian organizations outside of specified federal statutory authority. (c) Traditional Indian organizations recognized without formal federal approval of organizational structure. Some reservation boundaries transcend state boundaries (e.g., Navajo which is in Arizona, New Mexico, and Utah). For statistical convenience under "Number of Reservations", such reservations are counted in the state where population is predominant and/or tribal headquarters is located. (2) The acreages refer only to Indian lands which are either owned by the tribes or individual Indians, and held in trust by the U.S. government. Many of these parcels are located off reservations. Not all lands within reservation boundaries are necessarily trust lands. Many parcels are privately owned by tribes, individual Indians, and non-Indians. Also, some internal lands are the property of various governmental agencies. (3) Total Indian population in each state with reservation/trust lands, including those persons living outside of the BIA Service area. (4) Alaskan Indian Affairs are carried out under the Alaska Native Claims Settlement Act (Dec. 18, 1971). The Act provided for the establishment of regional and village corporations to conduct business for profit and non-profit purposes. There are 13 such regional corporations, each one with organized village corporations. The Annette Island Reservation remains the only federally recognized reservation in Alaska in the sense of specified reservation boundaries, trust lands, etc. (5) Aleuts and Eskimos are racially and linguistically related. Athapascans are related to the Navajo and Apache Indians. (6) Indian land status in Oklahoma is unique and there are no reservations except for Osage in the sense that the term is used elsewhere in the U.S. Likewise, many of the Oklahoma tribes are unique in their high degree of assimilation to the white culture.

NATIONS OF THE WORLD

As of mid-1993

Sources: U.S. Dept. of State; U.S. Census Bureau; *The World Factbook*; International Monetary Fund; *UN Statistical Yearbook*; *UN Demographic Yearbook*; International Iron and Steel Institute; *The Statesman's Year-Book*; *Encyclopaedia Britannica*; *Funk & Wagnalls New Encyclopedia*. Literacy rates are usually based on the ability to read and write on a lower elementary school level. The concept of literacy is changing in the industrialized countries, where literacy is defined as the ability to read instructions necessary for a job or a licence. By these standards, illiteracy may be more common than present rates suggest. Per person figures in communications and health sections are post-1988.

The nations of the world are listed in alphabetical order. Initials in the following articles include UN (United Nations), OAS (Org. of American States), NATO (North Atlantic Treaty Org.), EC (European Communities or Common Market), OAU (Org. of African Unity), ILO (Intl. Labour Org.), FAO (Food & Agriculture Org.), WHO (World Health Org.), IMF (Intl. Monetary Fund), GATT (General Agreement on Tarriffs & Trade), CIS (Commonwealth of Independent States). Note that most Commonwealth countries are represented by High Commissions rather than Embassies in the UK. The nearest embassy address is given for those countries not represented in the UK.

Afghanistan

Republic of Afghanistan

De Afghanistan Jamhuriat

People: Population (1992 est.): 16,095,000. **Pop. density:** 63 per sq. mi. **Urban** (1990): 18%. **Ethnic groups:** Pushtun 38%; Tajik 25%; Hazara 19%; Uzbek 6%. **Languages:** Pushtu, Dari Persian (spoken by Tajiks, Hazaras), Uzbek (Turkic). **Religions:** Sunni Muslim 74%, Shi'a Muslim 5%.

Geography: Area: 251,773 sq. mi., twice the size of the Br. Isles. **Location:** In SW Asia, NW of the Indian subcontinent. **Neighbors:** Pakistan on E, S, Iran on W, Turkmenistan, Tajikistan, Uzbekistan, on N; the NE tip touches China. **Topography:** The country is landlocked and mountainous, much of it over 4,000 ft. above sea level. The Hindu Kush Mts. tower 16,000 ft. above Kabul and reach a height of 25,000 ft. to the E. Trade with Pakistan flows through the 35-mile-long Khyber Pass. The climate is dry, with extreme temperatures, and there are large desert regions, though mountain rivers produce intermittent fertile valleys. **Capital:** Kabul, pop. (1988 est.) 1.4 mln.

Government: Type: In transition. **Head of state:** Pres. Burhanuddin Rabbani; in office Apr. 28, 1992. **Local divisions:** 30 provinces. **Defense** (1990): 15% of GDP.

Economy: Industries: Textiles, furniture, cement. **Chief crops:** Nuts, wheat, fruits. **Minerals:** Copper, coal, zinc, iron. **Other resources:** Wool, hides, karacul pelts. **Arable land:** 13%. **Livestock** (1990): 1.6 mln. cattle; 13 mln. sheep. **Electricity prod.** (1991): 1.4 bln. kWh. **Labor force:** agriculture supports about 80% of the population.

Finance: Monetary unit: Afghani (Mar. 1993: 50.60 = $1 US). **Gross domestic product** (1989): $3.1 bln. **Per capita GDP:** $220. **Imports** (1991): $874 mln.; partners: CIS 55%, Jap. 8%. **Exports** (1991): $236 mln.; partners: CIS 72%. **International reserves less gold** (Feb. 1992): $229 mln. **Gold:** 965,000 oz t. **Consumer prices** (change in 1991): 56%.

Transport: Motor vehicles (1990): 31,000 passenger cars, 30,000 comm. vehicles. **Civil aviation** (1989): 194 mln. passenger-km.

Communications: Television sets: 1 per 169 persons. **Radios:** 1 per 11 persons. **Telephones:** 1 per 443 persons. **Daily newspaper circ.** (1988): 10 per 1,000 pop.

Health: Life expectancy at birth (1992): 45 male; 43 female. **Births** (per 1,000 pop. 1992): 44. **Deaths** (per 1,000 pop. 1991): 20. **Natural increase:** 2.3%. **Hospital beds:** 1 per 2,054 persons. **Physicians:** 1 per 4,797 persons. **Infant mortality** (per 1,000 live births 1992): 164.

Education (1990): **Literacy:** 29%. **School:** Over 88% of adults have no formal schooling.

Major International Organizations: UN (World Bank, IMF)

Embassy: 31 Prince's Gate, London SW7 1QQ; 071-589 8891.

Afghanistan, occupying a favored invasion route since antiquity, has been variously known as Ariana or Bactria (in ancient times) and Khorasan (in the Middle Ages). Foreign empires alternated rule with local emirs and kings until the 18th century, when a unified kingdom was established. In 1973, a military coup ushered in a republic.

Pro-Soviet leftists took power in a bloody 1978 coup, and concluded an economic and military treaty with the USSR.

Late in Dec. 1979, the USSR began a massive military airlift into Kabul. The 3-month-old regime of Hafizullah Amin ended with a Soviet-backed coup, Dec. 27. He was replaced by Babrak Karmal, a more pro-Soviet leader. Soviet troops fanned out over Afghanistan, fighting Islamic rebels. Fighting continued for 9 years as the Soviets found themselves engaged in a protracted guerrilla war.

An UN-mediated agreement was signed Apr. 14, 1988 providing for the withdrawal of Soviet troops from Afghanistan, creation of a neutral Afghan state, and repatriation of millions of Afghan refugees. The U.S. and USSR pledged to serve as guarantors of the agreement. Afghan rebels rejected the pact and vowed to continue fighting while the "Soviets and their puppets" remained in Afghanistan.

The Soviets disclosed that during the war some 15,000 soldiers were killed. They completed their troop withdrawal Feb. 15, 1989; fighting between Afghan rebels and government forces ensued.

Communist Pres. Najibullah resigned Apr. 16, 1992 as competing guerrilla forces advanced on Kabul. The rebels achieved power, Apr. 28, ending 14 years of Soviet-backed regimes. Over 2 million Afghans had been killed and 6 million had fled the country since 1979.There were immediate clashes between moderates and Islamic fundamentalist forces. Burhanuddin Rabbani, a guerrilla leader, became president June 28. Fierce fighting continued around Kabul through 1993.

Albania

Republic of Albania

Republika e Shqipërisë

People: Population (1991 est.): 3,285,000. **Pop. density:** 295 per sq. mi. **Urban** (1991): 35%. **Ethnic groups:** Albanians (Gegs in N, Tosks in S) 90%, Greeks 8.0%. **Languages:** Albanian, Greek. **Religions:** Greek Orthodox 70%, Roman Catholic 10%.

Geography: Area: 11,100 sq. mi., slightly larger than the Highland region of Scotland. **Location:** On SE coast of Adriatic Sea. **Neighbors:** Greece on S, Yugoslavia on N, Macedonia on E. **Topography:** Apart from a narrow coastal plain, Albania consists of hills and mountains covered with scrub forest, cut by small E-W rivers. **Capital:** Tirana. **Cities** (1990 est.): Tirana 243,000; Durres 85,000; Elbasin 84,000.

Government: Type: Democracy. **Head of state:** Pres. Sali Berisha; in office Apr. 9, 1992. **Head of government:** Premier Alexander Meksi; in office Apr. 13, 1992. **Local divisions:** 26 districts. **Defense** (1990): 4.1% of GDP.

Economy: Industries: Cement, textiles, food processing. **Chief crops:** Corn, wheat, cotton, potatoes, tobacco, fruits. **Minerals:** Chromium, coal, oil. **Other resources:** Forests. **Arable land:** 21%. **Livestock** (1991): 650,000 cattle; 1.6 mln. sheep. **Electricity prod.** (1990): 5.0 bln. kWh. **Labor force:** 60% agric; 40% ind. & comm.

Finance: Monetary unit: Lek (Nov. 1992: 109 = $1 US). **Gross national product** (1991) $4.0 bln. **Per capita GNP** (1987): $1,300. **Imports** (1991): $147 mln.; partners: Czech., Yugoslavia, Rom. **Exports** (1991): $80 mln.; partners: Czech., Yugoslavia, Italy. **National budget** (1991): $1.4 bln. expenditure.

Transport: Chief ports: Durres, Vlone, Garande.

Communications: Television sets: 1 per 13 persons. **Radios:** 1 per 6 persons. **Daily newspaper circ.:** 48 per 1,000 pop.

Health: Life expectancy at birth (1992): 72 male; 79 female. **Births** (per 1,000 pop. 1992): 23. **Deaths** (per 1,000 pop. 1992): 5. **Natural increase:** 2.0%. **Hospital beds:** 1 per 176 persons. **Physicians:** 1 per 574 persons. **Infant mortality** (per 1,000 live births 1992): 27.

Education (1990): **Literacy:** 72%. **School:** Free and compulsory ages 7-15.

Ancient Illyria was conquered by Romans, Slavs, and Turks (15th century); the latter Islamized the population. Independent Albania was proclaimed in 1912, republic was formed in 1920. King Zog I ruled 1925-39, until Italy invaded.

Communist partisans took over in 1944, allied Albania with USSR, then broke with USSR in 1960 over de-Stalinization. Strong political alliance with China followed, leading to several billion dollars in aid, which was curtailed after 1974. China cut off aid in 1978 when Albania attacked its policies after the death of Chinese ruler Mao Tse-tung.

Large-scale purges of officials occurred during the 1970s. Enver Hoxha, the nation's ruler for 4 decades, died Apr. 11, 1985.

There was some liberalization in 1990, including measures providing for freedom to travel abroad and restoration of the right to practice religion.

In 1991, a general strike and urban opposition forced the communist cabinet to resign; a non-communist caretaker was installed. By March, over 40,000 Albanians had left their country and sailed to Italy. James Baker became the first U.S. secy. of state to visit Albania, June 22.

Albania's former Communists were routed in parliamentary elections May 1992, amid economic collapse and social unrest. Berisha was elected as the first non-Communist president since World War II. Inflation was about 150%, unemployment was estimated at 70% nationwide, and almost all food came from foreign aid.

Algeria

Democratic and Popular Republic of Algeria

al-Jumhuriya al-Jazâiriya ad-Dimuqratiya ash-Shabiya

People: Population (1992 est.): 26,666,000. **Age distrib.** (%): 0–14: 43.9; 15–59: 50.3; 60+: 5.8. **Pop. density:** 31 per sq. mi. **Urban** (1990): 51%. **Ethnic groups:** Arabs 75%, Berbers 25%. **Languages:** Arabic (official), Berber (indigenous language). **Religion:** Sunni Muslim (state religion).

Geography: Area: 918,497 sq. mi., more than 10 times the size of GB. **Location:** In NW Africa, from Mediterranean Sea into Sahara Desert. **Neighbors:** Morocco on W, Mauritania, Mali, Niger on S, Libya, Tunisia on E. **Topography:** The Tell, located on the coast, comprises fertile plains 50-100 miles wide, with a moderate climate and adequate rain. 2 major chains of the Atlas Mts., running roughly E-W, and reaching 7,000 ft., enclose a dry plateau region. Below lies the Sahara, mostly desert with major mineral resources. **Capital:** Algiers (El Djazair). **Cities** (1987 est.): El Djazair 1,483,000; Wahran 590,000; Qacentina 483,000.

Government: Type: Republic. **Head of state:** Pres. Ali Kafi; in office July 1, 1992. **Head of government:** Prime Min. Belaid Abdesalam; in office July 8, 1992. **Local divisions:** 48 provinces. **Defense** (1992): 1.8% of GDP.

Economy: Industries: Oil, light industry, food processing. **Chief crops:** Grains, wine-grapes, potatoes, dates, olives, oranges. **Minerals:** Mercury, iron, zinc, lead. **Crude oil reserves** (1987): 4.8 bln. bbls. **Other resources:** Cork trees. **Arable land:** 3%. **Livestock** (1988): 1.7 mln. cattle; 14 mln. sheep. **Electricity prod.** (1991): 16.7 bln. kWh. **Crude steel prod.** (1991): 767,000 metric tons. **Labor force:** 24% agric.; 4% ind. and commerce; 24% government, & services.

Finance: Monetary unit: Dinar (Mar. 1993: 23 = $1 US). **Gross domestic product** (1990): $54 bln. **Per capita GDP:** $2,130. **Imports** (1991): $9.2 bln.; partners: EC 64%. **Exports** (1991): $11.7 bln.; partners: EC 74%. **National budget** (1990): $17.3 bln. **International reserves less gold** (Mar. 1993): $1.8 bln. **Gold:** 5.5 mln. oz t. **Consumer prices** (change in 1990): 26%

Transport: Railroads (1991): 2,668 mi. long. **Motor vehicles** (1990): 750,000 passenger cars, 500,000 comm. vehicles. **Chief port:** El Djazair.

Communications: Television sets: 1 per 15 persons. **Radios:** 1 per 4 persons. **Telephones:** 1 per 23 persons. **Daily newspaper circ.** (1990): 53 per 1,000 pop.

Health: Life expectancy at birth (1992): 66 male; 68 female. **Births** (per 1,000 pop. 1992): 31. **Deaths** (per 1,000 pop. 1992): 7.0. **Natural increase:** 2.4%. **Hospital beds:** 1 per 393 persons. **Physicians:** 1 per 1,062 persons. **Infant mortality** (per 1,000 live births 1992): 57.

Education (1991): **Literacy:** 52%.

Major International Organizations: UN (FAO, IMF, WHO), OAU, Arab League, OPEC.

Embassy: 54 Holland Park, London W11 3RS; 071-221 7800.

Earliest known inhabitants were ancestors of Berbers, followed by Phoenicians, Romans, Vandals, and, finally, Arabs. Turkey ruled 1518 to 1830, when France took control.

Large-scale European immigration and French cultural inroads did not prevent an Arab nationalist movement from launching guerilla war. Peace, and French withdrawal, was negotiated with French Pres. Charles de Gaulle. One million Europeans left. Independence came July 5, 1962.

Ahmed Ben Bella was the victor of infighting and ruled 1962-65, when an army coup installed Col. Houari Boumedienne as leader.

In 1967, Algeria declared war with Israel, broke with U.S., and moved toward eventual military and political ties with the USSR. Some 500 died in riots protesting economic hardship in 1988. In 1989, voters approved a new constitution which cleared the way for a multiparty system and guaranteed "fundamental rights and freedoms" of Algerians.

The Government banned all non-religious activities at Algeria's 10,000 mosques, Jan. 22, 1992, after the fundamental Islamic Salvation Front (FIS) called for the overthrow of the government. Pres. Boudiaf was assassinated June 29. There were several attacks on high-ranking officials by militant Muslim fundamentalists in 1993.

Andorra

Principality of Andorra

Principat d'Andorra

People: Population (1992 est.): 54,000. **Age distrib.** (%): 0–14: 17.4; 14–59: 68.8; 60+: 13.8. **Pop. density:** 291 per sq. mi. **Ethnic groups:** Catalan 61%, Spanish 30%, Andorran 6%, French 3%. **Languages:** Catalan (official), Spanish, French. **Religion:** Roman Catholic.

Geography: Area: 185 sq. mi., slightly bigger than the Isle of Wight. **Location:** In Pyrenees Mtns. **Neighbors:** Spain on S, France on N. **Topography:** High mountains and narrow valleys over the country. **Capital:** Andorra la Vella.

Government: Type: Parliamentary democracy. **Head of government:** Oscar Ribas Reig; in office May 4, 1992. **Local divisions:** 7 parishes.

Economy: Industries: Tourism, tobacco products. **Labor force:** 20% agric.; 80% ind. and commerce; services; government.

Finance: Monetary unit: French franc, Spanish peseta.

Communications: Television sets: 1 per 8 persons. **Radios:** 1 per 4 persons. **Telephones:** 1 per 2 persons.

Health: Births (per 1,000 pop. 1992): 10. **Deaths** (per 1,000 pop. 1992): 4. **Natural increase:** 0.7%.

Education (1992): **Literacy:** 99%. **School:** Compulsory to age 16.

Major International Organizations: UN.

Delegation: 63 Westover Rd, London SW18 2RF; 081-874 4806.

Andorra was a co-principality, with joint sovereignty by France and the bishop of Urgel, from 1278 to 1993.

Tourism, especially skiing, is the economic mainstay. A free port, allowing for an active trading centre, draws some 10 million tourists annually. The ensuing economic prosperity, accompanied by Andorra's virtual law-free status, gave rise to calls for reform. Andorra voters chose to end a feudal system that had been in place for 715 years and adopt a parliamentary system of government Mar. 14, 1993.

Angola

Republic of Angola

República de Angola

People: Population (1991 est.): 8,902,000. **Pop. density:** 18 per sq. mi. **Urban** (1991): 29%. **Ethnic groups:** Ovimbundu 38%, Kimbundu 25%; Bakongo 13%. **Languages:** Portuguese (official), various Bantu languages. **Religions:** Roman Catholic 38%, Protestant 15%, indigenous beliefs 47%.

Geography: Area: 481,353 sq. mi., 5 times larger than the UK. **Location:** In SW Africa on Atlantic coast. **Neighbors:** Namibia on S, Zambia on E, Zaire on N; Cabinda, an enclave separated from rest of country by short Atlantic coast of Zaire, borders Congo Republic. **Topography:** Most of Angola consists of a plateau elevated 3,000 to 5,000 feet above sea level, rising from a narrow coastal strip. There is also a temperate highland area in the west-central region, a desert in the S, and a tropical rain forest covering Cabinda. **Capital:** Luanda, pop. (1988 est.) 1.1 mln.

Government: Type: Republic. **Head of state:** Pres. Jose Eduardo dos Santos b. Aug. 28, 1942; in office Sept. 20, 1979. **Head of government:** Prime Min. Marcolino Moco; in office Dec. 2, 1992. **Local divisions:** 18 provinces. **Defense** (1984): 14.3% of GDP.

Economy: Industries: Food processing, textiles, mining, tires, petroleum. **Chief crops:** Coffee, bananas. **Minerals:** Iron, diamonds (over 2 mln. carats a year), copper, phosphates, oil. **Livestock** (1991): 3.1 mln. cattle; 1 mln. goats. **Crude oil reserves** (1987): 1.9 bln. bbls. **Arable land:** 3%. **Fish catch** (1990): 178,000 metric tons. **Electricity prod.** (1991): 770 mln. kWh. **Labor force:** 85% agric., 15% industry.

Finance: Monetary unit: New Kwanza (Nov. 1992: 550 = $1 US). **Gross domestic product** (1991): $8.3 bln. **Per capita GDP:** $950. **Imports** (1991): $1.3 bln.; partners: Portugal 29%, Fra. 9%; U.S. 9%. **Exports** (1991): $3.4 bln.; partners: U.S. 56%.

Transport: Motor vehicles (1990): 130,000 passenger cars, 44,000 comm. vehicles. **Chief ports:** Cabinda, Lobito, Luanda.

Communications: Television sets: 1 per 200 persons. Radios: 1 per 22 persons. **Telephones:** 1 per 132 persons. **Daily newspaper circ.** (1984): 13 per 1,000 pop.

Health: Life expectancy at birth (1992): 43 male; 47 female. **Births** (per 1,000 pop. 1992): 46. **Deaths** (per 1,000 pop. 1992): 19. **Natural increase:** 2.7%. **Hospital beds:** 1 per 845 persons. **Physicians:** 1 per 15,136 persons. **Infant mortality** (per 1,000 live births 1992): 151.

Education (1992): **Literacy:** 40%.

Major International Organizations: UN (ILO, WHO), OAU.

Embassy: 98 Park Lane, London W1Y 3TA; 071-495 1752.

From the early centuries AD to 1500, Bantu tribes penetrated most of the region. Portuguese came in 1583, allied with the Bakongo kingdom in the north, and developed the slave trade. Large-scale colonization did not begin until the 20th century, when 400,000 Portuguese immigrated.

A guerrilla war begun in 1961 lasted until 1975, when Portugal granted independence. Fighting then erupted between three rival rebel groups—the National Front, based in Zaire, the Soviet-backed Popular Movement for the Liberation of Angola (MPLA), and the National Union for the Total Independence of Angola (UNITA), aided by the U.S. and S. Africa. The civil war killed thousands of blacks, drove most whites to emigrate, and completed economic ruin. Cuban troops and Soviet aid helped the MPLA win control of most of the country by 1976 and gain wide recognition as the government of Angola, but UNITA continued fighting.

An agreement was signed in Dec. 1988 between Angola, Cuba, and S. Africa on a timetable for withdrawal of Cuban troops, completed May 25, 1991. The 16-year war ended May 1, 1991, as the government and UNITA signed a peace agreement which would lead to democracy. Elections were held in Sept. 1992, but UNITA rejected the presidential election results and fighting again broke out and continued into 1993, with UNITA forces holding about 50% of the nation's territory.

The U.S. formally recognized the government of Angola, May 19, 1993, for the first time since independence.

Antigua and Barbuda

People: Population (1992 est.) 64,000 (incl. Redonda). **Urban** (1990): 32%. **Ethnic groups:** Mostly African. **Language:** English (official). **Religion:** Predominantly Church of England.

Geography: Area: 171 sq. mi., slightly larger than the Isle of Wight. **Location:** Eastern Caribbean. **Neighbors:** Approx. 30 mi. north of Guadeloupe. **Capital:** St. John's, pop. (1988 est.) 27,000.

Government: Type: Constitutional monarchy with British-style parliament. **Head of state:** Queen Elizabeth II; represented by Sir Wilfred E. Jacobs. **Head of government:** Prime Min. Vere Cornwall Bird; b. Dec. 7, 1910; in office Nov. 1, 1981.

Economy: Industries: Manufacturing, tourism. **Arable land:** 18%.

Finance: Monetary unit: East Caribbean dollar (June 1993: 2.70 = $1 US). **Gross domestic product** (1990): $350 mln.

Health: Infant mortality (per 1,000 live births 1992): 20.

Education (1990): **Literacy:** 90%.

Major International Organizations: UN, Commonwealth of Nations.

High Commission: 15 Thayer St, London W1M 5LD; 071-486 7073.

Columbus landed on Antigua in 1493. The British colonized it in 1632.

The British associated state of Antigua achieved independence as Antigua and Barbuda on Nov. 1, 1981. The government maintains close relations with the U.S., United Kingdom and Venezuela.

Argentina

Argentine Republic

República Argentina

People: Population (1992 est.): 32,901,000. **Age distrib.** (%): 0–14: 30.3; 15–59: 56.8; 60+: 12.9. **Pop. density:** 30 per sq. mi. **Urban** (1991): 87%. **Ethnic groups:** Europeans 95% (Spanish, Italian), Indians, Mestizos, Arabs. **Languages:** Spanish (official), Italian. **Religion:** Roman Catholic 92%.

Geography: Area: 1,065,189 sq. mi., 12 times the size of GB, second largest in S. America. **Location:** Occupies most of southern S. America. **Neighbors:** Chile on W, Bolivia, Paraguay on N, Brazil, Uruguay on NE. **Topography:** The mountains in W: the Andean, Central, Misiones, nd Southern. Aconcagua is the highest peak in the Western hemisphere, alt. 22,834 ft. E of the Andes are heavily wooded plains, called the Gran Chaco in the N, and the fertile, treeless Pampas in the central region. Patagonia, in the S, is bleak and arid. Rio de la Plata, 170 by 140 mi., is mostly fresh water, from 2,485-mi. Parana and 1,000-mi. Uruguay rivers. **Capital:** Buenos Aires. (The Senate has approved the moving of the capital to the Patagonia Region.) **Cities** (1991 est.): Buenos Aires (metro.) 12,582,000; Cordoba 1.1 mln.; Rosario (metro.) 1.0 mln.

Government: Type: Republic. **Head of state:** Pres. Carlos Saúl Menem; b. July 2, 1930; in office July 8, 1989. **Local divisions:** 28 provinces, 1 federal district. **Defense** (1991): 1.4% of GNP.

Economy: Industries: Food processing, flour milling, chemicals, textiles, machinery, autos. **Chief crops:** Grains, corn, grapes, linseed, sugar, tobacco, rice, soybeans, citrus fruits. **Minerals:** Oil, lead, zinc, iron, copper, tin, uranium. **Crude oil reserves** (1987): 2.1 bln. bbls. **Arable land:** 9%. **Livestock** (1991): 50 mln. cattle; 27 mln. sheep. **Fish catch** (1990): 555,000 metric tons. **Electricity prod.** (1991): 46.0 bln. kWh. **Crude steel prod.** (1991): 2.9 mln. metric tons. **Labor force:** 19% agric.; 36% ind. and comm.; 20% services.

Finance: Monetary unit: Peso (July 1993: .99 = $1 US). **Gross domestic product** (1991): $101.2 bln. **Per capita GDP:** $3,100. **Imports** (1991): $8.0 bln.; partners: U.S. 21%, W. Ger. 9%, Braz. 16%, Jap. 7%. **Exports** (1991): $12.3 bln.; partners: CIS 13%, Neth. 9%, U.S. 12%. **Tourism** (1990): $903 mln. receipts. **National budget** (1990): $17.3 bln. expenditures. **International reserves less gold** (Jan. 1992): $6.6 bln. **Gold:** 4.12 mln. oz t. **Consumer prices** (change in 1992): 24.9%.

Transport: Railroads (1988): 21,198 mi. long. **Motor vehicles** (1989): 4.0 mln. passenger cars, 1.5 mln. comm. vehicles. **Civil aviation** (1991): 8.2 mln. passenger-km; 1,473 airports. **Chief ports:** Buenos Aires, Bahia Blanca, La Plata.

Communications: Television sets: 1 per 4 persons. **Radios:** 1 per 1 person. **Telephones:** 1 per 9 persons. **Daily newspaper circ.** (1986): 88 per 1,000 pop.

Health: Life expectancy at birth (1992): 67 male; 74 female. **Births** (per 1,000 pop. 1992): 20. **Deaths** (per 1,000 pop. 1992): 9. **Natural increase:** 1.2%. **Hospital beds:** 1 per 150 persons. **Physicians:** 1 per 326 persons. **Infant mortality** (per 1,000 live births 1992): 31.

Education (1992): **Literacy:** 95%. **School:** Compulsory for 7 years.

Major International Organizations: UN (WHO, IMF, FAO), OAS.

Embassy: 53 Hans Place, London SW1X 0LB; 071-584 6494.

Nomadic Indians roamed the Pampas when Spaniards arrived, 1515-16, led by Juan Diaz de Solis. Nearly all the Indians were killed by the late 19th century. The colonists won independence, 1816, and a long period of disorders ended in a strong centralized government.

Large-scale Italian, German, and Spanish immigration in the decades after 1880 spurred modernization, making Argentina the most prosperous, educated, and industrialized of the major Latin American nations. Social reforms were enacted in the 1920s, but military coups prevailed 1930-46, until the election of Gen. Juan Peron as president.

Peron, with his wife Eva Duarte, effected labor reforms, but also suppressed speech and press freedoms, closed religious schools, and ran the country into debt. A 1955 coup exiled Peron, who was followed by a series of military and civilian regimes. Peron returned in 1973, and was once more elected president. He died 10 months later, succeeded by his wife, Isabel, who had been elected vice president, and who became the first woman head of state in the Western hemisphere.

A military junta ousted Mrs. Peron in 1976 amid charges of corruption. Under a continuing state of siege, the army battled guerrillas and leftists, killed 5,000 people, and jailed and tortured others. On Dec. 9, 1985, after a trial of 5 months and nearly 1,000 witnesses, 5 former junta members, including ex-presidents Jorge Videla and Gen. Roberto Eduardo Viola, were found guilty of murder and human rights abuses.

A severe worsening in economic conditions placed extreme pressure on the military government.

Argentine troops seized control of the British-held Falkland Islands on Apr. 2, 1982. Both countries had claimed sovereignty over the islands, located 250 miles off the Argentine coast, since 1833. The British dispatched a task force and declared a total air and sea blockade around the Falklands. Fighting began May 1; several hundred lost their lives as the result of the destruction of a British destroyer and the sinking of an Argentine cruiser.

British troops landed in force on East Falkland Island May 21. By June 2, the British had surrounded Stanley, the capital city and Argentine stronghold. The Argentine troops surrendered, June 14; Argentine President Leopoldo Galtieri resigned June 17.

Democratic rule returned to Argentina in 1983 as Raul Alfonsin's Radical Civic Union gained an absolute majority in the presidential electoral college and Congress. In 1989 the nation was plagued by severe financial problems as inflation reached crisis levels; over 6,000%. The hyperinflation sparked a week of looting and rioting in several cities; the government declared a 30-day state of siege May 29.

The government unveiled harsh economic measures in an effort to combat spiralling inflation, control government spending and restructure the foreign debt 1991–92.

Armenia

Republic of Armenia

Haikakan Hanrapetoutioun

People: Population (1992 est.): 3,415,000. **Pop. density:** 302 per sq. mi. **Urban** (1991): 70%. **Ethnic groups:** Armenian 93%.

Language: Armenian. **Religion:** Mostly Christian.

Geography: Area: 11,306 sq. mi., twice the size of N. Ireland. **Neighbors:** Georgia on N, Azerbaijan on E, Iran on S, Turkey on W. **Topography:** Mountains with many peaks above 10,000 ft. **Capital:** Yerevan.

Government: Type: Republic. **Head of state:** Pres. Levon Ter-Petrosyan; in office Oct. 16, 1991. **Head of government:** Gagik Arutyunyan.

Economy: Industries: Mining, chemicals. **Chief crops:** Cotton, figs, grain. **Minerals:** Copper, zinc. **Arable land:** 10%.

Finance: Monetary unit: Rouble.

Transport: Motor vehicles (1989): 230,000 passenger cars.

Communications: Television sets: 1 per 5 persons. **Radios:** 1 per 5 persons. **Telephones:** 1 per 6 persons. **Newspaper circ.:** 468 per 1,000 pop.

Health: Life expectancy at birth (1992): 68 male; 74 female. **Hospital beds:** 1 per 117 persons. **Physicians:** 1 per 246 persons. **Infant mortality** (per 1,000 live births 1992): 35.

Major International Organizations: UN (IMF), CIS.

Embassy: 25 Cheniston Gardens, London W8 6TG; 071-938 5435.

Armenia is an ancient country, parts of which are now in Turkey and Iran. Present-day Armenia was set up as a Soviet Republic Apr. 2, 1921. It joined Georgian and Azerbaijan SSRs Mar. 12, 1922 to form the Trans-caucasian SFSR, which became part of the USSR Dec. 30, 1922. Armenia became a constituent republic of the USSR Dec. 5, 1936. An earthquake struck Armenia Dec. 7, 1988; over 55,000 were killed and several cities and towns were left in ruins. Armenia declared independence Sept. 23, 1991, and became an independent state when the USSR disbanded Dec. 26, 1991.

Fighting between mostly Christian Armenia and mostly Muslim Azerbaijan escalated in 1992 and continued in 1993. Each country claimed Nagorno-Karabakh, an enclave in Azerbaijan that has a majority population of ethnic Armenians.

Australia

Commonwealth of Australia

People: Population (1992 est.): 17,576,000 (incl. Macquarie Island). **Age distrib.** (%): 0–14: 21.9; 15–59: 62.6; ; 59+: 15.5. **Pop. density:** 5.9 per sq. mi. **Urban** (1990): 85%. **Ethnic groups:** European 95%, Asian 4%, aborigines (including mixed) 1.5%. **Languages:** English, aboriginal languages. **Religions:** Anglican 26%, other Protestant 25%, Roman Catholic 25%.

Geography: Area: 2,966,200 sq. mi., almost as large as the continental U.S. **Location:** SE of Asia, Indian O. is W and S, Pacific O. (Coral, Tasman seas) is E; they meet N of Australia in Timor and Arafura seas: Tasmania lies 150 mi. S of Victoria state, across Bass Strait. **Neighbors:** Nearest are Indonesia, Papua New Guinea on N, Solomons, Fiji, and New Zealand on E. **Topography:** An island continent. The Great Dividing Range along the E coast has Mt. Kosciusko, 7,310 ft. The W plateau rises to 2,000 ft., with arid areas in the Great Sandy and Great Victoria deserts. The NW part of Western Australia and Northern Terr. are arid and hot. The NE has heavy rainfall and Cape York Peninsula has jungles. The Murray R. rises in New South Wales and flows 1,600 mi. to the Indian O. **Capital:** Canberra. **Cities** (1991 est.): Sydney 3,600,000; Melbourne 3,000,000; Brisbane 1,200,000; Perth 1,200,000; Adelaide 1,000,000.

Government: Type: Democratic, federal state system. **Head of state:** Queen Elizabeth II, represented by Gov.-Gen. William Hayden; in office: Feb. 16, 1989. **Head of government:** Prime Min. Paul Keating; b. Jan. 18, 1944; in office Dec. 20, 1991. **Local divisions:** 6 states, 2 territories. **Defense** (1992): 2.3% of GDP.

Economy: Industries: Iron, steel, textiles, electrical equip., chemicals, autos, aircraft, ships, machinery. **Chief crops:** Wheat (a leading export), barley, oats, corn, hay, sugar, wine, fruit, vegetables. **Minerals:** Coal, copper, iron, lead, tin, uranium, zinc. **Crude oil reserves** (1987): 1.6 bln. bbls. **Other resources:** Wool (30% of world output). **Arable land:** 9%. **Livestock** (1991): 22 mln. cattle; 162 mln. sheep; 2.5 mln. pigs. **Fish catch** (1990): 175,000 metric tons. **Electricity prod.** (1991): 155 bln. kWh. **Crude steel prod.** (1991): 6.1 mln. metric tons. **Labor force:** 6% agric.; 33% finance & services; 36% trade & manuf.

Finance: Monetary unit: Dollar (July 1993: 1.47 = $1 US). **Gross domestic product** (1991): $311 bln. **Per capita income** (1990): $18,054. **Imports** (1992): $43.7 bln; partners: U.S. 21%, Jap. 20%, UK 7%. **Exports** (1992): $42.4 bln.; partners: Jap. 27%, U.S. 11%, NZ 5%. **Tourism** (1990): $3.7 bln. receipts. **National budget** (1991): $93 bln. expenditures. **International reserves less gold** (Mar. 1993): $9.3 bln. **Gold:** 7.93 mln. oz t. **Consumer prices** (change in 1992): 1.0%.

Transport: Railroads (1991): 22,051 mi. long. **Motor vehicles** (1990): 7.6 mln. passenger cars, 2.1 mln. comm. vehicles. **Civil aviation** (1990): 23.0 mln. passenger-km.; 441 airports with scheduled flights. **Chief ports:** Sydney, Melbourne, Newcastle, Port Kembla, Fremantle, Geelong.

Communications: Television sets: 1 per 2 persons. **Radios:** 1 per 2 persons. **Telephones:** 1 per 2 persons. **Daily newspaper circ.** (1988): 405 per 1,000 pop.

Health: Life expectancy at birth (1992): 74 male; 80 female. **Births** (per 1,000 pop. 1992): 15. **Deaths** (per 1,000 pop. 1992): 8. **Natural increase:** .8%. **Hospital beds:** 1 per 199 persons. **Physicians:** 1 per 438 persons. **Infant mortality** (per 1,000 live births 1992): 8.

Education (1992): **Literacy:** 99%. **School:** Compulsory to age 15; attendance 94%.

Major International Organizations: UN and all its specialized agencies, OECD, Commonwealth of Nations.

High Commission: Australia House, Strand, London WC2B 4LA; 071-379 4334.

Capt. James Cook explored the E coast in 1770, when the continent was inhabited by a variety of different tribes. The first settlers, beginning in 1788, were mostly convicts, soldiers, and government officials. By 1830, Britain had claimed the entire continent, and the immigration of free settlers began to accelerate. The commonwealth was proclaimed Jan. 1, 1901. Northern Terr. was granted limited self-rule July 1, 1978.

States	Area (sq. mi.)	Population (1991 cen.)
New South Wales, Sydney	309,500	5,731,926
Victoria, Melbourne	87,900	4,243,719
Queensland, Brisbane	666,990	2,976,617
Western Aust., Perth	975,100	1,586,393
South Aust., Adelaide	379,900	1,400,656
Tasmania, Hobart	26,200	452,847
Aust. Capital Terr., Canberra	900	280,085
Northern Terr., Darwin	519,800	175,253

Australia's racially discriminatory immigration policies were abandoned in 1973, after 3 million Europeans (half British) had entered since 1945. The 50,000 aborigines and 150,000 part-aborigines are mostly detribalized, but there are several preserves in the Northern Territory. They remain economically disadvantaged.

Australia's agricultural success makes the country among the top exporters of beef, lamb, wool, and wheat. Major mineral deposits have been developed as well, largely for exports. Industrialization has been completed.

Australia harbors many plant and animal species not found elsewhere, including the kangaroo, koalas, platypus, dingo (wild dog), Tasmanian devil (racoon-like marsupial), wombat (bear-like marsupial), and barking and frilled lizards.

The nation suffered through a deep recession 1990–93. Unemployment was 11.1 per cent in Feb. 1993.

Australian External Territories

Norfolk Is., area 13½ sq. mi., pop. (1990) 1,800, was taken over, 1914. The soil is very fertile, suitable for citrus fruits, bananas, and coffee. Many of the inhabitants are descendants of the Bounty mutineers, moved to Norfolk 1856 from Pitcairn Is. Australia offered the island limited home rule, 1978.

Coral Sea Is. Territory, 1 sq. mi., is administered from Norfolk Is.

Territory of Ashmore and Cartier Is., area 2 sq. mi., in the Indian O. came under Australian authority 1934 and are administered as part of Northern Territory. **Heard** and **McDonald Is.** are administered by the Dept. of Science.

Cocos (Keeling) Is., 27 small coral islands in the Indian O. 1,750 mi. NW of Australia. Pop. (1990) 600, area: 5½ sq. mi. The residents voted to become part of Australia, Apr. 1984.

Kiritimati (Christmas Is.) 52 sq. mi., pop. (1991) 1,700, 230 mi. S of Java, was transferred by Britain in 1958. It has phosphate deposits.

Australian Antarctic Territory was claimed by Australia in 1933, including 2,362,000 sq. mi. of territory S of 60th parallel S Lat. and between 160th-45th meridians E Long. It does not include Adelie Coast.

Austria

Republic of Austria

Republik Österreich

People: Population (1992 est.): 7,867,000. **Age distrib.** (%): 0–14: 17.4; 15–59: 62.1; 60+: 20.5. **Pop. density:** 243 per sq. mi. **Urban** (1991): 54%. **Ethnic groups:** German 99%, Slovene, Croatian. **Language:** German. **Religion:** Roman Catholic 89%.

Geography: Area: 32,377 sq. mi., slightly larger than Scotland. **Location:** In S Central Europe. **Neighbors:** Switzerland, Liechtenstein on W, Germany, Czech Rep., Slovakia on N, Hungary on E, Slovenia, Italy on S. **Topography:** Austria is primarily mountainous, with the Alps and foothills covering the western and southern provinces. The eastern provinces and Vienna are located in the Danube River Basin. **Capital:** Vienna, pop. (1991 est.) 1,500,000.

Government: Type: Parliamentary democracy. **Head of state:** Pres. Thopmas Klestil; in office July 8, 1992. **Head of government:** Chancellor Franz Vranitzky; b. Oct. 4, 1937; in office June 16, 1986. **Local divisions:** 9 länder (states), each with a legislature. **Defense** (1990): 1.2% of GDP.

Economy: Industries: Steel, machinery, autos, electrical and optical equip., glassware, sport goods, paper, textiles, chemicals, cement. **Chief crops:** Grains, potatoes, beets. **Minerals:** Iron ore, oil, magnesite. **Other resources:** Forests, hydro power. **Arable land:** 17%. **Livestock** (1991): 2.5 mln. cattle; 3.6 mln. pigs. **Electricity prod.** (1991): 49.5 bln. kWh. **Crude steel prod.** (1991): 4.1 mln. metric tons. **Labor force:** 8% agric.; 35% ind. & comm.; 56% service.

Finance: Monetary unit: Schilling (June 1993: 11.90 = $1 US). **Gross domestic product** (1991): $164 bln. **Per capita GDP:** $20,895. **Imports** (1991): $54.1 bln.; partners: EC 70%. **Exports** (1992): $44.4 bln.; partners: EC 68%. **Tourism** (1990): $13.0 bln. receipts. **National budget** (1990): $49.6 bln. expenditures. **International reserves less gold** (Mar. 1993): $12.1 bln. **Gold:** 19.9 mln. oz t. **Consumer prices** (change in 1992): 4.0%.

Transport: Railroads (1991): 4,041 mi. long. **Motor vehicles** (1991): 2.9 mln. passenger cars, 256,000 comm. **Civil aviation** (1991): 2.9 bln. passenger-km; 6 airports with scheduled flights.

Communications: Television sets: 1 per 2.8 persons. **Radios:** 1 per 1.6 persons. **Telephones:** 1 per 1.8 persons. **Daily newspaper circ.** (1991): 445 per 1,000 pop.

Health: Life expectancy at birth (1991): 74 male; 81 female. **Births** (per 1,000 pop. 1992): 12. **Deaths** (per 1,000 pop. 1992): 11. **Natural increase:** –.1%. **Hospital beds:** 1 per 101 persons. **Physicians:** 1 per 334 persons. **Infant mortality** (per 1,000 live births 1992): 8.

Education (1992): **Literacy:** 99%. **School:** Compulsory for 9 years; attendance 95%.

Major International Organizations: UN and all of its specialized agencies, EFTA, OECD.

Embassy: 18 Belgrave Mews West, London SW1X 8HU; 071-235 3731.

Rome conquered Austrian lands from Celtic tribes around 15 BC. In 788 the territory was incorporated into Charlemagne's empire. By 1300, the House of Hapsburg had gained control; they added vast territories in all parts of Europe to their realm in the next few hundred years.

Austrian dominance of Germany was undermined in the 18th century and ended by Prussia by 1866. But the Congress of Vienna, 1815, confirmed Austrian control of a large empire in southeast Europe consisting of Germans, Hungarians, Slavs, Italians, and others.

The dual Austro-Hungarian monarchy was established in 1867, giving autonomy to Hungary and almost 50 years of peace.

World War I, started after the June 28, 1914 assassination of Archduke Franz Ferdinand, the Hapsburg heir, by a Serbian nationalist, destroyed the empire. By 1918 Austria was reduced to a small republic, with the borders it has today.

Nazi Germany invaded Austria Mar. 13, 1938. The republic was reestablished in 1945, under Allied occupation. Full independence and neutrality were restored in 1955.

Austria produces most of its food, as well as an array of industrial products. A large part of Austria's economy is controlled by state enterprises. Socialists have shared or alternated power with the conservative People's Party.

Azerbaijan

Azerbaijani Republic

Azerbaijchan Respublikasy

People: Population (1992 est.): 7,450,000. **Pop. density:** 223 per sq. mi. **Urban** (1991): 54%. **Ethnic groups:** Azerbaijani 82%, Russian 6%, Armenian 6%. **Languages:** Azeri, Turkish, Russian. **Religion:** Mostly Muslim.

Geography: Area: 33,400 sq. mi., slightly bigger than Scotland. **Neighbors:** Russia, Georgia on N, Iran on S, Armenia on W, Caspian Sea on E. **Capital:** Baku.

Government: Type: In transition. **Head of state:** Pres. Geidar A. Aliyev; in office June 30, 1993. **Head of government:** Prime Min. Surat Huseynov; in office June 30, 1993.

Economy: Industries: Oil refining. **Chief crops:** Grain, cotton, rice, silk. **Minerals:** Iron, copper, lead, zinc. **Livestock** (1989): 2.1 mln. cattle; 5.7 mln. goats & sheep. **Electricity prod.** (1991): 23.3 bln. kWh.

Finance: Monetary unit: Manat (Jan. 1993: 31.68 = $1 US).

Transport: Motor vehicles (1990): 240,000 passenger cars.

Communications: Newspaper circ. (1990): 73 per 1,000 pop.

Health: Life expectancy at birth (1992): 65 male; 73 female. **Births** (per 1,000 pop. 1992): 26. **Deaths** (per 1,000 pop. 1992): 7. **Natural increase:** 1.9%. **Hospital beds:** 1 per 98 persons. **Physicians:** 1 per 255 persons. **Infant mortality** (per 1,000 live births 1992): 45.

Major International Organizations: UN.

Azerbaijan was the home of Scythian tribes and part of the Roman Empire. It was overrun by Turks in the 11th century and conquered by Russia in 1806 and 1813. It joined the USSR Dec. 30, 1922, and became a constituent republic in 1936. Azerbaijan declared independence Aug. 30, 1991 and became an independent state when the Soviet Union disbanded Dec. 26, 1991.

Fighting between mostly Muslim Azerbaijan and mostly Christian Armenia escalated in 1992 and continued in 1993. Each country claimed Nagorno-Karabakh, an enclave in Azerbaijan with a majority population of ethnic Armenians.

A National Council ousted communist Pres. Mutaibov and took power May 19, 1992. Abulfez Elchibey became the nation's first democratically elected president June 7, but was ousted from office by Surat Huseynov, commander of a private militia, June 30, 1993. Huseynov became prime minister with expanded authority over the ministries of defence, interior and security.

The Bahamas

The Commonwealth of the Bahamas

People: Population (1992 est.): 255,000. **Age distrib.** (%): 0–14: 38.0; 15–59: 56.3; 60+: 5.7. **Pop. density:** 47 per sq. mi. **Urban** (1990): 60%. **Ethnic groups:** Black 85%, white (British, Canadian, U.S.) 15%. **Language:** English. **Religions:** Baptist 32%, Anglican 20%, Roman Catholic 19%.

Geography: Area: 5,380 sq. mi., about the size of N. Ireland. **Location:** In Atlantic O., E of Florida. **Neighbors:** Nearest are U.S. on W, Cuba on S. **Topography:** Nearly 700 islands (30 inhabited) and over 2,000 islets in the western Atlantic extend 760 mi. NW to SE. **Capital:** Nassau. **Cities** (1990 est.): New Providence 171,000; Freeport 25,000.

Government: Type: Independent commonwealth. **Head of state:** Queen Elizabeth II, represented by Gov.-Gen. Clifford Darling. **Head of government:** Prime Min. Hubert Ingraham; b. 1947; in office Aug. 21, 1992. **Local divisions:** 21 districts.

Economy: Industries: Tourism (50% of GDP), rum, banking, pharmaceuticals. **Chief crops:** Fruits, vegetables. **Minerals:** Salt. **Other resources:** Lobsters. **Arable land:** 2%. **Electricity prod.** (1991): 857 mln. kWh. **Labor force:** 5% agric.; 25% tourism, 30% government.

Finance: Monetary unit: Dollar (Apr. 1993: 1 = $1 US). **Gross domestic product** (1989): $2.4 bln. **Per capita income** (1988): $7,178. **Imports** (1991): $1.1 bln.; partners U.S. 35%, Nigeria 21%. **Exports** (1991): $306 mln.; partners: U.S. 41%, Norway 30%. **Tourism** (1990): $1.1 bln. receipts. **National budget** (1991): $727 mln. expenditures. **International reserves less gold** (Mar. 1993): $242 mln. **Consumer prices** (change in 1992): 5.7%.

Transport: Motor vehicles (1989): 67,000 passenger cars, 14,000 comm. vehicles. **Chief ports:** Nassau, Freeport.

Communications: Radios: 1 per 2 persons. **Television sets:** 1 per 4.6 persons. **Telephones:** 1 per 2 persons. **Daily newspaper circ.** (1991): 135 per 1,000 pop.

Health: Life expectancy at birth (1992): 69 male; 76 female. **Births** (per 1,000 pop. 1992): 19. **Deaths** (per 1,000 pop. 1992): 5. **Natural increase:** 1.4%. **Infant mortality** (per 1,000 live births 1992): 19.

Education (1992): **Literacy:** 95%. **School:** Compulsory through age 14.

Major International Organizations: UN (World Bank, IMF, WHO), OAS.

High Commission: 10 Chesterfield St, London W1X 8AH; 071-408 4488.

Christopher Columbus first set foot in the New World on San Salvador (Watling I.) in 1492, when Arawak Indians inhabited the islands. British settlement began in 1647; the islands became a British colony in 1783. Internal self-government was granted in 1964; full independence within the Commonwealth was attained July 10, 1973.

International banking and investment management has become a major industry alongside tourism, despite controversy over financial irregularities.

Bahrain

State of Bahrain

Dawlat al-Bahrayn

People: Population (1992 est.): 551,000. **Age distrib.** (%): 0-14: 32.7; 15-59: 64.2; 60+ 3.1. **Pop. density:** 2,055 per sq. mi.

Urban (1990): 82%. **Ethnic groups:** Bahraini 63%, Asian 13%, other Arab 10%, Iranian 6%. **Languages:** Arabic (official), Farsi, Urdu. **Religions:** Sunni Muslim 30%, Shi'ah Muslim 70%.

Geography: Area: 268 sq. mi., little bigger than the Isle of Man. **Location:** In Persian Gulf. **Neighbors:** Nearest are Saudi Arabia on W, Qatar on E. **Topography:** Bahrain Island, and several adjacent, smaller islands, are flat, hot and humid, with little rain. **Capital:** Manama, pop. (1988 est.) 151,000.

Government: Type: Traditional monarchy. **Head of state:** Amir Isa bin Sulman al-Khalifa; b. July 3, 1933; in office Nov. 2, 1961. **Head of government:** Prime Min. Kahlifa ibn Sulman al-Khalifa; b. 1935; in office Jan. 19, 1970. **Local divisions:** 12 districts. **Defense** (1990): 6.0% of GDP.

Economy: Industries: Oil products, aluminium smelting. **Chief crops:** Fruits, vegetables. **Minerals:** Oil, gas. **Crude oil reserves** (1985): 173 mln. bbls. **Arable land:** 5%. **Electricity prod.** (1991): 10.5 bln. kWh. **Labor force:** 5% agric.; 85% ind. and commerce; 5% services; 3% gov.

Finance: Monetary unit: Dinar (Mar. 1993: 1.00 = $2.66 US). **Gross domestic product** (1989): $3.4 bln. **Per capita income** (1989): $7,300. **Imports** (1991): $4.0 bln.; partners: Sau. Ar. 60%, UK 6%, U.S. 9%. **Exports** (1991): $3.4 bln.; partners: UAE 18%, Jap. 12%, Sing. 10%, U.S. 6%. **National budget** (1989): $1.3 bln. expenditures. **International reserves less gold** (Mar. 1993): $1.3 bln. **Gold:** 150,000 oz t. **Consumer prices** (change in 1992): 0.2%.

Transport: Motor vehicles (1990): 104,000 passenger cars, 23,000 comm. vehicles. **Chief port:** Sitra.

Communications: Television sets: 1 per 2.3 persons. **Radios:** 1 per 1.7 persons. **Telephones:** 1 per 3.4 persons.

Health: Life expectancy at birth (1992): 70 male; 75 female. **Births** (per 1,000 pop. 1992): 27. **Deaths** (per 1,000 pop. 1992): 3. **Natural increase:** 2.4. Medical services are free. **Infant mortality** (per 1,000 live births 1992): 21.

Education (1992): **Literacy:** 77%.

Major International Organizations: UN (GATT, IMF, WHO), Arab League.

Embassy: 98 Gloucester Rd, London SW7 4AU; 071-370 5132.

Long ruled by the Khalifa family, Bahrain was a British protectorate from 1861 to Aug. 15, 1971, when it regained independence.

Pearls, shrimp, fruits, and vegetables were the mainstays of the economy until oil was discovered in 1932. By the 1970s, oil reserves were depleted; international banking thrived.

Bahrain took part in the 1973-74 Arab oil embargo against the U.S. and other nations. The government bought controlling interest in the oil industry in 1975.

Bangladesh

People's Republic of Bangladesh

Gama Prajātantri Bangladesh

People: Population (1992 est.): 119,000,000. **Age distrib.** (%): 0-14: 44.3; 15-59: 50.4; 60+: 5.3. **Pop. density:** 2,132 per sq. mi. **Urban** (1990): 24%. **Ethnic groups:** Bengali 98%, Bihari, tribesmen. **Languages:** Bengali (official), Chakma, Magh. **Religions:** Muslim 83%, Hindu 16%.

Geography: Area: 55,813 sq. mi. slightly larger than England. **Location:** In S Asia, on N bend of Bay of Bengal. **Neighbors:** India nearly surrounds country on W, N, E; Myanmar on SE. **Topography:** The country is mostly a low plain cut by the Ganges and Brahmaputra rivers and their delta. The land is alluvial and marshy along the coast, with hills only in the extreme SE and NE. A tropical monsoon climate prevails, among the rainiest in the world. **Capital:** Dhaka. **Cities** (1991 metro. est.): Dhaka 6.1 mln.; Chittagong 2.1 mln.; Khulna 877,000.

Government: Type: Parliamentary democracy. **Head of state:** Pres. Abdur Rahman Biswas; in office Oct. 10, 1991. **Head of government:** Prime Min. Khaleda Zia; b. Nov. 1944; in office Mar. 20, 1991. **Local divisions:** 64 districts. **Defense** (1992): 1.5% of GDP.

Economy: Industries: Food processing, jute, textiles, fertilizers, petroleum products. **Chief crops:** Jute (most of world output), rice, tea. **Minerals:** Natural gas, offshore oil, coal. **Arable land:** 67%. **Livestock** (1991): 23 mln. cattle; 22 mln. goats. **Fish catch** (1990): 847,000 metric tons. **Electricity prod.** (1990): 5.7 bln. kWh. **Labor force:** 74% agric; 11% ind.; 15% services.

Finance: Monetary unit: Taka (Mar. 1993: 39 = $1 US). **Gross domestic product** (1991): $23.1 bln. **Per capita GDP:** $200. **Imports** (1991): $3.6 bln.; partners: Jap. 9%, U.S. 6%. **Exports** (1991): $1.6 bln.; partners: U.S. 31%, It. 9%; Pak 5%. **Tourism** (1990): $11.0 mln. receipts. **National budget** (1991): $3.7 bln. expenditures. **International reserves less gold** (Mar. 1993): $2.1 bln. **Gold:** 87,000 oz t. **Consumer prices** (change in 1992): 4.7%.

Transport: Railroads (1989): 1,750 mi. long. **Motor vehicles** (1990): 41,000 passenger cars, 53,000 comm. vehicles. **Chief ports:** Chittagong, Chalna.

Communications: Radios: 1 per 24 persons. **Television sets:** 1 per 315 persons. **Telephones in use:** 1 per 572 persons. **Daily newspaper circ.** (1988) 8 per 1,000 pop.

Health: Life expectancy at birth (1992): 55 male; 54 female. **Births** (per 1,000 pop. 1992): 36. **Deaths** (per 1,000 pop. 1992): 13. **Natural increase:** 2.3%. **Hospital beds:** 1 per 3,195 persons. **Physicians:** 1 per 5,500 persons. **Infant mortality** (per 1,000 live births 1992): 112.

Education (1992): **Literacy:** 73%. **School:** 73% attend primary school; 26% secondary school.

Major International Organizations: UN (GATT, IMF, WHO).

High Commission: 28 Queen's Gate, London SW7 5JA; 071-584 0081.

Muslim invaders conquered the formerly Hindu area in the 12th century. British rule lasted from the 18th century to 1947, when East Bengal became part of Pakistan.

Charging West Pakistani domination, the Awami League, based in the East, won National Assembly control in 1971. Assembly sessions were postponed; riots broke out. Pakistani troops attacked Mar. 25; Bangladesh independence was proclaimed the next day. In the ensuing civil war, one million died and 10 million fled to India.

War between India and Pakistan broke out Dec. 3, 1971. Pakistan surrendered in the East Dec. 15. Sheik Mujibur Rahman became prime minister. The country moved into the Indian and Soviet orbits, in response to U.S. support of Pakistan, and much of the economy was nationalized. Bangladesh adopted a parliamentary system of government in 1991.

In 1974, the government took emergency powers to curb widespread violence; Mujibur was assassinated and a series of coups followed.

Chronic destitution among the densely crowded population has been worsened by the decline of jute as a major world commodity.

On May 30, 1981, Pres. Ziaur Rahman was shot and killed in an unsuccessful coup attempt by army rivals. Vice President Abdus Sattar assumed the presidency but was ousted in a coup led by army chief of staff Gen. H.M. Ershad, Mar. 1982. Ershad declared Bangladesh an Islamic Republic in 1988. Bangladesh remains one of the world's poorest countries.

In 1988 and 1989, natural disasters and, monsoon rains brought devastation to Bangladesh: over 4,000 died, 30 million were made homeless. A cyclone struck Apr. 1991, killing over 131,000 people and caused $2.7 billion in damages. Some 7,500 U.S. military aided in the relief effort.

Barbados

People: Population (1992 est.): 254,000 **Age distrib.** (%): 0–14: 24.8%; 15–59: 60.6; 60+: 14.6. **Pop. density:** 1,530 per sq. mi. **Urban** (1992): 42%. **Ethnic groups:** African 80%, mixed 16%, Caucasian 4%. **Language:** English. **Religions:** Protestant 67%, Roman Catholic 4%.

Geography: Area: 166 sq. mi., little larger than the Isle of Wight. **Location:** In Atlantic, farthest E of W. Indies. **Neighbors:** Nearest are Trinidad, Grenada on SW. **Topography:** The island lies alone in the Atlantic almost completely surrounded by coral reefs. Highest point is Mt. Hillaby, 1,115 ft. **Capital:** Bridgetown, pop. (1990) 6,700.

Government: Type: Parliamentary democracy. **Head of state:** Queen Elizabeth II, represented by Gov.-Gen. Dame Nita Barrow in office June 6, 1990. **Head of government:** Prime Min. Erskine Sandiford; b. Mar. 24, 1937; in office June 1, 1987. **Local divisions:** 11 parishes and Bridgetown.

Economy: Industries: Sugar, tourism. **Chief crops:** Sugar, cotton. **Minerals:** Lime. **Other resources:** Fish. **Arable land:** 76%. **Electricity prod.** (1991): 539 mln. kwh. **Labor force:** 5% agric.; 17% ind. and comm.; 37% services and government.

Finance: Monetary unit: Dollar (June 1993: 2.01 = $1 US). **Gross domestic product** (1990): $1.7 bln. **Per capita GDP:** $6,500. **Imports** (1991): $694 mln.; partners: U.S. 35%, CARACOM 12%. **Exports** (1991): $205 mln.; partners: U.S. 21%, CARACOM 30%. **Tourism** (1990): $502 mln. receipts. **National budget** (1992): $615 mln. expenditures. **International reserves less gold** (Mar. 1993): $172 mln. **Consumer prices** (change in 1992): 6.1%.

Transport: Motor vehicles (1991): 38,000 passenger cars; 9,000 comm. vehicles. **Chief port:** Bridgetown.

Communications: Television sets: 1 per 3.9 persons. **Radios:** 1 per 1.1 persons. **Telephones:** 1 per 2.4 persons. **Daily newspaper circ.** (1990): 161 per 1,000 pop.

Health: Life expectancy at birth (1992): 70 male; 76 female. **Births** (per 1,000 pop. 1992): 16. **Deaths** (per 1,000 pop. 1992): 9. **Natural increase:** 0.7%. **Hospital beds:** 1 per 123 persons. **Physicians:** 1 per 1,042 persons. **Infant mortality** (per 1,000 live births 1992): 23.

Education (1992): **Literacy:** 99%. **School:** Compulsory to age 16.

Major International Organizations: UN (FAO, GATT, ILO, IMF, WHO), OAS.

High Commission: 1 Gt. Russell St, London WC1B 3NH; 071-631 4975.

Barbados was probably named by Portuguese sailors in reference to bearded fig trees. An English ship visited in 1605, and British settlers arrived on the uninhabited island in 1627. Slaves worked the sugar plantations until slavery was abolished in 1834.

Self-rule came gradually, with full independence proclaimed Nov. 30, 1966. British traditions have remained.

Republic of Belarus

Respublika Belarus

People: Population (1992 est.): 10,373,000. **Pop. density:** 129 per sq. mi. **Urban** (1991): 67%. **Ethnic groups:** Belarus 80%, Russian 13%. **Languages:** Belorussian, Russian.

Geography: Area: 80,134 sq. mi., slightly smaller than GB. **Neighbors:** Poland on W, Latvia, Lithuania on N, Russia on E, Ukraine on S. **Capital:** Minsk, pop. (1991) 1.6 mln. **Cities** (1991): Homel 503,000.

Government: Type: Republic. **Head of state:** Pres. Stanislav Shushkevich; in office Sept. 1991. **Head of government:** Prime Min. Vyacheslav Kebich. **Local divisions:** 6 Regions.

Economy: Industries: Food processing, chemicals, machine-tool & agricultural machinery. **Chief crops:** Grain, flax, potatoes, sugar beet. **Livestock** (1991): 6.3 mln. cattle; 4.7 mln. pigs. **Electricity prod.** (1991): 38.7 bln. kWh.

Finance: Monetary unit: Belarus rouble.

Transport: Railroads (1991): 3,472 mi. long. **Motor vehicles** (1990): 500,000 passenger cars.

Communications: Television sets: 1 per 3.3 persons. **Radios:** 1 per 1.3 persons. **Telephones:** 1 per 6.3 persons. **Newspaper circ.** (1990): 260 per 1,000 pop.

Health: Life expectancy at birth (1992): 66 male; 76 female. **Births** (per 1,000 pop. 1992): 15. **Deaths** (per 1,000 pop. 1992): 11. **Hospital beds:** 1 per 76 persons. **Physicians:** 1 per 248 persons. **Infant mortality** (per 1,000 live births 1992): 20.

Major International Organizations: UN, CIS.

The region was subject to Lithuanians and Poles in medieval times, and was a prize of war between Russia and Poland beginning in 1503. It became part of the USSR in 1922 although the west was controlled by Poland. The western part of the region was overrun by German armies in 1941; Belarus was recovered by Soviet troops in 1944. Following World War II, Belarus increased in area through Soviet annexation of part of NE Poland. Belarus declared independence Aug. 25, 1991. It became an independent state when the Soviet Union disbanded Dec. 25, 1991.

Belgium

Kingdom of Belgium

Koninkrijk België (Dutch)

Royaume de Belgique (French)

People: Population (1992 est.): 10,016,000. **Age distrib.** (%): 0–14: 18.2; 15–59: 61.7; 60+: 20.1. **Pop. density:** 848 per sq. mi. **Urban** (1992): 96%. **Ethnic groups:** Fleming 55%, Walloon 33%. **Languages:** Flemish (Dutch) 57%, French 33%, Italian, German. **Religion:** Roman Catholic 75%.

Geography: Area: 11,799 sq. mi., less than half the size of S. Ireland. **Location:** In NW Europe, on N. Sea. **Neighbors:** France on W, S, Luxembourg on SE, Germany on E, Netherlands on N. **Topography:** Mostly flat, the country is trisected by the Scheldt and Meuse, major commercial rivers. The land becomes hilly and forested in the SE (Ardennes) region. **Capital:** Brussels. **Cities** (1991 est.): Brussels (metro.) 970,000; Antwerp (metro.) 467,000; Ghent 233,000; Charleroi 209,000; Liège 195,000.

Government: Type: Parliamentary democracy under a constitutional monarch. **Head of state:** King Albert; in office Aug. 1, 1993. **Head of government:** Premier Jean-Luc Dehaene; b. Aug. 7, 1940; in office Mar. 7, 1992. **Local divisions:** 9 provinces; 3 regions; 3 cultural communities. **Defense** (1991): 2.7% of GDP.

Economy: Industries: Steel, glassware, diamond cutting, textiles, chemicals. **Chief crops:** Wheat, potatoes, sugar beets. **Minerals:** Coal. **Other resources:** Forests. **Arable land** (incl. Lux.): 26.5%. **Livestock** (1991): 3.1 mln cattle; 6.4 mln. pigs. **Fish catch** (1988): 23.3 metric tons. **Electricity prod.** (1991): 67 bln. kWh. **Crude steel prod.** (1991): 11.3 mln. metric tons. **Labor force:** 2% agric.; 26% ind. & comm.; 37% services & transportation; 23% public service.

Finance: Monetary unit: Franc (Aug. 1993: 35.50 = $1 US). **Gross domestic product** (1991): $171 bln. **Per capita GDP** $17,300. *Note:* the following trade and tourist data includes Luxembourg. **Imports** (1992): $120 bln.; partners: EC 73%. **Exports** (1992): $118 bln.; EC 74%. **Tourism** (1990): $3.5 bln receipts. **National budget** (1989): $51 bln. expenditures. **International reserves less gold** (Mar. 1993): $13.2 bln. **Gold:** 23.1 mln. oz t. **Consumer prices** (change in 1992): 2.4%.

Transport: Railroads (1990): 2,162 mi. long. **Motor vehicles** (1991): 3.9 mln. passenger cars, 596,000 comm. vehicles. **Civil aviation** (1990): 7.5 bln. passenger-km; 4 airports with scheduled flights. **Chief ports:** Antwerp, Zeebrugge, Ghent.

Communications: Television sets: 1 per 4.2 persons. **Radios:** 1 per 2.2 persons. **Telephones:** 1 per 1.9 persons. **Daily newspaper circ.** (1990): 213 per 1,000 pop.

Health: Life expectancy at birth (1992): 73 male; 80 female. **Births** (per 1,000 pop. 1992): 10. **Deaths** (per 1,000 pop. 1992): 10. **Natural increase** 0.2%. **Hospital beds:** 1 per 108 persons. **Physicians:** 1 per 317 persons. **Infant mortality** (per 1,000 live births 1992): 8.

Education (1992): **Literacy:** 98%. **School:** Compulsory to age 18.

Major International Organizations: UN and all of its specialized agencies, NATO, EC, OECD.

Embassy: 103 Eaton Sq, London SW1W 9AB; 071-235 5422

Belgium derives its name from the Belgae, the first recorded inhabitants, probably Celts. The land was conquered by Julius Caesar, and was ruled for 1800 years by conquerors, including Rome, the Franks, Burgundy, Spain, Austria, and France. After 1815, Belgium was made a part of the Netherlands, but it became an independent constitutional monarchy in 1830.

Belgian neutrality was violated by Germany in both world wars. King Leopold III surrendered to Germany, May 28, 1940. After the war, he was forced by political pressure to abdicate in favor of his son, King Baudouin.

The Flemings of northern Belgium speak Dutch while French is the language of the Walloons in the south. The language difference has been a perennial source of controversy and led to antagonism between the 2 groups. Parliament has passed measures aimed at transferring power from the central government to 3 regions—Wallonia, Flanders, and Brussels.

Belgium lives by its foreign trade; about 50% of its entire production is sold abroad.

Belize

People: Population (1992 est.): 189,000. **Age distrib.** (%): 0–14: 44.5; 15–59: 47.8; 60+: 7.6. **Pop. density:** 21 per sq. mi. **Ethnic groups:** Mestizo 43%, Creole 29%, Maya 8%. **Languages:** English (official), Spanish, native Creole dialects. **Religions:** Roman Catholic 57%, Protestant 28%.

Geography: Area: 8,867 sq. mi., the size of Wales. **Location:** Eastern coast of Central America. **Neighbors:** Mexico on N., Guatemala on W. and S. **Capital:** Belmopan. **Cities** (1991 est.): Belize City 44,000.

Government: Type: Parliamentary democracy. **Head of state:** Gov. Gen. Minita Gordon. **Head of government:** Prime Min. George Cadle Price; in office Sept. 8, 1989. **Local divisions:** 6 districts.

Economy: Sugar is the main export.

Finance: Monetary unit: Belize dollar (Mar. 1993: 2 = $1 US) **Gross domestic product** (1990): $290 mln. **Per capita GDP:** $1,637. **Imports** (1992): $273 mln.; partners: U.S. 55%, UK 8%. **Exports** (1992): $102 mln.; partners: U.S. 46%, UK 31%. **National budget** (1991): $123 mln. expenditures.

Health: Life expectancy at birth (1992): 67 male; 72 female. **Births** (per 1,000 pop. 1992): 31. **Deaths** (per 1,000 pop. 1992): 5. **Hospital beds:** 1 per 309 persons. **Physicians:** 1 per 1,543 persons. **Infant mortality** (per 1,000 live births, 1992): 30.

Education (1991): **Literacy:** 93%. **School:** Compulsory for 9 years; attendance 55%.

Major International Organizations: OAS, UN (IMF, World Bank), Commonwealth of Nations.

High Commission: 19a Cavendish Sq., London W1M 0JR; 071-499 9728.

Belize (formerly called British Honduras), was Great Britain's last colony on the American mainland, achieved independence on Sept. 21, 1981. British troops in Belize guarantee security.

Benin

Republic of Benin

République du Benin

People: Population (1992 est.): 4,997,000. **Age distrib.** (%): 0–14: 46.5; 15–59: 49.0; 60+: 4.5. **Pop. density:** 114 per sq. mi. **Urban** (1985): 20%. **Ethnic groups:** Fon, Adja, Bariba, Yoruba. **Languages:** French (official), Fon, Yoruba, Somba. **Religions:** Mainly animist with Christian, Muslim minorities.

Geography: Area: 43,483 sq. mi., slightly smaller than England.

Location: In W Africa on Gulf of Guinea. **Neighbors:** Togo on W, Burkina Faso, Niger on N, Nigeria on E. **Topography:** most of Benin is flat and covered with dense vegetation. The coast is hot, humid, and rainy. **Capital:** Porto–Novo. **Cities** (1984 est.): Cotonou 330,000.

Government: Type: Democracy. **Head of state:** Nicephore Soglo; in office Apr. 4, 1991. **Local divisions:** 6 provinces. **Defense** (1988): 2.1% of GDP.

Economy: Chief crops: Palm products, peanuts, cotton, coffee, tobacco. **Minerals:** Oil. **Arable land:** 12%. **Livestock** (1989): 890,000 sheep; 1.1 mln goats. **Fish catch** (1990): 39,000 metric tons. **Electricity prod.** (1991): 24 mln. kWh. **Labor force:** 60% agric; 38% serv. & comm.

Finance: Monetary unit: CFA franc (Mar. 1993: 273 = $1 US). **Gross domestic product** (1991): $1.7 bln. **Per capita GDP:** $400. **Imports** (1990): $428 mln.; partners: Fr. 34%. **Exports** (1990): $263 mln.; partners: EC. **National budget** (1990): $390 bln. expenditures. **International reserves less gold** (Feb. 1993): $245 mln.

Transport: Railroads (1992): 359 mi. long. **Chief port:** Cotonou.

Communications: Radios: 1 per 14 persons. **Televisions:** 1 per 281 persons. **Daily newspaper circ.** (1990): 3 per 1,000 pop.

Health: Life expectancy at birth (1992): 49 male; 52 female. **Births** (per 1,000 pop. 1992): 49. **Deaths** (per 1,000 pop. 1992): 16. **Natural increase:** 3.7%. **Hospital beds:** 1 per 749 persons. **Physicians:** 1 per 16,025 persons. **Infant mortality** (per 1,000 live births 1992): 115.

Education (1991): **Literacy:** 28%. **School:** Compulsory for 6 years; attendance 43%.

Major International Organizations: UN (GATT, IMF, WHO), OAU.

Embassy: 125 High St, Edgware; 081-951 1234.

The Kingdom of Abomey, rising to power in wars with neighboring kingdoms in the 17th century, came under French domination in the late 19th century, and was incorporated into French West Africa by 1904.

Under the name Dahomey, the country became independent Aug. 1, 1960. The name was changed to Benin in 1975. In the fifth coup since independence Col. Ahmed Kerekou took power in 1972; two years later he declared a socialist state with a " Marxist-Leninist" philosophy. In Dec. 1989, Kerekou announced that Marxism-Leninism would no longer be the state ideology. In 1991, Kerekou was defeated in Benin's first free presidential elections in 30 years by Nicephore Soglo.

The economy relies on the development of agriculturally based industries.

Bhutan

Kingdom of Bhutan

Druk-Yul

People: Population (1992 est.): 1,660,000. **Age distrib.** (%): 0–14: 39.8; 15–59: 53.8; over 60: 6.4 **Pop. density:** 91 per sq. mi. **Ethnic groups:** Bhote 60%, Nepalese 25%. **Languages:** Dzongkha (official), Gurung, Assamese. **Religions:** Buddhist (state religion) 75%, Hindu 25%.

Geography: Area: 18,147 sq. mi., one-third the size of England. **Location:** In eastern Himalayan Mts. **Neighbors:** India on W (Sikkim) and S, China on N. **Topography:** Bhutan is comprised of very high mountains in the N, fertile valleys in the center, and thick forests in the Duar Plain in the S. **Capital:** Thimphu (Paro Dzong is administrative capital), pop. (1987 est.) 20,000.

Government: Type: Monarchy. **Head of state:** King Jigme Singye Wangchuk; b. Nov. 11, 1955; in office July 21, 1972. **Local divisions:** 18 districts.

Economy: Industries: Handicrafts, chemicals. **Chief crops:** Rice, corn, wheat. **Other resources:** Timber. **Arable land:** 2%. **Labor force:** 93% agric.

Finance: Monetary unit: Ngultrum (Mar. 1993: 28.29 = $1 US) (Indian Rupee also used). **Gross domestic product** (1989): $273 mln. **Per capita GDP:** $199. **Tourism** (1990): 2.0 mln. receipts. **Imports** (1989): $138 mln.; partners India 67%. **Exports** (1989): $70 mln.; partners India 93%.

Communications: Radios: 1 per 64 persons. **Telephones:** 1 per 675 persons.

Health: Life expectancy at birth (1992): 50 male; 48 female. **Births** (per 1,000 pop. 1992): 40. **Deaths** (per 1,000 pop. 1992): 17. **Natural increase:** 2.3%. **Hospital beds:** 1 per 1,476 persons. **Physicians:** 1 per 9,686 persons. **Infant mortality** (per 1,000 live births 1992): 126.

Education (1989): **Literacy:** 15%. **School:** 25% attend.

Major International Organizations: UN (IMF, World Bank).

The region came under Tibetan rule in the 16th century. British influence grew in the 19th century. A monarchy, set up in 1907, became a British protectorate by a 1910 treaty. The country became independent in 1949, with India guiding foreign relations and supplying aid.

Links to India have been strengthened by airline service and a road network. Most of the population engages in subsistence agriculture.

Bolivia

Republic of Bolivia

República de Bolivia

People: Population (1992 est.): 7,323,000. **Age distrib.** (%): 0–14: 41.1; 15–59: 52.4; 60+: 5.5. **Pop. density:** 17 per sq. mi. **Urban** (1990): 51%. **Ethnic groups:** Quechua 30%, Aymara 25%, mixed 30%, European 14%. **Languages:** Spanish, Quechua, Aymara (all official). **Religion:** Roman Catholic 95%.

Geography: Area: 424,165 sq. mi., 3 times the size of the Br. Isles. **Location:** In central Andes Mtns. **Neighbors:** Peru, Chile on W, Argentina, Paraguay on S, Brazil on E and N. **Topography:** The great central plateau, at an altitude of 12,000 ft., over 500 mi. long, lies between two great cordilleras having 3 of the highest peaks in S. America. Lake Titicaca, on Peruvian border, is highest lake in world on which steamboats ply (12,506 ft.). The E central region has semitropical forests; the llanos, or Amazon-Chaco lowlands are in E. **Capitals:** Sucre (legal), La Paz (de facto). **Cities** (1989 est.): La Paz 1,669,000; Santa Cruz 529,000; Cochabamba 403,000.

Government: Type: Republic. **Head of state:** Pres. Gonzalo Sanchez de Lozada, in office Aug. 6, 1993. **Local divisions:** 9 departments. **Defence** (1990): 1.5% of GDP.

Economy: Industry: Textiles, food processing, mining, clothing. **Chief crops:** Potatoes, sugar, coffee, corn, coca (sold for cocaine processing). **Minerals:** Antimony, tin, tungsten, silver, zinc, oil, gas, iron. **Crude oil reserves** (1985): 157 mln. bbls. **Other resources:** Rubber, cinchona bark. **Arable land:** 3%. **Livestock** (1991): 12.3 mln. sheep; 5.3 mln. cattle; 1.6 mln. pigs. **Electricity prod.** (1991): 1.7 bln. kWh. **Labor force:** 50% agric., 10% ind. & comm, 26% serv. & govt.

Finance: Monetary unit: Bolivianos (Mar. 1993: 4.17 = $ 1 US). **Gross domestic product** (1990): $4.8 bln. **Per capita GDP** (1990): $690. **Imports** (1991): $760 mln.; partners: U.S. 20%, Jap. 10%, Arg. 14%, Braz. 20%. **Exports** (1991): $970 mln.; partners: U.S. 19%. **National budget** (1991): $825 mln. expenditures. **International reserves less gold** (Mar. 1993): $134 mln. **Gold:** 894,000 oz t. **Consumer prices** (change in 1991): 21%.

Transport: Railroads (1991): 2,269 mi. long. **Motor vehicles** (1988): 83,000 passenger cars, 150,000 comm. vehicles. **Civil aviation** (1990): 1.2 bln. passenger-km.; 19 airports with scheduled flights.

Communications: Television sets: 1 per 16 persons. **Radios:** 1 per 1.8 persons. **Telephones:** 1 per 37 persons. **Daily newspaper circ.** (1986): 35 per 1,000 pop.

Health: Life expectancy at birth (1992): 59 male; 64 female. **Births** (per 1,000 pop. 1992): 34. **Deaths** (per 1,000 pop. 1992): 19. **Natural increase:** 2.5%. **Hospital beds:** 1 per 686 persons. **Physicians:** 1 per 2,124 persons. **Infant mortality** (per 1,000 live births 1992): 83.

Education (1991): **Literacy:** 78%. **School:** Compulsory ages 7-14; attendance 82%.

Major International Organizations: UN (IMF, FAO, WHO), OAS.

Embassy: 106 Eaton Sq., London SW1W 9AA; 071-235 4248.

The Incas conquered the region from earlier Indian inhabitants in the 13th century. Spanish rule began in the 1530s, and lasted until Aug. 6, 1825. The country is named after Simon Bolivar, independence fighter.

In a series of wars, Bolivia lost its Pacific coast to Chile, the oilbearing Chaco to Paraguay, and rubber-growing areas to Brazil, 1879-1935.

Economic unrest, especially among the militant mine workers, has contributed to continuing political instability. A reformist government under Victor Paz Estenssoro, 1951-64, nationalized tin mines and attempted to improve conditions for the Indian majority, but was overthrown by a military junta. A series of coups and countercoups continued through 1981, until the military junta elected Gen. Villa as president.

In July 1982, the military junta assumed power amid a growing economic crisis and foreign debt difficulties. The junta resigned in October and allowed the Congress, elected democratically in 1980, to take power.

U.S. pressure on the government to reduce the country's output of coca, the raw material for cocaine, has led to clashes between police and coca growers and increased anti-U.S. feeling among Bolivians.

Bosnia and Herzegovina

Bosna i Hercegovina

People: Population (1992 est.): 4,365,000. **Pop. density:** 221 per sq. mi. **Ethnic groups:** Muslim Slavs 43%, Serbs 31%, Croats 17%. **Language:** Serbo-Croat (official). **Religions:** Muslim, Eastern Orthodox, Catholic.

Geography: Area: 19,741 sq. mi., one-third the size of England. **Location:** In SE Europe. **Neighbors:** Yugoslavia, Croatia, Adriatic Sea. **Topography:** Hilly with some mountains. About 50% of the land is forested. **Capital:** Sarajevo.

Government: Type: In transition. **Head of state:** Pres. Alija Izetbegovic.

Economy: Industries: Textiles, rugs, timber. **Chief crops:** Corn, wheat, oats, barley. **Minerals:** Bauxite, iron ore, coal.

Finance: Monetary unit: New Yugoslav Dinar (Dec. 1992): 225 = $1 US). **Gross domestic product** (1991): $14 bln.

Health: Hospital beds: 1 per 219 persons. **Physicians:** 1 per 624 persons.

Education: Literacy (1991): 90%.

International Organizations: UN.

Bosnia was ruled by Croatian kings *c.* A.D. 958, and by Hungary 1000–1200. It became organized *c.* 1200 and later took control of Herzegovina. The kingdom disintegrated from 1391, with the southern part becoming the independent duchy Herzegovina. It was conquered by Turks in 1463 and made a Turkish province. The area was placed under the control of Austria-Hungary in 1878, and made part of the province of **Bosnia and Herzegovina**, which was formally annexed to Austria-Hungary 1908, and it became a province of Yugoslavia in 1918. It was reunited with Herzegovina as a federated republic in the 1946 constitution.

The Bosnia and Herzegovina parliament adopted a declaration of sovereignty Oct. 15, 1991. A referendum for independence was passed Feb. 29, 1992. Ethnic Serbs' opposition to the referendum spurred violent clashes and bombings. The U.S. and EC recognized the republic as independent Apr. 7. Fierce fighting continued – interrupted by 2 ceasefires in June – as Serbs massacred many thousands of Bosnians, most of them civilians. Serb forces launched major offensives, July 13, marking the 100th day of the siege of Sarajevo, Bosnia's capital. By Sept. 1992, Serb nationalist forces occupied some 70% of Bosnia, with a small area under Croatian control.

The U.S. air-dropped relief supplies to Muslim towns under siege in E. Bosnia Feb. 28–Mar. 3, 1993. Bosnian Croats, Serbs and Muslims agreed in principle to the partitioning of the country into autonomous ethnic regions, July 30. Despite the accord, fierce fighting continued around Sarajevo and elsewhere in Bosnia. The mostly Muslim Bosnian Parliament rejected a specific partition plan, Aug. 29.

Botswana

Republic of Botswana

People: Population (1992 est.): 1,300,000. **Age distrib.** (%): 0–14: 39.6; 15–64: 48.3; 65+: 3.1. **Pop. density:** 5 per sq. mi. **Urban** (1991): 25%. **Ethnic groups:** Tswana, Kalanga, others. **Languages:** English (official), Setswana. **Religions:** Indigenous beliefs 50%, Christian 50%.

Geography: Area: 231,804 sq. mi., 2½ times bigger than UK. **Location:** In southern Africa. **Neighbors:** Namibia on N and W, S. Africa on S, Zimbabwe on NE; Botswana claims border with Zambia on N. **Topography:** The Kalahari Desert, supporting nomadic Bushmen and wildlife, spreads over SW; there are swamplands and farming areas in N, and rolling plains in E where livestock are grazed. **Capital:** Gaborone, pop. (1991) 138,000.

Government: Type: Parliamentary republic. **Head of state:** Pres. Quett Masire; b. 1925; in office July 13, 1980. **Local divisions:** 10 district councils and 4 town councils. **Defense** (1991): 4.4% of GDP.

Economy: Industries: Livestock processing, mining. **Chief crops:** Corn, sorghum, beans. **Minerals:** Copper, coal, nickel, diamonds. **Other resources:** Big game. **Arable land:** 2%. **Electricity prod.** (1991): 630 mln. kWh. **Labor force:** 70% agric.

Finance: Monetary unit: Pula (Mar. 1993: 2.38 = $1 US). **Gross domestic product** (1990): $3.1 bln. **Imports** (1991): $2.2 bln.; partners: S. Africa 88%. **Exports** (1991): $2.7 bln.; partners: Europe 67%, U.S. 17%, S. Africa 7%. **National budget** (1991): $1.7 bln. expenditures. **International reserves less gold** (Mar. 1993): $3.7 bln. **Consumer prices** (change in 1992): 16.2%.

Transport: Railroads (1991): 443 mi. long. **Motor vehicles** (1991): 26,000 passenger cars, 47,000 comm. vehicles.

Communications: Radios: 1 per 1.2 persons. **Telephones:** 1 per 26 persons. **Daily newspaper circ.** (1989): 22 per 1,000 pop.

Health: Life expectancy at birth (1992): 59 male; 65 female. **Births** (1,000 pop. 1992): 36. **Deaths** (per 1,000 pop. 1992): 9. **Natural increase:** 2.7%. **Hospital beds** (1990): 5,022. **Physicians:** 1 per 7,185 persons. **Infant mortality** (per 1,000 live births 1992): 43.

Education (1990): **Literacy:** 23%.

Major International Organizations: UN (GATT, IMF, WHO), OAU, Commonwealth of Nations.

High Commission: 6 Stratford Place, London W1N 9AE; 071-499 0031.

First inhabited by bushmen, then by Bantus, the region became the British protectorate of Bechuanaland in 1886, halting encroachment by Boers and Germans from the south and southwest. The country became fully independent Sept. 30, 1966, changing its name to Botswana.

Cattle-raising and mining (diamonds, copper, nickel) have contributed to the country's economic growth. The economy is closely tied to S. Africa.

Brazil

Federative Republic of Brazil

República Federativa do Brasil

People: Population (1992 cen.): 158,000,000. **Age distrib.** (%): 0–14: 35.2; 15–59: 57.7; 60+: 7.1. **Pop. density:** 48 per sq. mi. **Urban** (1989): 76%. **Ethnic groups:** Portuguese, Africans, and mulattoes make up the vast majority; Italians, Germans, Japanese, Indians, Jews, Arabs. **Languages:** Portuguese (official), English, German, Italian. **Religion:** Roman Catholic 89%.

Geography: Area: 3,286,470 sq. mi., larger than contiguous 48 U.S. states; largest country in S. America. **Location:** Occupies eastern half of S. America. **Neighbors:** French Guiana, Suriname, Guyana, Venezuela on N, Colombia, Peru, Bolivia, Paraguay, Argentina on W, Uruguay on S. **Topography:** Brazil's Atlantic coastline stretches 4,603 miles. In N is the heavily-wooded Amazon basin covering half the country. Its network of rivers navigable for 15,814 mi. The Amazon itself flows 2,093 miles in Brazil, all navigable. The NE region is semi-arid scrubland, heavily settled and poor. The S central region, favored by climate and resources, has almost half of the population, produces 75% of farm goods and 80% of industrial output. The narrow coastal belt includes most of the major cities. Almost the entire country has a tropical or semi-tropical climate. **Capital:** Brasilia. **Cities** (1991 metro. est.): Sao Paulo 15.2 mln.; Rio de Janeiro 6.0 mln.; Belo Horizonte 2.4 mln.; Salvador 2.0 mln.

Government: Type: Federal republic. **Head of state:** Pres. Itamar Franco; in office Dec. 29, 1992. **Local divisions:** 26 states, federal district (Brasilia). **Defense** (1990): 2.6% of GDP.

Economy: Industries: Steel, autos, ships, appliances, petrochemicals, machinery. **Chief crops:** Coffee (largest grower), cotton, soybeans, sugar, cocoa, rice, corn, fruits. **Minerals:** Chromium, iron, manganese, diamonds, gold, nickel, gem stones, tin, bauxite, oil. **Crude oil reserves** (1991): 2.8 bln. bbls. **Arable land:** 8%. **Livestock** (1989): 136 mln. cattle; 33 mln. pigs; 20 mln. sheep. **Fish catch** (1989): 850,000 metric tons. **Electricity prod.** (1991): 229 bln. kWh. **Crude steel prod.** (1991): 22.6 mln. metric tons. **Labor force:** 42% services; 31% agric.; 25% ind.

Finance: Monetary unit: Cruzeiro (June 1992: 3,059 = $1 US). **Gross domestic product** (1992): $388 bln. **Per capita GDP** (1990): $2,540. **Imports** (1992): $23 bln.; partners: U.S. 21%, EC 23%. **Exports** (1992): $36 bln.; partners: U.S. 26%, EC 27%. **Tourism** (1991): $1.4 bln. receipts. **National budget** (1991): $170 bln expenditures. **International reserves less gold** (Jan. 1993): $22.5 bln. **Gold:** 2.2 mln. oz t. **Consumer prices** (change in 1992): 1,100%.

Transport: Railroads (1990): 18,721 mi. long. **Motor vehicles** (1988): 14 mln. passenger cars, 1.6 mln. **Civil aviation** (1991): 17.2 bln. passenger-km.; 100 airports with scheduled flights. **Chief ports:** Santos, Rio de Janeiro, Vitoria, Salvador, Rio Grande, Recife.

Communications: Television sets: 1 per 5 persons. **Radios:** 1 per 2.5 persons. **Telephones:** 1 per 10 persons. **Daily newspaper circ.** (1990): 55 per 1,000 pop.

Health: Life expectancy at birth (1992): 62 male; 68 female. **Births** (per 1,000 pop. 1992): 26. **Deaths** (per 1,000 pop. 1992): 7. **Natural increase:** 1.9%. **Hospital beds:** 1 per 285 persons. **Physicians:** 1 per 684 persons. **Infant mortality** (per 1,000 live births 1992): 67.

Education (1991): **Literacy:** 81%.

Major International Organizations: UN and most of its specialized agencies, OAS.

Embassy: 32 Green St, London W1Y 4AT; 071-499 0877.

Pedro Alvares Cabral, a Portuguese navigator, is generally credited as the first European to reach Brazil, in 1500. The country was thinly settled by various Indian tribes. Only a few have survived to the present, mostly in the Amazon basin.

In the next centuries, Portuguese colonists gradually pushed inland, bringing along large numbers of African slaves. Slavery was not abolished until 1888.

The King of Portugal, fleeing before Napoleon's army, moved the seat of government to Brazil in 1808. Brazil thereupon became a kingdom under Dom Joao VI. After his return to Portugal, his son Pedro proclaimed the independence of Brazil, Sept. 7, 1822, and was acclaimed emperor. The second emperor, Dom Pedro II, was deposed in 1889, and a republic proclaimed, called the United States of Brazil. In 1967 the country was renamed the Federative Republic of Brazil.

A military junta took control in 1930; dictatorial power was assumed by Getulio Vargas, until finally forced out by the military in 1945. A democratic regime prevailed 1945-64, during which time the capital was moved from Rio de Janeiro to Brasilia in the interior.

In 1964 Pres. Joao Belchoir Marques Goulart instituted economic policies that aggravated Brazil's inflation; he was overthrown by an army revolt. The next 5 presidents were all military leaders. Censorship was imposed, and much of the opposition was suppressed amid charges of torture. In 1974 elections, the official opposition party made gains in the chamber of deputies; some relaxation of censorship occurred.

Since 1930, successive governments have pursued industrial and agricultural growth and the development of interior areas. Exploiting vast mineral resources, fertile soil in several regions, and a huge labor force, Brazil became the leading industrial power of Latin America by the 1970s, while agricultural output soared. Democratic presidential elections were held in 1985 as the nation returned to civilian rule. Fernando Collor de Mello was elected president in Dec. 1991.

However, income maldistribution and inflation have led to severe economic recession. Foreign debt is among the largest in the world. Brazil and its principal commercial bank lenders agreed to restructure the nation's $44 billion commercial debts, July 1992. The 1991 census revealed that population growth dipped below 2 percent for the first time in half a century.

Brazil unveiled a comprehensive environmental program for the Amazon region in 1989, amid an international outcry by environmentalists and others concerned about the ongoing destruction of the Amazon ecosystem. The Amazon rain forest was considered a global resource because of its impact on world weather patterns. Brazil hosted delegates from 178 countries at the Earth Summit June 3-14, 1992.

In Sept. 1992 Pres. Collor was impeached for corruption. He resigned on Dec. 29 as his trial was beginning, and Franco, who had been acting president, was sworn in as president.

Brunei Darussalam

State of Brunei Darussalam

Negara Brunei Darussalam

People: Population (1992 est.): 369,000. **Pop. density:** 165 per sq. mi. **Ethnic groups:** Malay 65%, Chinese 20%. **Languages:** Malay, English, (both official), Chinese. **Religions:** Muslim 60%, Buddhist 14%, Christian 10%.

Geography: Area: 2,226 sq. mi.; smaller than Lincolnshire. **Location:** On the north coast of the island of Borneo; it is surrounded on its landward side by the Malaysian state of Sarawak. **Capital:** Bandar Seri Begawan, pop. (1982 est.) 51,000.

Government: Type: Independent sultanate. **Head of government:** Sultan Sir Muda Hassanal Bolkiah Mu'izzadin Waddaulah; in office Jan. 1, 1984. **Local divisions:** 4 districts.

Economy: Industries: Petroleum (about 90% of revenue is derived from oil exports). **Chief crops:** Rice, bananas, cassava.

Finance: Monetary unit: Brunei dollar (Dec. 1992: 1.60 = $1 US). **Gross domestic product** (1989): $3.1 bln. **Per capita GDP** (1989): $9,600.

Transport: Motor vehicles (1990): 100,000 passenger cars, 12,000 comm. vehicles.

Communications: Television sets: 1 per 2.6 persons. **Radios:** 1 per 3 persons. **Telephones:** 1 per 6 persons.

Education (1987): **Literacy:** 95% among young.

Health: Life expectancy at birth (1992): 69 male; 73 female. **Infant mortality** (per 1,000 live births 1992): 26.

Major International Organizations: UN and some of its specialized agencies.

High Commission: 19 Belgrave Sq, London SW1X 8PG; 071-581 0521.

The Sultanate of Brunei was a powerful state in the early 16th century, with authority over all of the island of Borneo as well as parts of the Sulu Islands and the Philippines. In 1888, a treaty was signed which placed the state under the protection of Great Britain.

Brunei became a fully sovereign and independent state on Jan. 1, 1984.

The Sultan of Brunei donated $10 million to the Nicaraguan *contras* in 1987; the subsequent misplacement of the funds generated much media attention in the U.S.

Bulgaria

Republic of Bulgaria

Republika Bulgaria

People: Population (1992 est.): 8,868,000. **Age distrib.** (%): 0–14: 20.6; 15–59: 60.5; 60+: 18.9. **Pop. density:** 199 per sq. mi. **Urban** (1992): 67%. **Ethnic groups:** Bulgarian 85%, Turk 8.5%. **Languages:** Bulgarian (official), Turkish. **Religions:** Bulgarian Orthodox, 85%, Muslim 13%.

Geography: Area: 44,365 sq. mi., about half the size of GB. **Location:** In eastern Balkan Peninsula on Black Sea. **Neighbors:** Romania on N, Yugoslavia, Macedonia on W, Greece, Turkey on S. **Topography:** The Stara Planina (Balkan) Mts. stretch E-W across the center of the country, with the Danubian plain on N, the Rhodope Mts. on SW, and Thracian Plain on SE. **Capital:** Sofia. **Cities** (1991 est.): Sofia 1,200,000; Plovdiv 379,000; Varna 320,000.

Government: Type: Republic. **Head of state:** Pres. Zhelyu Zhelev; b. Mar. 3, 1935; in office Aug. 1, 1990. **Head of government:** Premier Lyuben Berov; in office Dec. 30, 1992. **Local divisions:** 9 provinces. **Defense** (1991): 4.4% of GNP.

Economy: Industries: Chemicals, machinery, metals, textiles, fur, leather goods, vehicles, processed food. **Chief crops:** Grains, fruit, corn, potatoes, tobacco. **Minerals:** Lead, manganese, lignite, coal. **Arable land:** 34%. **Livestock** (1990): 1.5 mln. cattle; 4.3 mln. pigs; 7.9 mln. sheep. **Fish catch** (1989): 121,000 metric tons. **Electricity prod.** (1990): 45 bln. kWh. **Crude steel prod.** (1991): 2.3 mln. metric tons. **Labor force:** 20% agric.; 33% ind.

Finance: Monetary unit: Leva (Dec. 1992: 25 = $1 US). **Gross national product** (1990): $47.3 bln. **Per capita GNP:** $5,300. **Imports** (1990): $9.6 bln.; partners: CIS 56%. **Exports** (1990): $8.4 bln.; partners: CIS 70%. **Tourism** (1989): $362 mln. revenues. **National budget** (1988): $28 bln. expenditures.

Transport: Railroads (1991): 4,106 km. long. **Motor vehicles** (1990): 1.3 mln. passenger cars, 200,000 comm. vehicles. **Civil aviation** (1990): 3.7 bln. passenger km.; 3 airports. **Chief ports:** Burgas, Varna.

Communications: Television sets: 1 per 3.9 persons. **Radios:** 1 per 4.8 persons. **Telephones:** 1 per 3.6 persons. **Daily newspaper circ.** (1988): 316 per 1,000 pop.

Health: Life expectancy at birth (1992): 69 male; 76 female. **Births** (per 1,000 pop. 1992): 13. **Deaths** (per 1,000 pop. 1992): 12. **Hospital beds:** 1 per 103 persons. **Physicians:** 1 per 337 persons. **Infant mortality** (per 1,000 live births 1992): 13.

Education (1990): **Literacy:** 98%.

Major International Organizations: UN.

Embassy: 186 Queen's Gate, London SW7 5HL; 071-584 9400.

Bulgaria was settled by Slavs in the 6th century. Turkic Bulgars arrived in the 7th century, merged with the Slavs, became Christians by the 9th century, and set up powerful empires in the 10th and 12th centuries. The Ottomans prevailed in 1396 and remained for 500 years.

A revolt in 1876 led to an independent kingdom in 1908. Bulgaria expanded after the first Balkan War but lost its Aegean coastline in World War I, when it sided with Germany. Bulgaria joined the Axis in World War II but withdrew in 1944. Communists took power with Soviet aid; the monarchy was abolished Sept. 8, 1946.

On Nov. 10, 1989, Communist party leader and head of state Todor Zhivkov, who had held power for 35 years, resigned. Zhivkov was imprisoned, Jan. 1990, and convicted, Sept. 1992, of corruption and abuse of power. In Jan. 1990, parliament voted to revoke the constitutionally guaranteed dominant role of the Communist Party.

Burkina Faso

People: Population (1992 est.): 9,653,000. **Pop. density:** 91 per sq. mi. **Urban** (1988): 8%. **Ethnic groups:** Voltaic groups (Mossi, Bobo), Mande. **Languages:** French (official), Sudanic tribal languages. **Religions:** animist 65%, Muslim 25%, Christian 10%.

Geography: Area: 105,869 sq. mi., slightly smaller than the Br. Isles. **Location:** In W. Africa, S of the Sahara. **Neighbors:** Mali on NW, Niger on NE, Benin, Togo, Ghana, Côte d'Ivoire on S. **Topography:** Landlocked Burkina Faso is in the savannah region of W. Africa. The N is arid, hot, and thinly populated. **Capital:** Ouagadougou. **Cities** (1990): Ouagadougou 500,000; Bobo-Dioulasso 250,000.

Government: Type: Military. **Head of state:** Pres. Blaise Compaoré; in office Oct. 15, 1987. **Head of government:** Prime Min. Youssouf Ouedraogo; in office June 16, 1992. **Local divisions:** 30 provinces. **Defense** (1988): 2.7% of GDP.

Economy: Chief crops: Millet, sorghum, rice, peanuts, grain. **Minerals:** Manganese, gold, limestone. **Arable land:** 10%. **Electricity prod.** (1991): 320 mln. kWh. **Labor force:** 82% agric.

Finance: Monetary unit: CFA franc (Mar. 1993: 273 = $1 US). **Gross domestic product** (1990): $2.9 bln. **Per capita GDP** (1989): $205. **Imports** (1989): $322 mln.; partners: EC, Côte d'Ivoire. **Exports** (1989): $95 mln.; partners: Côte d'Ivoire, EC, China. **International reserves less gold** (Jan. 1993): $345 mln. **Gold:** 11,000 oz t. **Consumer prices** (change in 1992): −1.4%.

Transport: Motor vehicles (1990): 12,000 passenger cars, 13,000 comm. vehicles.

Communications: Television sets: 1 per 223 persons. **Radios:** 1 per 44 persons. **Telephones:** 1 per 482 persons. **Daily newspaper circ.** (1989): 1 per 1,000 pop.

Health: Life expectancy at birth (1992): 52 male; 53 female. **Births** (per 1,000 pop. 1992): 50. **Deaths** (per 1,000 pop. 1992): 16. **Natural increase:** 3.4%. **Hospital beds:** 1 per 1,359 persons. **Physicians:** 1 per 29,914 persons. **Infant mortality** (per 1,000 live births 1992): 117.

Education (1991): **Literacy:** 18%. **School:** Only 8% attend.

Major International Organizations: UN and many of its specialized agencies, OAU.

Consulate: 5 Cinnamon Row, London SW11; 071-738 1800.

The Mossi tribe entered the area in the 11th to 13th centuries. Their kingdoms ruled until defeated by the Mali and Songhai empires.

French control came by 1896, but Upper Volta (name changed to Burkina Faso on Aug. 4, 1984) was not finally established as a separate territory until 1947. Full independence came Aug. 5, 1960, and a pro-French government was elected. The military seized power in 1980. A 1987 coup established the current regime, which restored limited democracy in the early 1990s.

Several hundred thousand farm workers migrate each year to Côte d'Ivoire and Ghana. Burkina Faso is heavily dependent on foreign aid.

Burma

(See Myanmar)

Burundi

Republic of Burundi

Republika y'Uburundi

People: Population (1992 est.): 6,022,000. **Age distrib.** (%): 0–14: 45.1; 15–59: 50.1; 60+: 4.8. **Pop. density:** 559 per sq. mi. **Urban** (1986): 8%. **Ethnic groups:** Hutu 85%, Tutsi 14%, Twa (pygmy) 1%. **Languages:** French, Rundi (both official). **Religions:** Roman Catholic 62%, traditional African 32%.

Geography: Area: 10,759 sq. mi., about the size of the Highland region of Scotland. **Location:** In central Africa. **Neighbors:** Rwanda on N, Zaire on W, Tanzania on E. **Topography:** Much of the country is grassy highland, with mountains reaching 8,900 ft. The southernmost source of the White Nile is located in Burundi. Lake Tanganyika is the second deepest lake in the world. **Capital:** Bujumbura, pop. (1991 est.) 240,000.

Government: Type: Republic. **Head of state:** Pres. Maj. Pierre Buyoya; in office Sept. 9, 1987. **Head of government:** Pres. Melchior Ndadaye; in office July 10, 1993. **Local divisions:** 15 provinces. **Defense** (1990): 19% of govt. budget.

Economy: Chief crops: Coffee (87% of exports), cotton, tea. **Minerals:** Nickel. **Arable land:** 43%. **Electricity prod.** (1991): 105 mln. kWh. **Labor force:** 93% agric.

Finance: Monetary unit: Franc (Apr. 1993: 236 = $1 US). **Gross domestic product** (1990): $1.2 bln. **Per capita GDP:** $200. **Imports** (1991): $248 mln.; partners: Belg.-Lux. 17%; W. Ger. 18%. **Exports** (1991): $90 mln; partners: W. Ger. 31%, Belg. 20%. **Tourism** (1990): $4 mln. receipts. **National budget** (1990): $203 mln. expenditures. **International reserves less gold** (Mar. 1993): $196 mln. **Gold:** 17,000 oz t. **Consumer prices** (change in 1992): 4.7%.

Transport: Motor vehicles (1990): 12,000 passenger cars, 12,000 comm. vehicles.

Communications: Radios: 1 per 11 persons. **Telephones:** 1 per 611 persons.

Health: Life expectancy at birth (1992): 51 male; 55 female. **Births** (per 1,000 pop. 1992): 46. **Deaths** (per 1,000 pop. 1992): 14. **Natural increase:** 3.2%. **Hospital beds:** 1 per 515 persons. **Physicians:** 1 per 31,777 persons. **Infant mortality** (per 1,000 live births 1992): 106.

Education (1991): **Literacy:** 50%. **School:** Compulsory for 6 years; attendance 45%.

Major International Organizations: UN (GATT, IMF, WHO), OAU.

Honorary Consulate: 19 Kenton Park Cres., Harrow, Middx; 081-907 8985.

The pygmy Twa were the first inhabitants, followed by Bantu Hutus, who were conquered in the 16th century by the Tutsi (Watusi), probably from Ethiopia. Under German control in 1899, the area fell to Belgium in 1916, which exercised successively a League of Nations mandate and UN trusteeship over Ruanda-Urundi (now the two countries of Rwanda and Burundi).

Independence came in 1962.

An unsuccessful Hutu rebellion in 1972-73 left 10,000 Tutsi and 150,000 Hutu dead. Over 100,000 Hutu fled to Tanzania and Zaire. In the 1980s Burundi's Tutsi-dominated regime pledged itself to ethnic reconciliation and democratic reform. In the nation's first democratic presidential election, in June 1993, a Hutu was elected. Burundi remains one of the poorest and most densely populated countries in Africa.

Cambodia

State of Cambodia

Roat Kampuchea

People: Population (1992 est.): 7,249,000. **Pop. density:** 103 per sq. mi. **Urban** (1990): 12%. **Ethnic groups:** Cambodian 90%, Vietnamese 4%, Chinese 5%. **Languages:** Khmer (official), French. **Religion:** Theravada Buddhism 95%.

Geography: Area: 70,238 sq. mi., about twice the size of Wales. **Location:** In Indochina Peninsula. **Neighbors:** Thailand on W, N, Laos on NE, Vietnam on E. **Topography:** The central area, formed by the Mekong R. basin and Tonle Sap lake, is level. Hills and mountains are in SE, a long escarpment separates the country from Thailand on NW. 75% of the area is forested. **Capital:** Phnom Penh, pop. (1990 est.) 800,000.

Government: Type: No single authority controls the whole country. **Head of state:** King Norodom Sihanouk; b. Oct. 31, 1922; in office June 3, 1993. **Head of government:** First Prime Min. Prince Norodom Ranariddh; in office Sept. 24, 1993. **Local divisions:** 19 provinces and 2 cities.

Economy: Industries: Rice milling, wood & rubber. **Chief crops:** Rice, corn. **Minerals:** Iron, copper, manganese. **Other resources:** Forests, rubber. **Arable land:** 16%. **Livestock** (1991): 2.0 mln. cattle; 1.5 mln. pigs. **Fish catch** (1991): 105,000 metric tons. **Electricity prod.** (1991): 200 mln. kWh. **Labor force:** 74% agric.

Finance: Monetary unit: Riel (Jan. 1993: 1,508 = $1 US). **Gross domestic product** (1991): $930 mln. **Per capita GDP:** $130. **Imports** (1988): $147 mln. **Exports** (1988): $32 mln.

Transport: Railroads (1989): 649 mi. long; 54 mln. passenger-miles. **Motor vehicles** (1988): 4,000 passenger cars, 7,000 trucks. **Chief ports:** Kompong Som.

Communications: Television sets: 1 per 125 persons. **Radios:** 1 per 10 persons. **Telephones:** 1 per 3,300 persons.

Health: Life expectancy at birth (1992): 48 male; 51 female. **Births** (per 1,000 pop. 1992): 37. **Deaths** (per 1,000 pop. 1992): 15. **Natural increase:** 2.2. **Hospital beds:** 1 per 632 persons. **Physicians:** 1 per 27,000 persons. **Infant mortality** (per 1,000 live births 1992): 121.

Education (1990): **Literacy:** 50%.

Major International Organizations: UN.

Early kingdoms dating from that of Funan in the 1st century AD culminated in the great Khmer empire which flourished from the 9th century to the 13th, encompassing present-day Thailand, Cambodia, Laos, and southern Vietnam. The peripheral areas were lost to invading Siamese and Vietnamese, and France established a protectorate in 1863. Independence came in 1953.

Prince Norodom Sihanouk, king 1941-1955 and head of state from 1960, tried to maintain neutrality. Relations with the U.S. were broken in 1965, after South Vietnam planes attacked Vietcong forces within Cambodia. Relations were restored in 1969, after Sihanouk charged Viet communists with arming Cambodian insurgents.

In 1970, pro-U.S. premier Lon Nol seized power, demanding removal of 40,000 North Viet troops; the monarchy was abolished. Sihanouk formed a government-in-exile in Peking, and open war began between the government and Khmer Rouge. The U.S. provided heavy military and economic aid.

Khmer Rouge forces captured Phnom Penh April 17, 1975. The new government evacuated all cities and towns, and shuffled the rural population, sending virtually the entire population to clear jungle, forest, and scrub, which covered half the country. Over one million people were killed in executions and enforced hardships.

Severe border fighting broke out with Vietnam in 1978; developed into a full-fledged Vietnamese invasion. The Vietnamese-backed Kampuchean National United Front for National Salvation, a Cambodian rebel movement, announced, Jan. 8, 1979, the formation of a government one day after the Vietnamese capture of Phnom Penh. Thousands of refugees flowed into Thailand and widespread starvation was reported.

On Jan. 10, 1983, Vietnam launched an offensive against rebel forces in the west. They overran a refugee camp, Jan. 31, driving 30,000 residents into Thailand. In March, Vietnam launched a major offensive against camps on the Cambodian-Thailand border, engaged Khmer Rouge guerrillas, and crossed the border instigating clashes with Thai troops. Vietnam announced that it would withdraw all its troops by Sept. 1989.

Following UN-sponsored elections that ended May 28, 1993, the 2 leading parties agreed to share power in an interim government June 18. The Khmer Rouge, who had boycotted the elections, agreed June 30 to merge their forces with the army of the government.

Cameroon

Republic of Cameroon

People: Population (1992 est.): 12,658,000. **Age distrib.** (%): 0–14: 46.1; 15–59: 48.3; 60+: 5.6. **Pop. density:** 70 per sq. mi. **Urban** (1990): 40%. **Ethnic groups:** Some 200 tribes; largest are Bamileke 30%, Fulani 7%. **Languages:** English, French (both official), numerous African groups. **Religions:** Animist 51%, Muslim 16%, Christian 33%.

Geography: Area: 179,714 sq. mi., twice the size of GB. **Location:** Between W and central Africa. **Neighbors:** Nigeria on NW, Chad, Central African Republic on E, Congo, Gabon, Equatorial Guinea on S. **Topography:** A low coastal plain with rain forests is in S; plateaus in centre lead to forested mountains in W, including Mt. Cameroon, 13,000 ft.; grasslands in N lead to marshes around Lake Chad. **Capital:** Yaounde. **Cities** (1988 est.): Douala 852,000; Yaounde 700,000.

Government: Type: Republic, one-party presidential regime. **Head of state:** Pres. Paul Biya; b. Feb. 13, 1933; in office Nov. 6, 1982. **Head of government:** Prime Min. Simon Achidi Achu; in office Apr. 9, 1992. **Local divisions:** 10 provinces. **Defense** (1990): 1.7% of GDP.

Economy: Industries: Aluminium processing, oil prod., palm products. **Chief crops:** Cocoa, coffee, cotton. **Crude oil reserves** (1985): 531 mln. bbls. **Other resources:** Timber. **Arable land:** 14%. **Livestock** (1989): 4.5 mln. cattle; 3.1 mln. sheep; 1.2 mln. pigs. **Fish catch** (1990): 77,000 metric tons. **Electricity prod.** (1991): 2.9 bln. kwh. **Labor force:** 74% agric., 11% ind. and commerce.

Finance: Monetary unit: CFA franc (Mar. 1993: 274 = $1 US). **Gross domestic product** (1991): $11.6 bln. **Per capita GDP:** $1,010. **Imports** (1990): 2.1 bln.; partners: Fr. 42%. **Exports** (1990): $2.1 bln.; partners: EC 50%. **National budget** (1990): $2.2 bln. **International reserves less gold** (Jan. 1993): $32.5 mln. **Gold:** 30,000 oz t.

Transport: Railroads (1990): 686 mi. long. **Motor vehicles** (1987): 78,000 passenger cars, 43,000 comm. vehicles. **Chief port:** Douala.

Communications: Radios: 1 per 6 persons. **Telephones:** 1 per 185 persons. **Daily newspaper circ.** (1991): 6 per 1,000 pop.

Health: Life expectancy at birth (1992): 55 male; 60 female. **Births** (per 1,000 pop. 1992): 44. **Deaths** (per 1,000 pop. 1992): 11. **Natural increase:** 3.1%. **Hospital beds:** 1 per 377 persons. **Physicians:** 1 per 12,540 persons. **Infant mortality** (per 1,000 live births 1992): 81.

Education (1991): **Literacy:** 65%. **School:** About 70% attend.

Major International Organizations: UN, OAU, EC (Associate).

Embassy: 84 Holland Pk, London W11 3SB; 071-727 0771.

Portuguese sailors were the first Europeans to reach Cameroon, in the 15th century. The European and American slave trade was very active in the area. German control lasted from 1884 to 1916, when France and Britain divided the territory, later receiving League of Nations mandates and UN trusteeships. French Cameroon became independent Jan. 1, 1960; one part of British Cameroon joined Nigeria in 1961, the other part joined Cameroon. Stability has allowed for development of roads, railways, agriculture, and petroleum production. Some 3,000 died in 1986 as a result of clouds of toxic gas of volcanic origin emanating from Lake Nyos.

Canada

People: Population (1992 est.): 27,351,000. **Age distrib.** (%): 0–14: 20.9; 15–59: 63.1; 60+: 16.0. **Pop. density:** 7 per sq. mi. **Urban** (1990): 77.0%. **Ethnic groups:** British 25%; French 24%; other European 16%; mixed 28%. **Languages:** English, French (both official). **Religions:** Roman Catholic 46%, Protestant 41%.

Geography: Area: 3,849,672 sq. mi., the largest country in land size in the Western Hemisphere. **Location:** Canada stretches 3,426 miles from east to west and extends southward from the North Pole to the U.S. border. Its seacoast includes 36,356 miles of mainland and 115,133 miles of islands, including the Arctic islands almost from Greenland to near the Alaskan border. Climate, while generally temperate, varies from freezing winter cold to blistering summer heat. **Capital:** Ottawa. **Cities** (1991 metro. est.): Montreal 3,100,000; Toronto 3,800,000; Vancouver 1,600,000; Ottawa-Hull 920,000; Edmonton 839,000; Calgary 754,000; Winnipeg 652,000; Quebec 645,000.

Government: Type: Confederation with parliamentary democracy. **Head of state:** Queen Elizabeth II, represented by Gov.-Gen. Ramon Hnatyshyn; in office Jan. 29, 1990. **Head of government:** Prime Min. Kim Campbell; b. Mar. 10, 1947; in office June 25, 1993. **Local divisions:** 10 provinces, 2 territories. **Defense** (1991): 2% of GDP.

Economy: Minerals: Nickel, zinc, copper, gold, lead, molybdenum, potash, silver. **Crude oil reserves** (1991): 6.4 bln. barrels. **Arable land:** 5%. **Livestock** (1990): 12.0 mln. cattle; 10.8 mln. pigs; 722,000 sheep. **Fish catch** (1989): 1.6 mln. metric tons. **Electricity prod.** (1991): 479 bln. kWh. **Crude steel prod.** (1991): 12.9 mln. metric tons. **Labor force:** 4% agric.; 52% ind. & comm., 28% services.

Finance: Monetary unit: Dollar (July 1993: 1.27 = $1 US). **Gross domestic product** (1991): $521 bln. **Per capita GDP:** $19,400. **Imports** (1992): $124 bln.; partners: U.S. 69%, EC 8%, Jap. 5%. **Exports** (1992): $134 bln.; partners: U.S. 75%, EC 9%, Jap. 5%. **Tourism** (1990): $6.3 bln. receipts. **National budget** (1990-91): $127 bln. expenditures. **International reserves less gold** (Mar. 1993): $12.7 bln. **Gold:** 9.1 mln. oz t. **Consumer prices** (change in 1992): 1.5%.

Transport: Railroads (1990): 56,771 mi. long. **Motor vehicles** (1989): 12.0 mln. passenger cars, 3.7 mln. comm. vehicles. **Civil aviation** (1990): 46.0 bln. passenger-km; 106 airports with scheduled flights.

Communications: Television sets: 1 per 1.7 persons. **Radios:** 1 per 1.2 persons. **Telephones:** 1 per 1.3 persons. **Daily newspaper circ.** (1991): 187 per 1,000 pop.

Health: Life expectancy at birth (1992): 74 male; 81 female. **Births** (per 1,000 pop. 1992): 14. **Deaths** (per 1,000 pop. 1992): 7. **Natural increase:** .7%. **Hospital beds:** 1 per 148 persons. **Physicians:** 1 per 449 persons. **Infant mortality** (per 1,000 live births 1992): 7.3.

Education (1991): **Literacy:** 99%.

Major International Organizations: UN and all of its specialized agencies, NATO, OECD, Commonwealth of Nations.

High Commission: Macdonald House, 1 Grosvenor Square, London W1X 0AB; 071-629 9492.

French explorer Jacques Cartier, who reached the Gulf of St. Lawrence in 1534, is generally regarded as the founder of Canada. But English seaman John Cabot sighted Newfoundland 37 years earlier, in 1497, and Vikings are believed to have reached the Atlantic coast centuries before either explorer.

Canadian settlement was pioneered by the French who established Quebec City (1608) and Montreal (1642) and declared New France a colony in 1663.

Britain, as part of its American expansion, acquired Acadia (later Nova Scotia) in 1717 and, through military victory over French forces in Canada (an extension of a European conflict between the 2 powers), captured Quebec (1759) and obtained control of the rest of New France in 1763. The French, through the Quebec Act of 1774, retained the rights to their own language, religion, and civil law.

The British presence in Canada increased during the American Revolution when many colonials, proudly calling themselves United Empire Loyalists, moved north to Canada.

Fur traders and explorers led Canadians westward across the continent. Sir Alexander Mackenzie reached the Pacific in 1793 and scrawled on a rock by the ocean, "from Canada by land."

In Upper and Lower Canada (later called Ontario and Quebec) and in the Maritimes, legislative assemblies appeared in the 18th century and reformers called for responsible government. But the War of 1812 intervened. The war, a conflict between Great Britain and the United States fought mainly in Upper Canada, ended in a stalemate in 1814.

In 1837 political agitation for more democratic government culminated in rebellions in Upper and Lower Canada. Britain sent Lord Durham to investigate and, in a famous report (1839), he recommended union of the 2 parts into one colony called Canada. The union lasted until Confederation, July 1, 1867, when proclamation of the British North America (BNA) Act launched the Dominion of Canada, consisting of Ontario, Quebec, and the former colonies of Nova Scotia and New Brunswick.

Since 1840 the Canadian colonies had held the right to internal self-government. The BNA act, which became the country's written constitution, established a federal system of government on the model of a British parliament and cabinet structure under the crown. Canada was proclaimed a self-governing Dominion within the British Empire in 1931.

In 1982 Canada severed its last formal legislative link with Britain by obtaining the right to amend its constitution (the British North America Act of 1867).

The Meech Lake Agreement was signed June 3, 1987. The

historic accord would have assured constitutional protection for Quebec's efforts to preserve its French language and culture. Critics of the accord charged that it did not make any provision for other minority groups and that it gave Quebec too much power, which might enable it to pass laws that conflicted with the nation's 1982 Charter of Rights and Freedoms. Its failure sparked a separatist revival in Quebec which culminated in Aug. 1992 in the Charlottetown Agreement. This called for changes to the constitution, such as recognition of Quebec as a "distinct society" within the Canadian Confederation and self-government for native peoples. The accord was defeated in a national referendum on Oct. 26, 1992.

In 1992 voters in the Northwest Territories approved the creation of a self-governing homeland for the 17,500 Inuit living in the territories. the area – to be known as Nunavut, "Our Land" – would cover an area of 136,493 sq miles and will take effect by 1999.

Canada became the first nation to ratify the North American Free Trade Agreement between Canada, Mexico and the U.S., June 23, 1993.

Canadian Provinces

	Sq. mi.	Population, 1991 cen.
Alberta	255,287	2,545,553
British Columbia	365,947	3,282,061
Manitoba	250,947	1,091,942
New Brunswick	28,355	723,900
Newfoundland	156,949	568,474
Nova Scotia	21,425	899,942
Ontario	412,581	10,084,885
Prince Edward Island	2,185	129,765
Quebec	594,860	6,895,963
Saskatchewan	251,866	988,928
Territories		
Northwest Territories	1,322,909	57,649
Yukon	186,661	27,797

Prime Ministers of Canada

Canada is a constitutional monarchy with a parliamentary system of government. It is also a federal state. Canada's official head of state is the King or Queen of England, represented by a resident Governor-General. However, in practice the nation is governed by the Prime Minister, leader of the party that commands the support of a majority of the House of Commons, dominant chamber of Canada's bicameral Parliament.

Name	Party	Term
Sir John A. MacDonald	Conservative	1867-1873
		1878-1891
Alexander Mackenzie	Liberal	1873-1878
Sir John J. C. Abbott	Conservative	1891-1892
Sir John S. D. Thompson	Conservative	1892-1894
Sir Mackenzie Bowell	Conservative	1894-1896
Sir Charles Tupper	Conservative	1896
Sir Wilfrid Laurier	Liberal	1896-1911
Sir Robert L. Borden	Cons. Union.	1911-1920
Arthur Meighen	Cons. Union.	1920-1921
W.L. Mackenzie King	Liberal	1921-1926[1]
		1926-1930
		1935-1948
R. B. Bennett	Conservative	1930-1935
Louis St. Laurent	Liberal	1948-1957
John G. Diefenbaker	Prog. Cons.	1957-1963
Lester B. Pearson	Liberal	1963-1968
Pierre Elliott Trudeau	Liberal	1968-1979
Joe Clark	Prog. Cons.	1979-1980
Pierre Elliott Trudeau	Liberal	1980-1984
John Turner	Liberal	1984
Brian Mulroney	Prog. Cons.	1984-1993
Kim Campbell	Prog. Cons.	1993-

(1) King's term was interrupted from June 26-Sept. 25, 1926, when Arthur Meighen again served as prime minister.

Cape Verde

Republic of Cape Verde

República de Cabo Verde

People: Population (1992 est.): 398,000. **Age distrib.** (%): 0–14: 45.6; 15–59: 47.7; 60+: 6.7. **Pop. density:** 255 per sq. mi. **Urban** (1991): 29%. **Ethnic groups:** Creole (mulatto) 71%, African 28%, European 1%. **Languages:** Portuguese (official), Crioulo. **Religion:** Roman Catholic 80%.

Geography: Area: 1,557 sq. mi., a bit larger than Suffolk. **Location:** In Atlantic O., off western tip of Africa. **Neighbors:** Nearest are Mauritania, Senegal. **Topography:** Cape Verde Islands are 15 in number, volcanic in origin (active crater on Fogo). The landscape is eroded and stark, with vegetation mostly in interior valleys. **Capital:** Praia. **Cities** (1990 est.): Mindelo 47,000; Praia 61,000.

Government: Type: Republic. **Head of state:** Pres. Antonio Mascarenhas Monteiro; in office Mar. 17, 1991. **Head of government:** Prime Min. Carlos Veiga; in office Apr. 4, 1991. **Local divisions:** 14 administrative districts.

Economy: Chief crops: Bananas, coffee, beats, corn, beans. **Minerals:** Salt. **Other resources:** Fish. **Arable land:** 10%. **Electricity prod.** (1991): 15 mln. kWh.

Finance: Monetary unit: Escudo (Mar. 1993: 77 = $1 US). **Gross domestic product** (1990): $310 mln. **Per capita GDP:** $800. **Imports** (1989): $108 mln.; partners: Port. 33%, Neth. 12%. **Exports** (1989): $10.9 mln.; partners: Port. 32%, Ang. 21%.

Transport: Motor vehicles: (1988): 13,000 passenger cars, 4,000 comm. vehicles. **Chief ports:** Mindelo, Praia.

Communications: Radios: 1 per 6.8 persons. **Telephones:** 1 per 76 persons.

Health: Life expectancy at birth (1992): 60 male; 64 female. **Births** (per 1,000 pop. 1992): 48. **Deaths** (per 1,000 pop. 1992): 11. **Natural increase:** 3.8%. **Hospital beds:** 1 per 550 persons. **Physicians:** 1 per 4,208 persons. **Infant mortality** (per 1,000 live births 1992): 61.

Education (1989): **Literacy:** 37%.

Major International Organizations: UN (GATT, IMF, WHO), OAU.

Embassy: 44 Konninginnegracht, 2514 AD, The Hague, Netherlands; 010 31 70 469623.

The uninhabited Cape Verdes were discovered by the Portuguese in 1456 or 1460. The first Portuguese colonists landed in 1462; African slaves were brought soon after, and most Cape Verdeans descend from both groups. Cape Verde independence came July 5, 1975. The islands have suffered from repeated extreme droughts and famines. Emphasis is placed on the development of agriculture and on fishing.

Antonio Mascarenhas Monteiro won the nation's first free presidential election in 1991.

Central African Republic

République Centrafricaine

People: Population (1992 est.): 3,029,000. **Pop. density:** 12 per sq. mi. **Urban** (1990): 47%. **Ethnic groups:** Banda 27%, Baya 34%, Mandja 21%, Sara 10%. **Languages:** French (official), local dialects. **Religions:** Protestant 25%, Roman Catholic 25%, traditional 24%.

Geography: Area: 240,534 sq. mi., about twice the size of the Br. Isles. **Location:** In central Africa. **Neighbors:** Chad on N, Cameroon on W, Congo, Zaire on S, Sudan on E. **Topography:** Mostly rolling plateau, average altitude 2,000 ft., with rivers draining S to the Congo and N to Lake Chad. Open, well-watered savanna covers most of the area, with an arid area in NE, and tropical rainforest in SW. **Capital:** Bangui, pop. (1988 metro. est.) 596,000.

Government: Type: Republic. (under military rule). **Head of state:** Gen. Andre Kolingba; in office Sept. 1, 1981. **Head of government:** Prime Min. Enoch Devant Lakove; in office Feb. 1993. **Local divisions:** 16 prefectures. **Defense** (1989): 2% of GDP.

Economy: Industries: Textiles, light manuf, mining. **Chief crops:** Cotton, coffee, peanuts, tobacco. **Minerals:** Diamonds (chief export), uranium. **Other resources:** Timber. **Arable land:** 3%. **Electricity prod.** (1991): 93 mln. kWh. **Labor force:** 72% agric.

Finance: Monetary unit: CFA franc (Mar. 1993: 273 = $1 US). **Gross domestic product** (1990): $1.3 bln. **Per capita GDP:** $440. **Imports** (1990): $214 mln.; partners: Fr. 44%. **Exports** (1990): $151 mln.; partners: Fr. 53%, Bel.-Lux. 23%. **National budget** (1991): $193 mln. expenditures. **International reserves less gold** (Jan. 1993): $103 mln. **Gold:** 12,000 oz t.

Transport: Motor vehicles (1989): 10,000 passenger cars, 8,000 comm. vehicles.

Communications: Radios: 1 per 5 persons. **Telephones:** 1 per 380 persons.

Health: Life expectancy at birth (1992): 46 male; 49 female. **Births** (per 1,000 pop. 1992): 44. **Deaths** (per 1,000 pop. 1992): 19. **Natural increase:** 2.5%. **Hospital beds:** 1 per 689 persons. **Physicians:** 1 per 17,292 persons. **Infant mortality** (per 1,000 live births 1992): 135.

Education (1991): **Literacy:** 27%. **School:** Primary school 79%; secondary school 18%.

Major International Organizations: UN (GATT, IMF, WHO), OAU.

Embassy: 30 rue des Perchamps, Paris 75016, France; 010 331 42244256.

Various Bantu tribes migrated through the region for centuries before French control was asserted in the late 19th century, when the region was named Ubangi-Shari. Complete independence was attained Aug. 13, 1960.

All political parties were dissolved in 1960, and the country became a center for Chinese political influence in Africa. Relations with China were severed after 1965. Elizabeth Domitien, premier 1975-76, was the first woman to hold that post in an African country. Pres. Jean-Bedel Bokassa, who seized power in a 1965 military coup, proclaimed himself constitutional emperor of the renamed Central African Empire Dec. 1976.

Bokassa's rule was characterized by ruthless and cruel authority and human rights violations. Bokassa was ousted in a bloodless coup aided by the French government, Sept. 20, 1979, and replaced by his cousin David Dacko, former president from 1960 to 1965. In 1981, the political situation deteriorated amid strikes and economic crisis. Gen. Kolingba replaced Dacko as head of state in a bloodless coup. Multiparty legislative and presidential elections were held in Oct. 1992 but were cancelled by the government when Kolingba was losing. New elections were scheduled for Oct. 1993.

Chad

Republic of Chad

République du Tchad

People: Population (1992 est.): 5,238,000. **Age distrib.** (%): 0–14: 42.5; 15–59: 51.7; 60+: 5.8. **Pop. density:** 10 per sq. mi. **Urban** (1990): 32%. **Ethnic groups:** 200 distinct groups. **Languages:** French, Arabic, (both official), some 100 other languages. **Religions:** Muslim 44%, Christian 33%, animist 23%.

Geography: Area: 495,755 sq. mi., four times the size of the Br. Isles. **Location:** In central N. Africa. **Neighbors:** Libya on N, Niger, Nigeria, Cameroon on W, Central African Republic on S, Sudan on E. **Topography:** Southern wooded savanna, steppe, and desert, part of the Sahara, in the N. Southern rivers flow N to Lake Chad, surrounded by marshland. **Capital:** N'Djamena, pop. (1992 est.) 500,000.

Government: Type: Republic. **Head of state:** Pres. Idriss Deby; in office Dec. 4, 1990. **Head of government:** Prime Min. Joseph Yodoyman; in office May 20, 1992. **Local divisions:** 14 prefectures. **Defense** (1990): 5.6% of GDP.

Economy: Chief crops: Cotton. **Minerals:** Uranium, salt. **Arable land:** 2%. **Fish catch** (1990): 115,000 metric tons. **Electricity prod.** (1991): 69 mln. kwh. **Labor force:** 85% agric.

Finance: Monetary unit: CFA franc (Mar. 1993: 273 = $1 US). **Gross domestic product** (1992): $1.0 bln. **Per capita GDP:** $190. **Imports** (1990): $264 mln.; partners: Fr. 47%. **Exports** (1990): $174 mln.; partners Fra. **International reserves less gold** (Jan. 1993): $74 mln. **Gold:** 11,000 oz t.

Transport: Motor vehicles (1989): 8,000 passenger cars, 6,000 comm. vehicles.

Communications: Radios: 1 per 4.3 persons. **Telephones:** 1 per 555 persons.

Health: Life expectancy at birth (1992): 39 male; 41 female. **Births** (per 1,000 pop. 1992): 42. **Deaths** (per 1,000 pop. 1992): 22. **Natural increase:** 2.0%. **Hospital beds** (1980): 3,500. **Physicians** (1980): 94. **Infant mortality** (per 1,000 live births 1992): 136.

Education (1991): **Literacy:** 30%.

Major International Organizations: UN, (GATT, IMF, WHO), OAU, EEC.

Embassy: Boulevard Lambermont 52, Brussels 1030, Belgium; 010 32 2 2151975.

Chad was the site of paleolithic and neolithic cultures before the Sahara Desest formed. A succesion of kingdoms and Arab slave traders dominated Chad until France took control around 1900. Independence came Aug. 11, 1960.

Northern Moslem rebels have fought animist and Christian southern government and French troops from 1966, despite numerous cease-fires and peace pacts.

Libyan troops entered the country at the request of the Chad government, December 1980. On Jan. 6, 1981 Libya and Chad announced their intention to unite. France together with several African nations condemned the agreement as a menace to African security. The Libyan troops were withdrawn from Chad in November 1981.

Rebel forces, led by Hissene Habre, captured the capital and forced Pres. Gioukouni Oueddei to flee the country in June 1982.

In 1983, France sent some 3,000 troops to Chad to assist Habre in opposing Libyan-backed rebels. France and Libya agreed to a simultaneous withdrawal of troops from Chad in September 1984, but Libyan forces remained in the north until Mar. 1987 when Chad forces drove them from their last major stronghold. In Dec. 1990 Pres. Hissene Habre was overthrown by a Libyan-supported insurgent group, the Patriotic Salvation Movement. The group's leader, Idriss Deby, assumed the presidency.

Chile

Republic of Chile

República de Chile

People: Population (1992 est.): 13,528,000. **Age distrib.** (%): 0–14: 30.9 15–59: 60.4; 60+: 7.7. **Pop. density:** 44 per sq. mi. **Urban** (1990): 84%. **Ethnic groups:** Mestizo 66%, Spanish 25%, Indian 5%. **Language:** Spanish. **Religions:** Roman Catholic 89%, Protestant 11%.

Geography: Area: 302,779 sq. mi., over 3 times larger than GB. **Location:** Occupies western coast of southern S. America. **Neighbors:** Peru on N, Bolivia on NE, Argentina on E. **Topography:** Andes Mtns. are on E border including some of the world's highest peaks; on W is 2,650-mile Pacific Coast. Width varies between 100 and 250 miles. In N is Atacama Desert, in center are agricultural regions, in S are forests and grazing lands. **Capital:** Santiago, pop. (1992 metro est.) 5,300,000.

Government: Type: Republic. **Head of state:** Pres. Patricio Aylwin Ozocar; b. Nov. 26, 1918; in office Mar. 11, 1990. **Local divisions:** 13 regions. **Defense** (1991): 3.4% of GNP.

Economy: Industries: Fish processing, wood products, iron, steel, textiles. **Chief crops:** Grain, onions, beans, potatoes, peas, fruits. **Minerals:** Copper (about half of export revenues), molybdenum, nitrates, iodine (half world output), iron, coal, oil, gas, gold, cobalt, zinc, manganese, borate, mica, mercury, salt, sulphur, marble, onyx. **Other resources:** Water, forests. **Arable land:** 7%. **Livestock** (1990): 3.3 mln. cattle; 6.5 mln. sheep; 1.1 mln. pigs. **Fish catch** (1991): 6.1 mln. metric tons. **Electricity prod.** (1991): 21.4 bln. kWh. **Labor force:** 19% agric., forestry, fishing; 34% ind. & comm.; 30% serv.

Finance: Monetary unit: Peso (July 1993: 392 = $1 US). **Gross domestic product** (1991): $29.2 bln. **Per capita GDP** (1990): $2,200. **Imports** (1991): $7.6 bln.; partners: U.S. 19%, EC 23%. **Exports** (1991): $9.0 bln.; partners: EC 34%, U.S. 18%. **Tourism** (1990): $548 mln. receipts. **National budget** (1991): $8.3 bln. expenditures. **International reserves less gold** (Mar. 1993): $9.7 bln. **Gold:** 1.86 mln. oz. t. **Consumer prices** (change in 1992): 15.4%.

Transport: Railroads (1990): 4,470 mi. long. **Motor vehicles** (1989): 690,000 passenger cars, 300,000 comm. vehicles. **Civil aviation** (1990): 2.9 bln. passenger-km.; 17 airports with scheduled flights. **Chief ports:** Valparaiso, Arica, Antofagasta.

Communications: Television sets: 1 per 4.1 persons. **Radios:** 1 per 3.3 persons. **Telephones:** 1 per 16 persons.

Health: Life expectancy at birth (1992): 71 male; 77 female. **Births** (per 1,000 pop. 1992): 21. **Deaths** (per 1,000 pop. 1992): 6. **Natural increase:** 1.5%. **Hospital beds:** 1 per 304 persons. **Physicians:** 1 per 919 persons. **Infant mortality** (per 1,000 live births 1992): 18.

Education (1991): **Literacy:** 92%. **School:** Compulsory from ages 6 to 14.

Major International Organizations: UN and all of its specialized agencies, OAS.

Embassy: 12 Devonshire St, London W1N 1FS; 071-580 6392.

Northern Chile was under Inca rule before the Spanish conquest, 1536-40. The southern Araucanian Indians resisted until the late 19th century. Independence was gained 1810-18, under Jose de San Martin and Bernardo O'Higgins; the latter, as supreme director 1817-23, sought social and economic reforms until deposed. Chile defeated Peru and Bolivia in 1836-39 and 1879-84, gaining mineral-rich northern land.

Eduardo Frei Montalva came into office in 1964, instituting social programs and gradual nationalization of foreign-owned mining companies. In 1970, Salvador Allende Gossens, a Marxist, became president with a third of the national vote.

The Allende government furthered nationalizations and improved conditions for the poor. But illegal and violent actions by extremist supporters of the government, the regime's failure to attain majority support, and poorly planned socialist economic programs led to political and financial chaos.

A military junta seized power Sept. 11, 1973, and said Allende killed himself. The junta named a mostly military cabinet and announced plans to "exterminate Marxism."

Repression continued during the 1980s with little sign of any political liberalization. In a plebiscite held Oct. 5, 1988, voters rejected junta-candidate Gen. Augusto Pinochet Ugarte who, if victorious, would have governed Chile until 1997. Pinochet accepted the rejection and called for presidential elections. In Dec. 1989 voters removed Pinochet from office and elected Patricio Aylwin as president. A 1991 report documented more than 2,200 deaths that were a result of human rights violations during Pinochet's rule.

Tierra del Fuego is the largest (18,800 sq. mi.) island in the archipelago of the same name at the southern tip of South America, an area of majestic mountains, tortuous channels, and high winds. It was discovered 1520 by Magellan and named the Land of Fire because of its many Indian bonfires. Part of the island is in Chile, part in Argentina. Punta Arenas, on a mainland peninsula, is a center of sheep-raising and the world's southernmost city (pop. about 70,000); Puerto Williams is the southernmost settlement.

China

People's Republic of China

Zhonghua Renmin Gonghe Guo

People: Population (1992 est.): 1,169,619,000. **Pop. density:** 315 per sq. mi. **Urban** (1990): 27%. **Ethnic groups:** Han Chinese 94%, Mongol, Korean, Manchu, others. **Languages:** Mandarin (official), Yue, Wu Hakka, Xiang, Gan, Min, Zhuang, Hui, Yi. **Religions:** officially atheist; Confucianism, Buddhism, Taoism are traditional.

Geography: Area: 3,696,100 sq. mi., slightly larger than the U.S. **Location:** Occupies most of the habitable mainland of E. Asia. **Neighbors:** Mongolia on N, Russia on NE and NW, Afghanistan, Pakistan, Tajikistan, Kazakhstan on W, India, Nepal, Bhutan, Myanmar, Laos, Vietnam on S, N. Korea on NE. **Topography:** Two-thirds of the vast territory is mountainous or desert, and only one-tenth is cultivated. Rolling topography rises to high elevations in the N in the Daxinganlingshanmai separating Manchuria and Mongolia; the Tienshan in Xinjiang; the Himalayan and Kunlunshanmai in the SW and in Tibet. Length is 1,860 mi. from N to S, width E to W is more than 2,000 mi. The eastern half of China is one of the best-watered lands in the world. Three great river systems, the Changjiang, the Huanghe, and the Xijiang provide water for vast farmlands. **Capital:** Beijing. **Cities** (1990 est.): Shanghai 7.7 mln.; Beijing 6.9 mln.; Tianjin 5.7 mln.; Canton 3.5 mln.; Shenyang 4.5 mln.; Wuhan 3.7 mln.

Government: Type: Communist Party-led state. **Head of state:** Pres. Jiang Zemin; in office Mar. 27, 1993. **Head of government:** Premier Li Peng; in office Apr. 9, 1989. **Local divisions:** 22 provinces, 5 autonomous regions, and 3 cities. **Defense** (1992): 3.0% of GNP.

Economy: Industries: Iron and steel, textiles, agriculture implements, trucks. **Chief crops:** Grain, rice, cotton, tea. **Minerals:** Tungsten, antimony, coal, iron, lead, manganese, molybdenum, tin. **Crude oil reserves** (1991): 30.8 bln. barrels. **Other resources:** Silk. **Arable land:** 11%. **Livestock** (1991): 81 mln. cattle; 369 mln. pigs; 112 mln. sheep. **Fish catch** (1990): 12.0 mln. metric tons. **Electricity prod.** (1991): 670 bln. kWh. **Crude steel prod.** (1991): 70.4 mln. metric tons. **Labor force:** 60% agric.; 25% ind. & comm.

Finance: Monetary unit: Yuan (July 1993: 5.71 = $1 US). **Gross national product** (1989): $393 bln. **Per capita GNP:** $360. **Imports** (1992): $76.3 bln.; partners: Jap. 20%, U.S. 11%, Hong Kong 20%. **Exports** (1992): $80.5 bln.; partners: Hong Kong 38%, Jap. 16%, U.S. 7%. **Tourism** (1991): $2.8 bln. receipts. **National budget** (1987): $66.1 bln. expenditures. **International reserves less gold** (Feb. 1993): $42.8 bln. **Gold:** 12.7 mln. oz t. **Consumer prices** (change in 1991): 2.1%.

Transport: Railroads (1990): 41,973 mi. long. **Motor vehicles** (1990): 1.6 mln. passenger cars, 4.1 mln. comm. vehicles. **Civil aviation** (1991): 30.1 bln. passenger-km, 90 airports with scheduled flights. **Chief ports:** Shanghai, Qinhuang-dao, Dalian, Canton.

Communications: Television sets: 1 per 8 persons. **Radios:** 1 per 9.1 persons. **Telephones:** 1 per 89 persons. **Daily newspaper circ.** (1989): 37 per 1,000 pop.

Health: Life expectancy at birth (1992): 69 male; 72 female. **Births** (per 1,000 pop. 1992): 22. **Deaths** (per 1,000 pop. 1992): 7. **Natural increase:** 1.5%. **Infant mortality** (per 1,000 live births 1992): 33. **Hospital beds:** 1 per 428 persons. **Physicians:** 1 per 646 persons.

Education (1987): **Literacy:** 70%. **School:** Compulsory for 9 years; first grade enrolment 93%.

Major International Organizations: UN (IMF, FAO, WHO).

Embassy: 5 Birch Grove, London W3 9SW; 081-993 0279.

History. Remains of various man-like creatures who lived as early as several hundred thousand years ago have been found in many parts of China. Neolithic agricultural settlements dotted the Huanghe basin from about 5000 BC. Their language, religion, and art were the sources of later Chinese civilization.

Bronze metallurgy reached a peak and Chinese pictographic writing, similar to today's, was in use in the more developed culture of the Shang Dynasty (c. 1500 BC-c. 1000 BC) which ruled much of North China.

A succession of dynasties and interdynastic warring kingdoms ruled China for the next 3,000 years. They expanded Chinese political and cultural domination to the south and west, and developed a brilliant technologically and culturally advanced society. Rule by foreigners (Mongols in the Yuan Dynasty, 1271-1368, and Manchus in the Ch'ing Dynasty, 1644-1911) did not alter the underlying culture.

A period of relative stagnation left China vulnerable to internal and external pressures in the 19th century. Rebellions left tens of millions dead, and Russia, Japan, Britain, and other powers exercised political and economic control in large parts of the country. China became a republic Jan. 1, 1912, following the Wuchang Uprising inspired by Dr. Sun Yat-sen.

For a period of 50 years, 1894-1945, China was involved in conflicts with Japan. In 1895, China ceded Korea, Taiwan, and other areas. On Sept. 18, 1931, Japan seized the Northeastern Provinces (Manchuria) and set up a puppet state called Manchukuo. The border province of Jehol was cut off as a buffer state in 1933. Japan invaded China proper July 7, 1937. After its defeat in World War II, Japan gave up all seized land.

Following World War II, internal disturbances arose involving the Kuomintang, communists, and other factions. China came under domination of communist armies, 1949-1950. The Kuomintang government moved to Taiwan, 90 mi. off the mainland, Dec. 8, 1949.

The People's Republic of China was proclaimed in Peking Sept. 21, 1949, by the Chinese People's Political Consultative Conference under Mao Zedong.

China and the USSR signed a 30-year treaty of "friendship, alliance and mutual assistance," Feb. 15, 1950.

The U.S. refused recognition of the new regime. On Nov. 26, 1950, the People's Republic sent armies into Korea against U.S. troops and forced a stalemate.

By the 1960s, relations with the USSR deteriorated, with disagreements on borders, ideology and leadership of world communism. The USSR cancelled aid accords, and China, with Albania, launched anti-Soviet propaganda drives.

On Oct. 25, 1971, the UN General Assembly ousted the Taiwan government from the UN and seated the People's Republic in its place. The U.S. had supported the mainland's admission but opposed Taiwan's expulsion.

U.S. Pres. Nixon visited China Feb. 21-28, 1972, on invitation from Premier Zhou Enlai, ending years of antipathy between the 2 nations. China and the U.S. opened liaison offices in each other's capitals, May-June 1973. The U.S., Dec. 15, 1978, formally recognized the People's Republic of China as the sole legal government of China; diplomatic relations between the 2 nations were established, Jan. 1, 1979.

Internal developments. After an initial period of consolidation, 1949-52, industry, agriculture, and social and economic institutions were forcibly molded according to Maoist ideals. However, frequent drastic changes in policy and violent factionalism interfered with economic development.

In 1957, Mao Zedong admitted an estimated 800,000 people had been executed 1949-54; opponents claimed much higher figures.

The Great Leap Forward, 1958-60, tried to force the pace of economic development through intensive labor on huge new rural communes, and through emphasis on ideological purity and enthusiasm. The program caused resistance and was largely abandoned. Serious food shortages developed, and the government was forced to buy grain from the West.

The Great Proletarian Cultural Revolution, 1965, was an attempt to oppose pragmatism and bureaucratic power and instruct a new generation in revolutionary principles. Massive purges took place. A program of forcibly relocating millions of urban teenagers into the countryside was launched.

By 1968 the movement had run its course; many purged officials returned to office in subsequent years, and reforms in education and industry that had placed ideology above expertise were gradually weakened.

In a continuing "reassessment" of the policies of Mao Zedong, Mao's widow, Jiang Quing, and other Gang of Four members were convicted of "committing crimes during the 'Cultural Revolution'," Jan. 25, 1981.

In the mid-1970s, factional and ideological fighting increased, and emerged into the open after the 1976 deaths of Mao and Premier Zhou Enlai. Mao's widow and 3 other leading leftists were purged and placed under arrest, after reportedly trying to seize power. The new ruling group modified Maoist policies in education, culture, and industry, and sought better ties with non-communist countries.

Relations with Vietnam deteriorated in 1978 as China charged persecution of ethnic Chinese. In retaliation for Vietnam's invasion of Cambodia, China attacked 4 Vietnamese border provinces Feb. 17, 1979; heavy border fighting ensued.

By the mid 1980's, China had enacted far-reaching economic reforms highlighed by the departure from rigid central planning and the stressing of market-oriented socialism.

Some 100,000 students and workers staged a march in Beijing to demand democratic reforms, May 4, 1989. The demonstrations continued during a visit to Beijing by Soviet leader Mikhail Gorbachev May 15-18. It was the first Sino-Soviet summit since 1959. A million people gathered in Beijing to demand democratic reforms and the removal of Deng and other leaders. There were protests in at least 20 other Chinese cities. Martial law was imposed, May 20, but was mostly ignored by the protesters.

Chinese army troops entered Beijing, June 3-4, and crushed the pro-democracy protests. Tanks and armored personnel carriers attacked Tiananmen Square, outside the Great Hall of the People, which was the main scene of the demonstrations and hunger strikes. It is estimated that 5,000 died, 10,000 were injured, and hundreds of students and workers arrested.

China's population, the world's largest, is still increasing, but with more couples following the government's one-child policy some experts predict that the nation's population will actually decline after peaking in the early 21st century.

Manchuria. Home of the Manchus, rulers of China 1644-1911, Manchuria has accommodated millions of Chinese settlers in the 20th century. Under Japanese rule 1931-45, the area became industrialized. China no longer uses the name Manchuria for the region, which is divided into the 3 NE provinces of Heilongjiang, Jilin, and Liaoning.

Guangxi is in SE China, bounded in N by Kweichow and Hunan provinces, E and S by Kwangtung, on SW by North Vietnam, and on W by Yunnan. Produces rice in the river valleys and has valuable forest products.

Inner Mongolia was organized by the People's Republic in 1947. Its boundaries have undergone frequent changes, reaching its greatest extent (and restored in 1979) in 1956, with an area of 454,000 sq. mi., allegedly in order to dilute the minority Mongol population. Chinese settlers outnumber the Mongols more than 10 to 1. Pop. (1990 cen.): 21.4 mln. Capital: Hohhot.

Xinjiang, in Central Asia, is 633,802 sq. mi., pop. (1990 cen.): 15.1 mln. (75% Uygurs, a Turkic Moslem group, with a heavy Chinese increase in recent years). Capital: Urumqi. It is China's richest region in strategic minerals.

Tibet, 470,000 sq. mi., is a thinly populated region of high plateaus and massive mountains, the Himalayas on the S, the Kunluns on the N. High passes connect with India and Nepal; roads lead into China proper. Capital: Lhasa. Average altitude is 15,000 ft. Jiachan, 15,870 ft., is believed to be the highest inhabited town on earth. Agriculture is primitive. Pop. (1990 cen.): 2.1 mln. (of whom about 500,000 are Chinese). Another 4 million Tibetans form the majority of the population of vast adjacent areas that have long been incorporated into China.

China ruled all of Tibet from the 18th century, but independence came in 1911. China reasserted control in 1951, and a communist government was installed in 1953, revising the theocratic Lamaist Buddhist rule. Serfdom was abolished, but all land remained collectivized.

A Tibetan uprising within China in 1956 spread to Tibet in 1959. The rebellion was crushed with Chinese troops, and Buddhism was almost totally suppressed. The Dalai Lama and 100,000 Tibetans fled to India.

Colombia

Republic of Colombia

República de Colombia

People: Population (1992 est.): 34,296,000. **Age distrib. (%):** 0–14: 36.1; 15–59: 57.8; 60+: 6.1. **Pop. density:** 77 per sq. mi. **Urban** (1983): 65.4%. **Ethnic groups:** Mestizo 58%, Caucasian 20%, Mulatto 14%. **Language:** Spanish. **Religion:** Roman Catholic 95%.

Geography: Area: 439,735 sq. mi., nearly 5 times bigger than the UK. **Location:** At the NW corner of S. America. **Neighbors:** Panama on NW, Ecuador, Peru on S, Brazil, Venezuela on E. **Topography:** Three ranges of Andes, the Western, Central, and Eastern Cordilleras, run through the country from N to S. The eastern range consists mostly of high table lands, densely populated. The Magdalena R. rises in Andes, flows N to Carribean, through a rich alluvial plain. Sparsely-settled plains in E are drained by Orinoco and Amazon systems. **Capital:** Bogotá. **Cities** (1992 est.): Bogotá 4,921,000; Medellín 1,581,000; Cali 1,624,000; Barranquilla 1,018,000.

Government: Type: Republic. **Head of state:** Pres. Cesar Gaviria Trujillo; b. Mar. 31, 1947; in office Aug. 7, 1990. **Local divisions:** 23 departments, 8 national territories, and special district of Bogotá. **Defense** (1991): 1.4% of GDP.

Economy: Industries: Textiles, processed goods, hides, steel, cement, chemicals. **Chief crops:** Coffee (50% of exports), rice, corn, cotton, sugar, bananas. **Minerals:** Oil, gas, emeralds (90% world output), gold, copper, lead, coal, iron, nickel, salt. **Crude oil reserves** (1991): 1.8 bln. bbls. **Other resources:** Rubber, balsam, dye-woods, copaiba, hydro power. **Arable land:** 5%. **Livestock** (1990): 24.6 mln. cattle; 2.6 mln. pigs; 2.6 mln. sheep. **Fish catch** (1990): 101,000 metric tons. **Electricity prod.** (1991): 38 bln. kWh. **Labor force:** 30% agric.; 24% ind.; 46% services.

Finance: Currency: Peso (July 1993: 678 = $1 US). **Gross domestic product** (1990): $43.0 bln. **Per capita GDP:** $1,300. **Imports** (1991): $6.1 bln.; partners: U.S. 36%, EC 16%, Jap. 11%. **Exports** (1991): $7.5 bln.; partners: U.S. 40%, EC 21%. **Tourism** (1990): $362 mln. receipts. **National budget** (1989): $3.9 bln. expenditures. **International reserves less gold** (Mar. 1993): $7.3 bln. **Gold:** 539,000 oz t. **Consumer prices** (change in 1992): 27.0%.

Transport: Railroads (1991): 79 mln. passenger-km. **Motor vehicles** (1989): 936,000 passenger cars, 364,000 comm. vehicles. **Civil aviation** (1991): 4.5 bln. passenger-km; airports with scheduled flights: 63. **Chief ports:** Buena Ventura, Santa Marta, Barranquilla, Cartagena.

Communications: Television sets: 1 per 5.6 persons. **Radios:** 1 per 7.3 persons. **Telephones:** 1 per 13 persons. **Daily newspaper circ.** (1992): 23 per 1,000 pop.

Health: Life expectancy at birth (1992): 69 male; 74 female. **Births** (per 1,000 pop. 1992): 24. **Deaths** (per 1,000 pop. 1992): 5. **Natural increase:** 1.9%. **Physicians:** 1 per 1,079 persons. **Infant mortality** (per 1,000 live births 1991): 37%.

Education (1990): **Literacy:** 80%. **School:** Only 28% finish primary school.

Major International Organizations: UN (World Bank, GATT), OAS.

Embassy: 3 Hans Crescent, London SW1X 0LN; 071-589 9177.

Spain subdued the local Indian kingdoms (Funza, Tunja) by the 1530s and ruled Colombia and neighboring areas as New Granada for 300 years. Independence was won by 1819. Venezuela and Ecuador broke away in 1829-30, and Panama withdrew in 1903.

One of the Latin American democracies, Colombia is plagued by rural and urban violence, though scaled down from "La Violencia" of 1948-58, which claimed 200,000 lives. Attempts at land and social reform and progress in industrialization have not succeeded in reducing massive social problems aggravated by a very high birth rate. In 1989, the government's increased activity against local drug traffickers sparked a series of retaliation killings. On Aug. 18, Luis Carlos Galán, the ruling party's presidential hopeful in the 1990 election, was assassinated. In 1990, 2 other presidential candidates were slain as the drug traffickers carried on a campaign of intimidation to stop the presidential election. Cesar Gaviria Trujillo, a strong advocate of maintaining the government's war against the nation's drug cartels, was elected president in May. His popularity greatly declined in 1992 when a drug boss escaped from prison in July, allegedly with aid from the military and prison officials, and the drug industry continued to grow.

Comoros

Federal Islamic Republic of the Comoros

Jumhurīyat al-Qumur al-Itthādīyah al-Islāmīyah

People: Population (1992 est.): 493,000. **Pop. density:** 588 per sq. mi. **Ethnic groups:** Arabs, Africans, East Indians. **Languages:** Arabic, French (both official). **Religions:** Sunni Muslim 86%, Roman Catholic 14%.

Geography: Area: 838 sq. mi., about the size of Nottinghamshire. **Location:** 3 islands (Grande Comore, Anjouan, and Moheli) in the Mozambique Channel between NW Madagascar and SE Africa. **Neighbors:** Nearest are Mozambique on W, Madagascar on E. **Topography:** The islands are of volcanic origin, with an active volcano on Grand Comoro. **Capital:** Moroni, pop. (1992 metro. est.) 30,000.

Government: Type: Republic. **Head of state:** Pres. Said Mohammed Djohar; in office Nov. 26, 1989. **Local divisions:** Each of the 3 main islands is a prefecture.

Economy: Industries: Perfume. **Chief crops:** Vanilla, copra, perfume plants, fruits. **Arable land:** 35%. **Electricity prod.** (1991): 24 mln. kWh. **Labor force:** 80% agric.

Finance: Monetary unit: CFA franc (Mar. 1993: 273 = $1 US). **Gross domestic product** (1991): $260 mln. **Per capita GDP:** $540. **Imports** (1990): $41 mln.; partners: Fr. 22%. **Exports** (1990): $16 mln.; partners: Fr. 41%, U.S. 53%.

Transport: Chief port: Dzaoudzi.

Communications: Radios: 1 per 9 persons. **Telephones:** 1 per 132 persons.

Health: Life expectancy at birth (1992): 55 male; 59 female. **Births** (per 1,000 pop. 1992): 47. **Deaths** (per 1,000 pop. 1992): 13. **Natural increase:** 3.5%. **Infant mortality** (per 1,000 live births 1992): 84.

Education: (1989): **Literacy:** 15%. **School:** Less than 20% attend secondary school.

Major International Organizations: UN (IMF, World Bank); OAU.

The islands were controlled by Muslim sultans until the French acquired them 1841-1909. They became a French overseas territory in 1947. A 1974 referendum favored independence, with only the Christian island of Mayotte preferring association with France. The French National Assembly decided to allow each of the islands to decide its own fate. The Comoro Chamber of Deputies declared independence July 6, 1975, with Ahmed Abdallah as president. In a referendum in 1976, Mayotte voted to remain French. A leftist regime that seized power from Abdallah in 1975 was deposed in a pro-French 1978 coup in which he regained the presidency.

In Nov. 1989 Pres. Abdallah was assassinated.

Congo

Republic of Congo

République du Congo

People: Population (1992 est.): 2,376,000. **Pop. density:** 17 per sq. mi. **Urban** (1990): 41%. **Ethnic groups:** Bakongo 45%, Bateke 20%, others. **Languages:** French (official), Kongo, Teke. **Religions:** Christian 50% (two-thirds Roman Catholic), animist 47%, Muslim 2%.

Geography: Area: 132,046 sq. mi., somewhat larger than the Br. Isles. **Location:** In western central Africa. **Neighbors:** Gabon, Cameroon on W, Central African Republic on N, Zaire on E, Angola on SW. **Topography:** Much of the Congo is covered by thick forests. A coastal plain leads to the fertile Niari Valley. The centre is a plateau; the Congo R. basin consists of flood plains in the lower and savanna in the upper portion. **Capital:** Brazzaville. **Cities** (1992 est.): Brazzaville (metro.) 937,000; Pointe-Noire 576,000; Loubomo 83,000.

Government: Type: Democracy. **Head of state:** Pres. Pascal Lissouba; in office Aug. 20, 1992. **Head of government:** Prime Min. Claude Antoine Dacosta; in office Dec. 6, 1992. **Local divisions:** 9 regions and capital district. **Defense** (1987): 4.6% of GNP.

Economy: Chief crops: Palm oil and kernels, cocoa, coffee, tobacco. **Minerals:** Gold, lead, copper, zinc. **Crude oil reserves** (1988): 750 mln. bbls. **Arable land:** 2%. **Fish catch** (1989): 19,000 metric tons. **Electricity prod.** (1991): 315 mln. kWh. **Labor force:** 90% agric.

Finance: Monetary unit: CFA franc (Mar. 1993: 273 = $1 US). **Gross domestic product** (1990): $2.4 bln. **Per capita GDP:** $1,070. **Imports** (1990): $621 mln.; partners: Fr. 62%. **Exports** (1990): $981 mln.; partners: U.S. 45%, Fr. 15%. **Tourism** (1990): $7 mln. receipts. **International reserves less gold** (Jan. 1993): $4.1 mln. **Gold:** 11,000 oz t.

Transport: Railroads (1989): 494 mi. long. **Motor vehicles** (1989): 26,000 passenger cars, 20,000 comm. vehicles. **Chief ports:** Pointe-Noire, Brazzaville.

Communications: Television sets: 1 per 402 persons. **Radios:** 1 per 9.4 persons. **Telephones:** 1 per 111 persons.

Health: Life expectancy at birth (1992): 52 male; 56 female. **Births** (per 1,000 pop. 1992): 43. **Deaths** (per 1,000 pop. 1992): 13. **Natural increase:** 3.0%. **Hospital beds:** 1 per 456 persons. **Physicians:** 1 per 3,873 persons. **Infant mortality** (per 1,000 live births 1992): 110.

Education (1991): **Literacy:** 57%. **School:** Compulsory for 10 years; attendance 80%.

Major International Organizations: UN (GATT, IMF, WHO), OAU.

Honorary Consulate: Livingstone House, 11 Carteret St, London SW1H 9DJ; 071-222 7575.

The Loango Kingdom flourished in the 15th century, as did the Anzico Kingdom of the Batekes; by the late 17th century they had become weakened. France established control by 1885. Independence came Aug. 15, 1960.

After a 1963 coup sparked by trade unions, the country adopted a Marxist-Leninist stance, with the USSR and China vying for influence. France remained a dominant trade partner and source of technical assistance, and French-owned private enterprise retained a major economic role. However, the government of Pres. Denis Sassou-Nguesso favored a strengthening of relations with the USSR; a socialist constitution was adopted, 1979.

In 1990, Marxism was renounced and opposition parties legalized. In 1991 the country's name was changed to Republic of Congo, and a new constitution was approved.

Costa Rica

Republic of Costa Rica

República de Costa Rica

People: Population (1992 est.): 3,187,000. **Age distrib.** (%): 0–14: 36.2; 15–49: 57.4; 50+: 6.4. **Pop. density:** 162 per sq. mi. **Urban** (1991): 50%. **Ethnic groups:** Spanish (with Mestizo minority). **Language:** Spanish (official). **Religion:** Roman Catholic 95%.

Geography: Area: 19,652 sq. mi., over twice the size of Wales. **Location:** In central America. **Neighbors:** Nicaragua on N, Panama on S. **Topography:** Lowlands by the Caribbean are tropical. The interior plateau, with an altitude of about 4,000 ft., is temperate. **Capital:** San Jose, pop. (1992 metro. est.) 890,000.

Government: Type: Democratic republic. **Head of state:** Pres. Rafael Angel Calderon; b. 1949; in office May 8, 1990. **Local divisions:** 7 provinces.

Economy: Industries: Furniture, food processing, aluminum, textiles, fertilizers, roofing, cement. **Chief crops:** Coffee (chief export), bananas, sugar, cocoa, cotton, hemp. **Minerals:** Gold, salt, sulphur, iron. **Other resources:** Fish, forests. **Arable land:** 12%. **Livestock** (1991): 1.7. mln. cattle. **Fish catch** (1990): 20,000 metric tons. **Electricity prod.** (1990): 2.9 bln. kWh. **Labor force:** 32% agric.; 25% ind. & comm.; 38% service and government.

Finance: Monetary unit: Colones (Mar. 1993: 138 = $1 US). **Gross domestic product** (1991): $5.6 bln. **Per capita GDP:** $1,810. **Imports** (1992): $2.5 bln.; partners: U.S. 38%, CACM 10%, Jap. 10%. **Exports** (1992): $1.8 bln.; partners: U.S. 45%, CACM 18%. **Tourism** (1989): $206 mln. receipts. **National budget** (1990): $1.0 bln. expenditures. **International reserves less gold** (Mar. 1993): $1.0 bln. **Gold:** 35,000 oz t. **Consumer prices** (change in 1992): 28.7%.

Transport: Motor vehicles (1990): 168,000 passenger cars, 94,000 comm. vehicles. **Civil aviation** (1991): 1.0 bln. passenger-km; 9 airports with scheduled flights. **Chief ports:** Limon, Puntarenas, Golfito.

Communications: Television sets: 1 per 4.9 persons. **Radios:** 1 per 11 persons. **Telephones:** 1 per 6.9 persons. **Daily newspaper circ.** (1990): 110 per 1,000 pop.

Health: Life expectancy at birth (1992): 75 male; 79 female. **Births** (per 1,000 pop. 1992): 27. **Deaths** (per 1,000 pop. 1992): 4. **Natural increase:** 2.3%. **Hospital beds:** 1 per 454 persons. **Physicians:** 1 per 798 persons. **Infant mortality** (per 1,000 live births 1992): 12.

Education (1992): **Literacy:** 93%. **School:** Compulsory for 6 years; attendance 99%.

Major International Organizations: UN (FAO, ILO, IMF, WHO), OAS.

Embassy: 19a Cavendish Sq, London W1M 0JR; 071-495 3985.

Guaymi Indians inhabited the area when Spaniards arrived, 1502. Independence came in 1821. Costa Rica seceded from the Central American Federation in 1838. Since the civil war of 1948-49, there has been little violent social conflict, and free political institutions have been preserved.

An earthquake in Apr. 1991 damaged the banana industry and shut down the port of Limon, adding pressure to a floundering economy.

Costa Rica, though still a largely agricultural country, has achieved a relatively high standard of living and social services, and land ownership is widespread, despite a troubled economy.

Côte d'Ivoire

Ivory Coast

République de la Côte d'Ivoire

People: Population (1992 est.): 13,497,000. **Age distrib.** (%): 0–14: 48.2; 15–59: 45.2; 60+: 6.6. **Pop. density:** 104 per sq. mi. **Urban** (1990): 40%. **Ethnic groups:** Baule 23%, Bete 18%, Senufo 15%, Malinke 11%, over 60 tribes. **Languages:** French (official), Akan, Kru, Voltaic, Malinke. **Religions:** Indigenous 63%, Muslim 25%, Christian 12%.

Geography: Area: 124,503 sq. mi., slightly larger than the UK. **Location:** On S. coast of W. Africa. **Neighbors:** Liberia, Guinea on W, Mali, Burkina Faso on N, Ghana on E. **Topography:** Forests cover the W half of the country, and range from a coastal strip to halfway to the N on the E. A sparse inland plain leads to low mountains in NW. **Capital:** Yamoussoukro (official); Abidjan (de facto), (1990 est.) 2.7 mln.

Government: Type: Republic. **Head of state:** Pres. Felix Houphouet-Boigny; b. Oct. 18, 1905; in office Aug. 7, 1960. **Head of government:** Prime Min. Alassane Ouattara. **Local divisions:** 49 departments.

Economy: Chief crops: Coffee, cocoa. **Minerals:** Diamonds, manganese. **Other resources:** Timber, rubber, petroleum. **Arable land:** 9%. **Livestock** (1990): 1.5 mln. goats; 1.5 mln. sheep; 991,000 cattle. **Fish catch** (1990): 108,000 metric tons. **Electricity prod.** (1991): 2.6 bln. kWh. **Labor force:** 85% agric., forestry.

Finance: Monetary unit: CFA franc (Mar. 1993: 273 = $1 US). **Gross domestic product** (1990): $10 bln. **Per capita GDP:** $800. **Imports** (1989): $2.1 bln.; partners: Fr. 31%, Jap. 5%, U.S. 5%. **Exports** (1989): $2.8 bln.; partners: Fr. 14%, Neth. 19%, U.S. 11%, It. 8%. **Tourism** (1990): $48 mln receipts; **International reserves less gold** (Jan. 1993): $6.9 mln. **Gold:** 45,000 oz t. **Consumer prices** (change in 1992): 3.5%.

Transport: Railroads (1989): 600 km. long. **Motor vehicles** (1989): 168,000 passenger cars, 90,000 comm. vehicles. **Chief ports:** Abidjan, Sassandra.

Communications: Television sets: 1 per 15 persons. **Radios:** 1 per 8.1 persons. **Telephones:** 1 per 143 persons. **Daily newspaper circ.** (1990): 12 per 1,000 pop.

Health: Life expectancy at birth (1992): 53 male; 57 female. **Births** (per 1,000 pop. 1992): 48. **Deaths** (per 1,000 pop. 1992): 12. **Natural increase:** 3.6%. **Hospital beds** (1982): 10,062. **Physicians** (1982): 502. **Infant mortality** (per 1,000 live births 1992): 94.

Education (1990): **Literacy:** 45%. **School:** Not compulsory; attendance 75%.

Major International Organizations: UN and all of its specialized agencies, OAU.

Embassy: 2 Upper Belgrave St, London SW1X 8BJ; 071-235 6991.

A French protectorate from 1842, Côte d'Ivoire became independent in 1960. It is the most prosperous of the tropical African nations, due to diversification of agriculture for export, close ties to France, and encouragement of foreign investment. About 20% of the population are workers from neighboring countries. Côte d'Ivoire officially changed its name from Ivory Coast in Oct. 1985.

Students and workers staged protests, Feb. 1990, demanding the ouster of Pres. Houphouet-Boigny and multiparty democracy. Côte d'Ivoire held its first multiparty presidential election in Oct. 1990.

Croatia

Republic of Croatia

Republika Hrvatska

People: Population (1992 est.): 4,784,000. **Pop. density:** 219 per sq. mi. **Ethnic groups:** Croats 78%; Serbs 12%. **Language:** Croatian. **Religion:** Mostly Roman Catholic 77%.

Geography: Area: 21,829 sq. mi., less than half the size of England. **Location:** in SE Europe. **Neighbors:** Slovenia, Bosnia and Herzegovina, Hungary, Yugoslavia, and the Adriatic Sea. Over 33% is forested. **Capital:** Zagreb.

Government: Type: Parliamentary democracy. **Head of state:** Pres. Franjo Tudjman; b. 1922; in office May 1990. **Head of government:** Prime Min. Hryoje Sarinic; in office Sept. 8, 1992. **Local divisions:** 102 districts.

Economy: Industries: Textiles, chemicals, aluminum prods., paper. **Chief crops:** Olives, wine. **Minerals:** Bauxite, copper, coal. **Arable land:** 32%. **Electricity prod.** (1991): 8.8 mln. kWh.

Finance: Monetary unit: Croatian Dinar (Jan. 1993: 365 = $1 US). **Gross domestic product** (1991): $26.3 bln. **Per capita GDP:** $5,600. **Imports** (1990): $4.4 bln. **Exports** (1990): $2.9 bln.

Transport: Motor vehicles (1990): 865,000 passenger cars, 72,000 comm. vehicles.

Communications: Television sets: 1 per 4 persons. **Radios:** 1 per 4 persons. **Telephones:** 1 per 4 persons. **Newspaper circ.** (1990): 150 per 1,000 pop.

Health: Life expectancy at birth (1990): 67 male; 74 female. **Births** (per 1,000 pop. 1992): 12. **Deaths** (per 1,000 pop. 1992): 11. **Hospital beds:** 1 per 133 persons. **Physicians:** 1 per 466 persons. **Infant mortality** (per 1,000 live births 1990): 10.

Education (1991): **Literacy:** 96%.

International Organizations: UN.

Republic Office: 18 Jermyn St, London SW1Y 6HP; 071-434 2946.

From the 7th century the area was inhabited by Croats, a south Slavic people. It was formed into a kingdom under Tomislav in 924, and joined with Hungary in 1102. The Croats became westernized and separated from Slavs under Serbian influence. The Croats retained autonomy under the Hungarian crown. Slavonia was taken by Turks in the 16th century, the northern part was restored by the Treaty of Karlowitz in 1699. Croatia helped Austria put down the Hungarian revolution 1848-49 and as a result was set up with Slavonia as the separate Austrian crownland of Croatia and Slavonia, which was reunited to Hungary as part of *Ausgleich* in 1867. It united with other Yugoslav areas to proclaim the kingdom of Serbs, Croats, and Slovenes in 1918. At the reorganization of Yugoslavia in 1929, Croatia and Slavonia became Savska county, which in 1939 was united with Primorje county to form the county of Croatia. A nominally independent state between 1941-45, it became a constituent republic in the 1946 constitution.

On June 25, 1991 Croatia declared independence from Yugoslavia. Fighting began between ethnic Serbs and Croats. There were clashes between Croats and Yugoslavian army units and their Serb supporters. Croatia was granted EC recognition Jan. 15, 1992. Fighting continued in 1992 and 1993 as some 30% of Croatia's territory remained under Serbian control.

Cuba

Republic of Cuba

República de Cuba

People: Population (1992 est.): 10,846,000. **Age distrib.** (%): 0-under 15: 23.3; 15–59: 64.9; 60+: 11.8. **Pop. density:** 245 per sq. mi. **Urban** (1991): 72%. **Ethnic groups:** Spanish, African. **Language:** Spanish. **Religions:** Roman Catholic 42%, none 49%.

Geography: Area: 44,218 sq. mi., about half the size of GB. **Location:** Westernmost of West Indies. **Neighbors:** Bahamas, U.S., on N, Mexico on W, Jamaica on S, Haiti on E. **Topography:** The coastline is about 2,500 miles. The N coast is steep and rocky, the S coast low and marshy. Low hills and fertile valleys cover more than half the country. Sierra Maestra in the E is the highest of 3 mountain ranges. **Capital:** Havana. **Cities** (1989 est.): Havana 2,077,000; Santiago de Cuba 397,000; Camaguey 274,000.

Government: Type: Communist state. **Head of state:** Pres. Fidel Castro Ruiz; b. Aug. 13, 1926; in office Dec. 3, 1976 (formerly Prime Min. since Feb. 16, 1959). **Local divisions:** 14 provinces, Havana. **Defense** (1989): 6.0% of GDP.

Economy: Industries: Cement, food processing, sugar. **Chief crops:** Sugar (75% of exports), tobacco, rice, coffee, tropical fruit. **Minerals:** Cobalt, nickel, iron, copper, manganese, salt. **Other resources:** Forests. **Arable land:** 29%. **Livestock** (1991): 4.9 mln. cattle; 1.9 mln. pigs. **Fish catch** (1991): 188,000 metric tons. **Electricity prod.** (1991): 16.2 bln. kWh. **Labor force:** 20% agric.; 33% ind. & comm.; 30% services & govt.

Finance: Monetary unit: Peso (Dec. 1992: .76 = $1 US). **Gross social product:** Economic measure not convertible to GNP. **Per capita income** (1990): $2,644. **Imports** (1991): $3.7 bln. **Exports** (1991): $3.6 bln. **Tourism** (1990): $250 mln. receipts.

National budget (1990): $14.4 bln. expenditures

Transport: Railroads (1990): 3,009 mi. long. **Motor vehicles** (1988): 241,000 passenger cars, 208,000 comm. vehicles. **Civil aviation** (1991): 3.1 bln. passenger-km.; 11 airports with scheduled flights. **Chief ports:** Havana, Matanzas, Cienfuegos, Santiago de Cuba.

Communications: Television sets: 1 per 5 persons. **Radios:** 1 per 3 persons. **Telephones:** 1 per 19 persons. **Daily newspaper circ.** (1988): 155 per 1,000 pop.

Health: Life expectancy at birth (1992): 74 male; 79 female. **Births** (per 1,000 pop. 1992): 18.0. **Deaths** (per 1,000 pop. 1992): 7. **Natural increase:** 1.1%. **Hospital beds:** 1 per 141 persons. **Physicians:** 1 per 303 persons. **Infant mortality** (per 1,000 live births 1992): 12.

Education (1992): **Literacy:** 99%. **School:** 92% of those aged 6–14 attend school.

Major International Organizations: UN (UNESCO, WHO).

Embassy: 167 High Holborn, London WC1; 071-240 2488.

Some 50,000 Indians lived in Cuba when it was reached by Columbus in 1492. Its name derives from the Indian Cubanacan. Except for British occupation of Havana, 1762-63, Cuba remained Spanish until 1898. A slave-based sugar plantation economy developed from the 18th century, aided by early mechanization of milling. Sugar remains the chief product and chief export despite government attempts to diversify.

A 10-year uprising ended in 1878 with guarantees of rights by Spain, which Spain failed to carry out. A full-scale movement under Jose Marti began Feb. 24, 1895.

The U.S. declared war on Spain in April, 1898, after the sinking of the U.S.S. Maine in Havana harbor, and defeated it in the Spanish-American War. Spain gave up all claims to Cuba. U.S. troops withdrew in 1902, but under 1903 and 1934 agreements, the U.S. leases a site at Guantanamo Bay in the SE as a naval base. U.S. and other foreign investments acquired a dominant role in the economy.

In 1952, former president Fulgencio Batista seized control and established a dictatorship, which grew increasingly harsh and corrupt. Fidel Castro assembled a rebel band in 1956; guerrilla fighting intensified in 1958. Batista fled Jan. 1, 1959, and in the resulting political vacuum Castro took power, becoming premier Feb. 16.

The government began a program of sweeping economic and social changes, without restoring promised liberties. Opponents were imprisoned and some were executed. Some 700,000 Cubans emigrated in the years after the Castro takeover, mostly to the U.S.

Cattle and tobacco lands were nationalized, while a system of cooperatives was instituted. By 1960 all banks and industrial companies had been nationalized, including over $1 billion worth of U.S.-owned properties, mostly without compensation.

Poor sugar crops resulted in collectivization of farms, stringent labor controls, and rationing, despite continued aid from the USSR and other communist countries.

The U.S. imposed an export embargo in 1962, severely damaging the economy. In 1961, some 1,400 Cubans, trained and backed by the U.S. Central Intelligence Agency, unsuccessfully tried to invade and overthrow the regime.

In the fall of 1962, the U.S. learned that the USSR had brought nuclear missiles to Cuba. After an Oct. 22 warning from Pres. Kennedy, the missiles were removed.

In 1977, Cuba and the U.S. signed agreements to exchange diplomats, without restoring full ties, and to regulate offshore fishing. In 1978, and again in 1980, the U.S. agreed to accept political prisoners released by Cuba some of whom, it was later discovered, were criminals and mental patients. A 1987 agreement provided for 20,000 Cubans to immigrate to the U.S. each year; Cuba agreed to take back some 2,500 jailed in the U.S. since the 1980 Mariel boat lift.

In 1975-78, Cuba sent troops to aid one faction in the Angola civil war. All Cuban troops were withdrawn by May 1991. Cuba's involvement in Central America, Africa, and the Caribbean contributed to poor relations with the U.S.

In 1983, 24 Cubans died and over 700 were captured, later repatriated, as a result of the U.S.-led invasion of Grenada.

Cuba resisted the social and economic reforms that took place in the late 1980s and 1990s in the Soviet Union and its successor states in Eastern Europe. The nation, whose economy had been heavily dependent on the Soviet Union, suffered severe economic difficulties in the 1990s.

A mystery illness of epidemic proportions struck Cuba in 1993. Over 43,000 people were diagnosed with the illness, which caused vision loss and impaired coordination. It was eventually discovered to be due to vitamin deficiency.

Cyprus

Republic of Cyprus

Kypriaki Dimokratia (Greek)

Kibris Cumhuriyeti (Turkish)

People: Population (1992 est.): 716,000. **Age distrib.** (%): 0–14: 25.4; 15–59: 60.4; 60+: 14.2. **Pop. density:** 200 per sq. mi. **Urban** (1991): 69%. **Ethnic groups:** Greeks 78%, Turks 18.7%, Armenians, Maronites. **Languages:** Greek, Turkish (both official), English. **Religions:** Orthodox 77%, Muslim 18%.

Geography: Area: 3,572 sq. mi., slightly bigger than the Grampian region of Scotland. **Location:** In eastern Mediterranean Sea, off Turkish coast. **Neighbors:** Nearest are Turkey on N, Syria, Lebanon on E. **Topography:** Two mountain ranges run E-W, separated by a wide, fertile plain. **Capital:** Nicosia, pop. (1992 est.) 166,000.

Government: Type: Republic. **Head of state:** Pres. Glafcos Clerides; in office Mar. 1, 1993. **Local divisions:** 6 districts. **Defense** (1990): 5% of GDP.

Economy: Industries: Light manuf. **Chief crops:** Grains, grapes, carobs, citrus fruits, potatoes, olives. **Minerals:** Copper, pyrites, asbetos. **Arable land:** 40%. **Electricity prod.** (1990): 1.6 mln. kWh. **Labor force:** 21% agric.; 20% ind., 18% comm., 19% serv.

Finance: Monetary unit: Pound (Mar. 1993: .48 = $1 US). **Gross domestic product** (1990): $5.3 bln. **Per capita GDP:** $7,585. **Imports** (1991): $2.2 bln.; partners: UK 13%, Itl. 12%. **Exports** (1991): $838 mln.; partners: UK 21%, Libya 9%. **Tourism** (1989): $990 mln. receipts. **National budget** (1991): $2.0 bln. expenditures. **International reserves less gold** (Mar. 1993): $1.1 bln. **Gold:** 459,000 oz. t. **Consumer prices** (change in 1992): 6.5%.

Transport: Motor vehicles (1989): 159,000 passenger cars, 54,000 comm. vehicles. **Civil aviation** (1991): 2.2 bln. passenger-km; one airport. **Chief ports:** Famagusta, Limassol.

Communications: Television sets: 1 per 3.4 persons. **Radios:** 1 per 2.7 persons. **Telephones:** 1 per 2.0 persons. **Daily newspaper circ.** (1991): 161 per 1,000 pop.

Health: Life expectancy at birth (1992): 74 male; 78 female. **Births** (per 1,000 pop. 1992): 18. **Deaths** (per 1,000 pop. 1992): 8. **Natural increase:** 1.0%. **Hospital beds:** 1 per 165 persons. **Physicians:** 1 per 480 persons. **Infant mortality** (per 1,000 live births 1992); 10.

Education (1991): **Literacy:** 95%. **School:** Compulsory for 9 years; attendance 99%.

Major International Organizations: UN (GATT, IMF, WHO), Commonwealth of Nations, EC (Assoc.).

High Commission: 93 Park St, London W1Y 4ET; 071-499 8272.

Agitation for enosis (union) with Greece increased after World War II, with the Turkish minority opposed, and broke into violence in 1955-56. In 1959, Britain, Greece, Turkey, and Cypriot leaders approved a plan for an independent republic, with constitutional guarantees for the Turkish minority and permanent division of offices on an ethnic basis. Greek and Turkish Communal Chambers dealt with religion, education, and other matters.

Archbishop Makarios III, formerly the leader of the enosis movement, was elected president, and full independence became final Aug. 16, 1960. Makarios was re-elected in 1968 and 1973.

Further communal strife led the United Nations to send a peace-keeping force in 1964; its mandate has been repeatedly renewed.

The Cypriot National Guard, led by officers from the army of Greece, seized the government July 15, 1974. Makarios fled the country. On July 20, Turkey invaded the island; Greece mobilized its forces but did not intervene. A cease-fire was arranged July 22. A peace conference collapsed Aug. 14; fighting resumed. By Aug. 16 Turkish forces had occupied the NE 40% of the island, despite the presence of UN peace-keeping forces. Makarios resumed the presidency in Dec., until his death, 1977.

Turkish Cypriots voted overwhelmingly, June 8, 1975, to form a separate Turkish Cypriot federated state. A president and assembly were elected in 1976. Some 200,000 Greeks have been expelled from the Turkish-controlled area, replaced by thousands of Turks, some from the mainland.

Turkish Republic of Northern Cyprus

A declaration of independence was announced by Turkish-Cypriot leader Rauf Denktash, Nov. 15, 1983. The new state is not internationally recognized although it does have trade relations with some countries. TRNC contains 1,295 sq mi., pop. (1992 est.): 176,000, 99% Turkish.

Czech Republic

(Figures prior to 1992 are for the Czech and Slovak Federal Republic)

People: Population (1992 est.): 10,400,000. **Age distrib.** (1990) (%): 0–14: 22.5; 15–59: 60.8; 60+: 16.7. **Pop. density:** 342 per sq. mi., slightly smaller than England. **Urban** (1990): 73%. **Ethnic groups:** Czech 94%, Slovak 4%.

Geography: Area: 30,449 sq. mi., slightly smaller than England. **Location:** In E central Europe. **Neighbors:** Poland on N, Germany on N, W, Austria on S, Slovakia on E, SE. **Topography:** Bohemia, in W, is a plateau surrounded by mountains; Moravia is hilly. **Capital:** Prague. **Cities** (1992 est.): Prague 1.2 mln.; Brno 391,000; Ostrava 331,000.

Government: Type: Republic. **Head of state:** Vaclav Havel; b. Oct. 5, 1936; in office Feb. 15, 1993. **Head of government:** Prime Min. Jan Strasky; in office July 3, 1992. **Defense** (1987): 6.8% of GNP.

Economy: Industries: Machinery, oil products, iron and steel, glass, chemicals, motor vehicles, cement. **Chief crops:** Wheat, sugar beets, potatoes, rye, corn, barley. **Minerals:** Coke, coal, iron. **Livestock** (1989): 5 mln. cattle; 7 mln. pigs; 1 mln. sheep. **Electricity prod.** (1989): 89.0 bln. kWh. **Crude steel prod.** (1991): 12.0 mln. metric tons. **Labor force:** 12% agric.; 37% ind.; 22% service, govt.

Finance: Monetary unit: Koruna (Aug. 1993: 29.43 = $1 US). **Gross domestic product** (1990): $120 bln. **Per capita GDP:** $7,700. **Imports** (1991): $10.4 bln.; partners: USSR 31%, E. Ger. 10%, Pol. 6%, W. Ger. 9%. **Exports** (1991): $10.8 bln.; partners: USSR 35%, E. Ger. 7%, Pol. 7%. **Tourism** (1989): $689 mln. receipts. **National budget** (1991): $16.8 bln. expenditures. **International reserves less gold** (Mar. 1993): $1.1 bln. **Gold:** 3.2 mln. oz t. **Consumer prices** (change in 1992): 8.2%.

Transport: Railroads (1990): 8,142 mi. long; 20.0 bln. passenger-km. **Motor vehicles** (1989): 3.1 mln. passenger cars, 327,000 comm. vehicles. **Civil aviation** (1991): 2.2 bln. passenger-km.; 8 airports.

Communications: Television sets: 1 per 2.7 persons. **Radios:** 1 per 3.3 persons. **Telephones:** 1 per 3.9 persons. **Daily newspaper circ.** (1990): 327 per 1,000 pop.

Health: Life expectancy at birth (1992): 69 male; 77 female. **Births** (per 1,000 pop. 1991): 14. **Deaths** (per 1,000 pop. 1991): 12. **Natural increase:** .2%. **Hospital beds:** 1 per 99 persons. **Physicians:** 1 per 317 persons. **Infant mortality** (per 1,000 live births 1991): 11.

Education (1992): **Literacy:** 99%.

Major International Organizations: UN (GATT, WHO).

Embassy: 25 Kensington Palace Gardens, London W8 4QY; 071-229 1255.

Bohemia and Moravia were part of the Great Moravian Empire in the 9th century and later became part of the Holy Roman Empire. Under the kings of Bohemia, Prague in the 14th century was the cultural center of Central Europe. Bohemia and Hungary became part of Austria-Hungary.

In 1914-1918 Thomas G. Masaryk and Eduard Benes formed a provisional government with the support of Slovak leaders including Milan Stefanik. They proclaimed the Republic of Czechoslovakia Oct. 28, 1918.

Czechoslovakia

By 1938 Nazi Germany had worked up disaffection among German-speaking citizens in Sudetenland and demanded its cession. Prime Min. Neville Chamberlain of Britain, backed by France, signed with Hitler at Munich, Sept. 30, 1938, an agreement to the cession, with a guarantee of peace by Hitler and Mussolini. Germany occupied Sudetenland Oct. 1-2.

Hitler, on Mar. 15, 1939, dissolved Czechoslovakia, made protectorates of Bohemia and Moravia, and supported the autonomy of Slovakia (proclaimed independent Mar. 14, 1939).

Soviet troops with some Czechoslovak contingents entered eastern Czechoslovakia in 1944 and reached Prague in May 1945; Benes returned as president. In May 1946 elections, the Communist Party won 38% of the votes, and Benes accepted Klement Gottwald, a communist, as prime minister.

In February 1948, the communists seized power in advance of scheduled elections. In May 1948 a new constitution was approved. Benes refused to sign it. On May 30 the voters were offered a one-slate ballot and the communists won full control. Benes resigned June 7 and Gottwald became president. A harsh Stalinist period followed, with complete and violent suppression of all opposition.

In Jan. 1968 a liberalization movement spread explosively through Czechoslovakia. Antonin Novotny, long the Stalinist ruler of the nation, was deposed as party leader and succeeded by Alexander Dubcek, a Slovak, who declared he intended to make communism democratic. On Mar. 22 Novotny resigned as president and was succeeded by Gen. Ludvik Svoboda. On Apr. 6, Premier Joseph Lenart resigned and was succeeded by Oldrich Cernik, whose new cabinet was pledged to carry out democratization and economic reforms.

In July 1968 the USSR and 4 Warsaw Pact nations demanded an end to liberalization. On Aug. 20 the Soviet, Polish, East German, Hungarian, and Bulgarian armies invaded Czechoslovakia.

Despite demonstrations and riots by students and workers, press censorship was imposed, liberal leaders were ousted from office and promises of loyalty to Soviet policies were made by some old-line Communist Party leaders.

On Apr. 17, 1969, Dubcek resigned as leader of the Communist Party and was succeeded by Gustav Husak. In Jan. 1970, Premier Cernik was ousted. Censorship was tightened, and the Communist Party expelled a third of its members. In 1973, amnesty was offered to some of the 40,000 who fled the country after the 1968 invasion, but repressive policies remained in force.

More than 700 leading Czechoslovak intellectuals and former party leaders signed a human rights manifesto in 1977, called Charter 77, prompting a renewed crackdown by the regime.

The police crushed the largest anti-government protests since 1968, when tens of thousands of demonstrators took to the streets of Prague, Nov. 17, 1989. As protesters demanded free elections, the Communist Party leadership resigned Nov. 24; millions went on strike Nov. 27.

On Dec. 10, 1989 the first Cabinet in 41 years without a communist majority took power; Vaclav Havel, playwright and human rights campaigner, was chosen president, Dec. 29. Havel failed to win re-election July 3, 1992; his bid was blocked by a Slovak-led coalition.

Slovakia declared sovereignty, July 17. Czech and Slovak leaders agreed, July 23, on a basic plan for a peaceful division of Czechoslovakia into 2 independent states.

Czech Republic

Czechoslovakia split into 2 separate states – the Czech Republic and Slovakia – on Jan. 1, 1993.

Denmark

Kingdom of Denmark

Kongeriget Danmark

People: Population (1992 est.): 5,163,000. **Age distrib.** (%): 0–14: 17.1; 15–59: 62.5; 60+: 20.4. **Pop. density:** 310 per sq. mi. **Urban** (1990): 86%. **Ethnic groups:** Almost all Scandinavian. **Language:** Danish. **Religion:** Evangelical Lutheran 90%.

Geography: Area: 16,633 sq. mi., half the size of Wales. **Location:** In northern Europe, separating the North and Baltic seas. **Neighbors:** Germany on S., Norway on NW, Sweden on NE. **Topography:** Denmark consists of the Jutland Peninsula and about 500 islands, 100 inhabited. The land is flat or gently rolling, and is almost all in productive use. **Capital:** Copenhagen, pop. (1991 metro.) 1.3 mln.

Government: Type: Constitutional monarchy. **Head of state:** Queen Margrethe II; b. Apr. 16, 1940; in office Jan. 14, 1972. **Head of government:** Prime Min. Poul Schluter; b. 1929; in office Sept. 10, 1982. **Local divisions:** 14 counties and one city (Copenhagen). **Defense** (1991): 2.0% of GDP.

Economy: Industries: Machinery, textiles, furniture, electronics. **Chief crops:** Dairy products. **Arable land:** 62%. **Livestock** (1987): 2.3 mln. cattle; 9.2 mln. pigs. **Fish catch** (1989): 1.9 mln. metric tons. **Electricity prod.** (1991): 31 bln. kWh. **Labor force:** 6% agric., 50% ind. & comm.; 11% serv.; 27% govt.

Finance: Monetary unit: Krone (July 1993: 6.56 = $1 US). **Gross domestic product** (1991): $91 bln. **Per capita GDP:** $17,700. **Imports** (1992): $32.3 bln.; partners: EC 52%, Swe. 10%. **Exports** (1992): $39.6 bln.; partners: EC 54%, Swe. 11%. **Tourism** (1991): $3.4 bln. receipts. **International reserves less gold** (Mar. 1993): $12.6 bln. **Gold:** 2.0 mln. oz t. **Consumer prices** (change in 1992): 2.1%.

Transport: Railroads (1990): 1,763 km. long. **Motor vehicles** (1990): 1.5 mln. passenger cars, 294,000 comm. vehicles. **Civil aviation** (1990): 4.2 bln. passenger-km; 12 airports with scheduled flights. **Chief ports:** Copenhagen, Alborg, Arhus, Odense.

Communications: Television sets: 1 per 2.7 persons. **Radios:** 1 per 2.4 persons. **Telephones:** 1 per 1.2 persons. **Daily newspaper circ.** (1991): 361 per 1,000 pop.

Health: Life expectancy at birth (1992): 72 male; 78 female. **Births** (per 1,000 pop. 1992): 12. **Deaths** (per 1,000 pop. 1992): 11. **Hospital beds:** 1 per 177 persons. **Physicians:** 1 per 360 persons. **Infant mortality** (per 1,000 live births 1992): 7.

Education (1991): **Literacy:** 99%. **School:** Compulsory for 9 years; attendance 100%.

Major International Organizations: UN and all of its specialized agencies, OECD, EC, NATO.

Embassy: 55 Sloane St, London SW1X 9SR; 071-333 0200.

The origin of Copenhagen dates back to ancient times, when the fishing and trading place named Havn (port) grew up on a cluster of islets, but Bishop Absalon (1128-1201) is regarded as the actual founder of the city.

Danes formed a large component of the Viking raiders in the early Middle Ages. The Danish kingdom was a major north European power until the 17th century, when it lost its land in southern Sweden. Norway was separated in 1815, and Schleswig-Holstein in 1864. Northern Schleswig was returned in 1920.

Voters ratified the Maastricht Treaty on greater European Community unity, May 1993, having rejected it in 1992.

The **Faeroe Islands** in the N. Atlantic, about 300 mi. NE of the Shetlands, and 850 mi. from Denmark proper, 18 inhabited, have an area of 540 sq. mi. and pop. (1992) of 48,000. They are self-governing in most matters.

Djibouti

Republic of Djibouti

Jumhouriyya Djibouti

People: Population (1992 est.): 390,000. **Pop. density:** 43 per sq. mi. **Urban** (1991): 81%. **Ethnic groups:** Somali 60%; Afar 35%. **Languages:** French, Arabic (both official), Afar, Somali. **Religion:** Sunni Muslim 94%.

Geography: Area: 8,950 sq. mi., about the size of Wales. **Location:** On E coast of Africa, separated from Arabian Peninsula by the strategically vital strait of Bab el-Mandeb. **Neighbors:** Ethiopia on W, NW, Eritrea on NW, Somalia on S. **Topography:** The territory, divided into a low coastal plain, mountains behind, and an interior plateau, is arid, sandy, and desolate. The climate is generally hot and dry. **Capital:** Djibouti, pop. (1988 metro.) 290,000.

Government: Type: Republic. **Head of state:** Pres. Hassan Gouled Aptidon, b. 1916; in office June 24, 1977. **Head of government:** Prem. Barkat Gourad Hamadou; in office Sept. 30, 1978. **Local divisions:** 5 districts.

Economy: Minerals: Salt. **Electricity prod.** (1991): 200 mln. kWh.

Finance: Monetary unit: Franc (Mar. 1993: 177=$1 US). **Gross domestic product** (1989): $344 mln. **Per capita GDP:** $1,030. **Imports** (1990): $311 mln.; partners: EC 36%. **Exports** (1990): $190 mln.; partners: Middle East 50%.

Transport: Motor vehicles (1989): 13,000 passenger cars, 13,000 comm. vehicles. **Chief port:** Djibouti.

Communications: Television sets: 1 per 38 persons. **Radios:** 1 per 18 persons. **Telephones:** 1 per 55 persons.

Health: Life expectancy at birth (1992): 47 male; 50 female. **Births** (per 1,000 pop. 1992): 43. **Deaths** (per 1,000 pop. 1992): 17. **Natural increase:** 2.6%. **Infant mortality** (per 1,000 live births 1992): 115.

Education (1991): **Literacy:** 48%.

Major International Organizations: UN, OAU, Arab League.

Embassy: 26 rue Emile Ménier, Paris 75116, France; 010 331 47274922.

France gained control of the territory in stages between 1862 and 1900.

Ethiopia and Somalia have renounced their claims to the area, but each has accused the other of trying to gain control. There were clashes between Afars (ethnically related to Ethiopians) and Issas (related to Somalis) in 1976. Immigrants from both countries continued to enter the country up to independence, which came June 27, 1977.

Unemployment is high and there are few natural resources. French aid is the mainstay of the economy, as well as assistance from the U.S.

Dominica

Commonwealth of Dominica

People: Population (1992 est.): 86,000. **Pop. density:** 296 per sq. mi. **Ethnic groups:** nearly all African or mulatto, Caribs. **Languages:** English (official), French creole. **Religion:** Roman Catholic 77%.

Geography: Area: 290 sq. mi., slightly larger than Merseyside. **Location:** In Eastern Caribbean, most northerly Windward Is. **Neighbors:** Guadeloupe to N, Martinique to S. **Topography:** Mountainous, a central ridge running from N to S, terminating in cliffs; volcanic in origin, with numerous thermal springs; rich deep topsoil on leeward side, red tropical clay on windward coast. **Capital:** Roseau, pop. (1987 est.) 22,000.

Government: Type: Parliamentary democracy. **Head of state:** Pres. Clarence Augustus Seignoret; in office: 1984. **Head of government:** Prime Min. Mary Eugenia Charles; b. 1919; in office: July 21, 1980. **Local divisions:** 10 parishes.

Economy: Industries: Agriculture, tourism. **Chief crops:** Bananas, citrus fruits, coconuts. **Minerals:** Pumice. **Other resources:** Forests. **Arable land:** 23%. **Electricity prod.** (1991): 16 mln. kWh. **Labor force:** 37% agric.; 20% ind & comm.; 30% services.

Finance: Monetary unit: East Caribbean dollar (May 1993: 2.70 = $1 US). **Gross domestic product** (1990): $170 mln. **Imports** (1992): $111 mln.; partners: UK 17%, U.S. 23%. **Exports** (1992): $56 mln.; partners: UK 70%. **Tourism** (1989): $19 mln. receipts. **Consumer prices** (change in 1991): 6.0%.

Transport: Chief port: Roseau.

Communications: Telephones: 1 per 11 persons.

Health: Life expectancy at birth (1992): 74 male; 79 female. **Births** (per 1,000 pop. 1992): 24. **Deaths** (per 1,000 pop. 1992): 5. **Natural increase:** 1.9%. **Hospital beds:** 1 per 247 persons. **Physicians:** 1 per 1,947 persons. **Infant mortality** (per 1,000 live births 1992): 11.

Education: Literacy: 90%.

Major International Organizations: UN, OAS.

High Commission: 1 Collingham Gdns, London SW5 0HW; 071-370 5194.

A British colony since 1805, Dominica was granted self government in 1967. Independence was achieved Nov. 3, 1978.

Hurricane David struck, Aug. 30, 1979, devastating the island and destroying the banana plantations, Dominica's economic mainstay. Coups were attempted in 1980 and 1981.

Dominica took a leading role in the instigation of the 1983 U.S.-led invasion of Grenada.

In 1992 the government instituted a controversial programme that offered passports to people from the Far East who agreed to invest large sums of money in the country.

Dominican Republic

República Dominicana

People: Population (1992 est.): 7,515,000. **Age distrib.** (%): 0–14: 37.9; 15–59: 56.6; 60+: 5.5. **Pop. density:** 401 per sq. mi. **Urban** (1990): 60%. **Ethnic groups:** Caucasian 16%, mixed 73%, black 11%. **Language:** Spanish. **Religion:** Roman Catholic 95%.

Geography: Area: 18,704 sq. mi., about one-third the size of England. **Location:** In West Indies, sharing I. of Hispaniola with Haiti. **Neighbors:** Haiti on W. **Topography:** The Cordillera Central range crosses the center of the country, rising to over 10,000 ft., highest in the Caribbean. The Cibao valley to the N is major agricultural area. **Capital:** Santo Domingo. **Cities** (1991 est.): Santo Domingo 2,400,000; Santiago de los Caballeros 490,000.

Government: Type: Representative democracy. **Head of state:** Pres. Joaquin Balaguer; in office: Aug. 16, 1986. **Local divisions:** 29 provinces and Santo Domingo. **Defense** (1990): 1.0% of GDP.

Economy: Industries: Sugar refining, cement, pharmaceuticals. **Chief crops:** sugar, cocoa, coffee, tobacco, rice. **Minerals:** Nickel, gold, silver. **Other resources:** Timber. **Arable land:** 23%. **Livestock** (1991): 2.2 mln. cattle; 431,000 pigs. **Electricity prod.** (1991): 4.4 bln. kWh. **Labor force:** 35% agric.; 13% ind.; 23% serv. & govt.

Finance: Monetary unit: Peso (Mar. 1993: 12.59 = $1 US). **Gross domestic product** (1991): $7.1 bln. **Per capita GDP:** $950. **Imports** (1991): $1.8 bln.; partners: U.S. 50%. **Exports** (1991): $775 mln.; partners: U.S. 59%, EC 19%. **Tourism** (1990): $750 mln. receipts. **National budget** (1990): $938 mln. expenditures. **International reserves less gold** (Mar. 1993): $508 mln. **Gold:** 18,000 oz t. **Consumer prices** (change in 1991): 53.9%

Transport: Motor vehicles (1989): 114,000 passenger cars, 72,000 comm. vehicles. **Civil aviation** (1988): 247 mln. passenger km.; 5 airports. **Chief ports:** Santo Domingo, San Pedro de Macoris, Puerto Plata.

Communications: Television sets: 1 per 10 persons. **Radios:** 1 per 6 persons. **Telephones:** 1 per 24 persons. **Daily newspaper circ.** (1990): 37 per 1,000 pop.

Health: Life expectancy at birth (1992): 66 male; 70 female. **Births** (per 1,000 pop. 1992): 27. **Deaths** (per 1,000 pop. 1992): 7. **Natural increase:** 2.0%. **Hospital beds:** 1 per 1,508 persons. **Physicians:** 1 per 934 persons. **Infant mortality** (per 1,000 live births 1992): 56.

Education (1991): **Literacy:** 83%. **School:** Compulsory for 6 years; attendance 70%.

Major International Organizations: UN (World Bank, IMF, GATT), OAS.

Hon. Consulate: 6 Queens Mansions, London W6 7EB; 071-602 1885.

Carib and Arawak Indians inhabited the island of Hispaniola when Columbus landed in 1492. The city of Santo Domingo, founded 1496, is the oldest settlement by Europeans in the hemisphere and has the supposed ashes of Columbus in an elaborate tomb in its ancient cathedral.

The western third of the island was ceded to France in 1697. Santo Domingo itself was ceded to France in 1795. Haitian leader Toussaint L'Ouverture seized it, 1801. Spain returned intermittently 1803-21, as several native republics came and went. Haiti ruled again, 1822-44, and Spanish occupation occurred 1861-63.

The country was occupied by U.S. Marines from 1916 to 1924, when a constitutionally elected government was installed.

In 1930, Gen. Rafael Leonidas Trujillo Molina was elected president. Trujillo ruled brutally until his assassination in 1961. Pres. Balaguer, appointed by Trujillo in 1960, resigned under pressure in 1962. Juan Bosch, elected president in the first free elections in 38 years, was overthrown in 1963.

On April 24, 1965, a revolt was launched by followers of Bosch and others, including a few communists. Four days later U.S. Marines intervened against the pro-Bosch forces. Token units were later sent by 5 So. American countries as a peace-keeping force.

A provisional government supervised a June 1966 election, in which Balaguer defeated Bosch by a 3-2 margin. The Inter-American Peace Force completed its departure Sept. 20, 1966.

Continued depressed world prices have affected the main export commodity, sugar.

Ecuador

Republic of Ecuador

República del Ecuador

People: Population (1992 est.): 10,933,000. **Age distrib.** (%): 0–14: 41.3; 15–64: 55.0; 65+: 3.7. **Pop. density:** 99 per sq. mi. **Urban** (1990): 54%. **Ethnic groups:** Indians 25%, Mestizo 55%, Spanish 10%, African 10%. **Languages:** Spanish (official), Quechuan, Jivaroan. **Religion:** Roman Catholic 95%.

Geography: Area: 109,483 sq. mi., about twice the size of England. **Location:** In NW S. America, on Pacific coast, astride Equator. **Neighbors:** Colombia to N, Peru to E and S. **Topography:** Two ranges of Andes run N and S, splitting the country into 3 zones: hot, humid lowlands on the coast; temperate highlands between the ranges, and rainy, tropical lowlands to the E. **Capital:** Quito. **Cities** (1991 est.): Guayaquil 2,000,000; Quito 1,500,000.

Government: Type: Republic. **Head of state:** Pres. Sixto Duran Ballen; b. 1922; in office Aug. 10, 1992. **Local divisions:** 21 provinces. **Defense** (1990): 1.6% of GDP.

Economy: Industries: Food processing, wood prods., textiles. **Chief crops:** Bananas (largest exporter), coffee, rice, sugar, corn. **Minerals:** Oil, copper, iron, lead, silver, sulphur. **Crude oil reserves** (1991): 1.8 bln. bbls. **Other resources:** Rubber, bark. **Arable land:** 6%. **Livestock** (1990): 3.8 mln. cattle; 4.1 mln. pigs; 2.1 mln. sheep. **Fish catch** (1989): 767,000 metric tons. **Electricity prod.** (1991): 6.4 bln. kWh. **Labor force:** 39% agric., 12% ind., 42% services.

Finance: Monetary unit: Sucre (July 1993: 1,875 = $1 US). **Gross domestic product** (1991): $11.5 bln. **Per capita GDP:** $1,070. **Imports** (1992): $2.4 bln.; partners: U.S. 34%. **Exports** (1992): $3.0 bln.; partners: U.S. 60%. **Tourism** (1990): $193 mln. receipts. **National budget** (1991): $2.2 bln. expenditures. **International reserves less gold** (Mar. 1993): $83 mln. **Gold:** 443,000 oz t. **Consumer prices** (change in 1992): 54.6%.

Transport: Railroads (1987): 965 km. long. **Motor vehicles** (1987): 272,000 passenger cars, 41,000 comm. vehicles. **Civil aviation** (1990): 1.2 bln. passenger-km. **Chief ports:** Guayaquil, Manta, Esmeraldas, Puerto Bolivar.

Communications: Television sets: 1 per 17 persons. **Radios:** 1 per 3.4 persons. **Telephones:** 1 per 28 persons. **Daily newspaper circ.** (1989): 87 per 1,000 pop.

Health: Life expectancy at birth (1992): 67 male, 72 female. **Births** (per 1,000 pop. 1992): 28. **Deaths** (per 1,000 pop. 1992): 6. **Natural increase:** 2.2%. **Hospital beds:** 1 per 610 persons. **Physicians** (1984): 11,000. **Infant mortality** (per 1,000 live births 1991): 60.

Education (1991): **Literacy:** 88%. **School:** Attendance to age 12–76% urban, 33% rural.

Major International Organizations: UN (IMF, WHO), OAS.

Embassy: 3 Hans Cres, London SW1 0LN; 071-584 1367.

Spain conquered the region, which was the northern Inca empire, in 1633. Liberation forces defeated the Spanish May 24, 1822, near Quito. Ecuador became part of the Great Colombia Republic but seceded, May 13, 1830.

Ecuador had been ruled by civilian and military dictatorships since 1968. A peaceful transfer of power from the military junta to the democratic civilian government took place, 1979.

Since 1972, the economy has revolved around its petroleum exports, which have declined since 1982 causing severe economic problems. Ecuador suspended interest payments for 1987 on its estimated $8.2 billion foreign debt following a Mar. 5-6 earthquake which left 20,000 homeless, and destroyed a stretch of the country's main oil pipeline.

Ecuadoran Indians staged a number of protests in 1991 to demand greater rights.

Ecuador and Peru have long disputed their Amazon Valley boundary.

The **Galapagos Islands,** 600 mi. to the W, are the home of huge tortoises and other unusual animals.

Egypt

Arab Republic of Egypt

Jumhūrīyah Misr al-Arabiya

People: Population (1992 est.): 56,386,000. **Age distrib (%)** 0-14: 41.8; 15-59: 52.7; 60+: 5.5. **Pop. density:** 146 per sq. mi. **Urban** (1986): 44%. **Ethnic groups:** Eastern Hamitic stock 90%, Bedouin, Nubian. **Languages:** Arabic (official), English. **Religion:** Sunni Muslim 94%.

Geography: Area: 386,650 sq. mi, about twice the size of England. **Location:** NE corner of Africa. **Neighbors:** Libya on W, Sudan on S, Israel on E. **Topography:** Almost entirely desolate and barren, with hills and mountains in E and along Nile. The Nile Valley, where most of the people live, stretches 550 miles. **Capital:** Cairo. **Cities** (1990 est.): Cairo 6,452,000; Alexandria 3,170,000; al-Jizah 2,156,000.

Government: Type: Republic. **Head of state:** Pres. Hosni Mubarak; b. 1929; in office Oct. 14, 1981. **Head of government:** Atef Sedki in office Nov. 10, 1986. **Local divisions:** 26 governorates. **Defense** (1991): 7.3% of GDP.

Economy: Industries: Textiles, chemicals, petrochemicals, food processing, cement. **Chief crops:** Cotton (one of largest producers), rice, beans, fruits, grains, vegetables, sugar, corn. **Minerals:** Oil, phosphates, gypsum, iron, manganese, limestone. **Crude oil reserves** (1991): 6.2 bln. bbls. **Arable land:** 4%. **Livestock** (1990): 1.9 mln. cattle; 1.3 mln. sheep. **Fish catch** (1990): 312,000 metric tons. **Electricity prod.** (1991): 45 bln. kWh. **Labor force:** 44% agric.; 22% services; 14% industry.

Finance: Monetary unit: Pound (Sept. 1993: 2.85 = $1 US). **Gross domestic product** (1991): $39.2 bln. **Per capita GDP:** $720. **Imports** (1991): $11.5 bln.; partners: U.S. 19%, W. Ger. 10%, It. 8%, France 8%. **Exports** (1991): $4.5 bln.; partners: It. 22%, Rom. 12%. **Tourism** (1990): $1.9 bln. receipts. **National budget** (1991): $16.7 bln. expenditures. **International reserves less gold** (Jan. 1993): $10.8 bln. **Gold:** 2.43 mln. oz t. **Consumer prices** (change in 1992): 13.6%.

Transport: Railroads (1991): 5,489 mi. long. **Motor vehicles** (1989): 826,000 passenger cars, 550,000 comm. vehicles. **Civil aviation** (1991): 5.2 bln. passenger-km.; 10 airports. **Chief ports:** Alexandria, Port Said, Suez.

Communications: Television sets: 1 per 15 persons. **Radios:** 1 per 3.9 persons. **Telephones:** 1 per 34 persons. **Daily newspaper circ.** (1991): 62 per 1,000 pop.

Health: Life expectancy at birth (1992): 58 male; 62 female. **Births** (per 1,000 pop. 1992): 33. **Deaths** (per 1,000 pop. 1992): 10. **Natural increase:** 2.3%. **Hospital beds:** 1 per 505 persons. **Physicians:** 1 per 616 persons. **Infant mortality** (per 1,000 live births 1992): 80.

Education (1990): **Literacy:** 44%. **School:** Compulsory ages 6-12.

Major International Organizations: UN (IMF, World Bank, GATT), OAU.

Embassy: 26 South St, London W1Y 6DD; 071-499 2401.

Archeological records of ancient Egyptian civilization date back to 4000 BC. A unified kingdom arose around 3200 BC, and extended its way south into Nubia and north as far as Syria. A high culture of rulers and priests was built on an economic base of serfdom, fertile soil, and annual flooding of the Nile banks.

Imperial decline facilitated conquest by Asian invaders (Hyksos, Assyrians). The last native dynasty fell in 341 BC to the Persians, who were in turn replaced by Greeks (Alexander and the Ptolemies), Romans, Byzantines, and Arabs, who introduced Islam and the Arabic language. The ancient Egyptian language is preserved only in the liturgy of the Coptic Christians.

Egypt was ruled as part of larger Islamic empires for several centuries. The Mamluks, a military caste of Caucasian origin, ruled Egypt from 1250 until defeat by the Ottoman Turks in 1517. Under Turkish sultans the khedive as hereditary viceroy had wide authority. Britain intervened in 1882 and took control of administration, though nominal allegiance to the Ottoman Empire continued until 1914.

The country was a British protectorate from 1914 to 1922. A 1936 treaty strengthened Egyptian autonomy, but Britain retained bases in Egypt and a condominium over the Sudan. Britain fought German and Italian armies from Egypt, 1940-42. In 1951 Egypt abrogated the 1936 treaty. The Sudan became independent in 1956.

The uprising of July 23, 1952, led by the Society of Free Officers, named Maj. Gen. Mohammed Naguib commander in chief and forced King Farouk to abdicate. When the republic was proclaimed June 18, 1953, Naguib became its first president and premier. Lt. Col. Gamal Abdel Nasser removed Naguib and became premier in 1954. In 1956, he was voted president. Nasser died in 1970 and was replaced by Vice Pres. Anwar Sadat.

The Aswan High Dam, completed 1971, provides irrigation for more than a million acres of land. Artesian wells, drilled in the Western Desert, reclaimed 43,000 acres, 1960-66.

When the state of Israel was proclaimed in 1948, Egypt joined other Arab nations invading Israel and was defeated.

After terrorist raids across its border, Israel invaded Egypt's Sinai Peninsula, Oct. 29, 1956. Egypt rejected a cease-fire demand by Britain and France; on Oct. 31 the 2 nations dropped bombs and on Nov. 5-6 landed forces. Egypt and Israel accepted a UN cease-fire; fighting ended Nov. 7.

A UN Emergency Force guarded the 117-mile long border between Egypt and Israel until May 19, 1967, when it was withdrawn at Nasser's demand. Egyptian troops entered the Gaza Strip and the heights of Sharm el Sheikh and 3 days later closed the Strait of Tiran to all Israeli shipping. Full-scale war broke out June 5 and before it ended under a UN cease-fire June 10, Israel had captured Gaza and the Sinai Peninsula, controlled the east bank of the Suez Canal and reopened the gulf.

Sporadic fighting with Israel continued almost daily, 1968-70. Israel and Egypt agreed, Aug. 7, 1970, to a cease-fire and peace negotiations proposed by the U.S. Negotiations failed to achieve results, but the cease-fire continued.

In a surprise attack Oct. 6, 1973, Egyptian forces crossed the Suez Canal into the Sinai. (At the same time, Syrian forces attacked Israelis on the Golan Heights.) Egypt was supplied by a USSR military airlift; the U.S. responded with an airlift to Israel. Israel counter-attacked, crossed the canal, surrounded Suez City. A UN cease-fire took effect Oct. 24.

A disengagement agreement was signed Jan. 18, 1974. Under it, Israeli forces withdrew from the canal's W bank; limited numbers of Egyptian forces occupied a strip along the E bank. A second accord was signed in 1975, with Israel yielding Sinai oil fields. Pres. Sadat's surprise visit to Jerusalem, Nov. 1977, opened the prospect of peace with Israel. On Mar. 26, 1979, Egypt and Israel signed a formal peace treaty, ending 30 years of war, and establishing diplomatic relations. Israel returned control of the Sinai to Egypt in April 1982.

Tension between Moslem fundamentalists and Christians in 1981 caused street riots and culminated in a nationwide security crackdown in Sept. Pres Sadat was assassinated on Oct. 6.

Egypt was a political and military supporter of the Allied forces in their defeat of Iraq in the Persian Gulf War, 1991.

Egypt saw a rising tide of Islamic fundamentalist violence in 1992 and 1993. Egyptian security forces conducted raids against Islamic militants Mar. 1993. Seven Islamic militants convicted of participating in 6 separate attacks on tourists were hanged June 8.

The **Suez Canal,** 103 mi. long, links the Mediterranean and Red seas. It was built by a French corporation 1859-69, but Britain obtained controlling interest in 1875. The last British troops were removed June 13, 1956. On July 26, Egypt nationalized the canal.

El Salvador

Republic of El Salvador

República de El Salvador

People: Population (1992 est.): 5,574,000. **Age distrib. (%):**

0–14; 44.4; 15–59: 49.9; 60+: 5.7. **Pop. density:** 686 per sq. mi. **Urban** (1991): 45%. **Ethnic groups:** Mestizo 89%, Indian 10%. **Language:** Spanish (official). **Religion:** Roman Catholic 75%.

Geography: Area: 8,124 sq. mi., the size of Wales. **Location:** In Central America. **Neighbors:** Guatemala on W, Honduras on N. **Topography:** A hot Pacific coastal plain in the south rises to a cooler plateau and valley region, densely populated. The N is mountainous, including many volcanoes. **Capital:** San Salvador, pop. (1993 est.) 1.4 mln.

Government: Type: Republic. **Head of state:** Pres., Alfredo Cristiani; b. Nov, 22, 1947; in office: June 1, 1989. **Local divisions:** 14 departments. **Defense** (1991): 3.6% of GDP.

Economy: Industries: Food and beverages, textiles, petroleum products. **Chief crops:** Coffee (21% of GDP), cotton, corn, sugar. **Other resources:** Rubber, forests. **Arable land:** 27%. **Livestock** (1990): 1.1 mln. cattle; 440,000 pigs. **Electricity prod.** (1991): 1.9 bln. kWh. **Labor force:** 40% agric.; 16% ind.; 27% services.

Finance: Monetary unit: Colon (Mar. 1993: 8.73 = $1 US). **Gross domestic product** (1992): $5.5 bln. **Per capita GDP:** $1,010. **Imports** (1992): $1.5 bln.; partners: U.S. 41%, CACM 22%. **Exports** (1992): $683 mln.; partners: U.S. 41%, EC 30%, CACM 10%. **Tourism** (1990): $70 mln. receipts. **National budget** (1990): $790 mln. expenditures. **International reserves less gold** (Mar. 1993): $458 mln. **Gold:** 469,000 oz t. **Consumer prices** (change in 1992): 20%.

Transport: Railroads (1991): 374 mi. long. **Motor vehicles** (1990): 80,000 passenger cars, 80,000 comm. vehicles. **Chief ports:** La Union, Acajutla.

Communications: Television sets: 1 per 12 persons. **Radios:** 1 per 2.6 persons. **Telephones:** 1 per 36 persons. **Daily newspaper circ.** (1991): 47 per 1,000 pop.

Health: Life expectancy at birth (1992): 68 male; 75 female. **Births** (per 1,000 pop. 1992): 33. **Deaths** (per 1,000 pop. 1992): 5. **Natural increase:** 2.8%. **Hospital beds:** 1 per 973 persons. **Physicians:** 1 per 1,322 persons. **Infant mortality** (per 1,000 live births 1992): 26.

Education (1991): **Literacy:** 75%. **School:** Compulsory for 6 years; attendance 82%.

Major International Organizations: UN (IMF, WHO, ILO), OAS, CACM.

Embassy: 5 Great James St, London WC1N 3DA; 071-430 2141.

El Salvador became independent of Spain in 1821, and of the Central American Federation in 1839.

A fight with Honduras in 1969 over the presence of 300,000 Salvadorean workers left 2,000 dead. Clashes were renewed 1970 and 1974.

A military coup overthrew the government of Pres. Carlos Humberto Romero in 1979, but the ruling military-civilian junta failed to quell a rebellion by leftist insurgents, armed by Cuba and Nicaragua. Extreme right-wing death squads organized to eliminate suspected leftists were blamed for thousands of deaths in the 1980s. The Reagan administration staunchly supported the government with military aid.

Voters turned out in large numbers in the May 1984 presidential election. Christian Democrat Jose Napoleon Duarte, a moderate, was victorious with 54% of the vote.

The 12-year civil war ended Jan. 16, 1992, as the government and leftist rebels signed a formal peace treaty. The civil war had taken the lives of some 75,000 people. The treaty provided for military and political reforms.

Nine soldiers, including 3 officers, were indicted Jan. 1990 in the Nov. 1989 slaying of 6 Jesuit priests at a university in San Salvador. Two of the officers received maximum 30-year jail sentences. They were released after serving 15 months of their sentences, Mar. 20, 1993, when the National Assembly passed a sweeping amnesty for those who had committed atrocities during the civil war.

Equatorial Guinea

Republic of Equatorial Guinea

República de Guinea Ecuatorial

People: Population (1992 est.): 388,000. **Age distrib.** (%): 0–14: 38.1; 15–59: 55.2; 60+: 6.7. **Pop. density:** 35 per sq. mi. **Ethnic groups:** Fangs 80%, Bubi 15%. **Languages:** Spanish (official), Fang, Bubi. **Religion:** Mostly Roman Catholic.

Geography: Area: 10,832 sq. mi., twice the size of N. Ireland. **Location:** Bioko Is. off W. Africa coast in Gulf of Guinea, and Rio Muni, mainland enclave. **Neighbors:** Gabon on S, Cameroon on E, N. **Topography:** Bioko Is. consists of 2 volcanic mountains and a connecting valley. Rio Muni, with over 90% of the area, has a coastal plain and low hills beyond. **Capital:** Malabo, (1989 est.) 38,000.

Government: Type: In transition. **Head of state:** Pres., Supreme Military Council, Teodoro Obiang Nguema Mbasogo; b. June 5, 1942; in office Oct. 10, 1979. **Head of government:** Prime Min. Silvestre Siale Bileka; in office Mar. 4, 1992. **Local divisions:** 7 provinces.

Economy: Chief crops: Cocoa, coffee, bananas, sweet potatoes. **Other resources:** Timber. **Arable land:** 8%. **Electricity prod.** (1991): 60 mln. kWh. **Labor force:** 50% agric.; 40% public sector.

Finance: Monetary unit: CFA franc (Mar. 1993: 278 = $1 US). **Gross domestic product** (1990): $136 mln. **Per capita GDP:** $430. **Imports** (1990): $68 mln.; partners: Fra. 26%, Sp. 21%. **Exports** (1990): $37 mln.; partners: Sp. 38%, Neth. 12%.

Transport: Chief ports: Malabo, Bata.

Communications: Radios: 1 per 3.5 persons.

Health: Life expectancy at birth (1992): 49 male; 53 female. **Births** (per 1,000 pop. 1992): 42. **Deaths** (per 1,000 pop. 1992): 15. **Natural increase:** 2.7%. **Hospital beds** (1982): 3,200. **Physicians:** 1 per 3,622 persons. **Infant mortality** (per 1,000 live births 1992): 107.

Education (1991): **Literacy:** 55%. **School:** About 65% attend primary school.

Major International Organizations: UN (IMF, World Bank), OAU.

Fernando Po (now Bioko) Island was reached by Portugal in the late 15th century and ceded to Spain in 1778. Independence came Oct. 12, 1968. Riots occurred in 1969 over disputes between the island and the more backward Rio Muni province on the mainland. Masie Nguema Biyogo, himself from the mainland, became president for life in 1972.

Masie's 11-year reign was one of the most brutal in Africa, resulting in a bankrupted nation. Most of the nation's 7,000 Europeans emigrated. In 1976, 45,000 Nigerian workers were evacuated amid charges of a reign of terror. Masie was ousted in a military coup, Aug. 1979. Mbasogo, leader of the coup, became president.

The nation is heavily dependent on external aid.

Eritrea

State of Eritrea

People: Population (1993 est.): 3,200,000. **Pop. density:** 88 per sq. mi. **Ethnic groups:** 9 different ethnic groups. **Languages:** 7 native languages. **Religions:** About evenly split between Muslim and Christian.

Geography: Area: 36,170 sq. mi., slightly larger than Scotland. **Location:** In E. Africa. **Neighbors:** Ethiopia on S, Djibouti on E, Sudan on W, Red Sea on N. **Topography:** Includes many islands of the Dahlak Archipelago; low coastal plains in S, mountain range with peaks to 9,000 ft. in N. **Capital:** Asmera.

Government: Type: In transition. **Head of state:** Issaias Afwerki; in office May 24, 1993.

Economy: No industry. **Chief crops:** Cotton, coffee, tobacco.

Transport: Chief ports: Masewa, Aseb.

Communications: No telephones outside the capital.

Major International Organizations: UN.

Eritrea was part of the ancient Ethiopian kingdom of Aksum. It was an Italian colony from 1890 to 1941, when it was captured by the British. Following a period of British and UN supervision, Eritrea was awarded to Ethiopia as part of a federation in 1952. Ethiopia annexed Eritrea as a province in 1962. This led to a 31-year struggle for independence, which ended when Eritrea formally declared itself an independent nation May 24, 1993.

Estonia

Republic of Estonia

Eesti Vabariik

People: Population (1992 est.): 1,607,000. **Pop. density:** 92 per sq. mi. **Urban:** (1991): 72%. **Ethnic groups:** Estonian 65%, Russian 30%. **Languages:** Estonian (official), Russian. **Religion:** Mostly Evangelical Lutheran.

Geography: Area: 17,413 sq. mi. **Neighbors:** bounded on N., W. by the Baltic Sea, E. by Russia, S. by Latvia. **Capital:** Tallinn, (1991 est.) 502,000.

Government: Type: Republic. **Head of state:** Pres. Lennart Meri; in office Oct. 5, 1992. **Head of government:** Prime Min. Mart Laar; in office Oct. 8, 1992. **Local divisions:** 15 districts, 33 towns, 26 urban settlements.

Economy: Industries: Agricultural machinery, electric motors. **Chief crops:** grain, vegetables. **Arable land:** 22%. **Livestock** (1990): 823,000 cattle, 138,000 sheep. **Electricity prod.** (1990): 17.2 mln. kWh. **Labor force:** Ind. & const. 42%, agric. 13%.

Finance: Monetary unit: Kroon (Jan. 1993: 11.26 = $1 US).

Transport: Railroads (1991): 640 mi. long. **Motor vehicles** (1989): 198,000 passenger cars. **Chief port:** Tallinn.

Communications: Television sets: 1 per 2.7 persons. **Radios:** 1 per 1.7 persons. **Telephones:** 1 per 5.1 persons.

Health: Life expectancy at birth (1992): 65 male; 75 female. **Hospital beds:** 1 per 83 persons. **Physicians:** 1 per 219 persons. **Infant mortality** (per 1,000 live births, 1992): 25.

Education: 11-year school curriculum.

Major international organizations: UN, IMF.

Embassy: 18 Chepstow Villas, London W11 2RB; 071-229 6700.

Estonia was a province of imperial Russia before World War I, was independent between World Wars I and II, but was conquered by the USSR in 1940. Estonia declared itself an "occupied territory", and proclaimed itself a free nation Mar. 1990. During an abortive Soviet coup, Estonia declared immediate full independence, Aug. 20, 1991; the Soviet Union recognized its independence in Sept. 1991.

The first free elections in over 50 years were held Sept. 20, 1992.

Ethiopia

(Figures prior to 1993 include Eritrea)

People: Population (1993 est.): 51,070,000. **Age distrib.** (%): 0–14: 46.5; 15–59: 47.3; 60+: 6.2. **Pop. density:** 117 per sq. mi. **Urban** (1992): 11%. **Ethnic groups:** Oromo 40%, Amhara 25%, Tigre 12%, Sidama 9%. **Languages:** Amharic (official), Tigre (Semitic languages); Galla (Hamitic). **Religions:** Orthodox Christian 40%, Muslim 40%.

Geography: Area: 435,606 sq. mi., nearly 4 times the size of the Br. Isles. **Location:** In E. Africa. **Neighbors:** Sudan on W, Kenya on S. Somalia, Djibouti on E, Eritrea on N. **Topography:** A high central plateau, between 6,000 and 10,000 ft. high, rises to higher mountains near the Great Rift Valley, cutting in from the SW. The Blue Nile and other rivers cross the plateau, which descends to plains on both W and SE. **Capital:** Addis Ababa, pop. (1984 est.) 1,412,000.

Government: Type: In transition. **Head of state:** Pres. Meles Zenawi; in office May 28, 1991. **Head of government:** Prime Min. Timirat Laynie; in office June 6, 1991. **Local divisions:** 13 provinces. **Defense** (1989): 8% of GDP.

Economy: Industries: Food processing, cement, textiles. **Chief crops:** Coffee (over 50% of export earnings), grains. **Minerals:** Platinum, gold, copper, potash. **Arable Land:** 13%. **Livestock** (1990): 30 mln. cattle; 23 mln. sheep. **Electricity prod.** (1991): 650 mln. kWh. **Labor force:** 80% agric.

Finance: Monetary unit: Birr (Mar. 1993: 5.00 = $1 US). **Gross domestic product** (1991): $6.6 bln. **Per capita GDP:** $130. **Imports** (1991): $472 mln.; partners: USSR 22%, U.S. 15%, Italy 10%, Jap. 6%, W.Ger. 10%. **Exports** (1991): $189 mln.; partners: U.S. 20%, W. Ger. 18%, Italy 7%. **National budget** (1989): $1.7 bln. expenditures. **International reserves less gold** (Mar. 1993): $252 mln. **Gold:** 113,000 oz t. **Consumer prices** (change in 1992): 10.5%.

Transport: Railroads (1989): 486 mi. long. **Motor vehicles** (1991): 38,000 passenger cars, 15,000 comm. vehicles. **Civil aviation** (1989): 1.6 bln. passenger-km; 29 airports with scheduled flights.

Communications: Television sets: 1 per 503 persons. **Radios:** 1 per 5.5 persons. **Telephones:** 1 per 320 persons. **Daily newspaper circ.** (1990): 1 per 1,000 pop.

Health: Life expectancy at birth (1992): 50 male; 53 female. **Births** (per 1,000 pop. 1992): 45. **Deaths** (per 1,000 pop. 1992): 15. **Natural increase:** 3.1%. **Hospital beds:** 1 per 3,873 persons. **Physicians:** 1 per 36,660 persons. **Infant mortality** (per 1,000 live births 1992): 113.

Education (1985): **Literacy:** 18%.

Major International Organizations: UN (IMF, WHO), OAU.

Embassy: 17 Princes Gate, London SW7 1PZ; 071-589 7212.

Ethiopian culture was influenced by Egypt and Greece. The ancient monarchy was invaded by Italy in 1880 but maintained its independence until another Italian invasion in 1936. British forces freed the country in 1941.

The last emperor, Haile Selassie I, established a parliament and judiciary system in 1931 but barred all political parties.

A series of droughts in the 1970s killed hundreds of thousands. An army mutiny, strikes, and student demonstrations led to the dethronement of Selassie in 1974. The ruling junta pledged to form a one-party socialist state and instituted a successful land reform; opposition was violently suppressed. The influence of the Coptic Church, embraced in AD 330, was curbed, and the monarchy was abolished in 1975.

The regime, torn by bloody coups, faced uprisings by tribal and political groups in part aided by Sudan and Somalia. Ties with the U.S., once a major arms and aid source, deteriorated, while cooperation accords were signed with the USSR in 1977. In 1978, Soviet advisors and Cuban troops helped defeat Somalia forces. Ethiopia and Somalia signed a peace agreement in 1988.

A world-wide relief effort began in 1984, as an extended drought caused millions to face starvation and death. In 1988, victories by Eritrean guerrillas forced the government to curtail the work of foreign aid workers in drought-stricken regions.

The Ethiopian People's Revolutionary Democratic Front (EPRDF), an umbrella group of 6 rebel armies, launched a major push against government forces, Feb. 1991. In May, Pres Mengistu Haile Mariam resigned and left the country. The EPRDF took possession of the capital and announced plans for a coalition government.

Eritrea, a province on the Red Sea, declared its independence May 24, 1993.

Fiji

Republic of Fiji

People: Population (1992 est.): 744,000. **Age distrib.** (%): 0–14: 38.2; 15–59: 56.9; 60+: 4.9. **Pop. density:** 105 per sq. mi. **Urban** (1986): 39%. **Ethnic groups:** Indian 48%, Fijian (Melanesian-Polynesian) 46%, European 2%. **Languages:** English (official), Fijian, Hindi. **Religions:** Christian 52%, Hindu 38%, Muslim 8%.

Geography: Area: 7,056 sq. mi., slightly smaller than Wales. **Location:** In western S. Pacific O. **Neighbors:** Nearest are Solomons on NW, Tonga on E. **Topography:** 322 islands (106 inhabited), many mountainous, with tropical forests and large fertile areas. Viti Levu, the largest island, has over half the total land area. **Capital:** Suva, pop. (1986 est.) 69,000.

Government: Type: Republic. **Head of state:** Pres. Penaia Ganilau; in office Dec. 5, 1987. **Head of government:** Prime Min. Ratu Sir Kamisese Mara; b. May 13, 1920; in office Oct. 10, 1970. **Local divisions:** 4 divisions, 1 dependency.

Economy: Industries: Sugar refining, light industry, tourism. **Chief crops:** Sugar, bananas, ginger. **Minerals:** Gold. **Other resources:** Timber. **Arable land:** 8%. **Electricity prod.** (1990): 325 mln. kWh. **Labor force:** 44% agric.

Finance: Monetary unit: Dollar (Mar. 1993: 1.53 = $1 US). **Gross domestic product** (1991): $1.3 bln. **Per capita GDP:** $1,700. **Imports** (1991): $840 mln.; partners: Austral. 29%, Jap. 12%, N.Z. 19%. **Exports** (1991): $646 mln.; partners: EC 32%, Aust. 21%. **Tourism** (1990): $320 mln. receipts. **National budget** (1992): $464 mln. expenditures. **International reserves less gold** (Mar. 1993): $283 mln. **Gold:** 10,000 oz t. **Consumer prices** (change in 1992): 4.9%.

Transport: Motor vehicles (1990): 40,000 passenger cars, 28,000 comm. vehicles. **Civil aviation** (1990): 882 mln. passenger-km; 17 airports with scheduled flights. **Chief ports:** Suva, Lautoka.

Communications: Television sets: 1 per 73 persons. **Radios:** 1 per 1.7 persons. **Telephones:** 1 per 10 persons. **Daily newspaper circ.** (1988): 56 per 1,000 pop.

Health: Life expectancy at birth (1992): 62 male; 67 female. **Births** (per 1,000 pop. 1992): 26. **Deaths** (per 1,000 pop. 1992): 7. **Natural increase:** 1.9%. **Hospital beds:** 1 per 413 persons. **Physicians:** 1 per 2,438 persons. **Infant mortality** (per 1,000 live births 1992): 19.

Education (1990): **Literacy:** 85%. **School:** 95% attend school.

Major International Organizations: UN (IMF, WHO).

Embassy: 34 Hyde Park Gate, London SW7 5DN; 071-584 3661.

A British colony since 1874, Fiji became an independent parliamentary democracy Oct. 10, 1970.

Cultural differences between the majority Indian community, descendants of contract laborers brought to the islands in the 19th century, and the less modernized native Fijians, who by law own 83% of the land in communal villages, have led to political polarization.

In 1987, a military coup ousted the government; order was restored May 21 when a compromise was reached granting Lt. Col. Rabuka, the coup's leader, increased power. Rabuka staged a second coup Sept. 25 and in Oct. declared Fiji a republic. A civilian government was restored to power in Dec., and a new constitution was drafted which protected the rights of all citizens.

Finland

Republic of Finland

Suomen Tasavalta

People: Population (1992 est.): 5,004,000. **Age distrib.** (%): 0–14: 19.3; 15–59: 62.9; 60+: 17.8. **Pop. density:** 38 per sq. mi. **Urban** (1992): 61%. **Ethnic groups:** Finns 94%, Swedes, Lapps. **Languages:** Finnish, Swedish (both official). **Religion:** Lutheran 97%.

Geography: Area: 130,119 sq. mi., slightly bigger than the Br. Isles. **Location:** In northern Europe. **Neighbors:** Norway on N, Sweden on W, Russia on E. **Topography:** South and central Finland are mostly flat areas with low hills and many lakes. The N has mountainous areas, 3,000-4,000 ft. **Capital:** Helsinki. **Cities** (1992 est.): Helsinki 490,000; Tampere 170,000; Turku 160,000.

Government: Type: Constitutional republic. **Head of state:** Pres. Mauno Koivisto; b. Nov. 25, 1923; in office: Jan. 27, 1982. **Head of government:** Prime Min. Esko Aho: b. 1954; in office: Apr. 26, 1991. **Local divisions:** 12 laanit (provinces). **Defense** (1989): 1.4% of GDP.

Economy: Industries: Machinery, metal, shipbuilding, textiles, clothing. **Chief crops:** Grains, potatoes, dairy prods. **Minerals:** Copper, iron, zinc. **Other resources:** Forests (40% of exports). **Arable land:** 8%. **Livestock** (1990): 1.3 mln. cattle; 1.3 mln. pigs. **Fish catch** (1989): 160,000 metric tons. **Electricity prod.** (1991): 49.3 bln. kWh. **Crude steel prod.** (1991): 2.8 mln. metric tons. **Labor force:** 9% agric.; 54% ind., comm. & finance; 25% services.

Finance: Monetary unit: Markka (June 1993: 5.62 = $1 US). **Gross domestic product** (1991): $80 bln. **Per capita GDP:** $16,200. **Imports** (1992): $21.2 bln.; partners: EC 45%. **Exports** (1992): $23.8 bln.; partners: EC 50%. **Tourism** (1991): $1.2 bln. receipts. **National budget** (1991): $41.5 bln. expenditures. **International reserves less gold** (Mar. 1993): $4.3 bln. **Gold** 2.0 mln. oz t. **Consumer prices** (change in 1992): 2.6%.

Transport: Railroads (1991): 3,656 mi. long. **Motor vehicles** (1990): 1.9 mln. passenger cars, 271,000 comm. vehicles. **Civil aviation** (1991): 9.8 bln. passenger-km; 25 airports. **Chief ports:** Helsinki, Turku.

Communications: Television sets: 1 per 2.7 persons. **Radios:** 1 per person. **Telephones:** 1 per 2.1 persons. **Daily newspaper circ.** (1990): 521 per 1,000 pop.

Health: Life expectancy at birth (1992): 72 male; 80 female. **Births** (per 1,000 pop. 1992): 12. **Deaths** (per 1,000 pop. 1992): 10. **Natural increase:** .02%. **Hospital beds:** 1 per 74 persons. **Physicians:** 1 per 503 persons. **Infant mortality** (per 1,000 live births 1992): 6.

Education (1991): **Literacy:** 99%. **School:** Compulsory for 9 years; attendance 99%.

Major International Organizations: UN (IMF, GATT), EFTA, OECD.

Embassy: 38 Chesham Place, London SW1X 8HW; 071-235 9531.

The early Finns probably migrated from the Ural area at about the beginning of the Christian era. Swedish settlers brought the country into Sweden, 1154 to 1809, when Finland became an autonomous grand duchy of the Russian Empire. Russian exactions created a strong national spirit; on Dec. 6, 1917, Finland declared its independence and in 1919 became a republic. On Nov. 30, 1939, the Soviet Union invaded, and the Finns were forced to cede 16,173 sq. mi., including the Karelian Isthmus, Viipuri, and an area on Lake Ladoga. After World War II, in which Finland tried to recover its lost territory, further cessions were exacted. In 1948, Finland signed a treaty of mutual assistance with the USSR; Finland and Russia nullified this treaty with a new pact in Jan. 1992. In 1956 Russia returned Porkkala, which had been ceded as a military base. In 1992 Finland's economy suffered because of changes in the former Soviet Union and Eastern Europe.

Aland, constituting an autonomous department, is a group of small islands, 590 sq. mi., in the Gulf of Bothnia, 25 mi. from Sweden, 15 mi. from Finland. Mariehamn is the principal port.

France

French Republic

République Française

People: Population (1992 est.): 57,287,000. **Age distrib.** (%): 0–14: 19.1; 15–60: 61.0; 60+: 19.9. **Pop. density:** 259 per sq. mi. **Urban** (1990): 74%. **Ethnic groups:** A mixture of various European and Mediterranean groups. **Languages:** French (official); minorities speak Breton, Alsatian German, Flemish, Italian, Basque, Catalan. **Religion:** Mostly Roman Catholic.

Geography: Area: 220,668 sq. mi., twice the size of the Br. Isles. **Location:** In western Europe, between Atlantic O. and Mediterranean Sea. **Neighbors:** Spain on S, Italy, Switzerland, Germany on E, Luxembourg, Belgium on N. **Topography:** A wide plain covers more than half of the country, in N and W, drained to W by Seine, Loire, Garonne rivers. The Massif Central is a mountainous plateau in center. In E are Alps (Mt. Blanc is tallest in W. Europe, 15,771 ft.), the lower Jura range, and the forested Vosges. The Rhone flows from Lake Geneva to Mediterranean. Pyrenees are in SW, on border with Spain. **Capital:** Paris. **Cities** (1990 est.): Paris 2,152,000; Marseille 801,000; Lyon 415,000; Toulouse 359,000; Nice 342,000; Strasbourg 252,000; Nantes 245,000; Bordeaux 201,000.

Government: Type: Republic. **Head of state:** Pres. François Mitterrand; b. Oct. 26, 1916; in office May 21, 1981. **Head of government:** Prime Min. Edouard Balladur; in office Mar. 29, 1993. **Local divisions:** 22 administrative regions containing 95 departments. **Defense** (1991): 3.6% of GDP.

Economy: Industries: Steel, chemicals, textiles, wine, perfume, aircraft, electronic equipment. **Chief crops:** Grains, corn, rice, fruits, vegetables. France is largest food producer, exporter, in W. Eur. **Minerals:** Bauxite, iron, coal. **Crude oil reserves** (1985): 221 mln. bbls. **Other resources:** Forests. **Arable land:** 32%. **Livestock** (1990): 21.1 mln. cattle; 12.2 mln. pigs; 10.3 mln. sheep. **Fish catch** (1990): 896,000 metric tons. **Electricity prod.** (1991): 399 bln. kWh. **Crude steel prod.** (1991): 18.4 mln. metric tons. **Labor force:** 9% agric.; 45% ind. & comm.; 46% services.

Finance: Monetary unit: Franc (July 1993: 5.79 = $1 US). **Gross domestic product** (1991). $1 trl. **Per capita GDP:** $18,300. **Imports** (1992): $239 bln.; partners: EC 51%. **Exports** (1992): $235 bln.; partners: EC 50%, U.S. 6%. **Tourism** (1990) $21.6 bln. receipts. **National budget** (1992): $246 bln. expenditures. **International reserves less gold** (Feb. 1993): $33.0 bln. **Gold:** 81.85 mln. oz t. **Consumer prices** (change in 1992): 2.4%.

Transport: Railroads (1991): 21,173 mi. long. **Motor vehicles** (1991): 23.8 mln. passenger cars, 5.1 mln. comm. vehicles. **Civil aviation** (1991): 32.5 bln. passenger-km; 64 airports with scheduled flights. **Chief ports:** Marseille, Le Havre, Nantes, Bordeaux, Rouen.

Communications: Television sets: 1 per 2.6 persons. **Radios:** 1 per 1.1 persons. **Telephones:** 1 per 1.7 persons. **Daily newspaper circ.** (1990): 176 per 1,000 pop.

Health: Life expectancy at birth (1992): 74 male; 82 female. **Births** (per 1,000 pop. 1992): 13. **Deaths** (per 1,000 pop. 1992): 9. **Natural increase:** .4%. **Hospital beds:** 1 per 80 persons. **Physicians:** 1 per 374 persons. **Infant mortality** (per 1,000 live births 1992): 7.

Education (1991): **Literacy:** 99%. **School:** Compulsory for 10 years.

Major International Organizations: UN and most of its specialized agencies, OECD, EC, NATO.

Embassy: 58 Knightsbridge, London SW1X 7JT; 071-235 8080.

Celtic Gaul was conquered by Julius Caesar 58-51 BC; Romans ruled for 500 years. Under Charlemagne, Frankish rule extended over much of Europe. After his death France emerged as one of the successor kingdoms.

The monarchy was overthrown by the French Revolution (1789-93) and succeeded by the First Republic; followed by the First Empire under Napoleon (1804-15), a monarchy (1814-48), the Second Republic (1848-52), the Second Empire (1852-70), the Third Republic (1871-1946), the Fourth Republic (1946-58), and the Fifth Republic (1958 to present).

France suffered severe losses in manpower and wealth in the first World War, 1914-18, when it was invaded by Germany. By the Treaty of Versailles, France exacted return of Alsace and Lorraine, French provinces seized by Germany in 1871. Germany invaded France again in May, 1940, and signed an armistice with a government based in Vichy. After France was liberated by the Allies Sept. 1944, Gen. Charles de Gaulle became head of the provisional government, serving until 1946.

De Gaulle again became premier in 1958, during a crisis over Algeria, and obtained voter approval for a new constitution, ushering in the Fifth Republic. Using strong executive powers, he promoted French economic and technological advances in the context of the European Economic Community and guarded French foreign policy independence.

France had withdrawn from Indochina in 1954, and from Morocco and Tunisia in 1956. Most of its remaining African territories were freed 1958-62.

In 1966, France withdrew all its troops from the integrated military command of NATO, though 60,000 remained stationed in Germany. France continued to attend political meetings of NATO.

In May 1968 rebellious students in Paris and other centers rioted, battled police, and were joined by workers who launched nationwide strikes. The government awarded pay increases to the strikers May 26. In elections to the Assembly in June, de Gaulle's backers won a landslide victory. Nevertheless, he resigned from office in April, 1969, after losing a nationwide referendum on constitutional reform.

On May 10, 1981, France elected François Mitterrand, a Socialist candidate, president. In September, the government nationalized 5 major industries and most private banks. In 1986, France began a privatization program in which many state-owned companies were sold. In 1993 the government completed the privatization program by selling stakes in 21 companies for about $54 billion. Mitterrand was elected to a second 7-year term in 1988.

France set tighter rules for entry into the country and made it easier for the government to expel foreigners in 1993.

The island of **Corsica,** in the Mediterranean W of Italy and N of Sardinia, is an official region of France comprising 2 departments. Area: 3,369 sq. mi.; pop. (1990 cen.): 249,700. The capital is Ajaccio, birthplace of Napoleon.

Overseas Departments

French Guiana is on the NE coast of South America with Suriname on the W and Brazil on the E and S. Its area is 43,740 sq. mi.; pop. (1992): 127,000. Guiana sends one senator and one deputy to the French Parliament. Guiana is administered by a prefect and has a Council General of 16 elected members; capital is Cayenne.

The famous penal colony, Devil's Island, was phased out between 1938 and 1951.

Immense forests of rich timber cover 90% of the land. Placer gold mining is the most important industry. Exports are shrimp, timber, and machinery.

Guadeloupe, in the West Indies' Leeward Islands, consists of 2 large islands, Basse-Terre and Grande-Terre, separated by the Salt River, plus Marie Galante and the Saintes group to the S and, to the N, Desirade, St. Barthelemy, and over half of St. Martin (the Netherlands portion is St. Maarten). A French possession since 1635, the department is represented in the French Parliament by 2 senators and 3 deputies; administration consists of a prefect (governor) and an elected general and regional councils.

Area of the islands is 660 sq. mi.; pop. (1991 est.) 395,000, mainly descendants of slaves; capital is Basse-Terre on Basse-Terre Is. The land is fertile; sugar, rum, and bananas are exported; tourism is an important industry.

Martinique, the northernmost of the Windward Islands, in the West Indies, has been a possession since 1635, and a department since March 1946. It is represented in the French Parliament by 2 senators and 3 deputies. The island was the birthplace of Napoleon's Empress Josephine.

It has an area of 425 sq. mi.; pop. (1991 est.) 365,000, mostly descendants of slaves. The capital is Fort-de-France (pop. 1991: 101,000). It is a popular tourist stop. The chief exports are rum, bananas, and petroleum products.

Mayotte, claimed by Comoros and administered by France, voted in 1976 to become a territorial collectivity of France. An island NW of Madagascar, its area is 144 sq. mi., pop. (1992 est.) 86,000.

Réunion is a volcanic island in the Indian O. about 420 mi. E of Madagascar, and has belonged to France since 1665. Area, 969 sq. mi.; pop. (1992 est.) 626,000, 30% of French extraction. Capital: Saint-Denis. The chief export is sugar. It elects 3 deputies, 2 senators to the French Parliament.

Territorial Collectivities

St. Pierre and Miquelon, formerly an Overseas Territory (1816–1976) and department (1976–85), made the transition to territorial collectivity in 1985. It consists of 2 groups of rocky islands near the SW coast of Newfoundland, inhabited by fishermen. The exports are chiefly fish products. The St. Pierre group has an area of 10 sq. mi.; Miquelon, 83 sq. mi. Total pop. (1992 est.), 6,513. The capital is St. Pierre. A deputy and a senator are elected to the French Parliament.

Overseas Territories

French Polynesia Overseas Territory, comprises 130 islands widely scattered among 5 archipelagos in the South Pacific; administered by a governor. Territorial Assembly and a Council with headquarters at Papeete, Tahiti, one of the **Society Islands** (which include the **Windward** and **Leeward** islands). A deputy and a senator are elected to the French Parliament.

Other groups are the **Marquesas Islands, the Tuamotu Archipelago,** including the **Gambier Islands,** and the **Austral Islands.**

Total area of the islands administered from Tahiti is 1,544 sq. mi.; pop. (1991 est.), 195,000, more than half on Tahiti. Tahiti is picturesque and mountainous with a productive coastline bearing coconut, banana and orange trees, sugar cane and vanilla.

Tahiti was visited by Capt. James Cook in 1769 and by Capt. Bligh in the *Bounty*, 1788-89. Its beauty impressed Herman Melville, Paul Gauguin, and Charles Darwin.

French Southern and Antarctic Lands Overseas Territory, comprises **Adelie Land,** on Antarctica, and 4 island groups in the Indian O. Adelie, reached 1840, has a research station, a coastline of 185 mi. and tapers 1,240 mi. inland to the South Pole. The U.S. does not recognize national claims in Antarctica. There are 2 huge glaciers, Ninnis, 22 mi. wide, 99 mi. long, and Mentz, 11 mi. wide, 140 mi. long. The Indian O. groups are:

Kerguelen Archipelago, visited 1772, consists of one large and 300 small islands. The chief is 87 mi. long, 74 mi. wide, and has Mt. Ross, 6,429 ft. tall. Principal research station is Port-aux-Francais. Seals often weigh 2 tons; there are blue whales, coal, peat, semiprecious stones. **Crozet Archipelago,** reached 1772, covers 195 sq. mi. Eastern Island rises to 6,560 ft. **Saint Paul,** in southern Indian O., has warm springs with earth at places heating to 120° to 390° F. **Amsterdam** is nearby; both produce cod and rock lobster.

New Caledonia and its dependencies, an overseas territory, are a group of islands in the Pacific O. about 1,115 mi. E of Australia and approx. the same distance NW of New Zealand. Dependencies are the **Loyalty Islands,** the **Isle of Pines, Huon Islands** and the **Chesterfield Islands.**

New Caledonia, the largest, has 6,530 sq. mi. Total area of the territory is 8,548 sq. mi.; population (1991 est.) 172,000. The group was acquired by France in 1853.

The territory is administered by a governor and government council. There is a popularly elected Territorial Assembly. A deputy and a senator are elected to the French Parliament. Capital: Noumea.

Mining is the chief industry. New Caledonia is one of the world's largest nickel producers. Other minerals found are chrome, iron, cobalt, manganese, silver, gold, lead, and copper. Agricultural products include coffee, copra, cotton, manioc (cassava), corn, tobacco, bananas and pineapples.

In 1987, New Caledonian voters chose by referendum to remain within the French Republic. There were clashes between French and Melanesians (Kanaks) in 1988.

Wallis and Futuna Islands, 2 archipelagos raised to status of overseas territory July 29, 1961, are in the SW Pacific S of the Equator between Fiji and Samoa. The islands have a total area of 106 sq. mi. and population (1988 est.) of 15,400. **Alofi,** attached to Futuna, is uninhabited. Capital: Mata-Utu. Chief products are copra, yams, taro roots, bananas. A senator and a deputy are elected to the French Parliament.

Gabon

Gabonese Republic

République Gabonaise

People: Population (1992 est.): 1,106,000. **Pop. density:** 10 per sq. mi. **Urban** (1990): 45%. **Ethnic groups:** Fang 25%, Bapounon 10%, others. **Languages:** French (official), Bantu dialects. **Religions:** Mostly Christian, a minority follow traditional beliefs.

Geography: Area: 103,346 sq. mi., slightly bigger than the UK. **Location:** On Atlantic coast of central Africa. **Neighbors:** Equatorial Guinea, Cameroon on N, Congo on E, S. **Topography:** Heavily forested, the country consists of coastal lowlands plateaus in N, E, and S, mountains in N, SE, and center. The Ogooue R. system covers most of Gabon. **Capital:** Libreville, pop. (1991 est.) 275,000.

Government: Type: Republic. **Head of state:** Pres. Omar Bongo; b. Dec. 30, 1935; in office: Dec. 2, 1967. **Head of government:** Prime Min. Casimir Oye Mba; in office: May 3, 1990. **Local divisions:** 9 provinces. **Defense** (1990): 3.2% of GDP.

Economy: Industries: Oil products. **Chief crops:** Cocoa, coffee, rice, peanuts, palm products, cassava, bananas. **Minerals:** Manganese, uranium, oil, iron, gas. **Crude oil reserves** (1985): 623 mln. bbls. **Other resources:** Timber. **Arable land:** 2%. **Electricity prod.** (1991): 995 mln. kWh. **Labor force:** 65% agric.; 30% ind. & comm.

Finance: Monetary unit: CFA franc (Mar. 1993: 273 = $1 US). **Gross domestic product** (1991) $5.3 bln. **Per capita GDP:** $4,400. **Imports** (1990): $780 mln.; partners: Fr. 51%. **Exports** (1990): $1.1 bln.; partners: Fr. 53%, U.S. 22%. **Tourism** (1990): $4 mln. receipts. **National budget** (1991): $1.8 bln. **International reserves less gold** (Jan. 1993): $167 mln. **Gold:** 13,000 oz t. **Consumer prices** (change in 1990): 8.0%.

Transport: Motor vehicles (1989): 19,000 passenger cars, 15,000 comm. vehicles. **Civil aviation** (1990): 445 mln. passenger-km. **Chief ports:** Port-Gentil, Owendo, Mayumba.

Communications: Television sets: 1 per 29 persons. **Radios:** 1 per 5 persons. **Telephones:** 1 per 64 persons.

Health: Life expectancy at birth (1992): 51 male; 56 female. **Births** (per 1,000 pop. 1992): 28. **Deaths** (per 1,000 pop. 1992): 15. **Natural increase:** 1.4%. **Hospital beds** (1985): 4,617. **Physicians** (1985): 265. **Infant mortality** (per 1,000 live births 1992): 100.

Education (1991): **Literacy:** 70%. **School:** Compulsory to age 16; attendance: 100% primary, 14% secondary.

Major International Organizations: UN (World Bank), OAU, OPEC.

Embassy: 27 Elvaston Place, London SW7 5NL; 071-823 9986.

France established control over the region in the second half of the 19th century. Gabon became independent Aug. 17, 1960. A multiparty political system was introduced in 1990, and a new constitution was enacted in 1991. It is one of the most prosperous black African countries, thanks to abundant natural resources, foreign private investment, and government development programs.

The Gambia

Republic of The Gambia

People: Population (1992 est.): 902,000. **Age distrib.** (%): 0–14: 45.9; 15–59: 54.4; 60+: 3.8. **Pop. density:** 218 per sq. mi. **Urban** (1990): 21%. **Ethnic groups:** Mandinka 42%, Fula 18%,

Wolof 16%, others. **Languages:** English (official), Mandinka, Wolof. **Religion:** Muslim 95%.

Geography: Area: 4,127 sq. mi., the size of Wales. **Location:** On Atlantic coast near western tip of Africa. **Neighbors:** Surrounded on 3 sides by Senegal. **Topography:** A narrow strip of land on each side of the lower Gambia. **Capital:** Banjul, pop. (1993 est.) 40,000.

Government: Type: Republic. **Head of state:** Pres. Dawda Kairaba Jawara; b. May 16, 1924; in office Apr. 24, 1970 (prime min. from June 12, 1962). **Local divisions:** 5 divisions and Banjul.

Economy: Industries: Tourism, peanut processing. **Chief crops:** Peanuts (main export), rice. **Arable land:** 16%. **Fish catch** (1989): 17,000 metric tons. **Electricity prod.** (1991): 65 mln. kWh. **Labor force:** 75% agric.; 18% ind. & comm.

Finance: Monetary unit: Dalasi (Mar. 1993: 9.14 = $1 US). **Gross domestic product** (1991): $207 mln. **Per capita GDP:** $235. **Imports** (1991): $167 mln.; partners: EC 53%. **Exports** (1991): $122 mln.; partners: Japan 60%. **Tourism** (1990): $26 mln. receipts. **National budget** (1990): $95 mln. expenditures. **International reserves less gold** (Jan. 1993): $64 mln. **Consumer prices** (change in 1992): 9.5%.

Transport: Motor vehicles (1989): 5,200 passenger cars, 1,000 comm. vehicles. **Chief port:** Banjul.

Communications: Radios: 1 per 6.1 persons. **Telephones:** 1 per 80 persons.

Health: Life expectancy at birth (1992): 47 male; 51 female. **Births** (per 1,000 pop. 1992): 47. **Deaths** (per 1,000 pop. 1992): 17. **Natural increase:** 3.0%. **Physicians:** 1 per 17,604 persons. **Infant mortality** (per 1,000 live births 1992): 129.

Education (1993): **Literacy:** 30%.

Major International Organizations: UN (GATT, IMF, WHO), OAU.

High Commission: 57 Kensington Court, London W8 5DG; 071-937 6316.

The tribes of Gambia were at one time associated with the West African empires of Ghana, Mali, and Songhay. The area became Britain's first African possession in 1588.

Independence came Feb. 18, 1965; republic status within the Commonwealth was achieved in 1970. After a coup attempt in 1981, The Gambia formed the confederation of Senegambia with Senegal that lasted until 1989. Gambia is one of the only functioning democracies in Africa. The country suffered from severe famine in the 1970s.

Georgia

Republic of Georgia

Sakartvelos Respublica

People: Population (1992 est.): 5,570,000. **Pop. density:** 206 per sq. mi. **Urban** (1991): 57%. **Ethnic groups:** Georgian 70%, Armenian 7%, Russian 6%. **Languages:** Georgian (official), Russian. **Religions:** Georgian Orthodox 65%, Russian Orthodox 10%.

Geography: Area: 26,911 sq. mi., the size of the Irish Rep. **Neighbors:** Black Sea on W, Russia on N, NE, Turkey, Armenia on S, Azerbaijan on SE. **Topography:** Separated from Russia on NE by main range of Caucasus mts. **Capital:** Tbilisi, pop. (1991) 1.2 mln.

Government: Type: In transition. **Head of state:** Pres. Eduard Shevardnadze; b. Jan. 25, 1928; in office Nov. 6, 1992.

Economy: Industries: Manganese mining. **Chief crops:** Citrus fruits, wheat, grapes. **Livestock** (1990): 1.5 mln. cattle; 1.9 mln. sheep.

Finance: Monetary unit: Rouble. **Imports** (1990): $1.5 bln. **Exports** (1990): $176 mln.

Transport: Railroads: 976 mi. long. **Motor vehicles:** 427,000 passenger cars.

Communications: Daily newspaper circ. (1990): 671 per 1,000 pop.

Health: Life expectancy at birth: 67 male; 73 female. **Births** (per 1,000 pop. 1992): 17. **Deaths** (per 1,000 pop. 1992): 9. **Infant mortality** (per 1,000 live births 1992): 34. **Hospital beds:** 1 per 90 persons. **Physicians:** 1 per 170 persons.

The region contained the ancient kingdoms of Colchis and Iberia. It was Christianized in the 4th century and conquered by Arabs in the 8th century. The region expanded to include the area from the Black Sea to the Caspian Sea and parts of Armenia and Persia before its disintegration under the impact of Mongol and Turkish invasions. The annexation to Russia in 1801 caused the Russian war with Persia, 1804-1813. Georgia entered the USSR in 1922 and became a constituent republic in 1936.

In 1989 strong nationalist feelings led the USSR to attempts at repression; Soviet troops attacked nationalist demonstrators in April, killing some 20 persons. Georgia declared independence Apr. 9, 1991. It became an independent state when the Soviet Union disbanded Dec. 26, 1991, although it did not join the Commonwealth of Independent States.

There was fighting during 1991 between rebel forces and loyalists of Pres. Zviad Gamsakhurdia, whom the rebels accused of aspiring to establish a dictatorship. Gamsakhurdia fled the capital Jan. 6, 1992. The ruling Military Council picked former Soviet Foreign Minister Eduard Shevardnadze to chair a newly created State Council. An attempted coup by forces loyal to ousted Pres. Gamsakhurdia was crushed June 24. Shevardnadze was elected Pres. Nov. 1992.

Georgia accused Russia of aiding rebels in Abkhazia, an autonomous region within Georgia, in 1993. The ethnic Abkhazis were in armed revolt to secure independence. Martial law was declared in parts of the region July 6.

Germany

Federal Republic of Germany

Bundesrepublik Deutschland

(Figures prior to 1990 for original 11 states)

People: Population (1992 est.): 80,387,000. **Age distrib.** (%): 0–14: 14.7; 15–59: 64.7; 60+: 20.6. **Pop. density:** 583 per sq. mi. **Urban** (1990): 86%. **Ethnic groups:** German 93%. **Language:** German. **Religions:** Protestant 44%, Roman Catholic 37%.

Geography: Area: 137,838 sq. mi., 3 times the size of England. **Location:** In central Europe. **Neighbors:** Denmark on N, Netherlands, Belgium, Luxembourg, France on W, Switzerland, Austria on S, Czech Rep., Poland on E. **Topography:** Germany is flat in N, hilly in center and W, and mountainous in Bavaria. Chief rivers are Elbe, Weser, Ems, Rhine, and Main, all flowing toward North Sea, and Danube, flowing toward Black Sea. **Capital:** Berlin. **Cities** (1991 est.): Berlin 3.0 mln.; Hamburg 1.6 mln.; Munich 1.3 mln.; Cologne 946,000; Essen 622,000; Frankfurt 635,000; Dortmund 575,000; Dusseldorf 593,000; Stuttgart 561,000; Leipzig 549,000; Dresden 521,000.

Government: Type: Federal republic. **Head of state:** Pres. Richard von Weizsäcker; b. Apr. 15, 1920; in office May 23, 1984. **Head of government:** Chan. Helmut Kohl; b. Apr. 3, 1930; in office Oct. 1, 1982. **Local divisions:** 16 laender (states) with substantial powers. **Defense** (1991): 2.5% of GDP.

Economy: Industries: Steel, ships, vehicles, machinery, electronics, coal, chemicals. **Chief crops:** Grains, potatoes, sugar beets. **Minerals:** Coal, potash, lignite, iron, uranium. **Arable land:** 35%. **Livestock** (1990): 15.3 mln. cattle; 10.0 mln. pigs; 1.2 mln. sheep. **Fish catch** (1990): 390,000 metric tons. **Electricity prod.** (1991): 580 bln. kWh. **Crude steel prod.** (1991): 42.1 mln. metric tons. **Labor force:** 5% agric.; 40% ind. & comm.; 54% services.

Finance: Monetary unit: Mark (Aug. 1993: 1.71 = $1 US). **Gross domestic product** (1991): $1,331 bln. **Per capita GDP:** $14,600. **Imports** (1992): $402 bln.; partners: EC 52%; other European 16%. **Exports** (1992): $422 bln.; partners: EC 55%; other European 19%. **Tourism** (1989): $8.6 bln. receipts. **National budget** (1990): $245 bln. expenditures. **International reserves less gold** (Mar. 1993): $70 bln. **Gold:** 95.18 mln. oz t. **Consumer prices** (change in 1992): 4.0%.

Transport: Railroads (1991): 56,397 mi. long. **Motor vehicles** (1990): 35.5 mln. passenger cars, 2.7 mln. comm. vehicles. **Civil aviation** (1988): 34.0 bln. passenger-km; 27 airports with scheduled flights. **Chief ports:** Hamburg, Bremen, Bremerhaven, Lubeck.

Communications: Television sets: 1 per 2.6 persons. **Radios:** 1 per 2.3 persons. **Telephones:** 1 per 1.5 persons. **Daily newspaper circ.** (1990): 401 per 1,000 pop.

Health: Life expectancy at birth (1992): 73 male; 79 female. **Births** (per 1,000 pop. 1992): 11.2. **Deaths** (per 1,000 pop. 1992): 11. **Hospital beds:** 1 per 95 persons. **Physicians:** 1 per 324 persons. **Infant mortality** (per 1,000 live births 1992): 7.

Education (1991): **Literacy:** 99%. **School:** Compulsory for 10 years; attendance 100%.

Major International Organizations: UN and all of its specialized agencies, EC, OECD, NATO.

Embassy: 23 Belgrave Square, London SW1X 8PZ; 071-235 5033.

Germany, prior to World War II, was a central European nation composed of numerous states which had a common language and traditions and which had been united in one country since 1871; since World War II until 1990, had been split in 2 parts.

History and government. Germanic tribes were defeated by Julius Caesar, 55 and 53 BC, but Roman expansion N of the Rhine was stopped in AD 9. Charlemagne, ruler of the Franks, consolidated Saxon, Bavarian, Rhenish, Frankish, and other lands; after him the eastern part became the German Empire. The Thirty Years' War, 1618-1648, split Germany into small principalities and kingdoms. After Napoleon, Austria contended with Prussia for dominance, but lost the Seven Weeks' War to Prussia, 1866. Otto von Bismarck, Prussian chancellor, formed the North German Confederation, 1867.

In 1870 Bismarck maneuvered Napoleon III into declaring war. After the quick defeat of France, Bismarck formed the **German Empire** and on Jan. 18, 1871, in Versailles, proclaimed King Wilhelm I of Prussia German emperor (Deutscher kaiser).

The German Empire reached its peak before World War I in 1914, with 208,780 sq. mi., plus a colonial empire. After that war Germany ceded Alsace-Lorraine to France; West Prussia and Posen (Poznan) province to Poland; part of Schleswig to Denmark; lost all of its colonies and the ports of Memel and Danzig.

Republic of Germany, 1919-1933, adopted the Weimar constitution; met reparation payments and elected Friedrich Ebert and Gen. Paul von Hindenburg presidents.

Third Reich, 1933-1945, Adolf Hitler led the National Socialist German Workers' (Nazi) party after World War I. In 1923 he attempted to unseat the Bavarian government and was imprisoned. Pres. von Hindenburg named Hitler chancellor Jan. 30, 1933; on Aug. 3, 1934, the day after Hindenburg's death, the cabinet joined the offices of president and chancellor and made Hitler *fuehrer* (leader). Hitler abolished freedom of speech and assembly, and began a long series of persecutions climaxed by the murder of millions of Jews and opponents.

Hitler repudiated the Versailles treaty and reparations agreements. He remilitarized the Rhineland 1936 and annexed Austria (Anschluss, 1938). At Munich he made an agreement with Neville Chamberlain, British prime minister, which permitted Hitler to annex part of Czechoslovakia. He signed a non-aggression treaty with the USSR, 1939. He declared war on Poland Sept. 1, 1939, precipitating World War II.

With total defeat near, Hitler committed suicide in Berlin Apr. 1945. The victorious Allies voided all acts and annexations of Hitler's Reich.

Postwar changes. The zones of occupation administered by the Allied Powers and later relinquished gave the USSR Saxony, Saxony-Anhalt, Thuringia, and Mecklenburg, and the former Prussian provinces of Saxony and Brandenburg.

The territory E of the Oder-Neisse line within 1937 boundaries comprising the provinces of Silesia, Pomerania, and the southern part of East Prussia, totaling about 41,220 sq. mi., was taken by Poland. Northern East Prussia was taken by the USSR.

The Western Allies ended the state of war with Germany in 1951. The USSR did so in 1955.

There was also created the area of Greater Berlin, within but not part of the Soviet zone, administered by the 4 occupying powers under the Allied Command. In 1948 the USSR withdrew, established its single command in East Berlin, and cut off supplies. The Allies utilized a gigantic airlift to bring food to West Berlin, 1948-1949. In Aug. 1961 the East Germans built a wall dividing Berlin, after over 3 million E. Germans had emigrated.

On Nov. 9, 1989 the E. German government announced the decision to open the border with the West signaling the end of the infamous Berlin Wall.

A new era: As communism was being rejected in E. Germany, talks began concerning German reunification. At a meeting in Ottawa, Feb. 1990, the foreign ministers of the World War II "Big Four" Allied nations—U.S., USSR, UK, and France—as well as the foreign ministers of E. Germany and W. Germany reached agreement on a format for high-level talks on German reunification.

In May, NATO ministers adopted a package of proposals on reunification, including the inclusion of the united Germany as a full member of NATO and the barring of the new Germany from having its own nuclear, chemical, or biological weapons. In July, the USSR agreed to conditions that would allow Germany to become a member of NATO.

The two nations agreed to monetary unification under the W. German mark beginning in July. The merger of the 2 Germanys took place on Oct. 3, 1990, and the first all-German elections since 1932 were held Dec. 2, 1990.

In 1992 neo-Nazi groups intensified their campaign against refugees. The Constitutional Protection Office reported 2,285 violent attacks by right-wingers in 1992. Parliament approved constitutional changes to restrict foreigners' rights to seek asylum in Germany, May 1993.

East Germany

The German Democratic Republic was proclaimed in the Soviet sector of Berlin Oct. 7, 1949. It was proclaimed fully sovereign in 1954, but Soviet troops remained on grounds of security and the 4-power Potsdam agreement.

Coincident with the entrance of W. Germany into the European Defense community in 1952, the East German government decreed a prohibited zone 3 miles deep along its 600-mile border with W. Germany and cut Berlin's telephone system in two. Berlin was further divided by erection of a fortified wall in 1961, but the exodus of refugees to the West continued, though on a smaller scale.

E. Germany suffered severe economic problems until the mid-1960s. A "new economic system" was introduced, easing the former central planning controls and allowing factories to make profits provided they were reinvested in operations or redistributed to workers as bonuses. By the early 1970s, the economy was highly industrialized. In May 1972 the few remaining private firms were ordered sold to the government. The nation was credited with the highest standard of living among Warsaw Pact countries. But growth slowed in the late 1970s, due to shortages of natural resources and labor, and a huge debt to lenders in the West. Comparison with the lifestyle in the West caused many of the young to leave the country.

The government firmly resisted following the USSR's policy of *glasnost*, but by Oct. 1989, was faced with nationwide demonstrations demanding reform. Pres. Erich Honecker, in office since 1976, was forced to resign, Oct. 18. On Nov. 4, the border with Czechoslovakia was opened and permission granted for refugees to travel on to the West, On Nov. 9, the decision was made to open the border with the West, signaling the end of the "Berlin Wall", which separated the 2 Germanys and was the supreme emblem of the cold war.

On Aug. 23, 1990, the E. German Parliament agreed to formal unification with W. Germany; this took place on Oct. 3.

West Germany

The Federal Republic of Germany was proclaimed May 23, 1949, in Bonn, after a constitution had been drawn up by a consultative assembly formed by representatives of the 11 laender (states) in the French, British, and American zones. Later reorganized into 9 units, the laender numbered 10 with the addition of the Saar, 1957. Berlin also was granted land (state) status, but the 1945 occupation agreements placed restrictions on it.

The occupying powers, the U.S., Britain, and France, restored the civil status, Sept. 21, 1949. The U. S. resumed diplomatic relations July 2, 1951. The powers lifted controls and the republic became fully independent May 5, 1955.

Dr. Konrad Adenauer, Christian Democrat, was made chancellor Sept. 15, 1949, re-elected 1953, 1957, 1961. Willy Brandt, heading a coalition of Social Democrats and Free Democrats, became chancellor Oct. 21, 1969.

In 1970 Brandt signed friendship treaties with the USSR and Poland. In 1971, the U.S., Britain, France, and the USSR signed an agreement on Western access to West Berlin. In 1972 the Bundestag approved the USSR and Polish treaties and East and West Germany signed their first formal treaty, implementing the agreement easing access to West Berlin. In 1973 a West Germany-Czechoslovakia pact normalized relations and nullified the 1938 "Munich Agreement".

In May 1974 Brandt resigned, saying he took full responsibility for "negligence" for allowing an East German spy to become a member of his staff.

West Germany experienced economic growth since the 1950s. The country led Europe in provisions for worker participation in the management of industry.

The NATO decision to deploy medium-range nuclear missiles in Western Europe sparked a demonstration by some 400,000 protesters in 1983. In 1989, Chanceller Kohl's call for early negotiations with the Soviets on reducing short-range missiles caused a rift with the NATO allies, especially the U.S. and Great Britain.

In 1989, the changes in the E. German government and the opening of the Berlin Wall sparked talk of reunification of the two Germanys. In 1990, under the leadership of Chanceller Kohl, W. Germany moved rapidly to reunite with E. Germany.

Helgoland, an island of 130 acres in the North Sea, was taken from Denmark by a British Naval Force in 1807 and later ceded to Germany to become a part of Schleswig-Holstein province in return for rights in East Africa. The heavily fortified island was surrendered to UK, May 23, 1945, demilitarized in 1947, and returned to W. Germany, Mar 1, 1952. It is a free port.

Ghana

Republic of Ghana

People: Population (1992 est.): 16,185,000. **Age distrib.** (%): 0–14: 46.6; 15-59: 48.9; 60+: 4.5. **Pop. density:** 175 per sq. mi. **Urban** (1990): 33%. **Ethnic groups:** Akan 44%, Moshi-Dagomba 16%, Ewe 13%, Ga 8%, others. **Languages:** English (official), Akan, Mossi, Ewe, Ga-Adangme. **Religions:** Traditional beliefs 38%, Muslim 30%, Christian 24%.

Geography: Area: 92,098 sq. mi., slightly smaller than the UK. **Location:** On southern coast of W. Africa. **Neighbors:** Côte d'Ivoire on W, Burkina Faso on N, Togo on E. **Topography:** Most of Ghana consists of low fertile plains and scrubland, cut by rivers and by the artificial Lake Volta. **Capital:** Accra, pop. (1988 est.) 949,000.

Government: Type: Military. **Head of government:** Pres. Jerry

Rawlings; b. 1947; in office: Dec. 31, 1981. **Local divisions:** 10 regions.

Economy: Industries: Aluminium, light industry. **Chief crops:** Cocoa, coffee. **Minerals:** Gold, manganese, industrial diamonds, bauxite. **Crude oil reserves:** (1980): 7 mln. bbls. **Other resources:** Timber, rubber. **Arable land:** 5%. **Livestock** (1990): 1.1 mln. cattle; 2.2 mln. sheep. **Fish catch** (1990): 360,000 metric tons. **Electricity prod.** (1991): 4.1 bln. kWh. **Labor force:** 55% agric.; 19% ind.

Finance: Monetary unit: Cedi (Mar. 1993: 555 = $1 US). **Gross domestic product** (1991): $6.2 bln. **Per capita GDP:** $400. **Imports** (1991): $1.2 bln.; partners: UK 10%, W. Ger. 12%, Nigeria 12%. **Exports** (1991): $843 mln.; partners: U.S. 23%, Neth. 9%, W. Ger. 9%. **International reserves less gold** (Mar. 1993): $399 mln. **Gold:** 275,000 oz t. **Consumer prices** (change in 1991): 18%.

Transport: Railroads (1991): 592 mi. long. **Motor vehicles** (1986): 26,000 passenger cars, 28,000 comm. vehicles. **Civil aviation** (1990): 407 mln. passenger-km; 3 airports with scheduled flights. **Chief ports:** Tema, Takoradi.

Communications: Television sets: 1 per 83 persons. **Radios:** 1 per 4.7 persons. **Telephones:** 1 per 191 persons.

Health: Life expectancy at birth (1992): 53 male; 56 female. **Births** (per 1,000 pop. 1992): 46. **Deaths** (per 1,000 pop. 1992): 13. **Natural increase:** 3.3%. **Physicians:** 1 per 22,127 persons. **Infant mortality** (per 1,000 live births 1992): 86.

Education (1991): **Literacy:** 60%.

Major International Organizations: UN and all of its specialized agencies, OAU.

Embassy: 13 Belgrave Sq, London SW1; 071-235 4142.

Named after an African empire along the Niger River, 400-1240 AD, Ghana was ruled by Britain for 113 years as the Gold Coast. The UN in 1956 approved merger with the British Togoland trust territory. Independence came March 6, 1957. Republic status within the Commonwealth was attained in 1960.

Pres. Kwame Nkrumah built hospitals and schools, promoted development projects like the Volta R. hydroelectric and aluminium plants but ran the country into debt, jailed opponents, and was accused of corruption. A 1964 referendum gave Nkrumah dictatorial powers and set up a one-party socialist state.

Nkrumah was overthrown in 1966 by a police-army coup, which expelled Chinese and East German teachers and technicians. Elections were held in 1969, but 4 further coups occurred in 1972, 1978, 1979, and 1981. The 1979 and 1981 coups, led by Flight Lieut. Jerry Rawlings, were followed by suspension of the constitution and banning of political parties. A new constitution, which allowed for multiparty politics, was approved in April 1992.

Greece

Hellenic Republic

Elliniki Dimokratia

People: Population (1992 est.): 10,064,000. **Age distrib.** (%): 0–14: 20.5; 15-59: 61.1; 60+: 20.4. **Pop. density:** 196 per sq. mi. **Urban** (1990): 63.0%. **Ethnic groups:** Greek 98.5%. **Language:** Greek. **Religion:** Greek Orthodox 97% (official).

Geography: Area: 51,146 sq. mi., about the size of England. **Location:** Occupies southern end of Balkan Peninsula in SE Europe. **Neighbors:** Albania, Macedonia, Bulgaria on N, Turkey on E. **Topography:** About 75% of Greece is non-arable, with mountains in all areas. Pindus Mts. run through the country N to S. The heavily indented coastline is 9,385 mi. long. Of over 2,000 islands, only 169 are inhabited, among them Crete, Rhodes, Milos, Corfu, Chios, Lesbos, Samos, Euboea, Delos, Mykonos. **Capital:** Athens. **Cities** (1991 est.): Athens 748,110; Thessaloniki 377,000; Patras 169,000.

Government: Type: Presidential parliamentary republic. **Head of state:** Pres. Konstantinos Karamanlis; in office May, 1990. **Head of government:** Prime Min. Konstantinos Mitsotakis; b. Oct. 18, 1918; in office Apr. 11, 1990. **Local divisions:** 51 prefectures. **Defense** (1991): 5.5% of GDP.

Economy: Industries: Textiles, chemicals, metals, wine, food processng, cement. **Chief crops:** Grains, corn, rice, cotton, tobacco, olives, citrus fruits, raisins, figs. **Minerals:** Bauxite, lignite, oil, manganese. **Crude oil reserves** (1985): 35 mln. bbls. **Arable land:** 23%. **Livestock** (1990): 11.0 mln. sheep; 5.6 mln. goats. **Fish catch** (1990): 128,000 metric tons. **Electricity prod.** (1991): 36.4 bln. kWh. **Labor force:** 28% agric.; 29% ind., 42% service.

Finance: Monetary unit: Drachma (Aug. 1993: 239 = $1 US). **Gross domestic product** (1991): $77 bln. **Per capita GDP:** $7,730. **Imports** (1991): $21.5 bln.; partners: Ger. 21%, It. 15%, Fr. 7%. **Exports** (1991): $8.6 bln.; partners: Ger. 20%, It. 17%, Fra. 10%. **Tourism** (1990): $2 bln. receipts. **National budget** (1991): $33 bln. expenditures. **International reserves less gold** (Mar. 1993): $4.7 bln. **Gold:** 3.4 mln. oz t. **Consumer prices** (change in 1992): 15.8%.

Transport: Railroads (1991): 1,540 mi. long. **Motor vehicles** (1990): 1.6 mln. passenger cars, 781,000 comm. vehicles. **Civil aviation** (1990): 7.7 bln. passenger-km; 33 airports with scheduled flights. **Chief ports:** Piraeus, Thessaloniki, Patrai.

Communications: Television sets: 1 per 4.5 persons. **Radios:** 1 per 2.2 persons. **Telephones:** 1 per 2.2 persons. **Daily newspaper circ.** (1986): 88 per 1,000 pop.

Health: Life expectancy at birth (1992): 75 male; 80 female. **Births** (per 1,000 pop. 1992): 11. **Deaths** (per 1,000 pop. 1992): 9. **Natural increase:** .2%. **Hospital beds:** 1 per 193 persons. **Physicians:** 1 per 327 persons. **Infant mortality** (per 1,000 live births 1992): 10.

Education (1991): **Literacy:** Men 96%, women 89%. **School:** Compulsory for 9 years.

Major International Organizations: UN (GATT, IMF, WHO, ILO), EC, NATO, OECD.

Embassy: 1a Holland Park, London W11 3TP; 071-727 8040.

The achievements of ancient Greece in art, architecture, science, mathematics, philosophy, drama, literature, and democracy became legacies for succeeding ages. Greece reached the height of its glory and power, particularly in the Athenian city-state, in the 5th century BC.

Greece fell under Roman rule in the 2d and 1st centuries BC. In the 4th century AD it became part of the Byzantine Empire and, after the fall of Constantinople to the Turks in 1453, part of the Ottoman Empire.

Greece won its war of independence from Turkey 1821-1829, and became a kingdom. A republic was established 1924; the monarchy was restored, 1935, and George II, King of the Hellenes, resumed the throne. In Oct., 1940, Greece rejected an ultimatum from Italy. Nazi support resulted in its defeat and occupation by Germans, Italians, and Bulgarians. By the end of 1944 the invaders withdrew. Communist resistance forces were defeated by Royalist and British troops. A plebiscite recalled King George II. He died Apr. 1, 1947, was succeeded by his brother, Paul I.

Communists waged guerrilla war 1947-49 against the government but were defeated with the aid of the U.S.

A period of reconstruction and rapid development followed, mainly with conservative governments under Premier Constantine Karamanlis. The Center Union led by George Papandreou won elections in 1963 and 1964. King Constantine, who acceded in 1964, forced Papandreou to resign. A period of political maneuvers ended in the military takeover of April 21, 1967, by Col. George Papadopoulos. King Constantine tried to reverse the consolidation of the harsh dictatorship Dec. 13, 1967, but failed and fled to Italy. Papadopoulos was ousted Nov. 25, 1973.

Greek army officers serving in the National Guard of Cyprus staged a coup on the island July 15, 1974. Turkey invaded Cyprus a week later, precipitating the collapse of the Greek junta, which was implicated in the Cyprus coup.

The 1981 victory of the Panhellenic Socialist Movement (Pasok) of Andreas Papandreou has brought about substantial changes in the internal and external policies that Greece has pursued for the past 5 decades. Greece has been victimized in the 1980s by incidents of international terrorism.

A scandal centered on George Kostokas, a banker and publisher, led to the arrest or investigation of about a dozen leading Socialists, implicated Papandreou, and led to the defeat of the Socialists at the polls in 1989. Following a period in the political wilderness, Papandreou and his Pasok party were re-elected in Oct. 1993.

Greenland

Kalaallit Nunaat

Greenland, a huge island between the N. Atlantic and the Polar Sea, is separated from the North American continent by Davis Strait and Baffin Bay. Its total area is 840,000 sq. mi., 84% of which is ice-capped. Most of the island is a lofty plateau 9,000 to 10,000 ft. in altitude. The average thickness of the cap is 1,000 ft. The population (1992) is 57,000. Under the 1953 Danish constitution the colony became an integral part of the realm with representatives in the Folketing. The Danish parliament, 1978, approved home rule for Greenland, effective May 1, 1979. Accepting home rule the islanders elected a socialist-dominated legislature, Apr. 4. With home rule, Greenlandic place names came into official use. The technically correct name for Greenland is now Kalaallit Nunaat; its capital is Nuuk, rather than Gothab. Fish is the principal export.

Grenada

People: Population (1992 est.): 84,000. **Pop. density:** 631 per sq. mi. **Ethnic groups:** Mostly African descent. **Languages:** English (official), French patois. **Religions:** Roman Catholic 64%, Anglican 22%.

Geography: Area: 133 sq. mi., about the size of the Isle of Wight. **Location:** 90 mi. N. of Venezuela. **Topography:** Main island is mountainous; country includes Carriacon and Petit Martinique islands. **Capital:** St. George's, pop. (1991 est.) 30,000.

Government: Type: Parliamentary democracy. **Head of state:** Queen Elizabeth II, represented by Gov.-Gen. Reginald Palmer. **Head of government:** Prime Min. Nicholas Brathwaite; in office Mar. 13, 1990. **Local divisions:** 6 parishes and one dependency.

Economy: Industries: Rum. **Chief crops:** Nutmegs, bananas, cocoa, mace. **Arable land:** 15%. **Electricity prod.** (1991): 26 mln. kWh. **Labor force:** 33% agric.; 31% services.

Finance: Monetary unit: East Caribbean dollar (Apr. 1993: 2.70 = $1 US). **Gross domestic product** (1989): $238 mln. **Per capita GDP:** $2,800. **Imports** (1989): $200 mln.; partners: UK 19%, Trin./Tob. 12%, U.S. 24%. **Exports** (1990): $26 mln.; partners: UK 23%, CARICOM countries 38%. **Tourism** (1991): $38 mln. receipts. **National budget** (1990): $77 mln. expenditures. **International reserves less gold** (Jan. 1993): $25 mln.

Transport: Chief port: St. George's.

Communications: Radios: 1 per 2.4 persons. **Telephones:** 1 per 19 persons.

Health: Life expectancy at birth (1992): 69 male; 74 female. **Births** (per 1,000 pop. 1992): 35. **Deaths** (per 1,000 pop. 1992): 7. **Natural increase:** 2.8%. **Infant mortality** (per 1,000 live births 1992): 28.

Education (1991): **Literacy:** 95%. **School:** Compulsory for 6 years.

Major International Organizations: UN (IMF, WHO), OAS.

High Commission: 1 Collingham Gdns, London SW5 0HW; 071-373 7808.

Columbus sighted the island 1498. First European settlers were French, 1650. The island was held alternately by France and England until final British occupation, 1784. Grenada became fully independent Feb. 7, 1974 during a general strike. It is the smallest independent nation in the Western Hemisphere.

On Oct. 14, 1983, a military coup ousted Prime Minister Maurice Bishop, who was put under house arrest, later freed by supporters, rearrested, and, finally, on Oct. 19, executed. U.S. forces, with a token force from 6 area nations, invaded Grenada, Oct. 25. Resistance from the Grenadian army and Cuban advisors was quickly overcome as most of the population welcomed the invading forces as liberators. U.S. troops left Grenada in June 1985.

Guatemala

Republic of Guatemala

República de Guatemala

People: Population (1992 est.): 9,784,000. **Age distrib.** (%): 0–14: 45.4; 15–59: 49.5; 60+: 5.1. **Pop. density:** 232 per sq. mi. **Urban** (1992): 39%. **Ethnic groups:** Maya 55%, Mestizos 44%. **Languages:** Spanish (official), Mayan languages. **Religion:** Mostly Roman Catholic.

Geography: Area: 42,042 sq. mi., about the size of Scotland and Wales combined. **Location:** In Central America. **Neighbors:** Mexico on N, W, El Salvador on S, Honduras, Belize on E. **Topography:** The central highland and mountain areas are bordered by the narrow Pacific coast and the lowlands and fertile river valleys on the Caribbean. There are numerous volcanoes in S, more than half a dozen over 11,000 ft. **Capital:** Guatemala City, pop. (1992 est.) 1,115,000.

Government: Type: Republic. **Head of state:** Pres. Ramiro de Leon Carpio; in office June 6, 1993. **Local divisions:** Guatemala City and 22 departments. **Defense** (1990): 1.0% of GDP.

Economy: Industries: Prepared foods, tyres, textiles. **Chief crops:** Coffee (one third of exports), sugar, bananas, cotton, corn. **Minerals:** Oil, nickel. **Crude oil reserves** (1985): 500 mln. bbls. **Other resources:** Rare woods, fish, chicle. **Arable land:** 12%. **Electricity prod.** (1991): 2.5 bln. kWh. **Labor force:** 36% agric.; 24% ind. & comm., 34% services.

Finance: Monetary unit: Quetzal (Apr. 1993: 5.47 = $1 US). **Gross domestic product** (1991): $11.7 bln. **Per capita GDP:** $1,260. **Imports** (1992): $2.4 bln.; partners: U.S. 37%, CACM 8%. **Exports** (1992): $1.0 bln.; partners: U.S. 28%, CACM 20%. **Tourism** (1990): $185 mln. receipts. **National budget** (1990): $1.1 bln. expenditures. **International reserves less gold** (Mar. 1993): $807 mln. **Gold:** 122,000 oz t. **Consumer prices** (change in 1992): 10.0%.

Transport: Motor vehicles (1990): 130,000 passenger cars, 100,000 comm. vehicles. **Civil aviation** (1990) 213 mln. passenger-km; 2 airports with scheduled flights. **Chief ports:** Puerto Barrios, San Jose.

Communications: Television sets: 1 per 18 persons. **Radios:** 1 per 22 persons. **Telephones:** 1 per 36 persons. **Daily newspaper circ.** (1989): 22 per 1,000 pop.

Health: Life expectancy at birth (1992): 61 male; 66 female. **Births** (per 1,000 pop. 1992): 34. **Deaths** (per 1,000 pop. 1992): 8. **Natural increase:** 2.6%. **Physicians:** 1 per 2,356 persons. **Infant mortality** (per 1,000 live births 1992): 56.

Education (1991): **Literacy:** 55%. **School:** Compulsory for 6 years; attendance 35%.

Major International Organizations: UN (IMF, World Bank), OAS.

Embassy: 13 Fawcett St, London SW10 9HN; 071-351 3042.

The old Mayan Indian empire flourished in what is today Guatemala for over 1,000 years before the Spanish.

Guatemala was a Spanish colony 1524-1821; briefly a part of Mexico and then of the U.S. of Central America, the republic was established in 1839.

Since 1945 when a liberal government was elected to replace the long-term dictatorship of Jorge Ubico, the country has seen a swing toward socialism, an armed revolt, renewed attempts at social reform, a military coup, and, in 1986, civilian rule. The Guerrilla Army of the Poor, an insurgent group founded 1975, led a military offensive by attacking army posts and succeeded in incorporating segments of the large Indian population in its struggle against the government.

Dissident army officers seized power, Mar. 23, 1982, denouncing the Mar. 7 presidential election as fraudulent and pledging to restore "authentic democracy" to the nation. Political violence has caused some 200,000 Guatemalans to seek refuge in Mexico. A second military coup occurred Oct. 8, 1983. The nation returned to civilian rule in 1986.

Pres. Jorge Serrano Elias was ousted by the military June 1, 1993. Ramiro de Leon Carpio was elected president by Congress June 6. De Leon fired the defence minister and reassigned several military commanders.

Guinea

Republic of Guinea

République de Guinée

People: Population (1992 est.): 7,783,000. **Pop. density:** 81 per sq. mi. **Urban** (1991): 26%. **Ethnic groups:** Foulah 35%, Malinké 30%, Soussous 20%, 15 other tribes. **Languages:** French (official), Peul, Mande. **Religions:** Muslim 85%, Christian 10%.

Geography: Area: 94,964 sq. mi., slightly bigger than the UK. **Location:** On Atlantic coast of W. Africa. **Neighbors:** Guinea-Bissau, Senegal, Mali on N, C te d'Ivoire on E, Liberia on S. **Topography:** A narrow coastal belt leads to the mountainous middle region, the source of the Gambia, Senegal, and Niger rivers. Upper Guinea, farther inland, is a cooler upland. The SE is forested. **Capital:** Conakry. **Cities** (1989 est.): Conakry 705,000; Labe 273,000; N'Zerekore 250,000; Kankan 278,000.

Government: Type: Republic. **Head of state:** Pres. Brig. Gen. Lansana Conte; b. 1944; in office: Apr. 5, 1984. **Local divisions:** 33 administrative regions. **Defense** (1988): 1.2% of GDP.

Economy: Chief crops: Bananas, pineapples, rice, corn, palm nuts, coffee, honey. **Minerals:** Bauxite, iron, diamonds. **Arable land:** 6%. **Electricity prod.** (1991) 300 mln. kWh. **Labor force:** 82% agric.; 9% ind. & comm.

Finance: Monetary unit: Franc (Jan. 1993: 811 = $1 US). **Gross domestic product** (1990): $3.0 bln. **Per capita GDP:** $410. **Imports** (1990): $692 mln.; partners: U.S. 16%. **Exports** (1990): $788 mln.; partners: U.S. 33%. **National budget** (1990): $708 mln.

Transport: Motor vehicles (1989): 13,000 passenger cars, 13,000 comm. vehicles. **Chief port:** Conakry.

Communications: Radios: 1 per 34 persons. **Telephones:** 1 per 355 persons.

Health: Life expectancy at birth (1992): 41 male; 45 female. **Births** (per 1,000 pop. 1992): 46. **Deaths** (per 1,000 pop. 1992): 21. **Natural increase:** 2.5%. **Physicians:** 1 per 9,732 persons. **Infant mortality** (per 1,000 live births 1992): 144.

Education (1989): **Literacy:** 35% (in French). **School:** Compulsory for 8 years; attendance: 36% primary, 15% secondary.

Major International Organizations: UN and most specialized agencies, OAU.

Embassy: 51 rue de la Faisanderie, Paris 75016, France; 010 331 47048148.

Part of the ancient West African empires, Guinea fell under French control 1849-98. Under Sekou Toure, it opted for full independence in 1958, and France withdrew all aid.

Toure turned to communist nations for support and set up a militant one-party state.

Thousands of opponents were jailed in the 1970s, in the aftermath of an unsuccessful Portuguese invasion. Many were tortured and killed.

The military took control of the government in a bloodless coup after the March 1984 death of Toure. A new constitution was approved in 1991, in which full democracy was promised by 1996. In 1992 movement towards democracy was slow; although political parties were made legal, political demonstrations were banned.

Guinea-Bissau

Republic of Guinea-Bissau

Republica da Guiné-Bissau

People: Population (1992 est.): 1,074,000. **Pop. density:** 77 per sq. mi. **Ethnic groups:** Balante 27%, Fula 23%, Manjaca 11%, Mandinka 12%. **Languages:** Portuguese (official), Crioulo, tribal languages. **Religions:** Traditional 54%, Muslim 38%, Christian 8%.

Geography: Area: 13,948 sq. mi. about the size of Wales and N. Ireland combined. **Location:** On Atlantic coast of W. Africa. **Neighbors:** Senegal on N, Guinea on E, S. **Topography:** A swampy coastal plain covers most of the country; to the east is a low savanna region. **Capital:** Bissau, pop. (1988 est.) 138,000.

Government: Type: Republic. **Head of state:** Brig.-Gen. João Bernardo Vieira; b. 1939; in office: Nov. 14,1980. **Head of government:** Prime Min. Carlos Correira; in office Dec. 27, 1991. **Local divisions:** 9 regions. **Defense** (1987): 3.3% of GDP.

Economy: Chief crops: Peanuts, cotton, rice. **Minerals:** Bauxite. **Arable land:** 10%. **Electricity prod.** (1991): 30 mln. kWh. **Labor force:** 90% agric.

Finance: Monetary unit: Peso (Jan. 1993: 4,491 = $1 US). **Gross domestic product** (1989): $154 mln. **Per capita GDP** (1991): $160. **Imports** (1989): $69 mln.; partners: Port. 20%, It. 27%. **Exports** (1989): $14 mln.; partners: Port. 35%. **National budget** (1989): $30 mln. expenditures.

Transport: Motor vehicles (1990): 3,000 passenger cars, 2,500 comm. vehicles.

Communications: Radios: 1 per 27 persons. **Daily newspaper circ.** (1990): 12 per 1,000 pop.

Health: Life expectancy at birth (1992): 45 male; 48 female. **Births** (per 1,000 pop. 1992): 42. **Deaths** (per 1,000 pop. 1992): 18. **Natural increase:** 2.4%. **Infant mortality** (per 1,000 live births 1992): 125.

Education (1991): **Literacy:** 36%. **School:** Compulsory for 4 years.

Major International Organizations: UN, OAU.

Consulate: 8 Palace Gate, London W8; 071-589 5253.

Portuguese mariners explored the area in the mid-15th century; the slave trade flourished in the 17th and 18th centuries, and colonization began in the 19th.

Beginning in the 1960s, an independence movement waged a guerrilla war and formed a government in the interior that achieved international support. Full independence came Sept. 10, 1974, after the Portuguese regime was overthrown.

The November 1980 coup gave Vieira absolute power. He has initiated political liberalization.

Guyana

Co-operative Republic of Guyana

People: Population (1992 est.): 739,000. **Age distrib.** (%): 0–14: 33.4; 5–59: 60.7; 60+: 5.9. **Pop. density:** 9 per sq. mi. **Urban** (1990): 35%. **Ethnic groups:** East Indian 51%, African 30%; mixed 14%. **Languages:** English (official), Amerindian dialects. **Religions:** Christian 46%, Hindu 37%; Muslim 9%.

Geography: Area: 83,000 sq. mi., about the size of England and Scotland combined. **Location:** On N coast of S. America. **Neighbors:** Venezuela on W, Brazil on S, Suriname on E. **Topography:** Dense tropical forests cover much of the land, although a flat coastal area up to 40 mi. wide, where 90% of the population lives, provides rich alluvial soil for agriculture. A grassy savanna divides the 2 zones. **Capital:** Georgetown, pop. (1985 est.) 170,000.

Government: Type: Republic. **Head of state:** Pres. Cheddi Jagan; in office Oct. 9, 1992. **Head of government:** Prime Min. Sam Hinds; in office Oct. 9, 1992. **Local divisions:** 10 regions. **Defense** (1989): 6% of GDP.

Economy: Industries: Mining, textiles. **Chief crops:** Sugar, rice, citrus and other fruits. **Minerals:** Bauxite, diamonds. **Other resources:** Timber, shrimp. **Arable land:** 2%. **Electricity prod.** (1991): 647 bln. kWh. **Labor force:** 33% agric.; 45% ind. & comm.; 22% services.

Finance: Monetary unit: Dollar (Mar. 1993: 126 = $1 US). **Gross domestic product** (1991): $250 mln. **Per capita GDP:** $300. **Imports** (1991): $246 mln.; partners: U.S. 33%, CARICOM 10%. **Exports** (1991): $189 mln.; partners: UK 31%, U.S. 23%. **National budget** (1990): $250 mln. **International reserves less gold** (Feb. 1993): $185 mln. **Consumer prices** (change in 1992): 10.0%.

Transport: Motor vehicles (1990): 24,000 passenger cars, 9,000 comm. vehicles. **Chief port:** Georgetown.

Communications: Radios: 1 per 2.5 persons. **Telephones:** 1 per 47 persons. **Daily newspaper circ.** (1991): 53 per 1,000 pop.

Health: Life expectancy at birth (1992): 61 male; 68 female. **Births** (per 1,000 pop. 1992): 21. **Deaths** (per 1,000 pop. 1992): 7. **Natural increase:** 1.4% **Hospital beds:** 1 per 341 persons. **Physicians:** 1 per 6,809 persons. **Infant mortality** (per 1,000 live births 1992): 51.

Education (1991): **Literacy:** 95%. **School:** Compulsory from ages 5 to 14.

Major International Organizations: UN (GATT, ILO, IMF, World Bank), Commonwealth of Nations, OAS.

Embassy: 3 Palace Court, London W2 4LP; 071-229 7684.

Guyana became a Dutch possession in the 17th century, but sovereignty passed to Britain in 1814. Indentured servants from India soon outnumbered African slaves. Ethnic tension has affected political life.

Guyana became independent May 26, 1966. A Venezuelan claim to the western half of Guyana was suspended in 1970 but renewed in 1982. The Suriname border is also disputed. The government has nationalized most of the economy which has remained severely depressed.

The Port Kaituma ambush of U.S. Rep. Leo J. Ryan and others investigating mistreatment of American followers of the Rev. Jim Jones' People's Temple cult triggered a mass suicide-execution of 911 cultists at Jonestown in the Guyana jungle, Nov. 18, 1978.

The People's National Congress, the party in power since Guyana became independent, was voted out of office with the election of Cheddi Jagan in Oct. 1992.

Haiti

Republic of Haiti

République d'Haïti

People: Population (1992 est.): 6,431,000. **Age distrib.** (%): 4–14: 40.2; 15–59: 53.6; 60+: 6.2. **Pop. density:** 607 per sq. mi. **Urban** (1990): 29%. **Ethnic groups:** African descent 95%. **Languages:** French, Creole (both official). **Religions:** Roman Catholic 80%, Protestant 10%; Voodoo widely practised.

Geography: Area: 10,579 sq. mi., one-third the size of Scotland. **Location:** In West Indies, occupies western third of island of Hispaniola. **Neighbors:** Dominican Republic on E, Cuba on W. **Topography:** About two-thirds of Haiti is mountainous. Much of the rest is semiarid. Coastal areas are warm and moist. **Capital:** Port-au-Prince, pop. (1992 est.) 752,000.

Government: Type: In transition. **Head of government:** Prime Min. Robert Malval; in office Aug. 30, 1993. **Local divisions:** 9 departments. **Defense** (1990): 1.5% of GDP.

Economy: Industries: Sugar refining, textiles. **Chief crops:** Coffee, sugar, bananas, cocoa, tobacco, rice. **Minerals:** Bauxite. **Other resources:** Timber. **Arable land:** 20%. **Livestock** (1989): 1.5 mln. cattle; 1.2 mln. goats. **Electricity prod.** (1991): 468 mln. kWh. **Labor force:** 66% agric.; 9% ind. & comm.; 25% services.

Finance: Monetary unit: Gourde (Dec. 1992: 5.00 = $1 US). **Gross domestic product** (1990): $2.7 bln. **Per capita GDP** (1991): $440. **Imports** (1991): $347 mln.; partners: U.S. 64%. **Exports** (1991): $103 mln.; partners: U.S. 84%. **Tourism** (1991): $66 mln. receipts. **National budget** (1990): $416 mln. expenditures. **International reserves less gold** (Mar. 1993): $17.3 mln. **Gold:** 18,000 oz t. **Consumer prices** (change in 1991): 15.4%.

Transport: Motor vehicles (1989): 32,000 passenger cars, 21,000 comm. vehicles. **Chief ports:** Port-au-Prince, Les Cayes.

Communications: Television sets: 1 per 265 persons. **Radios:** 1 per 2.2 persons. **Telephones:** 1 per 79 persons. **Daily newspaper circ.** (1990): 8 per 1,000 pop.

Health: Life expectancy at birth (1992): 53 male; 55 female. **Births** (per 1,000 pop. 1992): 43. **Deaths** (per 1,000 pop. 1992): 15. **Natural increase:** 2.8%. **Hospital beds:** 1 per 1,258 persons. **Physicians:** 1 per 6,039 persons. **Infant mortality rate** (per 1,000 live births, 1992): 104.

Education (1989): **Literacy:** 53%.

Major International Organizations: UN and some of its specialized agencies, OAS.

Embassy: Closed since Mar. 30, 1987.

Haiti, visited by Columbus, 1492, and a French colony from 1677, attained its independence, 1804, following the rebellion led by former slave Toussaint L'Ouverture. Following a period of political violence, the U.S. occupied the country 1915-34.

Dr. François Duvalier was voted president in 1957; in 1964 he was named president for life. Upon his death in 1971, he was succeeded by his son, Jean-Claude. Drought in 1975-77 brought famine, and Hurricane Allen in 1980 destroyed most of the rice, bean, and coffee crops.

Following several weeks of unrest, President Jean-Claude Duvalier fled Haiti aboard a U.S. Air Force jet Feb. 7, 1986, ending the 28-year dictatorship by the Duvalier family. A military-civilian council headed by Gen. Henri Namphy assumed control. In 1987, voters approved a new constitution.

The Jan. 17, 1988 elections led to Leslie Manigat being named president; opposition leaders charged widespread fraud. Gen. Namphy seized control, June 20, and named himself president of a military government. Namphy was ousted by a military coup in Sept. By mid-1990, there had been 5 governments since Duvalier fled. Father Jean-Bertrand Aristide was elected President Dec. 1990.

A coup led by leaders of the Tonton Macoutes, the private militia of the Duvalier family, was crushed by loyalist army forces, Jan. 1991. The attempted coup sparked riots that left some 70 dead. In Sept. 1991, Aristide was arrested by the military and expelled from the country.

Some 35,000 Haitian refugees were intercepted by the U.S. Coast Guard as they tried to enter the U.S., 1991-92. Most were returned to Haiti despite protests by U.S. human rights and legal organizations.

The UN imposed a worldwide oil, arms and financial embargo on Haiti, June 23, 1993. The embargo was later suspended when the military agreed to Aristide's return to power on Oct. 30.

Honduras

Republic of Honduras

República de Honduras

People: Population (1992 est.): 5,092,000. **Age distrib.** (%): 0–14: 44.6; 15–59: 50.5; 60+: 4.9. **Pop. density:** 117 per sq. mi. **Urban** (1991): 41%. **Ethnic groups:** Mestizo 90%, Indian 7%. **Language:** Spanish (official). **Religion:** Roman Catholic 95%.

Geography: Area: 43,277 sq. mi., about half the size of GB. **Location:** In Central America. **Neighbors:** Guatemala on W, El Salvador, Nicaragua on S. **Topography:** The Caribbean coast is 500 mi. long. Pacific coast, on Gulf of Fonseca, is 40 mi. long. Honduras is mountainous, with wide fertile valleys and rich forests. **Capital:** Tegucigalpa. **Cities** (1989 est.): Tegucigalpa 550,000; San Pedro Sula 399,000.

Government: Type: Democratic constitutional republic. **Head of state:** Pres. Rafael Leonardo Callejas; in office Jan. 27, 1990. **Local divisions:** 18 departments. **Defense** (1992): 1.0% of GDP.

Economy: Industries: Textiles, wood prods. **Chief crops:** Bananas (chief export), coffee, corn, beans. **Minerals:** Gold, silver, copper, lead, zinc, iron, antimony, coal. **Other resources:** Timber. **Arable land:** 16%. **Livestock** (1990): 2.8 mln. cattle. **Electricity prod.** (1990): 2.0 bln. kWh. **Labor force:** 62% agric.; 20% services; 9% manuf.

Finance: Monetary unit: Lempira (Apr. 1993: 5.86 = $1 US). **Gross domestic product** (1991): $2.5 bln. **Per capita GDP:** $516. **Imports** (1991): $880 mln.; partners: U.S. 39%, Jap. 8%. **Exports** (1991): $808 mln.; partners: U.S. 54%, Europe 34%. **Tourism** (1990): $28 mln. receipts. **International reserves less gold** (Mar. 1993): $159 mln. **Gold:** 21,000 oz t. **Consumer prices** (change in 1992): 8.8%.

Transport: Motor vehicles (1990): 88,000 passenger cars, 18,000 comm. vehicles. **Civil aviation** (1990): 516 mln. passenger-km; 9 airports with scheduled flights. **Chief ports:** Puerto Cortes, La Ceiba.

Communications: Television sets: 1 per 24 persons. **Radios:** 1 per 2.4 persons. **Telephones:** 1 per 46 persons. **Daily newspaper circ.** (1989): 51 per 1,000 pop.

Health: Life expectancy at birth (1992): 65 male; 68 female. **Births** (per 1,000 pop. 1992): 38. **Deaths** (per 1,000 pop. 1992): 7. **Natural increase:** 3.0%. **Hospital beds:** 1 per 818 persons. **Physicians:** 1 per 1,586 persons. **Infant mortality** (per 1,000 live births 1992): 54.

Education (1992): **Literacy:** 73%. **School:** Compulsory for 6 years; attendance 70%.

Major International Organizations: UN, (IMF, WHO, ILO), OAS.

Embassy: 115 Gloucester Place, London W1H 3PJ; 071-486 4880.

Mayan civilization flourished in Honduras in the 1st millennium AD. Columbus arrived in 1502. Honduras became independent after freeing itself from Spain, 1821 and from the Fed. of Central America, 1838.

Gen. Oswaldo Lopez Arellano, president for most of the period 1963-75 by virtue of one election and 2 coups, was ousted by the army in 1975 over charges of pervasive bribery by United Brands Co. of the U.S.

The government has resumed land distribution, raised minimum wages, and started a literacy campaign. An elected civilian government took power in 1982.

Honduras is one of the poorest countries in the Western Hemisphere, although the economy improved in 1992.

In Sept. 1992 the World Court awarded to Honduras two-thirds of the land in dispute on its border with El Salvador.

Hungary

Republic of Hungary

Magyar Köztársaság

People: Population (1992 est.): 10,333,000. **Age distrib.** (%): 0–14: 20.8; 15–59: 60.5; 60+: 18.7. **Pop. density:** 287 per sq. mi. **Urban** (1990): 62%. **Ethnic groups:** Magyar 92%, Gypsy 3%, German 2.5%. **Language:** Hungarian (Magyar). **Religions:** Roman Catholic 67%, Protestant 25%.

Geography: Area: 35,919 sq. mi., about the size of Scotland and N. Ireland combined. **Location:** In East Central Europe. **Neighbors:** Slovakia, Ukraine on N, Austria on W, Slovenia, Yugoslavia, Croatia on S, Romania on E. **Topography:** The Danube R. forms the Slovak border in the NW, then swings S to bisect the country. The eastern half of Hungary is mainly a great fertile plain, the Alfold; the W and N are hilly. **Capital:** Budapest. **Cities** (1991 est.): Budapest 2,016,000; Miskolc 196,000; Debrecen 212,000.

Government: Type: Parliamentary democracy. **Head of state:** Pres. Arpad Goncz; in office May 2, 1990. **Head of government:** Prime Min. Jozsef Antall; in office May 3, 1990. **Local divisions:** 19 counties, 1 capital. **Defense** (1992): 1.7% of GDP.

Economy: Industries: Iron and steel, machinery, pharmaceuticals, vehicles, communications equip., milling, distilling. **Chief crops:** Grains, vegetables, fruits, grapes. **Minerals:** Bauxite, coal, natural gas. **Arable land:** 54%. **Livestock** (1990): 1.6 mln. cattle; 7.6 mln. pigs; 2.0 mln. sheep. **Electricity prod.** (1990): 30.4 bln. kWh. **Crude steel prod.** (1991): 1.8 mln. metric tons. **Labor force:** 19% agric.; 48% ind. & comm.; 27% services.

Finance: Monetary unit: Forint (Mar. 1993: 88 = $1 US). **Gross domestic product** (1991): $60.1 bln. **Per capita GDP:** $5,700. **Imports** (1991): $11.7 bln.; partners: CIS 34%, EC 21%. **Exports** (1991): $10.2 bln.; partners: CIS 30%, EC 32%. **National budget** (1992): $13.6 bln. **Tourism** (1990): $1 bln. receipts. **Consumer prices** (change in 1991): 34.0%.

Transport: Railroads (1990): 8,221 mi. long. **Motor vehicles** (1989): 1.9 mln. passenger cars, 223,000 comm. vehicles. **Civil aviation** (1990): 1.5 bln. passenger-km; 1 airport with scheduled flights.

Communications: Television sets: 1 per 2.5 persons. **Radios:** 1 per 1.7 persons. **Telephones:** 1 per 5.5 persons. **Daily newspaper circ.** (1990): 237 per 1,000 pop.

Health: Life expectancy at birth (1992): 66 male; 75 female. **Births** (per 1,000 pop. 1992): 12. **Deaths** (per 1,000 pop. 1992): 14. **Natural increase:** –.2%. **Hospital beds:** 1 per 99 persons. **Physicians:** 1 per 306 persons. **Infant mortality** (per 1,000 live births 1992): 14.0.

Education (1992): **Literacy:** 98%. **School:** Compulsory to age 16; attendance 96%.

Major International Organizations: UN (IMF, World Bank, GATT).

Embassy: 35 Eaton Place, London SW1X 8BY; 071-235 4048.

Earliest settlers, chiefly Slav and Germanic, were overrun by Magyars from the east. Stephen I (997-1038) was made king by Pope Sylvester II in AD 1000. The country suffered repeated Turkish invasions in the 15th-17th centuries. After the defeats of the Turks, 1686-1697, Austria dominated, but Hungary obtained concessions until it regained internal independence in 1867, with the emperor of Austria as king of Hungary in a dual monarchy with a single diplomatic service. Defeated with the Central Powers in 1918, Hungary lost Transylvania to Romania, Croatia and Bacska to Yugoslavia, Slovakia and Carpatho-Ruthenia to Czechoslovakia, all of which had large Hungarian minorities. A republic under Michael Karolyi and a bolshevist revolt under Bela Kun were followed by a vote for a monarchy in 1920 with Admiral Nicholas Horthy as regent.

Hungary joined Germany in World War II, and was allowed to annex most of its lost territories. Russian troops captured the country, 1944-1945. By terms of an armistice with the Allied powers Hungary agreed to give up territory acquired by the 1938 dismemberment of Czechoslovakia and to return to its borders of 1937.

A republic was declared Feb. 1, 1946; Zoltan Tildy was elected president. In 1947 the communists forced Tildy out. Premier Imre Nagy, in office since mid-1953, was ousted for his moderate policy of favoring agriculture and consumer production, April 18, 1955.

In 1956, popular demands for the ousting of Erno Gero, Communist Party secretary, and for formation of a government by Nagy, resulted in the latter's appointment Oct. 23; demonstrations against communist rule developed into open revolt. On Nov. 4 Soviet forces launched a massive attack against Budapest with 200,000 troops, 2,500 tanks and armored cars.

About 200,000 persons fled the country. Nagy was executed and thousands were arrested. In the spring of 1963 the regime freed many anti-communists and captives from the 1956 revolt in a sweeping amnesty.

Hungarian troops participated in the 1968 Warsaw Pact invasion of Czechoslovakia. Major economic reforms were launched early in 1968, switching from a central planning system to one in which market forces and profit control much of production.

In 1989 parliament passed legislation legalizing freedom of assembly and association as Hungary shifted away from communism toward democracy. In Oct. the Communist Party was formally dissolved. The last Soviet troops left Hungary June 19, 1991.

Iceland

Republic of Iceland

Lýoveldio Island

People: Population (1992 est.): 259,000. **Age distrib.** (%): 0–14: 25.5; 15–59: 60.1; 60+: 14.4. **Pop. density:** 6 per sq. mi. **Urban** (1991): 90%. **Ethnic groups:** Homogeneous, descendants of Norwegians, Celts. **Language:** Icelandic (Islenska). **Religion:** Evangelical Lutheran 95%.

Geography: Area: 39,769 sq. mi., the size of Scotland and Wales combined. **Location:** At N end of Atlantic O. **Neighbors:** Nearest is Greenland. **Topography:** Iceland is of recent volcanic origin. Three-quarters of the surface is wasteland: glaciers, lakes, a lava desert. There are geysers and hot springs, and the climate is moderated by the Gulf Stream. **Capital:** Reykjavik, pop. (1991 est.) 97,000.

Government: Type: Constitutional republic. **Head of state:** Pres. Vigdis Finnbogadottir; b. Apr. 15, 1930; in office Aug. 1, 1980. **Head of government:** Prime Min. David Oddsson; in office Apr. 30, 1991. **Local divisions:** 23 counties, 14 ind. towns.

Economy: Industries: Fish products (some 80% of exports), aluminum. **Chief crops:** Potatoes, turnips, hay. **Arable land:** 0.5%. **Livestock** (1991): 549,000 sheep. **Fish catch** (1991): 991,000 metric tons. **Electricity prod.** (1991): 5.1 bln. kWh. **Labor force:** 11% agric.; 55% comm. & services, 14% fisheries.

Finance: Monetary unit: Kronur (Mar. 1993: 64.12 = $1 US). **Gross domestic product** (1991): $4.2 bln. **Per capita GDP:** $16,300. **Imports** (1992): $1.7 bln.; partners: EC 50%. **Exports** (1992): $1.6 bln.; partners: EC 67%. **Tourism** (1991): $223 mln. receipts. **National budget** (1991): $1.9 bln. expenditures. **International reserves less gold** (Mar. 1993): $443 mln. **Gold:** 49,000 oz t. **Consumer prices** (change in 1992): 4.0%.

Transport: Motor vehicles (1991): 121,000 passenger cars, 16,000 comm. vehicles. **Civil aviation** (1991): 1.8 bln. passenger-km; 21 airports with scheduled flights. **Chief port:** Reykjavik.

Communications: Television sets: 1 per 3.3 persons. **Radios:** 1 per 1.6 persons. **Telephones:** 1 per 2.2 persons. **Daily newspaper circ.** (1990): 518 per 1,000 pop.

Health: Life expectancy at birth (1992): 76 male; 81 female. **Births** (per 1,000 pop. 1992): 17. **Deaths** (per 1,000 pop. 1992): 7. **Natural increase:** 1.0%. **Hospital beds:** 1 per 73 persons. **Physicians:** 1 per 373 persons. **Infant mortality** (per 1,000 live births 1992): 4.

Education (1992): **Literacy:** 99%. **School:** Compulsory for 8 years; attendance 99%.

Major International Organizations: UN (GATT), NATO, OECD.

Embassy: 1 Eaton Terrace, London SW1W 8EY; 071-730 5131.

Iceland was an independent republic from 930 to 1262, when it joined with Norway. Its language has maintained its purity for 1,000 years. Danish rule lasted from 1380-1918; the last ties with the Danish crown were severed in 1941. The Althing, or assembly, is the world's oldest surviving parliament.

India

Republic of India

Bharat

People: Population (1992 est.): 886,362,000. **Age distrib.** (%): 0–14: 36.8; 15–59: 56.4; 60+: 5.8. **Pop. density:** 700 per sq. mi. **Urban** (1991): 28%. **Ethnic groups:** Indo-Aryan groups 72%, Dravidians 25%, Mongoloids 3%. **Languages:** 16 languages, including Hindi (official) and English (associate official). **Religions:** Hindu 83%, Muslim 11%, Christian 3%, Sikh 2%.

Geography: Area: 1,266,595 sq. mi., 10 times the size of the Br. Isles. **Location:** Occupies most of the Indian subcontinent in S. Asia. **Neighbors:** Pakistan on W, China, Nepal, Bhutan on N, Myanmar, Bangladesh on E. **Topography:** The Himalaya Mts., highest in world, stretch across India's northern borders. Below, the Ganges Plain is wide, fertile, and among the most densely populated regions of the world. The area below includes the Deccan Peninsula. Close to one quarter the area is forested. The climate varies from tropical heat in S to near-Arctic cold in N. Rajasthan Desert is in NW; NE Assam Hills get 400 in. of rain a year. **Capital:** New Delhi. **Cities** (1991 est.): Calcutta 10.8 mln.; Bombay 12.5 mln.; New Delhi 8.3 mln.; Madras 5.3 mln.; Bangalore 4.1 mln.; Hyderabad 4.2 mln.

Government: Type: Federal republic. **Head of state:** Pres. Ramaswamy Venkataraman; b. Dec. 4, 1910; in office July 25, 1987. **Head of government:** Prime Min. P. V. Narasimha Rao; b. June 28, 1921; in office June 21, 1991. **Local divisions:** 25 states, 7 union territories. **Defense** (1991): 3.5% of GDP.

Economy: Industries: Textiles, steel, processed foods, cement, machinery, chemicals, fertilizers, consumer appliances, autos. **Chief crops:** Rice, grains, coffee, sugar cane, spices, tea, cashews, cotton, copra, coir, juta, linseed. **Minerals:** Chromium, coal, iron, manganese, mica salt, bauxite, gypsum, oil. **Crude oil reserves** (1991): 4.2 bln. bbls. **Other resources:** Rubber, timber. **Arable land:** 57%. **Livestock** (1989): 195 mln. cattle; 55 mln. sheep. **Fish catch** (1990): 3.6 mln. metric tons. **Electricity prod.** (1991): 290 bln. kWh. **Crude steel prod.** (1991): 16.3 mln. metric tons. **Labor force:** 70% agric.; 19% ind. & comm.

Finance: Monetary unit: Rupee (Aug. 1993: 31.03 = $1 US). **Gross domestic product** (1992): $328 bln. **Per capita GDP:** $380. **Imports** (1991): $25.2 bln.; partners: Jap. 8%, U.S. 12%, EC 33%. **Exports** (1991): $20.2 bln.; partners: U.S. 16%, EC 25%, CIS 19%. **Tourism** (1991): $1.4 bln. receipts. **National budget** (1992): $53.4 bln. expenditures. **International reserves less gold** (Mar. 1993): $6.7 bln. **Gold:** 11.3 mln. oz. t. **Consumer prices** (change in 1992): 11.8%.

Transport: Railroads (1991): 38,752 mi. long. **Motor vehicles** (1990): 2.3 mln. passenger cars, 1.4 mln. comm. vehicles. **Civil aviation** (1990): 16.5 bln. passenger-km; 98 airports with scheduled flights. **Chief ports:** Calcutta, Bombay, Madras, Cochin, Vishakhapatnam.

Communications: Television sets: 1 per 44 persons. **Radios:** 1 per 15 persons. **Telephones:** 1 per 200 persons. **Daily newspaper circ.** (1988): 21 per 1,000 pop.

Health: Life expectancy at birth (1992): 57 male; 58 female. **Births** (per 1,000 pop. 1992): 30. **Deaths** (per 1,000 pop. 1992): 11. **Natural increase:** 1.9%. **Hospital beds:** 1 per 1,314 persons. **Physicians:** 1 per 2,337 persons. **Infant mortality** (per 1,000 live births 1992): 81.

Education (1991): **Literacy:** 48%. **School:** Compulsory to age 14.

Major International Organizations: UN (IMF, World Bank).

High Commission: India House, Aldwych, London WC2B 4NA; 071-836 8484.

India has one of the oldest civilizations in the world. Excavations trace the Indus Valley civilization back for at least 5,000 years. Paintings in the mountain caves of Ajanta, richly carved temples, the Taj Mahal in Agra, and the Kutab Minar in Delhi are among relics of the past.

Aryan tribes, speaking Sanskrit, invaded from the NW around 1500 BC, and merged with the earlier inhabitants to create classical Indian civilization.

Asoka ruled most of the Indian subcontinent in the 3d century BC, and established Buddhism. But Hinduism revived and eventually predominated. During the Gupta kingdom, 4th-6th century AD, science, literature, and the arts enjoyed a "golden age."

Arab invaders established a Muslim foothold in the W in the 8th century, and Turkish Muslims gained control of North India by 1200. The Mogul emperors ruled 1526-1857.

Vasco de Gama established Portuguese trading posts 1498-1503. The Dutch followed. The British East India Co. sent Capt. William Hawkins, 1609, to get concessions from the Mogul emperor for spices and textiles. Operating as the East India Co. the British gained control of most of India. The British parliament assumed political direction; under Lord Bentinck, 1828-35, rule by rajahs was curbed. After the Sepoy troops mutinied, 1857-58, the British supported the native rulers.

Nationalism grew rapidly after World War I. The Indian National Congress and the Muslim League demanded constitutional reform. A leader emerged in Mohandas K. Gandhi (called Mahatma, or Great Soul), born Oct. 2, 1869, assassinated Jan. 30, 1948. He advocated self-rule, non-violence, removal of untouchability. In 1930 he launched "civil disobedience," including boycott of British goods and rejection of taxes without representation.

In 1935 Britain gave India a constitution providing a bicameral federal congress. Mohammed Ali Jinnah, head of the Muslim League, sought creation of a Muslim nation, Pakistan.

The British government partitioned British India into the dominions of India and Pakistan. India became a self-governing member of the Commonwealth and a member of the UN. It became a democratic republic, Jan. 26, 1950.

More than 12 million Hindu & Muslim refugees crossed the India-Pakistan borders in a mass transferral of some of the 2 peoples during 1947; about 200,000 were killed in communal fighting.

After Pakistan troops began attacks on Bengali separatists in East Pakistan, Mar. 25, 1971, some 10 million refugees fled into India. India and Pakistan went to war Dec. 3, 1971, on both the East and West fronts. Pakistan troops in the east surrendered Dec. 16; Pakistan agreed to a cease-fire in the west Dec. 17. In Aug. 1973 India released 93,000 Pakistanis held prisoner since 1971. The 2 countries resumed full relations in 1976.

In 2 days of carnage, the Bengali population of the village of Mandai, Tripura State, 700 people, were massacred in a raid by indigenous tribal residents of the area, June 8-9, 1980. A similar year-long campaign against Bengali immigrants had been going on in Assam State.

Mrs. Indira Gandhi, was named prime minister Jan. 19, 1966. Threatened with adverse court rulings in a voting law case, and opposition protest campaign and strikes, Gandhi invoked emergency provisions of the constitution June, 1975. Thousands of opponents were arrested and press censorship imposed. Measures to control prices, protect small farmers, and improve productivity were adopted.

The emergency, especially enforcement of coercive birth control measures in some areas, and the prominent extra-constitutional role of Indira Gandhi's son Sanjay, was widely resented. Opposition parties, united in the Janata coalition, scored massive victories in federal and state parliamentary elections in 1977, turning Gandhi's New Congress Party from power.

Gandhi became prime minister for the second time, Jan. 14, 1980. She was assassinated by 2 of her Sikh bodyguards Oct. 31, 1984. Widespread rioting followed. Thousands of Sikhs were killed and some 50,000 left homeless. The assassination was in response to the government supression of a Sikh uprising in Punjab in June 1984 which included an assault on the Golden Temple, the holiest Sikh shrine. Rajiv, her son, replaced her as prime minister. He was swept from office in 1989 amid charges of incompetence and corruption. He was assassinated May 21, 1991 during an election campaign to regain the prime ministership.

Sikhs ignited several violent clashes during the 1980s. The government's May 1987 decision to bring the state of Punjab under the rule of the central government led to violence. Many died during a government siege of the Golden Temple at Amritsar, May 1988.

In the biggest wave of criminal violence in Indian history, a series of bombings jolted Bombay and Calcutta, Mar. 12–19, 1993, leaving over 300 dead and some 1,200 injured. The explosions came in the wake of nationwide riots prompted by the destruction of a 16th-century mosque by Hindu militants in Dec. 1992.

Sikkim, bordered by Tibet, Bhutan and Nepal, formerly British protected, became a protectorate of India in 1950. Area, 2,740 sq. mi.; pop. 1991 cen. 405,000; capital, Gangtok. In Sept. 1974 India's parliament voted to make Sikkim an associate Indian state, absorbing it into India.

Kashmir, a predominantly Muslim region in the NW, has been in dispute between India and Pakistan since 1947. A cease-fire was negotiated by the UN Jan. 1, 1949; it gave Pakistan control of one-third of the area, in the west and northwest, and India the remaining two-thirds, the Indian state of Jammu and Kashmir, which enjoys internal autonomy.

In 1990 and 1991, there were repeated clashes between Indian army troops and pro-independence demonstrators triggered by India's decision to impose central government rule. The clashes strained relations between India and Pakistan which India charged was aiding the Muslim separatists.

France, 1952-54, peacefully yielded to India its 5 colonies, former French India, comprising Pondicherry, Karikal, Mahe, Yanaon (which became Pondicherry Union Territory, area 185 sq. mi., pop. 1991, 807,000) and Chandernagor (which was incorporated into the state of West Bengal).

Indonesia

Republic of Indonesia

Republik Indonesia

People: Population (1992 est.): 195,000,000. **Age distrib.** (%): 0–14: 39.2; 15–59: 56.5; 60+: 5.3. **Pop. density:** 262 per sq. mi. **Urban** (1991): 31%. **Ethnic groups:** Malay, Chinese, Irianese. **Languages:** Bahasa Indonesian (Malay) (official), Javanese, other Austronesian languages. **Religion:** Muslim 88%.

Geography: Area: 735,268 sq. mi., about 6 times bigger than the Br. Isles. **Location:** Archipelago SE of Asia along the Equator. **Neighbors:** Malaysia on N, Papua New Guinea on E. **Topography:** Indonesia comprises some 17,000 islands, including Java (one of the most densely populated areas in the world with 1,500 persons to the sq. mi.), Sumatra, Kalimantan (most of Borneo), Sulawesi (Celebes), and West Irian (Irian Jaya, the W. half of New Guinea). Also: Bangka, Billiton, Madura, Bali, Timor. The mountains and plateaus on the major islands have a cooler climate than the tropical lowlands. **Capital:** Jakarta. **Cities** (1988 est.): Jakarta 8,800,000; Surabaya 2,500,000; Bandung 1,400,000; Medan 1,700,000.

Government: Type: Republic. **Head of state:** Pres. Suharto; b. June 8, 1921; in office Mar. 6, 1967. **Local divisions:** 24 provinces, 3 special regions. **Defense** (1992): 2.0% of GDP.

Economy: Industries: Food processing, textiles, cement, light industry. **Chief crops:** Rice, coffee, sugar. **Minerals:** Nickel, tin, oil, bauxite, copper, natural gas. **Crude oil reserves** (1991): 10.7 bln. bbls. **Other resources:** Rubber. **Arable land:** 8%. **Livestock** (1989): 6.5 mln. cattle; 5.4 mln. sheep. **Fish catch** (1990): 3.1 mln. metric tons. **Electricity prod.** (1991): 38 bln. kWh. **Crude steel prod.** (1991): 3 mln. metric tons. **Labor force:** 56% agric.; 23% ind. & comm.; 16% services.

Finance: Monetary unit: Rupiah (Aug. 1993: 2,096 = $1 US). **Gross domestic product** (1991): $122 bln. **Per capita GDP:** $630. **Imports** (1991): $25.8 bln.; partners: Jap. 23%, U.S. 12%, Sing. 6%. **Exports** (1991): $29.5 bln.; partners: Jap. 41%, U.S. 16%, Sing. 10%. **Tourism** (1990): $1.8 bln. receipts. **National budget** (1991): $23.4 bln. **International reserves less gold** (Feb. 1993): $10.8 bln. **Gold:** 3.11 mln. oz t. **Consumer prices** (change in 1992): 7.5%.

Transport: Railroads (1989): 7.8 bln. passenger-km. **Motor vehicles** (1991): 1.3 mln. passenger cars, 1.5 mln. comm. vehicles. **Civil aviation** (1991): 12.7 bln. passenger-km; 116 airports. **Chief ports:** Jakarta, Surabaya, Medan, Palembang, Semarang.

Communications: Television sets: 1 per 24 persons. **Radios:** 1 per 8 persons. **Telephones:** 1 per 172 persons.

Health: Life expectancy at birth (1992): 59 male; 64 female. **Births** (per 1,000 pop. 1992): 26. **Deaths** (per 1,000 pop. 1992): 8. **Natural increase:** 1.8%. **Hospital beds:** 1 per 1,485 persons. **Physicians:** 1 per 7,427 persons. **Infant mortality** (per 1,000 live births 1992): 70.

Education (1990): **Literacy:** 85%. **School:** 84% attend primary school.

Major International Organizations: UN and all of its specialized agencies, ASEAN, OPEC.

Embassy: 38 Grosvenor Sq, London W1X 9LL; 071-499 7661.

Hindu and Buddhist civilization from India reached the peoples of Indonesia nearly 2,000 years ago, taking root especially in Java. Islam spread along the maritime trade routes in the 15th century, and became predominant by the 16th century. The Dutch replaced the Portuguese as the most important European trade power in the area in the 17th century. They secured territorial control over Java by 1750. The outer islands were not finally subdued until the early 20th century, when the full area of present-day Indonesia was united under one rule for the first time.

Following Japanese occupation, 1942-45, nationalists led by Sukarno and Hatta proclaimed a republic. The Netherlands ceded sovereignty Dec. 27, 1949, after 4 years of fighting. West Irian, on New Guinea, remained under Dutch control.

After the Dutch in 1957 rejected proposals for new negotiations over West Irian, Indonesia stepped up the seizure of Dutch property. A U.S. mediator's plan was adopted in 1962. In 1963 the UN turned the area over to Indonesia, which promised a plebiscite. In 1969, voting by tribal chiefs favored staying with Indonesia, despite an uprising and widespread opposition.

Sukarno suspended Parliament in 1960, and was named president for life in 1963. Russian-armed Indonesian troops staged raids in 1964 and 1965 into Malaysia, whose formation Sukarno had opposed.

Indonesia's Communist Party tried to seize control in 1965; the army smashed the coup. In parts of Java, communists seized several districts before being defeated; over 300,000 communists were executed.

Gen. Suharto, head of the army, was named president in 1968 and was re-elected for a 6th consecutive 5-year term in 1993. A coalition of his supporters won a strong majority in House elections in 1971. Muslim opposition parties made gains in 1977 elections but lost ground in the 1982 elections. The military retains a predominant political role.

In 1966 Indonesia and Malaysia signed an agreement ending hostility.

Oil export earnings and political stability have made Indonesia's economy stable.

Iran

Islamic Republic of Iran

Jomhori-e-Islami-e-Irân

People: Population (1992 est.): 61,183,000. **Age distrib.** (%): 0–14: 43.8; 15–59: 50.4; 60+: 5.8. **Pop. density:** 96 per sq. mi. **Urban** (1990): 57%. **Ethnic groups:** Persian 51%, Azerbaijani 25%, Kurds 9%. **Languages:** Farsi (official), Turkmen, Kurdish, Arabic. **Religion:** Shi'a Muslim 95%.

Geography: Area: 636,293 sq. mi., 5 times larger than the Br. Isles. **Location:** Between the Middle East and S. Asia. **Neighbors:** Turkey, Iraq on W, Armenia, Azerbaijan, Turkmenistan on N, Afghanistan, Pakistan on E. **Topography:** Interior highlands and plains are surrounded by high mountains, up to 18,000 ft. Large salt deserts cover much of the area, but there are many oases and forest areas. Most of the population inhabits the N and NW. **Capital:** Tehran. **Cities** (1986 cen.): Tehran 6,022,000; Esfahan 1,001,000; Mashhad 1,466,000; Tabriz 994,000; Shiraz 848,000.

Government: Type: Islamic republic. **Religious head:** Ayatollah Sayyed Ali Khamenei; b. 1939; in office June 4, 1989. **Head of state:** Pres. Hashemi Rafsanjani; in office Aug 3, 1989. **Local divisions:** 24 provinces. **Defense** (1991): 15% of GNP.

Economy: Industries: Cement, sugar refining, carpets. **Chief crops:** Grains, rice, fruits, sugar beets, cotton, grapes. **Minerals:** Chromium, oil, gas. **Crude oil reserves** (1991): 63 bln. barrels. **Other resources:** Gums, wool, silk, caviar. **Arable land:** 9%. **Livestock** (1990): 8.3 mln. cattle; 34.0 mln. sheep. **Electricity prod.** (1990): 40 bln. kWh. **Labor force:** 33% agric.; 21% ind. & comm; 27% services.

Finance: Monetary unit: Rial (Mar. 1993: 67.07 = $1 US). **Gross national product** (1991): $90 bln. **Per capita GNP:** $1,500. **Imports** (1991): $21.6 bln.; partners: Ger. 20%, Jap. 10%, UK 6%. **Exports** (1991): $15.9 bln.; partners: Jap. 13%, Neth. 12%. **National budget** (1990): $80 bln. expenditures.

Transport: Motor vehicles (1990): 2.0 mln. passenger cars, 472,000 comm. vehicles. **Civil aviation** (1990): 5.5 bln. passenger-km.; 17 airports. **Chief port:** Bandar Abbas.

Communications: Television sets: 1 per 23 persons. **Radios:** 1 per 4.7 persons. **Telephones:** 1 per 25 persons. **Daily newspaper circ.** (1990): 13 per 1,000 pop.

Health: Life expectancy at birth (1992): 64 male; 66 female. **Births** (per 1,000 pop. 1992): 44. **Deaths** (per 1,000 pop. 1992): 10. **Natural increase:** 3.4%. **Hospital beds:** 1 per 653 persons. **Physicians:** 1 per 2,882 persons. **Infant mortality** (per 1,000 live births 1992): 66.

Education (1990): **Literacy:** 54%.

Major International Organizations: UN (IMF, WHO), OPEC.

Embassy: 27 Princes Gate, London SW7 1PX; 071-584 8101.

Iran was once called Persia. The Iranians, who supplanted an earlier agricultural civilization, came from the E during the 2d millennium BC; they were an Indo-European group related to the Aryans of India.

In 549 BC Cyrus the Great united the Medes and Persians in the Persian Empire, conquered Babylonia in 538 BC, restored Jerusalem to the Jews. Alexander the Great conquered Persia in 333 BC, but Persians regained their independence in the next century under the Parthians, themselves succeeded by Sassanian Persians in 226 AD. Arabs brought Islam to Persia in the 7th century, replacing the indigenous Zoroastrian faith. After Persian political and cultural autonomy was reasserted in the 9th century, the arts and sciences flourished for several centuries.

Turks and Mongols ruled Persia in turn from the 11th century to 1502, when a native dynasty reasserted full independence. The British and Russian empires vied for influence in the 19th century, and Afghanistan was severed from Iran by Britain in 1857.

Reza Khan abdicated as Shah, 1941, and was succeeded by his son, Mohammad Reza Pahlavi. Under his rule, Iran underwent economic and social change but political opposition was not tolerated.

Conservative Moslem protests led to 1978 violence. Martial law in 12 cities was declared Sept. 8. A military government was appointed Nov. 6 to deal with striking oil workers. Prime Min. Shahpur Bakhtiar was designated by the shah to head a regency council in his absence. The shah left Iran Jan. 16, 1979.

Exiled religious leader Ayatollah Ruhollah Khomeini named a provisional government council in preparation for his return to Iran, Jan. 31. Clashes between Khomeini's supporters and government troops culminated in a rout of Iran's elite Imperial Guard Feb. 11, leading to the fall of Bakhtiar's government.

The Iranian revolution was marked by revolts among the ethnic minorities and by a continuing struggle between the clerical forces and westernized intellectuals and liberals. The Islamic Constitution established final authority to be vested in a Faghi, the Ayatollah Khomeini.

Iranian militants seized the U.S. embassy, Nov. 4, 1979, and took hostages including 62 Americans. Despite international condemnations and U.S. efforts, including an abortive Apr., 1980, rescue attempt, the crisis continued. The U.S. broke diplomatic relations with Iran, Apr. 7th. The shah died in Egypt, July 27th. The hostage drama finally ended Jan. 21, 1981 when an accord, involving the release of frozen Iranian assets, was reached.

A dispute over the Shatt al-Arab waterway that divides the two countries brought Iran and Iraq, Sept. 22, 1980, into open warfare. Iraqi planes attacked Iranian air fields including Teheran airport. Iranian planes bombed Iraqi bases. Iraqi troops occupied Iranian territory including the port city of Khorramshahr in October. Iranian troops recaptured the city and drove Iraqi troops back across the border, May 1982. Iraq, and later Iran, attacked several oil tankers in the Persian Gulf during 1984. Saudi Arabian war planes shot down 2 Iranian jets, June 5, which they felt were threatening Saudi shipping. In Aug. 1988, Iran agreed to accept a UN resolution calling for a ceasefire.

In Nov. 1986, senior U.S. officials secretly visited Iran and exchanged arms for Iran's help in obtaining the release of U.S. hostages held by terrorists in Lebanon. The exchange sparked a major scandal in the Reagan administration.

A U.S. Navy warship shot down an Iranian commercial airliner, July 3, 1988, after mistaking it for an F-14 fighter jet; all 290 aboard the plane died.

A major earthquake struck northern Iran June 21, 1990, killing over 45,000, injuring 100,000, and leaving 400,000 homeless. A U.S. offer of assistance was accepted by the Iranian government.

Some one million Kurdish refugees crossed Iran's border to escape Iraqi forces following the Persian Gulf War.

Iraq

Republic of Iraq

al Jumhouriya al 'Iraqia

People: Population (1992 est.): 18,445,000. **Age distrib.** (%): 0–14: 44.5; 15–59: 50.3; 60+: 5.2. **Pop. density:** 109 per sq. mi. **Urban** (1991): 70%. **Ethnic groups:** Arabs, 75% Kurds, 15% Turks. **Languages:** Arabic (official), Kurdish. **Religions:** Muslim 95% (Shiites 60%, Sunnis 35%), Christian 5%.

Geography: Area: 167,924 sq. mi., 3 times bigger than England. **Location:** In the Middle East, occupying most of historic Mesopotamia. **Neighbors:** Jordan, Syria on W, Turkey on N, Iran on E, Kuwait, Saudi Arabia on S. **Topography:** Mostly an alluvial plain, including the Tigris and Euphrates rivers, descending from mountains in N to desert in SW. Persian Gulf region is marshland. **Capital:** Baghdad. **Cities** (1985 est.): Baghdad (metro.) 3,400,000, Basra 616,000, Mosul 570,000.

Government: Type: Republic. **Head of state:** Pres. Saddam Hussein At-Takriti, b. Apr. 29, 1937; in office July 16, 1979. **Local divisions:** 18 provinces. **Defense** (1990): 18% of GNP.

Economy: Industries: Textiles, petrochemicals, oil refining, cement. **Chief crops:** Grains, rice, dates, cotton. **Minerals:** Oil, gas. **Crude oil reserves** (1991): 100 bln. barrels. **Other resources:** Wool, hides. **Arable land:** 13%. **Livestock** (1991): 1.5 mln. cattle; 9.6 mln. sheep; 1.4 mln. goats. **Electricity prod.** (1991): 3.8 bln. kWh. **Labor force:** 48% services; 30% agric.; 22% ind.

Finance: Monetary unit: Dinar (Mar. 1993: .31 = $1 US). **Gross national product** (1989): $35 bln. **Per capita GNP:** $1,950. **Imports** (1990): $6.6 bln.; partners: Tur., U.S. **Exports** (1990): $10.4 bln.; partners: U.S., Tur., Jap. **National budget** (1990): $35 bln. expenditures.

Transport: Railroads (1991): 1,484 mi. long. **Motor vehicles** (1991): 744,000 passenger cars, 295,000 comm. vehicles. **Chief port:** Basra.

Communications: Television sets: 1 per 18 persons. **Radios:** 1 per 5 persons. **Telephones:** 1 per 25 persons. **Daily newspaper circ.** (1990): 32 per 1,000 pop.

Health: Life expectancy at birth (1992): 62 male; 64 female. **Births** (per 1,000 pop. 1992): 45. **Deaths** (per 1,000 pop. 1992): 8. **Natural increase:** 3.8%. **Hospital beds:** 1 per 586 persons. **Physicians:** 1 per 1,922 persons. **Infant mortality** (per 1,000 live births 1992): 84.

Major International Organizations: UN (IMF, ILO), Arab League, OPEC.

Education (1991): **Literacy:** 60%. **School:** Compulsory ages 6 to 12.

Embassy: 22 Queen's Gate, London SW7 5JE; 071-584 7141.

The Tigris-Euphrates valley, formerly called Mesopotamia, was the site of one of the earliest civilizations in the world. The Sumerian city-states of 3,000 BC originated the culture later developed by the Semitic Akkadians, Babylonians, and Assyrians.

Mesopotamia ceased to be a separate entity after the conquests of the Persians, Greeks, and Arabs. The latter founded Baghdad, from where the caliph ruled a vast empire in the 8th and 9th centuries. Mongol and Turkish conquests led to a decline in population, the economy, cultural life, and the irrigation system.

Britain secured a League of Nations mandate over Iraq after World War I. Independence under a king came in 1932. A leftist, pan-Arab revolution established a republic in 1958, which oriented foreign policy toward the USSR. Most industry has been nationalized, and large land holdings broken up.

A local faction of the international Baath Arab Socialist party has ruled by decree since 1968. Russia and Iraq signed an aid pact in 1972, and arms were sent along with several thousand advisers. The 1978 execution of 21 communists and a shift of trade to the West signalled a more neutral policy, straining relations with the USSR. In the 1973 Arab-Israeli war Iraq sent forces to aid Syria. Within a month of assuming power, Saddam Hussein instituted a bloody purge in the wake of a reported coup attempt against the new regime.

Years of battling with the Kurdish minority resulted in total defeat for the Kurds in 1975, when Iran withdrew support. The fighting led to Iraqi bombing of Kurdish villages in Iran, causing relations with Iran to deteriorate.

After skirmishing intermittently for 10 months over the sovereignty of the disputed Shatt al-Arab waterway that divides the two countries, Iraq and Iran, Sept. 22, 1980, entered into open warfare when Iraqi fighter-bombers attacked 10 Iranian airfields, including Teheran airport, and Iranian planes retaliated with strikes on 2 Iraqi bases. In the following days, there was heavy ground fighting around Abadan and the adjacent port of Khorramshahr as Iraq pressed its attack on Iran's oil-rich province of Khuzistan. In May 1982, Iraqi troops were driven back across the border.

Israeli airplanes destroyed a nuclear reactor near Baghdad on June 7, 1981, claiming that it could be used to produce nuclear weapons.

Iraq and Iran expanded their war to the Persian Gulf in Apr. 1984. There were several attacks on oil tankers. An Iraqi warplane launched a missile attack on the U.S.S. *Stark*, a U.S. Navy frigate on patrol in the Persian Gulf, May 17, 1987; 37 U.S. sailors died. Iraq apologized for the attack, claiming it was inadvertent. The fierce war ended Aug. 1988, when Iraq accepted a UN resolution for a ceasefire.

Iraq attacked and overran Kuwait Aug. 2, 1990, sparking an international crisis. The United Nations, Aug. 6, imposed a ban on all trade with Iraq and called on member countries to protect the assets of the legitimate government of Kuwait. Iraq declared Kuwait its 19th province, Aug. 28. A campaign of looting, murder, and pillage was mounted against Kuwaiti civilians. Westerners caught in Iraq and Kuwait were initially held as hostages, but by the end of 1990, all were released.

A U.S.-led coalition launched air and missile attacks on Iraq, Jan. 16, 1991, after the expiration of a UN Security Council deadline for Iraq to withdraw from Kuwait. Iraq retaliated by firing scud missiles at Saudi Arabia and Israel. The coalition began a ground attack to retake Kuwait Feb. 23. Iraqi forces showed little resistance and were soundly defeated in 4 days. Some 175,000 Iraqis were taken prisoner, and casualties were estimated at over 85,000. As part of the ceasefire agreement, Iraq agreed to scrap all poison gas and germ weapons and allow UN observers to inspect the sites. UN trade sanctions would remain in effect until Iraq complied.

Tensions heightened over the UN's efforts to dismantle Iraq's arms-production program, July 5, 1992, when a UN inspection team was denied entrance to a ministry building in Baghdad. Iraq allowed the inspection team access to the building July 26; the team found no arms-related evidence.

In the aftermath of the war, there were revolts against Pres. Saddam Hussein throughout Iraq. In Feb., Iraqi troops drove Kurdish insurgents and civilians to the Iran and Turkey borders, causing a refugee crisis. Britain and allies established havens inside Iraq for the Kurds.

The U.S. launched a missile attack aimed at Iraq's intelligence headquarters in Baghdad June 26, 1993. The U.S. justified the attack by citing evidence that Iraq had sponsored a plot to assassinate former Pres. George Bush during his visit to Kuwait in April.

Ireland

Eire

People: Population (1992 est.): 3,521,000. **Age distrib. (%):** 0–14: 30.5; 15–59: 54.5; 60+30 :15.0. **Pop. density:** 129 per sq. mi. **Urban** (1990): 57%. **Ethnic groups:** Celtic, English minority. **Languages:** English predominates, Irish (Gaelic) spoken by minority. **Religions:** Roman Catholic 95%, Anglican 3%.

Geography: Area: 27,558 sq. mi. **Location:** In the Atlantic O. just W of Great Britain. **Neighbors:** United Kingdom (Northern Ireland). **Topography:** Ireland consists of a central plateau surrounded by isolated groups of hills and mountains. The coastline is heavily indented by the Atlantic O. **Capital:** Dublin. **Cities** (1991 est.): Dublin 502,000; Cork (metro.) 133,000.

Government: Type: Parliamentary republic. **Head of state:** Pres. Mary Robinson; in office Dec. 3, 1990. **Head of government:** Prime Min. Albert Reynolds; b. 1935; in office Feb. 11, 1992. **Local divisions:** 26 counties. **Defense** (1990): 1.6% of GDP.

Economy: Industries: Food processing, textiles, chemicals, brewing, machinery, tourism. **Chief crops:** Potatoes, grain, sugar beets, fruits, vegetables. **Minerals:** Zinc, lead, silver, gas. **Arable land:** 14%. **Livestock** (1990): 5.6 mln. cattle; 961,000 pigs; 4.9 mln. sheep. **Fish catch** (1990): 247,000 metric tons. **Electricity prod.** (1991): 14.4 bln. kWh. **Labor force:** 15% agric.; 29% ind. 51% services.

Finance: Monetary unit: Punt (June 1993: .69 = $1 US). **Gross domestic product** (1991): $39.2 bln. **Per capita GDP:** $11,200. **Imports** (1991): $24.5 bln.; partners: UK 41%, U.S. 14%, other EC 25%. **Exports** (1991): $27.8 bln.; partners: UK 34%, other EC 40%, US 8%. **Tourism** (1990): $1.4 bln. receipts. **National budget** (1992): $12.6 bln. expenditures. **International reserves less gold** (Mar. 1993): $5.0 bln. **Gold:** 360,000 oz. t. **Consumer prices** (change in 1992): 3.2%.

Transport: Railroads (1991): 2,814 km. long. **Motor vehicles** (1990): 796,000 passenger cars, 147,000 comm. vehicles. **Civil aviation** (1990): 3.8 bln. passenger-km; 11 airports. **Chief ports:** Dublin, Cork.

Communications: Television sets: 1 per 3.8 persons. **Radios:** 1 per 1.7 persons. **Telephones:** 1 per 3.8 persons. **Daily newspaper circ.** (1991): 179 per 1,000 pop.

Health: Life expectancy at birth (1992): 72 male; 78 female. **Births** (per 1,000 pop. 1992): 15. **Deaths** (per 1,000 pop. 1992): 9. **Natural increase:** .6%. **Hospital beds:** 1 per 257 persons. **Physicians:** 1 per 681 persons. **Infant mortality** (per 1,000 live births 1992): 8.

Education (1991): **Literacy:** 99%. **School:** Compulsory for 9 years; attendance 91%.

Major International Organizations: UN (GATT, IMF, World Bank), EC, OECD.

Embassy: 17 Grosvenor Pl, London SW1X 7HR; 071-235 2171.

Celtic tribes invaded the islands about the 4th century BC; their Gaelic culture and literature flourished and spread to Scotland and elsewhere in the 5th century AD, the same century in which St. Patrick converted the Irish to Christianity. Invasions by Norsemen began in the 8th century, ended with defeat of the Danes by the Irish King Brian Boru in 1014. English invasions started in the 12th century; for over 700 years the Anglo-Irish struggle continued with bitter rebellions and savage repressions.

The Easter Monday Rebellion (1916) failed but was followed by guerrilla warfare and harsh reprisals by British troops, the "Black and Tans." The Dail Eireann, or Irish parliament, reaffirmed independence in Jan. 1919. The British offered dominion status to Ulster (6 counties) and southern Ireland (26 counties) Dec. 1921. The constitution of the Irish Free State, a British dominion, was adopted Dec. 11, 1922. Northern Ireland remained part of the United Kingdom.

A new constitution adopted by plebiscite came into operation Dec. 29, 1937. It declared the name of the state Eire in the Irish language (Ireland in the English) and declared it a sovereign democratic state.

On Dec. 21, 1948, an Irish law declared the country a republic rather than a dominion and withdrew it from the Commonwealth. The British Parliament recognized both actions, 1949, but reasserted its claim to incorporate the 6 northeastern counties in the United Kingdom. This claim has not been recognized by Ireland. *(See United Kingdom — Northern Ireland.)*

Irish governments have favoured peaceful unification of all Ireland. Ireland cooperated with Britain against terrorist groups.

Ireland suffered economic hardship in the 1980s; unemployment was over 20% in 1992.

Israel

State of Israel

Medinat Israel

People: Population (1992 est.): 4,748,000. **Age distrib.** (%): 0–14: 32.4; 15–59: 55.3; 60+: 13.3. **Pop. density:** 605 per sq. mi. **Urban** (1990): 89%. **Ethnic groups:** Jewish 83%, Arab 16%. **Languages:** Hebrew and Arabic (official). **Religions:** Jewish 83%, Muslim 13%.

Geography: Area: 7,847 sq. mi., about the size of Wales. **Location:** On eastern end of Mediterranean Sea. **Neighbors:** Lebanon on N, Syria, Jordan on E, Egypt on W. **Topography:** The Mediterranean coastal plain is fertile and well watered. In the center is the Judean Plateau. A triangular-shaped semi-desert region, the Negev, extends from south of Beersheba to an apex at the head of the Gulf of Aqaba. The eastern border drops sharply into the Jordan Rift Valley, including Lake Tiberias (Sea of Galilee) and the Dead Sea, which is 1,312 ft. below sea level, lowest point on the earth's surface. **Capital:** Jerusalem. Most countries maintain their embassy in Tel Aviv. **Cities** (1990 est.): Jerusalem 504,000; Tel Aviv-Yafo 321,000; Haifa 222,000.

Government: Type: Republic. **Head of state:** Pres. Chaim Herzog; b. Sept. 17, 1918; in office May 5, 1983. **Head of government:** Prime Min. Yitzhak Rabin; b. Mar. 1, 1922; in office July 13, 1992. **Local divisions:** 6 districts. **Defense** (1992): 12.1% of GDP.

Economy: Industries: Diamond cutting, textiles, electronics, machinery, food processing. **Chief crops:** Citrus fruit, vegetables. **Minerals:** Potash, copper, phosphate, manganese, sulphur. **Arable land:** 17%. **Livestock** (1991): 331,000 cattle; 375,000 sheep. **Fish catch** (1991): 26,000 metric tons. **Electricity prod.** (1991): 21.0 bln. kWh. **Labor force:** 6% agric.; 23% ind., 30% public services.

Finance: Monetary unit: New Sheqalim (Aug. 1993: 2.81 = $ 1 US). **Gross domestic product** (1991): $54.6 bln. **Per capita GDP:** $12,500. **Imports** (1991): $18.1 bln.; partners: U.S. 16%, W. Ger. 13%, UK 9%. **Exports** (1991): $12.1 bln.; partners: U.S. 30%, W. Ger. 5%, UK 7%. **Tourism** (1990): $1.4 bln. receipts. **National budget** (1992): $47.6 bln. expenditures. **International reserves less gold** (Jan. 1993): $4.6 bln. **Gold:** 9,000 oz t. **Consumer prices** (change in 1992): 11.6%.

Transport: Railroads (1990): 323 mi. long; 173 mln. passenger-km. **Motor vehicles** (1990): 786,000 passenger cars, 157,000 comm. vehicles. **Civil aviation** (1990): 7.0 mln. passenger-km; 7 airports with scheduled flights. **Chief ports:** Haifa, Ashdod, Eilat.

Communications: Television sets: 1 per 4.1 persons. **Radios:** 1 per 2.2 persons. **Telephones:** 1 per 2.1 persons. **Daily newspaper circ.** (1989): 357 per 1,000 pop.

Health: Life expectancy at birth (1992) Jewish pop. only: 76 male; 79 female. **Births** (per 1,000 pop. 1992): 21. **Deaths** (per 1,000 pop. 1992): 6%. **Natural increase:** 1.5%. **Hospital beds:** 1 per 161 persons. **Physicians:** 1 per 345 persons. **Infant mortality** (per 1,000 live births 1992): 9.

Education (1991): **Literacy:** 92% (Jewish), 70% (Arab).

Major International Organizations: UN (GATT).

Embassy: 2 Palace Green, London W8 4QB; 071-957 9500.

Occupying the SW corner of the ancient Fertile Crescent, Israel contains some of the oldest known evidence of agriculture and of primitive town life. A more advanced civilization emerged in the 3d millennium BC. The Hebrews probably arrived early in the 2d millennium BC. Under King David and his successors (c.1000 BC-597 BC), Judaism was developed and secured. After conquest by Babylonians, Persians, and Greeks, an independent Jewish kingdom was revived, 168 BC, but Rome took effective control in the next century, suppressed Jewish revolts in AD 70 and AD 135, and renamed Judea Palestine, after the earlier coastal inhabitants, the Philistines.

Arab invaders conquered Palestine in 636. The Arabic language and Islam prevailed within a few centuries, but a Jewish minority remained. The land was ruled from the 11th century as a part of non-Arab empires by Seljuks, Mamluks, and Ottomans (with a crusader interval, 1098-1291).

After 4 centuries of Ottoman rule, during which the population declined to a low of 350,000 (1785), the land was taken in 1917 by Britain, which in the Balfour Declaration that year pledged to support a Jewish national homeland there, as foreseen by the Zionists. In 1920 a British Palestine Mandate was recognized; in 1922 the land east of the Jordan was detached.

Jewish immigration, begun in the late 19th century, swelled in the 1930s with refugees from the Nazis; heavy Arab immigration from Syria and Lebanon also occurred. Arab opposition to Jewish immigration turned violent in 1920, 1921, 1929, and 1936. The UN General Assembly voted in 1947 to partition Palestine into an Arab and a Jewish state. Britain withdrew in May 1948.

Israel was declared an independent state May 14, 1948; the Arabs rejected partition. Egypt, Jordan, Syria, Lebanon, Iraq, and Saudi Arabia invaded, but failed to destroy the Jewish state, which gained territory. Separate armistices with the Arab nations were signed in 1949; Jordan occupied the West Bank, Egypt occupied Gaza, but neither granted Palestinian autonomy.

After persistent terrorist raids, Israel invaded Egypt's Sinai, Oct. 29, 1956, aided briefly by British and French forces. A UN cease-fire was arranged Nov. 6.

An uneasy truce between Israel and the Arab countries, supervised by a UN Emergency Force, prevailed until May 19, 1967, when the UN force withdrew at the demand of Egypt's Pres. Gamal Abdel Nasser. Egyptian forces reoccupied the Gaza Strip and closed the Gulf of Aqaba to Israeli shipping. In a 6-day war that started June 5, the Israelis took the Gaza Strip, occupied the Sinai Peninsula to the Suez Canal, and captured East Jerusalem, Syria's Golan Heights, and Jordan's West Bank. The fighting was halted June 10 by UN-arranged cease-fire agreements.

Egypt and Syria attacked Israel, Oct. 6, 1973 (Yom Kippur, most solemn day on the Jewish calendar). Israel counter-attacked, driving the Syrians back, and crossed the Suez Canal.

A cease fire took effect Oct. 24; a UN peace-keeping force went to the area. A disengagement agreement was signed Jan. 18, 1974. Israel withdrew from the canal's W bank. A second withdrawal was completed in 1976; Israel returned the Sinai to Egypt in 1982.

Israeli forces raided Entebbe, Uganda, July 3, 1976, and rescued 103 hostages seized by Arab and German terrorists.

In 1977, the conservative opposition, led by Menachem Begin, was voted into office for the first time. Egypt's Pres. Anwar al-Sadat visited Jerusalem Nov. 1977 and on Mar. 26, 1979. Egypt and Israel signed a formal peace treaty, ending 30 years of war, and establishing diplomatic relations.

Israel invaded S. Lebanon, March 1978, following a Lebanon-based terrorist attack in Israel. Israel withdrew in favor of a 6,000-man UN force, but continued to aid Christian militiamen. Violence on the Israeli-occupied West Bank rose in 1982 when Israel announced plans to build new Jewish settlements. Israel affirmed the entire city of Jerusalem as its capital, July 1980, encompassing the annexed East Jerusalem.

On June 7, 1981, Israeli jets destroyed an Iraqi atomic reactor near Baghdad that, Israel claimed, would have enabled Iraq to manufacture nuclear weapons.

Israeli jets bombed Palestine Liberation Organization (PLO) strongholds in Lebanon April, May 1982. In reaction to the wounding of the Israeli ambassador to Great Britain, Israeli forces in a coordinated land, sea, and air attack invaded Lebanon, June 6, to destroy PLO strongholds in that country. Israeli and Syrian forces engaged in the Bekaa Valley, June 9, but quickly agreed to a truce. Israeli forces encircled Beirut June 14. Following massive Israeli bombing of West Beirut, the PLO agreed to evacuate the city.

Israeli troops entered West Beirut after newly elected Lebanese president Bashir Gemayel was assassinated on Sept. 14. Israel received widespread condemnation when Lebanese Christian forces, Sept. 16, entered 2 West Beirut refugee camps and slaughtered hundreds of Palestinian refugees.

In 1989, violence continued over the Israeli military occupation of the West Bank and Gaza Strip; protesters and Israeli troops clashed frequently. Israeli police and stone-throwing Palestinians clashed, Oct. 8, 1990, around the al-Aqsa mosque on the Temple Mount in Jerusalem. Some 20 Palestinians died and 150 were injured.

The Knesset approved a new right-wing coalition government led by Prime Minister Yitzhak Shamir, June 11, 1990, following a 3-month political crisis that began with the fall of the previous "National Unity" government of Shamir and the Labor Party of Shimon Peres.

During the Persian Gulf War, Iraq fired a series of scud missiles at Israel; most were intercepted by U.S. Patriot missiles. Israel agreed in Aug. 1991 to take part in a U.S.-Soviet sponsored Middle East peace conference.

The Labour Party of Yitzhak Rabin won a clear victory in elections held June 23, 1992. Rabin called for peace and reconciliation with its Arab neighbors.

Israeli forces conducted air raids and artillery strikes against guerrilla bases and villages in S. Lebanon, July 25–29, 1993, in retaliation for attacks by a pro-Iranian group, Hezbollah, on N. Israel.

Israel and the Palestine Liberation Organization reached an agreement in principle in Aug. 1993 intended to lead to mutual recognition and a form of Palestinian self-rule in Gaza and the West Bank city of Jericho.

Italy

Italian Republic

Repubblica Italiana

People: Population (1992 est.): 57,904,000. **Age distrib.** (%): 0–14: 17.8; 15–59: 62.8; 60+: 19.4. **Pop. density:** 497 per sq. mi. **Urban** (1991): 67%. **Ethnic groups:** Italians, small minorities of Germans, Slovenes, Albanians. **Language:** Italian. **Religion:** Predominantly Roman Catholic.

Geography: Area: 116,303 sq. mi., slightly smaller than the Br. Isles. **Location:** In S Europe, jutting into Mediterranean S. **Neighbors:** France on W, Switzerland, Austria on N, Yugoslavia on E. **Topography:** Occupies a long boot-shaped peninsula, extending SE from the Alps into the Mediterranean, with the islands of Sicily and Sardinia offshore. The alluvial Po Valley drains most of N. The rest of the country is rugged and mountainous, except for intermittent coastal plains, like the Campania, S of Rome. Apennine Mts. run down through center of peninsula. **Capital:** Rome. **Cities** (1991 est.): Rome 2.8 mln.; Milan 1.4 mln.; Naples 1.2 mln.; Turin 1.0 mln.

Government: Type: Republic. **Head of state:** Pres. Oscar Luigi Scalfaro; in office May 28, 1992. **Head of government:** Prime Min. Carlo Azeglio Ciampi; in office Apr. 22, 1993. **Local divisions:** 20 regions with some autonomy, 94 provinces. **Defense** (1991): 2.2% of GDP.

Economy: Industries: Steel, machinery, autos, textiles, shoes, machine tools, chemicals. **Chief crops:** Grapes, olives, citrus fruits, vegetables, wheat, rice. **Minerals:** Mercury, potash, sulphur. **Crude oil reserves** (1991): 700 mln. bbls. **Arable land:** 32%. **Livestock** (1991): 8.7 mln. cattle; 9.5 mln. pigs; 11.6 mln. sheep. **Fish catch** (1990): 336,000 metric tons. **Electricity prod.** (1991): 235 bln. kWh. **Crude steel prod.** (1991): 25.4 mln. metric tons. **Labor force:** 10% agric.; 32% ind. and comm.; 58% services and govt.

Finance: Monetary unit: Lira (Sep. 1993: 1,611 = $1 US). **Gross domestic product** (1991): $965 bln. **Per capita GDP:** $16,700. **Imports** (1991): $181 bln.; partners: EC 58%, Fr. 15%, U.S. 7%. **Exports** (1991): $170 bln.; partners: EC 58%. **Tourism** (1990): $19.7 bln. receipts. **National budget** (1991): $565 bln. expenditures. **International reserves less gold** (Apr. 1993): $26 bln. **Gold:** 66.67 mln. oz t. **Consumer prices** (change in 1992): 5.4%.

Transport: Railroads (1990): 12,158 mi. long. **Motor vehicles** (1989): 24.3 mln. passenger cars, 2.0 mln. comm. vehicles. **Civil aviation** (1990): 22.7 bln. passenger-km; 30 airports. **Chief ports:** Genoa, Venice, Trieste, Taranto, Naples, La Spezia.

Communications: Television sets: 1 per 3.8 persons. **Radios:** 1 per 3.4 persons. **Telephones:** 1 per 1.8 persons. **Daily newspaper circ.** (1989): 142 per 1,000 pop.

Health: Life expectancy at birth (1992): 74 male; 81 female. **Births** (per 1,000 pop. 1992): 11. **Deaths** (per 1,000 pop. 1992): 10. **Natural increase:** .1%. **Hospital beds:** 1 per 135 persons. **Physicians:** 1 per 233 persons. **Infant mortality** (per 1,000 live births 1992): 8.

Education (1991): **Literacy:** 98%. **School:** Compulsory for 8 years.

Major International Organizations: UN and all of its specialized agencies, NATO, OECD, EC.

Embassy: 4 Grosvenor Sq, London W1X 9LA; 071-629 8200.

Rome emerged as the major power in Italy after 500 BC, dominating the more civilized Etruscans to the N and Greeks to the S. Under the Empire, which lasted until the 5th century AD, Rome ruled most of Western Europe, the Balkans, the Near East, and North Africa. In 1988, archeologists unearthed evidence showing Rome as a dynamic society in the 6th and 7th centuries B.C.

After the Germanic invasions, lasting several centuries, a high civilization arose in the city-states of the N, culminating in the Renaissance. But German, French, Spanish, and Austrian intervention prevented the unification of the country. In 1859 Lombardy came under the crown of King Victor Emmanuel II of Sardinia. By plebiscite in 1860, Parma, Modena, Romagna, and Tuscany joined, followed by Sicily and Naples, and by the Marches and Umbria. The first Italian parliament declared Victor Emmanuel king of Italy Mar. 17, 1861. Mantua and Venetia were added in 1866 as an outcome of the Austro-Prussian war. The Papal States were taken by Italian troops Sept. 20, 1870, on the withdrawal of the French garrison. The states were annexed to the kingdom by plebiscite. Italy recognized the State of Vatican City as independent Feb. 11, 1929.

Fascism appeared in Italy Mar. 23, 1919, led by Benito Mussolini, who took over the government at the invitation of the king Oct. 28, 1922. Mussolini acquired dictatorial powers. He made war on Ethiopia and proclaimed Victor Emmanuel III emperor, defied the sanctions of the League of Nations, sent troops to fight for Franco against the Republic of Spain and joined Germany in World War II.

After Fascism was overthrown in 1943, Italy declared war on Germany and Japan and contributed to the Allied victory. It surrendered conquered lands and lost its colonies. Mussolini was killed by partisans Apr. 28, 1945.

Victor Emmanuel III abdicated May 9, 1946; his son Humbert II was king until June 10, when Italy became a republic after a referendum, June 2-3. Reorganization of the Fascist party is forbidden.

Italy has enjoyed growth in industry and living standards since World War II, in part due to membership of the European Community. A wave of left-wing political violence began in the late 1970s with kidnappings and assassinations and continued into the 1980s. Christian Democratic leader and former Prime Min. Aldo Moro was murdered May 1978 by Red Brigade terrorists.

The Cabinet of Prime Min. Arnaldo Forlani resigned, May 26, 1981, in the wake of revelations that numerous high-ranking officials were members of an illegally secret Masonic lodge. The June 1983 elections saw Bettino Craxi chosen the nation's first Socialist premier. Craxi ended the longest tenure of an Italian leader since World War II by resigning Mar. 1987.

By mid-1991, some 20,000 Albanian refugees had entered Italy as the result of political unrest in their homeland. In Aug. an addition wave of 18,000 Alabanians reached Italy. They were rounded up and sent back to Albania.

In 1993 Italy's parliament and a referendum of Italian voters approved electoral reforms, amid growing political corruption scandals. Under the reforms, most members of parliament would be elected from single districts, rather than in a proportional representation system that fragmented power among several major parties.

Sicily, 9,926 sq. mi., pop. (1990) 5,172,000, is an island 180 by 120 mi., seat of a region that embraces the island of **Pantelleria,** 32 sq. mi., and the **Lipari** group, 44 sq. mi., pop. 14,000, including 2 active volcanoes: **Vulcano,** 1,637 ft. and **Stromboli,** 3,038 ft. From prehistoric times Sicily has been settled by various peoples; a Greek state had its capital at Syracuse. Rome took Sicily from Carthage 215 BC. **Mt. Etna,** 11,053 ft., is an active volcano and the tallest peak.

Sardinia, 9,301 sq. mi., pop. (1990) 1,657,000, lies in the Mediterranean, 115 mi. W of Italy and 7½ mi. S of Corsica. It is 160 mi. long, 68 mi. wide, and mountainous, with mining of coal, zinc, lead, copper. In 1720 Sardinia was added to the possessions of the Dukes of Savoy in Piedmont and Savoy to form the Kingdom of Sardinia. Giuseppe Garibaldi is buried on the nearby isle of Caprera. **Elba,** 86 sq. mi., lies 6 mi. W of Tuscany. Napoleon I lived in exile on Elba 1814-1815.

Trieste. An agreement, signed Oct. 5, 1954, by Italy and Yugoslavia, confirmed, Nov. 10, 1975, gave Italy provisional administration over the northern section and the seaport of Trieste, and Yugoslavia the part of Istrian peninsula it has occupied.

Jamaica

People: Population (1992 est.): 2,506,000. **Age distrib.** (%): 0–14: 33.7; 15–59: 56.4; 60+: 9.9. **Pop. density:** 592 per sq. mi. **Urban** (1990): 52%. **Ethnic groups:** African 76%, mixed 15%, Chinese, Caucasians, East Indians. **Languages:** English (official), Jamaican Creole. **Religion:** Protestant 60%.

Geography: Area: 4,232 sq. mi., slightly smaller than N. Ireland. **Location:** In West Indies. **Neighbors:** Nearest are Cuba on N, Haiti on E. **Topography:** The country is four-fifths covered by mountains. **Capital:** Kingston. **Cities** (1991 est.): St. Andrew 393,000, Kingston 100,000.

Government: Type: Parliamentary democracy. **Head of state:** Queen Elizabeth II, represented by Gov.-Gen. Howard Cooke. in office Aug. 1, 1991. **Head of government:** Prime Min. Percival J. Patterson; in office Mar. 30, 1992. **Local divisions:** 14 parishes; Kingston and St. Andrew corporate area. **Defense** (1991): 1.0% of GDP.

Economy: Industries: Rum, molasses, mining, tourism. **Chief crops:** Sugar cane, coffee, bananas, coconuts, citrus fruits. **Minerals:** Bauxite, limestone, gypsum. **Arable land:** 19%. **Livestock** (1991): 250,000 cattle; 440,000 goats. **Electricity prod.** (1991): 2.5 bln. kWh. **Labor force:** 31% agric.; 27% services; 41% ind.

Finance: Monetary unit: Dollar (Apr. 1993: 22.81 = $1 US). **Gross domestic product** (1991): $3.6 bln. **Per capita GDP:** $1,400. **Imports** (1991): $1.8 bln.; partners: U.S. 48%. **Exports** (1991): $1.2 bln.; partners: U.S. 36%. **Tourism** (1990): $740 mln. receipts. **National budget** (1991): $736 mln. **International reserves less gold** (Feb. 1993): $106 mln. **Consumer prices** (change in 1992): 99.9%.

Transport: Railroads (1989): 211 mi. long. **Motor vehicles** (1989): 93,000 passenger cars, 16,000 comm. vehicles. **Civil aviation** (1991): 1.3 bln. passenger km.; 6 airports with scheduled flights. **Chief ports:** Kingston, Montego Bay.

Communications: Television sets: 1 per 5.9 persons. **Radios:** 1 per 2.6 persons. **Telephones:** 1 per 13 persons. **Daily newspaper circ.** (1991): 51 per 1,000 pop.

Health: Life expectancy at birth (1992): 72 male; 76 female. **Births** (per 1,000 pop. 1992): 4. **Deaths** (per 1,000 pop. 1992): 6. **Natural increase:** 1.8%. **Hospital beds:** 1 per 468 persons. **Physicians:** 1 per 5,904 persons. **Infant mortality** (per 1,000 live births 1992): 17.

Education (1990): **Literacy:** 98%. **School:** Compulsory to age 14.

Major International Organizations: UN (World Bank, GATT), OAS.

High Commission: 1 Prince Consort Road, London SW7 2BQ; 071-823 9911.

Jamaica was visited by Columbus, 1494, and ruled by Spain (under whom Arawak Indians died out) until seized by Britain, 1655. Jamaica won independence Aug. 6, 1962.

In 1974 Jamaica sought an increase in taxes paid by U.S. and Canadian companies which mine bauxite on the island. The socialist government acquired 50% ownership of the companies' Jamaican interests in 1976, and was reelected that year. Rudimentary welfare state measures were passed. Relations with the U.S. improved greatly in the 1980s following the election of Edward Seaga.

Hurricane Gilbert struck Jamaica Sept. 12, 1988, killing some 45 and causing extensive damage including half the nation's houses.

Japan

Nippon

People: Population (1991 est.): 124,017,000. **Age distrib.** (%): 0–14: 18.0; 15–59: 64.3; 60+: 17.7. **Pop. density:** 850 per sq. mi. **Urban** (1990): 77%. **Ethnic groups:** Japanese 99.4%, Korean 0.5%. **Language:** Japanese. **Religions:** Buddhism, Shintoism shared by large majority.

Geography: Area: 145,856 sq. mi., one-third bigger than the UK. **Location:** Archipelago off E. coast of Asia. **Neighbors:** Russia on N, S. Korea on W. **Topography:** Japan consists of 4 main islands: Honshu ("mainland"), 87,805 sq. mi.; Hokkaido, 30,144 sq. mi.; Kyushu, 14,114 sq. mi.; and Shikoku, 7,049 sq. mi. The coast, deeply indented, measures 16,654 mi. The northern islands are a continuation of the Sakhalin Mts. The Kunlun range of China continues into southern islands, the ranges meeting in the Japanese Alps. In a vast transverse fissure crossing Honshu E-W rises a group of volcanoes, mostly extinct or inactive, including 12,388 ft. Fuji-San (Fujiyama) near Tokyo. **Capital:** Tokyo. **Cities** (1990 cen.): Tokyo 8.1 mln.; Osaka 2.6 mln.; Yokohama 3.2 mln.; Nagoya 2.1 mln.; Kyoto 1.4 mln.; Kobe 1.4 mln.; Sapporo 1.6 mln.; Kitakyushu 1 mln.; Kawasaki 1.1 mln; Fukuoka 1.2 mln.

Government: Type: Parliamentary democracy. **Head of state:** Emp. Akihito; b. Dec. 23, 1933; in office Jan. 7, 1989. **Head of**

government: Prime Min. Kiichi Miyazawa; in office Nov. 6, 1991. **Local divisions:** 47 prefectures. **Defense** (1991): Less than 1% of GNP.

Economy: Industries: Electrical & electronic equip., autos, machinery, chemicals. **Chief crops:** Rice, grains, vegetables, fruits. **Minerals:** negligible. **Crude oil reserves** (1985): 26 mln. bbls. **Arable land:** 13%. **Livestock** (1989): 4.6 mln. cattle; 11.7 mln. pigs. **Fish catch** (1989): 12.7 mln. metric tons. **Electricity prod.** (1990): 790 bln. kWh. **Crude steel prod.** (1990): 110.3 mln. metric tons. **Labor force:** 8% agric.; 32% manuf. & mining; 43% services & trade.

Finance: Monetary unit: Yen (June 1992: 127 = $1 US). **Gross national product** (1990): $2.1 trl. **Per capita GNP** (1990): $17,100. **Imports** (1991): $236 bln.; partners: U.S. 22%, Middle East 26%, SE Asia 22%, EC 6%. **Exports** (1991): $314 bln.; partners: U.S. 33%, EC 20%, SE Asia 23%. **Tourism** (1989): $3.1 bln. receipts. **National budget** (1990): $532 bln. expenditures. **International reserves less gold** (Mar. 1992): $72 bln. **Gold:** 24.23 mln. oz. t. **Consumer prices** (change in 1991): 3.3%.

Transport: Railroads (1988): 17,059 mi. long. **Motor vehicles** (1990): 36.6 mln. passenger cars, 22.2 mln. comm. vehicles. **Civil aviation** (1990): 95.3 bln. passenger-km; 71 airports with scheduled flights. **Chief ports:** Yokohama, Tokyo, Kobe, Osaka, Nagoya, Chiba, Kawasaki, Hakodate.

Communications: Television sets: 1 per 1.8 persons. **Radios:** 1 per 1.3 persons. **Telephones:** 1 per 2.3 persons. **Daily newspaper circ.** (1990): 429 per 1,000 pop.

Health: Life expectancy at birth (1991): 76 male; 82 female. **Births** (per 1,000 pop. 1991): 10. **Deaths** (per 1,000 pop. 1991): 7. **Natural increase:** 0.3%. **Hospital beds:** 1 per 77 persons. **Physicians:** 1 per 609 persons. **Infant mortality** (per 1,000 live births 1991): 4.

Education (1991): **Literacy:** 99%. **School:** Most attend school for 12 years.

Major International Organizations: UN (IMF, GATT, ILO), OECD.

Embassy: 101 Piccadilly, London W1V 9FN; 071-465 6500.

According to Japanese legend, the empire was founded by Emperor Jimmu, 660 BC, but earliest records of a unified Japan date from 1,000 years later. Chinese influence was strong in the formation of Japanese civilization. Buddhism was introduced before the 6th century.

A feudal system, with locally powerful noble families and their samurai warrior retainers, dominated from 1192. Central power was held by successive families of shoguns (military dictators), 1192-1867, until recovered by the Emperor Meiji, 1868. The Portuguese and Dutch had minor trade with Japan in the 16th and 17th centuries; U.S. Commodore Matthew C. Perry opened it to U.S. trade in a treaty ratified 1854. Japan fought China, 1894-95, gaining Taiwan. After war with Russia, 1904-05, Russia ceded S half of Sakhalin and gave concessions in China. Japan annexed Korea 1910. In World War I Japan ousted Germany from Shantung, took over German Pacific islands. Japan took Manchuria 1931, started war with China 1932. Japan launched war against the U.S. by attack on Pearl Harbor Dec. 7, 1941. Japan surrendered Aug. 14, 1945.

In a new constitution adopted May 3, 1947, Japan renounced the right to wage war; the emperor gave up claims to divinity; the Diet became the sole law-making authority.

The U.S. and 48 other non-communist nations signed a peace treaty and the U.S. a bilateral defense agreement with Japan, in San Francisco Sept. 8, 1951, restoring Japan's sovereignty as of April 28, 1952.

On June 26, 1968, the U.S. returned to Japanese control the Bonin Is., the Volcano Is. (including Iwo Jima) and Marcus Is. On May 15, 1972, Okinawa, the other Ryukyu Is. and the Daito Is. were returned to Japan by the U.S.; it was agreed the U.S. would continue to maintain military bases on Okinawa.

Industrialization was begun in the late 19th century. After World War II, Japan emerged as one of the most powerful economies in the world, and as a leader in technology.

The U.S. and EC member nations have criticized Japan for its restrictive policy on imports which has given Japan a substantial trade surplus.

In Apr. 1987, the U.S. imposed 100% tariffs on Japanese electronics imports in retaliation for what the U.S. considered various unfair trade practices.

The Recruit scandal, the nation's worst political scandal since World War II, which involved illegal political donations and stock trading, led to the resignation of Premier Noboru Takeshita in May 1989. A series of scandals rocked Japan's financial sector in 1991; one involved the largest bank, another the 4 largest securities firms.

Jordan

Hashemite Kingdom of Jordan

al Mamlaka al Urduniya al Hashemiyah

People: Population (1992 est.): 3,557,000. **Age distrib.** (%): 0–14: 48.1; 15–59: 46.9; 60+: 4.0. **Pop. density:** 94 per sq. mi. **Urban** (1990): 68%. **Ethnic groups:** Arab 98%. **Language:** Arabic (official). **Religions:** Sunni Muslim 92%, Christian 8%.

Geography: Area: 37,737 sq. mi., slightly smaller than Scotland and Wales combined. **Location:** In W Asia. **Neighbors:** Israel on W, Saudi Arabia on S, Iraq on E, Syria on N. **Topography:** About 88% of Jordan is arid. Fertile areas are in W. Only port is on short Aqaba Gulf coast. Country shares Dead Sea (1,296 ft. below sea level) with Israel. **Capital:** Amman. **Cities** (1989 est.): Amman 936,000; az-Zarqa 318,000; Irbid 161,000.

Government: Type: Constitutional monarchy. **Head of state:** King Hussein I; b. Nov. 14, 1935; in office Aug. 11, 1952. **Head of government:** Prime Min. Sharif Zaid ibn Shaker; in office Nov. 16, 1991. **Local divisions:** 8 governorates. **Defense** (1990): 9.5% of GDP.

Economy: Industries: Textiles, cement, food processing. **Chief crops:** Grains, olives, vegetables, fruits. **Minerals:** Phosphate, potash. **Arable land:** 5%. **Electricity prod.** (1991): 3.9 bln. kWh. **Labor force:** 20% agric. 20% manuf. & mining.

Finance: Monetary unit: Dinar (Mar. 1993: 1.00 = $1.43 US). **Gross domestic product** (1991): $3.6 bln. **Imports** (1991): $2.3 bln.; partners: Saudi Ar. 6%, U.S. 11%, Jap. 8%. **Exports** (1991): $1.0 bln.; partners: Saudi Ar. 12%, Ind. 13%, Iraq. 18%. **Tourism** (1989): $546 mln. receipts. **National budget** (1992): $1.8 bln. expenditures. **International reserves less gold** (Mar. 1993): $680 mln. **Gold:** 789,000 oz t. **Consumer prices** (change in 1992): 4.2%.

Transport: Motor vehicles (1990): 173,000 passenger cars, 68,000 comm. vehicles. **Civil aviation** (1990): 2.7 bln. passenger-km; 2 airports with scheduled flights. **Chief port:** Aqaba.

Communications: Television sets: 1 per 12 persons. **Radios:** 1 per 4.5 persons. **Telephones:** 1 per 10 persons. **Daily newspaper circ.** (1990): 73 per 1,000 pop.

Health: Life expectancy at birth (1991): 70 male; 73 female. **Births** (per 1,000 pop. 1990): 46.7. **Deaths** (per 1,000 pop. 1990): 5. **Natural increase:** 4.1%. **Hospital beds:** 1 per 502 persons. **Physicians:** 1 per 813 persons. **Infant mortality** (per 1,000 live births 1991): 38.

Education (1989): **Literacy:** 71%.

Major International Organizations: UN (WHO, IMF), Arab League.

Embassy: 6 Upper Phillimore Gdns, London W8 7HB; 071-937 3685.

From ancient times to 1922 the lands to the E of the Jordan were culturally and politically united with the lands to the W. Arabs conquered the area in the 7th century; the Ottomans took control in the 16th. Britain's 1920 Palestine Mandate covered both sides of the Jordan. In 1921, Abdullah, son of the ruler of Hejaz in Arabia, was installed by Britain as emir of an autonomous Transjordan, covering two-thirds of Palestine. An independent kingdom was proclaimed, 1946.

During the 1948 Arab-Israeli war the West Bank and old city of Jerusalem were added to the kingdom, which changed its name to Jordan. All these territories were lost to Israel in the 1967 war, which swelled the number of Arab refugees on the East Bank. A 1974 Arab summit conference designated the Palestine Liberation Organization as the sole representative of Arabs on the West Bank. Jordan accepted the move, and was granted an annual subsidy by Arab oil states.

In 1988 Jordan cut legal and administrative ties with the Israeli-occupied West Bank.

Some 700,000 refugees entered Jordan following Iraq's invasion of Kuwait, Aug. 1990. Jordan was viewed as supporting Iraq during the Gulf crisis.

Republic of Kazakhstan

Kazak Respublikasy

People: Population (1992 est.): 17,101,000. **Pop. density:** 16 per sq. mi. **Urban** (1991): 58%. **Ethnic groups:** Kazakh 40%, Russian 37%, German 6%, Ukrainian 5%. **Languages:** Kazakh, Russian, German. **Religion:** Muslim 47%.

Geography: Area: 1,049,200 sq. mi., 11 times larger than the UK. **Neighbors:** Russia on N, China on E, Kyrgyzstan, Uzbekistan, Turkmenistan on S, Caspian Sea on W. **Topography:** Extends from the lower reaches of Volga in Europe to the Altai mtns. on the Chinese border. **Capital:** Alma-Ata. **Cities** (1991): Alma-Ata 1.1 mln., Qaraghandy 608,000.

Government: Type: Republic. **Head of state:** Pres. Nursultan A.

Nazarbayev. **Head of government:** Prime Min. Sergei Tereshchenko.

Economy: Industries: Steel, cement, footwear, textiles. **Chief crops:** Grain, cotton. **Minerals:** Coal, tungsten, copper, lead, zinc. **Livestock** (1989): 9.7 mln. cattle; 36.5 mln. sheep; 3.2 mln. pigs.

Finance: Monetary unit: Rouble.

Transport: Railroads (1991): 9,040 mi. long. **Motor vehicles** (1989): 734,000 passenger cars. **Civil aviation** (1990): 13.3 bln. passenger-km., 5 airports with scheduled flights.

Communications: Telephones: 1 per 8.5 persons.

Health: Life expectancy at birth (1992): 63 male; 72 female. **Birth rate** (per 1,000 pop. 1992): 23. **Death rate** (per 1,000 pop. 1992): 8. **Hospital beds:** 1 per 74 persons. **Physicians:** 1 per 224 persons. **Infant mortality** (per 1,000 live births 1992): 26.

Major International Organizations: UN, CIS.

The region came under the Mongols in the 13th century and gradually came under Russian rule, 1730-1853. It was admitted to the USSR as a constituent republic 1936. Kazakhstan declared independence Dec. 16, 1991. It became an independent state when the Soviet Union dissolved Dec. 26, 1991.

Kenya

Republic of Kenya

Jamhuri ya Kenya

People: Population (1992 est.): 26,164,000. **Age distrib.** (%): 0–14: 49.6; 15–59: 50.0; 60+: 3.4. **Pop. density:** 116 per sq. mi. **Urban** (1991): 26%. **Ethnic groups:** Kikuyu 21%, Luo 13%, Luhya 14%, Kelenjin 11%, Kamba 11%, others, including Asians, Arabs, Europeans. **Languages:** Swahili (official), Kikuyu, Luhya, Luo, Meru. **Religions:** Protestant 38%, Roman Catholic 28%, Muslim 6%, others.

Geography: Area: 224,960 sq. mi., nearly twice the size of the Br. Isles. **Location:** On Indian O. coast of E. Africa. **Neighbors:** Uganda on W, Tanzania on S, Somalia on E, Ethopia, Sudan on N. **Topography:** The northern three-fifths of Kenya is arid. To the S, a low coastal area and a plateau varying from 3,000 to 10,000 ft. The Great Rift Valley enters the country N-S, flanked by high mountains. **Capital:** Nairobi. **Cities** (1987 est.): Nairobi 959,000; Mombasa 401,000.

Government: Type: Republic. **Head of state:** Pres. Daniel arap Moi, b. Sept., 1924; in office Aug. 22, 1978. **Local divisions:** Nairobi and 7 provinces. **Defense** (1989): 1.0% of GDP.

Economy: Industries: Tourism, light industry, petroleum prods. **Chief crops:** Coffee, corn, tea, cereals, cotton, sisal. **Minerals:** Gold, limestone, diatomite, salt, barytes, magnesite, felspar, sapphires, fluospar, garnets. **Other resources:** Timber, hides. **Arable land:** 4%. **Livestock** (1991): 13.7 mln. cattle. **Fish catch** (1990): 144,000 metric tons. **Electricity prod.** (1991): 2.8 bln. kWh. **Labor force:** 78% agric.

Finance: Monetary unit: Shilling (Mar. 1993: 45.52 = $1 US). **Gross domestic product** (1991): $9.7 bln. **Per capita GDP:** $385. **Imports** (1991): $1.9 bln.; partners: EC 45%. **Exports** (1991): $1.0 bln.; partners: EC 44%. **Tourism** (1992): $295 mln. receipts. **National budget** (1990): $2.8 bln expenditures. **International reserves less gold** (Mar. 1993): $77 mln. **Gold:** 80,000 oz t. **Consumer prices** (change in 1992): 35.5%.

Transport: Motor vehicles (1989): 133,000 passenger cars, 149,000 comm. vehicles. **Civil aviation** (1991): 1.4 bln. passenger-km; 16 airports with scheduled flights. **Chief port:** Mombasa.

Communications: Television sets: 1 per 100 persons. **Radios:** 1 per 6 persons. **Telephones:** 1 per 67 persons. **Daily newspaper circ.** (1991): 13 per 1,000 pop.

Health: Life expectancy at birth (1992): 60 male; 64 female. **Births** (per 1,000 pop. 1992): 44. **Deaths** (per 1,000 pop. 1992): 8. **Natural increase:** 3.6%. **Hospital beds:** 1 per 737 persons. **Physicians:** 1 per 7,313 persons. **Infant mortality** (per 1,000 live births 1992): 68.

Education (1989): **Literacy:** 50%. **School:** 86% attend primary school.

Major International Organizations: UN and all of its specialized agencies, OAU, Commonwealth of Nations.

High Commission: 24 New Bond St, London W1; 071-636 2371.

Arab colonies exported spices and slaves from the Kenya coast as early as the 8th century. Britain obtained control in the 19th century. Kenya won independence Dec. 12, 1963, 4 years after the end of the violent Mau Mau uprising.

Kenya had steady growth in industry and agriculture under a modified private enterprise system, and enjoyed a relatively free political life. But stability was shaken in 1974-5, with opposition charges of corruption and oppression.

Tribal clashes in the western provinces claimed some 2,000 lives and left 50,000 homeless in 1992. The unrest was the worst since independence in 1963. Several western nations issued travel advisories for Kenya.

In the 1990s Kenya suffered from widespread unemployment and high inflation. Pres. Moi suspended Parliament, Jan. 27, 1993, one day after it opened with its first opposition members since the early 1960s.

Kiribati

Republic of Kiribati

People: Population (1992 est.): 74,000. **Pop. density:** 278 per sq. mi. **Ethnic groups:** Nearly all Micronesian, some Polynesians. **Languages:** Gilbertese and English (official). **Religions:** Evenly divided between Protestant and Roman Catholic.

Geography: Area: 266 sq. mi., about the size of Merseyside. **Location:** 33 Micronesian islands (the Gilbert, Line, and Phoenix groups) in the mid-Pacific scattered in a 2-mln. sq. mi. chain around the point where the International Date Line cuts the Equator. **Neighbors:** Nearest are Nauru to SW, Tuvalu and Tokelau Is. to S. **Topography:** Except Banaba (Ocean) I., all are low-lying, with soil of coral sand and rock fragments, subject to erratic rainfall. **Capital:** Tarawa, (1990) 25,000.

Government: Type: Republic. **Head of state and of government:** Pres. Teateo Teannaki, b. Dec. 16, 1950; in office July 3, 1991.

Economy: Industries: Copra. **Chief crops:** Coconuts, breadfruit, pandanus, bananas, paw paw. **Other resources:** Fish. **Electricity prod.** (1990): 13 mln. kWh.

Finance: Monetary unit: Australian dollar. **Gross domestic product** (1990): $36 mln.

Transport: Chief port: Tarawa.

Communications: Radios: 1 per 7 persons. **Telephones:** 1 per 53 persons.

Health: Hospital beds: 1 per 231 persons. **Physicians:** 1 per 4,104 persons.

Education: Literacy (1985): 90%.

Honorary Consulate: Faith House, 7 Tufton St, London SW1P 3QN.

A British protectorate since 1892, the Gilbert and Ellice Islands colony was completed with the inclusion of the Phoenix Islands, 1937. Self-rule was granted 1971; the Ellice Islands separated from the colony 1975 and became independent Tuvalu, 1978. Kiribati (pronounced *Kiribass)* independence was attained July 12, 1979. Under a Treaty of Friendship the U.S. relinquished its claims to several of the Line and Phoenix islands, including Christmas, Canton, and Enderbury.

Tarawa Atoll was the scene of some of the bloodiest fighting in the Pacific during WW II.

North Korea

Democratic People's Republic of Korea

Chosun Minchu-chui Inmin Konghwa-guk

People: Population (1992 est.): 22,227,000. **Pop. density:** 477 per sq. mi. **Urban** (1990): 60%. **Ethnic groups:** Korean. **Languages:** Korean. **Religions:** Activities almost non-existent; traditionally Buddhism, Confucianism, Chondokyo.

Geography: Area: 46,540 sq. mi., about half the size of the UK. **Location:** In northern E. Asia. **Neighbors:** China, Russia on N, S. Korea on S. **Topography:** Mountains and hills cover nearly all the country, with narrow valleys and small plains in between. The N and the E coast are the most rugged areas. **Capital:** Pyongyang, (1987 est.) 2,355,000.

Government: Type: Communist state. **Head of state:** Pres. Kim Il-Sung; b. Apr. 15, 1912; in office Dec. 28, 1972. **Head of government:** Premier Kang Song San; in office Dec. 11, 1992. **Head of Communist Party:** Gen. Sec. Kim Il-Sung; in office: 1945. **Local divisions:** 9 provinces, 3 special cities. **Defense** (1991): 24% of GDP.

Economy: Industries: Textiles, petrochemicals, food processing. **Chief crops:** Corn, potatoes, fruits, vegetables, rice. **Minerals:** Coal, lead tungsten, graphite, magnesite, iron, copper, gold, phosphate, salt, fluorspar. **Arable land:** 19%. **Livestock** (1990): 1.2 mln. cattle; 3.1 mln. pigs. **Fish catch** (1990): 1.7 mln. metric tons. **Crude steel prod.** (1991) 7.0 mln. metric tons. **Electricity prod.** (1991): 36 bln. kWh. **Labor force:** 48% agric.

Finance: Monetary unit: Won (Mar. 1993: 2.15 = $1 US). **Gross domestic product** (1991): $23 bln. **Imports** (1990): $2.6 bln.; partners: China 17%, USSR 36%, Jap. 19%. **Exports** (1990): $2.0 bln.; partners: USSR 43% China 13%, Jap. 15%. **National budget** (1990): $17.7 bln expenditures.

Communications: Television sets: 1 per 90 persons. **Radios:** 1 per 6 persons.

Transport: Chief ports: Chonglin, Hamhung, Nampo.

Health: Life expectancy at birth (1992): 66 male; 72 female. **Births** (per 1,000 pop. 1991): 24. **Deaths** (per 1,000 pop. 1992): 6. **Natural increase:** 1.8%. **Hospital beds:** 1 per 74 persons. **Physicians:** 1 per 370 persons. **Infant mortality** (per 1,000 live births, 1992): 30.

Education (1991): **Literacy:** 99%. **School:** Compulsory for 11 years.

Major International Organizations: UN.

Embassy: 4 Palace Gate, London W8 5LY; 071-581 0247.

The Democratic People's Republic of Korea was founded May 1, 1948, in the zone occupied by Russian troops after World War II. Its armies tried to conquer the south, 1950. After 3 years of fighting, with Chinese and U.S. intervention, a cease-fire was proclaimed.

Industry, begun by the Japanese during their 1910-45 occupation, and nationalized in the 1940s, had grown substantially, using N. Korea's abundant mineral and hydroelectric resources.

In Mar. 1993 N. Korea became the first nation to formally withdraw from the Nuclear Non-proliferation Treaty, the international pact designed to limit the spread of nuclear weapons; the nation suspended its withdrawal in June in reaction to threats of UN economic sanctions.

South Korea

Republic of Korea

Taehan Min'guk

People: Population (1992 est.): 44,149,000. **Age distrib.** (%): 0–14: 27.3; 15–59: 65.5; 60+: 7.2. **Pop. density:** 1,161 per sq. mi. **Urban** (1988): 74%. **Ethnic groups:** Korean. **Language:** Korean. **Religions:** Christian 43%, Buddhist 18%.

Geography: Area: 38,025 sq. mi., about the size of Scotland and Wales combined. **Location:** In Northern E. Asia. **Neighbors:** N. Korea on N. **Topography:** The country is mountainous, with a rugged east coast. The western and southern coasts are deeply indented, with many islands and harbors. **Capital:** Seoul. **Cities** (1990 est.): Seoul 10.7 mln.; Pusan 3,800,000; Taegu 2,200,000; Inchon 1,600,000; Kwangju 1,200,000; Taejon 1,000,000.

Government: Type: Republic, with power centralized in a strong executive. **Head of state:** Pres. Kim Young Sam; in office Feb. 25, 1993. **Head of government:** Prime Min. Hwang In Sung; in office Feb. 22, 1993. **Local divisions:** 9 provinces and 6 special cities. **Defense** (1992): 4.5% of GDP.

Economy: Industries: Electronics, ships, textiles, clothing, motor vehicles. **Chief crops:** Rice, barley, vegetables, wheat. **Minerals:** Tungsten, coal, graphite. **Arable land:** 22%. **Livestock** (1990): 2.0 mln. cattle; 4.8 mln. pigs. **Fish catch:** (1990): 3.2 mln. metric tons. **Electricity prod.** (1991): 106 bln. kWh. **Crude steel prod.** (1991): 26.0 mln. metric tons. **Labor force:** 21% agric.; 27% manuf. & mining; 52% services.

Finance: Monetary unit: Won (Aug. 1993: 805 = $1 US). **Gross national product** (1991): $273 bln. **Per capita GNP:** $6,300. **Imports** (1992): $81 bln.; partners: Jap. 26%, U.S. 21%. **Exports** (1992): $72 bln.; partners: U.S. 26%, Jap. 18%. **Tourism** (1990): $3.5 bln. receipts. **National budget** (1992): $44.0 bln. expenditures. **International reserves less gold** (Mar. 1993): $18 bln. **Gold:** 323,000 oz t. **Consumer prices** (change in 1992): 6.2%.

Transport: Railroads (1990): 4,000 mi. long. **Motor vehicles** (1990): 2.0 mln passenger cars, 1.3 mln comm. vehicles. **Civil aviation** (1990): 18.7 bln. passenger-km; 12 airlines with scheduled flights. **Chief ports:** Pusan, Inchon.

Communications: Television sets: 1 per 4.9 persons. **Radios:** 1 per 1.0 persons. **Telephones:** 1 per 3.3 persons. **Daily newspaper circ.** (1990): 309 per 1,000 pop.

Health: Life expectancy at birth (1992): 67 male; 73 female. **Births** (per 1,000 pop. 1992): 15. **Deaths** (per 1,000 pop. 1992): 6. **Natural increase:** 0.9%. **Hospital beds:** 1 per 429 persons. **Physicians:** 1 per 1,007 persons. **Infant mortality** (per 1,000 live births 1992): 23.0.

Education (1991): **Literacy:** 96%. **School:** 90% attend high school, 14% college.

Major International Organizations: UN.

Embassy: 4 Palace Gate, London W8 5LY; 071-581 0247.

Korea, once called the Hermit Kingdom, has a recorded history since the 1st century BC. It was united in a kingdom under the Silla Dynasty, AD 668. It was at times associated with the Chinese empire; the treaty that concluded the Sino-Japanese war of 1894-95 recognized Korea's complete independence. In 1910 Japan forcibly annexed Korea as Chosun.

At the Potsdam conference, July, 1945, the 38th parallel was designated as the line dividing the Soviet and the American occupation. Russian troops entered Korea Aug. 10, 1945, U.S. troops entered Sept. 8, 1945. The Soviet military organized socialists and communists and blocked efforts to let the Koreans unite their country. *(See Index for Korean War.)*

The South Koreans formed the Republic of Korea in May 1948 with Seoul as the capital. Dr. Syngman Rhee was chosen president but a movement spearheaded by college students forced his resignation Apr. 26, 1960.

In an army coup May 16, 1961 Gen. Park Chung Hee became chairman of the ruling junta. He was elected president, 1963; a 1972 referendum allowed him to be reelected for 6 year terms unlimited times. Park was assassinated by the chief of the Korean CIA, Oct. 26, 1979. The calm of the new government was halted by the rise of Gen. Chun Doo Hwan, head of the military intelligence, who reinstated martial law, and reverted South Korea to the police state it was under Park.

In July 1972 South and North Korea agreed on a common goal of reunifying the 2 nations by peaceful means. But there was no sign of a thaw in relations between the two regimes until 1985 when they agreed to discuss economic issues. In 1988, radical students demanding reunification clashed with police.

On June 10, 1987 middle class office workers, shopkeepers, and business executives joined students in antigovernment protests in Seoul. They were protesting President Chun's decision to choose his successor and not allow the next president to be chosen by direct vote of the people. Following weeks of rioting and violence, Chun, July 1, agreed to permit election of the next president by direct popular vote and other constitutional reforms. In Dec., Roh Tae Woo was elected president. In 1990 the nation's 3 largest political parties merged; some 100,000 students demonstrated, charging that the merger was undemocratic.

Kim Young Sam took office in 1993 as the first civilian president since 1961.

Kuwait

State of Kuwait

Dowlat al-Kuwait

People: Population (1992 est.): 1,318,000. **Age distrib.** (%): 0–14: 35.5; 15–59: 62.1; 60+: 2.4. **Pop. density:** 191 per sq. mi. **Urban** (1990): 95%. **Ethnic groups:** Kuwaiti 50%, other Arab 35%, Iranians, Indians, Pakistanis. **Language:** Arabic (official). **Religion:** Muslim 85%.

Geography: Area: 6,880 sq. mi., slightly smaller than Wales. **Location:** In Middle East, at N end of Persian Gulf. **Neighbors:** Iraq on N, Saudi Arabia on S. **Topography:** The country is flat, very dry, and extremely hot. **Capital:** Kuwait. **Cities** (1985 est.): Hawalli 145,000; as-Salimiyah 153,000.

Government: Type: Constitutional monarchy. **Head of state:** Emir Shaikh Jabir al-Ahmad al-Jabir as-Sabah; b. 1928; in office: Jan. 1, 1978. **Head of government:** Prime Min. Shaikh Saad Abdulla as-Salim as-Sabah; in office: Feb. 8, 1978. **Local divisions:** 5 governorates. **Defense** (1991): 21% of GDP.

Economy: Industries: Oil products. **Minerals:** Oil, gas. **Crude oil reserves** (1990): 94 bln. barrels. **Cultivated land:** 1%. **Electricity prod.** (1991): 3.1 bln. kWh. **Labor force:** 45% social services; 20% construction.

Finance: Monetary unit: Dinar (Mar. 1993: 1.0 = $3.30 US). **Gross domestic product** (1991): $8.7 bln. **Per capita GDP:** $6,200. **Imports** (1991): $4.7 bln.; partners: Jap. 21%, U.S. 9%. **Exports** (1989): $11.4 bln.; partners: Jap. 16%, It. 10%. **Tourism** (1990): $80 mln. receipts. **National budget** (1992): $21 bln. expenditures. **International reserves less gold** (Mar. 1993): $4.2 bln. **Gold:** 2.53 mln. oz t.

Transport: Motor vehicles (1990): 500,000 passenger cars, 114,000 comm. vehicles. **Civil aviation** (1991): 1.8 mln. passenger-km; 1 airport with scheduled flights. **Chief port:** Mina al-Ahmadi.

Communications: Television sets: 1 per 2.6 persons. **Radios:** 1 per 1.8 persons. **Telephones:** 1 per 6.9 persons. **Daily newspaper circ.** (1992): 550 per 1,000 pop.

Health: Life expectancy at birth (1992): 72 male; 76 female. **Births** (per 1,000 pop. 1992): 32. **Deaths** (per 1,000 pop. 1992): 2. **Natural increase:** 3.0%. **Hospital beds:** 1 per 336 persons. **Physicians:** 1 per 695 persons. **Infant mortality** (per 1,000 live births 1992): 15.

Education (1989): **Literacy:** 71%. **School:** Compulsory for 8 years.

Major International Organizations: UN (World Bank, IMF, GATT), Arab League, OPEC.

Embassy: 45 Queen's Gate, London SW7 5HR; 071-589 4533.

Kuwait is ruled by the Al-Sabah dynasty, founded 1759. Britain ran foreign relations and defense from 1899 until independence in 1961. The majority of the population is non-Kuwaiti, with many Palestinians, and cannot vote.

Oil, first exported in 1946, is the fiscal mainstay, providing most of Kuwait's income. Oil pays for free medical care, education, and social security. There are no taxes, except customs duties.

Kuwaiti oil tankers have come under frequent attack by Iran because of Kuwait's support of Iraq in the Iran-Iraq War. In July 1987, U.S. Navy warships began escorting Kuwaiti tankers in the Persian Gulf.

In 1988, a Kuwaiti Airways jet was hijacked by pro-Iranian Shiite Muslim terrorists who demanded the release of 17 Shiite terrorists. The ordeal lasted 16 days as Kuwait refused to release them.

Kuwait was attacked and overrun by Iraqi forces Aug. 2, 1990. The Emir and senior members of the ruling family fled to Saudi Arabia to establish a government in exile. On Aug. 28, Iraq announced that Kuwait was its 19th province.

Following several weeks of aerial attacks on Iraq and Iraqi forces in Kuwait, a U.S.-led coalition began a ground attack Feb. 23, 1991. By Feb. 27, Iraqi forces were routed and Kuwait liberated.

Following liberation, there were reports of abuse of Palestinians and others suspected of collaborating with Iraqi occupiers.

Former U.S. President George Bush visited Kuwait, Apr. 14–16, 1993, and was honoured as the leader of the Persian Gulf War alliance that expelled Iraqi troops in 1991. Prior to the visit, Kuwaiti authorities arrested a group of Iraqis who had planned to assassinate Bush during his visit. An inquiry by the FBI substantiated accusations that the Iraqi government was involved in the plot.

Republic of Kyrgyzstan

Kyrgyz Respublikasy

People: Population (1992 est.): 4,567,000. **Pop. density:** 59 per sq. mi. **Urban.** (1991): 38%. **Ethnic groups:** Kyrghiz 52%, Russian 22%, Uzbec 13%.

Geography: Area: 76,642 sq. mi., slightly smaller than GB. **Neighbors:** Kazakhstan on N, China on E, Uzbekistan on W, Tajikistan on S. **Capital:** Bishkek. **Cities** (1991): Bishkek 631,000; Osh 218,000.

Government: Type: Republic. **Head of state:** Pres. Askar Akayev. **Head of government:** Prime Min. Tursunbek Chyngyshev. **Local divisions:** 6 oblasts.

Economy: Industries: Tanning, tobacco, textiles, mining. **Chief crops:** Wheat, sugar beets, tobacco. **Livestock** (1989): 1.2 mln. cattle; 10.4 mln. sheep.

Finance: Monetary unit: Som (May 1993): 4.16 = $1 US.

Transport: Railroads (1991): 490 mi. long. **Motor vehicles** (1990): 173,000 passenger cars. **Civil aviation** (1990): 3.7 bln. passenger-km; 1 airport.

Communications: Telephones: 1 per 14 persons. **Newspaper circ.** (1990): 367 per 1,000 pop.

Health: Life expectancy at birth (1992): 62 male; 71 female. **Birth rate** (per 1,000 pop. 1992): 31. **Death rate** (per 1,000 pop. 1992): 8. **Hospital beds:** 1 per 84 persons. **Physicians:** 1 per 275 persons. **Infant mortality** (1 per 1,000 live births 1992): 56.

Major International Organizations: UN (IMF), CIS.

The region was inhabited around the 13th century by the Kirghiz. It was annexed to Russia 1864. After 1917, it was nominally a Kara-Kirghiz autonomous area, which was reorganized 1926, and made a constituent republic of the USSR in 1936. Krygyzstan declared independence Aug. 31, 1991. It became an independent state when the Soviet Union disbanded Dec. 26, 1991.

Laos

Lao People's Democratic Republic

Sathalanalat Paxathipatai Paxax n Lao

People: Population (1992 est.): 4,440,000. **Pop. density:** 48 per sq. mi. **Urban** (1990): 19%. **Ethnic groups:** Lao 50%, Mon-Khmer tribes 25%, Thai 14%, Meo and Yao 13%, others. **Languages:** Lao (official), Palaung-Wa, Tai. **Religions:** Buddhism 80%, tribal 20%.

Geography: Area: 91,428 sq. mi., slightly smaller than the UK. **Location:** In Indochina Peninsula in SE Asia. **Neighbors:** Myanmar, China on N, Vietnam on E, Cambodia on S, Thailand on W. **Topography:** Landlocked, dominated by jungle. High mountains along the eastern border are the source of the E-W rivers slicing across the country to the Mekong R., which defines most of the western border. **Capital:** Vientiane, pop. (1985 cen.) 377,000.

Government: Type: Communist. **Head of state:** Pres. Nouhak Phoumsavan; in office Nov. 25, 1992. **Head of government:** Prime Min. Khamtai Siphandon; in office: Aug. 15, 1991. **Local divisions:** 17 provinces, municipality. **Defense** (1988): 3.8% of GDP.

Economy: Industries: Wood products, mining. **Chief crops:** Rice, corn, tobacco, cotton, opium, citrus fruits, coffee. **Minerals:** Tin. **Other resources:** Forests. **Arable land:** 4%. **Livestock** (1990): 1.3 mln. pigs. **Fish catch** (1990): 20,000 metric tons. **Electricity prod.** (1991): 1.1 bln. kWh. **Labor force:** 85% agric.; 6% ind.

Finance: Monetary unit: New kip (Dec. 1992: 714 = $1 US). **Gross domestic product** (1991): $800 mln. **Per capita GDP:** $200. **Imports** (1990): $240 mln.; partners: Thai. 45%, Jap. 20%. **Exports** (1990): $72 mln.; partners: Thai, Viet, USSR.

Transport: Motor vehicles (1989): 17,000 passenger cars, 3,500 comm. vehicles. **Civil Aviation** (1987): 18 mln. passenger km; 4 airports with scheduled flights.

Communications: Radios: 1 per 9 persons.

Health: Life expectancy at birth (1992): 49 male; 52 female. **Births** (per 1,000 pop. 1992): 44. **Deaths** (per 1,000 pop. 1992): 16. **Natural increase:** 2.8%. **Hospital beds:** 1 per 369 persons. **Physicians:** 1 per 6,495 persons. **Infant mortality** (per 1,000 live births, 1992): 107.

Education (1991): **Literacy:** 45%.

Major International Organizations: UN (FAO, IMF, WHO).

Laos became a French protectorate in 1893, but regained independence as a constitutional monarchy July 19, 1949.

Conflicts among neutralist, communist and conservative factions created a chaotic political situation. Armed conflict increased after 1960.

The 3 factions formed a coalition government in June 1962, with neutralist Prince Souvanna Phouma as premier. A 14-nation conference in Geneva signed agreements, 1962, guaranteeing neutrality and independence. By 1964 the Pathet Lao had withdrawn from the coalition, and, with aid from N. Vietnamese troops, renewed sporadic attacks. U.S. planes bombed the Ho Chi Minh trail, supply line from N. Vietnam to communist forces in Laos and S. Vietnam.

In 1970 the U.S. stepped up air support and military aid. After Pathet Lao military gains, Souvanna Phouma in May 1975 ordered government troops to cease fighting; the Pathet Lao took control. A Lao People's Democratic Republic was proclaimed Dec. 3, 1975.

Latvia

Republic of Latvia

Latvijas Republika

People: Population (1992 est.): 2,728,000. **Pop. density:** 109 per sq. mi. **Urban** (1991): 71%. **Ethnic groups:** Latvian 54%, Russian 33%. **Language:** Latvian. **Religion:** Mostly Evangelical Lutheran.

Geography: Area: 24,900 sq. mi., half the size of England. **Neighbors:** Estonia & Baltic Sea on N., Baltic Sea on W., Lithuania & Belarus on S., Russia on E. **Capital:** Riga, pop. (1991) 910,000.

Government: Type: Republic. **Head of state:** Anatolijs Gorbunovs. **Head of government:** Prime Min. Ivars Godmanis. **Local divisions:** 26 districts, 56 towns, 37 urban settlements.

Economy: Industries: Electric railway passenger cars, paper. **Chief crops:** oats, barley, potatoes. **Livestock** (1989): 1.5 mln. cattle. **Arable land:** 27%. **Electricity prod.** (1991): 5 bln. kWh. **Labor force:** 16% agric. & forestry; 41% ind. & comm.

Finance: Monetary unit: Latvian ruble. **Imports** (1990): 9.0 bln. **Exports** (1990): 239 mln.

Transport: Railroads (1991): 1,489 mi. long. **Motor vehicles** (1990): 271,000 passenger cars, 14,000 comm. vehicles. **Civil aviation** (1990): 3.7 bln. passenger-km.; 1 airport.

Communications: Telephones: 1 per 3.7 persons. **Newspaper circ.** (1990): 637 per 1,000 pop.

Health: Life expectancy at birth (1992): 64 male, 75 female. **Births** (per 1,000 pop. 1992): 15. **Deaths** (per 1,000 pop. 1992): 12. **Hospital beds:** 1 per 60 persons. **Physicians:** 1 per 200 persons. **Infant mortality** (per 1,000 live births 1992): 19.

Embassy: 72 Queensborough Terrace, London W2 3SP; 071-727 1698.

Prior to 1918, Latvia was occupied by the Russians and Germans. Was an independent republic 1918–39. The Aug. 1939 Soviet-German agreement assigned it to the Soviet sphere of influence. It was officially accepted as part of the USSR on Aug. 5, 1940. It was overrun by the German army, but retaken 1945. It attempted to establish independence 1990.

During an abortive Soviet coup, Latvia declared independence, Aug. 21, 1991. The Soviet Union recognized Latvia's independence in Sept. 1991.

Lebanon

Republic of Lebanon

al-Jumhouriya al-Lubnaniya

People: Population (1992 est.): 3,439,000. **Age distrib.** (%): 0–14: 37.0; 15–59: 55.1; 60+: 7.9. **Pop. density:** 856 per sq. mi. **Urban** (1990): 84%. **Ethnic groups:** Arab 85%, Palestinian 9%,

Armenian 4%. **Languages:** Arabic (official), French. **Religions:** Muslim 75%; Christian 25%.

Geography: Area: 4,015 sq. mi., smaller than Strathclyde. **Location:** On Eastern end of Mediterranean Sea. **Neighbors:** Syria on E. Israel on S. **Topography:** There is a narrow coastal strip, and 2 mountain ranges running N-S enclosing the fertile Beqaa Valley. The Litani R. runs S through the valley, turning W to empty into the Mediterranean. **Capital:** Beirut. **Cities** (1991 est.): Beirut 1,100,000; Tripoli 240,000.

Government: Type: Republic. **Head of state:** Pres. Elias Hrawi; in office Nov. 24, 1989. **Head of government:** Prime Min. Rafiq al-Hariri; in office Oct. 31, 1992. **Local divisions:** 5 governorates. **Defense** (1992): 8.2% of GDP.

Economy: Industries: Trade, food products, textiles, cement, oil products. **Chief crops:** Fruits, olives, tobacco, grapes, vegetables, grains. **Minerals:** Iron. **Arable land:** 21%. **Livestock** (1991): 400,000 goats; 205,000 sheep. **Electricity prod.** (1991): 3.8 bln. kWh. **Labor force:** 11% agric.; 79% ind., comm., services.

Finance: Monetary unit: Pound (Aug. 1993: 1,728 = $1 US). **Gross domestic product** (1991): $4.8 bln. **Per capita GDP:** $1,400. **Imports** (1990): $1.9 bln.; partners: It. 15%, Fr. 10%, U.S. 6%. **Exports** (1990): $700 mln.; partners: Saudi Ar. 16%, Jor. 6%, Kuw. 8%. **National budget** (1991): $1.3 bln. expenditures. **International reserves less gold** (Mar. 1993): $801.2 bln. **Gold:** 9.22 mln. oz t.

Transport: Motor vehicles (1985): 300,000 passenger cars, 50,000 comm. vehicles. **Civil aviation** (1990): 1.5 bln. passenger-km. **Chief ports:** Beirut, Tripoli, Sidon.

Communications: Television sets: 1 per 3.4 persons. **Radios:** 1 per 1.3 persons. **Telephones:** 1 per 18.4 persons. **Daily newspaper circ.** (1986): 211 per 1,000 pop.

Health: Life expectancy at birth (1992): 66 male; 71 female. **Births** (per 1,000 pop. 1992): 28. **Deaths** (per 1,000 pop. 1992): 7. **Natural increase:** 2.1%. **Hospital beds:** 1 per 263 persons. **Physicians:** 1 per 771 persons. **Infant mortality** (per 1,000 live births 1992): 43.

Education (1991): **Literacy:** 75%. **School:** Compulsory for 5 years; attendance 93%.

Major International Organizations: UN (IMF, ILO, WHO).

Embassy: 21 Kensington Palace Gardens, London W8 4QN; 071-229 7265.

Formed from 5 former Turkish Empire districts, Lebanon became an independent state Sept. 1, 1920, administered under French mandate 1920-41. French troops withdrew in 1946.

Under the 1943 National Covenant, all public positions were divided among the various religious communities, with Christians in the majority. By the 1970s, Muslims became the majority and demanded a larger political and economic role.

U.S. Marines intervened, May-Oct. 1958, during a Syrian-aided revolt. Continued raids against Israeli civilians, 1970-75, brought Israeli attacks against guerrilla camps and villages. Israeli troops occupied S. Lebanon, March 1978, and again in Apr. 1980.

An estimated 60,000 were killed and billions of dollars in damage inflicted in a 1975-76 civil war. Palestinian units and leftist Muslims fought against the Maronite militia, the Phalange, and other Christians. Several Arab countries provided political and arms support to the various factions, while Israel aided Christian forces. Up to 15,000 Syrian troops intervened in 1976, and fought Palestinian groups. Arab League troops from several nations tried to impose a cease-fire.

Clashes between Syrian troops and Christian forces erupted, Apr. 1, 1981, bringing to an end the ceasefire. By Apr. 22, fighting had also broken out between two Muslim factions. In July, Israeli air raids on Beirut killed or wounded some 800 persons.

Israeli forces invaded Lebanon June 6, 1982, in a coordinated land, sea, and air attack aimed at crushing strongholds of the Palestine Liberation Organization (PLO). Israeli and Syrian forces engaged in the Bekaa Valley. By June 14, Israeli troops had encircled Beirut. On Aug. 21, the PLO evacuated west Beirut following massive Israeli bombings of the city. Israeli troops entered west Beirut following the Sept. 14 assassination of newly elected Lebanese Pres. Bashir Gemayel. On Sept. 16, Lebanese Christian troops entered 2 refugee camps and massacred hundreds of Palestinian refugees. Israeli troops withdrew from Lebanon in June 1985.

In 1983, terrorist bombings became a way of life in Beirut as some 50 people were killed in an explosion at the U.S. Embassy, Apr. 18; 241 U.S. servicemen and 58 French soldiers died in separate Muslim suicide attacks, Oct. 23.

On Apr. 26, 1984, pro-Syrian Rashid Karami was appointed premier. The appointment failed to end virtual civil war in Beirut between Christian forces and Druse and Shiite Muslim militias. There was heavy fighting between Shiite militiamen and Palestinian guerrillas in May 1985. In June, Beirut Airport was the scene of a hostage crisis where Shiite terrorists held U.S. citizens for 17 days. Fierce artillery duels between Christian east Beirut and Muslim west Beirut, Mar.-Apr. 1989, left some 200 dead and 700 wounded.

Kidnapping of foreign nationals by Islamic militants became common in the 1980s. U.S., British, French, and Soviet citizens were victims. All were released by 1992.

A treaty signed May 22, 1991, between Lebanon and Syria recognized Lebanon as a separate and independent state for the first time since the 2 countries gained independence in 1943.

Israeli forces conducted air raids and artillery strikes against guerrilla bases and villages in S. Lebanon, causing over 200,000 to flee their homes July 25–29, 1993.

Lesotho

Kingdom of Lesotho

People: Population (1992 est.): 1,848,000. **Age distrib.** (%): 0–14: 42.3; 15–59: 52.2; 60+: 5.7. **Pop. density:** 157 per sq. mi. **Ethnic groups:** Sotho 99%. **Languages:** English, Sotho (both official). **Religions:** Roman Catholic 38%, Protestant 42%.

Geography: Area: 11,716 sq. mi., about twice the size of N. Ireland. **Location:** In Southern Africa. **Neighbors:** Completely surrounded by Republic of South Africa. **Topography:** Landlocked and mountainous, with altitudes ranging from 5,000 to 11,000 ft. **Capital:** Maseru, pop. (1990 est.) 109,000.

Government: Type: Parliamentary democracy & constitutional monarchy. **Head of state:** King Letsie III; in office Nov. 12, 1990. **Head of government:** Prime Min. Ntsu Mokhehle; in office: Apr. 1, 1993. **Local divisions:** 10 districts. **Defense** (1990): 8.6% of GDP.

Economy: Industries: Food processing. **Chief crops:** Corn, grains, peas, beans. **Other resources:** Diamonds. **Arable land:** 13%. **Labor force:** 40% agric.

Finance: Monetary unit: Maloti (Mar. 1993: 2.94 = $1 US). **Gross domestic product** (1990): $420 mln. **Per capita GDP:** $240. **Imports** (1990): $600 mln.; partners: mostly S. Afr. **Exports** (1990): $60 mln.; partners: mostly S. Afr. **National budget** (1991): $288 mln.

Transport: Motor vehicles (1987): 6,000 passenger cars, 15,000 comm. vehicles.

Communications: Radios: 1 per 5 persons. **Daily newspaper circ.** (1990): 5 per 1,000 pop.

Health: Life expectancy at birth (1992): 60 male; 63 female. **Births** (per 1,000 pop. 1992): 35. **Deaths** (per 1,000 pop. 1992): 10. **Natural increase:** 2.5%. **Hospital beds:** 1 per 672 persons. **Physicians:** 1 per 15,728 persons. **Infant mortality** (per 1,000 live births 1992): 74.

Education (1990): **Literacy:** 59%.

Major International Organizations: UN (IMF, UNESCO, WHO), OAU.

High Commission: 10 Collingham Rd, London SW5 0LT; 071-373 8581.

Lesotho (once called Basutoland) became a British protectorate in 1868 when Chief Moshesh sought protection against the Boers. Independence came Oct. 4, 1966. Elections were suspended in 1970. Most of Lesotho's GDP is provided by citizens working in S. Africa. Livestock raising is the chief industry; diamonds are the chief export.

South Africa imposed a blockade, Jan. 1, 1986, because of Lesotho's giving sanctuary to rebel groups fighting to overthrow the South African Government. The blockade sparked a Jan. 20 military coup, and was lifted, Jan. 25, when the new leaders agreed to expel the rebels.

In 1990 King Moshoeshoe was sent into exile by the military government. In Mar. 1993 Ntsu Mokhehle, a civilian, was elected prime minister, ending 23 years of military rule.

Liberia

Republic of Liberia

People: Population (1992 est.): 2,462,000. **Age distrib.** (%): 0–14: 46.8; 15–59: 48.3; 60+: 4.9. **Pop. density:** 64 per sq. mi. **Urban** (1990): 46%. **Ethnic groups:** Americo-Liberians 5%, indigenous tribes 95%. **Languages:** English (official), tribal dialects. **Religions:** Traditional beliefs 70%, Muslim 20%, Christian 10%.

Geography: Area: 38,250 sq. mi., about the size of Scotland and Wales combined. **Location:** On SW coast of W. Africa. **Neighbors:** Sierra Leone on W, Guinea on N, Côte d'Ivoire on E. **Topography:** Marshy Atlantic coastline rises to low mountains and plateaus in the forested interior; 6 major rivers flow in parallel courses to the ocean. **Capital:** Monrovia, (1987 est.) 400,000.

Government: Type: Civilian republic. **Head of state:** Pres. Amos Sawyer, act.; in office Nov. 22, 1990. **Local divisions:** 13 counties. **Defense** (1987): 3.8% of GDP.

Economy: Industries: Food processing, mining. **Chief crops:** Rice, cassava, coffee, cocoa, sugar. **Minerals:** Iron, diamonds, gold. **Other resources:** Rubber, timber. **Arable land:** 1%. **Fish catch** (1990): 16,000 metric tons. **Electricity prod.** (1991): 750 mln. kWh. **Labor force:** 82% agric.

Finance: Monetary unit: Dollar (May 1992: 1.00 = $1 US). **Gross domestic product** (1989): $1.0 bln. **Per capita GDP:** $440. **Imports** (1989): $394 mln.; partners: U.S. 32%, W. Ger. 10%, Jap. 6%, Neth. 7%. **Exports** (1989): $505 mln.; partners: W. Ger. 31%, U.S. 20%, It. 14%, Fr. 9%. **National budget** (1989): $435 mln. **International reserves less gold** (Feb. 1991): $7,000. **Consumer prices** (change in 1990): 5.8%.

Transport: Motor vehicles (1990): 8,000 passenger cars, 4,000 comm. vehicles. **Chief ports:** Monrovia, Buchanan, Greenville.

Communications: Television sets: 1 per 60 persons. **Radios:** 1 per 4.4 persons. **Telephones:** 1 per 278 persons. **Daily newspaper circ.** (1990): 11 per 1,000 pop.

Health: Life expectancy at birth (1992): 54 male; 59 female. **Births** (per 1,000 pop. 1992): 45. **Deaths** (per 1,000 pop. 1992): 13. **Natural increase:** 3%. **Hospital beds** (1981): 3,000. **Physicians** (1981): 236. **Infant mortality** (per 1,000 live births 1992): 119.

Education (1990): **Literacy:** 40%. **School:** 35% attend primary school.

Major International Organizations: UN and most specialized agencies, OAU.

Embassy: 2 Pembridge Place, London W2 4XB; 071-221 1036.

Liberia was founded in 1822 by U.S. black freedmen who settled at Monrovia with the aid of colonization societies. It became a republic July 26, 1847, with a constitution modeled on that of the U.S. Descendants of freedmen dominated politics.

Charging rampant corruption, an Army Redemption Council of enlisted men staged a bloody predawn coup, April 12, 1980, in which Pres. Tolbert was killed and replaced as head of state by Sgt. Samuel Doe. Doe was chosen president in a disputed election, and survived a subsequent coup, in 1985.

A civil war began Dec. 1989. Rebel forces seeking to depose Pres. Doe made major territorial gains and advanced on the capital, June 1990. In Sept., Doe was captured and put to death. A ceasefire was declared Feb. 13, 1991. More than half of the nation's population became refugees as a result of the civil war.

Libya

Socialist People's Libyan Arab Jamahiriya

al-Jamahiriyah al-Arabiya al-Libya al-Shabiya al-Ishtirakiya

People: Population: (1992 est.): 4,485,000. **Age distrib.** (%): 0–14: 45.0; 15–59: 51.2; 60+: 3.8. **Pop. density:** 6 per sq. mi. **Urban** (1990): 70%. **Ethnic groups:** Arab-Berber 97%. **Language:** Arabic. **Religion:** Sunni Muslim 97%.

Geography: Area: 679,359 sq. mi., nearly 6 times larger than the Br. Isles. **Location:** On Mediterranean coast of N. Africa. **Neighbors:** Tunisia, Algeria on W, Niger, Chad on S, Sudan, Egypt on E. **Topography:** Desert and semidesert regions cover 92% of the land, with low mountains in N, higher mountains in S, and a narrow coastal zone. **Capital:** Tripoli, (1988 est.) 591,000.

Government: Type: Islamic Arabic Socialist "Mass-State." **Head of state:** Col. Muammar al-Qaddafi; b. Sept. 1942; in office Sept. 1969. **Head of government:** Premier Abu Zaid Umar Dourda; in office Oct. 7, 1990. **Local divisions:** 25 municipalities. **Defense** (1987): 11.1% of GDP.

Economy: Industries: Carpets, textiles, petroleum. **Chief crops:** Dates, olives, citrus and other fruits, grapes, wheat. **Minerals:** Gypsum, oil, gas. **Crude oil reserves** (1987): 22 bln. bbls. **Arable land:** 2%. **Livestock** (1991): 5.5 mln. sheep; 1.0 mln. goats. **Electricity prod.** (1991): 13.6 bln. kWh. **Labor force:** 18% agric.; 31% ind.; 27% services; 24% govt.

Finance: Monetary unit: Dinar (Feb. 1993: 0.29 = $1 US). **Gross domestic product** (1990): $28.9 bln. **Per capita GDP:** $6,800. **Imports** (1990): $7.6 bln.; partners: It. 21%, W. Ger. 11%, Fr. 6%. **Exports** (1990): $11.0 bln.; partners: It. 57%, W. Ger. 27%, Sp. 13%. **National budget** (1989): $9.8 bln. expenditures. **International reserves less gold** (Mar. 1993): $6.1 bln. **Gold:** 3.6 mln. oz t.

Transport: Motor vehicles (1989): 448,000 passenger cars, 322,000 comm. vehicles. **Chief ports:** Tripoli, Benghazi.

Communications: Television sets: 1 per 8 persons. **Radios:** 1 per 4 persons. **Daily newspaper circ.** (1990): 10 per 1,000 pop.

Health: Life expectancy at birth (1992): 66 male; 71 female. **Births** (per 1,000 pop. 1992): 36. **Deaths** (per 1,000 pop. 1992): 6. **Natural increase:** 3.0%. **Hospital beds** (1982): 16,051. **Physicians** (1982): 5,200. **Infant mortality** (per 1,000 live births 1992): 60.

Education (1991): **Literacy:** 64%. **School:** Compulsory for 7 years; attendance 90%.

Major International Organizations: UN, Arab League, OAU, OPEC.

Libyan Interests Section: 119 Harley St, London W1N 1DH; 071-486 8250.

First settled by Berbers, Libya was ruled by Carthage, Rome, and Vandals, the Ottomans, Italy from 1912, and Britain and France after WW II. It became an independent constitutional monarchy Jan. 2, 1952. In 1969 a junta led by Col. Qaddafi seized power.

In the mid-1970s, Libya helped arm violent revolutionary groups in Egypt and Sudan, and aided international terrorists.

Libya and Egypt fought several air and land battles along their border in July, 1977. Chad charged Libya with military occupation of its uranium-rich northern region in 1977. Libyan troops were driven from their last major stronghold by Chad forces in 1987, leaving over $1 billion in military equipment behind.

On Jan. 7, 1986, the U.S. imposed economic sanctions against Libya, ordered all Americans to leave that country and froze all Libyan assets in the U.S. The U.S. commenced flight operations over the Gulf of Sidra, Jan. 27, and a U.S. Navy task force began conducting exercises in the Gulf, Mar. 23. When Libya fired antiaircraft missiles at American warplanes, the U.S. responded by sinking 2 Libyan ships and bombing a missile installation in Libya. The U.S. withdrew from the Gulf, Mar. 27.

The U.S. accused Libyan leader Qaddafi of having ordered the April 5 bombing of a West Berlin discotheque which killed 3, including a U.S. serviceman. After failing to get their European allies to join them in imposing economic sanctions against Libya, the U.S. sent warplanes to attack terrorist-related targets in Tripoli and Benghazi, Libya, Apr. 14.

The UN imposed limited sanctions, Apr. 15, 1992, for Libya's failure to extradite 2 intelligence agents linked to the 1988 bombing of Pan American World Airways flight 103 over Lockerbie, Scotland, and 4 others linked to an aeroplane bombing over Niger.

Liechtenstein

Principality of Liechtenstein

Fürstentum Liechtenstein

People: Population (1992 est.): 28,642. **Age distrib.** (%): 0–14: 20.1; 15–59: 66.3; 60+: 11.6. **Pop. density:** 461 per sq. mi. **Ethnic groups:** Alemannic 95%, Italian 5%. **Languages:** German (official), Alemannic dialect. **Religions:** Roman Catholic 87%, Protestant 8%.

Geography: Area: 62 sq. mi., about half the size of the Isle of Wight. **Location:** In the Alps. **Neighbors:** Switzerland on W, Austria on E. **Topography:** The Rhine Valley occupies one-third of the country, the Alps cover the rest. **Capital:** Vaduz. **Cities** (1989 cen.): Vaduz 4,874, Schaan 4,930.

Government: Type: Hereditary constitutional monarchy. **Head of state:** Prince Hans Adam; in office Nov. 13, 1989. **Head of government:** Hans Brunhart; b. Mar. 28, 1945; in office Apr. 26, 1978. **Local divisions:** 2 districts, 11 communities.

Economy: Industries: Machines, instruments, chemicals, furniture, ceramics. **Arable land:** 25%. **Labor force:** 54% industry, trade and building; 41% services; 4% agric., fishing, forestry.

Finance: Monetary unit: Swiss Franc. **Gross domestic product** (1990): $630 mln.

Communications: Radios: 1 per 2.9 persons. **Telephones:** 1 per 1.0 persons. **Daily newspaper circ.** (1990): 598 per 1,000 pop.

Health: Births (per 1,000 pop. 1992): 13. **Deaths** (per 1,000 pop. 1992): 7. **Natural increase:** .6%. **Infant mortality** (per 1,000 live births 1992): 5.

Education (1992): **Literacy:** 100%. **School:** Compulsory for 9 years; attendance 100%.

Embassy: Liechtenstein is represented in the UK by the Swiss Embassy.

Liechtenstein became sovereign in 1866. Austria administered the country's ports up to 1920; Switzerland has administered its postal services since 1921. Liechtenstein is united with Switzerland by a customs and monetary union. Taxes are low; many international corporations have headquarters there. Foreign workers comprise a third of the population.

The 1986 general elections were the first in which women were allowed to vote.

Lithuania

Republic of Lithuania

Lietuvos Respublika

People: Population (1992 est.): 3,788,000. **Pop. density:** 150 per sq. mi. **Urban** (1992): 68%. **Ethnic groups:** Lithuanian 80%, Russian 9%, Polish 7%. **Religion:** Mostly Roman Catholic.

Geography: Area: 25,170 sq. mi. **Neighbors:** Latvia on N., Belarus on E., S., Poland, Russia, & Baltic Sea on W. **Capital:** Vilnius. **Cities** (1992): Vilnius 597,000; Kaunas 433,000.

Government: Type: Republic. **Head of state:** Pres. Algirdas Brazauskas; in office Nov. 25, 1992. **Head of government:** Prime

Min. Bronislovas Lubys; in office Dec. 7, 1992.

Economy: Industries: Engineering, shipbuilding. **Chief crops:** grain, potatoes, vegetables. **Arable land:** 49%. **Livestock** (1991): 2.4 mln. cattle; 2.7 mln. pigs. **Electricity prod.** (1991): 25 mln. kWh. **Labor force:** 29% agric., 25% ind.

Finance: Monetary unit: Lit.

Transport: Railroads (1989): 1,951 mi. long. **Civil aviation** (1991): 2.3 mln. passenger-km. 3 airports. **Chief port:** Klaipeda.

Communications: Television sets: 1 per 2.9 persons. **Radios:** 1 per 1.2 persons. **Telephones:** 1 per 4.5 persons.

Health: Life expectancy at birth (1992): 66 male, 76 female. **Births** (per 1,000 pop. 1992): 15. **Deaths** (per 1,000 pop. 1992): 11. **Hospital beds:** 1 per 81 persons. **Physicians:** 1 per 262 persons. **Infant mortality rate** (per 1,000 live births 1992): 18.

Major International Organizations: UN.

Embassy: 17 Essex Villas, London W8 7BP; 071-938 2481.

Lithuania, was occupied by the German Army, 1914-18. It was annexed by the USSR, but the Soviets were overthrown, 1919. Lithuania was a democratic republic until 1926 when the regime was ousted by a coup. In 1939, the Soviet-German treaty assigned most of Lithuania to the Soviet sphere of influence. It became part of the USSR Aug. 3, 1940. Lithuania formally declared its independence from the Soviet Union Mar. 11, 1990. Soviet forces began large-scale maneuvers Mar. 18; border controls were tightened Mar. 21. The Soviets cut off oil and gas supplies Apr. 19. Lithuania agreed to suspend independence May 17, and the oil and gas supplies were renewed.

Soviet troops killed 15 protesters in Vilnius, Jan. 13, 1991, in a crackdown on pro-independence forces. During an abortive Soviet coup in Aug., Lithuania declared full independence, which was recognized by the Soviet Union in Sept. 1991.

In 1992 elections, former communists won an absolute majority in the legislature.

Luxembourg

Grand Duchy of Luxembourg

Grand-Duché de Luxembourg

People: Population: (1992 est.): 392,000. **Age distrib.** (%): 0–14: 17.3; 15–59: 64.5; 60+: 18.2. **Pop. density:** 400 per sq. mi. **Urban** (1991): 85%. **Ethnic groups:** Mixture of French and Germans predominate. **Languages:** French, German (both official), Luxembourgish. **Religion:** Roman Catholic 97%.

Geography: Area: 998 sq. mi., about the size of Co. Durham. **Location:** In W. Europe. **Neighbors:** Belgium on W, France on S, Germany on E. **Topography:** Heavy forests (Ardennes) cover N, S is a low, open plateau. **Capital:** Luxembourg, pop. (1990 est.) 75,000.

Government: Type: Constitutional monarchy. **Head of state:** Grand Duke Jean; b. Jan. 5, 1921; in office: Nov. 12, 1964. **Head of government:** Prime Min. Jacques Santer; in office: July 21, 1984. **Local divisions:** 3 districts. **Defense** (1991): 1.2% of GDP.

Economy: Industries: Steel, chemicals, beer, tires, tobacco, metal products, cement. **Chief crops:** Corn, wine. **Minerals:** Iron. **Arable land:** 25%. **Electricity prod.** (1991): 1.1 bln. kWh. **Labor force:** 1% agric.; 42% ind. & comm.; 45% services.

Finance: Monetary unit: Franc (Mar. 1993: 33.24 = $1 US). **Gross domestic product** (1991): $7.8 bln. **Per capita GDP:** $20,200. **Note:** trade and tourism data included in Belgian statistics. **Tourism** (1989): $286 mln. receipts. **Consumer prices** (change in 1992): 3.2%.

Transport: Railroads (1991): 169 mi. long. **Motor vehicles** (1991): 192,000 passenger cars, 18,000 comm. vehicles.

Communications: Television sets: 1 per 4.0 persons. **Radios:** 1 per 1.6 persons. **Telephones:** 1 per 2.3 persons. **Daily newspaper circ.** (1990): 340 per 1,000 pop.

Health: Life expectancy at birth (1992): 73 male; 80 female. **Births** (per 1,000 pop. 1992): 12. **Deaths** (per 1,000 pop. 1992): 11. **Hospital beds:** 1 per 85 persons. **Physicians:** 1 per 498 persons. **Infant mortality** (per 1,000 live births 1992): 7.

Education (1989): **Literacy:** 100%. **School:** Compulsory for 9 years; attendance 100%.

Major International Organizations: UN, OECD, EC, NATO.

Embassy: 27 Wilton Cres, London SW1X 8SD; 071-235 6961.

Luxembourg, founded about 963, was ruled by Burgundy, Spain, Austria, and France from 1448 to 1815. It left the Germanic Confederation in 1866. Overrun by Germany in 2 world wars, Luxembourg ended its neutrality in 1948, when a customs union with Belgium and Netherlands was adopted.

Macedonia

Republic of Macedonia

People: Population (1992 est.): 2,050,000. **Pop density:** 206 per sq. mi. **Ethnic groups:** Macedonian 68%, Albanian 20%. **Languages:** Macedonian, Albanian, Bulgarian, Greek. **Religions:** Mostly Eastern Orthodox; Muslim.

Geography: Area: 9,928 sq. mi., slightly larger than Wales. **Location:** In SE Europe. **Neighbours:** Bulgaria on E, Greece on S, Albania on W, Yugoslavia on N. **Capital:** Skopje. **Cities** (1991 metro. est.): Skopje 563,000, Tetovo 180,000.

Government: Type: Republic. **Head of state:** Pres. Kiro Gliforov. **Head of government:** Prime Min. Branko Crenkovski. **Local divisions:** 30 districts.

Economy: Industries: Steel, cement. **Chief crops:** Wheat, cotton, tobacco. **Livestock** (1992): 2.2 mln. sheep. **Electricity prod.** (1990): 5.7 bln. kWh.

Finance: Monetary unit: Denar. **Gross domestic product** (1990): $4.8 bln. **Per capita GDP:** $2,399.

Transport: Railroads (1990): 431 mi. long. **Motor vehicles** (1990): 230,000 passenger cars, 23,000 comm. vehicles. **Civil aviation:** 1 airport.

Communications: Television sets: 1 per 5.2 persons. **Radios:** 1 per 4.5 persons. **Telephones:** 1 per 5.7 persons. **Newspaper circ.** (1990): 26 per 1,000 pop.

Health: Hospital beds: 1 per 171 persons. **Physicians:** 1 per 464 persons. **Infant mortality** (per 1,000 live births 1990): 35.3.

Education (1990): Literacy: 90%.

Major International Organizations: UN.

Macedonia, as part of a larger region also called Macedonia, was ruled by Muslim Turks from 1389 to 1912, when native Greeks, Bulgarians and Slavs won independence. Serbia received the largest part of the territory with the rest going to Greece and Bulgaria. The area was incorporated into Serbia in 1918.

Macedonia declared its independence from Yugoslavia Sept. 8, 1991. At the request of Greece, the U.S. and most European nations have not recognized Macedonia as an independent nation until it changes its name and flag, which it has refused to do.

Macedonia was admitted to the UN under a provisional name in 1993. A UN force, which included 300 U.S. troops, was deployed in Macedonia in 1993 to deter the warring factions in Bosnia from carrying their dispute into other areas of the Balkans.

Madagascar

Democratic Republic of Madagascar

Repoblika Demokratika Malagasy

People: Population (1992 est.): 12,596,000. **Pop. density:** 55 per sq. mi. **Urban** (1990): 22%. **Ethnic groups:** 18 Malayan-Indonesian tribes (Merina 26%), with Arab and African presence. **Languages:** Malagasy, French (both official). **Religions:** Animist 52%, Christian 41%, Muslim 7%.

Geography: Area: 226,657 sq. mi., nearly twice the size of the Br. Isles. **Location:** In the Indian O., off the SE coast of Africa. **Neighbors:** Comoro Is., Mozambique (across Mozambique Channel). **Topography:** Humid coastal strip in the E, fertile valleys in the mountainous center plateau region, and a wider coastal strip on the W. **Capital:** Antananarivo, pop. (1990 est.) 802,000.

Government: Type: Republic. **Head of state:** Pres. Albert Zafy; in office Feb. 10, 1993. **Head of government:** Prime Min. Guy Razanamasy; in office Aug. 8, 1991. **Local divisions:** 6 provinces. **Defense** (1989): 2.2% of GDP.

Economy: Industries: Food processing, textiles. **Chief crops:** Coffee (over 50% of exports), cloves, vanilla, rice, sugar, sisal, tobacco, peanuts. **Minerals:** Chromium, graphite, coal, bauxite. **Arable land:** 5%. **Livestock** (1990): 10.4 mln. cattle; 1.3 mln. pigs. **Fish catch** (1990): 99,000 metric tons. **Electricity prod.** (1991): 450 mln. kWh. **Labor force:** 90% agric.

Finance: Monetary unit: Franc (Mar. 1993: 1,920 = $1 US). **Gross domestic product** (1991): $2.4 bln. **Per capita GDP:** $200. **Imports** (1991): $442 mln.; partners: Fr. 32%, U.S. 15%. **Exports** (1991): $305 mln.; partners: Fr. 34%, U.S. 14%. **Tourism** (1990): $28 mln. receipts. **National budget** (1990): $525 mln. **International reserves less gold** (Jan. 1993): $89 mln. **Consumer prices** (change in 1992): 14.5%.

Transport: Railroads (1990): 655 mi. long. **Motor vehicles** (1990): 46,000 passenger cars, 33,000 comm. vehicles. **Civil aviation** (1990): 512 mln. passenger-km; 50 airports with scheduled flights. **Chief ports:** Tamatave, Diego-Suarez, Majunga, Tulear.

Communications: Television sets: 1 per 95 persons. **Radios:** 1 per 8 persons. **Telephones:** 1 per 239 persons.

Health: Life expectancy at birth (1992): 51 male; 55 female. **Births** (per 1,000 pop. 1991): 47. **Deaths** (per 1,000 pop. 1991): 15. **Natural increase:** 3.2%. **Hospital beds** (1982): 20,800. **Phys-**

icians (1982): 940. **Infant mortality** (per 1,000 live births 1992): 93.

Education (1987): **Literacy:** 53%. **School:** Compulsory for 5 years; attendance 83%.

Major International Organizations: UN (GATT, WHO, IMF), OAU.

Consulate: Lanark Mansions, Pennard Rd, London W12 8DT; 081-746 0133.

Madagascar was settled 2,000 years ago by Malayan-Indonesian people, whose descendants still predominate. A unified kingdom ruled the 18th and 19th centuries. The island became a French protectorate, 1885, and a colony 1896. Independence came June 26, 1960.

Discontent with inflation and French domination led to a coup in 1972. The new regime nationalized French-owned financial interests, closed French bases and a U.S. space tracking station, and obtained Chinese aid. The government conducted a program of arrests, expulsion of foreigners, and repression of strikes, 1979.

In 1990, Madagascar ended a ban on multiparty politics that had been in place since 1975. Albert Zafy was elected president of Madagascar in 1993, ending the 17-year rule of Didier Ratsiraka, which was marked by a blend of socialism and authoritarianism.

Malawi

Republic of Malawi

People: Population (1992 est.): 9,605,000. **Age distrib.** (%): 0–14: 47.8; 15–59: 48.0; 60+: 4.2. **Pop. density:** 209 per sq. mi. **Urban** (1990): 15%. **Ethnic groups:** Chewa, 90%, Nyanja, Lomwe, other Bantu tribes. **Languages:** English, Chewa (both official), Lomwe, Yao. **Religions:** Christian 75%, Muslim 20%.

Geography: Area: 45,747 sq. mi., the size of Scotland, Wales and N. Ireland combined. **Location:** In SE Africa. **Neighbors:** Zambia on W, Mozambique on SE, Tanzania on N. **Topography:** Malawi stretches 560 mi. N-S along Lake Malawi (Lake Nyasa), most of which belongs to Malawi. High plateaus and mountains line the Rift Valley the length of the nation. **Capital:** Lilongwe. **Cities** (1987 est.): Blantyre 402,000; Lilongwe 220,000.

Government: Type: One-party state. **Head of state:** Pres. Hastings Kamuzu Banda, b. May 14, 1906; in office July 6, 1966. **Local divisions:** 24 districts. **Defense** (1989): 1.6% of GDP.

Economy: Industries: Textiles, sugar, cement. **Chief crops:** Tea, tobacco, sugar, coffee. **Other resources:** Rubber. **Arable land:** 25%. **Fish catch** (1990): 68 metric tons. **Electricity prod.** (1991): 535 mln. kWh. **Labor force:** 43% agric.; 23% ind. and comm.; 17% services.

Finance: Monetary unit: Kwacha (Mar. 1993): 4.40 = $1 US). **Gross domestic product** (1991): $1.9 bln. **Per capita GDP:** $200. **Imports** (1992): $720 mln.; partners: S. Afr. 29%, UK 24%, Jap. 6%. **Exports** (1992): $392 mln.; partners: UK 27%, S. Afr. 8%., Ger. 10%. **National budget** (1991): $510 mln. **International reserves less gold** (Mar. 1993): $45 mln. **Gold:** 13,000 oz t. **Consumer prices** (change in 1992): 12.4%.

Transport: Railroads (1987): 495 mi. long. **Motor vehicles** (1990): 16,000 passenger cars, 17,000 comm. vehicles. **Civil aviation** (1990) 86 mln. passenger-km; 5 airports with scheduled flights.

Communications: Radios: 1 per 4.3 persons. **Telephones:** 1 per 176 persons. **Daily newspaper circ.** (1991): 3 per 1,000 pop.

Health: Life expectancy at birth (1992): 48 male; 51 female. **Births** (per 1,000 pop. 1992): 52. **Deaths** (per 1,000 pop. 1992): 18. **Natural increase:** 3.4%. **Hospital beds:** 1 per 627 persons. **Physicians:** 1 per 27,094 persons. **Infant mortality** (per 1,000 live births 1992): 136.

Education (1989): **Literacy:** 25%. **School:** About 45% attend.

Major International Organizations: UN (World Bank, IMF), OAU, Commonwealth of Nations.

High Commission: 33 Grosvenor St, London W1X 9FG; 071-4172.

Bantus came in the 16th century, Arab slavers in the 19th. The area became the British protectorate Nyasaland, in 1891. It became independent July 6, 1964, and a republic in 1966.

Malaysia

People: Population (1992 est.): 18,410,000. **Age distrib.** (%): 0–14: 37.8; 15–59: 56.5; 60+: 5.7. **Pop. density:** 144 per sq. mi. **Urban** (1985): 38%. **Ethnic groups:** Malays 59%, Chinese 32%, Indian 9%. **Languages:** Malay (official), English, Chinese, Indian languages. **Religions:** Muslim, Hindu, Buddhist, Confucian, Taoist, local religions.

Geography: Area: 127,316 sq. mi., slightly larger than the Br. Isles. **Location:** On the SE tip of Asia, plus the N. coast of the island of Borneo. **Neighbors:** Thailand on N, Indonesia on S. **Topography:** Most of W. Malaysia is covered by tropical jungle, including the central mountain range that runs N-S through the peninsula. The western coast is marshy, the eastern, sandy. E. Malaysia has a wide, swampy coastal plain, with interior jungles and mountains. **Capital:** Kuala Lumpur, pop. (1991 est.) 1 mln.

Government: Type: Federal parliamentary democracy with a constitutional monarch. **Head of state:** Paramount Ruler Sultan Azlan Shah; in office Apr. 26, 1989. **Head of government:** Prime Min. Datuk Seri Mahathir bin Mohamad; b. Dec. 20, 1925; in office July 16, 1981. **Local divisions:** 13 states and 2 federal territories. **Defense** (1992): 5.0% of GDP.

Economy: Industries: Rubber goods, steel, electronics. **Chief crops:** Palm oil, copra, rice, pepper. **Minerals:** Tin (35% world output), iron. **Crude oil reserves** (1987): 3.2 bln. bbls. **Other resources:** Rubber (35% world output). **Arable land:** 13%. **Livestock** (1990): 2.2 mln. pigs. **Fish catch** (1990): 604,000 metric tons. **Electricity prod.** (1991): 16.5 bln. kWh. **Labor force:** 18% agric.; 11% tourism & trade; 10% govt.

Finance: Monetary unit: Ringgit (June 1993: 2.58 = $1 US). **Gross domestic product** (1991): $48 bln. **Per capita GDP:** $2,670. **Imports** (1991): $38.7 bln.; partners: Jap. 21%, U.S. 18%, Sing. 14%. **Exports** (1991): $35.4 bln.; partners: Jap. 20%, U.S. 17% Sing. 19%, Neth. 6%. **Tourism** (1990): $1.6 bln. receipts. **National budget** (1991): $11.8 bln. **International reserves less gold** (Mar. 1993): $19.4 bln. **Gold:** 2.22 mln. oz t. **Consumer prices** (change in 1992): 4.4%.

Transport: Railroads (incl. Singapore) (1991): 1,381 mi. long. **Motor vehicles** (1990): 1.8 mln. passenger cars, 407,000 comm. vehicles. **Civil aviation** (1990): 11.9 bln. passenger-km; 38 airports with scheduled flights. **Chief ports:** George Town, Kelang, Melaka, Kuching.

Communications: Television sets: 1 per 9 persons. **Radios:** 1 per 2.4 persons. **Telephones:** 1 per 8 persons. **Daily newspaper circ.** (1989): 145 per 1,000 pop.

Health: Life expectancy at birth (1992): 66 male; 71 female. **Births** (per 1,000 pop. 1992): 30. **Deaths** (per 1,000 pop. 1992): 6. **Natural increase:** 2.4%. **Hospital beds:** 1 per 457 persons. **Physicians:** 1 per 2,638 persons. **Infant mortality** (per 1,000 live births 1992): 27.

Education (1991): **Literacy:** 80%. **School:** 96% attend primary school, 65% attend secondary.

Major International Organizations: UN (World Bank, IMF, GATT), ASEAN.

High Commission: 45 Belgrave Sq, London SW1X 8QR; 071-235 8033.

European traders appeared in the 16th century; Britain established control in 1867. Malaysia was created Sept. 16, 1963. It included Malaya (which had become independent in 1957 after the suppression of Communist rebels), plus the formerly-British Singapore, Sabah (N Borneo), and Sarawak (NW Borneo). Singapore was separated in 1965, in order to end tensions between Chinese, the majority in Singapore, and Malays in control of the Malaysian government.

A monarch is elected by a council of hereditary rulers of the Malayan states every 5 years.

Abundant natural resources have assured prosperity, and foreign investment has aided industrialization.

Maldives

Republic of Maldives

Divehi Jumhuriya

People: Population (1992 est.): 226,000. **Age distrib.** (%): 0–14: 44.4; 15–59: 51.7; 60+: 3.9. **Pop. density:** 1,965 per sq. mi. **Urban** (1990): 26%. **Ethnic groups:** Sinhalese, Dravidian, Arab mixture. **Languages:** Divehi (Sinhalese dialect). **Religion:** Sunni Muslim.

Geography: Area: 115 sq. mi., half the size of the Isle of Man. **Location:** In the Indian O. SW of India. **Neighbors:** Nearest is India on N. **Topography:** 19 atolls with 1,087 islands, about 200 inhabited. None of the islands are over 5 sq. mi. in area, and all are nearly flat. **Capital:** Male, pop. (1991 est.) 55,000.

Government: Type: Republic. **Head of state:** Pres. Maumoon Abdul Gayoom; b. Dec. 29, 1939; in office Nov. 11, 1978. **Local divisions:** 19 districts.

Economy: Industries: Fish processing, tourism. **Chief crops:** Coconuts, fruit, millet. **Other resources:** Shells. **Arable land:** 10%. **Fish catch** (1990): 76,000 metric tons. **Electricity prod.** (1991): 11.0 mln. kWh. **Labor force:** 80% fishing, agriculture, & manufacturing.

Finance: Monetary unit: Rufiyaa (Mar. 1993: 10.48 = $1 US). **Gross domestic product** (1990): $174 mln. **Per capita GDP:** $770. **Imports** (1990): $128 mln.; partners: Sing., Ger., Sri Lan. **Exports** (1990): $52 mln.; partners: U.S., U.K. **Tourism** (1990): $142 mln. receipts.

Transport: Chief port: Male Atoll.

Communications: Radios: 1 per 8 persons. **Telephones:** 1 per 60 persons.

Health: Life expectancy at birth (1992): 62 male; 64 female. **Births** (per 1,000 pop. 1992): 45. **Deaths** (per 1,000 pop. 1992): 8. **Natural increase:** 3.7%. **Infant mortality** (per 1,000 live births 1992): 61.

Education (1989): **Literacy:** 93%. **School:** Only 6% of those aged 11-15 attend school.

Major International Organizations: UN.

The islands had been a British protectorate since 1887. The country became independent July 26, 1965. Long a sultanate, the Maldives became a republic in 1968. Natural resources and tourism are being developed; however, it remains one of the world's poorest countries.

Mali

Republic of Mali

République du Mali

People: Population (1992 est.): 8,641,000. **Age distrib.** (%): 0–14: 46.0; 15–59: 49.4; 60+: 4.6. **Pop. density:** 18 per sq. mi. **Urban** (1992): 25%. **Ethnic groups:** Mande (Bambara, Malinke, Sarakole) 50%, Peul 17%, Voltaic 12%, Songhai 6%, Tuareg and Moor, 5%. **Languages:** French (official), Bambara, Senufo. **Religion:** Muslim 90%.

Geography: Area: 478,764 sq. mi., 4 times the size of the Br. Isles. **Location:** In the interior of W. Africa. **Neighbors:** Mauritania, Senegal on W, Guinea, C te d'Ivoire, Burkina Faso on S, Niger on E, Algeria on N. **Topography:** A landlocked grassy plain in the upper basins of the Senegal and Niger rivers, extending N into the Sahara. **Capital:** Bamako, pop. (1989 metro. est.) 800,000.

Government: Type: Republic. **Head of state:** Pres. Alpha Oumar Konare; in office June 8, 1992. **Local divisions:** 8 regions. **Defense** (1989): 2.4% of GDP.

Economy: Chief crops: Millet, rice, peanuts, cotton. **Other resources:** Bauxite, iron, gold. **Arable land:** 2%. **Livestock** (1989): 5.7 mln. sheep; 4.8 mln. cattle. **Fish catch** (1990): 71,000 metric tons. **Electricity prod.** (1991): 750 mln. kWh. **Labor force:** 72% agric.; 12% ind. & comm.; 16% services.

Finance: Monetary unit: Franc (Mar. 1993: 273 = $1 US). **Gross domestic product** (1990): $2.2 bln. **Per capita GDP:** $265. **Imports** (1989): $513 mln.; partners: Fr. 22%, Ivory Coast 25%. **Exports** (1989): $285 mln.; partners: Belg.-Lux. 25%, Fr. 15%. **Tourism** (1990): $37 mln. receipts. **National budget** (1989): $519 mln. expenditures. **International reserves less gold** (Feb. 1993): $307 mln. **Gold:** 19,000 oz t.

Transport: Railroads (1991): 401 mi. long. **Motor vehicles** (1987): 29,000 passenger cars, 7,500 comm. vehicles.

Communications: Radios: 1 per 53 persons. **Telephones:** 1 per 730 persons.

Health: Life expectancy at birth (1992): 43 male; 47 female. **Births** (per 1,000 pop. 1992): 51. **Deaths** (per 1,000 pop. 1992): 21. **Natural increase:** 3.0%. **Hospital beds** (1983): 4,215. **Physicians** (1983): 283. **Infant mortality** (per 1,000 live births 1992): 110.

Education (1991): **Literacy:** 25%. **School:** 21% attend primary school.

Major International Organizations: UN and all of its specialized agencies, OAU, EC.

Embassy: 487 avenue Molière, Brussels 1060, Belgium; 010 32 2 3457432.

Until the 15th century the area was part of the great Mali Empire. Timbuktu was a center of Islamic study. French rule was secured, 1898. The Sudanese Rep. and Senegal became independent as the Mali Federation June 20, 1960, but Senegal withdrew, and the Sudanese Rep. was renamed Mali.

Mali signed economic agreements with France and, in 1963, with Senegal. In 1968, a coup ended the socialist regime. Famine struck in 1973-74, killing as many as 100,000 people. Drought conditions returned in the 1980s.

The military, Mar. 26, 1991, overthrew the government of Pres. Amadou Toumani Traore, who had been in power since 1968. A multiparty democracy was promised.

Malta

Repubblika Ta' Malta

People: Population (1992 est.): 354,000. **Age distrib.** (%): 0–14: 23.6; 15–59: 61.8; 60+: 14.6. **Pop. density:** 2,901 per sq. mi. **Ethnic groups:** Italian, Arab, French. **Languages:** Maltese, English (both official). **Religion:** Mainly Roman Catholic.

Geography: Area: 122 sq. mi., half the size of the Isle of Man. **Location:** In center of Mediterranean Sea. **Neighbors:** Nearest is Italy on N. **Topography:** Island of Malta is 95 sq. mi.; other islands in the group: Gozo, 26 sq. mi., Comino, 1 sq. mi. The coastline is heavily indented. Low hills cover the interior. **Capital:** Valletta. **Cities** (1990 est.): Birkirkara 21,000, Qormi 19,000.

Government: Type: Parliamentary democracy. **Head of state:** Pres. Censu Tabone; in office Apr. 4, 1989. **Head of government:** Prime Min. Edward Fenech-Adami; b. Feb. 7, 1934; in office May 12, 1987. **Local divisions:** 13 electoral districts. **Defense** (1990): 1.3% of GDP.

Economy: Industries: Textiles, machinery, food & beverages, tourism. **Chief crops:** Potatoes, tomatoes. **Arable land:** 38%. **Electricity prod.** (1991): $1.1 bln. kWh. **Labor force:** 2% agric.; 24% manuf.; 43% services; 29% gov.

Finance: Monetary unit: Maltese Lera (Mar. 1993: 0.37 = $1 US). **Gross domestic product** (1990): $2.5 bln. **Per capita GDP:** $7,000. **Imports** (1991): $2.1 bln.; partners: UK 16%, It. 30%, Ger. 14%, U.S. 4%. **Exports** (1991): $1.2 bln.; partners: Ger. 23%, UK 11%, It. 30%. **Tourism** (1989): $475 mln. receipts. **National budget** (1991): $1.3 bln. expenditures. **International reserves less gold** (Mar. 1992): 1.1 bln. **Gold:** 126,000 oz t. **Consumer prices** (change in 1992): 2.2% .

Transport: Motor vehicles (1990): 104,000 passenger cars, 19,000 comm. vehicles. **Civil aviation** (1990): 903 mln. passenger-km; 1 airport. **Chief port:** Valletta.

Communications: Television sets: 1 per 2.6 persons. **Radios:** 1 per 3.3 persons. **Telephones:** 1 per 2.1 persons.

Health: Life expectancy at birth (1992): 74 male; 79 female. **Births** (per 1,000 pop. 1992): 14. **Deaths** (per 1,000 pop. 1992): 8. **Natural increase:** .6%. **Hospital beds:** 1 per 108 persons. **Physicians:** 1 per 444 persons. **Infant mortality** (per 1,000 live births 1992): 7.

Education (1988): **Literacy:** 90%. **School:** Compulsory until age 16.

Major International Organizations: UN (GATT, WHO, IMF), Commonwealth of Nations.

High Commission: 16 Kensington Sq, London W8 5HL; 071-938 1712.

Malta was ruled by Phoenicians, Romans, Arabs, Normans, the Knights of Malta, France, and Britain (since 1814). It became independent Sept. 21, 1964. Malta became a republic in 1974. The withdrawal of the last of its sailors, Apr. 1, 1979, ended 179 years of British military presence on the island.

Marshall Islands

Republic of the Marshall Islands

People: Population (1992 est): 50,000. **Pop. density:** 714 per sq. mi. **Ethnic groups:** Marshallese 97%. **Languages:** English (official), Marshallese, Japanese. **Religion:** Protestant 90%.

Geography: Area: 70 sq. mi. **Location:** In central Pacific Ocean; comprising 2 800-mi.-long parallel chains of coral atolls. **Capital:** Dalap-Uliga-Darrit.

Government: Type: Republic. **Head of state:** Pres. Amata Kabua.

Economy: Agriculture and tourism are mainstays of the economy. **Electricity prod.** (1990): 80 mln. kWh.

Finance: Monetary unit: US dollar. **Gross domestic product** (1989): $63 mln. **Per capita GDP:** $1,500. **Imports** (1988): 34 mln. **Exports** (1988): $2 mln.

Transport: 24 airports with scheduled flights. **Port:** Majuro.

Communications: Telephones: 1 per 53 persons.

Health: Life expectancy at birth (1992): 61 male, 64 female. **Births** (per 1,000 pop. 1992): 47. **Deaths** (per 1,000 pop. 1992): 8. **Infant mortality** (per 1,000 live births 1992): 53.

Education (1990): **Literacy:** 86%.

Major International Organizations: UN.

The Marshall Islands were a German possession until World War 1 and administered by Japan between the world wars. After WW2, they were administered as part of the UN Trust Territory of the Pacific Islands by the U.S.

The Marshall Islands secured international recognition as an independent nation on Sept. 17, 1991.

Mauritania

Islamic Republic of Mauritania

République Islamique de Mauritanie

People: Population (1992 est.): 2,059,000. **Age distrib.** (%): 0–14: 46.4; 15–59: 49.0; 60+: 4.6. **Pop. density:** 5.5 per sq. mi. **Urban** (1987): 34%. **Ethnic groups:** Arab-Berber 80%, Negroes 20%. **Languages:** Arabic, French (both official), Hassanya Arabic (national). **Religion:** Nearly 100% Muslim.

Geography: Area: 419,212,954 sq. mi., about 3 times the size of the Br. Isles. **Location:** In W. Africa. **Neighbors:** Morocco on N,

Algeria, Mali on E, Senegal on S. **Topography:** The fertile Senegal R. valley in the S gives way to a wide central region of sandy plains and scrub trees. The N is arid and extends into the Sahara. **Capital:** Nouakchott. **Cities** (1992 est.): Nouakchott 550,000; Nouadhibou 70,000; Kaedi 74,000.

Government: Type: Islamic republic. **Head of state:** Pres. Maaouya Ould Sidi Ahmed Taya; in office Apr. 18, 1992. **Head of government:** Prime Min. Sidi Mohamed Ould Boubacar; in office Apr. 18, 1992. **Local divisions:** 12 regions, one capital district. **Defense** (1990): 4.2% of GDP.

Economy: Industries: Iron mining. **Chief crops:** Dates, grain. **Minerals:** Iron ore, gypsum. **Livestock** (1988): 4.1 mln. sheep; 3.9 mln. goats; 1.2 mln. cattle. **Fish catch** (1991): 92,000 metric tons. **Electricity prod.** (1991): 136 mln. kWh. **Labor force:** 47% agric., 14% ind. & comm., 29% services.

Finance: Monetary unit: Ouguiya (Mar. 1993: 116 = $1 US). **Gross domestic product** (1990): $1.0 bln. **Per capita GDP:** $520. **Imports** (1990): $639 mln.; partners: EC 60%. **Exports** (1990): $437 mln.; partners: EC 43%, Jap. 27%. **International reserves less gold** (Feb. 1993): $35 mln.

Transport: Motor vehicles (1990): 10,000 passenger cars, 5,000 comm. vehicles. **Chief ports:** Nouakchott, Nouadhibou.

Communications: Radios: 1 per 7.8 persons. **Television sets:** 1 per 1,100 persons.

Health: Life expectancy at birth (1992): 44 male; 50 female. **Births** (per 1,000 pop. 1992): 49. **Deaths** (per 1,000 pop. 1992): 19. **Natural increase:** 3.0%. **Hospital beds:** 1 per 1,217 persons. **Physicians:** 1 per 10,128 persons. **Infant mortality** (per 1,000 live births 1992): 89.

Education (1991): **Literacy:** 30%. **School:** 79% attend primary school, 18% attend secondary school.

Major International Organizations: UN (GATT, IMF, WHO), OAU, Arab League.

Embassy: 5 rue de Montevideo, Paris XVIe, France; 010 331 450 48854.

Mauritania was a French protectorate from 1903. It became independent Nov. 28, 1960. It annexed the south of former Spanish Sahara in 1976. Saharan guerrillas stepped up attacks in 1977; 8,000 Moroccan troops and French bomber raids aided the government. Mauritania signed a peace treaty with the Polisario Front, 1980, resumed diplomatic relations with Algeria while breaking a defense treaty with Morocco, and renounced sovereignty over its share of former Spanish Sahara. Morocco annexed the territory.

Mauritius

People: Population (1992 est.): 1,081,900. **Age distrib.** (%): 0–14: 36.3; 15–59: 57.2; 60+: 6.4. **Pop. density:** 1,313 per sq. mi. **Urban** (1990): 41%. **Ethnic groups:** Indo-Mauritian 68%, Creole 27%, others. **Languages:** English (official), French Creole, Bhojpuri. **Religions:** Hindu 51%, Christian 30%, Muslim 16%.

Geography: Area: 720 sq. mi., about the size of Warwickshire. **Location:** In the Indian O., 500 mi. E of Madagascar. **Neighbors:** Nearest is Madagascar on W. **Topography:** A volcanic island nearly surrounded by coral reefs. A central plateau is encircled by mountain peaks. **Capital:** Port Louis, pop. (1991 est.) 142,000.

Government: Type: Republic. **Head of state:** Pres. Cassam Uteem; in office June 30, 1992. **Head of government:** Prime Min. Aneerood Jugnauth; in office June 12, 1982. **Local divisions:** 9 districts, 3 dependencies.

Economy: Industries: Tourism, food processing. **Chief crops:** Sugar cane, tea. **Arable land:** 54%. **Electricity prod.** (1990): 423 mln. kWh. **Labor force:** 17% agric. & fishing; 32% manuf.; 14% govt. services.

Finance: Monetary unit: Rupee (Mar. 1993: 17.17 = $1 US). **Gross domestic product** (1991): $2.5 bln. **Per capita GDP:** $2,300. **Imports** (1991): $1.15 bln.; partners: UK 9%, Fr. 12%, S. Afr. 9%. **Exports** (1991): $1.1 bln.; partners: UK 50%, Fr. 22%, U.S. 8%. **Tourism** (1990): $264 mln. receipts. **National budget** (1990): $607 mln. **International reserves less gold** (Feb. 1993): $859 mln. **Gold:** 61,000 oz t. **Consumer prices** (change in 1992): 4.6%.

Transport: Motor vehicles (1990): 29,000 passenger cars, 6,000 comm. vehicles. **Chief port:** Port Louis.

Communications: Television sets: 1 per 8.2 persons. **Radios:** 1 per 4.2 persons. **Telephones:** 1 per 15 persons. **Daily newspaper circ.** (1989): 75 per 1,000 pop.

Health: Life expectancy at birth (1992): 66 male; 74 female. **Births** (per 1,000 pop. 1992): 19. **Deaths** (per 1,000 pop. 1992): 6. **Natural increase:** 1.3%. **Hospital beds:** 1 per 364 persons. **Physicians:** 1 per 1,118 persons. **Infant mortality** (per 1,000 live births 1992): 22.

Education (1989): **Literacy:** 94%. **School:** Almost all children attend school.

Major International Organizations: UN and all of its specialized agencies, OAU, Commonwealth of Nations.

High Commission: 32 Elvaston Place, London SW7 5NW; 071-581 0294.

Mauritius was uninhabited when settled in 1638 by the Dutch, who introduced sugar cane. France took over in 1721, bringing African slaves. Britain ruled from 1810 to Mar. 12, 1968, bringing Indian workers for the sugar plantations.

Mauritius formally severed its association with the British crown Mar. 12, 1992.

Mexico

United Mexican States

Estados Unidos Mexicanos

People: Population (1992 est.): 92,380,000. **Age distrib.** (%): 0–14: 36.5; 15–59: 57.8; 60+: 5.7. **Pop. density:** 121 per sq. mi. **Urban** (1990): 72%. **Ethnic groups:** Mestizo 60%, American Indian 29%, Caucasian 9%. **Languages:** Spanish (official), Amerindian languages. **Religion:** Roman Catholic 97%.

Geography: Area: 761,604 sq. mi., 6 times the size of the Br. Isles. **Location:** In southern N. America. **Neighbors:** U.S. on N, Guatemala, Belize on S. **Topography:** The Sierra Madre Occidental Mts. run NW-SE near the west coast; the Sierra Madre Oriental Mts., run near the Gulf of Mexico. They join S of Mexico City. Between the 2 ranges lies the dry central plateau, 5,000 to 8,000 ft. alt., rising toward the S, with temperate vegetation. Coastal lowlands are tropical. About 45% of land is arid. **Capital:** Mexico City. **Cities** (1991 metro. est.): Mexico City 20 mln.; Guadalajara 3 mln.; Monterrey 2.7 mln.

Government: Type: Federal republic. **Head of state:** Pres. Carlos Salinas de Gortari; b. Apr. 3, 1948; in office Dec. 1, 1988. **Local divisions:** Federal district and 31 states. **Defense** (1988): 1.0% of GDP.

Economy: Industries: Steel, chemicals, electric goods, textiles, rubber, petroleum, tourism. **Chief crops:** Cotton, coffee, wheat, rice, sugar cane, vegetables, corn. **Minerals:** Silver, lead, zinc, gold, oil, natural gas. **Crude oil reserves** (1991): 51 bln. barrels. **Arable land:** 13%. **Livestock** (1991): 31 mln. cattle; 15 mln. pigs; 6 mln. sheep. **Fish catch** (1991): 1.1 mln. metric tons. **Electricity prod.** (1991): 114 bln. kWh. **Crude steel prod.** (1991): 7.8 mln. metric tons. **Labor force:** 24% agric.; 19% manuf; 31% services; 14% comm.

Finance: Monetary unit: New Peso (July 1993: 3,122 = $1 US). **Gross domestic product** (1991): $289 bln. **Per capita GDP:** $3,200. **Imports** (1991): $36.7 bln.; partners: U.S. 69%, EC 13%. **Exports** (1991): $27.0 bln.; partners: U.S. 68%, EC 14%. **Tourism** (1992): $6.6 bln. receipts. **National budget** (1990): $47.9 bln. expenditures. **International reserves less gold** (Jan. 1993): $18.9 bln. **Gold:** 685,000 oz t. **Consumer prices** (change in 1992): 15.5%.

Transport: Railroads (1992): 16,363 mi. long. **Motor vehicles** (1990): 6.8 mln. passenger cars, 3.0 mln. comm. vehicles. **Civil aviation** (1991): 17.4 bln. passenger-km; 54 airports. **Chief ports:** Veracruz, Tampico, Mazatlan, Coatzacoalcos.

Communications: Television sets: 1 per 6.6 persons. **Radios:** 1 per 5.1 persons. **Telephones:** 1 per 7.6 persons. **Daily newspaper circ.** (1986): 142 per 1,000 pop.

Health: Life expectancy at birth (1992): 69 male; 76 female. **Births** (per 1,000 pop. 1992): 29. **Deaths** (per 1,000 pop. 1992): 5. **Natural increase:** 2.4%. **Hospital beds:** 1 per 1,298 persons. **Physicians:** 1 per 600 persons. **Infant mortality** (per 1,000 live births 1992): 29.

Education (1993): **Literacy:** 90%. **School:** Compulsory for 8 years.

Major International Organizations: UN (IMF, GATT), OAS.

Embassy: 42 Hertford St, London W1Y 7TF; 071-499 8586.

Mexico was the site of advanced Indian civilizations. The Mayas, an agricultural people, moved up from Yucatan, built immense stone pyramids, invented a calendar. The Toltecs were overcome by the Aztecs, who founded Tenochtitlan AD 1325, now Mexico City. Hernando Cortes, Spanish conquistador, destroyed the Aztec empire, 1519-1521.

After 3 centuries of Spanish rule the people rose, under Fr. Miguel Hidalgo y Costilla, 1810, Fr. Morelos y Payon, 1812, and Gen. Agustin Iturbide, who made himself emperor as Agustin I, 1821. A republic was declared in 1823.

Mexican territory extended into the present American Southwest and California until Texas revolted and established a republic in 1836; the Mexican legislature refused recognition but was unable to enforce its authority there. After numerous clashes, the U.S.-Mexican War, 1846-48, resulted in the loss by Mexico of the lands north of the Rio Grande.

French arms supported an Austrian archduke on the throne of Mexico as Maximilian I, 1864-67, but pressure from the U.S. forced France to withdraw. A dictatorial rule by Porfirio Diaz, president 1877-80, 1884-1911, led to fighting by rival forces until the new constitution of Feb. 5, 1917 provided social reform. Since then Mexico has developed large-scale programs of social security, labor protection, and school improvement. A constitutional provision requires management to share profits with labor.

The Institutional Revolutionary Party has been dominant in politics since 1929. Radical opposition, including some guerrilla activity, has been contained by strong measures.

The presidency of Luis Echeverria, 1970-76, was marked by a more leftist foreign policy and domestic rhetoric. Some land redistribution begun in 1976 was reversed under the succeeding administration.

Some gains in agriculture, industry, and social services have been achieved. The land is rich, but the rugged topography and lack of sufficient rainfall are major obstacles. Crops and farm prices are controlled, as are export and import. Economic prospects brightened with the discovery of vast oil reserves, perhaps the world's greatest. But much of the work force is jobless or underemployed.

Inflation and the drop in world oil prices caused economic problems in the 1980s. The peso was devalued and private banks were nationalized to restore financial stability.

Mexico reached agreement with the U.S. and Canada on the North American Free Trade Agreement, Aug. 12, 1992. The agreement required ratification by the 3 governments.

Micronesia

Federated States of Micronesia

People: Population (1992 est.): 111,000. **Pop. density:** 411 per sq. mi. **Ethnic groups:** Trukese 41%, Pohnpeian 26%. **Language:** English (official). **Religion:** Mostly Christian.

Geography: Area: 270 sq. mi., the size of Merseyside. The Federation consists of 607 islands in the W. Pacific Ocean. **Capital:** Palikir.

Government: Type: Republic. **Head of state:** Bailey Olter; in office May 21, 1991. **Local divisions:** 4 states.

Economy: Chief crops: Tropical fruits, vegetables, coconuts.

Finance: Monetary unit: US dollar. **Gross domestic product** (1989): $150 mln. **Imports** (1988): $67 mln. **Exports** (1988): $3 mln.

Transport: 4 airports with scheduled flights.

Communications: Television sets: 1 per 16 persons. **Radios:** 1 per 1.6 persons. **Telephones:** 1 per 61 persons.

Health: Life expectancy at birth (1992): 65 male, 69 female. **Births** (per 1,000 pop. 1992): 34. **Deaths** (per 1,000 pop. 1992): 5. **Hospital beds:** 1 per 280 persons. **Physicians:** 1 per 2,540 persons. **Infant mortality** (per 1,000 live births 1992): 39.

Education (1991): **Literacy:** 90%

Major International Organizations: UN.

The Federated States of Micronesia, formerly known as the Caroline Islands, were ruled successively by Spain, Germany, Japan and the US. They were internationally recognized as an independent nation on Sept. 17, 1991.

Republic of Moldova

Republica Moldoveneasca

People: Population (1992 est.): 4,458,000. **Pop. density:** 342 per sq. mi. **Urban** (1991): 48%. **Ethnic groups:** Moldovan 65%, Ukrainian 14%, Russian 13%. **Languages:** Romanian, Ukrainian. **Religion:** E. Orthodox 98%.

Geography: Area: 13,012 sq. mi., half the size of S. Ireland. **Neighbors:** Romania on W, Ukraine on N, E, and S. **Capital:** Kishinev. **Cities** (1991): Kishinev 753,000; Tiraspol 186,000.

Government: Type: Republic. **Head of state:** Pres. Mircea Snegur. **Head of government:** Prime Min. Andre Gangheli; in office July 1, 1992.

Economy: Industries: Canning, wine-making, textiles. **Chief crops:** Grain, grapes. **Minerals:** Lignite, gypsum. **Livestock** (1989): 1.1 mln. cattle; 1.9 mln. pigs; 1.3 mln. sheep. **Electricity prod.** (1991): 13 mln. kWh.

Finance: Monetary unit: Ruble.

Transport railroads (1991): 715 mi. long. **Motor vehicles** (1990): 177,000 passenger cars. **Civil aviation** (1990): 2.3 bln. passenger-km; 1 airport.

Communications: Telephones: 1 per 8 persons. **Newspaper circ.** (1990): 71 per 1,000 pop.

Health: Life expectancy at birth (1992): 64 male; 71 female. **Births** (per 1,000 pop. 1992): 19. **Deaths** (per 1,000 pop. 1992): 10. **Hospital beds:** 1 per 77 persons. **Physicians:** 1 per 251 persons. **Infant mortality** (per 1,000 live births 1992): 35.

Major International Organizations: UN, CIS.

In 1918 Romania annexed all of Bessarabia which Russia had acquired from Turkey in 1812 by the Treaty of Bucharest. In 1924 the Soviet Union established the Moldavian autonomous Soviet Socialist Republic on the eastern bank of the Dniester. It was merged with the Romanian-speaking districts of Bessarabia in 1940 to form the Moldavian SSR.

During World War II, Romania, allied with Germany, occupied the area. It was recaptured by the USSR in 1944. Moldova declared independence Aug. 27, 1991. It became an independent state when the Soviet Union disbanded Dec. 26, 1991. Fighting erupted between Moldovan security forces and Slavic separatists – ethnic Russians and ethnic Ukrainians – Mar. 1992. The Slavs feared that Moldovans, who are Romanian in language and culture, would merge with neighboring Romania.

Monaco

Principality of Monaco

People: Population (1992 est.): 29,712. **Age distrib.** (%): 0–14: 12.7; 15–59: 56.3 60+: 30.7. **Pop. density:** 49,520 per sq. mi. **Ethnic groups:** French 47%, Italian 16%, Monégasque 16%. **Language:** French (official). **Religion:** Predominantly Roman Catholic.

Geography: Area: 0.6 sq. mi. **Location:** On the NW Mediterranean coast. **Neighbors:** France to W, N, E. **Topography:** Monaco-Ville sits atop a high promontory, the rest of the principality rises from the port up the hillside. **Capital:** Monaco-Ville.

Government: Type: Constitutional monarchy. **Head of state:** Prince Rainier III; b. May 31, 1923; in office May 9, 1949. **Head of government:** Min. of State Jacques Dupont.

Economy: Industries: Tourism, gambling, chemicals, precision instruments, plastics.

Finance: Monetary unit: French franc or Monégasque franc.

Transport: Chief port: La Condamine.

Communications: Television sets (1984): 17,000. **Telephones** (1984): 18,000.

Health: Births (per 1,000 pop. 1992): 7. **Deaths** (per 1,000 pop. 1992): 7. **Infant mortality** (per 1,000 live births 1992): 8.

Education (1989): **Literacy:** 99%. **School:** Compulsory for 10 years; attendance 99%.

Major International Organizations: UN.

Consulate: 4 Cromwell Place, London SW7 2JE; 071-225 2679.

An independent principality for over 300 years, Monaco has belonged to the House of Grimaldi since 1297 except during the French Revolution. It was placed under the protectorate of Sardinia in 1815, and under that of France, 1861. The Prince of Monaco was an absolute ruler until a 1911 constitution.

Monaco's fame as a tourist resort is widespread. It is noted for its mild climate and magnificent scenery. The area has been extended by land reclamation.

Mongolia

People: Population (1992 est.): 2,305,000. **Pop. density:** 3 per sq. mi. **Urban** (1991): 58%. **Ethnic groups:** Mongol 90%. **Language:** Mongolian (official). **Religion:** Traditionally Lama Buddhism.

Geography: Area: 604,247 sq. mi., almost 5 times the size of the Br. Isles. **Location:** In E Central Asia. **Neighbors:** Russia on N, China on S. **Topography:** Mostly a high plateau with mountains, salt lakes, and vast grasslands. Arid lands in the S are part of the Gobi Desert. **Capital:** Ulaanbaatar. **Cities** (1991 est.): Ulaanbaatar 575,000, Darhan 90,000.

Government: Type: In transition. **Head of state:** Pres. Punsalmaagiyn Ochirbat; b. 1942; in office Mar. 21, 1990. **Head of government:** Prime Min. Puntsagiyn Jasray; in office July 21, 1992. **Local divisions:** 18 provinces, 3 municipalities. **Defense** (1984): 11.5% of GDP.

Economy: Industries: Food processing, textiles, chemicals, cement. **Chief crops:** Grain. **Minerals:** Coal, tungsten, copper, molybdenum, gold, tin. **Arable land:** 1%. **Livestock** (1990): 14.8 mln. sheep; 2.2 mln. cattle. **Electricity prod.** (1991): 3.7 bln. kWh. **Labor force:** 52% agric.; 10% manuf.

Finance: Monetary unit: Tugrik (Jan. 1993: 120 = $1 US). **Gross domestic product** (1991): $2.1 bln. **Per capita GDP:** $900. **Imports** (1991): $360 mln.; partners: CIS 91%. **Exports** (1991): $279 mln.; partners: CIS 80%.

Transport: Railroads (1991): 1,445 mi. long.

Communications: Television sets: 1 per 18 persons. **Radios:** 1 per 7.5 persons. **Telephones:** 1 per 32 persons. **Daily newspaper circ.** (1990): 106 per 1,000 pop.

Health: Life expectancy at birth (1992): 63 male; 68 female. **Births** (per 1,000 pop. 1992): 34. **Deaths** (per 1,000 pop. 1992): 8. **Natural increase:** 2.6%. **Hospital beds:** 1 per 79 persons. **Physicians:** 1 per 345 persons. **Infant mortality** (per 1,000 live births 1992): 47.

Major International Organizations: UN (ILO, WHO).

Education (1990): **Literacy:** 89%.

Embassy: 7 Kensington Court, London W8 5DL; 071-937 5238.

One of the world's oldest countries, Mongolia reached the zenith of its power in the 13th century when Genghis Khan and his successors conquered all of China and extended their influence as far W as Hungary and Poland. In later centuries, the empire dissolved and Mongolia became a province of China.

With the advent of the 1911 Chinese revolution, Mongolia, with Russian backing, declared its independence. A Mongolian Communist regime was established July 11, 1921.

Mongolia has been changed from a nomadic culture to one of settled agriculture and growing industries with aid from the USSR and East European nations.

In 1990, the Mongolian Communist Party surrendered its monopoly on power. Free elections were held July 1990; the communists were victorious.

Morocco

Kingdom of Morocco

al-Mamlaka al-Maghrebia

People: Population (1992 est.): 26,708,000. **Age distrib.** (%): 0–14: 41.2; 15–59: 53.7; 60+: 5.1. **Pop. density:** 154 per sq. mi. **Urban** (1992): 50%. **Ethnic groups:** Arab-Berber 99%. **Languages:** Arabic (official), Berber. **Religion:** Sunni Muslim 99%.

Geography: Area: 172,413 sq. mi., 50% bigger than the Br. Isles. **Location:** on NW coast of Africa. **Neighbors:** W. Sahara on S, Algeria on E. **Topography:** Consists of 5 natural regions: mountain ranges (Riff in the N, Middle Atlas, Upper Atlas, and Anti-Atlas); rich plains in the W; alluvial plains in SW; well-cultivated plateaus in the center; a pre-Sahara arid zone extending from SE. **Capital:** Rabat. **Cities** (1984): Casablanca 2,600,000; Fès 852,000; Rabat 556,000.

Government: Type: Constitutional monarchy. **Head of state:** King Hassan II; b. July 9, 1929; in office Mar. 3, 1961. **Head of government:** Prime Min. Mohammed Karim Lamrani; in office Aug. 11, 1992. **Local divisions:** 37 provinces, 5 municipalities. **Defense** (1992): 4.2% of GDP.

Economy: Industries: Carpets, clothing, leather goods, mining, tourism. **Chief crops:** Grain, fruits, dates, grapes. **Minerals:** Copper, cobalt, manganese, phosphates, lead, oil. **Crude oil reserves** (1980): 100 mln. bbls. **Arable land:** 18%. **Livestock** (1990): 3.5 mln. cattle; 17 mln. sheep; 5.9 mln. goats. **Fish catch** (1989): 551,000 metric tons. **Electricity prod.** (1991): 8.1 bln. kWh. **Labor force:** 50% agric., 26% services; 15% ind.

Finance: Monetary unit: Dirham (Mar. 1993: 9.09 = $1 US). **Gross domestic product** (1991): $27.3 bln. **Per capita GDP:** $1,060. **Imports** (1991): $6.0 bln.; partners: EC 53%, U.S. 11%. **Exports** (1991): $4.1 bln.; partners: EC 58%. **Tourism** (1990): $1.2 bln. receipts. **National budget** (1992): $7.7 bln. expenditures. **International reserves less gold** (Mar. 1993): $3.2 bln. **Gold:** 704,000 oz t. **Consumer prices** (change in 1992): 4.9%.

Transport: Railroads (1990): 1,893 km. long. **Motor vehicles** (1990): 666,000 passenger cars, 280,000 comm. vehicles. **Civil aviation** (1989): 2.7 bln. passenger-km; 15 airports. **Chief ports:** Tangier, Casablanca, Kenitra.

Communications: Television sets: 1 per 21 persons. **Radios:** 1 per 5.4 persons. **Telephones:** 1 per 62 persons. **Daily newspaper circ.** (1990): 15 per 1,000 pop.

Health: Life expectancy at birth (1992): 63 male; 67 female. **Births** (per 1,000 pop. 1992): 30. **Deaths** (per 1,000 pop. 1992): 8. **Natural increase:** 2.2%. **Hospital beds:** 1 per 959 persons. **Physicians:** 1 per 4,415 persons. **Infant mortality** (per 1,000 live births 1992): 56.

Education (1990): **Literacy:** 50%.

Major International Organizations: UN (ILO, IMF, WHO), OAU, Arab League.

Embassy: 49 Queen's Gate Gdns, London SW7 5NE; 071-581 5001.

Berbers were the original inhabitants, followed by Carthaginians and Romans. Arabs conquered in 683. In the 11th and 12th centuries, a Berber empire ruled all NW Africa and most of Spain from Morocco.

Part of Morocco came under Spanish rule in the 19th century; France controlled the rest in the early 20th. Tribal uprisings lasted from 1911 to 1933. The country became independent Mar. 2, 1956. Tangier, an internationalized seaport, was turned over to Morocco, 1956. Ifni, a Spanish enclave, was ceded in 1969.

Morocco annexed over 70,000 sq. mi. of phosphate-rich land Apr. 14, 1976, two-thirds of former Spanish Sahara, with the remainder annexed by Mauritania. Spain had withdrawn in February. Polisario, a guerrilla movement, proclaimed the region independent Feb. 27, and launched attacks with Algerian support. Morocco accepted U.S. military and economic aid. When Mauritania signed a treaty with the Polisario Front and gave up its portion of the former Spanish Sahara, Morocco occupied the area, 1980. Morocco accused Algeria of instigating Polisario attacks.

After years of bitter fighting, Morocco controlled the main urban areas, but the Polisario Front's guerrillas moved freely in the vast, sparsely populated deserts. The 2 sides signed a cease-fire agreement in 1990. The UN will conduct a referendum in Western Sahara on whether the territory should become independent or remain part of Morocco.

Mozambique

Republic of Mozambique

República de Mocambique

People: Population (1992 est.): 15,469,000. **Age distrib.** (%): 0–14: 45.3; 15–59: 50.6; 60+: 4.1. **Pop. density:** 50 per sq. mi. **Ethnic groups:** Bantu tribes. **Languages:** Portuguese (official), Makua, Malawi, Shona, Tsonga. **Religions:** Traditional beliefs 60%, Christian 30%, Muslim 10%.

Geography: Area: 303,769 sq. mi., 3 times bigger than the UK. **Location:** On SE coast of Africa. **Neighbors:** Tanzania on N, Malawi, Zambia, Zimbabwe on W, South Africa, Swaziland on S. **Topography:** Coastal lowlands comprise nearly half the country with plateaus rising in steps to the mountains along the western border. **Capital:** Maputo. **Cities** (1991 est.): Maputo 931,000, Beira 298,000.

Government: Type: Republic. **Head of state:** Pres. Joaquim Chissano; b. Oct. 22, 1939; in office Oct. 19, 1986. **Head of government:** Mario de Graca Machungo; in office July 17, 1986. **Local divisions:** 10 provinces. **Defense** (1987): 8.4% of GDP.

Economy: Industries: Cement, alcohol, textiles. **Chief crops:** Cashews, cotton, sugar, copra, tea. **Minerals:** Coal, titanium. **Arable land:** 4%. **Livestock** (1991): 1.3 mln. cattle. **Fish catch** (1990): 35,000 metric tons. **Electricity prod.** (1991): 1.7 bln. kWh. **Labor force:** 85% agric., 9% ind. & comm., 2% services.

Finance: Monetary unit: Metical (Mar. 1993: 2,982 = $1 US). **Gross domestic product** (1991): $1.7 bln. **Per capita GDP:** $120. **Imports** (1990): $870 mln.; partners: S. Afr. 11%, U.S. 8%, USSR 12%, It. 10%. **Exports** (1990): $117 mln.; partners: Sp. 21%, U.S. 16%, Jap. 15%. **National budget** (1989): $208 mln.

Transport: Railroads (1990): 2,033 mi. long. **Motor vehicles** (1990): 87,000 passenger cars, 24,000 comm. vehicles. **Chief ports:** Maputo, Beira, Nacala, Quelimane.

Communications: Television sets: 1 per 418 persons. **Radios:** 1 per 29 persons. **Telephones:** 1 per 217 persons. **Daily newspaper circ.** (1990): 3 per 1,000 pop.

Health: Life expectancy at birth (1992): 46 male; 49 female. **Births** (per 1,000 pop. 1992): 46. **Deaths** (per 1,000 pop. 1992): 17. **Natural increase:** 2.9%. **Hospital beds:** 1 per 1,227 persons. **Physicians:** 1 per 43,536 persons. **Infant mortality** (per 1,000 live births 1992): 134.

Education (1989): **Literacy:** 14%.

Major International Organizations: UN (IMF, World Bank), OAU.

Embassy: 21 Fitzroy Sq, London W1P 5HJ; 071-383 3800.

The first Portuguese post on the Mozambique coast was established in 1505, on the trade route to the East. Mozambique became independent June 25, 1975, after a ten-year war against Portuguese colonial domination. The 1974 revolution in Portugal paved the way for the orderly transfer of power to Frelimo (Front for the Liberation of Mozambique). Frelimo took over local administration Sept. 20, 1974, over the opposition, in part violent, of some blacks and whites. The new government, led by Maoist Pres. Samora Machel, promised a gradual transition to a communist system. Private schools were closed, rural collective farms organized, and private homes nationalized. Economic problems included the emigration of most of the country's whites, a politically untenable economic dependence on white-ruled South Africa, and a large external debt.

In the 1980s, severe drought and civil war caused famine and heavy loss of life.

Myanmar (formerly Burma)

Union of Myanmar

Pyidaungzu Myanma Naingngandaw

People: Population (1992 est.): 42,642,000. **Age distrib.** (%): 0–14: 41.2; 15–59: 52.8; 60+: 6.0. **Pop. density:** 162 per sq. mi. **Urban** (1991): 25%. **Ethnic groups:** Burmans (related to Tibetans) 68%; Shan 7%; Karen 4%; Rakhine 3%. **Languages:** Burmese (official), Karen, Shan. **Religions:** Buddhist 85%; animist, Christian.

Geography: Area: 261,789 sq. mi., 3 times larger than GB. **Location:** Between S. and S.E. Asia, on Bay of Bengal. **Neighbors:** Bangladesh, India on W, China, Laos, Thailand on E. **Topo-**

graphy: Mountains surround Myanmar on W, N, and E, and dense forests cover much of the nation. N-S rivers provide habitable valleys and communications, especially the Irrawaddy, navigable for 900 miles. The country has a tropical monsoon climate. **Capital:** Yangon. **Cities** (1983 est.): Yangon 2,458,712; Mandalay 458,000; Karbe (1973 cen.): 253,600; Moulmein 188,000.

Government: Type: Military. **Head of state and head of government:** Prime Min. Gen. Than Shwe; in office Apr. 24, 1992. **Local divisions:** 7 states and 7 divisions. **Defense** (1989): 3.0% of GDP.

Economy: Industries: Mining, textiles, footwear, petroleum refining. **Chief crops:** Rice, sugarcane, peanuts, beans. **Minerals:** Oil, lead, silver, tin, tungsten, precious stones. **Crude oil reserves** (1985): 733 mln. bbls. **Other resources:** Rubber, teakwood. **Arable land:** 15%. **Livestock.** (1991): 9.3 mln. cattle; 2.2 mln. pigs. **Fish catch** (1990): 743,000 metric tons. **Electricity prod.** (1991): 2.9 bln. kWh. **Labor force:** 66% agric; 12% ind.

Finance: Monetary unit: Kyat (Mar. 1993: 6.19 = $1 US). **Gross domestic product** (1991): $22.2 bln. **Per capita GDP:** $530. **Imports** (1991): $1.1 bln.; partners: Jap. 50%, EC 20%. **Exports** (1991): $568 mln.; partners: SE Asian countries 30%; EC 12%. **Tourism** (1990): $5 mln. receipts. **National budget** (1991): $9.3 bln. **International reserves less gold** (Mar. 1993): $294 mln. **Gold:** 251,000 oz t. **Consumer prices** (change in 1992): 23.5%.

Transport: Railroads (1990): 1,949 mi. long. **Motor vehicles** (1989): 27,000 passenger cars, 42,000 comm. vehicles. **Civil aviation** (1988): 214 mln. passenger-km.; 21 airports with scheduled flights. **Chief ports:** Yangon, Bassein, Moulmein.

Communications: Television sets: 1 per 592 persons. **Radios:** 1 per 13 persons. **Telephones:** 1 per 501 persons. **Daily newspaper circ.** (1989): 14 per 1,000 pop.

Health: Life expectancy at birth (1992): 57 male; 61 female. **Births** (per 1,000 pop. 1992): 29. **Deaths** (per 1,000 pop. 1992): 10. **Natural increase:** 1.9%. **Hospital beds:** 1 per 1,602 persons. **Physicians:** 1 per 3,389 persons. **Infant mortality** (per 1,000 live births 1992): 68.

Education (1990): **Literacy:** 81%. **School:** Compulsory for 4 years; attendance: 84%.

Major International Organizations: UN (World Bank, IMF, GATT).

Embassy: 19a Charles St, London W1X 8ER; 071-629 4486.

The Burmese arrived from Tibet before the 9th century, displacing earlier cultures, and a Buddhist monarchy was established by the 11th. Burma was conquered by the Mongol dynasty of China in 1272, then ruled by Shans as a Chinese tributary, until the 16th century.

Britain subjugated Burma in 3 wars, 1824-84, and ruled the country as part of India until 1937, when it became self-governing. Independence outside the Commonwealth was achieved Jan. 4, 1948.

Gen. Ne Win dominated politics from 1962 to 1988, when he abdicated power, following waves of anti-government demonstrations. He led a Revolutionary Council which drove Indians from the civil service and Chinese from commerce. Socialization of the economy was advanced, isolation from foreign countries enforced.

In 1987 Burma, once the richest nation in SE Asia, was granted less developed country status by the UN. Following Ne Win's resignation, Sein Lwin and later Maung Maung, a civilian, took power but rioting and street violence continued. In Sept., Gen. Saw Maung, a close associate of Ne Win, seized power.

In 1989 the country's name was changed to Myanmar.

The first free, multiparty elections in 30 years took place May 27, 1990, with the main opposition party winning a decisive victory, but the military rulers refused to hand over power.

Namibia

Republic of Namibia

People: Population (1992 est.): 1,574,000. **Pop density:** 4 per sq. mi. **Urban** (1991): 33%. **Ethnic groups:** Ovambo 50%, Kavango 10%, Herero 7%, Damara 7%. **Languages:** Afrikaans, English (official), several indigenous languages. **Religions:** Lutheran 50%, other Christian 30%.

Geography: Area: 317,818 sq. mi., more than 3 times bigger than UK. **Location:** In S. Africa on the coast of the Atlantic Ocean. Angola on the N., Botswana on the E., and South Africa on the S. **Capital:** Windhoek, pop. (1990 est.) 114,000.

Government: Type: Republic. **Head of state:** Pres. Sam Nujoma; in office Feb. 16, 1990. **Head of government:** Prime Min. Hage Geingob. **Local divisions:** 14 regions.

Economy: Mining accounts for over 40% of GDP. **Minerals:** Diamonds. **Fish catch** (1990): 289,000 metric tons. **Electricity prod.** (1991): 1.2 mln kWh.

Finance: Monetary unit: South African Rand. **Gross domestic product** (1991): $2.0 bln. **Per capita GDP:** $1,400. **Imports** (1989): $894 mln. **Exports** (1989): $1.0 bln. **National budget** (1992): $1.1 bln expenditures.

Transport: Railroads (1990): 1,480 mi. long.

Communications: Television sets: 1 per 42 persons. **Radios:** 1 per 5.8 persons. **Telephones:** 1 per 17 persons.

Health: Life expectancy at birth (1992): 58 male; 63 female. **Births** (per 1,000 pop. 1992): 45. **Deaths** (per 1,000 pop 1992): 10. **Natural increase:** 3.5. **Hospital beds:** 1 per 166 persons. **Physicians:** 1 per 4,450 persons. **Infant mortality** (per 1,000 live births 1992): 66.

Education (1989): **Literacy:** 16% nonwhite.

High Commission: 34 South Molton St, London W1Y 2BP; 071-408 2333.

Namibia was declared a protectorate by Germany in 1890 and officially called South-West Africa. South Africa seized the territory from Germany in 1915 during World War 1; the League of Nations gave South Africa a mandate over the territory in 1920. In 1966, the Marxist South-West Africa People's Organization (SWAPO) launched a guerrilla war for independence.

In 1968 the UN General Assembly gave the area the name Namibia.

In a 1977 referendum, white voters backed a plan for a multiracial interim government to lead to independence. SWAPO rejected the plan. Both S. Africa and Namibian rebels agreed to a UN plan for independence by the end of 1978. S. Africa rejected the plan, Sept. 20, 1978, and held elections for Namibia's constituent assembly, Dec., that were ignored by the major black opposition parties.

In 1982, So. African and SWAPO agreed in principle on a cease-fire and the holding of UN-supervised elections. So. Africa, however, insisted on the withdrawal of Cuban forces from Angola as a precondition to Namibian independence. On Jan. 18, 1983, South Africa dissolved the Namibian National Assembly and resumed direct control of the territory.

In 1988, A U.S. mediated plan was agreed upon by So. Africa, Angola, and Cuba, which called for withdrawal of Cuban troops from Angola and black majority rule in Namibia.

Namibia became an independent nation March 21, 1990.

Walvis Bay, the only deepwater port in the country, was turned over to South African administration in 1922. S. Africa said in 1978 it would discuss sovereignty only after Namibian independence. Discussions were held in 1991.

Nauru

Republic of Nauru

Naoero

People: Population (1992): 9,460. **Pop density:** 1,182 per sq. mi. **Ethnic groups:** Nauruans 57%, Pacific Islanders 26%, Chinese 8%, European 8%. **Language:** Nauruan (official). **Religion:** Predominantly Christian.

Geography: Area: 8 sq. mi. **Location:** In Western Pacific O. just S of Equator. **Neighbors:** Nearest are Solomon Is. **Topography:** Mostly a plateau bearing high grade phosphate deposits, surrounded by a coral cliff and a sandy shore in concentric rings. **Capital:** Yaren.

Government: Type: Republic. **Head of state:** Pres. Bernard Dowiyogo; in office Dec. 12, 1989. **Local divisions:** 14 districts.

Economy: Industries: Phosphate mining. **Electricity prod.** (1990): 48 mln. kWh.

Finance: Monetary unit: Australian dollar. **Gross national product** (1989): $60 mln.

Communications: Radios (1985): 4,000. **Telephones** (1980): 1,500.

Health: Births (per 1,000 pop. 1992): 19. **Deaths** (per 1,000 pop. 1992): 5. **Natural increase:** 1.4%. **Infant mortality** (per 1,000 live births 1992): 41.

Education (1988): **Literacy:** 99%. **School:** Compulsory from ages 6 to 16.

Govt. Offices: 3 Chesham St, London SW1X 8ND; 071-235 6911.

The island was discovered in 1798 by the British but was formally annexed to the German Empire in 1886. After World War I, Nauru became a League of Nations mandate administered by Australia. During World War II the Japanese occupied the island and shipped 1,200 Nauruans to the fortress island of Truk as slave laborers.

In 1947 Nauru was made a UN trust territory, administered by Australia. Nauru became an independent republic Jan. 31, 1968.

Phosphate exports provide one of the world's highest per capita revenues for the Nauru people.

Nepal

Kingdom of Nepal

Nepal Adhirajya

People: Population (1992 est.): 20,086,000. **Age distrib.** (%): –14: 42.2; 15–59: 52.9; 60+: 4.9. **Pop. density:** 357 per sq. mi. **Urban** (1987): 8%. **Ethnic groups:** The many tribes are descendants of Indian, Tibetan, and Central Asian migrants. **Languages:** Nepali (official, an Indic language), many others. **Religions:** Hindu (official) 90%, Buddhist 7%.

Geography: Area: 56,136 sq. mi., the size of England and N. Ireland combined. **Location:** Astride the Himalaya Mts. **Neighbors:** China on N, India on S. **Topography:** The Himalayas stretch across the N, the hill country with its fertile valleys extends across the center, while the southern border region is part of the flat, subtropical Ganges Plain. **Capital:** Kathmandu, (1987 est.) 422,000. **Cities:** Pokhara, Biratnagar, Birganj.

Government: Type: Parliamentary democracy. **Head of state:** King Birendra Bir Bikram Shah Dev; b. Dec. 28, 1945; in office Jan. 31, 1972. **Head of government:** Prime Min. Giriga Prasad Koirala; in office May 26, 1991. **Local divisions:** 14 zones. **Defense** (1992): 2.0% of GDP.

Economy: Industries: Sugar, jute mills, tourism. **Chief crops:** Jute, rice, grain. **Minerals:** Quartz. **Other resources:** Forests. **Arable land:** 17%. **Livestock** (1991): 6.3 mln. cattle. **Electricity prod.** (1990): 530 mln. kWh. **Labor force:** 93% agric.

Finance: Monetary unit: Rupee (Mar. 1993: 49 = $1 US). **Gross domestic product** (1991): $3.2 bln. **Per capita GDP:** $165. **Imports** (1991): $545 mln.; partners: India 47%, Jap. 25%. **Exports** (1991): $180 mln.; partners: India 68%. **Tourism** (1990): $57 mln. receipts. **National budget** (1992): $624 mln. **International reserves less gold** (Mar. 1993): $480 mln. **Gold:** 152,000 oz t. **Consumer prices** (change in 1992): 17.1%.

Transport: Civil aviation (1989): 408 mln. passenger-km.

Communications: Radios: 1 per 32 persons. **Telephones:** 1 per 415 persons.

Health: Life expectancy at birth (1992): 51 male; 51 female. **Births** (per 1,000 pop. 1992): 38. **Deaths** (per 1,000 pop. 1992): 14. **Natural increase:** 2.4%. **Hospital beds:** 1 per 3,960 persons. **Physicians:** 1 per 19,644 persons. **Infant mortality** (per 1,000 live births 1992): 90.

Education (1989): **Literacy:** 29%. **School:** Compulsory for 3 years; attendance: 79% primary, 22% secondary.

Major International Organizations: UN (IMF).

Embassy: 12a Kensington Palace Gdns, London W8 4QP; 071-229 1594.

Nepal was originally a group of petty principalities, the inhabitants of one of which, the Gurkhas, became dominant about 1769. In 1951 King Tribhubana Bir Bikram, member of the Shah family, ended the system of rule by hereditary premiers of the Ranas family, who had kept the kings virtual prisoners, and established a cabinet system of government.

Virtually closed to the outside world for centuries, Nepal is now linked to India and Pakistan by roads and air service and to Tibet by road. Polygamy, child marriage, and the caste system were officially abolished in 1963.

In response to numerous pro-democracy protests, the government, which had banned all political parties since 1960, announced the legalization of political parties in 1990. Multi-party elections were held in 1991.

Netherlands

Kingdom of the Netherlands

Koninkrijk der Nederlanden

People: Population (1992 est.) 15,112,000. **Age distrib.** (%): 0–14: 18.8; 15–60: 64.2; 60+: 17.0. **Pop. density:** 958 per sq. mi. **Urban** (1990): 88.3%. **Ethnic groups:** Dutch 97%. **Language:** Dutch. **Religions:** Roman Catholic 40%, Dutch Reformed 19.3%.

Geography: Area: 15,770 sq. mi., half the size of Scotland. **Location:** In NW Europe on North Sea. **Topography:** The land is flat, an average alt. of 37 ft. above sea level, with much land below sea level reclaimed and protected by some 1,500 miles of dykes. Since 1920 the government has been draining the IJsselmeer, formerly the Zuider Zee. **Capital:** Amsterdam. **Cities** (1990): Amsterdam 694,000; Rotterdam 576,100; The Hague 441,000.

Government: Type: Parliamentary democracy under a constitutional monarch. **Head of state:** Queen Beatrix; b. Jan. 31, 1938; in office Apr. 30, 1980. **Head of government:** Prime Min. Ruud Lubbers; in office Nov. 4, 1982. **Seat of govt.:** The Hague. **Local divisions:** 12 provinces. **Defense** (1991): 2.7% of GDP.

Economy: Industries: Metals, machinery, chemicals, oil refinery, diamond cutting, electronics, tourism. **Chief crops:** Grains, potatoes, sugar beets, vegetables, fruits, flowers. **Minerals:** Natural gas, oil. **Crude oil reserves** (1987): 195 mln. bbls. **Arable land:** 26%. **Livestock** (1990): 4.9 mln. cattle; 13.9 mln. pigs. **Fish catch** (1989): 421,000 metric tons. **Electricity prod.** (1991): 63.0 bln. kWh. **Crude steel prod.** (1991): 5.1 mln. metric tons. **Labor force:** 1% agric.; 30% ind., 44% services, 23% govt.

Finance: Monetary unit: Guilder (June 1993: 1.90 = $1 US). **Gross domestic product** (1991): $249 bln. **Per capita GDP:** $16,600. **Imports** (1992): $156 bln.; partners: Ger. 26%, Belg. 14%, U.S. 9%, U.K. 9%. **Exports** (1992): $160 bln.; partners: Ger. 26%, Belg. 14%, Fr. 10%, UK 9%. **Tourism** (1990): $3.6 bln. receipts. **National budget** (1991): $110 bln. expenditures. **International reserves less gold** (Mar. 1993): $27.2 bln. **Gold:** 31.09 mln. oz t. **Consumer prices** (change in 1992): 3.7%.

Transport: Railroads (1990): 2,828 km. long. **Motor vehicles** (1990): 5.5 mln. passenger cars, 555,000 comm. vehicles. **Civil aviation** (1990): 28.3 bln. passenger-km; 5 airports. **Chief ports:** Rotterdam, Amsterdam, Ijmuiden.

Communications: Television sets: 1 per 3.2 persons. **Radios:** 1 per 1.2 persons. **Telephones:** 1 per 1.6 persons. **Daily newspaper circ.** (1987): 312 per 1,000 pop.

Health: Life expectancy at birth (1992): 75 male; 81 female. **Births** (per 1,000 pop. 1992): 13. **Deaths** (per 1,000 pop. 1992): 9. **Natural increase:** .4%. **Hospital beds:** 1 per 164 persons. **Physicians:** 1 per 414 persons. **Infant mortality** (per 1,000 live births 1992): 7

Education (1991): **Literacy:** 99%. **School:** Compulsory for 10 years; attendance 100%.

Major International Organizations: UN and all of its specialized agencies, NATO, EC, OECD.

Embassy: 38 Hyde Park Gate, London SW7 5DP; 071-584 5040.

Julius Caesar conquered the region in 55 BC, when it was inhabited by Celtic and Germanic tribes.

After the empire of Charlemagne fell apart, the Netherlands (Holland, Belgium, Flanders) split among counts, dukes and bishops, passed to Burgundy and thence to Charles V of Spain. His son, Philip II, tried to check the Dutch drive toward political freedom and Protestantism (1568-1573). William the Silent, prince of Orange, led a confederation of the northern provinces, called Estates, in the Union of Utrecht, 1579. The Estates retained individual sovereignty, but were represented jointly in the States-General, a body that had control of foreign affairs and defense. In 1581 they repudiated allegiance to Spain. The rise of the Dutch republic to naval, economic, and artistic eminence came in the 17th century.

The United Dutch Republic ended 1795 when the French formed the Batavian Republic. Napoleon made his brother Louis king of Holland, 1806; Louis abdicated 1810 when Napoleon annexed Holland. In 1813 the French were expelled. In 1815 the Congress of Vienna formed a kingdom of the Netherlands, including Belgium, under William I. In 1830, the Belgians seceded and formed a separate kingdom.

The constitution, promulgated 1814, and subsequently revised, assures a hereditary constitutional monarchy.

The Netherlands maintained its neutrality in World War I, but was invaded and brutally occupied by Germany, 1940-45.

In 1949, after several years of fighting, the Netherlands granted independence to Indonesia, where it had ruled since the 17th century. In 1963, West New Guinea was turned over to Indonesia.

The independence of former Dutch colonies has instigated mass emigrations to the Netherlands.

Though the Netherlands has been heavily industrialized, its productive small farms export large quantities of pork and dairy foods. Rotterdam, located along the principal mouth of the Rhine, handles the most cargo of any ocean port in the world. Canals, of which there are over 3,400 are important in transportation.

Netherlands Antilles

The **Netherlands Antilles,** constitutionally on a level of equality with the Netherlands homeland within the kingdom, consist of 2 groups of islands in the West Indies. **Curaçao, Aruba,** and **Bonaire** are near the South American coast; **St. Eustatius, Saba,** and the southern part of **St. Maarten** are SE of Puerto Rico. Northern two-thirds of St. Maarten belong to French Guadeloupe; the French call the island St. Martin. Total area of the 2 groups is 385 sq. mi., including: Aruba 75, Bonaire 111, Curaçao 171, St. Eustatius 11, Saba 5, St. Maarten (Dutch part) 13.

Aruba was separated from The Netherlands Antilles on Jan. 1, 1986; it is an autonomous member of The Netherlands, the same status as the Netherland Antilles.

Total pop. (est. 1992) was 184,000. Willemstad, on Curacao, is the capital. Principal industry is the refining of crude oil from Venezuela. Tourism is an important industry, as is shipbuilding.

New Zealand

People: Population: (1991 est.): 3,347,000. **Age distrib.** (%): 0–14: 23.1, 15–59: 61.9; 60+30 : 15.0. **Pop. density:** 32 per sq. mi. **Urban** (1991): 76%. **Ethnic groups:** European (mostly British) 87%, Polynesian (mostly Maori) 9%. **Languages:** English, Maori (both official). **Religions:** Anglican 22%, Presbyterian 16%, Roman Catholic 15%, others.

Geography: Area: 103,736 sq. mi., slightly bigger than the UK. **Location:** In SW Pacific O. **Neighbors:** Nearest are Australia on W, Fiji, Tonga on N. **Topography:** Each of the 2 main islands (North and South Is.) is mainly hilly and mountainous. The east coasts consist of fertile plains, especially the broad Canterbury Plains on South Is. A volcanic plateau is in center of North Is. South Is. has glaciers and 15 peaks over 10,000 ft. **Capital:** Wellington. **Cities** (1991 est.): Auckland 315,000; Christchurch 292,000; Wellington 148,000; Manukau 224,000.

Government: Type: Parliamentary democracy. **Head of state:** Queen Elizabeth II, represented by Gov.-Gen. Dame Catherine Tizard. **Head of government:** Prime Min. Jim Bolger; b. 1935; in office Oct. 27, 1990. **Local divisions:** 93 counties, 12 towns & districts. **Defense** (1992): 2.0% of GDP.

Economy: Industries: Food processing, textiles, machinery, fish, forest prods. **Chief crops:** Grains, fruits. **Minerals:** Oil, gas, iron, coal. **Crude oil reserves** (1987): 182 mln. bbls. **Other resources:** Wool, timber. **Arable land:** 2%. **Livestock** (1991): 8.0 mln. cattle; 55 mln. sheep. **Fish catch** (1989): 509,000 metric tons. **Electricity prod.** (1991): 28.0 bln. kWh. **Labor force:** 11% agric. & mining; 41% ind. and comm., 47% services and govt.

Finance: Monetary unit: Dollar (June 1993: 1.85 = $1 US). **Gross domestic product** (1991): $46 bln. **Per capita GDP:** $14,000. **Imports** (1992): $9.2 bln.; partners: Austral. 22%, U.S. 16%, Jap. 20%. **Exports** (1992): $9.8 bln.; partners: UK 9%, U.S. 15%, Jap. 15%, Austral. 16%. **Tourism** (1990): $900,000 mln. receipts. **National budget** (1991): $18.3 bln. **International reserves less gold** (Feb. 1993): $3.0 bln. **Gold:** 1,000 oz t. **Consumer prices** (change in 1992): 1.0%.

Transport: Railroads (1990): 2,627 mi. long. **Motor vehicles** (1990): 1.5 mln. passenger cars; 310,000 comm. vehicles. **Civil aviation:** (1990): 10.5 bln. passenger-km, 36 airports. **Chief ports:** Auckland, Wellington, Lyttleton, Tauranga.

Communications: Television sets: 1 per 3.1 persons. **Radios:** 1 per 1.1 persons. **Telephones:** 1 per 1.4 persons. **Daily newspaper circ.** (1989): 306 per 1,000 pop.

Health: Life expectancy at birth (1992): 72 male; 80 female. **Births** (per 1,000 pop. 1992): 15. **Deaths** (per 1,000 pop. 1992): 8. **Natural increase:** .8%. **Hospital beds:** 1 per 111 persons. **Physicians:** 1 per 359 persons. **Infant mortality** (per 1,000 live births 1992): 10.

Education (1991): **Literacy:** 99%. **School:** Compulsory from ages 6 to 15; attendance 100%.

Major International Organizations: UN (GATT, World Bank, IMF), Commonwealth of Nations, OECD.

Embassy: New Zealand House, Haymarket, London SW1Y 4TQ; 071-930 8422.

The Maoris, a Polynesian group from the eastern Pacific, reached New Zealand before and during the 14th century. The first European to sight New Zealand was Dutch navigator Abel Janszoon Tasman, but Maoris refused to allow him to land. British Capt. James Cook explored the coasts, 1769-1770.

British sovereignty was proclaimed in 1840, with organized settlement beginning in the same year. Representative institutions were granted in 1853. Maori Wars ended in 1870 with British victory. The colony became a dominion in 1907, and is an independent member of the Commonwealth.

A labor tradition in politics dates back to the 19th century. Private ownership is basic to the economy, but state ownership or regulation affects many industries. Transportation, broadcasting, mining, and forestry are largely state-owned.

The native Maoris number about 325,000. Four of 97 members of the House of Representatives are elected directly by the Maori people.

New Zealand comprises **North Island,** 44,035 sq. mi.; **South Island,** 58,304 sq. mi.; **Stewart Island,** 674 sq. mi.; **Chatham Islands,** 372 sq. mi.

In 1965, the **Cook Islands** (pop. 1986 est., 17,185; area 93 sq. mi.) became self-governing although New Zealand retains responsibility for defense and foreign affairs. **Niue** attained the same status in 1974; it lies 400 mi. to W (pop. 1987 est., 2,500; area 100 sq. mi.). **Tokelau Is.,** (pop. 1987 est., 1,600; area 4 sq. mi.) are 300 mi. N of Samoa.

Ross Dependency, administered by New Zealand since 1923, comprises 160,000 sq. mi. of Antarctic territory.

Nicaragua

Republic of Nicaragua

República de Nicaragua

People: Population (1992 est.): 3,878,000. **Age distrib.** (%). 0–14: 45.8; 15–59: 49.9; 60+: 4.3. **Pop. density:** 77 per sq. mi. **Urban** (1990): 60%. **Ethnic groups:** Mestizo 69%, Caucasian 17%, black 9%, Indian 5%. **Language:** Spanish (official). **Religion:** Roman Catholic 88%.

Geography: Area: 50,193 sq. mi., slightly smaller than England. **Location:** In Central America. **Neighbors:** Honduras on N, Costa Rica on S. **Topography:** Both Atlantic and Pacific coasts are over 200 mi. long. The Cordillera Mtns., with many volcanic peaks, runs NW-SE through the middle of the country. Between this and a volcanic range to the E lie Lakes Managua and Nicaragua. **Capital:** Managua, pop. (1986) 1 mln.

Government: Type: Republic. **Head of Government:** Violeta Barrios de Chamorro; b. 1929; in office Apr. 25, 1990. **Local divisions:** 16 departments. **Defense** (1991): 3.8% of GDP.

Economy: Industries: Oil refining, food processing, chemicals, textiles. **Chief crops:** Bananas, cotton, fruit, yucca, coffee, sugar, corn, beans, cocoa, rice, sesame, tobacco, wheat. **Minerals:** Gold, silver, copper, tungsten. **Other resources:** Forests, shrimp. **Arable land:** 10%. **Livestock** (1991): 1.6 mln. cattle; 709,000 pigs. **Electricity prod.** (1991): 1.4 bln. kWh. **Labor force:** 44% agric.; 13% ind.; 43% services.

Finance: Monetary unit: Cordoba oro (May 1993: 5.00 = $1 US). **Gross domestic product** (1991): $1.7 bln. **Per capita GDP:** $425. **Imports** (1991): $738 mln.; partners US 25%, Latin Amer. 30%, EC 20%. **Exports** (1991): $342 mln.; partners OECD 75%, Comecon. **National budget** (1991): $499 mln. expenditures. **Consumer prices** (change in 1990): 11,000%.

Transport: Railroads (1991): 186 mi. long. **Motor vehicles** (1990): 31,000 passenger cars, 42,000 comm. vehicles. **Chief ports:** Corinto, Puerto Somoza, San Juan del Sur.

Communications: Television sets: 1 per 18 persons. **Radios:** 1 per 4.3 persons. **Telephones:** 1 per 82 persons. **Daily newspaper circ.** (1991): 28 per 1,000 pop.

Health: Life expectancy at birth (1992): 61 male; 66 female. **Births** (per 1,000 pop. 1992): 37. **Deaths** (per 1,000 pop. 1992): 8. **Natural increase:** 3.1%. **Hospital beds:** 1 per 761 persons. **Physicians:** 1 per 1,678 persons. **Infant mortality** (per 1,000 live births 1992): 57.

Education (1991): **Literacy:** 57%. **School:** Compulsory for 11 years or to 16 years old.

Major International Organizations: UN and all of its specialized agencies, OAS.

Embassy: 8 Gloucester Rd, London SW7 4RB; 071-584 4365.

Nicaragua, inhabited by various Indian tribes, was conquered by Spain in 1552. After gaining independence from Spain, 1821, Nicaragua was united for a short period with Mexico, then with the United Provinces of Central America, finally becoming an independent republic, 1838.

U.S. Marines occupied the country at times in the early 20th century, the last time from 1926 to 1933.

Gen. Anastasio Somoza Debayle was elected president 1967. He resigned 1972, but was elected president again in 1974. Martial law was imposed in Dec. 1974, after officials were kidnapped by the Marxist Sandinista guerrillas. Violent opposition spread to nearly all classes in 1978; nationwide strikes called against the government touched off a state of civil war. Months of simmering civil war ended when Somoza fled, July 19, 1979.

Relations with the U.S. were strained due to Nicaragua's aid to leftist guerrillas in El Salvador and the U.S. backing anti-Sandinista contra guerrilla groups.

In 1983, the contras launched their first major offensive; the Sandinistas imposed rule by decree. In 1985, the U.S. House rejected Pres. Reagan's request for military aid to the contras.

The diversion of funds to the contras from the proceeds of a secret arms sale to Iran caused a major scandal in the U.S. The plan, masterminded by the administration's national security advisor and his deputy, took place at a time when military aid to the contras was forbidden by law.

In a stunning upset, Violeta Barrios de Chamorro defeated Ortega in national elections, Feb. 25, 1990.

Niger

Republic of Niger

République du Niger

People: Population (1992 est.): 8,052,000. **Age distrib.** (%): 0–14: 46.7; 15–59: 48.5; 60+: 4.8. **Pop. density:** 16 per sq. mi. **Urban** (1988): 21%. **Ethnic groups:** Hausa 56%, Djerma 22%,

Fulani 8%, Tuareg 8%. **Languages:** French (official), Hausa, Fulani. **Religion:** Sunni Muslim 80%.

Geography: Area: 489,189 sq. mi., 4 times the size of the Br. Isles. **Location:** In the interior of N. Africa. **Neighbors:** Libya, Algeria on N, Mali, Burkina Faso on W, Benin, Nigeria on S, Chad on E. **Topography:** Mostly arid desert and mountains. A narrow savanna in the S and the Niger R. basin in the SW contain most of the population. **Capital:** Niamey, pop. (1987 est.) 350,000.

Government: Type: Republic; military in power. **Head of government:** Pres. Ali Seibou; in office Dec. 20, 1989. Prime Min. Amadou C. Heiffou; in office Oct. 27, 1991. **Local divisions:** 7 departments. **Defense** (1989): 0.8% of GDP.

Economy: Chief crops: Peanuts, cotton. **Minerals:** Uranium, coal, iron. **Arable land:** 3%. **Livestock** (1991): 2.2 mln. cattle; 3.5 mln. sheep; 4.8 mln. goats. **Electricity prod.** (1991): 230 mln. kWh. **Labor force:** 90% agric.

Finance: Monetary unit: CFA franc (Mar. 1993: 273 = $1 US). **Gross domestic product** (1991): $2.4 bln. **Per capita GDP:** $300. **Imports** (1990): $439 mln.; partners: Fr. 32%. **Exports** (1990): $320 mln.; partners: Fr. 65%, Nig. 11%. **National budget** (1989): $452 mln. expenditures. **International reserves less gold** (Jan. 1993): $225 mln. **Gold:** 11,000 oz t. **Consumer prices** (change in 1991): −7.8%.

Transport: Motor vehicles (1989): 16,000 passenger cars, 18,000 comm. vehicles.

Communications: Television sets: 1 per 321 persons. **Radios:** 1 per 19 persons. **Telephones:** 1 per 563 persons. **Daily newspaper cir.** (1991): 1 per 1,000 pop.

Health: Life expectancy at birth (1992): 42 male; 45 female. **Births** (per 1,000 pop. 1992): 58. **Deaths** (per 1,000 pop. 1992): 23. **Natural increase:** 3.5%. **Infant mortality** (per 1,000 live births 1992): 125.

Education (1991): **Literacy:** 28%. **School:** Compulsory for 6 years; attendance 15%.

Major International Organizations: UN (GATT, IMF, WHO, FAO), OAU.

Embassy: 154 rue de Longchamp, 75116 Paris, France; 010 331 45048060.

Niger was part of ancient and medieval African empires. European explorers reached the area in the late 18th century. The French colony of Niger was established 1900-22, after the defeat of Tuareg fighters, who had invaded the area from the N a century before. The country became independent Aug. 3, 1960. The next year it signed a bilateral agreement with France retaining close economic and cultural ties.

Nigeria

Federal Republic of Nigeria

People: Population (1991 cen.): 88,500,000. **Pop. density:** 248 per sq. mi. **Urban** (1990): 35%. **Ethnic groups:** Hausa 21%, Yoruba 20%, Ibo 17%, Fulani 9%, others. **Languages:** English (official), Hausa, Yoruba, Ibo. **Religions:** Muslim 50% (in N), Christian 40% (in S), others.

Geography: Area: 356,667 sq. mi., 3 times the size of the Br. Isles. **Location:** On the S coast of W. Africa. **Neighbors:** Benin on W, Niger on N, Chad, Cameroon on E. **Topography:** 4 E-W regions divide Nigeria: a coastal mangrove swamp 10-60 mi. wide, a tropical rain forest 50-100 mi. wide, a plateau of savanna and open woodland, and semi-desert in the N. **Capital:** Abuja. **Cities** (1992): Lagos 1,347,000; Ibadan 1,295,000.

Government: Type: In transition. **Head of state:** Pres. Ernest Shonekan; in office Aug. 26, 1993. **Local divisions:** 30 states plus federal capital territory. **Defense** (1990): 1.0% of GDP.

Economy: Industries: Crude oil (95% of export), food processing, assembly of vehicles, textiles. **Chief crops:** Cocoa (main export crop), tobacco, palm products, peanuts, cotton, soybeans. **Minerals:** Oil, gas, coal, iron, limestone, columbium, tin. **Crude oil reserves** (1991): 17.4 bln. bbls. **Other resources:** Timber, rubber, hides. **Arable land:** 31%. **Livestock** (1991): 14.5 mln. cattle; 23.6 mln. goats; 24 mln. sheep. **Fish catch** (1989): 315,000 metric tons. **Electricity prod.** (1991): 11.2 bln. kWh. **Labor force:** 54% agric., 19% ind., comm. and serv.

Finance: Monetary unit: Naira (Feb. 1993: 24.86 = $1 US). **Gross domestic product** (1990): $28 bln. **Per capita GDP:** $230. **Imports** (1990): $9.5 bln.; partners: U.S., EC. **Exports** (1990): $13.0 bln.; partners: U.S., EC. **Tourism** (1990): $21 mln. receipts. **National budget** (1992): $10.0 bln. expenditures. **International reserves less gold** (Jan. 1993): $966 mln. **Gold:** 687,000 oz t. **Consumer prices** (change in 1992): 53.9%.

Transport: Motor vehicles (1990): 785,000 passenger cars, 625,000 comm. vehicles. **Civil aviation** (1991): 774 mln. passenger-km; 14 airports. **Chief ports:** Port Harcourt, Lagos, Warri, Calabar.

Communications: Television sets: 1 per 30 persons. **Radios:** 1 per 12 persons. **Telephones:** 1 per 240 persons. **Daily newspaper circ.** (1990): 12 per 1,000 pop.

Health: Life expectancy at birth (1992): 48 male; 50 female. **Births** (per 1,000 pop. 1992): 46. **Deaths** (per 1,000 pop. 1992): 17. **Natural increase:** 2.9%. **Hospital beds:** 1 per 1,142 persons. **Physicians:** 1 per 6,900 persons. **Infant mortality** (per 1,000 live births 1992): 110.

Education (1991): **Literacy:** 51%. **School:** 42% attend primary school.

Major International Organizations: UN (GATT, IMO, WHO), OPEC, OAU, Commonwealth of Nations.

High Commission: Nigeria House, 9 Northumberland Ave, London WC2N 5BX; 071-839 1244.

Early cultures in Nigeria date back to at least 700 BC. From the 12th to the 14th centuries, more advanced cultures developed in the Yoruba area, at Ife, and in the north, where Muslim influence prevailed.

Portuguese and British slavers appeared from the 15th-16th centuries. Britain seized Lagos, 1861, during an anti-slave trade campaign, and gradually extended control inland until 1900. Nigeria became independent Oct. 1, 1960, and a republic Oct. 1, 1963.

On May 30, 1967, the Eastern Region seceded, proclaiming itself the Republic of Biafra, plunging the country into civil war. Casualties in the war were est. at over 1 million, including many "Biafrans" (mostly Ibos) who died of starvation despite international efforts to provide relief. The secessionists, after steadily losing ground, capitulated Jan. 12, 1970. Within a few years, the Ibos were reintegrated into national life.

Oil revenues have made possible a massive economic development program, largely using private enterprise, but agriculture has lagged.

After 13 years of military rule, the nation experienced a peaceful return to civilian government, Oct., 1979.

Military rule returned to Nigeria, Dec. 31, 1983 as a coup ousted the democratically elected government. The government had promised a return to civilian rule. However, the June 23, 1993 presidential election was voided by the incumbent president, Gen. Ibrahim Babangida, who rescinded his promise to surrender power to an elected civilian government. Babangida resigned and appointed a civilian to head an interim government, Aug. 26.

Norway

Kingdom of Norway

Kongeriket Norge

People: Population (1992 est.): 4,294,000. **Age distrib.** (%): 0–14: 19.0; 15–59: 59.9; 60+: 21.1. **Pop. density:** 34 per sq. mi. **Urban** (1990): 75%. **Ethnic groups:** Germanic (Nordic, Alpine, Baltic), minority Lapps. **Language:** Norwegian (official). **Religion:** Evangelical Lutheran 94%.

Geography: Area: 125,181 sq. mi., slightly larger than the Br. Isles. **Location:** Occupies the W part of Scandinavian peninsula in NW Europe (extends farther north than any European land). **Neighbors:** Sweden, Finland, Russia on E. **Topography:** A highly indented coast is lined with tens of thousands of islands. Mountains and plateaus cover most of the country, which is only 25% forested. **Capital:** Oslo. **Cities** (1992): Oslo 467,000; Bergen 215,000.

Government: Type: Hereditary constitutional monarchy. **Head of state:** King Harald V; b. Feb. 21, 1937; in office Jan. 17, 1991. **Head of government:** Prime Min. Gro Harlem Brundtland; in office Nov. 3, 1990. **Local divisions:** Oslo, Svalbard and 18 fylker (counties). **Defense** (1991): 3.2% of GDP.

Economy: Industries: Paper, shipbuilding, engineering, metals, chemicals, food processing oil, gas. **Chief crops:** Grains, potatoes, fruits. **Minerals:** Oil, copper, pyrites, nickel, iron, zinc, lead. **Crude oil reserves** (1987): 11.1 bln. bbls. **Other resources:** Timber. **Arable land:** 3%. **Livestock** (1991): 1.0 mln. sheep; 967,000 cattle; 721,000 pigs. **Fish catch** (1991): 1.9 mln. metric tons. **Electricity prod.** (1991): 121 bln. kWh. **Labor force:** 7% agric.; 47% ind., banking, comm.; 18% services; 26% govt.

Finance: Monetary unit: Kroner (July 1993: 7.18 = $1 US). **Gross domestic product** (1991): $72.9 bln. **Per capita GDP:** $17,100. **Imports** (1992): $25.9 bln.; partners: EC 47%. **Exports** (1992): $35.1 bln.; partners: EC 69%. **Tourism** (1990): $1.5 bln. receipts. **National budget** (1991): $52 bln. expenditures. **International reserves less gold** (Mar. 1993): $11.9 bln. **Gold:** 1.18 mln. oz t. **Consumer prices** (change in 1992): 2.3%.

Transport: Railroads (1990): 2,600 mi. long. **Motor vehicles** (1991): 1.6 mln. passenger cars, 383,000 comm. vehicles. **Civil aviation** (1990): 7.6 bln. passenger-km; 47 airports. **Chief ports:** Bergen, Stavanger, Oslo, Tonsberg.

Communications: Television sets: 1 per 2.9 persons. **Radios:** 1 per 1.3 persons. **Telephones:** 1 per 1.6 persons. **Daily newspaper circ.** (1991): 510 per 1,000 pop.

Health: Life expectancy at birth (1992): 74 male; 81 female. **Births** (per 1,000 pop. 1992): 14. **Deaths** (per 1,000 pop. 1992):

11. **Natural increase:** .3%. **Hospital beds:** 1 per 168 persons. **Physicians:** 1 per 309 persons. **Infant mortality** (per 1,000 live births 1992): 7.1.

Education (1991): **Literacy:** 99%. **School:** Compulsory for 9 years.

Major International Organizations: UN and all of its specialized agencies, NATO, OECD.

Embassy: 25 Belgrave Sq, London SW1X 8QD; 071-235 7151.

The first supreme ruler of Norway was Harald the Fairhaired who came to power in AD 872. Between 800 and 1000, Norway's Vikings raided and occupied widely dispersed parts of Europe.

The country was united with Denmark 1381-1814, and with Sweden, 1814-1905. In 1905, the country became independent with Prince Charles of Denmark as king.

Norway remained neutral during World War I. Germany attacked Norway Apr. 9, 1940, and held it until liberation May 8, 1945. The country abandoned its neutrality after the war, and joined the NATO alliance.

Abundant hydroelectric resources provided the base for Norway's industrialization, producing one of the highest living standards in the world.

Norway's merchant marine is one of the world's largest.

Svalbard is a group of mountainous islands in the Arctic Ocean, c. 23,957 sq. mi., pop. varying seasonally from 1,500 to 3,600. The largest, Spitsbergen (formerly called West Spitsbergen), 15,060 sq. mi., seat of governor, is about 370 mi. N of Norway. By a treaty signed in Paris, 1920, major European powers recognized the sovereignty of Norway, which incorporated it in 1925.

Oman

Sultanate of Oman

Saltanat 'Uman

People: Population (1992 est.): 1,587,000. **Pop. density:** 19 per sq. mi. **Urban** (1990): 10%. **Ethnic groups:** Omani/Arab 74%, Pakistani 21%. **Language:** Arabic (official). **Religions:** Ibadhi Muslim 75%, Sunni Muslim.

Geography: Area: 82,030 sq. mi., slightly smaller than GB. **Location:** On SE coast of Arabian peninsula. **Neighbors:** United Arab Emirates, Saudi Arabia, Yemen on W. **Topography:** Oman has a narrow coastal plain up to 10 mi. wide, a range of barren mountains reaching 9,900 ft., and a wide, stony, mostly waterless plateau, avg. alt. 1,000 ft. Also the tip of the Ruus-al-Jebal peninsula controls access to the Persian Gulf. **Capital:** Muscat, pop. (1990 est.) 85,000.

Government: Type: Absolute monarchy. **Head of state:** Sultan Qabus bin Said; b. Nov. 18, 1942; in office July 23, 1970. **Defense** (1992): 16% of GDP.

Economy: Chief crops: Dates, fruits vegetables, wheat, bananas. **Minerals:** Oil (95% of exports). **Crude oil reserves** (1987): 4.5 bln. bbls. **Fish catch** (1990): 110,000 metric tons. **Electricity prod.** (1991): 5.0 bln. kWh. **Labor force:** 60% agric. & fishing.

Finance: Monetary unit: Rial Omani (Mar. 1993: .38 = $1 US). **Gross domestic product** (1989): $7.7 bln. **Imports** (1990): $2.6 bln.; partners: Jap. 21%, UAE 17%, UK 14%. **Exports** (1990): $2.6 bln.; partners: Jap. 58%, Europe 30%. **National budget** (1990): $4.9 bln. revenues; $5.4 bln. expenditures. **International reserves less gold** (Mar. 1993): $1.6 bln. **Gold:** 289,000 oz t.

Transport: Motor vehicles (1990): 96,000 pasenger cars, 70,000 comm. vehicles. **Civil aviation** (1990): 1.6 bln. passenger-km; 6 airports. **Chief ports:** Matrah, Muscat.

Communications: Television sets: 1 per 1.4 persons. **Radios:** 1 per 1.6 persons. **Telephones:** 1 per 14 persons.

Health: Life expectancy at birth (1992): 65 male; 69 female. **Hospital beds:** 1 per 380 persons. **Physicians:** 1 per 1,071 persons. **Infant mortality** (per 1,000 live births 1992): 40.

Education (1989): **Literacy:** 20%. **School:** 80% at primary, 30% at secondary.

Major International Organizations: UN (World Bank, IMF), Arab League.

Embassy: 44 Montpelier Sq, London SW7 1JZ; 071-584 6782.

A long history of rule by other lands, including Portugal in the 16th century, ended with the ouster of the Persians in 1744. By the early 19th century, Muscat and Oman was one of the most important countries in the region, controlling much of the Persian and Pakistan coasts, and ruling far-away Zanzibar, which was separated in 1861 under British mediation.

British influence was confirmed in a 1951 treaty, and Britain helped suppress an uprising by traditionally rebellious interior tribes against control by Muscat in the 1950s.

On July 23, 1970, Sultan Said bin Taimur was overthrown by his son who changed the nation's name to Sultanate of Oman.

Oil is the major source of income.

Oman opened its air bases to Western forces following the Iraqi invasion of Kuwait on Aug. 2, 1990.

Pakistan

Islamic Republic of Pakistan

Islam-i Jamhuriya-e Pakistan

People: Population (1992 est.): 121,664,000. **Pop. density:** 391 per sq. mi. **Urban** (1988): 32%. **Ethnic groups:** Punjabi 66%, Sindhi 13%, Pathan 8.5%, Urdu 7.6%, Baluchi 2.5%, others. **Languages:** Urdu, (official), Punjabi, Sindhi, Pushtu, Baluchi, Brahvi. **Religion:** Muslim 97%.

Geography: Area: 310,403 sq. mi., over twice the size of the Br. Isles. **Location:** In W part of South Asia. **Neighbors:** Iran on W, Afghanistan, China on N, India on E. **Topography:** The Indus R. rises in the Hindu Kush and Himalaya mtns. in the N (highest is K2, or Godwin Austen, 28,250 ft., 2nd highest in world), then flows over 1,000 mi. through fertile valley and empties into Arabian Sea. Thar Desert, Eastern Plains flank Indus Valley. **Capital:** Islamabad. **Cities** (1992 est.): Karachi 7.0 mln.; Lahore 3.5 mln.; Faisalabad 2.0 mln.; Hyderabad 795,000; Rawalpindi 928,000.

Government: Type: Parliamentary democracy in a federal setting. **Head of state:** Pres. Ghulam Ishaq Khan; in office Dec. 12, 1988. **Head of government:** Prime Min. Benazir Bhutto; in office Oct. 1993. **Local divisions:** Federal capital, 4 provinces, tribal areas. **Defense** (1992): 6.4% of GDP.

Economy: Industries: Textiles, food processing, chemicals, petroleum products,**Chief crops:** Rice, wheat. **Minerals:** Natural gas, iron ore. **Crude oil reserves** (1987): 116 mln. bbls. **Other resources:** Wool. **Arable land:** 26%. **Livestock** (1990): 17.2 mln. cattle; 28.3 mln. sheep; 34.2 mln. goats. **Fish catch** (1990): 479,000 metric tons. **Electricity prod.** (1991): 35 bln. kWh. **Labor force:** 53% agric.; 13% ind; 33% services.

Finance: Monetary unit: Rupee (Aug. 1993: 29.75 = $1 US). **Gross domestic product** (1991): $45 bln. **Per capita GDP:** $380. **Imports** (1991): $7.9 bln.; partners: EC 21%, Jap. 13%, U.S. 16%. **Exports** (1991): $6.0 bln.; partners: EC 31%, Jap. 10%, U.S. 10%. **Tourism** (1990): $156 mln. receipts. **National budget** (1992): $10.0 bln. expenditures. **International reserves less gold** (Mar. 1993): $797 mln. **Gold:** 2.0 mln. oz t. **Consumer prices** (change in 1992): 9.5%.

Transport: Railroads (1990): 5,453 mi. long. **Motor vehicles** (1989): 738,000 passenger cars, 171,000 comm. vehicles. **Civil aviation** (1990): 9.3 bln. passenger-km; 35 airports with scheduled flights. **Chief port:** Karachi.

Communications: Television sets: 1 per 61 persons. **Radios:** 1 per 13 persons. **Telephones:** 1 per 131 persons. **Daily newspaper circ.** (1990): 9 per 1,000 pop.

Health: Life expectancy at birth (1992): 56 male; 57 female. **Births** (per 1,000 pop. 1992): 43. **Deaths** (per 1,000 pop. 1992): 14. **Natural increase:** 2.9%. **Hospital beds:** 1 per 1,706 persons. **Physicians:** 1 per 2,364 persons. **Infant mortality** (per 1,000 live births 1992): 105.

Education (1991): **Literacy:** 35%.

Major International Organizations: UN (GATT, ILO, IMF, WHO).

Embassy: 35 Lowndes Sq, London SW1X 9JN; 071-235 2044.

Present-day Pakistan shares the 5,000-year history of the India-Pakistan sub-continent. At present day Harappa and Mohenjo Daro, the Indus Valley Civilization, with large cities and elaborate irrigation systems, flourished c. 4,000-2,500 BC.

Aryan invaders from the NW conquered the region around 1,500 BC, forging a Hindu civilization that dominated Pakistan as well as India for 2,000 years.

Beginning with the Persians in the 6th century BC, and continuing with Alexander the Great and with the Sassanians, successive nations to the west ruled or influenced Pakistan, eventually separating the area from the Indian cultural sphere.

The first Arab invasion, AD 712, introduced Islam. Under the Mogul empire (1526-1857), Muslims ruled most of India, yielding to British encroachment and resurgent Hindus.

After World War I the Muslims of British India began agitation for minority rights in elections. Mohammad Ali Jinnah (1876-1948) was the principal architect of Pakistan. A leader of the Muslim League from 1916, he worked for dominion status for India; from 1940 he advocated a separate Muslim state.

When the British withdrew Aug. 14, 1947, the Islamic majority areas of India acquired self-government as Pakistan, with dominion status in the Commonwealth. Pakistan was divided into 2 sections, West Pakistan and East Pakistan. The 2 areas were nearly 1,000 mi. apart on opposite sides of India.

Pakistan became a republic in 1956. Pakistan had a National Assembly (legislature) with equal membership from East and West Pakistan, and 2 Provincial Assemblies. In Oct. 1958, Gen. Mohammad Ayub Khan took power in a coup. He was elected president in 1960, reelected in 1965.

Ayub resigned Mar. 25, 1969, after several months of violent rioting and unrest, most of it in East Pakistan, which demanded autonomy. The government was turned over to Gen. Agha Mohammad Yahya Khan and martial law was declared.

The Awami League, which sought regional autonomy for East Pakistan, won a majority in Dec. 1970 elections to a National Assembly which was to write a new constitution. In March, 1971 Yahya postponed the Assembly. Rioting and strikes broke out.

On Mar. 25, 1971, government troops launched attacks in the East. The Easterners, aided by India, proclaimed the independent nation of Bangladesh. In months of widespread fighting, countless thousands were killed. Some 10 million Easterners fled into India.

Full scale war between India and Pakistan had spread to both the East and West fronts by Dec. 3. Pakistan troops in the East surrendered Dec. 16; Pakistan agreed to a cease-fire in the West Dec. 17. On July 3, 1972, Pakistan and India signed a pact agreeing to withdraw troops from their borders and seek peaceful solutions to all problems.

Zulfikar Ali Bhutto, leader of the Pakistan People's Party, which had won the most West Pakistan votes in the Dec. 1970 elections, became president Dec. 20.

Bhutto was overthrown in a military coup July, 1977. Convicted of complicity in a 1974 political murder, Bhutto was executed Apr.4, 1979. Benazir Bhutto, his daughter, returned to Pakistan from exile in Europe in 1986. Her efforts to relaunch the Pakistan People's Party sparked violence and antigovernment riots.

Pres. Mohammad Zia ul-Haq was killed when his plane exploded in Aug. 1988. Following Nov. elections, Benazir Bhutto was named Prime Minister, the first woman leader of a Muslim nation. Her party was soundly defeated in the Oct. 1990 elections; there were charges of corruption against Bhutto.

Legislation was submitted in 1991 to adopt Islamic law in place of the current secular code.

Prime Min. Nawaz Sharif was ousted from office by Pres. Khan Apr. 18, 1993; he was reinstated by Pakistan's Supreme Court May 26. In Oct. 1993 elections Benazir Bhutto was again elected Prime Minister.

Panama

Republic of Panama

República de Panamá

People: Population (1992 est.): 2,529,000. **Age distrib.** (%): 0–14: 35.5; 15–59: 57.6; 60+: 6.9. **Pop. density:** 84 per sq. mi. **Urban** (1990): 53%. **Ethnic groups:** Mestizo 70%, West Indian 14%, Caucasian 10%, Indian 6%. **Languages:** Spanish (official), English. **Religions:** Roman Catholic 93%, Protestant 6%.

Geography: Area: 29,762 sq. mi., slightly larger than the Republic of Ireland. **Location:** In Central America. **Neighbors:** Costa Rica on W., Colombia on E. **Topography:** 2 mountain ranges run the length of the isthmus. Tropical rain forests cover the Caribbean coast and eastern Panama. **Capital:** Panama, (1990 est.) 411,000.

Government: Type: Constitutional democracy. **Head of state and head of government:** Pres. Guillermo Endara Galimany; in office Dec. 20, 1989. **Local divisions:** 9 provinces, 1 territory. **Defense** (1990): 1.5% of GDP.

Economy: Industries: Oil refining, international banking. **Chief crops:** Bananas, pineapples, cocoa, corn, coconuts, sugar. **Minerals:** Copper. **Other resources:** Forests (mahogany), shrimp. **Arable land:** 6%. **Livestock** (1990): 1.5 mln. cattle; 240,000 pigs. **Electricity prod.** (1991): 3.3 bln. kWh. **Labor force:** 26% agric., 28%, govt. & community services.

Finance: Monetary unit: Balboa (Apr. 1993: 1.00 = $1 US). **Gross domestic product** (1991): $5.2 bln. **Per capita GDP:** $1,150. **Imports** (1991): $1.5 bln.; partners: U.S. 37%. **Exports** (1991): $380 mln.; partners: U.S. 44%. **Tourism** (1990): $167 mln. receipts. **National budget** (1992): $1.7 bln. **International reserves less gold** (Jan. 1993): $553 mln. **Consumer prices** (change in 1992): 1.8%.

Transport: Motor vehicles (1990): 186,000 passenger cars, 49,000 comm. vehicles. **Civil aviation** (1990): 195 mln. passenger-km; 8 airports with scheduled flights. **Chief ports:** Balboa, Cristobal.

Communications: Television sets: 1 per 12 persons. **Radios:** 1 per 2.5 persons. **Telephones:** 1 per 9.3 persons. **Daily newspaper circ.** (1990): 60 per 1,000 pop.

Health: Life expectancy at birth (1992): 73 male; 77 female. **Births** (per 1,000 pop. 1992): 26. **Deaths** (per 1,000 pop. 1992): 5. **Natural increase:** 2.1%. **Hospital beds:** 1 per 330 persons. **Physicians:** 1 per 880 persons. **Infant mortality** (per 1,000 live births 1992): 17.

Education (1991): **Literacy:** 87%. **School:** Almost 100% attend primary school.

Major International Organizations: UN (IMF, IMO, World Bank), OAS.

Embassy: 119 Crawford St, London W1H 1AF; 071-487 5633.

The coast of Panama was sighted by Rodrigo de Bastidas, sailing with Columbus for Spain in 1501, and was visited by Columbus in 1502. Vasco Nunez de Balboa crossed the isthmus and "discovered" the Pacific O. Sept. 13, 1513. Spanish colonies were ravaged by Francis Drake, 1572-95, and Henry Morgan, 1668-71. Morgan destroyed the old city of Panama which had been founded in 1519. Freed from Spain, Panama joined Colombia in 1821.

Panama declared its independence from Colombia Nov. 3, 1903, with U.S. recognition. U.S. naval forces deterred action by Colombia. On Nov. 18, 1903, Panama granted use, occupation and control of the Canal Zone to the U.S. by treaty, ratified Feb. 26, 1904.

In 1978, a new treaty provided for a gradual takeover by Panama of the canal, and withdrawal of U.S. troops, to be completed by 1999. U.S. payments were substantially increased in the interim. The permanent neutrality of the canal was also guaranteed.

President Delvalle was ousted by the National Assembly, Feb. 26, 1988, after he tried to fire the head of the Panama Defense Forces, Gen. Manuel Antonio Noriega. Noriega had been indicted by 2 U.S. federal grand juries on drug charges. A general strike followed. Despite U.S.-imposed economic sanctions Noriega remained in power. Voters went to the polls to elect a new president May 7, 1989. Noriega claimed victory but foreign observers said that the opposition had won overwhelmingly and that Noriega was trying to steal the election. The government voided the election May 10, charging foreign interference. There was an attempted coup against Noriega Oct. 3.

U.S. troops invaded Panama Dec. 20 following a series of incidents, including the killing of a U.S. Marine by Panamanian soldiers. The operation had as its chief objective the capture of Noriega, who was wanted in the U.S. on drug trafficking charges. Noriega took refuge in the Vatican diplomatic mission, but surrendered after 10 days to U.S. officials, Jan. 3, 1990. He was convicted on 8 counts of racketeering & drug trafficking in a US District Court in Miami, Fla., Apr. 9, 1992.

Papua New Guinea

People: Population (1992 est.): 4,006,000. **Age distrib.** (%): 0–14: 41.6; 15–59: 52.8; 60+: 5.6. **Pop. density:** 22 per sq. mi. **Urban** (1990): 15.0%. **Ethnic groups:** Papuans (in S and interior), Melanesian (N,E), pygmies, minorities of Chinese, Australians, Polynesians. **Languages:** English (official), Melanesian languages, Papuan languages. **Religions:** Protestant 63%, Roman Catholic 31%, local religions.

Geography: Area: 178,260 sq. mi., twice the size of GB. **Location:** Occupies eastern half of island of New Guinea. **Neighbors:** Indonesia (West Irian) on W, Australia on S. **Topography:** Thickly forested mtns. cover much of the center of the country, with lowlands along the coasts. Included are some of the nearby islands of Bismarck and Solomon groups, including Admiralty Is., New Ireland, New Britain, and Bougainville. **Capital:** Port Moresby. **Cities** (1991): Port Moresby 193,000; Lae 80,000.

Government: Type: Parliamentary democracy. **Head of state:** Queen Elizabeth II, represented by Gov. Gen. Wiwa Korowi; in office Oct. 4, 1991. **Head of government:** Prime Min. Paias Wingti; in office July 17, 1992. **Local divisions:** 20 provinces. **Defense** (1989): Approx. 1.5% of GDP.

Economy: Chief crops: Coffee, coconuts, cocoa. **Minerals:** Gold, copper, silver. **Arable land:** 1%. **Livestock** (1990): 1.7 mln. pigs. **Electricity prod.** (1991): 1.5 bln. kWh. **Labor force:** 82% agric., 3% ind. and commerce, 8% services.

Finance: Monetary unit: Kina (Mar. 1993: 0.98 = $1 US). **Gross domestic product** (1991): $3.1 bln. **Per capita GDP:** $800. **Imports** (1992): $1.5 bln.; partners: Austral. 40%; Jap. 17%; U.S. 9%. **Exports** (1992): $1.8 bln.; partners: Jap. 26%, W. Ger. 36%, Austral. 8%. **National budget** (1992): $1.4 bln. **International reserves less gold** (Mar. 1993): $180 mln. **Gold:** 63,000 oz t. **Consumer prices** (change in 1992): 3.6%.

Transport: Motor vehicles (1989): 17,000 passenger cars, 26,000 comm. vehicles. **Chief ports:** Port Moresby, Lae.

Communications: Television sets: 1 per 375 persons. **Radios:** 1 per 15 persons. **Telephones:** 1 per 48 persons. **Daily newspaper circ.** (1988): 8 per 1,000 pop.

Health: Life expectancy at birth (1992): 55 male; 56 female. **Births** (per 1,000 pop. 1992): 34. **Deaths** (per 1,000 pop. 1992): 11. **Natural increase:** 2.3%. **Hospital beds:** 1 per 222 persons. **Physicians:** 1 per 11,904 persons. **Infant mortality** (per 1,000 live births 1992): 55.

Education (1991): **Literacy:** 52%. **School:** 65% at primary; 13% at secondary.

Major International Organizations: UN (GATT), Commonwealth of Nations.

High Commission: 14 Waterloo Place, London SW1Y 4AR; 071-930 0922.

Human remains have been found in the interior of New Guinea dating back at least 10,000 years and possibly much earlier. Successive waves of peoples probably entered the country from Asia through Indonesia. Europeans visited in the 15th century, but land claims did not begin until the 19th century, when the Dutch took control of the western half of the island.

The southern half of eastern New Guinea was first claimed by Britain in 1884, and transferred to Australia in 1905. The northern half was claimed by Germany in 1884, but captured in World War I by Australia, which was granted a League of Nations mandate and then a UN trusteeship over the area. The 2 territories were administered jointly after 1949, given self-government Dec. 1, 1973, and became independent Sept. 16, 1975.

The indigenous population consists of a huge number of tribes, many living in almost complete isolation with mutually unintelligible languages.

Paraguay

Republic of Paraguay

República del Paraguay

People: Population (1992 est.): 4,929,000. **Age distrib.** (%): 0–14: 41.0; 15–59: 52.0; 60+: 7.0. **Pop. density:** 31 per sq. mi. **Urban** (1990): 46%. **Ethnic groups:** Mestizo 95%, small Caucasian, Indian, black minorities. **Languages:** Spanish (official), Guarani. **Religion:** Roman Catholic (official) 97%.

Geography: Area: 157,047 sq. mi., slightly larger than the Br. Isles. **Location:** One of the 2 landlocked countries of S. America. **Neighbors:** Bolivia on N, Argentina on S, Brazil on E. **Topography:** Paraguay R. bisects the country. To E are fertile plains, wooded slopes, grasslands. To W is the Chaco plain, with marshes and scrub trees. Extreme W is arid. **Capital:** Asunción, pop. (1990 est.) 607,000.

Government: Type: Republic. **Head of state:** Pres. Juan Carlos Wasmosy; in office Aug. 15, 1993. **Local divisions:** 19 departments. **Defense** (1988): 1.0% of GDP.

Economy: Industries: Food processing, wood products, textiles, cement. **Chief crops:** Corn, cotton, beans, sugarcane. **Minerals:** Iron, manganese, limestone. **Other resources:** Forests. **Arable land:** 20%. **Livestock** (1991): cattle: 8.2 mln.; pigs: 2.4 mln. **Electricity prod.** (1991): 15.4 bln. kWh. **Labor force:** 44% agric., 34% ind. and commerce, 18% services.

Finance: Monetary unit: Guarani (Mar. 1993 1,631 = $1 US). **Gross domestic product** (1991): $7.0 bln. **Per capita GDP:** $1,460. **Imports** (1991): $1.8 bln., partners: Braz. 32%, EC 20%. **Exports** (1991): $642 mln.; partners: EC 37%, Braz. 25%. **Tourism** (1990): $113 mln. receipts. **National budget** (1991): $1.2 bln. expenditures. **International reserves less gold** (Mar. 1993): $561 mln. **Gold:** 35,000 oz t. **Consumer prices** (change in 1991): 27.3%.

Transport: Motor vehicles (1990): 117,000 passenger cars, 5,000 comm. vehicles. **Civil aviation** (1990): 571 mln. passenger-km; 1 airport with scheduled flight. **Chief port:** Asunción.

Communications: Television sets: 1 per 12 persons. **Radios:** 1 per 5.4 persons. **Telephones:** 1 per 42 persons. **Daily newspaper circ.** (1990): 29 per 1,000 pop.

Health: Life expectancy at birth (1992): 71 male; 74 female. **Births** (per 1,000 pop. 1992): 33. **Deaths** (per 1,000 pop. 1992): 5. **Natural increase:** 2.8%. **Hospital beds:** 1 per 931 persons. **Physicians:** 1 per 1,008 persons. **Infant mortality** (per 1,000 live births 1992): 28.

Education (1991): **Literacy:** 90%. **School:** Compulsory for 7 years; attendance 83%.

Major International Organizations: UN (IMF, WHO, ILO), OAS.

Embassy: Braemar Lodge, Cornwall Gdns, London SW7 4AQ; 071-937 1253.

The Guarani Indians were settled farmers speaking a common language before the arrival of Europeans.

Visited by Sebastian Cabot in 1527 and settled as a Spanish possession in 1535, Paraguay gained its independence from Spain in 1811. It lost much of its territory to Brazil, Uruguay, and Argentina in the War of the Triple Alliance, 1865-1870. Large areas were won from Bolivia in the Chaco War, 1932-35.

Gen. Alfredo Stroessner, who ruled since 1954, was ousted in a military coup led by Gen. Andres Rodriguez on Feb. 3, 1989. Rodriguez was elected president May 1. Juan Carlos Wasmosy was elected the nation's first civilian head of state in 1993.

Peru

Republic of Peru

República del Peru

People: Population (1992 est.): 22,767,000. **Age distrib.** (%): 0–14: 37.2; 15–59: 56.8; 60+: 6.0. **Pop. density:** 45 per sq. mi. **Urban** (1992): 70%. **Ethnic groups:** Indians 45%, Mestizos 37%, Caucasians 15%, blacks, Asians. **Languages:** Spanish, Quechua (both official), Aymara. **Religion:** Roman Catholic 90%.

Geography: Area: 496,222 sq. mi., 4 times larger than the Br. Isles. **Location:** On the Pacific coast of S. America. **Neighbors:** Ecuador, Colombia on N, Brazil, Bolivia on E, Chile on S. **Topography:** An arid coastal strip, 10 to 100 mi. wide, supports much of the population thanks to widespread irrigation. The Andes cover 27% of land area. The uplands are well watered, as are the eastern slopes reaching the Amazon basin, which covers half the country with its forests and jungles. **Capital:** Lima. **Cities** (1990 est.): Lima 5,826,000; Arequipa 634,000; Callao 589,000.

Government: Type: In transition. **Head of state:** Pres. Alberto Fujimori; b. July 28, 1938; in office July 28, 1990. **Head of government:** Prime Min. Oscar de la Plente Raygada; in office Apr. 6, 1992. **Local divisions:** 24 departments, 1 province. **Defense** (1991): 2.4% of GDP.

Economy: Industries: Fish meal, mineral processing, light industry, textiles. **Chief crops:** Cotton, sugar, coffee, corn. **Minerals:** Copper, lead, molybdenum, silver, zinc, iron, oil. **Crude oil reserves** (1987): 535 mln. bbls. **Other resources:** Wool, sardines. **Arable land:** 3%. **Livestock** (1991): 3.6 mln. cattle; 2.3 mln. pigs; 11.2 mln. sheep. **Fish catch** (1990): 6.1 mln. metric tons. **Electricity prod.** (1991): 15.8 bln. kWh. **Labor force:** 38% agric.; 17% ind. and mining; 45% govt. and other services.

Finance: Monetary unit: Nuevo Sol (July 1993: 2.01 = $1 US). **Gross domestic product** (1991): $20.6 bln. **Per capita GDP:** $920. **Imports** (1991): $3.5 bln.; partners: U.S. 32%, EC 17%. **Exports** (1991): $3.3 bln.; partners: U.S. 20%, EC 28%, Jap. 13%. **Tourism** (1990): $353 mln. receipts. **National budget** (1991): $1.8 bln. **International reserves less gold** (Mar. 1993): $2.9 bln. **Gold:** 1.8 mln. oz t. **Consumer prices** (change in 1992): 73.5%.

Transport: Railroads (1991): 2,157 mi. long. **Motor vehicles** (1990): 368,000 passenger cars, 237,000 comm. vehicles. **Civil aviation** (1990): 2.0 bln. passenger-km; 22 airports. **Chief ports:** Callao, Chimbate, Mollendo.

Communications: Television sets: 1 per 11 persons. **Radios:** 1 per 5.2 persons. **Telephones:** 1 per 28 persons. **Daily newspaper circ.** (1987): 57 per 1,000 pop.

Health: Life expectancy at birth (1992): 63 male; 67 female. **Births** (per 1,000 pop. 1992): 28. **Deaths** (per 1,000 pop. 1992): 8. **Natural increase:** 2.0%. **Hospital beds:** 1 per 625 persons. **Physicians:** 1 per 997 persons. **Infant mortality** (per 1,000 live births 1992): 59.

Education (1991): **Literacy:** 85%. **School:** Compulsory for 10 years.

Major International Organizations: UN and all its specialized agencies, OAS.

Embassy: 52 Sloane St, London SW1X 9SP; 071-235 1917.

The powerful Inca empire had its seat at Cuzco in the Andes covering most of Peru, Bolivia, and Ecuador, as well as parts of Colombia, Chile, and Argentina. Building on the achievements of 800 years of Andean civilization, the Incas had a high level of skill in architecture, engineering, textiles, and social organization.

A civil war had weakened the empire when Francisco Pizarro, Spanish conquistador, began raiding Peru for its wealth, 1532. In 1533 he had the seized ruling Inca, Atahualpa, fill a room with gold as a ransom, then executed him and enslaved the natives.

Lima was the seat of Spanish viceroys until the Argentine liberator, Jose de San Martin, captured it in 1821; Spain was defeated by Simon Bolivar and Antonio J. de Sucre; recognized Peruvian independence, 1824.

On Oct. 3, 1968, a military coup ousted Pres. Fernando Belaunde Terry. In 1968-74, the military government put through sweeping agrarian changes, and nationalized oil, mining, fishmeal, and banking industries.

Food shortages, escalating foreign debt, and strikes led to another coup, Aug. 29, 1976, and to a slowdown of socialist programs.

After 12 years of military rule, Peru returned to democratic leadership under former Pres. Belaunde Terry, July 1980.

Pres Fujimori dissolved the National Congress, suspended parts of the constitution and instituted press censorship, Apr. 5, 1992.

Philippines

Republic of the Philippines

People: Population (1992 est.): 67,114,000. **Age distrib.** (%): 0–14: 39.0; 15–59: 56.2; 60+: 4.8. **Pop. density:** 579 per sq. mi. **Urban** (1991): 43%. **Ethnic groups:** Malays the large majority, Chinese, Americans, Spanish are minorities. **Languages:** Pilipino (based on Tagalog), English (both official), Cebuano, Bicol, Ilocano, Pampango, many others. **Religions:** Roman Catholic 83%, Protestant 9%, Muslim 5%.

Geography: Area: 115,831 sq. mi., slightly smaller than the Br. Isles. **Location:** An archipelago off the SE coast of Asia. **Neighbors:** Nearest are Malaysia, Indonesia on S, Taiwan on N.

Topography: The country consists of some 7,100 islands stretching 1,100 mi. N-S. About 95% of area and population are on 11 largest islands, which are mountainous, except for the heavily indented coastlines and for the central plain on Luzon. **Capital:** Quezon City (Manila is de facto capital). **Cities** (1990 est.): Manila 1.8 mln.; Quezon City 1.5 mln.; Cebu 552,000.

Government: Type: Republic. **Head of state:** Pres. Fidel V. Ramos; b. 1928; in office June 30, 1992. **Local divisions:** 72 provinces, 61 cities. **Defense** (1991): 2.0% of GDP.

Economy: Industries: Food processing, textiles, clothing, drugs, wood prods., appliances. **Chief crops:** Sugar, rice, corn, pineapple, coconut. **Minerals:** Cobalt, copper, gold, nickel, silver, iron, petroleum. **Other resources:** Forests (42% of area). **Arable land:** 26%. **Livestock** (1990): 1.4 mln. cattle; 7.8 mln. pigs. **Fish catch** (1990): 2.0 mln. metric tons. **Electricity prod.** (1991): 31 bln. kWh. **Labor force:** 47% agric., 20% ind. and comm., 13% services.

Finance: Monetary unit: Peso (May 1993: 25.51 = $1 US). **Gross national product** (1991): $47 bln. **Per capita GNP:** $720. **Imports** (1991): $12.3 bln.; partners: U.S. 25%, Jap. 16%. **Exports** (1991): $8.7 bln.; partners: U.S. 35%, Jap. 17%, EC 19%. **Tourism** (1990): $1.3 bln. receipts. **National budget** (1991): $9.3 bln. expenditures. **International reserves less gold** (Mar. 1993): $5.7 bln. **Gold:** 2.8 mln. oz t. **Consumer prices** (change in 1992): 8.9%.

Transport: Railroads (1991): 658 mi. long. **Motor vehicles** (1990): 454,000 passenger cars, 783,000 comm. vehicles. **Civil aviation** (1991): 9.3 bln. passenger-km; 31 airports with scheduled flights. **Chief ports:** Cebu, Manila, Iloilo, Davao.

Communications: Television sets: 1 per 8.8 persons. **Radios:** 1 per 16 persons. **Telephones:** 1 per 60 persons. **Daily newspaper circ.** (1988): 44 per 1,000 pop.

Health: Life expectancy at birth (1992): 62 male; 68 female. **Births** (per 1,000 pop. 1992): 29. **Deaths** (per 1,000 pop. 1992): 7. **Natural increase:** 2.2%. **Hospital beds:** 1 per 683 persons. **Physicians:** 1 per 1,062 persons. **Infant mortality** (per 1,000 live births 1992): 54.0.

Education (1989): **Literacy:** 88%. **School:** Attendance 97% in elementary, 55% secondary.

Major International Organizations: UN (World Bank, IMF, GATT), ASEAN.

Embassy: 9a Palace Green, London W8 4QE; 071-937 1609.

The Malay peoples of the Philippine islands, whose ancestors probably migrated from Southeast Asia, were mostly hunters, fishers, and unsettled cultivators when first visited by Europeans.

The archipelago was visited by Magellan, 1521. The Spanish founded Manila, 1571. The islands, named for King Philip II of Spain, were ceded by Spain to the U.S. for $20 million, 1898, following the Spanish-American War. U.S. troops suppressed a guerrilla uprising in a brutal 6-year war, 1899-1905.

Japan attacked the Philippines Dec. 8, 1941 and occupied the islands during WW II.

On July 4, 1946, independence was proclaimed in accordance with an act passed by the U.S. Congress in 1934. A republic was established.

Riots by radical youth groups and terrorism by leftist guerrillas and outlaws, increased from 1970. On Sept. 21, 1972, President Marcos declared martial law. Ruling by decree, he ordered some land reform and stabilized prices. But opposition was suppressed, and a high population growth rate aggravated poverty and unemployment. Political corruption was widespread. On Jan. 17, 1973, Marcos proclaimed a new constitution with himself as president. His wife received wide powers in 1978 to supervise planning and development.

Government troops battled Moslem (Moro) secessionists, 1973-76, in southern Mindanao. Fighting resumed, 1977, after a Libyan-mediated agreement on autonomy was rejected by the region's mainly Christian voters.

Martial law was lifted Jan. 17, 1981. Marcos turned over legislative power to the National Assembly, released political prisoners, and said he would no longer rule by decree. He was reelected to a new 6-year term as president.

The assassination of prominent opposition leader Benigno S. Aquino Jr, Aug. 21, 1983, sparked demonstrations calling for the resignation of Marcos.

A bitter presidential election campaign ended Feb. 7, 1986 as elections were held amid allegations of widespread fraud. On Feb. 16, Marcos was declared the victor over Corazon Aquino, widow of slain opposition leader Benigno Aquino. Aquino declared herself president and announced a nonviolent "active resistance" to overthrow the Marcos government.

On Feb. 22, 2 leading military allies of Marcos quit their posts to protest the rigged elections. Marcos, Feb. 24, declared a state of emergency as his military and religious support continued to erode. That same day U.S. President Ronald Reagan urged Marcos to resign. Marcos ended his 20-year tenure as president Feb. 26 as he fled the country. Aquino was recognized immediately as president by the U.S. and other nations.

In 1987, Aquino announced the start of land reforms. Candidates endorsed by Aquino won large majorities in legislative elections held in May, attesting to her popularity. She was plagued, however, by a weak economy, widespread poverty, communist insurgents, and lukewarm support from the military.

Rebel troops seized military bases, TV stations, and bombed the presidential palace, Dec. 1, 1989. Government forces defeated the attempted coup with the aid of air cover provided by U.S. F-4s.

The US vacated the Subic Bay Naval Station at the end of 1992; the Philippine government served a notice of eviction following the collapse of talks on a gradual 3-year pull out.

The archipelago has a coastline of 10,850 mi. Manila Bay, with an area of 770 sq. mi., and a circumference of 120 mi., is the finest harbor in the Far East.

All natural resources of the Philippines belong to the state.

Poland

Republic of Poland

Rzeczpospolita Polska

People: Population (1992 est.): 38,385,000. **Age distrib.** (%): 0–14: 25.7; 15–59: 60.2; 60+: 14.1. **Pop. density:** 317 per sq. mi. **Urban** (1992): 62%. **Ethnic groups:** Polish 98%, Germans, Ukrainians, Byelorussians. **Language:** Polish. **Religion:** Roman Catholic 94%.

Geography: Area: 120,727 sq. mi., same size as the Br. Isles. **Location:** On the Baltic Sea in E Central Europe. **Neighbors:** Germany on W, Czech Rep., Slovakia on S, Lithuania, Belarus, Ukraine on E. **Topography:** Mostly lowlands forming part of the Northern European Plain. The Carpathian Mts. along the southern border rise to 8,200 ft. **Capital:** Warsaw. **Cities** (1991 est.): Warsaw 1.6 mln., Lodz 851,000, Kracow 748,000, Wroclaw 631,000, Poznan 570,000.

Government: Type: Democratic state. **Head of state:** Pres. Lech Walesa; in office Dec. 22, 1990. **Head of government:** Waldemar Pawlak. **Local divisions:** 49 provinces. **Defense** (1987): 6% of GDP.

Economy: Industries: Shipbuilding, chemicals, metals, autos, food processing. **Chief crops:** Grains, potatoes, sugar beets, tobacco, flax. **Minerals:** Coal, copper, zinc, silver, sulphur, natural gas. **Arable land:** 46%. **Livestock** (1991): 10.0 mln. cattle; 19.4 mln. pigs. **Fish catch** (1990): 473,000 metric tons. **Electricity prod.** (1991): 136 bln. kWh. **Crude steel prod.** (1991): 10.4 mln. metric tons. **Labor force:** 27% agric.; 36% ind. & comm.; 21% services.

Finance: Monetary unit: Zloty (July 1993: 17,225 = $1 US). **Gross domestic product** (1991): $162.7 bln. **Per capita GDP:** $4,300. **Imports** (1991): $15.7 bln.; partners: CIS 18%, Ger. 15%, Czech. 5%. **Exports** (1991): $14.9 bln.; partners: CIS 25%, E. Ger. 14%, Czech. 6%. **National budget** (1991): $22.4 bln. expenditures. **Tourism** (1990): $266 mln. receipts. **International reserves less gold** (Mar. 1993): $3.5 bln. **Gold:** 473,000 oz t. **Consumer prices** (change in 1992): 43.0%.

Transport: Railroads (1991): 25,848 km. long. **Motor vehicles** (1991): 5.2 mln. passenger cars, 1.1 mln. comm. vehicles. **Civil aviation** (1991): 3.4 bln. passenger-km; 12 airports. **Chief ports:** Gdansk, Gdynia, Szczecin.

Communications: Television sets: 1 per 3.9 persons. **Radios:** 1 per 3.6 persons. **Telephones:** 1 per 7.5 persons. **Daily newspaper circ.** (1991): 217 per 1,000 pop.

Health: Life expectancy at birth (1992): 68 male; 76 female. **Births** (per 1,000 pop. 1992): 14. **Deaths** (per 1,000 pop. 1992): 9. **Natural increase:** .5%. **Hospital beds:** 1 per 154 persons. **Physicians:** 1 per 471 persons. **Infant mortality** (per 1,000 live births 1992): 14.

Education (1991): **Literacy:** 98%. **School:** Compulsory for 8 years; attendance 97%.

Major International Organizations: UN (GATT, WHO).

Embassy: 47 Portland Place, London W1N 3AG; 071-580 4324.

Slavic tribes in the area were converted to Latin Christianity in the 10th century. Poland was a great power from the 14th to the 17th centuries. In 3 partitions (1772, 1793, 1795) it was apportioned among Prussia, Russia, and Austria. Overrun by the Austro-German armies in World War I, its independence, self-declared on Nov.11, 1918, was recognized by the Treaty of Versailles, June 28, 1919. Large territories to the east were taken in a war with Russia, 1921.

Germany and the USSR invaded Poland Sept. 1-27, 1939, and divided the country. During the war, some 6 million Polish citizens were killed by the Nazis, half of them Jews. With Germany's defeat, a Polish government-in-exile in London was recognized by the U.S., but the USSR pressed the claims of a rival group. The election of 1947 was completely dominated by the Communists.

In compensation for 69,860 sq. mi. ceded to the USSR, 1945, Poland received approx. 40,000 sq. mi. of German territory E of the

Oder-Neisse line comprising Silesia, Pomerania, West Prussia, and part of East Prussia.

In 12 years of rule by Stalinists, large estates were abolished, industries nationalized, schools secularized, and Roman Catholic prelates jailed. Farm production fell off. Harsh working conditions caused a riot in Poznan June 28-29, 1956.

A new Politburo, committed to development of a more independent Polish Communism, was named Oct. 1956, with Wladyslaw Gomulka as first secretary of the Communist Party. Collectivization of farms was ended and many collectives were abolished.

In Dec. 1970 workers in port cities rioted because of price rises and new incentive wage rules. On Dec. 20 Gomulka resigned as party leader; he was succeeded by Edward Gierek; the incentive rules were dropped, price rises were revoked.

Poland was the first communist state to get most-favored nation trade terms from the U.S.

A law promulgated Feb. 13, 1953, required government consent to high Roman Catholic church appointments. In 1956 Gomulka agreed to permit religious liberty and religious publications, provided the church kept out of politics. In 1961 religious studies in public schools were halted.

After 2 months of labor turmoil had crippled the country, the Polish government, Aug. 30, 1980, met the demands of striking workers at the Lenin Shipyard, Gdansk. Among the 21 concessions granted were the right to form independent trade unions and the right to strike — unprecedented political developments in the Soviet bloc. By 1981, 9.5 mln. workers had joined the independent trade union (Solidarity). Farmers won official recognition for their independent trade union in May. Solidarity leaders proposed, Dec. 12, a nationwide referendum on establishing a non-Communist government if the government failed to agree to a series of demands which included access to the mass media and free and democratic elections to local councils in the provinces.

Spurred by the fear of Soviet intervention, the government, Dec. 13, imposed martial law. Public gatherings, demonstrations, and strikes were banned and an internal and external blackout was imposed. Solidarity leaders called for a nationwide strike, but there were only scattered work stoppages. Lech Walesa and other Solidarity leaders were arrested. The U.S. imposed economic sanctions which were lifted when martial law was suspended Dec. 1982.

On Apr. 5, 1989, an accord was reached between the government and opposition factions on a broad range of political and economic reforms incl. free elections. In the first free elections in over 40 years, candidates endorsed by Solidarity swept the parliamentary elections, June 4. On Aug. 19, Tadeusz Mazowiecki became the first non-Communist to head an Eastern bloc nation, when he became prime minister.

The radical economic program designed to transform the economy into a free-market system drew protests from unions, farmers, and miners. In 1993 the government signed a privatization plan. Workers will get a 10% share in their companies and representation on non-executive boards of directors.

Portugal

Republic of Portugal

República Portuguesa

People: Population (1992 est.): 10,448,000 (incl. Azores & Madeira Islands). **Age distrib.** (%): 0–14: 22.7; 15–59: 59.9; 60+: 17.4. **Pop. density:** 287 per sq. mi. **Urban** (1990): 34%. **Ethnic groups:** Homogeneous Mediterranean stock with small African minority. **Language:** Portuguese. **Religion:** Roman Catholic 97%.

Geography: Area: 36,390 sq. mi., incl. the Azores and Madeira Islands, about the size of Scotland and N. Ireland combined. **Location:** At SW extreme of Europe. **Neighbors:** Spain on N, E. **Topography:** Portugal N of Tajus R, which bisects the country NE-SW, is mountainous, cool and rainy. To the S there are drier, rolling plains, and a warm climate. **Capital:** Lisbon. **Cities** (1987 metro. est.): Lisbon 2 mln., Oporto 1.5 mln.

Government: Type: Parliamentary democracy. **Head of state:** Pres. Mario Soares; b. Dec. 7, 1924; in office Mar. 9, 1986. **Head of government:** Prime Min. Anibal Cavaco Silva; in office Nov. 6, 1985. **Local divisions:** 18 districts, 2 autonomous regions, one dependency. **Defense** (1991): 2.8% of GDP.

Economy: Industries: Textiles, footwear, cork, chemicals, fish canning, wine, paper. **Chief crops:** Grains, potatoes, rice, grapes, olives, fruits. **Minerals:** Tungsten, uranium, copper, iron. **Other resources:** Forests (world leader in cork production). **Arable land:** 32%. **Livestock** (1991): 5.6 mln. sheep; 2.6 mln. pigs; 1.3 mln. cattle. **Fish catch** (1990): 321,000 metric tons. **Electricity prod.** (1991): 16 bln. kWh. **Labor force:** 19% agric.; 34% ind. and comm.; 46% services and govt.

Finance: Monetary unit: Escudo (July 1993: 166 = $1 US). **Gross domestic product** (1991): $87 bln. **Per capita GDP:** $8,400. **Imports** (1992): $30.0 bln.; partners: Ger. 12%, UK 8%, Fr. 11%. **Exports** (1992): $18.2 bln.; partners: UK 15%, Ger. 13%, Fr. 13%. **Tourism** (1990): $3.5 bln. receipts. **National budget** (1991): $33.9 bln. expenditures. **International reserves less gold** (Mar. 1993): $19.4 bln. **Gold:** 16.0 mln. oz t. **Consumer prices** (change in 1992): 8.9%.

Transport: Railroads (1991): 2,229 mi. long. **Motor vehicles** (1990): 3.2 mln. passenger cars, 189,000 comm. vehicles. **Civil aviation** (1990): 6.8 bln. passenger-km; 13 airports. **Chief ports:** Lisbon, Setubal, Leixoes.

Communications: Television sets: 1 per 5.8 persons. **Radios:** 1 per 4.2 persons. **Telephones:** 1 per 3.6 persons. **Daily newspaper circ.** (1991): 50 per 1,000 pop.

Health: Life expectancy at birth (1992): 71 male; 78 female. **Births** (per 1,000 pop. 1992): 12. **Deaths** (per 1,000 pop. 1992): 10. **Natural increase:** .5%. **Hospital beds:** 1 per 230 persons. **Physicians:** 1 per 352 persons. **Infant mortality** (per 1,000 live births 1992): 10.

Education (1990): **Literacy:** 83%. **School:** Compulsory for 6 years; attendance 60%.

Major International Organizations: UN (GATT, IMF, WHO), NATO, EC, OECD.

Embassy: 12 Belgrave Sq, London SW1X 8PN; 071-235 3688.

Portugal, an independent state since the 12th century, was a kingdom until a revolution in 1910 drove out King Manoel II and a republic was proclaimed.

From 1932 a strong, repressive government was headed by Premier Antonio de Oliveira Salazar. Illness forced his retirement in Sept. 1968.

On Apr. 25, 1974, the government was seized by a military junta led by Gen. Antonio de Spinola, who was named president.

The new government reached agreements providing independence for Guinea-Bissau, Mozambique, Cape Verde Islands, Angola, and Sao Tome and Principe. Despite a 64% victory for democratic parties in April 1975, the Soviet-supported Communist party increased its influence. Banks, insurance companies, and other industries were nationalized.

Parliament approved, June 1, 1989, a package of reforms that did away with the socialist economy and created a " democratic" economy and the denationalization of industries.

Azores Islands, in the Atlantic, 740 mi. W. of Portugal, have an area of 868 sq. mi. and a pop. (1992) of 236,000. A 1951 agreement gave the U.S. rights to use defense facilities in the Azores. The **Madeira Islands,** 350 mi. off the NW coast of Africa, have an area of 307 sq. mi. and a pop. (1992) of 253,000. Both groups were offered partial autonomy in 1976.

Macau, area of 6 sq. mi., is an enclave, a peninsula and 2 small islands, at the mouth of the Canton R. in China. Portugal granted broad autonomy in 1976. In 1987, Portugal and China agreed that Macau would revert to China in 1999. Macao, like Hong Kong, was guaranteed 50 years of noninterference in its way of life and capitalist system. Pop. (1992 est.): 367,000.

Qatar

State of Qatar

Dawlet al-Qatar

People: Population (1992 est.): 484,000. **Pop. density:** 113 per sq. mi. **Ethnic groups:** Arab 40%, Pakistani 18%, Iranian 14%, Indian 10%, others. **Languages:** Arabic (official), English. **Religion:** Muslim 95%.

Geography: Area: 4,247 sq. mi., smaller than N. Ireland. **Location:** Occupies peninsula on W coast of Persian Gulf. **Neighbors:** Saudi Arabia on W, United Arab Emirates on S. **Topography:** Mostly a flat desert, with some limestone ridges, vegetation of any kind is scarce. **Capital:** Doha, pop. (1987 est.) 250,000.

Government: Type: Traditional monarchy. **Head of state and head of government:** Emir & Prime Min. Khalifah ibn Hamad ath-Thani; b. 1932; in office Feb. 22, 1972 (amir), 1970 (prime min.). **Defense** (1989): 8.0% of GDP.

Economy: Arable land: 2.9%. **Electricity prod.** (1991): 4.2 bln. kWh. **Labor force:** 10% agric., 70% ind., services and commerce.

Finance: Monetary unit: Riyal (Mar. 1993: 3.64 = $1 US). **Gross domestic product** (1990): $7.4 bln. **Per capita GDP:** $15,000. **Imports** (1990): $1.4 bln.; partners: Jap. 11%, UK 13%, U.S. 9%. **Exports** (1990): $3.2 bln.; partners: Jap. 61%. **National budget** (1991): $3.2 bln. expenditures.

Transport: Chief ports: Doha, Musayid.

Communications: Television sets: 1 per 2.5 persons. **Radios:** 1 per 2.5 persons. **Telephones:** 1 per 3.4 persons.

Health: Life expectancy at birth (1992): 69 male; 74 female. **Hospital beds:** 1 per 399 persons. **Physicians:** 1 per 568 persons. **Infant mortality** (per 1,000 live births 1992): 24.

Education (1991): **Literacy:** 76%. **School:** Compulsory ages 6-16; attendance 98%.

Major International Organizations: UN (FAO, GATT, IMF, World Bank), Arab League, OPEC.

Embassy: 115 Queen's Gate, London SW7 5LP; 071-581 8611.

Qatar was under Bahrain's control until the Ottoman Turks took power, 1872 to 1915. In a treaty signed 1916, Qatar gave Great Britain responsibility for its defense and foreign relations. After Britain announced it would remove its military forces from the Persian Gulf area by the end of 1971, Qatar sought a federation with other British protected states in the area; this failed and Qatar declared itself independent, Sept. 1 1971.

Oil revenues give Qatar a per capita income among the highest in the world, but lack of skilled labor hampers development plans.

Romania

Republic of Romania

România

People: Population (1992 est.): 23,169,000. **Age distrib.** (%): 0–14: 24.7; 15–59: 60.9; 60+: 14.4. **Pop. density:** 252 per sq. mi. **Urban** (1992): 55%. **Ethnic groups:** Romanians 78%, Hungarians 11%. **Languages:** Romanian (official), Hungarian, German. **Religions:** Orthodox 80%, Roman Catholic 6%.

Geography: Area: 91,699 sq. mi., slightly smaller than the UK. **Location:** In SE Europe on the Black Sea. **Neighbors:** CIS on E (Moldova) and N (Ukraine), Hungary, Yugoslavia on W, Bulgaria on S. **Topography:** The Carpathian Mts. encase the north-central Transylvanian plateau. There are wide plains S and E of the mountains, through which flow the lower reaches of the rivers of the Danube system. **Capital:** Bucharest. **Cities** (1992 est.): Bucharest 2,064,000, Constanta 350,000, Iasi 342,000, Timisoara 333,000.

Government: Type: Republic. **Head of state:** Pres. Ion Iliescu; in office Dec. 25, 1989. **Head of government:** Prime Min. Nicolae Vacaroiu; in office Nov. 4, 1992. **Local divisions:** Bucharest and 40 counties. **Defense** (1985): 4.3% of GDP.

Economy: Industries: Steel, metals, machinery, oil products, chemicals, textiles, shoes, tourism. **Chief crops:** Grains, sunflower, vegetables, potatoes. **Minerals:** Oil, gas, coal. **Other resources:** Timber. **Arable land:** 45%. **Livestock** (1991): 6.2 mln. cattle; 11.6 mln. pigs; 15.4 mln. sheep. **Fish catch** (1990): 127,000 metric tons. **Electricity prod.** (1990): 64 bln. kWh. **Crude steel prod.** (1991): 7 mln. metric tons. **Labor force:** 28% agric.; 34% ind. & comm.

Finance: Monetary unit: Lei (Mar. 1993: 598 = $1 US). **Gross domestic product** (1991): $71.9 bln. **Per capita GDP:** $3,100. **Imports** (1991): $5.4 bln.; partners: CIS 50%. **Exports** (1991): $4.0 bln.; partners: CIS 30%. **Tourism** (1990): $106 mln. receipts. **National budget** (1991): $20 bln. expenditures.

Transport: Railroads (1991): 6,887 mi. long. **Motor vehicles** (1992): 1.3 mln passenger cars; 332,000 comm. vehicles. **Civil aviation** (1991): 1.6 bln. passenger-km; 14 airports. **Chief ports:** Constanta, Galati, Braila.

Communications: Television sets: 1 per 6.0 persons. **Radios:** 1 per 7.3 persons. **Telephones:** 1 per 7.7 persons. **Daily newspaper circ.** (1991): 134 per 1,000 pop.

Health: Life expectancy at birth (1992): 68 male; 74 female. **Births** (per 1,000 pop. 1992): 14. **Deaths** (per 1,000 pop. 1992): 10. **Hospital beds:** 1 per 107 persons. **Physicians:** 1 per 472 persons. **Infant mortality** (per 1,000 live births 1992): 22.

Education (1991): **Literacy:** 96%. **School:** Compulsory for 10 years; attendance 98%.

Major International Organizations: UN (World Bank, IMF, GATT).

Embassy: 4 Palace Green, London W8 4QD; 071-937 9666.

Romania's earliest known people merged with invading Proto-Thracians, preceding by centuries the Dacians. The Dacian kingdom was occupied by Rome, 106 AD-271 AD; people and language were Romanized. The principalities of Wallachia and Moldavia, dominated by Turkey, were united in 1859, became Romania in 1861. In 1877 Romania proclaimed independence from Turkey, became an independent state by the Treaty of Berlin, 1878, a kingdom, 1881, under Carol I. In 1886 Romania became a constitutional monarchy with a bicameral legislature.

Romania helped Russia in its war with Turkey, 1877-78. After World War I it acquired Bessarabia, Bukovina, Transylvania, and Banat. In 1940 it ceded Bessarabia and Northern Bukovina to the USSR, part of southern Dobrudja to Bulgaria, and northern Transylvania to Hungary.

In 1941, Romanian premier Marshal Ion Antonescu led his country in support of Germany against the USSR. In 1944 Antonescu was overthrown by King Michael and Romania joined the Allies.

With occupation by Soviet troops the communist-headed National Democratic Front displaced the National Peasant party. A People's Republic was proclaimed, Dec. 30, 1947; Michael was forced to abdicate. Land owners were dispossessed; most banks, factories and transportation units were nationalized.

On Aug. 22, 1965, a new constitution proclaimed Romania a Socialist, rather than a People's Republic.

Internal policies were oppressive. Ethnic Hungarians protested cultural and job discrimination, which has led to strained relations with Hungary.

Romania became industrialized, but lagged in consumer goods and in personal freedoms. All industry was state owned, and state farms and cooperatives owned almost all the arable land.

On Dec. 16, 1989, security forces opened fire on demonstrators in Timisoara; hundreds were buried in mass graves. President Nicolae Ceausescu declared a state of emergency as protests spread to other cities. By Dec. 21, the protests had spread to Bucharest where security forces fired on protestors. Army units joined the rebellion, Dec. 22, and a group known as the "Council of National Salvation" announced that it had overthrown the government. Fierce fighting took place between the army, which backed the new government, and forces loyal to Ceausescu.

Ceausescu was captured, Dec. 23 and, following a trial in which he and his wife were found guilty of genocide, was executed Dec. 25. The U.S. and USSR quickly recognized the new government.

Russia

Russian Federation

(Figures prior to 1990 are for the former USSR)

People: Population (1992 est.): 149,527,000. **Age distrib.** (%): 0–14: 23.1; 15–59: 61.5; 60+: 15.4. **Pop. density:** 22 per sq. mi. **Urban** (1991): 74%. **Ethnic groups:** Russians 82%, Tartar 3%. **Languages:** Russian (official), Ukrainian, Byelorussian, Uzbek, Armenian, Azerbaijani, Georgian, many others. **Religions:** Russian Orthodox 25%, non-religious 60%.

Geography: Area: 6,592,800 sq. mi., over 76% of the total area of the former USSR, and thus the largest country in the world. **Location:** Stretches from E. Europe across N Asia to the Pacific Ocean. **Neighbors:** Finland, Poland, Hungary, Norway, Estonia, Belarus, Ukraine on W, Georgia, Azerbaijan, Kazakhstan, China, Mongolia, N. Korea on S. **Topography:** Russia contains every type of climate except the distinctly tropical, and has a varied topography. The European portion is a low plain, grassy in S, wooded in N with Ural Mtns. on the E. Caucasus Mts. on the S. Urals stretch N-S for 2,500 mi. The Asiatic portion is also a vast plain, with mountains on the S and in the E; tundra covers extreme N, with forest belt below; plains, marshes are in W, desert in SW. **Capital:** Moscow. **Cities** (1991 est.): Moscow 8.8 mln.; St. Petersburg 4.4 mln.; Nizhniy Novgorod 1.4 mln.; Samara 1.2 mln.

Government: Type: Federation. **Head of state:** Pres. Boris Yeltsin; b. Feb. 1, 1931; in office July 10, 1991. **Head of government:** Prime Min. Viktor Chernomyrdin; in office Dec. 14, 1992. **Local divisions:** 20 autonomous republics, 49 oblasts, 6 krays. **Defense** (1991): 8% of GNP.

Economy: Industries: Steel, machinery, machine tools, vehicles, chemicals, cement, textiles, appliances, paper. **Chief crops:** Grain, cotton, sugar beets, potatoes, vegetables, sunflowers. **Minerals:** Manganese, mercury, potash, bauxite, cobalt, chromium, copper, coal, gold, lead, molybdenum, nickel, phosphates, silver, tin, tungsten, zinc, oil, potassium salts. **Other resources:** Forests. **Arable land:** 11%. **Livestock** (1990): 118 mln. cattle; 142 mln. sheep; 77 mln. pigs; 142 mln. goats. **Fish catch** (1989): 10.9 mln. metric tons. **Electricity prod.** (1991): 1,100 bln. kWh. **Crude steel prod.** (1988): 164 mln. metric tons. **Labor force:** 22% agric.; 29% industry, 26% services.

Finance: Monetary unit: Rouble (Aug. 1993: 987 = $1 US). **Gross domestic product** (1988): $2.5 trl. **Imports** (1991): $43.5 bln.; partners: EC, CIS. **Exports** (1991): $58.7 bln.; partners: EC, CIS. **National budget** (1989): $310 bln. expenditures. **Tourism** (1988): $216 mln. receipts.

Transport: Motor vehicles (1991): 8.9 mln. passenger cars, 484,000 comm. vehicles. **Civil aviation** (1990): 153 bln. passenger-km; 58 airports with scheduled flights. **Chief ports:** St. Petersburg, Murmansk, Tver, Archangelsk.

Communications: Television sets: 1 per 3.2 persons. **Radios:** 1 per 1.5 persons. **Telephones:** 1 per 6.7 persons. **Daily newspaper circ.** (1990): 112 per 1,000 pop.

Health: Life expectancy at birth (1992): 63 male; 74 female. **Births** (per 1,000 pop. 1992): 15. **Deaths** (per 1,000 pop. 1992): 11. **Natural increase:** .4%. **Hospital beds:** 1 per 77 persons. **Physicians:** 1 per 221 persons. **Infant mortality** (per 1,000 live births 1992): 31.

Education (1993): **Literacy:** 99%. **School:** Most receive 11 years of schooling.

Major International Organizations: UN (ILO, IMF, UNESCO, WHO), CIS.

Embassy: 15 Kensington Palace Gardens, London W8 4QG; 071-229 3628.

History. Slavic tribes began migrating into Russia from the W in the 5th century AD. The first Russian state, founded by Scandinavian chieftains, was established in the 9th century, centering in Novgorod and Kiev.

In the 13th century the Mongols overran the country. It recovered under the grand dukes and princes of Muscovy, or Moscow, and by 1480 freed itself from the Mongols. Ivan the Terrible was the first to be formally proclaimed Tsar (1547). Peter the Great (1682-1725) extended the domain and in 1721, founded the Russian Empire.

Western ideas and the beginnings of modernization spread through the huge Russian empire in the 19th and early 20th centuries. But political evolution failed to keep pace.

Military reverses in the 1905 war with Japan and in World War I led to the breakdown of the Tsarist regime. The 1917 Revolution began in March with a series of sporadic strikes for higher wages by factory workers. A provisional democratic government under Prince Georgi Lvov was established but was quickly followed in May by the second provisional government, led by Alexander Kerensky. The Kerensky government and the freely-elected Constituent Assembly were overthrown in a communist coup led by Vladimir Ilyich Lenin Nov. 7.

Soviet Union

Lenin's death Jan. 21, 1924, resulted in an internal power struggle from which Joseph Stalin eventually emerged the absolute ruler of Russia. Stalin secured his position at first by exiling opponents, but from the 1930s to 1953, he resorted to a series of "purge" trials, mass executions, and mass exiles to work camps. These measures resulted in millions of deaths, according to most estimates.

Germany and the Soviet Union signed a non-aggression pact Aug. 1939; Germany launched a massive invasion of the Soviet Union, June 1941. Notable heroic episode was the "900 days" siege of Leningrad, lasting to Jan. 1944, and causing a million deaths; the city was never taken. Russian winter counterthrusts, 1941 to '42 and 1942 to '43, stopped the German advance. Turning point was the failure of German troops to take and hold Stalingrad, Sept. 1942 to Feb. 1943. With British and U.S. Lend-Lease aid and sustaining great casualties, the Russians drove the German forces from eastern Europe and the Balkans in the next 2 years.

After Stalin died, Mar. 5, 1953, Nikita Khrushchev was elected first secretary of the Central Committee. In 1956 he condemned Stalin. "De-Stalinization" of the country on all levels was effected after Stalin's body was removed from the Lenin-Stalin tomb in Moscow.

Under Khrushchev the open antagonism of Poles and Hungarians toward domination by Moscow was brutally suppressed in 1956. He advocated peaceful co-existence with the capitalist countries, but continued arming the Soviet Union with nuclear weapons. He aided the Cuban revolution under Fidel Castro but withdrew Soviet missiles from Cuba during confrontation by U.S. Pres. Kennedy, Sept.-Oct. 1962.

Khrushchev was suddenly deposed, Oct. 1964, and replaced as party first secretary by Leonid I. Brezhnev.

In Aug. 1968 Russian, Polish, East German, Hungarian, and Bulgarian military forces invaded Czechoslovakia to put a curb on liberalization policies of the Czech government.

Massive Soviet military aid to North Vietnam in the late 1960s and early 1970s helped assure communist victories throughout Indo-China. Soviet arms aid and advisers were sent to several African countries in the 1970s, including Algeria, Angola, Somalia, and Ethiopia.

In 1979, Soviet forces entered Afghanistan to support that government against rebels. In 1988, the Soviets announced withdrawal of their troops, ending a futile 8-year war.

Mikhail Gorbachev was chosen Gen. Sec. of the Communist Party, Mar. 1985. He was the youngest member of the Politburo and signaled a change in Soviet leadership from those whose attitudes were shaped by Stalinism and World War II.

He held 4 summit meetings with U.S. Pres. Reagan. In 1987, in Washington, an INF treaty was signed.

In 1987, Gorbachev initiated a program of reforms, including expanded freedoms and the democratization of the political process, through openness (*glasnost*) and restructuring (*perestroika*). The reforms were opposed by some Eastern bloc countries and many old-line communists in the USSR. In 1989, the first Soviet Parliament was held since 1918.

Gorbachev faced economic problems as well as ethnic and nationalist unrest in the republics in 1990; the economy was in its worst state since WWII.

On Aug. 19, 1991, it was announced that the vice president had taken over the country due to Gorbachev's illness. A state of emergency was imposed for 6 months with all power resting with the State Committee on the State of Emergency. The Russian republic's Pres. Boris Yeltsin denounced the coup and called for a general strike. Some 50,000 demonstrated at the Russian parliament in support of Yeltsin. By Aug. 21, the coup had failed and Gorbachev was restored as pres. On Aug. 24, Gorbachev resigned as leader of the Communist Party and recommended that its central committee be disbanded. Several republics declared their independence including Russia, Ukraine, and Kazakhstan. On Aug. 29, the Soviet parliament voted to suspend all activities of the Communist Party.

On Sept. 2, Gorbachev declared that the nation was "on the brink of catastrophe", and proposed to transfer all central authority to himself, the leaders of 10 republics, and an appointed legislative council in order to form a new kind of Soviet Union.

The Soviet Union officially broke up Dec. 26, 1991, on the day after Gorbachev resigned. The Soviet hammer and sickle flying over the Kremlin was lowered and replaced by the flag of Russia, ending the domination of the Communist Party over all areas of national life since 1817.

Russian Federation

In the first major step in radical economic reform, Russia eliminated state subsidies on most goods and services, Jan. 1992. The effect was to allow prices to soar far beyond the means of ordinary workers. Pres. Yeltsin met with Pres. Bush in Washington, D.C., June 16-17. The two leaders agreed to massive arms reductions. Yeltsin addressed a joint session of Congress and appealed for economic aid for the CIS.

Russia launched a drive to privatize thousands of large and medium-sized state-owned enterprises in 1993. Pres. Yeltsin narrowly survived an impeachment vote by the Congress of People's Deputies Mar. 28. Yeltsin received strong support from voters in a country-wide referendum Apr. 25; 58 per cent of voters said they had confidence in him and his policies.

Rwanda

Republic of Rwanda

Republika y'u Rwanda

People: Population (1992 est.): 8,206,000. **Age distrib.** (%): 0–14: 48.7; 15–59: 47.1; 60+: 4.2. **Pop. density:** 806 per sq. mi. **Urban** (1991): 5%. **Ethnic groups:** Hutu 90%, Tutsi 9%, Twa (pygmies) 1%. **Languages:** French, Rwanda (both official). **Religions:** Christian 74%, traditional 25%, Muslim 1%.

Geography: Area: 10,169 sq. mi., slightly larger than Wales. **Location:** In E central Africa. **Neighbors:** Uganda on N, Zaire on W, Burundi on S, Tanzania on E. **Topography:** Grassy uplands and hills cover most of the country, with a chain of volcanoes in the NW. The source of the Nile R. has been located in the headwaters of the Kagera (Akagera) R., SW of Kigali. **Capital:** Kigali, pop. (1991 est.) 232,000.

Government: Type: Republic. **Head of state:** Pres. Juvenal Habyarimana; b. Mar. 8, 1937; in office July 5, 1973. **Head of government:** Prime Min. Dismas Nsengiyaremye; in office Apr. 2, 1992. **Local divisions:** 10 prefectures. **Defense** (1989): 1.6% of GDP.

Economy: Chief crops: Coffee, tea. **Minerals:** Tin, gold, wolframite. **Arable land:** 29%. **Electricity prod.** (1991): 130 mln. kWh. **Labor force:** 91% agric.

Finance: Monetary unit: Franc (Apr. 1993: 145 = $1 US). **Gross domestic product** (1989): $2.1 bln. **Per capita GDP:** $310. **Imports** (1990): $279.2 mln.; partners: Ken. 21%, Belg. 16%, Jap. 12%, W. Ger. 9%. **Exports** (1990): $111.7 mln.; partners: EC, Ugan. **National budget** (1989): $491 mln expenditures. **International reserves less gold** (Mar. 1993): $64 mln. **Consumer prices** (change in 1992): 9.5%.

Transport: Motor vehicles (1990): 8,000 passenger cars, 10,000 comm. vehicles.

Communications: Radios: 1 per 11 persons. **Telephones:** 1 per 497 persons.

Health: Life expectancy at birth (1992): 51 male; 55 female. **Births** (per 1,000 pop. 1992): 52. **Deaths** (per 1,000 pop. 1992): 15. **Natural increase:** 3.7%. **Hospital beds** (1984): 9,000. **Physicians** (1984): 177. **Infant mortality** (per 1,000 live births 1992): 108.

Education (1991): **Literacy:** 50%. **School:** Compulsory for 8 years; attendance 70%.

Major International Organizations: UN (GATT, IMF, WHO), OAU.

Embassy: 1 avenue des Fleurs, Woluwe Saint Pierre, Brussels 1150, Belgium; 010 32 2 7630702.

For centuries, the Tutsi (an extremely tall people) dominated the Hutus (90% of the population). A civil war broke out in 1959 and Tutsi power was ended. A referendum in 1961 abolished the monarchic system. Some 8,000 exiled Tutsi invaded Rwanda from Uganda, Sept. 1990. A new constitution was signed into effect in 1991 calling for multiparty politics, freedom of the press, and a limited presidential term. A peace accord between the government and the Tutsi rebels was signed in Aug. 1993.

Rwanda, which had been part of the Belgian UN trusteeship of Rwanda-Urundi, became independent July 1, 1962. The government was overthrown in a 1973 military coup. Rwanda is one of the most densely populated countries in Africa. All available arable land is being used, and is being subject to erosion.

St. Kitts and Nevis

Federation of St. Kitts & Nevis

People: Population (1992 est.): 40,293. **Pop. density:** 398 per sq. mi. **Ethnic groups:** black African 95%. **Language:** English. **Religion:** Protestant 76%.

Geography: Area: 101 sq. mi., half the size of the Isle of Man. **Location:** In the northern part of the Leeward group of the Lesser Antilles in the eastern Caribbean Sea. **Capital:** Basseterre, pop. (1989) 15,000.

Government: Constitutional monarchy. **Head of state:** Queen Elizabeth II represented by Sir Clement Arrindell. **Head of government:** Prime Minister Kennedy A. Simmonds; b. Apr. 12, 1936; in office Sept. 19, 1983.

Economy: Sugar is the principal industry.

Finance: Monetary unit: E. Caribbean dollar (Mar. 1993: 2.70 = $1 US). **Gross domestic product** (1990): $146 mln. **Tourism** (1990): $63 mln. receipts.

Communications: Telephones: 1 per 6 persons.

Health: Infant mortality (per 1,000 live births, 1992): 22.

Education (1991): **Literacy** : 98%.

High Commission: 10 Kensington Court, London W8 5DL; 071-937 9522.

St. Kitts (known locally as Liamuiga) and Nevis were reached (and named) by Columbus in 1493. They were settled by Britain in 1623, but ownership was disputed with France until 1713. They were part of the Leeward Islands Federation, 1871-1956, and the Federation of the W. Indies, 1958-62. The colony achieved self-government as an Associated State of the UK in 1967, and became fully independent Sept. 19, 1983.

St. Lucia

People: Population (1992 est.): 151,000. **Age distrib.** (%): 0–20: 44.5; 21–64: 47.5; 65+30 : 8.0. **Pop. density:** 634 per sq. mi. **Ethnic groups:** Predominantly African descent. **Languages:** English (official), French patois. **Religion:** Roman Catholic 90%.

Geography: Area: 238 sq. mi., about the size of the Isle of Man. **Location:** In Eastern Caribbean, 2nd largest of the Windward Is. **Neighbors:** Martinique to N, St. Vincent to SW. **Topography:** Mountainous, volcanic in origin; Soufrière, a volcanic crater, in the S. Wooded mountains run N-S to Mt. Gimie, 3,145 ft., with streams through fertile valleys. **Capital:** Castries, pop. (1989 est.) 55,000.

Government: Type: Parliamentary democracy. **Head of state:** Queen Elizabeth II, represented by Gov.-Gen. S.A. James. **Head of government:** Prime Min. John Compton; in office May 3, 1982. **Local divisions:** 11 quarters

Economy: Industries: Agriculture, tourism, manufacturing. **Chief crops:** Bananas, coconuts, cocoa, citrus fruits. **Other resources:** Forests. **Arable land:** 8%. **Electricity prod.** (1991): 112 mln. kWh. **Labor force:** 36% agric., 20% ind. & commerce, 18% services.

Finance: Monetary unit: East Caribbean dollar (Mar. 1993: 2.70 = $1 US). **Gross domestic product** (1990): $295 mln. **Per capita GDP:** $1,930. **Imports** (1990): $270 mln.; partners: U.S. 36%, UK 12%, Trin./Tob. 11%. **Exports** (1990): $127 mln.; partners: U.S. 19%, UK 51%. **Tourism** (1990): $155 mln. receipts.

Transport: Motor vehicles (1989): 7,000 passenger cars, 4,000 comm. vehicles. **Chief ports:** Castries, Vieux Fort.

Communications: Television sets: 1 per 6 persons. **Radios:** 1 per 1.5 persons. **Telephones:** 1 per 10 persons.

Health: Life expectancy at birth (1992): 70 male; 75 female. **Births** (per 1,000 pop. 1992): 26. **Deaths** (per 1,000 pop. 1992): 5. **Natural increase:** 2.1%. **Hospital beds:** 1 per 283 persons. **Physicians:** 1 per 2,521 persons. **Infant mortality** (per 1,000 live births 1992): 18.

Education (1989): **Literacy:** 78%. **School:** Compulsory ages 5-15; attendance 80%.

Major International Organizations: UN (IMF, ILO), CARICOM, OAS.

High Commission: 10 Kensington Court, London W8 5DL; 071-937 9522.

St. Lucia was ceded to Britain by France at the Treaty of Paris, 1814. Self government was granted with the West Indies Act, 1967. Independence was attained Feb. 22, 1979.

St. Vincent and the Grenadines

People: Population (1992 est.): 114,000. **Pop. density:** 760 per sq. mi. **Ethnic groups:** Mainly of African descent. **Language:** English. **Religions:** Methodist, Anglican, Roman Catholic.

Geography: Area: 150 sq. mi., the size of the Isle of Wight. **Location:** In the eastern Caribbean, St. Vincent (133 sq. mi.) and the northern islets of the Grenadines form a part of the Windward chain. **Neighbors:** St. Lucia to N, Barbados to E, Grenada to S. **Topography:** St. Vincent is volcanic, with a ridge of thickly wooded mountains running its length. **Capital:** Kingstown, pop. (1991 est.) 15,000.

Government: Type: Constitutional monarchy. **Head of state:** Queen Elizabeth II, represented by Gov.-Gen. David Jack; in office Sept. 20, 1989. **Head of government:** James Mitchell; in office July 30, 1984.

Economy: Industries: Agriculture, tourism. **Chief crops:** Bananas (62% of exports), arrowroot, coconuts. **Arable land:** 50%. **Electricity prod.** (1991): 63 mln. kWh. **Labor force:** 30% agric.

Finance: Monetary unit: East Caribbean dollar (Mar. 1993: 2.70 = $1 US). **Gross domestic product** (1989): $146 mln. **Per capita GDP** (1989): $1,315. **Tourism** (1991): $53 mln. receipts. **National budget** (1990): $67 mln. expenditures.

Transport: Motor vehicles (1991): 5,000 passenger cars, 2,800 comm. vehicles. **Chief port:** Kingstown.

Communications: Telephones: 1 per 6 persons.

Health: Life expectancy at birth (1992): 71 male; 74 female. **Births** (per 1,000 pop. 1992): 23. **Deaths** (per 1,000 pop. 1992): 5. **Natural increase:** 1.7%. **Infant mortality** (per 1,000 live births 1992): 19.

Education (1989): **Literacy:** 85%.

High Commission: 10 Kensington Court, London W8 5DL; 071-937 9522.

Columbus landed on St. Vincent on Jan. 22, 1498 (St. Vincent's Day). Britain and France both laid claim to the island in the 17th and 18th centuries; the Treaty of Versailles, 1783, finally ceded it to Britain. Associated State status was granted 1969; independence was attained Oct. 27, 1979.

The entire economic life of St. Vincent is dependent upon agriculture and tourism.

San Marino

Most Serene Republic of San Marino

Serenissima Repubblica di San Marino

People: Population (1992 est.): 23,000. **Age distrib.** (%): 0–14: 16.1; 15–59: 65.3; 60+: 16.1. **Pop. density:** 958 per sq. mi. **Urban** (1992): 90.5%. **Ethnic groups:** Sanmarinese 80%, Italian 18%. **Language:** Italian. **Religion:** Mostly Roman Catholic.

Geography: Area: 24 sq. mi., the size of Guernsey. **Location:** In N central Italy near Adriatic coast. **Neighbors:** Completely surrounded by Italy. **Topography:** The country lies on the slopes of Mt. Titano. **Capital:** San Marino, pop. (1991 est.) 4,643.

Government: Type: Republic. **Head of state:** Two co-regents appointed every 6 months. **Local divisions:** 9 municipalities.

Economy: Industries: Postage stamps, tourism, woollen goods, paper, cement, ceramics. **Arable land:** 17%.

Finance: Monetary unit: Italian lira. **Gross domestic product** (1991): $400 mln. **Tourism** (1991): 3.1 mln. arrivals.

Communications: Television sets: 1 per 3.4 persons. **Radios:** 1 per 1.8 persons. **Telephones:** 1 per 1.6 persons.

Births (per 1,000 pop. 1992): 8. **Deaths** (per 1,000 pop. 1992): 7. **Natural increase:** 0.1%. **Infant mortality** (per 1,000 live births 1992): 8.

Education (1991): **Literacy:** 97%. **School:** Compulsory for 8 years; attendance 93%.

Major International Organizations: UN.

San Marino claims to be the oldest state in Europe and to have been founded in the 4th century. A communist-led coalition ruled 1947-57; a similar coalition ruled 1978-86. It has had a treaty of friendship with Italy since 1862.

São Tomé and Príncipe

Democratic Republic of São Tomé and Príncipe

República Democrática de São Tomé e Príncipe

People: Population (1992 est.): 132,000. **Pop. density:** 354 per sq. mi. **Ethnic groups:** Portuguese-African mixture, African minority (Angola, Mozambique immigrants). **Language:** Portuguese. **Religion:** Christian 80%.

Geography: Area: 372 sq. mi., slightly smaller than the Orkney Islands. **Location:** In the Gulf of Guinea about 125 miles off W Central Africa. **Neighbors:** Gabon, Equatorial Guinea on E. **Topography:** São Tomé and Príncipe islands, part of an extinct volcano chain, are both covered by lush forests and croplands. **Capital:** São Tomé, pop. (1988 est.) 40,000.

Government: Type: Republic. **Head of state:** Pres. Miguel Trovoada; in office Apr. 3, 1991. **Head of government:** Prime Min. Norberto Jose d'Alva Costa Alegre; in office May 16, 1992. **Local divisions:** 2 districts.

Economy: Chief crops: Cocoa (82% of exports), coconut products. **Arable land:** 38%. **Electricity prod.** (1991): 10 mln. kWh.

Finance: Monetary unit: Dobra (Jan. 1993: 240 = $1 US). **Gross domestic product** (1989): $46 mln. **Per capita GDP:** $384. **Imports** (1990): $21.3 mln.; partners: Port. 61%, Angola 13%. **Exports** (1990): $4.4 mln.; partners: Neth. 52%, Port. 33%, Ger. 8%.

Transport: Chief ports: São Tomé, Santo Antonio.

Communications: Radios: 1 per 3.9 persons.

Health: Births (per 1,000 pop. 1992): 38. **Deaths** (per 1,000 pop. 1992): 7. **Natural increase:** 3.0%. **Physicians:** 1 per 2,819 persons. **Infant mortality** (per 1,000 live births 1992): 58.

Education (1988): **Literacy:** 50%.

Major International Organizations: UN, OAU.

Consulate: 42 North Audley St, London W1A 4PY; 071-499 1995.

The islands were uninhabited when discovered in 1471 by the Portuguese, who brought the first settlers — convicts and exiled Jews. Sugar planting was replaced by the slave trade as the chief economic activity until coffee and cocoa were introduced in the 19th century.

Portugal agreed, 1974, to turn the colony over to the Gabon-based Movement for the Liberation of São Tomé and Príncipe, which proclaimed as first president its East German-trained leader Manuel Pinto da Costa. Independence came July 12, 1975. Democratic reforms were instituted in 1987. In 1991 Miguel Trovoada won the first free presidential election following the withdrawal of Pres. Manuel Pinto da Costa, who had ruled the country since independence.

Agriculture and fishing are the mainstays of the economy.

Saudi Arabia

Kingdom of Saudi Arabia

al-Mamlaka al-'Arabiya as-Sa'udiya

People: Population (1992 cen.): 16,900,000. **Pop. density:** 20 per sq. mi. **Urban** (1990): 78%. **Ethnic groups:** Arab tribes, immigrants from other Arab and Muslim countries. **Language:** Arabic. **Religion:** Muslim 99%.

Geography: Area: 839,996 sq. mi., 7 times bigger than the Br. Isles. **Location:** Occupies most of Arabian Peninsula in Middle East. **Neighbors:** Kuwait, Iraq, Jordan on N, Yemen, Oman on S, United Arab Emirates, Qatar on E. **Topography:** The highlands on W, up to 9,000 ft., slope as an arid, barren desert to the Persian Gulf. **Capital:** Riyadh. **Cities** (1986 est.): Riyadh 1,380,000; Jidda 1,210,000; Mecca 463,000.

Government: Type: Monarchy with council of ministers. **Head of state and head of government:** King Fahd; b. 1922; in office June 13, 1982. **Local divisions:** 14 emirates. **Defense** (1992): 13% of GDP.

Economy: Industries: Oil products. **Chief crops:** Dates, wheat, barley, fruit. **Minerals:** Oil, gas, gold, copper, iron. **Crude oil reserves** (1990): 255 bln. barrels. **Arable land:** 2%. **Livestock** (1991): 5.6 mln. sheep; 3.5 mln. goats. **Electricity prod.** (1991): 60 bln. kWh. **Labor force:** 14% agric.; 11% ind; 53% serv., comm., & govt.; 20% construction.

Finance: Monetary unit: Riyal (July 1993: 3.70 = $1 US). **Gross domestic product** (1991): $104 bln. **Per capita GDP:** $5,800. **Imports** (1990): $21.5 bln.; partners: US 15%, Jap. 12%, UK 14%. **Exports** (1990): $44.3 bln.; partners: U.S. 22%, Jap., 20%. **National budget** (1992): $48 bln. expenditures. **International reserves less gold** (Mar. 1993): $6.5 bln. **Gold:** 4.59 mln. oz t. **Consumer prices** (change in 1992): 1.0%.

Transport: Railroads (1989): 555 mi. long. **Motor vehicles** (1990): 2.3 mln. passenger cars, 2.1 mln. comm. vehicles. **Civil aviation** (1990): 16.0 bln.; passenger-km.; 25 airports. **Chief ports:** Jidda, Ad-Dammam, Ras Tannurah.

Communications: Television sets: 1 per 3.5 persons. **Radios:** 1 per 3.3 persons. **Telephones:** 1 per 13 persons. **Daily newspaper circ.** (1989): 49 per 1,000 pop.

Health: Life expectancy at birth (1992): 65 male; 68 female. **Births** (per 1,000 pop. 1992): 38. **Deaths** (per 1,000 pop. 1991): 7. **Natural increase:** 3.1%. **Hospital beds:** 1 per 358 persons. **Physicians:** 1 per 623 persons. **Infant mortality** (per 1,000 live births 1992): 59.

Education (1990): **Literacy:** 62%.

Major International Organizations: UN (IMF, WHO, FAO), Arab League, OPEC.

Embassy: 30 Charles St, London W1X 7PN; 071-917 3000.

Arabia was united for the first time by Mohammed, in the early 7th century. His successors conquered the entire Near East and North Africa, bringing Islam and the Arabic language. But Arabia itself soon returned to its former status.

Nejd, long an independent state and center of the Wahhabi sect, fell under Turkish rule in the 18th century, but in 1913 Ibn Saud, founder of the Saudi dynasty, overthrew the Turks and captured the Turkish province of Hasa; took the Hejaz in 1925 and by 1926, most of Asir. The discovery of oil in the 1930s transformed the new country.

Crown Prince Khalid was proclaimed king on Mar. 25, 1975, after the assassination of King Faisal. Fahd became king on June 13, 1982 following Khalid's death. There is no constitution and no parliament. The king exercises authority together with a Council of Ministers. The Islamic religious code is the law of the land. Alcohol and public entertainments are restricted, and women have an inferior legal status.

Saudi units fought against Israel in the 1948 and 1973 Arab-Israeli wars. Many billions of dollars of advanced arms have been purchased from Britain, France, and the U.S., including jet fighters, missiles, and, in 1981, 5 airborne warning and control system (AWACS) aircraft from the U.S., despite strong opposition from Israel. Beginning with the 1967 Arab-Israeli war, Saudi Arabia provided large annual financial gifts to Egypt; aid was later extended to Syria, Jordan, and Palestinian guerrilla groups, as well as to other Muslim countries.

Faisal played a leading role in the 1973-74 Arab oil embargo against the U.S. and other nations in an attempt to force them to adopt an anti-Israel policy. Saudi Arabia joined most other Arab states, 1979, in condemning Egypt's peace treaty with Israel.

In the 1980s, Saudi Arabia's moderate position on crude oil prices often prevailed at OPEC meetings.

The Hejaz contains the holy cities of Islam — Medina where the Mosque of the Prophet enshrines the tomb of Mohammed, who died in the city June 7, 632, and Mecca, his birthplace. More than 600,000 Moslems from 60 nations pilgrimage to Mecca annually.

Two Saudi oil tankers were attacked May 1984, as Iran and Iraq began air attacks against shipping in the Persian Gulf. On May 29, the U.S., citing grave concern over the growing escalation of the Iran-Iraq war in the Persian Gulf, authorized the sale of 400 Stinger antiaircraft missiles.

In 1987, Iranians making a pilgrimage to Mecca clashed with anti-Iranian pilgrims and Saudi police; over 400 were killed. Saudi Arabia broke diplomatic relations with Iran in 1988. Some 1,426 Moslem pilgrims died July 2, 1990 when a stampede occurred in a pedestrian tunnel leading to Mecca.

Following Iraq's attack on Kuwait, Aug. 2, 1990, Saudi Arabia accepted the Kuwait royal family and over 400,000 Kuwaiti refugees. King Fahd invited Western and Arab troops to deploy on its soil in support of Saudi defense forces. During the Persian Gulf war, Iraq fired a series of Scud missiles at Saudi Arabia; most were intercepted by U.S. Patriot missiles, although 28 U.S. soldiers were killed when a scud hit their barracks in Dhahran, Feb. 25. The nation's northern Gulf coastline suffered severe pollution as a result of Iraqi sabotage of the Kuwaiti oil fields.

Senegal

Republic of Senegal

République du Sénégal

People: Population (1992 est.): 8,205,000. **Age distrib.** (%): 0–14: 47.5; 15–59: 47.5; 60+: 5.0. **Pop. density:** 108 per sq. mi. **Urban** (1986): 30%. **Ethnic groups:** Wolof 36%, Serer 17%, Fulani 17%, Diola 9%, Toucouleur 9%, Mandingo 6%. **Languages:** French (official), Wolof, Serer, Peul, Tukulor, others. **Religions:** Muslim 92%, Christian 2%.

Geography: Area: 75,750 sq. mi., slightly smaller than GB. **Location:** At western extreme of Africa. **Neighbors:** Mauritania on N, Mali on E, Guinea, Guinea-Bissau on S, Gambia surrounded on three sides. **Topography:** Low rolling plains cover most of Senegal, rising somewhat in the SE. Swamp and jungles are in SW. **Capital:** Dakar. **Cities** (1992): Dakar 1.7 mln.; Thies 201,000; Kaolack 179,000.

Government: Type: Republic. **Head of state:** Pres. Abdou Diouf; b. Sept. 7, 1935; in office Jan. 1, 1981. **Head of government:** Habib Thiam; in office Apr. 8, 1991. **Local divisions:** 10 regions. **Defense** (1989): 2.0% of GDP.

Economy: Industries: Food processing, fishing. **Chief crops:** Peanuts are chief export; millet, rice. **Minerals:** Phosphates. **Arable land:** 27%. **Livestock** (1991): 2.8 mln. cattle; 4.0 mln. sheep; 1.2 mln. goats. **Fish catch** (1989): 255,000 metric tons. **Electricity prod.** (1991): 758 mln. kWh. **Labor force:** 77% agric.

Finance: Monetary unit: CFA franc (Mar. 1993: 273 = $1 US). **Gross domestic product** (1990): $5.0 bln. **Per capita GDP:** $615. **Imports** (1990): $1.0 bln.; partners Fr. 37%, U.S. 6%. **Exports** (1990): $814 mln.; partners Fr. 25%, UK 6%. **Tourism** (1990): $152 mln. receipts. **National budget** (1989): 1.0 bln expenditures. **International reserves less gold** (Jan. 1993): $12.4 mln. **Gold:** 29,000 oz t. **Consumer prices** (change in 1991): –1.8%.

Transport: Railroads (1992): 562 mi. long. **Motor vehicles** (1989): 90,000 passenger cars, 36,000 comm. vehicles. **Chief ports:** Dakar, Saint-Louis.

Communications: Television sets: 1 per 125 persons. **Radios:** 1 per 8.7 persons. **Telephones:** 1 per 150 persons. **Daily newspaper circ.** (1990): 7 per 1,000 pop.

Health: Life expectancy at birth (1992): 54 male, 57 female. **Births** (per 1,000 pop. 1992): 44. **Deaths** (per 1,000 pop. 1992): 13. **Natural increase:** 2.9%. **Hospital beds:** 1 per 1,134 persons. **Physicians:** 1 per 17,072 persons. **Infant mortality** (per 1,000 live births 1992): 80.

Education (1988): **Literacy:** 10%. **School:** 48% at primary, 11% at secondary.

Major International Organizations: UN and all of its specialized agencies, OAU.

Embassy: 11 Phillimore Gdns, London W8 7QG; 071-937 0925.

Portuguese settlers arrived in the 15th century, but French control grew from the 17th century. The last independent Muslim state was subdued in 1893. Dakar became the capital of French West Africa.

Independence as part, along with the Sudanese Rep., of the Mali Federation, came June 20, 1960. Senegal withdrew Aug. 20. French political and economic influence is strong.

Senegal, Dec. 17, 1981, signed an agreement with The Gambia for confederation of the 2 countries under the name of Senegambia. The confederation began Feb. 1, 1982. The 2 nations retained their individual sovereignty but adopted joint defense and monetary policies. The confederation collapsed in 1989, although in 1991 the 2 nations signed a friendship and cooperation treaty.

In 1989, a border incident sparked ethnic violence against Senegalese in Mauritania and, in retaliation, against Mauritanians in Senegal.

Seychelles

Republic of Seychelles

People: Population (1992 est.): 68,000. **Age distrib.** (%): 0–14: 36.3; 15–64: 57.3; 65+: 6.4. **Pop. density:** 397 per sq. mi. **Urban** (1990): 60%. **Ethnic groups:** Creoles (mixture of Asians, Africans, and French) predominate. **Languages:** English, French (both official). **Religion:** Roman Catholic 90%.

Geography: Area: 171 sq. mi., slightly larger than the Isle of Wight. **Location:** In the Indian O. 700 miles NE of Madagascar. **Neighbors:** Nearest are Madagascar on SW, Somalia on NW. **Topography:** A group of 86 islands, about half of them composed of coral, the other half granite, the latter predominantly mountainous. **Capital:** Victoria, pop. (1986) 23,000.

Government: Type: Single party republic. **Head of state:** Pres. France-Albert René, b. Nov. 16, 1935; in office June 5, 1977. **Local divisions:** 23 districts. **Defense** (1990): 6.0% of GDP.

Economy: Industries: Food processing. **Chief crops:** Coconut products, cinnamon, vanilla, patchouli. **Electricity prod.** (1991): 80 mln. kWh. **Labor force:** 12% agric.; 19.4% tourism, comm.; 32% serv.; 40% govt.

Finance: Monetary unit: Rupee (Mar. 1993: 5.21 = $1 US). **Gross domestic product** (1991): $350 mln. **Per capita GDP:** $5,200. **Imports** (1991): $172 mln.; partners: UK 20%, So. Afr. 13%. **Exports** (1991): $48 mln.; partners: Pak. 38%; Jap. 26%. **National budget** (1989): $168 mln. expenditures. **Tourism** (1991): $97 mln. receipts. **International reserves less gold** (Mar. 1993): $26.5 mln. **Consumer prices** (change in 1992): 3.3%.

Transport: Motor vehicles (1989): 4,000 passenger cars, 1,300 comm. vehicles. **Chief port:** Victoria.

Communications: Radios: 1 per 3 persons. **Telephones:** 1 per 5 persons. **Daily newspaper circ.** (1990): 47 per 1,000 pop.

Health: Life expectancy at birth (1992): 65 male; 75 female. **Births** (per 1,000 pop. 1992): 23. **Deaths** (per 1,000 pop. 1992): 7. **Natural increase:** 1.6%. **Hospital beds:** 1 per 171 persons. **Physicians:** 1 per 992 persons. **Infant mortality** (per 1,000 live births 1992): 15.

Education (1991): **Literacy:** 85%. **School:** Compulsory for 9 years; attendance 98%.

Major International Organizations: UN, OAU, Commonwealth of Nations.

High Commission: 111 Eros House, Baker St, London W1M 1FE; 071-224 1660.

The islands were occupied by France in 1768, and seized by Britain in 1794. Ruled as part of Mauritius from 1814, the Seychelles became a separate colony in 1903. The ruling party had opposed independence as impractical, but pressure from the OAU and the UN became irresistible, and independence was declared June 29, 1976. The first president was ousted in a coup a year later by a socialist leader.

A new constitution, announced Mar. 1979, turned the country into a one-party state.

Sierra Leone

Republic of Sierra Leone

People: Population (1992 est.): 4,456,000. **Age distrib.** (%): 0–14: 41.4; 15–59: 53.5; 60+: 5.1. **Pop. density:** 159 per sq. mi. **Urban** (1991): 33%. **Ethnic groups:** Temne 30%, Mende 29%, others. **Languages:** English (official), tribal languages. **Religions:** Animist 30%, Muslim 30%, Christian 10%.

Geography: Area: 27,925 sq. mi., the size of the Rep. of Ireland. **Location:** On W coast of W. Africa. **Neighbors:** Guinea on N, E, Liberia on S. **Topography:** The heavily indented, 210-mi. coastline has mangrove swamps. Behind are wooded hills, rising to a plateau and mountains in the E. **Capital:** Freetown, pop. (1985 est.) 469,000. **Cities:** Bo, Kenema, Makeni.

Government: Type: Military. **Head of government:** Capt. Valentine E. M. Strasser; in office May 7, 1992. **Local divisions:** 4 provinces.

Economy: Industries: Mining, tourism. **Chief crops:** Cocoa, coffee, palm kernels, rice, ginger. **Minerals:** Diamonds, bauxite. **Arable land:** 25%. **Fish catch** (1990): 52,000 metric tons. **Electricity prod.** (1991): 185 mln. kWh. **Labor force:** 75% agric.; 15% ind. & serv.

Finance: Monetary unit: Leone (Mar. 1993: 561 = $1 US). **Gross domestic product** (1991): $1.4 bln. **Per capita GDP:** $330. **Imports** (1992): $131 mln.; partners: UK 22%, Fr. 11%. **Exports** (1992): $145 mln.; partners: Neth. 31%, UK 15%, U.S. 9%. **National budget** (1991): $181 mln. expenditures. **International reserves less gold** (Mar. 1993): $23 mln. **Consumer prices** (change in 1992): 65.5%.

Transport: Motor vehicles (1989): 29,000 passenger cars, 10,000 comm. vehicles. **Chief ports:** Freetown, Bonthe.

Communications: Television sets: 1 per 170 persons. **Radios:** 1 per 4.2 persons. **Telephones:** 1 per 160 persons. **Daily newspaper circ.** (1991): 3 per 1,000 pop.

Health: Life expectancy at birth (1992): 43 male; 48 female. **Births** (per 1,000 pop. 1992): 46. **Deaths** (per 1,000 pop. 1992): 21. **Natural increase:** 2.5%. **Hospital beds:** 1 per 980 persons. **Physicians:** 1 per 13,150 persons. **Infant mortality** (per 1,000 live births 1992): 148.

Education (1991): **Literacy:** 21%.

Major International Organizations: UN (GATT, IMF, WHO), Commonwealth of Nations, OAU.

Embassy: 33 Portland Place, London W1N 3AG; 071-636 6483.

Freetown was founded in 1787 by the British government as a haven for freed slaves. Their descendants, known as Creoles, number more than 60,000.

Successive steps toward independence followed the 1951 constitution. Full independence arrived Apr. 27, 1961. Sierra Leone became a republic Apr. 19, 1971. A one-party state approved by referendum 1978, brought political stability, but the economy has been plagued by inflation, corruption, and dependence upon the International Monetary Fund and creditors.

Mutinous soldiers ousted Pres. Momoh Apr. 30, 1992.

Singapore

Republic of Singapore

People: Population (1992 est.): 2,792,000. **Age distrib.** (%): 0–14: 23.4; 15–59: 68.4; 60+: 8.2. **Pop. density:** 12,464 per sq. mi. **Ethnic groups:** Chinese 77%, Malays 15%, Indians 6%. **Languages:** Chinese, Malay, Tamil, English all official. **Religions:** Buddhism 29%, Christian 19%, Muslim 16%, Taoism 13%.

Geography: Area: 224 sq. mi., the size of the Isle of Man. **Location:** Off tip of Malayan Peninsula in S.E. Asia. **Neighbors:** Nearest are Malaysia on N, Indonesia on S. **Topography:** Singapore is a flat, formerly swampy island. The nation includes 40 nearby islets. **Capital:** Singapore.

Government: Type: Republic. **Head of state:** Pres. Ong Teng Cheong; in office Sept. 2, 1993. **Head of government:** Prime Min. Goh Chok Tong; b. May 20, 1941; in office Nov. 28, 1990. **Defense** (1990): 4% of GDP.

Economy: Industries: Shipbuilding, oil refining, electronics, banking, textiles, food, rubber, lumber processing, tourism. **Arable land:** 11%. **Livestock** (1989): 321,000 pigs. **Electricity prod.** (1990): 14.4 bln. kWh. **Labor force:** 1% agric.; 58% ind. & comm.; 35% services.

Finance: Monetary unit: Dollar (May 1993: 1.64 = $1 US). **Gross domestic product** (1991): $38.3 bln. **Per capita GDP:** $13,900. **Imports** (1992): $72.1 bln.; partners: Jap. 18%, Malay. 13%, U.S. 17%, Sau. Ar. 9%. **Exports** (1992): $63.4 bln., partners: U.S. 20%, Malay. 16%, Jap. 11%, HK 6%. **Tourism** (1990): $4.3 bln. receipts. **National budget** (1991): $9.0 bln. expenditures. **Consumer prices** (change in 1992): 2.3%.

Transport: Motor vehicles (1991): 300,000 passenger cars, 127,000 comm. vehicles. **Civil aviation** (1991): 33.4 bln.

passenger-km; 1 airport.

Communications: Television sets: 1 per 4.9 persons. **Radios:** 1 per 4.2 persons. **Telephones:** 1 per 2.1 persons. **Daily newspaper circ.** (1990): 289 per 1,000 pop.

Health: Life expectancy at birth (1992): 73 male; 78 female. **Births** (per 1,000 pop. 1992): 18. **Deaths** (per 1,000 pop. 1992): 5. **Natural increase:** 1.3%. **Hospital beds:** 1 per 272 persons. **Physicians:** 1 per 779 persons. **Infant mortality** (per 1,000 live births 1992): 6.

Education (1990): **Literacy:** 87%. **School:** Not compulsory; attendance 94%.

Major International Organizations: UN (GATT, IMF, WHO), ASEAN.

High Commission: 9 Wilton Cres, London SW1X 8SA; 071-235 5441.

Founded in 1819 by Sir Thomas Stamford Raffles, Singapore was a British colony until 1959 when it became autonomous within the Commonwealth. On Sept. 16, 1963, it joined with Malaya, Sarawak and Sabah to form the Federation of Malaysia.

Tensions between Malayans, dominant in the federation, and ethnic Chinese, dominant in Singapore, led to an agreement under which Singapore became a separate nation, Aug. 9, 1965.

Singapore is one of the world's largest ports. Standards in health, education, and housing are high. International banking has grown.

Slovakia

Slovensko

People: Population (1993 est.): 5,300,000. **Pop. density:** 279 per sq. mi. **Ethnic groups:** Slovak 87%, Hungarian 10%.

Geography: Area: 18,932 sq. mi. **Location:** In E central Europe. **Neighbors:** Poland on N, Hungary on S, Austria, Czech Rep. on W, Ukraine on E. **Topography:** Mountains (Carpathians) in N, fertile Danube plane in S. **Capital:** Bratislava. **Cities** (1991 est.): Bratislava 440,000, Kosice 236,000.

Government: Type: Republic. **Head of state:** Pres. Michal Kovac; b. 1931; in office Feb. 2, 1993. **Head of government:** Prime Min. Vladimir Meciar; in office Jan. 1, 1993.

Economy: Industries: Iron and steel, glass, chemicals, cement. **Chief crops:** Wheat, potatoes, rye, corn.

Finance: Monetary unit: New Koruna (Feb. 1993: 29.00 = $1 US).

Education (1993): **Literacy:** 99%.

Major International Organizations: UN.

Slovakia was originally settled by Illyrian, Celtic and Germanic tribes and was incorporated into Great Moravia in the 9th century. It became part of Hungary in the 11th century. Overrun by Czech Hussites in the 15th century, it was restored to Hungarian rule in 1526. The Slovaks dissociated themselves from Hungary following World War I and joined the Czechs of Bohemia to form the Republic of Czechoslovakia, Oct. 28, 1918.

Germany invaded Czechoslovakia, 1939, and declared Slovakia an independent state. Slovakia rejoined Czechoslovakia in 1945.

Czechoslovakia split into 2 separate states—the Czech Republic and Slovakia—on Jan. 1, 1993.

Slovenia

Republic of Slovenia

Republica Slovenija

People: Population (1992 est.): 1,974,000. **Pop. density:** 252 per sq. mi. **Ethnic groups:** Slovenes 91%. **Languages:** Slovenian, Serbo-Croatian. **Religion:** Mostly Roman Catholic.

Geography: Area: 7,819 sq. mi., about the size of Wales. **Location:** In SE Europe. **Neighhbors:** Italy, Austria, Hungary, Croatia. **Topography:** Mostly hilly; 42% of the land is forested. **Capital:** Ljubljana, pop. (1991) 323,000.

Government: Type: Republic. **Head of state:** Pres. Milan Kucan. **Head of government:** Janez Drnovsek; in office May 14, 1992.

Economy: Industries: Steel, textiles. **Minerals:** Coal, mercury. **Chief crops:** Wheat, potatoes. **Livestock** (1991): 546,000 cattle; 576,000 pigs. **Electricity prod.** (1991): 12.2 bln. kWh.

Finance: Monetary unit: Tolar. **Gross domestic product** (1991): $21 bln. **Per capita GDP:** $10,700. **Imports** (1990): $4.6 bln. **Exports** (1990): $4.1 bln.

Transport: Motor vehicles (1990): 581,000 passenger cars.

Communications: Television sets: 1 per 3.7 persons. **Telephones:** 1 per 3 persons. **Newspaper circ.** (1990): 112 per 1,000 pop.

Health: Life expectancy at birth (1992): 70 male; 78 female. **Hospital beds:** 1 per 143 persons. **Physicians:** 1 per 481 persons. **Infant mortality** (per 1,000 live births 1991): 9.

Education: Literacy (1991): 90%.

Major International Organizations: UN.

Embassy: 2nd Floor, 49 Conduit Street, London W1R 9FB; 071-734 8870.

The Slovenes settled in their current territory in the period from the 6th to the 8th centuries. They fell under German domination as early as the 9th century. Modern Slovenian political history began after 1848 when the Slovenes, who were divided among several Austrian provinces, began their struggle for political and national unification. With the establishment of Yugoslavia in 1918, this unification was largely achieved when the majority of the Slovenes entered the new state, which became the Kingdom of the Serbs, Croats, and Slovenes.

Slovenia declared independence June 25, 1991.

Solomon Islands

People: Population (1992 est.): 360,000. **Age distrib.** (%): 0–14: 49; 15–59: 45.5; 60+: 5.5. **Pop. density:** 33 per sq. mi. **Urban** (1986): 15%. **Ethnic groups:** Melanesian 93%, Polynesian 4%. **Languages:** English (official), Papuan, Melanesian, Polynesian languages. **Religions:** Anglican 34%, Evangelical 24%, Roman Catholic 19%, traditional religions.

Geography: Area: 10,640 sq. mi., slightly larger than Wales. **Location:** Melanesian archipelago in the western Pacific O. **Neighbors:** Nearest is Papua New Guinea on W. **Topography:** 10 large volcanic and rugged islands and 4 groups of smaller ones. **Capital:** Honiara, pop. (1988) 30,000.

Government: Type: Parliamentary democracy within the Commonwealth of Nations. **Head of state:** Queen Elizabeth II, represented by Gov.-Gen. George Lepping. **Head of government:** Prime Min. Solomon Mamaloni; in office Mar. 28, 1989. **Local divisions:** 7 provinces and Honiara.

Economy: Industries: Fish canning. **Chief crops:** Coconuts, rice, bananas, yams. **Other resources:** Forests, marine shell. **Arable land:** 2%. **Fish catch** (1990): 25,000 metric tons. **Electricity prod.** (1991): 39 mln. kWh. **Labor force:** 32% agric., 32% services, 18% ind. & comm.

Finance: Monetary unit: Dollar (Mar. 1993: 3.16 = $1 US). **Gross domestic product** (1990): $200 mln. **Per capita GDP:** $600. **Imports** (1990): $92 mln.; partners: Austral. 31%, Jap. 14%, Sing. 18%. **Exports** (1990): $70 mln.; partners: Jap. 37%, UK 11%.

Communications: Radios: 1 per 4.6 persons. **Telephones:** 1 per 44 persons.

Health: Life expectancy at birth (1992): 67 male; 72 female. **Births** (per 1,000 pop. 1992): 41. **Deaths** (per 1,000 pop. 1992): 5. **Natural increase:** 3.6%. **Infant mortality** (per 1,000 live births 1992): 30.

Education (1989): **Literacy:** 60%. **School:** 78% attend primary school; 21% attend secondary school.

Major International Organizations: UN, Commonwealth of Nations.

Honorary Consulate: 17 Springfield Road, London SW19 7AL; 071-946 5552.

The Solomon Islands were sighted in 1568 by an expedition from Peru. Britain established a protectorate in the 1890s over most of the group, inhabited by Melanesians. The islands saw major World War II battles. Self-government came Jan. 2, 1976, and independence was formally attained July 7, 1978.

Somalia

Somali Democratic Republic

Jamhuriyadda Dimugradiga Somaliya

People: Population (1992 est.): 7,235,000. **Pop. density:** 29 per sq. mi. **Urban** (1990): 36%. **Ethnic groups:** Mainly Hamitic, others. **Languages:** Somali, Arabic (both official). **Religion:** Sunni Muslims 99%.

Geography: Area: 246,300 sq. mi., twice the size of the Br. Isles. **Location:** Occupies the eastern horn of Africa. **Neighbors:** Djibouti, Ethiopia, Kenya on W. **Topography:** The coastline extends for 1,700 mi. Hills cover the N; the centre and S are flat. **Capital:** Mogadishu, pop. (1986 est.) 700,000.

Government: Type: In transition. **Local divisions:** 16 regions.

Economy: Chief crops: Incense, sugar, bananas, sorghum, corn, gum. **Minerals:** Iron, tin, gypsum, bauxite, uranium. **Arable land:** 2%. **Livestock** (1991): 4.9 mln. cattle; 20 mln. goats; 14 mln. sheep. **Fish catch** (1990): 18,000 metric tons. **Electricity prod.** (1991): 60 mln. kWh. **Labor force:** 82% agric.

Finance: Monetary unit: Shilling (Dec. 1992: 2,615 = $1 US). **Gross domestic product** (1989): $1.7 bln. **Per capita GDP:** $170.

Imports (1990): $249 mln.; partners: It. 29%, Fra. 18%. **Exports** (1990): $58 mln.; partners: It. 17%. **Consumer prices** (change in 1990): 102%.

Transport: Motor vehicles (1990): 20,000 passenger cars, 12,000 comm. vehicles. **Chief ports:** Mogadishu, Berbera.

Communications: Radios: 1 per 20 persons.

Health: Life expectancy at birth (1992): 56 male; 56 female. **Births** (per 1,000 pop. 1992): 46. **Deaths** (per 1,000 pop. 1992): 13. **Natural increase:** 3.3%. **Hospital beds:** 1 per 1,053 persons. **Physicians:** 1 per 19,071 persons. **Infant mortality** (per 1,000 live births 1992): 116.

Education (1990): **Literacy:** 24%. **School:** 50% attend primary school, 7% attend secondary school.

Major International Organizations: UN, OAU, Arab League.

Embassy: 60 Portland Place, London W1N 3DG; 071-580 7148.

The UN in 1949 approved eventual creation of Somalia as a sovereign state and in 1950 Italy took over the trusteeship held by Great Britain since World War II.

British Somaliland was formed in the 19th century in the NW. Britain gave it independence June 26, 1960; on July 1 it joined with the former Italian part to create the independent Somali Republic.

On Oct. 21, 1969, a Supreme Revolutionary Council seized power in a bloodless coup, named a Council of Secretaries of State, and abolished the Assembly. In May, 1970, several foreign companies were nationalized.

Somalia has laid claim to Ogaden, the huge eastern region of Ethiopia, peopled mostly by Somalis. Ethiopia battled Somali rebels in 1977. Some 11,000 Cuban troops with Soviet arms defeated Somali army troops and ethnic Somali rebels in Ethiopia, 1978. As many as 1.5 mln. refugees entered Somalia. Guerrilla fighting in Ogaden continued until 1988 when a peace agreement was reached with Ethiopia.

Twenty-one years of one-man rule ended in Jan. 1991 with the flight of Gen. Muhamman Siyad Barrah from the capital. Fighting between rival factions caused 40,000 casualties in 1991 and 1992, and by mid-1992 the civil war combined with banditry to produce a famine that threatened some 1.5 million people with starvation. In July 1992 the UN secretary general declared Somalia to be a country without a government. In Dec. 1992 the UN accepted a U.S. offer of troops to safeguard the delivery of food to the starving. The UN took control of the multinational relief effort from the U.S. May 4, 1993, and sponsored negotiations among rival factions aimed at establishing an interim government. U.S. and UN forces carried out attacks against the forces of Gen. Mohammed Farah Aidid, the strongest Somali warlord, who opposed the UN role in Somalia.

South Africa

Republic of South Africa

Republiek van Suid-Afrika

People: Population (1992 est.): 41,688,000. **Age distrib.** (%): 0–14: 32.1; 15–59: 60.6; 60+: 7.3. **Pop. density:** 88 per sq. mi. **Urban** (1991): 60%. **Ethnic groups:** black 70%, white 16%, Coloured 8%, Asian 3%. **Religions:** Mainly Christian, Hindu, Muslim minorities. **Languages:** Afrikaans, English (both official), Nguni, Sotho languages.

Geography: Area: 472,359 sq. mi., about 4 times the size of the Br. Isles. **Location:** At the southern extreme of Africa. **Neighbors:** Namibia, Botswana, Zimbabwe on N, Mozambique, Swaziland on E; surrounds Lesotho. **Topography:** The large interior plateau reaches close to the country's 2,700-mi. coastline. There are few major rivers or lakes; rainfall is sparse in W, more plentiful in E. **Capitals:** Cape Town (legislative), Pretoria (administrative), and Bloemfontein (judicial). **Cities** (1990 metro.): Durban 1 mln; Cape Town 1.9 mln; Johannesburg 1.7 mln; Pretoria 850,000.

Government: Type: Republic with tricameral parliament, with one chamber each for whites, Coloureds (people of mixed race), and Asians; no franchise or parliamentary representation for blacks. **Head of state:** Pres. Frederik W. de Klerk; b. Mar. 18, 1936; in office Sept. 20, 1989. **Local divisions:** 4 provinces, 10 "homelands" for black Africans. **Defense** (1992): 3% of GDP.

Economy: Industries: Steel, tyres, motors, textiles, plastics. **Chief crops:** Corn, wool, dairy products, grain, tobacco, sugar, fruit, peanuts, grapes. **Minerals:** Gold (largest producer), chromium, antimony, coal, iron, manganese, nickel, phosphates, tin, uranium, gem diamonds, platinum, copper, vanadium. **Other resources:** Wool. **Arable land:** 12%. **Livestock** (1989): 11.8 mln. cattle; 30.3 mln. sheep. **Fish catch** (1989): 878,000 metric tons. **Electricity prod.** (1991): 180 bln. kWh. **Crude steel prod.** (1991): 9.3 mln. metric tons. **Labor force:** 25% agric.; 32% ind. and commerce; 34% serv.; 7% mining.

Finance: Monetary unit: Rand (Aug. 1993: 3.38 = $1 US). **Gross domestic product** (1991): $104 bln. **Per capita GDP:** $2,600. **Imports** (1992): $21.2 bln.; partners: Ger. 19%, U.S. 68%, UK. 12%. **Exports** (1992): $23.8 bln.; partners: U.S. 43%, Jap. 9%. **Tourism** (1990): $1.0 bln. receipts. **National budget** (1993): $35.0 bln. **International reserves less gold** (Mar. 1993): $1.5 bln. **Gold:** 5.6 mln. oz t. **Consumer prices** (change in 1992): 13.9%.

Transport: Railroads (1990): 15,793 mi. long. 15.1 bln. passenger-km. **Motor vehicles** (1990): 3.3 mln. passenger cars, 1.4 mln. comm. vehicles. **Civil aviation** (1991): 8.3 bln. passenger-km: 41 airports. **Chief ports:** Durban, Cape Town, East London, Port Elizabeth.

Communications: Television sets: 1 per 11 persons. **Radios:** 1 per 3.0 persons. **Telephones:** 1 per 6.1 persons. **Daily newspaper circ.** (1990): 48 per 1,000 pop.

Health: Life expectancy at birth (1992): 62 male; 67 female. **Births** (per 1,000 pop. 1992): 35. **Deaths** (per 1,000 pop. 1992): 8. **Natural increase:** 2.7%. **Physicians:** 1 per 1,320 persons. **Infant mortality** (per 1,000 live births 1992): 51.

Education (1990): **Literacy:** 99% (whites), 69% (Asians), 62% (Coloureds), 50% (Africans).

Major International Organizations: UN (GATT).

Embassy: South Africa House, Trafalgar Square, London WC2N 5DP; 071-930 4488.

Bushmen and Hottentots were the original inhabitants. Bantus, including Zulu, Xhosa, Swazi, and Sotho, had occupied the area from Transvaal to south of Transkei before the 17th century.

The Cape of Good Hope area was settled by Dutch, beginning in the 17th century. Britain seized the Cape in 1806. Many Dutch trekked north and founded 2 republics, the Transvaal and the Orange Free State. Diamonds were discovered, 1867, and gold, 1886. The Dutch (Boers) resented encroachments by the British and others; the Anglo-Boer War followed, 1899-1902. Britain won and, effective May 31, 1910, created the Union of South Africa, incorporating the British colonies of the Cape and Natal, the Transvaal and the Orange Free State. After a referendum, the Union became the Republic of South Africa, May 31, 1961, and withdrew from the Commonwealth.

With the election victory of Daniel Malan's National party in 1948, the policy of separate development of the races, or apartheid, already existing unofficially, became official. This called for separate development, separate residential areas, and ultimate political independence for the whites, Bantus, Asians, and Coloureds. In 1959 the government passed acts providing the eventual creation of several Bantu nations or Bantustans on 13% of the country's land area, though most black leaders opposed the plan.

Under apartheid, blacks were severely restricted to certain occupations, and paid far lower wages than whites for similar work. Only whites could vote or run for public office. There is an advisory Indian Council, partly elected, partly appointed. In 1969, a Colored People's Representative Council was created.

At least 600 persons, mostly Bantus, were killed in 1976 riots protesting apartheid. Black protests continued through the 1980s as violence broke out in several black townships. A new constitution was approved by referendum, Nov. 1983, which extended the parliamentary franchise to the Coloured and Asian minorities. Laws banning interracial sex and marriage were repealed in 1985.

In 1963, the Transkei, an area in the SE, became the first of these partially self-governing territories or "Homelands". Transkei became independent on Oct. 26, 1976, Bophuthatswana on Dec. 6, 1977, and Venda on Sept. 13, 1979; none received international recognition.

In 1981, So. Africa launched military operations in Angola and Mozambique to combat terrorist groups; So. African troops attacked the South West African People's Organization (SWAPO) guerrillas in Angola, March, 1982. South Africa and Mozambique signed a non-aggression pact in 1984.

In 1986, Nobel Peace Prize winner Bishop Desmond Tutu called for Western nations to apply sanctions against S. Africa to force an end to apartheid. President Botha announced in Apr. the end to the nation's system of racial pass laws and offered blacks an advisory role in government.

On May 19, S. Africa attacked 3 neighboring countries – Zimbabwe, Botswana, Zambia – to strike at guerrilla strongholds of the African National Congress.

A nationwide state of emergency was declared June 12, giving almost unlimited power to the security forces. On Apr. 22, 1987, a 6-week-old walkout by railway workers erupted into violence after the dismissal of 16,000 strikers. As confrontation between blacks and government increased, there was widespread support in Western nations for a complete trade embargo on S. Africa.

Some 2 million South African black workers staged a massive strike, June 6-8, 1988, to protest the government's new labor laws and the banning of political activity by trade unions and anti-apartheid groups. P.W. Botha, head of the government since 1978, resigned Aug. 14, 1989, and was replaced by Frederik W. de Klerk.

In 1990, the government lifted its bar on the African National Congress, the primary black group fighting to end white minority rule. On Feb. 11, black nationalist leader Nelson Mandela was freed after more than 27 years in prison. In Oct. the Separate Amenities Act was repealed, ending the legal basis of segregation in public places. In Feb. 1991 Pres. de Klerk announced plans to end all apartheid laws. In June the race registration law was repealed.

A band of marauders swept through the township of Boipatong, June 17, 1992, killing some 40 blacks and prompting the African National Congress to temporarily break off constitutional talks with the white-minority government. Violence involving rival black groups continued later in the year. Violence flared in several black townships following the assassination of Chris Hani, head of the South African Communist Party, Apr. 10, 1993. The nation's negotiating parties, June 3, settled upon Apr. 27, 1994, as the tentative date for South Africa's first elections in which all races can vote, which would choose a multiracial constituent assembly that would serve as an interim legislature and write a new constitution. Negotiators agreed, Sept. 7, on the creation of a multiracial transition committee to oversee government operations prior to the election.

Bophuthatswana: Population (1992 est.): 2,056,000. **Area:** 16,988 sq. mi., 6 discontinuous geographic units. **Capital:** Mmabatho. **Head of state:** Pres. Kgosi Lucas Manyane Mangope, b. Dec. 27, 1923; in office Dec. 6, 1977.

Ciskei: Population (1992 est.): 854,000. **Area:** 2,996 sq. mi. **Capital:** Bisho. **Head of state:** Brig. Joshua Oupa Gqozo.

Transkei: Population (1992 est.): 3,301,000. **Area:** 16,855 sq. mi., 3 discontinuous geographic units. **Capital:** Umtata. **Head of government:** Gen. Bantu Holomisa; in office Dec. 30, 1987.

Venda: Population (1992 est.): 567,000. **Area:** 2,771 sq. mi., 2 discontinuous geographic units. **Capital:** Thohoyandou. **Head of state:** Gabriel Ramushwana; in office Apr. 5, 1990.

Spain

España

People: Population (1992 est.): 39,118,000 (incl. Balearic & Canary Islands). **Age distrib.** (%): 0–14: 18.4; 15–59: 62.2; 60+: 19.4. **Pop. density:** 200 per sq. mi. **Urban** (1990): 79%. **Ethnic groups:** Spanish (Castilian, Valencian, Andalusian, Asturian) 72.8%, Catalan 16.4%, Galician 8.2%, Basque 2.3%. **Languages:** Spanish (official), Catalan, Galician, Basque. **Religion:** Roman Catholic 90%.

Geography: Area: 194,896 sq. mi., over twice the size of GB. **Location:** In SW Europe. **Neighbors:** Portugal on W. France on N. **Topography:** The interior is a high, arid plateau broken by mountain ranges and river valleys. The NW is heavily watered, the south has lowlands and a Mediterranean climate. **Capital:** Madrid. **Cities** (1991 est.): Madrid 2,909,000; Barcelona 1,623,000; Valencia 752,000; Seville 659,000.

Government: Type: Constitutional monarchy. **Head of state:** King Juan Carlos I de Borbon y Borbon, b. Jan. 5, 1938; in office Nov. 22, 1975. **Head of government:** Prime Min. Felipe Gonzalez Marquez; in office Dec. 2, 1982. **Local divisions:** 17 autonomous communities. **Defense** (1991): 2.0% of GDP.

Economy: Industries: Machinery, steel, textiles, shoes, autos, processed foods. **Chief crops:** Grains, olives, grapes, citrus fruits, vegetables, olives. **Minerals:** Lignite, uranium, lead, iron, copper, zinc, coal. **Other resources:** Forests (cork). **Arable land:** 31%. **Livestock** (1990): 4.9 mln. cattle; 16.9 mln. pigs; 23.7 mln. sheep. **Fish catch** (1989): 974,000 tons. **Electricity prod.** (1991): 157 bln. kWh. **Crude steel prod.** (1991): 12.7 mln. metric tons. **Labor force:** 16% agric.; 24% ind. and comm.; 52% serv.

Finance: Monetary unit: Peseta (July 1993: 133.29 = $1 US). **Gross domestic product** (1991): $487 bln. **Per capita GDP:** $12,400. **Imports** (1992): $99.7 bln.; partners: U.S. 8%, EC 57%. **Exports** (1992): $64.3 bln.; partners: EC 71%, U.S. 6%. **Tourism** (1990): $18.5 bln. receipts. **National budget** (1991): $115 bln. expenditures. **International reserves less gold** (Mar. 1993): $44.4 bln. **Gold:** 15.6 mln. oz t. **Consumer prices** (change in 1992): 5.8%.

Transport: Railroads (1991): 12,563 km. long. **Motor vehicles** (1990): 11.9 mln. passenger cars, 2.4 mln. comm. **Civil aviation** (1990): 22.1 bln. passenger-km; 25 airports with scheduled flights. **Chief ports:** Barcelona, Bilbao, Valencia, Cartagena, Gijon.

Communications: Television sets: 1 per 2.6 persons. **Radios:** 1 per 3.4 persons. **Telephones:** 1 per 2.5 persons. **Daily newspaper circ.** (1991): 76 per 1,000 pop.

Health: Life expectancy at birth (1992): 75 male; 82 female. **Births** (per 1,000 pop. 1992): 11. **Deaths** (per 1,000 pop. 1992): 8. **Natural increase:** .3%. **Hospital beds:** 1 per 198 persons. **Physicians:** 1 per 275 persons. **Infant mortality** (per 1,000 live births 1992): 6.

Education (1991): **Literacy:** 97%. **School:** Compulsory to age 16.

Major International Organizations: UN and all of its specialized agencies, NATO, OECD, EC.

Embassy: 24 Belgrave Sq, London SW1X 8QA; 071-235 5555.

Spain was settled by Iberians, Basques, and Celts, partly overrun by Carthaginians, conquered by Rome c.200 BC. The Visigoths, in power by the 5th century AD, adopted Christianity but by AD 711 lost to the Islamic invasion from Africa. Christian reconquest from the N led to a Spanish nationalism. In 1469 the kingdoms of Aragon and Castile were united by the marriage of Ferdinand II and Isabella I, and the last Moorish power was broken by the fall of the kingdom of Granada, 1492. Spain became a bulwark of Roman Catholicism.

Spain obtained a colonial empire with the discovery of America by Columbus, 1492, the conquest of Mexico by Cortes, and Peru by Pizarro. It also controlled the Netherlands and parts of Italy and Germany. Spain lost its American colonies in the early 19th century. It lost Cuba, the Philippines, and Puerto Rico during the Spanish-American War, 1898.

Primo de Rivera became dictator in 1923. King Alfonso XIII revoked the dictatorship, 1930, but was forced to leave the country 1931. A republic was proclaimed which disestablished the church, curtailed its privileges, and secularized education. A conservative reaction occurred 1933 but was followed by a Popular Front (1936-1939) composed of socialists, communists, republicans, and anarchists.

Army officers under Francisco Franco revolted against the government, 1936. In a destructive 3-year war, in which some one million died, Franco received massive help and troops from Italy and Germany, while the USSR, France, and Mexico supported the republic. War ended Mar. 28, 1939. Franco was named caudillo, leader of the nation. Spain was neutral in World War II but its relations with fascist countries caused its exclusion from the UN until 1955.

In July 1969, Franco and the Cortes designated Prince Juan Carlos as the future king and chief of state. After Franco's death, Nov. 20, 1975, Juan Carlos was sworn in as king. He presided over the formal dissolution of the institutions of the Franco regime. In free elections June 1977, moderates and democratic socialists emerged as the largest parties.

Catalonia and the Basque country were granted autonomy, Jan. 1980, following overwhelming approval in home-rule referendums. Basque extremists, however, have continued their campaign for independence.

The **Balearic Islands** in the western Mediterranean, 1,935 sq. mi., are a province of Spain; they include **Majorca** (Mallorca), with the capital, Palma; **Minorca, Cabrera, Ibiza** and **Formentera.** The **Canary Islands,** 2,807 sq. mi., in the Atlantic W of Morocco, form 2 provinces, including the islands of **Tenerife, Palma, Gomera, Hierro, Grand Canary, Fuerteventura,** and **Lanzarote** with Las Palmas and Santa Cruz thriving ports. **Ceuta** and **Melilla,** small enclaves on Morocco's Mediterranean coast, are part of Metropolitan Spain.

Spain has sought the return of Gibraltar, in British hands since 1704.

Sri Lanka

Democratic Socialist Republic of Sri Lanka

Sri Lanka Prajathanthrika Samajavadi Janarajaya

People: Population (1992 est.): 17,631,000. **Age distrib.** (%): 0–14: 35.3; 15–59: 58.1; 60+: 6.6. **Pop. density:** 695 per sq. mi. **Urban** (1991): 26%. **Ethnic groups:** Sinhalese 74%, Tamils 17%, Moors 7%. **Languages:** Sinhalese and Tamil (both official). **Religions:** Buddhist 69%, Hindu 15%, Christian 8%, Muslim 7%.

Geography: Area: 25,332 sq. mi. about the size of the Rep. of Ireland. **Location:** In Indian O. off SE coast of India. **Neighbors:** India on NW. **Topography:** The coastal area and the northern half are flat; the S-central area is hilly and mountainous. **Capital:** Colombo, pop. (1990): 615,000.

Government: Type: Republic. **Head of state:** Pres. Dingiri Banda Wijetunge; b. 1923; in office May 7, 1993. **Head of government:** Prime Minister Ranil Wickremasinghe; in office May 7, 1993. **Local divisions:** 9 provinces, 24 districts. **Defense** (1991): 5% of GDP.

Economy: Industries: Plywood, paper, milling, chemicals, textiles. **Chief crops:** Tea, coconuts, rice. **Minerals:** Graphite, limestone, gems, phosphate. **Other resources:** Forests, rubber. **Arable land:** 16%. **Livestock** (1991): 1.8 mln. cattle. **Fish catch** (1990): 165,000 metric tons. **Electricity prod.** (1991): 4.2 bln. kWh. **Labor force:** 46% agric.; 27% ind. and comm.; 26% serv.

Finance: Monetary unit: Rupee (Mar. 1993: 47 = $1 US). **Gross domestic product** (1991): $7.2 bln. **Per capita GDP:** $410. **Imports** (1991): $3.0 bln.; partners: Jap. 15%, UK 7%. **Exports** (1991): $2.3 bln.; partners: U.S. 22%, UK 7%. **Tourism** (1990): $125 mln. receipts. **National budget** (1992): $3.7 bln. expenditures. **International reserves less gold** (Mar. 1993): $1.0 bln. **Gold:** 160,000 oz t. **Consumer prices** (change in 1992): 11.4%.

Transport: Railroads (1990): 1,453 km. long. **Motor vehicles** (1990): 173,000 passenger cars, 146,000 comm. vehicles. **Civil aviation** (1991): 3.4 bln. passenger-km; 1 airport. **Chief ports:** Colombo, Trincomalee, Galle.

Communications: Television sets: 1 per 25 persons. **Radios:**

1 per 8 persons. **Telephones:** 1 per 102 persons.

Health: Life expectancy at birth (1992): 69 male; 74 female. **Births** (per 1,000 pop. 1992): 21. **Deaths** (per 1,000 pop. 1992): 6. **Natural increase:** 1.5%. **Hospital beds:** 1 per 356 persons. **Physicians:** 1 per 6,609 persons. **Infant mortality** (per 1,000 live births 1992): 21.

Education (1990): **Literacy:** 87%. **School:** Compulsory to age 12; attendance 98%.

Major International Organizations: UN (World Bank, IMF), Commonwealth of Nations.

High Commission: 13 Hyde Park Gdns, London W2 2LU; 071-262 1841.

The island was known to the ancient world as Taprobane (Greek for copper-coloured) and later as Serendip (from Arabic). Colonists from northern India subdued the indigenous Veddahs about 543 BC; their descendants, the Buddhist Sinhalese, still form most of the population. Hindu descendants of Tamil immigrants from southern India account for one-fifth of the population. Parts were occupied by the Portuguese in 1505 and by the Dutch in 1658. The British seized the island in 1796. As Ceylon it became an independent member of the Commonwealth in 1948. On May 22, 1972, Ceylon became the Republic of Sri Lanka.

Prime Min. W. R. D. Bandaranaike was assassinated Sept. 25, 1959. In new elections, the Freedom Party was victorious under Mrs. Sirimavo Bandaranaike, widow of the former prime minister.

After May 1970 elections, Mrs. Bandaranaike became prime minister again. In 1971 the nation suffered economic problems and terrorist activities by ultra-leftists, thousands of whom were executed. Massive land reform and nationalization of foreign-owned plantations was undertaken in the mid-1970s. Mrs. Bandaranaike was ousted in 1977 elections. A presidential form of government was installed in 1978 to restore stability.

Tension between the Sinhalese and Tamil separatists erupted into violence repeatedly in the 1980s. In 1987, hundreds died in an attack by Tamil rebels Apr. 17. Sri Lanka forces retaliated in June with attacks on the rebel-held Jaffna peninsula. Over 20,000 have died in the civil war, which continued into the 1990s. Pres. Ranasinghe Premadasa was assassinated, May 1, 1993, by a Tamil rebel.

Sudan

Republic of the Sudan

Jamhuryat as-Sudan

People: Population (1992 est.): 28,305,000. **Pop. density:** 29 sq. mi. **Urban** (1990): 22%. **Ethnic groups:** black 52%, Arab 39%, Beja 6%. **Languages:** Arabic (official), Dinka, Nubian, Nuer, Beja, others. **Religions:** Sunni Muslim 70%, animist 18%, Christian 5%.

Geography: Area: 966,757 sq. mi., the largest country in Africa, 8 times the size of the Br. Isles. **Location:** At the E end of Sahara desert zone. **Neighbors:** Egypt on N, Libya, Chad, Central African Republic on W, Zaire, Uganda, Kenya on S, Ethiopia and Eritrea on E. **Topography:** The N consists of the Libyan Desert in the W, and the mountainous Nubia desert in E, with narrow Nile valley between. The center contains large, fertile, rainy areas with fields, pasture, and forest. The S has rich soil, heavy rain. **Capital:** Khartoum. **Cities** (1983 est.): Khartoum 476,000; Omdurman 526,000; North Khartoum 341,000; Port Sudan 206,000.

Government: Type: Military. **Head of government:** Prime Min. Gen. Omar Al-Bashir; in office June 30, 1989. **Local divisions:** 9 states. **Defense** (1990): 7% of GDP.

Economy: Industries: Textiles, food processing. **Chief crops:** Gum arabic (principal world source), durra (sorghum), cotton (main export), sesame, peanuts, rice, coffee, sugar cane, wheat, dates. **Minerals:** Chrome, copper. **Other resources:** Mahogany. **Arable land:** 5%. **Livestock** (1991): 20 mln. cattle; 5 mln. sheep; 15 mln. goats. **Electricity prod.** (1991): 905 mln. kWh. **Labor force:** 78% agric.; 9% ind., comm.

Finance: Monetary unit: Dinar (Mar. 1993: 1.34 = $1 US). **Gross domestic product** (1991): $12.1 bln. **Per capita GDP:** $450. **Imports** (1991): $1.4 bln.; partners: EC 32%, US 13%. **Exports** (1991): $325 mln.; partners: EC 46%. **National budget** (1991): $2.1 bln. expenditures. **International reserves less gold** (Mar. 1993): $3.7 mln. **Consumer prices** (change in 1992): 112.6%.

Transport: Railroads (1988): 5,503 km. long. **Motor vehicles** (1990): 116,000 passenger cars, 56,000 comm. vehicles. **Civil aviation** (1991): 425 mln. passenger-km; 12 airports with scheduled flights. **Chief port:** Port Sudan.

Communications: Television sets: 1 per 117 persons. **Radios:** 1 per 4.6 persons. **Telephones:** 1 per 338 persons. **Daily newspaper circ.** (1990): 21 per 1,000 pop.

Health: Life expectancy at birth (1992): 53 male; 54 female. **Births** (per 1,000 pop. 1992): 44. **Deaths** (per 1,000 pop. 1992): 14. **Natural increase:** 3.0%. **Hospital beds:** 1 per 1,110 persons. **Physicians** (1983): 2,169. **Infant mortality** (per 1,000 live births 1992): 85.

Education (1991): **Literacy:** 27%. **School:** Compulsory for 9 years; attendance 50%.

Major International Organizations: UN (IMF, WHO, FAO), Arab League, OAU.

Embassy: 3 Cleveland Row, London SW1A 1DD; 071-839 8080.

Northern Sudan, ancient Nubia, was settled by Egyptians in antiquity, and was converted to Coptic Christianity in the 6th century. Arab conquests brought Islam in the 15th century.

In the 1820s Egypt took over the Sudan, defeating the last of earlier empires, including the Fung. In the 1880s a revolution was led by Mohammed Ahmed who called himself the Mahdi (leader of the faithful) and his followers, the dervishes.

In 1898 an Anglo-Egyptian force crushed the Mahdi's successors. In 1951 the Egyptian Parliament abrogated its 1899 and 1936 treaties with Great Britain, and amended its constitution, to provide for a separate Sudanese constitution.

Sudan voted for complete independence as a parliamentary government effective Jan. 1, 1956.

In 1969, a Revolutionary Council took power, but a civilian premier and cabinet were appointed; the government announced it would create a socialist state. The northern 12 provinces are predominantly Arab-Moslem and have been dominant in the central government. The 3 southern provinces are black Christians and animists. A 1972 peace agreement gave the South regional autonomy. The 2 halves of the nation began a civil war in 1988. Some 50,000 government soldiers launched a massive offensive against the southern rebels in 1992.

Economic problems plagued the nation in the 1980s, aggravated by a huge influx of refugees from neighboring countries. After 16 years in power, Pres. Nimeiry was overthrown in a bloodless military coup, Apr. 6, 1985. The Sudan held its first democratic parliamentary elections in 18 years in 1986. The elected government was overthrown in a bloodless coup June 30, 1989.

Sudan agreed to allow large-scale UN relief efforts in 1991, as some 7 million people were threatened with famine. The UN suspended aid to southern Sudan in 1992 because of the fighting. In 1993 Amnesty International accused Sudan of practising ethnic cleansing against the Nuba people of southern Sudan and of gross human rights violations in other war zones in the south.

Suriname

Republic of Suriname

People: Population (1992 est.): 410,000. **Pop. density:** 6 per sq. mi. **Ethnic groups** Hindustanis 37%, Creole 31%, Javanese 15%. **Languages:** Dutch (official), Sranantonga, English. **Religions:** Christian 47%, Hindu 27%, Muslim 19%.

Geography: Area: 63,037 sq. mi., about the size of England and Wales combined. **Location:** On N shore of S. America. **Neighbors:** Guyana on W, Brazil on S, French Guiana on E. **Topography:** A flat Atlantic coast, where dykes permit agriculture. Inland is a forest belt; to the S, largely unexplored hills cover 75% of the country. **Capital:** Paramaribo, pop. (1989) 192,000.

Government: Type: Republic. **Head of state:** Pres. Roland Venetiaan; in office Sept. 16, 1991. **Head of government:** Prime Min. Jules Adjodhia; in office Sept. 16, 1991. **Local divisions:** 10 districts.

Economy: Industries: Aluminium. **Chief crops:** Rice, sugar, fruits. **Minerals:** Bauxite. **Other resources:** Forests, shrimp. **Arable land:** 1%. **Electricity prod.** (1991): 2.0 bln. kWh. **Labor force:** 29% agric.; 15% ind. and commerce; 42% govt.

Finance: Monetary unit: Guilder (Mar. 1993: 1.78 = $1 US). **Gross domestic product** (1990): $472 mln. **Per capita GDP:** $3,400. **Imports** (1988): $370 mln.; partners: U.S. 37%, Neth. 15%, Trin./Tob. 9%. **Exports** (1990): $472 mln.; partners: Nor. 33%, U.S. 13%, Neth. 26%. **Tourism** (1990): $11 mln. receipts. **National budget** (1990): $716 mln. expenditures. **International reserves less gold** (Mar. 1993): $12.9 mln. **Gold:** 54,000 oz t.

Transport: Motor vehicles (1990): 36,000 passenger cars, 14,000 comm. vehicles. **Chief ports:** Paramaribo, Nieuw-Nickerie.

Communications: Television sets: 1 per 10 persons. **Radios:** 1 per 1.6 persons. **Telephones:** 1 per 8 persons. **Daily newspaper circ.** (1991): 43 per 1,000 pop.

Health: Life expectancy at birth (1992): 66 male; 71 female. **Births** (per 1,000 pop. 1992): 27. **Deaths** (per 1,000 pop. 1992): 5. **Natural increase:** 2.1%. **Infant mortality** (per 1,000 live births 1992): 34.

Education (1989): **Literacy:** 65%. **School:** Compulsory ages 6–12.

Major International Organizations: UN (WHO, ILO, FAO, World Bank, IMF), OAS.

Embassy: 2 Alexander Gogelweg, The Hague, Netherlands; 010 31 70 650844.

The Netherlands acquired Suriname in 1667 from Britain, in exchange for New Netherlands (New York). The 1954 Dutch constitution raised the colony to a level of equality with the Netherlands and the Netherlands Antilles. In the 1970s the Dutch government pressured for Suriname independence, which came Nov. 25, 1975, despite objections from East Indians. Some 40% of the population (mostly East Indians) emigrated to the Netherlands in the months before independence.

The National Military Council took over control of the government, Feb. 1982. The government came under democratic leadership in 1988.

Swaziland

Kingdom of Swaziland

People: Population (1992 est.): 913,000. **Age distrib.** (%): 0–14: 47.3; 15–59: 47.4; 60+: 5.3. **Pop. density:** 136 per sq. mi. **Urban** (1990): 30%. **Ethnic groups:** Swazi 90%, Zulu 2.3%, European 2.1%, other African, non-African groups. **Languages:** Swazi, English (both official). **Religion:** Christian 60%, indigenous beliefs 40%.

Geography: Area: 6,704 sq. mi., slightly smaller than Wales. **Location:** In southern Africa, near Indian O. coast. **Neighbors:** South Africa on N, W, S, Mozambique on E. **Topography:** The country descends from W-E in broad belts, becoming more arid in the lowveld region, then rising to a plateau in the E. **Capital:** Mbabane. **Cities** (1990 est.): Mbabane 46,000; Manzini 53,000.

Government: Type: Monarchy. **Head of state:** King Mswati III, in office Apr. 25, 1986. **Head of government:** Prime Min. Obed Dlamini; in office July 12, 1989. **Local divisions:** 4 districts, 2 municipalities, 40 regions.

Economy: Industries: Wood pulp. **Chief crops:** Sugar, corn, cotton, rice, pineapples, sugar, citrus fruits. **Minerals:** Asbestos, iron, coal. **Other resources:** Forests. **Arable land:** 8%. **Electricity prod.** (1991): 155 mln. kWh. **Labor force:** 53% agric.; 9% ind. and commerce; 9% serv.

Finance: Monetary unit: Lilangeni (Mar. 1993: 3.22 = $1 US). **Gross national product** (1990): $563 mln. **Per capita GDP:** $725. **Imports** (1992): $746 mln.; partners: S. Afr., 92%. **Exports** (1990): $543 mln.; partners: S. Afr. 40%. **National budget** (1993): $360 mln. expenditures. **International reserves less gold** (Feb. 1993): $256 mln. **Consumer prices** (change in 1991): 12.1%.

Transport: Motor vehicles (1991): 25,000 passenger cars, 8,000 comm. vehicles.

Communications: Radios: 1 per 6.3 persons. **Telephones:** 1 per 34 persons. **Daily newspaper circ.** (1990): 24 per 1,000 pop.

Health: Life expectancy at birth (1992): 52 male; 60 female. **Births** (per 1,000 pop. 1992): 44. **Deaths** (per 1,000 pop. 1992): 12. **Natural increase:** 3.2%. **Hospital beds** (1984): 1,608. **Physicians** (1984): 80. **Infant mortality** (per 1,000 live births 1992): 98.

Education (1990): **Literacy:** 65%. **School:** 82% attend primary school.

Major International Organizations: UN (IMF, WHO, FAO), OAU, Commonwealth of Nations.

High Commission: 58 Pont St, London SW1X 0AE; 071-581 4976.

The royal house of Swaziland traces back 400 years, and is one of Africa's last ruling dynasties. The Swazis, a Bantu people, were driven to Swaziland from lands to the north by the Zulus in 1820. Their autonomy was later guaranteed by Britain and Transvaal, with Britain assuming control after 1903. Independence came Sept. 6, 1968. In 1973 the king repealed the constitution and assumed full powers.

Under the constitution political parties are forbidden; parliament's role in government is limited to debate and advice.

Sweden

Kingdom of Sweden

Konungariket Sverige

People: Population (1992 est.): 8,602,000. **Age distrib.** (%): 0–14: 17.9; 15–59: 59.0; 60+: 23.1. **Pop. density:** 49 per sq. mi. **Urban** (1985): 85%. **Ethnic groups:** Swedish 91%, Finnish 3%, Lapps, European immigrants. **Language:** Swedish. **Religion:** Lutheran (official) 95%.

Geography: Area: 173,731 sq. mi., twice the size of the UK. **Location:** On Scandinavian Peninsula in N. Europe. **Neighbors:** Norway on W, Denmark on S (across Kattegat), Finland on E. **Topography:** Mountains along NW border cover 25% of Sweden, flat or rolling terrain covers the central and southern areas, which includes several large lakes. **Capital:** Stockholm. **Cities** (1992): Stockholm 679,000; Göteborg 433,000; Malmö 234,000.

Government: Type: Constitutional monarchy. **Head of state:** King Carl XVI Gustaf; b. Apr. 30, 1946; in office Sept. 19, 1973. **Head of government:** Prime Min. Carl Bildt; b. July 15, 1949; in office Oct. 3, 1991. **Local divisions:** 24 provinces. **Defense** (1991): 3.9% of GDP.

Economy: Industries: Steel, machinery, instruments, autos, shipbuilding, shipping, paper. **Chief crops:** Grains, potatoes, sugar beets. **Minerals:** Zinc, iron, lead, copper, gold, silver. **Other resources:** Forests (half the country) yield one quarter of exports. **Arable land:** 7%. **Livestock** (1990): 1.7 mln. cattle; 2.2 mln. pigs. **Fish catch** (1990): 240,000 metric tons. **Electricity prod.** (1991): 142 bln. kWh. **Crude steel prod.** (1992): 4.4 mln. metric tons. **Labor force:** 5% agric.; 24% manuf. & mining; 37% social services.

Finance: Monetary unit: Krona (July 1993: 7.97 = $1 US). **Gross domestic product** (1991): $147 bln. **Per capita GDP:** $17,200. **Imports** (1992): $49.7 bln.; partners: EC 56%. **Exports** (1992): $56.1 bln.; partners: EC 55%. **Tourism** (1990): $2.8 bln. receipts. **National budget** (1991): $78.7 bln. expenditures. **International reserves less gold** (Mar. 1993): $19.7 bln. **Gold:** 6.06 mln. oz t. **Consumer prices** (change in 1992): 2.3%.

Transport: Railroads (1990): 6,960 mi. long. **Motor vehicles** (1991): 3.6 mln. passenger cars, 324,000 comm. vehicles. **Civil aviation** (1990): 7.2 bln. passenger-km; 42 airports. **Chief ports:** Göteborg, Stockholm, Malmö.

Communications: Television sets: 1 per 2.4 persons. **Radios:** 1 per 1.2 persons. **Telephones:** 1 per 1.1 persons. **Daily newspaper circ.** (1990): 572 per 1,000 pop.

Health: Life expectancy at birth (1992): 75 male; 81 female. **Births** (per 1,000 pop. 1992): 13. **Deaths** (per 1,000 pop. 1992): 11. **Natural increase:** 2%. **Hospital beds:** 1 per 148 persons. **Physicians:** 1 per 320 persons. **Infant mortality** (per 1,000 live births 1992): 6.

Education (1991): **Literacy:** 99%. **School:** Compulsory for 12 years; attendance 100%.

Major International Organizations: UN and all of its specialized agencies, EFTA, OECD.

Embassy: 11 Montagu Place, London W1H 2AL; 071-724 2101.

The Swedes have lived in present-day Sweden for at least 5,000 years, longer than nearly any other European people. Gothic tribes from Sweden played a major role in the disintegration of the Roman Empire. Other Swedes helped create the first Russian state in the 9th century.

The Swedes were Christianized from the 11th century, and a strong centralized monarchy developed. A parliament, the Riksdag, was first called in 1435, the earliest parliament on the European continent, with all classes of society represented.

Swedish independence from rule by Danish kings (dating from 1397) was secured by Gustavus I in a revolt, 1521-23; he built up the government and military and established the Lutheran Church. In the 17th century Sweden was a major European power, gaining most of the Baltic seacoast, but its international position subsequently declined.

The Napoleonic wars, in which Sweden acquired Norway (it became independent 1905), were the last in which Sweden participated. Armed neutrality was maintained in both world wars.

Over 4 decades of Social Democratic rule was ended in 1976 parliamentary elections but the party was returned to power in the 1982 elections. Although 90% of the economy is in private hands, the government holds a large interest in water power production and the railroads are operated by a public agency.

Carl Bildt, a non-socialist, became Prime Minister Oct. 1991. His coalition government promised to turn the nation away from long-established economic and social programmes.

Switzerland

Swiss Confederation

People: Population (1992 est.): 6,828,000. **Age distrib.** (%): 0–14: 17.0; 15–59: 63.7; 60+: 19.3. **Pop. density:** 428 per sq. mi. **Urban** (1991): 60%. **Ethnic groups:** Mixed European stock. **Languages:** German, French, Italian (all official). **Religions:** Roman Catholic 49%, Protestant 48%.

Geography: Area: 15,941 sq. mi., half the size of Scotland. **Location:** In the Alps of Central Europe. **Neighbors:** France on W, Italy on S, Austria on E, Germany on N. **Topography:** The Alps cover 60% of the land area, the Jura, near France, 10%. Running between, from NE to SW, are midlands, 30%. **Capital:** Bern. **Cities** (1991): Zurich 342,000; Basel 171,200; Geneva 161,000, Bern 135,000.

Government: Type: Federal republic. **Head of government:** Pres. Adolf Ogi; in office Jan. 1, 1993. **Local divisions:** 20 full cantons, 6 half cantons. **Defense** (1990): 2.2% of GDP.

Economy: Industries: Machinery, machine tools, steel, instruments, watches, textiles, foodstuffs (cheese, chocolate), banking, tourism. **Chief crops:** Grains, potatoes, sugar beets, vegetables, tobacco. **Minerals:** Salt. **Other resources:** Hydro power potential. **Arable land:** 10%. **Livestock** (1991): 1.8 mln. cattle; 1.9 mln. pigs.

Electricity prod. (1991): 59 bln. kWh. **Crude steel prod.** (1988): 825,000 metric tons. **Labor force:** 39% ind. and commerce, 7% agric., 50% serv.

Finance: Monetary unit: Franc (July 1993: 1.49 = $1 US). **Gross domestic product** (1991): $147 bln. **Per capita GDP:** $21,700. **Imports** (1992): $61.7 bln.; partners: EC 71%. **Exports** (1992): $61.3 bln.; partners: EC 56%. **Tourism** (1990): $6.8 bln. receipts. **National budget** (1990): $23.8 bln. **International reserves less gold** (Mar. 1993): $31.3 bln. **Gold:** 83.28 mln. oz t. **Consumer prices** (change in 1992): 4.0%.

Transport: Railroads (1989): 3,119 mi. long. **Motor vehicles** (1990): 3.0 mln. passenger cars, 285,000 comm. vehicles. **Civil aviation** (1991): 15.1 bln. passenger-km; 6 airports with scheduled flights.

Communications: Television sets: 1 per 2.9 persons. **Radios:** 1 per 2.6 persons. **Telephones:** 1 per 1.2 persons. **Daily newspaper circ.** (1990): 471 per 1,000 pop.

Health: Life expectancy at birth (1992): 76 male; 83 female. **Births** (per 1,000 pop. 1992): 12. **Deaths** (per 1,000 pop. 1992): 10. **Natural increase:** .2%. **Physicians:** 1 per 317 persons. **Infant mortality** (per 1,000 live births 1992): 5.

Education (1991): **Literacy:** 99%. **School:** Compulsory for 9 years; attendance 100%.

Major International Organizations: Many UN specialized agencies (though not a member).

Embassy: 16 Montagu Place, London W1H 2BQ; 071-723 0701.

Switzerland, the Roman province of Helvetia, is a federation of 23 cantons (20 full cantons and 6 half cantons), 3 of which in 1291 created a defensive league and later were joined by other districts. Voters in the French-speaking part of Canton Bern voted for self-government, 1978; Canton Jura was created Jan. 1, 1979.

In 1648 the Swiss Confederation obtained its independence from the Holy Roman Empire. The cantons were joined under a federal constitution in 1848, with large powers of local control retained by each canton.

Switzerland has maintained an armed neutrality since 1815, and has not been involved in a foreign war since 1515. It is the seat of many UN and other international agencies.

Switzerland is a leading world banking center; stability of the currency brings funds from many quarters. The nation's famed secret bank accounts were phased out in 1992.

Syria

Syrian Arab Republic

al-Jumhuriyah al-Arabiyah

People: Population (1992 est.): 13,730,000. **Age distrib.** (%): 0–14: 49.3; 15–59: 44.2; 60+: 6.5. **Pop. density:** 192 per sq. mi. **Urban** (1990): 50%. **Ethnic groups:** Arab 90%, Kurd, Armenian, others. **Languages:** Arabic (official), Kurdish and Armenian. **Religions:** Sunni Muslim 74%, other Muslim 16%, Christian 10%.

Geography: Area: 71,498 sq. mi., the size of England and S. Ireland combined. **Location:** At eastern end of Mediterranean Sea. **Neighbors:** Lebanon, Israel on W, Jordan on S, Iraq on E, Turkey on N. **Topography:** Syria has a short Mediterranean coastline, then stretches E and S with fertile lowlands and plains, alternating with mountains and large desert areas. **Capital:** Damascus. **Cities** (1992 est.): Damascus 1,451,000; Aleppo 1,445,000; Homs 518,000.

Government: Type: Republic (under military regime). **Head of state:** Pres. Hafez al-Assad; b. Mar. 1930; in office Feb. 22, 1971. **Head of government:** Prime Min. Mahmoud Zuabi; in office Nov. 1, 1987. **Local divisions:** Damascus and 13 provinces. **Defense** (1989): 10.9% of GDP.

Economy: Industries: Oil products, textiles, tobacco, glassware, brassware. **Chief crops:** Cotton, grain, olives, fruits, vegetables. **Minerals:** Oil, phosphate, gypsum. **Crude oil reserves** (1987): 1.4 bln. bbls. **Other resources:** Wool. **Arable land:** 28%. **Livestock** (1990): 13 mln. sheep; 1 mln. goats. **Electricity prod.** (1991): 8 bln. kWh. **Labor force:** 32% agric.; 29% ind. & comm.; 39% services.

Finance: Monetary unit: Pound (Mar. 1993: 11.22 = $1 US). **Gross domestic product** (1991): $30.0 bln. **Per capita GDP:** $2,300. **Imports** (1991): $2.7 bln.; partners: EC 42%. **Exports** (1991): $3.6 bln.; partners: E. Europe 42%, EC 31%. **Tourism** (1990): $244 mln. receipts. **National budget** (1991): $7.5 bln. expenditures. **Consumer prices** (change in 1991): 7.7%.

Transport: Railroads (1991): 948 mi. long. **Motor vehicles** (1990): 117,000 passenger cars, 138,000 comm. vehicles. **Civil aviation** (1989): 833 mln. passenger-km; 5 airports with scheduled flights. **Chief ports:** Latakia, Tartus.

Communications: Television sets: 1 per 17 persons. **Radios:** 1 per 4.1 persons. **Telephones:** 1 per 17 persons. **Daily newspaper circ.** (1990): 21 per 1,000 pop.

Health: Life expectancy at birth (1992): 65 male; 67 female. **Births** (per 1,000 pop. 1992): 44. **Deaths** (per 1,000 pop. 1992): 7. **Natural increase:** 3.7%. **Hospital beds:** 1 per 840 persons. **Physicians:** 1 per 1,347 persons. **Infant mortality** (per 1,000 live births 1992): 45.

Education (1990): **Literacy:** 64% males. **School:** Compulsory for 6 years; attendance 94%.

Major International Organizations: UN (IMF, WHO, FAO), Arab League.

Syrian Interests Section: 8 Belgrave Sq, London SW1X 8PH; 071-245 9012.

Syria contains some of the most ancient remains of civilization. It was the center of the Seleucid empire, but later became absorbed in the Roman and Arab empires. Ottoman rule prevailed for 4 centuries, until the end of World War I.

The state of Syria was formed from former Turkish districts, made a separate entity by the Treaty of Sevres 1920 and divided into the states of Syria and Greater Lebanon. Both were administered under a French League of Nations mandate 1920-1941.

Syria was proclaimed a republic by the occupying French Sept. 16, 1941, and exercised full independence effective Apr. 17, 1946. Syria joined in the Arab invasion of Israel in 1948.

Syria joined with Egypt in Feb. 1958 in the United Arab Republic but seceded Sept. 30, 1961. The Socialist Baath party and military leaders seized power in Mar. 1963. The Baath, a pan-Arab organization, became the only legal party. The government has been dominated by members of the minority Alawite sect.

In the Arab-Israeli war of June 1967, Israel seized and occupied the Golan Heights area inside Syria, from which Israeli settlements had been shelled by Syria for years.

On Oct. 6, 1973, Syria joined Egypt in an attack on Israel. Arab oil states agreed in 1974 to give Syria $1 billion a year to aid anti-Israel moves. Some 30,000 Syrian troops entered Lebanon in 1976 to mediate in a civil war. They fought Palestinian guerrillas and, later, Christian militiamen. Syrian troops again battled Christian forces in Lebanon, Apr. 1981, ending a ceasefire that had been in place.

Following the June 6, 1982 Israeli invasion of Lebanon, Israeli planes destroyed 17 Syrian antiaircraft missile batteries in the Bekka Valley, June 9. Some 25 Syrian planes were downed during the engagement. Israel and Syria agreed to a cease fire June 11. In 1983, Syria backed the PLO rebels who ousted Yasir Arafat's forces from Tripoli.

Syria's role in promoting acts of international terrorism led to the breaking of diplomatic relations with Great Britain and the implementation of limited sanctions by the EC in 1986.

Syria condemned the Aug. 1990 Iraqi invasion of Kuwait and sent troops to help Allied Forces in the Gulf War.

In 1991, Syria accepted U.S. proposals for the terms of an Arab-Israeli peace conference.

Taiwan

Republic of China

Chung-hua Min-kuo

People: Population (1992 est.): 20,878,000. **Age distrib.** (%): 0-14: 27.1; 15-59: 63.2; 60+: 9.7. **Pop. density:** 1,503 per sq. mi. **Urban** (1990): 75%. **Ethnic groups:** Taiwanese 85%, Chinese 14%. **Languages:** Mandarin Chinese (official), Taiwan, Hakka dialects. **Religions:** Buddhism, Taoism, Confucianism prevail.

Geography: Area: 13,885 sq. mi., about the size of Wales and N. Ireland combined. **Location:** Off SE coast of China, between E. and S. China Seas. **Neighbors:** Nearest is China. **Topography:** A mountain range forms the backbone of the island; the eastern half is very steep and craggy, the western slope is flat, fertile, and well-cultivated. **Capital:** Taipei. **Cities** (1991): Taipei (metro.) 2,716,000; Kaohsiung 1,398,000; Taichung 777,000; Tainan 685,000.

Government: Type: Democracy. **Head of state and Nationalist Party chmn.:** Pres. Lee Teng-hui; b. Jan. 15, 1923; in office Jan. 13, 1988. **Head of government:** Prime Min. Lien Chan; in office Feb. 10, 1993. **Local divisions:** 16 counties, 5 cities, Taipei & Kao-Hsiung. **Defense** (1991): 4.6% of GDP.

Economy: Industries: Textiles, clothing, electronics, processed foods, chemicals, plastics. **Chief crops:** Rice, bananas, pineapples, sugarcane, sweet potatoes, peanuts. **Minerals:** Coal, limestone, marble. **Crude oil reserves** (1987): 10 mln. bbls. **Arable land:** 25%. **Livestock** (1989): 6.9 mln. pigs. **Fish catch** (1989): 1.2 mln. metric tons. **Electricity prod.** (1991): 76 bln. kWh. **Crude steel prod.** (1991): 10.9 mln. metric tons. **Labor force:** 15% agric.; 53% ind. & comm.; 22% services.

Finance: Monetary unit: New Taiwan dollar (July 1993: 26.28 = $1 US). **Gross national product** (1991): $180.1 bln. **Per capita GNP:** $8,790. **Imports** (1992): $72 bln.; partners: U.S. 23%, Jap. 30%. **Exports** (1992): $81 bln.; partners: U.S. 39%, Jap. 13%, Hong Kong 8%. **Tourism** (1990): $1.7 bln. receipts. **National budget** (1991): $30.1 bln.

Transport: Motor vehicles (1991): 2.6 mln. passenger cars, 653,000 commercial vehicles. **Civil aviation** (1991): 29.0 bln. passenger-km; 12 airports. **Chief ports:** Kaohsiung, Keelung, Hualien, Taichung.

Communications: Television sets: 1 per 3.2 persons. **Radios:** 1 per 1.5 persons. **Telephones:** 1 per 3 persons. **Daily newspaper circ.** (1989): 202 per 1,000 pop.

Health: Life expectancy at birth (1992): 72 male; 78 female. **Births** (per 1,000 pop. 1992): 16. **Deaths** (per 1,000 pop. 1992): 5. **Natural increase:** 1.1%. **Physicians:** 1 per 910 persons. **Hospital beds:** 1 per 227 persons. **Infant mortality** (per 1,000 live births 1992): 6.

Education (1991): **Literacy:** 90%. **School:** Compulsory for 9 years; attendance 99%.

Consulate: Free Chinese Centre, Dorland House, Regent St, London SW1Y 4PH; 071-930 5767.

Large-scale Chinese immigration began in the 17th century. The island came under mainland control after an interval of Dutch rule, 1620-62. Taiwan (also called Formosa) was ruled by Japan 1895-1945. Two million Kuomintang supporters fled to Taiwan in 1949. Both the Taipei and Peking governments consider Taiwan an integral part of China. Taiwan has rejected Peking's efforts at reunification, but unofficial dealings with the mainland have grown more flexible in the 1980s.

The U.S. upon its recognition of the People's Republic of China, Dec. 15, 1978, severed diplomatic ties with Taiwan. It maintains the unofficial American Institute in Taiwan, while Taiwan has established the Coordination Council for North American Affairs in Washington, D.C.

Land reform, government planning, U.S. aid and investment, and free universal education have brought huge advances in industry, agriculture, and mass living standards. In 1987, martial law was lifted after 38 years and in 1991, the 43-year period of emergency rule ended.

Taiwan has one of the world's strongest economies and is among the 10 leading capital exporters.

The Penghu (Pescadores), 50 sq. mi., pop. 120,000, lie between Taiwan and the mainland. **Quemoy** and **Matsu,** pop. (1990) 70,000 lie just off the mainland.

Tajikistan

Republic of Tajikistan

Respubliki i Tojikiston

People: Population (1992 est.): 5,680,000. **Pop. density:** 105 per sq. mi. **Urban** (1991): 32%. **Ethnic groups:** Tajik 62%, Uzbek 23%, Russian 8%. **Languages:** Tadzhik, Russian. **Religion:** Mostly Sunni Muslim.

Geography: Area: 54,019 sq. mi., about the size of England. **Neighbors:** Uzbekistan and Kyrgyzstan on N, and China on E, Afghanistan on S and E. **Topography:** Mountainous region which contains the Pamirs, Trans Alai mountain system. **Capital:** Dushanbe.

Government: Type: Parliamentary republic. **Head of state:** Pres. Imomali Rakhmonov; in office Nov. 20, 1992. **Head of government:** Vacant.

Economy: Industries: Cement, knitwear, footwear. **Chief crops:** Barley, cotton, wheat, vegetables. **Minerals:** Coal, lead, zinc. **Livestock** (1990): 1.3 mln. cattle; 3.3 mln. sheep. **Electricity prod.** (1991): 17 bln. kWh.

Finance: Monetary unit: Rouble. **Imports** (1990): $1.3 bln. **Exports** (1990): $706 mln.

Transport: Railroads (1990): 554 mi. long. **Civil aviation** (1990): 5.1 bln. passenger-km; 1 airport.

Communications: Television sets: 1 per 6 persons. **Telephones:** 1 per 10 persons. **Newspaper circ.** (1990): 298 per 1,000 pop.

Health: Life expectancy at birth (1992): 64 male; 70 female. **Births** (per 1,000 pop. 1992): 40. **Deaths** (per 1,000 pop. 1992): 8. **Hospital beds:** 1 per 93 persons. **Physicians:** 1 per 362 persons. **Infant mortality** (per 1,000 live births 1992): 74.

Major International Organizations: UN, CIS.

There were settled societies in the region from about 3000 BC. Throughout history the region has undergone invasions by Iranians, Arabs, who converted the population to Islam, Mongols, Uzbeks, Afghans, and Russians. In 1924 the Tadzhik ASSR was created within the Uzbek SSR. The Tadzhik SSR was proclaimed in 1929. Tajikistan declared independence Sept. 9, 1991. It became an independent state when the Soviet Union disbanded Dec. 26, 1991. The ruling Communist Party has retained power in Tajikistan. There were demonstrations by opposition forces – anti-communists and Islamic fundamentalists – in 1992.

Fighting between government forces and the rebels escalated in 1993; some 20,000 people were killed and over 500,000 displaced from their homes. Over 100,000 displaced people crossed as refugees into Afghanistan.

Tanzania

United Republic of Tanzania

Jamhuri ya Muungano wa Tanzania

People: Population (1992 est.) 27,791,000. **Pop. density:** 76 per sq. mi. **Urban** (1990): 32%. **Ethnic groups:** African. **Languages:** Swahili, English (both official), many others. **Religions:** Muslims 33%, Christian 33%, traditional beliefs 33%.

Geography: Area: 364,886 sq. mi., 3 times the the size of the Br. Isles. **Location:** On coast of E. Africa. **Neighbors:** Kenya, Uganda on N, Rwanda, Burundi, Zaire on W, Zambia, Malawi, Mozambique on S. **Topography:** Hot, arid central plateau, surrounded by the lake region in the W, temperate highlands in N and S, the coastal plains. Mt. Kilimanjaro, 19,340 ft., is highest in Africa. **Capital:** Dar-es-Salaam, pop. (1992) 1.4 mln.

Government: Type: Republic. **Head of state:** Pres. Ali Hassan Mwinyi; b. May 8, 1925; in office Nov. 5, 1985. **Head of government:** Prime Min. John Malecela; in office Nov. 9, 1990. **Local divisions:** 25 regions. **Defense** (1992): 3.9% of GDP.

Economy: Industries: Food processing, clothing. **Chief crops:** Sisal, cotton, coffee, tea, tobacco. **Minerals:** Diamonds, gold, nickel. **Other resources:** Hides. **Arable land:** 6%. **Livestock** (1991): 14 mln. cattle; 8.8 mln. goats; 3.5 mln. sheep. **Fish catch** (1989): 340,000 metric tons. **Electricity prod.** (1991): 905 mln. kWh. **Labor force:** 90% agric., 10% ind., comm. & govt.

Finance: Monetary unit: Shilling (Mar. 1993: 350 = $1 US). **Gross domestic product** (1991): $6.9 bln. **Per capita GDP:** $260. **Imports** (1991): $1.5 bln.; partners: UK 14%, Jap. 12%, Ger. 10%. **Exports** (1991): $478 mln.; partners: Ger. 15%, UK 13%. **Tourism** (1990): $63 mln. receipts. **National budget** (1990): $631 mln. expenditures. **International reserves less gold** (Jan. 1993): $204 mln. **Consumer prices** (change in 1992): 21.1%.

Transport: Motor vehicles (1990): 44,000 passenger cars; 52,000 comm. vehicles. **Civil aviation** (1991): $280 mln. passenger-km; 19 airports. **Chief ports:** Dar-es-Salaam, Mtwara, Tanga.

Communications: Radios: 1 per 6 persons. **Telephones:** 1 per 174 persons. **Daily newspaper circ.** (1989): 8 per 1,000 pop.

Health: Life expectancy at birth (1992): 50 male; 55 female. **Births** (per 1,000 pop. 1992): 50. **Deaths** (per 1,000 pop. 1992): 16. **Natural increase:** 3.4%. **Hospital beds** (1984): 22,800. **Physicians** (1984): 1,065. **Infant mortality** (per 1,000 live births 1992): 103.

Education (1987): **Literacy:** 85%. **School:** 87% attend primary school.

Major International Organizations: UN and all of its specialized agencies, OAU, Commonwealth of Nations.

High Commission: 43 Hertford St, London W1Y 8DB; 071-499 8951.

The Republic of Tanganyika in E. Africa and the island Republic of Zanzibar, off the coast of Tanganyika, joined into a single nation, the United Republic of Tanzania, Apr. 26, 1964. Zanzibar retains internal self-government.

Tanganyika. Arab colonization and slaving began in the 8th century AD; Portuguese sailors explored the coast by about 1500. Other Europeans followed.

In 1885 Germany established German East Africa of which Tanganyika formed the bulk. It became a League of Nations mandate and, after 1946, a UN trust territory, both under Britain. It became independent Dec. 9, 1961, and a republic within the Commonwealth a year later.

In 1967 the government set on a socialist course; it nationalized all banks and many industries. The government also ordered that Swahili, not English, be used in all official business.

Tanzanian forces drove Idi Amin from Uganda, Mar., 1979.

Zanzibar, the Isle of Cloves, lies 23 mi. off the coast of Tanganyika; its area is 621 sq. mi. The island of **Pemba,** 25 mi. to the NE, area 380 sq. mi., is included in the administration. The total population (1990 est.) is 375,000.

Chief industry is the production of cloves and clove oil of which Zanzibar and Pemba produce the bulk of the world's supply.

Zanzibar was for centuries the center for Arab slave-traders. Portugal ruled for 2 centuries until ousted by Arabs around 1700. Zanzibar became a British Protectorate in 1890; independence came Dec. 10, 1963. Revolutionary forces overthrew the Sultan Jan. 12, 1964. The new government ousted Western diplomats and newsmen, slaughtered thousands of Arabs, and nationalized farms. Union with Tanganyika followed, 1964. The ruling parties of Tanganyika and Zanzibar were united in 1977, as political tension eased.

Thailand

Kingdom of Thailand

Muang Thai or Prathet Thai

People: Population (1992 est.): 57,624,000. **Age distrib.** (%): 0–14: 45.0; 15–59: 49.0; 60+: 6.0. **Pop. density:** 290 per sq. mi. **Urban** (1990): 20%. **Ethnic groups:** Thai 75%, Chinese 14%, others 11%. **Languages:** Thai (official), Chinese, Malay, regional dialects. **Religions:** Buddhist 95%, Muslim 4%.

Geography: Area: 198,456 sq. mi., about twice the size of GB. **Location:** On Indochinese and Malayan Peninsulas in S.E. Asia. **Neighbors:** Myanmar on W. Laos on N, Cambodia on E, Malaysia on S. **Topography:** A plateau dominates the NE third of Thailand, dropping to the fertile alluvial valley of the Chao Phraya R. in the center. Forested mountains are in N, with narrow fertile valleys. The southern peninsula region is covered by rain forests. **Capital:** Bangkok, pop. (1991 metro. est.) 6.0 mln.

Government: Type: Constitutional monarchy. **Head of state:** King Bhumibol Adulyadej; b. Dec. 5, 1927; in office June 9, 1946. **Head of government:** Prime Min. Chuan Leekpai; in office Sept. 23, 1992. **Local divisions:** 72 provinces. **Defense** (1992): 3.0% of GDP.

Economy: Industries: Textiles, mining, wood prods., tourism. **Chief crops:** Rice (a major export), corn tapioca, sugarcane. **Minerals:** Antimony, tin (among largest producers), tungsten, iron, gas. **Other resources:** Forests (teak is exported), rubber. **Arable land:** 34%. **Livestock** (1991): 5.6 mln. cattle; 4.9 mln. pigs. **Fish catch** (1989): 2.3 mln. metric tons. **Electricity prod.** (1991): 37.5 bln. kWh. **Labor force:** 59% agric.; 26% ind. & comm.; 10% serv.; 8% govt.

Finance: Monetary unit: Baht (Mar. 1993: 25.36 = $1 US). **Gross national product** (1991): $92.6 bn. **Per capita GNP:** $1,630. **Imports** (1991): $39.0 bln.; partners: Jap. 30%, U.S. 11%. **Exports** (1991): $27.5 bln.; partners: Jap. 17%, U.S. 22%. **Tourism** (1990): $4.3 mln. receipts. **National budget** (1992): $17.9 bln. **International reserves less gold** (Mar. 1993): $21.4 bln. **Gold:** 2.47 mln. oz t. **Consumer prices** (change in 1991): 5.7%.

Transport: Railroads (1990): 2,399 mi. long. **Motor vehicles** (1990): 655,000 passenger cars, 1.5 mln. comm. vehicles. **Civil aviation** (1991): 18.2 bln. passenger-km; 24 airports with scheduled flights. **Chief ports:** Bangkok, Sattahip.

Communication: Television sets: 1 per 17 persons. **Radios:** 1 per 5.7 persons. **Telephones:** 1 per 41 persons. **Daily newspaper circ.** (1989): 50 per 1,000 pop.

Health: Life expectancy at birth (1992): 67 male; 71 female. **Births** (per 1,000 pop. 1992): 20. **Deaths** (per 1,000 pop. 1992): 7. **Natural increase:** 1.3%. **Hospital beds:** 1 per 597 persons. **Physicians:** 1 per 4,227 persons. **Infant mortality** (per 1,000 live births 1992): 35.

Education (1991): **Literacy:** 89%. **School:** Compulsory for 6 years; attendance 96%.

Major International Organizations: UN (GATT, World Bank).

Embassy: 30 Queen's Gate, London SW7 5JB; 071-589 0173.

Thais began migrating from southern China in the 11th century. Thailand is the only country in SE Asia never taken over by a European power, thanks to King Mongkut and his son King Chulalongkorn who ruled from 1851 to 1910, modernized the country, and signed trade treaties with both Britain and France. A bloodless revolution in 1932 limited the monarchy.

Japan occupied the country in 1941.

The military took over the government in a bloody 1976 coup. Kriangsak Chomanan, prime minister resigned, Feb. 1980, under opposition over soaring inflation, oil price increases, labor unrest and growing crime. Chatichai Choonhavan was chosen prime minister in a democratic election, Aug. 1988. In Feb. 1991, the military ousted Choonhavan in a bloodless coup. Elections were held Sept. 1992; Chuan Leekpai was chosen Prime Minister.

Vietnamese troops had crossed the border and been repulsed by Thai forces in the 1980s.

Togo

Republic of Togo

République Togolaise

People: Population (1992 est.): 3,958,000. **Age distrib.** (%): 0-14: 45.3; 15-59: 49.7; 60+: 5.0. **Pop. density:** 183 per sq. mi. **Urban** (1990): 25%. **Ethnic groups:** Ewe 35%, Mina 6%, Kabye 22%. **Languages:** French (official), Gur, Kwa. **Religions:** Traditional 50%, Christian 30%, Muslim 20%.

Geography: Area: 21,622 sq. mi., smaller than the Rep. of Ireland. **Location:** On S coast of W. Africa. **Neighbors:** Ghana on W, Burkina Faso on N, Benin on E. **Topography:** A range of hills running SW-NE splits Togo into 2 savanna plains regions. **Capital:** Lomé, pop. (1989 est.) 600,000.

Government: Type: In transition. **Head of state:** Pres. Gnassingbe Eyadema; b. Dec. 26, 1937; in office Apr. 14, 1967. **Head of government:** Prime Min. Joseph Kokou Koffgoh; in office Aug. 27, 1991. **Local divisions:** 21 prefectures.

Economy: Industries: Textiles, shoes. **Chief crops:** Coffee, cocoa, yams, manioc, millet, rice. **Minerals:** Phosphates. **Arable land:** 26%. **Electricity prod.** (1991): 209 mln. kWh. **Labor force:** 75% agric.; 20% industry.

Finance: Monetary unit: CFA franc (Mar. 1993: 273 = $1 US). **Gross domestic product** (1990): $1.5 bln. **Per capita GDP:** $400. **Imports** (1990): $502 mln.; partners: EC 61%. **Exports** (1990): $363 mln.; partners: EC 70%. **Tourism** (1990): $23 mln. receipts. **International reserves less gold** (Jan. 1993): $272 mln. **Gold:** 13,000 oz t. **Consumer prices** (change in 1991): 1.0%.

Transport: Railroads (1991): 326 mi. long. **Motor vehicles** (1990): 5,000 passenger cars. **Chief port:** Lomé.

Communications: Television sets: 1 per 156 persons. **Radios:** 1 per 5.0 persons. **Telephones:** 1 per 169 persons. **Daily newspaper circ.** (1991): 3 per 1,000 pop.

Health: Life expectancy at birth (1992): 54 male; 58 female. **Births** (per 1,000 pop. 1992): 48. **Deaths** (per 1,000 pop. 1992): 12. **Natural increase:** 3.6%. **Hospital beds:** 1 per 752 persons. **Physicians:** 1 per 12,992 persons. **Infant mortality** (per 1,000 live births 1992): 94.

Education (1990): **Literacy:** 45%.

Major International Organizations: UN (GATT, IMF), OAU.

Embassy: 30 Sloane Street, London SW1X 9NE; 071-235 0147.

The Ewe arrived in southern Togo several centuries ago. The country later became a major source of slaves. Germany took control in 1884. France and Britain administered Togoland as UN trusteeships. The French sector became the republic of Togo on Apr. 27, 1960.

The population is divided between Bantus in the S and Hamitic tribes in the N. Togo has actively promoted regional integration, as a means of stimulating the economy.

Some 25,000 people fled Togo to the neighbouring countries of Ghana and Benin as a result of civil unrest in 1993.

Tonga

Kingdom of Tonga

Pule 'anga Tonga

People: Population (1992 est.): 102,000. **Age distrib.** (%): 0–14: 44.4; 15–59: 50.5; 60+: 5.1. **Pop. density:** 377 per sq. mi. **Ethnic groups:** Tongans 98%, other Polynesian, European. **Languages:** Tongan, English (both official). **Religions:** Free Wesleyan 47%, Roman Catholic 14%, Free Church of Tonga 14%, Mormon 9%, Church of Tonga 9%.

Geography: Area: 270 sq. mi., the size of Co. Armagh. **Location:** In western S. Pacific O. **Neighbors:** Nearest is Fiji, on W, New Zealand, on S. **Topography:** Tonga comprises 169 volcanic and coral islands, 45 inhabited. **Capital:** Nuku'alofa, pop. (1986 metro.) 29,000.

Government: Type: Constitutional monarchy. **Head of state:** King Taufa'ahau Tupou IV; b. July 4, 1918; in office Dec. 16, 1965. **Head of government:** Prime Min. Baron Vaea; in office Aug. 21, 1991. **Local divisions:** 3 main island groups.

Economy: Industries: Tourism. **Chief crops:** Coconut products, bananas are exported. **Other resources:** Fish. **Arable land:** 25%. **Electricity prod.** (1991): 8 mln. kWh. **Labor force:** 45% agric, 27% services.

Finance: Monetary unit: Pa'anga (Apr. 1993: 1.36 = $1 US). **Gross domestic product** (1990): $92 mln. **Imports** (1991): $59 mln.; partners: NZ 39%, Aust. 25%. **Exports** (1991): $13 mln.; partners: Aust. 29%, NZ 56%. **Tourism** (1991): $7.6 mln. receipts.

Transport: Motor vehicles (1989): 1,400 passenger cars, 2,700 comm. vehicles. **Chief port:** Nuku'alofa.

Communications: Radios: 1 per 1.2 persons. **Telephones:** 1 per 18 persons.

Health: Life expectancy at birth (1992): 65 male; 70 female. **Births** (per 1,000 pop. 1992): 27. **Deaths** (per 1,000 pop. 1992): 5. **Natural increase:** 2.2%. **Infant mortality** (per 1,000 live births 1992): 23.

Education (1988): **Literacy:** 99%. **School:** Compulsory for 8 years; attendance 77%.

High Commission: 36 Molyneux St, London W1H 6AB; 071-724 5828.

The islands were first visited by the Dutch in the early 17th century. A series of civil wars ended in 1845 with establishment of the Tupou dynasty. In 1900 Tonga became a British protectorate. On June 4, 1970, Tonga became independent and a member of the Commonwealth.

Trinidad and Tobago

Republic of Trinidad and Tobago

People: Population (1992 est.): 1,285,000. **Age distrib.** (%): 0–14: 32.9; 15–59: 58.7; 60+: 8.4. **Pop. density:** 648 per sq. mi. **Ethnic groups:** Africans 43%, East Indians 40%, mixed 14%. **Language:** English (official). **Religions:** Roman Catholic 32%, Protestant 29%, Hindu 25%, Muslim 6%.

Geography: Area: 1,980 sq. mi., about the size of Northumberland. **Location:** Off eastern coast of Venezuela. **Neighbors:** Nearest is Venezuela on SW. **Topography:** Three low mountain ranges cross Trinidad E-W, with a well-watered plain between N and Central Ranges. Parts of E and W coasts are swamps. Tobago, 116 sq. mi., lies 20 mi. NE. **Capital:** Port-of-Spain. **Cities** (1990 metro. est.): Port-of-Spain 300,000; San Fernando 50,000.

Government: Type: Parliamentary democracy. **Head of state:** Pres. Noor Hassanali; in office Mar. 19, 1987. **Head of government:** Prime Min. Patrick Manning; in office Dec. 17, 1991. **Local divisions:** 8 counties, 3 municipalities.

Economy: Industries: Oil products, rum, cement, tourism. **Chief crops:** Sugar, cocoa, coffee, citrus fruits, bananas. **Minerals:** Asphalt, oil. **Crude oil reserves** (1987): 567 mln. bbls. **Arable land:** 14%. **Electricity prod.** (1991): 3.4 bln. kWh. **Labor force:** 18% construction-utilities, 14% manuf., mining, commerce, 47% services.

Finance: Monetary unit: Dollar (Mar. 1993: 4.25 = $1 US). **Gross domestic product** (1990): $4.9 bln. **Per capita GDP:** $3,600. **Imports** (1991): $1.6 bln.; partners: U.S. 51%, UK 8%. **Exports** (1991): $1.9 bln.; partners: U.S. 53%. **Tourism** (1990): $122 mln. receipts. **National budget** (1991): $1.7 bln. expenditures. **International reserves less gold** (Mar. 1993): $172 mln. **Gold:** 54,000 oz t. **Consumer prices** (change in 1992): 6.5%.

Transport: Motor vehicles (1989): 269,000 passenger cars, 68,000 comm. vehicles. **Civil aviation** (1990): 2.7 bln. passenger-km; 2 airports. **Chief port:** Port-of-Spain.

Communications: Television sets: 1 per 5 persons. **Radios:** 1 per 3.1 persons. **Telephones:** 1 per 5 persons. **Daily newspaper circ.** (1990): 140 per 1,000 pop.

Health: Life expectancy at birth (1992): 68 male; 73 female. **Births** (per 1,000 pop. 1992): 21. **Deaths** (per 1,000 pop. 1992): 6. **Natural increase:** 1.5%. **Hospital beds:** 1 per 318 persons. **Physicians:** 1 per 1,543 persons. **Infant mortality** (per 1,000 pop. 1992): 18.

Education (1988): **Literacy:** 97%. **School:** Compulsory for 8 years.

Major International Organizations: UN (GATT, IMF, WHO), Commonwealth of Nations, OAS.

High Commission: 42 Belgrave Sq, London SW1X 8NT; 071-245 9351.

Columbus sighted Trinidad in 1498. A British possession since 1802, Trinidad and Tobago won independence Aug. 31, 1962. It became a republic in 1976. The People's National Movement party has held control of the government since 1956.

The nation is one of the most prosperous in the Caribbean. Oil production has increased with offshore finds. Middle Eastern oil is refined and exported, mostly to the U.S.

In July 1990, some 120 Moslem extremists captured the parliament building and TV station and took about 50 hostages including Prime Minister Arthur Robinson, who was beaten, shot in the legs, and tied to explosives. After a 6-day siege, the rebels surrendered.

Tunisia

Republic of Tunisia

al Jumhuriyah at-Tunisiyah

People: Population (1992 est.): 8,445,000. **Age distrib.** (%) 0–14: 39.0; 15–59: 54.2; 60+: 6.8. **Pop. density:** 133 per sq. mi. **Ethnic groups:** Arab 98%. **Languages:** Arabic (official), French. **Religion:** Muslim 99%.

Geography: Area: 63,170 sq. mi., about the size of England, Wales and N. Ireland combined. **Location:** On N coast of Africa. **Neighbors:** Algeria on W, Libya on E. **Topography:** The N is wooded and fertile. The central coastal plains are given to grazing and orchards. The S is arid, approaching Sahara Desert. **Capital:** Tunis. **Cities** (1984 est.) Tunis 1,000,000, Sfax 475,000.

Government: Type: Republic. **Head of state:** Pres. Gen. Zine al-Abidine Ben Ali; b. Sept 3, 1936; in office Nov. 7, 1987. **Head of government:** Prime Min. Hamed Karoui; in office Sept. 27, 1989. **Local divisions:** 23 governorates. **Defense** (1992): 5.0% of GDP.

Economy: Industries: Food processing, textiles, oil products, mining, construction materials. **Chief crops:** Grains, dates, olives, citrus fruits, figs, vegetables, grapes. **Minerals:** Phosphates, iron, oil, lead, zinc. **Crude oil reserves** (1987): 1.7 bln. bbls. **Arable land:** 20%. **Livestock** (1990): 5.0 mln. sheep; 1 mln. goats. **Fish catch** (1990): 95,000 metric tons. **Electricity prod.** (1991): 4.2 bln. kWh. **Labor force:** 25% agric.; 34% industry; 40% serv.

Finance: Monetary unit: Dinar (Mar. 1993: 1.00 = $1 US). **Gross domestic product** (1991): $10.9 bln. **Per capita GDP:** $1,320. **Imports** (1992): $6.4 bln.; partners: EC 68%. **Exports** (1992): $4.0 bln.; partners: EC 73%. **Tourism** (1990): $953 mln. receipts. **National budget** (1992): $5.4 bln. expenditures. **International reserves less gold** (Mar. 1993): $730 mln. **Gold:** 215,000 oz t. **Consumer prices** (change in 1992): 5.4%.

Transport: Railroads (1990): 1,343 mi. long. **Motor vehicles** (1989): 321,000 passenger cars, 208,000 comm. vehicles. **Civil aviation** (1990): 1.5 bln. passenger-km; 5 airports. **Chief ports:** Tunis, Sfax, Bizerte.

Communications: Television sets: 1 per 13 persons. **Radios:** 1 per 4.7 persons. **Telephones:** 1 per 24 persons. **Daily newspaper circ.** (1991): 28 per 1,000 pop.

Health: Life expectancy at birth (1992): 70 male; 74 female. **Births** (per 1,000 pop. 1992): 26. **Deaths** (per 1,000 pop. 1992): 5. **Natural increase:** 2.1%. **Hospital beds:** 1 per 506 persons. **Physicians:** 1 per 1,834 persons. **Infant mortality** (per 1,000 pop. live births 1992): 38.

Education (1990): **Literacy:** 62%. **School:** Compulsory for 8 years; attendance 85%.

Major International Organizations: UN, Arab League, OAU.

Embassy: 29 Princes Gate, London SW7 1QG; 071-584 8117.

Site of ancient Carthage, and a former Barbary state under the suzerainty of Turkey, Tunisia became a protectorate of France under a treaty signed May 12, 1881. The nation became independent Mar. 20, 1956, and ended the monarchy the following year.

Tunisia has actively repressed Islamic fundamentalism.

Turkey

Republic of Turkey

Turkiye Cumhuriyeti

People: Population (1992 est.): 59,640,000. **Age distrib.** (%): 0–14: 38.5; 15–59: 54.9; 60+: 6.6. **Pop. density:** 197 per sq. mi. **Urban** (1990): 61%. **Ethnic groups:** Turks 80%, Kurds 17%. **Languages:** Turkish (official), Kurdish, Arabic. **Religion:** Muslim 98%.

Geography: Area: 301,381 sq. mi., 3 times the size of GB. **Location:** Occupies Asia Minor, between Mediterranean and Black Seas. **Neighbors:** Bulgaria, Greece on W, Georgia, Armenia on N, Iran on E, Iraq, Syria on S. **Topography:** Central Turkey has wide plateaus, with hot, dry summers and cold winters. High mountains ring the interior on all but W, with more than 20 peaks over 10,000 ft. Rolling plains are in W; mild, fertile coastal plains are in S, W. **Capital:** Ankara. **Cities** (1990 est.): Istanbul 6,700,000; Ankara 2,553,000; Izmir 1,700,000; Adana 931,000.

Government: Type: Republic. **Head of state:** Pres. Suleyman Demirel; in office May 16, 1993. **Head of government:** Prime Min. Tansu Ciller; in office July 5, 1993. **Local divisions:** 73 provinces. **Defense** (1992): 3.5% of GDP.

Economy: Industries: Iron, steel, machinery, metal prods., cars, processed foods. **Chief crops:** Tobacco, cereals, cotton, barley, corn, fruits, potatoes, sugar beets. **Minerals:** Chromium, mercury, boron, copper, coal. **Crude oil reserves** (1987): 139 mln. bbls. **Other resources:** Wool, silk, forests. **Arable land:** 30%. **Livestock** (1991): 12.0 mln. cattle; 31 mln. sheep. **Fish catch** (1989): 457,000 metric tons. **Electricity prod.** (1991): 44 bln. kWh. **Crude steel prod.** (1991): 9.2 mln. metric tons. **Labor force:** 56% agric.; 14% ind. and comm.; 29% serv.

Finance: Monetary unit: Lira (Aug. 1993: 11,366 = $1 US). **Gross domestic product** (1991): $198 bln. **Per capita GDP:** $3,400. **Imports** (1991): $21.0 bln.; partners: EC 49%, U.S. 7%. **Exports** (1991): $13.5 bln.; partners: EC 49%. **Tourism** (1991): $2.5 bln. receipts. **National budget** (1992): $49.7 bln. expenditures. **International reserves less gold** (Feb. 1993): $6.4 bln. **Gold:** 4.0 mln. oz t. **Consumer prices** (change in 1992): 70.1%.

Transport: Railroads (1991): 5,238 mi. long. **Motor vehicles** (1990): 1.6 mln. passenger cars, 584,000 comm. vehicles. **Civil aviation** (1991): 4.2 bln. passenger-km; 12 airports with scheduled flights. **Chief ports:** Istanbul, Izmir, Mersin, Samsun.

Communications: Television sets: 1 per 5 persons. **Radios:** 1 per 7.8 persons. **Telephones:** 1 per 7 persons.

Health: Life expectancy at birth (1992): 68 male; 72 female. **Births** (per 1,000 pop. 1992): 28. **Deaths** (per 1,000 pop. 1992): 6. **Natural increase:** 2.2%. **Hospital beds:** 1 per 465 persons. **Physicians:** 1 per 1,108 persons. **Infant mortality** (per 1,000 live births 1992): 54.

Education (1990): **Literacy:** 81%. **School:** Compulsory for 6 years; attendance 95%.

Major International Organizations: UN (GATT, WHO, IMF), NATO, OECD, EC.

Embassy: 43 Belgrave Sq, London SW1X 8PA; 071-235 5252.

Ancient inhabitants of Turkey were among the world's first agriculturalists. Such civilizations as the Hittite, Phrygian, and Lydian flourished in Asiatic Turkey (Asia Minor), as did much of Greek civilization. After the fall of Rome in the 5th century, Constantinople was the capital of the Byzantine Empire for 1,000 years. It fell in 1453 to Ottoman Turks, who ruled a vast empire for over 400 years.

Just before World War I, Turkey, or the Ottoman Empire, ruled what is now Syria, Lebanon, Iraq, Jordan, Israel, Saudi Arabia, Yemen, and islands in the Aegean Sea.

Turkey joined Germany and Austria in World War I and its defeat resulted in loss of much territory and fall of the sultanate. A republic was declared Oct. 29, 1923. The Caliphate (spiritual leadership of Islam) was renounced 1924.

Long embroiled with Greece over Cyprus, off Turkey's south coast, Turkey invaded the island July 20, 1974, after Greek officers seized the Cypriot government as a step toward unification with Greece. Turkey sought a new government for Cyprus, with Greek Cypriot and Turkish Cypriot zones. In reaction to Turkey's moves, the U.S. cut off military aid in 1975. Turkey, in turn, suspended the use of most U.S. bases. Aid was restored in 1978. There was a military takeover, Sept. 12, 1980.

Religious and ethnic tensions and active left and right extremists have caused endemic violence. Martial law, imposed in 1978, was lifted in 1984. The military formally transferred power to an elected parliament in 1983.

Turkey was a member of the Allied forces which ousted Iraq from Kuwait, 1991. In the aftermath of the war, millions of Kurdish refugees fled to Turkey's border to escape Iraqi forces.

Kurdish militants raided Turkish diplomatic missions in some 25 western European cities June 24, 1993. The militants were demanding an independent state for the Kurds.

Turkmenistan

Republic of Turkmenistan

People: Population (1992 est.): 3,838,000. **Pop. density:** 20 per sq. mi. **Urban** (1991): 46%. **Ethnic groups:** Turkmen 72%, Russian 9%, Uzbek 9%. **Languages:** Turkmen, Russian. **Religion:** Muslim 85%.

Geography: Area: 188,417 sq. mi., slightly smaller than the UK. **Neighbors:** Uzbekistan, Kazakhstan on N, NE, Afghanistan and Iran on S. The Kara Kum desert occupies 80% of the area. **Capital:** Ashkhabad, pop. (1991) 416,000.

Government: Type: Republic. **Head of state:** Pres. Saparmurad Niyazov. **Head of government:** Prime Min. Khan A. Akhmedov. **Local divisions:** 5 regions.

Economy: Industries: Mining, textiles. **Chief crops:** Grain, cotton, grapes. **Minerals:** Coal, sulphur, salt. **Livestock** (1990): 5.0 mln. Sheep. **Electricity prod.** (1991): 14.9 bln. kWh.

Finance: Monetary unit: Rouble. **Imports** (1990): $970 mln. **Exports** (1990): $239 mln.

Transport: Railroads (1990): 1,317 mi. long.

Communications: Telephones: 1 per 15 persons.

Health: Life expectancy at birth (1992): 59 male; 66 female. **Births** (per 1,000 pop. 1992): 36. **Deaths** (per 1,000 pop. 1992): 9. **Hospital beds:** 1 per 86 persons. **Physicians:** 1 per 274 persons. **Infant mortality** (per 1,000 live births 1992): 94.

Major International Organizations: UN, CIS.

The region has been inhabited by Turkmen tribes since the 10th century. It became part of Russian Turkistan 1881, and a constituent republic of the USSR 1925. Turkmenistan declared independence Oct. 27, 1991, and became an independent state when the Soviet Union disbanded Dec. 26, 1991.

Power rests mostly with the former Communist Party apparatus.

Tuvalu

People: Population (1992 est.): 9,494. **Pop. density:** 949 per sq. mi. **Ethnic group:** Polynesian. **Languages:** Tuvaluan, English. **Religion:** Mainly Protestant.

Geography: Area: 10 sq. mi., less than half the size of Guernsey. **Location:** 9 islands forming a NW-SE chain 360 mi. long in the SW Pacific O. **Neighbors:** Nearest are Samoa on SE, Fiji on S. **Topography:** The islands are all low-lying atolls, nowhere rising more than 15 ft. above sea level, composed of coral reefs. **Capital:** Funafuti, pop. (1985) 2,800.

Government: Head of state: Queen Elizabeth II, represented by Gov.-Gen. Toaripi Lauti; in office Oct. 1, 1990. **Head of government:** Prime Min. Bikenibeu Paeniu; in office Oct. 16, 1989. **Local divisions:** 8 island councils on the permanently inhabited islands.

Economy: Industries: Copra. **Chief crop:** Coconuts. **Labor force:** Approx. 1,500 Tuvaluans work overseas in the Gilberts' phosphate industry, or as overseas seamen.

Finance: Monetary unit: Australian dollar.

Transport: Chief port: Funafuti.

Health (including former Gilbert Is.): **Life expectancy at birth** (1992): 61 male; 64 female. **Births** (per 1,000 pop. 1992): 29. **Deaths** (per 1,000 pop. 1992): 10. **Natural increase:** 1.9%. **Infant mortality** (per 1,000 live births 1991): 33.

Education (1990): **Literacy:** 96%.

The Ellice Islands separated from the British Gilbert and Ellice Islands colony, 1975, and became independent Tuvalu Oct. 1, 1978.

Uganda

Republic of Uganda

People: Population (1992 est.): 19,386,000. **Age distrib.** (%): 0–14: 48.5; 15–59: 47.3; 60+: 4.2. **Pop. density:** 207 per sq. mi. **Urban** (1991): 11%. **Ethnic groups:** Bantu, Nilotic, Nilo-Hamitic, Sudanic tribes. **Languages:** English (official), Luganda, Swahili. **Religions:** Christian 63%, Muslim 6%, traditional beliefs.

Geography: Area: 93,354 sq. mi., slightly smaller than the UK. **Location:** In E. Central Africa. **Neighbors:** Sudan on N, Zaire on W, Rwanda, Tanzania on S, Kenya on E. **Topography:** Most of Uganda is a high plateau 3,000-6,000 ft. high, with high Ruwenzori range in W (Mt. Margherita 16,750 ft.), volcanoes in SW, NE is arid, W and SW rainy. Lakes Victoria, Edward, Albert form much of borders. **Capital:** Kampala, pop. (1991) 773,000.

Government: Type: Republic. **Head of state:** Pres. Yoweri Kaguta Museveni; b. 1944; in office: Jan. 29, 1986. **Head of government:** Prime Min. George Cosmas Adyebo; in office: Jan. 22, 1991. **Local divisions:** 10 provinces. **Defense** (1989): 1.5% of GDP.

Economy: Chief crops: Coffee, cotton, tea, corn, bananas, sugar. **Minerals:** Copper, cobalt. **Arable land:** 23%. **Livestock** (1991): 5.2 mln. cattle; 3.3 mln. goats; 1.9 mln. sheep. **Fish catch** (1990): 245,000 metric tons. **Electricity prod.** (1991): 312 mln. kWh. **Labor force:** 90% agric.

Finance: Monetary unit: Shilling (Mar. 1993: 1,217 = $1 US). **Gross domestic product** (1991): $5.6 bln. **Per capita GDP:** $300. **Imports** (1991): $196 mln.; partners: Kenya 24%, U.K. 17%. **Exports** (1991): $200 mln.; partners: U.S. 14%, U.K. 12%, Neth. 15%. **National budget** (1989): $790 mln. expenditures. **International reserves less gold** (Jan. 1993): $59 mln. **Consumer prices** (change in 1992): 52.4%.

Transport: Motor vehicles (1990): 35,000 passenger cars, 6,000 comm. vehicles.

Communications: Television sets: 1 per 191 persons. **Radios:** 1 per 5.1 persons. **Telephones:** 1 per 286 persons. **Daily newspaper circ.** (1990): 2 per 1,000 pop.

Health: Life expectancy at birth (1992): 50 male; 52 female. **Births** (per 1,000 pop. 1992): 51. **Deaths** (per 1,000 pop. 1992): 15. **Natural increase:** 3.6%. **Hospital beds:** 1 per 817 persons. **Physicians:** 1 per 20,000 persons. **Infant mortality** (per 1,000 live births 1992): 91.

Education (1989): **Literacy:** 52%. **School:** About 50% attend primary school.

Major International Organizations: UN (GATT, WHO, IMF), OAU, Commonwealth of Nations.

High Commission: Uganda House, 58 Trafalgar Sq, London WC2N 5DX; 071-839 5783.

Britain obtained a protectorate over Uganda in 1894. The country became independent Oct. 9, 1962, and a republic within the Commonwealth a year later. In 1967, the traditional kingdoms, including the powerful Buganda state, were abolished and the central government strengthened.

Gen. Idi Amin seized power from Prime Min. Milton Obote in 1971. As many as 300,000 of his opponents were reported killed in subsequent years. Amin was named president for life in 1976.

In 1972 Amin expelled nearly all of Uganda's 45,000 Asians. In 1973 the U.S. withdrew all diplomatic personnel.

Amid worsening economic and domestic crises, Uganda's troops exchanged invasion attacks with long-standing foe Tanzania, 1978 to 1979. Tanzanian forces, coupled with Ugandan exiles and rebels, ended the dictatorial rule of Amin, Apr. 11, 1979.

Ukraine

Ukrayina

People: Population (1992 est.): 51,994,000. **Age distrib.** (%): 0-19: 24.8; 20-59: 62.1; 60+: 13.0. **Pop. density:** 223 per sq. mi. **Urban** (1991): 68% **Ethnic groups:** Ukrainian 73%, Russian 22%. **Language:** Ukrainian (official). **Religions:** Orthodox 76%, Ukrainian Catholic 13.5%, Muslim 8.2%.

Geography: Area: 233,100 sq. mi., twice the size of the British Isles. **Location:** In SE Europe. **Neighbors:** Belarus on N, Russia on NE and E, Moldova and Romania on SW, Hungary, Slovakia and Poland on W. **Topography:** Part of the E. European plain. Mountainous areas include the Carpathians in the SW and the Crimean chain in the S. Arable black soil constitutes a large part of the country. **Capital:** Kyyiv. **Cities** (1991 est.): Kyyiv 2,637,000; Kharkiv 1,622,000; Donetsk 1,121,000; Odesa 1,104,000; Dnipropetrovsk 1,100,000.

Government: Type: Constitutional republic. **Head of state:** Pres. Leonid M. Kravchuk; b. 1934; in office Dec. 5, 1991. **Head of government:** Prime Min. Leonid Kuchma, b. 1932; in office Oct. 13, 1992. **Local divisions:** 24 provinces (oblasts), 1 autonomous province.

Economy: Industries: Steel, chemicals, machinery, vehicles, cement. **Chief crops:** Grains, sugar beets, potatoes. **Minerals:** Iron, manganese, chromium, copper, coal, lead, gold, nickel, potassium salts. **Other resources:** Forests. **Arable land:** 56%. **Fish catch** (1990): 550,000 metric tons. **Electricity prod.** (1990): 76.2 bln. kWh. **Crude steel prod.** (1990): 43.1 mln. metric tons. **Labor force:** 19% agric.; 41% ind. & comm.; 28% services.

Finance: Monetary unit: Karbovanet (May 1993: 3,000 = $1 US). **Gross national product** (1990): $47.6 bln. **Per capita income** (1987): $2,500. **Imports** (1990): $16.7 bln. **Exports** (1990): $13.5 bln. **National budget** (1990): $8 bln. expenditures.

Transport: Railroads (1990): 7.5 bln. passenger-km. **Civil aviation** (1990): 16.1 bln. passenger-km; 20 airports. **Chief ports:** Odessa, Kherson, Mykolayiv, Sevastopil, Berdiansk.

Communications: Television sets: 1 per 3 persons. **Radios:** 1 per 4 persons. **Daily newspaper circ.** (1990): 202 per 1,000 pop.

Health: Life expectancy at birth (1992): 65 male; 75 female. **Births** (per 1,000 pop. 1992): 14. **Deaths** (per 1,000 pop. 1992): 12. **Hospital beds:** 1 per 74 persons. **Physicians:** 1 per 229 persons. **Infant mortality** (per 1,000 live births 1992): 22.

Education (1990): **Literacy:** 99%.

Major International Organizations: UN, CIS.

The ancient ancestors of the Ukrainians, the Trypilians, flourished along the Dnipro River, Ukraine's main artery, from 6000–1000 BC. The Slavic ancestors of the Ukrainians inhabited modern Ukrainian territory well before the first century AD.

The princes of Kyyiv established a strong state called Kyyvian Rus in the 9th century. A strong dynasty was established, with ties to virtually all major European royal families. St. Volodymyr the Great, ruler of Kyyivan Ukraine, accepted Christianity as the national faith in 988. At the crossroads of major European trade routes, Kyyvian Rus reached its zenith during the reign of Iaroslav the Wise (1019–1054). While directly absorbing most of the Asian invasion of Europe in the 13th century, the Ukrainian state slowly disintegrated and was divided mainly between Russia and Poland.

The Ukrainian Cossack State, founded in the late 16th century, waged numerous wars of liberation against the occupiers of Ukraine: Russia, Poland, and Turkey. By the late 18th century, Ukrainian independence was lost. Ukraine's neighbors once again divided its territory. At the turn of the last century, Ukraine was occupied by 2 colonial powers, Russia and Austria–Hungary.

An independent Ukrainian National Republic was proclaimed on Jan. 22, 1918. In 1921 Ukraine's neighbors occupied and divided Ukrainian territory. In 1932–33 the Soviet government engineered a man-made famine in eastern Ukraine, resulting in the deaths of 7–10 million Ukrainians.

In March 1939 independent Carpatho–Ukraine was the first European state to wage war against Nazi-led aggression in the region. During WW2 the Ukrainian nationalist underground and its Ukrainian Insurgent Army (UPA) fought both Nazi German and Soviet forces. The restoration of Ukrainian independence was declared on June 30, 1941. Over 5 million Ukrainians lost their lives during the war. With the reoccupation of Ukraine by Soviet troops in 1944 came a renewed wave of mass arrests, executions and deportations of Ukrainians.

The world's worst nuclear power plant disaster occurred in Chernobyl, Ukraine, in April 1986.

Ukrainian independence was restored in 1991 with the dissolution of the Soviet Union. In a landslide national referendum, over 90% of Ukraine's population voted for independence on Dec. 1, 1991.

Ukraine suffered economic hardships in 1993; inflation hit 170% in the first quarter, and the GDP fell 10 per cent from the previous year.

United Arab Emirates

Ittihād al-Imarat al-Arabiyah

People: Population (1992 est.): 2,522,000. **Pop. density:** 78 per sq. mi. **Ethnic groups:** Arab, Iranian, Pakistani, Indian. **Languages:** Arabic (official), several others. **Religions:** Muslim 96%, Christian, Hindu.

Geography: Area: 32,000 sq. mi., the size of Scotland. **Location:** On the S shore of the Persian Gulf. **Neighbors:** Qatar on N, Saudi Ar. on W, S, Oman on E. **Topography:** A barren, flat coastal plain gives way to uninhabited sand dunes on the S. Hajar Mtns. are on E. **Capital:** Abu Dhabi. **Cities** (1990 est.): Abu Dhabi 722,000; Dubavy 266,000.

Government: Type: Federation of emirates. **Head of state:** Pres. Zaid ibn Sultan an-Nahayan b. 1923; in office Dec. 2, 1971. **Head of government:** Prime Min. Sheikh Maktum ibn Rashid al-Maktum; in office Nov. 20, 1990. **Local divisions:** 7 autonomous emirates: Abu Dhabi, Ajman, Dubai, Fujaira, Ras al-Khaimah, Sharjah, Umm al-Qaiwain. **Defense** (1989): 6.8% of GDP.

Economy: Chief crops: Vegetables, dates, limes. **Minerals:** Oil. **Crude oil reserves** (1991): 66 bln. barrels. **Arable land:** 1%. **Electricity prod.** (1991): 17.0 bln. kWh. **Labor force:** 5% agric.; 85% ind. and commerce; 5% serv.; 5% govt.

Finance: Monetary unit: Dirham (July 1993: 3,67 = $1 US). **Gross domestic product** (1989): $28.4 bln. **Per capita GDP:** $12,100. **Imports** (1992): $13.7 bln.; partners: Jap. 14%, UK 11%, Ger. 6%. **Exports** (1990): $21.3 bln.; partners: Jap. 36%. **International reserves less gold** (Feb. 1993): $5.5 bln. **Gold:** 797,000 oz t.

Transport: Motor vehicles (1990): 302,000 passenger cars; 157,000 comm. vehicles. **Civil aviation** (1991): 3.8 bln. passenger-km; 4 airports with scheduled flights. **Chief ports:** Dubavy, Abu Dhabi.

Communications: Television sets: 1 per 12 persons. **Radios:** 1 per 4.7 persons. **Telephones:** 1 per 4.3 persons.

Health: Life expectancy at birth (1992): 70 male, 74 female. **Hospital beds:** 1 per 442 persons. **Physicians:** 1 per 1,057 persons. **Infant mortality** (per 1,000 live births 1992): 23%.

Education (1989): **Literacy:** 68%. **School:** Compulsory ages 6-12.

Major International Organizations: UN (World Bank, IMF, ILO), Arab League, OPEC.

Embassy: 30 Princes Gate, London SW7 1PT; 071-581 3434.

The 7 "Trucial Sheikdoms" gave Britain control of defense and foreign relations in the 19th century. They merged to become an independent state Dec. 2, 1971.

The Abu Dhabi Petroleum Co. was fully nationalized in 1975. Oil revenues have given the UAE one of the highest per capita GDPs in the world. International banking has grown in recent years.

United Kingdom of Great Britain and Northern Ireland

People: Population (1992 est.): 57,797,800. **Age distrib.** (%): 0–14: 19.2; 15–59: 60.1; 60+: 20.7. **Pop. density:** 613 per sq. mi. **Urban** (1990): 90.0%. **Ethnic groups:** English 81.5%, Scottish 9.6%, Irish 2.4%, Welsh 1.9%, Ulster 1.8%; West Indian, Indian, Pakistani over 2%; others. **Languages:** English, Welsh spoken in western Wales. **Religions:** Church of England, Roman Catholic.

Geography: Area: 94,249 sq. mi. **Location:** Off the NW coast of Europe, across English Channel, Strait of Dover, and North Sea. **Neighbors:** Ireland to W, France to SE. **Topography:** England is mostly rolling land, rising to uplands of southern Scotland; Lowlands are in center of Scotland, granite Highlands are in N. Coast is heavily indented, especially on W. British Isles have milder climate than N Europe, due to the Gulf Stream, and ample rainfall. **Capital:** London. **Cities** (1991): London 6,378,600; Birmingham 934,900; Glasgow 689,210; Leeds 674,400; Sheffield 500,500; Bradford 449,100; Liverpool 448,300; Edinburgh 434,520; Manchester 397,400; Bristol 370,300.

Government: Type: Constitutional monarchy. **Head of state:** Queen Elizabeth II; b. Apr. 21, 1926; in office Feb. 6, 1952. **Head of government:** Prime Min. John Major; b. Mar. 29, 1943; in office Nov. 28, 1990. **Local divisions:** England and Wales: 54 non-metro counties, 6 metro counties, Greater London; Scotland: 9 regions, 3 island areas; N. Ireland: 6 counties divided into 26 districts. **Defense** (1991): 4.3% of GDP.

Economy: Industries: Steel, metals, vehicles, shipbuilding, banking, textiles, chemicals, electronics, aircraft, machinery, distilling. **Chief crops:** Grains, sugar beets, fruits, vegetables. **Minerals:** Coal, tin, oil, gas, limestone, iron, salt, clay. **Crude oil reserves** (1991): 4.0 bln. bbls. **Arable land:** 30%. **Livestock** (1991): 11.8 mln. cattle; 7.3 mln. pigs; 29.9 mln. sheep. **Fish catch** (1990): 803,000 metric tons. **Electricity prod.** (1991): 316 bln. kWh. **Crude steel prod.** (1991): 16.4 mln. metric tons. **Labor force:** 2.0% agric.; 26% manuf. & eng., 60% services.

Finance: Monetary unit: Pound (Sep. 1993: 0.67 = $1 US). **Gross domestic product** (1991): $915 bln. **Per capita GDP:** $15,900. **Imports** (1992): $221 bln. partners: EC 52%, U.S. 10%. **Exports** (1992): $190 bln.; partners: EC 53%, U.S. 13%. **Tourism** (1991): $18.8 bln. receipts. **National budget** (1992): $469 bln. expenditures. **International reserves less gold** (Mar. 1993): $38 bln. **Gold:** 19.0 mln. oz t. **Consumer prices** (change in 1992): 3.7%.

Transport: Railroads (1991): 23,518 mi. long. **Motor vehicles:** (1991): 19.7 mln. passenger cars, 2.7 mln. comm. vehicles. **Civil aviation** (1990): 79.5 bln. passenger-km; 56 airports with scheduled flights. **Chief ports:** London, Liverpool, Glasgow, Southampton, Cardiff, Belfast.

Communications: Television sets: 1 per 3 persons. **Radios:** 1 per person. **Telephones:** 1 per 1.9 persons. **Daily newspaper circ.** (1990): 388 per 1,000 pop.

Health: Life expectancy at birth (1992): 73 male; 79 female. **Births** (per 1,000 pop. 1992): 14.0. **Deaths** (per 1,000 pop. 1992): 11. **Natural increase:** 0.3%. **Hospital beds:** 1 per 138 persons. **Physicians:** 1 per 611 persons. **Infant mortality** (per 1,000 live births 1992): 8.

Education (1991): **Literacy:** 99%. **School:** Compulsory for 11 years; attendance 99%.

Major International Organizations: UN and all its specialized agencies, NATO, EC, OECD.

The United Kingdom of Great Britain and Northern Ireland comprises England, Wales, Scotland, and Northern Ireland.

Queen and Royal Family. The ruling sovereign is Elizabeth II of the House of Windsor, born Apr. 21, 1926, elder daughter of King George VI. She succeeded to the throne Feb. 6, 1952, and was crowned June 2, 1953. She was married Nov. 20, 1947, to Lt. Philip Mountbatten, born June 10, 1921, former Prince of Greece. He was created Duke of Edinburgh, Earl of Merioneth, and Baron Greenwich, and given the style H.R.H., Nov. 19, 1947; he was given the title Prince of the United Kingdom and Northern Ireland Feb. 22, 1957. Prince Charles Philip Arthur George, born Nov. 14, 1948, is the Prince of Wales and heir apparent. His son, William Philip Arthur Louis, born June 21, 1982, is second in line to the throne.

Parliament is the legislative governing body for the United Kingdom, with certain powers over dependent units. It consists of 2 houses. The **House of Lords** includes 763 hereditary and 314 life peers and peeresses, certain judges, 2 archbishops and 24 bishops of the Church of England. Total membership is over 1,000. The **House of Commons** has 650 members, who are elected by direct ballot and divided as follows: England 516; Wales 36; Scotland 71; Northern Ireland 12.

Resources and Industries. Great Britain's major occupations are manufacturing and trade. Metals and metal-using industries contribute more than 50% of the exports. Of about 60 million acres of land in England, Wales and Scotland, 46 million are farmed, of which 17 million are arable, the rest pastures.

Large oil and gas fields have been found in the North Sea. Commercial oil production began in 1975. There are large deposits of coal.

Britain imports all its cotton, rubber and sulphur, about 80% of its wool, half of its food and iron ore, also certain amounts of paper, tobacco and chemicals. Manufactured goods made from these basic materials have been exported since the industrial age began. Main exports are machinery, chemicals, woolen and synthetic textiles, clothing, autos and trucks, iron and steel, locomotives, ships, jet aircraft, farm machinery, drugs, radio, TV, radar and navigation equipment, scientific instruments, arms, whisky.

Religion and Education. The Church of England is Protestant Anglican. The Queen is its temporal head, with rights of appointments to archbishoprics, bishoprics, and other offices. There are 2 provinces, Canterbury and York, each headed by an archbishop. The most famous church is Westminster Abbey (1050-1760), site of coronations, tombs of Elizabeth I, Mary of Scots, kings, poets, and of the Unknown Warrior.

The most celebrated British universities are Oxford and Cambridge, each dating from the 13th century. There are about 75 other universities, 34 of which converted from polytechnic status in autumn 1992.

History. Britain was part of the continent of Europe until about 6,000 BC, but migration of peoples across the English Channel continued long afterward. Celts arrived 2,500 to 3,000 years ago. Their language survives in Welsh and Gaelic enclaves.

England was added to the Roman Empire in AD 43. After the withdrawal of Roman legions in 410, waves of Jutes, Angles, and Saxons arrived from German lands. They contended with Danish raiders for control from the 8th to 11th centuries.

The last successful invasion was by French-speaking Normans in 1066, who united the country with their dominions in France.

Opposition by nobles to royal authority forced King John to sign the Magna Carta in 1215, a guarantee of rights and the rule of law. In the ensuing decades, the foundations of the parliamentary system were laid.

English dynastic claims to large parts of France led to the Hundred Years War, 1338-1453, and the defeat of England. A long civil war, the War of the Roses, lasted 1455-85, and ended with the establishment of the powerful Tudor monarchy. A distinct English civilization flourished. The economy prospered over long periods of domestic peace unmatched in continental Europe. Religious independence was secured when the Church of England was separated from the authority of the Pope in 1534.

Under Queen Elizabeth I, England became a major naval power, leading to the founding of colonies in the New World and the expansion of trade with Europe and the Orient. Scotland was united with England when James VI of Scotland was crowned James I of England in 1603.

A struggle between Parliament and the Stuart kings led to a bloody civil war, 1642-49, and the establishment of a republic under the Puritan Oliver Cromwell. The monarchy was restored in 1660, but the "Glorious Revolution" of 1688 confirmed the sovereignty of Parliament: a Bill of Rights was granted 1689.

In the 18th century, parliamentary rule was strengthened. Technological and entrepreneurial innovations led to the Industrial Revolution. The 13 North American colonies were lost, but replaced by growing empires in Canada and India. Britain's role in the defeat of Napoleon, 1815, strengthened its position as the leading world power.

The extension of the franchise in 1832 and 1867, the formation of trade unions, and the development of universal public education were among the drastic social changes which accompanied the spread of industrialization and urbanization in the 19th century. Large parts of Africa and Asia were added to the empire during the reign of Queen Victoria, 1837-1901.

Though victorious in World War I, Britain suffered huge casualties and economic dislocation. Ireland became independent in 1921, and independence movements became active in India and other colonies.

The country suffered major bombing damage in World War II, but held out against Germany singlehandedly for a year after the fall of France in 1940.

Industrial growth continued in the postwar period, but Britain lost its leadership position to other powers. Labour governments passed socialist programs nationalizing some basic industries and expanding social security. Later Tory governments tried to increase the role of private enterprise.

The UK supported the UN resolutions against Iraq and sent military forces to the Persian Gulf war.

Wales

The Principality of Wales in western Britain has an area of 8,305 sq. mi. and a population (1991 cen.) of 2,798,000. Cardiff is the capital, pop. (1991 est.) 277,000.

England and Wales are administered as a unit. Less than 20% of the population of Wales speak both English and Welsh; about 32,000 speak only Welsh. A 1979 referendum rejected, 4-1, the creation of an elected Welsh Assembly.

Early Anglo-Saxon invaders drove Celtic peoples into the mountains of Wales, terming them Waelise (Welsh, or foreign). There they developed a distinct nationality. Members of the ruling house of Gwynedd in the 13th century fought England but were crushed, 1283. Edward of Caernarvon, son of Edward I of England, was created Prince of Wales, 1301.

Scotland

Scotland, a kingdom now united with England and Wales in Great Britain, occupies the northern 37% of the main British island, and the Hebrides, Orkney, Shetland and smaller islands. Length, 275 mi., breadth approx. 150 mi., area, 30,987 sq. mi., population (1991 cen.) 4,957,000.

The Lowlands, a belt of land approximately 60 mi. wide from the Firth of Clyde to the Firth of Forth, divide the farming region of the Southern Uplands from the granite Highlands of the North, contain 75% of the population and most of the industry. The Highlands, famous for hunting and fishing, have been opened to industry by many hydroelectric power stations.

Edinburgh, pop. (1991 est.) 438,232, is the capital. Glasgow, pop. (1991 est.) 725,100, is Britain's greatest industrial center. It is a shipbuilding complex on the Clyde and an ocean port. Aberdeen, pop. (1991 est.) 201,000, NE of Edinburgh, is a major port, center of granite industry, fish processing, and North Sea oil exploitation. Dundee, pop. (1991 est.) 166,000, NE of Edinburgh, is an industrial and fish processing center. About 90,000 persons speak Gaelic as well as English.

History. Scotland was called Caledonia by the Romans, who battled early Celtic tribes and occupied southern areas from the 1st to the 4th centuries. Missionaries from Britain introduced Christianity in the 4th century; St. Columba, an Irish monk, converted most of Scotland in the 6th century.

The Kingdom of Scotland was founded in 1018. William Wallace and Robert Bruce both defeated English armies 1297 and 1314, respectively.

In 1603 James VI of Scotland, son of Mary, Queen of Scots, succeeded to the throne of England as James I, and effected the Union of the Crowns. In 1707 Scotland received representation in the British Parliament, resulting from the union of former separate Parliaments. Its executive in the British cabinet is the Secretary of State for Scotland. The growing Scottish National Party urges independence. A 1979 referendum on the creation of an elected Scotland Assembly was defeated.

Memorials of Robert Burns, Sir Walter Scott, John Knox and Mary, Queen of Scots draw many tourists, as do the beauties of the Trossachs, Loch Katrine, Loch Lomond and abbey ruins.

Industries. Engineering products are the most important industry, with growing emphasis on office machinery, autos, electronics and other consumer goods. Oil has been discovered offshore in the North Sea, stimulating on-shore support industries.

Scotland produces fine woolens, worsteds, tweeds, silks, fine linens and jute. It is known for its special breeds of cattle and sheep. Fisheries have large hauls of herring, cod and whiting. Whisky is the biggest export.

The Hebrides are a group of c. 500 islands, 100 inhabited, off the W coast. The Inner Hebrides include **Skye, Mull,** and **Iona,** the last famous for the arrival of St. Columba, AD 563. The Outer Hebrides include **Lewis** and **Harris.** Industries include sheep raising and weaving. The **Orkney Islands,** c. 90, are to the NE. The capital is Kirkwall, on Pomona Is. Fish curing, sheep raising and weaving are occupations. NE of the Orkneys are the 200 **Shetland Islands,** 24 inhabited, home of Shetland ponies. The Orkneys and Shetlands have become centers for the North Sea oil industry.

Northern Ireland

Six of the 9 counties of Ulster, the NE corner of Ireland, constitute Northern Ireland, with the parliamentary boroughs of Belfast and Londonderry. Area 5,452 sq. mi., 1991 cen. pop. 1,570,000, capital and chief industrial center, Belfast (1991 est.) 297,000.

Industries. Shipbuilding, including large tankers, has long been an important industry, centered in Belfast, the largest port. Linen manufacture is also important, along with apparel, rope, and twine. Growing diversification has added engineering products, synthetic fibers, and electronics. There are large numbers of cattle, pigs, and sheep, potatoes, poultry, and dairy foods are also produced.

Government. An act of the British Parliament, 1920, divided Northern from Southern Ireland, each with a parliament and government. When Ireland became a dominion, 1921, and later a republic, Northern Ireland chose to remain a part of the United Kingdom. It elects 12 members to the British House of Commons.

During 1968-69, large demonstrations were conducted by Roman Catholics who charged they were discriminated against in voting rights, housing, and employment. The Catholics, a minority comprising about a third of the population, demanded abolition of property qualifications for voting in local elections. Violence and terrorism intensified, involving branches of the Irish Republican Army (outlawed in the Irish Republic), Protestant groups, police, and British troops.

A succession of Northern Ireland prime ministers pressed reform programs but failed to satisfy extremists on both sides. Over 2,000 were killed in over 15 years of bombings and shootings through 1990, many in England itself. Britain suspended the Northern Ireland parliament Mar. 30, 1972, and imposed direct British rule. A coalition government was formed in 1973 when moderates won election to a new one-house Assembly. But a Protestant general strike overthrew the government in 1974 and direct rule was resumed.

The turmoil and agony of Northern Ireland was dramatized in 1981 by the deaths of 10 imprisoned Irish nationalist hunger strikers in Maze Prison near Belfast. The inmates had starved themselves to death in an attempt to achieve status as political prisoners, but the British government refused to yield to their demands. In 1985, the Hillsborough agreement gave the Rep. of Ireland a voice in the governing of Northern Ireland; the accord was strongly opposed by Ulster loyalists.

Education and Religion. Northern Ireland is 2/3 Protestant, 1/3 Roman Catholic. Education is compulsory through age 16.

Channel Islands

The Channel Islands, area 75 sq. mi., est. pop. (1986) 145,000, off the NW coast of France, the only parts of the one-time Dukedom of Normandy belonging to England, are **Jersey, Guernsey** and the dependencies of Guernsey — **Alderney, Brechou, Great Sark, Little Sark, Herm, Jethou and Lihou.** Jersey and Guernsey have separate legal existences and lieutenant governors named by the Crown. The islands were the only British soil occupied by German troops in World War II.

Isle of Man

The Isle of Man, area 221 sq. mi., 1991 cen. pop. 69,788, is in the Irish Sea, 20 mi. from Scotland, 30 mi. from Cumberland. It is rich in lead and iron. The island has its own laws and a lieutenant governor appointed by the Crown. The Tynwald (legislature) consists of the Legislative Council, partly elected, and House of Keys, elected. Capital: Douglas. Farming, tourism, fishing (kippers, scallops) are chief occupations. Man is famous for the Manx tail-less cat.

Gibraltar

Gibraltar, a dependency on the southern coast of Spain, guards the entrance to the Mediterranean. The Rock has been in British possession since 1704. It is 2.75 mi. long, 3/4 of a mi. wide and 1,396 ft. in height; a narrow isthmus connects it with the mainland. Est. pop. (1992), 29,651.

In 1966 Spain called on Britain to give "substantial sovereignty" of Gibraltar to Spain and imposed a partial blockade. In 1967, residents voted for remaining under Britain. A new constitution, May 30, 1969, gave an elected House of Assembly more control in domestic affairs. A UN General Assembly resolution requested Britain to end Gibraltar's colonial status by Oct. 1, 1996. No settlement has been reached.

British West Indies

Swinging in a vast arc from the coast of Venezuela NE, then N and NW toward Puerto Rico are the Leeward Islands, forming a coral and volcanic barrier sheltering the Caribbean from the open Atlantic. Many of the islands are self-governing British possessions. Universal suffrage was instituted 1951-54; ministerial systems were set up 1956-1960.

The **Leeward Islands** still associated with the UK are **Montserrat** (1987 pop. 11,600, area 32 sq. mi., capital Plymouth), the small **British Virgin Islands** (pop. 1991 cen.: 16,749), and **Anguilla** (pop. 1990 est.: 7,000), the most northerly of the Leeward Islands.

The three **Cayman Islands,** a dependency, lie S of Cuba, NW of Jamaica. Pop. 23,000 (1987), most of it on Grand Cayman. It is a free port; in the 1970s Grand Cayman became a tax-free refuge for foreign funds and branches of many Western banks were opened there. Total area 102 sq. mi., capital Georgetown.

The **Turks and Caicos Islands,** at the SE end of the Bahama Islands, are a separate possession. There are about 30 islands, only 6 inhabited, pop. (1990 cen.) 11,696, area 193 sq. mi., capital Grand Turk. Salt, crayfish and conch shells are the main exports.

Bermuda

Bermuda is a British dependency governed by a royal governor and an assembly, dating from 1620, the oldest legislative body among British dependencies. Capital is Hamilton.

Bermuda comprises 360 small islands of coral formation, 20 inhabited, totalling 20.6 sq. mi. in the western Atlantic, 580 mi. E of North Carolina. Pop., 1992 est., was 60,213 (about 61% of African descent). Density is high.

The U.S. has air and naval bases under long-term lease, and a NASA tracking facility.

Bermuda boasts many resort hotels. The government raises most revenue from import duties. Exports: petroleum products, medicine.

South Atlantic

Falkland Islands and Dependencies, a British dependency, lie 300 mi. E of the Strait of Magellan at the southern end of South America.

The Falklands, or Islas Malvinas, include about 200 islands, area 4,700 sq. mi., pop. (1991 cen.) 2,121. Sheep-grazing is the main industry; wool is the principal export. There are indications of large oil and gas deposits. The islands are also claimed by Argentina, though 97% of inhabitants are of British origin. Argentina invaded the islands Apr. 2, 1982. The British responded by sending a task force to the area, landing their main force on the Falklands, May 21, and forcing an Argentine surrender at Port Stanley, June 14.

British Antarctic Territory, south of 60°S lat., was made a separate colony in 1962 and comprises mainly the **South Shetland Islands,** the **South Orkneys** and **Graham's Land.** A chain of meteorological stations is maintained.

St. Helena, an island 1,200 mi. off the W coast of Africa and 1,800 E of South America, has 47 sq. mi. and est. pop. in 1985 of 5,400. Flax, lace and rope making are the chief industries. After Napoleon Bonaparte was defeated at Waterloo the Allies exiled him to St. Helena, where he lived from Oct. 16, 1815, to his death, May 5, 1821. Capital is Jamestown.

Tristan da Cunha is the principal of a group of islands of volcanic origin, total area 40 sq. mi., half way between the Cape of Good Hope and South America. A volcanic peak 6,760 ft. high erupted in 1961. The 262 inhabitants were removed to England, but most returned in 1963. The islands are dependencies of St. Helena.

Ascension is an island of volcanic origin, 34 sq. mi. in area, 700 mi. NW of St. Helena, through which it is administered. It is a communications relay center for Britain, and has a U.S. satellite tracking center. Est. pop., 1985, was 1,500, half of them communications workers. The island is noted for sea turtles.

Hong Kong

A Crown Colony at the mouth of the Canton R. in China, 90 mi. S of Canton. Its nucleus is Hong Kong Is., 35 1/2 sq. mi., acquired from China 1841, on which is located Victoria, the capital. Opposite is Kowloon Peninsula, 3 sq. mi., and Stonecutters Is., 1/4 sq. mi., added, 1860. An additional 355 sq. mi. known as the New Territories, a mainland area and islands, were leased from China, 1898, for 99 years. Britain and China, Dec. 19, 1984, signed an agreement under which Hong Kong would be allowed to keep its capitalist system for 50 years after 1997, the year that the 99-year lease will expire. Total area of the colony is 409 sq. mi., with a population, 1992 est., of 5.8 million, including fewer than 20,000 British. From 1949 to 1962 Hong Kong absorbed more than a million refugees from China.

Hong Kong harbour was long an important British naval station and one of the world's great trans-shipment ports.

Principal industries are textiles and apparel; also tourism, $4.9 bln. expenditures (1991), shipbuilding, iron and steel, fishing, cement, and small manufactures.

Spinning mills, among the best in the world, and low wages compete with textiles elsewhere and have resulted in the protective measures in some countries. Hong Kong also has a booming electronics industry.

British Indian Ocean Territory

Formed Nov. 1965, embracing islands formerly dependencies of Mauritius or Seychelles: the Chagos Archipelago (including Diego Garcia), Aldabra, Farquhar and Des Roches. The last 3 were transferred to the Seychelles, which became independent in 1976. Area 22 sq mi. No civilian population remains.

Pacific Ocean

Pitcairn Island is in the Pacific, halfway between South America and Australia. The island was discovered in 1767 by Carteret but was not inhabited until 23 years later when the mutineers of the Bounty landed there. The area is 1.7 sq. mi. and pop. 1991, was 59. It is a British colony and is administered by a British Representative in New Zealand and a local Council. The uninhabited islands of **Henderson, Ducie** and **Oeno** are in the Pitcairn group.

United States of America

People: Population (1993 est.): 256,561,239 (incl. 50 states and District of Columbia). **Age distrib.** (%): 0–14: 21.7; 15–59: 61.4; 60+: 16.9. **Pop. density:** 70 per sq. mi. **Urban** (1990): 76%.

Geography: 3,618,770 sq. mi. (incl. 50 states and D. of C.) about half the size of Russia. Vast central plain, mountains in west, hills and low mountains in east.

Government: Federal republic, strong democratic tradition. **Head of state:** Bill Clinton; b. Aug. 19, 1946; in office Jan. 20, 1993. **Administrative divisions:** 50 states and Dist. of Columbia. **Defense** (1991): 5.7% of GNP.

Economy: Minerals: Coal, copper, lead, molybdenum, phosphates, uranium, bauxite, gold, iron, mercury, nickel, potash, silver, tungsten, zinc. **Crude oil reserves** (1991): 26 bln. barrels. **Arable land:** 21%. **Livestock** (1991): 98 mln. cattle; 54 mln. pigs; 11.3 mln. sheep. **Fish catch** (1991): 4.3 mln. metric tons. **Electricity prod.** (1991): 2,822 bln. kWh. **Crude steel prod.** (1991): 79.2 mln. metric tons.

Finance: Gross domestic product (1991): $5.6 trl. **Per capita GDP:** $22,470. **Imports** (1992): $553 bln.; partners: Can. 17%, Jap. 20%, Mex. 6%. **Exports** (1992): $447 bln.; partners: Can. 22%, Jap. 12%, Mex. 6%, UK 5%. **Tourism** (1991): $45.5 bln. receipts. **International reserves less gold** (Mar. 1993): $63.3 bln. **Gold:** 261.8 mln. oz t. **Consumer prices** (change in 1992): 3.0%.

Transport: Railroads (1990): 144,000 mi. long. **Motor vehicles:** (1990): 143 mln. passenger cars, 45 mln. comm. vehicles. **Civil aviation** (1990): 751 bln. passenger-km; 834 airports with scheduled flights.

Communications: Television sets: 1 per 1.3 persons. **Radios:** 1 per 0.5 persons. **Telephones:** 1 per 1.9 persons. **Daily newspaper circ.** (1990): 255 per 1,000 pop.

Health: Life expectancy at birth (1992): 72 male; 79 female. **Births** (per 1,000 pop. 1992): 14. **Deaths** (per 1,000 pop. 1992): 9. **Natural increase:** .5%. **Hospital beds:** 1 per 198 persons. **Physicians:** 1 per 404 persons. **Infant mortality** (per 1,000 live births 1992): 10.

Education (1991): **Literacy:** 97%. **School:** Compulsory ages 6–16.

Major International Organizations: UN (GATT, IMF, WHO, FAO), OAS, NATO, OECD.

Embassy: 24 Grosvenor Sq, London W1A 1AE; 071-499 9000.

The United States consists of 50 states and the Federal District of Columbia. The union is symbolized on the American flag by 50 stars; the 13 stripes symbolize the original 13 states of the union.

Government. The USA is a Federal Republic which has elections every 4 years. The legislative body (Congress) consists of 2 houses – the Senate and the House of Representatives. The president has power of veto over Congress decisions, unless they have passed with a two-thirds majority. The Senate has 100 members – 2 per state – who are elected by the people for a term of 6 years. The House of Representatives is composed of 435 representatives, plus delegates from the District of Columbia, American Samoa, Guam and the Virgin Islands. Puerto Rico is represented by a resident commissioner.

The president and the vice-president of the United States are the only elective federal officials not elected by direct vote of the people. They are elected by the members of the Electoral College. On presidential election day – the first Tuesday after the first Monday of every 4th year – each state chooses as many electors as it has senators and representatives in Congress. (The District of Columbia has 3 electors, so with 100 senators and 435 representatives, there are 538 members of the Electoral College.) A majority of 270 electoral votes are needed to elect the president and vice-president.

Resources and Industries. The United States is the world's greatest industrial producer, its major manufactures being machinery, transport, electronic equipment and consumer goods. The country is self-sufficient in many raw materials, but certain minerals and fuels, notably petroleum, are increasingly imported to supplement dwindling resources. Main exports are electrical goods, industrial machinery, chemicals, coal, timber, cigarettes, grain, fruit and vegetables. Agriculture is extremely important to the American economy, with around 983 million acres devoted to it. Over the last decade, however, it has been in decline and the number of farms has fallen from 2.4 million in 1982 to 2.1 million in 1991. The main crops produced are grain, cotton, tobacco, beans, peanuts, potatoes, rice, sugar, nuts and fruit.

Religion. The *1992 Yearbook of American and Canadian Churches* reported a total of 156,336,384 members of religious groups in the U.S. – 59% of the population; membership was up 5% on the previous year. Protestant churches (including such groups as Mormons and Jehovah's Witnesses) claim about 87 million adherents, Roman Catholics about 58.5 million, Muslims about 8 million, Jews about 6 million and Eastern churches about 4 million. Most recently the highest claims of church membership were found among those who said they were "born again" (82%). The regions with the highest proportions of their populations as church members were the Midwest (76%) and the South (74%). In the East membership was at the national average (69%), but in the West affiliation dipped to 54%. Women were somewhat more likely to be church members, by a margin of 72% to 66%.

Education. In 1991 62% of the 2.3 million high school graduates went on to full-time college education. Of the total enrolment figure, 67% were female and 58% were male. The rate for whites (65%) remained well above that of blacks (46%) and Hispanics (57%). The unemployment rate for 1991 high school graduates who were not enrolled in college was 25.3%, the highest in 8 years.

History. Tradition has it that Christopher Columbus discovered America in 1492, but there is evidence to suggest that the Vikings set foot there much earlier. Undisputed is the fact that the continent was already inhabited by "Indians" – now more accurately referred to as Native Americans.

Numerous European explorers followed Columbus and laid claim to various tracts of land on behalf of their countries. The first permanent English settlement was founded at Jamestown, Virginia in May, 1607. The first black laborers (indentured servants) were landed here by the Dutch in 1609. Chattel slavery was legally recognized in 1650.

The Plymouth Pilgrims arrived on the *Mayflower* at Cape Cod in 1620 and reached an agreement among themselves to form a government and abide by its laws. This was known as the Mayflower Compact.

Settlement of America continued apace, mainly by the Spanish, French and British. In the French and Indian War (1756-63), the French lost Canada and the Midwest to the British, who thus tightened their administrative hold in North America. Increasing dissatisfaction with British rule culminated in the American Revolution (1775-83). France and Spain sided with the Americans. Congress approved the Declaration of Independence July 4, 1776, but it was not accepted by the British cabinet until Nov. 30, 1782. Peace was eventually restored when Britain and the U.S. signed a peace treaty, Sept. 1783.

Napoleon, who had recovered Louisiana from Spain by secret treaty, sold it back to the U.S. in 1803 for $15 million. This doubled the area of the U.S. Western expansion was rapid, California being won through the Mexican War of 1846-48. The discovery of gold led to a huge influx of prospectors.

Slavery, which had been outlawed in 1808, became an increasing source of conflict between North and South. It led to the Civil War (1861-65), which the North won, and slavery was abolished. Rapid industrial and economic expansion followed: Alaska was purchased from Russia in 1867 and the Spanish-American War of 1898 led to the U.S. acquiring Guam, the Philippines, Puerto Rico and partial control of Cuba. It also annexed the independent republic of Hawaii. In 1916 the U.S. bought the Virgin Islands from Denmark.

The U.S., which had a policy of isolationism, reluctantly entered World War I (1914-18) in April 1917. The industrial boom of the

1920s ended in the Wall Street Crash of 1929 and a long period of Depression. The U.S. entered World War II (1939-45) in 1941, after the bombing of Pearl Harbor by the Japanese. Japan surrendered after an atomic bomb was dropped on Hiroshima, Aug. 6, 1945. The U.S. entered 2 more wars in an effort to stop the spread of communism – the Korean War (1950-53) and the Vietnam War (1954-75).

On the domestic front, race relations have been difficult, with riots breaking out in several cities since the 1960s. Like the rest of the developed world, the U.S. is currently suffering from recession. At mid-1992 unemployment stood at 7.5%.

Serious floods during the summer of 1993 rendered many people homeless and destroyed a huge amount of crops.

District of Columbia

Area: 69 sq. mi. **Population** (1992): 588,620. The city of Washington is coextensive with the District of Columbia.

The District of Columbia is the seat of the federal government of the United States. It lies on the west central edge of Maryland on the Potomac River, opposite Virginia. Its area was originally 100 sq. mi. taken from the sovereignty of Maryland and Virginia. Virginia's portion south of the Potomac was given back to that state in 1846.

The 23rd Amendment, ratified in 1961, granted residents the right to vote for president and vice president for the first time and gave them 3 members in the Electoral College. The first such votes were cast in Nov. 1964.

Congress, which has legislative authority over the District under the Constitution, established in 1878 a government of 3 commissioners appointed by the president. The Reorganization Plan of 1967 substituted a single commissioner (also called mayor), assistant, and 9-member City Council. Funds were still appropriated by Congress; residents had no vote in local government, except to elect school board members.

In Sept. 1970, Congress approved legislation giving the District one delegate to the House of Representatives. The delegate could vote in committee but not on the House floor. The first was elected 1971.

In May 1974 voters approved a charter giving them the right to elect their own mayor and a 13-member city council; the first took office Jan. 2, 1975. The district won the right to levy its own taxes but Congress retained power to veto council actions, and approve the city's annual budget.

Proposals for a "federal town" for the deliberations of the Continental Congress were made in 1783, 3 years before the adoption of the Constitution that gave the Confederation a national government. Rivalry between northern and southern delegates over the site appeared in the First Congress, 1789. John Adams, presiding officer of the Senate, cast the deciding vote of that body for Germantown, Pa. In 1790 Congress compromised by making Philadelphia the temporary capital for 10 years. The Virginia members of the House wanted a capital on the eastern bank of the Potomac; they were defeated by the Northerners, while the Southerners defeated the Northern attempt to have the nation assume the war debts on the 13 original states, the Assumption Bill fathered by Alexander Hamilton. Hamilton and Jefferson arranged a compromise: the Virginia men voted for the Assumption Bill, and the Northerners conceded the capital to the Potomac. President Washington chose the site in Oct. 1790 and persuaded landowners to sell their holdings to the government at £25, then about $66, an acre. The capital was named Washington.

Washington appointed Pierre Charles L'Enfant, a French engineer who had come over with Lafayette, to plan the capital on an area not over 10 mi. square. The L'Enfant plan, for streets 100 to 110 feet wide and one avenue 400 feet wide and a mile long, seemed grandiose and foolhardy. But Washington endorsed it. When L'Enfant ordered a wealthy landowner to remove his new manor house because it obstructed a vista, and demolished it when the owner refused, Washington stepped in and dismissed the architect. The official map and design of the city was completed by Benjamin Banneker, a distinguished black architect and astronomer, and Andrew Ellicott.

On Sept. 18, 1793, Pres. Washington laid the conerstone of the north wing of the Capitol. On June 3, 1800, Pres. John Adams moved to Washington and on June 10, Philadelphia ceased to be the temporary capital. The City of Washington was incorporated in 1802; the District of Columbia was created as a municipal corporation in 1871, embracing Washington, Georgetown, and Washington County.

Outlying U.S. Areas

American Samoa

Capital: Pago Pago, island of Tutuila. **Total area:** 84 sq. mi. **Population** (1992): 50,923.

Blessed with spectacular scenery and a delightful South Seas climate, American Samoa is the most southerly of all lands under U.S. sovereignty. It is an unincorporated territory consisting of 7 small islands of the Samoan group: **Tutuila, Aunu'u, Manu'a Group (Ta'u, Olosega and Ofu), Rose** and **Swain's Island**. The islands are 2,300 mi. SW of Honolulu.

A tripartate agreement between Great Britain, Germany and the U.S. in 1899 gave the U.S. sovereignty over the eastern islands of the Samoan group; these islands became American Samoa. Local chiefs officially ceded Tutuila and Aunu'u to the U.S. in April 1900 and the Manu'a group in July 1904; Swain's Island was annexed in 1925.

Samoa (Western), comprising the larger islands of the Samoan group, was a New Zealand mandate and UN Trusteeship until it became an independent nation Jan. 1, 1962 (*see index*).

Tutuila and Aunu'u have an area of 53 sq. mi. Ta'u has an area of 17 sq. mi., and the islets of Ofu and Olosega, 5 sq. mi. with a population of a few thousand. Swain's Island has nearly 2 sq. mi. and a population of about 100.

About 70% of the land is bush and mountains. Chief products and exports are fish products. Taro, bread-fruit, yams, coconuts, pineapples, oranges, and bananas are also produced.

From 1900-1951, American Samoa was under the jurisdiction of the U.S. Navy. Since 1951, it has been under the Interior Dept. On Jan. 3, 1978, the first popularly elected Samoan governor and lieutenant governor were inaugurated. Previously, the governor was appointed by the Secretary of the Interior. American Samoa has a bicameral legislature and elects its own member of Congress, who can introduce legislation and vote in committee, but not in the House.

The American Samoans are of Polynesian origin. They are nationals of the U.S.; approximately 20,000 live in Hawaii, 65,000 in California and Washington.

Guam

People: Population (1990): 133,152 – a 26% increase over the 1980 figure of 105,979. **Pop. density:** 631.6 per sq. mi. **Urban** (1980): 39.5%. **Major ethnic groups** (1990): Chamorro 43%, Filipino 28.6%, state-side immigrants 20%, remainder Micronesians. Native Guamanians, ethnically called Chamorros, are basically of Indonesian stock, with a mixture of Spanish and Filipino. In addition to the official language, they speak the native Chamorro. **Migration** (1990): About 52% of population were born elsewhere; of these 48% in Asia, 40% in U.S.

Geography: Total area: 217 sq. mi. land, 30 mi. long and 4 to 8.5 mi. wide. **Location:** largest and southernmost of the Mariana Islands in the West Pacific, 3,700 mi. W of Hawaii. **Climate:** Tropical, with temperatures from 70° to 90°F; avg. annual rainfall, about 70 in. **Topography:** Coralline limestone plateau in the N; southern chain of low volcanic mountains sloping gently to the W, more steeply to coastal cliffs on the E; general elevation, 500 ft.; highest pt., Mt. Lamlam, 1,334 ft. **Capital:** Agana.

Economy: Principal industries: Tourism, defence, construction, banking. **Principal manufactured goods:** Textiles, foods. **Agriculture: Chief crops:** Cabbages, eggplants, cucumber, long beans, tomatoes, bananas, coconuts, watermelon, yams, cantaloupe, papayas, maize, sweet potatoes. **Livestock** (1984): 2,000 cattle; 14,000 hogs/pigs. **Chief ports:** Apra Harbor. **International airport:** Tamuning. **Value of construction** (1980): $80.60 mln. **Employment distribution** (1987): 61.3% private sector; 38.7% govt. **Per capita income** (1986): $7,116. **Median household income** (1989): $30,755; persons per household 3.97; persons per family 4.26. **Unemployment** (1990): 3.8%. **Tourism** (1990): $550 mln. receipts.

Finance: Notable industries: Insurance, real estate, finance. **No. banks:** 13. **No. savings and loan assns.:** 2.

Federal government: No. federal employees (1990): 7,200. **Notable federal facilities:** Anderson AFB; naval, air and port bases.

History. Guam was probably settled by voyagers from the Indonesian–Philippine archipelago by at least the third century BC. Pottery, rice cultivation, and megalithic technology show strong East Asian cultural influence. Centralized, village clan-based communities engaged in agriculture and offshore fishing. The est. population by the early 16th century was between 50,000 and 75,000 inhabitants.

Magellan arrived in the Marianas Mar. 6, 1521. They were colonized in 1668 by Spanish missionaries who named them the Mariana islands in honor of Maria Anna, queen of Spain. When Spain ceded Guam to the U.S., it sold the other Marianas to Germany. Japan obtained a League of Nations mandate over the German islands in 1919; in Dec. 1941 it seized Guam; the island was retaken by the U.S. in July 1944.

Guam is a self-governing organized unincorporated U.S. territory. The Organic Act of 1950 provides for a governor and a 21-member unicameral legislature, elected biennially by the residents who are American citizens.

In 1972 a U.S. law gave Guam one delegate to the U.S. House of

Representatives; the delegate may vote in committee but not on the House floor.

Guam's quest to change its status to a U.S. Commonwealth began in the late 1970s. A Commission on Self-Determination, created in 1984, developed a Draft Commonwealth Act, which was submitted to Congress.

Commonwealth of Puerto Rico

Estado Libre Asociado de Puerto Rico

People: Population (1992): 3,580,332. **Pop. density:** 1,035 per sq. mi. **Urban** (1990): 66.8%. **Racial distribution** (1990): 99.9% Hispanic. **Language** On Jan. 28, 1993 the Govt. of Puerto Rico declared Spanish and English joint official languages.

Geography: Total area: 3,492 sq. mi. **Land area:** 3,427 sq. mi. **Location:** island lying between the Atlantic to the N and the Caribbean to the S; it is easternmost of the West Indies group called the Greater Antilles, of which Cuba, Hispaniola, and Jamaica are the larger islands. **Climate:** Mild, with a mean temperature of 77°F. **Topography:** Mountainous throughout three-fourths of its rectangular area, surrounded by a broken coastal plain; highest peak is Cero Puntita, 4,389 ft. **Capital:** San Juan.

Economy: Principal industries: Manufacturing. **Principal manufactured goods:** Pharmaceuticals, chemicals, machinery and metals, electric machinery and equipment, petroleum refining, food products, apparel. **Agriculture: Chief crops:** Coffee, plantains, pineapples, bananas, tomatoes, sugar cane, peppers, pumpkins, lettuce, tobacco, yams. **Livestock** (1990): 600,000 cattle; 206,000 pigs; 7.4 mln. poultry. **Nonfuel minerals** (1991): $119.2 mln., mostly cement. **Commercial fishing** (1992): $6.2 mln. **Chief ports/river shipping:** San Juan, Ponce, Mayaguez. **Major airports at:** San Juan, Ponce, Mayaguez, Aguadilla. **Value of construction** (1992): $2.7 bln. **Employment distribution** (1992): 22.5% public admin.; 19.8% trade; 16.8% mfg.; 3.4% agric. **Per capita income** (1992): $6,360. **Unemployment** (1992): 16.7%. **Tourism** (1992): $1.51 bln. receipts.

Finance: FDIC-insured commercial banks & trust companies (1992): 17. **Deposits:** $18.8 bln. **Savings institutions** (1992): 8. **Assets:** $4.1 bln.

Federal government: Civilian employees (1992): 10,000. **Notable federal facilities:** U.S. Naval Station at Roosevelt Roads, Ceiba; U.S. Army Training Area and Ft. Allen at Salinas; Sabana SECA Communications Center (U.S. Navy); Ft. Buchanan at Guaynabo.

Energy production (1992): 16,458 mln. kWh.

Education: Student-teacher ratio (1992): 21.0. **Avg. salary, public school teachers** (1992): $1,000 monthly.

History. Puerto Rico (or Borinquen, after the original Arawak Indian name Boriquen), was visited by Columbus on his second voyage, Nov. 19, 1493. In 1508 the Spanish arrived.

Sugar cane was introduced, 1515, and slaves were imported 3 years later. Gold mining petered out, 1570. Spaniards fought off a series of British and Dutch attacks; slavery was abolished, 1873. Under the treaty of Paris, Puerto Rico was ceded to the U.S. after the Spanish-American War, 1898. In 1952 the people voted in favor of Commonwealth status.

The Commonwealth of Puerto Rico is a self-governing part of the U.S. with a primary Hispanic culture. The current commonwealth political status of Puerto Rico gives the island's citizens virtually the same control over their internal affairs as the 50 states of the U.S. However, they do not vote in national elections, although they do vote in national primary elections.

Puerto Rico is represented in the U.S. Congress solely by a resident commissioner who has a voice but no vote, except in committees.

No federal income tax is collected from residents on income earned from local sources in Puerto Rico. Nevertheless, as part of the U.S. legal system, Puerto Rico is subject to the provisions of the U.S. Constitution; most federal laws apply as they do in the 50 states.

Puerto Rico's famous "Operation Bootstrap", begun in the late 1940s, succeeded in changing the island from "The Poorhouse of the Caribbean" to an area with the highest per capita income in Latin America. This pioneering program encouraged manufacturing and the development of the tourist trade by selective tax exemption, low-interest loans, and other incentives. Despite the marked success of Puerto Rico's development efforts over an extended period of time, per capita income in Puerto Rico is low in comparison to that of the U.S. Economic growth slowed in fiscal 1991 from the 2.2% of fiscal 1990.

Virgin Islands

St. John, St. Croix, St. Thomas

People: Population (1990): 101,809 (50,139, St. Croix; 48,166, St. Thomas; 3,504, St. John). **Pop. density:** 748.60 per sq. mi. **Urban** (1980): 39%. **Racial distribution** (1980): 15% White; 85% Black. **Major ethnic groups:** West Indian, French, Hispanic.

Geography: Total area: 151 sq. mi. **Land area:** 134 sq. mi. **Location:** 3 larger and 50 smaller islands and cays in the S and W of the V.I. group (British V.I. colony to the N and E) which is situated 70 mi. E of Puerto Rico, located W of the Anegada Passage, a major channel connecting the Atlantic Ocean and the Caribbean sea. **Climate:** Subtropical; the sun tempered by gentle trade winds; humidity is low; average temperature, 78°F. **Topography:** St. Thomas is mainly a ridge of hills running E and W, and has little tillable land; St. Croix rises abruptly in the N but slopes to the S to flatlands and lagoons; St. John has steep, lofty hills and valleys with little level tillable land. **Capital:** Charlotte Amalie, St. Thomas.

Economy: Principal industries: Tourism, rum, alumina prod., petroleum refining, watch industry, textiles, electronics. **Principal manufactured goods:** Rum, textiles, pharmaceuticals, perfumes. **Gross domestic product** (1987): $1.246 bln. **Agriculture: Chief crops:** Truck garden produce. **Minerals:** Sand, gravel. **Chief ports:** Cruz Bay, St. John; Frederiksted and Christiansted, St. Croix; Charlotte Amalie, St. Thomas. **International airports on:** St. Thomas, St. Croix. **Value of construction** (1987): $167.0 mln. **Per capita income** (1989): $11,052. **Unemployment** (1993): 2.8%. **Tourism** (1988): $662.6. **No. banks** (1990): 8.

History. The islands were visited by Columbus in 1493. Spanish forces, 1555, defeated the Caribes and claimed the territory; by 1596 the native population was annihilated. First permanent settlement in the U.S. territory, 1672, by the Danes; U.S. purchased the islands, 1917, for defense purposes.

The Virgin Islands has a republican form of government, headed by a governor and lieut. governor elected, since 1970, by popular vote for 4-year terms. There is a 15-member unicameral legislature, elected by popular vote. Residents of the V.I. have been U.S. citizens since 1927. Since 1973 they have elected a delegate to the U.S. House of Representatives, who may vote in committee but not in the House.

Navassa

This minor Caribbean island lies between Jamaica and Haiti, 100 miles south of Guantanamo Bay, Cuba; it covers about 3 sq. mi., is reserved by the U.S. for a lighthouse and is uninhabited. It is administered by the U.S. Coast Guard.

Wake, Midway, Other Islands

Wake Island, and its sister islands, **Wilkes** and **Peale**, lie in the Pacific Ocean on the direct route from Hawaii to Hong Hong, about 2,300 mi. W of Hawaii and 1,290 mi. E of Guam. The group is 4.5 mi. long, 1.5 mi. wide, and totals less than 3 sq. mi.

The U.S. flag was hoisted over Wake Island, July 4, 1898, formal possession taken Jan. 17, 1899; Wake has been administered by the U.S. Air Force since 1972. The population consists of about 200 persons.

The **Midway Islands**, acquired in 1867, are **Sand** and **Eastern**, in the North Pacific 1,150 mi. NW of Honolulu, with an area of about 3 sq. mi., administered by the U.S. Navy. There is no indigenous population; about 450 persons live there.

Johnston Atoll, 717 miles WSW of Honolulu, area 1 sq. mi., is operated by the Defense Nuclear Agency and the Fish and Wildlife Service, U.S. Dept. of the Interior; its population is about 1,200.

Kingman Reef, 920 miles S of Hawaii, is under Navy control.

Howland, Jarvis, and **Baker Islands**, 1,400–1,650 miles SW of Honolulu, uninhabited since World War II, are under the Interior Dept.

Palmyra is an atoll about 1,000 miles south of Hawaii, 2 sq. mi. Privately owned, it is under the Interior Dept.

Islands Under Trusteeship

The Trust Territory of the Pacific Islands was established in 1947, was the only strategic trusteeship of the 11 trusteeships established by the U.N. For nearly 4 decades, the territory had a heterogeneous population of about 140,000 people scattered among more than 2,100 islands and atolls in 3 major archipelagos: the Carolines, the Marshalls, and the Marianas. The entire geographic area is sometimes referred to as "Micronesia", meaning "little islands". The area of the Trust Territory covered some 3 million sq. miles of the Pacific Ocean, slightly larger than the continental U.S. However, its islands constituted a land area of only 715.8 sq. miles – about the size of Buckinghamshire. It formerly consisted of 7 districts and 4 political jurisdictions: The Commonwealth of the Northern Mariana Islands (CNMI), the Federated States of Micronesia (FSM), the Republic of the Marshall Islands (RMI), and Palau. As of Oct. 21, 1986, the RMI entered into free association with the U.S., as did the FSM effective Nov. 3, 1986. The CNMI became a commonwealth of the U.S., also effective Nov. 3. Only Palau remains under trusteeship.

Commonwealth of the Northern Mariana Islands

Located in the perpetually warm climes between Guam and the Tropic of Cancer, the 14 islands of the Northern Marianas form a 300-mile-long archipelago, comprising a total land area of 179.5 sq. miles. The native population, 1990, is 43,345, and is concentrated on the 3 largest of the 6 inhabited islands: **Saipan**, the seat of government and commerce (38,896), **Rota** (2,295), and **Tinian** (2,118).

The people of the Northern Marianas are predominantly of Chamorro cultural extraction, although numbers of Carolinians and immigrants from other areas of E. Asia and Micronesia have also settled in the islands. Pursuant to the Covenant of 1976, which established the Northern Marianas as a commonwealth in political union with the U.S., most natives and many domiciliaries of these islands achieved U.S. citizenship on Nov. 13, 1986, when the U.S. terminated its administration of the U.N. trusteeship as it affected the Northern Marianas. From July 18, 1947, the U.S. had administered the Northern Marianas under a trusteeship agreement with the U.N. Security Council. English is among the several languages commonly spoken.

The Northern Mariana Islands has been self-governing since 1978, when both a constitution drafted and adopted by the people became effective and a bicameral legislature with offices of governor and lieutenant governor was inaugurated. Commercial activity has increased steadily in recent years. In 1990, more than 417,146 tourists visited.

Palau

Palau (or Belau) consists of more than 200 islands in 16 states in the Caroline chain, of which 8 are permanently inhabited. The capital of Palau, Koror, lies 3,997 miles SW of Honolulu and 813 miles S of Guam. Population of Palau is 15,122 (1990), 10,501 (1990) in Koror. Average year-round temperature is 80°F, average annual rainfall 150 inches.

Until 1979, a High Commissioner appointed by the U.S. president, himself appointed a district administrator for Palau to oversee programs and administration there. In support of the islands' evolving political status, the U.S. recognized the Constitution of Palau and the establishment of the Government of Palau, consistent with U.S. responsibilities in Palau as the administering authority of the UN Trust Territory of the Pacific Islands (TTPI).

The Assistant Secretary of the Interior for Territorial and International Affairs has been delegated U.S. authority with respect to Palau and may suspend any newly enacted national law in Palau, as well as every newly enacted state law that involves finance or the expenditure of funds if the law is inconsistent with the trusteeship agreement or U.S. laws or regulations applicable to the TTPI. The Constitution became effective in 1980. The President and Vice President are elected by popular vote. A Council of Chiefs advises the President on matters concerning traditional law and custom. Palau has a bicameral national legislature composed of a House of Delegates and a Senate.

For more U.S. information see Index.

Uruguay

Republic of Uruguay

República del Uruguay

People: Population (1992 est.): 3,121,000. **Age distrib.** (%): 0–14: 26.9; 15–59: 57.7; 60+: 15.4. **Pop. density:** 45 per sq. mi. **Urban** (1990): 86.0%. **Ethnic groups:** Caucasians (Iberians, Italians) 89%, mestizos 10%, mulatto and black. **Language:** Spanish. **Religion:** Roman Catholic 66%.

Geography: Area: 68,037 sq. mi., slightly larger than England, Wales and N. Ireland combined. **Location:** In southern S. America, on the Atlantic O. **Neighbors:** Argentina on W, Brazil on N. **Topography:** Uruguay is composed of rolling, grassy plains and hills, well watered by rivers flowing W to Uruguay R. **Capital:** Montevideo, pop. (1991 est.) 1,400,000.

Government: Type: Republic. **Head of state:** Pres. Luis Alberto Lacalle; in office Nov. 26, 1989. **Local divisions:** 19 departments. **Defense:** (1989) 1.4% of GDP.

Economy: Industries: Meat-packing, textiles, wine, cement, oil products. **Chief crops:** Corn, wheat, citrus fruits, rice, oats, linseed. **Arable land:** 8%. **Livestock** (1990): 8.7 mln. cattle; 25.2 mln. sheep. **Fish catch** (1990): 88,000 metric tons. **Electricity prod.** (1991): 5.6 bln. kWh. **Labor force** 13% agric.; 22% manuf.; 16% serv.; 20% govt.; 17% comm.

Finance: Monetary unit: New Peso (May 1993: 3,621 = $1 US). **Gross domestic product** (1991): $9.1 bln. **Per capita GDP:** $2,935. **Imports** (1991): $1.3 bln.; partners: EC 27%, Braz. 17%, Arg. 14%, U.S. 8%. **Exports** (1991): $1.6 bln.; partners: Braz. 28%, U.S. 11%, EC 23%. **Tourism** (1990): $261 mln. receipts. **National budget** (1989): $1.5 bln. expenditures. **International reserves** less gold (Jan. 1993): $538 mln. **Gold:** 2.0 mln. oz t. **Consumer prices** (change in 1992): 68.5%.

Transport: Railroads (1989): 3,002 km. long. **Motor vehicles:** (1989): 190,000 passenger cars, 100,000 comm. vehicles. **Civil aviation** (1990): 471 mln. passenger-km; 7 airports. **Chief port:** Montevideo.

Communications: Television sets: 1 per 4.8 persons. **Radios:** 1 per person. **Telephones:** 1 per 5.8 persons. **Daily newspaper circ.** (1989): 227 per 1,000 pop.

Health: Life expectancy at birth (1992): 69 male; 76 female. **Births** (per 1,000 pop. 1992): 17. **Deaths** (per 1,000 pop. 1992): 10. **Natural increase:** .7%. **Hospital beds:** 1 per 127 persons. **Physicians:** 1 per 341 persons. **Infant mortality** (per 1,000 live births 1992): 22.

Education (1990): **Literacy:** 96%.

Major International Organizations: UN (GATT, IMF, WHO), OAS.

Embassy: 140 Brompton Rd, London SW3 1HY; 071-584 8192.

Spanish settlers did not begin replacing the indigenous Charrua Indians until 1624. Portuguese from Brazil arrived later, but Uruguay was attached to the Spanish Viceroyalty of Rio de la Plata in the 18th century. Rebels fought against Spain beginning in 1810. An independent republic was declared Aug. 25, 1825.

Socialist measures were adopted as far back as 1911. The state owns the power, telephone, railroad, cement, oil-refining and other industries.

Uruguay's standard of living was one of the highest in South America, and political and labor conditions among the freest. Economic stagnation, inflation, floods and drought, and a general strike in the late 1960s brought government attempts to strengthen the economy through devaluation of the peso and wage and price controls.

Terrorist activities led to Pres. Juan Maria Bordaberry agreeing to military control of his administration Feb. 1973. In June he abolished Congress and set up a Council of State in its place. Bordaberry was removed by the military in a 1976 coup. Civilian government was restored to the country in 1985.

Uzbekistan

Republic of Uzbekistan

Ǒzbekiston Republikasy

People: Population (1992 est.): 21,626,000. **Pop. density:** 125 per sq. mi. **Urban** (1991): 40%. **Ethnic groups:** Uzbek 70%, Russian 11%. **Religion:** Mostly Sunni Muslim.

Geography: Area: 172,700 sq. mi., twice the size of GB. **Neighbors:** Kazakhstan on N and W, Kyrgyzstan and Tajikistan on E, Afghanistan and Turkmenistan on S. **Topography:** Mostly plains and desert. **Capital:** Tashkent.

Government: Type: Republic. **Head of state:** Pres. Islam A. Karimov. **Head of government:** Prime Min. Abdulkhashim Mutalov; in ofice Jan. 8, 1992. **Local divisions:** 11 oblasts, autonomous republic.

Economy: Industries: Steel, tractors, cars, textiles. **Chief crops:** Cotton, rice. **Minerals:** Coal, copper. **Livestock** (1990): 4.1 mln. cattle; 8.7 mln sheep. **Electricity prod.** (1991): 54 bln. kWh. **Labor force:** 39% agric. & forestry; 39% ind. & construction.

Finance: Monetary unit: Rouble. **Imports** (1990): $3.5 bln. **Exports** (1990): $1.5 bln.

Transport: Railroads (1990): 4,225 mi. long. **Civil aviation** (1990): 11.0 bln passenger-km; 1 airport.

Communications: Television sets: 1 per 6 persons. **Telephones:** 1 per 15 persons.

Health: Life expectancy at birth (1992): 64 male; 70 female. **Births** (per 1,000 pop. 1992): 34. **Deaths** (per 1,000 pop. 1992): 7. **Hospital beds:** 1 per 82 persons. **Physicians:** 1 per 281 persons. **Infant mortality** (per 1,000 live births 1992): 65.

Major International Organizations: UN, CIS.

The region was overrun by the Mongols under Genghis Khan in 1220. In the 14th century, Uzbekistan became the center of a native empire – that of the Timurids. In later centuries Muslim feudal states emerged. Russian military conquest began in the 19th century.

The Uzbek SSR became a Soviet Union republic in 1925. Uzbekistan declared independence Aug. 29, 1991. It became an independent republic when the Soviet Union disbanded Dec. 26, 1991.

Vanuatu

Republic of Vanuatu

Ripablik Blong Vanuatu

People: Population (1992 est.): 174,000. **Pop. density:** 30 per sq. mi. **Ethnic groups:** Mainly Melanesian, some European, Polynesian, Micronesian. **Languages:** Bislama, French and English (all official). **Religions:** Presbyterian 40%, Roman Catholic 16%, animist 15%, Anglican 14%.

Geography: Area: 5,700 sq. mi. **Location:** SW Pacific, 1,200 mi NE of Brisbane, Australia. **Topography:** Dense forest with narrow coastal strips of cultivated land. **Capital:** Vila, pop. (1990) 19,000.

Government: Type: Republic. **Head of state:** Pres. Fred Timakata; in office government: Jan. 12, 1989. **Head of government:** Prime Min. Maxime Carlot Korman; in office Dec. 16, 1991.

Economy: Industries: Fish-freezing, meat canning, tourism. **Chief crops:** Copra (38% of exports), cocoa, coffee. **Minerals:** Manganese. **Other resources:** Forests, cattle. **Fish catch** (1990): 3.3 metric tons.

Finance: Monetary unit: Vatu (Mar. 1993: 120 = $1 US). **Gross domestic product** (1990): $142 mln. **Imports** (1990): $60 mln.; partners: Aus. 36%, Fr. 8%, Japan 13%. **Exports** (1990): $15 mln.; partners: Neth. 34%, Jap. 17%, Fr. 27%.

Health: Life expectancy at birth (1992): 67 male, 72 female. **Infant mortality** (per 1,000 live births 1992): 30.

Education: Literacy (1990): 90%. **School:** Not compulsory, but 85-90% of eligible children attend primary school.

High Commission: c/o Dept. for Foreign Affairs, Port Vila, Vanuatu.

The Anglo-French condominium of the New Hebrides, administered jointly by France and Great Britain since 1906, became the independent Republic of Vanuatu on July 30, 1980.

Vatican City

The Holy See

People: Population (1992 est.): 802. **Ethnic groups:** Italians, Swiss. **Languages:** Italian, Latin.

Geography: Area: 108.7 acres. **Location:** In Rome, Italy. **Neighbors:** Completely surrounded by Italy.

Monetary unit: Lira.

Apostolic Nunciature: 54 Parkside, London SW19 5NE; 081-946 1410.

The popes for many centuries, with brief interruptions, held temporal sovereignty over mid-Italy (the so-called Papal States), comprising an area of some 16,000 sq. mi., with a population in the 19th century of more than 3 million. This territory was incorporated in the new Kingdom of Italy, the sovereignty of the pope being confined to the palaces of the Vatican and the Lateran in Rome and the villa of Castel Gandolfo, by an Italian law, May 13, 1871. This law also guaranteed to the pope and his successors a yearly indemnity of over $620,000. The allowance, however, remained unclaimed.

A Treaty of Conciliation, a concordat and a financial convention were signed Feb. 11, 1929, by Cardinal Gasparri and Premier Mussolini. The documents established the independent state of Vatican City, and gave the Catholic religion special status in Italy. The treaty (Lateran Agreement) was made part of the Constitution of Italy (Article 7) in 1947. Italy and the Vatican reached preliminary agreement in 1976 on revisions of the concordat, that would eliminate Roman Catholicism as the state religion and end required religious education in Italian schools.

Vatican City includes St. Peter's, the Vatican Palace and Museum covering over 13 acres, the Vatican gardens, and neighboring buildings between Viale Vaticano and the Church. Thirteen buildings in Rome, outside the boundaries, enjoy extraterritorial rights; these buildings house congregations or officers necessary for the administration of the Holy See.

The legal system is based on the code of canon law, the apostolic constitutions and the laws especially promulgated for the Vatican City by the pope. The Secretariat of State represents the Holy See in its diplomatic relations. By the Treaty of Conciliation the pope is pledged to a perpetual neutrality unless his mediation is specifically requested. This, however, does not prevent the defense of the Church whenever it is persecuted.

The present sovereign of the State of Vatican City is the Supreme Pontiff John Paul II, Karol Wojtyla, born in Wadowice, Poland, May 18, 1920, elected Oct. 16, 1978 (the first non-Italian to be elected Pope in 456 years).

Venezuela

Republic of Venezuela

Republica de Venezuela

People: Population (1992 est.): 20,675,000. **Age distrib.** (%): 0–14: 38.3; 15–59: 56.0; 60+: 5.7. **Pop. density:** 58 per sq. mi. **Urban** (1990): 83%. **Ethnic groups:** Mestizo 69%, white (Spanish, Portuguese, Italian) 20%, black 9%, Indian 2%. **Language:** Spanish (official). **Religion:** Roman Catholic 92%.

Geography: Area: 352,143 sq. mi., nearly 3 times the size of Br. Isles. **Location:** On the Caribbean coast of S. America. **Neighbors:** Colombia on W, Brazil on S, Guyana on E. **Topography:** Flat coastal plain and Orinoco Delta are bordered by Andes Mtns. and hills. Plains, called llanos, extend between mountains and Orinoco. Guyana Highlands and plains are S of Orinoco, which stretches 1,600 mi. and drains 80% of Venezuela. **Capital:** Caracas. **Cities** (1990 est.): Caracas 1,290,000; Maracaibo 1,206,000; Barquisimeto 723,000; Valencia 955,000.

Government: Type: Federal republic. **Head of state:** Pres. Ramon Jose Velasquez; in office: June 5, 1993. **Local divisions:** 21 states, territory, federal district, federal dependency. **Defense** (1991): 4.3% of GDP.

Economy: Industries: Steel, oil products, textiles, containers, paper. **Chief crops:** Coffee, rice, fruits, sugar. **Minerals:** Oil, iron (extensive reserves and production), gold. **Crude oil reserves** (1991): 60 bln. barrels. **Arable land:** 4%. **Livestock** (1990): 13.8 mln. cattle. **Fish catch** (1990): 327,000 metric tons. **Electricity prod.** (1991): 55.7 bln. kWh. **Crude steel prod.** (1991): 3.2 mln. metric tons. **Labor force:** 6% agric.; 35% ind.; 26% services.

Finance: Monetary unit: Bolivar (Apr. 1993: 84.00 = $1 US). **Gross domestic product** (1991): $52.3 bln. **Per capita GDP:** $2,590. **Imports** (1991): $10.2 bln.; partners: U.S. 44%. **Exports** (1991): $15.1 bln.; partners: U.S. 50%. **Tourism** (1990): $359 mln. receipts. **National budget** (1991): $13.1 bln. expenditures. **International reserves less gold** (Mar. 1993): $8.5 bln. **Gold:** 11.46 mln. oz t. **Consumer prices** (change in 1992): 31.4%.

Transport: Railroads (1990): 226 mi. long. **Motor vehicles** (1990): 1.6 mln. passenger cars, 459 mln. comm. vehicles. **Civil aviation** (1990): 4.0 mln. passenger-km; 32 airports with scheduled flights. **Chief ports:** Maracaibo, La Guaira, Puerto Cabello.

Communications: Television sets: 1 per 5.6 persons. **Radios:** 1 per 2.4 persons. **Telephones:** 1 per 11 persons. **Daily newspaper circ.** (1989): 111 per 1,000 pop.

Health: Life expectancy at birth (1992): 71 male; 78 female. **Births** (per 1,000 pop. 1992): 28. **Deaths** (per 1,000 pop. 1992): 4. **Natural increase:** 2.4%. **Hospital beds:** 1 per 370 persons. **Physicians:** 1 per 576 persons. **Infant mortality** (per 1,000 live births 1992): 23.

Education (1991): **Literacy:** 88%. **School:** Compulsory for 8 years; attendance 82%.

Major International Organizations: UN (IMF, WHO, FAO), OAS, OPEC.

Embassy: 1 Cromwell Road, London SW7; 071-581 2776.

Columbus first set foot on the South American continent on the peninsula of Paria, Aug. 1498. Alonso de Ojeda, 1499, found Lake Maracaibo, called the land Venezuela, or Little Venice, because natives had houses on stilts. Venezuela was under Spanish domination until 1821. The republic was formed after secession from the Colombian Federation in 1830.

Military strongmen ruled Venezuela for most of the 20th century. They promoted the oil industry; some social reforms were implemented. Since 1959, the country has had democratically-elected governments.

Venezuela helped found the Organization of Petroleum Exporting States (OPEC). The government, Jan. 1, 1976, nationalized the oil industry with compensation. Oil accounts for much of total export earnings and the economy suffered a severe cash crisis in the 1980s as the result of falling oil revenues.

The government has attempted to reduce dependence on oil.

A coup attempt, led by mid-level military officers, was thwarted by loyalist troops Feb. 4, 1992. Pres. Perez announced a series of economic and political reforms Mar. 5. A second coup attempt was thwarted in Nov. Perez was suspended from office and charged with misappropriating government funds, May 1993.

Vietnam

Socialist Republic of Vietnam

Cong Hoa Xa Hoi Chu Nghia Viet Nam

People: Population (1992 est.): 68,964,000. **Age distrib.** (%): 0-14: 40.8; 15-59: 53.6; 60+: 5.6 **Pop. density:** 541 per sq. mi. **Urban** (1989): 20%. **Ethnic groups:** Vietnamese 84%, Chinese 2%, remainder Muong, Thai, Meo, Khmer, Man, Cham. **Lan-**

guages: Vietnamese (official), Chinese. **Religions:** Buddhists, Confucians, and Taoists most numerous, Roman Catholics, animists, Muslims, Protestants.

Geography: Area: 127,330 sq. mi., slightly bigger than the Br. Isles. **Location:** On the E coast of the Indochinese Peninsula in SE Asia. **Neighbors:** China on N, Laos, Cambodia on W. **Topography:** Vietnam is long and narrow, with a 1,400-mi. coast. About 24% of country is readily arable, including the densely settled Red R. valley in the N, narrow coastal plains in center, and the wide, often marshy Mekong R. Delta in the S. The rest consists of semi-arid plateaus and barren mountains, with some stretches of tropical rain forest. **Capital:** Hanoi. **Cities** (1992): Ho Chi Minh City 4.0 mln.; Hanoi 2.0 mln.

Government: Type: Communist. **Head of state:** Pres. Lee Duc Anh; in office Sept. 23, 1992. **Head of government:** Prime Min. Vo Van Kiet; in office Aug. 8, 1991. **Local divisions:** 50 provinces, 3 municipalities. **Defense** (1986): 19.4% of GNP.

Economy: Industries: Food processing, textiles, cement, chemical fertilizers. **Chief crops:** Rice, rubber, fruits and vegetables, corn, manioc, sugar cane. **Minerals:** Phosphates, coal, iron, manganese, bauxite, apatite, chromate. **Other resources:** Forests. **Arable land:** 23%. **Livestock** (1991): 3.2 mln. cattle; 12.5 mln. pigs. **Fish catch** (1990): 850,000 metric tons. **Electricity prod.** (1991): 9.2 bln. kWh. **Labor force:** 65% agric.; 35% ind. and service.

Finance: Monetary unit: Dong (Jan. 1993: 10,881 = $1 US). **Gross national product** (1991): $15.2 bln. **Per capita GNP:** $230. **Imports** (1991): $1.9 bln.; partners: CIS, Jap. **Exports** (1991): $1.8 bln.; partners: CIS. **National budget** (1990): $1.3 bln. expenditures.

Transport: Motor vehicles: (1976): 100,000 passenger cars, 200,000 comm. vehicles. **Civil aviation** (1988): 10.3 bln. passenger km; 3 airports with scheduled flights. **Chief ports:** Ho Chi Minh City, Haiphong, Da Nang.

Communications: Television sets: 1 per 31 persons. **Radios:** 1 per 10 persons. **Telephones:** 1 per 544 persons. **Daily newspaper circ.** (1990): 38 per 1,000 pop.

Health: Life expectancy at birth (1992): 63 male; 67 female. **Births** (per 1,000 pop. 1992): 29. **Deaths** (per 1,000 pop. 1992): 8. **Natural increase:** 2.1%. **Hospital beds:** 1 per 292 persons. **Physicians:** 1 per 3,096 persons. **Infant mortality** (per 1,000 live births 1992): 48.

Education (1989): **Literacy:** 88%.

Major International Organizations: UN (IMF, WHO).

Embassy: 12 Victoria Road, London W8 5RD; 071-937 1912.

Vietnam's recorded history began in Tonkin before the Christian era. Settled by Viets from central China, Vietnam was held by China, 111 BC-AD 939, and was a vassal state during subsequent periods. Vietnam defeated the armies of Kublai Khan, 1288. Conquest by France began in 1858 and ended in 1884 with the protectorates of Tonkin and Annam in the N. and the colony of Cochin-China in the S.

In 1940 Vietnam was occupied by Japan; nationalist aims gathered force. A number of groups formed the Vietminh (Independence) League, headed by Ho Chi Minh, communist guerrilla leader. In Aug. 1945 the Vietminh forced out Bao Dai, former emperor of Annam, head of a Japan-sponsored regime. France, seeking to reestablish colonial control, battled communist and nationalist forces, 1946-1954, and was finally defeated at Dienbienphu, May 8, 1954. Meanwhile, on July 1, 1949, Bao Dai had formed a State of Vietnam, with himself as chief of state, with French approval. China backed Ho Chi Minh.

A ceasefire accord signed in Geneva July 21, 1954, divided Vietnam along the Ben Hai R. It provided for a buffer zone, withdrawal of French troops from the North and elections to determine the country's future. Under the agreement the communists gained control of territory north of the 17th parallel, with its capital at Hanoi and Ho Chi Minh as president. South Vietnam came to comprise the 39 southern provinces. Some 900,000 North Vietnamese fled to South Vietnam.

On Oct. 26, 1955, Ngo Dinh Diem, premier of the interim government of South Vietnam, proclaimed the Republic of Vietnam and became its first president.

The North adopted a constitution, Dec. 31, 1959, based on communist principles and calling for reunification of all Vietnam. North Vietnam sought to take over South Vietnam beginning in 1954. Fighting persisted from 1956, with the communist Vietcong, aided by North Vietnam, pressing war in the South. Northern aid to Vietcong guerrillas was intensified in 1959, and large-scale troop infiltration began in 1964, with Soviet and Chinese arms assistance. Large Northern forces were stationed in border areas of Laos and Cambodia.

A serious political conflict arose in the South in 1963 when Buddhists denounced authoritarianism and brutality. This paved the way for a military coup Nov. 1-2, 1963, which overthrew Diem. Several military coups followed.

In 1964, the U.S. began air strikes against North Vietnam. Beginning in 1965, the raids were stepped up and U.S. troops became combatants. U.S. troop strength in Vietnam, which reached a high of 543,400 in Apr. 1969, was ordered reduced by President Nixon in a series of withdrawals, beginning in June 1969. U.S. bombings were resumed in 1972-73.

A ceasefire agreement was signed in Paris Jan. 27, 1973 by the U.S., North and South Vietnam, and the Vietcong. It was never implemented.

North Vietnamese forces launched attacks against remaining government outposts in the Central Highlands in the first months of 1975. Government retreats turned into a rout, and the Saigon regime surrendered April 30. North Vietnam assumed control, and began transforming society along communist lines. All businesses and farms were collectivized.

The war's toll included — Combat deaths: U.S. 47,369; South Vietnam over 200,000; other allied forces 5,225. Civilian casualties were over a million. Displaced war refugees in South Vietnam totaled over 6.5 million.

The first National Assembly of both parts of the country met and the country was officially reunited July 2, 1976. The Northern capital, flag, anthem, emblem, and currency were applied to the new state. Nearly all major government posts went to officials of the former Northern government.

Heavy fighting with Cambodia took place, 1977-80, amid mutual charges of aggression and atrocities against civilians. Increasing numbers of Vietnamese civilians, ethnic Chinese, escaped the country, via the sea, or the overland route across Cambodia. Vietnam launched an offensive against Cambodian refugee strongholds along the Thai-Cambodian border in 1985; they also engaged Thai troops.

Relations with China soured as 140,000 ethnic Chinese left Vietnam charging discrimination; China cut off economic aid. Reacting to Vietnam's invasion of Cambodia, China attacked 4 Vietnamese border provinces, Feb., 1979, instigating heavy fighting.

Vietnam announced a package of reforms aimed at reducing central control of the economy in 1987, as many of the old revolutionary followers of Ho Chi Minh were removed from office.

Progress has been made with the U.S. over the repatriating of "Amerasians", the children fathered by U.S. servicemen.

Western Samoa

Independent State of Western Samoa

Malotuto'atasi o Samoa i Sisifo

People: Population (1992 est.): 190,000. **Age distrib.** (%): 0–14: 50.4; 15–59: 45.4; 60+: 4.3. **Pop. density:** 167 per sq. mi. **Urban** (1981): 21.2%. **Ethnic groups:** Samoan (Polynesian) 88%, Euronesian (mixed) 10%, European, other Pacific Islanders. **Languages:** Samoan, English (both official). **Religions:** Protestant 70%, Roman Catholic 20%.

Geography: Area: 1,133 sq. mi., slightly bigger than Dorset. **Location:** In the S. Pacific O. **Neighbors:** Nearest are Fiji on W, Tonga on S. **Topography:** Main islands, Savai'i (670 sq. mi.) and Upolu (429 sq. mi.), both ruggedly mountainous, and small islands Manono and Apolima. **Capital:** Apia, pop. (1983 est.) 35,000.

Government: Type: Constitutional monarchy. **Head of state:** Malietoa Tanumafili II; b. Jan. 4, 1913; in office Jan. 1, 1962. **Head of government:** Prime Min. Toflau Eti Alesana; in office Apr. 11, 1988. **Local divisions:** 11 districts.

Economy: Chief crops: Cocoa, copra, bananas. **Other resources:** Hardwoods, fish. **Arable land:** 43%. **Electricity prod.** (1991): 45 mln. kWh. **Labor force:** 67% agric.

Finance: Monetary unit: Tala (Mar. 1993: 2.56 = $1 US). **Gross domestic product** (1990): $114 mln. **Per capita GDP** (1990): $690. **Imports** (1992): $113 mln.; partners: NZ 28% Austral. 20%, Jap. 13%, U.S. 5%. **Exports** (1992): $6.0 mln.; partners: EC 28%. **International reserves less gold** (Mar. 1993): $57 mln. **Consumer prices** (change in 1992): 8.5%.

Transport: Motor vehicles (1990): 2,500 passenger cars, 3,000 comm. vehicles. **Chief ports:** Apia, Asau.

Communications: Radios: 1 per 2.3 persons. **Telephones:** 1 per 29 persons.

Health: Life expectancy at birth (1992): 65 male; 70 female. **Births** (per 1,000 pop. 1992): 34. **Deaths** (per 1,000 pop. 1992): 7. **Natural increase:** 2.8%. **Hospital beds:** 1 per 255 persons. **Physicians:** 1 per 3,584 persons. **Infant mortality** (per 1,000 live births 1992): 40.

Education (1989): **Literacy:** 90%. **School:** 95% attend elementary school.

Major International Organizations: UN (IMF, World Bank), Commonwealth of Nations.

Embassy: Avenue Franklin D. Roosevelt 123, 1050 Brussels, Belgium; 010 32 2 6608454.

Western Samoa was a German colony, 1899 to 1914, when New Zealand landed troops and took over. It became a New Zealand mandate under the League of Nations and then, in 1945, a New

Zealand UN Trusteeship.

An elected local government took office in Oct. 1959 and the country became fully independent Jan. 1, 1962.

Yemen

Republic of Yemen

al-Jumhūrīyah al-Yamanīyah

People: Population (1992 est.): 10,394,000. **Pop. density:** 51 per sq. mi. **Urban** (1991): 29%. **Ethnic groups:** Arabs, Indians, some Negroids. **Language:** Arabic. **Religions:** Sunni Muslim 53%, Shiite Muslim 46%.

Geography: Area: 203,976 sq. mi., twice the size of the UK. **Location:** On the southern coast of the Arabian Peninsula. **Neighbors:** Saudi Arabia on NE, Oman on the E. **Topography:** A sandy coastal strip leads to well-watered fertile mountains in interior. **Capital:** Sana. **Cities** (1986 est.): Sana 427,000; Aden 250,000.

Government: Type: Republic. **Head of state:** Pres. Ali Abdullah Saleh, b. 1942; in office July 17, 1978. **Head of government:** Prime Min. Haydar Abu Bakr-al Attas; in office May 22, 1990. **Local divisions:** 17 provinces. **Defense** (1990): 20% of GDP.

Economy: Industries: Food processing, mining, petroleum refining. **Chief crops:** Wheat, sorghum, fruits, coffee, cotton. **Minerals:** Salt. **Crude oil reserves** (1984): 600 mln. bbls. **Arable land:** 6%. **Livestock** (1990): 3.1 mln. goats; 3.6 mln. sheep. **Fish catch** (1990): 89,000 metric tons. **Electricity prod.** (1990): 1 bln. kWh. **Labor force:** 64% agric.; 11% ind. and comm.; 25% serv.

Finance: Monetary unit: Rial (Jan. 1993: 16.50 = $1 US). **Gross domestic product** (1989): $5.3 bln. **Per capita GDP:** $545. **Imports** (1990): $2.1 bln.; partners: Saudi Ar. 20%, Fr. 8%, Jap. 16%. **Exports** (1990): $908 mln.; partners: Saudi Ar. 8%, Pak. 19%.

Transport: Motor vehicles (1990): 150,000 passenger cars, 220,000 comm. vehicles. **Civil aviation** (1990): 1.0 bln. Passenger-km.; 12 airports with scheduled flights. **Chief ports:** Al-Hudaydah, Al-Mukha, Aden.

Communications: Television sets: 1 per 38 persons. **Radios:** 1 per 35 persons. **Telephones:** 1 per 157 persons.

Health: Life expectancy at birth (1992): 49 male; 51 female. **Births** (per 1,000 pop. 1992): 51. **Deaths** (per 1,000 pop. 1992): 16. **Natural increase:** 3.5%. **Hospital beds:** 1 per 995 persons. **Physicians:** 1 per 5,531 persons. **Infant mortality** (per 1,000 live births 1992): 118.

Education (1990): **Literacy:** 38%. **School:** 59% attend primary school.

Major International Organizations: UN (IMF, WHO), Arab League.

Embassy: 41 South St, London W1Y 5PD; 071-629 9905.

Yemen's territory once was part of the ancient kindgom of Sheba, or Saba, a prosperous link in trade between Africa and India. A Biblical reference speaks of its gold, spices and precious stones as gifts borne by the Queen of Sheba to King Solomon.

Yemen became independent in 1918, after years of Ottoman Turkish rule, but remained politically and economically backward. Imam Ahmed ruled 1948-1962. Army officers headed by Brig. Gen. Abdullah al-Salal declared the country to be the Yemen Arab Republic.

The Imam Ahmed's heir, the Imam Mohamad al-Badr, fled to the mountains where tribesmen joined royalist forces; internal warfare between them and the republican forces continued. About 150,000 people died in the fighting.

There was a bloodless coup Nov. 5, 1967. In April 1970 hostilities ended with an agreement between Yemen and Saudi Arabia.

On June 13, 1974, an army group, led by Col. Ibrahim al-Hamidi, seized the government. He was assassinated in 1977.

Meanwhile, South Yemen won independence from Britain in 1967, formed out of the British colony of Aden and the British protectorate of South Arabia. It became the Arab world's only Marxist state, taking the name People's Democratic Republic of Yemen in 1970 and signing a 20-year friendship treaty with the USSR in 1979 that allowed for the stationing of Soviet troops in the south.

More than 300,000 Yemenis fled from the south to the north after independence, contributing to 2 decades of hostility between the 2 states that flared into warfare twice in the 1970s.

An Arab League-sponsored agreement between North and South Yemen on unification of the 2 countries was signed Mar. 29, 1979. An agreement providing for widespread political and economic cooperation was signed in 1988.

The 2 countries were formally united on May 21, 1990.

Yugoslavia

Federal Republic of Yugoslavia

Federativna Republika Jugoslavija

(Data prior to 1992 include former republics Croatia, Slovenia, Bosnia and Herzegovina, and Macedonia)

People: Population (1992 est): 10,337,000. **Age distrib.** (%): 0–14; 23.5; 15–59: 63.7; 60+: 12.8. **Pop. density:** 262 per sq. mi. **Urban** (1990): 50%. **Ethnic groups** (1992): Serbs 80%, Albanians 15%. **Languages:** Serbian (official), Macedonian, Hungarian, Albanian. **Religions:** Serbian Orthodox 80%, Roman Catholic, Muslim.

Geography: Area: 39,449 sq. mi. **Location:** On the Balkan Peninsula in SE Europe. Present-day Yugoslavia consists of the former republics of Serbia and Montenegro. **Neighbors:** Croatia, Bosnia and Herzegovina on W., Hungary on N., Romania, Bulgaria on E., Greece, Albania, Macedonia on S. **Capital:** Belgrade, pop. (1992 est.) 1,553,000.

Government Type: Republic. **Head of State:** Pres. Zoran Lilic; in office June 1993. **Local divisions:** 2 republics. **Defense** (1991): 4.6% of GDP.

Economy: Industries: Steel, wood products, computers. **Chief crops:** Corn, grains, tobacco, sugar beets. **Minerals:** Antimony, bauxite, lead, mercury, coal, iron, copper, chrome, zinc, salt. **Arable land:** 28%. **Livestock** (1991): 2.0 mln cattle; 4.5 mln pigs; 3.0 mln. sheep. **Fish catch** (1990): 8,000 metric tons. **Electricity prod.** (1990): 83.4 bln. kWh. **Crude steel prod.** (1990): 3.6 mln. metric tons. **Labor force:** 22% agric.; 70% ind.

Finance: Monetary unit: Dinar (Feb. 1993: 225 = $1 US). **Gross national product** (1990): $120.1 bln. **Per capita GNP:** $5,040. **Imports** (1990): $19.1 bln.; partners: EC 54%, USSR 15%. **Exports** (1990): $14.6 bln.; partners: EC 54% USSR 17%. **Tourism** (1990): $2.7 bln receipts. **National budget** (1990): $6.4 bln. expenditures. **International reserves less gold** (Mar. 1993): $1.4 bln. **Gold:** 1.90 mln. oz t. **Consumer prices** (change in 1991): 117.4%.

Transport: Motor vehicles (1990): 1.4 mln. passenger cars, 132,000 comm. vehicles. **Civil aviation** (1992): 7 airports.

Communications: Television sets: 1 per 3.6 persons. **Radios:** 1 per 6 persons. **Telephones:** 1 per 4.9 persons. **Daily newspaper circ.** (1990): 88 per 1,000 pop.

Health: Life expectancy at birth (1991): 70 male; 76 female. **Births** (per 1,000 pop. 1991): 14. **Deaths** (per 1,000 pop. 1991): 9. **Natural increase:** .5%. **Hospital beds:** 1 per 163 persons. **Physicians:** 1 per 490 persons. **Infant mortality** (per 1,000 live births 1991): 21.

Education (1991): **Literacy:** 90%. **School:** Almost all attend primary school.

Major International Organizations: UN (IMF, World Bank).

Embassy: 5 Lexham Gardens, London W8 5JJ; 071-370 6105.

Serbia, which had since 1389 been a vassal principality of Turkey, was established as an independent kingdom by the Treaty of Berlin, 1878. Montenegro, independent since 1389, also obtained international recognition in 1878. After the Balkan wars Serbia's boundaries were enlarged by the annexation of Old Serbia and Macedonia in 1913.

When the Austro-Hungarian empire collapsed after World War I, the Kingdom of the Serbs, Croats, and Slovenes was formed from the former provinces of Croatia, Dalmatia, Bosnia, Herzegovina, Slovenia, Vojvodina and the independent state of Montenegro. The name was later changed to Yugoslavia.

Nazi Germany invaded in 1941. Many Yugoslav partisan troops continued to operate. Among these were the Chetniks led by Draja Mikhailovich, who fought other partisans led by Josep Broz, known as Marshal Tito. Tito, backed by the USSR and Britain from 1943, was in control by the time the Germans had been driven from Yugoslavia in 1945. Mikhailovich was executed July 17, 1946, by the Tito regime.

A constituent assembly proclaimed Yugoslavia a republic Nov. 29, 1945. It became a federated republic Jan. 31, 1946, and Marshal Tito, a communist, became head of the government.

The Stalin policy of dictating to all communist nations was rejected by Tito. He accepted economic aid and military equipment from the U.S. and received aid in foreign trade also from France and Great Britain. Tito also supported the liberal government of Czechoslovakia in 1968 before the Soviet invasion.

A separatist movement among Croatians brought arrests and a change of leaders in the Croatian Republic in Jan. 1972. Violence by Croatian nationalists and fears of Soviet political intervention led to restrictions on political and intellectual dissent.

Beginning in 1965, reforms designed to decentralize the administration of economic development and to force industries to produce more efficiency in competition with foreign producers were introduced, and considerable trade with the West was developed.

Pres. Tito died May 4, 1980; with his death, the post as head of the Collective Presidency and also that as head of the League of Communists became a rotating system of succession among the members representing each republic.

On Jan. 22, 1990, a Communist Party conference renounced its constitutionally guaranteed leading role in society and called on parliament to enact "political pluralism, including a multiparty system".

Croatia and Slovenia formally declared independence June 25, 1991. In Croatia fighting began between Croats and ethnic Serbs. Serbia sent arms and medical supplies to the Serb rebels in Croatia. In Aug. there were numerous clashes between Croatian forces and Yugoslavian army units and their Serb supporters.

The republics of Serbia and Montenegro proclaimed a new "Federal Republic of Yugoslavia" Apr. 17, 1992. Serbia was the main supplier of arms to the ethnic Serb fighters in Bosnia and Herzegovina. The UN imposed sweeping international sanctions on Yugoslavia as a means of ending the bloodshed in Bosnia, May 30. Some 100,000 protesters in Belgrade called for the ousting of Serbian President Milosevic, June 28. As the result of UN trade sanctions and the nation's continued printing of money to support Serb forces in the Bosnian and Croatian conflicts, inflation was over 200 per cent and unemployment at 40 per cent, Feb. 1993.

Kosovo: An area of southern Serbia (4,203 sq. mi.), with a population of about 2,000,000, mostly Albanians. The capital is Pristina. The Albanian majority has declared its independence, which Serbia has not recognized.

Vojvodina: An area in northern Serbia (3,304 sq. mi.), with a population of about 2,000,000, mostly Serbian. The capital is Novi Sad.

Zaire

Republic of Zaire

République du Zaïre

People: Population (1992 est.): 39,084,000. **Pop. density:** 43 per sq. mi. **Urban** (1988): 44.2%. **Ethnic groups:** Bantu tribes 80%, over 200 other tribes. **Languages:** French (official), Kongo, Luba, Mongo, Rwanda, others. **Religions:** Christian 70%, Muslim 10%.

Geography: Area: 905,563 sq. mi., nearly 10 times bigger than the UK. **Location:** In central Africa. **Neighbors:** Congo on W, Central African Republic, Sudan on N, Uganda, Rwanda, Burundi, Tanzania on E, Zambia, Angola on S. **Topography:** Zaire includes the bulk of the Zaire (Congo) R. Basin. The vast central region is a low-lying plateau covered by rain forest. Mountainous terraces in the W, savannas in the S and SE, grasslands toward the N, and the high Ruwenzori Mtns. on the E surround the central region. A short strip of territory borders the Atlantic O. The Zaire R. is 2,718 mi. long. **Capital:** Kinshasa. **Cities** (1991 est.): Kinshasa 3,741,000; Lubumbashi 709,000.

Government: Type: Republic with strong presidential authority (in transition). **Head of state:** Pres. Mobutu Sese Seko; b. Oct. 14, 1930; in office Nov. 25, 1965. **Head of government:** Prime Min. Etienne Tshisekedi wa Mulumba; in office Aug. 15, 1992. **Local divisions:** 10 regions, Kinshasa. **Defense** (1988): 1% of GDP.

Economy: Chief crops: Coffee, rice, sugar cane, bananas, plantains, manioc, mangoes, tea, cocoa, palm oil. **Minerals:** Cobalt (60% of world reserves), copper, cadmium, gold, silver, tin, germanium, zinc, iron, manganese, uranium, radium. **Crude oil reserves** (1987): 111 mln. bbls. **Other resources:** Forests, rubber, ivory. **Arable land:** 3%. **Livestock** (1991): 1.6 mln. cattle; 2.9 mln. goats. **Fish catch** (1990): 162,000 metric tons. **Electricity prod.** (1991): 6.0 bln. kWh. **Labor force:** 75% agric..

Finance: Monetary unit: Zaire (Mar. 1993: 2,652 = $1 US). **Gross domestic product** (1990): $6.6 bln. **Per capita GDP:** $180. **Imports** (1991): $710 mln.; partners: Chi. 38%, Belg. 16%, Ger. 7%, Fra. 7%. **Exports** (1991): $828 mln.; partners: Belg.-Lux. 36%, U.S. 19%. **National budget** (1990): $1.1 bln. expenditures. **International reserves less gold** (Mar. 1993): $156 mln. **Gold:** 27,000 oz t. **Consumer prices** (change in 1992): 6,921%.

Transport: Railroads (1989): 3,193 mi. long. **Motor vehicles:** (1985): 24,000 passenger cars, 60,000 comm. vehicles. **Civil aviation** (1990): 487 mln. passenger-km; 26 airports with scheduled flights. **Chief ports:** Matadi, Boma.

Communications: Television sets: 1 per 1,707 persons. **Radios:** 1 per 9.7 persons. **Telephones:** 1 per 1,026 persons. **Daily newspaper circ.** (1988): 1 per 1,000 pop.

Health: Life expectancy at birth (1992): 52 male; 56 female. **Births** (per 1,000 pop. 1992): 45. **Deaths** (per 1,000 pop. 1992): 14. **Natural increase:** 3.1%. **Hospital beds:** 1 per 476 persons. **Physicians:** 1 per 23,193 persons. **Infant mortality** (per 1,000 live births 1992): 97.

Education (1990): **Literacy:** 72%.

Major International Organizations: UN and all of its specialized agencies, OAU.

Diplomatic Mission: 26 Chesham Place, London SW1X 8HH; 071-235 6137.

The earliest inhabitants of Zaire may have been the pygmies, followed by Bantus from the E and Nilotic tribes from the N. The large Bantu Bakongo kingdom ruled much of Zaire and Angola when Portuguese explorers visited in the 15th century.

Leopold II, king of the Belgians, formed an international group to exploit the Congo in 1876. In 1877 Henry M. Stanley explored the Congo and in 1878 the king's group sent him back to organize the region and win over the native chiefs. The Conference of Berlin, 1884-85, organized the Congo Free State with Leopold as king and chief owner. Exploitation of native laborers on the rubber plantations caused international criticism and led to granting of a colonial charter, 1908.

Belgian and Congolese leaders agreed Jan. 27, 1960, that the Congo would become independent June 30. In the first general elections, May 31, the National Congolese movement of Patrice Lumumba won 35 of 137 seats in the National Assembly. He was appointed premier June 21, and formed a coalition cabinet.

Widespread violence caused Europeans and others to flee. The UN Security Council Aug. 9, 1960, called on Belgium to withdraw its troops and sent a UN contingent. President Kasavubu removed Lumumba as premier; he was murdered in 1961.

The last UN troops left the Congo June 30, 1964, and Moise Tshombe became president.

On Sept. 7, 1964, leftist rebels set up a "People's Republic" in Stanleyville. Tshombe hired foreign mercenaries and sought to rebuild the Congolese Army. In Nov. and Dec. 1964 rebels slew scores of white hostages and thousands of Congolese; Belgian paratroops, dropped from U.S. transport planes, rescued hundreds. By July 1965 the rebels had lost their effectiveness.

In 1965 Gen. Joseph D. Mobutu was named president. He later changed his name to Mobutu Sese Seko. The country changed its name to Republic of Zaire on Oct. 27, 1971; in 1972 Zaireans with Christian names were ordered to change them to African names.

Serious economic difficulties, amid charges of corruption by government officials, plagued Zaire in the 1980s. In 1990 Pres. Mobutu announced an end to a 20-year ban on multiparty politics. In 1993 Prime Min. Etienne Tshisekedi wa Mulumba called for foreign military assistance in toppling Pres. Mobuto Sese Soto, who had held office for almost 28 years.

Zambia

Republic of Zambia

People: Population (1992 est.): 8,745,000. **Age distrib.** (%): 0–14: 48.2; 15–59: 47.8; 60+: 4.0. **Pop. density:** 30 per sq. mi. **Urban** (1990): 49%. **Ethnic groups:** Mostly Bantu tribes. **Languages:** English (official), Bantu dialects. **Religions:** Predominantly animist, Roman Catholic 21%, Protestant, Hindu, Muslim minorities.

Geography: Area: 290,586 sq. mi., 3 times larger than the UK. **Location:** In southern central Africa. **Neighbors:** Zaire on N, Tanzania, Malawi, Mozambique on E, Zimbabwe, Namibia on S, Angola on W. **Topography:** Zambia is mostly high plateau country covered with thick forests, and drained by several important rivers, including the Zambezi. **Capital:** Lusaka. **Cities** (1992): Lusaka 982,000; Kitwe 348,000; Ndola 376,000.

Government: Type: Republic. **Head of state:** Pres. Frederick Chiluba; b. 1943; in office Nov. 2, 1991. **Local divisions:** 9 provinces. **Defense** (1985): 6.8% of GDP.

Economy: Chief crops: Corn, tobacco, peanuts, cotton, sugar. **Minerals:** Cobalt, copper, zinc, gold, lead, vanadium, manganese, coal. **Other resources:** Rubber, ivory. **Arable land:** 7%. **Livestock** (1990): 2.8 mln. cattle. **Fish catch** (1989): 68,000 metric tons. **Electricity prod.** (1991): 12 bln. kWh. **Labor force:** 60% agric.; 40% ind. and comm.

Finance: Monetary unit: Kwacha (Mar. 1993: 100 = $1 US). **Gross domestic product** (1991): $4.2 bln. **Per capita GDP:** $380. **Imports** (1991): $1.3 bln.; S.Af. 13%, Ger. 6%, U.S. 7%. **Exports** (1991): $1.1 bln.; partners: Jap. 4%, UK 3%, U.S. 10%, Ger. 9%. **National budget** (1991): $1.5 bln. expenditures. **International reserves less gold** (Jan. 1992): $84 mln. **Gold:** 15,000 oz t. **Consumer prices** (change in 1991): 92%.

Transport: Motor vehicles (1982): 105,000 passenger cars, 97,000 comm. vehicles. **Civil aviation** (1991): 322 mln. passenger-km; 8 airports with scheduled flights.

Communications: Television sets: 1 per 44 persons. **Radios:** 1 per 14 persons. **Telephones:** 1 per 78 persons. **Daily newspaper circ.** (1989): 15 per 1,000 pop.

Health: Life expectancy at birth (1992): 55 male; 59 female. **Births** (per 1,000 pop. 1992): 48. **Deaths** (per 1,000 pop. 1992): 11. **Natural increase:** 3.7%. **Hospital beds:** 1 per 311 persons. **Physicians:** 1 per 8,437 persons. **Infant mortality** (per 1,000 live births 1992): 77.

Education (1991): **Literacy:** 54%. **School:** Less than 50% attend primary school.

Major International Organizations: UN (GATT, IMF, WHO), OAU, Commonwealth of Nations.

High Commission: 2 Palace Gate, London W8 5LY; 071-589 6655.

As Northern Rhodesia, the country was under the administration of the South Africa Company, 1889 until 1924, when the office of governor was established, and, subsequently, a legislature. The country became an independent republic within the Commonwealth Oct. 24, 1964.

After the white government of Rhodesia declared its independence from Britain Nov. 11, 1965, relations between Zambia and Rhodesia became strained.

As part of a program of government participation in major industries, a government corporation in 1970 took over 51% of the ownership of 2 foreign-owned copper mining companies. Privately-held land and other enterprises were nationalized in 1975, as were all newspapers. In the 1980s, decline in copper prices hurt the economy and severe drought caused famine.

Food riots erupted in June 1990, as the nation suffered its worst violence since independence.

Elections held Oct. 1991, resulted in an end to one-party rule.

Zimbabwe

Republic of Zimbabwe

People: Population (1992 est.): 11,033,000. **Age distrib.** (%): 0–14: 44.9; 15–59: 51.1; 60+: 4.0. **Pop. density:** 73 per sq. mi. **Urban** (1990): 25%. **Ethnic groups:** Shona 80%, Ndebele 19%. **Languages:** English (official), Shona, Sinde bele. **Religions:** Predominantly traditional tribal beliefs, Christian minority.

Geography: Area: 150,803 sq. mi., nearly 3 times larger than England. **Location:** In southern Africa. **Neighbors:** Zambia on N, Botswana on W, S. Africa on S, Mozambique on E. **Topography:** Zimbabwe is high plateau country, rising to mountains on eastern border, sloping down on the other borders. **Capital:** Harare. **Cities** (1988 est.): Harare 730,000; Bulawayo (metro.) 415,000.

Government: Type: Parliamentary democracy. **Head of state:** Pres. Robert Mugabe; b. Feb. 21, 1924; in office Jan. 1, 1988. **Local divisions:** 8 provinces. **Defense** (1991): 6.0% of GDP.

Economy: Industries: Clothing, chemicals, light industries. **Chief crops:** Tobacco, sugar, cotton, corn, wheat. **Minerals:** Chromium, gold, nickel, asbestos, copper, iron, coal. **Arable land:** 7%. **Livestock** (1991): 5.9 mln. cattle; 2.4 mln. goats. **Electricity prod.** (1991): 7.5 bln. kWh. **Labor force:** 74% agric.; 16% serv.

Finance: Monetary unit: Dollar (Mar. 1993: 6.6 = $1 US). **Gross domestic product** (1991): $7.1 bln. **Per capita GDP:** $660. **Imports** (1991): $1.6 bln. partners: EC 31%, S. Afr. 21%. **Exports** (1991): $1.8 bln.; partners: EC 40%. **National budget** (1991): $3.3 bln. expenditures. **Total reserves less gold** (Mar. 1992): $278.0 mln. **Consumer prices** (change in 1992): 46.3%.

Transport: Motor vehicles (1990): 178,000 passenger cars, 82,000 comm. vehicles. **Civil aviation** (1989): 709 mln. passenger-km.; 8 airports with scheduled flights.

Communications: Television sets: 1 per 70 persons. **Radios:** 1 per 18 persons. **Telephones:** 1 per 31 persons. **Daily newspaper circ.** (1990): 23 per 1,000 pop.

Health: Life expectancy at birth (1992): 60 male; 64 female. **Births** (per 1,000 pop. 1992): 41. **Deaths** (per 1,000 pop. 1992): 8. **Natural increase:** 3.3%. **Physicians:** 1 per 6,951 persons. **Infant mortality** (per 1,000 live births 1992): 59.

Education (1990): **Literacy:** 67%. **School:** 90% of Africans attend primary school, 15% secondary; attendance is higher for whites, Asians.

Major International Organizations: UN (IMF, World Bank), OAU, Commonwealth of Nations.

High Commission: Zimbabwe House, 429 Strand, London WC2R 0QE; 071-836 7755.

Britain took over the area as Southern Rhodesia in 1923 from the British South Africa Co. (which, under Cecil Rhodes, had conquered the area by 1897) and granted internal self-government. Under a 1961 constitution, voting was restricted to maintain whites in power. On Nov. 11, 1965, Prime Min. Ian D. Smith announced his country's unilateral declaration of independence. Britain termed the act illegal, and demanded Zimbabwe (known as Rhodesia until 1980) broaden voting rights to provide for eventual rule by the majority Africans.

Urged by Britain, the UN imposed sanctions, including embargoes on oil shipments to Zimbabwe. Some oil and gasoline reached Zimbabwe, however, from South Africa and Mozambique, before the latter became independent in 1975. In May 1968, the UN Security Council ordered a trade embargo.

A new constitution came into effect, Mar. 2, 1970. The election law effectively prevented full black representation through income tax requirements.

Intermittent negotiations between the government and various black nationalist groups failed to prevent increasing skirmishes. An "internal settlement" signed Mar. 1978 in which Smith and 3 popular black leaders share control until transfer of power to the black majority was rejected by guerrilla leaders.

In the country's first universal-franchise election, Apr. 21, 1979, Bishop Abel Muzorewa's United African National Council gained a bare majority control of the black-dominated parliament. Britain, 1979, began efforts to normalize its relationship with Zimbabwe. A British cease-fire was accepted by all parties, Dec. 5th. Independence was finally achieved Apr. 18, 1980.

Pres. Mugabe declared Zimbabwe's drought a national disaster and appealed to foreign donors for food, money and medicine Mar. 6, 1992.

Leading Countries in Population and Area in 1992

China has the highest population in the world, with 1.17 billion inhabitants, which is about 21% of the world's population. India has almost 900 million people and is expected to reach 1 billion by the end of the decade. The United States has the third largest population, with over 250 million, followed by Indonesia, Brazil and Russia. Russia is the largest country in area, with over 6.5 million square miles. The next largest countries are Canada, China, the United States and Brazil.

Area and Population of the World

Source: U.S. Bureau of the Census; prior to 1950, Rand McNally & Co.

			Population (est., thousands)							
Continent	**Area (1,000 sq. mi.)**	**% of Earth**	**1650**	**1750**	**1850**	**1900**	**1950[1]**	**1980[1]**	**1991[1]**	**% World Total, 1991[1]**
North America	9,400	16.2	5,000	5,000	39,000	106,000	166,000	252,000	279,000	5.1
South America	6,900	11.9	8,000	7,000	20,000	38,000	—	—	—	—
Latin America, Caribbean	—	—			—	—	166,000	364,000	458,000	8.4
Europe	3,800	6.6	100,000	140,000	265,000	400,000	392,000	484,000	502,000	9.2
Asia	17,400	30.1	335,000	476,000	754,000	932,000	1,368,000	2,494,000	3,046,000	56.2
Africa	11,700	20.2	100,000	95,000	95,000	118,000	281,000	594,000	817,000	15.0
USSR	—	—			—	—	180,000	266,000	293,000	5.4
Oceania, incl. Australia	3,300	5.7	2,000	2,000	2,000	6,000	12,000	23,000	27,000	0.4
Antarctica	5,400	9.3	Uninhabited							
World	**57,900**	**—**	**550,000**	**725,000**	**1,175,000**	**1,600,000**	**2,564,000**	**4,478,000**	**5,423,000**	**—**

(1) Figures do not add to total because of independent rounding.

Worldwide Illiteracy Shows a Decline

The number of illiterate people in the world has declined slightly in recent years. A report by the United Nations Educational, Scientific and Cultural Organization estimated the number of illiterate people to be 948 million in 1990, a slight drop from the 1985 estimate of 950 million.

(Continued)

The 948 million people represented 26.6% of the world's population. The report projected that the number of illiterate people will decrease to 935 million, or 21.8% of the population by the year 2000. While the report showed a significant decrease in the proportion of illiterate people—the number in 1970 was 890 million, or 38.5% of the adult population—it characterized progress in eradicating illiteracy as "painfully slow".

Population Projections, by Region and for Selected Countries: 2000 to 2020

Source: Bureau of the Census, U.S. Department of Commerce
(in thousands)

Region and Country	2000	2020
Sub-Saharan Africa[1]	**736,325**	**1,279,014**
Angola	11,424	19,153
Benin	6,509	11,901
Botswana	1,554	2,181
Burkina Faso	12,464	23,016
Burundi	7,731	13,725
Cameroon	14,453	23,487
Central African Republic	3,702	5,944
Chad	6,204	9,361
Congo	2,995	4,955
Côte d'Ivoire	18,144	33,581
Ethiopia	69,374	123,584
Ghana	20,527	35,579
Guinea	9,232	14,419
Guinea-Bissau	1,265	1,926
Kenya	34,259	57,265
Liberia	3,674	6,534
Madagascar	16,185	29,183
Malawi	11,892	22,235
Mali	10,667	19,169
Mauritania	2,652	4,849
Mozambique	20,936	35,443
Namibia	2,081	3,925
Niger	11,056	20,606
Nigeria	160,751	273,197
Rwanda	11,047	21,948
Senegal	10,482	18,466
Sierra Leone	5,399	8,919
Somalia	9,409	17,190
South Africa	51,375	82,882
Sudan	35,870	59,307
Tanzania	36,489	68,772
Togo	5,248	9,900
Uganda	25,802	48,393
Zaire	50,043	89,164
Zambia	11,572	21,973
Zimbabwe	13,806	21,338
Near East and North Africa[1]	**327,119**	**506,134**
Algeria	32,024	46,007
Cyprus	768	889
Egypt	66,498	97,505
Iraq	27,205	50,943
Israel	5,321	6,850
Jordan	4,880	8,987
Kuwait	2,879	4,564
Lebanon	4,058	5,755
Libya	5,599	8,549
Morocco	31,392	43,324
Oman	2,099	4,163
Saudi Arabia	25,003	45,836
Syria	18,212	35,761
Tunisia	9,713	12,597
Turkey	70,368	96,514
United Arab Emirates	3,598	6,182
Yemen	13,603	25,907
Asia[1]	**3,528,307**	**4,500,233**
Afghanistan	24,935	39,915
Bangladesh	143,226	209,898
Cambodia	8,498	11,947
China	1,303,342	1,541,143
India	1,018,092	1,316,989
Indonesia	223,820	287,289
Iran	78,246	143,230
Japan	128,144	127,716
Korea, North	25,491	30,969
Korea, South	45,962	48,649
Laos	4,964	6,923
Malaysia	21,950	31,598
Mongolia	2,836	4,390
Nepal	24,340	37,488
Myanmar (Burma)	49,787	67,689
Pakistan	149,147	251,305
Philippines	77,734	101,387
Singapore	3,021	3,401
Sri Lanka	19,296	23,283
Taiwan	22,441	25,059
Thailand	63,832	76,108
Vietnam	79,801	102,948
Latin America and the Caribbean[1]	**537,168**	**704,930**
Argentina	36,036	43,463
Belize	301	451
Bolivia	8,721	12,435
Brazil	180,536	231,672
Chile	15,025	18,484
Colombia	39,475	51,443
Costa Rica	3,803	5,294
Cuba	11,613	12,795
Dominican Republic	8,676	11,439
Ecuador	12,997	18,029
El Salvador	6,471	8,811
Guatemala	11,315	15,632
Haiti	7,649	11,374
Honduras	6,243	9,064
Jamaica	2,762	3,533
Mexico	108,754	147,911
Nicaragua	4,729	7,013
Panama	2,937	3,908
Paraguay	6,023	8,812
Peru	26,435	35,055
Trinidad and Tobago	1,425	1,761
Uruguay	3,289	3,620
Venezuela	24,596	34,357
North America, Europe and the former USSR[1]	**1,125,095**	**1,204,719**
Albania	3,824	4,677
Austria	7,762	7,488
Belgium	9,989	9,692
Bulgaria	9,004	9,071
Canada	29,301	33,128
Czechoslovakia (former)	16,303	16,9985
Denmark	5,147	4,980
Finland	5,075	5,024
France	58,548	60,149
Germany	81,532	81,883
Greece	10,166	9,902
Hungary	10,604	10,393
Ireland	3,509	3,837
Italy	58,592	56,068
Netherlands	15,642	15,698
Norway	4,411	4,497
Poland	38,889	41,698
Portugal	10,652	10,671
Romania	24,534	25,981
Spain	40,456	40,428
Sweden	8,761	8,646
Switzerland	7,018	6,843
USSR (former)	311,637	355,092
United Kingdom	58,719	59,431
United States	268,266	294,364
Yugoslavia (former)	25,112	26,349

(1) Includes countries not shown separately.

Population of World's Largest Cities

Source: Bureau of the Census, U.S. Dept. of Commerce

The table below represents one attempt at comparing the world's largest cities. The cities are defined as population clusters of continuous built-up areas with a population density of a least 5,000 persons per square mile. The boundary of the city was determined by examining detailed maps of each city in conjunction with the most recent official population statistics. Exclaves of areas exceeding the minimum population density were added to the city if the intervening gap was less than one mile. To the extent practical, non-residential areas,

(Continued)

such as parks, airports, industrial complexes and water, were excluded from the area reported for each city, thus making the population density reflective of the concentrations in the residential portions of the city. By using a consistent definition for the city, it is possible to make comparisons of the cities on the basis of total population, area, and population density.

The population of each city was projected based on projected country populations and the proportion of each city population to the total population of the country at the time of the last 2 censuses. Figures in the table below may differ from city population figures elsewhere in The World Almanac because of different methods of determining population.

City, Country	1991 (thousands)	2000 (thousands projected)	Area (sq. mi.)	Density 1991 (pop per sq. mi.)
Tokyo-Yokohama, Japan	27,245	29,971	1,089	25,019
Mexico City, Mexico	20,899	27,872	522	40,037
São Paulo, Brazil	18,701	25,354	451	41,466
Seoul, South Korea	16,792	21,976	342	49,101
New York, U.S.	14,625	14,648	1,274	11,480
Osaka-Kobe-Kyoto, Japan	13,872	14,287	495	28,025
Bombay, India	12,101	15,357	95	127,461
Calcutta, India	11,898	14,088	209	56,927
Rio de Janeiro, Brazil	11,688	14,169	260	44,952
Buenos Aires, Argentina	11,657	12,911	535	21,790
Moscow, Russia	10,446	11,121	379	27,562
Manila, Philippines	10,156	12,846	188	54,024
Los Angeles, U.S.	10,130	10,714	1,110	9,126
Cairo, Egypt	10,099	12,512	104	97,106
Jakarta, Indonesia	9,882	12,804	76	130,026
Tehran, Iran	9,779	14,251	112	87,312
London, U.K.	9,115	8,574	874	10,429
Delhi, India	8,778	11,849	138	63,612
Paris, France	8,720	8,803	432	20,185
Karachi, Pakistan	8,014	11,299	190	42,179
Lagos, Nigeria	7,998	12,528	56	142,821
Essen, Germany	7,452	7,239	704	10,585
Shanghai, China	6,936	7,540	78	88,924
Lima, Peru	6,815	9,241	120	56,794
Taipei, Taiwan	6,695	8,516	138	48,517
Istanbul, Turkey	6,678	8,875	165	40,476
Chicago, U.S.	6,529	6,568	762	8,568
Bangkok, Thailand	5,955	7,587	102	58,379
Bogotá, Colombia	5,913	7,935	79	74,851
Madras, India	5,896	7,384	115	51,270
Beijing, China	5,762	5,993	151	38,156
Hong Kong	5,693	5,956	23	247,501
Santiago, Chile	5,378	6,294	128	40,018
Pusan, S. Korea	5,008	6,700	54	92,735
Tianjin, China	4,850	5,298	49	98,990
Bangalore, India	4,802	6,764	50	96,041
Nagoya, Japan	4,791	5,303	307	15,606
Milan, Italy	4,749	4,839	344	13,806
St Petersburg, Russia	4,672	4,738	139	33,614
Madrid, Spain	4,513	5,104	66	68,385
Dhaka, Bangladesh	4,419	6,492	32	138,108
Lahore, Pakistan	4,376	5,864	57	76,779
Shenyang, China	4,289	4,684	39	109,974
Barcelona, Spain	4,227	4,834	87	48,584
Baghdad, Iran	4,059	5,239	97	41,843
Manchester, U.K.	4,030	3,827	357	11,287
Philadelphia, U.S.	4,003	3,979	471	8,499
San Francisco, U.S.	3,986	4,214	428	9,315
Belo Horizonte, Brazil	3,812	5,125	79	48,249
Kinshasa, Zaire	3,747	5,646	57	65,732
Ho Chi Minh City, Vietnam	3,725	4,481	31	120,168
Ahmadabad, India	3,709	4,837	32	115,893
Hyderabad, India	3,673	4,765	88	41,741
Sydney, Australia	3,536	3,708	338	10,460
Athens, Greece	3,507	3,866	116	30,237
Miami, U.S.	3,471	3,894	448	7,748
Guadalajara, Mexico	3,370	4,451	78	43,205
Guangzhou, China	3,360	3,652	79	42,537
Surabaya, Indonesia	3,248	3,632	43	75,544
Caracas, Venezuela	3,217	3,435	54	59,582
Wuhan, China	3,200	3,495	65	49,225
Toronto, Canada	3,145	3,296	154	20,420
Porto Alegre, Brazil	3,114	4,109	231	13,479
Rome, Italy	3,033	3,129	69	43,949
Berlin, Germany	3,021	3,006	274	11,026
Naples, Italy	2,978	3,134	62	48,032
Casablanca, Morocco	2,973	3,795	35	84,953
Detroit, U.S.(*)	2,969	2,735	468	6,343
Alexandria, Egypt	2,941	3,304	35	84,022
Monterrey, Mexico	2,939	3,974	77	38,169
Montreal, Canada	2,916	3,071	164	17,779
Melbourne, Australia	2,915	2,968	327	8,914
Ankara, Turkey	2,872	3,777	55	52,221
Yangon, Myanmar	2,864	3,332	47	60,927
Kiev, Ukraine	2,796	3,237	62	45,095
Dallas, U.S.	2,787	3,257	419	6,652
Singapore, Singapore	2,719	2,913	78	34,856
Taegu, South Korea	2,651	4,051	NA	NA
Harbin, China	2,643	2,887	30	88,110
Washington, U.S.	2,565	2,707	357	7,184
Poona, India	2,547	3,647	NA	NA
Boston, U.S.	2,476	2,485	303	8,172
Lisbon, Portugal	2,426	2,717	NA	NA
Tashkent, Uzbekistan	2,418	2,947	NA	NA
Chongqing, China	2,395	2,961	NA	NA
Chengdu, China	2,372	2,591	25	94,870
Vienna, Austria	2,344	2,647	NA	NA
Houston, U.S.	2,329	2,651	310	7,512
Budapest, Hungary	2,303	2,335	138	16,691
Salvador, Brazil	2,298	3,286	NA	NA

(*) Includes Windsor, Canada. NA = not available.

The World's Refugees

(as of 31 Dec. 1992)

Source: *World Refugee Survey 1993*, U.S. Committee for Refugees, a nonprofit corp. The refugees in this table include only those who are in need of protection and/or assistance, and do not include refugees who have resettled.

Country of Asylum	Mostly from	Number
Total Africa		**5,698,540**
Algeria	W. Sahara, Mali	165,000[1]
Angola	Zaire	9,000
Benin	Togo	4,300
Botswana	S. Africa, Angola	5,000
Burkina Faso	Mali	6,300
Burundi	Rwanda, Zaire	107,350[1]
Cameroon	Chad	1,500
Central African Rep.	Chad, Sudan	18,000
Congo	Chad, Angola	9,400
Côte d'Ivoire	Liberia	195,500
Djibouti	Ethiopia, Somalia	96,000
Egypt	Palestinians, Somalia	10,650
Ethiopia/Eritrea	Sudan, Somalia	416,000[1]
Gabon	various	200
Gambia, The	Senegal, Liberia	3,300
Ghana	Liberia, Togo	12,100
Guinea	Liberia, Sierra Leone	485,000[1]
Guinea-Bissau	Senegal	12,000
Kenya	Ethiopia, Sudan, Somalia	422,900[1]
Lesotho	South Africa	200
Liberia	Sierra Leone	100,000
Malawi	Mozambique	1,070,000
Mali	Mauritania	10,000
Mauritania	Mali	40,000
Morocco	various	800
Mozambique	various	250
Namibia	various	150
Niger	Chad	3,600
Nigeria	Chad, Liberia	2,900
Rwanda	Burundi	24,500
Senegal	Mauritania	55,100
Sierra Leone	Liberia	7,600
Somalia	Ethiopia/Eritrea	10,000[1]
S. Africa	Mozambique	250,000[1]
Sudan	Ethiopia/Eritrea, Chad	750,500[1]
Swaziland	South Africa, Mozambique	52,000
Tanzania	Burundi, Mozambique	257,800

(Continued)

Country of Asylum	Mostly from	Number
Togo	various	350
Uganda	Sudan, Rwanda	179,600[1]
Zaire	Angola, Burundi, Sudan	442,400
Zambia	Angola, Mozambique, Zaire	155,700
Zimbabwe	Mozambique	265,000[1]
Total East Asia/Pacific		**398,600**
Australia	various	24,000
China	Myanmar	12,500[1]
Hong Kong	Vietnam	45,300
Indonesia	Vietnam, Cambodia	15,600
Japan	Vietnam	700
Korea	Vietnam	150
Malaysia	Vietnam, Myanmar	16,700
Papua New Guinea	Indonesia	3,800
Philippines	Vietnam	5,600
Singapore	Vietnam	100
Taiwan	Vietnam	150
Thailand	Myanmar, Laos, Cambodia	255,000
Vietnam	Cambodia	19,000
Total Europe & N. America		**3,423,600**
Armenia	Azerbaijan	300,000[1]
Austria	former Yugoslavia	82,100
Azerbaijan	Armenia	246,000[1]
Belarus	various	3,700
Belgium	various	19,100
Bosnia and Herzegovina	former Yugoslavia	70,000[1]
Canada	various	37,700
Croatia	former Yugoslavia	420,000[1]
Czech Rep./Slovakia	former Yugoslavia	2,200
Denmark	former Yugoslavia	13,900
Finland	various	3,500
France	various	29,400
Germany	former Yugoslavia	536,000
Greece	various	1,900
Hungary	former Yugoslavia	40,000
Italy	former Yugoslavia	19,100
Luxembourg	former Yugoslavia	1,800
Macedonia	former Yugoslavia	32,700[1]
Netherlands	various	24,600
Norway	various	5,700
Poland	former Yugoslavia	1,500
Russia	various	460,000[1]
Slovenia	former Yugoslavia	68,900[1]
Spain	various	12,700
Sweden	former Yugoslavia	88,400
Switzerland	former Yugoslavia	81,700
Turkey	Iraq, former Yugoslavia	31,700
Ukraine	various	40,000[1]
United Kingdom	various	24,600
United States	various	103,700
Yugoslavia[2]	former Yugoslavia	621,000[1]
Total Latin America/Caribbean		**107,700**
Belize	El Salvador, Guatemala	6,100
Brazil	various	200
Colombia	various	400
Costa Rica	El Salvador, Nicaragua	34,350
Cuba	Haiti	1,100
Ecuador	various	200
El Salvador	various	250
French Guiana	Suriname	1,600
Guatemala	El Salvador, Nicaragua	4,900
Honduras	various	150
Mexico	Guatemala, El Salvador	47,300
Nicaragua	El Salvador	5,850
Panama	various	850
Peru	Cuba	400
Uruguay	various	100
Venezuela	Cuba, Haiti	1,350
Total Middle East/South & Central Asia		**7,938,550**
Afghanistan	Tajikistan	52,000
Bangladesh	Myanmar	245,000
India	Bangladesh, Tibet, Sri Lanka	378,000[1]
Iran	Afghanistan, Iraq	2,781,800[1]
Iraq	Iran	64,000
Nepal	Tibet, Bhutan	89,400
Pakistan	Afghanistan	1,577,000
Saudi Arabia	Iraq	27,400
Yemen	Somalia	52,500
Palestinians		
Gaza Strip		560,200
Jordan		1,010,850[3]
Lebanon		322,900[3]
Syria		307,400[3]
West Bank		459,100
Total Refugees		**17,556,900**

(1) Significant variance among sources in number reported. (2) Incl. Serbia/Montenegro. (3) Incl. some non-Palestinians.

Principal Sources of Refugees

Afghanistan	4,286,000[1]	Angola	404,200	Rwanda	201,500[1]
Palestinians	2,658,000[1]	Croatia	350,000	Sierra Leone	200,000
Mozambique	1,725,000[1]	Azerbaijan	350,000[1]	Burundi	184,000
Bosnia and Herzegovina	940,000[1]	Myanmar	333,700[1]	Sri Lanka	181,000
Somalia	864,800[1]	Sudan	263,000	Western Sahara	165,000[1]
Ethiopia/Eritrea	834,800[1]	Armenia	202,000[1]	Cambodia	148,600
Liberia	599,200[1]				

(1) Significant variance among sources in number reported.

Foreign Exchange Rates: 1970 to 1992

Source: International Monetary Fund

(National currency units per dollar, except as indicated; data are annual averages)

Year	Australia[1] (dollar)	Austria (schilling)	Belgium (franc)	Canada (dollar)	Denmark (krone)	France (franc)	Germany[2] (deutsch-mark)	Greece (drachma)
1970	1.1136	25.880	49.680	1.0103	7.489	5.5200	3.6480	30.00
1975	1.3077	17.443	36.799	1.0175	5.748	4.2876	2.4613	32.29
1980	1.1400	12.945	29.237	1.1693	5.634	4.2250	1.8175	42.62
1981	1.1495	15.948	37.194	1.1990	7.135	5.4396	2.2631	55.41
1983	.9014	17.968	51.121	1.2325	9.148	7.6203	2.5539	87.90
1984	.8794	20.009	57.784	1.2951	10.357	8.7391	2.8454	112.73
1985	.7003	20.690	59.378	1.3655	10.596	8.9852	2.9440	138.12
1986	.6709	15.267	44.672	1.3895	8.091	6.9261	2.1715	139.98
1987	.7009	12.643	37.334	1.3260	6.840	6.0107	1.7974	135.43
1988	.7842	12.243	36.768	1.2307	6.732	5.9569	1.7562	141.89
1989	.7925	13.231	39.404	1.1840	7.310	6.3801	1.8800	162.42
1990	.7813	11.370	33.418	1.1668	6.189	5.4453	1.6157	158.51
1991	.7791	11.676	34.148	1.1457	6.396	5.6421	1.6595	182.27
1992	.7353	10.989	32.150	1.2087	6.036	5.2938	1.5617	190.62

(Continued)

	India (rupee)	Ireland[1] (pound)	Italy (lira)	Japan (yen)	Malaysia (ringgit)	Netherlands (guilder)	Norway (kroner)	Portugal (escudo)
1970	7.576	2.3959	623	357.60	3.0900	3.5970	7.1400	28.75
1975	8.409	2.2216	653	296.78	2.4030	2.5293	5.2282	25.51
1980	7.887	2.0577	856	226.63	2.1767	1.9875	4.9381	50.08
1981	8.681	1.6132	1,138	220.63	2.3048	2.4998	5.7430	61.74
1983	10.104	1.2481	1,519	237.55	2.3204	2.8543	7.3012	111.61
1984	11.363	1.0871	1,756	237.52	2.3436	3.2087	8.1615	146.39
1985	12.369	1.0656	1,909	238.54	2.4830	3.3214	8.5972	170.39
1986	12.611	1.3415	1,490	168.52	2.5814	2.4500	7.3947	149.59
1987	12.962	1.4881	1,296	144.64	2.5196	2.0257	6.7375	140.88
1988	13.917	1.5261	1,301	128.15	2.6188	1.9766	6.5170	143.95
1989	16.226	1.4190	1,372	137.96	2.7088	2.1207	6.9045	157.46
1990	17.504	1.6585	1,198	144.79	2.7048	1.8209	6.2597	142.55
1991	22.742	1.6155	1,240	134.71	2.7501	1.8697	6.4829	144.48
1992	25.918	1.7053	1,232	126.65	2.5474	1.7885	6.2145	135.00

	Singapore (dollar)	South Korea (won)	Spain (peseta)	Sweden (krona)	Switzerland (franc)	Thailand (baht)	UK[1] (pound)
1970	3.0800	310.57	69.72	5.1700	4.3160	21.000	2.3959
1975	2.3713	484.00	57.43	4.1530	2.5839	20.379	2.2216
1980	2.1412	607.43	71.76	4.2309	1.6772	20.476	2.3243
1981	2.1053	681.03	92.40	5.0659	1.9674	21.731	2.0243
1983	2.1136	776.04	143.50	7.6717	2.1006	22.991	1.5159
1984	2.1331	805.69	160.78	8.2718	2.3497	23.639	1.3366
1985	2.2002	870.02	170.04	8.6039	2.4571	27.159	1.2963
1986	2.1774	881.45	140.04	7.1236	1.7989	26.299	1.4670
1987	2.1059	822.57	123.48	6.3404	1.4912	25.723	1.6389
1988	2.0124	731.57	116.49	6.1272	1.4633	25.294	1.7813
1989	1.9508	671.46	118.38	6.4469	1.6359	25.702	1.6897
1990	1.8125	707.76	101.93	5.9188	1.3892	25.585	1.7847
1991	1.7276	733.35	103.91	6.0475	1.4340	25.517	1.7694
1992	1.6290	780.65	102.38	5.8238	1.4062	25.400	1.7655

(1) Value of one unit of foreign currency in dollars. (2) W. Germany prior to 1991.

Major International Organizations

As of mid-1993

Association of Southeast Asian Nations (ASEAN) was formed in 1967 to promote economic, social, and cultural cooperation and development among the non-communist states of the region. Members in 1993 are Brunei Darussalam, Indonesia, Malaysia, Philippines, Singapore, Thailand. Annual ministerial meetings set policy; a central Secretariat in Jakarta and specialized intergovernmental committees work in trade, transportation, communications, agriculture, science, finance, and culture.

Caribbean Community and Common Market (Caricom) was established July 4, 1973. Its function is to further co-operation in economics, health, education, culture, science and technology, and tax administration, as well as the co-ordination of foreign policy. Members in 1993 are Antigua and Barbuda, Bahamas, Barbados, Belize, Dominica, Grenada, Guyana, Jamaica, Montserrat, St. Kitts and Nevis, St. Lucia, St. Vincent, Trinidad & Tobago.

Commonwealth of Independent States (CIS) was created Dec. 1991 upon the disbanding of the Soviet Union. It is made up of 10 of the 15 former Soviet constituent republics. Members are Armenia, Belarus, Kazakhstan, Kyrgyzstan, Moldova, Russia, Tajikistan, Turkmenistan, Ukraine and Uzbekistan. The commonwealth is not in itself a state, but an alliance of fully independent states. Commonwealth policy is set through coordinating bodies such as a Council of Heads of State and Council of Heads of Government. The capital of the commonwealth is Minsk, Belarus.

Commonwealth of Nations (see p. 303).

European Community (see p. 297).

European Free Trade Association (EFTA), was created May 3, 1960, to promote expansion of free trade. Current members are Austria, Finland, Iceland, Liechtenstein, Norway, Sweden and Switzerland. By Dec. 31, 1966, tariffs and quotas between member nations had been eliminated. Members of the association entered into free trade agreements with the EC in 1972 and 1973. In 1992 the EFTA and EC concluded an agreement to create a single market—with free flow of goods, services, capital and labour—encompassing the 19 nations of the 2 organizations.

Group of Seven (G-7) is an organization of 7 major industrial democracies who meet periodically to discuss world economic issues. Established Sep. 22, 1985, members are Canada, France, Germany, Italy, Japan, UK, and U.S.

International Criminal Police Organization (Interpol) was created June 13, 1956 to ensure and promote the widest possible mutual assistance between all police authorities within the limits of the law existing in the different countries and in the spirit of the Universal Declaration of Human Rights. There are 152 members in 1993.

League of Arab States (The Arab League) was created Mar. 22, 1945. Members in 1993 are Algeria, Bahrain, Djibouti, Egypt, Iraq, Jordan, Kuwait, Lebanon, Libya, Mauritania, Morocco, Oman, Qatar, The Palestine Liberation Org., Saudi Arabia, Somalia, Sudan, Syria, Tunisia, United Arab Emirates, Yemen. The League promotes economic, social, political and military cooperation, and mediates disputes among the Arab states; it represents Arab states in certain international negotiations. The League's headquarters is in Cairo.

North Atlantic Treaty Organization (NATO) was created by treaty (signed Apr. 4, 1949; in effect Aug. 24, 1949). Members in 1993 are Belgium, Canada, Denmark, France, Germany, Greece, Iceland, Italy, Luxembourg, Netherlands, Norway, Portugal, Spain, Turkey, United Kingdom, and the United States. The members agreed to settle disputes by peaceful means; to develop their individual and collective capacity to resist armed attack; to regard an attack on one as an attack on all; and to take necessary action to repel an attack under Article 51 of the United Nations Charter.

The NATO structure consists of a Council and a Military Committee of 3 commands (Allied Command Europe, Allied Command Atlantic, Allied Command Channel) and the Canada-U.S. Regional Planning Group.

With the dissolution of the Soviet Union and end of the cold war in the early 1990s, NATO members sought to modify the organization's mission, putting greater stress on political action and creating a rapid deployment force to react to local crises. Former Warsaw Pact members were no longer considered adversaries, and Hungary gained associate membership in 1991.

Organization of African Unity (OAU), formed May 25, 1963, by 32 African countries (51 in 1993) to promote peace and security as well as economic and social development. It holds annual conferences of heads of state. The headquarters is in Addis Ababa, Ethiopia.

Organization of American States (OAS) was formed in Bogotá, Colombia, Apr. 30, 1948. Headquarters is in Washington, D.C. It has a Permanent Council, Inter-American Economic and Social Council, Inter-American Council for Education, Science and Culture, Juridical Committee and Commission on Human Rights. The Permanent Council can call meetings of foreign ministers to deal with urgent security matters. A General Assembly meets annually. A secretary general and assistant are elected for 5-year terms. There are 35 members, each with one vote in the various organizations: Antigua and Barbuda, Argentina, the Bahamas, Barbados, Belize, Bolivia, Brazil, Chile, Colombia, Costa Rica, Cuba, Dominica, Dominican Republic, Ecuador, El Salvador, Grenada, Guatemala, Guyana, Haiti, Honduras, Jamaica, Mexico, Nicaragua, Panama, Paraguay, Peru, St. Kitts and Nevis, St. Lucia, St. Vincent and the Grenadines, Suriname, Trinidad & Tobago, United States, Uruguay, Venezuela. In 1962 the OAS excluded Cuba from OAS activities but not from membership.

Organization for Economic Cooperation and Development (OECD) was established Sept. 30, 1961 to promote economic and social welfare in member countries, and to stimulate and harmonize efforts on behalf of developing nations. The OECD collects and disseminates economic and environmental information. Members in 1993 are: Australia, Austria, Belgium, Canada, Denmark, Finland, France, Germany, Greece, Iceland, Ireland, Italy, Japan, Luxembourg, Netherlands, New Zealand, Norway, Portugal, Spain, Sweden, Switzerland, Turkey, United Kingdom, United States. Headquarters is in Paris.

Organization of Petroleum Exporting Countries (OPEC) was created Nov. 14, 1960. The group attempts to set world oil prices by controlling oil production. It is also involved in advancing members' interests in trade and development dealings with industrialized oil-consuming nations. Members in 1993 are Algeria, Gabon, Indonesia, Iran, Iraq, Kuwait, Libya, Nigeria, Qatar, Saudi Arabia, United Arab Emirates, Venezuela.

Geneva Conventions

The Geneva Conventions are 4 international treaties governing the protection of civilians in time of war, the treatment of prisoners of war, and the care of the wounded and sick in the armed forces. The first convention, covering the sick and wounded, was concluded in Geneva, Switzerland, in 1864; it was amended and expanded in 1906. A third convention, in 1929, covered prisoners of war. Outrage at the treatment of prisoners and civilians during World War II by some belligerents, notably Germany and Japan, prompted the conclusion, in August 1949, of 4 new conventions. Three of these restated and strengthened the previous conventions, and the fourth codified general principles of international law governing the treatment of civilians in wartime.

The 1949 convention for civilians provided for special safeguards for the wounded, children under 15, pregnant women, and the elderly. Discrimination was forbidden on racial, religious, national, or political grounds. Torture, collective punishment, reprisals, the unwarrented destruction of property, and the forced use of civilians for an occupier's armed forces were also prohibited.

Also included in the new 1949 treaties was a pledge to treat prisoners humanely, feed them adequately, and deliver relief supplies to them. They were not to be forced to disclose more than minimal information.

Most countries have formally accepted all or most of the humanitarian conventions as binding. A nation is not free to withdraw its ratification of the conventions during wartime. However, there is no permanent machinery in place to apprehend, try, or punish violators.

United Nations

The 48th regular session of the United Nations General Assembly opened in September 1993.

UN headquarters is in New York, N.Y., between First Ave. and Roosevelt Drive and E. 42d St. and E. 48th St. The General Assembly Bldg., Secretariat, Conference and Library bldgs. are interconnected.

A European office at Geneva includes Secretariat and agency staff members. Other offices of UN bodies and related organizations, with a staff of some 23,000 from some 150 countries, are scattered throughout the world.

The UN has a post office in New York originating

its own stamps.

Proposals to establish an organization of nations for maintenance of world peace led to the United Nations Conference on International Organization at San Francisco, Apr. 25-June 26, 1945, where the charter of the United Nations was drawn up. It was signed June 26 by 50 nations, and by Poland, one of the original 51 UN members, on Oct. 15, 1945. The charter came into effect Oct. 24, 1945, upon ratification by the permanent members of the Security Council and a majority of other signatories.

Purposes: To maintain international peace and security; to develop friendly relations among nations; to achieve international cooperation in solving economic, social, cultural, and humanitarian problems and in promoting respect for human rights and fundamental freedoms; to be a center for harmonizing the actions of nations in attaining these common ends.

Roster of the United Nations

(As of Sept. 1993)

The 184 members of the United Nations, with the years in which they became members.

Member	Year	Member	Year	Member	Year	Member	Year
Afghanistan	1946	Dominica	1978	Liberia	1945	Saint Vincent & the Grenadines	1980
Albania	1955	Dominican Rep.	1945	Libya	1955	San Marino	1992
Algeria	1962	Ecuador	1945	Liechtenstein	1990	São Tomé e Príncipe	1975
Andorra	1993	Egypt[3]	1945	Lithuania	1991	Saudi Arabia	1945
Angola	1976	El Salvador	1945	Luxembourg	1945	Senegal	1960
Antigua & Barbuda	1981	Equatorial Guinea	1968	Macedonia[5]	1993	Seychelles	1976
Argentina	1945	Eritrea	1993	Madagascar	1960	Sierra Leone	1961
Armenia	1992	Estonia	1991	Malawi	1964	Singapore[6]	1965
Australia	1945	Ethiopia	1945	Malaysia[6]	1957	Slovakia[2]	1993
Austria	1955	Fiji	1970	Maldives	1965	Slovenia	1992
Azerbaijan	1992	Finland	1955	Mali	1960	Solomon Islands	1978
Bahamas	1973	France	1945	Malta	1964	Somalia	1960
Bahrain	1971	Gabon	1960	Marshall Islands	1991	South Africa[7]	1945
Bangladesh	1974	Gambia, The	1965	Mauritania	1961	Spain	1955
Barbados	1966	Georgia	1992	Mauritius	1968	Sri Lanka	1955
Belarus	1945	Germany (E. & W.)	1973	Mexico	1945	Sudan	1956
Belgium	1945	Ghana	1957	Micronesia	1991	Suriname	1975
Belize	1981	Greece	1945	Moldova	1992	Swaziland	1968
Benin	1960	Grenada	1974	Monaco	1993	Sweden	1946
Bhutan	1971	Guatemala	1945	Mongolia	1961	Syria[3]	1945
Bolivia	1945	Guinea	1958	Morocco	1956	Tajikistan	1992
Botswana	1966	Guinea-Bissau	1974	Mozambique	1975	Tanzania[8]	1961
Bosnia & Herzegovina	1992	Guyana	1966	Myanmar (Burma)	1948	Thailand	1946
Brazil	1945	Haiti	1945	Namibia	1990	Togo	1960
Brunei Darussalam	1984	Honduras	1945	Nepal	1955	Trinidad & Tobago	1962
Bulgaria	1955	Hungary	1955	Netherlands	1945	Tunisia	1956
Burkina Faso	1960	Iceland	1946	New Zealand	1945	Turkey	1945
Burundi	1962	India	1945	Nicaragua	1945	Turkmenistan	1992
Cambodia	1955	Indonesia[4]	1950	Niger	1960	Uganda	1962
Cameroon	1960	Iran	1945	Nigeria	1960	Ukraine	1945
Canada	1945	Iraq	1945	Norway	1945	United Arab Emirates	1971
Cape Verde	1975	Ireland	1955	Oman	1971	United Kingdom	1945
Central Afr. Rep.	1960	Israel	1949	Pakistan	1947	United States	1945
Chad	1960	Italy	1955	Panama	1945	Uruguay	1945
Chile	1945	Jamaica	1962	Papua New Guinea	1975	Uzbekistan	1992
China[1]	1945	Japan	1956	Paraguay	1945	Vanuatu	1981
Colombia	1945	Jordan	1955	Peru	1945	Venezuela	1945
Comoros	1975	Kazakhstan	1992	Philippines	1945	Vietnam	1977
Congo	1960	Kenya	1963	Poland	1945	Western Samoa	1976
Costa Rica	1945	Korea, N.	1991	Portugal	1955	Yemen[9]	1947
Côte d'Ivoire	1960	Korea, S.	1991	Qatar	1971	Yugoslavia[10]	1945
Croatia	1992	Kuwait	1963	Romania	1955	Zaire	1960
Cuba	1945	Kyrgyzstan	1992	Russia	1945	Zambia	1964
Cyprus	1960	Laos	1955	Rwanda	1962	Zimbabwe	1980
Czech Rep.[2]	1993	Latvia	1991	Saint Kitts & Nevis	1983		
Denmark	1945	Lebanon	1945	Saint Lucia	1979		
Djibouti	1977	Lesotho	1966				

(1) The General Assembly voted in 1971 to expel the Chinese government on Taiwan and admit the Beijing government in its place. (2) Czechoslovakia, which split into the separate nations of the Czech Republic and Slovakia on Jan. 1, 1993, was a UN member from 1945 to 1992. (3) Egypt and Syria were original members of the UN. In 1958, the United Arab Republic was established by a union of Egypt and Syria and continued as a single member of the UN. In 1961, Syria resumed its separate membership. (4) Indonesia withdrew from the UN in 1965 and rejoined in 1966. (5) Admitted under the provisional name of The Former Yugoslav Republic of Macedonia. (6) Malaya joined the UN in 1957. In 1963, its name was changed to Malaysia following the accession of Singapore, Sabah, and Sarawak. Singapore became an independent UN member in 1965. (7) The General Assembly rejected the credentials of the South African delegates in 1974 and suspended the country from the Assembly. (8) Tanganyika was a member of the United Nations from 1961 and Zanzibar was a member from 1963. Following the ratification in 1964 of Articles of Union between Tanganyika and Zanzibar, the United Republic of Tanganyika and Zanzibar continued as a single member of the United Nations, later changing its name to United Republic of Tanzania. (9) The Yemen Arab Republic was admitted in 1947; the People's Democratic Republic of Yemen, in 1967. The two nations merged in 1990. (10) The Socialist Federal Republic of Yugoslavia became a member in 1945. After 4 of its 6 republics (Bosnia and Herzegovina, Croatia, Macedonia and Slovenia) declared independence in 1991–2, the two remaining republics, Montenegro and Serbia, reconstituted themselves as the Federal Republic of Yugoslavia, which assumed Yugoslavia's UN seat Apr. 8, 1992. The General Assembly suspended Yugoslavia in September 1992 for violating UN resolutions relating to the civil wars in the former Yugoslav republics.

Organization of the United Nations

The text of the UN Charter, and further information, may be obtained from the Office of Public Information, United Nations, New York, NY 10017.

General Assembly. The General Assembly is composed of representatives of all the member nations. Each nation is entitled to one vote.

The General Assembly meets in regular annual

sessions and in special session when necessary. Special sessions are convoked by the Secretary General at the request of the Security Council or of a majority of the members of the UN.

On important questions a two-thirds majority of members present and voting is required; on other questions a simple majority is sufficient.

The General Assembly must approve the budget and apportion expenses among members. A member in arrears will have no vote if the amount of arrears equals or exceeds the amount of the contributions due for the preceding two full years.

Security Council. The Security Council consists of 15 members, 5 with permanent seats. The remaining 10 are elected for 2-year terms by the General Assembly; they are not eligible for immediate reelection.

Permanent members of the Council are China, France, Russia, United Kingdom, United States.

Non-permanent members are Cape Verde, Hungary, Japan, Morocco, Venezuela (until Dec. 31, 1993); Brazil, Djibouti, New Zealand, Pakistan, Spain (until Dec. 31, 1994).

The Security Council has the primary responsibility within the UN for maintaining international peace and security. The Council may investigate any dispute that threatens international peace and security.

Any member of the UN at UN headquarters may participate in its discussions and a nation not a member of UN may appear if it is a party to a dispute.

Decisions on procedural questions are made by an affirmative vote of 9 members. On all other matters the affirmative vote of 9 members must include the concurring votes of all permanent members; it is this clause which gives rise to the so-called veto power of permanent members. A party to a dispute must refrain from voting.

The Security Council directs the various truce supervisory forces deployed throughout the world.

Economic and Social Council. The Economic and Social Council consists of 54 members elected by the General Assembly for 3-year terms of office. The council is responsible under the General Assembly for carrying out the functions of the United Nations with regard to international economic, social, cultural, educational, health and related matters. The council usually meets twice a year.

Trusteeship Council. The administration of trust territories is under UN supervision. The only remaining trust territory is Palau, administered by the U.S.

Secretariat. The Secretary General is the chief administrative officer of the UN. He may bring to the attention of the Security Council any matter that threatens international peace. He reports to the General Assembly.

Budget: The General Assembly approved a total budget for 1992-93 of $2.36 billion.

International Court of Justice (World Court). The International Court of Justice is the principal judicial organ of the United Nations. All members are *ipso facto* parties to the statute of the Court. Other states may become parties to the Court's statute.

The jurisdiction of the Court comprises cases which the parties submit to it and matters especially provided for in the charter or in treaties. The Court gives advisory opinions and renders judgments. Its decisions are binding only between the parties concerned and in respect to a particular dispute. If any party to a case fails to heed a judgment, the other party may have recourse to the Security Council.

The 15 judges are elected for 9-year terms by the General Assembly and the Security Council. Retiring judges are eligible for re-election. The Court remains permanently in session, except during vacations. All questions are decided by majority. The Court sits in The Hague, Netherlands.

United Nations Secretaries General

Year	Secretary, Nation	Year	Secretary, Nation	Year	Secretary, Nation
1946	Trygve Lie, Norway	1961	U Thant, Burma	1982	Javier Pérez de Cuéllar, Peru
1953	Dag Hammarskjöld, Sweden	1972	Kurt Waldheim, Austria	1992	Boutros Boutros-Ghali, Egypt

Visitors to the United Nations

United Nations headquarters is open to the public every day of the year except Christmas and New Year's Day. The public entrance is at 46th Street and First Avenue and opens at 9 a.m.

Guided tours begin from the main lobby of the General Assembly building and are given approximately every half hour from 9:15 a.m. to 4:45 p.m. daily. The tours last about one hour. Tours in languages other than English may be arranged.

Groups of 15 or more persons should make arrangements as far in advance as possible by writing to the Group Program Unit, Visitors' Service, Room GA-56, United Nations, New York, NY 10017, or telephone (212) 963-4440. Children under 5 are not permitted on tours.

UK Representatives to the United Nations

The UK representative to the United Nations holds the rank and status of Ambassador Extraordinary and Plenipotentiary.

Tenure	Representative	Tenure	Representative	Tenure	Representative
1946–50	Sir Alexander Cadogan	1964–70	Lord Caradon	1982–87	Sir John Thomson
1950–54	Sir Gladwyn Jebb	1970–74	Sir Colin Crowe	1987–90	Sir Crispin Tickell
1954–60	Sir Pierson Dixon	1974–79	Ivor Richards, QC	1990–	Sir David Hannay
1960–64	Sir Patrick Dean	1979–82	Sir Anthony Parsons		

British Missions & Delegations

- UK Mission to the United Nations, New York – Sir David Hannay, Amb.
- UK Mission to the Office of the United Nations & Other International Organizations at Geneva – M. R. Morland, Amb.
- UK Delegation to the Conference on Disarmament, Geneva – Sir Michael Weston, Amb.
- UK Delegation to the Organization for Economic Cooperation & Development, Paris – K. G. McInnes, Amb.
- UK Permanent Representative to the European Community, Brussels – Sir John Kerr, Amb.
- UK Delegation to the Council of Europe, Strasbourg – N. H. Marshall, Amb.
- UK Delegation to the International Monetary Fund & International Bank for Reconstruction & Development, Washington – D. Peretz, Exec. Director
- UK Delegation to the Negotiations on Conventional Arms Control in Europe, Vienna – P. Lever, Amb.
- UK Mission to the International Atomic Energy Agency, the UN Industrial Development Organization and the UN, Vienna – C. Hulse, Amb.
- United Nations Environment Programme, Nairobi – Sir Kieran Prendergast
- United Nations Centre for Human Settlements (Habitat), Nairobi – Sir Kieran Prendergast
- UK Representation on the Council of the Food & Agriculture Organization of the UN – J. R. Goldsack

Selected Specialized and Related Agencies

These agencies are autonomous, with their own memberships and organs, which have a functional relationship or working agreement with the UN (headquarters).

Food & Agriculture Organization (FAO) aims to increase production from farms, forests, and fisheries; improve food distribution and marketing, and nutrition and the living conditions of rural people. (Viale delle Terme di Caracalla, 00100 Rome, Italy)

General Agreement on Tariffs and Trade (GATT) is the only treaty setting rules for world trade; provides a forum for settling trade disputes and negotiating trade liberalization. (Centre William Rappard, 154 rue de Lausanne, 1211 Geneva 21, Switzerland)

International Atomic Energy Agency (IAEA) aims to promote the safe, peaceful uses of atomic energy. (Vienna International Centre, PO Box 100, A-1400, Vienna, Austria)

International Bank for Reconstruction and Development (IBRD) (World Bank) provides loans and technical assistance for economic development projects in developing member countries; encourages cofinancing for projects from other public and private sources. The **International Development Association (IDA)**, an affiliate of the Bank, provides funds for development projects on concessionary terms to the poorer developing member countries. The **International Finance Corporation (IFC)** an affiliate of the Bank, promotes the growth of the private sector in developing member countries; encourages the development of local capital markets; stimulates the international flow of private capital. (All at 1818 H St., NW, Washington, DC 20433)

International Civil Aviation Organization (ICAO) promotes international civil aviation standards and regulations. (1000 Sherbrooke St. W., Montreal, Quebec, Canada H3A 2R2)

International Fund for Agricultural Development (IFAD) aims to mobilize funds for agricultural and rural projects in developing countries. (107 Via del Serafico, Rome, Italy)

International Labour Organization (ILO) aims to promote employment; improve labour conditions and living standards. (4 route de Morillons, CH-1211, Geneva 22, Switzerland)

International Maritime Organization (IMO) aims to promote cooperation on technical matters affecting international shipping. (4 Albert Embankment, London SE1 7SR, England)

International Monetary Fund (IMF) aims to promote international monetary cooperation and currency stabilization and expansion of international trade. (700 19th St., NW, Washington, DC, 20431)

International Telecommunication Union (ITU) establishes international regulations for radio, telegraph, telephone and space radio-communications; allocates radio frequencies. (Place des Nations, 1211 Geneva 20, Switzerland)

United Nations Development Fund for Woman (UNIFEM) aims to assist women in their economic roles in Africa, Asia and Latin America. (304 E. 45th St., New York, NY 10017)

United Nations Educational, Scientific and Cultural Organization (UNESCO) aims to promote collaboration among nations through education, science, and culture. (9 Place de Fontenoy, 75700 Paris, France)

United Nations Children's Fund (UNICEF) provides aid and development assistance to programmes for children and mothers in developing countries. (1 UN Plaza, New York, NY 10017)

United Nations High Commissioner for Refugees (UNHCR) provides essential assistance for refugees. (Place des Nations, 1211 Geneva 10, Switzerland)

Universal Postal Union (UPU) aims to perfect postal services and promote international collaboration. (Weltpoststrasse 4, 3000 Berne, 15 Switzerland)

World Health Organization (WHO) aims to aid the attainment of the highest possible level of health. (1211 Geneva 27, Switzerland)

World Intellectual Property Organization (WIPO) seeks to protect, through international cooperation, literary, industrial, scientific, and artistic works. (34 Chemin des Colom Bettes, 1211 Geneva, Switzerland)

World Meteorological Org. (WMO) aims to coordinate and improve world meteorological work. (Case Postale 5, CH-1211, Geneva 20, Switzerland)

Ambassadors and Envoys
(as of 7 June 1993)

British embassies abroad are based in the capital city of the appropriate country. Britain does not have diplomatic relations with Iraq and Libya.

Amb. = Ambassador; **CG** = Consul General; **HC** = High Commissioner

Countries	Envoys from UK	Envoys to UK
Afghanistan	Staff withdrawn	Vacancy
Albania	Sir Patrick Fairweather, Amb.	Pavli Qesku, Amb.
Algeria	Christopher Battiscombe, Amb.	Abdelkrim Gheraieb, Amb.
Andorra	D. Joy, CG	Vacancy
Angola	A. R. Thomas, Amb.	José Primo, Amb.
Antigua & Barbuda	Emrys Davies, HC	James Thomas, HC
Argentina	Hon. Humphrey Maud, Amb.	Mario Campora, Amb.
Armenia	Sir Brian Fall, Amb.	Dr Armen Sarkissian, Amb.
Australia	Sir Brian Barder, HC	Richard Smith, HC
Austria	T. C. Wood, Amb.	Dr Walter Magrutsch, Amb.
Azerbaijan	Sir Brian Fall, Amb.	—
Bahamas	Brian Attewell, HC	Arthur Foulkes, HC
Bahrain	H. J. O. R. Tunnell, Consul	Karim Ebrahim Al Amb.
Bangladesh	Sir Colin Imray, HC	Dr A. F. M. Yusuf, HC
Barbados	Emrys Davies, HC	Sir William Douglas, HC
Belarus	Sir Brian Fall, Amb.	—
Belgium	J. W. D. Gray, Amb.	Herman Dehennin, Amb.
Belize	David Mackilligin, HC	Robert A. Leslie, HC
Benin	Christopher Macrae, HC	Vacancy
Bolivia	Richard Jackson, Amb.	Gen. Gary Prado Salmon, Amb.
Botswana	J. C. Edwards, HC	Margaret N. Nasha, HC
Brazil	P. W. Heap, Amb.	Paulo-Tarso Flecha de Lima,
Brunei	Adrian Sindall, HC	Pengiran Haji Mustapha, HC
Bulgaria	Richard Thomas, Amb.	Ivan Stancioff, Amb.
Burkina Faso	Margaret Rothwell, Amb.	Vacancy
Burundi	Kay Oliver, Chargé	Balthazar Habonimana, Amb.
Cameroon	William Quantrill, Amb.	Dr Gibering Bol-Alima, Amb.
Canada	Sir Nicholas Bayne, HC	Fredrik S. Eaton, HC
Cape Verde	Roger Beetham, Amb.	Vacancy
Central African Rep.	William Quantrill, Amb.	Auguste Magba, Amb.
Chad	William Quantrill, Amb.	Vacancy
Chile	Richard Neilson, Amb.	German Riesco, Amb.
China	Sir Robin McLaren, Amb.	Ma Yuzhen, Amb.
Colombia	Keith Morris, Amb.	Dr Virgilio Barco Vargas, Amb.
Comoros	P. J. Smith, Amb.	—
Congo	Embassy closed, 27/7/91	Jean-Marie Ewengue, Hon. Consul
Costa Rica	Miss L. M. Croll, Amb.	Luis Rafael Tinoco Amb.
Côte d'Ivoire	Margaret Rothwell, Amb.	Gervais Yao Attoungbré, Amb.
Croatia	Bryan Sparrow, Amb.	Prof. Zeljko Bujas, Amb.
Cuba	A. Leycester Coltman, Amb.	Maria A. Flores, Amb.
Cyprus	David Dain, HC	Angelos Angelides, HC
Czech Fed. Rep.	David Brighty, Amb.	Dr Karel Kühnl, Amb.
Denmark	Nigel Williams, Amb.	Rudolph Thorning-Petersen, Amb.
Djibouti	R. D. Gordon, Amb.	Ahmed Omar Farah, Amb.
Dominica	Emrys Davies, HC	Ashworth Elwin, HC
Dominican Rep.	J. G. Flynn, Amb.	Vacancy
Ecuador	Frank Wheeler, Amb.	Luis A. Davalos, Amb.
Egypt	C. W. Long, Amb.	Mohamed I. Shaker, Amb.
El Salvador	M. H. Connor, Amb.	Dr Mauricio Rosales-Rivera, Amb.
Equatorial Guinea	William Quantrill, Amb.	Vacancy
Estonia	B. B. Low, Amb.	Riivo Sinijäro, Amb.
Ethiopia	Michael Glaze, Amb.	Vacancy
Fiji	T. J. David, Amb.	Brig.-Gen. Ratu Epeli Nailatikau, Amb.
Finland	Neil Smith, Amb.	Leif Blomquist, Amb.
France	Sir Christopher Mallaby, Amb.	Bernard Dorin, Amb.
Gabon	Embassy closed 26/7/91	Vincent Boulé, Amb.
The Gambia	Alan Pover, HC	Vacancy
Georgia	Sir Brian Fall, Amb.	—
Germany	Sir Nigel Broomfield, Amb.	Baron Hermann von Richthofen, Amb.
Ghana	D. C. Walker, HC	K. B. Asante, HC
Greece	Sir David Miers, Amb.	George D. Papoulias, Amb.
Grenada	Emrys Davies, HC	Vacancy
Guatemala	Justin Nason, Amb.	Vacancy
Guinea	Roger Beetham, Amb.	Vacancy
Guinea-Bissau	Roger Beetham, Amb.	Vacancy
Guyana	D. J. Johnson, HC	Cecil S. Pilgrim, HC
Haiti	Derek Milton, HC	Embassy closed 30/3/87
Holy See	A. E. Palmer, Amb.	Archbishop Luigi Barbarito, Pro Nuncio
Honduras	Patrick Morgan, Amb.	Carlos M. Zeron, Amb.
Hungary	John Birch, Amb.	Tibor Antalpéter, Amb.
Iceland	P. F. M. Wogan, Amb.	Helgi Agústsson, Amb.
India	Sir Nicholas Fenn, HC	Dr L. M. Singhvi, HC
Indonesia	Roger Carrick, Amb.	Teuku Mohammad Hadi Thayeb, Amb.
Iran	D. N. Reddaway, Chargé	Seyed Shamseddin Khareghani, Min. Councellor
Irish Rep.	David Blatherwick, Amb.	Joseph Small, Amb.
Israel	R. A. Burns, Amb.	Yoav Biran, Amb.
Italy	Sir Patrick Fairweather, Amb.	Count Giacomo Attolico, Amb.
Jamaica	Derek Milton, HC	Ellen Gray Bogle, HC

(Continued)

Countries	Envoys from UK	Envoys to UK
Japan	Sir John Boyd, Amb	Hiroshi Kitamura, Amb.
Jordan	P. H. C. Eyers, Amb.	Fonad Ayoub, Amb.
Kazakhstan	Sir Brian Fall, Amb.	—
Kenya	Sir Kieran Prendergast, HC	Vacancy
Kiribati	F. McDermott, HC	Vacancy
Korean Rep.	David Wright, Amb.	Dr Hongkoo Lee, Amb.
Kuwait	W. H. Fullerton, Amb.	Ghazi M. A. Al-Rayes, Amb.
Kyrghyzstan	Sir Brian Fall, Amb.	—
Laos	C. C. W. Adams, Amb.	Vacancy
Latvia	R. C. Samuel, Chargé	Janis Lusis, Amb.
Lebanon	Maeve Fort, Amb.	Mahmoud Hammoud, Amb.
Lesotho	J. R. Cowling, HC	M. K. Tsekoa, HC
Liberia	Embassy closed 8/3/91	Vacancy
Liechtenstein	David Beattie, Amb.	Franz E. Muheim, Amb.
Lithuania	M. J. Peart, Amb.	Vincas Balickas Amb.
Luxembourg	Hon. Michael Pakenham, Amb.	Edouard Molitor, Amb.
Madagascar	P. J. Smith, Amb.	François de Paul Robotoson, Amb.
Malawi	Nigel Wenban-Smith, HC	Tony Kandiero, HC
Malaysia	Duncan Slater, HC	Tan Sri Wan Sidek, HC
Maldives	E. J. Field, HC	–
Mali	Roger Beetham, Amb.	Vacancy
Malta	Sir Peter Wallis, HC	Salvatore Stellini, HC
Marshall Islands	F. McDermott, HC	—
Mauritania	Sir Alan Ramsay, Amb.	Mohamed El Hanchi Ould Mohamed Saleh, Amb.
Mauritius	Michael Howell, HC	Dr Boodhun Teelock, HC
Mexico	Sir Roger Hervey, Amb.	Bernardo Amb.
Micronesia	F. McDermott, HC	—
Moldova	Sir Brian Fall, Amb.	—
Monaco	John Illman, CG	I. B. Ivanovic, CG
Mongolia	A. B. M. Morey, Amb.	Choisuregyn Batar, Amb.
Morocco	Sir Alan Ramsey, Amb.	Khalil Haddaoui, Amb.
Mozambique	R. J. S. Edis, Amb.	Lt. Gen. Armando Panguene, Amb.
Myanmar (Burma)	Julian Hartland-Swann, Amb.	U Hla Maung, Amb.
Namibia	Francis Richards, HC	Veiccoh K. Nghiwete, HC
Nauru	T. J. David, HC	–
Nepal	Timothy George, Amb.	Surya Prasad Shrestha, Amb.
Netherlands	Sir David Miers, Amb.	Joop Hoekman, Amb.
New Zealand	David Moss, HC	George F. Gair, HC
Nicaragua	J. H. Culver, Amb.	Fernando Zelay, Amb.
Niger	Margaret Rothwell, Amb.	Sandi Yacouba, Amb.
Nigeria	Christopher Macrae, HC	Alhaji Abubakar Alhaji, HC
Norway	David Ratford, Amb.	Kjell Eliassen, Amb.
Oman	Sir Terence Clark, Amb.	Abdulla Bin Mohamed Bin Ageel Al-Dhahab, Amb.
Pakistan	Sir Nicholas Barrington, HC	Mian Riaz Sanee, HC
Panama	T. H. Malcolmson, Amb	Theodoro F. Franco, Amb.
Papua New Guinea	John Guy, HC	Noel Levi, HC
Paraguay	Michael Dibben, Amb.	Antonio Espinoza, Amb.
Peru	Keith Haskell, Amb.	Arturo Garcia, Amb.
Philippines	A. G. Montgomery, Amb	Jesus P. Tanbunting, Amb.
Poland	Michael Llewellyn-Smith, Amb.	Tadeusz de Virion, Amb.
Portugal	J. S. Wall, Amb.	Antonio Val-Pereira, Amb.
Qatar	Graham Boyce, Amb.	Abdulrahman Abdulla Al-Wohaibi, Amb.
Romania	A. P. F. Bache, Amb.	Sergiu Celac, Amb.
Russian Federation	Sir Brian Fall, Amb.	Boris Pankin, Amb.
Rwanda	Kay Oliver, Chargé	François Ngarukiyintwali, Amb.
San Marino	Miss M. L. Croll, CG	Lord Forte, CG
São Tomé & Príncipe	A. R. Thomas, Amb.	Vacancy
Saudi Arabia	Hon. D. A. Gore-Booth, Amb.	Sheikh Nasser H. Almanqour, Amb.
Senegal	Roger Beetham, Amb.	Seydou Madani Sy, Amb.
Seychelles	E. J. Sharland, HC	Vacancy
Sierra Leone	David Sprague, HC	Vacancy
Singapore	Gordon Duggan, HC	Abdul Aziz Mahmood, HC
Slovakia	David Brighty, Amb.	Ján Vilikovský, Amb.
Slovenia	G. M. Johnston, Amb.	Matjerž Šintoveč, Amb.
Solomon Islands	Raymond Jones, HC	Lindsay F. Misros, HC
Somalia	Embassy closed	Ali Hassan Ali, Amb.
South Africa	Sir Anthony Reeve, Amb.	Kent D. S. Durr, Amb.
Spain	Sir Robin Fearn, Amb.	Felipe de la Morena, Amb.
Sri Lanka	E. J. Field, HC	Gen. D. S. Attygalle, HC
St Kitts & Nevis	Emrys Davies, HC	Richard Gunn, HC
St Lucia	Emrys Davies, HC	Richard Gunn, HC
St Vincent	Emrys Davies, HC	Richard Gunn, HC
Sudan	Peter Streams, Amb.	Sayed Ali Mohamed Osman Yassin, Amb.
Suriname	D. J. Johnson, Amb.	Cyril Bisoendat Ramkisor, Amb.
Swaziland	Brian Watkins, HC	Mboni N. Dlamini, HC
Sweden	R. L. B. Cormack, Amb.	Lennart Eckerberg, Amb.
Switzerland	David Beattie, Amb.	Franz E. Muheim, Amb.
Syria	Andrew Green, Amb.	Mohammad Khoder, Amb.
Tajikistan	Sir Brian Fall, Amb.	—
Tanzania	Roger Wesrtbrook, HC	Ali S. Mchumo, HC
Thailand	C. C. W. Adams, Amb.	Tongchan Jotikasthira, Amb.
Togo	D. C. Walker, HC.	Embassy closed
Tonga	William Cordiner, HC	S. M. Tuita, HC
Trinidad & Tobago	Brian Smith, HC	P. L. U. Cross, HC
Tunisia	M. L. Tait, Amb.	Mohamed Lessir, Amb.
Turkey	P. J. Goulden, Amb.	Candemir Önhon, Amb.
Turkmenistan	Sir Brian Fall, Amb.	—
Tuvalu	T. J. David, HC	—

(Continued)

Countries	Envoys from UK	Envoys to UK
Uganda	Charles Cullimore, HC	George Kirya, HC
Ukraine	S. N. P. Hemans, Amb.	Prof. Sergui Komisarenko, Amb.
United Arab Emirates	Graham Burton, Amb.	Easa Saleh, Al-Gurg, Amb.
United States	Sir Robin Kenwick, Amb.	Raymond G. H. Seitz, Amb.
Uruguay	Donald Lamont, Amb.	Luis Solé-Romeo, Amb.
Uzbekistan	Sir Brian Fall, Amb.	—
Vanuatu	T. J. Duggin, HC	Vacancy
Vatican City	Andrew Palmer, Amb.	Archbishop Luigi Barbarito, Pro Nuncio
Venezuela	J. G. Flynn, Amb.	Ignacio Arcaya, Amb.
Vietnam	Peter Williams, Amb.	Chau Phong, Amb.
Western Samoa	David Moss, HC	Afamasaga Toleafoa, HC
Yemen	R. D. Gordon, Amb.	Dr Shaya Mohsin Mohamed, Amb.
Yugoslavia, former	Michael Robinson, Chargé	Vacancy
Zaire	Kay Oliver, Chargé.	Liloo Nkema, Amb.
Zambia	Peter Hinchcliffe, HC	Edward H. Lubinda, HC
Zimbabwe	R. N. Dales, HC	Stephen C. Chiketa, HC

Diplomatic Officials – Forms of Address

Ambassador (British) – LETTERS *Superscription* (when in the country to which he is accredited only), "His Excellency (preceding all other ranks and titles), HM Ambassador to ——", *Commencement*, "Sir", or socially according to rank. *Conclusion*, "I have the honour to be Sir, Your Excellency's obedient servant". PERSONAL ADDRESS "Your Excellency".

Ambassador's Wife – She is not entitled to the style "Her Excellency" and is referred to and addressed by name, or conversationally as the Ambassadress.

Consuls (British) – LETTERS *Superscription*, "—— Esq, HM ('Consul-General', 'Consul', or 'Vice-Consul', as the case may be) ——". In other words as an Esquire (see p. 413).

Governor of a Country within the British Commonwealth is styled "His Excellency" (preceding all other ranks and titles) while actually administering a Government and within its boundary (also an office administering in his absence). If the Governor has not been knighted, he is styled "His Excellency Mr John Smith". Esquire should not be used with H.E.

Governor-General – The style of "His Excellency" precedes all other titles and ranks, and is used while actually administering a Government and within the territory administered. LETTERS *Superscription*, "His Excellency (Sir John) ——, Governor-General of ——" (also an officer administering in his absence). In other respects as for Governor.

Governor-General's Wife – The style of "Her Excellency" has, since 1924, been confined to the wives of the Govs-Gen. of Countries of the Commonwealth within the country administered by their husbands.

Governor's Wife – She is not accorded the style of "Her Excellency".

High Commissioner – *Superscription*, "His Excellency (preceding all other ranks, and titles) the High Commissioner for ——". Otherwise as for an Ambassador.

"Honourable" in Commonwealth Countries – The titles of "Honourable" is borne *for life* by all Members of the Queen's Privy Council in Canada, Members of the Canadian Senate, and Premiers and Lieutenant-Governors of Canadian Provinces, and of the Executive Councils of the Commonwealth of Australia and of the States of Victoria and Tasmania. In Canada the title of "Honourable" is borne *during office* by the following categories of Judges: Judges of Supreme and Exchequer Courts of Canada; the Chief Justices and Judges of the Supreme Courts of Ontario, Nova Scotia, New Brunswick, Alberta and Newfoundland; the Court of Queen's Bench and the Superior Court of Quebec; the Court of Appeal and the Court of Queen's Bench of Manitoba and Saskatchewan; the Court of Appeal and the Supreme Court of British Columbia; the Supreme Court of Judicature of Prince Edward Island; and the Territorial Courts of NW Territories and Yukon Territory. They are eligible to be personally recommended by the Governor-General for Her Majesty's permission to retain the title on retirement. Also in Commonwealth countries all Members of Executive Councils, all Members of Legislative Councils (other than Legislative Councils of Provinces of Canada), and by the Speaker of the Lower House of the Legislatures. It is also used locally by Members of the Executive and Legislative Councils of territories not possessing Responsible Government. The following in Commonwealth Countries are eligible to be recommended to retain the title of "Honourable" on retirement: Executive Councillors who have served for at least three years as Ministers or one year as Prime Minister; Presidents of Senates and Legislative Councils and Speakers of Legislative Assemblies on quitting office after having served three years in their respective offices; Senators and Members of the Legislative Councils on retirement or resignation after a continuous service of not less than ten years. (*See also* Judges in Commonwealth and Overseas Territories, p. 291).

Lieutenant-Governor – Isle of Man, Jersey and Guernsey, as for Governor. A Lt.-Gov. of a Canadian Province is "The Hon." (borne for life).

UK Customs Allowances

(as at July 1993)

Source: HM Customs & Excise

Goods Obtained in the EC

Duty-paid and tax-paid items bought in EC countries (not duty-free shops) incur no further tax in the UK, provided they are for your personal use. (Personal use includes gifts.) European Community law sets out guide levels, and if you bring in more than these levels, you must be able to show that the goods are for your personal use.

EC Guide levels

Cigarettes	800
Cigarillos	400
Cigars	200
Smoking tobacco	1 kg
Spirits	10 litres
Intermediate products, e.g. port & sherry	20 litres
Wine (not more than 60 litres may be sparkling)	90 litres
Beer	110 litres

(Continued)

Good obtained Outside the EC

Allowances	
Cigarettes, or	200
Cigarillos, or	100
Cigars, or	50
Tobacco	250g
Still table wine	2 litres
Spirits & strong liqueurs over 22% volume, or	1 litre
Fortified or sparkling wine, other liqueurs, or	2 litres
An additional still table wine allowance	2 litres
Perfume	60cc/ml
Toilet water	250cc/ml
All other goods, including gifts & souvenirs	£36 worth

Note: It is an offence to sell duty-free or duty-paid goods intended for personal use.

No one under 17 is entitled to tobacco or drinks allowances.

British Aid to Developing Countries

Bilateral Aid (country-to-country) accounts for about 60 per cent of the aid programme. Direct assistance to developing countries draws on special skills and expertise, in fields such as manpower and training, which are available in Britain. Some 76 per cent of British bilateral aid goes to the poorest countries. Commonwealth countries and British Dependencies receive 70 per cent of this aid, with India the largest recipient.

Multilateral Aid is channelled through international organizations and financial institutions such as the European Community, the World Bank and the United Nations agencies. It accounts for about 40 per cent of the aid programme.

UK Gross Bilateral Aid 1991/92

including Technical Cooperation (TC)

Source: Overseas Development Administration

AFRICA	£ thousand
Africa, North of Sahara	
Algeria	336
Egypt	12,383
Libya	–
Morocco	2,079
Tunisia	236
Total	**14,984**
Africa, South of Sahara	
Angola	1,278
Benin	113
Botswana	7,885
Burkina Faso	402
Burundi	182
Cameroon	3,056
Cape Verde Islands	113
Central African Republic	70
Chad	227
Comoros	18
Congo	353
Côte d'Ivoire	593
Djibouti	128
Equatorial Guinea	–
Ethiopia	18,915
Gabon	63
Gambia	4,876
Ghana	31,504
Guinea	606
Guinea-Bissau	32
Kenya	29,301
Lesotho	6,450
Liberia	497
Madagascar	501
Malawi	17,554
Mali	928
Mauritania	98
Mauritius	1,968
Mozambique	16,836
Namibia	2,362
Niger	340
Nigeria	14,453
Regional-EAC	1,171
Rwanda	214
São Tomé & Príncipe	–
Senegal	1,194
Seychelles	1,161
Sierra Leone	1,986
Somalia	2,975
South Africa[1]	9,330
St Helena & Dependencies	9,136
Sudan	17,461
Swaziland	2,943
Tanzania	25,066

AFRICA (Continued)	
Togo	299
Uganda	25,529
Zaire	397
Zambia	27,966
Zimbabwe	36,680
S. of Sahara unallocated	–
Total	**334,316**
Africa unallocated	2,487
TOTAL AFRICA	**351,787**

AMERICA	
America, Central	
Costa Rica	568
Cuba	5
El Salvador	66
Guatemala	57
Haiti	89
Honduras	1,451
Mexico	1,438
Nicaragua	206
Panama	850
Total	**4,729**
America, Caribbean	
Anguilla	1,732
Antigua & Barbuda	1,793
Bahamas	32
Barbados	384
Belize	2,902
Bermuda	2
British Virgin Islands	1,752
Cayman Islands	1
Dominica	1,986
Dominican Republic	25
Grenada	1,878
Guyana	5,529
Jamaica	4,173
Montserrat	2,969
St Kitts-Nevis	1,037
St Lucia	1,818
St Vincent	961
Suriname	1
Trinidad & Tobago	302
Turks & Caicos Islands	9,957
West Indies unallocated	2,763
Total	**41,994**
America, South	
Argentina	26
Bolivia	3,498
Brazil	2,706
Chile	692
Colombia	3,564
Ecuador	1,225

AMERICA (Continued)	
Falkland Islands	1,286
Paraguay	431
Peru	1,417
Uruguay	116
Venezuela	124
Total	**15,085**
America unallocated	997
TOTAL AMERICA	**62,805**

ASIA	
Asia, Middle East	
Iran	3,015
Iraq[2]	20,367
Israel	13
Jordan	3,122
Lebanon	182
Oman	1,044
Syria	3
West Bank & Gaza	1,526
Yemen	5,005
Middle East unallocated	104
Total	**34,381**
Asia, South	
Afghanistan	1,380
Bangladesh	54,121
Bhutan	775
India	128,547
Maldive Republic	650
Myanmar	53
Nepal	16,540
Pakistan	19,713
Sri Lanka	9,528
Total	**231,306**
Asia, Far East	
Brunei	8
Cambodia	709
China	21,036
Hong Kong	404
Indonesia	21,200
Korea, South	2
Laos	17
Malaysia	15,142
Mongolian	11
Philippines	1,934
Singapore	233
Thailand	2,270
Vietnam	379
Total	**63,346**
Asia unallocated	1,961
TOTAL ASIA	**330,994**

(Continued)

EUROPE	
Cyprus	498
Gibraltar	1,051
Malta	270
Turkey	16,796
Yugoslavia	319
TOTAL EUROPE	**18,933**
OCEANIA	
Cook Islands	8
Fiji	2,311
Kiribati	1,627
Papua New Guinea	163
Pitcairn Islands	41
OCEANIA (*Continued*)	
Solomon Islands	2,915
Tonga	238
Tuvalu	482
Vanuatu	5,111
Western Samoa	70
Total	**12,964**
Oceania unallocated	1,457
TOTAL OCEANIA	**14,421**
UNSPECIFIED	
World unallocated[1]	144,017
Exchequer advances to the CDC	60,000
ALL DEVELOPING COUNTRIES	
Commonwealth	**526,942**
of which	
Independent members	497,433
Dependencies	28,331
Other countries	1,178
Non-Commonwealth	**231,603**
Unallocable	**164,412**
TOTAL ALL DEVELOPING COUNTRIES	**982,957**

(1) There is no aid to the government of Iraq. The amounts recorded are humanitarian assistance provided through UN agencies and NGOs to North and South Iraq. (2) There is no aid to the government of South Africa. The amounts recorded are administered through NGOs, community groups and educational institutions for the benefit of the Black South African population. There is no involvement by the Government of South Africa. (3) The British Government has recognized Croatia, Slovenia and Bosnia-Herzegovina as independent republics. Flows reported here are primarily humanitarian aid to the former republics of Yugoslavia.

UK Gross Multilateral Aid 1991/92

Source: Overseas Development Administration

	£ thousand
UN AGENCIES	
General contributions	
World Food Programme: cash contributions	1,250
World Food Programme: food aid	19,014
Food and Agriculture Organization (FAO)	9,643
UN Development Programme (UNDP)	28,908
UN Children's Fund (UNICEF) General	9,047
UN Agency for Palestinian Refugees (UNRWA)	6,000
UN High Commission for Refugees (UNHCR)	17,556
International Fund for Agricultural Development (IFAD)	2,847
UN Population Fund (UNFPA)	7,500
UN Industrial Development Organization	2,734
Other	1,004
Specific programmes (not TC)	
Un Drug Control	584
UN Disaster Relief (Special Appeals)	19,996
UN Border Relief Operation (Thailand/Cambodia)	470
UN Technical Cooperation	
World Health Organization (WHO)	10,706
Other	614
TOTAL UN AGENCIES	**137,873**
WORLD BANK GROUP	
International Development Association (IDA)	215,866
International Bank for Reconstruction & Development (IBRD)	11,770
International Finance Corporation	430
World Bank TC	128
Multilateral Investment Guarantee Agency (MIGA)	–
TOTAL WORLD BANK GROUP	**288,194**

	£ thousand
REGIONAL DEVELOPMENT BANKS	
African Development Bank (inc TC)	1,771
African Development Fund	11,617
Asian Development Bank	708
Asian Development Fund	16,540
Caribbean Development Bank (CBD)	249
CDB Special Development Fund	2,438
Inter-American Development Bank (IADB)	503
IADB Fund for Special Operations	–
TOTAL REGIONAL DEVELOPMENT BANKS	**33,826**
EUROPEAN COMMUNITY	
European Development Fund	200,254
European Investment Bank	3,905
EC Technical Cooperation	205
Asian and Latin-American countries	26,961
Mediterranean countries	16,451
Food aid	65,018
Disaster relief	58,036
Other	42,592
TOTAL EUROPEAN COMMUNITY	**413,422**
RESEARCH ORGANIZATIONS	
International Maize & Wheat Improvement Centre	755
International Rice Research Institute	995
International Crop Research: Semi-Arid Tropics	960
Other agricultural research	5,506
Health & Population Research	367
TOTAL RESEARCH ORGANIZATIONS	**8,583**
OTHER INTERNATIONAL ORGANIZATIONS	
Commonwealth Fund for Technical Cooperation	6,605
Other	949
TOTAL OTHER ORGANIZATIONS	**7,554**
TOTAL MULTILATERAL CONTRIBUTIONS	**830,952**

NATIONAL DEFENCE

Service Personnel

At 1 April[1]

Source: CSO

Thousands

	1981	1982	1983	1984	1985	1986	1987	1988	1989	1990	1991	1992
UK service personnel												
All services:												
Male	316.8	311.9	305.2	309.7	309.8	306.5	303.7	300.9	295.4	288.5	279.5	273.8
Female	16.9	15.7	15.4	16.2	16.4	16.0	16.2	15.9	16.3	17.2	18.6	19.6
Total	333.8	327.6	320.6	325.9	326.2	322.5	319.8	316.9	311.6	305.7	298.1	293.4
Royal Naval Services[2]:												
Male	70.0	69.0	67.8	67.4	66.7	64.4	63.2	62.2	61.2	59.6	57.9	57.5
Female	4.1	4.0	3.9	3.9	3.7	3.4	3.4	3.3	3.5	3.6	4.2	4.6
Total	74.3	73.0	71.7	71.3	70.4	67.9	66.5	65.5	64.6	63.2	62.1	62.1
Army:												
Male	159.4	157.2	152.9	155.0	155.6	154.8	153.2	151.8	149.1	145.9	140.4	137.6
Female	6.6	6.0	6.1	6.6	6.8	6.6	6.5	6.3	6.5	6.9	7.2	7.8
Total	166.0	163.2	159.1	161.5	162.4	161.4	159.7	158.1	155.6	152.8	147.6	145.4
Royal Air Force:												
Male	87.2	85.7	84.5	87.3	87.5	87.2	87.3	87.0	85.1	83.0	81.2	78.7
Female	6.3	5.8	5.4	5.7	6.0	6.0	6.3	6.3	6.3	6.7	7.2	7.3
Total	93.5	91.5	89.8	93.1	93.4	93.2	93.6	93.3	91.4	89.7	88.4	86.0
Personnel locally entered overseas:												
Total	9.7	10.1	10.1	10.1	10.2	10.1	9.8	9.4	9.1	9.0	9.1	9.0
Regular Reserves:[1]												
Royal Naval Services[2]	28.9	26.9	26.1	25.8	25.6	26.5	26.8	27.1	27.6	28.4	28.5	27.5
Army	137.5	140.2	138.3	143.2	150.2	153.9	160.4	167.7	175.3	183.4	187.7	188.6
Royal Air Force	30.1	29.3	28.9	29.0	29.8	31.5	33.7	35.4	37.5	40.1	42.5	44.8
Total	196.5	196.4	193.4	198.0	205.5	211.6	220.9	230.2	240.4	252.0	258.7	260.8
Volunteer Reserves and Auxiliary Forces:												
Royal Naval Services[2]	6.4	6.4	6.5	6.3	6.4	6.7	6.8	6.8	6.8	7.0	7.0	5.8
Territorial Army	69.5	72.1	72.8	71.4	73.7	77.7	78.5	74.7	72.5	72.5	73.3	71.3
Ulster Defence Regiment	7.5	7.1	7.1	6.8	6.4	6.6	6.5	6.4	6.3	6.2	6.1	6.0
Home Service Force	–	–	0.3	0.3	0.9	3.0	3.3	3.1	3.0	3.2	3.4	2.9
Royal Air Force	0.6	0.6	0.8	1.1	1.2	1.4	1.6	1.8	1.7	1.7	1.8	2.2
Total[1]	84.0	86.3	87.5	85.9	88.6	95.4	96.8	92.8	90.4	90.6	91.6	88.3
Cadet Forces:[1,2]												
Royal Navy	31.1	28.7	29.4	28.4	28.4	28.0	27.5	27.1	26.5	26.2	27.0	27.0
Army	75.1	74.1	74.5	73.8	72.1	70.9	71.2	69.3	65.9	65.7	64.6	64.6
Royal Air Force	44.4	45.9	45.1	44.3	44.1	44.5	47.0	48.3	46.7	44.2	43.1	43.8
Total	**150.6**	**148.7**	**149.0**	**146.5**	**144.7**	**143.4**	**145.7**	**144.6**	**139.2**	**136.0**	**134.7**	**135.3**

(1) A few of the figures for reserves and cadets were collected at irregular intervals and do not necessarily refer to 1 April; they are the latest figures available at that date. (2) Royal Navy and Royal Marines figures have been combined under the Royal Naval Services heading. (3) Combined Cadet Force cadets are included under the relevant service.

Ranks in the Armed Forces

Army

Source: Army Information Office

General Officers & Staff

Field Marshal
General
Lieutenant General
Major General
Brigadier
Colonel

Regimental Officers

Lieutenant Colonel
Major
Captain
Lieutenant
Second Lieutenant

Warrant Officers & Non-Commissioned Officers

Warrant Officer Class 1 (Regimental Sergeant Major)
Warrant Officer Class 2 (Regimental Quartermaster Sergeant)
Warrant Officer Class 3 (Company Sergeant Major*)
Staff Sergeant*
Sergeant*
Corporal*
Lance Corporal
Private

*Some regiments and corps have different titles for these ranks.

Royal Navy

Source: Royal Navy & Royal Marines

Officers

Admiral of the Fleet
Admiral
Vice-Admiral
Rear-Admiral
Commodore (1st & 2nd Class)
Captain
Commander
Lieutenant-Commander
Lieutenant
Sub-Lieutenant
Acting Sub-Lieutenant
Midshipman

Ratings
Warrant Officer
Chief Petty Officer
Petty Officer
Leading Rating
Able Rating
Ordinary Rating

Women's Royal Navy Service

Officers
Chief Commandant
Commandant
Captain
Commander
Lieutenant-Commander
Lieutenant
Sub-Lieutenant

Ratings
Warrant Officer Wren
Chief Wren
Petty Officer Wren
Leading Wren
Able Rating
Ordinary Rating

Queen Alexandra's Royal Naval Nursing Service Officers
Matron-in-Chief and Director of Nursing Services
Principal Nursing Officer
Chief Nursing Officer
Superintending Nursing Officer
Senior Nursing Officer
Nursing Officer

Ratings
Warrant Officer RGN
Chief Petty Officer
Petty Officer
Leading Rating
Able Rating
Ordinary Rating

Royal Air Force
Source: RAF Museum, Hendon

Officers
Marshal of the RAF
Air Chief Marshal
Air Marshal
Air Vice-Marshal
Air Commodore
Group Captain
Wing Commander
Squadron Leader
Flight Lieutenant
Flying Officer
Pilot Officer

Non-commissioned ranks
Warrant Officer
Flight Sergeant
Sergeant
Corporal
Senior Aircraftman/woman
Leading Aircraftman/woman
Aircraftman/woman

Forces – forms of address

Naval, Military and Air Force Officers Professional rank should always precede any titles, e.g., "Adm. (the Right Hon.) the Earl of ——", "Gen. the (Right Hon.) Lord ——", "Air-Marshal Sir ——", but Lieutenants in the Army, and Flying Officers and Pilot Officers in the Air Force are addressed by their social and not their professional rank, e.g. "The Hon. Benjamin ——, Irish Guards", "George ——, Esq., 11th Hussars", or "William ——, Esq., RAF".

Military Orders, Decorations & Medals

(in order of precedence)
Source: Ministry of Defence

VC .... Victoria Cross
GC .... George Cross
KG .... Knight of the Order of the Garter
KT .... Knight of the Order of the Thistle
GCB ..... Knight Grand Cross or Dame Grand Cross of the Order of the Bath
OM .... Member of the Order of Merit
KCB ...... Knight Commander } of the Order of the Bath
CB .... Companion } of the Order of the Bath
GCSI ..... Knight Grand Commander } of the Order of the Star of India
KCSI ..... Knight Commander } of the Order of the Star of India
CSI ...... Companion } of the Order of the Star of India
GCMG ... Knight Grand Cross } of the Order of St Michael and St George
KCMG .... Knight Commander } of the Order of St Michael and St George
CMG ..... Companion } of the Order of St Michael and St George
GCIE ..... Knight Grand Commander } of the Order of the Indian Empire
KCIE ..... Knight Commander } of the Order of the Indian Empire
CIE ...... Companion } of the Order of the Indian Empire
CI .... Lady of the Imperial Order of the Crown of India
GCVO .... Knight Grand Cross or Dame Grand Cross } of the Royal Victorian Order
KCVO .... Knight Commander } of the Royal Victorian Order
DCVO .... Dame Commander } of the Royal Victorian Order
CVO ..... Commander } of the Royal Victorian Order
GBE ...... Knight Grand Cross or Dame Grand Cross of the Order of the British Empire
CH .... Member of the Order of the Companions of Honour
KBE ...... Knight Commander } of the Order of the British Empire
DBE ...... Dame Commander } of the Order of the British Empire
CBE ...... Commander } of the Order of the British Empire
DSO ..... Companion of the Distinguished Service Order
LVO ...... Lieutenant of the Royal Victorian Order
OBE ...... Officer of the Order of the British Empire
ISO ...... Companion of the Imperial Service Order
MVO ..... Member of the Royal Vic;torian Order
MBE ..... Member of the Order of the British Empire
RRC ..... Member of the Royal Red Cross
DSC ...... Distinguished Service Cross
MC .... Military Cross
DFC ...... Distinguished Flying Cross
AFC ...... Air Force Cross
ARRC .... Associate of the Royal Red Cross
DCM ..... Distinguished Conduct Medal
CGM ..... Conspicuous Gallantry Medal
GM .... George Medal
DSM ..... Distinguished Service Medal
MM ...... Military Medal
DFM ..... Distinguished Flying Medal
AFM ..... Air Force Medal
QGM ..... The Queen's Gallantry Medal
BEM ..... British Empire Medal
RVM ..... Royal Victoria Medal
ERD ...... Army Emergency Reserve Decoration
VD .... Volunteer Officers Decoration or Colonial Auxiliary Forces Officers Decoration
TD .... Territorial Decoration or Efficiency Decoration
RD .... Royal Navy Reserve Decoration
CD .... Canadian Forces Decoration
AK .... Knight of Australia
QSO ..... Queen's Service Order (New Zealand)
AE .... Air Efficiency Award
■ or * ..... Denotes the award of a bar to a decoration or medal for valour. The award of additional bars is indicated by the addition of a further similar symbol for each award.

Deployment of Service Personnel

At 1 July 1991

Source: CSO

Thousands

	1981	1982	1983	1984	1985	1986	1987	1988	1989	1990	1991
UK Service personnel, Regular Forces:											
In United Kingdom	245.0	215.2	228.8	230.4	229.6	228.3	228.1	226.2	220.2	215.9	207.9
England[1]	207.7	195.9	195.1	194.5	193.3	191.7	190.9	189.8	183.3	179.5	173.3
Wales[1]	6.3	6.1	6.1	6.2	6.3	6.3	6.1	5.8	5.4	5.3	5.2
Scotland[1]	18.9	19.0	18.7	20.6	20.1	19.7	19.6	19.3	20.0	19.3	18.2
Northern Ireland[2]	11.6	10.9	10.2	10.0	9.7	10.5	11.4	11.2	11.2	11.5	11.2
Overseas	91.3	109.8	94.0	96.1	96.9	94.1	91.3	90.4	88.4	88.9	89.3
Federal Republic of Germany[3]	70.4	69.8	67.0	66.7	67.3	66.7	66.8	65.6	63.9	63.2	69.7
Elsewhere in Continental Europe[4,7]	6.1	6.2	6.1	7.2	7.7	6.3	6.9	6.9	7.0	6.8	–
Gibraltar	2.2	2.7	2.0	2.1	2.4	2.3	2.1	1.8	1.6	1.8	1.0
Cyprus	4.9	4.8	4.9	4.8	4.7	4.9	4.6	4.5	4.8	4.8	5.2
Elsewhere in Mediterranean, Near East and Gulf	1.4	1.1	0.3	1.2	2.3	0.4	1.1	3.4	1.8	1.3	1.1
Hong Kong	2.5	2.5	2.4	2.5	2.4	2.4	2.3	2.3	2.1	2.1	2.3
Elsewhere in the Far East	0.3	0.3	0.7	0.6	0.4	0.3	0.3	0.3	0.6	0.5	0.5
Other locations[1,5]	3.5	22.4	10.5	11.3	9.8	10.9	7.0	5.6	6.6	8.4	9.5
Total	**334.3**	**324.3**	**321.7**	**325.9**	**325.8**	**321.7**	**318.7**	**315.8**	**307.8**	**303.1**	**297.2**
Locally entered service personnel:											
United Kingdom	1.3	0.6	1.2	1.2	1.2	1.3	1.2	1.3	1.2	1.4	1.4
Gibraltar	0.1	0.1	0.1	0.1	0.1	0.1	0.1	0.1	0.1	0.1	0.1
Hong Kong	6.7	6.6	6.6	6.7	6.7	6.4	6.0	5.8	5.5	5.5	5.5
Brunei	0.8	0.8	0.8	0.8	0.8	0.8	0.8	0.8	0.9	0.9	0.8
Nepal	1.2	1.3	1.4	1.3	1.3	1.4	1.5	1.4	1.4	1.1	1.3
Other locations[6]	–	0.6	–	–	–	–	–	–	–	–	–
Total	10.0	9.9	10.0	10.1	10.1	10.0	9.6	9.4	9.0	8.9	9.1

(1) From 1982 the England, Wales and Scotland national figures include personnel who were UK based but temporarily deployed in the South Atlantic. These have been included also in the overseas numbers against "Other locations". (2) The figures for Northern Ireland include all personnel from other parts of the United Kingdom and the British Army of the Rhine who are serving on emergency tours of duty, but exclude the Ulster Defence Regiment. (3) Army personnel serving in Northern Ireland on emergency tours of duty but remaining under the command of the Commander-in-Chief British Army of the Rhine are included in these figures. (4) These figures include personnel stationed in Berlin and Sardinia. (5) These figures include Defence Attachés/Advisers and their staff. (6) The 1982 figures comprise Gurkha troops serving in the Falkland Islands. (7) As from 1991 figures for Federal Republic of Germany and Elsewhere in Continental Europe are combined.

Search and Rescue Operations Within UK

Source: CSO

Number

	1980	1981	1982	1983	1984	1985	1986	1987	1988	1989	1990	1991
Call outs[1]												
of helicopters	1,090	1,168	1,164	1,224	1,211	1,215	1,251	1,486	1,734	1,736	1,851	1,779
of other aircraft	68	58	59	73	56	62	74	80	81	84	86	87
of marine craft[2]	9	6	8	7	8	1	–	–	–	–	–	5
of mountain rescue teams[3]	45	43	58	46	56	33	73	79	80	76	83	92
Persons rescued[4]: total	**859**	**859**	**898**	**969**	**1,061**	**883**	**811**	**950**	**1,234**	**1,275**	**1,866**	**1,458**
by helicopters	837	840	834	948	1,028	869	797	929	1,194	1,241	1,418	1,423
by marine craft[2]	1	–	1	3	2	–	–	–	–	–	–	–
by mountain rescue teams[3]	21	19	63	18	31	14	14	21	40	34	448	35
Incidents: total	**1,070**	**1,097**	**1,111**	**1,146**	**1,145**	**1,129**	**1,188**	**1,361**	**1,599**	**1,675**	**1,843**	**1,783**

(1) More than one element of the search and rescue services may be called out to a reported incident. (2) The RAF Marine craft unit was disbanded during 1986. Figures include HM Ships and Auxiliary Vessels on permanent standby. (3) Royal Air Force only. (4) Figures for persons rescued relate only to number of persons who were actually removed (alive) from a hazard or who were assisted in an urgent medical incident.

Formation of UK Armed Forces

At 1 April

Source: CSO

Number

	Unit[1]	1982	1983	1984	1985	1986	1987	1988	1989	1990	1991	1992
Royal Navy[2]												
Submarines	Vessels	22	21	22	24	26	26	24	26	24	24	20
Carriers and assault ships	Vessels	3	4	4	4	4	3	3	4	4	3	3
Cruisers and destroyers	Vessels	11	13	13	46	47	46	42	39	44	42	43
Frigates	Vessels	38	42	39								
Mine counter-measure	Vessels	33	36	34	32	39	36	35	36	37	35	31
Patrol ships and craft	Vessels	21	25	31	28	32	28	31	34	32	31	26
Fixed-wing aircraft	Squadrons	3	3	3	3	3	3	3	3	3	3	3
Helicopters	Squadrons	15	13	12	14	14	14	14	14	13	13	13
Royal Marines	Commandos	3	3	3	3	3	3	3	3	3	3	3
Army[3,4]												
Royal Armoured Corps	Regiments	19	19	19	19	19	19	19	19	19	19	19
Royal Artillery[5]	Regiments	22	22	22	22	22	22	22	22	22	22	21
Royal Engineers[6]	Regiments	11	12	12	13	13	13	13	13	13	13	13
Infantry[6]	Battalions	57	56	56	56	56	55	55	55	55	55	55
Special Air Service	Regiments	1	1	1	1	1	1	1	1	1	1	1
Army Air Corps[8]	Regiments	6	4	4	4	4	4	4	4	4	4	5
Royal Air Force												
Strike/attack	Squadrons	12	10	11	11	11	11	11	11	11	11	9
Offensive support	Squadrons	5	5	5	5	5	5	5	5	5	5	5

(Continued)

Number

	Unit[1]	1982	1983	1984	1985	1986	1987	1988	1989	1990	1991	1992
Air defence	Squadrons	9	9	8	9	9	9	9	9	9	11	9
Maritime patrol	Squadrons	4	4	4	4	4	4	4	4	4	4	4
Reconnaissance	Squadrons	3	2	3	3	3	3	3	3	2	4	5
Airborne early warning	Squadrons	1	1	1	1	1	1	1	1	1	1	1
Transport[7]	Squadrons	10	11	10	11	12	12	12	12	12	12	15
Tankers	Squadrons	2	3	3	3	4	3	3	3	3	3	3
Search and rescue	Squadrons	3	3	2	2	2	2	2	2	2	2	2
Surface-to-air missiles	Squadrons	8	8	8	8	8	8	8	8	7	7	6
Ground defence	Squadrons	6	6	5	5	5	5	5	6	6	5	5

(1) The number of personnel and the amount of equipment in each vessel, regiment, etc. varies according to the role currently assigned. (2) Excludes vessels undergoing construction, major refit, conversion, or on stand-by, etc. (3) Front-line Squadrons in the NATO area. (4) Combat Arm major units only. (5) The 1992 figure excludes the Training Regiment. (6) Includes Gurkhas. (7) Includes helicopters. This also includes 3 helicopter squadrons deployed outside the NATO area not previously shown. (8) A fifth Army Air Corps regiment (9AAC) was formed in 1991.

UK Defence Expenditure[1,2]

Source: CSO

£ million

	1980/81	1981/82	1982/83	1983/84	1984/85	1985/86	1986/87	1987/88	1988/89	1989/90	1990/91
Total expenditure at outturn prices[3]	11,182	12,607	14,412	15,487	17,122	17,943	18,163	18,856	19,072	20,755	22,298
of which:											
Expenditure on personnel	4,556	5,058	5,455	5,726	5,983	6,379	6,890	7,212	7,572	8,099	8,811
of the Armed Forces	2,460	2,728	2,914	3,076	3,236	3,510	3,787	4,032	4,300	4,539	4,811
of the retired Armed Forces	503	624	680	777	828	899	980	1,079	1,060	1,197	1,406
of civilian staff	1,593	1,706	1,861	1,873	1,919	1,970	2,123	2,101	2,212	2,363	2,594
Expenditure on equipment	4,885	5,638	6,297	6,939	7,838	8,193	7,885	8,270	8,038	8,536	8,838
Sea systems	1,513	1,624	1,730	1,849	2,228	2,499	2,494	2,797	2,633	2,890	2,955
Land systems	904	1,101	1,353	1,475	1,638	1,887	1,759	1,700	1,554	1,738	1,927
Air systems	2,059	2,458	2,640	3,057	3,474	3,296	3,090	3,230	3,085	3,102	3,197
Other	410	456	574	558	498	511	542	543	766	806	759
Other expenditure	1,741	1,910	2,659	2,822	3,302	3,370	3,387	3,374	3,462	4,120	4,649
Works, buildings and land	623	664	832	1,067	1,271	1,413	1,498	1,453	1,411	1,900	2,067
Miscellaneous stores and services	1,118	1,246	1,827	1,754	2,031	1,958	1,889	1,921	2,051	2,220	2,582
Total expenditure at constant (1989/90) prices[3]	**19,624**	**19,903**	**21,114**	**21,406**	**22,251**	**22,219**	**21,450**	**21,093**	**20,175**	**20,755**	**22,298**

(1) Expenditure as given in the annual Appropriation Accounts for the Defence Votes, Class 1. (2) Including expenditure of government departments other than the Ministry of Defence in years when these contributed to the Defence budget. (3) Because of changes in the responsibilities of the Ministry of Defence, expenditures in successive years are not necessarily comparable.

Percentage of Central Government Expenditures Spent on Defence, 1989

Source: U.S. Arms Control and Disarmament Agency

1. Afghanistan NA
2. Syria 69.8
3. Iraq NA
4. Yugoslavia 53.4
5. Cambodia NA
6. Qatar NA
7. Soviet Union 45.7
8. Vietnam NA
9. Mozambique 42.1
10. Oman 41.4
11. United Arab Emirates 40.7
12. Chad NA
13. Korea, North 39.5
14. Saudi Arabia 38.6
15. El Salvador 37.3
16. Nicaragua NA
17. Jordan 32.7
18. Burma 30.8
19. Ethiopia 30.5
20. Taiwan 30.4
21. Yemen (Senaa) 29.8
22. Bulgaria 29.7
23. Libya 29.2
24. Madagascar 28.9
25. Angola NA
26. United States 25.5
27. Bolivia 25.4
28. Israel 25.2
29. Yemen (Aden) NA
30. Pakistan 24.6

NA = not available.

The Largest Armed Forces in the World

Source: Russell Ash, *The Top Ten of Everything*

	Estimated active forces			
Country	Army	Navy	Air	Total
China	2,300,000	260,000	470,000	3,030,000
Russia	1,400,000	320,000	300,000	2,720,000[1]
USA	674,800	739,650[2]	499,300	1,913,750
India	1,100,000	55,000	110,000	1,265,000
North Korea	1,000,000	40,000	92,000	1,132,000
Vietnam	700,000	42,000	15,000	757,000
South Korea	520,000	60,000	53,000	633,000
Pakistan	515,000	20,000	45,000	580,000
Turkey	450,000	52,300	58,000	560,300
Iran	305,000	18,000	35,000	358,000

(1) Balance of total comprises Strategic Deterrent Forces, Paramilitary, National Guard, etc. (2) Navy 546,650, Marines 193,000.

Armed Forces Per 1,000 Persons, 1992[1]

Source: U.S. Arms Control and Disarmament Agency

Argentina	2.0	India	1.4	Pakistan	4.5
Australia	3.9	Indonesia	1.5	Philippines	1.7
Austria	6.6	Iran	8.9	Poland	7.7
Belgium	8.1	Iraq	20.3	Portugal	5.6
Bolivia	4.1	Israel	33.4	Romania	8.6
Brazil	2.0	Italy	6.2	Russia	18.2
Bulgaria	11.9	Japan	2.0	Singapore	19.9
Canada	3.0	Jordan	27.3	South Africa	1.9
Chile	6.8	Korea, North	50.9	Spain	5.6
China	2.6	Korea, South	14.5	Sweden	8.8
Colombia	4.1	Kuwait	9.8	Switzerland	0.2
Cuba	16.1	Lebanon	13.1	Syria	32.4
Denmark	5.7	Libya	19.1	Taiwan	17.4
Egypt	7.3	Mexico	2.1	Thailand	5.0
El Salvador	8.0	Mongolia	7.1	Turkey	9.6
Finland	6.5	Morocco	7.5	United Kingdom	5.1
France	7.5	Netherlands	6.1	United States	7.5
Germany	5.6	Nicaragua	3.6	Venezuela	3.7
Greece	15.5	Norway	7.6	Vietnam	12.4
Hungary	7.8	Oman	21.8		

(1) Includes active-duty personnel performing national security functions. Does not include reserves or paramilitary forces.

Nuclear Arms Treaties and Negotiations: An Historical Overview

Aug. 4, 1963 – Nuclear Test Ban Treaty signed in Moscow by the U.S., USSR, and Great Britain, prohibited testing of nuclear weapons in space, above ground, and under water.

Jan. 1967 – Outer Space Treaty banned the introduction of nuclear weapons into space.

1968 – Nuclear Non-proliferation Treaty, with U.S., USSR, and Great Britain as major signers, limited the spread of military nuclear technology by agreement not to assist non-nuclear nations in getting or making nuclear weapons.

May 26, 1972 – Strategic Arms Limitation Treaty (SALT I) signed in Moscow by U.S. and USSR. In the area of defensive nuclear weapons, the treaty limited antiballistic missiles to 2 sites of 100 antiballistic missile launchers in each country (amended in 1974 to one site in each country). The treaty also imposed a 5-year freeze on testing and deployment of intercontinental ballistic missiles and submarine-launched ballistic missiles. An interim short-term agreement putting a ceiling on numbers of offensive nuclear weapons was also signed. SALT I was in effect until Oct. 3, 1977.

July 3, 1974 – Protocol on antiballistic missile systems and a treaty and protocol on limiting underground testing of nuclear weapons was signed by U.S. and USSR in Moscow.

Sept. 1977 – U.S. and USSR agreed to continue to abide by SALT I, despite its expiration date.

June 18, 1979 – SALT II, signed in Vienna by the U.S. and USSR, constrained offensive nuclear weapons, limiting each side to 2,400 missile launchers and heavy bombers with that ceiling to apply until Jan. 1, 1985. The treaty also set a sub-ceiling of 1,320 ICBMs and SLBMs with multiple warheads on each side. Although approved by the U.S. Senate Foreign Relations Relations Committee, the treaty never reached the Senate floor for ratification because Pres. Jimmy Carter withdrew his support for the treaty following the December 1979 invasion of Afghanistan by Soviet troops.

Dec. 8, 1987 – Intermediate-Range Nuclear Forces Treaty (INF) signed in Washington, D.C. by USSR leader Mikhail Gorbachev and U.S. Pres. Ronald Reagan, eliminating all medium- and shorter-range nuclear missiles; ratified with conditions by U.S. Senate on May 27, 1988.

July 31, 1991 – Strategic Arms Reduction Treaty (START I) signed in Moscow by Soviet Pres. Mikhail Gorbachev and U.S. Pres. George Bush to reduce strategic offensive arms by approximately 30 percent in 3 phases over 7 years. START I was the first treaty to mandate reductions by the superpowers. The treaty was approved by the U.S. Senate Oct. 1, 1992. With the break-up of the Soviet Union in December 1991, 4 former Soviet republics became independent nations with strategic nuclear weapons on their territory – Russia, Ukraine, Kazakhstan and Belarus. The last 3 agreed in principle in 1992 to transfer their nuclear weapons to Russia and ratify START I. The Russian Supreme Soviet voted to ratify Nov. 4, 1992, but Russia decided not to provide the instruments of ratification until Ukraine, Kazakhstan and Belarus each ratified START I and acceded to the Nuclear Nonproliferation Treaty as non-nuclear nations. By late 1993, Belarus and Kazakhstan had ratified START I and acceded to the non-proliferation treaty. In September 1993, Ukrainian President Leonid Kravchuk agreed to a plan that could restart stalled negotiations on the transfer of nuclear weapons to Russia.

Jan. 3, 1992 – START II signed in Moscow by U.S. Pres. George Bush and Russian Pres. Boris Yeltsin. Potentially the broadest disarmament pact in history, it called for both sides to reduce their long-range nuclear arsenals to about one-third of their then-current levels within a decade and would entirely eliminate land-based multiple-warhead missiles. Action will not be taken on START II until START I is fully ratified. START II will require ratification only by the U.S. Senate and the legislature of Russia, which would, under the guidelines for START I finalization, be the only remaining nuclear republic of the former Soviet Union.

North Atlantic Treaty Organization International Commands

(as of mid-1993)

Supreme Allied Commander, Europe (SACEUR) — Gen. John Shalikashvili* (USA)
Deputy Supreme Allied Commander Europe (DSACEUR) — Gen. Sir John Waters (UKA)
Commander-in-Chief Allied Forces Northern Europe — Gen. Sir Garry Johnson (UKA)
Commander-in-Chief Allied Forces Central Europe — Gen. Henning von Ondarva (GEA)
Commander-in-Chief Allied Forces Southern Europe — Adm. Jeremy M. Boorda
Commander-in-Chief United Kingdom Air Forces — Gen. John Thomson (UKAF)
Chairman, NATO Military Committee — Field Marshal Sir Richard Vincent (UKA)

*Named by Pres. Bill Clinton, 11 Aug. 1993, to became chairman of the Joint Chiefs of Staff, effective 1 Oct. 1993.

Arms Glossary

Ballistic missile: a long-range missile that is guided by preset mechanisms in the first part of its flight, but, like an artillery shell, is a free-falling object as it approaches its target.
Cruise missile: a pilotless, warhead-equipped, miniature aircraft with its own guidance system.
Delivery vehicle: anything used to launch a warhead or cluster of warheads – such as a missile, aeroplane, or submarine.
Strategic nuclear weapon: nuclear weapons intended for use against a particular nation or region; tactical weapons are used on a battlefield in support of troops.
Throw-weight: a measure of how much "payload", or nuclear weaponry, can be "thrown" or carried by a missile to a distant target.
Verification: using various checks such as satellite photography and on-sight inspection to decide whether an arms control agreement has been violated.
Warhead: the part of a missile with the explosive charge.

Leading Arms Exporters, 1989

Source: U.S. Arms Control and Disarmament Agency

(millions of dollars)

1. Soviet Union	$19,600	6. W. Germany	$1,200	11. N. Korea	$400
2. United States	11,200	7. Czechoslovakia	875	12. Poland	400
3. United Kingdom	3,000	8. Israel	625	13. Egype	370
4. France	2,700	9. Sweden	575	14. E. Germany	330
5. China	2,000	10. Canada	410	15. Bulgaria	160

Based on a report delivered to Congress, July 1992, based on data supplied by the Defense Dept. and U.S. intelligence agencies, arms sales to the "third world" fell sharply in 1991. Total sales fell 40 percent, to $24.7 billion, the lowest level in 7 years. The U.S., which surpassed the Soviet Union as the biggest supplier in 1990, accounted for 57 percent of all sales in 1991. Saudi Arabia spent $5.6 billion, nearly 40 percent of total U.S. sales to the third world.

Leading Arms Importers, 1989

Source: U.S. Arms Control and Disarmament Agency

	Principal supplier[1]	$ millions Imports
1. Saudi Arabia	United Kingdom	$4,200
2. Afghanistan	Soviet Union	3,800
3. India	Soviet Union	3,500
4. Greece	United States	2,000
5. Iraq	Soviet Union	1,900
6. United States	—	1,600
7. Japan	United States	1,400
8. Iran	—	1,300
9. Vietnam	Soviet Union	1,300
10. Cuba	Soviet Union	1,200
11. Turkey	United States	$1,100
12. Syria	Soviet Union	1,00
13. Libya	Soviet Union	975
14. Ethiopia	Soviet Union	925
15. Soviet Union	Czechoslovakia	900
16. W. Germany	United States	875
17. United Arab Emirates	France	850
18. E. Germany	Soviet Union	825
19. Angola	Soviet Union	750
20. Spain	United States	750

(1) Supplies more than 50 percent of total value of imports.

DISASTERS

Some Notable Shipwrecks Since 1850

(Figures indicate estimated lives lost; as of mid-1993)

1854, Mar.—City of Glasgow; British steamer missing in North Atlantic; 480.

1854, Sept. 27—Arctic; U.S. (Collins Line) steamer sunk in collision with French steamer Vesta near Cape Race; 285-351.

1856, Jan. 23—Pacific; U.S. (Collins Line) steamer missing in North Atlantic; 186-286.

1858, Sept. 23—Austria; German steamer destroyed by fire in North Atlantic; 471.

1863, Apr. 27—Anglo-Saxon; British steamer wrecked at Cape Race; 238.

1865, Apr. 27—Sultana; a Mississippi River steamer blew up near Memphis, Tenn; 1,450.

1869, Oct. 27—Stonewall; steamer burned on Mississippi River below Cairo, Ill.; 200.

1870, Jan. 25—City of Boston; British (Inman Line) steamer vanished between New York and Liverpool; 177.

1870, Oct 19—Cambria; British steamer wrecked off northern Ireland; 196.

1872, Nov. 7—Mary Celeste; U.S. half-brig sailed from New York for Genoa; found abandoned in Atlantic 4 weeks later in mystery of sea; crew never heard from; loss of life unknown.

1873, Jan. 22—Northfleet; British steamer foundered off Dungeness, England; 300.

1873, Apr. 1—Atlantic; British (White Star) steamer wrecked off Nova Scotia; 585.

1873, Nov. 23—Ville du Havre; French steamer, sunk after collision with British sailing ship Loch Earn; 226.

1875, May 7—Schiller; German steamer wrecked off Scilly Isles; 312.

1875, Nov. 4—Pacific; U.S. steamer sunk after collision off Cape Flattery; 236.

1878, Sept. 3—Princess Alice; British steamer sank after collision in Thames River; 700.

1878, Dec. 18—Byzantin; French steamer sank after Dardanelles collision; 210.

1881, May 24—Victoria; steamer capsized in Thames River, Canada; 200.

1883, Jan. 19—Cimbria; German steamer sunk in collision with British steamer Sultan in North Sea; 389.

1887, Nov. 15—Wah Yeung; British steamer burned at sea; 400.

1890, Feb. 17—Duburg; British steamer wrecked, China Sea; 400.

1890, Sept. 19—Ertogrul; Turkish frigate foundered off Japan; 540.

1891, Mar. 17—Utopia; British steamer sank in collision with British ironclad Anson off Gibraltar; 562.

1895, Jan. 30—Elbe; German steamer sank in collision with British steamer Craithie in North Sea; 332.

1895, Mar. 11—Reina Regenta; Spanish cruiser foundered near Gibraltar; 400.

1898, Feb. 15—Maine; U.S. battleship blown up in Havana Harbor; 260.

1898, July 4—La Bourgogne; French steamer sunk in collision with British sailing ship Cromartyshire off Nova Scotia; 549.

1898, Nov. 26—Portland; U.S. steamer wrecked off Cape Cod; 157.

1904, June 15—General Slocum; excursion steamer burned in East River, New York City; 1,030.

1904, June 28—Norge; Danish steamer wrecked on Rockall Island, Scotland; 620.

1906, Aug. 4—Sirio; Italian steamer wrecked off Cape Palos, Spain; 350.

1908, Mar. 23—Matsu Maru; Japanese steamer sank in collision near Hakodate, Japan; 300.

1909, Aug. 1—Waratah; British steamer, Sydney to London, vanished; 300.

1910, Feb. 9—General Chanzy; French steamer wrecked off Minorca, Spain; 200.

1911, Sept. 25—Liberté; French battleship exploded at Toulon; 285.

1912, Mar. 5—Principe de Asturias; Spanish steamer wrecked off Spain; 500.

1912, Apr. 14-15—Titanic; British (White Star) steamer hit iceberg in North Atlantic; 1,503.

1912, Sept. 28—Kichemaru; Japanese steamer sank off Japanese coast; 1,000.

1914, May 29—Empress of Ireland; British (Canadian Pacific) steamer sunk in collision with Norwegian collier in St. Lawrence River; 1,014.

1915, May 7—Lusitania; British (Cunard Line) steamer torpedoed and sunk by German submarine off Ireland; 1,198.

1915, July 24—Eastland; excursion steamer capsized in Chicago River; 812.

1916, Feb. 26—Provence; French cruiser sank in Mediterranean; 3,100.

1916, Mar. 3—Principe de Asturias; Spanish steamer wrecked near Santos, Brazil; 558.

1916, Aug. 29—Hsin Yu; Chinese steamer sank off Chinese coast; 1,000.

1917, Dec. 6—Mont Blanc, Imo; French ammunition ship and Belgian steamer collided in Halifax Harbor; 1,600.

1918, Apr. 25—Kiang-Kwan Chinese steamer sank in collision off Hankow; 500.

1918, July 12—Kawachi; Japanese battleship blew up in Tokayama Bay; 500.

1918, Oct. 25—Princess Sophia; Canadian steamer sank off Alaskan coast; 398.

1919, Jan. 17—Chaonia; French steamer lost in Straits of Messina, Italy; 460.

1919, Sept. 9—Valbanera; Spanish steamer lost off Florida coast; 500.

1921, Mar. 18—Hong Kong; steamer wrecked in South China Sea; 1,000.

1922, Aug. 26—Niitaka; Japanese cruiser sank in storm off Kamchatka, USSR; 300.

1927, Oct. 25—Principessa Mafalda; Italian steamer blew up, sank off Porto Seguro, Brazil; 314.

1928, Nov. 12—Vestris; British steamer sank in gale off Virginia; 113.

1934, Sept. 8—Morro Castle; U.S. steamer, Havana to New York, burned off Asbury Park, N.J.; 134.

1939, May 23—Squalus; U.S. submarine sank off Portsmouth, N.H.; 26.

1939, June 1—Thetis; British submarine, sank in Liverpool Bay; 99.

1942, Feb. 18—Truxtun and Pollux; U.S. destroyer and cargo ship ran aground, sank off Newfoundland; 204.

1942, Oct. 2—Curacao; British cruiser sank after collision with liner Queen Mary; 338.

1944, Dec. 17-18—3 U.S. Third Fleet destroyers sank during typhoon in Philippine Sea; 790.

1947, Jan. 19—Himera; Greek steamer hit a mine off Athens; 392.

1947, Apr. 16—Grandcamp; French freighter exploded in Texas City, Tex., Harbor, starting fires; 510.

1948, Nov.—Chinese army evacuation ship exploded and sunk off S. Manchuria; 6,000.

1948, Dec. 3—Kiangya; Chinese refugee ship wrecked in explosion S. of Shanghai; 1,100+.

1949, Sept. 17—Noronic; Canadian Great Lakes Cruiser burned at Toronto dock; 130.

1952, Apr. 26—Hobson and Wasp; U.S. destroyer and aircraft carrier collided in Atlantic; 176.

1953, Jan. 31—Princess Victoria; British ferry sank in storm off northern Irish coast; 134.

1954, Sept. 26—Toya Maru; Japanese ferry sank in Tsugaru Strait, Japan; 1,172.

1956, July 26—Andrea Doria and Stockholm; Italian liner and Swedish liner collided off Nantucket; 51.

1957, July 14—Eshghabad; Soviet ship ran aground in Caspian Sea; 270.

1961, July 8—Save; Portuguese ship ran aground off Mozambique; 259.

1962, Apr. 8—Dara; British liner exploded and sunk in Persian Gulf; 236.

1963, Apr. 10—Thresher; U.S. Navy atomic submarine sank in North Atlantic; 129.

1964, Feb. 10—Voyager, Melbourne; Australian destroyer sank after collision with Australian aircraft carrier Melbourne off New South Wales; 82.

1965, Nov. 13—Yarmouth Castle; Panamanian registered cruise ship burned and sank off Nassau; 90.

1967, July 29—Forrestal; U.S. aircraft carrier caught fire off N. Vietnam; 134.

1968, Jan. 25—Dakar; Israeli submarine vanished in Mediterranean Sea; 69.

1968, Jan. 27—Minerve; French submarine vanished in Mediterranean; 52.

1968, late May—Scorpion; U.S. nuclear submarine sank in Atlantic near Azores; 99 (located Oct. 31).

1969, June 2—Evans; U.S. destroyer cut in half by Australian carrier Melbourne, S. China Sea; 74.

1970, Mar. 4—Eurydice; French submarine sank in Mediterranean near Toulon; 57.

1970, Dec. 15—Namyong-Ho; South Korean ferry sank in Korea Strait; 308.

1974, May 1— Motor launch capsized off Bangladesh; 250.

1974, Sept. 26— Soviet destroyer burned and sank in Black Sea; 200+.

1976, Oct. 20—George Prince and Frosta; ferryboat and Norwegian tanker collided on Mississippi R. at Luling, La.; 77.

1976, Dec. 25—Patria; Egyptian liner caught fire and sank in the Red Sea; c. 100.

1977, Jan. 11—Grand Zenith; Panamanian-registered tanker sank off Cape Cod, Mass.; 38.

1979, Aug. 14—23 yachts competing in Fastnet yacht race sunk or abandoned during storm in S. Irish Sea; 18.

1981, Jan. 27—Tamponas II; Indonesian passenger ship caught fire and sank in Java Sea; 580.

1981, May 26—Nimitz; U.S. Marine combat jet crashed on deck of U.S. aircraft carrier; 14.

1983, Feb. 12—Marine Electric; coal freighter sank during storm off Chincoteague, Va.; 33.

1983, May 25—10th of Ramadan; Nile steamer caught fire and sank in L. Nassar; 357.

1986, Aug. 31—Soviet passenger ship *Admiral Nakhimov* and Soviet freighter *Pyotr Vasev* collided in the Black Sea; 398.

1987, Mar. 6—Herald of Free Enterprise; British ferry capsized off Zeebrugge, Belgium; 188.

1987, Dec. 20—Dona Paz and **Victor;** Philippine ferry and oil tanker collided in the Tablas Strait; 3,000+.

1988, Aug. 6—Indian ferry capsized on Ganges R.; 400+.

1989, Apr. 7—Soviet submarine sank off Norway; 42.

1989, Apr. 19—USS Iowa; U.S. battleship; explosion in gun turret; 47.

1989, Aug. 20—Bowbelle and **Marchioness;** British barge struck British pleasure cruiser on Thames R. in central London; 56.

1989, Sept. 10—Romanian pleasure boat and Bulgarian barge collided on Danube R.; 161.

1991, Apr. 10—Auto ferry and oil tanker collided outside Livorno harbour, Italy; 140.

1991, Dec. 14—Salem Express; ferry rammed coral reef nr. Safaga, Egypt; 462.

1993, Feb. 17—Neptune; ferry capsized off Port-au-Prince, Haiti; 500+.

Some Notable Aircraft Disasters Since 1937

Date			Aircraft	Site of accident	Deaths
1937	May	6	German zeppelin Hindenburg	Burned at mooring, Lakehurst, N.J.	36
1944	Aug.	23	U.S. Air Force B-24	Hit school, Freckelton, England	76[1]
1945	July	28	U.S. Army B-25	Hit Empire State bldg., N.Y.C.	14[1]
1947	May	30	Eastern Air Lines DC-4	Crashed near Port Deposit, Md.	53
1952	Dec.	20	U.S. Air Force C-124	Fell, burned, Moses Lake, Wash.	87
1953	Mar.	3	Canadian Pacific Comet Jet	Karachi, Pakistan	11[2]
1953	June	18	U.S. Air Force C-124	Crashed, burned near Tokyo	129
1955	Nov.	1	United Air Lines DC-6B	Exploded, crashed near Longmont, Col.	44[3]
1956	June	20	Venezuelan Super-Constellation	Crashed in Atlantic off Asbury Park, N.J.	74
1956	June	30	TWA Super-Const., United DC-7	Collided over Grand Canyon, Arizona	128
1960	Dec.	16	United DC-8 jet, TWA Super-Const.	Collided over N.Y. City	134[4]
1962	Mar.	16	Flying Tiger Super-Const.	Vanished in Western Pacific	107
1962	June	3	Air France Boeing 707 jet	Crashed on takeoff from Paris	130
1962	June	22	Air France Boeing 707 jet	Crashed in storm, Guadeloupe, W.I.	113
1963	June	3	Chartered Northw. Airlines DC-7	Crashed in Pacific off British Columbia	101
1963	Nov.	29	Trans-Canada Airlines DC-8F	Crashed after takeoff from Montreal	118
1965	May	20	Pakistani Boeing 720-B	Crashed at Cairo, Egypt, airport	121
1966	Jan.	24	Air India Boeing 707 jetliner	Crashed on Mont Blanc, France-Italy	117
1966	Feb.	4	All-Nippon Boeing 727	Plunged into Tokyo Bay	133
1966	Mar.	5	BOAC Boeing 707 jetliner	Crashed on Mount Fuji, Japan	124
1966	Dec.	24	U.S. military-chartered CL-44	Crashed into village in So. Vietnam	129[1]
1967	Apr.	20	Swiss Britannia turboprop	Crashed at Nicosia, Cyprus	126
1967	July	19	Piedmont Boeing 727, Cessna 310	Collided in air, Hendersonville, N.C.	82
1968	Apr.	20	S. African Airways Boeing 707	Crashed on takeoff, Windhoek, SW Africa	122
1968	May	3	Braniff International Electra	Crashed in storm near Dawson, Tex.	85
1969	Mar.	16	Venezuelan DC-9	Crashed after takeoff from Maracaibo, Venezuela	155[5]
1969	Dec.	8	Olympia Airways DC-6B	Crashed near Athens in storm	93
1970	Feb.	15	Dominican DC-9	Crashed into sea on takeoff from Santo Domingo	102
1970	July	3	British chartered jetliner	Crashed near Barcelona, Spain	112
1970	July	5	Air Canada DC-8	Crashed near Toronto International Airport	108
1970	Aug.	9	Peruvian turbojet	Crashed after takeoff from Cuzco, Peru	101[1]
1970	Nov.	14	Southern Airways DC-9	Crashed in mountains near Huntington, W. Va.	75[6]
1971	July	30	All-Nippon Boeing 727 and Japanese Air Force F-86	Collided over Morioka, Japan	162[7]
1971	Sept.	4	Alaska Airlines Boeing 727	Crashed into mountain near Juneau, Alaska	111
1972	Aug.	14	E. German Ilyushin-62	Crashed on takeoff East Berlin	156
1972	Oct.	13	Aeroflot Ilyushin-62	E. German airline crashed near Moscow	176
1972	Dec.	3	Chartered Spanish airliner	Crashed on takeoff, Canary Islands	155
1972	Dec.	29	Eastern Airlines Lockheed Tristar	Crashed on approach to Miami Int'l. Airport	101
1973	Jan.	22	Chartered Boeing 707	Burst into flames during landing, Kano Airport, Nigeria	176
1973	Feb.	21	Libyan jetliner	Shot down by Israeli fighter planes over Sinai	108
1973	Apr.	10	British Vanguard turboprop	Crashed during snowstorm at Basel, Switzerland	104
1973	June	3	Soviet Supersonic TU-144	Crashed near Goussainville, France	14[8]
1973	July	11	Brazilian Boeing 707	Crashed on approach to Orly Airport, Paris	122
1973	July	31	Delta Airlines jetliner	Crashed, landing in fog at Logan Airport, Boston	89
1973	Dec.	23	French Caravelle jet	Crashed in Morocco	106
1974	Mar.	3	Turkish DC-10 jet	Crashed at Ermenonville near Paris	346
1974	Apr.	23	Pan American 707 jet	Crashed in Bali, Indonesia	107
1974	Dec.	1	TWA-727	Crashed in storm, Upperville, Va.	92
1974	Dec.	4	Dutch-chartered DC-8	Crashed in storm near Colombo, Sri Lanka	191
1975	Apr.	4	Air Force Galaxy C-5B	Crashed near Saigon, So. Vietnam, after takeoff with load of orphans	172
1975	June	24	Eastern Airlines 727 jet	Crashed in storm, JFK Airport, N.Y. City	113
1975	Aug.	3	Chartered 707	Hit mountainside, Agadir, Morocco	188
1976	Sept.	10	British Airways Trident, Yugoslav DC-9	Collided near Zagreb, Yugoslavia	176
1976	Sept.	19	Turkish 727	Hit mountain, southern Turkey	155
1976	Oct.	13	Bolivian 707 cargo jet	Crashed in Santa Cruz, Bolivia	100[9]
1977	Jan.	13	Aeroflot TU-104	Exploded and crashed at Alma-Ata, Central Asia	90
1977	Mar.	27	KLM 747, Pan American 747	Collided on runway, Tenerife, Canary Islands	582
1977	Nov.	19	TAP Boeing 727	Crashed on Madeira	130
1977	Dec.	4	Malaysian Boeing 737	Hijacked, then exploded in mid-air over Straits of Johore	100
1977	Dec.	13	U.S. DC-3	Crashed after takeoff at Evansville, Ind.	29[10]
1978	Jan.	1	Air India 747	Exploded, crashed into sea off Bombay	213
1978	Sept.	25	Boeing 727, Cessna 172	Collided in air, San Diego, Cal.	150

(Continued)

Date			Aircraft	Site of accident	Deaths
1978	Nov.	15	Chartered DC-8	Crashed near Colombo, Sri Lanka	183
1979	May	25	American Airlines DC-10	Crashed after takeoff at O'Hare Intl. Airport, Chicago	275[11]
1979	Aug.	17	Two Soviet Aeroflot jetliners	Collided over Ukraine	173
1979	Oct.	31	Western Airlines DC-10	Mexico City Airport	74
1979	Nov.	26	Pakistani Boeing 707	Crashed near Jidda, Saudi Arabia	156
1979	Nov.	28	New Zealand DC-10	Crashed into mountain in Antarctica	257
1980	Mar.	14	Polish Ilyushin 62	Crashed making emergency landing, Warsaw	87[12]
1980	Aug.	19	Saudi Arabian Tristar	Burned after emergency landing, Riyadh	301
1981	Dec.	1	Yugoslavian DC-9	Crashed into mountain in Corsica	174
1982	Jan.	13	Air Florida Boeing 737	Crashed into Potomac River after takeoff	78
1982	July	9	Pan-Am Boeing 727	Crashed after takeoff in Kenner, La.	153[13]
1982	Sept.	11	U.S. Army CH-47 Chinook helicopter	Crashed during air show in Mannheim, W. Germany	46
1983	Sept.	1	S. Korean Boeing 747	Shot down after violating Soviet airspace	269
1983	Nov.	27	Colombian Boeing 747	Crashed near Barajas Airport, Madrid	183
1985	Feb.	19	Spanish Boeing 727	Crashed into Mt. Oiz, Spain	148
1985	June	23	Air-India Boeing 747	Crashed into Atlantic Ocean S. of Ireland	329
1985	Aug.	2	Delta Air Lines jumbo jet	Crashed at Dallas-Ft. Worth Intl. Airport	133
1985	Aug.	12	Japan Air Lines Boeing 747	Crashed into Mt. Ogura, Japan	520[14]
1985	Dec.	12	Arrow Air DC 8	Crashed after takeoff in Gander, Newfoundland	256[15]
1986	Mar.	31	Mexican Boeing 727	Crashed NW of Mexico City	166
1986	Aug.	31	Aeromexico DC-9	Collided with Piper PA-28 over Cerritos, Cal.	82[16]
1987	May	9	Ilyushin 62M	Crashed after takeoff in Warsaw, Poland	183
1987	Aug.	16	Northwest Airlines MD-82	Crashed after takeoff in Romulus, Mich.	156
1988	July	3	Iranian A300 Airbus	Shot down by U.S. Navy warship *Vincennes* over Persian Gulf	290
1988	Dec.	21	Pan Am Boeing 747	Exploded and crashed in Lockerbie, Scotland	270[17]
1989	Feb.	8	Boeing 707	Crashed into mountain in Azores Islands off Portugal	144
1989	June	7	Suriname DC-8	Crashed near Paramaribo Airport, Suriname	168
1989	July	19	United Airlines DC-10	Crashed while landing with a disabled hydraulic system, Sioux City, Ia.	111
1989	Sept.	19	French DC-10	Exploded in air over Niger	171
1991	May	26	Austrian Boeing 767-300	Exploded over rural Thailand	223
1991	July	11	Nigerian DC-8	Crashed while landing at Jidda, Saudi Arabia	261
1992	July	22	Thai A300 Airbus	Crashed in Nepal	113
1992	Sept.	28	Pakistani A300 Airbus	Crashed in Himalayas	167
1992	Oct.	5	El Al cargo jet	Hit block of flats in Amsterdam	120

(1) Including those on the ground and in buildings. (2) First fatal crash of commercial jet plane. (3) Caused by bomb planted by John G. Graham in insurance plot to kill his mother, a passenger. (4) Including all 128 aboard the planes and 6 on ground. (5) Killed 84 on plane and 71 on ground. (6) Including 43 Marshall U. football players and coaches. (7) Airliner-fighter crash, pilot of fighter parachuted to safety, was arrested for negligence. (8) First supersonic plane crash killed 6 crewmen and 8 on the ground; there were no passengers. (9) Crew of 3 killed; 97, mostly children, killed on ground. (10) Including U. of Evansville basketball team. (11) Highest death toll in U.S. aviation history. (12) Including 22 members of U.S. boxing team. (13) Including 8 on ground. (14) Worst single-plane disaster. (15) Incl. 248 members of U.S. 101st Airborne Division. (16) Incl. 15 on the ground. (17) Incl. 11 on the ground.

Notable Rail Disasters

Date			Location	Deaths
1880	Aug.	11	Mays Landing, N. J.	40
1887	Aug.	10	Chatsworth, Ill.	81
1888	Oct.	10	Mud Run, Pa.	55
1891	June	14	Nr. Basel, Switzerland	100
1896	July	30	Atlantic City, N. J.	60
1903	Dec.	23	Laurel Run, Pa.	53
1904	Aug.	7	Eden, Col.	96
1904	Sept.	24	New Market Tenn.	56
1906	Mar.	16	Florence, Col.	35
1906	Oct.	28	Atlantic City, N. J.	40
1906	Dec.	30	Washington, D. C.	53
1907	Jan.	2	Volland, Kan.	33
1907	Jan.	19	Fowler, Ind.	29
1907	Feb.	16	New York, N.Y.	22
1907	Feb.	23	Colton, Cal.	26
1907	May	11	Lompoc, Cal.	36
1907	July	20	Salem, Mich.	33
1910	Mar.	1	Wellington, Wash.	96
1910	Mar.	21	Green Mountain, Ia.	55
1911	Aug.	25	Manchester, N. Y.	29
1912	July	4	East Corning, N. Y.	39
1912	July	5	Ligonier, Pa.	23
1914	Aug.	5	Tipton Ford, Mo.	43
1914	Sept.	15	Lebanon, Mo.	28
1915	May	22	Nr. Gretna, Scotland	227
1916	Mar.	29	Amherst, Oh.	27
1917	Sept.	28	Kellyville, Okla.	23
1917	Dec.	12	Modane, France	543[1]
1917	Dec.	20	Shepherdsville, Ky.	46
1918	June	22	Ivanhoe, Ind.	68
1918	July	9	Nashville, Tenn.	101
1918	Nov.	1	Brooklyn, N. Y.	97
1919	Jan.	12	South Byron, N. Y.	22
1919	July	1	Dunkirk, N. Y.	12
1919	Dec.	20	Onawa, Maine	23
1921	Feb.	27	Porter, Ind.	37
1921	Dec.	5	Woodmont, Pa.	27
1922	Aug.	5	Sulphur Spring, Mo.	34
1922	Dec.	13	Humble, Tex.	22
1923	Sept.	27	Lockett, Wy.	31
1925	June	16	Hackettstown, N. J.	50

Date			Location	Deaths
1926	Sept.	5	Waco, Col.	30
1928	Aug.	24	I.R.T. subway, Times Sq., N. Y.	18
1937	July	16	Nr. Patna, India	107
1938	June	19	Saugus, Mont.	47
1939	Aug.	12	Harney, Nev.	24
1939	Dec.	22	Nr. Magdeburg, Germany	132
1939	Dec.	22	Nr. Friedrichshafen, Germany	99
1940	Apr.	19	Little Falls, N. Y.	31
1940	July	31	Cuyahoga Falls, Oh.	43
1943	Aug.	29	Wayland, N. Y.	27
1943	Sept.	6	Frankford Junction, Philadelphia, Pa.	79
1943	Dec.	16	Between Rennert and Buie, N. C.	72
1944	Jan.	16	Leon Province, Spain	500
1944	Mar.	2	Salerno, Italy	521
1944	July	6	High Bluff, Tenn.	35
1944	Aug.	4	Near Stockton, Ga.	47
1944	Sept.	14	Dewey, Ind.	29
1944	Dec.	31	Bagley, Utah	50
1945	Aug.	9	Michigan, N. D.	34
1946	Mar.	20	Aracaju, Mexico	185
1946	Apr.	25	Naperville, Ill.	45
1947	Feb.	18	Gallitzin, Pa.	24
1949	Oct.	22	Nr. Dwor, Poland	200+
1950	Feb.	17	Rockville Centre, N. Y.	31
1950	Sept.	11	Coshocton, Oh.	33
1950	Nov.	22	Richmond Hill, N. Y.	79
1951	Feb.	6	Woodbridge, N. J.	84
1951	Nov.	12	Wyuta, Wyo.	17
1951	Nov.	25	Woodstock, Ala.	17
1952	Mar.	4	Nr. Rio de Janeiro, Brazil	119
1952	July	9	Rzepin, Poland	160
1952	Oct.	8	Harrow, England	112
1953	Mar.	27	Conneaut, Oh.	21
1955	Apr.	3	Guadalajara, Mexico	300
1956	Jan.	22	Los Angeles, Cal.	30
1956	Feb.	28	Swampscott, Mass.	13
1956	Sept.	5	Springer, N. M.	20
1957	June	11	Vroman, Col.	12
1957	Sept.	1	Kendal, Jamaica	178
1957	Sept.	29	Montgomery, W. Pakistan	250
1957	Dec.	4	London, England	90

(Continued)

Date			Location	Deaths
1958	May	8	Rio de Janeiro, Brazil	128
1958	Sept.	15	Elizabethport, N. J.	48
1960	Mar.	14	Bakersfield, Cal.	14
1960	Nov.	14	Pardubice, Czech.	110
1962	Jan.	8	Woerden, Netherlands	91
1962	May	3	Tokyo, Japan	163
1962	July	28	Steelton, Pa.	19
1964	July	26	Oporto, Portugal	94
1966	Dec.	28	Everett, Mass.	13
1970	Feb.	1	Buenos Aires, Argentina	236
1971	June	10	Salem, Ill.	11
1972	June	16	Vierzy, France	107
1972	July	21	Seville, Spain	76
1972	Oct.	6	Saltillo, Mexico	208
1972	Oct.	30	Chicago, Ill.	45
1974	Aug.	30	Zagreb, Yugoslavia	153
1977	Jan.	18	Granville, Australia	82
1977	Feb.	4	Chicago, Ill., elevated train	11
1981	June	6	Bihar, India	500+
1982	Jan.	27	El Asnam, Algeria	130
1982	July	11	Tepic, Mexico	120
1983	Feb.	19	Empalme, Mexico	100
1987	Jan.	4	Essex, Md.	16
1988	Dec.	12	Clapham, London	34
1989	Jan.	15	Maizdi Khan, Bangladesh	110+
1990	Jan.	4	Sindh Province, Pakistan	210+
1991	May	14	Shigaraki, Japan	42
1991	July	31	Camden, S.C.	7
1991	Aug.	28	N.Y. City subway	5

(1) World's worst train crash; passenger train derailed.

Hurricanes, Typhoons, Blizzards, Other Storms

Names of hurricanes and typhoons in italics – H. = hurricane; T. = typhoon

Date	Location	Deaths
1888 Mar. 11–14	Blizzard, Eastern U.S.	400
1900 Aug.–Sept.	H., Galveston, Tex.	6,000
1906 Sept. 21	H., La., Miss.	350
1906 Sept. 18	Typhoon, Hong Kong	10,000
1926 Sept. 11–22	H., Fla., Ala.	243
1926 Oct. 20	H., Cuba	600
1928 Sept. 6–20	H., So. Fla.	1,836
1930 Sept. 3	H., Dominican Rep.	2,000
1938 Sept. 21	H., Long, Island N.Y., New England	600
1940 Nov. 11–12	Blizzard, U.S. NE, Midwest	144
1942 Oct. 15–16	H., Bengal, India	40,000
1944 Sept. 9–16	H., N.C. to New Eng.	46
1952 Oct. 22	Typhoon, Philippines	440
1954 Aug. 30	H. *Carol*, Northeast U.S.	68
1954 Oct. 5–18	H. *Hazel*, Eastern, U.S., Haiti	347
1955 Aug. 12–13	H. *Connie*, Carolinas, Va., Md.	43
1955 Aug. 7–21	H. *Diane*, Eastern U.S.	400
1955 Sept. 19	H. *Hilda*, Mexico	200
1955 Sept. 22–28	H. *Janet*, Caribbean	500
1956 Feb. 1–29	Blizzard, Western Europe	1,000
1957 June 25–30	H. *Audrey*, Tex. to Ala.	390
1958 Feb. 15–16	Blizzard, NE U.S.	171
1959 Sept. 17–19	T. *Sarah*, Japan, S. Korea	2,000
1959 Sept. 26–27	T. *Vera*, Honshu, Japan	4,466
1960 Sept. 4–12	H. *Donna*, Caribbean, E. U.S.	148
1961 Sept. 11–14	H. *Carla*, Tex.	46
1961 Oct. 31	H. *Hattie*, Br. Honduras	400
1963 May 28–29	Windstorm, Bangladesh	22,000
1963 Oct. 4–8	H. *Flora*, Caribbean	6,000
1964 Oct. 4–7	H. *Hilda*, La., Miss., Ga.	38
1964 June 30	T. *Winnie*, N. Philippines	107
1964 Sept. 5	T. *Ruby*, Hong Kong and China	735
1965 May 11–12	Windstorm, Bangladesh	17,000
1965 June 1–2	Windstorm, Bangladesh	30,000
1965 Sept. 7–12	H. *Betsy*, Fla., Miss., La.	74
1965 Dec. 15	Windstorm, Bangladesh	10,000
1966 June 4–10	H. *Alma*, Honduras, SE U.S.	51
1966 Sept. 24–30	H. *Inez*, Carib., Fla., Mex.	293
1967 July 9	T. *Billie*, SW Japan	347
1967 Sept. 5–23	H. *Beulah*, Carib., Mex., Tex.	54
1967 Dec. 12–20	Blizzard, Southwest, U.S.	51
1968 Nov. 18–28	T. *Nina*, Philippines	63
1969 Aug. 17–18	H. *Camille*, Miss., La.	256
1970 July 30–Aug. 5	H. *Celia*, Cuba, Fla., Tex.	31
1970 Aug. 20–21	H. *Dorothy*, Martinique	42
1970 Sept. 15	T. *Georgia*, Philippines	300
1970 Oct. 14	T. *Sening*, Philippines	583
1970 Oct. 15	T. *Titang*, Philippines	526
1970 Nov. 13	Cyclone, Bangladesh	300,000
1971 Aug. 1	T. *Rose*, Hong Kong	130
1972 June 19–29	H. *Agnes*, Fla. to N.Y.	118
1972 Dec. 3	T. *Theresa*, Philippines	169
1973 June–Aug.	Monsoon rains in India	1,217
1974 June 11	Storm Dinah, Luzon Is., Philip.	71
1974 July 11	T. *Gilda*, Japan, S. Korea	108
1974 Sept. 19–20	H. *Fifi*, Honduras	2,000
1974 Dec. 25	Cyclone leveled Darwin, Aus.	50
1975 Sept. 13–27	H. *Eloise*, Caribbean, NE U.S.	71
1976 May 20	T. *Olga*, floods, Philippines	215
1977 July 25, 31	T. *Thelma*, T. *Vera*, Taiwan	39
1978 Oct. 27	T. *Rita*, Philippines	c. 400
1979 Aug. 30–Sept. 7	H. *David*, Caribbean, East. U.S.	1,100
1980 Aug. 4–11	H. *Allen*, Caribbean, Texas	272
1981 Nov. 25	T. *Irma*, Luzon Is., Philippines	176
1983 June	Monsoon rains in India	900
1983 Aug. 18	H. *Alicia*, southern Texas	17
1984 Sept. 2	T. *Ike*, southern Philippines	1,363
1985 May 25	Cyclone, Bangladesh	10,000
1985 Oct. 26–Nov. 6	H. *Juan*, SE U.S.	97
1987 Nov. 25	T. *Nina*, Philippines	650
1988 Sept. 10–17	H. *Gilbert*, Caribbean, Gulf of Mex.	260
1989 Sept. 16–22	H. *Hugo*, Caribbean, SE U.S.	504
1990 May 6–11	Cyclones, SE India	450
1991 Apr. 30	Cyclone, Bangladesh	70,000
1992 Aug. 24–26	H. *Andrew*, S. Florida, Louisiana	14
1993 Mar. 13–14	Blizzard, Eastern USA	200

Floods, Tidal Waves

Date		Location	Deaths
1228	....	Holland	100,000
1642	....	China	300,000
1887	....	Huang He River, China	900,000
1889	May 31	Johnstown, Pa.	2,200
1900	Sept. 8	Galveston, Tex.	5,000
1903	June 15	Heppner, Ore.	325
1911	....	Chang Jiang River, China	100,000
1913	Mar. 25–27	Ohio, Indiana	732
1915	Aug. 17	Galveston, Tex.	275
1928	Mar. 13	Collapse of St. Francis Dam, Saugus, Cal.	450
1928	Sept. 13	Lake Okeechobee, Fla.	2,000
1931	Aug.	Huang He River, China	3,700,000
1937	Jan. 22	Ohio, Miss. Valleys	250
1939	....	Northern China	200,000
1946	Apr. 1	Hawaii, Alaska	159
1947	....	Honshu Island, Japan	1,900
1951	Aug.	Manchuria	1,800
1953	Jan. 31	Western Europe	2,000
1954	Aug. 17	Farahzad, Iran	2,000
1955	Oct. 7–12	India, Pakistan	1,700
1959	Nov. 1	Western Mexico	2,000
1959	Dec. 2	Frejus, France	412
1960	Oct. 10	Bangladesh	6,000
1960	Oct. 31	Bangladesh	4,000
1962	Feb. 17	German North Sea coast	343
1962	Sept. 27	Barcelona, Spain	445
1963	Oct. 9	Dam collapse, Vaiont, Italy	1,800
1966	Nov. 3–4	Florence, Venice, Italy	113
1967	Jan. 18–24	Eastern Brazil	894
1967	Mar. 19	Rio de Janeiro, Brazil	436
1967	Nov. 26	Lisbon, Portugal	464
1968	Aug. 7–14	Gujarat State, India	1,000
1968	Oct. 7	Northeastern India	780
1969	Jan. 18–26	So. Cal.	100
1969	Mar. 17	Mundau Valley, Alagoas, Brazil	218
1969	Aug. 20–22	Western Virginia	189
1969	Sept. 15	South Korea	250
1969	Oct. 1–8	Tunisia	500
1970	May 20	Central Romania	160

(Continued)

Date		Location	Deaths
1970	July 22	Himalayas, India	500
1971	Feb. 26	Rio de Janeiro, Brazil	130
1972	Feb. 26	Buffalo Creek, W. Va.	118
1972	June 9	Rapid City, S.D.	236
1972	Aug. 7	Luzon Is., Philippines	454
1973	Aug. 19–31	Pakistan	1,500
1974	Mar. 29	Tubaro, Brazil	1,000
1974	Aug. 12	Monty–Long, Bangladesh	2,500
1976	June 5	Teton Dam collapse, Ida.	11
1976	July 31	Big Thompson Canyon, Col.	139
1976	Nov. 17	East Java, Indonesia	136
1977	July 19–20	Johnstown, Pa.	68
1978	June–Sept.	Northern India	1,200
1979	Jan.–Feb.	Brazil	204
1979	July 17	Lomblem Is., Indonesia	539
1979	Aug. 11	Morvi, India	5,000–15,000
1980	Feb. 13–22	So. Cal., Ariz.	26
1981	Apr.	Northern China	550
1981	July	Sichuan, Hubei Prov., China	1,300
1982	Jan. 23	Nr. Lima, Peru	600
1982	May 12	Guangdong, China	430
1982	June 6	So. Conn.	12
1982	Sept. 17–21	El Salvador, Guatemala	1,300+
1982	Dec. 2–9	Ill., Mo., Ark.	22
1983	Feb.–Mar.	Cal. coast	13
1983	Apr. 6–12	Ala., La., Miss., Tenn.	15
1984	May 27	Tulsa, Okla.	13
1984	Aug–Sept.	S. Korea	200+
1985	July 19	Northern Italy, dam burst	361
1987	Aug.–Sept.	Northern Bangladesh	1,000+
1988	Sept.	Northern India	1,000+
1991	Dec. 18–26	Texas	18
1992	Feb. 9–15	S. Cal.	13
1992	c. Sept. 8	Pakistan	?3,000
1992	Sept. 2	Vaucluse, France	80+
1993	July–Aug.	American Midwest	50+

Major Earthquakes

Magnitude of earthquakes (Mag.), distinct from deaths or damage caused, is measured on the Richter scale (see p. 235), on which each higher number represents a tenfold increase in energy measured in ground motion. Adopted in 1935, the scale has been applied in the following table to earthquakes as far back as reliable seismograms are available.

	Date	Location	Deaths	Mag.
526	May 20	Syria, Antioch	250,000	N.A.
856	....	Greece, Corinth	45,000	"
1057	....	China, Chihli	25,000	"
1268	....	Asia Minor, Cilicia	60,000	"
1290	Sept. 27	China, Chihli	100,000	"
1293	May 20	Japan, Kamakura	30,000	"
1531	Jan. 26	Portugal, Lisbon	30,000	"
1556	Jan. 24	China, Shaanxi	830,000	"
1667	Nov.	Caucasia, Shemaka	80,000	"
1693	Jan. 11	Italy, Catania	60,000	"
1730	Dec. 30	Japan, Hokkaido	137,000	"
1737	Oct. 11	India, Calcutta	300,000	"
1755	June 7	Northern Persia	40,000	"
1755	Nov. 1	Portugal, Lisbon	60,000	8.75*
1783	Feb. 4	Italy, Calabria	30,000	N.A.
1797	Feb. 4	Ecuador, Quito	41,000	"
1811-12		New Madrid, Mo. (series)	—	8.7*
1822	Sept. 5	Asia Minor, Aleppo	22,000	N.A.
1828	Dec. 28	Japan, Echigo	30,000	"
1868	Aug. 13-15	Peru and Ecuador	40,000	"
1875	May 16	Venezuela, Colombia	16,000	"
1886	Aug. 31	Charleston, S.C.	60	6.6
1896	June 15	Japan, sea wave	27,120	N.A.
1906	Apr. 18-19	San Francisco, Cal.	503	8.3
1906	Aug. 16	Chile, Valparaiso	20,000	8.6
1908	Dec. 28	Italy, Messina	83,000	7.5
1915	Jan. 13	Italy, Avezzano	29,980	7.5
1920	Dec. 16	China, Gansu	100,000	8.6
1923	Sept. 1	Japan, Yokohama	200,000	8.3
1927	May 22	China, Nan-Shan	200,000	8.3
1932	Dec. 26	China, Gansu	70,000	7.6
1933	Mar. 2	Japan	2,990	8.9
1933	Mar. 10	Long Beach, Cal.	115	6.2
1934	Jan. 15	India, Bihar-Nepal	10,700	8.4
1935	May 31	India, Quetta	50,000	7.5
1939	Jan. 24	Chile, Chillan	28,000	8.3
1939	Dec. 26	Turkey, Erzincan	30,000	7.9
1946	Dec. 21	Japan, Honshu	2,000	8.4
1948	June 28	Japan, Fukui	5,131	7.3
1949	Aug. 5	Ecuador, Pelileo	6,000	6.8
1950	Aug. 15	India, Assam	1,530	8.7
1953	Mar. 18	NW Turkey	1,200	7.2
1956	June 10-17	N. Afghanistan	2,000	7.7
1957	July 2	Northern Iran	2,500	7.4
1957	Dec. 13	Western Iran	2,000	7.1
1960	Feb. 29	Morocco, Agadir	12,000	5.8
1960	May 21-30	Southern Chile	5,000	8.3
1962	Sept. 1	Northwestern Iran	12,230	7.1
1963	July 26	Yugoslavia, Skopje	1,100	6.0
1964	Mar. 27	Alaska	131	8.4
1966	Aug. 19	Eastern Turkey	2,520	6.9
1968	Aug. 31	Northeastern Iran	12,000	7.4
1970	Jan. 5	Yunnan Province, China	10,000	7.7
1970	Mar. 28	Western Turkey	1,086	7.4
1970	May 31	Northern Peru	66,794	7.7
1971	Feb. 9	San Fernando Valley, Cal.	65	6.6
1972	Apr. 10	Southern Iran	5,057	6.9
1972	Dec. 23	Nicaragua	5,000	6.2
1974	Dec. 28	Pakistan (9 towns)	5,200	6.3
1975	Sept. 6	Turkey (Lice, etc.)	2,312	6.8
1976	Feb. 4	Guatemala	22,778	7.5
1976	May 6	Northeast Italy	946	6.5
1976	June 26	New Guinea, Irian Jaya	443	7.1
1976	July 28	China, Tangshan	242,000	8.2
1976	Aug. 17	Philippines, Mindanao	8,000	7.8
1976	Nov. 24	E. Turkey	4,000	7.9
1977	Mar. 4	Romania	1,541	7.5
1977	Aug. 19	Indonesia	200	8.0
1977	Nov. 23	Northwestern Argentina	100	8.2
1978	June 12	Japan, Sendai	21	7.5
1978	Sept. 16	Northeast Iran	25,000	7.7
1979	Sept. 12	Indonesia	100	8.1
1979	Dec. 12	Colombia, Ecuador	800	7.9
1980	Oct. 10	Northwestern Algeria	4,500	7.3
1980	Nov. 23	Southern Italy	4,800	7.2
1982	Dec. 13	North Yemen	2,800	6.0
1983	Mar. 31	Southern Colombia	250	5.5
1983	May 26	N. Honshu, Japan	81	7.7
1983	Oct. 30	Eastern Turkey	1,300	7.1
1985	Mar. 3	Chile	146	7.8
1985	Sept. 19, 21	Mexico City	4,200+	8.1
1987	Mar. 5-6	NE Ecuador	4,000+	7.3
1988	Aug. 20	India/Nepal border	1,000+	6.5
1988	Nov. 6	China/Burma border	1,000	7.3
1988	Dec. 7	NW Armenia	55,000+	6.8
1989	Oct. 17	San Francisco Bay area	62	6.9
1990	May 30	N. Peru	115	6.3
1990	June 21	NW Iran	40,000+	7.7
1990	July 16	Luzon, Philippines	1,621	7.7
1991	Feb. 1	Pakistan, Afghanistan border	1,200	6.8
1992	Mar. 13, 15	E. Turkey	4,000	6.2/6.0
1992	June 28	Yucca Valley, Cal.	1	7.4
1992	Oct. 12	Cairo, Egypt	450	5.9
1992	Dec. 12	Flores, Indonesia	2,500	7.5
1993	July 12	off Hokkaido, Japan	200+	7.8

(*) estimated from earthquake intensity. (N.A.) not available.

Some Recent Earthquakes

Source: Global Volcanism Network, Smithsonian Institution

Date	Location	Magnitude
Aug. 8, 1993	Agana, Guam	8.0
Jul. 12	off Hokkaido, Japan	7.8
Mar. 26	S. Greece	5.1
Mar. 12	Fiji	6.5
Mar. 6	Solomon Islands	6.5
Mar. 6	Fiji	6.7
Mar. 6	Santa Cruz Islands	7.1
Jan 15	Kushiro, Japan	7.0
Dec. 20, 1992	Banda Sea, Indonesia	7.0
Dec. 12	Flores, Indonesia	7.5

(Continued)

Date	Location	Magnitude
Nov. 8	Fiji	6.5
Oct. 23	Papua New Guinea	6.7
Oct. 17	Murindo, Colombia	7.2
Oct. 12	Cairo, Egypt	5.9
Sep. 11	SE Zaire	6.8
Sep. 2	Off Nicaragua	7.2
Aug. 19	Kyrgyzstan	7.5
Aug. 7	Gulf of Alaska	6.5
June 28	S. California	7.5/6.6
May 25	Cabo Cruz, Cuba	7.0

Fires

Date			Location	Deaths
1835	Dec.	16	New York City, 500 bldgs. destroyed	—
1845	May		Canton, China, theater	1,670
1871	Oct.	8	Chicago, $196 million loss	250
1871	Oct.	8	Peshtigo, Wis., forest fire	1,182
1872	Nov.	9	Boston, 800 bldgs. destroyed	—
1876	Dec.	5	Brooklyn (N.Y.), theater	295
1877	June	20	St. John, N. B., Canada	100
1881	Dec.	8	Ring Theater, Vienna	850
1887	May	25	Opéra Comique, Paris	200
1887	Sept.	4	Exeter, England, theater	200
1894	Sept.	1	Minn., forest fire	413
1897	May	4	Paris, charity bazaar	150
1900	June	30	Hoboken, N. J., docks	326
1902	Sept.	20	Birmingham, Ala., church	115
1903	Dec.	30	Iroquois Theater, Chicago	602
1908	Jan.	13	Rhoads Theater, Boyertown, Pa.	170
1908	Mar.	4	Collinwood, Oh., school	176
1911	Mar.	25	Triangle factory, N. Y. City	145
1913	Oct.	14	Mid Glamorgan, Wales, colliery	439
1918	Apr.	13	Norman Okla., state hospital	38
1918	Oct.	12	Cloquet, Minn., forest fire	400
1919	June	20	Mayaguez Theater, San Juan	150
1923	May	17	Camden, S. C., school	76
1924	Dec.	24	Hobart, Okla., school	35
1929	May	15	Cleveland, Oh., clinic	125
1930	Apr.	21	Columbus, Oh., penitentiary	320
1931	July	24	Pittsburgh, Pa., home for aged	48
1934	Dec.	11	Hotel Kerns, Lansing, Mich.	34
1938	May	16	Atlanta, Ga., Terminal Hotel	35
1940	Apr.	23	Natchez, Miss., dance hall	198
1942	Nov.	28	Cocoanut Grove, Boston	491
1942			St. John's, Newfoundland, hostel	100
1943	Sept.	7	Gulf Hotel, Houston	55
1944	July	6	Ringling Circus, Hartford	168
1946	June	5	LaSalle Hotel, Chicago	61
1946	Dec.	7	Winecoff Hotel, Atlanta	119
1946	Dec.	12	New York, ice plant, tenement	37
1949	Apr.	5	Effingham, Ill., hospital	77
1950	Jan.	7	Davenport, Ia., Mercy Hospital	41
1953	Mar.	29	Largo, Fla., nursing home	35
1953	Apr.	16	Chicago, metalworking plant	35
1957	Feb.	17	Warrenton, Mo., home for aged	72
1958	Mar.	19	New York City, loft building	24
1958	Dec.	1	Chicago, parochial school	95
1958	Dec.	16	Bogota, Colombia, store	83
1959	June	23	Stalheim, Norway, resort hotel	34
1960	Mar.	12	Pusan, Korea, chemical plant	68
1960	July	14	Guatemala City, mental hospital	225
1960	Nov.	13	Amude, Syria, movie theater	152
1961	Jan.	6	Thomas Hotel, San Francisco	20
1961	Dec.	8	Hartford, Conn., hospital	16
1961	Dec.	17	Niteroi, Brazil, circus	323
1963	May	4	Diourbel, Senegal, theater	64
1963	Nov.	18	Surfside Hotel, Atlantic City, N.J.	25
1963	Nov.	23	Fitchville, Oh., rest home	63
1963	Dec.	29	Roosevelt Hotel, Jacksonville, Fla.	22
1964	May	8	Manila, apartment bldg	30
1964	Dec.	18	Fountaintown, Ind., nursing home	20
1965	Mar.	1	LaSalle, Canada, apartment	28
1966	Mar.	11	Numata, Japan, 2 ski resorts	31
1966	Aug.	13	Melbourne, Australia, hotel	29
1966	Sept.	12	Anchorage, Alaska, hotel	14
1966	Oct.	17	N. Y. City bldg. (firemen)	12
1966	Dec.	7	Erzurum, Turkey, barracks	68
1967	Feb.	7	Montgomery, Ala., restaurant	25
1967	May	22	Brussels, Belgium, store	322
1967	July	16	Jay, Fla., state prison	37
1968	Feb.	26	Shrewsbury, England, hospital	22
1968	May	11	Vijayawada, India, wedding hall	58
1968	Nov.	18	Glasgow, Scotland, factory	24
1969	Jan.	26	Victoria Hotel, Dunnville, Ont.	13
1969	Dec.	2	Notre Dame, Can., nursing home	54
1970	Jan.	9	Marietta, Oh., nursing home	27
1970	Mar.	20	Seattle, Wash., hotel	19
1970	Nov.	1	Grenoble, France, dance hall	145
1970	Dec.	20	Tucson, Arizona, hotel	28
1971	Mar.	6	Burghoezli, Switzerland, psychiatric clinic	28
1971	Apr.	20	Hotel, Bangkok, Thailand	24
1971	Oct.	19	Honesdale, Pa., nursing home	15
1971	Dec.	25	Hotel, Seoul, So. Korea	162
1972	May	13	Osaka, Japan, nightclub	116
1972	July	5	Sherborne, England, hospital	30
1973	Feb.	6	Paris, France, school	21
1973	Nov.	6	Fukui, Japan, train	28
1973	Nov.	29	Kumamoto, Japan, department store	107
1973	Dec.	2	Seoul, Korea, theater	50
1974	Feb.	1	Sao Paulo, Brazil, bank building	189
1974	June	30	Port Chester, N. Y., discotheque	24
1974	Nov.	3	Seoul, So. Korea, hotel discotheque	88
1975	Dec.	12	Mina, Saudi Arabia, tent city	138
1976	Oct.	24	Bronx, N.Y., social club	25
1977	Feb.	25	Moscow, Rossiya hotel	45
1977	May	28	Southgate, Ky., nightclub	164
1977	June	9	Abidjan, Ivory Coast, nightclub	41
1977	June	26	Columbia, Tenn., jail	42
1977	Nov.	14	Manila, Philippines, hotel	47
1978	Jan.	28	Kansas City, Coates House Hotel	16
1979	July	14	Saragossa, Spain, hotel	80
1979	Dec.	31	Chapais, Quebec, social club	42
1980	May	20	Kingston, Jamaica, nursing home	157
1980	Nov.	21	MGM Grand Hotel, Las Vegas	84
1980	Dec.	4	Stouffer Inn, Harrison, N.Y.	26
1981	Jan.	9	Keansburg, N.J., boarding home	30
1981	Feb.	10	Las Vegas Hilton	8
1981	Feb.	14	Dublin, Ireland, discotheque	44
1982	Sept.	4	Los Angeles, apartment house	24
1982	Nov.	8	Biloxi, Miss., county jail	29
1983	Feb.	13	Turin, Italy, movie theater	64
1983	Dec.	17	Madrid, Spain, discotheque	83
1984	May	11	Great Adventure Amusement Park, N.J.	8
1985	Apr.	21	Tabaco, Philippines, movie theater	44
1985	Apr.	26	Buenos Aires, Argentina hospital	79
1985	May	11	Bradford, England, soccer stadium	53
1986	Dec.	31	Puerto Rico, Dupont Plaza Hotel	96
1987	May 6–June 2		Northern China forest fire	193
1987	Nov.	17	King's Cross, London	30
1990	Mar.	25	N.Y. City social club	87
1991	Sept.	3	Hamlet, N.C. chicken-processing plant	25
1991	Oct.	20–21	Oakland, Berkeley, Cal. wildfire	24
1992	Nov.	20	Windsor Castle, Berks	0
1993	Apr.	19	Waco, Tex., cult compound	72

Explosions

Date	Location	Deaths
1910 Oct. 1	Los Angeles Times Bldg.	21
1913 Mar. 7	Dynamite, Baltimore harbor	55
1915 Sept. 27	Gasoline tank car, Ardmore, Okla.	47
1917 Apr. 10	Munitions plant, Eddystone, Pa.	133
1917 Dec. 6	Halifax Harbor, Canada	1,654
1918 May 18	Chemical plant, Oakdale, Pa.	193
1918 July 1	Explosives factory, Chilwell, Notts	134
1918 July 2	Explosives, Split Rock, N.Y.	50
1918 Oct. 4	Shell plant, Morgan Station, N.J.	64
1919 May 22	Food plant, Cedar Rapids, Ia.	44
1920 Sept. 16	Wall Street, New York, bomb	30
1924 Jan. 3	Food plant, Pekin, Ill.	42
1928 April 13	Dance hall, West Plains, Mo.	40
1937 Mar. 18	New London, Tex., school	413
1940 Sept. 12	Hercules Powder, Kenvil, N.J.	55
1942 June 5	Ordnance plant, Elwood, Ill.	49

(Continued)

Date	Location	Deaths
1944 Apr. 14	Bombay, India, harbor	700
1944 July 17	Port Chicago, Cal., pier	322
1944 Oct. 21	Liquid gas tank, Cleveland	135
1947 Apr. 16	Texas City, Tex., pier	561
1948 July 28	Farben works, Ludwigshafen, Ger.	184
1950 May 19	Munitions barges, S. Amboy, N. J.	30
1956 Aug. 7	Dynamite trucks, Cali, Colombia	1,100
1958 Apr. 18	Sunken munitions ship, Okinawa	40
1958 May 22	Nike missiles, Leonardo, N.J.	10
1959 Apr. 10	World War II bomb, Philippines	38
1959 June 28	Rail tank cars, Meldrin, Ga.	25
1959 Aug. 7	Dynamite truck, Roseburg, Ore.	13
1959 Nov. 2	Jamuri Bazar, India, explosives	46
1959 Dec. 13	Dortmund, Ger., 2 apt. bldgs.	26
1960 Mar. 4	Belgian munitions ship, Havana	100
1960 Oct. 25	Gas, Windsor, Ont., store	11
1962 Jan. 16	Gas pipeline, Edson, Alberta, Canada	8
1962 Oct. 3	Telephone Co. office, N. Y. City	23
1963 Jan. 2	Packing plant, Terre Haute, Ind.	16
1963 Mar. 9	Dynamite plant, S. Africa	45
1963 Aug. 13	Explosives dump, Gauhiti, India	32
1963 Oct. 31	State Fair Coliseum, Indianapolis	73
1964 July 23	Bone, Algeria, harbor munitions	100
1965 Mar. 4	Gas pipeline, Natchitoches, La.	17
1965 Aug. 9	Missile silo, Searcy, Ark.	53
1965 Oct. 21	Bridge, Tila Bund, Pakistan	80
1965 Oct. 30	Cartagena, Colombia	48
1965 Nov. 24	Armory, Keokuk, Ia.	20
1966 Oct. 13	Chemical plant, La Salle, Que.	11
1967 Feb. 17	Chemical plant, Hawthorne, N.J.	11
1967 Dec. 25	Apartment bldg., Moscow	20
1968 Apr. 6	Sports store, Richmond, Ind.	43
1970 Apr. 8	Subway construction, Osaka, Japan	73
1971 June 24	Tunnel, Sylmar, Cal.	17
1971 June 28	School, fireworks, Pueblo, Mex.	13
1971 Oct. 21	Shopping center, Glasgow, Scot.	20
1973 Feb. 10	Liquified gas tank, Staten Is., N.Y.	40
1975 Dec. 27	Chasnala, India, mine	431
1976 Apr. 13	Lapua, Finland, munitions works	40
1977 Nov. 11	Freight train, Iri, S. Korea	57
1977 Dec. 22	Grain elevator, Westwego, La.	35
1978 Feb. 24	Derailed tank car, Waverly, Tenn.	12
1978 July 11	Propylene tank truck, Spanish coastal campsite	150
1980 Oct. 23	School, Ortuella, Spain	64
1982 Apr. 7	Tanker truck, tunnel, Oakland, Cal.	7
1982 Apr. 25	Antiques exhibition, Todi, Italy	33
1982 Nov. 2	Salang Tunnel, Afghanistan	1,000-3,000
1984 Feb. 25	Oil pipeline, Cubatao, Brazil	508
1984 June 21	Naval supply depot, Severomorsk, USSR	200+
1984 Nov. 19	Gas storage area, NE Mexico City	334
1984 Dec. 5	Coal mine, Taipei, Taiwan	94
1985 June 25	Fireworks factory, Hallett, Okla.	21
1988 July 6	Oil rig, North Sea	167
1989 June 3	Gas pipeline, between Ufa, Asha, USSR	650+
1992 Mar. 3	Coal mine, Kozlu, Turkey	270+
1992 Apr. 22	Sewer, Guadalajara, Mexico	190
1992 Sep. 1	Oil refinery, Athens, Greece	1
1993 May 14	Coal mine, Secunda, S. Africa	53

The Worst Mining Disasters in the World

Source: Russell Ash, *The Top Ten of Everything*

Location	Date	No. killed
Hinkeiko, China	26 April 1942	1,572
Courrières, France	10 March 1906	1,060
Omuta, Japan	9 November 1963	447
Senghenydd, Wales	14 October 1913	439
Coalbrook, South Africa	21 January 1960	437
Wankie, Rhodesia	6 June 1972	427
Bihar, India	28 May 1965	375
Chasnala, India	27 December 1975	372
Barnsley, Yorkshire	12 December 1866	361*
Monongah, West Virginia, USA	6 December 1907	361

*A further 28 were killed the following day while searching for survivors.

Notable Nuclear Accidents

Oct. 7, 1957 — A fire in the Windscale plutonium production reactor in Cumbria, UK, spread radioactive material throughout the countryside. In 1983, the British government said that 39 people probably died of cancer as a result.

1957 — A chemical explosion in Kasli, USSR, in tanks containing nuclear waste, spread radioactive material and forced a major evacuation.

Jan. 3, 1961 — An experimental reactor at a federal installation near Idaho Falls, Id. killed three workers—the only deaths in U.S. reactor operations. The plant had high radiation levels but damage was contained.

Oct. 5, 1966 — A sodium cooling system malfunction caused a partial core meltdown at the Enrico Fermi demonstration breeder reactor near Detroit, Mich. Radiation was contained.

Jan. 21, 1969 — A coolant malfunction from an experimental underground reactor at Lucens Vad, Switzerland resulted in the release of a large amount of radiation into a cavern, which was then sealed.

Mar. 22, 1975 — A technician checking for air leaks with a lighted candle caused a $100 million fire at the Brown's Ferry reactor in Decatur, Ala. The fire burned out electrical controls, lowering the cooling water to dangerous levels.

Mar. 28, 1979 — The worst commercial nuclear accident in the U.S. occurred as equipment failures and human mistakes led to a loss of coolant, and partial core meltdown at the Three Mile Island reactor in Middletown, Pa.

Feb. 11, 1981 — Eight workers were contaminated when over 100,000 gallons of radioactive coolant leaked into the containment building of the TVA's Sequoyah 1 plant in Tennessee.

Apr. 25, 1981 — Some 100 workers were exposed to radioactive material during repairs of a nuclear plant at Tsuruga, Japan.

Jan. 6, 1986 — A cylinder of nuclear material burst after being improperly heated at a Kerr-McGee plant at Gore, Okla. One worker died and 100 were hospitalized.

Apr. 26, 1986 — In the worst accident in the history of the nuclear power industry, fires and explosions resulting from an unauthorized experiment at the Chernobyl nuclear power plant near Kiev in the Soviet Union left at least 31 people dead in the immediate aftermath of the disaster and spread significant quantities of radioactive material over much of Europe. An estimated 135,000 people were evacuated from areas around Chernobyl, some of which were rendered uninhabitable for years. As a result of the radiation released into the atmosphere, tens of thousands of excess cancer deaths (as well as increased rates of birth defects) were expected in succeeding decades.

Record Oil Spills

As a rule, the number of tons can be multiplied by 7 to estimate the number of barrels spilled; the exact number of barrels in a ton varies with the type of oil. Each barrel contains 42 gallons.

Name, place	Date	Cause	Tons
Ixtoc I oil well, southern Gulf of Mexico	June 3, 1979	Blowout	600,000
Nowruz oil field, Persian Gulf	Feb., 1983	Blowout	600,000 (est.)
Atlantic Empress & Aegean Captain, off Trinidad & Tobago	July 19, 1979	Collision	300,000
Castillo de Bellver, off Cape Town, South Africa	Aug. 6, 1983	Fire	250,000
Amoco Cadiz, near Portsall, France	March 16, 1978	Grounding	223,000
Torrey Canyon, off Land's End, England	March 18, 1967	Grounding	119,000
Sea Star, Gulf of Oman	Dec. 19, 1972	Collision	115,000
Urquiola, La Coruna, Spain	May 12, 1976	Grounding	100,000
Hawaiian Patriot, northern Pacific	Feb. 25, 1977	Fire	99,000
Othello, Tralhavet Bay, Sweden	March 20, 1970	Collision	60,000-100,000

Other Notable Oil Spills

Name, place	Date	Cause	Gallons
Persian Gulf	Jan. 23, 1991 (began)	Spillage by Iraq	130,000,000*
Braer, off Shetland Islands	Jan. 5, 1993	Grounding	26,000,000
Atlantic Ocean, off northern Spain	Dec. 3, 1992	Unknown	21,500,000
World Glory, off South Africa	June 13, 1968	Hull failure	13,524,000
Burmah Agate, Galveston Bay, Tex.	Nov. 1, 1979	Collision	10,700,000
Exxon Valdez, Prince William Sound, Alas.	Mar. 24, 1989	Grounding	10,080,000
Keo, off Massachusetts	Nov. 5, 1969	Hull failure	8,820,000
Storage tank, Sewaren, N.J.	Nov. 4, 1969	Tank rupture	8,400,000
Ekofisk oil field, North Sea	Apr. 22, 1977	Well blowout	8,200,000
Argo Merchant, Nantucket, Mass.	Dec. 15, 1976	Grounding	7,700,000
Pipeline, West Delta, La.	Oct. 15, 1967	Dragging anchor	6,720,000
Tanker off Japan	Nov. 30, 1971	Ship broke in half	6,258,000
Storage tank, Monongahela River	Jan. 2, 1988	Tank rupture	3,800,000

* Estimated by Saudi Arabia. Some estimates are as low as 25,000,000 gallons.

Historic Assassinations Since 1865

1865—Apr. 14. U. S. Pres. Abraham Lincoln, shot by John Wilkes Booth in Washington, D. C.; died Apr. 15.

1881—Mar. 13. Alexander II, of Russia—July 2. U. S. Pres. James A. Garfield, shot by Charles J. Guiteau, Washington D.C.; died Sept. 19.

1900—July 29. Umberto I, king of Italy.

1901—Sept. 6. U. S. Pres. William McKinley in Buffalo, N. Y., died Sept. 14. Leon Czolgosz executed for the crime Oct. 29.

1913—Feb. 23. Mexican Pres. Francisco I. Madero and Vice Pres. Jose Pino Suarez.—Mar. 18. George, king of Greece.

1914—June 28. Archduke Francis Ferdinand of Austria-Hungary and his wife in Sarajevo, Bosnia (later part of Yugoslavia), by Gavrilo Princip.

1916—Dec. 30. Grigori Rasputin, politically powerful Russian monk.

1918—July 12. Grand Duke Michael of Russia, at Perm.—July 16. Nicholas II, abdicated as tsar of Russia; his wife, the Tsarina Alexandra, their son, Tsarevitch Alexis, and their daughters, Grand Duchesses Olga, Tatiana, Marie, Anastasia, and 4 members of their household were executed by Bolsheviks at Ekaterinburg.

1920—May 20. Mexican Pres. Gen. Venustiano Carranza in Tlaxcalantongo.

1922—Aug. 22. Michael Collins, Irish revolutionary.—Dec. 16. Polish President Gabriel Narutowicz in Warsaw by an anarchist.

1923—July 20. Gen. Francisco "Pancho" Villa, ex-rebel leader, in Parral, Mexico.

1928—July 17. Gen. Alvaro Obregon, president-elect of Mexico, in San Angel, Mexico.

1933—Feb. 15. In Miami, Fla., Joseph Zangara, anarchist, shot at Pres.-elect Franklin D. Roosevelt, but a woman seized his arm, and the bullet fatally wounded Mayor Anton J. Cermak, of Chicago, who died Mar. 6. Zangara was electrocuted on Mar. 20, 1933.

1934—July 25. In Vienna, Austrian Chancellor Engelbert Dollfuss by Nazis.

1935—Sept. 8. U.S. Sen. Huey P. Long, shot in Baton Rouge, La., by Dr. Carl Austin Weiss, who was slain by Long's bodyguards; Long died Sep. 10.

1940—Aug. 20. Leon Trotsky (Lev Bronstein), 63, exiled Russian war minister, near Mexico City. Killer identified as Ramon Mercador del Rio, a Spaniard, served 20 years in Mexican prison.

1948—Jan. 30. Mohandas K. Gandhi, 78, shot in New Delhi, India, by Nathuram Vinayak Godse.—Sept. 17. Count Folke Bernadotte, UN mediator for Palestine, ambushed in Jerusalem.

1951—July 20. King Abdullah ibn Hussein of Jordan.—Oct. 27. Prime Min. Liaquat Ali Khan of Pakistan shot in Rawalpindi.

1956—Sept. 21. Pres. Anastasio Somoza of Nicaragua, in Leon; died Sept. 29.

1957—July 26. Pres. Carlos Castillo Armas of Guatemala, in Guatemala City by one of his own guards.

1958—July 14. King Faisal of Iraq; his uncle, Crown Prince Abdullah; and July 15, Premier Nuri as-Said, by rebels in Baghdad.

1959—Sept. 25. Prime Minister Solomon Bandaranaike of Ceylon, by Buddhist monk in Colombo.

1961—Jan. 17. Ex-Premier Patrice Lumumba of the Congo, in Katanga Province—May 30. Dominican dictator Rafael Leonidas Trujillo Molina shot to death by assassins near Ciudad Trujillo.

1963—June 12. Medgar W. Evers, NAACP's Mississippi field secretary, in Jackson, Miss.—Nov. 2. Pres. Ngo Dinh Diem of the Republic of Vietnam and his brother, Ngo Dinh Nhu, in a military coup.—Nov. 22. U.S. Pres. John F. Kennedy fatally shot in Dallas, Tex.; accused Lee Harvey Oswald murdered by Jack Ruby while awaiting trial.

1965—Jan. 21. Iranian premier Hassan Ali Mansour fatally wounded by assassin in Tehran; 4 executed.—Feb. 21. Malcolm X, black nationalist, fatally shot in N. Y. City.

1966—Sept. 6. Prime Minister Hendrik F. Verwoerd of South Africa stabbed to death in parliament at Capetown.

1968—Apr. 4. Rev. Dr. Martin Luther King Jr. fatally shot in Memphis, Tenn. by James Earl Ray.—June 5. Sen. Robert F. Kennedy (D-N. Y.) fatally shot in Los Angeles; Sirhan Sirhan, resident alien, convicted of murder.

1971—Nov. 28. Jordan Prime Minister Wasfi Tal, in Cairo, by Palestinian guerrillas.

1973—Mar. 2. U. S. Ambassador Cleo A. Noel Jr., U. S. Chargé d'Affaires George C. Moore and Belgian Chargé d'Affaires Guy Eid killed by Palestinian guerrillas in Khartoum, Sudan.

1974—Aug. 19. U. S. Ambassador to Cyprus, Rodger P. Davies, killed by sniper's bullet in Nicosia.

1975—Feb. 11. Pres. Richard Ratsimandrava, of Madagascar, shot in Tananarive.—Mar. 25. King Faisal of Saudi Arabia shot by nephew Prince Musad Abdel Aziz, in royal palace, Riyadh.— Aug. 15. Bangladesh Pres. Sheik Mujibur Rahman killed in coup.

1976—Feb. 13. Nigerian head of state, Gen. Murtala Ramat Mohammed, slain by self-styled "young revolutionaries".

1977—Mar. 16. Kamal Jumblat, Lebanese Druse chieftain, was shot near Beirut.— Mar. 18. Congo Pres. Marien Ngouabi shot in Brazzaville.

1978—July 9. Former Iraqi Premier Abdul Razak Al-Naif shot in London.

1979—Feb. 14. U.S. Ambassador Adolph Dubs shot and killed by Afghan Muslim extremists in Kabul.— Aug. 27. Lord Mountbatten, WW2 hero, and 2 others were killed when a bomb exploded on his fishing boat off the coast of Co. Sligo, Ire. The IRA claimed responsibility. — Oct. 26. S. Korean President Park Chung Hee and 6 bodyguards fatally shot by Kim Jae Kyu, head of Korean CIA, and 5 aides in Seoul.

1980—Apr. 12. Liberian President William R. Tolbert slain in military coup.—Sept. 17. Former Nicaraguan President Anastasio Somoza Debayle shot in Paraguay.

1981— Oct. 6. Egyptian President Anwar el-Sadat fatally shot by a band of commandos while reviewing a military parade in Cairo.

1982—Sept. 14. Lebanese President-elect Bashir Gemayel killed by bomb in east Beirut.

1983— Aug. 21. Philippine opposition political leader Benigno Aquino Jr. fatally shot by a gunman at Manila International Airport.

1984—Oct. 31. Indian Prime Minister Indira Gandhi shot and killed by 2 of her bodyguards, who were members of the minority Sikh sect, in New Delhi.

1986—Feb. 28. Swedish Premier Olaf Palme shot and killed by a gunman in Stockholm.

1988—June 1. Lebanese Premier Rashid Karami killed when a bomb exploded aboard a helicopter in which he was travelling. —Apr. 16. PLO military chief Khalil Wazir (Abu Jihad) was gunned down by Israeli commandos in Tunisia.

1989—Aug. 18. Colombian Liberal Party presidential candidate Luis Carlos Galan was killed by Medellín cartel drug traffickers at a campaign rally in Bogotá.—Nov. 22. Lebanese president Rene Moawad was killed when a bomb exploded next to his motorcade.

1990—Mar. 22. Colombian Patriotic Union presidential candidate Bernando Jamamillo Ossa was shot by a gunman at an airport in Bogotá.

1991—May 21. Rajiv Gandhi, former prime minister of India, was killed when a bomb exploded during an election rally in Madras.

1992—June 29. Mohammed Boudiaf, President of Algeria, was shot by a gunman in Annaba.

1993—May 1. Ranasinghe Premadasa, president of Sri Lanka, killed by a bomb in Colombo.—Apr. 10. Chris Hani, S. African communist leader, shot by gunman in Boksburg.

Assassination Attempts

1910—Aug. 6. N. Y. City Mayor William J. Gaynor shot and seriously wounded by discharged city employee.

1912—Oct. 14. Former U. S. President Theodore Roosevelt shot and seriously wounded by demented man in Milwaukee, Wis.

1950—Nov. 1. In an attempt to assassinate President Truman, 2 members of a Puerto Rican nationalist movement—Griselio Torresola and Oscar Collazo—tried to shoot their way into Blair House. Torresola was killed, and a guard, Pvt. Leslie Coffelt, was fatally shot. Collazo was convicted Mar. 7, 1951, for the murder of Coffelt.

1970—Nov. 27. Pope Paul VI unharmed by knife-wielding assailant who attempted to attack him in Manila airport.

1972—May 15. Alabama Gov. George Wallace shot in Laurel, Md. by Arthur Bremer; seriously crippled.

1972—Dec. 7. Mrs. Ferdinand E. Marcos, wife of the Philippine president, was stabbed and seriously injured in Pasay City, Philippines.

1975—Sept. 5. Pres. Gerald R. Ford was unharmed when a Secret Service agent grabbed a pistol aimed at him by Lynette (Squeaky) Fromme, a Charles Manson follower, in Sacramento.

1975—Sept. 22. Pres. Gerald R. Ford escaped unharmed when Sara Jane Moore, a political activist, fired a revolver at him.

1980—Apr. 14. Indian Prime Minister Indira Gandhi was unharmed when a man threw a knife at her in New Delhi.

1980—May 29. Civil rights leader Vernon E. Jordan Jr. shot and wounded in Ft. Wayne, Ind.

1981—Jan. 16. Irish political activist Bernadette Devlin McAliskey and her husband were shot and seriously wounded by 3 members of a Protestant paramilitary group in Co. Tyrone, Ire.

1981—Mar. 30. Pres. Ronald Reagan, Press Secy. James Brady, Secret Service agent Timothy J. McCarthy, and Washington, D.C. policeman Thomas Delahanty were shot and seriously wounded by John W. Hinckley Jr. in Washington, D.C.

1981—May 13. Pope John Paul II and 2 bystanders were shot and wounded by Mehmet Ali Agca, an escaped Turkish murderer, in St. Peter's Square, Rome.

1982—May 12. Pope John Paul II was unharmed when a man with a knife was overpowered by guards, in Fatima, Portugal.

1982—June 3. Israel's ambassador to Britain Shlomo Argov was shot and seriously wounded by Arab terrorists in London.

1986—Sept. 7. Chilean President Gen. Augusto Pinochet Ugarte escaped unharmed when his motorcade was attacked by rebels using rockets, bazookas, grenades, and rifles.

RELIGIOUS INFORMATION

The Major World Religions

Buddhism

Founded: About 525 BC, near Benares, India.
Founder: Gautama Siddhartha (ca. 563-480), the Buddha, who achieved enlightenment through intense meditation.
Sacred Texts: The *Tripitaka,* a collection of the Buddha's teachings, rules of monastic life, and philosophical commentaries on the teachings; also a vast body of Buddhist teachings and commentaries, many of which are called *sutras.*
Organization: The basic institution is the *sangha* or monastic order through which the traditions are passed to each generation. Monastic life tends to be democratic and anti-authoritarian. Large lay organizations have developed in some sects.
Practice: Varies widely according to the sect and ranges from austere meditation to magical chanting and elaborate temple rites. Many practices, such as exorcism of devils, reflect pre-Buddhist beliefs.
Divisions: A wide variety of sects grouped into 3 primary branches: Therevada (sole survivor of the ancient Hinayana schools) which emphasizes the importance of pure thought and deed; Mahayana, which includes Zen and Soka-gakkai, ranges from philosophical schools to belief in the saving grace of higher beings or ritual practices, and to practical meditative disciplines; and Tantrism, an unusual combination of belief in ritual magic and sophisticated philosophy.
Location: Throughout Asia, from Ceylon to Japan. Zen and Soka-gakkai have several thousand adherents in the U.S.
Beliefs: Life is misery and decay, and there is no ultimate reality in it or behind it. The cycle of endless birth and rebirth continues because of desire and attachment to the unreal "self". Right meditation and deeds will end the cycle and achieve Nirvana, the Void, nothingness.

Hinduism

Founded: About 1500 BC by Aryan invaders of India where their Vedic religion intermixed with the practices and beliefs of the natives.
Sacred texts: The *Veda,* including the *Upanishads,* a collection of rituals and mythological and philosophical commentaries; a vast number of epic stories about gods, heroes and saints, including the *Bhagavadgita,* a part of the *Mahabharata,* and the *Ramayana;* and a great variety of other literature.
Organization: None, strictly speaking. Generally, rituals should be performed or assisted by Brahmins, the priestly caste, but in practice simpler rituals can be performed by anyone. Brahmins are the final judges of ritual purity, the vital element in Hindu life. Temples and religious organizations are usually presided over by Brahmins.
Practice: A variety of private rituals, primarily passage rites (eg. initiation, marriage, death, etc.) and daily devotions, and a similar variety of public rites in temples. Of the latter, the *puja,* a ceremonial dinner for a god, is the most common.
Divisions: There is no concept of orthodoxy in Hinduism, which presents a bewildering variety of sects, most of them devoted to the worship of one of the many gods. The 3 major living traditions are those devoted to the gods Vishnu and Shiva and to the goddess Shakti; each of them divided into further sub-sects. Numerous folk beliefs and practices, often in amalgamation with the above groups, exist side-by-side with sophisticated philosophical schools and exotic cults.
Location: Mainly India, Nepal, Malaysia, Guyana, Suriname, Sri Lanka.
Beliefs: There is only one divine principle; the many gods are only aspects of that unity. Life in all its forms is an aspect of the divine, but it appears as a separation from the divine, a meaningless cycle of birth and rebirth (*samsara*) determined by the purity or impurity of past deeds (*karma*). To improve one's *karma* or escape *samsara* by pure acts, thought, and/or devotion is the aim of every Hindu.

Islam

Founded: AD 622 in Medina, Arabian peninsula.
Founder: Mohammed (ca. 570-632), the Prophet.
Sacred texts: *Koran,* the words of God. *Hadith,* collections of the sayings of the Prophet.
Organization: Theoretically the state and religious community are one, administered by a caliph. In practice, Islam is a loose collection of congregations united by a very conservative tradition. Islam is basically egalitarian and non-authoritarian.
Practice: Every Moslem has 5 duties: to make the profession of faith ("There is no god but Allah . . ."), pray 5 times a day, give a regular portion of his goods to charity, fast during the day in the month of Ramadan, and make at least one pilgrimage to Mecca if possible.
Divisions: The 2 major sects of Islam are the Sunni (orthodox) and the Shi'ah. The Shi'ah believe in 12 *imams,* perfect teachers, who still guide the faithful from Paradise. Shi'ah practice tends toward the ecstatic, while the Sunni is staid and simple. The Shi'ah sect affirms man's free will; the Sunni is deterministic. The mystic tradition in Islam is Sufism. A Sufi adept believes he has acquired a special inner knowledge direct from Allah.
Location: From the west coast of Africa to the Philippines across a broad band that includes Tanzania, southern USSR and western China, India, Malaysia and Indonesia. Islam claims several million adherents in the U.S.
Beliefs: Strictly monotheistic. God is creator of the universe, omnipotent, just, and merciful. Man is God's highest creation, but limited and commits sins. He is misled by Satan, an evil spirit. God revealed the *Koran* to Mohammed to guide men to the truth. Those who repent and sincerely submit to God return to a state of sinlessness. In the end, the sinless go to Paradise, a place of physical and spiritual pleasure, and the wicked burn in Hell.

Judaism

Founded: About 1300 BCE.
Founder: Abraham is regarded as the founding patriarch, but the Torah of Moses is the basic source of the teachings.
Sacred Texts: The five books of Moses constitute the written Torah. Special sanctity is also assigned other writings of the Hebrew Bible—the teachings of oral Torah are recorded in the Talmud, the Midrash, and various commentaries.

(Continued p.560)

Major Christian Denominations:

Italics indicate that area which, generally speaking, most

Denomination	Origins	Organization	Authority	Special rites
Anglicans	Henry VIII separated English Catholic Church from Rome, 1534, for political reasons. The U.S. equivalent (Protestant Episcopal Church) was founded 1789.	*Bishops, in apostolic succession, are elected by diocesan representatives; part of Anglican Communion, symbolically headed by Archbishop of Canterbury.*	Scripture as interpreted by tradition, esp. *39 Articles* (1563); not dogmatic. Triannual convention of bishops, priests, and laymen.	Infant baptism, Holy Communion, others. Sacrament is symbolic, but has real spiritual effect.
Baptists	In radical Reformation objections to infant baptism, demands for church-state separation; John Smyth, English Separatist in 1609; Roger Williams, 1638, Providence, R.I.	Congregational, *i.e.*, each local church is autonomous.	Scripture; some Baptists, particularly in the South, interpret the Bible literally.	Baptism, after about age 12, by total immersion; Lord's Supper.
Church of Christ (Disciples)	Among evangelical Presbyterians in Ky. (1804) and Penn. (1809), in distress over Protestant factionalism and decline of fervor. Organized 1832.	Congregational.	*"Where the Scriptures speak, we speak; where the Scriptures are silent, we are silent."*	Adult baptism, Lord's Supper (weekly).
Lutherans	Martin Luther in Wittenberg, Germany, 1517, objected to Catholic doctrine of salvation by merit and sale of indulgences; break complete by 1519.	Varies from congregational to episcopal; in U.S. a combination of regional synods and congregational polities is most common.	*Scripture, and tradition as spelled out in Augsburg Confession (1530) and other creeds. These confessions of faith are binding although interpretations vary.*	Infant baptism, Lord's Supper. Christ's true body and blood present "in, with, and under the bread and wine."
Methodists	Rev. John Wesley began movement, 1738, within Church of England. First U.S. denomination Baltimore, 1784.	Conference and superintendent system. *In United Methodist Church, general superintendents are bishops—not a priestly order, only an office—who are elected for life.*	Scripture as interpreted by tradition, reason, and experience.	Baptism of infants or adults, Lord's Supper commanded. Other rites, inc. marriage, ordination, solemnize personal commitments.
Mormons	In visions of the Angel Moroni by Joseph Smith, 1827, in New York, in which he received a new revelation on golden tablets: *The Book of Mormon.*	Theocratic; all male adults are in priesthood which culminates in Council of 12 Apostles and 1st Presidency (1st President, 2 counselors).	*The Bible, Book of Mormon and other revelations to Smith, and certain pronouncements of the 1st Presidency.*	Baptism, at age 8, laying on of hands (which confers the gift of the Holy Spirit), Lord's Supper. Temple rites: baptism for the dead, marriage for eternity, others.
Orthodox	Original Christian proselytizing in 1st century; broke with Rome, 1054, after centuries of doctrinal disputes and diverging traditions.	Synods of bishops in autonomous, usually national, churches elect a patriarch, archbishop or metropolitan. These men, as a group, are the heads of the church.	Scripture, tradition, and the first 7 church councils up to Nicaea II in 787. Bishops in council have authority in doctrine and policy.	Seven sacraments: infant baptism and anointing, Eucharist (both bread and wine), ordination, penance, anointing of the sick, marriage.
Pentecostal	In Topeka, Kansas (1901), becoming popular in Wales (early 1900s), in reaction to loss of evangelical fervor among Methodists and other denominations.	Originally a movement, not a formal organization, Pentecostalism now has a variety of organized forms and continues also as a movement,	Scripture, individual charismatic leaders, the teachings of the Holy Spirit.	*Spirit baptism, esp. as shown in "speaking in tongues"; healing and sometimes exorcism; adult baptism, Lord's Supper.*
Presbyterians	In Calvinist Reformation in 1500s; differed with Lutherans over sacraments, church government. John Knox founded Scotch Presbyterian church about 1560.	*Highly structured representational system of ministers and laypersons (presbyters) in local, regional and national bodies (synods).*	Scripture.	Infant baptism, Lord's Supper; bread and wine symbolize Christ's spiritual presence.
Roman Catholics	Traditionally, by Jesus who named St. Peter the 1st Vicar; historically, in early Christian proselytizing and the conversion of imperial Rome in the 4th century.	Hierarchy with supreme power vested in Pope elected by cardinals. Councils of Bishops advise on matters of doctrine and policy.	*The Pope, when speaking for the whole church in matters of faith and morals, and tradition, which is partly recorded in scripture and expressed in church councils.*	Seven sacraments: baptism, contrition and penance, confirmation, Eucharist, marriage, ordination, and anointing of the sick (extreme unction).
United Church of Christ	*By ecumenical union, 1957, of Congregationalists and Evangelical & Reformed, representing both Calvinist and Lutheran traditions*	Congregational; a General Synod, representative of all congregations, sets general policy.	Scripture.	Infant baptism, Lord's Supper.

How Do They Differ?

distinguishes that denomination from any other.

Practice	Ethics	Doctrine	Other	Denomination
Formal, based on *Book of Common Prayer* (1549); services range from austerely simple to highly elaborate.	Tolerant; sometimes permissive; some social action programs.	*Apostles' Creed* is basic; otherwise, considerable variation ranges from rationalist and liberal to acceptance of most Roman Catholic dogma.	Strongly ecumenical, holding talks with all other branches of Christendom.	**Anglicans**
Worship style varies from staid to evangelistic. Extensive missionary activity.	Usually opposed to alcohol and tobacco; sometimes tends toward a perfectionist ethical standard.	*No creed; true church is of believers only, who are all equal.*	Since no authority can stand between the believer and God, the Baptists are strong supporters of church-state separation.	**Baptists**
Tries to avoid any rite or doctrine not explicitly part of the 1st century church. Some congregations may reject instrumental music.	Some tendency toward perfectionism; increasing interest in social action programs.	Simple New Testament faith; avoids any elaboration not firmly based on Scripture.	Highly tolerant in doctrinal and religious matters; strongly supportive of scholarly education.	**Church of Christ (Disciples)**
Relatively simple formal liturgy with emphasis on the sermon.	Generally, conservative in personal and social ethics; doctrine of "2 kingdoms" (worldly and holy) supports conservatism in secular affairs.	Salvation by faith alone through grace. Lutheranism has made major contributions to Protestant theology.	Though still somewhat divided along ethnic lines (German, Swede, etc.), main divisions are between fundamentalists and liberals.	**Lutherans**
Worship style varies widely by denomination, local church, geography.	Originally pietist and perfectionist; always strong social activist elements.	No distinctive theological development; 25 Articles abriged from Church of England's 39 not binding.	In 1968, United Methodist Church joined pioneer English- and German-speaking groups. UMs leaders in ecumenical movement.	**Methodists**
Staid service with hymns, sermon. Secret temple ceremonies may be more elaborate. Strong missionary activity.	Temperance; strict tithing. Combine a strong work ethic with communal self-reliance.	God is a material being; he created the universe out of pre-existing matter; all persons can be saved and many will become divine. Most other beliefs are traditionally Christian.	Mormons regard mainline churches as apostate, corrupt. Reorganized Church (founded 1860) rejects most Mormon doctrine and practice except Book of Mormon.	**Mormons**
Elaborate liturgy, usually in the vernacular, though extremely traditional. The liturgy is the essence of Orthodoxy. Veneration of icons.	Tolerant; very little social action; divorce, remarriage permitted in some cases. Priests need not be celibate; bishops are.	Emphasis on Christ's resurrection, rather than crucifixion; the Holy Spirit proceeds from God the Father only.	Orthodox Church in America, orginally under Patriarch of Moscow, was granted autonomy in 1970. Greek Orthodox do not recognize this autonomy.	**Orthodox**
Loosely structured service with rousing hymns and sermons, culminating in spirit baptism.	Usually, emphasis on perfectionism with varying degrees of tolerance.	Simple traditional beliefs, usually Protestant, with emphasis on the immediate presence of God in the Holy Spirit.	Once confined to lower-class "holy rollers", Pentecostalism now appears in mainline churches and has established middle-class congregations.	**Pentecostal**
A simple, sober service in which the sermon is central.	Traditionally, a tendency toward strictness with firm church- and self-discipline; otherwise tolerant.	Emphasizes the sovereignty and justice of God; no longer doctrinaire.	While traces of belief in predestination (that God has foreordained salvation for the "elect") remain, this idea is no longer a central element in Presbyterianism.	**Presbyterians**
Relatively elaborate ritual; wide variety of public and private rites, e.g. mass, rosary recitation, processions, novenas.	Theoretically very strict; tolerant in practice on most issues. Divorce and remarriage not accepted. Celibate clergy, except in Eastern rite.	Highly elaborated. Salvation by merit gained through faith. Unusual development of doctrines surrounding Mary. Dogmatic.	Roman Catholicism went through a period of relatively rapid change as a result of Vatican Council II.	**Roman Catholics**
Usually simple services with emphasis on the sermon.	Tolerant; some social action emphasis.	Standard Protestant; *Statement of Faith* (1959) is not binding.	The 2 main churches in the 1957 union represented earlier unions with small groups of almost every Protestant denomination.	**United Church of Christ**

Organization: Originally theocratic, Judaism has evolved a congregational polity. The basic institution is the local synagogue, operated by the congregation and led by a rabbi of their choice. Chief Rabbis in France and Great Britain have authority only over those who accept it; in Israel, the 2 Chief Rabbis have civil authority in family law.
Practice: Among traditional practitioners, almost all areas of life are governed by strict religious discipline. Sabbath and holidays are marked by special observances, and attendance at public worship is especially important then. The chief annual observances are Passover, celebrating the liberation of the Israelites from Egypt and marked by the ritual Seder meal in the home, and the 10 days from Rosh Hashana (New Year) to Yom Kippur (Day of Atonement), a period of fasting and penitence.
Divisions: Judaism is an unbroken spectrum from ultra conservative to ultra liberal, largely reflecting different points of view regarding the binding character of the prohibitions and duties—particularly the dietary and Sabbath observations—prescribed in the daily life of the Jew.
Location: Almost worldwide, with concentrations in Israel and the U.S.
Beliefs: Strictly monotheistic. God is the creator and absolute ruler of the universe. Men are free to choose to rebel against God's rule. God established a particular relationship with the Hebrew people: by obeying a divine law God gave them they would be a special witness to God's mercy and justice. The emphasis in Judaism is on ethical behavior (and, among the traditional, careful ritual obedience) as the true worship of God.

Religious Populations of the World

Source: *1993 Encyclopaedia Britannica Book of the Year*

	Africa	Asia	Europe	Latin America	Northern America	Oceania	Eurasia	World	%	Countries
Christians	327,204,000	285,365,000	413,756,000	435,811,000	239,004,000	22,628,000	109,254,000	**1,833,022,000**	33.4	270
Roman Catholics	122,907,000	123,597,000	262,638,000	405,623,000	97,022,000	8,208,000	5,590,000	**1,025,585,000**	18.7	259
Protestants	87,332,000	81,476,000	73,939,000	17,263,000	96,312,000	7,518,000	9,858,000	**373,698,000**	6.8	248
Orthodox	28,549,000	3,655,000	36,165,000	1,764,000	6,008,000	576,000	93,705,000	**170,422,000**	3.1	105
Anglicans	26,863,000	707,000	32,956,000	1,300,000	7,338,000	5,719,000	400	**74,883,400**	1.4	158
Other Christians	61,553,000	75,930,000	8,058,000	9,861,000	32,324,000	607,000	100,600	**188,433,600**	3.4	118
Muslims	278,250,800	636,976,000	12,574,500	1,350,500	2,847,000*	100,500	39,229,400	**971,328,700**	17.7	184
Nonreligious	1,896,000	691,144,000	52,411,000	17,159,000	25,265,000	3,291,000	85,066,000	**876,232,000**	16.0	236
Hindus	1,475,000	728,118,000	704,000	884,000	1,269,000	360,000	2,000	**732,812,000**	13.4	94
Buddhists	21,000	313,114,000	272,000	541,000	558,000	26,000	407,000	**314,939,000**	5.7	92
Atheists	316,000	161,414,000	17,604,000	3,224,000	1,319,000	535,000	55,898,000	**240,310,000**	4.4	139
Chinese folk religionists	13,000	186,817,000	60,000	73,000	122,000	21,000	1,000	**187,107,000**	3.4	60
New Religionists	21,000	141,382,000	50,000	530,000	1,421,000	10,000	1,000	**143,415,000**	2.6	27
Tribal religionists	70,588,000	24,948,000	1,000	936,000	41,000	67,000	0	**96,581,000**	1.8	104
Sikhs	26,000	18,272,000	231,000	8,000	254,000	9,000	500	**18,800,500**	0.3	21
Jews	337,000	5,587,000	1,469,000	1,092,000	7,003,000	98,000	2,236,000	**17,822,000**	0.3	134
Shamanists	1,000	10,233,000	2,000	1,000	1,000	1,000	254,000	**10,493,000**	0.2	11
Confucians	1,000	5,994,000	2,000	2,000	26,000	1,000	2,000	**6,028,000**	0.1	6
Baha'is	1,496,000	2,680,000	91,000	801,000	365,000	77,000	7,000	**5,517,000**	0.1	220
Jains	53,000	3,717,000	15,000	4,000	4,000	1,000	0	**3,794,000**	0.1	11
Shintoists	200	3,220,000	500	500	1,000	500	100	**3,222,800**	0.1	4
Other religionists	433,000	12,292,000	1,469,000	3,570,000	485,000	4,000	333,000	**18,586,000**	0.3	182
Total population	**652,132,000**	**3,231,273,000**	**500,712,000**	**465,987,000**	**279,985,000**	**27,230,000**	**292,691,000**	**5,480,010,000**	**100.0**	**270**

NOTES:
*This figure is disputed by the U.S. Muslim community, who claim 6 million adherents in the U.S. alone.
Continents: These follow current UN demographic practice. UN practice began in 1949 by dividing the world into 5 continents; then into 18 regions (1954); then into 8 major continental areas (called macro regions in 1987) and 24 regions (1983); and 7 major areas and 22 regions (1988). (See United Nations, *World Population Prospects 1990*, with populations of all continents, regions and countries covering the period 1950–2025.) The table above therefore now combines its former columns "East Asia" and "South Asia" into one single continent area. "Asia" (which excludes Eurasia [or European Asia]) is our provisional new term for the former USSR.
Countries: The last column enumerates sovereign and non-sovereign countries in which each religion or religious grouping has a significant following.
Rows: The list of religions is arranged by descending order of magnitude of global adherents in 1992 (last two columns but one); similarly for categories within "Christians".
Christians: Followers of Jesus Christ affiliated with churches (church members, including children: 1,692,466,000) plus persons professing in censuses or polls, though not so affiliated.
Other Christians: Catholics (non-Roman), marginal Protestants, crypto-Christians, and adherents of African, Asian, black and Latin-American indigenous churches.
Muslims: 83% Sunnis, 16% Shi'ites, 1% other schools. The definition excludes former ethnic Muslims who have now abandoned Islam, also followers of syncretistic religions combining Islam with other belief systems. In the U.S. a recent detailed survey showed that most Asian immigrants previously thought to be Muslims are now in fact Christians.
Nonreligious: Persons professing no religion, non-believers, agnostics, freethinkers, dereligionized secularists indifferent to all religion.
Hundus: 70% Vaishnavites, 25% Shaivites, 2% neo-Hindus and reform Hindus.
Buddhists: 56% Mahayana, 38% Theravada, 6% Tantrayana.
Atheists: Persons professing atheism, scepticism, disbelief, or irreligion, including anti-religious (opposed to all religion).
Chinese folk religionists: Followers of traditional Chinese religion (local deities, ancestor veneration, Confucian ethics, Taoism, universism, divination, some Buddhist elements).
New Religionists: Followers of Asian 20th-century New Religions. New Religious movements, radical new crisis religions and non-Christian syncretistic mass religions, all founded since 1800 and mostly since 1945.
Jews: 84% Ashkenazis, 10% Orientals, 4% Sephardis. The definition includes non-practising Jews, underground Jews, and crypto-Jews in Muslim countries.
Confucians: Non-Chinese followers of Confucius and Confucianism, mostly Koreans in Korea.
Other religionists: Including 50 minor world religions and a large number of spiritist religions, New Age religions, quasi religions, pseudo-religions, parareligions, religious or mystic systems, religious and semireligious brotherhoods of numerous varieties.
Total population: UN medium variant figures for mid-1992, as given in *World Population Prospects 1990* (New York: UN, 1991).

Church Membership, Ministers and Buildings: Estimates

United Kingdom

Source: CSO

	Adult members (millions)		Ministers (thousands)		Buildings (thousands)	
	1975	1990	1975	1990	1975	1990
Trinitarian Churches						
Anglican	2.27	1.84	15.9	14.1	19.8	18.3
Presbyterian	1.65	1.29	3.8	3.1	6.4	5.6
Methodist	0.61	0.48	4.2	2.3	9.1	7.5
Baptist	0.27	0.24	2.4	2.9	3.6	3.4
Other Protestant Churches	0.53	0.70	7.1	9.0	8.0	11.3
Roman Catholic	2.53	1.95	8.0	7.6	4.1	4.6
Orthodox	0.20	0.27	0.1	0.2	0.1	0.2
Total	**8.06**	**6.77**	**41.6**	**39.2**	**51.2**	**50.9**
Non-Trinitarian Churches						
Mormons	0.10	0.15	5.3	9.8	0.2	0.4
Jehovah's Witnesses	0.08	0.12	7.1	12.7	0.6	1.3
Spiritualists	0.06	0.06	0.2	0.4	0.6	0.6
Other Non-Trinitarian	0.09	0.13	0.9	1.5	1.1	1.1
Total	**0.33**	**0.46**	**13.5**	**24.4**	**2.5**	**3.4**
Other religions						
Muslims	0.40	0.99	1.0	2.3	0.2	1.0
Sikhs	0.12	0.39	0.1	0.2	0.1	0.2
Hindus	0.10	0.14	0.1	0.2	0.1	0.1
Jews	0.11	0.11	0.4	0.4	0.3	0.3
Others	0.08	0.23	0.4	1.2	0.1	0.4
Total	**0.81**	**1.86**	**2.0**	**4.3**	**0.8**	**2.0**

Percentage of the Population Attending Church Services: 1979 and 1989

England

Source: CSO

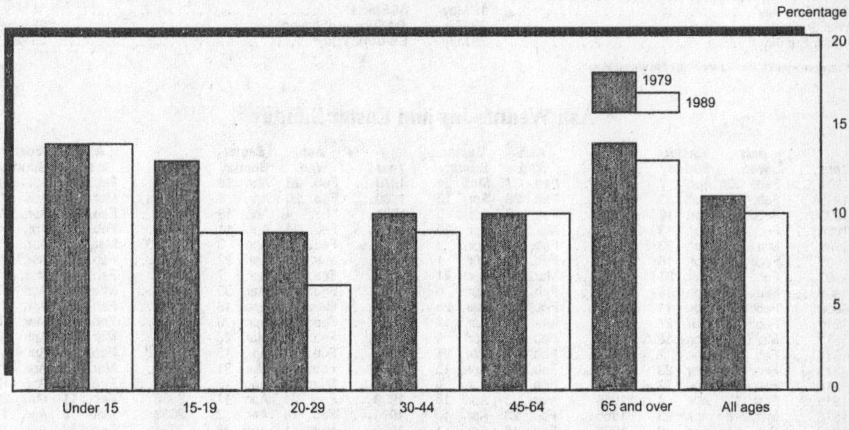

Anglican Calendar 1994

Where titles of days differ, the *Book of Common Prayer* (BCP) name appears first, followed by the *Alternative Service Book* (ASB) name in brackets. Note that Saints' Days are transferred when they fall on a Sunday or a greater holy day.

Jan.	1	Sa	Circumcision of Christ (Naming of Jesus)
	2	S	2nd after Christmas
	6	Th	Epiphany
	9	S	1st after Epiphany
	16	S	2nd after Epiphany
	23	S	3rd after Epiphany
	25	Tu	Conversion of St Paul
	30	S	Septuagesima (9th before Easter)
Feb.	2	W	Presentation of Christ
	6	S	Sexagesima (8th before Easter)
	13	S	Quinquagesima (7th before Easter)
	16	W	Ash Wednesday
	20	S	1st in Lent
	24	Th	St Matthias (BCP)
	27	S	2nd in Lent
Mar.	1	Tu	St David
	6	S	3rd in Lent
	13	S	4th in Lent; Mothering Sunday
	17	Th	St Patrick
	20	S	5th in Lent
	25	F	Annunciation to the Blessed Virgin Mary
	27	S	Palm Sunday
	31	Th	Maundy Thursday
Apr.	1	F	Good Friday
	2	Sa	Easter Eve
	3	S	Easter Day
	10	S	1st after Easter
	17	S	2nd after Easter

(Continued)

	23	Sa	St George
	24	S	3rd after Easter
	25	M	St Mark
May	1	S	4th after Easter
	2	M	St Philip and St James (transferred from 1st)
	8	S	5th after Easter; Rogation Sunday
	12	Th	Ascension Day
	14	Sa	St Matthias (ASB)
	15	S	Sunday after Ascension
	22	S	Whit Sunday (Pentecost)
	29	S	Trinity Sunday
Jun.	5	S	1st after Trinity (2nd after Pentecost)
	11	Sa	St Barnabas
	12	S	2nd after Trinity (3rd after Pentecost)
	19	S	3nd after Trinity (4th after Pentecost)
	24	F	Birth of St John the Baptist
	26	S	4th after Trinity (5th after Pentecost)
	29	W	St Peter
Jul.	3	S	St Thomas (ASB) 5th after Trinity (6th after Pentecost)
	10	S	6th after Trinity (7th after Pentecost)
	17	S	7th after Trinity (8th after Pentecost)
	22	F	St Mary Magdalen
	24	S	8th after Trinity (9th after Pentecost)
	25	M	St James
	31	S	9th after Trinity (10th after Pentecost)
Aug.	6	Sa	Transfiguration
	7	S	10th after Trinity (11th after Pentecost)
	14	S	11th after Trinity (12th after Pentecost)
	21	S	12th after Trinity (13th after Pentecost)
	28	S	13th after Trinity (14th after Pentecost)
Sep.	4	S	14th after Trinity (15th after Pentecost)
	8	Th	Blessed Virgin Mary (ASB)
	11	S	15th after Trinity (16th after Pentecost)
	18	S	16th after Trinity (17th after Pentecost)
	21	W	St Matthew
	25	S	17th after Trinity (18th after Pentecost)
	29	Th	St Michael and All Angels
Oct.	2	S	18th after Trinity (19th after Pentecost)
	9	S	19th after Trinity (20th after Pentecost)
	16	S	20th after Trinity (Last after Pentecost)
	18	Tu	St Luke
	23	S	21st after Trinity (9th before Christmas)
	28	F	St Simon and St Jude
	30	S	22nd after Trinity (8th before Christmas)
Nov.	1	Tu	All Saints' Day
	6	S	23rd after Trinity (7th before Christmas)
	13	S	24th after Trinity (6th before Christmas); Remembrance Sunday
	20	S	Sunday next before Advent (5th before Christmas)
	27	S	1st in Advent
	30	W	St Andrew
Dec.	4	S	2nd in Advent
	11	S	3rd in Advent
	18	S	4th in Advent
	21	W	St Thomas (BCP)
	24	Sa	Christmas Eve
	25	S	Christmas Day
	26	M	St Stephen
	27	Tu	St John the Evangelist
	28	W	Holy Innocents

Catholic Holy Days* & Movable Feasts, 1994

Epiphany*	6 Jan.
Ash Wednesday	16 Feb.
Easter Sunday	3 Apr.
Ascension Day*	12 May
Whit Sunday	22 May
Trinity Sunday	29 May
Corpus Christi*	2 Jun.
SS Peter & Paul*	29 Jun.
Assumption of the BVM*	15 Aug.
All Saints*	1 Nov.
1st Sunday of Advent	27 Nov.
Christmas Day*	25 Dec.

* Days on which Catholics are obliged to attend Mass.

Ash Wednesday and Easter Sunday

Year	Ash Wed.	Easter Sunday
1901	Feb. 20	Apr. 7
1902	Feb. 12	Mar. 30
1903	Feb. 25	Apr. 12
1904	Feb. 17	Apr. 3
1905	Mar. 8	Apr. 23
1906	Feb. 28	Apr. 15
1907	Feb. 13	Mar. 31
1908	Mar. 4	Apr. 19
1909	Feb. 24	Apr. 11
1910	Feb. 9	Mar. 27
1911	Mar. 1	Apr. 16
1912	Feb. 21	Apr. 7
1913	Feb. 5	Mar. 23
1914	Feb. 25	Apr. 12
1915	Feb. 17	Apr. 4
1916	Mar. 8	Apr. 23
1917	Feb. 21	Apr. 8
1918	Feb. 13	Mar. 31
1919	Mar. 5	Apr. 20
1920	Feb. 18	Apr. 4
1921	Feb. 9	Mar. 27
1922	Mar. 1	Apr. 16
1923	Feb. 14	Apr. 1
1924	Mar. 5	Apr. 20
1925	Feb. 25	Apr. 12
1926	Feb. 17	Apr. 4
1927	Mar. 2	Apr. 17
1928	Feb. 22	Apr. 8
1929	Feb. 13	Mar. 31
1930	Mar. 5	Apr. 20
1931	Feb. 18	Apr. 5
1932	Feb. 10	Mar. 27
1933	Mar. 1	Apr. 16
1934	Feb. 14	Apr. 1
1935	Mar. 6	Apr. 21
1936	Feb. 26	Apr. 12
1937	Feb. 10	Mar. 28
1938	Mar. 2	Apr. 17
1939	Feb. 22	Apr. 9
1940	Feb. 7	Mar. 24
1941	Feb. 26	Apr. 13
1942	Feb. 18	Apr. 5
1943	Mar. 10	Apr. 25
1944	Feb. 23	Apr. 9
1945	Feb. 14	Apr. 1
1946	Mar. 6	Apr. 21
1947	Feb. 19	Apr. 6
1948	Feb. 11	Mar. 28
1949	Mar. 2	Apr. 17
1950	Feb. 22	Apr. 9
1951	Feb. 7	Mar. 25
1952	Feb. 27	Apr. 13
1953	Feb. 18	Apr. 5
1954	Mar. 3	Apr. 18
1955	Feb. 23	Apr. 10
1956	Feb. 15	Apr. 1
1957	Mar. 6	Apr. 21
1958	Feb. 19	Apr. 6
1959	Feb. 11	Mar. 29
1960	Mar. 2	Apr. 17
1961	Feb. 15	Apr. 2
1962	Mar. 7	Apr. 22
1963	Feb. 27	Apr. 14
1964	Feb. 12	Mar. 29
1965	Mar. 3	Apr. 18
1966	Feb. 23	Apr. 10
1967	Feb. 8	Mar. 26
1968	Feb. 28	Apr. 14
1969	Feb. 19	Apr. 6
1970	Feb. 11	Mar. 29
1971	Feb. 24	Apr. 11
1972	Feb. 16	Apr. 2
1973	Mar. 7	Apr. 22
1974	Feb. 27	Apr. 14
1975	Feb. 12	Mar. 30
1976	Mar. 3	Apr. 18
1977	Feb. 23	Apr. 10
1978	Feb. 8	Mar. 26
1979	Feb. 28	Apr. 15
1980	Feb. 20	Apr. 6
1981	Mar. 4	Apr. 19
1982	Feb. 24	Apr. 11
1983	Feb. 16	Apr. 3
1984	Mar. 7	Apr. 22
1985	Feb. 20	Apr. 7
1986	Feb. 12	Mar. 30
1987	Mar. 4	Apr. 19
1988	Feb. 17	Apr. 3
1989	Feb. 8	Mar. 26
1990	Feb. 28	Apr. 15
1991	Feb. 13	Mar. 31
1992	Mar. 4	Apr. 19
1993	Feb. 24	Apr. 11
1994	Feb. 16	Apr. 3
1995	Mar. 1	Apr. 16
1996	Feb. 21	Apr. 7
1997	Feb. 12	Mar. 30
1998	Feb. 25	Apr. 12
1999	Feb. 17	Apr. 4
2000	Mar. 8	Apr. 23
2001	Feb. 28	Apr. 15
2002	Feb. 13	Mar. 31
2003	Mar. 5	Apr. 20
2004	Feb. 25	Apr. 11
2005	Feb. 9	Mar. 27
2006	Mar. 1	Apr. 16
2007	Feb. 21	Apr. 8
2008	Feb. 6	Mar. 23
2009	Feb. 25	Apr. 12
2010	Feb. 17	Apr. 4
2011	Mar. 9	Apr. 24
2012	Feb. 22	Apr. 8
2013	Feb. 13	Mar. 31
2014	Mar. 5	Apr. 20
2015	Feb. 18	Apr. 5
2016	Feb. 10	Mar. 27
2017	Mar. 1	Apr. 16
2018	Feb. 14	Apr. 1
2019	Mar. 6	Apr. 21
2020	Feb. 26	Apr. 12
2021	Feb. 17	Apr. 4
2022	Mar. 2	Apr. 17
2023	Feb. 22	Apr. 9
2024	Feb. 14	Mar. 31
2025	Mar. 5	Apr. 20
2026	Feb. 18	Apr. 5
2027	Feb. 10	Mar. 28
2028	Mar. 1	Apr. 16
2029	Feb. 14	Apr. 1
2030	Mar. 6	Apr. 21
2031	Feb. 26	Apr. 13
2032	Feb. 11	Mar. 28
2033	Mar. 2	Apr. 17
2034	Feb. 22	Apr. 9
2035	Feb. 7	Mar. 25
2036	Feb. 27	Apr. 13
2037	Feb. 18	Apr. 5
2038	Mar. 10	Apr. 25
2039	Feb. 23	Apr. 10
2040	Feb. 15	Apr. 1
2041	Mar. 6	Apr. 21
2042	Feb. 19	Apr. 6
2043	Feb. 11	Mar. 29
2044	Mar. 2	Apr. 17
2045	Feb. 22	Apr. 9
2046	Feb. 7	Mar. 25
2047	Feb. 27	Apr. 14
2048	Feb. 19	Apr. 5
2049	Mar. 3	Apr. 18
2050	Feb. 23	Apr. 10
2051	Feb. 15	Apr. 2
2052	Mar. 6	Apr. 21
2053	Feb. 19	Apr. 6
2054	Feb. 11	Mar. 29
2055	Mar. 3	Apr. 18
2056	Feb. 16	Apr. 2

(Continued)

Year	Ash Wed.	Easter Sunday	Year	Ash Wed.	Easter Sunday	Year	Ash Wed.	Easter Sunday	Year	Ash Wed.	Easter Sunday
2057...	Mar. 7	Apr. 22	2068...	Mar. 7	Apr. 22	2079...	Mar. 8	Apr. 23	2090...	Mar. 1	Apr. 16
2058...	Feb. 27	Apr. 14	2069...	Feb. 27	Apr. 14	2080...	Feb. 21	Apr. 7	2091...	Feb. 21	Apr. 8
2059...	Feb. 12	Mar. 30	2070...	Feb. 12	Mar. 30	2081...	Feb. 12	Mar. 30	2092...	Feb. 13	Mar. 30
2060...	Mar. 3	Apr. 18	2071...	Mar. 4	Apr. 19	2082...	Mar. 4	Apr. 19	2093...	Feb. 25	Apr. 12
2061...	Feb. 23	Apr. 10	2072...	Feb. 24	Apr. 10	2083...	Feb. 17	Apr. 4	2094...	Feb. 17	Apr. 4
2062...	Feb. 8	Mar. 26	2073...	Feb. 8	Mar. 26	2084...	Feb. 9	Mar. 26	2095...	Mar. 9	Apr. 24
2063...	Feb. 28	Apr. 15	2074...	Feb. 28	Apr. 15	2085...	Feb. 28	Apr. 15	2096...	Feb. 29	Apr. 15
2064...	Feb. 20	Apr. 6	2075...	Feb. 20	Apr. 7	2086...	Feb. 13	Mar. 31	2097...	Feb. 13	Mar. 31
2065...	Feb. 11	Mar. 29	2076...	Mar. 4	Apr. 19	2087...	Mar. 5	Apr. 20	2098...	Mar. 5	Apr. 20
2066...	Feb. 24	Apr. 11	2077...	Feb. 24	Apr. 11	2088...	Feb. 25	Apr. 11	2099...	Feb. 25	Apr. 12
2067...	Feb. 16	Apr. 3	2078...	Feb. 16	Apr. 3	2089...	Feb. 16	Apr. 3	2100...	Feb. 10	Mar. 28

Religious Beliefs

Source: SCPR's *British Social Attitudes* survey, 9th Report, ed. R. Jowell *et al.* (Dartmouth Publishing, 1992)

Percentages believing

	Britain	USA	Irish Republic	Northern Ireland
God	69	94	95	95
Life after death	55	78	80	78
Heaven	54	86	87	90
Religious miracles	45	73	73	77
Hell	28	71	53	74
The Devil	28	47	49	69
The Bible is the "actual" or "inspired word of God"	44	83	78	81

Religion and Public Life

Source: SCPR's *British Social Attitudes* survey, 9th Report, ed. R. Jowell *et al.* (Dartmouth Publishing, 1992)

Percentages agreeing

	Britain	USA	Irish Republic	Northern Ireland
Politicians who do not believe in God are unfit for public office.	31	59	35	52
Books and films that attack religions should be prohibited by law.	30	34	49	54
It would be better for the country if more people with strong religious beliefs held public office.	17	39	28	24
There should be daily prayers in all state schools.	70	73	83	87

Jewish Holy Days, Festivals and Fasts

	1993 (5753–54)	1994 (5754–55)	1995 (5755–56)	1996 (5756–57)	1997 (5757–58)
Tu B'Shvat	Feb. 6 Sat.	Jan. 27 Thu.	Jan. 16 Mon.	Feb. 5 Mon.	Jan. 23 Thu.
Ta'anis Esther (Fast of Esther)	Mar. 4 Thu.*	Feb. 24 Thu.	Mar. 15 Wed.	Mar. 4 Mon.	Mar. 20 Thu.*
Purim	Mar. 7 Sun.	Feb. 25 Fri.	Mar. 16 Thu.	Mar. 5 Tue.	Mar. 23 Sun.
Passover	Apr. 6 Tue.	Mar. 27 Sun.	Apr. 15 Sat.	Apr. 4 Thu.	Apr. 22 Tue.
	Apr. 13 Tue.	Apr. 3 Sun.	Apr. 22 Sat.	Apr. 11 Thu.	Apr. 29 Tue.
Lag B'Omer	May 9 Sun.	Apr. 29 Fri.	May 18 Thu.	May 7 Tue.	May 25 Sun.
Shavuot	May 26 Wed.	May 16 Mon.	June 4 Sun	May 24 Fri.	June 11 Sun.
	May 27 Thu.	May 17 Tue.	June 5 Mon.	May 25 Sat.	June 12 Mon.
Fast of the 17th Day of Tammuz	July 6 Tue.	June 26 Sun.	July 16 Sun.*	July 4 Thu.	July 22 Tue.
Fast of the 9th Day of Ac	July 27 Tue.	July 17 Sun.	Aug. 6 Sun.	July 25 Sat.	Aug. 12 Tue.
Rosh Hashanah	Sept. 16 Thu.	Sept. 6 Tue.	Sept. 25 Mon.	Sept. 14 Sat.	Oct. 2 Thu.
	Sept. 17 Fri.	Sept. 7 Wed.	Sept. 26 Tue.	Sept. 15 Sun.	Oct. 3 Fri.
Fast of Gedalya	Sept. 19 Sun.*	Sept. 8 Thu.	Sept. 27 Wed.	Sept. 16 Mon.	Oct. 5 Sun.*
Yom Kippur	Sept. 25 Sat.	Sept. 15 Thu.	Oct. 4 Wed.	Sept. 23 Mon.	Oct. 11 Sat.
Sukkot	Sept. 30 Thu.	Sept. 20 Tue.	Oct. 9 Mon.	Sept. 28 Sat.	Oct. 16 Thu.
	Oct. 6 Wed.	Sept. 26 Mon.	Oct. 15 Sun.	Oct. 4 Fri.	Oct. 22 Wed.
Shmini Atzeret	Oct. 7 Thu.	Sept. 27 Tue.	Oct. 16 Mon.	Oct. 5 Sat.	Oct. 23 Thu.
	Oct. 8 Fri.	Sept. 28 Wed.	Oct. 17 Tue.	Oct. 6 Sun.	Oct. 24 Fri.
Chanukah	Dec. 9 Thu.	Nov. 28 Mon.	Oct. 18 Mon.	Dec. 6 Fri.	Dec. 24 Wed.
	Dec. 16 Thu.	Dec. 5 Mon.	Oct. 25 Mon.	Dec. 13 Fri.	Dec. 31 Wed.
Fast of the 10th of Tevet	Dec. 24 Fri.	Dec. 13 Tue.	Jan. 2 Tue.	Dec. 20 Fri.	Jan. 8 Thu.

The months of the Jewish year are: (1) Tishri; (2) Cheshvan (also Marcheshvan); (3) Kislev; (4) Tebet (also Tebeth); (5) Shebat (also Shebhat); (6) Adar; 6a) Adar Sheni (II) added in leap years; (7) Nisan; (8) Iyar; (9) Sivan; (10) Tammuz; (11) Av (also Abh); (12) Elul. All Jewish holy days, etc., begin at sunset on the day previous. *Date changed to avoid Sabbath.

Greek Orthodox Movable Ecclesiastical Dates

	1993	1994	1995	1996	1997
Triódion begins	February 7	February 20	February 12	February 4	February 16
Sat. of Souls	February 20	March 5	February 25	February 17	March 1
Meat Fare	February 21	March 6	February 26	February 18	March 2
2nd Sat. of Souls	February 27	March 12	March 4	February 24	March 8
Lent begins	March 1	March 14	March 6	February 26	March 10
St. Theodore 3rd Sat. of Souls	March 6	March 19	March 11	March 2	March 15
Sunday of Orthodoxy	March 7	March 20	March 12	March 3	March 16
Sat. of Lazarus	April 10	April 23	April 15	April 6	April 19
Palm Sunday	April 11	April 24	April 16	April 7	April 20
Holy (Good) Friday	April 16	April 29	April 21	April 12	April 25
Western Easter	April 11	April 3	April 16	April 7	March 30
Orthodox Easter	April 18	May 1	April 23	April 14	April 27
Ascension	May 27	June 9	June 1	May 23	June 5
Sat. of Souls	June 5	June 18	June 10	June 1	June 14
Pentecost	June 6	June 19	June 11	June 2	June 15
All Saints	June 13	June 26	June 18	June 9	June 22

Islamic (Muslim) Calendar 1993–1997 (1414–1418)

The Islamic Calendar is a lunar reckoning from the year of the *hegira,* AD 622, when Muhammed moved from Mecca to Medina. It runs in cycles of 30 years, of which the 2nd, 5th, 7th, 10th, 13th, 16th, 18th, 21st, 24th, 26th and 29th are leap years; 1413 is the 3rd year, 1414 the 4th year of the cycle. Common years have 354 days, leap years 355, the extra day being added to the last month, Zu'lhijjah. Except for this case, the 12 months beginning with Muharram have alternately 30 and 29 days.

Year	Name of month	Month begins
1414	Jamada II	Nov. 16, 1993
1414	Rajab	Dec. 15, 1993
1414	Shaban	Jan. 14, 1994
1414	Ramadan	Feb. 12, 1994
1414	Shawwai	Mar. 14, 1994
1414	Zu'lkadah	Apr. 12, 1994
1414	Zu'lhijjah	May 12, 1994
1415	Muharram (New Year)	June 10, 1994
1415	Safar	July 10, 1994
1415	Rabia I	Aug. 8, 1994
1415	Rabia II	Sept. 7, 1994
1415	Jamada I	Oct. 6, 1994
1415	Jamada II	Nov. 5, 1994
1415	Rajab	Dec. 12, 1994
1415	Shaban	Jan. 3, 1995
1415	Ramadan	Feb. 2, 1995
1415	Shawwai	Mar. 3, 1995
1415	Zu'lkadah	Apr. 4, 1995
1415	Zu'lhijjah	May 1, 1995
1416	Muharram (New Year)	May 21, 1994
1416	Safar	June 30, 1994
1416	Rabia I	July 29, 1995
1416	Rabia II	Aug. 28, 1995
1416	Jamada I	Sept. 26, 1995
1416	Jamada II	Oct. 26, 1995
1416	Rajab	Nov. 24, 1995
1416	Shaban	Dec. 24, 1995
1416	Ramadan	Jan. 22, 1996
1416	Shawwai	Feb. 21, 1996
1416	Zu'lkadah	Mar. 21, 1996
1416	Zu'lhijjah	Apr. 20, 1996
1417	Muharram (New Year)	May 19, 1996
1417	Safar	June 18, 1996
1417	Rabia I	July 17, 1996
1417	Rabia II	Aug. 16, 1996
1417	Jamada I	Sept. 14, 1996
1417	Jamada II	Oct. 14, 1996
1417	Rajab	Nov. 12, 1996
1417	Shaban	Dec. 12, 1996
1417	Ramadan	Jan. 10, 1997
1417	Shawwai	Feb. 9, 1997
1417	Zu'lkadah	Mar. 10, 1997
1417	Zu'lhijjah	Apr. 9, 1997
1418	Muharram (New Year)	May 9, 1997
1418	Safar	June 8, 1997
1418	Rabia I	July 7, 1997
1418	Rabia II	Aug. 6, 1997
1418	Jamada I	Sept. 4, 1997
1418	Jamada II	Oct. 4, 1997
1418	Rajab	Nov. 2, 1997
1418	Shaban	Dec. 2, 1997
1418	Ramadan	Dec. 31, 1997
1418	Shawwai	Jan. 30, 1998
1418	Zu'lkadah	Feb. 27, 1998
1418	Zu'lhijjah	Mar. 30, 1998

Archbishops of Canterbury

Source: *Crockford's*

597 Augustine
604 Laurentius
619 Mellitus
624 Justus
627 Honorius
655 Deusdedit
668 Theodorus
693 Berhtwald
731 Tatwine
735 Nothelm
740 Cuthbert
761 Bregowine
765 Jaenberht
793 Æthelheard
805 Wulfred
832 Feologild
833 Ceolnoth
870 Æthelred
890 Plegmund
914 Æthelhelm
923 Wulfhelm
942 Oda
959 Ælfsige
959 Byrhthelm
960 Dunstan
c.988 Athelgar
990 Sigeric Serio
995 Ælfric
1005 Ælfheah
1013 Lyfing [Ælfstan]
1020 Æthelnoth
1038 Eadsige
1051 Robert of Jumièges
1052 Stigand
1070 Lanfranc
1093 Anselm
1114 Ralph d'Escures
1123 William de Corbeil
1139 Theobald of Bec
1162 Thomas Becket
1174 Richard [of Dover]
1184 Baldwin
1193 Hubert Walter
1207 Stephen Langton
1229 Richard le Grant
1234 Edmund Rich
1245 Boniface of Savoy
1273 Robert Kilwardby
1279 John Pecham
1294 Robert Winchelsey
1313 Walter Reynolds
1328 Simon Mepham
1333 John Stratford
1349 Thomas Bradwardine
1349 Simon Islip
1366 Simon Langham
1368 William Whittlesey
1375 Simon Sudbury
1381 William Courtenay
1396 Thomas Arundel[1]
1398 Roger Walden
1414 Henry Chichele
1443 John Stafford
1452 John Kempe
1454 Thomas Bourgchier
1486 John Morton
1501 Henry Deane
1503 William Warham
1533 Thomas Cranmer
1556 Reginald Pole
1559 Matthew Parker
1576 Edmund Grindal
1583 John Whitgift
1604 Richard Bancroft
1611 George Abbot
1633 William Laud
1660 William Juxon
1663 Gilbert Sheldon
1678 William Sancroft
1691 John Tillotson
1695 Thomas Tenison
1716 William Wake
1737 John Potter
1747 Thomas Herring
1757 Matthew Hutton
1758 Thomas Secker
1768 Frederick Cornwallis
1783 John Moore
1805 Charles Manners Sutton
1828 William Howley
1848 John Bird Sumner
1862 Charles Longley
1868 Archibald Campbell Tait
1883 Edward White Benson
1896 Frederick Temple
1903 Randall Davidson
1928 Cosmo Lang
1942 William Temple
1945 Geoffrey Fisher
1961 Michael Ramsey
1974 Donald Coggan
1980 Robert Runcie
1991 George Carey

(1) On 19 October 1399 Boniface IX annulled Arundel's translation to St Andrews and confirmed him in the See of Canterbury.

Anglican Hierarchy

Archbishops(*) and Bishops

Source: Church House, 6 Aug. 1993

England

Bath & Wells: James Thompson
Birmingham: Mark Santer
Blackburn: Alan Chesters
Bradford: David Smith
Bristol: Barry Rogerson
Canterbury: George Carey*
Carlisle: Ian Harland
Chelmsford: John Waine
Chester: Michael Baughen
Chichester: Eric Kemp
Coventry: Simon Barrington-Ward
Derby: Peter Dawes
Durham: David Jenkins
Ely: Stephen Sykes
Exeter: Hewlett Thompson
Gloucester: David Bentley
Guildford: Michael Adie
Hereford: John Oliver
Leicester: Thomas Butler
Lichfield: Keith Sutton
Lincoln: Robert Hardy
Liverpool: David Sheppard
London: David Hope
Manchester: Christopher Mayfield
Newcastle: Alec Graham
Norwich: Peter Nott
Oxford: Richard Harries
Peterborough: William Westwood
Portsmouth: Timothy Bavin
Ripon: David Young
Rochester: Michael Turnbull
Salisbury: David Stancliffe
Sheffield: David Lunn
Sodor & Man: Noel Jones
Southwark: Robert Williamson
Southwell: Patrick Harris
St Albans: John Taylor
St Edmundsbury & Ipswich: John Dennis
Truro: Michael Ball
Wakefield: Nigel McCulloch
Winchester: Colin James
Worcester: Philip Goodrich
York: John Habgood*

Wales

Bangor: Barry Morgan
Llandaff: Roy Davies
Monmouth: Rowan Williams
St Asaph: Alwyn Rice Jones*
St David's: Ivor Rees
Swansea & Brecon: Dewi Bridges

Scotland

Aberdeen & Orkney: Bruce Cameron
Argyll & the Isles: Douglas Cameron
Brechin: Robert Halliday
Edinburgh: Richard Holloway* (Primus)
Glasgow & Galloway: John Taylor
Moray, Ross & Caithness: George Sessford
St Andrews, Dunkeld & Dunblane: Michael Hare Duke

Ireland

Armagh: Robert Eames*
Cashel & Ossory: Noel Willoughby
Clogher: Brian Hannon
Connor: Samuel Poyntz
Cork, Cloyne & Ross: Robert Warke
Derry & Raphoe: James Mehaffy
Down & Dromore: Gordon McMullan
Dublin & Glendalough: Donald Caird*
Kilmore, Elphin & Ardagh: Michael Mayes
Limerick & Killaloe: Edward Darling
Meath & Kildare: Walton Empey
Tuam, Killala & Achonry: John Neill

Chronological List of Popes

Source: Annuario Pontificio. Table lists year of accession of each Pope.

The Apostle Peter, founder of the Church in Rome, arrived c. 42, was martyred c. 67, and raised to sainthood.

The Pope's temporal title is: Sovereign of the State of Vatican City. **The Pope's spiritual titles are:** Bishop of Rome, Vicar of Jesus Christ, Successor of St. Peter, Prince of the Apostles, Supreme Pontiff of the Universal Church, Patriarch of the West, Primate of Italy, Archbishop and Metropolitan of the Roman Province.

Anti-Popes, illegitimate claimants of or pretenders to the papal throne, are in *Italics*.

Year	Pope						
		235	St. Anterus	384	St. Siricius	535	St. Agapitus I
See		236	St. Fabian	399	St. Anastasius I	536	St. Silverius, Martyr
above.	St. Peter	251	St. Cornelius	401	St. Innocent I	537	Vigilius
67	St. Linus	*251*	*Novatian*	417	St. Zosimus	556	Pelagius I
76	St. Anacletus	253	St. Lucius I	418	St. Boniface I	561	John III
	or Cletus	254	St. Stephen I	*418*	*Eulalius*	575	Benedict I
88	St. Clement I	257	St. Sixtus II	422	St. Celestine I	579	Pelagius II
97	St. Evaristus	259	St. Dionysius	432	St. Sixtus III	590	St. Gregory I
105	St. Alexander I	269	St. Felix I	440	St. Leo I	604	Sabinian
115	St. Sixtus I	275	St. Eutychian	461	St. Hilary	607	Boniface III
125	St. Telesphorus	283	St. Gaius	468	St. Simplicius	608	St. Boniface IV
136	St. Hyginus	296	St. Marcellinus	483	St. Felix III (II)*	615	St. Deusdedit I or
140	St. Pius I	308	St. Marcellus I	492	St. Gelasius I		Adeodatus I
155	St. Anicetus	309	St. Eusebius	496	St. Anastasius II	619	Boniface V
166	St. Soter	311	St. Melchiades	498	St. Symmachus	625	Honorius I
175	St. Eleutherus	314	St. Sylvester I	*498*	*Lawrence (501-505)*	640	Severinus
189	St. Victor I	336	St. Marcus	514	St. Hormisdas	642	Theodore I
199	St. Zephyrinus	337	St. Julius I	523	St. John I, Martyr	649	St. Martin I, Martyr
217	St. Callistus I	352	Liberius	526	St. Felix IV (III)	654	St. Eugene I
217	*Hippolytus*	*355*	*Felix II**	530	Boniface II	657	St. Vitalian
222	St. Urban I	366	St. Damasus I	*530*	*Dioscorus*	672	Deusdedit II or
230	St. Pontian	*366*	*Ursinus*	533	John II		Adeodatus II

(Continued)

Year	Pope
676	Donus
678	St. Agatho
682	St. Leo II
684	St. Benedict II
685	John V
686	Conon
687	*Theodore*
687	*Paschal*
687	St. Sergius I
701	John VI
705	John VII
708	Sisinnius
708	Constantine
715	St. Gregory II
731	St. Gregory III
741	St. Zachary
752	Stephen II (III)†
757	St. Paul I
767	*Constantine*
768	*Philip*
768	Stephen III (IV)
772	Adrian I
795	St. Leo III
816	Stephen IV (V)
817	St. Paschal I
824	Eugene II
827	Valentine
827	Gregory IV
844	*John*
844	Sergius II
847	St. Leo IV
855	Benedict III
855	*Anastasius*
858	St. Nicholas I
867	Adrian II
872	John VIII
882	Marinus I
884	St. Adrian III
885	Stephen V (VI)
891	Formosus
896	Boniface VI
896	Stephen VI (VII)
897	Romanus
897	Theodore II
898	John IX
900	Benedict IV
903	Leo V
903	*Christopher*
904	Sergius III
911	Anastasius III
913	Landus
914	John X
928	Leo VI
928	Stephen VII (VIII)
931	John XI
936	Leo VII
939	Stephen VIII (IX)
942	Marinus II
946	Agapitus II
955	John XII
963	Leo VIII
964	Benedict V
965	John XIII
973	Benedict VI
974	*Boniface VII*
974	Benedict VII
983	John XIV
985	John XV
996	Gregory V
997	*John XVI*
999	Sylvester II
1003	John XVII
1004	John XVIII
1009	Sergius IV
1012	Benedict VIII
1012	*Gregory*
1024	John XIX
1032	Benedict IX
1045	Sylvester III
1045	Benedict IX
1045	Gregory VI
1046	Clement II
1047	Benedict IX
1048	Damasus II
1049	St. Leo IX
1055	Victor II
1057	Stephen IX (X)
1058	*Benedict X*
1059	Nicholas II
1061	Alexander II
1061	*Honorius II*
1073	St. Gregory VII
1080	*Clement III*
1086	Bl. Victor III
1088	Bl. Urban II
1099	Paschal II
1100	*Theodoric*
1102	*Albert*
1105	*Sylvester IV*
1118	Gelasius II
1118	*Gregory VIII*
1119	Callistus II
1124	Honorius II
1124	*Celestine II*
1130	Innocent II
1130	*Anacletus II*
1138	*Victor IV*
1143	Celestine II
1144	Lucius II
1145	Bl. Eugene III
1153	Anastasius IV
1154	Adrian IV**
1159	Alexander III
1159	*Victor IV*
1164	*Paschal III*
1168	*Callistus III*
1179	*Innocent III*
1181	Lucius III
1185	Urban III
1187	Clement III
1187	Gregory VIII
1191	Celestine III
1198	Innocent III
1216	Honorius III
1227	Gregory IX
1241	Celestine IV
1243	Innocent IV
1254	Alexander IV
1261	Urban IV
1265	Clement IV
1271	Bl. Gregory X
1276	Bl. Innocent V
1276	Adrian V
1276	John XXI
1277	Nicholas III
1281	Martin IV
1285	Honorius IV
1288	Nicholas IV
1294	St. Celestine V
1294	Boniface VIII
1303	Bl. Benedict XI
1305	Clement V
1316	John XXII
1328	*Nicholas V*
1334	Benedict XII
1342	Clement VI
1352	Innocent VI
1362	Bl. Urban V
1370	Gregory XI
1378	Urban VI
1378	*Clement VII*
1389	Boniface IX
1394	*Benedict XIII*
1404	Innocent VII
1406	Gregory XII
1409	*Alexander V*
1410	*John XXIII*
1417	Martin V
1431	Eugene IV
1439	*Felix V*
1447	Nicholas V
1455	Callistus III
1458	Pius II
1464	Paul II
1471	Sixtus IV
1484	Innocent VIII
1492	Alexander VI
1503	Pius III
1503	Julius II
1513	Leo X
1522	Adrian VI
1523	Clement VII
1534	Paul III
1550	Julius III
1555	Marcellus II
1555	Paul IV
1559	Pius IV
1566	St. Pius V
1572	Gregory XIII
1585	Sixtus V
1590	Urban VII
1590	Gregory XIV
1591	Innocent IX
1592	Clement VIII
1605	Leo XI
1605	Paul V
1621	Gregory XV
1623	Urban VIII
1644	Innocent X
1655	Alexander VII
1667	Clement IX
1670	Clement X
1676	Bl. Innocent XI
1689	Alexander VIII
1691	Innocent XII
1700	Clement XI
1721	Innocent XIII
1724	Benedict XIII
1730	Clement XII
1740	Benedict XIV
1758	Clement XIII
1769	Clement XIV
1775	Pius VI
1800	Pius VII
1823	Leo XII
1829	Pius VIII
1831	Gregory XVI
1846	Pius IX
1878	Leo XIII
1903	St. Pius X
1914	Benedict XV
1922	Pius XI
1939	Pius XII
1958	John XXIII
1963	Paul VI
1978	John Paul I
1978	John Paul II

*Felix II (355) was an anti-pope, so the numbers of subsequent Felixes are debatable. † The first Stephen elected in 752 died before being consecrated, so he is normally excluded from lists of popes. However, his existence makes the numbers of subsequent Stephens open to debate. ** The only English pope.

Roman Catholic Hierarchy

Source: U.S. Catholic Conference; Mid-year, 1993

Supreme Pontiff

At the head of the Roman Catholic Church is the Supreme Pontiff, Pope John Paul II, Karol Wojtyla, born at Wadowice (Krakow), Poland, May 18, 1920; ordained priest Nov. 1, 1946; appointed bishop July 4, 1958; promoted to archbishop of Krakow, Jan. 13, 1964; proclaimed cardinal June 26, 1967; elected pope as successor of Pope John Paul I Oct. 16, 1978; installed as pope Oct. 22, 1978.

College of Cardinals

Members of the Sacred College of Cardinals are chosen by the Pope to be his chief assistants and advisors in the administration of the church. Among their duties is the election of the Pope when the Holy See becomes vacant. The title of cardinal is a high honour, but does not represent any increase in the powers of holy orders.

In its present form, the College of Cardinals dates from the 12th century. The first cardinals, from about the 6th century, were deacons and priests of the leading churches of Rome, and bishops of neighbouring diocese. The title of cardinal was limited to members of the college in 1567. The number of cardinals was set at 70 in 1586 by Pope Sixtus V. From 1959 Pope John XXIII began to increase the number. However, the number of cardinals eligible to participate in papal elections was limited to 120. There were lay cardinals until 1918, when the Code of Canon Law specified that all cardinals must be priests. Pope John XXIII in 1962 established that all cardinals must be bishops. The first age limits were set in 1971 by Pope Paul VI, who decreed that at age 80 cardinals must retire from curial departments and offices and from participation in papal elections. They continue as members of the college, with all rights and privileges.

Archbishops (*) and Bishops

Source: *Catholic Yearbook*, Gabriel Communications Ltd.

England

Arundel & Brighton: Cormac Murphy-O'Connor
Birmingham: Maurice Couve de Murville*
Brentwood: Thomas McMahon
Clifton: Mervyn Alexander
East Anglia: Alan Clark
Lancaster: John Brewer
Leeds: David Konstant
Liverpool: Derek Worlock*
Middlesbrough: John Crowley
Northampton: Patrick McCartie
Nottingham: James McGuinness
Plymouth: Christopher Budd
Portsmouth: Crispian Hollis
Salford: Patrick Kelly
Shrewsbury: Joseph Gray
Southwark: Michael Bowen*
Westminster: Cardinal Basil Hume*

Wales

Cardiff: John Ward*
Menevia: Daniel Mullins
Wrexham: James Hannigan

Scotland

Aberdeen: Mario Conti
Argyll & the Isles: Roderick Wright
Dunkeld: Vincent Logan
Galloway: Maurice Taylor
Glasgow: Thomas Winning*
Motherwell: Joseph Devine
Paisley: John Mone
St Andrews & Edinburgh: Keith O'Brien*

Ireland

Achonry: Thomas Flynn
Ardagh & Clonmacnois: Colm O'Reilly
Armagh: Cahal Daly* (Primate of all Ireland)
Cashel & Emly: Dermot Clifford*
Clogher: Joseph Duffy
Clonfert: John Kirby
Cloyne: John Magee
Cork & Ross: Michael Murphy
Derry: Edward Daly
Down & Connor: Patrick Walsh
Dromore: Francis Brooks
Dublin: Desmond Connell*
Elphin: Dominic Conway
Ferns: Brendan Comiskey
Galway & Kilmacduagh: James McLoughlin
Kerry: Dermot O'Sullivan
Kildare & Leighlin: Laurence Ryan
Killala: Thomas Finnegan
Killaloe: Michael Harty
Kilmore: Francis McKiernan
Limerick: Jeremiah Newman
Meath: Michael Smith
Ossory: Laurence Forristal
Raphoe: Seamus Hegarty
Tuam: Joseph Cassidy*
Waterford & Lismore: Michael Russell

How to Address the Clergy

Source: *Crockford's* and *The Catholic Yearbook*

ANGLICAN	Envelope/formal listing	In writing (Dear . . .) and/or in speech	Referring to clergy
Archbishops	The Most Reverend (and Right Honourable*) the Lord Archbishop of X	Archbishop; more formally Your Grace	The Archbishop of X; the Archbishop; Archbishop Smith
Scottish Episcopal	The Most Reverend the Primus	Primus	The Primus
ANGLICAN	**Envelope/formal listing**	**In writing (Dear . . .) and/or in speech**	**Referring to clergy**
Assistant & Retired Bishops	The Right Reverend A.B. Smith	Bishop	Bishop
Bishops, Diocesan & Suffragan	The Right Reverend the Bishop of X; The Right Reverend (and Right Honourable*) the Lord Bishop of X *In the case of Privy Counsellors	Bishop; more formally My Lord	The Bishop of X; the Bishop; Bishop Smith
Deans & Provosts	The Very Reverend the Dean (Provost) of X	Dean (Provost); more formally Mr Dean (Mr Provost)	The Dean (Provost) of X; the Dean (Provost); Dean Smith (Provost Smith)
Archdeacons	The Venerable the Archdeacon of X, *occasionally* the Venerable A.B. Smith, Archdeacon of X	Archdeacon; more formally Mr Archdeacon	The Archdeacon of X; the Archdeacon; Archdeacon Smith
Canons (both residentiary & honorary)	The Reverend Canon A.B. Smith	Canon Smith	Canon Smith
Prebendaries	The Reverend A.B. Smith	Prebendary Smith	Prebendary Smith
Deacons (m/f) **& priests**	The reverend A. B. Smith; The Reverend Alan/Alice Smith	Mr/Mrs/Miss/Ms Smith (or Father Smith if a male priest prefers)	The Reverend A.B. Smith; Mr/Mrs/Miss/Ms Smith; Alan/Alice Smith (or Father Smith if a male priest prefers)
Chaplains to the Armed Forces	The Reverend A.B. Smith RN (or CF or RAF)	Padre; Padre Smith	the Padre; Padre Smith

(Continued)

ANGLICAN	Envelope/formal listing	In writing (Dear . . .) and/or in speech	Referring to clergy
Ordained members of religious orders	The Reverend Alan Smith XYZ; Brother Alan XYZ	Father; Father Smith; Brother Alan	The Reverend Alan; Father Alan Smith (XYZ); Father Smith; Brother Alan (XYZ)
ROMAN CATHOLIC			
The Pope	His Holiness the Pope, or His Holiness Pope John Paul II	Your Holiness or Most Holy Father	His Holiness
Cardinals	His Eminence the Cardinal Archbishop of X; His Eminence Cardinal John Brown, Archbishop of X	Your Eminence; Cardinal Brown	His Eminence
Archbishops	His Grace the Archbishop of X; the Most Reverend John Brown, Archbishop of X	Your Grace; Archbishop Brown	His Grace
Bishops	The Right Reverend John Brown, Bishop of X	Bishop Brown; *in speech* My Lord	His Lordship
Abbots	Right Reverend the Abbot of X, XYZ; The Right Reverend Dom John Brown, XYZ, Abbot of X	My Lord Abbot; Abbot; *in speech* Father Abbot	Abbot
Protonotaries Apostolic & Prelates of Honour	The Right Reverend Monsignor John Brown, *or* if he is also a Canon: The Right Reverend Monsignor Canon John Brown	Monsignor Brown; *in speech* Monsignor	Monsignor Brown
Chaplains of His Holiness	As for Prelates, but for Right Reverend read Very Reverend		
Provosts	As for Canons, but for Canon read Provost		
Canons	Very Reverend Canon John Brown	Canon Brown; *in speech* Canon	Canon Brown
Provincials	The Very Reverend Father Provincial XYZ	Father Provincial	Father Provincial
Priests	The Reverend John Brown	Father Brown; *in speech* Father	Father Brown
Deacons	The Reverend John Brown	Mr Brown	Mr Brown

Chief Rabbinate in Great Britain

Source: *The Jewish Handbook*

1704–1756	Aaron Hart
1756–1764	Hart Lyon
1765–1792	David Tevele Schiff
1802–1842	Solomon Herschell
1845–1890	Nathan Adler
1891–1911	Hermann Adler
1913–1946	Joseph Herman Hertz
1948–1965	Israel Brodie
1966–1991	Lord Jakobovits
1991–	Dr Jonathan Sacks

Office of the Chief Rabbi, Adler House, Tavistock Square, London WC1H 9HN; tel. 071-387 1066.

The Ten Commandments

According to Judaeo-Christian tradition, as related in the Bible, the Ten Commandments were revealed by God to Moses, and form the basic moral component of God's covenant with Israel. The Ten Commandments appear in two different places in the Old Testament—Exodus 20:1-17 and Deuteronomy 5:6-21—the phrasing similar but not identical. Most Protestant, Anglican and Orthodox Christians enumerate the commandments differently from Roman Catholics and Lutherans. Jewish tradition considers the introduction, "I am the Lord . . ." to be the first commandment and makes the prohibition against "other gods" and idolatry the second.

Abridged Text of the Ten Commandments in Exodus 20:1-17 is as follows:

I. I am the Lord your God, who brought you out of the land of Egypt, out of the house of bondage. You shall have no other gods before me.
II. You shall not make for yourself a graven image. You shall not bow down to them or serve them.
III. You shall not take the name of the Lord your God in vain.
IV. Remember the sabbath day, to keep it holy.
V. Honour your father and your mother.
VI. You shall not kill.
VII. You shall not commit adultery.
VIII. You shall not steal.
IX. You shall not bear false witness against your neighbour.
X. You shall not covet.

Books of the Bible

Old Testament – Standard Protestant English Versions

Genesis	II Chronicles	Daniel
Exodus	Ezra	Hosea
Leviticus	Nehemiah	Joel
Numbers	Esther	Amos
Deuteronomy	Job	Obadiah
Joshua	Psalms	Jonah
Judges	Proverbs	Micah
Ruth	Ecclesiastes	Nahum
I Samuel	Song of Solomon	Habakkuk
II Samuel	Isaiah	Zephaniah
I Kings	Jeremiah	Haggai
II Kings	Lamentations	Zechariah
I Chronicles	Ezekiel	Malachi

New Testament – Standard Protestant English Versions

Matthew	Ephesians	Hebrews
Mark	Phillippians	James
Luke	Colossians	I Peter
John	I Thessalonians	II Peter
Acts	II Thessalonians	I John
Romans	I Timothy	II John
I Corinthians	II Timothy	III John
II Corinthians	Titus	Jude
Galatians	Philemon	Revelation

Catholic Versions

All the Catholic books of the Bible (Old Testament and New Testament) have the same names as Protestant Versions. A Catholic Version (and Pre-Reformation Bibles) simply has the books **Tobit, Judith, Wisdom, Sirach (Ecclesiasticus), Baruch, I Maccabees,** and **II Maccabees** as part of the Old Testament. The Old Testament books that a Catholic Bible includes and a Protestant Bible does not are called "Deuterocanonical Books."

LANGUAGE

Sources for this section: *The World Almanac Guide to Good Word Usage; The Columbia Encyclopedia; Webster's Third New International Dictionary; The Oxford English Dictionary, 2nd ed.; The Associated Press Stylebook and Libel Manual; The Encyclopedia Americana.*

Neologisms

("New" words; from the Second Edition of the *Oxford English Dictionary*, Oxford Univ. Press, 1989.)

arcade game: a (mechanical or electronic) game of a type orig. popularized in amusement arcades.

assertiveness training: a technique by which diffident persons are trained to behave (more) assuredly.

astroturfed: carpeted with artificial turf.

birth parent: a natural (as opposed to an adoptive) parent.

build-down: a systematic reduction of nuclear armaments, by destroying two or more for each new one deployed.

bulimarexic: suffering from or characteristic of bulimia nervosa; one who suffers from bulimia nervosa.

camp-on: a facility of some telephone systems by which the caller of an engaged number can arrange for the system to ring it automatically as soon as it becomes free (in some cases ringing the caller also if he or she has replaced the receiver).

car-phone: a radio-telephone designed for use in a motor vehicle.

CD-ROM (compact disk – read only memory): a compact disk with data that can be viewed but not altered.

crack: a potent, crystalline form of cocaine, usually smoked for its stimulating effect.

debit card: a card issued by an organization, giving the holder access to an account, via an appropriate computer terminal, especially in order to authorize the transfer of funds to the account of another party when making a purchase, etc., without incurring revolving finance charges for credit.

designer drug: a drug synthesized to mimic a legally restricted or prohibited drug without itself being subject to restriction.

E-mail: colloquial shortening of electronic mail.

fast tracker: a high-flyer; an ambitious or thrusting person.

foodie: also foody. One who is particular about food, a gourmet.

gender gap: the difference in (esp. political) attitudes between men and women.

hate mail: letters (often anonymous) in which the senders express their hostility towards the recipient.

HIV (human immunodeficiency virus): either of 2 retroviruses (HIV-1, HIV-2) which cause AIDS.

microwavable: of food and food containers: suitable for cooking or heating in a microwave oven.

NIMBY, nimby: (not in my backyard): a slogan expressing objection to the siting of something considered unpleasant, such as nuclear waste, in one's own locality.

passive smoking: the inhalation of smoke involuntarily from the tobacco being smoked by others, considered as a health risk.

right to die: the alleged right of a brain-damaged or otherwise incurably ill person to the termination of life-sustaining treatment.

street credibility: popularity with, or accessibility to, ordinary people, esp. those involved in urban street culture; the appearance or fact of being "street-wise"; hence (apparent) familiarity with contemporary trends, fashions, social issues.

yuppiedom: the condition or fact of being a yuppie; the domain of yuppies; yuppies as a class.

Eponyms

(words named after people)

Bloody Mary – a vodka and tomato juice drink; after the nickname of Mary I, Queen of England, 1553-58, notorious for her persecution of Protestants.

Bloomers – full, loose trousers gathered at the knee; after Mrs. Amelia Bloomer, an American social reformer who advocated such clothing, 1851.

Bobbies – in Great Britain, police officers; after Sir Robert Peel, the statesman who organized the London police force, 1850.

Bowdlerize – to delete written matter considered indelicate; after Thomas Bowdler, British editor of an expurgated Shakespeare, 1825.

Boycott – to combine against in a policy of nonintercourse for economic or political reasons; after Charles C. Boycott, an English land agent in County Mayo, Ireland, ostracized in 1880 for refusing to reduce rents.

Braille – a system of writing for the blind; after Louis Braille, the French teacher of the blind who invented it, 1852.

Caesarean section – surgical removal of a child from the uterus through an abdominal incision; after Julius Caesar, born c. 102 B.C., in this manner, according to legend.

Casanova – a man who is a promiscuous and unscrupulous lover; after Giovanni Casanova, an Italian adventurer, 1725-98.

Chauvinist – excessively patriotic; after Nicolas Chauvin, a legendary French soldier devoted to Napoleon.

Derby – a stiff felt hat with a dome-shaped crown and rather narrow rolled brim; after Edward Stanley, 12th Earl of Derby, who in 1780 founded the Derby horse race at Epsom Downs, England, to which these hats are worn.

Gerrymander – to divide an election district in an unnatural way, to favor one political party; after Elbridge Gerry, and the salamander, for the salamander-like shape of a Mass. election district created, 1812, during Gerry's governorship.

Guillotine – a machine for beheading; after Joseph Guillotine, a French physician who proposed its use in 1789 as more humane than hanging.

Leotard – a close-fitting garment for the torso, worn by dancers, acrobats, and the like; after Julius Léotard, a 19th-century French aerial gymnast.

Silhouette – an outline image; from Etienne de Silhouette, the French finance minister, 1757, who advocated economies that included buying such paper portraits instead of painted miniatures.

Foreign Words and Phrases

(L = Latin; F = French; Y = Yiddish; R = Russian; G = Greek; I = Italian; S = Spanish)

ad hoc (L; *ad hok*): for the particular end or purpose at hand

ad infinitum (L; *ad in-fi-nite-um*): endless

ad nauseam (L; *ad nawz-ee-um*): to a sickening degree

apropos (L; *ap-ruh-poh*): to the point; appropriate

bête noire (F; *bet nwahr*): a thing or person viewed with particular dislike

bon appetit (F; *bon ap-uh-tee*): good appetite

bona fide (L; *boh nuh-fydee*): genuine

carte blanche (F; *kahrt blonnsh*): full discretionary power

cause célèbre (F; *kawz suh-leb-ruh*): a notorious incident

c'est la vie (F; *say lah vee*): that's life

chutzpah (Y; *khoot-spuh*): amazing nerve bordering on arrogance

coup de grâce (F; *kooh duh grahs*): the final blow

coup d'état (F; *kooh day tah*): forceful overthrow of a government

crème de la crème (F; *krem duh lah krem*): the best of the best

cum laude/magna cum laude/summa cum laude (L; *kuhm loud-ay; mag-nah . . .; soo-ma . . .*): with praise or honour; with great praise or honour; with the highest praise or honour

de facto (L; *day fak-toh*): in fact; generally agreed to without a formal decision

déjà vu (F; *day-zhah vooh*): the sensation that something happening has happened before

de jure (L; *day joor-ay*): determined by law, as opposed to de facto

de rigueur (F; *duh ree-gur*): necessary according to convention

détente (F; *day-tohnt*): an easing or relaxation of strained relations

éminence grise (F; *ay-mee-nohns greez*): one who wields power behind the scenes

enfant terrible (F; *ahnn-fahnn te-ree-bluh*): one whose unconventional behaviour causes embarrassment

en masse (F; *ahn mass*): in a large body

ergo (L; *air-goh*): therefore

esprit de corps (F; *es-pree duh kawr*): group spirit; feeling of camaraderie

eureka (G; *yoor-ee-kuh*): I have found it

ex post facto (L; *eks pohst fak-toh*): an explanation or regulation concocted after the event

fait accompli (F; *fayt uh-kom-plee*): an accomplished fact

faux pas (F; *fowe pah*): a social blunder

glasnost (R; *glahs-nost*): openness, candour

hoi polloi (G; *hoy puh-loy*): the masses

in loco parentis (L; *in loh-koh puh-ren-tis*): in place of a parent

in memoriam (L; *in muh-mawr-ee-uhm*): in memory of

in situ (L; *in sit-yooh*): in the original arrangement

in toto (L; *in toh-toh*): totally

je ne sais quoi (F; *zhuh nuh say kwah*): I don't know what; the little something that eludes description

joie de vivre (F; *zhwah duh veev-ruh*): joy of living, love of life

mea culpa (L; *may-uh cul-puh*): my fault

meshugga (Y; *meh-shoog-uh*): crazy

modus operandi (L; *moh-duhs op-uh-ran-dee*): method of operation

noblesse oblige (F; *noh-bles uh-bleezh*); the obligation of nobility to help the less fortunate

non compos mentis (L; *non kom-pos men-tis*): out of control of the mind; insane

nouveau riche (F; *nooh-voh reesh*); pejorative for recent rich who spend money conspicuously

perestroika (R; *pair-es-troy-kuh*): restructuring

persona non grata (L; *per-soh-nah non grah-tah*): unacceptable person

post-mortem (L; *pohst-more-tuhm*): after death; autopsy; analysis after event

prima donna (I; *pree-muh don-nuh*): temperamental person

pro tempore (L; *proh tem-puh-ray*): for the time being

que sera sera (S; *keh sair-ah sair-ah*): what will be, will be

quid pro quo (L; *kwid proh kwoh*): something given or received for something else

raison d'être (F; *ray-zohnn det-ruh*): reason for being

savoir-faire (F; *sav-wahr-fair*): dexterity in social and practical affairs

semper fidelis (L; *sem-puhr fee-day-lis*): always faithful

shlemiel (Y; *shleh-meel*): an unlucky, bungling person

status quo (L; *stay-tus qwoh*): existing order of things

tour de force (L; *toor duh fawrs*): feat accomplished through great skill

terra firma (L; *ter-uh fur-muh*): solid ground

verbatim (L; *ver-bay-tuhm*): word for word

vis-à-vis (F; *vee-zah-vee*): compared with

Foreign Idioms

English	Italian
Naked as a jaybird.	Naked as a worm. (Nudo come un verme.)
A bird in the hand is worth two in the bush.	Better a finch in hand than a thrush on a branch. (Meglio fringuello in man che tordo in frasca.)
To kill two birds with one stone.	To catch two pigeons with one bean. (Pigliare due piccioni con una fava.)
To eat humble pie.	To swallow the toad. (Inghiottire il rospo.)
To eat like a pig.	To eat like a buffalo. (Mangiare come un bufalo.)
Don't bite off more than you can chew.	Don't take a step longer than your leg. (Non fare il passo più lungo della gamba.)
Pride goes before a fall.	Pride rode out on horseback and came back on foot. (La superbia andò a cavallo e tornò a piedi.)
To go by fits and starts.	To go by hiccups. (Andare a singhiozzo.)
There is honour among thieves.	A dog doesn't eat a dog. (Cane non mangia cane.)
Once in a blue moon.	Every death of a pope. (Ad ogni morte di papa.)

English	French
Don't waste your breath!	Save your saliva! (Epargne ta salive!)
To turn up like a bad penny	To arrive like a hair in the soup. (Arriver comme un cheveu sur la soupe.)
To talk to yourself.	To talk to angels. (Parler aux anges.)
Let's get back to the subject.	Let's get back to our sheep. (Revenons à nos moutons.)
To pull a long face.	To make a funny nose. (Faire un drôle de nez.)
He laughs in your face.	He laughs in your nose. (Il vous rit au nez.)
By rule of thumb.	From the view of the nose. (A vue de nez.)
To be knock-kneed.	To have your legs in an X. (Avoir les jambes en X.)
Put that in your pipe and smoke it!	Put this in your pocket with your handkerchief on top! (Mets-le dans ta poche avec ton mouchoir dessus!)
It's all Greek to me!	It's Chinese! (C'est du chinois!)

English	Spanish
To hit the ceiling.	To scream at the sky. (Poner el grito en el cielo.)
Go fly a kite!	Go fry asparagus! (¡Véte a freír esparragos!)
There's always room for one more.	Where six can eat, seven can eat. (Donde comen seis, comen siete.)
To have the tables turned.	To go out for wool and come home shorn. (Ir por lana y volver esquilado.)
To cut off your nose to spite your face.	To throw stones at your own roof. (Tirar piedras contra su propio tejado.)
To slam the door in your face.	To slam the door on your nostrils. (Cerrarle la puerta en las narices.)
Give him an inch, he'll take a mile.	Give him a hand and he takes a foot. (Le da la mano y se toma el pie.)
To be alive and kicking.	To be alive and wagging your tail. (Estar vivo y coleando.)
You can't make a silk purse out of a sow's ear.	A monkey dressed in silk is still a monkey. (Aunque la mona se vista de seda, mona se queda.)
To swear a blue streak.	To toss out toads and snakes. (Echar sapos y culebras.)

Origins of Some Common English Idioms

dyed in the wool: to have traits deeply ingrained; from the fact that if wool is dyed before being made into yarn, or while still raw, the colour is more firmly fixed.

feet of clay: a blemish in the character of one previously held above reproach; from Daniel's interpretation of Nebuchanezzar's dream in the Old Testament. The king dreamed of an image made of precious metals, except for its feet, which were made of clay and iron. Daniel said that the feet symbolized human vulnerability to weakness and destruction.

hands down: effortlessly; incontestably; from the way a jockey, sure of victory, drops his hands, loosening his grip on the reins.

in seventh heaven: in a state of bliss; especially in Islamic beliefs, the heaven of heavens, the home of God and the highest angels.

kiss of death: something that seems good but is in reality the instrument of one's downfall; from the earlier phrase "Judas kiss", betraying Jesus to the authorities.

mad as a hatter: crazy; from the fact that mercury used in making felt hats often afflicted hatters with a violent twitching of the muscles as a result of its effects.

red herring: a herring cured by smoke; from the persistent odour, hence the use, trailed over the ground, from training a dog to follow this scent over any other.

red-letter day: a memorable day; from the custom of using red or purple colours to mark holy days on the calendar.

to bark up the wrong tree: to pursue a false lead; an Americanism that comes from hunting, some say specifically nocturnal racoon hunting, in which dogs often lost track of their quarry.

to buckle down: to adopt an attitude of effort and determination; probably from the act of buckling on armour to prepare for battle.

to go at it hammer and tongs: no holds barred; from the blacksmith who, with his tongs (long-handled pincers), took a piece of red-hot metal from the forge, laid it on the anvil and beat it into shape with his hammer.

to hold water: to pass a test for soundness; from testing a pitcher by filling it with water.

to knuckle under: to submit to another; from the time when one knelt before a conquerer, putting the "knuckles" of one's knees (the rounded part of the bone where the joint is bent) on the ground.

to make hay while the sun shines: to seize the opportunity; from hay's composition of mown grass dried for fodder, with the sun as the cheapest and most available drying agent.

to strike while the iron is hot: to seize the opportunity; from the blacksmith's need to swing the hammer while the metal on the anvil is glowing, or he must start up the forge again and reheat the iron.

Figures of Speech

anaphora – repetition of the first word or words from one sentence to another.

"Blessed are the poor in spirit: for theirs is the kingdom of heaven. Blessed are they that mourn: for they shall be comforted. Blessed are the meek for they shall inherit the earth." **Matthew 5:3**

"We shall fight in France, we shall fight on the seas and oceans, we shall fight with growing confidence and growing strength in the air, we shall defend our island, whatever the cost may be, we shall fight on the beaches, we shall fight on the landing grounds, we shall fight in the fields and in the streets, we shall fight in the hills; we shall never surrender." **Winston Churchill**

antihimeria – a type of enallage that substitutes one part of speech for another.

"Lord Angelo dukes it well." **Shakespeare,** *Measure for Measure*

"I am going in search of the great perhaps." **Rabelais**

antithesis – saying something two different ways, specifically by denying its contrary and asserting it.

"A man should be mourned at his birth, not at his death." **Montesquieu**

"The greatest crimes are caused by surfeit, not by want." **Aristotle**

catechresis – the substitution of one word with a seemingly inappropriate one.
"The Cold War" – **Bernard Baruch**
"And that White Sustenance – Despair" – **Emily Dickinson**

diacope – repetition of a word with another word interposing.
"Tomorrow, and tomorrow, and tomorrow . . ." **Shakespeare,** *Macbeth*
"A horse! a horse! my kingdom for a horse!" **Shakespeare,** *Richard III*

enallage – an effective grammatical error.
"We was robbed!" **Joe Jacobs**, professional prize fight manager
"Curiouser and curiouser" – **Lewis Carroll,** *Alice's Adventures in Wonderland*

epanepsis – ending a sentence or clause with the same word or phrase with which it began.
"Nothing can be created out of nothing." **Lucretius**
"Common sense is not so common." **Voltaire**

epanorthosis – a statement followed by a correction.
"Religion is a disease, but it is a noble disease." **Heraclitus**
"God make me pure, but not yet." **St Augustine**

epistrophe – repetition of the last word or words from one sentence to another.
"When I was a child, I spake as a child, I understood as a child, I thought as a child: but when I became a man, I put away childish things." **1 Cor. 13:11**
"Selfishness is not living as one wishes to live. It is asking others to live as one wishes to live." **Thomas Macaulay**

epizeuxis – the immediate repetition of a word or phrase.
"O dark, dark, dark, amid the blaze of noon." **John Milton**
"Then kill, kill, kill, kill, kill, kill." **Shakespeare,** *King Lear*

hyperbaton – any intentional deviation from normal word order.
"Whom God wishes to destroy, he first makes mad." **Euripides**
"Arms and the man I sing." **Virgil**

isolcolon – repetition of the same grammatical forms in different words.
"I speak Spanish to God, Italian to women, French to men, and German to my horse." **Charles V**
"The louder he talked of his honor, the faster we counted our spoons." **Ralph Waldo Emerson**

palindrome – repetition in which the sentence reads the same forwards or backwards.
"Able was I ere I saw Elba." **attributed to Napoleon**
"Madam, I'm Adam." **attributed to the first man addressing the first woman**

periphrasis – a roundabout means of expression.
"To meet the demands of nature." **Sallust**
"From pros and cons they fell to a warmer way of disputing." **Cervantes**

polyptoton – repetition of the same word or root with different grammatical forms or functions.
"Who shall stand guard to the guards themselves?" **Juvenal**
"Love is an irresistible desire to be irresistibly desired." **Robert Frost**

Commonly Confused English Words

adverse: unfavourable
averse: opposed

affect: to influence
effect: to cause

aggravate: to make worse
annoy: to irritate

allusion: an indirect reference
illusion: an unreal impression

anxious: apprehensive
eager: avid

capital: the seat of government
capitol: the building in which a legislative body meets

complement: to make complete; something that completes
compliment: to praise; praise

denote: to mean
connote: to suggest beyond the explicit meaning

elicit: to draw or bring out
illicit: illegal

emigrate: to leave for another place of residence
immigrate: to come to another place of residence

enquiry: question
inquiry: investigation

historic: an important occurrence
historical: any occurrence in the past

imminent: ready to take place
eminent: standing out

imply: to relay information but not explicitly
infer: to understand information that is not relayed explicitly

include: used when the items following are part of a whole
comprise: used when the items following are all of a whole

incredible: unbelievable
incredulous: sceptical

ingenious: clever
ingenuous: innocent

insidious: intended to trick
invidious: detrimental to reputation

less: a smaller amount (uncountables)
fewer: a smaller number (countables)

literally: actually
figuratively: metaphorically

oral: spoken, as opposed to written
verbal: referring to skill with language, as opposed to other skills

pestilence: a contagious or infectious epidemic disease
petulance: rudeness

practice: a repeated act
practise: to do regularly
(To remember difference between noun and verb think of *advice* and *advise.*)

prevaricate: to lie
procrastinate: to put off

prostrate: stretched out flat, face down
prostate: of or relating to the prostate gland

qualitative: relating to quality
quantitative: relating to number

Commonly Misspelled English Words

accidentally
accommodate
acquainted
all right
already
amateur
appearance
appropriate
bureau
character
commitment
conscious
conscientious
convenience
deceive
describe
description
desirable
despair
desperate
eliminate
embarrass
fascinating
foreign
forty
fulfil
government
grammar
humorous
incidentally
independent
indispensable
inoculate
iridescent
irresistible
laboratory
lightning
maintenance
marriage
miniature
mysterious
necessary
opportunity
permanent
phosphorus
rhythm
ridiculous
separate
similar
sincerely
sulphur
transferred

Some Common Abbreviations

Usage of full stops after abbreviations varies, but recently the tendency has been towards omission. Definitions preceding those in parentheses are in Latin or French. Abbreviations for awards and medals appear on p.543.

AA = Alcoholics Anonymous; Automobile Association
AC = alternating current
AD = anno Domini (in the year of the Lord)
AIDS = Acquired Immune Deficiency Syndrome
a.m. = ante meridiem (before noon)
anon. = anonymous
ASAP = as soon as possible
AWOL = Absent Without Leave
BA = Bachelor of Arts
BC = before Christ
BCE = before the Christian era
BMA = British Medical Association
BSc = Bachelor of Science
BST = British Summer Time
BTU = British thermal unit
bu = bushel
C = centigrade, Celsius
© = copyright
c. (or ca.) = circa (about)
CBI = Confederation of British Industry
CEO = chief executive officer
CI = Channel Islands
CIA = Central Intelligence Agency
CID = Criminal Investigation Department
cm = centimetre
COD = cash (or collect) on delivery
C of E = Church of England
CPR = cardio-pulmonary resuscitation
DC = direct current
DD = Doctor of Divinity
DDA = Dangerous Drugs Act
DES = Department of Education and Science
DNA = deoxyribonucleic acid
DOA = dead on arrival
DP = displaced person
ECU = European Currency Unit
ed = edited, edition, editor
e.g. = exempli gratia (for example)
EMS = European Monetary System
EMU = European Monetary Union
esp = especially
et al = et alii (and others)
etc. = et cetera (and so forth)
F = Fahrenheit
FBI = Federal Bureau of Investigation
fob = freight on board
FYI = for your information
GBH = grievous bodily harm
gdp = gross domestic product
gnp = gross national product
GP = general practitioner
HIV = Human Immunodeficiency Virus
Hon = the Honourable
HRH = His (Her) Royal Highness
i.e. = id est (that is)
IoW = Isle of Wight
IQ = Intelligence Quotient
IRA = Irish Republican Army
ISBN = International Standard Book Number
JP = Justice of the Peace
K = 1,000
kg = kilogram
km = kilometre
l = litre
lb = libra (pound)
lbw = leg before wicket
MA = Master of Arts
MEP = Member of the European Parliament
MD = Medicineae Doctor (Doctor of Medicine)
mfg = manufacturing
MIA = missing in action
ml = millilitre
mm = millimetre
mph = miles per hour
MSc = Master of Science
MS = manuscript
MSG = monosodium glutamate
Msgr = Monsignor
NCO = Non-commissioned Officer
No = numero (number)
NSPCC = National Society for the Prevention of Cruelty to Children
ODA = Overseas Development Administration
OECD = Organization for Economic Cooperation and Development
op = opus (work)
OPEC = Organization of Petroleum Exporting Countries
oz = ounce
p. = page (pp = pages)
p.m. = post meridiem (afternoon)
POW = prisoner of war
PS = post scriptum (postscript)
pt = pint(s), part, point
qt = quart(s)
R&D = research amd development
RDC = Rural District Council
REM = rapid eye movement
RIP = Requiescat in pace (May he rest in peace)
RN = Registered Nurse
ROTC = Reserve Officers' Training Corps
rpm = revolutions per minute
RSPCA = Royal Society for the Prevention of Cruelty to Animals
RSVP = Répondez s'il vous plaît (Please answer)
RUC = Royal Ulster Constabulary
SAE = stamped addressed envelope
SAYE = Save As You Earn
St = saint, street
TNT = trinitrotoluene
UFO = unidentified flying object
UHF = ultra high frequency
v. (or vs.) = versus (against)
VHF = very high frequency
w = watt

Latin and Greek Prefixes and Suffixes

Latin prefix/English meaning
a, abs/from
alti, alto/high
ambi/both
ante/before
aqui/water
arbori/tree
audio/hearing
avi/bird
brevi/short
centi/hundred
cerebro/brain
circum/around
ferri, ferro/iron
fissi/split
igni/fire
inter/between
juxta/close
lacto/milk
luni/moon
magni/great
mal/bad
multi/many
naso/nose
nati/birth
oculo/eye
oleo/oil
omni/all
ovi, ovo/egg
plano/flat
post/after
pre/before
pro/for
pulmo/lung
re/again
recti/straight
retro/backward
somni/sleep
stelli/star
sub/under
super/above
terri/land
trans/through
ultra/beyond
uni/one

Latin suffix/ English meaning
cide, cidal/kill
fid/split
fuge, fugal/flee from
grade/walking
pennale/wing
vorous/eating

Greek prefix/ English meaning
a/not
anti/against
astro/star
auto/self
biblio/book
bio/life
cardio/heart
chloro/green
chrono/time
cosmo/universe
ex/outside
geo/earth
geronto/old age
gluc/sweet
grapho/writing
helio/sun
hemi/half
hetero/different
homeo/similar
homo/same
hydro/water
hyper/above
kinesi/movement
litho/stone
logo/word
macro/large
mega/great
meso/middle
meta/beyond
micro/small
mono/one
necro/dead
neo/new
ornitho/bird
osteo/bone
pan/all
para/close
phono/sound
photo/light
poly/many
proto/first
pseudo/false
psycho/mind, spirit
pyro/fire
rhino/nose
theo/god
thermo/heat
toxico/poison
zoo/living

Greek suffix/ English meaning
algia/pain
archy/government
gamy/marriage
gnomy/knowledge
iasis/disease
itis/inflammation
lepsy/seizure
logy/science of
machy/battle
meter, metre/measure
oid/like
oma/tumour
phobe/fear
scope/observation
sect/cutting
soma/body
sophy/wisdom

A Collection of Animal Collectives

The English language boasts an abundance of names to describe groups of things, particularly pairs or aggregations of animals. Some of these words have fallen into comparative disuse, but many of them are still in service, helping to enrich the vocabularies of those who like their language to be precise, who tire of hearing a group referred to as "a bunch of," or who enjoy the sound of words that aren't overworked.

bale of turtles
band of gorillas
bed of clams, oysters
bevy of quail, swans
brace of ducks
brood of chicks
cast of hawks
cete of badgers
charm of goldfinches
cloud of gnats
clowder of cats
clutch of chicks
clutter of cats
colony of ants
congregation of plovers
covey of quail, partridge
crash of rhinoceri
cry of hounds
down of hares
drift of swine
drove of cattle, sheep
exaltation of larks
flight of birds
flock of sheep, geese
gaggle of geese
gam of whales
gang of elks
grist of bees
herd of elephants
horde of gnats
husk of hares
kindle or **kendle** of kittens
knot of toads
leap of leopards
leash of greyhounds, foxes
litter of pigs
mob of kangaroos
murder of crows
muster of peacocks
mute of hounds
nest of vipers
nest, nide of pheasants
pack of hounds, wolves
pair of horses
pod of whales, seals
pride of lions
school of fish
sedge or **siege** of cranes
shoal of fish, pilchards
skein of geese
skulk of foxes
sleuth of bears
sounder of boars, swine
span of mules
spring of teals
swarm of bees
team of ducks, horses
tribe or **trip** of goats
troop of kangaroos, monkeys
volery of birds
watch of nightingales
wing of plovers
yoke of oxen

Young Animal Names

The young of many animals, birds and fish have come to be called by special names, but many are often referred to simply as infants, babies, younglets, or younglings.

calf: cattle, elephant, antelope, rhino, hippo, whale, etc.
cheeper: grouse, partridge, quail.
chick, chicken: fowl.
cockerel: rooster.
codling, sprag: codfish.
colt: horse (male).
cub: lion, bear, shark, fox, etc.
cygnet: swan.
duckling: duck.
eaglet: eagle.
elver: eel.
eyas: hawk, others.
fawn: deer.
filly: horse (female).

fingerling: fish generally.
flapper: wild fowl.
fledgling: birds generally.
foal: horse, zebra, others.
fry: fish generally.
gosling: goose.
joey: kangaroo, others.
kid: goat.
kit: fox, beaver, rabbit, cat.
kitten, kitty, catling: cats, other fur-bearers.
lamb, lambkin, cosset, hog: sheep.
leveret: hare.
nestling: birds generally.
owlet: owl.
parr, smolt, grilse: salmon.
piglet, shoat, farrow, suckling: pig.
polliwog, tadpole: frog.
poult: turkey.
pullet: hen.
pup: dog, seal, sea lion, fox.
spike, blinker, tinker: mackerel.
squab: pigeon.
squeaker: pigeon, others.
whelp: dog, tiger, beasts of prey.
yearling: cattle, sheep, horse, etc.

The Principal Languages of the World

Source: Sidney S. Culbert, NI-25 — University of Washington, Seattle, WA 98195; data as of mid-1993

Languages With over 100 million Speakers

	Speakers (millions) Native	Total
Mandarin	827	930
Hindi	327	400
Spanish	326	371
English	319	463
Bengali	184	192
Arabic	182	214
Russian	172	291
Portuguese	167	179
Japanese	125	126
German	98	120
French	72	124
Malay-Indonesian	49	152

Languages With at Least 1 million Speakers (native plus non-native) as at mid-1993

Language	Millions
Achinese (N Sumatra, Indonesia)	3
Afrikaans (Sn. Africa)	10
Akan (or Twi-Fante) (Ghana)	7
Albanian (Albania; Yugoslavia)	5
Amharic (Ethiopia)	19
Arabic (see above)	214
Armenian (Armenia)	5
Assamese[1] (India; Bangladesh)	23
Aymara (Bolivia; Peru)	2
Azerbaijani (Azerbaijan)	15
Balinese (Bali, Indonesia)	3
Baluchi (Baluchistan, Pakistan)	5
Bashkir (Bashkortostan, in Russia)	1
Batak Toba (Indonesia)	4
Baule (Côte d' Ivoire)	2
Beja (Kassala, Sudan; Ethiopia)	1
Bemba (Zambia)	2
Bengali[1] (see above)	192
Berber[2]	
Beti (Cameroon; Gabon; Eq. Guinea)	2
Bhili (India)	3
Bikol (SE Luzon, Philippines)	4
Brahui (Pakistan; Afghan.; Iran)	2
Bugis (Indonesia; Malaysia)	4
Bulgarian (Bulgaria)	9
Burmese (Myanmar)	31
Buyi (S Guizhou, S China)	2
Byelorussian (Belarus)	10
Cantonese (China; Hong Kong)	65
Catalan (NE Spain; S France; Andorra)	9
Cebuano (Bohol Sea, Philippines)	13
Chagga (Kilimanjaro area, Tanzania)	1
Chiga (Ankole, Uganda)	1
Chinese[3]	
Chuvash (Chuvash, in Russia)	2
Czech (Czech Republic)	12
Danish (Denmark)	5
Dimli (EC Turkey)	1
Dogri (Jammu-Kashmir, C and E India)	1
Dong (SC China)	2
Dutch-Flemish (Netherlands; Belg.)	21
Dyerma (SW Niger)	2
Edo (Bendel, S Nigeria)	1
Efik (incl. Ibibio) (SE Nigeria)	6
English (see above)	463
Esperanto	2
Estonian (Estonia)	1
Ewe (SE Ghana; S Togo)	3

Language	Millions
Fang-Bulu (dialects of Beti, q.v.)	
Farsi (Iranian form of Persian, q.v.)	
Finnish (Finland; Sweden)	6
Fon (SC Benin; S Togo)	1
French (see above)	124
Fula (or Peulh) (Cameroon; Nigeria)	13
Fulakunda (Senegambia; Guinea Bissau)	2
Futa Jalon (NW Guinea; Sierra Leone)	3
Galician (Galicia, NW Spain)	4
Galla (see Oromo)	
Ganda (or Luganda) (S Uganda)	3
Georgian (Georgia)	4
German (see above)	120
Gilaki (Gilan, NW Iran)	2
Gogo (Rift Valley, Tanzania)	1
Gondi (C India)	2
Greek (Greece)	12
Guarani (Paraguay)	4
Gujarati[1] (WC India; S Pakistan)	40
Gusii (Kisii District, Nyanza, Kenya)	2
Hadiyya (Arusi, Ethiopia)	2
Hakka (or Kejia) (SE China)	34
Hani (S China)	1
Hausa (N Nigeria; Niger; Cameroon)	37
Haya (Kagera, NW Tanzania)	1
Hebrew (Israel)	4
Hindi[1,4] (see above)	400
Ho (Bihar and Orissa States, India)	1
Hungarian (or Magyar) (Hungary)	14
Iban (Indonesia; Malaysia)	1
Ibibio (see Efik)	
Igbo (or Ibo) (lower Niger, Nigeria)	17
Ijaw (Niger River delta, Nigeria)	2
Ilocano (NW Luzon, Philippines)	7
Indonesian (see Malay-Indonesian)	
Italian (Italy)	63
Japanese (see above)	126
Javanese (Java, Indonesia)	63
Kabyle (W Kabylia, N Algeria)	3
Kamba (E Kenya)	3
Kannada[1] (S India)	43
Kanuri (Nigeria; Niger; Chad; Cam.)	4
Karen (see Sgaw)	
Karo-Dairi (N Sumatra, Indonesia)	2
Kashmiri[1] (N India; NE Pakistan)	4
Kazakh (Kazakhstan)	8
Kenuzi-Dongola (S Egypt; Sudan)	1
Khalka (see Mongolian)	
Khmer (Kampuchea; Vietnam; Thailand)	8

Language	Millions
Khmer, Northern (Thailand)	1
Kikuyu (or Gekoyo) (WC Kenya)	5
Kituba (Bas-Zaire, Bandundu, Zaire)	4
Kongo (W Zaire; S Congo; NW Angola)	3
Konkani (Maharashtra and SW India)	4
Korean (Korea; China; Japan)	74
Kurdish (SW of Caspian Sea)	11
Kyrgyz (Kyrgyzstan)	2
Lao[5] (Laos)	4
Lampung (Sumatra, Indonesia)	2
Latvian (Latvia)	2
Lingala (including Bangala) (Zaire)	7
Lithuanian (Lithuania)	3
Luba-Lulua (or Chiluba) (Zaire)	7
Luba-Shaba (Shaba, Zaire)	1
Lubu (E Sumatra, Indonesia)	1
Luhya (W Kenya)	1
Luo (Kenya; Nyanza, Tanzania)	4
Luri (SW Iran; Iraq)	4
Lwena (E Angola; W Zambia)	2
Macedonian (Macedonia)	2
Madurese (Madura, Indonesia)	10
Magindanaon (S Philippines)	1
Makassar (S Sulawesi, Indonesia)	2
Makua (S Tanzania; N Mozambique)	4
Malagasy (Madagascar)	12
Malay-Indonesian (see above)	152
Malay, Pattani (SE Thailand)	1
Malayalam[1] (Kerala, India)	35
Malinke-Bambara-Dyula (W Africa)	9
Mandarin (see above)	930
Marathi[1] (Maharashtra, India)	68
Mazandarani (S Mazandaran, N Iran)	2
Mbundu (Benguela, Angola)	4
Mbundu (Luanda, Angola)	3
Meithei (NE India; Bangladesh)	1
Mende (Sierra Leone)	2
Meru (Eastern Province, C Tanzania)	1
Miao (or Hmong) (S China; SE Asia)	6
Mien (China; Viet.; Laos; Thailand)	2
Min (SE China; Taiwan; Malaysia)	50
Minangkabau (W Sumatra, Indon.)	6
Moldavian (included with Romanian)	
Mongolian (Mongolia; NE China)	6
Mordvin (Mordova, in Russia)	1
Moré (C Burkina Faso)	4
Nepali (Nepal; NE India; Bhutan)	16

Language	Millions
Ngulu (Mozambique; Malawi)	2
Nkole (Western Prov., Uganda)	1
Norwegian (Norway)	5
Nung (NE of Hanoi, Vietnam; China)	2
Nupe (Kwara, Niger States, Nigeria)	1
Nyamwezi-Sukuma (NW Tanzania)	5
Nyanja (Malawi; Zambia; Zimbabwe)	5
Oriya[1] (C and E India)	31
Oromo (W Ethiopia; N Kenya)	10
Pampangan (NW of Manila, Philip.)	2
Panay-Hiligaynon (Philippines)	7
Pangasinan (Lingayen G., Philip.)	2
Pashtu (Pakistan; Afghanistan; Iran)	21
Pedi (see Sotho, Northern)	
Persian (Iran; Afghanistan)	34
Polish (Poland)	44
Portuguese (see above)	179
Provençal (S France)	4
Punjabi[1] (Punjab, Pakistan; India)	92
Pushto (see Pashtu) (many spellings)	
Quechua A (Peru; Boliv.; Ec.; Arg.)	8
Rejang (SW Sumatra, Indonesia)	1
Riff (N Morocco; Algerian coast)	1
Romanian (Romania; Moldavia)	26
Romany (Vlach only) (Eur.; Amer.)	2
Ruanda (Rwanda; Uganda; Zaire)	8
Rundi (Burundi)	6
Russian (see above)	291
Samar-Leyte (C E Philippines)	3
Sango (C African Republic)	4
Santali (E India; Nepal)	5
Sasak (Lombok, Alas Strait, Indon.)	2
Serbo-Croatian (NW Balkan area)	20
Sgaw (SW Myanmar)	2
Shan (Shan, E Myanmar)	3
Shilha (W Algeria; S Morocco)	3
Shona (Zimbabwe)	8
Sidamo (Sidamo, S Ethiopia)	2
Sindhi[1] (SE Pakistan; W India)	18
Sinhalese (Sri Lanka)	13
Slovak (Slovakia)	5
Slovene (Slovenia)	2
Soga (Busoga, Uganda)	1
Somali (Som.; Eth.; Ken.; Djibouti)	6
Songye (Kasai Or., NW Shala, Zaire)	1
Soninke (Mali; countries to W S & E)	1
Sotho, Northern (Sn. Africa)	3
Sotho, Southern (Sn. Afr.; Lesotho)	4
Spanish (see above)	371
Sundanese (Sunda Strait, Indonesia)	26
Swahili (Kenya; Tanz.; Zaire; Uganda)	47
Swedish (Sweden; Finland)	9
Sylhetti (Bangladesh)	5
Tagalog (Philippines)	43
Tajiki (Tajikistan; Uzbek.; Kyrgyz.)	5
Tamazight (N Morocco; W Algeria)	3
Tamil[1] (Tamil Nadu, India; Sri Lanka)	68
Tatar (Tatarstan, in Russia)	8
Tausug (Philippines; Malaysia)	1
Telugu[1] (Andhra Pradesh, SE India)	72
Temne (C Sierra Leone)	2
Thai[5] (Thailand)	49
Tho (N Vietnam; S China)	2
Thonga (Mozambique; Sn. Africa)	3
Tibetan (SW China; N India; Nepal)	5
Tigrinya (S Eritrea, Tigre, Ethiopia)	4
Tiv (SE Nigeria; Cameroon)	2
Tong (see Dong)	
Tonga (SW Zambia; NW Zimbabwe)	2
Tswana (Botswana; Sn. Africa)	4
Tudza (N Vietnam; S China)	1
Tulu (S India)	2
Tumbuka (N Malawi; NE Zambia)	2
Turkish (Turkey)	58
Turkmen (Turkmenistan; Afghanistan)	3
Twi-Fante (see Akan)	
Uighur (Xinjiang, NW China)	8
Ukrainian (Ukraine; Russia; Poland)	46
Urdu[1,4] (Pakistan; India)	98
Uzbek (Uzbekistan)	14
Vietnamese (Vietnam)	63
Wolaytta (SW Ethiopia)	2
Wolof (Senegal)	7
Wu (Shanghai region, China)	65
Xhosa (SW Cape Prov., Sn. Africa)	8
Yao (see Mien)	
Yao (Malawi; Tanzania; Mozambique)	1
Yi (S and SW China)	7
Yiddish[6]	
Yoruba (SW Nigeria; Zou, Benin)	19
Zande (NE Zaire; SW Sudan)	1
Zhuang (S China)	15
Zulu (N Natal, Sn. Africa; Lesotho)	8

(1) One of the 15 languages of the Constitution of India. (2) See Kabyle, Riff, Shilha and Tamazight. (3) See Mandarin, Cantonese, Wu, Min and Hakka. The "common speech" (Putonghua) or the "national language" (Guoyu) is a standardized form of Mandarin as spoken in the area of Beijing. (4) Hindi and Urdu are essentially the same language, Hindustani. As the official language of Pakistan, it is written in a modified Arabic script and called Urdu. As the official language of India it is written in the Devanagari script and called Hindi. (5) The distinctions between some Thai dialects and Lao are political rather than linguistic. (6) Yiddish is usually considered a variant of German, though it has its own standard grammar and dictionaries, has a highly developed literature, and is written in Hebrew characters.

Naming Systems

Compiled by Ian Gordon, MA MLitt

There is an enormous variety of personal names around the world, but many of them can be identified as belonging to certain systematic patterns. It would be wrong for English speakers to assume that all other personal names follow the pattern we know. This section looks at five dominant systems around the world and explains how they work. While the information given is, inevitably, both general and selective, it will help readers to understand the logic and practice of the principal naming systems.

One generalization which can safely be made is that all the naming systems described here were developed in male-dominated cultures; names have apparently long been part of what people inherit through the male line. Indeed, a recurring term in this survey is "patronymic", meaning a name made from a father's name, such as Wilson, Jones or Macdonald.

Western European Names

Most readers of this book will belong to a society where the usual pattern is that each of us has an inherited family name preceded by at least one personal name given at birth. This pattern prevails throughout most of Europe and has, of course, been "exported" to North America, Australia, South Africa and elsewhere. In addition, we can often recognize where these names come from.

Given names mostly have either Biblical/Christian origins, e.g. David, Joseph, John, Peter and Paul, Mary, Elizabeth, Ann(e)/Anna/Hannah, or Germanic origins, e.g. Richard, William, Robert, Henry, Emma, Hilda. Furthermore, we can see these names or their equivalents in other countries of Europe. Maria, for example, is widespread, and it is fun to trace the various equivalents of John around Europe – Jean in France, Juan in Spain, Johann in Germany, Jan in Holland, Giovanni in Italy, and so on.

Family names mostly belong to one of four types – occupations, place names, patronymics (from fathers' names) and nicknames – and they have their equivalents in many languages.

English	French	German	Italian
Smith	Lefebvre/Forgeron	Schmidt	Fabbri/Ferrari
Miller	Meunier	Müller	Mugnaro/Molinari
Taylor	Tailleur/Couturier	Schneider	Sartori
Wood	Dubois	Wald	Bosco
Bridges	Dupont	Bruck	Ponti
Jones/Johnson	Jeanneau/Jeannot	Hansen/Johannsen	Giannini/Giovannetti
White	Blanc	Weiss	Bianco/Bianchi
Brown	Lebrun	Braun	Bruno
Read/Reed/Reid	Roux/Rousseau	Roth	Rossi

These European names and patterns can also be found in the USA and many countries to which they have been taken in recent centuries.

On the other hand, each country's, or rather culture's, set of names has its own distinctive features.

Danish and Norwegian family names are nearly all patronymics ending in *-sen*, e.g. Hansen, Nielsen, Jensen (Denmark's three commonest).

Swedish family names are mainly patronymics ending *-sson*, or compounds such as Lindberg (Linden-tree-mountain).

Dutch and Flemish family names often include particles: *de* (the) or *van (der)* (from the) in Dutch, e.g. de Kok (cook) and van der Berg (hill); *De* or *Van (den)* in Flemish, e.g. De Cock (the cook). Note that these particles are all lower case in Dutch, but have initial capitals in Flemish.

Greek family names often end *-poulos* (son), as in Papadopoulos (priest's son). Another common ending is *-ou*, as in Petrou (Peters).

Romanian family names often have a similar characteristic, such as the ending *-escu*, as in Popescu, which also means priest's son.

Three European countries stand apart in their naming systems.

Icelandic family names are true patronymics, so Jon Gudmundsson's sister in Gudrun Gudmundsdottir.

Finnish family names, uniquely, often have the adjectival ending *-nen*, and mostly relate to place names, as in Virtanen (brook) and Nieminen (cape). Given names are distinctive too, like Erkki and Pentti for boys, and Sari, Tuija and Usko for girls.

Hungarian names are unique in Europe in putting the family name first in both speech and writing. When outside Hungary, however, Hungarians change the order to the general European pattern. Common family names include Kovacs (smith), Nagy (large), Varga (shoemaker) and Szabo (tailor). Common given names include Ferenc, Laszlo, Istvan or Gyula for boys, and Ilona or Zsuzsa for girls.

Within the European pattern, two countries have developed systems of giving both parents' family names to children.

Spanish names append the mother's name to the father's. Thus, Fidel Castro (y) Ruiz is the son of Señor Castro, whose wife's maiden name was Ruiz. Although the complete name is usually reserved for formal usage, the tennis player Arantxa Sanchez Vicario, for example, has made a point of preserving her full name in daily use.

The *-ez* ending (equivalent to the "s" in Williams) is typical of many Spanish patronymics, e.g. Fernandez, Lopez, Martinez, Gomez and Rodriguez.

Portuguese names replace the Spanish *-ez* ending with *-es*, as in Fernandes and Rodrigues, and the mother's maiden name is included *before* the father's. The commonest Portuguese family names derive from places, such as Silva (wood) and Costa (shore).

Slav Names

Slav languages are spoken in Russia, Ukraine, Belarus, Poland, the Czech and Slovak republics, Bulgaria and the former Yugoslavia. A special feature of Slav family names is that they have separate masculine and feminine forms. The wife of the Czech athlete Emil Zatopek, for example, was Dana Zatopkova; in Poland Jerzy Cybulski's wife is Anna Cybulska; in Russia Vladimir Petrov's sister is Galina Petrova.

Another typical aspect of Slav names is a group of endings: the Polish *-(ow)ski*; the Ukrainian *-enko*; the Bulgarian patronymic endings *-ov* and *-ev*; the Russian *-ovich* and *-evich*; the Serbo-Croat *-ic* (pronounced "itch"), and the similar Polish ending *-wicz* (pronounced "vitch"). All these suffixes are added to male first names like Petr, Ivan, Mikhail and Boris.

Another practice in Russia is to give everyone three names, which follow a formal pattern:

given name, e.g. Stepan or Anna

patronymic (father's given name plus the suffix meaning son or daughter of), e.g. Arkadyevich or Arkadyevna

family name, e.g. Oblonsky or Oblonska.

The man's signature would read "S.A. Oblonsky"; friends and acquaintances would call him Stepan Arkadyevich; family would use a diminutive like Stiva or Stenya.

Islamic Names

Islamic names dominate North Africa, the Middle East, Pakistan and Bangladesh, and are found far beyond these regions. In the Islamic naming pattern almost all names have a religious significance, and many of them come from a limited repertoire. The apparent simplicity of this none the less has its complications. Often there are no fixed family names; titles combined with names may be used; and spellings vary, depending on the different dialects of Arabic and the different conventions of rendering them in the Roman alphabet.

It must be noted that some Islamic countries, notably Turkey and Iran, use non-Arabic family names that derive from their own languages.

Turkish family names (instituted in 1924) often begin *Öz-* (real), e.g Özturk, or end *-oglu* (son), e.g. Iskenderoglu (Sanderson).

Iranian family names are often characterized by the ending *-zadeh* (son of), as in Hosseinzadeh.

The main group of Islamic names is drawn from the Koran's list of the qualities of Allah, e.g. Ahmed (most praiseworthy), Ali (exalted), Aziz (mighty) and Rashid (chosen/chief). These names, with the suffix *-a*, may also apply to girls.

Another group of Islamic names honours the prophets and heroes of Islam, e.g. Hassan, Hussain and Abbas.

Complications set in when names are compounded. For example, Abdul is always prefixed to another name, as in Abdul Rahman (servant of the compassionate one); *al-* (the) is often prefixed to a geographical or occupational name, e.g Muammar (he who builds up) al-Gaddafy (of the Gaddafy tribe); *-(ud)din* (the faith) is a common suffix , e.g Salah al-Din (righteousness of faith).

The prefixed elements Abu and Umm celebrate the birth of a first son, as in Abu Hassan (father of Hassan) and Umm Hassan (mother of Hassan). The element *ibn* and the prefix *ben-* both mean "son of", while *binti* means "daughter of".

Titles or terms of honour include the name of the prophet Mohammed himself (not used as a separate personal name); Khan (prince); and Haji (one who has made the pilgrimage [*haj*] to Mecca).

Nowadays, many Muslims do add a final identifying name, often ending *-i*, which indicates family or geographical origins, e.g. Abbasi and Tehrani. A full Muslim name might therefore be lengthy and complicated, e.g. Sheikh Maktum ibn Rashid al-Maktum or Haidar Abu-Bakr al-Attas.

Chinese & Far Eastern Names

Chinese names offer a trap to the unwary because the family name always precedes the given name(s). For example, Deng Xiaoping's sons are Deng Zhifang and Deng Pufang, and his daughters are Deng Rong and Deng Nan. Nowadays, married Chinese women often retain their own family name.

It is said that Li Jun is the Eastern equivalent of John Smith, Li (or Lee) being the most widespread of the hundred or so standard family names, and Jun being a politically correct given name meaning "army". Other common family names include Chan (old), Chen (orange) and Wang (prince or yellow).

Given names usually consist of two parts (two characters in Chinese writing), e.g. Jian-guo (building up the country). Until recently these two-part names were hyphenated, so it was easy to recognize them for what they were. Since 1979, however, when new methods of transliterating Chinese were officially instituted, the two parts have been written together, e.g. Mao Zedong rather than Mao Tse-tung.

Korean and **Vietnamese** family names follow the Chinese pattern, but come from a more limited repertoire. The commonest Korean family name by far is Kim (gold), but other widespread names include Lee, Park, Ahn and Choe. In Vietnam the most common family name is Nguyen. In both cultures the two-part given name is hyphenated.

Japan is another country where the family name precedes the given name, although the Japanese reverse the order for the benefit of Westerners. Most of the family names were adopted about 100 years ago and are derived from the names of natural or geographical features. Common examples are the element *yama* (mountain), as in Nakayama and Yamamoto; *mura* or *muro* (village), as in Murakami and Nishimura; and the initial elements *fuji-* (wisteria), *ishi-* (stone) and *matsu-* (pine tree), as in Fujiyama, Ishimura and Matsushita. The commonest Japanese family names are reckoned to be Sato (village), Tanaka (rice field) and Suzuki (origin obscure).

India has a great complexity of religion and culture, so its names are extremely varied.

Hindu names follow a similar pattern to the Western one in that the family name is preceded by one or more given names, and a married woman adopts her husband's family name. Common family names include Patel (office-bearer), Desai (clerk), Gupta (protector), Kumar (prince), and Rao or Roy (king).

Hindu boys' names often begin with *raj-*, *nar-* or *sur-* and end in *esh* or *endra*, e.g. Naresh and Surendra. The names of deities, Ram, S(h)iva and Krishna, and combinations such as Sivaramakrishnan, also play a prominent part. The Punjabi honorific element *lal* may appear in various positions, as may *nath* (lord) and *das* (servant). Names given to girls include Indira, Leela, Meena and Rupa, long-established names originally implying splendour, play(fulness), fish and beauty respectively.

Sikh names are easily recognizable by the titles Singh (lion) for men and Kaur (princess) for women. These titles are borne by all Sikhs, but Singh is not exclusively a Sikh name; it may also be used by Hindus. The distinguishing name of a Sikh is the first, given name, which in the case of males often ends in *jit* or *inder*. The last, family name is often dropped. Thus Mohinder Singh Sandhu is known as Mohinder Singh, and his wife Gurmit may be called simply Gurmit Kaur.

African Names

North Africa has already been mentioned in the section on Islamic names. South of the Sahara there are many countries and cultures about which a few generalizations can be made. There is a mixture of African and European names because it is common to have a Christian given name (a legacy of missionary work) and an African name too, e.g. Nelson Mandela and Miriam Makeba.

The influence of the male line in most African cultures means that boys are given the names of one or more members of their father's family, but perhaps no fixed family name. Consequently, brothers may share no names, though both will have names found in the previous generations of their line. The same applies to girls, who have names from their mother's side.

It is difficult to generalize further, but there are recognizable elements in certain countries.

Kenyan peoples have different particles meaning "son of", such as *arap*, as in Daniel arap Moi, and *wa*, as in Ngugi wa Thiongo. Alternatively, the father's name may be prefixed with *kip-* for boys and *chep-* for girls, giving names as Kipkoech and Chepkoech.

Nigerian names include the initial elements *ade-*, *ogun-* and *olu/ola-*, meaning "crown", "fire-god" and "God" respectively. These elements are found in Yoruba-speakers' family names, such as Adeyemi, Ogundipe and Olatunji. Fixed family names are now in general use in Nigeria. Muslim names predominate in the north of the country.

Ghanaian names have a unique aspect in that each child is given a day name as well as a personal name and the family name.

Day	Boys' names	Girls' names
Sunday	Kwesi	Esi
Monday	Kojo	Adjua
Tuesday	Kwabena	Abena
Wednesday	Kweku	Akua
Thursday	Yao or Yaw	Yaa
Friday	Kofi	Efua
Saturday	Kwame	Ama

A full Ghanaian name might be John Kwame Bediako Dakwa, who would be known as Mr Bediako (after his father), Dakwa being his grandfather's name.

Angola and **Mozambique**, being former Portuguese territories, tend to use Portuguese family names as well as given names, e.g. Eduardo dos Santos and Argentina Paulino.

South Africa has a notable proportion of European names thanks to the Dutch (Afrikaans) and English settlers. From them come such names as Botha, Coetzee, Du Toit, Pretorius, van der Merwe, Smith and Jones – which bring us more or less full circle.

POSTAL INFORMATION

Source: Post Office

UK Domestic Services & Rates

(as at 1 Nov. 1993)

Letter Post

Weight not over	First Class	Second Class	Weight not over	First Class	Second Class
60g	25p	19p	500g	£1.20	93p
100g	36p	28p	600g	£1.50	£1.15
150g	45p	34p	700g	£1.80	£1.35
200g	54p	41p	750g	£1.95	£1.40
250g	64p	49p	800g	£2.05	Not
300g	74p	58p	900g	£2.25	admissible
350g	85p	66p	1000g	£2.40	over 750g
400g	96p	75p	Each extra 250g or		
450g	£1.08	84p	part thereof 60p		

The Royal Mail aims to deliver (Monday to Saturday) first class letters the day after collection and second class letters the third working day after collection, but actual service depends on time of posting and the destination of the letter.

Compensation in the ordinary post – The ordinary letter service is not designed as a compensation service, but compensation up to a maximum limit of £24 is payable if a letter is lost or damaged in the post due to the fault of the Post Office, its employees or agents. You are strongly urged, in your own interests, to obtain a Certificate of Posting (available free of charge) and keep it in safe custody so that it will be available as evidence of posting should you need to make a claim for compensation.

Compensation will not exceed the market value of things lost or the reduction in value of things damaged. It is not paid for ineligible articles (see the Post Office Guide) nor for damage to inadequately packed articles.

If you wish to send articles of higher value, eg money or jewellery, you are advised to use the Registered Post or Consequential Loss Insurance Services obtainable for an additional fee.

Surcharges – All unpaid or underpaid letters are treated as second class letters. Where the item is unpaid, or is underpaid at the applicable second class postage rate, the recipient will be charged with the amount of deficiency plus a fee of 14p per item.

Registered Post & Registered Plus

Registered Post is the secure way to send valuables through the post. Any first class letter may be registered and is guaranteed to be delivered the next day. Compensation for loss or damage is paid up to a maximum of £500. Registered post costs £3 per item (up to 2kg) plus first class postage. This cost includes 30p for a compensation premium, which must be added on the certificate of posting receipt.

If you are sending money or valuables above £500 and up to £2200, you should use Registered Plus – a guaranteed next-day delivery service with compensation for loss or damage up to £2200. Registered Plus costs £3.30 for items valued up to £1500, and £3.60 for items valued up to £2200 (in both cases up to 2kg). First class postage is additional.

If you are sending an item which could be worth more than its material value, you can take out Consequential Loss Insurance with cover of up to £10,000 for an extra fee.

Compensation up to	Fee*
£1,000	£0.45
£2,500	£0.60
£5,000	£0.85
£7,500	£1.10
£10,000	£1.35

*Plus the Registered or Registered Plus fee and first class postage.

Royal Mail Special Delivery

A priority service that offers you extra assurance of next-day delivery for your important letters, documents, contracts or other time-sensitive mail. Available at all post offices. Benefits include: special handling, proof of posting, signature on delivery, a special messenger delivery if items arrive too late for normal delivery, money-back guarantee. Fee £2.70 (in addition to first class postage)

Express Delivery

A similar service to Royal Mail Special Delivery, but for letters/packets being sent to the Isle of Man or the Channel Islands. Fee £1.95 (in addition to first class postage)

Recorded Delivery

Recorded Delivery is an optional extra facility available with the ordinary letter service; it is specially suitable for sending documents and items of little or no intrinsic value but NOT for sending money or valuables. It costs 55p in addition to first or second class postage, and provides for a Certificate of Post ing and a signature on delivery.

No compensation is payable for money, certain monetary articles or jewellery sent by Recorded Delivery.

Advice of Delivery

Proof of delivery can be returned to you, when using Registered or Recorded Delivery, by completing an Advice of Delivery form available at post offices. This service is available only at the time of posting. Fee: Registered or Recorded Delivery fee and postage plus 31p.

Late Posting Facility

Registered Post and Recorded Delivery letters are accepted on Travelling Post Offices.

The Registered Post or Recorded Delivery fee, normal postage and an additional charge of 12p must be paid by affixing stamps before the item is presented.

Faxmail (Facsimile/Courier Service)

With (or without) a fax machine you can reach 900 million people within hours. And you can do it even if they don't have a fax machine.

At a destination copies can be collected in person, courier delivered or prepared for normal delivery the next day.

UK Fax
The fax service is available to most towns and cities in the UK via a network of 110 strategically placed fax centres.

International Fax
The network is available to over 40 countries worldwide.

For the fastest, most cost-effective national and international fax/courier service, call the Electronic Mail Centre on 071-239 2495 or telephone FREEFONE INTELPOST.

Telemessage

Telemessage is British Telecom's electronic hard-copy messaging service, combining telecommunications with postal delivery. Telemessages can be sent at any hour from a telephone or telex machine in the UK.

To send a Telemessage by phone, dial 100 (190 in London, Birmingham or Glasgow) and ask for Telemessage.

By Telex, see your telex directory for the appropriate access codes.

To achieve next working day delivery, messages should be filed before 10pm Mondays to Saturdays (7pm Sundays and Bank Holidays).

For details of charges and further information, please call Telemessage Marketing FREE on 0800 282298.

Private Boxes (PO Boxes)

This facility enables you to call and collect your mail from your post office as many times a day as you like. Usually your mail will be handed to you when you call, but in some offices the mail will be placed in a locked box to which you hold a key, except for Registered, Recorded Delivery and certain other items which will still be handed to you when you call.

A standard fee of £48 per year for letters applies if you call during normal post office opening hours.

The following supplementary facilities are available to Post Office Box renters for an additional fee:

If you call at the post office after 6am but before the postman starts his first delivery, or before the post office opens to the public (whichever is the earlier), an additional fee of £48 per year for letters is charged.

If you need to call at night, when the post office is usually closed, we maybe able to make special arrangements, depending on local circumstances. An additional fee of £48 per year for letters is charged.

Only mail with the PO Box number included in the address will be sorted to the box.

If you would like the Royal Mail to deliver mail bearing your Private Box number to your address, there is an additional fee for each delivery of £48 per year for letters.

Alternatively, if you would like the Royal Mail to transfer mail bearing your normal address into your Private Box, there is an additional fee for each transfer from delivery of £48 per year for letters.

The charge for a replacement or duplicate key to a lockable Private Box is £1.05.

Special Search for Incoming Mail

At the request of the addressee, a special search will be made for a postal item at the office of delivery. The charge for this service is 22p (except for Poste Restante items – see below).

Poste Restante

If you are a traveller, you may have your correspondence addressed to any post office, except a town sub-office, for up to three months without charge. Items will normally be returned to the sender if not collected within two weeks (one month for items from abroad).

Special Service for the Visually Handicapped

This service offers special rates for the posting of periodicals, books and papers of any kind impressed in Braille and equipment designed specially for the use of the blind. The charges are:

By air to Europe:

Weight	Price
Up to 1 kg	Free postage
Over 1 kg up to 7 kg	First 1 kg: no charge
Each additional 50g (or part of)	1p

By air to countries Outside of Europe:

Weight	Price
Up to 500g	£0.10
Over 500g up to 1 kg	£0.20
Over 1 kg up to 7 kg	£0.20 per kg

By surface to all countries: Free postage up to 7 kg

UK Parcel Post

Same Day Datapost

Datapost provides you with a same-day service in and between most UK business centres. For a collection call free on **0800 88 44 22.**

Datapost

Guaranteed next-day delivery by 10am to all major UK business centres and by noon to almost everywhere else. For a Datapost collection, call free on **0800 88 44 22.**

Parcelforce

Guaranteed next-day delivery to 95% of all UK business addresses by close of business, with the additional option of delivery by 10am or noon if required.

Parcelforce 48

Guaranteed 2-day delivery to 95% of all UK business addresses with an inclusive weekly report providing a record of all despatches and deliveries.

Parcelforce Standard

A nationwide distribution service, with delivery normally in 2–3 working days. This includes Saturday delivery, at no extra cost.

Weight not over	Price	Weight not over	Price
1 kg	£2.60	8 kg	£5.50
2 kg	£3.25	10 kg	£6.50
4 kg	£4.25	30 kg	£8.10
6 kg	£4.80		

Size and Weight Limits – Individual parcels, except if addressed to Jersey, can weigh up to 30kg and measure up to 1.5m in length, and 3m in length and girth combined.

For parcels to Jersey the maximum weight is 10kg, while the maximum dimensions are 1.07m length and 2.0m length and girth combined.

Some Post Offices may not be able to accept parcels over 10kg.

Customs Declaration – A Parcelforce International Customs Pack (PFU5) must be affixed to all parcels for delivery to the Channel Islands.

Compensation – Parcelforce will, in certain circumstances, pay compensation for items that are lost or damaged in our system – providing you have a Certificate of Posting. The current level of compensation is up to £20 per parcel. You should obtain a Certificate of Posting which is available free of charge at the counter.

You can enjoy a higher level of compensation, if required, by completing a Compensation Fee Certificate of Posting, which you should present in the event of a claim. If your parcel is lost or damaged, compensation may be paid up to the specified limit according to the fee paid.

Compensation up to	Fee (in addition to postage)
£150	60p
£500	£1.10

Any compensation shall not exceed the market value of the items lost, or reduction in the value of items, damaged. Also, no compensation will be paid for prohibited items, including monetary items, or for items that have been inadequately packed. There is also no cover for consequential loss under this service.

The Compensation Fee facility can also be used in conjunction with Cash on Delivery.

Cash on Delivery

The Cash on Delivery facility provides you with a means of collecting a specific amount of money – up to a maximum invoice value of £500 – upon delivery of the parcel.

Fee (in addition to postage):

£1.70	Contract Customers
£2.00	Non-Contract Customers
£1.70	Enquiry Fee

When the parcel has been delivered and the specific amount collected, you should receive payment within two weeks of delivery.

However, if the amount to be collected exceeds £50, the parcel will be held and notice of the arrival sent to the addressee. The addressee will then be required to pay the Cash on Delivery amount at the delivery office, and, if they wish, collect the parcel at the same time.

Postage Forward Parcels

Available under licence, Postage Forward Parcels enables you to pay for parcels that your customers send you.

The customer is provided with an unstamped addressed label, special wrapper or container. The parcel is then sent, bearing this label, in the ordinary way but without payment being made at the counter. The licencee pays the charges on all parcels received in this way.

Fee: £40.00	Licence fee per address
17p	Fee per parcel delivered (in addition to postage)

This facility is not available for parcels sent to and from the Channel Islands or the Isle of Man.

Key to Postcode Map

Postcode	Area
AB	Aberdeen
AL	St. Albans
B	Birmingham
BA	Bath
BB	Blackburn
BD	Bradford
BH	Bournemouth
BL	Bolton
BN	Brighton
BR	Bromley
BS	Bristol
BT	Belfast
CA	Carlisle
CB	Cambridge
CF	Cardiff
CH	Chester
CM	Chelmsford
CO	Colchester
CR	Croydon
CT	Canterbury
CV	Coventry
CW	Crewe
DA	Dartford
DD	Dundee
DE	Derby
DG	Dumfries
DH	Durham
DL	Darlington
DN	Doncaster
DT	Dorchester
DY	Dudley
EH	Edinburgh
EN	Enfield
EX	Exeter
FK	Falkirk
FY	Blackpool
G	Glasgow
GL	Gloucester
GU	Guildford
HA	Harrow
HD	Huddersfield
HG	Harrogate
HP	Hemel Hempstead
HR	Hereford
HU	Hull
HX	Halifax
IG	Ilford
IP	Ipswich
IV	Inverness
JE	Jersey
KA	Kilmarnock
KT	Kingston-upon-Thames
KW	Kirkwall
KY	Kirkcaldy
L	Liverpool
LA	Lancaster
LD	Llandrindod Wells
LE	Leicester
LL	Llandudno
LN	Lincoln
LS	Leeds
LU	Luton
M	Manchester
ME	Medway
MK	Milton Keynes
ML	Motherwell
NE	Newcastle upon Tyne
NG	Nottingham
NN	Northampton
NP	Newport
NR	Norwich
OL	Oldham
OX	Oxford
PA	Paisley
PE	Peterborough
PH	Perth
PL	Plymouth
PO	Portsmouth
PR	Preston
RG	Reading
RH	Redhill
RM	Romford
S	Sheffield
SA	Swansea
SG	Stevenage
SK	Stockport
SL	Slough
SM	Sutton
SN	Swindon
SO	Southampton
SP	Salisbury
SR	Sunderland
SS	Southend-on-Sea
ST	Stoke-on-Trent
SY	Shrewsbury
TA	Taunton
TD	Galashiels
TF	Telford
TN	Tunbridge Wells
TQ	Torquay
TR	Truro
TS	Cleveland
TW	Twickenham
UB	Southall
WA	Warrington
WD	Watford
WF	Wakefield
WN	Wigan
WR	Worcester
WS	Walsall
WV	Wolverhampton
YO	York
ZE	Lerwick

Note: London area postcodes are not indicated. The Isle of Man has not been postcoded.

Postcode Areas of the UK

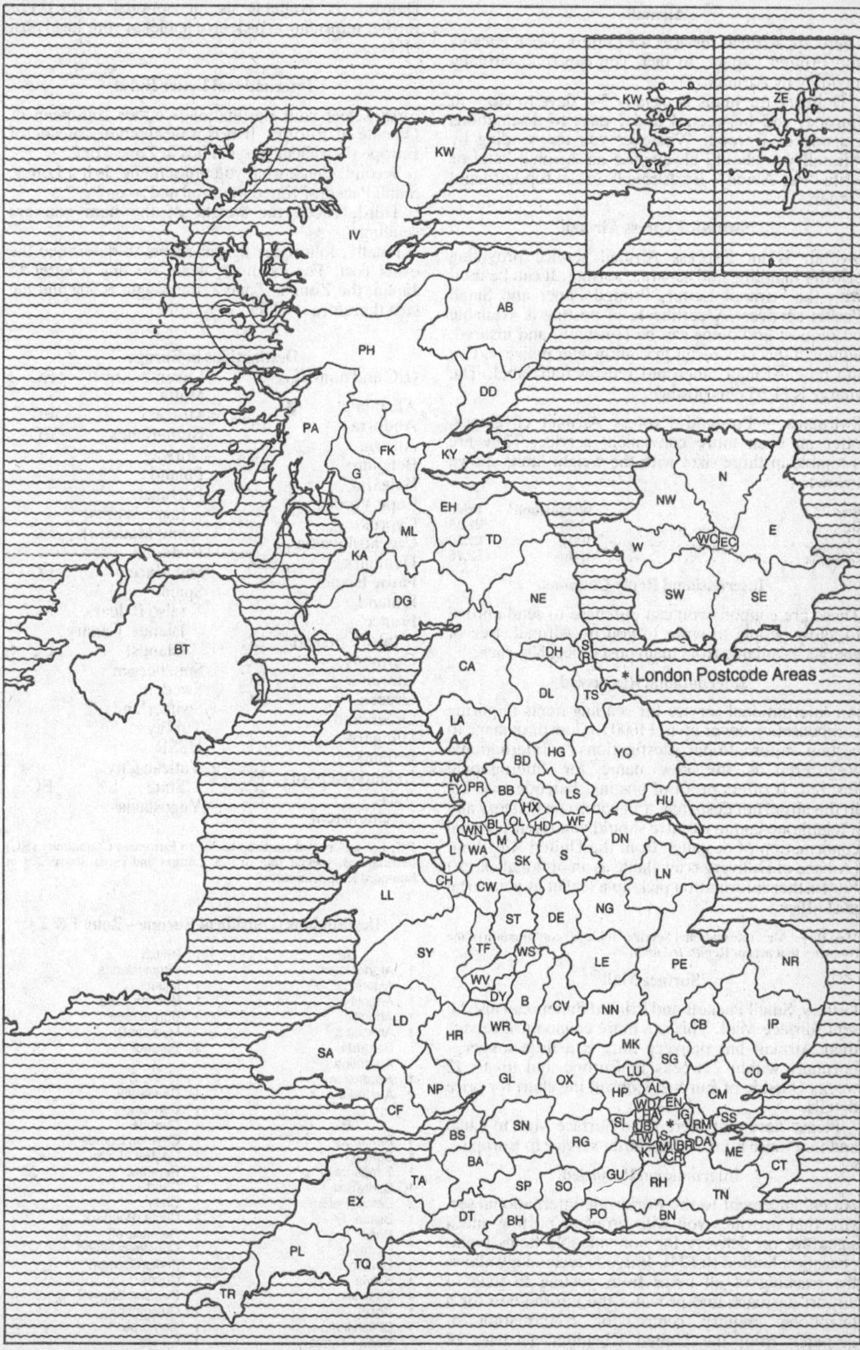

International Services

Airmail

There are Airmail services for Letters, Small Packets and Printed Papers. In fact, you can send virtually anything by Airmail.

Delivery for items is usually 3–4 days to cities in Europe, and between 4 and 7 days to destinations Outside of Europe. Whatever you are sending by Airmail you should always use an Airmail label or write "Par Avion – By Airmail" in the top left-hand corner.

Swiftair Express Airmail

Swiftair is an Express Airmail service providing priority handling and separate sorting. It can be used with the Airmail Letter, Printed Paper and Small Packet services. A certificate of posting is available on request and items can be registered and insured, although this may result in slightly later delivery. Use the blue Airmail label and red Swiftair label. The charge is £1.95 plus postage.

Swiftpack – Pre-paid Express Airmail envelopes, offer an even more convenient service. They are available in three sizes with the weight limits shown below:

Size	Weight limit	Price
DL	50g	£2.35
C5	100g	£2.50
C4	150g	£2.75

International Reply Coupons

These are coupons you can purchase to send abroad to allow people to write to you by Airmail, free of charge. Available from main post office, 60p each.

International Registered

An international service for sending items requiring compensation cover up to £1000 for loss or damage to certain international destinations.* International Registered is the new name for International Insured. It offers proof of posting, barcode tracking to the airport of despatch, a signature on delivery and a telephone enquiry centre should you require verbal confirmation of despatch from the United Kingdom. (Advice of Delivery is available as an optional extra.) For further information pick up a leaflet at your local post office.

*See Royal Mail International Service Guide for confirmation of the countries that accept Registered mail.

Surface Mail

Letters, Small Packets and Printed Papers can also be sent Surface Mail. This is a more economical service than Airmail but delivery time is a little longer – normally within 2 weeks in Europe and up to 12 weeks Outside of Europe. Consult the chart for price details.

Please note that there is no Surface Mail to Chad and that there is no Surface letter service to Europe.

International Recorded

An enhancement to the worldwide international service that provides you with proof of posting and a signature on delivery for non-valuable items (compensation limited to £24). Barcode technology allows the tracking of all items from posting to time of airport despatch and provides the information for a telephone enquiry centre for confirmation of despatch from the United Kingdom. (Advice of Delivery is available as an optional extra.) For further information pick up a leaflet at your local post office.

International Letter Rates

First, select your destination – either European or Outside of Europe. If it is a destination Outside of Europe then check to see if it is in Zone 1 or 2.

Second, check what you are sending. Is it a Letter, Small Packet, Printed Material and so on?

Third, check the weight of the item you are sending.

Finally, follow the figures across to determine the exact cost. For example, when sending a letter to Japan, the Zone is Zone 2, the weight is 30g and the cost therefore is £0.99.

Destinations in Europe

(EC and non-EC)

Albania	
Andorra	EC
Austria	
Belgium	EC
Bulgaria	
Cape Verde	
Cyprus	
Czechoslovakia	
Denmark	EC
Faroe Islands	
Finland	
France (also Corsica)	EC
Germany	EC
Gibraltar	EC
Greece	EC
Greenland	
Hungary	
Iceland	
Ireland (Rep. of)	EC
Italy	EC
Liechtenstein	
Luxembourg	EC
Malta	
Monaco	EC
Netherlands	EC
Norway	
Poland	
Portugal (also Azores and Madeira)	EC
Romania	
San Marino	EC
Spain (also Balearic Islands, Canary Islands)	EC
Spitzbergen	
Sweden	
Switzerland	
Turkey	
USSR	
Vatican City State	EC
Yugoslavia	

EC: For letters and cards up to 20g to European Community (EC) destinations, special rate of 24p. Letters and cards above 20g at Standard European rates.

Destinations (Outside of Europe – Zone 1 & 2

A

1	Afghanistan
1	Algeria
1	Angola
1	Anguilla
1	Antigua & Barbuda
1	Argentina
1	Ascension
2	Australia

B

1	Bahamas
1	Bahrain
1	Bangladesh
1	Barbados
2	Belau (Palau)
1	Belize
1	Benin
1	Bermuda
1	Bhutan
1	Bolvia
1	Boswana
1	Brazil
1	British Indian Ocean Territory
1	British Virgin Islands
1	Brunei
1	Burkina Faso
	Burma (see Myanmar)
1	Burundi

C

1	Cambodia
1	Cameroon
1	Canada
1	Cayman Islands
1	Central African Republic
1	Chad
1	Chile
2	China (People's Republic of)
1	Christmas Island (Indian Ocean)
1	Cocos (Keeling Islands)
1	Colombia
1	Comoros
1	Congo

(Continued)

1 Costa Rica
1 Côte d'Ivoire
1 Cuba

D
1 Djibouti
1 Dominica
1 Dominican Republic

E
1 Ecuador
2 East Timor
1 Egypt
1 El Salvador
1 Equatorial Guinea
1 Ethiopia

F
1 Falkland Islands & Dependencies
2 Fiji
1 French Guiana
2 French Polynesia
2 French Southern & Antarctic Territories (A)
1 French West Indies

G
1 Gabon
1 Gambia
1 Gaze & Khan Yunis
1 Ghana
1 Grenada
1 Guatemala
1 Guinea
1 Guinea-Bissau
1 Guyana

H
1 Haiti
1 Honduras
1 Hong Kong

I
1 India
1 Indonesia
1 Iran
1 Iraq
1 Israel
Ivory Coast (see Côte d'Ivoire)

J
1 Jamaica
2 Japan
1 Jordan

K
1 Kenya
2 Kiribati
2 Korea (Rep. of)
2 Korea (Democratic People's Rep. of)
1 Kuwait

L
1 Laos
1 Lebanon
1 Lesotho
1 Liberia
1 Libyan Soc Peoples' Arab Jamahiriya

M
1 Macao
1 Madagascar (Dem. Rep. of)
1 Malawi
1 Malaysia (B)
1 Maldives (Rep. of)
1 Mali
2 Marshall Islands
1 Mauritania
1 Mauritius
1 Mexico
2 Micronesia (Federal States of) – formerly Caroline Islands
2 Mongolia
1 Montserrat
1 Morocco
1 Mozambique
1 Myanmar (formerly Burma)

N
1 Namibia
2 Nauru Island
1 Nepal
1 Netherlands
Antilles & Aruba
2 New Caledonia
2 New Zealand
2 New Zealand Island Territories
1 Nicaragua
1 Nigeria
1 Niger Republic
2 Norfolk Island
2 Northern Mariana Islands

O
1 Oman

P
1 Pakistan
1 Panama
2 Papua New Guinea
1 Paraguay
1 Peru
2 Philippines
2 Pitcairn Island
1 Puerto Rico

Q
1 Qatar (State of)

R
1 Reunion
1 Rwanda

S
1 St Helena
1 St Kitts & Nevis
1 St Lucia
1 St Pierre & Miquelon
1 St Vincent & The Grenadines
2 Samoa, American
1 São Tomé & Príncipe
1 Saudi Arabia
1 Senegal
1 Seychelles
1 Sierra Leone
1 Singapore
2 Solomon Islands
1 Somalia (Dem. Rep.)
1 South Africa
1 Spanish
Territories of North Africa (Ceuta Chafarinas, Jadu & Melilla)
1 Sri Lanka
1 Sudan
1 Suriname
1 Swaziland
1 Syria

T
2 Taiwan
1 Tanzania
1 Thailand
1 Tibet
1 Togo (Rep. of)
2 Tonga
1 Trinidad & Tobago
1 Tristan da Cunha
1 Tunisia
1 Turks & Caicos Islands
2 Tuvalu

U
1 Uganda
1 United Arab Emirates (C)
1 USA
1 Uruguay

V
2 Vanuatu
1 Venezuela
1 Vietnam
1 Virgin Islands of USA

W
2 Wake Island
2 Wallis & Futuna Islands
2 Western Samoa

Y
1 Yemen (Rep. of)

Z
1 Zaire
1 Zambia
1 Zimbabwe

(A) There are no airmail services to the French, Southern and Antarctic Territories. (B) Malaya, Sabah and Sarawak. (C) Abu Dhabi, Ajman, Dubai, Fujarah, Ras al Khaimah, Sharjah, Umm of Quaiwan.

Airmail Prices
(Europe and Outside of Europe)

Weight (grammes) up to and including	Letters			Printed Papers and Newspapers				Small Packets		
	Europe	Zone 1	Zone 2	Europe	Zone 1 Printed Papers	Zone 1 News-papers	Zone 2 P Papers/ N papers	Europe	Zone 1	Zone 2
	£	£	£	£	£	£	£	£	£	£
10g	–	0.39	0.39	–	–	–	–	–	–	–
20g EC	0.24	0.57	0.57	0.28	0.37	0.37	0.40	–	–	–
Non EC	0.28	–	–	0.28	–	–	–	–	–	–
40g	0.39	0.89	0.99	0.34	0.52	0.48	0.58	–	–	–
60g	0.50	1.21	1.41	0.40	0.67	0.59	0.76	–	–	–
80g	0.61	1.53	1.83	0.46	0.82	0.70	0.94	–	–	–
100g	0.72	1.85	2.25	0.52	0.97	0.81	1.12	0.72	1.03	1.14
120g	0.83	2.17	2.67	0.58	1.12	0.92	1.30	0.80	1.19	1.32
140g	0.94	2.49	3.09	0.64	1.27	1.03	1.48	0.88	1.35	1.50
160g	1.05	2.81	3.51	0.70	1.42	1.14	1.66	0.96	1.51	1.68
180g	1.16	3.13	3.93	0.76	1.57	1.25	1.84	1.04	1.67	1.86
200g	1.27	3.45	4.35	0.82	1.72	1.36	2.02	1.12	1.83	2.04
220g	1.38	3.77	4.77	0.88	1.87	1.47	2.20	1.20	1.99	2.22
240g	1.49	4.09	5.19	0.94	2.02	1.58	2.38	1.28	2.15	2.40
260g	1.60	4.41	5.61	1.00	2.17	1.69	2.56	1.36	2.31	2.58
280g	1.71	4.73	6.03	1.06	2.32	1.80	2.74	1.44	2.47	2.76
300g	1.82	5.05	6.45	1.12	2.47	1.91	2.92	1.52	2.63	2.94
320g	1.93	5.37	6.87	1.18	2.62	2.02	3.10	1.60	2.79	3.12

(Continued)

Weight (grammes) up to and including	Letters Europe	Letters Zone 1	Letters Zone 2	Printed Papers and Newspapers Europe	Zone 1 Printed Papers	Zone 1 News-papers	Zone 2 P Papers/ N papers	Small Packets Europe	Small Packets Zone 1	Small Packets Zone 2
	£	£	£	£	£	£	£	£	£	£
340g	2.04	5.69	7.29	1.24	2.77	2.13	3.28	1.68	2.95	3.30
360g	2.15	6.01	7.71	1.30	2.92	2.24	3.46	1.76	3.11	3.48
380g	2.26	6.33	8.13	1.36	3.07	2.35	3.64	1.84	3.27	3.66
400g	2.37	6.65	8.55	1.42	3.22	2.46	3.82	1.92	3.43	3.84
420g	2.48	6.97	8.97	1.48	3.37	2.57	4.00	2.00	3.59	4.02
440g	2.59	7.29	9.39	1.54	3.52	2.68	4.18	2.08	3.75	4.20
460g	2.70	7.61	9.81	1.60	3.67	2.79	4.36	2.16	3.91	4.38
480g	2.81	7.93	10.23	1.66	3.82	2.90	4.54	2.24	4.07	4.56
500g	2.92	8.25	10.65	1.72	3.97	3.01	4.72	2.32	4.23	4.74
520g	3.03	8.57	11.07	1.78	4.12	3.12	4.90	2.40	4.39	4.92
540g	3.14	8.89	11.49	1.84	4.27	3.23	5.08	2.48	4.55	5.10
560g	3.25	9.21	11.91	1.90	4.42	3.34	5.26	2.56	4.71	5.28
580g	3.36	9.53	12.33	1.96	5.57	3.45	5.44	2.64	4.87	5.46
600g	3.47	9.85	12.75	2.02	4.72	3.56	5.62	2.72	5.03	5.64
620g	3.58	10.17	13.17	2.08	4.87	3.67	5.80	2.80	5.19	5.82
640g	3.69	10.49	13.59	2.14	5.02	3.78	5.98	2.88	5.35	6.00
660g	3.80	10.81	14.01	2.20	5.17	3.89	6.16	2.96	5.51	6.18
680g	3.91	11.13	14.43	2.26	5.32	4.00	6.34	3.04	5.67	6.36
700g	4.02	11.45	14.85	2.32	5.47	4.11	6.52	3.12	5.83	6.54
720g	4.13	11.77	15.27	2.38	5.62	4.22	6.70	3.20	5.99	6.72
740g	4.24	12.09	15.69	2.44	5.77	4.33	6.88	3.28	6.15	6.90
760g	4.35	12.41	16.11	2.50	5.92	4.44	7.06	3.36	6.31	7.08
780g	4.46	12.73	16.53	2.56	6.07	4.55	7.24	3.44	6.47	7.26
800g	4.57	13.05	16.95	2.62	6.22	4.66	7.42	3.52	6.63	7.44
820g	4.68	13.37	17.37	2.68	6.37	4.77	7.60	3.60	6.79	7.62
840g	4.79	13.69	17.79	2.74	6.52	4.88	7.78	3.68	6.95	7.80
860g	4.90	14.01	18.21	2.80	6.67	4.99	7.96	3.76	7.11	7.98
880g	5.01	14.33	18.63	2.86	6.82	5.10	8.14	3.84	7.27	8.16
900g	5.12	14.65	19.05	2.92	6.97	5.21	8.32	3.92	7.43	8.34
920g	5.23	14.97	19.47	2.98	7.12	5.32	8.50	4.00	7.59	8.52
940g	5.34	15.29	19.89	3.04	7.27	5.43	8.68	4.08	7.75	8.70
960g	5.45	15.61	20.31	3.10	7.42	5.54	8.86	4.16	7.91	8.88
980g	5.56	15.13	20.73	3.16	7.57	5.65	9.04	4.24	8.07	9.06
1000g	5.67	16.25	21.15	3.22	7.72	5.76	9.22	4.32	8.23	9.24
Each add. 20g	11p	32p	42p	6p*	15p	11p	18p*	8p†	16p†	18p†
Max. wgt	2kg	2kg	2kg	2kg	2kg	2kg	2kg	2kg	2kg	2kg

*Up to 5kg certain books and pamphlets. †Australia, Cuba, Myanmar and Papua New Guinea accept Small Packets only up to 500g. Italy accepts Small Packets only up to 1kg.

Surface Mail Prices

(Worldwide)

Weight (grammes) up to and including	Letters (outside Europe only)	Printed Papers	Small Packets
	£	£	£
20g	0.28	0.24	–
60g	0.48	0.35	–
100g	0.69	0.45	0.45
150g	0.92	0.60	0.60
200g	1.18	0.75	0.75
250g	1.42	0.90	0.90
300g	1.66	1.05	1.05
350g	1.92	1.20	1.20
400g	2.18	1.35	1.35
450g	2.44	1.50	1.50
500g	2.70	1.65	1.65
550g	2.96	1.78	1.78
600g	3.22	1.91	1.91
650g	3.48	2.04	2.04
700g	3.74	2.17	2.17
750g	4.00	2.30	2.30
800g	4.26	2.43	2.43
850g	4.52	2.56	2.56
900g	4.78	2.69	2.69
950g	5.04	2.82	2.82
1000g	5.30	2.95	2.95
1050g	5.56	3.07	3.07
1100g	5.82	3.19	3.19
1150g	6.08	3.31	3.31
1200g	6.34	3.43	3.43

Weight (grammes) up to and including	Letters (outside Europe only)	Printed Papers	Small Packets
	£	£	£
1250g	6.60	3.55	3.55
1300g	6.86	3.67	3.67
1350g	7.12	3.79	3.79
1400g	7.38	3.91	3.91
1450g	7.64	4.03	4.03
1500g	7.90	4.15	4.15
1550g	8.16	4.27	4.27
1600g	8.42	4.39	4.39
1650g	8.68	4.51	4.51
1700g	8.94	4.63	4.63
1750g	9.20	4.75	4.75
1800g	9.46	4.87	4.87
1850g	9.72	4.99	4.99
1900g	9.98	5.11	5.11
1950g	10.24	5.23	5.23
2000g	10.50	5.35	5.35
Max. wgt	2kg	2kg Except books and pamphlets which may weigh up to 5kg	2kg Except Australia, Cuba, Myanmar and Papua New Guinea (500g) and Italy (1kg)
Each add. 50g		12p	–

International Parcel Post

International Datapost

For guaranteed express delivery, to over 170 countries and territories worldwide. This service is not available at all Post Office counters. For your nearest acceptance point call the Parcelforce Enquiry Centre free on 0800 88 44 22.

Weight (kg)	0.5	1.0	1.5	2.0	2.5	3.0	3.5	4.0	4.5	5.0	Cost per extra 0.5kg
Zones										Cost (£)	
1	25.00	26.50	28.00	29.50	31.00	32.50	34.00	35.50	37.00	38.50	1.00
2	25.00	26.70	28.40	30.10	31.80	33.50	35.20	36.90	38.60	40.30	1.10
3	27.00	29.00	31.00	33.00	35.00	37.00	39.00	41.00	43.00	45.00	1.80
4	26.00	28.50	31.00	33.50	36.00	38.50	41.00	43.50	46.00	48.50	1.70
5	31.00	35.50	40.00	44.50	49.00	53.50	58.00	62.50	67.00	71.50	3.50
6	27.00	30.00	33.00	36.00	39.00	42.00	45.00	48.00	51.00	54.00	2.00
7	27.00	30.00	33.00	36.00	39.00	42.00	45.00	48.00	51.00	54.00	2.00

International Standard Service

For deliveries to over 200 countries and territories worldwide – Europe from 5 working days, and to the rest of the world from 7 working days.

Weight (kg)	0.5	1.0	1.5	2.0	2.5	3.0	3.5	4.0	4.5	5.0	Cost per extra 0.5kg
Zones										Cost (£)	
1	3.70	4.40	5.10	5.80	6.50	7.20	7.90	8.60	9.30	10.00	0.70
2	8.90	9.70	10.50	11.30	12.10	12.90	13.70	14.50	15.30	16.10	0.80
3	10.50	11.80	13.10	14.40	15.70	17.00	18.30	19.60	20.90	22.90	1.30
4	8.50	10.50	12.50	14.50	16.50	18.50	20.50	22.50	24.50	26.50	2.00
5	10.00	13.20	16.40	19.60	22.80	26.00	29.20	32.40	35.60	38.80	3.20
6	11.00	12.80	14.60	16.40	18.20	20.00	21.80	23.60	25.40	27.20	1.80
7	12.00	14.20	16.40	18.60	20.80	23.00	25.20	27.40	29.60	31.80	2.20

International Economy Service

For deliveries to most long-distance destinations at reduced rates (Europe from 10 working days, to the rest of the world from 20 working days).

Weight (kg)	0.5	1.0	1.5	2.0	2.5	3.0	3.5	4.0	4.5	5.0	Cost per extra 0.5kg
Zones										Cost (£)	
3	9.00	9.90	10.80	11.70	12.60	13.50	14.40	15.30	16.20	17.10	0.90
4	7.50	9.00	10.50	12.00	13.50	15.00	16.50	18.00	19.50	21.00	1.50
5	7.60	9.10	10.60	12.10	13.60	15.10	16.60	18.10	19.60	21.10	1.50
6	10.30	11.60	12.90	14.20	15.50	16.80	18.10	19.40	20.70	22.00	1.30
7	7.90	9.90	11.90	13.90	15.90	17.90	19.90	21.90	23.90	25.90	2.00

Note: Zones 1 & 2 are not served by Economy Service

Optional Extras

(Standard and Economy Service only)

Express delivery – Fastest possible delivery from post office in country of destination. Fee in addition to postage: £2.70.

Franc de Droits (FDD) – Pre-payment of foreign Customs charges to avoid inconveniencing recipient. Outward fee per parcel in addition to postage: £1.60. Inward delivery fee: £1.30.

Cash on delivery (C.O.D.) – parcels will not be delivered until a specified sum (the Trade Charge) has been collected on sender's behalf.

Cash on delivery (C.O.D.)

Outward parcels trade charge	Fee in addition to postage
Up to £200	£3.70
Over £200 up to £400	£7.00
Over £400 up to £600	£10.30
Over £600 up to £1000	£13.70
Over £1000 up to £1500	£16.80

Inward parcel delivery fee: £1.30

These are all available for an extra charge with standard and Economy Services only, to certain destinations. Further details from post offices.

Prices

To work out the price for any service, first find the Price Zone for the destination country in the Country Pricing Zones table. Then refer to the Price Tables for your chosen service and read off the price shown against your Price Zone and parcel weight. For every extra 0.5kg over 5kg, add the amount given in the supplementary table.

Country Pricing Zones

	Country	Zone
D	Afghanistan	5
D	Albania	3
	Algeria	5
E	Andorra	2
	Angola	5
	Anguilla	4
	Antigua & Barbuda	4
	Argentina	5
	Aruba	5
DS	Ascension	5
	Australia	7
	Austria	3
	Azores	3
	Bahamas	4
	Bahrain	5
	Balearic Isles	3
	Bangladesh	5
	Barbados	4
E	Belgium	2
	Belize	4
	Benin	5
	Bermuda	4
D	Bhutan	5
	Bolivia	5
	Botswana	5
	Brazil	5
	British Virgin Islands	4
	Brunei	6
	Bulgaria	3
	Burkina Faso	5
	Burundi	5
	Cameroon	5
	Canada	4
	Canary Islands	3
D	Cape Verde Islands	3
D	Caroline Islands	6
	Cayman Islands	4
	Central African Rep.	5
E	Chad	5
	Chile	5
	China (inc Tibet)	6
D	Christmas Is. (Ind. Ocn)	7
D	Cocos (Keeling) Island	7
	Colombia	5
	CIS (former USSR)	3
D	Comoros	5
	Congo (People's Rep. of)	5
E	Corsica	2
	Costa Rica	4
	Côte d'Ivoire	5
E	Cuba	4
	Cyprus	3
	Czech Republic	3
E	Denmark	2
	Djibouti	5
	Dominica	4
	Dominican Republic	4
E	East Timor	6
	Ecuador	5
	Egypt	5
	El Salvador	4
D	Equatorial Guinea	5
	Estonia	3
	Ethiopia	5
DS	Falkland Is. & Deps.	5
	Faroe Islands	2
D	Fiji	7
	Finland	3
E	France	2
	French Guiana	5
D	French Polynesia	7
	Gabon	5
	The Gambia	5
D	Gaza & Khan Yunis	5
	Georgia	3
E	Germany	2
	Ghana	5
	Gibraltar	3
	Greece	3
DE	Greenland	2
	Grenada	4
	Guadeloupe	4
	Guatemala	4
SE	Guernsey	2
	Guinea	5
	Guinea-Bissau	5
	Guyana	5
	Haiti	4
	Honduras	4
	Hong Kong	6
	Hungary	3
	Iceland	3
	India	5
	Indonesia	6
	Iran	5
	Iraq	5
E	Ireland Rep. of	1
	Israel	5
	Italy	3
	Jamaica	4
	Japan	6
SE	Jersey	2
	Jordan	5
	Kenya	5
D	Kiribati	7
	Korea (Rep. of)	6
	Kuwait	5
D	Laos	6
	Latvia	3
E	Lebanon	5
	Lesotho	5
	Liberia	5
D	Libya	5
E	Liechtenstein	2
	Lithuania	3
E	Luxembourg	2
	Macao	6
	Madagascar	5
	Madeira	3
	Malawi	5
	Malaysia	6
	Maldives	5
	Mali	5
	Malta	3
D	Mariana Islands	6
D	Marshall Islands	7
	Martinique	4
D	Mauritania	5
	Mauritius	5
	Mexico	4
E	Monaco	2
D	Mongolia	6
	Montserrat	4
	Morocco	5
	Mozambique	5
D	Myanmar (Burma)	6
	Namibia (SW Africa)	5
D	Nauru Island	7
D	Nepal	5
E	Netherlands	2
	Netherlands Antilles	4
	New Caledonia	7
	New Zealand	7
	New Zealand Is. Terr.	7
SE	New York City	2
	Nicaragua	4
	Niger Republic	5
	Nigeria	5
D	Norfolk Island	7
	Norway	3
	Oman	5
	Pakistan	5
	Panama	4
	Papua New Guinea	7
	Paraguay	5
	Peru	5
	Philippines	6
D	Pitcairn Island	7
	Poland	3
	Portugal	3
	Puerto Rico	4
	Qatar	5
	Reunion	5
	Romania	3
	Rwanda	5
D	Samoa (USA Terr)	7
D	San Marino	3
DS	St Helena	5
	St Kitts & Nevis	4
	St Lucia	4
	St Pierre & Miquelon	4
	St Vincent & Grenadines	4
D	São Tomé & Príncipe	5
	Sardinia	3
	Saudi Arabia	5
	Senegal	5
	Seychelles	5
	Sicily	3
	Sierra Leone	5
	Singapore	6
	Slovakia	3
	Solomon Islands	7
	Somalia Dem. Rep.	5
	South Africa	5
	Spain	3
D	Spanish Terr. (N. Africa)	5
DS	Spitzbergen	3
	Sri Lanka	5
	Sudan	5
	Suriname	5
	Swaziland	5
	Sweden	3
E	Switzerland	2
	Syria	5
	Taiwan	6
	Tanzania	5
	Thailand	6
	Togo	5
D	Tonga	7
	Trinidad & Tobago	5
D	Tristan da Cunha	5
	Tunisia	5
	Turkey	3
	Turks & Caicos Islands	4
D	Tuvalu	7
	Uganda	5
	United Arab Emirates	5
	Uruguay	5
	USA	4
	USSR, former (CIS)	3
	Vanuatu	7
D	Vatican City State	3
	Venezuela	5
	Vietnam	6
	Virgin Islands (USA)	4
D	Wake Island	7
D	Wallis & Futuna Island	7
D	Western Samoa	7
	Yemen	5
	Yugoslavia, former	3
	Zaire	5
	Zambia	5
	Zimbabwe	5

D *International Datapost service not available*

S *International Standard service not available*

E *International Economy service not available.*

Documentation for International Datapost
- datapost docket
- relevant customs documentation

including commercial invoices – ask at counter.

Documentation for International Standard or Economy Services
- customs pack
- standard service label

where applicable.

Size & Weight Limits – Many countries will accept parcels up to 30kg and 1.5m long. Ask at the counter or call 0800 22 44 66.

Insurance for International Datapost
Free insurance against loss or damage up to £5,000. Free consequential loss cover from £100 – £10,000.

Insurance for International Standard Service
Inclusive insurance against actual loss or damage up to £250 per parcel.

Insurance for International Economy Service
Limited discretionary compensation for loss or damage.

For details of exclusions and how to claim, ask at the counter or call 0800 22 44 66.

The Cost of Posting a Letter

Year	Cost
1840	1d
1918	1½d
1940	2½d
1957	3d
1965	4d
1968*	5d
1971	3p
1973	3½p
1974	4½p
1975	7p
1975 (September)	8½p
1977	9p
1979	10p
1980	12p
1981	14p
1982	15½p
1983	16p
1984	17p
1986	18p
1988	19p
1989	20p
1990	22p
1991	24p
1993	25p

*The two-tier postal system was introduced in 1968. Figures after this date are for first class post.

U.S. State Abbreviations

The 2-letter abbreviations below are approved by the U.S. Postal Service for use in addresses only. They do not replace the traditional abbreviations in other contexts.

State	Abbr.
Alabama	AL
Alaska	AK
American Samoa	AS
Arizona	AZ
Arkansas	AR
California	CA
Colorado	CO
Connecticut	CT
Delaware	DE
Dist. of Col.	DC
Federated States of Micronesia	FM
Florida	FL
Georgia	GA
Guam	GU
Hawaii	HI
Idaho	ID
Illinois	IL
Indiana	IN
Iowa	IA
Kansas	KS
Kentucky	KY
Louisiana	LA
Maine	ME
Marshall Islands	MH
Maryland	MD
Massachusetts	MA
Michigan	MI
Minnesota	MN
Missouri	MO
Mississippi	MS
Montana	MT
Nebraska	NE
Nevada	NV
New Hampshire	NH
New Jersey	NJ
New Mexico	NM
New York	NY
North Carolina	NC
North Dakota	ND
Northern Mariana Is.	MP
Ohio	OH
Oklahoma	OK
Oregon	OR
Pennsylvania	PA
Puerto Rico	PR
Rhode Island	RI
South Carolina	SC
South Dakota	SD
Tennessee	TN
Texas	TX
Utah	UT
Vermont	VT
Virginia	VA
Virgin Islands	VI
Washington	WA
West Virginia	WV
Wisconsin	WI
Wyoming	WY

Television Licences

The collection of monies to fund the BBC first began in 1922. The Postmaster General formed the television licensing business on instruction from the Home Office.

At that time only a radio licence was required, which cost just 10 shillings (50p). It was in 1946 that the radio and television licences were combined and then cost a grand total of £2.00.

Today, TV Licensing is a division of SSL (Subscription Services Limited), a Post Office enterprise company formed in 1991. 1500 staff are responsible for the collection and administration of the television licence fees on behalf of the BBC.

TV Licence Facts

- TV Licensing has on computer file 24 million addresses
- There are around 20 million television licence holders in the UK
- Watching television – whatever the channel (including Satellite and Cable) – without a TV licence is a criminal offence.
- Currently a colour television licence costs **£83** (less than 23p a day). A black/white licence is **£27.50**
- A colour licence is also required when you use a video recorder because it receives colour signals
- Television viewers watching without a licence can be fined up to £1000
- TV Licensing catches on average 1,000 evaders a day
- Revenue approaching £1.4 billion is collected for the BBC by TV Licensing
- Licence evasion costs the BBC £130 million in lost revenue per year
- On average TV Licensing sends out 1.5 million television licence reminders per month.
- Licensing operates from its headquarters in Bristol and 52 enquiry offices around the country

Payment

- direct at the post office
- direct by post
- by annual direct debit from a bank account or building society
- by savings stamps
- by four instalments from a bank/building society account

Postal Services and Television Licences

United Kingdom: Years ended 31 March[1]

Source: CSO

	Unit	1981	1982	1983	1984	1985	1986	1987	1988	1989[12]	1990	1991	1992
Letters and parcel post													
Letters, etc posted[2]	Millions	10,072	9,985	10,255	10,665	11,439	11,721	12,535	13,568	13,741	15,293	15,902	–
of which:													
Registered and insured	"	36.6	33.5	33.5	32.5	33.5	33.2	33.2	33.1	21.0	22.2	21.3	–
Airmail (Commonwealth and foreign)[3]	"	436.8	393.0	378.0	379.3	417.8	383.1	377.7	427.2	403.0	444.0	467.7	–
Business reply and freepost items	"	309.2	308.2	336.2	356.9	352.6	365.4	370.0	371.1	377.3	438.7	416.7	–
Parcels posted[4]	"	168.3	179.6	189.6	194.9	202.5	186.5	192.2	197.1	–	–	–	–
of which:													
Registered and insured[5, 13]	"	4.2	3.8	3.6	3.8	3.9	3.7	3.5	3.2	0.4	0.3	0.4	–
Inward and transit parcels handled	"	3.6	3.4	3.2	3.1	3.0	2.6	2.8	2.6	2.7	2.8	–	–
Postal orders													
Total issued[6]	Thousands	121,636	87,154	68,605	63,511	58,553	56,466	54,779	49,984	43,882	42,281	39,644	39,867
Telegrams and telephones[11]													
Telegrams: total	Thousands	13,662	11,521	7,694[10]	5,710	–	–	–	–	–	–	–	–
Inland	"	2,963	2,276	901[10]	–	–	–	–	–	–	–	–	–
Foreign (via Post Office system)[7]	"	10,699	9,245	6,793	5,710	–	–	–	–	–	–	–	–
Telex connections	Number	89,930	92,378	92,622	95,115	–	–	–	–	–	–	–	–
Telephone calls (Inland):													
total	Millions	20,175	20,806	21,403	22,686	–	–	–	–	–	–	–	–
Local	"	16,840	17,360	17,800	18,750	–	–	–	–	–	–	–	–
Trunk	"	3,335	3,446	3,603	3,936	–	–	–	–	–	–	–	–
Telephone calls (International): total	Thousands	116,533	132,255	148,478	172,746	–	–	–	–	–	–	–	–
Continental	"	79,467	86,352	93,109	104,065	–	–	–	–	–	–	–	–
Intercontinental	"	36,971	45,806	55,265	68,574	–	–	–	–	–	–	–	–
Maritime	"	95	97	104	107	–	–	–	–	–	–	–	–
Telephone stations[8]: total	Thousands	27,870	28,450	28,882	29,336	–	–	–	–	–	–	–	–
Public call offices	"	77	77	77	77	–	–	–	–	–	–	–	–
Private stations	"	27,793	28,373	28,805	29,259	–	–	–	–	–	–	–	–
Telephone exchanges[9]:													
total	Number	6,338	6,318	6,296	–	–	–	–	–	–	–	–	–
Automatic	"	6,338	6,318	6,296	–	–	–	–	–	–	–	–	–
Manual	"												
Television licences													
In force on 31 March	Thousands	18,667	18,554	18,494	18,632	18.716	18,705	18,953	19,396	19,396	19,645	19,546	19,631
of which:													
Colour	"	13,780	14,261	14,699	15,370	15,819	16,025	16,539	17,134	17,469	17,964	18,200	18,426

(1) Years ended 31 March for letter and parcel post, postal orders and telegrams sent. For all other items figures relate to 31 March in each year. (2) Including printed papers, newspapers, postcards and sample packets. (3) Including letters without special charge for air transport. (4) Includes Irish Republic inward traffic. (5) Includes compensation fee parcels. (6) Excluding those issued on HM ships, in many British possessions and in other places abroad. For 1980, 1981, 1984, 1986, 1987, 1988, 1989, 1990, 1991 and 1992 includes Overseas and Army. (7) Excluding those sent abroad via the private cable companies system. (8) A station is a telephone provided for the use of customer of renter. (9) Excluding auto-manual and trunk exchanges. (10) Inland telegram service ceased from 1 October 1982, therefore 1983 figures are not comparable with earlier years. (11) Any enquiries should be referred to British Telecom plc, 81 Newgate Street, London EC1A 7AJ. (12) Industrial action during year. (13) Registered Service to Irish Republic ceased in 1989.

CONSUMER INFORMATION

How to Get the Most for Your Money

Source: *Consumer's Resource Handbook*

Before Making a Purchase

(1) Analyse what you need and what features are important to you.

(2) Compare brands. Use word-of-mouth recommendations and formal product comparison reports. Check with your local library for magazines and other publications containing consumer information.

(3) Compare stores. Look for a store with a good reputation and take advantage of sales.

(4) Check for any additional charges, such as delivery and service costs.

(5) Compare warranties.

(6) Read terms of contracts carefully.

(7) Check the return or exchange policy.

After Your Purchase

(1) Follow proper use and care instructions for products.

(2) Read and understand the warranty provisions.

(3) If trouble develops, report the problem as soon as possible. Do not try to fix the product yourself as this may void the warranty.

(4) Keep a record of efforts to have your problem remedied. This record should include names of people you speak to, times, dates and other relevant information.

(5) Clearly state your problem and the solution you want.

(6) Include all relevant details, along with copies of documents (proof of purchase).

(7) Briefly describe what you have done to resolve the problem.

(8) Allow each person you contact a reasonable period of time to resolve your problem before contacting another source for assistance.

Handling Your Own Complaint

(1) Identify your problem and what you believe would be a fair settlement. Do you want your money back? Would you like the product repaired? Will an exchange do?

(2) Gather documentation regarding your complaint. Sales receipts, repair orders, warranties, cancelled cheques or contracts will back up your complaint and help the company to solve your problem.

(3) Go back to where you made the purchase. Contact the person who sold you the item or performed the service. Calmly and accurately explain the problem and what action you would like to be taken. If that person is not helpful, ask for the supervisor or manager and repeat your complaint. A large percentage of consumer problems are resolved at this level. Chances are yours will be too.

(4) Don't give up if you are not satisfied with the response. If the company operates nationally or the product is a national brand, write a letter to the person responsible for consumer complaints at the company's headquarters. If the company doesn't have a consumer office, direct your letter to the managing director of the company.

How to Write a Letter of Complaint

(1) If you have already contacted the person who sold you the product or service, or the company is out of town, you will need to write a letter to pursue your complaint.

(2) If you need the managing director's name and address of the company, first check in your phone directory to see if the company has a local office. If it does, call and ask for the information you need. If there is no local listing call Directory Enquiries.

Basic Tips on Letter Writing

(1) Include your name, address and home and work phone numbers.

(2) Type your letter if possible. If it is handwritten, make sure it is neat and easy to read.

(3) Make your letter brief and to the point. Include all important facts about your purchase, including the date and place where you made the purchase, and any information you can give about the product or service such as serial or model numbers or specific type of service.

(4) State exactly what you want done about the problem and how long you are willing to wait to get it resolved. Be reasonable.

(5) Include all documents regarding your problems. Be sure to send COPIES, not originals.

(6) Avoid writing an angry, sarcastic, or threatening letter. The person reading was probably not responsible for your problem, but may be very helpful in resolving it.

(7) Keep a copy of the letter for your records.

Buying on Credit

Source: Office of Fair Trading

Generally speaking, it's a bad idea to buy on credit. You'll pay a lot more than if you pay cash; you'll be paying off the debt for months or years ahead; and you'll be in trouble if you fall behind with the instalments.

Bear in mind the following points before you decide to buy on credit.

- Shop around for the best credit terms. You don't have to accept a shop's scheme; you may be able to borrow more cheaply elsewhere. The best deal is interest-free credit, which costs you nothing extra.
- Beware sales assistants who try to pressurize you into signing credit agreements on the spot with the offer of a free prize or special discount.
- Putting up your home as security may get you a cheaper loan, but if you fall behind with repayments, the company can sell your home to recoup its money.

Credit Brokers

A credit broker can help you to find a loan, but may charge a fee for this service. Discuss this before accepting the loan, as you might have to borrow extra to pay for it or may find it deducted from the loan.

Loans for buying a home and other loans up to £15,000 which are not taken up within 6 months incur a brokerage charge of only £3. If you have paid more, you can demand the return of the difference.

Cancelling Credit Agreements

Read the contract carefully before you sign to find out what rights of cancellation it allows you. The form should have a box headed "Your right to cancel".

You can cancel:

- If you have met the trader to discuss the deal and signed the form at home. In this case you do not have to accept the goods you were going to buy with the loan, and even if they have arrived, you can still cancel.

You cannot cancel:

- Deals arranged over the phone, even if you signed at home.
- If you signed the agreement in the trader's business premises.

Tips for Shopping by Mail, Telephone and Television

Source: *Consumer's Resource Handbook*

(1) Be suspicious of exaggerated product claims or very low prices, and read product descriptions very carefully – sometimes pictures or products are misleading.

(2) Ask about the firm's return policy. If it is not stated, ask before you order. For example, does the company pay charges for delivery and return? Is a warranty or guarantee available? Does the company sometimes substitute comparable goods for the product you want to order?

(3) Keep a complete record of your order including the company's name, address and telephone number, the price of the terms ordered, any handling or other charges, the date you posted (or telephoned) in the order, and your method of payment. Keep copies of cancelled cheques and/or statements.

(4) If you ordered by mail, your order should be shipped within 30 days after the company receives your complete order, unless another period is agreed upon when placing the order or is stated in an advertisement. If your order is delayed, a notice of delay should be sent to you within the promised shipping period along with an option to cancel the order.

(5) If you buy a product through a television shopping programme, check the cost of the same item sold by other sources, including local shops, catalogues, etc.

(6) If you want to buy a product based on a telephone call from a company, ask for the name, address and phone number where you can reach the caller after considering the offer.

(7) Never give your credit card number over the telephone as proof of your identity.

(8) For postal regulations about cash on delivery (C.O.D.) orders see p. 582.

Motoring Costs: Petrol Cars

(as at April 1993)

Source: AA

					Engine capacity (cc)
	Up to 1000	**1001 to 1400**	**1401 to 2000**	**2001 to 3000**	**3001 to 4500**
Standing charges per annum (£)					
Car licence	125.00	125.00	125.00	125.00	125.00
Insurance	622.49	802.45	968.00	1495.10	1544.53
Depreciation (based on 10,000 miles per annum)	833.50	1253.13	1752.02	3288.88	4287.00
Subscription	64.00	64.00	64.00	64.00	64.00
	1644.99	**2244.58**	**2909.02**	**4972.98**	**6020.53**
Cost per mile					**Pence**
5,000	32.90	44.89	58.18	99.46	120.41
10,000	16.45	22.45	29.09	49.73	60.21
15,000	12.08	16.63	21.73	37.54	45.85
20,000	10.73	14.98	19.80	34.73	42.96
25,000	9.91	13.99	18.64	33.05	41.23
30,000	8.26	11.66	15.54	27.54	34.36
Running cost per mile					**Pence**
Petrol*	5.69	6.50	7.58	10.34	11.37
Oil	0.53	0.53	0.57	0.63	1.03
Tyres	0.61	0.80	0.97	1.86	2.40
Servicing	1.20	1.20	1.20	1.62	2.43
Repairs & replacements	5.00	5.29	6.18	9.35	11.62
	13.03	**14.32**	**16.50**	**23.80**	**28.85**

* Unleaded petrol at £0.50 pence per litre.

Fuel Price Comparisons, UK

(as at May 1993)

Source: AA

Area	4-star	Unleaded 95 octane	Unleaded super	Diesel
	Pence per gallon			
Scotland & N. Ireland	252.83	230.36	249.03	229.45
North	247.76	225.03	242.31	225.21
Midlands	248.44	225.26	242.76	225.83
Wales	257.01	234.88	251.10	230.94
South	249.78	227.17	244.42	224.90
National average (gallons)	**250.61**	**227.99**	**245.25**	**226.57**
National average (litres)	**55.13**	**50.15**	**53.95**	**49.84**
(% taken as tax)	71.64	66.21	62.60	65.56
Supermarket average (gallons)	**237.08**	**214.35**	**223.89**	**211.85**
Supermarket average (litres)	**52.15**	**47.15**	**49.25**	**46.60**
(% taken as tax)	74.88	69.48	67.15	69.08

Fuel Price Comparisons, Europe

(as at 13 May 1993)

Source: AA

Country	Leaded	Unleaded	Diesel
	Pence per litre		
Austria	61.54	58.58	47.93
Belgium	67.82	60.30	51.37
Bulgaria	–	–	–
Croatia	–	–	–
Czech Rep.	–	–	–
Denmark	64.09	57.42	51.94
Finland	61.22	56.09	37.23
France	65.80	61.83	44.24
Germany	63.90	56.43	44.40
Greece	62.27	58.90	42.33
Holland	73.43	67.53	47.60
Hungary	–	–	–
Ireland	60.10	59.30	54.37
Italy	72.01	68.17	54.40
Luxembourg	50.34	43.12	36.88
Norway	80.61	72.97	30.26
Poland	–	–	–
Portugal	65.18	64.29	44.64
Romania	–	–	–
Serbia	–	–	–
Slovak Rep.	–	–	–
Spain	57.71	56.40	45.43
Sweden	71.98	68.24	50.62
Switzerland	59.12	54.97	56.81
Turkey	35.51	39.87	25.20
UK	55.13	50.15	49.84

Tips for Fuel-Efficient Driving

Source: U.S. Environmental Protection Agency

When Buying a New Vehicle

- **Buy the type of vehicle that best suits your needs.** Check *Which?* magazine to compare the fuel economy of similar models. In general, *larger displacement engines and higher horsepower ratings will result in lower fuel economy.* The additional power and torque may be useful for mountain driving or trailer towing situations, but your fuel economy will suffer during almost all types of driving. *Avoid unnecessary optional equipment* (especially heavy options such as four-wheel drive and options such as air conditioning that tax the engine). Extra equipment adds weight and decreases the fuel economy of the vehicle.

Conserving Fuel with Your Current Vehicle:

- **Drive your vehicle wisely.** *Avoid idles* of more than one minute (turn off your engine in traffic jams, limit vehicle warm-ups in winter). *Go easy on the brakes and accelerator* (anticipate stops and avoid "jack-rabbit" starts). Pay attention to speed. *You can improve your fuel economy about 15% by driving at 55 mph rather than 65 mph.* Put your vehicle's transmission into overdrive or a "fuel economy" position when cruising on motorways. *Do not carry unneeded items* that add weight. Reduce drag by placing items inside the vehicle or boot rather than on roof racks. *Use air conditioning only when necessary.*
- **Maintain your vehicle regularly.** *Periodic tune-ups improve vehicle fuel economy and performance.* Dragging brakes, low transmission fluid levels, out-of-tune engines, and old blocked fuel or air filters all hurt fuel economy. *Inflate tyres* to maximum recommended pressure and get periodic *wheel alignments.*
- **Keep track of your vehicle's fuel economy.** A marked increase in the amount of fuel you use could indicate the need for a tune-up, or serve as an early signal for necessary repairs.
- **Use your vehicle effectively.** *Use your vehicle only when necessary.* Combine errands into one trip. If you have access to more than one vehicle, drive the one that's most fuel efficient whenever possible. Consider car-sharing, bicycling, walking, or public transport.

Tips on Cutting Energy Costs in Your Home

Source: Con Edison Conservation Services, New York City

Heating

In many homes more energy is used for heating than anything else. Installing the right amount of insulation and double glazing pays off. Also consider the following advice:

- Make sure the thermostat and heating system are in good working order. An annual check-up is recommended.
- If your heating system has air filters, make sure they are clean.
- Set the thermostat no higher than 68 degrees. When no one is home, or when everyone is sleeping, the setting should be turned down to 60 degrees or lower. An automatic setback thermostat can raise and lower your home's temperature at times you specify.
- Close off and do not heat unused areas.
- If you do not have conventional double glazing, use sheets of plastic instead.
- Special glass fireplace doors help keep a room's heat from being drawn up the chimney when the fire is burning low. Close the damper when a fireplace is not in use.
- Use the sun's heat by opening blinds and curtains

on sunny days.

- Keep radiators and warm air outlets clean. Do not block them with furniture or curtains.

Water Heater

In many homes the water heater ranks second only to the heating system in total energy consumption.

- Put an insulation blanket on your water heater; when you go on holiday turn it to a minimum setting.
- If you have a dishwasher, set the water heater thermostat no higher than 140 degrees. If not, or if you have a separate water heater for baths, a setting as low as 110 degrees may be sufficient.
- Run the dishwasher and washing machine only when you have a full load. Use warm- or cold-water cycles for laundry when you can.
- Take showers instead of baths. About half as much hot water is used for a shower.
- Install a water-saver shower head.
- Install aerators or restrictors on all your taps.
- Do not leave the hot water running when rinsing dishes or shaving. Plug and partially fill the basin, or fill a bowl with water.
- Use the right size water heater for your needs. An oversized unit wastes energy heating unneeded water. An undersized unit will not deliver all the hot water you want when you need it.

Refrigerators and Freezers

The refrigerator operates 24 hours a day, every day, so it is one of the biggest users of energy in the home.

- Keep the condenser coils clean. The coils are on the back or at the bottom of the refrigerator. Carefully wipe, vacuum or brush the coils to remove dust and dirt at least once a year.
- Examine door gaskets and hinges regularly for air leaks. The doors should fit tightly. To check, place a piece of paper between the door and the cabinet. Close the door with normal force, then try to pull the paper straight out. There should be a slight resistance. Test all around the door, including the hinge side. If there are any places where the paper slides out easily, you need to adjust the hinges or replace the gasket, or both.
- Pause before opening your refrigerator door. Think of everything you will need before you open the door so you do not have to go back several times. When you open the door, close it quickly to keep the cool air in.
- Adjust the temperature-setting dial of the refrigerator as the manufacturer recommends. Use a thermometer to check the temperature (38 to 40 degrees is usually recommended for the refrigerator; zero degrees for the freezer). Settings that are too cold waste electricity.
- If you have a manual-defrost refrigerator, do not allow the ice to build up more than ¼ inch thick.
- Keep your refrigerator well stocked but allow room for air to circulate around the food.
- The freezer, on the other hand, should be packed full. If necessary, fill empty spaces with bags of ice cubes or fill milk cartons with water and freeze.
- When you are going to be away from home for a week or more, turn off and unplug the refrigerator, empty and clean it, and prop the door open.
- When shopping for a new refrigerator or freezer, eliminate those too large for your needs.

Cooking

- Cook as many dishes in the oven at one time as you can instead of cooking each separately. If recipes call for slightly different temperatures, say 325, 350, and 375 degrees, pick the middle temperature of 350 to cook all 3 dishes and remove each dish as it's done.

How to Get a Passport

Application forms for 10-year passports may be obtained from main post offices (except in Northern Ireland) or your area passport office (see below). Applications may be made by post or in person, but at least 1 month should be allowed for processing. (Allow 3 months if you apply during the busiest period, February–August.)

Documents required: All applications should be accompanied by a birth or adoption certification, and married women must also produce a marriage certificate or divorce documents.

Photographs: You must submit 2 full-face photos measuring 45×35mm, one of which must be verified as a true likeness by the person who countersigns the application.

Cost: A 32-page passport costs £18; a 48-page passport (designed for frequent travellers) costs £27.

Emergencies: If you have to travel urgently because of a death or serious illness, the Passport Office will do its best to expedite your application.

Passport Offices

Guernsey
White Rock
St Peter Port
Tel: 0481 726911

Isle of Man
Central Govt. Offices
Bucks Road
Douglas
Tel: 0624 685208

Jersey
Weighbridge
St Helier JE2 3ND
Tel: 0534 25377

Newport (N)
Olympia House
Upper Dock Street
Newport
Gwent NP9 1XA
Tel: 0633 244500/244292

Peterborough (P)
Aragon Court
Northminster Road
Peterborough
PE1 1QG
Tel: 0733 895555

Belfast
Hampton House
47–53 High Street
Belfast BT1 2QS
Tel: 0232 232371

Note: The London Office is a calling office only. Postal applications from Greater London and Middlesex should be sent to the Glasgow office.

If you live in Scotland, send your application to Glasgow.

If you live in Northern Ireland, send your application to Belfast.

Liverpool (Ll)
5th Floor
India Buildings
Water Street
Liverpool L2 0QZ
Tel: 051-237 3010

London (Personal callers only)
Clive House
70 Petty France
London SW1H 9HD
Tel: 071-279 3434

Glasgow (G)
3 Northgate
96 Milton Street,
Cowcaddens
Glasgow G4 0BT
Tel: 041-332 0271

Passport Office hours of business: Mondays to Fridays, 9 am to 4.30 pm, except the London Office which closes at 4.00 pm.

Areas Served

Avon N
Bedforshire P
Berkshire N
Buckingham P
Cambridgeshire P
Cheshire Li
Cleveland Li
Clwyd Li
Cornwall N
Cumbria Li
Derbyshire Li
Devon N
Dorset N
Durham Li
Dyfed N
East Sussex N
Essex (less London boroughs) P
Gloucestershire N
Greater London G
Greater Manchester Li
Gwent N
Gwynedd Li
Hampshire N
Hereford and Worcester N
Hertfordshire (less London boroughs) P
Humberside Li
Isle of Wight N
Kent (less London boroughs) P
Lancashire Li
Leicestershire P
Lincolnshire P
Merseyside Li
Middlesex G
Mid Glamorgan N
Norfolk P
Northamptonshire P
Northumberland Li
North Yorkshire Li
Nottinghamshire P
Oxfordshire N
Powys N
Shropshire N
Somerset N
South Glamorgan N
South Yorkshire Li
Staffordshire Li
Suffolk P
Surrey (less London boroughs) N
Tyne and Wear Li
Warwickshire P
West Glamorgan N
West Midlands P
West Sussex N
West Yorkshire Li
Wiltshire N

British Visitor's Passports

These are valid for 1 year only and may be used for holidays and unpaid business trips of up to 3 months. They are acceptable only in the following countries:

Andorra
Austria
Belgium
Bermuda
Denmark
Finland
France (including Corsica)
Germany
Gibraltar
Greece (including the Greek islands)
Iceland
Italy (including Elba, Sardinia and Sicily)
Liechtenstein
Luxembourg
Malta
Monaco
Netherlands
Norway
Portugal (including the Azores and Madeira)
San Marino
Spain (including the Balearics and the Canaries)
Sweden
Switzerland
Tunisia
Turkey
Yugoslavia

If in doubt, contact the embassies/consulates of the countries you wish to visit (*see* Nations section).

Availability: The holder and each person to be included in the passport must be at least 8 years old and a British citizen, a British Dependent Territories citizen or a British Overseas citizen lawfully resident in the UK.

Applications in England, Scotland and Wales should be made at a main post office. Applications in Northern Ireland, Jersey, Guernsey and the Isle of Man should be made at an area Passport Office (see above).

Documents required: One from each of the 2 groups below.

Group 1

- birth certificate or adoption certificate
- uncancelled British Visitor's Passport in present name
- certificate of naturalization or registration
- passport in which previously included as a child
- retirement pension book

Group 2

- NHS medical card
- driving licence
- valid bank cheque card or credit card
- recent electricity, gas or telephone bill
- child benefit book showing any children to be included

Photographs: 2 identical full-face photos for each adult; none required for children.

Cost: £12.00 (£18.00 if wife/husband is to be included).

TRAVELLERS' INFORMATION

Source: Department of Health

Medical Treatment in Non-EC Countries

Country	Documents needed to get medical treatment	What is normally free	What you pay charges for	Other information
Anguilla	Proof of UK residence (e.g. NHS medical card or UK driving licence).	Minor emergency treatment.	Hospital in-patient and out-patient treatment. Hospital accommodation. Dental treatment. Prescribed medicines. Ambulance travel.	Family-doctor-type treatment is available at out-patient clinics. A charge is made.
Australia	Proof of UK residence (e.g. UK passport or NHS medical card) and temporary entry permit.	Hospital treatment.	Treatment at some doctors' surgeries. Prescribed medicines. Ambulance travel.	You will need to enrol at a local Medicare office but this can be done after you get treatment. Some doctors' charges may be partially refunded by the Medicare scheme. Claim at the local office before you leave.

(Continued)

Country	Documents needed to get medical treatment	What is normally free	What you pay charges for	Other information
Austria	UK passport.	In-patient treatment in public ward of public hospitals, except for a nominal charge of about £2 per day.	Prescribed medicines. All other medical services including treatment at a hospital out-patient department or doctors' surgery. Private treatment or accommodation in a public hospital. Ambulance travel.	If you are an Austrian national resident in the UK, you will need to show your Austrian passport and UK NHS medical card.
Barbados	UK passport (or NHS medical card if not a UK national).	Hospital treatment. Treatment at polyclinics. Ambulance travel. Prescribed medicines for children and the elderly.	Dental treatment. Prescribed medicines.	
British Virgin Islands	Proof of UK residence (e.g. NHS medical card or UK driving licence).	Hospital and other medical treatment for persons aged 70 or over and school-age children.	Other visitors are charged for all services at rates applicable to residents.	
Bulgaria	UK passport and NHS medical card.	Hospital treatment. Other medical and dental treatment.	Prescribed medicines.	
Channel Islands (if staying less than 3 months)	Proof of UK residence (e.g. driving licence or NHS medical card).	*On Guernsey/Alderney:* Hospital treatment. Emergency dental treatment. Other medical care. Ambulance travel (Guernsey).	Some prescribed medicines.	No out-patient department at Guernsey General Hospital.
		On Jersey: Hospital in-patient and out-patient treatment. Ambulance travel. *On Sark:* Medical treatment.	Treatment at a doctor's surgery. Dental care. Prescribed medicines.	Free treatment at a family-doctor-type clinic is available most weekday mornings at the General Hospital. Hospital treatment provided in Guernsey.
Czech Republic	UK passport	Hospital treatment. Other medical care.	Prescribed medicines.	
Falkland Islands	Proof of UK residence (e.g. medical card or UK driving licence).	Hospital treatment. Dental treatment. Other medical treatment. Prescribed medicines. Ambulance travel.		
Finland	UK passport.	Consultation at health centre.	Hospital treatment. Dental treatment. Ambulance travel. Prescribed medicines.	Some charges may be partially refunded by Finnish Sickness Insurance Institution. Claim at the local office before leaving.
Hong Kong	NHS medical card and valid passport.	Emergency treatment at certain hospitals/clinics.*	Small charges are levied for all other services and treatment.	*List available from DH IRU Room 318, Hannibal House, Elephant and Castle, London SE1 6TE (for N. Ireland, see footnote 2).
Hungary	UK passport.	Treatment in hospital, polyclinic or at a doctor's surgery.	Dental & ophthalmic treatment. Prescribed medicines (flat-rate charge).	
Iceland	UK passport (or NHS medical card if not a UK national).	Hospital in-patient treatment. Emergency dental treatment for children aged 6–15.	Hospital out-patient treatment. Medical treatment. Prescribed medicines. Other dental treatment. Ambulance travel.	
Isle of Man	No documents needed.	Treatment as for UK National Health Service.	Dental treatment. Prescribed medicines.	
Malta (up to 30 days stay)	UK passport.	Immediately necessary medical treatment in a government hospital, area health centre (polyclinic) or district dispensary.	Non-government hospital dispensary or polyclinic treatment. Treatment at a private doctor's surgery. Prescribed medicines.	
Montserrat	Proof of UK residence (e.g. NHS medical card or UK driving licence).	Treatment at government institutions for persons aged over 65 and under 16. Dental treatment for school-age children.	Hospital in-patient and out-patient treatment. Hospital accommodation. Most prescribed medicines. Dental treatment. Ambulance travel.	Family-doctor-type treatment is available at government clinics and the hospital casualty department. A charge is made.

(Continued)

Country	Documents needed to get medical treatment	What is normally free	What you pay charges for	Other information
New Zealand	UK passport.	Dental treatment (persons under 19). Some prescribed medicines.	Treatment at hospitals. Treatment at a doctor's surgery. Some medicines.	Ask hospital or doctor if a refund is due. If not, claim at the local health office. Cash benefits from New Zealand Department of Health reduce charges.
Norway	UK passport.	Hospital in-patient treatment. Ambulance travel.	Other hospital treatment. Treatment at doctor's surgery. Dental treatment (except extractions). Prescribed medicines.	Some changes may be partially refunded by Norwegian social insurance scheme. Obtain receipt for payment and claim at social insurance office of district where treatment was obtained before you leave Norway.
Poland	NHS medical card.	Hospital treatment. Some dental treatment. Other medical treatment.	Doctor's visit (e.g. to your hotel). 30% of cost of prescribed medicines from a public pharmacy.	
Romania	UK passport and NHS medical card or UK driving licence.	Hospital Treatment. Some dental treatment. Other medical treatment.	Medicines supplied by public pharmacy.	
Slovak Republic	UK passport.	Hospital Treatment. Other medical care.	Prescribed medicines.	
St Helena	Proof of UK residence (e.g. UK passport or NHS medical card).	Hospital treatment in out-patient clinics during normal clinic times.	Hospital in-patient treatment. Dental treatment. Prescribed medicines. Ambulance travel.	Family-doctor-type treatment is available at the hospital out-patient clinic.
Sweden	UK passport.	Hospital in-patient treatment, including medicines. Dental treatment for children.	Hospital out-patient treatment. Other medical treatment. Prescribed medicines (except for certain chronic conditions). Ambulance travel.	Travelling expenses to hospital may be partially refunded.
Turks & Caicos Islands	Proof of UK residence (e.g. NHS medical card or UK driving licence).	All treatment to those under 16 and over 65. *On Grand Turk Island:* Dental treatment (at dental clinic). Prescribed medicines. Ambulance travel. *On Outer Islands:* Medical treatment at government clinics. Prescribed medicines.	*On Grand Turk Island:* Hospital in-patient treatment. Other medical treatment and the Town clinic.	*On Outer Islands:* No hospital services available on the outer islands.
USSR (former)	UK passport.	Hospital treatment. Some dental treatment. Other medical treatment.	Prescribed medicines.	This agreement applies to the following republics of the former USSR: Armenia, Azerbaijan, Belarus, Georgia, Kazakhstan, Kyrgyzstan, Moldova, Russia, Tajikistan, Turkmenistan, Uzbekistan, Ukraine.
Yugoslavia	UK passport if you are a UK national. If you are a UK resident but not a UK national you will need a certificate of insurance, obtainable from DSS Contributions Agency, Overseas Branch, Newcastle upon Tyne. NE98 1YX.	Hospital treatment. Some dental treatment. Other medical treatment.	Prescribed medicines.	If you are a Yugoslav national resident in the UK, you will need to show your Yugoslav passport and a certificate of UK social security insurance, obtainable from DSS Contributions Agency, Overseas Branch, Newcastle upon Tyne NE98 1YX (for N. Ireland see footnote 1). If you are not a UK/Yugoslav national but are the dependent of someone who is, you should also apply for a certificate. The agreement applies to all the successor republics.

(1) DHSS, Overseas Branch, Lindsay House, 8–14 Callender Street, Belfast BT1 5DP. (2) DHSS, Family Practitioner Services Branch, Room 909, Dundonald House, Upper Newtownards Road, Belfast BT4 3SF.

Immunization Recommendations

(as at mid-1993)

E = Immunization is an essential requirement for entry to the country concerned and you will require a certificate.
E1 = Immunization essential except for infants under 1 year (but note the advice above).
E2 = Immunization essential (except for infants under 1 year) unless arriving from non-infected areas and staying for less than 2 weeks. The UK is a non-infected area, but if travelling via equatorial Africa or South America, seek medical advice.
E3 = Vaccination essential if the traveller arrives from an infected country – i.e. where yellow fever is present. This will not apply if your journey is direct from the UK.
r = Immunization or tablets recommended for protection against disease, but note that for Yellow Fever pregnant women and infants under 9 months should not normally be immunized and therefore should avoid exposure to infection.
M = Meningitis, depending on area visited and time of year.
a) = Depends on area visited.
b) = Limited risk in São Tiàgo Island.
c) = Recommended for all travellers going to the Province of Darién.
d) = Certificate required only if leaving Paraguay to go to endemic areas.

Country	Hep. A Polio Typhoid*	Malaria	Yellow Fever	Other
Afghanistan	r	r	E3	–
Albania	–	–	E3	–
Algeria	r	r a)	E3	–
Angola	r	r	E3	–
Anguilla	–	–	–	–
Antigua/Barbuda	–	–	E3	–
Argentina	r	r a)	–	–
Armenia	–	–	–	–
Australia	–	–	E3	–
Austria	–	–	–	–
Azerbaijan	–	–	–	–
Bahamas	r	–	E3	–
Bahrain	r	–	E3	–
Bali	r	r	E3	–
Bangladesh	r	r	E3	–
Barbados	r	–	E3	–
Belarus	–	–	–	–
Belize	r	r	E3	–
Benin	r	r	E1	M
Bermuda	–	–	–	–
Bhutan	r	r	E3	–
Bolivia	r	r	E3 r	–
Bosnia & Herzegovina	r	–	–	–
Botswana	r	r	–	–
Brazil	r	r	E3 r	–
Brunei	r	–	E3	–
Bulgaria	r	–	–	–
Burkina Faso	r	r	E1	–
Burma (see Myanmar)	–	–	–	–
Burundi	r	r	E3 r	–
Cambodia	r	r	E3	–
Cameroon	r	r	E1	M
Canada	–	–	–	–
Cape Verde	r	r b)	E3	–
Cayman Islands	r	–	–	–
Central African Republic	r	r	E1	M
Chad	r	r	E1	M
Chile	r	–	–	–
China	r	r a)	E3	–
Colombia	r	r	r	–
Comoros	r	r	–	–
Congo	r	r	E1	–
Cook Islands	r	–	–	–
Costa Rica	r	r	–	–
Côte d'Ivoire	r	r	E1	M
Croatia	r	–	–	–
Cuba	r	–	–	–
Cyprus	–	–	–	–
Czech & Slovak Reps	r	–	–	–
Djibouti	r	r	E3	–
Dominica	r	–	E3	–
Dominican Republic	r	r	–	–
Ecuador	r	r	E3 r	–
Egypt	r	r a)	E3	–
El Salvador	r	r	E3	–
Equatorial Guinea	r	r	E3 r	–
Estonia	–	–	–	–
Ethiopia	r	r	E3 r	M
Falkland Islands	–	–	–	–
Fiji	r	–	E3	–
Finland	–	–	–	–
Gabon	r	r	E1	–
The Gambia	r	r	E3 r	M
Georgia	r	–	–	–
Ghana	r	r	E1	–
Greece	–	–	E3	–
Greenland	–	–	–	–
Grenada	r	–	E3	–
Guam	r	–	–	–
Guatemala	r	r	E3	–
Guiana, French	r	r	E1	–
Guinea	r	r	E3 r	–
Guinea-Bissau	r	r	E3 r	–
Guyana	r	r	E3 r	–
Haiti	r	r	E3	–
Honduras	r	r	E3	–
Hong Kong	r	r a)	–	–
Hungary	–	–	–	–
Iceland	–	–	–	–
India	r	r	E3	M
Indonesia	r	r	E3	–
Iran	r	r	E3	–
Iraq	r	r	E3	–
Israel	r	–	–	–
Ivory Coast (see Côte d'Ivoire)	–	–	–	–
Jamaica	r	–	E3	–
Japan	r	–	–	–
Jordan	r	–	E3	–
Kampuchea	r	r	E3	–
Kazakhstan	r	–	–	–
Kenya	r	r	E3	M
Kyrgyzstan	r	–	–	–
Kiribati	r	–	E3	–
Korea (North & South)	r	–	– –	
Kuwait	r	–	–	–
Laos	r	r	E3	–
Latvia	–	–	–	–
Lebanon	r	–	E3	–
Lesotho	r	–	E3 –	
Liberia	r	r	E1	M
Libya	r	r a)	E3	–
Lithuania	–	–	–	–
Macedonia	r	–	–	–
Madagascar	r	r	E3	–
Madeira	–	–	E3	–
Malawi	r	r	E3	–
Malaysia	r	r	E3	–
Maldives	r		E3	–
Mali	r	r	E1	M
Malta	–	–	E3	–
Mauritania	r	r	E2	–
Mauritius	r	r a)	E3	–
Mexico	r	r	E3	–
Moldova	r	–	–	–
Monaco	–	–	–	–
Mongolia	r	–	– –	
Montserrat	r	–	E3	–
Morocco	r	r a)	–	
Mozambique	r	r	E3	–

(Continued)

Country	Hep. A Polio Typhoid*	Malaria	Yellow Fever	Other
Myanmar (Burma)	r	r	E3	–
Namibia	r	r	E3 r	–
Nauru	r	–	E3	–
Nepal	r	r	E3	M
Netherlands, Antilles	r	–	E3	–
New Caledonia	r	–	E3	–
New Zealand	–	–	–	–
Nicaragua	r	r	E3	–
Niger	r	r	E1	M
Nigeria	r	r	E3 r	M
Niue	r	–	E3	–
Norway	–	–	–	–
Oman	r	r	E3	–
Pakistan	r	r	E3	M
Panama	r	r	c)	–
Papua New Guinea	r	r	E3	–
Paraguay	r	r	d)	–
Peru	r	r	E3 r	–
Philippines	r	r	E3	–
Pitcairn Island	r	–	E3	–
Poland	–	–	–	–
Polynesia, French (Tahiti)	r	–	E3	–
Puerto Rico	r	–	–	–
Qatar	r	–	E3	–
Réunion	r	–	E3	–
Romania	r	–	–	–
Russia	–	–	–	–
Rwanda	r	r	E1	–
St Helena	r	–	–	–
St Kitts & Nevis	r	–	E3	–
St Lucia	r	–	E3	–
St Vincent & Grenadines	r	–	E3	–
Samoa	r	–	E3	–
São Tome & Principe	r	r	E2	–
Saudi Arabia	r	r	E3	M
Senegal	r	r	E1	M
Seychelles	r	–	–	–
Sierra Leone	r	r	E3 r	M
Singapore	r	–	E3	–
Slovenia	r	–	–	–
Solomon Islands	r	r	E3	–
Somalia	r	r	E3 r	–
South Africa	r	r	E3	–
Sri Lanka	r	r	E3	–
Sudan	r	r	E3 r	M
Suriname	r	r	E3	–
Swaziland	r	r	E3	–
Sweden	–	–	–	–
Switzerland	–	–	–	–
Syria	r	r	E3	
Tahiti	r		E3	
Taiwan	r		E3	
Tajikistan	r	r	–	–
Tanzania	r	r	E3	
Thailand	r	r	E3	–
Togo	r	r	E1	M
Tonga	r		E3	
Trinidad & Tobago	r	–	E3	–
Tunisia	r	–	E3	–
Turkey	r	r a)	–	–
Turkmenistan	r	–	–	–
Turks & Caicos Islands	–	–	–	–
Tuvalu	r	–	E3	–
Uganda	r	r	E3 r	M
United Arab Emirates	r	r	–	–
Ukraine	–	–	–	–
Uruguay	r	–	–	–
USA	–	–	–	–
Uzbekistan	r	–	–	–
Vanuatu	r	r	–	–
Venezuela	r	r	r	–
Vietnam	r	r	E3	–
Virgin Islands	r	–	–	–
West Indies	r	–	E3	–
French West Indies	r		E3	
Yemen Arab Rep. (North)	r	r	E3	–
Yemen Dem. Rep. (South)	r	r	E3	–
Yugoslavia (former)	r	–	–	–
Zaire	r	r	E1	–
Zambia	r	r	r	–
Zimbabwe	r	r	E3	–

* Immunization against typhoid may be less important for short stays in 1st-class conditions.

Immunization Checklist

Recommended for all travellers:
If you have not previously been immunized against diphtheria, polio and tetanus, this is an ideal opportunity to get it done.

For all areas except North and West Europe, North America, Australia and New Zealand:
Poliomyelitis

For areas where standards of hygiene and sanitation may be less than ideal (in addition to close attention to food, water and personal hygiene):
Typhoid
Hepatitis A

For infected areas, as advised:
Anti-malarial tablets (and precautions against mosquito bites)
Yellow fever
Tuberculosis

In some circumstances:
Cholera
Rabies
Japanese encephalitis
Tick-encephalitis
Meningococcal meningitis

Note: Changes to these and other recommendations are notified on ISTEL.

The Department of Health produces a booklet called "Health Advice for Travellers", which is available free of charge – call the Health Literature Line any time on 0800 555 777.

Theme & Leisure Parks 1993

Source: British Tourist Authority

Alton Towers
Alton
Staffs ST10 4DB
Tel: 0538 702200

American Adventure
Ilkeston
Derbyshire DE7 5FX
Tel: 0773 531521

Blackgang Chine Fantasy Theme Park
Chale
Ventnor
Isle of Wight PO38 2HN
Tel: 0983 730330

Blackpool Pleasure Beach
525 Promenade
Blackpool
Lancs FT4 1EZ
Tel: 0253 41033

Camelot Theme Park
Charnock Richard
Chorley
Preston
Lancs PR7 5LP
Tel: 0257 453044

Chessington World of Adventure
Leatherhead Road
Chessington
Surrey KT9 2NE
Tel: 0372 725050

Dobwalls
Liskeard
Cornwall PL14 6HD
Tel: 0579 20325

Drayton Manor Park & Zoo
Tamworth
Staffs B78 3TW
Tel: 0827 287979

Dreamland White Knuckle Theme Park
Marine Terrace
Margate
Kent CT9 1XL
Tel: 0843 227011

Flambards Triple Theme Park
Culdrose Manor
Helston
Cornwall TR13 0GA
Tel: 0326 574549

Flamingo Land Zoo & Fun Park
Kirby Misperton
Malton
Yorks YO17 0UX
Tel: 065 386 287

Fort Fun
Royal Parade
Eastbourne
E. Sussex BN22 7LU
Tel: 0323 642833

Frontierland
Marine Road
Morecambe
Lancs LA4 4DG
Tel: 0524 410024

Funcoast World (Butlin's)
Skegness
Lincs PE25 1NJ
Tel: 0754 762311

Gulliver's Kingdom
Temple Walk
Matlock Bath
Derbyshire DE4 3PG
Tel: 0629 580540

Gulliver's World
Warrington
Warks
Tel: 0925 444888

Lightwater Valley Theme Park
North Stanley
Ripon
Yorks HG4 3HT
Tel: 0765 85321

Lowther Park
Hackthorpe
Penrith
Cumbria CA10 2HG
Tel: 093 12 523

Marvels Leisure & Amusement Park
Northstead Manor Gardens
North Bay
Scarborough
Yorks YO12 7UZ
Tel: 0723 372744

Metroland
MetroCentre
Gateshead
Tyne & Wear NE11 9YZ
Tel: 091–493 2048

New Palace Amusement Park
Marine Promenade
New Brighton
Merseyside L45 2JX
Tel: 051–639 6041

Once Upon a Time
Woolacombe
Devon EX34 7HH
Tel: 0271 867 474

Palms Tropical Oasis
92 London Road
Stapeley
Nantwich
Cheshire CW5 7LH
Tel: 0270 628628

Paultons Park
Ower
Romsey
Hampshire SO51 6AL
Tel: 0703 814442

Pleasureland Amusement Park
Esplanade
Southport
Lancs PR8 1RX
Tel: 0704 532717

Pleasurewood Hills American Theme Park
Corton Road
Lowestoft
Suffolk NR32 5DZ
Tel: 0502 513626

Rainbow's End
Hotham Park
Bognor Regis
W. Sussex PO21 1DB
Tel: 0243 825255

Rotunda Amusement Park
The Seafront
Folkestone
Kent CT20 1PX
Tel: 0303 53461

Smarts
Seafront
Littlehampton
W. Sussex BN17 5LL
Tel: 0903 721200

Southcoast World (Butlin's)
Bognor Regis
W. Sussex PO21 1JJ
Tel: 0243 822445

St Agnes Leisure Park
St Agnes
Cornwall
Tel: 087 255 2793

Thorpe Park
Staines Road
Chertsey
Surrey KT16 8PN
Tel: 0932 562633

Tower Park
Poole
Dorest
Tel: 0202 749094

Watermouth Castle
Ilfracombe
Devon EX34 9SL
Tel: 0271 863879

Watersplash World
North Bay
Scarborough
Yorks
Tel: 0723 372744

World in Miniature
Goonhavern
Cornwall
Tel: 0872 572828

Seaside Awards 1993

Source: British Tourist Authority

Developed by the Tidy Britain Group, the Seaside Award was designed to help raise standards of cleanliness and safety on British beaches.

Basic requirements

All beaches must be free of litter, industrial waste, sewage-related debris, oil pollution and large accumulations of rotting seaweed.

Resort beaches have to meet 28 different criteria, including the provision of fresh drinking water, toilets, parking, first aid, lifeguards or life-saving equipment and facilities for the disabled.

Rural beaches must provide easy access and appoint a special "guardian" who is responsible for ensuring that standards are maintained.

Water Quality

Water must meet the mandatory standard laid down by the EC Bathing Water Directive. This is indicated by a Seaside Award pale blue and yellow flag.

If the water meets the high guideline standard of the EC Directive, this is indicated by a Premier Seaside Award dark blue and yellow flag.

In all cases, the water must be sampled and tested at least 20 times a year.

Award Winners

P = Premier seaside award (for all beaches which meet EC water guideline and fulfil all land-based critera).
B = Blue Flag (a European award for resort beaches only, which allows comparison of standards between and within countries of the EC).

ENGLAND
Resort beaches

Beach Street, Sheerness **P/B**
Bexhill
Bognor Regis
Boscombe
Bournemouth **P/B**
Bridlington North
Bridlington South
Broadsands, Torbay
Colwell Bay **P/B**
Crinnis **P/B**
Dawlish Warren **P**
Eastbourne
Filey
Friars Cliff, Christchurch
Goodrington South Sands, Torbay
Hayling Island West **P/B**
Hunstanton **P/B**
Littlehampton
Lowestoft South
Margate
Meadfoot, Torquay **P/B**
Oddicombe, Torquay **P/B**
Paignton, Torbay
Poole Sandbanks **P/B**
Porthmeor **P/B**
Redgate, Torquay
Ryde East
Sandhaven
Sandown
Scarborough North
Scarborough South
Sennen Cove **P/B**
Southsea
Southwold **P/B**
Swanage Bay
Three Shells, Southend-on-Sea

(Continued)

England *contd.*
Resort beaches *contd.*
Tynemouth Longsands **P/B**
Viking Bay, Broadstairs
Wells-next-the-Sea
Weymouth Central
Whitby, West Cliff **P/B**
Woolacombe **P/B**

Rural beaches
Ainsdale
Aldeburgh **P**
Bamburgh **P**
Bantham **P**
Beadnall Bay **P**
Birling Gap **P**
Blackpool Sands **P**
Camber
Constantine Bay, St Merryn **P**
Crooklets, Bude **P**
Dymchurch
East Cowes
Harlyn Bay, St Merryn **P**
Highcliffe Castle, Christchurch
Kessingland **P**
Lepe Country Park
Maidencombe, Torquay **P**
Newton Haven **P**
Pembroke, Guernsey
Pevensey Bay
Polzeath **P**
Port Solf, Guernsey
Romney Sands, Littlestone-on-Sea
Runswick Bay
Sandsend **P**
Sandymouth, Bude **P**
Shoeburyness **P**
Snettisham
Springvale, IoW
St Helens, IoW
Strete Gate
Torcross **P**
Trebarwith Strand, Tintagel
Treyarnon, St Merryn **P**
Warkworth **P**
Watcombe, Torquay **P**
Widemouth Sand, Bude **P**
Winchelsea
Yaverland, IoW

NORTHERN IRELAND
Resort beaches
Benone **P/B**
West Bay Strand/ Portrush **P/B**

Rural Beaches
Cranfield Bay

SCOTLAND
Resort beaches
Fraserburgh
Nairn Central
Peterhead, Lido
St Andrews, West
Stonehaven

Rural Beaches
Dalmedie
Gullane Bents
Inverboyndie
Sandend

WALES
Resort beaches
Cefn Sidan, Pembrey Country Park **P/B**
Tenby North **P/B**
Traeth Y Gogledd, Aberystwyth
Whitesands, St Davids **P/B**

Rural Beaches
Aberdaron **P**
Abereiddy **P**
Amroth **P**
Barafundle **P**
Benllech
Borth
Broadhaven, Haverfordwest **P**
Broadhaven, South Pembroke **P**
Caerfal, St Davids **P**
Cel Bach
Cwmtydu
Dale
Gilfach Yr Halen
Llandanwg
Llangrannog
Lydstep **P**
Manorbier **P**
Morfa/Dinas Dinnie **P**
Mwnt **P**
Newgale **P**
Newport **P**
Penbryn
Port Eynon **P**
Poppit
Rest Bay, Porthcawl
Rhosneigr **P**
Skrinkle **P**
Southerndown
Tenby South
Traeth Y de, Aberaeron
Traeth Y Gogledd, Aberystwyth
Traethgwyn, Newquay
Trearddur Bay
Tresaith
West Angle Bay **P**
Yr Harbwr, Newquay

Hints for Home-Buyers

Source: Council of Mortgage Lenders

Who to approach for a mortgage

Many financial institutions undertake mortgage lending and would be pleased to give advice. These include building societies, banks, finance houses, insurance companies and specialist mortgage companies. They offer many different types of mortgage and you should compare the advantages of different mortgages before making up your mind.

When to consult a mortgage-lending institution

As soon as possible – even before you start looking at properties. Mortgage lenders are experienced in matters of house purchase and will tell you how much you can expect to borrow based on your income. It is also worthwhile considering what level of payments you think you can afford. Inspecting houses beyond your pocket only leads to disappointment.

If you make an offer to purchase, always be sure that it is initially verbal only and "subject to survey and contract". In any event, it is best to obtain the advice of a solicitor or a licensed conveyancer before signing any documents or putting anything in writing.

How much can you borrow?

This will mainly depend upon your financial position because neither you nor the mortgage lender will want the monthly repayments to overstrain your budget. As a general guide, you can expect to borrow about 3 times your gross annual income, i.e. before tax has been deducted. If people are borrowing jointly, the multiples may be 3 times the gross annual income of the higher earner, plus once the other income.

Although mortgage lending institutions will sometimes lend up to 100% of a property's value or purchase price, whichever is the lower, it is preferable for borrowers to have some stake in the property themselves. Loans of 90% and 95% are common for first-time buyers. If the advance is above 70–80% of the valuation, the lender will require some form of additional security. Usually this is a guarantee by an insurance company, which the mortgage lender will arrange, known as indemnity insurance. A single premium has to be paid by the borrower for this guarantee, and it may be possible for the fee to be added to the loan and repaid over the life of the mortgage.

How is your tax position affected?

The interest element in the repayment on the first £30,000 of a mortgage loan qualifies for income tax relief at the basic rate of tax (25% for 1992/93). Whether you have a repayment mortgage or an endowment loan (this is when you pay interest only to the mortgage lender, but at the same time contribute to an endowment insurance policy which is used to pay off the loan at the end of the mortgage term), the system by which you obtain your tax relief on the interest you pay is the same.

Your mortgage lender will calculate the amount of basic rate tax relief you are entitled to and deduct this from your monthly mortgage repayment figure. Thus the amount you pay your lender each month will be net of tax relief. The Inland Revenue will reimburse your lender with the difference between the net figure you have paid and the amount the lender would have asked you to pay had there been no tax relief on the interest element of your repayments. This arrangement is called Mortgage Interest Relief at Source (MIRAS). Borrowers with insufficient income to be subject to tax also benefit from the tax deduction system in the same way as a taxpayer and do not have to account to the Inland Revenue for deductions that have been made.

How much will you have to find in cash?

You will have to find, as your personal stake in the property, an amount equal to the difference between the purchase price and the loan from the lending institution. This will have to be paid at the time of purchase. The down-payment may prove a stumbling block and if you need to save towards this, you should choose a secure form of investment, such as a bank or building society account.

In addition to the immediate down-payment, you will have to pay the legal charges for the conveyance and the preparation of the mortgage, any Land Registry fee, stamp duty on the conveyance if the house costs more than £30,000 and the mortgage lender's valuation fee. The total of such initial costs on a £30,000 house with a 90% loan will be about £850. This figure does not allow for the costs of an independent structural survey or house-buyer's report, for removal expenses, or for the single premium to the insurance company for indemnity insurance on a higher-than-normal loan.

Is it worth getting an independent survey?

Yes, if you are in any doubt about the soundness of the property or about the reasonableness of the price. This will add to initial costs, but it may well pay you in the long run. The inspection by the mortgage lender's valuer may not reveal hidden faults. This is a valuation only and not a full structural survey. Lenders are not obliged to disclose their valuation report to borrowers but at the least you will be informed of any major defects noted by the valuer. If you know at the time you apply for your mortgage that you want a structural survey, tell your mortgage lender then. It may be possible for the lender's valuation to be done by a valuer who can simultaneously carry out the structural survey for you with some saving of cost. Some lenders offer a report on condition which costs less than a structural survey, yet will tell you more about the state of the property than a basic valuation.

What if the interest rate changes?

The mortgage rate is mainly determined by the rate which mortgage lenders have to pay in order to raise their funds. Since this rate varies, so does the rate normally charged to borrowers. However, you will always be given advance notice when your monthly repayment changes. It is sometimes possible to continue the same monthly repayment to the lender but if, when the rate goes up, you do not increase your repayments your total interest bill will be larger. The amount you pay your lender each month will also alter if the basic rate of tax relief is changed. Some lenders adjust the amount paid by the borrower on an annual basis, while others offer "fixed rate" loans, where the rate does not change for a given period.

What if you fall on hard times?

Naturally the mortgage lender will expect you to keep to your side of the contract and maintain your repayments regularly but, should you strike a bad patch, the lender will do everything possible to help you over it. The best plan is to take the lender into your confidence as soon as you think you cannot meet the monthly repayment; do not let arrears accumulate without getting in touch with your lender.

More detailed information and free leaflets may be obtained from BSA/CML Bookshop, 3 Savile Row, London W1X 1AF.

Home-Buyers' Glossary

Source: Council of Mortgage Lenders

Advance: The mortgage loan.
Bridging loan: Short-term loan enabling the borrower to bridge the gap between the purchase of a new house and the sale of the old.
Collateral: Property pledged as security against the repayment of the loan.
Completion: The final legal transfer of ownership of the property.
Contract: The written legal agreement between the seller and the buyer with regard to the property.
Conveyancer: Solicitor or licensed conveyancer who arranges the legal aspects of buying or selling property.
Conveyancing: The legal work in the sale and purchase of property.
Deeds: The legal documents which entitle the owner of the property to that property.
Disbursements: The fees such as stamp duty, Land Registry fees and search fees which are payable to the conveyancer by the buyer.
Equity: The difference between the value of the property and the amount of any loans secured against it.
Exchange of contracts: The point when both buyer and seller are legally bound to the transaction and the risk regarding the property passes to the buyer.
Freehold: Ownership of the property and the land on which it stands. This may also apply to flats if the leaseholders of a building form a limited company and buy the freehold jointly. In this case each leaseholder owns one share in the company.
Ground rent: Annual charge payable by leaseholders to the freeholder.
House-buyer's report: Surveyor's report on a property – less extensive than a structural survey.
Indemnity: Single payment for an insurance policy to cover the value of the property to lenders when they lend a high percentage of the purchase price.
Land Registry fee: A fee paid to the Land Registry to register ownership of a property.
Leasehold: Ownership of the property but not the land on which it stands, so that when the lease expires ownership of the property reverts to the freeholder.
Lessee: The person to whom a lease is granted.
Lessor: The person who grants a lease.
MIRAS: Mortgage Interest Relief At Source.
Mortgage: A loan made against the security of property.
Mortgagee: The person (or organization, e.g. a building society) lending the mortgage advance.
Mortgagor: The borrower, whose property stands as the security to the mortgage loan.
Principal: The amount of the loan on which interest is calculated.
Redemption: The final payment of a mortgage loan.
Redemption fee/Redemption interest: The charge made by some lenders if a mortgage redemption interest is ended early.
Stamp duty: A government tax of 1% on the purchase of a property costing £30,000 or more.
Subject to contract: Wording of any agreement before the exchange of contracts which allows either party to withdraw without incurring a penalty.
Survey: Full inspection of the property by a surveyor usually on behalf of the buyer.
Term: The length of time over which the mortgage loan is to be repaid.
Valuation: Inspection of the property to ascertain its acceptability to the lender as security against the mortgage loan, for which the borrower must pay.
Vendor: The person selling the property.

Average Regional House Prices at Mortgage Completion Stage (£)

Source: The Building Societies Association and Department of the Environment (5% sample survey of building society mortgage completions)

Period	Northern	Yorks & Humber	East Midlands	East Anglia	Greater London	South East (excl GL)	South West	West Midlands	North West	Wales	Scotland	Northern Ireland	UK
1980	17,710	17,689	18,928	22,808	30,968	29,832	25,293	21,663	20,092	19,363	21,754	23,656	23,596
1981	18,602	19,202	19,465	23,060	30,757	29,975	25,365	21,755	20,554	20,155	23,014	19,890	24,188
1982	18,071	18,180	19,487	23,358	30,712	29,676	25,514	20,992	20,744	19,662	22,522	20,177	23,644
1983	20,034	20,870	22,034	25,814	34,632	33,753	27,996	23,133	22,827	22,533	23,822	20,878	26,469
1984	22,604	22,356	24,377	28,296	39,346	37,334	30,612	24,989	24,410	23,665	25,865	21,455	29,106
1985	22,786	23,338	25,539	31,661	44,301	40,487	32,948	25,855	25,126	25,005	26,941	23,012	31,103
1986	24,333	25,607	28,483	36,061	54,863	48,544	38,536	28,437	27,503	27,354	28,242	25,743	36,276
1987	27,275	27,747	31,808	42,681	66,024	57,387	44,728	32,657	29,527	29,704	29,591	27,773	40,391
1988	30,193	32,685	40,521	57,295	77,697	72,561	58,457	41,700	34,074	34,244	31,479	29,875	49,355
1989	37,374	41,817	49,421	64,610	82,383	81,635	67,004	49,815	42,126	42,981	35,394	30,280	54,846
1990	43,655	47,231	52,620	61,427	83,821	80,525	65,378	54,694	50,005	46,464	41,744	31,849	59,785
1991	46,005	52,343	55,740	61,141	85,742	79,042	65,346	58,659	53,178	48,989	48,772	35,352	62,455
1992	48,347	52,278	54,599	56,770	78,254	74,347	61,460	57,827	56,377	49,685	49,224	37,775	60,821
1990 Q1	38,531	44,575	49,696	58,492	83,063	80,498	65,031	50,568	47,303	44,328	35,381	28,941	56,610
Q2	42,670	46,203	52,507	59,727	84,310	80,178	65,991	52,848	48,688	43,474	40,184	29,616	58,917
Q3	50,798	47,575	54,183	63,456	84,502	81,008	66,475	55,299	50,601	50,216	46,752	32,191	61,833
Q4	44,464	50,609	54,038	63,476	83,447	80,403	63,865	59,842	53,454	47,924	45,928	35,735	61,706
1991 Q1	45,556	47,424	52,625	61,861	87,455	78,382	64,312	54,378	50,262	47,336	47,296	32,162	60,625
Q2	44,177	52,728	55,835	59,442	84,863	77,356	62,826	58,721	52,185	45,952	47,887	33,273	61,047
Q3	46,369	52,943	57,277	63,760	86,356	79,769	68,322	60,578	55,049	51,414	48,910	37,197	63,926
Q4	47,375	54,883	56,523	59,131	84,513	80,034	65,268	58,726	54,516	50,463	50,634	38,166	63,489
1992 Q1	47,187	51,482	53,159	54,246	80,796	75,172	61,861	59,032	55,778	50,200	45,530	36,087	61,124
Q2	49,853	53,016	54,123	57,095	80,636	74,561	60,608	57,643	56,232	49,713	50,269	36,975	61,306
Q3	48,624	54,699	56,527	59,961	77,446	75,189	64,330	58,405	58,169	49,502	52,274	39,240	62,265
Q4	47,626	48,439	53,719	55,051	71,921	70,721	57,689	55,699	54,395	49,270	48,024	38,599	57,170

Mortgages

Source: Council of Mortgage Lenders

There are several types of mortgage available to borrowers.

Repayment Mortgage

This provides for regular monthly repayments such that, over the life of the mortgage (usually 20 or 25 years), the debt, together with interest, is entirely repaid.

The interest element in the repayments on the first £30,000 of a loan qualifies for income tax relief at the basic rate of tax. Most lenders calculate the repayments of borrowers with loans of up to £30,000 on a constant equal (unless the interest rate or the basic rate of tax changes) repayment basis taking into account the borrower's basic rate tax relief entitlement. Thus when the mortgage rate is 10% and tax relief is at the basic rate of 25%, a net rate of 7.5% will be applied. In this way a borrower pays a net rate directly to the lender which will recover the tax relief element from the Inland Revenue. Borrowers with insufficient income to pay tax will still benefit from the tax deduction system in the same way as a taxpayer and will not have to account to the Inland Revenue for deductions that have been made.

Instead of applying a net repayment system in which the repayments remain constant unless there is a change in the interest rate, or the basic rate of tax, some lenders may calculate payments on a repayment mortgage on an increasing net basis. This involves the lender calculating the tax relief due on the interest borrowers pay in a given year and deducting that from their gross repayments. In this way the mortgage repayments will be made net of tax relief and borrowers obtain the maximum tax relief in the first years of their mortgage. However, because the amount of interest they pay decreases as they pay back principal, the amount of tax relief they receive under this arrangement reduces accordingly. As a result they will be asked to increase their repayments each year to take this factor into account. The total amount paid over the whole period of the loan will be higher on this basis than under the constant net system.

The interest on repayment loans is normally charged on what is known as an annual rest basis. This means that the interest in the first year is charged on the initial loan for the period up to the end of the lender's financial year. In subsequent years interest is charged for the whole year on the debt outstanding at the beginning of the lender's financial year.

The initial mortgage term is relevant when mortgage rates change. When the rate rises borrowers are sometimes given the option of not increasing the repayment. The extent to which this can be done depends on the size of the increase in the rate and the outstanding term of the loan, the danger being that the current repayments will not suffice to meet the interest accruing on the amount. Thus there is far less scope to extend the term of a loan when the initial period is 30 years, where the interest element in the repayments is greater, than there is when it is 20 years. When mortgage rates fall borrowers may, if they wish, maintain their repayments and thus reduce the mortgage term.

Monthly Repayments on a £30,000 Loan*

Mortgage Rate %	20 Year Term £	25 Year Term £	30 Year Term £
7.00 (5.25 net)	204.90	182.10	167.40
7.50 (5.62 net)	211.80	189.00	174.60
8.00 (6.00 net)	218.10	195.60	181.80
8.50 (6.37 net)	225.00	202.80	189.30
9.00 (6.75 net)	231.60	210.00	196.50
9.50 (7.13 net)	238.80	217.50	204.60
10.00 (7.50 net)	245.40	224.40	211.80
10.50 (7.88 net)	252.90	232.20	220.20
11.00 (8.25 net)	259.50	239.40	227.40
11.50 (8.63 net)	267.30	247.50	236.10
12.00 (9.00 net)	273.90	254.70	243.60
12.50 (9.38 net)	282.00	261.00	252.30
13.00 (9.75 net)	288.90	270.30	259.80
13.50 (10.13 net)	296.70	278.70	268.80
14.00 (10.50 net)	303.90	286.20	276.60
14.50 (10.88 net)	312.00	294.30	285.00
15.00 (11.25 net)	319.20	302.40	293.40
15.50 (11.63 net)	327.60	311.10	302.40
16.00 (12.00 net)	334.80	318.90	310.50

*With Mortgage Interest Relief at Source.
Note: Figures assume annual rests for charging interest and no changes in the interest rate payable or in the basic rate of income tax relief at 25%.

Endowment Mortgage

A popular way of repaying a loan is to link it to an endowment assurance plan. During the life of the loan the borrower pays interest only to the lender, but simultaneously pays a monthly premium to an insurance company. At the end of the period of the mortgage the proceeds of the endowment policy are used to repay the mortgage loan and there may also be some money left over for the home-buyer. It should be noted that the interest and hence the tax relief on endowment loans remains constant because they are interest-only payments based on a mortgage debt which does not reduce.

One of the most popular types of endowment loan is a low-cost endowment mortgage. This assumes that the eventual proceeds of the policy (with bonuses) will be higher than the sum assured, and therefore provides for the initial sum assured to be lower than the size of the loan, thereby reducing the premium which has to be paid. At the end of the mortgage period the borrower can expect an additional capital sum, but if the proceeds of the policy (with bonuses) are less than the size of the loan, the borrower will have to find the difference.

Endowment mortgages have the advantage of providing for the loan to be paid off in full in the event of the borrower's death. In the case of non-profit and with-profits policies, the policy itself gives the necessary life cover. In the case of low-cost endowment mortgages, the cover is given partly through the endowment policy but, as this is not sufficient, also by a term insurance policy which is included in the "package" arranged by the insurance company.

One disadvantage of endowment loans is that when mortgage rates increase it is not usually possible for the borrower to extend the term of the loan; the higher repayments will need to be met in full. This point, together with the fact that endowment policies have a low "surrender" value in the early years, needs to be considered before a borrower chooses the endowment method of repayment.

It is not possible to give exact figures for the cost of an endowment mortgage because different insurance companies offer different terms (age and health are of course very relevant) and bonuses cannot be accurately predicted. However, the table below shows some typical monthly figures over 25 years. For comparison repayment loan figures are also shown.

Monthly Payments on a £30,000 Loan Over 25 Years

	Repayment Mortgage (10%)	Low-Cost With-Profits Endowment Mortgage (10%)	Low-Start Endowment Mortgage (10%)
Actual monthly repayment to mortgage lender net of tax relief...	£224.40	£187.50	£187.50
Insurance premium (example)	–	£40.90	£24.45
Total cost	£224.40	£228.40	£211.95
*Possible bonus	–	£14,000.00	£14,000.00

*These figures are based on the projected total value of the policies on maturity less £30,000 capital repaid to the mortgage lender.

Note: The insurance premiums on a low-start endowment mortgage will increase as the term passes.

Fixed-Rate Mortgage

The lender may offer a mortgage where the interest rate remains fixed, say, between 2 and 5 years, but sometimes longer. However, after the fixed rate term has expired, the interest rate will either change to the current variable rate or to a new fixed rate.

The advantage of a fixed-rate mortgage is that it guarantees the amount of the monthly repayment for a definite period. This may be useful if income will be limited for a time (for example, if a couple has a child and the woman stops working) so that repayments can be accurately budgeted for in advance. However, if general interest rates fall below the level of the fixed rate, it could work out an expensive option.

Deferred-Interest Mortgage

This type of loan offers a means of reducing repayments in the early years of the mortgage by deferring part of the interest payments until a later time. This is achieved by adding the interest the borrower has not paid to the amount of the loan, so the amount borrowed actually increases over time. After a certain fixed period the interest rate increases to the lender's standard level and there is a corresponding increase in the monthly repayment.

The disadvantages of such mortgages should be considered carefully. It is possible for borrowers to overcommit themselves for the future, anticipating a rise in income which can in fact prove to be insufficient to meet their increased repayments. Also, if interest rates have risen and the deposit on their property was small, borrowers may find that when their low-interest term expires, they have an outstanding loan which is greater than the actual value of their mortgaged home. These types of loan are also usually subject to substantial early redemption fees.

Some low-start mortgages simply offer borrowers a straightforward reduction in the interest rate for the first year or so and do not "roll up" the interest. This may provide a useful discount for the early part of the mortgage term.

Cap-and-Collar Mortgage

A cap-and-collar mortgage fixes the maximum and minimum rates of interest which may be charged on the loan for a given term. This has an obvious advantage during times of high interest rates, but at a time of low interest rates, the minimum limit may exceed current general rates so that repayments are higher than they would be with a variable rate mortgage.

Personal Equity Plan (PEP) Mortgage

With this type of loan the borrower repays interest only to the mortgage lender and simultaneously contributes to a Personal Equity Plan which is designed to repay the loan at the end of the mortgage term. The PEP is usually invested in unit trusts and is free from capital gains tax.

The advantage of a PEP mortgage is that it may bring high returns (more than sufficient to repay the mortgage loan) for relatively modest contributions.

The disadvantage is that it is a relatively high-risk option – unit trusts do not guarantee a certain level of return, and separate life cover will also be required by the lender.

Foreign Currency Mortgage

With a currency mortgage a loan is arranged in sterling which the lender then converts to the currency of a country with a lower interest rate than the UK.

However, foreign currency mortgages are a high-risk option since repayments are dependent on trends in international exchange rates.

Pension-Linked Loans

Home-buyers who are either self-employed or have a personal pension can elect to link a loan to a pension plan. During the life of the loan, the borrower pays interest only to the mortgage lender and, simultaneously, makes contributions to a personal pension plan. As tax relief is available on pension plan contributions as well as on the interest payments, this method is particularly attractive to those eligible. At the end of the mortgage the proceeds of the pension fund can be used to repay the mortgage loan and, additionally, provide a pension for retirement, although no lump sum will be available to supplement income from the pension.

Stamp Duty

Source: Council of Mortgage Lenders

Value of Property £	Stamp Duty £
Up to 60,000	–
60,000	–
62,000	620
66,000	660
70,000	700
74,000	740
78,000	780
82,000	820
86,000	860
90,000	900

Housing Associations

Source: Council of Mortgage Lenders

Housing associations are non-profit making organization which own and manage housing for people on low incomes or for special needs groups, e.g. the elderly or disabled. There are more than 2500 housing associations in England alone, and associations also operate in Scotland, Wales and Northern Ireland.

In England the Housing Corporation, a government agency, registers, funds, promotes and monitors housing associations. Since 1989, the agency Scottish Homes has performed these functions in Scotland, and Tai Cymru (Housing for Wales) does the same in Wales.

All housing associations are free to sell to their tenants should they so wish. Housing association tenants who cannot buy their dwellings are eligible for government grants to help them buy a home on the open market.

Housing associations are funded by a mixture of subsidies such as housing association grants (HAG) from the Housing Corporation and private finance, e.g. from building societies which lend them money on mortgage. The subsidy element is designed to make up the difference between the association's revenue from charging "affordable" rents and its actual costs.

Major housing associations include the Church Housing Association Ltd (families, the elderly, single homeless), the Guinness Trust (general housing), Jephson Homes (elderly, disabled, general), North British Housing Association Ltd (general), the Peabody Trust (the poor of London) and the Samuel Lewis Housing Trust (low income/homeless). There are thousands of others, many of them small or local associations serving a specific sector (e.g. the deaf). Most are registered with the Housing Corporation and are members of the National Federation of Housing Associations.

Useful Addresses

The Housing Corporation
149 Tottenham Court Road
London W1P 0BN
Tel: 071-387 9466

National Federation of Housing Associations
175 Grays Inn Road
London WC1X 8UP
Tel: 071-278 6571

Northern Ireland Federation of Housing Associations
Carlisle Memorial Centre
88 Clifton Street
Belfast BT13 1AB
Tel: 0232 230446

Scottish Federation of Housing Associations Ltd
40 Castle Street North
Edinburgh EH2 3BN
Tel: 031-226 6777

Scottish Homes
Thistle House
Haymarket Terrace
Edinburgh EH12

Tai Cymru (Housing for Wales)
25–30 Lambourne
Llanishen
Cardiff CF4 5ZJ
Tel: 0222 747979

The Welsh Federation of Housing Associations
Norbury House
Norbury Road
Fairwater
Cardiff CF5 3AS

Selected Advisory and Counselling Services

United Kingdom

Source: CSO

	Branch/centres (Numbers)			Clients (Thousands)		
	1971	1981	1991	1971	1981	1991
Al-Anon Family Groups	135	612	1,090	1.2	7.3	13.1
Alcoholics Anonymous[1]	420	1,550	2,800	6.3	30.0	45.0
Catholic Marriage Advisory Council	63	68	82	2.5	3.3	17.1
Citizens Advice Bureaux	512	914	2,111	1,500.0	4,514.6	7,648.9
Cruse Bereavement Care	13	73	185	5.0	9.1	22.5
Disablement Information and Advice Lines	–	44	100	–	40.0	75.0
Law Centres	1	41	60	1.0	155.0	452.4
Leukaemia Care Society	1	21	75	0.2	1.7	6.5

(Continued)

	Branch/centres (Numbers)			Clients (Thousands)		
	1971	1981	1991	1971	1981	1991
Relate[2]	141	178	133	21.6	38.3	70.0
Samaritans	127	180	185	89.0	314.7	470.0
Young People's Counselling and Advisory Service	–	55	125	–	30.0	113.0

(1) 1991 column contains 1990 data. (2) Including Marriage counselling in Scotland.

Citizens Advice Bureaux Enquiries

Source: CSO

Percentages

	England & Wales and Northern Ireland			Scotland		
	1980–81	1985–86	1991–92	1980–81	1985–86	1991–92
Types of enquiry						
Consumer, trade and business[1]	18.6	17.8	23.3	19.4	22.2	11.0
Housing, property and land	15.8	15.1	10.1	15.1	11.1	9.0
Social security	9.7	19.5	23.1	11.7	23.0	–
Family and personal	14.8	10.7	9.0	12.3	9.8	8.0
Employment	10.0	9.9	11.2	10.1	13.4	13.0
Taxes and Duties	2.7	2.5	5.0	2.7	–	–
Administration of justice	8.5	8.3	6.6	7.7	1.0	1.0
Holidays, travel and leisure	4.6	2.8	2.0	3.0	0.7	1.0
Health	3.6	3.0	2.1	3.6	–	–
Other	11.7	10.4	7.6	14.4	18.9	57.0

(1) Includes consumer debt.

Dangerous Dogs Act

Since 30 November 1991 it has been a legal requirement to register the following breeds of dog, unless you have a Certificate of Exemption:

- Pit Bull Terrier
- Japanese Tosa
- Dogo Argentino
- Fila Braziliero

In addition, it is a criminal offence to do the following:

- breed from your dog
- sell or exchange your dog, or offer or advertise your dog for sale or exchange
- give your dog as a gift, or offer to do so, or advertise your dog as a gift
- abandon your dog
- allow it to stray

When your dog is in a public place, it must be:

- muzzled so that it cannot bite anyone
- on a lead
- in the charge of someone who is at least 16 years old

Even if your dog is not one of the specified breeds, it is still an offence to allow it to be dangerously out of control in a public place. If actual injury is caused, the penalty is up to 2 years' imprisonment and/or an unlimited fine. Even when there is no injury, the penalty is a fine of up to £2000 and/or 6 months' imprisonment.

For further information contact the RSPCA (0403 64181).

Dog Breeds Registered with the Kennel Club

(as at 14 June 1993)

Source: The Kennel Club

Sporting Breeds

Hound Group
Afghan Hound
Basenji
Basset Hound
Basset Fauve de Bretagne
Bavarian Mountain Hound (Imported Register)
Beagle
Bloodhound
Borzoi
Dachshund (Long-haired)
Dachshund (Miniature Long-haired)
Dachshund (Smooth-haired)
Dachshund (Miniature Smooth-haired)
Dachshund (Wire-haired)
Dachshund (Miniature Wire-haired)
Deerhound
Elkhound
Finnish Spitz
Foxhound
Grand Basset Griffon Vendeen (Imported Register)
Grand Bleu de Gascogne (Imported Register)
Greyhound
Hamiltonstovare
Ibizan Hound
Irish Wolfhound
Norwegian Lundehund (Imported Register)
Otterhound
Petit Basset Griffon Vendeen
Pharoah Hound
Rhodesian Ridgeback
Saluki
Segugio Italiano (Imported Register)
Sloughi
Whippet

Gundog Group
Bracco Italiano (Imported Register)
Brittany
English Setter
German Short-haired Pointer
German Wire-haired Pointer
Gordon Setter
Hungarian Vizsla
Hungarian Wire-haired Vizsla
Irish Red & White Setter
Irish Setter
Italian Spinone
Kooikerhundje (Imported Register)
Large Munsterlander
Nova Scotia Duck Tolling Retreiver (Imported Register)
Pointer
Retriever (Chesapeake Bay)
Retriever (Curly Coated)
Retriever (Flat Coated)
Retriever (Golden)
Retriever (Labrador)
Spaniel (American Cocker)
Spaniel (Clumber)
Spaniel (Cocker)
Spaniel (English Springer)
Spaniel (Field)
Spaniel (Irish Water)
Spaniel (Sussex)
Spaniel (Welsh Springer)
Spanish Water Dog (Imported Register)
Weimaraner

Terrier Group
Airedale Terrier
Australian Terrier
Bedlington Terrier
Border Terrier
Bull Terrier
Bull Terrier (Miniature)
Cairn Terrier

(Continued)

Cesky Terrier (Imported Register)
Dandie Dinmont Terrier
Fox Terrier (Smooth)
Fox Terrier (Wire)
Glen of Imaal Terrier
Irish Terrier
Kerry Blue Terrier
Lakeland Terrier
Manchester Terrier
Norfolk Terrier
Norwich Terrier
Parson Jack Russell Terrier
Scottish Terrier
Sealyham Terrier
Skye Terrier
Soft-Coated Wheaten Terrier
Staffordshire Bull Terrier
Welsh Terrier
West Highland White Terrier

Non-Sporting Breeds

Utility Group
Boston Terrier
Bulldog
Canaan Dog
Chow Chow
Dalmatian
French Bulldog
German Spitz (Klein)
German Spitz (Mittel)
Japanese Akita
Japanese Shiba Inu
Japanese Spitz
Keeshond
Leonberger
Lhasa Apso
Mexican Hairless (Imported Register)
Miniature Schnauzer
Poodle (Miniature)
Poodle (Standard)
Poodle (Toy)
Schipperke
Schnauzer
Shar-Pei
Shih Tzu
Tibetan Spaniel
Tibetan Terrier

Working Group
Alaskan Malamute
Anatolian Shepherd Dog
Australian Cattle Dog
Bearded Collie
Belgian Shepherd Dog*
Bergamasco (Imported Register)
Bernese Mountain Dog
Border Collie
Bouvier des Flandres
Boxer
Briard
Bullmastiff
Collie (Rough)
Collie (Smooth)
Continental Landseer (ECT) (Imported Register)
Dobermann
Eskimo Dog
Estrela Mountain Dog
Finnish Lapphund (Imported Register)
German Shepherd Dog (Alsatian)
Giant Schnauzer
Great Dane
Hovawart
Hungarian Kuvasz
Hungarian Puli
Komondor
Lancashire Heeler
Maremma Sheepdog
Mastiff
Neapolitan Mastiff
Newfoundland
Norwegian Buhund
Old English Sheepdog
Pinscher
Polish Lowland Sheepdog
Portuguese Water Dog
Pyrenean Mountain Dog
Pyrenean Sheepdog (Imported Register)
Rottweiler
St Bernard
Samoyed
Shetland Sheepdog
Siberian Husky
Swedish Lapphund (Imported Register)
Swedish Vallhund
Tibetan Mastiff
Welsh Corgi (Cardigan)
Welsh Corgi (Pembroke)

Toy Group
Affenpinscher
Australian Silky Terrier
Bichon Frise
Bolognese (Imported Register)
Cavalier King Charles Spaniel
Chihuahua (Long Coat)
Chihuahua (Smooth Coat)
Chinese Crested
Coton de Tulear (Imported Register)
English Toy Terrier (Black and Tan)
Griffon Bruxellois
Italian Greyhound
Japanese Chin
King Charles Spaniel
Lowchen (Little Lion Dog)
Maltese
Miniature Pinscher
Papillon
Pekingese
Pomeranian
Pug
Yorkshire Terrier

* With effect from 1 January 1994 Belgian Shepherd Dogs will be classified as a single breed and will no longer form a sub-group.

Pedigree Cats Registered in 1992

Source: The Governing Council of the Cat Fancy

Breed	Number
Persian Long Hair	11,123
Siamese	5,624
Burmese	3,808
British Short Hair	3,605
Birman	2,047
Oriental Short Hair	1,275
Maine Coon	975
Abyssinian	663
Exotic Short Hair	607
Russian Blue	458
Devon Rex	452
Balinese	339
Somali	334
Tonkinese	307
Ragdoll	224
Turkish Van	193
Asian/Burmilla	186
Cornish Rex	145
Norwegian Forest	139
Others	108
Korat	95
Angora	60
Manx	35
Tiffanie	11
Total	**32,813**

Wedding Anniversaries

The traditional names for wedding anniversaries go back many years in social usage. As such names as wooden, crystal, silver and golden were applied, it was considered proper to present the married pair with gifts made of these products or of something related. The list of traditional gifts, with a few allowable revisions in parentheses, is presented below, followed by modern gifts in **bold face.**

1st – Paper, **clocks**
2rd – Cotton, **china**
3rd – Leather, **crystal & glass**
4th – Linen (silk), **electrical appliances**
5th – Wood, **silverware**
6th – Iron, **wood**
7th – Wool (copper), **desk sets**
8th – Bronze, **linens & lace**
9th – Pottery (china), **leather**
10th – Tin (aluminium), **diamond jewellery**
11th – Steel, **fashion jewellery, accessories**
12th – Silk, **pearls or coloured gems**
13th – Lace, **textiles & furs**
14th – Ivory, **gold jewellery**
15th – Crystal, **watches**
20th – China, **platinum**
25th – Silver, **sterling silver**
30th – Pearl, **diamond**
35th – Coral (jade), **jade**
40th – Ruby, **ruby**
45th – Sapphire, **sapphire**
50th – Gold, **gold**
55th – Emerald, **emerald**
60th – Diamond, **diamond**

Birthstones

Source: Jewelry Industry Council

Month	Ancient	Modern
January	Garnet	Garnet
February	Amethyst	Amethyst
March	Jasper	Bloodstone or Aquamarine
April	Sapphire	Diamond
May	Agate	Emerald
June	Emerald	Pearl, Moonstone, or Alexandrite
July	Onyx	Ruby
August	Carnelian	Sardonyx or Peridot
September	Chrysolite	Sapphire
October	Aquamarine	Opal or Tourmaline
November	Topaz	Topaz
December	Ruby	Turquoise or Zircon

Social Class Definitions

A Professionals such as doctors, surgeons, solicitors or dentists; chartered people like architects; fully qualified people with a large degree of responsibility such as senior editors, senior civil servants, town clerks, senior business executives and managers, and high-ranking grades of the Services.

B People with very responsible jobs such as university lecturers, matrons of hospitals, heads of local government departments; middle management in business; qualified scientists, bank managers and upper grades of the Services, police inspectors.

C1 All others doing non-manual jobs; nurses, technicians, pharmacists, salesmen, publicans, people in clerical positions and middle ranks of the Services, police sergeants.

C2 Skilled manual workers/craftsmen who have served apprenticeships; foremen, manual workers with special qualifications such as long-distance lorry drivers, security officers, police constables and lower grades of the Services.

D Semi-skilled and unskilled manual workers, including labourers and mates of occupations in the C2 grade and people serving apprenticeships; machine minders, farm labourers, bus and railway conductors, laboratory assistants, postmen, waiter/waitress, door-to-door and van salesmen.

E Those on lowest levels of subsistence including pensioners, casual workers, and others with minimum levels of income.

The UK's Top 50 Companies

Source: CBI

Rank	Company Name	Sector
1.	British Petroleum Company PLC	Oil & gas industry
2.	Shell Transport and Trading Company PLC	Oil & gas industry
3.	BAT Industries PLC	Tobacco industry
4.	British Telecommunications PLC	Telecommunications
5.	Mitsui & Co UK PLC	General trading company
6.	Imperial Chemical Industries PLC	Chemicals & pharmaceuticals
7.	British Aerospace PLC	Aerospace
8.	British Gas PLC	Public gas supply
9.	Grand Metropolitan PLC	Brewers & distillers
10.	Sainsbury (J) PLC	Food retailing
11.	Hanson PLC	Conglomerates
12.	Unilever PLC	Foods, detergents & personal products
13.	Sumimoto Corporation (UK) PLC	General trading company
14.	Ford Motor Co Ltd	Automobiles
15.	Tesco PLC	Food retailing
16.	BTR PLC	Industrial, construction & electrical, etc.
17.	General Electric Company PLC	Electronics & electricals
18.	Marks and Spencer PLC	Stores
19.	Esso UK PLC	Oil & gas industry
20.	Engelhard Ltd	Precious metals
21.	Allied-Lyons PLC	Brewers & distillers, food manufacturing
22.	British Airways PLC	Air transport
23.	Mitsubishi Corporation (UK)	Commodities trading
24.	Peninsular and Oriental Steam Navigation Company (P&O)	Shipping and construction
25.	Gallaher Ltd	Tobacco, distilling, housewares
26.	Argyll Group PLC	Food retailing & wholesaling
27.	Post Office	Postal services
28.	SmithKline Beecham PLC	Pharmaceuticals & healthcare
29.	Hillsdown Holdings PLC	Food manufacturing & household goods
30.	British Steel PLC	Steel industry
31.	Asda Group PLC	Food retailing
32.	Bass PLC	Brewing, pubs, hotels & leisure
33.	National Power PLC	Public electricity supply
34.	IBM United Kingdom Holdings Ltd	Information technology
35.	Texaco Ltd	Petroleum products
36.	Guinness PLC	Brewers & distillers
37.	Saatchi & Saatchi Company PLC	Advertising
38.	THORN EMI PLC	Rental & music business
39.	British Coal Corporation	Coal industry
40.	Ladbroke Group PLC	Hotels & leisure
41.	Dalgety PLC	Farming
42.	Boots Company PLC	Pharmaceuticals & healthcare
43.	Inchcape PLC	Automobiles
44.	RTZ Corporation PLC	Mining, metals & minerals
45.	Rolls-Royce PLC	Aerospace, power generation, engineering
46.	BICC PLC	Engineering, construction & metal-forming industries
47.	Glaxo Holdings PLC	Pharmaceutical products
48.	Kingfisher PLC	Stores
49.	Weston [George] Holdings Ltd	Food manufacturing
50.	Booker PLC	Agribusiness & food manufacturing

SPORT

For ease of reference this section is arranged as follows: Olympic Games information (summer and winter) appears first, arranged alphabetically by sport and alphabetically within by event. This is followed by other sports results for the 1992–93 season, and these too are arranged alphabetically by sport and event. Lists of champions are given for the principal events.

OLYMPIC GAMES

The modern Olympic Games, first held in Athens, Greece, in 1896*, were the result of efforts by Baron Pierre de Coubertin, a French educator, to promote interest in education and culture, also to foster better international understanding through the universal medium of youth's love of athletics.

His source of inspiration for the Olympic Games was the ancient Greek Olympic Games, most notable of the four Panhellenic celebrations. The games were combined patriotic, religious and athletic festivals held every four years. The first such recorded festival was held in 776 BC, the date from which the Greeks began to keep their calendar by "Olympiads", or four-year spans between the games.

The first Olympiad is said to have consisted merely of a 200-yard foot race near the small city of Olympia, but the games gained in scope and became demonstrations of national pride. Only Greek citizens – amateurs – were permitted to participate. Winners received laurel, wild olive and palm wreaths and were accorded many special privileges. Under the Roman emperors, the games deteriorated into professional carnivals and circuses. Emperor Theodosius banned them in AD 394.

Baron de Coubertin enlisted 9 nations to send athletes to the first modern Olympics in 1896; now more than 100 nations compete. Winter Olympic Games were started in 1924.

Olympic Information

Symbol: Five rings or circles, linked together to represent the sporting friendship of all peoples. The rings also symbolize the 5 continents – Europe, Asia, Africa, Australia and America. Each ring is a different colour – blue, yellow, black, green and red.

Flag: The symbol of the 5 rings on a plain white background.

Motto: "Citius, Altius, Fortius" – Latin meaning "faster, higher, braver", or the modern interpretation "swifter, higher, stronger". The motto was coined by Father Didon, a French educator, in 1895.

Creed: "The most important thing in the Olympic Games is not to win but to take part, just as the most important thing in life is not the triumph but the struggle. The essential thing is not to have conquered but to have fought well."

Oath: An athlete of the host country recites the following at the opening ceremony. "In the name of all competitors I promise that we will take part in these Olympic Games, respecting and abiding by the glory of sport and the honour of our team." Both the oath and the creed were composed by Pierre de Coubertin, the founder of the modern Games.

Flame: Symbolizes the continuity between the ancient and modern Games. The modern version of the flame was adopted in 1936. The torch used to kindle the flame is first lit by the sun's rays at Olympia, Greece, and then carried to the site of the Games by relays of runners. Ships and planes are used when necessary.

Sites of Olympic Games

1896 Athens, Greece
1900 Paris, France
1904 St. Louis, U.S.
1906 Athens, Greece*
1908 London, England
1912 Stockholm, Sweden
1920 Antwerp, Belgium
1924 Paris, France
1928 Amsterdam, Netherlands
1932 Los Angeles, U.S.
1936 Berlin, Germany
1948 London, England
1952 Helsinki, Finland
1956 Melbourne, Australia
1960 Rome, Italy
1964 Tokyo, Japan
1968 Mexico City, Mexico
1972 Munich, W. Germany
1976 Montreal, Canada
1980 Moscow, USSR
1984 Los Angeles, U.S.
1988 Seoul, S. Korea
1992 Barcelona, Spain
1996 Atlanta, U.S.
2000 Sydney, Australia

*Games not recognized by International Olympic Committee. The Games in 1916, 1940 and 1944 were not celebrated because of world wars. The 1980 games were boycotted by 62 nations, including the U.S. The 1984 games were boycotted by the USSR and most eastern bloc nations. East and West Germany competed separately 1968–88. The 1992 Unified Team consisted of 12 former Soviet republics. The 1992 Independent Olympic Participants (IOP) were athletes from Serbia, Montenegro and Macedonia.

Olympic Games Champions, 1896–1992

Athletics – Boxing – Swimming

(*Indicates Gold Medal-Winning Record)

Athletics – Men

100-Metre Run

1896	Thomas Burke, United States	12s
1900	Francis W. Jarvis, United States	11.0s
1904	Archie Hahn, United States	11s
1908	Reginald Walker, South Africa	10.8s
1912	Ralph Craig, United States	10.8s
1920	Charles Paddock, United States	10.8s
1924	Harold Abrahams, Great Britain	10.6s
1928	Percy Williams, Canada	10.8s
1932	Eddie Tolan, United States	10.3s
1936	Jesse Owens, United States	10.3s
1948	Harrison Dillard, United States	10.3s
1952	Lindy Remigino, United States	10.4s
1956	Bobby Morrow, United States	10.5s
1960	Armin Hary, Germany	10.2s

(Continued)

1964	Bob Hayes, United States	10.0s
1968	Jim Hines, United States	9.95s
1972	Valery Borzov, USSR	10.14s
1976	Hasely Crawford, Trinidad	10.06s
1980	Allan Wells, Great Britain	10.25s
1984	Carl Lewis, United States	9.99s
1988	Carl Lewis, United States	9.92s*
1992	Linford Christie, Great Britain	9.96s

200-Metre Run

1900	Walter Tewksbury, United States	22.2s
1904	Archie Hahn, United States	21.6s
1908	Robert Kerr, Canada	22.6s
1912	Ralph Craig, United States	21.7s
1920	Allan Woodring, United States	22s
1924	Jackson Scholz, United States	21.6s
1928	Percy Williams, Canada	21.8s
1932	Eddie Tolan, United States	21.2s
1936	Jesse Owens, United States	20.7s
1948	Mel Patton, United States	21.1s
1952	Andrew Stanfield, United States	20.7s
1956	Bobby Morrow, United States	20.6s
1960	Livio Berruti, Italy	20.5s
1964	Henry Carr, United States	20.3s
1968	Tommie Smith, United States	19.83s
1972	Valeri Borzov, USSR	20.00s
1976	Donald Quarrie, Jamaica	20.23s
1980	Pietro Mennea, Italy	20.19s
1984	Carl Lewis, United States	19.80s
1988	Joe DeLoach, United States	19.75s*
1992	Mike Marsh, United States	20.01s

400-Metre Run

1896	Thomas Burke, United States	54.2s
1900	Maxey Long, United States	49.4s
1904	Harry Hillman, United States	49.2s
1908	Wyndham Halswelle, Great Britain, walkover	50s
1912	Charles Reidpath, United States	48.2s
1920	Bevil Rudd, South Africa	49.6s
1924	Eric Liddell, Great Britain	47.6s
1928	Ray Barbuti, United States	47.8s
1932	William Carr, United States	46.2s
1936	Archie Williams, United States	46.5s
1948	Arthur Wint, Jamaica, B W I	46.2s
1952	George Rhoden, Jamaica, B W I	45.9s
1956	Charles Jenkins, United States	46.7s
1960	Otis Davis, United States	44.9s
1964	Michael Larrabee, United States	45.1s
1968	Lee Evans, United States	43.80s
1972	Vincent Matthews, United States	44.66s
1976	Alberto Juantorena, Cuba	44.26s
1980	Viktor Markin, USSR	44.60s
1984	Alonzo Babers, United States	44.27s
1988	Steven Lewis, United States	43.87s
1992	Quincy Watts, United States	43.50s*

800-Metre Run

1896	Edwin Flack, Australia	2m. 11s
1900	Alfred Tysoe, Great Britain	2m. 1.2s
1904	James Lightbody, United States	1m. 56s
1908	Mel Sheppard, United States	1m. 52.8s
1912	James Meredith, United States	1m. 51.9s
1920	Albert Hill, Great Britain	1m. 53.4s
1924	Douglas Lowe, Great Britain	1m. 52.4s
1928	Douglas Lowe, Great Britain	1m. 51.8s
1932	Thomas Hampson, Great Britain	1m. 49.8s
1936	John Woodruff, United States	1m. 52.9s
1948	Mal Whitfield, United States	1m. 49.2s
1952	Mal Whitfield, United States	1m. 49.2s
1956	Thomas Courtney, United States	1m. 47.7s
1960	Peter Snell, New Zealand	1m. 46.3s
1964	Peter Snell, New Zealand	1m. 45.1s
1968	Ralph Doubell, Australia	1m. 44.3s
1972	Dave Wottle, United States	1m. 45.9s
1976	Alberto Juantorena, Cuba	1m. 43.50s
1980	Steve Ovett, Great Britain	1m. 45.40s
1984	Joaquim Cruz, Brazil	1m. 43.00s*
1988	Paul Ereng, Kenya	1m. 43.45s
1992	William Tanui, Kenya	1m. 43.66s

1,500-Metre Run

1896	Edwin Flack, Australia	4m. 33.2s
1900	Charles Bennett, Great Britain	4m. 6.2s
1904	James Lightbody, United States	4m. 5.4s
1908	Mel Sheppard, United States	4m. 3.4s
1912	Arnold Jackson, Great Britain	3m. 56.8s
1920	Albert Hill, Great Britain	4m. 1.8s
1924	Paavo Nurmi, Finland	3m. 53.6s
1928	Harry Larva, Finland	3m. 53.2s
1932	Luigi Beccali, Italy	3m. 51.2s
1936	Jack Lovelock, New Zealand	3m. 47.8s
1948	Henri Eriksson, Sweden	3m. 49.8s
1952	Joseph Barthel, Luxemburg	3m. 45.2s
1956	Ron Delany, Ireland	3m. 41.2s
1960	Herb Elliott, Australia	3m. 35.6s
1964	Peter Snell, New Zealand	3m. 38.1s
1968	Kipchoge Keino, Kenya	3m. 34.9s
1972	Pekka Vasala, Finland	3m. 36.3s
1976	John Walker, New Zealand	3m. 39.17s
1980	Sebastian Coe, Great Britain	3m. 38.4s
1984	Sebastian Coe, Great Britain	3m. 32.53s*
1988	Peter Rono, Kenya	3m. 35.96s
1992	Fermin Cacho Ruiz, Spain	3m. 40.12s

3,000-Metre Steeplechase

1920	Percy Hodge, Great Britain	10m. 0.4s
1924	Willie Ritola, Finland	9m. 33.6s
1928	Toivo Loukola, Finland	9m. 21.8s
1932	Volmari Iso-Hollo, Finland (About 3,450 mtrs. extra lap by error)	10m. 33.4s
1936	Volmari Iso-Hollo, Finland	9m. 3.8s
1948	Thore Sjoestrand, Sweden	9m. 4.6s
1952	Horace Ashenfelter, United States	8m. 45.4s
1956	Chris Brasher, Great Britain	8m. 41.2s
1960	Zdzislaw Krzyszkowiak, Poland	8m. 34.2s
1964	Gaston Roelants, Belgium	8m. 30.8s
1968	Amos Biwott, Kenya	8m. 51s
1972	Kipchoge Keino, Kenya	8m. 23.6s
1976	Anders Garderud, Sweden	8m. 08.2s
1980	Bronislaw Malinowski, Poland	8m. 09.7s
1984	Julius Korir, Kenya	8m. 11.8s
1988	Julius Kariuki, Kenya	8m. 05.51s*
1992	Matthew Birir, Kenya	8m. 08.84s

5,000-Metre Run

1912	Hannes Kolehmainen, Finland	14m. 36.6s
1920	Joseph Guillemot, France	14m. 55.6s
1924	Paavo Nurmi, Finland	14m. 31.2s
1928	Willie Ritola, Finland	14m. 38s
1932	Lauri Lehtinen, Finland	14m. 30s
1936	Gunnar Hockert, Finland	14m. 22.2s
1948	Gaston Reiff, Belgium	14m. 17.6s
1952	Emil Zatopek, Czechoslovakia	14m. 6.6s
1956	Vladimir Kuts, USSR	13m. 39.6s
1960	Murray Halberg, New Zealand	13m. 43.4s
1964	Bob Schul, United States	13m. 48.8s
1968	Mohamed Gammoudi, Tunisia	14m. 05.0s
1972	Lasse Viren, Finland	13m. 26.4s
1976	Lasse Viren, Finland	13m. 24.76s
1980	Miruts Yifter, Ethiopia	13m. 21.0s
1984	Said Aouita, Morocco	13m. 05.59s*
1988	John Ngugi, Kenya	13m. 11.70s
1992	Dieter Baumann, Germany	13m. 12.52s

10,000-Metre Run

1912	Hannes Kolehmainen, Finland	31m. 20.8s
1920	Paavo Nurmi, Finland	31m. 45.8s
1924	Willie Ritola, Finland	30m. 23.2s
1928	Paavo Nurmi, Finland	30m. 18.8s
1932	Janusz Kusocinski, Poland	30m. 11.4s
1936	Ilmari Salminen, Finland	30m. 15.4s
1948	Emil Zatopek, Czechoslovakia	29m. 59.6s
1952	Emil Zatopek, Czechoslovakia	29m. 17.0s
1956	Vladimir Kuts, USSR	28m. 45.6s
1960	Pyotr Bolotnikov, USSR	28m. 32.2s
1964	Billy Mills, United States	28m. 24.4s
1968	Naftali Temu, Kenya	29m. 27.4s
1972	Lasse Viren, Finland	27m. 38.4s
1976	Lasse Viren, Finland	27m. 40.38s
1980	Miruts Yifter, Ethiopia	27m. 42.7s
1984	Alberto Cova, Italy	27m. 47.54
1988	Brahim Boutaib, Morocco	27m. 21.46s*
1992	Khalid Skah, Morocco	27m. 46.7s

Marathon

1896	Spiridon Loues, Greece	2h. 58m. 50s
1900	Michel Theato, France	2h. 59m. 45s
1904	Thomas Hicks, United States	3h. 28m. 63s
1908	John J. Hayes, United States	2h. 55m. 18.4s
1912	Kenneth McArthur, South Africa	2h. 36m. 54.8s
1920	Hannes Kolehmainen, Finland	2h. 32m. 35.8s
1924	Albin Stenroos, Finland	2h. 41m. 22.6s
1928	A.B. El Ouafi, France	2h. 32m. 57s
1932	Juan Zabala, Argentina	2h. 31m. 36s

(Continued)

1936	Kijung Son, Japan (Korean)	2h. 29m. 19.2s
1948	Delfo Cabrera, Argentina	2h. 34m. 51.6s
1952	Emil Zatopek, Czechoslovakia	2h. 23m. 03.2s
1956	Alain Mimoun, France	2h. 25m.
1960	Abebe Bikila, Ethiopia	2h. 15m. 16.2s
1964	Abebe Bikila, Ethiopia	2h. 12m. 11.2s
1968	Mamo Wolde, Ethiopia	2h. 20m. 26.4s
1972	Frank Shorter, United States	2h. 12m. 19.8s
1976	Waldemar Cierpinski, E. Germany	2h. 09m. 55s
1980	Waldemar Cierpinski, E. Germany	2h. 11m. 03s
1984	Carlos Lopes, Portugal	2h. 09m. 21s*
1988	Gelindo Bordin, Italy	2h. 10m. 32s
1992	Hwang Young-Cho, S. Korea	2h. 13m. 23s

20-Kilometre Walk

1956	Leonid Spirin, USSR	1h. 31m. 27.4s
1960	Vladimir Golubnichy, USSR	1h. 33m. 7.2s
1964	Kenneth Mathews, Great Britain	1h. 29m. 34.0s
1968	Vladimir Golubnichy, USSR	1h. 33m. 58.4s
1972	Peter Frenkel, E. Germany	1h. 26m. 42.4s
1976	Daniel Bautista, Mexico	1h. 24m. 40.6s
1980	Maurizio Damilano, Italy	1h. 23m. 35.5s
1984	Ernesto Canto, Mexico	1h. 23m. 13.0s
1988	Josef Pribilinec, Czech.	1h. 19m. 57.0s*
1992	Daniel Plaza Montero, Spain	1h. 21m. 45.0s

50-Kilometre Walk

1932	Thomas W. Green, Great Britain	4h. 50m. 10s
1936	Harold Whitlock, Great Britain	4h. 30m. 41.4s
1948	John Ljunggren, Sweden	4h. 41m. 52s
1952	Giuseppe Dordoni, Italy	4h. 28m. 07.8s
1956	Norman Read, New Zealand	4h. 30m. 42.8s
1960	Donald Thompson, Great Britain	4h. 25m. 30s
1964	Abdon Pamich, Italy	4h. 11m. 12.4s
1968	Christoph Hohne, E. Germany	4h. 20m. 13.6s
1972	Bern Kannenberg, W. Germany	3h. 56m. 11.6s
1980	Hartwig Gauter, E. Germany	3h. 49m. 24s
1984	Raul Gonzalez, Mexico	3h. 47m. 26s
1988	Vayachselav Ivanenko, USSR	3h. 38m. 29s*
1992	Andrei Perlov, Unified Team	3h. 50m. 13s

110-Metre Hurdles

1896	Thomas Curtis, United States	17.6s
1900	Alvin Kraenzlein, United States	15.4s
1904	Frederick Schule, United States	16s
1908	Forrest Smithson, United States	15s
1912	Frederick Kelly, United States	15.1s
1920	Earl Thomson, Canada	14.8s
1924	Daniel Kinsey, United States	15s
1928	Sydney Atkinson, South Africa	14.8s
1932	George Saling, United States	14.6s
1936	Forrest Towns, United States	14.2s
1948	William Porter, United States	13.9s
1952	Harrison Dillard, United States	13.7s
1956	Lee Calhoun, United States	13.5s
1960	Lee Calhoun, United States	13.8s
1964	Hayes Jones, United States	13.6s
1968	Willie Davenport, United States	13.3s
1972	Rod Milburn, United States	13.24s
1976	Guy Drut, France	13.30s
1980	Thomas Munkelt, E. Germany	13. 39s
1984	Roger Kingdom, United States	13.20s
1988	Roger Kingdom, United States	12.98s*
1992	Mark McCoy, Canada	13.12s

400-Metre Hurdles

1900	J.W.B. Tewksbury, United States	57.6s
1904	Harry Hillman, United States	53s
1908	Charles Bacon, United States	55s
1920	Frank Loomis, United States	54s
1924	F. Morgan Taylor, United States	52.6s
1928	Lord Burghley, Great Britain	53.4s
1932	Robert Tisdall, Ireland	51.7s
1936	Glenn Hardin, United States	52.4s
1948	Roy Cochran, United States	51.1s
1952	Charles Moore, United States	50.8s
1956	Glenn Davis, United States	50.1s
1960	Glenn Davis, United States	49.3s
1964	Rex Cawley, United States	49.6s
1968	Dave Hemery, Great Britain	48.12s
1972	John Akii-Bua, Uganda	47.82s
1976	Edwin Moses, United States	47.64s
1980	Volker Beck, E. Germany	48.70s
1984	Edwin Moses, United States	47.75s
1988	Andre Phillips, United States	47.19s
1992	Kevin Young, United States	46.78s*

High Jump

1896	Ellery Clark, United States	5ft. 11¼ in.
1900	Irving Baxter, United States	6ft. 2$\frac{4}{5}$ in.
1904	Samuel Jones, United States	5ft. 11 in.
1908	Harry Porter, United States	6ft. 3 in.
1912	Alma Richards, United States	6ft. 4 in.
1920	Richmond Landon, United States	6ft. 4 in.
1924	Harold Osborn, United States	6ft. 6 in.
1928	Robert W. King, United States	6ft. 4½ in.
1932	Duncan McNaughton, Canada	6ft. 5$\frac{5}{8}$ in.
1936	Cornelius Johnson, United States	6ft. 8 in.
1948	John L. Winter, Australia	6ft. 6 in.
1952	Walter Davis, United States	6ft. 8.32 in.
1956	Charles Dumas, United States	6ft. 11½ in.
1960	Robert Shavlakadze, USSR	7ft. 1 in.
1964	Valery Brumel, USSR	7ft. 1¾ in.
1968	Dick Fosbury, United States	7ft. 4¼ in.
1972	Yuri Tarmak, USSR	7ft. 3¾ in.
1976	Jacek Wszola, Poland	7ft. 4½ in.
1980	Gerd Wessig, E. Germany	7ft. 8¾ in.
1984	Dietmar Mogenburg, W. Germany	7ft. 8½ in.
1988	Guennadi Avdeenko, USSR	7ft. 9½ in.*
1992	Javier Sotomayor, Cuba	7ft. 8¼ in.

Long Jump

1896	Ellery Clark, United States	20ft. 10 in.
1900	Alvin Kraenzlein, United States	23ft. 6¾ in.
1904	Myer Prinstein, United States	24ft. 1 in.
1908	Frank Irons, United States	24ft. 6½ in.
1912	Albert Gutterson, United States	24ft. 11¼ in.
1920	William Petterssen, Sweden	23ft. 5½ in.
1924	DeHart Hubbard, United States	24ft. 5 in.
1928	Edward B. Hamm, United States	25ft. 4½ in.
1932	Edward Gordon, United States	25ft. ¾ in.
1936	Jesse Owens, United States	26ft. 5½ in.
1948	William Steele, United States	25ft. 8 in.
1952	Jerome Biffle, United States	24ft. 10 in.
1956	Gregory Bell, United States	25ft. 8¼ in.
1960	Ralph Boston, United States	26ft. 7¾ in.
1964	Lynn Davies, Great Britain	26ft. 5¾ in.
1968	Bob Beamon, United States	29ft. 2½ in.*
1972	Randy Williams, United States	27ft. ½ in.
1976	Arnie Robinson, United States	27ft. 4½ in.
1980	Lutz Dombrowski, E. Germany	28ft. ¼ in.
1984	Carl Lewis, United States	28ft. ¼ in.
1988	Carl Lewis, United States	28ft. 7¼ in.
1992	Carl Lewis, United States	28ft 5½ in.

400-Metre Relay

1912	Great Britain	42.4s
1920	United States	42.2s
1924	United States	41.0s
1928	United States	41.0s
1932	United States	40.0s
1936	United States	39.8s
1948	United States	40.6s
1952	United States	40.1s
1956	United States	39.5s
1960	Germany (U.S. disqualified)	39.5s
1964	United States	39.0s
1968	United States	38.2s
1972	United States	38.19s
1976	United States	38.33s
1980	USSR	38.26s
1984	United States	37.83s
1988	USSR (U.S. disqualified)	38.19s
1992	United States	37.4s*

1,600-Metre Relay

1908	United States	3m. 29.4s
1912	United States	3m. 16.6s
1920	Great Britain	3m. 22.2s
1924	United States	3m. 16s
1928	United States	3m. 14.2s
1932	United States	3m. 8.2s
1936	Great Britain	3m. 9s
1948	United States	3m. 10.4s
1952	Jamaica	3m. 03.9s
1956	United States	3m. 04.8s
1960	United States	3m. 02.2s
1964	United States	3m. 00.7s
1968	United States	2m. 56.16s
1972	Kenya	2m. 59.8s
1976	United States	2m. 58.65s
1980	USSR	3m. 01.1s
1984	United States	2m. 57.91s
1988	United States	2m. 56.16s

(Continued)

1992	United States	2m. 55.74s*

Pole Vault

1896	William Hoyt, United States	10ft. 10 in.
1900	Irving Baxter, United States	10ft. 10 in.
1904	Charles Dvorak, United States	11ft. 5¾ in.
1908	A. C. Gilbert, United States Edward Cook Jr., United States	12ft. 2 in.
1912	Harry Babcock, United States	12ft. 11½ in.
1920	Frank Foss, United States	13ft. 5 in.
1924	Lee Barnes, United States	12ft. 11½ in.
1928	Sabin W. Carr, United States	13ft. 9¼ in.
1932	William Miller, United States	14ft. 1¾ in.
1936	Earle Meadows, United States	14ft. 3¼ in.
1948	Guinn Smith, United States	14ft. 1¼ in.
1952	Robert Richards, United States	14ft. 11 in.
1956	Robert Richards, United States	14ft. 11½ in.
1960	Don Bragg, United States	15ft. 5 in.
1964	Fred Hansen, United States	16ft. 8¾ in.
1968	Bob Seagren, United States	17ft. 8½ in.
1972	Wolfgang Nordwig, E. Germany	18ft. 0½ in.
1976	Tadeusz Slusarski, Poland	18ft. 0½ in.
1980	Wladyslaw Kozakiewicz, Poland	18ft. 11½ in.
1984	Pierre Quinon, France	18ft. 10¼ in.
1988	Sergei Bubka, USSR	19ft. 9¼ in.*
1992	Maksim Tarassov, Unified Team	19ft. 0¼ in.

Hammer Throw

1900	John Flanagan, United States	163ft. 1 in.
1904	John Flanagan, United States	168ft. 1 in.
1908	John Flanagan, United States	170ft. 4¼ in.
1912	Matt McGrath, United States	179ft. 7⅛ in.
1920	Pat Ryan, United States	173ft. 5⅝ in.
1924	Fred Tootell, United States	174ft. 10⅛ in.
1928	Patrick O'Callaghan, Ireland	168ft. 7½ in.
1932	Patrick O'Callaghan, Ireland	176ft. 11⅛ in.
1936	Karl Hein, Germany	185ft. 4 in.
1948	Imre Nemeth, Hungary	183ft. 11½ in.
1952	Jozsef Csermak, Hungary	197ft. 11$\frac{9}{16}$ in.
1956	Harold Connolly, United States	207ft. 3½ in.
1960	Vasily Rudenkov, USSR	220ft. 1⅝ in.
1964	Romuald Klim, USSR	228ft. 9½ in.
1968	Gyula Zsivotsky, Hungary	240ft. 8 in.
1972	Anatoli Bondarchuk, USSR	247ft. 8 in.
1976	Yuri Syedykh, USSR	254ft. 4 in.
1980	Yuri Syedykh, USSR	268ft. 4½ in.
1984	Juha Tiainen, Finland	256ft. 2 in.
1988	Sergei Litinov, USSR	278ft. 2½ in.*
1992	Andrey Abduvaliyev, Unified Team	270ft. 9½ in.

Discus Throw

1896	Robert Garrett, United States	95ft. 7½ in.
1900	Rudolf Bauer, Hungary	118ft. 3 in.
1904	Martin Sheridan, United States	128ft. 10½ in.
1908	Martin Sheridan, United States	134ft. 2 in.
1912	Armas Taipale, Finland	148ft. 3 in.
	Both hands—Armas Taipale, Finland	271ft. 10¼ in.
1920	Elmer Niklander, Finland	146ft. 7 in.
1924	Clarence Houser, United States	151ft. 4 in.
1928	Clarence Houser, United States	155ft. 3 in.
1932	John Anderson, United States	162ft. 4 in.
1936	Ken Carpenter, United States	165ft. 7 in.
1948	Adolfo Consolini, Italy	173ft. 2 in.
1952	Sim Iness, United States	180ft. 6.85 in.
1956	Al Oerter, United States	184ft. 10½ in.
1960	Al Oerter, United States	194ft. 2 in.
1964	Al Oerter, United States	200ft. 1½ in.
1968	Al Oerter, United States	212ft. 6½ in.
1972	Ludvik Danek, Czechoslovakia	211ft. 3 in.
1976	Mac Wilkins, United States	221ft. 5.4 in.
1980	Viktor Rashchupkin, USSR	218ft. 8 in.
1984	Rolf Dannenberg, W. Germany	218ft. 6 in.
1988	Jurgen Schult, E. Germany	225ft. 9¼ in.*
1992	Romas Ubartas, Lithuania	213ft. 7¾ in.

Triple Jump

1896	James Connolly, United States	44ft. 11¾ in.
1900	Myer Prinstein, United States	47ft. 5¾ in.
1904	Myer Prinstein, United States	47 ft.
1908	Timothy Ahearne, Great Britain, Ireland	48ft. 11¼ in.
1912	Gustaf Lindblom, Sweden	48ft. 5¼ in.
1920	Vilho Tuulos, Finland	47ft. 7 in.
1924	Anthony Winter, Australia	50ft. 11¼ in.
1928	Mikio Oda, Japan	49ft. 11 in.
1932	Chuhei Nambu, Japan	51ft. 7 in.
1936	Naoto Tajima, Japan	52ft. 6 in.
1948	Arne Ahman, Sweden	50ft. 6¼ in.
1952	Adhemar da Silva, Brazil	53ft. 2¾ in.
1956	Adhemar da Silva, Brazil	53ft. 7¾ in.
1960	Jozef Schmidt, Poland	55ft. 2 in.
1964	Jozef Schmidt, Poland	55ft. 3½ in.
1968	Viktor Saneev, USSR	57ft. ¾ in.
1972	Viktor Saneev, USSR	56ft. 11 in.
1976	Viktor Saneev, USSR	56ft. 8¾ in.
1980	Jaak Uudmae, USSR	56ft. 11¼ in.
1984	Al Joyner, United States	56ft. 7½ in.
1988	Hristo Markov, Bulgaria	57ft. 9¼ in.
1992	Mike Conley, United States	59ft. 7½ in.*

16-lb. Shot Put

1896	Robert Garrett, United States	36ft. 9¾ in.
1900	Richard Sheldon, United States	46ft. 3¼ in.
1904	Ralph Rose, United States	48ft. 7 in.
1908	Ralph Rose, United States	46ft. 7½ in.
1912	Pat McDonald, United States	50ft. 4 in.
	Both hands—Ralph Rose, United States	90ft. 5½ in.
1920	Ville Porhola, Finland	48ft. 7¼ in.
1924	Clarence Houser, United States	49ft. 2¼ in.
1928	John Kuck, United States	52ft. ¾ in.
1932	Leo Sexton, United States	52ft. 6 in.
1936	Hans Woellke, Germany	53ft. 1¾ in.
1948	Wilbur Thompson, United States	56ft. 2 in.
1952	Parry O'Brien, United States	57ft. ½ in.
1956	Parry O'Brien, United States	60ft. 11¼ in.
1960	William Nieder, United States	64ft. 6¾ in.
1964	Dallas Long, United States	66ft. 8½ in.
1968	Randy Matson, United States	67ft. 4¾ in.
1972	Wladyslaw Komar, Poland	69ft. 6 in.
1976	Udo Beyer, E. Germany	69ft. ¾ in.
1980	Vladimir Kiselyov, USSR	70ft. ½ in.
1984	Alessandro Andrei, Italy	69ft. 9 in.
1988	Ulf Timmermann, E. Germany	73ft. 8¾ in.*
1992	Michael Stuice, United States	71ft. 2½ in.

Javelin

1908	Erik Lemming, Sweden	178ft. 7½ in.
	Held in middle—Erik Lemming, Sweden	179ft. 10½ in.
1912	Erik Lemming, Sweden	198ft. 11¼ in.
	Both hands, Julius Saaristo, Finland	358ft. 11⅞ in.
1920	Jonni Myyra, Finland	215ft. 9¾ in.
1924	Jonni Myyra, Finland	206ft. 6¾ in.
1928	Eric Lundkvist, Sweden	218ft. 6⅛ in.
1932	Matti Jarvinen, Finland	238ft. 6 in.
1936	Gerhard Stoeck, Germany	235ft. 8$\frac{5}{16}$ in.
1948	Tapio Rautavaara, Finland	228ft. 10½ in.
1952	Cy Young, United States	242ft. 0.79 in.
1956	Egil Danielson, Norway	281ft. 2¼ in.
1960	Viktor Tsibulenko, USSR	277ft. 8⅜ in.
1964	Pauli Nevala, Finland	271ft. 2½ in.
1968	Janis Lusis, USSR	295ft. 7¼ in.
1972	Klaus Wolfermann, W. Germany	296ft. 10 in.
1976	Miklos Nemeth, Hungary	310ft. 4 in.*
1980	Dainis Kula, USSR	299ft. 2⅜ in.
1984	Arto Haerkoenen, Finland	284ft. 8 in.
1988	Tapio Korjus, Finland	276ft. 6 in.
1992	Jan Zelezny, Czech	294ft. 2 in.

Decathlon

1912	Hugo Wieslander, Sweden	7,724.49 pts.(a)
1920	Helge Lovland, Norway	6,804.35 pts.
1924	Harold Osborn, United States	7,710.77 pts.
1928	Paavo Yrjola, Finland	8,053.29 pts.
1932	James Bausch, United States	8,462.23 pts.
1936	Glenn Morris, United States	7,900 pts.
1948	Robert Mathias, United States	7,139 pts.
1952	Robert Mathias, United States	7,887 pts.
1956	Milton Campbell, United States	7,937 pts.
1960	Rafer Johnson, United States	8,392 pts.
1964	Willi Holdorf, Germany	7,887 pts.(c)
1968	Bill Toomey, United States	8,193 pts.
1972	Nikolai Avilov, USSR	8,454 pts.
1976	Bruce Jenner, United States	8,617 pts.
1980	Daley Thompson, Great Britain	8,495 pts.
1984	Daley Thompson, Great Britain	8,798pts.(b)
1988	Christian Schenk, E. Germany	8,488 pts.
1992	Robert Zmelik, Czechoslovakia	8,611 pts.

(a) Jim Thorpe of the U.S. won the 1912 Decathlon with 8,413 pts. but was disqualified and had to return his medals because he had played professional baseball prior to the Olympic games. The medals were restored posthumously in 1982. (b) Scoring change effective Apr., 1985. (c) Former point systems used prior to 1964.

Athletics – Women

100-Metre Run

1928	Elizabeth Robinson, United States	12.2s
1932	Stella Walsh, Poland	11.9s
1936	Helen Stephens, United States	11.5s
1948	Francina Blankers-Koen, Netherlands	11.9s
1952	Marjorie Jackson, Australia	11.5s
1956	Betty Cuthbert, Australia	11.5s
1960	Wilma Rudolph, United States	11.0s
1964	Wyomia Tyus, United States	11.4s
1968	Wyomia Tyus, United States	11.0s
1972	Renate Stecher, E. Germany	11.07s
1976	Annegret Richter, W. Germany	11.08s
1980	Lyudmila Kondratyeva, USSR	11.6s
1984	Evelyn Ashford, United States	10.97s
1988	Florence Griffith-Joyner, United States	10.54s*
1992	Gail Devers, United States	10.82s

200-Metre Run

1948	Francina Blankers-Koen, Netherlands	24.4s
1952	Marjorie Jackson, Australia	23.7s
1956	Betty Cuthbert, Australia	23.4s
1960	Wilma Rudolph, United States	24.0s
1964	Edith McGuire, United States	23.0s
1968	Irena Szewinska, Poland	22.5s
1972	Renate Stecher, E. Germany	22.40s
1976	Barbel Eckert, E. Germany	22.37s
1980	Barbel Wockel, E. Germany	22.03
1984	Valerie Brisco-Hooks, United States	21.81s
1988	Florence Griffith-Joyner, United States	21.34s*
1992	Gwen Torrence, United States	21.81s

400-Metre Run

1964	Betty Cuthbert, Australia	52s
1968	Colette Besson, France	52s
1972	Monika Zehrt, E. Germany	51.08s
1976	Irena Szewinska, Poland	49.29s
1980	Marita Koch, E. Germany	48.88s
1984	Valerie Brisco-Hooks, United States	48.83s
1988	Olga Bryzgina, USSR	48.65s*
1992	Marie-Jose Perec, France	48.83s

800-Metre Run

1928	Lina Radke, Germany	2m. 16.8s
1960	Ludmila, Shetasova, USSR	2m. 4.3s
1964	Ann Packer, Great Britain	2m. 1.1s
1968	Madeline Manning, United States	2m. 0.9s
1972	Hildegard Falck, W. Germany	1m. 58.6s
1976	Tatyana Kazankina, USSR	1m. 54.94s
1980	Nadezhda Olizayrenko, USSR	1m. 53.5s*
1984	Doina Melinte, Romania	1m. 57.6s
1988	Sigrun Wodars, E. Germany	1m. 56.10s
1992	Ellen van Langen, Netherlands	1m. 55.54s.

1,500-Metre Run

1972	Lyudmila Bragina, USSR	4m. 01.4s
1976	Tatyana Kazankina, USSR	4m. 05.48s
1980	Tatyana Kazankina, USSR	3m. 56.6s
1984	Gabriella Dorio, Italy	4m. 03.25s
1988	Paula Ivan, Romania	3m. 53.96s*
1992	Hassiba Boulmerka, Algeria	3m. 55.3s

3,000-Metre Run

1984	Maricica Puica, Romania	8:35.96s
1988	Tatyana Samolenko, USSR	8:26.53s*
1992	Elena Romanova, Unified Team	8:46.04s

10,000-Metre Run

1988	Olga Boldarenko, USSR	31m. 44.69s
1992	Derartu Tulu, Ethiopia	31m. 06.02s*

400-Metre Relay

1928	Canada	48.4s
1932	United States	46.9s
1936	United States	46.9s
1948	Netherlands	47.5s
1952	United States	45.9s
1956	Australia	44.5s
1960	United States	44.5s
1964	Poland	43.6s
1968	United States	42.8s
1972	West Germany	42.81s
1976	East Germany	42.55s
1980	East Germany	41.60s*
1984	United States	41.65s
1988	United States	41.98s
1992	United States	42.11s

1,600-Metre Relay

1972	East Germany	3m. 23s
1976	East Germany	3m. 19.23s
1980	USSR	3m. 20.02s
1984	United States	3m. 18.29s
1988	USSR	3 m. 15.18s*
1992	Unified Team	3m. 20.20s

100-Metre Hurdles

1972	Annelie Ehrhardt, E. Germany	12.59s
1976	Johanna Schaller, E. Germany	12.77s
1980	Vera Komisova, USSR	12.56s
1984	Benita Brown-Fitzgerald, United States	12.84s
1988	Jordanka Donkova, Bulgaria	12.38s*
1992	Paraskevi Patoulidou, Greece	12.64s

400-Metre Hurdles

1984	Nawal el Moutawakil, Morocco	54.61s
1988	Debra Flintoff-King, Australia	53.17s*
1992	Sally Gunnell, Great Britain	53.23s

Heptathlon

1984	Glynis Nunn, Australia	6,390 pts.
1988	Jackie Joyner-Kersee, United States	7,215 pts.*
1992	Jackie Joyner-Kersee, United States	7,004 pts.

High Jump

1928	Ethel Catherwood, Canada	5ft. 2½ in.
1932	Jean Shiley, United States	5ft. 5¼ in.
1936	Ibolya Csak, Hungary	5ft. 3 in.
1948	Alice Coachman, United States	5ft. 6⅛ in.
1952	Esther Brand, South Africa	5ft. 5¾ in.
1956	Mildred L. McDaniel, United States	5ft. 9¼ in.
1960	Iolanda Balas, Romania	6ft. ¾ in.
1964	Iolanda Balas, Romania	6ft. 2¾ in.
1968	Miloslava Reskova, Czechoslovakia	5ft. 11½ in.
1972	Ulrike Meyfarth, W. Germany	6ft. 4 in.
1976	Rosemarie Ackermann, E. Germany	6ft. 3¾ in.
1980	Sara Simeoni, Italy	6ft. 5½ in.
1984	Ulrike Meyfarth, W. Germany	6ft. 7½ in.
1988	Louise Ritter, United States	6ft. 8 in.*
1992	Heike Henkel, Germany	6ft. 7½ in.

Discus Throw

1928	Helena Konopacka, Poland	129ft. 11¾ in.
1932	Lillian Copeland, United States	133ft. 2 in.
1936	Gisela Mauermayer, Germany	156ft. 3 in.
1948	Micheline Ostermeyer, France	137ft. 6½ in.
1952	Nina Romaschkova, USSR	168ft. 8 in.
1956	Olga Fikotova, Czechoslovakia	176ft. 1 in.
1960	Nina Ponomareva, USSR	180ft. 8¼ in.
1964	Tamara Press, USSR	187ft. 10 in.
1968	Lia Manoliu, Romania	191ft. 2 in.
1972	Faina Melnik, USSR	218ft. 7 in.
1976	Evelin Schlaak, E. Germany	226ft. 4 in.
1980	Evelin Jahl, E. Germany	229ft. 6 in.
1984	Ria Stalman, Netherlands	214ft. 5 in.
1988	Martina Hellmann, E. Germany	237ft. 2¼ in.*
1992	Maritza Marten Garcia, Cuba	229ft. 10 in.

Javelin

1932	"Babe" Didrikson, United States	143ft. 4 in.
1936	Tilly Fleischer, Germany	148ft. 2¾ in.
1948	Herma Bauma, Austria	149ft. 6 in.
1952	Dana Zatopkova, Czechoslovakia	165ft. 7 in.
1956	Inese Jaunzeme, USSR	176ft. 8 in.
1960	Elvira Ozolina, USSR	183ft. 8 in.
1964	Mihaela Penes, Romania	198ft. 7½ in.
1968	Angela Nemeth, Hungary	198ft. ½ in.
1972	Ruth Fuchs, E. Germany	209ft. 7 in.
1976	Ruth Fuchs, E. Germany	216ft. 4 in.
1980	Maria Colon, Cuba	224ft. 5 in.
1984	Tessa Sanderson, Great Britain	228ft. 2 in.
1988	Petra Felke, E. Germany	245ft.*
1992	Silke Renk, Germany	224ft. 2½ in.

Shot Put (8lb., 13oz.)

1948	Micheline Ostermeyer, France	45ft. 1½ in.
1952	Galina Zybina, USSR	50ft. 1¾ in.

(Continued)

1956	Tamara Tishkyevich, USSR	54ft. 5 in.
1960	Tamara Press, USSR	56ft. 10 in.
1964	Tamara Press, USSR	59ft. 6¼ in.
1968	Margitta Gummel, E. Germany	64ft. 4 in.
1972	Nadezhda Chizova, USSR	69ft.
1976	Ivanka Hristova, Bulgaria	69ft. 5¼ in.
1980	Ilona Slupianek, E. Germany	73ft. 6¼ in.*
1984	Claudia Losch, W. Germany	67ft. 2¼ in.
1988	Natalya Lisovskaya, USSR	72ft 11½ in.
1992	Svetlana Kriveleva, Unified Team	69ft. 1¼ in.

Long Jump

1948	Olga Gyarmati, Hungary	18ft. 8¼ in.
1952	Yvette Williams, New Zealand	20ft. 5¾ in.
1956	Elzbieta Krzeskinska, Poland	20ft. 9¾ in.
1960	Vyera Krepkina, USSR	20ft. 10¾ in.
1964	Mary Rand, Great Britain	22ft. 2¼ in.
1968	Viorica Viscopoleanu, Romania	22ft. 4½ in.
1972	Heidemarie Rosendahl, W. Germany	22ft. 3 in.
1976	Angela Voigt, E. Germany	22ft. ¾ in.
1980	Tatyana Kolpakova, USSR	23ft. 2 in.
1984	Anisoara Stanciu, Romania	22ft. 10 in.
1988	Jackie Joyner-Kersee, United States	24ft 3½ in.
1992	Heike Drechsler, Germany	25ft. 5¼ in.*

Marathon

1984	Joan Benoit, United States	2h. 24m. 52s*
1988	Rosa Mota, Portugal	2h. 25m. 40s
1992	Valentina Yegorova, Unified Team	2h. 32m. 41s

Boxing

Light Flyweight (106 lbs)

1968 Francisco Rodriguez, Venezuela
1972 Gyorgy Gedo, Hungary
1976 Jorge Hernandez, Cuba
1980 Shamil Sabyrov, USSR
1984 Paul Gonzalez, U.S.
1988 Ivailo Hristov, Bulgaria
1992 Rogelio Marcelo, Cuba

Flyweight (112½ lbs)

1904 George Finnegan, U.S.
1920 William Di Gennara, U.S.
1924 Fidel LaBarba, U.S.
1928 Antal Kocsis, Hungary
1932 Istvan Enekes, Hungary
1936 Willi Kaiser, Germany
1948 Pascual Perez, Argentina
1952 Nathan Brooks, U.S.
1956 Terence Spinks, Great Britain
1960 Gyula Torok, Hungary
1964 Fernando Atzori, Italy
1968 Ricardo Delgado, Mexico
1972 Georgi Kostadinov, Bulgaria
1976 Leo Randolph, U.S.
1980 Peter Lessov, Bulgaria
1984 Steve McCrory, U.S.
1988 Kim Kwang Sun, S. Korea
1992 Su Choi Choi, N. Korea

Bantamweight (119½ lbs)

1904 Oliver Kirk, U.S.
1908 A Henry Thomas, Great Britain
1920 Clarence Walker, South Africa
1924 William Smith, South Africa
1928 Vittorio Tamagnini, Italy
1932 Horace Gwynne, Canada
1936 Ulderico Sergo, Italy
1948 Tibor Csik, Hungary
1952 Pentti Hamalainen, Finland
1956 Wolfgang Behrendt, E. Germany
1960 Oleg Grigoryev, USSR
1964 Takao Sakurai, Japan
1968 Valery Sokolov, USSR
1972 Orlando Martinez, Cuba
1976 Yong-Jo Gu, N. Korea
1980 Juan Hernandez, Cuba
1984 Maurizio Stecca, Italy
1988 Kennedy McKinney, U.S.
1992 Joel Casamayor, Cuba

Featherweight (126 lbs)

1904 Oliver Kirk, U.S.
1908 Richard Gunn, Great Britain
1920 Paul Fritsch, France
1924 John Fields, U.S.
1928 Lambertus van Klaveren, Netherlands
1932 Carmelo Robledo, Argentina
1936 Oscar Casanovas, Argentina
1948 Ernesto Formenti, Italy
1952 Jan Zachara, Czech.
1956 Vladimir Safronov, USSR
1960 Francesco Musso, Italy
1964 Stanislav Stephashkin, USSR
1968 Antonin Roldan, Mexico
1972 Boris Kousnetsov, USSR
1976 Angel Herrera, Cuba
1980 Rudi Fink, E. Germany
1984 Meldrick Taylor, U.S.
1988 Giovanni Parisi, Italy
1992 Andreas Tews, Germany

Lightweight (132 lbs)

1904 Harry Spanger, U.S.
1908 Frederick Grace, Great Britain
1920 Samuel Mosberg, U.S.
1924 Hans Nielsen, Denmark
1928 Carlo Orlandi, Italy
1932 Lawrence Stevens, South Africa
1936 Imre Harangi, Hungary
1948 Gerald Dreyer, South Africa
1952 Aureliano Bolognesi, Italy
1956 Richard McTaggart, Great Britain
1960 Kazimierz Pazdzior, Poland
1964 Jozef Grudzien, Poland
1968 Ronald Harris, U.S.
1972 Jan Szczepanski, Poland
1976 Howard Davis, U.S.
1980 Angel Herrera, Cuba
1984 Pernell Whitaker, U.S.
1988 Andreas Zuelow, E. Germany
1992 Oscar De La Hoya, U.S.

Light Welterweight (140 lbs)

1952 Charles Adkins, U.S.
1956 Vladimir Yengibaryan, USSR
1960 Bohumil Nemecek, Czech.
1964 Jerzy Kulej, Poland
1968 Jerzy Kulej, Poland
1972 Ray Seales, U.S.
1976 Ray Leonard, U.S.
1980 Patrizio Oliva, Italy
1984 Jerry Page, U.S.
1988 Viatcheslav Janovski, USSR
1992 Hector Vinent, Cuba

Welterweight (148 lbs)

1904 Albert Young, U.S.
1920 Albert Schneider, Canada
1924 Jean Delarge, Belgium
1928 Edward Morgan, New Zealand
1932 Edward Flynn, U.S.
1936 Sten Suvio, Finland
1948 Julius Torma, Czech.
1952 Zygmunt Chychia, Poland
1956 Nicolae Linca, Romania
1960 Giovanni Benvenuti, Italy
1964 Marian Kasprzyk, Poland
1968 Manfred Wolke, E. Germany
1972 Emilio Correa, Cuba
1976 Jochen Bachfeld, E. Germany
1980 Andres Aldama, Cuba
1984 Mark Breland, U.S.
1988 Robert Wangila, Kenya
1992 Michael Carruth, Ireland

Light Middleweight (157 lbs)

1952 Laszlo Papp, Hungary
1956 Laszio Papp, Hungary
1960 Wilbert McClure, U.S.
1964 Boris Lagutin, USSR
1968 Boris Lagutin, USSR
1972 Dieter Kottysch, W. Germany
1976 Jerzy Rybicki, Poland
1980 Armando Martinez, Cuba
1984 Frank Tate, U.S.

(Continued)

1988 Park Si Hun, S. Korea
1992 Juan Lemus, Cuba

Middleweight (165½ lbs)

1904 Charles Mayer, U.S.
1908 John Douglas, Great Britain
1920 Harry Mallin, Great Britain
1924 Harry Mallin, Great Britain
1928 Piero Toscani, Italy
1932 Carmen Barth, U.S.
1936 Jean Despeaux, France
1948 Laszio Papp, Hungary
1952 Floyd Patterson, U.S.
1956 Gennady Schatkov, USSR
1960 Edward Crook, U.S.
1964 Valery Popenchenko, USSR
1968 Christopher Finnegan, Great Britain
1972 Vyacheslav Lemechev, USSR
1976 Michael Spinks, U.S.
1980 Jose Gomez, Cuba
1984 Joon-Sup Shin, S. Korea
1988 Henry Maske, E. Germany
1992 Ariel Hernandez, Cuba

Light Heavyweight (179 lbs)

1920 Edward Eagan, U.S.
1924 Harry Mitchell, Great Britain
1928 Victor Avendano, Argentina
1932 David Carstens, South Africa
1936 Roger Michelot, France
1948 George Hunter, South Africa
1952 Norvel Lee, U.S.
1956 James Boyd, U.S.
1960 Cassius Clay, U.S.
1964 Cosimo Pinto, Italy
1968 Dan Poznyak, USSR
1972 Mate Parlov, Yugoslavia
1976 Leon Spinks, U.S.
1980 Slobodan Kacar, Yugoslavia
1984 Anton Josipovic, Yugoslavia
1988 Andrew Maynard, U.S.
1992 Torsten May, Germany

Heavyweight (200½ lbs)

1984 Henry Tillman, U.S.
1988 Ray Mercer, U.S.
1992 Felix Savon, Cuba

Super Heavyweight (Unlimited)
(known as heavyweight from 1904-1980)

1904 Samuel Berger, U.S.
1908 Albert Oldham, Great Britain
1920 Ronald Rawson, Great Britain
1924 Otto von Porat, Norway
1928 Arturo Rodriguez Jurado, Argentina
1932 Santiago Lovell, Argentina
1936 Herbert Runge, Germany
1948 Rafael Inglesias, Argentina
1952 H. Edward Sanders, U.S.
1956 T. Peter Rademacher, U.S.
1960 Franco De Piccoli, Italy
1964 Joe Frazier, U.S.
1968 George Foreman, U.S.
1972 Teofilo Stevenson, Cuba
1976 Teofilo Stevenson, Cuba
1980 Teofilo Stevenson, Cuba
1984 Tyrell Biggs, U.S.
1988 Lennox Lewis, Canada
1992 Roberto Balado, Cuba

Swimming – Men

50-Metre Freestyle

1988	Matt Biondi, U.S.	22.14
1992	Aleksandr Popov, Unified Team	22.91*

100-Metre Freestyle

1896	Alfred Hajos, Hungary	1:22.2
1904	Zoltan de Halmay, Hungary (100 yards)	1:02.8
1908	Charles Daniels, U.S.	1:05.6
1912	Duke P. Kahanamoku, U.S.	1:03.4
1920	Duke P. Kahanamoku, U.S.	1:01.4
1924	John Weissmuller, U.S.	59.0
1928	John Weissmuller, U.S.	58.6
1932	Yasuji Miyazaki, Japan	58.2
1936	Ferenc Csik, Hungary	57.6
1948	Wally Ris, U.S.	57.3
1952	Clark Scholes, U.S.	57.4
1956	Jon Henricks, Australia	55.4
1960	John Devitt, Australia	55.2
1964	Don Schollander, U.S.	53.4
1968	Mike Wenden, Australia	52.2
1972	Mark Spitz, U.S.	51.22
1976	Jim Montgomery, U.S.	49.99
1980	Jorg Woithe, E. Germany	50.40
1984	Rowdy Gaines, U.S.	49.80
1988	Matt Biondi, United States	48.63*
1992	Aleksandr Popov, Unified Team	49.02

200-Metre Freestyle

1968	Mike Wenden, Australia	1:55.2
1972	Mark Spitz, U.S.	1:52.78
1976	Bruce Furniss, U.S.	1:50.29
1980	Sergei Kopliakov, USSR	1:49.81
1984	Michael Gross, W. Germany	1:47.44
1988	Duncan Armstrong, Australia	1:47.25
1992	Evgueni Sadovyi, Unified Team	1:46.70*

400-Metre Freestyle

1904	C. M. Daniels, U.S. (440 yards)	6:16.2
1908	Henry Taylor, Great Britain	5:36.8
1912	George Hodgson, Canada	5:24.4
1920	Norman Ross, U.S.	5:26.8
1924	John Weissmuller, U.S.	5:04.2
1928	Albert Zorilla, Argentina	5:01.6
1932	Clarence Crabbe, U.S.	4:48.4
1936	Jack Medica, U.S.	4:44.5
1948	William Smith, U.S.	4:41.0
1952	Jean Boiteux, France	4:30.7
1956	Murray Rose, Australia	4:27.3
1960	Murray Rose, Australia	4:18.3
1964	Don Schollander, U.S.	4:12.2
1968	Mike Burton, U.S.	4:09.0
1972	Brad Cooper, Australia	4:00.27
1976	Brian Goodell, U.S.	3:51.93
1980	Vladimir Salnikov, USSR	3:51.31
1984	George DiCarlo, U.S.	3:51.23
1988	Ewe Dassler, E. Germany	3:46.95
1992	Evgueni Sadovyi, Unified Team	3:45.00*

1,500-Metre Freestyle

1908	Henry Taylor, Great Britain	22:48.4
1912	George Hodgson, Canada	22:00.0
1920	Norman Ross, U.S.	22:23.2
1924	Andrew Charlton, Australia	20:06.6
1928	Arne Borg, Sweden	19:51.8
1932	Kusuo Kitamura, Japan	19:12.4
1936	Noboru Terada, Japan	19:13.7
1948	James McLane, U.S.	19:18.5
1952	Ford Konno, U.S.	18:30.3
1956	Murray Rose, Australia	17:58.9
1960	Jon Konrads, Australia	17:19.6
1964	Robert Windle, Australia	17:01.7
1968	Mike Burton, U.S.	16:38.9
1972	Mike Burton, U.S.	15:52.58
1976	Brian Goodell, U.S.	15:02.40
1980	Vladimir Salnikov, USSR	14:58.27
1984	Michael O'Brien, U.S.	15:05.20
1988	Vladimir Salnikov, USSR	15:00.40
1992	Kieren Perkins, Australia	14:43.48*

400-Metre Medley Relay

1960	United States	4:05.4
1964	United States	3:58.4
1968	United States	3:54.9
1972	United States	3:48.16
1976	United States	3:42.22
1980	Australia	3:45.70
1984	United States	3:39.30
1988	United States	3:36.93*
1992	United States	3:36.93*

400-Metre Freestyle Relay

1964	United States	3:31.2

(Continued)

1968	United States	3:31.7
1972	United States	3:26.42
1984	United States	3:19.03
1988	United States	3:16.53*
1992	United States	3:16.74

800-Metre Freestyle Relay

1908	Great Britain	10:55.6
1912	Australia	10:11.6
1920	United States	10:04.4
1924	United States	9:53.4
1928	United States	9:36.2
1932	Japan	8:58.4
1936	Japan	8:51.5
1948	United States	8:46.0
1952	United States	8:31.1
1956	Australia	8:23.6
1960	United States	8:10.2
1964	United States	7:52.1
1968	United States	7:52.33
1972	United States	7:35.78
1976	United States	7:23.22
1980	USSR	7:23.50
1984	United States	7:15.69
1988	United States	7:12.51
1992	Unified Team	7:11.95*

100-Metre Backstroke

1904	Walter Brack, Germany (100 yds.)	1:16.8
1908	Arno Bieberstein, Germany	1:24.6
1912	Harry Hebner, U.S.	1:21.2
1920	Warren Kealoha, U.S.	1:15.2
1924	Warren Kealoha, U.S.	1:13.2
1928	George Kojac, U.S.	1:08.2
1932	Masaji Kiyokawa, Japan	1:08.6
1936	Adolph Kiefer, U.S.	1:05.9
1948	Allen Stack, U.S.	1:06.4
1952	Yoshi Oyakawa, U.S.	1:05.4
1956	David Thiele, Australia	1:02.2
1960	David Thiele, Australia	1:01.9
1968	Roland Matthes, E. Germany	58.7
1972	Roland Matthes, E. Germany	56.58
1976	John Naber, U.S.	55.49
1980	Bengt Baron, Sweden	56.33
1984	Rick Carey, U.S.	55.79
1988	Daichi Suzuki, Japan	55.05
1988	Mark Tewksbury, Canada	53.98*

200-Metre Backstroke

1964	Jed Graef, U.S.	2:10.3
1968	Roland Matthes, E. Germany	2:09.6
1972	Roland Matthes, E. Germany	2:02.82
1976	John Naber, U.S.	1:59.19
1980	Sandor Wladar, Hungary	2:01.93
1984	Rick Carey, U.S.	2:00.23
1988	Igor Polianski, USSR	1:59.37
1992	Martin Lopez-Zubero, Spain	1:58.47*

100-Metre Breaststroke

1968	Don McKenzie, U.S.	1:07.7
1972	Nobutaka Taguchi, Japan	1:04.94
1976	John Hencken, U.S.	1:03.11
1980	Duncan Goodhew, Great Britain	1:03.44
1984	Steve Lundquist, U.S.	1:01.65
1988	Adrian Moorhouse, Great Britain	1:02.04
1992	Nelson Diebel, U.S.	1:01.50*

200-Metre Breaststroke

1908	Frederick Holman, Great Britain	3:09.2
1912	Walter Bathe, Germany	3:01.8
1920	Haken Malmroth, Sweden	3:04.4
1924	Robert Skelton, U.S.	2:56.6
1928	Yoshiyuki Tsuruta, Japan	2:48.8
1932	Yoshiyuki Tsuruta, Japan	2:45.4
1936	Tetsuo Hamuro, Japan	2:41.5
1948	Joseph Verdeur, U.S.	2:39.3
1952	John Davies, Australia	2:34.4
1956	Masura Furukawa, Japan	2:34.7
1960	William Mulliken, U.S.	2:37.4
1964	Ian O'Brien, Australia	2:27.8
1968	Felipe Munoz, Mexico	2:28.7
1972	John Hencken, U.S.	2:21.55
1976	David Wilkie, Great Britain	2:15.11
1980	Robertas Zhulpa, USSR	2:15.85
1984	Victor Davis, Canada	2:13.34
1988	Jozsef Szabo, Hungary	2:13.52
1992	Mike Barrowman, U.S.	2:10.16*

100-Metre Butterfly

1968	Doug Russell, U.S.	55.9
1972	Mark Spitz, U.S.	54.27
1976	Matt Vogel, U.S.	54.35
1980	Par Arvidsson, Sweden	54.92
1984	Michael Gross, W. Germany	53.08
1988	Anthony Nesty, Suriname	53.00*
1992	Pablo Morales, U.S.	53.32

200-Metre Butterfly

1956	William Yorzyk, U.S.	2:19.3
1960	Michael Troy, U.S.	2:12.8
1964	Kevin J. Berry, Australia	2:06.6
1968	Carl Robie, U.S.	2:08.7
1972	Mark Spitz, U.S.	2:00.70
1976	Mike Bruner, U.S.	1:59.23
1980	Sergei Fesenko, USSR	1:59.76
1984	Jon Sieben, Australia	1:57.04
1988	Michael Gross, W. Germany	1:56.94
1992	Mel Stewart, U.S.	1:56.26*

200-Metre Individual Medley

1968	Charles Hickcox, U.S.	2:12.0
1972	Gunnar Larsson, Sweden	2:07.17
1984	Alex Baumann, Canada	2:01.42
1988	Tamas Darnyi, Hungary	2:00.17*
1992	Tamas Darnyi, Hungary	2:00.76

400-Metre Individual Medley

1964	Dick Roth, U.S.	4:45.4
1968	Charles Hickcox, U.S.	4:48.4
1972	Gunnar Larsson, Sweden	4:31.98
1976	Rod Strachan, U.S.	4:23.68
1980	Aleksandr Sidorenko, USSR	4:22.89
1984	Alex Baumann, Canada	4:17.41
1988	Tamas Darnyi, Hungary	4:14.75
1992	Tamas Darnyi, Hungary	4:14.23*

	Springboard Diving	**Points**
1908	Albert Zurner, Germany	85.5
1912	Paul Guenther, Germany	79.23
1920	Louis Kuehn, U.S.	675.40
1924	Albert White, U.S.	97.46
1928	Pete Desjardins, U.S.	185.04
1932	Michael Galitzen, U.S.	161.38
1936	Richard Degener, U.S.	163.57
1948	Bruce Harlan, U.S.	163.64
1952	David Browning, U.S.	205.29
1956	Robert Clotworthy, U.S.	159.56
1960	Gary Tobian, U.S.	170.00
1964	Kenneth Sitzberger, U.S.	159.90
1968	Bernie Wrightson, U.S.	170.15
1972	Vladimir Vasin, USSR	594.09
1976	Phil Boggs, U.S.	619.52
1980	Aleksandr Portnov, USSR	905.02
1984	Greg Louganis, U.S.	754.41
1988	Greg Louganis, U.S.	730.80
1992	Mark Lenzi, U.S.	676.530

	Platform Diving	**Points**
1904	Dr. G.E. Sheldon, U.S.	12.75
1908	Hjalmar Johansson, Sweden	83.75
1912	Erik Adlerz, Sweden	73.94
1920	Clarence Pinkston, U.S.	100.67
1924	Albert White, U.S.	97.46
1928	Pete Desjardins, U.S.	98.74
1932	Harold Smith, U.S.	124.80
1936	Marshall Wayne, U.S.	113.58
1948	Sammy Lee, U.S.	130.05
1952	Sammy Lee, U.S.	156.28
1956	Joaquin Capilla, Mexico	152.44
1960	Robert Webster, U.S.	165.56
1964	Robert Webster, U.S.	148.58
1968	Klaus Dibiasi, Italy	164.18
1972	Klaus Dibiasi, Italy	504.12
1976	Klaus Dibiasi, Italy	600.51
1980	Falk Hoffmann, E. Germany	835.65
1984	Greg Louganis, U.S.	710.91
1988	Greg Louganis, U.S.	638.61
1992	Sun Shuwei, China	677.310

Swimming – Women

50-Metre Freestyle

1988	Kristin Otto, E. Germany	25.49
1992	Yang Wenyi, China	24.79*

100-Metre Freestyle

1912	Fanny Durack, Australia	1:22.2
1920	Ethelda Bleibtrey, U.S.	1:13.6
1924	Ethel Lackie, U.S.	1:12.4
1928	Albina Osipowich, U.S.	1:11.0
1932	Helene Madison, U.S.	1:06.8
1936	Hendrika Mastenbroek, Holland	1:05.9
1948	Greta Andersen, Denmark	1:06.3
1952	Katalin Szoke, Hungary	1:06.8
1956	Dawn Fraser, Australia	1:02.0
1960	Dawn Fraser, Australia	1:01.2
1964	Dawn Fraser, Australia	59.5
1968	Jan Henne, U.S.	1:00.0
1972	Sandra Neilson, U.S.	58.59
1976	Kornelia Ender, E. Germany	55.65
1980	Barbara Krause, E. Germany	54.79
1984	(tie) Carrie Steinseifer, U.S.	55.92
	Nancy Hogshead, U.S.	55.92
1988	Kristin Otto, E. Germany	54.93
1992	Zhuang Yong, China	54.64*

200-Metre Freestyle

1968	Debbie Meyer, U.S.	2:10.5
1972	Shane Gould, Australia	2:03.56
1976	Kornelia Ender, E. Germany	1:59.26
1980	Barbara Krause, E. Germany	1:58.33
1984	Mary Wayte, U.S.	1:59.23
1988	Heike Friedrich, E. Germany	1:57.65*
1992	Nicole Haislett, U.S.	1:57.90

400-Metre Freestyle

1924	Martha Norelius, U.S.	6:02.2
1928	Martha Norelius, U.S.	5:42.8
1932	Helene Madison, U.S.	5:28.5
1936	Hendrika Mastenbroek, Netherlands	5:26.4
1948	Ann Curtis, U.S.	5:17.8
1952	Valerie Gyenge, Hungary	5:12.1
1956	Lorraine Crapp, Australia	4:54.6
1960	Susan Chris von Saltza, U.S.	4:50.6
1964	Virginia Duenkel, U.S.	4:43.3
1968	Debbie Meyer, U.S.	4:31.8
1972	Shane Gould, Australia	4:19.44
1976	Petra Thuemer E. Germany	4:09.89
1980	Ines Diers, E. Germany	4:08.76
1984	Tiffany Cohen, U.S.	4:07.10
1988	Janet Evans, U.S.	4:03.85*
1992	Dagmar Hase, Germany	4:07.18

800-Metre Freestyle

1968	Debbie Meyer, U.S.	9:24.0
1972	Keena Rothhammer, U.S.	8:53.68
1976	Petra Thuemer, E. Germany	8:37.14
1980	Michelle Ford, Australia	8:28.90
1984	Tiffany Cohen, U.S.	8:24.95
1988	Janet Evans, U.S.	8:20.20*
1992	Janet Evans, U.S.	8:25.52

100-Metre Backstroke

1924	Sybil Bauer, U.S.	1:23.2
1928	Marie Braun, Netherlands	1:22.0
1932	Eleanor Holm, U.S.	1:19.4
1936	Dina Senff, Netherlands	1:18.9
1948	Karen Harup, Denmark	1:14.4
1952	Joan Harrison, South Africa	1:14.3
1956	Judy Grinham, Great Britain	1:12.9
1960	Lynn Burke, U.S.	1:09.3
1964	Cathy Ferguson, U.S.	1:07.7
1968	Kaye Hall, U.S.	1:06.2
1972	Melissa Belote, U.S.	1:05.78
1976	Ulrike Richter, E. Germany	1:01.83
1980	Rica Reinisch, E. Germany	1:00.86
1984	Theresa Andrews, U.S.	1:02.55
1988	Kristin Otto, E. Germany	1:00.89
1992	Krisztina Egerszegi, Hungary	1:00.68*

200-Metre Backstroke

1968	Pokey Watson, U.S.	2:24.8
1972	Melissa Belote, U.S.	2:19.19
1976	Ulrike Richter, E. Germany	2:13.43
1980	Rica Reinisch, E. Germany	2:11.77
1984	Jolanda De Rover, Netherlands	2:12.38
1988	Krisztina Egerszegi, Hungary	2:09.29
1992	Krisztina Egerszegi, Hungary	2:07.06*

100-Metre Breaststroke

1968	Djurdjica Bjedov, Yugoslavia	1:15.8
1972	Cathy Carr, U.S.	1:13.58
1976	Hannelore Anke, E. Germany	1:11:16
1980	Ute Geweniger, E. Germany	1:10.22
1984	Petra Van Staveren, Netherlands	1:09.88
1988	Tania Dangalakova, Bulgaria	1:07.95*
1992	Elena Roudkovskaia, Unified Team	1:08.00

200-Metre Breaststroke

1924	Lucy Morton, Great Britain	3:33.2
1928	Hilde Schrader, Germany	3:12.6
1932	Clare Dennis, Australia	3:06.3
1936	Hideko Maehata, Japan	3:03.6
1948	Nelly Van Vliet, Netherlands	2:57.2
1952	Eva Szekely, Hungary	2:51.7
1956	Ursula Happe, Germany	2:53.1
1960	Anita Lonsbrough, Great Britain	2:49.5
1964	Galina Prozumenschikova, USSR	2:46.4
1968	Sharon Wichman, U.S.	2:44.4
1972	Beverly Whitfield, Australia	2:41.71
1976	Marina Koshevaia, USSR	2:33.35
1980	Lina Kachushite, USSR	2:29.54
1984	Anne Ottenbrite, Canada	2:30.38
1988	Silke Hoerner, E. Germany	2:26.71
1992	Kyoko Iwasaki, Japan	2:26.65*

200-Metre Individual Medley

1968	Claudia Kolb, U.S.	2:24.7
1972	Shane Gould, Australia	2:23.07
1984	Tracy Caulkins, U.S.	2:12.64
1988	Daniela Hunger, E. Germany	2:12.59
1992	Lin Li, China	2:11.65*

400-Metre Individual Medley

1964	Donna de Varona, U.S.	5:18.7
1968	Claudia Kolb, U.S.	5:08.5
1972	Gail Neall, Australia	5:02.97
1976	Ulrike Tauber, E. Germany	4:42.77
1980	Petra Schneider, E. Germany	4:36.29*
1984	Tracy Caulkins, U.S.	4:39.24
1988	Janet Evans, U.S.	4:37.76
1992	Krisztina Egerszegi, Hungary	4:36.73

100-Metre Butterfly

1956	Shelley Mann, U.S.	1:11.0
1960	Carolyn Schuler, U.S.	1:09.5
1964	Sharon Stouder, U.S.	1:04.7
1968	Lynn McClements, Australia	1:05.5
1972	Mayumi Aoki, Japan	1:03.34
1976	Kornelia Ender, E. Germany	1:00.13
1980	Caren Metschuck, E. Germany	1:00.42
1984	Mary T. Meagher, U.S.	59.26
1988	Kristin Otto, E. Germany	59.00
1992	Qian Hong, China	58.62*

200-Metre Butterfly

1968	Ada Kok, Netherlands	2:24.7
1972	Karen Moe, U.S.	2:15.57
1976	Andrea Pollack, E. Germany	2:11.41
1980	Ines Geissler, E. Germany	2:10.44
1984	Mary T. Meagher, U.S.	2:06.90*
1988	Kathleen Nord, E. Germany	2:09.51
1992	Summer Sanders, U.S.	2:08.67

400-Metre Medley Relay

1960	United States	4:41.1
1960	United States	4:33.9
1968	United States	4:28.3
1972	United States	4:20.75
1976	East Germany	4:07.95
1980	East Germany	4:06.67
1984	United States	4:08.34
1988	E. Germany	4:03.74
1992	United States	4:02.54*

400-Metre Freestyle Relay

1912	Great Britain	5:52.8
1920	United States	5:11.6
1924	United States	4:58.8
1928	United States	4:47.6

(Continued)

1932	United States	4:38.0
1936	Netherlands	4:36.0
1948	United States	4:29.2
1952	Hungary	4:24.4
1956	Australia	4:17.1
1960	United States	4:08.9
1964	United States	4:03.8
1968	United States	4:02.5
1972	United States	3:55.19
1976	United States	3:44.82
1980	East Germany	3:42.71
1984	United States	3:43.43
1988	E. Germany	3:40.63
1992	United States	3:39.46*

	Springboard Diving	Points
1920	Aileen Riggin, U.S.	539.90
1924	Elizabeth Becker, U.S.	474.50
1928	Helen Meany, U.S.	78.62
1932	Georgia Coleman U.S.	87.52
1936	Marjorie Gestring, U.S.	89.27
1948	Victoria M. Draves, U.S.	108.74
1952	Patricia McCormick, U.S.	147.30
1956	Patricia McCormick, U.S.	142.36
1960	Ingrid Kramer, Germany	155.81
1964	Ingrid Engel-Kramer, Germany	145.00
1968	Sue Gossick, U.S.	150.77
1972	Micki King, U.S.	450.03
1976	Jenni Chandler, U.S.	506.19
1980	Irina Kalinina, USSR	725.91
1984	Sylvie Bernier, Canada	536.70
1988	Gao Min, China	580.23
1992	Gao Min, China	572.400

	Platform Diving	Points
1912	Greta Johansson, Sweden	39.90
1920	Stefani Fryland-Clausen, Denmark	34.60
1924	Caroline Smith, U.S.	33.20
1928	Elizabeth B. Pinkston, U.S.	31.60
1932	Dorothy Poynton, U.S.	40.26
1936	Dorothy Poynton Hill, U.S.	33.93
1948	Victoria M. Draves, U.S.	68.87
1952	Patricia McCormick, U.S.	79.37
1956	Patricia McCormick, U.S.	84.85
1960	Ingrid Kramer, Germany	91.28
1964	Lesley Bush, U.S.	99.80
1968	Milena Duchkova, Czech	109.59
1972	Ulrika Knape, Sweden	390.00
1976	Elena Vaytsekhouskaya, USSR	406.59
1980	Martina Jaschke, E. Germany	596.25
1984	Zhou Jihong, China	435.51
1988	Xu Yanmei, China	445.20
1992	Fu Mingxia, China	461.430

25TH SUMMER OLYMPICS

Barcelona, Spain, 25 July–9 Aug. 1992

Over 14,000 athletes gathered in Barcelona, Spain, in July and August for 16 days to compete in the Games of the XXV Olympiad. The athletes represented a record 172 nations, 11 more than participated in any previous Olympics, and competed for medals in 257 events.

The 1992 games will be remembered mostly for Linford Christie's thrilling performance in the 100-metre run, which gained him his first Olympic gold medal. Other notable events at the games were Sally Gunnell's victory in the 400-metre hurdles, Carl Lewis's success in the long jump (his third consecutive gold medal in the event), the near-perfect diving of the Chinese women, and the domination of men's gymnastics by Vitaly Shcherbo of the Unified Team. The games also saw the appearance of South African athletes for the first time in 28 years. On the negative side, world-record holder Sergei Bubka of Ukraine failed to win a medal in the pole vault, and Liz McColgan came a disappointing 6th in the 10,000-metres run – an event she was tipped to win.

The Unified Team made up of athletes of 12 republics of the former Soviet Union won the most gold medals (45) and the most medals over all (112). Great Britain came 12th, with 5 gold medals and 20 medals over all.

Final Medals Standing

	Gold	Silver	Bronze	Total
Unified Team[1]	45	38	29	112
United States	37	34	37	108
Germany	33	21	28	82
China	16	22	16	54
Cuba	14	6	11	31
Hungary	11	12	7	30
South Korea	12	5	12	29
France	8	5	16	29
Australia	7	9	11	27
Spain	13	7	2	22
Japan	3	8	11	22
Great Britain	5	3	12	20
Italy	6	5	8	19
Poland	3	6	10	19
Canada	6	5	7	18
Romania	4	6	8	18
Bulgaria	3	7	6	16
Netherlands	2	6	7	15
Sweden	1	7	4	12
New Zealand	1	4	5	10
North Korea	4	0	5	9
Kenya	2	4	2	8
Czechoslovakia	4	2	1	7
Norway	2	4	1	7
Turkey	2	2	2	6
Denmark	1	1	4	6
Indonesia	2	2	1	5
Finland	1	2	2	5
Jamaica	0	3	1	4
Nigeria	0	3	1	4
Brazil	2	1	0	3
Morocco	1	1	1	3
Ethiopia	1	0	2	3
Latvia	0	2	1	3
Croatia	0	1	2	3
Belgium	0	1	2	3
Iran	0	1	2	3
I.O.P.[2]	0	1	2	3
Greece	2	0	0	2
Ireland	1	1	0	2
Algeria	1	0	1	2
Estonia	1	0	1	2
Lithuania	1	0	1	2
Austria	0	2	0	2
Namibia	0	2	0	2
South Africa	0	2	0	2
Israel	0	1	1	2
Mongolia	0	0	2	2
Slovenia	0	0	2	2
Switzerland	1	0	0	1
Mexico	0	1	0	1
Peru	0	1	0	1
Taiwan	0	1	0	1
Argentina	0	0	1	1
Bahamas	0	0	1	1
Colombia	0	0	1	1
Ghana	0	0	1	1
Malaysia	0	0	1	1
Pakistan	0	0	1	1
Philippines	0	0	1	1
Puerto Rico	0	0	1	1
Qatar	0	0	1	1
Suriname	0	0	1	1
Thailand	0	0	1	1

(1) Athletes from 12 former Soviet republics. (2) Independent Olympic Participants (athletes from Serbia, Montenegro and Macedonia).

1992 Summer Olympics Medal Winners
(Gold, Silver, Bronze)

Archery

Men's 70-metre Individual – Sebastien Flute, France; Chung Jae Hun, S. Korea; Simon Terry, Great Britain.

Men's Team – Spain; Finland; Great Britain.

Women's 70-Metre Individual – Cho Youn Jeong, S. Korea; Kim Soo Nyung, S. Korea; Natalia Valeeva, Unified Team.

Women's Team – S. Korea; China; Unified Team.

Athletics

Men

100m – Linford Christie, Great Britain; Frankie Fredericks, Namibia; Dennis Mitchell, U.S.

200m – Mike Marsh, U.S.; Frankie Fredericks, Namibia; Michael Bates, U.S.

400m – Quincy Watts, U.S.; Steve Lewis, U.S.; Samson Kitur, Kenya.

800m – William Tanui, Kenya; Nixon Kiprotich, Kenya; Johnny Gray, U.S.

1,500m – Fermin Cacho Ruiz, Spain; Rachid El-Basir, Morocco; Mohamed Ahmed Sulaiman, Qatar.

5,000m – Dieter Baumann, Germany; Paul Bitok, Kenya; Fita Bayisa, Ethiopia.

10,000m – Khalid Skah, Morocco; Richard Chelimo, Kenya; Addis Abebe, Ethiopia.

110m Hurdles – Mark McKoy, Canada; Tony Dees, U.S.; Jack Pierce, U.S.

400m Hurdles – Kevin Young, U.S.; Winthrop Graham, Jamaica; Kriss Akabusi, Great Britian.

4×100m Relay – U.S.; Nigeria; Cuba.

4×400m Relay – U.S.; Cuba; Great Britain.

Shot Put – Michael Stulce, U.S.; James Doehring, U.S.; Viacheslav Lykho, Unified Team.

Triple Jump – Mike Conley, U.S.; Charles Simpkins, U.S.; Frank Rutherford, U.S.

Javelin – Jan Zelezny, Czechoslovakia; Seppo Raty, Finland; Steve Backley, Great Britain.

High Jump – Javier Sotomayor, Cuba; Patrik Sjoeberg, Sweden; (tie) Artur Partyka, Poland, Timothy Forsythe, Australia, Hollis Conway, U.S.

Hammer Throw – Andrey Abduvaliyev, Unified Team; Igor Astapkovich, Unified Team; Igor Nikulin, Unified Team.

Long Jump – Carl Lewis, U.S.; Mike Powell, U.S.; Joe Greene, U.S.

Pole Vault – Maksim Tarassov, Unified Team; Igor Trandenkov, Unified Team; Javier Garcia Chico, Spain.

Decathlon – Robert Zmelik, Czechoslovakia; Antonio Penalver, Spain; Dave Johnson, U.S.

Discus – Romas Ubartas, Lithuania; Jurgen Schult, Germany; Roberto Moya, Cuba.

20-km Walk – Daniel Plaza Montero, Spain; Guillaume Leblanc, Canada; Giovanni de Benedictis, Italy.

50-km Walk – Andrei Perlov, Unified Team; Carlos Mercenario Carbajal, Mexico; Ronald Weigel, Germany.

3,000m Steeplechase – Mathew Birir, Kenya; Patrick Sang, Kenya; William Mutwol; Kenya.

Marathon – Hwang Young-Cho, S. Korea; Koitchi Morishita, Japan; Stephan Freigang, Germany.

Women

100m – Gail Devers, U.S.; Juliet Cuthbert, Jamaica; Irina Privalova, Unified Team.

200m – Gwen Torrance, U.S.; Juliet Cuthbert; Merlene Ottey, Jamaica.

400m – Marie-Jose Perec, France; Olga Bryzgina, Unified Team; Ximena Restrepo Gaviria, Colombia.

800m – Ellen van Langen, Netherlands; Lilia Nurutdinova, Unified Team; Ana Quirot, Cuba.

1,500m – Hassiba Boulmerka, Algeria; Lyudmila Rogacheva, Unified Team; Qu Yunxia, China.

3,000m – Yelina Romanova, Unified Team; Tatyana Dorovskikh, Unified Team; Angela Frances Chalmers, Canada.

10,000m – Derartu Tulu, Ethiopia; Elana Meyer, South Africa; Lynn Jennings, U.S.

100m Hurdles – Paraskevi Patoulidou, Greece; LaVonna Martin, U.S.; Yordanka Donkova, Bulgaria.

400m Hurdles – Sally Gunnell, Great Britain; Sandra Farmer-Patrick, U.S.; Janeene Vickers, U.S.

4×100m Relay – U.S.; Unified Team; Nigeria.

4×400m Relay – Unified Team; U.S.; Great Britain.

Javelin – Silke Renk, Germany; Natalia Shikolenko, Unified Team; Karen Forkel, Germany.

Long Jump – Heike Drechsler, Germany; Inessa Kravets, Unified Team; Jackie Joyner-Kersee, U.S.

High Jump – Heike Henkel, Germany; Galina Astafei, Romania; Joanet Quintero, Cuba.

Shot Put – Svetlana Kriveleva, Unified Team; Huang Zhihong, China; Kathrin Neimke, Germany.

Heptathlon – Jackie Joyner-Kersee, U.S.; Irina Belova, Unified Team; Sabine Braun, Germany.

10-km Walk – Chen Yueling, China; Yelina Nikolaeva, Unified Team; Li Chunxiu, China.

Discus – Maritza Marten Garcia, Cuba; Tzvetanka Mintcheva Khristova, Bulgaria; Daniela Costian, Australia.

Marathon – Valentina Yegorova, Unified Team; Yuko Arimori, Japan; Lorraine Moller, New Zealand.

Badminton

Men

Men's Singles – Alan Budi Kusuma, Indonesia; Ardy Wiranata, Indonesia; (tie) Thomas Stuer-Lauridsen, Denmark, & Hermawan Susanto, Indonesia.

Men's Doubles – Kim Moon Soo and Park Joo Bong, S. Korea; Eddy Hartono and Rudy Gunawan, Indonesia; (tie) Li Yongbo and Tian Bingyi, China, & Sidek Razig and Sidek Jalani, Malaysia.

Women

Women's Singles – Susi Susanti, Indonesia; Bang Soo Hyun, S. Korea; (tie) Huang Hua, China, & Tang Jiuhong, China.

Women's Doubles – Hwang Hye Young and Chung So-Young, S. Korea; Guan Weizhen and Nong Qunhua, China; (tie) Gil Young Ah and Shim Eun Jung, S. Korea, & Lin Yanfen and Yao Fen, China.

Baseball

Cuba; Taiwan; Japan.

Basketball

Men – U.S.; Croatia; Lithuania.

Women – Cuba; China; US.

Boxing

106 Pounds – Rogelio Marcelo, Cuba; Daniel Bojinov, Bulgaria; (tie) Jan Quast, Germany, & Roel Velasco, Philippines.

112 Pounds – Su Choi Choi, N. Korea; Raul Gonzalez, Cuba; (tie) Timothy Austin, U.S., & Istvan Kovacs, Hungary.

119 Pounds – Joel Casamayor, Cuba; Wayne McCullough, Ireland; (tie) Li Gwang Sik, N. Korea, & Mohamed Achik, Morocco.

126 Pounds – Andreas Tews, Germany; Faustino Reyes, Spain; (tie) Hocine Soltani, Algeria, & Ramazi Paliani, Unified Team.

132 Pounds – Oscar De La Hoya, U.S.; Marco Rudolph, Germany; (tie) Hong Sung Sik, N. Korea, & Namjil Bayarsaikhan, Mongolia.

140 Pounds – Hector Vinent, Cuba; Mark Leduc, Canada; (tie) Jyri Kjall, Finland, & Leonard Doroftei, Romania.

148 Pounds – Michael Carruth, Ireland; Juan Hernandez, Cuba; (tie) Anibal Acevedo Santiago, Puerto Rico, & Arkom Chenglai, Thailand.

157 Pounds – Juan Lemus, Cuba; Orhan Delibas, Netherlands; (tie) Gyorgy Mizsei, Hungary, & Robin Reid, Great Britain.

165 Pounds – Ariel Hernandez, Cuba; Chris Byrd, U.S.; (tie) Chris Johnson, Canada, & Lee Seung Bae, S. Korea.

179 Pounds – Torsten May, Germany; Rostislav Zaoulitchnyi, Unified Team; (tie) Zoltan Beres, Hungary, & Wojciech Bartnik, Poland.

201 Pounds – Felix Savon, Cuba; David Izonritei, Nigeria; (tie) Arnold Van Der Lijde, Netherlands, & David Tua, New Zealand.

(Continued)

Over 201 Pounds – Roberto Balado, Cuba; Richard Igbineghu, Nigeria; (tie) Brian Nielsen, Denmark, & Svilen Roussinov, Bulgaria.

Canoe/Kayak

Men

Single Kayak Slalom – Pierpaolo Ferrazzi, Italy; Sylvain Curinier, France; Jochen Lettmann, Germany.

Kayak 500m Singles – Mikko Yrjoe Kolehmainen, Finland; Zsolt Gyulay, Hungary; Knut Holmann, Norway.

Kayak 500m Doubles – Germany; Poland; Italy.

Kayak 1,000m Singles – Clint Robinson, Australia; Knut Holmann, Norway; Greg Barton, U.S.

Kayak 1,000m Doubles – Germany; Sweden; Poland.
Kayak 1,000m Fours – Germany; Hungary; Australia.

Double Canoe Slalom – U.S.; Czechoslovakia; France.

Canoe Slalom – Lukas Pollert, Czechoslovakia; Gareth Marriott, Great Britain; Jacky Avril, France.

Canoe 500m Singles – Nikolai Boukhalov, Bulgaria; Mikhail Slivinski, Unified Team; Olaf Heukrodt, Germany.

Canoe 500m Doubles – Unified Team; Germany; Bulgaria.

Canoe 1,000m Singles – Nikolai Boukhalov, Bulgaria; Ivans Klementjevs, Latvia; Gyorgy Zala, Hungary.

Canoe 1,000m Doubles – Germany; Denmark; France.

Women

Kayak Slalom – Elisabeth Micheler, Germany; Danielle Anne Woodward, Australia; Dana Chladek, U.S.

Kayak 500m Singles – Birgit Schmidt, Germany; Rita Koban, Hungary; Izabella Dylewska, Poland.

Kayak 500m Doubles – Germany; Sweden; Hungary.

Kayak 500m Fours – Hungary; Germany; Sweden.

Cycling

Men

Individual Road Race – Fabio Casartelli, Italy; Erik Dekker, Netherlands; Dainis Ozols, Latvia.

Sprint – Jens Fiedler, Germany; Garry Neiwand, Australia; Curtis Harnett, Canada.

Individual Points Race – Giovanni Lombardi, Italy; Leon Van Bon, Netherlands; Cedric Mathy, Belgium.

4,000-m Team Pursuit – Germany; Australia; Denmark.

4-km Individual Pursuit – Chris Boardman, Great Britain; Jens Lehmann, Germany; Gary Anderson, New Zealand.

1-km Time Trial – Jose Moreno, Spain; Shane Kelly, Australia; Erin Hartwell, U.S.

Road Race – Germany; Italy; France.

Women

Sprint – Erika Salumae, Estonia; Annet Neumann, Germany; Ingrid Haringa, Netherlands.

Individual Pursuit – Petra Rossner, Germany; Kathryn Watt, Australia; Rebecca Twigg, U.S.

Individual Road Race – Kathryn Watt, Australia; Jeannie Longo-Ciprelli, France; Monique Knol, Netherlands.

Diving

Men's Platform – Sun Shuwei, China; Scott Donie, U.S.; Xiong Ni, China.

Men's Springboard – Mark Lenzi, U.S.; Tan Liangde, China; Dmitri Saoutine, Unified Team.

Women's Platform – Fu Mingxia, China; Yelina Mirochina, Unified Team; Mary Ellen Clark, U.S.

Women's Springboard – Gao Min, China; Irina Lachko, Unified Team; Brita Pia Baldus, Germany.

Equestrianism

Individual 3-Day Event – Matthew Ryan, Australia; Herbert Blocker, Germany; Robert Tait, New Zealand.

Team 3-Day Event – Australia; New Zealand; Germany.

Individual Dressage – Nicole Uphoff, Germany; Isabelle Regina Werth, Germany; Klaus Balkenhol, Germany.

Team Dressage – Germany; Netherlands; U.S.

Individual Jumping – Ludger Beerbaum, Germany; Piet Raymakers, Netherlands; Norman Dello Joio, U.S.

Team Jumping – Netherlands; Austria; France.

Fencing

Men

Individual Foil – Philippe Omnes, France; Serguei Goloubitski, Unified Team; Elvis Gregory Gil, Cuba.

Team Foil – Germany; Cuba; Poland.

Individual Sabre – Bence Szabo, Hungary; Marco Marin, Italy; Jean-François Lamour, France.

Team Sabre – Unified Team; Hungary; France.

Individual Épée – Eric Srecki, France; Pavel Kolobkov, Unified Team; Jean-Michel Henry, France.

Team Épée – Germany; Hungary; Unified Team.

Women

Individual Foil – Giovanna Trillini, Italy; Wang Huifeng, China; Tatiana Sadovskaia, Unified Team.

Team Foil – Italy; Germany; Romania.

Gymnastics

Men

Floor Exercise – Li Xiaosahuang, China; (tie) Grigori Misutin, Unified Team, & Yukio Iketani, Japan.

Horizontal Bar – Trent Dimas, U.S.; (tie) Andreas Wecker, Germany, & Grigori Misutin, Unified Team.

Parallel Bars – Vitaly Shcherbo, Unified Team; Li Jing, China; (tie) Igor Korobtchinski, Unified Team, Guo Linyao, China, & Masayuki Matsunaga, Japan.

Pommel Horse – (tie) Vitaly Shcherbo, Unified Team, & Pae Gil Su, N. Korea; Andreas Wecker, Germany.

Rings – Vitaly Shcherbo, Unified Team; Li Jing, China; (tie) Andreas Wecker, Germany, & Li Xiaosahuang, China.

Vault – Vitaly Shcherbo, Unified Team; Grigori Misutin, Unified Team; Yoo Ok Ryul, S. Korea.

Individual All-round – Vitaly Shcherbo, Unified Team; Grigori Misiutin, Unified Team; Valeri Belenki, Unified Team.

Team – Unified Team; China; Japan.

Women

Balance Beam – Tatiana Lisenko, Unified Team; (tie) Lu Li, China, & Shannon Miller, U.S.

Floor Exercise – Lavinia Corina Milosovici, Romania; Henrietta Onodi, Hungary; (tie) Shannon Miller, U.S., Cristina Bontas, Romania, & Tatiana Gutsu, Unified Team.

Uneven Bars – Lu Li, China; Tatiana Gutsu, Unified Team; Shannon Miller, U.S.

Vault – (tie) Henrietta Onodi, Hungary, & Lavinia Corina Milosovici, Romania; Tatiana Lisenko, Unified Team.

All-round – Tatiana Gutsu, Unified Team; Shannon Miller, U.S.; Lavinia Corina Milosovici, Romania.

Team Artistic – Unified Team; Romania; U.S.

Rhythmic Gymnastics

Alexandra Timoshenko, Unified Team; Carolina Pascual Gracia, Spain; Oksana Skaldina, Unified Team.

Hockey

Men – Germany; Australia; Pakistan.

Women – Spain; Germany; Great Britain.

Judo

Men

132 Pounds – Nazim Gousseinov, Unified Team; Yoon Hyun, S. Korea; (tie) Tadanori Koshino, Japan, & Richard Trautmann, Germany.

143 Pounds – Rogerio Sampaio Cardoso, Brazil; Josef Csak, Hungary; (tie) Udo Gunter Quellmalz, Germany, & Israel Hernandez Planas, Cuba.

157 Pounds – Toshihiko, Japan; Bertalan Hajtos, Hungary; (tie) Chung Hoon, S. Korea, & Shay Oren Smadga, Israel.

172 Pounds – Hidehiko Yoshida, Japan; Jason Morris, U.S.; (tie) Bertrand Damaisin, France, & Kim Byung Joo, S. Korea.

198 Pounds – Waldemar Legien, Poland; Pascal Tayot, France; (tie) Hirotaka Okada, Japan, & Nicolas Gill, Canada.

209 Pounds – Antal Kovacs, Hungary; Raymond Stevens, Great Britain; (tie) Dmitri Sergeev, Unified Team, & Theo Meijer, Netherlands.

(Continued)

Heavyweight – David Khakhaleichvili, Unified Team; Naoya Ogawa, Japan; (tie) David Douillet, France, & Imre Csosz, Hungary.

Women

106 Pounds – Cecile Nowak, France; Ryoko Tamura, Japan; (tie) Hulya Senyurt, Turkey, & Amarilis Savon, Cuba.

115 Pounds – Almudena Munoz Martinez, Spain; Moriko Mizoguchi, Japan; (tie) Li Zhongyun, China, & Sharon Rendle, Great Britain.

123 Pounds – Miriam Blasco Soto, Spain; Nicola Fairbrother, Great Britain; (tie) Chiyori Tateno, Japan, & Driulis Gonzalez, Cuba.

134 Pounds – Catherine Fleury, France; Yael Arad, Israel; (tie) Zhang Di, China, & Yelina Petrova, Unified Team.

146 Pounds – Odalis Reve Jimenez, Cuba; Emanuela Pierantozzi, Italy; (tie) Kate Howey, Great Britain, & Heidi Rakels, Belgium.

159 Pounds – Kim Mi Jung, S. Korea; Yoko Tanabe, Japan; (tie) Irene De Kok, Netherlands, & Laetitia Meignan, France.

Over 159 Pounds – Zhuang Xiaoyan, China; Estela Rodriguez Villaneuva, Cuba; (tie) Natalia Lupino, France, & Yoko Sakaue, Japan.

Modern Pentathlon

Individual – Arkadiusz Skrzypaszek, Poland; Attila Mizser, Hungary; Eduard Zenovka, Unified Team.

Team – Poland; Unified Team; Italy.

Rowing

Men

Single Sculls – Thomas Lange, Germany; Vaclav Chalupa, Czechoslovakia; Kajetan Broniewski, Poland.

Double Sculls – Australia; Austria; Netherlands.

Coxless Pairs – Great Britain; Germany; Slovenia.

Coxed Pairs – Great Britain; Italy; Romania.

Coxed Fours – Romania; Germany; Poland.

Coxless Fours – Australia; U.S.; Slovenia.

Quadruple Sculls – Germany; Norway; Italy.

Coxed Eights – Canada; Romania; Germany.

Women

Single Sculls – Elisabeta Lipa, Romania; Annelies Bredael, Belgium; Silken Suzette Laumann, Canada.

Double Sculls – Germany; Romania; China.

Coxless Pairs – Canada; Germany; U.S.

Coxless Fours – Canada; U.S.; Germany.

Quadruple Sculls – Germany; Romania; Unified Team.

Coxed Eights – Canada; Romania; Germany.

Shooting

Men

Running Game Target – Michael Jakosits, Germany; Anatoly Asrabaev, Unified Team; Lubos Racansky, Czechoslovakia.

Rapid Fire Pistol – Ralf Schumann, Germany; Afanasijs Kuzmins, Latvia; Vladimir Vokhmianine, Unified Team.

Three-Position Rifle – Gratchia Petikiane, Unified Team; Bob Foth, U.S.; Ryohei Koba, Japan.

Free Rifle – Lee Eun Chul, S. Korea; Harald Stenvaag, Norway; Stevan Pletikosic, I.O.P.

Air Pistol – Wang Yifu, China; Serguei Pyjianov, Unified Team; Sorin Babili, Romania.

Air Rifle – Iouri Fedkine, Unified Team; Franck Badiou, France; Johann Riederer, Germany.

Free Pistol – Konstantine Loukachik, Unified Team; Wang Yifu, China; Ragnar Skanaker, Sweden.

Women

Air Pistol – Marina Logvinenko, Unified Team; Jasna Sekaric, I.O.P.; Maria Zdravkova Grousdeva, Bulgaria.

Three-Position Rifle – Launi Meili, U.S.; Nonka Detcheva Matova, Bulgaria; Malgorzata Ksaizkiewicz, Poland.

Sport Pistol – Marina Logvinenko, Unified Team; Li Duihong, China; Dorzhsuren Munkhbayar, Mongolia.

Air Rifle – Yeo Kab Soon, S. Korea; Vesela Letcheva, Bulgaria; Aranka Binder, I.O.P.

Mixed

Trap – Petr Hrdlicka, Czechoslovakia; Kazumi Watanabe, Japan; Marco Venturini, Italy.

Skeet – Zhang Shan, China; Juan Jorge Giha Yarur, Peru; Bruno Mario Rossetti, Italy.

Soccer

Spain; Poland; Ghana.

Swimming

Men

50m Freestyle – Aleksandr Popov, Unified Team; Matt Biondi, U.S.; Tom Jager, U.S.

100m Freestyle – Aleksandr Popov, Unified Team; Gustavo Borges, Brazil; Stephan Caron, France.

200m Freestyle – Evgueni Sadovyi, Unified Team; Anders Holmertz, Sweden; Antti Alexander Kasvio, Finland.

400m Freestyle – Evgueni Sadovyi, Unified Team; Kieren Perkins, Australia; Anders Holmertz, Sweden.

1,500m Freestyle – Kieren Perkins, Australia; Glen Housman, Australia; Joerg Hoffmann, Germany.

100m Breaststroke – Nelson Diebel, U.S.; Norbert Rozsa, Hungary; Philip Rogers, Australia.

200m Breaststroke – Mike Barrowman, U.S.; Norbert Rozsa, Hungary; Nick Gillingham, Great Britain.

100m Butterfly – Pablo Morales, U.S.; Rafal Szukala, Poland; Anthony Conrad Nesty, Suriname.

200m Butterfly – Mel Stewart, U.S.; Danyon Loader, New Zealand; Franck Esposito, France.

100m Backstroke – Mark Tewksbury, Canada; Jeff Rouse, U.S.; David Berkoff, U.S.

200m Backstroke – Martin Lopez-Zubero, Spain; Vladimir Selkov, Unified Team; Stefano Battistelli, Italy.

200m Individual Medley – Tamas Darnyi, Hungary; Greg Burgess, U.S.; Attila Czene, Hungary.

400m Individual Medley – Tamas Darnyi, Hungary; Eric Namesnik, U.S.; Luca Sacchi, Italy.

400m Freestyle Relay – U.S.; Unified Team; Germany.

800m Freestyle Relay – Unified Team; Sweden; U.S.

400m Medley Relay – U.S.; Unified Team; Canada.

Women

50m Freestyle – Yang Wenyi, China; Zhuang Yong, China; Angel Martino, U.S.

100m Freestyle – Zhuang Yong, China; Jenny Thompson, U.S.; Franziska van Almsick, Germany.

200m Freestyle – Nicole Haislett, U.S.; Franziska van Almsick Germany; Kerstin Kielgass, Germany.

400m Freestyle – Dagmar Hase, Germany; Janet Evans, U.S.; Hayley Lewis, Australia.

800m Freestyle – Janet Evans, U.S.; Hayley Lewis, Australia; Jana Henke, Germany.

100m Breaststroke – Yelina Roudkovskaia, Unified Team; Anita Nall, U.S.; Samantha Riley, Australia.

200m Breaststroke – Kyoko Iwasaki, Japan; Lin Li, China; Anita Nall, U.S.

100m Backstroke – Krisztina Egerszegi, Hungary; Tunde Szabo, Hungary; Lea Loveless, U.S.

200m Backstroke – Krisztina Egerszegi, Hungary; Dagmar Hase, Germany; Nicole Stevenson, Australia.

100m Butterfly – Qian Hong, China; Christine Ahmann-Leighton, U.S.; Catharine Plewinski, France.

200m Butterfly – Summer Sanders, U.S.; Wang Xiaohong, China; Susan O'Neill; Australia.

200m Individual Medley – Lin Li, China; Summer Sanders, U.S.; Daniela Hunger, Germany.

400m Individual Medley – Krisztina Egerszegi, Hungary; Lin Li, China; Summer Sanders, U.S.

400m Freestyle Relay – U.S.; China; Germany.

400m Medley Relay – U.S.; Germany; Unified Team.

Synchronized Swimming

Solo – Kristen Babb-Sprague, U.S.; Sylvie Frechette, Canada; Fumiko Okuno, Japan.

(Continued)

Duet – Karen Josephson and Sarah Josephson, U.S.; Penny Vilagos and Vicky Vilagos, Canada; Fumiko Okuno and Aki Takayama, Japan.

Table Tennis

Men's Singles – Jan Waldner, Sweden; Jean-Philippe Gatien, France; Kim Taek Soo, S. Korea.

Men's Doubles – Lu Lin and Wang Tao, China; Steffen Fetzner and Jorg Rosskopf, Germany; (tie) Kang Hee Chan and Lee Chul Seung, S. Korea, & Kim Taek Soo and Yoo Nam Kyu, S. Korea.

Women's Singles – Deng Yaping, China; Qiao Hong, China; (tie) Hyun Jung Hwa, S. Korea, & Li Bun Hui, N. Korea.

Women's Doubles – Deng Yaping and Qiao Hong, China; Chen Zihe and Gao Jun, China; (tie) Li Bun Hui and Yu Sun Bok, N. Korea, & Hong Cha Ok and Hyun Jung Hwa, S. Korea.,

Team Handball

Men – Unified Team; Sweden; France.

Women – S. Korea; Norway; Unified Team.

Tennis

Men's Singles – Marc Rosset, Switzerland; Jordi Arrese, Spain; (tie) Goran Ivanisevic, Croatia, & Andrei Cherkasov, Unified Team.

Men's Doubles – Boris Becker and Michael Stich, Germany; Wayne Ferreira and Piet Norval, South Africa; (tie) Goran Ivanisevic and Goran Prpic, Croatia, & Javier Frana and Christian Carlos Miniussi, Argentina.

Women's Singles – Jennifer Capriati, U.S.; Steffi Graf, Germany; (tie) Aranxta Sanchez Vicario, Spain, & Mary Joe Ferandez, U.S.

Women's Doubles – Gigi Fernandez and Mary Joe Fernandez, U.S.; Conchita Martinez and Aranxta Sanchez Vicario, Spain; (tie) Natalya Zvereva and Leila Meskhi, Unified Team, & Rachel McQuillan and Nicole Provis, Australia.

Volleyball

Men – Brazil; Netherlands; U.S.

Women – Cuba; Unified Team; U.S.

Water Polo

Italy; Spain; Unified Team.

Weight Lifting

115 Pounds – Ivan Ivanov, Bulgaria; Lin Qisheng, China; Traian Ciharean, Romania.

123 Pounds – Chun Byung Kwan, S. Korea; Liu Shoubin, China; Luo Jianming, China.

132 Pounds – Naim Suleymanoglu, Turkey; Nikolai Peshalov, Bulgaria; He Yingqiang, China.

148 Pounds – Israel Militossian, Unified Team; Yoto Yotov, Bulgaria; Andreas Behm, Germany.

165 Pounds – Fedor Kassapu, Unified Team; Pablo Lara, Cuba; Kim Myong Nam, N. Korea.

180 Pounds – Pyrros Dimas, Greece; Krzysztof Siemion, Poland; None awarded, Ibragim Samadov of the Unified Team refused medal.

198 Pounds – Kakhi Kakhlachvili, Unified Team; Serguei Syrtsov, Unified Team; Sergiusz Wolczaniecki, Poland.

220 Pounds – Victor Tregoubov, Unified Team; Timour Taimazov, Unified Team; Waldemar Malak, Poland.

243 Pounds – Ronny Weller, Germany; Artour Akoev, Unified Team; Stefan Botev, Bulgaria.

Over 243 Pounds – Aleksandr Kourlovitch, Unified Team; Leonid Taranenko, Unified Team; Manfred Nerlinger, Germany.

Wrestling

Freestyle

106 Pounds – Kim Il, N. Korea; Kim Jong Shin, S. Korea; Vougar Oroudjov, Unified Team.

115 Pounds – Li Hak Son, S. Korea; Zeke Jones, U.S.; Valentin Jordanov, Bulgaria.

126 Pounds – Alejandro Puerto Diaz, Cuba; Serguei Smal, Unified Team; Kim Yong Sik, N. Korea.

137 Pounds – John Smith, U.S.; Asgari Mohammadian, Iran; Lazaro Reinoso Martinez, Cuba.

150 Pounds – Arsen Fadzaev, Unified Team; Valentin Dotchev Getzov, Bulgaria; Kosei Akaishi, Japan.

163 Pounds – Park Jang Soon, S. Korea; Kenny Monday, U.S.; Amir Reza Khadem Azghadi, Iran.

182 Pounds – Kevin Jackson, U.S.; Elmadi Jabraijlov, Unified Team; Rasul Khadem Azghadi, Iran.

198 Pounds – Makharbek Khadartsev, Unified Team; Kenan Simsek, Turkey; Chris Campbell, U.S.

220 Pounds – Leri Khabelov, Unified Team; Heiko Balz, Germany; Ali Kayali, Turkey.

286 Pounds – Bruce Baumgartner, U.S.; Jeff Thue, Canada; David Gobedjichvili, Unified Team.

Greco-Roman

106 Pounds – Oleg Koutherenko, Unified Team; Vincenzo Maenza, Italy; Wilber Sanchez, Cuba.

115 Pounds – Jon Ronningen, Norway; Alfred Ter-Mkrttchian, Unified Team; Min Kyung Kap, S. Korea.

126 Pounds – An Han Bong, S. Korea; Rifat Yildiz, Germany; Sheng Zetian, China.

137 Pounds – M. Akif Pirim, Turkey; Serguei Martynov, Unified Team; Juan Luis Maren Delis, Cuba.

150 Pounds – Attila Repka, Hungary; Islam Dougoutchiev, Unified Team; Rodney Smith, U.S.

163 Pounds – Mnatsakan Iskandarian, Unified Team; Jozef Tracz, Poland; Torbjorn Johansson, Sweden.

181 Pounds – Peter Farkas, Hungary; Piotr Stepien, Poland; Daoulet Tourlykhanov, Unified Team;

198 Pounds – Maik Bullmann, Germany; Hakki Basar, Turkey; Gogui Kogouachvili, Unified Team.

220 Pounds – Hector Milian Perez, Cuba; Dennis Marvin Koslowski, U.S.; Serguei Demiachkievitch, Unified Team.

286 Pounds – Aleksandr Karelin, Unified Team; Tomas Johansson, Sweden; Ioan Grigoras, Romania.

Yachting

Soling – Denmark; U.S.; Great Britain.

Finn – Jose van der Ploeg, Spain; Brian Ledbetter, U.S.; Craig Monk, New Zealand.

Tornado – France; U.S.; Australia.

Europe – Linda Anderson, Norway; Natalia Via Dufresne, Spain; Julia Trotman, U.S.

Flying Dutchman – Spain; U.S.; Denmark.

Star – U.S.; New Zealand; Canada.

Men's Sailboard – Franck David, France; Mike Gebhardt, U.S.; Lars Kleppich, Australia.

Women's Sailboard – Barbara Kendall, New Zealand; Zhang Xiaodong, China; Dorien de Vries, Netherlands.

Men's 470 – Spain; U.S.; Estonia.

Women's 470 – Spain; New Zealand; U.S.

WINTER OLYMPICS

Sites of Games

1924 Chamonix, France
1928 St. Moritz, Switzerland
1932 Lake Placid, N.Y.
1936 Garmisch-Partenkirchen, Germany
1948 St. Moritz, Switzerland
1952 Oslo, Norway
1956 Cortina d'Ampezzo, Italy
1960 Squaw Valley, Cal.
1964 Innsbruck, Austria
1968 Grenoble, France
1972 Sapporo, Japan
1976 Innsbruck, Austria
1980 Lake Placid, N.Y.
1984 Sarajevo, Yugoslavia
1988 Calgary, Alberta
1992 Albertville, France
1994 Lillehammer, Norway
1998 Nagano, Japan

In 1992 the Unified Team represented the former Soviet republics of Russia, Ukraine, Belarus, Kazakhstan and Uzbekistan.

Winter Olympic Games Champions, 1924–1992

Bobsledding

4-Man Bob

(Driver in parentheses)		Time
1924	Switzerland (Eduard Scherrer)	5:45.54
1928	United States (William Fiske) (5-man)	3:20.50
1932	United States (William Fiske)	7:53.68
1936	Switzerland (Pierre Musy)	5:19.85
1948	United States (Francis Tyler)	5:20.10
1952	Germany (Andreas Ostler)	5:07.84
1956	Switzerland (Franz Kapus)	5:10.44
1964	Canada (Victor Emery)	4:14.46
1968	Italy (Eugenio Monti) (2 races)	2:17.39
1972	Switzerland (Jean Wicki)	4:43.07
1976	E. Germany (Meinhard Nehmer)	3:40.43
1980	E. Germany (Meinhard Nehmer)	3:59.92
1984	E. Germany (Wolfgang Hoppe)	3:20.22
1988	Switzerland (Ekkehard Fasser)	3:47.51
1992	Austria (Ingo Appelt)	3:53.90

2-Man Bob

		Time
1932	United States (Hubert Stevens)	8:14.74
1936	United States (Ivan Brown)	5:29.29
1948	Switzerland (F. Endrich)	5:29.20
1952	Germany (Andreas Ostler)	5:24.54
1956	Italy (Dalla Costa)	5:30.14
1964	Great Britain (Anthony Nash)	4:21.90
1968	Italy (Eugenio Monti)	4:41.54
1972	W. Germany (Wolfgang Zimmerer)	4:57.07
1976	E. Germany (Meinhard Nehmer)	3:44.42
1980	Switzerland (Erich Schaerer)	4:09.36
1984	E.Germany (Wolfgang Hoppe)	3:25.56
1988	USSR (Janis Kipours)	3:54.19
1992	Switzerland (Gustav Weber)	4:03.26

Luge

Men's singles

		Time
1964	Thomas Keohler, Germany	3:26.77
1968	Manfred Schmid, Austria	2:52.48
1972	Wolfgang Scheidel, E. Germany	3:27.58
1976	Detlef Guenther, E. Germany	3:27.688
1980	Bernhard Glass, E. Germany	2:54.796
1984	Paul Hildgartner, Italy	3:04.258
1988	Jens Mueller, E. Germany	3:05.548
1992	Georg Hackl, Germany	3:02.363

Men's Pairs

		Time
1964	Austria	1:41.62
1968	E. Germany	1:35.85
1972	Italy, E. Germany (tie)	1:28.35
1976	E. Germany	1:25.604
1980	E. Germany	1:19.331
1984	W. Germany	1:23.620
1988	E. Germany	1:31.940
1992	Germany	1:32.053

Women's Singles

		Time
1964	Ortun Enderlein, Germany	3:24.67
1968	Erica Lechner, Italy	2:28.66
1972	Anna M. Muller, E. Germany	2:59.18
1976	Margit Schumann, E. Germany	2:50.621
1980	Vera Zozulya, USSR	2:36.537
1984	Steffi Martin, E. Germany	2:46.570
1988	Steffi Walter, E. Germany	3:03.973
1992	Doris Neuner, Austria	3:06.696

Biathlon

Men's 10 Kilometres

		Time
1980	Frank Ullrich, E. Germany	32:10.69
1984	Eirik Kvalfoss, Norway	30:53.80
1988	Frank-Peter Roetsch, E. Germany	25:08.10
1992	Mark Kirchner, Germany	26.02:30

Men's 20 Kilometres

		Time
1960	Klas Lestander,Sweden	1:33:21.6
1964	Vladimir Melanin, USSR	1:20:26.8
1968	Magnar Solberg, Norway	1:13:45.9
1972	Magnar Solberg, Norway	1:15:55.50
1976	Nikolai Kruglov, USSR	1:14:12.26
1980	Anatoly Aljabiev, USSR	1:08:16.31
1984	Peter Angerer, W. Germany	1:11:52.7
1988	Frank-Peter Roetsch, E. Germany	0:56:33.33
1992	Yevgeny Redkine, Unified Team	0:57:34.4

Men's 30-km Relay

		Time
1968	USSR, Norway, Sweden	2:13:02.4
1972	USSR, Finland, E. Germany	1:51:44.92
1976	USSR, Finland, E. Germany	1:57:55.64
1980	USSR, E. Germany, W. Germany (30 km.)	1:34:03.27
1984	USSR, Norway, W. Germany	1:38:51.70
1988	USSR, W. Germany, Italy	1:22:30.00
1992	Germany, Unified Team, Sweden	1:24:43.50

Women's 7.5 Kilometres

		Time
1992	Anfissa Restsova, Unified Team	24:29.20

Women's 15 Kilometres

		Time
1992	Antje Misersky, Germany	51:47.2

Women's 22.5-km Relay

		Time
1992	France, Germany, Unified Team	1:15:55.6

Figure Skating

Men's Singles

1908 Ulrich Salchow, Sweden
1920 Gillis Grafstrom, Sweden
1924 Gillis Grafstrom, Sweden
1928 Gillis Grafstrom, Sweden
1932 Karl Schaefer, Austria
1936 Karl Schaefer, Austria
1948 Richard Button, U.S.
1952 Richard Button, U.S.
1956 Hayes Alan Jenkins, U.S.
1960 David W. Jenkins, U.S.
1964 Manfred Schnelldorfer, Germany
1968 Wolfgang Schwartz, Austria
1972 Ondrej Nepela, Czechoslovakia
1976 John Curry, Great Britain
1980 Robin Cousins, Great Britain
1984 Scott Hamilton, U.S.
1988 Brian Boitano, U.S.
1992 Viktor Petrenko, Unified Team

Women's Singles

1908 Madge Syers, Great Britain
1920 Magda Julin-Mauroy, Sweden
1924 Herma von Szabo-Planck, Austria
1928 Sonja Henie, Norway
1932 Sonja Henie, Norway
1936 Sonja Henie, Norway
1948 Barbara Ann Scott, Canada
1952 Jeanette Altwegg, Great Britain
1956 Tenley Albright, U.S.
1960 Carol Heiss, U.S.
1964 Sjoukje Dijkstra, Netherlands
1968 Peggy Fleming, U.S.
1972 Beatrix Schuba, Austria
1976 Dorothy Hamill, U.S.
1980 Anett Poetzsch, E. Germany
1984 Katarina Witt, E. Germany
1988 Katarina Witt, E. Germany
1992 Kristi Yamaguchi, U.S.

Pairs

1908 Anna Hubler & Heinrich Burger, Germany
1920 Ludovika & Walter Jakobsson, Finland
1924 Helene Engelman & Alfred Berger, Austria
1928 Andree Joly & Pierre Brunet, France
1932 Andree Joly & Pierre Brunet, France
1936 Maxi Herber & Ernst Baier, Germany
1948 Micheline Lannoy & Pierre Baugniet, Belgium
1952 Ria and Paul Falk, Germany
1956 Elisabeth Schwartz & Kurt Oppelt, Austria
1960 Barbara Wagner & Robert Paul, Canada
1964 Ludmila Beloussova & Oleg Protopopov, USSR
1968 Ludmila Beloussova & Oleg Protopopov, USSR
1972 Irina Rodnina & Alexei Ulanov, USSR
1976 Irina Rodnina & Aleksandr Zaitzev, USSR
1980 Irina Rodnina & Aleksandr Zaitzev, USSR
1984 Elena Valova & Oleg Vassiliev, USSR
1988 Ekaterina Gordeeva & Sergei Grinkov, USSR
1992 Natalia Mishkutienok & Artur Dmitriev, Unified Team

Ice Dancing

1976 Ludmila Pakhomova & Aleksandr Gorschkov, USSR
1980 Natalya Linichuk & Gennadi Karponosov, USSR
1984 Jayne Torvill & Christopher Dean, Great Britain

(Continued)

1988	Natalia Bestemianova & Andrei Bukin, USSR
1992	Marina Klimova & Sergei Ponomarenko, Unified Team

Ice Hockey

1920	Canada, U.S., Czechoslovakia
1924	Canada, U.S., Great Britain
1928	Canada, Sweden, Switzerland
1932	Canada, U.S., Germany
1936	Great Britain, Canada, U.S.
1948	Canada, Czechoslovakia, Switzerland
1952	Canada, U.S., Sweden
1956	USSR, U.S., Canada
1960	U.S., Canada, USSR
1964	USSR, Sweden, Czechoslovakia
1968	USSR, Czechoslovakia, Canada
1972	USSR, U.S., Czechoslovakia,
1976	USSR, Czechoslovakia, W. Germany
1980	U.S., USSR, Sweden
1984	USSR, Czechoslovakia, Sweden
1988	USSR, Finland, Sweden
1992	Unified Team, Canada, Czechoslovakia

Skiing, Alpine

Men's Downhill

		Time
1948	Henri Oreiller, France	2:55.0
1952	Zeno Colo, Italy	2:30.8
1956	Anton Sailer, Austria	2:52.2
1960	Jean Vuarnet, France	2:06.0
1964	Egon Zimmermann, Austria	2:18.16
1968	Jean-Claude Killy, France	1:59.85
1972	Bernhard Russi, Switzerland	1:51.43
1976	Franz Klammer, Austria	1:45.73
1980	Leonhard Stock, Austria	1:45.50
1984	Bill Johnson, U.S.	1:45:59
1988	Pirmin Zurbriggen, Switzerland	1:59.63
1992	Patrick Ortlieb, Austria	1:50.37

Men's Super Giant Slalom

		Time
1988	Franck Piccard, France	1:39.66
1992	Kjetil-Andre Aamodt, Norway	1:13.04

Men's Giant Slalom

		Time
1952	Stein Eriksen, Norway	2:25.0
1956	Anton Sailer, Austria	3:00.1
1960	Roger Staub, Switzerland	1:48.3
1964	Francois Bonlieu, France	1:46.71
1968	Jean-Claude Killy, France	3:29.28
1972	Gustavo Thoeni, Italy	3:09.62
1976	Heini Hemmi, Switzerland	3:26.97
1980	Ingemar Stenmark, Sweden	2:40.74
1984	Max Julen, Switzerland	2:41.18
1988	Alberto Tomba, Italy	2:06:37
1992	Alberto Tomba, Italy	2:06.98

Men's Slalom

		Time
1948	Edi Reinalter, Switzerland	2:10.3
1952	Othmar Schneider, Austria	2:00.0
1956	Anton Sailer, Austria	194.7 pts.
1960	Ernst Hinterseer, Austria	2:08.9
1964	Josef Stiegler, Austria	2:11.13
1968	Jean-Claude Killy, France	1:39.73
1972	Francisco Fernandez Ochoa, Spain	1:49.27
1976	Piero Gros, Italy	2:03.29
1980	Ingemar Stenmark, Sweden	1:44.26
1984	Phil Mahre, U.S.	1:39.41
1988	Alberto Tomba, Italy	1:39.47
1992	Finn Christian Jagge, Norway	1:44.39

Men's Combined

		Points
1988	Hubert Strolz, Austria	36.55
1992	Josef Polig, Italy	14.58

Women's Downhill

		Time
1948	Hedi Schlunegger, Switzerland	2:28.3
1952	Trude Jochum-Beiser, Austria	1:47.1
1956	Madeleine Berthod, Switzerland	1:40.7
1960	Heidi Biebl, Germany	1:37.6
1964	Christl Haas, Austria	1:55.39
1968	Olga Pall, Austria	1:40.87
1972	Marie Therese Nadig, Switzerland	1:36.68
1976	Rosi Mittermaier, W. Germany	1:46.16
1980	Annemarie Proell Moser, Austria	1:37.52
1984	Michela Figini, Switzerland	1:13.36
1988	Marina Kiehl, W. Germany	1:25.86
1992	Kerrin Lee-Gartner, Canada	1:52.55

Women's Super Giant Slalom

		Time
1988	Sigrid Wolf, Austria	1:19.03
1992	Deborah Compagnoni, Italy	1:21.22

Women's Giant Slalom

		Time
1952	Andrea Mead Lawrence, U.S.	2:06.8
1956	Ossi Reichert, Germany	1:56.5
1960	Yvonne Ruegg, Switzerland	1:39.9
1964	Marielle Goitschel, France	1:52.24
1968	Nancy Greene, Canada	1:51.97
1972	Marie Therese Nadig, Switzerland	1:29.90
1976	Kathy Kreiner, Canada	1:29.13
1980	Hanni Wenzel, Liechtenstein (2 runs)	2:41.66
1984	Debbie Armstrong, U.S.	2:20.98
1988	Vreni Schneider, Switzerland	2:06.49
1992	Pernilla Wiberg, Sweden	2:12.74

Women's Slalom

		Time
1948	Gretchen Fraser, U.S.	1:57.2
1952	Andrea Mead Lawrence, U.S.	2:10.6
1956	Renee Colliard, Switzerland	112.3 pts.
1960	Anne Heggtveigt, Canada	1:49.6
1964	Christine Goitschel, France	1:29.86
1968	Marielle Goitschel, France	1:25.86
1972	Barbara Cochran, U.S.	1:31.24
1976	Rosi Mittermaier, W. Germany	1:30.54
1980	Hanni Wenzel, Liechtenstein	1:25.09
1984	Paoletta Magoni, Italy	1:36.47
1988	Vreni Schneider, Switzerland	1:36.69
1992	Petra Kronberger, Austria	1:32.68

Women's Combined

		Points
1988	Anita Wachter, Austria	29.25
1992	Petra Kronberger, Austria	2.55

Skiing, Cross-Country

Men's 10 Kilometres (6.2 miles)

		Time
1992	Vegard Ulvang, Norway	27:36.0

Men's 15 kilometres (9.3 miles)

		Time
1924	Thorleif Haug, Norway	1:14:31
1928	Johan Grottumsbraaten, Norway	1:37:01
1932	Sven Utterstrom, Sweden	1:23:07
1936	Erik-August Larsson, Sweden	1:14:38
1948	Martin Lundstrom, Sweden	1:13:50
1952	Hallgeir Brenden, Norway	1:01:34
1956	Hallgeir Brenden, Norway	49:39.0
1960	Haakon Brusveen, Norway	51:55.5
1964	Eero Maentyranta, Finland	50:54.1
1968	Harald Groenningen, Norway	47:54.2
1972	Sven-Ake Lundback, Sweden	45:28.24
1976	Nikolai Balukov, USSR	43:58.47
1980	Thomas Wassberg, Sweden	41:57.63
1984	Gunde Svan, Sweden	41:25.6
1988	Mikhail Deviatiarov, USSR	41:18.9
1992	Bjorn Dahlie, Norway	38:01.9

(Note: approx. 18-km. course 1924–1952)

Men's 30 kilometres (18.6 miles)

		Time
1956	Veikko Hakulinen, Finland	1:44:06.0
1960	Sixten Jernberg, Sweden	1:51:03.9
1964	Eero Maentyranta, Finland	1:30:50.7
1968	Franco Nones, Italy	1:35:39.2
1972	Vyacheslav Vedenine, USSR	1:36:31.15
1976	Sergei Saveliev, USSR	1:30:29.38
1980	Nikolai Zimyatov, USSR	1:27:02.80
1984	Nikolai Zimyatov, USSR	1:28:56.3
1988	Aleksei Prokourorov, USSR	1:24:26.3
1992	Vegard Ulvang, Norway	1:22.27.8

Men's 50 kilometres (31.2 miles)

		Time
1924	Thorleif Haug, Norway	3:44:32.0
1928	Per Erik Hedlund, Sweden	4:52:03.0
1932	Veli Saarinen, Finland	4:28:00.0
1936	Elis Wiklund, Sweden	3:30:11.0
1948	Nils Karlsson, Sweden	3:47:48.0
1952	Veikko Hakulinen, Finland	3:33:33.0
1956	Sixten Jernberg, Sweden	2:50:27.0
1960	Kalevi Hamalainen, Finland	2:59:06.3
1964	Sixten Jernberg, Sweden	2:43:52.6
1968	Ole Ellefsaeter, Norway	2:28:45.8
1972	Paal Tyldum, Norway	2:43:14.75

(Continued)

1976	Ivar Formo, Norway	2:37:30.05
1980	Nikolai Zimyatov, USSR	2:27:24.60
1984	Thomas Wassberg, Sweden	2:15:55.8
1988	Gunde Svan, Sweden	2:04:30.9
1992	Bjorn Dahlie, Norway	2:03:41.5

Men's 40-km Relay — Time

1936	Finland, Norway, Sweden	2:41:33.0
1948	Sweden, Finland, Norway	2:32:08.0
1952	Finland, Norway, Sweden	2:20:16.0
1956	USSR, Finland, Sweden	2:15:30.0
1960	Finland, Norway, USSR	2:18:45.6
1964	Sweden, Finland, USSR	2:18:34.6
1968	Norway, Sweden, Finland	2:08:33.5
1972	USSR, Norway, Switzerland	2:04:47.94
1976	Finland, Norway, USSR	2:07:59.72
1980	USSR, Norway, Finland	1:57:03.46
1984	Sweden, USSR, Finland	1:55:06.30
1988	Sweden, USSR, Czechoslovakia	1:43:58.60
1992	Norway, Italy, Finland	1:39:26.00

Men's Combined Cross-Country & Jumping — Points

1924	Thorleif Haug, Norway	453.800
1928	Johan Grottumsbraaten, Norway	427.800
1932	Johan Grottumsbraaten, Norway	446.000
1936	Oddbjorn Hagen, Norway	430.300
1948	Heikki Hasu, Finland	448.800
1952	Simon Slattvik, Norway	451.621
1956	Sverre Stenersen, Norway	455.000
1960	Georg Thoma, Germany	457.952
1964	Tormod Knutsen, Norway	469.280
1968	Franz Keller, W. Germany	449.040
1972	Ulrich Wehling, E. Germany	413.340
1976	Ulrich Wehling, E. Germany	423.390
1980	Ulrich Wehling, E. Germany	432.200
1984	Tom Sandberg, Norway	422.595
1988	Hippolyt Kempf, Switzerland	235.800
1992	Fabrice Guy, France	426.470

Men's Nordic Team Combined — Time

1988	W. Germany, Switzerland, Austria	1:20:46.0
1992	Japan, Norway, Austria	1:23:36.5

Women's 5 kilometres (approx. 3.1 miles) — Time

1964	Claudia Boyarskikh, USSR	17:50.5
1968	Toini Gustafsson, Sweden	16:45.2
1972	Galina Koulacova, USSR	17:00.50
1976	Helena Takalo, Finland	15:48.69
1980	Raisa Smetanina, USSR	15:06.92
1984	Marja-Liisa Haemaelainen, Finland	17:04.0
1988	Marjo Matikainen, Finland	15:04.0
1992	Marjut Lukkarinen	14:13.8

Women's 10 kilometres (6.2 miles) — Time

1952	Lydia Wideman, Finland	41:40.0
1956	Lyubov Kosyreva, USSR	38:11.0
1960	Maria Gusakova, USSR	39:46.6
1964	Claudia Boyarskikh, USSR	40:24.3
1968	Toini Gustafsson, Sweden	36:46.5
1972	Galina Koulacova, USSR	34:17.82
1976	Raisa Smetanina, USSR	30:13.41
1980	Barbara Petzold, E. Germany	30:31.54
1984	Marja-Liisa Haemaelainen, Finland	31:44.2
1988	Vida Ventsene, USSR	30:08.3
1992	Lyubov Yegorova, Unified Team	25:53.7

Women's 15 kilometres (9.3 miles) — Time

1992	Lyubov Yegorova, Unified Team	42:20.8

Women's 30 kilometres (18.6 miles) — Time

1984	Marja-Liisa Haemaelainen, Finland	1:01:45.0
1988	Tamara Tikhonova, USSR	55:53.6
1992	Stefania Belmondo, Italy	1:22:30.1

Women's 20-km Relay — Time

1956	Finland, USSR, Sweden (15 km.)	1:09:01.0
1960	Sweden, USSR, Finland (15 km.)	1:04:21.4
1964	USSR, Sweden, Finland (15 km.)	59:20.2
1968	Norway, Sweden, USSR (15 km.)	57:30.0
1972	USSR, Finland, Norway (15 km.)	48:46.15
1976	USSR, Finland, E. Germany	1:07:49.75
1980	E. Germany, USSR, Norway	1:02:11.10
1984	Norway, Czechoslovakia, Finland	1:06:49.70
1988	USSR, Norway, Finland	59:51.1
1992	Unified Team, Norway, Italy	59:34.8

Skiing, Freestyle

Men's Moguls — Points

1992	Edgar Grospiron, France	25.81

Women's Moguls — Points

1992	Donna Weinbrecht, U.S.	23.69

Ski Jumping

Men's Team (90 metres) — Points

1988	Finland, Yugoslavia, Norway	634.4
1992	Finland, Austria, Czechoslovakia	644.4

Men's 90 metres — Points

1924	Jacob Thams, Norway	227.5
1928	Alfred Andersen, Norway	230.5
1932	Birger Ruud, Norway	228.1
1936	Birger Ruud, Norway	232.0
1948	Petter Hugsted, Norway	228.1
1952	Arnfinn Bergmann, Norway	226.0
1956	Antti Hyvarinen, Finland	227.0
1960	Helmut Recknagel, Germany	227.2
1964	Toralf Engan, Norway	230.7
1968	Vladimir Beloussov, USSR	231.3
1972	Wojiech Fortuna, Poland	219.9
1976	Karl Schnabl, Austria	234.8
1980	Jouko Tormanen, Finland	271.0
1984	Matti Nykaenen, Finland	231.2
1988	Matti Nykaenen, Finland	224.0
1992	Ernst Vettori, Austria	222.8

Men's 120 metres — Points

1992	Toni Nieminen, Finland	239.5

Speed Skating

Men's 500 metres — Time

1924	Charles Jewtraw, U.S.	0:44.0
1928	Thunberg, Finland & Evensen, Norway (tie)	0:43.4
1932	John A. Shea, U.S.	0:43.4
1936	Ivar Ballangrud, Norway	0:43.4
1948	Finn Helgesen, Norway	0:43.1
1952	Kenneth Henry, U.S.	0:43.2
1956	Evgeniy Grishin, USSR	0:40.2
1960	Evgeniy Grishin, USSR	0:40.2
1964	Terry McDermott, U.S.	0:40.1
1968	Erhard Keller, W. Germany	0:40.3
1972	Erhard Keller, W. Germany	0:39.44
1976	Evgeny Kulikov, USSR	0:39.17
1980	Eric Heiden, U.S.	0:38.03
1984	Sergei Fokichev, USSR	0:38.19
1988	Uwe-Jens Mey, E. Germany	0:36.45
1992	Uwe-Jens Mey, Germany	0:37.14

Men's 1,000 metres — Time

1976	Peter Mueller, U.S.	1:19.32
1980	Eric Heiden, U.S.	1:15.18
1984	Gaetan Boucher, Canada	1:15.80
1988	Nikolai Guiliaev, USSR	1:13.03
1992	Olaf Zinke, Germany	1:14.85

Men's 1,500 metres — Time

1924	Clas Thunberg, Finland	2:20.8
1928	Clas Thunberg, Finland	2:21.1
1932	John A. Shea, U.S.	2:57.5
1936	Charles Mathiesen, Norway	2:19.2
1948	Sverre Farstad, Norway	2:17.6
1952	Hjalmar Andersen, Norway	2:20.4
1956	Grishin, & Mikhailov, both USSR (tie)	2:08.6
1960	Aas, Norway & Grishin, USSR (tie)	2:10.4
1964	Ants Anston, USSR	2:10.3
1968	Cornetis Verkerk, Netherlands	2:03.4
1972	Ard Schenk, Netherlands	2:02.96
1976	Jan Egil Storholt, Norway	1:59.38
1980	Eric Heiden, U.S.	1:55.44
1984	Gaetan Boucher, Canada	1:58.36
1988	Andre Hoffmann, E. Germany	1:52.06
1992	Johann Koss, Norway	1:54.81

Men's 5,000 metres — Time

1924	Clas Thunberg, Finland	8:39.0
1928	Ivar Ballangrud, Norway	8:50.5
1932	Irving Jaffee, U.S.	9:40.8
1936	Ivar Ballangrud, Norway	8:19.6
1948	Reidar Liaklev, Norway	8:29.4

(Continued)

1952	Hjalmar Andersen, Norway	8:10.6
1956	Boris Shilkov, USSR	7:48.7
1960	Viktor Kosichkin, USSR	7:51.3
1964	Knut Johannesen, Norway	7:38.4
1968	F. Anton Maier, Norway	7:22.4
1972	Ard Schenk, Netherlands	7:23.61
1976	Sten Stensen, Norway	7:24.48
1980	Eric Heiden, U.S.	7:02.29
1984	Sven Tomas Gustafson, Sweden	7:12:28
1988	Tomas Gustafson, Sweden	6:44:63
1992	Geir Karlstad, Norway	6:59.97

Men's 10,000 metres

		Time
1924	Julius Skutnabb, Finland	18:04.8
1928	Event not held, thawing of ice	
1932	Irving Jaffee, U.S.	19:13.6
1936	Ivar Ballangrud, Norway	17:24.3
1948	Ake Seyffarth, Sweden	17:26.3
1952	Hjalmar Andersen, Norway	16:45.8
1956	Sigvard Ericsson, Sweden	16:35.9
1960	Knut Johannesen, Norway	15:46.6
1964	Jonny Nilsson, Sweden	15:50.1
1968	Jonny Hoeglin, Sweden	15:23.6
1972	Ard Schenk, Netherlands	15:01.35
1976	Piet Kleine, Netherlands	14:50.59
1980	Eric Heiden, U.S.	14:28.13
1984	Igor Malkov, USSR	14:39.90
1988	Tomas Gustafson, Sweden	13:48.20
1992	Bart Veldkamp, Netherlands	14:12.12

Women's 500 metres

		Time
1960	Helga Haase, Germany	0:45.9
1964	Lydia Skoblikova, USSR	0:45.0
1968	Ludmila Titova, USSR	0:46.1
1972	Anne Henning, U.S.	0:43.33
1976	Sheila Young, U.S.	0:42.76
1980	Karin Enke, E. Germany	0:41.78
1984	Christa Rothenburger, E. Germany	0:41.02
1988	Bonnie Blair, U.S.	0:39.10
1992	Bonnie Blair, U.S.	0:40.33

Women's 1,000 metres

		Time
1960	Klara Guseva, USSR	1:34.1
1964	Lydia Skoblikova, USSR	1:33.2
1968	Carolina Geijssen, Netherlands	1:32.6
1972	Monika Pflug, W. Germany	1:31.40
1976	Tatiana Averina, USSR	1:28.43
1980	Natalya Petruseva, USSR	1:24.10
1984	Karin Enke, E. Germany	1:21.61
1988	Christa Rothenburger, E. Germany	1:17.65
1992	Bonnie Blair, U.S.	1:21.90

Women's 1,500 metres

		Time
1960	Lydia Skoblikova, USSR	2:52.2
1964	Lydia Skoblikova, USSR	2:22.6
1968	Kaija Mustonen, Finland	2:22.4
1972	Dianne Holum, U.S.	2:20.85
1976	Galina Stepanskaya, USSR	2:16.58
1980	Anne Borckink, Netherlands	2:10.95
1984	Karin Enke, E. Germany	2:03.42
1988	Yvonne van Gennip, Netherlands	2:00.68
1992	Jacqueline Boerner, Germany	2:05.87

Women's 3,000 metres

		Time
1960	Lydia Skoblikova, USSR	5:14.3
1964	Lydia Skoblikova, USSR	5:14.9
1968	Johanna Schut, Netherlands	4:56.2
1972	Christina Baas-Kaiser, Netherlands	4:52.14
1976	Tatiana Averina, USSR	4:45.19
1980	Bjoerg Eva Jensen, Norway	4:32.13
1984	Andrea Schoene, E. Germany	4:24.79
1988	Yvonne van Gennip, Netherlands	4:11.94
1992	Gunda Niemann, Germany	4:19.90

Women's 5,000 metres

		Time
1988	Yvonne van Gennip, Netherlands	7:14:13
1992	Gunda Niemann, Germany	7:31.57

Short Track Speed Skating

Men's 1,000 metres

		Time
1992	Kim Ki-Hoon, S. Korea	1:30.76

Men's 5,000-metre Relay

		Time
1992	S. Korea, Canada, Japan	7:14.02

Women's 500 metres

		Time
1992	Cathy Turner, U.S.	47.04

Women's 3,000-metre Relay

		Time
1992	Canada, U.S., Unified Team	4:36.62

16TH WINTER OLYMPICS

Albertville, France, 8–23 Feb. 1992

The 16th Olympics winter games in Albertville, France, featured a record 2,174 athletes from 63 countries competing for medals. Germany, whose athletes won a games-high 26 medals, competed as a single team for the first time since 1964. The Unified Team, made up of some former Soviet Republics, finished second with 233 medals.

Medal Winners

	Gold	Silver	Bronze	Total
Germany	10	10	6	26
Unified Team	9	6	8	23
Austria	6	7	8	21
Norway	9	6	5	20
Italy	4	6	4	14
United States	5	4	2	11
France	3	5	1	9
Canada	2	3	2	7
Finland	3	1	3	7
Japan	1	2	4	7
The Netherlands	1	1	2	4
South Korea	2	1	1	4
Sweden	1	0	3	4
China	0	3	0	3
Czechoslovakia	0	0	3	3
Switzerland	1	0	2	3
Luxembourg	0	2	0	2
New Zealand	0	1	0	1
North Korea	0	0	1	1
Spain	0	0	1	1

Individual Medal Winners

(Gold, Silver, Bronze)

Alpine Skiing

Women's Combined: Petra Kronberger, Austria; Anita Wachter, Austria; Florence Masnada, France.

Women's Downhill: Kerrin-Lee-Gartner, Canada; Hilary Lindh, U.S.; Veronika Wallinger, Austria.

Women's Giant Slalom: Pernilla Wiberg, Sweden; Diana Roffe, U.S.; Anita Wachter, Austria.

Women's Slalom: Petra Kronberger, Austria; Annelise Corberger, New Zealand; Blanca Fernández-Ochoa, Spain.

Women's Super Giant Slalom: Deborah Compagnoni, Italy; Carole Merle, France; Katja Seizinger, Germany.

Men's Combined: Josef Polig, Italy; Gianfranco Martin, Italy; Steve Locher, Switzerland.

Men's Downhill: Patrick Ortlieb, Austria; Franck Piccard, France; Günther Mader, Austria.

Men's Giant Slalom: Alberto Tomba, Italy; Marc Girardelli, Luxembourg; Kjetil-Andre Aamodt, Norway.

(Continued)

Men's Super Giant Slalom: Kjetil Andre Aamodt, Norway; Marc Girardelli, Luxembourg; Jan Einar Thorsen, Norway.

Men's Slalom: Finn Christian Jagge, Norway; Alberto Tomba, Italy; Michael Tritscher, Austria.

Biathlon

Women's 15km: Antje Misersky, Germany; Svetlana Pecherskaia, Unified Team; Myriam Bedard, Canada.

Women's 7.5km: Anfissa Restsova, Unified Team; Antje Misersky, Germany; Yelena Belova, Unified Team.

Men's 10km: Mark Kirchner, Germany; Ricco Gross, Germany; Harri Eloranta, Finland.

Men's 20km: Yevgeny Redkine, Unified Team; Mark Kirchner, Germany; Mikael Lofgren, Sweden.

Cross-country Skiing

Women's 5km: Marjut Lukkarinen, Finland; Lyubov Yegorova, Unified Team; Yelena Valbe, Unified Team.

Women's 10km: Lyubov Yegorova, Unified Team; Stefania Belmondo, Italy; Yelena Valbe, Unified Team.

Women's 15km: Lyubov Yegorova, Unified Team; Marjut Lukkarinen, Finland; Yelena Valbe, Unified Team.

Women's 30km: Stefania Belmondo, Italy; Lyubov Yegorova, Unified Team; Yelena Valbe, Unified Team.

Men's 10km: Vegard Ulvang, Norway; Marco Alvarello, Italy; Christer Majback, Sweden.

Men's 15km: Bjorn Dahlie, Norway; Vegard Ulvang, Norway; Giorgio Vanzetta, Italy.

Men's 30km: Vegard Ulvang, Norway; Bjorn Dahlie, Norway; Terje Langli, Norway.
Men's 50km: Bjorn Dahlie, Norway; Maurilio De Zolt, Italy; Giorgio Vanzetta, Italy.

Cross-country Combined

Individual: Fabrice Guy, France; Sylvain Guillaume, France; Klaus Sulzenbacher, Austria.

Figure Skating

Men: Viktor Petrenko, Unified Team; Paul Wylie, U.S.; Petr Bama, Czechoslovakia.

Ice Dancing: Klimova/Ponomarenko, Unified Team; Duchesnay/Duchesnay, France; Usova/Zhulin, Unified Team.

Pairs: Mishkutienok/Dmitriev, Unified Team; Bechke/Petrov, Unified Team; Brasseur/Eisler, Canada.

Women: Kristi Yamaguchi, U.S.; Midori Ito, Japan; Nancy Kerrigan, U.S.

Freestyle Skiing

Women's Moguls: Donna Weinbrecht, U.S.; Elizaveta Kojevnikova, Unified Team; Stine Hattestad, Norway.

Men's Moguls: Edgar Grospiron, France; Olivier Allamand, France; Nelson Carmichael, U.S.

Luge

Women's Singles: Doris Neuner, Austria; Angelica Neuner, Austria; Susi Erdmann, Germany.

Men's Singles: Georg Hackl, Germany; Markus Prock, Austria; Markus Schmidt, Austria.

Men's Doubles: Stefan Krausse/Jan Behrendt, Germany; Yves Mankel/Thomas Rudolph, Germany; Hansjorg Raffi/Norbert Huber, Italy.

Ski Jumping

Individual, 120m: Toni Nieminen, Finland; Martin Höllwarth, Austria; Heinz Kuttin, Austria.

Individual, Normal Hill: Ernst Vettori, Austria; Martin Höllwarth, Austria; Toni Nieminen, Finland.

Speed Skating

LONG TRACK

Women's 500m: Bonnie Blair, U.S.; Ye Qiaobo, China; Christa Luding, Germany.

Women's 1,000m: Bonnie Blair, U.S.; Ye Qiaobo, China; Monique Gatbrecht, Germany.

Women's 1,500m: Jacqueline Börner, Germany; Gunda Niemann, Germany; Seiko Hashimoto, Japan.

Women's 3,000m: Gunda Niemann, Germany; Heike Warnicke, Germany; Emese Hunyady, Austria.

Women's 5,000m: Gunda Niemann, Germany; Heike Warnicke, Germany; Claudia Pechstein, Germany.

Men's 500m: Uwe-Jens Mey, Germany; Toshiyuki Kuroiwa, Japan; Juniohi Inoue, Japan.

Men's 1,000m: Olaf Zinke, Germany; Kim Yoon Man, South Korea; Yukinori Miyabe, Japan.

Men's 1,500m: Johann Koss, Norway; Adne Sondral, Norway; Leo Visser, Netherlands.

Men's 5,000m: Geir Karlstad, Norway; Falco Zandstra, Netherlands; Leo Visser, Netherlands.

Men's 10,000m: Bart Veldkamp, Netherlands; Johann Koss, Norway; Geir Karlstad, Norway.

SHORT TRACK

Women's 500m: Cathy Turner, U.S.; Li Yan, China; Hwang Ok Sil, North Korea.

Men's 1,000m: Kim Ki Hoon, South Korea; Frederic Blackburn, Canada; Lee Yoon Ho, South Korea.

AMERICAN FOOTBALL

Super Bowl Champions

Year	Winner	Loser
1967	Green Bay Packers, 35	Kansas City Chiefs, 10
1968	Green Bay Packers, 33	Oakland Raiders, 14
1969	New York Jets, 16	Baltimore Colts, 7
1970	Kansas City Chiefs, 23	Minnesota Vikings, 7
1971	Baltimore Colts, 16	Dallas Cowboys, 13
1972	Dallas Cowboys, 24	Miami Dolphins, 3
1973	Miami Dolphins, 14	Washington Redskins, 7
1974	Miami Dolphins, 24	Minnesota Vikings, 7
1975	Pittsburgh Steelers, 16	Minnesota Vikings, 6
1976	Pittsburgh Steelers, 21	Dallas Cowboys, 17
1977	Oakland Raiders, 32	Minnesota Vikings, 14
1978	Dallas Cowboys, 27	Denver Broncos, 10
1979	Pittsburgh Steelers, 35	Dallas Cowboys, 31
1980	Pittsburgh Steelers, 31	Los Angeles Rams, 19

Year	Winner	Loser
1981	Oakland Raiders, 27	Philadelphia Eagles, 10
1982	San Francisco 49ers, 26	Cincinnati Bengals, 21
1983	Washington Redskins, 27	Miami Dolphins, 17
1984	Los Angeles Raiders, 38	Washington Redskins, 9
1985	San Francisco 49ers, 38	Miami Dolphins, 16
1986	Chicago Bears, 46	New England Patriots, 10
1987	New York Giants, 39	Denver Broncos, 20
1988	Washington Redskins, 42	Denver Broncos, 10
1989	San Francisco 49ers, 20	Cincinnati Bengals, 16
1990	San Francisco 49ers, 55	Denver Broncos, 10
1991	New York Giants, 20	Buffalo Bills, 19
1992	Washington Redskins, 37	Buffalo Bills, 24
1993	Dallas Cowboys, 52	Buffalo Bills, 17

ANGLING

IGFA Freshwater & Saltwater All-Tackle World Records

Source: International Game Fish Association. Records confirmed to May 1993

Saltwater Fish

Species	Weight	Where caught	Date	Angler
Albacore	88 lbs. 2 oz.	Pt. Mogan, Canary Islands	Nov. 19, 1977	Siegfried Dickemann
Amberjack, greater	155 lbs. 10 oz.	Bermuda	June 24, 1981	Joseph Dawson
Barracuda, great	85 lbs.	Christmas Island	Apr. 11, 1992	John Helfrich
Barracuda, Mexican	21 lbs.	Costa Rica	Mar. 27, 1987	E. Greg Kent
Barracuda, Pacific	6 lbs. 3 oz.	Pt. Loma, San Diego, Cal.	Apr. 4, 1992	James Seibert
Bass, barred sand	13 lbs. 3 oz.	Huntington Beach, Cal.	Aug. 29, 1988	Robert Halal
Bass, black sea	9 lbs. 8 oz.	Virginia Beach, Va.	Jan. 9, 1987	Joe Mizelle Jr.
Bass, black sea	9 lbs. 8 oz.	Virginia Beach, Va.	Dec. 22, 1990	Jack Stallings Jr.
Bass, giant sea	563 lbs. 8 oz.	Anacaba Island, Cal.	Aug. 20, 1968	James D. McAdam Jr.
Bass, striped	78 lbs. 8 oz.	Atlantic City, N.J.	Sept. 21, 1982	Albert McReynolds
Bass, white	6 lbs. 3 oz.	L. Orange, Va.	July 31, 1989	Ronald Sprouse
Bluefish	31 lbs. 12 oz.	Hatteras Inlet, N.C.	Jan. 30, 1972	James M. Hussey
Bonefish	19 lbs.	Zululand, S. Africa	May 26, 1962	Brian W. Batchelor
Bonito, Atlantic	18 lbs. 14 oz.	Fayal I., Azores	July 8, 1953	D. G. Higgs
Bonito, Pacific	14 lbs. 12 oz.	San Benitos Is., Mex.	Oct. 12, 1980	Jerome Rilling
Cabezon	23 lbs.	Juan De Fuca Strait, Wash.	Aug. 4, 1990	Wesley Hunter
Cobia	135 lbs. 9 oz.	Shark Bay, Australia	July 9, 1985	Peter W. Goulding
Cod, Atlantic	98 lbs. 12 oz.	Isle of Shoals, N.H.	June 8, 1969	Alphonse Bielevich
Cod, Pacific	30 lbs.	Andrew Bay, Alaska	June 7, 1984	Donald Vaughn
Conger	110 lbs. 8 oz.	Plymouth, England	Aug. 20, 1991	Hans Clausen
Dolphin	87 lbs.	Papagallo Gulf, Costa Rica	Sept. 25, 1976	Manual Salazar
Drum, black	113 lbs. 1 oz.	Lewes, Del.	Sept. 15, 1975	Gerald Townsend
Drum, red	94 lbs. 2 oz.	Avon, N.C.	Nov. 7, 1984	David Deuel
Eel, American	8 lb. 8 oz.	Brewster, Mass.	May 17, 1992	Gerald Lapierre
Eel, marbled	36 lbs. 1 oz.	Hazelmere Dam, S. Africa	June 10, 1984	Ferdie van Nooten
Flounder, southern	20 lb. 9 oz.	Nassau Sound, Fla.	Dec. 23, 1983	Larenza Mungin
Flounder, summer	22 lbs. 7 oz.	Montauk, N.Y.	Sept. 15, 1975	Charles Nappi
Grouper, Warsaw	436 lbs. 12 oz.	Gulf of Mexico, Destin, Fla.	Dec. 22, 1985	Steve Haeusler
Halibut, Atlantic	255 lbs. 4 oz.	Gloucester, Mass.	July 28, 1989	Sonny Manley
Halibut, California	53 lbs. 4 oz.	Santa Rosa Is., Cal.	July 7, 1988	Russell Harmon
Halibut, Pacific	368 lbs.	Gustavus, Alaska	July 5, 1991	Celia Devitt
Jack, crevalle	54 lbs. 7oz.	Pt. Michel, Gabon	Jan. 15, 1982	Thomas Gibson Jr.
Jack, horse-eye	24 lbs. 8 oz.	Miami, Fla.	Dec. 20, 1982	Tito Schnau
Jack, Pacific crevalle	26 lbs. 12 oz.	Golfito, Costa Rica	Aug. 2, 1992	Jerome Matthews
Jewfish	680 lbs.	Fernandina Beach, Fla.	May 20, 1961	Lynn Joyner
Kawakawa	29 lbs.	Clarion Is., Mexico	Dec. 17, 1986	Ronald Nakamura
Lingcod	69 lbs.	Langara Is., B.C.	June 16, 1992	Murray Romer
Mackerel, cero	17 lbs. 2 oz.	Islamorada, Fla.	Apr. 5, 1986	G. Michael Mills
Mackerel, king	90 lbs.	Key West, Fla.	Feb. 16, 1976	Norton Thornton
Mackeral, Spanish	13 lbs.	Ocracoke Inlet, N.C.	Nov. 4, 1987	Robert Cranton
Marlin, Atlantic blue	1,402 lbs. 2 oz.	Vitoria, Brazil	Feb. 29, 1992	Paulo Amorin
Marlin, black	1,560 lbs.	Cabo Blanco, Peru	Aug. 4, 1953	A. C. Glassell Jr.
Marlin, Pacific blue	1,376 lbs.	Kaaiwa Pt., Hawaii	May. 31, 1982	J.W. deBeaubien
Marlin, striped	494 lbs.	Tutukaka, New Zealand	Jan. 16, 1986	Bill Boniface
Marlin, white	181 lbs. 14 oz.	Vitoria, Brazil	Dec. 8, 1979	Evandro Luiz Caser
Permit	51 lbs. 8 oz.	Lake Worth, Fla.	Apr. 28, 1978	William M. Kenney
Pollack	27 lbs. 6 oz.	Devon, England	Jan. 16, 1986	Robert Milkins
Pollock	46 lbs. 10 oz.	Perkins Cove, Me.	Oct. 24, 1990	Linda Paul
Pompano, African	50 lbs. 8 oz.	Daytona Beach, Fla.	Apr. 21, 1990	Tom Sargent
Roosterfish	114 lbs.	La Paz, Mexico	June 1, 1960	Abe Sackheim
Runner, blue	8 lbs. 4 oz.	Bimini, Bahamas	Sept. 9, 1990	Brent Rowland
Runner, rainbow	37 lbs. 9 oz.	Clarion Is., Mexico	Nov. 21, 1991	Tom Pfleger
Sailfish, Atlantic	135 lbs. 5 oz.	Lagos, Nigeria	Nov. 10, 1991	Ron King
Sailfish, Pacific	221 lbs.	Santa Cruz Is., Ecuador	Feb. 12, 1947	C. W. Stewart
Seabass, white	83 lbs. 12 oz.	San Felipe, Mexico	Mar. 31, 1953	L.C. Baumgardner
Seatrout, spotted	16 lbs.	Mason's Beach, Va.	May 28, 1977	William Katko
Shark, bigeye thresher	802 lbs.	Tutukaka, New Zealand	Feb. 8, 1981	Dianne North
Shark, blue	437 lbs.	Catherine Bay, N.S.W. Australia	Oct. 2, 1976	Peter Hyde
Shark, great hammerhead	991 lbs.	Sarasota, Fla.	May 30, 1982	Allen Ogle
Shark, Greenland	1,708 lbs. 9 oz.	Trondheim, Norway	Oct. 18, 1987	Terje Nordtvedt
Shark, man-eater or white	2,664 lbs.	Ceduna, Australia	Apr. 21, 1959	Alfred Dean
Shark, porbeagle	465 lbs.	Cornwall, England	July 23, 1976	Jorge Potier
Shark, shortfin mako	1,115 lbs.	Black R., Mauritius	Nov. 16, 1988	Patrick Guillanton
Shark, tiger	1,780 lbs.	Cherry Grove, S.C.	June 14, 1964	Walter Maxwell
Skipjack, black	26 lbs.	Baja, Mexico	Oct. 23, 1991	Clifford Hamishi
Snapper, cubera	121 lbs. 8 oz.	Cameron, La.	July 5, 1982	Mike Hebert
Snook	53 lbs. 10 oz.	Costa Rica	Oct. 18, 1978	Gilbert Ponzi
Spearfish, Mediterranean	90 lbs. 13 oz.	Madeira Island, Portugal	June 2, 1980	Joseph Larkin
Swordfish	1,182 lbs.	Iquique, Chile	May 7, 1953	L. Marron
Tarpon	283 lbs. 4 oz.	Sierra Leone	Apr. 16, 1991	Yvon Sebag
Tautog	24 lbs.	Wachapreagee, Va.	Aug. 25, 1987	Gregory Bell
Tope	72 lbs. 12 oz.	Parengarenga Harbor, New Zealand	Dec. 19, 1986	Melanie Feldman
Trevally, bigeye	15 lbs. 8 oz.	Waianae, Hawaii	Mar. 6, 1992	Darryl Bailey
Trevally, giant	145 lbs. 8 oz.	Makena, Hawaii	Mar. 28, 1991	Russell Mori
Tuna, Atlantic bigeye	375 lbs. 8 oz.	Ocean City, Md.	Aug. 26, 1977	Cecil Browne
Tuna, blackfin	42 lbs.	Bermuda	June 2, 1978	Alan J. Card
		Bermuda	July 18, 1989	Gilbert Pearman
Tuna, bluefin	1,496 lbs.	Aulds Cove, Nova Scotia	Oct. 26, 1979	Ken Fraser
Tuna, longtail	79 lbs. 2 oz.	Montague Is., N.S.W., Australia	Apr. 12, 1982	Tim Simpson
Tuna, Pacific bigeye	435 lbs.	Cabo Blanco, Peru	Apr. 17, 1957	Dr. Russel Lee

(Continued)

Species	Weight	Where caught	Date	Angler
Tuna, skipjack	41 lbs. 14 oz.	Mauritius	Nov. 12, 1985	Edmund Heinzen
Tuna, southern bluefin	348 lbs. 5 oz.	Whakatane, New Zealand	Jan. 16, 1981	Rex Wood
Tuna, yellowfin	388 lbs. 12 oz.	San Benedicto Island, Mexico	Apr. 1, 1977	Curt Wiesenhutter
Tunny, little	35 lbs. 2 oz.	Cap de Garde, Algeria	Dec. 14, 1988	Jean Yves Chatard
Wahoo	155 lbs. 8 oz.	Bahamas	Apr. 3, 1990	William Bourne
Weakfish	19 lbs. 2 oz.	Jones Beach Inlet, N.Y.	Oct. 11, 1984	Dennis Rooney
		Delaware Bay, Delaware	May 20, 1989	William Thomas
Yellowtail, California	79 lbs. 4 oz.	Alijos Rocks, Mexico	July 2, 1991	Robert Walker
Yellowtail, southern	114 lbs. 10 oz.	Tauranga, New Zealand	Feb. 5, 1984	Mike Godfrey

Freshwater Fish

Species	Weight	Where caught	Date	Angler
Barramundi	63 lbs. 2 oz.	Normah R., Australia	Apr. 28, 1991	Scott Barnsley
Bass, largemouth	22 lbs. 4 oz.	Montgomery Lake, Ga.	June 2, 1932	George W. Perry
Bass, peacock	26 lbs. 8 oz.	Matevini R., Colombia	Jan. 26, 1982	Rod Neubert
Bass, redeye	8 lbs. 3 oz.	Flint River, Ga.	Oct. 23, 1977	David A. Hubbard
Bass rock	lbs.	York River, Ont.	Aug. 1, 1974	Peter Gulgin
Bass, smallmouth	11 lbs. 15 oz.	Dale Hollow Lake, Ky.	July 9, 1955	David L. Hayes
Bass, Suwannee	3 lbs. 14 oz.	Suwannee River, Fla.	Mar. 2, 1985	Ronnie Everett
Bass, white	6 lbs. 13 oz.	L. Orange, Va.	July 31, 1989	Ronald Sprouse
Bass, whiterock	24 lbs. 3 oz.	Leesville L., Va.	May 12, 1989	David Lambert
Bass, yellow	2 lbs. 4 oz.	Lake Monroe, Ind.	Mar. 27, 1977	Donald L. Stalker
Bluegill	4 lbs. 12 oz.	Ketona Lake, Ala.	Apr. 9, 1950	T.S. Hudson
Bowfin	21 lbs. 8 oz.	Florence, S.C.	Jan. 29, 1980	Robert Harmon
Buffalo, bigmouth	70 lbs. 5 oz.	Bastrop, La.	Apr. 21, 1980	Delbert Sisk
Buffalo, black	55 lbs. 8 oz.	Cherokee L., Tenn.	May 3, 1984	Edward McLain
Buffalo, smallmouth	68 lbs. 8 oz.	L. Hamilton, Ark.	May 16, 1984	Jerry Dolezal
Bullhead, brown	5 lbs. 8 oz.	Veal Pond, Ga.	May 22, 1975	Jimmy Andrews
Bullhead, yellow	4 lbs. 4 oz.	Mormon Lake, Ariz.	May 11, 1984	Emily Williams
Burbot	18 lbs. 4 oz.	Pickford, Mich.	Jan. 31, 1980	Thomas Courtemanche
Carp	75 lbs. 11 oz.	Lac de St. Cassien, France	May 21, 1987	Leo van der Gugten
Catfish, blue	109 lbs. 4 oz.	Cooper R., S.C.	Mar. 14, 1991	George Lijewski
Catfish, channel	58 lbs.	Santee-Cooper Res., S.C.	July 7, 1964	W.B. Whaley
Catfish, flathead	91 lbs. 4 oz.	L. Lewisville, Tex.	Mar. 28, 1982	Mike Rogers
Catfish, white	18 lbs. 14 oz.	Withlacoochee R., Fla.	Sept. 21, 1991	Jim Miller
Char, Arctic	32 lbs. 9 oz.	Tree River, Canada	July 30, 1981	Jeffrey Ward
Crappie, white	5 lbs. 3 oz.	Enid Dam, Miss.	July 31, 1957	Fred L. Bright
Dolly Varden	16 lbs. 12 oz.	Mashutuk R., Alaska	July 21, 1991	Gary King Jr.
Dorado	51 lbs. 5 oz.	Corrientes, Argentina	Sept. 27, 1984	Armando Giudice
Drum, freshwater	54 lbs. 8 oz.	Nickajack Lake, Tenn.	Apr. 20, 1972	Benny E. Hull
Gar, alligator	279 lbs.	Rio Grande River, Tex.	Dec. 2, 1951	Bill Valverde
Gar, Florida	21 lbs. 3 oz.	Boca Raton, Fla.	June 3, 1981	Jeff Sabol
Gar, longnose	50 lbs. 5 oz.	Trinity River, Tex.	July 30, 1954	Townsend Miller
Gar, shortnose	5 lbs.	Sally Jones L., Oklahoma	Apr. 26, 1985	Buddy Croslin
Gar, spotted	8 lbs. 12 oz.	Tennessee R., Ala.	Aug. 26, 1987	Winston Baker
Grayling, Arctic	5 lbs. 15 oz.	Katseyedie River, N.W.T.	Aug. 16, 1967	Jeanne P. Branson
Inconnu	53 lbs.	Pah R., Alaska	Aug. 20, 1986	Lawrence Hudnall
Kokanee	9 lbs. 6 oz.	Okanagan Lake, Vernon, B.C.	June 18, 1988	Norm Kuhn
Muskellunge	65 lbs.	Blackstone Harbor, Ont.	Oct. 16, 1988	Kenneth O'Brien
Muskellunge, tiger	51 lbs. 3 oz.	Lac Vieux-Desert, Wis., Mich.	July 16, 1919	John Knobla
Perch, Nile	191 lbs. 8 oz.	L. Victoria, Kenya	Sept. 5, 1991	Andy Davison
Perch, white	4 lbs. 12 oz.	Messalonskee Lake, Me.	June 4, 1949	Mrs. Earl Small
Perch, yellow	4 lbs. 3 oz.	Bordentown, N.J.	May, 1865	Dr. C.C. Abbot
Pickerel, chain	9 lbs. 6 oz.	Homerville, Ga.	Feb. 17, 1961	Baxley McQuaig Jr.
Pike, northern	55 lbs. 1 oz.	Lake of Grefeern, W., Germany	Oct. 16, 1986	Lothar Louis
Redhorse, greater	9 lbs. 3 oz.	Salmon R., Pulaski, N.Y.	May 11, 1985	Jason Wilson
Redhorse, silver	11 lbs. 7 oz.	Plum Creek, Wis.	May 29, 1985	Neal Long
Salmon, Atlantic	79 lbs. 2 oz.	Tana River, Norway	1928	Henrik Henriksen
Salmon, chinook	97 lbs. 4 oz.	Kenai R., Alas.	May 17, 1985	Les Anderson
Salmon, chum	32 lbs.	Behm Canal, Alas.	June 7, 1985	Fredrick Thynes
Salmon, coho	33 lbs. 4 oz.	Salmon R., Pulaski, N.Y.	Sept. 27, 1989	Jerry Lifton
Salmon, pink	13 lbs. 1 oz.	St. Mary's R., Ont.	Sept. 23, 1992	Ray Higaki
Salmon, sockeye	15 lbs. 3 oz.	Kenai R., Alaska	Aug. 9, 1987	Stan Roach
Sauger	8 lbs. 12 oz.	Lake Sakakawea, N.D.	Oct. 6, 1971	Mike Fischer
Shad, American	11 lbs. 4 oz.	Connecticut R., Mass.	May 19, 1986	Bob Thibodo
Sturgeon, white	468 lbs.	Benicia, Cal.	July 9, 1983	Joey Pallotta 3d
Sunfish, green	2 lbs. 2 oz.	Stockton Lake, Mo.	June 18, 1971	Paul M. Dilley
Sunfish, redbreast	1 lb. 12 oz.	Suwannee R., Fla.	May 29, 1984	Alvin Buchanan
Sunfish, redear	4 lbs. 13 oz.	Marianna, Fla.	Mar. 13, 1986	Joey Floyd
Tigerfish, giant	97 lbs.	Zaire R., Kinshasa, Zaire	July 9, 1988	Raymond Houtmans
Tilapia	6 lbs.	L. Okeechobee, Fla.	June 24, 1989	Joseph M. Tucker
Trout, Apache	5 lb. 3 oz.	Apache Res., Ariz.	May 29, 1991	John Baldwin
Trout, brook	14 lbs. 8 oz.	Nipigon River, Ont.	July 1916	Dr. W.J. Cook
Trout, brown	40 lbs. 4 oz.	Little Red R., Ark.	May 9, 1992	Howard Collins
Trout, bull	32 lbs.	L. Pend Oreille, Ida.	Oct. 27, 1949	N.L. Higgins
Trout, cutthroat	41 lbs.	Pyramid Lake, Nev.	Dec. 1925	J. Skimmerhorn
Trout, golden	11 lbs.	Cook's Lake, Wyo.	Aug. 5, 1948	Charles S. Reed
Trout, lake	66 lbs. 8 oz.	Great Bear Lake, N.W.T.	July 19, 1991	Rodney Harback
Trout, rainbow	42 lbs. 2 oz.	Bell Island, Alas.	June 22, 1970	David Robert White
Trout, tiger	20 lbs. 13 oz.	Lake Michigan, Wis.	Aug. 12, 1978	Pete Friedland
Walleye	25 lbs.	Old Hickory Lake, Tenn.	Aug. 1, 1960	Mabry Harper
Warmouth	2 lbs. 7 oz.	Yellow R., Holt, Fla.	Oct. 19, 1985	Tony D. Dempsey
Whitefish, lake	14 lbs. 6 oz.	Meaford, Ont.	May 21, 1984	Dennis Laycock
Whitefish, mountain	5 lbs. 6 oz.	Rioh R., Sask.	June 15, 1988	John Bell
Whitefish, river	11 lbs. 2 oz.	Nymoua, Sweden	Dec. 9, 1984	Jorgen Larsson
Whitefish, round	6 lbs.	Putahow R., Manitoba	June 14, 1984	Allen Ristori
Zander	22 lbs. 2 oz.	Trosa, Sweden	June 12, 1986	Harry Lee Tennison

National League First Division Champions

Year	Individual	Team
1906	F. Beales	Boston Association
1907	A. Croft	Sheffield Amal. AA
1908	J. Mason	Sheffield & Dist.
1909	J. H. R. Bazley	Leeds AAA
1910	A. Blackman	Leeds AAA
1911	W. Lowe	Sheffield AAA
1912	G. Beales	Boston Association
1913	W. Gough	Nottingham Association
1914	A. Sharrett	Leeds AAA
1915–18	No contest	
1919	T. Hill	Boston Association
1920	R. Barlow	County Palatine
1921	J. Wakefield	Derby Association
1922	B. Hobday	Lincoln Association
1923	J. W. Cauldwell	County Palatine
1924	W. T. Willcocks	Castleford & Dist.
1925	G. Allen	Long Eaton Federation
1926	A. Fletcher	Lincoln AA
1927	J. H. R. Bazley	Grimsby & Dist.
1928	W. Tetley	Leeds & Dist Amal.
1929	J. Sykes	Boston
1930	C. Muddimer	Sheffield Amal.
1931	W. Daddy	Hull Amal.
1932	H. Sallis	Loughborough
1933	E. Dabill	Sheffield & Dist. AA
1934	H. Smith	Sheffield Amal. AS
1935	A. Kellett	Lincoln AA
1936	A. E. Bryant	Lincoln
1937	H. Jones	G & W Salford
1938	G. Wright	Hull Amal.
1939–45	No contest	
1946	G. Laybourne	Hull & Dist. AAA
1947	W. Edwards	Worksop & Dist. AA
1948	W. Thompson	Leeds Amal AA
1949	R. Woodhall	Leeds Amal AA
1950	W. Rockley	Peterborough AA
1951	S. Buxton	Doncaster & Dist. AA
1952	H. Seed	Leeds Amal AA
1953	N. Hazelwood	Lincoln AA
1954	R. Lye	Hull APS
1955	J. Carr	Sheffield Amal.
1956	R. Lusby	Coventry AA
1957	H. Storey	Nottingham AA
1958	W. Hughes	Coventry AA
1959	J. Sharp	Bedford AC
1960	K. Smith	King's Lynn AA
1961	J. Blakey	Coventry AA
1962	V. Baker	Lincoln AA
1963	R. Sims	Northampton Nene
1964	C. Burch	Kidderminster & DAA
1965	D. Burr	Rugby Federation
1966	R. Jarvis	Boston & Dist.
1967	E. Townsin	Derby Railway Inst.
1968	D. Groom	Leighton Buzzard
1969	R. Else	Stoke City & Dist.
1970	B. Lakey	Cambridge Fish PF
1971	R. Harris	Leicester AS
1972	P. Coles	Birmingham AS
1973	A. Wright	Grimsby & Dist.
1974	P. Anderson	Leicester AS
1975	M. Hoad-Reddick	Birmingham AA
1976	N. Wells	Birmingham AA
1977	R. Foster	Coventry
1978	D. Harris	Coleshill
1979	M. Cullen	Barnsley & Dist.
1980	P. Burrell	Notts Federation
1981	D. Steer	Essex County
1982	A. Mayer	Rotheram
1983	D. Howl	Notts Fed.
1984	C. Gregg	Coleshill
1985	B. Oliver	ABC
1985	M. Stabler	Izaak Walton Staffs
1986	J. Robinson	Nottingham & Dist.
1988	S. Hall	Redditch Fed of Ang.
1989	B. Wickens	Reading & Dist. AA
1990	S. Cheetham	Trevs AS
1991	P. Hargreaves	Izaak Walton Preston
1992	K. Gregory	Nottingham & Dist.
1993	S. Canty	Liverpool & Dist.

World Freshwater Champions

Year	Individual	Team
1957	Mandelli (Ita)	Italy
1958	Garroit (Bel)	Belgium
1959	Tesse (Fra)	France
1960	Tesse (Fra)	Belgium
1961	Legogue (Fra)	E. Germany
1962	Tedesco (Ita)	Italy
1963	Lane (Eng)	France
1964	Fontanet (Fra)	France
1965	Tesse (Fra)	Romania
1966	Guiheneuf (Fra)	France
1967	Isenbaert (Bel)	Belgium
1968	Grebenstein (W. Ger)	France
1969	Harris (Eng)	Netherlands
1970	Van den Eynde (Bel)	Belgium
1971	Bassi (Ita)	Italy
1972	Levels (Neth)	France
1973	Michiels (Bel)	Belgium
1974	Richter (W. Ger)	France
1975	Heaps (Eng)	France
1976	Bassi (Ita)	Italy
1977	Mainil (Bel)	Luxembourg
1978	J. P. Fourgeat (Fra)	France
1979	Heulard (Fra)	France
1980	W. R. Kremkus (W. Ger)	W. Germany
1981	D. Thomas (Eng)	France
1982	K. Ashurst (Eng)	Netherlands
1983	W. R. Kremkus (W. Ger)	Belgium
1984	B. Smithers (Ire)	Luxembourg
1985	D. Roper (Eng)	England
1986	L. Wever (Neth)	Italy
1987	C. Branson (Wales)	England
1988	J.-P. Fouquet (Fra)	England
1989	T. Pickering (Eng)	France
1990	R. Nudd (Eng)	France
1991	R. Nudd (Eng)	England
1992	D. Wesson (Aust)	Italy
1993	Mario Barros (Por)	Italy

ASSOCIATION FOOTBALL

Barclays League Final Tables 1992–93

Premier Division	Home				Goals		Away			Goals			
	P	W	D	L	F	A	W	D	L	F	A	Pts	GD
1 Manchester U	42	14	5	2	39	14	10	7	4	28	17	84	+36
2 Aston Villa	42	13	5	3	36	16	8	6	7	21	24	74	+17
3 Norwich C	42	13	6	2	31	19	8	3	10	30	46	72	−4
4 Blackburn R	42	13	4	4	38	18	7	7	7	30	28	71	+22
5 QPR	42	11	5	5	41	32	6	7	8	22	23	63	+8
6 Liverpool	42	13	4	4	41	18	3	7	11	21	37	59	+7
7 Sheffield W	42	9	8	4	34	26	6	6	9	21	25	59	+4
8 Tottenham H	42	11	5	5	40	25	5	6	10	20	41	59	−6
9 Manchester C	42	7	8	6	30	25	8	4	9	26	26	57	+5
10 Arsenal	42	8	6	7	25	20	7	5	9	15	18	56	+2
11 Chelsea	42	9	7	5	29	22	5	7	9	22	32	56	−3
12 Wimbledon	42	9	4	8	32	23	5	8	8	24	32	54	+1
13 Everton	42	7	6	8	26	27	8	2	11	27	28	53	−2
14 Sheffield U	42	10	6	5	33	19	4	4	13	21	34	52	+1
15 Coventry C	42	7	4	10	29	28	6	9	6	23	29	52	−5
16 Ipswich T	42	8	9	4	29	22	4	7	10	21	33	52	−5
17 Leeds U	42	12	8	1	40	17	0	7	14	17	45	51	−5
18 Southampton	42	10	6	5	30	21	3	5	13	24	40	50	−7
19 Oldham Ath	42	10	6	5	43	30	3	4	14	20	44	49	−11
10 Crystal Palace	42	6	9	6	27	25	5	7	9	21	36	49	−13
21 Middlesbrough	42	8	5	8	33	27	3	6	12	21	48	44	−21
22 Nottingham F	42	6	4	11	17	25	4	6	11	24	37	40	−21

First Division	Home				Goals		Away			Goals			
	P	W	D	L	F	A	W	D	L	F	A	Pts	GLS
1 Newcastle U	46	16	6	1	58	15	13	3	7	34	23	96	(92)
2 West Ham U	46	16	5	2	50	17	10	5	8	31	24	88	(81)
3 Portsmouth	46	19	2	2	48	9	9	7	8	32	37	88	(80)

(Continued)

First Division

		Home			Goals		Away			Goals			
	P	W	D	L	F	A	W	D	L	F	A	Pts	GLS
4 Tranmere R	46	15	4	4	48	24	8	6	9	24	32	79	(72)
5 Swindon T	46	15	5	3	41	23	6	8	9	33	36	76	(74)
6 Leicester C	46	14	5	4	43	24	8	5	10	28	40	76	(71)
7 Millwall	46	14	6	3	46	21	4	10	9	19	32	70	(65)
8 Derby Co	46	11	2	10	40	33	8	7	8	28	24	66	(68)
9 Grimsby T	46	12	6	5	33	25	7	1	15	25	32	64	(58)
10 Peterborough U	46	7	11	5	30	26	9	3	11	25	37	62	(55)
11 Wolverhampton W	46	11	6	6	37	26	5	7	11	20	30	61	(57)
12 Charlton Ath	46	10	8	5	28	19	6	5	12	21	27	61	(49)
13 Barnsley	46	12	4	7	29	19	5	5	13	27	41	60	(56)
14 Oxford U	46	8	7	8	29	21	6	7	10	24	35	56	(56)
15 Bristol C	46	10	7	6	29	25	4	7	12	20	42	56	(49)
16 Watford	46	8	7	8	27	30	6	6	11	30	41	55	(57)
17 Notts Co	46	10	7	6	33	21	2	9	12	22	49	52	(55)
18 Southend U	46	9	8	6	33	22	4	5	14	21	42	52	(54)
19 Birmingham C	46	10	4	9	30	32	3	8	12	20	40	51	(50)
20 Luton T	46	6	13	4	26	26	4	8	11	22	36	51	(48)
21 Sunderland	46	9	6	8	34	28	4	5	14	16	36	50	(50)
22 Brentford	46	7	6	10	28	30	6	4	13	24	41	49	(52)
23 Cambridge U	46	8	6	9	29	32	3	10	10	19	37	49	(48)
24 Bristol R	46	6	6	11	30	42	4	5	14	25	45	41	(55)

Second Division

		Home			Goals		Away			Goals			
	P	W	D	L	F	A	W	D	L	F	A	Pts	GLS
1 Stoke C	46	17	4	2	41	13	10	8	5	32	21	93	(73)
2 Bolton W	46	18	2	3	48	14	9	7	7	32	27	90	(80)
3 Port Vale	46	14	7	2	44	17	12	4	7	35	27	89	(79)
4 WBA	46	17	3	3	56	22	8	7	8	32	32	85	(88)
5 Swansea C	46	12	7	4	38	17	8	6	9	27	30	73	(65)
6 Stockport Co	46	11	11	1	47	18	8	4	11	34	39	72	(81)
7 Leyton Orient	46	16	4	3	49	20	5	5	13	20	33	72	(69)
8 Reading	46	14	4	5	44	20	4	11	8	22	31	69	(66)
9 Brighton & HA	46	13	4	6	36	24	7	5	11	27	35	69	(63)
10 Bradford C	46	12	5	6	36	24	6	9	8	33	43	68	(69)
11 Rotherham U	46	9	7	7	30	27	8	7	8	30	33	65	(60)
12 Fulham	46	9	9	5	28	22	7	8	8	29	33	65	(57)
13 Burnley	46	11	8	4	38	21	4	8	11	19	38	61	(57)
14 Plymouth Arg	46	11	6	6	38	28	5	6	12	21	36	60	(59)
15 Huddersfield T	46	10	6	7	30	22	7	3	13	24	39	60	(54)
16 Hartlepool U	46	8	6	9	19	23	6	6	11	23	37	54	(42)
17 AFC Bournemouth	46	7	10	6	28	34	5	7	11	17	28	53	(45)
18 Blackpool	46	9	9	5	40	30	3	6	14	23	45	51	(63)
19 Exeter C	46	5	8	10	26	30	6	9	8	28	39	50	(54)
20 Hull C	46	9	5	9	28	26	4	6	13	18	43	50	(46)
21 Preston NE	46	8	5	10	41	47	5	3	15	24	47	47	(65)
22 Mansfield T	46	7	8	8	34	34	4	3	16	18	46	44	(52)
23 Wigan Ath	46	6	6	11	26	34	4	5	14	17	38	41	(43)
24 Chester C	46	6	2	15	30	47	2	3	18	19	55	29	(49)

Third Division

		Home			Goals		Away			Goals			
	P	W	D	L	F	A	W	D	L	F	A	Pts	GLS
1 Cardiff C	42	13	7	1	42	20	12	1	8	35	27	83	(77)
2 Wrexham	42	14	3	4	48	26	9	8	4	27	26	80	(75)
3 Barnet	42	16	4	1	45	19	7	6	8	21	29	79	(66)
4 York C	42	13	6	2	41	15	8	6	7	31	30	75	(66)
5 Walsall	42	11	6	4	42	31	11	1	9	34	30	73	(76)
6 Crewe Alex	42	13	3	5	47	23	8	4	9	28	33	70	(75)
7 Bury	42	10	7	4	36	19	8	2	11	27	36	63	(63)
8 Lincoln C	42	10	6	5	31	20	8	3	10	26	33	63	(57)
9 Shrewsbury T	42	11	3	7	36	30	6	8	7	21	22	62	(57)
10 Colchester U	42	13	3	5	38	26	5	2	14	29	50	59	(67)
11 Rochdale	42	10	3	8	38	29	6	7	8	32	41	58	(70)
12 Chesterfield	42	11	3	7	32	28	4	8	9	27	35	56	(59)
13 Scarborough	42	7	7	7	32	30	8	2	11	34	41	54	(66)
14 Scunthorpe U	42	8	7	6	38	25	6	5	10	19	29	54	(57)
15 Darlington	42	5	6	10	23	31	7	8	6	25	22	50	(48)
16 Doncaster R	42	6	5	10	22	28	5	9	7	20	29	47	(42)
17 Hereford U	42	7	9	5	31	27	3	6	12	16	33	45	(47)
18 Carlisle U	42	7	5	9	29	27	4	6	11	22	38	44	(51)
19 Torquay U	42	6	4	11	18	26	6	3	12	27	41	43	(45)
20 Northampton T	42	6	5	10	19	28	5	3	13	29	46	41	(48)
21 Gillingham	42	9	4	8	32	28	0	9	12	16	36	40	(48)
22 Halifax T	42	3	5	13	20	35	6	4	11	25	33	36	(45)

Coca-Cola Cup 1992–93
(formerly Rumbelows Cup)

First Round, First Leg

Bolton W	2	Port Vale	1
Cardiff C	1	Bristol C.	0
Carlisle U	4	Burnley	1
Chesterfield	2	York C	0
Colchester U	1	Brighton & HA	1
Crewe Alex	4	Rochdale	1
Darlington	1	Scunthorpe U	1
Doncaster R	0	Lincoln C	3
Exeter C	0	Birmingham C	0
Fulham	0	Brentford	2
Gillingham	2	Northampton T	1
Halifax T	1	Hartlepool U	2
Hereford U	2	Torquay U	2
Hull C	2	Rotherham U	2
Leyton Orient	2	Millwall	2
Oxford U	3	Swansea C	0
Peterborough U	4	Barnet	0
Preston NE	2	Stoke C	1
Shrewsbury T	1	Wigan Ath	2
Stockport Co	1	Chester C	1
Sunderland	2	Huddersfield T	3
Wrexham	1	Bury	1
Grimsby T	1	Barnsley	1
Newcastle U	2	Mansfield T	1
Scarborough	3	Bradford C	0
Tranmere R	3	Blackpool	0
Walsall	1	Bournemouth	1
WBA	1	Plymouth Arg	0

First Round, Second Leg

Barnet	2	Peterborough U	2
Barnsley	1	Grimsby T	1*
Birmingham C	1	Exeter C	4
Blackpool	4	Tranmere R	0
Bournemouth	0	Walsall	1
Brentford	2	Fulham	0
Bristol C	5	Cardiff C	1
Burnley	1	Carlisle U	1
Bury	4	Wrexham	3
Chester C	1	Stockport Co	2
Hartlepool U	3	Halifax T	2
Lincoln	1	Doncaster R	1
Mansfield T	0	Newcastle U	0
Plymouth Arg	2	WBA	0
Port Vale	1	Bolton W	1
Rochdale	1	Crewe Alex	2
Rotherham U	1	Hull C	0
Scunthorpe U	2	Darlington	0
Swansea C	1	Oxford U	0
Torquay U	5	Hereford U	0
Wigan Ath ††	0	Shrewsbury T	1*
York C	0	Chesterfield	0
Bradford C	3	Scarborough	5
Brighton & HA	1	Colchester U	0
Huddersfield T ††	0	Sunderland	1*
Millwall	3	Leyton Orient	0
Stoke C	4	Preston NE	0*
Northampton T	0	Gillingham	2

Second Round, First Leg

Tottenham H	3	Brentford	1
Arsenal	1	Millwall	1
Bolton W	1	Wimbledon	3
Bristol C	2	Sheffield U	1
Bury	0	Charlton Ath	0
Cambridge U	2	Stoke C	2
Carlisle U	2	Norwich C	2
Crystal Palace	3	Lincoln C	1
Exeter C	0	Oldham Ath	1
Leeds U	4	Scunthorpe U	1
Liverpool	4	Chesterfield	4
Notts Co	3	Wolverhampton W	2
Watford	2	Reading	2
Wigan Ath	2	Ipswich T	2
Blackpool	0	Portsmouth	4
Brighton & HA	1	Manchester U	1
Coventry C	2	Scarborough	0
Gillingham	0	Southampton	0
Huddersfield T	1	Blackburn R	1
Leicester C	2	Peterborough U	0
Luton T	2	Plymouth Arg	2
Manchester C	0	Bristol R	0
Newcastle U	0	Middlesbrough	0
Oxford U	1	Aston Villa	2

(Continued)

(Coca-Cola Cup contd.)

QPR	2	Grimsby T	1
Rotherham U	1	Everton	0
Sheffield W	3	Hartlepool U	0
Southend U	1	Derby Co	0
Stockport Co	2	Nottingham F	3
Torquay U	0	Swindon T	6
Walsall	0	Chelsea	3
West Ham U	0	Crewe Alex	0

Second Round, Second Leg

Blackburn R	4	Huddersfield	3*
Chesterfield	1	Liverpool	4
Grimsby T	2	QPR †	1*
Hartlepool U	2	Sheffield W	2
Ipswich T	4	Wigan Ath	0
Lincoln C	1	Crystal Palace	1
Peterborough U	2	Leicester C	1
Plymouth Arg	3	Luton T	2
Portsmouth	2	Blackpool	0
Swindon T	3	Torquay U	2
Wimbledon	0	Bolton W	1
Aston Villa	2	Oxford U	1
Brentford	2	Tottenham H	4
Bristol R	1	Manchester C	2*
Charlton Ath	0	Bury	1
Chelsea	1	Walsall	0
Crewe Alex	2	West Ham U	0
Derby Co	7	Southend U	0
Everton	3	Rotherham U	0
Manchester U	1	Brighton & HA	0
Middlesbrough	1	Newcastle U	3
Millwall	1	Arsenal †	1*
Norwich C	2	Carlisle	0
Nottingham F	2	Stockport Co	1
Oldham Ath	0	Exeter C	0
Reading	0	Watford	2
Scarborough	3	Coventry C	0
Sheffield U	4	Bristol C	1
Southampton	3	Gillingham	0
Stoke C	1	Cambridge U	2
Wolverhampton W	0	Notts Co	1
Scunthorpe U	2	Leeds U	2

Third Round

Bury	0	QPR	2
Notts Co	2	Cambridge U	3
Plymouth Arg	3	Scarborough	3
Portsmouth	0	Ipswich T	1
Sheffield W	7	Leicester C	1
Swindon T	0	Oldham	1
Aston Villa	1	Manchester U	0
Blackburn R	2	Norwich C	0
Chelsea	2	Newcastle U	1
Crewe Alex	0	Nottingham F	1
Derby Co	1	Arsenal	1
Everton	0	Wimbledon	0
Manchester C	0	Tottenham H	1
Sheffield U	0	Liverpool	0
Southampton	0	Crystal Palace	2
Watford	2	Leeds U	1

Third Round Replays

Wimbledon	0	Everton	1
Liverpool	3	Sheffield U	0
Scarborough	2	Plymouth Arg	1
Arsenal	2	Derby Co	1

Fourth Round

Cambridge U	1	Oldham Ath	0
Liverpool	1	Crystal Palace	1
Aston Villa	2	Ipswich T	2
Everton	2	Chelsea	2
Nottingham F	2	Tottenham H	0
Sheffield W	4	QPR	0
Blackburn R	6	Watford	1
Scarborough	0	Arsenal	1

Fourth Round Replays

Ipswich T	1	Aston Villa	0
Chelsea	1	Everton	0
Crystal Palace	2	Liverpool	1*

Fifth Round

Blackburn R	3	Cambridge U	2
Crystal Palace	3	Chelsea	1
Arsenal	2	Nottingham F	0
Ipswich T	1	Sheffield W	1

Fifth Round Replay

Sheffield W	1	Ipswich T	0

Semi-final, First Leg

Crystal Palace	1	Arsenal	3
Blackburn R	2	Sheffield W	4

Semi-final, Second Leg

Arsenal	2	Crystal Palace	0
Sheffield W	2	Blackburn R	1

Final at Wembley

Arsenal	2	Sheffield W	1

*after extra time †won on penalties ††won on away goals

European Champions

Year	Winners	Score	Runners-up	Venue
1960	USSR	2-1	Yugoslavia	Paris
1964	Spain	2-1	USSR	Madrid
1968	Italy	2-0	Yugoslavia	Rome
		(after 1-1 draw)		
1972	W. Germany	3-0	USSR	Brussels
1976	Czechoslovakia	2-2	W. Germany	Belgrade
		(Czechoslovakia won 5-3 on penalties)		
1980	W. Germany	2-1	Belgium	Rome
1984	France	2-0	Spain	Paris
1988	Holland	2-0	USSR	Munich
1992	Denmark	2-0	W. Germany	Gothenburg

European Cup 1992–93

Preliminary Round, First Leg

K1 Klaksvikar	1	Skonto Riga	3
Olimpija Ljubljana	3	Norma Tallinn	0
Shelbourne	0	Tavria Simferopol	0
Valletta	1	Maccabi Tel Aviv	2

Preliminary Round, Second Leg

Maccabu Tel Aviv	1	Valletta	0
Norma Tallinn	0	Olimpija Ljubljana	2
Skonto Riga	3	K1 Klaksvikar	0
Tavria Simferopol	2	Shelbourne	0

First Round, First Leg

AEK Athens	1	Apoel	1
FK Austria	3	CSKA Sofia	1
Barcelona	1	Viking Stavanger	0
Glentoran	0	Marseille	5
IFK Gothenberg	2	Besiktas	0
Kuusysi	1	Dinamo Bucharest	0
Lech Poznan	2	Skonto Riga	0
Maccabi Tel Aviv	0	FC Brugge	1
AC Milan	4	Olimpija Ljubljana	0
PSV Eindhoven	6	Zalgiris Vilnius	0
Rangers	2	Lyngby	0
Sion	4	Tavria Simferopol	1
Slovan Bratislava	4	Ferencvaros	1
Stuttgart	3	Leeds U	0
Union Luxembourg	1	FC Porto	4
Vikingur	0	CSKA Moscow	1

First Round, Second Leg

Apoel	2	AEK Athens	2
Besiktas	2	IFK Gothenburg	1
FC Brugge	3	Maccabi Tel Aviv	0
CSKA Moscow	4	Vikingur	0
CSKA Sofia	3	FK Austria	2
Dinamo Bucharest	2	Kuusysi	0
Ferencvaros	0	Slovan Bratislava	0
Leeds U	4	Stuttgart	1

(Leeds U awarded match 3-0 on forfeit as Stuttgart included fourth foreign player)

Replay: Leeds U	2	Stuttgart	1
Lyngby	0	Rangers	1
Marseille	3	Glentoran	0
Olimpija Ljubljana	0	AC Milan	3
FC Porto	5	Union Luxembourg	0
Skonto Riga	0	Lech Poznan	0
Tavria Simferopol	1	Sion	3
Viking Stavanger	0	Barcelona	0
Zalgiris Vilnius	0	PSV Eindhoven	2

Second Round, First Leg

AEK Athens	1	PSV Eindhoven	0
FC Brugge	2	FK Austria	0
CSKA Moscow	1	Barcelona	1
Dinamo Bucharest	0	Marseille	0
IFK Gothenburg	1	Lech Poznan	0
Rangers	2	Leeds U	1
Sion	2	FC Porto	2
Slovan Bratislava	0	AC Milan	1

Second Round, Second Leg

FK Austria	3	FC Brugge	1
Barcelona	2	CSKA Moscow	3
Lech Poznan	0	IFK Gothenburg	3
Leeds U	1	Rangers	2
Marseille	2	Dinamo Bucharest	0
AC Milan	4	Slovan Bratislava	0
FC Porto	4	Sion	0
PSV Eindhoven	3	AEK Athens	0

Semi-finals, Group A

FC Brugge	1	CSKA Moscow	0
Rangers	2	Marseille	2
CSKA Moscow	0	Rangers	1
Marseille	3	FC Brugge	0
FC Brugge	1	Rangers	1
CSKA Moscow	1	Marseille	1
Marseille	6	CSKA Moscow	0
Rangers	2	FC Brugge	1
CSKA Moscow	1	FC Brugge	2
Marseille	1	Rangers	1
FC Brugge	0	Marseille	1
Rangers	0	CSKA Moscow	0

Semi-finals, Group B

AC Milan	4	IFK Gothenburg	0
FC Porto	2	PSV Eindhoven	2
IFK Gothenburg	1	FC Porto	0
PSV Eindhoven	1	AC Milan	2
PSV Eindhoven	1	IFK Gothenburg	3
FC Porto	0	AC Milan	1
IFK Gothenburg	3	PSV Eindhoven	0
AC Milan	1	FC Porto	0
IFK Gothenburg	0	AC Milan	1
PSV Eindhoven	0	FC Porto	1
AC Milan	2	PSV Eindhoven	0
FC Porto	2	IFK Gothenburg	0

Final

Marseille	1	AC Milan	0

European Cup Champions

Year	Winners	Score	Runners-up
1956	Real Madrid	4-3	Rheims
1957	Real Madrid	2-0	Fiorentina
1958	Real Madrid	3-2	AC Milan
1959	Real Madrid	2-0	Rheims
1960	Real Madrid	7-3	Eintracht Frankfurt
1961	Benfica	3-2	Barcelona
1962	Benfica	5-3	Real Madrid
1963	AC Milan	2-1	Benfica
1964	Inter-Milan	3-1	Real Madrid
1965	Inter-Milan	1-0	Benfica
1966	Real Madrid	2-1	Partizan Belgrade
1967	Celtic	2-1	Inter-Milan
1968	Manchester U	4-1	Benfica
1969	AC Milan	4-1	Ajax
1970	Feyenoord	2-1	Celtic
1971	Ajax	2-0	Panathinaikos
1972	Ajax	2-0	Inter-Milan
1973	Ajax	1-0	Juventus
1974	Bayern Munich	4-0	Atletico Madrid
		(after 1-1 draw)	
1975	Bayern Munich	2-0	Leeds U
1976	Bayern Munich	1-0	St. Etienne
1977	Liverpool	3-1	B.M/gladbach
1978	Liverpool	1-0	FC Bruges
1979	Nottingham F	1-0	Malmo
1980	Nottingham F	1-0	SV Hamburg
1981	Liverpool	1-0	Real Madrid
1982	Aston Villa	1-0	Bayern Munich
1983	SV Hamburg	1-0	Juventus
1984	Liverpool	1-1	AS Roma
	(Liverpool won 4-2 on penalties)		
1985	Juventus	1-0	Liverpool
1986	Steaua Bucharest	0-0	Barcelona
	(Steaua won 2-0 on penalties)		
1987	FC Porto	2-1	Bayern Munich
1988	PSV Eindhoven	0-0	Benfica
	(Eindhoven won 6-5 on penalties)		
1989	AC Milan	4-0	Steaua Bucharest
1990	AC Milan	1-0	Benfica
1991	Red Star Belgrade	0-0	Olympique Marseille
	(Red Star won 5-3 on penalties)		
1992	Barcelona	1-0	Sampdoria
1993	Marseille	1-0	AC Milan

European Cup-Winners' Cup 1992–93

Preliminary Round, First Leg

Avenir Beggen	1	B36 Torshavn	0
Branik Maribor	4	Hamrun Spartans	0
Stromsgodset	0	Hapoel Tel Aviv	2
Vaduz	0	Chernomoretz Odessa	5

Preliminary Round, Second Leg

Chernomoretz Odessa	7	Vaduz	1
Hamrun Spartans	2	Branik Maribor	1
Harpoel Tel Aviv	2	Stromsgodset	0
B36 Torshavn	1	Avenir Beggen	1

First Round, First Leg

AIK Stockholm	3	Aarhus	3
Airdrieonians	0	Sparta Prague	1
Bohemians	0	Steaua Bucharest	0
Branik Maribor	0	Atletico Madrid	3
Cardiff C	1	Admira Wacker	1
Feyenoord	1	Harpoel Tel Aviv	0
Glenavon	1	Antwerp	1
Levski Sofia	2	Lucerne	1
Liverpool	6	Apollon Limassol	1
Miedz Legnica	0	Monaco	1
Moscow Spartak	0	Avenir Beggen	0
Olympiakos	0	Chernomoretz Odessa	1
Parma	1	Ujpest	0
Trabzonspor	2	TPSTurku	0
Valur	0	Boavista	0
Werder Bremen	3	Hannover	1

First Round, Second Leg

Aarhus	1	AIK Stockholm	1
Admira Wecker	1	Cardiff C	0
Apollon Limassol	1	Liverpool	2
Antwerp	1	Glenavon	1
	(Antwerp won 3-1 on penalties.)		
Atletico Madrid	6	Branik Maribor	1
Avenir Beggen	1	Moscow Spartak	5
Boavista	3	Valur	0
Chernomoretz Odessa	0	Olympiakos	3
Hannover	2	Werder Bremen	1
Harpoel Tel Aviv	2	Feyenoord	1
Lucerne	1	Levski Sofia	0
Monaco	0	Miedz Legnica	0
Sparta Prague	2	Airdrieonians	1
Steaua Bucharest	4	Bohemians	0
TPS Turku	2	Trabzonspor	2
Ujpest	1	Parma	1

Second Round, First Leg

Aarhus	3	Steaua Bucharest	2
Admira Wecker	2	Antwerp	4
Lucerne	1	Feyenoord	0
Monaco	0	Olympiakos	1
Parma	0	Boavista	0
Spartak Moscow	4	Liverpool	2
Trabzonspor	0	Atletico Madrid	2
Werder Bremen	2	Sparta Prague	3

Second Round, Second Leg

Antwerp	3	Admira Wecker	4
Atletico Madrid	0	Trabzonspor	0
Boavista	0	Parma	2
Feyenoord	4	Lucerne	1
Liverpool	0	Moscow Spartak	2
Olympiakos	0	Monaco	0
Sparta Prague	1	Werder Bremen	0
Steaua Bucharest	2	Aarhus	1

Quarter-finals, First Leg

Antwerp	0	Steaua Bucharest	0
Feyenoord	0	Moscow Spartak	1
Olympiakos	1	Atletico Madrid	1
Sparta Prague	0	Parma	0

Quarter-finals, Second Leg

Atletico Madrid	3	Olympiakos	1
Moscow Spartak	3	Feyenoord	1
Parma	2	Sparta Prague	0
Steaua Bucharest	1	Antwerp	1

Semi-finals, First Leg

Atletico Madrid	1	Parma	2
Moscow Spartak	1	Antwerp	0

Semi-finals, Second Leg

Antwerp	3	Moscow Spartak	1
Parma	0	Atletico Madrid	1

Final

Parma	3	Antwerp	1

European Cup-Winners' Cup Champions

Year	Winners	Score	Runners-up
1961	Rangers	0-2	Fiorentina
	Fiorentina	2-1	Rangers
	(Fiorentina won 4-1 on aggregate)		
1962	Atletico Madrid	3-0	Fiorentina
	(after 1-1 draw)		
1963	Tottenham H	5-1	Atletico Madrid
1964	Sporting Lisbon	1-0	MTK Budapest
	(after 3-3 draw)		
1965	West Ham U	2-0	Munich 1860
1966	B. Dortmund	2-1	Liverpool
1967	Bayern Munich	1-0	Rangers
1968	AC Milan	2-0	SV Hamburg
1969	Slovan Brat.	3-2	Barcelona
1970	Manchester C	2-1	Gornik Zabrze
1971	Chelsea	2-1	Real Madrid
	(after 1-1 draw)		
1972	Rangers	3-2	Moscow Dynamo
1973	AC Milan	1-0	Leeds U
1974	FC Magdeburg	2-0	AC Milan
1975	Dynamo Kiev	3-0	Ferencvaros
1976	Anderlecht	4-2	West Ham U
1977	SV Hamburg	2-0	Anderlecht
1978	Anderlecht	4-0	Austria/WAC
1979	Barcelona	4-3	Fortuna Dusseldorf
1980	Valencia	0-0	Arsenal
	(Valencia won 5-4 on penalties)		
1981	Dynamo Tbilisi	2-1	Carl Zeiss Jena
1982	Barcelona	2-1	Standard Liège
1983	Aberdeen	2-1	Real Madrid
1984	Juventus	2-1	FC Porto
1985	Everton	3-1	R. Vienna
1986	Dynamo Kiev	3-0	Atletico Madrid
1987	Ajax	1-0	Lokomotiv Leipzig
1988	Mechelen	1-0	Ajax
1989	Barcelona	2-0	Sampdoria
1990	Sampdoria	2-0	Anderlecht
1991	Manchester U	2-1	Barcelona
1992	Werder Bremen	2-0	Monaco
1993	Parma	3-1	Antwerp

European Super Cup Champions

Played annually between the winners of the European Champions' Cup and the European Cup-Winners' Cup.

Year	Winners	Score	Runners-up
1972	Ajax	3-1, 3-2	Rangers
1973	Ajax	0-1, 6-0	Milan
1974	Not contested		
1975	Dynamo Kiev	1-0, 2-0	Bayern Munich
1976	Anderlecht	4-1, 1-2	Bayern Munich
1977	Liverpool	1-1, 6-0	Hamburg
1978	Anderlecht	3-1, 1-2	Liverpool
1979	Nottingham F	1-0, 1-1	Barcelona
1980	Valencia	1-0, 1-2	Nottingham F
1981	Not contested		
1982	Aston Villa	0-1, 3-0	Barcelona
1983	Aberdeen	0-0, 2-0	Hamburg
1984	Juventus	2-0	Liverpool
1985	Juventus v Everton not contested due to UEFA ban on English clubs		
1986	Steaua Bucharest	1-0	Dynamo Kiev
1987	FC Porto	1-0, 1-0	Ajax
1988	KV Mechelen	3-0, 0-1	PSV Eindhoven
1989	AC Milan	1-1, 1-0	Barcelona
1990	AC Milan	1-1, 2-0	Sampdoria
1991	Manchester U	1-0	Red Star Belgrade
1992	Werder Bremen	1–0	Barcelona

FA Cup 1992–93

First Round

Accrington S	3	Gateshead	2
Blackpool	1	Rochdale	1
Blyth S	1	Southport	1
Bolton W	2	Sutton Cd	1
Bournemouth	0	Barnet	0
Bradford C	1	Preston NE	1
Brighton & HA	2	Hayes	0
Burnley	2	Scarborough	1
Bury	2	Witton Alb	0
Cardiff C	2	Bath C	3
Chester C	1	Altrincham	1
Colchester U	4	Slough	0
Crewe Alex	6	Wrexham	1
Dagenham & Redbge	4	Leyton Orient	5
Darlington	1	Hull C	2
Doncaster R	1	Hartlepool U	2
Exeter C	1	Kidderminster H	0
Gillingham	3	Kettering T	2
Kingstonian	1	Peterborough U	1
Lincoln C	0	Stafford R	0
Macclesfield	0	Chesterfield	0
Marine	4	Halifax T	1
Marlow	3	Salisbury	3
Northampton T	3	Fulham	1
Rotherham U	4	Walsall	0
Scunthorpe U	0	Huddersfield T	0
Shrewsbury T	3	Mansfield T	1
Solihull	2	VS Rugby	2
St Albans	1	Cheltenham T	2
Sutton U	1	Hereford U	2
Torquay U	2	Yeovil	5
WBA	8	Aylesbury	0
Wigan Ath	3	Carlisle U	1
Woking	3	Nuneaton	1
Wycombe W	3	Merthyr T	1
York C	1	Stockport Co	3
Dorking	2	Plymouth Arg	3
Reading	1	Birmingham C	0
Stoke C	0	Port Vale	0

First Round Replays

Port Vale	3	Stoke C	1
Altrincham	2	Chester	0
Barnet	1	Bournemouth	2
Chesterfield	2	Macclesfield	2*
Huddersfield T	2	Scunthorpe U	1
Peterborough U	9	Kingstonian	1

(Replay ordered after missile from crowd hit Kingstonian goalkeeper)

(Continued)

Preston NE	4	Bradford C	5
Rochdale	1	Blackpool	0
VS Rugby	2	Solihull	1
Stafford R	2	Lincoln C	1
Peterborough U	1	Kingstonian	0
Salisbury	2	Marlow	2*

Second Round

Accrington S	1	Crewe Alex	6
Altrincham	1	Port Vale	4
Bolton W	4	Rochdale	0
Brighton & HA	1	Woking	1
Burnley	1	Shrewsbury T	1
Cheltenham T	1	Bournemouth	1
Gillingham	1	Colchester U	1
Macclesfield	0	Stockport Co	2
Marine	3	Stafford R	2
Reading	3	Leyton Orient	0
Rotherham U	1	Hull C	0
Yeovil	0	Hereford U	0
Bath C	2	Northampton T	2
Bradford C	0	Huddersfield T	2
Hartlepool U	4	Southport	0
Wycombe W	2	WBA	2
Plymouth Arg	3	Peterborough U	2
VS Rugby	0	Marlow	0
Exeter C	2	Swansea C	5
Wigan Ath	1	Bury	1

Second Round Replays

Northampton T	3	Bath C	0
Shrewsbury T	1	Burnley	2
WBA	1	Wycombe W	0
Bournemouth	3	Cheltenham T	0
Colchester	2	Gillingham	3
Hereford U	1	Yeovil	2
Marlow	2	VS Rugby	0
Woking	1	Brighton & HA	2
Bury	1	Wigan Ath	0

Third Round

Aston Villa	1	Bristol R	1
Blackburn R	3	Bournemouth	1
Brentford	0	Grimsby T	2
Brighton & HA	1	Portsmouth	0
Derby Co	2	Stockport Co	1
Gillingham	0	Huddersfield T	0
Hartlepool U	1	Crystal Palace	0
Leeds U	1	Charlton Ath	1
Manchester C	1	Reading	1
Marlow	1	Tottenham H	5
Newcastle U	4	Port Vale	0
Oldham Ath	2	Tranmere R	2
Sheffield U	2	Burnley	2
Swansea C	1	Oxford U	1
Watford	1	Wolverhampton W	4
WBA	0	West Ham U	2
Wimbledon	0	Everton	0
Yeovil	1	Arsenal	3
Bolton W	2	Liverpool	2
Nottingham F	2	Southampton	1
QPR	3	Swindon T	0
Manchester U	2	Bury	0
Crewe Alex	3	Marine	1
Ipswich T	3	Plymouth Arg	1
Northampton T	0	Rotherham U	1
Notts Co	0	Sunderland	2
Cambridge U	1	Sheffield W	2
Leicester C	2	Barnsley	2
Middlesbrough	2	Chelsea	1
Norwich C	1	Coventry	0
Southend U	1	Millwall	0
Luton T	2	Bristol C	0

Third Round Replays

Burnley	2	Sheffield U	4
Everton	1	Wimbledon	2
Oxford U	2	Swansea C	2*
Tranmere R	3	Oldham Ath	0
Charlton Ath	1	Leeds U	3
Huddersfield T	2	Gillingham	1
Liverpool	0	Bolton W	2
Reading	0	Manchester C	4
Barnsley	1*	Leicester C	1
Bristol R	0	Aston Villa	3

Fourth Round

Aston Villa	1	Wimbledon	1
Crewe Alex	0	Blackburn R	3
Huddersfield T	1	Southend U	2
Luton T	1	Derby Co	5
Manchester U	1	Brighton & HA	0
Nottingham F	1	Middlesbrough	1
QPR	1	Manchester C	2
Rotherham U	1	Newcastle U	1
Sheffield U	1	Hartlepool U	0
Tranmere R	1	Ipswich T	2
Barnsley	4	West Ham U	1
Norwich C	0	Tottenham H	2
Sheffield W	1	Sunderland	0
Wolverhampton W	0	Bolton W	2
Arsenal	2	Leeds U	2
Swansea C	0	Grimsby T	0

Fourth Round Replays

Leeds U	2	Arsenal	3
Middlesbrough	0	Nottingham F	3
Newcastle U	2	Rotherham	0
Wimbledon	0*	Aston Villa	0
Grimsby T	2	Swansea C	0

Fifth Round

Arsenal	2	Nottingham F	0
Blackburn R	1	Newcastle U	0
Derby Co	3	Bolton W	1
Ipswich T	4	Grimsby T	0
Manchester C	2	Barnsley	0
Sheffield W	2	Southend U	0
Sheffield U	2	Manchester U	1
Tottenham H	3	Wimbledon	0

Sixth Round

Sheffield U	0	Blackburn R	0
Ipswich T	2	Arsenal	4
Manchester C	2	Tottenham H	4
Derby Co	3	Sheffield W	3

Sixth Round Replays

Sheffield W	1	Derby Co	0
Blackburn R	0	Sheffield U	0*

Semi-finals

Sheffield U	1	Sheffield W	2
Arsenal	1	Tottenham H	0

Final

Arsenal	1	Sheffield W	1

Replay

Arsenal	2	Sheffield W	1

*Won on penalties

FA Cup Winners

Double winners in **bold**.

Year	Winners	Score	Runners-up
1871–72	Wanderers	1-0	Royal Engineers
1872–73	Wanderers	2-0	Oxford University
1873–74	Oxford University	2-0	Royal Engineers
1874–75	Royal Engineers	1-1, 2-0	Old Etonians
1875–76	Wanderers	1-1, 3-0	Old Etonians
1876–77	Wanderers	2-1	Oxford University
1877–78	Wanderers	3-1	Royal Engineers
1878–79	Old Etonians	1-0	Clapham Rovers
1879–80	Clapham Rovers	1-0	Oxford University
1880–81	Old Carthusians	3-0	Old Etonians
1881–82	Old Etonians	1-0	Blackburn Rovers
1882–83	Blackburn Olympic	2-1	Old Etonians
1883–84	Blackburn Rovers	2-1	Queen's Park
1884–85	Blackburn Rovers	2-0	Queen's Park
1885–86	Blackburn Rovers	0-0, 2-0	West Bromwich A
1886–87	Aston Villa	2-0	West Bromwich A
1887–88	West Bromwich A	2-1	Preston NE
1888–89	**Preston NE**	3-0	Wolverhampton W

(Continued)

(FA Cup Winners contd.)

Year	Winners	Score	Runners-up
1889–90	Blackburn R	6-1	Sheffield W
1890–91	Blackburn R	3-1	Notts County
1891–92	West Bromwich A	3-0	Aston Villa
1892–93	Wolverhampton W	1-0	Everton
1893–94	Notts County	4-1	Bolton County
1894–95	Aston Villa	1-0	West Bromwich A
1895–96	Sheffield W	2-1	Wolverhampton
1896–97	**Aston Villa**	3-2	Everton
1897–98	Nottingham F	3-1	Derby County
1898–99	Sheffield U	4-1	Derby County
1899–00	Bury	4-0	Southampton
1900–01	Tottenham H	2-2, 3-1	Sheffield U
1901–02	Sheffield U	1-1, 2-1	Southampton
1902–03	Bury	6-0	Derby County
1903–04	Manchester City	1-0	Bolton Wanderers
1904–05	Aston Villa	2-0	Newcastle U
1905–06	Everton	1-0	Newcastle U
1906–07	Sheffield W	2-1	Everton
1907–08	Wolverhampton	3-1	Newcastle U
1908–09	Manchester U	1-0	Bristol City
1909–10	Newcastle U	1-1, 2-0	Barnsley
1910–11	Bradford City	0-0, 1-0	Newcastle
1911–12	Barnsley	0-0, 1-0	West Bromwich A
1912–13	Aston Villa	1-0	Sunderland
1913–14	Burnley	1-0	Liverpool
1914–15	Sheffield U	3-0	Chelsea
1919–20	Aston Villa	1-0	Huddersfield T
1920–21	Tottenham H	1-0	Wolverhampton
1921–22	Huddersfield T	1-0	Preston NE
1922–23	Bolton Wanderers	2-0	West Ham U
1923–24	Newcastle U	2-0	Aston Villa
1924–25	Sheffield U	1-0	Cardiff City
1925–26	Bolton Wanderers	1-0	Manchester City
1926–27	Cardiff City	1-0	Arsenal
1927–28	Blackburn R	3-1	Huddersfield T
1928–29	Bolton Wanderers	2-0	Portsmouth
1929–30	Arsenal	2-0	Huddersfield T
1930–31	West Bromwich A	2-1	Birmingham
1931–32	Newcastle U	2-1	Arsenal
1932–33	Everton	3-0	Manchester City
1933–34	Manchester City	2-1	Portsmouth
1934–35	Sheffield W	4-2	West Bromwich A
1935–36	Arsenal	1-0	Sheffield U
1936–37	Sunderland	3-1	Preston NE
1937–38	Preston NE	1-0	Huddersfield T
1938–39	Portsmouth	4-1	Wolverhampton
1945–46	Derby County	4-1	Charlton Athletic
1946–47	Charlton Athletic	1-0	Burnley
1947–48	Manchester U	4-2	Blackpool
1948–49	Wolverhampton	3-1	Leicester City
1949–50	Arsenal	2-0	Liverpool
1950–51	Newcastle U	2-0	Blackpool
1951–52	Newcastle U	1-0	Arsenal
1952–53	Blackpool	4-3	Bolton Wanderers
1953–54	West Bromwich A	3-2	Preston NE
1954–55	Newcastle U	3-1	Manchester City
1955–56	Manchester City	3-1	Birmingham City
1956–57	Aston Villa	2-1	Manchester U
1957–58	Bolton W	2-0	Manchester U
1958–59	Nottingham F	2-1	Luton T
1959–60	Wolverhampton	3-0	Blackburn R
1960–61	**Tottenham H**	2-0	Leicester City
1961–62	Tottenham H	3-1	Burnley
1962–63	Manchester U	3-1	Leicester City
1963–64	West Ham U	3-2	Preston NE
1964–65	Liverpool	2-1	Leeds U
1965–66	Everton	3-2	Sheffield W
1966–67	Tottenham H	2-1	Chelsea
1967–68	West Bromwich A	1-0	Everton
1968–69	Manchester City	1-0	Leicester City
1969–70	Chelsea	2-2, 2-1	Leeds U
1970–71	**Arsenal**	2-1	Liverpool
1971–72	Leeds U	1-0	Arsenal
1972–73	Sunderland	1-0	Leeds U
1973–74	Liverpool	3-0	Newcastle U
1974–75	West Ham U	2-0	Fulham
1975–76	Southampton	1-0	Manchester U
1976–77	Manchester U	2-1	Liverpool
1977–78	Ipswich T	1-0	Arsenal
1978–79	Arsenal	3-2	Manchester U
1979–80	West Ham U	1-0	Arsenal
1980–81	Tottenham H	1-1, 3-2	Manchester City
1981–82	Tottenham H	1-1, 1-0	Queen's Park R
1982–83	Manchester U	2-2, 4-0	Brighton & Hove A
1983–84	Everton	2-0	Watford
1984–85	Manchester U	1-0	Everton
1985–86	**Liverpool**	3-1	Everton
1986–87	Coventry City	3-2	Tottenham H
1987–88	Wimbledon	1-0	Liverpool
1988–89	Liverpool	3-2	Everton
1989–90	Manchester U	3-3, 1-0	Crystal Palace
1990–91	Tottenham H	2-1	Nottingham F
1991–92	Liverpool	2-0	Sunderland
1992–93	Arsenal	2-1	Sheffield W

Women's FA Cup Winners

Year	Winners	Score	Runners-up
1970–71	Southampton	4-1	Stewarton & Thistle
1971–72	Southampton	3-2	Lee's Ladies
1972–73	Southampton	2-0	Westhorn United
1973–74	Fodens	2-1	Southampton
1974–75	Southampton	4-2	Warminster
1975–76	Southampton	2-1	Queens Park Rangers
1976–77	Queens Park Rangers	1-0	Southampton
1977–78	Southampton	8-2	Queens Park Rangers
1978–79	Southampton	1-0	Lowestoft
1979–80	St Helens	1-0	Preston North End
1980–81	Southampton	4-2	St Helens
1981–82	Lowestoft	2-0	Cleveland Spartans
1982–83	Doncaster Belles	3-2	St Helens
1983–84	Howbury Grange	4-2	Doncaster Belles
1984–85	Friends of Fulham	2-0	Doncaster Belles
1985–86	Norwich	4-3	Doncaster Belles
1986–87	Doncaster Belles	2-0	St Helens
1987–88	Doncaster Belles	3-1	Leasowe Pacific
1988–89	Leasowe Pacific	3-2	Friends of Fulham
1989–90	Doncaster Belles	1-0	Friends of Fulham
1990–91	Doncaster Belles	1-0	Millwall Lionesses
1991–92	Doncaster Belles	4-0	Red Star Southampton
1992–93	Arsenal	3-0	Doncaster Belles

Football League Champions

Double winners in bold.

Year	Winners	Pts	Runners-up	Pts
1888–89	**Preston NE**	40	Aston Villa	29
1889–90	Preston NE	33	Everton	31
1890–91	Everton	29	Preston NE	27
1891–92	Sunderland	42	Preston NE	37
1892–93	Sunderland	48	Preston NE	37
1893–94	Aston Villa	44	Sunderland	38
1894–95	Sunderland	47	Everton	42
1895–96	Aston Villa	45	Derby City	41
1896–97	**Aston Villa**	47	Sheffield U	36
1897–98	Sheffield U	42	Sunderland	37
1898–99	Aston Villa	45	Liverpool	43
1899–1900	Aston Villa	50	Sheffield U	48
1900–01	Liverpool	45	Sunderland	43
1901–02	Sunderland	44	Everton	41
1902–03	Sheffield W	42	Aston Villa	41
1903–04	Sheffield W	47	Manchester City	44
1904–05	Newcastle U	48	Everton	47
1905–06	Liverpool	51	Preston NE	47
1906–07	Newcastle U	51	Bristol City	48
1907–08	Manchester U	52	Aston Villa	43
1908–09	Newcastle U	53	Everton	46
1909–10	Aston Villa	53	Liverpool	48
1910–11	Manchester U	52	Aston Villa	51
1911–12	Blackburn R	49	Everton	46
1912–13	Sunderland	54	Aston Villa	50
1913–14	Blackburn R	51	Aston Villa	44
1914–15	Everton	46	Oldham Athletic	45
1919–20	West Bromwich A	60	Burnley	51
1920–21	Burnley	59	Manchester City	54
1921–22	Liverpool	57	Tottenham	51
1922–23	Liverpool	60	Sunderland	54
1923–24	Huddersfield T	57	Cardiff City	57
1924–25	Huddersfield T	58	West Bromwich A	56
1925–26	Huddersfield T	57	Arsenal	52

(Continued)

Year	Winners	Pts	Runners-up	Pts
1926–27	Newcastle U	56	Huddersfield T	51
1927–28	Everton	53	Huddersfield T	51
1928–29	Sheffield W	52	Leicester City	51
1929–30	Sheffield W	60	Derby County	50
1930–31	Arsenal	66	Aston Villa	59
1931–32	Everton	56	Arsenal	54
1932–33	Arsenal	58	Aston Villa	54
1933–34	Arsenal	59	Huddersfield T	56
1934–35	Arsenal	58	Sunderland	54
1935–36	Sunderland	56	Derby County	48
1936–37	Manchester City	57	Charlton Athletic	54
1937–38	Arsenal	52	Wolverhampton	51
1938–39	Everton	59	Wolverhampton	55
1940–46	–			
1946–47	Liverpool	57	Manchester U	56
1947–48	Arsenal	59	Manchester U	52
1948–49	Portsmouth	58	Manchester U	53
1949–50	Portsmouth	53	Wolverhampton	53
1950–51	Tottenham H	60	Manchester U	56
1951–52	Manchester U	57	Tottenham H	53
1952–53	Arsenal	54	Preston NE	54
1953–54	Wolverhampton	57	West Bromwich A	53
1954–55	Chelsea	52	Wolverhampton	48
1955–56	Manchester U	60	Blackpool	49
1956–57	Manchester U	64	Tottenham H	56
1957–58	Wolverhampton	64	Preston NE	59
1958–59	Wolverhampton	61	Manchester U	55
1959–60	Burnley	55	Wolverhampton	54
1960–61	**Tottenham H**	66	Sheffield W	58
1961–62	Ipswich T	56	Burnley	53
1962–63	Everton	61	Tottenham H	55

Year	Winners	Pts	Runners-up	Pts
1963–64	Liverpool	57	Manchester U	53
1964–65	Manchester U	61	Leeds U	61
1965–66	Liverpool	61	Leeds U	55
1966–67	Manchester U	60	Nottingham F	56
1967–68	Manchester City	58	Manchester U	56
1968–69	Leeds U	67	Liverpool	61
1969–70	Everton	66	Leeds U	57
1970–71	**Arsenal**	65	Leeds U	57
1971–72	Derby County	58	Leeds U	57
1972–73	Liverpool	60	Arsenal	57
1973–74	Leeds U	62	Liverpool	57
1974–75	Derby County	53	Liverpool	51
1975–76	Liverpool	60	QPR	59
1976–77	Liverpool	57	Manchester City	56
1977–78	Nottingham F	64	Liverpool	57
1978–79	Liverpool	68	Nottingham F	60
1979–80	Liverpool	60	Manchester U	58
1980–81	Aston Villa	60	Ipswich T	56
1981–82	Liverpool	87	Ipswich T	83
1982–83	Liverpool	82	Watford	71
1983–84	Liverpool	80	Southampton	77
1984–85	Everton	90	Liverpool	77
1985–86	**Liverpool**	88	Everton	86
1986–87	Everton	86	Liverpool	77
1987–88	Liverpool	90	Manchester U	81
1988–89	Arsenal	76	Liverpool	76
1989–90	Liverpool	79	Aston Villa	70
1990–91	Arsenal	83	Liverpool	76
1991–92	Leeds U	82	Manchester U	78
1992–93	Manchester U	84	Aston Villa	74

Football League Cup Winners

Year	Winners	Score	Runners-up
1961	Aston Villa	3-0*, 0-2	Rotherham U
1962	Norwich City	3-0, 1-0	Rochdale
1963	Birmingham City	3-1, 0-0	Aston Villa
1964	Leicester City	1-1, 3-2	Stoke City
1965	Chelsea	3-2, 0-0	Leicester City
1966	West Bromwich A	1-2, 4-1	West Ham U
1967	QPR	3-2	West Bromwich A
1968	Leeds U	1-0	Arsenal
1969	Swindon T	3-1	Arsenal
1970	Manchester City	2-1	West Bromwich A
1971	Tottenham H	2-0	Aston Villa
1972	Stoke City	2-1	Chelsea
1973	Tottenham H	1-0	Norwich City
1974	Wolverhampton W	2-1	Manchester City
1975	Aston Villa	1-0	Norwich City
1976	Manchester City	2-1	Newcastle U
1977	Aston Villa	0-0, 1-1*, 3-2	Everton
1978	Nottingham F	0-0*, 1-0	Liverpool
1979	Nottingham F	3-2	Southampton
1980	Wolverhampton W	1-0	Nottingham F
1981	Liverpool	1-1*, 2-1	West Ham U
1982	Liverpool	3-1*	Tottenham H
1983	Liverpool	2-1*	Manchester U
1984	Liverpool	0-0*, 1-0	Everton
1985	Norwich City	1-0	Sunderland
1986	Oxford U	3-0	QPR
1987	Arsenal	2-1	Liverpool
1988	Luton T	3-2	Arsenal
1989	Nottingham F	3-1	Luton T
1990	Nottingham F	1-0	Oldham Athletic
1991	Sheffield W	1-0	Manchester U
1992	Manchester U	1-0	Nottingham F
1993	Arsenal	2-1	Sheffield W

*After extra time.

Tennents Charity Shield

(7 Aug. 1993)

The year's league winner plays the year's FA Cup winner.

Arsenal .... 1 Manchester U 1

(United won 5-4 on penalties)

UEFA Cup 1992–93

First Round, First Leg

Benfica	3	Belvedur Izola	0
Caen	3	Zaragoza	2
Cologne	2	Celtic	0
FC Copenhagen	5	MP Mikkeli	0
Electroputere Craiova	0	Panathinaikos	6
Fenerbahce	3	Botev Plovdiv	1
Floriana	0	Borussia Dortmund	1
Fram	0	Kaiserslautern	3
Grasshoppers	1	Sporting Lisbon	2
Hibernian	2	Anderlecht	2
Juventus	6	Anorthosis	1
GKS Katowice	0	Galatasaray	0
Kiev Dynamo	1	Rapid	0
Lokomotiv Plovdiv	2	Auxerre	2
Manchester U	0	Moscow Torpedo	0
Mechelen	2	Orebro	1
Moscow Dynamo	5	Rosenborg	1
Neuchatel Xamax	2	Frem	2
Norrkoping	1	Torino	0
Paris St Germain	2	PAOK Salonika	0
Politechnica Timisoara	1	Real Madrid	1
Salzburg	0	Ajax	3
Sheffield W	8	Spora Luxembourg	1
Sigma Olomouc	1	Uni Craiova	0
Slavia Prague	1	Hearts	0
Standard Liege	5	Portadown	0
Vac Izzo	1	Groningen	0
Valencia	1	Napoli	5
Vitesse	3	Derry City	0
Wacker Innsbruck	1	Roma	4
Widzew Lodz	2	Eintracht Frankfurt	2
Vitoria Guimaraes	3	Real Sociedad	0

First Round, Second Leg

Ajax	3	Salzburg	1
Anderlecht	1	Hibernian	1
Anorthosis	0	Juventus	4
Auxerre	7	Lokomotiv Plovdiv	1
Belvedur Izola	0	Benfica	5
Borussia Dortmund	7	Floriana	2
Botev Plovdiv	2		
Celtic	3	Cologne	0
Derry City	1	Vitesse	2
Eintracht Frankfurt	9	Widzew Lodz	0
Frem	4	Neuchatel Xamax	1

(Continued)

(UEFA Cup contd.)

Galatasaray	2	GKS Katowice	1
Groningen	1	Vac Izzo	1
Hearts	4	Slavia Prague	2
Kaiserslautern	4	Frem	0
Moscow Torpedo	0	Manchester U	0

(Moscow Torpedo won 4-3 on penalties)

MP Mikkeli	1	FC Copenhagen	5
Napoli	1	Valencia	1
Orebro	0	Mechelen	0
Panathinaikos	4	Electroputere Craiova	0
PAOK Salonika	0	Paris St Germain	2

(Abandoned after 46 minutes: crowd trouble))

Portadown	0	Standard Liege	0
Rapid	3	Kiev Dynamo	2
Real Madrid	4	Politechnica Timisoara	0
Real Sociedad	2	Vitoria Guimaraes	0
Roma	1	Wacker Innsbruck	0
Rosenborg	2	Moscow Dynamo	0
Spora Luxembourg	1	Sheffield W	2
Sporting Lisbon	1	Grasshoppers	3
Torino	3	Norrkoping	0
Uni Craiova	1	Sigma Olomouc	2
Zaragoza	2	Caen	0

Second Round, First Leg

Anderlecht	4	Kiev Dynamo	2
Auxerre	5	FC Copenhagen	0
Benfica	5	Vac Izzo	1
Borussia Dortmund	1	Celtic	0
Eintracht Frankfurt	0	Galatasaray	0
Fenerbahce	1	Sigma Olomouc	0
Frem	0	Zaragoza	1
Hearts	0	Standard Liege	1
Kaiserslautern	3	Sheffield W	1
Napoli	0	Paris St Germain	2
Panathinaikos	0	Juventus	1
Real Madrid	5	Moscow Torpedo	2
Roma	3	Grasshoppers	0
Torino	1	Moscow Dynamo	2
Vitesse	1	Mechelen	0
Vitoria Guimaraes	0	Ajax	3

Second Round, Second Leg

Ajax	2	Vitoria Guimaraes	1
Celtic	1	Borussia Dortmund	2
FC Copenhagen	0	Auxerre	2
Galatasaray	1	Eintracht Frankfurt	0
Grasshoppers	4	Roma	3
Juventus	0	Panathinaikos	0
Kiev Dynamo	0	Anderlecht	3
Mechelen	0	Vitesse	1
Moscow Dynamo	0	Torino	0
Moscow Torpedo	3	Real Madrid	2
Paris St Germain	0	Napoli	0
Sheffield W	2	Kaiserslautern	2
Sigma Olomouc	7	Fenerbahce	1
Standard Liege	1	Hearts	0
Vac Izzo	0	Benfica	1
Zaragoza	5	Frem	1

Third Round, First Leg

Ajax	2	Kaiserslautern	0
Borussia Dortmund	3	Zaragoza	1
Moscow Dynamo	2	Benfica	2
Paris St Germain	0	Anderlecht	0
Roma	3	Galatasaray	1
Sigma Olomouc	1	Juventus	2
Standard Liege	2	Auxerre	2
Vitesse	0	Real Madrid	1

Third Round, Second Leg

Anderlecht	1	Paris St Germain	1
Auxerre	2	Standard Liege	1
Benfica	2	Moscow Dynamo	0
Galatasaray	3	Roma	2
Juventus	5	Sigma Olomouc	0
Kaiserslautern	0	Ajax	1
Real Madrid	2	Vitesse	0
Zaragoza	2	Borussia Dortmund	1

Quarter-finals, First Leg

Auxerre	4	Ajax	2
Benfica	2	Juventus	1
Real Madrid	3	Paris St Germain	1
Roma	1	Borussia Dortmund	0

Quarter-finals, Second Leg

Ajax	1	Auxerre	0
Borussia Dortmund	2	Roma	0
Juventus	3	Benfica	0
Paris St Germain	4	Real Madrid	1

Semi-finals, First Leg

Borussia Dortmund	2	Auxerre	0
Juventus	2	Paris St Germain	1

Semi-finals, Second Leg

Auxerre	2	Borussia Dortmund	0

(Borussia Dortmund won 6-5 on penalties)

Paris St Germain	0	Juventus	1

Final, First Leg

Borussia Dortmund	1	Juventus	3

Final, Second Leg

Juventus	3	Borussia Dortmund	0

UEFA Cup Winners

Year	Winners	Score	Runners-up
1958	Barcelona	6-0 2-2	London
1960	Barcelona	4-1 0-0	Birmingham City
1961	AS Roma	2-0 2-2	Birmingham City
1962	Valencia	6-2 1-1	Barcelona
1963	Valencia	2-1 2-0	Dynamo Zagreb
1964	Real Zaragoza	2-1	Valencia
1965	Ferencvaros	1-0	Juventus
1966	Barcelona	4-2 0-1	Real Zaragoza
1967	Dynamo Zagreb	2-0 6-0	Leeds U
1968	Leeds U	1-0 0-0	Ferencvaros
1969	Newcastle U	3-0 3-2	Ujpest Dozsa
1970	Arsenal	3-0 1-3	Anderlecht
1971	Leeds U	1-1 2-2*	Juventus
1972	Tottenham H	2-1 1-1	Wolverhampton W
1973	Liverpool	3-0 0-2	B.M/gladbach
1974	Feyenoord	2-0 2-2	Tottenham H
1975	B.M/gladbach	5-1 0-0	Twente Enschede
1976	Liverpool	3-2 1-1	FC Bruges
1977	Juventus	1-0 1-2*	Ath. Bilbao
1978	PSV Eindhoven	3-0 0-0	Bastia
1979	B.M/gladbach	1-0 1-1	Red Star B'grade
1980	Eintracht Frankfurt	1-0 2-3*	B.M/gladbach
1981	Ipswich T	3-0 2-4	AZ 67 Alkmaar
1982	IFK Gothenburg	1-0 3-0	SV Hamburg
1983	Anderlecht	1-0 1-1	Benfica
1984	Tottenham H	1-1 1-1†	Anderlecht
1985	Real Madrid	3-0 0-1	Videoton
1986	Real Madrid	5-1 0-2	Cologne
1987	IFK Gothenburg	1-0 1-1	Dundee U
1988	Bayer Leverskusen	0-3 3-0†	Espanol
1989	Napoli	2-1 3-3	VFB Stuttgart
1990	Juventus	3-1 0-0	Fiorentina
1991	Inter-Milan	2-0 0-1	AS Roma
1992	Ajax	0-0 2-2	Torino
1993	Juventus	3-1 3-0	Borussia Dortmund

*Won on away goals. †Won on penalties.

SCOTTISH FOOTBALL

B & Q Cup 1992–93

First Round

Ayr U	2	St Mirren	1
Berwick R	2	East Stirling	2*

(Berwick R won 5-4 on penalties)

Dumbarton	0	Hamilton Ac	3
Forfar Ath	2	Morton	5
Kilmarnock	2	Clyde	1
Queen's Park	2	Montrose	3*
Stenhousemuir	2	Cowdenbeath	4
Stranraer	3	Alloa	2

(Continued)

Meadowbank T	1	East Fife	0*
Arbroath	3	Dunfermline Ath	0

Second Round

Albion R	0	Hamilton Ac	2
Berwick R	1	Arbroath	0
Brechin C	1	Morton	2
Cowdenbeath	0	Montrose	4
Kilmarnock	1	Ayr U	0
Raith R	0	Meadowbank T	0*

(Meadowbank T won 4-2 on penalties)

Stirling Alb	2	Clydebank	1
Stranraer	0	Queen of the S	2

Quarter-finals

Stirling Alb	0	Montrose	1
Hamilton Ac	5	Berwick R	2
Kilmarnock	1	Morton	2
Meadowbank T	3	Queen of the S	2

Semi-finals

Morton	3	Montrose	1*
Hamilton Ac	1	Meadowbank T	1*

(Hamilton Ac won 2-1 on penalties)

Final

Hamilton Ac	3	Morton	2

*After extra time

Scottish Cup 1992–93

First Round

Huntly	4	Stranraer	2
Inverness T	3	Civil Service Strollers	1
Queen of the S	3	Spartans	0
Queens Park	1	Clyde	1
Cove R	2	Peterhead	0
Forfar Ath	5	Albion R	0

Second Round

Clyde	3	Brechin C	1
Cove R	2	Montrose	0
East Fife	1	Alloa	1
Gala Fairydean	1	Arbroath	1
Vale of Leithen	2	East Stirling	2
Inverness T	0	Berwick R	1
Stenhousemuir	2	Forfar Ath	3
Huntly	2	Queen of the S	1

Second Round Replays

Alloa	1	East Fife	1

(East Fife won 6-5 on penalties aet)

Arbroath	2	Gala Fairydean	0
East Stirling	3	Vale of Leithen	2

Third Round

Aberdeen	4	Hamilton Ac	1
Airdrieonians	0	Clydebank	0
Arbroath	3	Morton	0
Clyde	0	Celtic	0
Cove R	2	East Stirling	2
Dundee U	3	Meadowbank T	1
Dunfermline Ath	1	Ayr U	2
Hearts	6	Huntly	0
Hibernian	5	St Mirren	2
Kilmarnock	5	Raith R	0
Motherwell	0	Rangers	2
Partick Thistle	0	Cowdenbeath	1
St Johnstone	6	Forfar Ath	0
Stirling Albion	1	East Fife	2
Dundee	2	Dumbarton	0
Falkirk	5	Berwick R	2

Third Round Replays

Clydebank	2	Airdrieonians	0
Celtic	1	Clyde	0
East Stirling	2	Cove R	1

Fourth Round

Arbroath	0	East Fife	0
Ayr U	0	Rangers	2
Cowdenbeath	0	Hibernian	0
Falkirk	2	Celtic	0
Hearts	2	Dundee	0
Kilmarnock	0	St Johnstone	0
Aberdeen	2	Dundee U	0
East Stirling	1	Clydebank	2

Fourth Round Replays

Hibernian	1	Cowdenbeath	0
St Johnstone	1	Kilmarnock	0
East Fife	1	Arbroath	4

Quarter-finals

Aberdeen	1	Clydebank	1
Arbroath	0	Rangers	3
Hearts	2	Falkirk	0
Hibernian	2	St Johnstone	0

Quarter-final Replay

Clydebank	3	Aberdeen	4

Semi-finals

Hibernian	0	Aberdeen	1
Rangers	2	Hearts	1

Final

Rangers	2	Aberdeen	1

Scottish Cup Champions

Year	Winners	Score	Runners-up
1873–74	Queen's Park	2-0	Clydesdale
1874–75	Queen's Park	3-0	Renton
1875–76	Queen's Park	1-1 2-0	Third Lanark
1876–77	Vale of Leven	1-1 1-1 3-2	Rangers
1877–78	Vale of Leven	1-0	Third Lanark
1878–79	Cup awarded to Vale of Leven when Rangers failed to appear for replay after 1-1 draw.		
1879–80	Queen's Park	3-0	Thornlibank
1880–81	Queen's Park	3-1	Dumbarton
1881–82	Queen's Park	2-2 4-1	Dumbarton
1882–83	Dumbarton	2-2 2-1	Vale of Leven
1883–84	Cup awarded to Queen's Park when Vale of Leven failed to appear for the final.		
1884–85	Renton	0-0 3-1	Vale of Leven
1885–86	Queen's Park	3-1	Renton
1886–87	Hibernian	2-1	Dumbarton
1887–88	Renton	6-1	Cambuslang
1888–89	Third Lanark	2-1	Celtic
1889–90	Queen's Park	1-1 2-1	Vale of Leven
1890–91	Hearts	1-0	Dumbarton
1891–92	Celtic	5-1	Queen's Park
1892–93	Queen's Park	2-1	Celtic
1893–94	Rangers	3-1	Celtic
1894–95	St Bernard's	2-1	Renton
1895–96	Hearts	3-1	Hibernian
1896–97	Rangers	5-1	Dumbarton
1897–98	Rangers	2-0	Kilmarnock
1898–99	Celtic	2-0	Rangers
1899–00	Celtic	4-3	Queen's Park
1900–01	Hearts	4-3	Celtic
1901–02	Hibernian	1-0	Celtic
1902–03	Rangers	1-1 0-0 2-0	Hearts
1903–04	Celtic	3-2	Rangers
1904–05	Third Lanark	0-0 3-1	Rangers
1905–06	Hearts	1-0	Third Lanark
1906–07	Celtic	3-0	Hearts
1907–08	Celtic	5-1	St Mirren
	(Cup withdrawn following a riot after 2 drawn matches)		
1909–10	Dundee	2-2 0-0 2-1	Clyde
1910–11	Celtic	0-0 2-0	Hamilton Ac
1911–12	Celtic	2-0	Clyde
1912–13	Falkirk	2-0	Raith R
1913–14	Celtic	0-0 4-1	Hibernian
1919–20	Kilmarnock	3-2	Albion R

(Continued)

(Scottish Cup Champions contd.)

Year	Winners	Score	Runners-up
1920–21	Partick Thistle	1-0	Rangers
1921–22	Morton	1-0	Rangers
1922–23	Celtic	1-0	Hibernian
1923–24	Airdrieonians	2-0	Hibernian
1924–25	Celtic	2-1	Dundee
1925–26	St Mirren	2-0	Celtic
1926–27	Celtic	3-1	East Fife
1927–28	Rangers	4-0	Celtic
1928–29	Kilmarnock	2-0	Rangers
1929–30	Rangers	0-0 2-1	Partick This
1930–31	Celtic	2-2 4-2	Motherwell
1931–32	Rangers	1-1 3-0	Kilmarnock
1932–33	Celtic	1-0	Motherwell
1933–34	Rangers	5-0	St Mirren
1934–35	Rangers	2-1	Hamilton Ac
1935–36	Rangers	1-0	Third Lanark
1936–37	Celtic	2-1	Aberdeen
1937–38	East Fife	1-1 4-2	Kilmarnock
1938–39	Clyde	4-0	Motherwell
1946–47	Aberdeen	2-1	Hibernian
1947–48	Rangers	1-1 1-0	Morton
1948–49	Rangers	4-1	Clyde
1949–50	Rangers	3-0	East Fife
1950–51	Celtic	1-0	Motherwell
1951–52	Motherwell	4-0	Dundee
1952–53	Rangers	1-1 1-0	Aberdeen
1953–54	Celtic	2-1	Aberdeen
1954–55	Clyde	1-1 1-0	Celtic
1955–56	Hearts	3-1	Celtic
1956–57	Falkirk	1-1 2-1	Kilmarnock
1957–58	Clyde	1-0	Hibernian
1958–59	St Mirren	3-1	Aberdeen
1959–60	Rangers	2-0	Kilmarnock
1960–61	Dunfermline A	0-0 2-0	Celtic
1961–62	Rangers	2-0	St Mirren
1962–63	Rangers	1-1 3-0	Celtic
1963–64	Rangers	3-1	Dundee
1964–65	Celtic	3-2	Dunfermline A
1965–66	Rangers	0-0 1-0	Celtic
1966–67	Celtic	2-0	Aberdeen
1967–68	Dunfermline A	3-1	Hearts
1968–69	Celtic	4-0	Rangers
1969–70	Aberdeen	3-1	Celtic
1970–71	Celtic	1-1 2-1	Rangers
1971–72	Celtic	6-1	Hibernian
1972–73	Rangers	3-2	Celtic
1973–74	Celtic	3-0	Dundee United
1974–75	Celtic	3-1	Airdrieonians
1975–76	Rangers	3-1	Hearts
1976–77	Celtic	1-0	Rangers
1977–78	Rangers	2-1	Aberdeen
1978–79	Rangers	0-0 0-0 3-2	Hibernian
1979–80	Celtic	1-0	Rangers
1980–81	Rangers	0-0 4-1	Dundee United
1981–82	Aberdeen	4-1	Rangers
1982–83	Aberdeen	1-0	Rangers
1983–84	Aberdeen	2-1	Celtic
1984–85	Celtic	2-1	Dundee United
1985–86	Aberdeen	3-0	Hearts
1986–87	St Mirren	1-0	Dundee United
1987–88	Celtic	2-1	Dundee United
1988–89	Celtic	1-0	Rangers
1989–90	Aberdeen	0-0	Celtic
	(Aberdeen won 9-8 on penalties)		
1990–91	Motherwell	4-3	Dundee United
1991–92	Rangers	2-1	Airdrieonians
1992–93	Rangers	2-1	Aberdeen

Scottish League
Final Tables 1992–93

		Home			Goals		Away			Goals			
Premier Division	P	W	D	L	F	A	W	D	L	F	A	GD	Pts
Rangers	44	20	2	0	52	11	13	5	4	45	24	+62	73
Aberdeen	44	13	7	2	41	13	14	3	5	46	23	+51	64
Celtic	44	13	5	4	37	18	11	7	4	31	23	+27	60
Dundee U	44	8	7	7	25	27	11	2	9	31	22	+7	47
Hearts	44	12	6	4	26	15	3	8	11	11	20	–5	44
St Johnstone	44	8	10	4	29	27	2	10	10	23	39	–14	40
Hibernian	44	8	8	6	32	28	4	5	13	22	36	–10	37
Partick Thistle	44	5	6	11	26	41	7	6	9	24	30	–21	36
Motherwell	44	7	4	11	27	37	4	9	9	19	25	–16	35
Dundee	44	7	4	11	25	34	4	8	10	23	34	–20	34
Falkirk	44	7	5	10	40	39	4	2	16	20	47	–26	26
Airdrieonians	44	4	9	9	22	27	2	8	12	13	43	–35	29

		Home			Goals		Away			Goals			
First Division	P	W	D	L	F	A	W	D	L	F	A	GD	Pts
Raith R	44	17	5	0	54	14	8	10	4	31	27	+44	65
Kilmarnock	44	13	6	3	43	14	8	6	8	24	26	+27	54
Dunfermline Ath.	44	10	5	7	33	27	12	3	7	31	20	+17	52
St Mirren	44	11	5	6	33	20	10	4	8	29	32	+10	51
Hamilton Ac	44	11	7	4	36	23	8	5	9	29	22	+20	50
Morton	44	11	3	8	36	27	8	7	7	29	29	+9	48
Ayr U	44	9	9	4	27	19	5	9	8	22	25	+5	46

		Home			Goals		Away			Goals			
First Division	P	W	D	L	F	A	W	D	L	F	A	GD	Pts
Clydebank	44	10	8	4	42	22	6	5	11	29	44	+5	45
Dumbarton	44	10	3	9	30	30	5	4	13	26	41	–15	37
Stirling Albion	44	7	5	10	23	31	4	8	10	21	30	–17	35
Meadowbank T	44	6	6	10	23	32	5	4	13	28	48	–29	32
Cowdenbeath	44	0	5	17	18	55	3	2	17	15	54	–76	13

		Home			Goals		Away			Goals			
Second Division	P	W	D	L	F	A	W	D	L	F	A	GD	Pts
Clyde	39	11	5	4	37	18	11	5	3	40	24	+35	54
Brechin C	39	13	3	3	37	13	10	4	6	25	19	+30	53
Stranraer	39	8	9	2	33	21	11	6	3	36	23	+25	53
Forfar Ath	39	10	5	4	47	30	8	5	7	27	24	+20	46
Alloa	39	8	4	7	25	28	8	8	4	38	26	+9	44
Arbroath	39	8	6	6	34	26	10	2	7	25	24	+9	44
Stenhousemuir	39	9	3	8	30	25	6	7	6	29	23	+11	40
Berwick R	39	8	5	6	30	25	8	2	10	26	39	–8	39
East Fife	39	6	6	8	32	33	8	4	7	38	31	+6	38
Queen of the S	39	5	4	11	27	37	7	5	7	30	35	–15	33
Queen's Park	39	6	6	7	29	32	2	6	12	22	41	–22	28
Montrose	39	5	3	12	24	35	5	4	10	22	36	–25	27
East Stirling	39	4	4	12	24	39	4	5	10	26	46	–35	25
Albion R	39	4	5	10	22	36	2	5	13	14	40	–40	22

Scottish League Champions

Year	Winners	Pts	Runners-up	Pts
1890–91	Dumbarton/ Rangers	29	–	
1891–92	Dumbarton	37	Celtic	35
1892–93	Celtic	29	Rangers	28
	Division 1			
1893–94	Celtic	29	Hearts	26
1894–95	Hearts	31	Celtic	26
1895–96	Celtic	30	Rangers	26
1896–97	Hearts	28	Hibernian	26
1897–98	Celtic	33	Rangers	29
1898–99	Rangers	36	Hearts	26
1899–00	Rangers	32	Celtic	25
1900–01	Rangers	35	Celtic	29
1901–02	Rangers	28	Celtic	26
1902–03	Hibernian	37	Dundee	31
1903–04	Third Lanark	43	Hearts	39
1904–05	Celtic	41	Rangers	41
1905–06	Celtic	49	Hearts	43
1906–07	Celtic	55	Dundee	48
1907–08	Celtic	55	Falkirk	51
1908–09	Celtic	51	Dundee	50
1909–10	Celtic	54	Falkirk	52
1910–11	Rangers	52	Aberdeen	48
1911–12	Rangers	51	Celtic	45
1912–13	Rangers	53	Celtic	49
1913–14	Celtic	65	Rangers	59
1914–15	Celtic	65	Hearts	61
1915–16	Celtic	67	Rangers	56
1917–18	Rangers	56	Celtic	55
1919–20	Rangers	71	Celtic	68

(Continued)

Year	Winners	Pts	Runners-up	Pts
1920–21	Rangers	76	Celtic	66
1921–22	Celtic	67	Rangers	66
1922–23	Rangers	55	Airdrieonians	50
1923–24	Rangers	59	Airdrieonians	50
1924–25	Rangers	60	Airdrieonians	57
1925–26	Celtic	58	Airdrieonians	50
1926–27	Rangers	56	Motherwell	51
1927–28	Rangers	60	Celtic	55
1928–29	Rangers	67	Celtic	51
1929–30	Rangers	60	Motherwell	55
1930–31	Rangers	60	Celtic	58
1931–32	Motherwell	66	Rangers	61
1932–33	Rangers	62	Motherwell	59
1933–34	Rangers	66	Motherwell	62
1934–35	Rangers	55	Celtic	52
1935–36	Celtic	66	Rangers	61
1936–37	Rangers	61	Aberdeen	54
1937–38	Celtic	61	Hearts	58
1938–39	Rangers	59	Celtic	48
1946–47	Rangers	46	Hibernian	44
1947–48	Hibernian	48	Rangers	46
1948–49	Rangers	46	Dundee	45
1949–50	Rangers	50	Hibernian	49
1950–51	Hibernian	48	Rangers	38
1951–52	Hibernian	45	Rangers	41
1952–53	Rangers	43	Hibernian	43
1953–54	Celtic	43	Hearts	38
1954–55	Aberdeen	49	Celtic	46
1955–56	Rangers	52	Aberdeen	46
1956–57	Rangers	55	Hearts	53
1957–58	Hearts	62	Rangers	49
1958–59	Rangers	50	Hearts	48
1959–60	Hearts	54	Kilmarnock	50
1960–61	Rangers	51	Kilmarnock	50
1961–62	Dundee	54	Rangers	51
1962–63	Rangers	57	Kilmarnock	48
1963–64	Rangers	55	Kilmarnock	49
1964–65	Kilmarnock	50	Hearts	50
1965–66	Celtic	57	Rangers	55
1966–67	Celtic	58	Rangers	55
1967–68	Celtic	63	Rangers	61
1968–69	Celtic	54	Rangers	49
1969–70	Celtic	57	Rangers	45
1970–71	Celtic	56	Aberdeen	54
1971–72	Celtic	60	Aberdeen	50
1972–73	Celtic	57	Rangers	56
1973–74	Celtic	53	Hibernian	49
1974–75	Rangers	56	Hibernian	49
	Premier Division			
1975–76	Rangers	54	Celtic	48
1976–77	Celtic	55	Rangers	46
1977–78	Rangers	55	Aberdeen	53
1978–79	Celtic	48	Rangers	45
1979–80	Aberdeen	48	Celtic	47
1980–81	Celtic	56	Aberdeen	49
1981–82	Celtic	55	Aberdeen	53
1982–83	Dundee U	56	Celtic	55
1983–84	Aberdeen	57	Celtic	50
1984–85	Aberdeen	59	Celtic	52
1985–86	Celtic	50	Hearts	50
1986–87	Rangers	69	Celtic	63
1987–88	Celtic	72	Hearts	62
1988–89	Rangers	56	Aberdeen	50
1989–90	Rangers	51	Aberdeen	44
1990–91	Rangers	55	Aberdeen	53
1991–92	Rangers	72	Hearts	63
1992–93	Rangers	73	Aberdeen	64

Skol Cup 1992–93

First Round

East Stirling	0	Alloa	1
Stranraer	0	East Fife	0
(Stranraer won 5-4 on penalties)			
Stenhousemuir	2	Arbroath	3
Brechin C	2	Albion R	1
Queen's Park	1	Clyde	3
Queen of the S	3	Berwick R	0

Second Round

Alloa	1	St Johnstone	3
Airdrieonians	2	Stranraer	3*
Brechin C	4	Hamilton Ac	2
Dumbarton	0	Rangers	5
Dundee U	6	Queen of the S	0
Morton	2	Kilmarnock	3*
Motherwell	4	Clyde	2
Partick Thistle	2	Ayr U	0
Meadowbank T	0	Dundee	3
Falkirk	4	Forfar Ath	1
Hearts	1	Clydebank	0
Hibernian	4	Raith R	1
Montrose	0	Dunfermline Ath	6
St Mirren	1	Cowdenbeath	0
Arbroath	0	Aberdeen	4
Stirling Alb	0	Celtic	3

Third Round

Dundee U	3	St Mirren	0
Kilmarnock	3	Hibernian	1*
Aberdeen	1	Dunfermline Ath	0*
Brechin C	1	Hearts	2*
Celtic	1	Dundee	0
Motherwell	0	Falkirk	1
St Johnstone	2	Partick Thistle	2*
(St Johnstone won 4-3 on penalties)			
Stranraer	0	Rangers	5

Quarter-finals

Kilmarnock	1	St Johnstone	3
Dundee U	2	Rangers	3*
Falkirk	1	Aberdeen	4
Hearts	1	Celtic	2

Semi-finals

St Johnstone	1	Rangers	3
Celtic	0	Aberdeen	1

Final

Aberdeen	1	Rangers	2*

*After extra time

Skol Cup Champions

Formerly Scottish League Cup

Year	Winners	Score	Runners-up
1946–47	Rangers	4-0	Aberdeen
1947–48	East Fife	1-1 4-1	Falkirk
1948–49	Rangers	2-0	Raith Rovers
1949–50	East Fife	3-0	Dunfermline
1950–51	Motherwell	3-0	Hibernian
1951–52	Dundee	3-2	Rangers
1952–53	Dundee	2-0	Kilmarnock
1953–54	East Fife	3-2	Partick Thistle
1954–55	Hearts	4-2	Motherwell
1955–56	Aberdeen	2-1	St Mirren
1956–57	Celtic	0-0 3-0	Partick Thistle
1957–58	Celtic	7-1	Rangers
1958–59	Hearts	5-1	Partick Thistle
1959–60	Hearts	2-1	Third Lanark
1960–61	Rangers	2-0	Kilmarnock
1961–62	Rangers	1-1 3-1	Hearts
1962–63	Hearts	1-0	Kilmarnock
1963–64	Rangers	5-0	Morton
1964–65	Rangers	2-1	Celtic
1965–66	Celtic	2-1	Rangers
1966–67	Celtic	1-0	Rangers
1967–68	Celtic	5-3	Dundee
1968–69	Celtic	6-2	Hibernian
1969–70	Celtic	1-0	St Johnstone
1970–71	Rangers	1-0	Celtic
1971–72	Partick Thistle	4-1	Celtic
1972–73	Hibernian	2-1	Celtic
1973–74	Dundee U	1-0	Celtic

(Continued)

(Skol Cup Champions contd.)

Year	Winners	Score	Runners-up
1974–75	Celtic	6-3	Hibernian
1975–76	Rangers	1-0	Celtic
1976–77	Aberdeen	2-1	Celtic
1977–78	Rangers	2-1	Celtic
1978–79	Rangers	2-1	Aberdeen
1979–80	Dundee U	0-0 3-0	Aberdeen
1980–81	Dundee U	3-0	Dundee
1981–82	Rangers	2-1	Dundee U
1982–83	Celtic	2-1	Rangers
1983–84	Rangers	3-2	Celtic
1984–85	Rangers	1-0	Dundee U
1985–86	Aberdeen	3-0	Hibernian
1986–87	Rangers	2-1	Celtic
1987–88	Rangers	3-3	Aberdeen
	(Rangers won 5-3 on penalties)		
1988–89	Rangers	3-2	Aberdeen
1989–90	Aberdeen	2-1	Rangers
1990–91	Rangers	2-1	Celtic
1991–92	Hibernian	2-0	Dunfermline Ath.
1992–93	Rangers	2-1	Aberdeen

World Club Champions

Year	Winners	Score	Runners-up
1960	Real Madrid (Spa)	5-1	Penarol (Uru)
1961	Penarol (Uru)	7-2*	Benfica (Por)
1962	Santos (Bra)	8-4	Benfica (Por)
1963	Santos (Bra)	7-6*	AC Milan (Ita)
1964	Inter Milan (Ita)	3-1*	Independiente (Arg)
1965	Inter Milan (Ita)	3-0	Independiente (Arg)
1966	Penarol (Uru)	4-0	Real Madrid (Spa)
1967	Racing Club (Arg)	3-2*	Celtic (Sco)
1968	Estudiantes (Arg)	2-1	Manchester U (Eng)
1969	AC Milan (Ita)	4-2	Estudiantes (Arg)
1970	Feyenoord (Hol)	3-2	Estudiantes (Arg)
1971	Nacional (Uru)	3-2	Panathanaikos (Gre)
1972	Ajax (Hol)	4-1	Independiente (Arg)
1973	Independiente (Arg)	1-0	Juventus (Ita)
1974	Atletico Madrid (Spa)	2-1	Independiente (Arg)
1975	Not held		
1976	Bayern Munich (FRG)	2-0	Cruzeiro (Bra)
1977	Boca Juniors (Arg)	5-2	B. M/gladbach (FRG)
1978	Not held		
1979	Olimpia (Par)	3-1	Malmo (Swe)
1980	Nacional (Uru)	1-0	Nottingham F (Eng)
1981	Flamengo (Bra)	3-0	Liverpool (Eng)
1982	Penarol (Uru)	2-0	Aston Villa (Eng)
1983	Gremio (Bra)	2-1	SV Hamburg (FRG)
1984	Independiente (Arg)	1-0	Liverpool (Eng)
1985	Juventus (Ita)	2-2	Argentinos Jr (Arg)
	(Juventus won 4-2 on penalties)		
1986	River Plate (Arg)	1-0	Steaua Buch. (Rom)
1987	FC Porto (Por)	2-1	Penarol (Uru)
1988	Nacional (Uru)	2-2	PSV Eindhoven (Hol)
	(Nacional won 7-6 on penalties)		
1989	AC Milan (Ita)	1-0	Atletico Nacional (Col)
1990	AC Milan (Ita)	3-0	Olimpia (Par)
1991	Red Star Belgrade (Yug)	3-0	Colo Colo (Bra)
1992	Sao Paolo (Bra)	2-1	Barcelona (Spa)

*Including a play-off match.

The World Cup

The World Cup, emblematic of international soccer supremacy, was won by West Germany on July 8, 1990, with a 1-0 victory over defending champion Argentina on a penalty shot in the 84th minute. It was the lowest-scoring final in the 60 years of World Cup play. It was the third World Cup title for West Germany, equalling Brazil and Italy. In 1994 the U.S. will host the tournament for the first time. Winners and sites of previous World Cup matches follow:

Year	Winner	Score	Runner-up	Venue
1930	Uruguay	4-2	Argentina	Montevideo
1934	Italy	2-1	Czechoslovakia	Rome
1938	Italy	4-2	Hungary	Paris
1950	Uruguay	2-1	Brazil	Rio de Janeiro
1954	W. Germany	3-2	Hungary	Berne
1958	Brazil	5-2	Sweden	Stockholm
1962	Brazil	3-1	Czechoslovakia	Santiago
1966	England	4-2	W. Germany	London
1970	Brazil	4-1	Italy	Mexico City
1974	W. Germany	2-1	Holland	Munich
1978	Argentina	3-1	Holland	Buenos Aires
1982	Italy	3-1	W. Germany	Madrid
1986	Argentina	3-2	W. Germany	Mexico City
1990	W. Germany	1-0	Argentina	Rome

ATHLETICS

AAA Championships

Birmingham, July 1993

Finals – Men

100m	L. Christie	10.13s
200m	J. Williams	20.47s
400m	O. Kennedy	45.32s
800m	M. Steele	1m 47.83s
1500m	M. Yates	3m 38.75s
3000m	J. Kester	7m 56.39s
5000m	J. Brown	13m 35.67s
110m hurdles	C. Jackson	13.15s
400m hurdles	G. Cadogan	50.60s
3000m steeplechase	C. Walker	8m 33.45s
10,000m walk	M. Bell	42m 29.63s
High jump	T. Forsyth	2.32m
Long jump	F. Salle	7.72m
Triple jump	F. Agyepong	16.05m
Pole vault	S. Arkell	5.60m
Discus	R. Weir	57.44m
Hammer	P. Head	72.32m
Javelin	C. Mackenzie	81.44m
Shot	M. Simson	18.79m

Finals – Women

100m	B. Kinch	11.44s
200m	C. Freeman	22.71s
400m	P. Smith	52.15s
800m	K. Holmes	2m 02.69s
1500m	A. Wyeth	4m 11.03s
110m hurdles	S. Gunnell	13.08s
400m hurdles	J. Parker	58.14s
5000m walk	V. Lupton	22m 34.50s
High jump	D. Marti	1.86m
Long jump	N. Boegman	6.50m
Triple jump	L. Espergen	13.43m
Pole vault	K. Staples	3.20m
Discus	D. Costigan	61.58m
Hammer	D. Sosimenko	56.86m
Javelin	S. Holroyd	60.10m
Shot	M. Augee	17.24m

Cross Country World Champions

Men

Year	Individual	Team
1973	Pekka Päivärinta (Fin)	Belgium
1974	Eric de Beck (Bel)	Belgium
1975	Ian Stewart (Scot)	New Zealand
1976	Carlos Lopes (Por)	England
1977	Leon Schots (Bel)	Belgium
1978	John Treacy (Irl)	France
1979	John Treacy (Irl)	England
1980	Craig Virgin (USA)	England
1981	Craig Virgin (USA)	Ethiopia
1982	Mohamed Kedir (Eth)	Ethiopia
1983	Bekele Debele (Eth)	Ethiopia
1984	Carlos Lopes (Por)	Ethiopia
1985	Carlos Lopes (Por)	Ethiopia
1986	John Ngugi (Ken)	Kenya
1987	John Ngugi (Ken)	Kenya
1988	John Ngugi (Ken)	Kenya
1989	John Ngugi (Ken)	Kenya
1990	Khalid Skah (Mor)	Kenya
1991	Khalid Skah (Mor)	Kenya
1992	John Ngugi (Ken)	Kenya
1993	William Sigei (Ken)	Kenya

Women

Year	Individual	Team
1973	Paola Cacchi (Ita)	England
1974	Paola Pigni (Ita)	England
1975	Julie Brown (USA)	USA
1976	Carmen Valero (Spa)	USSR
1977	Carmen Valero (Spa)	USSR
1978	Grete Waitz (Nor)	Romania
1979	Grete Waitz (Nor)	USA
1980	Grete Waitz (Nor)	USSR
1981	Grete Waitz (Nor)	USSR
1982	Maricica Puica (Rom)	USSR
1983	Greta Waitz (Nor)	United States
1984	Maricica Puica (Rom)	United States
1985	Zola Budd (Eng)	United States
1986	Zola Budd (Eng)	England
1987	Annette Sergent (Fra)	United States
1988	Ingrid Kristiansen (Nor)	USSR
1989	Annette Sergent (Fra)	USSR
1990	Lynn Jennings (US)	USSR
1991	Lynn Jennings (US)	Ethiopia/Kenya
1992	Lynn Jennings (US)	Kenya
1993	Albertina Dias (Por)	Kenya

Europa Cup

Rome, June 1993

Men

100m	L. Christie (GB)	10.22s
200m	J. Regis (GB)	20.38s
400m	D. Grindley (GB)	44.75s
800m	A. Bulkovsky (Ukr)	1m 47.32s
1500m	A. Bulkovsky (Ukr)	3m 37.51s
5000m	R. Denmark (GB)	13m 30.02s
10,000m	T. Pantel (Fra)	28m 02.71s
4×100m relay	Great Britain	38.53s
4×400m relay	Great Britain	3m 00.25s
110m hurdles	C. Jackson (GB)	13.10s
400m hurdles	S. Diagana (Fra)	48.08s
3000m steeplechase	S. Brand (Ger)	8m 17.77s
High jump	A. Partyaka (Pol)	2.30m
Long jump	G. Evangelisti (Ita)	8.04m
Triple jump	P. Camara (Fra)	17.46m
Pole vault	R. Gataullin (Rus)	6.00m
Discus	L. Riedel (Ger)	66.30m
Hammer	S. Litvinov (Rus)	80.78m
Javelin	J. Zelezny (Cz Rep)	89.84m
Shot	A. Bagach (Ukr)	20.15m

Final Standings

1 Russia **2** Great Britain **3** France

Women

100m	I. Privalova (Rus)	11.08s
200m	I. Privalova (Rus)	20.30s
400m	E. Ruzina (Rus)	51.54s
800m	E. Kovacs (Rom)	*
1500m	V. Chuvashova (Rus)	4m 16.03s
3000m	M. Keszek (Rom)	8m 51.88s
10,000m	V. Nenasheva (Rus)	32m 38.46s
4×100m relay	Russia	42.79s
4×400m relay	Russia	3m 24.23s
110m hurdles	M. Azyabina (Rus)	12.63s
400m hurdles	S. Gunnell (GB)	53.73s
High jump	G. Astafei (Rom)	2.00m
Long jump	H. Drechsler (Ger)	7.02m
Triple jump	Y. Chen (Rus)	14.34m
Discus	L. Korotkevich (Rus)	64.58m
Javelin	F. Tirlea (Rom)	62.68m
Shot	A. Romanova (Rus)	19.43m

*Official time unavailable because of mechanical failure.

Final Standings

1 Russia **2** Romania **3** Ukraine

Marathons 1992–93

Men

Place	Winner	Nationality	Time
Berlin	David Tsebe	S.Af	2:08.07
Boston	Cosmas N-Deti	Ken	2:09.33
Fukuoka (Tokyo)	Tena-Negere	Eth	2:09.04
London	Eamonn Martin	GB	2:10.50
New York	Willie Mtolo	S.Af	2:09.29
Rotterdam	Dionicio Ceron	Mex	2:11.08

Women

Place	Winner	Nationality	Time
Berlin	Uta Pippig	Ger	2:30.22
Boston	Olga Markova	Rus	2:25.27
London	Katrine Doerre	Ger	2:27.09
New York	Liza Nodiek	Aus	2:24.40
Rotterdam	Anna Van Schuppen	Neth	2:31.05
Tokyo	Liz McColgan	GB	2:27.38

London Marathon Champions

Men

1981	Dick Beardsley (US) & Inge Simonsen (Nor)	2h 11m 48s

(London Marathon Champions continued)

1982	Hugh Jones (GB)	2h 09m 24s
1983	Mike Gratton (GB)	2h 09m 43s
1984	Charlie Spedding (GB)	2h 09m 57s
1985	Steve Jones (GB)	2h 08m 16s
1986	Toshihiko Seko (Jap)	2h 10m 02s
1987	Hiromi Taniguchi (Jap)	2h 09m 50s
1988	Henryk Jorgensen (Den)	2h 10m 20s
1989	Douglas Wakiihuri (Ken)	2h 09m 03s
1990	Allister Hutton (GB)	2h 10m 10s
1991	Iakov Tolstikov (USSR)	2h 09m 17s
1992	Antonio Pinto (Por)	2h 10m 02s
1993	Eamonn Martin (GB)	2h 10m 50s

Women

1981	Joyce Smith (GB)	2h 29m 57s
1982	Joyce Smith (GB)	2h 29m 43s
1983	Grete Waitz (Nor)	2h 25m 29s
1984	Ingrid Kristiansen (Nor)	2h 24m 26s
1985	Ingrid Kristiansen (Nor)	2h 21m 06s
1986	Grete Waitz (Nor)	2h 24m 54s
1987	Ingrid Kristiansen (Nor)	2h 22m 48s
1988	Ingrid Kristiansen (Nor)	2h 25m 41s
1989	Veronique Marot (GB)	2h 25m 56s
1990	Wanda Panfil (Pol)	2h 26m 31s
1991	Rosa Mota (Por)	2h 26m 14s
1992	Katrine Doerre (Ger)	2h 29m 38s
1993	Katrine Doerre (Ger)	2h 27m 09s

World Athletics Championships

Stuttgart, Aug. 1993

Finals – Men

100m	Linford Christie (GB)	09.87s
200m	Frank Fredericks (Nam)	19.85s
400m	Michael Johnson (US)	43.65s
800m	Paul Ruto (Ken)	1m 44.71s
1500m	Noureddine Morceli (Alg)	3m 34.24s
5000m	Ismael Kirui (Ken)	13m 02.75s
10,000m	Haile Gabresiliasie (Eth)	27m 46.02s
Marathon	Mark Plaatjes (US)	2h 13m 57s
3000m steeple	Moses Kiptanui (Ken)	8m 06.36s
110m hurdles	Colin Jackson (GB)	12.91s
400m hurdles	Kevin Young (US)	47.18s
High jump	Javier Sotomayor (Cub)	2.40m
Pole vault	Sergei Bubka (Ukr)	6.00m
Long jump	Mike Powell (US)	8.59m
Triple jump	Mike Conley (US)	17.86m
Shot put	Werner Günthör (Swi)	21.97m
Discus throw	Lars Riedel (Ger)	67.72m
Hammer throw	Andrei Abduvaliyev (Taj)	81.64m
Javelin throw	Jan Zelezny (Cze)	85.98m
Decathlon	Dan O'Brien (US)	8,817 pts
20km walk	Valenti Massana (Spa)	1h 22m 31s
50km walk	Jesus Angel Garcia (Spa)	3h 41m 41s
4×100m relay	United States	37.48s
4×400m relay	United States	2m 54.29s

Finals – Women

100m	Gail Devers (US)	10.82s
200m	Merlene Ottey (Jam)	21.98s
400m	Jearl Miles (US)	49.82s
800m	Maria Mutola (Moz)	1m 55.43s
1500m	Liu Dong (Chi)	4m 00.50s
3000m	Qu Yunxia (Chi)	8m 28.71s
10,000m	Wang Junxia (Chi)	30m 49.30s
Marathon	Junko Asari (Jap)	2h 30m 03s
100m hurdles	Gail Devers (US)	12.46s
400m hurdles	Sally Gunnell (GB)	52.74s
High jump	Ioamnet Quintero (Cub)	1.99m
Long jump	Heike Drechsler (Ger)	7.11m
Triple jump	Ana Biryukova (Rus)	15.09m
Shot put	Huang Zhihong (Chi)	20.57m
Discus throw	Olga Burova (Rus)	67.40m
Javelin throw	Trine Hattestad (Nor)	69.18m
Heptathlon	Jackie Joyner-Kersee (US)	6,837 pts
10km walk	Sari Essayah (Fin)	42m 59s
4×100m relay	Russia	41.49s
4×400m relay	United States	3m 16.71s

World Athletics Indoor Records

As of Sept. 1993

The International Amateur Athletic Federation began recognizing world indoor athletic records as official on January 1, 1987. Prior to that, there were only unofficial world indoor bests. World indoor bests set prior to January 1, 1987 are subject to approval as world records provided they meet the prescribed IAAF world records criteria, including drug testing. To be accepted as a world indoor record, a performance must meet the same criteria as a world record outdoors, except that a track performance cannot be set on an indoor track larger than 200 metres. * = Record pending.

Men

Event	Record	Holder	Country	Date	Where made
50 metres	5.61	Manfred Kokot	E. Germany	Feb. 4, 1973	E. Berlin
60 metres	6.41	Andre Cason	U.S.	Feb. 14, 1992	Madrid
200 metres	20.36	Bruno Marie-Rose	France	Feb. 22, 1987	Lievin, France
400 metres	45.02	Danny Everett	U.S.	Feb. 2, 1992	Germany
800 metres	1:44.84	Paul Ereng	Kenya	Mar. 4, 1989	Budapest
1000 metres	2:15.26	Noureddine Morceli	Algeria	Feb. 22, 1992	Birmingham, Eng.
1500 metres	3:34.16	Noureddine Morceli	Algeria	Feb. 28, 1991	Seville, Spain
1 Mile	3:49.78	Eamonn Coghlan	Ireland	Feb. 27, 1983	E. Rutherford, N.J.
3000 metres	7:37.31	Moses Kiptanui	Kenya	Feb. 20, 1992	Seville, Spain
5000 metres	13:20.40	Suleiman Nyambui	Tanzania	Feb. 6, 1981	New York
50-metre hurdles	6.25	Mark McKoy	Canada	Jan. 27, 1985	Rosemont, Ill.
60-metre hurdles	7.36	Greg Foster	U.S.	Jan. 16, 1987	Los Angeles
High Jump	7 ft. 11½ in.	Javier Sotomayor	Cuba	Mar. 4, 1989	Budapest
Pole Vault	20 ft. 2 in.	Sergei Bubka	Ukraine	Feb. 21, 1993	Ukraine
Long Jump	28 ft. 10¼ in.	Carl Lewis	U.S.	Feb. 27, 1984	New York
Triple Jump	58 ft. 3¼ in.	Mike Conley	U.S.	Feb. 27, 1987	New York
Shot Put	74 ft. 4¼ in.	Randy Barnes	U.S.	Jan. 20, 1989	Los Angeles

Women

Event	Record	Holder	Country	Date	Where made
50 metres	*6.00	Irina Privalova	Russia	Feb. 2, 1993	Moscow
60 metres	*6.95	Gail Devers	U.S.	Mar. 12, 1993	Toronto
200 metres	*21.87	Merlene Ottey	Jamaica	Feb. 13, 1993	Lievin, France
400 metres	49.59	Jarmila Kratochvilova	Czechoslovakia	Mar. 7, 1982	Milan
800 metres	1:56.40	Christine Wachtel	E. Germany	Feb. 13, 1988	Vienna
1000 metres	2:34.67	Lilia Nurutdinova	Russia	Feb. 7, 1992	Moscow
1500 metres	4:00.27	Doina Melinte	Romania	Feb. 9, 1990	E. Rutherford, N.J.
1 Mile	4:17.13	Doina Melinte	Romania	Feb. 9, 1990	E. Rutherford, N.J.
3000 metres	8:33.82	Elly Van Hulst	Netherlands	Feb. 8, 1986	England
5000 metres	15:03.17	Liz McColgan	G. Britain	Feb. 22, 1992	Birmingham, Eng.
50-metre hurdles	6:58	Cornelia Oschkenat	E. Germany	Feb. 20, 1988	Berlin
60-metre hurdles	*7.63	Lyudmila Narozhi-Lenko	Russia	Mar. 4, 1993	Seville, Spain
High Jump	6 ft. 9½ in.	Heike Henkel	Germany	Feb. 8, 1992	Germany
Long Jump	24 ft. 2¼ in.	Heike Dreschler	E. Germany	Feb. 13, 1988	Vienna
Triple Jump	47 ft. 4½ in.	Inessa Kravets	USSR	Mar. 9, 1991	Seville, Spain
Shot Put	73 ft. 10 in.	Helena Fibingerova	Czechoslovakia	Feb. 19, 1977	Czechoslovakia

BADMINTON

All-England Champions

Post-war winners

Singles

Year	Men	Women
1947	Conny Jepsen (Swe)	Marie Ussing (Den)
1948	Jörn Skaarup (Den)	Kirsten Thorndahl (Den)
1949	Dave Freeman (US)	Aase Jacobsen (Den)
1950	Wong Peng Soon (Mal)	Tonny Olsen-Ahm (Den)
1951	Wong Peng Soon (Mal)	Aase Jacobsen (Den)
1952	Wong Peng Soon (Mal)	Tonny Olsen-Ahm (Den)
1953	Eddie Choong (Mal)	Marie Ussing (Den)
1954	Eddie Choong (Mal)	Judy Devlin (US)
1955	Wong Peng Soon (Mal)	Margaret Varner (US)
1956	Eddie Choong (Mal)	Margaret Varner (US)
1957	Eddie Choong (Mal)	Judy Devlin (US)
1958	Erland Kops (Den)	Judy Devlin (US)
1959	Tan Joe Hok (Indo)	Heather Ward (Eng)
1960	Erland Kops (Den)	Judy Devlin (US)
1961	Erland Kops (Den)	Judy Hashman (US)
1962	Erland Kops (Den)	Judy Hashman (US)
1963	Erland Kops (Den)	Judy Hashman (US)
1964	Knud Nielsen (Den)	Judy Hashman (US)
1965	Erland Kops (Den)	Ursula Smith (Eng)
1966	Tan Aik Huang (Mal)	Judy Hashman (US)
1967	Erland Kops (Den)	Judy Hashman (US)
1968	Rudy Hartono (Indo)	Eva Twedberg (Swe)
1969	Rudy Hartono (Indo)	Hiroe Yuki (Jap)
1970	Rudy Hartono (Indo)	Etsuko Takenaka (Jap)
1971	Rudy Hartono (Indo)	Eva Twedberg (Swe)
1972	Rudy Hartono (Indo)	Noriko Nakayama (Jap)
1973	Rudy Hartono (Indo)	Margaret Beck (Eng)
1974	Rudy Hartono (Indo)	Hiroe Yuki (Jap)
1975	Sven Pri (Den)	Hiroe Yuki (Jap)
1976	Rudy Hartono (Indo)	Gillian Gilks (Eng)
1977	Flemming Delfs (Den)	Hiroe Yuki (Jap)
1978	Liem Swie King (Indo)	Gillian Gilks (Eng)
1979	Liem Swie King (Indo)	Lene Köppen (Den)
1980	Prakash Padukone (Indo)	Lene Köppen (Den)
1981	Liem Swie King (Indo)	Sun Ai Hwang (S Kor)
1982	Morten Frost (Den)	Zang Ailing (Chi)
1983	Luan Jin (Chi)	Zang Ailing (Chi)
1984	Morten Frost (Den)	Li Lingwei (Chi)
1985	Zhao Jianhua (Chi)	Han Aiping (Chi)
1986	Morten Frost (Den)	Kim Yun Ja (S Kor)
1987	Morten Frost (Den)	Kirsten Larsen (Den)
1988	Ib Frederiksen (Den)	Gu Jiaming (Chi)
1989	Yang Yang (Chi)	Li Lingwei (Chi)
1990	Zhao Jianhua (Chi)	Susi Susanti (Indo)
1991	Ardi Wiranata (Indo)	Susi Susanti (Indo)
1992	Liu Jun (Chi)	Tang Jiuhong (Chi)
1993	Heryanto Arbi (Indo)	Susi Susanti (Indo)

Men's Doubles

1980	Tjun Tjun & Johan Wahjudi (Indo)
1981	Kartono & Rudy Heryanto (Indo)
1982	Jalani Sidek & Razis Sidek (Mal)
1983	Thomas Kihlström & Stefan Karlsson (Swe)
1984	Rudy Heryanto & Kartono (Indo)
1985	Kim Moon-Soo & Park Joon Bong (Kor)
1986	Kim Moon-Soo & Park Joon Bong (Kor)
1987	Li Yongbo & Tian Bingyi (Chi)
1988	Li Yongbo & Tian Bingyi (Chi)
1989	Lee Sang Bok & Park Joo Bong (S Kor)
1990	Kim Moon Soo & Park Joo Bong (S Kor)
1991	Li Yongbo & Tian Bingyi (Chi)
1992	Rudy Gunawan & Eddie Hartono (Indo)
1993	Jon Holst-Christensen & Thomas Lund (Den)

Women's Doubles

1980	Gillian Gilks & Nora Perry (Eng)
1981	Nora Perry & Jane Webster (Eng)
1982	Lin Ying & Wu Dixi (Chi)
1983	Xu Rong & Wu Jiangui (Chi)
1984	Lin Ying & Wu Dixi (Chi)
1985	Han Aiping & Li Lingwei (Chi)
1986	Chung Myung-Hee & Hwang Hye-Younge (Kor)
1987	Chung Myung Hee & Hwang Hye Young (S Kor)
1988	Chung So Young & Kim Yun Ja (S Kor)
1989	Chung Myung Hee & Chung So Young (S Kor)
1990	Chung Myung Hee & Hwang Hye Young (S Kor)
1991	Chung So Young & Hwang Hye Young (S Kor)
1992	Lin Yanfen & Yao Fen (Chi)
1993	Chung So Young & Gil Young Ah (S Kor)

Mixed Doubles

1980	Mike Tredgett & Nora Perry (Eng)
1981	Mike Tredgett & Nora Perry (Eng)
1982	Martin Dew & Gillian Gilks (Eng)
1983	Thomas Kihlström (Swe) & Nora Perry (Eng)
1984	Martin Dew & Gillian Gilks (Eng)
1985	Billy Gilliland (Sco) & Nora Perry (Eng)
1986	Park Joo-Bong & Chung Myung Hee (Kor)
1987	Lee Deuk-Choon & Chung Myung Hee (S Kor)
1988	Wang Pengrin & Shi Fangjing (Chi)
1989	Park Joo Bong & Chung Myung Hee (S Kor)
1990	Park Joo Bong & Chung Myung Hee (S Kor)
1991	Park Joo Bong & Chung Myung Hee (S Kor)
1992	Thomas Lund & Pernille Dupont (Den)
1993	Jon Holst-Christensen & Grete Morgensen (Den)

European Champions

Singles

Year	Men	Women
1968	Sture Johnsson (Swe)	Iringard Latz (W Ger)
1970	Sture Johnsson (Swe)	Ewa Twedberg (Swe)
1972	Wolfgang Bochow (W Ger)	Margaret Beck (Eng)
1974	Sture Johnsson (Swe)	Gillian Gilks (Eng)
1976	Flemming Delfs (Den)	Gillian Gilks (Eng)
1978	Flemming Delfs (Den)	Lene Køppen (Den)
1980	Flemming Delfs (Den)	Liselotte Blumer (Swi)
1982	Jens Peter Nierhoff (Den)	Lene Køppen (Den)
1984	Morten Frost (Den)	Helen Troke (Eng)
1986	Morten Frost (Den)	Helen Troke (Eng)
1988	Darren Hall (Eng)	Kirsten Larsen (Den)
1990	Steve Baddeley (Eng)	Pernille Nedergaard (Den)
1992	Poul-Erik Hoyer-Larsen (Den)	Pernille Nedergaard (Den)

Men's Doubles

1968	David Eddy & Roger Powell (Eng)
1970	Elo Hansen & Par Walsöe (Den)
1972	Willi Braun & Roland Maywald (W Ger)
1974	Willi Braun & Roland Maywald (W Ger)
1976	Ray Stevens & Mike Tredgett (Eng)
1978	Ray Stevens & Mike Tredgett (Eng)
1980	Claes Nordin & Stefan Karlsson (Swe)
1982	Stefan Karlsson & Thomas Kihlström (Swe)
1984	Martin Dew & Mike Tredgett (Eng)
1986	Steen Fladberg & Jesper Helledie (Den)
1988	Jens Pieter Nierhoff & Michael Kjeldsen (Den)
1990	Jan Paulsen & Henrik Swarrer (Den)
1992	Jon Holst-Christensen & Thomas Lund (Den)

Women's Doubles

1968	Margaret Boxall & Susan Whetnall (Eng)
1970	Margaret Boxall & Susan Whetnall (Eng)
1972	Gillian Gilks & Judy Hashman (Eng)
1974	Gillian Gilks & Margaret Beck (Eng)
1976	Gillian Gilks & Susan Whetnall (Eng)
1978	Nora Perry & Anne Statt (Eng)
1980	Jane Webster & Nora Perry (Eng)
1982	Gillian Gilks & Gillian Clark (Eng)
1984	Karen Chapman & Gillian Clark (Eng)
1986	Gillian Clark & Gillian Gowers (Eng)
1988	Dorte Kjaer & Nettie Nielsen (Den)
1990	Dorte Kjaer & Nettie Nielsen (Den)
1992	Lim Xao Quing & Christine Magnussen (Swe)

Mixed Doubles

1968	Tony Jordan & Susan Whetnall (Eng)
1970	David Eddy & Margaret Beck (Eng)
1972	Derek Talbot & Gillian Gilks (Eng)
1974	Derek Talbot & Gillian Gilks (Eng)
1976	Derek Talbot & Gillian Gilks (Eng)
1978	Mike Tredgett & Nora Perry (Eng)
1980	Mike Tredgett & Nora Perry (Eng)
1982	Martin Dew & Gillian Gilks (Eng)
1984	Martin Dew & Gillian Gilks (Eng)
1986	Martin Dew & Gillian Gilks (Eng)
1988	Steen Fladberg & Gillian Clark (Den & Eng)
1990	Jon Holst-Christensen & Grete Morgensen (Den)
1992	Thomas Lund & Pernille Dupont (Den)

Team

1972	England	1980	Denmark	1988	Denmark
1974	England	1982	England	1990	Denmark
1976	Denmark	1984	England	1992	Sweden
1978	England	1986	Denmark	1993	

World Champions

Singles

Year	Men	Women
1977	Flemming Delfs (Den)	Lene Køppen (Den)
1980	Rudy Hartono (Indo)	Verawaty Wiharjo (Indo)
1983	Icuk Sugiarto (Indo)	Li Lingwei (Chi)
1985	Hang Jian (Chi)	Han Aiping (Chi)
1987	Yang Yang (Chi)	Han Aiping (Chi)
1989	Yang Yang (Chi)	Li Lingwei (Chi)
1991	Zhao Jianhua (Chi)	Tang Jiuhong (Chi)
1993	Joko Suprianto (Indo)	Susi Susanti (Indo)

Men's Doubles

1977	Tjun Tjun & Johan Wahjudi (Indo)
1980	Christian Hadinata & Ade Chandra (Indo)
1983	Steen Fladberg & Jesper Helledie (Den)
1985	Joo Bong Park & Moon Soo Kim (Kor)
1987	Li Yongbo & Tian Bingyi (Chi)
1989	Li Yongbo & Tian Bingyi (Chi)
1991	Joo Bong Park & Moon Soo Kim (Kor)
1993	Ricky Subagja & Rudy Gunawan (Indo)

Women's Doubles

1977	Etsuko Toganoo & Emiko Veno (Jap)
1980	Nora Perry & Jane Webster (Eng)
1983	Lin Ying & Wu Dixi (Chi)
1985	Han Aiping & Li Lingwei (Chi)
1987	Lin Ying & Guan Weizhen (Chi)
1989	Ling Ying & Guan Weizhen (Chi)
1991	Guan Weizhen & Nong Qunhua (Chi)
1993	Nong Qunhua & Zhou Lei (Chi)

Mixed Doubles

1977	Steen Skovgaard & Lene Køppen (Den)
1980	Christian Hadinata & Imelda Wigoeno (Indo)
1983	Thomas Kihlström (Swe) & Nora Perry (Eng)
1985	Joo Bong Park & Sang Hee Yoo (Kor)
1987	Wang Pengren & Shi Fangjing (Chi)
1989	Joo Bong Park & Myeong Hee Chung (Kor)
1991	Joo Bong Park & Myeong Hee Chung (Kor)
1993	Thomas Lund (Den) & Catrine Bengtsson (Swe)

BASKETBALL

English Basketball Association National Champions

Year	Men	Year	Women
1981	Sunderland	1981	Southgate
1982	Crystal Palace	1982	Southgate
1983	Sunderland	1983	Southgate
1984	Solent	1984	A.C. Northampton
1985	Manchester United	1985	A.C. Northampton
1986	Kingston	1986	Crystal Palace
1987	BCP London	1987	A.C. Northampton
1988	Murray Livingston	1988	Stockport
1989	Glasgow Rangers	1989	Northampton
1990	Kingston	1990	Northampton
1991	Kingston	1991	Crystal Palace
1992	Kingston	1992	Thames Valley
1993	Woking	1993	Sheffield

European Champions

Year	Men	Year	Women
1935	Latvia	1938	Italy
1937	Lithuania	–	–
1939	Lithuania	–	–
1946	Czechoslovakia	–	–
1947	USSR	–	–
1949	Egypt	1950	USSR
1951	USSR	1952	USSR
1953	USSR	1954	USSR
1955	Hungary	1956	USSR
1957	USSR	1958	Bulgaria
1959	USSR	1960	USSR
1961	USSR	1962	USSR
1963	USSR	1964	USSR
1965	USSR	1966	USSR
1967	USSR	1968	USSR
1969	USSR	1970	USSR
1971	USSR	1972	USSR
1973	Yugoslavia	1974	USSR
1975	Yugoslavia	1976	USSR
1977	Yugoslavia	1978	USSR
1979	USSR	1980	USSR
1981	USSR	1981	USSR
1983	Italy	1983	USSR
1985	USSR	1985	USSR
1987	Greece	1987	USSR
1989	Yugoslavia	1989	USSR
1991	Yugoslavia	1991	USSR
1993	Germany	1993	Spain

World Champions

Year	Men	Year	Women
1950	Argentina	1953	USA
1954	USA	1957	USA
1959	Brazil	1959	USSR
1963	Brazil	1964	USSR
1967	USSR	1967	USSR
1970	Yugoslavia	1971	USSR
1974	USSR	1975	USSR
1978	Yugoslavia	1979	USA
1982	USSR	1983	USSR
1986	USA	1987	USA
1990	Yugoslavia	1990	USA

BOXING

Boxing Champions by Classes

As of Aug. 1992 the only generally accepted title holder was in the heavyweight division. There are numerous governing bodies in boxing, including the World Boxing Council, the World Boxing Assn., the International Boxing Federation, the United States Boxing Assn., the North American Boxing Federation and the European Boxing Union. Other organizations are recognized by TV networks and the print media. All the governing bodies have their own champions and assorted boxing divisions. The following are the recognized champions in the principal divisions of the World Boxing Association, the World Boxing Council, the International Boxing Federation and the World Boxing Organization.

Class	WBA	WBC	IBF	WBO
Heavyweight	Riddick Bowe (US)	Lennox Lewis (GB)	Riddick Bowe (US)	Tony Morrison (US)
Cruiserweight	Bobby Cruz (US)	Anaciet Wamba (Fr)	Alfred Cole (US)	Nestor Giovannini (Arg)
Light Heavyweight	Vergil Hill (US)	Jeff Harding (Aus)	Henry Maske (Ger)	Leon Leonzer-Barber (US)
Super Middleweight	Michael Nunn (US)	Nigel Benn (GB)	Chris Eubank (GB)	Chris Eubank (GB)
Middleweight	Reggie Johnson (US)	Gerald McClellan (US)	Roy Jones (US)	Chris Pyatt (GB)
Junior Middleweight	Julio Caesar Vasquez (Arg)	Terry Norris (US)	Gianfranco Rossi (It)	—
Welterweight	Christiano España (Ven)	Buddy McGirt (US)	Felix Trinidad (PR)	Gert Bow Jacobsen (Den)
Junior Welterweight	Juan Coggi (Arg)	Pernell Whitaker (US)	Charles Murray (US)	Zack Padilla (PR)
Lightweight............	Dingaan Thobela (SA)	Miguel Angel Gonzalez (Mex)	Freddie Pendleton (US)	Giovanni Paris (It)

(Continued)

Class	WBA	WBC	IBF	WBO
Junior Lightweight.....	Enaro Hernandez (US)	vacant	John-John Molina (PR)	—
Featherweight........	Yung Kyun Park (Kor)	Gregorio Vargas (Mex)	Tom Johnson (US)	Steve Robinson (GB)
Junior Featherweight ..	Wilfredo Vasquez (Pu Ri)	Tracey Patterson (US)	Kennedy McKinney (US)	—
Super Bantamweight ..	—	—	—	Daniel Jimenez (PR)
Bantamweight........	Jorge E. Julio (Col)	Jungil Byon (S Kor)	Orlando Canizales (US)	Rafael del Valle (PR)
Flyweight............	David Griman (Ven)	Yuri Arbachakov (Jap)	Pichit Sithbang (Thai)	Jacob Mantala (SA)

Ring Champions by Years

*Abandoned title

Heavyweights

1882-1892	John L. Sullivan (a)
1892-1897	James J. Corbett (b)
1897-1899	Robert Fitzsimmons
1899-1905	James J. Jeffries (c)
1905-1906	Marvin Hart
1906-1908	Tommy Burns
1908-1915	Jack Johnson
1915-1919	Jess Willard
1919-1926	Jack Dempsey
1926-1928	Gene Tunney*
1928-1930	vacant
1930-1932	Max Schmeling
1932-1933	Jack Sharkey
1933-1934	Primo Carnera
1934-1935	Max Baer
1935-1937	James J. Braddock
1937-1949	Joe Louis*
1949-1951	Ezzard Charles
1951-1952	Joe Walcott
1952-1956	Rocky Marciano*
1956-1959	Floyd Patterson
1959-1960	Ingemar Johansson
1960-1962	Floyd Patterson
1962-1964	Sonny Liston
1964-1967	Cassius Clay* (Muhammad Ali) (d)
1970-1973	Joe Frazier
1973-1974	George Foreman
1974-1978	Muhammad Ali
1978-1979	Leon Spinks (e), Muhammad Ali*
1978	Ken Norton (WBC, Larry Holmes (WBC) (f)
1979	John Tate (WBA)
1980	Mike Weaver (WBA)
1982	Michael Dokes (WBA)
1983	Gerrie Coetzee (WBA)
1984	Tim Witherspoon (WBC); Pinklon Thomas (WBC); Greg Page (WBA)
1985	Tony Tubbs (WBA); Michael Spinks (IBF)
1986	Tim Witherspoon (WBA); Trevor Berbick (WBC); Mike Tyson (WBC); James (Bone-Crusher) Smith (WBA).
1987	Mike Tyson (WBA).
1990	James "Buster" Douglas (WBA, WBC, IBF)
1990	Evander Holyfield (WBA, WBC, IBF)
1993	Riddick Bowe (WBA, IBF, WBC); Lennox Lewis (WBC)(g); Tony Morrison (WBO)

(a) London Prize Ring (bare knuckle champion. (b) First Marquis of Queensberry champion. (c) Jeffries abandoned the title (1905) and designated Marvin Hart and Jack Root as logical contenders. Hart defeated Root in 12 rounds (1905) and in turn was defeated by Tommy Burns (1906) who laid claim to the title. Jack Johnson defeated Burns (1908) and was recognized as champion. He clinched the title by defeating Jeffries in an attempted comeback (1910). (d) Title declared vacant by the WBA and other groups in 1967 after Clay's refusal to fulfil his military obligation. Joe Frazier was recognized as champion by 6 states, Mexico, and S. America. Jimmy Ellis was declared champion by the WBA. Frazier KOd Ellis, Feb. 16, 1970. (e) After Spinks defeated Ali, the WBC recognized Ken Norton as champion. Norton subsequently lost his title to Larry Holmes. (f) Holmes was stripped of his WBC title in 1984. He was the IBF champion when he lost to Michael Spinks. (g) Lewis was named WBC champion when Bowe refused to fight him.

Light Heavyweights

1903	Jack Root, George Gardner
1903-1905	Bob Fitzsimmons
1905-1912	Philadelphia Jack O'Brien*
1912-1916	Jack Dillon
1916-1920	Battling Levinsky
1920-1922	George Carpentier
1922-1923	Battling Siki
1923-1925	Mike McTigue
1925-1926	Paul Berlenbach
1926-1927	Jack Delaney*
1927-1929	Tommy Loughran*
1930-1934	Maxey Rosenbloom
1934-1935	Bob Olin
1935-1939	John Henry Lewis*
1939	Melio Bettina
1939-1941	Billy Conn*
1941	Anton Christoforidis (won NBA title)
1941-1948	Gus Lesnevich, Freddie Mills
1948-1950	Freddie Mills
1950-1952	Joey Maxim
1952-1960	Archie Moore
1961-1962	vacant
1962-1963	Harold Johnson
1963-1965	Willie Pastrano
1965-1966	Jose Torres
1966-1968	Dick Tiger
1968-1974	Bob Foster*, John Conteh (WBA)
1975-1977	John Conteh (WBC), Miguel Cuello (WBC), Victor Galindez (WBA)
1978	Mike Rossman (WBA), Mate Parlov (WBC), Marvin Johnson (WBC)
1979	Victor Galindez (WBA), Matthew Saad Muhammac (WBC)
1980	Eddie Mustava Muhammad (WBA)
1981	Michael Spinks (WBA), Dwight Braxton (WBC)
1983	Michael Spinks
1986	Marvin Johnson (WBA); Dennis Andries (WBC)
1987	Thomas Hearns (WBC); Leslie Stewart (WBA); Virgil Hill (WBA); Don Lalonde (WBC).
1988	Ray Leonard* (WBC)
1989	Jeff Harding (WBC)
1990	Dennis Andries (WBC)
1991	Thomas Hearns (WBA); Jeff Harding (WBC)
1992	Iran Barkley (WBA)
1993	Vergil Hill (WBA); Jeff Harding (WBC); Henry Maske (IBF); Leon Leonzer-Barber (WBO)

Middleweights

1884-1891	Jack "Nonpareil" Dempsey
1891-1897	Bob Fitzsimmons*
1897-1907	Tommy Ryan*
1907-1908	Stanley Ketchel, Billy Papke
1908-1910	Stanley Ketchel
1911-1913	vacant
1913	Frank Klaus, George Chip
1914-1917	Al McCoy
1917-1920	Mike O'Dowd
1920-1923	Johnny Wilson
1923-1926	Harry Greb
1926-1931	Tiger Flowers, Mickey Walker
1931-1932	Gorilla Jones (NBA)
1932-1937	Marcel Thil
1938	Al Hostak (NBA), Solly Krieger (NBA)
1939-1940	Al Hostak (NBA)
1941-1947	Tony Zale
1947-1948	Rocky Graziano
1948	Tony Zale, Marcel Cerdan
1949-1951	Jake LaMotta
1951	Ray Robinson, Randy Turpin, Ray Robinson*
1953-1955	Carl (Bobo) Olson
1955-1957	Ray Robinson
1957	Gene Fullmer, Ray Robinson, Carmen Basilio
1958	Ray Robinson
1959	Gene Fullmer (NBA); Ray Robinson (N.Y.)
1960	Gene Fullmer (NBA); Paul Pender (New York and Mass.)
1961	Gene Fullmer (NBA); Terry Downes (New York, Mass., Europe)
1962	Gene Fullmer, Dick Tiger (NBA), Paul Pender (New York and Mass.)*
1963	Dick Tiger (universal).
1963-1965	Joey Giardello
1965-1966	Dick Tiger
1966-1967	Emile Griffith
1967	Nino Benvenuti
1967-1968	Emile Griffith
1968-1970	Nino Benvenuti
1970-1977	Carlos Monzon*
1977-1978	Rodrigo Valdez

(Continued)

(Ring Champions by Years contd.)

1978-1979	Hugo Corro
1979-1980	Vito Antuofermo
1980	Alan Minter, Marvin Hagler
1987	Ray Leonard* (WBC); Thomas Hearns (WBC); Sumbu Kalambay (WBA.
1988	Iran Barkley (WBC)
1989	Mike McCallum (WBA); Roberto Duran (WBC)
1991	Julian Jackson (WBC)
1992	Reggie Johnson (WBA)
1993	Reggie Johnson (WBA); Gerald McClellan (WBC); Roy Jones (IBF); Chris Pyatt (WBO)

Welterweights

1892-1894	Mysterious Billy Smith
1894-1896	Tommy Ryan
1896	Kid McCoy*
1900	Rube Ferns, Matty Matthews
1901	Rube Ferns
1901-1904	Joe Walcott
1904-1906	Dixie Kid, Joe Walcott, Honey Mellody
1907-1911	Mike Sullivan
1911-1915	vacant
1915-1919	Ted Lewis
1919-1922	Jack Britton
1922-1926	Mickey Walker
1926	Pete Latzo
1927-1929	Joe Dundee
1929	Jackie Fields
1930	Jack Thompson, Tommy Freeman
1931	Freeman, Thompson, Lou Brouillard
1932	Jackie Fields
1933	Young Corbett, Jimmy McLarnin
1934	Barney Ross, Jimmy McLarnin
1935-1938	Barney Ross
1938-1940	Henry Armstrong
1940-1941	Fritzie Zivic
1941-1946	Fred Cochrane
1946-1948	Marty Servo*; Ray Robinson (a)
1948-1950	Ray Robinson*
1951	Johnny Bratton (NBA)
1951-1954	Kid Gavilan
1954-1955	Johnny Saxton
1955	Tony De Marco, Carmen Basilio
1956	Carmen Basilio, Johnny Saxton, Basilio
1957	Carmen Basilio*
1958-1960	Virgil Akins, Don Jordan
1960	Benny Paret
1961	Emile Griffith, Benny Paret
1962	Emile Griffith
1963	Luis Rodriguez, Emile Griffith
1964-1966	Emile Griffith*
1966-1969	Curtis Cokes
1969-1970	Jose Napoles, Billy Backus
1971-1975	Jose Napoles
1975-1976	John Stracey (WBC), Angel Espada (WBA)
1976-1979	Carlos Palomino (WBC), Jose Cuevas (WBA)
1979	Wilfredo Benitez (WBC), Sugar Ray Leonard (WBC)
1980	Roberto Duran (WBC), Thomas Hearns (WBA), Sugar Ray Leonard (WBC)
1981-1982	Sugar Ray Leonard*
1983	Donald Curry (WBA); Milton McCrory (WBC)
1985	Donald Curry
1986	Lloyd Honeyghan (WBC)
1987	Mark Breland (WBA); Marlon Starling (WBA); Jorge Vaca (WBC).
1988	Tomas Molinares (WBA); Lloyd Honeyghan (WBC).
1989	Marlon Starling (WBC); Mark Breland (WBA)
1990	Maurice Blocker (WBC); Aaron Davis (WBA)
1991	Meldrick Taylor (WBA); Simon Brown (WBC); Buddy McGirt (WBC)
1993	Christiano España (WBA); Buddy McGirt (WBC); Felix Trinidad (IBF); Gert Bow Jacobsen (WBO)

(a) Robinson gained the title by defeating Tommy Bell in an elimination agreed to by the NY Commission and the NBA. Both claimed Robinson waived his title when he won the middleweight crown from LaMotta in 1951.

Lightweights

1896-1899	Kid Lavigne
1899-1902	Frank Erne
1902-1908	Joe Gans
1908-1910	Battling Nelson
1910-1912	Ad Wolgast
1912-1914	Willie Ritchie
1914-1917	Freddie Welsh
1917-1925	Benny Leonard*
1925	Jimmy Goodrich, Rocky Kansas
1926-1930	Sammy Mandell
1930	Al Singer, Tony Canzoneri
1930-1933	Tony Canzoneri
1933-1935	Barney Ross*
1935-1936	Tony Canzoneri
1936-1938	Lou Ambers
1938	Henry Armstrong
1939	Lou Ambers
1940	Lew Jenkins
1941-1943	Sammy Angott
1944	S. Angott (NBA), J. Zurita (NBA)
1945-1951	Ike Williams (NBA: later universal)
1951-1952	James Carter
1952	Lauro Salas, James Carter
1953-1954	James Carter
1954	Paddy De Marco; James Carter
1955	James Carter; Bud Smith
1956	Bud Smith, Joe Brown
1956-1962	Joe Brown
1962-1965	Carlos Ortiz
1965	Ismael Laguna
1965-1968	Carlos Ortiz
1968-1969	Teo Cruz
1969-1970	Mando Ramos
1970	Ismael Laguna, Ken Buchanan (WBA)
1971	Mando Ramos (WBC), Pedro Carrasco (WBC)
1972-1979	Roberto Duran* (WBA)
1972	Pedro Carrasco, Mando Ramos, Chango Carmona, Rodolfo Gonzalez (all WBC)
1974-1976	Guts Ishimatsu (WBC)
1976-1977	Esteban De Jesus (WBC)
1979	Jim Watt (WBC), Ernesto Espana (WBA)
1980	Hilmer Kenty (WBA)
1981	Alexis Arguello (WBC), Sean O'Grady (WBA), Arturo Frias (WBA)
1982-1984	Ray Mancini (WBA)
1983	Edwin Rosario (WBC)
1984	Livingstone Bramble (WBA); Jose Luis Ramirez (WBC)
1985	Hector (Macho) Camacho (WBC)
1986	Edwin Rosario (WBA); Jose Luis Ramirez (WBC).
1987	Julio Cesar Chavez (WBA).
1989	Edwin Rosario (WBA); Pernell Whitaker (WBC).
1990	Juan Nazario (WBA); Pernell Whitaker (WBA)
1992	Joey Gamache (WBA)
1993	Miguel Angel Gonzalez (WBC); Dingaan Thobela (WBA); Freddie Pendleton (IBF); Giovanni Paris (WBO)

Featherweights

1892-1900	George Dixon (disputed)
1900-1901	Terry McGovern, Young Corbett*
1901-1912	Abe Attell
1912-1923	Johnny Kilbane
1923	Eugene Criqui, Johnny Dundee
1923-1925	Johnny Dundee*
1925-1927	Kid Kaplan*
1927-1928	Benny Bass, Tony Canzoneri
1928-1929	Andre Routis
1929-1932	Battling Battalino*
1932-1934	Tommy Paul (NBA)
1933-1936	Freddie Miller
1936-1937	Petey Sarron
1937-1938	Henry Armstrong*
1938-1940	Joey Archibald (b)
1940-1941	Harry Jeffra
1942-1948	Willie Pep
1948-1949	Sandy Saddler
1949-1950	Willie Pep
1950-1957	Sandy Saddler*
1957-1959	Hogan (Kid) Bassey
1959-1963	Davey Moore
1963-1964	Sugar Ramos
1964-1967	Vicente Saldivar*
1968-1971	Paul Rojas (WBA), Sho Saljo (WBA)
1971	Antonio Gomez (WBA), Kuniaki Shibada (WBC)
1972	Ernesto Marcel* (WBA), Clemente Sanchez* (WBC), Jose Legra (WBC)
1973	Eder Jofre (WBC)
1974	Ruben Olivares (WBA), Alexis Arguello (WBA), Bobby Chacon (WBC)
1975	Ruben Olivares (WBC), David Kotey (WBC)
1976	Danny Lopez (WBC)
1977	Rafael Ortega (WBA)
1978	Cecilio Lastra (WBA), Eusebio Pedrosa (WBA)
1980	Salvador Sanchez (WBC)
1982	Juan LaPorte (WBC)

1984	Wilfredo Gomez (WBC); Azumah Nelson (WBC)
1985	Barry McGuigan (WBA)
1986	Steve Cruz (WBA)
1987	Antonio Esparragoza (WBA)
1988	Jeff Fenech (WBC)
1990	Marcos Villasana (WBC)
1991	Yung Kyun Park (WBA)
1991	Paul Hodkinson (WBA)
1993	Gregorio Vargas (WBC); Yung Kyun Park (WBA); Tom Johnson (IBF); Steve Robinson (WBO)

(b) After Petey Scalzo knocked out Archibald in an overweight match and was refused a title bout, the NBA named Scalzo champion. The NBA title succession: Scalzo, 1938-1941; Richard Lemos, 1941; Jackie Wilson, 1941-1943; Jackie Callura, 1943; Phil Terranova, 1943-1944; Sal Bartolo, 1944-1946.

British Champions 1992–93

Weight	Champions as at Aug. 10, 1993
Heavyweight	Herbie Hide
Cruiserweight	Carl Thompson
Light-heavyweight	Maurice Core
Super-middleweight	Vacant
Middleweight	Frank Grant
Light-middleweight	Andy Till
Welterweight	Gary Jacobs
Light-welterweight	Andy Holligan
Lightweight	Paul Burke
Super-featherweight	Neil Haddock
Featherweight	Vacant
Bantamweight	Drew Doherty
Flyweight	Francis Ampofo

Commonwealth Champions 1992–93

Weight	Champions as at Aug. 10, 1993
Heavyweight	Henry Akinwande (GB)
Cruiserweight	Vacant
Light-heavyweight	Brent Kosolofski (Can)
Super-middleweight	Henry Wharton (GB)
Middleweight	Richie Woodhall (GB)
Light-middleweight	Lloyd Honeyghan (GB)
Welterweight	Eamonn Loughran (GB)
Light-welterweight	Andy Holligan (GB)
Lightweight	Paul Burke (GB)
Super-featherweight	Tony Pep (Can)
Featherweight	Billy Hardy (GB)
Bantamweight	John Armour (GB)
Flyweight	Francis Ampofo (GB)

European Champions 1992–93

Weight	Champions as at Aug. 10, 1993
Heavyweight	Henry Akinwande (GB)
Cruiserweight	Massimiliano Duran (Ita)
Light-heavyweight	Eddie Smulders (Neth)
Super-middleweight	Ray Close (GB)
Middleweight	Agostino Cardamone (Ita)
Light-middleweight	Laurent Boudovani (Fra)
Welterweight	Gary Jacobs (GB)
Light-welterweight	Valery Kayumba (Fra)
Lightweight	Jean-Baptiste Mendy (Fra)
Super-featherweight	Jacobin Yoma (Fra)
Featherweight	Maurizio Stecca (Ita)
Bantamweight	Vincenzo Belcastro (Ita)
Flyweight	Vacant

History of Heavyweight Championship Bouts

*Title Changed Hands

1889—July 8—John L. Sullivan def. Jake Kilrain, 75, Richburg, Miss. Last championship bare knuckles bout.

***1892**—Sept. 7—James J. Corbett def. John L. Sullivan, 21, New Orleans. Big gloves used for first time.

1894—Jan. 25—James J. Corbett KOd Charley Mitchell, 3, Jacksonville, Fla.

***1897**—Bob Fitzsimmons def. James J. Corbett, 14, Carson City, Nev.

***1899**—June 9—James J. Jeffries def. Bob Fitzsimmons, 11, Coney Island, N.Y.

1899—Nov. 3—James J. Jeffries def. Tom Sharkey, 25, Coney Island, N.Y.

1900—May 11—James J. Jeffries KOd James J. Corbett, 23, Coney Island, N.Y.

1901—Nov. 15—James J. Jeffries KOd Gus Ruhlin, 5, San Francisco.

1902—July 25—James J. Jeffries KOd Bob Fitzsimmons, 8, San Francisco.

1903—Aug. 14—James J. Jeffries KOd James J. Corbett, 10, San Francisco.

1904—Aug. 26—James J. Jeffries KOd Jack Monroe, 2, San Francisco.

***1905**—James J. Jeffries retired, July 3—Marvin Hart KOd Jack Root, 12, Reno. Jeffries refereed and presented the title to the victor. Jack O'Brien also claimed the title.

***1906**—Feb. 23—Tommy Burns def. Marvin Hart, 20, Los Angeles.

1906—Nov. 28—Philadelphia Jack O'Brien and Tommy Burns, 20, draw, Los Angeles.

1907—May 8—Tommy Burns def. Jack O'Brien, 20, Los Angeles.

1907—July 4—Tommy Burns KOd Bill Squires, 1, Colma, Cal.

1907—Dec. 2—Tommy Burns KOd Gunner Moir, 10, London.

1908—Feb. 10—Tommy Burns KOd Jack Palmer, 4, London.

1908—March 17—Tommy Burns KOd Jem Roche, 1, Dublin.

1908—April 18—Tommy Burns KOd Jewey Smith, 5, Paris.

1908—June 13—Tommy Burns KOd Bill Squires, 8, Paris.

1908—Aug. 24—Tommy Burns KOd Bill Squires, 13, Sydney, New South Wales.

1908—Sept. 2—Tommy Burns KOd Bill Lang, 2, Melbourne, Australia.

***1908**—Dec. 26—Jack Johnson KOd Tommy Burns, 14, Sydney, Australia. Police halted contest.

1909—May 19—Jack Johnson and Jack O'Brien, 6, draw, Philadelphia.

1909—June 30—Jack Johnson and Tony Ross, 6, draw, Pittsburgh.

1909—Sept. 9—Jack Johnson and Al Kaufman, 10, draw, San Francisco.

1909—Oct. 16—Jack Johnson KOd Stanley Ketchel, 12, Colma, Cal.

1910—July 4—Jack Johnson KOd Jim Jeffries, 15, Reno, Nev. Jeffries came back from retirement.

1912—July 4—Jack Johnson def. Jim Flynn, 9, Las Vegas, N.M. Contest stopped by police.

1913—Nov. 28—Jack Johnson KOd Andre Spaul, 2, Paris.

1913—Dec. 9—Jack Johnson and Jim Johnson, 10, draw, Paris. Bout called a draw when Jack Johnson declared he had broken his arm.

1914—June 27—Jack Johnson def. Frank Moran, 20, Paris.

***1915**—April 5—Jess Willard KOd Jack Johnson, 26, Havana. Cuba.

1916—March 25—Jess Willard and Frank Moran, 10, draw, New York.

***1919**—July 4—Jack Dempsey KOd Jess Willard, Toledo, Oh. Willard failed to answer bell for 4th round.

1920—Sept. 6—Jack Dempsey KOd Billy Miske, 3, Benton Harbor, Mich.

1920—Dec. 14—Jack Dempsey KOd Bill Brennan, 12, New York.

(Continued)

(Heavyweight Championship Bouts contd.)

1921—July 2—Jack Dempsey KOd George Carpentier, 4, Boyle's Thirty Acres, Jersey City, N.J. Carpentier had held the so-called white heavyweight title since July 16, 1914, in a series established in 1913, after Jack Johnson's exile in Europe late in 1912.

1923—July 4—Jack Dempsey def. Tom Gibbons, 15, Shelby, Mont.

1923—Sept. 14—Jack Dempsey KOd Luis Firpo, 2, New York.

*1926—Sept. 23—Gene Tunney def. Jack Dempsey, 10, Philadelphia.

1927—Sept. 22—Gene Tunney def. Jack Dempsey, 10, Chicago.

1928—July 26—Gene Tunney KOd Tom Heeney, 11, New York; soon afterward he announced his retirement.

*1930—June 12—Max Schmeling def. Jack Sharkey, 4, New York. Sharkey fouled Schmeling in a bout which was generally considered to have resulted in the election of a successor to Gene Tunney, New York.

1931—July 3—Max Schmeling KOd Young Stribling, 15, Cleveland.

*1932—June 21—Jack Sharkey def. Max Schmeling, 15, New York.

*1933—June 29— Primo Carnera KOd Jack Sharkey, 6, New York.

1933—Oct. 22—Primo Carnera def. Paulino Uzcudun, 15, Rome.

1934—March 1—Primo Carnera def. Tommy Loughran, 15, Miami.

*1934—June 14—Max Baer KOd Primo Carnera, 11, New York.

*1935—June 13—James J. Braddock def. Max Baer, 15, New York.

*1937—June 22—Joe Louis KOd James J. Braddock, 8, Chicago.

1937—Aug. 30—Joe Louis def. Tommy Farr, 15, New York.

1938—Feb. 23—Joe Louis KOd Nathan Mann, 3, New York.

1938—April 1—Joe Louis KOd Harry Thomas, 5, Chicago.

1938—June 22—Joe Louis KOd Max Schmeling, 1, New York.

1939—Jan. 25—Joe Louis KOd John H. Lewis, 1, New York.

1939—April 17—Joe Louis KOd Jack Roper, 1, Los Angeles.

1939—June 28—Joe Louis KOd Tony Galento, 4, New York.

1939—Sept. 20—Joe Louis KOd Bob Pastor, 11, Detroit.

1940—February 9—Joe Louis def. Arturo Godoy, 15, New York.

1940—March 29—Joe Louis KOd Johnny Paycheck, 2, New York.

1940—June 20—Joe Louis KOd Arturo Godoy, 8, New York.

1940—Dec. 16—Joe Louis KOd Al McCoy, 6, Boston.

1941—Jan. 31—Joe Louis KOd Red Burman, 5, New York.

1941—Feb. 17—Joe Louis KOd Gus Dorzalo, 2, Philadelphia.

1941—March 21—Joe Louis KOd Abe Simon, 13, Detroit.

1941—April 8—Joe Louis KOd Tony Musto, 9, St. Louis.

1941—May 23—Joe Louis def. Buddy Baer, 7, Washington, D.C., on a disqualification.

1941—June 18—Joe Louis KOd Billy Conn, 13, New York.

1941—Sept. 29—Joe Louis KOd Lou Nova, 6, New York.

1942—Jan. 9—Joe Louis KOd Buddy Baer, 1, New York.

1942—March 27—Joe Louis KOd Abe Simon, 6, New York.

1946—June 19—Joe Louis KOd Billy Conn, 8, New York.

1946—Sept. 18—Joe Louis KOd Tami Mauriello, 1, New York.

1947—Dec. 5—Joe Louis def. Joe Walcott, 15, New York.

1948—June 25—Joe Louis KOd Joe Walcott, 11, New York.

*1949—June 22—Following Joe Louis's retirement Ezzard Charles def. Joe Walcott, 15, Chicago, NBA recognition only.

1949—Aug. 10—Ezzard Charles KOd Gus Lesnevich, 7, New York.

1949—Oct. 14—Ezzard Charles KOd Pat Valentino, 8, San Francisco; clinched American title.

1950—Aug. 15—Ezzard Charles KOd Freddy Beshore, 14, Buffalo.

1950—Sept. 27—Ezzard Charles def. Joe Louis in latter's attempted comeback, 15, New York; universal recognition.

1950—Dec. 5—Ezzard Charles KOd Nick Barone, 11, Cincinnati.

1951—Jan. 12—Ezzard Charles KOd Lee Oma, 10, New York.

1951—March 7—Ezzard Charles def. Joe Walcott, 15, Detroit.

1951—May 30—Ezzard Charles def. Joey Maxim, light heavyweight champion, 15, Chicago.

*1951—July 18—Joe Walcott KOd Ezzard Charles, 7, Pittsburgh.

1952—June 5—Joe Walcott def. Ezzard Charles, 15, Philadelphia.

*1952—Sept. 23—Rocky Marciano KOd Joe Walcott, 13, Philadelphia.

1953—May 15—Rocky Marciano KOd Joe Walcott, 1, Chicago.

1953—Sept. 24—Rocky Marciano KOd Roland LaStarza, 11, New York.

1954—June 17—Rocky Marciano def. Ezzard Charles, 15, New York.

1954—Sept. 17—Rocky Marciano KOd Ezzard Charles, 8, New York.

1955—May 16—Rocky Marciano KOd Don Cockell, 9, San Francisco.

1955—Sept. 21—Rocky Marciano KOd Archie Moore, 9, New York. Marciano retired undefeated, Apr. 27, 1956.

*1956—Nov. 30—Floyd Patterson KOd Archie Moore, 5, Chicago.

1957—July 29—Floyd Patterson KOd Hurricane Jackson, 10, New York.

1957—Aug. 22—Floyd Patterson KOd Pete Rademacher, 6, Seattle.

1958—Aug. 18—Floyd Patterson KOd Roy Harris, 12, Los Angeles.

1959—May 1—Floyd Patterson KOd Brian London, 11, Indianapolis.

*1959—June 26—Ingemar Johansson KOd Floyd Patterson, 3, New York.

*1960—June 20—Floyd Patterson KOd Ingemar Johansson, 5, New York. First heavyweight in boxing history to regain title.

1961—Mar. 13—Floyd Patterson KOd Ingemar Johansson, 6, Miami Beach.

1961—Dec. 4—Floyd Patterson KOd Tom McNeeley, 4, Toronto.

*1962—Sept. 25—Sonny Liston KOd Floyd Patterson, 1, Chicago.

1963—July 22—Sonny Liston KOd Floyd Patterson, 1, Las Vegas.

*1964—Feb. 25—Cassius Clay KOd Sonny Liston, 7, Miami Beach.

1965—May 25—Cassius Clay KOd Sonny Liston, 1, Lewiston, Maine.

1965—Nov. 11—Cassius Clay KOd Floyd Patterson, 12, Las Vegas.

1966—Mar. 29—Cassius Clay def. George Chuvalo, 15, Toronto.

1966—May 21—Cassius Clay KOd Henry Cooper, 6, London.

1966—Aug. 6—Cassius Clay KOd Brian London, 3, London.

1966—Sept. 10—Cassius Clay KOd Karl Mildenberger, 12, Frankfurt, Germany.

1966—Nov. 14—Cassius Clay KOd Cleveland Williams, 3, Houston.

1967—Feb. 6—Cassius Clay def. Ernie Terrell, 15, Houston.

1967—Mar. 22—Cassius Clay KOd Zora Folley, 7, New York. Clay was stripped of his title by the WBA and others for refusing military service.

*1970—Feb. 16—Joe Frazier KOd Jimmy Ellis, 5, New York.

1970—Nov. 18—Joe Frazier KOd Bob Foster, 2, Detroit.

1971—Mar. 8—Joe Frazier def. Cassius Clay (Muhammad Ali), 15, New York.

1972—Jan. 15—Joe Frazier KOd Terry Daniels, 4, New Orleans.

1972—May 25—Joe Frazier KOd Ron Stander, 5, Omaha.

*1973—Jan. 22—George Foreman KOd Joe Frazier, 2, Kingston, Jamaica.

1973—Sept. 1—George Foreman KOd Joe Roman, 1, Tokyo.

1974—Mar. 3—George Foreman KOd Ken Norton, 2, Caracas.

*1974—Oct. 30—Muhammad Ali KOd George Foreman, 8, Zaire.

1975—Mar. 24—Muhammad Ali KOd Chuck Wepner, 15, Cleveland.

1975—May 16—Muhammad Ali KOd Ron Lyle, 11, Las Vegas.

1975—June 30—Muhammad Ali def. Joe Bugner, 15, Malaysia.

1975—Oct. 1—Muhammad Ali KOd Joe Frazier, 14, Manila.

1976—Feb. 20—Muhammad Ali KOd Jean-Pierre Coopman, 5, San Juan.

1976—Apr. 30—Muhammad Ali def. Jimmy Young, 15, Landover, Md.

1976—May 25—Muhammad Ali KOd Richard Dunn, 5, Munich.

1976—Sept. 28—Muhammad Ali def. Ken Norton, 15, New York.

1977—May 16—Muhammad Ali def. Alfredo Evangelista, 15, Landover, Md.

1977—Sept. 29—Muhammad Ali def. Earnie Shavers, 15, New York.

*1978—Feb. 15—Leon Spinks def. Muhammad Ali, 15, Las Vegas.

*1978—Sept. 15—Muhammad Ali def. Leon Spinks, 15, New Orleans. Ali retired in 1979.

(Bouts when title changed hands only)

*1978—June 9—(WBC) Larry Holmes def. Ken Norton, 15, Las Vegas.

*1980—Mar. 31—(WBA) Mike Weaver KOd John Tate, 15, Knoxville.

*1982—Dec. 10—(WBA) Michael Dokes KOd Mike Weaver, 1, Las Vegas.

*1983—Sept. 23—(WBA) Gerrie Coetzee KOd Michael Dokes, 10, Richfield, Oh.

*1984—Mar. 10—(WBC) Tim Witherspoon def. Greg Page, 12, Las Vegas, Nev.

*1984—Aug. 31—(WBC) Pinklon Thomas def. Tim Witherspoon, 12, Las Vegas, Nev.

*1984—Dec. 2—(WBA) Greg Page KOd Gerrie Coetzee, 8, Sun City, Bophuthatswana

*1985—Apr. 29—(WBA) Tony Tubbs def. Greg Page, 15, Buffalo, N.Y.

(Continued)

*1985—Sept. 21—(IBF) Michael Spinks def. Larry Holmes, 15, Las Vegas, Nev.

*1986—Jan. 17—(WBA) Tim Witherspoon def. Tony Tubbs, 15, Atlanta, Ga.

*1986—Mar. 23—(WBC) Trevor Berbick def. Pinklon Thomas, 12, Miami, Fla.

*1986—Nov. 22—(WBC) Mike Tyson KOd Trevor Berbick, 2, Las Vegas.

*1986—Dec. 12—(WBA) James (Bonecrusher) Smith KOd Tim Witherspoon, 1, New York.

*1987—Mar. 7—(WBA) Mike Tyson def. James (Bonecrusher) Smith, 12, Las Vegas.

*1988—June 27—(IBF) Mike Tyson KOd Michael Spinks, 1, Atlantic City.

*1990—Feb. 11—(WBA, WBC, IBF) James "Buster" Douglas KOd Mike Tyson, 10, Tokyo.

*1990—Oct. 25—(WBA, WBC, IBF) Evander Holyfield KOd James "Buster" Douglas, 3, Las Vegas.

1992—Nov. 13—(WBA, WBC, IBF) Riddick Bowe def. Evander Holyfield, 12, Las Vegas.

1993—Oct. 2—(WBC) Lennox Lewis def. Frank Bruno, 7, Cardiff.

CHESS

British Chess Federation Champions

Year and Venue		Men	Women
1904	Hastings	W. E. Napier	Miss K. B. Finn
1905	Southport	H. E. Atkins	Miss K. B. Finn
1906	Shrewsbury	H. E. Atkins	Mrs F. D. Herring
1907	Crystal Palace	H. E. Atkins	Mrs F. D. Herring
1908	Tunbridge W.	H. E. Atkins	Mrs A. L. Curling
1909	Scarborough	H. E. Atkins	Mrs D. L. Anderson
1910	Oxford	H. E. Atkins	Mrs H. M. Houlding
1911	Glasgow	H. E. Atkins	Mrs H. M. Houlding
1912	Richmond	R. C. Griffith	Mrs D. L. Anderson
1913	Cheltenham	F. D. Yates	Mrs A. N. G. Moseley
1914	Chester	F. D. Yates	Mrs H. M. Houlding
1915–18		No contest	No contest
1919	Hastings	No contest	Mrs S. J. Holloway
1920	Edinburgh	R. H. V. Scott	Mrs A. Stephenson
1921	Malvern	F. D. Yates	Mrs D. L. Anderson
1922	London	No contest	Miss E. C. Price
1923	Southsea	Sir G. A. Thomas, Bt.	Miss E. C. Price
1924	Southport	H. E. Atkins	Miss E. C. Price
1925	Stratford on A.	H. E. Atkins	Mrs A. Stephenson
1926	Edinburgh	F. D. Yates	Mrs A. Stephenson
1927	London	No contest	No contest
1928	Tenby	F. D. Yates	Miss E. C. Price
1929	Ramsgate	Mir Sultan Khan	Miss M. D. Gilchrist
1930	Scarborough	No contest	Mrs A. Stephenson
1931	Worcester	F. D. Yates	Mrs R. P. Michell & Mrs T. Wheelwright
1932	London	Mir Sultan Khan	Mrs R. P. Michell
1933	Hastings	Mir Sultan Khan	Miss Fatima
1934	Chester	Sir G. A. Thomas, Bt.	Miss M. D. Gilchrist
1935	Yarmouth	W. Winter	Mrs R. P. Michell
1936	Bournemouth	W. Winter	Mrs S. J. Holloway
1937	Blackpool	W. A. Fairhurst	Miss R. M. Drew
1938	Brighton	C. H. O'D. Alexander	Miss M. Musgrave
1939	Bournemouth	No contest	Miss E. Saunders
1940–45		No contest	No contest
1946	Nottingham	R. F. Combe	Miss E. Saunders
1947	Harrogate	H. Golombek	Miss E. Tranmer
1948	London	R. J. Broadbent	Miss E. C. Price
1949	Felixstowe	H. Golombek	Miss E. Tranmer
1950	Buxton	R. J. Broadbent	Mrs R. M. Bruce
1951	Swansea	E. Klein	Mrs R. M. Bruce
1952	Chester	R. G. Wade	No contest
1953	Hastings	D. A. Yanofsky	Miss E. Tranmer
1954	Nottingham	L. W. Barden & A. Phillips	Mrs R. M. Bruce
1955	Aberystwyth	H. Golombek	Miss J. F. Doulton & Mrs R. M. Bruce
1956	Blackpool	C. H. O'D. Alexander	Mrs E. Pritchard
1957	Leamington	J. Penrose	Capt P. A. Sunnucks
1958	Plymouth	Dr S. Fazekas	Capt P. A. Sunnucks
1959	York	J. Penrose	Mrs R. M. Bruce
1960	Leicester	J. Penrose	Mrs R. M. Bruce
1961	Aberystwyth	J. Penrose	Miss E. Tranmer
1962	Whitby	J. Penrose	Mrs R. M. Bruce
1953	Bath	J. Penrose	Mrs R. M. Bruce
1964	Whitby	M. J. Haygarth	Capt P. A. Sunnucks
1965	Hastings	P. N. Lee	Mrs E. Pritchard
1966	Sunderland	Dr J. Penrose	Mrs M. E. E. Clarke & Miss G. Moore
1967	Oxford	Dr J. Penrose	Mrs R. M. Bruce & Miss D. Dobson
1968	Bristol	Dr J. Penrose	Miss D. Dobson
1969	Rhyl	Dr J. Penrose	Mrs R. M. Bruce & Miss D. Dobson
1970	Coventry	R. G. Wade	Mrs J. Hartston
1971	Blackpool	R. D. Keene	Mrs J. Hartston
1972	Brighton	B. R. Eley	Mrs J. Hartston
1973	Eastbourne	W. R. Hartston	Mrs J. Hartston
1974	Clacton	G. S. Botterill	Mrs J. Hartston
1975	Morecambe	W. R. Hartston	Miss S. Jackson
1976	Portsmouth	A. J. Mestel	Dr J. Hartston
1977	Brighton	G. S. Botterill	Dr J. Hartston
1978	Ayr	J. S. Speelman	Miss S. Jackson
1979	Chester	R. Bellin	Dr J. Miles
1980	Brighton	Dr J. D. M. Nunn	Miss S. Jackson
1981	Morecambe	P. E. Littlewood	Miss S. Jackson
1982	Torquay	A. J. Miles	Miss J. Garwell
1983	Southport	A. J. Mestel	Mrs R. Hamid & Mrs H. Milligan
1984	Brighton	N. D. Short	Miss B. Sathe & Mrs V. Unni
1985	Edinburgh	J. S. Speelman	Mrs R. Hamid
1986	Southampton	J. S. Speelman	Mrs S. K. Arkell
1987	Swansea	N. D. Short	Miss C. Forbes
1988	Blackpool	A. J. Mestel	Miss C. Forbes
1989	Plymouth	M. Adams	Mrs R. Hamid
1990	Eastbourne	H. J. Plaskett	Mrs S. K. Arkell
1991	Eastbourne	J. M. Hodgson	Mrs S. K. Arkell
1992	Plymouth	J. M. Hodgson	Mrs S. K. Arkell
1993	Dundee	M. Hennigan	Miss S. Dahr

World Champions

Men

The best players of their time, regarded by later generations as world champions, were François Philidor, Alexandre Deschappelles, Louis de la Bourdonnais, all France; Howard Staunton, England; Adolph Anderssen, Germany and Paul Morphy, U.S. In 1866 Wilhelm Steinitz defeated Adolph Anderssen and claimed the world champion title. Official world champions since the title was first used follow:

1866–1894	Wilhelm Steinitz, Austria
1894–1921	Emanuel Lasker, Germany
1921–1927	Jose R. Capablanca, Cuba
1927–1935	Alexander A. Alekhine, France
1935–1937	Max Euwe, Netherlands
1937–1946	Alexander A. Alekhine, France
1948–1957	Mikhail Botvinnik, USSR
1957–1958	Vassily Smyslov, USSR
1958–1959	Mikhail Botvinnik, USSR
1960–1961	Mikhail Tal, USSR
1961–1963	Mikhail Botvinnik, USSR
1963–1969	Tigran Petrosian, USSR
1969–1972	Boris Spassky, USSR
1972–1975	Bobby Fischer, U.S. (a)
1975–1985	Anatoly Karpov, USSR
1985	Gary Kasparov, USSR

(a) Defaulted championship after refusal to accept International Chess Federation rules for a championship match, April 1975.

(World Chess Champions contd.)

Women

1927–1939	Vera Menchik, USSR	**1958–1962**	Elizaveta Bikova, USSR
1949–1953	Ludmila Rudenko, USSR	**1962–1978**	Nona Gaprinandashvili, USSR
1953–1956	Elizaveta Bikova, USSR	**1978–1991**	Maya Chiburdanidze, USSR
1956–1958	Olga Rubtsova, USSR	**1991**	Xie Jun, China

CRICKET

Benson and Hedges Cup Winners

Year	Winner	Runner-up	Margin	Year	Winner	Runner-up	Margin
1972	Leicestershire	Yorkshire	5 wickets	1984	Lancashire	Warwickshire	6 wickets
1973	Kent	Worcestershire	39 runs	1985	Leicestershire	Essex	5 wickets
1974	Surrey	Leicestershire	27 runs	1986	Middlesex	Kent	2 runs
1975	Leicestershire	Middlesex	5 wickets	1987	Yorkshire	Northants	Fewer wickets lost (scores level)
1976	Kent	Worcestershire	43 runs				
1977	Gloucestershire	Kent	64 runs				
1978	Kent	Derbyshire	6 wickets	1988	Hampshire	Derbyshire	7 wickets
1979	Essex	Surrey	35 runs	1989	Nottinghamshire	Essex	3 wickets
1980	Northants	Essex	6 runs	1990	Lancashire	Worcestershire	69 runs
1981	Somerset	Surrey	7 wickets	1991	Worcestershire	Lancashire	65 runs
1982	Somerset	Nottinghamshire	9 wickets	1992	Hampshire	Kent	41 runs
1983	Middlesex	Essex	4 runs	1993	Derbyshire	Lancashire	6 runs

County Champions

1864	Surrey	1890	Surrey	1926	Lancashire	1962	Yorkshire
1865	Nottinghamshire	1891	Surrey	1927	Lancashire	1963	Yorkshire
1866	Middlesex	1892	Surrey	1928	Lancashire	1964	Worcestershire
1867	Yorkshire	1893	Yorkshire	1929	Nottinghamshire	1965	Worcestershire
1868	Nottinghamshire	1894	Surrey	1930	Lancashire	1966	Yorkshire
1869	Nottinghamshire & Yorkshire (shared)	1895	Surrey	1931	Yorkshire	1967	Yorkshire
		1896	Yorkshire	1932	Yorkshire	1968	Yorkshire
1870	Yorkshire	1897	Lancashire	1933	Yorkshire	1969	Glamorgan
1871	Nottinghamshire	1898	Yorkshire	1934	Lancashire	1970	Kent
1872	Nottinghamshire	1899	Surrey	1935	Yorkshire	1971	Surrey
1873	Gloucestershire & Nottinghamshire (shared)	1900	Yorkshire	1936	Derbyshire	1972	Warwickshire
		1901	Yorkshire	1937	Yorkshire	1973	Hampshire
		1902	Yorkshire	1938	Yorkshire	1974	Worcestershire
1874	Gloucestershire	1903	Middlesex	1939	Yorkshire	1975	Leicestershire
1875	Nottinghamshire	1904	Lancashire	1940–45	Not held	1976	Middlesex
1876	Gloucestershire	1905	Yorkshire	1946	Yorkshire	1977	Kent & Middlesex (shared)
1877	Gloucestershire	1906	Kent	1947	Middlesex		
1878	Undecided	1907	Nottinghamshire	1948	Glamorgan	1978	Kent
1879	Lancashire & Nottinghamshire (shared)	1908	Yorkshire	1949	Middlesex & Yorkshire (shared)	1979	Essex
		1909	Kent			1980	Middlesex
		1910	Kent	1950	Lancashire & Surrey (shared)	1981	Nottinghamshire
1880	Nottinghamshire	1911	Warwickshire			1982	Middlesex
1881	Lancashire	1912	Yorkshire	1951	Warwickshire	1983	Essex
1882	Lancashire & Nottinghamshire (shared)	1913	Kent	1952	Surrey	1984	Essex
		1914	Surrey	1953	Surrey	1985	Middlesex
		1915–18	Not held	1954	Surrey	1986	Essex
1883	Nottinghamshire	1919	Yorkshire	1955	Surrey	1987	Nottinghamshire
1884	Nottinghamshire	1920	Middlesex	1956	Surrey	1988	Worcestershire
1885	Nottinghamshire	1921	Middlesex	1957	Surrey	1989	Worcestershire
1886	Nottinghamshire	1922	Yorkshire	1958	Surrey	1990	Middlesex
1887	Surrey	1923	Yorkshire	1959	Yorkshire	1991	Essex
1888	Surrey	1924	Yorkshire	1960	Yorkshire	1992	Essex
1889	Lancashire, Nottinghamshire & Surrey (shared)	1925	Yorkshire	1961	Hampshire	1993	Middlesex

Minor Counties Champions

1895	Norfolk Durham Worcestershire	1906 1907 1908	Staffordshire Lancashire II Staffordshire	1928 1929 1930	Berkshire Oxfordshire Durham	1950 1951 1952	Surrey II Kent II Buckinghamshire
1896	Worcestershire	1909	Wiltshire	1931	Leicestershire II	1953	Berkshire
1897	Worcestershire	1910	Norfolk	1932	Buckinghamshire	1954	Surrey II
1898	Worcestershire	1911	Staffordshire	1933	Undecided	1955	Surrey II
1899	Northamptonshire Buckinghamshire	1912 1913	In abeyance Norfolk	1934 1935	Lancashire II Middlesex II	1956 1957	Kent II Yorkshire II
1900	Glamorgan Durham Northamptonshire	1920 1921 1922	Staffordshire Staffordshire Buckinghamshire	1936 1937 1938	Hertfordshire Lancashire II Buckinghamshire	1958 1959 1960	Yorkshire II Warwickshire II Lancashire II
1901	Durham	1923	Buckinghamshire	1939	Surrey II	1961	Somerset II
1902	Wiltshire	1924	Berkshire	1946	Suffolk	1962	Warwickshire II
1903	Northamptonshire	1925	Buckinghamshire	1947	Yorkshire II	1963	Cambridgeshire
1904	Northamptonshire	1926	Durham	1948	Lancashire II	1964	Lancashire II
1905	Norfolk	1927	Staffordshire	1949	Lancashire II	1965	Somerset II

(Continued)

1966	Lincolnshire	1973	Shropshire	1980	Durham	1987	Buckinhamshire
1967	Cheshire	1974	Oxfordshire	1981	Durham	1988	Cheshire
1968	Yorkshire II	1975	Hertfordshire	1982	Oxfordshire	1989	Oxfordshire
1969	Buckinghamshire	1976	Durham	1983	Hertfordshire	1990	Hertfordshire
1970	Bedfordshire	1977	Suffolk	1984	Durham	1991	Staffordshire
1971	Yorkshire II	1978	Devon	1985	Cheshire	1992	Staffordshire
1972	Bedfordshire	1979	Suffolk	1986	Cumberland	1993	Staffordshire

NatWest Trophy Holders

Year	Winner	Runner-up	Margin
1963	Sussex	Worcestershire	14 runs
1964	Sussex	Warwickshire	8 wickets
1965	Yorkshire	Surrey	175 runs
1966	Warwickshire	Worcestershire	5 wickets
1967	Kent	Somerset	32 runs
1968	Warwickshire	Sussex	4 wickets
1969	Yorkshire	Derbyshire	69 runs
1970	Lancashire	Sussex	6 wickets
1971	Lancashire	Kent	24 runs
1972	Lancashire	Warwickshire	4 wickets
1973	Gloucestershire	Sussex	40 runs
1974	Kent	Lancashire	4 wickets
1975	Lancashire	Middlesex	7 wickets
1976	Northants	Lancashire	4 wickets
1977	Middlesex	Glamorgan	5 wickets
1978	Sussex	Somerset	5 wickets
1979	Somerset	Northants	45 runs
1980	Middlesex	Surrey	7 wickets
1981	Derbyshire	Northants	Fewer wickets lost (scores level)
1982	Surrey	Warwickshire	9 wickets
1983	Somerset	Kent	24 runs
1984	Middlesex	Kent	4 wickets
1985	Essex	Nottinghamshire	1 run
1986	Sussex	Lancashire	7 wickets
1987	Nottinghamshire	Northants	3 wickets
1988	Middlesex	Worcestershire	3 wickets
1989	Warwickshire	Middlesex	4 wickets
1990	Lancashire	Northants	7 wickets
1991	Hampshire	Surrey	4 wickets
1992	Northants	Leicestershire	8 wickets
1993	Warwickshire	Sussex	5 wickets

TEST CRICKET

Cornhill Tests

First Cornhill Test
(Old Trafford, 3 June 1993)

Australia won by 179 runs.
Australia 289 and 432-5 dec. England 210 and 332.

Second Cornhill Test
(Lord's, 17 June 1993)

Australia won by an innings and 62 runs.
Australia 632-4 dec. England 205 and 365.

Third Cornhill Test
(Trent Bridge, 11 July 1993)

Match drawn.
England 321 and 422-6 dec. Australia 373 and 202-6.

Fourth Cornhill Test
(Headingley, 22 July 1993)

Australia won by an innings and 148 runs.
Australia 653-4 dec. England 200 and 305.

Fifth Cornhill Test
(Edgbaston, 5 Aug. 1993)

Australia won by 8 wickets.
England 276 and 251. Australia 408 and 120-2.

Sixth Cornhill Test
(The Oval, 19 Aug. 1993)

England won by 161 runs.
England 380 and 313. Australia 303 and 229.

Other Tests

Zimbabwe v. India
(Harare, 18–22 Oct. 1992)

Match drawn.
Zimbabwe 456 and 146-4 dec. India 307.

Zimbabwe v. New Zealand

First Test
(Bulawayo, 1–5 Nov. 1992)

Match drawn.
New Zealand 325-3 dec. and 222-5 dec. Zimbabwe 219 and 197-1.

Second Test
(Harare, 7–12 Nov. 1992)

New Zealand won by 177 runs.
New Zealand 335 and 262-5 dec. Zimbabwe 283-9 dec. and 137.

South Africa v. India

First Test
(Durban, 13–17 Nov. 1992)

Match drawn.
South Africa 254 and 176-3. India 277.

Second Test
(Johannesburg, 26–30 Nov. 1992)

Match drawn.
South Africa 292 and 252. India 227 and 141-4.

Third Test
(Port Elizabeth, 26–29 Dec. 1992)

South Africa won by 9 wickets.
India 212 and 215. South Africa 275 and 155-1.

Fourth Test
(Cape Town, 2–6 Jan. 1993)

Match drawn.
South Africa 360-9 dec. and 130-6 dec. India 276 and 29-1.

Australia v. West Indies

First Test
(Brisbane, 27 Nov.–1 Dec. 1992)

Match drawn.
Australia 293 and 308. West Indies 371 and 133-8.

Second Test
(Melbourne, 26–30 Dec. 1992)

Australia won by 139 runs.
Australia 395 and 196. West Indies 233 and 219.

Third Test
(Sydney, 2–6 Jan. 1993)

Match drawn.
Australia 503-9 dec. and 117-0. West Indies 606.

Fourth Test
(Adelaide, 23–26 Jan. 1993)

West Indies won by 1 run.
West Indies 252 and 146. Australia 213 and 184.

Fifth Test
(Perth, 30 Jan.–1 Feb. 1993)

West Indies won by an innings and 25 runs.
Australia 119 and 178. West Indies 322.

(Continued)

Sri Lanka v. New Zealand

First Test
(Moratuwa, 27 Nov.–2 Dec. 1992)

Match drawn.
New Zealand 288 and 195-5. Sri Lanka 327-6 dec.

Second Test
(Colombo, 6–9 Dec. 1992)

Sri Lanka won by 9 wickets.
Sri Lanka 394 and 70-1. New Zealand 102 and 361.

New Zealand v. Pakistan

(Hamilton, 2–5 Jan. 1993)

Pakistan won by 33 runs.
Pakistan 216 and 174. New Zealand 264 and 93.

India v. England

First Test
(Calcutta, 29 Jan.–2 Feb. 1993)

India won by 8 wickets.
India 371 and 82-2. England 163 and 286.

Second Test
(Madras, 11–15 Feb. 1993)

India won by an innings and 22 runs.
India 560-6 dec. England 286 and 252.

Third Test
(Bombay, 19–23 Feb. 1993)

India won by an innings and 15 runs.
England 347 and 229. India 591.

Texaco Trophy

England v. Australia

First Match
(Old Trafford, 19 May 1993)

Australia won by 4 runs.
Australia 258-9. England 254.

Second Match
(Edgbaston, 21 May 1993)

Australia won by 3 runs.
England 277-5. Australia 280-4.

Third Match
(Lord's, 23 May 1993)

Australia won by 19 runs.
Australia 230-5. England 211.

World Cup
(March 1992)

Australia v. England – England won by 8 wickets.
Australia v. India – Australia won by 1 run.
Australia v. Sri Lanka – Australia won by 7 wickets.
England v. Sri Lanka – England won by 106 runs.
India v. New Zealand – New Zealand won by 4 wickets.
India v. Pakistan – India won by 43 runs.
India v. South Africa – South Africa won by 6 wickets.
India v. Zimbabwe – India won by 55 runs.
New Zealand v. England – New Zealand won by 7 wickets.
New Zealand v. Zimbabwe – New Zealand won by 48 runs.
Pakistan v. Australia – Pakistan won by 48 runs.
Pakistan v. England – No result.
Pakistan v. Sri Lanka – Pakistan won by 4 wickets.
South Africa v. England – England won by 3 wickets.
South Africa v. New Zealand – New Zealand won by 7 wickets.
South Africa v. Pakistan – Pakistan won by 20 runs.
South Africa v. Sri Lanka – Sri Lanka won by 3 wickets.
South Africa v. West Indies – South Africa won by 54 runs.
South Africa v. Zimbabwe – South Africa won by 7 wickets.
West Indies v. India – West Indies won by 5 wickets.
West Indies v. New Zealand – New Zealand won by 5 wickets.
West Indies v. Sri Lanka – West Indies won by 91 runs.
West Indies v. Zimbabwe – West Indies won by 75 runs.

Semi-finals

England v. South Africa – England won by 19 runs.
New Zealand v. Pakistan – Pakistan won by 4 wickets.

Final

Pakistan v. England – Pakistan won by 22 runs.

World Cup Champions

Men

Year	Winner	Runner-up	Margin
1975	West Indies	Australia	17 runs
1979	West Indies	England	92 runs
1983	India	West Indies	43 runs
1987	Australia	England	7 runs
1992	Pakistan	England	22 runs

Women

Year	Winner	Runner-up	Margin
1973	England	Australia	League Table
1978	Australia	England	8 wickets
1982	Australia	England	3 wickets
1988	Australia	England	8 wickets
1993	England	New Zealand	67 runs

CYCLING

Milk Race Champions

1951	Ian Steel (GB)
1952	Ken Russell (GB)
1953	Gordon Thomas (GB)
1954	Eugène Tamburlini (Fra)
1955	Anthony Hewson (GB)
1958	Richard Durlacher (Aut)
1959	Bill Bradley (GB)
1960	Bill Bradley (GB)
1961	Billy Holmes (GB)
1962	Eugen Pokorny (Pol)
1963	Peter Chisman (GB)
1964	Arthur Metcalfe (GB)
1965	Les West (GB)
1966	Josef Gawliczek (Pol)
1967	Les West (GB)
1968	Gosta Pettersson (Swe)
1969	Fedor Den Hertog (Hol)
1970	Jiri Mainus (Cze)
1971	Fedor Den Hertog (Hol)
1972	Hennie Kuiper (Hol)
1973	Piet van Katwijk (Hol)
1974	Roy Schuiten (Hol)
1975	Bernt Johansson (Swe)
1976	Bill Nickson (GB)
1977	Said Gusseinov (USSR)
1978	Jan Brzezny (Pol)
1979	Yuriy Kashirin (USSR)
1980	Ivan Mitchtenko (USSR)
1981	Sergey Krivocheyev (USSR)
1982	Yuriy Kashirin (USSR)
1983	Matt Eaton (US)
1984	Oleg Czougeda (USSR)
1985	Eric van Lancker (Bel)
1986	Joey McLoughlin (GB)
1987	Malcolm Elliott (GB)
1988	Vasiliy Zhdanov (USSR)
1989	Brian Walton (Can)
1990	Shane Sutton (Aus)
1991	Chris Walker (GB)
1992	Conor Henry (Ire)
1993	Chris Lillywhite (GB)

Paris–Nice Champions

1933	Alfons Schepers (Bel)
1934	Gaston Rebry (Bel)
1935	René Vietto (Fra)
1936	Maurice Archambaud (Fra)
1937	Roger Lapebie (Fra)
1938	Jules Lowie (Bel)
1939	Maurice Archambaud (Fra)
1946	Fermo Camellini (Ita)
1951[1]	Roger Decock (Bel)
1952[1]	Louison Bobet (Fra)
1953[1]	Jean-Pierre Munch (Fra)
1954	Raymond Impanis (Bel)
1955	Jean Bobet (Fra)
1956	Fred Debruyne (Bel)
1957	Jacques Anquetil (Fra)
1958	Fred Debruyne (Bel)
1959[2]	Jean Graczyck (Fra)
1960	Raymond Impanis (Bel)
1961	Jacques Anquetil (Fra)
1962	Jozef Planckaert (Bel)
1963	Jacques Anquetil (Fra)
1964	Jan Janssen (Neth)
1965	Jacques Anquetil (Fra)
1966	Jacques Anquetil (Fra)
1967	Tom Simpson (GB)
1968	Rolf Wolfshohl (Ger)
1969	Eddy Merckx (Bel)
1970	Eddy Merckx (Bel)
1971	Eddy Merckx (Bel)
1972	Raymond Poulidor (Fra)
1973	Raymond Poulidor (Fra)
1974	Joop Zoetemelk (Neth)
1975	Joop Zoetemelk (Neth)
1976	Michel Laurent (Fra)
1977	Freddy Maertens (Bel)
1978	Gerrie Knetemann (Neth)
1979	Joop Zoetemelk (Neth)
1980	Gilb. Duclos-Lassalle (Fra)
1981	Stephen Roche (Irl)
1982	Sean Kelly (Irl)
1983	Sean Kelly (Irl)
1984	Sean Kelly (Irl)
1985	Sean Kelly (Irl)
1986	Sean Kelly (Irl)
1987	Sean Kelly (Irl)
1988	Sean Kelly (Irl)
1989	Miguel Indurain (Spa)
1990	Miguel Indurain (Spa)
1991	Tony Rominger (Swi)
1992	Jean-François Bernard (Fra)
1993	Alex Zuelle (Swi)

(1) Paris–Côte d'Azur. (2) Paris–Nice–Rome.

Tour of Britain Champions

1987	Joey McLoughlin (GB)
1988	Malcolm Elliott (GB)
1989	Robert Millar (GB)
1990	Michel Dernies (Bel)
1991	Phil Anderson (Aus)
1992	Max Sciandri (Ita)
1993	Phil Anderson (Aus)

Tour de France Champions

1903	Maurice Garin (Fra)
1904	Henri Cornet (Fra)
1905	Louis Trousselier (Fra)
1906	René Pottier (Fra)
1907	Lucien Petit-Breton (Fra)
1908	Lucien Petit-Breton (Fra)
1909	François Faber (Lux)
1910	Octave Lapize (Fra)
1911	Gustave Garrigou (Fra)
1912	Odile Defraye (Bel)
1913	Philippe Thys (Bel)
1914	Philippe Thys (Bel)
1919	Firmin Lambot (Bel)
1920	Philippe Thys (Bel)
1921	Leon Scieur (Bel)
1922	Firmin Lambot (Bel)
1923	Henri Pelissier (Fra)
1924	Ottavio Bottecchia (Ita)
1925	Ottavio Bottechia (Ita)
1926	Lucien Buysse (Bel)
1927	Nicholas Frantz (Lux)
1928	Nicholas Frantz (Lux)
1929	Maurice de Waele (Bel)
1930	André Leducq (Fra)
1931	Antonin Magne (Fra)
1932	André Leducq (Fra)
1933	Georges Speicher (Fra)
1934	Antonin Magne (Fra)
1935	Romain Maes (Bel)
1936	Sylvère Maes (Bel)
1937	Roger Lapebie (Fra)
1938	Gino Bartali (Ita)
1939	Sylvère Maes (Bel)
1947	Jean Robic (Fra)
1948	Gino Bartali (Ita)
1949	Fausto Coppi (Ita)
1950	Ferdinand Kebler (Swi)
1951	Hugo Koblet (Swi)
1952	Fausto Coppi (Ita)
1953	Louison Bobet (Fra)
1954	Louison Bobet (Fra)
1955	Louison Bobet (Fra)
1956	Roger Walkowiak (Fra)
1957	Jacques Anquetil (Fra)
1958	Charly Gaul (Lux)
1959	Federico Dahamontès (Spa)
1960	Gastone Nencini (Ita)
1961	Jacques Anquetil (Fra)
1962	Jacques Anquetil (Fra)
1963	Jacques Anquetil (Fra)
1964	Jacques Anquetil (Fra)
1965	Felice Gimondi (Ita)
1966	Lucien Aimar (Fra)
1967	Roger Pingeon (Fra)
1968	Jan Janssen (Hol)
1969	Eddy Merckx (Bel)
1970	Eddy Merckx (Bel)
1971	Eddy Merckx (Bel)
1972	Eddy Merckx (Bel)
1973	Luis Ocana (Spa)
1974	Eddy Merckx (Bel)
1975	Bernard Thevenet (Fra)
1976	Lucien van Impe (Bel)
1977	Bernard Thevenet (Fra)
1978	Bernard Hinault (Fra)
1979	Bernard Hinault (Fra)
1980	Joop Zoetemelk (Hol)
1981	Bernard Hinault (Fra)
1982	Bernard Hinault (Fra)
1983	Laurent Fignon (Fra)
1984	Laurent Fignon (Fra)
1985	Bernard Hinault (Fra)
1986	Greg LeMond (US)
1987	Stephen Roche (Ire)
1988	Pedro Delgado (Spa)
1989	Greg LeMond (US)
1990	Greg LeMond (US)
1991	Miguel Indurain (Spa)
1992	Miguel Indurain (Spa)
1993	Miguel Indurain (Spa)

Tour of Italy Champions

1947	Fausto Coppi (Ita)
1948	Fiorenzo Magni (Ita)
1949	Fausto Coppi (Ita)
1950	Hugo Koblet (Swi)
1951	Fiorenzo Magni (Ita)
1952	Fausto Coppi (Ita)
1953	Fausto Coppi (Ita)
1954	Carlo Clerici (Swi)
1955	Fiorenzo Magni (Ita)
1956	Charly Gaul (Lux)
1957	Gastone Nencini (Ita)
1958	Ercole Baldini (Ita)
1959	Charly Gaul (Lux)
1960	Jacques Anquetil (Fra)
1961	Arn Pambianco (Ita)
1962	Franco Balmamion (Ita)
1963	Franco Balmanion (Ita)
1964	Jacques Anquetil (Fra)
1965	Vittorio Ardoni (Ita)
1966	Gianni Motta (Ita)
1967	Felice Gimondi (Ita)
1968	Eddy Merckx (Bel)
1969	Felice Gimondi (Ita)
1970	Eddy Merckx (Bel)
1971	Gosta Pettersson (Swe)
1972	Eddy Merckx (Bel)
1973	Eddy Merckx (Bel)
1974	Eddy Merckx (Bel)
1975	F. Bertoglio (Ita)
1976	Felice Gimondi (Ita)
1977	Michel Pollentier (Bel)
1978	Johan De Muynck (Bel)
1979	Giuseppe Saronni (Ita)
1980	Bernard Hinault (Fra)
1981	Giovanni Bartaglin (Ita)
1982	Bernard Hinault (Fra)
1983	Giuseppe Saronni (Ita)
1984	Francesco Moser (Ita)
1985	Bernard Hinault (Fra)
1986	Roberto Visentini (Ita)
1987	Stephen Roche (Ire)
1988	Andy Hampsten (US)
1989	Laurent Fignon (Fra)
1990	Gianni Bugno (Ita)
1991	Franco Chioccioli (Ita)
1992	Miguel Indurain (Spa)
1993	Miguel Indurain (Spa)

Tour of Spain Champions

1947	Edourd Van Dyck (Bel)
1948	Bernardo Ruiz (Spa)
1950	Emilio Rodriquez (Spa)
1955	J. Dotto (Fra)
1956	A. Contero (Ita)
1957	Jesus Lorono (Spa)
1958	Jean Stablinski (Fra)
1959	Antonio Suarez (Spa)
1960	F. de Mulder (Bel)
1961	Angelino Soler (Spa)
1962	Rudi Altig (FRG)
1963	Jacques Anquetil (Fra)
1964	Raymond Poulidor (Fra)
1965	Rolf Wolfshohl (FRG)
1966	Francisco Gabicagogeascoa (Spa)
1967	Jan Janssen (Hol)
1968	Felice Gimondi (Ita)
1969	Roger Pingeon (Fra)
1970	Luis Ocana (Spa)
1971	F. Bracke (Bel)
1972	José-Manuel Fuente (Spa)
1973	Eddy Merckx (Bel)
1974	José-Manuel Fuente (Spa)
1975	G. Tamames (Spa)
1976	J. Pesarrodona (Spa)
1977	Freddy Maertens (Bel)
1978	Bernard Hinault (Fra)
1979	Joop Zoetemelk (Hol)
1980	Faustino Ruperez (Spa)
1981	Giovanni Bartaglin (Ita)

(Continued)

(Tour of Spain Champions contd.)

1982	Marino Lejaretta (Spa)
1983	Bernard Hinault (Fra)
1984	Eric Caritoux (Fra)
1985	Pedro Delgado (Spa)
1986	Alvaro Pino (Spa)
1987	Luis Herrera (Col)
1988	Sean Kelly (Ire)
1989	Pedro Delgado (Spa)
1990	Marco Giovannetti (Ita)
1991	Melchor Mauri (Spa)
1992	Tony Rominger (Swi)
1993	Tony Rominger (Swi)

DARTS

World Professional Champions*

Year	Winner	Runner-up
1978	Leighton Rees	John Lowe
1979	John Lowe	Leighton Rees
1980	Eric Bristow	Bobby George
1981	Eric Bristow	John Lowe
1982	Jocky Wilson	John Lowe
1983	Keith Deller	Eric Bristow
1984	Eric Bristow	Dave Whitcombe
1985	Eric Bristow	John Lowe
1986	Eric Bristow	Dave Whitcombe
1987	John Lowe	Eric Bristow
1988	Bob Anderson	John Lowe
1989	Jocky Wilson	Eric Bristow
1990	Phil Taylor	Eric Bristow
1991	Dennis Priestley	Eric Bristow
1992	Phil Taylor	Mike Gregory
1993	John Lowe	Alan Warriner

*All winners British.

EQUESTRIANISM

European Champions

Show Jumping

Individual

	Men	Horse
1957	Hans-Günter Winkler (FRG)	Sonnenglanz
1958	Fritz Thiedemann (FRG)	Meteor
1959	Piero d'Inzeo (Ita)	Uruguay
1961	David Broome (GB)	Sunsalve
1962	David Barker (GB)	Mister Softee
1963	Graziano Mancinelli (Ita)	Rockette
1965	Hermann Schridde (FRG)	Dozent
1966	Nelson Pessoa (Bra)	Gran Geste
1967	David Broome (GB)	Mister Softee
1969	David Broome (GB)	Mister Softee
1971	Hartwig Steenken (FRG)	Simona
1973	Paddy McMahon (GB)	Penwood Forge Mill

	Women	Horse
1957	Pat Smythe (GB)	Flanagan
1958	Giulia Serventi (Ita)	Doly
1959	Ann Townsend (GB)	Bandit
1960	Susan Cohen (GB)	Clare Castle
1961	Pat Smythe (GB)	Flanagan
1962	Pat Smythe (GB)	Flanagan
1963	Pat Smythe (GB)	Flanagan
1966	Janou Lefèbvre (Fra)	Kenavo
1967	Kathy Kusner (US)	Untouchable
1968	Anneli Drummond-Hay (GB)	Merely-a-Monarch
1969	Iris Kellett (Ire)	Morning Light
1971	Ann Moore (GB)	Psalm
1973	Ann Moore (GB)	Psalm

	Rider*	Horse
1975	Alwin Schockemohle (FRG)	Warwick
1977	Johan Heins (Hol)	Seven Valleys
1979	Gerd Wiltfang (FRG)	Roman
1981	Paul Schockemohle (FRG)	Deister
1983	Paul Schockemohle (FRG)	Deister
1985	Paul Schockemohle (FRG)	Deister
1987	Pierre Durand (Fra)	Jappeloup
1989	John Whitaker (GB)	Next Milton
1991	Erik Navet (Fra)	Waiti Quito de Baussy
1993	Willi Melliger (Swi)	Quinta C

*The women's event merged with the men's after 1973.

Team

1975	West Germany
1977	Holland
1979	Britain
1981	West Germany
1983	Switzerland
1985	Britain
1987	Britain
1989	Britain
1991	Holland
1993	Switzerland

Three-Day Event

Individual

	Rider	Horse
1953	Lawrence Rook (GB)	Starlight
1954	Albert Hill (GB)	Crispin
1955	Frank Weldon (GB)	Kilbarry
1957	Sheila Willcox (GB)	High and Mighty
1959	Hans Schwarzenbach (Swi)	Burn Trout
1962	James Templar (GB)	M'Lord Connolly
1965	Marian Babirecki (Pol)	Volt
1967	Eddie Boylan (Ire)	Durlas Eile
1969	Mary Gordon-Watson (GB)	Cornishman V
1971	HRH Princess Anne (GB)	Doublet
1973	Aleksandr Yevdokimov (USSR)	Jeger
1975	Lucinda Prior-Palmer (GB)	Be Fair
1977	Lucinda Prior-Palmer (GB)	George
1979	Nils Haagensen (Den)	Monaco
1981	Hansueli Schmutz (Swi)	Oran
1983	Rachel Bayliss (GB)	Mystic Minstrel
1985	Virginia Holgate (GB)	Priceless
1987	Virginia Leng (née Holgate) (GB)	Night Cap
1989	Virginia Leng (GB)	Master Craftsman
1991	Ian Stark (GB)	Glenburnie
1993	Jean-Lou Bigot (Fra)	Twist la Beige

Team

1953	Britain
1954	Britain
1955	Britain
1957	Britain
1959	West Germany
1962	USSR
1965	USSR
1967	Britain
1969	Britain
1971	Britain
1973	West Germany
1975	USSR
1977	Britain
1979	Ireland
1981	Britain
1983	Sweden
1985	Britain
1987	Britain
1989	Britain
1991	Britain
1993	Sweden

Horse of the Year Show
(Wembley, Oct. 1992)

Coomes Speed Stakes

1. Henderson Grannusch (J. Whitaker) clear 50.20sec; 2. Ancit Feedback (D. Broome) clear 52.00.

Daily Mail Christy Beaufort Championship

(Leading junior showjumper of the year): 1. Strawberry Mojo (N. Bingham) clear 34.23sec; 2. Flaxlands Major Decision (H. Mason) clear 35.56; 3. CR Operation Charlie (E. Edwards) clear 36.02.

DHL London Classic

1. Henderson Grannusch (J. Whitaker) clear 31.51sec; 2. Corona (G. Billington) clear 32.70; 3. Rock Du Taillon (J. Lessens, Bel) 33.67.

DHL Puissance

1. Henderson Gammon (J. Whitaker) clear at 6ft 10in.

Everest Championship

1. Henderson Hopscotch (J. Whitaker) clear 35.30sec; 2. Terrenova Lapaz (M. McCourt) 4 faults 37.01; 3. Bluebird (J. Popley) 4 faults 39.34.

(Continued)

Everest Derby

1. Henderson My Mesieur (M. Whitaker) clear 33.59sec; 2. Henderson Gammon (J. Whitaker) clear 36.11; 3. Ancit Countryman (D. Broome) clear 41.58; 4. Diamond Exchange (Jessica Chesney) 4 faults 34.59.

Fordyce Curry Consolation International Stakes

1. Early Edition (P. Murphy) clear 51.04sec; 2. Bluebird (J. Popeley) clear 52.47; 3. Corella (M. Armstrong) clear 52.96.

M & A Outdoor Clothing Accumulator

1. Roby Foulards Payday (P. Lejeune, Bel) 21pts, 28.62sec; 2. Senator Hudson Boy (M. Lucas) 21, 28.82; 3. Bowriver Queen (J. Fisher) 21, 28.92.

National Grade B Championship

1. Gold Run II (P. Charles) clear 27.19sec; 2. It's the Business (G. Glazzard) retired in jump-off. (Four horses were equal third with four first-round faults.)

National 138 Centimetres Championship

1. Ferry Bound (Nicola Western) clear 30.70sec; 2. Coniston Lad (D. Woolley) clear 31.83; 3. Millstreet Shadow (Sara Rust) clear 33.64.

Nigerian Ports Leading Jumper of the Year

1. Henderson Gammon (J. Whitaker) clear 32.05sec; 2. Roby Foulards Shogun (P. Lejeune, Bel) clear 33.45; 3. Faldo (P. Murphy) 3 faults 36.02.

Olympic Star Spotters Championship

1. The Legal Venture II (M. Edwards) 4 faults 37.61sec; 2. Endeavour (A. Bradley) 4 faults 38.56; 3. Katy's Choice (A. Saywell) 4 faults 46.88.

Osborne Refrigeration Knock-out Semi-finals

Panacee DuThot (Alexandra Ledermann, Fr) beat Ancit Feedback (D. Broome); Paradise Peppermill (J. Harris) beat Rossport Aquila (M. McCourt).

Paul Fabrications Foxhunter Championship

1. Itziweeni (M. Pyrah) clear 35.10sec; 2. Electrik II (G. Goosen) clear 35.66; 3. JJ II (S. Bowen) clear 39.03.

Senator Junior Foxhunter Championship

1. Dovecote Holly (M. Cowan) clear 28.75sec; 2. Village Cobbler (C. Vinnicombe) clear 29.35; 3. Frosty Mop (L. Henderson) clear 31.63.

Woodhouse Challenge

1. Monterrey (J. Fisher) clear 48.99sec; 2. Rossport Aquila (M. McCourt) clear 50.34; 3. Wessex Fields of Athenry (P. Sutton) clear 52.00.

Woodhouse Stakes

1=. The Waysider (J. Turi), Corona (G. Billington) clear 30.62sec; 3. Bowriver Queen (J. Fisher) clear 31.64.

Nations Cup, 1993

Venue	Winning Team
Rome, Italy	Germany
Kiskuhnlaus, Hungary	Great Britain
Hickstead, Great Britain	Great Britain
Saint Gallen, Switzerland	France
Gera, Germany	Denmark
Aachen, Germany	Switzerland
Drammen, Norway	Netherlands
Luxembourg, Luxembourg	Switzerland
Falsterbo, Sweden	Netherlands
La Baule, France	France
Dublin, Ireland	United States
Rotterdam, Netherlands	Netherlands
Calgary, Canada	France
Plovdiv, Bulgaria	Greece
San Marino, San Marino	Germany
Linz, Austria	Germany
Lanaken, Belgium	Switzerland
Prague, Czech Republic	Germany
Barcelona, Spain	Cancelled

Olympia International Horse Show
(December 1992)

Christmas Carol Stakes

1. Albertino (T. Fruhmann, Aus) clear 29.22sec; 2. Everest Limited Edition (Skelton) clear 29.49; 3. Akai Sarcelle de Sisse (H. Godignon, Fr) clear 31.09.

Christmas Eve Six Bar

1=. Everest Major Wager (N. Skelton), San Patrignano Dorina (F. Sloothaak, Ger); 3=. Optiebeurs Easy Jumper (J. Lansink, Neth), Robin (P. Eriksson, Swe).

Christmas Hamper

1. Everest My Mesieur (M. Whitaker, GB) 43.66sec; 2. Everest Major Wager (N. Skelton, GB) 43.96; 3. John Blunt (R. Tebbel, Ger) 44.70.

Everest Brandy Butter Stakes

1. Everest Sure Thing (M. Edgar, GB) clear 26.74sec; 2. Everest Florida (N. Skelton, GB) clear 26.75; 3. Ancit Countryman (D. Broome, GB) clear 27.29.

Everest Christmas Knockout

1. Everest Florida (N. Skelton); 2. Everest Fonda (J. Whitaker); 3=. Lysco (H. Lanner, Swe), Lakeside (P. Charles, Ire).

Everest Mince Pie Stakes

1. President Papillon Bose (R-Y. Bost, Fr) clear 39.66sec; 2. Everest Minka (M. Edgar, GB) clear 46.35; 3. Springbok (G. Gullikson, Nor) clear 48.34.

Everest Snowman Stakes

1. Everest Fire One/Cloud Chase (G. Luckett, GB) 72.64sec; 2. Delsey/JJ (D. Bowen, GB) 77.52; 3. Everest Unique/Minka (M. Edgar, GB) 80.79.

Mistletoe Stakes

1. Everest My Mesieur (M. Whitaker, GB) clear 20.19sec; 2. President Papillon Bose (R-Y. Bost) clear 21.74; 3. Lucilla (R. Smith, GB) clear 21.78.

MSS Christmas Pudding Stakes

1. Raspail (R-Y. Bost, Fr) 47.82sec; 2. Everest Florida (N. Skelton, GB) 48.96; 3. Home James (M. Michaels, US) 51.28.

MSS Bareback Puissance

1=. Robin (P. Eriksson, Swe), Ever If Ever (J. Turi, GB), Alonso (G. Billington, GB).

Olympia Grand Prix

1. Everest Midnight Madness (M. Whitaker) clear 29.64sec; 2. Almox Rattina (Beerbaum) clear 30.32; 3. Akai Quidam de Revel (H. Godignon, Fr) clear 30.44.

Puissance

1. Golo (R. Tebbell); 2=. Tommy (R. Tebell), Everest Percival (M. Whitaker, GB), Robin (P. Eriksson, Swe), Akai Sarcelle de Sisse (H. Godignon, Fr), Almox Alex (L. Beerbaum, Ger).

Standings European League

1. L. Beerbaum (Ger) 58pts; 2. H. Luther (Ger) 56; 3. C. M. de Irujo (Sp) 53.

Volvo World Cup Qualifier

1. Almox Ratina (L. Beerbaum, Ger) clear 32.78sec; 2. Royal Chocolate (P. Charles, Ire) clear 36.13; 3. Bockmann's Genius (T. Fruhmann, Aus) clear 36.78.

Royal International Horse Show
(May 1993)

Bond International Chase

Everest Fire One, ridden by Geoff Luckett.

Bond International July Stakes

Giulietta, ridden by A. Pollman-Schweckhorst.

(Continued)

Bond International Speed Challenge

Dun Equity, ridden by Keith Shore.

Bond International Speed Classic

Everest Fire One, ridden by Geoff Luckett.

Bond International Stakes

Donna Carara, ridden by Dietmar Gugler.

Bond International Sussex Stakes

Gold, ridden by Harvey Smith.

King George V Gold Cup

Everest Limited Edition, ridden by Nick Skelton.

Queen Elizabeth II Cup

Bond Xtra, ridden by Tina Cassan.

Royal Windsor Horse Show

(May 1993)

De Lage Landen Grand Prix

1. Corella (M. Armstrong) 4 faults 57.83sec; 2. Wessex Zakatak (P. Sutton) 4 faults 58.20; 3. Everest Twostep (M. Whitaker) 5 faults 59.56.

Grade A

1. Everest Unique (M. Edgar) clear 44.8sec; 2. Alfredo (K. Brown) clear 45.1; 3. Wessex Field of Athonry (P. Sutton) clear 45.26.

Harrods International Driving Grand Prix

Leading horse teams (after dressage): 1. G. Bowman (GB) 37.3pts; 2. J-E. Pahlsson (Swe) 39.3; 3. T. Eriksson (Swe) 44.7.

Leverton Accumulator

1. Everest Florida (N. Skelton) 36pts, 41.55sec; 2. McBumble Bee (P. Charles) 36, 42.35; 3. Everest Monsanta (M. Whitaker) 36, 43.51.

Leverton Speed Classic

1. Everest Hopscotch (J. Whitaker 52.95sec); 2. Everest Radiant (L. Edgar 54.37); 3. Supergrass (M. Lewis 54.50).

Lucas Ladies National

1. Everest Fol Amour (V. Whitaker) clear 47.48sec; 2. Finance (J. Cleeland) 4 faults 53.14; Mr Ross Poldark (A. Kent) 8 faults 52.45.

Pony Teams Dressage

1. P. Gammell (GB) 37.0sec; 2. A. Unmussig (Ger) 45.0; 3. Prince Philip (GB) 51.3.

Toyota Grade A

1. Winstar (M. Edgar) clear 42.04sec; 2. Pacifica (V. Roberts) clear 45.0; 3. Saigon (W. Funnell) clear 47.02.

Walwyn Novice

1. Everest Calibre (G. Luckett) clear 39.4sec; 2. Money More (C. Edwards) clear 40.98; 3=. Hazelpar Houdini (N. Warwick); Renville (J. Fisher); Alpine Mist (K. Doyle); Toy (M. Aasen) 4 faults in first round.

World Champions

Show Jumping

Individual

Year	Men	Horse
1953	Francisco Goyoago (Spa)	Quorum
1954	Hans-Günter Winkler (FRG)	Halla
1955	Hans-Günter Winkler (FRG)	Halla
1956	Raimondo d'Inzeo (Ita)	Merano
1960	Raimondo d'Inzeo (Ita)	Gowran Girl
1966	Pierre d'Oriola (Fra)	Pomone
1970	David Broome (GB)	Beethoven
1974	Hartwig Steenken (FRG)	Simona

Year	Women	Horse
1965	Marion Coakes (GB)	Stroller
1970	Janou Lefèbvre (Fra)	Rocket
1974	Janou Tissot (née Lefèbvre) (Fra)	Rocket

Year	Rider*	Horse
1978	Gerd Wiltfang (FRG)	Roman
1982	Norbert Koof (FRG)	Fire II
1986	Gail Greenhough (Can)	Mr T
1990	Eric Navet (Fr)	Malesan Quito de Baussy

*The women's event merged with the men's after 1974.

Team

1978	Britain	1986	United States
1982	France	1990	France

Three-Day Event

Individual

Year	Rider	Horse
1966	Carlos Moratorio (Arg)	Chalon
1970	Mary Gordon-Watson (GB)	Cornishman V
1974	Bruce Davidson (US)	Irish Cap
1978	Bruce Davidson (US)	Might Tango
1982	Lucinda Green (GB)	Regal Realm
1986	Virginia Leng (GB)	Priceless
1990	Blyth Tait (NZ)	Messiah

Team

1966	Ireland	1982	Great Britain
1970	Great Britain	1986	Great Britain
1974	United States	1990	New Zealand
1978	Canada		

Dressage

Individual

Year	Rider	Horse
1966	Josef Neckermann (FRG)	Mariano
1970	Yelena Petouchkova (USSR)	Popel
1974	Reiner Klimke (FRG)	Mehmed
1978	Christine Stuckelberger (Swi)	Granat
1982	Reiner Klimke (FRG)	Ahlerich
1986	Anne Grethe Jensen (Den)	Marzog
1990	Nicole Uphoff (FRG)	Rembrandt

Team

1966	West Germany	1982	West Germany
1970	USSR	1986	West Germany
1974	West Germany	1990	West Germany
1978	West Germany		

Endurance

Individual

Year	Rider	Horse
1986	Cassandra Schuler (US)	Skikos Omar
1988	Becky Hart (US)	RO Grand Sultan
1990	Becky Hart (US)	RO Grand Sultan
1992	Becky Hart (US)	RO Grand Sultan

Team

1986	Great Britain	1990	Great Britain
1988	United States	1992	France

Vaulting

Men's Individual

1986	Dietmar Ott (FRG)	1990	Michael Lehner (FRG)
1988	Christopher Pensing (FRG)	1992	Christophe Lensing (Ger)

Women's Individual

1986	Silke Bernhard (FRG)	1990	Silke Bernhard (FRG)
1988	Silke Bernhard (FRG)	1992	Barbara Strobel (Ger)

Team

1986	West Germany	1988	West Germany
1990	Switzerland	1992	Germany

Carriage Driving

Year	Individual	Team
1972	Auguste Dubey (Swi)	Great Britain
1974	Sandor Fulop (Hun)	Great Britain
1976	Imre Abonyi (Hun)	Hungary
1978	Gyorgy Bardos (Hun)	Hungary
1980	Gyorgy Bardos (Hun)	Great Britain
1982	Tjeerd Velstra (Hol)	Holland
1984	Laszlo Juhasz (Hun)	Hungary
1986	Tjeerd Velstra (Hol)	Holland
1988	Ijsbrand Chardon (Hol)	Holland
1990	Ad Aarts (Hol)	Holland
1992	Ijsbraud Chardon (Hol)	Germany

GOLF

Professional Golf Tournaments 1992–93

(PGA European Tour)

Men

Tournament	Winner
Austrian Open	Ronan Rafferty (Ire)
Benson & Hedges International	Paul Broadhurst (Eng)
Cannes Open	Rodger Davis (Aus)
Dubai Desert Classic	Wayne Westner (SA)
Dunhill British Masters	Peter Baker (Eng)
Dutch Open	Colin Montgomerie (Scot)
English Open	Ian Woosnam (Wales)
European Masters	Barry Lane (Eng)
European Open	Gordon Brand Jr (Eng)
French Open	Constantino Rocca (Ita)
German Masters	Barry Lane (Eng)
International Open	Peter Fowler (Aus)
Irish Open	Nick Faldo (Eng)
Johnnie Walker Classic	Nick Faldo (Eng)
Monte Carlo Open	Cancelled
Open Golf Championship	Greg Norman (Aus)
Scandinavian Masters	Peter Baker (Eng)
Scottish Open	Jesper Parnevik (Swe)
Spanish Open	Joakim Haeggman (Swe)
Volvo PGA	Bernhard Langer (Ger)

Women

Tournament	Winner
Ford Golf Classic	Federica Dassu (Ita)
Italian Ladies' Open	Laura Davies (Eng)
Leiden Ladies' Open	Corinne Dibnah (Aus)
European Masters'	Helen Dobson (Eng)
Slovenian Ladies' Open	Karen Lunn (Aus)
Hennessy Ladies' Cup	Liselotte Neumann (Swe)
Women's British Open	Patty Sheehan (US)

British Open Golf Champions

Men

Year	Winner	Year	Winner	Year	Winner	Year	Winner
1872	T. Morris Jr. (GB)	1901	J. Braid (GB)	1934	T. Cotton (GB)	1968	G. Player (SA)
1873	T. Kidd (GB)	1902	A. Herd (GB)	1935	A. Perry (GB)	1969	A. Jacklin (GB)
1874	M. Park (GB)	1903	H. Vardon (GB)	1936	A. Padgham (GB)	1970	J. Nicklaus (USA)
1875	W. Park (GB)	1904	J. White (GB)	1937	T. Cotton (GB)	1971	L. Trevino (USA)
1876	B. Martin (GB)	1905	J. Braid (GB)	1938	R. Whitcombe (GB)	1972	L. Trevino (USA)
1877	J. Anderson (GB)	1906	J. Braid (GB)	1939	R. Burton (GB)	1973	T. Weiskopf (USA)
1878	J. Anderson (GB)	1907	A. Massy (GB)	1940–45	Not played	1974	G. Player (SA)
1879	J. Anderson (GB)	1908	J. Braid (GB)	1946	S. Snead (USA)	1975	T. Watson (USA)
1880	B. Ferguson (GB)	1909	J. Taylor (GB)	1947	F. Daly (GB)	1976	J. Miller (USA)
1881	B. Ferguson (GB)	1910	J. Braid (GB)	1948	T. Cotton (GB)	1977	T. Watson (USA)
1882	B. Ferguson (GB)	1911	H. Vardon (GB)	1949	A. Locke (SA)	1978	J. Nicklaus (USA)
1883	W. Fernie (GB)	1912	E. Ray (GB)	1950	A. Locke (SA)	1979	S. Ballesteros (Spa)
1884	J. Simpson (GB)	1913	J. Taylor (GB)	1951	M. Faulkner (GB)	1980	T. Watson (USA)
1885	B. Martin (GB)	1914	H. Vardon (GB)	1952	A. Locke (SA)	1981	B. Rogers (USA)
1886	D. Brown (GB)	1915–19	Not played	1953	B. Hogan (USA)	1982	T. Watson (USA)
1887	W. Park (GB)	1920	G. Duncan (GB)	1954	P. Thomson (Aust)	1983	T. Watson (USA)
1888	J. Burns (GB)	1921	J. Hutchison (USA)	1955	P. Thomson (Aust)	1984	S. Ballesteros (Spa)
1889	W. Park Jr. (GB)	1922	W. Hagen (USA)	1956	P. Thomson (Aust)	1985	A. Lyle (GB)
1890	J. Ball* (GB)	1923	A. Havers (GB)	1957	A. Locke (SA)	1986	G. Norman (Aust)
1891	H. Kirkaldy (GB)	1924	W. Hagen (USA)	1958	P. Thomson (Aust)	1987	N. Faldo (GB)
1892	H. Hilton* (GB)	1925	J. Barnes (USA)	1959	G. Player (SA)	1988	S. Ballesteros (Spa)
1893	W. Auchterlonie (GB)	1926	R. Jones* (USA)	1960	K. Nagle (Aust)	1989	M. Calcavecchia (USA)
1894	J. Taylor (GB)	1927	R. Jones* (USA)	1961	A. Palmer (USA)	1990	N. Faldo (GB)
1895	J. Taylor (GB)	1928	W. Hagen (USA)	1962	A. Palmer (USA)	1991	I. Baker-Finch (Aust)
1896	H. Vardon (GB)	1929	W. Hagen (USA)	1963	R. Charles (NZ)	1992	N. Faldo (GB)
1897	H. Hilton (GB)	1930	R. Jones* (USA)	1964	T. Lema (USA)	1993	G. Norman (Aust)
1898	H. Vardon (GB)	1931	T. Armour (USA)	1965	P. Thomson (Aust)		
1899	H. Vardon (GB)	1932	G. Sarazen (USA)	1966	J. Nicklaus (USA)		
1900	J. Taylor (GB)	1933	D. Shute (USA)	1967	R. De Vicenzo (Arg)		

*Amateur

Women

Year	Winner	Year	Winner	Year	Winner	Year	Winner
1976	J. Lee Smith (GB)	1981	D. Massey (USA)	1986	L. Davies (GB)	1990	H. Alfredsson (Swe)
1977	V. Saunders (GB)	1982	Figueras-Dotti (Spa)	1987	A. Nicholas (GB)	1991	P. Grice-Whittaker (GB)
1978	J. Melville (GB)	1983	Not played	1988	C. Dibnah (Aust) / S. Little (SA)	1992	P. Sheehan (USA)
1979	A. Sheard (SA)	1984	A. Okamoto (Jap)	1989	J. Geddes (USA)	1993	K. Lunn (Aust)
1980	D. Massey (USA)	1985	B. King (USA)				

Ryder Cup Champions

United States versus Great Britain 1927–71; Great Britain and Ireland 1973–77; Europe 1979–.

Year	Venue	Running Scores Day 1 Eur US	Day 2 Eur US	Day 3 Eur US
1927	Worcester, Massachusetts	1–3	2½–9½	–
1929	Moortown, Yorks	1½–2½	7–5	–
1931	Scioto, Ohio	1–3	3–9	–
1933	Southport and Ainsdale	2½–1½	6½–5½	–
1935	Ridgewood, New Jersey	1–3	3–9	–
1937	Southport and Ainsdale	1½–2½	4–8	–
1947	Portland, Oregon	0–4	1–11	–
1949	Ganton, Yorks	3–1	5–7	–
1951	Pinehurst, North Carolina	1–3	2½–9½	–
1953	Wentworth, Surrey	1–3	5½–6½	–
1955	Thunderbird, Calif.	1–3	4–8	–
1957	Lindrick Club, Yorks	1–3	7½–4½	–
1959	Elorado CC, California	1½–2½	3½–8½	–
1961	Royal Lytham & St Annes	2–6	9½–14½	–
1963	Atlanta, Georgia	2–6	4–23	9–23
1965	Royal Birkdale, Southport	4–4	7–9	12½–19½
1967	Houston, Texas	2½–5½	3–13	8½–23½
1969	Royal Birkdale, Southport	4½–3½	8–7½	16–16
1971	St Louis, Missouri	4½–3½	6–12½	13½–18½
1973	Muirfield, Scotland	5½–2½	8–8	13–19
1975	Laurel Valley, Pennsylvania	1½–6½	3½–12½	11–21
1977	Royal Lytham & St Annes	1½–3½	2½–7½	7½–12½
1979	Greenbrier, West Virginia	2½–5½	7½–8½	11–17
1981	Walton Heath GC, Surrey	4½–3½	5½–10½	9½–18½
1983	PGA National GC, Florida	4½–3½	8–8	13½–14½
1985	The Belfry, Sutton Coldfield	3½–4½	9–7	16½–11½
1987	Muirfield Village, Columbus	6–2	10½–5½	15–13
1989	The Belfry, Sutton Coldfield	5–3	9–7	14–14
1991	Kiawah Island, South Carolina	4½–3½	8–8	13½–14½
1993	The Belfry, Sutton Coldfield	4½–3½	8½–7½	13–15

Score: US 23, Great Britain/Europe 5, Halved 2

Solheim Cup

Year	Venue	Winner
1990	Lake Nona Golf Club, Florida	USA
1992	Delmahoy Country Club, Edinburgh	Europe

Sunrise Cup

Year	Venue	Winner
1992	Sunrise Country Club, Taipei	Sweden

US Masters Champions

Year	Winner	Year	Winner	Year	Winner	Year	Winner
1934	Horton Smith	1951	Ben Hogan	1966	Jack Nicklaus	1980	Severiano Ballesteros
1935	Gene Sarazen	1952	Sam Snead	1967	Gay Brewer Jr	1981	Tom Watson
1936	Horton Smith	1953	Ben Hogan	1968	Bob Goalby	1982	Craig Stadler
1937	Byron Nelson	1954	Sam Snead	1969	George Archer	1983	Severiano Ballesteros
1938	Henry Picard	1955	Cary Middlecoff	1970	Billy Casper	1984	Ben Crenshaw
1939	Ralph Guldahl	1956	Jack Burke	1971	Charles Coody	1985	Bernhard Langer
1940	Jimmy Demaret	1957	Doug Ford	1972	Jack Nicklaus	1986	Jack Nicklaus
1941	Craig Wood	1958	Arnold Palmer	1973	Tommy Aaron	1987	Larry Mize
1942	Byren Nelson	1959	Art Wall Jr	1974	Gary Player	1988	Sandy Lyle
1943–45	Not played	1960	Arnold Palmer	1975	Jack Nicklaus	1989	Nick Faldo
1946	Herman Keiser	1961	Gary Player	1976	Ray Floyd	1990	Nick Faldo
1947	Jimmy Demaret	1962	Arnold Palmer	1977	Tom Watson	1991	Ian Woosnam
1948	Claude Harmon	1963	Jack Nicklaus	1978	Gary Player	1992	Fred Couples
1949	Sam Snead	1964	Arnold Palmer	1979	Fuzzy Zoeller	1993	Bernhard Langer
1950	Jimmy Demaret	1965	Jack Nicklaus				

US Open Champions

Men

Year	Winner	Year	Winner	Year	Winner	Year	Winner
1903	Willie Anderson	1917–18	Not played	1932	Gene Sarazen	1949	Cary Middlecoff
1904	Willie Anderson	1919	Walter Hagen	1933	John Goodman*	1950	Ben Hogan
1905	Willie Anderson	1920	Edward Ray	1934	Olin Dutra	1951	Ben Hogan
1906	Alex Smith	1921	Jim Barnes	1935	Sam Parks Jr	1952	Julius Boros
1907	Alex Ross	1922	Gene Sarazen	1936	Tony Manero	1953	Ben Hogan
1908	Fred McLeod	1923	Bobby Jones*	1937	Ralph Guldahl	1954	Ed Furgol
1909	George Sargent	1924	Cyril Walker	1938	Ralph Guldahl	1955	Jack Fleck
1910	Alex Smith	1925	Willie MacFarlane	1939	Byron Nelson	1956	Cary Middlecoff
1911	John McDermott	1926	Bobby Jones*	1940	Lawson Little	1957	Dick Mayer
1912	John McDermott	1927	Tommy Armour	1941	Craig Wood	1958	Tommy Bolt
1913	Francis Quimet*	1928	John Farrell	1942–45	Not played	1959	Billy Casper
1914	Walter Hagen	1929	Bobby Jones*	1946	Lloyd Mangrum	1960	Arnold Palmer
1915	Jerome Travers*	1930	Bobby Jones*	1947	L. Worsham	1961	Gene Littler
1916	Chick Evans*	1931	William Burke	1948	Ben Hogan	1962	Jack Nicklaus

(Continued)

Year	Winner	Year	Winner	Year	Winner	Year	Winner
1963	Julius Boros	1971	Lee Trevino	1979	Hale Irwin	1987	Scott Simpson
1964	Ken Venturi	1972	Jack Nicklaus	1980	Jack Nicklaus	1988	Curtis Strange
1965	Gary Player	1973	Johnny Miller	1981	David Graham	1989	Curtis Strange
1966	Billy Casper	1974	Hale Irwin	1982	Tom Watson	1990	Hale Irwin
1967	Jack Nicklaus	1975	Lou Graham	1983	Larry Nelson	1991	Payne Stewart
1968	Lee Trevino	1976	Jerry Pate	1984	Fuzzy Zoeller	1992	Tom Kite
1969	Orville Moody	1977	Hubert Green	1985	Andy North	1993	Lee Janzen
1970	Tony Jacklin	1978	Andy North	1986	Ray Floyd		

Women

Year	Winner	Year	Winner	Year	Winner	Year	Winner
1948	"Babe" Zaharias	1960	Betsy Rawls	1972	Susie Maxwell Berning	1983	Jan Stephenson
1949	Louise Suggs	1961	Mickey Wright	1973	Susie Maxwell Berning	1984	Hollis Stacy
1950	"Babe" Zaharias	1962	Murle Lindstrom	1974	Sandra Haynie	1985	Kathy Baker
1951	Betsy Rawls	1963	Mary Mills	1975	Sandra Palmer	1986	Jane Geddes
1952	Louise Suggs	1964	Mickey Wright	1976	JoAnne Carner	1987	Laura Davies
1953	Betsy Rawls	1965	Carol Mann	1977	Hollis Stacy	1988	Liselotte Neumann
1954	"Babe" Zaharias	1966	Sandra Spuzich	1978	Hollis Stacy	1989	Betsy King
1955	Fay Crocker	1967	Catherine Lacoste*	1979	Jerilyn Britz	1990	Betsy King
1956	Mrs. K. Cornelius	1968	Susie Maxwell Berning	1980	Amy Alcott	1991	Meg Mallon
1957	Betsy Rawls	1969	Donna Caponi	1981	Pat Bradley	1992	Patty Sheehan
1958	Mickey Wright	1970	Donna Caponi	1982	Janet Alex	1993	Lauri Merten
1959	Mickey Wright	1971	JoAnne Carner				

*Amateur

US PGA Champions

Year	Winner	Year	Winner	Year	Winner	Year	Winner
1922	Gene Sarazen	1940	Byron Nelson	1958	Dow Finsterwald	1976	Dave Stockton
1923	Gene Sarazen	1941	Victor Ghezzi	1959	Bob Rosburg	1977	Lanny Wadkins
1924	Walter Hagen	1942	Sam Snead	1960	Jay Hebert	1978	John Mahaffey
1925	Walter Hagen	1943	Not played	1961	Jerry Barber	1979	David Graham
1926	Walter Hagen	1944	Bob Hamilton	1962	Gary Player	1980	Jack Nicklaus
1927	Walter Hagen	1945	Byron Nelson	1963	Jack Nicklaus	1981	Larry Nelson
1928	Leo Diegel	1946	Ben Hogan	1964	Bob Nichols	1982	Ray Floyd
1929	Leo Diegel	1947	Jim Ferrier	1965	Dave Marr	1983	Hal Sutton
1930	Tommy Armour	1948	Ben Hogan	1966	Al Geiberger	1984	Lee Trevino
1931	Tom Creavy	1949	Sam Snead	1967	Don January	1985	Hubert Green
1932	Olin Dutra	1950	Chandler Harper	1968	Julius Boros	1986	Bob Tway
1933	Gene Sarazen	1951	Sam Snead	1969	Ray Floyd	1987	Larry Nelson
1934	Paul Runyan	1952	James Turnesa	1970	Dave Stockton	1988	Jeff Sluman
1935	Johnny Revolta	1953	Walter Burkemo	1971	Jack Nicklaus	1989	Payne Stewart
1936	Denny Shute	1954	Melvin Harbert	1972	Gary Player	1990	Wayne Grady
1937	Denny Shute	1955	Doug Ford	1973	Jack Nicklaus	1991	John Daly
1938	Paul Runyan	1956	Jack Burke	1974	Lee Trevino	1992	Nick Price
1939	Henry Picard	1957	Lionel Hebert	1975	Jack Nicklaus	1993	Paul Azinger

World Cup of Golf
(Until 1966 called Canada Cup)

Year	Winner	Year	Winner	Year	Winner	Year	Winner
1953	Argentina	1964	United States	1974	South Africa	1984	Spain
1954	Australia	1965	South Africa	1975	United States	1985	Canada
1955	United States	1966	United States	1976	Spain	1986	Not played
1956	United States	1967	United States	1977	Spain	1987	Wales
1957	Japan	1968	Canada	1978	United States	1988	United States
1958	Ireland	1969	United States	1979	United States	1989	Australia
1959	Australia	1970	Australia	1980	Canada	1990	Germany
1960	United States	1971	United States	1981	Not played	1991	Sweden
1961	United States	1972	Taiwan	1982	Spain	1992	United States
1962	United States	1973	United States	1983	United States		
1963	United States						

HORSE RACING

Major Horse Races 1992–93

Race	Horse	Jockey
Cheltenham Gold Cup	Jodami	Mark Dwyer
Derby	Commander-in-Chief	Mick Kinane
Grand National	Race void	
Oaks	Intrepidity	Michael Roberts
One Thousand Guineas	Sayyedati	Walter Swinburn
St Leger	User Friendly	George Duffield
Two Thousand Guineas	Zafonic	Pat Eddery
French Derby	Hernando	Cash Asmussen
French One Thousand Guineas	Madeleine's Dream	Cash Asmussen

(Continued)

(Major Horse Races 1992–93 contd.)

Race	Horse	Jockey
French Two Thousand Guineas	Kingmambo	Cash Asmussen
Prix de l'Arc de Triomphe	Subotica	Thierry Jarnet
Irish Derby	Commander-in-Chief	Pat Eddery
Irish Grand National	Ebony Jane	Charly Swan
Irish One Thousand Guineas	Nicer	Michael Hills
Irish Two Thousand Guineas	Barathea	Michael Roberts

Arc de Triomphe Champions

Year	Horse	Year	Horse
1920	Comrade	1957	Oreso
1921	Ksar	1958	Ballymoss
1922	Ksar	1959	Saint Crespin
1923	Parth	1960	Pussaint Chef
1924	Massine	1961	Molvedo
1925	Priori	1962	Soltikoff
1926	Biribi	1963	Exbury
1927	Mon Talisman	1964	Prince Royal II
1928	Kantar	1965	Sea Bird II
1929	Ortello	1966	Bon Mot
1930	Motrico	1967	Topyo
1931	Pearl Cap	1968	Vaguely Noble
1932	Motrico	1969	Levmoss
1933	Crapom	1970	Sassafras
1934	Brantome	1971	Mill Reef
1935	Samos	1972	San San
1936	Corrida	1973	Rheingold
1937	Corrida	1974	Allez France
1938	Eclair au Chocolat	1975	Star Appeal
1939	–	1976	Ivanjica
1940	–	1977	Alleged
1941	La Pacha	1978	Alleged
1942	Djebel	1979	Three Troikas
1943	Verso II	1980	Detroit
1944	Ardan	1981	Gold River
1945	Nikellora	1982	Akiyda
1946	Caracella	1983	All Along
1947	Le Paillon	1984	Sagace
1948	Migoli	1985	Rainbow Quest
1949	Coronation	1986	Dancing Brave
1950	Tantieme	1987	Trempolino
1951	Tantieme	1988	Tony Bin
1952	Nuccio	1989	Carroll House
1953	La Sorellina	1990	Saumarez
1954	Sica Boy	1991	Suave Dancer
1955	Ribot	1992	Suave Dancer
1956	Ribot	1993	Subotica

Cheltenham Gold Cup Winners

Year	Horse	Year	Horse
1924	Red Splash	1959	Roddy Owen
1925	Balinode	1960	Pas Seul
1926	Koko	1961	Saffron Tartan
1927	Thrown In	1962	Mandarin
1928	Patron Saint	1963	Mill House
1929	Easter Hero	1964	Arkle
1930	Easter Hero	1965	Arkle
1931	–	1966	Arkle
1932	Golden Miller	1967	Woodland Venture
1933	Golden Miller	1968	Fort Leney
1934	Golden Miller	1969	What a Myth
1935	Golden Miller	1970	L'Escargot
1936	Golden Miller	1971	L'Escargot
1937	–	1972	Glencaraig Lady
1938	Morse Code	1973	The Dikler
1939	Brendan's Cottage	1974	Captain Christy
1940	Roman Hackle	1975	Ten Up
1941	Poet Prince	1976	Royal Frolic
1942	Medoc II	1977	Davy Lad
1943	–	1978	Midnight Court
1944	–	1979	Alverton
1945	Red Rower	1980	Master Smudge
1946	Prince Regent	1981	Little Owl
1947	Fortina	1982	Silver Buck
1948	Cottage Rake	1983	Bregawn
1949	Cottage Rake	1984	Burrough Hill Lad
1950	Cottage Rake	1985	Forgive N'Forget
1951	Silver Fame	1986	Dawn Run
1952	Mont Tremblant	1987	The Thinker
1953	Knock Hard	1988	Charter Party
1954	Four Ten	1989	Desert Orchid
1955	Gay Donald	1990	Norton's Coin
1956	Limber Hill	1991	Garrison Savannah
1957	Linwell	1992	Cool Ground
1958	Kerstin	1993	Jodami

Derby Winners

Year	Horse	Year	Horse
1780	Diomed	1856	Ellington
1781	Young Eclipse	1857	Blink Bonny
1782	Assassin	1858	Beadsman
1783	Saltram	1859	Musjid
1784	Sergeant	1860	Thormanby
1785	Aimwell	1861	Kettledrum
1786	Noble	1862	Caractacus
1787	Sir Peter Teazle	1863	Marconi
1788	Sir Thomas	1864	Blair Atholl
1789	Skyscraper	1865	Gladiateur
1790	Rhadamanthus	1866	Lord Lyon
1791	Eager	1867	Hermit
1792	John Bull	1868	Blue Gown
1793	Waxy	1869	Pretender
1794	Daedalus	1870	Kingcraft
1795	Spread Eagle	1871	Favonius
1796	Didelot	1872	Cremorne
1797	(Unnamed colt)	1873	Doncaster
1798	Sir Harry	1874	George Frederick
1799	Archduke	1875	Galopin
1800	Champion	1876	Kisber
1801	Eleanor	1877	Silvio
1802	Tyrant	1878	Sefton
1803	Ditto	1879	Sir Bevys
1804	Hannibal	1880	Bend Or
1805	Cardinal Beaufort	1881	Iroquois
1806	Paris	1882	Shotover
1807	Election	1883	St Blaise
1808	Pan	1884	St Gatien* / Harvester*
1809	Pope		
1810	Whalebone	1885	Melton
1811	Phantom	1886	Ormonde
1812	Octavius	1887	Merry Hampton
1813	Smolensko	1888	Ayrshire
1814	Blucher	1889	Donovan
1815	Whisker	1890	Sainfoin
1816	Prince Leopold	1891	Common
1817	Azor	1892	Sir Hugo
1818	Sam	1893	Isinglass
1819	Tiresias	1894	Ladas
1820	Sailor	1895	Sir Visto
1821	Gustavus	1896	Persimmon
1822	Moses	1897	Galtee More
1823	Emilius	1898	Jeddah
1824	Cedric	1899	Flying Fox
1825	Middleton	1900	Diamond Jubilee
1826	Lapdog	1901	Volodyovski
1827	Mameluke	1902	Ard Patrick
1828	Cadland	1903	Rock Sand
1829	Frederick	1904	St Amant
1830	Priam	1905	Cicero
1831	Spaniel	1906	Spearmint
1832	St Giles	1907	Orby
1833	Dangerous	1908	Signorinetta
1834	Plenipotentiary	1909	Minoru
1835	Mundig	1910	Lemberg
1836	Bay Middleton	1911	Sunstar
1837	Phosphorus	1912	Tagalie
1838	Amato	1913	Aboyeur
1839	Bloomsbury	1914	Durbar II
1840	Little Wonder	1915	Pommern
1841	Coronation	1916	Fifinella
1842	Attila	1917	Gay Crusader
1843	Cotherstone	1918	Gainsborough
1844	Orlando	1919	Grand Parade
1845	The Merry Monarch	1920	Spion Kop
1846	Pyrrhus the First	1921	Humorist
1847	Cossack	1922	Captain Cuttle
1848	Surplice	1923	Papyrus
1849	The Flying Dutchman	1924	Sansovino
1850	Voltigeur	1925	Manna
1851	Teddington	1926	Coronach
1852	Daniel O'Rourke	1927	Call Boy
1853	West Australian	1928	Felstead
1854	Andover	1929	Trigo
1855	Wild Dayrell	1930	Blenheim

(Continued)

(Derby Winners contd.)

Year	Horse	Year	Horse
1931	Cameronian	1963	Relko
1932	April the Fifth	1964	Santa Claus
1933	Hyperion	1965	Sea Bird II
1934	Windsor Lad	1966	Charlottown
1935	Bahram	1967	Royal Palace
1936	Mahmoud	1968	Sir Ivor
1937	Mid-day Sun	1969	Blakeney
1938	Bois Roussel	1970	Nijinsky
1939	Blue Peter	1971	Mill Reef
1940	Pont l'Eveque	1972	Roberto
1941	Owen Tudor	1973	Morston
1942	Watling Street	1974	Snow Knight
1943	Straight Deal	1975	Grundy
1944	Ocean Swell	1976	Empery
1945	Dante	1977	The Minstrel
1946	Airborne	1978	Shirley Heights
1947	Pearl Diver	1979	Troy
1948	My Love	1980	Henbit
1949	Nimbus	1981	Shergar
1950	Galcador	1982	Golden Fleece
1951	Arctic Prince	1983	Teenoso
1952	Tulyar	1984	Secreto
1953	Pinza	1985	Slip Anchor
1954	Never Say Die	1986	Shahrastani
1955	Phil Drake	1987	Reference Point
1956	Lavandin	1988	Kahyasi
1957	Crepello	1989	Nashwan
1958	Hard Ridden	1990	Quest for Fame
1959	Parthia	1991	Generous
1960	St Paddy	1992	Dr Devious
1961	Psidium	1993	Commander-in-Chief
1962	Larkspur		

*Dead heat.

Grand National Winners

Year	Horse	Year	Horse
1836	The Duke	1886	Old Joe
1837	The Duke	1887	Gamecock
1838	Sir William	1888	Playfair
1839	Lottery	1889	Frigate
1840	Jerry	1890	Ilex
1841	Charity	1891	Come Away
1842	Gay Lad	1892	Father O'Flynn
1843	Vanguard	1893	Cloister
1844	Discount	1894	Why Not
1845	Cureall	1895	Wild Man from Borneo
1846	Pioneer	1896	Soarer
1847	Matthew	1897	Manifesto
1848	Chandler	1898	Drogheda
1849	Peter Simple	1899	Manifesto
1850	Abd-el-Kader	1900	Ambush II
1851	Abd-el-Kader	1901	Grudon
1852	Miss Mowbray	1902	Shannon Lass
1853	Peter Simple	1903	Drumcree
1854	Bourton	1904	Moifaa
1855	Wanderer	1905	Kirkland
1856	Freetrader	1906	Ascetic's Silver
1857	Emigrant	1907	Eremon
1858	Little Charley	1908	Rubio
1859	Half Caste	1909	Lutteur III
1860	Anatis	1910	Jenkinstown
1861	Jealousy	1911	Glenside
1862	Huntsman	1912	Jerry M
1863	Emblem	1913	Covetcoat
1864	Emblematic	1914	Sunloch
1865	Alcibiade	1915	Ally Sloper
1866	Salamander	1916	Vermouth
1867	Cortolvin	1917	Ballymacad
1868	The Lamb	1918	Poethlyn
1869	The Colonel	1919	Poethlyn
1870	The Colonel	1920	Troytown
1871	The Lamb	1921	Shaun Spadah
1872	Casse Tete	1922	Music Hall
1873	Disturbance	1923	Sergeant Murphy
1874	Reugny	1924	Master Robert
1875	Pathfinder	1925	Double Chance
1876	Regal	1926	Jack Horner
1877	Austerlitz	1927	Sprig
1878	Shifnal	1928	Tipperary Tim
1879	The Liberator	1929	Gregalach
1880	Empress	1930	Shaun Goilin
1881	Woodbrook	1931	Grakle
1882	Seaman	1932	Forbra
1883	Zoedone	1933	Kellsboro' Jack
1884	Voluptuary	1934	Golden Miller
1885	Roquefort	1935	Reynoldstown

(Grand National Winners contd.)

Year	Horse	Year	Horse
1936	Reynoldstown	1968	Reg Alligator
1937	Royal Mail	1969	Highland Wedding
1938	Battleship	1970	Gay Trip
1939	Workman	1971	Specify
1940	Bogskar	1972	Well To Do
1946	Lovely Cottage	1973	Red Rum
1947	Caughoo	1974	Red Rum
1948	Sheila's Cottage	1975	L'Escargot
1949	Russian Hero	1976	Rag Trade
1950	Freebooter	1977	Red Rum
1951	Nickel Coin	1978	Lucius
1952	Teal	1979	Rubstic
1953	Early Mist	1980	Ben Nevis
1954	Royal Tan	1981	Aldaniti
1955	Quare Times	1982	Grittar
1956	E.S.B.	1983	Corbiere
1957	Sundrew	1984	Hallo Dandy
1958	Mr What	1985	Last Suspect
1959	Oxo	1986	West Tip
1960	Merryman II	1987	Maori Venture
1961	Nicolaus Silver	1988	Rhyme N'Reason
1962	Kilmore	1989	Little Polveir
1963	Ayala	1990	Mr Frisk
1964	Team Spirit	1991	Seagram
1965	Jay Trump	1992	Party Politics
1966	Anglo	1993	Race void
1967	Foinavon		

Irish Derby Champions

Year	Horse	Year	Horse
1866	Selim	1922	Spike Island
1867	Golden Plover	1923	Waygood
1868	Madeira	1924	Zodiac/Haine
1869	The Scout	1925	Zionist
1870	Billy Pitt	1926	Embargo
1871	Maid of Athens	1927	Knight of the Grail
1872	Trickstress	1928	Baytown
1873	Kyrle Daly	1929	Kopi
1874	Ben Battle	1930	Rock Star
1875	Innishowen	1931	Sea Serpent
1876	Umpire	1932	Dastur
1877	Redskin	1933	Harninero
1878	Madame Dubarry	1934	Primero/Patriot King
1879	Soulouque	1935	Museum
1880	King of the Bees	1936	Raeburn
1881	Master Ned	1937	Phidias
1882	Sortie	1938	Rosewell
1883	Sylph	1939	Mondragon
1884	Theologian	1940	Turkham
1885	St Kevin	1941	Sol Oriens
1886	Theodemir	1942	Windsor Slipper
1887	Pet Fox	1943	The Phoenix
1888	Theodolite	1944	Slide On
1889	Tragedy	1945	Piccadilly
1890	Kentish Fire	1946	Bright News
1891	Narraghmore	1947	Sayajirao
1892	Roy Neil	1948	Nathoo
1893	Bowline	1949	Hindostan
1894	Blairfinds	1950	Dark Warrior
1895	Portmarnock	1951	Fraise du Bois II
1896	Gulsalberk	1952	Thirteen of Diamonds
1897	Wales	1953	Chamier
1898	Noble Howard	1954	Zarathustra
1899	Oppressor	1955	Panaslipper
1900	Gallinaria	1956	Talgo
1901	Carrigavalla	1957	Ballymoss
1902	St Brendan	1958	Sindon
1903	Lord Rossmore	1959	Fidalgo
1904	Royal Arch	1960	Chamour
1905	Flax Pack	1961	Your Highness
1906	Killeagh	1962	Tambourine II
1907	Orby	1963	Ragusa
1908	Wilde Bouquet	1964	Santa Claus
1909	Bachelor's Double	1965	Meadow Court
1910	Aviator	1966	Sodium
1911	Shanballymore	1967	Ribocco
1912	Civility	1968	Ribero
1913	Bachelors Wedding	1969	Prince Regent
1914	Land of Song	1970	Nijinsky
1915	Ballaghtobin	1971	Irish Ball
1916	Furore	1972	Steel Pulse
1917	First Flyer	1973	Weaver's Hall
1918	King John	1974	English Prince
1919	Loch Lomond	1975	Grundy
1920	He Goes	1976	Malacate
1921	Ballyheron	1977	The Minstrel

(Continued)

(Irish Derby Champions contd.)

Year	Horse	Year	Horse
1978	Shirley Heights	1986	Shahrastani
1979	Troy	1987	Sir Harry Lewis
1980	Tyrnavos	1988	Kahyasi
1981	Shergar	1989	Old Vic
1982	Assert	1990	Salsabil
1983	Shareef Dancer	1991	Generous
1984	El Gran Senor	1992	St Jovite
1985	Law Society	1993	Commander-in-Chief

Oaks Champions

Year	Horse	Year	Horse
1779	Bridget	1852	Songstress
1780	Tetoum	1853	Catherine Hayes
1781	Faith	1854	Mincemeat
1782	Ceres	1855	Marchioness
1783	Maid of the Oaks	1856	Mincepie
1784	Stella	1857	Blink Bonny
1785	Trifle	1858	Governess
1786	Yellow Filly	1859	Summerside
1787	Annette	1860	Butterfly
1788	Nightshade	1861	Brown Duchess
1789	Tag	1862	Fue de Joie
1790	Hippolyta	1863	Queen Bertha
1791	Portia	1864	Fille de l'Air
1792	Volante	1865	Regalia
1793	Caelia	1866	Tormentor
1794	Hermione	1867	Hippia
1795	Platina	1868	Formosa
1796	Pasiot	1869	Brigantine
1797	Nike	1870	Gamos
1798	Bellissima	1871	Hannah
1799	Bellina	1872	Reine
1800	Ephemera	1873	Marie Stuart
1801	Eleanor	1874	Apology
1802	Scotia	1875	Spinaway
1803	Theophania	1876	Enguerrande† / Camelia†
1804	Pelisse		
1805	Meteora	1877	Placida
1806	Bronze	1878	Jannette
1807	Briseis	1879	Wheel of Fortune
1808	Morel	1880	Jenny Howlet
1809	Maid of Orleans	1881	Thebais
1810	Oriana	1882	Geheimniss
1811	Sorcery	1883	Bonny Jean
1812	Manuella	1884	Busybody
1813	Music	1885	Lonely
1814	Medora	1886	Miss Jummy
1815	Minuet	1887	Reve d'Or
1816	Landscape	1888	Seabreeze
1817	Neva	1889	L'Abbesse de Jouarre
1818	Corinne	1890	Memoir
1819	Shoveler	1891	Mimi
1820	Caroline	1892	La Fleche
1821	Augusta	1893	Mrs Butterwick
1822	Pastille	1894	Amiable
1823	Zinc	1895	La Sagesse
1824	Cobweb	1896	Canterbury Pilgrim
1825	Wings	1897	Limasol
1826	Lilias	1898	Airs and Graces
1827	Gulnare	1899	Musa
1828	Turquoise	1900	La Roche
1829	Green Mantle	1901	Caps and Bells II
1830	Variation	1902	Sceptre
1831	Oxygen	1903	Our Lassie
1832	Galata	1904	Pretty Polly
1833	Vespa	1905	Cherry Lass
1834	Pussy	1906	Keystone II
1835	Queen of Trumps	1907	Glass Doll
1836	Cyprian	1908	Signorinetta
1837	Miss Letty	1909	Perola
1838	Industry	1910	Rosedrop
1839	Deception	1911	Cherimoya
1840	Crucifix	1912	Mirska
1841	Ghuznee	1913	Jest
1842	Our Nell	1914	Princess Dorrie
1843	Poison	1915	Snow Marten
1844	The Princess	1916	Fifinella
1845	Refraction	1917	Sunny Jane
1846	Mendicant	1918	My Dear
1847	Miami	1919	Bayuda
1848	Cymba	1920	Charlebelle
1849	Lady Evelyn	1921	Love in Idleness
1850	Rhedycina	1922	Pogrom
1851	Iris	1923	Brownhylda

(Oaks Champions contd.)

Year	Horse	Year	Horse
1924	Straitlace	1959	Petite Etoile*
1925	Saucy Sue	1960	Never Too Late*
1926	Short Story	1961	Sweet Solera*
1927	Beam	1962	Monade
1928	Toboggan	1963	Noblesse
1929	Pennycomequick	1964	Homeward Bound
1930	Rose of England	1965	Long Look
1931	Brulette	1966	Valoris
1932	Udaipur	1967	Pia
1933	Chatelaine	1968	La Lagune
1934	Light Brocade	1969	Sleeping Partner
1935	Quashed	1970	Lupe
1936	Lovely Rosa	1971	Altesse Royale*
1937	Exhibitionist	1972	Ginevra
1938	Rockfel	1973	Mysterious*
1939	Galatea II	1974	Polygamy
1940	Godiva	1975	Juliette Marny
1941	Commotion	1976	Pawneese
1942	Sun Chariot	1977	Dunfermline*
1943	Why Hurry	1978	Fari Salinia
1944	Hycilla	1979	Scintillate
1945	Sun Stream	1980	Bireme
1946	Steady Aim	1981	Blue Wind
1947	Imprudence*	1982	Time Charter
1948	Masaka	1983	Sun Princess*
1949	Musidora*	1984	Circus Plume
1950	Asmena	1985	Oh So Sharp*
1951	Neasham Belle	1986	Midway Lady*
1952	Frieze	1987	Unite
1953	Ambiguity	1988	Diminuendo
1954	Sun Cap	1989	Snow Bride
1955	Meld*	1990	Salsabil*
1956	Sicarelle	1991	Jet Ski Lady
1957	Carrozza	1992	User Friendly
1958	Bella Paola*	1993	Intrepidity

†Dead heat. *Won more than one classic.

One Thousand Guineas Champions

Year	Horse	Year	Horse
1814	Charlotte	1859	Mayonaise
1815	Unnamed filly	1860	Sagitta
1816	Rhoda	1861	Nemesis
1817	Neva	1862	Hurricane
1818	Corinne	1863	Lady Augusta
1819	Catgut	1864	Tomato
1820	Rowena	1865	Siberia
1821	Zeal	1866	Repulse
1822	Whizgig	1867	Achievement
1823	Zinc	1868	Formosa
1824	Cobweb	1869	Scottish Queen
1825	Tontine	1870	Hester
1826	Problem	1871	Hannah
1827	Arab	1872	Reine
1828	Zoe	1873	Cecilia
1829	Young Mouse	1874	Apology
1830	Charlotte West	1875	Spinaway
1831	Galantine	1876	Camelia
1832	Galata	1877	Belphoebe
1833	Tarantella	1878	Pilgrimage
1834	May-Day	1879	Wheel of Fortune
1835	Preserve	1880	Elizabeth
1836	Destiny	1881	Thebais
1837	Chapeau d'Espagne	1882	St Marguerite
1838	Barcarolle	1883	Hauteur
1839	Cara	1884	Busybody
1840	Crucifix	1885	Farewell
1841	Potentia	1886	Miss Jummy
1842	Firebrand	1887	Reve d'Or
1843	Extempore	1888	Briarroot
1844	Sorella	1889	Minthe
1845	Picnic	1890	Semolina
1846	Mendicant	1891	Mimi
1847	Clementina	1892	La Fleche
1848	Canezou	1893	Siffleuse
1849	The Flea	1894	Amiable
1850	Lady Orford	1895	Galeottia
1851	Aphrodite	1896	Thias
1852	Kate	1897	Chelandry
1853	Mentmore Lass	1898	Nun Nicer
1854	Virage	1899	Sibola
1855	Habena	1900	Winifreda
1856	Manganese	1901	Aida
1857	Imperieuse	1902	Sceptre
1858	Governess	1903	Quintessence

(Continued)

(1,000 Guineas Champions contd.)

Year	Horse	Year	Horse
1904	Pretty Polly	1949	Musidora
1905	Cherry Lass	1950	Camaree
1906	Flair	1951	Belle of All
1907	Witch Elm	1952	Zabara
1908	Rhodora	1953	Happy Laughter
1909	Electra	1954	Festoon
1910	Winkipop	1955	Meld
1911	Atmah	1956	Honeylight
1912	Tagalie	1957	Rose Royale II
1913	Jest	1958	Bella Paola
1914	Princess Dorrie	1959	Petite Etoile
1915	Vaucluse	1960	Never Too Late
1916	Canyon	1961	Sweet Solera
1917	Diadem	1962	Abermaid
1918	Ferry	1963	Hula Dancer
1919	Roseway	1964	Pourparler
1920	Cinna	1965	Night Off
1921	Bettina	1966	Glad Rags
1922	Silver Urn	1967	Fleet
1923	Tranquil	1968	Caergwrle
1924	Plack	1969	Full Dress II
1925	Saucy Sue	1970	Humble Duty
1926	Pillion	1971	Altesse Royale
1927	Cresta Run	1972	Waterloo
1928	Scuttle	1973	Mysterious
1929	Taj Mah	1974	Highclere
1930	Fair Isle	1975	Nocturnal Spree
1931	Four Course	1976	Flying Water
1932	Kandy	1977	Mrs McArdy
1933	Bety Brown	1978	Enstone Spark
1934	Campanula	1979	One in a Million
1935	Mesa	1980	Quick as Lightning
1936	Tide-Way	1981	Fairy Footsteps
1937	Exhibitionist	1982	On the House
1938	Rockfel	1983	Ma Biche
1939	Galatea II	1984	Pebbles
1940	Godiva	1985	Oh So Sharp
1941	Dancing Time	1986	Midway Lady
1942	Sun Chariot	1987	Miesque
1943	Herringbone	1988	Ravinella
1944	Picture Play	1989	Musical Bliss
1945	Sun Stream	1990	Salsabil
1946	Hypericum	1991	Shadayid
1947	Imprudence	1992	Hatoof
1948	Queenpot	1993	Sayeddati

St Leger Champions

Year	Horse	Year	Horse
1776	Allabaculia	1813	Altisidora
1777	Bourbon	1814	William
1778	Hollandaise	1815	Fihlo da Puta
1779	Tommy	1816	The Duchess
1780	Ruler	1817	Ebor
1781	Serina	1818	Reveller
1782	Imperatrix	1819	Antonio
1783	Phenomenon	1820	St Patrick
1784	Omphale	1821	Jack Spigot
1785	Cowslip	1822	Theodore
1786	Paragon	1823	Barefoot
1787	Spadille	1824	Jerry
1788	Young Flora	1825	Memnon
1789	Pewett	1826	Tarrare
1790	Ambidexter	1827	Matilda
1791	Young Traveller	1828	The Colonel
1792	Tartar	1829	Rowton
1793	Ninety-Three	1830	Birmingham
1794	Beningbrough	1831	Chorister
1795	Hambletonian	1832	Margrave
1796	Ambrosio	1833	Rockingham
1797	Lounger	1834	Touchstone
1798	Symmetry	1835	Queen of Trumps
1799	Cockfighter	1836	Elis
1800	Champion	1837	Mango
1801	Quiz	1838	Don John
1802	Orville	1839	Charles the Twelfth
1803	Remembrancer	1840	Launcelot
1804	Sancho	1841	Satirist
1805	Staveley	1842	The Blue Bonnet
1806	Fyldener	1843	Nutwith
1807	Paulina	1844	Foig a Ballagh
1808	Petronius	1845	The Baron
1809	Ashton	1846	Sir Tatton Sykes
1810	Octavian	1847	Van Tromp
1811	Soothsayer	1848	Surplice
1812	Otterington	1849	The Flying Dutchman

(St Leger Champions contd.)

Year	Horse	Year	Horse
1850	Voltigeur	1922	Royal Lancer
1851	Newminster	1923	Tranquil
1852	Stockwell	1924	Salmon-Trout
1853	West Australian	1925	Solario
1854	Knight of St George	1926	Coronach
1855	Saucebox	1927	Book Law
1856	Warlock	1928	Fairway
1857	Imperieuse	1929	Trigo
1858	Sunbeam	1930	Singapore
1859	Gamester	1931	Sandwich
1860	St Albans	1932	Firdaussi
1861	Caller Ou	1933	Hyperion
1862	The Marquis	1934	Windsor Lad
1863	Lord Clifden	1935	Bahram
1864	Blair Athol	1936	Boswell
1865	Gladiateur	1937	Chumleigh
1866	Lord Lyon	1938	Scottish Union
1867	Achievement	1939	No race
1868	Formosa	1940	Turkham
1869	Pero Gomez	1941	Sun Castle
1870	Hawthornden	1942	Sun Chariot
1871	Hannah	1943	Herringbone
1872	Wenlock	1944	Tehran
1873	Marie Stuart	1945	Chamossaire
1874	Apology	1946	Airborne
1875	Craig Millar	1947	Sayajirao
1876	Petrarch	1948	Black Tarquin
1877	Silvio	1949	Ridge Wood
1878	Jannette	1950	Scratch II
1879	Rayon d'Or	1951	Talma II
1880	Robert the Devil	1952	Tulyar
1881	Iroquois	1953	Premonition
1882	Dutch Oven	1954	Never Say Die
1883	Ossian	1955	Meld
1884	The Lambkin	1956	Cambremer
1885	Melton	1957	Ballymoss
1886	Ormonde	1958	Alcide
1887	Kitwarlin	1959	Cantelo
1888	Seabreeze	1960	St Paddy
1889	Donovan	1961	Aurelius
1890	Memoir	1962	Hethersett
1891	Common	1963	Ragusa
1892	La Fleche	1964	Indiana
1893	Isinglass	1965	Provoke
1894	Throstle	1966	Sodium
1895	Sir Visto	1967	Ribocco
1896	Persimmon	1968	Ribero
1897	Galtee More	1969	Intermezzo
1898	Wildfowler	1970	Nijinsky
1899	Flying Fox	1971	Athens Wood
1900	Diamond Jubilee	1972	Boucher
1901	Doricles	1973	Peleid
1902	Sceptre	1974	Bustino
1903	Rock Sand	1975	Bruni
1904	Pretty Polly	1976	Crow
1905	Challacombe	1977	Dunfermline
1906	Troutbeck	1978	Julio Mariner
1907	Wool Winder	1979	Son of Love
1908	Your Majesty	1980	Light Cavalry
1909	Bayardo	1981	Cut Above
1910	Swynford	1982	Touching Wood
1911	Prince Palatine	1983	Sun Princess
1912	Tracery	1984	Commanche Run
1913	Night Hawk	1985	Oh So Sharp
1914	Black Jester	1986	Moon Madness
1915	Pommern	1987	Reference Point
1916	Hurry On	1988	Minster Son
1917	Gay Crusader	1989	Michelozzo
1918	Gainsborough	1990	Snurge
1919	Keysoe	1991	Toulon
1920	Caligula	1992	User Friendly
1921	Polemarch	1993	Bob's Return

Two Thousand Guineas Champions

Year	Horse	Year	Horse
1809	Wizard	1820	Pindarrie
1810	Hephestion	1821	Reginald
1811	Trophonius	1822	Pastille
1812	Cwrw	1823	Nicolo
1813	Smolensko	1824	Schahriar
1814	Olive	1825	Enamel
1815	Tigris	1826	Devise
1816	Nectar	1827	Turcoman
1817	Manfred	1828	Cadland
1818	Interpreter	1829	Patron
1819	Antar	1830	Augustus

(Continued)

(2,000 Guineas Champions contd.)

Year	Horse	Year	Horse	Year	Horse	Year	Horse
1831	Riddlesworth	1871	Bothwell	1912	Sweeper II	1953	Nearula
1832	Archibald	1872	Prince Charlie	1913	Louvis	1954	Darius
1833	Clearwell	1873	Gang Forward	1914	Kennymore	1955	Our Babu
1834	Glencoe	1874	Atlantic	1915	Pommern	1956	Gilles de Retz
1835	Ibrahim	1875	Camballo	1916	Clarissimus	1957	Crepello
1836	Bay Middleton	1876	Petrarch	1917	Gay Crusader	1958	Pall Mall
1837	Achmet	1877	Chamant	1918	Gainsborough	1959	Taboun
1838	Grey Momus	1878	Pilgrimage	1919	The Panther	1960	Martial
1839	The Corsair	1879	Charibert	1920	Tetratema	1961	Rockavon
1840	Crucifix	1880	Petronel	1921	Criag an Eran	1962	Privy Councillor
1841	Ralph	1881	Peregrine	1922	St Louis	1963	Only for Life
1842	Meteor	1882	Shotover	1923	Ellangowan	1964	Baldric II
1843	Cotherstone	1883	Galliard	1924	Diophon	1965	Niksar
1844	The Ugly Buck	1884	Scot Free	1925	Manna	1966	Kashmir II
1845	Idas	1885	Paradox	1926	Colorado	1967	Royal Palace
1846	Sir Tatton Sykes	1886	Ormonde	1927	Adam's Apple	1968	Sir Ivor
1847	Conyngham	1887	Enterprise	1928	Flamingo	1969	Right Tack
1848	Flatcatcher	1888	Ayrshire	1929	Mr Jinks	1970	Nijinsky
1849	Nunnykirk	1889	Enthusiast	1930	Diolite	1971	Brigadier Gerard
1850	Pitsford	1890	Surefoot	1931	Cameronian	1972	High Top
1851	Hernandez	1891	Common	1932	Orwell	1973	Mon Fils
1852	Stockwell	1892	Bona Vista	1933	Rodosto	1974	Nonoalco
1853	West Australian	1893	Isinglass	1934	Colombo	1975	Bolkonski
1854	The Hermit	1894	Ladas	1935	Bahram	1976	Wollow
1855	Lord of the Isles	1895	Kirkconnel	1936	Pay Up	1977	Nebbiolo
1856	Fazzoletto	1896	St Frusquin	1937	Le Ksar	1978	Roland Gardens
1857	Vedette	1897	Galtee More	1938	Pasch	1979	Tap On Wood
1858	Fitzroland	1898	Disraeli	1939	Blue Peter	1980	Known Fact
1859	Promised Land	1899	Flying Fox	1940	Djebel	1981	To-Agori-Mou
1860	The Wizard	1900	Diamond Jubilee	1941	Lambert Simnel	1982	Zino
1861	Diophantus	1901	Handicapper	1942	Big Game	1983	Lomond
1862	The Marquis	1902	Sceptre	1943	Kingsway	1984	El Gran Senor
1863	Marconi	1903	Rock Sand	1944	Garden Path	1985	Shaheed
1864	General Peel	1904	St Amant	1945	Court Martial	1986	Dancing Brave
1865	Gladiateur	1905	Vedas	1946	Happy Knight	1987	Don't Forget Me
1866	Lord Lyon	1906	Gorgos	1947	Tudor Minstrel	1988	Doyoun
1867	Vauban	1907	Slieve Gallion	1948	My Babu	1989	Nashwan
1868	Moslem* / Formosa*	1908	Norman III	1949	Nimbus	1990	Tirol
		1909	Minoru	1950	Palestine	1991	Mystiko
1869	Pretender	1910	Neil Gow	1951	Ki Ming	1992	Rodrigo de Triano
1870	Macgregor	1911	Sunstar	1952	Thunderhead II	1993	Zafonic

*Dead heat

ICE HOCKEY

British Champions

Year	Winners	Year	Winners
1982	Dundee Rockets	1988	Durham Wasps
1983	Dundee Rockets	1989	Nottingham Panthers
1984	Dundee Rockets	1990	Cardiff Devils
1985	Fife Flyers	1991	Durham Wasps
1986	Murrayfield Racers	1992	Durham Wasps
1987	Durham Wasps	1993	Cardiff Devils

European Cup Winners

Year	Team	Year	Team
1966	ZKL Brno	1980	CSKA Moscow
1967	ZKL Brno	1981	CSKA Moscow
1968	ZKL Brno	1982	CSKA Moscow
1969	CSKA Moscow	1983	CSKA Moscow
1970	CSKA Moscow	1984	CSKA Moscow
1971	CSKA Moscow	1985	CSKA Moscow
1972	CSKA Moscow	1986	CSKA Moscow
1973	CSKA Moscow	1987	CSKA Moscow
1974	CSKA Moscow	1988	CSKA Moscow
1975	Wings of the Soviet	1989	CSKA Moscow
1976	CSKA Moscow	1990	CSKA Moscow
1977	Poldi Kladno	1991	Djurgarden Stockholm
1978	CSKA Moscow	1992	Djurgarden Stockholm
1979	CSKA Moscow	1993	Malmö IF

World Champions

Year	Team	Year	Team
1920	Canada	1964	USSR
1924	Canada	1965	USSR
1928	Canada	1966	USSR
1930	Canada	1967	USSR
1931	Canada	1968	USSR
1932	Canada	1970	USSR
1933	United States	1971	USSR
1934	Canada	1972	Czechoslovakia
1935	Canada	1973	USSR
1936	Great Britain	1974	USSR
1937	Canada	1975	USSR
1938	Canada	1976	Czechoslovakia
1939	Canada	1977	Czechoslovakia
1947	Czechoslovakia	1978	USSR
1948	Canada	1979	USSR
1949	Czechoslovakia	1980	United States
1950	Canada	1981	USSR
1951	Canada	1982	USSR
1952	Canada	1983	USSR
1953	Sweden	1984	USSR
1954	USSR	1985	Czechoslovakia
1955	Canada	1986	USSR
1956	USSR	1987	Sweden
1957	Sweden	1988	USSR
1958	Canada	1989	USSR
1959	Canada	1990	USSR
1960	United States	1991	Sweden
1961	Canada	1992	Sweden
1962	Sweden	1993	Sweden
1963	USSR		

ICE SKATING

European Figure Skating Champions

Year	Men	Women	Pairs
1930	Karl Schäfer (Aus)	Fritzi Burger (Aus)	Organista & Szalay (Hun)
1931	Karl Schäfer (Aus)	Sonja Henie (Nor)	Organista & Szalay (Hun)
1932	Karl Schäfer (Aus)	Sonja Henie (Nor)	Andrée & Brunet (Fr)
1933	Karl Schäfer (Aus)	Sonja Henie (Nor)	Papez & Zwack (Aus)
1934	Karl Schäfer (Aus)	Sonja Henie (Nor)	Rotter & Szolls (Hun)
1935	Karl Schäfer (Aus)	Sonja Henie (Nor)	Herber & Baier (Ger)
1936	Karl Schäfer (Aus)	Sonja Henie (Nor)	Herber & Baier (Ger)
1937	Felix Kaspar (Aus)	Cecilia Colledge (GB)	Herber & Baier (Ger)
1938	Felix Kaspar (Aus)	Cecilia Colledge (GB)	Herber & Baier (Ger)
1939	Graham Sharp (GB)	Cecilia Colledge (GB)	Herber & Baier (Ger)
1947	Hans Gerschwiler (Swi)	Barbara Ann Scott (Can)	Lannoy & Baugniet (Bel)
1948	Richard T. Button (USA)	Barbara Ann Scott (Can)	Kekessy & Kiraly (Hun)
1949	Edi Rada (Aus)	Eva Pawlik (Aus)	Kekessy & Kiraly (Hun)
1950	Ede Kiraly (Hun)	Alena Vrzanova (Cze)	Nagy & Nagy (Hun)
1951	Helmut Seibt (Aus)	Jeanette Altwegg (GB)	Baran & Falk (FRG)
1952	Helmut Seibt (Aus)	Jeanette Altwegg (GB)	Falk & Falk (FRG)
1953	Carlo Fassi (Ita)	Valda Osborn (GB)	Nicks & Nicks (GB)
1954	Carlo Fassi (Ita)	Gundi Busch (FRG)	Grandjean & Grandjean (Swi)
1955	Alain Giletti (Fra)	Hanna Eigel (Aus)	Nagy & Nagy (Hun)
1956	Alain Giletti (Fra)	Ingrid Wendel (Aus)	Schwarz & Oppelt (Aus)
1957	Alain Giletti (Fra)	Hanna Eigel (Aus)	Suchankova & Dolezal (Cze)
1958	Karol Divin (Cze)	Ingrid Wendel (Aus)	Suchankova & Dolezal (Cze)
1959	Karol Divin (Cze)	Hanna Walter (Aus)	Kilius & Bäumler (FRG)
1960	Alain Giletti (Fra)	Sjoukje Dijkstra (Neth)	Kilius & Bäumler (FRG)
1961	Alain Giletti (Fra)	Sjoukje Dijkstra (Neth)	Kilius & Bäumler (FRG)
1962	Alain Calmat (Fra)	Sjoukje Dijkstra (Neth)	Kilius & Bäumler (FRG)
1963	Alain Calmat (Fra)	Sjoukje Dijkstra (Neth)	Kilius & Bäumler (FRG)
1964	Alain Calmat (Fra)	Sjoukje Dijkstra (Neth)	Kilius & Bäumler (FRG)
1965	Emmerich Danzer (Aus)	Regina Heitzer	Belousova & Protopopov (USSR)
1966	Emmerich Danzer (Aus)	Regina Heitzer	Belousova & Protopopov (USSR)
1967	Emmerich Danzer (Aus)	Gabriele Seyfert (GDR)	Belousova & Protopopov (USSR)
1968	Emmerich Danzer (Aus)	Hanna Maskova (Cze)	Belousova & Protopopov (USSR)
1969	Ondrej Nepela (Cze)	Gabriele Seyfert (GDR)	Rodnina & Ulanov (USSR)
1970	Ondrej Nepela (Cze)	Gabriele Seyfert (GDR)	Rodnina & Ulanov (USSR)
1971	Ondrej Nepela (Cze)	Beatrix Schuba (Aus)	Rodnina & Ulanov (USSR)
1972	Ondrej Nepela (Cze)	Beatrix Schuba (Aus)	Rodnina & Ulanov (USSR)
1973	Ondrej Nepela (Cze)	Christine Errath (GDR)	Rodnina & Zaitsev (USSR)
1974	Jan Hoffmann (GDR)	Christine Errath (GDR)	Rodnina & Zaitsev (USSR)
1975	Vladimir Kovalev (USSR)	Christine Errath (GDR)	Rodnina & Zaitsev (USSR)
1976	John Curry (GB)	Dianne de Leeuw (Neth)	Rodnina & Zaitsev (USSR)
1977	Jan Hoffmann (GDR)	Anett Poetzsch (GDR)	Rodnina & Zaitsev (USSR)
1978	Jan Hoffmann (GDR)	Annet Poetzsch (GDR)	Rodnina & Zaitsev (USSR)
1979	Jan Hoffmann (GDR)	Annet Poetzsch (GDR)	Tscherkasova & Shakhrai (USSR)
1980	Robin Cousins (GB)	Anett Poetzsch (GDR)	Rodnina & Zaitsev (USSR)
1981	Igor Bobrin (USSR)	Denise Bielmann (Swi)	Vorobjeva & Lisovski (USSR)
1982	Norbert Schramm (FRG)	Claudia Kristofics-B. (Aus)	Baess & Thierbach (GDR)
1983	Norbert Schramm (FRG)	Katarina Witt (GDR)	Baess & Thierbach (GDR)
1984	Alexandr Fadeev (USSR)	Katarina Witt (GDR)	Valova & Vasiliev (USSR)
1985	Jozef Sabovcik (Cze)	Katarina Witt (GDR)	Valova & Vasiliev (USSR)
1986	Jozef Sabovcik (Cze)	Katarina Witt (GDR)	Valova & Vasiliev (USSR)
1987	Alexandr Fadeev (USSR)	Katarina Witt (GDR)	Selezneva & Makarov (USSR)
1988	Alexandr Fadeev (USSR)	Katarina Witt (GDR)	Gordeeva & Grinkov (USSR)
1989	Alexandr Fadeev (USSR)	Claudia Leistner (FRG)	Selezneva & Makarov (USSR)
1990	Viktor Petrenko (USSR)	Evelyn Grossmann (GDR)	Gordeeva & Grinkov (USSR)
1991	Viktor Petrenko (USSR)	Surya Bonaly (Fra)	Mishkuteniok & Dmitriev (USSR)
1992	Petr Barna (Cze)	Surya Bonaly (Fra)	Mishkuteniok & Dmitriev (CIS)

UK Figure Skating Champions

Year	Men	Women	Pairs
1975	J. Curry	K. Richardson	
1976	R. J. Cousins	K. Richardson	A. Beckwith & R. Lindsey
1977	R. J. Cousins	K. Richardson	A. Beckwith & R. Lindsey
1978	R. J. Cousins	D. Cottrill	R. Daw & S. Garland
1979	R. J. Cousins	K. Richardson	R. Daw & S. Garland
1980	C. Howarth	K. Wood	R. Daw & S. Garland
1981	M. Pepperday	D. Cottrill	I. Jenkins & S. Garland
1982	M. Pepperday	K. Wood	I. Jenkins & S. Garland
1983	M. Pepperday	S. Jackson	I. Jenkins & S. Garland
1984	S. Pickavance	S. Jackson	L. Cushley & N. Cushley
1985	S. Pickavance	J. Conway	C. Peake & A. Naylor
1986	P. Robinson	J. Conway	C. Peake & A. Naylor
1987	P. Robinson	J. Conway	C. Peake & A. Naylor
1988	C. Newberry	J. Conway	C. Peake & A. Naylor
1989	S. Cousins	E. Murdoch	C. Peake & A. Naylor
1990	S. Cousins	J. Conway	C. Peake & A. Naylor
1991	S. Cousins	J. Conway	K. Pritchard & J. Briggs
1992	S. Cousins	C. von Sayer	V. Pearce & C. Shorten

World Figure Skating Champions

Year	Men	Women	Pairs
1952	Dick Button, U.S.	Jacqueline du Bief, France	Falk & Falk, E. Germany
1953	Hayes Jenkins, U.S.	Tenley Albright, U.S.	Nicks & Nicks, GB
1954	Hayes Jenkins, U.S.	Gundi Busch, W. Germany	Dafoe & Bowden, Canada
1955	Hayes Jenkins, U.S.	Tenley Albright, U.S.	Dafoe & Bowden, Canada
1956	Hayes Jenkins, U.S.	Carol Heiss, U.S.	Schwarz & Oppelt, Austria
1957	Dave Jenkins, U.S.	Carol Heiss, U.S.	Wagner & Paul, Canada
1958	Dave Jenkins, U.S.	Carol Heiss, U.S.	Wagner & Paul, Canada
1959	Dave Jenkins, U.S.	Carol Heiss, U.S.	Wagner & Paul, Canada
1960	Alain Giletti, France	Carol Heiss, U.S.	Wagner & Paul, Canada
1961	none	none	none
1962	Don Jackson, Canada	Sjoukje Dijkstra, Neth.	Jelinek & Jelinek, Canada
1963	Don McPherson, Canada	Sjoukje Dijkstra, Neth.	Kilius & Bäumler, E. Germany
1964	Manfred Schnelldorfer, W. Germany	Sjoukje Dijkstra, Neth.	Kilius & Bäumler, E. Germany
1965	Alain Calmat, France	Petra Burka, Canada	Belousova & Protopopov, USSR
1966	Emmerich Danzer, Austria	Peggy Fleming, U.S.	Belousova & Protopopov, USSR
1967	Emmerich Danzer, Austria	Peggy Fleming, U.S.	Belousova & Protopopov, USSR
1968	Emmerich Danzer, Austria	Peggy Fleming, U.S.	Belousova & Protopopov, USSR
1969	Tim Wood, U.S.	Gabriele Seyfert, E. Germany	Rodnina & Ulanov, USSR
1970	Tim Wood, U.S.	Gabriele Seyfert, E. Germany	Rodnina & Ulanov, USSR
1971	Ondrej Nepela, Czech.	Beatrix Schuba, Austria	Rodnina & Ulanov, USSR
1972	Ondrej Nepela, Czech.	Beatrix Schuba, Austria	Rodnina & Ulanov, USSR
1973	Ondrej Nepela, Czech.	Karen Magnussen, Canada	Rodnina & Zaitsev, USSR
1974	Jan Hoffmann, E. Germany	Christine Errath, E. Germany	Rodnina & Zaitsev, USSR
1975	Sergei Volkov, USSR	Dianne de Leeuw, Neth.-U.S.	Rodnina & Zaitsev, USSR
1976	John Curry, Gt. Britain	Dorothy Hamill, U.S.	Rodnina & Zaitsev, USSR
1977	Vladimir Kovalev, USSR	Linda Fratianne, U.S.	Rodnina & Zaitsev, USSR
1978	Charles Tickner, U.S.	Anett Potzsch, E. Germany	Rodnina & Zaitsev, USSR
1979	Vladimir Kovalev, USSR	Linda Fratianne, U.S.	Babilonia & Gardner, US
1980	Jan Hoffmann, E. Germany	Anett Potzsch, E. Germany	Tscherkasova & Shakhrai, USSR
1981	Scott Hamilton, U.S.	Denise Biellmann, Switzerland	Vorobieva & Lisovski
1982	Scott Hamilton, U.S.	Elaine Zayak, U.S.	Baess & Thierbach, W. Germany
1983	Scott Hamilton, U.S.	Rosalynn Sumners, U.S.	Valova & Vasiliev, USSR
1984	Scott Hamilton, U.S.	Katarina Witt, E. Germany	Underhill & Martini, Canada
1985	Aleksandr Fadeev, USSR	Katarina Witt, E. Germany	Valova & Vasiliev, USSR
1986	Brian Boitano, U.S.	Debi Thomas, U.S.	Gordeeva & Grinkov, USSR
1987	Brian Orser, Canada	Katarina Witt, E. Germany	Gordeeva & Grinkov, USSR
1988	Brian Boitano, U.S.	Katarina Witt, E. Germany	Valova & Vasiliev, USSR
1989	Kurt Browning, Canada	Midori Ito, Japan	Gordeeva & Grinkov, USSR
1990	Kurt Browning, Canada	Jill Trenary, U.S.	Gordeeva & Grinkov, USSR
1991	Kurt Browning, Canada	Kristi Yamaguchi, U.S.	Mishkuteniok & Dmitriev, USSR
1992	Viktor Petrenko, Ukraine	Kristi Yamaguchi, U.S.	Mishkuteniok & Dmitriev, CIS
1993	Kurt Browning, Canada	Oksana Baiul, Ukraine	Brasseur & Eisler (Can)

British Ice Dancing Champions

1937	R. Wilkie & Miss D. Wallis
1938	R. Wilkie & Miss D. Wallis
1939	R. Wilkie & Miss D. Wallis
1947	A. Edmonds & Miss P. Borrajo
1948	A. Edmonds & Miss P. Borrajo
1949	R. Hudson & Miss S. Cooke
1950	R. Hudson & Miss S. Cooke
1951	J. Slater & Miss J. Dewhirst
1952	J. Slater & Miss J. Dewhirst
1953	J. Slater & Miss J. Dewhirst
1954	L. Demmy & Miss J. Westwood
1955	P. Thomas & Miss P. Weight
1956	C. Jones & Miss J. Markham
1957	C. Jones & Miss J. Markham
1958	C. Jones & Miss D. Denny
1959	C. Jones & Miss D. Denny
1960	C. Jones & Miss D. Denny
1961	M. Phillips & Miss L. Shearman
1962	M. Phillips & Miss L. Shearman
1963	D. Hickinbottom & Miss J. Sawbridge
1964	D. Hickinbottom & Miss J. Sawbridge
1965	B. Ford & Miss D. Towler
1966	B. Ford & Miss D. Towler
1967	B. Ford & Miss D. Towler
1968	B. Ford & Miss D. Towler
1969	R. Bradshaw & Miss S. Getty
1970	R. Bradshaw & Miss S. Getty
1971	P. Dalby & Miss J. Sawbridge
1972	G. Watts & Miss H. Green
1973	G. Watts & Miss H. Green
1974	G. Watts & Miss H. Green
1975	G. Watts & Miss H. Green
1976	W. Maxwell & Miss J. Thompson
1977	W. Maxwell & Miss J. Thompson
1978	C. Dean & Miss J. Torvill
1979	C. Dean & Miss J. Torvill
1980	C. Dean & Miss J. Torvill
1981	C. Dean & Miss J. Torvill
1982	C. Dean & Miss J. Torvill
1983	C. Dean & Miss J. Torvill
1984	N. Slater & Miss K. Barber
1985	P. Askham & Miss S. Jones
1986	P. Askham & Miss S. Jones
1987	P. Askham & Miss S. Jones
1988	P. Askham & Miss S. Jones
1989	A. Place & Miss L. Burton
1990	J. Blomfield & Miss A. Hall
1991	A. Place & Miss M. Bruce
1992	J. Lanning & Miss M. Humphreys

European Ice Dancing Champions

1954	Westwood & Demmy, GB
1955	Westwood & Demmy, GB
1956	Weight & Thomas, GB
1957	Markham & Jones, GB
1958	Markham & Jones, GB
1959	Denny & Jones, GB
1960	Denny & Jones, GB
1961	Denny & Jones, GB
1962	Guhel & Guhel, Fra
1963	Shearman & Philipps, GB
1964	Romanova & Roman, Cze
1965	Romonova & Roman, Cze
1966	Towler & Ford, GB
1967	Towler & Ford, GB
1968	Towler & Ford, GB
1969	Towler & Ford, GB
1970	Pakhomova & Gorshkov, USSR
1971	Pakhomova & Gorshkov, USSR
1972	Buck & Buck, FRG
1973	Pakhomova & Gorshkov, USSR
1974	Pakhomova & Gorshkov, USSR
1975	Pakhomova & Gorshkov, USSR
1976	Pakhomova & Gorshkov, USSR
1977	Moiseeva & Minenkov, USSR
1978	Moiseeva & Minenkov, USSR
1979	Linichuk & Karponosov, USSR
1980	Linichuk & Karponosov, USSR
1981	Torvill & Dean, GB
1982	Torvill & Dean, GB
1983	Bestemianova & Bukin, USSR
1984	Torvill & Dean, GB
1985	Bestemianova & Bukin, USSR
1986	Bestemianova & Bukin, USSR
1987	Bestemianova & Bukin, USSR
1988	Bestemianova & Bukin, USSR
1989	Klimova & Ponomarenko, USSR
1990	Klimova & Ponomarenko, USSR
1991	Klimova & Ponomarenko, USSR
1992	Klimova & Ponomarenko, CIS
1993	Usova & Zhulin (Rus)

World Ice Dancing Champions

1953	Westwood & Demmy, GB	1967	Towler & Ford, GB	1981	Torvill & Dean, GB
1954	Westwood & Demmy, GB	1968	Towler & Ford, GB	1982	Torvill & Dean, GB
1955	Westwood & Demmy, GB	1969	Towler & Ford, GB	1983	Torvill & Dean, GB
1956	Westwood & Demmy, GB	1970	Pakhomova & Gorshkov, USSR	1984	Torvill & Dean, GB
1957	Weight & Thomas, GB	1971	Pakhomova & Gorshkov, USSR	1985	Bestemianova & Bukin, USSR
1958	Markham & Jones, GB	1972	Pakhomova & Gorshkov, USSR	1986	Bestemianova & Bukin, USSR
1959	Markham & Jones, GB	1973	Pakhomova & Gorshkov, USSR	1987	Bestemianova & Bukin, USSR
1960	Denny & Jones, GB	1974	Pakhomova & Gorshkov, USSR	1988	Bestemianova & Bukin, USSR
1961	Denny & Jones, GB	1975	Moiseeva & Minenkov, USSR	1989	Klimova & Ponomarenko, USSR
1962	Romanova & Roman, Cze	1976	Pakhomova & Gorshkov, USSR	1990	Klimova & Ponomarenko, USSR
1963	Romanova & Roman, Cze	1977	Moiseeva & Minenkov, USSR	1991	Duchesnay & Duchesnay, Fr
1964	Romanova & Roman, Cze	1978	Linichuk & Karponosov, USSR	1992	Klimova & Ponomarenko, CIS
1965	Romanova & Roman, Cze	1979	Linichuk & Karponosov, USSR	1993	Usova & Zhulin (Rus)
1966	Towler & Ford, GB	1980	Regöczy & Sally, Hun		

MOTOR CYCLING

World Championship Grand Prix, 1992–93

GP	Rider	Nationality	Machine
Australian			
500cc	Kevin Schwantz	U.S.	Suzuki
250cc	Tetsuya Harada	Japanese	Yamaha
125cc	Dirk Raudies	German	Honda
Austrian			
500cc	Kevin Schwantz	U.S.	Suzuki
250cc	Doriano Romboni	Italian	Honda
125cc	Takeshi Tsujimura	Japanese	Honda
British			
500cc	Luca Cadalora	Italian	Yamaha
250cc	Jean-Philippe Ruggia	French	Aprilia
125cc	Dirk Raudies	German	Honda
Dutch			
500cc	Kevin Schwantz	U.S.	Suzuki
250cc	Loris Capirossi	Italian	Honda
125cc	Dirk Raudies	German	Honda
European			
500c	Wayne Rainey	U.S.	Yamaha
250cc	Massimiliano Biaggi	Italian	Honda
125cc	Noboru Ueda	Japanese	Honda
German			
500cc	Daryl Beattie	Australian	Honda
250cc	Doriano Romboni	Italian	Honda
125cc	Dirk Raudies	German	Honda
Japanese			
500cc	Wayne Rainey	U.S.	Yamaha
250cc	Tetsuya Harada	Japanese	Yamaha
125cc	Dirk Raudies	German	Honda
Malaysian			
500cc	Wayne Rainey	U.S.	Yamaha
250cc	Noboatsu Aoki	Japanese	Honda
125cc	Dirk Raudies	German	Honda
San Marino			
500cc	Mick Doohan	Australian	Honda
250cc	Loris Capirossi	Italian	Honda
125cc	Dirk Raudies	German	Honda
Spanish			
500cc	Kevin Schwantz	U.S.	Suzuki
250cc	Tetsuya Harada	Japanese	Yamaha
125cc	Kazuto Sakata	Japanese	Honda

British Grand Prix 500cc Champions

Year	Winner	Machine
1949	Harold Daniel (UK)	Norton
1950	Geoff Duke (UK)	Norton
1951	Geoff Duke (UK)	Norton
1952	Reg Armstrong (Ire)	Norton
1953	Ray Amm (S. Rho)	Norton
1954	Ray Amm (S. Rho)	Norton
1955	Geoff Duke (UK)	Gilera
1956	John Surtees (UK)	MV Agusta
1957	Bob McKintyre (UK)	Gilera
1958	John Surtees (UK)	MV Agusta
1959	John Surtees (UK)	MV Agusta
1960	John Surtees (UK)	MV Agusta
1961	Mike Hailwood (UK)	Norton
1962	Gary Hocking (S. Rho)	MV Agusta
1963	Mike Hailwood (UK)	MV Agusta
1964	Mike Hailwood (UK)	MV Agusta
1965	Mike Hailwood (UK)	MV Agusta
1966	Mike Hailwood (UK)	Honda
1967	Mike Hailwood (UK)	Honda
1968	Giacomo Agostini (Ita)	MV Agusta
1969	Giacomo Agostini (Ita)	MV Agusta
1970	Giacomo Agostini (Ita)	MV Agusta
1971	Giacomo Agostini (Ita)	MV Agusta
1972	Giacomo Agostini (Ita)	MV Agusta
1973	Jack Findlay (Aus)	Suzuki
1974	Phil Carpenter (UK)	Yamaha
1975	Mike Grant (UK)	Kawasaki
1976	Tom Herron (UK)	Yamaha
1977	Pat Hennen (US)	Suzuki
1978	Kenny Roberts (US)	Yamaha
1979	Kenny Roberts (US)	Yamaha
1980	Randy Mamola (US)	Suzuki
1981	Jack Middleburg (Neth)	Suzuki
1982	Franco Uncini (Ita)	Suzuki
1983	Kenny Roberts (US)	Yamaha
1984	Randy Mamola (US)	Honda
1985	Freddie Spencer (US)	Honda
1986	Wayne Gardner (US)	Honda
1987	Eddie Lawson (US)	Yamaha
1988	Wayne Rainey (US)	Suzuki
1989	Kevin Schwantz (US)	Suzuki
1990	Kevin Schwantz (US)	Suzuki
1991	Wayne Gardner (Aus)	Honda
1992	Wayne Gardner (Aus)	Honda
1993	Luca Cadalora (Ita)	Yamaha

Isle of Man – Senior TT Champions*

Year	Rider, Machine	Speed
1911	Oliver Godfrey, Indian	47.63mph
1912	Frank Applebee, Scott,	48.69mph
1913	Tim Wood, Scott	48.27mph
1914	Cyril Pullin, Rudge	49.49mph
1915–19	Not held	
1920	Tommy De La Hay, Sunbeam	51.48mph
1921	Howard Davies, AJS	54.50mph
1922	Alec Bennett, Sunbeam	58.31mph
1923	Tom Sinard, Douglas	55.55mph
1924	Alec Bennett, Norton	61.64mph
1925	Howard Davies, HRD	66.13mph
1926	Stanley Woods, Norton	67.54mph
1927	Alec Bennett, Norton	68.41mph
1928	Charlie Dodson, Sunbeam	62.98mph
1929	Charlie Dodson, Sunbeam	72.05mph
1930	Wal Handley, Rudge Whitworth	72.24mph
1931	Tim Hunt, Norton	77.90mph
1932	Stanley Woods, Norton	79.38mph
1933	Stanley Woods, Norton	77.16mph
1934	Jimmy Guthrie, Norton	78.01mph

(Continued)

(Isle of Man TT Champions contd.)

Year	Rider, Machine	Speed
1935	Stanley Woods, Moto Guzzi	84.68mph
1936	Jimmy Guthrie, Norton	85.80mph
1937	Freddie Frith, Norton	88.21mph
1938	Harold Daniell, Norton	89.11mph
1939	Georg Meir (Ger), BMW	89.38mph
1940–46	Not held	
1947	Harold Daniell, Norton	82.81mph
1948	Artie Bell, Norton	84.97mph
1949	Harold Daniell, Norton	86.93mph
1950	Geoff Duke, Norton	92.27mph
1951	Geoff Duke, Norton	93.83mph
1952	Reg Armstrong, Norton	92.97mph
1953	Ray Amm (S.Rho), Norton	93.85mph
1954	Ray Amm (S.Rho), Norton	88.12mph
1955	Geoff Duke, Norton	97.93mph
1956	John Surtees, MV Agusta	96.57mph
1957	Bob McIntyre, Gilera	98.99mph
1958	John Surtees, MV Agusta	98.63mph
1959	John Surtees, MV Agusta	87.94mph
1960	John Surtees, MV Agusta	102.44mph
1961	Mike Hailwood, Norton	100.60mph
1962	Gary Hocking (S.Rho), MV Agusta	103.51mph
1963	Mike Hailwood, MV Agusta	104.64mph
1964	Mike Hailwood, MV Agusta	100.95mph
1965	Mike Hailwood, MV Agusta	91.69mph
1966	Mike Hailwood, Honda	103.11mph
1967	Mike Hailwood, Honda	105.62mph
1968	Giacomo Agostini (Ita), MV Agusta	101.63mph
1969	Giacomo Agostini (Ita), MV Agusta	104.75mph
1970	Giacomo Agostini (Ita), MV Agusta	101.52mph
1971	Giacomo Agostini (Ita), MV Agusta	102.59mph
1972	Giacomo Agostini (Ita), MV Agusta	104.02mph
1973	Jack Findlay (Aus), Suzuki	101.55mph
1974	Phil Carpenter, Yamaha	96.99mph
1975	Mick Grant, Kawasaki	100.27mph
1976	Tom Herron, Yamaha	105.16mph
1977	Phil Read, Suzuki	106.98mph
1978	Tom Herron, Suzuki	111.74mph
1979	Mike Hailwood, Suzuki	111.75mph
1980	Graeme Crosby (NZ), Suzuki	109.65mph
1981	Mick Grant, Suzuki	106.14mph
1982	Norman Brown, Suzuki	110.98mph
1983	Not held	
1984	Rob McElnea, Suzuki	115.66mph
1985	Joey Dunlop, Honda	113.69mph
1986	Roger Burnett, Honda	113.98mph
1987	Joey Dunlop, Honda	99.85mph
1988	Joey Dunlop, Honda	117.38mph
1989	Steve Hislop, Honda	118.23mph
1990	Carl Fogarty, Honda	110.95mph
1991	Steve Hislop, Honda	121.09mph
1992	Steve Hislop, Norton	121.28mph
1993	Philip McCallen, Honda	154.47mph

*All winners from British Isles, unless stated.

World Champions

Class	Rider	Machine
1949		
125cc	Nello Pagani (Ita)	Mondial
250cc	Bruno Ruffo (Ita)	Guzzi
350cc	Freddie Frith (GB)	Velocette
500cc	Leslie Graham (GB)	AJS
Sidecar	Eric Oliver (GB)	Norton
1950		
125cc	Bruno Ruffo (Ita)	Mondial
250cc	Dario Ambrosini (Ita)	Benelli
350cc	Bob Foster (GB)	Velocette
500cc	Umberto Masetti (Ita)	Gilera
Sidecar	Eric Oliver (GB)	Norton
1951		
125cc	Carlo Ubbiali (Ita)	Mondial
250cc	Bruno Ruffo (Ita)	Guzzi
350cc	Geoff Duke (GB)	Norton
500cc	Geoff Duke (GB)	Norton
Sidecar	Eric Oliver (GB)	Norton
1952		
125cc	Cecil Sandford (GB)	MV
250cc	Enrico Lorensetti (Ita)	Guzzi
350cc	Geoff Duke (UK)	Norton
500cc	Umberto Masetti (Ita)	Gilera
Sidecar	Cyril Smith (GB)	Norton
1953		
125cc	Werner Haas (FRG)	NSU
250cc	Werner Haas (FRG)	NSU
350cc	Fergus Anderson (GB)	Guzzi
500cc	Geoff Duke (GB)	Gilera
Sidecar	Eric Oliver (GB)	Norton
1954		
125cc	Rupert Hollaus (Austria)	NSU
250cc	Werner Haas (FRG)	NSU
350cc	Fergus Anderson (GB)	Guzzi
500cc	Geoff Duke (GB)	Gilera
Sidecar	Wilhelm Noll (FRG)	BMW
1955		
125cc	Carlo Ubbiali (Ita)	MV
250cc	Herman Muller (FRG)	NSU
350cc	Bill Lomas (GB)	Guzzi
500cc	Geoff Duke (GB)	Gilera
Sidecar	Wilhelm Faust (FRG)	BMW
1956		
125cc	Carlo Ubbiali (Ita)	MV
250cc	Carlo Ubbiali (Ita)	MV
350cc	Bill Lomas (GB)	Guzzi
500cc	John Surtees (GB)	MV
Sidecar	Wilhelm Noll (FRG)	BMW
1957		
125cc	Tarquinio Provini (Ita)	Mondial
250cc	Cecil Sandford (GB)	Mondial
350cc	Keith Campbell (Aus)	Guzzi
500cc	Libero Liberati (Ita)	Gilera
Sidecar	Fritz Hillebrand (FRG)	BMW
1958		
125cc	Carlo Ubbiali (Ita)	MV
250cc	Tarquinio Provini (Ita)	MV
350cc	John Surtees (GB)	MV
500cc	John Surtees (GB)	MV
Sidecar	Walter Schneider (FRG)	BMW
1959		
125cc	Carlo Ubbiali (Ita)	MV
250cc	Carlo Ubbiali (Ita)	MV
350cc	John Surtees (GB)	MV
500cc	John Surtees (GB)	MV
Sidecar	Walter Schneider (FRG)	BMW
1960		
125cc	Carlo Ubbiali (Ita)	MV
250cc	Carlo Ubbiali (Ita)	MV
350cc	John Surtees (GB)	MV
500cc	John Surtees (GB)	MV
Sidecar	Helmut Fath (FRG)	BMW
1961		
125cc	Tom Phillis (Aus)	Honda
250cc	Mike Hailwood (GB)	Honda
350cc	Gary Hocking (Rho)	MV
500cc	Gary Hocking Rho)	MV
Sidecar	Max Deubel (FRG)	BMW
1962		
50cc	Ernst Degner (FRG)	Suzuki
125cc	Luigi Taveri (Swi)	Honda
250cc	Jim Redman (Rho)	Honda
350cc	Jim Redman (Rho)	Honda
500cc	Mike Hailwood (GB)	MV
Sidecar	Max Deubel (FRG)	BMW
1963		
50cc	Hugh Anderson (NZ)	Suzuki
100cc	Hugh Anderson (NZ)	Suzuki
125cc	Hugh Anderson (NZ)	Suzuki
250cc	Jim Redman (Rho)	Honda
350cc	Jim Redman (Rho)	Honda
500cc	Mike Hailwood (GB)	MV
Sidecar	Max Deubel (FRG)	BMW
1964		
50cc	Hugh Anderson (NZ)	Suzuki
125cc	Luigi Taveri (Swi)	Honda
250cc	Phil Read (GB)	Yamaha
350cc	Jim Redman (Rho)	Honda
500cc	Mike Hailwood (GB)	MV
Sidecar	Max Deubel (FRG)	BMW

1965	Rider	Machine
50cc	Ralph Bryans (Ire)	Honda
125cc	Hugh Anderson (NZ)	Suzuki
250cc	Phil Read (GB)	Yamaha
350cc	Jim Redman (Rho)	Honda
500cc	Mike Hailwood (GB)	MV
Sidecar	Fritz Scheidegger (Swi)	BMW

1966		
50cc	Hans-Georg Anscheidt (FRG)	Suzuki
125cc	Luigi Taveri (Swi)	Honda
250cc	Mike Hailwood (GB)	Honda
350cc	Mike Hailwood (GB)	Honda
500cc	Giacomo Agostini (Ita)	MV
Sidecar	Fritz Scheidegger (Swi)	BMW

1967		
50cc	Hans-Georg Anscheidt (FRG)	Suzuki
125cc	Bill Ivy (GB)	Yamaha
250cc	Mike Hailwood (GB)	Honda
350cc	Mike Hailwood (GB)	Honda
500cc	Giacomo Agostini (Ita)	MV
Sidecar	Klaus Enders (FRG)	BMW

1968		
50cc	Hans-Georg Anscheidt (FRG)	Suzuki
125cc	Phil Read (GB)	Yamaha
250cc	Phil Read (GB)	Yamaha
350cc	Giacomo Agostini (Ita)	MV
500cc	Giacomo Agostini (Ita)	MV
Sidecar	Helmut Fath (FRG)	URS

1969		
50cc	Angel Nieto (Spa)	Derbi
125cc	Dave Simmonds (GB)	Kawasaki
250cc	Kel Carruthers (Aus)	Benelli
350cc	Giacomo Agostini (Ita)	MV
500cc	Giacomo Agostini (Ita)	MV
Sidecar	Klaus Enders (FRG)	BMW

1970		
50cc	Angel Nieto (Spa)	Derbi
125cc	Dieter Braun (FRG)	Suzuki
250cc	Rod Gould (GB)	Yamaha
350cc	Giacomo Agostini (Ita)	MV
500cc	Giacomo Agostini (Ita)	MV
Sidecar	Klaus Enders (FRG)	BMW

1971		
50cc	Jan de Vries (Hol)	Kreidler
125cc	Angel Nieto (Spa)	Derbi
250cc	Phil Read (GB)	Yamaha
350cc	Giacomo Agostini (Ita)	MV
500cc	Giacomo Agostini (Ita)	MV
Sidecar	Horst Owesle (FRG)	Munch

1972		
50cc	Angel Nieto (Spa)	Derbi
125cc	Angel Nieto (Spa)	Derbi
250cc	Jarno Saarinen (Fin)	Yamaha
350cc	Giacomo Agostini (Ita)	MV
500cc	Giacomo Agostini (Ita)	MV
Sidecar	Klaus Enders (FRG)	BMW

1973		
50cc	Jan de Vries (Hol)	Kreidler
125cc	Kent Andersson (Swe)	Yamaha
250cc	Dieter Braun (FRG)	Yamaha
350cc	Giacomo Agostini (Ita)	MV
500cc	Phil Read (GB)	MV
Sidecar	Klaus Enders (FRG)	BMW

1974		
50cc	Henk van Kessell (Hol)	Kreidler
125cc	Kent Andersson (Swe)	Yamaha
250cc	Walter Villa (Ita)	H-Davidson
350cc	Giacomo Agostini (Ita)	Yamaha
500cc	Phil Read (GB)	MV
Sidecar	Klaus Enders (FRG)	Busch BMW

1975		
50cc	Angel Nieto (Spa)	Kreidler
125cc	Paolo Pileri (Ita)	Morbidelli
250cc	Walter Villa (Ita)	H-Davidson
350cc	Johnny Cecotto (Ven)	Yamaha
500cc	Giacomo Agostini (Ita)	Yamaha
Sidecar	Rolf Steinhausen (FRG)	Konig

1976	Rider	Machine
50cc	Angel Nieto (Spa)	Bultaco
125cc	Pier-Paolo Bianchi (Ita)	Morbidelli
250cc	Walter Villa (Ita)	H-Davidson
350cc	Walter Villa (Ita)	H-Davidson
500cc	Barry Sheene (GB)	Suzuki
Sidecar	Rolf Steinhausen (FRG)	Busch Konig

1977		
50cc	Angel Nieto (Spa)	Bultaco
125cc	Pier-Paolo Bianchi (Ita)	Morbidelli
250cc	Mario Lega (Ita)	Morbidelli
350cc	Takazumi Katayama (Jap)	Yamaha
500cc	Barry Sheene (GB)	Suzuki
750cc	Steve Baker (US)	Yamaha
F1	Phil Read (GB)	Honda
Sidecar	George O'Dell (GB)	Yamaha

1978		
50cc	Ricardo Tormo (Spa)	Bultaco
125cc	Eugenio Lazzarini (Ita)	MBA
250cc	Kork Ballington (SAf)	Kawasaki
350cc	Kork Ballington (SAf)	Kawasaki
500cc	Kenny Roberts (US)	Yamaha
750cc	Johnny Cecotto (Ven)	Yamaha
F1	Mike Hailwood (GB)	Ducati
Sidecar	Rolf Biland (Swi)	Yamaha

1979		
50cc	Eugenio Lazzarini (Ita)	Kreidler
125cc	Angel Nieto (Spa)	Morbidelli
250cc	Kork Ballington (SAf)	Kawasaki
350cc	Kork Ballington (SAf)	Kawasaki
500cc	Kenny Roberts (US)	Yamaha
750cc	Patrick Pons (Fra)	Yamaha
F1	Ron Haslam (GB)	Honda
Sidecar	Rolf Biland (Swi)	Yamaha

1980		
50cc	Eugenio Lazzarini (Ita)	Kreidler
125cc	Pier-Paolo Bianchi (Ita)	MBA
250cc	Anton Mang (FRG)	Kawasaki
350cc	John Ekerold (SAf)	Yamaha
500cc	Kenny Roberts (US)	Yamaha
F1	Graeme Crosby (NZ)	Suzuki
Sidecar	Jock Taylor (GB)	Yamaha

1981		
50cc	Ricardo Tormo (Spa)	Bultaco
125cc	Angel Nieto (Spa)	Minarelli
250cc	Anton Mang (FRG)	Kawasaki
350cc	Anton Mang (FRG)	Kawasaki
500cc	Marco Lucchinelli (Ita)	Suzuki
F1	Graeme Crosby (NZ)	Suzuki
Sidecar	Rolf Biland (Swi)	Yamaha

1982		
50cc	Stefan Dorflinger (Swi)	MBA
125cc	Angel Nieto (Spa)	Garelli
250cc	Jean-Louis Tournadre (Fra)	Yamaha
350cc	Anton Mang (FRG)	Kawasaki
500cc	Franco Uncini (Ita)	Suzuki
F1	Joey Dunlop (Ire)	Honda
Sidecar	Werner Schwarzel (FRG)	Yamaha

1983		
50cc	Stefan Dorflinger (Swi)	Kreidler
125cc	Angel Nieto (Spa)	Garelli
250cc	Carlos Lavado (Ven)	Yamaha
500cc	Freddie Spencer (US)	Honda
F1	Joey Dunlop (Ire)	Honda
Sidecar	Rolf Biland (Swi)	Yamaha

1984		
80cc	Stefan Dorflinger (Swi)	Zundapp
125cc	Angel Nieto (Spa)	Garelli
250cc	Christain Sarron (Fra)	Yamaha
500cc	Eddie Lawson (US)	Yamaha
F1	Joey Dunlop (Ire)	Honda
Sidecar	Egbert Streuer (Hol)	Yamaha

1985		
80cc	Stefan Dorflinger (Swi)	Krauser
125cc	Fausto Gresini (Ita)	Garelli
250cc	Freddie Spencer (US)	Honda
500cc	Freddie Spencer (US)	Honda
F1	Joey Dunlop (Ire)	Honda
Sidecar	Egbert Streuer (Hol)	Yamaha

(Continued)

(Motor Cycling World Champions contd.)

1986	Rider	Machine
80cc	Jorge Martinez (Spa)	Derbi
125cc	Luca Cadalora (Ita)	Garelli
250cc	Carlos Lavado (Ven)	Yamaha
500cc	Eddie Lawson (US)	Yamaha
F1	Joey Dunlop (Ire)	Honda
Sidecar	Egbert Streuer (Hol)	Yamaha
1987		
80cc	Jorge Martinez (Spa)	Derbi
125cc	Fausto Gresini (Ita)	Garelli
250cc	Anton Mang (FRG)	Honda
500cc	Wayne Gardner (Aus)	Honda
F1	Virginio Ferrari (Ita)	Yamaha
Sidecar	Steve Webster (GB)	LCR Krauser
1988		
80cc	Jorge Martinez (Spa)	Derbi
125cc	Jorge Martinez (Spa)	Derbi
250cc	Sito Pons (Spa)	Honda
500cc	Eddie Lawson (US)	Yamaha
F1	Carl Fogarty (GB)	Honda
Sidecar	Steve Webster (GB)	LCR Krauser
1989		
80cc	Champi Herreros (Spa)	Derbi
125cc	Alex Crivelle (Spa)	Cobas
250cc	Sito Pons (Spa)	Honda
500cc	Eddie Lawson (US)	Honda
Sidecar	Steve Webster (GB)	Krauser
1990	**Rider**	**Machine**
125cc	Loris Capirossi (Ita)	Honda
250cc	John Kocinski (US)	Yamaha
500cc	Wayne Rainey (US)	Yamaha
Sidecar	Alain Michel (Fra)	Krauser
1991		
125cc	Loris Capirossi (Ita)	Honda
250cc	Luca Cadalora (US)	Honda
500cc	Wayne Rainey (US)	Yamaha
Sidecar	Steve Webster (GB)	LCR
1992		
125cc	Alessando Granigni (Ita)	Aprilia
250cc	Luca Cadalora (US)	Honda
500cc	Wayne Rainey (US)	Yamaha
Sidecar	Rolf Biland (Swi)	LCR
1993		
125cc	Ralf Waldmann (Ger)	Aprilia
250cc	Tetsuya Harada (Jap)	Honda
500cc	Kevin Schwantz (US)	Yamaha
Sidecar	Rolf Biland (Swi)	LCR-Krauser

MOTOR RACING

Formula One Grand Prix Winners, 1992–3

Grand Prix	Winner	Car
Australian	Gerhard Berger	McLaren
Brazilian	Ayrton Senna	McLaren
British	Alain Prost	Williams
Canadian	Alain Prost	Williams
European	Ayrton Senna	McLaren
French	Alain Prost	Williams
German	Alain Prost	Williams
Hungarian	Damon Hill	Williams
Italian	Ayrton Senna	McLaren
Japanese	Ricardo Patrese	Williams
Monaco	Ayrton Senna	McLaren
Portuguese	Michael Schumacher	Benetton-Ford
San Marino	Alain Prost	Williams
Spanish	Alain Prost	Williams

British Grand Prix Winners

Year	Winner	Car
1950	Giuseppe Farina (Ita)	Alfa Romeo
1951	Jose Froilan Gonzalez (Arg)	Ferrari
1952	Alberto Ascari (Ita)	Ferrari
1953	Alberto Ascari (Ita)	Ferrari
1954	Jose Froilan Gonzalez (Arg)	Ferrari
1955	Stirling Moss (GB)	Mercedes-Benz
1956	Juan Manuel Fangio (Arg)	Lancia-Ferrari
1957	Stirling Moss (GB) & Tony Brooks (GB)	Vanwall
1958	Peter Collins (GB)	Ferrari
1959	Jack Brabham (Aus)	Cooper-Climax
1960	Jack Brabham (Aus)	Cooper-Climax
1961	Wolfgang Von Trips (FRG)	Ferrari
1962	Jim Clark (GB)	Lotus-Climax
1963	Jim Clark (GB)	Lotus-Climax
1964	Jim Clark (GB)	Lotus-Climax
1965	Jim Clark (GB)	Lotus-Climax
1966	Jack Brabham (Aus)	Brabham-Repco
1967	Jim Clark (GB)	Lotus-Ford
1968	Jo Siffert (Swi)	Lotus-Ford
1969	Jackie Stewart (GB)	Matra-Ford
1970	Jochen Rindt (Aut)	Lotus-Ford
1971	Jackie Stewart (GB)	Tyrrell-Ford
1972	Emerson Fittipaldi (Bra)	Lotus-Ford
1973	Peter Revson (US)	McLaren-Ford
1974	Jody Scheckter (SA)	Tyrrell-Ford
1975	Emerson Fittipaldi (Bra)	McLaren-Ford
1976	Niki Lauda (Aut)	Ferrari

(British GP Winners contd.)

Year	Winner	Car
1977	James Hunt (GB)	McLaren-Ford
1978	Carlos Reutemann (Arg)	Ferrari
1979	Clay Regazzoni (Swi)	Williams-Ford
1980	Alan Jones (Aus)	Williams-Ford
1981	John Watson (GB)	McLaren-Ford
1982	Niki Lauda (Aut)	McLaren-Ford
1983	Alain Prost (Fra)	Renault
1984	Niki Lauda (Aut)	McLaren-TAG
1985	Alain Prost (Fra)	McLaren-TAG
1986	Nigel Mansell (GB)	Williams-Honda
1987	Nigel Mansell (GB)	Williams-Honda
1988	Ayrton Senna (Bra)	McLaren-Honda
1989	Alain Prost (Fra)	McLaren-Honda
1990	Alain Prost (Fra)	Ferrari
1991	Nigel Mansell (GB)	Williams-Renault
1992	Nigel Mansell (GB)	Williams
1993	Alain Prost (Fra)	Williams

Indianapolis 500 Winners

Year	Winner, Car	mph
1911	Ray Harroun, Marmon Wasp	74.59
1912	Joe Dawson, National	78.72
1913	Jules Goux, Peugeot	75.933
1914	Rene Thomas, Delage	82.47
1915	Ralph DePalma, Mercedes	89.84
1916	Dario Resta, Peugeot	84.00
1917-18	race not held	
1919	Howdy Wilcox, Peugeot	88.05
1920	Gaston Chevrolet, Monroe	88.16
1921	Tommy Milton, Frontenac	89.62
1922	Jimmy Murphy, Murphy Special	94.48
1923	Tommy Milton, H.C.S.	90.95
1924	L.L. Corum-Joe Boyer, Duesenberg	98.23
1925	Pete DePaolo, Duesenberg	101.13
1926	Frank Lockhart, Miller	95.904
1927	George Souders, Duesenberg)	97.545
1928	Louis Meyer, Miller	99.482
1929	Ray Keech, Simplex	97.585
1930	Billy Arnold, Miller-Hartz	100.448
1931	Louis Schneider, Bowes Seal Fast	96.629
1932	Fred Frame, Miller-Hartz	104.144
1933	Louis Meyer, Tydol	104.162
1934	Bill Cummings, Boyle Products	104.863
1935	Kelly Petillo, Gilmore Speedway	106.240
1936	Louis Meyer, Ring Free	109.069
1937	Wilbur Shaw, Shaw-Gilmore	113.580
1938	Floyd Roberts, Burd Piston Ring	117.200
1939	Wilbur Shaw, Boyle	115.035
1940	Wilbur Shaw, Boyle	114.277

Year	Winner, Car	mph
1941	Floyd Davis-Mauri Rose, Knock-Out-Hose Clip	115.117
1942-45	race not held	
1946	George Robson, Thorne Engineering	114.820
1947	Mauri Rose, Blue Crown Special	116.338
1948	Mauri Rose, Blue Crown Special	119.814
1949	Bill Holland, Blue Crown Special	121.327
1950	Johnny Parsons, Wynn Kurtis Kraft	124.002
1951	Lee Wallard, Belanger	126.224
1952	Troy Ruttman, Agajanian	128.922
1953	Bill Vukovich, Fuel Injection	128.740
1954	Bill Vukovich, Fuel Injection	130.840
1955	Bob Sweikert, John Zink Special	128.209
1956	Pat Flaherty, John Zink Special	128.490
1957	Sam Hanks, Belond Exhaust	135.601
1958	Jimmy Bryan, Belond A.P.	133.791
1959	Rodger Ward, Leader Card Special	135.857
1960	Jim Rathmann, Ken Paul Special	138.767
1961	A.J. Foyt, Bowes Seal Fast	139.130
1962	Rodger Ward, Leader Card Special	140.293
1963	Parnelli Jones, Agajanian Special	143.137
1964	A.J. Foyt, Sheraton-Thompson Special	147.350
1965	Jim Clark, Lotus-Ford	150.686
1966	Graham Hill, American Red Ball	144.317
1967	A.J. Foyt, Sheraton-Thompson Special	151.207
1968	Bobby Unser, Rislone Special	152.882
1969	Mario Andretti, STP Oil Treatment Special	156.867
1970	Al Unser, Johnny Lightning Special	155.749
1971	Al Unser, Johnny Lightning Special	157.735
1972	Mark Donohue, Sunoco McLaren	162.962
1973	Gordon Johncock, STP Double Oil Filter	159.036
1974	Johnny Rutherford, McLaren	158.589
1975	Bobby Unser, Jorgenson Eagle	149.213
1976	Johnny Rutherford, Hygain McLaren	148.725
1977	A.J. Foyt, Gilmore Coyote-Ford	161.331
1978	Al Unser, Lola Cosworth	161.363
1979	Rick Mears, Penske-Cosworth	158.899
1980	Johnny Rutherford, Chaparral-Cosworth	142.862
1981	Bobby Unser, Penske-Cosworth	139.085
1982	Gordon Johncock, Wildcat-Cosworth	162.026
1983	Tom Sneva, March-Cosworth	162.117
1984	Rick Mears, March-Cosworth	163.621
1985	Danny Sullivan, March-Cosworth	152.982
1986	Bobby Rahal, March-Cosworth	170.722
1987	Al Unser, March-Cosworth	162.175
1988	Rick Mears, Penske-Chevy V8	144.809
1989	Emerson Fittipaldi, Penske PC 18-Chevy	167.581
1990	Arie Luyendyk, Lola-Chevy	185.984
1991	Rick Mears, Penske-Chevy	176.457
1992	Al Unser, Galmer-Chevy A	134.477
1993	Emerson Fittipaldi, Penske-Chevy C	157.207

The race was less than 500 miles in the following years: 1916 (300 mi.) ...., 1926 (400 mi.), 1950 (345 mi.), 1973 (332.5 mi.), 1975 (435 mi.), 1976 (255 mi.). Race record – 185.984 mph, Arie Luyendyk, 1990.

Le Mans 24-Hour Champions

1982	Derek Bell (GB)/Jacky Ickx (Bel) Porsche
1983	Hurley Haywood/Al Holbert (both US)/Vern Schuppan (Aut) Porsche
1984	Klaus Ludwig (FRG)/Henri Pescarolo (Fra) Porsche
1985	Paulo Barilla (Ita)/Klaus Ludwig/John Winter (both FRG) Porsche
1986	Derek Bell (GB)/Al Holbert (US)/Hans Stuck (FRG) Porsche
1987	Derek Bell (GB)/Al Holbert (US)/Hans Stuck (FRG) Porsche
1988	Jan Lammers (Neth)/Johnny Dumfries/Andy Wallace (both GB) Jaguar
1989	Stanley Dickens (Swe)/Jochen Mass/Manuel Reuter (both FRG) Mercedes
1990	John Nielsen (Den)/Price Cobb (US)/Martin Brundle (GB) Jaguar
1991	Volker Weidler (Ger)/Johnny Herbert (GB)/Bertrand Gachot (Bel) Mazda
1992	Derek Warwick (GB)/Yannick Daimas (Fra)/Mark Blundell (GB) Peugeot
1993	Christophe Bouchut/Eric Helary (both Fra)/Geoff Brabham (Aus) Peugeot

Notable One-Mile Speed Records

Date	Driver	Car	mph
26/1/06	Marriott	Stanley (Steam)	127.659
16/3/10	Oldfield	Benz	131.724
23/4/11	Burman	Benz	141.732
12/2/19	DePalma	Packard	149.875
27/4/20	Milton	Duesenberg	155.046
28/4/26	Parry-Thomas	Thomas Spl.	170.624
29/3/27	Seagrave	Sunbeam	203.790
22/4/28	Keech	White Triplex	207.552
11/3/29	Seagrave	Irving-Napier	231.446
5/2/31	Campbell	Napier-Campbell	246.086
24/2/32	Campbell	Napier-Campbell	253.96
22/2/33	Campbell	Napier-Campbell	272.109
3/9/35	Campbell	Bluebird Special	301.13
19/11/37	Eyston	Thunderbolt 1	311.42
16/9/38	Eyston	Thunderbolt 1	357.5
23/8/39	Cobb	Railton	368.9
16/9/47	Cobb	Railton-Mobil	394.2
5/8/63	Breedlove	Spirit of America	407.45
27/10/64	Arfons	Green Monster	536.71
15/11/65	Breedlove	Spirit of America	600.601
23/10/70	Gabelich	Blue Flame	622.407
9/10/79	Barrett	Budweiser Rocket	638.637*
4/10/83	Noble	Thrust 2	633.6

*Not recognized as official by sanctioning bodies.

World Grand Prix Champions

Year	Driver
1951	Juan Fangio, Argentina
1952	Alberto Ascari, Italy
1953	Alberto Ascari, Italy
1954	Juan Fangio, Argentina
1955	Juan Fangio, Argentina
1956	Juan Fangio, Argentina
1957	Juan Fangio, Argentina
1958	Mike Hawthorne, England
1959	Jack Brabham, Australia
1960	Jack Brabham, Australia
1961	Phil Hill, United States
1962	Graham Hill, England
1963	Jim Clark, Scotland
1964	John Surtees, England
1965	Jim Clark, Scotland
1966	Jack Brabham, Australia
1967	Denis Hulme, New Zealand
1968	Graham Hill, England
1969	Jackie Stewart, Scotland
1970	Jochen Rindt, Austria
1971	Jackie Stewart, Scotland
1972	Emerson Fittipaldi, Brazil
1973	Jackie Stewart, Scotland
1974	Emerson Fittipaldi, Brazil
1975	Niki Lauda, Austria
1976	James Hunt, England
1977	Niki Lauda, Austria
1978	Mario Andretti, U.S.
1979	Jody Scheckter, So. Africa
1980	Alan Jones, Australia
1981	Nelson Piquet, Brazil
1982	Keke Rosberg, Finland
1983	Nelson Piquet, Brazil
1984	Niki Lauda, Austria
1985	Alain Prost, France
1986	Alain Prost, France
1987	Nelson Piquet, Brazil
1988	Ayrton Senna, Brazil
1989	Alain Prost, France
1990	Ayrton Senna, Brazil
1991	Ayrton Senna, Brazil
1992	Nigel Mansell, England
1993	Alain Prost, France

MOTOR RALLYING

Motor Rally Winners, 1992–93

Rally	Winner	Car
Acropolis	Miki Biasion (Ita)	Ford Escort Cosworth
Argentinian	Juha Kankkunen (Fin)	Toyota Celica
Australian	Didier Auriol (Fra)	Lancia Delta Integrale
French	François Delecour (Fra)	Ford Escort Cosworth
Italian	Andrea Aghini (Ita)	Lancia Delta Integrale
Ivory Coast	Kejiro Shinozuka (Jap)	Mitsubishi Gallant
Monte Carlo	Didier Auriol (Fra)	Toyota Celica
New Zealand	Colin McRae (GB)	Subaru Legacy
Portuguese	François Delecour (Fra)	Ford Escort Cosworth
RAC	Carlos Sainz (Spa)	Toyota Celica
Safari	Juha Kankkunen (Fin)	Toyota Celica
Spanish	Carlos Sainz (Spa)	Toyota Celica
Swedish	Mats Jonsson (Swe)	Toyota Celica

Monte Carlo Rally Champions

Year	Driver	Car
1982	Walter Rohrl (FRG)	Opel
1983	Walter Rohrl (FRG)	Opel
1984	Walter Rohrl (FRG)	Audi
1985	Ari Vatanen (Fin)	Peugeot
1986	Henri Toivonen (Fin)	Lancia
1987	Miki Biasion (Ita)	Lancia
1988	Bruno Saby (Fra)	Lancia
1989	Miki Biasion (Ita)	Lancia
1990	Didier Auriol (Fra)	Lancia
1991	Carlos Sainz (Spa)	Toyota
1992	Didier Auriol (Fra)	Lancia
1993	Didier Auriol (Fra)	Toyota

RAC Rally Champions

Year	Driver	Car
1982	Hannu Mikkola (Fin)	Audi
1983	Stig Blomqvist (Swe)	Audi
1984	Ari Vatanen (Fin)	Peugeot
1985	Henri Toivonen (Fin)	Lancia
1986	Timo Salonen (Fin)	Peugeot
1987	Juha Kankkunen (Fin)	Lancia
1988	Markku Alen (Fin)	Lancia
1989	Pentti Arikkala (Fin)	Mitsubishi
1990	Carlos Sainz (Spa)	Toyota
1991	Juha Kankkunen (Fin)	Lancia
1992	Carlos Sainz (Spa)	Toyota

World Rally Driving Champions

Year	Driver	Country
1977	Sandro Munari	Italy
1978	Markku Alen	Finland
1979	Bjorn Waldegaard	Sweden
1980	Walter Rohrl	W. Germany
1981	Ari Vatanen	Finland
1982	Walter Rohrl	W. Germany
1983	Hannu Mikkola	Finland
1984	Stig Blomqvist	Sweden
1985	Timo Salonen	Finland
1986	Juha Kankkunen	Finland
1987	Juha Kankkunen	Finland
1988	Miki Biasion	Italy
1989	Miki Biasion	Italy
1990	*Men:* Carlos Sainz	Spain
	Women: Louise Aitken-Walker	G. Britain
1991	*Men:* Juha Kankkunen	Finland
	Women: Minna Sillankavva	Finland
1992	*Men:* Carlos Sainz	Spain
	Women: Eija Jurvanen	Finland

ROWING

Head of the River Race Champions

Year	Winning team
1926–36	London RC
1937	No race
1938	Goldie BC
1939	London RC
1940–45	No race
1946–48	Imperial College BC
1949–50	London RC
1951–52	Jesus College BC
1953	Thames RC
1954	RAF
1955–56	Thames RC
1957	Isis BC
1958–62	Barn Cottage
1963–66	University of London
1967–72	Tideway Scullers School
1973	Leander
1974	Tideway
1975–76	ARA National Squad
1977	Leander 1
1978	London 1
1979	ARA National Squad 1
1980	ARA National Squad 2
1981	Thames Tradesmen's 1
1982	ARA National Squad
1983	Thames Tradesmen's 1
1984–87	ARA National Squad 1
1988	GB National Squad 2
1989	GB National Squad 1
1990	GB National Squad
1991	Leander 1
1992	Molesey 1
1993	Munster (Germany)

Henley Grand Challenge Cup Winners

(Winners British, unless stated otherwise)

Year	Winning team
1839	First Trinity BC, Cambridge
1840	Leander Club
1841–42	Cambridge Subscription Rooms
1843	Oxford University BC
1844–55	Etonian Club, Oxford
1845	Cambridge University BC
1846	Thames Club, London
1847–48	Oxford University BC
1849	Wadham College, Oxford
1850–53	Oxford University BC
1854	First Trinity BC, Cambridge
1844	Cambridge University BC
1856	Royal Chester RC
1857	London RC
1858	Cambridge University BC
1859	London RC
1860–61	First Trinity BC, Cambridge
1862	London RC
1863	University College, Oxford
1864–65	Kingston RC
1866–67	Etonian Club, Oxford
1868	London RC
1869–71	Etonian Club, Oxford
1872–74	London RC
1875	Leander Club
1876	Thames RC
1877	London RC
1878	Thames RC
1879	Jesus College, Cambridge
1880	Leander Club
1881	London RC
1882	Exeter College, Oxford
1883–84	London RC
1885	Jesus College, Cambridge
1886–87	Trinity Hall, Cambridge
1888–89	Thames RC
1890	London RC
1891–94	Leander Club
1895	Trinity Hall, Cambridge
1896	Leander Club
1897	New College, Oxford
1898–1901	Leander Club

Year	Winning team	Year	Winning team
1902	Third Trinity BC, Cambridge	1957	Cornell University (US)
1903–05	Leander Club	1958	Trud Club (USSR)
1906	Club Nautique de Gand (Bel)	1959	Harvard University (US)
1907	Sport Nautique de Gand (Bel)	1960	Molesey BC
1908	Christ Church, Oxford	1961	Central Sport Club of the USSR Navy (USSR)
1909	Royal Club Nautique de Gand (Bel)	1962	Central Sport Club of the USSR Navy (USSR)
1910	Magdalen College, Oxford	1963	University of London
1911	Magdalen College, Oxford	1964	Zjalghiris Viljnjus (USSR)
1912	Sydney RC (Aust)	1965	Ratzeburger RC (Ger)
1913	Leander Club	1966	TSC Berlin (Ger)
1914	Harvard Athletic Assoc. BC (US)	1967	SC Wissenschaft DHfK (Ger)
1920	Magdalen College, Oxford	1968	University of London
1921	Magdalen College, Oxford	1969	SC Einheit, Dresden (Ger)
1922	Leander Club	1970	ASK Vorwärts (W Ger)
1923	Thames RC	1971	Tideway Scullers' School
1924–26	Leander Club	1972	WMF Moscow (USSR)
1927–28	Thames RC	1973	Trud Kolomna (USSR)
1929	Leander Club	1974	Trud Club (USSR)
1930–31	London RC	1975	Leander Club & Thames Tradesmen's RC
1932	Leander Club	1976	Thames Tradesmen's RC
1933	London RC	1977	University of Washington (US)
1934	Leander Club	1978	Trakia Club, Bulgaria
1935	Pembroke College, Cambridge	1979	Thames Tradesmen's RC/London RC
1936	FC Zürich Ruder Club (Swi)	1980	Charles River Rowing Association (US)
1937	R. Viking (Ger)	1981	Oxford University BC/Thames Tradesmen's RC
1938	London RC	1982	Leander/London RC (GB)
1939	Harvard University (US)	1983	London RC/University of London (GB)
1946	Leander Club	1984	Leander/London RC (GB)
1947	Jesus College, Cambridge	1985	Harvard University (US)
1948	Thames RC	1986	Nautilus (GB)
1949	Leander Club	1987	Soviet Army (USSR)
1950	Harvard University (US)	1988	Leander/University of London (GB)
1951	Lady Margaret BC, Cambridge	1989	RC Hansa Dortmund (FRG)
1952–53	Leander Club	1990	RC Hansa Dortmund (FRG)
1954	Club Krylia Sovetov (USSR)	1991	Leander & Star
1955	University of Pennsylvania (US)	1992	University of London
1956	Centre Sportif des Forces de l'Armée Française (Fra)	1993	Dortmund (Ger)

University Boat Race Winners

(Putney–Mortlake)

Cambridge: 70 wins. **Oxford:** 67 wins.

Year	Winner	Time	Distance	Year	Winner	Time	Distance
1829	Oxford	14m 30s	Easily	1886	Cambridge	22m 30s	⅔ length
1836	Cambridge	36m 0s	1m	1887	Cambridge	20m 52s	2½ lengths
1839	Cambridge	31m 0s	1m 45s	1888	Cambridge	20m 48s	7 lengths
1840	Cambridge	29m 30s	¾ length	1889	Cambridge	20m 14s	3 lengths
1841	Cambridge	32m 30s	1m 5s	1890	Oxford	22m 3s	1 length
1842	Oxford	30m 10s	13s	1891	Oxford	21m 48s	½ length
1845	Cambridge	23m 30s	30s	1892	Oxford	19m 10s	2¼ lengths
1846	Cambridge	21m 5s	3 lengths	1893	Oxford	18m 45s	1 length 4 ft
1849	Cambridge	22m 0s	Easily	1894	Oxford	21m 39s	3½ lengths
1849	Oxford	—	Foul	1895	Oxford	20m 50s	2¼ lengths
1852	Oxford	21m 36s	27s	1896	Oxford	20m 1s	⅖ length
1854	Oxford	25m 29s	11 strokes	1897	Oxford	19m 12s	2½ lengths
1856	Cambridge	25m 45s	½ length	1898	Oxford	22m 15s	Easily
1857	Oxford	22m 50s	32s	1899	Cambridge	21m 4s	3¼ lengths
1858	Cambridge	21m 23s	22s	1900	Cambridge	18m 45s	20 lengths
1859	Oxford	24m 40s	Camb. sank	1901	Oxford	22m 31s	⅖ length
1860	Cambridge	26m 5s	1 length	1902	Cambridge	19m 9s	5 lengths
1861	Oxford	23m 30s	47s	1903	Cambridge	19m 33s	6 lengths
1862	Oxford	24m 40s	30s	1904	Cambridge	21m 37s	4½ lengths
1863	Oxford	23m 6s	45s	1905	Oxford	20m 35s	3 lengths
1864	Oxford	21m 40s	27s	1906	Cambridge	19m 25s	3½ lengths
1865	Oxford	21m 24s	4 lengths	1907	Cambridge	20m 26s	4½ lengths
1866	Oxford	25m 35s	3 lengths	1908	Cambridge	19m 20s	2½ lengths
1867	Oxford	22m 39s	½ length	1909	Oxford	19m 50s	3½ lengths
1868	Oxford	20m 56s	6 lengths	1910	Oxford	20m 14s	3½ lengths
1869	Oxford	20m 4s	3 lengths	1911	Oxford	18m 29s	2¾ lengths
1870	Cambridge	22m 4s	1½ lengths	1912	Oxford	22m 5s	6 lengths
1871	Cambridge	23m 10s	1 length	1913	Oxford	20m 53s	¾ length
1872	Cambridge	21m 15s	2 lengths	1914	Cambridge	20m 23s	4½ lengths
1873	Cambridge	19m 35s	3 lengths	1920	Cambridge	21m 11s	4 lengths
1874	Cambridge	22m 35s	3½ lengths	1921	Cambridge	19m 45s	1 length
1875	Oxford	22m 2s	10 lengths	1922	Cambridge	19m 27s	4½ lengths
1876	Cambridge	20m 20s	Easily	1923	Oxford	20m 54s	¾ length
1877	Dead heat	24m 8s	—	1924	Cambridge	18m 41s	4½ lengths
1878	Oxford	22m 15s	10 lengths	1925	Cambridge	21m 50s	Oxford sank
1879	Cambridge	21m 18s	3 lengths	1926	Cambridge	19m 29s	5 lengths
1880	Oxford	21m 23s	3¾ lengths	1927	Cambridge	20m 14s	3 lengths
1881	Oxford	21m 51s	3 lengths	1928	Cambridge	20m 25s	10 lengths
1882	Oxford	20m 12s	7 lengths	1929	Cambridge	19m 24s	7 lengths
1883	Oxford	21m 18s	3½ lengths	1930	Cambridge	19m 9s	2 lengths
1884	Cambridge	21m 39s	2½ lengths	1931	Cambridge	19m 26s	2½ lengths
1885	Oxford	21m 36s	2½ lengths	1932	Cambridge	19m 11s	5 lengths

(Continued)

(University Boat Race contd.)

Year	Winner	Time	Distance
1933	Cambridge	20m 57s	2¼ lengths
1934	Cambridge	18m 3s	4¼ lengths
1935	Cambridge	19m 48s	4½ lengths
1936	Cambridge	21m 6s	5 lengths
1937	Oxford	22m 39s	3 lengths
1938	Oxford	20m 30s	2 lengths
1939	Cambridge	19m 3s	4 lengths
1946	Oxford	19m 54s	3 lengths
1947	Cambridge	23m 1s	10 lengths
1948	Cambridge	17m 50s	5 lengths
1949	Cambridge	18m 57s	¼ length
1950	Cambridge	20m 15s	3½ lengths
1951	Cambridge	20m 50s	12 lengths
1952	Oxford	20m 23s	Canvas
1953	Cambridge	19m 54s	8 lengths
1954	Oxford	20m 23s	4½ lengths
1955	Cambridge	19m 10s	16 lengths
1956	Cambridge	18m 36s	1¼ lengths
1957	Cambridge	19m 1s	2 lengths
1958	Cambridge	18m 15s	3½ lengths
1959	Oxford	18m 52s	6 lengths
1960	Oxford	18m 59s	1¼ lengths
1961	Cambridge	19m 22s	4¼ lengths
1962	Cambridge	19m 46s	5 lengths
1963	Oxford	20m 47s	5 lengths
1964	Cambridge	19m 18s	6½ lengths
1965	Oxford	18m 7s	4 lengths
1966	Oxford	19m 12s	3¾ lengths

Year	Winner	Time	Distance
1967	Oxford	18m 52s	3¼ lengths
1968	Cambridge	18m 22s	3½ lengths
1969	Cambridge	18m 4s	4 lengths
1970	Cambridge	20m 22s	3½ lengths
1971	Cambridge	17m 58s	10 lengths
1972	Cambridge	18m 36s	9½ lengths
1973	Cambridge	19m 21s	13 lengths
1974	Oxford	17m 35s	5½ lengths
1975	Cambridge	19m 27s	3¾ lengths
1976	Oxford	16m 58s	6½ lengths
1977	Oxford	19m 28s	7 lengths
1978	Oxford	18m 58s	Camb. sank
1979	Oxford	20m 33s	3½ lengths
1980	Oxford	19m 20s	Canvas
1981	Oxford	18m 11s	8 lengths
1982	Oxford	18m 21s	3¼ lengths
1983	Oxford	19m 7s	4½ lengths
1984	Oxford	16m 45s	4 lengths
1985	Oxford	17m 11s	4¾ lengths
1986	Cambridge	17m 58s	5 lengths
1987	Oxford	19m 59s	4 lengths
1988	Oxford	17m 35s	5½ lengths
1989	Oxford	18m 27s	2½ lengths
1990	Oxford	17m 15s	2¼ lengths
1991	Oxford	16m 59s	4¾ lengths
1992	Oxford	17m 44s	1¼ lengths
1993	Cambridge	17m 00s	3½ lengths

World Champions

(Not held in Olympic years)

Men

Single Sculls

1985 Pertti Karppinen (Fin)
1986 Peter-Michael Kolbe (FRG)
1987 Thomas Lange (GDR)
1989 Thomas Lange (GDR)
1990 Yuri Janson (USSR)
1991 Thomas Lange (Ger)
1993 Derek Porter (Can)

Double Sculls

1985 Thomas Lange/Uwe Heppner (GDR)
1986 Alberto Belgori/Igor Pescialli (Ita)
1987 Danayl Yordanov/Vassil Radev (Bul)
1989 Lars Bjoeness/Rol Bent Thorsen (Nor)
1990 Arnold Junke/Christopher Zerbst (Hol)
1991 Nicolaas Rienks/H. Zwolle (Hol)
1993 Yves Lamarque/Samuel Barathay (Fra)

Coxless Pairs

1985 Nikolay Pimenov/Yuriy Pimenov (USSR)
1986 Nikolay Pimenov/Yuriy Pimenov (USSR)
1987 Andrew Holmes/Steven Redgrave (GB)
1989 Thomas Jung/Uwe Kellner (GDR)
1990 Thomas Jung/Uwe Kellner (GDR)
1991 Steven Redgrave/Matthew Pinsent (GB)
1993 Steven Redgrave/Matthew Pinsent (GB)

Coxed Pairs

1985	Italy	1990	Italy
1986	Great Britain	1991	Italy
1987	Italy	1993	Great Britain
1989	Italy		

Coxless Fours

1985	West Germany	1990	Australia
1986	United States	1991	Australia
1987	East Germany	1993	France
1989	East Germany		

Coxed Fours

1985	USSR	1990	East Germany
1986	East Germany	1991	Germany
1987	East Germany	1993	Romania
1989	Romania		

Quadruple Sculls

1985	Canada	1990	USSR
1986	Canada	1991	USSR
1987	USSR	1993	Germany
1989	Holland		

Eights

1985	USSR	1990	West Germany
1986	Australia	1991	Germany
1987	United States	1993	Germany
1989	West Germany		

Women

Single Sculls

1985 Cornelia Linse (GDR)
1986 Jutta Hampe (GDR)
1987 Magdalena Georgieva (Bul)
1989 Elisabeta Lipa (Rom)
1990 Brigit Peter (GDR)
1991 Silke Laumann (Can)
1993 Jana Thieme (Ger)

Double Sculls

1985 Sylvia Schurabe/Martina Schroter (GDR)
1986 Sylvia Schurabe/Beate Schramm (GDR)
1987 Steska Madina/Violeta Ninova (Bul)
1989 Jana Sorgers/Beate Schramm (GDR)
1990 Kathrin Boron/Beate Schramm (GDR)
1991 Beate Schramm/K. Boron (Ger)
1993 Philippa Baker/Brenda Lawson (NZ)

Coxless Pairs

1985 Rodica Arba/Elena Florea (Rom)
1986 Rodica Arba/Olga Homeghi (Rom)
1987 Rodica Arba/Olga Homeghi (Rom)
1989 Kathrin Haaker/Judith Zeidler (GDR)
1990 Stephani Worromior/Ingeburg Althoss (FRG)
1991 McBean/K. Heddle (Can)
1993 Christine Gosse/Helene Cortin (Fra)

Quadruple Sculls

1985	East Germany	1990	East Germany
1986	East Germany	1991	Germany
1987	East Germany	1993	China
1989	East Germany		

Coxed Fours

1985	East Germany	1990	Romania
1986	Romania	1993	No race
1987	Romania		

Coxless Fours

1986	United States	1990	Romania
1987	–	1991	Canada
1989	East Germany	1993	China

Eights

1985	USSR	1990	Romania
1986	USSR	1991	Canada
1987	Romania	1993	Romania
1989	Romania		

RUGBY LEAGUE

Internationals 1992–93

Winner	Runner-up	Venue	Date
Australia 10	Great Britain 6	Wembley	Oct. 1992
England 36	Wales 11	Swansea	Nov. 1992
Wales 19	France 18	Perpignan	Dec. 1992
Great Britain 48	France 6	Carcassonne	Mar. 1993
Great Britain 72	France 6	Leeds	Apr. 1993

Challenge Cup Winners

Year	Winners		Runners-up	
1897	Batley	10	St Helens	3
1898	Batley	7	Bradford	0
1899	Oldham	19	Hunslet	9
1900	Swinton	16	Salford	8
1901	Batley	6	Warrington	0
1902	Broughton R.	25	Salford	0
1903	Halifax	7	Salford	0
1904	Halifax	8	Warrington	3
1905	Warrington	6	Hull K.R.	0
1906	Bradford	5	Salford	0
1907	Warrington	17	Oldham	3
1908	Hunslet	14	Hull	0
1909	Wakefield T.	17	Hull	0
1910	Leeds	7	Hull	7
Replay	Leeds	26	Hull	12
1911	Broughton R.	4	Wigan	0
1912	Dewsbury	8	Oldham	5
1913	Huddersfield	9	Warrington	5
1914	Hull	6	Wakefield T.	0
1915	Huddersfield	37	St Helens	3
1916-19	Competition suspended			
1920	Huddersfield	21	Wigan	10
1921	Leigh	13	Halifax	0
1922	Rochdale H.	10	Hull	9
1923	Leeds	28	Hull	3
1924	Wigan	21	Oldham	4
1925	Oldham	16	Hull K.R.	3
1926	Swinton	9	Oldham	3
1927	Oldham	26	Swinton	7
1928	Swinton	5	Warrington	3
1929	Wigan	13	Dewsbury	2
1930	Widnes	10	St Helens	3
1931	Halifax	22	York	8
1932	Leeds	11	Swinton	8
1933	Huddersfield	21	Warrington	17
1934	Hunslet	11	Widnes	5
1935	Castleford	11	Huddersfield	8
1936	Leeds	18	Warrington	2
1937	Widnes	18	Keighley	5
1938	Salford	7	Barrow	4
1939	Halifax	20	Salford	3
1940	No competition			
1941	Leeds	19	Halifax	2
1042	Leeds	15	Halifax	10
1943	Dewsbury	16	Leeds	9
	Dewsbury	0	Leeds	6
	(Dewsbury won on aggregate 16-15)			
1944	Bradford	0	Wigan	3
	Bradford	8	Wigan	0
	(Bradford won on aggregate 8-3)			
1945	Huddersfield	7	Bradford N.	4
	Huddersfield	6	Bradford N.	5
	(Huddersfield won on aggregate 13-9)			
1946	Wakefield T.	13	Wigan	12
1947	Bradford N.	8	Leeds	4
1948	Wigan	8	Bradford N.	3
1949	Bradford N.	12	Halifax	0
1950	Warrington	19	Widnes	0
1951	Wigan	10	Barrow	0
1952	Workington T.	18	Featherstone R.	10
1953	Huddersfield	15	St Helens	10
1954	Warrington	4	Halifax	4
Replay	Warrington	8	Halifax	4
1955	Barrow	21	Workington T.	12
1956	St Helens	13	Halifax	2
1957	Leeds	9	Barrow	7
1958	Wigan	13	Workington T.	9
1959	Wigan	30	Hull	13
1960	Wakefield T.	38	Hull	5
1961	St Helens	12	Wigan	6
1962	Wakefield T.	12	Huddersfield	6
1963	Wakefield T.	25	Wigan	10
1964	Widnes	13	Hull K.R.	5
1965	Wigan	20	Hunslet	16
1966	St Helens	21	Wigan	2
1967	Featherstone R.	17	Barrow	12
1968	Leeds	11	Wakefield T.	10
1969	Castleford	11	Salford	6
1970	Castleford	7	Wigan	2
1971	Leigh	24	Leeds	7
1972	St Helens	16	Leeds	13
1973	Featherstone R.	33	Bradford N.	14
1974	Warrington	24	Featherstone R.	9
1975	Widnes	14	Warrington	7
1976	St Helens	20	Widnes	5
1977	Leeds	16	Widnes	7
1978	Leeds	14	St Helens	12
1979	Widnes	12	Wakefield T.	3
1980	Hull K.R.	10	Hull	5
1981	Widnes	18	Hull K.R.	9
1982	Hull	14	Widnes	14
Replay	Hull	18	Widnes	9
1983	Featherstone R.	14	Hull	12
1984	Widnes	19	Wigan	6
1985	Wigan	28	Hull	24
1986	Castleford	15	Hull K.R.	14
1987	Halifax	19	St Helens	18
1988	Wigan	32	Halifax	12
1989	Wigan	27	St Helens	0
1990	Wigan	36	Warrington	14
1991	Wigan	13	St Helens	8
1992	Wigan	28	Castleford	12
1993	Wigan	20	Widnes	14

Lancashire Cup Winners

Season	Winners		Runners-up	
1905–06	Wigan	0	Leigh	0
Replay	Wigan	8	Leigh	0
1906–07	Broughton R.	15	Warrington	6
1907–08	Oldham	16	Broughton R.	9
1908–09	Wigan	10	Oldham	9
1909–10	Wigan	22	Leigh	5
1910–11	Oldham	4	Swinton	3
1911–12	Rochdale H.	12	Oldham	5
1912–13	Wigan	21	Rochdale H.	5
1913–14	Oldham	5	Wigan	0
1914–15	Rochdale H.	3	Wigan	2
1915–18	Competition suspended			
1918–19	Rochdale H.	22	Oldham	0
1919–20	Oldham	7	Rochdale H.	0
1920–21	Broughton R.	6	Leigh	3
1921–22	Warrington	7	Oldham	5
1922–23	Wigan	20	Leigh	2
1923–24	St Helens Recs.	17	Swinton	0
1924–25	Oldham	10	St Helens Recs.	0
1925–26	Swinton	15	Wigan	11
1926–27	St Helens	10	St Helens Recs.	2
1927–28	Swinton	5	Wigan	2
1928–29	Wigan	5	Widnes	4
1929–30	Warrington	15	Salford	2
1930–31	St Helens Recs.	18	Wigan	3
1931–32	Salford	10	Swinton	8
1932–33	Warrington	10	St Helens	9
1933–34	Oldham	12	St Helens Rec.	0
1934–35	Salford	21	Wigan	12
1935–36	Salford	15	Wigan	7
1936–37	Salford	5	Wigan	2
1937–38	Warrington	8	Barrow	4
1938–39	Wigan	10	Salford	7
1939–40*	Swinton	5	Widnes	4
	Swinton	16	Widnes	11
	(Swinton won on aggregate 21-15)			
1940–45	Competition suspended			
1945–46	Widnes	7	Wigan	3
1946–47	Wigan	9	Belle Vue R.	3
1947–48	Wigan	10	Belle Vue R.	7
1948–49	Wigan	14	Warrington	8
1949–50	Wigan	20	Leigh	7
1950–51	Wigan	28	Warrington	5
1951–52	Wigan	14	Leigh	6
1952–53	Leigh	22	St Helens	5
1953–54	St Helens	16	Wigan	8
1954–55	Barrow	12	Oldham	2

(Continued)

(Lancashire Cup Winners contd.)

Year	Winners		Runners-up	
1955–56	Leigh	26	Widnes	9
1956–57	Oldham	10	St Helens	3
1957–58	Oldham	13	Wigan	8
1958–59	Oldham	12	St Helens	2
1959–60	Warrington	5	St Helens	4
1960–61	St Helens	15	Swinton	9
1961–62	St Helens	25	Swinton	9
1962–63	St Helens	7	Swinton	4
1963–64	St Helens	15	Leigh	4
1964–65	St Helens	12	Swinton	4
1965–66	Warrington	16	Rochdale H.	5
1966–67	Wigan	16	Oldham	13
1967–68	St Helens	2	Warrington	2
Replay	St Helens	13	Warrington	10
1968–69	St Helens	30	Oldham	2
1969–70	Swinton	11	Leigh	2
1970–71	Leigh	7	St Helens	4
1971–72	Wigan	15	Widnes	8
1972–73	Salford	25	Swinton	11
1973–74	Wigan	19	Salford	9
1974–75	Widnes	6	Salford	2
1975–76	Widnes	16	Salford	7
1976–77	Widnes	16	Workington T.	11
1977–78	Workington T.	16	Wigan	13
1978–79	Widnes	15	Workington T.	13
1979–80	Widnes	11	Workington T.	0
1980–81	Warrington	26	Wigan	10
1981–82	Leigh	8	Widnes	3
1982–83	Warrington	16	St Helens	0
1983–84	Barrow	12	Widnes	8
1984–85	St Helens	26	Wigan	18
1985–86	Wigan	34	Warrington	8
1986–87	Wigan	27	Oldham	6
1987–88	Wigan	28	Warrington	16
1988–89	Wigan	22	Salford	17
1989–90	Warrington	24	Oldham	16
1990–91	Widnes	24	Salford	18
1991–92	St Helens	24	Rochdale H.	14
1992–93	Wigan	5	St Helens	4

* Emergency war-time competition.

Stones Bitter Premiership

Season	Winners		Runners-up	
1975	Leeds	26	St Helens	11
1976	St Helens	15	Salford	2
1977	St Helens	32	Warrington	20
1978	Bradford N.	17	Widnes	8
1979	Leeds	24	Bradford N.	2
1980	Widnes	19	Bradford N.	5
1981	Hull K.R.	11	Hull	7
1982	Widnes	23	Hull	8
1983	Widnes	22	Hull	10
1984	Hull K.R.	18	Castleford	10
1985	St Helens	36	Hull K.R.	16
1986	Warrington	38	Halifax	10
1987	Wigan	8	Warrington	0
1988	Widnes	38	St Helens	14
1989	Widnes	18	Hull	10
1990	Widnes	28	Bradford N.	6
1991	Hull	14	Widnes	4
1992	Wigan	48	St Helens	16

Yorkshire Cup Winners

Season	Winners		Runners-up	
1905–06	Hunslet	13	Halifax	3
1906–07	Bradford	8	Hull K.R.	5
1907–08	Hunslet	17	Halifax	0
1908–09	Halifax	9	Hunslet	5
1909–10	Huddersfield	21	Batley	0
1910–11	Wakefield T.	8	Huddersfield	2
1911–12	Huddersfield	22	Hull K.R.	10
1912–13	Batley	17	Hull	3
1913–14	Huddersfield	19	Bradford N.	3
1914–15	Huddersfield	31	Hull	0
1918–19	Huddersfield	14	Dewsbury	8
1919–20	Huddersfield	24	Leeds	5
1920–21	Hull K.R.	2	Hull	0
1921–22	Leeds	11	Dewsbury	3
1922–23	York	5	Batley	0
1923–24	Hull	10	Huddersfield	4
1924–25	Wakefield T.	9	Batley	8
1925–26	Dewsbury	2	Huddersfield	0
1926–27	Huddersfield	10	Wakefield T.	3
1927–28	Dewsbury	8	Hull	2
1928–29	Leeds	5	Featherstone R.	0
1929–30	Hull K.R.	13	Hunslet	7
1930–31	Leeds	10	Huddersfield	2
1931–32	Huddersfield	4	Hunslet	2
1932–33	Leeds	8	Wakefield T.	0
1933–34	York	10	Hull K.R.	4
1934–35	Leeds	5	Wakefield T	5
Replay	Leeds	2	Wakefield T.	2
Replay	Leeds	13	Wakefield T.	0
1935–36	Leeds	3	York	0
1936–37	York	9	Wakefield T.	2
1937–38	Leeds	14	Huddersfield	8
1938–39	Huddersfield	18	Hull	10
1939–40	Featherstone R.	12	Wakefield T.	9
1940–41	Bradford N.	15	Dewsbury	5
1941–42	Bradford N.	24	Halifax	0
1942–43	Dewsbury	7	Huddersfield	0
	Huddersfield	2	Dewsury	0
	(Dewsbury won on aggregate 7-2)			
1943–44	Bradford N.	5	Keighley	2
	Keighley	5	Bradford N.	5
	(Bradford N. won on aggregate 10-7)			
1944–45	Hunslet	3	Halifax	12
	Halifax	2	Hunslet	0
	(Halifax won on aggregate 14-3)			
1945–46	Bradford N.	5	Wakefield T.	2
1946–47	Wakefield T.	10	Hull	0
1947–48	Wakefield T.	7	Leeds	7
Replay	Wakefield T.	8	Leeds	7
1948–49	Bradford N.	18	Castleford	9
1949–50	Bradford N.	11	Huddersfield	4
1950–51	Huddersfield	16	Castleford	3
1951–52	Wakefield T.	17	Keighley	3
1952–53	Huddersfield	18	Batley	8
1953–54	Bradford N.	7	Hull	2
1954–55	Halifax	22	Hull	14
1955–56	Halifax	10	Hull	10
Replay	Halifax	7	Hull	0
1956–57	Wakefield T.	23	Hunslet	5
1957–58	Huddersfield	15	York	8
1958–59	Leeds	24	Wakefield T.	20
1959–60	Featherstone R.	15	Hull	14
1960–61	Wakefield T.	16	Huddersfield	10
1961–62	Wakefield T.	19	Leeds	9
1962–63	Hunslet	12	Hull K.R.	2
1963–64	Halifax	10	Featherstone R.	0
1964–65	Wakefield T.	18	Leeds	2
1965–66	Bradford N.	17	Hunslet	8
1966–67	Hull K.R.	25	Featherstone R.	12
1967–68	Hull K.R.	8	Hull	7
1968–69	Leeds	22	Castleford	11
1969–70	Hull	12	Featherstone R.	9
1970–71	Leeds	23	Featherstone R.	7
1971–72	Hull K.R.	11	Castleford	7
1972–73	Leeds	36	Dewsbury	9
1973–74	Leeds	7	Wakefield T.	2
1974–75	Hull K.R.	16	Wakefield T.	13
1975–76	Leeds	15	Hull K.R.	11
1976–77	Leeds	16	Featherstone R.	12
1977–78	Castleford	17	Featherstone R.	7
1978–79	Bradford N.	18	York	8
1979–80	Leeds	15	Halifax	6
1980–81	Leeds	8	Hull K.R.	7
1981–82	Castleford	10	Bradford N.	5
1982–83	Hull	18	Bradford N.	7
1983–84	Hull	13	Castleford	2
1984–85	Hull	29	Hull K.R.	12
1985–86	Hull K.R.	22	Castleford	18
1986–87	Castleford	31	Hull	24
1987–88	Bradford N.	12	Castleford	12
Replay	Bradford N.	11	Castleford	2
1988–89	Leeds	33	Castleford	12
1989–90	Bradford N.	20	Featherstone R.	14
1990–91	Castleford	11	Wakefield T.	8
1991–92	Castleford	28	Bradford N.	6
1992–93	Wakefield T.	29	Sheffield Eagles	16

RUGBY UNION

British Lions Tour of New Zealand

First Test
(Christchurch, 12 June 1993)

New Zealand	20	British Isles	18

Second Test
(Wellington, 26 June 1993)

New Zealand	7	British isles	20

Third Test
(Auckland, 3 July 1993)

Year		Winners	
New Zealand	30	British Isles	13

County Champions

Year	Winners	Year	Winners
1889	Yorkshire	1940-46	Not held
1890	Yorkshire	1947	Lancashire
1891	Lancashire	1948	Lancashire
1892	Yorkshire	1949	Lancashire
1893	Yorkshire	1950	Cheshire
1894	Yorkshire	1951	East Midlands
1895	Yorkshire	1952	Middlesex
1896	Yorkshire	1953	Yorkshire
1897	Kent	1954	Middlesex
1898	Northumberland	1955	Lancashire
1899	Devon	1956	Middlesex
1900	Durham	1957	Devon
1901	Devon	1958	Warwickshire
1902	Durham	1959	Warwickshire
1903	Durham	1960	Warwickshire
1904	Kent	1961	Cheshire
1905	Durham	1962	Warwickshire
1906	Devon	1963	Warwickshire
1907	Devon & Durham (shared)	1964	Warwickshire
		1965	Warwickshire
1908	Cornwall	1966	Middlesex
1909	Durham	1967	Surrey & Durham
1910	Gloucestershire	1968	Middlesex
1911	Devon	1969	Lancashire
1912	Devon	1970	Staffordshire
1913	Gloucestershire	1971	Surrey
1914	Midlands	1972	Gloucestershire
1915-19	Not held	1973	Lancashire
1920	Gloucestershire	1974	Gloucestershire
1921	Gloucestershire	1975	Gloucestershire
1922	Gloucestershire	1976	Glouchestershire
1923	Somerset	1977	Lancashire
1924	Cumberland	1978	North Midlands
1925	Leicestershire	1979	Middlesex
1926	Yorkshire	1980	Lancashire
1927	Kent	1981	Northumberland
1928	Yorkshire	1982	Lancashire
1929	Middlesex	1983	Gloucestershire
1930	Gloucestershire	1984	Gloucestershire
1931	Gloucestershire	1985	Middlesex
1932	Gloucestershire	1986	Warwickshire
1933	Hampshire	1987	Yorkshire
1934	East Midlands	1988	Lancashire
1935	Lancashire	1989	Durham
1936	Hampshire	1990	Lancashire
1937	Gloucestershire	1991	Cornwall
1938	Lancashire	1992	Lancashire
1939	Warwickshire	1993	Lancashire

Five-Nations Championship

(16 Jan. 1993)

England	16	France	15
Scotland	15	Ireland	3

(6 Feb. 1993)

Wales	10	England	9
France	11	Scotland	3

(20 Feb. 1993)

Ireland	6	France	21
Scotland	20	Wales	0

(6 Mar. 1993)

England	26	Scotland	12
Wales	14	Ireland	19

(20 Mar. 1993)

France	26	Wales	10
Ireland	17	England	3

Final Table

	P	W	D	L	F	A	Pts
France	4	3	0	1	73	35	6
Scotland	4	2	0	2	50	40	4
England	4	2	0	2	54	54	4
Ireland	4	2	0	2	45	53	4
Wales	4	1	0	3	34	74	2

Pilkington Cup Winners

Year	Winners		Runners-up	
1980	Leicester	21	London Irish	9
1981	Leicester	22	Gosforth	15
1982	Gloucester*	12	Moseley	12
1983	Bristol	28	Leicester	22
1984	Bath	10	Bristol	9
1985	Bath	24	London Welsh	15
1986	Bath	25	Wasps	7
1987	Bath	19	Wasps	12
1988	Harlequins	28	Bristol	22
1989	Bath	10	Leicester	6
1990	Bath	48	Gloucester	6
1991	Harlequins	25	Northampton	13
1992	Bath	15	Harlequins	12
1993	Leicester	23	Harlequins	16

* Shared.

Sevens Tournaments 1992–93

Tournament	Winners	Runners-up
Hong Kong International Sevens	Western Samoa 17	Fiji 14
Middlesex Sevens	Wasps 26	Northampton 24

University Rugby Champions

(No scores given for 1871–1904, as modern scoring values were not adopted until 1905. Matches played at the Oval 1873–80, at Blackheath 1880–87, at Queen's Club 1887–1921, then Twickenham. War matches (1939–45) played at Oxford and Cambridge.)

111 matches played. Oxford 47, Cambridge 51. 13 draws.

1871–72	Oxford	1875–76	Oxford	1879–80	Cambridge	1883–84	Oxford
1872–73	Cambridge	1876–77	Cambridge	1880–81	Drawn	1884–85	Oxford
1873–74	Drawn	1877–78	Oxford	1881–82	Oxford	1885–86	Cambridge
1874–75*	Drawn	1878–79	Drawn	1882–83	Oxford	1886–87	Cambridge

(Continued)

(University Rugby Champions contd.)

1887–88	Cambridge	1913–14	Cambridge 13-3	1941–42	Cambridge 9-6	1965–66	Drawn 5-5
1888–89	Cambridge	1914–19	Not played		Cambridge 17-8	1966–67	Oxford 8-6
1889–90	Oxford	1919–20	Cambridge 7-5	1942–43	Cambridge 9-0	1967–68	Cambridge 6-0
1890–91	Drawn	1920–21	Oxford 17-14		Cambridge 16-3	1968–69	Cambridge 9-6
1891–92	Cambridge	1921–22	Oxford 11-5	1943–44	Cambridge 13-4	1969–70	Oxford 9-6
1892–93	Drawn	1922–23	Cambridge 21-8		Oxford 6-5	1970–71	Oxford 14-3
1893–94	Oxford	1923–24	Oxford 21-4	1944–45	Drawn 3-3	1971–72	Oxford 21-3
1894–95	Drawn	1924–25	Oxford 11-6		Cambridge 16-4	1972–73	Cambridge 16-6
1895–96	Cambridge	1925–26	Cambridge 33-3	1945–46	Cambridge 11-8	1973–74	Cambridge 14-12
1896–97	Oxford	1926–27	Cambridge 30-5	1946–47	Oxford 15-5	1974–75	Cambridge 16-15
1897–98	Oxford	1927–28	Cambridge 22-14	1947–48	Cambridge 6-0	1975–76	Cambridge 34-12
1898–99	Cambridge	1928–29	Cambridge 14-10	1948–49	Oxford 14-8	1976–77	Cambridge 15-0
1899–1900	Cambridge	1929–30	Oxford 9-0	1949–50	Oxford 3-0	1977–78	Oxford 16-10
1900–01	Oxford	1930–31	Drawn 3-3	1950–51	Oxford 8-0	1978–79	Cambridge 25-7
1901–02	Oxford	1931–32	Oxford 10-3	1951–52	Oxford 13-0	1979–80	Oxford 9-3
1902–03	Drawn	1932–33	Oxford 8-3	1952–53	Cambridge 6-5	1980–81	Cambridge 13-9
1903–04	Oxford	1933–34	Oxford 5-3	1953–54	Drawn 6-6	1981–82	Cambridge 9-6
1904–05	Cambridge	1934–35	Cambridge 29-4	1954–55	Cambridge 3-0	1982–83	Cambridge 20-13
1905–06	Cambridge 15-13	1935–36	Drawn 0-0	1955–56	Oxford 9-5	1983–84	Cambridge 20-9
1906–07	Oxford 12-8	1936–37	Cambridge 6-5	1956–57	Cambridge 14-9	1984–85	Cambridge 32-6
1907–08	Oxford 17-0	1937–38	Oxford 17-4	1957–58	Oxford 3-0	1985–86	Oxford 7-6
1908–09	Drawn 5-5	1938–39	Cambridge 8-6	1958–59	Cambridge 17-6	1986–87	Oxford 15-10
1909–10	Oxford 35-3	1939–40	Oxford 15-3	1959–60	Oxford 9-3	1987–88	Cambridge 15-10
1910–11	Oxford 23-18		Cambridge 14-13	1960–61	Cambridge 13-0	1988–89	Oxford 27-7
1911–12	Oxford 19-0	1940–41	Cambridge 11-9	1961–62	Cambridge 9-3	1989–90	Cambridge 22-13
1912–13	Cambridge 10-3		Cambridge 3-0	1962–63	Cambridge 14-0	1990–91	Oxford 21-12
				1963–64	Cambridge 19-11	1991–92	Cambridge 17-11
				1964–65	Oxford 19-6	1992–93	Cambridge 19-11

Welsh Cup Winners

Year	Winners		Runners-up	
1980	Bridgend	15	Swansea	9
1981	Cardiff	14	Bridgend	6
1982	Cardiff*	12	Bridgend	12
1983	Pontypool	18	Swansea	6
1984	Cardiff	24	Neath	19
1985	Llanelli	15	Cardiff	14
1986	Cardiff	28	Newport	21
1987	Cardiff	16	Swansea	15 aet
1988	Llanelli	28	Neath	13
1989	Neath	14	Llanelli	13
1990	Neath	16	Bridgend	10
1991	Llanelli	24	Pontypool	9
1992	Llanelli	6	Swansea	7
1993	Llanelli	21	Neath	18

* Winners on most tries rule.

World Cup

(Oct. 1991)

Pool 1

England	12	New Zealand	18
Italy	30	US	9
New Zealand	46	United States	6
England	36	Italy	6
England	37	US	9
New Zealand	31	Italy	21

Pool 2

Scotland	47	Japan	9
Ireland	55	Zimbabwe	11
Scotland	51	Zimbabwe	12
Ireland	32	Japan	16
Scotland	24	Ireland	15
Zimbabwe	8	Japan	52

Pool 3

Australia	32	Argentina	19
Wales	13	W. Samoa	16
Australia	32	Argentina	19
Australia	9	W. Samoa	3
Wales	16	Argentina	7
Wales	3	Australia	38
Argentina	12	W. Samoa	35

Pool 4

France	30	Romania	3
Canada	13	Fiji	3
France	33	Fiji	9
Canada	19	Romania	11
Fiji	15	Romania	17
France	19	Canada	13

Quarter-finals

(18 Oct. 1991)

Scotland	28	W. Samoa	6
France	10	England	19
Ireland	18	Australia	19
New Zealand	29	Canada	13

Semi-finals

(27 Oct. 1991)

Scotland	6	England	9
New Zealand	6	Australia	16

Third place play-off

(30 Oct. 1991)

New Zealand	13	Scotland	6

Final

(2 Nov. 1991)

England	6	Australia	12

World Cup Winners

Year	Winners		Runners-up	
1987	New Zealand	29	France	9
1992	Australia	12	England	6

World Cup Sevens

(16–18 Apr. 1993)

Pool A

Final standings	P	W	D	L	F	A	Pts
South Africa	5	5	0	0	175	43	15
Fiji	5	4	0	1	150	60	13
Wales	5	3	0	2	135	78	11
Japan	5	2	0	3	67	120	9
Romania	5	1	0	4	44	133	7
Latvia	5	0	0	5	31	168	5

Pool B

Final standings	P	W	D	L	F	A	Pts
New Zealand	5	5	0	0	157	24	15
Ireland	5	4	0	1	128	45	13

Final standings	P	W	D	L	F	A	Pts
South Korea	5	3	0	2	80	98	11
France	5	1	0	4	50	85	7
Netherlands	5	1	0	4	47	167	7
United States	5	1	0	4	62	105	7

Pool C

Final standings	P	W	D	L	F	A	Pts
Australia	5	4	0	1	141	29	13
Tonga	5	4	0	1	117	34	13
Argentina	5	3	0	2	67	79	11
Scotland	5	3	0	2	96	64	11
Italy	5	1	0	4	41	123	7
Taiwan	5	0	0	5	24	157	5

Pool D

Final standings	P	W	D	L	F	A	Pts
Western Samoa	5	5	0	0	193	31	15
England	5	4	0	1	138	38	13
Canada	5	2	0	3	75	87	9
Spain	5	2	0	3	59	114	9
Hong Kong	5	1	0	4	43	161	7
Namibia	5	1	0	4	55	132	7

Quarter Finals

Pool E

Western Samoa	0	Ireland	17
Tonga	7	Fiji	21
Western Samoa	12	Fiji	14
Tonga	12	Ireland	14
Western Samoa	42	Tonga	7
Fiji	31	Ireland	7

Pool F

South Africa	5	Australia	7
New Zealand	12	England	21
South Africa	7	England	14
New Zealand	42	Australia	0
South Africa	31	New Zealand	14
England	12	Australia	21

Semi-finals

Fiji	7	England	21
Ireland	19	Australia	21

Final

England	21	Australia	17

SAILING

Admiral's Cup 1993

	Team	Yacht Names
1	Germany	Pinta Rubin XII Container
2	Australia	Ninja Great News II Ragamuffin
3	France	Corum Diamant Corum Rubis Corum Saphir
4	Italy	Brava Q8 Larouge Mandrake
5	Japan	Nipon Swing Champosa
6	United Kingdom	GBE International Provezza Source Indulgence
7	Ireland	Jameson I Jameson 2 Jameson 3
8	Netherlands	Ace Promotion VII

The America's Cup

Competition for the America's Cup grew out of the first contest to establish a world yachting championship, one of the carnival features of the London Exposition of 1851. The race, open to all classes of yachts from all over the world, covered a 60-mile course around the Isle of Wight; the prize was a cup worth about $500, donated by the Royal Yacht Squadron of England, known as the "America's Cup" because it was first won by the United States yacht *America*. The next competition is in San Diego in 1995.

Year	Winner
1851	*America*
1870	*Magic* defeated *Cambria*, England, (1-0)
1871	*Columbia* (first three races) and *Sappho* (last two races) defeated *Livonia*, England, (4-1)
1876	*Madeline* defeated *Countess of Dufferin*, Canada, (2-0)
1881	*Mischief* defeated *Atalanta*, Canada, (2-0)
1885	*Puritan* defeated *Genesta*, England, (2-0)
1886	*Mayflower* defeated *Galatea*, England, (2-0)
1887	*Volunteer* defeated *Thistle*, Scotland, (2-0)
1893	*Vigilant* defeated *Valkyrie II*, England, (3-0)
1895	*Defender* defeated *Valkyrie III*, England, (3-0)
1899	*Columbia* defeated *Shamrock*, England, (3-0)
1901	*Columbia* defeated *Shamrock II*, England, (3-0)
1903	*Reliance* defeated *Shamrock III*; England, (3-0)
1920	*Resolute* defeated *Shamrock IV*, England, (3-2)
1930	*Enterprise* defeated *Shamrock V*, England, (4-0)
1934	*Rainbow* defeated *Endeavour*, England, (4-2)
1937	*Ranger* defeated *Endeavour II*, England, (4-0)
1958	*Columbia* defeated *Sceptre*, England, (4-0)
1962	*Weatherly* defeated *Gretel*, Australia, (4-1)
1964	*Constellation* defeated *Sovereign*, England, (4-0)
1967	*Intrepid* defeated *Dame Pattie*, Australia, (4-0)
1970	*Intrepid* defeated *Gretel II*, Australia, (4-1)
1974	*Courageous* defeated *Southern Cross*, Australia, (4-0)
1977	*Courageous* defeated *Australia*, Australia, (4-0)
1980	*Freedom* defeated *Australia*, Australia, (4-1)
1983	*Australia II*, Australia, defeated *Liberty* (4-3)
1987	*Stars & Stripes* defeated *Kookaburra III*, Australia, (4-0)
1988	*Stars & Stripes* defeated *New Zealand*, New Zealand, (2-0)
1992	*America³* defeated *Il Moro di Venezia*, Italy (4–1)

Cowes Week 1993

Class	Winning Yacht
IMS Class A	Magic
CHS Class 1	Camp Freddie
CHS Class 2	Local Hero
CHS Class 3	Kozmos
CHS Class 4	Owl
CHS Class 5	Pawky Goo
CHS Class 6	Charlotte Sometimes
International J-24	Head Case
Contessa 32	Trader Jo
Sigma 38	Arbitrator
Sigma 33	Shadowfax
International Etchell	Arbitrator
South Coast One Design	Tuonela
National Sonata	Cadenza
Daring	Dauntless
Dragon Lady	Dragon Lady
Solent Sunbeam	Santa Baby
International Flying 15	Forrader
Redwing	Quail
National Swallow	Kingfisher
Seaview Mermaid	Rosemary
National Squib	Atom
X One Design	Zoe
Victory	Steadfast

Fastnet Race 1993

Trophy	Winning Craft
Alf Loomis	Indulgence
Battler Beedle Quaich	Twee Gesusters
Bloodhound Cup	Twee Gesusters
Bobbin Lowein Wheel	Dolphin and Youth
Buckley Memorial	Encore
Cas Van Dam Memorial	Eagle
Catherine Green and Founders Cup	Galicia 93 Pescanova
Clarion Cup	Eagle
Clarke Cup	Ragamuffin
Cordon Rouge	Sunstone
Culdrose	Kindamagic
Eerivale Cup	Ole
Errol Bruce Cup	Indulgence
Fastnet Challenge Cup	Indulgence
Fastnet Rock	Encore
Favona Cup	Buckshot
Figaro	Corum Saphir
Foxhound Cup	Twee Gesusters
Galley Slave	Stratos
Hong Kong Cup	New Zealand Endeavour
Inter-Regiment Cup	Kindamagic
Iolaire Cup	Ole
Iolaire Block	Stormy Weather
Jolie Brise Cup	Ole
Keith Ludlow	Encore
Norlethe Cup	Eagle
Philip Whitehead Cup	Galicia 93 Pescanova
Quailo Cup	Sunstone
RORC Bowl	Assuage
RORC Prize	Anahita/Antwerp Express/Eagle
Royal Thames Spirit Cup	Galicia 93 Pescanova
Seth Smith	Lutine
Swinburn Cup	Jameson 2
Veritas Performance Cup	Encore
West Mersea Yacht Club	Eagle
Whirlwind	Assuage

Whitbread Round the World Champions

Year	Yacht	Country
1973–74	Sayula II	Mexico
1977–78	Flyer	Netherlands
1981–82	Flyer	Netherlands
1985–86	L'Esprit d'equipe	France
1989–90	Steinlager II	New Zealand

SKIING

World Cup Alpine Champions

Men

Year	Winner
1967	Jean Claude Killy, France
1968	Jean Claude Killy, France
1969	Karl Schranz, Austria
1970	Karl Schranz, Austria
1971	Gustavo Thoeni, Italy
1972	Gustavo Thoeni, Italy
1973	Gustavo Thoeni, Italy
1974	Piero Gros, Italy
1975	Gustavo Thoeni, Italy
1976	Ingemar Stenmark, Sweden
1977	Ingemar Stenmark, Sweden
1978	Ingemar Stenmark, Sweden
1979	Peter Luescher, Switzerland
1980	Andreas Wenzel, Liechtenstein
1981	Phil Mahre, U.S.
1982	Phil Mahre, U.S.
1983	Phil Mahre, U.S.
1984	Pirmin Zurbriggen, Switzerland
1985	Marc Girardelli, Luxembourg
1986	Marc Girardelli, Luxembourg
1987	Pirmin Zurbriggen, Switzerland
1988	Pirmin Zurbriggen, Switzerland
1989	Marc Girardelli, Luxembourg
1990	Pirmin Zurbriggen, Switzerland
1991	Marc Girardelli, Luxembourg
1992	Paul Accola, Switzerland
1993	Marc Girardelli, Luxembourg

Women

Year	Winner
1967	Nancy Greene, Canada
1968	Nancy Greene, Canada
1969	Gertrud Gabl, Austria
1970	Michele Jacot, France
1971	Annemarie Proell, Austria
1972	Annemarie Proell, Austria
1973	Annemarie Proell, Austria
1974	Annemarie Proell, Austria
1975	Annemarie Proell, Austria
1976	Rose Mittermaier, W. Germany
1977	Lise-Marie Morerod, Switzerland
1978	Hanni Wenzel, Liechtenstein
1979	Annemarie Proell Moser, Austria
1980	Hanni Wenzel, Liechtenstein
1981	Marie-Theres Nadig, Switzerland
1982	Erika Hess, Switzerland
1983	Tamara McKinney, U.S.
1984	Erika Hess, Switzerland
1985	Michela Figini, Switzerland
1986	Maria Walliser, Switzerland
1987	Maria Walliser, Switzerland
1988	Michela Figini, Switzerland
1989	Vreni Schneider, Switzerland
1990	Petra Kronberger, Austria
1991	Petra Kronberger, Austria
1992	Petra Kronberger, Austria
1993	Anita Wachter, Austria

SNOOKER

Major Tournaments 1992–93

Tournament	Winner
Asian Open	Dave Harold (Eng)
British Open	Steve Davis (Eng)
Dubai Duty Free	John Parrott (Eng)
European Open	Steve Davis (Eng)
Grand Prix	Jimmy White (Eng)
International Open*	Stephen Hendry (Scot)
Regal Welsh	Ken Doherty (Irl)
UK Championship	Jimmy White (Eng)
World Championship	Stephen Hendry (Scot)
Benson and Hedges Masters	Stephen Hendry (Scot)
World Matchplay Champion	Gary Wilkinson (Eng)

* Replaces Mercantile Credit Classic

Benson & Hedges Champions

(British, unless specified)

Year	Winner	Year	Winner
1975	John Spencer	1985	Cliff Thorburn (Can)
1976	Ray Reardon	1986	Cliff Thorburn (Can)
1977	Doug Mountjoy	1987	Dennis Taylor
1978	Alex Higgins	1988	Steve Davis
1979	Perrie Mans (S Af)	1989	Stephen Hendry
1980	Terry Griffiths	1990	Stephen Hendry
1981	Alex Higgins	1991	Stephen Hendry
1982	Steve Davis	1992	Stephen Hendry
1983	Cliff Thorburn (Can)	1993	Stephen Hendry
1984	Jimmy White		

British Open Champions

(British, unless specified)

Year	Winner	Year	Winner
1985	Silvino Francisco (S Af)	1990	Bob Chaperon (Can)
1986	Steve Davis	1991	Stephen Hendry
1987	Jimmy White	1992	Jimmy White
1988	Stephen Hendry	1993	Steve Davis
1989	Tony Meo		

European Open Champions

Year	Winner	Year	Winner
1989	John Parrott	1992	Jimmy White
1990	John Parrott	1993	Steve Davis
1991	Tony Jones		

UK Open Champions

Year	Winner	Year	Winner
1984	Steve Davis	1989	Stephen Hendry
1985	Steve Davis	1990	Stephen Hendry
1986	Steve Davis	1991	Stephen Hendry
1987	Steve Davis	1992	Jimmy Parrott
1988	Doug Mountjoy	1993	Jimmy White

World Champions

(British, unless specified)

Year	Winner	Score	Runners-up
1976	Ray Reardon	27-16	Alex Higgins
1977	John Spencer	25-21	Cliff Thorburn (Can)
1978	Ray Reardon	25-18	Perrie Mans (S Af)
1979	Terry Griffiths	24-16	Dennis Taylor
1980	Cliff Thorburn (Can)	18-16	Alex Higgins
1981	Steve Davis	18-12	Doug Mountjoy
1982	Alex Higgins	18-15	Ray Reardon
1983	Steve Davis	18-6	Cliff Thornburn (Can)
1984	Steve Davis	18-16	Jimmy White
1985	Dennis Taylor	18-17	Steve Davis
1986	Joe Johnson	18-12	Steve Davis
1987	Steve Davis	18-14	Joe Johnson
1988	Steve Davis	18-11	Terry Griffiths
1989	Steve Davis	18-3	John Parrott
1990	Stephen Hendry	18-12	Jimmy White
1991	John Parrott	18-11	Jimmy White
1992	Stephen Hendry	18-14	Jimmy White
1993	Stephen Hendry	18-5	Jimmy White

World Matchplay Champions

Year	Winner	Year	Winner
1988	Steve Davis	1991	Gary Wilkinson
1989	Jimmy White	1992	Gary Wilkinson
1990	Jimmy White		

SQUASH

British Open Champions

Men		Women	
1971	Jonah Barrington (GB)	1971	Heather McKay (Aus)
1972	Jonah Barrington (GB)	1972	Heather McKay (Aus)
1973	Jonah Barrington (GB)	1973	Heather McKay (Aus)
1974	Geoff Hunt (Aus)	1974	Heather McKay (Aus)
1975	Qamar Zaman (Pak)	1975	Heather McKay (Aus)
1976	Geoff Hunt (Aus)	1976	Heather McKay (Aus)
1977	Geoff Hunt (Aus)	1977	Heather McKay (Aus)
1978	Geoff Hunt (Aus)	1978	Susan Newman (Aus)
1979	Geoff Hunt (Aus)	1979	Barbara Well (Aus)
1980	Geoff Hunt (Aus)	1980	Vicki Hoffman (Aus)
1981	Geoff Hunt (Aus)	1981	Vicki Hoffman (Aus)
1982	Jahangir Khan (Pak)	1982	Vicki Cardwell (née Hoffman) (Aus)
1983	Jahangir Khan (Pak)	1983	Vicki Cardwell (Aus)
1984	Jahangir Khan (Pak)	1984	Susan Devoy (NZ)
1985	Jahangir Khan (Pak)	1985	Susan Devoy (NZ)
1986	Jahangir Khan (Pak)	1986	Susan Devoy (NZ)
1987	Jahangir Khan (Pak)	1987	Susan Devoy (NZ)
1988	Jahangir Khan (Pak)	1988	Susan Devoy (NZ)
1989	Jahangir Khan (Pak)	1989	Susan Devoy (NZ)
1990	Jahangir Khan (Pak)	1990	Susan Devoy (NZ)
1991	Jahangir Khan (Pak)	1991	Lisa Opie (GB)
1992	Jansher Khan (Pak)	1992	Susan Devoy (NZ)
1993	Jansher Khan (Pak)	1993	Michelle Martin (Aus)

European Champions

Individual

Year	Men	Women
1990	Chris Walker (Eng)	Senga Macfie (Eng)
1991	Chris Walker (Eng)	Martine Lemoignan (Eng)
1992	Chris Walker (Eng)	Corinne Castets (Fra)

Team

Men			
1973–79	England	1987–91	England
1980	Sweden	1992	Scotland
1981–82	England	1993	England
1983–86	Sweden	**Women**	
		1978–93	England

World Open Champions

Men

1975	Geoff Hunt (Aus)	1991	Rodney Martin (Aus)
1977	Geoff Hunt (Aus)	1992	Jansher Khan (Pak)
1979	Geoff Hunt (Aus)		
1980	Geoff Hunt (Aus)		
1981	Jahangir Khan (Pak)		
1982	Jahangir Khan (Pak)		
1983	Jahangir Khan [Pak)		
1984	Jahangir Khan (Pak)		
1985	Jahangir Khan (Pak)		
1986	Ross Norman (NZ)		
1987	Jansher Khan (Pak)		
1988	Jahangir Khan (Pak)		
1989	Jansher Khan (Pak)		
1990	Jansher Khan (Pak)		

Women

1976	Heather McKay (Aus)
1979	Heather McKay (Aus)
1981	Rhonda Thorne (Aus)
1983	Vicki Cardwell (Aus)
1985	Susan Devoy (NZ)
1987	Susan Devoy (NZ)
1989	Martine Lemoignan (Eng)
1990	Susan Devoy (NZ)
1992	Susan Devoy (NZ)
1993	Michelle Martin (Aus)

World Team Champions

Men

1967	Australia	1981	Pakistan
1969	Australia	1983	Pakistan
1971	Australia	1985	Pakistan
1973	Australia	1987	Pakistan
1975	Great Britain	1989	Australia
1977	Pakistan	1991	Australia
1979	Great Britain		

Women

1979	Great Britain	1987	England
1981	Australia	1989	England
1983	Australia	1990	England
1985	England	1992	Australia

SWIMMING

Swimming Records

As of Aug. 1993

Men's Records

Distance	Time	Holder	Country	Where made	Date
Freestyle					
50 metres	**0:21.81**	Tom Jager	U.S.	Nashville	Mar. 24, 1990
100 metres	**0:48.42**	Matt Biondi	U.S.	Austin, Tex.	Aug. 10, 1988
200 metres	**1:46.69**	Giorgio Lamberti	Italy	Bonn	Aug. 15, 1989
400 metres	**3:45.00**	Evgueni Sadovyi	Unified Team	Barcelona	July 29, 1992
800 metres	**7:47.85**	Keiren Perkins	Australia	Edmonton	Aug 25,, 1991
1,500 metres	**14:43.48**	Keiren Perkins	Australia	Barcelona	July 31, 1992
Breaststroke					
100 metres	**1:00.95**	Karoly Guttler	Hungary	Sheffield	Aug. 3, 1993
200 metres	**2:10.16**	Mike Barrowman	U.S.	Barcelona	July 29, 1992
Butterfly					
100 metres	**0:52.84**	Pablo Morales	U.S.	Orlando, Fla.	June 23, 1986
200 metres	**1:55.69**	Melvin Stewart	U.S.	Perth, Australia	Jan. 12, 1991
Backstroke					
100 metres	**0:53.86**	Jeff Rouse	U.S.	Barcelona	July 29, 1992
200 metres	**1:56.57**	Martin Lopez-Zubero	Spain	Tuscaloosa, Ala.	Nov. 23, 1991
Individual Medley					
200 metres	**1:56.62**	Jani Sievinen	Finland	Paris	Feb. 6, 1993
400 metres	**4:12.36**	Tamas Darnyi	Hungary	Perth, Australia	Jan. 8, 1991
Freestyle Relays					
400 m (4×100)	**3:16.53**	Jacobs, Dalbey, Jager, Biondi	U.S.	Seoul	Sept. 23, 1988
800 m (4×200)	**7:11.95**	Lepikov, Pychnenko, Taianovitch, Sadovyi	Unified Team	Barcelona	July 27, 1992
Medley Relays					
400 m (4×100)	**3:36.93**	Berkoff, Schroeder, Jacobs, Biondi	U.S.	Seoul	Sept. 25, 1988
		Rouse, Diebel, Morales, Olsen	U.S.	Barcelona	July 31, 1992

Women's Records

Distance	Time	Holder	Country	Where made	Date
Freestyle					
50 metres	**0:24.79**	Yang Wenyi	China	Barcelona	Aug. 31, 1992
100 metres	**0:54.48**	Jenny Thompson	U.S.	Indianapolis	Mar. 1, 1992
200 metres	**1:57.55**	Heike Friedrich	E. Germany	Berlin	June 18, 1986
400 metres	**4:03.85**	Janet Evans	U.S.	Seoul	Sept. 22, 1988
800 metres	**8:16.22**	Janet Evans	U.S.	Tokyo	Aug. 20, 1989
1,500 metres	**15:52.10**	Janet Evans	U.S.	Orlando, Fla.	Mar. 26, 1988
Breaststroke					
100 metres	**1:07.91**	Silke Hoerner	E. Germany	Strasbourg, France	Aug. 21, 1987
200 metres	**2:25.35**	Anita Hall	U.S.	Indianapolis	Mar. 2, 1992
Butterfly					
100 metres	**0:57.93**	Mary T. Meagher	U.S.	Brown Deer, Wis.	Aug. 16, 1981
200 metres	**2:05.96**	Mary T. Meagher	U.S.	Brown Deer, Wis.	Aug. 13, 1981
Backstroke					
100 metres	**1:00.31**	Krisztina Egerszegi	Hungary	Athens	Aug. 22, 1991
200 metres	**2:06.62**	Kristina Egerszegi	Hungary	Athens	Aug. 25, 1991
Individual Medley					
200 metres	**2:11.65**	Lin Li	China	Barcelona	July 30, 1992
400 metres	**4:36.10**	Petra Schneider	E. Germany	Ecuador	Aug. 1, 1982
Freestyle Relays					
400 m (4×100)	**3:39.46**	Haislett, Torres, Martino, Thompson	U.S.	Barcelona	July 28, 1992
800 m (4×200)	**7:11.95**	Lepikov, Pychnenko, Taianovitch, Sadovyi	Unified Team	Barcelona	July 27, 1992
Medley Relays					
400 m (4×100)	**4:02.54**	Loveless, Nall, Ahmann-Leighton, Thompson	U.S.	Barcelona	July 30, 1992

TENNIS

All-England Champions, Wimbledon

Men's Singles

Year	Champion	Final opponent
1877	Spencer Gore	William Marshall
1878	Patrick Hadow	Spencer Gore
1879	John Hartley	Vere St Leger Goold
1880	John Hartley	Herbert Lawford
1881	William Renshaw	John Hartley
1882	William Renshaw	Ernest Renshaw
1883	William Renshaw	Ernest Renshaw
1884	William Renshaw	Herbert Lawford
1885	William Renshaw	Herbert Lawford
1886	William Renshaw	Herbert Lawford
1887	Herbert Lawford	Ernest Renshaw
1888	Ernest Renshaw	Herbert Lawford
1889	William Renshaw	Ernest Renshaw
1890	Willoughby Hamilton	William Renshaw
1891	Wilfred Baddeley	Joshua Pim
1892	Wilfred Baddeley	Joshua Pim
1893	Joshua Pim	Wilfred Baddeley
1894	Joshua Pim	Wilfred Baddeley
1895	Wilfred Baddeley	Wilberforce Eaves
1896	Harold Mahony	Wilfred Baddeley
1897	Reggie Doherty	Harold Mahony
1898	Reggie Doherty	Laurie Doherty
1899	Reggie Doherty	Arthur Gore
1900	Reggie Doherty	Sydney Smith
1901	Arthur Gore	Reggie Doherty
1902	Laurie Doherty	Arthur Gore
1903	Laurie Doherty	Frank Riseley
1904	Laurie Doherty	Frank Riseley
1905	Laurie Doherty	Norman Brookes
1906	Laurie Doherty	Frank Riseley
1907	Norman Brookes	Arthur Gore
1908	Arthur Gore	Herbert Roper Barrett
1909	Arthur Gore	Josiah Ritchie
1910	Tony Wilding	Arthur Gore
1911	Tony Wilding	Herbert Roper Barrett
1912	Tony Wilding	Arthur Gore
1913	Tony Wilding	Maurice McLaughlin
1914	Norman Brookes	Tony Wilding
1915-18	Not held	
1919	Gerald Patterson	Norman Brookes
1920	Bill Tilden	Gerald Patterson
1921	Bill Tilden	Brian Norton
1922	Gerald Patterson	Randolph Lycett
1923	William Johnston	Francis Hunter
1924	Jean Borotra	René Lacoste
1925	René Lacoste	Jean Borotra
1926	Jean Borotra	Howard Kinsey
1927	Henri Cochet	Jean Borotra
1928	René Lacoste	Henri Cochet
1929	Henri Cochet	Jean Borotra
1930	Bill Tilden	Wilmer Allison
1931	Sydney Woods	Frank Shields
1932	Ellsworth Vines	Bunny Austin
1933	Jack Crawford	Ellsworth Vines
1934	Fred Perry	Jack Crawford
1935	Fred Perry	Gottfried von Cramm
1936	Fred Perry	Gottfried von Cramm
1937	Donald Budge	Gottfried von Cramm
1938	Donald Budge	Wilfred Austin
1939	Bobby Riggs	Elwood Cooke
1940-45	Not held	
1946	Yvon Petra	Geoff E. Brown
1947	Jack Kramer	Tom P. Brown
1948	Bob Falkenburg	John Bromwich
1949	Ted Schroeder	Jaroslav Drobny
1950	Budge Patty	Frank Sedgman
1951	Dick Savitt	Ken McGregor
1952	Frank Sedgman	Jaroslav Drobny
1953	Vic Seixas	Kurt Nielsen
1954	Jaroslav Drobny	Ken Rosewall
1955	Tony Trabert	Kurt Nielsen
1956	Lew Hoad	Ken Rosewall
1957	Lew Hoad	Ashley Cooper
1958	Ashley Cooper	Neale Fraser
1959	Alex Olmedo	Rod Laver
1960	Neale Fraser	Rod Laver
1961	Rod Laver	Chuck McKinley
1962	Rod Laver	Martin Mulligan
1963	Chuck McKinley	Fred Stolle
1964	Roy Emerson	Fred Stolle
1965	Roy Emerson	Fred Stolle
1966	Manuel Santana	Dennis Ralston
1967	John Newcombe	Wilhelm Bungert
1968	Rod Laver	Tony Roche
1969	Rod Laver	John Newcombe
1970	John Newcombe	Ken Rosewall
1971	John Newcombe	Stan Smith
1972	Stan Smith	Ilie Nastase
1973	Jan Kodes	Alex Metreveli
1974	Jimmy Connors	Ken Rosewall
1975	Arthur Ashe	Jimmy Connors
1976	Bjorn Borg	Ilie Nastase
1977	Bjorn Borg	Jimmy Connors
1978	Bjorn Borg	Jimmy Connors
1979	Bjorn Borg	Roscoe Tanner
1980	Bjorn Borg	John McEnroe
1981	John McEnroe	Bjorn Borg
1982	Jimmy Connors	John McEnroe
1983	John McEnroe	Chris Lewis
1984	John McEnroe	Jimmy Connors
1985	Boris Becker	Kevin Curren
1986	Boris Becker	Ivan Lendl
1987	Pat Cash	Ivan Lendl
1988	Stefan Edberg	Boris Becker
1989	Boris Becker	Stefan Edberg
1990	Stefan Edberg	Boris Becker
1991	Michael Stich	Boris Becker
1992	Andre Agassi	Goran Ivanisevic
1993	Pete Sampras	Jim Courier

Women's Singles

Year	Champion	Final opponent
1884	Maud Watson	Lilian Watson
1885	Maud Watson	Blanche Bingley
1886	Blanche Bingley	Maud Watson
1887	Lottie Dod	Blanche Bingley
1988	Lotttie Dod	Blanche Hillyard
1889	Blanche Hillyard	Lena Rice
1890	Lena Rice	Miss M. Jacks
1891	Lottie Dod	Blanche Hillyard
1892	Lottie Dod	Blanche Hillyard
1893	Lottie Dod	Blanche Hillyard
1894	Blanche Hillyard	Lucy Austin
1895	Charlotte Cooper	Helen Jackson
1896	Charlotte Cooper	Alice Pickering
1897	Blanche Hillyard	Charlotte Cooper
1898	Charlotte Cooper	Louise Martin
1899	Blanche Hillyard	Charlotte Cooper
1900	Blanche Hillyard	Charlotte Cooper
1901	Charlotte Sterry	Blanche Hillyard
1902	Muriel Robb	Charlotte Sterry
1903	Dorothea Douglass	Ethel Thomson
1904	Dorothea Douglass	Charlotte Sterry
1905	May Sutton	Dorothea Douglass
1906	Dorothea Douglass	May Sutton
1907	May Sutton	Dorothea Lambert Chambers
1908	Charlotte Sterry	Agatha Morton
1909	Dora Boothby	Agatha Morton
1910	Dorothea Lambert Chambers	Dora Boothby
1911	Dorothea Lambert Chambers	Dora Boothby
1912	Ethel Larcombe	Charlotte Sterry
1913	Dorothea Lambert Chambers	Winifred McNair
1914	Dorothea Lambert Chambers	Ethel Larcombe
1915-18	Not held	
1919	Suzanne Lenglen	Dorothea Lambert Chambers
1920	Suzanne Lenglen	Dorothea Lambert Chambers
1921	Suzanne Lenglen	Elizabeth Ryan
1922	Suzanne Lenglen	Molla Mallory
1923	Suzanne Lenglen	Kitty McKane
1924	Kitty McKane	Helen Wills
1925	Suzanne Lenglen	Joan Fry
1926	Kitty Godfree	Lili de Alvarez
1927	Helen Wills	Lili de Alvarez
1928	Helen Wills	Lili de Alvarez
1929	Helen Wills	Helen Jacobs
1930	Helen Wills Moody	Elizabeth Ryan
1930	Cilly Aussem	Hilda Krahwinkel
1932	Helen Wills Moody	Helen Jacobs
1933	Helen Wills Moody	Dorothy Round
1934	Dorothy Round	Helen Jacobs
1935	Helen Wills Moody	Helen Jacobs
1936	Helen Jacobs	Hilda Sperling
1937	Dorothy Round	Jadwiga Jedrzejowska

(Continued)

(Wimbledon Champions contd.)

Year	Champion	Final opponent
1938	Helen Wills Moody	Helen Jacobs
1939	Alice Marble	Kay Stammers
1940-45	Not held	
1946	Pauline Betz	Louise Brough
1947	Margaret Osborne	Doris Hart
1948	Louise Brough	Doris Hart
1949	Louise Brough	Margaret du Pont
1950	Louise Brough	Margaret du Pont
1951	Doris Hart	Shirley Fry
1952	Maureen Connolly	Louise Brough
1953	Maureen Connolly	Doris Hart
1954	Maureen Connolly	Louise Brough
1955	Louise Brough	Beverly Fleitz
1956	Shirley Fry	Angela Buxton
1957	Althea Gibson	Darlene Hard
1958	Althea Gibson	Angela Mortimer
1959	Maria Bueno	Darlene Hard
1960	Maria Bueno	Sandra Reynolds
1961	Angela Mortimer	Christine Truman
1962	Karen Hantze-Susman	Vera Sukova
1963	Margaret Smith	Billie Jean Moffitt
1964	Maria Bueno	Margaret Smith
1965	Margaret Smith	Maria Bueno
1966	Billie Jean King	Maria Bueno
1967	Billie Jean King	Ann Jones
1968	Billie Jean King	Judy Tegart
1969	Ann Jones	Billie Jean King
1970	Margaret Court	Billie Jean King
1971	Evonne Goolagong	Margaret Court
1872	Billie Jean King	Evonne Goolagong
1973	Billie Jean King	Chris Evert
1974	Chris Evert	Olga Morozova
1975	Billie Jean King	Evonne Cawley
1976	Chris Evert	Evonne Cawley
1977	Virginia Wade	Betty Stove
1978	Martina Navratilova	Chris Evert Lloyd
1979	Martina Navratilova	Chris Evert Lloyd
1980	Evonne Cawley	Chris Evert Lloyd
1981	Chris Evert Lloyd	Hana Mandlikova
1982	Martina Navratilova	Chris Evert Lloyd
1983	Martina Navratilova	Andrea Jaeger
1984	Martina Navratilova	Chris Evert Lloyd
1985	Martina Navratilova	Chris Evert Lloyd
1986	Martina Navratilova	Hana Mandlikova
1987	Martina Navratilova	Steffi Graf
1988	Steffi Graf	Martina Navratilova
1989	Steffi Graf	Martina Navratilova
1990	Martina Navratilova	Zena Garrison
1991	Steffi Graf	Gabriella Sabatini
1992	Steffi Graf	Monica Seles
1993	Steffi Graf	Jana Novotna

Australian Open Champions

Year	Men	Women
1969	Rod Laver	Margaret Court
1970	Arthur Ashe	Margaret Court
1971	Ken Rosewall	Margaret Court
1972	Ken Rosewall	Virginia Wade
1973	John Newcombe	Margaret Court
1974	Jimmy Connors	Evonne Goolagong
1975	John Newcombe	Evonne Goolagong
1976	Mark Edmonson	Evonne Cawley
1977*	Roscoe Tanner	Kerry Reid
	Vitas Gerulaitis	Evonne Cawley
1978	Guillermo Vilas	Chris O'Neill
1979	Guillermo Vilas	Barbara Jordan
1980	Brian Teacher	Hana Mandlikova
1981	Johan Kriek	Martina Navratilova
1982	Johan Kriek	Chris Evert Lloyd
1983	Mats Wilander	Martina Navratilova
1984	Mats Wilander	Chris Evert Lloyd
1985	Stefan Edberg	Martina Navratilova
1986†	Not held	Not held
1987	Stefan Edberg	Hana Mandlikova
1988	Mats Wilander	Steffi Graf
1989	Ivan Lendl	Steffi Graf
1990	Ivan Lendl	Steffi Graf
1991	Boris Becker	Monica Seles
1992	Jim Courier	Monica Seles
1993	Jim Courier	Monica Seles

* Two tournaments were held in 1977 (Jan. and Dec.).
† Tournament turned back to Jan in 1987, so no championship was decided 1986.

Davis Cup Challenge Round

Year	Result	
1900	United States 5	British Isles 0
1901	Not played	
1902	United States 3	British Isles 2
1903	British Isles 4	United States 1
1904	British Isles 5	Belgium 0
1905	British Isles 5	United States 0
1906	British Isles 5	United States 0
1907	Australia 3	British Isles 2
1908	Australasia 3	United States 2
1909	Australasia 5	United States 0
1910	(not played)	
1911	Australasia 5	United States 0
1912	British Isles 3	Australasia 2
1913	United States 3	British Isles 2
1914	Australasia 3	United States 2
1915-18	Not played	
1919	Australasia 4	British Isles 1
1920	United States 5	Australasia 0
1921	United States 5	Japan 0
1922	United States 4	Australasia 1
1923	United States 4	Australasia 1
1924	United States 5	Australasia 0
1925	United States 5	France 0
1926	United States 4	France 1
1927	France 3	United States 2
1928	France 4	United States 1
1929	France 3	United States 2
1930	France 4	United States 1
1931	France 3	Great Britain 2
1932	France 3	United States 2
1933	Great Britain 3	France 2
1934	Great Britain 4	United States 1
1935	Great Britain 5	United States 0
1936	Great Britain 3	Australia 2
1937	United States 4	Great Britain 1
1938	United States 3	Australia 2
1939	Australia 3	United States 2
1940-45	Not played	
1946	United States 5	Australia 0
1947	United States 4	Australia 1
1948	United States 5	Australia 0
1949	United States 4	Australia 1
1950	Australia 4	United States 1
1951	Australia 3	United States 2
1952	Australia 4	United States 1
1953	Australia 3	United States 2
1954	United States 3	Australia 2
1955	Australia 5	United States 0
1956	Australia 5	United States 0
1957	Australia 3	United States 2
1958	United States 3	Australia 2
1959	Australia 3	United States 2
1960	Australia 4	Italy 1
1961	Australia 5	Italy 0
1962	Australia 5	Mexico 0
1963	United States 3	Australia 2
1964	Australia 3	United States 2
1965	Australia 4	Spain 1
1966	Australia 4	India 1
1967	Australia 4	Spain 1
1968	United States 4	Australia 1
1969	United States 5	Romania 0
1970	United States 5	W. Germany 0
1971	United States 3	Romania 2
1972	United States 3	Romania 2
1973	Australia 5	United States 0
1974	South Africa (default by India)	
1975	Sweden 3	Czech. 2
1976	Italy 4	Chile 1
1977	Australia 3	Italy 1
1978	United States 4	Great Britain 1
1979	United States 5	Italy 0
1980	Czechoslovakia 4	Italy 1
1981	United States 3	Argentina 1
1982	United States 3	France 0
1983	Australia 3	Sweden 1
1984	Sweden 3	United States 0
1985	Sweden 3	W. Germany 2
1986	Australia 3	Sweden 2
1987	Sweden 5	India 0
1988	W. Germany 4	Sweden 1
1989	W. Germany 3	Sweden 2
1990	United States 3	Australia 2
1991	France 3	United States 1
1992	United States 3	Switzerland 1

French Open Champions

Year	Men	Women
1969	Rod Laver	Margaret Court
1970	Jan Kodes	Margaret Court
1971	Jan Kodes	Evonne Goolagong
1972	Andres Gimeno	Billie Jean King
1973	Ilie Nastase	Margaret Court
1974	Bjorn Borg	Chris Evert
1975	Bjorn Borg	Chris Evert
1976	Adriano Panatta	Sue Barker
1977	Guillermo Vilas	Mima Jausovec
1978	Bjorn Borg	Virginia Ruzici
1979	Bjorn Borg	Chris Evert Lloyd
1980	Bjorn Borg	Chris Evert Lloyd
1981	Bjorn Borg	Hana Mandlikova
1982	Mats Wilander	Martina Navratilova
1983	Yannick Noah	Chris Evert Lloyd
1984	Ivan Lendl	Martina Navratilova
1985	Mats Wilander	Chris Evert Lloyd
1986	Ivan Lendl	Chris Evert Lloyd
1987	Ivan Lendl	Steffi Graf
1988	Mats Wilander	Steffi Graf
1989	Michael Chang	Arantxa Sanchez
1990	Andres Gomez	Monica Seles
1991	Jim Courier	Monica Seles
1992	Jim Courier	Monica Seles
1993	Sergi Bruguera	Steffi Graf

U.S. Open Champions

Men's Singles

Year	Champion	Final opponent
1910	William Larned	T. C. Bundy
1911	William Larned	Maurice McLoughlin
1912	Maurice McLoughlin	Wallace Johnson
1913	Maurice McLoughlin	Richard Williams
1914	Richard Williams	Maurice McLoughlin
1915	William Johnston	Maurice McLoughlin
1916	Richard Williams	William Johnston
1917	Richard Murray	N. W. Niles
1918	Richard Murray	Bill Tilden
1919	William Johnston	Bill Tilden
1920	Bill Tilden	William Johnston
1921	Bill Tilden	Wallace Johnson
1922	Bill Tilden	William Johnston
1923	Bill Tilden	William Johnston
1924	Bill Tilden	William Johnston
1925	Bill Tilden	William Johnston
1926	René Lacoste	Jean Borotra
1927	René Lacoste	Bill Tilden
1928	Henri Cochet	Francis Hunter
1929	Bill Tilden	Francis Hunter
1930	John Doeg	Francis Shields
1931	H. Ellsworth Vines	George Lott
1932	H. Ellsworth Vines	Henri Cochet
1933	Fred Perry	John Crawford
1934	Fred Perry	Wilmer Allison
1935	Wilmer Allison	Sidney Wood
1936	Fred Perry	Don Budge
1937	Don Budge	Baron G. von Cramm
1938	Don Budge	C. Gene Mako
1939	Robert Riggs	S. Welby Van Horn
1940	Don McNeill	Robert Riggs
1941	Robert Riggs	F. L. Kovacs
1942	F. R. Schroeder Jr.	Frank Parker
1943	Joseph Hunt	Jack Kramer
1944	Frank Parker	William Talbert
1945	Frank Parker	William Talbert
1946	Jack Kramer	Thomas Brown Jr.
1947	Jack Kramer	Frank Parker
1948	Pancho Gonzales	Eric Sturgess
1949	Pancho Gonzales	F. R. Schroeder Jr.
1950	Arthur Larsen	Herbert Flam
1951	Frank Sedgman	E. Victor Seixas Jr.
1952	Frank Sedgman	Gardnar Mulloy
1953	Tony Trabert	E. Victor Seixas Jr.
1954	E. Victor Seixas Jr.	Rex Hartwig
1955	Tony Trabert	Ken Rosewall
1956	Ken Rosewall	Lewis Hoad
1957	Malcolm Anderson	Ashley Cooper
1958	Ashley Cooper	Malcolm Anderson
1959	Neale A. Fraser	Alejandro Olmedo
1960	Neale A. Fraser	Rod Laver
1961	Roy Emerson	Rod Laver
1962	Rod Laver	Roy Emerson
1963	Rafael Osuna	F. A. Froehling 3d
1964	Roy Emerson	Fred Stolle
1965	Manuel Santana	Cliff Drysdale
1966	Fred Stolle	John Newcombe
1967	John Newcombe	Clark Graebner
1968	Arthur Ashe	Tom Okker
1969	Rod Laver	Tony Roche
1970	Ken Rosewall	Tony Roche
1971	Stan Smith	Jan Kodes
1972	Ilie Nastase	Arthur Ashe
1973	John Newcombe	Jan Kodes
1974	Jimmy Connors	Ken Rosewall
1975	Manuel Orantes	Jimmy Connors
1976	Jimmy Connors	Bjorn Borg
1977	Guillermo Vilas	Jimmy Connors
1978	Jimmy Connors	Bjorn Borg
1979	John McEnroe	Vitas Gerulaitis
1980	John McEnroe	Bjorn Borg
1981	John McEnroe	Bjorn Borg
1982	Jimmy Connors	Ivan Lendl
1983	Jimmy Connors	Ivan Lendl
1984	John McEnroe	Ivan Lendl
1985	Ivan Lendl	John McEnroe
1986	Ivan Lendl	Miloslav Mecir
1987	Ivan Lendl	Mats Wilander
1988	Mats Wilander	Ivan Lendl
1989	Boris Becker	Ivan Lendl
1990	Pete Sampras	Andre Agassi
1991	Stefan Edberg	Jim Courier
1992	Stefan Edberg	Pete Sampras
1993	Pete Sampras	Cedric Pioline

Women's Singles

Year	Champion	Final opponent
1926	Molla B. Mallory	Elizabeth Ryan
1927	Helen Wills	Betty Nuthall
1928	Helen Wills	Helen Jacobs
1929	Helen Wills	M. Watson
1930	Betty Nuthall	L. A. Harper
1931	Helen Wills Moody	E. B. Whittingstall
1932	Helen Jacobs	Carolin A. Babcock
1933	Helen Jacobs	Helen Wills Moody
1934	Helen Jacobs	Sarah H. Palfrey
1935	Helen Jacobs	Sarah P. Fabyan
1936	Alice Marble	Helen Jacobs
1937	Anita Lizana	Jadwiga Jedrzejowska
1938	Alice Marble	Nancye Wynne
1939	Alice Marble	Helen Jacobs
1940	Alice Marble	Helen Jacobs
1941	Sarah Palfrey Cooke	Pauline Betz
1942	Pauline Betz	Louise Brough
1943	Pauline Betz	Louise Brough
1944	Pauline Betz	Margaret Osborne
1945	Sarah P. Cooke	Pauline Betz
1946	Pauline Betz	Doris Hart
1947	Louise Brough	Margaret Osborne
1948	Margaret Osborne duPont	Louise Brough
1949	Margaret Osborne duPont	Doris Hart
1950	Margaret Osborne duPont	Doris Hart
1951	Maureen Connolly	Shirley Fry
1952	Maureen Connolly	Doris Hart
1953	Maureen Connolly	Doris Hart
1954	Doris Hart	Louise Brough
1955	Doris Hart	Patricia Ward
1956	Shirley Fry	Althea Gibson
1957	Althea Gibson	Louise Brough
1958	Althea Gibson	Darlene Hard
1959	Maria Bueno	Christine Truman
1960	Darlene Hard	Maria Bueno
1961	Darlene Hard	Ann Haydon
1962	Margaret Smith	Darlene Hard
1963	Maria Bueno	Margaret Smith
1964	Maria Bueno	Carole Graebner
1965	Margaret Smith	Billie Jean Moffitt
1966	Maria Bueno	Nancy Richey

(Continued)

(U.S. Open Champions contd.)

Year	Champion	Final opponent	Year	Champion	Final opponent
1967	Billie Jean King	Ann Haydon Jones	1981	Tracy Austin	Martina Navratilova
1968	Virginia Wade	Billie Jean King	1982	Chris Evert Lloyd	Hana Mandlikova
1969	Margaret Court	Nancy Richey	1983	Martina Navratilova	Chris Evert Lloyd
1970	Margaret Court	Rosemary Casals	1984	Martina Navratilova	Chris Evert Lloyd
1971	Billie Jean King	Rosemary Casals	1985	Hana Mandlikova	Martina Navratilova
1972	Billie Jean King	Kerry Melville	1986	Martina Navratilova	Helena Sukova
1973	Margaret Court	Evonne Goolagong	1987	Martina Navratilova	Steffi Graf
1974	Billie Jean King	Evonne Goolagong	1988	Steffi Graf	Gabriela Sabatini
1975	Chris Evert	Evonne Cawley	1989	Steffi Graf	Martina Navratilova
1976	Chris Evert	Evonne Cawley	1990	Gabriela Sabatini	Steffi Graf
1977	Chris Evert	Wendy Turnbull	1991	Monica Seles	Martina Navratilova
1978	Chris Evert	Pam Shriver	1992	Monica Seles	Arantxa Sanchez Vicario
1979	Tracy Austin	Chris Evert Lloyd	1993	Steffi Graf	Helena Sukova
1980	Chris Evert Lloyd	Hana Mandlikova			

NOTABLE SPORTS STORIES

Sep. 1992–Aug. 1993

Real Men Cry

Gary Herbert became the first cox to be honoured for services to rowing when he was made an MBE in the New Year honours list, along with the oarsmen Greg and Johnny Searle. Together they won the coxed pairs gold medal at the Barcelona Olympics. The plucky 8-stoner touched the hearts of the nation by blubbing through the national anthem at the presentation ceremony.

Taking the Mick

Nobody gave Ireland a hope when they faced England at the end of the Five Nations Championship. But, sustained by the home crowd, they produced an inspirational performance to win 17-3. They also produced the best quote of the season: "I was going to keep this a secret, but we spent a weekend at Lourdes," said coach Gerry Murphy. Mind you, this appears as cheap and showy Blarney when contrasted with the bulldog laconicism of Bobby Gould: "Football," gritted the Coventry City manager, "is about football."

Board Senseless

In February England's Nigel Short won the 13th game against Dutch champion Jan Timman, and the right to challenge Gary Kasparov for the world chess championship. Short, aged 27 but looking all of 13, got straight in there. "Kasparov is a thoroughly unpleasant character who can't deal with human beings . . . he looks like an ape." Clearly a classical opening – attack as defence. Kasparov modestly countered that he could beat Short and Timman simultaneously.

Take the Money and Run

In a contrived head-to-head 100 metres sprint at Gateshead in July, Linford Christie and Carl Lewis earned themselves roughly £1,000 per step, each. Christie easily won the hugely hyped event, with Lewis, looking not entirely interested, finishing third. A promotional disaster was narrowly avoided when Jon Drummond came from nowhere to finish on Christie's shoulder, 0.04 of a second behind him.

Bad Sports

The FA fined Wimbledon hard man Vinnie Jones £20,000 and imposed a 6-month ban suspended for 3 months for his part in a video demonstrating the niceties of fouling. Mr Jones – "Mosquito Brain" to his manager – confessed himself "totally gutted".

And while his father's team kept up the rhetoric against football hooligans, the Prime Minister's son collected 4 red cards last season, 2 during the week in which he celebrated his 18th birthday. Major Minor complained that referees were victimizing him.

Bernhard Langer marked his partner Nick Faldo's card a par 4, when Faldo had scored 5. Faldo verified the card, handed it in without realizing the mistake, and was promptly disqualified as the law demands. This was during the Million Dollar Challenge in Sun City, South Africa, the world's richest golf tournament. Faldo said that he had no hard feelings towards Langer.

In March the IAAF imposed a life ban from athletics on the Canadian sprinter Ben Johnson. In 1988 Johnson won the 100 metres in the Seoul Olympics but was subsequently banned for 2 years when anabolic steroids were found in his system, He returned in 1992 and reached the semi-finals in Barcelona. In 1993 he was tested at a meeting in Montreal and found to have an unacceptably high level of testosterone. Johnson did not contest the decision.

Starters Orders

And – they're off! No they're not – yes they are . . . The Grand National got off famously. The elasticated starting-tape snagged one or two of the runners, but they shook it off quickly. The starter waved his red flag, 100 yards or so down the course the recall man shook his, and the riders pulled up. The second attempt was more serious. The tape snared the legs of one horse and caught around the neck of jockey Richard Dunwoody. The starter didn't unfurl his flag properly and it is unclear whether the recall man responded, but off shot all the field bar nine. Much contention flew between officials. After a stewards' inquiry and consultation with trainers, it was decided that the 1993 Grand National would not be rerun as it was impractical "from a horse point of view". The punters were reimbursed, and the Government lost £6 million in betting tax. Wits suggested that the next year, Group Four be given the contract – "then they'd be sure to get away first time".

Stable Condition

During the Breeders' Cup in Florida last November, the horse Mr Brooks threw his rider Lester Piggott and rolled on him. The horse was swiftly put down and the 57-year-old jockey taken to hospital. If only such fine discrimination had been used at Aintree.

Anyone For?

During the summer William Hill were offering merely 500-1 against conclusive proof of extra-terrestrial life or the return of Elvis Presley. The odds against the appointment of a female pope, the Archbishop of Canterbury confirming (no pun intended) a Second Coming, or somebody British winning a Wimbledon singles title were 1000-1. Nothing very unusual happened in the event, especially at Wimbledon, except that the weather stayed fine, and two Americans slugged out the men's singles decider on a sun-bathed Fourth of July.

On a more worrying note, erotomania was stalking the professional tennis circuit. At the end of April, Monica Seles was stabbed in the shoulder at a Hamburg tournament by a man who wanted to improve the chances of Steffi Graf. Conversely, police ejected and banned from Wimbledon a man whose deluded attachment to Seles led him to hound and pester Graf.

Triumph of the Wheel

There was an epic passage by Scotland's Robert Millar during the eleventh stage of the Tour de France. Attacking at the foot of the Col de la Bonette, he stormed the 15-mile climb up Europe's highest road to breast the peak ahead of the eventual winner Miguel Indurain. It brought Millar nothing in the end, but he became a well-respected footnote in the race's history. Next year the tour will include a 2-day stage in England. Town and county councils in Kent, East Sussex and Hampshire are to pay £½ million for the privilege, and this year sent officers to the Midi in order to find out how the convoy and attendant circus is managed.

Another Scot on a bicycle to make an impression in July was Graeme Obree. He broke the world hour record, which had stood for nine years, by covering 51.596 kilometres – 445 metres up on the record. Obree's finest hour came at Hamar in Norway. His home-made machine included parts of a spin dryer and a child's BMX.

Women in White

While the men stumbled from defeat to unrelieved humiliation, England's women cricketers won the World Cup. Along the way they even dispatched the counterparts of the males' tormentors – Australia.

Mere Statistics

By coincidence both the League Cup and the FA Cup finals were contested by the same teams and decided by the same result. In both cases Arsenal beat Sheffield Wednesday 2-1. Unfortunately, that was about the most interesting feature of these attritional, end-of-season confrontations, especially the FA Cup, which was eventually settled after 239 minutes of what a commentator tersely termed "industrial football". Slightly less congruent, but more pleasing, was England's defeat of Australia to win the inaugural rugby World Sevens, a result which turned the 1991 World Cup final on its head.

Arms and the Men

After being brought on as substitute in the FA Cup final, Steve Morrow scored the winning goal. Upon surrendering to the lusty embrace of his captain, he stumbled over and broke his arm. A writhing Morrow was stretchered off while his apparently insouciant team-mates scampered away to collect their medals.

While playing for Middlesex against the Australians at Lord's, Mike Gatting was run out on 32. In a state of heightened emotion he approached the dressing-room door, missed the wooden part of it altogether, and put his left arm through the glass. Gatting received a large number of stitches but was back in fettle for the First Test . . . during which England captain Graham Gooch, batting to save the match, was given out for handling the ball. He played one down in the conventional way only to see it bounce straight up and hover over leg stump, where he swatted it away with the back of his hand. The last Englishman to thus dismiss himself was Gubby Allen, in the "Bodyline" series against Australia.

When Rory Met Tony

The Springboks were back at Twickenham last November for the first time since their tour was disrupted by anti-apartheid demonstrators 24 years ago. England fielded two brothers – an Underwood on each wing – for the first time since the inter-war years. Rory gave Tony a scoring pass, as England beat their visitors 33-6.

A Sign of the Times

Henry Cooper, ex-heavyweight champion, the man who floored Cassius Clay and the only British boxer ever to win 3 Lonsdale belts outright, had to sell them in July. Wanting to cover losses incurred as a Lloyd's name, our 'Enry had to let the belts go for £42,000, which was less than anticipated.

Goodbye

The retirement of Roy Race – "Roy of the Rovers" – after 39 years, man, boy and player-manager at Melchester, was announced on Feb. 16. Roy had transferred from *The Tiger* to his own magazine, which was to close in March.

It could have been an omen. On Feb. 24 Bobby Moore died after a two-year struggle with cancer. As talismanic a presence in real football as Roy was in the comics, he had captained England's World Cup-winning team in 1966. According to his peers, he was a class act and a gentleman. "Of all the defenders I have challenged, he was the fairest, the best and the most honourable," said Pele.

To complete the odd sequence, Tofik Bakhramov died the next month. Readers of a certain age will recognize the moustachioed, baggy-shorted Azerbaijani linesman who confirmed England's controversial goal when the ball bounced from crossbar to goal-line in the 1966 World Cup Final.

Peter Scudamore, the most successful jockey in the history of National Hunt racing, retired in April. His final tally was 1,677 winners, half as many again as his nearest rival.

Another spiritual relative of Roy Race bade farewell in July. Ian Botham, a.k.a. Beefy, a.k.a. Guy the Gorilla, retired to the squirarchy. In 102 Test Matches he scored 5,200 runs, took 383 wickets and held 128 catches.

Hello again

It's official: Jayne Torvill and Christopher Dean formally confirmed that they will return for the 1994 Winter Olympics in Lillehammer, Norway. The pair won the ice-dance Gold Medal at Sarajevo in 1984 with a sensuous performance to Ravel's *Bolero*.

VITAL STATISTICS

This section aims to give an idea of the British character by presenting various statistics about the way we live – such things as how much exercise we take, what foods we eat, how we spend our spare time, our opinions on racial prejudice and our views on the meaning of life.

Household Size

Source: CSO

Percentages and number

	1961	1971	1981	1991
1 person	12	18	22	26
2 people	30	32	32	34
3 people	23	19	17	17
4 people	19	17	18	16
5 people	9	8	7	6
6 or more people	7	6	4	2
Number of households[1] (=100%) (thousands)	16,189	18,317	19,492	9,955
Average household size (number of people)	3.09	2.89	2.71	2.48

(1) 1961, 1971, 1981 Census data; 1991 General Household Survey. 1991 column shows sample size.

Composition of Households

Source: CSO

Percentages

Type of household	1961	1971	1981	1991
Living alone	3.9	6.3	8.0	10.7
Married couple, no children	17.8	19.3	19.5	23.0
Married couple with dependent children[1]	52.2	51.7	47.4	41.1
Married couple with non-dependent children only	11.6	10.0	10.3	10.8
Lone parent with dependent children[1]	2.5	3.5	5.8	10.0
Other households	12.0	9.2	9.0	4.3
All people in private households[2]	49,545	52,347	52,760	24,607

(1) These family types may also include non-dependent children. (2) 1961, 1971, 1981 Census data; 1991 General Household Survey. 1991 column contains sample size.

Homeless Households in Temporary Accommodation[1,2]

Source: CSO

Thousands

	1986	1990	1991
Bed and breakfast	9	12	13
Hostels, including women's refuges	5	10	12
Short-life tenancies and other accommodation	8	27	40
Total in temporary accommodation	23	48	64

(1) At end of year. (2) Includes households awaiting outcome of homelessness enquiries.

Dwelling Price Indices[1,2]

Source: CSO

Indices (1985=100)

	1981	1989	1990	1991	1992[3]
United Kingdom	73	202	199	195	188
North	79	170	193	193	205
Yorkshire & Humberside	78	194	211	222	221
East Midlands	74	207	207	200	200
East Anglia	72	221	197	186	180
Greater London	66	203	199	191	172
Rest of South East	70	216	198	186	172
South West	74	219	198	188	181
West Midlands	81	219	223	224	222
North West	80	184	212	215	217
England	73	207	203	198	190
Wales	77	193	201	187	192
Scotland	74	144	161	170	181
Northern Ireland	81	124	131	134	142

(1) Based on a sample of building societies advances completed for house purchases. Continues to include Abbey National plc from quarter 3 1989. (2) Indices have been adjusted to take account of changes in the mix of dwellings being bought with building societies mortgages. They also exclude those dwellings bought at non-market prices. (3) Second quarter (April to June).

Domestic Responsibilities in Britain

Who usually does the following jobs around the house?

Source: SCPR's *British Social Attitudes* survey, 9th Report, ed. R. Jowell *et al.* (Dartmouth Publishing, 1992)

Percentages

Task	All households	Households where man works and ... woman works full-time	... woman works part-time	... woman is not in paid work
Household shopping				
mainly man	8	4	5	5
mainly woman	45	42	51	57
shared equally	47	53	44	37
Making evening meal				
mainly man	9	7	5	3
mainly woman	70	60	75	81
shared equally	20	32	20	16
Washing evening dishes				
mainly man	28	28	20	18
mainly woman	33	24	41	37
shared equally	37	46	38	42
Household cleaning				
mainly man	4	5	–	–
mainly woman	68	63	82	82
shared equally	27	30	18	17
Washing and ironing				
mainly man	3	3	–	1
mainly woman	84	78	91	91
shared equally	12	17	9	8

(Continued)

Percentages

Task	All households	Households where man works and ... ... woman works full-time	... woman works part-time	... woman is not in paid work
Repairing household equipment				
mainly man	82	84	85	81
mainly woman	6	3	7	8
shared equally	10	10	8	10
Organizing household money and bills				
mainly man	31	27	29	40
mainly women	40	44	41	36
shared equally	28	28	30	23

UK Household Expenditure

Source: CSO

	1976	1981	1985	1986	1990	1991 Indices/ per-centages	1991 £ million (current prices)
Indices at constant 1985 prices							
Food	96	99	100	103	109	109	44,053
Alcoholic drink	93	95	100	100	105	101	23,555
Tobacco	126	117	100	97	96	94	9,746
Clothing and footwear	68	79	100	109	118	116	21,034
Housing	83	91	100	104	111	111	51,614
Fuel and power	93	97	100	103	100	108	14,272
Household goods and services							
Household durables	83	86	100	107	130	128	11,495
Other	89	89	100	110	123	119	11,301
Transport and communication							
Purchase of vehicles	65	78	100	109	133	108	16,426
Running of vehicles	81	90	100	107	132	128	26,710
Other travel	82	92	100	107	135	132	12,610
Post and telecommunications	62	85	100	108	135	135	6,833
Recreation, entertainment and education							
TV, video, etc	50	67	100	113	138	141	7,710
Books, newspapers, etc	111	112	100	103	112	108	4,805
Other	82	94	100	105	140	137	22,400
Other goods and services							
Catering (meals, etc)	90	89	100	108	149	144	31,049
Other goods	89	88	100	107	142	140	13,398
Other services	56	73	100	114	171	164	26,555
Less expenditure by foreign tourists, etc	87	74	100	96	99	86	−8,207
Household expenditure abroad	47	94	100	112	155	147	8,978
Total household expenditure	82	90	100	106	125	122	356,337
Percentage of total household expenditure at current prices							
Food	19.2	16.3	14.4	14.0	12.3	12.4	44,053
Alcoholic drink	7.6	7.3	7.4	6.9	6.4	6.6	23,555
Tobacco	4.1	3.6	3.3	3.2	2.6	2.7	9,746
Clothing and footwear	7.7	6.7	7.0	7.1	6.1	5.9	21,034
Housing	13.6	14.9	15.4	15.5	14.0	14.5	51,614
Fuel and power	4.7	5.1	4.9	4.6	3.6	4.0	14,272
Household goods and services	7.6	6.9	6.7	6.7	6.5	6.4	22,796
Transport and communication	15.4	17.2	17.4	17.1	18.5	17.6	62,579
Recreation, entertainment and education	9.2	9.4	9.4	9.4	9.9	9.8	34,915
Other goods, services and adjustments	10.8	12.5	14.1	15.5	20.1	20.1	71,773
Total	100.0	100.0	100.0	100.0	100.0	100.0	356,337

Regional Differences in Household Expenditure

United Kingdom

Source: CSO

Percentages and £ per week

	Percentage of expenditure: Housing	Fuel, light & power	Food	Alcohol and tobacco	Clothing and footwear	Household goods & services	Motoring & fares	Leisure goods & services	Other goods & services, miscel-laneous	Average total expen-diture (£ per week) (=100%)
United Kingdom	18.7	4.6	18.0	6.1	6.3	12.9	15.7	13.3	4.4	253.11
North	17.2	5.4	19.6	7.7	6.7	12.5	15.2	11.6	4.2	210.53
Yorkshire & Humberside	17.8	5.4	18.8	7.1	6.3	12.5	14.7	12.8	4.6	221.38
East Midlands	18.6	4.5	17.7	5.8	6.2	12.5	17.2	13.1	4.2	257.25
East Anglia	20.2	4.8	18.7	4.9	5.4	13.5	14.3	12.9	5.1	241.68
South East	20.0	4.0	17.2	5.2	5.9	13.4	15.4	14.3	4.6	291.49

(Continued)

Percentages and £ per week

	Percentage of expenditure									Average total expenditure (£ per week) (=100%)
	Housing	Fuel, light & power	Food	Alcohol and tobacco	Clothing and footwear	Household goods & services	Motoring & fares	Leisure goods & services	Other goods & services, Miscellaneous	
South West	19.4	4.4	17.0	5.2	5.8	12.7	17.4	13.6	4.6	266.24
West Midlands	20.0	4.6	18.3	6.1	6.3	12.5	17.1	11.1	4.0	242.34
North West	17.9	4.8	17.6	7.5	6.9	12.1	15.6	13.5	4.1	245.87
England	19.3	4.5	17.9	6.0	6.2	12.7	16.0	13.0	4.5	257.31
Wales	16.3	5.2	18.9	6.8	6.4	13.2	15.9	12.9	4.5	224.38
Scotland	15.4	5.4	19.4	7.3	7.3	13.7	14.4	13.0	4.2	219.56
Northern Ireland	15.3	6.7	20.8	6.0	8.4	11.9	16.3	11.0	3.8	222.29

Household Expenditure: International Comparison, 1990

Source: CSO

Percentages

	Percentage of total expenditure in each category							
	Food, beverages, tobacco[1]	Clothing and footwear	Rent, fuel and power	Furniture, furnishings, household equipment	Medical care and health expenses	Transport and communication	Recreation, entertainment, education, culture	Miscellaneous goods and services
United Kingdom	21.5	6.2	18.5	6.7	1.5	17.9	7.5	18.0
Belgium	19.0	7.8	16.7	10.8	11.2	13.6	6.6	15.5
Denmark	21.2	5.3	27.8	6.5	2.1	16.3	9.8	10.9
France	19.1	6.4	19.1	7.9	9.4	16.6	7.5	14.1
Germany (Fed. Rep.)[2]	16.6	7.7	18.4	8.8	14.3	15.1	9.0	10.2
Greece	37.9	8.7	11.6	8.2	3.8	14.3	5.6	9.9
Irish Republic[2]	37.6	7.1	10.8	8.4	3.8	12.7	10.5	9.2
Italy	20.7	10.3	14.6	9.5	6.4	12.2	9.4	17.0
Japan[2]	20.5	6.4	19.2	6.1	10.8	10.2	10.2	16.7
Luxembourg	19.2	6.2	20.9	10.0	7.6	18.1	4.0	14.0
Netherlands	18.1	6.9	18.7	8.5	12.5	11.0	9.9	14.5
Portugal[3]	37.2	10.3	4.9	8.6	4.5	15.4	5.7	13.4
Spain	21.8	8.9	12.6	6.6	3.8	15.4	6.5	24.4
United States[2]	13.1	6.6	19.3	5.6	15.3	14.5	10.1	15.6

(1) Includes for the UK, Ireland and Greece expenditure on food (Ireland and Greece only) alcoholic and non-alcoholic drinks and tobacco in restaurants, cafes and hotels. For other countries these are classified as miscellaneous goods and services. (2) Data are for 1988. (3) Data for 1986.

Estimated Household Food Consumption: Great Britain

Source: CSO

Ounces per person per week

	1982	1983	1984	1985	1986	1987	1988	1989	1990	1991
Liquid whole milk[1] (pints)	3.95	3.80	3.61	3.32	3.04	2.88	2.66	2.42	2.17	1.94
Other milk (pints or equivalent pints)	0.43	0.49	0.67	0.79	1.08	1.19	1.35	1.50	1.65	1.80
Cheese	3.80	4.01	3.84	3.91	4.16	4.09	4.13	4.07	4.00	4.11
Butter	3.17	3.27	2.87	2.83	2.27	2.14	2.00	1.75	1.61	1.54
Margarine	4.33	4.08	4.08	3.76	4.10	3.98	3.78	3.47	3.19	3.14
All other oils and fats (fl oz for oils)	3.48	3.33	3.34	3.47	4.12	3.92	4.07	4.25	4.20	4.07
Eggs (number)	3.51	3.53	3.21	3.15	3.01	2.89	2.67	2.29	2.20	2.25
Preserves and honey	1.99	2.05	1.95	1.87	1.96	1.88	1.85	1.76	1.69	1.79
Sugar	10.31	9.84	9.15	8.41	8.04	7.48	6.94	6.46	6.03	5.88
Beef and veal	7.06	6.57	6.27	6.51	6.58	6.77	6.35	6.03	5.25	5.35
Mutton and lamb	3.59	3.87	3.32	3.27	3.01	2.65	2.78	2.99	2.91	3.02
Pork	4.02	3.53	3.29	3.45	3.64	3.17	3.29	3.15	2.97	2.88
Bacon and ham, uncooked	3.95	4.02	3.58	3.69	3.68	3.46	3.48	3.35	3.03	3.00
Bacon and ham, cooked (including canned)	1.15	1.09	1.11	1.14	1.13	1.15	1.13	1.22	1.15	1.15
Poultry and cooked chicken	6.85	6.99	7.24	6.90	7.30	8.14	8.09	7.76	7.95	7.63
Other cooked and canned meats	2.51	2.65	2.45	2.60	2.59	2.45	2.62	2.48	2.18	2.11
Offal	0.97	0.84	0.83	0.79	0.74	0.69	0.63	0.55	0.51	0.47
Sausages, uncooked	3.33	3.33	3.00	2.97	2.73	2.66	2.48	2.53	2.41	2.18
Other meat products	5.19	5.18	5.44	5.42	5.67	5.84	5.72	5.89	5.78	6.14
Fish, fresh and processed	2.75	2.81	2.64	2.53	2.66	2.62	2.60	2.60	2.41	2.29
Canned fish	0.63	0.77	0.70	0.71	0.84	0.91	0.90	0.95	1.03	1.06
Fish and fish products, frozen	1.65	1.55	1.56	1.67	1.64	1.57	1.56	1.66	1.65	1.53
Potatoes (excluding processed)	41.11	39.88	39.82	40.96	38.76	37.68	36.43	35.59	35.17	33.81
Fresh green vegetables	11.24	10.78	10.83	9.78	11.11	9.97	10.42	10.23	9.78	9.13
Other fresh vegetables	15.66	15.71	15.26	15.70	16.82	16.67	16.81	17.13	16.18	16.26
Frozen vegetables	5.25	4.92	5.19	5.97	6.28	6.72	6.53	6.70	6.56	7.04
Canned beans	4.16	4.45	4.45	4.43	4.79	4.59	4.64	4.44	4.37	4.35
Other canned vegetables	5.17	5.08	4.76	5.37	5.41	4.86	4.88	4.53	4.33	4.45

(Continued)

Ounces per person per week

	1982	1983	1984	1985	1986	1987	1988	1989	1990	1991
Apples	7.02	7.08	6.84	6.93	7.26	7.05	7.17	7.26	7.10	6.70
Bananas	2.94	2.86	2.91	2.81	3.06	3.21	3.58	4.00	4.39	4.55
Oranges	2.70	2.82	2.70	2.48	3.10	2.70	3.13	2.99	2.82	2.67
All other fresh fruit	6.09	6.87	6.55	6.31	6.91	7.30	7.14	7.20	7.03	7.61
Canned fruit	2.65	2.42	2.28	2.05	2.22	2.06	2.15	2.15	1.83	1.85
Dried fruit, nuts and fruit and nut products	1.21	1.43	1.27	1.23	1.38	1.49	1.30	1.24	1.28	1.37
Fruit juices (fl oz)	4.30	5.20	5.28	5.21	6.34	7.17	7.43	7.52	7.11	8.80
Flour	5.28	4.97	4.34	4.05	4.14	3.93	3.59	3.28	3.19	2.84
Bread	31.03	30.74	30.57	30.99	30.79	30.60	30.28	29.43	28.10	26.53
Buns, scones and teacakes	1.02	0.97	0.98	1.01	1.05	1.09	1.11	1.15	1.19	1.37
Cakes and pastries	2.74	2.62	2.58	2.48	2.55	2.61	2.56	2.45	2.47	2.78
Biscuits	5.66	5.47	5.29	5.22	5.42	5.32	5.28	5.25	5.26	5.18
Breakfast cereals	3.54	3.83	4.13	4.04	4.38	4.42	4.47	4.45	4.47	4.72
Oatmeal and oat products	0.37	0.45	0.42	0.49	0.55	0.49	0.63	0.55	0.52	0.69
Tea	2.02	2.04	1.80	1.74	1.74	1.71	1.65	1.61	1.52	1.48
Instant coffee	0.51	0.53	0.54	0.54	0.55	0.52	0.53	0.50	0.48	0.53
Canned soups	2.66	2.69	2.68	2.70	2.54	2.81	2.78	2.71	2.41	2.45
Pickles and sauces	1.97	2.15	2.10	2.14	2.18	2.09	2.30	2.34	2.37	2.44

(1) Including also school and welfare milk.

Households with Durable Goods: Great Britain, 1990

Source: CSO

Percentages and numbers

	Economically active					All economically active heads of households	Economically inactive heads of households	All heads of households
	Professional	Employers and managers	Other non-manual	Skilled manual[1]	Unskilled manual			
Percentage of households with:								
Deep-freezer[2]	89	92	86	88	79	88	70	81
Washing machine	95	96	91	93	88	93	77	87
Tumble drier	65	67	53	54	44	57	28	46
Microwave oven	68	69	57	63	50	63	29	50
Dishwasher	36	33	14	10	4	18	4	13
Telephone	98	98	92	86	71	91	84	88
Television	98	99	98	99	99	99	98	99
Colour	93	98	94	96	94	96	91	94
Black and white only	5	1	4	3	6	3	8	5
Video	81	86	76	82	70	81	36	64
Home computer	45	35	30	24	12	29	5	20
CD player	35	34	29	25	18	28	8	21
Sample size (=100%) (numbers)	447	1,304	1,209	2,666	185	5,811	3,614	9,425

(1) Includes semi-skilled manual. (2) Includes fridge-freezers.

UK Household Expenditure on Selected Leisure Items

Source: CSO

£ and percentages

	1981	1986	1991
Average weekly household expenditure (£)			
Alcoholic drink consumed away from home[1]	5.39[2]	5.93	7.57
Meals consumed out[2]	..	4.38	6.01
Books, newspapers, magazines, etc	2.00	2.73	3.67
Television, video, radio, audio and musical instruments (purchases, rentals, licence fees)[3]	3.26	4.85	6.30
Home computers	..	..	0.52
Purchase of materials for home repairs, etc	1.57	3.06	3.92
Holidays	3.08	5.39	9.84
Hobbies	0.08	0.06	0.13
Cinema admissions	0.14	0.10	0.19
Dance admissions	0.12	0.12	..
Theatre, concert, etc. admissions	0.17	0.29	0.51
Subscription and admission charges to participant sports	0.43	0.71	1.06
Football match admissions	0.06	0.08	0.18 (combined)
Admissions to other spectator sports	0.02	0.04	
Sports goods (excluding clothes)	0.26	0.37	0.43
Other entertainment	0.24	0.41	0.81
Total weekly expenditure on above[4]	**16.82**[3]	**28.52**	**41.14**
Expenditure on above items as a percentage of total household expenditure	13.4	16.0	15.9

(1) Includes home consumption for 1991. (2) Eaten on the premises, excluding state school meals and workplace meals. (3) A slight change in the component parts of this sub-group has been made for 1991, and the data modified for earlier years where necessary. (4) The total for 1981 is not comparable with later years since the figure for the category "Meals consumed out" is not available.

Participation in Home-based Leisure Activities

Great Britain

Source: CSO

Percentages and numbers

	1977	1980	1983	1986	1987	1990
Percentage participating in each activity in the 4 weeks before interview						
Watching TV	97	98	98	98	99	99
Visiting or entertaining friends or relatives	91	91	91	94	95	96
Listening to radio	87	88	87	86	88	89
Listening to records or tapes	62	64	63	67	73	76
Reading books	54	57	56	59	60	62
Gardening	42	43	44	43	46	48
DIY	35	37	36	39	43	43
Dressmaking, needlework or knitting	29	28	27	27	27	23
Sample size (=100%) (numbers)	23,171	22,599	19,050	19,209	19,529	17,574

Time Use in a Typical Week: Great Britain, 1991–92

Source: CSO

Hours

	Full-time employees		Part-time employees		
	Males	Females	Females	Housewives	Retired
Weekly hours spent on:					
Employment and travel[1]	48.9	43.7	21.1	0.4	0.2
Essential activities[2]	26.8	42.3	57.0	65.5	36.0
Sleep[3]	49.0	49.0	49.0	49.0	49.0
Free time	46.5	33.0	41.0	53.5	83.0
Free time per weekday	4.8	3.3	4.7	7.0	11.6
Free time per weekend day	11.3	8.3	8.7	9.0	12.6

(1) Travel to and from place of work. (2) Essential domestic work and personal care, including essential shopping, child care, cooking, personal hygiene and appearance. (3) An average of 7 hours sleep per night is assumed.

Participation in Indoor Sports, Games and Physical Exercise: Great Britain, 1990

Source: CSO

Percentages and numbers

	Professional	Employers and managers	Intermediate and junior non-manual	Skilled manual and own account non professional	Semi-skilled manual and personal service	Unskilled manual	All groups[1]
Percentage in each group participating in each activity in the 4 weeks before interview							
Snooker, pool, billiards	14	13	10	19	12	8	14
Swimming	19	13	15	9	9	5	12
Keep fit, yoga	11	10	17	6	9	6	12
Darts	5	6	5	11	7	6	7
Weight lifting, training	7	5	4	5	3	2	5
Tenpin bowling or skittles	5	4	4	3	3	1	4
Badminton	5	3	4	2	1	1	3
Squash	9	5	2	2	1	–	3
Soccer	4	2	1	2	1	1	2
Table tennis	2	2	2	1	1	1	2
Carpet bowls	1	2	1	1	1	1	1
Self defence	1	1	1	1	–	–	1
Ice skating	1	–	1	–	1	–	1
Basketball	–	–	–	–	–	–	1
Sample size (=100%) (numbers)	680	2,355	5,666	3,602	3,302	970	17,574

Participation in Outdoor Sports, Games and Physical Activities: Great Britain, 1990

Source: CSO

Percentages and numbers

	Professional	Employers and managers	Intermediate and junior non-manual	Skilled manual and own account non-professional	Semi-skilled manual and personal service	Unskilled manual	All groups[1]
Percentage in each group participating in each activity in the 4 weeks before interview							
Walking	51	45	43	40	35	31	41
Cycling	13	8	9	9	9	8	9

(Continued)

Percentages and numbers

	Professional	Employers and managers	Intermediate and junior non-manual	Skilled manual and own account non-professional	Semi-skilled manual and personal service	Unskilled manual	All groups[1]
Percentage in each group participating in each activity in the 4 weeks before interview							
Golf	13	10	4	5	2	1	5
Running (incl. jogging, etc.)	11	6	5	4	3	2	5
Swimming	8	5	4	4	2	2	4
Soccer	6	3	3	5	2	2	4
Tennis	4	3	2	1	1	1	2
Fishing	3	2	1	3	2	2	2
Lawn bowls	1	2	1	2	1	1	1
Water sports (excl. sailing)	3	2	1	1	–	–	1
Cricket	2	1	1	1	–	–	1
Horse riding	1	1	1	1	1	–	1
Field sports	1	2	–	1	–	–	1
Sailing	3	1	1	1	–	–	1
Hockey	1	1	1	–	–	–	1
Sample size (=100%) (numbers)	680	2,355	5,666	3,602	3,302	970	17,574

(1) Includes full-time students, members of the Armed Forces, people who have never worked, and inadequately described occupations.

Britain's Favourite Places

Source: British Tourist Authority

(NA = Not available; F = Free admission; * = Estimated visitor numbers)

Top 20 Attractions Charging Admission	1990 visits	1991 visits	1992 visits
1. Alton Towers, Staffordshire	2,070,000	1,968,000	2,501,379
2. Madame Tussaud's, London	2,547,447	2,248,956	2,263,994
3. Tower of London	2,296,683	1,923,520	2,235,199
4. Natural History Museum, London	1,527,815	1,571,681	1,700,000
5. St Paul's Cathedral, London†	NA	1,500,000*	1,400,000
6. Tower World, Blackpool	1,426,000	1,300,000	1,300,000
7. Science Museum, London	1,303,345	1,327,503	1,212,504
8. Chessington World of Adventures	1,514,790	1,410,000	1,170,000
9. Thorpe Park, Surrey	974,000	921,014	1,026,000
10. Royal Academy, London	1,308,500	807,962	1,018,114
11. Flamingo Land, North Yorkshire	1,138,000	1,087,000	991,000
12. Edinburgh Castle	1,078,120	973,620	986,305
13. Kew Gardens	1,196,346	988,000	953,250
14. Drayton Manor Park, Staffordshire	989,500	990,000	950,000
15. London Zoo	1,243,655	1,116,247	939,597
16. Roman Baths and Pump Room, Bath	950,472	827,214	895,948
17. American Adventure, Ilkeston	750,000	1,000,000	860,000
18. Jorvik Viking Centre, York	846,228	791,225	785,028
19. Windsor Castle, State Apartments	855,239	627,213	769,298
20. Chester Zoo	904,000	880,378	768,100

† In April 1991 St Paul's Cathedral introduced an admission charge

Top 10 Historic Properties	1990 visits	1991 visits	1992 visits
1. Tower of London	2,296,683	1,923,520	2,235,199
2. St Paul's Cathedral	NA	1,500,000*	1,400,000*
3. Edinburgh Castle	1,078,120	973,620	986,305
4. Roman Baths and Pump Room, Bath	950,472	827,214	895,948
5. Windsor Castle, State Apartments	855,239	627,213	690,000
6. Warwick Castle	685,000	682,621	769,298
7. Stonehenge, Wiltshire	703,221	615,377	649,442
8. Hampton Court Palace	520,995	502,377	486,100
9. Shakespeare's Birthplace, Stratford	603,899	516,623	580,440
10. Blenheim Palace, Oxfordshire	511,630	503,328	577,704

Top 10 Gardens	1990 visits	1991 visits	1992 visits
1. Hampton Court Gardens	NA	1,000,000	1,086,450 (F)
2. Tropical World, Roundhay Park, Leeds	863,024	1,062,654*	1,100,000* (F)
3. Kew Gardens	1,196,346	988,000	953,250
4. Royal Botanical Gardens, Edinburgh	785,591	765,909	662,459 (F)
5. Wisley Gardens, Surrey	640,000	630,000	616,970
6. Botanic Gardens, Belfast	350,000*	350,000	400,000* (F)
7. Sir Thomas and Lady Dixon Park, Belfast	300,000*	320,000	282,000* (F)
8. Botanic Gardens, Glasgow	350,000*	350,000	400,000* (F)
9. University of Oxford Botanic Gardens	NA	324,800	350,000* (F)
10. Stourhead Gardens, Wiltshire	Na	228,209	239,261

Top 10 Museums and Galleries	1990 visits	1991 visits	1992 visits
1. British Museum, London	4,769,439	5,061,287	6,309,349 (F)
2. National Gallery, London	3,682,233	4,280,139	4,313,988 (F)

(Continued)

Top 10 Museums and Galleries

	1990 visits	1991 visits	1992 visits
3. Natural History Museum, London	1,527,815	1,571,682	1,575,637 (F)
4. Tate Gallery, London	1,562,431	1,816,421	1,700,000
5. Science Museum, London	1,303,345	1,327,503	1,212,504
6. Victoria and Albert Museum, London	901,362	1,066,428	1,182,402 (F)
7. Royal Academy, London	1,308,500	807,962	874,688 (F)
8. Glasgow Art Gallery and Museum	1,008,180	892,865	1,018,114
9. Jorvik Viking Centre, York	846,228	791,225	785,028
10. National Museum of Photography, Bradford	NA	753,981	775,139 (F)

Top 10 Wildlife Attractions

	1990 visits	1991 visits	1992 visits
1. London Zoo	1,243,655	1,116,247	939,587
2. Chester Zoo	904,000	880,378	768,100
3. Sea Life Centre, Blackpool	320,000	680,000	595,000
4. Lotherton Bird Garden, W. Yorks	490,000*	500,000	500,000* (F)
5. Edinburgh Zoo	542,020	486,324	496,084
6. Whipsnade Wild Animal Park, Beds	530,000	566,008	406,789
7. Birmingham Nature Centre	NA	328,428	398,349 (F)
8. Twycross Zoo, Atherstone	462,383	426,308	378,583
9. Cotswold Wildlife Park, Burford	376,412	354,255	314,700
10. Cricket St Thomas Wildlife Park, Somerset	NA	333,790	309,466

Top 10 Country Parks

	1990 visits	1991 visits	1992 visits
1. Strathclyde Country Park, Motherwell	4,200,000*	4,220,000*	4,220,000* (F)
2. Bradgate Park, Leicestershire	1,300,000*	1,300,000*	1,300,000* (F)
3. Sandwell Valley Country Park, West Bromwich	1,250,000*	1,250,000*	1,100,000* (F)
4. Clent Hills Country Park, Romsley	1,000,000*	1,000,000*	1,000,000* (F)
5. Clumber Park, Worksop	1,000,000*	1,000,000*	1,000,000* (F)
6. Crawfordsburn Country Park, Belfast	1,000,000*	1,000,000*	1,000,000* (F)
7. Sherwood Forest Country Park, Notts	1,000,000*	1,000,000*	1,000,000* (F)
8. Thetford Forest Park	NA	1,000,000*	1,000,000* (F)
9. Dunstable Downs Country Park, Beds	850,000*	900,000*	800,000* (F)
10. Elvaston Castle Country park, Derbyshire	NA	800,000*	800,000* (F)

Top 10 Leisure Parks and Piers

	1990 visits	1991 visits	1992 visits
1. Blackpool Pleasure Beach	6,500,000*	6,500,000*	6,500,000* (F)
2. Palace Pier, Brighton	3,500,000*	3,500,000*	3,500,000* (F)
3. Alton Towers, Staffs	2,070,000	1,968,000	2,501,379
4. Pleasure Beach, Great Yarmouth	2,600,000*	2,500,000*	2,250,000* (F)
5. Pleasureland, Southport	1,500,000*	1,750,000*	2,000,000* (F)
6. Tower World, Blackpool	1,426,000	1,300,000	1,300,000
7. Frontierland, Morecambe	1,300,000*	1,300,000*	1,300,000* (F)
8. Chessington World of Adventures	1,514,790	1,410,000	1,170,000
9. Thorpe Park, Surrey	NA	921,014	1,026,000
10. Peter Pan's Playground, Southend-on-Sea	NA	NA	1,000,000* (F)

Top London Attractions*

Source: London Tourist Board

Millions

	1990	1991	1992
1. British Museum	4.8	5.1	6.3
2. National Gallery	3.7	4.3	4.3
3. Madame Tussaud's	2.5	2.2	2.3
4. Tower of London	2.3	1.9	2.2
5. Tate Gallery	1.5	1.8	1.6
6. St Paul's Cathedral	–	1.5	1.4
7. Natural History Museum	1.5	1.6	1.3
8. Chessington World of Adventures	1.5	1.4	1.2
9. Science Museum	1.3	1.3	1.2
10. Victoria and Albert Museum	1.0	1.1	1.2
11. Royal Botanic Gardens	1.2	1.0	1.0
12. London Zoo	1.2	1.1	0.9
13. Royal Chapels, Westminster Abbey†	0.9	0.7	0.8
14. National Portrait Gallery	0.6	0.6	0.6
15. Rock Circus, Piccadilly	0.5	0.5	0.6
16. Hampton Court Palace	0.5	0.5	0.6
17. National Maritime Museum	0.6	0.6	0.5

* Excludes Royal Academy of Arts and Hayward Gallery where attendance depends on annual programme of exhibitions.
† The estimated attendance for all of Westminster Abbey in 1992 was 2.75 million.

Visitors to London

Source: London Tourist Board

Millions

	1990	1991	1992*	1993*
Visits				
Domestic	7.0	6.5	6.5	7.0
Overseas	10.3	8.9	9.8	10.3
All	17.3	15.4	16.3	17.3
Expenditure				£ millions
Domestic	680	720	735	760
Overseas	4,270	3,800	4,100	4,550
All	4,950	4,520	4,835	5,310

* Estimated figures.

Overseas Visitors to the UK

Source: London Tourist Board

Thousands

		Areas of residence		
Year	Total visits	North America	Western Europe	Other areas
1987	15,566	3,394	9,317	2,855
1988	15,799	3,272	9,669	2,859
1989	17,338	3,481	10,689	3,168
1990	18,021	3,749	10,645	3,627
1991	16,705	2,747	11,057	3,001
1992 (P)	18,100	–	11,560	–
% change 1991/90	+9	–27	+5	–17

P = Provisional. Constituent items may not add exactly to totals because of rounding.

Major Attractions in Scotland 1992

Source: Scottish Tourist Board

Attractions with free admission	Visitors 1991	Visitors 1992
Glasgow Art Gallery & Museum	892,865	874,688
Royal Botanic Gardens, Edinburgh	765,909	662,459
Museum of Transport, Glasgow	493,239	492,978
Royal Museum of Scotland, (Chambers Street) Edinburgh	457,207	460,249
The Burrell Collection, Glasgow	486,085	425,380
New Lanark Village	275,000*	400,000*
National Gallery of Scotland, Edinburgh	315,154	358,235
Glasgow Botanical Gardens	350,000*	350,000*
Aberdeen Art Gallery	356,937	349,936
People's Palace, Glasgow	298,668	313,078

Attractions with paid admission	Visitors 1991	Visitors 1992
Edinburgh Castle	973,620	986,305
Edinburgh Zoo	486,324	496,084
Culzean Castle & Country Park, Maybole	385,781	353,204
Stirling Castle	254,614	263,546
Palace of Holyroodhouse, Edinburgh	273,429	254,782
Blair Castle, Blair Atholl	241,623	248,679
Urquhart Castle, nr. Drumnadrochit	177,928	170,551
Blair Drummond Safari & Leisure Park, Stirling	195,018	169,224
Glencoe Visitor Centre	160,226	160,633
Sea Life Centre, St Andrews	165,500	145,259
Total (all attractions)	**30,181,742**	**30,004,542**

* Estimate.

Visitors to Northern Ireland 1992

Source: N.I. Tourist Board

Great Britain	726,500
England & Wales	530,400
Scotland	196,100
Republic of Ireland	352,000
Europe	86,100
Germany	32,400
France	17,400
Holland	9,400
Italy	5,600
Other Europe	21,300
North America	60,300
USA	39,600
Canada	20,700
Australia/New Zealand	17,800
Other Overseas	11,800
TOTAL VISITORS	1,254,500

Major Attractions in Northern Ireland 1992

Source: N.I. Tourist Board

1.	Ulster Museum	442,831 F*
2.	Giant's Causeway	350,000 F
3.	Craft Village, Londonderry	180,000 F
4.	Belfast Zoo	174,498
5.	Ulster Folk and Transport Museum	135,634
6.	Ulster American Folk Park	131,625
7.	Cranfield Beach	120,000
8.	Waterworld	108,162
9.	Shane's Castle	100,000
10.	Belleek Pottery	90,000
11.	Portstewart Strand	81,084
12.	Causeway Safari Park	80,000
13.	Old Bushmills Distillery	69,164 F
14.	Northern Ireland Aquarium	61,157
15.	Newry Arts Centre	56,212 F
16.	Carrickfergus Castle	55,947
17.	North Down Heritage Centre	55,248 F
18.	Buttermarket	53,000 F
19.	Marble Arch Caves	53,000
20.	Carrick-a-Rede Rope Bridge	51,411

* Special exhibitions, such as the Dinosaur Exhibition during 1992, were charged.

Foreign Holidays by UK Residents

Source: CSO

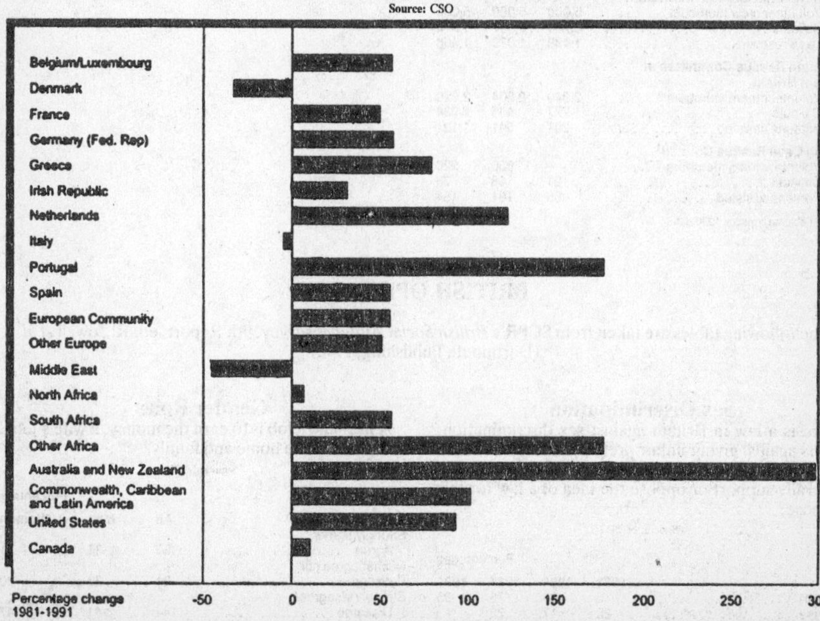

Income of Selected UK Charities, 1990[1]

Source: CSO

£ million

	Total income	Total voluntary income
National Trust	104.3	55.7
Oxfam	62.1	45.0
Barnardo's	69.6	29.9
Salvation Army	70.2	39.0
Save the Children Fund	52.2	38.6
Spastics Society	49.2	19.1
Imperial Cancer Research Fund	52.9	42.1
Royal National Lifeboat Institution	52.7	47.4
British Red Cross Society	43.9	21.8
Cancer Research Campaign	49.3	40.3
Royal National Institute for the Blind	46.9	19.9
Guide Dogs for the Blind Association	32.8	24.4
National Society for the Prevention of Cruelty to Children	28.6	22.6
Christian Aid	31.2	18.7
Charity Projects Limited	6.9	2.5
Royal Society for the Prevention of Cruelty to Animals	27.9	23.8
British Heart Foundation	29.0	23.8
Help the Aged	28.3	24.5
Marie Curie Memorial Foundation	24.8	19.7
Action Aid	21.9	16.2
Royal British Legion	18.7	12.2
Tear Fund	14.9	13.9
Royal Society for the Protection of Birds	22.4	14.8
People's Dispensary for Sick Animals	16.3	13.4
Cancer Relief Macmillan Fund	16.2	14.8

(1) Accounting periods ending in 1990; although 12-month periods covered may differ.

UK Voluntary Rescue Work

Source: CSO

Numbers

	1971	1981	1991
Royal National Lifeboat Institution			
Volunteer crew members	5,000	5,000	5,000
Callouts	2,789	3,017	4,972
Lives rescued	1,438	1,076	1,408
Mountain Rescue Committee of Great Britain			
Volunteer team members	2,340	2,804	2,920
Callouts	277	485	1,034
Persons assisted	207	541	1,121
British Cave Rescue Council[1]			
Volunteer team members	–	900	920
Callouts	21	48	73
Persons assisted	66	101	154

(1) 1991 column contains 1990 data.

Membership of Selected Organizations for Young People (UK)

Source: CSO

Thousands

	1971	1981	1991
Membership			
Cub Scouts[1]	265	309	349
Brownie Guides[2,3]	376	427	385
Scouts[4]	215	234	192
Girl Guides[3,5]	316	348	225
Sea Cadet Corps	18	19	16
Army Cadet Force	39	46	39
Air Training Corps	33	35	34
Combined Cadet Force	45	44	40
Boys Brigade	140	154	103
Girls Brigade	97	94	40
Methodist Association of Youth Clubs	115	127	40
National Association of Boys Clubs	164	186	155
Youth Clubs UK – Boys	179	430[7]	310
– Girls	140	341[7]	290
National Federation of Young Farmers' Clubs[6]			
– Males	24	28	18
– Females	16	23	15
Young Men's Christian Association[7]			
Registered members			
– Males	35	36	43
– Females	13	19	32
Rotaract Clubs	1	10	10
Duke of Edinburgh's Award			
Participants	122	170	200
Awards gained			
Bronze	18	23	35
Silver	7	10	13
Gold	3	5	6

(1) Includes Beaver Scouts (6–8 years). (2) Includes Rainbow Guides (4 or 5–7 years). (3) Includes Guides in the Channel Islands, Isle of Man and British Guides in foreign countries. (4) Includes Venture Scouts (15.5–20 years). (5) Includes Ranger Guides (14–18 years) and young leaders (15–18 years). (6) Figures relate to England, Wales and the Channel Islands, and to young people aged between 10 and 25 in 1971, and between 10 and 26 in 1981. (7) Figures relate to persons aged under 25.

BRITISH OPINIONS

The following tables are taken from SCPR's *British Social Attitudes* survey, 9th Report, ed. R. Jowell *et al.* (Dartmouth Publishing, 1992).

Sex Discrimination

There is a law in Britain against sex discrimination; that is against giving unfair preference to men – or to women – in employment, pay and so on. Do you generally support or oppose the idea of a law for this purpose?

Source: SCPR

Percentages

	1983	1984	1987	1991
Support	76	80	75	85
Oppose	22	17	22	13

Gender Roles

A husband's job is to earn the money, a wife's job is to look after the home and family.

Source: SCPR

Percentage

	All	Men	Women
Strongly agree/ Agree	33	35	31
Neither agree nor disagree	21	23	20
Strongly disagree/ Disagree	44	41	47

Attitudes Towards Home Ownership

Source: SCPR

	Percentage agreeing		
	1984	1987	1991
'Positive' statements			
Buying a home works out cheaper than paying rent.	44	33	30
Owning a home gives you freedom to alter it.	40	31	22
Your own home will be something to leave to your family.	39	34	26
Owning a home makes it easier to move.	27	19	16
'Negative' statements			
Couples who buy their own home would be wise to wait before starting a family.	59	61	61
Owning a home is too much of a risk for couples without secure jobs.	59	64	69
Owning your home is just too much of a responsibility.	12	10	10
Owning your home can be a risky investment.	25	34	43
Owning your home ties up money you may need for other things.	35	37	35
Owning your home is a big financial burden to repair and maintain.	50	55	57

Racial Prejudice

Do you think there is a lot of prejudice against Asians and black people in Britain today?

Source: SCPR

Percentages

	Asians			Blacks		
	1983	1987	1991	1983	1987	1991
A lot	54	62	58	50	57	50
A little	37	30	35	40	33	41
Hardly any	6	6	4	7	7	7
Don't know/other answer	3	2	3	3	2	3

Working Women

Do you perceive any improvement in recent years in employment opportunities, incomes and promotion prospects for women?

Source: SCPR

	Percentage agreeing		
	1984	1987	1991
Job opportunities are:			
Better for women	7	6	7
No different for men and women	37	34	23
Worse for women	51	54	62
Income and wages are:			
Better for women	2	1	2
No different for men and women	31	27	23
Worse for women	61	66	65

Social Class

Most people see themselves as belonging to a particular social class. Which social class would you say you belong to?

Source: SCPR

Percentages

	1983	1984	1985	1986	1987	1989	1991
Upper middle	1	2	2	1	2	1	2
Middle	24	25	26	24	26	28	27
Upper working	23	19	19	21	21	21	18
Working	46	48	47	48	46	44	46
Poor	3	3	4	3	3	3	4
Don't know	3	2	2	2	1	2	2

The British Conscience

(a) Suppose a law was being considered by Parliament which you thought was really unjust and harmful. Which, if any, of the following things do you think you would do?

(b) And have you ever done any of the following things about a government action which you thought was unjust and harmful?

Source: SCPR

Percentages

	(a) Would do	(b) Ever done
Contact my MP	48.4	16.7
Speak to influential person	17.0	5.3
Contact a government department	11.3	4.3
Contact radio, TV or newspaper	13.5	3.8
Sign a petition	77.8	52.5
Raise the issue in an organization I already belong to	9.3	4.8
Go on a protest or demonstration	13.6	9.1
Form a group of like-minded people	6.6	1.7
No, none of these	6.4	36.5

Corporate Conduct

Do you think there is anything wrong with the following business activities?

Source: SCPR

Percentages

	Nothing wrong	A bit wrong	Wrong	Seriously wrong	Very seriously wrong
A British firm competing for a contract in a foreign country offers large gifts of money to officials.	7	10	33	28	20
A tobacco manufacturer sponsors a national event popular with young people to get publicity.	16	11	33	19	19
Two large breweries get together and agree to raise their prices at the same time.	17	10	36	20	14
A company provides its directors with expensive company cars even though they are hardly ever used for work.	13	11	40	21	13
A private taxi firm puts up its fares during a public transport strike.	7	13	42	25	12

Sexual Relationships

Do you think it is wrong or not wrong if a man and a woman have sexual relations before marriage?

Source: SCPR

	Percentages
Always wrong	11.1
Almost always wrong	6.5
Wrong only sometimes	14.4
Not wrong at all	61.6
Can't choose	5.7

What about a married person having sexual relations with someone other than his or her husband or wife?

	Percentages
Always wrong	58.1
Almost always wrong	24.6
Wrong only sometimes	10.7
Not wrong at all	2.6
Can't choose	3.5

And what about sexual relations between two adults of the same sex?

	Percentages
Always wrong	52.0
Almost always wrong	7.1
Wrong only sometimes	10.1
Not wrong at all	18.8
Can't choose	11.3

Abortion

Source: SCPR

Percentage agreeing

	1983	1985	1987	1989	1990
The law should allow an abortion if the couple agree they do not wish to have the child.	46	55	59	59	62
The law should allow an abortion if the woman decides on her own she does not wish to have the child.	38	49	54	49	56

How Happy Are the British?

If you were to consider your life in general these days, how happy or unhappy would you say you are, on the whole?

Source: SCPR

	Percentage
Very happy	32.5
Fairly happy	57.0
Not very happy	7.5
Not at all happy	1.4
Can't choose	0.8

Attitudes Towards the Meaning of Life

Do you agree with the following statements?

Source: SCPR

Percentage agreeing

	Britain	USA	Irish Republic	Northern Ireland
There is little that people can do to change the course of their lives.	22	13	24	27
Life is meaningful only because God exists.	21	49	50	54
Life does not serve any purpose.	14	8	9	11
The course of our lives is decided by God.	20	40	58	54
We each make our own fate.	61	62	66	51
I am very happy these days.	33	37	41	37

OBITUARIES

1 Sep. 1992–31 Aug. 1993

A

Abe, Kobo, 68; Japanese novelist & poet; Jan. 22.
Adler, Stella, 91; U.S. acting teacher whose students included Marlon Brando, Candice Bergen and Warren Beatty; Dec. 21.
Adley, Robert, 58; British Conservative politician noted for his maverick views; May 13.
Alexander, Donald, 79; British documentary film-maker (*Wealth of a Nation*); Jul. 20.
Anderson, Marian, 91; U.S. opera singer, first black to be permanent member of New York Met; Apr. 8.
Andrews, Dana, 83; U.S. film actor (*Laura, Fallen Angel, Beyond a Reasonable Doubt*); Dec. 17.
Argyll, Margaret Duchess of, 80; British socialite; July 26.
Ashe, Arthur, 49; U.S. tennis player, won Wimbledon singles, 1975; Feb. 6.

B

Baudouin, King, 62; Belgian monarch, reigned for 42 years; Jul. 31.
Bauza, Mario, 82; Cuban-born musician, leader of Afro-Cuban Jazz Orchestra; Jul. 11.
Benson, Ivy, 79; British bandleader, founder of All Girl Orchestra; May 6.
Bernstein, Lord (Sidney), 94; British impresario, founder of Granada Television; Feb. 5.
Booth, Shirley, 94; U.S. actress, star of TV series *Hazel* and Oscar-winner for *Come Back Little Sheba*; Oct. 16.
Braden, Bernard, 76; Canadian actor/broadcaster who found fame in Britain (*Braden's Beat, Bedtime with Braden*); Feb. 2.
Brandt, Willy, 78; German chancellor, winner of 1971 Nobel Peace Prize; Oct. 9.
Bresslaw, Bernard, 59; British actor who found fame in *The Army Game* and the *Carry On* films; Jun. 11.
Budd, Roy, 46; British jazz pianist, writer of film scores (*Soldier Blue, Who Dares Wins, The Wild Geese*); Aug. 7.
Butts, Alfred, 93; U.S. inventor of Scrabble board game; Apr. 4.

C

Cahn, Sammy, 79; U.S. lyricist ("Come Fly With Me", "Love and Marriage", "My Kind of Town"); Jan. 15.
Cansdale, George, 83; British zoologist & television presenter, 1950s; Aug. 24.
Cantinflas, Mexican comic actor (*Around the World in 80 Days*); Apr. 20.
Carey, Joyce, 94; British stage & film actress (*This Happy Breed, Brief Encounter*); Mar. 2.
Charteris, Leslie, 85; British/U.S. author, creator of The Saint; Apr. 15.
Chavez, Cesar, 66; U.S.–Hispanic union leader, organizer of national grape boycott; Apr. 23.
Christoff, Boris, 75; Bulgarian-born bass singer regarded as all-round operatic performer; Jun. 28.
Connally, John, 76; U.S. politician, wounded during the assassination of President John Kennedy; Jun. 15.
Connors, Chuck, 71; U.S. actor, most often cast as a rugged tough guy (*Rifleman, The Big Country*); Nov. 10.
Craven, Danie, 82; South African rugby official, who fought apartheid through sport; Jan. 4.
Crosby, Bob, 80; U.S. swing-era band-leader; Mar. 9.
Culliford, Pierre, 64; Belgian cartoonist, creator of "Smurf" characters; Dec. 24.

D

Dawson, Les, 59; British comedian noted for lugubrious appearance; Jun. 10.
De Rita, Joe, 83; U.S. comedian, last of the Three Stooges; Jul. 3.
Desmond, Florence, 87; British music-hall star who specialized in impersonation; Jan. 16.
Dessauer, John, 88; U.S. pioneer of photocopying, co-founder of Xerox Corporation; Aug. 12.
Donald James, 76; British stage & film actor of the 1940s and 1950s (*The Great Escape, In Which We Serve, Lust for Life*); Aug. 3.
Dorsey, Tommy, 93; U.S. pianist known as the father of gospel music; Jan. 23.
Dubcek, Alexander, 70; Czech politician who instrumented socialism with a human face; Nov. 8.

E

Eckstine, Billy, 78; U.S. singer and band-leader, promoter of "bebop"; Mar. 8.
Elliott, Denholm, 70; British actor, *Trading Places, A Room with a View*; Oct. 6.
Ewart-Biggs, Baroness Jane, 63; British Labour peer; Oct. 7.
Evans, Sir Geraint, 70, British opera singer, famous for Verdi's *Falstaff*; Sep. 12.

F

Fermoy, Ruth Lady, 84; British aristocrat, grandmother of the Princess of Wales; Jul. 6.
Franks, Lord (Oliver), 87; British academic, former ambassador in Washington, co-creator of Marshall Plan and NATO; Oct. 15.

G

Gardenia, Vincent, 70; U.S. stage & film actor (*Moonstruck, The Front Page*); Dec. 9.
Gillespie, Dizzy, 75; U.S. jazz trumpeter, creator of "bebop"; Jan. 6.
Gilliatt, Penelope, 61; British novelist & critic; May. 9.
Gish, Lillian, 96; U.S. actress noted for "sweet" roles (*The Birth of a Nation, The Night of the Hunter*); Feb. 27.
Goldberg, Szymon, 84; Polish-born violinist particularly noted for performances of Mozart sonatas; Jul. 19.
Golding, William, 81; British author (*Lord of the Flies*), winner of Nobel prize for literature; Jun. 19.
Gormley, Joe, 75; British trade union leader, head of the National Union of Mineworkers; May 27.
Granger, Stewart, 80; British film actor (*King Solomon's Mines, Beau Brummel, Bhowani Junction*); Aug. 16.
Grundy, Bill, 69; British TV personality, *Today* programme; Feb. 10.
Gwynne, Fred, 66; U.S. actor, best known as Herman Munster; Jul. 2.

H

Hani, Chris, 50; South African political leader within ANC; Apr. 10.
Hayes, Helen, 92; U.S. actress (*The Sin of Madelon Claudet, A Farewell to Arms*); Mar. 17.
Hearst, William Jr, 85; U.S. newspaper baron and journalist; May 14.
Hepburn, Audrey, 63; Belgian-born film actress (*Gigi, Roman Holiday, Breakfast at Tiffany's*); Jan. 20.
Hibbert, Eleanor (Jean Plaidy/Victoria Holt), 82; British writer, best known for historical novels; Jan. 18.
Holloway, Sterling, 87; U.S. actor, voice of Winnie the Pooh; Nov. 22.
Home, William Douglas, 80; British playwright (*The Reluctant Debutante*); Sep. 28.
Horszowski, Mieczyslaw, 100; Polish pianist who performed up to the time of his death; May 22.
Howe, Irving, 72; U.S. literary and social critic; May 5.
Hunt, James, 45; British racing driver, one-time world champion; Jun. 14.

I

Inglis, Brian, 76; British journalist, author & broadcaster (*All Our Yesterdays, What the Papers Say*); Feb. 11.

J

Jacob, Sir Ian, 93; British army general who became director-general of the BBC; Apr. 24.
Johnson, Marvin, 54; U.S. singer, "I'll Pick a Rose for My Rose"; May 15.
Juan, Prince, 79; Spanish aristocrat, father of King Juan Carlos; Apr. 1.

K

Kanin, Michael, 83; U.S. screenwriter, producer & director; Mar. 12.
Keeler, Ruby, 83; U.S. film actress, star of many Busby Berkeley musicals; Feb. 28.
Kendricks, Eddie, 52; U.S. singer, leader of The Temptations ("The Way You Do the Things You Do", "Just My Imagination"); Oct. 5.

L

Lamborghini, Ferruccio, 76; Italian founder of sports car company; Feb. 20.

M

MacMillan, Sir Kenneth, 62; British choreographer, head of Royal Ballet; Oct. 29.
Mankiewicz, Joseph, 83; U.S. film director/writer (*All About Eve, A Letter to Three Wives, Cleopatra*); Feb. 5.
Mann, Sunnie, 79; British horse-trainer who came to prominence when her husband was kidnapped in Beirut; Nov. 30.
Marshall, Thurgood (Thoroughgood), 84; U.S. lawyer, first black member of the Supreme Court; Jan. 24.
Maskell, Dan, 84; British broadcaster, "the voice of tennis"; Dec. 10.
Mikardo, Ian, 84; British Labour politician; May 6.
Mills, Nat, 93; British music hall star partnered by wife, Bobbie, 1920s–40s; Aug. 13.
Milstein, Nathan, 88; Russian-born violin virtuoso; Dec. 21.
Moore, Bobby, 51; British footballer, captain of 1966 World Cup-winning side; Feb. 24.
Mori, Taikichiro, 88; Japanese businessman, reputedly the richest in the world (£8.8 billion); Jan. 30.

N

Negulesco, Jean, 93; Romanian-born film director (*How to Marry a Millionaire*, *Humoresque*); Jul. 18.

Nixon, Patricia, 81; U.S. "First Lady" – wife of former president Richard Nixon; Jun. 22.

Nolan, Sir Sidney, 75; Australian painter inspired by the landscape and folk heroes of his country; Nov. 28.

Norman, Leslie, 82; British film-maker, director of many Ealing productions; Feb. 20.

Nureyev, Rudolf, 54; Russian ballet dancer, acknowledged to be the greatest of the 20th century; Jan. 6.

O

Ozal, Turgut, 66; Turkish president; Apr. 17.

P

Parker, Cecilia, 88; U.S. actress, best known as Marian, the big sister of Andy Hardy; Jul. 25.

Pasternak, Josephine, 92; Russian poet (*In Memoriam Pedro*); Feb. 17.

Perkins, Anthony, 60; U.S. actor, best remembered for his role in *Psycho*; Sep. 12.

Premadasa, Ranasinghe, 68; Sri Lankan president; May 1.

Pulitzer, Joseph Jr, 80; U.S. journalist and newspaper publisher; Jun. 2.

Pyke, Magnus, 83; British food scientist and TV pundit; Oct. 20.

R

Radford, Winifred, 91; British opera singer & scholar; Apr. 15.

Ridley, Lord (Nicholas), 64; British politician, dedicated supporter of "Thatcherism"; Mar. 5.

Robinson, Cardew, 75; British actor/writer, best known for roles as a chinless silly ass; Dec. 27.

Roach, Hal, 100; U.S. film-maker, pioneer in comedy; Nov. 2.

Ronson, Mick, 47; British rock guitarist with David Bowie and Mott the Hoople; Apr. 30.

Rootstein, Adel, 62; South African-born window-dresser, creator of mannequins based on real people; Sep. 23.

Ryan, Paul, 44; British singer/songwriter of 1960s ("Eloise"); Nov. 29.

S

Sabin, Albert, 86; U.S. researcher on viruses; developed polio vaccine; Mar. 3.

Salisbury, Harrison, 84; U.S. journalist, *New York Times*, author of *Nine Hundred Days*; Jul. 6.

Scott-Moore, Elizabeth, 90; British water-colourist; Aug. 12.

Sharaff, Irene, 83; U.S. costume designer who won 5 Oscars; Aug. 16.

Sharkey, Ray, 40; U.S. film & TV actor; June 11.

Shawn, William, 85; U.S. editor of the *New Yorker*, 1952–87; Dec. 8.

Shirley, Anne, 75; U.S. actress (*Anne of Green Gables*, *Stella Dallas*, *Murder My Sweet*); Jul. 4.

Smith, Alexis, 72; U.S. film actress (*Gentleman Jim*, *Rhapsody in Blue*); Jun. 9.

Smith, T. Dan, 78; British political activist, imprisoned for taking bribes from John Poulson in housing scam; Jul. 27.

Sobell, Sir Michael, 100; British businessman & philanthropist; Aug. 31.

Stark, Dame Freya, 100; intrepid British travel writer (*The Valleys of the Assassins*, *A Winter in Arabia*); May 9.

T

Tambo, Oliver, 75; South African lawyer, leader of ANC during Nelson Mandela's imprisonment; Apr. 24.

Thomas, James "Sonny", 66; U.S. blues musician; Jun. 26.

Thompson, E(dward) P(almer), 69; British historian, "greatest of the 20th century"; Aug. 28.

Todd, Ann, 82; British actress (*The Seventh Veil*, *The Passionate Friends*, *Madeleine*); May 6.

Troyanos, Tatiana, 54; U.S. opera singer with commanding stage presence; Aug. 22.

Twitty, Conway, 59; U.S. country singer; Jun. 5.

V

Vaughan, Dame Janet, 93; British scientist, principal of Somerville College, Oxford; Jan. 9.

W

Warris, Ben, 83; British comedian whose career spanned variety theatre, radio and television; Jan. 16.

Westall, Robert, 63; British children's author (*The Machine-Gunners*); Apr. 15.

Willis, Lord (Ted), 78; British writer for film, stage and television, creator of *Dixon of Dock Green*; Dec. 22.

Woddis, Roger, 76; British poet and parodist; Jul. 16.

Y

Yates, Jess, 74; British entertainer and TV presenter, *Stars on Sunday*; Apr. 9.

OFFBEAT NEWS STORIES OF 1993

Too Many Balls

While Jim Meade searched for his golf ball in woods off the 16th fairway, another one came through the trees and hit him between the eyes. As friends rushed to help him to his feet, another firmly driven ball smacked him in the back. "I'd love to know the odds on being hit twice by a golf ball," said Mr Meade.

Not Enough Balls

The bawdy Second World War song about Hitler's manhood could be right after all according to Dr Fritz Redlich, a medical historian. "Hitler was a difficult and uncooperative patient who refused clinical examinations of his lower abdomen and genitals, as well as X-rays of his chest and abdomen." Dr Redlich reached his conclusion after interviewing people who knew Hitler and studying letters and diaries written by Hitler's physician, Dr Theodor Morell.

EC Directives on Hot Air

Such is the power of suggestion that the EC has appointed a 4-strong team in Brussels to stem the tide of tall stories about the Commission, many of which are reproduced in the British press. It is, apparently, a foul libel that donkeys on British beaches will have to wear nappies; that trawlermen will have to wear hairnets and carry condoms; that paddling pools will need lifeguards; and that charity shops will be unable to sell secondhand books and prams. The cost of dispelling these "Euromyths and Misunderstandings" is put at £18,000 a year.

Abstracting the Mickey

A "blob" painting by 4-year-old Carly Johnson was submitted as a joke to the Manchester Academy of Fine Arts annual show, but was among the 150 chosen for display from 1000 submissions. It was subsequently bought by an Irish art collector for £295. "I don't feel in the least embarrassed about it," said Glenys Latham, president of the academy. "Technical skill can get in the way of instinctive response." As for the buyer, he described it as "sheer, innocent poetry".

Boozy Bodice-Ripper

Emma Blair, creator of *A Most Determined Woman* and *Where No Man Cries*, was undone by a drop too many and "unfrocked" after an orgy of destruction in a quiet country village. Emma, otherwise known as Ian Blair, a burly 50-year-old Glaswegian, had been drinking for 3 days in an attempt to overcome writer's block. Magistrates, who heard that "she" had crashed into 3 cars in the space of as many minutes, imposed a £3500 fine and a 3-year ban from driving.

To Boldly Go . . .

Americans worried about the cost of the space programme had plenty to brood on when told that the tricky problem of using a toilet in zero gravity had been solved. The Improved Waste Collection Facility (IWCF), which involves the user strapping himself to the toilet with thigh bars and foot restraints, cost $30 million to develop – a far cry from spending a penny.

Emotional Incontinence

What do Mozart and Dr Johnson have in common, apart from profound creativity? According to Dr Benjamin Simkin of Cedars-Sinai Medical Center in Los Angeles the answer is Tourette's syndrome. Both men were prone to hyperactivity, bursts of foul language, bodily tics and an obsession with anal function, all of which are symptoms of the syndrome. "The concept of 'incontinence of the emotions' might well serve as the connecting link between two of the intellectual giants of the 18th century."

Running Joke

The installation of a fountain in the reception area of Slough Town Hall had an unforeseen effect on visitors. The sound of running water increased the number of times they had to visit the toilet. A local councillor said he was "sorry to hear that members of the public have been inconvenienced by this".

Horseplay

The White Horse of Kilburn, North Yorkshire, which is carved into a chalk hillside, underwent "cosmetic surgery" at the hands of practical jokers. Black binliners were fixed to the monument, temporarily changing the horse into a zebra.

Power of Love

A lovers' quarrel, in which Caroline Love and Luis Moreno chased each other in vans through northern Sydney, Australia, came to an abrupt end when both plunged over the same cliff. They were later said to be in a "satisfactory condition" in hospital.

Parrot No More

Driven to distraction by his neighbour's noisy parrots, one of which had been trained to repeat his first name, Mark Leach could stand no more. He knocked down a fence, entered the aviary and strangled the offending bird. Oxford Crown Court heard that council officers had recorded parrot sound levels of 89 decibels – the equivalent of heavy traffic or thunder. Fined £600 with £350 costs and bound over to keep the peace, Mr Leach said he was pursuing civil proceedings to end the "parrot menace".

Rien ne va plus

As Monsieur X bent over to flush the toilet on a French super-speed train, his wallet fell in and was swallowed up. When he attempted to fish it out, the metal jaws of the loo clamped fast round his wrist and refused to let go. Somehow he managed to pull the alarm signal and the train came to an emergency stop near Tours. Firemen raced to the scene to cut him free, and television cameras later arrived to show an enthralled nation Mr X being carried away on a stretcher with his wallet in one hand and the recalcitrant toilet bowl still clamped to his wrist.

Top Wrigglers

The tenth annual worm-charming championship was won by the ladies of St Theresa's Cheshire Home. Using cold tea and a worm song, they encouraged 72 appearances from the 12-ft square plot of earth in 15 minutes. This was well short of the record (139 worms) but locals blamed poor conditions.

SOUNDBITES 1992–93

"I'm not an expert on the economy."
Norman Lamont, *Today*

"I always get my threes and fives muddled up."
Norman Lamont, *Daily Express*

"The Americans don't really understand what's going on in Bosnia. To them it's the unspellables killing the unpronouncables."
P. J. O'Rourke, *The Sun*

"I want William Shakespeare in our classroom, not Ronald McDonald."
John Patten, Minister for Education

"I fed Robert Maxwell three times when he came to the factory on flying visits. By heck, I wish I'd poisoned him."
Ivy Needham, former works canteen manageress and Maxwell pensioner, *Daily Mail*

"This page is dedicated to Michael Heseltine. It represents all that he understands about the worries and fears of the ordinary working-class people in depression-hit Britain. Nothing. Absolutely nothing."
Blank front page, *The Sun*

"There's this myth that the Royal Family is worth £6 billion. Its madness . . . where is it all, that's what I'd like to know."
Prince Edward, *The Sun*

"The Government is giving my party a bad name. I am ready if the country needs me."
Lord Sutch, leader of the Official Monster Raving Loony Party, *Daily Mail*

"I always say: 'A woman is like a teabag; you never know how strong she is until she gets into hot water.'"
Ivana Trump, *Hello!*

"I don't hate the press: I find a lot of it very unpalatable. But if that's the way they want to behave . . ."
Prince Philip, *Independent on Sunday*

"Many people don't drink enough when they go out because they're frightened the toilets will be so filthy they won't want to use them."
Susan Cunningham of the pressure group All Mod Cons, *Independent*

"Given the choice between a free private showing of the hard-core porn video *Red Hot Dutch* (X) in committee room 19, and a live performance on the floor of the House by Mr Tony Newton (PG) many MPs took the view that their responsibilities to their constituents demanded that, however painful the duty, they sit through the whole disgusting video."
Matthew Parris, *The Times*

"We may have people into bestiality in the military, but they don't bring their goats into the barracks."
Harry Summers, retired US Army Colonel, on allowing homosexuals into the armed forces, *Today*, Radio 4

"I have as my ideal the life of Jesus."
Richard Nixon in *Nixon, a Life* by Jonathan Aitken

"For Bush, suicide is the best remedy."
Al-Jumhouriyah, Iraqi government newspaper

"He is brighter and sharper than most of his Cabinet colleagues. But then so is Trigger."
Richard Littlejohn on Kenneth Clarke, *The Sun*

"Society needs to condemn a little more and understand a little less."
John Major on the rising number of young offenders

"The England cricket team – failing, morally shifty, globally insignificant, distracted by irrelevant attention to demeanour, run by discredited leaders insolently continuing in office – may not be a credit to the nation, but is a perfect reflection of it."
Mark Lawson, *Independent*

"When it comes to culture, you'll find more on a month-old carton of yoghurt than between the ears of the Princess of Wales."
Richard Littlejohn, *The Sun*

"It's not affected my work – how healthy do you have to be to play Da Do Ron Ron?"
Kenny Everett, disc jockey, confirms he is HIV positive, *The Sun*

"The trouble with this Government is that we don't have enough dukes in it."
Sir John Stokes, *Sunday Times*

"You can't have been here that long – you haven't got a pot belly."
Prince Philip to a British tourist in Hungary, *Daily Express*

"Do you think Sir Norman Fowler is spending enough time with his family?"
Letter, *Financial Times*

"Ideally a Chief Secretary to the Treasury should be flinty-faced, stone-hearted and odious. I believe that I fit the bill."
Michael Portillo, *Hansard*

"She is short on looks, deprived of any dress sense, has a figure like a Jurassic monster, is very greedy when it comes to loot, no tact and wants to up-stage everyone else."
Sir Nicholas Fairbairn MP, on the Duchess of York

"Doesn't she feel the slightest bit of shame that she should now be spitting at everything in which she once believed?"
John Junor on Lady Thatcher, *Mail on Sunday*

"Mr Gummer is not greatly liked even on his own side."
Doug Henderson, Labour MP, *Daily Mirror*

"It's very hard for an actor to open his gob without whatever he says sounding risible. If you even whisper a murmur of complaint, you're labelled a po-faced git who can't see the funny side of things."
Kenneth Branagh